College Edition

HARPER COLLINS
ITALIAN
DICTIONARY

ITALIAN · ENGLISH   ENGLISH · ITALIAN

HarperCollinsPublishers

by/a cura di
Catherine E. Love, Michela Clari

American language consultant/inglese americano
Dennis Allen

editorial staff/segreteria di redazione
Angela Campbell, Vivian Marr,
Anne Bradley, Elspeth Anderson,
Anne Marie Banks, Susan Dunsmore

ISBN 0-06-275506-4
ISBN 0-06-276508-6 (pbk)

96 97 98 RRD 10 9 8 7 6

INDICE

CONTENTS

Introduzione	vii
Elenco delle abbreviazioni	viii
Trascrizione fonetica	x
La pronuncia dell'italiano	xii
Verbi italiani	xiii
Verbi inglesi	xviii
I numeri	xx
ITALIANO–INGLESE	
INGLESE–ITALIANO	

Introduction	vii
Abbreviations used in the dictionary	viii
Phonetic transcription	x
Italian pronunciation	xii
Italian verb forms	xiii
English verb forms	xviii
Numbers	xx
ITALIAN–ENGLISH	
ENGLISH–ITALIAN	

I marchi registrati

I termini che a nostro parere costituiscono un marchio registrato sono stati designati come tali. In ogni caso, né la presenza né l'assenza di tale designazione implicano alcuna valutazione del loro reale stato giuridico.

Note on trademarks

Words which we have reason to believe constitute trademarks have been designated as such. However, neither the presence nor the absence of such designation should be regarded as affecting the legal status of any trademark.

INTRODUZIONE

Per capire l'inglese

Questo nuovo ed aggiornatissimo dizionario si rivolge alle esigenze del mondo moderno, con un ampio lemmario che rispecchia la lingua inglese di oggi e comprende, naturalmente, anche la terminologia in uso nel mondo degli affari e dell'informatica, nonché un'ampia scelta di abbreviazioni, sigle, acronimi e termini geografici che compaiono di frequente nella stampa. Per una facile consultazione, le forme irregolari di verbi e sostantivi compaiono come lemmi principali con un rimando alla forma di partenza, dove viene fornita la traduzione.

Per esprimersi in inglese

Per aiutarvi ad esprimervi in un inglese corretto ed idiomatico, abbiamo inserito un sistema di indicatori, una preziosa "guida" al vostro servizio, per chiarirvi il senso e l'ambito d'uso di ciascuna traduzione ed orientarvi verso la scelta che più si adatta al vostro contesto. Tutti i termini d'uso corrente sono stati trattati in modo dettagliato ed esauriente ed illustrati da esempi tipici.

Un compagno di lavoro

L'attenzione e la cura che hanno accompagnato la creazione di questo nuovo dizionario Collins ne fanno uno strumento di facile consultazione, prezioso ed affidabile per lo studio ed il lavoro. Ci auguriamo che costituirà un fedele compagno al servizio di tutte le vostre esigenze linguistiche.

INTRODUCTION

Understanding Italian

This new and thoroughly up-to-date dictionary provides the user with wide-ranging, practical coverage of current usage, including terminology relevant to business and office automation, and a comprehensive selection of abbreviations, acronyms and geographical names commonly found in the press. You will also find, for ease of consultation, irregular forms of Italian verbs and nouns with a cross-reference to the basic form where a translation is given.

Self-expression in Italian

To help you express yourself correctly and idiomatically in Italian, numerous indications – think of them as signposts – guide you to the most appropriate translation for your context. All the most commonly used words are given detailed treatment, with many examples of typical usage.

A working companion

Much care has been taken to make this new Collins dictionary thoroughly reliable, easy to use and relevant to your work and study. We hope it will become a long-serving companion for all your foreign language needs.

ABBREVIAZIONI

ABBREVIATIONS

aggettivo	**a**	adjective
abbreviazione	**abbr**	abbreviation
avverbio	**ad**	adverb
amministrazione	**ADMIN**	administration
aeronautica, viaggi aerei	**AER**	flying, air travel
aggettivo	**ag**	adjective
agricoltura	**AGR**	agriculture
amministrazione	**AMM**	administration
anatomia	**ANAT**	anatomy
architettura	**ARCHIT**	architecture
astronomia, astrologia	**ASTR**	astronomy, astrology
l'automobile	**AUT**	automobiles
avverbio	**av**	adverb
aeronautica, viaggi aerei	**AVIAT**	flying, air travel
biologia	**BIOL**	biology
botanica	**BOT**	botany
inglese di Gran Bretagna	**Brit**	British English
consonante	**C**	consonant
chimica	**CHIM, CHEM**	chemistry
congiunzione	**cj**	conjunction
familiare (! da evitare)	**col(!)**	colloquial usage (! particularly offensive)
commercio, finanza, banca	**COMM**	commerce, finance, banking
informatica	**COMPUT**	computing
congiunzione	**cong**	conjunction
edilizia	**CONSTR**	building
sostantivo usato come aggettivo, non può essere usato né come attributo, né dopo il sostantivo qualificato	**cpd**	compound element: noun used as adjective and which cannot follow the noun it qualifies
cucina	**CUC, CULIN**	cookery
davanti a	**dav**	before
determinante: articolo, aggettivo dimostrativo o indefinito etc	**det**	determiner: article, demonstrative etc
diritto	**DIR**	law
economia	**ECON**	economics
edilizia	**EDIL**	building
elettricità, elettronica	**ELETTR, ELEC**	electricity, electronics
esclamazione, interiezione	**escl, excl**	exclamation, interjection
specialmente	**esp**	especially
femminile	**f**	feminine
familiare (! da evitare)	**fam(!)**	colloquial usage (! particularly offensive)
ferrovia	**FERR**	railroad
figurato	**fig**	figurative use
fisiologia	**FISIOL**	physiology
fotografia	**FOT**	photography
(verbo inglese) la cui particella è inseparabile dal verbo	**fus**	(phrasal verb) where the particle cannot be separated from main verb
nella maggior parte dei sensi; generalmente	**gen**	in most or all senses; generally
geografia, geologia	**GEO**	geography, geology
geometria	**GEOM**	geometry
impersonale	**impers**	impersonal
informatica	**INFORM**	computing
insegnamento, sistema scolastico e universitario	**INS**	education, schools and universities

ABBREVIAZIONI

ABBREVIATIONS

invariabile	inv	invariable
irregolare	irg	irregular
grammatica, linguistica	LING	grammar, linguistics
maschile	m	masculine
matematica	MAT(H)	mathematics
termine medico, medicina	MED	medical term, medicine
il tempo, meteorologia	METEOR	the weather, meteorology
maschile o femminile, secondo il sesso	m/f	either masculine or feminine depending on sex
esercito, lingua militare	MIL	military matters
musica	MUS	music
sostantivo	n	noun
nautica	NAUT	sailing, navigation
numerale (aggettivo, sostantivo)	num	numeral adjective or noun
	o.s.	oneself
peggiorativo	peg, pej	derogatory, pejorative
fotografia	PHOT	photography
fisiologia	PHYSIOL	physiology
plurale	pl	plural
politica	POL	politics
participio passato	pp	past participle
preposizione	prep	preposition
psicologia, psichiatria	PSIC, PSYCH	psychology, psychiatry
tempo del passato	pt	past tense
sostantivo che non si usa al plurale	q	uncountable noun: not used in the plural
qualcosa	qc	
qualcuno	qn	
religione, liturgia	REL	religions, church service
sostantivo	s	noun
	sb	somebody
insegnamento, sistema scolastico e universitario	SCOL	education, schools and universities
singolare	sg	singular
soggetto (grammaticale)	sog	(grammatical) subject
	sth	something
congiuntivo	sub	subjunctive
soggetto (grammaticale)	subj	(grammatical) subject
termine tecnico, tecnologia	TECN, TECH	technical term, technology
telecomunicazioni	TEL	telecommunications
tipografia	TIP	typography, printing
televisione	TV	television
tipografia	TYP	typography, printing
inglese degli Stati Uniti	US	American English
vocale	V	vowel
verbo	vb	verb
verbo o gruppo verbale con funzione intransitiva	vi	verb or phrasal verb used intransitively
verbo riflessivo	vr	reflexive verb
verbo o gruppo verbale con funzione transitiva	vt	verb or phrasal verb used transitively
zoologia	ZOOL	zoology
marchio registrato	®	registered trademark
introduce un'equivalenza culturale	≈	introduces a cultural equivalent

TRASCRIZIONE FONETICA

CONSONANTI

CONSONANTS

NB. **p, b, t, d, k, g** sono seguiti
da un'aspirazione in inglese.

NB. **p, b, t, d, k, g** are not
aspirated in Italian.

*p*adre	p	*p*uppy
*b*am*b*ino	b	*b*aby
*t*u*tt*o	t	*t*en*t*
*d*a*d*o	d	*d*og ro*d*
cane *che*	k	*c*ork *k*iss *ch*ord
gola *ghiro*	g	*g*a*g* *gu*ess
*s*ano	s	*s*o ri*c*e ki*ss*
*s*vago e*s*ame	z	cou*s*in bu*zz*
*sc*ena	sh	*sh*eep *s*ugar
surmena*g*e	zh	plea*s*ure vi*s*ion
pe*c*e lan*c*iare	ch	*ch*ur*ch*
*gi*ro *gi*oco	j	*j*udge *g*eneral
a*f*a *f*aro	f	*f*arm hal*f*
*v*ero bra*v*o	v	*v*ery e*v*e
*th*riller	th	*th*in bo*th*
	th	*th*at o*th*er
*l*etto a*l*a	l	*l*ittle ba*ll*
*gl*i	lyi	
*r*ete a*r*co	r	*r*at b*r*at
*r*amo ma*d*re	m	*m*ove co*mb*
*n*o fu*m*ante	n	*n*o ra*n*
*gn*omo	ny	
Be*ring*	ng	si*ng*ing ba*nk*
*h*andicap	h	*h*at re*h*eat
bu*i*o p*i*acere	y	*y*et
*u*omo g*u*aio	w	*w*all a*w*ay

VARIE

MISCELLANEOUS

indica che la vocale precedente è una nasale, come in a*m*pere, bido*n*ville, lapi*n*	ṅ	shows that the preceding vowel is nasal, as in French sal*on*
segue la sillaba accentata	'	follows the stressed syllable
indica che due consonanti si pronunciano separatamente	·	shows where two consonants should be pronounced separately
indica l'allungamento della vocale cui è posposto	:	shows where a vowel should be lengthened

PHONETIC TRANSCRIPTION

VOCALI

NB. La messa in equivalenza di certi suoni indica solo una rassomiglianza approssimativa.

VOWELS

NB. The pairing of some vowel sounds only indicates approximate equivalence.

camping manager	a	add map laugh
mamma amore	à	
	â	palm father odd
stella edera	ā	ace rate gauge
	är	care air
epoca eccetto	e	set tent
vino idea	ē	heel bead
atelier	ə	darken above
ping-pong	i	hit pity
	ī	ice dime aisle
rosa occhio	o	
	ô	law dog order
ponte ognuno	ō	open so
utile zucca	o͞o	pool food
	o͝o	took full
piuccheperfetto	yo͞o	use few
montgomery	u	fun done up
peluche wurstel	ü	
	ûr	urn term
tailleur	o͞e	
föhn	œ	

DITTONGHI

DIPHTHONGS

	oi	oil boy
	ou	out now

ITALIAN PRONUNCIATION

VOWELS

Where the vowel ā or the vowel ō appears in a stressed syllable it can be either open [e], [o] or closed [ā], [ō]. As the open or closed pronunciation of these vowels is subject to regional variation, the distinction is of little importance to the user of this dictionary. Phonetic transcription for headwords containing these vowels will therefore only appear where other pronunciation difficulties are present.

CONSONANTS

c before "e" or "i" is pronounced *tch*.

ch is pronounced like the "k" in "kit".

g before "e" or "i" is pronounced like the "j" in "jet".

gh is pronounced like the "g" in "get".

gl before "e" or "i" is normally pronounced like the "lli" in "million", and in a few cases only like the "gl" in "glove".

gn is pronounced like the "ny" in "canyon".

sc before "e" or "i" is pronounced *sh*.

z is pronounced like the "ts" in "stetson", or like the "d's" in "bird's-eye".

Headwords containing the above consonants and consonantal groups have been given full phonetic transcription in this dictionary.

NB. All double written consonants in Italian are fully sounded: e.g. the *tt* in "tutto" is pronounced as in "ha*t* *t*rick".

ITALIAN VERBS

1 Gerundio *2* Participio passato *3* Presente *4* Imperfetto *5* Passato remoto *6* Futuro *7* Condizionale *8* Congiuntivo presente *9* Congiuntivo passato *10* Imperativo

accadere *like* **cadere**
accedere *like* **concedere**
accendere 2 acceso 5 accesi, accendesti
accludere *like* **alludere**
accogliere *like* **cogliere**
accondiscendere *like* **scendere**
accorgersi *like* **scorgere**
accorrere *like* **correre**
accrescere *like* **crescere**
addirsi *like* **dire**
addurre *like* **ridurre**
affiggere 2 affisso 5 affissi, affiggesti
affliggere 2 afflitto 5 afflissi, affliggesti
aggiungere *like* **giungere**
alludere 2 alluso 5 allusi, alludesti
ammettere *like* **mettere**
andare 3 vado, vai, va, andiamo, andate, vanno 6 andrò *etc* 8 vada *10* va'!, vada!, andate!, vadano!
annettere 2 annesso 5 annessi *or* annettei, annettesti
apparire 2 apparso 3 appaio, appari *o* apparisci, appare *o* apparisce, appaiono *o* appariscono 5 apparvi *o* apparsi, apparisti, apparve *o* apparì *o* apparse, apparvero *o* apparirono *o* apparsero 8 appaia *o* apparisca
appartenere *like* **tenere**
appendere 2 appeso 5 appesi, appendesti
apporre *like* **porre**
apprendere *like* **prendere**
aprire 2 aperto 3 apro 5 aprii *o* apersi, apristi 8 apra
ardere 2 arso 5 arsi, ardesti
ascendere *like* **scendere**
aspergere 2 asperso 5 aspersi, aspergesti
assalire *like* **salire**
assistere 2 assistito
assolvere 2 assolto 5 assolsi *o* assolvei *o* assolvetti, assolvesti
assumere 2 assunto 5 assunsi, assumesti
astenersi *like* **tenere**
attendere *like* **tendere**
attingere *like* **tingere**
AVERE 3 ho, hai, ha, abbiamo, avete, hanno 5 ebbi, avesti, ebbe, avemmo, aveste, ebbero 6 avrò *etc* 8 abbia *etc 10* abbi!, abbia!, abbiate!, abbiano!
avvedersi *like* **vedere**
avvenire *like* **venire**
avvincere *like* **vincere**
avvolgere *like* **volgere**
benedire *like* **dire**
bere *1* bevendo 2 bevuto 3 bevo *etc* 4 bevevo *etc* 5 bevvi *o* bevetti, bevesti 6

berrò *etc* 8 beva *etc* 9 bevessi *etc*
cadere 5 caddi, cadesti 6 cadrò *etc*
chiedere 2 chiesto 5 chiesi, chiedesti
chiudere 2 chiuso 5 chiusi, chiudesti
cingere 2 cinto 5 cinsi, cingesti
cogliere 2 colto 3 colgo, colgono 5 colsi, cogliesti 8 colga
coincidere 2 coinciso 5 coincisi, coincidesti
coinvolgere *like* **volgere**
commettere *like* **mettere**
commuovere *like* **muovere**
comparire *like* **apparire**
compiacere *like* **piacere**
compiangere *like* **piangere**
comporre *like* **porre**
comprendere *like* **prendere**
comprimere 2 compresso 5 compressi, comprimesti
compromettere *like* **mettere**
concedere 2 concesso *o* conceduto 5 concessi *o* concedei *o* concedetti, concedesti
concludere *like* **alludere**
concorrere *like* **correre**
condurre *like* **ridurre**
confondere *like* **fondere**
congiungere *like* **giungere**
connettere *like* **annettere**
conoscere 2 conosciuto 5 conobbi, conoscesti
consistere *like* **assistere**
contendere *like* **tendere**
contenere *like* **tenere**
contorcere *like* **torcere**
contraddire *like* **dire**
contraffare *like* **fare**
contrarre *like* **trarre**
convenire *like* **venire**
convincere *like* **vincere**
coprire *like* **aprire**
correggere *like* **reggere**
correre 2 corso 5 corsi, corresti
corrispondere *like* **rispondere**
corrompere *like* **rompere**
costringere *like* **stringere**
costruire 5 costrussi, costruisti
crescere 2 cresciuto 5 crebbi, crescesti
cuocere 2 cotto 3 cuocio, cociamo, cuociono 5 cossi, cocesti
dare 3 do, dai, dà, diamo, date, danno 5 diedi *o* detti, desti 6 darò *etc* 8 dia *etc* 9 dessi *etc 10* da'!, dai!, date!, diano!
decidere 2 deciso 5 decisi, decidesti
decrescere *like* **crescere**
dedurre *like* **ridurre**

deludere *like* alludere
deporre *like* porre
deprimere *like* comprimere
deridere *like* ridere
descrivere *like* scrivere
desumere *like* assumere
detergere *like* tergere
devolvere 2 devoluto
difendere 2 difeso 5 difesi, difendesti
diffondere *like* fondere
dipendere *like* appendere
dipingere *like* tingere
dire *1* dicendo 2 detto 3 dico, dici, dice, diciamo, dite, dicono 4 dicevo *etc* 5 dissi, dicesti 6 dirò *etc* 8 dica, diciamo, diciate, dicano 9 dicessi *etc* 10 di'!, dica!, dite!, dicano!
dirigere 2 diretto 5 diressi, dirigesti
discendere *like* scendere
dischiudere *like* chiudere
disciogliere *like* sciogliere
discorrere *like* correre
discutere 2 discusso 5 discussi, discutesti
disfare *like* fare
disilludere *like* alludere
disperdere *like* perdere
dispiacere *like* piacere
disporre *like* porre
dissolvere 2 dissolto *o* dissoluto 5 dissolsi *o* dissolvetti *o* dissolvei, dissolvesti
dissuadere *like* persuadere
distendere *like* tendere
distinguere 2 distinto 5 distinsi, distinguesti
distogliere *like* togliere
distrarre *like* trarre
distruggere *like* struggere
divenire *like* venire
dividere 2 diviso 5 divisi, dividesti
dolere 3 dolgo, duoli, duole, dolgono 5 dolsi, dolesti 6 dorrò *etc* 8 dolga
DORMIRE *1* GERUNDIO dormendo
2 PARTICIPIO PASSATO dormito
3 PRESENTE dormo, dormi, dorme, dormiamo, dormite, dormono
4 IMPERFETTO dormivo, dormivi, dormiva, dormivamo, dormivate, dormivano
5 PASSATO REMOTO dormii, dormisti, dormì, dormimmo, dormiste, dormirono
6 FUTURO dormirò, dormirai, dormirà, dormiremo, dormirete, dormiranno
7 CONDIZIONALE dormirei, dormiresti, dormirebbe, dormiremmo, dormireste, dormirebbero
8 CONGIUNTIVO PRESENTE dorma, dorma, dorma, dormiamo, dormiate, dormano
9 CONGIUNTIVO PASSATO dormissi, dormissi, dormisse, dormissimo, dormiste, dormissero
10 IMPERATIVO dormi!, dorma!, dormite!, dormano!

dovere 3 devo *o* debbo, devi, deve, dobbiamo, dovete, devono *o* debbono 6 dovrò *etc* 8 debba, dobbiamo, dobbiate, devano *o* debbano
eccellere 2 eccelso 5 eccelsi, eccellesti
eludere *like* alludere
emergere 2 emerso 5 emersi, emergesti
emettere *like* mettere
erigere *like* dirigere
escludere *like* alludere
esigere 2 esatto
esistere 2 esistito
espellere 2 espulso 5 espulsi, espellesti
esplodere 2 esploso 5 esplosi, esplodesti
esporre *like* porre
esprimere *like* comprimere
ESSERE 2 stato 3 sono, sei, è, siamo, siete, sono 4 ero, eri, era, eravamo, eravate, erano 5 fui, fosti, fu, fummo, foste, furono 6 sarò *etc* 8 sia *etc* 9 fossi, fossi, fosse, fossimo, foste, fossero 10 sii!, sia!, siate!, siano!
estendere *like* tendere
estinguere *like* distinguere
estrarre *like* trarre
evadere 2 evaso 5 evasi, evadesti
evolvere 2 evoluto
fare *1* facendo 2 fatto 3 faccio, fai, fa, facciamo, fate, fanno 4 facevo *etc* 5 feci, facesti 6 farò *etc* 8 faccia *etc* 9 facessi *etc* 10 fa'!, faccia!, fate!, facciano!
fingere *like* cingere
FINIRE *1* GERUNDIO finendo
2 PARTICIPIO PASSATO finito
3 PRESENTE finisco, finisci, finisce, finiamo, finite, finiscono
4 IMPERFETTO finivo, finivi, finiva, finivamo, finivate, finivano
5 PASSATO REMOTO finii, finisti, finì, finimmo, finiste, finirono
6 FUTURO finirò, finirai, finirà, finiremo, finirete, finiranno
7 CONDIZIONALE finirei, finiresti, finirebbe, finiremmo, finireste, finirebbero
8 CONGIUNTIVO PRESENTE finisca, finisca, finisca, finiamo, finiate, finiscano
9 CONGIUNTIVO PASSATO finissi, finissi, finisse, finissimo, finiste, finissero
10 IMPERATIVO finisci!, finisca!, finite!, finiscano!

flettere 2 flesso
fondere 2 fuso 5 fusi, fondesti
friggere 2 fritto 5 frissi, friggesti
fungere 2 funto 5 funsi, fungesti
giacere 3 giaccio, giaci, giace, giac-(c)iamo, giacete, giacciono 5 giacqui, giacesti 8 giaccia *etc* 10 giaci!, giaccia!, giac(c)iamo!, giacete!, giacciano!
giungere 2 giunto 5 giunsi, giungesti
godere 6 godrò *etc*
illudere *like* alludere

immergere *like* emergere
immettere *like* mettere
imporre *like* porre
imprimere *like* comprimere
incidere *like* decidere
includere *like* alludere
incorrere *like* correre
incutere *like* discutere
indulgere 2 indulto 5 indulsi, indulgesti
indurre *like* ridurre
inferire[1] 2 inferto 5 infersi, inferisti
inferire[2] 2 inferito 5 inferii, inferisti
infliggere *like* affliggere
infrangere 2 infranto 5 infransi, infrangesti
infondere *like* fondere
insistere *like* assistere
intendere *like* tendere
interdire *like* dire
interporre *like* porre
interrompere *like* rompere
intervenire *like* venire
intraprendere *like* prendere
introdurre *like* ridurre
invadere *like* evadere
irrompere *like* rompere
iscrivere *like* scrivere
istruire *like* costruire
ledere 2 leso 5 lesi, ledesti
leggere 2 letto 5 lessi, leggesti
maledire *like* dire
mantenere *like* tenere
mettere 2 messo 5 misi, mettesti
mordere 2 morso 5 morsi, mordesti
morire 2 morto 3 muoio, muori, muore, moriamo, morite, muoiono 6 morirò *o* morrò *etc* 8 muoia
mungere 2 munto 5 munsi, mungesti
muovere 2 mosso 5 mossi, movesti
nascere 2 nato 5 nacqui, nascesti
nascondere 2 nascosto 5 nascosi, nascondesti
nuocere 2 nuociuto 3 nuoccio, nuoci, nuoce, nociamo *o* nuociamo, nuocete, nuocciono 4 nuocevo *etc* 5 nocqui, nuocesti 6 nuocerò *etc* 7 nuoccia
occorrere *like* correre
offendere *like* difendere
offrire 2 offerto 3 offro 5 offersi *o* offrii, offristi 8 offra
omettere *like* mettere
opporre *like* porre
opprimere *like* comprimere
ottenere *like* tenere
parere 2 parso 3 paio, paiono 5 parvi *o* parsi, paresti 6 parrò *etc* 8 paia, paiamo, paiate, paiano
PARLARE *1* GERUNDIO parlando
2 PARTICIPIO PASSATO parlato
3 PRESENTE parlo, parli, parla, parliamo, parlate, parlano
4 IMPERFETTO parlavo, parlavi, parlava, parlavamo, parlavate, parlavano
5 PASSATO REMOTO parlai, parlasti, parlò, parlammo, parlaste, parlarono
6 FUTURO parlerò, parlerai, parlerà, parleremo, parlerete, parleranno
7 CONDIZIONALE parlerei, parleresti, parlerebbe, parleremmo, parlereste, parlerebbero
8 CONGIUNTIVO PRESENTE parli, parli, parli, parliamo, parliate, parlino
9 CONGIUNTIVO PASSATO parlassi, parlassi, parlasse, parlassimo, parlaste, parlassero
10 IMPERATIVO parla!, parli!, parlate!, parlino!
percorrere *like* correre
percuotere 2 percosso 5 percossi, percotesti
perdere 2 perso *o* perduto 5 persi *o* perdei *o* perdetti, perdesti
permettere *like* mettere
persuadere 2 persuaso 5 persuasi, persuadesti
pervenire *like* venire
piacere 2 piaciuto 3 piaccio, piacciamo, piacciono 5 piacqui, piacesti 8 piaccia *etc*
piangere 2 pianto 5 piansi, piangesti
piovere 5 piovve
porgere 2 porto 5 porsi, porgesti
porre *1* ponendo *2* posto *3* pongo, poni, pone, poniamo, ponete, pongono *4* ponevo *etc* 5 posi, ponesti 6 porrò *etc* 8 ponga, poniamo, poniate, pongano 9 ponessi *etc*
posporre *like* porre
possedere *like* sedere
potere *3* posso, puoi, può, possiamo, potete, possono 6 potrò *etc* 8 possa, possiamo, possiate, possano
prediligere 2 prediletto 5 predilessi, prediligesti
predire *like* dire
prefiggersi *like* affiggere
preludere *like* alludere
prendere 2 preso 5 presi, prendesti
preporre *like* porre
prescrivere *like* scrivere
presiedere *like* sedere
presumere *like* assumere
pretendere *like* tendere
prevalere *like* valere
prevedere *like* vedere
prevenire *like* venire
produrre *like* ridurre
proferire *like* inferire[2]
profondere *like* fondere
promettere *like* mettere
promuovere *like* muovere
proporre *like* porre
prorompere *like* rompere
proscrivere *like* scrivere

proteggere *2* protetto *5* protessi, proteggesti
provenire *like* **venire**
provvedere *like* **vedere**
pungere *2* punto *5* punsi, pungesti
racchiudere *like* **chiudere**
raccogliere *like* **cogliere**
radere *2* raso *5* rasi, radesti
raggiungere *like* **giungere**
rapprendere *like* **prendere**
ravvedersi *like* **vedere**
recidere *like* **decidere**
redigere *2* redatto
redimere *2* redento *5* redensi, redimesti
reggere *2* retto *5* ressi, reggesti
rendere *2* reso *5* resi, rendesti
reprimere *like* **comprimere**
rescindere *like* **scindere**
respingere *like* **spingere**
restringere *like* **stringere**
ricadere *like* **cadere**
richiedere *like* **chiedere**
riconoscere *like* **conoscere**
ricoprire *like* **coprire**
ricorrere *like* **correre**
ridere *2* riso *5* risi, ridesti
ridire *like* **dire**
ridurre *1* riducendo *2* ridotto *3* riduco *etc 4* riducevo *etc 5* ridussi, riducesti *6* ridurrò *etc 8* riduca *etc 9* riducessi *etc*
riempire *1* riempiendo *3* riempio, riempi, riempie, riempiono
rifare *like* **fare**
riflettere *2* riflettuto *o* riflesso
rifrangere *like* **infrangere**
rimanere *2* rimasto *3* rimango, rimangono *5* rimasi, rimanesti *6* rimarrò *etc 8* rimanga
rimettere *like* **mettere**
rimpiangere *like* **piangere**
rinchiudere *like* **chiudere**
rincrescere *like* **crescere**
rinvenire *like* **venire**
ripercuotere *like* **percuotere**
riporre *like* **porre**
riprendere *like* **prendere**
riprodurre *like* **ridurre**
riscuotere *like* **scuotere**
risolvere *like* **assolvere**
risorgere *like* **sorgere**
rispondere *2* risposto *5* risposi, rispondesti
ritenere *like* **tenere**
ritrarre *like* **trarre**
riuscire *like* **uscire**
rivedere *like* **vedere**
rivivere *like* **vivere**
rivolgere *like* **volgere**
rodere *2* roso *5* rosi, rodesti
rompere *2* rotto *5* ruppi, rompesti
salire *3* salgo, sali, salgono *8* salga
sapere *3* so, sai, sa, sappiamo, sapete,

sanno *5* seppi, sapesti *6* saprò *etc 8* sappia *etc 10* sappi!, sappia!, sappiate!, sappiano!
scadere *like* **cadere**
scegliere *2* scelto *3* scelgo, scegli, sceglie, scegliamo, scegliete, scelgono *5* scelsi, scegliesti *8* scelga, scegliamo, scegliate, scelgano *10* scegli!, scelga!, scegliamo!, scegliete!, scelgano!
scendere *2* sceso *5* scesi, scendesti
schiudere *like* **chiudere**
scindere *2* scisso *5* scissi, scindesti
sciogliere *2* sciolto *3* sciolgo, sciolgi, scioglie, sciogliamo, scegliete, sciolgono *5* sciolsi, sciogliesti *8* sciolga, sciogliamo, sciogliate, sciolgano *10* sciogli!, sciolga!, sciogliamo!, sciogliete!, sciolgano!
scommettere *like* **mettere**
scomparire *like* **apparire**
scomporre *like* **porre**
sconfiggere *2* sconfitto *5* sconfissi, sconfiggesti
sconvolgere *like* **volgere**
scoprire *like* **aprire**
scorgere *2* scorto *5* scorsi, scorgesti
scorrere *like* **correre**
scrivere *2* scritto *5* scrissi, scrivesti
scuotere *2* scosso *3* scuoto, scuoti, scuote, scotiamo, scotete, scuotono *5* scossi, scotesti *6* scoterò *etc 8* scuota, scotiamo, scotiate, scuotano *10* scuoti!, scuota!, scotiamo!, scotete!, scuotano!
sedere *3* siedo, siedi, siede, siedono *8* sieda
seppellire *2* sepolto
smettere *like* **mettere**
smuovere *like* **muovere**
socchiudere *like* **chiudere**
soccorrere *like* **correre**
soddisfare *like* **fare**
soffriggere *like* **friggere**
soffrire *2* sofferto *5* soffersi *o* soffrii, soffristi
soggiungere *like* **giungere**
solere *2* solito *3* soglio, suoli, suole, sogliamo, solete, sogliono *8* soglia, sogliamo, sogliate, sogliano
sommergere *like* **emergere**
sopprimere *like* **comprimere**
sorgere *2* sorto *3* sorsi, sorgesti
sorprendere *like* **prendere**
sorreggere *like* **reggere**
sorridere *like* **ridere**
sospendere *like* **appendere**
sospingere *like* **spingere**
sostenere *like* **tenere**
sottintendere *like* **tendere**
spandere *2* spanto
spargere *2* sparso *5* sparsi, spargesti
sparire *5* sparii *o* sparvi, sparisti
spegnere *2* spento *3* spengo, spengono *5*

spensi, spegnesti *8* spenga
spendere *2* speso *5* spesi, spendesti
spingere *2* spinto *5* spinsi, spingesti
sporgere *like* **porgere**
stare *2* stato *3* sto, stai, sta, stiamo, state, stanno *5* stetti, stesti *6* starò *etc 8* stia *etc 9* stessi *etc 10* sta'!, stia!, state!, stiano!
stendere *like* **tendere**
storcere *like* **torcere**
stringere *2* stretto *5* strinsi, stringesti
struggere *2* strutto *5* strussi, struggesti
succedere *like* **concedere**
supporre *like* **porre**
svenire *like* **venire**
svolgere *like* **volgere**
tacere *2* taciuto *3* taccio, tacciono *5* tacqui, tacesti *8* taccia
tendere *2* teso *5* tesi, tendesti *etc*
tenere *3* tengo, tieni, tiene, tengono *5* tenni, tenesti *6* terrò *etc 8* tenga
tingere *2* tinto *5* tinsi, tingesti
togliere *2* tolto *3* tolgo, togli, toglie, togliamo, togliete, tolgono *5* tolsi, togliesti *8* tolga, togliamo, togliate, tolgano *10* togli!, tolga!, togliamo!, togliete!, tolgano!
torcere *2* torto *5* torsi, torcesti
tradurre *like* **ridurre**
trafiggere *like* **sconfiggere**
transigere *like* **esigere**
trarre *1* traendo *2* tratto *3* traggo, trai, trae, traiamo, traete, traggono *4* traevo *etc 5* trassi, traesti *6* trarrò *etc 8* tragga *9* traessi *etc*
trascorrere *like* **correre**
trascrivere *like* **scrivere**
trasmettere *like* **mettere**
trasparire *like* **apparire**
trattenere *like* **tenere**

uccidere *2* ucciso *5* uccisi, uccidesti
udire *3* odo, odi, ode, odono *8* oda
ungere *2* unto *5* unsi, ungesti
uscire *3* esco, esci, esce, escono *8* esca
valere *2* valso *3* valgo, valgono *5* valsi, valesti *6* varrò *etc 8* valga
vedere *2* visto *o* veduto *5* vidi, vedesti *6* vedrò *etc*
VENDERE *1* GERUNDIO vendendo
  2 PARTICIPIO PASSATO venduto
  3 PRESENTE vendo, vendi, vende, vendiamo, vendete, vendono
  4 IMPERFETTO vendevo, vendevi, vendeva, vendevamo, vendevate, vendevano
  5 PASSATO REMOTO vendei *o* vendetti, vendesti, vendé *o* vendette, vendemmo, vendeste, venderono *o* vendettero
  6 FUTURO venderò, venderai, venderà, venderemo, venderete, venderanno
  7 CONDIZIONALE venderei, venderesti, venderebbe, venderemmo, vendereste, venderebbero
  8 CONGIUNTIVO PRESENTE venda, venda, venda, vendiamo, vendiate, vendano
  9 CONGIUNTIVO PASSATO vendessi, vendessi, vendesse, vendessimo, vendeste, vendessero
  10 IMPERATIVO vendi!, venda!, vendete!, vendano!
venire *2* venuto *3* vengo, vieni, viene, vengono *5* venni, venisti *6* verrò *etc 8* venga
vincere *2* vinto *5* vinsi, vincesti
vivere *2* vissuto *5* vissi, vivesti
volere *3* voglio, vuoi, vuole, vogliamo, volete, vogliono *5* volli, volesti *6* vorrò *etc 8* voglia *etc 10* vogli!, voglia!, vogliate!, vogliano!
volgere *2* volto *5* volsi, volgesti

VERBI INGLESI

present	pt	pp	present	pt	pp
arise (arising)	arose	arisen	eat	ate	eaten
awake (awaking)	awoke	awaked	fall	fell	fallen
be (am, is, are, being)	was, were	been	feed	fed	fed
			feel	felt	felt
			fight	fought	fought
			find	found	found
bear	bore	born(e)	flee	fled	fled
beat	beat	beaten	fling	flung	flung
become (becoming)	became	become	fly (flies)	flew	flown
befall	befell	befallen	forbid (forbidding)	forbade	forbidden
begin (beginning)	began	begun	forecast	forecast	forecast
behold	beheld	beheld	forego	forewent	foregone
bend	bent	bent	foresee	foresaw	foreseen
beseech	besought	besought	foretell	foretold	foretold
beset (besetting)	beset	beset	forget (forgetting)	forgot	forgotten
bet (betting)	bet (*also* betted)	bet (*also* betted)	forgive (forgiving)	forgave	forgiven
bid (bidding)	bid (*also* bade)	bid (*also* bidden)	forsake (forsaking)	forsook	forsaken
bind	bound	bound	freeze (freezing)	froze	frozen
bite (biting)	bit	bitten	get (getting)	got	got, (*US*) gotten
bleed	bled	bled			
blow	blew	blown	give (giving)	gave	given
break	broke	broken	go (goes)	went	gone
breed	bred	bred	grind	ground	ground
bring	brought	brought	grow	grew	grown
build	built	built	hang	hung (*also* hanged)	hung (*also* hanged)
burn	burned (*also* burnt)	burned (*also* burnt)	have (has; having)	had	had
burst	burst	burst	hear	heard	heard
buy	bought	bought	hide (hiding)	hid	hidden
can	could	(been able)	hit (hitting)	hit	hit
cast	cast	cast	hold	held	held
catch	caught	caught	hurt	hurt	hurt
choose (choosing)	chose	chosen	keep	kept	kept
cling	clung	clung	kneel	knelt (*also* kneeled)	knelt (*also* kneeled)
come (coming)	came	come	know	knew	known
cost	cost	cost	lay	laid	laid
creep	crept	crept	lead	led	led
cut (cutting)	cut	cut	lean	leaned (*also* leant)	leaned (*also* leant)
deal	dealt	dealt	leap	leaped (*also* leapt)	leaped (*also* leapt)
dig (digging)	dug	dug			
do (3rd person: he/ she/it/does)	did	done	learn	learned (*also* learnt)	learned (*also* learnt)
draw	drew	drawn	leave (leaving)	left	left
dream	dreamed (*also* dreamt)	dreamed *also* dreamt)	lend	lent	lent
			let (letting)	let	let
drink	drank	drunk	lie (lying)	lay	lain
drive (driving)	drove	driven	light	lighted (*also* lit)	lighted (*also* lit)
dwell	dwelt	dwelt	lose (losing)	lost	lost

present	pt	pp	present	pt	pp
make (making)	made	made	**spell**	spelled (*also* spelt)	spelled (*also* spelt)
may	might	—	**spend**	spent	spent
mean	meant	meant	**spill**	spilled (*also* spilt)	spilled (*also* spilt)
meet	met	met			
mistake (mistaking)	mistook	mistaken	**spin** (spinning)	spun	spun
mow	mowed	mowed (*also* mown)	**spit** (spitting)	spat	spat
			split (splitting)	split	split
must	(had to)	(had to)			
pay	paid	paid	**spoil**	spoiled (*also* spoilt)	spoiled (*also* spoilt)
put (putting)	put	put			
quit (quitting)	quit (*also* quitted)	quit (*also* quitted)	**spread**	spread	spread
			spring	sprang	sprung
read	read	read	**stand**	stood	stood
rend	rent	rent	**steal**	stole	stolen
rid (ridding)	rid	rid	**stick**	stuck	stuck
ride (riding)	rode	ridden	**sting**	stung	stung
ring	rang	rung	**stink**	stank	stunk
rise (rising)	rose	risen	**stride** (striding)	strode	stridden
run (running)	ran	run			
saw	sawed	sawn	**strike** (striking)	struck	struck (*also* stricken)
say	said	said			
see	saw	seen	**strive** (striving)	strove	striven
seek	sought	sought	**swear**	swore	sworn
sell	sold	sold	**sweep**	swept	swept
send	sent	sent	**swell**	swelled	swelled (*also* swollen)
set (setting)	set	set			
shake (shaking)	shook	shaken	**swim** (swimming)	swam	swum
shall	should	—	**swing**	swung	swung
shear	sheared	sheared (*also* shorn)	**take** (taking)	took	taken
			teach	taught	taught
shed (shedding)	shed	shed	**tear**	tore	torn
shine (shining)	shone	shone	**tell**	told	told
			think	thought	thought
shoot	shot	shot	**throw**	threw	thrown
show	showed	shown	**thrust**	thrust	thrust
shrink	shrank	shrunk	**tread**	trod	trodden
shut (shutting)	shut	shut	**wake** (waking)	woke (*also* waked)	waked (*also* woken)
sing	sang	sung	**waylay**	waylaid	waylaid
sink	sank	sunk	**wear**	wore	worn
sit (sitting)	sat	sat	**weave** (weaving)	wove (*also* weaved)	woven (*also* weaved)
slay	slew	slain			
sleep	slept	slept	**wed** (wedding)	wedded	wedded (*also* wed)
slide (sliding)	slid	slid			
sling	slung	slung	**weep**	wept	wept
slit (slitting)	slit	slit	**win** (winning)	won	won
smell	smelled (*Brit* smelt)	smelled (*Brit* smelt)	**wind**	wound	wound
			withdraw	withdrew	withdrawn
sow	sowed	sown (*also* sowed)	**withhold**	withheld	withheld
			withstand	withstood	withstood
speak	spoke	spoken	**wring**	wrung	wrung
speed	sped (*also* speeded)	sped (*also* speeded)	**write** (writing)	wrote	written

I NUMERI

NUMBERS

uno(a)	1	one
due	2	two
tre	3	three
quattro	4	four
cinque	5	five
sei	6	six
sette	7	seven
otto	8	eight
nove	9	nine
dieci	10	ten
undici	11	eleven
dodici	12	twelve
tredici	13	thirteen
quattordici	14	fourteen
quindici	15	fifteen
sedici	16	sixteen
diciassette	17	seventeen
diciotto	18	eighteen
diciannove	19	nineteen
venti	20	twenty
ventuno	21	twenty-one
ventidue	22	twenty-two
ventitré	23	twenty-three
ventotto	28	twenty-eight
trenta	30	thirty
quaranta	40	forty
cinquanta	50	fifty
sessanta	60	sixty
settanta	70	seventy
ottanta	80	eighty
novanta	90	ninety
cento	100	a hundred, one hundred
cento uno	101	a hundred and one
duecento	200	two hundred
mille	1 000	a thousand, one thousand
milleduecentodue	1 202	one thousand two hundred and two
cinquemila	5 000	five thousand
un milione	1 000 000	a million, one million

I NUMERI

NUMBERS

primo(a), 1°	first, 1st
secondo(a), 2°	second, 2nd
terzo(a), 3°	third, 3rd
quarto(a)	fourth, 4th
quinto(a)	fifth, 5th
sesto(a)	sixth, 6th
settimo(a)	seventh
ottavo(a)	eighth
nono(a)	ninth
decimo(a)	tenth
undicesimo(a)	eleventh
dodicesimo(a)	twelfth
tredicesimo(a)	thirteenth
quattordicesimo(a)	fourteenth
quindicesimo(a)	fifteenth
sedicesimo(a)	sixteenth
diciassettesimo(a)	seventeenth
diciottesimo(a)	eighteenth
diciannovesimo(a)	nineteenth
ventesimo(a)	twentieth
ventunesimo(a)	twenty-first
ventiduesimo(a)	twenty-second
ventitreesimo(a)	twenty-third
ventottesimo(a)	twenty-eighth
trentesimo(a)	thirtieth
centesimo(a)	hundredth
centunesimo(a)	hundred-and-first
millesimo(a)	thousandth
milionesimo(a)	millionth

ITALIANO-INGLESE
ITALIAN-ENGLISH

A

A, a |à| *sf o m inv* (*lettera*) A, a; **A come Ancona** ≈ A for Able; **dalla a alla z** from a to z.

A *abbr* (= *altezza*) h; (= *area*) A; (= *autostrada*) ≈ I (*US*), M (*Brit*).

a *prep* (*a + il* = **al**, *a + lo* = **allo**, *a + l'* = **all'**, *a + la* = **alla**, *a + i* = **ai**, *a + gli* = **agli**, *a + le* = **alle**) (*stato in luogo, tempo*) at; in; (*moto a luogo, complemento di termine*) to; (*mezzo*) with, by; (*scopo, fine*) for, to; **essere ~ Roma/alla posta/~ casa** to be in Rome/at the post office/at home; **~ 18 anni** at 18 (years of age); **~ mezzanotte/Natale** at midnight/Christmas; **alle 3** at 3 (o'clock); **~ maggio** in May; **~ giorni** in a few days; **~ piedi/cavallo** on foot/horseback; **pagato ~ ore/giornata** paid by the hour/day; **una barca ~ motore** a motorboat; **alla milanese** the Milanese way, in the Milanese fashion; **~ 500 lire il chilo** 500 lire a *o* per kilo; **viaggiare ~ 100 chilometri l'ora** to travel at 100 kilometres an *o* per hour; **~ 10 chilometri da Firenze** 10 kilometres from Florence; **restare ~ cena** to stay for dinner; **~ domani!** see you tomorrow!; **~ uno ~ uno** one by one.

AA *sigla* = Alto Adige.

AAS *sigla f* = **Azienda Autonoma di Soggiorno**.

AA.VV. *abbr* = autori vari.

aba'te *sm* abbot.

abbacchia'to, a |àbbàkkyà'tō| *ag* downhearted, in low spirits.

abbacina're |àbbàchčnà'rä| *vt* to dazzle.

abbaglian'te |àbbàlyàn'tä| *ag* dazzling; **~i** *smpl* (*AUT*): **accendere gli ~i** to put one's headlights on high (*US*) *o* full (*Brit*) beam.

abbaglia're |àbbàlyà'rä| *vt* to dazzle; (*illudere*) to delude.

abba'glio |àbbàl'yō| *sm* blunder; **prendere un ~** to blunder, make a blunder.

abbaia're *vi* to bark.

abbai'no *sm* dormer window; (*soffitta*) attic room.

abbandona're *vt* to leave, abandon, desert; (*trascurare*) to neglect; (*rinunciare a*) to abandon, give up; **~rsi** *vr* to let o.s. go; **~ il campo** (*MIL*) to retreat; **~ la presa** to let go; **~rsi a** (*ricordi, vizio*) to give o.s. up to.

abbandona'to, a *ag* (*casa*) deserted; (*miniera*) disused; (*trascurato: terreno, podere*) neglected; (*bambino*) abandoned.

abbando'no *sm* abandoning; neglecting; (*stato*) abandonment; neglect; (*SPORT*) withdrawal; (*fig*) abandon; **in ~** (*edificio, giardino*) neglected.

abbarbicar'si *vr*: **~ (a)** (*anche fig*) to cling (to).

abbassamen'to *sm* lowering; (*di pressione, livello dell'acqua*) fall; (*di prezzi*) reduction; **~ di temperatura** drop in temperature.

abbassa're *vt* to lower; (*radio*) to turn down; **~rsi** *vr* (*chinarsi*) to stoop; (*livello, sole*) to go down; (*fig: umiliarsi*) to demean o.s.; **~ i fari** (*AUT*) to dim (*US*) *o* dip (*Brit*) one's lights; **~ le armi** (*MIL*) to lay down one's arms.

abbas'so *escl*: **~ il re!** down with the king!

abbastan'za |àbbàstàn'tsä| *av* (*a sufficienza*) enough; (*alquanto*) quite, rather, fairly; **non è ~ furbo** he's not shrewd enough; **un vino ~ dolce** quite a sweet wine, a fairly sweet wine; **averne ~ di qn/qc** to have had enough of sb/sth.

abbat'tere *vt* (*muro, casa, ostacolo*) to knock down; (*albero*) to fell; (*: sog: vento*) to bring down; (*bestie da macello*) to slaughter; (*cane, cavallo*) to destroy, put down; (*selvaggina, aereo*) to shoot down; (*fig: sog: malattia, disgrazia*) to lay low; **~rsi** *vr* (*avvilirsi*) to lose heart; **~rsi a terra** *o* **al suolo** to fall to the ground; **~rsi su** (*sog: maltempo*) to beat down on; (*: disgrazia*) to hit, strike.

abbattimen'to *sm* knocking down; felling; (*di casa*) demolition; (*prostrazione: fisica*) exhaustion; (*: morale*) despondency.

abbattu'to, a *ag* despondent, depressed.

abbazi'a |àbbàttsč'à| *sf* abbey.

abbeceda'rio |àbbàchàdà'ryō| *sm* primer.

abbellimen'to *sm* embellishment.

abbelli're *vt* to make beautiful; (*ornare*) to embellish.

abbevera're *vt* to water; **~rsi** *vr* to drink.

abbeverato'io *sm* drinking trough.

ab'bi, ab'bia, abbia'mo, ab'biano, abbia'te *vb vedi* **avere**.

abbicci |àbbčchč'| *sm inv* alphabet; (*sillabario*) primer; (*fig*) basics *pl*.

abbien'te *ag* well-to-do, well-off.

abbiet'to, a *ag* = **abietto**.

abbigliamen'to |àbbčlyàmàn'tō| *sm* dress *q*;

(*indumenti*) clothes *pl*; (*industria*) clothing industry.

abbiglia're [àbbēlyà'rā] *vt* to dress up.

abbinamen'to *sm* combination; linking; matching.

abbina're *vt*: ~ (**con** *o* **a**) (*gen*) to combine (with); (*nomi*) to link (with); ~ **qc a qc** (*colori etc*) to match sth with sth.

abbindola're *vt* (*fig*) to cheat, trick.

abboccamen'to *sm* (*colloquio*) talks *pl*, meeting; (*TECN: di tubi*) connection.

abbocca're *vt* (*tubi, canali*) to connect, join up ♦ *vi* (*pesce*) to bite; (*tubi*) to join; ~ (**all'amo**) (*fig*) to swallow the bait.

abbocca'to, a *ag* (*vino*) sweetish.

abbonamen'to *sm* subscription; (*alle ferrovie etc*) commutation (*US*) *o* season (*Brit*) ticket; **in** ~ for subscribers only; for commutation ticket holders only; **fare l'**~ (**a**) to take out a subscription (to); to buy a commutation *o* season ticket (for).

abbona're *vt* (*cifra*) to deduct; (*fig: perdonare*) to forgive; ~**rsi** *vr*: ~**rsi a un giornale** to take out a subscription to a newspaper; ~**rsi al teatro/alle ferrovie** to buy a commutation (*US*) *o* season (*Brit*) ticket for the theater/the train.

abbona'to, a *sm/f* subscriber; commutation- *o* season-ticket holder; **elenco degli** ~**i** telephone directory.

abbondan'te *ag* abundant, plentiful; (*giacca*) roomy.

abbondan'za [àbbōndàn'tsà] *sf* abundance; plenty.

abbonda're *vi* to abound, be plentiful; ~ **in** *o* **di** to be full of, abound in.

abborda'bile *ag* (*persona*) approachable; (*prezzo*) reasonable.

abborda're *vt* (*nave*) to board; (*persona*) to approach; (*argomento*) to tackle; ~ **una curva** to take a curve.

abbottona're *vt* to button up, do up; ~**rsi** *vr* to button (up).

abbottona'to, a *ag* (*camicia etc*) buttoned (up); (*fig*) reserved.

abbottonatu'ra *sf* buttons *pl*; **questo cappotto ha l'**~ **da uomo/da donna** this coat buttons on the man's/woman's side.

abbozza're [àbbōttsà'rā] *vt* to sketch, outline; (*SCULTURA*) to rough-hew; ~ **un sorriso** to give a hint of a smile.

abboz'zo [àbbot'tsō] *sm* sketch, outline; (*DIR*) draft.

abbraccia're [àbbràchà'rā] *vt* to embrace; (*persona*) to hug, embrace; (*professione*) to take up; (*contenere*) to include; ~**rsi** *vr* to hug *o* embrace (one another).

abbrac'cio [àbbràch'chō] *sm* hug, embrace.

abbrevia're *vt* to shorten; (*parola*) to abbreviate, shorten.

abbreviazio'ne [àbbrāvyàttsyō'nā] *sf* abbreviation.

abbronzan'te [àbbrōndzàn'tā] *ag* tanning, sun *cpd*.

abbronza're [àbbrōndzà'rā] *vt* (*pelle*) to tan; (*metalli*) to bronze; ~**rsi** *vr* to tan, get a tan.

abbronza'to, a [àbbrōndzà'tō] *ag* (*sun*)tanned.

abbronzatu'ra [àbbrōndzàtōō'rà] *sf* tan, suntan.

abbrustoli're *vt* (*pane*) to toast; (*caffè*) to roast.

abbrutimen'to *sm* exhaustion; degradation.

abbruti're *vt* (*snervare, stancare*) to exhaust; (*degradare*) to degrade; **essere abbrutito dall'alcool** to be ruined by drink.

abbuffar'si *vr* (*fam*): ~ (**di qc**) to stuff o.s. (with sth).

abbuffa'ta *sf* (*fam*) nosh-up; **farsi un'**~ to stuff o.s.

abbuona're *vt* = **abbonare**.

abbuo'no *sm* (*COMM*) allowance, discount; (*SPORT*) handicap.

abdica're *vi* to abdicate; ~ **a** to give up, renounce.

abdicazio'ne [àbdēkàttsyō'nā] *sf* abdication.

aberrazio'ne [àbārràttsyō'nā] *sf* aberration.

abeta'ia *sf* fir wood.

abe'te *sm* fir (tree); ~ **bianco** silver fir; ~ **rosso** spruce.

abiet'to, a *ag* despicable, abject.

a'bile *ag* (*idoneo*): ~ (**a qc/a fare qc**) fit (for sth/to do sth); (*capace*) able; (*astuto*) clever; (*accorto*) skilful; ~ **al servizio militare** fit for military service.

abilità *sf inv* ability; cleverness; skill.

abilitan'te *ag* qualifying; **corsi** ~**i** (*INS*) ≈ teacher training *sg*.

abilita're *vt*: ~ **qn a qc/a fare qc** to qualify sb for sth/to do sth; **è stato abilitato all'insegnamento** he has qualified to teach.

abilita'to, a *ag* qualified; (*TEL*) which has an outside line.

abilitazio'ne [àbēlētàttsyō'nā] *sf* qualification.

abissa'le *ag* abysmal; (*fig: senza limiti*) profound.

abissi'no, a *ag, sm/f* Abyssinian.

abis'so *sm* abyss, gulf.

abitabilità *sf*: **licenza di** ~ *document stating that a property is fit for habitation*.

abita'colo *sm* (*AER*) cockpit; (*AUT*) inside; (*di camion*) (driver's) cab.

abitan'te *sm/f* inhabitant.

abita're *vt* to live in, dwell in ♦ *vi*: ~ **in campagna/a Roma** to live in the country/in Rome.

abita'to, a *ag* inhabited; lived in ♦ *sm* (*anche*: **centro** ~) built-up area.

abitazio'ne [àbētàttsyō'nā] *sf* residence; house.

a'bito *sm* dress *q*; (*da uomo*) suit; (*da donna*) dress; (*abitudine, disposizione, REL*) habit;

~i *smpl* (*vestiti*) clothes; **in** ~ **da cerimonia** in formal dress; **in** ~ **da sera** in evening dress; **"è gradito l'~ scuro"** "dress formal"; ~ **mentale** way of thinking.

abitua'le *ag* usual, habitual; (*cliente*) regular.

abitualmen'te *av* usually, normally.

abitua're *vt*: ~ **qn a** to get sb used *o* accustomed to; ~**rsi a** to get used to, accustom o.s. to.

abitudina'rio, a *ag* of fixed habits ♦ *sm/f* creature of habit.

abitu'dine *sf* habit; **aver l'~ di fare qc** to be in the habit of doing sth; **d'~** usually; **per** ~ from *o* out of habit.

abiura're *vt* to renounce.

abnegazio'ne [àbnāgàttsyō'nā] *sf* (self-) abnegation, self-denial.

abnor'me *ag* (*enorme*) extraordinary; (*anormale*) abnormal.

aboli're *vt* to abolish; (*DIR*) to repeal.

abolizio'ne [àbōlēttsyō'nā] *sf* abolition; repeal.

abomine'vole *ag* abominable.

abori'geno [àbōrē'jānō] *sm* aborigine.

aborri're *vt* to abhor, detest.

aborti're *vi* (*MED: accidentalmente*) to miscarry, have a miscarriage; (*: deliberatamente*) to have an abortion; (*fig*) to miscarry, fail.

abor'to *sm* miscarriage; abortion; (*fig*) freak; ~ **clandestino** backstreet abortion.

abrasio'ne *sf* abrasion.

abrasi'vo, a *ag*, *sm* abrasive.

abroga're *vt* to repeal, abrogate.

abrogazio'ne [àbrōgàttsyō'nā] *sf* repeal.

abruzze'se [àbrōōttsā'sā] *ag* of (*o* from) the Abruzzi.

Abruz'zo [àbrōōt'tsō] *sm*: **l'~, gli** ~**i** the Abruzzi.

ab'side *sf* apse.

A'bu Dha'bi *sf* Abu Dhabi.

abu'lico, a, ci, che *ag* lacking in willpower.

abusa're *vi*: ~ **di** to abuse, misuse; (*approfittare, violare*) to take advantage of; ~ **dell'alcool/dei cibi** to drink/eat to excess.

abusivi'smo *sm* (*anche*: ~ **edilizio**) unlawful building.

abusi'vo, a *ag* unauthorized, unlawful; (**occupante**) ~ (*di una casa*) squatter.

abu'so *sm* abuse, misuse; excessive use; **fare** ~ **di** (*stupefacenti, medicine*) to abuse.

a.C. *abbr av* (= *avanti Cristo*) BC.

ac'ca *sf* letter H; **non capire un'**~ not to understand a thing.

accad'de *vb vedi* **accadere**.

accade'mia *sf* (*società*) learned society; (*scuola: d'arte, militare*) academy; ~ **di Belle Arti** art school.

accade'mico, a, ci, che *ag* academic ♦ *sm* academician.

accade're *vi* to happen, occur.

accadu'to *sm* event; **raccontare l'**~ to describe what has happened.

accalappiaca'ni *sm inv* dogcatcher.

accalappia're *vt* to catch; (*fig*) to trick, dupe.

accalca're *vt*, ~**rsi** *vr* to crowd, throng.

accaldar'si *vr* to grow hot.

accalorar'si *vr* (*fig*) to get excited.

accampamen'to *sm* camp.

accampa're *vt* to encamp; (*fig*) to put forward, advance; ~**rsi** *vr* to camp; ~ **scuse** to make excuses.

accanimen'to *sm* fury; (*tenacia*) tenacity, perseverance.

accanir'si *vr* (*infierire*) to rage; (*ostinarsi*) to persist.

accanitamen'te *av* fiercely; assiduously.

accani'to, a *ag* (*odio, gelosia*) fierce, bitter; (*lavoratore*) assiduous; (*giocatore*) inveterate; (*tifoso, sostenitore*) keen; **fumatore** ~ chain smoker.

accan'to *av* near, nearby; ~ **a** *prep* near, beside, close to; **la casa** ~ the house next door.

accantona're *vt* (*problema*) to shelve; (*somma*) to set aside.

accaparramen'to *sm* (*COMM*) cornering, buying up.

accaparra're *vt* (*COMM*) to corner, buy up; (*versare una caparra*) to pay a deposit on; ~**rsi** *vr*: ~**rsi qc** (*fig: simpatia, voti*) to secure sth (for o.s.).

accapigliar'si [àkkàpēlyàr'sē] *vr* to come to blows; (*fig*) to quarrel.

accappato'io *sm* bathrobe.

accappona're *vi*: **far** ~ **la pelle a qn** (*fig*) to bring sb out in goose pimples.

accarezza're [àkkàrāttsà'rā] *vt* to caress, stroke, fondle; (*fig*) to toy with.

accartoccia're [àkkàrtōchá'rā] *vt* (*carta*) to roll up, screw up; ~**rsi** *vr* (*foglie*) to curl up.

accasar'si *vr* to set up house; to get married.

accasciar'si [àkkàshàr'sē] *vr* to collapse; (*fig*) to lose heart.

accatasta're *vt* to stack, pile.

accattonag'gio [àkkàttōnàd'jō] *sm* begging.

accatto'ne, a *sm/f* beggar.

accavalla're *vt* (*gambe*) to cross; ~**rsi** *vr* (*sovrapporsi*) to overlap; (*addensarsi*) to gather.

acceca're [àchākà'rā] *vt* to blind ♦ *vi* to go blind.

acce'dere [àche'dārā] *vi*: ~ **a** to enter; (*richiesta*) to grant, accede to; (*fonte*) to gain access to.

accelera're [àchālārà'rā] *vt* to speed up ♦ *vi* (*AUT*) to accelerate; ~ **il passo** to quicken one's pace.

accelera'to, a [àchālàrà'tō] *ag* quick, rapid ♦ *sm* (*FERR*) local train, stopping train.

accelerato're [àchālàràtō'rā] *sm* (*AUT*) accelerator.

accelerazio'ne [àchālàrȧttsyō'nä] *sf* acceleration.

accen'dere [àchen'därä] *vt* (*fuoco, sigaretta*) to light; (*luce, televisione*) to put o switch o turn on; (*AUT: motore*) to switch on; (*COMM: conto*) to open; (: *debito*) to contract; (: *ipoteca*) to raise; (*fig: suscitare*) to inflame, stir up; **~rsi** *vr* (*luce*) to come o go on; (*legna*) to catch fire, ignite; (*fig: lotta, conflitto*) to break out.

accendi'no [àchāndē'nō], **accendisi'garo** [àchāndēsē'gàrō] *sm* (cigarette) lighter.

accenna're [àchānnà'rä] *vt* to indicate, point out; (*MUS*) to pick out the notes of; to hum ♦ *vi*: **~ a** (*fig: alludere a*) to hint at; (: *far atto di*) to make as if; **~ un saluto** (*con la mano*) to make as if to wave; (*col capo*) to half nod; **~ un sorriso** to half smile; **accenna a piovere** it looks as if it's going to rain.

accen'no [àchān'nō] *sm* (*cenno*) sign; nod; (*allusione*) hint.

accensio'ne [àchānsyō'nä] *sf* (*vedi accendere*) lighting; switching on; opening; (*AUT*) ignition.

accenta're [àchāntà'rä] *vt* (*parlando*) to stress; (*scrivendo*) to accent.

accentazio'ne [àchāntàttsyō'nä] *sf* accentuation; stressing.

accen'to [àchen'tō] *sm* accent; (*FONETICA, fig*) stress; (*inflessione*) tone (of voice).

accentramen'to [àchāntràmàn'tō] *sm* centralization.

accentra're [àchāntrà'rä] *vt* to centralize.

accentrato're, tri'ce [àchāntrátō'rä] *ag* (*persona*) unwilling to delegate; **politica ~trice** policy of centralization.

accentua're [àchāntōōà'rä] *vt* to stress, emphasize; **~rsi** *vr* to become more noticeable.

accerchia're [àchārkyà'rä] *vt* to surround, encircle.

accertamen'to [àchārtàmàn'tō] *sm* check; assessment.

accerta're [àchārtà'rä] *vt* to ascertain; (*verificare*) to check; (*reddito*) to assess; **~rsi** *vr*: **~rsi (di qc/che)** to make sure (of sth/that).

acce'so, a [àchā'sō] *pp di* **accendere** ♦ *ag* lit; on; open; (*colore*) bright; **~ di** (*ira, entusiasmo etc*) burning with.

accessi'bile [àchāssē'bēlä] *ag* (*luogo*) accessible; (*persona*) approachable; (*prezzo*) reasonable; (*idea*): **~ a qn** within the reach of sb.

acces'so [àches'sō] *sm* (*anche INFORM*) access; (*MED*) attack, fit; (*impulso violento*) fit, outburst; **programmi dell'~** (*TV*) educational programmes; **tempo di ~** (*INFORM*) access time; **~ casuale/seriale/sequenziale** (*INFORM*) random/serial/sequential access.

accessoria'to, a [àchàssōryà'tō] *ag* with accessories.

accesso'rio, a [àchàsso'ryō] *ag* secondary, of secondary importance; **~i** *smpl* accessories.

accet'ta [àchāt'tä] *sf* hatchet.

accetta'bile [àchättà'bēlä] *ag* acceptable.

accetta're [àchättà'rä] *vt* to accept; **~ di fare qc** to agree to do sth.

accettazio'ne [àchāttàttsyō'nä] *sf* acceptance; (*locale di servizio pubblico*) reception; **~ bagagli** (*AER*) check-in (desk); **~ con riserva** qualified acceptance.

accet'to, a [àchet'tō] *ag* (*persona*) welcome; **(ben) ~ a tutti** well-liked by everybody.

accezio'ne [àchāttsyō'nä] *sf* meaning.

acchiappa're [àkkyàppà'rä] *vt* to catch; (*afferrare*) to seize.

acchi'to [àkkē'tō] *sm*: **a primo ~** at first sight.

acciacca'to, a [àchàkkà'tō] *ag* (*persona*) full of aches and pains; (*abito*) crushed.

acciac'co, chi [àchàk'kō] *sm* ailment; **~chi** *smpl* aches and pains.

acciaieri'a [àchàyàrē'à] *sf* steelworks *sg*.

accia'io [àchà'yō] *sm* steel; **~ inossidabile** stainless steel.

accidenta'le [àchēdàntà'lä] *ag* accidental.

accidentalmen'te [àchēdàntàlmàn'tä] *av* (*per caso*) by chance; (*non deliberatamente*) accidentally, by accident.

accidenta'to, a [àchēdàntà'tō] *ag* (*terreno etc*) uneven.

acciden'te [àchēden'tä] *sm* (*caso imprevisto*) accident; (*disgrazia*) mishap; **~i!** (*fam: per rabbia*) damn (it)!; (: *per meraviglia*) good heavens!; **~i a lui!** damn him!; **non vale un ~** it's not worth a damn; **non capisco un ~** it's as clear as mud to me; **mandare un ~ a qn** to curse sb.

acci'dia [àchē'dyà] *sf* (*REL*) sloth.

acciglia'to, a [àchēlyà'tō] *ag* frowning.

accin'gersi [àchēn'jàrsē] *vr*: **~ a fare** to be about to do.

acciottola'to [àchōttōlà'tō] *sm* cobbles *pl*.

acciuffa're [àchōōffà'rä] *vt* to seize, catch.

acciu'ga, ghe [àchōō'gà] *sf* anchovy; **magro come un'~** as thin as a rake.

acclama're *vt* (*applaudire*) to applaud; (*eleggere*) to acclaim.

acclamazio'ne [àkklàmàttsyō'nä] *sf* applause; acclamation.

acclimata're *vt* to acclimatize; **~rsi** *vr* to become acclimatized.

acclimatazio'ne [àkklēmàtàttsyō'nä] *sf* acclimatization.

acclu'dere *vt* to enclose.

acclu'so, a *pp di* **accludere** ♦ *ag* enclosed.

accoccolar'si *vr* to crouch.

accodar'si *vr* to follow, tag on (behind).

accoglien'te [àkkōlyen'tä] *ag* welcoming,

friendly.

accoglien'za |àkkōlyen'tsà| *sf* reception; welcome; **fare una buona ~ a qn** to welcome sb.

acco'gliere |àkkol'yārā| *vt* (*ricevere*) to receive; (*dare il benvenuto*) to welcome; (*approvare*) to agree to, accept; (*contenere*) to hold, accommodate.

accol'go *etc vb vedi* **accogliere.**

accolla're *vt* (*fig*): **~ qc a qn** to force sth on sb; **~rsi** *vr*: **~rsi qc** to take sth upon o.s., shoulder sth.

accolla'to, a *ag* (*vestito*) high-necked.

accol'si *etc vb vedi* **accogliere.**

accoltella're *vt* to knife, stab.

accol'to, a *pp di* **accogliere.**

accomandi'ta *sf* (*DIR*) limited partnership.

accomiata're *vt* to dismiss; **~rsi** *vr*: **~rsi (da)** to take one's leave (of).

accomodamen'to *sm* agreement, settlement.

accomodan'te *ag* accommodating.

accomoda're *vt* (*aggiustare*) to repair, mend; (*riordinare*) to tidy; (*sistemare: questione, lite*) to settle; **~rsi** *vr* (*sedersi*) to sit down; (*fig: risolversi: situazione*) to work out; **si accomodi!** (*venga avanti*) come in!; (*si sieda*) take a seat!

accompagnamen'to |àkkōmpànyàmān'tō| *sm* (*MUS*) accompaniment; (*COMM*): **lettera di ~** accompanying letter.

accompagna're |àkkōmpànyà'rā| *vt* to accompany, come *o* go with; (*MUS*) to accompany; (*unire*) to couple; **~rsi** *vr* (*armonizzarsi*) to go well together; **~ qn a casa** to see sb home; **~ qn alla porta** to show sb out; **~ un regalo con un biglietto** to put in *o* send a card with a present; **~ qn con lo sguardo** to follow sb with one's eyes; **~ la porta** to close the door gently; **~rsi a** (*frequentare*) to frequent; (*colori*) to go with, match; (*cibi*) to go with.

accompagnato're, tri'ce |àkkōmpànyàtō'rā| *sm/f* companion, escort; (*guida turistica*) courier; (*MUS*) accompanist; (*SPORT*) team manager.

accomuna're *vt* to pool, share; (*avvicinare*) to unite.

acconciatu'ra |àkkōnchàtōō'rà| *sf* hairstyle.

accondiscenden'te |àkkōndēshànden'tā| *ag* affable.

accondiscen'dere |àkkōndēshàn'dārā| *vi*: **~ a** to agree *o* consent to.

accondisce'so, a |àkkōndēshà'sō| *pp di* **accondiscendere.**

acconsenti're *vi*: **~ (a)** to agree *o* consent (to); **chi tace acconsente** silence means consent.

accontenta're *vt* to satisfy; **~rsi** *vr*: **~rsi di** to be satisfied with, content o.s. with; **chi si accontenta gode** there's no point in com-

plaining.

accon'to *sm* part payment; **pagare una somma in ~** to pay a sum of money as a deposit; **~ di dividendo** interim dividend.

accoppiamen'to *sm* pairing off; mating; (*ELETTR, INFORM*) coupling.

accoppia're *vt* to couple, pair off; (*BIOL*) to mate; **~rsi** *vr* to pair off; to mate.

accoppiato're *sm* (*TECN*) coupler; **~ acustico** (*INFORM*) acoustic coupler.

accora'to, a *ag* heartfelt.

accorcia're |àkkōrchà'rā| *vt* to shorten; **~rsi** *vr* to become shorter; (*vestiti: nel lavaggio*) to shrink.

accorda're *vt* to reconcile; (*colori*) to match; (*MUS*) to tune; (*LING*): **~ qc con qc** to make sth agree with sth; (*DIR*) to grant; **~rsi** *vr* to agree, come to an agreement; (*colori*) to match.

accor'do *sm* agreement; (*armonia*) harmony; (*MUS*) chord; **essere d'~** to agree; **andare d'~** to get on well together; **d'~!** all right!, agreed!; **mettersi d'~ (con qn)** to agree *o* come to an agreement with sb; **prendere ~i con ~** to reach an agreement with; **~ commerciale** trade agreement; **A~ generale sulle tariffe ed il commercio** General Agreement on Tariffs and Trade, GATT.

accor'gersi |àkkor'jàrsē| *vr*: **~ di** to notice; (*fig*) to realize.

accorgimen'to |àkkōrjēmān'tō| *sm* shrewdness *q*; (*espediente*) trick, device.

accor'rere *vi* to run up.

accor'si *vb vedi* **accorgersi**; **accorrere.**

accor'so, a *pp di* **accorrere.**

accortez'za |àkkōrtāt'tsà| *sf* (*avvedutezza*) good sense; (*astuzia*) shrewdness.

accor'to, a *pp di* **accorgersi** ♦ *ag* shrewd; **stare ~** to be on one's guard.

accostamen'to *sm* (*di colori etc*) combination.

accosta're *vt* (*avvicinarsi a*) to approach; (*socchiudere: imposte*) to half-close; (: *porta*) to leave ajar ♦ *vi*: **~ (a)** (*NAUT*) to come alongside; (*AUT*) to draw up (at); **~rsi** *vr*: **~rsi a** to draw near, approach; (*somigliare*) to be like, resemble; (*fede, religione*) to turn to; (*idee politiche*) to come to agree with; **~ qc a** (*avvicinare*) to bring sth near to, put sth near to; (*colori, stili*) to match sth with; (*appoggiare: scala etc*) to lean sth against.

accovacciar'si |àkkōvàchàr'sē| *vr* to crouch.

accozza'glia |àkkōttsàl'yà| *sf* (*peg: di idee, oggetti*) jumble, hodgepodge; (: *di persone*) odd assortment.

accreb'bi *etc vb vedi* **accrescere.**

accredita're *vt* (*notizia*) to confirm the truth of; (*COMM*) to credit; (*diplomatico*) to accredit; **~rsi** *vr* (*fig*) to gain credit.

accre'dito *sm* (*COMM*: *atto*) crediting; (: *effetto*) credit.

accre'scere [àkkrāsh'shārā] *vt* to increase; ~**rsi** *vr* to increase, grow.

accrescimen'to [àkkrāshēmān'tō] *sm* increase, growth.

accresciti'vo, a [àkkrāshētē'vō] *ag, sm* (*LING*) augmentative.

accresciu'to, a [àkkrāshōō'tō] *pp di* **accrescere**.

accucciar'si [àkkōōchàr'sē] *vr* (*cane*) to lie down; (*persona*) to crouch down.

accudi're *vi:* ~ **a**, *vt* to attend to; to look after.

acculturazio'ne [àkkōōltōōráttsyō'nā] *sf* (*SOCIOLOGIA*) integration.

accumula're *vt* to accumulate; ~**rsi** *vr* to accumulate; (*FINANZA*) to accrue.

accumulato're *sm* (*ELETTR*) accumulator.

accumulazio'ne [àkkōōmōōlàttsyō'nā] *sf* accumulation.

accu'mulo *sm* accumulation.

accuratez'za [àkkōōrátāt'tsà] *sf* care; accuracy.

accura'to, a *ag* (*diligente*) careful; (*preciso*) accurate.

accu'sa *sf* accusation; (*DIR*) charge; **l'~, la pubblica** ~ (*DIR*) the prosecution; **mettere qn sotto** ~ to indict sb; **in stato di** ~ committed for trial.

accusa'bile *ag* (*DIR*) chargeable.

accusa're *vt* (*sentire: dolore*) to feel; ~ **qn di qc** to accuse sb of sth; (*DIR*) to charge sb with sth; ~ **ricevuta di** (*COMM*) to acknowledge receipt of; ~ **la fatica** to show signs of exhaustion; **ha accusato il colpo** (*anche fig*) you could see that he had felt the blow.

accusa'to, a *sm/f* accused.

accusato're, tri'ce *ag* accusing ♦ *sm/f* accuser ♦ *sm* (*DIR*) prosecutor.

acer'bo, a [àcher'bō] *ag* bitter; (*frutta*) sour, unripe; (*persona*) immature.

a'cero [à'chārō] *sm* maple.

acer'rimo, a [àcher'rēmō] *ag* very fierce.

aceta'to [àchātà'tō] *sm* acetate.

ace'to [àchā'tō] *sm* vinegar; **mettere sotto** ~ to pickle.

aceto'ne [àchātō'nā] *sm* nail polish remover.

A.'C.I. [à'chē] *sigla m* (= *Automobile Club d'Italia*) ≈ AAA (*US*), AA (*Brit*).

acidità [àchēdētà'] *sf* acidity; sourness; ~ **(di stomaco)** heartburn.

a'cido, a [à'chēdō] *ag* (*sapore*) acid, sour; (*CHIM*) acid ♦ *sm* (*CHIM*) acid.

aci'dulo, a [àchē'dōōlō] *ag* slightly sour, slightly acid.

a'cino [à'chēnō] *sm* berry; ~ **d'uva** grape.

A'CLI *sigla fpl* (= *Associazioni Cristiane dei Lavoratori Italiani*) *Christian Trade Union Association.*

ac'me *sf* (*fig*) acme, peak; (*MED*) crisis.

ac'ne *sf* acne.

ac'qua *sf* water; (*pioggia*) rain; ~**e** *sfpl* waters; **fare** ~ (*NAUT*) to leak, take in water; **essere con** *o* **avere l'~ alla gola** to be in great difficulty; **tirare** ~ **al proprio mulino** to feather one's own nest; **navigare in cattive** ~**e** (*fig*) to be in deep water; ~ **in bocca!** mum's the word!; ~ **corrente** running water; ~ **dolce** fresh water; ~ **di mare** sea water; ~ **minerale** mineral water; ~ **ossigenata** hydrogen peroxide; ~ **piovana** rain water; ~ **potabile** drinking water; ~ **salata** *o* **salmastra** salt water; ~ **tonica** tonic water.

acquafor'te, *pl* **acquefor'ti** *sf* etching.

acqua'io *sm* sink.

acquara'gia [àkkwárà'jà] *sf* turpentine.

acqua'rio *sm* aquarium; (*dello zodiaco*): **A~** Aquarius; **essere dell'A~** to be Aquarius.

acquartiera're *vt* (*MIL*) to quarter.

acquasan'ta *sf* holy water.

acqua'tico, a, ci, che *ag* aquatic; (*sport, sci*) water *cpd*.

acquattar'si *vr* to crouch (down).

acquavi'te *sf* brandy.

acquazzo'ne [àkkwáttsō'nā] *sm* cloudburst, heavy shower.

acquedot'to *sm* aqueduct; waterworks *pl*, water system.

ac'queo, a *ag:* **vapore** ~ water vapor (*US*) *o* vapour (*Brit*); **umore** ~ aqueous humor (*US*) *o* humour (*Brit*).

acquerel'lo *sm* watercolor (*US*), watercolour (*Brit*).

acqueru'giola [àkkwārōō'jōlà] *sf* drizzle.

acquieta're *vt* to appease; (*dolore*) to ease; ~**rsi** *vr* to calm down.

acquiren'te *sm/f* purchaser, buyer.

acquisi're *vt* to acquire.

acquisizio'ne [àkkwēzēttsyō'nā] *sf* acquisition.

acquista're *vt* to purchase, buy; (*fig*) to gain ♦ *vi* to improve; ~ **in bellezza** to become more beautiful; **ha acquistato in salute** his health has improved.

acqui'sto *sm* purchase; **fare** ~**i** to go shopping; **ufficio** ~**i** (*COMM*) purchasing department; ~ **rateale** installment (*US*) *o* hire purchase (*Brit*).

acquitri'no *sm* bog, marsh.

acquoli'na *sf:* **far venire l'~ in bocca a qn** to make sb's mouth water.

acquo'so, a *ag* watery.

a'cre *ag* acrid, pungent; (*fig*) harsh, biting.

acre'dine *sf* (*fig*) bitterness.

acri'lico, a, ci, che *ag, sm* acrylic.

acro'bata, i, e *sm/f* acrobat.

acroba'tico, a, ci, che *ag* (*ginnastica*) acrobatic; (*AER*) aerobatic ♦ *sf* acrobatics *sg*.

acrobazi'a [àkrōbáttsē'á] *sf* acrobatic feat; ~**e**

aeree aerobatics.

acro'nimo *sm* acronym.

acro'poli *sf inv*: **l'A~** the Acropolis.

acui're *vt* to sharpen; **~rsi** *vr* (*gen*) to increase; (*crisi*) to worsen.

acu'leo *sm* (*ZOOL*) sting; (*BOT*) prickle.

acu'me *sm* acumen, perspicacity.

acumina'to, a *ag* sharp.

acu'stico, a, ci, che *ag* acoustic ♦ *sf* (*scienza*) acoustics *sg*; (*di una sala*) acoustics *pl*; **apparecchio ~** 'hearing aid; **cornetto ~** ear trumpet.

acutez'za |àkōōtāt'tsà| *sf* sharpness; shrillness; acuteness; high pitch; intensity; keenness.

acutizza're |àkōōtēddzà'rā| *vt* (*fig*) to intensify; **~rsi** *vr* (*fig: crisi, malattia*) to become worse, worsen.

acu'to, a *ag* (*appuntito*) sharp, pointed; (*suono, voce*) shrill, piercing; (*MAT, LING, MED*) acute; (*MUS*) high-pitched; (*fig: dolore, desiderio*) intense; (: *perspicace*) acute, keen ♦ *sm* (*MUS*) high note.

ad *prep* (*dav V*) = **a**.

adagia're |àdàjà'rā| *vt* to lay *o* set down carefully; **~rsi** *vr* to lie down, stretch out.

ada'gio |àdà'jō| *av* slowly ♦ *sm* (*MUS*) adagio; (*proverbio*) adage, saying.

adami'tico, a, ci, che *ag*: **in costume ~** in one's birthday suit.

adatta'bile *ag* adaptable.

adattabilità *sf* adaptability.

adattamen'to *sm* adaptation; **avere spirito di ~** to be adaptable.

adatta're *vt* to adapt; (*sistemare*) to fit; **~rsi** *vr*: **~rsi (a)** (*ambiente, tempi*) to adapt (to); (*essere adatto*) to be suitable (for); (*accontentarsi*): **~rsi a qc/a fare qc** to make the best of sth/of doing sth.

adattato're *sm* (*ELETTR*) adapter, adaptor.

adat'to, a *ag*: **~ (a)** suitable (for), right (for).

addebita're *vt*: **~ qc a qn** to debit sb with sth; (*fig: incolpare*) to blame sb for sth.

adde'bito *sm* (*COMM*) debit.

addensamen'to *sm* thickening; gathering.

addensa're *vt* to thicken; **~rsi** *vr* to thicken; (*nuvole*) to gather.

addenta're *vt* to bite into.

addentrar'si *vr*: **~ in** to penetrate, go into.

adden'tro *av* (*fig*): **essere molto ~ in qc** to be well-versed in sth.

addestramen'to *sm* training; **~ aziendale** company training.

addestra're *vt*, **~rsi** *vr* to train; **~rsi in qc** to practice (*US*) *o* practise (*Brit*) sth.

addet'to, a *ag*: **~ a** (*persona*) assigned to; (*oggetto*) intended for ♦ *sm* employee; (*funzionario*) attaché; **~ commerciale/stampa** commercial/press attaché; **~ al telex** telex operator; **gli ~i ai lavori** authorized

personnel; (*fig*) those in the know; **"vietato l'ingresso ai non ~i ai lavori"** "authorized personnel only".

addì *av* (*AMM*): **~ 3 luglio 1989** on July 3rd 1989.

addiac'cio |àddyàch'chō| *sm* (*MIL*) bivouac; **dormire all'~** to sleep in the open.

addie'tro *av* (*indietro*) behind; (*nel passato, prima*) before, ago.

addi'o *sm, escl* goodbye, farewell.

addirittu'ra *av* (*veramente*) really, absolutely; (*perfino*) even; (*direttamente*) directly, right away.

addir'si *vr*: **~ a** to suit, be suitable for.

Ad'dis Abe'ba *sf* Addis Ababa.

addita're *vt* to point out; (*fig*) to expose.

additi'vo *sm* additive.

addiziona'le |àddēttsyōnà'lā| *ag* additional ♦ *sf* (*anche*: **imposta ~**) surtax.

addiziona're |àddēttsyōnà'rā| *vt* (*MAT*) to add (up).

addizio'ne |àddēttsyō'nā| *sf* addition.

addobba're *vt* to decorate.

addob'bo *sm* decoration.

addolci're |àddōlchē'rā| *vt* (*caffè etc*) to sweeten; (*acqua, fig: carattere*) to soften; **~rsi** *vr* (*fig*) to mellow, soften; **~ la pillola** (*fig*) to sugar the pill.

addolora're *vt* to pain, grieve; **~rsi** *vr*: **~rsi (per)** to be distressed (by).

addolora'to, a *ag* distressed, upset; **l'A~a** (*REL*) Our Lady of Sorrows.

addo'me *sm* abdomen.

addomestica're *vt* to tame.

addomina'le *ag* abdominal; (**muscoli** *mpl*) **~i** stomach muscles.

addormenta're *vt* to put to sleep; **~rsi** *vr* to fall asleep, go to sleep.

addormenta'to, a *ag* sleeping, asleep; (*fig: tardo*) stupid, dopey.

addossa're *vt* (*appoggiare*): **~ qc a qc** to lean sth against sth; (*fig*): **~ la colpa a qn** to lay the blame on sb; **~rsi** *vr*: **~rsi qc** (*responsabilità etc*) to shoulder sth.

addos'so *av* (*sulla persona*) on; **~ a** *prep* (*sopra*) on; (*molto vicino*) right next to; **mettersi ~ il cappotto** to put one's coat on; **andare** (*o* **venire**) **~ a** (*AUT: altra macchina*) to run into; (: *pedone*) to run over; **non ho soldi ~** I don't have any money on me; **stare ~ a qn** (*fig*) to breathe down sb's neck; **dare ~ a qn** (*fig*) to attack sb; **mettere gli occhi ~ a qn/qc** to take quite a fancy to sb/sth; **mettere le mani ~ a qn** (*picchiare*) to hit sb; (*catturare*) to seize sb; (*molestare: donna*) to feel sb up.

addot'to, a *pp di* **addurre**.

addu'co *etc vb vedi* **addurre**.

addur're *vt* (*DIR*) to produce; (*citare*) to cite.

addus'si *etc vb vedi* **addurre**.

adegua're *vt*: ~ **qc a** to adjust sth to; ~**rsi** *vr* to adapt.

adeguatez'za |àdàgwàtāt'tsà| *sf* adequacy; suitability; fairness.

adegua'to, a *ag* adequate; *(conveniente)* suitable; *(equo)* fair.

adem'piere *vt* to fulfill *(US)*, fulfil *(Brit)*, carry out; *(comando)* to carry out.

adempimen'to *sm* fulfillment *(US)*, fulfilment *(Brit)*; carrying out; **nell'~ del proprio dovere** in the performance of one's duty.

adempi're *vt* = **adempiere**.

A'den: il golfo di ~ *sm* the Gulf of Aden.

adeno'idi *sfpl* adenoids.

adep'to *sm* disciple, follower.

aderen'te *ag* adhesive; *(vestito)* close-fitting ♦ *sm/f* follower.

aderen'za |àdārcn'tsà| *sf* adhesion; ~**e** *sfpl* *(fig)* connections, contacts.

aderi're *vi* *(stare attaccato)* to adhere, stick; ~ **a** to adhere to, stick to; *(fig: società, partito)* to join; *(: opinione)* to support; *(richiesta)* to agree to.

adesca're *vt* *(attirare)* to lure, entice; *(TECN: pompa)* to prime.

adesio'ne *sf* adhesion; *(fig: assenso)* agreement, acceptance; *(appoggio)* support.

adesi'vo, a *ag, sm* adhesive.

ades'so *av* *(ora)* now; *(or ora, poco fa)* just now; *(tra poco)* any moment now; **da ~ in poi** from now on; **per ~** for the moment, for now.

adiacen'te |àdyàchen'tā| *ag* adjacent.

adibi're *vt* *(usare)*: ~ **qc a** to turn sth into.

A'dige |à'dējà| *sm*: **l'~** the Adige.

a'dipe *sm* fat.

adirar'si *vr*: ~ **(con** *o* **contro qn per qc)** to get angry (with sb over sth).

adira'to, a *ag* angry.

adi're *vt* *(DIR)*: ~ **le vie legali** to take legal proceedings; ~ **un'eredità** to take legal possession of an inheritance.

a'dito *sm*: **dare ~ a** *(sospetti)* to give rise to.

ADN *sigla m* (= *acido deossiribonucleico)* DNA.

adocchia're |àdōkkyà'rā| *vt* *(scorgere)* to catch sight of; *(occhieggiare)* to eye.

adolescen'te |àdōlāshen'tā| *ag, sm/f* adolescent.

adolescen'za |àdōlāshen'tsà| *sf* adolescence.

adolescenzia'le |àdōlāshāntsyà'lā| *ag* adolescent.

adombra're *vt* *(fig)* to veil, conceal; ~**rsi** *vr* *(cavallo)* to shy; *(persona)* to grow suspicious; *(: aversene a male)* to be offended.

adopera're *vt* to use; ~**rsi** *vr* to strive; ~**rsi per qn/qc** to do one's best for sb/sth.

adora're *vt* to adore; *(REL)* to adore, worship.

adorazio'ne |àdōràttsyō'nā| *sf* adoration; worship.

adorna're *vt* to adorn.

ador'no, a *ag*: ~ **(di)** adorned (with).

adotta're *vt* to adopt; *(decisione, provvedimenti)* to pass.

adotti'vo, a *ag* *(genitori)* adoptive; *(figlio, patria)* adopted.

adozio'ne |àdōttsyō'nā| *sf* adoption.

adria'tico, a, ci, che *ag* Adriatic ♦ *sm*: **l'A~, il mare A~** the Adriatic, the Adriatic Sea.

adula're *vt* to flatter.

adulato're, tri'ce *sm/f* flatterer.

adulato'rio, a *ag* flattering.

adulazio'ne |àdōōlàttsyō'nā| *sf* flattery.

adultera're *vt* to adulterate.

adulte'rio *sm* adultery.

adul'tero, a *ag* adulterous ♦ *sm/f* adulterer/adulteress.

adul'to, a *ag* adult; *(fig)* mature ♦ *sm* adult, grown-up.

adunan'za |àdōōnàn'tsà| *sf* assembly, meeting.

aduna're *vt*, ~**rsi** *vr* to assemble, gather.

aduna'ta *sf* *(MIL)* parade, muster.

adun'co, a, chi, che *ag* hooked.

AEDA *sigla mpl* (= *Autori Editori Associati)* association of authors and publishers.

aerazio'ne |àāràttsyō'nā| *sf* ventilation; *(TECN)* aeration.

ae'reo, a *ag* air *cpd*; *(radice)* aerial ♦ *sm* aerial; *(aeroplano)* plane; ~ **da caccia** fighter (plane); ~ **di linea** airliner; ~ **a reazione** jet (plane).

aero'bica *sf* aerobics *sg*.

aerodina'mico, a, ci, che *ag* aerodynamic; *(affusolato)* streamlined ♦ *sf* aerodynamics *sg*.

aeromodel'lo *sm* model aircraft.

aerona'utica *sf* *(scienza)* aeronautics *sg*; ~ **militare** air force.

aeronava'le *ag* *(forze, manovre)* air and sea *cpd*.

aeropla'no *sm* (air)plane *(US)*, (aero)plane *(Brit)*.

aeropor'to *sm* airport.

aeroportua'le *ag* airport *cpd*.

aerosca'lo *sm* airstrip.

aerosol' *sm inv* aerosol.

aerospazia'le |àārōspàttsyà'lā| *ag* aerospace.

aerosta'tico, a, ci, che *ag* aerostatic; **pallone ~** hot air balloon.

A.F. *abbr* (= *alta frequenza)* HF; *(AMM)* = **assegni familiari.**

a'fa *sf* sultriness.

affa'bile *ag* affable.

affabilità *sf* affability.

affaccendar'si |àffàchāndàr'sē| *vr*: ~ **intorno a qc** to busy o.s. with sth.

affaccenda'to, a *ag* busy.

affacciar'si |àffàchàr'sē| *vr*: ~ **(a)** to appear (at); ~ **alla vita** to come into the world.

affama'to, a *ag* starving; *(fig)*: ~ **(di)** eager

(for).

affanna're vt to leave breathless; (fig) to worry; ~**rsi** vr: ~**rsi per qn/qc** to worry about sb/sth.

affan'no sm breathlessness; (fig) anxiety, worry.

affannosamen'te av with difficulty; anxiously.

affanno'so, a ag (respiro) difficult; (fig) troubled, anxious.

affa're sm (faccenda) matter, affair; (COMM) piece of business, (business) deal; (occasione) bargain; (DIR) case; (fam: cosa) thing; ~**i** smpl (COMM) business sg; ~ **fatto!** done!, it's a deal!; **sono ~i miei** that's my business; **bada agli ~i tuoi!** mind your own business!; **uomo d'~i** businessman; **ministro degli A~i Esteri** Secretary of State (US), Foreign Secretary (Brit).

affari'sta, i sm profiteer, unscrupulous businessman.

affascinan'te |àffàshčnàn'tā| ag fascinating.

affascina're |àffàshčná'rā| vt to bewitch; (fig) to charm, fascinate.

affaticamen'to sm tiredness.

affatica're vt to tire; ~**rsi** vr (durar fatica) to tire o.s. out.

affat'to av completely; **non** ... ~ not ... at all; **niente** ~ not at all.

afferma're vi (dire di sì) to say yes ♦ vt (dichiarare) to maintain, affirm; ~**rsi** vr to assert o.s., make one's name known.

affermativamen'te av in the affirmative, affirmatively.

affermati'vo, a ag affirmative.

affermazio'ne |àffàrmáttsyō'nā| sf affirmation, assertion; (successo) achievement.

afferra're vt to seize, grasp; (fig: idea) to grasp; ~**rsi** vr: ~**rsi a** to cling to.

Aff. Est. abbr = Affari Esteri.

affetta're vt (tagliare a fette) to slice; (ostentare) to affect.

affetta'to, a ag sliced; affected ♦ sm sliced cold meat.

affettatri'ce |àffàttàtrč'chā| sf meat slicer.

affettazio'ne |àffàttàttsyō'nā| sf affectation.

affetti'vo, a ag emotional, affective.

affet'to, a ag: **essere ~ da** to suffer from ♦ sm affection; **gli ~i familiari** one's nearest and dearest.

affettuosamen'te av affectionately; (nelle lettere): (ti saluto) ~, **Maria** love, Maria.

affettuosità sf inv affection; ~ sfpl (manifestazioni) demonstrations of affection.

affettuo'so, a ag affectionate.

affezionar'si |àffàttsyōnàr'sč| vr: ~ **a** to grow fond of.

affeziona'to, a |àffàttsyōná'tō| ag: ~ **a qn/qc** fond of sb/sth; (attaccato) attached to sb/sth.

affezio'ne |àffàttsyō'nā| sf (affetto) affection;

(MED) ailment, disorder.

affianca're vt to place side by side; (MIL) to flank; (fig) to support; ~ **qc a qc** to place sth next to o beside sth; ~**rsi** vr: ~**rsi a qn** to stand beside sb.

affiatamen'to sm understanding.

affiatar'si vr to get on well together.

affibbia're vt to buckle, do up; (fig: dare) to give.

affidabilità sf reliability.

affidamen'to sm (DIR: di bambino) custody; (fiducia): **fare** ~ **su qn** to rely on sb; **non dà nessun** ~ he's not to be trusted.

affida're vt: ~ **qc o qn a qn** to entrust sth o sb to sb; ~**rsi** vr: ~**rsi a** to place one's trust in.

affievolir'si vr to grow weak.

affig'gere |àffčd'jàrā| vt to stick up, post up.

affila're vt to sharpen.

affila'to, a ag (gen) sharp; (volto, naso) thin.

affilia're vt to affiliate; ~**rsi** vr: ~**rsi a** to become affiliated to.

affina're vt to sharpen.

affinché |àffčnkā'| cong in order that, so that.

affi'ne ag similar.

affinità sf inv affinity.

affiora're vi to emerge.

affis'si etc vb vedi **affiggere**.

affis'so sm billposting.

affis'so, a pp di **affiggere** ♦ sm bill, poster; (LING) affix.

affittaca'mere sm/f inv landlord/landlady.

affitta're vt (dare in affitto) to rent (out), let (Brit); (prendere in affitto) to rent.

affit'to sm rent; (contratto) lease; **dare in** ~ to rent (out), let; **prendere in** ~ to rent.

affittua'rio sm lessee.

afflig'gere |àfflčd'jàrā| vt to torment; ~**rsi** vr to grieve.

afflis'si etc vb vedi **affliggere**.

afflit'to, a pp di **affliggere**.

afflizio'ne |àfflčttsyō'nā| sf distress, torment.

afflosciar'si |àfflōshàr'sč| vr to go limp; (frutta) to go soft.

affluen'te sm tributary.

affluen'za |àfflōōcn'tsà| sf flow; (di persone) crowd.

afflui're vi to flow; (fig: merci, persone) to pour in.

afflus'so sm influx.

affoga're vt, vi to drown; ~**rsi** vr to drown; (deliberatamente) to drown o.s.

affoga'to, a ag drowned; (CUC: uova) poached.

affollamen'to sm crowding; (folla) crowd.

affolla're vt, ~**rsi** vr to crowd.

affolla'to, a ag crowded.

affondamen'to sm (di nave) sinking.

affonda're vt to sink.

affranca're vt to free, liberate; (AMM) to redeem; (*lettera*) to stamp; (: *meccanicamente*) to meter (*US*), frank (*Brit*); ~**rsi** *vr* to free o.s.

affrancatri'ce |àffrànkàtrē'chā| *sf* postage meter (*US*), franking machine (*Brit*).

affrancatu'ra *sf* (*di francobollo*) stamping; metering (*US*), franking (*Brit*); (*tassa di spedizione*) postage; ~ **a carico del destinatario** postage paid.

affran'to, a *ag* (*esausto*) worn out; (*abbattuto*) overcome.

affre'sco, schi *sm* fresco.

affretta're *vt* to quicken, speed up; ~**rsi** *vr* to hurry; ~**rsi a fare qc** to hurry o hasten to do sth.

affretta'to, a *ag* (*veloce: passo, ritmo*) quick, fast; (*frettoloso: decisione*) hurried, hasty; (: *lavoro*) rushed.

affronta're *vt* (*pericolo etc*) to face; (*assalire: nemico*) to confront; ~**rsi** *vr* (*reciproco*) to confront each other.

affron'to *sm* affront, insult; **fare un** ~ **a qn** to insult sb.

affumica're *vt* to fill with smoke; to blacken with smoke; (*alimenti*) to smoke.

affusola'to, a *ag* tapering.

afga'no, a *ag*, *sm/f* Afghan.

Afgha'nistan |àfgà'nēstàn| *sm*: **l'**~ Afghanistan.

a.f.m. *abbr* (*COMM*: = *a fine mese*) e.o.m. (= end of month).

afo'so, a *ag* sultry, close.

A'frica *sf*: **l'**~ Africa.

african'der *sm inv* Afrikaner.

africa'no, a *ag*, *sm/f* African.

afroasia'tico a, ci, che *ag* Afro-Asian.

afrodisi'aco, a, ci, che *ag*, *sm* aphrodisiac.

AG *sigla* = Agrigento.

agen'da |àjɛn'dà| *sf* diary; ~ **tascabile/da tavolo** pocket/desk diary.

agen'te |àjɛn'tà| *sm* agent; ~ **di cambio** stockbroker; ~ **di custodia** prison officer; ~ **marittimo** shipping agent; ~ **di polizia** police officer; ~ **provocatore** agent provocateur; ~ **delle tasse** tax inspector; ~ **di vendita** sales agent; **resistente agli** ~**i atmosferici** weather-resistant.

agenzi'a |àjàntsē'à| *sf* agency; (*succursale*) branch; ~ **di collocamento** employment agency; ~ **immobiliare** real estate agency (*US*), estate agent's (office) (*Brit*); **A**~ **Internazionale per l'Energia Atomica (AIEA)** International Atomic Energy Agency (IAEA); ~ **matrimoniale** ≈ dating service (*US*), marriage bureau (*Brit*); ~ **pubblicitaria** advertising agency; ~ **di stampa** press agency; ~ **viaggi** travel agency.

agevola're |àjàvōlà'rā| *vt* to facilitate, make easy.

agevolazio'ne |àjàvōlàttsyō'nā| *sf* (*facilitazio-*

ne economica) facility; ~ **di pagamento** payment on easy terms; ~**i creditizie** easy credit (terms); ~**i fiscali** tax concessions.

age'vole |àjā'vōlā| *ag* easy; (*strada*) smooth.

aggancia're |àggànchà'rā| *vt* to hook up; (*FERR*) to couple; ~**rsi** *vr*: ~**rsi a** to hook up to; (*fig: pretesto*) to seize on.

aggan'cio |àggàn'chō| *sm* (*TECN*) coupling; (*fig: conoscenza*) contact.

aggeg'gio |àdjād'jō| *sm* gadget, contraption.

aggetti'vo |àdjāttē'vō| *sm* adjective.

agghiacciante |àggyàchàn'tā| *ag* (*fig*) chilling.

agghiaccia're |àggyàchà'rā| *vt* to freeze; (*fig*) to make one's blood run cold; ~**rsi** *vr* to freeze.

agghindar'si |àggēndàr'sē| *vr* to deck o.s. out.

aggioga're |àdjōgà'rā| *vt* (*buoi*) to yoke; (*popolo*) to subjugate.

aggiornamen'to |àdjōrnàmàn'tō| *sm* updating; revision; postponement; **corso di** ~ refresher course.

aggiorna're |àdjōrnà'rā| *vt* (*opera, manuale*) to bring up-to-date; (: *rivedere*) to revise; (*listino*) to maintain, up-date; (*seduta etc*) to postpone; ~**rsi** *vr* to bring (o keep) o.s. up-to-date.

aggiorna'to, a |àdjōrnà'tō| *ag* up-to-date.

aggiotag'gio |àdjōtàd'jō| *sm* (*ECON*) rigging the market.

aggira're |àdjērà'rā| *vt* to go round; (*fig: ingannare*) to trick; ~**rsi** *vr* to wander about; **il prezzo s'aggira sul milione** the price is around the million mark.

aggiudica're |àdjōōdēkà'rā| *vt* to award; (*all'asta*) to knock down; ~**rsi qc** to win sth.

aggiun'gere |àdjōōn'jàrā| *vt* to add.

aggiun'si |àdjōōn'sē| *etc vb vedi* **aggiungere**.

aggiun'to, a |àdjōōn'tō| *pp di* **aggiungere** ♦ *ag* assistant *cpd* ♦ *sm* assistant ♦ *sf* addition; **sindaco** ~ deputy mayor; **in** ~**a** ... what's more ....

aggiusta're |àdjōōstà'rā| *vt* (*accomodare*) to mend, repair; (*riassettare*) to adjust; (*fig: lite*) to settle; ~**rsi** *vr* (*arrangiarsi*) to make do; (*con senso reciproco*) to come to an agreement; **ti aggiusto io!** I'll fix you!

agglomera'to *sm* (*di rocce*) conglomerate; (*di legno*) particleboard (*US*), chipboard (*Brit*); ~ **urbano** built-up area.

aggrappar'si *vr*: ~ **a** to cling to.

aggravamen'to *sm* worsening.

aggravan'te *ag* (*DIR*) aggravating ♦ *sf* aggravation.

aggrava're *vt* (*aumentare*) to increase; (*appesantire: anche fig*) to weigh down, make heavy; (*fig: pena*) to make worse; ~**rsi** *vr* (*fig*) to worsen, become worse.

aggra'vio *sm*: ~ **di costi** increase in costs.

aggrazia'to, a |àggràttsyà'tō| *ag* graceful.

aggredi're *vt* to attack, assault.

aggrega're vt: ~ qn a qc to admit sb to sth; ~rsi vr to join; ~rsi a to join, become a member of.

aggrega'to, a ag associated ♦ sm aggregate; ~ urbano built-up area.

aggressio'ne sf aggression; (atto) attack, assault; ~ a mano armata armed assault.

aggressività sf aggressiveness.

aggressi'vo, a ag aggressive.

aggresso're sm aggressor, attacker.

aggrotta're vt: ~ le sopracciglia to frown.

aggroviglia're |àggrōvēlyà'rā| vt to tangle; ~rsi vr (fig) to become complicated.

agguanta're vt to catch, seize.

aggua'to sm trap; (imboscata) ambush; tendere un ~ a qn to set a trap for sb.

agguerri'to, a ag (sostenitore, nemico) fierce.

agiatez'za |àjàtàt'tsà| sf prosperity.

agia'to, a |àjà'tō| ag (vita) easy; (persona) well-off, well-to-do.

a'gile |à'jēlà| ag agile, nimble.

agilità |àjēlētà'| sf agility, nimbleness.

a'gio |à'jō| sm ease, comfort; ~i smpl comforts; mettersi a proprio ~ to make o.s. at home o comfortable; dare ~ a qn di fare qc to give sb the chance of doing sth.

agi're |àjē'rā| vi to act; (esercitare un'azione) to take effect; (TECN) to work, function; ~ contro qn (DIR) to take action against sb.

agita're |àjētà'rā| vt (bottiglia) to shake; (mano, fazzoletto) to wave; (fig: turbare) to disturb; (: incitare) to stir (up); ~rsi vr (mare) to be rough; (malato, dormitore) to toss and turn; (bambino) to fidget; (emozionarsi) to get upset; (POL) to agitate.

agita'to, a |àjētà'tō| ag rough; restless; fidgety; upset, perturbed.

agitato're, tri'ce |àjētàtō'rā| sm/f (POL) agitator.

agitazio'ne |àjētàttsyō'nā| sf agitation; (POL) unrest, agitation; mettere in ~ qn to upset o distress sb.

a'git-'prop |à'jēt'prop| abbr m (= agitatore-propagandista) communist agitator.

a'gli |àl'yē| prep + det vedi a.

a'glio |àl'yō| sm garlic.

agnel'lo |ànyєl'lō| sm lamb.

agno'stico, a, ci, che |ànyo'stēkō| ag, sm/f agnostic.

a'go, pl a'ghi sm needle; ~ da calza knitting needle.

ago. abbr (= agosto) Aug.

agoni'a sf agony.

agoni'stico, a, ci, che ag athletic; (fig) competitive.

agonizzan'te |àgōnēddzàn'tà| ag dying.

agonizza're |àgōnēddzà'rā| vi to be dying.

agopuntu'ra sf acupuncture.

ago'sto sm August; per fraseologia vedi luglio.

agra'rio, a ag agrarian, agricultural; (riforma) land cpd ♦ sm landowner ♦ sf agriculture.

agri'colo, a ag agricultural, farm cpd.

agricolto're sm farmer.

agricoltu'ra sf agriculture, farming.

agrifo'glio |àgrēfol'yō| sm holly.

agrimenso're sm land surveyor.

agrituri'smo sm farm vacations pl.

a'gro, a ag sour, sharp.

agrodol'ce |àgrōdōl'chā| ag bittersweet; (salsa) sweet and sour.

agru'me sm (spesso al pl: pianta) citrus; (: frutto) citrus fruit.

agrume'to sm citrus grove.

aguzza're |àgōōttsà'rā| vt to sharpen; ~ gli orecchi to prick up one's ears; ~ l'ingegno to use one's wits.

aguzzi'no, a |àgōōddzē'nō| sm/f jailer; (fig) tyrant.

aguz'zo, a |àgōōt'tsō| ag sharp.

a'hi escl (dolore) ouch!

ahimè escl alas!

a'i prep + det vedi a.

A'ia sf: L'~ The Hague.

a'ia sf threshing floor.

AIDDA sigla f (= Associazione Imprenditrici Donne Dirigenti d'Azienda) association of women entrepreneurs and managers.

AIE sigla f (= Associazione Italiana degli Editori) publishers' association.

AIEA sigla f vedi Agenzia Internazionale per l'Energia Atomica.

AIED sigla f = Associazione Italiana Educazione Demografica.

AIG sigla f = Associazione Italiana Alberghi per la Gioventù.

aio'la sf = aiuola.

AIPI sigla f = Associazione Italiana Protezione Infanzia.

airo'ne sm heron.

aitan'te ag robust.

aiuo'la sf flower bed.

aiutan'te sm/f assistant ♦ sm (MIL) adjutant; (NAUT) master-at-arms; ~ di campo aide-de-camp.

aiuta're vt to help; ~ qn (a fare) to help sb (to do).

aiu'to sm help, assistance, aid; (aiutante) assistant; venire in ~ di qn to come to sb's aid; ~ chirurgo assistant surgeon.

aizza're |àēttsà'rā| vt to incite; ~ i cani contro qn to set the dogs on sb.

al prep + det vedi a.

a.l. abbr = anno luce.

a'la, pl a'li sf wing; fare ~ to fall back, make way; ~ destra/sinistra (SPORT) right/left wing.

alabas'tro sm alabaster.

a'lacre ag quick, brisk.

alacrità *sf* promptness, speed.
alambic'co, chi *sm* still (*CHIM*).
ala'no *sm* Great Dane.
ala're *ag* wing *cpd*; **~i** *smpl* andirons.
Ala'ska *sf*: **l'~** Alaska.
ala'to, a *ag* winged.
al'ba *sf* dawn; **all'~** at dawn.
albane'se *ag*, *sm/f*, *sm* Albanian.
Albani'a *sf*: **l'~** Albania.
al'batro *sm* albatross.
albeggia're |àlbādjà'rā| *vi*, *vb impers* to dawn.
albera'to, a *ag* (*viale*, *piazza*) lined with trees, tree-lined.
alberatu'ra *sf* (*NAUT*) masts *pl*.
alberga're *vt* (*dare albergo*) to accommodate ♦ *vi* (*poetico*) to dwell.
albergato're, tri'ce *sm/f* hotelier, hotel-keeper.
alberghie'ro, a |àlbārgyc'rō| *ag* hotel *cpd*.
alber'go, ghi *sm* hotel; **~ diurno** *public toilets with washing and shaving facilities etc*; **~ della gioventù** youth hostel.
al'bero *sm* tree; (*NAUT*) mast; (*TECN*) shaft; **~ a camme** camshaft; **~ genealogico** family tree; **~ a gomiti** crankshaft; **~ maestro** mainmast; **~ di Natale** Christmas tree; **~ di trasmissione** transmission shaft.
albicoc'ca, che *sf* apricot.
albicoc'co, chi *sm* apricot tree.
al'bo *sm* (*registro*) register, roll; (*AMM*) bulletin board.
al'bum *sm* album; **~ da disegno** sketch book.
albu'me *sm* albumen; (*bianco d'uovo*) egg white.
albumi'na *sf* albumin.
al'ce |àl'chā| *sm* elk.
alchi'mia |àlkē'myà| *sf* alchemy.
alchimi'sta, i |àlkēmē'stà| *sm* alchemist.
al'col *sm inv* = **alcool**.
alcolicità |àlkōlēchētà'| *sf* alcohol(ic) content.
alco'lico, a, ci, che *ag* alcoholic ♦ *sm* alcoholic drink.
alcoli'smo *sm* alcoholism.
alcoli'sta, i, e *sm/f* alcoholic.
alcolizza'to, a |àlkōlēddzà'tō| *sm/f* alcoholic.
al'cool *sm inv* alcohol; **~ denaturato** wood alcohol (*US*), methylated spirits *pl* (*Brit*); **~ etilico** ethyl alcohol; **~ metilico** methyl alcohol.
alcotest' *sm inv* Breathalyzer ®.
alco'va *sf* alcove.
alcu'no, a *det* (*dav sm*: **alcun** + *C*, *V*, **alcuno** + *s impura*, *gn*, *pn*, *ps*, *x*, *z*; *dav sf*: **alcuna** + *C*, **alcun'** +*V*) (*nessuno*): **non ... ~** no, not any; **~i(e)** *det pl*, *pronome pl* some, a few; **non c'è ~a fretta** there's no hurry, there isn't any hurry; **senza alcun riguardo** without any consideration.
aldilà *sm inv*: **l'~** the hereafter, the after-life.
aleato'rio, a *ag* (*incerto*) uncertain.

aleggia're |àlādjà'rā| *vi* (*fig*: *profumo*, *sospetto*) to be in the air.
Alessan'dria *sf* (*anche*: **~ d'Egitto**) Alexandria.
alet'ta *sf* (*TECN*) fin; tab.
Aleuti'ne *sfpl*: **le isole ~** the Aleutian Islands.
alfabe'tico, a, ci, che *ag* alphabetical.
alfabe'to *sm* alphabet.
alfanume'rico, a, ci, che *ag* alphanumeric.
alfie're *sm* standard-bearer; (*SCACCHI*) bishop.
alfi'ne *av* finally, in the end.
al'ga, ghe *sf* seaweed *q*, alga.
al'gebra |àl'jàbrà| *sf* algebra.
Alge'ri |àljà'rē| *sf* Algiers.
Algeri'a |àljàrē'à| *sf*: **l'~** Algeria.
algeri'no, a |àljàrē'nō| *ag*, *sm/f* Algerian.
algorit'mo *sm* algorithm.
ALI *sigla f* (= *Associazione Librai Italiani*) booksellers' association.
alian'te *sm* (*AER*) glider.
a'libi *sm inv* alibi.
ali'ce |àlē'chā| *sf* anchovy.
aliena're *vt* (*DIR*) to transfer; (*rendere ostile*) to alienate; **~rsi qn** to alienate sb.
aliena'to, a *ag* alienated; transferred; (*fuor di senno*) insane ♦ *sm* lunatic, insane person.
alienazio'ne |àlyānàttsyō'nā| *sf* alienation; transfer; insanity.
alie'no, a *ag* (*avverso*): **~ (da)** opposed (to), averse (to) ♦ *sm/f* alien.
alimenta're *vt* to feed; (*TECN*) to feed, supply; (*fig*) to sustain ♦ *ag* food *cpd*; **~i** *smpl* foodstuffs; (*anche*: **negozio di ~i**) grocery store (*US*), grocer's shop (*Brit*); **regime ~** diet.
alimentazio'ne |àlēmāntàttsyō'nā| *sf* feeding; (*cibi*) diet; **~ di fogli** (*INFORM*) sheet feed.
alimen'to *sm* food; **~i** *smpl* food *sg*; (*DIR*) alimony.
ali'quota *sf* share; **~ d'imposta** tax rate; **~ minima** (*FISCO*) basic rate.
alisca'fo *sm* hydrofoil.
a'lito *sm* breath.
all., alleg. *abbr* (= *allegato*) enc., encl.
al'la *prep* + *det vedi* **a**.
allacciamen'to |àllàchàmān'tō| *sm* (*TECN*) connection.
allaccia're |àllàchà'rā| *vt* (*scarpe*) to tie, lace (up); (*cintura*) to do up, fasten; (*due località*) to link; (*luce*, *gas*) to connect; (*amicizia*) to form; **~rsi** *vr* (*vestito*) to fasten; **~ o ~rsi la cintura** to fasten one's belt.
allacciatu'ra |àllàchàtōō'rà| *sf* fastening.
allagamen'to *sm* flooding *q*; flood.
allaga're *vt*, **~rsi** *vr* to flood.
allampana'to, a *ag* lanky.
allarga're *vt* to widen; (*vestito*) to let out; (*aprire*) to open; (*fig*: *dilatare*) to extend; **~rsi** *vr* (*gen*) to widen; (*scarpe*, *pantaloni*) to

stretch; (*fig: problema, fenomeno*) to spread.
allarma're *vt* to alarm; **~rsi** *vr* to become alarmed.
allar'me *sm* alarm; **mettere qn in ~** to alarm sb; **~ aereo** air-raid warning.
allarmi'smo *sm* scaremongering.
allarmi'sta, i, e *sm/f* scaremonger, alarmist.
allatta're *vt* (*sog: donna*) to (breast-)feed; (*: animale*) to suckle; **~ artificialmente** to bottle-feed.
al'le *prep + det vedi* **a**.
allean'za |àllààn'tsá| *sf* alliance.
allear'si *vr* to form an alliance.
allea'to, a *ag* allied ♦ *sm/f* ally.
allega're (*accludere*) to enclose; (*DIR: citare*) to cite, adduce; (*denti*) to set on edge.
allega'to, a *ag* enclosed ♦ *sm* enclosure; **in ~** enclosed; **in ~ Vi inviamo ...** please find enclosed ....
alleggeri're |àllàdjàrē'rā| *vt* to lighten, make lighter; (*fig: sofferenza*) to alleviate, lessen; (*: lavoro, tasse*) to reduce.
allegori'a *sf* allegory.
allegri'a *sf* gaiety, cheerfulness.
alle'gro, a *ag* cheerful, merry; (*un po' brillo*) merry, tipsy; (*vivace: colore*) bright ♦ *sm* (*MUS*) allegro.
allenamen'to *sm* training.
allena're *vt*, **~rsi** *vr* to train.
allenato're *sm* (*SPORT*) trainer, coach.
allenta're *vt* to slacken; (*disciplina*) to relax; **~rsi** *vr* to become slack; (*ingranaggio*) to work loose.
allergi'a, gi'e |àllàrjē'á| *sf* allergy.
aller'gico, a, ci, che |àllcr'jčkō| *ag* allergic.
allestimen'to *sm* preparation, setting up; **in ~** in preparation.
allesti're *vt* (*cena*) to prepare; (*esercito, nave*) to equip, fit out; (*spettacolo*) to stage.
allettan'te *ag* attractive, alluring.
alletta're *vt* to lure, entice.
allevamen'to *sm* breeding, rearing; (*luogo*) stock farm; **pollo d'~** battery hen.
alleva're *vt* (*animale*) to breed, rear; (*bambino*) to bring up.
allevato're *sm* breeder.
allevia're *vt* to alleviate.
allibi're *vi* to turn pale; (*essere turbato*) to be disconcerted.
allibi'to, a *ag* pale; disconcerted.
allibrato're *sm* bookmaker.
allieta're *vt* to cheer up, gladden.
allie'vo *sm* pupil; (*apprendista*) apprentice; **~ ufficiale** cadet.
alligato're *sm* alligator.
allineamen'to *sm* alignment.
allinea're *vt* (*persone, cose*) to line up; (*TIP*) to align; (*fig: economia, salari*) to adjust, align; **~rsi** *vr* to line up; (*fig: a idee*): **~rsi a** to come into line with.

allinea'to, a *ag* aligned, in line; **paesi non ~i** (*POL*) non-aligned countries.
al'lo *prep + det vedi* **a**.
alloc'co, a, chi, che *sm* tawny owl ♦ *sm/f* oaf.
allocuzio'ne |àllōkōōttsyō'nā| *sf* address, solemn speech.
allo'dola *sf* (sky)lark.
alloggia're |àllōdjà'rā| *vt* to accommodate ♦ *vi* to live.
allog'gio |àllod'jō| *sm* accommodations (*US*), accommodation (*Brit*); (*appartamento*) apartment.
allontanamen'to *sm* removal; dismissal; estrangement.
allontana're *vt* to send away, send off; (*impiegato*) to dismiss; (*pericolo*) to avert, remove; (*estraniare*) to alienate; **~rsi** *vr*: **~rsi (da)** to go away (from); (*estraniarsi*) to become estranged (from).
allo'ra *av* (*in quel momento*) then ♦ *cong* (*in questo caso*) well then; (*dunque*) well then, so; **la gente d'~** people then *o* in those days; **da ~ in poi** from then on; **e ~?** (*che fare?*) what now?; (*e con ciò?*) so what?
allorché' |àllōrkā'| *cong* (*formale*) when, as soon as.
allo'ro *sm* laurel; **riposare** *o* **dormire sugli ~i** to rest on one's laurels.
al'luce |àl'lōōchā| *sm* big toe.
allucinan'te |àllōōchēnàn'tā| *ag* (*scena, spettacolo*) awful, terrifying; (*fam: incredibile*) amazing.
allucina'to, a |àllōōchēnà'tō| *ag* terrified; (*fuori di sé*) bewildered, confused.
allucinazio'ne |àllōōchēnàttsyō'nā| *sf* hallucination.
allu'dere *vi*: **~ a** to allude to, hint at.
allumi'nio *sm* aluminum (*US*), aluminium (*Brit*).
allunag'gio |àllōōnàd'jō| *sm* moon landing.
alluna're *vi* to land on the moon.
allunga're *vt* to lengthen; (*distendere*) to prolong, extend; (*diluire*) to water down; **~rsi** *vr* to lengthen; (*ragazzo*) to stretch, grow taller; (*sdraiarsi*) to lie down, stretch out; **~ le mani** (*rubare*) to pick pockets; **gli allungò uno schiaffo** he gave him a swipe at him.
allu'si *etc vb vedi* **alludere**.
allusio'ne *sf* hint, allusion.
allu'so, a *pp di* **alludere**.
alluvio'ne *sf* flood.
almanac'co, chi *sm* almanac.
alme'no *av* at least ♦ *cong*: **(se) ~** if only; **(se) ~ piovesse!** if only it would rain!
alo'geno, a |àlo'jänō| *ag*: **lampada ~a** halogen lamp.
alo'ne *sm* halo.
alpes'tre *ag* (*delle alpi*) alpine; (*montuoso*) mountainous.
Al'pi *sfpl*: **le ~** the Alps.

alpini'smo *sm* mountaineering, climbing.

alpini'sta, i, e *sm/f* mountaineer, climber.

alpi'no, a *ag* Alpine; mountain *cpd*; ~i *smpl* (*MIL.*) Italian Alpine troops.

alquan'to *av* rather, a little; ~, **a** *det* a certain amount of, some ♦ *pronome* a certain amount, some; ~i(e) *det pl*, *pronome pl* several, quite a few.

Alsa'zia [àlsàt'tsyà] *sf* Alsace.

alt *escl* halt!, stop! ♦ *sm*: **dare l'**~ to call a halt.

altale'na *sf* (*a funi*) swing; (*in bilico, anche fig*) seesaw.

alta're *sm* altar.

altera're *vt* to alter, change; (*cibo*) to adulterate; (*registro*) to falsify; (*persona*) to irritate; ~**rsi** *vr* to alter; (*cibo*) to go bad; (*persona*) to lose one's temper.

alterazio'ne [àltàràttsyō'nā] *sf* alteration, change; adulteration; falsification; annoyance.

alter'co, chi *sm* altercation, wrangle.

alternan'za [àltārnàn'tsà] *sf* alternation; (*AGR*) rotation.

alterna're *vt*, ~**rsi** *vr* to alternate.

alternati'vo, a *ag* alternative ♦ *sf* alternative; **non abbiamo** ~**e** we have no alternative.

alterna'to, a *ag* alternate; (*ELETTR*) alternating.

alternato're *sm* alternator.

alter'no, a *ag* alternate; **a giorni** ~i on alternate days, every other day.

alte'ro, a *ag* proud.

altez'za [àltāt'tsà] *sf* (*di edificio, persona*) height; (*di tessuto*) width, breadth; (*di acqua, pozzo*) depth; (*di suono*) pitch; (*GEO*) latitude; (*titolo*) highness; (*fig: nobiltà*) greatness; **essere all'**~ **di** to be on a level with; (*fig*) to be up to *o* equal to; **all'**~ **della farmacia** near the chemist's.

altezzo'so, a [àltāttsō'sō] *ag* haughty.

altic'cio, a, ci, ce [àltēch'chō] *ag* tipsy.

altipia'no *sm* = **altopiano**.

altisonan'te *ag* (*fig*) high-sounding, pompous.

altitu'dine *sf* altitude.

al'to, a *ag* high; (*persona*) tall; (*tessuto*) wide, broad; (*sonno, acque*) deep; (*suono*) high (-pitched); (*GEO*) upper; (*: settentrionale*) northern ♦ *sm* top (part) ♦ *av* high; (*parlare*) aloud, loudly; **il palazzo è** ~ **20 metri** the building is 20 meters high; **il tessuto è** ~ **70 cm** the material is 70 cm wide; **ad** ~**a voce** aloud; **a notte** ~**a** in the dead of night; **in** ~ up, upwards; at the top; **mani in** ~! hands up!; **dall'**~ **in** *o* **al basso** up and down; **degli** ~**i e bassi** (*fig*) ups and downs; **andare a testa** ~**a** (*fig*) to carry one's head high; **essere in** ~ **mare** (*fig*) to be far from a solution; ~**a fedeltà** high fidelity, hi-fi; ~**a moda** haute couture; **l'A**~ **Medioevo** the Early Middle Ages; **l'**~ **Po** the upper reaches of the Po.

altoatesi'no, a *ag* of (*o* from) the Alto Adige.

altofor'no *sm* blast furnace.

altoloca'to, a *ag* of high rank, highly placed.

altoparlan'te *sm* loudspeaker.

altopia'no, *pl* **altipia'ni** *sm* upland plain, plateau.

Al'to Vol'ta *sm*: **l'**~ Upper Volta.

altrettan'to, a *ag, pronome* as much; (*pl*) as many ♦ *av* equally; **tanti auguri! — grazie,** ~ all the best! — thank you, the same to you.

al'tri *pronome inv* (*qualcuno*) somebody; (*: in espressioni negative*) anybody; (*un'altra persona*) another (person).

altrimen'ti *av* otherwise.

al'tro, a *det* other; **un** ~ **libro** (*supplementare*) another book, one more book; (*diverso*) another book, a different book; **un** ~ another (one); **l'**~ the other (one); **gli** ~**i** (*la gente*) others, other people; **desidera** ~? do you want anything else?; **aiutarsi l'un l'**~ to help one another; **l'uno e l'**~ both (of them); **l'**~ **giorno** the other day; **l'**~ **ieri** the day before yesterday; **domani l'**~ the day after tomorrow; **quest'**~ **mese** next month; **da un giorno all'**~ from day to day; (*qualsiasi giorno*) any day now; **d'**~**a parte** on the other hand; **tra l'**~ among other things; **ci mancherebbe** ~! that's all we need!; **non faccio** ~ **che studiare** I do nothing but study; **sei contento?** — ~ **che!/tutt'**~! are you pleased? — and how!/on the contrary!; **noi/voi** ~**i** us/you (lot).

altroché [àltrōkā'] *escl* certainly!, and how!

altron'de *av*: **d'**~ on the other hand.

altro've *av* elsewhere, somewhere else.

altru'i *ag inv* other people's ♦ *sm*: **l'**~ other people's belongings *pl*.

altrui'smo *sm* altruism.

altrui'sta, i, e *ag* altruistic ♦ *sm/f* altruist.

altu'ra *sf* (*rialto*) height, high ground; (*alto mare*) open sea; **pesca d'**~ deep-sea fishing.

alun'no, a *sm/f* pupil.

alvea're *sm* hive.

al'veo *sm* riverbed.

alzabandie'ra [àltsàbàndyā'rà] *sm inv* (*MIL.*): **l'**~ the raising of the flag.

alza're [àltsà'rā] *vt* to raise, lift; (*issare*) to hoist; (*costruire*) to build, erect; ~**rsi** *vr* to rise; (*dal letto*) to get up; (*crescere*) to grow tall (*o* taller); ~ **le spalle** to shrug one's shoulders; ~ **le carte** to cut the cards; ~ **il gomito** to drink too much; ~ **le mani su qn** to raise one's hand to sb; ~ **i tacchi** to take to one's heels; ~**rsi in piedi** to stand up, get to one's feet; ~**rsi col piede sbagliato** to get out of bed on the wrong side.

alza'ta [àltsà'tà] *sf* lifting, raising; **un'**~ **di spalle** a shrug.

A.M. *abbr* = **aeronautica militare**.

ama'bile *ag* lovable; (*vino*) sweet.

A'MAC *sigla f* = *Aeronautica Militare-Aviazione Civile*.

ama'ca, che *sf* hammock.

amalgama're *vt.* **~rsi** *vr* to amalgamate.

aman'te *ag*: **~ di** (*musica etc*) fond of ♦ *sm/f* lover/mistress.

amaran'to *sm* (*BOT*) love-lies-bleeding ♦ *ag inv*: **color ~** reddish purple.

ama're *vt* to love; (*amico, musica, sport*) to like.

amareggia're |àmàràdjà'rà| *vt* to sadden, upset; **~rsi** *vr* to get upset; **~rsi la vita** to make one's life a misery.

amareggia'to, a |àmàràdjà'tō| *ag* upset, saddened.

amare'na *sf* sour black cherry.

amaret'to *sm* (*dolce*) macaroon; (*liquore*) bitter liqueur made with almonds.

amarez'za |àmàràt'tsà| *sf* bitterness.

ama'ro, a *ag* bitter ♦ *sm* bitterness; (*liquore*) bitters *pl*.

amaro'gnolo, a |àmàrōn'yōlō| *ag* slightly bitter.

ama'to, a *ag* beloved, loved, dear ♦ *sm/f* loved one.

amato're, tri'ce *sm/f* (*amante*) lover; (*intenditore: di vini etc*) connoisseur; (*dilettante*) amateur.

amaz'zone |àmàd'dzōnà| *sf* (*MITOLOGIA*) Amazon; (*cavallerizza*) horsewoman; (*abito*) riding habit; **cavalcare all'~** to ride side-saddle; **il Rio delle A~i** the (river) Amazon.

amazzo'nico, a, ci, che |àmàddzo'nčkō| *ag* Amazonian; **Amazon** *cpd*.

ambasceri'a |àmbàshàrč'à| *sf* embassy.

ambascia'ta |àmbàshà'tà| *sf* embassy; (*messaggio*) message.

ambasciato're, tri'ce |àmbàshàtō'rà| *sm/f* ambassador/ambassadress.

ambedu'e *ag inv*: **~ i ragazzi** both boys ♦ *pronome inv* both.

ambides'tro, a *ag* ambidextrous.

ambienta'le *ag* environmental; (*temperatura*) ambient *cpd*.

ambienta're *vt* to acclimatize; (*romanzo, film*) to set; **~rsi** *vr* to get used to one's surroundings.

ambientazio'ne |àmbyàntàttsyō'nà| *sf* setting.

ambien'te *sm* environment; (*fig: insieme di persone*) milieu; (*stanza*) room.

ambiguità *sf inv* ambiguity.

ambi'guo, a *ag* ambiguous; (*persona*) shady.

ambi're *vt* (*anche: vi*: **~ a**) to aspire to; **un premio molto ambito** a much sought-after prize.

am'bito *sm* sphere, field.

ambivalen'te *ag* ambivalent; **questo apparecchio è ~** this is a dual-purpose device.

ambizio'ne |àmbčttsyō'nà| *sf* ambition.

ambizio'so, a |àmbčttsyō'sō| *ag* ambitious.

am'bo *ag inv* both.

am'bra *sf* amber; **~ grigia** ambergris.

ambulan'te *ag* travelling, itinerant.

ambulan'za |àmbōōlàn'tsà| *sf* ambulance.

ambulatoria'le *ag* (*MED*) outpatient(s) *cpd*; **operazione ~** operation as an outpatient; **visita ~** visit to the doctor's office (*US*) *o* surgery (*Brit*).

ambulato'rio *sm* (*studio medico*) doctor's office (*US*), surgery (*Brit*).

AM'DI *sigla f* = *Associazione Medici Dentisti Italiani*.

A'ME *sigla m* = *Accordo Monetario Europeo*.

ame'ba *sf* amoeba, ameba (*US*).

amenità *sf inv* pleasantness *q*; (*facezia*) pleasantry.

ame'no, a *ag* pleasant; (*strano*) funny, strange; (*spiritoso*) amusing.

Ame'rica *sf*: **l'~** America; **l'~ latina** Latin America; **l'~ del sud** South America.

americana'ta *sf* (*peg*): **le Olimpiadi sono state una vera ~** the Olympics were a typically vulgar American extravaganza.

americani'smo *sm* Americanism; (*ammirazione*) love of America.

america'no, a *ag, sm/f* American.

ameti'sta *sf* amethyst.

amian'to *sm* asbestos.

ami'ca *sf vedi* **amico**.

amiche'vole |àmčkà'vōlà| *ag* friendly.

amici'zia |àmčchčt'tsyà| *sf* friendship; **~e** *sfpl* (*amici*) friends; **fare ~ con qn** to make friends with sb.

ami'co, a, ci, che *sm/f* friend; (*amante*) boyfriend/girlfriend; **~ del cuore** *o* **intimo** bosom friend; **~ d'infanzia** childhood friend.

a'mido *sm* starch.

ammacca're *vt* (*pentola*) to dent; (*persona*) to bruise; **~rsi** *vr* to bruise.

ammaccatu'ra *sf* dent; bruise.

ammaestra're *vt* (*animale*) to train; (*persona*) to teach.

ammaina're *vt* to lower, haul down.

ammalar'si *vr* to get sick (*US*), fall ill (*Brit*).

ammala'to, a *ag* ill, sick ♦ *sm/f* sick person; (*paziente*) patient.

ammalia're *vt* (*fig*) to enchant, charm.

ammaliato're, tri'ce *sm/f* enchanter/enchantress.

amman'co, chi *sm* (*ECON*) deficit.

ammanetta're *vt* to handcuff.

ammanicatu'ra *sf* string-pulling.

ammansi're *vt* (*animale*) to tame; (*fig: persona*) to calm down, placate.

ammantar'si *vr*: **~ di** (*persona*) to wrap o.s. in; (*fig: prato etc*) to be covered in.

ammarag'gio |àmmàràd'jō| *sm* (*sea*) landing; splashdown.

ammara're *vi* (*AER*) to make a sea landing;

(*astronave*) to splash down.

ammassa're *vt* (*ammucchiare*) to amass; (*raccogliere*) to gather together; ~**rsi** *vr* to pile up; to gather.

ammas'so *sm* mass; (*mucchio*) pile, heap; (*ECON*) stockpile.

ammatti're *vi* to go mad.

ammazza're |àmmàttsà'rā| *vt* to kill; ~**rsi** *vr* (*uccidersi*) to kill o.s.; (*rimanere ucciso*) to be killed; ~**rsi di lavoro** to work o.s. to death.

ammen'da *sf* amends *pl*; (*DIR, SPORT*) fine; **fare** ~ **di qc** to make amends for sth.

ammes'so, a *pp di* **ammettere** ♦ *cong*: ~ **che** supposing that.

ammet'tere *vt* to admit; (*riconoscere: fatto*) to acknowledge, admit; (*permettere*) to allow, accept; (*supporre*) to suppose; **ammettiamo che ...** let us suppose that ....

ammezza'to |àmmāddzà'tō| *sm* (*anche*: **piano** ~) entresol, mezzanine.

ammicca're *vi*: ~ (**a**) to wink (at).

amministra're *vt* to run, manage; (*REL, DIR*) to administer.

amministrati'vo, a *ag* administrative.

amministrato're *sm* administrator; (*COMM*) director; ~ **aggiunto** associate director; ~ **delegato** managing director; ~ **fiduciario** trustee; ~ **unico** sole director.

amministrazio'ne |àmmēnēstràttsyō'nā| *sf* management; administration; **consiglio d'**~ board of directors; **l'**~ **comunale** local government; ~ **fiduciaria** trust.

ammira'glia |àmmērāl'yà| *sf* flagship.

ammiraglia'to |àmmērālyà'tō| *sm* admiralty.

ammira'glio |àmmērāl'yō| *sm* admiral.

ammira're *vt* to admire.

ammirato're, tri'ce *sm/f* admirer.

ammirazio'ne |àmmēràttsyō'nā| *sf* admiration.

ammi'si *etc vb vedi* **ammettere**.

ammissi'bile *ag* admissible, acceptable.

ammissio'ne *sf* admission; (*approvazione*) acknowledgment.

Amm.ne *abbr* = **amministrazione**.

ammobilia're *vt* to furnish.

ammoderna're *vt* to modernize.

ammo'do, a mo'do *av* properly ♦ *ag inv* respectable, nice.

ammoglia're |àmmōlyà'rā| *vt* to find a wife for; ~**rsi** *vr* to marry, take a wife.

ammol'lo *sm*: **lasciare in** ~ to leave to soak.

ammoni'aca *sf* ammonia.

ammonimen'to *sm* warning; admonishment.

ammoni're *vt* (*avvertire*) to warn; (*rimproverare*) to admonish; (*DIR*) to caution.

ammonizio'ne |àmmōnēttsyō'nā| *sf* (*monito: anche SPORT*) warning; (*rimprovero*) reprimand; (*DIR*) caution.

ammonta're *vi*: ~ **a** to amount to ♦ *sm* (*totale*) amount.

ammonticchia're |àmmōntĕkkyà'rā| *vt* to pile up, heap up.

ammorba're *vt* (*diffondere malattia*) to infect; (*sog: odore*) to taint, foul.

ammorbiden'te *sm* fabric softener.

ammorbidi're *vt* to soften.

ammortamen'to *sm* redemption; amortization; ~ **fiscale** capital allowance.

ammorta're *vt* (*FINANZA: debito*) to pay off, redeem; (: *spese d'impianto*) to write off.

ammortizza're |àmmōrtĕddzà'rā| *vt* (*FINANZA*) to pay off, redeem; (: *spese d'impianto*) to write off; (*AUT, TECN*) to absorb, deaden.

ammortizzato're |àmmōrtĕddzàtō'rā| *sm* (*AUT, TECN*) shock absorber.

Amm.re *abbr* = **amministratore**.

ammucchia're |àmmōōkkyà'rā| *vt*, ~**rsi** *vr* to pile up, accumulate.

ammuffi're *vi* to go moldy (*US*) *o* mouldy (*Brit*).

ammutinamen'to *sm* mutiny.

ammutinar'si *vr* to mutiny.

ammutina'to, a *ag* mutinous ♦ *sm* mutineer.

ammutoli're *vi* to be struck dumb.

amnesi'a *sf* amnesia.

amnisti'a *sf* amnesty.

a'mo *sm* (*PESCA*) hook; (*fig*) bait.

amora'le *ag* amoral.

amo're *sm* love; ~**i** *smpl* love affairs; **il tuo bambino è un** ~ your baby's a darling; **fare l'**~ *o* **all'**~ to make love; **andare d'**~ **e d'accordo con qn** to get on very well with sb; **per** ~ **o per forza** by hook or by crook; **amor proprio** self-esteem, pride.

amoreggia're |àmōrādjà'rā| *vi* to flirt.

amore'vole *ag* loving, affectionate.

amor'fo, a *ag* amorphous; (*fig: persona*) lifeless.

amori'no *sm* cupid.

amoro'so, a *ag* (*affettuoso*) loving, affectionate; (*d'amore: sguardo*) amorous; (: *poesia, relazione*) love *cpd*.

ampe're |àñpcr'| *sm inv* amp(ère).

ampiez'za |àmpyāt'tsà| *sf* width, breadth; spaciousness; (*fig: importanza*) scale, size; ~ **di vedute** broad-mindedness.

am'pio, a *ag* wide, broad; (*spazioso*) spacious; (*abbondante: vestito*) loose; (: *gonna*) full; (: *spiegazione*) ample, full.

amples'so *sm* (*sessuale*) intercourse.

ampliamen'to *sm* (*di strada*) widening; (*di aeroporto*) expansion; (*fig*) broadening.

amplia're *vt* (*allargare*) to widen; (*fig: discorso*) to enlarge on; ~**rsi** *vr* to grow, increase; ~ **la propria cultura** to broaden one's mind.

amplifica're *vt* to amplify; (*magnificare*) to extol.

amplificato're *sm* (*TECN, MUS*) amplifier.

amplificazio'ne [ámplēfēkàttsyō'nä] *sf* amplification.

ampol'la *sf* (*vasetto*) cruet.

ampollo'so, a *ag* bombastic, pompous.

amputa're *vt* (*MED*) to amputate.

amputazio'ne [ámpōōtàttsyō'nä] *sf* amputation.

Arn'sterdam *sf* Amsterdam.

AN *sigla* = *Ancona*.

A'NA *sigla f* (*MIL*) = *Associazione Nazionale Alpini*.

ANAAO *sigla f* (= *Associazione Nazionale Aiuti e Assistenti Ospedalieri*) *trade union for hospital workers*.

anabbaglian'te [ánàbbàlyàn'tä] *ag* (*AUT*) dimmed (*US*), dipped (*Brit*); **~i** *smpl* dimmed *o* dipped headlights.

anacroni'smo *sm* anachronism.

ana'grafe *sf* (*registro*) register of births, marriages and deaths; (*ufficio*) office of vital statistics (*US*), registry office (*Brit*).

anagra'fico, a, ci, che *ag* (*AMM*): **dati ~ci** personal data; **comune di residenza ~a** district where resident.

anagram'ma, i *sm* anagram.

analco'lico, a, ci, che *ag* non-alcoholic ♦ *sm* soft drink; **bevanda ~a** soft drink.

analfabe'ta, i, e *ag, sm/f* illiterate.

analfabeti'smo *sm* illiteracy.

analge'sico, a, ci, che [ánálje'zēkō] *ag, sm* analgesic.

ana'lisi *sf inv* analysis; (*MED: esame*) test; **in ultima ~** in conclusion, in the final analysis; **~ grammaticale** parsing; **~ del sangue** blood test; **~ dei sistemi/costi** systems/cost analysis.

anali'sta, i, e *sm/f* analyst; (*PSIC*) (psycho)analyst; **~ finanziario** financial analyst; **~ di sistemi** systems analyst.

anali'tico, a, ci, che *ag* analytic(al).

analizza're [ánálēddzá'rä] *vt* to analyze (*US*), analyse (*Brit*); (*MED*) to test.

analogi'a, gi'e [ánálōjē'á] *sf* analogy.

analo'gico, a, ci, che [ánálo'jēkō] *ag* analogical; (*calcolatore, orologio*) analog(ue).

ana'logo, a, ghi, ghe *ag* analogous.

a'nanas *sm inv* pineapple.

anarchi'a [ánárkē'á] *sf* anarchy.

anar'chico, a, ci, che [ánár'kēkō] *ag* anarchic(al) ♦ *sm/f* anarchist.

A.'N.A.S. *sigla f* (= *Azienda Nazionale Autonoma delle Strade*) *national road(s) department*.

anate'ma, i *sm* anathema.

anatomi'a *sf* anatomy.

anato'mico, a, ci, che *ag* anatomical; (*sedile*) ergonomically designed.

a'natra *sf* duck; **~ selvatica** mallard.

anatroc'colo *sm* duckling.

AN'CA *sigla f* = *Associazione Nazionale Cooperative Agricole*.

an'ca, che *sf* (*ANAT*) hip; (*ZOOL*) haunch.

AN'CAB *sigla f* (= *Associazione Nazionale delle Cooperative di Abitazione*) *national association of housing cooperatives*.

ANCC *sigla f* = *Associazione Nazionale Carabinieri*.

AN'CE [án'chä] *sigla f* (= *Associazione Nazionale Costruttori Edili*) *national association of builders*.

an'che [án'kä] *cong* also; (*perfino*) even; **vengo anch'io!** I'm coming too!; **~ se** even if; **~ volendo, non finiremmo in tempo** even if we wanted to, we wouldn't finish in time.

ancheggia're [ánkādjá'rä] *vi* to wiggle (one's hips).

anchilosa'to, a [ánkēlōzà'tō] *ag* stiff.

AN'CI [án'chē] *sigla f* (= *Associazione Nazionale dei Comuni Italiani*) *national confederation of local authorities*.

anconeta'no, a *ag* of (*o* from) Ancona.

anco'ra *av* still; (*di nuovo*) again; (*di più*) some more; (*persino*): **~ più forte** even stronger; **non ~** not yet; **~ una volta** once more, once again; **~ un po'** a little more; (*di tempo*) a little longer.

an'cora *sf* anchor; **gettare/levare l'~** to cast/weigh anchor; **~ di salvezza** (*fig*) last hope.

ancorag'gio [ánkōrád'jō] *sm* anchorage.

ancora're *vt*, **~rsi** *vr* to anchor.

ANCR *sigla f* (= *Associazione Nazionale Combattenti e Reduci*) *servicemen's and ex-servicemen's association*.

Andalusi'a *sf*: **l'~** Andalusia.

andalu'so, a *ag, sm/f* Andalusian.

andamen'to *sm* (*di strada, malattia*) course; (*del mercato*) state.

andan'te *ag* (*corrente*) current; (*di poco pregio*) cheap, second-rate ♦ *sm* (*MUS*) andante.

anda're *sm*: **a lungo ~** in the long run; **con l'andar del tempo** with the passing of time; **racconta storie a tutto ~** she's forever talking rubbish ♦ *vi* (*gen*) to go; (*essere adatto*): **~ a** to suit; (*piacere*): **il suo comportamento non mi va** I don't like the way he behaves; **ti va di ~ al cinema?** do you feel like going to the movies?; **~ a cavallo** to ride; **~ in macchina/aereo** to go by car/plane; **~ a fare qc** to go and do sth; **~ a pescare/sciare** to go fishing/skiing; **andarsene** to go away; **vado e vengo** I'll be back in a minute; **~ per i 50** (*età*) to be going on 50; **~ a male** to go bad; **~ fiero di qc/qn** to be proud of sth/sb; **~ perduto** to be lost; **come va?** (*lavoro, progetto*) how are things?; **come va? — bene, grazie!** how are you? — fine, thanks!; **va fatto entro oggi** it has to be done today; **ne va della nostra vita** our lives are at stake; **se non vado errato** if I'm not mistaken; **le**

mele vanno molto apples are selling well; **va da sé** (*è naturale*) it goes without saying; **per questa volta vada** let's say no more about it this time.

anda'ta *sf* (*viaggio*) outward journey; **biglietto di sola** ~ one-way *o* single (*Brit*) ticket; **biglietto di** ~ **e ritorno** round-trip (*US*) *o* return (*Brit*) ticket.

andatu'ra *sf* (*modo di andare*) walk, gait; (*SPORT*) pace; (*NAUT*) tack.

andaz'zo [àndàt'tsō] *sm* (*peg*): **prendere un brutto** ~ to take a turn for the worse.

An'de *sfpl*: **le** ~ the Andes.

andi'no, a *ag* Andean.

andirivie'ni *sm inv* coming and going.

an'dito *sm* corridor, passage.

Andor'ra *sf* Andorra.

andrò *etc vb vedi* **andare**.

andro'ne *sm* entrance hall.

ANDS *sigla f* (= *Associazione Nazionale Docenti Subalterni*) *teachers' union*.

AN'DU *sigla f* (= *Associazione Nazionale Docenti Universitari*) *association of university teachers*.

aned'doto *sm* anecdote.

anela're *vi*: ~ **a** (*fig*) to long for, yearn for.

ane'lito *sm* (*fig*): ~ **di** longing *o* yearning for.

anel'lo *sm* ring; (*di catena*) link.

anemi'a *sf* anemia (*US*), anaemia (*Brit*).

ane'mico, a, ci, che *ag* anemic (*US*), anaemic (*Brit*).

ane'mone *sm* anemone.

anestesi'a *sf* anesthesia (*US*), anaesthesia (*Brit*).

anestesi'sta, i, e *sm/f* anesthesiologist (*US*), anaesthetist (*Brit*).

aneste'tico, a, ci, che *ag*, *sm* anesthetic (*US*), anaesthetic (*Brit*).

anestetizza're [ànàstātĕddzà'rā] *vt* to anesthetize (*US*), anaesthetize (*Brit*).

anfi'bio, a *ag* amphibious ♦ *sm* amphibian; (*AUT*) amphibious vehicle.

anfitea'tro *sm* amphitheater (*US*), amphitheatre (*Brit*).

anfitrio'ne *sm* host.

an'fora *sf* amphora.

anfrat'to *sm* ravine.

ange'lico, a, ci, che [ànje'lēkō] *ag* angelic(al).

an'gelo [àn'jàlō] *sm* angel; ~ **custode** guardian angel; **l'~ del focolare** (*fig*) the perfect housewife.

angheri'a [àngārē'à] *sf* vexation.

angi'na [ànjē'nà] *sf* tonsillitis; ~ **pectoris** angina.

anglica'no, a *ag* Anglican.

anglici'smo [ànglēchĕz'mō] *sm* anglicism.

anglo'filo, a *ag* anglophilic ♦ *sm/f* anglophile.

anglosas'sone *ag* Anglo-Saxon.

Ango'la *sf*: **l'~** Angola.

angola'no, a *ag*, *sm/f* Angolan.

angola're *ag* angular.

angolatu'ra *sf* angle.

angolazio'ne [àngōlàttsyō'nā] *sf* (*di angolo*) angulation; (*FOT, CINEMA, TV, fig*) angle.

an'golo *sm* corner; (*MAT*) angle; ~ **cottura** (*di appartamento etc*) cooking area; **fare** ~ **con** (*strada*) to run into; **dietro l'~** (*anche fig*) round the corner.

angolo'so, a *ag* (*oggetto*) angular; (*volto, corpo*) angular, bony.

ango'scia, sce [àngosh'shà] *sf* deep anxiety, anguish *q*.

angoscia're [àngōshà'rā] *vt* to cause anguish to; ~**rsi** *vr*: ~**rsi (per)** (*preoccuparsi*) to become anxious (about); (*provare angoscia*) to get upset (about *o* over).

angoscio'so, a [àngōshō'sō] *ag* (*d'angoscia*) anguished; (*che dà angoscia*) distressing, painful.

anguil'la *sf* eel.

angu'ria *sf* watermelon.

angu'stia *sf* (*ansia*) anguish, distress; (*povertà*) poverty, want.

angustia're *vt* to distress; ~**rsi** *vr*: ~**rsi (per)** to worry (about).

angu'sto, a *ag* (*stretto*) narrow; (*fig*) mean, petty.

a'nice [à'nēchā] *sm* (*CUC*) aniseed; (*BOT*) anise; (*liquore*) anisette.

anidri'de *sf* (*CHIM*): ~ **carbonica/solforosa** carbon/sulphur dioxide.

a'nima *sf* soul; (*abitante*) inhabitant; ~ **gemella** soul mate; **un'~ in pena** (*anche fig*) a tormented soul; **non c'era** ~ **viva** there wasn't a living soul; **volere un bene dell'~ a qn** to be extremely fond of sb; **rompere l'~ a qn** to drive sb mad; **il nonno buon'~** ... Grandfather, God rest his soul ....

anima'le *sm*, *ag* animal.

animale'sco, a, schi, sche *ag* (*gesto, atteggiamento*) animal-like.

anima're *vt* to give life to, liven up; (*incoraggiare*) to encourage; ~**rsi** *vr* to become animated, come to life.

anima'to, a *ag* animate; (*vivace*) lively, animated; (: *strada*) busy.

animato're, tri'ce *sm/f* guiding spirit; (*CINEMA*) animator; (*di festa*) life and soul.

animazio'ne [ànēmàttsyō'nā] *sf* liveliness; (*strada*) bustle; (*CINEMA*) animation; ~ **teatrale** amateur theater (*US*) *o* dramatics (*Brit*).

a'nimo *sm* (*mente*) mind; (*cuore*) heart; (*coraggio*) courage; (*disposizione*) character, disposition; **avere in** ~ **di fare qc** to intend *o* have a mind to do sth; **farsi** ~ to pluck up courage; **fare qc di buon/mal** ~ to do sth willingly/unwillingly; **perdersi d'~** to lose heart.

animosità *sf* animosity.

ANI'TA *sigla f* = *Associazione Nazionale dell'Industria dei Trasporti Automobilistici; Associazione Naturista Italiana.*

a'nitra *sf* = **anatra.**

An'kara *sf* Ankara.

ANM *sigla f* (= *Associazione Nazionale dei Magistrati*) *national association of magistrates.*

ANMI *sigla f* (= *Associazione Nazionale Marinai d'Italia*) *national association of seamen.*

ANMIG *sigla f* (= *Associazione Nazionale fra Mutilati e Invalidi di Guerra*) *national association for disabled ex-servicemen.*

annacqua're *vt* to water down, dilute.

annaffia're *vt* to water.

annaffiato'io *sm* watering can.

anna'li *smpl* annals.

annaspa're *vi* (*nell'acqua*) to flounder; (*fig: nel buio, nell'incertezza*) to grope.

anna'ta *sf* year; (*importo annuo*) annual amount; **vino di** ~ vintage wine.

annebbia're *vt* (*fig*) to cloud; ~**rsi** *vr* to become foggy; (*vista*) to become dim.

annegamen'to *sm* drowning.

annega're *vt, vi* to drown; ~**rsi** *vr* (*accidentalmente*) to drown; (*deliberatamente*) to drown o.s.

anneri're *vt* to blacken ♦ *vi* to become black.

annessio'ne *sf* (*POL*) annexation.

annes'so, a *pp di* **annettere** ♦ *ag* attached; (*POL*) annexed; **... e tutti gli** ~**i e connessi** ... and so on and so forth.

annet'tere *vt* (*POL*) to annex; (*accludere*) to attach.

annichila're, annichili're |ȧnnĕkĕlȧ'rȧ, ȧnnĕkĕlĕ'rȧ| *vt* to annihilate.

annidar'si *vr* to nest.

annientamen'to *sm* annihilation, destruction.

annienta're *vt* to annihilate, destroy.

anniversa'rio *sm* anniversary.

an'no *sm* year; **quanti** ~**i hai?** — **ho 40** ~**i** how old are you? — I'm 40 (years old); **gli** ~**i 20** the 20s; **porta bene gli** ~**i** she doesn't look her age; **porta male gli** ~**i** she looks older than she is; ~ **commerciale** business year; ~ **giudiziario** legal year; ~ **luce** light-year; **gli** ~**i di piombo** the Seventies in Italy, characterized by terrorist attacks and killings.

annoda're *vt* to knot, tie; (*fig: rapporto*) to form.

annoia're *vt* to bore; (*seccare*) to annoy; ~**rsi** *vr* to be bored; to be annoyed.

anno'so, a *ag* (*albero*) old; (*fig: problema etc*) age-old.

annota're *vt* (*registrare*) to note; (*commentare*) to annotate.

annotazio'ne |ȧnnōtȧttsyō'nȧ| *sf* note; annotation.

annovera're *vt* to number.

annua'le *ag* annual.

annualmen'te *av* annually, yearly.

annua'rio *sm* yearbook.

annui're *vi* to nod; (*acconsentire*) to agree.

annullamen'to *sm* annihilation, destruction; cancellation; annulment; quashing.

annulla're *vt* to annihilate, destroy; (*contratto, francobollo*) to cancel; (*matrimonio*) to annul; (*sentenza*) to quash; (*risultati*) to declare void.

annul'lo *sm* (*AMM*) cancelling.

annuncia're |ȧnnōōnchȧ'rȧ| *vt* to announce; (*dar segni rivelatori*) to herald.

annunciato're, tri'ce |ȧnnōōnchȧtō'rȧ| *sm/f* (*RADIO, TV*) announcer.

Annunciazio'ne |ȧnnōōnchȧttsyō'nȧ| *sf* (*REL*): **l'**~ the Annunciation.

annun'cio |ȧnnōōn'chō| *sm* announcement; (*fig*) sign; ~ **pubblicitario** advertisement; ~**i economici** classified advertisements; **piccoli** ~**i** classified ads; ~**i mortuari** (*colonna*) obituary column.

an'nuo, a *ag* annual, yearly.

annusa're *vt* to sniff, smell; ~ **tabacco** to take snuff.

annuvolamen'to *sm* clouding (over).

annuvola're *vt* to cloud; ~**rsi** *vr* to become cloudy, cloud over.

a'no *sm* anus.

a'nodo *sm* anode.

anomali'a *sf* anomaly.

ano'malo, a *ag* anomalous.

anonima'to *sm* anonymity; **conservare l'**~ to remain anonymous.

ano'nimo, a *ag* anonymous ♦ *sm* (*autore*) anonymous writer (*o painter etc*); **un tipo** ~ (*peg*) a colorless (*US*) *o* colourless (*Brit*) character.

anorma'le *ag* abnormal ♦ *sm/f* subnormal person; (*eufemismo*) homosexual.

anormalità *sf inv* abnormality.

AN'SA *sigla f* (= *Agenzia Nazionale Stampa Associata*) *national press agency.*

an'sa *sf* (*manico*) handle; (*di fiume*) bend, loop.

ansan'te *ag* out of breath, panting.

AN'SEA *sigla f* (= *Associazione delle Nazioni del Sud-Est asiatico*) ASEAN.

an'sia *sf* anxiety; **stare in** ~ (**per qn/qc**) to be anxious (about sb/sth).

ansietà *sf* anxiety.

ansima're *vi* to pant.

ansio'so, a *ag* anxious.

an'ta *sf* (*di finestra*) shutter; (*di armadio*) door.

antagoni'smo *sm* antagonism.

antagoni'sta, i, e *sm/f* antagonist.

antar'tico, a, ci, che *ag* Antarctic ♦ *sm*: **l'A**~ the Antarctic.

Antar'tide *sf*: **l'**~ Antarctica.

antebel'lico, a, ci, che *ag* prewar *cpd*.

anteceden'te |àntāchādcn'tā| *ag* preceding, previous.

antefat'to *sm* previous events *pl*; previous history.

anteguer'ra *sm* pre-war period.

antena'to *sm* ancestor, forefather.

anten'na *sf* (*RADIO, TV*) aerial; (*ZOOL*) antenna, feeler; **rizzare le ~e** (*fig*) to prick up one's ears.

antepor're *vt*: **~ qc a qc** to place *o* put sth before sth.

antepo'sto, a *pp di* **anteporre**.

antepri'ma *sf* preview.

anterio're *ag* (*ruota, zampa*) front *cpd*; (*fatti*) previous, preceding.

antesigna'no |àntāsēnyà'nō| *sm* (*STORIA*) standard-bearer; (*fig*) forerunner.

antiae'reo, a *ag* antiaircraft *cpd*.

antiato'mico, a, ci, che *ag* anti-nuclear; **rifugio ~** fallout shelter.

antibio'tico, a, ci, che *ag, sm* antibiotic.

antica'glia |àntēkàl'yà| *sf* junk *q*.

antica'mera *sf* anteroom; **fare ~** to be kept waiting; **non mi passerebbe neanche per l'~ del cervello** it wouldn't even cross my mind.

antica'rie *ag inv* which fights tooth decay.

antichità |àntēkētà'| *sf inv* antiquity; (*oggetto*) antique.

anticiclo'ne |àntēchēklō'nā| *sm* anticyclone.

anticipa're |àntēchēpà'rā| *vt* (*consegna, visita*) to bring forward, anticipate; (*somma di denaro*) to pay in advance; (*notizia*) to disclose ♦ *vi* to be ahead of time.

anticipa'to, a |àntēchēpà'tō| *ag* (*prima del previsto*), early; **pagamento ~** payment in advance.

anticipazio'ne |àntēshēpàttsyō'nā| *sf* anticipation; (*di notizia*) advance information; (*somma di denaro*) advance.

anti'cipo |àntē'chēpō| *sm* anticipation; (*di denaro*) advance; **in ~** early, in advance; **con un sensibile ~** well in advance.

anti'co, a, chi, che *ag* (*quadro, mobili*) antique; (*dell'antichità*) ancient; **all'~a** old-fashioned.

anticonceziona'le |àntēkōnchàttsyōnà'lā| *sm* contraceptive.

anticonformi'sta, i, e *ag, sm/f* nonconformist.

anticongelan'te |àntēkōnjàlàn'tā| *ag, sm* antifreeze.

anticongiuntura'le |àntēkōnjōōntōōrà'lā| *ag* (*ECON*) **misure ~i** measures to remedy the economic situation.

anticor'po *sm* antibody.

anticostituziona'le |àntēkōstētōōttsyōnà'lā| *ag* unconstitutional.

antido'ping *sm inv* (*SPORT*) drug test.

anti'doto *sm* antidote.

antidro'ga *ag inv* anti-drug(s) *cpd*.

antieste'tico, a, ci, che *ag* unsightly.

anti'fona *sf* (*MUS. REL*) antiphon; **capire l'~** (*fig*) to take the hint.

antifur'to *sm* anti-theft device.

antige'lo |àntējc'lō| *ag inv* antifreeze *cpd* ♦ *sm* (*per motore*) antifreeze; (*per cristalli*) de-icer.

antigie'nico, a, ci, che |àntējc'nēkō| *ag* unhygienic.

Antil'le *sfpl*: **le ~** the West Indies.

anti'lope *sf* antelope.

antima'fia *ag inv* anti-mafia *cpd*.

antincen'dio |àntēnchcn'dyō| *ag inv* fire *cpd*; **bombola ~** fire extinguisher.

antineb'bia *sm inv* (*anche*: **faro ~**: *AUT*) fog light.

antinevral'gico, a, ci, che |àntēnàvràl'jčkō| *ag* painkilling ♦ *sm* painkiller.

antiora'rio *ag*: **in senso ~** in a counterclockwise direction, counterclockwise.

antipa'sto *sm* hors d'œuvre.

antipati'a *sf* antipathy, dislike.

antipa'tico, a, ci, che *ag* unpleasant, disagreeable.

Anti'podi *smpl*: **gli ~** the Antipodes; **essere agli a~** (*fig*) to be poles apart.

antiquaria'to *sm* antique trade; **un pezzo d'~** an antique.

antiqua'rio *sm* antique dealer.

antiqua'to, a *ag* antiquated, old-fashioned.

antirifles'so *ag inv* (*schermo*) non-glare *cpd*.

antirug'gine |àntērōōd'jēnā| *ag* anti-rust *cpd* ♦ *sm inv* rust-preventer.

antisemi'ta, i, e *ag* anti-semitic.

antisemiti'smo *sm* anti-semitism.

antiset'tico, a, ci, che *ag, sm* antiseptic.

antistami'nico, a, ci, che *ag, sm* antihistamine.

antistan'te *ag* opposite.

antiterrori'smo *sm* anti-terrorist measures *pl*.

anti'tesi *sf* antithesis.

antologi'a, gi'e |àntōlōjē'à| *sf* anthology.

antonoma'sia *sf* antonomasia; **per ~** par excellence.

an'tro *sm* cavern.

antropo'fago, gi *sm* cannibal.

antropologi'a |àntrōpōlōjē'à| *sf* anthropology.

antropolo'gico, a, ci, che |àntrōpōlo'jčkō| *ag* anthropological.

antropo'logo, a, gi, ghe *sm/f* anthropologist.

anula're *ag* ring *cpd* ♦ *sm* ring finger.

Anver'sa *sf* Antwerp.

an'zi |àn'tsē| *av* (*invece*) on the contrary; (*o meglio*) or rather, or better still.

anzianità |àntsyànētà'| *sf* old age; (*AMM*) seniority.

anzia'no, a |àntsyà'nō| *ag* old; (*AMM*) senior ♦ *sm/f* old person; senior member.

anziché |àntsēkà'| *cong* rather than.

anzitem'po |àntsētcm'pō| *av* (*in anticipo*) early.

anzitut'to |àntsētōōt'tō| *av* first of all.

AO *sigla* = *Aosta.*

aosta'no, a *ag* of (*o* from) Aosta.

AP *sigla* = *Ascoli Piceno.*

apar'theid |àpár'thāēt| *sm* apartheid.

aparti'tico, a, ci, che *ag* (*POL*) non-party *cpd.*

apati'a *sf* apathy, indifference.

apa'tico, a, ci, che *ag* apathetic, indifferent.

a.p.c. *abbr* = **a pronta cassa.**

a'pe *sf* bee.

aperiti'vo *sm* aperitif.

apertamen'te *av* openly.

aper'to, a *pp di* **aprire** ♦ *ag* open ♦ *sm*: **all'~** outdoors; **rimanere a bocca ~a** (*fig*) to be taken aback.

apertu'ra *sf* opening; (*ampiezza*) width, spread; (*POL*) approach; (*FOT*) aperture; **~ alare** wing span; **~ mentale** openmindedness; **~ di credito** (*COMM*) granting of credit.

API *sigla f* = *Associazione Piccole e Medie Industrie.*

a'pice |à'pēchā| *sm* apex; (*fig*) height.

apicolto're *sm* beekeeper.

apicoltu'ra *sf* beekeeping.

apne'a *sf*: **immergersi in ~** to dive without breathing apparatus.

apocalis'se *sf* apocalypse.

apo'lide *ag* stateless.

apoli'tico, a, ci, che *ag* (*neutrale*) nonpolitical; (*indifferente*) apolitical.

apoplessi'a *sf* (*MED*) apoplexy.

apo'stolo *sm* apostle.

apostrofa're *vt* (*parola*) to write with an apostrophe; (*persona*) to address.

apos'trofo *sm* apostrophe.

app. *abbr* (= *appendice*) app.

appagamen'to *sm* satisfaction; fulfilment.

appaga're *vt* to satisfy; (*desiderio*) to fulfil; **~rsi** *vr*: **~rsi di** to be satisfied with.

appaia're *vt* to couple, pair.

appa'io *etc vb vedi* **apparire.**

Appala'chi |àppálá'kē| *smpl*: **i Monti ~** the Appalachian Mountains.

appallottola're *vt* (*carta, foglio*) to crumple into a ball; **~rsi** *vr* (*gatto*) to roll up into a ball.

appaltato're *sm* contractor.

appal'to *sm* (*COMM*) contract; **dare/prendere in ~ un lavoro** to let out/undertake a job on contract.

appannag'gio |àppànnàd'jō| *sm* (*compenso*) annuity; (*fig*) privilege, prerogative.

appanna're *vt* (*vetro*) to mist; (*metallo*) to tarnish; (*vista*) to dim; **~rsi** *vr* to mist over; to tarnish; to grow dim.

appara'to *sm* equipment, machinery; (*ANAT*) apparatus; **~ scenico** (*TEATRO*) props *pl.*

apparecchia're |àppárākkyà'rā| *vt* to prepare; (*tavola*) to set ♦ *vi* to set the table.

apparecchiatu'ra |àppárākkyàtōō'rá| *sf* equipment; (*macchina*) machine, device.

apparec'chio |àppárāk'kyō| *sm* piece of apparatus, device; (*aeroplano*) aircraft *inv*; **~i sanitari** bathroom *o* sanitary appliances; **~ televisivo/telefonico** television set/telephone.

apparen'te *ag* apparent.

apparentemen'te *av* apparently.

apparen'za |àppárcn'tsà| *sf* appearance; **in** *o* **all'~** apparently, to all appearances.

appari're *vi* to appear; (*sembrare*) to seem, appear.

appariscen'te |àppárēshcn'tā| *ag* (*colore*) garish, gaudy; (*bellezza*) striking.

apparizio'ne |àppárcttsyō'nā| *sf* apparition.

appar'so, a *pp di* **apparire.**

appartamen'to *sm* apartment.

appartar'si *vr* to withdraw.

apparta'to, a *ag* (*luogo*) secluded.

appartenen'za |àppártāncn'tsà| *sf*: **~ (a)** (*gen*) belonging (to); (*a un partito, club*) membership (of).

appartene're *vi*: **~ a** to belong to.

appar'vi *etc vb vedi* **apparire.**

appassionan'te *ag* thrilling, exciting.

appassiona're *vt* to thrill; (*commuovere*) to move; **~rsi** *vr*: **~rsi a qc** to take a great interest in sth; to be deeply moved by sth.

appassiona'to, a *ag* passionate; (*entusiasta*): **~ (di)** keen (on).

appassi're *vi* to wither.

appellar'si *vr* (*ricorrere*): **~ a** to appeal to; (*DIR*): **~ contro** to appeal against.

appel'lo *sm* roll-call; (*implorazione, DIR*) appeal; (*sessione d'esame*) exam session; **fare ~ a** to appeal to; **fare l'~** (*INS*) to call the register *o* roll; (*MIL*) to call the roll.

appe'na *av* (*a stento*) hardly, scarcely; (*solamente, da poco*) just ♦ *cong* as soon as; **(non) ~ furono arrivati ...** as soon as they had arrived ...; **~ ... che** *o* **quando** no sooner ... than.

appen'dere *vt* to hang (up).

appendia'biti *sm inv* hook, peg; (*mobile*) hall tree (*US*), hall stand (*Brit*).

appendi'ce |àppándē'chā| *sf* appendix; **romanzo d'~** popular serial.

appendici'te |àppándēchē'tā| *sf* appendicitis.

Appenni'ni *smpl*: **gli ~** the Apennines.

appesanti're *vt* to make heavy; **~rsi** *vr* to grow stout.

appe'so, a *pp di* **appendere.**

appeti'to *sm* appetite.

appetito'so, a *ag* appetising; (*fig*) attractive, desirable.

appezzamen'to |àppāttsámàn'tō| *sm* (*anche*: **~ di terreno**) plot, piece of ground.

appiana're *vt* to level; (*fig*) to smooth away,

iron out; ~**rsi** *vr* (*divergenze*) to be ironed out.

appiatti're *vt* to flatten; ~**rsi** *vr* to become flatter; (*farsi piatto*) to flatten o.s.; ~**rsi al suolo** to lie flat on the ground.

appicca're *vt*: ~ **il fuoco a** to set fire to, set on fire.

appiccica're |àppĕchĕkà'rā| *vt* to stick; (*fig*): ~ **qc a qn** to palm sth off on sb; ~**rsi** *vr* to stick; (*fig: persona*) to cling.

appiccicatic'cio, a, ci, ce |àppĕchĕkátĕch'chō| *ag*, **appiccico'so, a** |àppĕchĕkō'sō| *ag* sticky; (*fig: persona*): **essere ~** to cling like a leech.

appieda'to, a *ag*: **rimanere ~** to be left without means of transport.

appie'no *av* fully.

appigliar'si |àppēlyár'sē| *vr*: ~ **a** (*afferrarsi*) to take hold of; (*fig*) to cling to.

appi'glio |àppēl'yō| *sm* hold; (*fig*) pretext.

appioppa're *vt*: ~ **qc a qn** (*nomignolo*) to pin sth on sb; (*compito difficile*) to saddle sb with sth; **gli ha appioppato un pugno sul muso** he punched him in the face.

appisolar'si *vr* to doze off.

applaudi're *vt, vi* to applaud.

appla'uso *sm* applause *no pl*.

applica'bile *ag*: ~ **(a)** applicable (to).

applica're *vt* to apply; (*regolamento*) to enforce; ~**rsi** *vr* to apply o.s.

applica'to, a *ag* (*arte, scienze*) applied ♦ *sm* (*AMM*) clerk.

applicazio'ne |àppĕkáttsyō'nā| *sf* application; enforcement; ~**i tecniche** (*INS*) vocational education classes (*US*), practical subjects (*Brit*).

appoggia're |àppōdjà'rā| *vt* (*mettere contro*): ~ **qc a qc** to lean *o* rest sth against sth; (*fig: sostenere*) to support; ~**rsi** *vr*: ~**rsi a** to lean against; (*fig*) to rely upon.

appog'gio |àppod'jō| *sm* support.

appollaiar'si *vr* (*anche fig*) to perch.

appon'go, appo'ni *etc vb vedi* **apporre**.

appor're *vt* to affix.

apporta're *vt* to bring.

appor'to *sm* (*gen, FINANZA*) contribution.

appo'si *etc vb vedi* **apporre**.

appositamen'te *av* (*apposta*) on purpose; (*specialmente*) specially.

appo'sito, a *ag* appropriate.

appo'sta *av* on purpose, deliberately; **neanche a farlo ~,** ... by sheer coincidence, ...

apposta're *vt* to lie in wait for; ~**rsi** *vr* to lie in wait.

appo'sto, a *pp di* **apporre**.

appren'dere *vt* (*imparare*) to learn; (*comprendere*) to grasp.

apprendimen'to *sm* learning.

apprendi'sta, i, e *sm/f* apprentice.

apprendista'to *sm* apprenticeship.

apprensio'ne *sf* apprehension.

apprensi'vo, a *ag* apprehensive.

appre'so, a *pp di* **apprendere**.

appres'so *av* (*accanto, vicino*) close by, near; (*dietro*) behind; (*dopo, più tardi*) after, later ♦ *ag inv* (*dopo*): **il giorno ~** the next day; ~ **a** *prep* (*vicino a*) near, close to.

appresta're *vt* to prepare, get ready; ~**rsi** *vr*: ~**rsi a fare qc** to prepare *o* get ready to do sth.

appret'to *sm* starch.

apprezza'bile |àpprāttsá'bēlā| *ag* (*notevole*) noteworthy, significant; (*percepibile*) appreciable.

apprezzamen'to |àpprāttsàmán'tō| *sm* appreciation; (*giudizio*) opinion; (*commento*) comment.

apprezza're |àpprāttsá'rā| *vt* to appreciate.

approc'cio |àpproch'chō| *sm* approach.

approda're *vi* (*NAUT*) to land; (*fig*): **non ~ a nulla** to come to nothing.

appro'do *sm* landing; (*luogo*) landing place.

approfitta're *vi*: ~ **di** (*persona, situazione*) to take advantage of; (*occasione, opportunità*) to make the most of, profit by.

approfondi're *vt* to deepen; (*fig*) to study in depth; ~**rsi** *vr* (*gen, fig*) to deepen; (*peggiorare*) to get worse.

appronta're *vt* to prepare, get ready.

appropriar'si *vr*: ~ **di qc** to appropriate sth, take possession of sth; ~ **indebitamente di** to embezzle.

appropria'to, a *ag* appropriate.

appropriazio'ne |àpprōpryáttsyō'nā| *sf* appropriation; ~ **indebita** (*DIR*) embezzlement.

approssima're *vt* (*cifra*): ~ **per eccesso/per difetto** to round up/down; ~**rsi** *vr*: ~**rsi a** to approach, draw near.

approssimati'vo, a *ag* approximate, rough; (*impreciso*) inexact, imprecise.

approssimazio'ne |àpprōssēmáttsyō'nā| *sf* approximation; **per ~** approximately, roughly.

approva're *vt* (*condotta, azione*) to approve of; (*candidato*) to pass; (*progetto di legge*) to approve.

approvazio'ne |àpprōváttsyō'nā| *sf* approval.

approvvigionamen'to |àpprōvvējōnámán'tō| *sm* supplying; stocking up; ~**i** *smpl* (*MIL*) supplies.

approvvigiona're |àpprōvvējōnà'rā| *vt* to supply; ~**rsi** *vr* to lay in provisions, stock up; ~ **qn di qc** to supply sb with sth.

appuntamen'to *sm* appointment; (*amoroso*) date; **darsi ~** to arrange to meet (one another).

appunta're *vt* (*rendere aguzzo*) to sharpen; (*fissare*) to pin, fix; (*annotare*) to note down.

appunta'to *sm* (*CARABINIERI*) corporal.

appunti'no *av* perfectly.

appunti're *vt* to sharpen.

appun'to *sm* note; *(rimprovero)* reproach ♦ *av (proprio)* exactly, just; **per l'~!, ~!** exactly!

appura're *vt* to check, verify.

apr. *abbr* (= *aprile)* Apr.

apribotti'glie |àprēbōttēl'yä| *sm inv* bottle-opener.

apri'le *sm* April; **pesce d'~!** April Fool!; *per fraseologia vedi* **luglio.**

apri're *vt* to open; *(via, cadavere)* to open up; *(gas, luce, acqua)* to turn on ♦ *vi* to open; **~rsi** *vr* to open; **~ le ostilità** *(MIL)* to start up *o* begin hostilities; **~ una sessione** *(IN-FORM)* to log on; **~rsi a qn** to confide in sb, open one's heart to sb; **mi si è aperto lo stomaco** I'm hungry; **apriti cielo!** heaven forbid!

aprisca'tole *sm inv* can *o* tin *(Brit)* opener.

APT *sigla f* (= *Azienda di Promozione Turistica)* ≈ tourist board.

AQ *sigla* = *Aquila.*

aqua'rio *sm* = **acquario.**

a'quila *sf (ZOOL)* eagle; *(fig)* genius.

aquilo'ne *sm (giocattolo)* kite; *(vento)* North wind.

AR *sigla* = *Arezzo.*

Ara'bia Saudi'ta *sf:* **l'~** Saudi Arabia.

ara'bico, a, ci, che *ag:* **il Deserto ~** the Arabian Desert.

ara'bile *ag* arable.

a'rabo, a *ag, sm/f* Arab ♦ *sm (LING)* Arabic; **parlare ~** *(fig)* to talk incomprehensibly.

ara'chide |árá'kēdä| *sf* peanut.

arago'sta *sf* spiny lobster.

aral'dica *sf* heraldry.

aral'do *sm* herald.

arance'to |àránchā'tō| *sm* orange grove.

aran'cia, ce |àràn'chà| *sf* orange.

arancia'ta |àránchá'tà| *sf* orangeade.

aran'cio |àràn'chō| *sm (BOT)* orange tree; *(colore)* orange ♦ *ag inv (colore)* orange; **fiori di ~** orange blossom *sg.*

arancio'ne |àránchō'nä| *ag inv:* **(color) ~** bright orange.

ara're *vt* to plow *(US)*, plough *(Brit).*

arato're *sm* plowman *(US)*, ploughman *(Brit).*

ara'tro *sm* plow *(US)*, plough *(Brit).*

aratu'ra *sf* plowing *(US)*, ploughing *(Brit).*

araz'zo |àrát'tsō| *sm* tapestry.

arbitrag'gio |àrbētrád'jō| *sm (SPORT)* refereeing; umpiring; *(DIR)* arbitration; *(COMM)* arbitrage.

arbitra're *vt (SPORT)* to referee; to umpire; *(DIR)* to arbitrate.

arbitra'rio, a *ag* arbitrary.

arbitra'to *sm* arbitration.

arbi'trio *sm* will; *(abuso, sopruso)* arbitrary act.

ar'bitro *sm* arbiter, judge; *(DIR)* arbitrator; *(SPORT)* referee; *(: TENNIS, CRICKET)* umpire.

arboscel'lo |àrbōshcl'lō| *sm* sapling.

arbu'sto *sm* shrub.

ar'ca, che *sf (sarcofago)* sarcophagus; **l'~ di Noè** Noah's ark.

arca'ico, a, ci, che *ag* archaic.

arcan'gelo |àrkán'jälō| *sm* archangel.

arca'no, a *ag* arcane, mysterious ♦ *sm* mystery.

arca'ta *sf (ARCHIT, ANAT)* arch; *(ordine di archi)* arcade.

archeologi'a |àrkāōlōjē'á| *sf* arch(a)eology.

archeolo'gico, a, ci, che |àrkāolo'jckō| *ag* arch(a)eological.

archeo'logo, a, gi, ghe |àrkāo'lōgō| *sm/f* arch(a)eologist.

arche'tipo |àrke'tēpō| *sm* archetype.

archet'to |àrkāt'tō| *sm (MUS)* bow.

architetta're |àrkētättà'rä| *vt (fig: ideare)* to devise; *(: macchinare)* to plan, concoct.

architet'to |àrkētät'tō| *sm* architect.

architetto'nico, a, ci, che |àrkētätto'nckō| *ag* architectural.

architettu'ra |àrkētättōō'rá| *sf* architecture.

archivia're |àrkēvyà'rä| *vt (documenti)* to file; *(DIR)* to dismiss.

archiviazio'ne |àrkēvyáttsyō'nä| *sf* filing; dismissal.

archi'vio |àrkē'vyō| *sm* archives *pl; (INFORM)* file; **~ principale** *(INFORM)* master file.

archivi'sta, i, e |àrkēvē'stà| *sm/f (AMM)* archivist; *(in ufficio)* filing clerk.

AR'CI |àr'chē| *sigla f* (= *Associazione Ricreativa Culturale Italiana)* cultural society.

arcie're |àrchc'rä| *sm* archer.

arci'gno, a |àrchēn'yō| *ag* grim, severe.

arcio'ne |àrchō'nä| *sm* saddlebow.

Arcip. *abbr* = **arcipelago.**

arcipe'lago, ghi |àrchēpc'làgō| *sm* archipelago.

arcive'scovo |àrchēvä'skōvō| *sm* archbishop.

ar'co, chi *sm (arma, MUS)* bow; *(ARCHIT)* arch; *(MAT)* arc; **nell'~ di 3 settimane** within the space of 3 weeks; **~ costituzionale** *political parties involved in formulating Italy's post-war constitution.*

arcobale'no *sm* rainbow.

arcua'to, a *ag* curved, bent; **dalle gambe ~e** bow-legged.

arden'te *ag* burning; *(fig)* burning, ardent.

ar'dere *vt, vi* to burn; **legna da ~** firewood.

arde'sia *sf* slate.

ardimen'to *sm* daring.

ardi're *vi* to dare ♦ *sm* daring.

ardi'to, a *ag* brave, daring, bold; *(sfacciato)* bold.

ardo're *sm* blazing heat; *(fig)* ardour, fervour.

ar'duo, a *ag* arduous, difficult.

a'rea *sf* area; *(EDIL)* land, ground; **nell'~ dei partiti di sinistra** among the parties of the left; ~ **fabbricabile** building land; ~ **di rigore** (*SPORT*) penalty area; ~ **di servizio** (*AUT*) service area.

are'na *sf* arena; (*per corride*) bullring; (*sabbia*) sand.

arena'ria *sf* sandstone.

arenar'si *vr* to run aground; (*fig: trattative*) to come to a standstill.

areopla'no *sm* = **aeroplano**.

areti'no, a *ag* of (*o* from) Arezzo.

ar'gano *sm* winch.

argenta'to, a |àrjàntà'tō| *ag* silver-plated; (*colore*) silver, silvery; (*capelli*) silver (-grey).

argen'teo, a |àrjen'tāō| *ag* silver, silvery.

argenteri'a |àrjāntārē'à| *sf* silverware, silver.

argentie're |àrjàntyc'rā| *sm* silversmith.

Argenti'na |àrjàntē'nà| *sf*: **l'~** Argentina.

argenti'no, a |àrjàntē'nō| *ag, sm/f* (*dell'Argentina*) Argentinian ♦ *sf* crewneck sweater.

argen'to |àrjen'tō| *sm* silver; ~ **vivo** quicksilver; **avere l'~ (vivo) addosso** (*fig*) to be fidgety.

argil'la |àrjēl'là| *sf* clay.

argina're |àrjēnà'rā| *vt* (*fiume, acque*) to embank; (: *con diga*) to dike up; (*fig: inflazione, corruzione*) to check; (: *spese*) to limit.

ar'gine |àr'jēnā| *sm* embankment, bank; (*diga*) dike, dyke; **far ~ a, porre un ~ a** (*fig*) to check, hold back.

argomenta're *vi* to argue.

argomen'to *sm* argument; (*materia, tema*) subject; **tornare sull'~** to bring the matter up again.

argui're *vt* to deduce.

argu'to, a *ag* sharp, quick-witted; (*spiritoso*) witty.

argu'zia |àrgōōt'tsyà| *sf* wit; (*battuta*) witty remark.

a'ria *sf* air; (*espressione, aspetto*) air, look; (*MUS: melodia*) tune; (: *di opera*) aria; **all'~ aperta** in the open (air); **manca l'~** it's stuffy; **andare all'~** (*piano, progetto*) to come to nothing; **mandare all'~ qc** to ruin *o* upset sth; **darsi delle ~e** to put on airs; **ha la testa per ~** his head is in the clouds; **che ~ tira?** (*fig: atmosfera*) what's the atmosphere like?

aridità *sf* aridity, dryness; (*fig*) lack of feeling.

a'rido, a *ag* arid.

arieggia're |àryèdjà'rā| *vt* (*cambiare aria*) to air; (*imitare*) to imitate.

arie'te *sm* ram; (*MIL*) battering ram; (*dello zodiaco*): **A~** Aries; **essere dell'A~** to be Aries.

arin'ga, ghe *sf* herring *inv*; ~ **affumicata** smoked herring, kipper; ~ **marinata** pickled herring.

a'rista *sf* (*CUC*) chine of pork.

aristocra'tico, a, ci, che *ag* aristocratic.

aristocrazi'a |àrēstōkràttsē'à| *sf* aristocracy.

aritme'tica *sf* arithmetic.

arlecchi'no |àrlākkē'nō| *sm* harlequin.

ar'ma, i *sf* weapon, arm; (*parte dell'esercito*) arm; **alle ~i!** to arms!; **chiamare alle ~i** to draft (*US*), call up (*Brit*); **sotto le ~i** in the army (*o* armed forces); **combattere ad ~i pari** (*anche fig*) to fight on equal terms; **essere alle prime ~i** (*fig*) to be a novice; **passare qn per le ~i** to execute sb; **battersi all'~ bianca** to fight with blades; ~ **a doppio taglio** (*anche fig*) double-edged weapon; ~ **da fuoco** firearm.

arma'dio *sm* cupboard; (*per abiti*) wardrobe; ~ **a muro** built-in cupboard.

armamenta'rio *sm* equipment, instruments *pl*.

armamen'to *sm* (*MIL*) armament; (: *materiale*) arms *pl*, weapons *pl*; (*NAUT*) fitting out; manning; **la corsa agli ~i** the arms race.

arma're *vt* to arm; (*arma da fuoco*) to cock; (*NAUT: nave*) to rig, fit out; to man; (*EDIL: volta, galleria*) to prop up, shore up; **~rsi** *vr* to arm o.s.; (*MIL*) to take up arms.

arma'to, a *ag*: ~ **(di)** (*anche fig*) armed (with) ♦ *sf* (*MIL*) army; (*NAUT*) fleet; **rapina a mano ~a** armed robbery.

armato're *sm* shipowner.

armatu'ra *sf* (*struttura di sostegno*) framework; (*impalcatura*) scaffolding; (*STORIA*) armor *q* (*US*), armour *q* (*Brit*), suit of armo(u)r.

armeggia're |àrmādjà'rā| *vi* (*affaccendarsi*): ~ **(intorno a qc)** to mess about (with sth).

Arme'nia *sf*: **l'~** Armenia.

arme'no, a *ag, sm/f, sm* Armenian.

armeri'a *sf* (*deposito*) armory (*US*), armoury (*Brit*); (*collezione*) collection of arms.

armisti'zio |àrmēstēt'tsyō| *sm* armistice.

armoni'a *sf* harmony.

armo'nico, a, ci, che *ag* harmonic; (*fig*) harmonious ♦ *sf* (*MUS*) harmonica; **~a a bocca** mouth organ.

armonio'so, a *ag* harmonious.

armonizza're |àrmōnēddzà'rā| *vt* to harmonize; (*colori, abiti*) to match ♦ *vi* to be in harmony; to match.

arne'se *sm* tool, implement; (*oggetto indeterminato*) thing, contraption; **male in ~** (*malvestito*) badly dressed; (*di salute malferma*) in poor health; (*di condizioni economiche*) down-at-the-heels.

ar'nia *sf* hive.

aro'ma, i *sm* aroma; fragrance; **~i** *smpl* herbs and spices; **~i naturali/artificiali** natural/artificial flavoring *sg* (*US*) *o* flavouring *sg* (*Brit*).

aroma'tico, a, ci, che *ag* aromatic; (*cibo*) spicy.

aromatizza're |àrōmàtĕddzà'rā| *vt* to season, flavor (*US*), flavour (*Brit*).

ar'pa *sf* (*MUS*) harp.

arpeg'gio |àrpàd'jō| *sm* (*MUS*) arpeggio.

arpi'a *sf* (*anche fig*) harpy.

arpio'ne *sm* (*gancio*) hook; (*cardine*) hinge; (*PESCA*) harpoon.

arrabattar'si *vr* to do all one can, strive.

arrabbia're *vi* (*cane*) to be affected with rabies; **~rsi** *vr* (*essere preso dall'ira*) to get angry, fly into a rage.

arrabbia'to, a *ag* (*cane*) rabid, with rabies; (*persona*) furious, angry.

arrabbiatu'ra *sf*: **prendersi un'~ (per qc)** to become furious (over sth).

arraffa're *vt* to snatch, seize; (*sottrarre*) to pinch.

arrampicar'si *vr* to climb (up); **~ sui vetri** *o* **sugli specchi** (*fig*) to clutch at straws.

arrampica'ta *sf* climb.

arrampicato're, tri'ce *sm/f* (*gen, SPORT*) climber; **~ sociale** (*fig*) social climber.

arranca're *vi* to limp, hobble; (*fig*) to struggle along.

arrangi'are |àrrànjà'rā| *vt* to arrange; **~rsi** *vr* to manage, do the best one can.

arreca're *vt* to bring; (*causare*) to cause.

arredamen'to *sm* (*studio*) interior design; (*mobili etc*) furnishings *pl*.

arreda're *vt* to furnish.

arredato're, tri'ce *sm/f* interior designer.

arre'do *sm* fittings *pl*, furnishings *pl*; **~ per uffici** office furnishings.

arrembag'gio |àrrāmbàd'jō| *sm* (*NAUT*) boarding.

arren'dersi *vr* to surrender; **~ all'evidenza (dei fatti)** to face (the) facts.

arrende'vole *ag* (*persona*) yielding, compliant.

arrendevolez'za |àrrāndāvōlàt'tsà| *sf* compliancy.

arre'so, a *pp di* **arrendersi**.

arresta're *vt* (*fermare*) to stop, halt; (*catturare*) to arrest; **~rsi** *vr* (*fermarsi*) to stop.

arresta'to, a *sm/f* person under arrest.

arre'sto *sm* (*cessazione*) stopping; (*fermata*) stop; (*cattura, MED*) arrest; (*COMM: in produzione*) stoppage; **subire un ~** to come to a stop *o* standstill; **mettere agli ~i** to place under arrest; **~i domiciliari** (*DIR*) house arrest.

arretra're *vt, vi* to withdraw.

arretra'to, a *ag* (*lavoro*) behind schedule; (*paese, bambino*) backward; (*numero di giornale*) back *cpd*; **~i** *smpl* arrears; **gli ~i dello stipendio** back pay *sg*.

arricchimen'to |àrrĕkkĕmān'tō| *sm* enrich-ment.

arricchi're |àrrĕkkē'rā| *vt* to enrich; **~rsi** *vr* to become rich.

arricchi'to, a |àrrĕkkē'tō| *sm/f* nouveau riche.

arriccia're |àrrĕchà'rā| *vt* to curl; **~ il naso** to turn up one's nose.

arri'dere *vi*: **~ a qn** (*fortuna, successo*) to smile on sb.

arrin'ga, ghe *sf* harangue; (*DIR*) address by counsel.

arrischia're |àrrĕskyà'rā| *vt* to risk; **~rsi** *vr* to venture, dare.

arrischia'to, a |àrrĕskyà'tō| *ag* risky; (*temerario*) reckless, rash.

arri'so, a *pp di* **arridere**.

arriva're *vi* to arrive; (*avvicinarsi*) to come; (*accadere*) to happen, occur; **~ a** (*livello, grado etc*) to reach; **lui arriva a Roma alle 7** he gets to *o* arrives at Rome at 7; **~ a fare qc** to manage to do sth, succeed in doing sth; **non ci arrivo** I can't reach it; (*fig: non capisco*) I can't understand it.

arriva'to, a *ag* (*persona: di successo*) successful ♦ *sm/f*: **essere un ~** to have made it; **nuovo ~** newcomer; **ben ~!** welcome!; **non sono l'ultimo ~!** (*fig*) I'm no fool!

arriveder'ci |àrrēvàdàr'chĕ| *escl* goodbye!

arriveder'la *escl* (*forma di cortesia*) goodbye!

arrivi'smo *sm* (*ambizione*) ambitiousness; (*sociale*) social climbing.

arrivi'sta, i, e *sm/f* go-getter.

arri'vo *sm* arrival; (*SPORT*) finish, finishing line.

arrogan'te *ag* arrogant.

arrogan'za |àrrōgàn'tsà| *sf* arrogance.

arroga're *vt*: **~rsi il diritto di fare qc** to assume the right to do sth; **~rsi il merito di qc** to claim credit for sth.

arrola're *vb* = **arruolare**.

arrossamen'to *sm* reddening.

arrossa're *vt* (*occhi, pelle*) to redden, make red; **~rsi** *vr* to go *o* become red.

arrossi're *vi* (*per vergogna, timidezza*) to blush; (*per gioia*) to flush, blush.

arrosti're *vt* to roast; (*pane*) to toast; (*ai ferri*) to grill.

arro'sto *sm, ag inv* roast; **~ di manzo** roast beef.

arrota're *vt* to sharpen; (*investire con un veicolo*) to run over.

arroti'no *sm* knife grinder.

arrotola're *vt* to roll up.

arrotonda're *vt* (*forma, oggetto*) to round; (*stipendio*) to add to; (*somma*) to round off.

arrovellar'si *vr* (*anche*: **~ il cervello**) to rack one's brains.

arroventa'to, a *ag* red-hot.

arruffa're *vt* to ruffle; (*fili*) to tangle; (*fig: questione*) to confuse.

arruggini're |àrrōōdjĕnē'rā| *vt* to rust; **~rsi** *vr* to rust; (*fig*) to become rusty.

arruolamen'to *sm* (*MIL*) enlistment.

arruola're *vt* (*MIL*) to enlist; ~**rsi** *vr* to enlist, join up.

arsena'le *sm* (*MIL*) arsenal; (*cantiere navale*) dockyard.

arse'nico *sm* arsenic.

ar'si *vb vedi* **ardere**.

ar'so, a *pp di* **ardere** ♦ *ag* (*bruciato*) burnt; (*arido*) dry.

arsu'ra *sf* (*calore opprimente*) burning heat; (*siccità*) drought.

art. *abbr* (= *articolo*) art.

ar'te *sf* art; (*abilità*) skill; **a regola d'**~ (*fig*) perfectly; **senz'**~ **né parte** penniless and out of a job.

artefat'to, a *ag* (*stile, modi*) affected; (*cibo*) adulterated.

arte'fice [àrtā'fēchā] *sm/f* craftsman/woman; (*autore*) author.

arte'ria *sf* artery.

arteriosclero'si *sf* arteriosclerosis, hardening of the arteries.

arterio'so, a *ag* arterial.

ar'tico, a, ci, che *ag* Arctic ♦ *sm*: **l'A**~ the Arctic; **il Circolo polare** ~ the Arctic Circle; **l'Oceano** ~ the Arctic Ocean.

articola're *ag* (*ANAT*) of the joints, articular ♦ *vt* to articulate; (*suddividere*) to divide, split up; ~**rsi** *vr*: ~**rsi in** (*discorso, progetto*) to be divided into.

articola'to, a *ag* (*linguaggio*) articulate; (*AUT*) articulated.

articolazio'ne [àrtēkōláttsyō'nā] *sf* (*ANAT. TECN*) joint; (*di voce, concetto*) articulation.

arti'colo *sm* article; ~ **di fondo** (*STAMPA*) leader, leading article; ~**i di marca** branded goods; **un bell'**~ (*fig*) a real character.

Ar'tide *sm*: **l'**~ the Arctic.

artificia'le [àrtēfēchà'lā] *ag* artificial.

artificie're [àrtēfēche'rā] *sm* (*MIL*) artificer; (: *per disinnescare bombe*) bomb-disposal expert.

artifi'cio [àrtēfē'chō] *sm* (*espediente*) trick, artifice; (*ricerca di effetto*) artificiality.

artificio'so, a [àrtēfēchō'sō] *ag* cunning; (*non spontaneo*) affected.

artigiana'le [àrtējàná'lā] *ag* craft *cpd*.

artigiana'to [àrtējàná'tō] *sm* craftsmanship; craftsmen *pl*.

artigia'no, a [àrtējá'nō] *sm/f* craftsman/woman.

artiglie're [àrtēlye'rā] *sm* artilleryman.

artiglieri'a [àrtēlyārē'à] *sf* artillery.

arti'glio [àrtē'lyō] *sm* claw; (*di rapaci*) talon; **sfoderare gli** ~**i** (*fig*) to show one's claws.

arti'sta, i, e *sm/f* artist; **un lavoro da** ~ (*fig*) a professional piece of work.

arti'stico, a, ci, che *ag* artistic.

ar'to *sm* (*ANAT*) limb.

artri'te *sf* (*MED*) arthritis.

artro'si *sf* osteoarthritis.

arzigogola'to, a [àrdzēgōgōlà'tō] *ag* tortuous.

arzigo'golo [àrdzēgo'gōlō] *sm* tortuous expression.

arzil'lo, a [àrdzēl'lō] *ag* lively, sprightly.

ascel'la [àshel'là] *sf* (*ANAT*) armpit.

ascenden'te [àshānden'tā] *sm* ancestor; (*fig*) ascendancy; (*ASTR*) ascendant.

ascen'dere [àshān'dārā] *vi*: ~ **al trono** to ascend the throne.

ascensio'ne [àshānsyō'nā] *sf* (*ALPINISMO*) ascent; (*REL*): **l'A**~ the Ascension; **isola dell'A**~ Ascension Island.

ascenso're [àshānsō'rā] *sm* elevator (*US*), lift (*Brit*).

asce'sa [àshā'sà] *sf* ascent; (*al trono*) accession; (*al potere*) rise.

asce'si [àshe'zē] *sf* asceticism.

asce'so, a [àshā'sō] *pp di* **ascendere**.

asces'so [àshes'sō] *sm* (*MED*) abscess.

asce'ta, i [àshe'tà] *sm* ascetic.

a'scia, pl a'sce [àsh'shà] *sf* axe.

asciugacapel'li [àshōōgákàpāl'lē] *sm* hair dryer.

asciugama'no [àshōōgàmá'nō] *sm* towel.

asciuga're [àshōōgà'rā] *vt* to dry; ~**rsi** *vr* to dry o.s.; (*diventare asciutto*) to dry.

asciugatri'ce [àshōōgàtrē'chā] *sf* dryer.

asciuttez'za [àshōōttāt'tsà] *sf* dryness; leanness; curtness.

asciut'to, a [àshōōt'tō] *ag* dry; (*fig: magro*) lean; (: *burbero*) curt ♦ *sm*: **restare all'**~ (*fig*) to be left penniless; **restare a bocca** ~**a** (*fig*) to be disappointed.

ascola'no, a *ag* of (o from) Ascoli.

ascolta're *vt* to listen to; ~ **il consiglio di qn** to listen to o heed sb's advice.

ascoltato're, tri'ce *sm/f* listener.

ascol'to *sm*: **essere** o **stare in** ~ to be listening; **dare** o **prestare** ~ **(a)** to pay attention (to); **indice di** ~ (*TV. RADIO*) audience rating.

AS. COM. *sigla f* = *Associazione Commercianti*.

ascrit'to, a *pp di* **ascrivere**.

ascri'vere *vt* (*attribuire*): ~ **qc a qn** to attribute sth to sb; ~ **qc a merito di qn** to give sb credit for sth.

aset'tico, a, ci, che *ag* aseptic.

asfalta're *vt* to asphalt.

asfal'to *sm* asphalt.

asfissi'a *sf* asphyxia, asphyxiation.

asfissian'te *ag* (*gas*) asphyxiating; (*fig: calore, ambiente*) stifling, suffocating; (: *persona*) tiresome.

asfissia're *vt* to asphyxiate, suffocate; (*fig: opprimere*) to stifle; (: *infastidire*) to get on sb's nerves ♦ *vi* to suffocate, asphyxiate.

A'sia *sf*: **l'**~ Asia.

asia'tico, a, ci, che *ag, sm/f* Asiatic, Asian.

asi'lo *sm* refuge, sanctuary; ~ **(d'infanzia)** nursery (school); ~ **nido** crèche; ~ **politico** political asylum.

asimme'trico, a, ci, che *ag* asymmetric(al).

a'sino *sm* donkey, ass; **la bellezza dell'**~ *(fig: di ragazza)* the beauty of youth; **qui casca l'**~! there's the rub!

a'sma *sf* asthma.

asma'tico, a, ci, che *ag, sm/f* asthmatic.

asocia'le |àsōchá'lā| *ag* antisocial.

a'sola *sf* buttonhole.

aspa'rago, gi *sm* asparagus *q.*

asper'gere |àsper'jārā| *vt:* ~ **(di** *o* **con)** to sprinkle (with).

asperità *sf inv* roughness *q;* *(fig)* harshness *q.*

asper'si *etc vb vedi* **aspergere.**

asper'so, a *pp di* **aspergere.**

aspetta're *vt* to wait for; *(anche COMM)* to await; *(aspettarsi)* to expect; *(essere in serbo: notizia, evento etc)* to be in store for, lie ahead of ♦ *vi* to wait; ~**rsi qc** to expect sth; ~ **un bambino** to be expecting (a baby); **questo non me l'aspettavo** I wasn't expecting this; **me l'aspettavo!** I thought as much!

aspettati'va *sf* expectation; **inferiore all'**~ worse than expected; **essere/mettersi in** ~ *(AMM)* to be on/take leave of absence.

aspet'to *sm* *(apparenza)* aspect, appearance, look; *(punto di vista)* point of view; **di bell'**~ good-looking.

aspiran'te *ag* *(attore etc)* aspiring ♦ *sm/f* candidate, applicant.

aspirapol'vere *sm inv* vacuum cleaner.

aspira're *vt* *(respirare)* to breathe in, inhale; *(sog: apparecchi)* to suck (up) ♦ *vi:* ~ **a** to aspire to.

aspirato're *sm* extractor fan.

aspirazio'ne |àspēràttsyō'nā| *sf* *(TECN)* suction; *(anelito)* aspiration.

aspiri'na *sf* aspirin.

asporta're *vt* *(anche MED)* to remove, take away.

asprez'za |àsprāt'tsà| *sf* sourness, tartness; pungency; harshness; roughness; rugged nature.

as'pro, a *ag* *(sapore)* sour, tart; *(odore)* acrid, pungent; *(voce, clima, fig)* harsh; *(superficie)* rough; *(paesaggio)* rugged.

Ass. *abbr* = **assicurazione; assicurata; assegno.**

assaggia're |àssàdjà'rā| *vt* to taste.

assaggi'ni |àssàdjē'nē| *smpl* *(CUC)* selection of first courses.

assag'gio |àssàd'jō| *sm* tasting; *(piccola quantità)* taste; *(campione)* sample.

assa'i *av* *(molto)* a lot, much; *(: con ag)* very; *(a sufficienza)* enough ♦ *ag inv* *(quantità)* a lot of, much; *(numero)* a lot of, many; ~ **contento** very pleased.

assal'go *etc vb vedi* **assalire.**

assali're *vt* to attack, assail.

assalito're, tri'ce *sm/f* attacker, assailant.

assalta're *vt* *(MIL)* to storm; *(banca)* to raid; *(treno, diligenza)* to hold up.

assal'to *sm* attack, assault; **prendere d'**~ *(fig: negozio, treno)* to storm; *(: personalità)* to besiege; **d'**~ *(editoria, giornalista etc)* aggressive.

assapora're *vt* to savor *(US)*, savour *(Brit)*.

assassina're *vt* to murder; *(POL)* to assassinate; *(fig)* to ruin.

assassi'nio *sm* murder; assassination.

assassi'no, a *ag* murderous ♦ *sm/f* murderer; assassin.

as'se *sm* *(TECN)* axle; *(MAT)* axis ♦ *sf* board; ~ **da stiro** ironing board.

asseconda're *vt:* ~ **qn (in qc)** to go along with sb (in sth); ~ **i desideri di qn** to go along with sb's wishes; ~ **i capricci di qn** to give in to sb's whims.

assedia're *vt* to besiege.

asse'dio *sm* siege.

assegna're |àssānyà'rā| *vt* to assign, allot; *(premio)* to award.

assegnata'rio |àssānyàtá'ryō| *sm* *(DIR)* assignee; *(COMM)* recipient; **l'**~ **del premio** the person awarded the prize.

assegnazio'ne |àssānyàttsyō'nā| *sf* *(di casa, somma)* allocation; *(di carica)* assignment; *(di premio, borsa di studio)* awarding.

asse'gno |àssān'yō| *sm* allowance; *(anche:* ~ **bancario)** check *(US)*, cheque *(Brit)*; **contro** ~ cash on delivery; ~ **circolare** bank draft; ~ **di invalidità** *o* **di malattia** injury *o* sickness benefit; ~ **post-datato** post-dated check; ~ **sbarrato** ≈ check for deposit only *(US)*, crossed cheque *(Brit)*; ~ **non sbarrato** ≈ negotiable check *(US)*, uncrossed cheque *(Brit)*; ~ **di studio** study grant; **"**~ **non trasferibile"** "non transferable" *(US)*, "account payee only" *(Brit)*; ~ **di viaggio** travel(l)er's check; ~ **a vuoto** bad check *(US)*, dud cheque *(Brit)*; ~**i alimentari** alimony *sg;* ~**i familiari** ≈ child welfare *sg* *(US)*, ≈ child benefit *sg* *(Brit)*.

assemblag'gio |àssāmblàd'jō| *sm* *(INDUSTRIA)* assembly.

assembla're *vt* to assemble.

assemble'a *sf* assembly; *(raduno, adunanza)* meeting.

assembramen'to *sm* public gathering; **divieto di** ~ ban on public meetings.

assenna'to, a *ag* sensible.

assen'so *sm* assent, consent.

assentar'si *vr* to go out.

assen'te *ag* absent; *(fig)* faraway, vacant ♦ *sm/f* absentee.

assentei'smo *sm* absenteeism.

assentei'sta, i, e *sm/f* *(dal lavoro)* absentee.

assenti're *vi*: ~ **(a)** to agree (to), assent (to).

assen'za |àssen'tsà| *sf* absence.

asseri're *vt* to maintain, assert.

asserragliar'si |àssàrràlyàr'sē| *vr*: ~ **(in)** to barricade o.s. (in).

asservi're *vt* to enslave; (*fig: animo, passioni*) to subdue; ~**rsi** *vr*: ~**rsi (a)** to submit (to).

asserzio'ne |àssārtsyō'nā| *sf* assertion.

assessora'to *sm* councillorship.

assesso're *sm* councillor.

assestamen'to *sm* (*sistemazione*) arrangement; (*EDIL, GEO*) settlement.

assesta're *vt* (*mettere in ordine*) to put in order, arrange; ~**rsi** *vr* to settle in; (*GEO*) to settle; ~ **un colpo a qn** to deal sb a blow.

asseta'to, a *ag* thirsty, parched.

asset'to *sm* order, arrangement; (*NAUT, AER*) trim; **in ~ di guerra** on a war footing; ~ **territoriale** land management.

assicura're *vt* (*accertare*) to ensure; (*infondere certezza*) to assure; (*fermare, legare*) to make fast, secure; (*fare un contratto di assicurazione*) to insure; ~**rsi** *vr* (*accertarsi*): ~**rsi (di)** to make sure (of); (*contro il furto etc*): ~**rsi (contro)** to insure o.s. (against).

assicura'to, a *ag* insured ♦ *sf* (*anche*: **lettera** ~**a**) registered letter.

assicurato're, tri'ce *ag* insurance *cpd* ♦ *sm/f* insurance agent; **società** ~**trice** insurance company.

assicurazio'ne |àssēkōōràttsyō'nā| *sf* assurance; insurance; ~ **multi-rischio** comprehensive insurance.

assideramen'to *sm* exposure.

assidera're *vt* to freeze; ~**rsi** *vr* to freeze; **morire assiderato** to die of exposure.

assi'duo, a *ag* (*costante*) assiduous; (*regolare*) regular.

assie'me *av* (*insieme*) together ♦ *prep*: ~ **a** (together) with.

assillan'te *ag* (*dubbio, pensiero*) nagging; (*creditore*) pestering.

assilla're *vt* to pester, torment.

assil'lo *sm* (*fig*) worrying thought.

assimila're *vt* to assimilate.

assimilazio'ne |àssēmēlàttsyō'nā| *sf* assimilation.

assio'ma, i *sm* axiom.

assioma'tico, a, ci, che *ag* axiomatic.

assi'se *sfpl* (*DIR*) assizes; **corte** *f* **d'**~ court of assizes.

assisten'te *sm/f* assistant; ~ **sociale** social worker; ~ **universitario** (assistant) lecturer; ~ **di volo** (*AER*) flight attendant.

assisten'za |àssēsten'tsà| *sf* assistance; ~ **legale** legal aid; ~ **ospedaliera** free hospital treatment; ~ **sanitaria** health service; ~ **sociale** welfare services *pl*.

assistenzia'le |àssēstāntsyà'lā| *ag* (*ente, orga-*

nizzazione) welfare *cpd*; (*opera*) charitable.

assistenziali'smo |àssēstāntsyàlēz'mō| *sm* (*peg*) excessive state aid.

assi'stere *vt* (*aiutare*) to assist, help; (*curare*) to treat ♦ *vi*: ~ **(a qc)** (*essere presente*) to be present (at sth), attend (sth).

assisti'to, a *pp di* **assistere**.

as'so *sm* ace; **piantare qn in** ~ to leave sb in the lurch.

associa're |àssōchá'rā| *vt* to associate; (*rendere partecipe*): ~ **qn a** (*affari*) to take sb into partnership in; (*partito*) to make sb a member of; ~**rsi** *vr* to enter into partnership; ~**rsi a** to become a member of, join; (*dolori, gioie*) to share in; ~ **qn alle carceri** to take sb to prison.

associazio'ne |àssōchàttsyō'nā| *sf* association; ~ **di categoria** trade association; ~ **a** *o* **per delinquere** (*DIR*) criminal association; **A**~ **Europea di Libero Scambio** European Free Trade Association, EFTA; ~ **in partecipazione** (*COMM*) joint venture.

assoda're *vt* (*muro, posizione*) to strengthen; (*fatti, verità*) to ascertain.

assoda'to, a *ag* well-founded.

assoggetta're |àssōdjàttà'rā| *vt* to subject, subjugate; ~**rsi** *vr*: ~**rsi a** to submit to.

assola'to, a *ag* sunny.

assolda're *vt* to recruit.

assol'si *etc vb vedi* **assolvere**.

assol'to, a *pp di* **assolvere**.

assolutamen'te *av* absolutely.

assolu'to, a *ag* absolute.

assoluzio'ne |àssōlōōttsyō'nā| *sf* (*DIR*) acquittal; (*REL*) absolution.

assol'vere *vt* (*DIR*) to acquit; (*REL*) to absolve; (*adempiere*) to carry out, perform.

assomiglia're |àssōmēlyá'rā| *vi*: ~ **a** to resemble, look like.

assonna'to, a *ag* sleepy.

assopir'si *vr* to doze off.

assorben'te *ag* absorbent ♦ *sm*: ~ **igienico** sanitary napkin (*US*) *o* towel (*Brit*); ~ **interno** tampon.

assorbi're *vt* to absorb; (*fig: far proprio*) to assimilate.

assorda're *vt* to deafen.

assortimen'to *sm* assortment.

assorti'to, a *ag* assorted; (*colori*) matched, matching.

assor'to, a *ag* absorbed, engrossed.

assottiglia're |àssōttēlyà'rā| *vt* to make thin, thin; (*aguzzare*) to sharpen; (*ridurre*) to reduce; ~**rsi** *vr* to grow thin; (*fig: ridursi*) to be reduced.

A.S.S.T. *sigla f* (= *Azienda di Stato per i Servizi Telefonici*) *state-run telecommunications company*.

assuefa're *vt* to accustom; ~**rsi** *vr*: ~**rsi a** to get used to, accustom o.s. to.

assuefat'to, a *pp di* **assuefare.**

assuefazio'ne |àssōōāfáttsyō'nā| *sf* (*MED*) addiction.

assu'mere *vt* (*impiegato*) to take on, engage; (*responsabilità*) to assume, take upon o.s.; (*contegno, espressione*) to assume, put on; (*droga*) to consume.

assun'si *etc vb vedi* **assumere.**

assun'to, a *pp di* **assumere** ♦ *sm* (*tesi*) proposition.

assunzio'ne |àssōōntsyō'nā| *sf* (*di impiegati*) employment, engagement; (*REL*): **l'A**~ the Assumption.

assurdità *sf inv* absurdity; **dire delle** ~ to talk nonsense.

assur'do, a *ag* absurd.

a'sta *sf* pole; (*modo di vendita*) auction.

astan'te *sm* bystander.

astanteri'a *sf* emergency (*US*) o casualty (*Brit*) department.

aste'mio, a *ag* teetotal ♦ *sm/f* teetotaller.

astener'si *vr*: ~ **(da)** to abstain (from), refrain (from); (*POL*) to abstain (from).

astensio'ne *sf* abstention.

astensioni'sta, i, e *sm/f* (*POL*) abstentionist.

asteri'sco, schi *sm* asterisk.

astero'ide *sm* asteroid.

a'stice |à'stēchā| *sm* lobster.

astigia'no, a |àstējà'nō| *ag* of (*o* from) Asti.

astinen'za |àstēncn'tsá| *sf* abstinence; **essere in crisi di** ~ to suffer from withdrawal symptoms.

a'stio *sm* rancour, resentment.

astratti'smo *sm* (*ARTE*) abstract art.

astrat'to, a *ag* abstract.

as'tro *sm* star.

astrologi'a |àstrōlōjē'á| *sf* astrology.

astrolo'gico, a, ci, che |àstrōlo'jēkō| *ag* astrological.

astro'logo, a, ghi, ghe *sm/f* astrologer.

astrona'uta, i, e *sm/f* astronaut.

astrona'utica *sf* astronautics *sg*.

astrona've *sf* space ship.

astronomi'a *sf* astronomy.

astrono'mico, a, ci, che *ag* astronomic(al).

astro'nomo *sm* astronomer.

astuc'cio |àstōōch'chō| *sm* case, box, holder.

astu'to, a *ag* astute, cunning, shrewd.

astu'zia |àstōōt'tsyà| *sf* astuteness, shrewdness; (*azione*) trick.

AT *sigla* = *Asti.*

A.T. *abbr* (= *alta tensione*) HT.

ATA *sigla f* = *Associazione Turistica Albergatori.*

ata'vico, a, ci, che *ag* atavistic.

atei'smo *sm* atheism.

atelier |àtəlyā'| *sm inv* (*laboratorio*) workshop; (*studio*) studio; (*sartoria*) fashion house.

Ate'ne *sf* Athens.

atene'o *sm* university.

atenie'se *ag, sm/f* Athenian.

a'teo, a *ag, sm/f* atheist.

ati'pico, a, ci, che *ag* atypical.

atlan'te *sm* atlas; **i Monti dell'A**~ the Atlas Mountains.

atlan'tico, a, ci, che *ag* Atlantic ♦ *sm*: **l'A**~, **l'Oceano A**~ the Atlantic, the Atlantic Ocean.

atle'ta, i, e *sm/f* athlete.

atle'tica *sf* athletics *sg*; ~ **leggera** track and field events *pl*; ~ **pesante** weightlifting and wrestling.

ATM *sigla f* = *Azienda Tranviaria Municipale.*

atmosfe'ra *sf* atmosphere.

atmosfe'rico, a, ci, che *ag* atmospheric.

atol'lo *sm* atoll.

ato'mico, a, ci, che *ag* atomic; (*nucleare*) atomic, atom *cpd*, nuclear.

atomizzato're |àtōmēddzàtō'rā| *sm* (*di acqua, lacca*) spray; (*di profumo*) atomizer.

a'tomo *sm* atom.

a'tono, a *ag* (*FONETICA*) unstressed.

a'trio *sm* entrance hall, lobby.

atro'ce |àtrō'chā| *ag* (*che provoca orrore*) dreadful; (*terribile*) atrocious.

atrocità |àtrōchētá| *sf inv* atrocity.

atrofi'a *sf* atrophy.

attaccabri'ghe |àttàkkàbrē'gā| *sm/f inv* quarrelsome person.

attaccamen'to *sm* (*fig*) attachment, affection.

attaccapan'ni *sm* hook, peg; (*mobile*) hall stand.

attacca're *vt* (*unire*) to attach; (*cucendo*) to sew on; (*far aderire*) to stick (on); (*appendere*) to hang (up); (*assalire: anche fig*) to attack; (*iniziare*) to begin, start; (*fig: contagiare*) to pass on ♦ *vi* to stick, adhere; ~**rsi** *vr* to stick, adhere; (*trasmettersi per contagio*) to be contagious; (*afferrarsi*): ~**rsi (a)** to cling (to); (*fig: affezionarsi*): ~**rsi (a)** to become attached (to); ~ **discorso** to start a conversation; **con me non attacca!** that won't work with me!

attaccatic'cio, a, ci, ce |àttàkkàtēch'chō| *ag* sticky.

attaccatu'ra *sf* (*di manica*) join; ~ **(dei capelli)** hairline.

attac'co, chi *sm* (*azione offensiva: anche fig*) attack; (*MED*) attack, fit; (*SCI*) binding; (*ELETTR*) socket.

attanaglia're |àttànàlyà'rā| *vt* (*anche fig*) to grip.

attardar'si *vr*: ~ **a fare qc** (*fermarsi*) to stop to do sth; (*stare più a lungo*) to stay behind to do sth.

attecchi're |àttākkē'rā| *vi* (*pianta*) to take root; (*fig*) to catch on.

atteggiamen'to *sm* attitude.

atteggiar'si |àttādjàr'sē| *vr*: ~ **a** to pose as.

attempa'to, a *ag* elderly.

attenden'te *sm* (*MIL.*) orderly.

atten'dere *vt* to wait for, await ♦ *vi*: ~ **a** to attend to.

attendi'bile *ag* (*scusa, storia*) credible; (*fonte, testimone, notizia*) reliable; (*persona*) trustworthy.

attener'si *vr*: ~ **a** to keep o stick to.

attenta're *vi*: ~ **a** to make an attempt on.

attenta'to *sm* attack; ~ **alla vita di qn** attempt on sb's life.

atten'to, a *ag* attentive; (*accurato*) careful, thorough ♦ *escl* be careful!; **stare** ~ **a qc** to pay attention to sth; **~i!** (*MIL.*) attention!; **~i al cane** beware of the dog.

attenuan'te *sf* (*DIR*) extenuating circumstance.

attenua're *vt* to alleviate, ease; (*diminuire*) to reduce; **~rsi** *vr* to ease, abate.

attenuazio'ne |àttānōōàttsyō'nā| *sf* alleviation; easing; reduction.

attenzio'ne |àttāntsyō'nā| *sf* attention ♦ *escl* watch out!, be careful!; **coprire qn di ~i** to lavish attention on sb.

atterrag'gio |àttārràd'jō| *sm* landing; ~ **di fortuna** emergency landing.

atterra're *vt* to bring down ♦ *vi* to land.

atterri're *vt* to terrify.

atte'sa *sf* vedi **atteso**.

atte'si *etc* *vb* vedi **attendere**.

atte'so, a *pp* *di* **attendere** ♦ *sf* waiting; (*tempo trascorso aspettando*) wait; **essere in ~a di qc** to be waiting for sth; **in ~a di una vostra risposta** (*COMM*) awaiting your reply; **restiamo in ~a di Vostre ulteriori notizie** (*COMM*) we look forward to hearing (further) from you.

attesta're *vt*: ~ **qc/che** to testify to sth/(to the fact) that.

attesta'to *sm* certificate.

attestazio'ne |àttāstàttsyō'nā| *sf* (*certificato*) certificate; (*dichiarazione*) statement.

at'tico, ci *sm* attic.

atti'guo, a *ag* adjacent, adjoining.

attilla'to, a *ag* (*vestito*) close-fitting, tight; (*persona*) dressed up.

at'timo *sm* moment; **in un** ~ in a moment.

attinen'te *ag*: ~ **a** relating to, concerning.

attinen'za |àttēncn'tsà| *sf* connection.

attin'gere |àttēn'jārā| *vt*: ~ **a** o **da** (*acqua*) to draw from; (*denaro, notizie*) to obtain from.

attin'to, a *pp* *di* **attingere**.

attira're *vt* to attract; **~rsi delle critiche** to incur criticism.

attitu'dine *sf* (*disposizione*) aptitude; (*atteggiamento*) attitude.

attiva're *vt* to activate; (*far funzionare*) to set going, start.

attivi'sta, i, e *sm/f* activist.

attività *sf* *inv* activity; (*COMM*) assets *pl*; ~ **liquide** (*COMM*) liquid assets.

atti'vo, a *ag* active; (*COMM*) profit-making ♦ *sm* (*COMM*) assets *pl*; **in** ~ in credit; **chiudere in** ~ to show a profit; **avere qc al proprio** ~ (*fig*) to have sth to one's credit.

attizza're |àttēttsà'rā| *vt* (*fuoco*) to poke; (*fig*) to stir up.

attizzato'io |àttēttsàtō'yō| *sm* poker.

at'to, a *ag*: ~ **a** fit for, capable of ♦ *sm* act; (*azione, gesto*) action, act, deed; (*DIR: documento*) deed, document; **~i** *smpl* (*di congressi etc*) proceedings; **essere in** ~ to be under way; **mettere in** ~ to put into action; **fare** ~ **di fare qc** to make as if to do sth; **all'~ pratico** in practice; **dare** ~ **a qn di qc** to give sb credit for sth; ~ **di nascita/morte** birth/death certificate; ~ **di proprietà** title deed; ~ **pubblico** official document; ~ **di vendita** bill of sale; **~i osceni** (**in luogo pubblico**) (*DIR*) indecent exposure; **~i verbali** transactions.

atto'nito, a *ag* dumbfounded, astonished.

attorciglia're |àttōrchēlyà'rā| *vt*, **~rsi** *vr* to twist.

atto're, tri'ce *sm/f* actor/actress.

attornia're *vt* (*circondare*) to surround; **~rsi** *vr*: **~rsi di** to surround o.s. with.

attor'no *av*, ~ **a** *prep* round, around, about.

attracca're *vt, vi* (*NAUT*) to dock, berth.

attrac'co, chi *sm* (*NAUT: manovra*) docking, berthing; (*luogo*) berth.

attra'e *etc vb vedi* **attrarre**.

attraen'te *ag* attractive.

attrag'go *etc vb vedi* **attrarre**.

attrar're *vt* to attract.

attras'si *etc vb vedi* **attrarre**.

attratti'va *sf* attraction, charm.

attrat'to, a *pp* *di* **attrarre**.

attraversamen'to *sm* crossing; ~ **pedonale** pedestrian crossing.

attraversa're *vt* to cross; (*città, bosco, fig: periodo*) to go through; (*sog: fiume*) to run through.

attraver'so *prep* through; (*da una parte all'altra*) across.

attrazio'ne |àttràttsyō'nā| *sf* attraction.

attrezza're |àttrāttsà'rā| *vt* to equip; (*NAUT*) to rig.

attrezzatu'ra |àttrāttsàtōō'rà| *sf* equipment *q*; rigging; **~e per uffici** office equipment.

attrez'zo |àttrāt'tsō| *sm* tool, instrument; (*SPORT*) piece of equipment.

attribui're *vt*: ~ **qc a qn** (*assegnare*) to give o award sth to sb; (*quadro etc*) to attribute sth to sb.

attribu'to *sm* attribute.

attri'ce |àttrē'chā| *sf* vedi **attore**.

attri'to *sm* (*anche fig*) friction.

attua'bile *ag* feasible.

attuabilità *sf* feasibility.

attua'le *ag* (*presente*) present; (*di attualità*)

topical; (*che è in atto*) actual.

attualità *sf inv* topicality; (*avvenimento*) current event; **notizie d'~** (*TV*) the news *sg*.

attualizza're [àttōōáléddzà'rā] *vt* to update, bring up to date.

attualmen'te *av* at the moment, at present.

attua're *vt* to carry out; **~rsi** *vr* to be realized.

attuazio'ne [àttōōáttsyō'nā] *sf* carrying out.

attuti're *vt* to deaden, reduce; **~rsi** *vr* to die down.

A.U. *abbr* = **allievo ufficiale.**

auda'ce [àōōdà'chā] *ag* audacious, daring, bold; (*provocante*) provocative; (*sfacciato*) impudent, bold.

auda'cia [àōōdà'chá] *sf* audacity, daring; boldness; provocativeness; impudence.

a'udio *sm* (*TV, RADIO, CINEMA*) sound.

audiocasset'ta *sf* (audio) cassette.

audiole'so, a *sm/f* person who is hard of hearing.

audiovisi'vo, a *ag* audiovisual.

audito'rio *sm* auditorium.

audizio'ne [àōōdēttsyō'nā] *sf* hearing; (*MUS*) audition.

a'uge [à'ōōjā] *sf* (*della gloria, carriera*) height, peak; **essere in ~** to be at the top.

augura'le *ag*: **messaggio ~** greeting; **biglietto ~** greeting(s) card.

augura're *vt* to wish; **~rsi qc** to hope for sth.

augu'rio *sm* (*presagio*) omen; (*voto di benessere etc*) (good) wish; **essere di buon/ cattivo ~** to be of good omen/be ominous; **fare gli ~i a qn** to give sb one's best wishes; **tanti ~i!** all the best!

a'ula *sf* (*scolastica*) classroom; (*universitaria*) lecture hall; (*di edificio pubblico*) hall; **~ magna** main hall; **~ del tribunale** courtroom.

aumenta're *vt, vi* to increase; **~ di peso** (*persona*) to put on weight; **la produzione è aumentata del 50%** production has increased by 50%.

aumen'to *sm* increase.

a'ureo, a *ag* (*di oro*) gold *cpd*; (*fig: colore, periodo*) golden.

aure'ola *sf* halo.

auro'ra *sf* dawn.

ausilia're *ag, sm, sm/f* auxiliary.

ausi'lio *sm* aid.

auspica'bile *ag* desirable.

auspica're *vt* to call for, express a desire for.

auspi'cio [àōōspē'chō] *sm* omen; (*protezione*) patronage; **sotto gli ~i di** under the auspices of; **è di buon ~** it augurs well.

austerità *sf inv* austerity.

auste'ro, a *ag* austere.

austra'le *ag* southern.

Austra'lia *sf*: **l'~** Australia.

australia'no, a *ag, sm/f* Australian.

A'ustria *sf*: **l'~** Austria.

austri'aco, a, ci, che *ag, sm/f* Austrian.

autar'chico, a, ci, che [àōōtàr'kēkō] *ag* (*sistema*) self-sufficient, autarkic; (*prodotto*) home *cpd*, home-produced.

a'ut a'ut *sm inv* ultimatum.

autentica're *vt* to authenticate.

autenticità [àōōtāntēchētà'] *sf* authenticity.

auten'tico, a, ci, che *ag* (*quadro, firma*) authentic, genuine; (*fatto*) true, genuine.

auti'sta, i *sm* driver; (*personale*) chauffeur.

a'uto *sf inv* car.

autoadesi'vo, a *ag* self-adhesive ♦ *sm* sticker.

autoarticola'to *sm* semi(trailer) (*US*), articulated lorry (*Brit*).

autobiografi'a *sf* autobiography.

autobiogra'fico, a, ci, che *ag* autobiographic(al).

autoblin'da *sf* armored (*US*) *o* armoured (*Brit*) car.

autobom'ba *sf inv* car bomb.

autobot'te *sf* tanker.

a'utobus *sm inv* bus.

autocar'ro *sm* truck.

autocister'na [àōōtōchēster'nà] *sf* tanker.

autocolon'na *sf* convoy.

autocontrol'lo *sm* self-control.

autocopiati'vo, a *ag*: **carta ~a** carbonless paper.

autocorrie'ra *sf* coach, bus.

autocra'tico, a, ci, che *ag* autocratic.

autocri'tica, che *sf* self-criticism.

autoc'tono, a *ag, sm/f* native.

autodemolizio'ne [àōōtōdāmōlēttsyō'nā] *sf* wrecking (*US*) *o* breaker's (*Brit*) yard.

autodidat'ta, i, e *sm/f* autodidact, self-taught person.

autodife'sa *sf* self-defence.

autoferrotranvia'rio, a *ag* public transport *cpd*.

autogestio'ne [àōōtōjāstyō'nā] *sf* worker management.

autogesti'to, a [àōōtōjāstē'tō] *ag* under worker management.

auto'grafo, a *ag, sm* autograph.

autogrill' *sm inv* roadside restaurant.

autolesioni'smo *sm* (*fig*) self-destruction.

autoli'nea *sf* bus route.

auto'ma, i *sm* automaton.

automa'tico, a, ci, che *ag* automatic ♦ *sm* (*bottone*) snap fastener; (*fucile*) automatic; **selezione ~a** (*TEL*) direct dialling.

automazio'ne [àōōtōmáttsyō'nā] *sf*: **~ delle procedure d'ufficio** office automation.

automez'zo [àōōtōmcd'dzō] *sm* motor vehicle.

automo'bile *sf* (motor) car; **~ da corsa** race car (*US*), racing car (*Brit*).

automobili'smo *sm* (*gen*) motoring; (*SPORT*) motor racing.

automobili'sta, i, e *sm/f* motorist.
automobili'stico, a, ci, che *ag* automobile *cpd*, car *cpd*; (*sport*) motor *cpd*.
autonoleg'gio [àōōtōnōlàd'jō] *sm* car rental (*US*), car hire (*Brit*).
autonomi'a *sf* autonomy; (*di volo*) range.
auto'nomo, a *ag* autonomous; (*sindacato, pensiero*) independent.
autopar'co, chi *sm* (*parcheggio*) parking lot (*US*), car park (*Brit*); (*insieme di automezzi*) transport fleet.
autopom'pa *sf* fire engine.
autopsi'a *sf* post-mortem (examination), autopsy.
autora'dio *sf inv* (*apparecchio*) car radio; (*autoveicolo*) radio car.
auto're, tri'ce *sm/f* author; **l'~ del furto** the person who committed the robbery; **diritti d'~** copyright *sg*; (*compenso*) royalties.
autoregolamentazio'ne [àōōtōràgōlàmàntàt-tsyō'nà] *sf* self-regulation.
autore'vole *ag* authoritative; (*persona*) influential.
autorilevazio'ne [àōōtōrēlàvàttsyō'nà] *sf:* **~ di errori** (*INFORM*) automatic error detection.
autorimes'sa *sf* garage.
autorità *sf inv* authority.
autoritrat'to *sm* self-portrait.
autorizza're [àōōtōrēddzà'rà] *vt* to authorize, give permission for.
autorizzazio'ne [àōōtōrēddzàttsyō'nà] *sf* authorization.
autoscat'to *sm* (*FOT*) timer.
autoscon'tro *sm* bumper car.
autoscuo'la *sf* driving school.
autosnoda'to *sm* articulated vehicle.
autostop' *sm* hitchhiking.
autostoppi'sta, i, e *sm/f* hitchhiker.
autostra'da *sf* freeway (*US*), motorway (*Brit*).
autosufficien'te [àōōtōsōōffēchen'tà] *ag* self-sufficient.
autotassazio'ne [àōōtōtàssàttsyō'nà] *sf system of taxation where individual himself assesses and pays tax due.*
autotre'no *sm* semi(trailer) (*US*), articulated lorry (*Brit*).
autovei'colo *sm* motor vehicle.
autovettu'ra *sf* (motor) car.
autunna'le *ag* (*di autunno*) autumn *cpd*; (*da autunno*) autumnal.
autun'no *sm* autumn.
AV *sigla* = *Avellino.*
a/v *abbr* = **a vista.**
avalla're *vt* (*FINANZA*) to guarantee; (*fig: sostenere*) to back; (*: confermare*) to confirm.
aval'lo *sm* (*FINANZA*) guarantee.
avambrac'cio, *pl(f)* **-cia** [àvàmbràch'chō] *sm* forearm.

avampo'sto *sm* (*MIL*) outpost.
Ava'na *sf:* **l'~** Havana.
ava'na *sm inv* (*sigaro*) Havana (cigar); (*colore*) Havana brown.
avanguar'dia *sf* vanguard; (*ARTE*) avant-garde.
avanscoper'ta *sf* (*MIL*) reconnaissance; **andare in ~** to reconnoitre.
avan'ti *av* (*stato in luogo*) in front; (*moto: andare, venire*) forward; (*tempo: prima*) before ♦ *prep* (*luogo*): **~ a** before, in front of; (*tempo*): **~ Cristo** before Christ ♦ *escl* (*entrate*) come (o go) in!; (*MIL*) forward!; (*coraggio*) come on! ♦ *sm inv* (*SPORT*) forward; **il giorno ~** the day before; **~ e indietro** backwards and forwards; **andare ~** to go forward; (*continuare*) to go on; (*precedere*) to go (on) ahead; (*orologio*) to be fast; **essere ~ negli studi** to be well advanced with one's studies; **mandare ~ la famiglia** to provide for one's family; **mandare ~ un'azienda** to run a business; **~ il prossimo!** next please!
avantre'no *sm* (*AUT*) front chassis.
avanzamen'to [àvàntsàmàn'tō] *sm* (*gen*) advance; (*fig*) progress; promotion.
avanza're [àvàntsà'rà] *vt* (*spostare in avanti*) to move forward, advance; (*domanda*) to put forward; (*promuovere*) to promote; (*essere creditore*): **~ qc da qn** to be owed sth by sb ♦ *vi* (*andare avanti*) to move forward, advance; (*fig: progredire*) to make progress; (*essere d'avanzo*) to be left, remain; **basta e avanza** that's more than enough.
avanza'to, a [àvàntsà'tō] *ag* (*teoria, tecnica*) advanced ♦ *sf* (*MIL*) advance; **in età ~a** advanced in years, up in years.
avan'zo [àvàn'tsō] *sm* (*residuo*) remains *pl*, left-overs *pl*; (*MAT*) remainder; (*COMM*) surplus; (*eccedenza di bilancio*) profit carried forward; **averne d'~ di qc** to have more than enough of sth; **~ di cassa** cash in hand; **~ di galera** (*fig*) jailbird.
avari'a *sf* (*guasto*) damage; (*: meccanico*) breakdown.
avaria'to, a *ag* (*merce*) damaged; (*cibo*) off.
avari'zia [àvàrēt'tsyà] *sf* avarice; **crepi l'~!** to hang with the expense!
ava'ro, a *ag* avaricious, miserly ♦ *sm* miser.
ave'na *sf* oats *pl*.
ave're *sm* (*COMM*) credit; **~i** *smpl* (*ricchezza*) wealth *sg*, possessions ♦ *vt*, *vb ausiliare* to have; **~ da mangiare/bere** to have something to eat/drink; **~ da o a fare qc** to have to do sth; **~ (a) che fare** *o* **vedere con qn/qc** to have to do with sb/sth; **ho 28 anni** I am 28 (years old); **cos'hai?** what's wrong *o* what's the matter (with you)?; **avercela con qn** to have something against sb; **quanti ne abbiamo oggi?** what's the date today?; **ne ha ancora per molto?** have you got much longer

to go?; **averne fin sopra i capelli** *o* **piene le tasche** (*fam*) to be fed up to the teeth; *vedi anche* **fame, freddo** *etc*.

a'vi *smpl* ancestors, forefathers.

aviato're, tri'ce *sm/f* aviator, pilot.

aviazio'ne [àvyáttsyō'nā] *sf* aviation; (*MIL*) air force; ~ **civile** civil aviation.

avicoltu'ra *sf* bird breeding; (*di pollame*) poultry farming.

avidità *sf* eagerness; greed.

a'vido, a *ag* eager; (*peg*) greedy.

avie're *sm* (*MIL*) airman.

avitamino'si *sf* vitamin deficiency.

avoca'do *sm* avocado.

avo'rio *sm* ivory.

avul'so, a *ag*: **parole** ~**e dal contesto** words out of context; ~ **dalla società** (*fig*) cut off from society.

Avv. *abbr* = **avvocato**.

avvaler'si *vr*: ~ **di** to avail o.s. of.

avvallamen'to *sm* sinking *q*; (*effetto*) depression.

avvalora're *vt* to confirm.

avvantaggia're [àvvántádjá'rā] *vt* to favor (*US*), favour (*Brit*); ~**rsi** *vr* (*trarre vantaggio*): ~**rsi di** to take advantage of; (*prevalere*): ~**rsi negli affari/sui concorrenti** to get ahead in business/of one's competitors.

avveder'si *vr*: ~ **di qn/qc** to notice sb/sth.

avvedu'to, a *ag* (*accorto*) prudent; (*scaltro*) astute.

avvelenamen'to *sm* poisoning.

avvelena're *vt* to poison.

avvenen'te *ag* attractive, charming.

avven'go *etc vb vedi* **avvenire**.

avvenimen'to *sm* event.

avveni're *vi*, *vb impers* to happen, occur ♦ *sm* future.

avven'ni *etc vb vedi* **avvenire**.

avventar'si *vr*: ~ **su** *o* **contro qn/qc** to hurl o.s. *o* rush at sb/sth.

avventa'to, a *ag* rash, reckless.

avventi'zio, a [àvvāntēt'tsyō] *ag* (*impiegato*) temporary; (*guadagno*) casual.

avven'to *sm* advent, coming; (*REL*): **l'A**~ Advent.

avvento're *sm* customer.

avventu'ra *sf* adventure; (*amorosa*) affair; **avere spirito d'**~ to be adventurous.

avventurar'si *vr* to venture.

avventurie'ro, a *sm/f* adventurer/adventuress.

avventuro'so, a *ag* adventurous.

avvenu'to, a *pp di* **avvenire**.

avverar'si *vr* to come true.

avver'bio *sm* adverb.

avverrò *etc vb vedi* **avvenire**.

avversa're *vt* to oppose.

avversa'rio, a *ag* opposing ♦ *sm* opponent, adversary.

avversio'ne *sf* aversion.

avversità *sf inv* adversity, misfortune.

avver'so, a *ag* (*contrario*) contrary; (*sfavorevole*) unfavorable (*US*), unfavourable (*Brit*).

avverten'za [àvvārten'tsá] *sf* (*ammonimento*) warning; (*cautela*) care; (*premessa*) foreword; ~**e** *sfpl* (*istruzioni per l'uso*) instructions.

avvertimen'to *sm* warning.

avverti're *vt* (*avvisare*) to warn; (*rendere consapevole*) to inform, notify; (*percepire*) to feel.

avvez'zo, a [àvvāt'tsō] *ag*: ~ **a** used to.

avviamen'to *sm* (*atto*) starting; (*effetto*) start; (*AUT*) starting; (*: dispositivo*) starter; (*COMM*) goodwill.

avvia're *vt* (*mettere sul cammino*) to direct; (*impresa, trattative*) to begin, start; (*motore*) to start; ~**rsi** *vr* to set off, set out.

avvicendamen'to [àvvēchāndámān'tō] *sm* alternation; (*AGR*) rotation; **c'è molto** ~ **di personale** there is a high turnover of staff.

avvicenda're [àvvēchāndá'rā] *vt*, ~**rsi** *vr* to alternate.

avvicinamen'to [àvvēchēnámān'tō] *sm* approach.

avvicina're [àvvēchēná'rā] *vt* to bring near; (*trattare con: persona*) to approach; ~**rsi** *vr*: ~**rsi (a qn/qc)** to approach (sb/sth), draw near (to sb/sth); (*somigliare*) to be similar (to sb/sth), be close (to sb/sth).

avvilen'te *ag* (*umiliante*) humiliating; (*scoraggiante*) discouraging, disheartening.

avvilimen'to *sm* humiliation; disgrace; discouragement.

avvili're *vt* (*umiliare*) to humiliate; (*degradare*) to disgrace; (*scoraggiare*) to dishearten, discourage; ~**rsi** *vr* (*abbattersi*) to lose heart.

avviluppa're *vt* (*avvolgere*) to wrap up; (*ingarbugliare*) to entangle.

avvinazza'to, a [àvvēnàttsà'tō] *ag* drunk.

avvin'cere [àvvēn'chārā] *vt* to charm, enthral.

avvinghia're [àvvēngyá'rā] *vt* to clasp; ~**rsi** *vr*: ~**rsi a** to cling to.

avvin'si *etc vb vedi* **avvincere**.

avvin'to, a *pp di* **avvincere**.

avvi'o *sm* start, beginning; **dare l'**~ **a qc** to start sth off; **prendere l'**~ to get going, get under way.

avvisa'glia [àvvēzál'yà] *sf* (*sintomo: di temporale etc*) sign; (*di malattia*) manifestation, sign, symptom; (*scaramuccia*) skirmish.

avvisa're *vt* (*far sapere*) to inform; (*mettere in guardia*) to warn.

avvisato're *sm* (*apparecchio d'allarme*) alarm; ~ **acustico** horn; ~ **d'incendio** fire alarm.

avvi'so *sm* warning; (*annuncio*) announcement; (*affisso*) notice; (*inserzione pubblici-*

taria) advertisement; **a mio** ~ in my opinion; **mettere qn sull'**~ to put sb on their guard; **fino a nuovo** ~ until further notice; ~ **di consegna/spedizione** (*COMM*) delivery/consignment notice (*US*) *o* note (*Brit*); ~ **di pagamento** (*COMM*) payment advice.

avvista're *vt* to sight.

avvita're *vt* to screw down (*o* in).

avvizzi're |àvvēttsē'rā| *vi* to wither.

avvoca'to, es'sa *sm/f* (*DIR*) lawyer, barrister (*Brit*); (*fig*) defender, advocate; ~ **di parte civile** counsel for the plaintiff; ~ **difensore** counsel for the defence.

avvol'gere |àvvol'jārā| *vt* to roll up; (*bobina*) to wind up; (*avviluppare*) to wrap up; ~**rsi** *vr* (*avvilupparsi*) to wrap o.s. up.

avvolgi'bile |àvvōljē'bēlā| *sm* blind.

avvolgimen'to |àvvōljēmān'tō| *sm* winding.

avvol'si *etc vb vedi* **avvolgere**.

avvol'to, a *pp di* **avvolgere**.

avvolto'io *sm* vulture.

azale'a |àddzále'à| *sf* azalea.

azien'da |àddzyen'dà| *sf* business, firm, concern; ~ **agricola** farm; ~ (**autonoma**) **di soggiorno** tourist board; ~ **a partecipazione statale** *business in which the State has a financial interest*; ~**e pubbliche** public corporations.

azienda'le |àddzyàndà'lā| *ag* company *cpd*; **organizzazione** ~ business administration.

aziona're |àttsyōnà'rā| *vt* to activate.

aziona'rio, a |àttsyōnà'ryō| *ag* share *cpd*; **capitale** ~ share capital; **mercato** ~ stock market.

azio'ne |àttsyō'nā| *sf* action; (*COMM*) share; ~ **sindacale** union action (*US*), industrial action (*Brit*); ~**i preferenziali** preferred stock *sg* (*US*), preference shares (*Brit*).

azioni'sta, i, e |àttsyōnē'stà| *sm/f* (*COMM*) shareholder.

azo'to |àddzo'tō| *sm* nitrogen.

azte'co, a, ci, che |àstc'kō| *ag, sm/f* Aztec.

azzanna're |àttsànnà'rā| *vt* to sink one's teeth into.

azzarda're |àddzàrdà'rā| *vt* (*soldi, vita*) to risk, hazard; (*domanda, ipotesi*) to hazard, venture; ~**rsi** *vr*: ~**rsi a fare** to dare (to) do.

azzarda'to, a |àddzàrdà'tō| *ag* (*impresa*) risky; (*risposta*) rash.

azzar'do |àddzár'dō| *sm* risk; **gioco d'**~ game of chance.

azzecca're |àttsàkkà'rā| *vt* (*bersaglio*) to hit, strike; (*risposta, pronostico*) to get right; (*fig: indovinare*) to guess.

azzeramen'to |àddzàràmàn'tō| *sm* (*INFORM*) reset.

azzera're |àddzàrà'rā| *vt* (*MAT, FISICA*) to make equal to zero, reduce to zero; (*TECN: strumento*) to (re)set to zero.

az'zimo, a |àd'dzēmō| *ag* unleavened ♦ *sm* un-

leavened bread.

azzoppa're |àttsōppá'rā| *vt* to lame, make lame.

Azzor're |àddzōr'rā| *sfpl*: **le** ~ the Azores.

azzuffar'si |àttsōōffár'sē| *vr* to come to blows.

azzur'ro, a |àddzōōr'rō| *ag* blue ♦ *sm* (*colore*) blue; **gli** ~**i** (*SPORT*) the Italian national team.

azzurro'gnolo, a |àddzōōrrōn'yōlō| *ag* bluish.

B

B, b |bē| *sf o m inv* (*lettera*) B, b; ~ **come Bologna** ≈ B for Baker.

BA *sigla* = *Bari*.

baba'u *sm inv* ogre, bogeyman.

babbe'o *sm* simpleton.

bab'bo *sm* (*fam*) dad, daddy; **B**~ **Natale** Santa Claus.

babbuc'cia, ce |bàbbōōch'chà| *sf* slipper; (*per neonati*) bootee.

babbui'no *sm* baboon.

babor'do *sm* (*NAUT*) port side.

baca'to, a *ag* worm-eaten, rotten; (*fig: mente*) diseased; (: *persona*) corrupt.

bac'ca, che *sf* berry.

baccalà *sm* dried salted cod; (*fig: peg*) dummy.

bacca'no *sm* din, clamor (*US*), clamour (*Brit*).

baccel'lo |bàchcl'lō| *sm* pod.

bacchet'ta |bàkkāt'tà| *sf* (*verga*) stick, rod; (*di direttore d'orchestra*) baton; (*di tamburo*) drumstick; **comandare a** ~ to rule with a rod of iron; ~ **magica** magic wand.

bache'ca, che |bàkc'kà| *sf* (*mobile*) showcase, display case; (*UNIVERSITÀ, in ufficio*) bulletin board.

baciama'no |bàchàmá'nō| *sm*: **fare il** ~ **a qn** to kiss sb's hand.

bacia're |bàchá'rā| *vt* to kiss; ~**rsi** *vr* to kiss (one another).

bacil'lo |bàchēl'lō| *sm* bacillus, germ.

bacinel'la |bàchēncl'là| *sf* basin.

baci'no |bàchē'nō| *sm* basin; (*MINERALOGIA*) field, bed; (*ANAT*) pelvis; (*NAUT*) dock; ~ **carbonifero** coalfield; ~ **di carenaggio** dry dock; ~ **petrolifero** oilfield.

ba'cio |bá'chō| *sm* kiss.

ba'co, chi *sm* worm; ~ **da seta** silkworm.

ba'da *sf*: **tenere qn a** ~ (*tener d'occhio*) to keep an eye on sb; (*tenere a distanza*) to hold sb at bay.

bada're *vi* (*fare attenzione*) to take care, be careful; ~ **a** (*occuparsi di*) to look after, take care of; (*dar ascolto*) to pay attention to; **è un tipo che non bada a spese** money is no object to him; **bada ai fatti tuoi!** mind your own business!

badi'a *sf* abbey.

badi'le *sm* shovel.

baf'fi *smpl* mustache *sg*, moustache *sg* (*Brit*); (*di animale*) whiskers; **leccarsi i** ~ to lick one's lips; **ridere sotto i** ~ to laugh up one's sleeve.

bagaglia'io [bàgàlyà'yō] *sm* baggage car (*US*) *o* van (*Brit*); (*AUT*) trunk (*US*), boot (*Brit*).

baga'glio [bàgàl'yō] *sm* luggage *q*, baggage *q*; **fare/disfare i** ~**i** to pack/unpack; ~ **a mano** hand luggage.

bagattel'la *sf* trifle, trifling matter.

Bagdad' *sf* Baghdad.

baggiana'ta [bàdjànà'tà] *sf* foolish action; **dire** ~**e** to talk nonsense.

baglio're [bàlyō'rà] *sm* flash, dazzling light; **un** ~ **di speranza** a sudden ray of hope.

bagnan'te [bànyàn'tà] *sm/f* bather.

bagna're [bànyà'rà] *vt* to wet; (*inzuppare*) to soak; (*innaffiare*) to water; (*sog: fiume*) to flow through; (: *mare*) to wash, bathe; (*brindare*) to drink to, toast; ~**rsi** *vr* (*al mare*) to go swimming *o* bathing; (*in vasca*) to have a bath.

bagna'to, a [bànyà'tō] *ag* wet; **era come un pulcino** ~ he looked like a drowned rat.

bagni'no [bànyē'nō] *sm* lifeguard.

ba'gno [bàn'yō] *sm* bath; (*locale*) bathroom; ~**i** *smpl* (*stabilimento*) baths; **fare il** ~ to have a bath; (*nel mare*) to go swimming; **fare il** ~ **a qn** to give sb a bath; **mettere a** ~ to soak; ~ (**di**) **schiuma** bubble bath.

bagnomari'a [bànyōmàrē'à] *sm:* **cuocere a** ~ to cook in a double boiler (*US*) *o* double saucepan (*Brit*).

Baha'ma [bàà'mà] *sfpl:* **le** ~ the Bahamas.

Bahre'in [bàrà'ēn] *sm:* **il** ~ Bahrain *o* Bahrein.

ba'ia *sf* bay.

baionet'ta *sf* bayonet.

ba'ita *sf* mountain hut.

balaustra'ta *sf* balustrade.

balbetta're *vi* to stutter, stammer; (*bimbo*) to babble ♦ *vt* to stammer out.

balbu'zie [bàlbōōt'tsyà] *sf* stammer.

balbuzien'te [bàlbōōttsycn'tà] *ag* stuttering, stammering.

Balca'ni *smpl:* **i** ~ the Balkans.

balca'nico, a, ci, che *ag* Balkan.

balco'ne *sm* balcony.

baldacchi'no [bàldàkkē'nō] *sm* canopy; **letto a** ~ four-poster (bed).

baldan'za [bàldàn'tsà] *sf* self-confidence; boldness.

bal'do, a *ag* bold, daring.

baldo'ria *sf:* **fare** ~ to have a riotous time.

Balea'ri *sfpl:* **le isole** ~ the Balearic Islands.

bale'na *sf* whale.

balena're *vb impers:* **balena** there's lightning ♦ *vi* to flash; **mi balenò un'idea** an idea flashed through my mind.

balenie'ra *sf* (*per la caccia*) whaler, whaling ship.

bale'no *sm* flash of lightning; **in un** ~ in a flash.

bale'ra *sf* (*locale*) dance hall; (*pista*) dance floor.

bales'tra *sf* crossbow.

ba'lia *sf* wet-nurse; ~ **asciutta** nanny.

bali'a *sf:* **in** ~ **di** at the mercy of; **essere lasciato in** ~ **di se stesso** to be left to one's own devices.

balil'la *sm inv* (*STORIA*) member of Fascist youth group.

bali'stico, a, ci, che *ag* ballistic ♦ *sf* ballistics *sg*; **perito** ~ ballistics expert.

bal'la *sf* (*di merci*) bale; (*fandonia*) (tall) story.

balla'bile *sm* dance number, dance tune.

balla're *vt, vi* to dance.

balla'ta *sf* ballad.

ballato'io *sm* (*terrazzina*) gallery.

balleri'na *sf* dancer; ballet dancer; (*scarpa*) pump; ~ **di rivista** chorus girl.

balleri'no *sm* dancer; ballet dancer.

ballet'to *sm* ballet.

bal'lo *sm* dance; (*azione*) dancing *q*; ~ **in maschera** *o* **mascherato** fancy-dress ball; **essere in** ~ (*fig: persona*) to be involved; (: *cosa*) to be at stake; **tirare in** ~ **qc** to bring sth up, raise sth.

ballottag'gio [bàllōttàd'jō] *sm* (*POL*) second ballot.

balnea're *ag* seaside *cpd*; (*stagione*) bathing.

baloc'co, chi *sm* toy.

balor'do, a *ag* stupid, senseless.

balsa'mico, a, ci, che *ag* (*aria, brezza*) balmy; **pomata** ~**a** balsam.

bal'samo *sm* (*aroma*) balsam; (*lenimento, fig*) balm.

bal'tico, a, ci, che *ag* Baltic; **il (mar) B**~ the Baltic (Sea).

baluar'do *sm* bulwark.

bal'za [bàl'tsà] *sf* (*dirupo*) crag; (*di stoffa*) frill.

balza'no, a [bàltsà'nō] *ag* (*persona, idea*) queer, odd.

balza're [bàltsà'rà] *vi* to bounce; (*lanciarsi*) to jump, leap; **la verità balza agli occhi** the truth of the matter is obvious.

bal'zo [bàl'tsō] *sm* bounce; jump, leap; (*del terreno*) crag; **prendere la palla al** ~ (*fig*) to seize one's opportunity.

bamba'gia [bàmbà'jà] *sf* (*ovatta*) absorbent cotton (*US*), cotton wool (*Brit*); (*cascame*) cotton waste; **tenere qn nella ~** (*fig*) to mollycoddle sb.

bambi'na *sf vedi* **bambino**.

bambina'ia *sf* nanny, nurse(maid).

bambi'no, a *sm/f* child; **fare il ~** to behave childishly.

bamboc'cio |bàmboch'chō| *sm* plump child; (*pupazzo*) rag doll.

bam'bola *sf* doll.

bambolot'to *sm* male doll.

bambù *sm* bamboo.

bana'le *ag* banal, commonplace.

banalità *sf inv* banality.

bana'na *sf* banana.

bana'no *sm* banana tree.

ban'ca, che *sf* bank; **~ d'affari** commercial bank (*US*), merchant bank (*Brit*); **~ (di) dati** data bank.

bancarel'la *sf* stall.

banca'rio, a *ag* banking, bank *cpd* ♦ *sm* bank clerk.

bancarot'ta *sf* bankruptcy; **fare ~** to go bankrupt.

bancarottie're *sm* bankrupt.

banchet'to |bànkàt'tō| *sm* banquet.

banchie're |bànkye'rà| *sm* banker.

banchi'na |bànkē'nà| *sf* (*di porto*) quay; (*per pedoni, ciclisti*) path; (*di stazione*) platform; **~ cedevole** (*AUT*) soft shoulder (*US*) *o* verge (*Brit*); **~ spartitraffico** (*AUT*) median (strip) (*US*), central reservation (*Brit*).

banchi'sa |bànkē'zà| *sf* ice pack (*US*), pack ice (*Brit*).

ban'co, chi *sm* bench; (*di negozio*) counter; (*di mercato*) stall; (*di officina*) (work-) bench; (*GEO, banca*) bank; **sotto ~** (*fig*) under the counter; **tenere il ~** (*nei giochi*) to be (the) banker; **tener ~** (*fig*) to monopolize the conversation; **~ di chiesa** pew; **~ di corallo** coral reef; **~ degli imputati** dock; **~ del Lotto** lottery-ticket office; **~ di prova** (*fig*) testing ground; **~ dei testimoni** witness stand.

bancogi'ro |bànkōjē'rō| *sm* credit transfer.

Ban'comat ® *sm inv* automated banking; (*tessera*) cash card.

bancono'ta *sf* banknote.

ban'da *sf* band; (*di stoffa*) band, stripe; (*lato, parte*) side; (*di calcolatore*) tape; **~ perforata** punch tape.

banderuo'la *sf* (*METEOR*) weathercock, weathervane; **essere una ~** (*fig*) to be fickle.

bandie'ra *sf* flag, banner; **battere ~ italiana** (*nave etc*) to fly the Italian flag; **cambiare ~** (*fig*) to change sides; **~ di comodo** flag of convenience.

bandi're *vt* to proclaim; (*esiliare*) to exile; (*fig*) to dispense with.

bandi'to *sm* outlaw, bandit.

bandito're *sm* (*di aste*) auctioneer.

ban'do *sm* proclamation; (*esilio*) exile, banishment; **mettere al ~ qn** to exile sb; (*fig*) to freeze sb out; **~ alle ciance!** that's enough talk!

ban'dolo *sm* (*di matassa*) end; **trovare il ~ della matassa** (*fig*) to find the key to the problem.

Bangkok' |bànkok'| *sf* Bangkok.

Bangladesh' |bànglàdesh'| *sm*: **il ~** Bangladesh.

bar *sm inv* bar.

ba'ra *sf* coffin.

barac'ca, che *sf* shed, hut; (*peg*) hovel; **mandare avanti la ~** to keep things going; **piantare ~ e burattini** to throw everything up.

baracca'to, a *sm/f person living in temporary camp*.

baracchi'no |bàràkkē'nō| *sm* (*chiosco*) stall; (*apparecchio*) CB radio.

baracco'ne *sm* booth, stall; **~i** *smpl* (*luna park*) carnival, amusement park; **fenomeno da ~** circus freak.

baracco'poli *sf inv* shanty town.

baraon'da *sf* hubbub, bustle.

bara're *vi* to cheat.

ba'ratro *sm* abyss.

baratta're *vt*: **~ qc con** to barter sth for, swap sth for.

barat'to *sm* barter.

barat'tolo *sm* (*di latta*) tin; (*di vetro*) jar; (*di coccio*) pot.

bar'ba *sf* beard; **farsi la ~** to shave; **farla in ~ a qn** (*fig*) to fool sb; **servire qn di ~ e capelli** (*fig*) to teach sb a lesson; **che ~!** what a bore!

barbabie'tola *sf* beet (*US*), beetroot (*Brit*); **~ da zucchero** sugar beet.

Barba'dos *sfpl*: **le ~** Barbados *sg*.

barba'rico, a, ci, che *ag* (*invasione*) barbarian; (*usanze, metodi*) barbaric.

barba'rie *sf* barbarity.

bar'baro, a *ag* barbarous; **~i** *smpl* barbarians.

bar'becue |bà:'bēkyōō:| *sm inv* barbecue.

barbie're *sm* barber.

barbitu'rico, a, ci, che *ag* barbituric ♦ *sm* barbiturate.

barbo'ne *sm* (*cane*) poodle; (*vagabondo*) tramp.

barbu'to, a *ag* bearded.

bar'ca, che *sf* boat; **una ~ di** (*fig*) heaps of, tons of; **mandare avanti la ~** (*fig*) to keep things going; **~ a remi** rowboat (*US*), rowing boat (*Brit*); **~ a vela** sailboat (*US*), sailing boat (*Brit*).

barcaio'lo *sm* boatman.

barcamenar'si *vr* (*nel lavoro*) to get by; (*a parole*) to beat around the bush.

Barcello'na |bàrchàllō'nà| *sf* Barcelona.

barcolla're *vi* to stagger.

barco'ne *sm* (*per ponti di barche*) pontoon.

barel'la *sf* (*lettiga*) stretcher.

Ba'rents: il mar di ~ *sm* the Barents Sea.

bare'se *ag* of (*o* from) Bari.

baricen'tro [bárĕchen'trō] *sm* center (*US*) *o* centre (*Brit*) of gravity.

bari'le *sm* barrel, cask.

bari'sta, i, e *sm/f* bartender; bar owner.

bari'tono *sm* baritone.

barlu'me *sm* glimmer, gleam.

ba'ro *sm* (*CARTE*) cardsharp.

baroc'co, a, chi, che *ag*, *sm* baroque.

baro'metro *sm* barometer.

baro'ne *sm* baron; **i** ~**i della medicina** (*fig peg*) the top brass in the medical faculty.

barones'sa *sf* baroness.

bar'ra *sf* bar; (*NAUT*) helm; (*segno grafico*) stroke.

barrica're *vt* to barricade.

barrica'ta *sf* barricade; **essere dall'altra parte della** ~ (*fig*) to be on the other side of the fence.

barrie'ra *sf* barrier; (*GEO*) reef; **la Grande B~ Corallina** the Great Barrier Reef.

barroc'cio [bárroch'chō] *sm* cart.

baruf'fa *sf* scuffle; **fare** ~ to squabble.

barzellet'ta [bárdzāllāt'tá] *sf* joke, funny story.

basamen'to *sm* (*parte inferiore, piedestallo*) base; (*TECN*) bed, base plate.

basa're *vt* to base, found; ~**rsi** *vr*: ~**rsi su** (*sog: fatti, prove*) to be based *o* founded on; (*: persona*) to base one's arguments on.

ba'sco, a, schi, sche *ag* Basque ♦ *sm/f* Basque ♦ *sm* (*lingua*) Basque; (*copricapo*) beret.

bascul'la *sf* weighing machine, weighbridge.

ba'se *sf* base; (*fig: fondamento*) basis; (*POL*) rank and file; **di** ~ basic; **in** ~ **a** on the basis of, according to; **in** ~ **a ciò** ... on that basis ...; **a** ~ **di caffè** coffee-based; **essere alla** ~ **di qc** to be at the root of sth; **gettare le** ~**i per qc** to lay the basis *o* foundations for sth; **avere buone** ~**i** (*INS*) to have a sound educational background.

ba'seball [bā'ēsbo:l] *sm* baseball.

baset'ta *sf* sideburn.

basila're *ag* basic, fundamental.

Basile'a *sf* Basle.

basi'lica, che *sf* basilica.

basi'lico *sm* basil.

bassez'za [bássāt'tsá] *sf* (*d'animo, di sentimenti*) baseness; (*azione*) base action.

bas'so, a *ag* low; (*di statura*) short; (*meridionale*) southern ♦ *sm* bottom, lower part; (*MUS*) bass; **a occhi** ~**i** with eyes lowered; **a** ~ **prezzo** cheap; **scendere da** ~ to go downstairs; **cadere in** ~ (*fig*) to come down in the world; **la** ~**a Italia** southern Italy; **il** ~ **Medioevo** the late Middle Ages.

bassofon'do, *pl* **bassifon'di** *sm* (*GEO*) shallows *pl*; **i** ~**i** (**della città**) the seediest parts of the town.

bassorilie'vo *sm* bas-relief.

bassot'to, a *ag* squat ♦ *sm* (*cane*) dachshund.

bastar'do, a *ag* (*animale, pianta*) hybrid, crossbreed; (*persona*) illegitimate, bastard (*peg*) ♦ *sm/f* illegitimate child, bastard (*peg*); (*cane*) mongrel.

basta're *vi, vb impers* to be enough, be sufficient; ~ **a qn** to be enough for sb; ~ **a se stesso** to be self-sufficient; **basta chiedere** *o* **che chieda a un vigile** you have only to *o* need only ask a policeman; **basti dire che** ... suffice it to say that ...; **basta!** that's enough!, that will do!; **punto e basta!** and that's that!

bastian' *sm*: ~ **contrario** awkward customer.

bastimen'to *sm* ship, vessel.

bastona're *vt* to beat, thrash; **avere l'aria di un cane bastonato** to look crestfallen.

bastona'ta *sf* blow (with a stick); **prendere qn a** ~**e** to give sb a good beating.

bastonci'no [bástōnchē'nō] *sm* (*piccolo bastone*) small stick; (*TECN*) rod; (*SCI*) ski pole; ~**i di pesce** (*CUC*) fish sticks (*US*), fish fingers (*Brit*).

basto'ne *sm* stick; ~**i** *smpl* (*CARTE*) suit in Neapolitan pack of cards; ~ **da passeggio** walking stick; **mettere i** ~**i fra le ruote a qn** to put a spoke in sb's wheel.

batta'ge [bátàzh'] *sm inv*: ~ **promozionale** *o* **pubblicitario** publicity campaign.

batta'glia [báttál'yá] *sf* battle.

batta'glio [báttál'yō] *sm* (*di campana*) clapper; (*di porta*) knocker.

battaglio'ne [báttályō'nā] *sm* battalion.

battel'lo *sm* boat.

batten'te *sm* (*imposta: di porta*) wing, flap; (*: di finestra*) shutter; (*per bussare*) knocker; (*di orologio*) hammer; **chiudere i** ~**i** (*fig*) to shut up shop.

bat'tere *vt* to beat; (*grano*) to thresh; (*percorrere*) to scour; (*rintoccare: le ore*) to strike ♦ *vi* (*bussare*) to knock; (*urtare*): ~ **contro** to hit *o* strike against; (*pioggia, sole*) to beat down; (*cuore*) to beat; (*TENNIS*) to serve; ~**rsi** *vr* to fight; ~ **le mani** to clap; ~ **i piedi** to stamp one's feet; ~ **su un argomento** to hammer home an argument; ~ **a macchina** to type; ~ **il marciapiede** (*peg*) to walk the streets; ~ **un rigore** (*CALCIO*) to take a penalty; ~ **in testa** (*AUT*) to knock; **in un batter d'occhio** in the twinkling of an eye; **senza** ~ **ciglio** without batting an eye (*US*) *o* an eyelid (*Brit*); **battersela** to run off.

batte'ri *smpl* bacteria.

batteri'a *sf* battery; (*MUS*) drums *pl*; ~ **da cucina** pots and pans *pl*.

batteriologi'a [báttāryōlōjē'á] *sf* bacteriology.

batte'simo *sm* (*sacramento*) baptism; (*rito*)

baptism, christening; **tenere qn a** ~ to be godfather (o godmother) to sb.

battezza're |bàttăddzà'rà| *vt* to baptize; to christen.

battibale'no *sm*: **in un** ~ in a flash.

battibec'co, chi *sm* squabble.

batticuo're *sm* palpitations *pl*; **avere il** ~ to be frightened to death.

batti'gia |bàttē'jà| *sf* water's edge.

battima'no *sm* applause.

battipan'ni *sm inv* carpet beater.

battiste'ro *sm* baptistry.

battistra'da *sm inv* (*di pneumatico*) tread; (*di gara*) pacemaker.

battitappe'to *sm inv* upright vacuum cleaner.

bat'tito *sm* beat, throb; ~ **cardiaco** heartbeat; ~ **della pioggia/dell'orologio** beating of the rain/ticking of the clock.

battito're *sm* (*BASEBALL*) batter; (*CRICKET*) batsman; (*CACCIA*) beater.

battitu'ra *sf* (*anche*: ~ **a macchina**) typing; (*del grano*) threshing.

battu'ta *sf* blow; (*di macchina da scrivere*) stroke; (*MUS*) bar; beat; (*TEATRO*) cue; (*di caccia*) beating; (*POLIZIA*) combing, scouring; (*TENNIS*) service; **fare una** ~ to crack a joke, make a witty remark; **aver la** ~ **pronta** (*fig*) to have a ready answer; **è ancora alle prime** ~**e** it's just started.

batuf'folo *sm* wad.

bau'le *sm* trunk; (*AUT*) trunk (*US*), boot (*Brit*).

bauxi'te |bàōōksē'tà| *sf* bauxite.

ba'va *sf* (*di animale*) slaver, slobber; (*di lumaca*) slime; (*di vento*) breath.

bavagli'no |bàvàlyē'nō| *sm* bib.

bava'glio |bàvàl'yō| *sm* gag.

bavare'se *ag, sm/f* Bavarian.

ba'vero *sm* collar.

Bavie'ra *sf* Bavaria.

bazar' |bàddzàr'| *sm inv* bazaar.

bazze'cola |bàddzā'kōlà| *sf* trifle.

bazzica're |bàttsēkà'rà| *vt* (*persona*) to hang about with; (*posto*) to hang about ♦ *vi*: ~ **in/con** to hang about/hang about with.

bear'si *vr*: ~ **di qc/a fare qc** to delight in sth/ in doing sth; ~ **alla vista di** to enjoy looking at.

beatitu'dine *sf* bliss.

bea'to, a *ag* blessed; (*fig*) happy; ~ **te!** lucky you!

bebè *sm inv* baby.

beccac'cia, ce |bākkách'chà| *sf* woodcock.

becca're *vt* to peck; (*fig: raffreddore*) to pick up, catch; ~**rsi** *vr* (*fig*) to squabble.

becca'ta *sf* peck.

beccheggia're |bākkādjà'rà| *vi* to pitch.

beccherò *etc* |bākkāro'| *vb vedi* **beccare**.

becchi'me |bākkē'mà| *sm* birdseed.

becchi'no |bākkē'nō| *sm* gravedigger.

bec'co, chi *sm* beak, bill; (*di caffettiera etc*) spout; lip; (*fig fam*) cuckold; **mettere** ~ (*fam*) to butt in; **chiudi il** ~! (*fam*) shut your mouth!, shut your trap!; **non ho il** ~ **di un quattrino** (*fam*) I'm broke.

Befa'na *sf old woman who, according to legend, brings children their presents at the Epiphany*; (*Epifania*) Epiphany; (*donna brutta*): **b**~ hag, witch.

bef'fa *sf* practical joke; **farsi** ~ *o* ~**e di qn** to make a fool of sb.

beffar'do, a *ag* scornful, mocking.

beffa're *vt* (*anche*: ~**rsi di**) to make a fool of, mock.

be'ga, ghe *sf* quarrel.

be'gli |bel'yē|, **be'i** *ag vedi* **bello**.

beige |bezh| *ag inv* beige.

Beirut' *sf* Beirut.

bel *ag vedi* **bello**.

bela're *vi* to bleat.

bela'to *sm* bleating.

bel'ga, gi, ghe *ag, sm/f* Belgian.

Bel'gio |bel'jō| *sm*: **il** ~ Belgium.

Belgra'do *sf* Belgrade.

bel'la *sf vedi* **bello**.

bellez'za |bāllāt'tsà| *sf* beauty; **chiudere** *o* **finire qc in** ~ to finish sth with a flourish; **che** ~! fantastic!; **ho pagato la** ~ **di 60.000 lire** I paid 60,000 lire, no less.

bellico'so, a *ag* warlike.

belligeran'te |bāllējàràn'tā| *ag* belligerent.

bellimbu'sto *sm* dandy.

bel'lo, a *ag* (*dav sm* **bel** +*C*, **bell'** +*V*, **bello** + *s impura, gn, pn, ps, x, z, pl* **bei** +*C*, **begli** + *s impura etc o V*) beautiful, fine, lovely; (*uomo*) handsome ♦ *sm* (*bellezza*) beauty; (*tempo*) fine weather ♦ *sf* beauty, belle; (*innamorata*) sweetheart; (*anche*: ~**a copia**) fair copy; (*SPORT, CARTE*) deciding match ♦ *av*: **fa** ~ the weather is fine, it's fine; **una** ~**a cifra** a considerable sum of money; **un bel niente** absolutely nothing; **è una truffa** ~**a e buona!** it's a real fraud!; **è bell'e finito** it's already finished; **adesso viene il** ~ now comes the best part; **proprio sul più** ~ at that very moment; **farsi** ~ **di qc** (*vantarsi*) to show off about sth; **fare la** ~**a vita** to lead an easy life; **cosa fa di** ~? are you doing anything interesting?; **alla bell'e meglio** somehow or other; **oh** ~**a!, anche questa è** ~**a!** (*ironico*) that's nice!; **le B**~**e Arti** fine arts.

bellune'se *ag* of (o from) Belluno.

bel'va *sf* wild animal.

belvede're *sm inv* panoramic viewpoint.

benché |bānkā'| *cong* although.

ben'da *sf* bandage; (*per gli occhi*) blindfold.

benda're *vt* to bandage; to blindfold.

bendispo'sto, a *ag*: ~ **a qn/qc** well-disposed

towards sb/sth.

be'ne *av* well; (*completamente*, *affatto*): **è ben difficile** it's very difficult ♦ *ag inv*: **gente ~** well-to-do people ♦ *sm* good; (*COMM*) asset; **~i** *smpl* (*averi*) property *sg*, estate *sg*; **io sto ~/poco ~** I'm well/not very well; **va ~** all right; **ben più lungo/caro** much longer/more expensive; **lo spero ~** I certainly hope so; **volere un ~ dell'anima a qn** to love sb very much; **un uomo per ~ a** respectable man; **fare ~** to do the right thing; **fare ~ a** (*salute*) to be good for; **fare del ~ a qn** to do sb a good turn; **di ~ in meglio** better and better; **~i ambientali** environmental assets; **~i di consumo** consumer goods; **~i di consumo durevole** consumer durables; **~i culturali** cultural heritage; **~i immateriali** immaterial *o* intangible assets; **~i patrimoniali** fixed assets; **~i privati** private property *sg*; **~i pubblici** public property *sg*; **~i reali** tangible assets.

benedet'to, a *pp di* **benedire** ♦ *ag* blessed, holy.

benedi're *vt* to bless; to consecrate; **l'ho mandato a farsi ~** (*fig*) I told him to go to hell.

benedizio'ne |bānādēttsyō'nā| *sf* blessing.

beneduca'to, a *ag* well-mannered.

benefatto're, tri'ce *sm/f* benefactor/ benefactress.

beneficen'za |bānāfēchen'tsà| *sf* charity.

beneficia're |bānāfēchà'rā| *vi*: **~ di** to benefit by, benefit from.

beneficia'rio, a |bānāfēchà'ryō| *ag*, *sm/f* beneficiary.

benefi'cio |bānāfē'chō| *sm* benefit; **con ~ d'inventario** (*fig*) with reservations.

bene'fico, a, ci, che *ag* beneficial; charitable.

Be'nelux *sm*: **il ~** Benelux, the Benelux countries.

benemeren'za |bānāmārcn'tsà| *sf* merit.

beneme'rito, a *ag* meritorious.

benepla'cito |bānāplá'chētō| *sm* (*approvazione*) approval; (*permesso*) permission.

benes'sere *sm* well-being.

benestan'te *ag* well-to-do.

benesta're *sm* consent, approval.

benevolen'za |bānāvōlcn'tsá| *sf* benevolence.

bene'volo, a *ag* benevolent.

bengo'di *sm* land of plenty.

beniami'no, a *sm/f* favorite (*US*), favourite (*Brit*).

beni'gno, a |bānēn'yō| *ag* kind, kindly; (*critica etc*) favorable (*US*), favourable (*Brit*); (*MED*) benign.

benintenziona'to, a |bānēntāntsyōnà'tō| *ag* well-meaning.

beninte'so *av* of course; **~ che** *cong* provided that.

benpensan'te *sm/f* conformist.

benservi'to *sm*: **dare il ~ a qn** (*sul lavoro*) to fire sb; (*fig*) to send sb packing.

bensì *cong* but (rather).

benvenu'to, a *ag*, *sm* welcome; **dare il ~ a qn** to welcome sb.

benvi'sto, a *ag*: **essere ~ (da)** to be well thought of (by).

benvole're *vt*: **farsi ~ da tutti** to win everybody's affection; **prendere a ~ qn/qc** to take a liking to sb/sth.

benzi'na |bāndzē'nà| *sf* gas (*US*), petrol (*Brit*); **fare ~** to get gas *o* petrol; **rimanere senza ~** to run out of gas *o* petrol.

benzina'io |bāndzēnà'yō| *sm* gas station (*US*) *o* petrol pump (*Brit*) attendant.

beo'ne *sm* heavy drinker.

be're *vt* to drink; (*assorbire*) to soak up; **questa volta non me la dai a ~!** I won't be taken in this time!

bergama'sco, a, schi, sche *ag* of (*o* from) Bergamo.

Be'ring |bā'rēng|: **il mar di ~** *sm* the Bering Sea.

berli'na *sf* (*AUT*) sedan (*US*), saloon (car) (*Brit*); **mettere alla ~** (*fig*) to hold up to ridicule.

Berli'no *sf* Berlin; **~ est/ovest** East/West Berlin.

Bermu'da *sfpl*: **le ~** Bermuda *sg*.

bermu'da *smpl* (*calzoncini*) Bermuda shorts.

Ber'na *sf* Bern.

bernoc'colo *sm* bump; (*inclinazione*) flair.

berrò *etc vb vedi* **bere**.

bersaglia're |bārsályà'rā| *vt* to shoot at; (*colpire ripetutamente*, *fig*) to bombard; **bersagliato dalla sfortuna** dogged by ill fortune.

bersaglie're |bārsályc'rā| *sm member of rifle regiment in Italian army*.

bersa'glio |bārsàl'yō| *sm* target.

bestem'mia *sf* curse; (*REL*) blasphemy.

bestemmia're *vi* to curse, swear; to blaspheme ♦ *vt* to curse, swear at; to blaspheme; **~ come un turco** to swear like a trooper.

be'stia *sf* animal; **lavorare come una ~** to work like a dog; **andare in ~** (*fig*) to fly into a rage; **una ~ rara** (*fig*: *persona*) an oddball; **~ da soma** beast of burden.

bestia'le *ag* bestial, brutish; (*fam*): **fa un caldo ~** it's terribly hot; **fa un freddo ~** it's bitterly cold.

bestialità *sf inv* (*qualità*) bestiality; **dire/fare una ~ dopo l'altra** to say/do one idiotic thing after another.

bestia'me *sm* livestock; (*bovino*) cattle *pl*.

Betlem'me *sf* Bethlehem.

betonie'ra *sf* cement mixer.

bet'tola *sf* (*peg*) dive.

betul'la *sf* birch.

bevan'da *sf* drink, beverage.
bevito're, tri'ce *sm/f* drinker.
be'vo *etc vb vedi* **bere**.
bevu'to, a *pp di* **bere** ♦ *sf* drink.
bev'vi *etc vb vedi* **bere**.
BG *sigla* = *Bergamo*.
BI *sigla f* = *Banca d'Italia*.
bia'da *sf* fodder.
biancheri'a |byànkārē'à| *sf* linen; ~ **intima** underwear; ~ **da donna** ladies' underwear, lingerie.
bian'co, a, chi, che *ag* white; (*non scritto*) blank ♦ *sm* white; (*intonaco*) whitewash ♦ *sm/f* white, white man/woman; **in** ~ (*foglio, assegno*) blank; **in** ~ **e nero** (*TV, FOT*) black and white; **mangiare in** ~ to follow a bland diet; **pesce in** ~ boiled fish; **andare in** ~ (*non riuscire*) to fail; (*in amore*) to be rejected; **notte** ~**a** *o* **in** ~ sleepless night; **voce** ~**a** (*MUS*) treble (voice); **votare scheda** ~**a** to return a blank voting slip; ~ **dell'uovo** egg-white.
biancose'gno |byànkōsān'yō| *sm* signature to a blank document.
biancospi'no *sm* hawthorn.
biascica're |byàshčkà'rā| *vt* to mumble.
biasima're *vt* to disapprove of, censure.
bia'simo *sm* disapproval, censure.
bib'bia *sf* bible.
biberon' *sm inv* feeding bottle.
bi'bita *sf* (soft) drink.
bibliografi'a *sf* bibliography.
bibliote'ca, che *sf* library; (*mobile*) bookcase.
biblioteca'rio, a *sm/f* librarian.
bicamera'le *ag* (*POL*) bicameral, two-chamber *cpd*.
bicarbona'to *sm*: ~ (**di sodio**) bicarbonate (of soda).
bicchie're |bĕkkyc'rā| *sm* glass; **è (facile) come bere un bicchier d'acqua** it's as easy as pie.
biciclet'ta |bēchēklāt'tà| *sf* bicycle; **andare in** ~ to cycle.
bici'pite |bēchē'pētā| *sm* bicep.
bidé *sm inv* bidet.
bidel'lo, a *sm/f* (*INS*) janitor.
bidireziona'le |bēdērāttsyōnà'lā| *ag* bidirectional.
bidona're *vt* (*fam: piantare in asso*) to let down; (: *imbrogliare*) to cheat, swindle.
bidona'ta *sf* (*fam*) swindle.
bido'ne *sm* drum, can; (*anche:* ~ **dell'immondizia**) trash can (*US*), (dust)bin (*Brit*); (*fam: truffa*) swindle; **fare un** ~ **a qn** (*fam*) to let sb down; to cheat sb.
bidonvil'le |bēdónvēl'| *sf inv* shanty town.
bie'co, a, chi, che *ag* sinister.
biel'la *sf* (*TECN*) connecting rod.
bienna'le *ag* biennial ♦ *sf*: **la B**~ **di Venezia** the Venice Arts Festival.

bien'nio *sm* period of two years.
bier're *sm/f member of the Red Brigades*.
bie'tola *sf* beet.
bifoca'le *ag* bifocal.
bifol'co, a, chi, che *sm/f* (*peg*) bumpkin, yokel.
bi'fora *sf* (*ARCHIT*) mullioned window.
biforcar'si *vr* to fork.
biforcazio'ne |bēčōrkàttsyō'nā| *sf* fork.
biforcu'to, a *ag* (*anche fig*) forked.
bigami'a *sf* bigamy.
bi'gamo, a *ag* bigamous ♦ *sm/f* bigamist.
bighellona're |bēgàllōnà'rā| *vi* to loaf (around).
bighello'ne, a |bēgàllō'nā| *sm/f* loafer.
bigiotteri'a |bējōttārē'à| *sf* costume jewelry (*US*) *o* jewellery (*Brit*); (*negozio*) jewelry store (*US*) *o* jeweller's (shop) (*Brit*) (*selling only costume jewelry*).
bigliar'do |bēlyár'dō| *sm* = **biliardo**.
biglietta'io, a |bēlyàttà'yō| *sm/f* (*nei treni*) conductor (*US*), ticket inspector (*Brit*); (*in autobus etc*) conductor/conductress; (*CINEMA, TEATRO*) box-office attendant.
biglietteri'a |bēlyāttārē'à| *sf* (*di stazione*) ticket office; **booking office**; (*di teatro*) box office.
bigliet'to |bēlyāt'tō| *sm* (*per viaggi, spettacoli etc*) ticket; (*cartoncino*) card; (*anche:* ~ **di banca**) (bank)note; ~ **d'auguri/da visita** greetings/visiting card; ~ **d'andata e ritorno** round-trip (*US*) *o* return (*Brit*) ticket; ~ **omaggio** complimentary ticket.
bignè |bēnyc'| *sm inv* cream puff.
bigodi'no *sm* roller, curler.
bigot'to, a *ag* over-pious ♦ *sm/f* church fiend.
biki'ni *sm inv* bikini.
bilan'cia, ce |bēlàn'chà| *sf* (*pesa*) scales *pl*; (: *di precisione*) balance; (*dello zodiaco*): **B**~ Libra; **essere della B**~ to be Libra; ~ **commerciale/dei pagamenti** balance of trade/payments.
bilancia're |bēlànchà'rā| *vt* (*pesare*) to weigh; (: *fig*) to weigh up; ~ **le uscite e le entrate** (*COMM*) to balance expenditure and revenue.
bilan'cio |bēlàn'chō| *sm* (*COMM*) balance (-sheet); (*statale*) budget; **far quadrare il** ~ to balance the books; **chiudere il** ~ **in attivo/passivo** to make a profit/loss; **fare il** ~ **di** (*fig*) to assess; ~ **consolidato** consolidated balance; ~ **consuntivo** (final) balance; ~ **preventivo** budget; ~ **pubblico** national budget; ~ **di verifica** trial balance.
bi'le *sf* bile; (*fig*) rage, anger.
biliar'do *sm* billiards *sg*; (*tavolo*) billiard table.
bi'lico, chi *sm*: **essere in** ~ to be balanced; (*fig*) to be undecided; **tenere qn in** ~ to keep sb in suspense.
bilin'gue *ag* bilingual.

bilio'ne *sm* (*mille milioni*) billion (*US*), thousand million; (*milione di milioni*) trillion (*US*), billion (*Brit*).

bim'bo, a *sm/f* little boy/girl.

bimensi'le *ag* fortnightly.

bimestra'le *ag* two-monthly, bimonthly.

bimes'tre *sm* two-month period; **ogni ~ every two months.

bina'rio, a *ag* binary ♦ *sm* (railway) track *o* line; (*piattaforma*) platform; **~ morto** dead-end track.

bino'colo *sm* binoculars *pl.*

**bio... *prefisso* bio....

biochi'mica |bēōkē'mēkä| *sf* biochemistry.

biodegrada'bile *ag* biodegradable.

biofi'sica *sf* biophysics *sg.*

biografi'a *sf* biography.

biogra'fico, a, ci, che *ag* biographical.

bio'grafo, a *sm/f* biographer.

biologi'a |bēōlōjē'ä| *sf* biology.

biolo'gico, a, ci, che |bēōlo'jēkō| *ag* biological.

bio'logo, a, ghi, ghe *sm/f* biologist.

bion'do, a *ag* blond, fair.

bio'nica *sf* bionics *sg.*

biopsi'a *sf* biopsy.

biorit'mo *sm* biorhythm.

biparti'to, a (*POL*) two-party *cpd* ♦ *sm* (*POL*) bipartisan *o* two-party alliance.

bir'ba *sf* rascal, rogue.

birban'te *sm* rascal, rogue.

birbona'ta *sf* naughty trick.

birbo'ne, a *ag* (*bambino*) naughty ♦ *sm/f* little rascal.

birichi'no, a |bērēkē'nō| *ag* mischievous ♦ *sm/f* scamp, little rascal.

biril'lo *sm* pin (*US*), skittle (*Brit*); **~i** *smpl* (*gioco*) bowling *q* (*US*), skittles *sg* (*Brit*).

Birma'nia *sf*: **la ~** Burma.

birma'no, a *ag*, *sm/f* Burmese (*inv*).

bi'ro ® *sf inv* biro ®.

bir'ra *sf* beer; **~ scura** stout; **a tutta ~** (*fig*) at top speed.

birreri'a *sf* (*locale*) ≈ beer bar; (*fabbrica*) brewery.

bis *escl, sm inv* encore ♦ *ag inv* (*treno, autobus*) additional; (*numero*): **12 ~** 12a.

bisac'cia, ce |bēzäch'chä| *sf* knapsack.

Bisan'zio |bēzän'tsyō| *sf* Byzantium.

bisbe'tico, a, ci, che *ag* ill-tempered, crabby.

bisbiglia're |bēzbēlyä'rä| *vt, vi* to whisper.

bisbi'glio |bēzbēl'yō| *sm* whisper; (*notizia*) rumor (*US*), rumour (*Brit*).

bisbiglı'o |bēzbēlyē'ō| *sm* whispering.

bisboc'cia, ce |bēzboch'chä| *sf* binge, spree; **fare ~** to have a binge.

bi'sca, sche *sf* gambling house.

Bisca'glia |bēskäl'yä| *sf*: **il golfo di ~** the Bay of Biscay.

bis'chero |bē'skärō| *sm* (*MUS*) peg; (*fam*:

toscano) fool, idiot.

bi'scia, sce |bēsh'shä| *sf* snake; **~ d'acqua** water snake.

biscotta'to, a *ag* crisp; **fette ~e** rusks.

biscot'to *sm* cookie (*US*), biscuit (*Brit*).

bisesti'le *ag*: **anno ~** leap year.

bisezio'ne |bēsättsyō'nä| *sf* dichotomy.

bislac'co, a, chi, che *ag* odd, weird.

bislun'go, a, ghi, ghe *ag* oblong.

bisnon'no, a *sm/f* great-grandfather/grandmother.

bisogna're |bēzōnyä'rä| *vb impers*: **bisogna che tu parta/lo faccia** you'll have to go/do it; **bisogna parlargli** we'll (*o* I'll) have to talk to him ♦ *vi* (*esser utile*) to be necessary.

biso'gno |bēzōn'yō| *sm* need; **~i** *smpl* (*necessità corporali*): **fare i propri ~i** to relieve o.s.; **avere ~ di qc/di fare qc** to need sth/to do sth; **al ~, in caso di ~** if need be.

bisogno'so, a |bēzōnyō'sō| *ag* needy, poor; **~ di** in need of, needing.

bison'te *sm* (*ZOOL*) bison.

bistec'ca, che *sf* steak, beefsteak; **~ al sangue/ai ferri** rare/grilled steak.

bisticcia're |bēstēchä'rä| *vi*, **~rsi** *vr* to quarrel, bicker.

bistic'cio |bēstēch'chō| *sm* quarrel, squabble; (*gioco di parole*) pun.

bistratta're *vt* to maltreat.

bi'sturi *sm inv* scalpel.

bisun'to, a *ag* very greasy.

bitor'zolo |bētōr'tsōlō| *sm* (*sulla testa*) bump; (*sul corpo*) lump.

bit'ter *sm inv* bitters *pl.*

bivacca're *vi* (*MIL*) to bivouac; (*fig*) to bed down.

bivac'co, chi *sm* bivouac.

bi'vio *sm* fork; (*fig*) dilemma.

bizanti'no, a |bēddzäntē'nō| *ag* Byzantine.

biz'za |bēd'dzä| *sf* tantrum; **fare le ~e** to throw a tantrum.

bizzar'ro, a |bēddzär'rō| *ag* bizarre, strange.

bizzef'fe |bēddzef'fä|: **a ~** *av* in plenty, galore.

BL *sigla* = Belluno.

blandi're *vt* to soothe; to flatter.

blan'do, a *ag* mild, gentle.

blasfe'mo, a *ag* blasphemous ♦ *sm/f* blasphemer.

blaso'ne *sm* coat of arms.

blatera're *vi* to chatter.

blat'ta *sf* cockroach.

blinda'to, a *ag* armored (*US*), armoured (*Brit*); **camera ~a** strong room; **vetro ~** bulletproof glass.

blocca're *vt* to block; (*isolare*) to isolate, cut off; (*porto*) to blockade; (*prezzi, beni*) to freeze; (*meccanismo*) to jam; **~rsi** *vr* (*motore*) to stall; (*freni, porta*) to jam, stick; (*ascensore*) to get stuck, stop; **ha bloccato la macchina** (*AUT*) he jammed on the brakes.

bloccaster'zo [blŏkkàster'tsō] *sm* (*AUT*) steering lock.

bloccherò *etc* [blŏkkàro'] *vb vedi* **bloccare**.

blocchet'to [blŏkkàt'tō] *sm* notebook.

bloc'co, chi *sm* block; (*MIL*) blockade; (*dei fitti*) restriction; (*quadernetto*) pad; (*fig: unione*) coalition; (*il bloccare*) blocking; isolating, cutting-off; blockading; freezing; jamming; **in** ~ (*nell'insieme*) as a whole; (*COMM*) in bulk; ~ **cardiaco** cardiac arrest.

bloc-no'tes [bloknot'] *sm inv* notebook, notepad.

blu *ag inv, sm inv* dark blue.

bluffa're *vi* (*anche fig*) to bluff.

blu'sa *sf* (*camiciotto*) smock; (*camicetta*) blouse.

BMT *sigla m* = **bollettino meteorologico**.

BN *sigla* = *Benevento*.

BO *sigla* = *Bologna*.

bo'a *sm inv* (*ZOOL*) boa constrictor; (*sciarpa*) feather boa ♦ *sf* buoy.

boa'to *sm* rumble, roar.

bob [bob] *sm inv* bobsleigh.

bobi'na *sf* reel, spool; (*di pellicola*) spool; (*di film*) reel; (*ELETTR*) coil.

boc'ca, che *sf* mouth; **essere di buona** ~ to be a hearty eater; (*fig*) to be easily satisfied; **essere sulla** ~ **di tutti** (*persona, notizia*) to be the talk of the town; **rimanere a** ~ **asciutta** to have nothing to eat; (*fig*) to be disappointed; **in** ~ **al lupo!** good luck!; ~ **di leone** (*BOT*) snapdragon.

boccac'cia, ce [bŏkkàch'chà] *sf* (*malalingua*) gossip; (*smorfia*) **fare le** ~**ce** to pull faces.

bocca'glio [bŏkkàl'yō] *sm* (*TECN*) nozzle; (*di respiratore*) mouthpiece.

bocca'le *sm* jug; ~ **da birra** tankard.

boccasce'na [bŏkkàshe'nà] *sm inv* proscenium.

bocca'ta *sf* mouthful; (*di fumo*) puff; **prendere una** ~ **d'aria** to go out for a breath of (fresh) air.

boccet'ta [bŏchàt'tà] *sf* small bottle.

boccheggia're [bŏkkàdjà'rà] *vi* to gasp.

bocchi'no [bŏkkē'nō] *sm* (*di sigaretta, sigaro: cannella*) cigarette-holder; cigar-holder; (*di pipa, strumenti musicali*) mouthpiece.

boc'cia, ce [bŏch'chà] *sf* bottle; (*da vino*) decanter, carafe; (*palla di legno, metallo*) boccie ball (*US*), bowl (*Brit*); **gioco delle** ~**ce** boccie (*US*), bowls *sg* (*Brit*).

boccia're [bŏchà'rà] *vt* (*proposta, progetto*) to reject; (*INS*) to fail; (*BOCCE*) to hit.

bocciatu'ra [bŏchàtōō'rà] *sf* failure.

boccio'lo [bŏcho'lō] *sm* bud.

boc'colo *sm* curl.

bocco'ne *sm* mouthful, morsel; **mangiare un** ~ to have a bite to eat.

bocco'ni *av* face downwards.

Boe'mia *sf* Bohemia.

boe'mo, a *ag, sm/f* Bohemian.

bofonchia're [bōfōnkyà'rà] *vi* to grumble.

Bogotá *sf* Bogotá.

bo'ia *sm inv* executioner; hangman; **fa un freddo** ~ (*fam*) it's cold as hell; **mondo** ~!, ~ **d'un mondo ladro!** (*fam*) damn!, blast!

boia'ta *sf* botch.

boicottag'gio [bōēkŏttàd'jō] *sm* boycott.

boicotta're *vt* to boycott.

bol'gia, ge [bol'jà] *sf* (*fig*): **c'era una tale** ~ **al cinema** the cinema was absolutely mobbed.

bo'lide *sm* (*ASTR*) meteor; (*macchina: da corsa*) race car (*US*), racing car (*Brit*); (: *elaborata*) performance car; **come un** ~ like a flash, at top speed; **entrare/uscire come un** ~ to charge in/out.

Boli'via *sf*: **la** ~ Bolivia.

bolivia'no, a *ag, sm/f* Bolivian.

bol'la *sf* bubble; (*MED*) blister; (*COMM*) bill, receipt; **finire in una** ~ **di sapone** (*fig*) to come to nothing; ~ **di accompagnamento** waybill; ~ **di consegna** delivery note; ~ **papale** papal bull.

bolla're *vt* to stamp; (*fig*) to brand.

bollen'te *ag* boiling; boiling hot; **calmare i** ~**i spiriti** to sober up, calm down.

bollet'ta *sf* bill; (*ricevuta*) receipt; **essere in** ~ to be hard up; ~ **di consegna** delivery note; ~ **doganale** clearance certificate; ~ **di trasporto aereo** air waybill.

bollet'tino *sm* bulletin; (*COMM*) note; ~ **meteorologico** weather forecast; ~ **di ordinazione** order form; ~ **di spedizione** consignment note.

bolli're *vt, vi* to boil; **qualcosa bolle in pentola** (*fig*) there's something brewing.

bolli'to *sm* (*CUC*) boiled meat.

bollito're *sm* (*TECN*) boiler; (*CUC*: *per acqua*) kettle; (: *per latte*) milk pan.

bollitu'ra *sf* boiling.

bol'lo *sm* stamp; **imposta di** ~ stamp duty; ~ **auto** road tax; ~ **per patente** driving licence tax; ~ **postale** postmark.

bollo're *sm*: **dare un** ~ **a qc** to bring sth to a boil (*US*) *o* the boil (*Brit*); **i** ~**i della gioventù** youthful enthusiasm *sg*.

bologne'se [bōlōnyà'sà] *ag* Bolognese; **spaghetti alla** ~ spaghetti bolognese.

bom'ba *sf* bomb; **tornare a** ~ (*fig*) to get back to the point; **sei stato una** ~! you were tremendous!; ~ **atomica** atom bomb; ~ **a mano** hand grenade; ~ **ad orologeria** time bomb.

bombardamen'to *sm* bombardment; bombing.

bombarda're *vt* to bombard; (*da aereo*) to bomb.

bombardie're *sm* bomber.

bombet'ta *sf* derby (*US*), bowler (hat) (*Brit*).

bom'bola *sf* cylinder; ~ **del gas** gas cylinder.

bombonie'ra *sf* box of candy *(US) o* sweets *(Brit)* *(as souvenir at weddings, first communions etc)*.

bonac'cia, ce |bŏnách'chá| *sf* dead calm.

bonaccio'ne, a |bŏnàchŏ'nä| *ag* good-natured, easy-going ♦ *sm/f* good-natured sort.

bona'rio, a *ag* good-natured, kind.

boni'fica, che *sf* reclamation; reclaimed land.

boni'fico, ci *sm (riduzione, abbuono)* discount; *(versamento a terzi)* credit transfer.

Bonn *sf* Bonn.

bontà *sf* goodness; *(cortesia)* kindness; **aver la ~ di fare qc** to be good *o* kind enough to do sth.

bo'nus-'malus *sm inv* no-claims discount *(US) o* bonus *(Brit)*.

borbo'nico, a, ci, che *ag* Bourbon; *(fig)* backward, out of date.

borbotta're *vi* to mumble; *(stomaco)* to rumble.

borbotti'o, ii *sm* mumbling; rumbling.

bor'chia |bŏr'kyá| *sf* stud.

bordatu'ra *sf (SARTORIA)* border, trim.

borde'aux |bŏrdo'| *sm (colore)* burgundy, maroon; *(vino)* Bordeaux.

bordel'lo *sm* brothel.

bor'do *sm (NAUT)* ship's side; *(orlo)* edge; *(striscia di guarnizione)* border, trim; **a ~ di** *(nave, aereo)* aboard, on board; *(macchina)* in; **sul ~ della strada** at the roadside; **persona d'alto ~** *(fig)* VIP.

bordu'ra *sf* border.

borga'ta *sf* hamlet; *(a Roma)* working-class suburb.

borghe'se |bŏrgä'zä| *ag (spesso peg)* middle-class; bourgeois; **abito ~** civilian dress; **poliziotto in ~** plainclothes policeman.

borghesi'a |bŏrgäzē'á| *sf* middle classes *pl*; bourgeoisie.

bor'go, ghi *sm (paesino)* village; *(quartiere)* district; *(sobborgo)* suburb.

bo'ria *sf* self-conceit, arrogance.

borio'so, a *ag* arrogant.

borlot'to *sm* kidney bean.

Bor'neo *sm:* **il ~** Borneo.

borotal'co *sm* talcum powder.

borrac'cia, ce |bŏrrách'chá| *sf* canteen, water-bottle.

bor'sa *sf* bag; *(anche: ~ da signora)* purse *(US)*, handbag *(Brit)*; *(ECON)*: **la B~ (valori)** the Stock Exchange; **~ dell'acqua calda** hot-water bottle; **B~ merci** commodity exchange; **~ nera** black market; **~ della spesa** shopping bag; **~ di studio** grant.

borsaio'lo *sm* pickpocket.

borseg'gio |bŏrsäd'jŏ| *sm* pickpocketing.

borselli'no *sm* purse.

borsel'lo *sm* men's handbag.

borset'ta *sf* handbag.

borsi'sta, i, e *sm/f (ECON)* speculator; *(INS)*

grant-holder.

bosca'glia |bŏskál'yá| *sf* woodlands *pl*.

boscaio'lo *sm* woodcutter; forester.

boschet'to |bŏskät'tŏ| *sm* copse, grove.

bo'sco, schi *sm* wood.

bosco'so, a *ag* wooded.

bos'solo *sm* cartridge case.

Bot, bot *sigla m inv vedi* **buono ordinario del Tesoro**.

bota'nico, a, ci, che *ag* botanical ♦ *sm* botanist ♦ *sf* botany.

bo'tola *sf* trap door.

Botswa'na |bŏtsvá'ná| *sm:* **il ~** Botswana.

bot'ta *sf* blow; *(rumore)* bang; **dare (un sacco di) ~e a qn** to give sb a good thrashing; **~ e risposta** *(fig)* cut and thrust.

bot'te *sf* barrel, cask; **essere in una ~ di ferro** *(fig)* to be as safe as houses; **volere la ~ piena e la moglie ubriaca** to want to have one's cake and eat it too.

botte'ga, ghe *sf* shop; *(officina)* workshop; **stare a ~ (da qn)** to serve one's apprenticeship (with sb); **le B~ghe Oscure** *headquarters of the Italian Communist party*.

bottega'io, a *sm/f* shopkeeper.

botteghi'no |bŏttägē'nŏ| *sm* ticket office; *(del lotto)* public lottery office.

botti'glia |bŏttēl'yá| *sf* bottle.

bottiglieri'a |bŏttēlyärē'á| *sf* wine shop.

botti'no *sm (di guerra)* booty; *(di rapina, furto)* loot; **fare ~ di qc** *(anche fig)* to make off with sth.

bot'to *sm* bang; crash; **di ~** suddenly; **d'un ~** *(fam)* in a flash.

botto'ne *sm* button; *(BOT)* bud; **stanza dei ~i** control room; *(fig)* nerve centre; **attaccare (un) ~ a** *o* **con qn** to buttonhole sb; **botton d'oro** buttercup.

bovi'no, a *ag* bovine; **~i** *smpl* cattle.

box |boks| *sm inv (per cavalli)* horsetrailer *(US)*, horsebox *(Brit)*; *(per macchina)* garage; *(per macchina da corsa)* pit; *(per bambini)* playpen.

boxe |boks| *sf* boxing.

boz'za |bot'tsá| *sf* draft; *(TIP)* proof; **~ di stampa/impaginata** galley/page proof.

bozzet'to |bŏttsät'tŏ| *sm* sketch.

boz'zolo |bot'tsŏlŏ| *sm* cocoon.

BR *sigla fpl* = **Brigate Rosse** ♦ *sigla* = Brindisi.

bra'ca, che *sf (gamba di pantalone)* trouser leg; **~che** *sfpl (fam)* pants *(US)*, trousers; *(mutandoni)* drawers; **calare le ~che** *(fig fam)* to chicken out.

bracca're *vt* to hunt.

braccet'to |brächät'tŏ| *sm:* **a ~** arm in arm.

braccherò *etc* |bråkkåro'| *vb vedi* **braccare**.

braccia'le |brächá'lä| *sm* bracelet; *(distintivo)* armband.

braccialet'to |brächálät'tŏ| *sm* bracelet,

bangle.

braccian'te [bràchàn'tà] *sm* (AGR) day laborer (US) *o* labourer (Brit).

braccia'ta [bràchá'tà] *sf* armful; (nel nuoto) stroke.

brac'cio [bràch'chō] *sm* (pl(f) **braccia**: ANAT) arm; (pl(m) **bracci**: di gru, fiume) arm; (: di edificio) wing; **camminare sotto** ~ to walk arm in arm; **è il suo** ~ **destro** he's his right-hand man; ~ **di ferro** (anche fig) trial of strength; ~ **di mare** sound.

braccio'lo [bràcho'lō] *sm* (appoggio) arm.

brac'co, chi *sm* hound.

bracconie're *sm* poacher.

bra'ce [brà'chā] *sf* embers pl.

bracie're [bràche'rà] *sm* brazier.

bracio'la [bràcho'là] *sf* (CUC) chop.

bra'dipo *sm* (ZOOL) sloth.

bra'do, a *ag*: **allo stato** ~ in the wild *o* natural state.

bra'ma *sf*: ~ (**di/di fare**) longing (for/to do), yearning (for/to do).

brama're *vt*: ~ (**qc/di fare qc**) to long (for sth/to do sth), yearn (for sth/to do sth).

bramosi'a *sf*: ~ (**di**) longing (for), yearning (for).

bran'ca, che *sf* branch.

bran'chia [bràn'kyà] *sf* (ZOOL) gill.

bran'co, chi *sm* (di cani, lupi) pack; (di uccelli, pecore) flock; (peg: di persone) gang, pack.

brancola're *vi* to grope, feel one's way.

bran'da *sf* camp bed.

brandel'lo *sm* scrap, shred; **a ~i** in tatters, in rags; **fare a ~i** to tear to shreds.

brandi'na *sf* cot (US), camp bed (Brit).

brandi're *vt* to brandish.

bra'no *sm* piece; (di libro) passage.

brasa're *vt* to braise.

brasa'to *sm* braised beef.

Brasi'le *sm*: **il** ~ Brazil.

Brasi'lia *sf* Brasilia.

brasilia'no, a *ag*, *sm/f* Brazilian.

brava'ta *sf* (azione spavalda) act of bravado.

bra'vo, a *ag* (abile) clever, capable, skilful; (buono) good, honest; (: bambino) good; (coraggioso) brave; ~! well done!; (al teatro) bravo!; **su da ~!** (fam) there's a good boy!; **mi sono fatto le mie ~e 8 ore di lavoro** I put in a full 8 hours' work.

bravu'ra *sf* cleverness, skill.

brec'cia, ce [bràch'chà] *sf* breach; **essere sulla** ~ (fig) to be going strong; **fare** ~ **nell'animo** *o* **nel cuore di qn** to find the way to sb's heart.

Bre'ma *sf* Bremen.

bresa'ola *sf* kind of dried salted beef.

brescia'no, a [bràshà'nō] *ag* of (o from) Brescia.

Breta'gna [bràtàn'yà] *sf*: **la** ~ Brittany.

bretel'la *sf* (AUT) link; **~e** *sfpl* suspenders (US), braces (Brit).

bret'tone *ag*, *sm/f* Breton.

bre've *ag* brief, short; **in** ~ in short; **per farla** ~ to cut a long story short; **a** ~ (COMM) short-term.

brevetta're *vt* to patent.

brevet'to *sm* patent; ~ **di pilotaggio** pilot's license (US) *o* licence (Brit).

brevità *sf* brevity.

brez'za [bràd'dzà] *sf* breeze.

bric'co, chi *sm* jug; ~ **del caffè** coffeepot.

briccona'ta *sf* mischievous trick.

bricco'ne, a *sm/f* rogue, rascal.

bri'ciola [brà'chōlà] *sf* crumb.

bri'ciolo [brà'chōlō] *sm* (specie fig) bit.

bridge [brèj] *sm* bridge.

bri'ga, ghe *sf* (fastidio) trouble, bother; **attaccar** ~ to start a quarrel; **pigliarsi la** ~ **di fare qc** to take the trouble to do sth.

brigadie're *sm* (dei carabinieri etc) ≈ sergeant.

brigan'te *sm* bandit.

briga'ta *sf* (MIL) brigade; (gruppo) group, party; **le B~e Rosse** (POL) the Red Brigades.

brigati'smo *sm* phenomenon of the Red Brigades.

brigati'sta, i, e *sm/f* (POL) member of the Red Brigades.

bri'glia [brèl'yà] *sf* rein; **a** ~ **sciolta** at full gallop; (fig) at full speed.

brillan'te *ag* bright; (anche fig) brilliant; (che luccica) shining ♦ *sm* diamond.

brillanti'na *sf* hair cream.

brilla're *vi* to shine; (mina) to blow up ♦ *vt* (mina) to set off.

bril'lo, a *ag* merry, tipsy.

bri'na *sf* hoarfrost.

brinda're *vi*: ~ **a qn/qc** to drink to *o* toast sb/sth.

brin'disi *sm inv* toast.

bri'o *sm* liveliness, go.

brio'che [brèosh'] *sf inv* brioche (bun).

brio'so, a *ag* lively.

bri'scola *sf* type of card game; (seme vincente) trump(s); (carta) trump card.

britan'nico, a, ci, che *ag* British ♦ *sm/f* Briton; **i B~ci** the British pl.

bri'vido *sm* shiver; (di ribrezzo) shudder; (fig) thrill; **racconti del** ~ suspense stories.

brizzola'to, a [brèttsōlà'tō] *ag* (persona) going gray; (barba, capelli) graying.

broc'ca, che *sf* jug.

brocca'to *sm* brocade.

broc'colo *sm* broccoli q.

broda'glia [brōdàl'yà] *sf* (peg) dishwater.

bro'do *sm* broth; (per cucinare) stock; ~ **ristretto** consommé; **lasciare (cuocere) qn nel suo** ~ to let sb stew (in his own juice); **tutto**

fa ~ every little bit helps.
brogliac'cio |brōlyách'chō| *sm* scratch note (*US*), scribbling pad (*Brit*).
bro'glio |brol'yō| *sm*: ~ **elettorale** gerrymandering; **~i** *smpl* (*DIR*) malpractices.
bronchi'te |brōnkē'tā| *sf* (*MED*) bronchitis.
bron'cio |brōn'chō| *sm* sulky expression; **tenere il** ~ to sulk.
bron'co, chi *sm* bronchial tube.
brontola're *vi* to grumble; (*tuono, stomaco*) to rumble.
brontolo'ne, a *ag* grumbling ♦ *sm/f* grumbler.
bronzi'na |brōndzē'nā| *sf* (*TECN*) bush.
bron'zo |brōn'dzō| *sm* bronze; **che faccia di** ~! what nerve!
bross. *abbr* = **in brossura.**
brossu'ra *sf*: **in** ~ (*libro*) paperback.
bruca're *vt* to browse on, nibble at.
brucherà *etc* |brōōkārā'| *vb vedi* **brucare.**
bruciacchia're |brōōchákkyá'rā| *vt* to singe, scorch; **~rsi** *vr* to become singed *o* scorched.
bruciape'lo |brōōchápā'lō|: **a** ~ *av* pointblank.
brucia're |brōōchá'rā| *vt* to burn; (*scottare*) to scald ♦ *vi* to burn; ~ **gli avversari** (*SPORT, fig*) to leave the rest of the field behind; ~ **le tappe** *o* **i tempi** (*SPORT, fig*) to shoot ahead; **~rsi la carriera** to put an end to one's career.
bruciato're |brōōchátō'rā| *sm* burner.
bruciatu'ra |brōōchátōō'rá| *sf* (*atto*) burning *q*; (*segno*) burn; (*scottatura*) scald.
brucio're |brōōchō'rā| *sm* burning *o* smarting sensation.
bru'co, chi *sm* grub; (*di farfalla*) caterpillar.
bru'folo *sm* pimple, spot.
brughie'ra |brōōgyc'rā| *sf* heath, moor.
brulica're *vi* to swarm.
brul'lo, a *ag* bare, bleak.
bru'ma *sf* mist.
bru'no, a *ag* brown, dark; (*persona*) dark(-haired).
bru'sco, a, schi, sche *ag* (*sapore*) sharp; (*modi, persona*) brusque, abrupt; (*movimento*) abrupt, sudden.
brusi'o *sm* buzz, buzzing.
bruta'le *ag* brutal.
brutalità *sf inv* brutality.
bru'to, a *ag* (*forza*) brute *cpd* ♦ *sm* brute.
brut'ta *sf vedi* **brutto.**
bruttez'za |brōōttā'tsá| *sf* ugliness.
brut'to, a *ag* ugly; (*cattivo*) bad; (*malattia, strada, affare*) nasty, bad ♦ *sm*: **guardare qn di** ~ to give sb a nasty look ♦ *sf* rough copy, first draft; ~ **tempo** bad weather; **passare un** ~ **quarto d'ora** to have a nasty time of it; **vedersela** **~a** (*per un attimo*) to have a nasty moment; (*per un periodo*) to have a bad time of it.
bruttu'ra *sf* (*cosa brutta*) ugly thing; (*sudi-*

ciume) filth; (*azione meschina*) mean action.
Bruxel'les |brüscl'| *sf* Brussels.
BS *sigla* = *Brescia.*
B.T. *abbr* (= *bassa tensione*) LT ♦ *sigla m inv* = **buono del Tesoro.**
btg *abbr* = **battaglione.**
bu'ca, che *sf* hole; (*avvallamento*) hollow; ~ **delle lettere** mailbox (*US*), letterbox (*Brit*).
bucane've *sm inv* snowdrop.
buca're *vt* (*forare*) to make a hole (*o* holes) in; (*pungere*) to pierce; (*biglietto*) to punch; **~rsi** *vr* (*con eroina*) to mainline; ~ **una gomma** to have a flat tire (*US*) *o* puncture (*Brit*); **avere le mani bucate** (*fig*) to be a spendthrift.
Bu'carest *sf* Bucharest.
buca'to *sm* (*operazione*) washing; (*panni*) wash, washing.
buc'cia, ce |bōōch'chà| *sf* skin, peel; (*corteccia*) bark.
bucherella're |bōōkārállá'rā| *vt* to riddle with holes.
bucherò *etc* |bōōkāro'| *vb vedi* **bucare.**
bu'co, chi *sm* hole; **fare un** ~ **nell'acqua** to fail, draw a blank; **farsi un** ~ (*fam: drogarsi*) to have a fix.
Bu'dapest *sf* Budapest.
buddi'smo *sm* Buddhism.
budel'lo *sm* intestine; (*fig: tubo*) tube; (*vicolo*) alley; **~a** *sfpl* bowels, guts.
budi'no *sm* pudding.
bu'e, *pl* **buo'i** *sm* ox; (*anche:* **carne di ~**) beef; **uovo all'occhio di** ~ fried egg.
Bue'nos A'ires *sf* Buenos Aires.
bu'falo *sm* buffalo.
bufe'ra *sf* storm.
buffet'to *sm* flick.
buf'fo, a *ag* funny; (*TEATRO*) comic.
buffona'ta *sf* (*azione*) prank, jest; (*parola*) jest.
buffo'ne *sm* buffoon.
buggera're |bōōdjārā'rā| *vt* to swindle, cheat.
bugi'a, gi'e |bōōjē'á| *sf* lie; (*candeliere*) candleholder.
bugiar'do, a |bōōjár'dō| *ag* lying, deceitful ♦ *sm/f* liar.
bugigat'tolo |bōōjēgát'tōlō| *sm* poky little room.
bu'io, a *ag* dark ♦ *sm* dark, darkness; **fa** ~ **pesto** it's pitch-dark.
bul'bo *sm* (*BOT*) bulb; ~ **oculare** eyeball.
Bulgari'a *sf*: **la** ~ Bulgaria.
bul'garo, a *ag, sm/f, sm* Bulgarian.
bul'lo *sm* (*persona*) tough.
bullo'ne *sm* bolt.
buo'i *smpl di* **bue.**
buonafe'de *sf* good faith.
buona'nima *sf* = **buon'anima;** *vedi* **anima.**
buonanot'te *escl* good night! ♦ *sf*: **dare la** ~ **a** to say good night to.

buonase'ra *escl* good evening!

buoncostu'me *sm* public morality; **la (squadra del)** ~ (*POLIZIA*) the vice squad.

buondi *escl* hello!

buongior'no |bwŏnjŏr'nō| *escl* good morning (*o* afternoon)!

buongra'do *av*: **di** ~ willingly.

buongusta'io, a *sm/f* gourmet.

buongu'sto *sm* good taste.

buo'no, a *ag* (*dav sm* **buon** + *C o V*, **buono** + *s impura, gn, pn, ps, x, z*; *dav sf* **buona** + *C*, **buon'** +*V*) good; (*benevolo*): ~ **(con)** good (to), kind (to); (*adatto*): ~ **a/da** fit for/to ♦ *sm* good; (*COMM*) voucher, coupon; **alla buona** *ag* simple ♦ *av* in a simple way, without any fuss; **è un tipo alla buona** he's an easy-going sort; **che Dio ce la mandi buona!** here's hoping!; **accetterà con le buone o con le cattive** he'll have to accept whether he wants to or not; **essere un poco di** ~ to be a nasty piece of work; **buon compleanno!** happy birthday!; **buon divertimento!** have a nice time!; **buona fortuna!** good luck!; **buon riposo!** sleep well!; **buon viaggio!** bon voyage!, have a good trip!; **tante buone cose!** all the best!; ~ **d'acquisto** credit note, credit slip; ~ **di cassa** cash voucher; ~ **di consegna** delivery note; **ad ogni buon conto** in any case; ~ **fruttifero** interest-bearing bond; ~ **d'imbarco** shipping note; ~ **d'imposta** *special credit instrument for tax-relief purposes*; **di buon mattino** early in the morning; **a buon mercato** cheap; **di buon'ora** early; ~ **a nulla** good-for-nothing; ~ **ordinario del Tesoro (Bot, bot)** short-term treasury bond; ~ **postale fruttifero** interest-bearing bond (*issued by Italian Post Office*); **buon senso** common sense; ~ **del Tesoro** treasury bill; **deciditi una buona volta!** make up your mind once and for all!; **fare buon viso a cattivo gioco** to put a good face on things.

buonsen'so *sm* = **buon senso.**

buontempo'ne, a *sm/f* jovial person.

buonusci'ta |bwŏnŏŏshē'tà| *sf* (*INDUSTRIA*) (*large*) sum given to employee on retirement or on leaving a company; (*di affitti*) sum paid for the relinquishing of tenancy rights.

buratti'no *sm* puppet.

bur'bero, a *ag* surly, gruff.

bur'la *sf* prank, trick.

burla're *vt*: ~ **qc/qn**, ~**rsi di qc/qn** to make fun of sth/sb.

buro'crate *sm* bureaucrat.

burocra'tico, a, ci, che *ag* bureaucratic.

burocrazi'a |bŏŏrŏkràttsē'à| *sf* bureaucracy.

burra'sca, sche *sf* storm.

burrasco'so, a *ag* stormy.

bur'ro *sm* butter.

burro'ne *sm* ravine.

busca're *vt* (*anche*: ~**rsi**: *raffreddore*) to get,

catch; **buscarle** (*fam*) to get a hiding.

buscherò *etc* |bŏŏskàro'| *vb vedi* **buscare.**

bussa're *vi* to knock; ~ **a quattrini** (*fig*) to ask for money.

bus'sola *sf* compass; **perdere la** ~ (*fig*) to lose one's bearings.

bu'sta *sf* (*da lettera*) envelope; (*astuccio*) case; **in** ~ **aperta/chiusa** in an unsealed/sealed envelope; ~ **paga** pay packet.

bustarel'la *sf* bribe, backhander.

busti'na *sf* (*piccola busta*) envelope; (*di cibi, farmaci*) sachet; (*MIL*) garrison cap (*US*), forage cap (*Brit*); ~ **di tè** tea bag.

bu'sto *sm* bust; (*indumento*) corset, girdle; **a mezzo** ~ (*fotografia, ritratto*) half-length.

buta'no *sm* butane.

butta're *vt* to throw; (*anche*: ~ **via**) to throw away; ~**rsi** *vr* (*saltare*) to jump; ~ **giù** (*scritto*) to scribble down, dash off; (*cibo*) to gulp down; (*edificio*) to pull down, demolish; (*pasta, verdura*) to put into boiling water; **ho buttato là una frase** I mentioned it in passing; **buttiamoci!** (*saltiamo*) let's jump!; (*rischiamo*) let's go for it!; ~**rsi dalla finestra** to jump out of the window.

buz'zo |bŏŏd'dzō| *sm* (*fam*: *pancia*) belly, paunch; **di** ~ **buono** (*con impegno*) with a will.

C

C, c |chē| *sf o m inv* (*lettera*) C, c ♦ *abbr* (*GEO*) = **capo**; (= *Celsius, centigrado*) C; (= *conto*) a/c; ~ **come Como** ≈ C for Charlie.

CA *sigla* = *Cagliari.*

c.a. *abbr* (*ELETTR*) *vedi* **corrente alternata**; (*COMM*) = **corrente anno.**

cab. *abbr* = **cablogramma.**

cabaret' |kàbàrc'| *sm inv* cabaret.

cabi'na *sf* (*di nave*) cabin; (*da spiaggia*) beach hut; (*di autocarro, treno*) cab; (*di aereo*) cockpit; (*di ascensore*) cage; ~ **di proiezione** (*CINEMA*) projection booth; ~ **di registrazione** recording booth; ~ **telefonica** telephone box.

cabina'to *sm* cabin cruiser.

cablag'gio |kàblàd'jō| *sm* wiring.

cablogram'ma *sm* cable(gram).

caca'o *sm* cocoa.

cac'ca *sf* (*fam*: *anche fig*) shit (*!*).

cac'cia |kàch'chà| *sf* hunting; (*con fucile*) shooting; (*inseguimento*) chase; (*cacciagione*) game ♦ *sm inv* (*aereo*) fighter; (*nave*) destroyer; **andare a ~** to go hunting; **andare a ~ di guai** to be asking for trouble; **~ grossa** big-game hunting; **~ all'uomo** manhunt.

cacciabombardie're |kàchàbŏmbàrdyc'rà| *sm* fighter-bomber.

cacciagio'ne |kàchàjŏ'nà| *sf* game.

caccia're |kàchá'rà| *vt* to hunt; (*mandar via*) to chase away; (*ficcare*) to shove, stick ♦ *vi* to hunt; **~rsi** *vr* (*fam: mettersi*): **~rsi tra la folla** to plunge into the crowd; **dove s'è cacciata la mia borsa?** where has my bag got to?; **~rsi nei guai** to get into trouble; **~ fuori qc** to whip *o* pull sth out; **~ un urlo** to let out a yell.

cacciato'ra |kàchàtŏ'rà| *sf* (*giacca*) hunting jacket; (*CUC*): **pollo** *etc* **alla ~** chicken *etc* cacciatore.

cacciato're |kàchàtŏ'rà| *sm* hunter; **~ di frodo** poacher; **~ di dote** fortune-hunter.

cacciatorpedinie're |kàchàtŏrpàdĕnyc'rà| *sm* destroyer.

cacciavi'te |kàchàvĕ'tà| *sm inv* screwdriver.

cachemi're |kàshmĕr'| *sm inv* cashmere.

cachet |kàshe'| *sm* (*MED*) capsule; (*: compressa*) tablet; (*compenso*) fee; (*colorante per capelli*) rinse.

ca'chi |kà'kĕ| *sm inv* (*albero, frutto*) persimmon; (*colore*) khaki ♦ *ag inv* khaki.

ca'cio |kà'chŏ| *sm* cheese; **essere come il ~ sui maccheroni** (*fig*) to turn up at the right moment.

cac'tus *sm inv* cactus.

cada'vere *sm* (dead) body, corpse.

cadave'rico, a, ci, che *ag* (*fig*) deathly pale.

cad'di *etc vb vedi* **cadere**.

caden'te *ag* falling; (*casa*) tumbledown; (*persona*) decrepit.

caden'za |kàden'tsà| *sf* cadence; (*andamento ritmico*) rhythm; (*MUS*) cadenza.

cade're *vi* to fall; (*denti, capelli*) to fall out; (*tetto*) to fall in; **questa gonna cade bene** this skirt hangs well; **lasciar ~** (*anche fig*) to drop; **~ dal sonno** to be falling asleep on one's feet; **~ ammalato** to fall ill; **~ dalle nuvole** (*fig*) to be taken aback.

cadet'to *sm* cadet.

cadrò *etc vb vedi* **cadere**.

cadu'to, a *ag* (*morto*) dead ♦ *sm* dead soldier ♦ *sf* fall; **monumento ai ~i** war memorial; **~a di temperatura** drop in temperature; **la ~a dei capelli** hair loss; **~a del sistema** (*INFORM*) system failure.

caffè *sm inv* coffee; (*locale*) café; **~ corretto** coffee with liqueur; **~ in grani** coffee beans; **~ macchiato** coffee with a dash of milk; **~ macinato** ground coffee.

caffei'na *sf* caffeine.

caffellat'te *sm inv* café au lait (*US*); white coffee (*Brit*).

caffetteri'a *sf* coffee shop.

caffettie'ra *sf* coffeepot.

cafo'ne *sm* (*contadino*) peasant; (*peg*) boor.

cagiona're |kàjŏnà'rà| *vt* to cause, be the cause of.

cagione'vole |kàjŏnà'vŏlà| *ag* delicate, weak.

caglia're |kàlyá'rà| *vi* to curdle.

cagliarita'no, a |kàlyàrĕtà'nŏ| *ag* of (*o* from) Cagliari.

ca'gna |kàn'yà| *sf* (*ZOOL, peg*) bitch.

cagna'ra |kànyà'rà| *sf* (*fig*) uproar.

cagne'sco, a, schi, sche |kànyà'skŏ| *ag* (*fig*): **guardare qn in ~** to scowl at sb.

CAI *sigla m = Club Alpino Italiano*.

Ca'iro *sm*: **il ~** Cairo.

calabre'se *ag, smf* Calabrian.

calabro'ne *sm* hornet.

Calaha'ri |kàlàà'rĕ|: **il Deserto di ~** *sm* the Kalahari Desert.

calama'io *sm* inkpot; inkwell.

calama'ro *sm* squid.

calami'ta *sf* magnet.

calamità *sf inv* calamity, disaster; **~ naturale** natural disaster.

cala're *vt* (*far discendere*) to lower; (*MAGLIA*) to decrease ♦ *vi* (*discendere*) to go (*o* come) down; (*tramontare*) to set, go down; **~ di peso** to lose weight.

cala'ta *sf* (*invasione*) invasion.

cal'ca *sf* throng, press.

calca'gno |kàlkàn'yŏ| *sm* heel.

calca're *sm* limestone ♦ *vt* (*premere coi piedi*) to tread, press down; (*premere con forza*) to press down; (*mettere in rilievo*) to stress; **~ la mano** to overdo it, exaggerate; **~ le scene** (*fig*) to be on the stage; **~ le orme di qn** (*fig*) to follow in sb's footsteps.

cal'ce |kàl'chà| *sm*: **in ~** at the foot of the page ♦ *sf* lime; **~ viva** quicklime.

calcestruz'zo |kàlchàstrŏŏt'tsŏ| *sm* concrete.

calcherò *etc* |kàlkàro'| *vb vedi* **calcare**.

calcia're |kàlchá'rà| *vt, vi* to kick.

calciato're |kàlchàtŏ'rà| *sm* (football) player.

calci'na |kàlchĕ'nà| *sf* (lime) mortar.

calcinac'cio |kàlchĕnách'chŏ| *sm* flake of plaster.

cal'cio |kàl'chŏ| *sm* (*pedata*) kick; (*sport*) football, soccer; (*di pistola, fucile*) butt; (*CHIM*) calcium; **~ d'angolo** (*SPORT*) corner (kick); **~ di punizione** (*SPORT*) free kick.

cal'co, chi *sm* (*ARTE*) casting, molding (*US*), moulding (*Brit*); cast, mo(u)ld.

calcola're *vt* to calculate, work out, reckon; (*ponderare*) to weigh (up).

calcolato're, tri'ce *ag* calculating ♦ *sm* calculator; (*fig*) calculating person ♦ *sf* (*anche*: **macchina calcolatrice**) calculator; **~ digitale** digital computer; **~ elettronico** computer; **~ da tavolo** desktop computer.

cal'colo *sm* (*anche MAT*) calculation; (*infinite-*

simale etc) calculus; *(MED)* stone; **fare il ~ di qc** to work sth out; **fare i propri ~i** *(fig)* to weigh the pros and cons; **per ~** out of self-interest.

calda'ia *sf* boiler.

caldarro'sta *sf* roast chestnut.

caldeggia're |kăldădjá'rā| *vt* to support.

cal'do, a *ag* warm; *(molto ~)* hot; *(fig: appassionato)* keen ♦ *sm* heat; **ho ~** I'm warm; I'm hot; **fa ~** it's warm; it's hot; **non mi fa né ~ né freddo** I couldn't care less; **a ~** *(fig)* in the heat of the moment.

caleidosco'pio *sm* kaleidoscope.

calenda'rio *sm* calendar.

calen'de *sfpl* calends; **rimandare qc alle ~ greche** to put sth off indefinitely.

cales'se *sm* gig.

ca'libro *sm (di arma)* caliber *(US)*, calibre *(Brit)*, bore; *(TECN)* callipers *pl*; *(fig)* caliber; **di grosso ~** *(fig)* prominent.

ca'lice |ká'lēchă| *sm* goblet; *(REL)* chalice.

cali'gine |kălē'jēnā| *sf* fog; *(mista con fumo)* smog.

calligrafi'a *sf (scrittura)* handwriting; *(arte)* calligraphy.

cal'lo *sm* callus; *(ai piedi)* corn; **fare il ~ a qc** to get used to sth.

cal'ma *sf* calm; **faccia con ~** take your time.

calman'te *sm* sedative, tranquillizer.

calma're *vt* to calm; *(lenire)* to soothe; **~rsi** *vr* to grow calm, calm down; *(vento)* to abate; *(dolori)* to ease.

calmie're *sm* controlled price.

cal'mo, a *ag* calm, quiet.

ca'lo *sm (COMM: di prezzi)* fall; *(: di volume)* shrinkage; *(: di peso)* loss.

calo're *sm* warmth; *(intenso, FISICA)* heat; **essere in ~** *(ZOOL)* to be on heat.

calori'a *sf* calorie.

calori'fero *sm* radiator.

caloro'so, a *ag* warm; **essere ~** not to feel the cold.

calpesta're *vt* to tread on, trample on; **"è vietato ~ l'erba"** "keep off the grass".

calun'nia *sf* slander; *(scritta)* libel.

calva'rio *sm (fig)* affliction, cross.

calvi'zie |kálvēt'tsyā| *sf* baldness.

cal'vo, a *ag* bald.

cal'za |kál'tsá| *sf (da donna)* stocking; *(da uomo)* sock; **fare la ~** to knit; **~e di nailon** nylons, (nylon) stockings.

calzama'glia |kăltsámál'yá| *sf* tights *pl*; *(per danza, ginnastica)* leotard.

calza're |kăltsá'rā| *vt (scarpe, guanti: mettersi)* to put on; *(: portare)* to wear ♦ *vi* to fit; **~ a pennello** to fit like a glove.

calzatu'ra |kăltsátōō'rá| *sf* footwear.

calzaturifi'cio |kăltsátōōrēfē'chō| *sm* shoe *o* footwear factory.

calzet'ta |kăltsăt'tá| *sf* ankle sock; **una mezza ~** *(fig)* a nobody.

calzetto'ne |kăltsăttō'nā| *sm* heavy knee-length sock.

calzi'no |kăltsē'nō| *sm* sock.

calzola'io |kăltsōlá'yō| *sm* shoemaker; *(che ripara scarpe)* cobbler.

calzoleri'a |kăltsōlārē'á| *sf (negozio)* shoe shop; *(arte)* shoemaking.

calzonci'ni |kăltsōnchē'nē| *smpl* shorts; **~ da bagno** (swimming) trunks.

calzo'ne |kăltsō'nā| *sm* trouser leg; *(CUC)* savoury turnover made with pizza dough; **~i** *smpl* pants *(US)*, trousers *(Brit)*.

camaleon'te *sm* chameleon.

cambia'le *sf* bill (of exchange); *(pagherò cambiario)* promissory note; **~ di comodo** *o* **di favore** accommodation bill.

cambiamen'to *sm* change.

cambia're *vt* to change; *(modificare)* to alter, change; *(barattare)*: **~ (qc con qn/qc)** to exchange (sth with sb/for sth) ♦ *vi* to change, alter; **~rsi** *vr (variare abito)* to change; **~ casa** to move (house); **~ idea** to change one's mind; **~ treno** to change trains; **~ le carte in tavola** *(fig)* to change one's tune; **~ (l')aria in una stanza** to air a room; **è ora di ~ aria** *(andarsene)* it's time to move on.

cambiavalu'te *sm inv* exchange office.

cam'bio *sm* change; *(modifica)* alteration, change; *(scambio, COMM)* exchange; *(corso dei cambi)* rate (of exchange); *(TECN, AUT)* gears *pl*; **in ~ di** in exchange for; **dare il ~ a qn** to take over from sb; **fare il** *o* **un ~** to change (over); **~ a termine** *(COMM)* forward exchange *(Brit)*.

Cam'bital *sigla m = Ufficio Italiano dei Cambi.*

Cambo'gia |kámbo'já| *sf:* **la ~** Cambodia.

cambogia'no, a |kámbōjá'nō| *ag, sm/f* Cambodian.

cambu'sa *sf* storeroom.

ca'mera *sf* room; *(anche:* **~ da letto)** bedroom; *(POL)* chamber, house; **~ ardente** mortuary chapel; **~ d'aria** inner tube; *(di pallone)* bladder; **~ blindata** strongroom; **C~ di Commercio** Chamber of Commerce; **C~ dei Deputati** Chamber of Deputies, ≈ House of Representatives *(US)*, ≈ House of Commons *(Brit)*; **~ a gas** gas chamber; **~ del lavoro** labor union center *(US)*, trades union centre *(Brit)*; **~ a un letto/a due letti/matrimoniale** single/twin-bedded/double room; **~ oscura** *(FOT)* dark room; **~ da pranzo** dining room.

camera'ta, i, e *sm/f* companion ♦ *sf* dormitory.

camerati'smo *sm* comradeship.

camerie'ra *sf (domestica)* maid; *(che serve a tavola)* waitress; *(che fa le camere)* chambermaid.

camerie're *sm* (man)servant; (*di ristorante*) waiter.

cameri'no *sm* (*TEATRO*) dressing room.

Ca'merun *sm*: **il** ~ Cameroon.

ca'mice |kà'mēchā| *sm* (*REL*) alb; (*per medici etc*) lab coat.

camicet'ta |kàmēchāt'tà| *sf* blouse.

cami'cia, cie |kàmē'chà| *sf* (*da uomo*) shirt; (*da donna*) blouse; **nascere con la** ~ (*fig*) to be born lucky; **sudare sette** ~**cie** (*fig*) to have a hell of a time; ~ **di forza** straitjacket; ~ **da notte** (*da donna*) nightgown; (*da uomo*) nightshirt; **C**~ **nera** (*fascista*) Blackshirt.

camicia'io, a |kàmēchà'yō| *sm/f* (*sarto*) shirtmaker; (*che vende camicie*) shirtseller.

camicio'la |kàmēcho'là| *sf* vest.

camiciot'to |kàmēchot'tō| *sm* casual shirt; (*per operai*) smock.

caminet'to *sm* hearth, fireplace.

cami'no *sm* chimney; (*focolare*) fireplace, hearth.

ca'mion *sm inv* truck.

camionci'no |kàmyōnchē'nō| *sm* van.

camionet'ta *sf* jeep.

camioni'sta, i *sm* truck driver.

cam'ma *sf* cam; **albero a** ~**e** camshaft.

cammel'lo *sm* (*ZOOL*) camel; (*tessuto*) camel hair.

camme'o *sm* cameo.

cammina're *vi* to walk; (*funzionare*) to work, go; ~ **a carponi** *o* **a quattro zampe** to go on all fours.

cammina'ta *sf* walk; **fare una** ~ to go for a walk.

cammi'no *sm* walk; (*sentiero*) path; (*itinerario, direzione, tragitto*) way; **mettersi in** ~ to set *o* start off; **cammin facendo** on the way; **riprendere il** ~ to continue on one's way.

camomil'la *sf* camomile; (*infuso*) camomile tea.

camor'ra *sf* Camorra; (*fig*) racket.

camorri'sta, i, e *sm/f* member of the Camorra; (*fig*) racketeer.

camo'scio |kàmōsh'shō| *sm* chamois.

campa'gna |kàmpàn'yà| *sf* country, countryside; (*POL, COMM, MIL*) campaign; **in** ~ in the country; **andare in** ~ to go to the country; **fare una** ~ to campaign; ~ **promozionale vendite** sales campaign.

campagno'lo, a |kàmpànyo'lō| *ag* country *cpd* ♦ *sf* (*AUT*) cross-country vehicle.

campa'le *ag* field *cpd*; (*fig*): **una giornata** ~ a hard day.

campa'na *sf* bell; (*anche:* ~ **di vetro**) bell jar; **sordo come una** ~ as deaf as a doorpost; **sentire l'altra** ~ (*fig*) to hear the other side of the story.

campanel'la *sf* small bell; (*di tenda*) curtain ring.

campanel'lo *sm* (*all'uscio, da tavola*) bell.

campani'le *sm* bell tower, belfry.

campanili'smo *sm* parochialism.

campa'no, a *ag* of (*o* from) Campania.

campa're *vi* to live; (*tirare avanti*) to get by, manage; ~ **alla giornata** to live from day to day.

campa'to, a *ag*: ~ **in aria** unsound, unfounded.

campeggia're |kàmpàdjà'rā| *vi* to camp; (*risaltare*) to stand out.

campeggiato're, tri'ce |kàmpàdjàtō'rā| *sm/f* camper.

campeg'gio |kàmpàd'jō| *sm* camping; (*terreno*) camp site; **fare (del)** ~ to go camping.

campes'tre *ag* country *cpd*, rural; **corsa** ~ cross-country race.

cam'ping |kam'pēng| *sm inv* camp site.

campiona'rio, a *ag*: **fiera** ~**a** a trade fair ♦ *sm* collection of samples.

campiona'to *sm* championship.

campionatu'ra *sf* (*COMM*) production of samples; (*STATISTICA*) sampling.

campio'ne, es'sa *sm/f* (*SPORT*) champion ♦ *sm* (*COMM*) sample; ~ **gratuito** free sample; **prelievi di** ~ product samples.

cam'po *sm* (*gen*) field; (*MIL*) field; (*: accampamento*) camp; (*spazio delimitato: sportivo etc*) ground; field; (*di quadro*) background; **i** ~**i** (*campagna*) the countryside; **padrone del** ~ (*fig*) victor; ~ **da aviazione** airfield; ~ **di concentramento** concentration camp; ~ **di golf** golf course; ~ **lungo** (*CINEMA, TV, FOT*) long shot; ~ **da tennis** tennis court; ~ **visivo** field of vision.

camposan'to, pl campisan'ti *sm* cemetery.

camuffa're *vt* to disguise; ~**rsi** *vr*: ~**rsi (da)** to disguise o.s. (as); (*per ballo in maschera*) to dress up (as).

CAN *abbr* (= *Costo, Assicurazione e Nolo*) CIF.

Can. *abbr* (*GEO*) = **canale**.

Ca'nada *sm*: **il** ~ Canada.

canade'se *ag, sm/f* Canadian ♦ *sf* (*anche:* **tenda** ~) ridge tent.

cana'glia |kànál'yà| *sf* rabble, mob; (*persona*) scoundrel, rogue.

cana'le *sm* (*anche fig*) channel; (*artificiale*) canal.

ca'napa *sf* hemp; ~ **indiana** cannabis.

Cana'rie *sfpl*: **le (isole)** ~ the Canary Islands, the Canaries.

canari'no *sm* canary.

Canber'ra *sf* Canberra.

cancella're |kànchēllà'rā| *vt* (*con la gomma*) to erase; (*con la penna*) to strike out; (*annullare*) to annul, cancel; (*disdire*) to cancel.

cancella'ta |kànchēllà'tà| *sf* fence.

cancelleri'a |kànchēllàrē'à| *sf* chancery;

(quanto necessario per scrivere) stationery.

cancellie're |kànchàllyc'rä| *sm* chancellor; *(di tribunale)* court clerk *(US)*, clerk of the court *(Brit)*.

cancel'lo |kànchcl'lō| *sm* gate.

cancero'geno, a |kànchàro'jänō| *ag* carcinogenic ♦ *sm* carcinogen.

cancero'logo, a, gi, ghe |kànchàro'lōgō| *sm/f* cancer specialist.

cancero'so, a |kànchàrō'sō| *ag* cancerous ♦ *sm/f* cancer patient.

cancre'na *sf* gangrene.

can'cro *sm* (*MED*) cancer; *(dello zodiaco)*: **C~** Cancer; **essere del C~** to be Cancer.

candeggia're |kàndädjà'rä| *vt* to bleach.

candeggi'na |kàndädjē'nà| *sf* bleach.

cande'la *sf* candle; **~ (di accensione)** (*AUT*) spark plug; **una lampadina da 100 ~e** (*ELETTR*) a 100 watt bulb; **a lume di ~** by candlelight; **tenere la ~** *(fig)* to act as chaperone.

candela'bro *sm* candelabra.

candelie're *sm* candlestick.

candelot'to *sm* candle; **~ di dinamite** stick of dynamite; **~ lacrimogeno** tear gas grenade.

candidar'si *vr*: **~ (per)** (*POL*) to present o.s. as candidate (for).

candida'to, a *sm/f* candidate; *(aspirante a una carica)* applicant.

candidatu'ra *sf* candidacy; application.

can'dido, a *ag* white as snow; *(puro)* pure; *(sincero)* sincere, candid.

candi'to, a *ag* candied.

cando're *sm* brilliant white; purity; sincerity, candor *(US)*, candour *(Brit)*.

ca'ne *sm* dog; *(di pistola, fucile)* cock; **fa un freddo ~** it's bitterly cold; **non c'era un ~** there wasn't a soul; **quell'attore è un ~** he's a rotten actor; **~ da caccia** hunting dog; **~ da guardia** guard dog; **~ lupo** alsatian; **~ da salotto** lap dog; **~ da slitta** husky.

canes'tro *sm* basket; **fare un ~** (*SPORT*) to shoot a basket.

cangian'te |kànjàn'tä| *ag* iridescent; **seta ~** shot silk.

cangu'ro *sm* kangaroo.

cani'cola *sf* scorching heat.

cani'le *sm* kennel; *(di allevamento)* kennels *pl*; **~ municipale** dog pound.

cani'no, a *ag, sm* canine.

can'na *sf* *(pianta)* reed; *(: indica, da zucchero)* cane; *(bastone)* stick, cane; *(di fucile)* barrel; *(di organo)* pipe; *(DROGA: gergo)* joint; **~ fumaria** chimney flue; **~ da pesca** (fishing) rod; **~ da zucchero** sugar cane.

cannel'la *sf* (*CUC*) cinnamon; *(di conduttura; botte)* tap.

cannello'ni *smpl* *pasta tubes stuffed with sauce and baked.*

canne'to *sm* bed of reeds.

canni'bale *sm* cannibal.

cannocchia'le |kànnōkkyà'lä| *sm* telescope.

cannona'ta *sf*: **è una vera ~!** *(fig)* it's (o he's *etc*) fantastic!

canno'ne *sm* (*MIL*) gun; *(: STORIA)* cannon; *(tubo)* pipe, tube; *(piega)* box pleat; *(fig)* ace; **donna ~** fat woman.

cannonie're *sm* (*NAUT*) gunner; *(CALCIO)* goal scorer.

cannuc'cia, ce |kànnōōch'chà| *sf* (drinking) straw.

cano'a *sf* canoe.

ca'none *sm* canon, criterion; *(mensile, annuo)* rent; fee; **legge dell'equo ~** fair rent act.

cano'nica, che *sf* presbytery.

cano'nico, ci *sm* (*REL*) canon.

canonizza're |kànōnēddzà'rä| *vt* to canonize.

cano'ro, a *ag* *(uccello)* singing, song *cpd*.

canottag'gio |kànōttàd'jō| *sm* rowing.

canottie'ra *sf* undershirt *(US)*, vest *(Brit)*.

canot'to *sm* small boat, dinghy; canoe.

canovac'cio |kànōvàch'chō| *sm* *(tela)* canvas; *(strofinaccio)* duster; *(trama)* plot.

cantan'te *sm/f* singer.

canta're *vt, vi* to sing; **~ vittoria** to crow; **fare ~ qn** *(fig)* to make sb talk.

cantasto'rie *sm/f inv* storyteller.

cantauto're, tri'ce *sm/f* singer-composer.

canterella're *vt, vi* to hum, sing to o.s.

canticchia're |kàntēkkyà'rä| *vt, vi* to hum, sing to o.s.

cantie're *sm* *(EDIL)* (building) site; *(anche:* **~ navale)** shipyard.

cantile'na *sf* *(filastrocca)* lullaby; *(fig)* sing-song voice.

canti'na *sf* *(locale)* cellar; *(bottega)* wine shop.

can'to *sm* song; *(arte)* singing; *(REL)* chant; chanting; *(poesia)* poem, lyric; *(parte di una poesia)* canto; *(parte, lato)*: **da un ~** on the one hand; **d'altro ~** on the other hand.

cantona'ta *sf* *(di edificio)* corner; **prendere una ~** *(fig)* to blunder.

canto'ne *sm* *(in Svizzera)* canton.

cantonie'ra *ag*: **(casa) ~** road inspector's house.

cantuc'cio |kàntōōch'chō| *sm* corner, nook.

canu'to, a *ag* white, whitehaired.

canzona're |kàntsōnà'rä| *vt* to tease.

canzonatu'ra |kàntsōnàtōō'rà| *sf* teasing; *(beffa)* joke.

canzo'ne |kàntsō'nä| *sf* song; *(POESIA)* canzone.

canzonie're |kàntsōnyc'rä| *sm* (*MUS*) songbook; *(LETTERATURA)* collection of poems.

ca'os *sm inv* chaos.

cao'tico, a, ci, che *ag* chaotic.

CAP *sigla m vedi* **codice di avviamento posta-**

le.
cap. *abbr* (= *capitolo*) ch.
capa'ce [kápá'chā] *ag* able, capable; (*ampio, vasto*) large, capacious; **sei ~ di farlo?** can you o are you able to do it?; **~ d'intendere e di volere** (*DIR*) in full possession of one's faculties.
capacità [kápáchētā'] *sf inv* ability; (*DIR, di recipiente*) capacity; **~ produttiva** production capacity.
capacitar'si [kápáchētár'sē] *vr*: **~ di** to make out, understand.
capan'na *sf* hut.
capannel'lo *sm* knot (of people).
capan'no *sm* (*di cacciatori*) hide; (*da spiaggia*) cabana (*US*), bathing hut (*Brit*).
capanno'ne *sm* (*AGR*) barn; (*fabbricato industriale*) (factory) shed.
caparbietà *sf* stubbornness.
capar'bio, a *ag* stubborn.
capar'ra *sf* deposit, down payment.
capati'na *sf*: **fare una ~ da qn/in centro** to pop in on sb/into town.
capeggia're [kápēdjá'rā] *vt* (*rivolta etc*) to head, lead.
capel'lo *sm* hair; **~i** *smpl* (*capigliatura*) hair *sg*; **averne fin sopra i ~i di qc/qn** to be fed up to the (back) teeth with sth/sb; **mi ci hanno tirato per i ~i** (*fig*) they dragged me into it; **tirato per i ~i** (*spiegazione*) farfetched.
capello'ne, a *sm/f* hippie.
capellu'to, a *ag*: **cuoio ~** scalp.
capezza'le [kápāttsá'lā] *sm* bolster; (*fig*) bedside.
capez'zolo [kápāt'tsōlō] *sm* nipple.
capien'te *ag* capacious.
capien'za [kápyen'tsá] *sf* capacity.
capigliatu'ra [kápēlyátōō'rá] *sf* hair.
capi're *vt* to understand; **~ al volo** to understand immediately; **si capisce!** (*certamente!*) of course!, certainly!
capita'le *ag* (*mortale*) capital; (*fondamentale*) main *cpd*, chief *cpd* ♦ *sf* (*città*) capital ♦ *sm* (*ECON*) capital; **~ azionario** equity capital, share capital; **~ d'esercizio** working capital; **~ fisso** capital assets, fixed capital; **~ immobile** real estate; **~ liquido** cash assets *pl*; **~ mobile** movables *pl*; **~ di rischio** risk capital; **~ sociale** (*di società*) authorized capital; (*di club*) funds *pl*; **~ di ventura** venture capital, risk capital.
capitali'smo *sm* capitalism.
capitali'sta, i, e *ag, sm/f* capitalist.
capitalizza're [kápētáleēddzá'rā] *vt* to capitalize.
capitalizzazio'ne [kápētáleēddzáttsyō'nā] *sf* capitalization.
capitana're *vt* to lead; (*CALCIO*) to captain.
capitaneri'a *sf*: **~ (di porto)** port authorities

capita'no *sm* captain; **~ di lungo corso** master mariner; **~ di ventura** (*STORIA*) mercenary leader.
capita're *vi* (*giungere casualmente*) to happen to go, find o.s.; (*accadere*) to happen; (*presentarsi: cosa*) to turn up, present itself ♦ *vb impers* to happen; **~ a proposito/bene/male** to turn up at the right moment/at a good time/at a bad time; **mi è capitato un guaio** I've had some trouble.
capitel'lo *sm* (*ARCHIT*) capital.
capitola're *vi* to capitulate.
capitolazio'ne [kápētōláttsyō'nā] *sf* capitulation.
capi'tolo *sm* chapter; **~i** *smpl* (*COMM*) items; **non ho voce in ~** (*fig*) I have no say in the matter.
capitom'bolo *sm* headlong fall, tumble.
ca'po *sm* (*ANAT*) head; (*persona*) head, leader; (*: in ufficio*) head, boss; (*: in tribù*) chief; (*estremità: di tavolo, scale*) head, top; (*: di filo*) end; (*GEO*) cape; **andare a ~** to start a new paragraph; **"punto a ~"** "full stop — new paragraph"; **da ~** over again; **in ~ a** (*tempo*) within; **da un ~ all'altro** from one end to the other; **fra ~ e collo** (*all'improvviso*) out of the blue; **un discorso senza né ~ né coda** a senseless o meaningless speech; **~ d'accusa** (*DIR*) charge; **~ di bestiame** head *inv* of cattle; **C~ di Buona Speranza** Cape of Good Hope; **~ di vestiario** item of clothing.
capoban'da, *pl* **capiban'da** *sm* (*MUS*) bandmaster; (*di malviventi, fig*) gang leader.
capoc'cia [kápoch'chá] *sm inv* (*di lavoranti*) overseer; (*peg: capobanda*) boss.
capoclas'se, *pl(m)* **capiclas'se,** *pl(f) inv sm/f* (*INS*) = class president (*US*), form captain (*Brit*).
capocuo'co, chi *sm* head cook.
Capodan'no *sm* New Year.
capofami'glia, *pl(m)* **capifami'glia,** *pl(f) inv* [kápōfámēl'yá] *sm/f* head of the family.
capofit'to: a ~ *av* headfirst, headlong.
capogi'ro [kápōjē'rō] *sm* dizziness *q*; **da ~** (*fig*) astonishing, staggering.
capogrup'po, *pl(m)* **capigrup'po,** *pl(f) inv sm/f* group leader.
capolavo'ro, i *sm* masterpiece.
capoli'nea, *pl* **capili'nea** *sm* terminus.
capoli'no *sm*: **far ~** to peep out (*o in etc*).
capoli'sta, *pl(m)* **capili'sta,** *pl(f) inv sm/f* (*POL*) top candidate on electoral list.
capoluo'go, *pl* **ghi** *o* **capiluo'ghi** *sm* chief town, administrative center (*US*) o centre (*Brit*).
capomas'tro, *pl* **i** *o* **capimas'tri** *sm* master builder.
capora'le *sm* (*MIL*) private first class (*US*),

lance corporal (*Brit*).

caporepar'to, *pl*(*m*) **capirepar'to,** *pl*(*f*) *inv sm/f* (*di operai*) foreman; (*di ufficio, negozio*) head of department.

caposa'la *sf inv* (*MED*) head nurse (*US*), ward sister (*Brit*).

caposal'do, *pl* **capisal'di** *sm* stronghold; (*fig: fondamento*) basis, cornerstone.

caposqua'dra, *pl* **capisqua'dra** *sm* (*di operai*) foreman, ganger; (*MIL*) squad leader; (*SPORT*) team captain.

capostazio'ne, *pl* **capistazio'ne** [kåpōståt'tsyōnå] *sm* station master.

caposti'pite *sm* progenitor; (*fig*) earliest example.

capota'vola, *pl*(*m*) **capita'vola,** *pl*(*f*) *inv sm/f* (*persona*) head of the table; **sedere a ~** to sit at the head of the table.

capo'te [kåpot'] *sf inv* (*AUT*) soft top, hood (*Brit*).

capotre'no, *pl* **capitre'no** *o* **capotre'ni** *sm* conductor (*US*), guard (*Brit*).

capouffi'cio, *pl*(*m*) **capiuffi'cio,** *pl*(*f*) *inv* [kåpōōōffē'chō] *sm/f* head clerk.

Ca'po Ver'de *sm*: **il ~** Cape Verde.

capover'so *sm* (*di verso, periodo*) first line; (*TIP*) indent; (*paragrafo*) paragraph; (*DIR*: *comma*) section.

capovol'gere [kåpōvōl'jårå] *vt* to overturn; (*fig*) to reverse; **~rsi** *vr* to overturn; (*barca*) to capsize; (*fig*) to be reversed.

capovolgimen'to [kåpōvōljēmån'tō] *sm* (*fig*) reversal, complete change.

capovol'to, a *pp di* **capovolgere** ♦ *ag* upside down; (*barca*) capsized.

cap'pa *sf* (*mantello*) cape, cloak; (*del camino*) hood.

cappel'la *sf* (*REL*) chapel.

cappella'no *sm* chaplain.

cappel'lo *sm* hat; **ti faccio tanto di ~!** (*fig*) I take my hat off to you!; **~ a bombetta** derby (*US*), bowler (hat) (*Brit*); **~ a cilindro** top hat.

cap'pero *sm* caper.

cappo'ne *sm* capon.

cappotta're *vi* (*AUT*) to overturn.

cappot'to *sm* (over)coat.

cappucci'no [kåpōōchē'nō] *sm* (*frate*) Capuchin monk; (*bevanda*) frothy white coffee.

cappuc'cio [kåpōōch'chō] *sm* (*copricapo*) hood; (*della biro*) cap.

ca'pra *sf* (she-)goat.

capre'se *ag* from (*o* of) Capri.

capret'to *sm* kid.

capric'cio [kåprēch'chō] *sm* caprice, whim; (*bizza*) tantrum; **fare i ~i** to be very naughty; **~ della sorte** quirk of fate.

capriccio'so, a [kåprēchō'sō] *ag* capricious, whimsical; naughty.

Capricor'no *sm* Capricorn; **essere del ~**

(*dello zodiaco*) to be Capricorn.

caprifo'glio [kåprēfol'yō] *sm* honeysuckle.

caprio'la *sf* somersault.

caprio'lo *sm* roe deer.

ca'pro *sm* billy-goat; **~ espiatorio** (*fig*) scapegoat.

capro'ne *sm* billy-goat.

cap'sula *sf* capsule; (*di arma, per bottiglie*) cap.

capta're *vt* (*RADIO, TV*) to pick up; (*cattivarsi*) to gain, win.

CAR *sigla m = Centro Addestramento Reclute.*

carabi'na *sf* rifle.

carabinie're *sm* member of Italian military police force.

Cara'cas *sf* Caracas.

caraf'fa *sf* carafe.

Carai'bi *smpl*: **il mar dei ~** the Caribbean (Sea).

carai'bico, a, ci, che *ag* Caribbean.

caramel'la *sf* candy (*US*), sweet (*Brit*).

caramel'lo *sm* caramel.

cara'to *sm* (*di oro, diamante etc*) carat.

carat'tere *sm* character; (*caratteristica*) characteristic, trait; **avere un buon ~** to be good-natured; **informazione di ~ tecnico/confidenziale** information of a technical/confidential nature; **essere in ~ con qc** (*intonarsi*) to be in harmony with sth.

caratteri'no *sm* difficult nature *o* character.

caratteri'stico, a, ci, che *ag* characteristic ♦ *sf* characteristic, feature; **segni ~ci** (*su passaporto etc*) distinguishing marks.

caratterizza're [kåråttårēddzå'rå] *vt* to characterize, distinguish.

carboidra'to *sm* carbohydrate.

carbona'io *sm* (*chi fa carbone*) charcoal-burner; (*commerciante*) coalman, coal merchant.

carbo'ne *sm* coal; **~ fossile** (pit) coal; **essere o stare sui ~i ardenti** to be like a cat on hot bricks.

carbo'nio *sm* (*CHIM*) carbon.

carbonizza're [kårbōnēddzà'rå] *vt* (*legna*) to carbonize; (: *parzialmente*) to char; **morire carbonizzato** to be burned to death.

carburan'te *sm* (motor) fuel.

carburato're *sm* carburetor (*US*), carburettor (*Brit*).

carcas'sa *sf* carcass; (*fig: peg: macchina etc*) (old) wreck.

carcera'to, a [kårchårå'tō] *sm/f* prisoner.

car'cere [kår'chårå] *sm* prison; (*pena*) imprisonment; **~ di massima sicurezza** maximum-security prison.

carcerie're, a [kårchåryc'rå] *sm/f* (*anche fig*) jailer.

carcio'fo [kårcho'fō] *sm* artichoke.

cardelli'no *sm* goldfinch.

cardi'aco, a, ci, che *ag* cardiac, heart *cpd*.

cardina'le *ag*, *sm* cardinal.
car'dine *sm* hinge.
cardiologi'a [kàrdyōlōjē'à] *sf* cardiology.
cardio'logo, gi *sm* heart specialist, cardiologist.
car'do *sm* thistle.
caren'te *ag*: ~ **di** lacking in.
caren'za [kàren'tsà] *sf* lack, scarcity; (*vitaminica*) deficiency.
caresti'a *sf* famine; (*penuria*) scarcity, dearth.
carez'za [kàràt'tsà] *sf* caress; **dare** *o* **fare una** ~ **a** (*persona*) to caress; (*animale*) to stroke, pat.
carezza're [kàràttsà'rà] *vt* to caress, stroke, fondle.
carezze'vole [kàràttsā'vōlā] *ag* sweet, endearing.
car'go, ghi *sm* (*nave*) cargo boat, freighter; (*aereo*) freighter.
cariar'si *vr* (*denti*) to decay.
ca'rica *sf vedi* **carico**.
caricabatteri'e *sm inv* (*ELETTR*) battery charger.
carica're *vt* to load; (*aggravare: anche fig*) to weigh down; (*orologio*) to wind up; (*batteria, MIL*) to charge; ~**rsi** *vr*: ~**rsi di** to burden *o* load o.s. with; (*fig: di responsabilità, impegni*) to burden o.s. with.
caricatu'ra *sf* caricature.
ca'rico, a, chi, che *ag* (*che porta un peso*): ~ **di** loaded *o* laden with; (*fucile*) loaded; (*orologio*) wound up; (*batteria*) charged; (*colore*) deep; (*caffè, tè*) strong ♦ *sm* (*il caricare*) loading; (*ciò che si carica*) load; (*COMM*) shipment; (*fig: peso*) burden, weight ♦ *sf* (*mansione ufficiale*) office, position; (*MIL. TECN. ELETTR*) charge; ~ **di debiti** up to one's ears in debt; **persona a** ~ dependent; **essere a** ~ **di qn** (*spese etc*) to be charged to sb; (*accusa, prova*) to be against sb; **testimone a** ~ witness for the prosecution; **farsi** ~ **di** (*problema, responsabilità*) to take on; **a** ~ **del cliente** at the customer's expense; ~ **di lavoro** (*di ditta, reparto*) workload; ~ **utile** payload; **capacità di** ~ cargo capacity; **entrare/essere in** ~**a** to come into/be in office; **ricoprire** *o* **rivestire una** ~**a** to hold a position; **uscire di** ~**a** to leave office; **dare la** ~**a a** (*orologio*) to wind up; (*fig: persona*) to back up; **tornare alla** ~**a** (*fig*) to insist, persist; **ha una forte** ~**a di simpatia** he's very likeable.
ca'rie *sf* (*dentaria*) decay.
cari'no, a *ag* lovely, pretty, nice; (*simpatico*) nice.
cari'sma [kàrēz'mà] *sm* charisma.
carità *sf* charity; **per** ~! (*escl di rifiuto*) good heavens, no!
caritate'vole *ag* charitable.

carnagio'ne [kàrnájō'nā] *sf* complexion.
carna'le *ag* (*amore*) carnal; (*fratello*) blood cpd.
car'ne *sf* flesh; (*bovina, ovina etc*) meat; **in** ~ **e ossa** in the flesh, in person; **essere (bene) in** ~ to be well padded, be plump; **non essere né** ~ **né pesce** (*fig*) to be neither fish nor fowl; ~ **di manzo/maiale/pecora** beef/pork/mutton; ~ **in scatola** canned meat; ~ **tritata** hamburger meat (*US*), mince (*Brit*).
carne'fice [kàrnā'fēchā] *sm* executioner; hangman.
carnefici'na [kàrnāfēchē'nà] *sf* carnage; (*fig*) disaster.
carneva'le *sm* carnival.
carni'voro, a *ag* carnivorous.
carno'so, a *ag* fleshy; (*pianta, frutto, radice*) pulpy; (*labbra*) full.
ca'ro, a *ag* (*amato*) dear; (*costoso*) dear, expensive; **se ti è** ~**a la vita** if you value your life.
caro'gna [kàrōn'yà] *sf* carrion; (*fig fam*) swine.
carosel'lo *sm* merry-go-round.
caro'ta *sf* carrot.
carova'na *sf* caravan.
carovi'ta *sm* high cost of living.
car'pa *sf* carp.
Carpa'zi [kàrpàt'sē] *smpl*: **i** ~ the Carpathian Mountains.
carpenteri'a *sf* carpentry.
carpentie're *sm* carpenter.
carpi're *vt*: ~ **qc a qn** (*segreto etc*) to get sth out of sb.
carpo'ni *av* on all fours.
carra'bile *ag* suitable for vehicles; **"passo** ~**"** "keep clear".
carra'io, a *ag*: **passo** ~ vehicle entrance.
carreggia'ta [kàrrēdjà'tà] *sf* roadway, carriageway (*Brit*); **rimettersi in** ~ (*fig: recuperare*) to catch up; **tenersi in** ~ (*fig*) to keep to the right path.
carrella'ta *sf* (*CINEMA. TV: tecnica*) tracking; (*: scena*) running shot; ~ **di successi** medley of hit tunes.
carrel'lo *sm* trolley; (*AER*) undercarriage; (*CINEMA*) dolly; (*di macchina da scrivere*) carriage.
carret'ta *sf*: **tirare la** ~ (*fig*) to plod along.
carret'to *sm* handcart.
carrie'ra *sf* career; **fare** ~ to get on; **ufficiale di** ~ (*MIL*) regular officer; **a gran** ~ at full speed.
carrio'la *sf* wheelbarrow.
car'ro *sm* cart, wagon; **il Gran/Piccolo C**~ (*ASTR*) the Great/Little Bear; **mettere il** ~ **avanti ai buoi** (*fig*) to put the cart before the horse; ~ **armato** tank; ~ **attrezzi** (*AUT*) tow truck (*US*), breakdown van (*Brit*); ~ **funebre** hearse; ~ **merci/bestiame** (*FERR*)

freight/cattle car.

carroz'za [kàrrot'tsà] *sf* carriage, coach; ~ **letto** (*FERR*) sleeper; ~ **ristorante** (*FERR*) dining car.

carrozzel'la [kàrrŏttsel'là] *sf* (*per bambini*) baby carriage (*US*), pram (*Brit*); (*per invalidi*) wheelchair.

carrozzeri'a [kàrrŏttsàrē'à] *sf* body, coachwork (*Brit*); (*officina*) body shop.

carrozzie're [kàrrŏttsye'rà] *sm* (*AUT: progettista*) car designer; (: *meccanico*) coachbuilder.

carrozzi'na [kàrrŏttsē'nà] *sf* baby carriage (*US*), pram (*Brit*).

carrozzo'ne [kàrrŏttsŏ'nà] *sm* (*da circo, di zingari*) caravan.

carru'cola *sf* pulley.

car'ta *sf* paper; (*al ristorante*) menu; (*GEO*) map; plan; (*documento, da gioco*) card; (*costituzione*) charter; ~**e** *sfpl* (*documenti*) papers, documents; **alla** ~ (*al ristorante*) à la carte; **cambiare le ~e in tavola** (*fig*) to shift one's ground; **fare ~e false** (*fig*) to go to great lengths; ~ **assegni** bank card; ~ **assorbente** blotting paper; ~ **bollata** *o* **da bollo** (*AMM*) official stamped paper; ~ **di credito** credit card; ~ **di debito** debit (*US*) *o* cash (*Brit*) card; ~ (**geografica**) map; ~ **d'identità** identity card; ~ **igienica** toilet paper; ~ **d'imbarco** (*AER. NAUT*) boarding card, boarding pass; ~ **da lettere** writing paper; ~ **libera** (*AMM*) unstamped paper; ~ **millimetrata** graph paper; ~ **oleata** wax (*US*) *o* waxed (*Brit*) paper; ~ **da pacchi**, ~ **da imballo** wrapping paper, brown paper; ~ **da parati** wallpaper; ~ **verde** (*AUT*) *international insurance certificate*; ~ **vetrata** sandpaper; ~ **da visita** business card.

cartacarbo'ne, *pl* **cartecarbo'ne** *sf* carbon paper.

cartac'cia, **ce** [kàrtàch'chà] *sf* waste paper.

cartamone'ta *sf* paper money.

cartape'cora *sf* parchment.

cartape'sta *sf* papier-mâché.

cartastrac'cia [kàrtàstràch'chà] *sf* waste paper.

carteg'gio [kàrtàd'jŏ] *sm* correspondence.

cartel'la *sf* (*scheda*) card; (*custodia: di cartone*) folder; (: *di uomo d'affari etc*) briefcase; (: *di scolaro*) schoolbag, satchel; ~ **clinica** (*MED*) case sheet.

cartelli'no (*etichetta*) label; (*su porta*) notice; (*scheda*) card; **timbrare il** ~ (*all'entrata*) to punch (*US*) *o* clock (*Brit*) in; (*all'uscita*) to punch (*US*) *o* clock (*Brit*) out; ~ **di presenza** timecard.

cartel'lo *sm* sign; (*pubblicitario*) poster; (*stradale*) sign, signpost; (*in dimostrazioni*) placard; (*ECON*) cartel.

cartello'ne *sm* (*pubblicitario*) advertising poster; (*della tombola*) scoring frame; (*TEA-*

TRO) playbill; **tenere il** ~ (*spettacolo*) to have a long run.

cartie'ra *sf* paper mill.

cartila'gine [kàrtēlà'jēnà] *sf* cartilage.

carti'na *sf* (*AUT. GEO*) map.

cartoc'cio [kàrtoch'chŏ] *sm* paper bag; **cuocere al** ~ (*CUC*) to bake in tinfoil.

cartografi'a *sf* cartography.

cartola'io, **a** *sm/f* stationer.

cartoleri'a *sf* stationery store (*US*), stationer's (shop (*Brit*)).

cartoli'na *sf* postcard; ~ **di auguri** greetings card; ~ **precetto** *o* **rosa** (*MIL*) draft card (*US*), call-up card (*Brit*).

cartoman'te *sm/f* fortune-teller (*using cards*).

cartonci'no [kàrtŏnchē'nŏ] *sm* (*materiale*) thin cardboard; (*biglietto*) card; ~ **della società** compliments slip.

carto'ne *sm* cardboard; (*del latte, dell'aranciata*) carton; (*ARTE*) cartoon; ~**i animati** (*CINEMA*) cartoons.

cartuc'cia, **ce** [kàrtŏŏch'chà] *sf* cartridge; ~ **a salve** blank cartridge; **mezza** ~ (*fig: persona*) good-for-nothing.

ca'sa *sf* house; (*specialmente la propria* ~) home; (*COMM*) firm, house; **essere a** ~ to be at home; **vado a** ~ **mia/tua** I'm going home/ to your house; ~ **di correzione** reformatory (*US*), community home (*Brit*); ~ **di cura** nursing home; ~ **editrice** publishing house; ~ **dello studente** student hostel; ~ **di tolleranza**, ~ **d'appuntamenti** brothel; ~**e popolari** ≈ public housing units (*US*), ≈ council houses (*o* flats) (*Brit*).

Casablan'ca *sf* Casablanca.

casac'ca, **che** *sf* military coat; (*di fantino*) blouse.

casa'le *sm* (*gruppo di case*) hamlet; (*casa di campagna*) farmhouse.

casalin'go, a, ghi, ghe *ag* household, domestic; (*fatto a casa*) home-made; (*semplice*) homely; (*amante della casa*) home-loving ♦ *sf* housewife; ~**ghi** *smpl* (*oggetti*) household articles; **cucina** ~**a** plain home cooking.

casa'ta *sf* family lineage.

casa'to *sm* family name.

Casc. *abbr* (*GEO*) = **cascata**.

cascamor'to *sm* woman-chaser; **fare il** ~ to chase women.

casca're *vi* to fall; ~ **bene/male** (*fig*) to land lucky/unlucky; ~ **dalle nuvole** (*fig*) to be taken aback; ~ **dal sonno** to be falling asleep on one's feet; **caschi il mondo** no matter what; **non cascherà il mondo se ...** it won't be the end of the world if ....

casca'ta *sf* fall; (*d'acqua*) cascade, waterfall.

cascherò *etc* [kàskàro'] *vb vedi* **cascare**.

casci'na [kàshē'nà] *sf* farmstead.

cascina'le [kàshēnà'là] *sm* (*casolare*) farmhouse; (*cascina*) farmstead.

ca'sco, schi *sm* helmet; *(del parrucchiere)* hair-dryer; *(di banane)* bunch; **i ~schi blu** the UN peace-keeping troops.

caseggia'to |kásādjá'tō| *sm* *(edificio)* large apartment building *(US)* o block of flats *(Brit)*; *(gruppo di case)* group of houses.

caseifi'cio |kázăēfē'chō| *sm* creamery.

casel'la *sf* pigeonhole; **~ postale (C.P.)** post office box (P.O. box).

casella'rio *sm* *(mobile)* filing cabinet; *(raccolta di pratiche)* files *pl*; **~ giudiziale** court records *pl*; **~ penale** police files *pl*.

casel'lo *sm* *(di autostrada)* tollgate.

caserec'cio, a, ci, ce |kásărāch'chō| *ag* homemade.

caser'ma *sf* barracks *pl*.

caserta'no, a *ag* of (o from) Caserta.

casi'no *sm* *(disordine)* mess; *(baccano)* racket; *(casa di prostituzione)* brothel.

casinò *sm* *inv* casino.

casi'stica *sf* *(MED)* record of cases; **secondo la ~ degli incidenti stradali** according to road accident data.

ca'so *sm* chance; *(fatto, vicenda)* event, incident; *(possibilità)* possibility; *(MED, LING)* case; **a ~** at random; **per ~** by chance, by accident; **in ogni ~, in tutti i ~i** in any case, at any rate; **in ~ contrario** otherwise; **al ~** should the opportunity arise; **nel ~ che** in case; **~ mai** if by chance; **far ~ a qc/qn** to pay attention to sth/sb; **fare o porre o mettere il ~ che** to suppose that; **guarda ~ ...** strangely enough ...; **è il ~ che ce ne andiamo** we'd better go; **~ limite** borderline case.

casola're *sm* cottage.

Ca'spio *sm*: **il mar ~** the Caspian Sea.

ca'spita *escl* *(di sorpresa)* good heavens!; *(di impazienza)* for goodness' sake!

cas'sa *sf* case, crate, box; *(bara)* coffin; *(mobile)* chest; *(involucro: di orologio etc)* case; *(macchina)* cash register; *(luogo di pagamento)* cash desk, checkout (counter); *(fondo)* fund; *(istituto bancario)* bank; **battere ~** *(fig)* to come looking for money; **~ automatica prelievi** cash dispenser; **~ continua** night deposit *(US)* o safe *(Brit)*; **mettere in ~ integrazione** ≈ to lay off; **C~ del Mezzogiorno** *development fund for the South of Italy*; **~ mutua** o **malattia** health insurance plan; **~ di risonanza** *(MUS)* soundbox; *(fig)* platform; **~ di risparmio** savings bank; **~ rurale e artigiana** credit institution *(serving farmers and craftsmen)*; **~ toracica** *(ANAT)* chest.

cassafor'te, pl cassefor'ti *sf* safe.

cassapan'ca, pl cassapan'che o **cassepan'che** *sf* settle.

casseruo'la, cassero'la *sf* saucepan.

casset'ta *sf* box; *(per registratore)* cassette; *(CINEMA, TEATRO)* box-office takings *pl*;

pane a o **in ~** sandwich bread; **film di ~** *(commerciale)* box-office draw; **far ~** to be a box-office success; **~ delle lettere** mailbox *(US)*, letterbox *(Brit)*; **~ di sicurezza** strongbox.

casset'to *sm* drawer.

cassetto'ne *sm* chest of drawers.

cassie're, a *sm/f* cashier; *(di banca)* teller.

cassintegra'to, a *sm/f person who has been laid off.*

casso'ne *sm* *(cassa)* large case, large chest.

Cast. *abbr* = **castello**.

ca'sta *sf* caste.

casta'gna |kástán'yà| *sf* chestnut; **prendere qn in ~** *(fig)* to catch sb in the act.

casta'gno |kástán'yō| *sm* chestnut (tree).

casta'no, a *ag* chestnut (brown).

castel'lo *sm* castle; *(TECN)* scaffolding.

castiga're *vt* to punish.

castiga'to, a *ag* *(casto, modesto)* pure, chaste; *(emendato: prosa, versione)* expurgated, amended.

casti'go, ghi *sm* punishment.

castità *sf* chastity.

ca'sto, a *ag* chaste, pure.

casto'ro *sm* beaver.

castran'te *ag* frustrating.

castra're *vt* to castrate; to geld; to fix *(US)*, doctor *(Brit)*; *(fig: iniziativa)* to frustrate.

castroneri'a *sf* *(fam)*: **dire ~e** to talk rubbish.

casua'le *ag* chance *cpd*.

casu'pola *sf* simple little cottage.

catacom'ba *sf* catacomb.

catafa'scio |kátáfásh'shō| *sm*: **andare a ~** to collapse; **mandare a ~** to wreck.

catalizzato're |kátálēddzátō'rā| *sm* *(anche fig)* catalyst.

cata'logo, ghi *sm* catalog *(US)*, catalogue *(Brit)*; **~ dei prezzi** price list.

Catalo'nia *sf*: **la ~** Catalonia.

catane'se *ag* of (o from) Catania.

catapec'chia |kátápāk'kyà| *sf* hovel.

catapul'ta *sf* catapult.

catarifrangen'te |kátárēfrànjen'tā| *sm* *(AUT)* reflector.

catar'ro *sm* catarrh.

cata'sta *sf* stack, pile.

cata'sto *sm* land register; land registry office.

catas'trofe *sf* catastrophe, disaster.

catastro'fico, a, ci, che *ag* *(evento)* catastrophic; *(persona, previsione)* pessimistic.

catechi'smo |kátākēz'mō| *sm* catechism.

categori'a *sf* category; *(di albergo)* class.

catego'rico, a, ci, che *ag* categorical.

cate'na *sf* chain; **reazione a ~** chain reaction; **susseguirsi a ~** to happen in quick succession; **~ di montaggio** assembly line; **~e da neve** *(AUT)* snow chains.

catenac'cio |kátānách'chō| *sm* bolt.

catenel'la *sf* (*ornamento*) chain; (*di orologio*) watch chain; (*di porta*) door chain.

caterat'ta *sf* cataract; (*chiusa*) sluice gate.

cater'va *sf* (*di cose*) loads *pl*, heaps *pl*; (*di persone*) horde.

catete're *sm* (*MED*) catheter.

catinel'la *sf*: **piovere a ~e** to pour, rain cats and dogs.

cati'no *sm* basin.

cato'dico, a, ci, che *ag*: **tubo a raggi ~ci** cathode-ray tube.

cator'cio [kátor'chō] *sm* (*peg*) old wreck.

catra'me *sm* tar.

cat'tedra *sf* teacher's desk; (*di università*) chair; **salire** *o* **montare in ~** (*fig*) to pontificate.

cattedra'le *sf* cathedral.

cattedra'tico, a, ci, che *ag* (*insegnamento*) university *cpd*; (*ironico*) pedantic ♦ *sm/f* professor.

cattive'ria *sf* (*qualità*) wickedness; (*di bambino*) naughtiness; (*azione*) wicked action; **fare una ~** to do something wicked; **to be naughty.**

cattività *sf* captivity.

catti'vo, a *ag* bad; (*malvagio*) bad, wicked; (*turbolento: bambino*) bad, naughty; (*: mare*) rough; (*odore, sapore*) nasty, bad ♦ *sm/f* bad *o* wicked person; **farsi ~ sangue** to worry, get in a state; **farsi un ~ nome** to earn o.s. a bad reputation; **i ~i** (*nei film*) the bad guys.

cattolice'simo [káttōlēchā'zēmō] *sm* Catholicism.

catto'lico, a, ci, che *ag*, *sm/f* (Roman) Catholic.

cattu'ra *sf* capture.

cattura're *vt* to capture.

cauca'sico, a, ci, che *ag*, *sm/f* Caucasian.

Ca'ucaso *sm*: **il ~** the Caucasus.

caucciù [káōōchōō'] *sm* rubber.

ca'usa *sf* cause; (*DIR*) lawsuit, case, action; **a ~ di** because of; **per ~ sua** because of him; **fare** *o* **muovere ~ a qn** to take legal action against sb; **parte in ~** litigant.

causa'le *ag* (*LING*) causal ♦ *sf* cause, reason.

causa're *vt* to cause.

ca'ustico, a, ci, che *ag* caustic.

caute'la *sf* caution, prudence.

cautela're *vt* to protect; **~rsi** *vr*: **~rsi (da** *o* **contro)** to take precautions (against).

ca'uto, a *ag* cautious, prudent.

cauziona're [káōōttsyōnà'rā] *vt* to guarantee.

cauzio'ne [káōōttsyō'nā] *sf* security; (*DIR*) bail; **rilasciare dietro ~** to release on bail.

cav. *abbr* = **cavaliere.**

ca'va *sf* quarry.

cavalca're *vt* (*cavallo*) to ride; (*muro*) to sit astride; (*sog: ponte*) to span.

cavalca'ta *sf* ride; (*gruppo di persone*) riding party.

cavalcavi'a *sm inv* overpass.

cavalcio'ni [káválchō'nē]: **a ~ di** *prep* astride.

cavalie're *sm* rider; (*feudale, titolo*) knight; (*soldato*) cavalryman; (*al ballo*) partner.

cavallere'sco, a, schi, sche *ag* chivalrous.

cavalleri'a *sf* chivalry; (*milizia a cavallo*) cavalry.

cavalleriz'zo, a [kávàllārēt'tsō] *sm/f* riding instructor; circus rider.

cavallet'ta *sf* grasshopper; (*dannosa*) locust.

cavallet'to *sm* (*FOT*) tripod; (*da pittore*) easel.

cavalli'na *sf* (*GINNASTICA*) horse; (*gioco*) leap-frog; **correre la ~** (*fig*) to sow one's wild oats.

caval'lo *sm* horse; (*SCACCHI*) knight; (*AUT: anche: ~ vapore*) horsepower; (*dei pantaloni*) crotch; **a ~** on horseback; **a ~ di** astride, straddling; **siamo a ~** (*fig*) we've made it; **da ~** (*fig: dose*) drastic; (*: febbre*) raging; **vivere a ~ tra due periodi** to straddle two periods; **~ di battaglia** (*TEATRO*) tour de force; (*fig*) hobbyhorse; **~ da corsa** racehorse; **~ a dondolo** rocking horse; **~ da sella** saddle horse; **~ da soma** packhorse.

cava're *vt* (*togliere*) to draw out, extract, take out; (*: giacca, scarpe*) to take off; (*: fame, sete, voglia*) to satisfy; **~rsi** *vr*: **~rsi da** (*guai, problemi*) to get out of; **cavarsela** to get away with it; to manage, get on all right; **non ci caverà un bel nulla** you'll get nothing out of it (*o* him *etc*).

cavatap'pi *sm inv* corkscrew.

caver'na *sf* cave.

caverno'so, a *ag* (*luogo*) cavernous; (*fig: voce*) deep; (*: tosse*) raucous.

cavez'za [kàvāt'tsà] *sf* halter.

ca'via *sf* guinea pig.

cavia'le *sm* caviar.

cavi'glia [kàvēl'yá] *sf* ankle.

cavilla're *vi* to quibble.

cavil'lo *sm* quibble.

cavillo'so, a *ag* quibbling, hair-splitting.

cavità *sf inv* cavity.

ca'vo, a *ag* hollow ♦ *sm* (*ANAT*) cavity; (*grossa corda*) rope, cable; (*ELETTR, TEL*) cable.

cavola'ta *sf* (*fam*) stupid thing, foolish thing.

cavolfio're *sm* cauliflower.

ca'volo *sm* cabbage; **non m'importa un ~** (*fam*) I don't give a hoot; **che ~ vuoi?** (*fam*) what the heck do you want?; **~ di Bruxelles** Brussels sprout.

cazza'ta [káttsà'tá] *sf* (*fam!*: *stupidaggine*) stupid thing, something stupid.

caz'zo [kát'tsō] *sm* (*fam!*: *pene*) prick (!); **non gliene importa un ~** (*fig fam!*) he doesn't give a damn about it; **fatti i ~i tuoi** (*fig fam!*) mind your own damn business.

cazzot'to |kåttsot'tō] *sm* punch; **fare a ∼i** to come to blows.

cazzuo'la |kåttswo'lå] *sf* trowel.

CB *sigla = Campobasso.*

CC *abbr = Carabinieri.*

cc *abbr (= centimetro cubico)* cc.

C.C. *abbr =* **codice civile.**

c.c. *abbr (= conto corrente)* c/a, a/c; *(ELETTR) vedi* **corrente continua.**

c/c *abbr (= conto corrente)* c/a, a/c.

CCI *sigla f (= Camera di Commercio Internazionale)* ICC *(= International Chamber of Commerce).*

CCIAA *sigla f = Camera di Commercio Industria, Agricoltura e Artigianato.*

CCT *sigla m vedi* **certificato di credito del Tesoro.**

C.D. *abbr (= Corpo Diplomatico)* CD.

c.d. *abbr =* **cosiddetto.**

c.d.d. *abbr (= come dovevasi dimostrare)* QED *(= quod erat demonstrandum).*

C.d.M. *abbr =* **Cassa del Mezzogiorno.**

CE *sigla = Caserta.*

ce |chā] *pronome, av vedi* **ci.**

C.E. *sigla =* **Consiglio d'Europa.**

CECA *sigla f (= Comunità Europea del Carbone e dell'Acciaio)* ECSC *(= European Coal and Steel Community).*

cecchi'no |chākkē'nō] *sm* sniper; *(POL) member of parliament who votes against his own party.*

ce'ce |chā'chā] *sm* chickpea, garbanzo *(esp US).*

cecità |chāchētå'] *sf* blindness.

ce'co, a, chi, che |chc'kō] *ag, sm/f, sm* Czech.

Cecoslovac'chia |chākōzlōvák'kyå] *sf:* **la ∼** Czechoslovakia.

cecoslovac'co, a, chi, che |chākōzlōvák'kō] *ag, sm/f* Czechoslovakian.

CED |ched] *sigla m =* **centro elaborazione dati.**

ce'dere |che'dārā] *vt (concedere: posto)* to give up; *(DIR)* to transfer, make over ♦ *vi (cadere)* to give way, subside; **∼ (a)** to surrender to, yield (to), give in (to); **∼ il passo (a qn)** to let (sb) pass in front; **∼ il passo a qc** *(fig)* to give way to sth; **∼ la parola (a qn)** to hand over (to sb).

cede'vole |chādā'vōlā] *ag (terreno)* soft; *(fig)* yielding.

ce'dola |che'dōlå] *sf (COMM)* coupon; voucher.

cedra'ta |chādrá'tá] *sf* citron juice.

ce'dro |che'drō] *sm* cedar; *(albero da frutto, frutto)* citron.

CE'E |che'ā] *sigla f vedi* **Comunità Economica Europea.**

cef'fo |chef'fō] *sm (peg)* ugly mug.

ceffo'ne |chāffō'nā] *sm* slap, smack.

cela're |chālá'rā] *vt* to conceal; **∼rsi** *vr* to hide.

celebra're |chālābrá'rā] *vt* to celebrate; *(ce-*

rimonia) to hold; **∼ le lodi di qc/qn** to sing the praises of sth/sb.

celebrazio'ne |chālābráttsyō'nā] *sf* celebration.

ce'lebre |chc'lābrā] *ag* famous, celebrated.

celebrità |chālābrētá'] *sf inv* fame; *(persona)* celebrity.

ce'lere |chc'lārā] *ag* fast, swift; *(corso)* crash *cpd* ♦ *sf (POLIZIA)* riot police.

cele'ste |chālc'stā] *ag* celestial; heavenly; *(colore)* sky-blue.

ce'lia |chclyå] *sf* joke; **per ∼** for a joke.

celiba'to |chālēbá'tō] *sm* celibacy.

ce'libe |chc'lēbā] *ag* single, unmarried ♦ *sm* bachelor.

cel'la |chel'lá] *sf* cell; **∼ di rigore** punishment cell.

cellopha'ne ® |sclōfán'] *sm* cellophane ®.

cel'lula |chel'lōōlá] *sf (BIOL, ELETTR, POL)* cell.

cellula're |chāllōōlá'rā] *ag* cellular ♦ *sm (furgone)* police van; **segregazione ∼** *(DIR)* solitary confinement.

celluli'te |chāllōōlē'tā] *sf* cellulitis.

cel'ta |chel'tá] *sm/f* Celt.

cel'tico, a, ci, che |chel'tēkō] *ag, sm* Celtic.

cem'balo |chām'bálō] *sm (MUS)* harpsichord.

cementa're |chāmántá'rā] *vt (anche fig)* to cement.

cemen'to |chāmán'tō] *sm* cement; **∼ armato** reinforced concrete.

ce'na |chā'nå] *sf* dinner; *(leggera)* supper.

cena'colo |chāná'kōlō] *sm (circolo)* coterie, circle; *(REL, dipinto)* Last Supper.

cena're |chāná'rā] *vi* to dine, have dinner.

cen'cio |chān'chō] *sm* piece of cloth, rag; *(per spolverare)* duster; **essere bianco come un ∼** to be as white as a sheet.

ce'nere |chā'nārā] *sf* ash.

Ceneren'tola |chānárcn'tōlá] *sf (anche fig)* Cinderella.

cen'no |chān'nō] *sm (segno)* sign, signal; *(gesto)* gesture; *(col capo)* nod; *(con la mano)* wave; *(allusione)* hint, mention; *(breve esposizione)* short account; **far ∼ di sì/no** to nod (one's head)/shake one's head; **∼ d'intesa** sign of agreement; **∼i di storia dell'arte** an outline of the history of art.

censimen'to |chānscmán'tō] *sm* census.

CEN'SIS |chān'sēs] *sigla m (= Centro Studi Investimenti Sociali) independent institute carrying out research on Italy's social and cultural welfare.*

censo're |chānsō'rā] *sm* censor.

censu'ra |chānsōō'rá] *sf* censorship; censor's office; *(fig)* censure.

censura're |chānsōōrá'rā] *vt* to censor; to censure.

cent. *abbr =* **centesimo.**

centellina're |chāntāllēná'rā] *vt* to sip; *(fig)* to savor *(US),* savour *(Brit).*

centena'rio, a |chāntānà'ryō| *ag (che ha cento anni)* hundred-year-old; *(che ricorre ogni cento anni)* centennial, centenary *cpd* ♦ *sm/f* centenarian ♦ *sm* centenary.

cente'simo, a |chānte'zēmō| *ag, sm* hundredth; **essere senza un** ~ to be penniless.

centi'grado, a |chāntē'grädō| *ag* centigrade; **20 gradi** ~**i** 20 degrees centigrade.

centi'litro |chāntē'lētrō| *sm* centiliter *(US)*, centilitre *(Brit)*.

centi'metro |chāntē'mātrō| *sm* centimeter *(US)*, centimetre *(Brit)*; *(nastro)* tape measure *(in centimeters)*.

centina'io, *pl(f)* **-aia** |chāntēnà'yō| *sm*: **un** ~ **(di)** a hundred; about a hundred.

cen'to |chcn'tō| *num* a hundred, one hundred; **per** ~ per cent; **al** ~ **per** ~ a hundred per cent; ~ **di questi giorni!** many happy returns (of the day)!

centodie'ci |chāntōdyc'chē| *num* one hundred and ten; **laurearsi con** ~ **e lode** *(UNIVERSITÀ)* ≈ to graduate summa cum laude *(US)* o with first-class honours *(Brit)*.

centomi'la |chāntōmē'là| *num* a o one hundred thousand; **te l'ho detto** ~ **volte** *(fig)* I've told you a thousand times.

Centra'frica |chāntrà'frēkà| *sm*: **il** ~ the Central African Republic.

centra'le |chāntrà'lā| *ag* central ♦ *sf*: ~ **elettrica** electric power station; ~ **del latte** dairy; ~ **di polizia** police headquarters *pl*; ~ **telefonica** (telephone) exchange; **sede** ~ head office.

centralini'sta |chāntrālēnē'stá| *sm/f* operator.

centrali'no |chāntrālē'nō| *sm* (telephone) exchange; *(di albergo etc)* switchboard.

centralizza're |chāntrālēddzà'rā| *vt* to centralize.

centra're |chāntrà'rā| *vt* to hit the center *(US)* o centre *(Brit)* of; *(TECN)* to center; ~ **una risposta** to get the right answer; **ha centrato il problema** you've hit the nail on the head.

centravan'ti |chāntrávàn'tē| *sm inv* center forward.

centri'fuga |chāntrē'fōōgà| *sf* spin-dryer.

cen'tro |chcn'trō| *sm* center *(US)*, centre *(Brit)*; **fare** ~ to hit the bull's eye; *(CALCIO)* to score; *(fig)* to hit the nail on the head; ~ **balneare** seaside resort; ~ **commerciale** shopping center; *(città)* business district; ~ **di costo** cost center; ~ **elaborazione dati** data-processing unit; ~ **ospedaliero** hospital complex; ~ **sociale** community center; ~**i vitali** *(anche fig)* vital organs.

centromedia'no |chāntrōmādyà'nō| *sm (CALCIO)* center half.

cep'po |chāp'pō| *sm (di albero)* stump; *(pezzo di legno)* log.

ce'ra |chā'rà| *sf* wax; *(aspetto)* appearance, look; ~ **per pavimenti** floor polish.

ceralac'ca |chārálàk'kà| *sf* sealing wax.

cera'mica, che |chārà'mēkà| *sf* ceramic; *(ARTE)* ceramics *sg*.

cerbiat'to |chārbyàt'tō| *sm* fawn.

cer'ca |chār'kà| *sf*: **in** o **alla** ~ **di** in search of.

cercaperso'ne |chārkápārsō'nà| *sm inv* beeper.

cerca're |chārkà'rā| *vt* to look for, search for ♦ *vi*: ~ **di fare qc** to try to do sth.

cercherò *etc* |chārkāro'| *vb vedi* **cercare.**

cer'chia |chār'kyà| *sf* circle.

cerchia'to, a |chārkyà'tō| *ag*: **occhiali** ~**i d'osso** horn-rimmed spectacles; **avere gli occhi** ~**i** to have dark rings under one's eyes.

cer'chio |chār'kyō| *sm* circle; *(giocattolo, di botte)* hoop; **dare un colpo al** ~ **e uno alla botte** *(fig)* to keep two things going at the same time.

cerchio'ne |chārkyō'nà| *sm* (wheel)rim.

cerea'le |chārāà'lā| *sm* cereal.

cerebra'le |chārābrà'lā| *ag* cerebral.

cerimo'nia |chārēmo'nyà| *sf* ceremony; **senza tante** ~**e** *(senza formalità)* informally; *(bruscamente)* unceremoniously, without so much as a by-your-leave.

cerimonia'le |chārēmōnyà'lā| *sm* etiquette; ceremonial.

cerimonie're |chārēmōnyc'rā| *sm* master of ceremonies.

cerimonio'so, a |chārēmōnyō'sō| *ag* formal, ceremonious.

ceri'no |chārē'nō| *sm* wax match.

CERN |chārn| *sigla m (= Comitato Europeo di Ricerche Nucleari)* CERN.

cer'nia |chcr'nyá| *sf (ZOOL)* stone bass.

cernie'ra |chārnyc'rá| *sf* hinge; ~ **lampo** zipper *(US)*, zip (fastener) *(Brit)*.

cer'nita |chcr'nētà| *sf* selection; **fare una** ~ **di** to select.

ce'ro |chā'rō| *sm* (church) candle.

cero'ne |chārō'nà| *sm (trucco)* greasepaint.

cerot'to |chārot'tō| *sm* Band-Aid ® *(US)*, sticking plaster *(Brit)*.

certamen'te |chārtámān'tā| *av* certainly, surely.

certez'za |chārtāt'tsà| *sf* certainty.

certifica're |chārtēfēkà'rā| *vt* to certify.

certifica'to |chārtēfēkà'tō| *sm* certificate; ~ **medico/di nascita** medical/birth certificate; ~ **di credito del Tesoro (CCT)** treasury bill.

certificazio'ne |chārtēfēkàttsyō'nà| *sf* certification; ~ **di bilancio** *(COMM)* external audit.

cer'to, a |chcr'tō| *ag* certain; *(sicuro)*: ~ **(di/che)** certain o sure (of/that) ♦ *det certain* ♦ *av* certainly, of course; ~**i** *pronome pl* some; **un** ~ **non so che** an indefinable something; **di una** ~**a età** past one's prime, not so young; **sì** ~ yes indeed; **no** ~ certainly not; **di** ~ certainly.

certosi'no |chārtōzē'nō| *sm* Carthusian monk;

(liquore) chartreuse; **è un lavoro da** ~ it's a persnickety job.

certu'ni [chārtŏŏ'nē] *pronome pl* some (people).

ceru'me [chārŏŏ'mā] *sm* (ear) wax.

cervel'lo, *pl* **i** *(anche: pl(f)* **a** *o* **e)** [chārvel'lŏ] *sm* brain; ~ **elettronico** computer; **avere il** *o* **essere un** ~ **fino** to be sharp-witted; **è uscito di** ~, **gli è dato di volta il** ~ he's gone off his head.

cervica'le [chārvēkā'lā] *ag* cervical.

cer'vo, a [cher'vŏ] *sm/f* stag/hind ♦ *sm* deer; ~ **volante** stag beetle.

cesella're [chāzāllā'rā] *vt* to chisel; *(incidere)* to engrave.

cesel'lo [chāzel'lŏ] *sm* chisel.

CE'SIS [chā'sēs] *sigla m* (= *Comitato Esecutivo per i Servizi di Informazione e di Sicurezza) committee on intelligence and security matters, reporting to the Prime Minister.*

ceso'ie [chāzŏ'yā] *sfpl* shears.

cespu'glio [chāspŏŏl'yŏ] *sm* bush.

cessa're [chāssā'rā] *vi, vt* to stop, cease; ~ **di fare qc** to stop doing sth; **"cessato allarme"** "all clear".

cessa'te il fuo'co [chāssā'tā-] *sm* ceasefire.

cessazio'ne [chāssáttsyŏ'nā] *sf* cessation; *(interruzione)* suspension.

cessio'ne [chāssyŏ'nā] *sf* transfer.

ces'so [ches'sŏ] *sm (fam: gabinetto)* john *(US)*, bog *(Brit)*.

ce'sta [chā'stá] *sf* (large) basket.

cestel'lo [chāstel'lŏ] *sm (per bottiglie)* crate; *(di lavatrice)* basket *(US)*, drum *(Brit)*.

cestina're [chāstēnā'rā] *vt* to throw away; *(fig: proposta)* to turn down; *(: romanzo)* to reject.

cesti'no [chāstē'nŏ] *sm* basket; *(per la carta straccia)* wastepaper basket; ~ **da viaggio** *(FERR)* box *(US)* o packed *(Brit)* lunch (o dinner).

ce'sto [chā'stŏ] *sm* basket.

cesu'ra [chāzŏŏ'rá] *sf* caesura.

ceta'ceo [chātá'chāŏ] *sm* sea mammal.

ce'to [che'tŏ] *sm* (social) class.

ce'tra [chā'trá] *sf* zither; *(fig: di poeta)* lyre.

cetrioli'no [chātrēŏlē'nŏ] *sm* gherkin.

cetrio'lo [chātrēo'lŏ] *sm* cucumber.

Cf., Cfr. *abbr (= confronta)* cf.

CFS *sigla m* (= *Corpo Forestale dello Stato) body responsible for the planting and management of forests.*

cg *abbr (= centigrammo)* cg.

C.G.I.L. *sigla f* (= *Confederazione Generale Italiana del Lavoro) trades union organization.*

CH *sigla = Chieti.*

chalet' [shále'] *sm inv* chalet.

champa'gne [shâṅpány'] *sm inv* champagne.

chance [shâṅs] *sf inv* chance.

charme [shárm] *sm* charm.

char'ter [chā:'tər] *ag inv (volo)* charter *cpd*; *(aereo)* chartered ♦ *sm inv* chartered plane.

che [kā] *pronome (relativo: persona: soggetto)* who; *(: oggetto)* whom; *(: cosa)* which, that; *(interrogativo, esclamativo)* what; **l'uomo** ~ **io vedo** the man (whom) I see; **il libro** ~ **è sul tavolo** the book which *o* that is on the table; **il giorno** ~ ... the day (that) ...; **la sera** ~ **ti ho visto** the evening I saw you; ~ **(cosa) fai?** what are you doing?; **a** ~ **(cosa) pensi?** what are you thinking about?; **non sa** ~ **fare** he doesn't know what to do ♦ *det* what; *(di numero limitato)* which; ~ **vestito ti vuoi mettere?** what (o which) dress do you want to put on?; ~ **tipo di film hai visto?** what sort of film did you see?; ~ **bel vestito!** what a lovely dress!; ~ **buono!** how delicious! ♦ *cong* that; **so** ~ **tu c'eri** I know (that) you were there; **voglio** ~ **tu studi** I want you to study; *(affinché)*: **vieni qua,** ~ **ti veda** come here, so that I can see you; *(temporale)*: **arrivai** ~ **eri già partito** you had already left when I arrived; **sono anni** ~ **non lo vedo** I haven't seen him in years; *(in frasi imperative)*: ~ **venga pure** let him come by all means; **non** ~ **sia stupido** not that he's stupid; ~ **tu venga o no, noi partiamo lo stesso** we're leaving whether you come or not; *vedi* **non, più, meno** *etc*.

chec'ca, che [kāk'kā] *sf (fam: omosessuale)* fairy.

chef [shef] *sm inv* chef.

cherose'ne [kārŏze'nā] *sm* kerosene.

cherubi'no [kārŏŏbē'nŏ] *sm* cherub.

cheta're [kātá'rā] *vt* to hush, silence; ~**rsi** *vr* to quieten down, fall silent.

chetichel'la [kātēkel'lá]: **alla** ~ *av* stealthily, unobtrusively; **andarsene alla** ~ to slip away.

che'to, a [kā'tŏ] *ag* quiet, silent.

chi [kē] *pronome (interrogativo: soggetto)* who; *(: oggetto)*: **di** ~ **è questo libro?** whose book is this?; **con** ~ **parli?** to whom are you talking?, who are you talking to?; *(relativo: colui/colei che)* he/she who; *(: complemento)*: **dillo a** ~ **vuoi** tell it to whoever you like; ~ **dice una cosa** ~ **un'altra** some say one thing some another; **lo riferirò a** ~ **di dovere** I'll pass it on to the relevant person; **so io di** ~ **parlo** I'm naming no names; ~ **si somiglia si piglia** birds of a feather flock together; **si salvi** ~ **può** every man for himself.

chiacchiera're [kyàkkyārā'rā] *vi* to chat; *(discorrere futilmente)* to chatter; *(far pettegolezzi)* to gossip.

chiacchiera'ta [kyàkkyārā'tá] *sf* chat; **farsi una** ~ to have a chat.

chiac'chiere [kyàk'kyārā] *sfpl* chatter *q*; gossip *q*; **fare due** *o* **quattro** ~ to have a chat; **perdersi in** ~ to waste time talking.

chiacchiero'ne, a |kyàkkyārō'nā| *ag* talkative, chatty; gossipy ♦ *sm/f* chatterbox; gossip.

chiama're |kyàmà'rā| *vt* to call; (*rivolgersi a qn*) to call (in), send for; **~rsi** *vr* (*aver nome*) to be called; **mi chiamo Paolo** my name is Paolo; **mandare a ~ qn** to send for sb, call sb in; **~ alle armi** to call up; **~ in giudizio** to summon; **~ qn da parte** to take sb aside.

chiama'ta |kyàmà'tà| *sf* (*TEL*) call; (*MIL*) call-up; **~ interurbana** long-distance call; **~ con preavviso** person-to-person call; **~ alle urne** (*POL*) election.

chiap'pa |kyàp'pà| *sf* (*fam: natica*) cheek; **~e** *sfpl* bottom *sg*.

chia'ra |kyà'rà| *sf* egg white.

chiarez'za |kyàràt'tsà| *sf* clearness; clarity.

chiarifica're |kyàrēfēkà'rā| *vt* (*anche fig*) to clarify.

chiarificazio'ne |kyàrēfēkàttsyō'nā| *sf* clarification.

chiarimen'to |kyàrēmān'tō| *sm* clarification *q*, explanation.

chiari're |kyàrē'rā| *vt* to make clear; (*fig: spiegare*) to clear up, explain; **~rsi** *vr* to become clear; **si sono chiariti** they've sorted things out.

chia'ro, a |kyà'rō| *ag* clear; (*luminoso*) clear, bright; (*colore*) pale, light ♦ *av* (*parlare, vedere*) clearly; **si sta facendo ~** the day is dawning; **sia ~a una cosa** let's get one thing straight; **mettere in ~ qc** (*fig*) to clear sth up; **parliamoci ~** let's be frank.

chiaro're |kyàrō'rā| *sm* (diffuse) light.

chiaroveggen'te |kyàrōvādjen'tā| *sm/f* clairvoyant.

chias'so |kyàs'sō| *sm* uproar, row; **far ~** to make a din; (*fig*) to make a fuss; (: *scalpore*) to cause a stir.

chiasso'so, a |kyàssō'sō| *ag* noisy, rowdy; (*vistoso*) showy, gaudy.

chi'atta |kyàt'tà| *sf* barge.

chia've |kyà'và| *sf* key ♦ *ag inv* key *cpd*; **chiudere a ~** to lock; **~ d'accensione** (*AUT*) ignition key; **~ a forcella** fork spanner; **~ inglese** monkey wrench; **in ~ politica** in political terms; **~ di volta** (*anche fig*) keystone; **~i in mano** (*contratto*) turn-key *cpd*; **prezzo ~i in mano** (*di macchina*) street (*US*) *o* on-the-road (*Brit*) price.

chiavistel'lo |kyàvēstel'lō| *sm* bolt.

chiaz'za |kyàt'tsà| *sf* stain, splash.

chiazza're |kyàttsà'rā| *vt* to stain, splash.

chic |shēk| *ag inv* chic, elegant.

chicchessi'a |kēkkàssē'à| *pronome* anyone, anybody.

chic'co, chi |kēk'kō| *sm* (*di cereale, riso*) grain; (*di caffè*) bean; **~ di grandine** hailstone; **~ d'uva** grape.

chie'dere |kyc'dārā| *vt* (*per sapere*) to ask; (*per avere*) to ask for ♦ *vi*: **~ di qn** to ask after sb; (*al telefono*) to ask for *o* want sb; **~rsi** *vr*: **~rsi (se)** to wonder (whether); **~ qc a qn** to ask sb sth; to ask sb for sth; **~ scusa a qn** to apologize to sb; **~ l'elemosina** to beg; **non chiedo altro** that's all I want.

chierichet'to |kyàrēkàt'tō| *sm* altar boy.

chie'rico, ci |kyc'rēkō| *sm* cleric; altar boy.

chie'sa |kyc'zà| *sf* church.

chie'si *etc* |kyc'zē| *vb vedi* **chiedere.**

chie'sto, a |kyc'stō| *pp di* **chiedere.**

Chi'gi |kē'jē|: **palazzo ~** *sm* (*POL*) *offices of the Italian Prime Minister.*

chi'glia |kēl'yà| *sf* keel.

chi'lo |kē'lō| *sm* kilo.

chilogram'mo |kēlōgràm'mō| *sm* kilogram.

chilometrag'gio |kēlōmàtràd'jō| *sm* (*AUT*) = mileage.

chilome'trico, a, ci, che |kēlōmc'trēkō| *ag* kilometric; (*fig*) endless.

chilo'metro |kēlo'mātrō| *sm* kilometer (*US*), kilometre (*Brit*).

chi'mico, a, ci, che |kē'mēkō| *ag* chemical ♦ *sm/f* chemist ♦ *sf* chemistry.

chimo'no |kēmo'nō| *sm inv* kimono.

chi'na |kē'nà| *sf* (*pendio*) slope, descent; (*BOT*) cinchona; (**inchiostro di**) ~ Indian ink; **risalire la ~** (*fig*) to be on the road to recovery.

china're |kēnà'rā| *vt* to lower, bend; **~rsi** *vr* to stoop, bend.

chincaglieri'a |kēnkàlyàrē'à| *sf* variety store (*US*), gift shop (*Brit*); **~e** *sfpl* knick-knacks.

chini'no |kēnē'nō| *sm* quinine.

chi'no, a |kē'nō| *ag*: **a capo ~, a testa ~a** head bent *o* bowed.

chioc'cia, ce |kyoch'chà| *sf* brooding hen.

chioc'cio, a, ci, ce |kyoch'chō| *ag* (*voce*) clucking.

chioc'ciola |kyoch'chōlà| *sf* snail; **scala a ~** spiral staircase.

chio'do |kyo'dō| *sm* nail; (*fig*) obsession; **~ scaccia ~** (*proverbio*) one problem drives away another; **roba da ~i!** it's unbelievable!; **~ di garofano** (*CUC*) clove.

chio'ma |kyo'mà| *sf* (*capelli*) head of hair; (*di albero*) foliage.

chio'sco, schi |kyo'skō| *sm* kiosk, stall.

chios'tro |kyos'trō| *sm* cloister.

chiroman'te |kērōmàn'tā| *sm/f* palmist; (*indovino*) fortune-teller.

chirurgi'a |kērōōrjē'à| *sf* surgery.

chirur'gico, a, ci, che |kērōōr'jēkō| *ag* surgical.

chirur'go, ghi *o* **gi** |kērōōr'gō| *sm* surgeon.

chissà |kēssà'| *av* who knows, I wonder.

chitar'ra |kētàr'rà| *sf* guitar.

chitarri'sta, i, e |kētàrrē'stà| *sm/f* guitarist, guitar player.

chiu'dere [kyōō'dārā] *vt* to close, shut; *(luce, acqua)* to turn off; *(definitivamente: fabbrica)* to close down, shut down; *(strada)* to close; *(recingere)* to enclose; *(porre termine)* to end ♦ *vi* to close, shut; to close down, shut down; to end; **~rsi** *vr* to shut, close; *(ritirarsi: anche fig)* to shut o.s. away; *(ferita)* to close up; **~ un occhio su** *(fig)* to turn a blind eye to; **chiudi la bocca!** *o* **il becco!** *(fam)* shut up!

chiun'que [kēōōn'kwā] *pronome (relativo)* whoever; *(indefinito)* anyone, anybody; **~ sia** whoever it is.

chi'usi *etc* [kyōō'sē] *vb vedi* **chiudere.**

chiu'so, a [kyōō'sō] *pp di* **chiudere** ♦ *ag (porta)* shut, closed; (: *a chiave)* locked; *(senza uscita: strada etc)* blocked off; *(rubinetto)* off; *(persona)* uncommunicative; *(ambiente, club)* exclusive ♦ *sm:* **stare al ~** *(fig)* to be shut up ♦ *sf (di corso d'acqua)* sluice, lock; *(recinto)* enclosure; *(di discorso etc)* conclusion, ending; "**~**" *(negozio etc)* "closed"; "**~ al pubblico**" "no admittance to the public".

chiusu'ra [kyōōsōō'rā] *sf* closing; shutting; closing *o* shutting down; enclosing; putting *o* turning off; ending; *(dispositivo)* catch; fastening; fastener; **orario di ~** closing time; **~ lampo** ® zipper *(US)*, zip (fastener) *(Brit)*.

ci [chē] *(dav lo, la, li, le, ne diventa* **ce**) *pronome (personale)* us; (: *complemento di termine)* (to) us; (: *riflessivo)* ourselves; (: *reciproco)* one another; *(dimostrativo: di ciò, su ciò, in ciò etc)* about *(o* on *o* of) it ♦ *av (qui)* here; *(lì)* there; **~ siamo divertiti** we enjoyed ourselves; **~ amiamo** we love one another; **non so cosa far~** I don't know what to do about it; **che c'entro io?** what have I got to do with it?; **~ puoi giurare, ~ puoi scommettere** you can bet on it; **~ puoi contare** you can depend on it; **~ sei?** (sei pronto) are you ready?; *(hai capito)* do you follow?; **esser~** *vedi* **essere.**

C.ia *abbr* (= *compagnia*) Co.

ciabat'ta [chābát'tá] *sf* mule, slipper.

ciabatti'no [chábáttē'nō] *sm* cobbler.

ciac [chàk] *sm* *(CINEMA)* clapper board; **~, si gira!** action!

Ciad' [chàd] *sm:* **il ~** Chad.

cial'da [chàl'dá] *sf (CUC)* wafer.

cialtro'ne [cháltrō'nā] *sm* good-for-nothing.

ciambel'la [chámbel'lá] *sf (CUC)* ring-shaped cake; *(salvagente)* life-saver *(US)*, rubber ring *(Brit)*.

cian'cia, ce [chàn'chá] *sf* gossip *q*, tittle-tattle *q*.

cianfrusa'glie [chànfrōōzál'yā] *sfpl* bits and pieces.

cianu'ro [chánōō'rō] *sm* cyanide.

cia'o [chá'ō] *escl (all'arrivo)* hello!; *(alla partenza)* bye!

ciarla're [chàrlà'rā] *vi* to chatter; *(peg)* to gossip.

ciarlata'no [chárlátá'nō] *sm* charlatan.

ciascu'no, a [cháskōō'nō] *(dav sm:* **ciascun** +C, V, **ciascuno** +s *impura, gn, pn, ps, x, z; dav sf:* **ciascuna** +C, **ciascun'** +V) *det, pronome* each.

cibar'si [chēbár'sē] *vr:* **~ di** *(anche fig)* to live on.

ciberne'tica [chēbārnc'tēkà] *sf* cybernetics *sg*.

ci'bo [chē'bō] *sm* food.

cica'la [chēkà'lá] *sf* cicada.

cicatri'ce [chēkátrē'chā] *sf* scar.

cicatrizzar'si [chēkátrēddzár'sē] *vr* to form a scar, heal (up).

cic'ca, che [chēk'kà] *sf* cigarette end; *(fam: sigaretta)* fag; **non vale una ~** *(fig)* it's worthless.

cic'cia [chēch'chá] *sf (fam: carne)* meat; (: *grasso umano)* fat, flesh.

ciccio'ne, a [chēchō'nā] *sm/f (fam)* fatty.

cicero'ne [chēchārō'nā] *sm* guide.

ciclami'no [chēklámē'nō] *sm* cyclamen.

cicli'smo [chēklēz'mō] *sm* cycling.

cicli'sta, i, e [chēklē'stá] *sm/f* cyclist.

ci'clo [chē'klō] *sm* cycle; *(di malattia)* course.

ciclomoto're [chēklōmōtō'rā] *sm* moped.

ciclo'ne [chēklō'nā] *sm* cyclone.

ciclosti'le [chēklōstē'lā] *sm* cyclostyle.

cico'gna [chēkōn'yá] *sf* stork.

cico'ria [chēko'ryá] *sf* chicory.

CI'DA [chē'dá] *sigla f* = *Confederazione Italiana Dirigenti d'Azienda.*

cie'co, a, chi, che [chc'kō] *ag* blind ♦ *sm/f* blind man/woman; **alla ~a** *(anche fig)* blindly.

cie'lo [chc'lō] *sm* sky; *(REL)* heaven; **toccare il ~ con un dito** *(fig)* to walk on air; **per amor del ~!** for heavens' sake!

ci'fra [chē'frá] *sf (numero)* figure, numeral; *(somma di denaro)* sum, figure; *(monogramma)* monogram, initials *pl*; *(codice)* code, cipher.

cifra're [chēfrá'rā] *vt (messaggio)* to code; *(lenzuola etc)* to embroider with a monogram.

ci'glio [chēl'yō] *sm (margine)* edge, verge; *(pl(f)* **ciglia**: *delle palpebre)* (eye)lash; *(sopracciglio)* eyebrow; **non ha battuto ~** *(fig)* he didn't bat an eyelid.

ci'gno [chēn'yō] *sm* swan.

cigolan'te [chēgōlán'tā] *ag* squeaking, creaking.

cigola're [chēgōlá'rā] *vi* to squeak, creak.

CIIS *sigla m* (= *Comitato Interparlamentare per l'Informazione e la Sicurezza*) all-party committee on intelligence and security.

Ci'le [chē'lā] *sm:* **il ~** Chile.

cilec'ca |chĕlāk'ká| *sf*: **far ~ to** fail.
cile'no, a |chĕlc'nō| *ag*, *sm/f* Chilean.
cilie'gia, gie *o* **ge** |chĕlyc'jà| *sf* cherry.
cilie'gio |chĕlyc'jō| *sm* cherry tree.
cilindra'ta |chĕlĕndrá'tá| *sf* (AUT) (cubic) capacity; **una macchina di grossa ~ a** big-engined car.
cilin'dro |chĕlĕn'drō| *sm* cylinder; (*cappello*) top hat.
CIM |chĕm| *sigla m* = *centro d'igiene mentale*.
ci'ma |chĕ'má| *sf* (*sommità*) top; (*di monte*) top, summit; (*estremità*) end; (*fig*: *persona*) genius; **in ~ a** at the top of; **da ~ a fondo** from top to bottom; (*fig*) from beginning to end.
cime'lio |chĕmc'lyō| *sm* relic.
cimenta're |chĕmăntà'rā| *vt* to put to the test; **~rsi** *vr*: **~rsi in qc** to undertake sth.
ci'mice |chĕ'mĕchă| *sf* (ZOOL) bug; (*puntina*) thumbtack (US), drawing pin (Brit).
ciminie'ra |chĕmĕnyc'rá| *sf* chimney; (*di nave*) funnel.
cimite'ro |chĕmĕtc'rō| *sm* cemetery.
cimur'ro |chĕmōōr'rō| *sm* (*di cani*) distemper.
Ci'na |chĕ'ná| *sf*: **la ~** China.
cincin', cin cin |chĕnchĕn'| *escl* cheers!
cincischia're |chĕnchĕskyà'rā| *vi* to mess about, fiddle about.
ci'ne |chĕ'nā| *sm inv* (*fam*) cinema.
cinea'sta, i, e |chĕnăà'stá| *sm/f* person in the film industry; film-maker.
cinegiorna'le |chĕnājōrnà'lā| *sm* newsreel.
ci'nema |chĕ'nāmá| *sm inv* cinema; **~ muto** silent films; **~ d'essai** (*locale*) avant-garde cinema, experimental cinema.
cinepre'sa |chĕnāprà'sá| *sf* cinecamera.
cine'se |chĕnā'sā| *ag*, *sm/f*, *sm* Chinese *inv*.
cinete'ca, che |chĕnātc'ká| *sf* (*collezione*) film collection, film library; (*locale*) film library.
cine'tico, a, ci, che |chĕnc'tĕkō| *ag* kinetic.
cin'gere |chĕn'jārā| *vt* (*attorniare*) to surround, encircle; **~ la vita con una cintura** to put a belt round one's waist; **~ d'assedio** to besiege, lay siege to.
cin'ghia |chĕn'gyá| *sf* strap; (*cintura*, TECN) belt; **tirare la ~** (*fig*) to tighten one's belt.
cinghia'le |chĕngyà'lā| *sm* wild boar.
cinguetta're |chĕngwăttá'rā| *vi* to twitter.
ci'nico, a, ci, che |chĕ'nĕkō| *ag* cynical ♦ *sm/f* cynic.
cini'smo |chĕnĕz'mō| *sm* cynicism.
cinquan'ta |chĕnkwán'tá| *num* fifty.
cinquantena'rio |chĕnkwàntáná'ryō| *sm* fiftieth anniversary.
cinquanten'ne |chĕnkwántc'nā| *sm/f* fifty-year-old man/woman.
cinquante'simo, a |chĕnkwántc'zĕmō| *num* fiftieth.
cinquanti'na |chĕnkwántc'ná| *sf* (*serie*): **una ~ (di)** about fifty; (*età*): **essere sulla ~** to be about fifty.

cin'que |chĕn'kwā| *num* five; **avere ~ anni** to be five (years old); **il ~ dicembre 1988** the fifth of December 1988; **alle ~** (*ora*) at five (o'clock); **siamo in ~** there are five of us.
cinquecente'sco, a, schi, sche |chĕnkwāchāntá'skō| *ag* sixteenth-century.
cinquecen'to |chĕnkwāchcn'tō| *num* five hundred ♦ *sm*: **il C~** the sixteenth century.
cinquemi'la |chĕnkwāmĕ'lá| *num* five thousand.
cin'si *etc* |chĕn'sĕ| *vb vedi* **cingere**.
cin'ta |chĕn'tá| *sf* (*anche*: **~ muraria**) city walls *pl*; **muro di ~** (*di giardino etc*) surrounding wall.
cinta're |chĕntá'rā| *vt* to enclose.
cin'to, a |chĕn'tō| *pp di* **cingere**.
cin'tola |chĕn'tōlá| *sf* (*cintura*) belt; (*vita*) waist.
cintu'ra |chĕntōō'rá| *sf* belt; **~ di salvataggio** life preserver (US), lifebelt (Brit); **~ di sicurezza** (AUT, AER) safety *o* seat belt.
cinturi'no |chĕntōōrĕ'nō| *sm* strap; **~ dell'orologio** watch band (US) *o* strap (Brit).
CIO *sigla m* (= *Comitato Internazionale Olimpico*) IOC (= *International Olympic Committee*).
ciò |cho| *pronome* this; that; **~ che** what; **~ nonostante** *o* **nondimeno** nevertheless, in spite of that; **con tutto ~** for all that, in spite of everything.
cioc'ca, che |chok'ká| *sf* (*di capelli*) lock.
cioccola'ta |chōkkōlá'tá| *sf* chocolate; (*bevanda*) (hot) chocolate; **~ al latte/fondente** milk/plain chocolate.
cioccolati'no |chōkkōlátĕ'nō| *sm* chocolate.
cioccola'to |chōkkōlá'tō| *sm* chocolate.
cioè |chōc'| *av* that is (to say).
ciondola're |chōndōlá'rā| *vt* (*far dondolare*) to dangle, swing ♦ *vi* to dangle; (*fig*) to loaf (around).
cion'dolo |chōn'dōlō| *sm* pendant; **~ portafortuna** charm.
ciondolo'ni |chōndōlō'nĕ| *av*: **con le braccia/gambe ~** with arms/legs dangling.
ciononostan'te |chōnōnōstán'tā| *av* nonetheless, nevertheless.
cio'tola |cho'tōlá| *sf* bowl.
ciot'tolo |chot'tōlō| *sm* pebble; (*di strada*) cobble(stone).
cipi'glio |chĕpĕl'yō| *sm* frown.
cipol'la |chĕpōl'lá| *sf* onion; (*di tulipano etc*) bulb.
cipres'so |chĕprcs'sō| *sm* cypress (tree).
ci'pria |chĕp'ryá| *sf* (face) powder.
ciprio'ta, i, e |chĕprĕō'tá| *ag*, *sm/f* Cypriot.
Ci'pro |chĕ'prō| *sm* Cyprus.
cir'ca |chĕr'ká| *av* about, roughly ♦ *prep* about, concerning; **a mezzogiorno ~** around noon.
cir'co, chi |chĕr'kō| *sm* circus.

circola're [chērkōlá'rā] *vi* to circulate; (*AUT*) to drive (along), move (along) ♦ *ag* circular ♦ *sf* (*AMM*) circular; (*di autobus*) circle (line); **circola voce che** ... there is a rumor going around that ...; **assegno** ~ bank draft.

circolazio'ne [chērkōláttsyō'nā] *sf* circulation; (*AUT*): **la** ~ (the) traffic; **libretto di** ~ log book, registration book; **tassa di** ~ road tax (*Brit*).

cir'colo [chēr'kōlō] *sm* circle; **entrare in** ~ (*ANAT*) to enter the bloodstream.

circoncisio'ne [chērkōnchēzyō'nā] *sf* circumcision.

circonda're [chērkōndá'rā] *vt* to surround.

circondaria'le [chērkōndáryá'lā] *ag*: **casa di pena** ~ ≈ county jail (*US*), ≈ district prison (*Brit*).

circonda'rio [chērkōndá'ryō] *sm* (*DIR*) administrative district; (*zona circostante*) neighborhood (*US*), neighbourhood (*Brit*).

circonferen'za [chērkōnfāren'tsá] *sf* circumference.

circonvallazio'ne [chērkōnválláttsyō'nā] *sf* beltway (*US*), ring road (*Brit*); (*per evitare una città*) by-pass.

circoscrit'to, a [chērkōskrēt'tō] *pp di* **circoscrivere**.

circoscri'vere [chērkōskrē'vārā] *vt* to circumscribe; (*fig*) to limit, restrict.

circoscrizio'ne [chērkōskrēttsyō'nā] *sf* (*AMM*) district, area; ~ **elettorale** constituency.

circospet'to, a [chērkōspet'tō] *ag* circumspect, cautious.

circostan'te [chērkōstán'tā] *ag* surrounding, neighboring (*US*), neighbouring (*Brit*).

circostan'za [chērkōstán'tsá] *sf* circumstance; (*occasione*) occasion; **parole di** ~ words suited to the occasion.

circui're [chērkōō'rā] *vt* (*fig*) to fool, take in.

circu'ito [chērkōō'ētō] *sm* circuit; **andare in** *o* **fare corto** ~ to short-circuit; ~ **integrato** integrated circuit.

ciril'lico, a, ci, che [chērēl'lēkō] *ag* Cyrillic.

C.I.'S.A.L. [chē'sál] *sigla f* (= *Confederazione Italiana Sindacati Autonomi dei Lavoratori*) trades union organization.

C.I.S.L. [chēsl] *sigla f* (= *Confederazione Italiana Sindacati Lavoratori*) trades union organization.

C.I.'S.N.A.L. [chē'snál] *sigla f* (= *Confederazione Italiana Sindacati Nazionali dei Lavoratori*) trades union organization.

ci'ste [chē'stā] *sf* = **cisti**.

cister'na [chēster'ná] *sf* tank, cistern.

ci'sti [chē'stē] *sf inv* cyst.

cisti'te [chēstē'tā] *sf* cystitis.

C.I.T. [chēt] *sigla f* = *Compagnia Italiana Turismo*.

cit. *abbr* (= *citato, citata*) cit.

cita're [chētá'rā] *vt* (*DIR*) to summon; (*autore*) to quote; (*a esempio, modello*) to cite; ~ **qn per danni** to sue sb.

citazio'ne [chētáttsyō'nā] *sf* summons *sg*; quotation; (*di persona*) mention.

cito'fono [chēto'fōnō] *sm* entry phone; (*in uffici*) intercom.

citolo'gico, a, ci, che [chētōlo'jēkō] *ag*: **esame** ~ test for detection of cancerous cells.

ci'trico, a, ci, che [chē'trēkō] *ag* citric.

città [chēttá'] *sf inv* town; (*importante*) city; ~ **universitaria** university campus; **C~ del Capo** Cape Town.

cittadel'la [chēttádél'lá] *sf* citadel, stronghold.

cittadinan'za [chēttádēnán'tsá] *sf* citizens *pl*, inhabitants *pl* of a town (*o* city); (*DIR*) citizenship.

cittadi'no, a [chēttádē'nō] *ag* town *cpd*; city *cpd* ♦ *sm/f* (*di uno Stato*) citizen; (*abitante di città*) town dweller, city dweller.

ciuc'cio [chōōch'chō] *sm* (*fam*) pacifier (*US*), dummy (*Brit*).

ciu'co, a, chi, che [chōō'kō] *sm/f* ass.

ciuf'fo [chōōf'fō] *sm* tuft.

ciur'ma [chōōr'má] *sf* (*di nave*) crew.

civet'ta [chēvát'tá] *sf* (*ZOOL*) owl; (*fig: donna*) coquette, flirt ♦ *ag inv*: **auto/nave** ~ decoy car/ship; **fare la** ~ **con qn** to flirt with sb.

civetta're [chēváttá'rā] *vi* to flirt.

civetteri'a [chēvāttārē'á] *sf* coquetry, coquettishness.

civettuo'lo, a [chēváttwo'lō] *ag* flirtatious.

ci'vico, a, ci, che [chē'vēkō] *ag* civic; (*museo*) municipal, town *cpd*; **guardia** ~**a** city (*US*) *o* town (*Brit*) policeman; **senso** ~ public spirit.

civi'le [chēvē'lā] *ag* civil; (*non militare*) civilian; (*nazione*) civilized ♦ *sm* civilian; **stato** ~ marital status; **abiti** ~**i** civvies.

civili'sta, i, e [chēvēlē'stá] *sm/f* (*avvocato*) civil lawyer; (*studioso*) expert in civil law.

civilizza're [chēvēlēddzá'rā] *vt* to civilize.

civilizzazio'ne [chēvēlēddzáttsyō'nā] *sf* civilization.

civiltà [chēvēltá'] *sf* civilization; (*cortesia*) civility.

civi'smo [chēvēz'mō] *sm* public spirit.

CL *sigla* = *Caltanissetta*.

cl *abbr* (= *centilitro*) cl.

clac'son *sm inv* (*AUT*) horn.

clamo're *sm* (*frastuono*) din, uproar; (*fig*) outcry.

clamoro'so, a *ag* noisy; (*fig*) sensational.

clandestinità *sf* (*di attività*) secret nature; **vivere nella** ~ to live in hiding; (*ricercato politico*) to live underground.

clandesti'no, a *ag* clandestine; (*POL*) underground, clandestine ♦ *sm/f* stowaway.

clarinet'to *sm* clarinet.

clas'se *sf* class; **di** ~ (*fig*) with class; of excellent quality; ~ **turistica** (*AER*) economy class.

classici'smo |klássĕchēz'mō| *sm* classicism.

clas'sico, a, ci, che *ag* classical; (*tradizionale: moda*) classic(al) ♦ *sm* classic; classical author; (*anche:* **liceo** ~) *secondary school with emphasis on the humanities.*

classi'fica, che *sf* classification; (*SPORT*) placings *pl*; (*di dischi*) charts *pl*, hit parade.

classifica're *vt* to classify; (*candidato, compito*) to grade; **~rsi** *vr* to be placed.

classificato're *sm* filing cabinet.

classificazio'ne |klássĕfĕkáttsyō'nă| *sf* classification; grading.

classi'sta, i, e *ag* class-conscious ♦ *sm/f* class-conscious person.

claudican'te *ag* (*zoppo*) lame; (*fig: prosa*) halting.

cla'usola *sf* (*DIR*) clause.

clausu'ra *sf* (*REL*): **monaca di** ~ nun belonging to an enclosed order; **fare una vita di** ~ (*fig*) to lead a cloistered life.

cla'va *sf* club.

clavicem'balo |klávĕchăm'bálō| *sm* harpsichord.

clavi'cola *sf* (*ANAT*) collarbone.

clemen'te *ag* merciful; (*clima*) mild.

clemen'za |klămĕn'tsá| *sf* mercy, clemency; mildness.

clepto'mane *sm/f* kleptomaniac.

clerica'le *ag* clerical.

cle'ro *sm* clergy.

clessi'dra *sf* (*a sabbia*) hourglass; (*ad acqua*) water clock.

cliché |klēshā'| *sm inv* (*TIP*) plate; (*fig*) cliché.

clien'te *sm/f* customer, client.

cliente'la *sf* customers *pl*, clientèle.

clienteli'smo *sm*: ~ **politico** political nepotism.

cli'ma, i *sm* climate.

clima'tico, a, ci, che *ag* climatic; **stazione ~a** health resort.

climatizzazio'ne |klēmátĕddzàttsyō'nă| *sf* air conditioning.

cli'nico, a, ci, che *ag* clinical ♦ *sm* (*medico*) clinician ♦ *sf* (*scienza*) clinical medicine; (*casa di cura*) clinic, nursing home; (*settore d'ospedale*) clinic; **quadro** ~ anamnesis; **avere l'occhio** ~ (*fig*) to have an expert eye.

cliste're *sm* (*MED*) enema; (: *apparecchio*) *device used to give an enema.*

cloa'ca, che *sf* sewer.

cloche |klosh| *sf inv* (*AER*) control stick, joy-stick; **cambio a** ~ (*AUT*) floor-mounted gear lever.

clo'ro *sm* chlorine.

clorofil'la *sf* chlorophyll.

clorofor'mio *sm* chloroform.

club *sm inv* club.

cm *abbr* (= *centimetro*) cm.

c.m. *abbr* (= *corrente mese*) inst.

CN *sigla* = *Cuneo.*

c/n *abbr* = *conto nuovo.*

CNEN *sigla m* (= *Comitato Nazionale per l'Energia Nucleare*) ≈ AEC (*US*), AEA (*Brit*).

CNIOP *sigla m* = *Centro Nazionale per l'Istruzione e l'Orientamento Professionale.*

CNR *sigla m* (= *Consiglio Nazionale delle Ricerche*) *science research council.*

CNRN *sigla m* = *Comitato Nazionale Ricerche Nucleari.*

CO *sigla* = *Como.*

Co. *abbr* (= *compagnia*) Co.

coabita're *vi* to live together, live under the same roof.

coagula're *vt* to coagulate ♦ *vi*, **~rsi** *vr* to coagulate; (*latte*) to curdle.

coalizio'ne |kōălĕttsyō'nă| *sf* coalition.

coat'to, a *ag* (*DIR*) compulsory, forced; **condannare al domicilio** ~ to place under house arrest.

CO'BAS *sigla mpl* (= *Comitati di base*) *independent trades unions.*

co'bra *sm inv* cobra.

cocai'na *sf* cocaine.

coccar'da *sf* cockade.

cocchie're |kōkkyĕ'rā| *sm* coachman.

coc'chio |kok'kyō| *sm* (*carrozza*) coach; (*biga*) chariot.

coccinel'la |kōchĕncl'lá| *sf* ladybug (*US*), ladybird (*Brit*).

coc'cio |koch'chō| *sm* earthenware; (*vaso*) earthenware pot; **~i** *smpl* fragments (of pottery).

cocciutag'gine |kōchōōtàd'jĕnă| *sf* stubbornness, pig-headedness.

cocciu'to, a |kōchōō'tō| *ag* stubborn, pig-headed.

coc'co, chi *sm* (*pianta*) coconut palm; (*frutto*): **noce di** ~ coconut ♦ *sm/f* (*fam*) darling; **è il** ~ **della mamma** he's mummy's darling.

coccodril'lo *sm* crocodile.

coccola're *vt* to cuddle, fondle.

cocen'te |kōchen'tă| *ag* (*anche fig*) burning.

cocerò *etc* |kōchăro'| *vb vedi* **cuocere.**

coco'mero *sm* watermelon.

cocuz'zolo |kōkōōt'tsōlō| *sm* top; (*di capo, cappello*) crown.

cod. *abbr* = **codice.**

co'da *sf* tail; (*fila di persone, auto*) line (*US*), queue (*Brit*); (*di abiti*) train; **con la** ~ **dell'occhio** out of the corner of one's eye; **mettersi in** ~ to line up (*US*), queue (up) (*Brit*); to join the line *o* queue; ~ **di cavallo** (*acconciatura*) ponytail; **avere la** ~ **di paglia** (*fig*) to have a guilty conscience; ~ **di rospo** (*CUC*) frogfish tail.

codar'do, a *ag* cowardly ♦ *sm/f* coward.

code'sto, a *ag, pronome* (*poetico*) this; that.

co'dice |ko'dĕchă| *sm* code; (*manoscritto anti-*

co) codex; ~ **di avviamento postale (CAP)** zip code *(US)*, postcode *(Brit)*; ~ **a barre** bar code; ~ **civile** civil code; ~ **fiscale** tax code; ~ **penale** penal code; ~ **della strada** highway code.

codi'fica *sf* codification; *(INFORM: di programma)* coding.

codifica're *vt (DIR)* to codify; *(cifrare)* to code.

codificazio'ne |kōdĕfĕkáttsyō'nā| *sf* coding.

coercizio'ne |kōārchĕttsyō'nā| *sf* coercion.

coeren'te *ag* coherent.

coeren'za |kōārcn'tsá| *sf* coherence.

coesio'ne *sf* cohesion.

coesi'stere *vi* to coexist.

coeta'neo, a *ag, sm/f* contemporary; **essere ~ di qn** to be the same age as sb.

cofanet'to *sm* casket; ~ **dei gioiélli** jewelry box *(US)*, jewel case *(Brit)*.

co'fano *sm (AUT)* hood *(US)*, bonnet *(Brit)*; *(forziere)* chest.

cof'fa *sf (NAUT)* top.

co'gli |kōl'yē| *prep + det vedi* **con.**

co'gliere |kol'yārā| *vt (fiore, frutto)* to pick, gather; *(sorprendere)* to catch, surprise; *(bersaglio)* to hit; *(fig: momento opportuno etc)* to grasp, seize, take; *(: capire)* to grasp; ~ **l'occasione (per fare)** to take the opportunity (to do); ~ **sul fatto** *o* **in flagrante/alla sprovvista** to catch redhanded/unprepared; ~ **nel segno** *(fig)* to hit the nail on the head.

coglio'ne |kōlyō'nā| *sm (fam!: testicolo)*: ~**i** balls *(!)*; *(: fig: persona sciocca)* jerk; **rompere i ~i a qn** to get on sb's tits *(!)*.

cognac' |konyák'| *sm inv* cognac.

cogna'to, a |kōnyá'tō| *sm/f* brother-/sister-in-law.

cognizio'ne |kōnyĕttsyō'nā| *sf* knowledge; **con ~ di causa** with full knowledge of the facts.

cogno'me |kōnyō'mā| *sm* surname.

co'i *prep + det vedi* **con.**

coiben'te *ag* insulating.

coinciden'za |kōĕnchĕden'tsá| *sf* coincidence; *(FERR, AER, di autobus)* connection.

coinci'dere |kōĕnchē'dārā| *vi* to coincide.

coinci'so, a |kōĕnchē'zō| *pp di* **coincidere.**

coinquili'no *sm* fellow tenant.

cointeressen'za |kōĕntārāssen'tsá| *sf (COMM)*: **avere una ~ in qc** to own shares in sth; ~ **dei lavoratori** profit sharing.

coinvol'gere |kōĕnvol'jārā| *vt*: ~ **in** to involve in.

coinvolgimen'to |kōĕnvōljĕmān'tō| *sm* involvement.

coinvol'to, a *pp di* **coinvolgere.**

col *prep + det vedi* **con.**

Col. *abbr (= colonnello)* Col.

colà *av* there.

colabro'do *sm inv* strainer.

colapa'sta *sm inv* colander.

cola're *vt (liquido)* to strain; *(pasta)* to drain; *(oro fuso)* to pour ♦ *vi (sudore)* to drip; *(botte)* to leak; *(cera)* to melt; ~ **a picco** *vt, vi (nave)* to sink.

cola'ta *sf (di lava)* flow; *(FONDERIA)* casting.

colazio'ne |kōláttsyō'nā| *sf (anche: prima ~)* breakfast; *(anche: seconda ~)* lunch; **fare ~** to have breakfast *(o lunch)*; ~ **di lavoro** working lunch.

Coldiret'ti *abbr f (= Confederazione nazionale coltivatori diretti)* federation of Italian farmers.

cole'i *pronome vedi* **colui.**

cole'ra *sm (MED)* cholera.

colestero'lo *sm* cholesterol.

COLF *abbr f =* **collaboratrice familiare.**

col'go *etc vb vedi* **cogliere.**

colibrì *sm* hummingbird.

co'lica *sf (MED)* colic.

coli'no *sm* strainer.

col'la *prep + det vedi* **con** ♦ *sf* glue; *(di farina)* paste.

collabora're *vi* to collaborate; ~ **a** to collaborate on; *(giornale)* to contribute to.

collabora'to, tri'ce *sm/f* collaborator; contributor; ~ **esterno** freelance; ~**trice familiare** maid.

collaborazio'ne |kōlläbōráttsyō'nā| *sf* collaboration; contribution.

colla'na *sf* necklace; *(collezione)* collection, series.

collant' |kolán'| *sm inv* pantihose *pl (US)*, tights *pl (Brit)*.

colla're *sm* collar.

collas'so *sm (MED)* collapse.

collatera'le *ag* collateral; **effetti ~i** side effects.

collauda're *vt* to test, try out.

colla'udo *sm* testing *q*; test.

col'le *prep + det vedi* **con** ♦ *sm* hill.

colle'ga, ghi, ghe *sm/f* colleague.

collegamen'to *sm* connection; *(MIL)* liaison; *(RADIO)* link(-up); **ufficiale di ~** liaison officer.

collega're *vt* to connect, join, link; ~**rsi** *vr (RADIO, TV)* to link up; ~**rsi con** *(TEL)* to get through to.

collegia'le |kōlläjá'lā| *ag (riunione, decisione)* collective; *(INS)* boarding school *cpd* ♦ *sm/f* boarder; *(fig: persona timida e inesperta)* schoolboy/girl.

colle'gio |kōllc'jō| *sm* college; *(convitto)* boarding school; ~ **elettorale** *(POL)* constituency.

col'lera *sf* anger; **andare in ~** to get angry.

colle'rico, a, ci, che *ag* quick-tempered, irascible.

collet'ta *sf* collection.

collettività *sf* community.

colletti'vo, a *ag* collective; *(interesse)* general, everybody's; *(biglietto, visita etc)* group *cpd* ♦ *sm (POL.)* (political) group; **società in nome ~** *(COMM)* partnership.

collet'to *sm* collar; **~i bianchi** *(fig)* white-collar workers.

colleziona're [kōllāttsyōná'rā] *vt* to collect.

collezio'ne [kōllāttsyō'nā] *sf* collection.

collima're *vi* to correspond, coincide.

colli'na *sf* hill.

collina're *ag* hill *cpd*.

colli'rio *sm* eyewash.

collisio'ne *sf* collision.

col'lo *prep + det vedi* **con** ♦ *sm* neck; *(di abito)* neck, collar; *(pacco)* parcel; **~ del piede** instep.

collocamen'to *sm (impiego)* employment; *(disposizione)* placing, arrangement; **ufficio di ~** ≈ state *(o* federal) employment agency; **~ a riposo** retirement.

colloca're *vt (libri, mobili)* to place; *(persona: trovare un lavoro per)* to find a job for, place; *(COMM: merce)* to find a market for; **~ qn a riposo** to retire sb.

collocazio'ne [kōllōkàttsyō'nā] *sf* placing; *(di libro)* classification.

colloquia'le *ag (termine etc)* colloquial; *(tono)* informal.

collo'quio *sm* conversation, talk; *(ufficiale, per un lavoro)* interview; *(INS)* preliminary oral exam; **avviare un ~ con qn** *(POL etc)* to start talks with sb.

collo'so, a *ag* sticky.

collot'tola *sf* nape *o* scruff of the neck; **afferrare qn per la ~** to grab sb by the scruff of the neck.

collusio'ne *sf (DIR)* collusion.

colluttazio'ne [kōllōōttàttsyō'nā] *sf* scuffle.

colma're *vt:* **~ di** *(anche fig)* to fill with; *(dare in abbondanza)* to load *o* overwhelm with; **~ un divario** *(fig)* to bridge a gap.

col'mo, a *ag:* **~ (di)** full (of) ♦ *sm* summit, top; *(fig)* height; **al ~ della disperazione** in the depths of despair; **è il ~!** it's the last straw!; **e per ~ di sfortuna ...** and to cap it all ....

colom'ba *sf vedi* **colombo.**

Colom'bia *sf:* **la ~** Colombia.

colombia'no, a *ag, sm/f* Colombian.

colom'bo, a *sm/f* dove; pigeon; **~i** *(fig fam)* lovebirds.

Colo'nia *sf* Cologne.

colo'nia *sf* colony; *(per bambini)* holiday camp; **(acqua di) ~** (eau de) cologne.

colonia'le *ag* colonial ♦ *sm/f* colonist, settler.

colo'nico, a, ci, che *ag:* **casa ~a** farmhouse.

colonizza're [kōlōnēddzà'rā] *vt* to colonize.

colon'na *sf* column; **~ sonora** *(CINEMA)* sound track; **~ vertebrale** spine, spinal column.

colonnel'lo *sm* colonel.

colo'no *sm (coltivatore)* tenant farmer.

coloran'te *sm* coloring *(US)*, colouring *(Brit)*.

colora're *vt* to color *(US)*, colour *(Brit)*; *(disegno)* to colo(u)r in.

colo're *sm* color *(US)*, colour *(Brit)*; *(CARTE)* suit; **a ~i** in colo(u)r, colo(u)r *cpd*; **la gente di ~** colo(u)red people; **diventare di tutti i ~i** to turn scarlet; **farne di tutti i ~i** to get up to all sorts of mischief *(Brit)*; **passarne di tutti i ~i** to go through all sorts of problems.

colori'to, a *ag* colored *(US)*, coloured *(Brit)*; *(viso)* rosy, pink; *(linguaggio)* colorful *(US)*, colourful *(Brit)* ♦ *sm (tinta)* color *(US)*, colour *(Brit)*; *(carnagione)* complexion.

colo'ro *pronome pl vedi* **colui.**

colossa'le *ag* colossal, enormous.

colos'so *sm* colossus.

col'pa *sf* fault; *(biasimo)* blame; *(colpevolezza)* guilt; *(azione colpevole)* offence; *(peccato)* sin; **di chi è la ~?** whose fault is it?; **è ~ sua** it's his fault; **per ~ di** through, owing to; **senso di ~** sense of guilt; **dare la ~ a qn di qc** to blame sb for sth.

colpe'vole *ag* guilty.

colpevolizza're [kōlpāvōlēddzà'rā] *vt:* **~ qn** to make sb feel guilty.

colpi're *vt* to hit, strike; *(fig)* to strike; **rimanere colpito da qc** to be amazed *o* struck by sth; **è stato colpito da ordine di cattura** there is a warrant out for his arrest; **~ nel segno** *(fig)* to hit the nail on the head.

col'po *sm (urto)* knock; *(fig: affettivo)* blow, shock; *(: aggressivo)* blow; *(di pistola)* shot; *(MED)* stroke; *(furto)* raid; **di ~, tutto d'un ~** suddenly; **fare ~** to make a strong impression; **il motore perde ~i** *(AUT)* the engine is misfiring; **è morto sul ~** he died instantly; **mi hai fatto venire un ~!** what a fright you gave me!; **ti venisse un ~!** *(fam)* drop dead!; **~ d'aria** chill; **~ in banca** bank job *o* raid; **~ basso** *(PUGILATO, fig)* hit below the belt; **~ di fulmine** love at first sight; **~ di grazia** coup de grâce; *(fig)* finishing blow; **~ d'occhio** at a glance; **~ di scena** *(TEATRO)* coup de théâtre; *(fig)* dramatic turn of events; **~ di sole** sunstroke; **~i di sole** *(nei capelli)* highlights; **~ di Stato** coup d'état; **~ di telefono** phone call; **~ di testa** (sudden) impulse *o* whim; **~ di vento** gust (of wind).

colpo'so, a *ag:* **omicidio ~** manslaughter.

col'si *etc vb vedi* **cogliere.**

coltella'ta *sf* stab.

coltel'lo *sm* knife; **avere il ~ dalla parte del manico** *(fig)* to have the whip hand; **~ a serramanico** clasp knife.

coltiva're *vt* to cultivate; *(verdura)* to grow, cultivate.

coltivato're *sm* farmer; **~ diretto** small independent farmer.

coltivazio'ne [kōltēvåttsyō'nā] sf cultivation; growing; ~ **intensiva** intensive farming.

col'to, a pp di **cogliere** ♦ ag (istruito) cultured, educated.

col'tre sf blanket.

coltu'ra sf cultivation; ~ **alternata** crop rotation.

colu'i, cole'i, pl **colo'ro** pronome the one; ~ **che parla** the one o the man o the person who is speaking; **colei che amo** the one o the woman o the person (whom) I love.

com. abbr = **comunale; commissione.**

co'ma sm inv coma.

comandamen'to sm (REL) commandment.

comandan'te sm (MIL) commander, commandant; (di reggimento) commanding officer; (NAUT, AER) captain.

comanda're vi to be in command ♦ vt to command; (imporre) to order, command; ~ **a qn di fare** to order sb to do.

coman'do sm (ingiunzione) order, command; (autorità) command; (TECN) control; ~ **generale** general headquarters pl; ~ **a distanza** remote control.

coma're sf (madrina) godmother; (donna pettegola) gossip.

coma'sco, a, schi, sche ag of (o from) Como.

combacia're [kōmbáchá'rā] vi to meet; (fig: coincidere) to coincide, correspond.

combatten'te ag fighting ♦ sm combatant; **ex-~** ex-serviceman.

combat'tere vt to fight; (fig) to combat, fight against ♦ vi to fight.

combattimen'to sm fight; fighting q; (di pugilato) match; **mettere fuori** ~ to knock out.

combatti'vo, a ag pugnacious.

combattu'to, a ag (incerto: persona) uncertain, undecided; (gara, partita) hard fought.

combina're vt to combine; (organizzare) to arrange; (fam: fare) to make, cause ♦ vi (corrispondere): ~ **(con)** to correspond (with).

combinazio'ne [kōmbēnáttsyō'nā] sf combination; (caso fortuito) coincidence; **per** ~ by chance.

combric'cola sf (gruppo) party; (banda) gang.

combusti'bile ag combustible ♦ sm fuel.

combustio'ne sf combustion.

combut'ta sf (peg) gang; **in** ~ in league.

co'me av (gen) like; (in qualità di) as; (interrogativo, esclamativo) how; (che cosa, prego): ~? pardon?, sorry? ♦ cong as; (che, in quale modo) how; (appena che, quando) as soon as; ~ **sta?** how are you?; ~ **sei cresciuto!** how you've grown!; ~ **se** as if, as though; **ora** ~ **ora** right now; **oggi** ~ **oggi** at the present time; ~ **mai?** how come?; **com'è il tuo amico?** what's your friend like?;

attento a ~ **parli!** mind your tongue!; ~ **non detto** let's forget it; **com'è vero Dio** as God is my witness; vedi **cosi.**

CO'MECON abbr m (= Consiglio di Mutua Assistenza Economica) COMECON.

comedo'ne sm blackhead.

come'ta sf comet.

co'mico, a, ci, che ag (TEATRO) comic; (buffo) comical ♦ sm (attore) comedian, comic actor; (comicità) comic spirit, comedy.

comi'gnolo [kōmēn'yōlō] sm chimney top.

comincia're [kōmēnchá'rā] vt, vi to begin, start; ~ **a fare/col fare** to begin to do/by doing; **cominciamo bene!** (ironico) we're off to a fine start!

comita'to sm committee; ~ **direttivo** steering committee; ~ **di gestione** works council.

comiti'va sf party, group.

comi'zio [kōmēt'tsyō] sm (POL) meeting, assembly; ~ **elettorale** election rally.

com'ma, i sm (DIR) subsection.

comman'do sm inv commando (squad).

comme'dia sf comedy; (opera teatrale) play; (: che fa ridere) comedy; (fig) playacting q.

commedian'te sm/f (peg) third-rate actor/ actress; (: fig) sham.

commedio'grafo, a sm/f (autore) comedy writer.

commemora're vt to commemorate.

commemorazio'ne [kōmmāmōrầttsyō'nā] sf commemoration.

commendato're sm official title awarded for services to one's country.

commensa'le sm/f table companion.

commenta're vt to comment on; (testo) to annotate; (RADIO, TV) to give a commentary on.

commentato're, tri'ce sm/f commentator.

commen'to sm comment; (a un testo, RADIO, TV) commentary; ~ **musicale** (CINEMA) background music.

commercia'le [kōmmárchà'lā] ag commercial, trading; (peg) commercial.

commerciali'sta, i, e [kōmmárchálē'stá] sm/f (laureato) graduate in economics and commerce; (consulente) business consultant.

commercializza're [kōmmárchálēddzà'rā] vt to market.

commercializzazio'ne [kōmmárchálēddzàttsyō'nā] sf marketing.

commercian'te [kōmmárchán'tā] sm/f trader, dealer; (negoziante) shopkeeper; ~ **all'ingrosso** wholesaler; ~ **in proprio** proprietor (US), sole trader (Brit).

commercia're [kōmmárchá'rā] vi: ~ **in,** vt to deal o trade in.

commer'cio [kōmmer'chō] sm trade, commerce; **essere in** ~ (prodotto) to be on the market o on sale; **essere nel** ~ (persona) to be in business; ~ all'ingrosso/al minuto wholesale/retail trade.

commes'so, a *pp di* commettere ♦ *sm/f* sales clerk *(US)*, shop assistant *(Brit)* ♦ *sm (impiegato)* clerk ♦ *sf (COMM)* order; ~ viaggiatore traveling salesman.

commesti'bile *ag* edible; ~i *smpl* foodstuffs.

commet'tere *vt* to commit; *(ordinare)* to commission, order.

commia'to *sm* leave-taking; prendere ~ da qn to take one's leave of sb.

commina're *vt (DIR)* to make provision for.

commisera're *vt* to sympathize with, commiserate with.

commiserazio'ne [kōmmēzărăttsyō'nā] *sf* commiseration.

commi'si *etc vb vedi* commettere.

commissaria'to *sm (AMM)* commissionership; *(: sede)* commissioner's office; *(: di polizia)* police station.

commissa'rio *sm* commissioner; *(di pubblica sicurezza)* ≈ (police) captain *(US)*, (police) superintendent *(Brit)*; *(SPORT)* steward; *(membro di commissione)* member of a committee *o* board; alto ~ high commissioner; ~ di bordo *(NAUT)* purser; ~ d'esame member of an examining board; ~ di gara race official; ~ tecnico *(SPORT)* national coach.

commissiona're *vt* to order, place an order for.

commissiona'rio *sm (COMM)* agent, broker.

commissio'ne *sf (incarico)* errand; *(comitato, percentuale)* commission; *(COMM: ordinazione)* order; ~i *sfpl (acquisti)* shopping *sg*; ~ d'esame examining board; ~ permanente standing committee; ~i bancarie bank charges.

committen'te *sm/f (COMM)* purchaser, customer.

commos'so, a *pp di* commuovere.

commoven'te *ag* moving.

commozio'ne [kōmmōttsyō'nā] *sf* emotion, deep feeling; ~ cerebrale *(MED)* concussion.

commuo'vere *vt* to move, affect; ~rsi *vr* to be moved.

commuta're *vt (pena)* to commute; *(ELETTR)* to change *o* switch over.

commutazio'ne [kōmmōōtăttsyō'nā] *sf (DIR, ELETTR)* commutation.

comò *sm inv* chest of drawers.

comodi'no *sm* bedside table.

comodità *sf inv* comfort; convenience.

co'modo, a *ag* comfortable; *(facile)* easy; *(conveniente)* convenient; *(utile)* useful, handy ♦ *sm* comfort; convenience; con ~ at one's convenience *o* leisure; fare il proprio ~ to do as one pleases; far ~ to be useful *o* handy; stia ~! don't bother to get up!

compaesa'no, a *sm/f* fellow-countryman/

woman; person from the same town.

compa'gine [kōmpă'jēnā] *sf (squadra)* team.

compagni'a [kōmpănyē'ă] *sf* company; *(gruppo)* gathering; fare ~ a qn to keep sb company; essere di ~ to be sociable.

compa'gno, a [kōmpăn'yō] *sm/f (di classe, gioco)* companion; *(POL)* comrade; ~ di lavoro workmate; ~ di scuola classmate; ~ di viaggio fellow traveler.

compa'io *etc vb vedi* comparire.

compara're *vt* to compare.

comparati'vo, a *ag, sm* comparative.

comparazio'ne [kōmpărăttsyō'nā] *sf* comparison.

compa're *sm (padrino)* godfather; *(complice)* accomplice; *(fam: amico)* old pal, old mate.

compari're *vi* to appear; ~ in giudizio *(DIR)* to appear before the court.

comparizio'ne [kōmpărēttsyō'nā] *sf (DIR)* appearance; mandato di ~ summons *sg*.

compar'so, a *pp di* comparire ♦ *sf* appearance; *(TEATRO)* walk-on; *(CINEMA)* extra.

compartecipa're [kōmpărtāchēpă'rā] *vi (COMM)*: ~ a to have a share in.

compartecipazio'ne [kōmpărtāchēpăttsyō'nā] *sf* sharing; *(quota)* share; ~ agli utili profit-sharing; in ~ jointly.

compartimen'to *sm* compartment; *(AMM)* district.

compar'vi *etc vb vedi* comparire.

compassa'to, a *ag (persona)* composed; freddo e ~ cool and collected.

compassio'ne *sf* compassion, pity; avere ~ di qn to feel sorry for sb, pity sb; fare ~ to arouse pity.

compassione'vole *ag* compassionate.

compas'so *sm* (pair of) compasses *pl*; callipers *pl*.

compati'bile *ag (scusabile)* excusable; *(conciliabile, INFORM)* compatible.

compatimen'to *sm* compassion; indulgence; con aria di ~ with a condescending air.

compati're *vt (aver compassione di)* to sympathize with, feel sorry for; *(scusare)* to make allowances for.

compatrio'ta, i, e *sm/f* compatriot.

compattez'za [kōmpăttăt'tsă] *sf (solidità)* compactness; *(fig: unità)* solidarity.

compat'to, a *ag* compact; *(roccia)* solid; *(folla)* dense; *(fig: gruppo, partito)* united, close-knit.

compen'dio *sm* summary; *(libro)* compendium.

compensa're *vt (equilibrare)* to compensate for, make up for; ~rsi *vr (reciproco)* to balance each other out; ~ qn di *(rimunerare)* to pay *o* remunerate sb for; *(risarcire)* to pay compensation to sb for; *(fig: fatiche, dolori)* to reward sb for.

compensa'to *sm (anche: legno ~)* plywood.

compen'so *sm* compensation; payment, remuneration; reward; **in** ~ (*d'altra parte*) on the other hand.

com'pera *sf* purchase; **fare le** ~**e** to do the shopping.

compera're *vt* = **comprare**.

competen'te *ag* competent; (*mancia*) apt, suitable; (*capace*) qualified; **rivolgersi all'ufficio** ~ to apply to the office concerned.

competen'za [kōmpāten'tsà] *sf* competence; (*DIR: autorità*) jurisdiction; (*TECN, COMM*) expertise; ~**e** *sfpl* (*onorari*) fees; **definire le** ~**e** to establish responsibilities.

compe'tere *vi* to compete, vie; (*DIR: spettare*): ~ **a** to lie within the competence of.

competito're, tri'ce *sm/f* competitor.

competizio'ne [kōmpātēttsyō'nà] *sf* competition; **spirito di** ~ competitive spirit.

compiacen'te [kōmpyàchen'tā] *ag* courteous, obliging.

compiacen'za [kōmpyàchen'tsà] *sf* courtesy.

compiace're [kōmpyàchā'rā] *vi*: ~ **a** to gratify, please ♦ *vt* to please; ~**rsi** *vr* (*provare soddisfazione*): ~**rsi di** *o* **per qc** to be delighted at sth; (*rallegrarsi*): ~**rsi con qn** to congratulate sb; (*degnarsi*): ~**rsi di fare** to be so good as to do.

compiacimen'to [kōmpyàchēmān'tō] *sm* satisfaction.

compiaciu'to, a [kōmpyàchōō'tō] *pp di* **compiacere**.

compian'gere [kōmpyàn'jārā] *vt* to sympathize with, feel sorry for.

compian'to, a *pp di* **compiangere** ♦ *ag*: **il** ~ **presidente** the late lamented president ♦ *sm* mourning, grief.

com'piere *vt* (*concludere*) to finish, complete; (*adempiere*) to carry out, fulfil; ~**rsi** *vr* (*avverarsi*) to be fulfilled, come true; ~ **gli anni** to have one's birthday.

compila're *vt* to compile; (*modulo*) to complete.

compilato're, tri'ce *sm/f* compiler.

compilazio'ne [kōmpēlàttsyō'nà] *sf* compilation; completion.

compimen'to *sm* (*termine, conclusione*) completion, fulfilment; **portare a** ~ **qc** to conclude sth, bring sth to a conclusion.

compi're *vb* = **compiere**.

compita're *vt* to spell out.

com'pito *sm* (*incarico*) task, duty; (*dovere*) duty; (*INS*) exercise; (*: a casa*) piece of homework; **fare i** ~**i** to do one's homework.

compi'to, a *ag* well-mannered, polite.

compiutez'za [kōmpyōōtāt'tsà] *sf* (*completezza*) completeness; (*perfezione*) perfection.

compiu'to, a *pp di* **compiere** ♦ *ag*: **a 20 anni** ~**i** at 20 years of age, at age 20; **un fatto** ~ a fait accompli.

complean'no *sm* birthday.

complementa're *ag* complementary; (*INS: materia*) subsidiary.

complemen'to *sm* complement; (*MIL*) reserve (troops); ~ **oggetto** (*LING*) direct object.

complessa'to, a *ag, sm/f*: **essere (un)** ~ to be full of complexes *o* hang-ups (*fam*).

complessità *sf* complexity.

complessivamen'te *av* (*nell'insieme*) on the whole; (*in tutto*) altogether.

complessi'vo, a *ag* (*globale*) comprehensive, overall; (*totale: cifra*) total; **visione** ~**a** overview.

comples'so, a *ag* complex ♦ *sm* (*PSIC, EDIL*) complex; (*MUS: corale*) ensemble; (*: orchestrina*) band; (*: di musica pop*) group; **in** *o* **nel** ~ on the whole.

completamen'to *sm* completion.

completa're *vt* to complete.

comple'to, a *ag* complete; (*teatro, autobus*) full ♦ *sm* suit; **al** ~ full; (*tutti presenti*) all present; **essere al** ~ (*teatro*) to be sold out; ~ **da sci** ski suit.

complica're *vt* to complicate; ~**rsi** *vr* to become complicated.

complicazio'ne [kōmplēkàttsyō'nà] *sf* complication; **salvo** ~**i** unless any difficulties arise.

com'plice [kom'plēchà] *sm/f* accomplice.

complimentar'si *vr*: ~ **con** to congratulate.

complimen'to *sm* compliment; ~**i** *smpl* (*cortesia eccessiva*) ceremony *sg*; ~**i!** congratulations!; **senza** ~**i!** don't stand on ceremony!; make yourself at home!; help yourself!

complotta're *vi* to plot, conspire.

complot'to *sm* plot, conspiracy.

compo'ne *etc vb vedi* **comporre**.

componen'te *sm/f* member ♦ *sm* component.

compon'go *etc vb vedi* **comporre**.

componi'bile *ag* (*mobili, cucina*) fitted.

componimen'to *sm* (*DIR*) settlement; (*INS*) composition; (*poetico, teatrale*) work.

compor're *vt* (*musica, testo*) to compose; (*mettere in ordine*) to arrange; (*DIR: lite*) to settle; (*TIP*) to set; (*TEL*) to dial; **comporsi** *vr*: **comporsi di** to consist of, be composed of.

comportamenta'le *ag* behavioral (*US*), behavioural (*Brit*).

comportamen'to *sm* behavior (*US*), behaviour (*Brit*); (*di prodotto*) performance.

comporta're *vt* (*implicare*) to involve, entail; (*consentire*) to permit, allow (of); ~**rsi** *vr* (*condursi*) to behave.

compo'si *etc vb vedi* **comporre**.

composito're, tri'ce *sm/f* composer; (*TIP*) compositor, typesetter.

composizio'ne [kōmpōzēttsyō'nà] *sf* composition; (*DIR*) settlement.

compo'sta *sf vedi* **composto**.

compostez'za |kōmpōstāt'tsä| *sf* composure; decorum.

compo'sto, a *pp di* **comporre** ♦ *ag (persona)* composed, self-possessed; *(: decoroso)* dignified; *(formato da più elementi)* compound *cpd* ♦ *sm* compound; *(cuc etc)* mixture ♦ *sf (cuc)* stewed fruit *q; (AGR)* compost.

compra're *vt* to buy; *(corrompere)* to bribe.

comprato're, tri'ce *sm/f* buyer, purchaser.

compraven'dita *sf (COMM)* (contract of) sale; **un atto di** ~ a deed of sale.

compren'dere *vt (contenere)* to comprise, consist of; *(capire)* to understand.

comprendo'nio *sm*: **essere duro di** ~ to be slow on the uptake.

comprensi'bile *ag* understandable.

comprensio'ne *sf* understanding.

comprensi'vo, a *ag (prezzo)*: ~ **di** inclusive of; *(indulgente)* understanding.

compreso'rio *sm* area, territory; *(AMM)* district.

compre'so, a *pp di* **comprendere** ♦ *ag (incluso)* included; **tutto** ~ all inclusive, all in.

compres'sa *sf vedi* **compresso**.

compressio'ne *sf* compression.

compres'so, a *pp di* **comprimere** ♦ *ag (vedi comprimere)* pressed; compressed; repressed ♦ *sf (MED: garza)* compress; *(: pastiglia)* tablet.

compresso're *sm* compressor; *(anche:* **rullo** ~) steamroller.

comprima'rio, a *sm/f (TEATRO)* supporting actor/actress.

compri'mere *vt (premere)* to press; *(FISICA)* to compress; *(fig)* to repress.

compromes'so, a *pp di* **compromettere** ♦ *sm* compromise.

compromet'tere *vt* to compromise; ~**rsi** *vr* to compromise o.s.

comproprietà *sf (DIR)* joint ownership.

comprova're *vt* to confirm.

compun'to, a *ag* contrite; **con fare** ~ with a solemn air.

compunzio'ne |kōmpōōntsyō'nä| *sf* contrition; solemnity.

computa're *vt* to calculate; *(addebitare)*: ~ **qc a qn** to debit sb with sth.

compu'ter |kəmpyōō:'tər| *sm inv* computer.

computerizza'to, a |kōmpōōtārĕddzä'tō| *ag* computerized.

computisteri'a *sf* accounting, book-keeping.

com'puto *sm* calculation; **fare il** ~ **di** to count.

comuna'le *ag* municipal, town *cpd*; **consiglio/palazzo** ~ town council/hall; **è un impiegato** ~ he works for the local council.

comu'ne *ag* common; *(consueto)* common, everyday; *(di livello medio)* average; *(ordi-*

nario) ordinary ♦ *sm (AMM)* town council; *(: sede)* town hall ♦ *sf (di persone)* commune; **fuori del** ~ out of the ordinary; **avere in** ~ to have in common, share; **mettere in** ~ to share; **un nostro** ~ **amico** a mutual friend of ours; **fare cassa** ~ to pool one's money.

comunica're *vt (notizia)* to pass on, convey; *(malattia)* to pass on; *(ansia etc)* to communicate; *(trasmettere: calore etc)* to transmit, communicate; *(REL)* to administer communion to ♦ *vi* to communicate; ~**rsi** *vr (propagarsi)*: ~**rsi a** to spread to; *(REL)* to receive communion.

comunicati'vo, a *ag (sentimento)* infectious; *(persona)* communicative ♦ *sf* communicativeness.

comunica'to *sm* communiqué; ~ **stampa** press release.

comunicazio'ne |kōmōōnĭkàttsyō'nä| *sf* communication; *(annuncio)* announcement; *(TEL)*: ~ **(telefonica)** (telephone) call; **dare la** ~ **a qn** to put sb through; **ottenere la** ~ to get through; **salvo** ~**i contrarie da parte Vostra** unless we hear from you to the contrary.

comunio'ne *sf* communion; ~ **dei beni** *(DIR: tra coniugi)* joint ownership of property.

comuni'smo *sm* communism.

comuni'sta, i, e *ag, sm/f* communist.

comunità *sf inv* community; **C~ Economica Europea (CEE)** European Economic Community (EEC).

comunita'rio, a *ag* community *cpd*.

comun'que *cong* however, no matter how ♦ *av (in ogni modo)* in any case; *(tuttavia)* however, nevertheless.

con *prep (nei seguenti casi* **con** *può fondersi con l'articolo definito:* **con** + **il** = **col**, **con** + **la** = **colla**, **con** + **gli** = **cogli**, **con** + **i** = **coi**, **con** + **le** = **colle)** with; **partire col treno** to leave by train; ~ **mio grande stupore** to my great astonishment; ~ **la forza** by force; ~ **questo freddo** in this cold weather; ~ **il 1° di ottobre** as of October 1st; ~ **tutto ciò** in spite of that, for all that; ~ **tutto che era arrabbiato** even though he was angry, in spite of the fact that he was angry; **e** ~ **questo?** so what?

cona'to *sm*: ~ **di vomito** retching.

con'ca, che *sf (GEO)* valley.

concatena're *vt* to link up, connect; ~**rsi** *vr* to be connected.

con'cavo, a *ag* concave.

conce'dere |kōnche'därä| *vt (accordare)* to grant; *(ammettere)* to admit, concede; ~**rsi qc** to treat o.s. to sth, allow o.s. sth.

concentramen'to |kōnchänträmän'tō| *sm* concentration.

concentra're |kōnchäntrà'rä| *vt*, ~**rsi** *vr* to concentrate.

concentra'to |kōnchäntrà'tō| *sm* concentrate;

~ **di pomodoro** tomato paste.

concentrazio'ne |kōnchāntráttsyō'nā| *sf* concentration; ~ **orizzontale/verticale** (*ECON*) horizontal/vertical integration.

concen'trico, a, ci, che |kōnchen'trēkō| *ag* concentric.

concepi'bile |kōnchāpē'bēlā| *ag* conceivable.

concepimen'to |kōnchāpēmān'tō| *sm* conception.

concepi're |kōnchāpē'rā| *vt* (*bambino*) to conceive; (*progetto, idea*) to conceive (of); (*metodo, piano*) to devise; (*situazione*) to imagine, understand.

concer'nere |kōnchēr'nārā| *vt* to concern; **per quanto mi concerne** as far as I'm concerned.

concerta're |kōnchārtá'rā| *vt* (*MUS*) to harmonize; (*ordine*) to devise, plan; ~**rsi** *vr* to agree.

concerti'sta, i, e |kōnchārtē'stā| *sm/f* (*MUS*) concert performer.

concer'to |kōncher'tō| *sm* (*MUS*) concert; (*: componimento*) concerto.

conces'si *etc* |kōnchcs'sē| *vb vedi* **concedere.**

concessiona'rio |kōnchāssyōnā'ryō| *sm* (*COMM*) agent, dealer; ~ **esclusivo (di)** sole agent (for).

concessio'ne |kōnchāssyō'nā| *sf* concession.

conces'so, a |kōnches'sō| *pp di* **concedere.**

concet'to |kōnchct'tō| *sm* (*pensiero, idea*) concept; (*opinione*) opinion; **è un impiegato di** ~ ≈ he's a white-collar worker.

concezio'ne |kōnchāttsyō'nā| *sf* conception; (*idea*) view, idea.

conchi'glia |kōnkēl'yá| *sf* shell.

con'cia |kōn'chá| *sf* (*di pelli*) tanning; (*di tabacco*) curing; (*sostanza*) tannin.

concia're |kōnchá'rā| *vt* (*pelli*) to tan; (*tabacco*) to cure; (*fig: ridurre in cattivo stato*) to beat up; ~**rsi** *vr* (*sporcarsi*) to get in a mess; (*vestirsi male*) to dress badly; **ti hanno conciato male** *o* **per le feste!** they've really beaten you up!

concilia'bile |kōnchēlyá'bēlā| *ag* compatible.

concilia'bolo |kōnchēlyá'bōlō| *sm* secret meeting.

concilian'te |kōnchēlyán'tā| *ag* conciliatory.

concilia're |kōnchēlyá'rā| *vt* to reconcile; (*contravvenzione*) to pay on the spot; (*favorire: sonno*) to be conducive to, induce; (*procurare: simpatia*) to gain; ~**rsi qc** to gain *o* win sth (for o.s.); ~**rsi qn** to win sb over; ~**rsi con** to be reconciled with.

conciliazio'ne |kōnchēlyáttsyō'nā| *sf* reconciliation; (*DIR*) settlement; **la C**~ (*STORIA*) the Lateran Pact.

conci'lio |kōnchē'lyō| *sm* (*REL*) council.

concima're |kōnchēmá'rā| *vt* to fertilize; (*con letame*) to manure.

conci'me |kōnchē'mā| *sm* manure; (*chimico*) fertilizer.

concisio'ne |kōnchēzyō'nā| *sf* concision, conciseness.

conci'so, a |kōnchē'zō| *ag* concise, succinct.

concita'to, a |kōnchētá'tō| *ag* excited, emotional.

concittadi'no, a |kōnchēttádē'nō| *sm/f* fellow citizen.

concla've *sm* conclave.

conclu'dere *vt* to conclude; (*portare a compimento*) to conclude, finish, bring to an end; (*operare positivamente*) to achieve ♦ *vi* (*essere convincente*) to be conclusive; ~**rsi** *vr* to come to an end, close.

conclusio'ne *sf* conclusion; (*risultato*) result.

conclusi'vo, a *ag* conclusive; (*finale*) final.

conclu'so, a *pp di* **concludere.**

concomitan'za |kōnkōmētán'tsá| *sf* (*di circostanze, fatti*) combination.

concordan'za |kōnkōrdán'tsá| *sf* (*anche LING*) agreement.

concorda're *vt* (*prezzo*) to agree on; (*LING*) to make agree ♦ *vi* to agree; ~ **una tregua** to agree to a truce.

concorda'to *sm* agreement; (*REL*) concordat.

concor'de *ag* (*d'accordo*) in agreement; (*simultaneo*) simultaneous.

concor'dia *sf* harmony, concord.

concorren'te *ag* competing; (*MAT*) concurrent ♦ *sm/f* (*SPORT, COMM*) competitor; (*a un concorso di bellezza*) contestant.

concorren'za |kōnkōrrcn'tsá| *sf* competition; ~ **sleale** unfair competition; **a prezzi di** ~ at competitive prices.

concorrenzia'le |kōnkōrrāntsyá'lā| *ag* competitive.

concor'rere *vi:* ~ **(in)** (*MAT*) to converge *o* meet (in); ~ **(a)** (*competere*) to compete (for); (*: INS: a una cattedra*) to apply (for); (*partecipare: a un'impresa*) to take part (in), contribute (to).

concor'so, a *pp di* **concorrere** ♦ *sm* competition; (*esame*) competitive examination; ~ **di bellezza** beauty contest; ~ **di circostanze** combination of circumstances; ~ **di colpa** (*DIR*) contributory negligence; **un** ~ **ippico** a showjumping event; ~ **in reato** (*DIR*) complicity in a crime; ~ **per titoli** competitive examination for qualified candidates.

concre'to, a *ag* concrete ♦ *sm:* **in** ~ in reality.

concubi'na *sf* concubine ♦ *sm:* **sono** ~**i** they are living together.

concussio'ne *sf* (*DIR*) extortion.

condan'na *sf* condemnation; sentence; conviction; ~ **a morte** death sentence.

condanna're *vt* (*disapprovare*) to condemn; (*DIR*): ~ **a** to sentence to; ~ **per** to convict of.

condanna'to, a *sm/f* convict.

condensa're *vt*, ~**rsi** *vr* to condense.

condensato're *sm* capacitor.
condensazio'ne [kōndānsàttsyō'nā] *sf* condensation.
condimen'to *sm* seasoning; dressing.
condi're *vt* to season; (*insalata*) to dress.
condiscenden'te [kōndēshānden'tā] *ag* obliging; compliant.
condiscenden'za [kōndēshānden'tsà] *sf* (*disponibilità*) obligingness; (*arrendevolezza*) compliance.
condiscen'dere [kōndēshān'dārā] *vi*: ~ **a** to agree to.
condisce'so, a [kōndēshā'sō] *pp di* **condiscendere**.
condivi'dere *vt* to share.
condivi'so, a *pp di* **condividere**.
condiziona'le [kōndēttsyōnà'lā] *ag* conditional ♦ *sm* (*LING*) conditional ♦ *sf* (*DIR*) suspended sentence.
condizionamen'to [kōndēttsyōnàmàn'tō] *sm* conditioning; ~ **d'aria** air conditioning.
condiziona're [kōndēttsyōnà'rā] *vt* to condition; **ad aria condizionata** air-conditioned.
condizio'ne [kōndēttsyō'nā] *sf* condition; ~i *sfpl* (*di pagamento etc*) terms, conditions; **a** ~ **che** on condition that, provided that; **a nessuna** ~ on no account; ~**i a convenirsi** terms to be arranged; ~**i di lavoro** working conditions; ~**i di vendita** sales terms.
condoglian'ze [kōndōlyàn'tsā] *sfpl* condolences.
condominia'le *ag*: **riunione** ~ residents' meeting; **spese** ~**i** common charges.
condomi'nio *sm* joint ownership; (*edificio*) jointly-owned building.
condo'mino *sm* joint owner.
condona're *vt* (*DIR*) to remit.
condo'no *sm* remission; ~ **fiscale** *conditional amnesty for people evading tax*.
condot'ta *sf vedi* **condotto**.
condot'to, a *pp di* **condurre** ♦ *ag*: **medico** ~ local authority doctor (*in country district*) ♦ *sm* (*canale, tubo*) pipe, conduit; (*ANAT*) duct ♦ *sf* (*modo di comportarsi*) conduct, behavior (*US*), behaviour (*Brit*); (*di un affare etc*) handling; (*di acqua*) piping; (*incarico sanitario*) *country medical practice controlled by a local authority*.
conducen'te [kōndōōchen'tā] *sm* driver.
condu'co *etc vb vedi* **condurre**.
condur're *vt* to conduct; (*azienda*) to manage; (*accompagnare: bambino*) to take; (*automobile*) to drive; (*trasportare: acqua, gas*) to convey, conduct; (*fig*) to lead ♦ *vi* to lead; **condursi** *vr* to behave, conduct o.s.; ~ **a termine** to conclude.
condus'si *etc vb vedi* **condurre**.
condutto're, tri'ce *ag*: **filo** ~ (*fig*) thread; **motivo** ~ leitmotiv ♦ *sm* (*di mezzi pubblici*) driver; (*FISICA*) conductor.

conduttu'ra *sf* (*gen*) pipe; (*di acqua, gas*) main.
conduzio'ne [kōndōōttsyō'nā] *sf* (*di affari, ditta*) management; (*DIR*: *locazione*) lease; (*FISICA*) conduction.
confabula're *vi* to confab.
confacen'te [kōnfáchen'tā] *ag*: ~ **a qn/qc** suitable for sb/sth; **clima** ~ **alla salute** healthy climate.
Confagricoltu'ra *abbr f* (= *Confederazione generale dell'Agricoltura Italiana*) *confederation of Italian farmers*.
CONFA'PI *sigla f* = *Confederazione Nazionale della Piccola Industria*.
confar'si *vr*: ~ **a** to suit, agree with.
Confartigiana'to [kōnfártējànà'tō] *abbr f* = *Confederazione Generale dell'Artigianato Italiano*.
confat'to, a *pp di* **confarsi**.
Confcommer'cio [kōnfkōmmer'chō] *abbr f* = *Confederazione Generale del Commercio*.
confederazio'ne [kōnfàdāràttsyō'nā] *sf* confederation; ~ **imprenditoriale** employers' association.
conferen'za [kōnfāren'tsà] *sf* (*discorso*) lecture; (*riunione*) conference; ~ **stampa** press conference.
conferenzie're, a [kōnfàrāntsye'rā] *sm/f* lecturer.
conferimen'to *sm* conferring, awarding.
conferi're *vt*: ~ **qc a qn** to give sth to sb, confer sth on sb ♦ *vi* to confer.
confer'ma *sf* confirmation.
conferma're *vt* to confirm.
confessa're *vt*, ~**rsi** *vr* to confess; **andare a** ~**rsi** (*REL*) to go to confession.
confessiona'le *ag*, *sm* confessional.
confessio'ne *sf* confession; (*setta religiosa*) denomination.
confes'so, a *ag*: **essere reo** ~ to have pleaded guilty.
confesso're *sm* confessor.
confet'to *sm* sugared almond; (*MED*) pill.
confettu'ra *sf* (*gen*) jam; (*di arance*) marmalade.
confeziona're [kōnfàttsyōnà'rā] *vt* (*vestito*) to make (up); (*merci, pacchi*) to package.
confezio'ne [kōnfàttsyō'nā] *sf* (*di abiti*: *da uomo*) tailoring; (: *da donna*) dressmaking; (*imballaggio*) packaging; ~ **regalo** gift pack; ~ **risparmio** economy size; ~ **da viaggio** travel pack; ~**i per signora** ladies' wear *q*; ~**i da uomo** menswear *q*.
conficca're *vt*: ~ **qc in** to hammer *o* drive sth into; ~**rsi** *vr* to stick.
confida're *vi*: ~ **in** to confide in, rely on ♦ *vt* to confide; ~**rsi con qn** to confide in sb.
confiden'te *sm/f* (*persona amica*) confidant/confidante; (*informatore*) informer.
confiden'za [kōnfēden'tsà] *sf* (*familiarità*) inti-

macy, familiarity; (*fiducia*) trust, confidence; (*rivelazione*) confidence; **prendersi (troppe) ~e** to take liberties; **fare una ~ a qn** to confide something to sb.

confidenzia'le [kōnfēdăntsyá'lā] *ag* familiar, friendly; (*segreto*) confidential; **in via ~** confidentially.

configurar'si *vr*: **~ a** to assume the shape *o* form of.

configurazio'ne [kōnfēgōōráttsyō'nā] *sf* configuration.

confinan'te *ag* neighboring (*US*), neighbouring (*Brit*).

confina're *vi*: **~ con** to border on ♦ *vt* (*POL*) to intern; (*fig*) to confine; **~rsi** *vr* (*isolarsi*): **~rsi in** to shut o.s. up in.

confina'to, a *ag* interned ♦ *smf* internee.

Confindus'tria *sigla f* (= *Confederazione Generale dell'Industria Italiana*) *employers' association*.

confi'ne *sm* boundary; (*di paese*) border, frontier; **territorio di ~** border zone.

confi'no *sm* internment.

confi'sca *sf* confiscation.

confisca're *vt* to confiscate.

conflagrazio'ne [kōnflăgráttsyō'nā] *sf* conflagration.

conflit'to *sm* conflict; **essere in ~ con qc** to clash with sth; **essere in ~ con qn** to be at loggerheads with sb.

conflittua'le *ag*: **rapporto ~** relationship based on conflict.

conflittualità *sf* conflicts *pl*.

confluen'za [kōnflōōen'tsá] *sf* (*di fiumi*) confluence; (*di strade*) junction.

conflui're *vi* (*fiumi*) to flow into each other, meet; (*strade*) to meet.

confon'dere *vt* to mix up, confuse; (*imbarazzare*) to embarrass; **~rsi** *vr* (*mescolarsi*) to mingle; (*turbarsi*) to be confused; (*sbagliare*) to get mixed up; **~ le idee a qn** to mix sb up, confuse sb.

conforma're *vt* (*adeguare*): **~ a** to adapt *o* conform to; **~rsi** *vr*: **~rsi (a)** to conform (to).

confor'me *ag*: **~ a** (*simile*) similar to; (*corrispondente*) in keeping with.

conformemen'te *av* accordingly; **~ a** in accordance with.

conformi'smo *sm* conformity.

conformi'sta, i, e *smf* conformist.

conformità *sf* conformity; **in ~ a** in conformity with.

conforta're *vt* to comfort, console.

conforte'vole *ag* (*consolante*) comforting; (*comodo*) comfortable.

confor'to *sm* (*consolazione, sollievo*) comfort, consolation; (*conferma*) support; **a ~ di qc** in support of sth; **i ~i (religiosi)** the last sacraments.

confrater'nita *sf* brotherhood.

confronta're *vt* to compare; **~rsi** *vr* (*scontrarsi*) to have a confrontation.

confron'to *sm* comparison; (*DIR. MIL. POL*) confrontation; **in *o* a ~ di** in comparison with, compared to; **nei miei** (*o* **tuoi** *etc*) **~i** towards me (*o* you *etc*).

confu'si *etc vb vedi* **confondere**.

confusio'ne *sf* confusion; (*imbarazzo*) embarrassment; **far ~** (*disordine*) to make a mess; (*chiasso*) to make a racket; (*confondere*) to confuse things.

confu'so, a *pp di* **confondere** ♦ *ag* (*vedi confondere*) confused; embarrassed.

confuta're *vt* to refute.

congeda're [kōnjādá'rā] *vt* to dismiss; (*MIL*) to demobilize; **~rsi** *vr* to take one's leave.

conge'do [kōnjá'dō] *sm* (*anche MIL*) leave; **prendere ~ da qn** to take one's leave of sb; **~ assoluto** (*MIL*) discharge.

congegna're [kōnjānyá'rā] *vt* to construct, put together.

conge'gno [kōnjān'yō] *sm* device, mechanism.

congelamen'to [kōnjálámān'tō] *sm* (*gen*) freezing; (*MED*) frostbite; **~ salariale** wage freeze.

congela're [kōnjálá'rā] *vt*, **~rsi** *vr* to freeze.

congelato're [kōnjálátō'rā] *sm* freezer.

conge'nito, a [kōnje'nētō] *ag* congenital.

conge'rie [kōnje'ryā] *sf inv* (*di oggetti*) heap; (*di idee*) muddle, jumble.

congestiona're [kōnjāstyōná'rā] *vt* to congest; **essere congestionato** (*persona, viso*) to be flushed; (*zona: per traffico*) to be congested.

congestio'ne [kōnjāstyō'nā] *sf* congestion.

congettu'ra [kōnjāttōō'rà] *sf* conjecture, supposition.

congi'ungere [kōnjōōn'jārā] *vt*, **~rsi** *vr* to join (together).

congiuntivi'te [kōnjōōntēvē'tā] *sf* conjunctivitis.

congiunti'vo [kōnjōōntē'vō] *sm* (*LING*) subjunctive.

congiun'to, a [kōnjōōn'tō] *pp di* **congiungere** ♦ *ag* (*unito*) joined ♦ *smf* (*parente*) relative.

congiuntu'ra [kōnjōōntōōrá'rà] *sf* (*giuntura*) junction, join; (*ANAT*) joint; (*circostanza*) juncture; (*ECON*) economic situation.

congiuntura'le [kōnjōōntōōrá'lā] *ag* of the economic situation; **crisi ~** economic crisis.

congiunzio'ne [kōnjōōntsyō'nā] *sf* (*LING*) conjunction.

congiu'ra [kōnjōō'rá] *sf* conspiracy.

congiura're [kōnjōōrá'rā] *vi* to conspire.

conglomera'to *sm* (*GEO*) conglomerate; (*fig*) conglomeration; (*EDIL*) concrete.

Con'go *sm*: **il ~** the Congo.

congole'se *ag, smf* Congolese *inv*.

congratular'si *vr*: **~ con qn per qc** to congratulate sb on sth.

congratulazio'ni [kōngrátōōláttsyō'nē] *sfpl*

congratulations.

congre'ga, ghe *sf* band, bunch.

congregazio'ne |kŏngrāgáttsyŏ'nä| *sf* congregation.

congressi'sta, i, e *sm/f* participant at a congress.

congres'so *sm* congress.

con'gruo, a *ag* (*prezzo, compenso*) adequate, fair; (*ragionamento*) coherent, consistent.

conguaglia're |kŏngwályá'rä| *vt* to balance; (*stipendio*) to adjust.

congua'glio |kŏngwál'yŏ| *sm* balancing; adjusting; (*somna di denaro*) balance; **fare il ~ di** to balance; to adjust.

conia're *vt* to mint, coin; (*fig*) to coin.

coniazio'ne |kŏnyáttsyŏ'nä| *sf* mintage.

co'nico, a, ci, che *ag* conical.

coni'fera *sf* conifer.

coniglie'ra |kŏnēlyc'rà| *sf* (*gabbia*) rabbit hutch; (*più grande*) rabbit run.

conigliet'to |kŏnēlyāt'tŏ| *sm* bunny.

coni'glio |kŏnēl'yŏ| *sm* rabbit; **sei un ~!** (*fig*) you're chicken!

coniuga'le *ag* (*amore, diritti*) conjugal; (*vita*) married, conjugal.

coniuga're *vt* (*LING*) to conjugate; **~rsi** *vr* to get married.

coniuga'to, a *ag* (*AMM*) married.

coniugazio'ne |kŏnyŏōgáttsyŏ'nä| *sf* (*LING*) conjugation.

co'niuge |ko'nyŏōjä| *sm/f* spouse.

connatura'to, a *ag* inborn.

connaziona'le |kŏnnáttsyŏnà'lä| *sm/f* fellow-countryman/woman.

connessio'ne *sf* connection.

connes'so, a *pp di* **connettere.**

connet'tere *vt* to connect, join ♦ *vi* (*fig*) to think straight.

connetto're *sm* (*ELETTR*) connector.

conniven'te *ag* conniving.

connota'ti *smpl* distinguishing marks; **rispondere ai ~i** to fit the description; **cambiare i ~i a qn** (*fam*) to beat sb up.

connu'bio *sm* (*matrimonio*) marriage; (*fig*) union.

co'no *sm* cone; **~ gelato** ice-cream cone.

conob'bi *etc vb vedi* **conoscere.**

conoscen'te |kŏnŏshcn'tä| *sm/f* acquaintance.

conoscen'za |kŏnŏshcn'tsà| *sf* (*il sapere*) knowledge *q*; (*persona*) acquaintance; (*facoltà sensoriale*) consciousness *q*; **essere a ~ di qc** to know sth; **portare qn a ~ di qc** to inform sb of sth; **per vostra ~** for your information; **fare la ~ di qn** to make sb's acquaintance; **perdere ~** to lose consciousness; **~ tecnica** know-how.

cono'scere |kŏnŏsh'shärä| *vt* to know; **ci siamo conosciuti a Firenze** we (first) met in Florence; **~ qn di vista** to know sb by sight; **farsi ~** (*fig*) to make a name for o.s.

conoscito're, tri'ce |kŏnŏshctŏ'rä| *sm/f* connoisseur.

conosciu'to, a |kŏnŏshŏō'tŏ| *pp di* **conoscere** ♦ *ag* well-known.

conqui'sta *sf* conquest.

conquista're *vt* to conquer; (*fig*) to gain, win.

conquistato're, tri'ce *sm/f* (*in guerra*) conqueror ♦ *sm* (*seduttore*) lady-killer.

cons. *abbr* = **consiglio.**

consacra're *vt* (*REL*) to consecrate; (: *sacerdote*) to ordain; (*dedicare*) to dedicate; (*fig: uso etc*) to sanction; **~rsi a** to dedicate o.s. to.

consangui'neo, a *sm/f* blood relation.

consape'vole *ag*: **~ di** aware o conscious of.

consapevolez'za |kŏnsàpávŏlät'tsà| *sf* awareness, consciousness.

con'scio, a, sci, sce |kon'shŏ| *ag*: **~ di** aware o conscious of.

consecuti'vo, a *ag* consecutive; (*successivo: giorno*) following, next.

conse'gna |kŏnsän'yà| *sf* delivery; (*merce consegnata*) consignment; (*custodia*) care, custody; (*MIL: ordine*) orders *pl*; (: *punizione*) confinement to barracks; **alla ~** on delivery; **dare qc in ~ a qn** to entrust sth to sb; **passare le ~e a qn** to hand over to sb; **~ a domicilio** home delivery; **in contrassegno, pagamento alla ~** cash on delivery; **~ sollecita** prompt delivery.

consegna're |kŏnsänyá'rä| *vt* to deliver; (*affidare*) to entrust, hand over; (*MIL*) to confine to barracks.

consegnata'rio |kŏnsänyàtà'ryŏ| *sm* consignee.

conseguen'te *ag* consequent.

conseguentemen'te *av* consequently.

conseguen'za |kŏnsāgwcn'tsà| *sf* consequence; **per o di ~** consequently.

conseguimen'to *sm* (*di scopo, risultato etc*) achievement, attainment; **al ~ della laurea** on graduation.

consegui're *vt* to achieve ♦ *vi* to follow, result; **~ la laurea** to graduate, obtain one's degree.

consen'so *sm* approval, consent.

consensua'le *ag* (*DIR*) by mutual consent.

consenti're *vi*: **~ a** to consent o agree to ♦ *vt* to allow, permit; **mi si consenta di ringraziare ...** I would like to thank ....

consenzien'te |kŏnsäntsycn'tä| *ag* (*gen, DIR*) consenting.

conser'to, a *ag*: **a braccia ~e** with one's arms folded.

conser'va *sf* (*CUC*) preserve; **~ di frutta** jam; **~ di pomodoro** tomato paste; **~e alimentari** (*canned o bottled*) foods.

conserva're *vt* (*CUC*) to preserve; (*custodire*) to keep; (: *dalla distruzione etc*) to preserve, conserve; **~rsi** *vr* to keep.

conservato're, tri'ce _ag, sm/f_ (_POL_) conservative.

conservato'rio _sm_ (_di musica_) conservatory.

conservatori'smo _sm_ (_POL_) conservatism.

conservazio'ne [kōnsārváttsyō'nā] _sf_ preservation; conservation; **istinto di** ~ instinct for self-preservation; **a lunga** ~ (_latte, panna_) long-life _cpd_.

conses'so _sm_ (_assemblea_) assembly; (_riunione_) meeting.

considera'bile _ag_ worthy of consideration.

considera're _vt_ to consider; (_reputare_) to consider, regard; ~ **molto qn** to think highly of sb.

considera'to, a _ag_ (_prudente_) cautious, careful; (_stimato_) highly thought of, esteemed.

considerazio'ne [kōnsēdāráttsyō'nā] _sf_ (_esame, riflessione_) consideration; (_stima_) regard, esteem; (_pensiero, osservazione_) observation; **prendere in** ~ to take into consideration.

considere'vole _ag_ considerable.

consiglia'bile [kōnsēlyá'bēlā] _ag_ advisable.

consiglia're [kōnsēlyá'rā] _vt_ (_persona_) to advise; (_metodo, azione_) to recommend, advise, suggest; ~**rsi** _vr:_ ~**rsi con qn** to ask sb for advice.

consiglie're, a [kōnsēlye'rā] _sm/f_ adviser ♦ _sm:_ ~ **d'amministrazione** board member; ~ **comunale** town councilor (_US_) o councillor (_Brit_); ~ **delegato** (_COMM_) managing director.

consi'glio [kōnsēl'yō] _sm_ (_suggerimento_) advice _q_, piece of advice; (_assemblea_) council; ~ **d'amministrazione** board; **C~ d'Europa** Council of Europe; ~ **di fabbrica** work council; **il C~ dei Ministri** (_POL_) ≈ the Cabinet; **C~ di stato** _advisory body to the Italian government on administrative matters and their legal implications_; **C~ superiore della magistratura** _state body responsible for judicial appointments and regulations_.

consi'mile _ag_ similar.

consisten'te _ag_ solid; (_fig_) sound, valid.

consisten'za [kōnsēsten'tsā] _sf_ (_di impasto_) consistency; (_di stoffa_) texture; **senza** ~ (_sospetti, voci_) ill-founded, groundless; ~ **di cassa/di magazzino** cash/stock in hand; ~ **patrimoniale** financial solidity.

consi'stere _vi:_ ~ **in** to consist of.

consisti'to, a _pp di_ consistere.

CON'SOB _sigla f_ (= _Commissione nazionale per le società e la borsa_) _regulatory body for the Italian Stock Exchange_.

consociar'si [kōnsōchàr'sē] _vr_ to go into partnership.

consocia'to, a [kōnsōchà'tō] _ag_ associated ♦ _sm/f_ associate.

consolan'te _ag_ consoling, comforting.

consola're _ag_ consular ♦ _vt_ (_confortare_) to

console, comfort; (_rallegrare_) to cheer up; ~**rsi** _vr_ to be comforted; to cheer up.

consola'to _sm_ consulate.

consolazio'ne [kōnsōláttsyō'nā] _sf_ consolation, comfort.

con'sole _sm_ consul ♦ _sf_ [kōńsol'] (_quadro di comando_) console.

consolidamen'to _sm_ strengthening; consolidation.

consolida're _vt_ to strengthen, reinforce; (_MIL, terreno_) to consolidate; ~**rsi** _vr_ to consolidate.

consolidazio'ne [kōnsōlēdáttsyō'nā] _sf_ strengthening; consolidation.

consommé [kōńsomā'] _sm inv_ consommé.

consonan'te _sf_ consonant.

consonan'za [kōnsōnán'tsá] _sf_ consonance.

con'sono, a _ag:_ ~ **a** consistent with, consonant with.

consor'te _sm/f_ consort.

consor'zio [kōnsor'tsyō] _sm_ consortium; ~ **agrario** farmers' cooperative; ~ **di garanzia** (_COMM_) underwriting syndicate.

consta're _vi:_ ~ **di** to consist of ♦ _vb impers:_ **mi consta che** it has come to my knowledge that, it appears that; **a quanto mi consta** as far as I know.

constata're _vt_ to establish, verify; (_notare_) to notice, observe.

constatazio'ne [kōnstátáttsyō'nā] _sf_ observation; ~ **amichevole** (_in incidenti_) _jointly-agreed statement for insurance purposes_.

consue'to, a _ag_ habitual, usual ♦ _sm:_ **come di** ~ as usual.

consuetudina'rio, a _ag:_ **diritto** ~ (_DIR_) common law.

consuetu'dine _sf_ habit; (_usanza_) custom.

consulen'te _sm/f_ consultant; ~ **aziendale/tecnico** management/technical consultant.

consulen'za [kōnsōōlen'tsá] _sf_ consultancy; ~ **medica/legale** medical/legal advice; **ufficio di** ~ **fiscale** tax consultancy office; ~ **tecnica** technical consultancy o advice.

consulta're _vt_ to consult; ~**rsi** _vr:_ ~**rsi con qn** to seek the advice of sb.

consultazio'ne [kōnsōōltáttsyō'nā] _sf_ consultation; ~**i** _sfpl_ (_POL_) talks, consultations; **libro di** ~ reference book.

consulti'vo, a _ag_ consultative.

consulto'rio _sm:_ ~ **familiare** o **matrimoniale** marriage guidance centre; ~ **pediatrico** children's clinic.

consuma're _vt_ (_logorare: abiti, scarpe_) to wear out; (_usare_) to consume, use up; (_mangiare, bere_) to consume; (_DIR_) to consummate; ~**rsi** _vr_ to wear out; to be used up; (_anche fig_) to be consumed; (_combustibile_) to burn out.

consuma'to, a _ag_ (_vestiti, scarpe, tappeto_) worn; (_persona: esperto_) accomplished.

consumato're sm consumer.
consumazio'ne [kōnsōōmáttsyō'nā] sf (bibita) drink; (spuntino) snack; (DIR) consummation.
consumi'smo sm consumerism.
consu'mo sm consumption; wear; use; generi o beni di ~ consumer goods; beni di largo ~ basic commodities; imposta sui ~i tax on consumer goods.
consunti'vo sm (ECON) final balance.
consun'to, a ag worn-out; (viso) wasted.
con'ta sf (nei giochi): fare la ~ to see who is going to be "it".
conta'bile ag accounts cpd, accounting ♦ sm/f accountant.
contabilità sf (attività, tecnica) accounting, accountancy; (insieme dei libri etc) books pl, accounts pl; (ufficio) ~ accounting (US) o accounts (Brit) department; ~ finanziaria financial accounting; ~ di gestione management accounting.
contachilo'metri [kōntákēlo'mātrē] sm inv ≈ odometer (US), ≈ mileometer (Brit).
contadi'no, a sm/f countryman/woman; farm worker; (peg) peasant.
contagia're [kōntàjá'rā] vt to infect.
conta'gio [kōntà'jō] sm infection; (per contatto diretto) contagion; (epidemia) epidemic.
contagio'so, a [kōntàjō'sō] ag infectious; contagious.
contagi'ri [kōntàjē'rē] sm inv (AUT) tachometer (US), rev counter (Brit).
contagoc'ce [kōntàgōch'chā] sm inv dropper.
contamina're vt to contaminate.
contaminazio'ne [kōntàmēnáttsyō'nā] sf contamination.
contan'te sm cash; pagare in ~i to pay cash.
conta're vt to count; (considerare) ♦ vi to count, be of importance; ~ su qn to count o rely on sb; ~ di fare qc to intend to do sth; ha i giorni contati, ha le ore contate his days are numbered; la gente che conta people who matter.
contascat'ti sm inv telephone meter.
contato're sm meter.
contatta're vt to contact.
contat'to sm contact; essere in ~ con qn to be in touch with sb; fare ~ (ELETTR: fili) to touch.
con'te sm count.
conte'a sf (STORIA) earldom; (AMM) county.
conteggia're [kōntādjá'rā] vt to charge, put on the bill.
conteg'gio [kōntád'jō] sm calculation.
conte'gno [kōntán'yō] sm (comportamento) behavior (US), behaviour (Brit); (atteggiamento) attitude; darsi un ~ (ostentare disinvoltura) to act nonchalant; (ricomporsi) to pull o.s. together.

contegno'so, a [kōntányō'sō] ag reserved, dignified.
contempla're vt to contemplate, gaze at; (DIR) to make provision for.
contemplati'vo, a ag contemplative.
contemplazio'ne [kōntámpláttsyō'nā] sf contemplation.
contem'po sm: nel ~ meanwhile, in the meantime.
contemporaneamen'te av simultaneously; at the same time.
contempora'neo, a ag, sm/f contemporary.
contenden'te sm/f opponent, adversary.
conten'dere vi (competere) to compete; (litigare) to quarrel ♦ vt: ~ qc a qn to contend with o be in competition with sb for sth.
contene're vt to contain; ~rsi vr to contain o.s.
contenito're sm container.
contenta'bile ag: difficilmente ~ difficult to please.
contenta're vt to please, satisfy; ~rsi vr: ~rsi di to be satisfied with, content o.s. with; si contenta di poco he is easily satisfied.
contentez'za [kōntāntāt'tsà] sf contentment.
contenti'no sm sop.
conten'to, a ag pleased, glad; ~ di pleased with.
contenu'to ag (ira, entusiasmo) restrained, suppressed; (forza) contained ♦ sm contents pl; (argomento) content.
contenzio'so, a [kōntāntsyo'sō] ag (DIR) contentious ♦ sm (AMM: ufficio) legal department.
conte'so, a pp di contendere ♦ sf dispute, argument.
contes'sa sf countess.
contesta're vt (DIR) to notify; (fig) to dispute; ~ il sistema to protest against the system.
contestato're, tri'ce ag anti-establishment ♦ sm/f protester.
contestazio'ne [kōntāstáttsyō'nā] sf (DIR: disputa) dispute; (: notifica) notification; (POL) anti-establishment activity; in caso di ~ if there are any objections.
conte'sto sm context.
conti'guo, a ag: ~ (a) adjacent (to).
continenta'le ag continental.
continen'te ag continent ♦ sm (GEO) continent; (: terra ferma) mainland.
continen'za [kōntēnen'tsá] sf continence.
contingen'te [kōntēnjen'tā] ag contingent ♦ sm (COMM) quota; (MIL) contingent.
contingen'za [kōntēnjen'tsà] sf circumstance; (indennità di) ~ cost-of-living allowance.
continuamen'te av (senza interruzione) continuously, nonstop; (ripetutamente) continually.
continua're vt to continue (with), go on with

♦ *vi* to continue, go on; ~ **a fare qc** to go on
o continue doing sth; **continua a nevicare/a
fare freddo** it's still snowing/cold.

continuati'vo, a *ag* (*occupazione*) permanent; (*periodo*) consecutive.

continuazio'ne |kōntēnōōáttsyō'nä| *sf* continuation.

continuità *sf* continuity.

conti'nuo, a *ag* (*numerazione*) continuous;
(*pioggia*) continual, constant; (*ELETTR: corrente*) direct; **di** ~ continually.

con'to *sm* (*calcolo*) calculation; (*COMM,
ECON*) account; (*di ristorante, albergo*) bill;
(*fig: stima*) consideration, esteem; **avere un**
~ **in sospeso (con qn)** to have an outstanding account (with sb); (*fig*) to have a score to
settle (with sb); **fare i** ~**i con qn** to settle
one's account with sb; **fare** ~ **su qn** to count
o rely on sb; **fare** ~ **che** (*supporre*) to
suppose that; **rendere** ~ **a qn di qc** to be
accountable to sb for sth; **rendersi** ~ **di qc/
che** to realize sth/that; **tener** ~ **di qn/qc** to
take sb/sth into account; **tenere qc da** ~ to
take great care of sth; **ad ogni buon** ~ in
any case; **di poco/nessun** ~ of little/no
importance; **per** ~ **di** on behalf of; **per** ~
mio as far as I'm concerned; (*da solo*) on
my own; **a** ~**i fatti, in fin dei** ~**i** all things
considered; **mi hanno detto strane cose sul
suo** ~ I've heard some strange things about
him; ~ **capitale** capital account; ~ **cifrato**
numbered account; ~ **corrente** checking
account (*US*), current account (*Brit*); ~
corrente postale Post Office account; ~ **economico** profit and loss account; ~ **in partecipazione** joint account; ~ **passivo** account
payable; ~ **profitti e perdite** profit and loss
account; ~ **alla rovescia** countdown; ~ **valutario** foreign currency account.

contor'cere |kōntor'chärä| *vt* to twist; (*panni*)
to wring (out); ~**rsi** *vr* to twist, writhe.

contorna're *vt* to surround; ~**rsi** *vr*: ~**rsi di**
to surround o.s. with.

contor'no *sm* (*linea*) outline, contour; (*ornamento*) border; (*CUC*) vegetables *pl*; **fare da**
~ **a** to surround.

contorsio'ne *sf* contortion.

contor'to, a *pp di* **contorcere.**

contrabbanda're *vt* to smuggle.

contrabbandie're, a *sm/f* smuggler.

contrabban'do *sm* smuggling, contraband;
merce di ~ contraband, smuggled goods *pl*.

contrabbas'so *sm* (*MUS*) (double) bass.

contraccambia're *vt* (*favore etc*) to return;
vorrei ~ I'd like to show my appreciation.

contraccetti'vo, a |kōntràchättē'vō| *ag, sm*
contraceptive.

contraccol'po *sm* rebound; (*di arma da fuoco*) recoil; (*fig*) repercussion.

contra'da *sf* street; district.

contraddet'to, a *pp di* **contraddire.**

contraddi're *vt* to contradict; ~**rsi** *vr* to contradict o.s.; (*uso reciproco: persone*) to contradict each other *o* one another; (: *testimonianze etc*) to be contradictory.

contraddistin'guere *vt* (*merce*) to mark;
(*fig: atteggiamento, persona*) to distinguish.

contraddistin'to, a *pp di* **contraddistinguere.**

contraddit'to'rio, a *ag* contradictory; (*sentimenti*) conflicting ♦ *sm* (*DIR*) crossexamination.

contraddizio'ne |kōntràddēttsyō'nä| *sf* contradiction; **cadere in** ~ to contradict o.s.; **essere in** ~ (*tesi, affermazioni*) to contradict one
another; **spirito di** ~ argumentativeness.

contra'e *etc vb vedi* **contrarre.**

contraen'te *sm* contractor.

contrae'rea *sf* (*MIL*) anti-aircraft artillery.

contraffa're *vt* (*persona*) to mimic; (*voce*) to
disguise; (*firma*) to forge, counterfeit.

contraffat'to, a *pp di* **contraffare** ♦ *ag*
counterfeit.

contraffazio'ne |kōntràffáttsyō'nä| *sf* mimicking *q*; disguising *q*; forging *q*; (*cosa contraffatta*) forgery.

contraffor'te *sm* (*ARCHIT*) buttress; (*GEO*)
spur.

contrag'go *etc vb vedi* **contrarre.**

contral'to *sm* (*MUS*) contralto.

contrappel'lo *sm* (*MIL*) second roll call.

contrappesa're *vt* to counterbalance; (*fig*:
decisione) to weigh up.

contrappe'so *sm* counterbalance, counterweight.

contrappor're *vt*: ~ **qc a qc** to counter sth
with sth; (*paragonare*) to compare sth with
sth; **contrapporsi** *vr*: **contrapporsi a qc** to
contrast with sth, be opposed to sth.

contrappo'sto, a *pp di* **contrapporre.**

contrariamen'te *av*: ~ **a** contrary to.

contraria're *vt* (*contrastare*) to thwart,
oppose; (*irritare*) to annoy, bother; ~**rsi** *vr*
to get annoyed.

contraria'to, a *ag* annoyed.

contrarietà *sf* adversity; (*fig*) aversion.

contra'rio, a *ag* opposite; (*sfavorevole*) unfavorable (*US*), unfavourable (*Brit*) ♦ *sm* opposite; **essere** ~ **a qc** (*persona*) to be against
sth; **al** ~ on the contrary; **in caso** ~ otherwise; **avere qualcosa in** ~ to have an objection; **non ho niente in** ~ I have no objection.

contrar're *vt* (*malattia, debito*) to contract;
(*muscoli*) to tense; (*abitudine, vizio*) to pick
up; (*accordo, patto*) to enter into; **contrarsi**
vr to contract; ~ **matrimonio** to marry.

contrassegna're |kōntrássänyá'rä| *vt* to mark.

contrasse'gno |kōntrássän'yō| *sm* (*distintivo*)
distinguishing mark; **spedire in** ~ (*COMM*) to
send COD.

contras'si *etc vb vedi* **contrarre.**

contrastan'te *ag* contrasting.

contrasta're *vt* (*avversare*) to oppose; (*impedire*) to bar; (*negare: diritto*) to contest, dispute ♦ *vi*: ~ **(con)** (*essere in disaccordo*) to contrast (with); (*lottare*) to struggle (with).

contra'sto *sm* contrast; (*conflitto*) conflict; (*litigio*) dispute.

contrattac'co *sm* counterattack; **passare al** ~ (*fig*) to fight back.

contratta're *vt*, *vi* to negotiate.

contrattem'po *sm* hitch.

contrat'to, a *pp di* **contrarre** ♦ *sm* contract; ~ **di acquisto** purchase agreement; ~ **di affitto**, ~ **di locazione** lease; ~ **collettivo di lavoro** collective agreement; ~ **di lavoro** contract of employment; ~ **a termine** forward contract.

contrattua'le *ag* contractual; **forza** ~ (*di sindacato*) bargaining power.

contravveni're *vi*: ~ **a** (*legge*) to contravene; (*obbligo*) to fail to meet.

contravvento're, tri'ce *sm/f* offender.

contravvenu'to, a *pp di* **contravvenire.**

contravvenzio'ne [kōntrâvvântsyō'nâ] *sf* contravention; (*ammenda*) fine.

contrazio'ne [kōntrâttsyō'nâ] *sf* contraction; (*di prezzi etc*) reduction.

contribuen'te *sm/f* taxpayer; property tax payer (*US*), ratepayer (*Brit*).

contribui're *vi* to contribute.

contributi'vo, a *ag* contributory.

contribu'to *sm* contribution; (*sovvenzione*) subsidy, contribution; (*tassa*) tax; **~i previdenziali** ≈ welfare (*US*) *o* national insurance (*Brit*) contributions; **~i sindacali** trade union dues.

contri'to, a *ag* contrite, penitent.

con'tro *prep* against; ~ **di me/lui** against me/him; **pastiglie** ~ **la tosse** throat lozenges; ~ **pagamento** (*COMM*) on payment; ~ **ogni mia aspettativa** contrary to my expectations; **per** ~ on the other hand.

controbat'tere *vt* (*fig: a parole*) to answer back; (: *confutare*) to refute.

controbilancia're [kōntrōbēlânchâ'râ] *vt* to counterbalance.

controcorren'te *av*: **andare** ~ (*anche fig*) to swim against the tide.

controcultu'ra *sf* counterculture.

controffensi'va *sf* counteroffensive.

controfigu'ra *sf* (*CINEMA*) double.

controfirma're *vt* to countersign.

controlla're *vt* (*accertare*) to check; (*sorvegliare*) to watch, control; (*tenere nel proprio potere, fig: dominare*) to control; **~rsi** *vr* to control o.s.

controlla'ta *sf* (*COMM: società*) associated company.

control'lo *sm* check; watch; control; **base di** ~ (*AER*) ground control; **telefono sotto** ~ tapped telephone; **visita di** ~ (*MED*) checkup; ~ **doganale** customs inspection; ~ **di gestione** management control; ~ **delle nascite** birth control; ~ **di qualità** quality control.

controllo're *sm* (*FERR, AUTOBUS*) conductor (*US*), (ticket) inspector (*Brit*); ~ **di volo** *o* **del traffico aereo** air traffic controller.

controlu'ce [kōntrōlōō'châ] *sf inv* (*FOT*) backlit shot ♦ *av*: **(in)** ~ against the light; (*fotografare*) into the light.

controma'no *av*: **guidare** ~ to drive on the wrong side of the road; (*in un senso unico*) to drive the wrong way up a one-way street.

controparti'ta *sf* (*fig: compenso*): **come** ~ in return.

contropie'de *sm* (*SPORT*): **azione di** ~ sudden counter-attack; **prendere qn in** ~ (*fig*) to catch sb off his (*o* her) guard.

controproducen'te [kōntrōprōdōōchen'tâ] *ag* counterproductive.

contror'dine *sm* counter-order; **salvo** ~ unless I (*o* you *etc*) hear to the contrary.

controsen'so *sm* (*contraddizione*) contradiction in terms; (*assurdità*) nonsense.

controspionag'gio [kōntrōspēōnâd'jō] *sm* counterespionage.

controvalo're *sm* equivalent (value).

controven'to *av* against the wind; **navigare** ~ (*NAUT*) to sail to windward.

controver'sia *sf* controversy; (*DIR*) dispute; ~ **sindacale** industrial dispute.

controver'so, a *ag* controversial.

controvo'glia [kōntrōvol'yâ] *av* unwillingly.

contuma'ce [kōntōōmá'châ] *ag* (*DIR*): **rendersi** ~ to default, fail to appear in court ♦ *sm/f* (*DIR*) defaulter.

contuma'cia [kōntōōmá'châ] *sf* (*DIR*) default.

contunden'te *ag*: **corpo** ~ blunt instrument.

conturban'te *ag* (*sguardo, bellezza*) disturbing.

conturba're *vt* to disturb, upset.

contusio'ne *sf* (*MED*) bruise.

convalescen'te [kōnvâlâshen'tâ] *ag*, *sm/f* convalescent.

convalescen'za [kōnvâlâshen'tsâ] *sf* convalescence.

convalida're *vt* (*AMM*) to validate; (*fig: sospetto, dubbio*) to confirm.

conve'gno [kōnvân'yō] *sm* (*incontro*) meeting; (*congresso*) convention, congress; (*luogo*) meeting place.

convene'voli *smpl* civilities.

convenien'te *ag* suitable; (*vantaggioso*) profitable; (: *prezzo*) cheap.

convenien'za [kōnvânyen'tsâ] *sf* suitability; advantage; cheapness; **~e** *sfpl* social conventions.

conveni're *vt* to agree upon ♦ *vi* (*riunirsi*) to gather, assemble; (*concordare*) to agree;

(*tornare utile*) to be worthwhile ♦ *vb impers*: **conviene fare questo** it is advisable to do this; **conviene andarsene** we should go; **ne convengo** I agree; **come convenuto** as agreed; **in data da** ~ on a date to be agreed; **come (si) conviene ad una signorina** as befits a young lady.

conventi'cola *sf* (*cricca*) clique; (*riunione*) secret meeting.

conven'to *sm* (*di frati*) monastery; (*di suore*) convent.

convenu'to, a *pp di* **convenire** ♦ *sm* (*cosa pattuita*) agreement ♦ *sm/f* (*DIR*) defendant; **i** ~**i** (*i presenti*) those present.

convenziona'le [kōnvāntsyōnā'lā] *ag* conventional.

convenziona'to, a [kōnvāntsyōnā'tō] *ag* (*ospedale, clinica*) providing free health care, ≈ National Health Service *cpd* (*Brit*).

convenzio'ne [kōnvāntsyō'nā] *sf* (*DIR*) agreement; (*nella società*) convention; **le** ~**i (sociali)** social conventions.

convergen'te [kōnvārjen'tā] *ag* convergent.

convergen'za [kōnvārjen'tsà] *sf* convergence.

conver'gere [kōnver'jārā] *vi* to converge.

conver'sa *sf* (*REL*) lay sister.

conversa're *vi* to have a conversation, converse.

conversazio'ne [kōnvārsàttsyō'nā] *sf* conversation; **fare** ~ (*chiacchierare*) to chat, have a chat.

conversio'ne *sf* conversion; ~ **ad U** (*AUT*) U-turn.

conver'so, a *pp di* **convergere**; **per** ~ *av* conversely.

converti're *vt* (*trasformare*) to change; (*POL, REL*) to convert; ~**rsi** *vr*: ~**rsi (a)** to be converted (to).

converti'to, a *sm/f* convert.

convertito're *sm* (*ELETTR*) converter.

conves'so, a *ag* convex.

convincen'te [kōnvēnchen'tā] *ag* convincing.

convin'cere [kōnvēn'chārā] *vt* to convince; ~ **qn di qc** to convince sb of sth; (*DIR*) to prove sb guilty of sth; ~ **qn a fare qc** to persuade sb to do sth.

convin'to, a *pp di* **convincere** ♦ *ag*: **reo** ~ (*DIR*) convicted criminal.

convinzio'ne [kōnvēntsyō'nā] *sf* conviction, firm belief.

convissu'to, a *pp di* **convivere**.

convita'to, a *sm/f* guest.

convit'to *sm* (*INS*) boarding school.

conviven'za [kōnvēven'tsà] *sf* living together; (*DIR*) cohabitation.

convi'vere *vi* to live together.

convivia'le *ag* convivial.

convoca're *vt* to call, convene; (*DIR*) to summon.

convocazio'ne [kōnvōkàttsyō'nā] *sf* meeting;

summons *sg*; **lettera di** ~ (letter of) notification to appear *o* attend.

convoglia're [kōnvōlyà'rā] *vt* to convey; (*dirigere*) to direct, send.

convo'glio [kōnvol'yō] *sm* (*di veicoli*) convoy; (*FERR*) train; ~ **funebre** funeral procession.

convola're *vi*: ~ **a (giuste) nozze** (*scherzoso*) to tie the knot.

convulsio'ne *sf* convulsion.

convul'so, a *ag* (*pianto*) violent, convulsive; (*attività*) feverish.

COOP. *abbr f* = **cooperativa.**

coopera're *vi*: ~ **(a)** to cooperate (in).

cooperati'va *sf* cooperative.

cooperazio'ne [kōōpāràttsyō'nā] *sf* cooperation.

coordina're *vt* to coordinate.

coordina'te *sfpl* (*MAT, GEO*) coordinates.

coordina'ti *smpl* (*MODA*) coordinates.

coordinazio'ne [kōōrdēnàttsyō'nā] *sf* coordination.

Copenha'gen [kōpānà'gàn] *sf* Copenhagen.

coper'chio [kōper'kyō] *sm* cover; (*di pentola*) lid.

coper'ta *sf* cover; (*di lana*) blanket; (*da viaggio*) lap robe (*US*), rug (*Brit*); (*NAUT*) deck.

coperti'na *sf* (*STAMPA*) cover, jacket.

coper'to, a *pp di* **coprire** ♦ *ag* covered; (*cielo*) overcast ♦ *sm* place setting; (*posto a tavola*) place; (*al ristorante*) cover charge; ~ **di** covered in *o* with.

coperto'ne *sm* (*telo impermeabile*) tarpaulin; (*AUT*) rubber tire.

copertu'ra *sf* (*anche ECON, MIL*) cover; (*di edificio*) roofing; **fare un gioco di** ~ (*SPORT*) to play a defensive game; ~ **assicurativa** insurance coverage (*US*) *o* cover (*Brit*).

co'pia *sf* copy; (*FOT*) print; **brutta/bella** ~ rough/final copy; ~ **conforme** (*DIR*) certified copy; ~ **omaggio** presentation copy.

copia're *vt* to copy.

copiatri'ce [kōpyàtrē'chà] *sf* copier, copying machine.

copio'ne *sm* (*CINEMA, TEATRO*) script.

cop'pa *sf* (*bicchiere*) goblet; (*per frutta, gelato*) dish; (*trofeo*) cup, trophy; ~**e** *sfpl* (*CARTE*) suit in Neapolitan pack of cards; ~ **dell'olio** oil pan (*US*) *o* sump (*Brit*).

cop'pia *sf* (*di persone*) couple; (*di animali, SPORT*) pair.

coprica'po *sm* headgear; (*cappello*) hat.

coprifuo'co, chi *sm* curfew.

coprilet'to *sm* bedspread.

copri're *vt* to cover; (*occupare: carica, posto*) to hold; ~**rsi** *vr* (*cielo*) to cloud over; (*vestirsi*) to wrap up, cover up; (*ECON*) to cover o.s.; ~**rsi di** (*macchie, muffa*) to become covered in; ~ **qn di baci** to smother sb with kisses; ~ **le spese** to break even; ~**rsi**

le spalle (*fig*) to cover o.s.

coque |kok| *sf*: **uovo alla** ~ boiled egg.

corag'gio |kōrád'jō| *sm* courage, bravery; ~! (*forza!*) come on!; (*animo!*) cheer up!; **farsi** ~ to pluck up courage; **hai un bel** ~! (*sfacciataggine*) you've got a nerve *o* a cheek!

coraggio'so, a |kōrádjō'sō| *ag* courageous, brave.

cora'le *ag* choral; (*approvazione*) unanimous.

coral'lo *sm* coral; **il mar dei C**~**i** the Coral Sea.

cora'no *sm* (*REL*) Koran.

coraz'za |kōrát'tsá| *sf* armor (*US*), armour (*Brit*); (*di animali*) carapace, shell; (*MIL*) armo(u)r(-plating).

corazza'to, a |kōráttsà'tō| *ag* (*MIL*) armored (*US*), armoured (*Brit*) ♦ *sf* battleship.

corazzie're |kōráttsyc'rā| *sm* (*STORIA*) cuirassier; (*guardia presidenziale*) *carabiniere of the President's guard*.

corbelleri'a *sf* stupid remark; ~**e** *sfpl* (*sciocchezze*) nonsense *q*.

cor'da *sf* cord; (*fune*) rope; (*spago, MUS*) string; **dare** ~ **a qn** (*fig*) to let sb have his (*o* her) way; **tenere sulla** ~ **qn** (*fig*) to keep sb on tenterhooks; **tagliare la** ~ (*fig*) to slip away, sneak off; **essere giù di** ~ to feel down; ~**e vocali** vocal cords.

corda'ta *sf* (*ALPINISMO*) roped party.

cordia'le *ag* cordial, warm ♦ *sm* (*bevanda*) cordial.

cordialità *sf inv* warmth, cordiality; ~ *sfpl* (*saluti*) best wishes.

cordo'glio |kōrdol'yō| *sm* grief; (*lutto*) mourning.

cordo'ne *sm* cord, string; (*linea: di polizia*) cordon; ~ **ombelicale** umbilical cord; ~ **sanitario** quarantine line.

Core'a *sf*: **la** ~ Korea; **la** ~ **del Nord/Sud** North/South Korea.

corea'no, a *ag*, *sm/f* Korean.

coreografi'a *sf* choreography.

coreo'grafo, a *sm/f* choreographer.

coria'ceo, a |kōryà'chāō| *ag* (*BOT, ZOOL*) coriaceous; (*fig*) tough.

corian'dolo *sm* (*BOT*) coriander; ~**i** *smpl* (*per carnevale etc*) confetti *q*.

corica're *vt* to put to bed; ~**rsi** *vr* to go to bed.

coricherò *etc* |kōrēkàro'| *vb vedi* **coricare**.

Corin'to *sf* Corinth.

cori'sta, i, e *sm/f* (*REL*) choir member, chorister; (*TEATRO*) member of the chorus.

cor'na *sfpl vedi* **corno**.

cornac'chia |kōrnàk'kyà| *sf* crow.

cornamu'sa *sf* bagpipes *pl*.

cor'nea *sf* (*ANAT*) cornea.

cor'ner *sm inv* (*CALCIO*) corner (kick); **salvarsi in** ~ (*fig: in gara, esame etc*) to get

through by the skin of one's teeth.

cornet'ta *sf* (*MUS*) cornet; (*TEL*) receiver.

cornet'to *sm* (*CUC*) croissant; ~ **acustico** ear trumpet.

corni'ce |kōrnc'chā| *sf* frame; (*fig*) background, setting.

cornicio'ne |kōrnēchō'nā| *sm* (*di edificio*) ledge; (*ARCHIT*) cornice.

cor'no *sm* (*ZOOL*: *pl*(*f*) ~**a**, *MUS*) horn; (*fam*): **fare le** ~**a a qn** to be unfaithful to sb; **dire peste e** ~**a di qn** to call sb every name under the sun; **un** ~! not on your life!

Cornova'glia |kōrnōvàl'yà| *sf*: **la** ~ Cornwall.

cornu'to, a *ag* (*con corna*) horned; (*fam!*: *marito*) cuckolded ♦ *sm* (*fam!*) cuckold; (*: insulto*) bastard (*!*).

co'ro *sm* chorus; (*REL*) choir.

corolla'rio *sm* corollary.

coro'na *sf* crown; (*di fiori*) wreath.

coronamen'to *sm* (*di impresa*) completion; (*di carriera*) crowning achievement; **il** ~ **dei propri sogni** the fulfilment of one's dreams.

corona're *vt* to crown.

corona'ria *sf* coronary artery.

cor'po *sm* body; (*cadavere*) (dead) body; (*militare, diplomatico*) corps *inv*; (*di opere*) corpus; **prendere** ~ to take shape; **darsi anima e** ~ **a** to give o.s. heart and soul to; **a** ~ **a** ~ hand-to-hand; ~ **d'armata** army corps; ~ **di ballo** corps de ballet; ~ **dei carabinieri** ≈ police force; ~ **celeste** heavenly body; ~ **di guardia** (*soldati*) guard; (*locale*) guardroom; ~ **insegnante** teaching staff; ~ **del reato** material evidence.

corpora'le *ag* bodily; (*punizione*) corporal.

corporatu'ra *sf* build, physique.

corporazio'ne |kōrpōráttsyō'nā| *sf* corporation.

corpo'reo, a *ag* bodily, physical.

corpo'so, a *ag* (*vino*) full-bodied.

corpulen'to, a *ag* stout, corpulent.

corpulen'za |kōrpōōlcn'tsà| *sf* stoutness, corpulence.

corpu'scolo *sm* corpuscle.

correda're *vt*: ~ **di** to provide *o* furnish with; **domanda corredata dai seguenti documenti** application accompanied by the following documents.

corre'do *sm* equipment; (*di sposa*) trousseau.

correg'gere |kōrrcd'jārā| *vt* to correct; (*compiti*) to correct, mark.

corren'te *ag* (*fiume*) flowing; (*acqua del rubinetto*) running; (*moneta, prezzo*) current; (*comune*) everyday ♦ *sm*: **essere al** ~ **(di)** to be well-informed (about) ♦ *sf* (*movimento di liquido*) current, stream; (*spiffero*) draught; (*ELETTR, METEOR*) current; (*fig*) trend, tendency; **mettere al** ~ **(di)** to inform (of); **la vostra lettera del 5** ~ **mese** (*in lettere commerciali*) in your letter of the 5th inst.;

articoli di qualità ~ average-quality products; ~ **alternata (c.a.)** alternating current (AC); ~ **continua (c.c.)** direct current (DC).

correntemen'te av (comunemente) commonly; **parlare una lingua** ~ to speak a language fluently.

correnti'sta, i, e sm/f (checking (US) o current (Brit)) account holder.

corre'o, a sm/f (DIR) accomplice.

cor'rere vi to run; (precipitarsi) to rush; (partecipare a una gara) to race, run; (fig: diffondersi) to go round ♦ vt (SPORT: gara) to compete in; (rischio) to run; (pericolo) to face; ~ **dietro a qn** to run after sb; **corre voce che** ... it is rumoured that ....

corresponsabilità sf joint responsibility; (DIR) joint liability.

corresponsio'ne sf payment.

corres'si etc vb vedi **correggere.**

correttez'za [kŏrrăttăt'tsá] sf (di comportamento) correctness; (SPORT) fair play.

corret'to, a pp di **correggere** ♦ ag (comportamento) correct, proper; **caffè** ~ **al cognac** coffee laced with brandy.

corretto're, tri'ce sm/f: ~ **di bozze** proofreader ♦ sm: **(liquido)** ~ correction fluid.

correzio'ne [kŏrrăttsyŏ'nă] sf correction; marking; ~ **di bozze** proofreading.

corri'da sf bullfight.

corrido'io sm corridor; **manovre di** ~ (POL) lobbying sg.

corrido're sm (SPORT) runner; (: su veicolo) racer.

corrie'ra sf bus, coach (Brit).

corrie're sm (diplomatico, di guerra) courier; (posta) mail, post (Brit); (spedizioniere) carrier.

corrima'no sm handrail.

corrispetti'vo sm amount due; **versare a qn il** ~ **di una prestazione** to pay sb the amount due for his (o her) services.

corrisponden'te ag corresponding ♦ sm/f correspondent.

corrisponden'za [kŏrrĕspŏndĕn'tsá] sf correspondence; ~ **in arrivo/partenza** incoming/ outgoing mail.

corrispon'dere vi (equivalere): ~ **(a)** to correspond (to); (per lettera): ~ **con** to correspond with ♦ vt (stipendio) to pay; (fig: amore) to return.

corrispo'sto, a pp di **corrispondere.**

corrobora're vt to strengthen, fortify; (fig) to corroborate, bear out.

corro'dere vt, ~**rsi** vr to corrode.

corrom'pere vt to corrupt; (comprare) to bribe.

corrosio'ne sf corrosion.

corrosi'vo, a ag corrosive.

corro'so, a pp di **corrodere.**

corrot'to, a pp di **corrompere** ♦ ag corrupt.

corrucciar'si [kŏrrŏŏchàr'sē] vr to grow angry o vexed.

corruga're vt to wrinkle; ~ **la fronte** to knit one's brows.

corrup'pi etc vb vedi **corrompere.**

corrutte'la sf corruption, depravity.

corruzio'ne [kŏrrŏŏttsyŏ'nă] sf corruption; bribery; ~ **di minorenne** (DIR) contributing to the delinquency of a minor (US), corruption of a minor (Brit).

cor'sa sf running q; (gara) race; (di autobus, taxi) journey, trip; **fare una** ~ to run, dash; (SPORT) to run a race; **andare** o **essere di** ~ to be in a hurry; ~ **ad ostacoli** (IPPICA) steeplechase; (ATLETICA) hurdles race.

corsa'ro, a ag: **nave** ~**a** privateer ♦ sm privateer.

cor'si etc vb vedi **correre.**

corsi'a sf (AUT, SPORT) lane; (di ospedale) ward; ~ **preferenziale** ≈ bus lane; ~ **di sorpasso** (AUT) passing (US) o overtaking (Brit) lane.

Cor'sica sf: **la** ~ Corsica.

corsi'vo sm cursive (writing); (TIP) italics pl.

cor'so, a pp di **correre** ♦ ag, sm/f Corsican ♦ sm course; (strada cittadina) principal street; (di unità monetaria) circulation; (di titoli, valori) rate, price; **dar libero** ~ **a** to give free expression to; **in** ~ in progress, under way; (annata) current; ~ **d'acqua** river; stream; (artificiale) waterway; ~ **serale** evening class; **aver** ~ **legale** to be legal tender.

cor'te sf (court)yard; (DIR, regale) court; **fare la** ~ **a qn** to court sb; ~ **d'appello** court of appeal, appellate court (US); ~ **di cassazione** final court of appeal; **C**~ **dei Conti** State audit court; **C**~ **Costituzionale** special court dealing with constitutional and ministerial matters; ~ **marziale** court-martial.

cortec'cia, ce [kŏrtăch'chá] sf bark.

corteggiamen'to [kŏrtădjámăn'tŏ] sm courtship.

corteggia're [kŏrtădjá'rá] vt to court.

corteggiato're [kŏrtădjátŏ'rá] sm suitor.

corte'o sm procession; ~ **funebre** funeral cortège.

corte'se ag courteous.

cortesi'a sf courtesy; **fare una** ~ **a qn** to do sb a favour; **per** ~, **dov'è** ...? excuse me, please, where is ...?

cortigia'no, a [kŏrtĕjá'nŏ] sm/f courtier ♦ sf courtesan.

corti'le sm (court)yard.

corti'na sf curtain; (anche fig) screen.

cortiso'ne sm cortisone.

cor'to, a ag short ♦ av: **tagliare** ~ to come straight to the point; **essere a** ~ **di qc** to be short of sth; **essere a** ~ **di parole** to be at a loss for words; **la settimana** ~**a** the 5-day week; ~ **circuito** short-circuit.

cortocircu'ito [kŏrtōchĕrkōō'ētō] *sm* ≐ **corto circuito**.

cortometrag'gio [kōrtōmātrád'jō] *sm* short (feature film).

corvi'no, a *ag* (*capelli*) jet-black.

cor'vo *sm* raven.

co'sa *sf* thing; (*faccenda*) affair, matter, business *q*; **(che) ~?** what?; **(che) cos'è?** what is it?; **a ~ pensi?** what are you thinking about?; **tante belle ~e!** all the best!; **ormai è ~ fatta!** (*positivo*) it's in the bag!; (*negativo*) it's done now!; **a ~e fatte** when it's all over.

co'sca, sche *sf* (*di mafiosi*) clan.

co'scia, sce [kosh'shá] *sf* thigh; **~ di pollo** (*CUC*) chicken leg.

coscien'te [kōshen'tā] *ag* conscious; **~ di** conscious *o* aware of.

coscien'za [kōshen'tsá] *sf* conscience; (*consapevolezza*) consciousness; **~ politica** political awareness.

coscienzio'so, a [kōshāntsyō'sō] *ag* conscientious.

cosciot'to [kōshot'tō] *sm* (*CUC*) leg.

coscrit'to *sm* (*MIL*) conscript.

coscrizio'ne [kōskrēttsyō'nā] *sf* conscription.

così *av* so; (*in questo modo*) like this, like that ♦ *ag inv* (*tale*): **non ho mai visto un film ~** I've never seen such a film ♦ *cong* (*perciò*) so, therefore; **~ lontano** so far away; **un ragazzo ~ intelligente** such an intelligent boy; **~ ... come** as ... as; **non è ~ bravo come te** he's not as good as you; **come stai? — ~** how are you? — so-so; **non ho detto ~** I didn't say that; **e ~ via** and so on; **per ~ dire** so to speak.

cosicché [kōsēkkā'] *cong* so (that).

cosiddet'to, a *ag* so-called.

cosme'si *sf* (*scienza*) cosmetics *sg*; (*prodotti*) cosmetics *pl*; (*trattamento*) beauty treatment.

cosme'tico, a, ci, che *ag, sm* cosmetic.

co'smico, a, ci, che *ag* cosmic.

co'smo *sm* cosmos.

cosmona'uta, i, e *sm/f* cosmonaut.

cosmopoli'ta, i, e *ag* cosmopolitan.

co'so *sm* (*fam*: *oggetto*) thing, thingumajig; (: *aggeggio*) contraption; (: *persona*) what's his name, thingumajig.

cospar'gere [kōspár'jārā] *vt*: **~ di** to sprinkle with.

cospar'so, a *pp di* **cospargere**.

cospet'to *sm*: **al ~ di** in front of; in the presence of.

cospicuità *sf* vast quantity.

cospi'cuo, a *ag* considerable, large.

cospira're *vi* to conspire.

cospirato're, tri'ce *sm/f* conspirator.

cospirazio'ne [kōspēráttsyō'nā] *sf* conspiracy.

cos'si *etc vb vedi* **cuocere**.

Cost. *abbr* = **costituzione**.

co'sta *sf* (*tra terra e mare*) coast(line); (*litorale*) shore; (*pendio*) slope; (*ANAT*) rib; **navigare sotto ~** to hug the coast; **la C~ Azzurra** the French Riviera; **la C~ d'Avorio** the Ivory Coast; **velluto a ~e** corduroy.

costà *av* there.

costan'te *ag* constant; (*persona*) steadfast ♦ *sf* constant.

costan'za [kōstán'tsá] *sf* (*gen*) constancy; (*fermezza*) constancy, steadfastness; **il Lago di C~** Lake Constance.

costa're *vi, vt* to cost; **~ caro** to be expensive, cost a lot; **~ un occhio della testa** to cost a fortune; **costi quel che costi** no matter what.

Co'sta Ri'ca *sf*: **la ~** Costa Rica.

costa'ta *sf* (*CUC*: *di manzo*) ≈ rib roast (*US*), large chop (*Brit*).

costa'to *sm* (*ANAT*) ribs *pl*.

costeggia're [kōstādjá'rā] *vt* to be close to; to run alongside.

coste'i *pronome vedi* **costui**.

costellazio'ne [kōstāllāttsyō'nā] *sf* constellation.

costerna're *vt* to dismay.

costerna'to, a *ag* dismayed.

costernazio'ne [kōstārnáttsyō'nā] *sf* dismay, consternation.

costie'ro, a *ag* coastal, coast *cpd* ♦ *sf* stretch of coast.

costipa'to, a *ag* (*stitico*) constipated.

costitui're *vt* (*comitato, gruppo*) to set up, form; (*collezione*) to put together, build up; (*sog: elementi, parti*: *comporre*) to make up, constitute; (*rappresentare*) to constitute; (*DIR*) to appoint; **~rsi** *vr*: **~rsi (alla polizia)** to give o.s. up (to the police); **~rsi parte civile** (*DIR*) to associate in an action with the public prosecutor for damages; **il fatto non costituisce reato** this is not a crime.

costituti'vo, a *ag* constituent, component; **atto ~** (*DIR*: *di società*) memorandum of association.

costituziona'le [kōstētōōttsyōná'lā] *ag* constitutional.

costituzio'ne [kōstētōōttsyō'nā] *sf* setting up; building up; constitution.

co'sto *sm* cost; **sotto ~** for less than cost price; **a ogni** *o* **qualunque ~, a tutti i ~i** at all costs; **~i di esercizio** running costs; **~i fissi** fixed costs; **~i di gestione** operating costs; **~i di produzione** production costs.

co'stola *sf* (*ANAT*) rib; **ha la polizia alle ~e** the police are hard on his heels.

costolet'ta *sf* (*CUC*) cutlet.

costo'ro *pronome pl vedi* **costui**.

costo'so, a *ag* expensive, costly.

costret'to, a *pp di* **costringere**.

costrin'gere [kōstrēn'jārā] *vt*: ~ **qn a fare qc** to force sb to do sth.

costritti'vo, a *ag* coercive.

costrizio'ne [kōstrēttsyō'nā] *sf* coercion.

costrui're *vt* to construct, build.

costrutti'vo, a *ag* (*EDIL*) building *cpd*; (*fig*) constructive.

costruzio'ne [kōstrōōttsyō'nā] *sf* construction, building; **di ~ inglese** British-made.

costu'i, coste'i, *pl* **costo'ro** *pronome* (*soggetto*) he/she; *pl* they; (*complemento*) him/her; *pl* them; **si può sapere chi è ~?** (*peg*) just who is that fellow?

costu'me *sm* (*uso*) custom; (*foggia di vestire, indumento*) costume; **il buon ~** public morality; **donna di facili ~i** woman of easy morals; **~ da bagno** swimsuit; (*da uomo*) swimming *o* bathing trunks *pl*.

costumi'sta, i, e *sm/f* costume maker, costume designer.

coten'na *sf* bacon rind.

coto'gna [kōtōn'yà] *sf* quince.

cotolet'ta *sf* (*di maiale, montone*) chop; (*di vitello, agnello*) cutlet.

cotona're *vt* (*capelli*) to rat (*US*), backcomb (*Brit*).

coto'ne *sm* cotton; **~ idrofilo** absorbent cotton (*US*), cotton wool (*Brit*).

cotonifi'cio [kōtōnēfē'chō] *sm* cotton mill.

cot'ta *sf* (*REL*) surplice; (*fam: innamoramento*) crush.

cot'timo *sm*: **lavorare a ~** to do piecework.

cot'to, a *pp di* **cuocere** ♦ *ag* cooked; (*fam: innamorato*) head-over-heels in love ♦ *sm* brickwork; **~ a puntino** cooked to perfection; **dirne di ~e e di crude a qn** to call sb every name under the sun; **farne di ~e e di crude** to get in *o* (*US*) *o* up to (*Brit*) all kinds of mischief; **mattone di ~** fired brick; **pavimento in ~** tile floor.

cottu'ra *sf* cooking; (*in forno*) baking; (*in umido*) stewing; **~ a fuoco lento** simmering; **angolo (di) ~** cooking area.

cova're *vt* to hatch; (*fig: malattia*) to be sickening for; (*: odio, rancore*) to nurse ♦ *vi* (*fuoco, fig*) to smolder (*US*), smoulder (*Brit*).

cova'ta *sf* (*anche fig*) brood.

co'vo *sm* den; **~ di terroristi** terrorist base.

covo'ne *sm* sheaf.

coz'za [kot'tsà] *sf* mussel.

cozza're [kōttsà'rā] *vi*: **~ contro** to bang into, collide with.

coz'zo [kot'tsō] *sm* collision.

C.P. *abbr* (= *cartolina postale*) pc; (*POSTA*) *vedi* **casella postale**; (*NAUT*) = **capitaneria (di porto)**; (*DIR*) = **codice penale**.

Craco'via *sf* Cracow.

cram'po *sm* cramp.

cra'nio *sm* skull.

crate're *sm* crater.

cravat'ta *sf* tie; **~ a farfalla** bow tie.

cravatti'no *sm* bow tie.

crean'za [krāān'tsà] *sf* manners *pl*; **per buona ~** out of politeness.

crea're *vt* to create.

creativltà *sf* creativity.

crea'to *sm* creation.

creato're, tri'ce *ag* creative ♦ *sm/f* creator; **un ~ di alta moda** fashion designer; **andare al C~** to go to meet one's maker.

creatu'ra *sf* creature; (*bimbo*) baby, infant.

creazio'ne [krāáttsyō'nā] *sf* creation; (*fondazione*) foundation, establishment.

creb'bi *etc vb vedi* **crescere**.

creden'te *sm/f* (*REL*) believer.

creden'za [krāden'tsà] *sf* belief; (*armadio*) sideboard.

credenzia'li [krādāntsyà'lē] *sfpl* credentials.

cre'dere *vt* to believe ♦ *vi*: **~ in, ~ a** to believe in; **~ qn onesto** to believe sb (to be) honest; **~ che** to believe *o* think that; **~rsi furbo** to think one is clever; **lo credo bene!** I can well believe it!; **fai quello che credi** *o* **come credi** do as you please.

credi'bile *ag* credible, believable.

credibilità *sf* credibility.

crediti'zio, a [krādētēt'tsyō] *ag* credit.

cre'dito *sm* (*anche COMM*) credit; (*reputazione*) esteem, repute; **comprare a ~** to buy on credit; **~ agevolato** easy credit terms; **~ d'imposta** tax credit.

credito're, tri'ce *sm/f* creditor.

cre'do *sm inv* creed.

cre'dulo, a *ag* credulous.

credulo'ne, a *sm/f* simpleton, sucker (*fam*).

cre'ma *sf* cream; (*con uova, zucchero etc*) custard; **~ idratante** moisturizing cream; **~ pasticciera** confectioner's custard; **~ solare** suntan lotion.

crema're *vt* to cremate.

cremato'rio *sm* crematorium.

cremazio'ne [krāmáttsyō'nā] *sf* cremation.

cre'misi *ag inv, sm inv* crimson.

Cremli'no *sm*: **il ~** the Kremlin.

cremone'se *ag* of (*o* from) Cremona.

cremo'so, a *ag* creamy.

cre'pa *sf* crack.

crepac'cio [krāpách'chō] *sm* large crack, fissure; (*di ghiacciaio*) crevasse.

crepacuo're *sm* broken heart.

crepapel'le *av*: **ridere a ~** to split one's sides laughing.

crepa're *vi* (*fam: morire*) to kick the bucket; **~ dalle risa** to split one's sides laughing; **~ dall'invidia** to be green with envy.

crepita're *vi* (*fuoco*) to crackle; (*pioggia*) to patter.

crepiti'o, ii *sm* crackling; pattering.

crepu'scolo *sm* twilight, dusk.

crescen'do [krāshen'dō] *sm* (*MUS*) crescendo.

crescen'te [krāshen'tā] *ag* (*gen*) growing, increasing; (*luna*) waxing.

cre'scere [kresh'shārā] *vi* to grow ♦ *vt* (*figli*) to raise.

cresci'one [krāshō'nā] *sm* watercress.

cre'scita [krāsh'shētā] *sf* growth.

cresciu'to, a [krāshōō'tō] *pp di* **crescere**.

cre'sima *sf* (*REL*) confirmation.

cresima're *vt* to confirm.

cre'spo, a *ag* (*capelli*) frizzy; (*tessuto*) puckered ♦ *sm* crêpe.

cre'sta *sf* crest; (*di polli, uccelli*) crest, comb; **alzare la ~** (*fig*) to become cocky; **abbassare la ~** (*fig*) to climb down; **essere sulla ~ dell'onda** (*fig*) to be riding high.

Cre'ta *sf* Crete.

cre'ta *sf* (*gesso*) chalk; (*argilla*) clay.

crete'se *ag, sm/f* Cretan.

cretina'ta *sf* (*fam*): **dire/fare una ~** to say/do a stupid thing.

creti'no, a *ag* stupid ♦ *sm/f* idiot, fool.

CRI *sigla f* = **Croce Rossa Italiana**.

cric *sm inv* (*TECN*) jack.

cric'ca, che *sf* clique.

cric'co, chi *sm* = **cric**.

crice'to [krēche'tō] *sm* hamster.

crimina'le *ag, sm/f* criminal.

Cri'minalpol. *abbr* = **polizia criminale**.

cri'mine *sm* (*DIR*) crime.

criminologi'a [krēmēnōlōjē'ā] *sf* criminology.

crimino'so, a *ag* criminal.

crina'le *sm* ridge.

cri'ne *sm* horsehair.

crinie'ra *sf* mane.

crip'ta *sf* crypt.

crisante'mo *sm* chrysanthemum.

cri'si *sf inv* crisis; (*MED*) attack, fit; **essere in ~** (*partito, impresa etc*) to be in a state of crisis; **~ energetica** energy crisis; **~ di nervi** attack *o* fit of nerves.

cristalleri'a *sf* (*fabbrica*) crystal glassworks *sg*; (*oggetti*) crystalware.

cristalli'no, a *ag* (*MINERALOGIA*) crystalline; (*fig: suono, acque*) crystal clear ♦ *sm* (*ANAT*) crystalline lens.

cristallizza're [krēstāllēddzā'rā] *vi*, **~rsi** *vr* to crystallize; (*fig*) to become fossilized.

cristal'lo *sm* crystal.

cristiane'simo *sm* Christianity.

cristianità *sf* Christianity; (*i cristiani*) Christendom.

cristia'no, a *ag, sm/f* Christian; **un povero ~** (*fig*) a poor soul *o* beggar; **comportarsi da ~** (*fig*) to behave in a civilized manner.

cri'sto *sm*: **C~** Christ; **(un) povero ~** (a) poor beggar.

crite'rio *sm* criterion; (*buon senso*) (common) sense.

cri'tica, che *sf vedi* **critico**.

critica're *vt* to criticize.

cri'tico, a, ci, che *ag* critical ♦ *sm* critic ♦ *sf* criticism; **la ~a** (*attività*) criticism; (*persone*) the critics *pl*.

critico'ne, a *sm/f* faultfinder.

crivella're *vt*: **~ (di)** to riddle (with).

crivel'lo *sm* riddle.

croccan'te *ag* crisp, crunchy ♦ *sm* (*CUC*) almond crunch.

croc'chia [krok'kyā] *sf* chignon, bun.

croc'chio [krok'kyō] *sm* (*di persone*) small group, cluster.

cro'ce [krō'chā] *sf* cross; **in ~** (*di traverso*) crosswise; (*fig*) on tenterhooks; **mettere in ~** (*anche fig: criticare*) to crucify; (: *tormentare*) to nag to death; **la C~ Rossa** the Red Cross; **~ uncinata** swastika.

crocefig'gere *etc* [krōchāfēd'jārā] = **crocifiggere** *etc*.

crocerossi'na [krōchārōssē'nā] *sf* Red Cross nurse.

crocevi'a [krōchāvē'ā] *sm inv* crossroads *sg*.

crocia'to, a [krōchā'tō] *ag* cross-shaped ♦ *sm* (*anche fig*) crusader ♦ *sf* crusade.

crocic'chio [krōchēk'kyō] *sm* crossroads *sg*.

crocie'ra [krōche'rā] *sf* (*viaggio*) cruise; (*ARCHIT*) transept; **altezza di ~** (*AER*) cruising height; **velocità di ~** (*AER, NAUT*) cruising speed.

crocifig'gere [krōchēfēd'jārā] *vt* to crucify.

crocifissio'ne [krōchēfēssyō'nā] *sf* crucifixion.

crocifis'so, a [krōchēfēs'sō] *pp di* **crocifiggere** ♦ *sm* crucifix.

crogiolar'si [krōjōlār'sē] *vr*: **~ al sole** to bask in the sun.

crogio'lo [krōjo'lō] *sm* crucible; (*fig*) melting pot.

crolla're *vi* to collapse.

crol'lo *sm* collapse; (*di prezzi*) slump, sudden fall.

cro'ma *sf* (*MUS*) eighth note (*US*), quaver (*Brit*).

croma'to, a *ag* chromium-plated.

cro'mo *sm* chrome, chromium.

cromoso'ma, i *sm* chromosome.

cro'naca, che *sf* chronicle; (*STAMPA*) news *sg*; (: *rubrica*) column; (*TV, RADIO*) commentary; **fatto** *o* **episodio di ~** news item; **~ nera** crime news *sg*; crime column.

cro'nico, a, ci, che *ag* chronic.

croni'sta, i *sm* (*STAMPA*) reporter, columnist.

cronisto'ria *sf* chronicle; (*fig: ironico*) blow-by-blow account.

cronologi'a [krōnōlōjē'ā] *sf* chronology.

cronometra're *vt* to time.

crono'metro *sm* chronometer; (*a scatto*) stopwatch.

cro'sta *sf* crust; (*MED*) scab; (*ZOOL*) shell; (*di ghiaccio*) layer; (*fig peg: quadro*) daub.

crosta'cei [krōstā'chāē] *smpl* shellfish.

crosta'ta *sf* (*CUC*) tart.

crosti'no *sm.* (*CUC*) croûton; (: *da antipasto*) canapé.

cruccia're [krōōchá'rā] *vt* to torment, worry; **~rsi** *vr*: **~rsi per** to torment o.s. over.

cruc'cio [krōōch'chō] *sm* worry, torment.

crucia'le [krōōchà'lā] *ag* crucial.

cruciver'ba [krōōchĕvcr'bá] *sm inv* crossword (puzzle).

crude'le *ag* cruel.

crudeltà *sf* cruelty.

cru'do, a *ag* (*non cotto*) raw; (*aspro*) harsh, severe.

cruen'to, a *ag* bloody.

crumi'ro *sm* (*peg*) scab, blackleg (*Brit*).

cru'na *sf* eye (of a needle).

cru'sca *sf* bran.

cruscot'to *sm* (*AUT*) dashboard.

CS *sigla* = *Cosenza*.

C.S. *sigla* (*MIL*) = *comando supremo*; (*AUT*) = *codice della strada*.

c.s. *abbr* = *come sopra*.

CT *sigla* = *Catania*.

c.t. *abbr* = **commissario tecnico**.

Cu'ba *sf* Cuba.

cuba'no, a *ag*, *sm/f* Cuban.

cubet'to *sm* (small) cube; **~ di ghiaccio** ice cube.

cu'bico, a, ci, che *ag* cubic.

cu'bo, a *ag* cubic ♦ *sm* cube; **elevare al ~** (*MAT*) to cube.

cucca'gna [kōōkkàn'yà] *sf*: **paese della ~** land of plenty; **albero della ~** greasy pole (*fig*).

cuccet'ta [kōōchāt'tá] *sf* (*FERR*) couchette; (*NAUT*) berth.

cucchiaia'ta [kōōkkyàyá'tá] *sf* spoonful; table-spoonful.

cucchiai'no [kōōkkyāč'nō] *sm* teaspoon; coffee spoon.

cucchia'io [kōōkkyà'yō] *sm* spoon; (*da tavola*) tablespoon; (*cucchiaiata*) spoonful; table-spoonful.

cuc'cia, ce [kōōch'chà] *sf* dog's bed; **a ~!** down!

cucciola'ta [kōōchōlá'tá] *sf* litter.

cuc'ciolo [kōōch'chōlō] *sm* cub; (*di cane*) puppy.

cuci'na [kōōchē'nà] *sf* (*locale*) kitchen; (*arte culinaria*) cooking, cookery; (*le vivande*) food, cooking; (*apparecchio*) stove; **di ~** (*le-zione*) cooking *cpd*; **~ componibile** fitted kitchen; **~ economica** kitchen range.

cucina're [kōōchēnà'rā] *vt* to cook.

cucini'no [kōōchēnē'nō] *sm* kitchenette.

cuci're [kōōchē'rā] *vt* to sew, stitch; **~ la bocca a qn** (*fig*) to shut sb up.

cuci'to, a [kōōchē'tō] *sm* sewing; (*INS*) sewing, needlework.

cucitri'ce [kōōchētrē'chā] *sf* (*TIP*: *per libri*) stitching machine; (*per fogli*) stapler.

cucitu'ra [kōōchētōō'rà] *sf* sewing, stitching; (*costura*) seam.

cucù *sm inv*, **cucu'lo** *sm* cuckoo.

cuf'fia *sf* bonnet, cap; (*da infermiera*) cap; (*da bagno*) swimming cap; (*per ascoltare*) headphones *pl*, headset.

cugi'no, a [kōōjē'nō] *sm/f* cousin.

cu'i *pronome* (*nei complementi indiretti*): **la persona a ~ accennava** the person you were referring to *o* to whom you referred; **il libro di ~ parlavo** the book I was talking about *o* about which I was talking; **il quartiere in ~ abito** the district where I live; (*inserito tra l'articolo e il sostantivo*) whose; **il ~ nome** whose name; **la ~ madre** whose mother; **per ~** (*perciò*) therefore, so.

culina'ria *sf* cookery.

cul'la *sf* cradle.

culla're *vt* to rock; (*fig: idea, speranza*) to cherish; **~rsi** *vr* (*gen*) to sway; **~rsi in vane speranze** (*fig*) to cherish fond hopes; **~rsi nel dolce far niente** (*fig*) to sit back and relax.

culminan'te *ag*: **posizione ~** (*ASTR*) highest point; **punto** *o* **momento ~** (*fig*) climax.

culmina're *vi*: **~ in** *o* **con** to culminate in.

cul'mine *sm* top, summit.

cu'lo *sm* (*fam!*) ass (*US!*), arse (*Brit!*); (: *fig: fortuna*): **aver ~** to have the luck of the devil; **prendere qn per il ~** to jerk sb around (*US!*), take the piss out of sb (*Brit!*).

cul'to *sm* (*religione*) religion; (*adorazione*) worship, adoration; (*venerazione: anche fig*) cult.

cultu'ra *sf* (*gen*) culture; (*conoscenza*) educa-tion, learning; **di ~** (*persona*) cultured; (*isti-tuto*) cultural, of culture; **~ generale** general knowledge; **~ di massa** mass culture.

cultura'le *ag* cultural.

culturi'smo *sm* body-building.

cumula're *vt* to accumulate, amass.

cumulati'vo, a *ag* cumulative; (*prezzo*) inclu-sive; (*biglietto*) group *cpd*.

cu'mulo *sm* (*mucchio*) pile, heap; (*METEOR*) cumulus; **~ dei redditi** (*FISCO*) combined in-comes; **~ delle pene** (*DIR*) consecutive sentences.

cu'neo *sm* wedge.

cunet'ta *sf* (*di strada etc*) bump; (*scolo: nelle strade di città*) gutter; (: *di campagna*) ditch.

cuni'colo *sm* (*galleria*) tunnel; (*di miniera*) pit, shaft; (*di talpa*) hole.

cuo'ca *sf vedi* **cuoco**.

cuo'cere [kwo'chārā] *vt* (*alimenti*) to cook; (*mattoni etc*) to fire ♦ *vi* to cook; **~ in umido/a vapore/in padella** to stew/steam/fry; **~ al forno** (*pane*) to bake; (*arrosto*) to roast.

cuo'co, a, chi, che *sm/f* cook; (*di ristorante*) chef.

cuoia'me *sm* leather goods *pl.*

cuo'io *sm* leather; ~ **capelluto** scalp; **tirare le ~a** *(fam)* to kick the bucket.

cuo're *sm* heart; **~i** *smpl* (CARTE) hearts; **avere buon** ~ to be kind-hearted; **stare a ~ a qn** to be important to sb; **un grazie di ~** heartfelt thanks; **ringraziare di ~** to thank sincerely; **nel profondo del** ~ in one's heart of hearts; **avere la morte nel** ~ to be sick at heart.

cupidi'gia [kōōpēdē'jà] *sf* greed, covetousness.

cu'po, a *ag* dark; *(suono)* dull; *(fig)* gloomy, dismal.

cu'pola *sf* dome; *(più piccola)* cupola.

cu'ra *sf* care; (MED: *trattamento)* (course of) treatment; **aver ~ di** *(occuparsi di)* to look after; **a ~ di** *(libro)* edited by; **fare una ~** to follow a course of treatment; **~ dimagrante** diet.

cura'bile *ag* curable.

curan'te *ag*: **medico** ~ doctor (in charge of a patient).

cura're *vt* *(malato, malattia)* to treat; (: *guarire)* to cure; *(aver cura di)* to take care of; *(testo)* to edit; **~rsi** *vr* to take care of o.s.; (MED) to follow a course of treatment; **~rsi di** to pay attention to; *(occuparsi di)* to look after.

cura'to *sm* parish priest; *(protestante)* vicar, minister.

curato're, tri'ce *sm/f* (DIR) trustee; *(di antologia etc)* editor; ~ **fallimentare** (official) receiver.

cu'ria *sf* (REL): **la ~ romana** the Roman curia; ~ **notarile** notaries' association *o* guild.

curiosag'gine [kōōryōsàd'jēnā] *sf* nosiness.

curiosa're *vi* to look round, wander round; *(tra libri)* to browse; ~ **nei negozi** to look *o* wander round the shops; ~ **nelle faccende altrui** to poke one's nose into other people's affairs.

curiosità *sf inv* curiosity; *(cosa rara)* curio, curiosity.

curio'so, a *ag* *(che vuol sapere)* curious, inquiring; *(ficcanaso)* curious, inquisitive; *(bizzarro)* strange, curious ♦ *sm/f* busybody, nosy parker; **essere ~ di** to be curious about; **una folla di ~i** a crowd of onlookers.

curri'culum *sm inv*: ~ **(vitae)** curriculum vitae.

curso're *sm* (INFORM) cursor.

cur'va *sf* curve; *(stradale)* bend, curve.

curva're *vt* to bend ♦ *vi* *(veicolo)* to take a bend; *(strada)* to bend, curve; **~rsi** *vr* to bend; *(legno)* to warp.

cur'vo, a *ag* curved; *(piegato)* bent.

CUS *sigla m = Centro Universitario Sportivo.*

cuscinet'to [kōōshēnàt'tō] *sm* pad; (TECN) bearing ♦ *ag inv*: **stato ~** buffer state; ~ **a sfere** ball bearing.

cusci'no [kōōshē'nō] *sm* cushion; *(guanciale)* pillow.

cu'spide *sf* (ARCHIT) spire.

custo'de *sm/f* *(di museo)* keeper, custodian; *(di parco)* warden; *(di casa)* concierge; *(di fabbrica, carcere)* guard.

custo'dia *sf* care; (DIR) custody; *(astuccio)* case, holder; **avere qc in** ~ to look after sth; **dare qc in** ~ **a qn** to entrust sth to sb's care; **agente di** ~ prison guard; ~ **delle carceri** prison security; ~ **cautelare** (DIR) custody.

cu'te *sf* (ANAT) skin.

cuti'cola *sf* cuticle.

C.V. *abbr = cavallo vapore.*

c.v.d. *abbr (= come volevasi dimostrare)* QED *(= quod erat demonstrandum)*.

c.vo *abbr =* **corsivo**.

CZ *sigla = Catanzaro.*

D

D, d [dē] *sf o m inv (lettera)* D, d; **D come Domodossola** ≈ D for Dog.

D *abbr (= destra)* R; (FERR) = **diretto.**

da *prep (da + il =* **dal,** *da + lo =* **dallo,** *da + l' =* **dall',** *da + la =* **dalla,** *da + i =* **dai,** *da + gli =* **dagli,** *da + le =* **dalle)** *(agente)* by; *(provenienza)* from; *(causale)* with; *(moto a luogo: riferito a persone)*: **vado ~ Pietro/dal giornalaio** I'm going to Pietro's (house)/to the newsagent's; *(stato in luogo: riferito a persone)*: **sono ~ Pietro** I'm at Pietro's (house); *(moto per luogo)* through; *(fuori da)* out of, from; *(tempo)*: **vivo qui ~ un anno** I have been living here for a year; **è dalle 3 che ti aspetto** I've been waiting for you since 3 (o'clock); ~ **bambino piangevo molto** I cried a lot as a *o* when I was a child; **qualcosa ~ bere/mangiare** something to drink/eat; **comportarsi ~ bambino** to behave like a child; **una ragazza dai capelli biondi** a girl with blonde hair; **un vestito ~ 100.000 lire** a 100,000 lire dress; **è una cosa ~ poco** it's nothing special; ~ **... a** from ... to; ~ **oggi in poi** from today onwards; **d'ora in poi** *o* **in avanti** from now on; **l'ho fatto ~ me** I did it myself; **non è ~ lui** it's not like him; **macchina ~ corsa** racing car.

dà *vb vedi* **dare.**

dabbe'ne *ag inv* honest, decent.

Dac'ca *sf* Dacca.

dacca'po, da ca'po *av* (*di nuovo*) (once) again; (*dal principio*) all over again, from the beginning.

dacché [dàkkā'] *cong* since.

da'do *sm* (*da gioco*) dice *o* die (*pl* dice); (*CUC*) bouillon cube (*US*), stock cube (*Brit*); (*TECN*) (screw) nut; **~i** *smpl* (game of) dice.

daffa're, da fa're *sm* work, toil; **avere un gran ~** to be very busy.

da'gli [dàl'yē], **dai** *prep + det vedi* **da**.

da'ino *sm* (fallow) deer *inv*; (*pelle*) buckskin.

Dakar' *sf* Dakar.

dal *prep + det vedi* **da**.

dal. *abbr* (= *decalitro*) dal.

dall', dal'la, dal'le, dal'lo *prep + det vedi* **da**.

dalto'nico, a, ci, che *ag* colorblind (*US*), colour-blind (*Brit*).

dam. *abbr* (= *decametro*) dam.

da'ma *sf* lady; (*nei balli*) partner; (*gioco*) checkers *sg* (*US*), draughts *sg* (*Brit*); **far ~** (*nel gioco*) to make a crown; **~ di compagnia** lady's companion; **~ di corte** lady-in-waiting.

Dama'sco *sf* Damascus.

damigel'la [dàmējel'lā] *sf* (*STORIA*) damsel; (*: titolo*) mistress; **~ d'onore** (*di sposa*) bridesmaid.

damigia'na [dàmējá'nà] *sf* demijohn.

damme'no *ag inv*: **per non essere ~ di qn** so as not to be outdone by sb.

DAMS *sigla m* (= *Disciplina delle Arti, della Musica, dello Spettacolo*) *study of the performing arts*.

dana'ro *sm* = **denaro**.

danaro'so, a *ag* wealthy.

dane'se *ag* Danish ♦ *sm/f* Dane ♦ *sm* (*LING*) Danish.

Danimar'ca *sf*: **la ~** Denmark.

danna're *vt* (*REL*) to damn; **~rsi** *vr*: **~rsi (per)** (*fig: tormentarsi*) to be worried to death (by); **far ~ qn** to drive sb mad; **~rsi l'anima per qc** (*affannarsi*) to work o.s. to death for sth; (*tormentarsi*) to worry o.s. to death over sth.

danna'to, a *ag* damned.

dannazio'ne [dànnàttsyō'nā] *sf* damnation.

danneggia're [dànnàdjà'rā] *vt* to damage; (*rovinare*) to spoil; (*nuocere*) to harm; **la parte danneggiata** (*DIR*) the injured party.

dan'no *vb vedi* **dare** ♦ *sm* damage; (*a persona*) harm, injury; **~i** *smpl* (*DIR*) damages; **a ~ di qn** to sb's detriment; **chiedere/risarcire i ~i** to sue for/pay damages.

danno'so, a *ag*: **~ (a *o* per)** harmful (to), bad (for).

dante'sco, a, schi, sche *ag* Dantesque; **l'opera ~a** Dante's work.

Danu'bio *sm*: **il ~** the Danube.

dan'za [dàn'tsà] *sf*: **la ~** dancing; **una ~** a dance.

danzan'te [dàntsàn'tā] *ag* dancing; **serata ~** dance.

danza're [dàntsà'rā] *vt, vi* to dance.

danzato're, tri'ce [dàntsàtō'rā] *sm/f* dancer.

dappertut'to *av* everywhere.

dappo'co *ag inv* inept; worthless.

dappri'ma *av* at first.

Dardanel'li *smpl*: **i ~** the Dardanelles.

dar'do *sm* dart.

da're *sm* (*COMM*) debit ♦ *vt* to give; (*produrre: frutti, suono*) to produce ♦ *vi* (*guardare*): **~ su** to look (out) onto; **~rsi** *vr*: **~rsi a** to dedicate o.s. to; **quanti anni mi dai?** how old do you think I am?; **danno ancora quel film?** is that film still showing?; **~ da mangiare a qn** to give sb something to eat; **~ per certo qc** to consider sth certain; **~ ad intendere a qn che ...** to lead sb to believe that ...; **~ per morto qn** to give sb up for dead; **~ qc per scontato** to take sth for granted; **~rsi ammalato** to report sick; **~rsi alla bella vita** to have a good time; **~rsi al bere** to take to drink; **~rsi al commercio** to go into business; **~rsi da fare per fare qc** to go to a lot of bother to do sth; **~rsi per vinto** to give in; **può ~rsi** maybe, perhaps; **si dà il caso che ...** it so happens that ...; **darsela a gambe** to take to one's heels; **il ~ e l'avere** (*ECON*) debits and credits *pl*.

Dar-es-Sala'am *sf* Dar-es-Salaam.

dar'sena *sf* dock.

da'ta *sf* date; **in ~ da destinarsi** on a date still to be announced; **in ~ odierna** as of today; **amicizia di lunga *o* vecchia ~** long-standing friendship; **~ di emissione** date of issue; **~ di nascita** date of birth; **~ di scadenza** expiration (*US*) *o* expiry (*Brit*) date.

data're *vt* to date ♦ *vi*: **~ da** to date from.

da'to, a *ag* dated.

da'to, a *ag* (*stabilito*) given ♦ *sm* datum; **~i** *smpl* data *pl*; **~ che** given that; **in ~i casi** in certain cases; **è un ~ di fatto** it's a fact.

dato're, tri'ce *sm/f*: **~ di lavoro** employer.

dat'tero *sm* date (*BOT*).

dattilografa're *vt* to type.

dattilografi'a *sf* typing.

dattilo'grafo, a *sm/f* typist.

dattiloscrit'to *sm* typescript.

davan'ti *av* in front; (*dirimpetto*) opposite ♦ *ag inv* front ♦ *sm* front; **~ a** *prep* in front of; (*dirimpetto a*) facing, opposite; (*in presenza di*) before, in front of.

davanza'le [dàvàntsà'lā] *sm* windowsill.

davan'zo, d'avan'zo [dàvàn'tsō] *av* more than enough.

davve'ro *av* really, indeed; **dico ~** I mean it.

dazia'rio, a [dàttsyà'ryō] *ag* excise *cpd*.

da'zio [dàt'tsyō] *sm* (*somma*) duty; (*luogo*) customs *pl*; **~ d'importazione** import duty.

db *abbr* (= *decibel*) dB.

DC *sigla f* = **Democrazia Cristiana**.

d.C. *av abbr* (= *dopo Cristo*) A.D.

DD *abbr* (*FERR*) = **direttissimo**.

D.D.T. *abbr m* (= *dicloro-difenil-tricloroetano*) D.D.T.

de'a *sf* goddess.

deb'bo *etc vb vedi* **dovere**.

debella're *vt* to overcome, conquer.

debilita're *vt* to debilitate.

debitamen'te *av* duly, properly.

de'bito, a *ag* due, proper ♦ *sm* debt; (*COMM: dare*) debit; **a tempo ~** at the right time; **portare a ~ di qn** to debit sb with; **~ consolidato** consolidated debt; **~ d'imposta** tax liability; **~ pubblico** national debt.

debito're, tri'ce *smf* debtor.

de'bole *ag* weak, feeble; (*suono*) faint; (*luce*) dim ♦ *sm* weakness.

debolez'za [dābōlāt'tsà] *sf* weakness.

debuttan'te *smf* (*gen*) beginner, novice; (*TEATRO*) actor/actress at the beginning of his (*o* her) career.

debutta're *vi* to make one's début.

debut'to *sm* début.

de'cade *sf* period of ten days.

decaden'te *ag* decadent.

decaden'za [dākáden'tsà] *sf* decline; (*DIR*) loss, forfeiture.

decadu'to, a *ag* (*persona*) impoverished; (*norma*) lapsed.

decaffeina'to, a *ag* decaffeinated.

deca'logo *sm* (*fig*) rulebook.

deca'no *sm* (*REL*) dean.

decanta're *vt* (*virtù, bravura etc*) to praise; (*persona*) to sing the praises of.

decapita're *vt* to decapitate, behead.

decappotta'bile *ag, sf* convertible.

decedu'to, a [dāchādōo'tō] *ag* deceased.

decelera're [dāchālārá'rā] *vt, vi* to decelerate, slow down.

decenna'le [dāchānnà'lā] *ag* (*che dura 10 anni*) ten-year *cpd*; (*che ricorre ogni 10 anni*) ten-yearly, every ten years ♦ *sm* (*ricorrenza*) tenth anniversary.

decen'ne [dāchen'nā] *ag*: **un bambino ~** a ten-year-old child, a child of ten.

decen'nio [dāchen'nyō] *sm* decade.

decen'te [dāchen'tā] *ag* decent, respectable, proper; (*accettabile*) satisfactory, decent.

decentralizza're [dāchāntrálēddzá'rā] *vt* (*AMM*) to decentralize.

decentramen'to [dāchāntrámān'tō] *sm* decentralization.

decentra're [dāchāntrá'rā] *vt* to decentralize, move out of *o* away from the center.

decen'za [dāchen'tsà] *sf* decency, propriety.

deces'so [dāches'sō] *sm* death; **atto di ~** death certificate.

deci'dere [dāchē'dārā] *vi* to decide, make up one's mind ♦ *vt*: **~ qc** to decide on sth; (*questione, lite*) to settle sth; **~rsi** *vr*: **~rsi (a fare)** to decide (to do), make up one's mind (to do); **~ di fare/che** to decide to do/that; **~ di qc** (*sog: cosa*) to determine sth.

decifra're [dāchēfrá'rā] *vt* to decode; (*fig*) to decipher, make out.

deci'litro [dāchē'lētrō] *sm* deciliter (*US*), decilitre (*Brit*).

decima'le [dāchēmá'lā] *ag* decimal.

decima're [dāchēmá'rā] *vt* to decimate.

de'cimo, a [de'chēmō] *num* tenth.

deci'na [dāchē'nà] *sf* ten; (*circa dieci*): **una ~ (di)** about ten.

deci'si [dāchē'zē] *etc vb vedi* **decidere**.

decisiona'le [dāchēzyōná'lā] *ag* decision-making *cpd*.

decisio'ne [dāchēzyō'nā] *sf* decision; **prendere una ~** to make a decision; **con ~** decisively, resolutely.

decisi'vo, a [dāchēzē'vō] *ag* (*gen*) decisive; (*fattore*) deciding.

deci'so, a [dāchē'zō] *pp di* **decidere** ♦ *ag* (*persona, carattere*) determined; (*tono*) firm, resolute.

declassa're *vt* to downgrade; to lower in status; **1ª declassata** (*FERR*) first-class carriage which may be used by second-class passengers.

declina're *vi* (*pendio*) to slope down; (*fig: diminuire*) to decline; (*tramontare*) to set, go down ♦ *vt* to decline; **~ le proprie generalità** (*fig*) to give one's particulars; **~ ogni responsabilità** to disclaim all responsibility.

declinazio'ne [dāklēnáttsyō'nā] *sf* (*LING*) declension.

decli'no *sm* decline.

decli'vio *sm* (downward) slope.

decodifica're *vt* to decode.

decolla're *vi* (*AER*) to take off.

décolleté [dākōltā'] *ag inv* (*abito*) low-necked, low-cut ♦ *sm* (*di abito*) low neckline; (*di donna*) cleavage.

decol'lo *sm* take-off.

decolora're *vt* to bleach.

decompor're *vt*, **decomporsi** *vr* to decompose.

decomposizio'ne [dākōmpōzēttsyō'nā] *sf* decomposition.

decompo'sto, a *pp di* **decomporre**.

decompressio'ne *sf* decompression.

decongela're [dākōnjālā'rā] *vt* to defrost.

decongestiona're [dākōnjāstyōná'rā] *vt* (*MED, traffico*) to relieve congestion in.

decora're *vt* to decorate.

decorati'vo, a *ag* decorative.

decorato're, tri'ce *smf* (interior) decorator.

decorazio'ne [dākōráttsyō'nā] *sf* decoration.

deco'ro *sm* decorum.

decoro'so, a *ag* decorous, dignified.

decorren'za [dākōrren'tsá] *sf*: **con** ~ **da** (as) from.

decor'rere *vi* to pass, elapse; (*avere effetto*) to run, have effect.

decor'so, a *pp di* **decorrere** ♦ *sm* (*evoluzione: anche MED*) course.

decreb'bi *etc vb vedi* **decrescere**.

decre'pito, a *ag* decrepit.

decre'scere [dākrāsh'shārā] *vi* (*diminuire*) to decrease, diminish; (*acque*) to subside, go down; (*prezzi*) to go down.

decresciu'to, a [dākrāshōō'tō] *pp di* **decrescere**.

decreta're *vt* (*norma*) to decree; (*mobilitazione*) to order; ~ **lo stato d'emergenza** to declare a state of emergency; ~ **la nomina di qn** to decide on the appointment of sb.

decre'to *sm* decree; ~ **legge** *decree with the force of law*; ~ **di sfratto** eviction order.

decurta're *vt* (*debito, somma*) to reduce.

decurtazio'ne [dākōōrtáttsyō'nā] *sf* reduction.

de'dalo *sm* maze, labyrinth.

de'dica, che *sf* dedication.

dedica're *vt* to dedicate; ~**rsi** *vr*: ~**rsi a** (*votarsi*) to devote o.s. to.

dedicherò *etc* [dādēkāro'] *vb vedi* **dedicare**.

de'dito, a *ag*: ~ **a** (*studio etc*) dedicated *o* devoted to; (*vizio*) addicted to.

dedot'to, a *pp di* **dedurre**.

dedu'co *etc vb vedi* **dedurre**.

dedur're *vt* (*concludere*) to deduce; (*defalcare*) to deduct.

dedus'si *etc vb vedi* **dedurre**.

defalca're *vt* to deduct.

defenestra're *vt* to throw out of the window; (*fig*) to remove from office.

deferen'te *ag* respectful, deferential.

deferi're *vt* (*DIR*): ~ **a** to refer to.

defezio'ne [dāfättsyō'nā] *sf* defection, desertion.

deficien'te [dāfēchen'tā] *ag* (*mancante*): ~ **di** deficient in; (*insufficiente*) insufficient ♦ *sm/f* mental defective; (*peg: cretino*) idiot.

deficien'za [dāfēchen'tsá] *sf* deficiency; (*carenza*) shortage; (*fig: lacuna*) weakness.

de'ficit [de'fēchēt] *sm inv* (*ECON*) deficit.

defini're *vt* to define; (*risolvere*) to settle; (*questione*) to finalize.

definiti'vo, a *ag* definitive, final ♦ *sf*: **in ~a** (*dopotutto*) when all is said and done; (*dunque*) well then.

defini'to, a *ag* definite; **ben** ~ clear, clear cut.

definizio'ne [dāfēnēttsyō'nā] *sf* (*gen*) definition; (*di disputa, vertenza*) settlement; (*di tempi, obiettivi*) establishment.

deflagrazio'ne [dāflágráttsyō'nā] *sf* explosion.

deflazio'ne [dāflāttsyō'nā] *sf* (*ECON*) deflation.

defletto're *sm* (*AUT*) deflector (*US*), quarter-

light (*Brit*).

deflui're *vi*: ~ **da** (*liquido*) to flow away from; (*fig: capitali*) to flow out of.

deflus'so *sm* (*della marea*) ebb.

deforma're *vt* (*alterare*) to put out of shape; (*corpo*) to deform; (*pensiero, fatto*) to distort; ~**rsi** *vr* to lose its shape.

deformazio'ne [dāfōrmáttsyō'nā] *sf* (*MED*) deformation; **questa è** ~ **professionale!** that's force of habit because of your (*o* his *etc*) job!

defor'me *ag* deformed; disfigured.

deformità *sf inv* deformity.

defrauda're *vt*: ~ **qn di qc** to defraud sb of sth, cheat sb out of sth.

defun'to, a *ag* late *cpd* ♦ *sm/f* deceased.

degenera're [dājānārá'rā] *vi* to degenerate.

degenerazio'ne [dājānāráttsyō'nā] *sf* degeneration.

dege'nere [dājc'nārā] *ag* degenerate.

degen'te [dājen'tā] *sm/f* bedridden person; (*ricoverato in ospedale*) in-patient.

degen'za [dājen'tsá] *sf* confinement to bed; ~ **ospedaliera** period in hospital.

de'gli [dāl'yē] *prep + det vedi* **di**.

degluti're *vt* to swallow.

degnar'si [dānyár'sē] *vr*: ~ **di fare** to deign *o* condescend to do.

de'gno, a [dān'yō] *ag* dignified; ~ **di** worthy of; ~ **di lode** praiseworthy.

degrada're *vt* (*MIL*) to demote; (*privare della dignità*) to degrade; ~**rsi** *vr* to demean o.s.

degra'do *sm*: ~ **urbano** urban decline.

degusta're *vt* to sample, taste.

degustazio'ne [dāgōōstáttsyō'nā] *sf* sampling, tasting; ~ **di vini** (*locale*) specialty (*US*) *o* specialist (*Brit*) wine bar; ~ **di caffè** (*locale*) specialty (*US*) *o* specialist (*Brit*) coffee shop.

de'i *smpl di* **dio** ♦ *prep + det vedi* **di**.

del *prep + det vedi* **di**.

delato're, tri'ce *sm/f* police informer.

de'lega, ghe *sf* (*procura*) proxy; **per** ~ **notarile** ≈ through a lawyer.

delega're *vt* to delegate.

delega'to *sm* delegate.

delegazio'ne [dālāgáttsyō'nā] *sf* delegation.

delegherò *etc* [dālāgáro'] *vb vedi* **delegare**.

delete'rio, a *ag* deleterious, noxious.

delfi'no *sm* (*ZOOL*) dolphin; (*STORIA*) dauphin; (*fig*) probable successor.

Del'hi [de'lē] *sf* Delhi.

deli'bera *sf* decision.

delibera're *vt* to come to a decision on ♦ *vi* (*DIR*): ~ (**su qc**) to rule (on sth).

delicatez'za [dālēkátát'tsá] *sf* delicacy; frailty; thoughtfulness; tactfulness.

delica'to, a *ag* delicate; (*salute*) delicate, frail; (*fig: gentile*) thoughtful, considerate; (*: che dimostra tatto*) tactful.

delimita're *vt* (*anche fig*) to delimit.

delinea're *vt* to outline; ~**rsi** *vr* to be outlined; (*fig*) to emerge.

delinquen'te *sm/f* criminal, delinquent.

delinquen'za |dālēnkwcn'tsá| *sf* criminality, delinquency; ~ **minorile** juvenile delinquency.

deli'quio *sm* (*MED*) swoon; **cadere in** ~ to swoon.

deliran'te *ag* (*MED*) delirious; (*fig: folla*) frenzied; (: *discorso, mente*) insane.

delira're *vi* to be delirious, rave; (*fig*) to rave.

deli'rio *sm* delirium; (*ragionamento insensato*) raving; (*fig*): **andare/mandare in** ~ to go/send into a frenzy.

delit'to *sm* crime; ~ **d'onore** *crime committed to avenge one's honor*.

delittuo'so, a *ag* criminal.

deli'zia |dālēt'tsyá| *sf* delight.

delizia're |dālēttsyà'rā| *vt* to delight; ~**rsi** *vr*: ~**rsi di qc/a fare qc** to take delight in sth/in doing sth.

delizio'so, a |dālēttsyō'sō| *ag* delightful; (*cibi*) delicious.

dell', del'la, del'le, del'lo *prep* + *det vedi* **di**.

del'ta *sm inv* delta.

deltapla'no *sm* hang-glider; **volo col** ~ hang-gliding.

delucidazio'ne |dālōōchēdàttsyō'nā| *sf* clarification *q*.

deluden'te *ag* disappointing.

delu'dere *vt* to disappoint.

delu'si *etc vb vedi* **deludere**.

delusio'ne *sf* disappointment.

delu'so, a *pp di* **deludere** ♦ *ag* disappointed.

demago'gico, a, ci, che |dāmàgo'jēkō| *ag* popularity-seeking, demagogic.

demago'go, ghi *sm* demagogue.

dema'nio *sm* government property.

demen'te *ag* (*MED*) demented, mentally deranged; (*fig*) crazy, mad.

demen'za |dāmen'tsá| *sf* dementia; madness; ~ **senile** senile dementia.

demenzia'le |dāmàntsyá'lā| *ag* insane.

dem'mo *vb vedi* **dare**.

democra'tico, a, ci, che *ag* democratic.

democrazi'a |dāmōkràttsē'á| *sf* democracy; **la D~ Cristiana** the Christian Democrat Party.

democristia'no, a *ag, sm/f* Christian Democrat.

demografi'a *sf* demography.

demogra'fico, a, ci, che *ag* demographic; **incremento** ~ increase in population.

demoli're *vt* to demolish.

demolizio'ne |dāmōlēttsyō'nā| *sf* demolition.

de'mone *sm* demon.

demo'nio *sm* demon, devil; **il D~** the Devil.

demoralizza're |dāmōrálēddzà'rā| *vt* to demoralize; ~**rsi** *vr* to become demoralized.

demotiva're *vt*: ~ **qn** to take away sb's motivation.

demotiva'to, a *ag* unmotivated, lacking motivation.

dena'ro *sm* money; ~**i** *smpl* (*CARTE*) suit in *Neapolitan pack of cards*.

denatura'to, a *ag vedi* **alcool**.

denigra're *vt* to denigrate, run down.

denomina're *vt* to name; ~**rsi** *vr* to be named *o* called.

denominato're *sm* (*MAT*) denominator.

denominazio'ne |dānōmēnàttsyō'nā| *sf* name; denomination; ~ **di origine controllata** (**D.O.C.**) *label guaranteeing the quality and origin of a wine*.

denota're *vt* to denote, indicate.

densità *sf inv* density; (*di nebbia*) thickness, denseness; **ad alta/bassa** ~ **di popolazione** densely/sparsely populated.

den'so, a *ag* thick, dense.

denta'le *ag* dental.

denta'rio, a *ag* dental.

dentatu'ra *sf* set of teeth, teeth *pl*; (*TECN: di ruota*) serration.

den'te *sm* tooth; (*di forchetta*) prong; (*GEO: cima*) jagged peak; **al** ~ (*CUC: pasta*) *cooked so as to be firm when eaten*; **mettere i** ~**i** to teethe; **mettere qc sotto i** ~**i** to have a bite to eat; **avere il** ~ **avvelenato contro** *o* **con qn** to bear sb a grudge; ~ **di leone** (*BOT*) dandelion; ~**i del giudizio** wisdom teeth.

den'tice |dcn'tēchā| *sm* (*ZOOL*) sea bream.

dentie'ra *sf* (set of) false teeth *pl*.

dentifri'cio |dāntēfrē'chō| *sm* toothpaste.

denti'sta, i, e *sm/f* dentist.

den'tro *av* inside; (*in casa*) indoors; (*fig: nell'intimo*) inwardly ♦ *prep*: ~ **(a)** in; **piegato in** ~ folded over; **qui/là** ~ in here/there; ~ **di sé** (*pensare, brontolare*) to oneself; **tenere tutto** ~ to keep everything bottled up (inside o.s.); **darci** ~ (*fig fam*) to slog away, work hard.

denuclearizza'to, a |dānōōklàārēddzà'tō| *ag* denuclearized, nuclear-free.

denuda're *vt* (*persona*) to strip; (*parte del corpo*) to bare; ~**rsi** *vr* to strip.

denun'cia, ce *o* **cie** |dānōōn'chà|, **denun'zia** |dā'nōōntsyà| *sf* denunciation; declaration; **fare una** ~ *o* **sporgere** ~ **contro qn** (*DIR*) to report sb to the police; ~ **del reddito** (*income*) tax return.

denuncia're |dānōōnchá'rā|, **denunzia're** |dānōōn'tsyàrā| *vt* to denounce; (*dichiarare*) to declare; ~ **qn/qc (alla polizia)** to report sb/sth to the police.

denutri'to, a *ag* undernourished.

denutrizio'ne |dānōōtrēttsyō'nā| *sf* malnutrition.

deodoran'te *sm* deodorant.

deontologi'a |dāōntōlōjē'á| *sf* (*professionale*) professional code of conduct.

depenalizzazio'ne |dāpānálēddzàttsyō'nā| *sf*

decriminalization.

dépendan'ce [dāpåńdåńs'] *sf inv* outbuilding.

deperi'bile *ag* perishable; **merce** ~ perishables *pl*, perishable goods *pl*.

deperimen'to *sm* (*di persona*) wasting away; (*di merci*) deterioration.

deperi're *vi* to waste away.

depilato'rio, a *ag* hair-removing, depilatory ♦ *sm* hair remover, depilatory.

depilazio'ne [dāpēlåttsyō'nå] *sf* hair removal, depilation.

dépliant' [dāplēåń'] *sm inv* leaflet; (*opuscolo*) brochure.

deplora're *vt* to deplore; to lament.

deplore'vole *ag* deplorable.

depo'ne, depon'go *etc vb vedi* **deporre**.

depor're *vt* (*depositare*) to put down; (*rimuovere: da una carica*) to remove; (*: re*) to depose; (*DIR*) to testify; ~ **le armi** (*MIL*) to lay down arms; ~ **le uova** to lay eggs.

deporta're *vt* to deport.

deporta'to *smf* deportee.

deportazio'ne [dāpōrtåttsyō'nå] *sf* deportation.

depo'si *etc vb vedi* **deporre**.

depositan'te *sm* (*COMM*) depositor.

deposita're *vt* (*gen, GEO, ECON*) to deposit; (*lasciare*) to leave; (*merci*) to store; ~**rsi** *vr* (*sabbia, polvere*) to settle.

deposita'rio *sm* (*COMM*) depository.

depo'sito *sm* deposit; (*luogo*) warehouse; depot; (*: MIL*) depot; ~ **bagagli** checkroom (*US*), left-luggage office (*Brit*); ~ **di munizioni** ammunition dump.

deposizio'ne [dāpōzēttsyō'nå] *sf* deposition; (*da una carica*) removal; **rendere una falsa** ~ to perjure o.s.

depo'sto, a *pp di* **deporre**.

deprava're *vt* to corrupt, pervert.

deprava'to, a *ag* depraved ♦ *smf* degenerate.

depreca're *vt* to deprecate, deplore.

depreda're *vt* to rob, plunder.

depressio'ne *sf* depression; **area** *o* **zona di** ~ (*METEOR*) area of low pressure; (*ECON*) depressed area.

depres'so, a *pp di* **deprimere** ♦ *ag* depressed.

deprezzamen'to [dāprāttsåmån'tō] *sm* depreciation.

deprezza're [dāprāttså'rå] *vt* (*ECON*) to depreciate.

deprimen'te *ag* depressing.

depri'mere *vt* to depress.

depura're *vt* to purify.

depurato're *sm*: ~ **d'acqua** water purifier; ~ **di gas** scrubber.

deputa'to, a *o* **es'sa** *smf* (*POL*) deputy.

deputazio'ne [dāpōōtåttsyō'nå] *sf* deputation; (*POL*) position of deputy.

deragliamen'to [dārålyåmån'tō] *sm* derailment.

deraglia're [dārålyå'rå] *vi* to be derailed; **far**

~ to derail.

derapa're *vi* (*veicolo*) to skid; (*SCI*) to sideslip.

derattizzazio'ne [dārāttēddzåttsyō'nå] *sf* rodent control.

deregolamenta're *vt* to deregulate.

deregolamentazio'ne [dārāgōlåmåntåttsyō'nå] *sf* deregulation.

derelit'to, a *ag* derelict.

dereta'no *sm* (*fam*) bottom, buttocks *pl*.

deri'dere *vt* to mock, deride.

deri'si *etc vb vedi* **deridere**.

derisio'ne *sf* derision, mockery.

deri'so, a *pp di* **deridere**.

deriso'rio, a *ag* (*gesto, tono*) mocking.

deri'va *sf* (*NAUT, AER*) drift; (*dispositivo*: *AER*) fin; (*: NAUT*) centerboard (*US*), centreboard (*Brit*); **andare alla** ~ (*anche fig*) to drift.

deriva're *vi*: ~ **da** to derive from ♦ *vt* to derive; (*corso d'acqua*) to divert.

deriva'to, a *ag* derived ♦ *sm* (*CHIM, LING*) derivative; (*prodotto*) by-product.

derivazio'ne [dārēvåttsyō'nå] *sf* derivation; diversion.

dermati'te *sf* dermatitis.

dermatologi'a [dārmåtōlōjē'å] *sf* dermatology.

dermato'logo, a, gi, ghe *smf* dermatologist.

de'roga, ghe *sf* (special) dispensation; **in** ~ **a** as a (special) dispensation to.

deroga're *vi*: ~ **a** (*DIR*) to repeal in part.

derra'te *sfpl* commodities; ~ **alimentari** foodstuffs.

deruba're *vt* to rob.

descrit'to, a *pp di* **descrivere**.

descri'vere *vt* to describe.

descrizio'ne [dāskrēttsyō'nå] *sf* description.

deser'to, a *ag* deserted ♦ *sm* (*GEO*) desert; **isola** ~**a** desert island.

desidera'bile *ag* desirable.

desidera're *vt* to want, wish for; (*sessualmente*) to desire; ~ **fare/che qn faccia** to want *o* wish to do/sb to do; **desidera fare una passeggiata?** would you like to go for a walk?; **farsi** ~ (*fare il prezioso*) to play hard to get; (*farsi aspettare*) to take one's time; **lascia molto a** ~ it leaves a lot to be desired.

deside'rio *sm* wish; (*più intenso, carnale*) desire.

desidero'so, a *ag*: ~ **di** longing *o* eager for.

designa're [dāsēnyå'rå] *vt* to designate, appoint; (*data*) to fix; **la vittima designata** the intended victim.

designazio'ne [dāsēnyåttsyō'nå] *sf* designation, appointment.

desina're *vi* to dine, have dinner ♦ *sm* dinner.

desinen'za [dāzēnen'tså] *sf* (*LING*) ending, inflexion.

desi'stere *vi*: ~ **da** to give up, desist from.

desisti'to, a *pp di* **desistere**.

desolan'te *ag* distressing.

desola'to, a *ag* (*paesaggio*) desolate; (*persona: spiacente*) sorry.

desolazio'ne |dāzōlàttsyō'nā| *sf* desolation.

de'spota, i *sm* despot.

des'si *etc vb vedi* **dare**.

destabilizza're |dāstàbclčddzà'rā| *vt* to destabilize.

desta're *vt* to wake (up); (*fig*) to awaken, arouse; ~**rsi** *vr* to wake (up).

de'ste *etc vb vedi* **dare**.

destina're *vt* to destine; (*assegnare*) to appoint, assign; (*indirizzare*) to address; ~ **qc a qn** to intend to give sth to sb, intend sb to have sth.

destinata'rio, a *sm/f* (*di lettera*) addressee; (*di merce*) consignee; (*di mandato*) payee.

destinazio'ne |dāstēnàttsyō'nā| *sf* destination; (*uso*) purpose.

desti'no *sm* destiny, fate.

destitui're *vt* to dismiss, remove.

destituzio'ne |dāstētōōttsyō'nā| *sf* dismissal, removal.

de'sto, a *ag* (wide) awake.

des'tra *sf vedi* **destro**.

destreggiar'si |dāstrādjár'sē| *vr* to maneuver (*US*), manoeuvre (*Brit*).

destrez'za |dāstrāt'tsà| *sf* skill, dexterity.

des'tro, a *ag* right, right-hand; (*abile*) skillful (*US*), skilful (*Brit*), adroit ♦ *sf* (*mano*) right hand; (*parte*) right (side); (*POL*): **la** ~**a** the right ♦ *sm* (*BOXE*) right; **a** ~**a** (*essere*) on the right; (*andare*) to the right; **tenere la** ~**a** to keep to the right.

desu'mere *vt* (*dedurre*) to infer, deduce; (*trarre: informazioni*) to obtain.

desun'to, a *pp di* **desumere**.

detassa're *vt* to remove the duty (*o* tax) from.

detene're *vt* (*incarico, primato*) to hold; (*proprietà*) to have, possess; (*in prigione*) to detain, hold.

deten'go, deten'ni *etc vb vedi* **detenere**.

detenti'vo, a *ag*: **mandato** ~ imprisonment order; **pena** ~**a** prison sentence.

detento're, tri'ce *sm/f* (*di titolo, primato etc*) holder.

detenu'to, a *sm/f* prisoner.

detenzio'ne |dātāntsyō'nā| *sf* holding; possession; detention.

detergen'te |dātārjcn'tā| *ag* detergent; (*crema, latte*) cleansing ♦ *sm* detergent.

deter'gere |dātcr'jārā| *vt* (*gen*) to clean; (*pelle, viso*) to cleanse; (*sudore*) to wipe (away).

deterioramen'to *sm*: ~ (**di**) deterioration (in).

deteriora're *vt* to damage; ~**rsi** *vr* to deteriorate.

deterio're *ag* (*merce*) second-rate; (*significa-*

to) pejorative; (*tradizione letteraria*) lesser, minor.

determinan'te *ag* decisive, determining.

determina're *vt* to determine.

determinati'vo, a *ag* determining; **articolo** ~ (*LING*) definite article.

determina'to, a *ag* (*gen*) certain; (*particolare*) specific; (*risoluto*) determined, resolute.

determinazio'ne |dātārmēnàttsyō'nā| *sf* determination; (*decisione*) decision.

deterren'te *ag, sm* deterrent.

deterrò *etc vb vedi* **detenere**.

detersi'vo *sm* detergent; (*per bucato*: **in polvere**) powdered soap (*US*), washing powder (*Brit*).

deter'so, a *pp di* **detergere**.

detesta're *vt* to detest, hate.

detie'ne *etc vb vedi* **detenere**.

detona're *vi* to detonate.

detonato're *sm* detonator.

detonazio'ne |dātōnàttsyō'nā| *sf* (*di esplosivo*) detonation, explosion; (*di arma*) bang; (*di motore*) knocking, pinging (*US*).

detra'e, detrag'go *etc vb vedi* **detrarre**.

detrar're *vt*: ~ (**da**) to deduct (from), take away (from).

detras'si *etc vb vedi* **detrarre**.

detrat'to, a *pp di* **detrarre**.

detrazio'ne |dātràttsyō'nā| *sf* deduction; ~ **d'imposta** tax allowance.

detrimen'to *sm* detriment, harm; **a** ~ **di** to the detriment of.

detri'to *sm* (*GEO*) detritus.

detronizza're |dātrōnēddzà'rā| *vt* to dethrone.

det'ta *sf*: **a** ~ **di** according to.

dettaglian'te |dāttàlyàn'tā| *sm/f* (*COMM*) retailer.

dettaglia're |dāttàlyà'rā| *vt* to detail, give full details of.

dettagliatamen'te |dāttàlyátàmàn'tā| *av* in detail.

detta'glio |dāttàl'yō| *sm* detail; (*COMM*): **il** ~ retail; **al** ~ (*COMM*) retail; separately.

detta'me *sm* dictate, precept.

detta're *vt* to dictate; ~ **legge** (*fig*) to lay down the law.

detta'to *sm* dictation.

dettatu'ra *sf* dictation.

det'to, a *pp di* **dire** ♦ *ag* (*soprannominato*) called, known as; (*già nominato*) abovementioned ♦ *sm* saying; ~ **fatto** no sooner said than done; **presto** ~! it's easier said than done!

deturpa're *vt* to disfigure; (*moralmente*) to sully.

devastan'te *ag* (*anche fig*) devastating.

devasta're *vt* to devastate; (*fig*) to ravage.

devastazio'ne |dāvàstàttsyō'nā| *sf* devastation, destruction.

devia're *vi*: ~ (**da**) to turn off (from) ♦ *vt* to

divert.

deviazio'ne [dăvyăttsyō'nă] *sf* (*anche AUT*) diversion; **fare una** ~ to make a detour.

de'vo *etc vb vedi* **dovere.**

devolu'to, a *pp di* **devolvere.**

devoluzio'ne [dăvōlōōttsyō'nă] *sf* (*DIR*) devolution, transfer.

devol'vere *vt* (*DIR*) to transfer, devolve; ~ **qc in beneficenza** to give sth to charity.

devo'to, a *ag* (*REL*) devout, pious; (*affezionato*) devoted.

devozio'ne [dăvōttsyō'nă] *sf* devoutness; (*anche REL*) devotion.

dg *abbr* (= *decigrammo*) dg.

di *prep* (*di* + *il* = **del,** *di* + *lo* = **dello,** *di* + *l'* = **dell',** *di* + *la* = **della,** *di* + *i* = **dei,** *di* + *gli* = **degli,** *di* + *le* = **delle**) of; (*causa*) with; for; of; (*mezzo*) with; (*provenienza*) from ♦ *det*: **del pane** (some) bread; **dei libri** (some) books; **la sorella** ~ **mio padre** my father's sister; **un sacchetto** ~ **plastica/orologio d'oro** a plastic bag/gold watch; **tremare** ~ **paura** to tremble with fear; **un bambino** ~ **tre anni** a child of three, a three-year-old child; **una commedia** ~ **Goldoni** a comedy by Goldoni; **il nome** ~ **Maria** the name Mary; ~ **primavera/giugno** in spring/June; ~ **mattina/sera** in the morning/evening; ~ **notte** by night; at night; in the night; ~ **domenica** on Sundays; ~ ... **in** from ... to; *vedi* **più, meno** *etc*.

dì *sm* day; **buon** ~! hallo!; **a** ~ = **addì.**

diabe'te *sm* diabetes *sg*.

diabe'tico, a, ci, che *ag*, *sm/f* diabetic.

diabo'lico, a, ci, che *ag* diabolical.

dia'cono *sm* (*REL*) deacon.

diade'ma, i *sm* diadem; (*di donna*) tiara.

diafram'ma, i *sm* (*divisione*) screen; (*ANAT, FOT, contraccettivo*) diaphragm.

dia'gnosi [dĕăn'yōzĕ] *sf* diagnosis *sg*.

diagnostica're [dĕănyōstĕkă'ră] *vt* to diagnose.

diagno'stico, a, ci, che [dĕănyo'stĕkō] *ag* diagnostic; **aiuti** ~**ci** (*INFORM*) debugging aids.

diagona'le *ag*, *sf* diagonal.

diagram'ma, i *sm* diagram; ~ **a barre** bar chart; ~ **di flusso** flow chart.

dialetta'le *ag* dialectal; **poesia** ~ poetry in dialect.

dialet'to *sm* dialect.

dia'lisi *sf* dialysis.

dialogan'te *ag*: **unità** ~ (*INFORM*) interactive terminal.

dialoga're *vi*: ~ (**con**) to have a dialogue (with); (*conversare*) to converse (with) ♦ *vt* (*scena*) to write the dialogue for.

dia'logo, ghi *sm* dialogue.

diaman'te *sm* diamond.

dia'metro *sm* diameter.

dia'mine *escl*: **che** ~ ...**?** what on earth ...?

diapositi'va *sf* transparency, slide.

dia'ria *sf* daily (expense) allowance.

dia'rio *sm* diary; ~ **di bordo** (*NAUT*) log(book); ~ **di classe** (*INS*) class register; ~ **degli esami** (*INS*) exam timetable.

diarre'a *sf* diarrhoea.

diatri'ba *sf* diatribe.

diavoleri'a *sf* (*azione*) act of mischief; (*aggeggio*) weird contraption.

dia'volo *sm* devil; **è un buon** ~ he's a good sort; **avere un** ~ **per capello** to be in a foul temper; **avere una fame/un freddo del** ~ to be ravenously hungry/frozen stiff; **mandare qn al** ~ (*fam*) to tell sb to go to hell; **fare il** ~ **a quattro** to kick up a fuss.

dibat'tere *vt* to debate, discuss; ~**rsi** *vr* to struggle.

dibattimen'to *sm* (*dibattito*) debate, discussion; (*DIR*) hearing.

dibat'tito *sm* debate, discussion.

dic. *abbr* (= *dicembre*) Dec.

dicaste'ro *sm* ministry.

di'ce [dē'chă] *vb vedi* **dire.**

dicem'bre [dēchem'bră] *sm* December; *per fraseologia vedi* **luglio.**

dicembri'no, a [dēchămbrē'nō] *ag* December *cpd*.

diceri'a [dēchārē'á] *sf* rumor (*US*), rumour (*Brit*), piece of gossip.

dichiara're [dēkyárá'rā] *vt* to declare; ~**rsi** *vr* to declare o.s.; (*innamorato*) to declare one's love; **si dichiara che** ... it is hereby declared that ...; ~**rsi vinto** to acknowledge defeat.

dichiara'to, a [dēkyárá'tō] *ag* (*nemico, ateo*) avowed.

dichiarazio'ne [dēkyárăttsyō'nă] *sf* declaration; ~ **dei redditi** statement of income; (*modulo*) tax return.

dicianno've [dēchánno'vă] *num* nineteen.

diciannoven'ne [dēchánnōven'nă] *ag*, *sm/f* nineteen-year-old.

diciasset'te [dēchásset'tă] *num* seventeen.

diciassetten'ne [dēchássätten'nă] *ag*, *sm/f* seventeen-year-old.

diciotten'ne [dēchōtten'nă] *ag*, *sm/f* eighteen-year-old.

diciot'to [dēchot'tō] *num* eighteen ♦ *sm inv* (*INS*) minimum satisfactory mark awarded in Italian universities.

dicitu'ra [dēchĕtōō'rá] *sf* words *pl*, wording.

di'co *etc vb vedi* **dire.**

didascali'a *sf* (*di illustrazione*) caption; (*CINEMA*) subtitle; (*TEATRO*) stage directions *pl*.

didat'tico, a, ci, che *ag* didactic; (*metodo, programma*) teaching; (*libro*) educational ♦ *sf* didactics *sg*; teaching methodology.

diden'tro *av* inside, indoors.

didie'tro *av* behind ♦ *ag inv* (*ruota, giardino*) back, rear *cpd* ♦ *sm* (*di casa*) rear; (*fam*:

sedere) backside.
die'ci |dye'chē| *num* ten.
diecimi'la |dyechēmē'là| *num* ten thousand.
dieci'na |dyāchē'nà| *sf* = **decina**.
die'di *etc vb vedi* **dare**.
di'esel |dē:'zəl| *sm inv* diesel engine.
die'ta *sf* diet; **essere a ~** to be on a diet.
dieto'logo, a, gi, ghe *sm/f* dietician.
die'tro *av* behind; (*in fondo*) at the back ♦ *prep* behind; (*tempo: dopo*) after ♦ *sm* (*di foglio, giacca*) back; (*di casa*) back, rear ♦ *ag inv* back *cpd*; **le zampe di ~** the hind legs; **~ ricevuta** against receipt; **~ richiesta** on demand; (*scritta*) on application; **andare ~ a** (*anche fig*) to follow; **stare ~ a qn** (*sorvegliare*) to keep an eye on sb; (*corteggiare*) to hang around sb; **portarsi ~ qn/qc** to bring sb/sth with one, bring sb/sth along; **gli hanno riso/parlato ~** they laughed at/ talked about him behind his back.
die'tro front' *escl* about face! (*US*), about turn! (*Brit*) ♦ *sm* (*MIL*) about-face, about-turn; (*fig*) volte-face, about-face, about-turn; **fare ~** (*MIL, fig*) to about-face, about-turn; (*tornare indietro*) to turn round.
difat'ti *cong* in fact, as a matter of fact.
difen'dere *vt* to defend; **~rsi** *vr* (*cavarsela*) to get by; **~rsi da/contro** to defend o.s. from/against; **~rsi dal freddo** to protect o.s. from the cold; **sapersi ~** to know how to look after o.s.
difensi'vo, a *ag* defensive ♦ *sf*: **stare sulla ~a** (*anche fig*) to be on the defensive.
difenso're, a *sm/f* defender; **avvocato ~** counsel for the defense (*US*) *o* defence (*Brit*).
dife'sa *sf vedi* **difeso**.
dife'si *etc vb vedi* **difendere**.
dife'so, a *pp di* **difendere** ♦ *sf* defense (*US*), defence (*Brit*); **prendere le ~e di qn** to defend sb, take sb's part.
difetta're *vi* to be defective; **~ di** to be lacking in, lack.
difetti'vo, a *ag* defective.
difet'to *sm* (*mancanza*): **~ di** lack of; (*di fabbricazione*) fault, flaw, defect; (*morale*) fault, failing, defect; (*fisico*) defect; **far ~** to be lacking; **in ~** at fault; **in the wrong.**
difetto'so, a *ag* defective, faulty.
diffama're *vt* (*a parole*) to slander; (*per iscritto*) to libel.
diffamato'rio, a *ag* slanderous; libellous.
diffamazio'ne |dēffámáttsyō'nā| *sf* slander; libel.
differen'te *ag* different.
differen'za |dēffārēn'tsà| *sf* difference; **a ~ di** unlike; **non fare ~ (tra)** to make no distinction (between).
differenzia'le |dēffārāntsyà'lā| *ag, sm* differential; **classi ~i** (*INS*) special classes (*for backward children*).

differenzia're |dēffārāntsyà'rā| *vt* to differentiate; **~rsi da** to differentiate o.s. from; to differ from.
differi're *vt* to postpone, defer ♦ *vi* to be different.
diffi'cile |dēffē'chēlā| *ag* difficult; (*persona*) hard to please, difficult (to please); (*poco probabile*): **è ~ che sia libero** it is unlikely that he'll be free ♦ *sm/f*: **fare il(la) ~** to be difficult, be awkward ♦ *sm* difficult part; difficulty; **essere ~ nel mangiare** to be fussy about one's food.
difficilmen'te |dēffēchēlmān'tā| *av* (*con difficoltà*) with difficulty; **~ verrà** he's unlikely to come.
difficoltà *sf inv* difficulty.
difficolto'so, a *ag* (*compito*) difficult, hard; (*persona*) difficult, hard to please; **digestione ~a** poor digestion.
diffi'da *sf* (*DIR*) warning, notice.
diffida're *vi*: **~ di** to be suspicious *o* distrustful of ♦ *vt* (*DIR*) to warn; **~ qn dal fare qc** to warn sb not to do sth, caution sb against doing sth.
diffiden'te *ag* suspicious, distrustful.
diffiden'za |dēffēden'tsà| *sf* suspicion, distrust.
diffon'dere *vt* (*luce, calore*) to diffuse; (*notizie*) to spread, circulate; **~rsi** *vr* to spread.
diffu'si *etc vb vedi* **diffondere**.
diffusio'ne *sf* diffusion; spread; (*anche di giornale*) circulation; (*FISICA*) scattering.
diffu'so, a *pp di* **diffondere** ♦ *ag* (*FISICA*) diffuse; (*notizia, malattia etc*) widespread; **è opinione ~a che ...** it's widely held that ....
difila'to *av* (*direttamente*) straight, directly; (*subito*) right away.
difteri'te *sf* diphtheria.
di'ga, ghe *sf* dam; (*portuale*) breakwater.
digeren'te |dējārēn'tā| *ag* (*apparato*) digestive.
digeri're |dējārē'rā| *vt* to digest.
digestio'ne |dējāstē'nā| *sf* digestion.
digesti'vo, a |dējāstē'vō| *ag* digestive ♦ *sm* (*after-dinner*) liqueur.
Digio'ne |dējō'nā| *sf* Dijon.
digita'le |dējētá'lā| *ag* digital; (*delle dita*) finger *cpd*, digital ♦ *sf* (*BOT*) foxglove.
digita're |dējētà'rā| *vt* (*dati*) to key (in); (*tasto*) to press.
digiuna're |dējōōnà'rā| *vi* to starve o.s.; (*REL*) to fast.
digiu'no, a |dējōō'nō| *ag*: **essere ~** not to have eaten ♦ *sm* fast; **a ~** on an empty stomach.
dignità |dēnyētá'| *sf inv* dignity.
dignita'rio |dēnyētá'ryō| *sm* dignitary.
dignito'so, a |dēnyētō'sō| *ag* dignified.
DI'GOS *sigla f* (= *Divisione Investigazioni Generali e Operazioni Speciali*) *police department dealing with political security*.

digressio'ne *sf* digression.

digrigna're |dēgrēnyà'rā| *vt:* ~ **i denti** to grind one's teeth.

dilaga're *vi* to flood; (*fig*) to spread.

dilania're *vt* to tear to pieces.

dilapida're *vt* to squander, waste.

dilata're *vt* to dilate; (*gas*) to cause to expand; (*passaggio, cavità*) to open (up); ~**rsi** *vr* to dilate; (*FISICA*) to expand.

dilatazio'ne |dēlàtàttsyō'nā| *sf* (*ANAT*) dilation; (*di gas, metallo*) expansion.

dilaziona're |dēlàttsyōnà'rā| *vt* to delay, defer.

dilazio'ne |dēlàttsyō'nā| *sf* deferment.

dileggia're |dēlàdjà'rā| *vt* to mock, deride.

dilegua're *vi*, ~**rsi** *vr* to vanish, disappear.

dilem'ma, i *sm* dilemma.

dilettan'te *sm/f* dilettante; (*anche* SPORT) amateur.

diletta're *vt* to give pleasure to, delight; ~**rsi** *vr:* ~**rsi di** to take pleasure in, enjoy.

dilette'vole *ag* delightful.

dilet'to, a *ag* dear, beloved ♦ *sm* pleasure, delight.

diligen'te |dēlējen'tā| *ag* (*scrupoloso*) diligent; (*accurato*) careful, accurate.

diligen'za |dēlējen'tsà| *sf* diligence; care; (*carrozza*) stagecoach.

dilui're *vt* to dilute.

dilungar'si *vr* (*fig*): ~ **su** to talk at length on *o* about.

diluvia're *vb impers* to pour (down).

dilu'vio *sm* downpour; (*inondazione, fig*) flood; **il** ~ **universale** the Flood.

dimagran'te *ag* slimming *cpd*.

dimagri're *vi* to get thinner, lose weight.

dimena're *vt* to wave, shake; ~**rsi** *vr* to toss and turn; (*fig*) to struggle; ~ **la coda** (*sog: cane*) to wag its tail.

dimensio'ne *sf* dimension; (*grandezza*) size; **considerare un discorso nella sua** ~ **politica** to look at a speech in terms of its political significance.

dimentican'za |dēmàntēkàn'tsà| *sf* forgetfulness; (*errore*) oversight, slip; **per** ~ inadvertently.

dimentica're *vt* to forget; ~**rsi** *vr:* ~**rsi di qc** to forget sth.

dimenticato'io *sm* (*scherzoso*): **cadere/ mettere nel** ~ to sink into/consign to oblivion.

dimen'tico, a, chi, che *ag:* ~ **di** (*che non ricorda*) forgetful of; (*incurante*) oblivious of, unmindful of.

dimes'so, a *pp di* **dimettere** ♦ *ag* (*voce*) subdued; (*uomo, abito*) modest, humble.

dimestichez'za |dēmàstēkàt'tsà| *sf* familiarity.

dimet'tere *vt:* ~ **qn da** to dismiss sb from; (*dall'ospedale*) to discharge sb from; ~**rsi** *vr:* ~**rsi (da)** to resign (from).

dimezza're |dēmàddzà'rā| *vt* to halve.

diminui're *vt* to reduce, diminish; (*prezzi*) to bring down, reduce ♦ *vi* to decrease, diminish; (*rumore*) to die down, die away; (*prezzi*) to fall, go down.

diminuti'vo, a *ag, sm* diminutive.

diminuzio'ne |dēmēnōōttsyō'nā| *sf* decreasing, diminishing; **in** ~ on the decrease; ~ **della produttività** fall in productivity.

dimi'si *etc vb vedi* **dimettere**.

dimissiona'rio, a *ag* outgoing, resigning.

dimissio'ni *sfpl* resignation *sg;* **dare** *o* **presentare le** ~ to resign, hand in one's resignation.

dimo'ra *sf* residence; **senza fissa** ~ of no fixed address *o* abode.

dimora're *vi* to reside.

dimostran'te *sm/f* (*POL*) demonstrator.

dimostra're *vt* to demonstrate, show; (*provare*) to prove, demonstrate; ~**rsi** *vr:* ~**rsi molto abile** to show o.s. *o* prove to be very clever; **non dimostra la sua età** he doesn't look his age; **dimostra 30 anni** he looks about 30 (years old).

dimostrati'vo, a *ag* (*anche* LING) demonstrative.

dimostrazio'ne |dēmōstràttsyō'nā| *sf* demonstration; proof.

dina'mico, a, ci, che *ag* dynamic ♦ *sf* dynamics *sg.*

dinami'smo *sm* dynamism.

dinamitar'do, a *ag:* **attentato** ~ dynamite attack ♦ *sm/f* dynamiter.

dinami'te *sf* dynamite.

di'namo *sf inv* dynamo.

dinan'zi |dēnàn'tsē|: ~ **a** *prep* in front of.

dinasti'a *sf* dynasty.

dinie'go, ghi *sm* (*rifiuto*) refusal; (*negazione*) denial.

dinoccola'to, a *ag* lanky; **camminare** ~ to walk with a slouch.

dinosa'uro *sm* dinosaur.

dintor'no *av* round, (round) about; ~**i** *smpl* outskirts; **nei** ~**i di** in the vicinity *o* neighborhood of.

di'o, *pl* **de'i** *sm* god; **D**~ God; **gli dei** the gods; **si crede un** ~ he thinks he's wonderful; **D**~ **mio!** my God!; **D**~ **ce la mandi buona** let's hope for the best; **D**~ **ce ne scampi e liberi!** God forbid!

dio'cesi |dēo'chàzē| *sf inv* diocese.

diossi'na *sf* dioxin.

dipana're *vt* (*lana*) to wind into a ball; (*fig*) to disentangle, sort out.

dipartimen'to *sm* department.

dipenden'te *ag* dependent ♦ *sm/f* employee.

dipenden'za |dēpànden'tsà| *sf* dependence; **essere alle** ~**e di qn** to be employed by sb *o* in sb's employ.

dipen'dere *vi:* ~ **da** to depend on; (*finanziariamente*) to be dependent on; (*derivare*) to come from, be due to.

dipe'si *etc vb vedi* **dipendere.**

dipe'so, a *pp di* **dipendere.**

dipin'gere [dčpēn'jārā] *vt* to paint.

dipin'si *etc vb vedi* **dipingere.**

dipin'to, a *pp di* **dipingere** ♦ *sm* painting.

diplo'ma, i *sm* diploma.

diploma're *vt* to graduate (*US*), award a diploma to ♦ *vi* to graduate (*US*), obtain a diploma.

diploma'tico, a, ci, che *ag* diplomatic ♦ *sm* diplomat.

diploma'to, a *ag* qualified ♦ *sm/f* qualified person, holder of a diploma.

diplomazi'a [dēplōmáttsē'á] *sf* diplomacy.

dipor'to *sm*: **imbarcazione** *f* **da** ~ pleasure craft.

dirada're *vt* to thin (out); (*visite*) to reduce, make less frequent; **~rsi** *vr* to disperse; (*nebbia*) to clear (up).

dirama're *vt* to issue ♦ *vi*, **~rsi** *vr* (*strade*) to branch.

di're *vt* to say; (*segreto, fatto*) to tell; ~ **qc a qn** to tell sb sth; ~ **a qn di fare qc** to tell sb to do sth; ~ **di sì/no** to say yes/no; **si dice che ...** they say that ...; **mi si dice che ...** I am told that ...; **si direbbe che ...** it looks (*o* sounds) as though ...; **dica, signora?** (*in un negozio*) are you being helped, ma'am (*US*)?, yes, Madam, can I help you (*Brit*)?; **sa quello che dice** he knows what he's talking about; **lascialo** ~ (*esprimersi*) let him have his say; (*ignoralo*) just ignore him; **come sarebbe a** ~? what do you mean?; **che ne diresti di andarcene?** how about leaving?; **chi l'avrebbe mai detto!** who would have thought it!; **si dicono esperti** they say they are experts; **per così** ~ so to speak; **a dir poco** to say the least; **non c'è che** ~ there's no doubt about it; **non dico di no** I can't deny it; **il che è tutto** ~ need I say more?

dires'si *etc vb vedi* **dirigere.**

direttamen'te *av* (*immediatamente*) directly, straight; (*personalmente*) directly; (*senza intermediari*) direct, straight.

direttis'sima *sf* (*tragitto*) most direct route; (*DIR*): **processo per** ~ summary trial.

direttis'simo *sm* (*FERR*) fast (through) train.

diretti'vo, a *ag* (*POL, AMM*) executive; (*COMM*) managerial, executive ♦ *sm* leadership, leaders *pl* ♦ *sf* directive, instruction.

diret'to, a *pp di* **dirigere** ♦ *ag* direct ♦ *sm* (*FERR*) through train ♦ *sf*: **in** (**linea**) **~a** (*RADIO, TV*) live; **il mio** ~ **superiore** my immediate superior.

diretto're, tri'ce *sm/f* (*di azienda*) director; manager/ess; (*di scuola elementare*) principal (*US*), head (teacher) (*Brit*); ~ **amministrativo** corporate executive secretary (*US*), company secretary (*Brit*); ~ **del carcere**

prison warden (*US*) *o* governor (*Brit*); ~ **di filiale** branch manager; ~ **d'orchestra** conductor; ~ **di produzione** (*CINEMA*) producer; ~ **sportivo** team manager; ~ **tecnico** (*SPORT*) trainer, coach.

direzio'ne [dērāttsyō'nā] *sf* (*senso: anche fig*) direction; (*conduzione: gen*) running; (: *di partito*) leadership; (: *di società*) management; (: *di giornale*) editorship; (*direttori*) management; **in** ~ **di** in the direction of, towards.

dirigen'te [dērējen'tā] *ag* managerial ♦ *sm/f* executive; (*POL*) leader; **classe** ~ ruling class.

dirigen'za [dērējen'tsá] *sf* management; (*POL*) leadership.

dirigenzia'le [dērējántsyá'lā] *ag* managerial.

diri'gere [dērē'jārā] *vt* to direct; (*impresa*) to run, manage; (*MUS*) to conduct; **~rsi** *vr*: **~rsi verso** *o* **a** to make *o* head for; ~ **i propri passi verso** to make one's way towards; **il treno era diretto a Pavia** the train was heading for Pavia.

dirigi'bile [dērējē'bēlā] *sm* airship.

dirimpet'to *av* opposite; ~ **a** *prep* opposite, facing.

dirit'to, a *ag* straight; (*onesto*) straight, upright ♦ *av* straight, directly ♦ *sm* right side; (*TENNIS*) forehand; (*MAGLIA*) plain stitch, knit stitch; (*prerogativa*) right; (*leggi, scienza*): **il** ~ law; **stare** ~ to stand up straight; **aver** ~ **a qc** to be entitled to sth; **punto** ~ plain (stitch); **andare** ~ to go straight on; **a buon** ~ quite rightly; **~i** (**d'autore**) royalties; ~ **di successione** right of succession.

dirittu'ra *sf* (*SPORT*) straight; (*fig*) rectitude.

dirocca'to, a *ag* tumbledown, in ruins.

dirompen'te *ag* (*anche fig*) explosive.

dirottamen'to *sm*: ~ (**aereo**) hijack.

dirotta're *vt* (*nave, aereo*) to change the course of; (*aereo: sotto minaccia*) to hijack; (*traffico*) to divert ♦ *vi* (*nave, aereo*) to change course.

dirottato're, tri'ce *sm/f* hijacker.

dirot'to, a *ag* (*pioggia*) torrential; (*pianto*) unrestrained; **piovere a** ~ to pour, rain cats and dogs; **piangere a** ~ to cry one's heart out.

diru'po *sm* crag, precipice.

disabita'to, a *ag* uninhabited.

disabituar'si *vr*: ~ **a** to get out of the habit of.

disaccor'do *sm* disagreement.

disadatta'to, a *ag* (*PSIC*) maladjusted.

disador'no, a *ag* plain, unadorned.

disaffezio'ne [dēzáffāttsyō'nā] *sf* disaffection.

disage'vole [dēsājā'vōlā] *ag* (*scomodo*) uncomfortable; (*difficile*) difficult.

disagia'to, a [dēzájā'tō] *ag* poor, needy; (*vita*)

hard.

disa'gio [dēzà'jō] *sm* discomfort; (*disturbo*) inconvenience; (*fig: imbarazzo*) embarrassment; **~i** *smpl* hardship *sg*, poverty *sg*; **essere a ~** to be ill at ease.

disa'mina *sf* close examination.

disapprova're *vt* to disapprove of.

disapprovazio'ne [dēzàpprōvàttsyō'nà] *sf* disapproval.

disappun'to *sm* disappointment.

disarciona're [dēzàrchōnà'rà] *vt* to unhorse.

disarman'te *ag* (*fig*) disarming.

disarma're *vt, vi* to disarm.

disar'mo *sm* (*MIL*) disarmament.

disas'tro *sm* disaster.

disastro'so, a *ag* disastrous.

disatten'to, a *ag* inattentive.

disattenzio'ne [dēzàttàntsyō'nà] *sf* carelessness, lack of attention.

disattiva're *vt* (*bomba*) to deactivate, defuse.

disavan'zo [dēzàvàn'tsō] *sm* (*ECON*) deficit.

disavventu'ra *sf* misadventure, mishap.

disbri'go, ghi *sm* (prompt) clearing up *o* settlement.

disca'pito *sm*: **a ~ di** to the detriment of.

disca'rica, che *sf* (*di rifiuti*) dump.

discenden'te [dēshànden'tà] *ag* descending ♦ *sm/f* descendant.

discen'dere [dēshen'dàrà] *vt* to go (*o come*) down ♦ *vi* to go (*o come*) down; (*smontare*) to get off; **~ da** (*famiglia*) to be descended from; **~ dalla macchina/dal treno** to get out of the car/out of *o* off the train; **~ da cavallo** to dismount, get off one's horse.

disce'polo, a [dēshà'pōlō] *sm/f* disciple.

discer'nere [dēsher'nàrà] *vt* to discern.

discernimen'to [dēshàrnēmàn'tō] *sm* discernment.

disce'so, a [dēshà'sō] *pp di* **discendere** ♦ *sf* descent; (*pendio*) slope; **in ~a** (*strada*) downhill *cpd*, sloping; **~a libera** (*SCI*) downhill race.

dischiu'dere [dēskyōō'dàrà] *vt* (*aprire*) to open; (*fig: rivelare*) to disclose, reveal.

dischiu'si *etc* [dēskyōō'sē] *vb vedi* **dischiudere.**

dischiu'so, a [dēskyōō'sō] *pp di* **dischiudere.**

discin'to, a [dēshēn'tō] *ag* (*anche*: **in abiti ~i**) half-undressed.

discio'gliere [dēshol'yàrà] *vt*, **~rsi** *vr* to dissolve; (*fondere*) to melt.

disciol'to, a [dēshol'tō] *pp di* **disciogliere.**

discipli'na [dēshēplē'nà] *sf* discipline.

disciplina're [dēshēplēnà'rà] *ag* disciplinary ♦ *vt* to discipline.

di'sco, schi *sm* disc, disk; (*SPORT*) discus; (*fonografico*) record; (*INFORM*) disk; **~ magnetico** (*INFORM*) magnetic disk; **~ orario** (*AUT*) parking disc; **~ rigido** (*INFORM*) hard disk; **~ volante** flying saucer.

discografi'a *sf* (*tecnica*) recording, record-making; (*industria*) record industry.

discogra'fico, a, ci, che *ag* record *cpd*, recording *cpd* ♦ *sm* record producer; **casa ~a** record(ing) company.

di'scolo, a *ag* (*bambino*) undisciplined, unruly ♦ *sm/f* rascal.

discolpa're *vt* to clear of blame; **~rsi** *vr* to clear o.s., prove one's innocence; (*giustificarsi*) to excuse o.s.

discono'scere [dēskōnōsh'shàrà] *vt* (*figlio*) to disown; (*meriti*) to ignore, disregard.

disconosciu'to, a [dēskōnōshōō'tō] *pp di* **disconoscere.**

disconti'nuo, a *ag* (*linea*) broken; (*rendimento, stile*) irregular; (*interesse*) sporadic.

discor'de *ag* conflicting, clashing.

discor'dia *sf* discord; (*dissidio*) disagreement, clash.

discor'rere *vi*: **~ (di)** to talk (about).

discor'so, a *pp di* **discorrere** ♦ *sm* speech; (*conversazione*) conversation, talk.

disco'sto, a *ag* faraway, distant ♦ *av* far away; **~ da** *prep* far from.

discote'ca, che *sf* (*raccolta*) record library; (*luogo di ballo*) disco(thèque).

discrepan'za [dēskràpàn'tsà] *sf* discrepancy.

discre'to, a *ag* discreet; (*abbastanza buono*) reasonable, fair.

discrezio'ne [dēskràttsyō'nà] *sf* discretion; (*giudizio*) judgment, discernment; **a ~ di** at the discretion of.

discriminan'te *ag* (*fattore, elemento*) decisive ♦ *sf* (*DIR*) extenuating circumstance.

discrimina're *vt* to discrimate.

discriminazio'ne [dēskrēmēnàttsyō'nà] *sf* discrimination.

discus'si *etc vb vedi* **discutere.**

discussio'ne *sf* discussion; (*litigio*) argument; **mettere in ~** to bring into question; **fuori ~** out of the question.

discus'so, a *pp di* **discutere.**

discu'tere *vt* to discuss, debate; (*contestare*) to question, dispute ♦ *vi* (*conversare*): **~ (di)** to discuss; (*litigare*) to argue.

discuti'bile *ag* questionable.

disdegna're [dēzdànyà'rà] *vt* to scorn.

disde'gno [dēzdàn'yō] *sm* scorn, disdain.

disdegno'so, a [dēzdànyō'sō] *ag* disdainful, scornful.

disdet'to, a *pp di* **disdire** ♦ *sf* cancellation; (*sfortuna*) bad luck.

disdice'vole [dēzdēchà'vōlà] *ag* improper, unseemly.

disdi're *vt* (*prenotazione*) to cancel; **~ un contratto d'affitto** (*DIR*) to give notice.

disegna're [dēsànyà'rà] *vt* to draw; (*progettare*) to design; (*fig*) to outline.

disegnato're, tri'ce [dēsànyàtō'rà] *sm/f* designer.

dise'gno [dēzān'yō] *sm* drawing; (*su stoffa etc*) design; (*fig: schema*) outline; ~ **industriale** industriale design; ~ **di legge** (*DIR*) bill.

diserban'te *sm* weed-killer.

disereda're *vt* to disinherit.

diserta're *vt, vi* to desert.

diserto're *sm* (*MIL*) deserter.

diserzio'ne [dēzārtsyō'nā] *sf* (*MIL*) desertion.

disfacimen'to [dēsfáchēmān'tō] *sm* (*di cadavere*) decay; (*fig: di istituzione, impero, società*) decline, decay; **in** ~ in decay.

disfa're *vt* to undo; (*valigie*) to unpack; (*meccanismo*) to take to pieces; (*lavoro, paese*) to destroy; (*neve*) to melt; ~**rsi** *vr* to come undone; (*neve*) to melt; ~ **il letto** to strip the bed; ~**rsi di qn** (*liberarsi*) to get rid of sb.

disfat'ta *sf vedi* **disfatto**.

disfatti'sta, i, e *sm/f* defeatist.

disfat'to, a *pp di* **disfare** ♦ *ag* (*gen*) undone, untied; (*letto*) unmade; (*persona: sfinito*) exhausted, worn-out; (: *addolorato*) grief-stricken ♦ *sf* (*sconfitta*) rout.

disfunzio'ne [dēsfōōntsyō'nā] *sf* (*MED*) dysfunction; ~ **cardiaca** heart trouble.

disgela're [dēzjālá'rā] *vt, vi*, ~**rsi** *vr* to thaw.

disge'lo [dēzje'lō] *sm* thaw.

disgra'zia [dēzgrát'tsyà] *sf* (*sventura*) misfortune; (*incidente*) accident, mishap.

disgrazia'to, a [dēzgráttsyà'tō] *ag* unfortunate ♦ *sm/f* wretch.

disgrega're *vt*, ~**rsi** *vr* to break up.

disgui'do *sm* hitch; ~ **postale** error in postal delivery.

disgusta're *vt* to disgust; ~**rsi** *vr*: ~**rsi di** to be disgusted by.

disgu'sto *sm* disgust.

disgusto'so, a *ag* disgusting.

disidrata're *vt* to dehydrate.

disidrata'to, a *ag* dehydrated.

disillu'dere *vt* to disillusion, disenchant.

disillusio'ne *sf* disillusion, disenchantment.

disimpara're *vt* to forget.

disimpegna're [dēzēmpānyà'rā] *vt* (*persona: da obblighi*): ~ **da** to release from; (*oggetto dato in pegno*) to redeem, get out of pawn; ~**rsi** *vr*: ~**rsi da** (*obblighi*) to release o.s. from, free o.s. from.

disincaglia're [dēzēnkàlyá'rā] *vt* (*barca*) to refloat; ~**rsi** *vr* to get afloat again.

disincanta'to, a *ag* disenchanted, disillusioned.

disincentiva're [dēzēnchāntēvá'rā] *vt* to discourage.

disinfesta're *vt* to disinfest.

disinfestazio'ne [dēzēnfāstáttsyō'nā] *sf* disinfestation.

disinfettan'te *ag, sm* disinfectant.

disinfetta're *vt* to disinfect.

disinfezio'ne [dēzēnfāttsyō'nā] *sf* disinfection.

disinganna're *vt* to disillusion.

disingan'no *sm* disillusion.

disinibi'to, a *ag* uninhibited.

disinnesca're *vt* to defuse.

disinnesta're *vt* (*marcia*) to disengage.

disinquina're *vt* to free from pollution.

disintegra're *vt, vi* to disintegrate.

disinteressar'si *vr*: ~ **di** to take no interest in.

disinteres'se *sm* indifference; (*generosità*) unselfishness.

disintossica're *vt* (*alcolizzato, drogato*) to treat for alcoholism (*o* drug addiction); ~**rsi** *vr* to clear out one's system; (*alcolizzato, drogato*) to be treated for alcoholism (*o* drug addiction).

disintossicazio'ne [dēzēntōssēkáttsyō'nā] *sf* treatment for alcoholism (*o* drug addiction).

disinvol'to, a *ag* casual, free and easy.

disinvoltu'ra *sf* casualness, ease.

dislessi'a *sf* dyslexia.

dislivel'lo *sm* difference in height; (*fig*) gap.

disloca're *vt* to station, position.

dismisu'ra *sf* excess; **a** ~ to excess, excessively.

disobbedi're *etc* = **disubbidire** *etc*.

disoccupa'to, a *ag* unemployed ♦ *sm/f* unemployed person.

disoccupazio'ne [dēzōkkōōpáttsyō'nā] *sf* unemployment.

disonestà *sf* dishonesty.

disone'sto, a *ag* dishonest.

disonora're *vt* to dishonor (*US*), dishonour (*Brit*), bring disgrace upon.

disono're *sm* dishonor (*US*), dishonour (*Brit*), disgrace.

diso'pra *av* (*con contatto*) on top; (*senza contatto*) above; (*al piano superiore*) upstairs ♦ *ag inv* (*superiore*) upper ♦ *sm inv* top, upper part; **la gente** ~ the people upstairs; **il piano** ~ the floor above.

disordina're *vt* to mess up, disarrange; (*MIL*) to throw into disorder.

disordina'to, a *ag* untidy; (*privo di misura*) irregular, wild.

disor'dine *sm* (*confusione*) disorder, confusion; (*sregolatezza*) debauchery; ~**i** *smpl* (*POL etc*) disorder *sg*; (*tumulti*) riots.

disorga'nico, a, ci, che *ag* incoherent, disorganized.

disorientamen'to *sm* (*fig*) confusion, bewilderment.

disorienta're *vt* to disorientate; ~**rsi** *vr* (*fig*) to get confused, lose one's bearings.

disorienta'to, a *ag* disorientated.

disossa're *vt* (*CUC*) to bone.

disot'to *av* below, underneath; (*in fondo*) at the bottom; (*al piano inferiore*) downstairs ♦ *ag inv* (*inferiore*) lower; bottom *cpd* ♦ *sm* *inv* (*parte inferiore*) lower part; bottom; **la gente** ~ the people downstairs; **il piano** ~ the floor below.

dispac'cio [dēspàch'chō] *sm* dispatch.

dispara'to, a *ag* disparate.

di'spari *ag inv* odd, uneven.

disparità *sf inv* disparity.

dispar'te: in ~ *av* (*da lato*) aside, apart; **tenersi** *o* **starsene in** ~ to keep to o.s., hold aloof.

dispen'dio *sm* (*di denaro, energie*) expenditure; (: *spreco*) waste.

dispendio'so, a *ag* expensive.

dispen'sa *sf* pantry, larder; (*mobile*) sideboard; (*DIR*) exemption; (*REL*) dispensation; (*fascicolo*) number, issue.

dispensa're *vt* (*elemosine, favori*) to distribute; (*esonerare*) to exempt.

dispera're *vi*: ~ **(di)** to despair (of); ~**rsi** *vr* to despair.

dispera'to, a *ag* (*persona*) in despair; (*caso, tentativo*) desperate.

disperazio'ne [dēspāràttsyō'nā] *sf* despair.

disper'dere *vt* (*disseminare*) tò disperse; (*MIL*) to scatter, rout; (*fig: consumare*) to waste, squander; ~**rsi** *vr* to disperse; to scatter.

dispersio'ne *sf* dispersion, dispersal; (*FISICA, CHIM*) dispersion.

dispersi'vo, a *ag* (*lavoro etc*) disorganized.

disper'so, a *pp di* **disperdere** ♦ *sm/f* missing person; (*MIL*) missing soldier.

dispet'to *sm* spite *q*, spitefulness *q*; **fare un** ~ **a qn** to play a (nasty) trick on sb; **a** ~ **di** in spite of; **con suo grande** ~ much to his annoyance.

dispetto'so, a *ag* spiteful.

dispiace're [dēspyàchā'rā] *sm* (*rammarico*) regret, sorrow; (*dolore*) grief ♦ *vi*: ~ **a** to displease ♦ *vb impers*: **mi dispiace (che)** I am sorry (that); ~**i** *smpl* (*preoccupazioni*) troubles, worries; **se non le dispiace, me ne vado adesso** if you don't mind, I'll go now.

dispiaciu'to, a [dēspyàchōō'tō] *pp di* **dispiacere** ♦ *ag* sorry.

dispo'ne, dispon'go *etc vb vedi* **disporre.**

disponi'bile *ag* available.

dispor're *vt* (*sistemare*) to arrange; (*preparare*) to prepare; (*DIR*) to order; (*persuadere*): ~ **qn a** to incline *o* dispose sb towards ♦ *vi* (*decidere*) to decide; (*usufruire*): ~ **di** to use, have at one's disposal; (*essere dotato*): ~ **di** to have; **disporsi** *vr* (*ordinarsi*) to place o.s., arrange o.s.; **disporsi a fare** to get ready to do; **disporsi all'attacco** to prepare for an attack; **disporsi in cerchio** to form a circle.

dispo'si *etc vb vedi* **disporre.**

dispositi'vo *sm* (*meccanismo*) device; (*DIR*) pronouncement; ~ **di controllo** *o* **di comando** control device; ~ **di sicurezza** (*gen*) safety device; (*di arma da fuoco*) safety catch.

disposizio'ne [dēspōzēttsyō'nā] *sf* arrangement, layout; (*stato d'animo*) mood; (*tendenza*) bent, inclination; (*comando*) order; (*DIR*) provision, regulation; **a** ~ **di qn** at sb's disposal; **per** ~ **di legge** by law; ~ **testamentaria** provisions of a will.

dispo'sto, a *pp di* **disporre** ♦ *ag* (*incline*): ~ **a fare** disposed *o* prepared to do.

dispo'tico, a, ci, che *ag* despotic.

dispoti'smo *sm* despotism.

disprezza're [dēsprāttsà'rā] *vt* to despise.

disprez'zo [dēsprēt'tsō] *sm* contempt; **con** ~ **del pericolo** with a total disregard for the danger involved.

di'sputa *sf* dispute, quarrel.

disputa're *vt* (*contendere*) to dispute, contest; (*SPORT: partita*) to play; (: *gara*) to take part in ♦ *vi* to quarrel; ~ **di** to discuss; ~**rsi qc** to fight for sth.

dissacra're *vt* to desecrate.

dissanguamen'to *sm* loss of blood.

dissangua're *vt* (*fig: persona*) to bleed white; (: *patrimonio*) to suck dry; ~**rsi** *vr* (*MED*) to lose blood; (*fig*) to ruin o.s.; **morire dissanguato** to bleed to death.

dissapo're *sm* slight disagreement.

dis'se *vb vedi* **dire.**

disseca're *vt* to dissect.

dissecca're *vt,* ~**rsi** *vr* to dry up.

dissemina're *vt* to scatter; (*fig: notizie*) to spread.

dissen'so *sm* dissent; (*disapprovazione*) disapproval.

dissenteri'a *sf* dysentery.

dissenti're *vi*: ~ **(da)** to disagree (with).

disseppelli're *vt* (*esumare: cadavere*) to disinter, exhume; (*dissotterrare: anche fig*) to dig up, unearth; (: *rancori*) to resurrect.

dissertazio'ne [dēssārtàttsyō'nā] *sf* dissertation.

disservi'zio [dēssārvēt'tsyō] *sm* inefficiency.

dissesta're *vt* (*ECON*) to ruin.

dissesta'to, a *ag* (*fondo stradale*) uneven; (*economia, finanze*) shaky; **"strada ~a"** (*per lavori in corso*) "road out" (*US*), "road up" (*Brit*).

disse'sto *sm* (financial) ruin.

dissetan'te *ag* refreshing.

disseta're *vt* to quench the thirst of; ~**rsi** *vr* to quench one's thirst.

dissezio'ne [dēssāttsyō'nā] *sf* dissection.

dis'si *vb vedi* **dire.**

dissiden'te *ag*, *sm/f* dissident.

dissi'dio *sm* disagreement.

dissi'mile *ag* different, dissimilar.

dissimula're *vt* (*fingere*) to dissemble; (*nascondere*) to conceal.

dissimulato're, tri'ce *sm/f* dissembler.

dissimulazio'ne |dēssēmōōlàttsyō'nā| *sf* dissembling; concealment.

dissipa're *vt* to dissipate; (*scialacquare*) to squander, waste.

dissipatez'za |dēssēpátāt'tsà| *sf* dissipation.

dissipa'to, a *ag* dissolute, dissipated.

dissipazio'ne |dēssēpáttsyō'nā| *sf* squandering.

dissocia're |dēssōchá'rā| *vt* to dissociate.

dissol'to, a *pp di* **dissolvere.**

dissolu'bile *ag* soluble.

dissolutez'za |dēssōlōōtāt'tsà| *sf* dissoluteness.

dissoluti'vo, a *ag* (*forza*) divisive; **processo** ~ (*anche fig*) process of dissolution.

dissolu'to, a *pp di* **dissolvere** ♦ *ag* dissolute, licentious.

dissolven'za |dēssōlven'tsà| *sf* (*CINEMA*) fading.

dissol'vere *vt* to dissolve; (*neve*) to melt; (*fumo*) to disperse; ~**rsi** *vr* to dissolve; to melt; to disperse.

dissonan'te *ag* discordant.

dissonan'za |dēssōnán'tsà| *sf* (*fig: di opinioni*) clash.

dissotterra're *vt* (*cadavere*) to disinter, exhume; (*tesori, rovine*) to dig up, unearth; (*fig: sentimenti, odio*) to bring up again, resurrect.

dissua'dere *vt*: ~ **qn da** to dissuade sb from.

dissuasio'ne *sf* dissuasion.

dissua'so, a *pp di* **dissuadere.**

distaccamen'to *sm* (*MIL*) detachment.

distacca're *vt* to detach, separate; (*SPORT*) to leave behind; ~**rsi** *vr* to be detached; (*fig*) to stand out; ~**rsi da** (*fig: allontanarsi*) to grow away from.

distac'co, chi *sm* (*separazione*) separation; (*fig: indifferenza*) detachment; (*SPORT*): **vincere con un** ~ **di ...** to win by a distance of ....

distan'te *av* far away ♦ *ag* distant, far away; **essere** ~ (**da**) to be a long way (from); **è** ~ **da qui?** is it far from here?; **essere** ~ **nel tempo** to be in the distant past.

distan'za |dēstán'tsà| *sf* distance; **comando a** ~ remote control; **a** ~ **di 2 giorni** 2 days later; **tener qn a** ~ to keep sb at arm's length; **prendere le** ~**e da qc/qn** to dissociate o.s. from sth/sb; **tenere** *o* **mantenere le** ~**e** to keep one's distance; ~ **focale** focal length; ~ **di sicurezza** safe distance; (*AUT*) braking distance; ~ **di tiro** range; ~ **di visibilità** visibility.

distanzia're |dēstántsyá'rā| *vt* to space out, place at intervals; (*SPORT*) to outdistance; (*fig: superare*) to outstrip, surpass.

dista're *vi*: **distiamo pochi chilometri da Roma** we are only a few kilometers (away) from Rome; **dista molto da qui?** is it far (away) from here?; **non dista molto** it's not far (away).

disten'dere *vt* (*coperta*) to spread out; (*gambe*) to stretch (out); (*mettere a giacere*) to lay; (*rilassare: muscoli, nervi*) to relax; ~**rsi** *vr* (*rilassarsi*) to relax; (*sdraiarsi*) to lie down.

distensio'ne *sf* stretching; relaxation; (*POL*) détente.

distensi'vo, a *ag* (*gen*) relaxing, restful; (*farmaco*) tranquillizing; (*POL*) conciliatory.

diste'so, a *pp di* **distendere** ♦ *ag* (*allungato: persona, gamba*) stretched out; (*rilassato: persona, atmosfera*) relaxed ♦ *sf* expanse, stretch; **avere un volto** ~ to look relaxed.

distilla're *vt* to distil.

distilla'to *sm* distillate.

distillazio'ne |dēstēllàttsyō'nā| *sf* distillation.

distilleri'a *sf* distillery.

distin'guere *vt* to distinguish; ~**rsi** *vr* (*essere riconoscibile*) to be distinguished; (*emergere*) to stand out, be conspicuous, distinguish o.s.; **un vino che si distingue per il suo aroma** a wine with a distinctive bouquet.

distin'guo *sm inv* distinction.

distin'ta *sf* (*nota*) note; (*elenco*) list; ~ **di pagamento** receipt; ~ **di versamento** deposit slip.

distinti'vo, a *ag* distinctive; distinguishing ♦ *sm* badge.

distin'to, a *pp di* **distinguere** ♦ *ag* (*dignitoso ed elegante*) distinguished; ~**i saluti** (*in lettera*) yours faithfully.

distinzio'ne |dēstēntsyō'nā| *sf* distinction; **non faccio** ~**i** (*tra persone*) I don't discriminate; (*tra cose*) it's all the same to me; **senza** ~ **di razza/religione ...** no matter what one's race/creed ....

disto'gliere |dēstol'yārā| *vt*: ~ **da** to take away from; (*fig*) to dissuade from.

distol'to, a *pp di* **distogliere.**

distor'cere |dēstor'chārā| *vt* to twist; (*fig*) to twist, distort; ~**rsi** *vr* (*contorcersi*) to twist.

distorsio'ne *sf* (*MED*) sprain; (*FISICA, OTTICA*) distortion.

distor'to, a *pp di* **distorcere.**

distrar're *vt* to distract; (*divertire*) to entertain, amuse; **distrarsi** *vr* (*non fare attenzione*) to be distracted, let one's mind wander; (*svagarsi*) to amuse *o* enjoy o.s.; ~ **lo sguardo** to look away; **non distrarti!** pay attention!

distrattamen'te *av* without thinking.

distrat'to, a *pp di* **distrarre** ♦ *ag* absentminded; (*disattento*) inattentive.

distrazio'ne |dēstráttsyō'nā| *sf* absentmindedness; inattention; (*svago*) distraction, entertainment; **errori di** ~ careless mistakes.

distret'to *sm* district.

distribui're *vt* to distribute; (*CARTE*) to deal (out); (*consegnare: posta*) to deliver; (*lavoro*) to allocate, assign; (*ripartire*) to share out.

distributo're sm (di benzina) gas (US) o petrol (Brit) pump; (AUT, ELETTR) distributor; (automatico) vending machine.

distribuzio'ne [dēstrēbōōttsyō'nā] sf distribution; delivery; allocation, assignment; sharing out.

districa're vt to disentangle, unravel; ~rsi vr (tirarsi fuori): ~rsi da to get out of, disentangle o.s. from; (fig: cavarsela) to manage, get by.

distrofi'a sf dystrophy.

distrug'gere [dēstrōōd'jārā] vt to destroy.

distrutti'vo, a ag destructive.

distrut'to, a pp di **distruggere**.

distruzio'ne [dēstrōōttsyō'nā] sf destruction.

disturba're vt to disturb, trouble; (sonno, lezioni) to disturb, interrupt; ~rsi vr to put o.s. out; **non si disturbi** please don't bother.

distur'bo sm trouble, bother, inconvenience; (indisposizione) (slight) disorder, ailment; ~i smpl (RADIO, TV) static sg; ~ **della quiete pubblica** (DIR) disturbance of the peace; ~i **di stomaco** stomach trouble sg.

disubbidien'te ag disobedient.

disubbidien'za [dēzōōbbēdyen'tsā] sf disobedience; ~ **civile** civil disobedience.

disubbidi're vi: ~ **(a qn)** to disobey (sb).

disuguaglian'za [dēzōōgwālyān'tsā] sf inequality.

disugua'le ag unequal; (diverso) different; (irregolare) uneven.

disumanità sf inhumanity.

disuma'no, a ag inhuman; **un grido** ~ a terrible cry.

disunio'ne sf disunity.

disuni're vt to divide, disunite.

disu'so sm: **andare** o **cadere in** ~ to fall into disuse.

di'ta sfpl di **dito**.

dita'le sm thimble.

dita'ta sf (colpo) jab (with one's finger); (segno) fingermark.

di'to, pl(f) **di'ta** sm finger; (misura) finger, finger's breadth; ~ **(del piede)** toe; **mettersi le ~a nel naso** to pick one's nose; **mettere il ~ sulla piaga** (fig) to touch a sore spot; **non ha mosso un ~ (per aiutarmi)** he didn't lift a finger (to help me); **ormai è segnato a ~** everyone knows about him now.

dit'ta sf firm, business; **macchina della ~** company car.

ditta'fono sm Dictaphone ®.

dittato're sm dictator.

dittatu'ra sf dictatorship.

ditton'go, ghi sm diphthong.

diur'no, a ag day cpd, daytime cpd ♦ sm (anche: albergo ~) public toilets with washing and shaving facilities etc; **ore ~e** daytime sg; **spettacolo** ~ matinee; **turno** ~ day shift.

di'va sf vedi **divo**.

divaga're vi to digress.

divagazio'ne [dēvāgáttsyō'nā] sf digression; ~i **sul tema** variations on a theme.

divampa're vi to flare up, blaze up.

diva'no sm sofa; (senza schienale) divan; ~ **letto** sofa bed.

divarica're vt to open wide.

diva'rio sm difference.

diven'go etc vb vedi **divenire**.

diveni're vi = **diventare**.

diven'ni etc vb vedi **divenire**.

diventa're vi to become; ~ **famoso/ professore** to become famous/a teacher; ~ **vecchio** to grow old; **c'è da ~ matti** it's enough to drive you crazy.

divenu'to, a pp di **divenire**.

diver'bio sm altercation.

divergen'te [dēvārjen'tā] ag divergent.

divergen'za [dēvārjen'tsā] sf divergence; ~ **d'opinioni** difference of opinion.

diver'gere [dēver'jārā] vi to diverge.

diverrò etc vb vedi **divenire**.

diversamen'te av (in modo differente) differently; (altrimenti) otherwise; ~ **da quanto stabilito** contrary to what had been decided.

diversifica're vt to diversify, vary; ~rsi vr: ~rsi **(per)** to differ (in).

diversificazio'ne [dēvārsēfēkáttsyō'nā] sf diversification; difference.

diversio'ne sf diversion.

diversità sf inv difference, diversity; (varietà) variety.

diversi'vo, a ag diversionary ♦ sm diversion, distraction; **fare un'azione** ~a to create a diversion.

diver'so, a ag (differente): ~ **(da)** different (from) ♦ sm (omosessuale) homosexual; ~i, **e** det pl several, various; (COMM) sundry ♦ pronome pl several (people), many (people).

diverten'te ag amusing.

divertimen'to sm amusement, pleasure; (passatempo) pastime, recreation; **buon** ~! enjoy yourself!

diverti're vt to amuse, entertain; ~rsi vr to amuse o enjoy o.s.; **divertiti!** enjoy yourself, have a good time!; ~rsi **alle spalle di qn** to have a laugh at sb's expense.

diverti'to, a ag amused.

divezza're [dēvāttsā'rā] vt (anche fig): ~ **(da)** to wean (from).

dividen'do sm dividend.

divi'dere vt (anche MAT) to divide; (distribuire, ripartire) to divide (up), split (up); ~rsi vr (persone) to separate, part; (coppia) to separate; ~rsi **(in)** (scindersi) to divide (into), split up (into); (ramificarsi) to fork; **è diviso dalla moglie** he's separated from his wife; **si divide tra casa e lavoro** he divides his time between home and work.

divie'to *sm* prohibition; "~ **di accesso**" "no entry"; "~ **di caccia**" "no hunting"; "~ **di parcheggio**" "no parking"; "~ **di sosta**" (*AUT*) "no waiting".

divincolar'si *vr* to wriggle, writhe.

divinità *sf inv* divinity.

divi'no, a *ag* divine.

divi'sa *sf* (*MIL etc*) uniform; (*COMM*) foreign currency.

divi'si *etc vb vedi* **dividere**.

divisio'ne *sf* division; ~ **in sillabe** syllable division; (*a fine riga*) hyphenation.

divi'smo *sm* (*esibizionismo*) playing to the crowd.

divi'so, a *pp di* **dividere**.

diviso'rio, a *ag* (*siepe, muro esterno*) dividing; (*muro interno*) dividing, partition *cpd* ♦ *sm* (*in una stanza*) partition.

di'vo, a *sm/f* star; **come una** ~**a** like a prima donna.

divora're *vt* to devour; ~ **qc con gli occhi** to eye sth greedily.

divorzia're [dēvōrtsyá'rā] *vi*: ~ **(da qn)** to divorce (sb).

divorzia'to, a [dēvōrtsyá'tō] *ag* divorced ♦ *sm/f* divorcee.

divor'zio [dēvor'tsyō] *sm* divorce.

divulga're *vt* to divulge, disclose; (*rendere comprensibile*) to popularize; ~**rsi** *vr* to spread.

divulgazio'ne [dēvōōlgáttsyō'nā] *sf* (*vedi vb*) disclosure; popularization; spread.

diziona'rio [dēttsyōná'ryō] *sm* dictionary.

dizio'ne [dēttsyō'nā] *sf* diction; pronunciation.

Djakar'ta [jákár'tá] *sf* Djakarta.

dl *abbr* (= *decilitro*) dl.

dm *abbr* (= *decimetro*) dm.

DNA *sigla m* (*BIOL*) DNA.

do *sm* (*MUS*) C; (: *solfeggiando la scala*) do(h).

dobbia'mo *vb vedi* **dovere**.

D.O.C. [dok] *sigla vedi* **denominazione di origine controllata**.

doc. *abbr* = **documento**.

doc'cia, ce [dōch'chá] *sf* (*bagno*) shower; (*condotto*) pipe; **fare la** ~ to take a shower; ~ **fredda** (*fig*) slap in the face.

docen'te [dōchen'tā] *ag* teaching ♦ *sm/f* teacher; (*di università*) lecturer.

docen'za [dōchen'tsá] *sf* university teaching *o* lecturing; **ottenere la libera** ~ to become a lecturer.

D.O.C.G. *sigla* (= *denominazione di origine controllata e garantita*) *label guaranteeing the quality and origin of a wine*.

do'cile [do'chēlā] *ag* docile.

documenta're *vt* to document; ~**rsi** *vr*: ~**rsi (su)** to gather information *o* material (about).

documenta'rio, a *ag*, *sm* documentary.

documentazio'ne [dōkōōmāntáttsyō'nā] *sf* documentation.

documen'to *sm* document; ~**i** *smpl* (*d'identità etc*) papers.

Dodecanne'so *sm*: **le Isole del** ~ the Dodecanese Islands.

dodicen'ne [dōdēchen'nā] *ag*, *sm/f* twelve-year-old.

dodice'simo, a [dōdēche'zēmō] *num* twelfth.

do'dici [dō'dēchē] *num* twelve.

doga'na *sf* (*ufficio*) customs *pl*; (*tassa*) (customs) duty; **passare la** ~ to go through customs.

dogana'le *ag* customs *cpd*.

doganie're *sm* customs officer.

do'glie [dol'yā] *sfpl* (*MED*) labor *sg* (*US*), labour *sg* (*Brit*), labo(u)r pains.

dog'ma, i *sm* dogma.

dogma'tico, a, ci, che *ag* dogmatic.

dol'ce [dōl'chā] *ag* sweet; (*colore*) soft; (*carattere, persona*) gentle, mild; (*fig: mite: clima*) mild; (*non ripido: pendio*) gentle ♦ *sm* (*sapore* ~) sweetness, sweet taste; (*CUC: portata*) sweet, dessert; (: *torta*) cake; **il** ~ **far niente** sweet idleness.

dolcez'za [dōlchāt'tsá] *sf* sweetness; softness; mildness; gentleness.

dolcia'rio, a [dōlchá'ryō] *ag* confectionery *cpd*.

dolcias'tro, a [dōlchás'trō] *ag* (*sapore*) sweetish.

dolcifican'te [dōlchēfēkán'tā] *ag* sweetening ♦ *sm* sweetener.

dolciu'mi [dōlchōō'mē] *smpl* candies.

dolen'te *ag* sorrowful, sad.

dole're *vi* to be sore, hurt, ache; ~**rsi** *vr* to complain; (*essere spiacente*): ~**rsi di** to be sorry for; **mi duole la testa** my head aches, I've got a headache.

dol'go *etc vb vedi* **dolere**.

dol'laro *sm* dollar.

do'lo *sm* (*DIR*) malice; (*frode*) fraud, deceit.

Dolomi'ti *sfpl*: **le** ~ the Dolomites.

doloran'te *ag* aching, sore.

dolo're *sm* (*fisico*) pain; (*morale*) sorrow, grief; **se lo scoprono sono** ~**i!** if they find out there'll be trouble!

doloro'so, a *ag* painful; sorrowful, sad.

dolo'so, a *ag* (*DIR*) malicious; **incendio** ~ arson.

dol'si *etc vb vedi* **dolere**.

dom. *abbr* (= *domenica*) Sun.

doman'da *sf* (*interrogazione*) question; (*richiesta*) demand; (: *cortese*) request; (*DIR: richiesta scritta*) application; (*ECON*): **la** ~ demand; **fare una** ~ **a qn** to ask sb a question; **fare** ~ (**per un lavoro**) to apply (for a job); **far regolare** ~ (**di qc**) to apply through the proper channels (for sth); **fare** ~ **all'autorità giudiziaria** to apply to the courts; ~ **di divorzio** divorce petition; ~ **di matri-**

monio proposal.

domanda're *vt* (*per avere*) to ask for; (*per sapere*) to ask; (*esigere*) to demand; ~**rsi** *vr* to wonder, ask o.s.; ~ **qc a qn** to ask sb for sth; to ask sb sth.

doma'ni *av* tomorrow ♦ *sm* (*l'indomani*) next day, following day; **il** ~ (*il futuro*) the future; (*il giorno successivo*) the next day; **un** ~ some day; ~ **l'altro** the day after tomorrow; ~ **(a) otto** a week tomorrow; **a** ~! see you tomorrow!

doma're *vt* to tame!

domato're, tri'ce *sm/f* (*gen*) tamer; ~ **di cavalli** horsebreaker; ~ **di leoni** lion tamer.

domatti'na *av* tomorrow morning.

dome'nica, che *sf* Sunday; *per fraseologia vedi* **martedì**.

domenica'le *ag* Sunday *cpd*.

domenica'no, a *ag, sm/f* Dominican.

dome'stica, che *vedi* **domestico**.

dome'stico, a, ci, che *ag* domestic ♦ *sm/f* servant, domestic; **le pareti** ~**che** one's own four walls; **animale** *m* ~ pet; **una** ~**a a ore** a daily (woman).

domicilia're [dōmēchēlyá'rā] *ag vedi* **arresto**.

domiciliar'si [dōmēchēlyár'sē] *vr* to take up residence.

domici'lio [dōmēchē'lyō] *sm* (*DIR*) domicile, place of residence; **visita a** ~ (*MED*) house call; "**recapito a** ~" "deliveries"; **violazione di** ~ (*DIR*) breaking and entering.

dominan'te *ag* (*colore, nota*) dominant; (*opinione*) prevailing; (*idea*) main *cpd*, chief *cpd*; (*posizione*) dominating *cpd*; (*classe, partito*) ruling *cpd*.

domina're *vt* to dominate; (*fig: sentimenti*) to control, master ♦ *vi* to be in the dominant position; ~**rsi** *vr* (*controllarsi*) to control o.s.; ~ **su** (*fig*) to surpass, outclass.

dominato're, tri'ce *ag* ruling *cpd* ♦ *sm/f* ruler.

dominazio'ne [dōmēnáttsyō'nā] *sf* domination.

dominica'no, a *ag*: **la Repubblica D~a** the Dominican Republic.

domi'nio *sm* dominion; (*fig: campo*) field, domain; ~**i coloniali** colonies; **essere di** ~ **pubblico** (*notizia etc*) to be common knowledge.

dona're *vt* to give, present; (*per beneficenza etc*) to donate ♦ *vi* (*fig*): ~ **a** to suit, become; ~ **sangue** to give blood.

donato're, tri'ce *sm/f* donor; ~ **di sangue/di organi** blood/organ donor.

donazio'ne [dōnáttsyō'nā] *sf* donation; **atto di** ~ (*DIR*) deed of gift.

don'de *av* (*poetico*) whence.

dondola're *vt* (*cullare*) to rock; ~**rsi** *vr* to swing, sway.

don'dolo *sm*: **sedia/cavallo a** ~ rocking chair/horse.

dongiovan'ni [dōnjōvàn'nē] *sm* Don Juan, ladies' man.

don'na *sf* woman; (*titolo*) Donna; (*CARTE*) queen; **figlio di buona** ~! (*fam*) son of a bitch!; ~ **di casa** housewife; ~ **a ore** daily (help *o* woman); ~ **delle pulizie** cleaning lady, cleaner; ~ **di servizio** maid; ~ **di vita** *o* **di strada** prostitute, streetwalker.

donnaio'lo *sm* ladykiller.

donne'sco, a, schi, sche *ag* women's, woman's.

don'nola *sf* weasel.

do'no *sm* gift.

do'po *av* (*tempo*) afterwards; (: *più tardi*) later; (*luogo*) after, next ♦ *prep* after ♦ *cong* (*temporale*): ~ **aver studiato** after having studied ♦ *ag inv*: **il giorno** ~ the following day; ~ **mangiato** *o* **a dormire** after having eaten *o* after a meal he goes and takes a nap; **un anno** ~ a year later; ~ **di me/lui** after me/him; ~ **che** = **dopoché**.

dopobar'ba *sm inv* after-shave.

dopoché [dōpōkā'] *cong* after, when.

dopodiché [dōpōdēkā'] *av* after which.

dopodoma'ni *av* the day after tomorrow.

dopoguer'ra *sm* postwar years *pl*.

dopolavo'ro *sm* recreational club.

dopopran'zo [dōpōprán'dzō] *av* after lunch (*o* dinner).

doposci [dōpōshē'] *sm inv* après-ski outfit.

doposcuo'la *sm inv* school club offering extra tuition and recreational facilities.

dopotut'to *av* after all.

doppiag'gio [dōppyàd'jō] *sm* (*CINEMA*) dubbing.

doppia're *vt* (*NAUT*) to round; (*SPORT*) to lap; (*CINEMA*) to dub.

doppiato're, tri'ce *sm/f* dubber.

doppiet'ta *sf* (*fucile*) double-barreled (*US*) *o* double-barrelled (*Brit*) shotgun; (*sparo*) shot from both barrels; (*CALCIO*) double; (*PUGILATO*) one-two; (*AUT*) double-clutch (*US*), double-declutch (*Brit*).

doppiez'za [dōppyāt'tsà] *sf* (*fig: di persona*) duplicity, double-dealing.

dop'pio, a *ag* double; (*fig: falso*) double-dealing, deceitful ♦ *sm* (*quantità*): **il** ~ (**di**) twice as much (*o* many), double the amount (*o* number) of; (*SPORT*) doubles *pl* ♦ *av* double; **battere una lettera in** ~**a copia** to type a letter with a carbon copy; **fare il** ~ **gioco** (*fig*) to play a double game; **chiudere a** ~**a mandata** to double-lock; ~ **senso** double entendre; **frase a** ~ **senso** sentence with a double meaning; **un utensile a** ~ **uso** a dual-purpose utensil.

doppiofon'do *sm* (*di valigia*) false bottom; (*NAUT*) double hull.

doppio'ne *sm* duplicate (copy).

doppiopet'to *sm* double-breasted jacket.

doppi'sta *sm/f* (*TENNIS*) doubles player.

dora're *vt* to gild; *(CUC)* to brown; ~ **la pillola** *(fig)* to sugar the pill.

dora'to, a *ag* golden; *(ricoperto d'oro)* gilt, gilded.

doratu'ra *sf* gilding.

dormicchia're |dŏrmĕkkyà'rā| *vi* to doze.

dormien'te *ag* sleeping ♦ *sm/f* sleeper.

dormiglio'ne, a |dŏrmēlyŏ'nā| *sm/f* sleepyhead.

dormi're *vi* to sleep; *(essere addormentato)* to be asleep, be sleeping; **il caffè non mi fa** ~ coffee keeps me awake; ~ **come un ghiro** to sleep like a log; ~ **della grossa** to sleep soundly, be dead to the world; ~ **in piedi** *(essere stanco)* to be asleep on one's feet.

dormi'ta *sf:* **farsi una** ~ to have a good sleep.

dormito'rio *sm* dormitory; ~ **pubblico** flophouse *(US)* o doss house *(Brit)* *(run by local authority)*.

dormive'glia |dŏrmēvāl'yà| *sm* drowsiness.

dorrò *etc vb vedi* **dolere**.

dorsa'le *ag:* **spina** ~ backbone, spine.

dor'so *sm* back; *(di montagna)* ridge, crest; *(di libro)* spine; *(NUOTO)* backstroke; **a** ~ **di cavallo** on horseback.

dosag'gio |dŏzàd'jŏ| *sm* *(atto)* measuring out; **sbagliare il** ~ to get the proportions wrong.

dosa're *vt* to measure out; *(MED)* to dose.

do'se *sf* quantity, amount; *(MED)* dose.

dossier' |dŏsyā'| *sm inv* dossier, file.

dos'so *sm* *(rilievo)* rise; *(: di strada)* bump; *(dorso):* **levarsi di** ~ **i vestiti** to take one's clothes off; **levarsi un peso di** ~ *(fig)* to take a weight off one's mind.

dota're *vt:* ~ **di** to provide o supply with; *(fig)* to endow with;

dota'to, a *ag:* ~ **di** *(attrezzature)* equipped with; *(bellezza, intelligenza)* endowed with; **un uomo** ~ a gifted man.

dotazio'ne |dŏtàttsyŏ'nā| *sf* *(insieme di beni)* endowment; *(di macchine etc)* equipment; **dare qc in** ~ **a qn** to issue sb with sth, issue sth to sb; **i macchinari in** ~ **alla fabbrica** the machinery in use in the factory.

do'te *sf* *(di sposa)* dowry; *(assegnata a un ente)* endowment; *(fig)* gift, talent.

Dott. *abbr* (= *dottore*) Dr.

dot'to, a *ag* *(colto)* learned ♦ *sm* *(sapiente)* scholar; *(ANAT)* duct.

dottora'to *sm* degree; ~ **di ricerca** doctorate, doctor's degree.

dotto're, es'sa *sm/f* doctor.

dottri'na *sf* doctrine.

Dott.ssa *abbr* (= *dottoressa*) Dr.

double-fa'ce |dōōblfàs'| *ag inv* reversible.

do've *av* where; *(in cui)* where, in which; *(dovunque)* wherever ♦ *sm:* **per ogni** ~ everywhere; **di dov'è?** where are you from?; **da** ~ **abito vedo tutta la città** I can see the whole city from where I live; **per** ~ **si passa?**
which way should we go?; **le dò una mano fin** ~ **posso** I'll help you as much as I can.

dove're *sm* *(obbligo)* duty ♦ *vt* *(essere debitore)*: ~ **qc (a qn)** to owe (sb) sth ♦ *vi* *(seguito dall'infinito: obbligo)* to have to; **lui deve farlo** he has to do it, he must do it; **è dovuto partire** he had to leave; **ha dovuto pagare** he had to pay; *(: intenzione)*: **devo partire domani** I'm (due) to leave tomorrow; *(: probabilità)* **dev'essere tardi** it must be late; **doveva accadere** it was bound to happen; **avere il senso del** ~ to have a sense of duty; **rivolgersi a chi di** ~ to apply to the appropriate authority o person; **a** ~ *(bene)* properly; *(debitamente)* as he (o she *etc*) deserves; **come si deve** *(bene)* properly; *(meritatamente)* properly, as he (o she *etc*) deserves; **una persona come si deve** a respectable person.

dovero'so, a *ag* (right and) proper.

dovrò *etc vb vedi* **dovere**.

dovun'que *av* *(in qualunque luogo)* wherever; *(dappertutto)* everywhere; ~ **io vada** wherever I go.

dovutamen'te *av* *(debitamente:* redigere, compilare) correctly; *(: rimproverare)* as he (o she *etc*) deserves.

dovu'to, a *ag* *(causato):* ~ **a** due to ♦ *sm* due; **nel modo** ~ in the proper way; **ho lavorato più del** ~ I worked more than was necessary.

dozzi'na |dŏddzē'nà| *sf* dozen; **una** ~ **di uova** a dozen eggs; **di** o **da** ~ *(scrittore, spettacolo)* second-rate.

dozzina'le |dŏddzēnà'lā| *ag* cheap, second-rate.

DP *sigla f* (= *Democrazia Proletaria*) *political party.*

dra'ga, ghe *sf* dredger.

draga're *vt* to dredge.

draghe'rò *etc* |dràgàro'| *vb vedi* **dragare**.

dra'go, ghi *sm* dragon; *(fig fam)* genius.

dram'ma, i *sm* drama; **fare un** ~ **di qc** to make a drama out of sth.

dramma'tico, a, ci, che *ag* dramatic.

drammatizza're |dràmmàtēddzà'rā| *vt* to dramatize.

drammatur'go, ghi *sm* playwright, dramatist.

drappeggia're |dràppàdjà'rā| *vt* to drape.

drappeg'gio |dràppàd'jŏ| *sm* *(tessuto)* drapery; *(di abito)* folds.

drappel'lo *sm* *(MIL)* squad; *(gruppo)* band, group.

drap'po *sm* cloth.

dra'stico, a, ci, che *ag* drastic.

drenag'gio |drānàd'jŏ| *sm* drainage.

drena're *vt* to drain.

Dre'sda *sf* Dresden.

dribbla're *vi* *(CALCIO)* to dribble ♦ *vt*

(*avversario*) to dodge, avoid.

drit'to, a *ag, av* = **diritto** ♦ *sm/f* (*fam: furbo*): **è un** ~ he's a crafty *o* sly one ♦ *sf* (*destra*) right, right hand; (*NAUT*) starboard; **a** ~**a e a manca** (*fig*) on all sides, right, left and center.

drizza're |drĕttsá'rā| *vt* (*far tornare diritto*) to straighten; (*volgere: sguardo, occhi*) to turn, direct; (*innalzare: antenna, muro*) to erect; ~**rsi** *vr* to stand up; ~ **le orecchie** to prick up one's ears; ~**rsi in piedi** to rise to one's feet; ~**rsi a sedere** to sit up.

dro'ga, ghe *sf* (*sostanza aromatica*) spice; (*stupefacente*) drug; ~**ghe pesanti/leggere** hard/soft drugs.

droga're *vt* to season, spice; to drug, dope; ~**rsi** *vr* to take drugs.

droga'to, a *sm/f* drug addict.

drogheri'a |drōgārĕ'á| *sf* grocery (store) (*US*), grocer's (shop) (*Brit*).

drogherò *etc* |drōgáro'| *vb vedi* **drogare**.

droghie're, a |drōgyc'rā| *sm/f* grocer.

dromeda'rio *sm* dromedary.

D.T. *abbr* = **direttore tecnico**.

dub'bio, a *ag* (*incerto*) doubtful, dubious; (*ambiguo*) dubious ♦ *sm* (*incertezza*) doubt; **avere il** ~ **che** to be afraid that, suspect that; **essere in** ~ **fra** to hesitate between; **mettere in** ~ **qc** to question sth; **nutrire seri** ~**i su qc** to have grave doubts about sth; **senza** ~ doubtless, no doubt.

dubbio'so, a *ag* doubtful, dubious.

dubita're *vi*: ~ **di** (*onestà*) to doubt; (*risultato*) to be doubtful of; ~ **di qn** to mistrust sb; ~ **di sé** to be unsure of o.s.

Dubli'no *sf* Dublin.

du'ca, chi *sm* duke.

du'ce |dōō'chā| *sm* (*STORIA*) captain; (*: del fascismo*) duce.

duches'sa |dōōkās'sá| *sf* duchess.

du'e *num* two; **a** ~ **a** ~ two at a time, two by two; **dire** ~ **parole** to say a few words; **ci metto** ~ **minuti** I'll have it done in a jiffy.

duecente'sco, a, schi, sche |dōōáchántá'skō| *ag* thirteenth-century.

duecen'to |dōōáchcn'tō| *num* two hundred ♦ *sm*: **il D**~ the thirteenth century.

duella're *vi* to fight a duel.

duel'lo *sm* duel.

duemi'la *num* two thousand ♦ *sm inv*: **il** ~ **the** year two thousand.

duepez'zi |dōōápct'tsē| *sm* (*costume da bagno*) two-piece swimsuit; (*abito femminile*) two-piece suit.

duet'to *sm* duet.

dul'cis in fun'do |dōōl'chēsēn'fōōndō| *av* to cap it all.

du'na *sf* dune.

dun'que *cong* (*perciò*) so, therefore; (*riprendendo il discorso*) well (then) ♦ *sm inv*:

venire al ~ to come to the point.

du'o *sm inv* (*MUS*) duet; (*TEATRO, CINEMA, fig*) duo.

duo'le *etc vb vedi* **dolere**.

duo'mo *sm* cathedral.

du'plex *sm inv* (*TEL*) party line.

duplica'to *sm* duplicate.

du'plice |dōō'plēchā| *ag* double, twofold; **in** ~ **copia** in duplicate.

duplicità |dōōplĕchĕtá'| *sf* (*fig*) duplicity.

duran'te *prep* during; **vita natural** ~ for life.

dura're *vi* to last; **non può** ~! this can't go on any longer!; ~ **fatica a** to have difficulty in; ~ **in carica** to remain in office.

dura'ta *sf* length (of time); duration; **per tutta la** ~ **di** throughout; ~ **media della vita** life expectancy.

duratu'ro, a *ag*, **dure'vole** *ag* (*ricordo*) lasting; (*materiale*) durable.

durez'za |dōōrát'tsá| *sf* hardness; stubbornness; harshness; toughness.

du'ro, a *ag* (*pietra, lavoro, materasso, problema*) hard; (*persona: ostinato*) stubborn, obstinate; (*: severo*) harsh, hard; (*voce*) harsh; (*carne*) tough ♦ *sm/f* (*persona*) tough one ♦ *av*: **tener** ~ (*resistere*) to stand firm, hold out; **avere la pelle** ~**a** (*fig: persona*) to be tough; **fare il** ~ to act tough; ~ **di comprendonio** slow-witted; ~ **d'orecchi** hard of hearing.

duro'ne *sm* hard skin.

dut'tile *ag* (*sostanza*) malleable; (*fig: carattere*) docile, biddable; (*: stile*) adaptable.

D.V. *abbr* (= *Deo volente*) DV.

E

E, e |ā| *sf o m inv* (*lettera*) E, e; **E come Empoli** ≈ E for Easy.

E *abbr* (= *est*) E; (*AUT*) = *itinerario europeo*.

e, *dav V spesso* **ed** *cong* and; (*avversativo*) but; (*eppure*) and yet; ~ **lui?** what about him?; ~ **compralo!** well buy it then!

è *vb vedi* **essere**.

E.A. *abbr* = **ente autonomo**.

E.A.D. *sigla f vedi* **elaborazione automatica dei dati**.

ebanisteri'a *sf* cabinetmaking; (*negozio*) cabinet (*US*) *o* cabinet-maker's (*Brit*) shop.

e'bano *sm* ebony.

ebbe'ne *cong* well (then).

eb'bi *etc vb vedi* **avere**.

ebbrez'za |ábbrāt'tsá| *sf* intoxication.

eb'bro, a *ag* drunk; ~ **di** (*gioia etc*) beside o.s. *o* wild with.

e'bete *ag* stupid, idiotic.

ebeti'smo *sm* stupidity.

ebollizio'ne [ābōllēttsyō'nā] *sf* boiling; **punto di** ~ boiling point.

ebra'ico, a, ci, che *ag* Hebrew, Hebraic ♦ *sm* (*LING*) Hebrew.

ebre'o, a *ag* Jewish ♦ *sm/f* Jew/Jewess.

E'bridi *sfpl*: **le (isole)** ~ the Hebrides.

ebur'neo, a *ag* ivory *cpd*.

E/C *abbr* = **estratto conto**.

ecatom'be *sf* (*strage*) slaughter, massacre.

ecc *abbr av* (= *eccetera*) etc.

ecceden'te [āchāden'tā] *sm* surplus.

ecceden'za [āchāden'tsā] *sf* excess, surplus; (*INFORM*) overflow.

ecce'dere [āche'dārā] *vt* to exceed ♦ *vi* to go too far; ~ **nel bere/mangiare** to indulge in drink/food to excess.

eccellen'te [āchāllen'tā] *ag* excellent.

eccellen'za [āchālen'tsā] *sf* excellence; (*titolo*): **Sua E~** His Excellency.

eccel'lere [āchel'lārā] *vi*: ~ **(in)** to excel (at); ~ **su tutti** to surpass everyone.

eccel'so, a [āchel'sō] *pp di* **eccellere** ♦ *ag* (*cima, montagna*) high; (*fig: ingegno*) great, exceptional.

eccen'trico, a, ci, che [āchen'trēkō] *ag* eccentric.

eccessi'vo, a [āchāssē'vō] *ag* excessive.

ecces'so [āches'sō] *sm* excess; **all'~** (*gentile, generoso*) to excess, excessively; **dare in** ~**i** to fly into a rage; ~ **di velocità** (*AUT*) speeding; ~ **di zelo** overzealousness.

ecce'tera [āche'tārā] *av* et cetera, and so on.

eccet'to [āchet'tō] *prep* except, with the exception of; ~ **che** *cong* except, other than; ~ **che (non)** unless.

eccettua're [āchāttōōā'rā] *vt* to except; **eccettuati i presenti** present company excepted.

ecceziona'le [āchāttsyōnā'lā] *ag* exceptional; **in via del tutto** ~ in this instance, exceptionally.

eccezio'ne [āchāttsyō'nā] *sf* exception; (*DIR*) objection; **a** ~ **di** with the exception of, except for; **d'**~ exceptional; **fare un'**~ **alla regola** to make an exception to the rule.

ecchi'mosi [ākkē'mōzē] *sf inv* bruise.

ecci'dio [āchē'dyō] *sm* massacre.

eccitan'te [āchētán'tā] *ag* (*gen*) exciting; (*sostanza*) stimulating ♦ *sm* stimulant.

eccita're [āchētā'rā] *vt* (*curiosità, interesse*) to excite, arouse; (*folla*) to incite; ~**rsi** *vr* to get excited; (*sessualmente*) to become aroused.

eccitazio'ne [āchētāttsyō'nā] *sf* excitement.

ecclesia'stico, a, ci, che *ag* ecclesiastical, church *cpd*; clerical ♦ *sm* ecclesiastic.

ec'co *av* (*per dimostrare*): ~ **il treno!** here's *o* here comes the train!; (*dav pronome*): ~**mi!** here I am!; ~**ne uno!** here's one (of them)!; (*dav pp*): ~ **fatto!** there, that's done!

ecco'me *av* rather; **ti piace?** — ~! do you like it? — I'll say! *o* and how! *o* rather! (*Brit*).

ECG *sigla m* = **elettrocardiogramma**.

echeggia're [ākādjā'rā] *vi* to echo.

eclet'tico, a, ci, che *ag, sm/f* eclectic.

ecletti'smo *sm* eclecticism.

eclissa're *vt* to eclipse; (*fig*) to eclipse, overshadow; ~**rsi** *vr* (*persona: scherzoso*) to slip away.

eclis'si *sf* eclipse.

e'co, *pl*(m) e'chi *sm o f* echo; **suscitò** *o* **ebbe una profonda** ~ it caused quite a stir.

ecografi'a *sf* (*MED*) ultrasound.

ecologi'a [ākōlōjē'á] *sf* ecology.

ecolo'gico, a, ci, che [ākōlo'jēkō] *ag* ecological.

eco'logo, a, gi, ghe *sm/f* ecologist.

economa'to *sm* (*INS*) bursar's office.

economi'a *sf* economy; (*scienza*) economics *sg*; (*risparmio: azione*) saving; **fare** ~ to economize, make economies; **l'**~ **sommersa** underground (*US*) *o* the black (*Brit*) economy.

econo'mico, a, ci, che *ag* economic; (*poco costoso*) economical; **edizione** ~**a** economy edition.

economi'sta, i *sm* economist.

economizza're [ākōnōmēddzá'rā] *vt, vi* to save.

eco'nomo, a *ag* thrifty ♦ *sm/f* (*INS*) bursar.

E'CU *abbr m inv* (= *European Currency Unit*) ECU.

E'cuador *sm*: **l'**~ Ecuador.

ecume'nico, a, ci, che *ag* ecumenical.

ecze'ma [ākdze'má] *sm* eczema.

ed *cong vedi* **e**.

Ed. *abbr* = **editore**.

ed. *abbr* = **edizione**.

e'dera *sf* ivy.

edi'cola *sf* newspaper kiosk *o* stand (*US*).

edicolan'te *sm/f* news dealer (*US*) *o* vendor (*Brit*) (*in kiosk*).

edifican'te *ag* edifying.

edifica're *vt* to build; (*fig: teoria, azienda*) to establish; (*indurre al bene*) to edify.

edifi'cio [ādēfē'chō] *sm* building; (*fig*) structure.

edi'le *ag* building *cpd*.

edili'zio, a [ādēlēt'tsyō] *ag* building *cpd* ♦ *sf* building, building trade.

Edimbur'go *sf* Edinburgh.

e'dito, a *ag* published.

edito're, tri'ce *ag* publishing *cpd* ♦ *sm/f* publisher; (*curatore*) editor.

editori'a *sf* publishing.

editoria'le *ag* publishing *cpd* ♦ *sm (articolo di fondo)* editorial, leader.

edit'to *sm* edict.

edizio'ne [ādēttsyō'nā] *sf* edition; *(tiratura)* printing; ~ **a tiratura limitata** limited edition.

edoni'smo *sm* hedonism.

edot'to, a *ag* informed; **rendere qn ~ su qc** to inform sb about sth.

educan'da *sf* boarder.

educa're *vt* to educate; *(gusto, mente)* to train; ~ **qn a fare** to train sb to do.

educati'vo, a *ag* educational.

educa'to, a *ag* polite, well-mannered.

educazio'ne [ādōōkáttsyō'nā] *sf* education; *(familiare)* upbringing; *(comportamento)* (good) manners *pl*; **per ~** out of politeness; **questa è pura mancanza d'~!** this is sheer bad manners!; ~ **fisica** *(INS)* physical training *o* education.

educherò *etc* [ādōōkáro'] *vb vedi* **educare**.

E.E.D. *sigla f vedi* **elaborazione elettronica dei dati**.

EEG *sigla m* = **elettroencefalogramma**.

efe'lide *sf* freckle.

effemina'to, a *ag* effeminate.

effera'to, a *ag* brutal, savage.

effervescen'te [āffārvāshen'tā] *ag* effervescent.

effettivamen'te *av (in effetti)* in fact; *(a dire il vero)* really, actually.

effetti'vo, a *ag (reale)* real, actual; *(impiegato, professore)* permanent; *(MIL)* regular ♦ *sm (MIL)* strength; *(di patrimonio etc)* sum total.

effet'to *sm* effect; *(COMM: cambiale)* bill; *(fig: impressione)* impression; **far ~** *(medicina)* to take effect, (start to) work; **cercare l'~** to seek attention; **in ~i** in fact; ~**i attivi** *(COMM)* bills receivable; ~**i passivi** *(COMM)* bills payable; ~**i personali** personal effects, personal belongings.

effettua're *vt* to effect, carry out.

effica'ce [āffēká'chā] *ag* effective.

effica'cia [āffēká'chá] *sf* effectiveness.

efficien'te [āffēchen'tā] *ag* efficient.

efficienti'smo [āffēchāntēz'mō] *sm* maximum efficiency.

efficien'za [āffēchen'tsá] *sf* efficiency.

effigia're [āffējá'rā] *vt* to represent, portray.

effi'gie [āffē'jā] *sf inv* effigy.

effi'mero, a *ag* ephemeral.

efflu'vio *sm (anche peg, ironico)* scent, perfume.

effusio'ne *sf* effusion.

e.g. *abbr (= exempli gratia)* e.g.

egemoni'a [ājāmōnē'á] *sf* hegemony.

Ege'o [āje'ō] *sm*: **l'~, il mare ~** the Aegean (Sea).

e'gida [e'jēdà] *sf*: **sotto l'~ di** under the aegis of.

Egit'to [ājēt'tō] *sm*: **l'~** Egypt.

egizia'no, a [ājēttsyà'nō] *ag, sm/f* Egyptian.

egi'zio, a [ājēt'tsyō] *ag, sm/f (ancient)* Egyptian.

e'gli [āl'yē] *pronome* he; ~ **stesso** he himself.

e'go *sm inv (PSIC)* ego.

egocen'trico, a, ci, che [āgōchen'trēkō] *ag* egocentric(al) ♦ *sm/f* self-centered *(US) o* self-centred *(Brit)* person.

egocentri'smo [āgōchāntrēz'mō] *sm* egocentricity.

egoi'smo *sm* selfishness, egoism.

egoi'sta, i, e *ag* selfish, egoistic ♦ *sm/f* egoist.

egoi'stico, a, ci, che *ag* egoistic, selfish.

egoti'smo *sm* egotism.

egoti'sta, i, e *ag* egotistic ♦ *sm/f* egotist.

Egr. *abbr* = **Egregio**.

egre'gio, a, gi, gie [āgre'jō] *ag* distinguished; *(nelle lettere)*: **E~ Signore** Dear Sir.

eguaglian'za *etc* [āgwályàn'tsá] *vedi* **uguaglianza** *etc*.

egualita'rio, a *ag, sm/f* egalitarian.

E.I. *abbr* = *Esercito Italiano*.

elabora're *vt (progetto)* to work out, elaborate; *(dati)* to process; *(digerire)* to digest.

elaborato're *sm (INFORM)*: ~ **elettronico** computer.

elaborazio'ne [ālábōráttsyō'nā] *sf* elaboration; processing; digestion; ~ **automatica dei dati (E.A.D.)** *(INFORM)* automatic data processing (A.D.P.); ~ **elettronica dei dati (E.E.D.)** *(INFORM)* electronic data processing (E.D.P.); ~ **testi** *(INFORM)* text processing.

elargi're [ālárjē'rā] *vt* to hand out.

elargizio'ne [ālárjēttsyō'nā] *sf* donation.

elasticizza'to, a [ālástēchēddzá'tō] *ag (tessuto)* stretch *cpd*.

ela'stico, a, ci, che *ag* elastic; *(fig: andatura)* springy; (: *decisione, vedute)* flexible ♦ *sm (gommino)* rubber band; *(per il cucito)* elastic *q*.

elefan'te *sm* elephant.

elegan'te *ag* elegant.

elegan'za [ālāgán'tsá] *sf* elegance.

eleg'gere [āled'jārā] *vt* to elect.

elementa're *ag* elementary; **le (scuole)** ~**i** grade *(US) o* primary *(Brit)* school; **prima ~** first year of primary school, ≈ 1st grade *(US)*, ≈ infants' class *(Brit)*.

elemen'to *sm* element; *(parte componente)* element, component, part; ~**i** *smpl (della scienza etc)* elements, rudiments.

elemo'sina *sf* charity, alms *pl*; **chiedere l'~** to beg.

elemosina're *vt* to beg for, ask for ♦ *vi* to beg.

elenca're *vt* to list.

elencherò *etc* [ālānkáro'] *vb vedi* **elencare**.

elen'co, chi *sm* list; ~ **nominativo** list of names; ~ **telefonico** telephone directory.
eles'si *etc vb vedi* **eleggere.**
eletti'vo, a *ag* (*carica etc*) elected.
elet'to, a *pp di* **eleggere ♦** *sm/f* (*nominato*) elected member.
elettora'le *ag* electoral, election *cpd*.
elettora'to *sm* electorate.
eletto're, tri'ce *sm/f* voter, elector.
elettra'uto *sm inv* workshop for car electrical repairs; (*tecnico*) car electrician.
elettrici'sta, i [ālāttrēchē'stá] *sm* electrician.
elettricità [ālāttrēchētá'] *sf* electricity.
elet'trico, a, ci, che *ag* electric(al).
elettrifica're *vt* to electrify.
elettrizzan'te [ālāttrēddzàn'tā] *ag* (*fig*) electrifying, thrilling.
elettrizza're [ālāttrēddzá'rā] *vt* to electrify; ~**rsi** *vr* to become charged with electricity; (*fig: persona*) to be thrilled.
elet'tro... *prefisso* electro....
elettrocardiogram'ma, i *sm* electrocardiogram.
elet'trodo *sm* electrode.
elettrodome'stico, a, ci, che *ag:* **apparecchi** ~**ci** domestic (electrical) appliances.
elettroencefalogram'ma, i [ālāttrōānchāfàlōgràm'má] *sm* electroencephalogram.
elettro'geno, a [ālāttro'jānō] *ag:* **gruppo** ~ generator.
elettro'lisi *sf* electrolysis.
elettromagne'tico, a, ci, che [ālāttrōmánye'tēkō] *ag* electromagnetic.
elettromotri'ce [ālāttrōmōtrē'chā] *sf* electric train.
elettro'ne *sm* electron.
elettro'nico, a, ci, che *ag* electronic **♦** *sf* electronics *sg*.
elettroshock' [ālāttrōshok'] *sm inv* (electro)shock treatment.
elettrotec'nico, a, ci, che *ag* electrotechnical **♦** *sm* electrical engineer.
eleva're *vt* to raise; (*edificio*) to erect; (*multa*) to impose; ~ **un numero al quadrato** to square a number.
elevatez'za [ālāvátāt'tsá] *sf* (*altezza*) elevation; (*di animo, pensiero*) loftiness.
eleva'to, a *ag* (*gen*) high; (*cime*) high, lofty; (*fig: stile, sentimenti*) lofty.
elevazio'ne [ālāváttsyō'nā] *sf* elevation; (*l'elevare*) raising.
elezio'ne [ālāttsyō'nā] *sf* election; ~**i** *sfpl* (*POL*) election(s); **patria d'**~ chosen country.
e'lica, che *sf* propeller.
elicot'tero *sm* helicopter.
eli'dere *vt* (*FONETICA*) to elide; ~**rsi** *vr* (*forze*) to cancel each other out, neutralize each other.
elimina're *vt* to eliminate.
eliminato'ria *sf* eliminating round.

eliminazio'ne [ālēmēnáttsyō'nā] *sf* elimination.
e'lio *sm* helium.
elipor'to *sm* heliport.
elisabettia'no, a *ag* Elizabethan.
elisir' *sm inv* elixir.
eli'so, a *pp di* **elidere.**
elita'rio, a *ag* elitist.
éli'te [ālēt'] *sf inv* élite.
el'la *pronome* she; (*forma di cortesia*) you; ~ **stessa** she herself; you yourself.
ellis'se *sf* ellipse.
ellit'tico, a, ci, che *ag* elliptic(al).
elmet'to *sm* helmet.
el'mo *sm* helmet.
elogia're [ālōjá'rā] *vt* to praise.
elogiati'vo, a [ālōjátē'vō] *ag* laudatory.
elo'gio [ālo'jō] *sm* (*discorso, scritto*) eulogy; (*lode*) praise; ~ **funebre** funeral oration.
eloquen'te *ag* eloquent; **questi dati sono** ~**i** these facts speak for themselves.
eloquen'za [ālōkwen'tsá] *sf* eloquence.
elo'quio *sm* speech, language.
elucubra're *vt* (*piano*) to ponder about, ponder over.
elucubrazio'ni [ālōōkōōbráttsyō'nē] *sfpl* (*anche ironico*) cogitations, ponderings.
elu'dere *vt* to evade.
elu'si *etc vb vedi* **eludere.**
elusio'ne *sf:* ~ **d'imposta** tax evasion.
elusi'vo, a *ag* evasive.
elu'so, a *pp di* **eludere.**
elve'tico, a, ci, che *ag* Swiss.
emacia'to, a [āmáchá'tō] *ag* emaciated.
emana're *vt* to send out, give off; (*fig: leggi*) to promulgate; (*: decreti*) to issue **♦** *vi:* ~ **da** to come from.
emanazio'ne [āmánáttsyō'nā] *sf* (*di raggi, calore*) emanation; (*di odori*) exhalation; (*di legge*) promulgation; (*di ordine, circolare*) issuing.
emancipa're [āmánchēpá'rā] *vt* to emancipate; ~**rsi** *vr* (*fig*) to become liberated o emancipated.
emancipazio'ne [āmánchēpáttsyō'nā] *sf* emancipation.
emargina're [āmárjēná'rā] *vt* (*fig: socialmente*) to cast out.
emargina'to, a [āmárjēná'tō] *sm/f* outcast.
ematologi'a [āmátōlōjē'á] *sf* hematology (*US*), haematology (*Brit*).
emato'ma, i *sm* hematoma (*US*), haematoma (*Brit*).
emble'ma, i *sm* emblem.
emblema'tico, a, ci, che *ag* emblematic; (*fig: atteggiamento, parole*) symbolic.
emboli'a *sf* embolism.
embrio'ne *sm* embryo.
emendamen'to *sm* amendment.
emenda're *vt* to amend.
emergen'te [āmārjen'tā] *ag* emerging.

emergen'za [āmārjen'tsà] *sf* emergency; **in caso di** ~ in an emergency.
emer'gere [āmer'jārā] *vi* to emerge; (*sommergibile*) to surface; (*fig: distinguersi*) to stand out.
eme'rito, a *ag* (*insigne*) distinguished; **è un** ~ **cretino!** he's a complete idiot!
emer'si *etc vb vedi* **emergere**.
emer'so, a *pp di* **emergere** ♦ *ag* (*GEO*): **terre** ~**e** lands above sea level.
emes'so, a *pp di* **emettere**.
emet'tere *vt* (*suono, luce*) to give out, emit; (*onde radio*) to send out; (*assegno, franco-bollo, ordine*) to issue; (*fig: giudizio*) to express, voice; ~ **la sentenza** (*DIR*) to pass sentence.
emicra'nia *sf* migraine.
emigran'te *ag, sm/f* emigrant.
emigra're *vi* to emigrate.
emigra'to, a *ag* emigrant ♦ *sm/f* emigrant; (*STORIA*) émigré.
emigrazio'ne [āmēgràttsyō'nā] *sf* emigration.
emilia'no, a *ag* of (*o* from) Emilia.
eminen'te *ag* eminent, distinguished.
eminen'za [āmēnen'tsà] *sf* eminence; ~ **grigia** (*fig*) éminence grise.
emira'to *sm* emirate; **gli E**~**i Arabi Uniti** the United Arab Emirates.
emisfe'ro *sm* hemisphere; ~ **boreale/australe** northern/southern hemisphere.
emi'si *etc vb vedi* **emettere**.
emissa'rio *sm* (*GEO*) outlet, effluent; (*inviato*) emissary.
emissio'ne *sf* (*vedi emettere*) emission; sending out; issue; (*RADIO*) broadcast.
emitten'te *ag* (*banca*) issuing; (*RADIO*) broadcasting, transmitting ♦ *sf* (*RADIO*) transmitter.
emofili'a *sf* hemophilia (*US*), haemophilia (*Brit*).
emofili'aco, a, ci, che *ag, sm/f* hemophiliac (*US*), haemophiliac (*Brit*).
emoglobi'na *sf* hemoglobin (*US*), haemoglobin (*Brit*).
emorragi'a, gi'e [āmōrràjē'à] *sf* hemorrhage (*US*), haemorrhage (*Brit*).
emorro'idi *sfpl* hemorrhoids (*US*), haemorrhoids (*Brit*).
emosta'tico, a, ci, che *ag* hemostatic (*US*), haemostatic (*Brit*); **laccio** ~ tourniquet; **ma-tita** ~**a** styptic pencil.
emotività *sf* emotionalism.
emoti'vo, a *ag* emotional.
emozionan'te [āmōttsyōnán'tā] *ag* exciting, thrilling.
emoziona're [āmōttsyōnà'rā] *vt* (*appassio-nare*) to thrill, excite; (*commuovere*) to move; (*innervosire*) to upset; ~**rsi** *vr* to be excited; to be moved; to be upset.
emozio'ne [āmōttsyō'nā] *sf* emotion; (*agita-*

zione) excitement.
em'pio, a *ag* (*sacrilego*) impious; (*spietato*) cruel, pitiless; (*malvagio*) wicked, evil.
empo'rio *sm* general store.
emula're *vt* to emulate.
e'mulo, a *sm/f* imitator.
emulsio'ne *sf* emulsion.
EN *sigla = Enna.*
enci'clica, che [ānchē'klēkà] *sf* (*REL*) encycli-cal.
enciclopedi'a [ānchēklōpādē'à] *sf* ency-clop(a)edia.
encomia'bile *ag* commendable, praiseworthy.
encomia're *vt* to commend, praise.
enco'mio *sm* commendation; ~ **solenne** (*MIL*) mention in dispatches.
endoveno'so, a *ag* (*MED*) intravenous ♦ *sf* in-travenous injection.
ENE'A *sigla f = Comitato nazionale per la ri-cerca e lo sviluppo dell'Energia Nucleare e delle Energie Alternative.*
E.'N.E.L. *sigla m* (= *Ente Nazionale per l'Energia Elettrica*) *national electricity company.*
energe'tico, a, ci, che [ānārje'tēkō] *ag* (*ri-sorse, crisi*) energy *cpd*; (*sostanza, alimento*) energy-giving.
energi'a, gi'e [ānārjē'à] *sf* (*FISICA*) energy; (*fig*) energy, vigor (*US*), vigour (*Brit*).
ener'gico, a, ci, che [ānēr'jēkō] *ag* energetic, vigorous.
en'fasi *sf* emphasis; (*peg*) bombast, pompos-ity.
enfa'tico, a, ci, che *ag* emphatic; pompous.
enfatizza're [ānfátēddzà'rā] *vt* to emphasize, stress.
enfise'ma *sm* emphysema.
E'NI *sigla m = Ente Nazionale Idrocarburi.*
enig'ma, i *sm* enigma.
enigma'tico, a, ci, che *ag* enigmatic.
E'NIT *sigla m* (= *Ente Nazionale Italiano per il Turismo*) *Italian tourist authority.*
enne'simo, a *ag* (*MAT, fig*) nth; **per l'**~**a volta** for the umpteenth time.
enologi'a [ānōlōjē'à] *sf* enology.
eno'logo, gi *sm* wine expert.
enor'me *ag* enormous, huge.
enormità *sf inv* enormity, huge size; (*assurdi-tà*) absurdity; **non dire** ~! don't talk non-sense!
enote'ca, che *sf* (*negozio*) wine bar.
E.'N.P.A. *sigla m* (= *Ente Nazionale Prote-zione Animali*) ≈ SPCA (*US*), ≈ RSPCA (*Brit*).
E.'N.P.A.S. *sigla m* (= *Ente Nazionale di Pre-videnza e Assistenza per i Dipendenti Statali*) *welfare organization for State employees.*
en'te *sm* (*istituzione*) body, board, corpora-tion; (*FILOSOFIA*) being; ~ **locale** local government (*US*), local authority (*Brit*); ~

pubblico public body; ~ **di ricerca** research organization.

enteri'te *sf* enteritis.

entità *sf* (*FILOSOFIA*) entity; (*di perdita, danni, investimenti*) extent; (*di popolazione*) size; **di molta/poca** ~ (*avvenimento, incidente*) of great/little importance.

entram'bi, e *pronome pl* both (of them) ♦ *ag pl*: ~ **i ragazzi** both boys, both of the boys.

entran'te *ag* (*prossimo: mese, anno*) next, coming.

entra're *vi* to enter, go (*o come*) in; ~ **in** (*luogo*) to enter, go (*o come*) into; (*trovar posto, poter stare*) to fit into; (*essere ammesso a: club etc*) to join, become a member of; ~ **in automobile** to get into the car; **far** ~ **qn** (*visitatore etc*) to show sb in; ~ **in società/in commercio con qn** to go into partnership/business with sb; **questo non c'entra** (*fig*) that's got nothing to do with it.

entra'ta *sf* entrance, entry; ~**e** *sfpl* (*COMM*) receipts, takings; (*ECON*) income *sg*; **"~ libera"** "admission free"; **con l'~ in vigore dei nuovi provvedimenti ...** once the new measures come into effect ...; ~**e tributarie** tax revenue *sg*.

en'tro *prep* (*temporale*) within; ~ **domani** by tomorrow; ~ **e non oltre il 25 aprile** no later than 25th April.

entroter'ra *sm inv* hinterland.

entusiasman'te *ag* exciting.

entusiasma're *vt* to excite, fill with enthusiasm; ~**rsi** *vr*: ~**rsi (per qc/qn)** to become enthusiastic (about sth/sb).

entusia'smo *sm* enthusiasm.

entusia'sta, i, e *ag* enthusiastic ♦ *sm/f* enthusiast.

entusia'stico, a, ci, che *ag* enthusiastic.

enuclea're *vt* (*formale: chiarire*) to explain.

enumera're *vt* to enumerate, list.

enuncia're [ānōōnchà'rā] *vt* (*teoria*) to enunciate, set out.

enzi'ma, i *sm* enzyme.

epa'tico, a, ci, che *ag* hepatic; **cirrosi** ~**a** cirrhosis of the liver.

epati'te *sf* hepatitis.

e'pico, a, ci, che *ag* epic.

epidemi'a *sf* epidemic.

epider'mico, a, ci, che *ag* (*ANAT*) skin *cpd*; (*fig: interesse, impressioni*) superficial.

epider'mide *sf* skin, epidermis.

Epifani'a *sf* Epiphany.

epi'gono *sm* imitator.

epi'grafe *sf* epigraph; (*su libro*) dedication.

epilessi'a *sf* epilepsy.

epilet'tico, a, ci, che *ag, sm/f* epileptic.

epi'logo, ghi *sm* conclusion.

episo'dico, a, ci, che *ag* (*romanzo, narrazione*) episodic; (*fig: occasionale*) occasional.

episo'dio *sm* episode; **sceneggiato a** ~**i** serial.

epi'stola *sf* epistle.

epistola're *ag* epistolary; **essere in rapporto** *o* **relazione** ~ **con qn** to correspond *o* be in correspondence with sb.

epi'teto *sm* epithet.

e'poca, che *sf* (*periodo storico*) age, era; (*tempo*) time; (*GEO*) age; **mobili d'**~ period furniture; **fare** ~ (*scandalo*) to cause a stir; (*cantante, moda*) to mark a new era.

epope'a *sf* (*anche fig*) epic.

eppu're *cong* and yet, nevertheless.

EPT *sigla m* (= *Ente Provinciale per il Turismo*) *district tourist bureau*.

epura're *vt* (*POL*) to purge.

equa'nime *ag* (*imparziale*) fair, impartial.

equato're *sm* equator.

equazio'ne [ākwättsyō'nā] *sf* (*MAT*) equation.

eques'tre *ag* equestrian.

equila'tero, a *ag* equilateral.

equilibra're *vt* to balance.

equilibra'to, a *ag* (*carico, fig: giudizio*) balanced; (*vita*) well-regulated; (*persona*) stable, well-balanced.

equili'brio *sm* balance, equilibrium; **perdere l'**~ to lose one's balance; **stare in** ~ **su** (*persona*) to balance on; (*oggetto*) to be balanced on.

equilibri'smo *sm* tightrope walking; (*fig*) juggling.

equi'no, a *ag* horse *cpd*, equine.

equino'zio [ākwēnot'tsyō] *sm* equinox.

equipaggiamen'to [ākwēpàdjámān'tō] *sm* (*operazione: di nave*) equipping, fitting out; (: *di spedizione, esercito*) equipping; (*attrezzatura*) equipment.

equipaggia're [ākwēpàdjá'rā] *vt* to equip; ~**rsi** *vr* to equip o.s.

equipag'gio [ākwēpàd'jō] *sm* crew.

equipara're *vt* to make equal.

équi'pe [ākēp'] *sf* (*SPORT, gen*) team.

equità *sf* equity, fairness.

equitazio'ne [ākwētáttsyō'nā] *sf* (horse-)riding.

equivalen'te *ag, sm* equivalent.

equivalen'za [ākwēvàlen'tsá] *sf* equivalence.

equivale're *vi*: ~ **a** to be equivalent to; ~**rsi** *vr* (*forze etc*) to counterbalance each other; (*soluzioni*) to amount to the same thing; **equivale a dire che ...** that is the same as saying that ...

equival'so, a *pp di* **equivalere**.

equivoca're *vi* to misunderstand.

equi'voco, a, ci, che *ag* equivocal, ambiguous; (*sospetto*) dubious ♦ *sm* misunderstanding; **a scanso di** ~**ci** to avoid any misunderstanding; **giocare sull'**~ to equivocate.

e'quo, a *ag* fair, just.

e'ra *sf* era.

e'ra *etc vb vedi* **essere**.

eraria'le *ag*: **ufficio** ~ ≈ tax office; **imposte** ~**i** revenue taxes; **spese** ~**i** public expenditure *sg*.

era'rio *sm*: **l'**~ ≈ the Treasury.

er'ba *sf* grass; (*aromatica, medicinale*) herb; **in** ~ (*fig*) budding; **fare di ogni** ~ **un fascio** (*fig*) to lump everything (*o* everybody) together.

erbac'cia, ce [ārbách'chá] *sf* weed.

erbet'te *sfpl* beet tops.

erbori'sta, i, e *sm/f* herbalist.

erboristeri'a *sf* (*scienza*) study of medicinal herbs; (*negozio*) herbalist's (shop).

erbo'so, a *ag* grassy.

ere'de *sm/f* heir; ~ **legittimo** heir at law.

eredità *sf* (*DIR*) inheritance; (*BIOL*) heredity; **lasciare qc in** ~ **a qn** to leave *o* bequeath sth to sb.

eredita're *vt* to inherit.

eredita'rio, a *ag* hereditary.

ereditie'ra *sf* heiress.

eremi'ta, i *sm* hermit.

eremitag'gio [ārāmētád'jō] *sm* hermitage.

e'remo *sm* hermitage; (*fig*) retreat.

eresi'a *sf* heresy.

eres'si *etc vb vedi* **erigere**.

ere'tico, a, ci, che *ag* heretical ♦ *sm/f* heretic.

eret'to, a *pp di* **erigere** ♦ *ag* erect, upright.

erezio'ne [ārāttsyō'nā] *sf* (*FISIOL*) erection.

ergastola'no, a *sm/f* prisoner serving a life sentence, lifer (*fam*).

erga'stolo *sm* (*DIR*: *pena*) life imprisonment; (: *luogo di pena*) prison (*for those serving life sentences*).

ergono'mico, a, ci, che *ag* ergonomic(al).

e'rica *sf* heather.

eri'gere [ārē'jārā] *vt* to erect, raise; (*fig*: *fondare*) to found.

erite'ma *sm* (*MED*) inflammation, erythema; ~ **solare** sunburn.

ermelli'no *sm* ermine.

erme'tico, a, ci, che *ag* hermetic.

er'nia *sf* (*MED*) hernia; ~ **del disco** slipped disc.

e'ro *vb vedi* **essere**.

ero'dere *vt* to erode.

ero'e *sm* hero.

eroga're *vt* (*somme*) to distribute; (*gas, servizi*) to supply.

erogazio'ne [ārōgáttsyō'nā] *sf* distribution; supply.

ero'ico, a, ci, che *ag* heroic.

eroi'na *sf* heroine; (*droga*) heroin.

eroi'smo *sm* heroism.

erosio'ne *sf* erosion.

ero'so, a *pp di* **erodere**.

ero'tico, a, ci, che *ag* erotic.

eroti'smo *sm* eroticism.

er'pete *sm* herpes *sg*.

er'pice [ār'pēchā] *sm* (*AGR*) harrow.

erra're *vi* (*vagare*) to wander, roam; (*sbagliare*) to be mistaken.

erro'neo, a *ag* erroneous, wrong.

erro're *sm* error, mistake; (*morale*) error; **per** ~ by mistake; ~ **giudiziario** miscarriage of justice.

er'to, a *ag* (very) steep ♦ *sf* steep slope; **stare all'**~**a** to be on the alert.

erudi're *vt* to teach, educate.

erudi'to, a *ag* learned, erudite.

erutta're *vt* (*sog*: *vulcano*) to throw out, belch.

eruzio'ne [ārōōttsyō'nā] *sf* eruption; (*MED*) rash.

E.S. *sigla m* (= *elettroshock*) ECT.

esacerba're [āzáchārbá'rā] *vt* to exacerbate.

esagera're [āzájārá'rā] *vt* to exaggerate ♦ *vi* to exaggerate; (*eccedere*) to go too far; **senza** ~ without exaggeration.

esagera'to, a [āzájārá'tō] *ag* (*notizia, proporzioni*) exaggerated; (*curiosità, pignoleria*) excessive; (*prezzo*) exorbitant ♦ *sm/f*: **sei il solito** ~ you are exaggerating as usual.

esagerazio'ne [āsájārāttsyō'nā] *sf* exaggeration.

esagona'le *ag* hexagonal.

esa'gono *sm* hexagon.

esala're *vt* (*odori*) to give off ♦ *vi*: ~ **(da)** to emanate (from); ~ **l'ultimo respiro** (*fig*) to breathe one's last.

esalazio'ne [āzálāttsyō'nā] *sf* (*emissione*) exhalation; (*odore*) fumes *pl*.

esaltan'te *ag* exciting.

esalta're *vt* to exalt; (*entusiasmare*) to excite, stir; ~**rsi** *vr*: ~**rsi** **(per qc)** to grow excited (about sth).

esalta'to, a *sm/f* fanatic.

esaltazio'ne [āzáltāttsyō'nā] *sf* (*elogio*) extolling, exalting; (*nervosa*) intense excitement; (*mistica*) exaltation.

esa'me *sm* examination; (*INS*) exam, examination; **fare** *o* **dare un** ~ to sit *o* take an exam; **fare un** ~ **di coscienza** to search one's conscience; ~ **di guida** driving test; ~ **del sangue** blood test.

esamina're *vt* to examine.

esan'gue *ag* bloodless; (*fig*: *pallido*) pale, wan; (: *privo di vigore*) lifeless.

esa'nime *ag* lifeless.

esaspera're *vt* to exasperate; (*situazione*) to exacerbate; ~**rsi** *vr* to become annoyed *o* exasperated.

esasperazio'ne [āzáspārāttsyō'nā] *sf* exasperation.

esattamen'te *av* exactly; accurately, precisely.

esattez'za [āzáttāt'tsá] *sf* exactitude, accuracy, precision; **per l'**~ to be precise.

esat'to, a *pp di* **esigere** ♦ *ag* (*calcolo, ora*) correct, right, exact; (*preciso*) accurate, precise; (*puntuale*) punctual.

esatto're *sm* (*di imposte etc*) collector.

esattori'a *sf*: ~ **comunale** district assessor's office (*US*) *o* rates office (*Brit*).

esaudi're *vt* to grant, fulfil (*US*), fulfil (*Brit*).

esaurien'te *ag* exhaustive.

esaurimen'to *sm* exhaustion; ~ **nervoso** nervous breakdown; **svendita (fino) ad ~ della merce** clearance sale.

esauri're *vt* (*stancare*) to exhaust, wear out; (*provviste, miniera*) to exhaust; ~**rsi** *vr* to exhaust o.s., wear o.s. out; (*provviste*) to run out.

esauri'to, a *ag* exhausted; (*merci*) sold out; (*libri*) out of print; **essere ~** (*persona*) to be run down; **registrare il tutto ~** (*TEATRO*) to have a full house.

esa'usto, a *ag* exhausted.

esautora're *vt* (*dirigente, funzionario*) to deprive of authority.

esazio'ne [āzáttsyō'nã] *sf* collection (of taxes).

e'sca, pl es'che *sf* bait.

escamota'ge [eskámotázh'] *sm* subterfuge.

escandescen'za [āskándãshen'tsã] *sf*: **dare in** ~**e** to lose one's temper, fly into a rage.

e'sce [csh'shã] *vb vedi* **uscire**.

eschime'se [āskēmã'sã] *ag, sm/f, sm* Eskimo.

e'sci [csh'shē] *vb vedi* **uscire**.

escl. *abbr* (= *escluso*) excl.

esclama're *vi* to exclaim, cry out.

esclamazio'ne [āsklámáttsyō'nã] *sf* exclamation.

esclu'dere *vt* to exclude.

esclu'si *etc vb vedi* **escludere**.

esclusio'ne *sf* exclusion; **a ~ di, fatta ~ per** except (for), apart from; **senza ~ (alcuna)** without exception; **procedere per ~** to follow a process of elimination; **senza ~ di colpi** (*fig*) with no holds barred.

esclusi'va *sf vedi* **esclusivo**.

esclusivamen'te *av* exclusively, solely.

esclusi'vo, a *ag* exclusive ♦ *sf* (*DIR. COMM*) exclusive *o* sole rights *pl*.

esclu'so, a *pp di* **escludere** ♦ *ag*: **nessuno ~** without exception; **IVA ~a** ≈ excluding sales tax, ≈ exclusive of sales tax.

e'sco *vb vedi* **uscire**.

escogita're [āskōjētá'rã] *vt* to devise, think up.

e'scono *vb vedi* **uscire**.

escoriazio'ne [āskōryáttsyō'nã] *sf* abrasion, graze.

escremen'ti *smpl* excrement *sg*, faeces.

escursio'ne *sf* (*gita*) excursion, trip; (: *a piedi*) hike, walk; (*METEOR*): ~ **termica** temperature range.

escursioni'sta, i, e *sm/f* (*gitante*) (day) excursionist (*US*) *o* tripper (*Brit*); (: *a piedi*) hiker, walker.

esecra're *vt* to loathe, abhor.

esecuti'vo, a *ag, sm* executive.

esecuto're, tri'ce *sm/f* (*MUS*) performer; (*DIR*) executor.

esecuzio'ne [āzākōōttsyō'nã] *sf* execution, carrying out; (*MUS*) performance; ~ **capitale** execution.

esege'ta, i [āzãje'tá] *sm* commentator.

esegui're *vt* to carry out, execute; (*MUS*) to perform, execute.

esem'pio *sm* example; **per ~** for example, for instance; **fare un ~** to give an example.

esempla're *ag* exemplary ♦ *sm* example; (*copia*) copy; (*BOT, ZOOL, GEO*) specimen.

esemplifica're *vt* to exemplify.

esenta're *vt*: ~ **qn/qc da** to exempt sb/sth from.

esentas'se *ag inv* tax-free.

esen'te *ag*: ~ **da** (*dispensato da*) exempt from; (*privo di*) free from.

esenzio'ne [āzãntsyō'nã] *sf* exemption.

ese'quie *sfpl* funeral rites; funeral service *sg*.

esercen'te [āzãrchen'tã] *sm/f* trader, dealer; shopkeeper.

esercita're [āzãrchētã'rã] *vt* (*professione*) to practice (*US*), practise (*Brit*); (*allenare: corpo, mente*) to exercise, train; (*diritto*) to exercise; (*influenza, pressione*) to exert; ~**rsi** *vr* to practise; ~**rsi nella guida** to practise one's driving.

esercitazio'ne [āzãrchētáttsyō'nã] *sf* (*scolastica, militare*) exercise; ~**i di tiro** target practice *sg*.

eser'cito [āzer'chētō] *sm* army.

eserci'zio [āzãrchēt'tsyō] *sm* practice; (*compito, movimento*) exercise; (*azienda*) business, concern; (*ECON*): ~ **finanziario** fiscal (*US*) *o* financial (*Brit*) year; **in ~** (*medico etc*) practicing (*US*), practising (*Brit*); **nell'~ delle proprie funzioni** in the execution of one's duties.

esibi're *vt* to exhibit, display; (*documenti*) to produce, present; ~**rsi** *vr* (*attore*) to perform; (*fig*) to show off.

esibizio'ne [āzēbēttsyō'nã] *sf* exhibition; (*di documento*) presentation; (*spettacolo*) show, performance.

esibizioni'sta, i, e [āzēbēttsyōnē'stá] *sm/f* exhibitionist.

esigen'te [āzējen'tã] *ag* demanding.

esigen'za [āzējen'tsá] *sf* demand, requirement.

esi'gere [āzē'jārā] *vt* (*pretendere*) to demand; (*richiedere*) to demand, require; (*imposte*) to collect.

esi'guo, a *ag* small, slight.

esilaran'te *ag* hilarious; **gas ~** laughing gas.

e'sile *ag* (*persona*) slender, slim; (*stelo*) thin; (*voce*) faint.

esilia're *vt* to exile.

esilia'to, a *ag* exiled ♦ *sm/f* exile.

esi'lio *sm* exile.

esi'mere *vt*: ~ **qn/qc da** to exempt sb/sth

from; **~rsi** *vr*: **~rsi da** to get out of.

esisten'te *ag* existing; (*attuale*) present, current.

esisten'za [āzēsten'tsá] *sf* existence.

esistenziali'smo [āzēstāntsyálēz'mō] *sm* existentialism.

esi'stere *vi* to exist.

esisti'to, a *pp di* **esistere**.

esitan'te *ag* hesitant; (*voce*) faltering.

esita're *vi* to hesitate.

esitazio'ne [āzētáttsyō'nā] *sf* hesitation.

e'sito *sm* result, outcome.

e'skimo *sm* (*giaccone*) parka.

e'sodo *sm* exodus.

eso'fago, gi *sm* esophagus (*US*), oesophagus (*Brit*).

esonera're *vt*: **~ qn da** to exempt sb from.

esorbitan'te *ag* exorbitant, excessive.

esorci'smo [āzōrchēz'mō] *sm* exorcism.

esorcizza're [āzōrchēddzá'rā] *vt* to exorcize.

esordien'te *sm/f* beginner.

esor'dio *sm* debut.

esordi're *vi* (*nel teatro*) to make one's debut; (*fig*) to start out, begin (one's career); **esordì dicendo che** ... he began by saying (that) ....

esorta're *vt*: **~ qn a fare** to urge sb to do.

esortazio'ne [āzōrtáttsyō'nā] *sf* exhortation.

eso'so, a *ag* (*prezzo*) exorbitant; (*persona*: *avido*) grasping.

esote'rico, a, ci, che *ag* esoteric.

eso'tico, a, ci, che *ag* exotic.

espan'dere *vt* to expand; (*confini*) to extend; (*influenza*) to extend, spread; **~rsi** *vr* to expand.

espansio'ne *sf* expansion.

espansività *sf* expansiveness.

espansi'vo, a *ag* expansive, communicative.

espan'so, a *pp di* **espandere**.

espatria're *vi* to leave one's country.

espa'trio *sm* expatriation; **permesso di ~** authorization to leave the country.

espedien'te *sm* expedient; **vivere di ~i** to live by one's wits.

espel'lere *vt* to expel.

esperien'za [āspāryen'tsá] *sf* experience; (*SCIENZA*: *prova*) experiment; **parlare per ~** to speak from experience.

esperimen'to *sm* experiment; **fare un ~** to carry out *o* do an experiment.

esper'to, a *ag*, *sm/f* expert.

espia're *vt* to atone for.

espiazio'ne [āspēáttsyō'nā] *sf*: **~ (di)** expiation (of), atonement (for).

espira're *vt*, *vi* to breathe out.

espletamen'to *sm* (*AMM*) carrying out.

espleta're *vt* (*AMM*) to carry out.

esplica're *vt* (*attività*) to carry out, perform.

esplicati'vo, a *ag* explanatory.

espli'cito, a [āsplē'chētō] *ag* explicit.

esplo'dere *vi* (*anche fig*) to explode ♦ *vt* to

fire.

esplora're *vt* to explore.

esplorato're, tri'ce *sm/f* explorer; (*anche*: **giovane ~**) (boy) scout/(girl) scout *o* guide (*Brit*) ♦ *sm* (*NAUT*) scout (ship).

esplorazio'ne [āsplōráttsyō'nā] *sf* exploration; **mandare qn in ~** (*MIL*) to send sb to scout ahead.

esplosio'ne *sf* explosion.

esplosi'vo, a *ag*, *sm* explosive.

esplo'so, a *pp di* **esplodere**.

espo'ne *etc vb vedi* **esporre**.

esponen'te *sm/f* (*rappresentante*) representative.

esponenzia'le [āspōnāntsyá'lā] *ag* (*MAT*) exponential.

espon'go, espo'ni *etc vb vedi* **esporre**.

espor're *vt* (*merci*) to display; (*quadro*) to exhibit, show; (*fatti, idee*) to explain, set out; (*porre in pericolo*, *FOT*) to expose; **esporsi** *vr*: **esporsi a** (*sole, pericolo*) to expose o.s. to; (*critiche*) to lay o.s. open to.

esporta're *vt* to export.

esportato're, tri'ce *ag* exporting ♦ *sm* exporter.

esportazio'ne [āspōrtáttsyō'nā] *sf* (*azione*) exportation, export; (*insieme di prodotti*) exports *pl*.

espo'se *etc vb vedi* **esporre**.

esposi'metro *sm* exposure meter.

esposizio'ne [āspōzēttsyō'nā] *sf* displaying; exhibiting; setting out; (*anche FOT*) exposure; (*mostra*) exhibition; (*narrazione*) explanation, exposition.

espo'sto, a *pp di* **esporre** ♦ *ag*: **~ a nord** facing north, north-facing ♦ *sm* (*AMM*) statement, account; (: *petizione*) petition.

espressio'ne *sf* expression.

espressi'vo, a *ag* expressive.

espres'so, a *pp di* **esprimere** ♦ *ag* express ♦ *sm* (*lettera*) express letter; (*anche*: **treno ~**) express train; (*anche*: **caffè ~**) espresso.

espri'mere *vt* to express; **~rsi** *vr* to express o.s.

espropria're *vt* (*terreni, edifici*) to expropriate; (*persona*) to dispossess.

espropriazio'ne [āsprōpryáttsyō'nā] *sf*, **espro'prio** *sm* expropriation.

espugna're [āspōōnyá'rā] *vt* to take by force, storm.

espul'si *etc vb vedi* **espellere**.

espulsio'ne *sf* expulsion.

espul'so, a *pp di* **espellere**.

es'sa *pronome f*, **es'se** *pronome fpl vedi* **esso**.

essen'za [āssen'tsá] *sf* essence.

essenzia'le [āssāntsyá'lā] *ag* essential ♦ *sm*: **l'~** the main *o* most important thing.

es'sere *sm* being; **~ umano** human being ♦ *vi*, *vb con attributo* to be ♦ *vb ausiliare* to have (*o qualche volta* be); **è giovane/**

professore he is young/a teacher; **è l'una** it's one o'clock; **sono le otto** it's eight o'clock; **esserci: c'è/ci sono** there is/there are; **che c'è?** what's wrong?; **ci siamo!** here we are!; (*fig*) this is it!; (*: siamo alle solite*) here we go again!; ~ **di** (*appartenenza*) to belong to; (*origine*) to be from; **è di mio fratello** it belongs to my brother, it's my brother's; **è venuto?** has he come?, did he come?; **è stato fabbricato in India** it was made in India; **è da fare subito** it must be *o* to be done immediately; **non è da te** it's not like you; **sarà quel che sarà** what will be will be; **come se niente fosse** as if nothing had happened; **sia quel che sia, io me ne vado** whatever happens I'm off; **c'era una volta** ... once upon a time there was ....

es'si *pronome mpl vedi* **esso**.

essicca're *vt* (*gen*) to dry; (*legname*) to season; (*cibi*) to desiccate; (*bacino, palude*) to drain; ~**rsi** *vr* (*fiume, pozzo*) to dry up; (*vernice*) to dry (out).

es'so, a *pronome* it; (*riferito a persona: soggetto*) he/she; (*: complemento*) him/her; ~**i, e** *pronome pl* they; (*complemento*) them.

est *sm* east; **i paesi dell'E**~ the Eastern bloc *sg*.

e'stasi *sf* ecstasy.

estasia're *vt* to send into raptures; ~**rsi** *vr*: ~**rsi (davanti a)** to go into ecstasies (over), go into raptures (over).

esta'te *sf* summer.

esta'tico, a, ci, che *ag* ecstatic.

estempora'neo, a *ag* (*discorso*) extempore, impromptu; (*brano musicale*) impromptu.

esten'dere *vt* to extend; ~**rsi** *vr* (*diffondersi*) to spread; (*territorio, confini*) to extend.

estensio'ne *sf* extension; (*di superficie*) expanse; (*di voce*) range.

estenuan'te *ag* wearing, tiring.

estenua're *vt* (*stancare*) to wear out, tire out.

esterio're *ag* outward, external.

esteriorità *sf inv* outward appearance.

esteriorizza're [āstāryōrĕddzá'rā] *vt* (*gioia etc*) to show.

esterna're *vt* to express; ~ **un sospetto** to voice a suspicion.

ester'no, a *ag* (*porta, muro*) outer, outside; (*scala*) outside; (*alunno, impressione*) external ♦ *sm* outside, exterior ♦ *sm/f* (*allievo*) day pupil; "**per uso** ~" "for external use only"; **gli** ~**i sono stati girati a Boston** (*CINEMA*) the location shots were taken in Boston.

e'stero, a *ag* foreign ♦ *sm*: **all'**~ abroad; **Ministero degli E**~**i, gli E**~**i** Ministry for Foreign Affairs, ≈ State Department (*US*), ≈ Foreign Office (*Brit*).

esterofili'a *sf excessive love of foreign things.*

esterrefat'to, a *ag* (*costernato*) horrified;

(*sbalordito*) astounded.

este'si *etc vb vedi* **estendere**.

este'so, a *pp di* **estendere** ♦ *ag* extensive, large; **scrivere per** ~ to write in full.

este'tico, a, ci, che *ag* aesthetic ♦ *sf* (*disciplina*) aesthetics *sg*; (*bellezza*) attractiveness; **chirurgia** ~**a** cosmetic surgery; **cura** ~**a** beauty treatment.

esteti'sta, i, e *sm/f* beautician.

e'stimo *sm* valuation; (*disciplina*) surveying.

estin'guere *vt* to extinguish, put out; (*debito*) to pay off; (*conto*) to close; ~**rsi** *vr* to go out; (*specie*) to become extinct.

estin'si *etc vb vedi* **estinguere**.

estin'to, a *pp di* **estinguere**.

estinto're *sm* (*fire*) extinguisher.

estinzio'ne [āstēntsyō'nā] *sf* putting out; (*di specie*) extinction; (*di debito*) payment; (*di conto*) closing.

estirpa're *vt* (*pianta*) to uproot, pull up; (*dente*) to extract; (*tumore*) to remove; (*fig: vizio*) to eradicate.

esti'vo, a *ag* summer *cpd*.

Esto'nia *sf*: **l'**~ Estonia.

estor'cere [āstor'chārā] *vt*: ~ **qc (a qn)** to extort sth (from sb).

estorsio'ne *sf* extortion.

estor'to, a *pp di* **estorcere**.

estrada're *vt* to extradite.

estradizio'ne [āstrádĕttsyō'nā] *sf* extradition.

estra'e, estrag'go *etc vb vedi* **estrarre**.

estra'neo, a *ag* foreign; (*discorso*) extraneous, unrelated ♦ *sm/f* stranger; **rimanere** ~ **a qc** to take no part in sth; **sentirsi** ~ **a** (*famiglia, società*) to feel alienated from; "**ingresso vietato agli** ~**i**" "no admittance to unauthorized personnel".

estraniar'si *vr*: ~ **(da)** to cut o.s. off (from).

estrar're *vt* to extract; (*minerali*) to mine; (*sorteggiare*) to draw; ~ **a sorte** to draw lots.

estras'si *etc vb vedi* **estrarre**.

estrat'to, a *pp di* **estrarre** ♦ *sm* extract; (*di documento*) abstract; ~ **conto** (*bank*) statement; ~ **di nascita** birth certificate.

estrazio'ne [āstráttsyō'nā] *sf* extraction; mining; drawing *q*; draw.

estremamen'te *av* extremely.

estremi'sta, i, e *sm/f* extremist.

estremità *sf inv* extremity, end ♦ *sfpl* (*ANAT*) extremities.

estre'mo, a *ag* extreme; (*ultimo: ora, tentativo*) final, last ♦ *sm* extreme; (*di pazienza, forza*) limit, end; ~**i** *smpl* (*DIR*) essential elements; (*AMM: dati essenziali*) details, particulars; **l'E**~ **Oriente** the Far East.

estrinseca're *vt* to express, show.

es'tro *sm* (*capriccio*) whim, fancy; (*ispirazione creativa*) inspiration.

estromes'so, a *pp di* **estromettere**.

estromet'tere vt: ~ **(da)** (partito, club etc) to expel (from); (discussione) to exclude (from).

estromissio'ne sf expulsion.

estro'so, a ag whimsical, capricious; inspired.

estrover'so, a ag, sm extrovert.

estua'rio sm estuary.

esuberan'te ag exuberant; (COMM) laid-off.

esuberan'za [āzōōbārán'tsá] sf (di persona) exuberance; ~ **di personale** (COMM) over-staffing (US), overmanning (Brit).

esula're vi: ~ **da** (competenza) to be beyond; (compiti) not to be part of.

e'sule sm/f exile.

esultan'za [āzōōltán'tsá] sf exultation.

esulta're vi to exult.

esuma're vt (salma) to exhume, disinter; (fig) to unearth.

età sf inv age; **all'~ di 8 anni** at the age of 8, at 8 years of age; **ha la mia ~** he (o she) is the same age as me o as I am; **di mezza ~** middle-aged; **raggiungere la maggiore ~** to come of age; **essere in ~ minore** to be under age; **in ~ avanzata** advanced in years.

etano'lo sm ethanol.

e'tere sm ether.

ete'reo, a ag ethereal.

eternità sf eternity.

eter'no, a ag eternal; (interminabile: lamenti, attesa) never-ending; **in ~** for ever, eternally.

eteroge'neo, a [ātārōje'nāō] ag heterogeneous.

e'tica sf vedi **etico**.

etichet'ta [ātēkāt'tá] sf label; (cerimoniale): **l'~** etiquette.

e'tico, a, ci, che ag ethical ♦ sf ethics sg.

etimologi'a, gi'e [ātēmōlōjē'á] sf etymology.

eti'ope ag, sm/f Ethiopian.

Etio'pia sf: **l'~** Ethiopia.

etio'pico, a, ci, che ag, sm (LING) Ethiopian.

Et'na sm: **l'~** Etna.

et'nico, a, ci, che ag ethnic.

etru'sco, a, schi, sche ag, sm/f Etruscan.

et'taro sm hectare (= 10,000 m²).

et'to sm abbr = **ettogrammo**.

ettogram'mo sm hectogram(me) (= 100 grams).

etto'litro sm hectoliter (US), hectolitre (Brit).

EU abbr = **Europa**.

eucalip'to sm eucalyptus.

Eucaristi'a sf: **l'~** the Eucharist.

eufemi'smo sm euphemism.

eufori'a sf euphoria.

Eura'sia sf Eurasia.

eurasia'tico, a, ci, che ag, sm/f Eurasian.

Euratom' sigla f (= Comunità Europea dell'Energia Atomica) Euratom.

eurodeputa'to sm Euro MP.

eurodivi'sa sf Eurocurrency.

eurodol'laro sm Eurodollar.

euromerca'to sm Euromarket.

Euro'pa sf: **l'~** Europe.

europe'o, a ag, sm/f European.

eutanasi'a sf euthanasia.

E.V. abbr = Eccellenza Vostra.

evacua're vt to evacuate.

evacuazio'ne [āvákōōáttsyō'nā] sf evacuation.

eva'dere vi (fuggire): ~ **da** to escape from ♦ vt (sbrigare) to deal with, dispatch; (tasse) to evade.

evange'lico, a, ci, che [āvánje'lēkō] ag evangelical.

evangeli'sta, i [āvánjālē'stá] sm evangelist.

evapora're vi to evaporate.

evaporazio'ne [āvápōráttsyō'nā] sf evaporation.

eva'si etc vb vedi **evadere**.

evasio'ne sf (vedi evadere) escape; dispatch; **dare ~ ad un ordine** to carry out o execute an order; **letteratura d'~** escapist literature; **~ fiscale** tax evasion.

evasi'vo, a ag evasive.

eva'so, a pp di **evadere** ♦ sm escapee.

evaso're sm: ~ **(fiscale)** tax evader.

evenien'za [āvānyen'tsá] sf: **nell'~ che ciò succeda** should that happen; **essere pronto ad ogni ~** to be ready for anything o any eventuality.

even'to sm event.

eventua'le ag possible.

eventualità sf inv eventuality, possibility; **nell'~ di** in the event of.

eventualmen'te av if need be, if necessary.

E'verest sm: **l'~, il Monte ~** (Mount) Everest.

eversio'ne sf subversion.

eversi'vo, a ag subversive.

eviden'te ag evident, obvious.

evidentemen'te av evidently; (palesemente) obviously, evidently.

eviden'za [āvēden'tsá] sf obviousness; **mettere in ~** to point out, highlight; **tenere in ~ qc** to bear sth in mind.

evidenziato're [āvēdántsyátō'rā] sm (penna) highlighter.

evira're vt to castrate.

evita'bile ag avoidable.

evita're vt to avoid; ~ **di fare** to avoid doing; ~ **qc a qn** to spare sb sth.

e'vo sm age, epoch.

evoca're vt to evoke.

evocati'vo, a ag evocative.

evocherò etc [āvōkáro'] vb vedi **evocare**.

evoluti'vo, a ag (gen, BIOL) evolutionary; (MED) progressive.

evolu'to, a pp di **evolversi** ♦ ag (popolo, civiltà) (highly) developed, advanced; (persona: emancipato) independent; (: senza pregiudizi) broad-minded.

evoluzio'ne [āvōlōōttsyō'nā] sf evolution.

evol'versi *vr* to evolve; **con l'~ della situazione** as the situation develops.

evvi'va *escl* hurrah!; **~ il re!** long live the king!, hurrah for the king!

ex *prefisso* ex-, former ♦ *sm/f inv* ex-boyfriend/ girlfriend.

ex a'equo [egze'kwō] *av*: **classificarsi primo ~** to come joint first, come equal first.

ex'tra *ag inv*, *sm inv* extra.

extraconiuga'le *ag* extramarital.

extraparlamenta're *ag* extraparliamentary.

extrasensoria'le *ag*: **percezione** *f* **~** extrasensory perception.

extraurba'no, a *ag* suburban.

F

F, f [āf'fā] *sf ō m inv* (*lettera*) F, f; **F come Firenze** ≈ F for Fox.

F *abbr* (= *Fahrenheit*) F.

F. *abbr* (= *fiume*) R.

fa *vb vedi* **fare** ♦ *sm inv* (*MUS*) F; (: *solfeggiando la scala*) fa ♦ *av*: **10 anni ~** 10 years ago.

fabbiso'gno [fàbbēzōn'yō] *sm* needs *pl*, requirements *pl*; **il ~ nazionale di petrolio** the country's oil requirements; **~ del settore pubblico** government debt borrowing (*US*), public sector borrowing requirement (*Brit*).

fab'brica *sf* factory.

fabbrican'te *sm* manufacturer, maker.

fabbrica're *vt* to build; (*produrre*) to manufacture, make; (*fig*) to fabricate, invent.

fabbrica'to *sm* building.

fabbricazio'ne [fàbbrēkàttsyō'nā] *sf* building, fabrication; making, manufacture, manufacturing.

fab'bro *sm* (black)smith.

faccen'da [fàchen'dá] *sf* matter, affair; (*cosa da fare*) task, chore; **le ~e domestiche** the housework *sg*.

faccet'ta [fàchāt'tá] *sf* (*di pietra preziosa*) facet.

facchi'no [fàkkē'nō] *sm* porter.

fac'cia, ce [fách'chá] *sf* face; (*di moneta, medaglia*) side; **~ a ~** face to face; **di ~ a** opposite, facing; **avere la ~ (tosta) di dire/ fare qc** to have the cheek *o* nerve to say/do sth; **fare qc alla ~ di qn** to do sth to spite sb; **leggere qc in ~ a qn** to see sth written all over sb's face.

faccia'ta [fàchá'tá] *sf* façade; (*di pagina*) side.

fac'cio *etc* [fách'chō] *vb vedi* **fare**.

facen'te [fàchān'tá]: **~ funzione** *sm* (*AMM*) deputy.

faces'si *etc* [fàchās'sē] *vb vedi* **fare**.

face'to, a [fàchā'tō] *ag* witty, humorous.

face'vo *etc* [fàchā'vō] *vb vedi* **fare**.

face'zia [fàchet'tsyá] *sf* witticism, witty remark.

fachi'ro [fàkē'rō] *sm* fakir.

fa'cile [fà'chēlā] *ag* easy; (*affabile*) easy-going; (*disposto*): **~ a** inclined to, prone to; (*probabile*): **è ~ che piova** it's likely to rain; **donna di ~i costumi** woman of easy virtue, loose woman.

facilità [fàchēlētà'] *sf* easiness; (*disposizione, dono*) aptitude.

facilita're [fàchēlētà'rā] *vt* to make easier.

facilitazio'ne [fàchēlētàttsyō'nā] *sf* (*gen*) facilities *pl*; **~i di pagamento** easy terms, credit facilities.

facilmen'te [fàchēlmān'tā] *av* (*gen*) easily; (*probabilmente*) probably.

facilo'ne, a [fàchēlō'nā] *sm/f* (*peg*) happy-go-lucky person.

facinoro'so, a [fàchēnōrō'sō] *ag* violent.

facoltà *sf inv* faculty; (*CHIM*) property; (*autorità*) power.

facoltati'vo, a *ag* optional; (*fermata d'autobus*) request *cpd*.

facolto'so, a *ag* wealthy, rich.

facsi'mile *sm* facsimile.

fag'gio [fàd'jō] *sm* beech.

fagia'no [fàjà'nō] *sm* pheasant.

fagioli'no [fàjōlē'nō] *sm* string bean.

fagio'lo [fàjo'lō] *sm* bean; **capitare a ~** to come at the right time.

fagocita're [fàgōchētà'rā] *vt* (*fig: industria etc*) to absorb, swallow up; (*scherzoso: cibo*) to devour.

fagot'to *sm* bundle; (*MUS*) bassoon; **far ~** (*fig*) to pack up and go.

fa'i *vb vedi* **fare**.

fa'ida *sf* feud.

fai'na *sf* (*ZOOL*) stone marten.

Fa'hrenheit [fà':rɔnhāēt] *sm* Fahrenheit.

falan'ge [fàlàn'jā] *sf* (*ANAT, MIL*) phalanx.

falca'ta *sf* stride.

fal'ce [fàl'chā] *sf* scythe; **~ e martello** (*POL*) hammer and sickle.

falcet'to [fàlchāt'tō] *sm* sickle.

falcia're [fàlchá'rā] *vt* to cut; (*fig*) to mow down.

falciatri'ce [fàlchátrē'chā] *sf* (*per fieno*) reaping machine; (*per erba*) mowing machine.

fal'co, chi *sm* hawk.

falco'ne *sm* falcon.

fal'da *sf* (*GEO*) layer, stratum; (*di cappello*) brim; (*di cappotto*) tails *pl*; (*di monte*) lower slope; (*di tetto*) pitch; (*di neve*) flake; **abito a ~e** tails *pl*.

falegna'me [fàlānyà'mā] *sm* joiner.

fale'na *sf* (*ZOOL*) moth.
Fal'kland [fàl'klànd] *sfpl*: **le isole ~** the Falkland Islands.
falla'ce [fàllà'chā] *ag* misleading, deceptive.
fal'lico, a, ci, che *ag* phallic.
fallimenta're *ag* (*COMM*) bankruptcy *cpd*; **bilancio ~** negative balance, deficit; **diritto ~** bankruptcy law.
fallimen'to *sm* failure; bankruptcy.
falli're *vi* (*non riuscire*): **~ (in)** to fail (in); (*DIR*) to go bankrupt ♦ *vt* (*colpo, bersaglio*) to miss.
falli'to, a *ag* unsuccessful; bankrupt ♦ *sm/f* bankrupt.
fal'lo *sm* error, mistake; (*imperfezione*) defect, flaw; (*SPORT*) foul; fault; (*ANAT*) phallus; **senza ~** without fail; **cogliere qn in ~** to catch sb out; **mettere il piede in ~** to slip.
fallo'crate *sm* male chauvinist.
falò *sm inv* bonfire.
falsa're *vt* to distort, misrepresent.
falsari'ga, ghe *sf* lined page, ruled page; **sulla ~ di ...** (*fig*) along the lines of ....
falsa'rio *sm* forger; counterfeiter.
falsifica're *vt* to forge; (*monete*) to forge, counterfeit.
falsità *sf inv* (*di persona, notizia*) falseness; (*bugia*) falsehood, lie.
fal'so, a *ag* false; (*errato*) wrong; (*falsificato*) forged; fake; (: *oro, gioielli*) imitation *cpd* ♦ *sm* forgery; **essere un ~ magro** to be heavier than one looks; **giurare il ~** to commit perjury; **~ in atto pubblico** forgery (of a legal document).
fa'ma *sf* fame; (*reputazione*) reputation, name.
fa'me *sf* hunger; **aver ~** to be hungry; **fare la ~** (*fig*) to starve, exist at subsistence level.
fame'lico, a, ci, che *ag* ravenous.
famigera'to, a [fàmējàrà'tō] *ag* notorious, ill-famed.
fami'glia [fàmēl'yà] *sf* family.
familia're *ag* (*della famiglia*) family *cpd*; (*ben noto*) familiar; (*rapporti, atmosfera*) friendly; (*LING*) informal, colloquial ♦ *sm/f* relative, relation; **una vettura ~** a family car.
familiarità *sf* familiarity; friendliness; informality.
familiarizza're [fàmēlyàrēddzà'rā] *vi*: **~ con qn** to get to know sb; **abbiamo familiarizzato subito** we got on well together from the start.
famo'so, a *ag* famous, well-known.
fana'le *sm* (*AUT*) light, lamp (*Brit*); (*luce stradale, NAUT*) light; (*di faro*) beacon.
fana'tico, a, ci, che *ag* fanatical; (*del teatro, calcio etc*): **~ di o per** mad o crazy about ♦ *sm/f* fanatic; (*tifoso*) fan.
fanciullez'za [fànchōōllàt'tsà] *sf* childhood.

fanciul'lo, a [fànchōōl'lō] *sm/f* child.
fando'nia *sf* tall story; **~e** *sfpl* nonsense *sg*.
fanfa'ra *sf* brass band; (*musica*) fanfare.
fanfaro'ne *sm* braggart.
fanghi'glia [fàngēl'yà] *sf* mire, mud.
fan'go, ghi *sm* mud; **fare i ~ghi** (*MED*) to take a course of mud baths.
fango'so, a *ag* muddy.
fan'no *vb vedi* fare.
fannullo'ne, a *sm/f* idler, loafer.
fantascien'za [fàntàshen'tsà] *sf* science fiction.
fantasi'a *sf* fantasy, imagination; (*capriccio*) whim, caprice ♦ *ag inv*: **vestito ~** patterned dress.
fantasio'so, a *ag* (*dotato di fantasia*) imaginative; (*bizzarro*) fanciful, strange.
fanta'sma, i *sm* ghost, phantom.
fantastica're *vi* to daydream.
fantasticheri'a [fàntàstēkàrē'à] *sf* daydream.
fanta'stico, a, ci, che *ag* fantastic; (*potenza, ingegno*) imaginative.
fan'te *sm* infantryman; (*CARTE*) jack, knave (*Brit*).
fanteri'a *sf* infantry.
fanti'no *sm* jockey.
fantoc'cio [fàntoch'chō] *sm* puppet.
fantoma'tico, a, ci, che *ag* (*nave, esercito*) phantom *cpd*; (*personaggio*) mysterious.
FAO *sigla f* FAO (= *Food and Agriculture Organization*).
farabut'to *sm* crook.
farao'na *sf* guinea fowl.
farao'ne *sm* (*STORIA*) Pharaoh.
farao'nico, a, ci, che *ag* of the Pharaohs; (*fig*) enormous, huge.
farci're [fàrchē'rà] *vt* (*carni, peperoni etc*) to stuff; (*torte*) to fill.
fard [fàr] *sm inv* blusher.
fardel'lo *sm* bundle; (*fig*) burden.
fa're *vt* to make; (*operare, agire*) to do; (*TEATRO*) to act; **~ l'avvocato/il medico** to be a lawyer/doctor; **~ del tennis** to play tennis; **~ il morto/l'ignorante** to act dead/the fool; **non fa niente** it doesn't matter; **2 più 2 fa 4** 2 and 2 are o make 4; **farcela** to succeed, manage; **non ce la faccio più** I can't go on any longer; **farla a qn** to get the better of sb; **farla finita con qc** to have done with sth; **ti facevo più intelligente** I thought you were more intelligent ♦ *vi* (*essere adatto*) to be suitable; (*stare per*): **fece per parlare quando ...** he was about to speak when ...; **~ in modo di** to act in such a way that; **faccia pure!** go ahead!; **~ da** (~ *le funzioni di*) to act as; **ci sa ~** he's very capable; **fa proprio al caso nostro** it's just what we need; **"davvero?" — fece** "really?" — he said ♦ *vb impers*: *vedi* **bello, freddo** *etc*; **piangere/ridere qn** to make sb cry/laugh; **~ venire qn** to send for sb; **fammi vedere** let me see;

~**rsi** *vr* (*diventare*) to become; ~**rsi la macchina** to get a car for o.s.; ~**rsi avanti** to come forward; ~**rsi notare** to get o.s. noticed; **fatti più in là!** move along a bit!

fare'tra *sf* quiver.

farfal'la *sf* butterfly.

farfuglia're [fàrfŏŏlyá'rā] *vt, vi* to mumble, mutter.

fari'na *sf* flour; ~ **gialla** corn (*US*) *o* maize (*Brit*) flour; ~ **integrale** whole-wheat flour; **questa non è** ~ **del tuo sacco** (*fig*) this isn't your own idea (*o* work).

farina'cei [fàrēnà'chāē] *smpl* starches.

farin'ge [fàrēn'jā] *sf* (*ANAT*) pharynx.

farino'so, a *ag* (*patate*) floury; (*neve, mela*) powdery.

farmace'utico, a, ci, che [fàrmáchā'ōōtēkō] *ag* pharmaceutical.

farmaci'a, ci'e [fàrmáchē'á] *sf* pharmacy; (*negozio*) pharmacy, chemist's (shop) (*Brit*).

farmaci'sta, i, e [fàrmáchē'stá] *sm/f* pharmacist, chemist (*Brit*).

far'maco, ci *o* **chi** *sm* drug, medicine.

farnetica're *vi* to rave, be delirious.

fa'ro *sm* (*NAUT*) lighthouse; (*AER*) beacon; (*AUT*) headlight, headlamp (*Brit*).

farragino'so, a [fàrràjēnō'sō] *ag* (*stile*) muddled, confused.

far'sa *sf* farce.

farse'sco, a, schi, sche *ag* farcical.

fasc. *abbr* = **fascicolo**.

fa'scia, sce [fàsh'shá] *sf* band, strip; (*MED*) bandage; (*di sindaco, ufficiale*) sash; (*parte di territorio*) strip, belt; (*di contribuenti etc*) group, band; **essere in** ~**sce** (*anche fig*) to be in one's infancy; ~ **oraria** time band.

fascia're [fàshá'rā] *vt* to bind; (*MED*) to bandage; (*bambino*) to put a diaper (*US*) *o* nappy (*Brit*) on.

fasciatu'ra [fàshátōō'rà] *sf* (*azione*) bandaging; (*fascia*) bandage.

fasci'colo [fàshē'kōlō] *sm* (*di documenti*) file, dossier; (*di rivista*) issue, number; (*opuscolo*) booklet, pamphlet.

fa'scino [fàsh'shēnō] *sm* charm, fascination.

fa'scio [fàsh'shō] *sm* bundle, sheaf; (*di fiori*) bunch; (*di luce*) beam; (*POL*): **il F**~ the Fascist Party.

fasci'smo [fàshēz'mō] *sm* fascism.

fasci'sta, i, e [fàshē'stá] *ag, sm/f* fascist.

fa'se *sf* phase; (*TECN*) stroke; **in** ~ **di espansione** in a period of expansion; **essere fuori** ~ (*motore*) to run roughly; (*fig*) to feel rotten.

fasti'dio *sm* bother, trouble; **dare** ~ **a qn** to bother *o* annoy sb; **sento** ~ **allo stomaco** my stomach's upset; **avere** ~**i con la polizia** to have trouble *o* bother with the police.

fastidio'so, a *ag* annoying, tiresome; (*schifiltoso*) fastidious.

fa'sto *sm* pomp, splendor (*US*), splendour (*Brit*).

fasto'so, a *ag* sumptuous, lavish.

fasul'lo, a *ag* (*gen*) fake; (*dichiarazione, persona*) false; (*pretesto*) bogus.

fa'ta *sf* fairy.

fata'le *ag* fatal; (*inevitabile*) inevitable; (*fig*) irresistible.

fatali'smo *sm* fatalism.

fatalità *sf inv* inevitability; (*avversità*) misfortune; (*fato*) fate, destiny.

fata'to, a *ag* (*spada, chiave*) magic; (*castello*) enchanted.

fati'ca, che *sf* hard work, toil; (*sforzo*) effort; (*di metalli*) fatigue; **a** ~ with difficulty; **respirare a** ~ to have difficulty (in) breathing; **fare** ~ **a fare qc** to find it difficult to do sth; **animale da** ~ beast of burden.

faticac'cia, ce [fàtēkách'chá] *sf*: **fu una** ~ it was hard work, it was a hell of a job (*fam*).

fatica're *vi* to toil; ~ **a fare qc** to have difficulty doing sth.

fatica'ta *sf* hard work.

fati'chi *etc* [fàtē'kē] *vb vedi* **faticare**.

fatico'so, a *ag* (*viaggio, camminata*) tiring, exhausting; (*lavoro*) laborious.

fati'dico, a, ci, che *ag* fateful.

fa'to *sm* fate, destiny.

Fatt. *abbr* (= *fattura*) inv.

fattac'cio [fàttàch'chō] *sm* foul deed.

fattez'ze [fàttāt'tsá] *sfpl* features.

fatti'bile *ag* feasible, possible.

fattispe'cie [fàttēspe'chā] *sf*: **nella** *o* **in** ~ in this case *o* instance.

fat'to, a *pp di* **fare** ♦ *ag*: **un uomo** ~ a grown man ♦ *sm* fact; (*azione*) deed; (*avvenimento*) event, occurrence; (*di romanzo, film*) action, story; ~ **a mano/in casa** hand-/homemade; **è ben** ~**a** she has a nice figure; **cogliere qn sul** ~ to catch sb red-handed; **il** ~ **sta** *o* **è che** the fact remains *o* is that; **in** ~ **di** as for, as far as ... is concerned; **fare i** ~**i propri** to mind one's own business; **è uno che sa il** ~ **suo** he knows what he's about; **gli ho detto il** ~ **suo** I told him what I thought of him; **porre qn di fronte al** ~ **compiuto** to present sb with a fait accompli.

fatto're *sm* (*AGR*) farm manager; (*MAT*) *elemento costitutivo*) factor.

fattori'a *sf* farm; (*casa*) farmhouse.

fattori'no *sm* errand boy; (*di ufficio*) office boy; (*d'albergo*) porter.

fattucchie'ra [fàttōōkkye'rà] *sf* witch.

fattu'ra *sf* (*COMM*) invoice; (*di abito*) tailoring; (*malia*) spell; **pagamento contro presentazione** ~ payment on invoice.

fattura're *vt* (*COMM*) to invoice; (*prodotto*) to produce; (*vino*) to adulterate.

fattura'to *sm* (*COMM*) turnover.

fatturazio'ne [fàttōōràttsyō'nā] *sf* billing, invoicing.

fa'tuo, a *ag* vain, fatuous; **fuoco** ~ (*anche fig*) will-o'-the-wisp.

fa'uci [fà'ōōchē] *sfpl* (*di leone etc*) jaws; (*di vulcano*) mouth *sg*.

fa'una *sf* fauna.

fa'usto, a *ag* (*formale*) happy; **un** ~ **presagio** a good omen.

fauto're, tri'ce *sm/f* advocate, supporter.

fa'va *sf* broad bean.

favel'la *sf* speech.

favil'la *sf* spark.

fa'vo *sm* (*di api*) honeycomb.

fa'vola *sf* (*fiaba*) fairy tale; (*d'intento morale*) fable; (*fandonia*) yarn; **essere la** ~ **del paese** (*oggetto di critica*) to be the talk of the town; (*zimbello*) to be a laughing stock.

favolo'so, a *ag* fabulous; (*incredibile*) incredible.

favo're *sm* favor (*US*), favour (*Brit*); **per** ~ please; **prezzo/trattamento di** ~ preferential price/treatment; **condizioni di** ~ (*COMM*) favo(u)rable terms; **fare un** ~ **a qn** to do sb a favo(u)r; **col** ~ **delle tenebre** under cover of darkness.

favoreggiamen'to [fàvōrādjàmān'tō] *sm* (*DIR*) aiding and abetting.

favore'vole *ag* favorable (*US*), favourable (*Brit*).

favori're *vt* to favor (*US*), favour (*Brit*); (*il commercio, l'industria, le arti*) to promote, encourage; **vuole** ~**?** won't you help yourself?; **favorisca in salotto** please come into the sitting room; **mi favorisca i documenti** please may I see your papers?

favoriti'smo *sm* favoritism (*US*), favouritism (*Brit*).

favori'to, a *ag, sm/f* favorite (*US*), favourite (*Brit*).

fazio'ne [fàttsyō'nā] *sf* faction.

faziosità [fàttsyōsētà'] *sf* sectarianism.

fazzolet'to [fàttsōlāt'tō] *sm* handkerchief; (*per la testa*) (head)scarf.

F.C. *abbr* = **fuoricorso**.

f.co *abbr* = **franco**.

FE *sigla* = Ferrara.

febb. *abbr* (= *febbraio*) Feb.

febbra'io *sm* February; *per fraseologia vedi* **luglio.**

feb'bre *sf* fever; **aver la** ~ to have a high temperature; ~ **da fieno** hay fever.

febbri'le *ag* (*anche fig*) feverish.

fec'cia, ce [fāch'chà] *sf* dregs *pl*.

fe'ci [fe'chē] *sfpl* f(a)eces, excrement *sg*.

fe'ci *etc* [fe'chē] *vb vedi* **fare.**

fe'cola *sf* potato flour.

feconda're *vt* to fertilize.

fecondazio'ne [fākōndàttsyō'nā] *sf* fertilization; ~ **artificiale** artificial insemination.

fecondità *sf* fertility.

fecon'do, a *ag* fertile.

Fed'com *sigla m* = *Fondo Europeo di Cooperazione Monetaria.*

fe'de *sf* (*credenza*) belief, faith; (*REL*) faith; (*fiducia*) faith, trust; (*fedeltà*) loyalty; (*anello*) wedding ring; (*attestato*) certificate; **aver** ~ **in qn** to have faith in sb; **tener** ~ **a** (*ideale*) to remain loyal to; (*giuramento, promessa*) to keep; **in buona/cattiva** ~ in good/bad faith; **"in** ~**"** (*DIR*) "in witness whereof".

fede'le *ag* (*leale*): ~ **(a)** faithful (to); (*veritiero*) true, accurate ♦ *sm/f* follower; **i** ~**i** (*REL*) the faithful.

fedeltà *sf* faithfulness; (*coniugale*) fidelity; (*esattezza: di copia, traduzione*) accuracy; **alta** ~ (*RADIO*) high fidelity.

fe'dera *sf* pillowslip, pillowcase.

federa'le *ag* federal.

federazio'ne [fādàràttsyō'nā] *sf* federation.

Federcac'cia [fādārkàch'chà] *abbr f* (= *Federazione Italiana della Caccia*) hunting federation.

Federcal'cio [fādārkàl'chō] *abbr m* (= *Federazione Italiana Gioco Calcio*) Italian football association.

Federconsor'zi [fādārkōnsor'tsē] *abbr f* (= *Federazione Italiana dei Consorzi Agrari*) federation of farmers' cooperatives.

fedi'frago, a, ghi, ghe *ag* faithless, perfidious.

fedi'na *sf* (*DIR*): ~ **(penale)** record; **avere la** ~ **penale sporca** to have a police record.

fe'gato *sm* liver; (*fig*) guts *pl*, nerve; **mangiarsi** *o* **rodersi il** ~ to be consumed with rage.

fel'ce [fāl'chā] *sf* fern.

feli'ce [fālē'chā] *ag* happy; (*fortunato*) lucky.

felicità [fālēchētà'] *sf* happiness.

felicitar'si [fālēchētàr'sē] *vr* (*congratularsi*): ~ **con qn per qc** to congratulate sb on sth.

felicitazio'ni [fālēchētàttsyō'nē] *sfpl* congratulations.

feli'no, a *ag, sm* feline.

felpa'to, a *ag* (*tessuto*) brushed; (*passo*) stealthy; **con passo** ~ stealthily.

fel'tro *sm* felt.

fem'mina *sf* (*ZOOL, TECN*) female; (*figlia*) girl, daughter; (*spesso peg*) woman.

femmini'le *ag* feminine; (*sesso*) female; (*lavoro, giornale*) woman's, women's; (*moda*) women's ♦ *sm* (*LING*) feminine.

femminilità *sf* femininity.

femmini'smo *sm* feminism.

femmini'sta, i, e *ag, sm/f* feminist.

fe'more *sm* thighbone, femur.

fen'dere *vt* to cut through.

fendineb'bia *sm* (*AUT*) fog lamp.

finditu'ra *sf* (*gen*) crack; (*di roccia*) cleft, crack.

feno'meno *sm* phenomenon.

fe'retro *sm* coffin.

feria'le *ag*: **giorno** ~ weekday, working day.

fe'rie *sfpl* vacation *sg* (*US*), holidays (*Brit*); **andare in** ~ to go on vacation *o* holiday; **25 giorni di** ~ **pagate** 25 days' vacation *o* holiday with pay.

ferimen'to *sm* wounding.

feri're *vt* to injure; (*deliberatamente*: *MIL etc*) to wound; (*colpire*) to hurt; ~**rsi** *vr* to hurt o.s., injure o.s.

feri'to, a *sm/f* wounded *o* injured man/woman ♦ *sf* injury; wound.

ferito'ia *sf* slit.

fer'ma *sf* (*MIL*) (period of) service; (*CACCIA*): **cane da** ~ pointer.

fermacar'te *sm inv* paperweight.

fermacravat'ta *sm inv* tie tack (*US*), tiepin (*Brit*).

ferma'glio [fărmál'yō] *sm* clasp; (*gioiello*) brooch; (*per documenti*) clip.

fermamen'te *av* firmly.

ferma're *vt* to stop, halt; (*POLIZIA*) to detain, hold; (*bottone etc*) to fasten, fix ♦ *vi* to stop; ~**rsi** *vr* to stop, halt; ~**rsi a fare qc** to stop to do sth.

ferma'ta *sf* stop; ~ **dell'autobus** bus stop.

fermentazio'ne [fărmăntáttsyō'nă] *sf* fermentation.

fermen'to *sm* (*anche fig*) ferment; (*lievito*) yeast.

fermez'za [fărmăt'tsă] *sf* (*fig*) firmness, steadfastness.

fer'mo, a *ag* still, motionless; (*veicolo*) stationary; (*orologio*) not working; (*saldo*: *anche fig*) firm; (*voce, mano*) steady ♦ *escl* stop!; keep still! ♦ *sm* (*chiusura*) catch, lock; (*DIR*): ~ **di polizia** police detention; ~ **restando che** ... it being understood that ....

fer'mo po'sta *av, sm inv* general delivery (*US*), poste restante (*Brit*).

fero'ce [făro'chă] *ag* (*animale*) wild, fierce, ferocious; (*persona*) cruel, fierce; (*fame, dolore*) raging.

fero'cia, cie [făro'chă] *sf* ferocity.

Ferr. *abbr* = **ferrovia**.

ferra'glia [fărrál'yà] *sf* scrap iron.

ferrago'sto *sm* (*festa*) feast of the Assumption; (*periodo*) August vacation (*US*) *o* holidays *pl* (*Brit*).

ferramen'ta *sfpl* hardware *sg*, ironmongery *sg* (*Brit*); **negozio di** ~ hardware shop *o* store (*US*).

ferra're *vt* (*cavallo*) to shoe.

ferra'to, a *ag* (*FERR*): **strada** ~**a** railroad line (*US*), railway line (*Brit*); (*fig*): **essere** ~ **in** (*materia*) to be well up in.

ferravec'chio [fărrăvek'kyō] *sm* scrap merchant.

fer'reo, a *ag* iron *cpd*.

ferrie'ra *sf* ironworks *sg o pl*.

fer'ro *sm* iron; **una bistecca ai** ~**i** a grilled steak; **mettere a** ~ **e fuoco** to put to the sword; **essere ai** ~**i corti** (*fig*) to be at daggers drawn; **tocca** ~! knock on (*US*) *o* touch (*Brit*) wood!; ~ **battuto** wrought iron; ~ **di cavallo** horseshoe; ~ **da stiro** iron; ~**i da calza** knitting needles; **i** ~**i del mestiere** the tools of the trade.

ferrotranvia'rio, a *ag* public transport *cpd*.

Ferrotranvie'ri *abbr f* (= *Federazione Nazionale Lavoratori Autoferrotranvieri e Internavigatori) transport workers' union.*

ferrovi'a *sf* railroad (*US*), railway (*Brit*).

ferrovia'rio, a *ag* railroad *cpd* (*US*), railway *cpd* (*Brit*).

ferrovie're *sm* railroad man (*US*), railwayman (*Brit*).

fer'tile *ag* fertile.

fertilità *sf* fertility.

fertilizzan'te [fărtĕlĕddzán'tă] *sm* fertilizer.

fertilizza're [fărtĕlĕddzá'ră] *vt* to fertilize.

ferven'te *ag* fervent, ardent.

fer'vere *vi*: **fervono i preparativi per** ... they are making feverish preparations for ....

fer'vido, a *ag* fervent, ardent.

fervo're *sm* fervor (*US*), fervour (*Brit*); (*punto culminante*) height.

fe'sa *sf* (*CUC*) rump of veal.

fesseri'a *sf* stupidity; **dire** ~**e** to talk nonsense.

fes'so, a *pp di* **fendere** ♦ *ag* (*fam*: *sciocco*) crazy, cracked.

fessu'ra *sf* crack, split; (*per gettone, moneta*) slot.

fe'sta *sf* (*religiosa*) feast; (*pubblica*) holiday; (*compleanno*) birthday; (*onomastico*) name day; (*ricevimento*) celebration, party; **far** ~ to have a holiday; (*far baldoria*) to live it up; **far** ~ **a qn** to give sb a warm welcome; **essere vestito a** ~ to be dressed up to the nines; ~ **comandata** (*REL*) holiday of obligation; **la** ~ **della mamma/del papà** Mother's/Father's Day.

festeggiamen'ti [făstădjámăn'tĕ] *smpl* celebrations.

festeggia're [făstădjà'ră] *vt* to celebrate; (*persona*) to have a celebration for.

festi'no *sm* party; (*con balli*) ball.

festi'vo, a *ag* (*atmosfera*) festive; **giorno** ~ holiday.

festo'so, a *ag* merry, joyful.

feten'te *ag* (*puzzolente*) fetid; (*comportamento*) disgusting ♦ *sm/f* (*fam*) stinker, rotter (*Brit*).

fetic'cio [fătĕch'chō] *sm* fetish.

fe'to *sm* fetus.

feto're *sm* stench, stink.

fet'ta *sf* slice.

fettuc'cia, ce [făttōōch'chă] *sf* tape, ribbon.

fettucci'ne [făttōōchĕ'nă] *sfpl* (*CUC*) ribbon-shaped pasta.

feuda'le *ag* feudal.

fe'udo *sm* (*STORIA*) fief; (*fig*) stronghold.

ff *abbr* (*AMM*) = **facente funzione**; (= *fogli*) pp.

FF.AA *abbr* = **forze armate**.

FF.SS. *abbr* (= *Ferrovie dello Stato*) *Italian railways*.

FG *sigla* = *Foggia*.

FI *sigla* = *Firenze*.

fia'ba *sf* fairy tale.

fiabe'sco, a, schi, sche *ag* fairy-tale *cpd*.

fiac'ca *sf* weariness; (*svogliatezza*) listlessness; **battere la** ~ to shirk.

fiacca're *vt* to weaken.

fiaccherò *etc* [fyàkkāro'] *vb vedi* **fiaccare**.

fiac'co, a, chi, che *ag* (*stanco*) tired, weary; (*svogliato*) listless; (*debole*) weak; (*mercato*) slack.

fiac'cola *sf* torch.

fiaccola'ta *sf* torchlight procession.

fia'la *sf* phial.

fiam'ma *sf* flame; (*NAUT*) pennant.

fiamman'te *ag* (*colore*) flaming; **nuovo** ~ brand new.

fiamma'ta *sf* blaze.

fiammeggia're [fyàmmādjà'rā] *vi* to blaze.

fiammi'fero *sm* match.

fiammin'go, a, ghi, ghe *ag* Flemish ♦ *sm/f* Fleming ♦ *sm* (*LING*) Flemish; (*ZOOL*) flamingo; **i** ~**ghi** the Flemish.

fianca'ta *sf* (*di nave etc*) side; (*NAUT*) broadside.

fiancheggia're [fyànkādjà'rā] *vt* to border; (*fig*) to support, back (up); (*MIL*) to flank.

fian'co, chi *sm* side; (*di persona*) hip; (*MIL*) flank; **di** ~ sideways, from the side; **a ~ a ~** side by side; **prestare il proprio** ~ **alle critiche** to leave o.s. open to criticism; ~ **destr/sinistr!** (*MIL*) right/left turn!

Fian'dre *sfpl:* **le** ~ Flanders *sg*.

fiaschetteri'a [fyàskāttārē'à] *sf* wine shop.

fia'sco, schi *sm* flask; (*fig*) fiasco; **fare** ~ to be a fiasco.

fiata're *vi* (*fig: parlare*): **senza** ~ without saying a word.

fia'to *sm* breath; (*resistenza*) stamina; ~**i** *smpl* (*MUS*) wind instruments; **avere il** ~ **grosso** to be out of breath; **prendere** ~ to catch one's breath; **bere qc tutto d'un** ~ to drink sth in one gulp.

fib'bia *sf* buckle.

fi'bra *sf* fiber (*US*), fibre; (*fig*) constitution; ~ **ottica** optical fibre; ~ **di vetro** fiberglass (*US*), fibreglass (*Brit*).

ficcana'so, *pl(m)* ~**i,** *pl(f) inv sm/f* busybody.

ficca're *vt* to push, thrust, drive; ~**rsi** *vr* (*andare a finire*) to get to; ~ **il naso negli affari altrui** (*fig*) to poke *o* stick one's nose into other people's business; ~**rsi nei pasticci**

o **nei guai** to get into hot water *o* a fix.

ficcherò *etc* [fēkkāro'] *vb vedi* **ficcare**.

fiche [fēsh] *sf inv* (*nei giochi d'azzardo*) chip.

fi'co, chi *sm* (*pianta*) fig tree; (*frutto*) fig; ~ **d'India** prickly pear; ~ **secco** dried fig.

fidanzamen'to [fēdàntsàmān'tō] *sm* engagement.

fidanzar'si [fēdàntsàr'sē] *vr* to get engaged.

fidanza'to, a [fēdàntsà'tō] *sm/f* fiancé/fiancée.

fidar'si *vr:* ~ **di** to trust; ~**rsi è bene non** ~**rsi è meglio** (*proverbio*) better safe than sorry.

fida'to, a *ag* reliable, trustworthy.

fideiusso're *sm* (*DIR*) guarantor.

fi'do, a *ag* faithful, loyal ♦ *sm* (*COMM*) credit.

fidu'cia [fēdōō'chà] *sf* confidence, trust; **incarico di** ~ position of trust, responsible position; **persona di** ~ reliable person; **è il mio uomo di** ~ he is my right-hand man; **porre la questione di** ~ (*POL*) to ask for a vote of confidence.

fiducio'so, a [fēdōōchō'sō] *ag* trusting.

fie'le *sm* (*MED*) bile; (*fig*) bitterness.

fieni'le *sm* hayloft.

fie'no *sm* hay.

fie'ra *sf* fair; (*animale*) wild beast; ~ **di beneficenza** charity bazaar; ~ **campionaria** trade fair.

fierez'za [fyārāt'tsà] *sf* pride.

fie'ro, a *ag* proud; (*crudele*) fierce, cruel; (*audace*) bold.

fie'vole *ag* (*luce*) dim; (*suono*) weak.

fi'fa *sf* (*fam*): **aver** ~ to have the jitters.

fifo'ne, a *sm/f* (*fam, scherzoso*) coward.

fig. *abbr* (= *figura*) fig.

FIGC *sigla f* (= *Federazione Italiana Gioco Calcio*) *Italian football association*.

Fi'gi [fē'jē] *sfpl:* **le isole** ~ Fiji, the Fiji Islands.

fi'glia [fēl'yà] *sf* daughter; (*COMM*) counterfoil (*Brit*), stub.

figlia're [fēlyà'rā] *vi* to give birth.

figlias'tro, a [fēlyàs'trō] *sm/f* stepson/daughter.

fi'glio [fēl'yō] *sm* son; (*senza distinzione di sesso*) child; ~ **d'arte: essere** ~ **d'arte** to come from a theatrical (*o* musical *etc*) family; ~ **di puttana** (*fam!*) son of a bitch (*!*); ~ **unico** only child.

figlioc'cio, a, ci, ce [fēlyoch'chō] *sm/f* godchild, godson/daughter.

figlio'la [fēlyo'là] *sf* daughter; (*fig: ragazza*) girl.

figlio'lo [fēlyo'lō] *sm* (*anche fig: ragazzo*) son.

figu'ra *sf* figure; (*forma, aspetto esterno*) form, shape; (*illustrazione*) picture, illustration; **far** ~ to look smart; **fare una brutta** ~ to make a bad impression; **che** ~**!** how embarrassing!

figurac'cia, ce [fēgōōràch'chà] *sf:* **fare una** ~ to create a bad impression.

figura're *vi* to appear ♦ *vt*: ~**rsi qc** to imagine sth; ~**rsi** *vr*: **figurati!** imagine that!; **ti do noia? — ma figurati!** am I disturbing you? — not at all!

figurati'vo, a *ag* figurative.

figuri'na *sf* (*statuetta*) figurine; (*cartoncino*) picture card.

figurini'sta, i, e *sm/f* dress designer.

figuri'no *sm* fashion sketch.

figu'ro *sm*: **un losco** ~ a suspicious character.

figuro'ne *sm*: **fare un** ~ (*persona, oggetto*) to look terrific; (*persona: con un discorso etc*) to make an excellent impression.

fi'la *sf* row, line; (*coda*) queue; (*serie*) series, string; **di** ~ in succession; **fare la** ~ to queue; **in** ~ **indiana** in single file.

filamen'to *sm* filament.

filan'ca ® *sf stretch material.*

filan'da *sf* spinning mill.

filan'te *ag*: **stella** ~ (*stella cadente*) shooting star; (*striscia di carta*) streamer.

filantropi'a *sf* philanthropy.

filantro'pico, a, ci, che *ag* philanthropic(al).

filan'tropo *sm* philanthropist.

fila're *vt* to spin; (*NAUT*) to pay out ♦ *vi* (*baco, ragno*) to spin; (*formaggio fuso*) to go stringy; (*liquido*) to trickle; (*discorso*) to hang together; (*fam: amoreggiare*) to go steady; (*muoversi a forte velocità*) to go at full speed; (*andarsene lestamente*) to make o.s. scarce ♦ *sm* (*di alberi etc*) row, line; ~ **diritto** (*fig*) to toe the line.

filarmo'nico, a, ci, che *ag* philharmonic.

filastroc'ca, che *sf* nursery rhyme.

filateli'a *sf* philately, stamp collecting.

fila'to, a *ag* spun ♦ *sm* yarn ♦ *av*: **vai dritto** ~ **a casa** go straight home; **3 giorni** ~**i** 3 days running *o* on end.

filatu'ra *sf* spinning; (*luogo*) spinning mill.

filet'to *sm* (*ornamento*) braid, trimming; (*di vite*) thread; (*di carne*) fillet.

filia'le *ag* filial ♦ *sf* (*di impresa*) branch.

filibustie're *sm* pirate; (*fig*) adventurer.

filigra'na *sf* (*in oreficeria*) filigree; (*su carta*) watermark.

filip'pica *sf* invective.

Filippi'ne *sfpl*: **le** ~ the Philippines.

filippi'no, a *ag, sm/f* Filipino.

film *sm inv* film.

filma're *vt* to film.

filma'to *sm* short film.

filmi'no *sf* film strip.

fi'lo *sm* (*anche fig*) thread; (*filato*) yarn; (*metallico*) wire; (*di lama, rasoio*) edge; **con un** ~ **di voce** in a whisper; **un** ~ **d'aria** (*fig*) a breath of air; **dare del** ~ **da torcere a qn** to create difficulties for sb, make life difficult for sb; **fare il** ~ **a qn** (*corteggiare*) to be after sb, chase sb; **per** ~ **e per segno** in de-

tail; ~ **d'erba** blade of grass; ~ **di perle** string of pearls; ~ **di Scozia** fine cotton yarn; ~ **spinato** barbed wire.

filoamerica'no, a *ag* pro-American.

fi'lobus *sm inv* trolley bus.

filodiffusio'ne *sf* rediffusion.

filodramma'tico, a, ci, che *ag*: (**compagnia**) ~**a** amateur dramatic society ♦ *sm/f* amateur actor/actress.

filonci'no [fēlōnchē'nō] *sm* ≈ French bread.

filo'ne *sm* (*di minerali*) seam, vein; (*pane*) ≈ French bread; (*fig*) trend.

filosofi'a *sf* philosophy.

filoso'fico, a, ci, che *ag* philosophical.

filo'sofo, a *sm/f* philosopher.

filosovie'tico, a, ci, che *ag* pro-Soviet.

filovi'a *sf* (*linea*) trolley line; (*bus*) trolley bus.

filtra're *vt, vi* to filter.

fil'tro *sm* filter; (*pozione*) potion; ~ **dell'olio** (*AUT*) oil filter.

fil'za [fēl'tsá] *sf* (*anche fig*) string.

FIN *sigla f* = *Federazione Italiana Nuoto*.

fin *av, prep* = **fino.**

fina'le *ag* final ♦ *sm* (*di libro, film*) end, ending; (*MUS*) finale ♦ *sf* (*SPORT*) final.

finali'sta, i, e *sm/f* finalist.

finalità *sf* (*scopo*) aim, purpose.

finalizza're [fēnálēddzà'rā] *vt*: ~ **a** to direct towards.

finalmen'te *av* finally, at last.

finan'za [fēnán'tsá] *sf* finance; ~**e** *sfpl* (*di individuo, Stato*) finances; (**Guardia di**) ~ (*di frontiera*) ≈ Customs Service (*US*), ≈ Customs and Excise (*Brit*); (**Intendenza di**) ~ ≈ Internal Revenue Service (*US*), ≈ Inland Revenue (*Brit*); **Ministro delle** ~**e** Minister of Finance, ≈ Secretary of the Treasury (*US*), ≈ Chancellor of the Exchequer (*Brit*).

finanziamen'to [fēnántsyàmàn'tō] *sm* (*azione*) financing; (*denaro fornito*) funds *pl.*

finanzia're [fēnántsyà'rā] *vt* to finance, fund.

finanzia'rio, a [fēnántsyà'ryō] *ag* financial ♦ *sf* (*anche*: **società** ~**a**) investment company.

finanziato're, tri'ce [fēnántsyàtō'rē] *ag*: **ente** ~, **società** ~**trice** backer ♦ *sm/f* backer.

finanzie're [fēnántsye'rā] *sm* financier; (*guardia di finanza: doganale*) customs officer; (*: tributaria*) Internal Revenue official (*US*), Inland Revenue official (*Brit*).

finché [fēnkà'] *cong* (*per tutto il tempo che*) as long as; (*fino al momento in cui*) until; ~ **vorrai** as long as you like; **aspetta** ~ **non esca** wait until he goes (*o* comes) out.

fi'ne *ag* (*lamina, carta*) thin; (*capelli, polvere*) fine; (*vista, udito*) keen, sharp; (*persona: raffinata*) refined, distinguished; (*osservazione*) subtle ♦ *sf* end ♦ *sm* aim, purpose; (*esito*) result, outcome; **in** *o* **alla** ~ in the end, finally; **alla fin** ~ at the end of the day, in the end; **che ~ ha fatto?** what became of him?; **buona ~ e buon principio!** (auguri) happy New Year!; **a fin di bene** with the best of intentions; **al ~ di fare qc** (in order) to do sth; **condurre qc a buon ~** to bring sth to a successful conclusion; **secondo ~** ulterior motive.

fi'ne settima'na sm o f inv weekend.

fines'tra sf window.

finestri'no sm (di treno, auto) window.

finez'za [fēnāt'tsā] sf thinness; fineness; keenness, sharpness; refinement; subtlety.

fin'gere [fēn'jārā] vt to feign; (supporre) to imagine, suppose; **~rsi** vr: **~rsi ubriaco/pazzo** to pretend to be drunk/crazy; **~ di fare** to pretend to do.

finimen'ti smpl (di cavallo etc) harness sg.

finimon'do sm pandemonium.

fini're vt to finish ♦ vi to finish, end ♦ sm: **sul ~ della festa** towards the end of the party; **~ di fare** (compiere) to finish doing; (smettere) to stop doing; **~ in galera** to end up o finish up in prison; **farla finita** (con la vita) to put an end to one's life; **com'è andata a ~?** what happened in the end?; **finiscila!** stop it!

finitu'ra sf finish.

finlande'se ag Finnish ♦ sm/f Finn ♦ sm (LING) Finnish.

Finlan'dia sf: **la ~** Finland.

fi'no, a ag (capelli, seta) fine; (oro) pure; (fig: acuto) shrewd ♦ av (spesso troncato in **fin**: pure, anche) even ♦ prep (spesso troncato in **fin**: tempo): **fin quando?** till when?; (: luogo): **fin qui** as far as here; **~ a** (tempo) until, till; (luogo) as far as, (up) to; **fin da domani** from tomorrow onwards; **fin da ieri** since yesterday; **fin dalla nascita** from o since birth.

finoc'chio [fēnok'kyō] sm fennel; (fam peg: pederasta) queer.

fino'ra av up till now.

fin'si etc vb vedi **fingere**.

fin'to, a pp di **fingere** ♦ ag (capelli, dente) false; (fiori) artificial; (cuoio, pelle) imitation cpd; (fig: simulato: pazzia etc) feigned, sham ♦ sf pretense (US), pretence (Brit), sham; (SPORT) feint; **far ~a (di fare)** to pretend (to do); **l'ho detto per ~a** I was only pretending; (per scherzo) I was only kidding.

finzio'ne [fēntsyō'nā] sf pretense (US), pretence (Brit), sham.

fiocca're vi (neve) to fall; (fig: insulti etc) to fall thick and fast.

fioc'co, chi sm (di nastro) bow; (di stoffa, lana) flock; (di neve) flake; (NAUT) jib; **coi ~chi** (fig) first-rate; **~chi di granoturco** cornflakes.

fio'cina [fyo'chēnā] sf harpoon.

fio'co, a, chi, che ag faint, dim.

fion'da sf catapult.

fiora'io, a sm/f florist,

fiordali'so sm (BOT) cornflower.

fior'do sm fjord.

fio're sm flower; **~i** smpl (CARTE) clubs; **nel ~ degli anni** in one's prime; **a fior d'acqua** on the surface of the water; **a fior di labbra** in a whisper; **aver i nervi a fior di pelle** to be on edge; **fior di latte** cream; **è costato fior di soldi** it cost a pretty penny; **il fior ~ della società** the cream of society; **~i di campo** wild flowers.

fioren'te ag (industria, paese) flourishing; (salute) blooming; (petto) ample.

fiorenti'no, a ag, sm/f Florentine ♦ sf (CUC) T-bone steak.

fioret'to sm (SCHERMA) foil.

fiori're vi (rosa) to flower; (albero) to blossom; (fig) to flourish.

fiori'sta, i, e sm/f florist.

fioritu'ra sf (di pianta) flowering, blooming; (di albero) blossoming; (fig: di commercio, arte) flourishing; (insieme dei fiori) flowers pl; (MUS) fioritura.

fiot'to sm (di lacrime) flow, flood; (di sangue) gush, spurt.

FI'PE sigla f = Federazione Italiana Pubblici Esercizi.

Firen'ze [fēren'tsā] sf Florence.

fir'ma sf signature; (reputazione) name.

firmamen'to sm firmament.

firma're vt to sign.

firma'rio, a sm/f signatory.

fisarmo'nica, che sf accordion.

fisca'le ag fiscal, tax cpd; (meticoloso) punctilious; **medico ~** doctor employed by Social Security to verify cases of sick leave.

fiscali'sta, i, e sm/f tax consultant.

fiscalizza're [fēskálēddzá'rā] vt to exempt from taxes.

fischia're [fēskyá'rā] vi to whistle ♦ vt to whistle; (attore) to boo, hiss; **mi fischian le orecchie** my ears are singing; (fig) my ears are burning.

fischietta're [fēskyāttá'rā] vi, vt to whistle.

fischiet'to [fēskyāt'tō] sm (strumento) whistle.

fis'chio [fēs'kyō] sm whistle; **prendere ~i per fiaschi** to get hold of the wrong end of the stick.

fi'sco sm tax authorities pl, ≈ Internal Revenue Service (US), ≈ Inland Revenue (Brit).

fi'sica sf vedi **fisico**.

fisicamen'te av physically.

fi'sico, a, ci, che ag physical ♦ sm/f physicist ♦ sm physique ♦ sf physics sg.

fi'sima sf fixation.

fisiologi'a [fēzyōlōjē'á] sf physiology.

fisionomi'a sf face, physiognomy.

fisioterapi'a sf physiotherapy.

fissag'gio [fēssád'jō] sm (FOT) fixing.

fissa're vt to fix, fasten; (guardare intensa-

mente) to stare at; (*data, condizioni*) to fix, establish, set; (*prenotare*) to book; ~**rsi** *vr*: ~**rsi su** (*sog: sguardo, attenzione*) to focus on; (*fig: idea*) to become obsessed with.

fissazio'ne [fēssáttsyō'nā] *sf* (*PSIC*) fixation.

fissio'ne *sf* fission.

fis'so, a *ag* fixed; (*stipendio, impiego*) regular ♦ *av:* **guardar** ~ **qn/qc** to stare at sb/sth; **avere un ragazzo** ~ to have a steady boyfriend; **senza** ~**a dimora** of no fixed abode.

fit'ta *sf vedi* **fitto**.

fitta'volo *sm* tenant.

fitti'zio, a [fēttēt'tsyō] *ag* fictitious, imaginary.

fit'to, a *ag* thick, dense; (*pioggia*) heavy ♦ *sm* (*affitto, pigione*) rent ♦ *sf* sharp pain; **una** ~**a al cuore** (*fig*) a pang of grief; **nel** ~ **del bosco** in the heart *o* depths of the wood.

fiuma'na *sf* torrent; (*fig*) stream, flood.

fiu'me *sm* river ♦ *ag inv:* **processo** ~ long-running trial; **scorrere a** ~**i** (*acqua, sangue*) to flow in torrents.

fiuta're *vt* to smell, sniff; (*sog: animale*) to scent; (*fig: inganno*) to get wind of, smell; ~ **tabacco** to take snuff; ~ **cocaina** to snort cocaine.

fiu'to *sm* (sense of) smell; (*fig*) nose.

flac'cido, a [flàch'chēdō] *ag* flabby.

flaco'ne *sm* bottle.

flagella're [flàjàllà'rā] *vt* to flog, scourge; (*sog: onde*) to beat against.

flagel'lo [flàjel'lō] *sm* scourge.

flagran'te *ag* flagrant; **cogliere qn in** ~ to catch sb red-handed.

flanel'la *sf* flannel.

flash [flàsh] *sm inv* (*FOT*) flash; (*giornalistico*) newsflash.

fla'uto *sm* flute.

fle'bile *ag* faint, feeble.

flem'ma *sf* (*calma*) coolness, phlegm; (*MED*) phlegm.

flemma'tico, a, ci, che *ag* phlegmatic, cool.

flessi'bile *ag* pliable; (*fig: che si adatta*) flexible.

flessio'ne *sf* (*gen*) bending; (*GINNASTICA:* a terra) sit-up; (: *in piedi*) forward bend; (: *sulle gambe*) knee-bend; (*diminuzione*) slight drop, slight fall; (*LING*) inflection; **fare una** ~ to bend; **una** ~ **economica** a downward trend in the economy.

fles'so, a *pp di* **flettere**.

flessuo'so, a *ag* supple, lithe; (*andatura*) flowing, graceful.

flet'tere *vt* to bend.

flip'per [flēp'pār] *sm inv* pinball machine.

flirt [flə:t] *sm inv* brief romance, flirtation.

F.lli *abbr* (= *fratelli*) Bros.

flo'ra *sf* flora.

flo'rido, a *ag* flourishing; (*fig*) glowing with health.

flo'scio, a, sci, sce [flosh'shō] *ag* (*cappello*) floppy, soft; (*muscoli*) flabby.

flot'ta *sf* fleet.

flu'ido, a *ag, sm* fluid.

flui're *vi* to flow.

fluorescen'te [flōōōrāshen'tā] *ag* fluorescent.

fluo'ro *sm* fluorine.

fluoru'ro *sm* fluoride.

flus'so *sm* flow; (*FISICA, MED*) flux; ~ **e riflusso** ebb and flow; ~ **di cassa** (*COMM*) cash flow.

fluttua're *vi* to rise and fall; (*ECON*) to fluctuate.

fluvia'le *ag* river *cpd*, fluvial.

FM *abbr vedi* **modulazione di frequenza**.

FMI *sigla m vedi* **Fondo Monetario Internazionale**.

FO *sigla* = *Forlì*.

fobi'a *sf* phobia.

fo'ca, che *sf* (*ZOOL*) seal.

focac'cia, ce [fōkách'chà] *sf kind of pizza*; (*dolce*) sweet roll (*US*), bun (*Brit*); **rendere pan per** ~ to get one's own back, give tit for tat.

foca'le *ag* focal.

focalizza're [fōkálēddzà'rā] *vt* (*FOT: immagine*) to get into focus; (*fig: situazione*) to get into perspective; ~ **l'attenzione su** to focus one's attention on.

fo'ce [fō'chà] *sf* (*GEO*) mouth.

fochi'sta, i [fōkē'stà] *sm* (*FERR*) stoker, fireman.

focola'io *sm* (*MED*) center (*US*) *o* centre (*Brit*) of infection; (*fig*) hotbed.

focola're *sm* hearth, fireside; (*TECN*) furnace.

foco'so, a *ag* fiery; (*cavallo*) mettlesome, fiery.

fo'dera *sf* (*di vestito*) lining; (*di libro, poltrona*) cover.

fodera're *vt* to line; to cover.

fo'dero *sm* (*di spada*) scabbard; (*di pugnale*) sheath; (*di pistola*) holster.

fo'ga *sf* enthusiasm.

fog'gia, ge [fod'jà] *sf* (*maniera*) style; (*aspetto*) form, shape; (*moda*) fashion, style.

foggia're [fōdjà'rā] *vt* to shape; to style.

fo'glia [fol'yà] *sf* leaf; **ha mangiato la** ~ (*fig*) he's caught on; ~ **d'argento/d'oro** silver/gold leaf.

foglia'me [fōlyà'mā] *sm* foliage, leaves *pl*.

fogliet'to [fōlyāt'tō] *sm* (*piccolo foglio*) slip of paper, piece of paper; (*manifestino*) leaflet, handout.

fo'glio [fol'yō] *sm* (*di carta*) sheet (of paper); (*di metallo*) sheet; (*documento*) document; (*banconota*) (bank)note; ~ **rosa** (*AUT*) provisional licence; ~ **di via** (*DIR*) expulsion order; ~ **volante** pamphlet.

fo'gna [fōn'yà] *sf* drain, sewer.

fognatu'ra [fōnyàtōō'rà] *sf* drainage, sewerage.

föhn |fœːn| *sm inv* hair-dryer.
fola'ta *sf* gust.
folclo're *sm* folklore.
folgora're *vt* (*sog: fulmine*) to strike down; (: *alta tensione*) to electrocute.
folgorazio'ne |fōlgŏráttsyŏ'nä| *sf* electrocution; **ebbe una** ~ (*fig: idea*) he had a brainstorm (*US*) *o* brainwave (*Brit*).
fol'gore *sf* thunderbolt.
fol'la *sf* crowd, throng.
fol'le *ag* mad, insane; (*TECN*) idle; **in** ~ (*AUT*) in neutral.
folleggia're |fōllädjá'rä| *vi* (*divertirsi*) to paint the town red.
follet'to *sm* elf.
folli'a *sf* folly, foolishness; foolish act; (*pazzia*) madness, lunacy; **amare qn alla** ~ to love sb to distraction; **costare una** ~ to cost a fortune.
fol'to, a *ag* thick.
fomenta're *vt* to stir up, foment.
fon *sm inv* = **föhn**.
fonda'le *sm* (*del mare*) bottom; (*TEATRO*) backdrop; **il** ~ **marino** the sea bed.
fondamenta'le *ag* fundamental, basic.
fondamen'to *sm* foundation; ~**a** *sfpl* (*EDIL*) foundations.
fonda're *vt* to found; (*fig: dar base*): ~ **qc su** to base sth on; ~**rsi** *vr* (*teorie*): ~**rsi** (**su**) to be based (on).
fondatez'za |fōndátät'tsá| *sf* soundness.
fondazio'ne |fōndáttsyŏ'nä| *sf* foundation.
fon'dere *vt* (*neve*) to melt; (*metallo*) to fuse, melt; (*fig: colori*) to merge, blend; (: *imprese, gruppi*) to merge ♦ *vi* to melt; ~**rsi** *vr* to melt; (*fig: partiti, correnti*) to unite, merge.
fonderi'a *sf* foundry.
fondia'rio, a *ag* land *cpd*.
fondi'na *sf* (*piatto fondo*) soup plate; (*portapistola*) holster.
fon'do, a *ag* deep ♦ *sm* (*di recipiente, pozzo*) bottom; (*di stanza*) back; (*quantità di liquido che resta, deposito*) dregs *pl*; (*sfondo*) background; (*unità immobiliare*) property, estate; (*somma di denaro*) fund; (*SPORT*) long-distance race; ~**i** *smpl* (*denaro*) funds; **a notte** ~**a** at dead of night; **in** ~ **a** at the bottom of; at the back of; (*strada*) at the end of; **laggiù in** ~ (*lontano*) over there; (*in profondità*) down there; **in** ~ (*fig*) after all, all things considered; **andare fino in** ~ **a** (*fig*) to examine thoroughly; **andare a** ~ (*nave*) to sink; **conoscere a** ~ to know inside out; **dar** ~ **a** (*fig: provvisti, soldi*) to use up; **toccare il** ~ (*fig*) to plumb the depths; **a** ~ **perduto** (*COMM*) without security; ~ **comune di investimento** investment trust; **F**~ **Monetario Internazionale (FMI)** International Monetary Fund (IMF); ~ **di previdenza** social insurance fund; ~ **di riserva** reserve fund; ~ **tinta**

(*cosmetico*) foundation; ~ **urbano** town property; ~**i di caffè** coffee grounds; ~**i d'esercizio** working capital *sg*; ~**i liquidi** liquid assets; ~**i di magazzino** old *o* unsold stock *sg*; ~**i neri** slush fund *sg*.
fone'tica *sf* phonetics *sg*.
fonta'na *sf* fountain.
fontanel'la *sf* drinking fountain.
fon'te *sf* spring, source; (*fig*) source ♦ *sm*: ~ **battesimale** (*REL*) font.
fo'oting |fŏō'tĕng| *sm* jogging.
forag'gio |fōrád'jŏ| *sm* fodder, forage.
fora're *vt* to pierce, make a hole in; (*pallone*) to burst; (*pneumatico*) to puncture; (*biglietto*) to punch; ~**rsi** *vr* (*gen*) to develop a hole; (*AUT, pallone, timpano*) to burst; ~ **una gomma** to burst a tire.
foratu'ra *sf* piercing; bursting; puncturing; punching.
for'bici |for'bēchē| *sfpl* scissors.
forbici'na |fōrbēchē'ná| *sf* earwig.
forbi'to, a *ag* (*stile, modi*) polished.
for'ca, che *sf* (*AGR*) fork, pitchfork; (*patibolo*) gallows *sg*.
forcel'la |fōrchĕl'lá| *sf* (*TECN*) fork; (*di monte*) pass.
forchet'ta |fōrkät'tá| *sf* fork; **essere una buona** ~ to enjoy one's food.
forci'na |fōrchē'ná| *sf* hairpin.
for'cipe |for'chēpä| *sm* forceps *pl*.
forco'ne *sm* pitchfork.
foren'se *ag* (*linguaggio*) legal; **avvocato** ~ lawyer, barrister (*Brit*).
fore'sta *sf* forest; **la F**~ **Nera** the Black Forest.
foresta'le *ag* forest *cpd*; **guardia** ~ forester.
foresteri'a *sf* (*di convento, palazzo etc*) guest rooms *pl*, guest quarters *pl*.
forestie'ro, a *ag* foreign ♦ *sm/f* foreigner.
forfa'it |forfc'| *sm inv*: (**prezzo a**) ~ fixed price, set price; **dichiarare** ~ (*SPORT*) to withdraw; (*fig*) to give up.
forfeta'rio, a *ag*: **prezzo** ~ (*da pagare*) fixed *o* set price; (*da ricevere*) lump sum.
for'fora *sf* dandruff.
for'gia, ge |for'já| *sf* forge.
forgia're |fōrjá'rä| *vt* to forge.
for'ma *sf* form; (*aspetto esteriore*) form, shape; (*DIR: procedura*) procedure; (*per calzature*) last; (*stampo da cucina*) mold (*US*), mould (*Brit*); ~**e** *sfpl* (*del corpo*) figure, shape; **le** ~**e** (*convenzioni*) appearances; **errori di** ~ stylistic errors; **essere in** ~ to be in good shape; **tenersi in** ~ to keep fit; **in** ~ **ufficiale/privata** officially/privately; **una** ~ **di formaggio** a (whole) cheese.
formaggi'no |fōrmádjē'nŏ| *sm* processed cheese.
formag'gio |fōrmád'jŏ| *sm* cheese.
forma'le *ag* formal.

formalità *sf inv* formality.

formalizza're |fŏrmálĕddzà'rā| *vt* to formalize.

forma're *vt* to form, shape, make; (*nunero di telefono*) to dial; (*fig*: *carattere*) to form, mould (*US*), mould (*Brit*); ~**rsi** *vr* to form, take shape; **il treno si forma a Milano** the train starts from Milan.

forma'to *sm* format, size.

formattazio'ne |fŏrmáttàttsyŏ'nā| *sf* (*INFORM*) formatting.

formazio'ne |fŏrmáttsyŏ'nā| *sf* formation; (*fig*: *educazione*) training; ~ **professionale** vocational training.

formi'ca, che *sf* ant.

formica'io *sm* anthill.

formicola're *vi* (*gamba, braccio*) to tingle; (*brulicare*: *anche fig*): ~ **di** to be swarming with; **mi formicola la gamba** I've got pins and needles in my leg, my leg's tingling.

formicoli'o *sm* pins and needles *pl*; swarming.

formida'bile *ag* powerful, formidable; (*straordinario*) remarkable.

formo'so, a *ag* shapely.

for'mula *sf* formula; ~ **di cortesia** (*nelle lettere*) letter ending.

formula're *vt* to formulate.

forna'ce |fŏrná'chā| *sf* (*per laterizi etc*) kiln; (*per metalli*) furnace.

forna'io *sm* baker.

fornel'lo *sm* (*elettrico, a gas*) ring; (*di pipa*) bowl.

forni're *vt*: ~ **qn di qc, ~ qc a qn** to provide *o* supply sb with sth, supply sth to sb; ~**rsi** *vr*: ~**rsi di** (*procurarsi*) to provide o.s. with.

forni'to, a *ag*: **ben ~** (*negozio*) well-stocked.

fornito're, tri'ce *ag*: **ditta ~trice di** ... company supplying ... ♦ *sm/f* supplier.

fornitu'ra *sf* supply.

for'no *sm* (*di cucina*) oven; (*panetteria*) bakery; (*TECN*: *per calce etc*) kiln; (: *per metalli*) furnace; **fare i ~i** (*MED*) to undergo heat treatment.

fo'ro *sm* (*buco*) hole; (*STORIA*) forum; (*tribunale*) (law) court.

for'se *av* perhaps, maybe; (*circa*) about; **essere in ~** to be in doubt.

forsenna'to, a *ag* mad, crazy, insane.

for'te *ag* strong; (*suono*) loud; (*spesa*) considerable, great ♦ *av* strongly; (*velocemente*) fast; (*a voce alta*) loud(ly); (*violentemente*) hard ♦ *sm* (*edificio*) fort; (*specialità*) forte, strong point; **piatto ~** (*CUC*) main dish; **avere un ~ mal di testa/raffreddore** to have a bad headache/cold; **essere ~ in qc** to be good at sth; **farsi ~ di qc** to make use of *o* avail o.s. of sth; **dare man ~ a qn** to back sb up, support sb; **usare le maniere ~i** to use strong-arm tactics.

fortez'za |fŏrtät'tsà| *sf* (*morale*) strength;

(*luogo fortificato*) fortress.

fortifica're *vt* to fortify, strengthen.

fortu'ito, a *ag* fortuitous, chance *cpd*.

fortu'na *sf* (*destino*) fortune, luck; (*buona sorte*) success, fortune; (*eredità, averi*) fortune; **per ~** luckily, fortunately; **di ~** makeshift, improvised; **atterraggio di ~** emergency landing.

fortuna'le *sm* storm.

fortunatamen'te *av* luckily, fortunately.

fortuna'to, a *ag* lucky, fortunate; (*coronato da successo*) successful.

fortuno'so, a *ag* (*vita*) eventful; (*avvenimento*) unlucky.

forun'colo *sm* (*MED*) boil.

forvia're *vt, vi* = **fuorviare**.

for'za |for'tsà| *sf* strength; (*potere*) power; (*FISICA*) force ♦ *escl* come on!; ~**e** *sfpl* (*fisiche*) strength *sg*; (*MIL*) forces; **per ~** against one's will; (*naturalmente*) of course; **per ~ di cose** by force of circumstances; **a viva ~** by force; **a ~ di** by dint of; **farsi ~** (*coraggio*) to pluck up one's courage; **bella ~!** (*ironico*) how clever of you (*o* him *etc*)!; ~ **lavoro** work force, manpower; **per causa di ~ maggiore** (*DIR*) by reason of an act of God; (*per estensione*) due to circumstances beyond one's control; **la ~ pubblica** the police *pl*; ~ **di vendita** (*COMM*) sales force; ~ **di volontà** willpower; **le ~e armate** the armed forces.

forza're |fŏrtsá'rā| *vt* to force; (*cassaforte, porta*) to force (open); (*voce*) to strain; ~ **qn a fare** to force sb to do.

forza'to, a |fŏrtsá'tŏ| *ag* forced ♦ *sm* (*DIR*) prisoner sentenced to hard labor.

forzie're |fŏrtsye'rā| *sm* strongbox; (*di pirati*) treasure chest.

forzu'to, a |fŏrtsŏŏ'tŏ| *ag* big and strong.

foschi'a |fŏskĕ'à| *sf* mist, haze.

fo'sco, a, schi, sche *ag* dark, gloomy; **dipingere qc a tinte ~sche** (*fig*) to paint a gloomy picture of sth.

fosfa'to *sm* phosphate.

fosforescen'te |fŏsfŏrāshen'tā| *ag* phosphorescent; (*lancetta dell'orologio etc*) luminous.

fo'sforo *sm* phosphorous.

fos'sa *sf* pit; (*di cimitero*) grave; ~ **biologica** septic tank; ~ **comune** mass grave.

fossa'to *sm* ditch; (*di fortezza*) moat.

fosset'ta *sf* dimple.

fos'si *etc vb vedi* **essere**.

fos'sile *ag, sm* fossil (*cpd*).

fos'so *sm* ditch; (*MIL*) trench.

fo'ste *etc vb vedi* **essere**.

fo'to *sf inv* photo; ~ **ricordo** souvenir photo; ~ **tessera** passport(-type) photo.

foto... *prefisso* photo....

fotocomposito're *sm* filmsetter.

fotocomposizio'ne |fŏtŏkŏmpŏzĕttsyŏ'nā| *sf*

film setting.
fotoco'pia *sf* photocopy.
fotocopia're *vt* to photocopy.
fotoge'nico, a, ci, che [fōtōjeˈnēkō] *ag* photogenic.
fotografa're *vt* to photograph.
fotografi'a *sf* (*procedimento*) photography; (*immagine*) photograph; **fare una** ~ to take a photograph; **una** ~ **a colori/in bianco e nero** a color/black and white photograph.
fotogra'fico, a, ci, che *ag* photographic; **macchina** ~**a** camera.
foto'grafo, a *sm/f* photographer.
fotogram'ma, i *sm* (*CINEMA*) frame.
fotomodel'lo, a *sm/f* fashion model.
fotomontag'gio [fōtōmōntádˈjō] *sm* photomontage.
fotorepor'ter *sm/f inv* newspaper (*o* magazine) photographer.
fotoroman'zo [fōtōrōmánˈdzō] *sm* photo romance (*US*), romantic picture story (*Brit*).
fotosin'tesi *sf* photosynthesis.
fot'tere *vt* (*fam!*: *avere rapporti sessuali*) to fuck(*!*), screw(*!*); (: *rubare*) to pinch, swipe; (: *fregare*): **mi hanno fottuto** they played a dirty trick on me; **vai a farti** ~! fuck off!(*!*)
fottu'to, a *ag* (*fam!*) fucking(*!*).
foulard [fōōlárˈ] *sm inv* scarf.
FR *sigla* = *Frosinone*.
fr. *abbr* (*COMM*) = **franco**.
fra *prep* = **tra**.
fracassa're *vt* to shatter, smash; ~**rsi** *vr* to shatter, smash; (*veicolo*) to crash.
fracas'so *sm* smash; crash; (*baccano*) din, racket.
fra'dicio, a, ci, ce [fráˈdēchō] *ag* (*guasto*) rotten; (*molto bagnato*) soaking (wet); **ubriaco** ~ blind drunk.
fra'gile [fráˈjēlā] *ag* fragile; (*salute*) delicate; (*nervi, vetro*) brittle.
fragilità [frájēlētáˈ] *sf* (*vedi ag*) fragility; delicacy; brittleness.
fra'gola *sf* strawberry.
frago're *sm* (*di cascate, carro armato*) roar; (*di tuono*) rumble.
fragoro'so, a *ag* deafening; **ridere in modo** ~ to roar with laughter.
fragran'te *ag* fragrant.
frainten'dere *vt* to misunderstand.
frainte'so, a *pp di* **fraintendere**.
frammen'to *sm* fragment.
frammi'sto, a *ag*: ~ **a** interspersed with, mixed with.
fra'na *sf* landslide; (*fig*: *persona*): **essere una** ~ to be useless, be a walking disaster area.
frana're *vi* to slip, slide down.
francamen'te *av* frankly.
france'se [fránchāˈzā] *ag* French ♦ *sm/f* Frenchman/woman ♦ *sm* (*LING*) French; **i F**~**i** the French.

franchez'za [fránkātˈtsá] *sf* frankness, openness.
franchi'gia, gie [fránkēˈjá] *sf* (*AMM*) exemption; (*DIR*) franchise; (*NAUT*) shore leave; ~ **doganale** exemption from customs duty.
Fran'cia [fránˈchá] *sf*: **la** ~ France.
fran'co, a, chi, che *ag* (*COMM*) free; (*sincero*) frank, open, sincere ♦ *sm* (*moneta*) franc; **farla** ~**a** (*fig*) to get off scot-free; ~ **a bordo** free on board; ~ **di dogana** duty-free; ~ **a domicilio** delivered free of charge; ~ **fabbrica** ex factory, ex works; **prezzo** ~ **fabbrica** ex-works price; ~ **magazzino** ex warehouse; ~ **di porto** carriage free; ~ **vagone** free on rail; ~ **tiratore** sm sniper; (*POL*) member of parliament who votes against his own party.
francobol'lo *sm* (postage) stamp.
franco-canade'se *ag, sm/f* French Canadian.
Francofor'te *sf* Frankfurt.
frangen'te [fránjenˈtā] *sm* (*onda*) breaker; (*scoglio emergente*) reef; (*circostanza*) situation, circumstance.
fran'gia, ge [fránˈjá] *sf* fringe.
frangiflut'ti [fránjēflōōtˈtē] *sm inv* breakwater.
frangiven'to [fránjēvenˈtō] *sm* windbreak.
franto'io *sm* (*AGR*) olive press; (*TECN*) crusher.
frantuma're *vt*, ~**rsi** *vr* to break into pieces, shatter.
frantu'mi *smpl* pieces, bits; (*schegge*) splinters; **andare in** ~, **mandare in** ~ to shatter, smash to pieces *o* smithereens.
frappé *sm* (*CUC*) milk shake.
frasa'rio *sm* (*gergo*) vocabulary, language.
fra'sca, sche *sf* (leafy) branch; **saltare di palo in** ~ to jump from one subject to another.
fra'se *sf* (*LING*) sentence; (*locuzione, espressione, MUS*) phrase; ~ **fatta** set phrase.
fraseologi'a [frázāōlōjēˈá] *sf* phraseology.
fras'sino *sm* ash (tree).
frastaglia'to, a [frástályáˈtō] *ag* (*costa*) indented, jagged.
frastorna're *vt* (*intontire*) to daze; (*confondere*) to bewilder, befuddle.
frastorna'to, a *ag* dazed; bewildered.
frastuo'no *sm* hubbub, din.
fra'te *sm* friar, monk.
fratellan'za [frátāllánˈtsá] *sf* brotherhood; (*associazione*) fraternity.
fratellas'tro *sm* stepbrother.
fratel'lo *sm* brother; ~**i** *smpl* brothers; (*nel senso di fratelli e sorelle*) brothers and sisters.
frater'no, a *ag* fraternal, brotherly.
fratrici'da, i, e [frátrēchēˈdá] *ag* fratricidal ♦ *sm/f* fratricide; **guerra** ~ civil war.
fratta'glie [fráttálˈyā] *sfpl* (*CUC*: *gen*) offal *sg*; (: *di pollo*) giblets.
frattan'to *av* in the meantime, meanwhile.
frattem'po *sm*: **nel** ~ in the meantime,

meanwhile.

frattu'ra *sf* fracture; *(fig)* split, break.

fraudolen'to, a *ag* fraudulent.

frazionamen'to [fráttsyōnámān'tō] *sm* division, splitting up.

frazio'ne [fráttsyō'nā] *sf* fraction; *(borgata)*: ~ **di comune** hamlet.

frec'cia, ce [frāch'chá] *sf* arrow; ~ **di direzione** *(AUT)* turn signal (indicator) *(US)*, indicator *(Brit)*.

frecci'ata [frāchá'tá] *sf:* **lanciare una** ~ to make a cutting remark.

fredda're *vt* to shoot dead.

freddez'za [frāddāt'tsá] *sf* coldness.

fred'do, a *ag, sm* cold; **fa** ~ it's cold; **aver** ~ to be cold; **soffrire il** ~ to feel the cold; **a** ~ *(fig)* deliberately.

freddolo'so, a *ag* sensitive to the cold.

freddu'ra *sf* pun.

frega're *vt* to rub; *(fam: truffare)* to take in, cheat; (: *rubare*) to swipe, pinch; **fregarsene** *(fam!)*: **chi se ne frega?** who gives a damn (about it)?

frega'ta *sf* rub; *(fam)* swindle; *(NAUT)* frigate.

fregatu'ra *sf (fam: imbroglio)* rip-off; (: *delusione*) let-down.

fregherò *etc* [frāgáro'] *vb vedi* **fregare**.

fre'gio [frā'jō] *sm (ARCHIT)* frieze; *(ornamento)* decoration.

fre'mere *vi:* ~ **di** to tremble *o* quiver with; ~ **d'impazienza** to be champing at the bit.

fre'mito *sm* tremor, quiver.

frena're *vt (veicolo)* to slow down; *(cavallo)* to rein in; *(lacrime)* to restrain, hold back ♦ *vi* to brake; **~rsi** *vr (fig)* to restrain o.s., control o.s.

frena'ta *sf:* **fare una** ~ to brake.

frenesi'a *sf* frenzy.

frene'tico, a, ci, che *ag* frenetic.

fre'no *sm* brake; *(morso)* bit; **tenere a** ~ *(passioni etc)* to restrain; **tenere a** ~ **la lingua** to hold one's tongue; ~ **a disco** disc brake; ~ **a mano** handbrake.

frequenta're *vt (scuola, corso)* to attend; *(locale, bar)* to go to, frequent; *(persone)* to see (often).

frequenta'to, a *ag (locale)* busy.

frequen'te *ag* frequent; **di** ~ frequently.

frequen'za [frākwen'tsá] *sf* frequency; *(INS)* attendance.

fresa're *vt (TECN)* to mill.

freschez'za [frāskāt'tsá] *sf* freshness.

fre'sco, a, schi, sche *ag* fresh; *(temperatura)* cool; *(notizia)* recent, fresh ♦ *sm:* **godere il** ~ to enjoy the cool air; ~ **di bucato** straight from the wash, newly washed; **stare** ~ *(fig)* to be in for it; **mettere al** ~ to put in a cool place; *(fig: in prigione)* to put inside *o* in the cooler.

frescu'ra *sf* cool.

fre'sia *sf* freesia.

fret'ta *sf* hurry, haste; **in** ~ in a hurry; **in** ~ **e furia** in a mad rush; **aver** ~ to be in a hurry; **far** ~ **a qn** to hurry sb.

frettolosamen'te *av* hurriedly, in a rush.

frettolo'so, a *ag (persona)* in a hurry; *(lavoro etc)* hurried, rushed.

fria'bile *ag (terreno)* friable; *(pasta)* crumbly.

frig'gere [frēd'jārā] *vt* to fry ♦ *vi (olio etc)* to sizzle; **vai a farti ~!** *(fam)* get lost!

frigidità [frējēdētá'] *sf* frigidity.

fri'gido, a [frē'jēdō] *ag (MED)* frigid.

frigna're [frēnyá'rā] *vi* to whine, snivel.

frigno'ne, a [frēnyō'nā] *sm/f* whiner, sniveller.

fri'go, ghi *sm* fridge.

frigori'fero, a *ag* refrigerating ♦ *sm* refrigerator; **cella** ~**a** cold storage.

fringuel'lo *sm* chaffinch.

fris'si *etc vb vedi* **friggere**.

fritta'ta *sf* omelet(te); **fare una** ~ *(fig)* to make a mess of things.

frittel'la *sf (CUC)* pancake; (: *ripiena*) fritter.

frit'to, a *pp di* **friggere** ♦ *ag* fried ♦ *sm* fried food; **ormai siamo ~i!** *(fig fam)* now we've had it!; **è un argomento** ~ **e rifritto** that's old hat; ~ **misto** mixed fry.

frittu'ra *sf (cibo)* fried food; ~ **di pesce** mixed fried fish.

friula'no, a *ag* of *(o* from) Friuli.

fri'volo, a *ag* frivolous.

frizio'ne [frēttsyō'nā] *sf* friction; *(di pelle)* rub, rub-down; *(AUT)* clutch.

frizzan'te [frēddzàn'tā] *ag (anche fig)* sparkling.

friz'zo [frēd'dzō] *sm* witticism.

froda're *vt* to defraud, cheat.

fro'de *sf* fraud; ~ **fiscale** tax evasion.

fro'do *sm:* **di** ~ illegal, contraband; **pescatore di** ~, **cacciatore di** ~ poacher.

fro'gia, gie [fro'já] *sf (di cavallo etc)* nostril.

frol'lo, a *ag (carne)* tender; (: *di selvaggina)* high; *(fig: persona)* soft; **pasta ~a** short-(crust) pastry.

fron'da *sf* (leafy) branch; *(di partito politico)* internal opposition; ~**e** *sfpl (di albero)* foliage *sg*.

fronta'le *ag* frontal; *(scontro)* head-on.

fron'te *sf (ANAT)* forehead; *(di edificio)* front, façade ♦ *sm (MIL, POL, METEOR)* front; **a** ~, **di** ~ facing, opposite; **di** ~ **a** *(posizione)* opposite, facing, in front of; *(a paragone di)* compared with; **far** ~ **a** *(nemico, problema)* to confront; *(responsabilità)* to face up to; *(spese)* to cope with.

fronteggia're [frōntādjá'rā] *vt (avversari, difficoltà)* to face, stand up to; *(spese)* to cope with.

frontespi'zio [frōntāspēt'tsyō] *sm (ARCHIT)* frontispiece; *(di libro)* title page.

frontie'ra *sf* border, frontier.
fronto'ne *sm* pediment.
fron'zolo |frōn'dzōlō| *sm* frill.
frot'ta *sf* crowd; **in ~, a ~e** in their hundreds, in droves.
frot'tola *sf* fib; **raccontare un sacco di ~e** to tell a pack of lies.
fruga'le *ag* frugal.
fruga're *vi* to rummage ♦ *vt* to search.
frugherò *etc* |froogà'rō| *vb vedi* **frugare**.
fruito're *sm* user.
fruizio'ne |frōōēttsyō'nā| *sf* use.
frulla're *vt* (*CUC*) to whisk ♦ *vi* (*uccelli*) to flutter; **cosa ti frulla in mente?** what is going on in that mind of yours?
frulla'to *sm* (*CUC*) milk shake; (: *con solo frutta*) fruit drink.
frullato're *sm* blender.
frulli'no *sm* whisk.
frumen'to *sm* wheat.
fruscia're |froōshà'rā| *vi* to rustle.
frusci'o |frooshē'ō| *sm* rustle; rustling.
fru'sta *sf* whip; (*CUC*) whisk.
frusta're *vt* to whip.
frusta'ta *sf* lash.
frusti'no *sm* riding crop.
frustra're *vt* to frustrate.
frustrazio'ne |frooostráttsyō'nā| *sf* frustration.
frut'ta *sf* fruit; (*portata*) dessert; **~ candita/ secca** candied/dried fruit.
frutta're *vi* (*investimenti*, *deposito*) to bear dividends, give a return; **il mio deposito in banca (mi) frutta il 10%** my bank deposits bring (me) in 10%; **quella gara gli fruttò la medaglia d'oro** he won the gold medal in that competition.
frutte'to *sm* orchard.
frutticoltu'ra *sf* fruit growing.
frutti'fero, a *ag* (*albero etc*) fruit-bearing; (*fig: che frutta*) fruitful, profitable; **deposito ~** interest-bearing deposit.
fruttiven'dolo, a *sm/f* produce dealer (*US*), greengrocer (*Brit*).
frut'to *sm* fruit; (*fig: risultato*) result(s); (*ECON: interesse*) interest; (: *reddito*) income; **è ~ della tua immaginazione** it's a figment of your imagination; **~i di mare** seafood *sg*.
fruttuo'so, a *ag* fruitful, profitable.
FS *abbr* (= *Ferrovie dello Stato*) Italian railways.
f.t. *abbr* = **fuori testo**.
f.to. *abbr* (= *firmato*) signed.
fu *vb vedi* **essere** ♦ *ag inv*: **il ~ Paolo Bianchi** the late Paolo Bianchi.
fucila're |foōchēlà'rā| *vt* to shoot.
fucila'ta |foōchēlà'tà| *sf* rifle shot.
fucilazio'ne |foōchēlàttsyō'nā| *sf* execution (by firing squad).
fuci'le |foōchē'lā| *sm* rifle, gun; (*da caccia*)

shotgun, gun; **~ a canne mozze** sawed-off shotgun.
fuci'na |foōchē'ná| *sf* forge.
fu'co, chi *sm* drone.
fuc'sia *sf* fuchsia.
fu'ga, ghe *sf* escape, flight; (*di gas, liquidi*) leak; (*MUS*) fugue; **mettere qn in ~** to put sb to flight; **~ di cervelli** brain drain.
fuga'ce |foōgà'chā| *ag* fleeting, transient.
fuga're *vt* (*dubbi, incertezze*) to dispel, drive out.
fugge'vole |foōdjä'vōlā| *ag* fleeting.
fuggia'sco, a, schi, sche |foōdjà'skō| *ag, sm/f* fugitive.
fuggifug'gi |foōdjēfoōd'jē| *sm* scramble, stampede.
fuggi're |foōdjē'rā| *vi* to flee, run away; (*fig: passar veloce*) to fly ♦ *vt* to avoid.
fuggiti'vo, a |foōdjētē'vō| *sm/f* fugitive, runaway.
fu'i *vb vedi* **essere**.
fulgo're *sm* brilliance, splendor (*US*), splendour (*Brit*).
fulig'gine |foōlēd'jēnā| *sf* soot.
fulmina're *vt* (*sog: elettricità*) to electrocute; (*con arma da fuoco*) to shoot dead; **~rsi** *vr* (*lampadina*) to go, blow; (*fig: con lo sguardo*): **mi fulminò (con uno sguardo)** he looked daggers at me.
ful'mine *sm* bolt of lightning; **~i** *smpl* lightning *sg*; **~ a ciel sereno** bolt from the blue.
fulmi'neo, a *ag* (*fig: scatto*) rapid; (: *minaccioso*) threatening.
ful'vo, a *ag* tawny.
fumaio'lo *sm* (*di nave*) funnel; (*di fabbrica*) chimney.
fuman'te *ag* (*piatto etc*) steaming.
fuma're *vi* to smoke; (*emettere vapore*) to steam ♦ *vt* to smoke.
fuma'rio, a *ag*: **canna ~a** flue.
fuma'ta *sf* (*segnale*) smoke signal; **farsi una ~** to have a smoke; **~ bianca/nera** (*in Vaticano*) signal that a new pope has/has not been elected.
fumato're, tri'ce *sm/f* smoker.
fumet'to *sm* comic strip; **giornale** *m* **a ~i** comic.
fum'mo *vb vedi* **essere**.
fu'mo *sm* smoke; (*vapore*) steam; (*il fumare tabacco*) smoking; **~i** *smpl* (*industriali etc*) fumes; **vendere ~** to deceive, cheat; **è tutto ~ e niente arrosto** it has no substance to it; **i ~i dell'alcool** (*fig*) the after-effects of drink.
fumo'geno, a |foōmo'jänō| *ag* (*candelotto*) smoke *cpd* ♦ *sm* smoke bomb; **cortina ~a** smoke screen.
fumo'so, a *ag* smoky; (*fig*) muddled.
funam'bolo, a *sm/f* tightrope walker.
fu'ne *sf* rope, cord; (*più grossa*) cable.
fu'nebre *ag* (*rito*) funeral; (*aspetto*) gloomy,

funereal.

funera'le *sm* funeral.

fune'sto, a *ag* (*incidente*) fatal; (*errore, decisione*) fatal, disastrous; (*atmosfera*) gloomy, dismal.

fun'gere |fōōn'jārā| *vi*: ~ **da** to act as.

fun'go, ghi *sm* fungus; (*commestibile*) mushroom; ~ **velenoso** toadstool; **crescere come i ~ghi** (*fig*) to spring up overnight.

funicola're *sf* funicular railway.

funivi'a *sf* cable railway.

fun'si *etc vb vedi* **fungere**.

fun'to, a *pp di* **fungere**.

funziona're |fōōntsyōnä'rā| *vi* to work, function; (*fungere*): ~ **da** to act as.

funziona'rio |fōōntsyōnä'ryō| *sm* official; ~ **statale** civil servant.

funzio'ne |fōōntsyō'nā| *sf* function; (*carica*) post, position; (*REL*) service; **in** ~ (*meccanismo*) in operation; **in** ~ **di** (*come*) as; **vive in** ~ **dei figli** he lives for his children; **far** ~ **di** to act as; **fare la** ~ **di qn** (*farne le veci*) to take sb's place.

fuo'co, chi *sm* fire; (*fornello*) ring; (*FOT, FISICA*) focus; **dare** ~ **a qc** to set fire to sth; **far** ~ (*sparare*) to fire; **prendere** ~ to catch fire; ~ **d'artificio** firework; ~ **di paglia** flash in the pan; ~ **sacro** *o* **di Sant'Antonio** (*MED fam*) shingles *sg*.

fuorché |fwōrkā'| *cong, prep* except.

FUO'RI *sigla m* (= *Fronte Unitario Omosessuale Rivoluzionario Italiano*) *gay liberation movement*.

fuo'ri *av* outside; (*all'aperto*) outdoors, outside; (~ *di casa, SPORT*) out; (*esclamativo*) get out! ♦ *prep*: ~ (**di**) out of, outside ♦ *sm* outside; **essere in** ~ (*sporgere*) to stick out; **lasciar** ~ **qc/qn** to leave sth/sb out; **far** ~ (*fam*: *soldi*) to spend; (: *cioccolatini*) to eat up; (: *rubare*) to nick; **far** ~ **qn** (*fam*) to kill sb, do sb in; **essere tagliato** ~ (*da un gruppo, ambiente*) to be excluded; **essere** ~ **di sé** to be beside oneself; ~ **luogo** (*inopportuno*) out of place, uncalled for; ~ **mano** out of the way, remote; ~ **pasto** between meals; ~ **pericolo** out of danger; ~ **dai piedi!** get out of the way!; ~ **servizio** out of order; ~ **stagione** out of season; **illustrazione** ~ **testo** (*STAMPA*) plate; ~ **uso** out of use.

fuoribor'do *sm inv* speedboat (with outboard motor); outboard motor.

fuoribu'sta *sm inv* unofficial payment.

fuoriclas'se *sm/f inv* (undisputed) champion.

fuoricor'so *ag inv* (*moneta*) no longer in circulation; (*INS*): (**studente**) ~ *undergraduate who has not completed a course in due time.*

fuorigio'co |fwōrējo'kō| *sm* offside.

fuorileg'ge |fwōrēlād'jā| *sm/f inv* outlaw.

fuorise'rie *ag inv* (*auto etc*) custom-built ♦ *sf* custom-built car.

fuoristra'da *sm* (*AUT*) cross-country vehicle.

fuorusci'to, a, fuoriusci'to, a |fwōr(ē)ōōshē'tō| *sm/f* exile ♦ *sf* (*di gas*) leakage, escape; (*di sangue, linfa*) seepage.

fuorvia're *vt* to mislead; (*fig*) to lead astray ♦ *vi* to go astray.

furbacchio'ne, a |fōōrbàkkyō'nā| *sm/f* cunning old devil.

furbi'zia |fōōrbēt'tsyà| *sf* (*vedi ag*) cleverness; cunning; **una** ~ a cunning trick.

fur'bo, a *ag* clever, smart; (*peg*) cunning ♦ *sm/f*: **fare il** ~ to (try to) be clever *o* smart; **fatti** ~! show a bit of sense!

furen'te *ag*: ~ (**contro**) furious (with).

fureri'a *sf* (*MIL*) orderly room.

furet'to *sm* ferret.

furfan'te *sm* rascal, scoundrel.

furgonci'no |fōōrgōnchē'nō| *sm* panel truck (*US*), small van (*Brit*).

furgo'ne *sm* truck.

fu'ria *sf* (*ira*) fury, rage; (*fig: impeto*) fury, violence; (*fretta*) rush; **a** ~ **di** by dint of; **andare su tutte le** ~**e** to fly into a rage.

furibon'do, a *ag* furious.

furie're *sm* quartermaster.

furio'so, a *ag* furious; (*mare, vento*) raging.

fu'rono *vb vedi* **essere**.

furo're *sm* fury; (*esaltazione*) frenzy; **far** ~ to be all the rage.

furti'vo, a *ag* furtive.

fur'to *sm* theft; ~ **con scasso** burglary.

fu'sa *sfpl*: **fare le** ~ to purr.

fuscel'lo |fōōshel'lō| *sm* twig.

fu'si *etc vb vedi* **fondere**.

fusi'bile *sm* (*ELETTR*) fuse.

fusio'ne *sf* (*di metalli*) fusion, melting; (*colata*) casting; (*COMM*) merger; (*fig*) merging.

fu'so, a *pp di* **fondere** ♦ *sm* (*FILATURA*) spindle; **diritto come un** ~ as stiff as a board; ~ **orario** time zone.

fusolie'ra *sf* (*AER*) fuselage.

fusta'gno |fōōstàn'yō| *sm* corduroy.

fustel'la *sf* (*su scatola di medicinali*) tear-off tab.

fustiga're *vt* (*frustare*) to flog; (*fig: costumi*) to censure, denounce.

fusti'no *sm* (*di detersivo*) bucket (*US*), tub (*Brit*).

fu'sto *sm* stem; (*ANAT, di albero*) trunk; (*recipiente*) drum, can; (*fam*) he-man.

fu'tile *ag* vain, futile.

futilità *sf inv* futility.

futuri'smo *sm* futurism.

futu'ro, a *ag, sm* future.

G

G, g [jē] *sf o m inv* (*lettera*) G, g; **G come Genova** ≈ G for George.

g. *abbr* (= *grammo*) g.

gabardi'ne [gàbárdēn'] *sm* (*tessuto*) gabardine; (*soprabito*) gabardine raincoat.

gabba're *vt* to take in, dupe; **~rsi** *vr:* **~rsi di qn** to make fun of sb.

gab'bia *sf* cage; (*DIR*) dock; (*da imballaggio*) crate; **la ~ degli accusati** (*DIR*) the dock; **~ dell'ascensore** elevator (*US*) o lift (*Brit*) shaft; **~ toracica** (*ANAT*) rib cage.

gabbia'no *sm* (sea)gull.

gabinet'to *sm* (*MED etc*) examination (*US*) o consulting (*Brit*) room; (*POL*) ministry; (*di decenza*) lavatory; (*INS: di fisica etc*) laboratory.

Gabon' *sm:* **il ~** Gabon.

gae'lico, a, ci, che *ag, sm* Gaelic.

gaffe [gàf] *sf inv* blunder, faux pas.

gagliar'do, a [gàlyár'dō] *ag* strong, vigorous.

gaiez'za [gàyāt'tsà] *sf* gaiety, cheerfulness.

ga'io, a *ag* cheerful.

ga'la *sf* (*sfarzo*) pomp; (*festa*) gala.

galan'te *ag* gallant, courteous; (*avventura, poesia*) amorous.

galanteri'a *sf* gallantry.

galantuo'mo, *pl* **galantuo'mini** *sm* gentleman.

galas'sia *sf* galaxy.

galate'o *sm* (good) manners *pl*, etiquette.

galeot'to *sm* (*rematore*) galley slave; (*carcerato*) convict.

gale'ra *sf* (*NAUT*) galley; (*prigione*) prison.

gal'la *sf:* **a ~** afloat; **venire a ~** to surface, come to the surface; (*fig: verità*) to come out.

galleggiamen'to [gàllādjàmān'tō] *sm* floating; **linea di ~** (*di nave*) waterline.

galleggian'te [gàllādjàn'tā] *ag* floating ♦ *sm* (*natante*) barge; (*di pescatore, lenza, TECN*) float.

galleggia're [gàllādjà'rā] *vi* to float.

galleri'a *sf* (*traforo*) tunnel; (*ARCHIT, d'arte*) gallery; (*TEATRO*) circle; (*strada coperta con negozi*) arcade; **~ del vento** o **aerodinamica** (*AER*) wind tunnel.

Gal'les *sm:* **il ~** Wales.

galle'se *ag* Welsh ♦ *sm/f* Welshman/woman ♦ *sm* (*LING*) Welsh; **i G~i** the Welsh.

gallet'ta *sf* cracker; (*NAUT*) ship (*US*) o ship's (*Brit*) biscuit.

gallet'to *sm* young cock, cockerel; (*fig*) cocky young man; **fare il ~** to play the gallant.

Gal'lia *sf:* **la ~** Gaul.

galli'na *sf* hen; **andare a letto con le ~e** to go to bed early.

galli'smo *sm* machismo.

gal'lo *sm* cock; **al canto del ~** at daybreak, at cockcrow; **fare il ~** to play the gallant.

gallo'ne *sm* piece of braid; (*MIL*) stripe; (*unità di misura*) gallon.

galoppa're *vi* to gallop.

galoppi'no *sm* errand boy; (*POL*) canvasser.

galop'po *sm* gallop; **al** o **di ~** at a gallop.

galvanizza're [gàlvánēddzà'rā] *vt* to galvanize.

gam'ba *sf* leg; (*asta: di lettera*) stem; **in ~** (*in buona salute*) well; (*bravo, sveglio*) bright, smart; **prendere qc sotto ~** (*fig*) to treat sth too lightly; **scappare a ~e levate** to take to one's heels; **~e!** scatter!

gamba'le *sm* legging.

gamberet'to *sm* shrimp.

gam'bero *sm* (*di acqua dolce*) crayfish; (*di mare*) prawn.

Gam'bia *sf:* **la ~** the Gambia.

gam'bo *sm* stem; (*di frutta*) stalk.

gamel'la *sf* mess tin.

gam'ma *sf* (*MUS*) scale; (*di colori, fig*) range; **~ di prodotti** product range.

gana'scia, sce [gànàsh'shà] *sf* jaw; **~sce del freno** (*AUT*) brake shoes.

gan'cio [gàn'chō] *sm* hook.

Gan'ge [gàn'jā] *sm:* **il ~** the Ganges.

gan'gheri [gàn'gārē] *smpl:* **uscire dai ~** (*fig*) to fly into a temper.

gangre'na *sf* = **cancrena.**

ga'ra *sf* competition; (*SPORT*) competition; contest; match; (*: corsa*) race; **fare a ~** to compete, vie; **~ d'appalto** (*COMM*) tender.

gara'ge [gàràzh'] *sm inv* garage.

garan'te *sm/f* guarantor.

garanti're *vt* to guarantee; (*debito*) to stand surety for; (*dare per certo*) to assure.

garanti'smo *sm* protection of civil liberties.

garanzi'a [gàràntsē'à] *sf* guarantee; (*pegno*) security; **in ~** under guarantee.

garba're *vi:* **non mi garba** I don't like it (o him *etc*).

garbatez'za [gàrbàtāt'tsà] *sf* courtesy, politeness.

garba'to, a *ag* courteous, polite.

gar'bo *sm* (*buone maniere*) politeness, courtesy; (*di vestito etc*) grace, style.

garbu'glio [gàrbōōl'yō] *sm* tangle; (*fig*) muddle, mess.

gareggia're [gàrādjà'rā] *vi* to compete.

garganel'la *sf:* **a ~** from the bottle.

gargari'smo *sm* gargle; **fare i ~** to gargle.

garit'ta *sf* (*di caserma*) sentry box.

garo'fano *sm* carnation; **chiodo di ~** clove.

garret'to sm hock.

garri're vi to chirp.

gar'rulo, a ag (uccello) chirping; (persona: loquace) garrulous, talkative.

gar'za [gárˈdzà] sf (per bende) gauze.

garzo'ne [gárdzōˈnā] sm (di negozio) boy.

gas sm inv gas; **a tutto** ~ at full speed; **dare** ~ (AUT) to accelerate; ~ **lacrimogeno** tear gas; ~ **naturale** natural gas.

gasa're etc = **gassare** etc.

gasa'to, a sm/f (fam: persona) freak.

gasdot'to sm gas pipeline.

gaso'lio sm diesel (oil).

gas(s)a're vt to aerate, carbonate; (asfissiare) to gas; ~**rsi** vr (fam) to get excited.

gas(s)a'to, a ag (bibita) carbonated, fizzy.

gasso'so, a ag gaseous; gassy ♦ sf fizzy drink.

gas'trico, a, ci, che ag gastric.

gastroenteri'te sf gastroenteritis.

gastronomi'a sf gastronomy.

gastro'nomo, a sm/f gourmet, gastronome.

gat'ta sf cat, she-cat; **una** ~ **da pelare** (fam) a thankless task; **qui** ~ **ci cova!** I smell a rat!, there's something fishy going on here!

gattabu'ia sf (fam scherzoso: prigione) clink.

gatti'no sm kitten.

gat'to sm cat, tomcat; ~ **delle nevi** (AUT. SCI) snowcat; ~ **a nove code** cat-o'-nine-tails; ~ **selvatico** wildcat.

gattopar'do sm: ~ **africano** serval; ~ **americano** ocelot.

gattuc'cio [gáttōōchˈchō] sm dogfish.

gauden'te sm/f pleasure-seeker.

ga'udio sm joy, happiness.

gavet'ta sf (MIL) mess tin; **venire dalla** ~ (MIL, fig) to rise from the ranks.

gaz'za [gádˈdzà] sf magpie.

gazzar'ra [gáddzárˈrà] sf racket, din.

gazzel'la [gáddzelˈlà] sf gazelle; (dei carabinieri) (high-speed) police car.

gazzet'ta [gáddzātˈtà] sf news sheet; **G~ Ufficiale** official publication containing details of new laws.

gazzo'so, a [gáddzōˈsō] ag = **gassoso**.

Gazz. Uff. abbr = **Gazzetta Ufficiale.**

GB sigla (= Gran Bretagna) GB.

G.C. abbr = **genio civile.**

G.d.F. abbr = **guardia di finanza.**

GE sigla = Genova.

gel [jel] sm inv gel.

gela're [jālàˈrà] vt, vi, vb impers to freeze; **mi ha gelato il sangue** (fig) it made my blood run cold.

gela'ta [jālàˈtà] sf frost.

gelateri'a [jālàtārēˈà] sf ice-cream shop.

gelati'na [jālàtēˈnà] sf gelatine; ~ **esplosiva** gelignite; ~ **di frutta** fruit jelly.

gelatino'so, a [jālàtēnōˈsō] ag gelatinous, jelly-like.

gela'to, a [jālàˈtō] ag frozen ♦ sm ice-cream.

ge'lido, a [jeˈlēdō] ag icy, ice-cold.

ge'lo [jeˈlō] sm (temperatura) intense cold; (brina) frost; (fig) chill.

gelo'ne [jālōˈnā] sm chilblain.

gelosi'a [jālōsēˈà] sf jealousy.

gelo'so, a [jālōˈsō] ag jealous.

gel'so [jelˈsō] sm mulberry (tree).

gelsomi'no [jālsōmēˈnō] sm jasmine.

gemellag'gio [jāmālládˈjō] sm twinning.

gemella're [jāmāllàˈrà] ag twin cpd ♦ vt (città) to twin.

gemel'lo, a [jāmelˈlō] ag, sm/f twin; ~**i** smpl (di camicia) cufflinks; (dello zodiaco): **G~i** Gemini sg; **essere dei G~i** to be Gemini.

ge'mere [jeˈmārā] vi to moan, groan; (cigolare) to creak; (gocciolare) to drip, ooze.

ge'mito [jeˈmētō] sm moan, groan.

gem'ma [jemˈmà] sf (BOT) bud; (pietra preziosa) gem.

Gen abbr (MIL: = generale) Gen.

gen. abbr (= generale, generalmente) gen.

gendar'me [jāndàrˈmà] sm policeman; (fig) martinet.

ge'ne [jeˈnà] sm gene.

genealogi'a, gi'e [jānààlōjēˈà] sf genealogy.

genealo'gico, a, ci, che [jānààloˈjēkō] ag genealogical; **albero** ~ family tree.

genera'le [jānàràˈlā] ag, sm general; **in** ~ (per sommi capi) in general terms; (di solito) usually, in general; **a** ~ **richiesta** by popular request.

generalità [jānàràlētáˈ] sfpl (dati d'identità) particulars.

generalizza're [jānàràlēddzàˈrà] vt, vi to generalize.

generalizzazio'ne [jānàràlēddzàttsyōˈnā] sf generalization.

generalmen'te [jānàràlmānˈtā] av generally.

genera're [jānàràˈrà] vt (dar vita) to give birth to; (produrre) to produce; (causare) to arouse; (TECN) to produce, generate.

generato're [jānàràtōˈrā] sm (TECN) generator.

generazio'ne [jānàràttsyōˈnā] sf generation.

ge'nere [jeˈnàrā] sm kind, type, sort; (BIOL) genus; (merce) article, product; (LING) gender; (ARTE, LETTERATURA) genre; **in** ~ generally, as a rule; **cose del o di questo** ~ such things; **il** ~ **umano** mankind; ~**i alimentari** foodstuffs; ~**i di consumo** consumer goods; ~**i di prima necessità** basic essentials.

gene'rico, a, ci, che [jāneˈrēkō] ag generic; (vago) vague, imprecise; **medico** ~ general practitioner.

ge'nero [jeˈnàrō] sm son-in-law.

generosità [jānārōsētáˈ] sf generosity.

genero'so, a [jānàrōˈsō] ag generous.

ge'nesi [jeˈnàzē] sf genesis.

gene'tico, a, ci, che [jāne'tĕkō] *ag* genetic ♦ *sf* genetics *sg*.

gengi'va [jānjē'và] *sf* (ANAT) gum.

geni'a [jānē'à] *sf* (*peg*) mob, gang.

genia'le [jānyà'lā] *ag* (*persona*) of genius; (*idea*) ingenious, brilliant.

ge'nio [je'nyō] *sm* genius; (*attitudine, talento*) talent, flair, genius; **andare a ~ a qn** to be to sb's liking, appeal to sb; **~ civile** civil engineers *pl*; **il ~ (militare)** the Engineers.

genita'le [jānĕtà'lā] *ag* genital; **~i** *smpl* genitals.

genito're [jānētō'rā] *sm* parent, father *o* mother; **~i** *smpl* parents.

genn. *abbr* (= *gennaio*) Jan.

genna'io [jānnà'yō] *sm* January; *per fraseologia vedi* **luglio.**

genoci'dio [jānōchē'dyō] *sm* genocide.

Ge'nova [je'nòvà] *sf* Genoa.

genove'se [jānōvà'sā] *ag, sm/f* Genoese (*pl inv*).

genta'glia [jāntál'yà] *sf* (*peg*) rabble.

gen'te [jen'tà] *sf* people *pl*.

genti'le [jāntē'lā] *ag* (*persona, atto*) kind; (: *garbato*) courteous, polite; (*nelle lettere*): **G~ Signore** Dear Sir; (: *sulla busta*): **G~ Signor Fernando Villa** Mr. Fernando Villa.

gentilez'za [jāntēlāt'tsà] *sf* kindness; courtesy, politeness; **per ~** (*per favore*) please.

gentiluo'mo, *pl* **gentiluo'mini** [jāntē'lwomō] *sm* gentleman.

genuflessio'ne [jānōōflāssyō'nā] *sf* genuflection.

genui'no, a [jānōōē'nō] *ag* (*prodotto*) natural; (*persona, sentimento*) genuine, sincere.

geografi'a [jāōgràfē'à] *sf* geography.

geogra'fico, a, ci, che [jāōgrà'fēkō] *ag* geographic(al).

geo'grafo, a [jāo'gràfō] *sm/f* geographer.

geologi'a [jāōlōjē'à] *sf* geology.

geolo'gico, a, ci, che [jāōlo'jēkō] *ag* geologic(al).

geo'metra, i, e [jāo'mātrà] *sm/f* (*professionista*) surveyor.

geometri'a [jāōmātrē'à] *sf* geometry.

geome'trico, a, ci, che [jāōme'trēkō] *ag* geometric(al).

geopoli'tico, a, ci, che [jāōpōlē'tēkō] *ag* geopolitical.

gera'nio [jārà'nyō] *sm* geranium.

gerar'ca, chi [jāràr'kà] *sm* (STORIA: *nel fascismo*) party official.

gerarchi'a [jārárkē'à] *sf* hierarchy.

gerar'chico, a, ci, che [jāràr'kēkō] *ag* hierarchical.

geren'te [jàren'tà] *sm/f* manager/manageress.

geren'za [jàren'tsà] *sf* management.

ger'go, ghi [jer'gō] *sm* jargon; slang.

geriatri'a [jàryàtrē'à] *sf* geriatrics *sg*.

geria'trico, a, ci, che [jàryà'trēkō] *ag* geriatric.

ge'rla [je'rlà] *sf* conical wicker basket.

Germa'nia [jārmà'nyà] *sf*: **la ~** Germany; **la ~ occidentale/orientale** West/East Germany.

ger'me [jer'mā] *sm* germ; (*fig*) seed.

germinazio'ne [jārmēnàttsyō'nā] *sf* germination.

germoglia're [jārmōlyà'rā] *vi* (*emettere germogli*) to sprout; (*germinare*) to germinate.

germo'glio [jārmōl'yō] *sm* shoot; (*gemma*) bud.

gerogli'fico, ci [jārōglē'fēkō] *sm* hieroglyphic.

geronto'logo, a, gi, ghe [jārōnto'lōgō] *sm/f* specialist in geriatrics.

gerun'dio [jārōōn'dyō] *sm* gerund.

Gerusalem'me [jārōōzàlem'mā] *sf* Jerusalem.

ges'so [jes'sō] *sm* chalk; (SCULTURA, MED, EDIL) plaster; (*statua*) plaster figure; (*minerale*) gypsum.

ge'sta [je'stà] *sfpl* (*letterario*) deeds, feats.

gestan'te [jāstàn'tà] *sf* expectant mother.

gestazio'ne [jāstàttsyō'nā] *sf* gestation.

gesticola're [jāstēkōlà'rā] *vi* to gesticulate.

gestiona'le [jāstyōnà'lā] *ag* administrative, management *cpd*.

gestio'ne [jāstyō'nā] *sf* management; **~ di magazzino** stock control; **~ patrimoniale** investment management.

gesti're [jāstē'rā] *vt* to run, manage.

ge'sto [je'stō] *sm* gesture.

gesto're [jāstō'rā] *sm* manager.

Gesù [jāzōō'] *sm* Jesus; **~ bambino** the Christ Child.

gesui'ta, i [jāzōōē'tà] *sm* Jesuit.

getta're [jāttà'rā] *vt* to throw; (*anche*: **~ via**) to throw away *o* out; (SCULTURA) to cast; (EDIL) to lay; (*acqua*) to spout; (*grido*) to utter; **~rsi** *vr*: **~rsi in** (*impresa*) to throw o.s. into; (*mischia*) to hurl o.s. into; (*sog*: *fiume*) to flow into; **~ uno sguardo su** to take a quick look at.

getta'ta [jāttà'tà] *sf* (*di cemento, gesso, metalli* cast; (*diga*) jetty.

get'tito [jet'tētō] *sm* revenue.

get'to [jet'tō] *sm* (*di gas, liquido,* AER) jet; (BOT) shoot; **a ~ continuo** uninterruptedly; **di ~** (*fig*) straight off.

getto'ne [jāttō'nā] *sm* token; (*per giochi*) counter; (: *roulette etc*) chip; **~ di presenza** attendance fee; **~ telefonico** telephone token.

gettonie'ra [jāttōnyc'rà] *sf* telephone-token dispenser.

gey'ser [gà'ēzə] *sm inv* geyser.

Gha'na [gà'nà] *sm*: **il ~** Ghana.

ghen'ga, ghe [gen'gà] *sf* (*fam*) gang, crowd.

ghepar'do [gāpàr'dō] *sm* cheetah.

ghermi're [gārmē'rā] *vt* to grasp, clasp, clutch.

ghet'ta [gāt'tà] *sf* (*gambale*) gaiter.

ghettizza're [gāttēddzà'rā] *vt* to segregate.

ghet'to [gāt'tō] *sm* ghetto.

ghiaccia'ia [gyàchà'yà] *sf* (*anche fig*) icebox.

ghiaccia'io [gyáchá'yō] *sm* glacier.

ghiaccia're [gyáchá'rā] *vt* to freeze; (*fig*): ~ **qn** to make sb's blood run cold ♦ *vi* to freeze, ice over.

ghiaccia'to, a [gyáchá'tō] *ag* frozen; (*bevanda*) ice-cold.

ghiac'cio [gyách'chō] *sm* ice.

ghiacc'io'lo [gyácho'lō] *sm* icicle; (*tipo di gelato*) popsicle ® (*US*), ice lolly (*Brit*).

ghia'ia [gyá'yá] *sf* gravel.

ghian'da [gyán'dá] *sf* (*BOT*) acorn.

ghian'dola [gyán'dōlá] *sf* gland.

ghiandola're [gyándōlá'rā] *ag* glandular.

ghigliotti'na [gēlyōttē'ná] *sf* guillotine.

ghigna're [gēnyá'rā] *vi* to sneer.

ghi'gno [gēn'yō] *sm* (*espressione*) sneer; (*risata*) mocking laugh.

ghin'gheri [gēn'gārē] *smpl*: **in** ~ all dolled up; **mettersi in** ~ to put on one's Sunday best.

ghiot'to, a [gyōt'tō] *ag* greedy; (*cibo*) delicious, appetizing.

ghiotto'ne, a [gyōttō'nā] *sm/f* glutton.

ghiottoneri'a [gyōttōnārē'á] *sf* greed, gluttony; (*cibo*) delicacy, tidbit (*US*), titbit (*Brit*).

ghiribiz'zo [gērēbēd'dzō] *sm* whim.

ghirigo'ro [gērēgo'rō] *sm* scribble, squiggle.

ghirlan'da [gērlán'dá] *sf* garland, wreath.

ghi'ro [gē'rō] *sm* dormouse.

ghi'sa [gē'zá] *sf* cast iron.

G.I. *abbr* = **giudice istruttore**.

già [já] *av* already; (*ex, in precedenza*) formerly ♦ *escl* of course!, yes indeed!; ~ **che ci sei** ... while you are at it ....

giac'ca, che [ják'ká] *sf* jacket; ~ **a vento** windbreaker (*US*), windcheater (*Brit*).

giacché [jákkā'] *cong* since, as.

giacchet'ta [jákkāt'tá] *sf* (light) jacket.

gi'accio *etc* [jách'chō] *vb vedi* **giacere**.

giacco'ne [jákkō'nā] *sm* heavy jacket.

giacen'za [jáchen'tsá] *sf*: **merce in** ~ goods in stock; **capitale in** ~ uninvested capital; ~**e di magazzino** unsold stock.

giace're [jáchá'rā] *vi* to lie.

giacimen'to [jáchēmán'tō] *sm* deposit.

giacin'to [jáchēn'tō] *sm* hyacinth.

giaciu'to, a [jáchōō'tō] *pp di* **giacere**.

gia'da [já'dá] *sf* jade.

giaggio'lo [jádjo'lō] *sm* iris.

giagua'ro [jágwá'rō] *sm* jaguar.

giallas'tro, a [jállás'trō] *ag* yellowish; (*carnagione*) sallow.

gial'lo [jál'lō] *ag* yellow; (*carnagione*) sallow ♦ *sm* yellow; (*anche*: **romanzo** ~) detective novel; (*anche*: **film** ~) detective film; ~ **dell'uovo** yolk; **il mar G**~ the Yellow Sea.

giallo'gnolo, a [jállōn'yōlō] *ag* yellowish, dirty yellow.

Giama'ica [jámá'ēká] *sf*: **la** ~ Jamaica.

giamaica'no, a [jàmáčká'nō] *ag*, *sm/f* Jamaican.

giamma'i [jámmá'ē] *av* never.

Giappo'ne [jáppō'nā] *sm*: **il** ~ Japan.

giappone'se [jáppōnā'sá] *ag*, *sm/f*, *sm* Japanese *inv*.

gia'ra [já'rá] *sf* jar.

giardinag'gio [járdēnád'jō] *sm* gardening.

giardinet'ta [járdēnāt'tá] *sf* station wagon (*US*), estate car (*Brit*).

giardinie're, a [járdēnyc'rā] *sm/f* gardener ♦ *sf* (*misto di sottaceti*) mixed pickles *pl*; (*automobile*) = **giardinetta**.

giardi'no [járdē'nō] *sm* garden; ~ **d'infanzia** nursery school; ~ **pubblico** public gardens *pl*, (public) park; ~ **zoologico** zoo.

giarrettie'ra [járráttyc'rá] *sf* garter.

Gia'va [já'vá] *sf* Java.

giavellot'to [jávállot'tō] *sm* javelin.

gibbo'so, a [jēbbō'sō] *ag* (*superficie*) bumpy; (*naso*) crooked.

Gibilter'ra [jēbēlter'rá] *sf* Gibraltar.

gigan'te, es'sa [jēgán'tā] *sm/f* giant ♦ *ag* giant, gigantic; (*COMM*) giant-size.

gigante'sco, a, schi, sche [jēgántā'skō] *ag* gigantic.

gigantografi'a [jēgántōgráfē'á] *sf* (*FOT*) blow-up.

gi'glio [jēl'yō] *sm* lily.

gilè [jēlc'] *sm inv* waistcoat.

gin [jēn] *sm inv* gin.

ginca'na [jēnká'ná] *sf* gymkhana.

ginecologi'a [jēnākōlōjē'á] *sf* gynecology (*US*), gynaecology (*Brit*).

gineco'logo, a, gi, ghe [jēnāko'lōgō] *sm/f* gynecologist (*US*), gynaecologist (*Brit*).

gine'pro [jēnā'prō] *sm* juniper.

gines'tra [jēnes'trá] *sf* (*BOT*) broom.

Gine'vra [jēnā'vrá] *sf* Geneva; **il Lago di** ~ Lake Geneva.

gingillar'si [jēnjēllár'sē] *vr* to fritter away one's time; (*giocare*): ~ **con** to fiddle with.

gingil'lo [jēnjēl'lō] *sm* plaything.

ginna'sio [jēnná'zyō] *sm the 4th and 5th year of secondary school in Italy*.

ginna'sta, i, e [jēnná'stá] *sm/f* gymnast.

ginna'stica [jēnná'stēká] *sf* gymnastics *sg*; (*esercizio fisico*) fitness exercises *pl*; (*INS*) physical education.

gin'nico, a, ci, che [jē'nēkō] *ag* gymnastic.

ginoc'chio [jēnok'kyō], *pl(m)* **ginoc'chi** *o pl(f)* **ginoc'chia** *sm* knee; **stare in** ~ to kneel, be on one's knees; **mettersi in** ~ to kneel (down).

ginocchio'ni [jēnōkkyō'nē] *av* on one's knees.

gioca're [jōká'rā] *vt* to play; (*scommettere*) to stake, wager, bet; (*ingannare*) to take in ♦ *vi* to play; (*a roulette etc*) to gamble; (*fig*) to play a part, be important; (*TECN: meccanismo*) to be loose; ~ **a** (*gioco, sport*) to play; (*cavalli*) to bet on; ~ **d'astuzia** to be crafty; ~**rsi la carriera** to put one's career at risk; ~**rsi tutto** to risk everything; **a che gioco giochiamo?** what are you playing at?

giocato're, tri'ce |jōkátō'rā| *sm/f* player; gambler.

giocat'tolo |jōkát'tōlō| *sm* toy.

giocherella're |jōkārállá'rā| *vi*: ~ **con** (*giocattolo*) to play with; (*distrattamente*) to fiddle with.

giocherò *etc* |jōkāro'| *vb vedi* **giocare**.

giochet'to |jōkāt'tō| *sm* (*gioco*) game; (*tranello*) trick; (*fig*): **è un** ~ it's child's play.

gio'co, chi |jo'kō| *sm* game; (*divertimento,* *TECN*) play; (*al casinò*) gambling; (*CARTE*) hand; (*insieme di pezzi etc necessari per un* *gioco*) set; **per** ~ for fun; **fare il doppio** ~ **con qn** to double-cross sb; **prendersi** ~ **di qn** to pull sb's leg; **stare al** ~ **di qn** to play along with sb; **è in** ~ **la mia reputazione** my reputation is at stake; ~ **d'azzardo** game of chance; ~ **della palla** ball game; ~ **degli** **scacchi** chess set; **i G~chi Olimpici** the Olympic Games.

giocofor'za |jōkōfor'tsá| *sm*: **essere** ~ to be inevitable.

giocolie're |jōkōlye'rā| *sm* juggler.

gioco'so, a |jōkō'sō| *ag* playful, jesting.

gioga'ia |jōgá'yá| *sf* (*GEO*) range of mountains.

gio'go, ghi |jō'gō| *sm* yoke.

gio'ia |jo'yá| *sf* joy, delight; (*pietra preziosa*) jewel, precious stone.

gioielleri'a |jōyāllārē'á| *sf* jeweler's (*US*) *o* jeweller's (*Brit*) craft; (*negozio*) jewelry store (*US*), jeweller's (shop) (*Brit*).

gioiellie're, a |jōyállye'rā| *sm/f* jeweler (*US*), jeweller (*Brit*).

gioiel'lo |jōyēl'lō| *sm* jewel, piece of jewelry (*US*) *o* jewellery (*Brit*); ~**i** *smpl* (*gioie*) jewel(le)ry *sg*.

gioio'so, a |jōyō'sō| *ag* joyful.

Giorda'nia |jōrdá'nyá| *sf*: **la** ~ Jordan.

Giorda'no |jōrdá'nō| *sm*: **il** ~ the Jordan.

giorda'no, a |jōrdá'nō| *ag, sm/f* Jordanian.

giornala'io, a |jōrnálá'yō| *sm/f* newsdealer (*US*), newsagent (*Brit*).

giorna'le |jōrná'lā| *sm* (news)paper; (*diario*) journal, diary; (*COMM*) journal; ~ **di bordo** (*NAUT*) ship's log; ~ **radio** radio news *sg*.

giornalet'to |jōrnálát'tō| *sm* (children's) comic.

giornalie'ro, a |jōrnálye'rō| *ag* daily; (*che varia: umore*) changeable ♦ *sm* day laborer (*US*) *o* labourer (*Brit*).

giornali'no |jōrnálē'nō| *sm* children's comic.

giornali'smo |jōrnálēz'mō| *sm* journalism.

giornali'sta, i, e |jōrnálē'stá| *sm/f* journalist.

giornali'stico, a, ci, che |jōrnálē'stēkō| *ag* journalistic; **stile** ~ journalese.

giornalmen'te |jōrnálmán'tā| *av* daily.

giorna'ta |jōrná'tá| *sf* day; (*paga*) day's wages, day's pay; **durante la** ~ **di ieri** yesterday; **fresco di** ~ (*uovo*) freshly laid; **vivere alla** ~ to live from day to day; ~ **lavorativa** working day.

gior'no |jōr'nō| *sm* day; (*opposto alla notte*) day, daytime; (*luce del* ~) daylight; **al** ~ per day; **di** ~ by day; ~ **per** ~ day by day; **al** ~ **d'oggi** nowadays; **tutto il santo** ~ all day long.

gios'tra |jos'trá| *sf* (*per bimbi*) merry-go-round; (*torneo storico*) joust.

giostra're |jōstrá'rā| *vi* (*STORIA*) to joust, tilt; ~**rsi** *vr* to manage.

giov. *abbr* (= *giovedì*) Thur(s).

giovamen'to |jōvámán'tō| *sm* benefit, help.

gio'vane |jō'vánā| *ag* young; (*aspetto*) youthful ♦ *sm/f* youth/girl, young man/woman; **i** ~**i** young people; **è** ~ **del mestiere** he's new to the job.

giovanet'to, a |jōvánāt'tō| *sm/f* young man/ woman.

giovani'le |jōvánē'lā| *ag* youthful; (*scritti*) early; (*errore*) of youth.

giovanot'to |jōvánot'tō| *sm* young man.

giova're |jōvá'rā| *vi*: ~ **a** (*essere utile*) to be useful to; (*far bene*) to be good for ♦ *vb impers* (*essere bene, utile*) to be useful; ~**rsi** *vr*: ~**rsi di qc** to make use of sth; **a che giova prendersela?** what's the point of getting upset?

Gio've |jo'vā| *sm* (*MITOLOGIA*) Jove; (*ASTR*) Jupiter.

giovedì |jōvādē'| *sm inv* Thursday; *per fraseologia vedi* **martedì**.

gioven'ca, che |jōvēn'ká| *sf* heifer.

gioventù |jōvántōō'| *sf* (*periodo*) youth; (*i giovani*) young people *pl*, youth.

giovia'le |jōvyá'lā| *ag* jovial, jolly.

giovinas'tro |jōvēnás'trō| *sm* young thug.

giovincel'lo |jōvēnchel'lō| *sm* young lad.

giovinez'za |jōvēnāt'tsá| *sf* youth.

giradis'chi |jērádē'skē| *sm inv* record player.

giraf'fa |jēráf'fá| *sf* giraffe; (*TV, CINEMA,* *RADIO*) boom.

giramen'to |jērámán'tō| *sm*: ~ **di testa** dizzy spell.

giramon'do |jērámōn'dō| *sm/f inv* globe-trotter.

giran'dola |jērán'dōlá| *sf* (*fuoco d'artificio*) Catherine wheel; (*giocattolo*) toy windmill; (*banderuola*) weather vane, weathercock.

giran'te |jērán'tā| *sm/f* (*chi gira un assegno*) endorser.

gira're |jērá'rā| *vt* (*far ruotare*) to turn; (*percorrere, visitare*) to go round; (*CINEMA*) to shoot; (*: film: come regista*) to make; (*COMM*) to endorse ♦ *vi* to turn; (*più veloce*) to spin; (*andare in giro*) to wander, go around; **~rsi** *vr* to turn; **~ attorno a** to go round; to revolve round; **si girava e rigirava nel letto** he tossed and turned in bed; **far ~ la testa a qn** to make sb dizzy; (*fig*) to turn sb's head; **gira al largo** keep your distance; **girala come ti pare** (*fig*) look at it whichever way you like; **gira e rigira ...** after a lot of driving (*o* walking) about ...; (*fig*) whichever way you look at it; **cosa ti gira?** (*fam*) what's got into you?; **mi ha fatto ~ le scatole** (*fam*) he drove me crazy.

girarro'sto [jĕrárro'stŏ] *sm* (*CUC*) spit.

giraso'le [jĕrásŏ'lā] *sm* sunflower.

gira'ta [jĕrà'tá] *sf* (*passeggiata*) stroll; (*con veicolo*) drive; (*COMM*) endorsement.

girata'rio, a [jĕrátá'ryŏ] *sm/f* endorsee.

giravol'ta [jĕrávŏl'tá] *sf* twirl, turn; (*curva*) sharp bend; (*fig*) about-turn.

girel'lo [jĕrel'lŏ] *sm* (*di bambino*) go-cart (*US*), Babywalker ® (*Brit*); (*taglio di carne*) top round (*US*), topside (*Brit*).

giret'to [jĕrät'tŏ] *sm* (*passeggiata*) walk, stroll; (: *in macchina*) drive, spin; (: *in bicicletta*) ride.

gire'vole [jĕrā'vŏlā] *ag* revolving, turning.

giri'no [jĕrē'nŏ] *sm* tadpole.

gi'ro [jē'rŏ] *sm* (*circuito, cerchio*) circle; (*di chiave, manovella*) turn; (*viaggio*) tour, excursion; (*passeggiata*) stroll, walk; (*in macchina*) drive; (*in bicicletta*) ride; (*SPORT: della pista*) lap; (*di denaro*) circulation; (*CARTE*) hand; (*TECN*) revolution; **fare un ~** to go for a walk (*o* a drive *o* a ride); **fare il ~ di** (*parco, città*) to go round; **andare in ~** (*a piedi*) to walk around; **guardarsi in ~** to look around; **prendere in ~ qn** (*fig*) to take sb for a ride; **a stretto ~ di posta** by return mail (*US*) *o* return of post (*Brit*); **nel ~ di un mese** in a month's time; **essere nel ~** (*fig*) to belong to a circle (of friends); **~ d'affari** (*viaggio*) business tour; (*COMM*) turnover; **~ di parole** circumlocution; **~ di prova** (*AUT*) test drive; **~ turistico** sightseeing tour; **~ vita** waist measurement.

girocol'lo [jĕrŏkol'lŏ] *sm*: **a ~** crewneck *cpd*.

girocon'to [jĕrŏkŏn'tŏ] *sm* (*ECON*) credit transfer.

giro'ne [jĕrŏ'nā] *sm* (*SPORT*) series of games; **~ di andata/ritorno** (*CALCIO*) first/second half of the season.

gironzola're [jĕrŏndzŏlá'rā] *vi* to stroll about.

giroton'do [jĕrŏtŏn'dŏ] *sm* ring-around-the-rosey (*US*), ring-a-ring-o'roses (*Brit*); **in ~** in a circle.

girovaga're [jĕrŏvágá'rā] *vi* to wander about.

giro'vago, a, ghi, ghe [jĕrŏ'vágŏ] *sm/f* (*vagabondo*) tramp; (*venditore*) peddler; **una compagnia di ~ghi** (*attori*) a company of strolling actors.

gi'ta [jē'tá] *sf* excursion, trip; **fare una ~** to go for a trip, go on an outing.

gita'no, a [jĕtá'nŏ] *sm/f* gipsy.

gitan'te [jĕtán'tā] *sm/f* member of a tour.

giù [jōō] *av* down; (*dabbasso*) downstairs; **in ~** downwards, down; **la mia casa è un po' più in ~** my house is a bit further on; **~ di lì** (*pressappoco*) thereabouts; **bambini dai 6 anni in ~** children aged 6 and under; **cadere ~ per le scale** to fall down the stairs; **~ le mani!** hands off!; **essere ~** (*fig*: *di salute*) to be run down; (: *di spirito*) to be depressed; **quel tipo non mi va ~** I can't stand that guy.

giub'ba [jōōb'bá] *sf* jacket.

giubbot'to [jōōbbot'tŏ] *sm* jerkin; **~ antiproiettile** bulletproof vest.

giubila're [jōōbēlá'rā] *vi* to rejoice.

giu'bilo [jōō'bēlŏ] *sm* rejoicing.

giudica're [jōōdēká'rā] *vt* to judge; (*accusato*) to try; (*lite*) to arbitrate in; **~ qn/qc bello** to consider sb/sth (to be) beautiful.

giudica'to [jōōdēká'tŏ] *sm* (*DIR*): **passare in ~** to pass final judgment.

giu'dice [jōō'dēchā] *sm* judge; **~ collegiale** member of the court; **~ conciliatore** justice of the peace; **~ istruttore** committing (*US*) *o* examining (*Brit*) magistrate; **~ popolare** member of a jury.

giudizia'le [jōōdēttsyá'lā] *ag* judicial.

giudizia'rio, a [jōōdēttsyá'ryŏ] *ag* legal, judicial.

giudi'zio [jōōdēt'tsyŏ] *sm* judgment; (*opinione*) opinion; (*DIR*) judgment, sentence; (: *processo*) trial; (: *verdetto*) verdict; **aver ~** to be wise *o* prudent; **essere in attesa di ~** to be awaiting trial; **citare in ~** to summons; **l'imputato è stato rinviato a ~** the accused has been committed for trial.

giudizio'so, a [jōōdēttsyŏ'sŏ] *ag* prudent, judicious.

giug'giola [jōōd'jŏlá] *sf*: **andare in brodo di ~e** (*fam*) to be over the moon.

giu'gno [jōōn'yŏ] *sm* June; *per fraseologia vedi* **luglio.**

giuli'vo, a [jōōlē'vŏ] *ag* merry.

giulla're [jōōllá'rā] *sm* jester.

giumen'ta [jōōmān'tá] *sf* mare.

giun'co, chi [jōōn'kŏ] *sm* (*BOT*) rush.

giun'gere [jōōn'jārā] *vi* to arrive ♦ *vt* (*mani etc*) to join; **~ a** to arrive at, reach; **~ nuovo a qn** to come as news to sb; **~ in porto** to reach harbor; (*fig*) to be brought to a successful outcome.

giun'gla [jōōn'glá] *sf* jungle.

giun'si *etc* [jōōn'sē] *vb vedi* **giungere.**

giun'to, a [jōōn'tŏ] *pp di* **giungere** ♦ *sm* (*TECN*) coupling, joint ♦ *sf* addition; (*organo esecutivo, amministrativo*) council, board; **per ~a** into the bargain, in addition; **~a militare** military junta.

giuntu'ra [jōōntōō'rà] *sf* joint.

giuoca're [jwŏkà'rà] *vt, vi* = **giocare**.

giuo'co [jwo'kō] *sm* = **gioco**.

giuramen'to [jōōràmàn'tō] *sm* oath; ~ **falso** perjury.

giura're [jōōrà'rà] *vt* to swear ♦ *vi* to swear, take an oath; **gliel'ho giurata** I swore I would get even with him.

giura'to, a [jōōrà'tō] *ag*: **nemico** ~ sworn enemy ♦ *sm/f* juror, juryman/woman.

giuri'a [jōōrē'à] *sf* jury.

giuri'dico, a, ci, che [jōōrē'dēkō] *ag* legal.

giurisdizio'ne [jōōrēzdēttsyō'nà] *sf* jurisdiction.

giurispruden'za [jōōrēsprōōden'tsà] *sf* jurisprudence.

giuri'sta, i, e [jōōrē'stà] *sm/f* jurist.

giustappor're [jōōstàppōr'rà] *vt* to juxtapose.

giustapposizio'ne [jōōstàppōzēttsyō'nà] *sf* juxtaposition.

giustappo'sto, a [jōōstàppō'stō] *pp di* **giustappore**.

giustifica're [jōōstēfēkà'rà] *vt* to justify; ~**rsi** *vr*: ~**rsi di** *o* **per qc** to justify *o* excuse o.s. for sth.

giustificati'vo, a [jōōstēfēkàtē'vō] *ag* (*AMM*): **nota** *o* **pezza** ~**a** receipt.

giustificazio'ne [jōōstēfēkàttsyō'nà] *sf* justification; (*INS*) (note of) excuse.

giusti'zia [jōōstēt'tsyà] *sf* justice; **farsi** ~ **(da sé)** (*vendicarsi*) to take the law into one's own hands.

giustizia're [jōōstēttsyà'rà] *vt* to execute, put to death.

giustizie're [jōōstēttsyc'rà] *sm* executioner.

giu'sto, a [jōō'stō] *ag* (*equo*) fair, just; (*vero*) true, correct; (*adatto*) right, suitable; (*preciso*) exact, correct ♦ *av* (*esattamente*) exactly, precisely; (*per l'appunto, appena*) just; **arrivare** ~ to arrive just in time; **ho** ~ **bisogno di te** you're just the person I need.

gla'bro, a *ag* hairless.

glacia'le [glàchà'là] *ag* glacial.

gladi'olo *sm* gladiolus.

glan'dola *sf* = **ghiandola**.

glas'sa *sf* (*CUC*) icing.

gli [lyē] *det mpl* (*dav V, s impura, gn, pn, ps, x, z*) the ♦ *pronome* (*a lui*) to him; (*a esso*) to it; (*in coppia con lo, la, li, le, ne: a lui, a lei, a loro etc*): **gliele do** I'm giving them to him (*o her o them*); **gliene ho parlato** I spoke to him (*o her o them*) about it; *vedi anche* **il**.

gliceri'na [glēchàrē'nà] *sf* glycerine.

gli'cine [glē'chēnà] *sm* wistaria.

glie'la *etc* [lyà'là] *vedi* **gli**.

globa'le *ag* overall; (*vista*) global.

glo'bo *sm* globe.

glo'bulo *sm* (*ANAT*): ~ **rosso/bianco** red/white corpuscle.

glo'ria *sf* glory; **farsi** ~ **di qc** to pride o.s. on sth, take pride in sth.

gloriar'si *vr*: ~ **di qc** to pride o.s. on sth, glory *o* take pride in sth.

glorifica're *vt* to glorify.

glorio'so, a *ag* glorious.

glossa'rio *sm* glossary.

gluco'sio *sm* glucose.

glu'teo *sm* gluteus; ~**i** *smpl* buttocks.

GM *abbr* = **genio militare**.

GN *abbr* = **gratifica natalizia**.

G.N. *abbr* = **gas naturale**.

gnoc'chi [nyok'kē] *smpl* (*CUC*) small dumplings made of semolina pasta or potato.

gno'mo [nyo'mō] *sm* gnome.

gnor'ri [nyor'rē] *sm/f inv*: **non fare lo** ~! stop acting as if you didn't know anything about it!

GO *sigla* = **Gorizia**.

go'al [gō'ōōl] *sm inv* (*SPORT*) goal.

gob'ba *sf* (*ANAT*) hump; (*protuberanza*) bump.

gob'bo, a *ag* hunchbacked; (*ricurvo*) round-shouldered ♦ *sm/f* hunchback.

Go'bi *smpl*: **il Deserto dei** ~ the Gobi Desert.

goc'cia, ce [gōch'chà] *sf* drop; ~ **di rugiada** dewdrop; **somigliarsi come due** ~**ce d'acqua** to be as like as two peas in a pod; **è la** ~ **che fa traboccare il vaso!** it's the last straw!

goc'cio [gōch'chō] *sm* drop, spot.

gocciola're [gōchōlà'rà] *vi, vt* to drip.

goccioli'o [gōchōlē'ō] *sm* dripping.

gode're *vi* (*compiacersi*): ~ **(di)** to be delighted (at), rejoice (at); (*trarre vantaggio*): ~ **di** to enjoy, benefit from ♦ *vt* to enjoy; ~**rsi la vita** to enjoy life; **godersela** to have a good time, enjoy o.s.

godimen'to *sm* enjoyment.

godrò *etc vb vedi* **godere**.

goffag'gine [gōffàd'jēnà] *sf* clumsiness.

gof'fo, a *ag* clumsy, awkward.

go'gna [gōn'yà] *sf* pillory.

gol *sm inv* = **goal**.

go'la *sf* (*ANAT*) throat; (*golosità*) gluttony, greed; (*di camino*) flue; (*di monte*) gorge; **fare** ~ (*anche fig*) to tempt; **ricacciare il pianto** *o* **le lacrime in** ~ to swallow one's tears.

golet'ta *sf* (*NAUT*) schooner.

golf *sm inv* (*SPORT*) golf; (*maglia*) cardigan.

gol'fo *sm* gulf.

goliar'dico, a, ci, che *ag* (*canto, vita*) student *cpd*.

golo'so, a *ag* greedy.

gol'pe *sm inv* (*POL*) coup.

gomita'ta *sf*: **dare una** ~ **a qn** to elbow sb; **farsi avanti a (forza** *o* **furia di)** ~**e** to elbow one's way through; **fare a** ~**e per qc** to fight to get sth.

go'mito *sm* elbow; (*di strada etc*) sharp

bend.

gomi'tolo *sm* ball.

gom'ma *sf* rubber; (*colla*) gum; (*per cancellare*) eraser; (*di veicolo*) tire (*US*), tyre (*Brit*); ~ **da masticare** chewing gum; ~ **a terra** flat (tire).

gommapiu'ma ® *sf* foam rubber.

gommi'no *sm* rubber tip; (*rondella*) rubber washer.

gommi'sta, i, e *sm/f* tire (*US*) *o* tyre (*Brit*) specialist; (*rivenditore*) tire *o* tyre merchant.

gommo'ne *sm* rubber dinghy.

gommo'so, a *ag* rubbery.

gon'dola *sf* gondola.

gondolie're *sm* gondolier.

gonfalo'ne *sm* banner.

gonfia're *vt* (*pallone*) to blow up, inflate; (*dilatare, ingrossare*) to swell; (*fig: notizia*) to exaggerate; ~**rsi** *vr* to swell; (*fiume*) to rise.

gon'fio, a *ag* swollen; (*stomaco*) bloated; (*palloncino, gomme*) inflated, blown up; (*con pompa*) pumped up; (*vela*) full; **occhi ~i di pianto** eyes swollen with tears; ~ **di orgoglio** (*persona*) puffed up (with pride); **avere il portafoglio ~** to have a bulging wallet.

gonfio're *sm* swelling.

gongola're *vi* to look pleased with o.s.; ~ **di gioia** to be overjoyed.

gon'na *sf* skirt; ~ **pantalone** culottes *pl*.

gon'zo [gŏn'dzŏ] *sm* simpleton, fool.

gorgheggia're [gŏrgādjà'rā] *vi* to warble; to trill.

gorgheg'gio [gŏrgād'jŏ] *sm* (*MUS, di uccello*) trill.

gor'go, ghi *sm* whirlpool.

gorgoglia're [gŏrgŏlyà'rā] *vi* to gurgle.

gorgogli'o [gŏrgŏlyē'ŏ] *sm* gurgling.

goril'la *sm inv* gorilla; (*guardia del corpo*) bodyguard.

go'tico, a, ci, che *ag, sm* Gothic.

got'ta *sf* gout.

governan'te *sm/f* ruler ♦ *sf* (*di bambini*) governess; (*donna di servizio*) housekeeper.

governa're *vt* (*stato*) to govern, rule; (*pilotare, guidare*) to steer; (*bestiame*) to tend, look after.

governati'vo, a *ag* (*politica, decreto*) government *cpd*, governmental; (*stampa*) pro-government.

governato're *sm* governor.

gover'no *sm* government.

goz'zo [gŏt'tsŏ] *sm* (*ZOOL*) crop; (*MED*) goitre; (*fig fam*) throat.

gozzoviglia're [gŏttsŏvēlyà'rā] *vi* to make merry, carouse.

gpm *abbr* (= *giri per minuto*) rpm.

GR *sigla* = *Grosseto* ♦ *sigla m* = **giornale radio**.

gracchia're [gràkkyà'rā] *vi* to caw.

gracida're [gràchēdà'rā] *vi* to croak.

gracidi'o, ii [gràchēdē'ŏ] *sm* croaking.

gra'cile [grà'chēlā] *ag* frail, delicate.

gradas'so *sm* boaster.

gradatamen'te *av* gradually, by degrees.

gradazio'ne [gràdàttsyŏ'nā] *sf* (*sfumatura*) gradation; ~ **alcolica** alcoholic content, strength.

grade'vole *ag* pleasant, agreeable.

gradimen'to *sm* pleasure, satisfaction; **essere di mio** (*o* **tuo** *etc*) ~ to be to my (*o* your *etc*) liking.

gradina'ta *sf* flight of steps; (*in teatro, stadio*) tiers *pl*.

gradi'no *sm* step; (*ALPINISMO*) foothold.

gradi're *vt* (*accettare con piacere*) to accept; (*desiderare*) to wish, like; **gradisce una tazza di tè?** would you like a cup of tea?

gradi'to, a *ag* welcome.

gra'do *sm* (*MAT, FISICA etc*) degree; (*stadio*) degree, level; (*MIL, sociale*) rank; **essere in ~ di fare** to be in a position to do; **di buon ~** willingly; **per ~i** by degrees; **un cugino di primo/secondo ~** a first/second cousin; **subire il terzo ~** (*anche fig*) to be given the third degree.

gradua'le *ag* gradual.

gradua're *vt* to grade.

gradua'to, a *ag* (*esercizi*) graded; (*scala, termometro*) graduated ♦ *sm* (*MIL*) non-commissioned officer.

graduato'ria *sf* (*di concorso*) list; (*per la promozione*) order of seniority.

graduazio'ne [gràdōōàttsyŏ'nā] *sf* graduation.

graf'fa *sf* (*gancio*) clip; (*segno grafico*) brace.

graffet'ta *sf* paper clip.

graffia're *vt* to scratch.

graffiatu'ra *sf* scratch.

graf'fio *sm* scratch.

graffi'ti *smpl* graffiti.

grafi'a *sf* spelling; (*scrittura*) handwriting.

gra'fico, a, ci, che *ag* graphic ♦ *sm* graph; (*persona*) graphic designer ♦ *sf* graphic arts *pl*; ~ **a torta** pie chart.

grami'gna [gràmēn'yà] *sf* weed; couch grass.

gramma'tica, che *sf* grammar.

grammatica'le *ag* grammatical.

gram'mo *sm* gram(me).

gra'mo, a *ag* (*vita*) wretched.

gran *ag vedi* **grande**.

gra'na *sf* (*granello, di minerali, corpi spezzati*) grain; (*fam: seccatura*) trouble; (: *soldi*) cash ♦ *sm inv* cheese similar to Parmesan.

grana'glie [grànàl'yà] *sfpl* corn *sg*, seed *sg*.

grana'io *sm* granary, barn.

grana'ta *sf* (*frutto*) pomegranate; (*pietra preziosa*) garnet; (*proiettile*) grenade.

granatie're *sm* (*MIL*) grenadier; (*fig*) fine figure of a man.

Gran Breta'gna [grànbrātàn'yà] *sf*: **la ~** Great Britain.

grancas'sa *sf* (*MUS*) bass drum.
gran'chio [grán'kyō] *sm* crab; (*fig*) blunder; **prendere un ~** (*fig*) to blunder.
grandangola're *sm* wide-angle lens *sg*.
gran'de *ag* (*qualche volta* **gran** +*C*, **grand'** +*V*) (*grosso, largo, vasto*) big, large; (*alto*) tall; (*lungo*) long; (*in sensi astratti*) great ♦ *sm/f* (*persona adulta*) adult, grown-up; (*chi ha ingegno e potenza*) great man/woman; **mio fratello più ~** my big *o* older brother; **il gran pubblico** the general public; **di gran classe** (*prodotto*) high-class; **cosa farai da ~?** what will you be *o* do when you grow up?; **fare le cose in ~** to do things in style; **fare il ~** (*strafare*) to act big; **una gran bella donna** a very beautiful woman; **non è una gran cosa** *o* **un gran che** it's nothing special; **non ne so gran che** I don't know very much about it.
grandeggia're [grándādjá'rá] *vi* (*emergere per grandezza*): **~ su** to tower over; (*darsi arie*) to put on airs.
grandez'za [grándāt'tsá] *sf* (*dimensione*) size; (*fig*) greatness; **in ~ naturale** lifesize; **manie di ~** delusions of grandeur.
grandina're *vb impers* to hail.
gran'dine *sf* hail.
grandio'so, a *ag* grand, grandiose.
grandu'ca, chi *sm* grand duke.
granduca'to *sm* grand duchy.
granduches'sa [grándōōkás'sá] *sf* grand duchess.
granel'lo *sm* (*di cereali, uva*) seed; (*di frutta*) pip; (*di sabbia, sale etc*) grain.
grani'ta *sf kind of water ice.*
grani'to *sm* granite.
gra'no *sm* (*in quasi tutti i sensi*) grain; (*frumento*) wheat; (*di rosario, collana*) bead; **~ di pepe** peppercorn.
grantur'co *sm* maize.
gra'nulo *sm* granule; (*MED*) pellet.
grap'pa *sf rough, strong brandy.*
grap'polo *sm* bunch, cluster.
gra'spo *sm* bunch (of grapes).
grasset'to *sm* (*TIP*) bold-face.
gras'so, a *ag* fat; (*cibo*) fatty; (*pelle*) greasy; (*terreno*) rich; (*fig: guadagno, annata*) plentiful; (: *volgare*) coarse, lewd ♦ *sm* (*di persona, animale*) fat; (*sostanza che unge*) grease.
grassoc'cio, a, ci, ce [grássoch'chō] *ag* plump.
grasso'ne, a *sm/f* (*fam: persona*) dumpling.
gra'ta *sf* grating.
gratic'cio [grátēch'chō] *sm* trellis; (*stuoia*) mat.
grati'cola *sf* grill.
grati'fica, che *sf* bonus; **~ natalizia** Christmas bonus.
gratificazio'ne [grátēfēkáttsyō'ná] *sf* (*soddisfazione*) satisfaction, reward.

gratina're *vt* (*CUC*) to cook au gratin.
gra'tis *av* free, for nothing.
gratitu'dine *sf* gratitude.
gra'to, a *ag* grateful.
grattaca'po *sm* worry, headache.
grattacie'lo [gráttáche'lō] *sm* skyscraper.
gratta're *vt* (*pelle*) to scratch; (*raschiare*) to scrape; (*pane, formaggio, carote*) to grate; (*fam: rubare*) to pinch ♦ *vi* (*stridere*) to grate; (*AUT*) to grind; **~rsi** *vr* to scratch o.s.; **~rsi la pancia** (*fig*) to twiddle one's thumbs.
gratta'ta *sf* scratch; **fare una ~** (*AUT: fam*) to grind the gears.
grattu'gia, gie [gráttōō'já] *sf* grater.
grattugia're [gráttōōjá'rá] *vt* to grate; **pane *m* grattugiato** breadcrumbs *pl*.
gratuità *sf* (*fig*) gratuitousness.
gratu'ito, a *ag* free; (*fig*) gratuitous.
grava'me *sm* táx; (*fig*) burden, weight.
grava're *vt* to burden ♦ *vi*: **~ su** to weigh on.
gra've *ag* (*danno, pericolo, peccato etc*) grave, serious; (*responsabilità*) heavy, grave; (*contegno*) grave, solemn; (*voce, suono*) deep, low-pitched; (*LING*): **accento ~** grave accent ♦ *sm* (*FISICA*) (heavy) body; **un malato ~** a person who is seriously ill.
gravidan'za [grávēdán'tsá] *sf* pregnancy.
gra'vido, a *ag* pregnant.
gravità *sf* seriousness; (*anche FISICA*) gravity.
gravita're *vi* (*FISICA*): **~ intorno a** to gravitate around.
gravo'so, a *ag* heavy, onerous.
gra'zia [grát'tsyá] *sf* grace; (*favore*) favor (*US*), favour (*Brit*); (*DIR*) pardon; **di ~** (*ironico*) if you please; **troppa ~!** (*ironico*) you're too generous!; **quanta ~ di Dio!** what abundance!; **entrare nelle ~e di qn** to win sb's favour; **Ministero di G~ e Giustizia** Ministry of Justice, ≈ Department of Justice (*US*), ≈ Lord Chancellor's Office (*Brit*).
grazia're [gráttsyá'rá] *vt* (*DIR*) to pardon.
gra'zie [grát'tsyá] *escl* thank you!; **~ mille!** *o* **tante!** *o* **infinite!** thank you very much!; **~ a** thanks to.
grazio'so, a [gráttsyō'sō] *ag* charming, delightful; (*gentile*) gracious.
Gre'cia [gre'chá] *sf*: **la ~** Greece.
gre'co, a, ci, che *ag, sm/f, sm* Greek.
grega'rio *sm* (*CICLISMO*) supporting rider.
greg'ge, *pl* (*f*) **i [gräd'já] *sm* flock.
greg'gio, a, gi, ge [gräd'jō] *ag* raw, unrefined; (*diamante*) rough, uncut; (*tessuto*) unbleached ♦ *sm* (*anche*: **petrolio ~**) crude (oil).
grembiu'le *sm* apron; (*sopravveste*) overall.
grem'bo *sm* lap; (*ventre della madre*) womb.
gremi'to, a *ag*: **~ (di)** packed *o* crowded (with).
gre'to *sm* (exposed) gravel bed of a river.

gret'to, a *ag* mean, stingy; *(fig)* narrow-minded.

gre've *ag* heavy.

grez'zo, a |grād'dzō| *ag* = **greggio**.

grida're *vi (per chiamare)* to shout, cry (out); *(strillare)* to scream, yell ♦ *vt* to shout (out), yell (out); ~ **aiuto** to cry *o* shout for help.

gri'do, *pl(m)* **i** *o pl(f)* **a** *sm* shout, cry; scream, yell; *(di animale)* cry; **di** ~ famous; **all'ultimo** ~ in the latest style.

gri'gio, a, gi, gie |grē'jō| *ag, sm* gray *(US)*, grey *(Brit)*.

gri'glia |grēl'yá| *sf (per arrostire)* grill; *(ELETTR)* grid; *(inferriata)* grating; **alla** ~ *(CUC)* grilled.

griglia'ta |grēlyá'tá| *sf (CUC)* grill.

grillet'to *sm* trigger.

gril'lo *sm (ZOOL)* cricket; *(fig)* whim; **ha dei** ~**i per la testa** his head is full of nonsense.

grimaldel'lo *sm* picklock.

grin'fia *sf*: **cadere nelle** ~**e di qn** *(fig)* to fall into sb's clutches.

grin'ta *sf* grim expression; *(SPORT)* fighting spirit; **avere molta** ~ to be very determined.

grin'za |grēn'tsà| *sf* crease, wrinkle; *(ruga)* wrinkle; **il tuo ragionamento non fa una** ~ your argument is faultless.

grinzo'so, a |grēntsō'sō| *ag* wrinkled; creased.

grippa're *vi (TECN)* to seize.

grissi'no *sm* bread-stick.

groenlande'se *ag* Greenland *cpd* ♦ *sm/f* Greenlander.

Groenlan'dia *sf*: **la** ~ Greenland.

gron'da *sf* eaves *pl.*

gronda'ia *sf* gutter.

grondan'te *ag* dripping.

gronda're *vi* to pour; *(essere bagnato)*: ~ **di** to be dripping with ♦ *vt* to drip with.

grop'pa *sf (di animale)* back, rump; *(fam: dell'uomo)* back, shoulders *pl.*

grop'po *sm* tangle; **avere un** ~ **alla gola** *(fig)* to have a lump in one's throat.

gros'sa *sf (unità di misura)* gross.

grossez'za |grōssāt'tsá| *sf* size; thickness.

grossi'sta, i, e *sm/f (COMM)* wholesaler.

gros'so, a *ag* big, large; *(di spessore)* thick; *(grossolano: anche fig)* coarse; *(grave, insopportabile)* serious, great; *(tempo, mare)* rough ♦ *sm*: **il** ~ **di** the bulk of; **un pezzo** ~ *(fig)* a VIP, a bigwig; **farla** ~**a** to do something very stupid; **dirle** ~**e** to tell tall tales *(US)* o stories *(Brit)*; **questa è** ~**a!** that's a good one!; **sbagliarsi di** ~ to be completely wrong; **dormire della** ~**a** to sleep like a log.

grossolanità *sf* coarseness.

grossola'no, a *ag* rough, coarse; *(fig)* coarse, crude; *(: errore)* stupid.

grossomo'do *av* roughly.

grot'ta *sf* cave; grotto.

grotte'sco, a, schi, sche *ag* grotesque.

grovie'ra *sm o f* gruyère (cheese).

grovi'glio |grōvēl'yō| *sm* tangle; *(fig)* muddle.

gru *sf inv* crane.

gruc'cia, ce |grōōch'chá| *sf (per camminare)* crutch; *(per abiti)* coat-hanger.

grugni're |grōōnyē'rā| *vi* to grunt.

grugni'to |grōōnyē'tō| *sm* grunt.

gru'gno |grōōn'yō| *sm* snout; *(fam: faccia)* mug.

grul'lo, a *ag* silly, stupid.

gru'mo *sm (di sangue)* clot; *(di farina etc)* lump.

grumo'so, a *ag* lumpy.

grup'po *sm* group; ~ **sanguigno** blood group.

gruvie'ra *sm o f* = **groviera**.

gruz'zolo |grōōt'tsōlō| *sm (di denaro)* hoard.

GT *abbr (AUT:* = *gran turismo)* GT.

G.U. *abbr* = **Gazzetta Ufficiale**.

guadagna're |gwádányá'rā| *vt (ottenere)* to gain; *(soldi, stipendio)* to earn; *(vincere)* to win; *(raggiungere)* to reach; **tanto di guadagnato!** so much the better!

guada'gno |gwádán'yō| *sm* earnings *pl*; *(COMM)* profit; *(vantaggio, utile)* advantage, gain; ~ **di capitale** capital gains *pl*; ~ **lordo/netto** gross/net earnings *pl*.

guada're *vt* to ford.

gua'do *sm* ford; **passare a** ~ to ford.

gua'i *escl*: ~ **a te** *(o* **lui** *etc)*! woe betide you *(o him etc)*!

guai'na *sf (fodero)* sheath; *(indumento per donna)* girdle.

gua'io *sm* trouble, mishap; *(inconveniente)* trouble, snag.

guai're *vi* to whine, yelp.

guai'to *sm (di cane)* yelp, whine; *(il guaire)* yelping, whining.

guan'cia, ce |gwàn'chá| *sf* cheek.

guancia'le |gwánchá'lā| *sm* pillow; **dormire fra due** ~**i** *(fig)* to sleep easy, have no worries.

guan'to *sm* glove; **trattare qn con i** ~**i** *(fig)* to handle sb with kid gloves; **gettare/raccogliere il** ~ *(fig)* to throw down/take up the gauntlet.

guanto'ne *sm* boxing glove.

guardabos'chi |gwárdábo'skē| *sm inv* forest ranger.

guardacac'cia |gwárdákàch'chá| *sm inv* gamekeeper.

guardaco'ste *sm inv* coastguard; *(nave)* coastguard patrol vessel.

guardali'nee *sm inv (SPORT)* linesman.

guardamac'chine |gwárdàmák'kēnā| *sm/f inv* parking lot *(US)* o car-park *(Brit)* attendant.

guarda're *vt (con lo sguardo: osservare)* to look at; *(film, televisione)* to watch; *(custodire)* to look after, take care of ♦ *vi* to look; *(badare)*: ~ **a** to pay attention to; *(luoghi: esser orientato)*: ~ **a** to face; ~**rsi** *vr* to look at o.s.; ~ **di** to try to; ~**rsi da** *(astenersi)* to refrain from; (*stare in guardia*) to beware of; ~**rsi da fare** to take care not to do; **ma guarda un po'**! good heavens!; **e guarda caso** ... as if by coincidence ...; ~ **qn dall'alto in basso** to look down on sb; **non** ~ **in faccia a nessuno** (*fig*) to have no regard for anybody; ~ **di traverso** to scowl *o* frown at; ~ **a vista qn** to keep a close watch on sb.

guardaro'ba *sm inv* wardrobe; (*locale*) cloakroom.

guardarobie're, a *sm/f* cloakroom attendant.

guardasigil'li [gwàrdàsêjĉl'lĉ] *sm inv* ≈ Attorney General (*US*), ≈ Lord Chancellor (*Brit*).

guar'dia *sf* (*individuo, corpo*) guard; (*sorveglianza*) watch; **fare la** ~ **a qc/qn** to guard sth/sb; **stare in** ~ (*fig*) to be on one's guard; **il medico di** ~ the doctor on call; **il fiume ha raggiunto il livello di** ~ the river has reached the high-water mark; ~ **carceraria** (prison) guard (*US*) *o* warder (*Brit*); ~ **del corpo** bodyguard; ~ **di finanza** (*corpo*) customs *pl*; (*persona*) customs officer; ~ **forestale** forest ranger; ~ **giurata** security guard; ~ **medica** emergency doctor service; ~ **municipale** town policeman; ~ **notturna** night security guard; ~ **di pubblica sicurezza** policeman.

guardia'no, a *sm/f* (*di carcere*) guard (*US*), warder (*Brit*); (*di villa etc*) caretaker; (*di museo*) custodian; (*di zoo*) keeper; ~ **notturno** night watchman.

guardi'na *sf* cell.

guardin'go, a, ghi, ghe *ag* wary, cautious.

guardio'la *sf* porter's lodge; (*MIL*) look-out tower.

guarigio'ne [gwàrêjô'nã] *sf* recovery.

guari're *vt* (*persona, malattia*) to cure; (*ferita*) to heal ♦ *vi* to recover, be cured; to heal (up).

guarnigio'ne [gwárnêjô'nã] *sf* garrison.

guarni're *vt* (*ornare: abiti*) to trim; (*CUC*) to garnish.

guarnizio'ne [gwàrnĉttsyô'nã] *sf* trimming; garnish; (*TECN*) gasket.

guastafe'ste *sm/f inv* spoilsport.

guasta're *vt* to spoil, ruin; (*meccanismo*) to break; ~**rsi** *vr* (*cibo*) to go bad; (*meccanismo*) to break down; (*tempo*) to change for the worse; (*amici*) to quarrel, fall out.

gua'sto, a *ag* (*non funzionante*) broken; (: *telefono etc*) out of order; (*andato a male*) bad, rotten; (: *dente*) decayed, bad; (*fig: corrotto*) depraved ♦ *sm* breakdown; (*avaria*) failure; ~ **al motore** engine failure.

Guatema'la *sm*: **il** ~ Guatemala.

guatemalte'co, a, ci, che *ag, sm/f* Guatemalan.

guaz'za [gwàt'tsà] *sf* heavy dew.

guazzabu'glio [gwàttsàbōōl'yô] *sm* muddle.

guer'cio, a, ci, ce [gwãr'chô] *ag* cross-eyed.

guer'ra *sf* war; (*tecnica: atomica, chimica etc*) warfare; **fare la** ~ **(a)** to wage war (against); ~ **mondiale** world war.

guerrafonda'io *sm* warmonger.

guerreggia're [gwãrrãdjá'rã] *vi* to wage war.

guerre'sco, a, schi, sche *ag* (*di guerra*) war *cpd*; (*incline alla guerra*) warlike.

guerrie'ro, a *ag* warlike ♦ *sm* warrior.

guerri'glia [gwãrrĉl'yà] *sf* guerrilla warfare.

guerriglie'ro [gwãrrĉlyc'rô] *sm* guerrilla.

gu'fo *sm* owl.

gu'glia [gōōl'yà] *sf* (*ARCHIT*) spire; (*di roccia*) needle.

Guia'na *sf*: **la** ~ **francese** French Guiana.

gui'da *sf* guide; (*comando, direzione*) guidance, direction; (*AUT*) driving; (: *sterzo*) steering; (*tappeto, di tenda, cassetto*) runner; ~ **a destra/sinistra** (*AUT*) right-/left-hand drive; **essere alla** ~ **di** (*governo*) to head; (*spedizione, paese*) to lead; **far da** ~ **a qn** (*mostrare la strada*) to show sb the way; (*in una città*) to show sb (a)round; ~ **telefonica** telephone directory.

guida're *vt* to guide; (*condurre a capo*) to lead; (*auto*) to drive; (*aereo, nave*) to pilot; **sa** ~? can you drive?

guidato're, tri'ce *sm/f* (*conducente*) driver.

Guine'a *sf*: **la Repubblica di** ~ the Republic of Guinea; **la** ~ **Equatoriale** Equatorial Guinea.

guinza'glio [gwĉntsál'yô] *sm* leash, lead.

gui'sa *sf*: **a** ~ **di** like, in the manner of.

guizza're [gwĉttsà'rã] *vi* to dart; to flicker; to leap; ~ **via** (*fuggire*) to slip away.

guiz'zo [gwĉt'tsô] *sm* (*di animali*) dart; (*di fulmine*) flash.

gu'scio [gōōsh'shô] *sm* shell.

gusta're *vt* (*cibi*) to taste; (: *assaporare con piacere*) to enjoy, savor (*US*), savour (*Brit*); (*fig*) to enjoy, appreciate ♦ *vi*: ~ **a** to please; **non mi gusta affatto** I don't like it at all.

gustati'vo, a *ag*: **papille** *fpl* ~**e** taste buds.

gu'sto *sm* (*senso*) taste; (*sapore*) taste, flavor (*US*), flavour (*Brit*); (*godimento*) enjoyment; **al** ~ **di fragola** strawberry-flavo(u)red; **di** ~ **barocco** in the baroque style; **mangiare di** ~ to eat heartily; **prenderci** ~: **ci ha preso** ~ he's acquired a taste for it.

gusto'so, a *ag* tasty; (*fig*) agreeable.

guttura'le *ag* guttural.

Guya'na [gōōyá'nà] *sf*: **la** ~ Guyana.

H

H, h [àk'kà] *sf o m inv (lettera)* H, h ♦ *abbr (= ora)* hr; *(= etto, altezza)* h; **H come hotel** ≈ H for How.

ha, ha'i [à, àč] *vb vedi* **avere.**

Hai'ti [àč'tč] *sf* Haiti.

haitia'no, a [àčtyà'nō] *ag, sm/f* Haitian.

hall [ho:l] *sf inv* hall, foyer.

han'dicap [hàn'dčkáp] *sm inv* handicap.

handicappa'to, a [àndčkàppà'tō] *ag* handicapped ♦ *sm/f* handicapped person, disabled person.

han'no [àn'nō] *vb vedi* **avere.**

hascisc' [àshčsh'] *sm* hashish.

hawaia'no, a [àvàyà'nō] *ag, sm/f* Hawaiian.

Hawa'ii [àvà'č] *sfpl:* **le ~** Hawaii *sg.*

Hel'sinki [čl'sčnkč] *sf* Helsinki.

her'pes [cr'pàs] *sm (MED)* herpes *sg;* **~ zoster** shingles *sg.*

hg *abbr (= ettogrammo)* hg.

hi'-fi [hà'čfàč] *sf inv, ag inv* hi-fi.

Himala'ia [čmàlà'yà] *sm:* **l'~** the Himalayas *pl.*

hl *abbr (= ettolitro)* hl.

ho [o] *vb vedi* **avere.**

hobby' [ho'bč] *sm inv* hobby.

hoc'key [ho'kč] *sm* hockey; **~ su ghiaccio** ice hockey.

hol'ding [hō'ōōldčng] *sf inv* holding company.

Hondu'ras [ōndōō'ràs] *sm* Honduras.

Hong' Kong [òn'kòng] *sf* Hong Kong.

Honolu'lu [ōnōlōō'lōō] *sf* Honolulu.

ho'stess [hō'ōōstčs] *sf inv* air stewardess.

hotel' [ōtcl'] *sm inv* hotel.

Hz *abbr (= hertz)* Hz.

I

I, i [č] *sf o m inv (lettera)* I, i; **I come Imola** ≈ I for Item.

i *det mpl* the; *vedi anche* **il.**

IACP *sigla m (= Istituto Autonomo per le Case Popolari) public housing association.*

ia'to *sm* hiatus.

ibe'rico, a, ci, che *ag* Iberian; **la Penisola l~a** the Iberian Peninsula.

iberna're *vi* to hibernate ♦ *vt (MED)* to induce hypothermia in.

ibernazio'ne [čbàrnàttsyō'nà] *sf* hibernation.

ibid. *abbr (= ibidem)* ib(id).

i'brido, a *ag, sm* hybrid.

I'CE [č'chà] *sigla m (= Istituto nazionale per il Commercio Estero)* overseas trade board.

ico'na *sf* icon.

id *abbr (= idem)* do.

Iddi'o *sm* God.

ide'a *sf* idea; *(opinione)* opinion, view; *(ideale)* ideal; **avere le ~e chiare** to know one's mind; **cambiare ~** to change one's mind; **dare l'~ di** to seem, look like; **neanche** *o* **neppure per ~!** certainly not!, no way!; **~ fissa** obsession.

idea'le *ag, sm* ideal.

ideali'smo *sm* idealism.

ideali'sta, i, e *sm/f* idealist.

ideali'stico, a, ci, che *ag* idealistic.

idealizza're [čdàálčddzà'rà] *vt* to idealize.

idea're *vt (immaginare)* to think up, conceive; *(progettare)* to plan.

ideato're, tri'ce *sm/f* author.

iden'tico, a, ci, che *ag* identical.

identifica're *vt* to identify.

identificazio'ne [čdàntčfčkàttsyō'nà] *sf* identification.

identità *sf inv* identity.

ideologi'a, gi'e [čdàōlōjč'à] *sf* ideology.

ideolo'gico, a, ci, che [čdàōlo'jčkō] *ag* ideological.

idil'lico, a, ci, che *ag* idyllic.

idil'lio *sm* idyll; **tra di loro è nato un ~** they have fallen in love.

idio'ma, i *sm* idiom, language.

idioma'tico, a, ci, che *ag* idiomatic; **frase** *f* **~a** idiom.

idiosincrasi'a *sf* idiosyncrasy.

idio'ta, i, e *ag* idiotic ♦ *sm/f* idiot.

idiozi'a [čdyōttsč'à] *sf* idiocy; *(atto, discorso)* idiotic thing to do (*o* say).

idola'tra, i, e *ag* idolatrous ♦ *sm/f* idolater.

idolatra're *vt* to worship; *(fig)* to idolize.

idolatri'a *sf* idolatry.

i'dolo *sm* idol.

idoneità *sf* suitability; **esame** *m* **di ~** qualifying examination.

ido'neo, a *ag:* **~ a** suitable for, fit for; *(MIL)* fit for; *(qualificato)* qualified for.

idran'te *sm* hydrant.

idratan'te *ag (crema)* moisturizing ♦ *sm* moisturizer.

idrata're *vt (pelle)* to moisturize.

idratazio'ne [čdràtàttsyō'nà] *sf* moisturizing.

idra'ulico, a, ci, che *ag* hydraulic ♦ *sm* plumber ♦ *sf* hydraulics *sg.*

i'drico, a, ci, che *ag* water *cpd.*

idrocarbu'ro *sm* hydrocarbon.

idroelet'trico, a, ci, che *ag* hydroelectric.

idro'filo, a *ag*: **cotone** *m* ~ absorbent cotton (*US*), cotton wool (*Brit*).

idrofobi'a *sf* rabies *sg*.

idro'fobo, a *ag* rabid; (*fig*) furious.

idro'geno [ēdro'jānō] *sm* hydrogen.

idropor'to *sm* (*AER*) seaplane base.

idrorepellen'te *ag* water-repellent.

idrosca'lo *sm* = **idroporto**.

idrovolan'te *sm* seaplane.

iel'la *sf* bad luck.

iella'to, a *ag* plagued by bad luck.

ie'na *sf* hyena.

iera'tico, a, ci, che *ag* (*REL*: *scrittura*) hieratic; (*fig*: *atteggiamento*) solemn.

ie'ri *av*, *sm* yesterday; **il giornale di** ~ yesterday's paper; ~ **l'altro** the day before yesterday; ~ **sera** yesterday evening.

iettato're, tri'ce *sm/f* jinx.

igie'ne [ējē'nā] *sf* hygiene; **norme d'**~ sanitary regulations; **ufficio d'**~ public health office; ~ **mentale** mental health; ~ **pubblica** public health.

igie'nico, a, ci, che [ējc'nēkō] *ag* hygienic; (*salubre*) healthy.

IGM *sigla m* (= *Ispettorato Generale della Motorizzazione*) road traffic inspectorate.

igna'ro, a [ēnyá'rō] *ag*: ~ **di** unaware of, ignorant of.

igni'fugo, a, ghi, ghe [ēnyē'fōōgō] *ag* flame-resistant, fireproof.

igno'bile [ēnyo'bēlā] *ag* despicable, vile.

ignomi'nia [ēnyōmē'nyā] *sf* ignominy.

ignoran'te [ēnyōrán'tā] *ag* ignorant.

ignoran'za [ēnyōrán'tsā] *sf* ignorance.

ignora're [ēnyōrá'rā] *vt* (*non sapere, conoscere*) to be ignorant o unaware of, not to know; (*fingere di non vedere, sentire*) to ignore.

igno'to, a [ēnyo'tō] *ag* unknown ♦ *sm/f*: **figlio di** ~i child of unknown parentage; **il Milite I**~ the Unknown Soldier.

il *det m* (*pl* (*m*) **i**; *diventa* **lo** (*pl* **gli**) *davanti a s impura, gn, pn, ps, x, z*; *f* **la** (*pl* **le**)) (*gen*) the; (*generalizzazione, l'astrazione*) *generalmente non tradotto*; ~ **libro/lo studente/ l'acqua** the book/the student/the water; ~ **coraggio/l'amore/la giovinezza** courage/love/ youth; ~ **venerdi** *etc* (*abitualmente*) on Fridays *etc*; (*quel giorno*) on (the) Friday *etc*; **la settimana prossima** next week; **2.500 lire** ~ **chilo/paio** 2,500 lire a o per kilo/pair; **rompersi la gamba** to break one's leg; **avere i capelli neri/il naso rosso** to have dark hair/a red nose.

i'lare *ag* cheerful.

ilarità *sf* hilarity, mirth.

ill. *abbr* (= *illustrazione*; *illustrato*) ill.

illanguidi're *vi* to grow weak o feeble.

illazio'ne [ēllāttsyō'nā] *sf* inference, deduction.

ille'cito, a [ēllā'chētō] *ag* illicit.

illega'le *ag* illegal.

illegalità *sf* illegality.

illeggi'bile [ēllādjē'bēlā] *ag* illegible.

illegittimità [ēllājēttēmētá'] *sf* illegitimacy.

illegit'timo, a [ēllājēt'tēmō] *ag* illegitimate.

ille'so, a *ag* unhurt, unharmed.

illettera'to, a *ag* illiterate.

illibatez'za [ēllēbátāt'tsā] *sf* (*di donna*) virginity.

illiba'to, a *ag*: **donna** ~a virgin.

illimita'to, a *ag* boundless; unlimited.

illividi're *vi* (*volto, mani*) to turn livid; (*cielo*) to grow leaden.

ill.mo *abbr* = **illustrissimo**.

illo'gico, a, ci, che [ēllo'jēkō] *ag* illogical.

illu'dere *vt* to deceive, delude; ~**rsi** *vr* to deceive o.s., delude o.s.

illumina're *vt* to light up, illuminate; (*fig*) to enlighten; ~**rsi** *vr* to light up; ~ **a giorno** (*con riflettori*) to floodlight.

illumina'to, a *ag* (*fig*: *sovrano, spirito*) enlightened.

illuminazio'ne [ēllōōmēnáttsyō'nā] *sf* lighting; illumination; floodlighting; (*fig*) flash of inspiration.

illumini'smo *sm* (*STORIA*): **l'I**~ the Enlightenment.

illu'si *etc vb vedi* **illudere**.

illusio'ne *sf* illusion; **farsi delle** ~i to delude o.s.

illusioni'smo *sm* conjuring.

illusioni'sta, i, e *sm/f* conjurer.

illu'so, a *pp di* **illudere**.

illuso'rio, a *ag* illusory.

illustra're *vt* to illustrate.

illustrati'vo, a *ag* illustrative.

illustrazio'ne [ēllōōstráttsyō'nā] *sf* illustration.

illus'tre *ag* eminent, renowned.

illustris'simo, a *ag* (*negli indirizzi*) very revered.

I'LOR *sigla f vedi* **imposta locale sui redditi**.

IM *sigla* = *Imperia*.

imbacucca're *vt*, ~**rsi** *vr* to wrap up.

imbaldanzi're [ēmbáldántsē'rā] *vt* to give confidence to; ~**rsi** *vr* to grow bold.

imballag'gio [ēmbállád'jō] *sm* packing *q*.

imballa're *vt* to pack; (*AUT*) to race; ~**rsi** *vr* (*AUT*) to race.

imbalsama're *vt* to embalm.

imbambola'to, a *ag* (*sguardo, espressione*) vacant, blank.

imbandi're *vt*: ~ **un banchetto** to prepare a lavish feast.

imbandi'to, a *ag*: **tavola** ~a lavishly o sumptuously decked table.

imbarazzan'te [ēmbárāttsán'tā] *ag* embarrassing, awkward.

imbarazza're [ēmbárāttsá'rā] *vt* (*mettere a di-*

sagio) to embarrass; (*ostacolare*: *movimenti*) to hamper; (: *stomaco*) to lie heavily on; ~**rsi** *vr* to become embarrassed.

imbarazza'to, a |ĕmbàráttsà'tō| *ag* embarrassed; **avere lo stomaco** ~ to have an upset stomach.

imbaraz'zo |ĕmbàrát'tsō| *sm* (*disagio*) embarrassment; (*perplessità*) puzzlement, bewilderment; **essere** *o* **trovarsi in** ~ to be in an awkward situation *o* predicament; **mettere in** ~ to embarrass; ~ **di stomaco** indigestion.

imbarcade'ro *sm* landing stage.

imbarca're *vt* (*passeggeri*) to embark; (*merci*) to load; ~**rsi** *vr*: ~**rsi su** to board; ~**rsi per l'America** to sail for America; ~**rsi in** (*fig*: *affare*) to embark on.

imbarcazio'ne |ĕmbàrkàttsyō'nā| *sf* (small) boat, (small) craft *inv*; ~ **di salvataggio** lifeboat.

imbar'co, chi *sm* embarkation; loading; boarding; (*banchina*) landing stage; **carta d'**~ boarding card.

imbastardi're *vt* to bastardize, debase; ~**rsi** *vr* to degenerate, become debased.

imbasti're *vt* (*cucire*) to tack; (*fig*: *abbozzare*) to sketch, outline.

imbat'tersi *vr*: ~ **in** (*incontrare*) to bump *o* run into.

imbatti'bile *ag* unbeatable, invincible.

imbavaglia're |ĕmbàvàlyà'rā| *vt* to gag.

imbecca're *vt* (*uccelli*) to feed; (*fig*) to prompt, put words into sb's mouth.

imbecca'ta *sf* (*TEATRO*) prompt; **dare l'**~ **a qn** to prompt sb; (*fig*) to give sb their cue.

imbecil'le |ĕmbāchēl'lā| *ag* idiotic ♦ *sm/f* idiot; (*MED*) imbecile.

imbecillità |ĕmbāchēllētà'| *sf inv* (*MED*, *fig*) imbecility, idiocy; **dire** ~ to talk nonsense.

imbelletta're *vt* (*viso*) to make up, put make-up on; ~**rsi** *vr* to make o.s. up, put on one's make-up.

imbelli're *vt* to adorn, embellish ♦ *vi* to grow more beautiful.

imber'be *ag* beardless; **un giovanotto** ~ a callow youth.

imbestiali're *vt* to infuriate; ~**rsi** *vr* to become infuriated, fly into a rage.

imbe'vere *vt* to soak; ~**rsi** *vr*: ~**rsi di** to soak up, absorb.

imbianca're *vt* to whiten; (*muro*) to whitewash ♦ *vi* to become *o* turn white.

imbiancatu'ra *sf* (*di muro*: con bianco di calce) whitewashing; (: con altre pitture) painting.

imbianchi'no |ĕmbyánkē'nō| *sm* (house) painter, painter and decorator.

imbiondi're *vt* (*capelli*) to lighten; (*CUC*: *cipolla*) to brown; ~**rsi** *vr* (*capelli*) to lighten, go blonde, go fair; (*messi*) to turn golden,

ripen.

imbizzarrir'si |ĕmbēddzàrrēr'sē| *vr* (*cavallo*) to become frisky.

imbocca're *vt* (*bambino*) to feed; (*entrare*: *strada*) to enter, turn into ♦ *vi*: ~ **in** (*sog*: *strada*) to lead into; (: *fiume*) to flow into.

imboccatu'ra *sf* mouth; (*di strada, porto*) entrance; (*MUS, del morso*) mouthpiece.

imboc'co, chi *sm* entrance.

imbonito're *sm* (*di spettacolo, circo*) barker.

imborghesir'si |ĕmbōrgāzēr'sē| *vr* to become bourgeois.

imbosca're *vt* to hide; ~**rsi** *vr* (*MIL*) to evade military service.

imbosca'ta *sf* ambush.

imbosca'to *sm* draft dodger.

imboschimen'to |ĕmbōskēmān'tō| *sm* afforestation.

imbottiglia're |ĕmbōttēlyà'rā| *vt* to bottle; (*NAUT*) to blockade; (*MIL*) to hem in; ~**rsi** *vr* to be stuck in a traffic jam.

imbotti're *vt* to stuff; (*giacca*) to pad; ~**rsi** *vr*: ~**rsi di** (*rimpinzarsi*) to stuff o.s. with.

imbotti'to, a *ag* (*sedia*) upholstered; (*giacca*) padded ♦ *sf* quilt.

imbottitu'ra *sf* stuffing; padding.

imbraccia're |ĕmbràchà'rā| *vt* (*fucile*) to shoulder; (*scudo*) to grasp.

imbrana'to, a *ag* clumsy, awkward ♦ *sm/f* clumsy person.

imbrattacar'te *sm/f* (*peg*) scribbler.

imbratta're *vt* to dirty, smear, daub; ~**rsi** *vr*: ~**rsi (di)** to dirty o.s. (with).

imbrattate'le *sm/f* (*peg*) dauber.

imbriglia're |ĕmbrēlyà'rā| *vt* to bridle.

imbrocca're *vt* (*fig*) to guess correctly.

imbroglia're |ĕmbrōlyà'rā| *vt* to mix up; (*fig*: *raggirare*) to deceive, cheat; (: *confondere*) to confuse, mix up; ~**rsi** *vr* to get tangled; (*fig*) to become confused.

imbro'glio |ĕmbrol'yō| *sm* (*groviglio*) tangle; (*situazione confusa*) mess; (*truffa*) swindle, trick.

imbroglio'ne, a |ĕmbrōlyō'nā| *sm/f* cheat, swindler.

imbroncia're |ĕmbrōnchà'rā| *vi* (*anche*: ~**rsi**) to sulk.

imbroncia'to, a |ĕmbrōnchà'tō| *ag* (*persona*) sulky; (*cielo*) cloudy, threatening.

imbruni're *vi, vb impers* to grow dark; **all'**~ at dusk.

imbrutti're *vt* to make ugly ♦ *vi* to become ugly.

imbuca're *vt* to post.

imburra're *vt* to butter.

imbutifor'me *ag* funnel-shaped.

imbu'to *sm* funnel.

ime'ne *sm* hymen.

imita're *vt* to imitate; (*riprodurre*) to copy; (*assomigliare*) to look like.

imitato're, tri'ce *sm/f* (*gen*) imitator; (*TEATRO*) impersonator, impressionist.

imitazio'ne [ĭmētáttsyō'nä] *sf* imitation.

immacola'to, a *ag* spotless; immaculate.

immagazzina're [ĭmmágáddzĕnä'rä] *vt* to store.

immagina'bile [ĭmmájĕnä'bĕlä] *ag* imaginable.

immagina're [ĭmmäjĕnä'rä] *vt* to imagine; (*supporre*) to suppose; (*inventare*) to invent; **s'immagini!** don't mention it!, not at all!

immagina'rio, a [ĭmmäjĕnä'ryō] *ag* imaginary.

immaginati'va [ĭmmäjĕnätĕ'vä] *sf* imagination.

immaginazio'ne [ĭmmäjĕnättsyō'nä] *sf* imagination; (*cosa immaginata*) fancy.

imma'gine [ĭmmä'jĕnä] *sf* image; (*rappresentazione grafica, mentale*) picture.

immagino'so, a [ĭmmäjĕnō'sō] *ag* (*linguaggio, stile*) fantastic.

immalinconi're *vt* to sadden, depress; **~rsi** *vr* to become depressed, become melancholy.

immanca'bile *ag* unfailing.

immancabilmen'te *av* without fail, unfailingly.

immanen'te *ag* (*FILOSOFIA*) inherent, immanent.

immangia'bile [ĭmmänjá'bĕlä] *ag* inedible.

immatricola're *vt* to register; **~rsi** *vr* (*INS*) to matriculate, enrol.

immatricolazio'ne [ĭmmätrēkōláttsyō'nä] *sf* registration; matriculation; enrolment.

immaturità *sf* immaturity.

immatu'ro, a *ag* (*frutto*) unripe; (*persona*) immature; (*prematuro*) premature.

immedesimar'si *vr*: **~ in** to identify with.

immediatamen'te *av* immediately, at once.

immediatez'za [ĭmmädyátät'tsä] *sf* immediacy.

immedia'to, a *ag* immediate.

immemora'bile *ag* immemorial; **da tempo ~** from time immemorial.

imme'more *ag*: **~ di** forgetful of.

immensità *sf* immensity.

immen'so, a *ag* immense.

immer'gere [ĭmmĕr'järä] *vt* to immerse, plunge; **~rsi** *vr* to plunge; (*sommergibile*) to dive, submerge; (*dedicarsi a*): **~rsi in** to immerse o.s. in.

immerita'to, a *ag* undeserved.

immerite'vole *ag* undeserving, unworthy.

immersio'ne *sf* immersion; (*di sommergibile*) submersion, dive; (*di palombaro*) dive; **linea di ~** (*NAUT*) water line.

immer'so, a *pp di* **immergere.**

immes'so, a *pp di* **immettere.**

immet'tere *vt*: **~ (in)** to introduce (into); **~ dati in un computer** to enter data on a computer.

immigran'te *ag, sm/f* immigrant.

immigra're *vi* to immigrate.

immigra'to, a *sm/f* immigrant.

immigrazio'ne [ĭmmēgráttsyō'nä] *sf* immigration.

imminen'te *ag* imminent.

imminen'za [ĭmmĕncn'tsä] *sf* imminence.

immischia're [ĭmmĕskyá'rä] *vt*: **~ qn in** to involve sb in; **~rsi** *vr*: **~rsi in** to interfere o meddle in.

immiserimen'to *sm* impoverishment.

immissa'rio *sm* (*GEO*) affluent, tributary.

immissio'ne *sf* (*gen*) introduction; (*di aria, gas*) intake; **~ di dati** (*INFORM*) data entry.

immo'bile *ag* motionless, still; (**beni**) **~i** *smpl* real estate *sg*.

immobilia're *ag* (*DIR*) property *cpd*; **patrimonio ~** real estate; **società ~** real estate company.

immobili'smo *sm* inertia.

immobilità *sf* immobility.

immobilizza're [ĭmmōbēlēddzá'rä] *vt* to immobilize; (*ECON*) to lock up.

immobiliz'zo [ĭmmōbēlēd'dzō] *sm*: **spese d'~** capital expenditure.

immode'stia *sf* immodesty.

immode'sto, a *ag* immodest.

immola're *vt* to sacrifice.

immondezza'io [ĭmmōndättsá'yō] *sm* rubbish dump.

immondi'zia [ĭmmōndĕt'tsyá] *sf* dirt, filth; (*spesso al pl: spazzatura, rifiuti*) rubbish *q*, refuse *q*.

immon'do, a *ag* filthy, foul.

immora'le *ag* immoral.

immoralità *sf* immorality.

immortala're *vt* to immortalize.

immorta'le *ag* immortal.

immortalità *sf* immortality.

immu'ne *ag* (*esente*) exempt; (*MED, DIR*) immune.

immunità *sf* immunity; **~ parlamentare** parliamentary privilege (*Brit*).

immunizza're [ĭmmōōnĕddzá'rä] *vt* (*MED*) to immunize.

immunizzazio'ne [ĭmmōōnĕddzáttsyō'nä] *sf* immunization.

immunolo'gico, a, ci, che [ĭmmōōnōlo'jĕkō] *ag* immunological.

immuta'bile *ag* immutable; unchanging.

impacca're *vt* to pack.

impacchetta're [ĭmpákkättä'rä] *vt* to pack up.

impaccia're [ĭmpáchá'rä] *vt* to hinder, hamper.

impaccia'to, a [ĭmpáchá'tō] *ag* awkward, clumsy; (*imbarazzato*) embarrassed.

impac'cio [ĭmpách'chō] *sm* obstacle; (*imbarazzo*) embarrassment; (*situazione imbarazzante*) awkward situation.

impac'co, chi *sm* (*MED*) compress.

impadronir'si *vr*: ~ **di** to seize, take possession of; (*fig*: *apprendere a fondo*) to master.

impaga'bile *ag* priceless.

impagina're [ĕmpájĕnà'rā] *vt* (*TIP*) to paginate, page (up).

impaginazio'ne [ĕmpájĕnàttsyō'nā] *sf* pagination.

impaglia're [ĕmpàlyà'rā] *vt* to stuff (with straw).

impala'to, a *ag* (*fig*) stiff as a board.

impalcatu'ra *sf* scaffolding; (*anche fig*) framework.

impallidi're *vi* to turn pale; (*fig*) to fade.

impana're *vt* (*CUC*) to dip (*o* roll) in breadcrumbs.

impantanar'si *vr* to sink (in the mud); (*fig*) to get bogged down.

impaperar'si *vr* to stumble over a word.

impappinar'si *vr* to stammer, falter.

impara're *vt* to learn; **così impari!** that'll teach you!

imparatic'cio [ĕmpàrátĕch'chō] *sm* half-baked notions *pl*.

impareggia'bile [ĕmpàràdjá'bĕlā] *ag* incomparable.

imparentar'si *vr*: ~ **con** to marry into.

im'pari *ag inv* (*disuguale*) unequal; (*dispari*) odd.

imparti're *vt* to bestow, give.

imparzia'le [ĕmpàrtsyà'lā] *ag* impartial, unbiased.

imparzialità [ĕmpàrtsyálĕtá'] *sf* impartiality.

impassi'bile *ag* impassive.

impasta're *vt* (*pasta*) to knead; (*colori*) to mix.

impasticcar'si *vr* to pop pills.

impa'sto *sm* (*l'impastare*: *di pane*) kneading; (: *di cemento*) mixing; (*pasta*) dough; (*anche fig*) mixture.

impat'to *sm* impact.

impauri're *vt* to scare, frighten ♦ *vi* (*anche*: ~**rsi**) to become scared *o* frightened.

impa'vido, a *ag* intrepid, fearless.

impazien'te [ĕmpáttsyen'tā] *ag* impatient.

impazien'za [ĕmpáttsyen'tsá] *sf* impatience.

impazza'ta [ĕmpáttsà'tá] *sf*: **all'~** (*precipitosamente*) at breakneck speed; (*colpire*) wildly.

impazzi're [ĕmpáttsē'rā] *vi* to go mad; ~ **per qn/qc** to be crazy about sb/sth.

impecca'bile *ag* impeccable.

impedimen'to *sm* obstacle, hindrance.

impedi're *vt* (*vietare*): ~ **a qn di fare** to prevent sb from doing; (*ostruire*) to obstruct; (*impacciare*) to hamper, hinder.

impegna're [ĕmpànyà'rā] *vt* (*dare in pegno*) to pawn; (*onore etc*) to pledge; (*prenotare*) to book, reserve; (*obbligare*) to oblige; (*occupare*) to keep busy; (*MIL*: *nemico*) to engage; ~**rsi** *vr* (*vincolarsi*): ~**rsi a fare** to undertake to do; (*mettersi risolutamente*):

~**rsi in qc** to devote o.s. to sth; ~**rsi con qn** (*accordarsi*) to come to an agreement with sb.

impegnati'vo, a [ĕmpānyátē'vō] *ag* binding; (*lavoro*) demanding, exacting.

impegna'to, a [ĕmpānyá'tō] *ag* (*occupato*) busy; (*fig*: *romanzo, autore*) committed, engagé.

impe'gno [ĕmpān'yō] *sm* (*obbligo*) obligation; (*promessa*) promise, pledge; (*zelo*) diligence, zeal; (*compito, d'autore*) commitment; ~**i di lavoro** business commitments.

impegolar'si *vr* (*fig*): ~ **in** to get heavily involved in.

impelagar'si *vr* = **impegolarsi**.

impellen'te *ag* pressing, urgent.

impenetra'bile *ag* impenetrable.

impennar'si *vr* (*cavallo*) to rear up; (*AER*) to go into a climb; (*fig*) to bridle.

impenna'ta *sf* (*di cavallo*) rearing up; (*di aereo*) climb, nose-up; (*fig*: *scatto d'ira*) burst of anger.

impensa'bile *ag* (*inaccettabile*) unthinkable; (*difficile da concepire*) inconceivable.

impensa'to, a *ag* unforeseen, unexpected.

impensieri're *vt*, ~**rsi** *vr* to worry.

imperan'te *ag* prevailing.

impera're *vi* (*anche fig*) to reign, rule.

imperati'vo, a *ag*, *sm* imperative.

imperato're, tri'ce *sm/f* emperor/empress.

impercetti'bile [ĕmpārchāttē'bĕlā] *ag* imperceptible.

imperdona'bile *ag* unforgivable, unpardonable.

imperfet'to, a *ag* imperfect ♦ *sm* (*LING*) imperfect (tense).

imperfezio'ne [ĕmpārfāttsyō'nā] *sf* imperfection.

imperia'le *ag* imperial.

imperiali'smo *sm* imperialism.

imperio'so, a *ag* (*persona*) imperious; (*motivo, esigenza*) urgent, pressing.

imperitu'ro, a *ag* everlasting.

imperi'zia [ĕmpārēt'tsyà] *sf* lack of experience.

impermali're *vt* to take offence.

impermea'bile *ag* waterproof ♦ *sm* raincoat.

impernia're *vt*: ~ **qc su** to hinge sth on; (*fig*: *discorso, relazione etc*) to base sth on; ~**rsi** *vr* (*fig*): ~**rsi su** to be based on.

impe'ro *sm* empire; (*forza, autorità*) rule, control.

imperscruta'bile *ag* inscrutable.

imperso'na'le *ag* impersonal.

impersona're *vt* to personify; (*TEATRO*) to play, act (the part of); ~**rsi** *vr*: ~**rsi in un ruolo** to get into a part, live a part.

imperter'rito, a *ag* unperturbed.

impertinen'te *ag* impertinent.

impertinen'za [ĕmpārtēnen'tsá] *sf* impertinence.

imperturba'bile *ag* imperturbable.
imperversa're *vi* to rage.
imper'vio, a *ag* (*luogo*) inaccessible; (*strada*) impassable.
im'peto *sm* (*moto, forza*) force, impetus; (*assalto*) onslaught; (*fig: impulso*) impulse; (: *slancio*) transport; **con ~** (*parlare*) forcefully, energetically.
impetra're *vt* to beg for, beseech.
impetti'to, a *ag* stiff, erect; **camminare ~** to strut.
impetuo'so, a *ag* (*vento*) strong, raging; (*persona*) impetuous.
impianta're *vt* (*motore*) to install; (*azienda, discussione*) to establish, start.
impian'to *sm* (*installazione*) installation; (*apparecchiature*) plant; (*sistema*) system; **~ elettrico** wiring; **~ sportivo** sports complex; **~i di risalita** (*SCI*) ski lifts.
impiastra're, impiastriccia're [ēmpyástrēchá'-rā] *vt* to smear, dirty.
impias'tro *sm* poultice; (*fig fam: persona*) nuisance.
impiccagio'ne [ēmpēkkájō'nā] *sf* hanging.
impicca're *vt* to hang; **~rsi** *vr* to hang o.s.
impiccia're [ēmpēchá'rā] *vt* to hinder, hamper; **~rsi** *vr* to meddle, interfere; **impicciati degli affari tuoi!** mind your own business!
impic'cio [ēmpēch'chō] *sm* (*ostacolo*) hindrance; (*seccatura*) trouble, bother; (*affare imbrogliato*) mess; **essere d'~** to be in the way; **cavare** *o* **togliere qn dagli ~i** to get sb out of trouble.
impiccio'ne, a [ēmpēchō'nā] *sm/f* busybody.
impiega're *vt* (*usare*) to use, employ; (*assumere*) to employ, take on; (*spendere: denaro, tempo*) to spend; (*investire*) to invest; **~rsi** *vr* to get a job, obtain employment; **impiego un quarto d'ora per andare a casa** it takes me *o* I take a quarter of an hour to get home.
impiegati'zio, a [ēmpyāgátēt'tsyō] *ag* clerical, white-collar *cpd*; **lavoro/ceto ~** clerical *o* white-collar work/workers *pl*.
impiega'to, a *sm/f* employee; **~ statale** government employee.
impie'go, ghi *sm* (*uso*) use; (*occupazione*) employment; (*posto di lavoro*) (regular) job, post; (*ECON*) investment; **~ pubblico** job in the public sector.
impietosi're *vt* to move to pity; **~rsi** *vr* to be moved to pity.
impieto'so, a *ag* pitiless, cruel.
impietri're *vt* (*anche fig*) to petrify.
impiglia're [ēmpēlyá'rā] *vt* to catch, entangle; **~rsi** *vr* to get caught up *o* entangled.
impigri're *vt* to make lazy ♦ *vi* (*anche:* **~rsi**) to grow lazy.
impingua're *vt* (*maiale etc*) to fatten; (*fig:*

tasche, casse dello Stato) to stuff with money.
impiomba're *vt* (*pacco*) to seal (with lead); (*dente*) to fill.
implaca'bile *ag* implacable.
implica're *vt* to imply; (*coinvolgere*) to involve; **~rsi** *vr*: **~rsi (in)** to become involved (in).
implicazio'ne [ēmplēkáttsyō'nā] *sf* implication.
impli'cito, a [ēmplē'chētō] *ag* implicit.
implora're *vt* to implore.
impolvera're *vt* to cover with dust; **~rsi** *vr* to get dusty.
impomata're *vt* (*pelle*) to put ointment on; (*capelli*) to pomade; (*baffi*) to wax; **~rsi** *vr* (*fam*) to get spruced up.
impo'ne *etc vb vedi* **imporre**.
imponen'te *ag* imposing, impressive.
impon'go *etc vb vedi* **imporre**.
imponi'bile *ag* taxable ♦ *sm* taxable income.
impopola're *ag* unpopular.
impopolarità *sf* unpopularity.
impor're *vt* to impose; (*costringere*) to force, make; (*far valere*) to impose, enforce; **imporsi** *vr* (*persona*) to assert o.s.; (*cosa: rendersi necessario*) to become necessary; (*aver successo: moda, attore*) to become popular; **~ a qn di fare** to force sb to do, make sb do.
importan'te *ag* important.
importan'za [ēmpōrtàn'tsá] *sf* importance; **dare ~ a qc** to attach importance to sth; **darsi ~** to give o.s. airs.
importa're *vt* (*introdurre dall'estero*) to import ♦ *vi* to matter, be important ♦ *vb impers* (*essere necessario*) to be necessary; (*interessare*) to matter; **non importa!** it doesn't matter!; **non me ne importa!** I don't care!
importato're, tri'ce *ag* importing ♦ *sm/f* importer.
importazio'ne [ēmpōrtàttsyō'nā] *sf* importation; (*merci importate*) imports *pl*.
impor'to *sm* (*total*) amount.
importuna're *vt* to bother.
importu'no, a *ag* irksome, annoying.
impo'si *etc vb vedi* **imporre**.
imposizio'ne [ēmpōzēttsyō'nā] *sf* imposition; (*ordine*) order, command; (*onere, imposta*) tax.
impossessar'si *vr*: **~ di** to seize, take possession of.
impossi'bile *ag* impossible; **fare l'~** to do one's utmost, do all one can.
impossibilità *sf* impossibility; **essere nell'~ di fare qc** to be unable to do sth.
impossibilita'to, a *ag*: **essere ~ a fare qc** to be unable to do sth.
impo'sta *sf* (*di finestra*) shutter; (*tassa*) tax; **~ indiretta sui consumi** excise duty *o* tax; **~ locale sui redditi** (*ILOR*) tax on unearned in-

come; ~ **patrimoniale** property tax; ~ **sul reddito** income tax; ~ **sul reddito delle persone fisiche (IRPEF)** personal income tax; ~ **di successione** inheritance tax (*US*), capital transfer tax (*Brit*); ~ **sugli utili** tax on profits; ~ **sul valore aggiunto (I.V.A.)** sales tax, value added tax.

imposta're *vt* (*imbucare*) to post; (*servizio, organizzazione*) to set up; (*lavoro*) to organize, plan; (*resoconto, rapporto*) to plan; (*problema*) to set out, formulate; (*TIP: pagina*) to lay out; ~ **la voce** (*MUS*) to pitch one's voice.

impostazio'ne |ĕmpōstàttsyō'nä| *sf* (*di lettera*) mailing (*US*), posting (*Brit*); (*di problema, questione*) formulation, statement; (*di lavoro*) organization, planning; (*di attività*) setting up; (*MUS*: *di voce*) pitch.

impo'sto, *a pp di* **imporre.**

imposto're, a *sm/f* impostor.

impoten'te *ag* weak, powerless; (*anche MED*) impotent.

impoten'za |ĕmpōten'tsä| *sf* weakness, powerlessness; impotence.

impoveri're *vt* to impoverish ♦ *vi* (*anche*: ~**rsi**) to become poor.

impratica'bile *ag* (*strada*) impassable; (*campo da gioco*) unplayable.

impratichi're |ĕmpráttkē'rä| *vt* to train; ~**rsi** *vr*: ~**rsi in qc** to practice (*US*) *o* practise (*Brit*) sth.

impreca're *vi* to curse, swear; ~ **contro** to hurl abuse at.

imprecisa'to, a |ĕmprächĕzà'tō| *ag* (*non preciso: quantità, numero*)· indeterminate.

imprecisio'ne |ĕmprächĕzyō'nä| *sf* imprecision; inaccuracy.

impreci'so, a |ĕmprächĕ'zō| *ag* imprecise, vague; (*calcolo*) inaccurate.

impregna're |ĕmpränyá'rä| *vt*: ~ **(di)** (*imbevere*) to soak *o* impregnate (with); (*riempire: anche fig*) to fill (with).

imprendito're *sm* (*industriale*) entrepreneur; (*appaltatore*) contractor; **piccolo** ~ small businessman.

imprenditori'a *sf* enterprise; (*imprenditori*) entrepreneurs *pl*.

imprenditoria'le *ag* (*ceto, classe*) entrepreneurial.

imprepara'to, a *ag*: ~ **(a)** (*gen*) unprepared (for); (*lavoratore*) untrained (for); **cogliere qn** ~ to catch sb unawares.

impreparazio'ne |ĕmpràpárättsyō'nä| *sf* lack of preparation.

impre'sa *sf* (*iniziativa*) enterprise; (*azione*) exploit; (*azienda*) firm, concern; ~ **familiare** family firm; ~ **pubblica** state-owned enterprise.

impresa'rio *sm* (*TEATRO*) manager, impresario; ~ **di pompe funebri** funeral director.

imprescindi'bile |ĕmprāshĕndē'bēlä| *ag* not to be ignored.

impres'si *etc vb vedi* **imprimere.**

impressionan'te *ag* impressive; upsetting.

impressiona're *vt* to impress; (*turbare*) to upset; (*FOT*) to expose; ~**rsi** *vr* to be easily upset.

impressio'ne *sf* impression; (*fig: sensazione*) sensation, feeling; (*stampa*) printing; **fare** ~ (*colpire*) to impress; (*turbare*) to frighten, upset; **fare buona/cattiva** ~ **a** to make a good/bad impression on.

impres'so, a *pp di* **imprimere.**

impresta're *vt*: ~ **qc a qn** to lend sth to sb.

imprevedi'bile *ag* unforeseeable; (*persona*) unpredictable.

impreviden'te *ag* lacking in foresight.

impreviden'za |ĕmprāvēden'tsä| *sf* lack of foresight.

imprevi'sto, a *ag* unexpected, unforeseen ♦ *sm* unforeseen event; **salvo** ~**i** unless anything unexpected happens.

impreziosi're |ĕmprättsyōsē'rä| *vt*: ~ **di** to embellish with.

imprigionamen'to |ĕmprējōnàmän'tō| *sm* imprisonment.

imprigiona're |ĕmprējōná'rä| *vt* to imprison.

impri'mere *vt* (*anche fig*) to impress, stamp; (*comunicare: movimento*) to transmit, give.

improba'bile *ag* improbable, unlikely.

im'probo, a *ag* (*fatica, lavoro*) hard, laborious.

impron'ta *sf* imprint, impression, sign; (*di piede, mano*) print; (*fig*) mark, stamp; ~ **digitale** fingerprint.

imprope'rio *sm* insult.

improponi'bile *ag* which cannot be proposed *o* suggested.

impro'prio, a *ag* improper; **arma** ~**a** offensive weapon.

improroga'bile *ag* (*termine*) that cannot be extended.

improvvisamen'te *av* suddenly; unexpectedly.

improvvisa're *vt* to improvise; ~**rsi** *vr*: ~**rsi cuoco** to (decide to) act as cook.

improvvisa'ta *sf* (*pleasant*) surprise.

improvvisazio'ne |ĕmprōvvĕzàttsyō'nä| *sf* improvisation; **spirito d'**~ spirit of invention.

improvvi'so, a *ag* (*imprevisto*) unexpected; (*subitaneo*) sudden; **all'**~ unexpectedly; suddenly.

impruden'te *ag* foolish, imprudent; (*osservazione*) unwise.

impruden'za |ĕmprōōden'tsä| *sf* foolishness, imprudence; **è stata un'**~ that was a foolish *o* an imprudent thing to do.

impuden'te *ag* impudent.

impuden'za |ĕmpōōden'tsä| *sf* impudence.

impudici'zia |ĕmpōōdēchēt'tsyä| *sf* immodesty.

impudi'co, a, chi, che *ag* immodest.

impugna're [ēmpōōnyá'rā] *vt* to grasp, grip; (*DIR*) to contest.

impugnatu'ra [ēmpōōnyátōō'rä] *sf* grip, grasp; (*manico*) handle; (: *di spada*) hilt.

impulsività *sf* impulsiveness.

impulsi'vo, a *ag* impulsive.

impul'so *sm* impulse; **dare un ~ alle vendite** to boost sales.

impunemen'te *av* with impunity.

impunità *sf* impunity.

impuni'to, a *ag* unpunished.

impuntar'si *vr* to stop dead, refuse to budge; (*fig*) to be obstinate.

impurità *sf inv* impurity.

impu'ro, a *ag* impure.

imputa're *vt* (*ascrivere*): **~ qc a** to attribute sth to; (*DIR*: *accusare*): **~ qn di** to charge sb with, accuse sb of.

imputa'to, a *smf* (*DIR*) accused, defendant.

imputazio'ne [ēmpōōtáttsyō'nā] *sf* (*DIR*) charge; (*di spese*) allocation.

imputridi're *vi* to rot.

in *prep* (*in* + *il* = **nel**, *in* + *lo* = **nello**, *in* + *l'* = **nell'**, *in* + *la* = **nella**, *in* + *i* = **nei**, *in* + *gli* = **negli**, *in* + *le* = **nelle**) in; (*moto a luogo*) to; (: *dentro*) into; (*mezzo*): **~ autobus/ treno** by bus/train; (*composizione*): **~ marmo** made of marble, marble *cpd*; **essere ~ casa** to be at home; **andare ~ Austria** to go to Austria; **Maria Bianchi ~ Rossi** Maria Rossi née Bianchi; **siamo ~ quattro** there are four of us.

ina'bile *ag*: **~ a** incapable of; (*fisicamente*, *MIL*) unfit for.

inabilità *sf*: **~ (a)** unfitness (for).

inabita'bile *ag* uninhabitable.

inabita'to, a *ag* uninhabited.

inaccessi'bile [ēnáchāssē'bēlā] *ag* (*luogo*) inaccessible; (*persona*) unapproachable; (*mistero*) unfathomable.

inaccetta'bile [ēnáchāttá'bēlā] *ag* unacceptable.

inacerbi're [ēnáchārbē'rā] *vt* to exacerbate; **~rsi** *vr* (*persona*) to become embittered.

inacidi're [ēnáchēdē'rā] *vt* (*persona*, *carattere*) to embitter; **~rsi** *vr* (*latte*) to go sour; (*fig*: *persona*, *carattere*) to become sour, become embittered.

inadat'to, a *ag*: **~ (a)** unsuitable *o* unfit (for).

inadegua'to, a *ag* inadequate.

inadempien'te *ag* defaulting ♦ *smf* defaulter.

inadempien'za [ēnádāmpyen'tsä] *sf*: **~ a un contratto** non-fulfilment of a contract; **dovuto alle ~e dei funzionari** due to negligence on the part of the officials.

inadempimen'to *sm* non-fulfilment.

inafferra'bile *ag* elusive; (*concetto*, *senso*) difficult to grasp.

l'NAIL *sigla m* (= *Istituto Nazionale per l'Assicurazione contro gli Infortuni sul Lavoro*) state body providing sickness benefit in the event of accidents at work.

inala're *vt* to inhale.

inalato're *sm* inhaler.

inalazio'ne [ēnálättsyō'nä] *sf* inhalation.

inalbera're *vt* (*NAUT*) to hoist, raise; **~rsi** *vr* (*fig*) to flare up, fly off the handle.

inaltera'bile *ag* unchangeable; (*colore*) fast, permanent; (*affetto*) constant.

inaltera'to, a *ag* unchanged.

inamida're *vt* to starch.

inamida'to, a *ag* starched.

inammissi'bile *ag* inadmissible.

inanima'to, a *ag* inanimate; (*senza vita*: *corpo*) lifeless.

inappaga'bile *ag* insatiable.

inappella'bile *ag* (*decisione*) final, irrevocable; (*DIR*) final, not open to appeal.

inappeten'za [ēnáppäten'tsä] *sf* (*MED*) lack of appetite.

inappunta'bile *ag* irreproachable, flawless.

inarca're *vt* (*schiena*) to arch; (*sopracciglia*) to raise; **~rsi** *vr* to arch.

inaridimen'to *sm* (*anche fig*) drying up.

inaridi're *vt* to make arid, dry up ♦ *vi* (*anche*: **~rsi**) to dry up, become arid.

inarresta'bile *ag* (*processo*) irreversible; (*emorragia*) that cannot be stemmed; (*corsa del tempo*) relentless.

inascolta'to, a *ag* unheeded, unheard.

inaspettatamen'te *av* unexpectedly.

inaspetta'to, a *ag* unexpected.

inaspri're *vt* (*disciplina*) to tighten up, make harsher; (*carattere*) to embitter; (*rapporti*) to make worse; **~rsi** *vr* to become harsher; to become bitter; to become worse.

inattacca'bile *ag* (*anche fig*) unassailable; (*alibi*) cast-iron.

inattendi'bile *ag* unreliable.

inatte'so, a *ag* unexpected.

inatti'vo, a *ag* inactive, idle; (*CHIM*) inactive.

inattua'bile *ag* impracticable.

inaudi'to, a *ag* unheard of.

inaugura'le *ag* inaugural.

inaugura're *vt* to inaugurate, open; (*monumento*) to unveil.

inaugurazio'ne [ēnáōōgōōráttsyō'nä] *sf* inauguration; unveiling.

inavvedu'to, a *ag* careless, inadvertent.

inavverten'za [ēnávvärten'tsä] *sf* carelessness, inadvertence.

inavvertitamen'te *av* inadvertently, unintentionally.

inavvicina'bile [ēnávvēchēná'bēlā] *ag* unapproachable.

In'ca *ag inv*, *smf inv* Inca.

incaglia're [ēnkályá'rā] *vi* (*NAUT*: *anche*: **~rsi**) to run aground.

incalcola'bile *ag* incalculable.

incalli'to, a *ag* calloused; (*fig*) hardened, inveterate; (: *insensibile*) hard.

incalzan'te |ĕnkáltsàn'tā| *ag* urgent, insistent; (*crisi*) imminent.

incalza're |ĕnkáltsà'rā| *vt* to follow *o* pursue closely; (*fig*) to press ♦ *vi* (*urgere*) to be pressing; (*essere imminente*) to be imminent.

incamera're *vt* (*DIR*) to expropriate.

incammina're *vt* (*fig: avviare*) to start up; ~**rsi** *vr* to set off.

incanala're *vt* (*anche fig*) to channel; ~**rsi** *vr* (*folla*): ~**rsi verso** to converge on.

incancrenir'si *vr* to become gangrenous.

incandescen'te |ĕnkándāshcn'tā| *ag* incandescent, white-hot.

incanta're *vt* to enchant, bewitch; ~**rsi** *vr* (*rimanere intontito*) to be spellbound; to be in a daze; (*meccanismo: bloccarsi*) to jam.

incantato're, tri'ce *ag* enchanting, bewitching ♦ *sm/f* enchanter/enchantress.

incante'simo *sm* spell, charm.

incante'vole *ag* charming, enchanting.

incan'to *sm* spell, charm, enchantment; (*asta*) auction; **come per ~** as if by magic; **ti sta d'~!** (*vestito etc*) it really suits you!; **mettere all'~** to put up for auction.

incanuti're *vi* to go white.

incapa'ce |ĕnkápá'chā| *ag* incapable.

incapacità |ĕnkápáchĕtá'| *sf* inability; (*DIR*) incapacity; ~ **d'intendere e di volere** diminished responsibility.

incaponir'si *vr* to be stubborn, be determined.

incappa're *vi*: ~ **in qc/qn** (*anche fig*) to run into sth/sb.

incappuccia're |ĕnkáppōōchá'rā| *vt* to put a hood on; ~**rsi** *vr* (*persona*) to put on a hood.

incapricciar'si |ĕnkáprĕchár'sĕ| *vr*: ~ **di** to take a fancy to *o* for.

incapsula're *vt* (*dente*) to crown.

incarcera're |ĕnkárchárá'rā| *vt* to imprison.

incarica're *vt*: ~ **qn di fare** to give sb the responsibility of doing; ~**rsi** *vr*: ~**rsi di** to take care *o* charge of.

incarica'to, a *ag*: ~ **(di)** in charge (of), responsible (for) ♦ *sm/f* delegate, representative; **docente ~** (*di università*) teacher (*US*) *o* lecturer (*Brit*) without tenure; ~ **d'affari** (*POL*) chargé d'affaires.

inca'rico, chi *sm* task, job; (*INS*) temporary post.

incarna're *vt* to embody; ~**rsi** *vr* to be embodied; (*REL*) to become incarnate.

incarnazio'ne |ĕnkárnàttsyō'nā| *sf* incarnation; (*fig*) embodiment.

incartamen'to *sm* dossier, file.

incartapecori'to, a *ag* (*pelle*) wrinkled.

incarta're *vt* to wrap (in paper).

incasella're *vt* (*posta*) to sort; (*fig: nozioni*) to pigeonhole.

incassa're *vt* (*merce*) to pack (in cases); (*gemma: incastonare*) to set; (*ECON: riscuotere*) to collect; (*PUGILATO: colpi*) to take, stand up to.

incas'so *sm* cashing, encashment; (*introito*) takings *pl*.

incastona're *vt* to set.

incastonatu'ra *sf* setting.

incastra're *vt* to fit in, insert; (*fig: intrappolare*) to catch; ~**rsi** *vr* (*combaciare*) to fit together; (*restare bloccato*) to become stuck.

incas'tro *sm* slot, groove; (*punto di unione*) joint; **gioco a ~** interlocking puzzle.

incatena're *vt* to chain up.

incatrama're *vt* to tar.

incattivi're *vt* to make wicked; ~**rsi** *vr* to turn nasty.

inca'uto, a *ag* imprudent, rash.

incava're *vt* to hollow out.

incava'to, a *ag* hollow; (*occhi*) sunken.

inca'vo *sm* hollow; (*solco*) groove.

incavolar'si *vr* (*fam*) to lose one's temper, get annoyed.

incazzar'si |ĕnkáttsár'sĕ| *vr* (*fam!*) to get steamed up.

ince'dere |ĕnchc'dārā| *vi* (*poetico*) to advance solemnly ♦ *sm* solemn gait.

incendia're |ĕnchāndyà'rā| *vt* to set fire to; ~**rsi** *vr* to catch fire, burst into flames.

incendia'rio, a |ĕnchāndyà'ryō| *ag* incendiary ♦ *sm/f* arsonist.

incen'dio |ĕnchen'dyō| *sm* fire.

inceneri're |ĕnchānārē'rā| *vt* to burn to ashes, incinerate; (*cadavere*) to cremate; ~**rsi** *vr* to be burnt to ashes.

incenerito're |ĕnchānārētō'rā| *sm* incinerator.

incen'so |ĕnchen'sō| *sm* incense.

incensura'to, a |ĕnchānsōōrá'tō| *ag* (*DIR*): **essere ~** to have a clean record.

incentiva're |ĕnchāntĕvá'rā| *vt* (*produzione, vendite*) to boost; (*persona*) to motivate.

incenti'vo |ĕnchāntĕ'vō| *sm* incentive.

incentrar'si |ĕnchāntrár'sĕ| *vr*: ~ **su** (*fig*) to center (*US*) *o* centre (*Brit*) on.

inceppa're |ĕnchāppá'rā| *vt* to obstruct, hamper; ~**rsi** *vr* to jam.

incera'ta |ĕnchārá'tá| *sf* (*tela*) tarpaulin; (*impermeabile*) oilskins *pl*.

incertez'za |ĕnchārtāt'tsá| *sf* uncertainty.

incer'to, a |ĕncher'tō| *ag* uncertain; (*irresoluto*) undecided, hesitating ♦ *sm* uncertainty; **gli ~i del mestiere** the risks of the job.

incespica're |ĕnchāspēká'rā| *vi*: ~ **(in qc)** to trip (over sth).

incessan'te |ĕnchāssán'tā| *ag* incessant.

ince'sto |ĕnche'stō| *sm* incest.

incet'ta |ĕnchet'tá| *sf* buying up; **fare ~ di qc** to buy up sth.

inchie'sta |ĕnkye'stá| *sf* investigation, inquiry.

inchina're [ĕnkĕnà'rā] *vt* to bow; **~rsi** *vr* to bend down; (*per riverenza*) to bow; (*: donna*) to curtsy.

inchi'no [ĕnkĕ'nō] *sm* bow; curtsy.

inchioda're [ĕnkyōdà'rā] *vt* to nail (down); **~ la macchina** (*AUT*) to jam on the brakes.

inchios'tro [ĕnkyos'trō] *sm* ink; **~ simpatico** invisible ink.

inciampa're [ĕnchámpá'rā] *vi* to trip, stumble.

inciam'po [ĕnchàm'pō] *sm* obstacle; **essere d'~ a qn** (*fig*) to be in sb's way.

incidenta'le [ĕnchĕdántá'lā] *ag* incidental.

incidentalmen'te [ĕnchĕdántálmän'tā] *av* (*per caso*) by chance; (*per inciso*) incidentally, by the way.

inciden'te [ĕnchĕden'tā] *sm* accident; (*episodio*) incident; **e con questo l'~ è chiuso** and that is the end of the matter; **~ d'auto** car accident; **~ diplomatico** diplomatic incident.

inciden'za [ĕnchĕden'tsá] *sf* incidence; **avere una forte ~ su qc** to affect sth greatly.

inci'dere [ĕnchĕ'dārā] *vi* **~ su** to bear upon, affect ♦ *vt* (*tagliare incavando*) to cut into; (*ARTE*) to engrave; to etch; (*canzone*) to record.

incin'ta [ĕnchĕn'tà] *ag f* pregnant.

incipien'te [ĕnchĕpyen'tā] *ag* incipient.

incipria're [ĕnchĕpryá'rā] *vt* to powder.

incir'ca [ĕnchĕr'kà] *av*: **all'~** more or less, very nearly.

inci'si *etc* [ĕnchĕ'zĕ] *vb vedi* **incidere**.

incisio'ne [ĕnchĕzyō'nā] *sf* cut; (*disegno*) engraving; etching; (*registrazione*) recording; (*MED*) incision.

incisi'vo, a [ĕnchĕzĕ'vō] *ag* incisive; (*ANAT*): **(dente) ~** incisor.

inci'so, a [ĕnchĕ'zō] *pp di* **incidere** ♦ *sm*: **per ~** incidentally, by the way.

inciso're [ĕnchĕzō'rā] *sm* (*ARTE*) engraver.

incitamen'to [ĕnchĕtámän'tō] *sm* incitement.

incita're [ĕnchĕtá'rā] *vt* to incite.

incivi'le [ĕnchĕvĕ'lā] *ag* uncivilized; (*villano*) impolite.

incivili're [ĕnchĕvĕlĕ'rā] *vt* to civilize.

inciviltà [ĕnchĕvĕltá'] *sf* (*di popolazione*) barbarism; (*fig: di trattamento*) barbarity; (*: maleducazione*) incivility, rudeness.

incl. *abbr* (= *incluso*) encl.

inclemen'te *ag* (*giudice*, *sentenza*) severe, harsh; (*fig: clima*) harsh; (*: tempo*) inclement.

inclemen'za [ĕnklämen'tsá] *sf* severity; harshness; inclemency.

inclina'bile *ag* (*schienale*) reclinable.

inclina're *vt* to tilt ♦ *vi* (*fig*): **~ a qc/a fare** to incline towards sth/doing; **~ a** to tend towards sth/to do; **~rsi** *vr* (*barca*) to list; (*aereo*) to bank.

inclina'to, a *ag* sloping.

inclinazio'ne [ĕnklĕnáttsyō'nā] *sf* slope; (*fig*) inclination, tendency.

incli'ne *ag*: **~ a** inclined to.

inclu'dere *vt* to include; (*accludere*) to enclose.

inclusio'ne *sf* inclusion.

inclusi'vo, a *ag*: **~ di** inclusive of.

inclu'so, a *pp di* **includere** ♦ *ag* included; enclosed.

incoeren'te *ag* incoherent; (*contraddittorio*) inconsistent.

incoeren'za [ĕnkōáren'tsá] *sf* incoherence; inconsistency.

inco'gnito, a [ĕnkon'yĕtō] *ag* unknown ♦ *sm*: **in ~** incognito ♦ *sf* (*MAT, fig*) unknown quantity.

incolla're *vt* to glue; (*unire con colla*) to stick together; **~ gli occhi addosso a qn** (*fig*) to fix one's eyes on sb.

incollatu'ra *sf* (*IPPICA*): **vincere/perdere di un'~** to win/lose by a head.

incolonna're *vt* to draw up in columns.

incolo're *ag* colorless (*US*), colourless (*Brit*).

incolpa're *vt*: **~ qn di** to charge sb with.

incol'to, a *ag* (*terreno*) uncultivated; (*trascurato: capelli*) neglected; (*persona*) uneducated.

inco'lume *ag* safe and sound, unhurt.

incolumità *sf* safety.

incomben'te *ag* (*pericolo*) imminent, impending.

incomben'za [ĕnkōmben'tsá] *sf* duty, task.

incom'bere *vi* (*sovrastare minacciando*): **~ su** to threaten, hang over.

incomincia're [ĕnkōmĕnchá'rā] *vi, vt* to begin, start.

incomoda're *vt* to trouble, inconvenience; **~rsi** *vr* to put o.s. out.

inco'modo, a *ag* uncomfortable; (*inopportuno*) inconvenient ♦ *sm* inconvenience, bother.

incompati'bile *ag* incompatible.

incompatibilità *sf* incompatibility; **~ di carattere** (mutual) incompatibility.

incompeten'te *ag* incompetent.

incompeten'za [ĕnkōmpäten'tsá] *sf* incompetence.

incompiu'to, a *ag* unfinished, incomplete.

incomple'to, a *ag* incomplete.

incomprensi'bile *ag* incomprehensible.

incomprensio'ne *sf* incomprehension.

incompre'so, a *ag* not understood; misunderstood.

inconcepi'bile [ĕnkōnchápĕ'bĕlā] *ag* inconceivable.

inconcilia'bile [ĕnkōnchĕlyá'bĕlā] *ag* irreconcilable.

inconcluden'te *ag* inconclusive; (*persona*) ineffectual.

incondiziona'to, a [ĕnkōndĕttsyōná'tō] *ag* unconditional.

inconfessa'bile *ag* (*pensiero, peccato*) unmentionable.

inconfondi'bile *ag* unmistakable.

inconfuta'bile *ag* irrefutable.

incongruen'te *ag* inconsistent.

incongruen'za |ēnkōngrōōen'tsà| *sf* inconsistency.

incon'gruo, a *ag* incongruous.

inconsape'vole *ag*: ~ **di** unaware of, ignorant of.

inconsapevolez'za |ēnkōnsápávōlàt'tsà| *sf* ignorance, lack of awareness.

incon'scio, a, sci, sce |ēnkon'shō| *ag* unconscious ♦ *sm* (*PSIC*): **l'**~ the unconscious.

inconsisten'te *ag* (*patrimonio*) insubstantial; (*dubbio*) unfounded; (*ragionamento, prove*) tenuous, flimsy.

inconsisten'za |ēnkōnsēsten'tsà| *sf* insubstantial nature; lack of foundation; flimsiness.

inconsola'bile *ag* inconsolable.

inconsue'to, a *ag* unusual.

inconsul'to, a *ag* rash.

incontenta'bile *ag* (*desiderio, avidità*) insatiable; (*persona: capriccioso*) hard to please, very demanding.

incontesta'bile *ag* incontrovertible, indisputable.

incontinen'za |ēnkōntēnen'tsà| *sf* incontinence.

incontra're *vt* to meet; (*difficoltà*) to meet with; ~**rsi** *vr* to meet.

incontra'rio *av*: **all'**~ (*sottosopra*) upside down; (*alla rovescia*) back to front; (*all'indietro*) backwards; (*nel senso contrario*) the other way round.

incontrasta'bile *ag* incontrovertible, indisputable.

incontrasta'to, a *ag* (*successo, vittoria, verità*) uncontested, undisputed.

incon'tro *av*: ~ **a** (*verso*) towards ♦ *sm* meeting; (*SPORT*) match; meeting; (*fortuito*) encounter; **venire** ~ **a** (*richieste, esigenze*) to comply with; ~ **di calcio** soccer game.

incontrolla'bile *ag* uncontrollable.

inconvenien'te *sm* drawback, snag.

incoraggiamen'to |ēnkōrádjàmàn'tō| *sm* encouragement; **premio d'**~ consolation prize.

incoraggia're |ēnkōrádjà'rà| *vt* to encourage.

incorna're *vt* to gore.

incornicia're |ēnkōrnēchà'rà| *vt* to frame.

incorona're *vt* to crown.

incoronazio'ne |ēnkōrōnáttsyō'nà| *sf* coronation.

incorpora're *vt* to incorporate; (*fig: annettere*) to annex.

incorreggi'bile |ēnkōrrádjē'bēlà| *ag* incorrigible.

incor'rere *vi*: ~ **in** to meet with, run into.

incorrutti'bile *ag* incorruptible.

incor'so, a *pp di* **incorrere**.

incoscien'te |ēnkōshen'tà| *ag* (*inconscio*) unconscious; (*irresponsabile*) reckless, thoughtless.

incoscien'za |ēnkōshen'tsà| *sf* unconsciousness; recklessness, thoughtlessness.

incostan'te *ag* (*studente, impiegato*) inconsistent; (*carattere*) fickle, inconstant; (*rendimento*) sporadic.

incostan'za |ēnkōstán'tsà| *sf* inconstancy, fickleness.

incostituziona'le |ēnkōstētōōttsyōnà'là| *ag* unconstitutional.

incredi'bile *ag* incredible, unbelievable.

incredulità *sf* incredulity.

incre'dulo, a *ag* incredulous, disbelieving.

incrementa're *vt* to increase; (*dar sviluppo a*) to promote.

incremen'to *sm* (*sviluppo*) development; (*aumento numerico*) increase, growth.

increscio'so, a |ēnkráshō'sō| *ag* (*spiacevole*) unpleasant; regrettable.

increspar'si *vr* (*acqua*) to ripple; (*capelli*) to go frizzy; (*pelle, tessuto*) to wrinkle.

incrimina're *vt* (*DIR*) to charge.

incriminazio'ne |ēnkrēmēnáttsyō'nà| *sf* (*atto d'accusa*) indictment, charge.

incrina're *vt* to crack; (*fig: rapporti, amicizia*) to cause to deteriorate; ~**rsi** *vr* to crack; to deteriorate.

incrinatu'ra *sf* crack; (*fig*) rift.

incrocia're |ēnkrōchà'rà| *vt* to cross; (*incontrare*) to meet ♦ *vi* (*NAUT, AER*) to cruise; ~**rsi** *vr* (*strade*) to cross, intersect; (*persone, veicoli*) to pass each other; ~ **le braccia/le gambe** to fold one's arms/cross one's legs.

incrociato're |ēnkrōchátō'rà| *sm* cruiser.

incro'cio |ēnkrō'chō| *sm* (*anche FERR*) crossing; (*di strade*) crossroads.

incrolla'bile *ag* (*fede*) unshakeable, firm.

incrosta're *vt* to encrust; ~**rsi** *vr*: ~**rsi di** to become encrusted with.

incrostazio'ne |ēnkrōstáttsyō'nà| *sf* encrustation; (*di calcare*) scale; (*nelle tubature*) fur (*Brit*), scale.

incruen'to, a *ag* (*battaglia*) without bloodshed, bloodless.

incubatri'ce |ēnkōōbátrē'chà| *sf* incubator.

incubazio'ne |ēnkōōbáttsyō'nà| *sf* incubation.

in'cubo *sm* nightmare.

incu'dine *sf* anvil; **trovarsi** *o* **essere tra l'**~ **e il martello** (*fig*) to be between the devil and the deep blue sea.

inculca're *vt*: ~ **qc in** to inculcate sth into, instill sth into.

incunea're *vt* to wedge.

incura'bile *ag* incurable.

incuran'te *ag*: ~ **(di)** heedless (of), careless (of).

incu'ria *sf* negligence.

incuriosi're *vt* to make curious; ~**rsi** *vr* to be-

come curious.
incursio'ne *sf* raid.
incurva're *vt*, ~**rsi** *vr* to bend, curve.
incus'so, a *pp di* **incutere.**
incustodi'to, a *ag* unguarded, unattended;
  passaggio a livello ~ unmanned level crossing.
incu'tere *vt* to arouse; ~ **timore/rispetto a**
  qn to strike fear into sb/command sb's respect.
in'daco *sm* indigo.
indaffara'to, a *ag* busy.
indaga're *vt* to investigate.
indagato're, tri'ce *ag* (*sguardo*, *domanda*)
  searching; (*mente*) inquiring.
inda'gine [ēndá'jēnā] *sf* investigation, inquiry;
  (*ricerca*) research, study; ~ **di mercato**
  market survey.
indebitamen'te *av* (*immeritatamente*) unde-
  servedly; (*erroneamente*) wrongfully.
indebitar'si *vr* to run o get into debt.
inde'bito, a *ag* undeserved; wrongful.
indebolimen'to *sm* weakening; (*debolezza*)
  weakness.
indeboli're *vt*, *vi* (*anche:* ~**rsi**) to weaken.
indecen'te [ēndāchen'tā] *ag* indecent.
indecen'za [ēndāchen'tsá] *sf* indecency; **è**
  un'~**!** (*vergogna*) it's scandalous!, it's a disgrace!
indecifra'bile [ēndāchēfrá'bēlā] *ag* indecipherable.
indecisio'ne [ēndāchēzyō'nā] *sf* indecisive-
  ness; indecision.
indeci'so, a [ēndāchē'zō] *ag* indecisive; (*irre-
  soluto*) undecided.
indecoro'so, a *ag* (*comportamento*) indeco-
  rous, unseemly.
indefes'so, a *ag* untiring, indefatigable.
indefini'bile *ag* indefinable.
indefini'to, a *ag* (*anche LING*) indefinite; (*impreciso, non determinato*) undefined.
indeforma'bile *ag* crushproof.
inde'gno, a [ēndān'yō] *ag* (*atto*) shameful;
  (*persona*) unworthy.
indele'bile *ag* indelible.
indelicatez'za [ēndālēkátát'tsá] *sf* tactlessness.
indelica'to, a *ag* (*domanda*) indiscreet, tactless.
indemonia'to, a *ag* possessed (by the devil).
inden'ne *ag* unhurt, uninjured.
indennità *sf inv* (*rimborso: di spese*)
  allowance; (*: di perdita*) compensation, indemnity; ~ **di contingenza** cost-of-living
  allowance; ~ **di fine rapporto** severance payment (*on retirement, when laid off, or when
  taking up other employment*); ~ **di trasferta**
  travel expenses *pl*.
indennizza're [ēndānnēddzá'rā] *vt* to
  compensate.
indenniz'zo [ēndānnēd'dzō] *sm* (*somma*)

compensation, indemnity.
inderoga'bile *ag* binding.
indescrivi'bile *ag* indescribable.
indesidera'bile *ag* undesirable.
indesidera'to, a *ag* unwanted.
indeterminatez'za [ēndātārmēnátát'tsá] *sf*
  vagueness.
indeterminati'vo, a *ag* (*LING*) indefinite.
indetermina'to, a *ag* indefinite, indeterminate.
indet'to, a *pp di* **indire.**
In'dia *sf*: **l'**~ India; **le** ~**e occidentali** the
  West Indies.
india'no, a *ag* Indian ♦ *sm/f* Indian; **l'Oceano**
  I~ the Indian Ocean.
indiavola'to, a *ag* possessed (by the devil);
  (*vivace, violento*) wild.
indica're *vt* (*mostrare*) to show, indicate; (*:
  col dito*) to point to, point out; (*consigliare*)
  to suggest, recommend.
indicati'vo, a *ag* indicative ♦ *sm* (*LING*) indicative (mood).
indica'to, a *ag* (*consigliato*) advisable;
  (*adatto*): ~ **per** suitable for, appropriate for.
indicato're, tri'ce *ag* indicating ♦ *sm* (*elenco*)
  guide; directory; (*TECN*) gauge; indicator;
  cartello ~ sign; ~ **della benzina** fuel gauge;
  ~ **di velocità** (*AUT*) speedometer; (*AER*) air-
  speed indicator.
indicazio'ne [ēndēkáttsyō'nā] *sf* indication;
  (*informazione*) piece of information; ~**i per**
  l'uso instructions for use.
in'dice [ēn'dēchā] *sm* (*ANAT: dito*) index
  finger, forefinger; (*lancetta*) needle, pointer;
  (*fig: indizio*) sign; (*TECN, MAT, nei libri*) index; ~ **azionario** share index; ~ **di gradimento** (*RADIO, TV*) popularity rating; ~ **dei**
  prezzi al consumo ≈ retail price index.
indicherò *etc* [ēndēkáro'] *vb vedi* **indicare.**
indici'bile [ēndēchē'bēlā] *ag* inexpressible.
indicizza're [ēndēchēddzá'rā] *vt*: ~ **al costo**
  della vita to index (*US*), index-link (*Brit*).
indicizza'to, a [ēndēchēddzá'tō] *ag* (*polizza,
  salario etc*) indexed (*US*), index-linked (*Brit*).
indicizzazio'ne [ēndēchēddzáttsyō'nā] *sf* index-
  ing.
indietreggia're [ēndyātrádjá'rā] *vi* to draw
  back, retreat.
indie'tro *av* back; (*guardare*) behind, back;
  (*andare, cadere: anche:* **all'**~) backwards;
  rimanere ~ to be left behind; **essere** ~ (*col
  lavoro*) to be behind; (*orologio*) to be slow;
  rimandare qc ~ to send sth back; **non vado**
  né avanti né ~ (*fig*) I'm not getting anywhere, I'm getting nowhere.
indife'so, a *ag* (*città, confine*) undefended;
  (*persona*) defenseless (*US*), defenceless
  (*Brit*), helpless.
indifferen'te *ag* indifferent ♦ *sm*: **fare l'**~ to
  pretend to be indifferent, be o act casual;

(fingere di non vedere o sentire) to pretend not to notice.

indifferen'za |ĕndĕffãren'tsà| *sf* indifference.

indi'geno, a |ĕndē'jãnō| *ag* indigenous, native ♦ *sm/f* native.

indigen'te |ĕndējen'tã| *ag* poverty-stricken, destitute.

indigen'za |ĕndējen'tsà| *sf* extreme poverty.

indigestio'ne |ĕndējãstyō'nã| *sf* indigestion.

indige'sto, a |ĕndēje'stō| *ag* indigestible.

indigna're |ĕndēnyá'rã| *vt* to fill with indignation; **~rsi** *vr* to be (*o* get) indignant.

indignazio'ne |ĕndēnyãttsyō'nã| *sf* indignation.

indimentica'bile *ag* unforgettable.

in'dio, a *ag, sm/f* (South American) Indian.

indipenden'te *ag* independent.

indipendentemen'te *av* independently; **~ dal fatto che gli piaccia o meno, verrà!** he's coming, whether he likes it or not!

indipenden'za |ĕndēpãnden'tsà| *sf* independence.

indi're *vt* (*concorso*) to announce; (*elezioni*) to call.

indiret'to, a *ag* indirect.

indirizza're |ĕndērĕttsà'rã| *vt* (*dirigere*) to direct; (*mandare*) to send; (*lettera*) to address; **~ la parola a qn** to address sb.

indirizza'rio |ĕndērĕttsà'ryō| *sm* mailing list.

indiriz'zo |ĕndērĕt'tsō| *sm* address; (*direzione*) direction; (*avvio*) trend, course; **~ assoluto** (*INFORM*) absolute address.

indiscipli'na |ĕndĕshĕplē'nà| *sf* indiscipline.

indisciplina'to, a |ĕndĕshĕplēnà'tō| *ag* undisciplined, unruly.

indiscre'to, a *ag* indiscreet.

indiscrezio'ne |ĕndĕskrãttsyō'nã| *sf* indiscretion.

indiscrimina'to, a *ag* indiscriminate.

indiscus'so, a *ag* unquestioned.

indiscuti'bile *ag* indisputable, unquestionable.

indispensa'bile *ag* indispensable, essential.

indispetti're *vt* to irritate, annoy ♦ *vi* (*anche*: **~rsi**) to get irritated *o* annoyed.

indisponen'te *ag* irritating, annoying.

indispor're *vt* to antagonize.

indisposizio'ne |ĕndĕspōzĕttsyō'nã| *sf* (slight) indisposition.

indispo'sto, a *pp di* **indisporre** ♦ *ag* indisposed, unwell.

indissolu'bile *ag* indissoluble.

indistintamen'te *av* (*senza distinzioni*) indiscriminately, without exception; (*in modo indefinito: vedere, sentire*) vaguely, faintly.

indistin'to, a *ag* indistinct.

indistrutti'bile *ag* indestructible.

indi'via *sf* endive.

individua'le *ag* individual.

individuali'smo *sm* individualism.

individuali'sta, i, e *sm/f* individualist.

individualità *sf* individuality.

individualmen'te *av* individually.

individua're *vt* (*dar forma distinta a*) to characterize; (*determinare*) to locate; (*riconoscere*) to single out.

indivi'duo *sm* individual.

indivisi'bile *ag* indivisible; **quei due sono ~i** (*fig*) those two are inseparable.

indivi'so, a *ag* undivided.

indizia're |ĕndĕttsyà'rã| *vt*: **~ qn di qc** to cast suspicion on sb for sth.

indizia'to, a |ĕndĕttsyà'tō| *ag* suspected ♦ *sm/f* suspect.

indi'zio |ĕndĕt'tsyō| *sm* (*segno*) sign, indication; (*POLIZIA*) clue; (*DIR*) piece of evidence.

Indoci'na |ĕndōchē'nà| *sf*: **l'~** Indochina.

in'dole *sf* nature, character.

indolen'te *ag* indolent.

indolen'za |ĕndōlen'tsà| *sf* indolence.

indolenzi're |ĕndōlãntsē'rã| *vt* (*gambe, braccia etc*) to make stiff, cause to ache; (: *intorpidire*) to numb; **~rsi** *vr* to become stiff; to go numb.

indolenzi'to, a |ĕndōlãntsē'tō| *ag* stiff, aching; (*intorpidito*) numb.

indolo're *ag* painless.

indoma'ni *sm*: **l'~** the next day, the following day.

Indone'sia *sf*: **l'~** Indonesia.

indonesia'no, a *ag, sm/f, sm* Indonesian.

indora're *vt* (*rivestire in oro*) to gild; (*CUC*) to dip in egg yolk; **~ la pillola** (*fig*) to sugar the pill.

indossa're *vt* (*mettere indosso*) to put on; (*avere indosso*) to have on.

indossato're, tri'ce *sm/f* model.

indot'to, a *pp di* **indurre**.

indottrina're *vt* to indoctrinate.

indovina're *vt* (*scoprire*) to guess; (*immaginare*) to imagine, guess; (*il futuro*) to foretell; **tirare a ~** to make a shot in the dark.

indovina'to, a *ag* successful; (*scelta*) inspired.

indovinel'lo *sm* riddle.

indovi'no, a *sm/f* fortuneteller.

indù *ag, sm/f* Hindu.

indubbiamen'te *av* undoubtedly.

indub'bio, a *ag* certain, undoubted.

indu'co *etc vb vedi* **indurre**.

indugia're |ĕndōōjà'rã| *vi* to take one's time, delay.

indu'gio |ĕndōō'jō| *sm* (*ritardo*) delay; **senza ~** without delay.

indulgen'te |ĕndōōljen'tã| *ag* indulgent; (*giudice*) lenient.

indulgen'za |ĕndōōljen'tsà| *sf* indulgence; leniency.

indul'gere |ĕndōōl'jãrã| *vi*: **~ a** (*accondiscendere*) to comply with; (*abbandonarsi*) to indulge in.

indul'to, a *pp di* **indulgere** ♦ *sm* (*DIR*) pardon.

indumen'to *sm* article of clothing, garment; ~**i** *smpl* (*vestiti*) clothes; ~**i intimi** underwear *sg*.

indurimen'to *sm* hardening.

induri're *vt* to harden ♦ *vi* (*anche:* ~**rsi**) to harden, become hard.

indur're *vt*: ~ **qn a fare qc** to induce *o* persuade sb to do sth; ~ **qn in errore** to mislead sb; ~ **in tentazione** to lead into temptation.

indus'si *etc vb vedi* **indurre**.

indus'tria *sf* industry; **la piccola/grande** ~ small/big business.

industria'le *ag* industrial ♦ *sm* industrialist.

industrializza're |ĕndōōstryálĕddzá'rä| *vt* to industrialize.

industrializzazio'ne |ĕndōōstryálĕddzáttsyō'nä| *sf* industrialization.

industriar'si *vr* to do one's best, try hard.

industrio'so, a *ag* industrious, hard-working.

induzio'ne |ĕndōōttsyō'nä| *sf* induction.

inebeti'to, a *ag* dazed, stunned.

inebria're *vt* (*anche fig*) to intoxicate; ~**rsi** *vr* to become intoxicated.

ineccepi'bile |ĕnáchápĕ'bĕlä| *ag* unexceptionable.

ine'dia *sf* starvation.

ine'dito, a *ag* unpublished.

ineffica'ce |ĕnäffĕká'chä| *ag* ineffective.

ineffica'cia |ĕnäffĕká'chá| *sf* inefficacy, ineffectiveness.

inefficien'te |ĕnäffĕchen'tä| *ag* inefficient.

inefficien'za |ĕnäffĕchen'tsä| *sf* inefficiency.

ineguaglia'bile |ĕnägwályá'bĕlä| *ag* incomparable, matchless.

ineguaglian'za |ĕnägwályán'tsä| *sf* (*sociale*) inequality; (*di superficie, livello*) unevenness.

inegua'le *ag* unequal; (*irregolare*) uneven.

inelutta'bile *ag* inescapable.

ineluttabilità *sf* inescapability.

inenarra'bile *ag* unutterable.

inequivoca'bile *ag* unequivocal.

ineren'te *ag*: ~ **a** concerning, regarding.

iner'me *ag* unarmed, defenseless (*US*), defenceless (*Brit*).

inerpicar'si *vr*: ~ (**su**) to clamber (up).

iner'te *ag* inert; (*inattivo*) indolent, sluggish.

iner'zia |ĕner'tsyä| *sf* inertia; indolence, sluggishness.

inesattez'za |ĕnäzáttät'tsä| *sf* inaccuracy.

inesat'to, a *ag* (*impreciso*) inaccurate, inexact; (*erroneo*) incorrect; (*AMM: non riscosso*) uncollected.

inesauri'bile *ag* inexhaustible.

inesisten'te *ag* non-existent.

inesora'bile *ag* inexorable, relentless.

inesorabilmen'te *av* inexorably.

inesperien'za |ĕnäspáryen'tsä| *sf* inexperience.

inesper'to, a *ag* inexperienced.

inesplica'bile *ag* inexplicable.

inesplora'to, a *ag* unexplored.

inesplo'so, a *ag* unexploded.

inespressi'vo, a *ag* (*viso*) expressionless, inexpressive.

inespres'so, a *ag* unexpressed.

inesprimi'bile *ag* inexpressible.

inespugna'bile |ĕnáspōōnyá'bĕlä| *ag* (*fortezza, torre etc*) impregnable.

inesteti'smo *sm* beauty problem.

inestima'bile *ag* inestimable; (*valore*) incalculable.

inestirpa'bile *ag* ineradicable.

inettitu'dine *sf* ineptitude.

inet'to, a *ag* (*incapace*) inept; (*che non ha attitudine*): ~ (**a**) unsuited (to).

ineva'so, a *ag* (*ordine, corrispondenza*) outstanding.

inevita'bile *ag* inevitable.

inevitabilmen'te *av* inevitably.

ine'zia |ĕnct'tsyä| *sf* trifle, thing of no importance.

infagotta're *vt* to bundle up, wrap up; ~**rsi** *vr* to wrap up.

infalli'bile *ag* infallible.

infallibilità *sf* infallibility.

infaman'te *ag* (*accusa*) defamatory, slanderous.

infama're *vt* to defame.

infa'me *ag* infamous; (*fig: cosa, compito*) awful, dreadful.

infa'mia *sf* infamy.

infanti'le *ag* child *cpd*; childlike; (*adulto, azione*) childish; **letteratura** ~ children's books *pl*.

infan'zia |ĕnfán'tsyä| *sf* childhood; (*bambini*) children *pl*; **prima** ~ babyhood, infancy.

infarina're *vt* to cover with (*o* sprinkle with *o* dip in) flour; ~ **di zucchero** to sprinkle with sugar.

infarinatu'ra *sf* (*fig*) smattering.

infar'to *sm* (*MED*): ~ (**cardiaco**) coronary.

infastidi're *vt* to annoy, irritate; ~**rsi** *vr* to get annoyed *o* irritated.

infatica'bile *ag* tireless, untiring.

infat'ti *cong* as a matter of fact, in fact, actually.

infatuar'si *vr*: ~ **di** *o* **per** to become infatuated with, fall for.

infatuazio'ne |ĕnfátōōáttsyō'nä| *sf* infatuation.

infa'usto, a *ag* unfavorable (*US*), unfavourable (*Brit*).

infecondità *sf* infertility.

infecon'do, a *ag* infertile.

infede'le *ag* unfaithful.

infedeltà *sf* infidelity.

infeli'ce |ĕnfälĕ'chä| *ag* unhappy; (*sfortunato*) unlucky, unfortunate; (*inopportuno*) inopportune, ill-timed; (*mal riuscito: lavoro*) bad, poor.

infelicità |ēnfālēchētá'| *sf* unhappiness.

infeltri're *vi*, ~**rsi** *vr* (*lana*) to become matted.

inferen'za |ēnfārcn'tsá| *sf* inference.

inferio're *ag* lower; (*per intelligenza, qualità*) inferior ♦ *sm/f* inferior; ~ **a** (*numero, quantità*) less *o* smaller than; (*meno buono*) inferior to; ~ **alla media** below average.

inferiorità *sf* inferiority.

inferi're *vt* (*dedurre*) to infer, deduce.

infermeri'a *sf* infirmary; (*di scuola, nave*) sick bay.

infermie're, a *sm/f* nurse.

infermità *sf inv* illness; infirmity; ~ **di mente** mental illness.

infer'mo, a *ag* (*ammalato*) ill; (*debole*) infirm; ~ **di mente** mentally ill.

inferna'le *ag* infernal; (*proposito, complotto*) diabolical; **un tempo** ~ (*fam*) hellish weather.

infer'no *sm* hell; **soffrire le pene dell'**~ (*fig*) to go through hell.

inferoci're |ēnfārōchē'rā| *vt* to make fierce ♦ *vi*, ~**rsi** *vr* to become fierce.

inferria'ta *sf* grating.

infervora're *vt* to arouse enthusiasm in; ~**rsi** *vr* to get excited, get carried away.

infesta're *vt* to infest.

infetta're *vt* to infect; ~**rsi** *vr* to become infected.

infetti'vo, a *ag* infectious.

infet'to, a *ag* infected; (*acque*) polluted, contaminated.

infezio'ne |ēnfāttsyō'nā| *sf* infection.

infiacchi're |ēnfyákkē'rā| *vt* to weaken ♦ *vi* (*anche:* ~**rsi**) to grow weak.

infiamma'bile *ag* inflammable.

infiamma're *vt* to set on fire; (*fig, MED*) to inflame; ~**rsi** *vr* to catch fire; (*MED*) to become inflamed; (*fig*): ~**rsi di** to be fired with.

infiammazio'ne |ēnfyámmáttsyō'nā| *sf* (*MED*) inflammation.

infiasca're *vt* to bottle.

inficia're |ēnfēchà'rā| *vt* (*DIR*: *atto, dichiarazione*) to challenge.

infi'do, a *ag* unreliable, treacherous.

infieri're *vi*: ~ **su** (*fisicamente*) to attack furiously; (*verbalmente*) to rage at; (*epidemia*) to rage over.

infig'gere |ēnfēd'jārā| *vt*: ~ **qc in** to thrust *o* drive sth into.

infila're *vt* (*ago*) to thread; (*mettere: chiave*) to insert; (*: vestito*) to slip *o* put on; (*strada*) to turn into, take; ~**rsi** *vr*: ~**rsi in** to slip into; (*indossare*) to slip on; ~ **un anello al dito** to slip a ring on one's finger; ~ **l'uscio** to slip in; to slip out; ~**rsi la giacca** to put on one's jacket.

infiltrar'si *vr* to penetrate, seep through; (*MIL*) to infiltrate.

infiltra'to, a *sm/f* infiltrator.

infiltrazio'ne |ēnfēltráttsyō'nā| *sf* infiltration.

infilza're |ēnfēltsá'rā| *vt* (*infilare*) to string together; (*trafiggere*) to pierce.

in'fimo, a *ag* lowest; **un albergo di** ~ **ordine** a third-rate hotel.

infi'ne *av* finally; (*insomma*) in short.

infingar'do, a *ag* lazy ♦ *sm/f* slacker.

infinità *sf* infinity; (*in quantità*): **un'**~ **di** an infinite number of.

infinitesima'le *ag* infinitesimal.

infini'to, a *ag* infinite; (*LING*) infinitive ♦ *sm* infinity; (*LING*) infinitive; **all'**~ (*senza fine*) endlessly; (*LING*) in the infinitive.

infinocchia're |ēnfēnōkkyá'rā| *vt* (*fam*) to hoodwink.

infiorescen'za |ēnfyōrāshcn'tsá| *sf* inflorescence.

infirma're *vt* (*DIR*) to invalidate.

infischiar'si |ēnfēskyár'sē| *vr*: ~ **di** not to care about.

infis'so, a *pp di* **infiggere** ♦ *sm* fixture; (*di porta, finestra*) frame.

infitti're *vt, vi* (*anche:* ~**rsi**) to thicken.

inflaziona're |ēnfláttsyōná'rā| *vt* to inflate.

inflazio'ne |ēnfláttsyō'nā| *sf* inflation.

inflazioni'stico, a, ci, che |ēnfláttsyōnē'stēkō| *ag* inflationary.

inflessi'bile *ag* inflexible; (*ferreo*) unyielding.

inflessio'ne *sf* inflexion.

inflig'gere |ēnfēd'jārā| *vt* to inflict.

inflis'si *etc vb vedi* **infliggere**.

inflit'to, a *pp di* **infliggere**.

influen'te *ag* influential.

influen'za |ēnflōōen'tsá| *sf* influence; (*MED*) influenza, flu.

influenza're |ēnflōōāntsá'rā| *vt* to influence, have an influence on.

influi're *vi*: ~ **su** to influence.

influs'so *sm* influence.

INFN *sigla m* = *Istituto Nazionale di Fisica Nucleare*.

infoca'to, a *ag* (*metallo etc*) red-hot; (*sabbia, guance*) burning; (*discorso*) heated, passionate.

infognar'si |ēnfōnyár'sē| *vr* (*fam*) to get into a mess; ~ **in un mare di debiti** to be up to one's *o* the eyes in debt.

infolti're *vt, vi* to thicken.

infonda'to, a *ag* unfounded, groundless.

infon'dere *vt*: ~ **qc in qn** to instill sth in sb; ~ **fiducia in qn** to inspire sb with confidence.

inforca're *vt* to fork (up); (*bicicletta, cavallo*) to get on; (*occhiali*) to put on.

informa'le *ag* informal.

informa're *vt* to inform, tell; ~**rsi** *vr*: ~**rsi (di** *o* **su)** to inquire (about); **tenere informato qn** to keep sb informed.

informa'tico, a, ci, che *ag* (*settore*) computer *cpd* ♦ *sf* computer science.

informati'vo, a *ag* informative; **a titolo** ~ **for** information only.

informatizza're [ēnfōrmátēddzá'rā] *vt* to computerize.

informato're *sm* informer.

informazio'ne [ēnfōrmáttsyō'nā] *sf* piece of information; ~**i** *sfpl* information *sg*; **chiedere un'**~ to ask for (some) information.

infor'me *ag* shapeless.

informicolar'si *vr*, **informicolir'si** *vr*: **mi si è informicolata una gamba** my leg's asleep.

inforna're *vt* to put in the oven.

inforna'ta *sf* (*anche fig*) batch.

infortunar'si *vr* to injure o.s., have an accident.

infortuna'to, a *ag* injured, hurt ♦ *sm/f* injured person.

infortu'nio *sm* accident; ~ **sul lavoro** industrial accident, accident at work.

infortuni'stica *sf* study of (industrial) accidents.

infossar'si *vr* (*terreno*) to sink; (*guance*) to become hollow.

infossa'to, a *ag* hollow; (*occhi*) deep-set; (*: per malattia*) sunken.

infradicia're [ēnfrádēchá'rā] *vt* (*inzuppare*) to soak, drench; (*marcire*) to rot; ~**rsi** *vr* to get soaked, get drenched; to rot.

infran'gere [ēnfrán'jārā] *vt* to smash; (*fig: legge, patti*) to break; ~**rsi** *vr* to smash, break.

infrangi'bile [ēnfránjē'bēlā] *ag* unbreakable.

infran'to, a *pp di* **infrangere** ♦ *ag* broken.

infraros'so, a *ag*, *sm* infrared.

infrasettimana'le *ag* midweek *cpd*.

infrastruttu'ra *sf* infrastructure.

infrazio'ne [ēnfráttsyō'nā] *sf*: ~ **a** breaking of, violation of.

infreddatu'ra *sf* slight cold.

infreddoli'to, a *ag* cold, chilled.

infrequen'te *ag* infrequent, rare.

infrolli're *vi*, ~**rsi** *vr* (*selvaggina*) to become high.

infruttuo'so, a *ag* fruitless.

infuo'ri *av* out; **all'**~ outwards; **all'**~ **di** (*eccetto*) except, with the exception of.

infuria're *vi* to rage; ~**rsi** *vr* to fly into a rage.

infusio'ne *sf* infusion.

infu'so, a *pp di* **infondere** ♦ *ag*: **scienza** ~**a** (*anche ironico*) innate knowledge ♦ *sm* infusion; ~ **di camomilla** camomile tea.

Ing. *abbr* = **ingegnere.**

ingaggia're [ēngádjá'rā] *vt* (*assumere con compenso*) to take on, hire; (*SPORT*) to sign on; (*MIL*) to engage.

ingag'gio [ēngád'jō] *sm* hiring; signing on.

ingagliardi're [ēngályárdē'rā] *vt* to strengthen, invigorate ♦ *vi* (*anche:* ~**rsi**) to grow stronger.

inganna're *vt* to deceive; (*coniuge*) to be unfaithful to; (*fisco*) to cheat; (*eludere*) to dodge, elude; (*fig: tempo*) to while away ♦ *vi* (*apparenza*) to be deceptive; ~**rsi** *vr* to be mistaken, be wrong.

ingannato're, tri'ce *ag* deceptive; (*persona*) deceitful.

inganne'vole *ag* deceptive.

ingan'no *sm* deceit, deception; (*azione*) trick; (*menzogna, frode*) cheat, swindle; (*illusione*) illusion.

ingarbuglia're [ēngárbōōlyá'rā] *vt* to tangle; (*fig*) to confuse, muddle; ~**rsi** *vr* to become confused o muddled.

ingarbugli'ato, a [ēngárbōōlyá'tō] *ag* tangled; confused, muddled.

ingegnar'si [ēnjānyár'sē] *vr* to do one's best, try hard; ~ **per vivere** to live by one's wits; **basta** ~ **un po'** you just need a bit of ingenuity.

ingegne're [ēnjānye'rā] *sm* engineer; ~ **civile/navale** civil/naval engineer.

ingegneri'a [ēnjānyārē'á] *sf* engineering.

inge'gno [ēnjān'yō] *sm* (*intelligenza*) intelligence, brains *pl*; (*capacità creativa*) ingenuity; (*disposizione*) talent.

ingegnosità [ēnjānyōsētá'] *sf* ingenuity.

ingegno'so, a [ēnjānyō'sō] *ag* ingenious, clever.

ingelosi're [ēnjālōsē'rā] *vt* to make jealous ♦ *vi* (*anche:* ~**rsi**) to become jealous.

ingen'te [ēnjen'tā] *ag* huge, enormous.

ingentili're [ēnjāntēlē'rā] *vt* to refine, civilize; ~**rsi** *vr* to become more refined, become more civilized.

ingenuità [ēnjānōōētá'] *sf* ingenuousness.

inge'nuo, a [ēnje'nōō] *ag* ingenuous, naïve.

ingeren'za [ēnjāren'tsá] *sf* interference.

ingeri're [ēnjārē'rā] *vt* to ingest.

ingessa're [ēnjāssá'rā] *vt* (*MED*) to put a cast on.

ingessatu'ra [ēnjāssátōō'rá] *sf* plaster.

Inghilter'ra [ēngēlter'rá] *sf*: **l'**~ England.

inghiotti're [ēngyōttē'rā] *vt* to swallow.

inghip'po [ēngēp'pō] *sm* trick.

ingialli're [ēnjállē'rā] *vi* to go yellow.

ingiganti're [ēnjēgántē'rā] *vt* to enlarge, magnify ♦ *vi* to become gigantic o enormous.

inginocchiar'si [ēnjēnōkkyár'sē] *vr* to kneel (down).

inginocchiato'io [ēnjēnōkkyátō'yō] *sm* priedieu.

ingioiella're [ēnjōyállá'rā] *vt* to bejewel, adorn with jewels.

ingiù [ēnjōō'] *av* down, downwards.

ingiun'gere [ēnjōōn'jārā] *vt*: ~ **a qn di fare qc** to enjoin o order sb to do sth.

ingiun'to, a [ēnjōōn'tō] *pp di* **ingiungere.**

ingiunzio'ne [ēnjōōntsyō'nā] *sf* injunction, command; ~ **di pagamento** final demand.

ingiu'ria [ĕnjōō'ryá] *sf* insult; (*fig: danno*) damage.

ingiuria're [ĕnjōōryá'rä] *vt* to insult, abuse.

ingiurio'so, a [ĕnjōōryō'sō] *ag* insulting, abusive.

ingiustamen'te [ĕnjōōstámän'tä] *av* unjustly.

ingiustifica'bile [ĕnjōōstĕfĕká'bĕlä] *ag* unjustifiable.

ingiustifica'to, a [ĕnjōōstĕfĕká'tō] *ag* unjustified.

ingiusti'zia [ĕnjōōstĕt'tsyá] *sf* injustice.

ingiu'sto, a [ĕnjōō'stō] *ag* unjust, unfair.

ingle'se *ag* English ♦ *sm/f* Englishman/woman ♦ *sm* (*LING*) English; **gli l~i** the English; **andarsene** *o* **filare all'~** to take French leave.

ingobbi're *vi*, **~rsi** *vr* to become stooped.

ingoia're *vt* to gulp (down); (*fig*) to swallow (up); **ha dovuto ~ il rospo** (*fig*) he had to accept the situation.

ingolfa're *vt*, **~rsi** *vr* (*motore*) to flood.

ingolosi're *vt*: **~ qn** to make sb's mouth water; (*fig*) to attract sb ♦ *vi* (*anche:* **~rsi**): **~ (di)** (*anche fig*) to become greedy (for).

ingombran'te *ag* cumbersome.

ingombra're *vt* (*strada*) to block; (*stanza*) to clutter up.

ingom'bro, a *ag*: **~ di** (*strada*) blocked by; (*stanza*) cluttered up with ♦ *sm* obstacle; **essere d'~** to be in the way; **per ragioni di ~** for reasons of space.

ingordi'gia [ĕngōrdĕ'já] *sf*: **~ (di)** greed (for); avidity (for).

ingor'do, a *ag*: **~ di** greedy for; (*fig*) greedy *o* avid for ♦ *sm/f* glutton.

ingorga're *vt* to block; **~rsi** *vr* to be blocked up, be choked up.

ingor'go, ghi *sm* blockage, obstruction; (*anche:* **~ stradale**) traffic jam.

ingozza're [ĕngōttsá'rä] *vt* (*animali*) to fatten; (*fig: persona*) to stuff; **~rsi** *vr*: **~rsi (di)** to stuff o.s. (with).

ingranag'gio [ĕngránád'jō] *sm* (*TECN*) gear; (*di orologio*) mechanism; **gli ~i della burocrazia** the bureaucratic machinery.

ingrana're *vi* to mesh, engage ♦ *vt* to engage; **~ la marcia** to get into gear.

ingrandimen'to *sm* enlargement; extension; magnification; growth; expansion.

ingrandi're *vt* (*anche FOT*) to enlarge; (*estendere*) to extend; (*OTTICA, fig*) to magnify ♦ *vi* (*anche:* **~rsi**) to become larger *o* bigger; (*aumentare*) to grow, increase; (*espandersi*) to expand.

ingrandito're *sm* (*FOT*) enlarger.

ingrassag'gio [ĕngrássád'jō] *sm* greasing.

ingrassa're *vt* to make fat; (*animali*) to fatten; (*AGR: terreno*) to manure; (*lubrificare*) to grease ♦ *vi* (*anche:* **~rsi**) to get fat, put on weight.

ingratitu'dine *sf* ingratitude.

ingra'to, a *ag* ungrateful; (*lavoro*) thankless, unrewarding.

ingrazia're [ĕngráttsyá'rä] *vt*: **~rsi qn** to ingratiate o.s. with sb.

ingredien'te *sm* ingredient.

ingres'so *sm* (*porta*) entrance; (*atrio*) hall; (*l'entrare*) entrance, entry; (*facoltà di entrare*) admission; **"~ libero"** "admission free"; **~ principale** main entrance; **~ di servizio** tradesmen's entrance.

ingrossa're *vt* to increase; (*folla, livello*) to swell ♦ *vi* (*anche:* **~rsi**) to increase; to swell.

ingros'so *av*: **all'~** (*COMM*) wholesale; (*all'incirca*) roughly, about.

ingrugna'to, a [ĕngrōōnyá'tō] *ag* grumpy.

inguaiar'si *vr* to get into trouble.

inguaina're *vt* to sheathe.

ingualci'bile [ĕngwálchĕ'bĕlä] *ag* crease-resistant.

inguari'bile *ag* incurable.

in'guine *sm* (*ANAT*) groin.

ingurgita're [ĕngōōrjĕtá'rä] *vt* to gulp down.

inibi're *vt* to forbid, prohibit; (*PSIC*) to inhibit.

inibi'to, a *ag* inhibited ♦ *sm/f* inhibited person.

inibito'rio, a *ag* (*PSIC*) inhibitory, inhibitive; (*provvedimento, misure*) restrictive.

inibizio'ne [ĕnĕbĕttsyō'nä] *sf* prohibition; inhibition.

inietta're *vt* to inject; **~rsi** *vr*: **~rsi di sangue** (*occhi*) to become bloodshot.

iniezio'ne [ĕnyáttsyō'nä] *sf* injection.

inimica're *vt* to alienate, make hostile; **~rsi** *vr*: **~rsi con qn** to fall out with sb; **si è inimicato gli amici di un tempo** he has alienated his old friends.

inimici'zia [ĕnĕmĕchĕt'tsyá] *sf* animosity.

inimita'bile *ag* inimitable.

inimmagina'bile [ĕnĕmmájĕná'bĕlä] *ag* unimaginable.

ininfiamma'bile *ag* non-flammable.

inintelligi'bile [ĕnĕntállĕjĕ'bĕlä] *ag* unintelligible.

ininterrottamen'te *av* non-stop, continuously.

ininterrot'to, a *ag* (*fila*) unbroken; (*rumore*) uninterrupted.

iniquità *sf inv* iniquity; (*atto*) wicked action.

ini'quo, a *ag* iniquitous.

inizia'le [ĕnĕttsyá'lä] *ag*, *sf* initial.

inizializza're [ĕnĕttsyálĕddzá'rä] *vt* (*INFORM*) to boot.

inizialmen'te [ĕnĕttsyálmän'tä] *av* initially, at first.

inizia're [ĕnĕttsyá'rä] *vi*, *vt* to begin, start; **~ qn a** to initiate sb into; (*pittura etc*) to introduce sb to; **~ a fare qc** to start doing sth.

iniziati'va [ĕnĕttsyátĕ'vá] *sf* initiative; **~ privata** private enterprise.

iniziato're, tri'ce [ĕnĕttsyátō'rä] *sm/f* initiator.

ini'zio [ĕnĕt'tsyō] *sm* beginning; **all'~** at the

beginning, at the start; **dare** ~ **a qc** to start sth, get sth going; **essere agli** ~**i** (*progetto, lavoro etc*) to be in the initial stages.

innaffia're *etc* = **annaffiare** *etc*.

innalza're [ēnnáltsá'rā] *vt* (*sollevare, alzare*) to raise; (*rizzare*) to erect; ~**rsi** *vr* to rise.

innamoramen'to *sm* falling in love.

innamora're *vt* to enchant, charm; ~**rsi** *vr*: ~**rsi (di qn)** to fall in love (with sb).

innamora'to, a *ag* (*che nutre amore*): ~ **(di)** in love (with); (*appassionato*): ~ **di** very fond of ♦ *sm/f* lover; (*anche scherzoso*) sweetheart.

innan'zi [ēnnán'tsē] *av* (*stato in luogo*) in front, ahead; (*moto a luogo*) forward, on; (*tempo: prima*) before ♦ *prep* (*prima*) before: ~ **a** in front of; **d'ora** ~ from now on; **farsi** ~ to step forward; ~ **tempo** ahead of time; ~ **tutto** above all.

inna'to, a *ag* innate.

innatura'le *ag* unnatural.

innega'bile *ag* undeniable.

inneggia're [ēnnādjà'rā] *vi*: ~ **a** to sing hymns to; (*fig*) to sing the praises of.

innervosi're *vt*: ~ **qn** to get on sb's nerves; ~**rsi** *vr* to get irritated *o* upset.

innesca're *vt* to prime.

inne'sco, schi *sm* primer.

innesta're *vt* (*BOT, MED*) to graft; (*TECN*) to engage; (*inserire: presa*) to insert.

inne'sto *sm* graft; grafting *q*; (*TECN*) clutch; (*ELETTR*) connection.

in'no *sm* hymn; ~ **nazionale** national anthem.

innocen'te [ēnnōchen'tā] *ag* innocent.

innocen'za [ēnnōchen'tsà] *sf* innocence.

inno'cuo, a *ag* innocuous, harmless.

innomina'to, a *ag* unnamed.

innova're *vt* to change, make innovations in.

innovati'vo, a *ag* innovative.

innovazio'ne [ēnnōváttsyō'nā] *sf* innovation.

innumere'vole *ag* innumerable.

inocula're *vt* (*MED*) to inoculate.

inodo'ro, a *ag* odorless (*US*), odourless (*Brit*).

inoffensi'vo, a *ag* harmless.

inoltra're *vt* (*AMM*) to pass on, forward; ~**rsi** *vr* (*addentrarsi*) to advance, go forward.

inoltra'to, a *ag*: **a notte** ~**a** late at night; **a primavera** ~**a** late in the spring.

inol'tre *av* besides, moreover.

inol'tro *sm* (*AMM*) forwarding.

inonda're *vt* to flood.

inondazio'ne [ēnōndáttsyō'nā] *sf* flooding *q*; flood.

inopero'so, a *ag* inactive, idle.

inopina'to, a *ag* unexpected.

inopportu'no, a *ag* untimely, ill-timed; (*poco adatto*) inappropriate; (*momento*) inopportune.

inoppugna'bile [ēnōppōōnyá'bēlā] *ag* incontrovertible.

inorga'nico, a, ci, che *ag* inorganic.

inorgogli're [ēnōrgōlyē'rā] *vt* to make proud ♦ *vi* (*anche*: ~**rsi**) to become proud; ~**rsi di qc** to pride o.s. on sth.

inorridi're *vt* to horrify ♦ *vi* to be horrified.

inospita'le *ag* inhospitable.

inosservan'te *ag*: **essere** ~ **di** to fail to comply with.

inosserva'to, a *ag* (*non notato*) unobserved; (*non rispettato*) not observed, not kept; **passare** ~ to go unobserved, escape notice.

inossida'bile *ag* stainless.

INPS *sigla m* (= *Istituto Nazionale Previdenza Sociale*) social security service.

inquadra're *vt* (*foto, immagine*) to frame; (*fig*) to situate, set.

inquadratu'ra *sf* (*CINEMA, FOT: atto*) framing; (: *immagine*) shot; (: *sequenza*) sequence.

inqualifica'bile *ag* unspeakable.

inquietan'te *ag* disturbing, worrying.

inquieta're *vt* (*turbare*) to disturb, worry; ~**rsi** *vr* to worry, become anxious; (*impazientirsi*) to get upset.

inquie'to, a *ag* restless; (*preoccupato*) worried, anxious.

inquietu'dine *sf* anxiety, worry.

inquili'no, a *sm/f* tenant.

inquinamen'to *sm* pollution.

inquina're *vt* to pollute.

inquiren'te *ag* (*DIR*): **magistrato** ~ committing (*US*) *o* examining (*Brit*) magistrate; **commissione** ~ commission of inquiry.

inquisi're *vt, vi* to investigate.

inquisito're, tri'ce *ag* (*sguardo*) inquiring.

inquisizio'ne [ēnkwēzēttsyō'nā] *sf* inquisition.

insabbiamen'to *sm* (*fig*) shelving.

insabbia're *vt* (*fig: pratica*) to shelve; ~**rsi** *vr* (*barca*) to run aground; (*fig: pratica*) to be shelved.

insacca're *vt* (*grano, farina etc*) to bag, put into sacks; (*carne*) to put into sausage skins.

insacca'ti *smpl* (*CUC*) sausages.

insala'ta *sf* salad; (*pianta*) lettuce; ~ **mista** mixed salad.

insalatie'ra *sf* salad bowl.

insalu'bre *ag* unhealthy.

insana'bile *ag* (*piaga*) which cannot be healed; (*situazione*) irremediable; (*odio*) implacable.

insanguina're *vt* to stain with blood.

insa'nia *sf* insanity.

insapona're *vt* to soap; ~**rsi le mani** to soap one's hands.

insapona'ta *sf*: **dare un'**~ **a qc** to give sth a (quick) soaping.

insapori're *vt* to flavor (*US*), flavour (*Brit*); (*con spezie*) to season; ~**rsi** *vr* to acquire flavo(u)r.

insapo'ro, a *ag* tasteless, insipid.

insapu'ta *sf*: **all'~ di qn** without sb knowing.

insazia'bile |ēnsáttsyá'bēlá| *ag* insatiable.

inscatola're *vt* (*frutta, carne*) to can.

inscena're |ēnshāná'rā| *vt* (*TEATRO*) to stage, put on; (*fig*) to stage.

inscindi'bile |ēnshēndē'bēlā| *ag* (*fattori*) inseparable; (*legame*) indissoluble.

insecchi're |ēnsākkē'rā| *vt* (*seccare*) to dry up; (: *piante*) to wither ♦ *vi* to dry up, become dry; to wither.

insediamen'to *sm* (*AMM: in carica, ufficio*) installation; (*villaggio, colonia*) settlement.

insedia're (*AMM*) to install; **~rsi** *vr* (*AMM*) to take up office; (*colonia, profughi etc*) to settle; (*MIL*) to take up positions.

inse'gna |ēnsān'yá| *sf* sign; (*emblema*) sign, emblem; (*bandiera*) flag, banner; **~e** *sfpl* (*decorazioni*) insignia *pl*.

insegnamen'to |ēnsānyámān'tō| *sm* teaching; **trarre ~ da un'esperienza** to learn from an experience, draw a lesson from an experience; **che ti serva da ~** let this be a lesson to you.

insegnan'te |ēnsānyán'tā| *ag* teaching ♦ *sm/f* teacher.

insegna're |ēnsānyá'rā| *vt, vi* to teach; **~ a qn qc** to teach sb sth; **~ a qn a fare qc** to teach sb (how) to do sth; **come lei ben m'insegna** ... (*ironico*) as you will doubtless be aware ....

inseguimen'to *sm* pursuit, chase; **darsi all'~ di qn** to give chase to sb.

insegui're *vt* to pursue, chase.

inseguito're, tri'ce *sm/f* pursuer.

insella're *vt* to saddle.

inselvatichi're |ēnsálvátēkē'rā| *vt* (*persona*) to make unsociable ♦ *vi* (*anche*: **~rsi**) to grow wild; (*persona*) to become unsociable.

inseminazio'ne |ēnsāmēnáttsyō'nā| *sf* insemination.

insenatu'ra *sf* inlet, creek.

insensa'to, a *ag* senseless, stupid.

insensi'bile *ag* (*anche fig*) insensitive.

insensibilità *sf* insensitivity, insensibility.

insepara'bile *ag* inseparable.

insepol'to, a *ag* unburied.

inserimen'to *sm* (*gen*) insertion; **problemi di ~** (*di persona*) adjustment problems.

inseri're *vt* to insert; (*ELETTR*) to connect; (*allegare*) to enclose; **~rsi** *vr* (*fig*): **~rsi in** to become part of; **~ un annuncio sul giornale** to put o place an advertisement in the newspaper.

inser'to *sm* (*pubblicazione*) insert; **~ filmato** (*film*) clip.

inservi'bile *ag* useless.

inservien'te *sm/f* attendant.

inserzio'ne |ēnsārtsyō'nā| *sf* insertion; (*avviso*) advertisement; **fare un'~ sul giornale** to put an advertisement in the newspaper.

inserzioni'sta, i, e |ēnsārtsyōnē'stá| *sm/f* advertiser.

insettici'da, i |ēnsāttēchē'dá| *sm* insecticide.

inset'to *sm* insect.

insicurez'za |ēnsēkōōrát'tsá| *sf* insecurity.

insicu'ro, a *ag* insecure.

insi'dia *sf* snare, trap; (*pericolo*) hidden danger; **tendere un'~ a qn** to lay o set a trap for sb.

insidia're *vt* (*MIL*) to harass; **~ la vita di qn** to make an attempt on sb's life.

insidio'so, a *ag* insidious.

insie'me *av* together; (*contemporaneamente*) at the same time ♦ *prep*: **~ a o con** together with ♦ *sm* whole; (*MAT, servizio, assortimento*) set; (*MODA*) ensemble, outfit; **tutti ~** all together; **tutto ~** all together; (*in una volta*) at one go; **nell'~** on the whole; **d'~** (*veduta etc*) overall.

insi'gne |ēnsēn'yā| *ag* (*persona*) famous, distinguished, eminent; (*città, monumento*) notable.

insignifican'te |ēnsēnyēfēkán'tā| *ag* insignificant.

insigni're |ēnsēnyē'rā| *vt*: **~ qn di** to confer on sb.

insince'ro, a |ēnsēnche'rō| *ag* insincere.

insindaca'bile *ag* unquestionable.

insinuan'te *ag* (*osservazione, sguardo*) insinuating; (*maniere*) ingratiating.

insinua're *vt* (*introdurre*): **~ qc in** to slip o slide sth into; (*fig*) to insinuate, imply; **~rsi** *vr*: **~rsi in** to seep into; (*fig*) to creep into; to worm one's way into.

insinuazio'ne |ēnsēnōōáttsyō'nā| *sf* (*fig*) insinuation.

insi'pido, a *ag* insipid.

insisten'te *ag* insistent; (*pioggia, dolore*) persistent.

insisten'za |ēnsēsten'tsá| *sf* insistence; persistence.

insi'stere *vi*: **~ su qc** to insist on sth; **~ in qc/a fare** (*perseverare*) to persist in sth/in doing.

insisti'to, a *pp di* insistere.

in'sito, a *ag*: **~ (in)** inherent (in).

insoddisfat'to, a *ag* dissatisfied.

insoddisfazio'ne |ēnsōddēsfáttsyō'nā| *sf* dissatisfaction.

insofferen'te *ag* intolerant.

insofferen'za |ēnsōffären'tsá| *sf* impatience.

insolazio'ne |ēnsōláttsyō'nā| *sf* (*MED*) sunstroke.

insolen'te *ag* insolent.

insolenti're *vi* to grow insolent ♦ *vt* to insult, be rude to.

insolen'za |ēnsōlen'tsá| *sf* insolence.

inso'lito, a *ag* unusual, out of the ordinary.

insolu'bile *ag* insoluble.

insolu'to, a *ag* (*non risolto*) unsolved; (*non*

pagato) unpaid, outstanding.
insolven'te *ag* (*DIR*) insolvent.
insolven'za |ēnsōlven'tsá| *sf* (*DIR*) insolvency.
insolvi'bile *ag* insolvent.
insom'ma *av* (*in breve, in conclusione*) in short; (*dunque*) well ♦ *escl* for heaven's sake!
insonda'bile *ag* unfathomable.
inson'ne *ag* sleepless.
inson'nia *sf* insomnia, sleeplessness.
insonnoli'to, a *ag* sleepy, drowsy.
insonorizzazio'ne |ēnsōnōrēddzàttsyō'nã| *sf* soundproofing.
insopporta'bile *ag* unbearable.
insopprimi'bile *ag* insuppressible.
insorgen'za |ēnsōrjen'tsá| *sf* (*di malattia*) onset.
insor'gere |ēnsōr'jārā| *vi* (*ribellarsi*) to rise up, rebel; (*apparire*) to come up, arise.
insormonta'bile *ag* (*ostacolo*) insurmountable, insuperable.
insor'si *etc vb vedi* **insorgere**.
insor'to, a *pp di* **insorgere** ♦ *sm/f* rebel, insurgent.
insospetta'bile *ag* (*al di sopra di ogni sospetto*) above suspicion; (*inatteso*) unsuspected.
insospetta'to, a *ag* unsuspected.
insospetti're *vt* to make suspicious ♦ *vi* (*anche:* ~**rsi**) to become suspicious.
insosteni'bile *ag* (*posizione, teoria*) untenable; (*dolore, situazione*) intolerable, unbearable; **le spese di manutenzione sono** ~**i** the maintenance costs are excessive.
insostitui'bile *ag* (*persona*) irreplaceable; (*aiuto, presenza*) invaluable.
insozza're |ēnsōttsà'rā| *vt* (*pavimento*) to make dirty; (*fig: reputazione, memoria*) to tarnish, sully; ~**rsi** *vr* to get dirty.
inspera'bile *ag*: **la guarigione/salvezza era** ~ there was no hope of a cure/of rescue; **abbiamo ottenuto risultati** ~**i** the results we achieved were far better than we had hoped.
inspera'to, a *ag* unhoped-for.
inspiega'bile *ag* inexplicable.
inspira're *vt* to breathe in, inhale.
insta'bile *ag* (*carico, indole*) unstable; (*tempo*) unsettled; (*equilibrio*) unsteady.
instabilità *sf* instability; (*di tempo*) changeability.
installa're *vt* to install; ~**rsi** *vr* (*sistemarsi*): ~**rsi in** to settle in.
installazio'ne |ēnstāllāttsyō'nã| *sf* installation.
instanca'bile *ag* untiring, indefatigable.
instaura're *vt* to introduce, institute.
instilla're *vt* to instil.
instrada're *vt* = **istradare**.
insù *av* up, upwards; **guardare all'**~ to look up *o* upwards; **naso all'**~ turned-up nose.
insubordinazio'ne |ēnsōōbōrdēnàttsyō'nã| *sf*

insubordination.
insucces'so |ēnsōōches'sō| *sm* failure, flop.
insudicia're |ēnsōōdēchá'rā| *vt* to dirty; ~**rsi** *vr* to get dirty.
insufficien'te |ēnsōōffēchen'tā| *ag* insufficient; (*compito, allievo*) inadequate.
insufficien'za |ēnsōōffēchen'tsá| *sf* insufficiency; inadequacy; (*INS*) fail; ~ **di prove** (*DIR*) lack of evidence.
insula're *ag* insular.
insuli'na *sf* insulin.
insul'so, a *ag* (*sciocco*) inane, silly; (*persona*) dull, insipid.
insulta're *vt* to insult, affront.
insul'to *sm* insult, affront.
insupera'bile *ag* (*ostacolo, difficoltà*) insuperable, insurmountable; (*eccellente: qualità, prodotto*) unbeatable; (*: persona, interpretazione*) unequalled.
insuperbi're *vt* to make proud, make arrogant; ~**rsi** *vr* to become arrogant.
insurrezio'ne |ēnsōōrrāttsyō'nã| *sf* revolt, insurrection.
insussisten'te *ag* non-existent.
intacca're *vt* (*fare tacche*) to cut into; (*corrodere*) to corrode; (*fig: cominciare ad usare: risparmi*) to break into; (*: ledere*) to damage.
intaglia're |ēntālyá'rā| *vt* to carve.
intagliato're, tri'ce |ēntālyátō'rā| *sm/f* engraver.
inta'glio |ēntàl'yō| *sm* carving.
intangi'bile |ēntànjē'bēlā| *ag* (*bene, patrimonio*) untouchable; (*fig: diritto*) inviolable.
intan'to *av* (*nel frattempo*) meanwhile, in the meantime; (*per cominciare*) just to begin with; ~ **che** *cong* while.
intar'sio *sm* inlaying *q*, marquetry *q*; inlay.
intasamen'to *sm* (*ostruzione*) blockage, obstruction; (*AUT: ingorgo*) traffic jam.
intasa're *vt* to choke (up), block (up); (*AUT*) to obstruct, block; ~**rsi** *vr* to become choked *o* blocked.
intasca're *vt* to pocket.
intat'to, a *ag* intact; (*puro*) unsullied.
intavola're *vt* to start, enter into.
integer'rimo, a |ēntājer'rēmō| *ag* honest, upright.
integra'le *ag* complete; (*pane, farina*) wholewheat; **film in versione** ~ uncut version of a film; **calcolo** ~ (*MAT*) integral calculus; **edizione** ~ unabridged edition.
integran'te *ag*: **parte** *f* ~ integral part.
integra're *vt* to complete; (*MAT*) to integrate; ~**rsi** *vr* (*persona*) to become integrated.
integrati'vo, a *ag* (*assegno*) supplementary; (*INS*): **esame** ~ *assessment test given when changing schools*.
integrazio'ne |ēntāgrāttsyō'nã| *sf* integration.
integrità *sf* integrity.

in'tegro, a _ag (intatto, intero)_ complete, whole; _(retto)_ upright.

intelaiatu'ra _sf_ frame; _(fig)_ structure, framework.

intellet'to _sm_ intellect.

intellettua'le _ag, sm/f_ intellectual.

intellettualo'ide _(peg) ag_ pseudo-intellectual ♦ _sm/f_ pseudo-intellectual, would-be intellectual.

intelligen'te |ēntāllējcn'tā| _ag_ intelligent.

intelligen'za |ēntāllējcn'tsá| _sf_ intelligence.

intellighen'zia |ēntāllēgcn'tsyá| _sf_ intelligentsia.

intelligi'bile |ēntāllējē'bēlā| _ag_ intelligible.

intemera'to, a _ag (persona, vita)_ blameless, irreproachable; _(coscienza)_ clear; _(fama)_ unblemished.

intemperan'te _ag_ intemperate, immoderate.

intemperan'za |ēntāmpāràn'tsá| _sf_ intemperance; **~e** _sfpl (eccessi)_ excesses.

intempe'rie _sfpl_ bad weather _sg._

intempesti'vo, a _ag_ untimely.

intenden'te _sm:_ **~ di Finanza** internal _(US)_ o inland _(Brit)_ revenue officer.

intenden'za |ēntāndcn'tsá| _sf:_ **~ di Finanza** internal _(US)_ o inland _(Brit)_ revenue office.

inten'dere _vt (avere intenzione):_ **~ fare qc** to intend _o_ mean to do sth; _(comprendere)_ to understand; _(udire)_ to hear; _(significare)_ to mean; **~rsi** _vr (conoscere):_ **~rsi di** to know a lot about, be a connoisseur of; _(accordarsi)_ to get on (well); **~rsi con qn su qc** to come to an agreement with sb about sth; **intendersela con qn** _(avere una relazione amorosa)_ to have an affair with sb; **mi ha dato a ~ che ...** he led me to believe that ...; **non vuole ~ ragione** he won't listen to reason; **s'intende** naturally!, of course!; **intendiamoci** let's get it quite clear; **ci siamo intesi?** is that clear?, is that understood?

intendimen'to _sm (intelligenza)_ understanding; _(proposito)_ intention.

intendito're, tri'ce _sm/f_ connoisseur, expert; **a buon intenditor poche parole** _(proverbio)_ a word is enough to the wise.

inteneri're _vt (fig)_ to move (to pity); **~rsi** _vr (fig)_ to be moved.

intensifica're _vt,_ **~rsi** _vr_ to intensify.

intensità _sf_ intensity; _(del vento)_ force, strength.

intensi'vo, a _ag_ intensive.

inten'so, a _ag (luce, profumo)_ strong; _(colore)_ intense, deep.

intenta're _vt (DIR):_ **~ causa contro qn** to start _o_ institute proceedings against sb.

intenta'to, a _ag:_ **non lasciare nulla d'~** to leave no stone unturned, try everything.

inten'to, a _ag (teso, assorto):_ **~ (a)** intent (on), absorbed (in) ♦ _sm_ aim, purpose; **fare qc con l'~ di** to do sth with the intention of;

riuscire nell'~ to achieve one's aim.

intenziona'le |ēntāntsyōná'lā| _ag_ intentional; _(DIR: omicidio)_ premeditated; **fallo ~** _(SPORT)_ deliberate foul.

intenziona'to, a |ēntāntsyōná'tō| _ag:_ **essere ~ a fare qc** to intend to do sth, have the intention of doing sth; **ben ~** well-meaning, well-intentioned; **mal ~** ill-intentioned.

intenzio'ne |ēntāntsyō'nā| _sf_ intention; _(DIR)_ intent; **avere ~ di fare qc** to intend to do sth, have the intention of doing sth.

interagi're |ēntārájē'rā| _vi_ to interact.

interamen'te _av_ entirely, completely.

interatti'vo, a _ag_ interactive.

interazio'ne |ēntārāttsyō'nā| _sf_ interaction.

intercala're _sm_ pet phrase, stock phrase ♦ _vt_ to insert.

intercape'dine _sf_ gap, cavity.

interce'dere |ēntārchc'dārā| _vi_ to intercede.

intercessio'ne |ēntārchāssyō'nā| _sf_ intercession.

intercetta're |ēntārchāttā'rā| _vt_ to intercept.

intercettazio'ne |ēntārchāttáttsyō'nā| _sf:_ **~ telefonica** telephone tapping.

interconnet'tere _vt_ to interconnect.

intercor'rere _vi (esserci)_ to exist; _(passare: tempo)_ to elapse.

intercor'so, a _pp di_ **intercorrere.**

interdet'to, a _pp di_ **interdire** ♦ _ag_ forbidden, prohibited; _(sconcertato)_ dumbfounded ♦ _sm (REL)_ interdict; **rimanere ~** to be taken aback.

interdi're _vt_ to forbid, prohibit, ban; _(REL)_ to interdict; _(DIR)_ to deprive of civil rights.

interdizio'ne |ēntārdēttsyō'nā| _sf_ prohibition, ban.

interessamen'to _sm_ interest; _(intervento)_ intervention, good offices _pl._

interessan'te _ag_ interesting; **essere in stato ~** to be expecting (a baby).

interessa're _vt_ to interest; _(concernere)_ to concern, be of interest to; _(far intervenire):_ **~ qn a** to draw sb's attention to ♦ _vi:_ **~ a** to interest, matter to; **~rsi** _vr (mostrare interesse):_ **~rsi a** to take an interest in, be interested in; _(occuparsi):_ **~rsi di** to take care of; **precipitazioni che interessano le regioni settentrionali** rainfall affecting the north; **si è interessato di farmi avere quei biglietti** he took the trouble to get me those tickets.

interessa'to, a _ag (coinvolto)_ interested, involved; _(peg):_ **essere ~** to act out of pure self-interest ♦ _sm/f (coinvolto)_ person concerned; **a tutti gli ~i** to all those concerned, to all interested parties.

interes'se _sm (anche COMM)_ interest; _(tornaconto):_ **fare qc per ~** to do sth out of self-interest; **~ maturato** _(ECON)_ accrued interest; **~ privato in atti di ufficio** _(AMM)_ abuse of public office.

interessen'za [ēntārăssen'tsá] *sf* (*ECON*) profit sharing.

interfac'cia, ce [ēntārfàch'chá] *sf* (*INFORM*) interface; ~ **utente** user interface.

interferen'za [ēntārfären'tsá] *sf* interference.

interferi're *vi* to interfere.

interfo'no *sm* intercom; (*apparecchio*) internal phone.

interiezio'ne [ēntāryăttsyō'nā] *sf* exclamation, interjection.

in'terim *sm inv* (*periodo*) interim, interval; **ministro ad** ~ acting *o* interim minister; (*incarico*) temporary appointment.

interio'ra *sfpl* entrails.

interio're *ag* inner *cpd*; **parte** *f* ~ inside.

interiorità *sf* inner being.

interiorizza're [ēntāryōrēddzà'rā] *vt* to internalize.

interli'nea *sf* (*DATTILOGRAFIA*) spacing; (*TIP*) leading; **doppia** ~ double spacing.

interlocuto're, tri'ce *sm/f* speaker.

interlocuto'rio, a *ag* interlocutory.

interlu'dio *sm* (*MUS*) interlude.

intermedia'rio, a *ag*, *sm/f* intermediary.

intermediazio'ne [ēntārmādyáttsyō'nā] *sf* mediation.

interme'dio, a *ag* intermediate.

intermez'zo [ēntārmed'dzō] *sm* (*intervallo*) interval; (*breve spettacolo*) intermezzo.

intermina'bile *ag* interminable, endless.

intermitten'te *ag* intermittent.

intermitten'za [ēntārmĕtten'tsá] *sf*: **ad** ~ intermittent.

internamen'to *sm* internment; confinement (to a mental hospital).

interna're *vt* (*arrestare*) to intern; (*MED*) to confine to a mental hospital.

interna'to, a *ag* interned; confined (to a mental hospital) ♦ *sm/f* internee; inmate (of a mental hospital) ♦ *sm* (*collegio*) boarding school; (*MED*) period as an intern (*US*) *o* a houseman (*Brit*).

internaziona'le [ēntārnăttsyōná'lā] *ag* international.

interni'sta, i, e *sm/f* specialist in internal medicine.

inter'no, a *ag* (*di dentro*) internal, interior, inner; (*: mare*) inland; (*nazionale*) domestic; (*allievo*) boarding ♦ *sm* inside, interior; (*di paese*) interior; (*fodera*) lining; (*di appartamento*) apartment (number); (*TEL*) extension ♦ *sm/f* (*INS*) boarder; ~**i** *smpl* (*CINEMA*) interior shots; **commissione** ~**a** (*INS*) internal examination board; **"per uso** ~**"** (*MED*) "to be taken internally"; **all'**~ inside; **Ministero degli I**~**i** Ministry of the Interior, ≈ Department of the Interior (*US*), ≈ Home Office (*Brit*); **notizie dall'**~ (*STAMPA*) home news.

inte'ro, a *ag* (*integro, intatto*) whole, entire; (*completo, totale*) complete; (*numero*) whole; (*non ridotto: biglietto*) full.

interpellan'za [ēntārpăllàn'tsá] *sf*: **presentare un'**~ (*POL*) to ask a (parliamentary) question; ~ **parlamentare** interpellation.

interpella're *vt* to consult; (*POL*) to question.

Interpol' *sf* Interpol.

interpor're *vt* (*ostacolo*): ~ **qc a qc** to put sth in the way of sth; (*influenza*) to use; **interporsi** *vr* to intervene; ~ **appello** (*DIR*) to appeal; **interporsi fra** (*mettersi in mezzo*) to come between.

interpo'sto, a *pp di* **interporre**.

interpreta're *vt* (*spiegare, tradurre*) to interpret; (*MUS, TEATRO*) to perform; (*personaggio, sonata*) to play; (*canzone*) to sing.

interpretaria'to *sm* interpreting.

interpretazio'ne [ēntārprātáttsyō'nā] *sf* interpretation.

inter'prete *sm/f* interpreter; (*TEATRO*) actor/actress, performer; (*MUS*) performer; **farsi** ~ **di** to act as a spokesman for.

interpunzio'ne [ēntārpōōntsyō'nā] *sf* punctuation; **segni di** ~ punctuation marks.

interra're *vt* (*seme, pianta*) to plant; (*tubature etc*) to lay underground; (*MIL*: *pezzo d'artiglieria*) to dig in; (*riempire di terra*: *canale*) to fill in.

interroga're *vt* to question; (*INS*) to test.

interrogati'vo, a *ag* (*occhi, sguardo*) questioning, inquiring; (*LING*) interrogative ♦ *sm* question; (*fig*) mystery.

interroga'to'rio, a *ag* interrogatory, questioning ♦ *sm* (*DIR*) questioning *q*.

interrogazio'ne [ēntārrōgáttsyō'nā] *sf* questioning *q*; (*INS*) oral test; (*POL*): ~ **(parlamentare)** question.

interrom'pere *vt* to interrupt; (*studi, trattative*) to break off, interrupt; ~**rsi** *vr* to break off, stop.

interrot'to, a *pp di* **interrompere**.

interrutto're *sm* switch.

interruzio'ne [ēntārrōōttsyō'nā] *sf* (*vedi interrompere*) interruption; break; ~ **di gravidanza** termination of pregnancy.

interseca're *vt*, ~**rsi** *vr* to intersect.

intersti'zio [ēntārstēt'tsyō] *sm* interstice, crack.

interurba'no, a *ag* inter-city; (*TEL*: *chiamata*) long-distance; (*: telefono*) long-distance ♦ *sf* long-distance call, trunk call (*Brit*).

interval'lo *sm* interval; (*spazio*) space, gap; ~ **pubblicitario** (*TV*) commercial break.

interveni're *vi* (*partecipare*): ~ **a** to take part in; (*intromettersi: anche POL*) to intervene; (*MED: operare*) to operate.

interven'to *sm* participation; (*intromissione*) intervention; (*MED*) operation; (*breve discorso*) speech; **fare un** ~ **nel corso di** (*dibattito, programma*) to take part in.

intervenu'to, a *pp di* **intervenire** ♦ *sm*: **gli** ~**i**

intervi'sta *sf* interview.

intervista're *vt* to interview.

intervistato're, tri'ce *sm/f* interviewer.

inte'so, a *pp di* **intendere** ♦ *ag* agreed ♦ *sf* understanding; *(accordo)* agreement, understanding; **resta** ~ **che** ... it is understood that ...; **non darsi per** ~ **di qc** to take no notice of sth; **uno sguardo d'**~**a** a knowing look.

intesta're *vt (lettera)* to address; *(proprietà)*: ~ **a** to register in the name of; ~ **un assegno a qn** to make out a check to sb.

intestata'rio, a *sm/f* holder.

intestazio'ne |ĕntāstáttsyō'nā| *sf* heading; *(su carta da lettere)* letterhead; *(registrazione)* registration.

intestina'le *ag* intestinal.

intesti'no, a *ag (lotte)* internal, civil ♦ *sm* (*ANAT*) intestine.

intiepidi're *vt (riscaldare)* to warm (up); *(raffreddare)* to cool (down); *(fig: amicizia etc)* to cool; ~**rsi** *vr* to warm (up); to cool (down); to cool.

intimamen'te *av* intimately; **sono** ~ **convinto che** ... I'm firmly o deeply convinced that ...; **i due fatti sono** ~ **connessi** the two events are closely connected.

intima're *vt* to order, command; ~ **la resa a qn** (*MIL*) to call upon sb to surrender.

intimazio'ne |ĕntēmàttsyō'nā| *sf* order, command.

intimidato'rio, a *ag* threatening.

intimidazio'ne |ĕntēmēdáttsyō'nā| *sf* intimidation.

intimidi're *vt* to intimidate ♦ *vi (anche:* ~**rsi***)* to grow shy.

intimità *sf* intimacy; privacy; *(familiarità)* familiarity.

in'timo, a *ag* intimate; *(affetti, vita)* private; *(fig: profondo)* inmost ♦ *sm (persona)* intimate o close friend; *(dell'animo)* bottom, depths *pl*; **parti** ~**e** (*ANAT*) private parts; **rapporti** ~**i** *(sessuali)* intimate relations.

intimori're *vt* to frighten; ~**rsi** *vr* to become frightened.

intin'gere |ĕntēn'jārā| *vt* to dip.

intin'golo *sm* sauce; *(pietanza)* stew.

intin'to, a *pp di* **intingere**.

intirizzi're |ĕntērēddzē'rā| *vt* to numb ♦ *vi (anche:* ~**rsi***)* to go numb.

intitola're *vt* to give a title to; *(dedicare)* to dedicate; ~**rsi** *vr (libro, film)* to be called.

intollera'bile *ag* intolerable.

intolleran'te *ag* intolerant.

intolleran'za |ĕntōllārán'tsá| *sf* intolerance.

intonaca're *vt* to plaster.

into'naco, ci o **chi** *sm* plaster.

intona're *vt (canto)* to start to sing; *(armonizzare)* to match; ~**rsi** *vr (colori)* to go together; ~**rsi a** *(carnagione)* to suit; *(abito)*

to go with, match.

intonazio'ne |ĕntōnàttsyō'nā| *sf* intonation.

intonti're *vt* to stun, daze ♦ *vi*, ~**rsi** *vr* to be stunned o dazed.

intonti'to, a *ag* stunned, dazed; ~ **dal sonno** stupid with sleep.

intop'po *sm* stumbling block, obstacle.

intorbida're *vt (liquido)* to make turbid; *(mente)* to cloud; ~ **le acque** *(fig)* to muddy the waters.

intor'no *av* around; ~ **a** *prep (attorno a)* around; *(riguardo, circa)* about.

intorpidi're *vt* to numb; *(fig)* to make sluggish ♦ *vi (anche:* ~**rsi***)* to grow numb; *(fig)* to become sluggish.

intossica're *vt* to poison.

intossicazio'ne |ĕntōssēkáttsyō'nā| *sf* poisoning.

intraduci'bile |ĕntrádōōchē'bēlā| *ag* untranslatable.

intralcia're |ĕntrálchá'rā| *vt* to hamper, hold up.

intral'cio |ĕntrál'chō| *sm* hitch.

intrallazza're |ĕntrállàttsá'rā| *vi* to intrigue, scheme.

intrallaz'zo |ĕntrállát'tsō| *sm (POL)* intrigue, maneuver *(US)*, manoeuvre *(Brit)*; *(traffico losco)* racket.

intramonta'bile *ag* timeless.

intramuscola're *ag* intramuscular.

intransigen'te |ĕntránsējen'tā| *ag* intransigent, uncompromising.

intransigen'za |ĕntránsējen'tsá| *sf* intransigence.

intransiti'vo, a *ag*, *sm* intransitive.

intrappola're *vt* to trap; **rimanere intrappolato** to be trapped; **farsi** ~ to get caught.

intraprenden'te *ag* enterprising, go-ahead; *(con le donne)* forward, bold.

intraprenden'za |ĕntràprándēn'tsá| *sf* audacity, initiative; *(con le donne)* boldness.

intrapren'dere *vt* to undertake; *(carriera)* to embark (up)on.

intrapre'so, a *pp di* **intraprendeɾe**.

intratta'bile *ag* intractable.

intrattene're *vt (divertire)* to entertain; *(chiacchierando)* to engage in conversation; *(rapporti)* to have, maintain; ~**rsi** *vr* to linger; ~**rsi su qc** to dwell on sth.

intrattenimen'to *sm* entertainment.

intravede're *vt* to catch a glimpse of; *(fig)* to foresee.

intreccia're |ĕntráchá'rā| *vt (capelli)* to plait, braid; *(intessere: anche fig)* to weave, interweave, intertwine; ~**rsi** *vr* to intertwine, become interwoven; ~ **le mani** to clasp one's hands; ~ **una relazione amorosa** *(fig)* to begin an affair.

intrec'cio |ĕntrách'chō| *sm (fig: trama)* plot, story.

intre'pido, a *ag* fearless, intrepid.

intrica're *vt* (*fili*) to tangle; (*fig: faccenda*) to complicate; **~rsi** *vr* to become tangled; to become complicated.

intri'co, chi *sm* (*anche fig*) tangle.

intrigan'te *ag* scheming ♦ *sm/f* schemer, intriguer.

intriga're *vi* to scheme.

intri'go, ghi *sm* plot, intrigue.

intrin'seco, a, ci, che *ag* intrinsic.

intri'so, a *ag*: **~ (di)** soaked (in).

intristi're *vi* (*persona: diventare triste*) to grow sad; (*pianta*) to wilt.

introdot'to, a *pp di* **introdurre**.

introdur're *vt* to introduce; (*chiave etc*): **~ qc in** to insert sth into; (*persona: far entrare*) to show in; **introdursi** *vr* (*moda, tecniche*) to be introduced; **introdursi in** (*persona: penetrare*) to enter; (: *entrare furtivamente*) to steal *o* slip into.

introduzio'ne [ĕntrŏdōŏttsyō'nä] *sf* introduction.

intro'ito *sm* income, revenue.

intromes'so, a *pp di* **intromettersi**.

intromet'tersi *vr* to interfere, meddle; (*interporsi*) to intervene.

intromissio'ne *sf* interference, meddling; intervention.

introspezio'ne [ĕntrŏspättsyō'nä] *sf* introspection.

introva'bile *ag* (*persona, oggetto*) who (*o* which) cannot be found; (*libro etc*) unobtainable.

introver'so, a *ag* introverted ♦ *sm/f* introvert.

intrufolar'si *vr*: **~ (in)** (*stanza*) to sneak in(to), slip in(to); (*conversazione*) to butt in (on).

intru'glio [ĕntrōōl'yō] *sm* concoction.

intrusio'ne *sf* intrusion; interference.

intru'so, a *sm/f* intruder.

intui're *vt* to perceive by intuition; (*rendersi conto*) to realize.

intu'ito *sm* intuition; (*perspicacia*) perspicacity.

intuizio'ne [ĕntōōĕttsyō'nä] *sf* intuition.

inturgidi're [ĕntōōrjēdē'rä] *vi*, **~rsi** *vr* to swell.

inumanità *sf inv* inhumanity.

inuma'no, a *ag* inhuman.

inuma're *vt* (*seppellire*) to bury, inter.

inumazio'ne [ĕnōōmättsyō'nä] *sf* burial, interment.

inumidi're *vt* to dampen, moisten; **~rsi** *vr* to become damp *o* wet.

inurbamen'to *sm* urbanization.

inusita'to, a *ag* unusual.

inu'tile *ag* useless; (*superfluo*) pointless, unnecessary; **è stato tutto ~!** it was all in vain!

inutilità *sf* uselessness; pointlessness.

inutilizza'bile [ĕnōōtēlĕddzä'bēlä] *ag* unusable.

inutilmen'te *av* (*senza risultato*) fruitlessly; (*senza utilità, scopo*) unnecessarily, needlessly; **l'ho cercato ~** I looked for him in vain; **ti preoccupi ~** there's nothing for you to worry about, there's no need for you to worry.

invaden'te *ag* (*fig*) intrusive.

invaden'za [ĕnvádĕn'tsä] *sf* intrusiveness.

inva'dere *vt* to invade; (*affollare*) to swarm into, overrun; (*sog: acque*) to flood.

invaditri'ce [ĕnvádĕtrĕ'chä] *ag f vedi* **invasore**.

invaghir'si [ĕnvägĕr'sĕ] *vr*: **~ di** to take a fancy to.

invalica'bile *ag* (*montagna*) impassable.

invalida're *vt* to validate.

invalidità *sf* infirmity; disability; (*DIR*) invalidity.

inva'lido, a *ag* (*inferno*) infirm; (*al lavoro*) disabled; (*DIR: nullo*) invalid ♦ *sm/f* invalid; disabled person; **~ di guerra** disabled exserviceman; **~ del lavoro** industrially disabled person.

inval'so, a *ag* (*diffuso*) established.

inva'no *av* in vain.

invaria'bile *ag* invariable.

invaria'to, a *ag* unchanged.

invasa're *vt* (*pianta*) to pot.

invasa'to, a *ag* possessed (by the devil) ♦ *sm/f* person possessed by the devil; **urlare come un ~** to shout like a madman.

invasio'ne *sf* invasion.

inva'so, a *pp di* **invadere**.

invaso're, invaditri'ce [ĕnvádĕtrĕ'chä] *ag* invading ♦ *sm* invader.

invecchiamen'to [ĕnvĕkkyämän'tō] *sm* growing old; ageing; **questo whisky ha un ~ di 12 anni** this whisky has been aged (*US*) *o* matured (*Brit*) for 12 years.

invecchia're [ĕnvĕkkyä'rä] *vi* (*persona*) to grow old; (*vino, popolazione*) to age; (*moda*) to become dated ♦ *vt* to age; (*far apparire più vecchio*) to make look older; **lo trovo invecchiato** I find he has aged.

inve'ce [ĕnvā'chä] *av* instead; (*al contrario*) on the contrary; **~ di** *prep* instead of.

invei're *vi*: **~ contro** to rail against.

inveleni're *vt* to embitter; **~rsi** *vr* to become bitter.

invendu'to, a *ag* unsold.

inventa're *vt* to invent; (*pericoli, pettegolezzi*) to make up, invent.

inventaria're *vt* to make an inventory of, inventory.

inventa'rio *sm* inventory; (*COMM*) stocktaking *q*.

inventi'vo, a *ag* inventive ♦ *sf* inventiveness.

invento're, tri'ce *sm/f* inventor.

invenzio'ne [ĕnvāntsyō'nä] *sf* invention; (*bugia*) lie, story.

inverecon'dia *sf* shamelessness, immodesty.

inverna'le *ag* winter *cpd*; *(simile all'inverno)* wintry.

inver'no *sm* winter; **d'~** in (the) winter.

inverosi'mile *ag* unlikely ♦ *sm:* **ha dell'~** it's hard to believe, it's incredible.

inversio'ne *sf* inversion; **"divieto d'~"** *(AUT)* "no U-turns".

inver'so, a *ag* opposite; *(MAT)* inverse ♦ *sm* contrary, opposite; **in senso ~** in the opposite direction; **in ordine ~** in reverse order.

invertebra'to, a *ag, sm* invertebrate.

inverti're *vt* to invert; *(disposizione, posti)* to change; *(ruoli)* to exchange; **~ la marcia** *(AUT)* to do a U-turn; **~ la rotta** *(NAUT)* to go about; *(fig)* to do a U-turn.

inverti'to, a *sm/f* homosexual.

investiga're *vt, vi* to investigate.

investigati'vo, a *ag:* **squadra ~a** detective squad.

investigato're, tri'ce *sm/f* investigator, detective.

investigazio'ne [ēnvāstēgáttsyō'nā] *sf* investigation, inquiry.

investimen'to *sm* *(ECON)* investment; *(di veicolo)* crash, collision; *(di pedone)* knocking down.

investi're *vt* *(denaro)* to invest; *(sog: veicolo: pedone)* to hit; *(: altro veicolo)* to crash into; *(apostrofare)* to assail; *(incaricare):* **~ qn di** to invest sb with; **~rsi** *vr* *(fig):* **~rsi di una parte** to enter thoroughly into a role.

investito're, tri'ce *sm/f* driver responsible for an accident.

investitu'ra *sf* investiture.

invetera'to, a *ag* inveterate.

invetti'va *sf* invective.

invia're *vt* to send.

invia'to, a *sm/f* envoy; *(STAMPA)* correspondent.

invi'dia *sf* envy; **fare ~ a qn** to make sb envious.

invidia'bile *ag* enviable.

invidia're *vt:* **~ qn (per qc)** to envy sb (for sth); **~ qc a qn** to envy sb sth; **non aver nulla da ~ a nessuno** to be as good as the next one.

invidio'so, a *ag* envious.

invinci'bile [ēnvēnchē'bēlā] *ag* invincible.

invi'o, vi'i *sm* sending; *(insieme di merci)* consignment.

inviola'bile *ag* inviolable.

inviola'to, a *ag* *(diritto, segreto)* inviolate; *(foresta)* virgin *cpd*; *(montagna, vetta)* unscaled.

inviperi're *vi,* **~rsi** *vr* to become furious, fly into a temper.

inviperi'to, a *ag* furious.

invischi'are [ēnvēskyà'rā] *vt* *(fig):* **~ qn in qc** to involve sb in sth, mix sb up in sth; **~rsi** *vr:* **~rsi (con qn/in qc)** to get mixed up *o* involved (with sb/in sth).

invisi'bile *ag* invisible.

invi'so, a *ag:* **~ a** unpopular with.

invitan'te *ag* *(proposta, odorino)* inviting; *(sorriso)* appealing, attractive.

invita're *vt* to invite; **~ qn a fare** to invite sb to do.

invita'to, a *sm/f* guest.

invi'to *sm* invitation; **dietro ~ del sig. Rossi** at Mr Rossi's invitation.

invoca're *vt* *(chiedere: aiuto, pace)* to cry out for; *(appellarsi: la legge, Dio)* to appeal to, invoke.

invoglia're [ēnvōlyá'rā] *vt:* **~ qn a fare** to tempt sb to do, induce sb to do.

involonta'rio, a *ag* *(errore)* unintentional; *(gesto)* involuntary.

involti'no *sm* *(CUC)* roulade.

invol'to *sm* *(pacco)* parcel; *(fagotto)* bundle.

invo'lucro *sm* cover, wrapping.

involuti'vo, a *ag:* **subire un processo ~** to regress.

involu'to, a *ag* involved, intricate.

involuzio'ne [ēnvōlōōttsyō'nā] *sf* *(di stile)* convolutedness; *(regresso):* **subire un'~** to regress.

invulnera'bile *ag* invulnerable.

inzacchera're [ēntsàkkàrà'rā] *vt* to spatter with mud; **~rsi** *vr* to get muddy.

inzuppa're [ēntsōōppá'rā] *vt* to soak; **~rsi** *vr* to get soaked; **inzuppò i biscotti nel latte** he dipped the biscuits in the milk.

i'o *pronome* I ♦ *sm inv:* **l'~** the ego, the self; **~ stesso(a)** I myself; **sono ~** it's me.

io'dio *sm* iodine.

io'gurt *sm inv* = yoghurt.

io'ne *sm* ion.

lo'nio *sm:* **lo ~, il mar ~** the Ionian (Sea).

i'osa: a ~ *av* in abundance, in great quantity.

I'PAB *sigla fpl* (= *Istituzioni pubbliche di Assistenza e Beneficenza)* charitable institutions.

iper'bole *sf* *(LETTERATURA)* hyperbole; *(MAT)* hyperbola.

iperbo'lico, a, ci, che *ag* *(LETTERATURA, MAT)* hyperbolic(al); *(fig: esagerato)* exaggerated.

ipermerca'to *sm* large supermarket.

ipersensi'bile *ag* *(persona)* hypersensitive; *(FOT: lastra, pellicola)* hypersensitized.

ipertensio'ne *sf* high blood pressure, hypertension.

ipno'si *sf* hypnosis.

ipno'tico, a, ci, che *ag* hypnotic.

ipnoti'smo *sm* hypnotism.

ipnotizza're [ēpnōtēddzà'rā] *vt* to hypnotize.

ipoaller'gico, a, ci, che [ēpōàller'jēkō] *ag* hypoallergenic.

ipocondri'a *sf* hypochondria.

ipocondri'aco, a, ci, che *ag, sm/f* hypochondriac.

ipocrisi'a *sf* hypocrisy.
ipo'crita, i, e *ag* hypocritical ♦ *sm/f* hypocrite.
ipote'ca, che *sf* mortgage.
ipoteca're *vt* to mortgage.
ipo'tesi *sf inv* hypothesis; **facciamo l'~ che ..., ammettiamo per ~ che ...** let's suppose *o* assume that ...; **nella peggiore/migliore delle ~i** at worst/best; **nell'~ che venga** should he come, if he comes; **se per ~ io partissi ...** just supposing I were to leave ....
ipote'tico, a, ci, che *ag* hypothetical.
ipotizza're |ĕpōtĕddzá'rā| *vt:* ~ **che** to form the hypothesis that.
ip'pico, a, ci, che *ag* horse *cpd* ♦ *sf* horse-racing.
ippocasta'no *sm* horse chestnut.
ippo'dromo *sm* racecourse.
ippopo'tamo *sm* hippopotamus.
ip'silon *sf o m inv* (*lettera*) Y, y; (: *dell'alfabeto greco*) upsilon.
IPSO'A *sigla m* (= *Istituto Post-Universitario per lo Studio dell'Organizzazione Aziendale*) postgraduate institute of business administration.
i'ra *sf* anger, wrath.
irache'no, a |ĕràkc'nō| *ag, sm/f* Iraqi.
Iran' *sm:* **l'~** Iran.
irania'no, a *ag, sm/f* Iranian.
Iraq' *sm:* **l'~** Iraq.
IR'CE |ĕr'chā| *sigla m* = *Istituto per le relazioni culturali con l'Estero*.
l'RI *sigla m* (= *Istituto per la Ricostruzione Industriale*) state-controlled industrial investment office.
i'ride *sf* (*arcobaleno*) rainbow; (*ANAT, BOT*) iris.
Irlan'da *sf:* **l'~** Ireland; **l'~ del Nord** Northern Ireland, Ulster; **la Repubblica d'~** Eire, the Republic of Ireland; **il mar d'~** the Irish Sea.
irlande'se *ag* Irish ♦ *sm/f* Irishman/woman; **gli l~i** the Irish.
ironi'a *sf* irony.
iro'nico, a, ci, che *ag* ironic(al).
ironizza're |ĕrōnĕddzà'rā| *vt, vi:* ~ **su** to be ironical about.
iro'so, a *ag* (*sguardo, tono*) angry, wrathful; (*persona*) irascible.
IR'PEF *sigla f vedi* **imposta sul reddito delle persone fisiche**.
irpi'no, a *ag* of (*o* from) Irpinia.
irradia're *vt* to radiate; (*sog: raggi di luce: illuminare*) to shine on ♦ *vi* (*diffondersi: anche:* **~rsi**) to radiate.
irradiazio'ne |ĕrràdyàttsyō'nā| *sf* radiation.
irraggiungi'bile |ĕrràdjōōnjĕ'bēlā| *ag* unreachable; (*fig: meta*) unattainable.
irragione'vole |ĕrràjōnà'vōlā| *ag* (*privo di ragione*) irrational; (*fig: persona, pretese, prezzo*) unreasonable.

irraziona'le |ĕrràttsyōnà'lā| *ag* irrational.
irrea'le *ag* unreal.
irrealizza'bile |ĕrrāàlĕddzà'bēlā| *ag* (*sogno, desiderio*) unattainable, unrealizable; (*progetto*) unworkable, impracticable.
irrealtà *sf* unreality.
irrecupera'bile *ag* (*gen*) irretrievable; (*fig: persona*) irredeemable.
irrecusa'bile *ag* (*offerta*) not to be refused; (*prova*) irrefutable.
irredenti'sta, i, e *ag, sm/f* (*STORIA*) Irredentist.
irrefrena'bile *ag* uncontrollable.
irrefuta'bile *ag* irrefutable.
irregola're *ag* irregular; (*terreno*) uneven.
irregolarità *sf inv* irregularity; unevenness *q*.
irremovi'bile *ag* (*fig*) unshakeable, unyielding.
irrepara'bile *ag* irreparable; (*fig*) inevitable.
irreperi'bile *ag* nowhere to be found.
irreprensi'bile *ag* irreproachable.
irrequie'to, a *ag* restless.
irresisti'bile *ag* irresistible.
irresolu'to, a *ag* irresolute.
irrespira'bile *ag* (*aria*) unbreathable; (*fig: opprimente*) stifling, oppressive; (: *malsano*) unhealthy.
irresponsa'bile *ag* irresponsible.
irrestringi'bile |ĕrràstrĕnjĕ'bēlā| *ag* unshrinkable.
irreversi'bile *ag* irreversible.
irrevoca'bile *ag* irrevocable.
irriconosci'bile |ĕrrĕkōnōshĕ'bēlā| *ag* unrecognizable.
irriduci'bile |ĕrrĕdōōchĕ'bēlā| *ag* irreducible; (*fig*) unshakeable.
irriflessi'vo, a *ag* thoughtless.
irriga're *vt* (*annaffiare*) to irrigate; (*sog: fiume etc*) to flow through.
irrigazio'ne |ĕrrĕgàttsyō'nā| *sf* irrigation.
irrigidimen'to |ĕrrĕjĕdĕmàn'tō| *sm* stiffening; hardening; tightening.
irrigidi're |ĕrrĕjĕdĕ'rā| *vt* to stiffen; (*disciplina*) to tighten; **~rsi** *vr* to stiffen; (*posizione, atteggiamento*) to harden.
irriguardo'so, a *ag* disrespectful.
irri'guo, a *ag* (*terreno*) irrigated; (*acque*) irrigation *cpd*.
irrilevan'te *ag* (*trascurabile*) insignificant.
irrinuncia'bile |ĕrrĕnōōnchà'bēlā| *ag* vital; which cannot be abandoned.
irripeti'bile *ag* unrepeatable.
irrisol'to, a *ag* (*problema*) unresolved.
irriso'rio, a *ag* derisory.
irrispetto'so, a *ag* disrespectful.
irrita'bile *ag* irritable.
irritan'te *ag* (*atteggiamento*) irritating, annoying; (*MED*) irritant.
irrita're *vt* (*mettere di malumore*) to irritate, annoy; (*MED*) to irritate; **~rsi** *vr* (*stizzirsi*)

to become irritated o annoyed; (*MED*) to become irritated.

irritazio'ne |črrētáttsyō'nā| *sf* irritation; annoyance.

irriveren'te *ag* irreverent.

irrobusti're *vt* (*persona*) to make stronger, make more robust; (*muscoli*) to strengthen; ~**rsi** *vr* to become stronger.

irrom'pere *vi*: ~ **in** to burst into.

irrora're *vt* to sprinkle; (*AGR*) to spray.

irrot'to, a *pp di* **irrompere**.

irruen'te *ag* (*fig*) impetuous, violent.

irruen'za |črrōōcn'tsá| *sf* impetuousness; **con** ~ impetuously.

irrup'pi *etc vb vedi* **irrompere**.

irruvidi're *vt* to roughen ♦ *vi* (*anche*: ~**rsi**) to become rough.

irruzio'ne |črrōōttsyō'nā| *sf*: **fare** ~ **in** to burst into; (*sog*: *polizia*) to raid.

irsu'to, a *ag* (*petto*) hairy; (*barba*) bristly.

ir'to, a *ag* bristly; ~ **di** bristling with.

Is. *abbr* (= *isola*) I.

iscris'si *etc vb vedi* **iscrivere**.

iscrit'to, a *pp di* **iscrivere** ♦ *sm/f* member; **gli** ~**i alla gara** the competitors; **per** o **in** ~ in writing.

iscri'vere *vt* to register, enter; (*persona*): ~ **(a)** to register (in), enrol (in); ~**rsi** *vr*: ~**rsi (a)** (*club, partito*) to join; (*università*) to register o enrol (at); (*esame, concorso*) to register o enter (for).

iscrizio'ne |čskrĕttsyō'nā| *sf* (*epigrafe etc*) inscription; (*a scuola, società etc*) enrolment; registration.

I'SEF *sigla m* = *Istituto Superiore di Educazione Fisica*.

Islam' *sm*: **l'**~ Islam.

isla'mico, a, ci, che *ag* Islamic.

Islan'da *sf*: **l'**~ Iceland.

islande'se *ag* Icelandic ♦ *sm/f* Icelander ♦ *sm* (*LING*) Icelandic.

i'sola *sf* island; ~ **pedonale** (*AUT*) mall (*US*), pedestrian precinct (*Brit*).

isolamen'to *sm* isolation; (*TECN*) insulation; **essere in cella di** ~ to be in solitary confinement; ~ **acustico** soundproofing; ~ **termico** thermal insulation.

isola'no, a *ag* island *cpd* ♦ *sm/f* islander.

isolan'te *ag* insulating ♦ *sm* insulator.

isola're *vt* to isolate; (*TECN*) to insulate; (*acusticamente*) to soundproof.

isola'to, a *ag* isolated; insulated ♦ *sm* (*edificio*) block.

isolazioni'smo |čsōláttsyōnč'smō| *sm* isolationism.

iso'topo *sm* isotope.

ispessimen'to *sm* thickening.

ispessi're *vt* to thicken; ~**rsi** *vr* to get thicker, thicken.

ispettora'to *sm* inspectorate.

ispetto're, tri'ce *sm/f* inspector; (*COMM*) supervisor; ~ **di zona** (*COMM*) area supervisor o manager; ~ **di reparto** floor walker (*US*), shop walker (*Brit*).

ispeziona're |čspáttsyōná'rā| *vt* to inspect.

ispezio'ne |čspáttsyō'nā| *sf* inspection.

i'spido, a *ag* bristly, shaggy.

ispira're *vt* to inspire; ~**rsi** *vr*: ~**rsi a** to draw one's inspiration from; (*conformarsi*) to be based on; **l'idea m'ispira** the idea appeals to me.

ispirato're, tri'ce *ag* inspiring ♦ *sm/f* inspirer; (*di ribellione*) instigator.

ispirazio'ne |čspáttsyō'nā| *sf* inspiration; **secondo l'**~ **del momento** according to the mood of the moment.

Israe'le *sm*: **l'**~ Israel.

israelia'no, a *ag, sm/f* Israeli.

israeli'ta, i, e *sm/f* Jew/Jewess; (*STORIA*) Israelite.

israeli'tico, a, ci, che *ag* Jewish.

issa're *vt* to hoist; ~ **l'ancora** to weigh anchor.

I'stanbul *sf* Istanbul.

istanta'neo, a *ag* instantaneous ♦ *sf* (*FOT*) snapshot.

istan'te *sm* instant, moment; **all'**~, **sull'**~ instantly, immediately.

istan'za |čstàn'tsá| *sf* petition, request; **giudice di prima** ~ (*DIR*) judge of the court of first instance; **giudizio di seconda** ~ judgment on appeal; **in ultima** ~ (*fig*) finally; ~ **di divorzio** petition for divorce.

I'STAT *sigla m* = *Istituto Centrale di Statistica*.

I'STEL *sigla f* = *Indagine sull'ascolto delle televisioni in Italia*.

iste'rico, a, ci, che *ag* hysterical.

isterili're *vt* (*terreno*) to render infertile; (*fig*: *fantasia*) to dry up; ~**rsi** *vr* to become infertile; to dry up.

isteri'smo *sm* hysteria.

istiga're *vt* to incite.

istigazio'ne |čstēgáttsyō'nā| *sf* instigation; ~ **a delinquere** (*DIR*) incitement to crime.

istinti'vo, a *ag* instinctive.

istin'to *sm* instinct.

istitui're *vt* (*fondare*) to institute, found; (*porre*: *confronto*) to establish; (*intraprendere*: *inchiesta*) to set up.

istitu'to *sm* institute; (*di università*) department; (*ente, DIR*) institution; ~ **di bellezza** beauty salon; ~ **di credito** bank, banking institution; ~ **tecnico commerciale** ≈ business college; ~ **tecnico industriale statale** ≈ technical college.

istituto're, tri'ce *sm/f* (*fondatore*) founder; (*precettore*) tutor/governess.

istituzio'ne |čstētōōttsyō'nā| *sf* institution; ~**i** *sfpl* (*DIR*) institutes; **lotta alle** ~**i** struggle

against the Establishment.
is'tmo *sm* (*GEO*) isthmus.
istogram'ma, i *sm* histogram.
istrada're *vt* (*fig: persona*): ~ **(a/verso)** to direct (to/towards).
istria'no, a *ag, sm/f* Istrian.
is'trice |ēs'trēchā| *sm* porcupine.
istrio'ne *sm* (*peg*) ham (actor).
istrui're *vt* (*insegnare*) to teach; (*ammaestrare*) to train; (*informare*) to instruct, inform; (*DIR*) to prepare.
istrui'to, a *ag* educated.
istrutti'vo, a *ag* instructive.
istrutto're, tri'ce *sm/f* instructor ♦ *ag*: **giudice** ~ committing (*US*) *o* examining (*Brit*) magistrate.
istrutto'ria *sf* (*DIR*) (preliminary) investigation and hearing; **formalizzare un'~** to proceed to a formal hearing.
istruzio'ne |ēstrōōttsyō'nā| *sf* (*gen*) training; (*INS, cultura*) education; (*direttiva*) instruction; (*DIR*) = **istruttoria; Ministero della Pubblica I~** Ministry of Education; **~i di spedizione** forwarding instructions; **~i per l'uso** instructions (for use).
istupidi're *vt* (*sog: colpo*) to stun, daze; (: *droga, stanchezza*) to stupefy; **~rsi** *vr* to become stupid.
I'SVE *sigla m* (= *Istituto di Studi per lo Sviluppo Economico*) institute for research into economic development.
Ita'lia *sf*: **l'~** Italy.
italia'no, a *ag* Italian ♦ *sm/f* Italian ♦ *sm* (*LING*) Italian; **gli l~i** the Italians.
ITC *sigla m* = **istituto tecnico commerciale.**
i'ter *sm* passage, course; **l'~ burocratico** the bureaucratic process.
itineran'te *ag* wandering, itinerant; **mostra ~** touring exhibition; **spettacolo ~** touring show.
itinera'rio *sm* itinerary.
I'TIS *sigla m* = **istituto tecnico industriale statale.**
itteri'zia |ēttārēt'tsyā| *sf* (*MED*) jaundice.
it'tico, a, ci, che *ag* fish *cpd*; fishing *cpd*.
Iugosla'via *sf* = **Jugoslavia.**
iugosla'vo, a *ag, sm/f* = **jugoslavo, a.**
iu'ta *sf* jute.
I.'V.A. *sigla f vedi* **imposta sul valore aggiunto.**
i'vi *av* (*formale, poetico*) therein; (*nelle citazioni*) ibid.

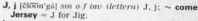

J

J, j |clōōn'gà| *sm o f inv* (*lettera*) J, j; ~ **come Jersey** ≈ J for Jig.
jazz |jàz| *sm* jazz.
jazzi'sta, i |jàddzē'stà| *sm* jazz player.
jeans |jēnz| *smpl* jeans.
jeep |jēp| *sm inv* jeep.
jer'sey |jcr'zē| *sm inv* jersey (cloth).
joc'key |jo'kē| *sm inv* (*CARTE*) jack; (*fantino*) jockey.
jog'ging |jo'gēng| *sm* jogging; **fare ~** to go jogging.
jolly' |jo'lē| *sm inv* joker.
jr. *abbr* (= *junior*) Jr., jr.
judo' |jōōdo'| *sm* judo.
Jugosla'via |yōōgōzlà'vyà| *sf*: **la ~** Yugoslavia.
jugosla'vo, a *ag, sm/f* Yugoslav(ian).
ju'ke box' |jōōk'boks'| *sm inv* jukebox.
ju'ta |yōō'tà| *sf* = **iuta.**

K

K, k |kàp'pà| *sf o m inv* (*lettera*) K, k ♦ *abbr* (= *kilo-, chilo-*) k; (*INFORM*) K; **K come Kursaal** ≈ K for King.
Kampa'la *sf* Kampala.
karaki'ri *sm* harakiri.
karatè |kàràtc'| *sm* karate.
Kas'hmir |kàsh'mēr| *sm*: **il ~** Kashmir.
kayak' |kàyàk'| *sm inv* kayak.
kenia'no, a, kenio'ta, i, e *ag, sm/f* Kenyan.
Ken'ya |kā'nyà| *sm*: **il ~** Kenya.
kerose'ne |kārōzc'nā| *sm* = **cherosene.**
kg *abbr* (= *chilogrammo*) kg.
kibbutz' |kēbbōōts'| *sm inv* kibbutz.
Kilimangia'ro |kēlēmànjà'rō| *sm*: **il ~** Kilimanjaro.
kil'ler |kēl'làr| *sm inv* gunman, hired gun.
ki'lo *etc* = **chilo** *etc*.
kilt |kēlt| *sm inv* kilt.
kimo'no |kēmo'nō| *sm* = **chimono.**
kitsch |kēch| *sm* kitsch.
km *abbr* (= *chilometro*) km.

kmq *abbr* (= *chilometro quadrato*) km².
koa'la |kōá'là| *sm inv* koala (bear).
krap'fen |kràp'fən| *sm inv* doughnut.
Kua'la Lumpur' *sf* Kuala Lumpur.
Kuwa'it |kōōvá'ēt| *sm*: **il ~** Kuwait.
kW *abbr* (= *kilowatt, chilowatt*) kW.
kWh *abbr* (= *kilowattora*) kW/h.

L

L, l |eI'lä| *sf o m inv* (*lettera*) L, l ♦ *abbr* (= *lira*) L; **L come Livorno** ≈ L for Love.
l' *det vedi* **la, lo.**
la *det f* (*dav V* **l'**) the ♦ *pronome* (*dav V* **l'**) (*oggetto: persona*) her; (: *cosa*) it; (: *forma di cortesia*) you ♦ *sm inv* (*MUS*) A; (: *solfeggiando la scala*) la; *vedi anche* **il.**
là *av* there; **di ~** (*da quel luogo*) from there; (*in quel luogo*) in there; (*dall'altra parte*) over there; **di ~ di** beyond; **per di ~** that way; **più in ~** further on; (*tempo*) later on; **~ dentro/sopra/sotto** in/up (*o* on)/under there; **~ per ~** (*sul momento*) there and then; **essere in ~ con gli anni** to be getting on (in years); **essere più di ~ che di qua** to be more dead than alive; **va' ~!** come off it!; **stavolta è andato troppo in ~** this time he's gone too far; *vedi anche* **quello.**
lab'bro *sm* (*pl(f)*: **labbra**: *solo nel senso* ANAT) lip.
la'bile *ag* fleeting, ephemeral.
labirin'to *sm* labyrinth, maze.
laborato'rio *sm* (*di ricerca*) laboratory; (*di arti, mestieri*) workshop; **~ linguistico** language laboratory.
laborio'so, a *ag* (*faticoso*) laborious; (*attivo*) hard-working.
laburi'sta, i, e *ag* Labour *cpd* (*Brit*) ♦ *sm/f* Labour Party member (*Brit*).
lac'ca, che *sf* lacquer; (*per unghie*) nail polish.
lacca're *vt* (*mobili*) to varnish, lacquer.
lac'cio |làch'chō| *sm* noose; (*legaccio, tirante*) lasso; (*di scarpa*) lace; **~ emostatico** (MED) tourniquet.
laceran'te |làchàràn'tä| *ag* (*suono*) piercing, shrill.
lacera're |làchàrà'rä| *vt* to tear to shreds, lacerate; **~rsi** *vr* to tear.
la'cero, a |là'chārō| *ag* (*logoro*) torn, tattered; (MED) lacerated; **ferita ~-contusa** injury with lacerations and bruising.
laco'nico, a, ci, che *ag* laconic, brief.

la'crima *sf* tear; (*goccia*) drop; **in ~e** in tears.
lacrima're *vi* to water.
lacrime'vole *ag* heartrending, pitiful.
lacrimo'geno, a |làkrēmo'jānō| *ag*: **gas ~** tear gas.
lacrimo'so, a *ag* tearful.
lacu'na *sf* (*fig*) gap.
lacus'tre *ag* lake *cpd*.
laddo've *cong* whereas.
la'dro *sm* thief; **al ~!** stop thief!
ladroci'nio |làdrōchē'nyō| *sm* theft, robbery.
ladrun'colo, a *sm/f* petty thief.
laggiù |làdjōō'| *av* down there; (*di là*) over there.
la'gna |làn'yà| *sf* (*fam: persona, cosa*) drag, bore; **fare la ~** to whine, moan.
lagnan'za |lànyàn'tsà| *sf* complaint.
lagnar'si |lànyàr'sē| *vr*: **~ (di)** to complain (about).
la'go, ghi *sm* lake.
La'gos |là'gōs| *sf* Lagos.
la'grima *etc* = **lacrima** *etc.*
lagu'na *sf* lagoon.
laguna're *ag* lagoon *cpd.*
la'ico, a, ci, che *ag* (*apostolato*) lay; (*vita*) secular; (*scuola*) non-denominational ♦ *sm/f* layman/woman ♦ *sm* lay brother.
la'ido, a *ag* filthy, foul; (*fig: osceno*) obscene, filthy.
la'ma *sf* blade ♦ *sm inv* (ZOOL) llama; (REL) lama.
lambicca're *vt* to distil; **~rsi il cervello** to rack one's brains.
lambi're *vt* (*fig: sog: fiamme*) to lick; (: *acqua*) to lap.
lambret'ta ® *sf* scooter.
lamel'la *sf* (*di metallo etc*) thin sheet, thin strip; (*di fungo*) gill.
lamenta're *vt* to lament; **~rsi** *vr* (*emettere lamenti*) to moan, groan; (*rammaricarsi*): **~rsi (di)** to complain (about).
lamente'la *sf* complaining *q.*
lamente'vole *ag* (*voce*) complaining, plaintive; (*stato*) lamentable, pitiful.
lamen'to *sm* moan, groan; (*per la morte di qn*) lament.
lamento'so, a *ag* plaintive.
lamet'ta *sf* razor blade.
lamie'ra *sf* sheet metal.
la'mina *sf* (*lastra sottile*) thin sheet (*o* layer *o* plate); **~ d'oro** gold leaf; gold foil.
lamina're *vt* to laminate.
lamina'to, a *ag* laminated; (*tessuto*) lamé ♦ *sm* laminate.
lam'pada *sf* lamp; **~ a petrolio/a gas** oil/gas lamp; **~ a spirito** blowtorch; **~ a stelo** floor lamp, standard lamp (*Brit*); **~ da tavolo** table lamp.
lampada'rio *sm* chandelier.

lampadi'na *sf* light bulb; ~ **tascabile** flashlight.

lampan'te *ag* (*fig*: *evidente*) crystal clear, evident.

lampa'ra *sf* fishing lamp; (*barca*) boat for fishing by lamplight (*in Mediterranean*).

lampeggia're [lámpādjá'rā] *vi* (*luce*, *fari*) to flash ♦ *vb impers*: **lampeggia** there's lightning.

lampeggiato're [lámpādjátō'rā] *sm* (*AUT*) indicator.

lampio'ne *sm* street light *o* lamp (*Brit*).

lam'po *sm* (*METEOR*) flash of lightning; (*di luce*, *fig*) flash ♦ *ag inv*: **cerniera** ~ zipper (*US*), zip (fastener) (*Brit*); **guerra** ~ blitzkrieg; ~**i** *smpl* (*METEOR*) lightning *q*; **passare come un** ~ to flash past *o* by.

lampo'ne *sm* raspberry.

la'na *sf* wool; ~ **d'acciaio** steel wool; **pura** ~ **vergine** virgin (*US*) *o* pure new (*Brit*) wool; ~ **di vetro** glass wool.

lancet'ta [lánchāt'tá] *sf* (*indice*) pointer, needle; (*di orologio*) hand.

lan'cia, ce [lán'chá] *sf* (*arma*) lance; (: *picca*) spear; (*di pompa antincendio*) nozzle; (*imbarcazione*) launch; **partire** ~ **in resta** (*fig*) to set off ready for battle; **spezzare una** ~ **in favore di qn** (*fig*) to come to sb's defence; ~ **di salvataggio** lifeboat.

lanciabom'be [lánchábōm'bā] *sm inv* (*MIL*) mortar.

lanciafiam'me [láncháfyám'mā] *sm inv* flamethrower.

lanciamis'sili [lánchámēs'sēlē] *ag inv* missile-launching ♦ *sm inv* missile launcher.

lanciaraz'zi [lánchárád'dzē] *ag inv* rocket-launching ♦ *sm inv* rocket launcher.

lancia're [lánchá'rā] *vt* to throw, hurl, fling; (*SPORT*) to throw; (*far partire: automobile*) to get up to full speed; (*bombe*) to drop; (*razzo*, *prodotto*, *moda*) to launch; (*emettere: grido*) to give out; ~**rsi** *vr*: ~**rsi contro/su** to throw *o* hurl *o* fling o.s. against/on; ~**rsi in** (*fig*) to embark on; ~ **un cavallo** to give a horse his head; ~ **il disco** (*SPORT*) to throw the discus; ~ **il peso** (*SPORT*) to put the shot; ~**rsi all'inseguimento di qn** to set off in pursuit of sb; ~**rsi col paracadute** to parachute.

lanciasilu'ri [lánchásēlōō'rē] *sm inv* torpedo tube.

lancia'to, a [lánchá'tō] *ag* (*affermato: attore*, *prodotto*) well-known, famous; (*veicolo*) speeding along, racing along.

lancinan'te [lánchēnán'tā] *ag* (*dolore*) shooting, throbbing; (*grido*) piercing.

lan'cio [lán'chō] *sm* throwing *q*; throw; dropping *q*; drop; launching *q*; launch; ~ **del disco** (*SPORT*) throwing the discus; ~ **del peso** (*SPORT*) putting the shot.

lan'da *sf* (*GEO*) moor.

lan'guido, a *ag* (*fiacco*) languid, weak; (*tenero*, *malinconico*) languishing.

langui're *vi* to languish; (*conversazione*) to flag.

languo're *sm* weakness, languor.

lanie'ro, a *ag* wool *cpd*.

lanifi'cio [lánēfē'chō] *sm* wool (*US*) *o* woollen (*Brit*) mill.

lanoli'na *sf* lanolin(e).

lano'so, a *ag* woolly.

lanter'na *sf* lantern; (*faro*) lighthouse.

lanterni'no *sm*: **cercarsele col** ~ to be asking for trouble.

lanu'gine [lánōō'jēnā] *sf* down.

La'os *sm* Laos.

lapalissia'no, a *ag* self-evident.

La Paz' [lápás'] *sf* La Paz.

lapida're *vt* to stone.

lapida'rio, a *ag* (*fig*) terse.

la'pide *sf* (*di sepolcro*) tombstone; (*commemorativa*) plaque.

lapin' [lápán'] *sm inv* coney.

la'pis *sm inv* pencil.

lap'pone *ag*, *sm/f*, *sm* Lapp.

Lappo'nia *sf*: **la** ~ Lapland.

lap'sus *sm inv* slip.

lar'do *sm* bacon fat, lard.

larghez'za [lárgāt'tsá] *sf* width; breadth; looseness; generosity; ~ **di vedute** broadmindedness.

largi're [lárjē'rā] *vt* to give generously.

lar'go, a, ghi, ghe *ag* wide, broad; (*maniche*) wide; (*abito: troppo ampio*) loose; (*fig*) generous ♦ *sm* width; breadth; (*mare aperto*): **il** ~ the open sea ♦ *sf*: **stare** *o* **tenersi alla** ~**a (da qn/qc)** to keep one's distance (from sb/sth), keep away (from sb/sth); ~ **due metri** two meters wide; ~ **di spalle** broadshouldered; **di** ~**ghe vedute** broad-minded; **in** ~**a misura** to a great *o* large extent; **su** ~**a scala** on a large scale; **di manica** ~**a** generous, open-handed; **al** ~ **di Genova** off the coast of Genoa; **farsi** ~ **tra la folla** to push one's way through the crowd.

la'rice [lá'rēchā] *sm* (*BOT*) larch.

larin'ge [lárēn'jā] *sf* larynx.

laringi'te [lárēnjē'tā] *sf* laryngitis.

laringoia'tra, i, e *sm/f* (*medico*) throat specialist.

lar'va *sf* larva; (*fig*) shadow.

lasa'gne [lázán'yā] *sfpl* lasagna *sg*.

lasciapassa're [láshápássá'rā] *sm inv* pass, permit.

lascia're [láshá'rā] *vt* to leave; (*abbandonare*) to leave, abandon, give up; (*cessare di tenere*) to let go of ♦ *vb ausiliare*: ~ **qn fare qc** to let sb do sth ♦ *vi*: ~ **di fare** (*smettere*) to stop doing; ~**rsi andare/truffare** to let o.s. go/be cheated; ~ **andare** *o* **correre** *o* **perdere**

to let things go their own way; ~ **stare qc/qn** to leave sth/sb alone; ~ **qn erede** to make sb one's heir; ~ **la presa** to lose one's grip; ~ **il segno (su qc)** to leave a mark (on sth); (*fig*) to leave one's mark (on sth); ~ **(molto) a desiderare** to leave much to be desired; **ci ha lasciato la vita** it cost him his life.

la'scito [làsh'shētō] *sm* (*DIR*) legacy.

lasci'via [làshē'vyá] *sf* lust, lasciviousness.

lasci'vo, a [làshē'vō] *ag* lascivious.

la'ser [là'zār] *ag, sm inv*: (**raggio**) ~ laser (beam).

lassati'vo, a *ag, sm* laxative.

lassi'smo *sm* laxity.

las'so *sm*: ~ **di tempo** interval, lapse of time.

lassù *av* up there.

las'tra *sf* (*di pietra*) slab; (*di metallo, FOT*) plate; (*di ghiaccio, vetro*) sheet; (*radiografica*) X-ray (plate).

lastrica're *vt* to pave.

lastrica'to *sm* paving.

las'trico, ci *o* **chi** *sm* paving; **essere sul ~** (*fig*) to be penniless; **gettare qn sul ~** (*fig*) to leave sb destitute.

lastro'ne *sm* (*ALPINISMO*) sheer rock face.

laten'te *ag* latent.

latera'le *ag* lateral, side *cpd*; (*uscita, ingresso etc*) side *cpd* ♦ *sm* (*CALCIO*) half-back.

lateralmen'te *av* sideways.

lateri'zio [làtārēt'tsyō] *sm* (perforated) brick.

latifondi'sta, i, e *sm/f* large agricultural landowner.

latifon'do *sm* large estate.

lati'no, a *ag, sm* Latin.

lati'noameri'cano, a *ag, sm/f* Latin-American.

latitan'te *sm/f* fugitive (from justice).

latitan'za [làtētàn'tsà] *sf*: **darsi alla ~** to go into hiding.

latitu'dine *sf* latitude.

la'to, a *ag*: **in senso ~** broadly speaking ♦ *sm* side; (*fig*) aspect, point of view; **d'altro ~** (*d'altra parte*) on the other hand.

latra're *vi* to bark.

latri'na *sf* rest room (*US*), public lavatory (*Brit*).

latroci'nio [làtrōchē'nyō] *sm* = **ladrocinio**.

lat'ta *sf* tin (plate); (*recipiente*) tin can.

latta'io, a *sm/f* (*distributore*) milkman/ woman; (*commerciante*) dairyman/woman.

lattan'te *ag* unweaned ♦ *sm/f* breast-fed baby.

lat'te *sm* milk; **fratello di ~** foster brother; **avere ancora il ~ alla bocca** (*fig*) to be still wet behind the ears; **tutto ~ e miele** (*fig*) all smiles; ~ **detergente** cleansing lotion; ~ **intero** whole (*US*) *o* full-cream (*Brit*) milk; ~ **magro** *o* **scremato** skimmed milk; ~ **secco** *o* **in polvere** dried *o* powdered milk.

lat'teo, a *ag* milky; (*dieta, prodotto*) milk *cpd*.

latteri'a *sf* dairy.

lattici'ni [làttēchē'nē] *smpl* dairy products.

latti'na *sf* (*di birra etc*) can.

lattu'ga, ghe *sf* lettuce.

la'urea *sf* degree.

laurean'do, a *sm/f* final-year student.

laurea're *vt* to confer a degree on; ~**rsi** *vr* to graduate.

laurea'to, a *ag, sm/f* graduate.

la'uro *sm* laurel.

la'uto, a *ag* (*pranzo, mancia*) lavish; ~**i guadagni** handsome profits.

la'va *sf* lava.

lavabiancheri'a [làvàbyánkārē'à] *sf inv* washing machine.

lava'bo *sm* washbasin.

lavag'gio [làvàd'jō] *sm* washing *q*; ~ **del cervello** brainwashing *q*.

lava'gna [làvàn'yà] *sf* (*GEO*) slate; (*di scuola*) blackboard; ~ **luminosa** overhead projector.

lavan'da *sf* (*anche MED*) wash; (*BOT*) lavender; **fare una ~ gastrica a qn** to pump sb's stomach.

lavanda'ia *sf* washerwoman.

lavanderi'a *sf* (*di ospedale, caserma etc*) laundry; ~ **automatica** launderette; ~ **a secco** dry-cleaner's.

lavandi'no *sm* sink; (*del bagno*) washbasin.

lavapiat'ti *sm/f* dishwasher.

lava're *vt* to wash; ~**rsi** *vr* to wash, freshen up; ~ **a secco** to dry-clean; ~ **i panni sporchi in pubblico** (*fig*) to wash one's dirty linen in public; ~**rsi le mani/i denti** to wash one's hands/clean one's teeth.

lavasec'co *sm o f inv* dry-cleaner's.

lavastovi'glie [làvàstōvēl'yā] *sm o f inv* (*macchina*) dishwasher.

lava'ta *sf* wash; (*fig*): **dare una ~ di capo a qn** to give sb a good telling-off.

lavati'vo *sm* (*clistere*) enema; (*buono a nulla*) good-for-nothing, idler.

lavato'io *sm* (public) washhouse.

lavatri'ce [làvàtrē'chā] *sf* washing machine.

lavatu'ra *sf* washing *q*; ~ **di piatti** dishwater.

lavel'lo *sm* (kitchen) sink.

lavi'na *sf* snowslide.

lavoran'te *sm/f* worker.

lavora're *vi* to work; (*fig: bar, studio etc*) to do good business ♦ *vt* to work; ~ **a** to work on; ~ **a maglia** to knit; ~ **di fantasia** (*suggestionarsi*) to imagine things; (*fantasticare*) to let one's imagination run free; ~**rsi qn** (*fig: convincere*) to work on sb.

lavorati'vo, a *ag* working.

lavorato're, tri'ce *sm/f* worker ♦ *ag* working.

lavorazio'ne [làvōràttsyō'nā] *sf* (*gen*) working; (*di legno, pietra*) carving; (*di film*) making; (*di prodotto*) manufacture; (*modo di esecuzione*) workmanship.

lavori'o *sm* intense activity.

lavo'ro *sm* work; *(occupazione)* job, work *q*; *(opera)* piece of work, job; *(ECON)* labor *(US)*, labour *(Brit)*; **Ministero del L~** Department of Labor *(US)*, Department of Employment *(Brit)*; **(fare) i ~i di casa** (to do) the housework *sg*; **~i forzati** hard labor *sg*; **i ~i del parlamento** the parliamentary session *sg*; **~i pubblici** public works.

lazia'le [làttsyà'lā] *ag* of (*o* from) Lazio.

lazzaret'to [làddzárāt'tō] *sm* leper hospital.

lazzaro'ne [làddzárō'nā] *sm* scoundrel.

laz'zo [làd'dzō] *sm* jest.

LE *sigla* = *Lecce*.

le *det fpl* the ♦ *pronome* *(oggetto)* them; (: *a lei, a essa*) (to) her; (: *forma di cortesia*) (to) you; *vedi anche* **il**.

lea'le *ag* loyal; *(sincero)* sincere; *(onesto)* fair.

leali'sta, i, e *sm/f* loyalist.

lealtà *sf* loyalty; sincerity; fairness.

le'asing [lē:'zēng] *sm* leasing; lease.

leb'bra *sf* leprosy.

lebbro'so, a *ag* leprous ♦ *sm/f* leper.

lec'ca lec'ca *sm inv* lollipop.

leccapie'di *sm/f inv* *(peg)* toady, bootlicker.

lecca're *vt* to lick; *(sog: gatto: latte etc)* to lick *o* lap up; *(fig)* to flatter; **~rsi** *vr* *(fig)* to preen o.s.; **~rsi i baffi** to lick one's lips.

lecca'to, a *ag* affected ♦ *sf* lick.

lecche'rò etc [làkkāro'] *vb vedi* **leccare**.

lec'cio [làch'chō] *sm* holm oak, ilex.

leccorni'a *sf* titbit, delicacy.

le'cito, a [lā'chētō] *ag* permitted, allowed; **se mi è ~** if I may; **mi sia ~ far presente che** ... may I point out that ....

le'dere *vt* to damage, injure; **~ gli interessi di qn** to be prejudicial to sb's interests.

le'ga, ghe *sf* league; *(di metalli)* alloy; **metallo di bassa ~** base metal; **gente di bassa ~** common *o* vulgar people.

legac'cio [làgàch'chō] *sm* string, lace.

lega'le *ag* legal ♦ *sm* lawyer; **corso ~ delle monete** official exchange rate; **medicina ~** forensic medicine; **studio ~** lawyer's office.

legalità *sf* legality, lawfulness.

legalizza're [làgàlēddzà'rā] *vt* to authenticate; *(regolarizzare)* to legalize.

lega'me *sm* *(corda, fig: affettivo)* tie, bond; *(nesso logico)* link, connection; **~ di sangue** *o* **di parentela** family tie.

lega're *vt* *(prigioniero, capelli, cane)* to tie (up); *(libro)* to bind; *(CHIM)* to alloy; *(fig: collegare)* to bind, join ♦ *vi* *(far lega)* to unite; *(fig)* to get on well; **è pazzo da ~** *(fam)* he should be locked up.

legata'rio, a *sm/f* *(DIR)* legatee.

lega'to *sm* *(REL)* legate; *(DIR)* legacy, bequest.

legatori'a *sf* *(attività)* bookbinding; *(negozio)* bookbinder's.

legatu'ra *sf* *(di libro)* binding; *(MUS)* ligature.

legazio'ne [làgàttsyō'nā] *sf* legation.

legen'da [làjen'dà] *sf* *(di carta geografica etc)* = **leggenda**.

leg'ge [làd'jā] *sf* law; **~ procedurale** procedural law.

leggen'da [làdjen'dà] *sf* *(narrazione)* legend; *(di carta geografica etc)* key, legend.

leggenda'rio, a [làdjàndà'ryō] *ag* legendary.

leg'gere [led'jārā] *vt, vi* to read; **~ il pensiero di qn** to read sb's mind *o* thoughts.

leggerez'za [làdjārāt'tsà] *sf* lightness; thoughtlessness; fickleness.

legge'ro, a [làdje'rō] *ag* light; *(agile, snello)* nimble, agile, light; *(tè, caffè)* weak; *(fig: non grave, piccolo)* slight; (: *spensierato*) thoughtless; (: *incostante*) fickle; free and easy; **una ragazza ~a** *(fig)* a flighty girl; **alla ~a** thoughtlessly.

leggia'dro, a [làdjà'drō] *ag* pretty, lovely; *(movimenti)* graceful.

leggi'bile [làdjē'bēlā] *ag* legible; *(libro)* readable, worth reading.

leggi'o, gi'i [làdjē'ō] *sm* lectern; *(MUS)* music stand.

legherò etc [làgāro'] *vb vedi* **legare**.

legifera're [làjēfàrà'rā] *vi* to legislate.

legiona'rio [làjōnà'ryō] *sm* *(romano)* legionary; *(volontario)* legionnaire.

legio'ne [làjō'nā] *sf* legion; **~ straniera** foreign legion.

legislati'vo, a [làjēclàtē'vō] *ag* legislative.

legislato're [làjēclàtō'rā] *sm* legislator.

legislatu'ra [làjēclàtōō'rà] *sf* legislature.

legislazio'ne [làjēclàttsyō'nā] *sf* legislation.

legittima're [làjēttēmà'rā] *vt* *(figlio)* to legitimize; *(comportamento etc)* to justify.

legittimità [làjēttēmētà'] *sf* legitimacy.

legit'timo, a [làjēt'tēmō] *ag* legitimate; *(fig: giustificato, lecito)* justified, legitimate; **~a difesa** *(DIR)* self-defense *(US)*, self-defence *(Brit)*.

le'gna [làn'yà] *sf* firewood.

legna'ia [lànyà'yà] *sf* woodshed.

legnaio'lo [lànyàyo'lō] *sm* woodcutter.

legna'me [lànyà'mā] *sm* wood, timber.

legna'ta [lànyà'tà] *sf* hit *(US)* *o* blow *(Brit)* with a stick; **dare a qn un sacco di ~e** to give sb a good hiding.

le'gno [làn'yō] *sm* wood; *(pezzo di ~)* piece of wood; **di ~** wooden; **~ compensato** plywood.

legno'so, a [lànyō'sō] *ag* *(di legno)* wooden; *(come il legno)* woody; *(carne)* tough.

legu'mi *smpl* *(BOT)* pulses.

le'i *pronome* *(soggetto)* she; *(oggetto: per dare rilievo, con preposizione)* her; *(forma di cortesia: anche:* **L~**) you; *(forma di cortesia: anche:* **L~**) you ♦ *sm*: **la mia ~** my beloved ♦ *sm*: **dare del ~ a qn** to address sb as "lei"; **~ stessa** she herself; you yourself; **è ~** it's her.

lem'bo *sm* (*di abito, strada*) edge; (*striscia sottile*: *di terra*) strip.

lem'ma, i *sm* headword.

lem'me lem'me *av* (very) very slowly.

le'na *sf* (*fig*) energy, stamina; **di buona ~** (*lavorare, camminare*) at a good pace.

Leningra'do *sf* Leningrad.

leni're *vt* to soothe.

len'te *sf* (*OTTICA*) lens *sg*; **~ d'ingrandimento** magnifying glass; **~i a contatto, ~i corneali** contact lenses.

lentez'za |lāntāt'tsá| *sf* slowness.

lentic'chia |lāntēk'kyà| *sf* (*BOT*) lentil.

lentig'gine |lāntēd'jēnā| *sf* freckle.

len'to, a *ag* slow; (*molle: fune*) slack; (*non stretto: vite, abito*) loose ♦ *sm* (*ballo*) slow dance.

len'za |len'tsá| *sf* fishing line.

lenzuo'lo |lāntswo'lō| *sm* sheet; **~a** *sfpl* pair of sheets; **~ funebre** shroud.

leonci'no |lāōnchē'nō| *sm* lion cub.

leo'ne *sm* lion; (*dello zodiaco*): **L~** Leo; **essere del L~** to be Leo.

leopar'do *sm* leopard.

lepori'no, a *ag*: **labbro ~** harelip.

le'pre *sf* hare.

ler'cio, a, ci, ce |ler'chō| *ag* filthy.

lerciu'me |lārchōō'mā| *sm* filth.

le'sbico, a, ci, che *ag, sf* lesbian.

le'si *etc vb vedi* **ledere**.

lesina're *vt* to be stingy with ♦ *vi*: **~ (su)** to skimp (on), be stingy (with).

lesio'ne *sf* (*MED*) lesion; (*DIR*) injury, damage; (*EDIL*) crack.

lesi'vo, a *ag*: **~ (di)** damaging (to), detrimental (to).

le'so, a *pp di* **ledere** ♦ *ag* (*offeso*) injured; **parte ~a** (*DIR*) injured party; **~a maestà** lese-majesty.

Lesot'ho |lāsō'tō| *sm* Lesotho.

lessa're *vt* (*CUC*) to boil.

les'si *etc vb vedi* **leggere**.

lessica'le *ag* lexical.

les'sico, ci *sm* vocabulary; (*dizionario*) lexicon.

lessicografi'a *sf* lexicography.

les'so, a *ag* boiled ♦ *sm* boiled meat.

le'sto, a *ag* quick; (*agile*) nimble; **~ di mano** (*per rubare*) light-fingered; (*per picchiare*) free with one's fists.

lestofan'te *sm* swindler, con man.

leta'le *ag* lethal, deadly.

letama'io *sm* dunghill.

leta'me *sm* manure, dung.

letar'go, ghi *sm* lethargy; (*ZOOL*) hibernation.

leti'zia |lātēt'tsyà| *sf* joy, happiness.

let'ta *sf*: **dare una ~ a qc** to glance *o* look through sth.

let'tera *sf* letter; **~e** *sfpl* (*letteratura*) lit-

erature *sg*; (*studi umanistici*) arts (subjects); **alla ~** literally; **in ~e** in words, in full; **diventar ~ morta** (*legge*) to become a dead letter; **restar ~ morta** (*consiglio, invito*) to go unheeded; **~ di accompagnamento** accompanying letter; **~ assicurata** registered letter; **~ di cambio** (*COMM*) bill of exchange; **~ di credito** (*COMM*) letter of credit; **~ di intenti** letter of intent; **~ di presentazione** *o* **raccomandazione** letter of introduction; **~ raccomandata** certified (*US*) *o* recorded delivery (*Brit*) letter; **~ di trasporto aereo** (*COMM*) air waybill.

lettera'le *ag* literal.

letteralmen'te *av* literally.

lettera'rio, a *ag* literary.

lettera'to, a *ag* well-read, scholarly.

letteratu'ra *sf* literature.

letti'ga, ghe *sf* (*portantina*) litter; (*barella*) stretcher.

letti'no *sm* crib (*US*), cot (*Brit*).

let'to, a *pp di* **leggere** ♦ *sm* bed; **andare a ~** to go to bed; **~ a castello** bunk beds *pl*; **~ a una piazza/a due piazze** *o* **matrimoniale** single/double bed.

Letto'nia *sf*: **la ~** Latvia.

lettora'to *sm* (*INS*) lectorship, assistantship; (*REL*) lectorate.

letto're, tri'ce *sm/f* reader; (*INS*) (foreign) teaching assistant (*US*), (foreign language) assistant (*Brit*) ♦ *sm*: **~ ottico** (*di caratteri*) optical character reader.

lettu'ra *sf* reading.

leucemi'a |lāōōchāmē'à| *sf* leukaemia.

le'va *sf* lever; (*MIL*) conscription; **far ~ su qn** to work on sb; **essere di ~** to be due for call-up; **~ del cambio** (*AUT*) gear lever.

levan'te *sm* east; (*vento*) East wind; **il L~** the Levant.

leva're *vt* (*occhi, braccio*) to raise; (*sollevare, togliere*: *tassa, divieto*) to lift; (: *indumenti*) to take off, remove; (*rimuovere*) to take away; (: *dal di sopra*) to take off; (: *dal di dentro*) to take out; **~rsi** *vr* to get up; (*sole*) to rise; **~ le tende** (*fig*) to pack up and leave; **~rsi il pensiero** to put one's mind at rest; **levati di mezzo** *o* **di lì** *o* **di torno!** get out of my way!

leva'ta *sf* (*di posta*) collection.

levatac'cia, ce |lāvàtách'chà| *sf* early rise.

levato'io, a *ag*: **ponte ~** drawbridge.

levatri'ce |lāvàtrē'chā| *sf* midwife.

levatu'ra *sf* intelligence, mental capacity.

leviga're *vt* to smooth; (*con carta vetrata*) to sand.

leviga'to, a *ag* (*superficie*) smooth; (*fig*: *stile*) polished; (: *viso*) flawless.

levità *sf* lightness.

levrie're *sm* greyhound.

lezio'ne |lāttsyō'nā| *sf* lesson; (*all'università,*

sgridata) lecture; **fare** ~ to teach; to lecture.
lezio'so, a |lāttsyō'sō| *ag* affected; simpering.
lez'zo |lād'dzō| *sm* stench, stink.
lg *abbr* (= *lira sterlina*) £.
Ll *sigla* = *Livorno*.
li *pronome pl* (*oggetto*) them.
lì *av* there; **di** *o* **da** ~ from there; **per di** ~ that way; **di** ~ **a pochi giorni** a few days later; ~ **per** ~ there and then; at first; **essere** ~ **(~) per fare** to be on the point of doing, be about to do; ~ **dentro** in there; ~ **sotto** under there; ~ **sopra** on there; up there; **tutto** ~ that's all; *vedi anche* **quello**.
libagio'ne |lēbăjō'nā| *sf* libation.
libane'se *ag, sm/f* Lebanese *inv*.
Liba'no *sm:* **il** ~ the Lebanon.
lib'bra *sf* (*peso*) pound.
libec'cio |lēbāch'chō| *sm* south-west wind.
libel'lo *sm* libel.
libel'lula *sf* dragonfly.
libera'le *ag, sm/f* liberal.
liberalizza're |lēbārălĕddzà'rā| *vt* to liberalize.
libera're *vt* (*rendere libero: prigioniero*) to release; (: *popolo*) to free, liberate; (*sgombrare: passaggio*) to clear; (: *stanza*) to vacate; (*produrre: energia*) to release; **~rsi** *vr:* **~rsi di qc/qn** to get rid of sth/sb.
liberato're, tri'ce *ag* liberating ♦ *sm/f* liberator.
liberazio'ne |lēbārāttsyō'nā| *sf* liberation; release; freeing.
liber'colo *sm* (*peg*) worthless book.
Libe'ria *sf:* **la** ~ Liberia.
liberia'no, a *ag, sm/f* Liberian.
liberi'smo *sm* (*ECON*) laissez-faire.
li'bero, a *ag* free; (*strada*) clear; (*non occupato: posto etc*) vacant, free; (*TEL*) not engaged; ~ **di fare qc** free to do sth; ~ **da** free from; **una donna dai** ~**i costumi** a woman of loose morals; **avere via** ~**a** to have a free hand; **dare via** ~**a a qn** to give sb the go-ahead; **via** ~**a!** all clear!; ~ **arbitrio** free will; ~ **professionista** self-employed professional person; ~ **scambio** free trade; ~**a uscita** (*MIL*) leave.
liberoscambi'smo *sm* (*ECON*) free trade.
libertà *sf inv* freedom; (*tempo disponibile*) free time ♦ *sfpl* (*licenza*) liberties; **essere in** ~ **provvisoria/vigilata** to be released without bail/be on probation; ~ **di riunione** right to hold meetings.
liberta'rio, a *ag* libertarian.
liberti'no, a *ag, sm/f* libertine.
li'berty |lē'bārtĕ| *ag inv, sm* art nouveau.
Li'bia *sf:* **la** ~ Libya.
li'bico, a, ci, che *ag, sm/f* Libyan.
libi'dine *sf* lust.
libidino'so, a *ag* lustful, libidinous.
libi'do *sf* libido.
libra'io *sm* bookseller.

libra'rio, a *ag* book *cpd*.
librar'si *vr* to hover.
libreri'a *sf* (*bottega*) bookstore; (*stanza*) library; (*mobile*) bookcase.
libret'to *sm* booklet; (*taccuino*) notebook; (*MUS*) libretto; ~ **degli assegni** checkbook (*US*), chequebook (*Brit*); ~ **di circolazione** (*AUT*) logbook; ~ **di deposito** (bank) deposit book; ~ **di risparmio** (savings) bankbook, passbook; ~ **universitario** student's report book.
li'bro *sm* book; ~ **bianco** (*POL*) white paper; ~ **di cassa** cash book; ~ **di consultazione** reference book; ~ **mastro** ledger; ~ **paga** payroll; ~ **tascabile** paperback; ~ **di testo** textbook; ~**i contabili** (account) books; ~**i sociali** company records.
lican'tropo *sm* werewolf.
licea'le |lēchāā'lā| *ag* high school *cpd* (*US*), secondary school *cpd* (*Brit*) ♦ *sm/f* high school *o* secondary school pupil.
licen'za |lēchen'tsā| *sf* (*permesso*) permission, leave; (*di pesca, caccia, circolazione*) permit, license (*US*), licence (*Brit*); (*MIL*) leave; (*INS*) graduation (*US*) *o* school-leaving (*Brit*) certificate; (*libertà*) liberty; (*sfrenatezza*) licentiousness; **andare in** ~ (*MIL*) to go on leave; **su** ~ **di ...** (*COMM*) under license from ...; ~ **di esportazione** export license; ~ **di fabbricazione** manufacturer's license; ~ **poetica** poetic license.
licenziamen'to |lēchāntsyāmăn'tō| *sm* dismissal.
licenzia're |lēchāntsyà'rā| *vt* (*impiegato*) to dismiss; (*INS*) to award a certificate to; **~rsi** *vr* (*impiegato*) to resign, hand in one's notice; (*INS*) to obtain one's graduation (*US*) *o* school-leaving (*Brit*) certificate.
licenziosità |lēchāntsyōsĕtà'| *sf* licentiousness.
licenzio'so, a |lēchāntsyō'sō| *ag* licentious.
lice'o |lēche'ō| *sm* (*INS*) high school (*for 14- to 19-year-olds*); ~ **classico/scientifico** high school specializing in classics/scientific subjects.
liche'ne |lēke'nā| *sm* (*BOT*) lichen.
li'do *sm* beach, shore.
Li'echtenstein |lĕk'tənstăĕn| *sm:* **il** ~ Liechtenstein.
lie'to, a *ag* happy, glad; **"molto ~"** (*nelle presentazioni*) "pleased to meet you"; **a** ~ **fine** with a happy ending.
lie've *ag* light; (*di poco conto*) slight; (*sommesso: voce*) faint, soft.
lievita're *vi* (*anche fig*) to rise ♦ *vt* to leaven.
lie'vito *sm* yeast; ~ **di birra** brewer's yeast.
li'gio, a, gi, gie |lē'jō| *ag* faithful, loyal.
lignag'gio |lēnyàd'jō| *sm* descent, lineage.
li'gure *ag* Ligurian; **la Riviera L~** the Italian Riviera.
lil'la, lillà *sm inv* lilac.

Li'ma *sf* Lima.

li'ma *sf* file; ~ **da unghie** nail file.

limaccio'so, a [lēmáchō'sō] *ag* muddy.

lima're *vt* to file (down); *(fig)* to polish.

lim'bo *sm* (*REL*) limbo.

limet'ta *sf* nail file.

limita're *vt* to limit, restrict; *(circoscrivere)* to bound, surround.

limitatamen'te *av* to a limited extent; ~ **alle mie possibilità** in so far as I am able.

limitati'vo, a *ag* limiting, restricting.

limita'to, a *ag* limited, restricted.

limitazio'ne [lēmētáttsyō'nā] *sf* limitation, restriction.

li'mite *sm* limit; *(confine)* border, boundary ♦ *ag inv:* **caso** ~ extreme case; **al** ~ if worst comes to worst; ~ **di velocità** speed limit.

limi'trofo, a *ag* neighboring (*US*), neighbouring (*Brit*).

li'mo *sm* mud, slime; (*GEO*) silt.

limona'ta *sf* lemon soda (*US*), lemonade (*Brit*); *(spremuta)* lemonade (*US*), lemon squash (*Brit*).

limo'ne *sm* *(pianta)* lemon tree; *(frutto)* lemon.

limpidez'za [lēmpēdāt'tsá] *sf* clearness; *(di discorso)* clarity.

lim'pido, a *ag (acqua)* limpid, clear; *(cielo)* clear; *(fig: discorso)* clear, lucid.

lin'ce [lēn'chā] *sf* lynx.

lincia're [lēnchá'rā] *vt* to lynch.

lin'do, a *ag* tidy, spick and span; *(biancheria)* clean.

li'nea *sf (gen)* line; *(di mezzi pubblici di trasporto: itinerario)* route; (: *servizio)* service; *(di prodotto: collezione)* collection; (: *stile)* style; **a grandi** ~**e** in outline; **mantenere la** ~ to look after one's figure; **è caduta la** ~ *(TEL)* I (o you *etc*) have been cut off; **di** ~: **aereo di** ~ airliner; **nave di** ~ liner; **volo di** ~ scheduled flight; **in** ~ **diretta da** *(TV. RADIO)* coming to you direct from; ~ **aerea** airline; ~ **continua** solid line; ~ **di partenza/d'arrivo** *(SPORT)* starting/finishing line; ~ **punteggiata** dotted line; ~ **di tiro** line of fire.

lineamen'ti *smpl* features; *(fig)* outlines.

linea're *ag* linear; *(fig)* coherent, logical.

lineet'ta *sf (trattino)* dash; *(d'unione)* hyphen.

lin'fa *sf (BOT)* sap; *(ANAT)* lymph; ~ **vitale** *(fig)* lifeblood.

lingot'to *sm* ingot, bar.

lin'gua *sf (ANAT, CUC)* tongue; *(idioma)* language; **mostrare la** ~ to stick out one's tongue; **di** ~ **italiana** Italian-speaking; ~ **madre** mother tongue; **una** ~ **di terra** a spit of land.

linguac'cia [lēngwàch'chá] *sf (fig)* spiteful gossip.

linguacciu'to, a [lēngwàchōō'tō] *ag* gossipy.

linguag'gio [lēngwàd'jō] *sm* language; ~ **giuridico** legal language; ~ **macchina** *(INFORM)* machine language; ~ **di programmazione** *(INFORM)* programming language.

linguet'ta *sf (di strumento)* reed; *(di scarpa, TECN)* tongue; *(di busta)* flap.

lingui'sta, i, e *sm/f* linguist.

lingui'stico, a, ci, che *ag* linguistic ♦ *sf* linguistics *sg*.

linimen'to *sm* liniment.

li'no *sm (pianta)* flax; *(tessuto)* linen.

lino'leum *sm inv* linoleum, lino.

liofilizza're [lēōfēlēddzá'rā] *vt* to freeze-dry.

liofilizza'ti [lēōfēlēddzá'tē] *smpl* freeze-dried foods.

Lio'ne *sf* Lyons.

LI'PU *sigla f* (= *Lega Italiana Protezione Uccelli*) *society for the protection of birds.*

liqua'me *sm* liquid sewage.

liquefa're *vt (render liquido)* to liquefy; *(fondere)* to melt; ~**rsi** *vr* to liquefy; to melt.

liquefat'to, a *pp di* **liquefare**.

liquida're *vt (società, beni; persona: uccidere)* to liquidate; *(persona: sbarazzarsene)* to get rid of; *(conto, problema)* to settle; *(COMM: merce)* to sell off, clear.

liquidazio'ne [lēkwēdáttsyō'nā] *sf (di società, persona)* liquidation; *(di conto)* settlement; *(di problema)* settling; *(COMM: di merce)* clearance sale; *(AMM)* severance pay *(on retirement, or when laid off, or when taking up other employment)*.

liquidità *sf* liquidity.

li'quido, a *ag, sm* liquid; **denaro** ~ cash, ready money; ~ **per freni** brake fluid.

liquigas' ® *sm inv* butane, Calor gas ® (*Brit*).

liquiri'zia [lēkwērēt'tsyá] *sf* licorice.

liquo're *sm* liqueur.

liquoro'so, a *ag:* **vino** ~ dessert wine.

li'ra *sf (unità monetaria)* lira; *(MUS)* lyre; ~ **sterlina** pound sterling.

li'rico, a, ci, che *ag* lyric(al); *(MUS)* lyric ♦ *sf (poesia)* lyric poetry; *(componimento poetico)* lyric; *(MUS)* opera; **cantante/teatro** ~ opera singer/house.

liri'smo *sm* lyricism.

Lisbo'na *sf* Lisbon.

li'sca, sche *sf (di pesce)* fishbone.

liscia're [lēshá'rā] *vt* to smooth; *(fig)* to flatter; ~**rsi i capelli** to straighten one's hair.

li'scio, a, sci, sce [lēsh'shō] *ag* smooth; *(capelli)* straight; *(mobile)* plain; *(bevanda alcolica)* straight; *(fig)* straightforward, simple ♦ *av:* **andare** ~ to go smoothly; **passarla** ~**a** to get away with it.

lise'use [lēzœz'] *sf inv* bed jacket.

li'so, a *ag* worn out, threadbare.

li'sta *sf (striscia)* strip; *(elenco)* list; ~

elettorale electoral roll; ~ **delle vivande** menu.

lista're vt: ~ **(di)** to edge (with), border (with).

listi'no sm list; ~ **di borsa** the Stock Exchange list; ~ **dei cambi** (foreign) exchange rate; ~ **dei prezzi** price list.

litani'a sf litany.

li'te sf quarrel, argument; (DIR) lawsuit.

litiga're vi to quarrel; (DIR) to litigate.

liti'gio [lētē'jō] sm quarrel.

litigio'so, a [lētējō'sō] ag quarrelsome; (DIR) litigious.

litografi'a sf (sistema) lithography; (stampa) lithograph.

litogra'fico, a, ci, che ag lithographic.

litora'le ag coastal, coast cpd ♦ sm coast.

litora'neo, a ag coastal.

li'tro sm liter (US), litre (Brit).

litto'rio, a ag (STORIA) lictorial; **fascio** ~ fasces pl.

Litua'nia sf: **la** ~ Lithuania.

liturgi'a, gi'e [lētōōrjē'à] sf liturgy.

liu'to sm lute.

livel'la sf level; ~ **a bolla d'aria** spirit level.

livella're vt to level, make level; **~rsi** vr to become level; (fig) to level out, balance out.

livellatri'ce [lēvāllàtrē'chā] sf steamroller.

livel'lo sm level; (fig) level, standard; **ad alto** ~ (fig) high-level; **a** ~ **mondiale** world-wide; **a** ~ **di confidenza** confidentially; ~ **di magazzino** stock level; ~ **del mare** sea level; **sul** ~ **del mare** above sea level; ~ **occupazionale** level of employment; ~ **retributivo** salary level.

li'vido, a ag livid; (per percosse) bruised, black and blue; (cielo) leaden ♦ sm bruise.

livo're sm malice, spite.

Livor'no sf Livorno, Leghorn.

livre'a sf livery.

liz'za [lēt'tsà] sf lists pl; **essere in** ~ **per** (fig) to compete for; **scendere in** ~ (anche fig) to enter the lists.

lo det m (dav s impura, gn, pn, ps, x, z; dav V **l'**) the ♦ pronome (dav V **l'**) (oggetto: persona) him; (: cosa) it; ~ **sapevo** I knew it; ~ **so** I know; **sii buono, anche se lui non** ~ **è** be good, even if he isn't; vedi anche **il**.

lob'bia sf homburg.

lobbi'sta, i, e sm/f lobbyist.

lo'bo sm lobe; ~ **dell'orecchio** ear lobe.

loca'le ag local ♦ sm room; (luogo pubblico) premises pl; ~ **notturno** nightclub.

località sf inv locality.

localizza're [lōkàlēddzà'rā] vt (circoscrivere) to confine, localize; (accertare) to locate, place.

locan'da sf inn.

locandie're, a sm/f innkeeper.

locandi'na sf (TEATRO) poster.

loca're vt (casa) to rent out, let; (macchina) to rent (out).

locata'rio, a sm/f tenant.

locati'vo, a ag (DIR) rentable.

locato're, tri'ce sm/f landlord/lady.

locazio'ne [lōkàttsyō'nā] sf (da parte del locatario) renting q; (da parte del locatore) renting out q, letting q; **(contratto di)** ~ lease; **(canone di)** ~ rent; **dare in** ~ to rent out, let.

locomoti'va sf locomotive.

locomoto're sm electric locomotive.

locomozio'ne [lōkōmōttsyō'nā] sf locomotion; **mezzi di** ~ vehicles, means of transport.

lo'culo sm burial recess.

locu'sta sf locust.

locuzio'ne [lōkōōttsyō'nā] sf phrase, expression.

loda're vt to praise.

lo'de sf praise; (INS): **laurearsi con 110 e** ~ ≈ to graduate summa cum laude (US), ≈ to graduate with first-class honours (Brit).

lo'den sm inv (stoffa) loden; (cappotto) loden overcoat.

lode'vole ag praiseworthy.

logarit'mo sm logarithm.

log'gia, ge [lod'jà] sf (ARCHIT) loggia; (circolo massonico) lodge.

loggio'ne [lōdjō'nā] sm (di teatro): **il** ~ the Gods sg.

logicamen'te [lōjēkàmàn'tā] av naturally, obviously.

logicità [lōjēchētà'] sf logicality.

lo'gico, a, ci, che [lo'jēkō] ag logical ♦ sf logic.

logi'stica [lōjē'stēkà] sf logistics sg.

lo'go sm inv logo.

logoramen'to sm (di vestiti etc) wear.

logoran'te ag exhausting.

logora're vt to wear out; (sciupare) to waste; **~rsi** vr to wear out; (fig) to wear o.s. out.

logori'o sm wear and tear; (fig) strain.

lo'goro, a ag (stoffa) worn out, threadbare; (persona) worn out.

Lo'ira sf: **la** ~ the Loire.

lombag'gine [lōmbàd'jēnā] sf lumbago.

Lombardi'a sf: **la** ~ Lombardy.

lombar'do, a ag, sm/f Lombard.

lomba're ag (ANAT, MED) lumbar.

lomba'ta sf (taglio di carne) loin.

lom'bo sm (ANAT) loin.

lombri'co, chi sm earthworm.

londine'se ag London cpd ♦ sm/f Londoner.

Lon'dra sf London.

longa'nime ag forbearing.

longevità [lōnjàvētà'] sf longevity.

longe'vo, a [lōnjà'vō] ag long-lived.

longili'neo, a [lōnjēlē'nāō] ag long-limbed.

longitu'dine [lōnjētōō'dēnà] sf longitude.

lontanamen'te av remotely; **non ci pensavo neppure** ~ it didn't even occur to me.

lontanan'za [lōntánàn'tsá] *sf* distance; absence.

lonta'no, a *ag* (*distante*) distant, faraway; (*assente*) absent; (*vago: sospetto*) slight, remote; (*tempo: remoto*) far-off, distant; (*parente*) distant, remote ♦ *av* far; **è ~a la casa?** is it far to the house?, is the house far from here?; **è ~ un chilometro** it's a kilometer away *o* a kilometer from here; **più ~** farther; **da** *o* **di ~** from a distance; **~ da** a long way from; **alla ~a** slightly, vaguely.

lon'tra *sf* otter.

loqua'ce [lōkwá'chā] *ag* talkative, loquacious; (*fig: gesto etc*) eloquent.

lor'do, a *ag* dirty, filthy; (*peso, stipendio*) gross; **~ d'imposta** pre-tax.

Lore'na *sf* (GEO) Lorraine.

lo'ro *pronome pl* (*oggetto, con preposizione*) them; (*complemento di termine*) to them; (*soggetto*) they; (*forma di cortesia: anche:* **L~**) you; to you; **il(la) ~, i(le) ~** *det* their; (*forma di cortesia: anche:* **L~**) your ♦ *pronome* theirs; (*forma di cortesia: anche:* **L~**) yours ♦ *sm inv*: **il ~** their (*o* your) money ♦ *sf inv*: **la ~** (*opinione*) their (*o* your) view; **i ~** (*famiglia*) their (*o* your) family; (*amici etc*) their (*o* your) own people; **un ~ amico** a friend of theirs; **è dalla ~** he's on their (*o* your) side; **ne hanno fatto un'altra delle ~** they've (*o* you've) done it again; **~ stessi(e)** they themselves; you yourselves.

losan'ga, ghe *sf* diamond, lozenge.

Losan'na *sf* Lausanne.

lo'sco, a, schi, sche *ag* (*fig*) shady, suspicious.

lot'ta *sf* struggle, fight; (SPORT) wrestling; **essere in ~ (con)** to be in conflict (with); **fare la ~ (con)** to wrestle (with); **~ armata** armed struggle; **~ di classe** (POL) class struggle; **~ libera** (SPORT) freestyle (US) *o* all-in (*Brit*) wrestling.

lotta're *vi* to fight, struggle; to wrestle.

lottato're, tri'ce *sm/f* wrestler.

lotteri'a *sf* lottery; (*di gara ippica*) sweepstake.

lottizza're [lōttēddzà'rā] *vt* to divide into plots.

lottizzazio'ne [lōttēddzàttsyō'nā] *sf* division into plots.

lot'to *sm* (*gioco*) (state) lottery; (*parte*) lot; (EDIL) site; **vincere un terno al ~** (*anche fig*) to hit the jackpot.

lozio'ne [lōttsyō'nā] *sf* lotion.

L.st. *abbr* (= *lire sterline*) £.

LT *sigla* = *Latina.*

LU *sigla* = *Lucca.*

lubrifican'te *sm* lubricant.

lubrifica're *vt* to lubricate.

luca'no, a *ag* of (*o* from) Lucania.

lucchet'to [lōōkkàt'tō] *sm* padlock.

luccica're [lōōchēkà'rā] *vi* to sparkle; (*oro*) to glitter; (*stella*) to twinkle; (*occhi*) to glisten.

luccichi'o [lōōchēkē'ō] *sm* sparkling; glittering; twinkling; glistening.

luccico'ne [lōōchēkō'nā] *sm*: **avere i ~i agli occhi** to have tears in one's eyes.

luc'cio [lōōch'chō] *sm* (ZOOL) pike.

luc'ciola [lōōch'chōlá] *sf* (ZOOL) firefly; glowworm.

lu'ce [lōō'chā] *sf* light; (*finestra*) window; **alla ~ di** by the light of; **fare qc alla ~ del sole** (*fig*) to do sth in the open; **dare alla ~** (*bambino*) to give birth to; **fare ~ su qc** (*fig*) to shed *o* throw light on sth; **~ del sole/della luna** sun/moonlight.

lucen'te [lōōchen'tā] *ag* shining.

lucentez'za [lōōchāntāt'tsá] *sf* shine.

lucer'na [lōōcher'nà] *sf* oil lamp.

lucerna'rio [lōōchàrnà'ryō] *sm* skylight.

lucer'tola [lōōcher'tōlá] *sf* lizard.

lucida're [lōōchēdá'rā] *vt* to polish; (*ricalcare*) to trace.

lucidatri'ce [lōōchēdàtrē'chā] *sf* floor polisher.

lucidità [lōōchēdētá'] *sf* lucidity.

lu'cido, a [lōō'chēdō] *ag* shining, bright; (*lucidato*) polished; (*fig*) lucid ♦ *sm* shine; (*per scarpe etc*) polish; (*disegno*) tracing.

luci'gnolo [lōōchē'nyōlō] *sm* wick.

lucrati'vo, a *ag* lucrative; **a scopo ~** for gain.

lu'cro *sm* profit, gain; **a scopo di ~** for gain; **organizzazione senza scopo di ~** non-profit (US) *o* non-profit-making (*Brit*) organization.

lucro'so, a *ag* lucrative, profitable.

lucullia'no, a *ag* (*pasto*) sumptuous.

ludi'brio *sm* mockery *q*; (*oggetto di scherno*) laughing stock.

lu'e *sf* syphilis.

lu'glio [lōōl'yō] *sm* July; **nel mese di ~** in July, in the month of July; **il primo ~** the first of July; **arrivare il 2 ~** to arrive on the 2nd of July; **all'inizio/alla fine di ~** at the beginning/at the end of July; **durante il mese di ~** during July; **a ~ del prossimo anno** in July of next year; **ogni anno a ~** every July; **che fai a ~?** what are you doing in July?; **ha piovuto molto a ~ quest'anno** July was very wet this year.

lu'gubre *ag* gloomy.

lu'i *pronome* (*soggetto*) he; (*oggetto: per dare rilievo, con preposizione*) him ♦ *sm inv*: **il mio ~** my beloved; **~ stesso** he himself; **è ~** it's him.

luma'ca, che *sf* slug; (*chiocciola*) snail.

lumaco'ne *sm* (*large*) slug; (*fig*) slowpoke (US), slowcoach (*Brit*).

lu'me *sm* light; (*lampada*) lamp; **~ a olio** oil lamp; **chiedere ~i a qn** (*fig*) to ask sb for advice; **a ~ di naso** (*fig*) by rule of thumb.

lumici'no [lōōmēchē'nō] *sm* small *o* faint light; **essere (ridotto) al ~** (*fig*) to be at death's door.

lumie'ra *sf* chandelier.

lumina're *sm* luminary.
lumina'ria *sf* (*per feste*) illuminations *pl*.
luminescen'te [lōōmēnāshen'tā] *ag* luminescent.
lumi'no *sm* small light; ~ **da notte** nightlight; ~ **per i morti** candle for the dead.
lumino'so, a *ag* (*che emette luce*) luminous; (*cielo, colore, stanza*) bright; (*sorgente*) of light, light *cpd*; (*fig: sorriso*) bright, radiant; **insegna** ~**a** illuminated sign.
lun. *abbr* (= *lunedì*) Mon.
lu'na *sf* moon; ~ **nuova/piena** new/full moon; **avere la** ~ to be in a bad mood; ~ **di miele** honeymoon.
lu'na park *sm inv* amusement park.
luna're *ag* lunar, moon *cpd*.
luna'rio *sm* almanac; **sbarcare il** ~ to make ends meet.
luna'tico, a, ci, che *ag* whimsical, temperamental.
lunedì *sm inv* Monday; *per fraseologia vedi* **martedì**.
lungag'gine [lōōngād'jēnā] *sf* slowness; ~**i della burocrazia** red tape.
lungamen'te *av* (*a lungo*) for a long time; (*estesamente*) at length.
lungar'no *sm* embankment along the Arno.
lunghez'za [lōōngět'tsā] *sf* length; ~ **d'onda** (*FISICA*) wavelength.
lun'gi [lōōn'jē] *av*: ~ **da** *prep* far from.
lungimiran'te [lōōnjēmērān'tā] *ag* far-sighted.
lun'go, a, ghi, ghe *ag* long; (*lento: persona*) slow; (*diluito: caffè, brodo*) weak, watery, thin ♦ *sm* length ♦ *prep* along; ~ **3 metri** 3 meters long; **avere la barba** ~**a** to be unshaven; **a** ~ for a long time; **a** ~ **andare** in the long run; **di gran** ~**a** (*molto*) by far; **andare in** ~ *o* **per le lunghe** to drag on; **saperla** ~**a** to know what's what; **in** ~ **e in largo** far and wide, all over; ~ **il corso dei secoli** throughout the centuries; **navigazione di** ~ **corso** ocean-going navigation.
lungofiu'me *sm* embankment.
lungola'go *sm* road round a lake.
lungoma're *sm* boardwalk (*US*), promenade (*Brit*).
lungometrag'gio [lōōngōmātrād'jō] *sm* (*CINEMA*) feature film.
lungote'vere *sm* embankment along the Tiber.
lunot'to *sm* (*AUT*) rear *o* back window; ~ **termico** rear window defroster (*US*), heated rear window (*Brit*).
luo'go, ghi *sm* place; (*posto: di incidente etc*) scene, site; (*punto, passo di libro*) passage; **in** ~ **di** instead of; **in primo** ~ in the first place; **aver** ~ to take place; **dar** ~ **a** to give rise to; ~ **comune** commonplace; ~ **del delitto** scene of the crime; ~ **geometrico** locus; ~ **di nascita** birthplace; (*AMM*) place of birth; ~ **di pena** prison, penitentiary; ~ **di provenienza** place of origin.
luogotenen'te *sm* (*MIL*) lieutenant.
lupacchiot'to [lōōpākkyot'tō] *sm* (*ZOOL*) (wolf) cub.
lupa'ra *sf* sawed-off shotgun.
lupet'to *sm* (*ZOOL*) (wolf) cub; (*negli scouts*) cub scout.
lu'po, a *sm/f* wolf/she-wolf; **cane** ~ German shepherd (dog); **tempo da** ~**i** filthy weather.
lup'polo *sm* (*BOT*) hop.
lu'rido, a *ag* filthy.
luridu'me *sm* filth.
lusin'ga, ghe *sf* (*spesso al pl*) flattery *q*.
lusinga're *vt* to flatter.
lusinghie'ro, a [lōōzēngye'rō] *ag* flattering, gratifying.
lussa're *vt* (*MED*) to dislocate.
lussazio'ne [lōōssāttsyō'nā] *sf* (*MED*) dislocation.
lussemburghe'se [lōōssāmbōōrgā'sā] *ag* of (*o* from) Luxembourg ♦ *sm/f* native (*o* inhabitant) of Luxembourg.
Lussembur'go *sm* (*stato*): **il** ~ Luxembourg ♦ *sf* (*città*) Luxembourg.
lus'so *sm* luxury; **di** ~ luxury *cpd*.
lussuo'so, a *ag* luxurious.
lussureggia're [lōōssōōrādjá'rā] *vi* to be luxuriant.
lussu'ria *sf* lust.
lussurio'so, a *ag* lascivious, lustful.
lustra're *vt* to polish, shine.
lustrascar'pe *sm/f inv* shoeshine.
lustri'no *sm* sequin.
lus'tro, a *ag* shiny; (*pelliccia*) glossy ♦ *sm* shine, gloss; (*fig*) préstige, glory; (*quinquennio*) five-year period.
lut'to *sm* mourning; **essere in/portare il** ~ to be in/wear mourning.
luttuo'so, a *ag* mournful, sad.

M

M, m [em'mā] *sf o m inv* (*lettera*) M, m; **M come Milano** ≈ M for Mike.
m. *abbr* = **mese; metro; miglia; monte.**
ma *cong* but; ~ **insomma!** for goodness sake!; ~ **no!** of course not!
ma'cabro, a *ag* gruesome, macabre.
macché [mākkā'] *escl* not at all!, certainly not!
macchero'ni [mākkārō'nē] *smpl* macaroni *sg*.
mac'chia [mäk'kyä] *sf* stain, spot; (*chiazza di*

diverso colore) spot; splash, patch; (*tipo di boscaglia*) scrub; ~ **d'inchiostro** ink stain; **estendersi a** ~ **d'olio** (*fig*) to spread rapidly; **darsi/vivere alla** ~ (*fig*) to go into/live in hiding.

macchia're [mákkyà'rā] *vt* (*sporcare*) to stain, mark; ~**rsi** *vr* (*persona*) to get o.s. dirty; (*stoffa*) to stain; to get stained *o* marked; ~**rsi di un delitto** to be guilty of a crime.

macchia'to, a [màkkyà'tō] *ag* (*pelle, pelo*) spotted; ~ **di** stained with; **caffè** ~ coffee with a dash of milk.

macchiet'ta [mákkyāt'tà] *sf* (*disegno*) sketch, caricature; (*TEATRO*) caricature; (*fig: persona*) character.

mac'china [màk'kēnà] *sf* machine; (*motore, locomotiva*) engine; (*automobile*) car; (*fig: meccanismo*) machinery; **andare in** ~ (*AUT*) to go by car; (*STAMPA*) to go to press; **salire in** ~ to get into the car; **venire in** ~ to come by car; **sala** ~**e** (*NAUT*) engine room; ~ **da cucire** sewing machine; ~ **fotografica** camera; ~ **da presa** cinecamera; ~ **da scrivere** typewriter; ~ **utensile** machine tool; ~ **a vapore** steam engine.

macchinalmen'te [mákkēnàlmān'tā] *av* mechanically.

macchina're [mákkēnà'rā] *vt* to plot.

macchina'rio [mákkēnà'ryō] *sm* machinery.

macchinazio'ne [mákkēnàttsyō'nā] *sf* plot, machination.

macchinet'ta [mákkēnāt'tà] *sf* (*fam: caffettiera*) percolator; (*: accendino*) lighter.

macchini'sta, i [mákkēnē'stà] *sm* (*di treno*) engineer (*US*), engine-driver (*Brit*); (*di nave*) engineer; (*TEATRO, TV*) stagehand.

macchino'so, a [mákkēnō'sō] *ag* complex, complicated.

macedo'nia [máchādo'nyà] *sf* fruit salad.

macella'io [máchàllà'yō] *sm* butcher.

macella're [máchàllà'rā] *vt* to slaughter, butcher.

macellazio'ne [máchàllàttsyō'nā] *sf* slaughtering, butchering.

macelleri'a [máchàllārē'à] *sf* meat market (*US*), butcher's (shop) (*Brit*).

macel'lo [máchel'lō] *sm* (*mattatoio*) slaughterhouse, abattoir (*Brit*); (*fig*) slaughter, massacre; (*: disastro*) shambles *sg*.

macera're [máchārà'rā] *vt* to macerate; (*CUC*) to marinate; ~**rsi** *vr* to waste away; (*fig*): ~**rsi in** to be consumed with.

macerazio'ne [máchàràttsyō'nā] *sf* maceration.

mace'rie [máche'ryà] *sfpl* rubble *sg*, debris *sg*.

ma'cero [mà'chārō] *sm* (*operazione*) pulping; (*stabilimento*) pulping mill; **carta da** ~ paper for pulping.

machiavel'lico, a, ci, che [mákyàvel'lēkō] *ag* (*anche fig*) Machiavellian.

maci'gno [máchēn'yō] *sm* (*masso*) rock, boulder.

macilen'to, a [máchēlcn'tō] *ag* emaciated.

ma'cina [mà'chēnà] *sf* (*pietra*) millstone; (*macchina*) grinder.

macinacaffè [máchēnàkàffc'] *sm inv* coffee grinder.

macinape'pe [máchēnàpà'pā] *sm inv* peppermill.

macina're [máchēnà'rā] *vt* to grind; (*carne*) to grind (*US*), mince (*Brit*).

macina'to [máchēnà'tō] *sm* meal, flour; (*carne*) ground (*US*) *o* minced (*Brit*) meat.

macini'no [máchēnē'nō] *sm* (*per caffè*) coffee grinder; (*per pepe*) peppermill; (*scherzoso: macchina*) clunker (*US*), old banger (*Brit*).

maciulla're [máchōōllà'rā] *vt* (*canapa, lino*) to brake; (*fig: braccio etc*) to crush.

ma'cro... *prefisso* macro....

macula'to, a *ag* (*pelo*) spotted.

Mada'ma: palazzo ~ *sm* (*POL*) seat of the *Italian Chamber of Senators*.

Made'ra *sf* (*GEO*) Madeira ♦ *sm inv* (*vino*) Madeira.

ma'dido, a *ag*: ~ (**di**) wet *o* moist (with).

Madon'na *sf* (*REL*) Our Lady.

madorna'le *ag* enormous, huge.

ma'dre *sf* mother; (*matrice di bolletta*) counterfoil ♦ *ag inv* mother *cpd*; **ragazza** ~ unmarried mother; **scena** ~ (*TEATRO*) principal scene; (*fig*) terrible scene.

madrelin'gua *sf* mother tongue, native language.

madrepa'tria *sf* mother country, native land.

madreper'la *sf* mother-of-pearl.

Madrid' *sf* Madrid.

madriga'le *sm* madrigal.

madrile'no, a *ag* of (*o* from) Madrid ♦ *sm/f* person from Madrid.

madri'na *sf* godmother.

maestà *sf inv* majesty; **Sua M**~ **la Regina** Her Majesty the Queen.

maestosità *sf* majesty.

maesto'so, a *ag* majestic.

maes'tra *sf vedi* **maestro**.

maestra'le *sm* north-west wind.

maestran'ze [máàstrán'tsà] *sfpl* workforce *sg*.

maestri'a *sf* mastery, skill.

maes'tro, a *sm/f* (*INS: anche*: ~ **di scuola** *o* **elementare**) grade (*US*) *o* primary (*Brit*) school teacher; (*esperto*) expert ♦ *sm* (*artigiano, fig: guida*) master; (*MUS*) maestro ♦ *ag* (*principale*) main; (*di grande abilità*) masterly; **un colpo da** ~ (*fig*) a masterly move; **muro** ~ main wall; **strada** ~**a** main road; ~**a d'asilo** nursery teacher; ~ **di ballo** dancing master; ~ **di cerimonie** master of ceremonies; ~ **d'orchestra** leader (*US*), conductor; ~ **di scherma** fencing master; ~ **di sci** ski instructor.

ma'fia _sf_ Mafia.
mafio'so _sm_ member of the Mafia.
ma'ga, ghe _sf_ sorceress.
maga'gna [mágán'yá] _sf_ defect, flaw, blemish; (_noia, guaio_) problem.
maga'ri _escl_ (_esprime desiderio_): ~ **fosse vero!** if only it were true!; **ti piacerebbe andare in Scozia? — ~!** would you like to go to Scotland? — and how! ♦ _av_ (_anche_) even; (_forse_) perhaps.
magazzinag'gio [mágáddzēnád'jō] _sm_: (**spese di**) ~ storage charges _pl_, warehousing charges _pl_.
magazzinie're [mágáddzēnye'rá] _sm_ warehouseman.
magazzi'no [mágáddzē'nō] _sm_ warehouse; **grande** ~ department store; ~ **doganale** bonded warehouse.
mag'gio [mád'jō] _sm_ May; _per fraseologia vedi_ **luglio**.
maggiora'na [mádjōrá'ná] _sf_ (_BOT_) (sweet) marjoram.
maggioran'za [mádjōrán'tsá] _sf_ majority; **nella** ~ **dei casi** in most cases.
maggiora're [mádjōrá'rá] _vt_ to increase, raise.
maggiorazio'ne [mádjōráttsyō'ná] _sf_ (_COMM_) rise, increase.
maggiordo'mo [mádjōrdo'mō] _sm_ butler.
maggio're [mádjō'rá] _ag_ (_comparativo: più grande_) bigger, larger; taller; greater; (_: più vecchio: sorella, fratello_) older, elder; (_: di grado superiore_) senior; (_: più importante_, _MIL_, _MUS_) major; (_superlativo_) biggest, largest; tallest; greatest; oldest, eldest ♦ _sm/f_ (_di grado_) superior; (_di età_) elder; (_MIL_) major; (_: AER_) squadron leader; **la maggior parte** the majority; **andare per la** ~ (_cantante, attore etc_) to be very popular, be "in".
maggioren'ne [mádjōren'ná] _ag_ of age ♦ _sm/f_ person who has come of age.
maggiorita'rio, a [mádjōrētá'ryō] _ag_ majority _cpd_.
maggiormen'te [mádjōrmán'tá] _av_ much more; (_con senso superlativo_) most.
magi'a [májē'á] _sf_ magic.
ma'gico, a, ci, che [má'jēkō] _ag_ magic; (_fig_) fascinating, charming, magical.
ma'gio [má'jō] _sm_ (_REL_): **i re Magi** the Magi, the Three Wise Men.
magiste'ro [májēste'rō] _sm_ teaching; (_fig: maestria_) skill; (_INS_): **Facoltà di M~** ≈ teachers' training college.
magistra'le [májēstrá'lá] _ag_ grade school (_US_) _o_ primary (_Brit_) teachers', grade school _o_ primary teaching _cpd_; (_abile_) skillful (_US_), skilful (_Brit_); **istituto** ~ _secondary school for the training of primary teachers_.
magistra'to [májēstrá'tō] _sm_ magistrate.
magistratu'ra [májēstrátōō'rá] _sf_ magis-

trature; (_magistrati_): **la** ~ the Bench.
ma'glia [mál'yá] _sf_ stitch; (_lavoro ai ferri_) knitting _q_; (_tessuto, SPORT_) jersey; (_maglione_) jersey, sweater; (_di catena_) link; (_di rete_) mesh; **avviare/diminuire le** ~**e** to cast on/cast off; **lavorare a** ~, **fare la** ~ to knit; ~ **diritta/rovescia** knit/purl.
maglia'ia [mályá'yá] _sf_ knitter.
maglieri'a [mályārē'á] _sf_ knitwear; (_negozio_) knitwear shop; **macchina per** ~ knitting machine.
magliet'ta [mályát'tá] _sf_ (_canottiera_) undershirt (_US_), vest (_Brit_); (_tipo camicia_) T-shirt.
maglifi'cio [mályēfē'chō] _sm_ knitwear factory.
magli'na [mályē'ná] _sf_ (_tessuto_) jersey.
ma'glio [mál'yō] _sm_ mallet; (_macchina_) power hammer.
maglio'ne [mályō'ná] _sm_ jersey, sweater.
mag'ma _sm_ magma; (_fig_) mass.
magnac'cia [mányách'chá] _sm inv_ (_peg_) pimp.
magnanimità [mányánēmētá'] _sf_ magnanimity.
magna'nimo, a [mányá'nēmō] _ag_ magnanimous.
magna'te [mányá'tá] _sm_ tycoon, magnate.
magne'sia [mánye'zyá] _sf_ (_CHIM_) magnesia.
magne'sio [mánye'zyō] _sm_ (_CHIM_) magnesium; **al** ~ (_lampada, flash_) magnesium _cpd_.
magne'te [mánye'tá] _sm_ magnet.
magne'tico, a, ci, che [mánye'tēkō] _ag_ magnetic.
magneti'smo [mányātēz'mō] _sm_ magnetism.
magnetizza're [mányātēddzá'rá] _vt_ (_FISICA_) to magnetize; (_fig_) to mesmerize.
magneto'fono [mányátō'fōnō] _sm_ tape recorder.
magnificamen'te [mányēfēkámán'tá] _av_ magnificently, extremely well.
magnificen'za [mányēfēchen'tsá] _sf_ magnificence, splendor (_US_), splendour (_Brit_).
magni'fico, a, ci, che [mányē'fēkō] _ag_ magnificent, splendid; (_ospite_) generous.
ma'gno, a [mán'yō] _ag_: **aula** ~**a** main hall.
magno'lia [mányo'lyá] _sf_ magnolia.
ma'go, ghi _sm_ (_stregone_) magician, wizard; (_illusionista_) magician.
magrez'za [mágrát'tsá] _sf_ thinness.
ma'gro, a _ag_ (_very_) thin, skinny; (_carne_) lean; (_formaggio_) low-fat; (_fig: scarso, misero_) meager (_US_), meagre (_Brit_), poor; (_: meschino: scusa_) poor, lame; **mangiare di** ~ not to eat meat.
ma'i _av_ (_nessuna volta_) never; (_talvolta_) ever; **non ...** ~ never; ~ **più** never again; **come** ~**?** why (_o_ how) on earth?; **chi/dove/ quando** ~**?** whoever/wherever/whenever?
maia'le _sm_ (_ZOOL_) pig; (_carne_) pork.
maio'lica _sf_ majolica.
maione'se _sf_ mayonnaise.

Maior'ca *sf* Majorca.

ma'is *sm* corn (*US*), maize (*Brit*).

maiu'scolo, a *ag* (*lettera*) capital ♦ *sf* capital letter ♦ *sm* capital letters *pl*; (*TIP*) upper case; **scrivere tutto (in)** ~ to write everything in capitals *o* in capital letters.

mal *av, sm vedi* **male**.

ma'la *sf* (*gergo*) underworld.

malaccor'to, a *ag* rash, careless.

malafe'de *sf* bad faith.

malaffa're: di ~ *ag* (*gente*) shady, dishonest; **donna di** ~ prostitute.

malage'vole |málájä'võlä| *ag* difficult, hard.

malagra'zia |málágrát'tsyá| *sf*: **con** ~ with bad grace, impolitely.

malalin'gua, *pl* **malalin'gue** *sf* gossip (*person*).

malamen'te *av* badly; (*sgarbatamente*) rudely.

malanda'to, a *ag* (*persona: di salute*) in poor health; (*: di condizioni finanziarie*) badly off; (*trascurato*) shabby.

mala'nimo *sm* ill will, malevolence; **di** ~ unwillingly.

malan'no *sm* (*disgrazia*) misfortune; (*malattia*) ailment.

malape'na *sf*: **a** ~ hardly, scarcely.

mala'ria *sf* malaria.

mala'rico, a, ci, che *ag* malarial.

malasor'te *sf* bad luck.

malatic'cio, a |málátéch'chõ| *ag* sickly.

mala'to, a *ag* ill, sick; (*gamba*) bad; (*pianta*) diseased ♦ *sm/f* sick person; (*in ospedale*) patient; **darsi** ~ (*sul lavoro etc*) to go sick.

malatti'a *sf* (*infettiva etc*) illness, disease; (*cattiva salute*) illness, sickness; (*di pianta*) disease; **mettersi in** ~ to go on sick leave; **fare una** ~ **di qc** (*fig: disperarsi*) to get in a state about sth.

malaugura'to, a *ag* ill-fated, unlucky.

malaugu'rio *sm* bad *o* ill omen; **uccello del** ~ bird of ill omen.

malavi'ta *sf* underworld.

malavito'so, a *sm/f* gangster.

malavo'glia |málávol'yá|: **di** ~ *av* unwillingly, reluctantly.

Mala'wi |málá'vē| *sm*: **il** ~ Malawi.

Malaysi'a *sf* Malaysia.

malaysia'no, a *ag, sm/f* Malaysian.

malcapita'to, a *ag* unlucky, unfortunate ♦ *sm/f* unfortunate person.

malcon'cio, a, ci, ce |málkōn'chō| *ag* in a sorry state.

malconten'to *sm* discontent.

malcostu'me *sm* immorality.

maldes'tro, a *ag* (*inabile*) inexpert, inexperienced; (*goffo*) awkward.

maldicen'te |máldēchen'tā| *ag* slanderous.

maldicen'za |máldēchen'tsá| *sf* malicious gossip.

maldispo'sto, a *ag*: ~ **(verso)** ill-disposed (towards).

Maldi've *sfpl*: **le** ~ the Maldives.

ma'le *av* badly ♦ *sm* (*ciò che è ingiusto, disonesto*) evil; (*danno, svantaggio*) harm; (*sventura*) misfortune; (*dolore fisico, morale*) pain, ache; **sentirsi** ~ to feel ill; **aver mal di cuore/fegato** to have a heart/liver complaint; **aver mal di denti/d'orecchi/di testa** to have toothache/earache/a headache; **aver mal di gola** to have a sore throat; **aver** ~ **ai piedi** to have sore feet; **far** ~ (*dolere*) to hurt; **far** ~ **alla salute** to be bad for one's health; **far del** ~ **a qn** to hurt *o* harm sb; **parlar** ~ **di qn** to speak ill of sb; **restare** *o* **rimanere** ~ to be sorry; to be disappointed; to be hurt; **trattar** ~ **qn** to ill-treat sb; **andare a** ~ to go off *o* bad; **come va?** — **non c'è** ~ how are you? — not bad; **di** ~ **in peggio** from bad to worse; **per** ~ **che vada** however badly things go; **non avertene a** ~, **non prendertela a** ~ don't take it to heart; **mal comune mezzo gaudio** (*proverbio*) a trouble shared is a trouble halved; **mal d'auto** carsickness; **mal di mare** seasickness.

maledet'to, a *pp di* **maledire** ♦ *ag* cursed, damned; (*fig fam*) damned, blasted.

maledi're *vt* to curse.

maledizio'ne |málādēttsyō'nä| *sf* curse; ~! damn it!

maleduca'to, a *ag* rude, ill-mannered.

maleducazio'ne |málādōōkáttsyō'nä| *sf* rudeness.

malefat'ta *sf* misdeed.

malefi'cio |málāfē'chō| *sm* witchcraft.

male'fico, a, ci, che *ag* (*aria, cibo*) harmful, bad; (*influsso, azione*) evil.

male'se *ag, sm/f* Malay(an) ♦ *sm* (*LING*) Malay.

Male'sia *sf* Malaya.

males'sere *sm* indisposition, slight illness; (*fig*) uneasiness.

malevolen'za |málāvōlen'tsá| *sf* malevolence.

male'volo, a *ag* malevolent.

malfama'to, a *ag* notorious.

malfat'to, a *ag* (*persona*) deformed; (*oggetto*) badly made; (*lavoro*) badly done.

malfatto're, tri'ce *sm/f* wrongdoer.

malfer'mo, a *ag* unsteady, shaky; (*salute*) poor, delicate.

malformazio'ne |málfōrmáttsyō'nä| *sf* malformation.

mal'ga, ghe *sf* Alpine hut.

malgover'no *sm* maladministration.

malgra'do *prep* in spite of, despite ♦ *cong* although; **mio** (*o* **tuo** *etc*) ~ against my (*o* your *etc*) will.

mali'a *sf* spell; (*fig: fascino*) charm.

maliar'do, a *ag* (*occhi, sorriso*) bewitching ♦ *sf* enchantress.

malignamen'te [málēnyámān'tā] *av* maliciously.

maligna're [málēnyá'rā] *vi:* ~ **su** to malign, speak ill of.

malignità [málēnyētá'] *sf inv* (*qualità*) malice, spite; (*osservazione*) spiteful remark; **con** ~ spitefully, maliciously.

mali'gno, a [málēn'yō] *ag* (*malvagio*) malicious, malignant; (*MED*) malignant.

malinconi'a *sf* melancholy, gloom.

malinco'nico, a, ci, che *ag* melancholy.

malincuo're: a ~ *av* reluctantly, unwillingly.

malinforma'to, a *ag* misinformed.

malintenziona'to, a [málēntāntsyōná'tō] *ag* ill-intentioned.

malinte'so, a *ag* misunderstood; (*riguardo, senso del dovere*) mistaken, wrong ♦ *sm* misunderstanding.

mali'zia [málēt'tsyà] *sf* (*malignità*) malice; (*furbizia*) cunning; (*espediente*) trick.

malizio'so, a [málēttsyō'sō] *ag* malicious; cunning; (*vivace, birichino*) mischievous.

mallea'bile *ag* malleable.

mallevado're *sm* guarantor.

malleveri'a *sf* guarantee, surety.

mallop'po *sm* (*fam: refurtiva*) loot.

malmena're *vt* to beat up; (*fig*) to ill-treat.

malmes'so, a *ag* shabby.

malnutri'to, a *ag* undernourished.

malnutrizio'ne [málnōōtrēttsyō'nā] *sf* malnutrition.

ma'lo, a *ag:* **in** ~ **modo** badly.

maloc'chio [málok'kyō] *sm* evil eye.

malo'ra *sf* (*fam*): **andare in** ~ to go to the dogs; **va in** ~! go to hell!

malo're *sm* (sudden) illness.

malridot'to, a *ag* (*abiti, scarpe, persona*) in a sorry state; (*casa, macchina*) dilapidated, in a poor state of repair.

malsa'no, a *ag* unhealthy.

malsicu'ro, a *ag* unsafe.

Mal'ta *sf* Malta.

mal'ta *sf* (*EDIL*) mortar.

maltem'po *sm* bad weather.

maltenu'to, a *ag* badly looked after, badly kept.

malte'se *ag, sm/f, sm* Maltese *inv*.

mal'to *sm* malt.

maltol'to *sm* ill-gotten gains *pl*.

maltrattamen'to *sm* ill treatment.

maltratta're *vt* to mistreat.

malumo're *sm* bad mood; (*irritabilità*) bad temper; (*discordia*) ill feeling; **di** ~ in a bad mood.

mal'va *sf* (*BOT*) mallow ♦ *ag, sm inv* mauve.

malva'gio, a, gi, gie [málvá'jō] *ag* wicked, evil.

malvagità [málvájētá'] *sf inv* (*qualità*) wickedness; (*azione*) wicked deed.

malversazio'ne [málvārsáttsyō'nā] *sf* (*DIR*) embezzlement.

malvesti'to, a *ag* badly dressed, ill-clad.

malvi'sto, a *ag:* ~ **(da)** disliked (by), unpopular (with).

malviven'te *sm* criminal.

malvolentie'ri *av* unwillingly, reluctantly.

malvole're *vt:* **farsi** ~ **da qn** to make o.s. unpopular with sb ♦ *sm:* **prendere qn a** ~ to take a dislike to sb.

mam'ma *sf* mom (*US*), mum(my) (*Brit*); ~ **mia!** my goodness!

mamma'rio, a *ag* (*ANAT*) mammary.

mammel'la *sf* (*ANAT*) breast; (*di vacca, capra etc*) udder.

mammi'fero *sm* mammal.

mammi'smo *sm* excessive attachment to one's mother.

mam'mola *sf* (*BOT*) violet.

ma'nager [ma'nējə] *sm inv* manager.

manageria'le [mànájáryà'lā] *ag* managerial.

mana'ta *sf* (*colpo*) slap; (*quantità*) handful.

man'ca *sf* left (hand); **a destra e a** ~ left, right and center, on all sides.

mancamen'to *sm* (*di forze*) (feeling of) faintness, weakness.

mancan'za [mànkàn'tsà] *sf* lack; (*carenza*) shortage, scarcity; (*fallo*) fault; (*imperfezione*) failing, shortcoming; **per** ~ **di tempo** through lack of time; **in** ~ **di meglio** for lack of anything better; **sentire la** ~ **di qc/qn** to miss sth/sb.

manca're *vi* (*essere insufficiente*) to be lacking; (*venir meno*) to fail; (*sbagliare*) to be wrong, make a mistake; (*non esserci*) to be missing, not to be there; (*essere lontano*): ~ **(da)** to be away (from) ♦ *vt* to miss; ~ **di** to lack; ~ **a** (*promessa*) to fail to keep; **tu mi manchi** I miss you; **mancò poco che morisse** he very nearly died; **mancano ancora 10 dollari** we're still $10 short; **manca un quarto alle 6** it's a quarter to 6; **non mancherò** I won't forget, I'll make sure I do so; **ci mancherebbe altro!** of course I (*o* you *etc*) will!; ~ **da casa** to be away from home; ~ **di rispetto a** *o* **verso qn** to be lacking in respect towards sb, be disrespectful towards sb; ~ **di parola** not to keep one's word, go back on one's word; **sentirsi** ~ to feel faint.

manca'to, a *ag* (*tentativo*) unsuccessful; (*artista*) failed.

manche [mânsh] *sf inv* (*SPORT*) heat.

mancherò *etc* [mànkáro'] *vb vedi* **mancare**.

manche'vole [mànkā'vōlā] *ag* (*insufficiente*) inadequate, insufficient.

manchevolez'za [mànkāvōlāt'tsà] *sf* (*scorrettezza*) fault, shortcoming.

man'cia, ce [màn'chá] *sf* tip; ~ **competente** reward.

mancia'ta [mànchá'tá] *sf* handful.

manci'no, a [mànchē'nō] *ag* (*braccio*) left;

(*persona*) left-handed; (*fig*) underhand.

man'co *av* (*nemmeno*): ~ **per sogno** *o* **per idea!** not on your life!

mandan'te *sm/f* (*DIR*) principal; (*istigatore*) instigator.

mandaran'cio [màndàrán'chō] *sm* clementine.

manda're *vt* to send; (*far funzionare: macchina*) to drive; (*emettere*) to send out; (: *grido*) to give, utter, let out; ~ **avanti** (*persona*) to send ahead; (*fig: famiglia*) to provide for; (: *ditta*) to look after, run; (: *pratica*) to attend to; ~ **a chiamare qn** to send for sb; ~ **giù** to send down; (*anche fig*) to swallow; ~ **in onda** (*RADIO, TV*) to broadcast; ~ **in rovina** to ruin; ~ **via** to send away; (*licenziare*) to fire.

mandari'no *sm* mandarin (orange); (*cinese*) mandarin.

manda'ta *sf* (*quantità*) lot, batch; (*di chiave*) turn; **chiudere a doppia** ~ to double-lock.

mandata'rio *sm* (*DIR*) representative, agent.

manda'to *sm* (*incarico*) commission; (*DIR: provvedimento*) warrant; (*di deputato etc*) mandate; (*ordine di pagamento*) postal *o* money order; ~ **d'arresto**, ~ **di cattura** warrant for arrest; ~ **di comparizione** summons *sg*; ~ **di perquisizione** search warrant.

mandi'bola *sf* mandible, jaw.

mandoli'no *sm* mandolin(e).

man'dorla *sf* almond.

mandorla'to *sm* nut brittle.

man'dorlo *sm* almond tree.

man'dria *sf* herd.

mandria'no *sm* cowherd, herdsman.

mandri'no *sm* (*TECN*) mandrel.

manegge'vole [mànādjà'vōlā] *ag* easy to handle.

maneggia're [mànādjà'rā] *vt* (*creta, cera*) to mold (*US*), mould (*Brit*), work, fashion; (*arnesi, utensili*) to handle; (: *adoperare*) to use; (*fig: persone, denaro*) to handle, deal with.

maneg'gio [mànād'jō] *sm* molding (*US*), moulding (*Brit*); handling; use; (*intrigo*) plot, scheme; (*per cavalli*) riding school.

mane'sco, a, schi, sche *ag* free with one's fists.

manet'te *sfpl* handcuffs.

manganel'lo *sm* club.

manga'ne'se *sm* manganese.

mangerec'cio, a, ci, ce [mànjārāch'chō] *ag* edible.

mangia'bile [mànjá'bēlā] *ag* edible, eatable.

mangiadis'chi [mànjàdē'skē] *sm inv* record player.

mangianas'tri [mànjànás'trē] *sm inv* cassette-recorder.

mangia're [mànjá'rā] *vt* to eat; (*intaccare*) to eat into *o* away; (*CARTE, SCACCHI etc*) to

take ♦ *vi* to eat ♦ *sm* eating; (*cibo*) food; (*cucina*) cooking; **fare da** ~ to do the cooking; **~rsi le parole** to mumble; **~rsi le unghie** to bite one's nails.

mangiasol'di [mànjàsol'dē] *ag inv* (*fam*): **macchinetta** ~ one-armed bandit.

mangiato'ia [mànjátō'yá] *sf* feeding-trough.

mangi'me [mànjē'mā] *sm* fodder.

mangiucchia're [mànjōōkkyá'rā] *vt* to nibble.

man'go, ghi *sm* mango.

mani'a *sf* (*PSIC*) mania; (*fig*) obsession, craze; **avere la** ~ **di fare qc** to have a habit of doing sth; ~ **di persecuzione** persecution complex *o* mania.

maniaca'le *ag* (*PSIC*) maniacal; (*fanatico*) fanatical.

mani'aco, a, ci, che *ag* suffering from a mania; ~ (**di**) obsessed (by), crazy (about).

ma'nica, che *sf* sleeve; (*fig: gruppo*) gang, bunch; (*GEO*): **la M~, il Canale della M~** the (English) Channel; **senza ~che** sleeveless; **essere in ~che di camicia** to be in one's shirt sleeves; **essere di** ~ **larga/stretta** to be easy-going/strict; ~ **a vento** (*AER*) wind sock.

manicaret'to *sm* tidbit (*US*), titbit (*Brit*).

manichet'ta [mànēkāt'tá] *sf* (*TECN*) hose.

manichi'no [mànēkē'nō] *sm* (*di sarto, vetrina*) dummy.

ma'nico, ci *sm* handle; (*MUS*) neck; ~ **di scopa** broomstick.

manico'mio *sm* mental hospital; (*fig*) madhouse.

manicot'to *sm* muff; (*TECN*) coupling; sleeve.

manicu're *sm o f inv* manicure ♦ *sf inv* manicurist.

manie'ra *sf* way, manner; (*stile*) style, manner; **~e** *sfpl* manners; **in** ~ **che** so that; **in** ~ **da** so as to; **alla** ~ **di** in *o* after the style of; **in una** ~ **o nell'altra** one way or another; **in tutte le ~e** at all costs; **usare buone ~e con qn** to be polite to sb; **usare le ~e forti** to use strong-arm tactics.

maniera'to, a *ag* affected.

manie'ro *sm* manor.

manifattu'ra *sf* (*lavorazione*) manufacture; (*stabilimento*) factory.

manifatturie'ro, a *ag* manufacturing.

manifestan'te *sm/f* demonstrator.

manifesta're *vt* to show, display; (*esprimere*) to express; (*rivelare*) to reveal, disclose ♦ *vi* to demonstrate; **~rsi** *vr* to show o.s.; **~rsi amico** to prove o.s. (to be) a friend.

manifestazio'ne [mànēfāstáttsyō'nā] *sf* show, display; expression; (*sintomo*) sign, symptom; (*dimostrazione pubblica*) demonstration; (*cerimonia*) event.

manifesti'no *sm* leaflet.

manife'sto, a *ag* obvious, evident ♦ *sm* poster, bill; (scritto ideologico) manifesto.

mani'glia [mánēl'yá] sf handle; (sostegno: negli autobus etc) strap.

Mani'la sf Manila.

manipola're vt to manipulate; (alterare: vino) to adulterate.

manipolazio'ne [mánēpōláttsyō'nā] sf manipulation; adulteration.

mani'polo sm (drappello) handful.

maniscal'co, chi sm blacksmith.

man'na sf (REL) manna.

manna'ia sf (del boia) (executioner's) ax (US) o axe (Brit); (per carni) cleaver.

manna'ro, a ag: **lupo ~** werewolf.

ma'no, i sf hand; (strato: di vernice etc) coat; **a ~** by hand; **cucito a ~** hand-sewn; **fatto a ~** handmade; **alla ~** (persona) easygoing; **fuori ~** out of the way; **di prima ~** (notizia) first-hand; **di seconda ~** secondhand; **man ~** little by little, gradually; **man ~ che** as; **a piene ~i** (fig) generously; **spendere le ~i bucate** to spend money like water; **aver le ~i in pasta** to be in the know; **avere qc per le ~i** (progetto, lavoro) to have sth in hand; **dare una ~ a qn** to lend sb a hand; **dare una ~ di vernice a qc** to give sth a coat of paint; **darsi la ~** to shake hands; **forzare la ~** to go too far; **mettere ~ a qc** to have a hand in sth; **mettere le ~i avanti** (fig) to safeguard o.s.; **restare a ~i vuote** to be left empty-handed; **venire alle ~i** to come to blows; **~i in alto!** hands up!

manodo'pera sf labor (US), labour (Brit).

manomes'so, a pp di **manomettere**.

mano'metro sm gauge, manometer.

manomet'tere vt (alterare) to tamper with; (aprire indebitamente) to break open illegally.

manomissio'ne sf (di prove etc) tampering; (di lettera) opening.

mano'pola sf (dell'armatura) gauntlet; (guanto) mitt; (di impugnatura) hand-grip; (pomello) knob.

manoscrit'to, a ag handwritten ♦ sm manuscript.

manovalan'za [mánōválán'tsá] sf unskilled workers pl.

manova'le sm laborer (US), labourer (Brit).

manovel'la sf handle; (TECN) crank.

mano'vra sf maneuver (US), manoeuvre (Brit); (FERR) shunting; **~e di corridoio** palace intrigues.

manovra're vt (veicolo) to maneuver (US), manoeuvre (Brit); (macchina, congegno) to operate; (fig: persona) to manipulate ♦ vi to maneuver.

manrove'scio [mánrōvcsh'shō] sm slap (with back of hand).

mansar'da sf attic.

mansio'ne sf task, duty, job.

mansue'to, a ag (animale) tame; (persona) gentle, docile.

mansuetu'dine sf tameness; gentleness, docility.

mantel'lo sm cloak; (fig: di neve etc) blanket, mantle; (TECN: involucro) casing, shell; (ZOOL) coat.

mantene're vt to maintain; (adempiere: promesse) to keep, abide by; (provvedere a) to support, maintain; **~rsi** vr: **~rsi calmo/giovane** to stay calm/young; **~ i contatti con qn** to keep in touch with sb.

mantenimen'to sm maintenance.

mantenu'to, a sm/f gigolo/kept woman.

man'tice [mán'tēchā] sm bellows pl; (di carrozza, automobile) top (US), hood (Brit).

man'to sm cloak; **~ stradale** road surface.

Man'tova sf Mantua.

mantova'no, a ag of (o from) Mantua.

manua'le ag manual ♦ sm (testo) manual, handbook.

manuali'stico, a, ci, che ag textbook cpd.

manualmen'te av manually, by hand.

manu'brio sm handle; (di bicicletta etc) handlebars pl; (SPORT) dumbbell.

manufat'to sm manufactured article; **~i** smpl manufactured goods.

manutenzio'ne [mánōōtántsyō'nā] sf maintenance, upkeep; (d'impianti) maintenance, servicing.

man'zo [mán'dzō] sm (ZOOL) steer; (carne) beef.

Maomet'to sm Mohammed.

map'pa sf (GEO) map.

mappamon'do sm map of the world; (globo girevole) globe.

mara'sma, i sm (fig) decay, decline.

marato'na sf marathon.

mar'ca, che sf mark; (bollo) stamp; (COMM: di prodotti) brand; (contrassegno, scontrino) ticket, check; **prodotti di (gran) ~** high-class products; **~ da bollo** official stamp.

marca're vt (munire di contrassegno) to mark; (a fuoco) to brand; (SPORT: gol) to score; (: avversario) to mark; (accentuare) to stress; **~ visita** (MIL) to report sick.

marca'to, a ag (lineamenti, accento etc) pronounced.

Mar'che [már'kā] sfpl: **le ~** the Marches (region of central Italy).

marcherò etc [márkāro'] vb vedi **marcare**.

marche'se, a [márkā'zā] sm/f marquis o marquess/marchioness.

marchia'no, a [márkyá'nō] ag (errore) glaring, gross.

marchia're [márkyá'rā] vt to brand.

marchigia'no, a [márkčjá'nō] ag of (o from) the Marches.

mar'chio [már'kyō] sm (di bestiame, COMM, fig) brand; **~ deposato** registered trademark; ~ **di fabbrica** trademark.

mar'cia, ce [màr'chá] *sf (anche MUS, MIL)*
march; *(funzionamento)* running; *(il camminare)* walking; *(AUT)* gear; **mettere in** ~ to
start; **mettersi in** ~ to get moving; **far** ~
indietro *(AUT)* to reverse; *(fig)* to backpedal; ~ **forzata** forced march; ~ **funebre**
funeral march.

marciapie'de [màrchápye'dā] *sm (di strada)*
sidewalk *(US)*, pavement *(Brit)*; *(FERR)* platform.

marcia're [màrchá'rā] *vi* to march; *(andare:
treno, macchina)* to go; *(funzionare)* to run,
work.

mar'cio, a, ci, ce [màr'chō] *ag (frutta, legno)*
rotten, bad; *(MED)* festering; *(fig)* corrupt,
rotten ♦ *sm*: **c'è del** ~ **in questa storia** *(fig)*
there's something fishy about this business;
avere torto ~ to be utterly wrong.

marci're [màrchē'rā] *vi (andare a male)* to go
bad, rot; *(suppurare)* to fester; *(fig)* to rot.

marciu'me [màrchōō'mā] *sm (parte guasta: di
cibi etc)* rotten part, bad part; *(di radice,
pianta)* rot; *(fig: corruzione)* rottenness, corruption.

mar'co, chi *sm (unità monetaria)* mark.

ma're *sm* sea; **di** ~ *(brezza, acqua, uccelli,
pesce)* sea *cpd*; **in** ~ at sea; **per** ~ by sea;
sul ~ *(barca)* on the sea; *(villaggio, località)*
by *o* beside the sea; **andare al** ~ *(in vacanza
etc)* to go to the seaside; **il mar Caspio** the
Caspian Sea; **il mar Morto** the Dead Sea; **il
mar Nero** the Black Sea; **il** ~ **del Nord** the
North Sea; **il mar Rosso** the Red Sea; **il mar
dei Sargassi** the Sargasso Sea; **i** ~**i del Sud**
the South Seas.

mare'a *sf* tide; **alta/bassa** ~ high/low tide.

mareggia'ta [màrādjá'tá] *sf* heavy sea.

marem'ma *sf (GEO)* swampy coastal area.

maremma'no, a *ag (zona, macchia)*
swampy; *(della Maremma)* of *(o* from) the
Maremma.

maremo'to *sm* seaquake.

marescial'lo [màrāshàl'lō] *sm (MIL)* marshal;
(: sottufficiale) warrant officer.

marezza'to, a [màrāddzá'tō] *ag (seta etc)* wa-
tered, moiré; *(legno)* veined; *(carta)* mar-
bled.

margari'na *sf* margarine.

margheri'ta [màrgārē'tá] *sf* (ox-eye) daisy,
marguerite; *(di stampante)* daisy wheel.

margheriti'na [màrgārētē'ná] *sf* daisy.

margina'le [màrjēná'lā] *ag* marginal.

mar'gine [màr'jēnā] *sm* margin; *(di bosco,
via)* edge; border; **avere un buon** ~ **di
tempo/denaro** to have plenty of time/money;
~ **di guadagno** *o* **di utile** profit margin; ~ **di
sicurezza** safety margin.

marijua'na [marēwà:'nə] *sf* marijuana.

mari'na *sf* navy; *(costa)* coast; *(quadro)*

seascape; ~ **mercantile** merchant marine
(US) o navy *(Brit)*; ~ **militare (M.M.)** ≈
Navy *(US)*, Royal Navy (RN) *(Brit)*.

marina'io *sm* sailor.

marina're *vt (CUC)* to marinate; ~ **la scuola**
to play truant.

marina'ro, a *ag (tradizione, popolo)* sea-
faring; *(CUC)* with seafood; **alla** ~**a** *(vestito,
cappello)* sailor *cpd*; **borgo** ~ district where
fishing folk live.

marina'ta *sf* marinade.

mari'no, a *ag* sea *cpd*, marine.

marionet'ta *sf* puppet.

marita're *vt* to marry; ~**rsi** *vr*: ~**rsi a** *o* **con
qn** to marry sb, get married to sb.

marita'to, a *ag* married.

mari'to *sm* husband; **prendere** ~ to get
married; **ragazza (in età) da** ~ girl of
marriageable age.

marit'timo, a *ag* maritime, sea *cpd*.

marma'glia [màrmál'yá] *sf* mob, riff-raff.

marmella'ta *sf* jam; *(di agrumi)* marmalade.

marmit'ta *sf (recipiente)* pot; *(AUT)* silencer.

mar'mo *sm* marble.

marmoc'chio [màrmok'kyō] *sm (fam)* (little)
kid.

marmot'ta *sf (ZOOL)* marmot.

marocchi'no, a [màrōkkē'nō] *ag, sm/f* Moroccan.

Maroc'co *sm*: **il** ~ Morocco.

maro'so *sm* breaker.

mar'ra *sf* hoe.

Marrakesh' [màrràkāsh'] *sf* Marrakesh.

marro'ne *ag inv* brown ♦ *sm (BOT)* chestnut.

marsa'la *sm inv (vino)* Marsala (wine).

Marsi'glia [màrsēl'yá] *sf* Marseilles.

marsi'na *sf* tails *pl*, tail coat.

marsu'pio *sm (ZOOL)* pouch, marsupium.

mart. *abbr* (= *martedì*) Tue(s).

Mar'te *sm (ASTR, MITOLOGIA)* Mars.

martedì *sm inv* Tuesday; **di** *o* **il** ~ on Tues-
days; **oggi è** ~ **3 aprile** (the date) today is
Tuesday April 3rd; ~ **stavo male** I wasn't
well on Tuesday; **il giornale di** ~ Tuesday's
newspaper; ~ **grasso** Shrove Tuesday.

martellan'te *ag (fig: dolore)* throbbing.

martella're *vt* to hammer ♦ *vi (pulsare)* to
throb; *(: cuore)* to thump.

martellet'to *sm (di pianoforte)* hammer; *(di
macchina da scrivere)* typebar; *(di giudice,
nelle vendite all'asta)* gavel; *(MED)* percussion hammer.

martel'lo *sm* hammer; *(di uscio)* knocker;
suonare a ~ *(fig: campane)* to sound the
tocsin; ~ **pneumatico** pneumatic drill.

martinet'to *sm (TECN)* jack.

martinga'la *sf (di giacca)* half-belt; *(di cavallo)* martingale.

mar'tire *sm/f* martyr.

marti'rio *sm* martyrdom; *(fig)* agony, torture.

mar'tora *sf* marten.
martoria're *vt* to torment, torture.
marxi'smo *sm* Marxism.
marxi'sta, i, e *ag, sm/f* Marxist.
marzapa'ne [màrtsàpà'nä] *sm* marzipan.
marzia'le [màrtsyà'lä] *ag* martial.
mar'zo [màr'tsō] *sm* March; *per fraseologia vedi* **luglio.**
marzoli'no, a [màrtsōlē'nō] *ag* March *cpd.*
mascalzona'ta [màskàltsōnà'tà] *sf* dirty trick.
mascalzo'ne [màskàltsō'nä] *sm* rascal, scoundrel.
masca'ra *sm inv* mascara.
mascarpo'ne *sm soft cream cheese often used in desserts.*
mascel'la [màshel'lä] *sf* (*ANAT*) jaw.
mas'chera [mà'skàrà] *sf* mask; (*travestimento*) disguise; (: *per un ballo etc*) fancy dress; (*TEATRO, CINEMA*) usher/usherette; (*personaggio del teatro*) stock character; **in ~** (*mascherato*) masked; **ballo in ~** fancy-dress ball; **gettere la ~** (*fig*) to reveal o.s.; **~ antigas/subacquea** gas/diving mask; **~ di bellezza** face pack.
maschera're [màskàrà'rä] *vt* to mask; (*travestire*) to disguise; to dress up; (*fig: celare*) to hide, conceal; (*MIL*) to camouflage; **~rsi** *vr:* **~rsi da** to disguise o.s. as; to dress up as; (*fig*) to masquerade as.
mascheri'na [màskàrē'nà] *sf* (*piccola maschera*) mask; (*di animale*) patch; (*di scarpe*) toe-cap; (*AUT*) radiator grill.
maschi'le [màskē'lä] *ag* masculine; (*sesso, popolazione*) male; (*abiti*) men's; (*per ragazzi: scuola*) boys'.
mas'chio, a [màs'kyō] *ag* (*BIOL*) male; (*virile*) manly ♦ *sm* (*anche ZOOL. TECN*) male; (*uomo*) man; (*ragazzo*) boy; (*figlio*) son.
mascoli'no, a *ag* masculine.
mascot'te [màskot'] *sf inv* mascot.
masochi'smo [màzōkēz'mō] *sm* masochism.
masochi'sta, i, e [màzōkē'stá] *ag* masochistic ♦ *sm/f* masochist.
mas'sa *sf* mass; (*di errori etc*): **una ~ di** heaps of, masses of; (*di gente*) mass, multitude; (*ELETTR*) ground (*US*), earth (*Brit*); **in ~** (*COMM*) in bulk; (*tutti insieme*) en masse; **adunata in ~** mass meeting; **manifestazione/cultura di ~** mass demonstration/culture; **produrre in ~** to mass-produce; **la ~ (del popolo)** the masses *pl.*
massacran'te *ag* exhausting, gruelling.
massacra're *vt* to massacre, slaughter.
massa'cro *sm* massacre, slaughter; (*fig*) mess, disaster.
massaggia're [màssàdjà'rä] *vt* to massage.
massaggiato're, tri'ce [màssàdjàtō'rä] *sm/f* masseur/masseuse.
massag'gio [màssàd'jō] *sm* massage.
massa'ia *sf* housewife.

masseri'a *sf* large farm.
masseri'zie [màssārēt'tsyä] *sfpl* (household) furnishings.
massic'cio, a, ci, ce [màssēch'chō] *ag* (*oro, legno*) solid; (*palazzo*) massive; (*corporatura*) stout ♦ *sm* (*GEO*) massif.
mas'sima *sf vedi* **massimo.**
massima'le *sm* maximum; (*COMM*) ceiling, limit.
mas'simo, a *ag, sm* maximum ♦ *sf* (*sentenza, regola*) maxim; (*METEOR*) maximum temperature; **in linea di ~a** generally speaking; **arrivare entro il tempo ~** to arrive within the time limit; **al ~** at (the) most; **sfruttare qc al ~** to make full use of sth; **arriverò al ~ alle 5** I'll arrive at 5 at the latest; **erano presenti le ~e autorità** all the most important dignitaries were there; **il ~ della pena** (*DIR*) the maximum penalty.
massi'vo, a *ag* (*intervento*) en masse; (*emigrazione*) mass; (*emorragia*) massive.
mas'so *sm* rock, boulder.
masso'ne *sm* freemason.
massoneri'a *sf* freemasonry.
masso'nico, a, ci, che *ag* masonic.
mastel'lo *sm* tub.
mastica're *vt* to chew.
ma'stice [mà'stēchä] *sm* mastic; (*per vetri*) putty.
masti'no *sm* mastiff.
masturbazio'ne [màstōōrbàttsyō'nä] *sf* masturbation.
matas'sa *sf* skein.
matema'tico, a, ci, che *ag* mathematical ♦ *sm/f* mathematician ♦ *sf* mathematics *sg.*
materassi'no *sm* mat; **~ gonfiabile** inflatable mattress.
materas'so *sm* mattress; **~ a molle** spring mattress.
mate'ria *sf* (*FISICA*) matter; (*TECN, COMM*) material, matter *q*; (*disciplina*) subject; (*argomento*) subject matter, material; **prima di entrare in ~ ...** before discussing the matter in hand ...; **un esperto in ~ (di musica etc)** an expert on the subject (of music etc); **sono ignorante in ~** I know nothing about it; **~ cerebrale** cerebral matter; **~ grassa** fat; **~ grigia** (*anche fig*) grey matter; **~e plastiche** plastics; **~e prime** raw materials.
materia'le *ag* material; (*fig: grossolano*) rough, rude ♦ *sm* material; (*insieme di strumenti etc*) equipment *q*, materials *pl*; **~ da costruzione** building materials *pl.*
materiali'sta, i, e *ag* materialistic ♦ *sm/f* materialist.
materializzar'si [màtāryàlēddzàr'sē] *vr* to materialize.
materialmen'te *av* (*fisicamente*) materially; (*economicamente*) financially.

maternità *sf* motherhood, maternity; (*clinica*) birthing center (*US*), maternity hospital (*Brit*); **in (congedo di)** ~ on maternity leave.

mater'no, a *ag* (*amore, cura etc*) maternal, motherly; (*nonno*) maternal; (*lingua, terra*) mother *cpd*; **scuola** ~**a** nursery school.

mati'ta *sf* pencil; ~**e colorate** crayons; ~ **per gli occhi** eyeliner (pencil).

matri'ce |mátrē'chă| *sf* matrix; (*COMM*) counterfoil; (*fig: origine*) background.

matri'cola *sf* (*registro*) register; (*numero*) registration number; (*nell'università*) freshman, fresher (*Brit fam*).

matri'gna |mátrēn'yă| *sf* stepmother.

matrimonia'le *ag* matrimonial, marriage *cpd*; **camera/letto** ~ double room/bed.

matrimo'nio *sm* marriage, matrimony; (*durata*) marriage, married life; (*cerimonia*) wedding.

matro'na *sf* (*fig*) matronly woman.

mattato'io *sm* slaughterhouse, abattoir (*Brit*).

matti'na *sf* morning; **la** *o* **alla** *o* **di** ~ in the morning; **di prima** ~, **la** ~ **presto** early in the morning; **dalla** ~ **alla sera** (*continuamente*) from morning to night; (*improvvisamente: cambiare*) overnight.

mattina'ta *sf* morning; (*spettacolo*) matinée, afternoon performance; **in** ~ in the course of the morning; **nella** ~ in the morning; **nella tarda** ~ at the end of the morning; **nella tarda** ~ **di sabato** late on Saturday morning.

mattinie'ro, a *ag*: **essere** ~ to be an early riser.

matti'no *sm* morning; **di buon** ~ early in the morning.

mat'to, a *ag* mad, crazy; (*fig: falso*) false, imitation; (: *opaco*) matt, dull ♦ *sm/f* madman/woman; **avere una voglia** ~**a di qc** to be dying for sth; **far diventare** ~ **qn** to drive sb mad *o* crazy; **una gabbia di** ~**i** (*fig*) a madhouse.

matto'ne *sm* brick; (*fig*): **questo libro/film è un** ~ this book/film is heavy going.

mattonel'la *sf* tile.

mattuti'no, a *ag* morning *cpd*.

matura're *vi* (*anche:* ~**rsi**) (*frutta, grano*) to ripen; (*ascesso*) to come to a head; (*fig: persona, idea, ECON*) to mature ♦ *vt* to ripen; to (make) mature; ~ **una decisione** to come to a decision.

maturità *sf* maturity; (*di frutta*) ripeness, maturity; (*INS*) graduation (*US*) *o* school-leaving (*Brit*) examination.

matu'ro, a *ag* mature; (*frutto*) ripe, mature.

matu'sa *sm/f inv* (*scherzoso*) old fogey.

Maurita'nia *sf*: **la** ~ Mauritania.

Mauri'zio |máōōrēt'tsyō| *sf*: **(l'isola di)** ~ Mauritius.

mausole'o *sm* mausoleum.

max. *abbr* (= *massimo*) max.

ma'xi... *prefisso* maxi....

maz'za |mát'tsă| *sf* (*bastone*) club; (*martello*) sledge-hammer; (*SPORT: da golf*) club; (: *da baseball, cricket*) bat.

mazza'ta |máttsă'tă| *sf* (*anche fig*) heavy blow.

mazzet'ta |máttsāt'tă| *sf* (*di banconote etc*) bundle.

maz'zo |mát'tsō| *sm* (*di fiori, chiavi etc*) bunch; (*di carte da gioco*) pack.

MC *sigla* = Macerata.

ME *sigla* = Messina.

me *pronome* me; **sei bravo quanto** ~ you are as clever as I (am) *o* as me.

mean'dro *sm* meander.

M.E.C. |mek| *abbr m* = **Mercato Comune Europeo.**

Mec'ca *sf* (*anche fig*): **La** ~ Mecca.

meccanicamen'te *av* mechanically.

mecca'nico, a, ci, che *ag* mechanical ♦ *sm* mechanic ♦ *sf* mechanics *sg*; (*attività tecnologica*) mechanical engineering; (*meccanismo*) mechanism; **officina** ~**a** garage.

meccani'smo *sm* mechanism.

meccanizza're |mākkánēddzá'rā| *vt* to mechanize.

meccanizzazio'ne |mākkánēddzáttsyō'nā| *sf* mechanization.

meccanografi'a *sf* (*mechanical*) data processing.

meccanogra'fico, a, ci, che *ag*: **centro** ~ data processing department.

mecena'te |māchānă'tā| *sm* patron.

mèche |mesh| *sf inv* streak; **farsi le** ~ to have one's hair streaked.

meda'glia |mādál'yă| *sf* medal; ~ **d'oro** (*oggetto*) gold medal; (*persona*) gold medalist (*US*) *o* medallist (*Brit*).

medaglio'ne |mādályō'nā| *sm* (*ARCHIT*) medallion; (*gioiello*) locket.

mede'simo, a *ag* same; (*in persona*): **io** ~ I myself.

me'dia *sf vedi* **medio.**

mediamen'te *av* on average.

media'no, a *ag* median; (*valore*) mean ♦ *sm* (*CALCIO*) half-back.

median'te *prep* by means of.

media're *vt* (*fare da mediatore*) to act as mediator in; (*MAT*) to average.

media'to, a *ag* indirect.

mediato're, tri'ce *sm/f* mediator; (*COMM*) middle man, agent; **fare da** ~ **fra** to mediate between.

mediazio'ne |mādyáttsyō'nā| *sf* mediation; (*COMM: azione, compenso*) brokerage.

medicamen'to *sm* medicine, drug.

medica're *vt* to treat; (*ferita*) to dress.

medica'to, a *ag* (*garza, shampoo*) medicated.

medicazio'ne |mādēkáttsyō'nā| *sf* treatment,

medication; dressing; **fare una** ~ **a qn** to dress sb's wounds.

medici'na [mādēchē'nà] *sf* medicine; ~ **legale** forensic medicine.

medicina'le [mādēchēnà'lā] *ag* medicinal ♦ *sm* drug, medicine.

me'dico, a, ci, che *ag* medical ♦ *sm* doctor; ~ **di bordo** ship's doctor; ~ **di famiglia** family doctor; ~ **fiscale** *doctor who examines patients signed off sick for a lengthy period by their private doctor*; ~ **generico** general practitioner, GP.

medieva'le *ag* medieval.

me'dio, a *ag* average; (*punto, ceto*) middle; (*altezza, statura*) medium ♦ *sm* (*dito*) middle finger ♦ *sf* average; (*MAT*) mean; (*INS: voto*) ≈ grade point average (*US*), end-of-term average (*Brit*); ~**e** *sfpl, scuola* ~**a** *first 3 years of high school*; **licenza** ~**a** *leaving certificate awarded at the end of 3 years of secondary education*; **in** ~**a** on average; **al di sopra/sotto della** ~**a** above/below average; **viaggiare ad una** ~**a di ...** to travel at an average speed of ...; **il M**~ **Oriente** the Middle East.

medio'cre *ag* (*gen*) mediocre; (*qualità, stipendio*) poor.

mediocrità *sf* mediocrity; poorness.

medioeva'le *ag* = **medievale**.

Medioe'vo *sm* Middle Ages *pl*.

meditabon'do, a *ag* thoughtful.

medita're *vt* to ponder over, meditate on; (*progettare*) to plan, think out ♦ *vi* to meditate.

medita'to, a *ag* (*gen*) meditated; (*parole*) carefully-weighed; (*vendetta*) premeditated; **ben** ~ (*piano*) well worked-out, neat.

meditazio'ne [mādētàttsyō'nā] *sf* meditation.

mediterra'neo, a *ag* Mediterranean; **il (mare) M**~ the Mediterranean (Sea).

me'dium *sm/f inv* medium.

medu'sa *sf* (*ZOOL*) jellyfish.

mega'fono *sm* megaphone.

megalo'mane *ag, sm/f* megalomaniac.

mege'ra [māje'rà] *sf* (*peg: donna*) shrew.

me'glio [mel'yō] *av, ag inv* better; (*con senso superlativo*) best ♦ *sm* (*la cosa migliore*): **il** ~ the best (thing); **faresti** ~ **ad andartene** you had better leave; **alla** ~ as best one can; **andar di bene in** ~ to get better and better; **fare del proprio** ~ to do one's best; **per il** ~ for the best; **aver la** ~ **su qn** to get the better of sb.

me'la *sf* apple; ~ **cotogna** quince.

melagra'na *sf* pomegranate.

melanza'na [mālàndzà'nà] *sf* eggplant.

melas'sa *sf* molasses *sg*.

melen'so, a *ag* dull, stupid.

melli'fluo, a *ag* (*peg*) sugary, honeyed.

mel'ma *sf* mud, mire.

me'lo *sm* apple tree.

melodi'a *sf* melody.

melo'dico, a, ci, che *ag* melodic.

melodio'so, a *ag* melodious.

melodram'ma, i *sm* melodrama.

melo'ne *sm* (musk) melon.

mem'bra *sfpl vedi* **membro**.

membra'na *sf* membrane.

mem'bro *sm* member; (*pl(f)* ~**a**: *arto*) limb.

memora'bile *ag* memorable.

memoran'dum *sm inv* memorandum.

me'more *ag*: ~ **di** (*ricordando*) mindful of; (*riconoscente*) grateful for.

memo'ria *sf* (*anche INFORM*) memory; ~**e** *sfpl* (*opera autobiografica*) memoirs; **a** ~ (*imparare, sapere*) by heart; **a** ~ **d'uomo** within living memory; ~ **di sola lettura** (*INFORM*) read-only memory; ~ **tampone** (*INFORM*) buffer.

memoria'le *sm* (*raccolta di memorie*) memoirs *pl*; (*DIR*) memorial.

memorizza're [māmōrēddzà'rā] *vt* (*gen*) to memorize; (*INFORM*) to store.

memorizzazio'ne [māmōrēddzàttsyō'nā] *sf* memorization; storage.

me'na *sf* scheme.

menadi'to: a ~ *av* perfectly, thoroughly; **sapere qc a** ~ to have sth at one's fingertips.

menagra'mo *sm/f inv* jinx.

mena're *vt* to lead; (*picchiare*) to hit, beat; (*dare: colpi*) to deal; ~ **la coda** (*cane*) to wag its tail; ~ **qc per le lunghe** to drag sth out; ~ **il can per l'aia** (*fig*) to beat around the bush.

mendican'te *sm/f* beggar.

mendica're *vt* to beg for ♦ *vi* to beg.

menefreghi'smo [mānāfrāgēz'mō] *sm* (*fam*) couldn't-care-less attitude.

menin'ge [mānēn'jā] *sf* (*MED*) meninx; **spremersi le** ~**i** to rack one's brains.

meningi'te [mānēnjē'tā] *sf* meningitis.

meni'sco *sm* (*ANAT, MAT, FISICA*) meniscus.

me'no *av* less; (*in frasi comparative*): ~ **freddo che** not as cold as, less cold than; (: *seguito da nome, pronome*): ~ **alto di** not as tall as, less tall than; (*in frasi superlative*): **il(la)** ~ **bravo(a)** the least clever; (*di temperatura*) below (zero), minus; (*MAT*) minus, less; (*l'ora*): **sono le 8** ~ **un quarto** it's a quarter of eight (*US*) *o* to eight ♦ *ag inv* (*tempo, denaro*) less; (*errori, persone*) fewer ♦ *prep* except (for) ♦ *sm inv* (*la parte minore*): **il** ~ the least; (*MAT*) minus; **i** ~ (*la minoranza*) the minority; **a** ~ **che** *cong* unless; **essere da** ~ **di** to be outdone by; **fare a** ~ **di qc** (*privarsene*) to do without sth; (*rinunciarvi*) to give sth up; **fare a** ~ **di fumare** to give up smoking; **non potevo fare a** ~ **di ridere** I couldn't help laughing; **mille lire in** ~ a thousand lire less; ~ **male** so much the better; thank goodness.

menoma're *vt* (*danneggiare*) to maim, disable.

menoma'to, a *ag* (*persona*) disabled ♦ *sm/f* disabled person.

menomazio'ne [mānōmàttsyō'nā] *sf* disablement.

menopa'usa *sf* menopause.

men'sa *sf* (*locale*) canteen; (: *MIL*) mess; (: *nelle università*) cafeteria (*US*), refectory (*Brit*).

mensi'le *ag* monthly ♦ *sm* (*periodico*) monthly (magazine); (*stipendio*) monthly salary.

mensilmen'te *av* (*ogni mese*) every month; (*una volta al mese*) monthly.

men'sola *sf* bracket; (*ripiano*) shelf; (*ARCHIT*) corbel.

men'ta *sf* mint; (*anche*: ~ **piperita**) peppermint; (*bibita*) peppermint cordial; (*caramella*) mint, peppermint.

menta'le *ag* mental.

mentalità *sf inv* mentality.

mentalmen'te *av* mentally.

men'te *sf* mind; **imparare/sapere qc a** ~ to learn/know sth by heart; **avere in** ~ **qc** to have sth in mind; **avere in** ~ **di fare qc** to intend to do sth; **fare venire in** ~ **qc a qn** to remind sb of sth; **mettersi in** ~ **di fare qc** to make up one's mind to do sth; **passare di** ~ **a qn** to slip sb's mind; **tenere a** ~ **qc** to bear sth in mind; **a** ~ **fredda** objectively; **lasciami fare** ~ **locale** let me think.

mentecat'to, a *ag* half-witted ♦ *sm/f* half-wit, imbecile.

menti're *vi* to lie.

menti'to, a *ag*: **sotto** ~**e spoglie** under false pretenses (*US*) *o* pretences (*Brit*).

men'to *sm* chin; **doppio** ~ double chin.

mento'lo *sm* menthol.

men'tre *cong* (*temporale*) while; (*avversativo*) whereas ♦ *sm*: **in quel** ~ at that very moment.

menù *sm inv* (set) menu; ~ **turistico** standard *o* tourists' menu.

menziona're [màntsyōnà'rā] *vt* to mention.

menzio'ne [màntsyō'nā] *sf* mention; **fare** ~ **di** to mention.

menzo'gna [màntson'yá] *sf* lie.

menzogne'ro, a [màntsōnye'rō] *ag* false, untrue.

meravi'glia [màràvēl'yá] *sf* amazement, wonder; (*persona, cosa*) marvel, wonder; **a** ~ perfectly, wonderfully.

meraviglia're [màràvēlyá'rā] *vt* to amaze, astonish; ~**rsi** *vr*: ~**rsi (di)** to marvel (at); (*stupirsi*) to be amazed (at), be astonished (at); **mi meraviglio di te!** I'm surprised at you!; **non c'è da** ~**rsi** it's not surprising.

meraviglio'so, a [màràvēlyō'sō] *ag* wonderful, marvelous (*US*), marvellous (*Brit*).

merc. *abbr* (= *mercoledì*) Wed.

mercan'te *sm* merchant; ~ **d'arte** art dealer; ~ **di cavalli** horse dealer.

mercanteggia're [màrkàntādjá'rā] *vt* (*onore, voto*) to sell ♦ *vi* to bargain, haggle.

mercanti'le *ag* commercial, mercantile; (*nave, marina*) merchant *cpd* ♦ *sm* (*nave*) merchantman.

mercanzi'a [màrkàntsē'á] *sf* merchandise, goods *pl*.

mercati'no *sm* (*rionale*) local street market; (*ECON*) unofficial stock market.

merca'to *sm* market; **di** ~ (*economia, prezzo, ricerche*) market *cpd*; **mettere** *o* **lanciare qc sul** ~ to launch sth on the market; **a buon** ~ *ag, av* cheap; ~ **dei cambi** exchange market; **M**~ **Comune (Europeo)** (European) Common Market; ~ **del lavoro** labor market, job market; ~ **nero** black market; ~ **al rialzo/al ribasso** (*BORSA*) sellers'/buyers' market; ~ **a termine** forward market, futures market.

mer'ce [mer'chā] *sf* goods *pl*, merchandise; ~ **deperibile** perishable goods *pl*.

mercé [màrchā'] *sf* mercy; **essere alla** ~ **di qn** to be at sb's mercy.

mercena'rio, a [màrchānà'ryō] *ag*, *sm* mercenary.

merceri'a [màrchārē'á] *sf* (*articoli*) notions *pl* (*US*), haberdashery (*Brit*); (*bottega*) notions store (*US*), haberdasher's shop (*Brit*).

mercoledì *sm inv* Wednesday; ~ **delle Ceneri** Ash Wednesday; *per fraseologia vedi* **martedì**.

mercu'rio *sm* mercury.

mer'da *sf* (*fam!*) shit (*!*).

meren'da *sf* afternoon snack.

meridia'no, a *ag* (*di mezzogiorno*) midday *cpd*, noonday ♦ *sm* meridian ♦ *sf* (*orologio*) sundial.

meridiona'le *ag* southern ♦ *sm/f* southerner.

meridio'ne *sm* south.

merin'ga, ghe *sf* (*CUC*) meringue.

merita're *vt* to deserve, merit ♦ *vb impers* (*valere la pena*): **merita andare** it is worth going; **non merita neanche parlarne** it's not worth talking about; **per quel che merita** for what it's worth.

merite'vole *ag* worthy.

me'rito *sm* merit; (*valore*) worth; **dare** ~ **a qn di** to give sb credit for; **finire a pari** ~ to tie first (*o* second *etc*); to tie; **in** ~ **a** as regards, with regard to; **entrare nel** ~ **di una questione** to go into a matter; **non so niente in** ~ I don't know anything about it.

meritocrazi'a [màrētōkràttsē'á] *sf* meritocracy.

merito'rio, a *ag* praiseworthy.

merlet'to *sm* lace.

mer'lo *sm* (*ZOOL*) blackbird; (*ARCHIT*) battlement.

merluz'zo [mārlōōt'tsŏ] *sm* (*ZOOL*) cod.

me'scere [māsh'shārā] *vt* to pour (out).

meschinità [māskēnētá'] *sf* wretchedness; meagreness; meanness; narrow-mindedness.

meschi'no, a [māskē'nŏ] *ag* wretched; (*scarso*) meager (*US*), meagre (*Brit*); (*persona*: *gretta*) mean; (: *limitata*) narrow-minded, petty; **fare una figura** ~**a** to cut a poor figure.

me'scita [māsh'shētá] *sf* wine shop.

mesciu'to, a [māshōō'tŏ] *pp di* **mescere.**

mescolan'za [māskōlán'tsá] *sf* mixture.

mescola're *vt* to mix; (*vini, colori*) to blend; (*mettere in disordine*) to mix up, muddle up; (*carte*) to shuffle; ~**rsi** *vr* to mix; to blend; to get mixed up; (*fig*): ~**rsi in** to get mixed up in, meddle in.

me'se *sm* month; **il** ~ **scorso** last month; **il corrente** ~ this month.

mes'sa *sf* (*REL*) mass; (*il mettere*): ~ **a fuoco** focusing; ~ **in moto** starting; ~ **in piega** (*acconciatura*) set; ~ **a punto** (*TECN*) adjustment; (*AUT*) tune-up (*US*), tuning (*Brit*); (*fig*) clarification; ~ **in scena** = **messinscena.**

messaggeri'e [māssádjārē'á] *sfpl* (*ditta*: *di distribuzione*) distributors; (: *di trasporto*) freight company.

messagge'ro [māssádjɇ'rŏ] *sm* messenger.

messag'gio [māssád'jŏ] *sm* message.

messa'le *sm* (*REL*) missal.

mes'se *sf* harvest.

Messi'a *sm inv* (*REL*): **il** ~ the Messiah.

messica'no, a *ag, sm/f* Mexican.

Mes'sico *sm*: **il** ~ Mexico; **Città del** ~ Mexico City.

messinsce'na [māssēnshc'nà] *sf* (*TEATRO*) production.

mes'so, a *pp di* **mettere** ♦ *sm* messenger.

mestieran'te *sm/f* (*peg*) money-grubber; (: *scrittore*) hack.

mestie're *sm* (*professione*) job; (: *manuale*) trade; (: *artigianale*) craft; (*fig: abilità nel lavoro*) skill, technique; **di** ~ by *o* to trade; **essere del** ~ to know the tricks of the trade.

mesti'zia [māstēt'tsyá] *sf* sadness, melancholy.

me'sto, a *ag* sad, melancholy.

me'stola *sf* (*CUC*) ladle; (*EDIL*) trowel.

me'stolo *sm* (*CUC*) ladle.

mestrua'le *ag* menstrual.

mestruazio'ne [māstrŏŏáttsyŏ'nā] *sf* menstruation; **avere le** ~**i** to have one's period.

me'ta *sf* destination; (*fig*) aim, goal.

metà *sf inv* half; (*punto di mezzo*) middle; **dividere qc a** *o* **per** ~ to divide sth in half, halve sth; **fare a** ~ **(di qc con qn)** to go halves (with sb in sth); **a** ~ **prezzo** at half price; **a** ~ **settimana** midweek; **a** ~ **strada** halfway; **verso la** ~ **del mese** halfway

through the month, towards the middle of the month; **dire le cose a** ~ to leave some things unsaid; **fare le cose a** ~ to leave things half-done; **la mia dolce** ~ (*fam scherzoso*) my better half.

metaboli'smo *sm* metabolism.

metafi'sica *sf* metaphysics *sg*.

meta'fora *sf* metaphor.

metal'lico, a, ci, che *ag* (*di metallo*) metal *cpd*; (*splendore, rumore etc*) metallic.

metallizza'to, a [mātállēddzà'tŏ] *ag* (*verniciatura*) metallic.

metal'lo *sm* metal; **di** ~ metal *cpd*.

metallurgi'a [mātállōōrjē'á] *sf* metallurgy.

metalmecca'nico, a, ci, che *ag* engineering *cpd* ♦ *sm* engineering worker.

metamor'fosi *sf* metamorphosis.

meta'no *sm* methane.

mete'ora *sf* meteor.

meteori'te *sm* meteorite.

meteorologi'a [mātāŏrōlŏjē'á] *sf* meteorology.

meteorolo'gico, a, ci, che [mātāŏrŏlŏ'jēkŏ] *ag* meteorological, weather *cpd*.

meteoro'logo, a, ghi, ghe *sm/f* meteorologist.

metic'cio, a, ci, ce [mātēch'chŏ] *sm/f* half-caste, half-breed.

meticolo'so, a *ag* meticulous.

meto'dico, a, ci, che *ag* methodical.

me'todo *sm* method; (*manuale*) manual, tutor (*Brit*); **far qc con/senza** ~ to do sth methodically/unmethodically.

metrag'gio [mātrád'jŏ] *sm* (*SARTORIA*) length; (*CINEMA*) footage; **film a lungo** ~ feature film; **film a corto** ~ short film.

metratu'ra *sf* length.

me'trico, a, ci, che *ag* metric; (*POESIA*) metrical ♦ *sf* metrics *sg*.

me'tro *sm* meter (*US*), metre (*Brit*); (*nastro*) tape measure; (*asta*) (meter) ruler (*US*) *o* rule (*Brit*).

metrò *sm inv* subway (*US*), underground (*Brit*).

metronot'te *sm inv* night security guard.

metro'poli *sf* metropolis.

metropolita'no, a *ag* metropolitan ♦ *sf* subway (*US*), underground (*Brit*).

met'tere *vt* to put; (*abito*) to put on; (: *portare*) to wear; (*installare: telefono*) to put in; (*fig: provocare*): ~ **fame/allegria a qn** to make sb hungry/happy; (*supporre*): **mettiamo che** ... let's suppose *o* say that ...; ~**rsi** *vr* (*persona*) to put o.s.; (*oggetto*) to go; (*disporsi: faccenda*) to turn out; ~**rsi a piangere/ridere** to start crying/laughing, start *o* begin to cry/laugh; ~**rsi a sedere** to sit down; ~**rsi al lavoro** to set to work; ~**rsi a letto** to get into bed; (*per malattia*) to take to one's bed; ~**rsi il cappello** to put on one's hat; ~**rsi sotto** to get down to things; ~**rsi in so-**

cietà to set o.s. up in business; **si sono messi insieme** (coppia) they've started going out together; **~rci: ~rci molta cura/molto tempo** to take a lot of care/a lot of time; **mettercela tutta** to do one's best; **ci ho messo 3 ore per venire** it's taken me 3 hours to get here; **un annuncio sul giornale** to place an advertisement in the paper; **~ a confronto** to compare; **~ in conto** (somma etc) to put on account; **~ in luce** (problemi, errori) to stress, highlight; **~ a tacere qn/qc** to keep sb/sth quiet; **~ su casa** to set up house; **~ su un negozio** to open a store; **~ su peso** to put on weight; **~ via** to put away.

mezza'dro [māddzá'drō] sm (AGR) share-cropper.

mezzalu'na [māddzálōō'nà], pl **mezzelu'ne** sf (dell'islamismo) crescent; (coltello) (semicircular) chopping knife.

mezzani'no [māddzánē'nō] sm mezzanine (floor).

mezza'no, a [māddzá'nō] ag (medio) average, medium; (figlio) middle cpd ♦ sm/f (intermediario) go-between; (ruffiano) pimp.

mezzanot'te [māddzánot'tā] sf midnight.

mez'zo, a [med'dzō] ag half; **un ~ litro/panino** half a liter/roll ♦ av half-; **~ morto** half-dead ♦ sm (metà) half; (parte centrale: di strada etc) middle; (per raggiungere un fine) means sg; (veicolo) vehicle; (nell'indicare l'ora): **le nove e ~** half past nine; **mezzogiorno e ~** half past twelve ♦ sf: **la ~a** half-past twelve (in the afternoon); **~i** smpl (possibilità economiche) means; **di ~a età** middle-aged; **aver una ~a idea di fare qc** to have half a mind to do sth; **è stato un ~ scandalo** it almost caused a scandal; **un soprabito di ~a stagione** a spring (o autumn) coat; **a ~a voce** in an undertone; **una volta e ~ più grande** one and a half times bigger; **di ~** middle, in the middle; **andarci di ~** (patir danno) to suffer; **esserci di ~** (ostacolo) to be in the way; **levarsi o togliersi di ~** to get out of the way; **mettersi di ~** to interfere; **togliere di ~** (persona, cosa) to get rid of; (fam: uccidere) to bump off; **non c'è una via di ~** there's no middle course; **in ~ a** in the middle of; **nel bel ~ (di)** right in the middle (of); **per o a ~ di** by means of; **a ~ corriere** by carrier; **~i di comunicazione di massa** mass media pl; **~i pubblici** public transportation sg; **~i di trasporto** means of transport.

mezzogior'no [māddzōjōr'nō] sm midday, noon; (GEO) south; **a ~** at 12 (o'clock) o midday o noon; **il ~ d'Italia** southern Italy.

mezz'o'ra, mezzo'ra [māddzō'rà] sf half-hour, half an hour.

MI sigla = Milano.

mi pronome (dav lo, la, li, le, ne diventa **me**)

(oggetto) me; (complemento di termine) (to) me; (riflessivo) myself ♦ sm (MUS) E; (: solfeggiando la scala) mi; **~ aiuti?** will you help me?; **me ne ha parlato** he spoke to me about it, he told me about it; **~ servo da solo** I'll help myself.

mi'a vedi **mio**.

miagola're vi to miaow, mew.

mi'ca sf (CHIM) mica ♦ av (fam): **non ... ~** not ... at all; **non sono ~ stanco** I'm not a bit tired; **non sarà ~ partito?** he wouldn't have left, would he?; **~ male** not bad.

mic'cia, ce [mēch'chá] sf fuse.

micidia'le [mēchēdyà'lā] ag fatal; (dannosissimo) deadly.

mi'cio, a, ci, cie [mē'chō] sm/f pussy (cat).

microbiologi'a [mēkrōbēōlōjē'á] sf microbiology.

mi'crobo sm microbe.

microcircu'ito [mēkrōchērkōō'ētō] sm microcircuit.

microfilm' sm inv microfilm.

micro'fono sm microphone.

microinforma'tica [mēkrō...] sf microcomputing.

microon'da sf microwave.

microprocesso're [mēkrōprōchàssō'rā] sm microprocessor.

microsco'pico, a, ci, che ag microscopic.

microsco'pio sm microscope.

microsol'co, chi a (solco) microgroove; (disco: a 33 giri) long-playing record, LP; (: a 45 giri) extended-play record, EP.

microspi'a sf hidden microphone, bug (fam).

midol'lo, pl(f) ~a sm (ANAT) marrow; **~ spinale** spinal cord.

mi'e, mie'i vedi **mio**.

mie'le sm honey.

mie'tere vt (AGR) to reap, harvest; (fig: vite) to take, claim.

mietitrebbiatri'ce [myātētrābbyàtrē'chà] sf combine harvester.

mietitri'ce [myātētrē'chà] sf (macchina) combine (US), harvester (Brit).

mietitu'ra sf (raccolto) harvest; (lavoro) harvesting; (tempo) harvest-time.

mi'glia [mēl'yà] sfpl di **miglio**.

miglia'io [mēlyá'yō], pl(f) **~a** sm thousand; **un ~ (di)** about a thousand; **a ~a** by the thousand, in thousands.

mi'glio [mēl'yō] sm (BOT) millet; (pl(f) **~a**: unità di misura) mile; **~ marino o nautico** nautical mile.

miglioramen'to [mēlyōràmān'tō] sm improvement.

migliora're [mēlyōrà'rà] vt, vi to improve.

miglio're [mēlyō'rà] ag (comparativo) better; (superlativo) best ♦ sm: **il ~** the best (thing) ♦ sm/f: **il(la) ~** the best (person); **il miglior vino di questa regione** the best wine in this area; **i ~i auguri** best wishes.

migliori'a |mēlyōrē'á| sf improvement.
mi'gnolo |mēn'yōlō| sm (ANAT) little finger, pinkie; (: dito del piede) little toe.
migra're vi to migrate.
migrazio'ne |mēgráttsyō'nà| sf migration.
mi'la pl di **mille**.
milane'se ag Milanese ♦ sm/f person from Milan; **i ~i** the Milanese; **cotoletta alla ~** (CUC) Wiener schnitzel; **risotto alla ~** (CUC) risotto with saffron.
Mila'no sf Milan.
miliarda'rio, a ag, sm/f millionaire.
miliar'do sm billion (US), thousand million (Brit).
milia're ag: **pietra ~** milestone.
miliona'rio, a ag, sm/f millionaire.
milio'ne sm million; **un ~ di lire** a million lire.
militan'te ag, sm/f militant.
militan'za |mēlētán'tsá| sf militancy.
milita're vi (MIL) to be a soldier, serve; (fig: in un partito) to be a militant ♦ ag military ♦ sm serviceman; **fare il ~** to do one's military service; **~ di carriera** regular (soldier).
militare'sco, a, schi, sche ag (portamento) military cpd.
mi'lite sm soldier.
mili'zia |mēlēt'tsyá| sf (corpo armato) militia.
milizia'no |mēlēttsyá'nō| sm militiaman.
millantato're, tri'ce sm/f boaster.
millanteri'a sf (qualità) boastfulness.
mil'le num (pl **mila**) a o one thousand; **dieci-mila** ten thousand.
millefo'glie |mēllāfol'yā| sm inv (CUC) napoleon (US), cream o vanilla slice (Brit).
millen'nio sm millennium.
millepie'di sm inv centipede.
mille'simo, a ag, sm thousandth.
milligram'mo sm milligram(me).
milli'litro sm milliliter (US), millilitre (Brit).
milli'metro sm millimeter (US), millimetre (Brit).
mil'za |mēl'tsá| sf (ANAT) spleen.
mime'tico, a, ci, che ag (arte) mimetic; **tuta ~a** (MIL) camouflage.
mimetizza're |mēmātēddzá'rá| vt to camouflage; **~rsi** vr to camouflage o.s.
mi'mica sf (arte) mime.
mi'mo sm (attore, componimento) mime.
mimo'sa sf mimosa.
min. abbr (= minuto, minimo) min.
mi'na sf (esplosiva) mine; (di matita) lead.
minac'cia, ce |mēnách'chà| sf threat; **sotto la ~ di** under threat of.
minaccia're |mēnáchá'rá| vt to threaten; **~ qn di morte** to threaten to kill sb; **~ di fare qc** to threaten to do sth; **minaccia di piovere** it looks like rain.
minaccio'so, a |mēnáchō'sō| ag threatening.
mina're vt (MIL) to mine; (fig) to undermine.

minato're sm miner.
minato'rio, a ag threatening.
minchio'ne, a |mēnkyō'nà| (fam) ag idiotic ♦ sm/f idiot.
minera'le ag, sm mineral.
mineralogi'a |mēnārálōjē'á| sf mineralogy.
minera'rio, a ag (delle miniere) mining; (dei minerali) ore cpd.
mines'tra sf soup; **~ in brodo** noodle soup; **~ di verdura** vegetable soup.
minestro'ne sm thick vegetable and pasta soup.
mingherli'no, a |mēngārlē'nō| ag thin, slender.
mi'ni ag inv mini ♦ sf inv miniskirt.
miniatu'ra sf miniature.
minielaborato're sm minicomputer.
minie'ra sf mine; **~ di carbone** coalmine; (impresa) coalmine.
minigon'na sf miniskirt.
minimizza're |mēnēmēddzá'rá| vt to minimize.
mi'nimo, a ag minimum, least, slightest; (piccolissimo) very small, slight; (il più basso) lowest, minimum ♦ sm minimum; **al ~** at least; **girare al ~** (AUT) to idle; **il ~ indispensabile** the bare minimum; **il ~ della pena** the minimum sentence.
ministe'ro sm (POL, REL) ministry; (governo) government; (DIR): **Pubblico M~** State Prosecutor; **~ delle Finanze** ministry of finance, ≈ Treasury.
minis'tro sm (POL, REL) minister; **~ delle Finanze** minister of finance.
minoran'za |mēnōrán'tsá| sf minority; **essere in ~** to be in the minority.
minora'to, a ag handicapped ♦ sm/f physically (o mentally) handicapped person.
minorazio'ne |mēnōráttsyō'nà| sf handicap.
Minor'ca sf Minorca.
mino're ag (comparativo) less; (: più piccolo) smaller; (: numero) lower; (: inferiore) lower, inferior; (: meno importante) minor; (: più giovane) younger; (superlativo) least; smallest; lowest; least important; youngest ♦ sm/f (minorenne) minor, person under age; **in misura ~** to a lesser extent; **questo è il male ~** this is the lesser evil.
minoren'ne ag under age ♦ sm/f minor, person under age.
minori'le ag juvenile; **carcere ~** reformatory (US), young offenders' institution (Brit); **delinquenza ~** juvenile delinquency.
minorita'rio, a ag minority cpd.
minu'scolo, a ag (scrittura, carattere) small; (piccolissimo) tiny ♦ sf small letter ♦ sm small letters pl; (TIP) lower case; **scrivere tutto (in) ~** to write everything in small letters.
minu'ta sf rough copy, draft.
minu'to, a ag tiny, minute; (pioggia) fine;

(*corporatura*) delicate, fine; (*lavoro*) detailed ♦ *sm* (*unità di misura*) minute; **al ~** (*COMM*) retail; **avere i ~i contati** to have very little time.

minu'zia [mēnōōt'tsyà] *sf* (*cura*) meticulousness; (*particolare*) detail.

minuziosamen'te [mēnōōttsyōsàmän'tä] *av* meticulously; in minute detail.

minuzio'so, a [mēnōōttsyō'sō] *ag* (*persona*, *descrizione*) meticulous; (*esame*) minute.

mi'o, mi'a, mie'i, mi'e *det*: **il ~, la mia** *etc* my ♦ *pronome*: **il ~, la mia** *etc* mine ♦ *sm*: **ho speso del ~** I spent my own money ♦ *sf*: **la mia** (*opinione*) my view; **i miei** my family; **un ~ amico** a friend of mine; **per amor ~** for my sake; **è dalla mia** he is on my side; **anch'io ho avuto le mie** (*disavventure*) I've had my problems too; **ne ho fatta una delle mie!** (*sciocchezze*) I've done it again!; **cerco di stare sulle mie** I try to keep myself to myself.

mi'ope *ag* short-sighted.

miopi'a *sf* short-sightedness, myopia; (*fig*) short-sightedness.

mi'ra *sf* (*anche fig*) aim; **avere una buona/cattiva ~** to be a good/bad shot; **prendere la ~** to take aim; **prendere di ~ qn** (*fig*) to pick on sb.

mira'bile *ag* admirable, wonderful.

mira'colo *sm* miracle.

miracolo'so, a *ag* miraculous.

mirag'gio [mèràd'jō] *sm* mirage.

mira're *vi*: **~ a** to aim at.

miri'ade *sf* myriad.

miri'no *sm* (*TECN*) sight; (*FOT*) viewer, viewfinder.

mirtil'lo *sm* blueberry, whortleberry.

mir'to *sm* myrtle.

misan'tropo, a *sm/f* misanthropist.

misce'la [mēshe'là] *sf* mixture; (*di caffè*) blend.

miscella'nea [mēshàllà'nàà] *sf* miscellany.

mis'chia [mēs'kyà] *sf* scuffle; (*RUGBY*) scrum, scrummage.

mischia're [mēskyà'rà] *vt*, **~rsi** *vr* to mix, blend.

miscono'scere [mēskōnōsh'shàrà] *vt* (*qualità*, *coraggio etc*) to fail to appreciate.

miscreden'te *ag* (*REL*) misbelieving; (: *incredulo*) unbelieving ♦ *sm/f* misbeliever; unbeliever.

miscu'glio [mēskōōl'yō] *sm* mixture, hodgepodge, jumble.

mi'se *vb vedi* **mettere**.

misera'bile *ag* (*infelice*) miserable, wretched; (*povero*) poverty-stricken; (*di scarso valore*) miserable.

mise'ria *sf* extreme poverty; (*infelicità*) misery; **~e** *sfpl* (*del mondo etc*) misfortunes, troubles; **costare una ~** to cost next to noth-

ing; **piangere ~** to plead poverty; **ridursi in ~** to be reduced to poverty; **porca ~!** (*fam*) hell!

misericor'dia *sf* mercy, pity.

misericordio'so, a *ag* merciful.

mi'sero, a *ag* miserable, wretched; (*povero*) poverty-stricken; (*insufficiente*) miserable.

misfat'to *sm* misdeed, crime.

mi'si *vb vedi* **mettere**.

miso'gino [mēzo'jēnō] *sm* misogynist.

mis'sile *sm* missile; **~ cruise** *o* **di crociera** cruise missile; **~ terra-aria** surface-to-air missile.

missiona'rio, a *ag*, *sm/f* missionary.

missio'ne *sf* mission.

misterio'so, a *ag* mysterious.

miste'ro *sm* mystery; **fare ~ di qc** to make a mystery out of sth; **quanti ~i!** why all the mystery?

mi'stico, a, ci, che *ag* mystic(al) ♦ *sm* mystic.

mistifica're *vt* to fool, bamboozle.

mi'sto, a *ag* mixed; (*scuola*) mixed, coeducational ♦ *sm* mixture; **un tessuto in ~ lino** a linen mix.

mistu'ra *sf* mixture.

misu'ra *sf* measure; (*misurazione*, *dimensione*) measurement; (*taglia*) size; (*provvedimento*) measure, step; (*moderazione*) moderation; (*MUS*) time; (: *divisione*) bar; (*fig*: *limite*) bounds *pl*, limit; **in ~** in accordance with, according to; **nella ~ in cui** inasmuch as, insofar as; **in giusta ~** moderately; **oltre ~** beyond measure; **su ~** custom made (*US*), made to measure (*Brit*); **in ugual ~** equally, in the same way; **a ~ d'uomo** on a human scale; **passare la ~** to overstep the mark, go too far; **prendere le ~e a qn** to take sb's measurements, measure sb; **prendere le ~e di qc** to measure sth; **ho preso le mie ~** I've taken the necessary steps; **non ha il senso della ~** he doesn't know when to stop; **~ di lunghezza/capacità** measure of length/capacity; **~e di sicurezza/prevenzione** safety/precautionary measures.

misura're *vt* (*ambiente*, *stoffa*) to measure; (*terreno*) to survey; (*abito*) to try on; (*pesare*) to weigh; (*fig*: *parole etc*) to weigh up; (: *spese, cibo*) to limit ♦ *vi* to measure; **~rsi** *vr*: **~rsi con qn** to have a confrontation with sb; (*competere*) to compete with sb.

misura'to, a *ag* (*ponderato*) measured; (*prudente*) cautious; (*moderato*) moderate.

misurazio'ne [mēzōōràttsyō'nä] *sf* measuring; (*di terreni*) surveying.

mi'te *ag* mild; (*prezzo*) moderate, reasonable.

mi'tico, a, ci, che *ag* mythical.

mitiga're *vt* to mitigate, lessen; (*lenire*) to soothe, relieve; **~rsi** *vr* (*odio*) to subside;

(*tempo*) to become milder.
mi'tilo *sm* mussel.
mi'to *sm* myth.
mitologi'a, gi'e [mētōlōjē'á] *sf* mythology.
mitolo'gico, a, ci, che [mētōlo'jēkō] *ag* mythological.
mi'tra *sf* (*REL*) miter (*US*), mitre (*Brit*) ♦ *sm inv* (*arma*) sub-machine gun.
mitraglia're [mētrályá'rā] *vt* to machine-gun.
mitragliato're, tri'ce [mētrályátō'rā] *ag*: **fucile** *m* ~ sub-machine gun ♦ *sf* machine gun.
mitteleurope'o,.a *ag* Central European.
mitten'te *sm/f* sender.
ml *abbr* (= *millilitro*) ml.
MLD *sigla m vedi* **Movimento per la Liberazione della Donna**.
MM *abbr* = *Metropolitana Milanese*.
mm *abbr* (= *millimetro*) mm.
M.M. *abbr vedi* **marina militare**.
MN *sigla* = *Mantova*.
M/N, m/n *abbr* (= *motonave*) MV.
MO *sigla* = *Modena*.
M.O. *abbr* = **Medio Oriente**.
mo' *sm*: **a** ~ **di** *prep* like; **a** ~ **di esempio** by way of example.
mo'bile *ag* mobile; (*parte di macchina*) moving; (*DIR: bene*) movable, personal ♦ *sm* (*arredamento*) piece of furniture; ~**i** *smpl* furniture *sg*.
mobi'lia *sf* furniture.
mobilia're *ag* (*DIR*) personal, movable.
mobi'lio *sm* = **mobilia**.
mobilità *sf* mobility.
mobilita're *vt* to mobilize; ~ **l'opinione pubblica** to rouse public opinion.
mobilitazio'ne [mōbēlētáttsyō'nā] *sf* mobilization.
mocassi'no *sm* moccasin.
moccio'so, a [mōchō'sō] *sm/f* (*bambino piccolo*) little kid; (*peg*) snot-nosed (*US*) *o* snottynosed (*Brit*) kid.
moc'colo *sm* (*di candela*) candle end; (*fam: bestemmia*) oath; (: *moccio*) snot; **reggere il** ~ to act as chaperon(e).
mo'da *sf* fashion; **alla** ~, **di** ~ fashionable, in fashion.
modalità *sf inv* formality; **seguire attentamente le** ~ **d'uso** to follow the instructions carefully; ~ **giuridiche** legal procedures; ~ **di pagamento** method of payment.
model'la *sf* model.
modella're *vt* (*creta*) to model, shape; ~**rsi** *vr*: ~**rsi su** to model o.s. on.
model'lo *sm* model; (*stampo*) mold (*US*), mould (*Brit*) ♦ *ag inv* model *cpd*.
mo'dem *sm inv* modem.
modene'se *ag* of (*o* from) Modena.
modera're *vt* to moderate; ~**rsi** *vr* to restrain o.s.; ~ **la velocità** to reduce speed; ~ **i termini** to weigh one's words.

modera'to, a *ag* moderate.
moderato're, tri'ce *sm/f* moderator.
moderazio'ne [mōdāráttsyō'nā] *sf* moderation.
modernizza're [mōdārnēddzà'rā] *vt* to bring up to date, modernize; ~**rsi** *vr* to get up to date.
moder'no, a *ag* modern.
mode'stia *sf* modesty; ~ **a parte** ... in all modesty ..., though I say it myself ....
mode'sto, a *ag* modest.
mo'dico, a, ci, che *ag* reasonable, moderate.
modi'fica, che *sf* modification; **subire delle** ~**che** to undergo some modifications.
modifica're *vt* to modify, alter; ~**rsi** *vr* to alter, change.
modi'sta *sf* milliner.
mo'do *sm* way, manner; (*mezzo*) means, way; (*occasione*) opportunity; (*LING*) mood; (*MUS*) mode; ~**i** *smpl* (*maniere*) manners; **a suo** ~, **a** ~ **suo** in his own way; **ad** *o* **in ogni** ~ anyway; **di** *o* **in** ~ **che** so that; **in** ~ **da** so as to; **in tutti i** ~**i** at all costs; (*comunque sia*) anyway; (*in ogni caso*) in any case; **in un certo qual** ~ in a way, in some ways; **in qualche** ~ somehow or other; **oltre** ~ extremely; ~ **di dire** turn of phrase; **per** ~ **di dire** so to speak; **fare a** ~ **proprio** to do as one likes; **fare le cose a** ~ to do things properly; **una persona a** ~ a well-mannered person; **c'è** ~ **e** ~ **di farlo** there's a right way and a wrong way of doing it.
modula're *vt* to modulate ♦ *ag* modular.
modulazio'ne [mōdōōláttsyō'nā] *sf* modulation; ~ **di frequenza** (**FM**) frequency modulation (**FM**).
mo'dulo *sm* (*modello*) form; (*ARCHIT, lunare, di comando*) module; ~ **di domanda** application form; ~ **d'iscrizione** enrolment form; ~ **di versamento** deposit slip.
Mogadi'scio [mōgádēsh'shō] *sm* Mogadishu.
mo'gano *sm* mahogany.
mo'gio, a, gi, gie [mo'jō] *ag* down in the dumps, dejected.
mo'glie [mōl'yā] *sf* wife.
moha'ir [mocr'] *sm* mohair.
moi'ne *sfpl* cajolery *sg*; (*leziosità*) affectation *sg*; **fare le** ~ **a qn** to cajole sb.
mo'la *sf* millstone; (*utensile abrasivo*) grindstone.
mola're *vt* to grind ♦ *ag* (*pietra*) mill *cpd* ♦ *sm* (*dente*) molar.
mo'le *sf* mass; (*dimensioni*) size; (*edificio grandioso*) massive structure; **una** ~ **di lavoro** loads of work.
mole'cola *sf* molecule.
molesta're *vt* to bother, annoy.
mole'stia *sf* annoyance, bother; **recar** ~ **a qn** to bother sb.
mole'sto, a *ag* annoying.
molisa'no, a *ag* of (*o* from) Molise.

mol'la *sf* spring; ~**e** *sfpl* (*per camino*) tongs; **prendere qn con le** ~**e** to treat sb with kid gloves.

molla're *vt* to release, let go; (*NAUT*) to ease; (*fig*: *ceffone*) to give ♦ *vi* (*cedere*) to give in; ~ **gli ormeggi** (*NAUT*) to cast off; ~ **la presa** to let go.

mol'le *ag* soft; (*muscoli*) flabby; (*fig*: *debole*) weak, feeble.

molleggia'to, a [mōllādjá'tō] *ag* (*letto*) sprung; (*auto*) with good suspension.

molleg'gio [mōllād'jō] *sm* (*per veicoli*) suspension; (*elasticità*) springiness; (*GINNA-STICA*) knee-bends *pl*.

mollet'ta *sf* (*per capelli*) bobby pin (*US*), hairgrip (*Brit*); (*per panni stesi*) clothes pin (*US*) *o* peg (*Brit*); ~**e** *sfpl* (*per zucchero*) tongs.

mollez'za [mōllēt'tsá] *sf* softness; flabbiness; weakness, feebleness; ~**e** *sfpl*: **vivere nelle** ~**e** to live in the lap of luxury.

molli'ca, che *sf* crumb, soft part.

mollic'cio, a, ci, ce [mōllēch'chō] (*terreno, impasto*) soggy; (*frutta*) soft; (*floscio: mano*) limp; (: *muscolo*) flabby.

mollu'sco, schi *sm* mollusc.

mo'lo *sm* jetty, pier.

molte'plice [mōltá'plēchā] *ag* (*formato di più elementi*) complex; ~**i** *pl* (*svariati: interessi, attività*) numerous, various.

molteplicità [mōltáplēchētá'] *sf* multiplicity.

moltiplica're *vt* to multiply; ~**rsi** *vr* to multiply; (*richieste*) to increase in number.

moltiplicato're *sm* multiplier.

moltiplicazio'ne [mōltēplēkáttsyō'nā] *sf* multiplication.

moltitu'dine *sf* multitude; **una** ~ **di** a vast number *o* a multitude of.

mol'to, a *det* much, a lot of; (*con sostantivi al plurale*): ~**i(e)** many, a lot of; (*lungo: tempo*) long ♦ *av* a lot; (*in frasi negative*) much; (*intensivo*) very ♦ *pronome* much, a lot; ~**i(e)** *pronome pl* many, a lot; ~ **meglio** much *o* a lot better; ~ **buono** very good; ~**a gente** a lot of people, many people; **per** ~ (**tempo**) for a long time; **ci vuole** ~ (**tempo**)? will it take long?; **arriverà fra non** ~ he'll arrive soon.

momentaneamen'te *av* at the moment, at present.

momenta'neo, a *ag* momentary, fleeting.

momen'to *sm* moment; **da un** ~ **all'altro** at any moment; (*all'improvviso*) suddenly; **al** ~ **di fare** just as I was (*o* you were *o* he was etc) doing; **a** ~**i** (*da un* ~ *all'altro*) any time *o* moment now; (*quasi*) nearly; **per il** ~ for the time being; **dal** ~ **che** ever since; (*dato che*) since; ~ **culminante** climax.

mo'naca, che *sf* nun.

Mo'naco *sf* Monaco; ~ (**di Baviera**) Munich.

mo'naco, ci *sm* monk.

monar'ca, chi *sm* monarch.

monarchi'a [mōnárkē'á] *sf* monarchy.

monar'chico, a, ci, che [mōnár'kēkō] *ag* (*stato, autorità*) monarchic; (*partito, fede*) monarchist ♦ *sm/f* monarchist.

monaste'ro *sm* (*di monaci*) monastery; (*di monache*) convent.

mona'stico, a, ci, che *ag* monastic.

mon'co, a, chi, che *ag* maimed; (*fig*) incomplete; ~ **d'un braccio** one-armed.

monco'ne *sm* stump.

monda'na *sf* prostitute.

mondanità *sf* (*frivolezza*) worldliness; **le** ~ (*piaceri*) the pleasures of the world.

monda'no, a *ag* (*anche fig*) worldly; (*dell'alta società*) society *cpd*; fashionable.

monda're *vt* (*frutta, patate*) to peel; (*piselli*) to shell; (*pulire*) to clean.

mondezza'io [mōndáttsá'yō] *sm* garbage (*US*) *o* rubbish (*Brit*) dump.

mondia'le *ag* (*campionato, popolazione*) world *cpd*; (*influenza*) world-wide; **di fama** ~ world famous.

mon'do *sm* world; (*grande quantità*): **un** ~ **di** lots of, a host of; **il gran** *o* **bel** ~ high society; **per niente al** ~, **per nessuna cosa al** ~ not for all the world; **da che** ~ **è** ~ since time *o* the world began; **mandare qn all'altro** ~ to kill sb; **mettere/venire al** ~ to bring/come into the world; **vivere fuori dal** ~ to be out of touch with the real world; (**sono**) **cose dell'altro** ~! it's incredible!; **com'è piccolo il** ~! it's a small world!

monega'sco, a, schi, sche *ag*, *sm/f* Monegasque.

monel'lo, a *sm/f* street urchin; (*ragazzo vivace*) scamp, imp.

mone'ta *sf* coin; (*ECON: valuta*) currency; (*denaro spicciolo*) (small) change; ~ **estera** foreign currency; ~ **legale** legal tender.

moneta'rio, a *ag* monetary.

Mongo'lia *sf*: **la** ~ Mongolia.[*l*]

mongo'lico, a, ci, che *ag* Mongolian.

mongoli'smo *sm* mongolism, Down's syndrome.

mon'golo, a *ag* Mongolian ♦ *sm/f*, *sm* Mongol, Mongolian.

mongolo'ide *ag*, *sm/f* (*MED*) mongol.

mo'nito *sm* warning.

mo'nitor *sm inv* (*TECN, TV*) monitor.

mono'colo *sm* (*lente*) monocle, eyeglass.

monocolo're *ag* (*POL*): **governo** ~ one-party government.

monogami'a *sf* monogamy.

mono'gamo, a *ag* monogamous ♦ *sm* monogamist.

monografi'a *sf* monograph.

monogram'ma, i *sm* monogram.

monolin'gue *ag* monolingual.

mono'logo, ghi *sm* monologue.
monopat'tino *sm* scooter.
monopo'lio *sm* monopoly; **~ di stato** government monopoly.
monopolizza're [mōnōpōlēddzà'rā] *vt* to monopolize.
monosil'labo, a *ag* monosyllabic ♦ *sm* monosyllable.
monotoni'a *sf* monotony.
mono'tono, a *ag* monotonous.
monsigno're [mōnsēnyō'rā] *sm* (*REL: titolo*) Your (*o* His) Grace.
monso'ne *sm* monsoon.
montaca'richi [mōntàkà'rēkē] *sm inv* hoist, freight elevator (*US*), goods lift (*Brit*).
montag'gio [mōntàd'jō] *sm* (*TECN*) assembly; (*CINEMA*) editing.
monta'gna [mōntàn'yà] *sf* mountain; (*zona montuosa*): **la ~** the mountains *pl*; **andare in ~** to go to the mountains; **aria/strada di ~** mountain air/road; **casa di ~** house in the mountains; **~e russe** roller coaster *sg*, big dipper *sg* (*Brit*).
montagno'so, a [mōntànyō'sō] *ag* mountainous.
montana'ro, a *ag* mountain *cpd* ♦ *sm/f* mountain dweller.
monta'no, a *ag* mountain *cpd*.
montan'te *sm* (*di porta*) jamb; (*di finestra*) upright; (*CALCIO: palo*) post; (*PUGILATO*) upper cut; (*COMM*) total amount.
monta're *vt* to eat *o* (*o* come) up; (*cavallo*) to ride; (*apparecchiatura*) to set up, assemble; (*CUC*) to whip; (*ZOOL*) to cover; (*incastonare*) to mount, set; (*CINEMA*) to edit; (*FOT*) to mount ♦ *vi* to go (*o* come) up; (*a cavallo*) to mount; **~ bene/male** to ride well/badly; (*aumentare di livello, volume*) to rise; **~rsi** *vr* to become big-headed; **~ qc** to exaggerate sth; **~ qn** *o* **la testa a qn** to turn sb's head; **~rsi la testa** to become big-headed; **~ in bicicletta/macchina/treno** to get on a bicycle/into a car/on a train; **~ a cavallo** to get on *o* mount a horse; **~ la guardia** (*MIL*) to mount guard.
montatu'ra *sf* assembling *q*; (*di occhiali*) frames *pl*; (*di gioiello*) mounting, setting; (*fig*): **~ pubblicitaria** publicity stunt.
montavivan'de *sm inv* dumbwaiter.
mon'te *sm* mountain; **a ~** upstream; **andare a ~** (*fig*) to come to nothing; **mandare a ~ qc** (*fig*) to upset sth, cause sth to fail; **il M~ Bianco** Mont Blanc; **il M~ Everest** Mount Everest; **~ di pietà** pawnshop; **~ premi** prize.
Montecito'rio [mōntàchētō'ryō] *sm*: **palazzo ~** (*POL*) seat of the Italian Chamber of Deputies.
montgo'mery [məntgu'mərē] *sm inv* duffel coat.
monto'ne *sm* (*ZOOL*) ram; (*anche*: **giacca di**

~) sheepskin (jacket); **carne di ~** mutton.
montuosità *sf* mountainous nature.
montuo'so, a *ag* mountainous.
monumen'to *sm* monument.
moquet'te [moket'] *sf* wall-to-wall carpet.
mo'ra *sf* (*del rovo*) blackberry; (*del gelso*) mulberry; (*DIR*) delay; (: *somma*) arrears *pl*.
mora'le *ag* moral ♦ *sf* (*scienza*) ethics *sg*, moral philosophy; (*complesso di norme*) moral standards *pl*, morality; (*condotta*) morals *pl*; (*insegnamento morale*) moral ♦ *sm* morale; **la ~ della favola** the moral of the tale; **essere giù di ~** to be feeling down; **aver il ~ alto/a terra** to be in good/low spirits.
morali'sta, i, e *ag* moralistic ♦ *sm/f* moralist.
moralità *sf* morality; (*condotta*) morals *pl*.
morato'ria *sf* (*DIR*) moratorium.
morbidez'za [mōrbēdàt'tsà] *sf* softness; smoothness; tenderness.
mor'bido, a *ag* soft; (*pelle*) soft, smooth; (*carne*) tender.
morbil'lo *sm* (*MED*) measles *sg*.
mor'bo *sm* disease.
morbo'so, a *ag* (*fig*) morbid.
mor'chia [mor'kyà] *sf* (*residuo grasso*) dregs *pl*; oily deposit.
morda'ce [mōrdà'chā] *ag* biting, cutting.
morden'te *sm* (*fig: di satira, critica*) bite; (: *di persona*) drive.
mor'dere *vt* to bite; (*addentare*) to bite into; (*corrodere*) to eat into.
mordicchia're [mōrdēkkyà'rā] *vt* (*gen*) to chew at.
moren'te *ag* dying ♦ *sm/f* dying man/woman.
morfi'na *sf* morphine.
mori'a *sf* high mortality.
moribon'do, a *ag* dying, moribund.
morigera'to, a [mōrējàrà'tō] *ag* of good morals.
mori're *vi* to die; (*abitudine, civiltà*) to die out; **~ di dolore** to die of a broken heart; **~ di fame** to die of hunger; (*fig*) to be starving; **~ di freddo** to freeze to death; (*fig*) to be frozen; **~ d'invidia** to be green with envy; **~ di noia/paura** to be bored/scared to death; **~ dalla voglia di fare qc** to be dying to do sth; **fa un caldo da ~** it's terribly hot.
mormora're *vi* to murmur; (*brontolare*) to grumble; **si mormora che ...** it's rumored (*US*) *o* rumoured (*Brit*) that ...; **la gente mormora** people are talking.
mormori'o *sm* murmuring; grumbling.
mo'ro, a *ag* dark(-haired); dark(-complexioned); **i M~i** *smpl* (*STORIA*) the Moors.
moro'so, a *ag* in arrears ♦ *sm/f* (*fam: innamorato*) sweetheart.
mor'sa *sf* (*TECN*) vise (*US*), vice (*Brit*); (*fig: stretta*) grip.

morset'to *sm* (*TECN*) clamp; (*ELETTR*) terminal.

morsica're *vt* to nibble (at), gnaw (at); (*sog: insetto*) to bite.

mor'so, a *pp di* **mordere** ♦ *sm* bite; (*di insetto*) sting; (*parte della briglia*) bit; **dare un ~ a qc/qn** to bite sth/sb; **i ~i della fame** pangs of hunger.

mortadel'la *sf* (*CUC*) mortadella (*type of salted pork meat*).

morta'io *sm* mortar.

morta'le *ag, sm* mortal.

mortalità *sf* mortality; (*STATISTICA*) mortality, death rate.

mor'te *sf* death; **in punto di ~** at death's door; **ferito a ~** (*soldato*) mortally wounded; (*in incidente*) fatally injured; **essere annoiato a ~** to be bored to death *o* to tears; **avercela a ~ con qn** to be bitterly resentful of sb; **avere la ~ nel cuore** to have a heavy heart.

mortifica're *vt* to mortify.

mor'to, a *pp di* **morire** ♦ *ag* dead ♦ *sm/f* dead man/woman; **i ~i** the dead; **fare il ~** (*nell'acqua*) to float on one's back; **un ~ di fame** (*fig peg*) a down-and-out; **le campane suonavano a ~** the funeral bells were tolling.

morto'rio *sm* (*anche fig*) funeral.

mosa'ico, ci *sm* mosaic; **l'ultimo tassello del ~** (*fig*) the last piece of the puzzle.

Mo'sca *sf* Moscow.

mo'sca, sche *sf* fly; **rimanere** *o* **restare con un pugno di ~sche** (*fig*) to be left empty-handed; **non si sentiva una ~** (*fig*) you could have heard a pin drop; **~ cieca** blind-man's buff.

mosca'to *sm* muscatel (wine).

mosceri'no [mōshārē'nō] *sm* midge, gnat.

mosche'a [mōske'à] *sf* mosque.

moschet'to [mōskāt'tō] *sm* musket.

moschetto'ne [mōskāttō'nā] *sm* (*gancia*) spring clip; (*ALPINISMO*) carabiner, snaplink.

moschici'da, i, e [mōskēchē'dà] *ag* fly *cpd*; **carta ~** flypaper.

mo'scio, a, sci, sce [mōsh'shō] *ag* (*fig*) lifeless; **ha la "r" ~a** he can't roll his "r"'s.

mosco'ne *sm* (*ZOOL*) bluebottle; (*barca*) pedalo; (*: a remi*) *kind of pedalo with oars*.

moscovi'ta, i, e *ag, sm/f* Muscovite.

mos'sa *sf* movement; (*nel gioco*) move; **darsi una ~** (*fig*) to give o.s. a shake; **prendere le ~e da qc** to come about as the result of sth.

mos'si *etc vb vedi* **muovere**.

mos'so, a *pp di* **muovere** ♦ *ag* (*mare*) rough; (*capelli*) wavy; (*FOT*) blurred; (*ritmo, prosa*) animated.

mostar'da *sf* mustard.

mo'sto *sm* must.

mos'tra *sf* exhibition, show; (*ostentazione*) show; **in ~** on show; **far ~ di** (*fingere*) to

pretend; **far ~ di sé** to show off; **mettersi in ~** to draw attention to o.s.

mostra're *vt* to show ♦ *vi*: **~ di fare** to pretend to do; **~rsi** *vr* to appear; **~ la lingua** to stick out one's tongue.

mos'tro *sm* monster.

mostruo'so, a *ag* monstrous.

motel' *sm inv* motel.

motiva're *vt* (*causare*) to cause; (*giustificare*) to justify, account for.

motivazio'ne [mōtēvàttsyō'nā] *sf* justification; (*PSIC*) motivation.

moti'vo *sm* (*causa*) reason, cause; (*movente*) motive; (*letterario*) (central) theme; (*disegno*) motif, design, pattern; (*MUS*) motif; **per quale ~?** why?, for what reason?; **per ~i di salute** for health reasons, on health grounds; **~i personali** personal reasons.

mo'to *sm* (*anche FISICA*) motion; (*movimento, gesto*) movement; (*esercizio fisico*) exercise; (*sommossa*) rising, revolt; (*commozione*) feeling, impulse ♦ *sf inv* (*motocicletta*) motorbike; **fare del ~** to take some exercise; **un ~ d'impazienza** an impatient gesture; **mettere in ~** to set in motion; (*AUT*) to start up.

motocar'ro *sm* three-wheeled van.

motociclet'ta [mōtōchēklàt'tà] *sf* motorcycle.

motocicli'smo [mōtōchēklēz'mō] *sm* motorcycling, motorcycle racing.

motocicli'sta, i, e [mōtōchēklē'stà] *sm/f* motorcyclist.

motona've *sf* motor vessel.

motopescherec'cio [mōtōpàskārāch'chō] *sm* motor fishing vessel.

moto're, tri'ce *ag* motor; (*TECN*) driving ♦ *sm* engine, motor ♦ *sf* (*TECN*) engine, motor; **albero ~** drive shaft; **forza ~trice** driving force; **a ~** motor *cpd*, power-driven; **~ a combustione interna/a reazione** internal combustion/jet engine.

motori'no *sm* moped; **~ di avviamento** (*AUT*) starter.

motorizza'to, a [mōtōrēddzà'tō] *ag* (*truppe*) motorized; (*persona*) having a car *o* transport.

motorizzazio'ne [mōtōrēddzàttsyō'nā] *sf* (*ufficio tecnico e organizzativo*): **(ufficio della) ~** road traffic office.

motosca'fo *sm* motorboat.

motovedet'ta *sf* motor patrol vessel.

motri'ce [mōtrē'chà] *sf vedi* **motore**.

motteg'gio [mōttàd'jō] *sm* banter.

mot'to *sm* (*battuta scherzosa*) witty remark; (*frase emblematica*) motto, maxim.

moven'te *sm* motive.

moven'za [mōven'tsà] *sf* movement.

movimenta're *vt* to liven up.

movimenta'to, a *ag* (*festa, partita*) lively; (*riunione*) animated; (*strada, vita*) busy;

(*soggiorno*) eventful.

movimen'to *sm* movement; (*fig*) activity, hustle and bustle; (*MUS*) tempo, movement; **essere sempre in ~** to be always on the go; **fare un po' di ~** (*esercizio fisico*) to exercise; **c'è molto ~ in città** the town is very busy; **~ di capitali** movement of capital; **M~ per la Liberazione della Donna (MLD)** Women's Movement.

movio'la *sf* moviola; **rivedere qc alla ~** to see an instant (*US*) o action (*Brit*) replay of sth.

Mozambi'co [mŏddzámbē'kŏ] *sm*: **il ~** Mozambique.

mozio'ne [mŏttsyŏ'nā] *sf* (*POL*) motion; **~ d'ordine** (*POL*) point of order.

mozzafia'to [mŏttsáfyà'tŏ] *ag inv* breathtaking.

mozza're [mŏttsá'rā] *vt* to cut off; (*coda*) to dock; **~ il fiato** *o* **il respiro a qn** (*fig*) to take sb's breath away.

mozzarel'la [mŏttsárcl'lá] *sf* mozzarella (*a moist Neapolitan curd cheese*).

mozzico'ne [mŏttsēkŏ'nā] *sm* stub, butt, end; (*anche*: **~ di sigaretta**) cigarette butt.

moz'zo *sm* [mod'dzŏ] (*MECCANICA*) hub; [mŏt'tsŏ] (*NAUT*) ship's boy; **~ di stalla** stable boy.

mq *abbr* (= *metro quadro*) sq.m.

MS *sigla* = *Massa Carrara.*

ms. *abbr* (= *manoscritto*) ms.

Mti *abbr* = *monti.*

muc'ca, che *sf* cow.

muc'chio [mōōk'kyŏ] *sm* pile, heap; (*fig*): **un ~ di** lots of, heaps of.

mu'co, chi *sm* mucus.

muco'sa *sf* mucous membrane.

muf'fa *sf* mold (*US*), mould (*Brit*), mildew; **fare la ~** to go moldy.

mugghia're [mōōggyá'rā] *vi* (*fig*: *mare, tuono*) to roar; (: *vento*) to howl.

muggi're [mōōdjē'rā] *vi* (*vacca*) to low, moo; (*toro*) to bellow; (*fig*) to roar.

muggi'to [mōōdjē'tŏ] *sm* low, moo; bellow; roar.

mughet'to [mōōgāt'tŏ] *sm* lily of the valley.

mugna'io, a [mōōnyá'yŏ] *sm/f* miller.

mugola're *vi* (*cane*) to whimper, whine; (*fig*: *persona*) to moan.

mugugna're [mōōgōōnyà'rā] *vi* (*fam*) to mutter, mumble.

mulattie'ra *sf* mule track.

mulat'to, a *ag, sm/f* mulatto.

mulina're *vi* to whirl, spin (round and round).

mulinel'lo *sm* (*moto vorticoso*) eddy, whirl; (*di canna da pesca*) reel; (*NAUT*) windlass.

muli'no *sm* mill; **~ a vento** windmill.

mu'lo *sm* mule.

mul'ta *sf* fine.

multa're *vt* to fine.

multicolo're *ag* multicolored (*US*), multicoloured (*Brit*).

multifor'me *ag* (*paesaggio, attività, interessi*) varied; (*ingegno*) versatile.

multimedia'le *ag* multimedia *cpd.*

multinaziona'le [mōōltēnàttsyŏnà'lā] *ag, sf* multinational.

mul'tiplo, a *ag, sm* multiple.

multiuten'za [mōōltēōōtcn'tsà] *sf* (*INFORM*) time sharing.

mum'mia *sf* mummy.

mun'gere [mōōn'jārā] *vt* (*anche fig*) to milk.

mungitu'ra [mōōnjētōō'rà] *sf* milking.

municipa'le [mōōnēchēpà'lā] *ag* (*gen*) municipal; **palazzo ~** town hall; **autorità ~i** local government *sg.*

munici'pio [mōōnēchē'pyŏ] *sm* town council; (*edificio*) town hall; **sposarsi in ~** ≈ to have a civil marriage.

muni'fico, a, ci, che *ag* munificent, generous.

muni're *vt*: **~ qc/qn di** to equip sth/sb with; **~ di firma** (*documento*) to sign.

munizio'ni [mōōnēttsyŏ'nē] *sfpl* (*MIL*) ammunition *sg.*

mun'si *etc vb vedi* **mungere.**

mun'to, a *pp di* **mungere.**

muo'io *etc vb vedi* **morire.**

muo'vere *vt* to move; (*ruota, macchina*) to drive; (*sollevare*: *questione, obiezione*) to raise, bring up; (: *accusa*) to make, bring forward; **~rsi** *vr* to move; **~ causa a qn** (*DIR*) to take legal action against sb; **~ a compassione** to move to pity; **~ guerra a** *o* **contro qn** to wage war against sb; **~ mari e monti** to move heaven and earth; **~ al pianto** to move to tears; (*fig*) to be starting out; **muoviti!** hurry up!, get a move on!

mu'ra *sfpl vedi* **muro.**

mura'glia [mōōrál'yà] *sf* (high) wall.

mura'le *ag* wall *cpd*; mural.

mura're *vt* (*persona, porta*) to wall up.

mura'rio, a *ag* building *cpd*; **arte ~a** masonry.

murato're *sm* (*con pietre*) mason; (*con mattoni*) bricklayer.

muratu'ra *sf* (*lavoro murario*) masonry; **casa in ~** (*di pietra*) stonebuilt house; (*di mattoni*) brick house.

mu'ro *sm* wall; **~a** *sfpl* (*cinta cittadina*) walls; **a ~** wall *cpd*; (*armadio etc*) built-in; **mettere al ~** (*fucilare*) to shoot o execute (by firing squad); **~ di cinta** surrounding wall; **~ divisorio** dividing wall; **~ del suono** sound barrier.

mu'sa *sf* muse.

mus'chio [mōōs'kyŏ] *sm* (*ZOOL*) musk; (*BOT*) moss.

muscola're *ag* muscular, muscle *cpd.*

muscolatu'ra *sf* muscle structure.

mu'scolo *sm* (*ANAT*) muscle.

muse'o *sm* museum.
museruo'la *sf* muzzle.
mu'sica *sf* music; ~ **da ballo/camera** dance/ chamber music.
musica'le *ag* musical.
musicasset'ta *sf* (pre-recorded) cassette.
musici'sta, i, e |mōōzēchē'stá| *sm/f* musician.
musico'mane *sm/f* music lover.
mu'so *sm* muzzle; (*di auto, aereo*) nose; **te- nere il** ~ to sulk.
muso'ne, a *sm/f* sulky person.
mus'sola *sf* muslin.
mus(s)ulma'no, a *ag, sm/f* Muslim, Moslem.
mu'ta *sf* (*di animali*) molting (*US*), moulting (*Brit*); (*di serpenti*) sloughing; (*per immer- sioni subacquee*) diving suit; (*gruppo di cani*) pack.
muta'bile *ag* changeable.
mutamen'to *sm* change.
mutan'de *sfpl* (*da uomo*) (under)pants.
mutandi'ne *sfpl* (*da donna, bambino*) briefs (*Brit*), pants; ~ **di plastica** plastic pants.
muta're *vt, vi* to change, alter.
mutazio'ne |mōōtàttsyō'nā| *sf* change, al- teration; (*BIOL*) mutation.
mute'vole *ag* changeable.
mutila're *vt* to mutilate, maim; (*fig*) to muti- late, deface.
mutila'to, a *sm/f* disabled person (*through loss of limbs*); ~ **di guerra** disabled war vet- eran (*US*) o ex-serviceman (*Brit*).
mutilazio'ne |mōōtēlàttsyō'nā| *sf* mutilation.
muti'smo *sm* (*MED*) mutism; (*atteg- giamento*) (stubborn) silence.
mu'to, a *ag* (*MED*) dumb; (*emozione, dolore, CINEMA*) silent; (*LING*) silent, mute; (*carta geografica*) blank; ~ **per lo stupore** *etc* speechless with amazement *etc*; **ha fatto sce- na** ~**a** he didn't utter a word.
mu'tua *sf* (*anche*: **cassa** ~) health insurance plan; **medico della** ~ doctor who works in a health insurance plan.
mutua're *vt* (*fig*) to borrow.
mutua'to, a *sm/f* member of a health insur- ance plan.
mu'tuo, a *ag* (*reciproco*) mutual ♦ *sm* (*ECON*) (long-term) loan; ~ **ipotecario** mortgage.

N

N, n |cn'nā| *sf o m* (*lettera*) N, n; **N come Na- poli** ≈ N for Nan.
N *abbr* (= *nord*) N.

n *abbr* (= *numero*) no.
NA *sigla* = *Napoli*.
nabab'bo *sm* (*anche fig*) nabob.
nac'chere |nàk'kārā| *sfpl* castanets.
NAD *sigla m* = **nucleo anti-droga**.
nadir' *sm* (*ASTR*) nadir.
naf'ta *sf* naphtha; (*per motori diesel*) diesel oil.
naftali'na *sf* (*CHIM*) naphthalene; (*tarmicida*) mothballs *pl*.
na'ia *sf* (*ZOOL*) cobra; (*MIL*) slang term for national service.
naïf' |nàēf'| *ag inv* naïve.
na'ilon *sm* = **nylon**.
Nairo'bi *sf* Nairobi.
nan'na *sf* (*linguaggio infantile*): **andare a** ~ to go (to) beddy-bye(s).
na'no, a *ag, sm/f* dwarf.
napoleta'no, a *ag, sm/f* Neapolitan ♦ *sf* (*mac- chinetta da caffè*) Neapolitan coffee pot.
Na'poli *sf* Naples.
nap'pa *sf* tassel.
narci'so |nàrchē'zō| *sm* narcissus.
narco'si *sf* general anaesthesia, narcosis.
narco'tico, ci *sm* narcotic.
nari'ce |nàrē'chā| *sf* nostril.
narra're *vt* to tell the story of, recount.
narrati'vo, a *ag* narrative ♦ *sf* (*branca lette- raria*) fiction.
narrato're, tri'ce *sm/f* narrator.
narrazio'ne |nàrràttsyō'nā| *sf* narration; (*racconto*) story, tale.
nasa'le *ag* nasal.
nascen'te |nàshen'tā| *ag* (*sole, luna*) rising.
na'scere |nàsh'shārā| *vi* (*bambino*) to be born; (*pianta*) to come o spring up; (*fiume*) to rise, have its source; (*sole*) to rise; (*dente*) to come through; (*fig: derivare, conseguire*): ~ **da** to arise from, be born out of; **è nata nel 1952** she was born in 1952; **da cosa nasce cosa** one thing leads to another.
na'scita |nàsh'shētà| *sf* birth.
nascitu'ro, a |nàshētōō'rō| *sm/f* future child; **come si chiamerà il** ~? what's the baby going to be called?
nascon'dere *vt* to hide, conceal; ~**rsi** *vr* to hide.
nascondi'glio |nàskōndēl'yō| *sm* hiding place.
nascondi'no *sm* (*gioco*) hide-and-seek.
nasco'si *etc vb vedi* **nascondere**.
nasco'sto, a *pp di* **nascondere** ♦ *ag* hidden; **di** ~ secretly.
nasel'lo *sm* (*ZOOL*) hake.
na'so *sm* nose.
Nassa'u *sf* Nassau.
nas'tro *sm* ribbon; (*magnetico, isolante, SPORT*) tape; ~ **adesivo** adhesive tape; ~ **trasportatore** conveyor belt.
nastur'zio |nàstōōr'tsyō| *sm* nasturtium.
nata'le *ag* of one's birth ♦ *sm* (*REL*): **N**~

Christmas; (*giorno della nascita*) birthday; ~i *smpl*: **di illustri/umili** ~i of noble/humble birth.

natalità *sf* birth rate.

natali'zio, a [nátálḗt'tsyō] *ag* (*del Natale*) Christmas *cpd*.

natan'te *sm* craft *inv*, boat.

na'tica, che *sf* (*ANAT*) buttock.

nati'o, a, ti'i, ti'e *ag* native.

Natività *sf* (*REL*) Nativity.

nati'vo, a *ag*, *sm/f* native.

na'to, a *pp di* **nascere** ♦ *ag*: **un attore** ~ a born actor; ~**a Pieri** née Pieri.

N.A.'T.O. *sigla f* NATO (= *North Atlantic Treaty Organization*).

natu'ra *sf* nature; **pagare in** ~ to pay in kind; ~ **morta** still life.

natura'le *ag* natural ♦ *sm*: **al** ~ (*alimenti*) served plain; (*ritratto*) life-size; **(ma) è** ~! (*in risposte*) of course!; **a grandezza** ~ life-size; **acqua** ~ spring water.

naturalez'za [nátōōrálát'tsá] *sf* naturalness.

naturali'sta, i, e *sm/f* naturalist.

naturalizza're [nátōōrálḗddzà'rā] *vt* to naturalize.

naturalmen'te *av* naturally; (*certamente, sì*) of course.

naturi'smo *sm* naturism.

naturi'sta, i, e *ag*, *sm/f* naturist.

naufraga're *vi* (*nave*) to be wrecked; (*persona*) to be shipwrecked; (*fig*) to fall through.

naufra'gio [nàōōfrá'jō] *sm* shipwreck; (*fig*) ruin, failure.

na'ufrago, ghi *sm* castaway, shipwreck victim.

na'usea *sf* nausea; **avere la** ~ to feel sick; **fino alla** ~ ad nauseam.

nauseabon'do, a *ag*, **nausean'te** *ag* nauseating, sickening.

nausea're *vt* to nauseate, make (feel) sick.

na'utico, a, ci, che *ag* nautical ♦ *sf* (art of) navigation; **salone** ~ (*mostra*) boat show.

nava'le *ag* naval; **battaglia** ~ naval battle; (*gioco*) battleships *pl*.

nava'ta *sf* (*anche:* ~ **centrale**) nave; (*anche:* ~ **laterale**) aisle.

na've *sf* ship, vessel; ~ **da carico** cargo ship, freighter; ~ **cisterna** tanker; ~ **da guerra** warship; ~ **di linea** liner; ~ **passeggeri** passenger ship; ~ **portaerei** aircraft carrier; ~ **spaziale** spaceship.

navet'ta *sf* shuttle; (*servizio di collegamento*) shuttle (service).

navicel'la [nàvḗchel'là] *sf* (*di aerostato*) gondola; ~ **spaziale** spaceship.

naviga'bile *ag* navigable.

navigan'te *sm* sailor, seaman.

naviga're *vi* to sail; ~ **in cattive acque** (*fig*) to be in deep water.

naviga'to, a *ag* (*fig: esperto*) experienced.

navigato're, tri'ce *sm/f* (*gen*) navigator; ~ **solitario** single-handed sailor.

navigazio'ne [nàvḗgàttsyō'nà] *sf* navigation; **dopo una settimana di** ~ after a week at sea.

navi'glio [nàvēl'yō] *sm* fleet, ships *pl*; (*canale artificiale*) canal; ~ **da pesca** fishing fleet.

Na'zaret(h) [nád'dzàrāt] *sf* Nazareth.

naziona'le [nàttsyōnà'lā] *ag* national ♦ *sf* (*SPORT*) national team.

nazionali'smo [nàttsyōnàlēz'mō] *sm* nationalism.

nazionali'sta, i, e [nàttsyōnàlē'stá] *ag*, *sm/f* nationalist.

nazionalità [nàttsyōnàlētá'] *sf inv* nationality.

nazionalizza're [nàttsyōnàlēddzà'rā] *vt* to nationalize.

nazionalizzazio'ne [nàttsyōnàlēddzàttsyō'nā] *sf* nationalization.

nazio'ne [nàttsyō'nà] *sf* nation.

nazi'smo [nàttsēz'mō] *sm* Nazism.

nazi'sta, i, e [nàttsē'stá] *ag*, *sm/f* Nazi.

NB *abbr* (= *nota bene*) NB.

N.d.A. *abbr* (= *nota dell'autore*) author's note.

N.d.D. *abbr* = *nota della direzione*.

N.d.E. *abbr* (= *nota dell'editore*) publisher's note.

N.d.R. *abbr* (= *nota della redazione*) editor's note.

N.d.T. *abbr* (= *nota del traduttore*) translator's note.

ne *av* (*moto da luogo*) from there ♦ *pronome* of him/her/it/them; about him/her/it/them; ~ **riconosco la voce** I recognize his (o her) voice; **non parliamone più!** let's not talk about him (o her o it o them) any more!; ~ **deduco che l'avete trovato** I gather you've found it; ~ **consegue che ...** it follows therefore that ...; (*con valore partitivo*): **hai dei libri?** — **si,** ~ **ho** have you any books? — yes, I have (some); **hai del pane?** — **no, non** ~ **ho** have you any bread? — no, I don't have any; **quanti anni hai?** — ~ **ho 17** how old are you? — I'm 17.

né *cong*: ~ ... ~ neither ... nor; ~ **l'uno** ~ **l'altro lo vuole** neither of them wants it; ~ **più** ~ **meno** no more no less; **non parla** ~ **l'italiano** ~ **il tedesco** he speaks neither Italian nor German, he doesn't speak either Italian or German; **non piove** ~ **nevica** it isn't raining or snowing.

N.E. *abbr* (= *nordest*) NE.

nean'che [nàn'kā] *av, cong* not even; **non ...** ~ not even; ~ **se volesse potrebbe venire** he couldn't come even if he wanted to; **non l'ho visto** — **neanch'io** I didn't see him — neither did I o I didn't either; ~ **per idea** o **sogno!** not on your life!; **non ci penso** ~! I wouldn't dream of it!; ~ **a pagarlo lo farebbe** he wouldn't do it even if you paid him.

neb'bia *sf* fog; (*foschia*) mist.

nebbio'so, a *ag* foggy; misty.

nebulizzato're [nāb͞oōlĕddzàtō'rā] *sm* atomizer.

nebulo'sa *sf* nebula.

nebulosità *sf* haziness.

nebulo'so, a *ag* (*atmosfera*, *cielo*) hazy; (*fig*) hazy, vague.

nécessa'ire [nāscser'] *sm inv*: ~ **da viaggio** overnight case *o* bag.

necessariamen'te [nāchāssàryámān'tā] *av* necessarily.

necessa'rio, a [nāchāssà'ryō] *ag* necessary ♦ *sm*: **fare il** ~ to do what is necessary; **lo stretto** ~ the bare essentials *pl*.

necessità [nāchāssētà'] *sf inv* necessity; (*povertà*) need, poverty; **trovarsi nella** ~ **di fare qc** to be forced *o* obliged to do sth, have to do sth.

necessita're [nāchāssētà'rā] *vt* to require ♦ *vi* (*aver bisogno*): ~ **di** to need.

necrolo'gio [nākrōlo'jō] *sm* obituary notice; (*registro*) register of deaths.

nefan'do, a *ag* infamous, wicked.

nefa'sto, a *ag* inauspicious, ill-omened.

nega're *vt* to deny; (*rifiutare*) to deny, refuse; ~ **di aver fatto/che** to deny having done/that.

negativamen'te *av* negatively; **rispondere** ~ to give a negative response.

negati'vo, a *ag*, *sf*, *sm* negative.

negazio'ne [nāgàttsyō'nā] *sf* negation.

negherò *etc* [nāgāro'] *vb vedi* **negare.**

neglet'to, a [nāglet'tō] *ag* (*trascurato*) neglected.

ne'gli [nāl'yē] *prep + det vedi* **in.**

négligé' [nāglēzhā'] *sm inv* negligee.

negligen'te [nāglējen'tā] *ag* negligent, careless.

negligen'za [nāglējen'tsá] *sf* negligence, carelessness.

negozia'bile [nāgōttsyà'bēlā] *ag* negotiable.

negozian'te [nāgōttsyán'tā] *sm/f* trader, dealer; (*bottegaio*) storekeeper (*US*), shopkeeper (*Brit*).

negozia're [nāgōttsyà'rā] *vt* to negotiate ♦ *vi*: ~ **in** to trade *o* deal in.

negozia'to [nāgōttsyà'tō] *sm* negotiation.

negoziato're, tri'ce [nāgōttsyátō'rā] *sm/f* negotiator.

nego'zio [nāgot'tsyō] *sm* (*locale*) store (*US*), shop (*Brit*); (*affare*) (piece of) business *q*; (*DIR*): ~ **giuridico** legal transaction.

ne'gro, a *ag*, *sm/f* Negro.

negroman'te *sm/f* necromancer.

negromanzi'a [nāgrōmántsē'á] *sf* necromancy.

ne'i, nel, nell', nel'la, nel'le, nel'lo *prep + det vedi* **in.**

nem'bo *sm* (*METEOR*) nimbus.

nemi'co, a, ci, che *ag* hostile; (*MIL*) enemy *cpd* ♦ *sm/f* enemy; **essere** ~ **di** to be strongly averse *o* opposed to.

nemme'no *av*, *cong* = **neanche.**

ne'nia *sf* dirge; (*motivo monotono*) monotonous tune.

ne'o *sm* mole; (*fig*) (slight) flaw.

ne'o... *prefisso* neo....

neofasci'sta, i, e [nāōfáshē'stá] *sm/f* neofascist.

neologi'smo [nāōlōjēz'mō] *sm* neologism.

ne'on *sm* (*CHIM*) neon.

neona'to, a *ag* newborn ♦ *sm/f* newborn baby.

neozelande'se [nāōddzālándā'sā] *ag* New Zealand *cpd* ♦ *sm/f* New Zealander.

Nepal' *sm*: **il** ~ Nepal.

neppu're *av*, *cong* = **neanche.**

nerba'ta *sf* (*colpo*) blow; (*sferzata*) whiplash.

ner'bo *sm* lash; (*fig*) strength, backbone.

nerboru'to, a *ag* muscular; robust.

neret'to *sm* (*TIP*) bold type.

ne'ro, a *ag* black; (*scuro*) dark ♦ *sm* black; **nella miseria più** ~**a** in utter *o* abject poverty; **essere di umore** ~, **essere** ~ to be in a filthy mood; **mettere qc** ~ **su bianco** to put sth down in black and white; **vedere tutto** ~ to look on the black side (of things).

nerofu'mo *sm* lampblack.

nervatu'ra *sf* (*ANAT*) nervous system; (*BOT*) veining; (*ARCHIT, TECN*) rib.

ner'vo *sm* (*ANAT*) nerve; (*BOT*) vein; **avere i** ~**i** to be on edge; **dare sui** ~**i a qn** to get on sb's nerves; **tenere/avere i** ~**i saldi** to keep/ be calm; **che** ~**i!** damn (it)!

nervosi'smo *sm* (*PSIC*) nervousness; (*irritazione*) irritability.

nervo'so, a *ag* nervous; (*irritabile*) irritable ♦ *sm* (*fam*): **far venire il** ~ **a qn** to get on sb's nerves; **farsi prendere dal** ~ to let o.s. get irritated.

ne'spola *sf* (*BOT*) medlar; (*fig*) blow, punch.

ne'spolo *sm* medlar tree.

nes'so *sm* connection, link.

nessu'no, a *det* (*dav sm* **nessun** + *C*, *V*, **nessuno** + *s impura*, *gn*, *pn*, *ps*, *x*, *z*; *dav sf* **nessuna** + *C*, **nessun'** + *V*) (*non uno*) no, espressione negativa + any; (*qualche*) any ♦ *pronome* (*non uno*) no one, nobody, espressione negativa + any(one); (: *cosa*) none, espressione negativa + any; (*qualcuno*) anyone, anybody; (*qualcosa*) anything; **non c'è nessun libro** there isn't any book, there is no book; **hai** ~**a obiezione?** do you have any objections?; ~ **è venuto, non è venuto** ~ nobody came; **nessun altro** no one else, nobody else; **nessun'altra cosa** nothing else; **in nessun luogo** nowhere.

netta're *vt* to clean ♦ *sm* [net'tárā] nectar.

nettez'za [nāttāt'tsá] *sf* cleanness, cleanliness; ~ **urbana** department of sanitation (*US*), cleansing department (*Brit*).

net'to, a *ag* (*pulito*) clean; (*chiaro*) clear,

clear-cut; (*deciso*) definite; (*ECON*) net; **tagliare qc di** ~ to cut sth clean off; **taglio** ~ **col passato** (*fig*) clean break with the past.

netturbi'no *sm* garbage collector (*US*), dustman (*Brit*).

neurochirurgi'a [nāōōrōkĕrōōrjĕ'á] *sf* neurosurgery.

neurologi'a [nāōōrōlōjĕ'á] *sf* neurology.

neurolo'gico, a, ci, che [nāōōrōlo'jĕkō] *ag* neurological.

neuro'logo a, gi, ghe *sm/f* neurologist.

neuro'si *sf inv* = **nevrosi**.

neutra'le *ag* neutral.

neutralità *sf* neutrality.

neutralizza're [nāōōtrálĕddzá'rā] *vt* to neutralize.

ne'utro, a *ag* neutral; (*LING*) neuter ♦ *sm* (*LING*) neuter.

neutro'ne *sm* neutron.

neva'io *sm* snowfield.

ne've *sf* snow; **montare a** ~ (*CUC*) to whip up; ~ **carbonica** dry ice.

nevica're *vb impers* to snow.

nevica'ta *sf* snowfall.

nevis'chio [nāvēs'kyō] *sm* sleet.

nevo'so, a *ag* snowy; snow-covered.

nevralgi'a [nāvráljĕ'á] *sf* neuralgia.

nevral'gico, a, ci, che [nāvrál'jĕkō] *ag*: **punto** ~ (*MED*) nerve centre; (*fig*) crucial point.

nevraste'nico, a, ci, che *ag* (*MED*) neurasthenic; (*fig*) hot-tempered ♦ *sm/f* neurasthenic; hot-tempered person.

nevro'si *sf inv* neurosis.

nevro'tico, a, ci, che *ag, sm/f* (*anche fig*) neurotic.

Niaga'ra *sm*: **le cascate del** ~ the Niagara Falls.

nib'bio *sm* (*ZOOL*) kite.

Nicara'gua *sm*: **il** ~ Nicaragua.

nicaraguen'se *ag, sm/f* Nicaraguan.

nic'chia [nēk'kyá] *sf* niche; (*naturale*) cavity, hollow; ~ **di mercato** (*COMM*) market niche.

nicchia're [nēkkyá'rā] *vi* to shilly-shally, hesitate.

ni'chel [nē'kāl] *sm* nickel.

nichili'smo [nēkēlēz'mō] *sm* nihilism.

Nicosi'a *sf* Nicosia.

nicoti'na *sf* nicotine.

nidia'ta *sf* (*di uccelli, fig: di bambini*) brood; (*di altri animali*) litter.

nidifica're *vi* to nest.

ni'do *sm* nest ♦ *ag inv*: **asilo** ~ day nursery, crèche; **a** ~ **d'ape** (*tessuto etc*) honeycomb *cpd*.

nien'te *pronome* (*nessuna cosa*) nothing; (*qualcosa*) anything; **non ...** ~ nothing, espressione negativa + anything ♦ *sm* nothing ♦ *av* (*in nessuna misura*): **non è** ~ **buono** it's not good at all; **una cosa da** ~ a trivial thing; **poco o** ~ next to nothing; ~ **affatto**

not at all, not in the least; **nient'altro** nothing else; **nient'altro che** nothing but; just, only; ~ **di** ~ absolutely nothing; **per** ~ (*invano, gratuitamente*) for nothing; **non ... per** ~ not ... at all; ~ **male!** not bad at all!; ~ **paura!** never fear!; **e** ~ **scuse!** don't try to make excuses!; **basta un** ~ **per farla piangere** the slightest thing is enough to make her cry.

nientedime'no, nienteme'no *av* actually, even ♦ *escl* really!, I say!

Ni'ger [nē'jār] *sm*: **il** ~ Niger; (*fiume*) the Niger.

Nige'ria [nēje'ryà] *sf* Nigeria.

nigeria'no, a [nējāryá'nō] *ag, sm/f* Nigerian.

Ni'lo *sm*: **il** ~ the Nile.

nim'bo *sm* halo.

nin'fa *sf* nymph.

ninfe'a *sf* water lily.

ninfo'mane *sf* nymphomaniac.

ninnanan'na *sf* lullaby.

nin'nolo *sm* (*balocco*) plaything; (*gingillo*) knick-knack.

nipo'te *sm/f* (*di zii*) nephew/niece; (*di nonni*) grandson/daughter, grandchild.

nippo'nico, a, ci, che *ag* Japanese.

nitidez'za [nētēdāt'tsá] *sf* (*gen*) clearness; (*di stile*) clarity; (*FOT, TV*) sharpness.

ni'tido, a *ag* clear; (*immagine*) sharp, well-defined.

nitra'to *sm* nitrate.

ni'trico, a, ci, che *ag* nitric.

nitri're *vi* to neigh.

nitri'to *sm* (*di cavallo*) neighing *q*; neigh; (*CHIM*) nitrite.

nitrogliceri'na [nētrōglēchārē'ná] *sf* nitroglycerine.

ni'veo, a *ag* snow-white.

Niz'za [nēt'tsá] *sf* Nice.

nn *abbr* (= *numeri*) nos.

NO *sigla* = *Novara*.

no *av* (*risposta*) no; **vieni o** ~? are you coming or not?; **come** ~! of course!, certainly!; **perché** ~? why not?

N.O. *abbr* (= *nordovest*) NW.

nobildon'na *sf* noblewoman.

no'bile *ag* noble ♦ *sm/f* noble, nobleman/woman.

nobilia're *ag* noble.

nobilita're *vt* (*anche fig*) to ennoble; ~**rsi** *vr* (*rendersi insigne*) to distinguish o.s.

nobiltà *sf* nobility; (*di azione etc*) nobleness.

nobiluo'mo *sm, pl* **-uo'mini** nobleman.

noc'ca, che *sf* (*ANAT*) knuckle.

noc'cio *etc* [nōch'chō] *vb vedi* **nuocere**.

noccio'la [nōcho'lá] *sf* hazelnut ♦ *ag inv* (*anche*: **color** ~) hazel, light brown.

noccioli'na [nōchōlē'ná] *sf* (*anche*: ~ **americana**) peanut.

noc'ciolo [noch'chōlō] *sm* (*di frutto*) stone; (*fig*) heart, core; [nōcho'lō] (*albero*) hazel.

no'ce [nō'chā] *sm* (*albero*) walnut tree ♦ *sf* (*frutto*) walnut; **una ~ di burro** (*CUC*) a dab of butter; **~ di cocco** coconut; **~ moscata** nutmeg.

nocepe'sca, sche [nōchāpe'skà] *sf* nectarine.

noce'vo *etc* [nōchā'vō] *vb vedi* **nuocere.**

nociu'to [nōchoō'tō] *pp di* **nuocere.**

noci'vo, a [nōchē'vō] *ag* harmful, noxious.

noc'qui *etc vb vedi* **nuocere.**

no'do *sm* (*di cravatta, legname, NAUT*) knot; (*AUT, FERR*) junction; (*MED, ASTR, BOT*) node; (*fig: legame*) bond, tie; (*: punto centrale*) heart, crux; **avere un ~ alla gola** to have a lump in one's throat; **tutti i ~i vengono al pettine** (*proverbio*) your sins will find you out.

nodo'so, a *ag* (*tronco*) gnarled.

no'dulo *sm* (*ANAT, BOT*) nodule.

no'i *pronome* (*soggetto*) we; (*oggetto: per dare rilievo, con preposizione*) us; **~ stessi(e)** we ourselves; (*oggetto*) ourselves; **da ~** (*nel nostro paese*) in our country, where we come from; (*a casa nostra*) at our house.

no'ia *sf* boredom; (*disturbo, impaccio*) bother *q*, trouble *q*; **avere qn/qc a ~** not to like sb/ sth; **mi è venuto a ~** I'm tired of it; **dare ~ a** to annoy; **avere delle ~e con qn** to have trouble with sb.

noial'tri *pronome* we.

noio'so, a *ag* boring; (*fastidioso*) annoying, troublesome.

noleggia're [nōlādjá'rā] *vt* (*prendere a noleggio*) to rent, hire (*Brit*); (*dare a noleggio*) to rent out, hire out (*Brit*); (*aereo, nave*) to charter.

noleggiato're, tri'ce [nōlādjàtō'rā] *sm/f* renter; charterer.

noleg'gio [nōlād'jō] *sm* rental; charter.

nolen'te *ag:* **volente o ~** whether one likes it or not, willy-nilly.

no'lo *sm* rental; charter; (*per trasporto merci*) freight; **prendere/dare a ~ qc** to rent/rent out sth, hire/hire out sth (*Brit*).

no'made *ag* nomadic ♦ *sm/f* nomad.

nomadi'smo *sm* nomadism.

no'me *sm* name; (*LING*) noun; **in o a ~ di** in the name of; **di o per ~** (*chiamato*) called, named; **conoscere qn di ~** to know sb by name; **fare il ~ di qn** to name sb; **faccia pure il mio ~** feel free to mention my name; **~ d'arte** stage name; **~ di battesimo** Christian name; **~ depositato** trade name; **~ di famiglia** surname; **~ da ragazza** maiden name; **~ da sposata** married name.

nome'a *sf* notoriety.

nomi'gnolo [nōmēn'yōlō] *sm* nickname.

no'mina *sf* appointment.

nomina'le *ag* nominal; (*LING*) noun *cpd*.

nomina're *vt* to name; (*eleggere*) to appoint; (*citare*) to mention; **non l'ho mai sentito ~**

I've never heard of it (o him).

nominati'vo, a *ag* (*LING*) nominative; (*COMM*) registered ♦ *sm* (*LING: anche:* **caso ~**) nominative (case); (*COMM, AMM*) name.

non *av* not ♦ *prefisso* non-; **grazie — ~ c'è di che** thank you — don't mention it; **i ~ credenti** the unbelievers; *vedi* **affatto, appena** *etc.*

nonché [nōnkā'] *cong* (*tanto più, tanto meno*) let alone; (*e inoltre*) as well as.

nonconformi'sta, i, e *ag, sm/f* nonconformist.

noncuran'te *ag:* **~ (di)** careless (of), indifferent (to); **con fare ~** with a nonchalant air.

noncuran'za [nōnkoōràn'tsà] *sf* carelessness, indifference; **un'aria di ~** a nonchalant air.

nondime'no *cong* (*tuttavia*) however; (*nonostante*) nevertheless.

non'no, a *sm/f* grandfather/mother; (*in senso più familiare*) grandma/grandpa; **~i** *smpl* grandparents.

nonnul'la *sm inv:* **un ~** nothing, a trifle.

no'no, a *num* ninth.

nonostan'te *prep* in spite of, notwithstanding ♦ *cong* although, even though.

non plus ul'tra *sm inv:* **il ~ (di)** the last word (in).

nontiscordardimé *sm inv* (*BOT*) forget-me-not.

nord *sm* north ♦ *ag inv* north; (*regione*) northern; **verso ~** north, northwards; **l'America del N~** North America.

nordest *sm* north-east.

nor'dico, a, ci, che *ag* nordic, northern European.

nordi'sta, i, e *ag, sm/f* Yankee.

nordo'vest *sm* north-west.

Norimber'ga *sf* Nuremberg.

nor'ma *sf* (*principio*) norm; (*regola*) regulation, rule; (*consuetudine*) custom, rule; **di ~** normally; **a ~ di legge** according to law, as laid down by law; **al di sopra della ~** above average, above the norm; **per sua ~ e regola** for your information; **proporsi una ~ di vita** to set o.s. rules to live by; **~e di sicurezza** safety regulations; **~e per l'uso** instructions for use.

norma'le *ag* normal.

normalità *sf* normality.

normalizza're [nōrmálēddzà'rā] *vt* to normalize, bring back to normal.

normalmen'te *av* normally.

Normandi'a *sf:* **la ~** Normandy.

norman'no, a *ag, sm/f* Norman.

normati'vo, a *ag* normative ♦ *sf* regulations *pl.*

norvege'se [nōrvājā'sā] *ag, sm/f, sm* Norwegian.

Norve'gia [nōrvā'jà] *sf:* **la ~** Norway.

nosoco'mio *sm* hospital.

nostalgi'a [nōstáljč'á] *sf* (*di casa, paese*) homesickness; (*del passato*) nostalgia.

nostal'gico, a, ci, che [nōstàl'jčkō] *ag* homesick; nostalgic ♦ *sm/f* (*POL*) *person who hopes for the return of Fascism.*

nostra'no, a *ag* local; (*pianta, frutta*) homeproduced.

nos'tro, a *det*: **il(la) ~(a)** *etc* our ♦ *pronome*: **il(la) ~(a)** *etc* ours ♦ *sm*: **abbiamo speso del ~** we spent our own money ♦ *sf*: **la ~a** (*opinione*) our view; **i ~i** our family; our own people; **è dei ~i** he's one of us; **è dalla ~a** (*parte*) he's on our side; **anche noi abbiamo avuto le ~e** (*disavventure*) we've had our problems too; **alla ~a!** (*brindisi*) to us!

nostro'mo *sm* boatswain.

no'ta *sf* (*segno*) mark; (*comunicazione scritta, MUS*) note; (*fattura*) bill; (*elenco*) list; **prendere ~ di qc** to note sth, make a note of sth, write sth down; (*fig: fare attenzione*) to note sth, take note of sth; **degno di ~** noteworthy, worthy of note; **~e caratteristiche** distinguishing marks *o* features; **~e a piè di pagina** footnotes.

nota'bile *ag* notable; (*persona*) important ♦ *sm* prominent citizen.

nota'io *sm* notary.

nota're *vt* (*segnare: errori*) to mark; (*registrare*) to note (down), write down; (*rilevare, osservare*) to note, notice; **farsi ~** to get o.s. noticed.

notari'le *ag*: **atto ~** legal document (*authorized by a notary*); **studio ~** notary's office.

notazio'ne [nōtàttsyō'nā] *sf* (*MUS*) notation.

note'vole *ag* (*talento*) notable, remarkable; (*peso*) considerable.

noti'fica, che *sf* notification.

notifica're *vt* (*DIR*): **~ qc a qn** to notify sb of sth, give sb notice of sth.

notificazio'ne [nōtčfčkàttsyō'nā] *sf* notification.

noti'zia [nōtčt'tsyà] *sf* (*piece of*) news *sg*; (*informazione*) piece of information; **~e** *sfpl* news *sg*; information *sg*.

notizia'rio [nōtčttsyá'ryō] *sm* (*RADIO, TV, STAMPA*) news *sg*.

no'to, a *ag* (well-)known.

notorietà *sf* fame; notoriety.

noto'rio, a *ag* well-known; (*peg*) notorious.

nottam'bulo, a *sm/f* night owl (*fig*).

notta'ta *sf* night.

not'te *sf* night; **di ~** at night; (*durante la ~*) in the night, during the night; **questa ~** (*passata*) last night; (*che viene*) tonight; **nella ~ dei tempi** in the mists of time; **come va? — peggio che andar di ~** how are things? — worse than ever; **~ bianca** sleepless night.

nottetem'po *av* at night; during the night.

not'tola *sf* (*ZOOL*) noctule.

nottur'no, a *ag* nocturnal; (*servizio, guardiano*) night *cpd* ♦ *sf* (*SPORT*) night game (*US*), evening fixture (*Brit*).

nov. *abbr* (= *novembre*) Nov.

novan'ta *num* ninety.

novanten'ne *ag, sm/f* ninety-year-old.

novante'simo, a *num* ninetieth.

novanti'na *sf*: **una ~ (di)** about ninety.

no've *num* nine.

novecente'sco, a, schi, sche [nōvàchāntà'skō] *ag* twentieth-century.

novecen'to [nōvàchen'tō] *num* nine hundred ♦ *sm*: **il N~** the twentieth century.

novel'la *sf* (*LETTERATURA*) short story.

novelli'no, a *ag* (*pivello*) green, inexperienced.

novelli'sta, i, e *sm/f* short-story writer.

novelli'stica *sf* (*arte*) short-story writing; (*insieme di racconti*) short stories *pl*.

novel'lo, a *ag* (*piante, patate*) new; (*insalata, verdura*) early; (*sposo*) newly-married.

novem'bre *sm* November; *per fraseologia vedi* **luglio**.

novembri'no, a *ag* November *cpd*.

novemi'la *num* nine thousand.

novenna'le *ag* (*che dura 9 anni*) nine-year *cpd*; (*ogni 9 anni*) nine-yearly.

novilu'nio *sm* (*ASTR*) new moon.

novità *sf inv* novelty; (*innovazione*) innovation; (*cosa originale, insolita*) something new; (*notizia*) (piece of) news *sg*; **le ~ della moda** the latest fashions.

novizia'to [nōvčttsyà'tō] *sm* (*REL*) novitiate; (*tirocinio*) apprenticeship.

novi'zio, a [nōvčt'tsyō] *sm/f* (*REL*) novice; (*tirocinante*) beginner, apprentice.

nozio'ne [nōttsyō'nā] *sf* notion, idea; **~i** *sfpl* (*rudimenti*) basic knowledge *sg*, rudiments.

nozioni'smo [nōttsyōnčz'mō] *sm* superficial knowledge.

nozioni'stico, a, ci, che [nōttsyōnč'stčkō] *ag* superficial.

noz'ze [not'tsā] *sfpl* wedding *sg*, marriage *sg*; **~ d'argento/d'oro** silver/golden wedding *sg*.

N.P.A. *abbr* = **nave portaerei**.

ns. *abbr* (*COMM*) = **nostro**.

NU *sigla* = *Nuoro*.

N.U. *sigla* (= *Nazioni Unite*) UN.

nu'be *sf* cloud.

nubifra'gio [nōōbčfrà'jō] *sm* cloudburst.

nu'bile *ag* (*donna*) unmarried, single.

nu'ca, che *sf* nape of the neck.

nuclea're *ag* nuclear.

nu'cleo *sm* nucleus; (*gruppo*) team, unit, group; (*MIL, POLIZIA*) squad; **~ antidroga** anti-drugs squad; **il ~ familiare** the family unit.

nudi'smo *sm* nudism.

nudi'sta, i, e *sm/f* nudist.

nudità *sf inv* nudity, nakedness; (*di pae-*

saggio) bareness ♦ *sfpl* (*parti nude del corpo*) nakedness *sg*.

nu'do, a *ag* (*persona*) bare, naked, nude; (*membra*) bare, naked; (*montagna*) bare ♦ *sm* (*ARTE*) nude; **a occhio ~** to the naked eye; **a piedi ~i** barefoot; **mettere a ~** (*cuore, verità*) to lay bare; **gli ha detto ~ e crudo che ...** he told him bluntly that ....

nu'golo *sm*: **un ~ di** a whole host of.

nul'la *pronome, av* = **niente** ♦ *sm*: **il ~** nothing; **svanire nel ~** to vanish into thin air; **basta un ~ per farlo arrabbiare** he gets annoyed over the slightest thing.

nullao'sta *sm inv* authorization.

nullatenen'te *ag*: **essere ~** to own nothing ♦ *smf* person with no property.

nullità *sf inv* nullity; (*persona*) nonentity.

nul'lo, a *ag* useless, worthless; (*DIR*) null (and void); (*SPORT*): **incontro ~** draw.

numera'le *ag, sm* numeral.

numera're *vt* to number.

numerazio'ne [nōōmărättsyō'nä] *sf* numbering; (*araba, decimale*) notation.

nume'rico, a, ci, che *ag* numerical.

nu'mero *sm* number; (*romano, arabo*) numeral; (*di spettacolo*) act, turn; **dare i ~i** (*farneticare*) not to be all there; **tanto per fare ~ invitiamo anche lui** why don't we invite him to make up the numbers?; **ha tutti i ~i per riuscire** he's got what it takes to succeed; **che ~ tuo fratello!** your brother is a real character!; **~ civico** house number; **~ chiuso** (*UNIVERSITÀ*) selective entry system; **~ doppio** (*di rivista*) issue with supplement; **~ di scarpe** size of shoe.

numero'so, a *ag* numerous, many; (*folla, famiglia*) large.

nun'zio [nōōn'tsyō] *sm* (*REL*) nuncio.

nuoc'cio *etc* [nwoch'chō] *vb vedi* **nuocere**.

nuo'cere [nwo'chärä] *vi*: **~ a** to harm, damage; **il tentar non nuoce** (*proverbio*) there's no harm in trying.

nuociu'to, a [nwōchōō'tō] *pp di* **nuocere**.

nuo'ra *sf* daughter-in-law.

nuota're *vi* to swim; (*galleggiare: oggetti*) to float; **~ a rana/sul dorso** to do the breast stroke/backstroke.

nuota'ta *sf* swim.

nuotato're, tri'ce *smf* swimmer.

nuo'to *sm* swimming.

nuo'va *sf vedi* **nuovo**.

nuovamen'te *av* again.

Nuo'va York *sf* New York.

Nuo'va Zelan'da [-dzälän'dä] *sf*: **la ~** New Zealand.

nuo'vo, a *ag* new ♦ *sf* (*notizia*) (piece of) news *sg*; **come ~** as good as new; **di ~** again; **fino a ~ ordine** until further notice; **il suo volto non mi è ~** I know his face; **rimettere a ~** (*cosa, macchina*) to make it

like new; **anno ~, vita ~a!** it's time to turn over a new leaf!; **~ fiammante** *o* **di zecca** brand-new; **la N~a Guinea** New Guinea; **la N~a Inghilterra** New England; **la N~a Scozia** Nova Scotia.

nutri'ce [nōōtrē'chä] *sf* wet-nurse.

nutrien'te *ag* nutritious, nourishing.

nutrimen'to *sm* food, nourishment.

nutri're *vt* to feed; (*fig: sentimenti*) to harbor (*US*), harbour (*Brit*), nurse.

nutriti'vo, a *ag* nutritional; (*alimento*) nutritious.

nutri'to, a *ag* (*numeroso*) large; (*fitto*) heavy; **ben/mal ~** well/poorly fed.

nutrizio'ne [nōōtrēttsyō'nä] *sf* nutrition.

nu'volo, a *ag* cloudy ♦ *sf* cloud.

nuvolosità *sf* cloudiness.

nuvolo'so, a *ag* cloudy.

nuzia'le [nōōttsyà'lä] *ag* nuptial; wedding *cpd*.

nylon' [nà'ēlən] *sm* nylon.

O

O, o [o] *sf o m inv* (*lettera*) O, o; **~ come Otranto** ≈ O for Oboe.

o *cong* (*dav V spesso* **od**) or; **~ ... ~** either ... or; **~ l'uno ~ l'altro** either (of them); **~ meglio** or rather.

O. *abbr* (= *ovest*) W.

o'asi *sf inv* oasis.

obbedien'te *etc vedi* **ubbidiente** *etc*.

obbietta're *etc vedi* **obiettare** *etc*.

obbliga're *vt* (*costringere*): **~ qn a fare** to force *o* oblige sb to do; (*DIR*) to bind; **~rsi** *vr*: **~rsi a fare** to undertake to do; **~rsi per qn** (*DIR*) to stand surety for sb, act as guarantor for sb.

obbligatis'simo, a *ag* (*ringraziamento*): **~!** much obliged!

obbliga'to, a *ag* (*costretto, grato*) obliged; (*percorso, tappa*) set, fixed; **passaggio ~** (*fig*) essential requirement.

obbligato'rio, a *ag* compulsory, obligatory.

obbligazio'ne [ōbblēgàttsyō'nä] *sf* obligation; (*COMM*) bond, debenture; **~ dello Stato** government bond; **~i convertibili** convertible loan stock, convertible debentures.

obbligazioni'sta, i, e [ōbblēgàttsyōnē'stà] *smf* bond-holder.

ob'bligo, ghi *sm* obligation; (*dovere*) duty; **avere l'~ di fare, essere nell'~ di fare** to be obliged to do; **essere d'~** (*discorso, applauso*) to be called for; **avere degli ~ghi con** *o* verso qn to be under an obligation to sb, be indebted to sb; **le formalità d'~** the necessary formalities.

obb.mo *abbr* = **obbligatissimo.**

obbro'brio *sm* disgrace; (*fig*) mess, eyesore.

obeli'sco, schi *sm* obelisk.

obera'to, a *ag*: **~ di** (*lavoro*) overloaded *o* overburdened with; (*debiti*) crippled with.

obesità *sf* obesity.

obe'so, a *ag* obese.

obietta're *vt*: **~ che** to object that; **~ su qc** to object to sth, raise objections concerning sth.

obiettivamen'te *av* objectively.

obiettività *sf* objectivity.

obietti'vo, a *ag* objective ♦ *sm* (*OTTICA, FOT*) lens *sg*, objective; (*MIL, fig*) objective.

obietto're *sm* objector; **~ di coscienza** conscientious objector.

obiezio'ne [ōbyāttsyō'nā] *sf* objection.

obito'rio *sm* morgue.

obli'quo, a *ag* oblique; (*inclinato*) slanting; (*fig*) devious, underhand; **sguardo ~** sidelong glance.

oblitera're *vt* (*francobollo*) to cancel; (*biglietto*) to stamp.

obliteratri'ce [ōblētārátrē'chā] *sf* (*anche:* **macchina ~**) cancelling machine; stamping machine.

oblò *sm inv* porthole.

oblun'go, a, ghi, ghe *ag* oblong.

o'boe *sm* oboe.

obsolescen'za [ōbsōlāshen'tsā] *sf* (*ECON*) obsolescence.

obsole'to, a *ag* obsolete.

OC *abbr* (= *onde corte*) SW.

o'ca, pl o'che *sf* goose.

ocag'gine [ōkàd'jēnā] *sf* silliness, stupidity.

occasiona'le *ag* (*incontro*) chance; (*cliente, guadagni*) casual, occasional.

occasio'ne *sf* (*caso favorevole*) opportunity; (*causa, motivo, circostanza*) occasion; (*COMM*) bargain; **all'~** should the need arise; **alla prima ~** at the first opportunity; **d'~** (*a buon prezzo*) bargain *cpd*; (*usato*) secondhand.

occhia'ia [ōkkyà'yà] *sf* eye socket; **~e** *sfpl* (*sotto gli occhi*) shadows (under the eyes).

occhia'li [ōkkyà'lē] *smpl* glasses, spectacles; **~ da sole** sunglasses.

occhia'ta [ōkkyà'tà] *sf* look, glance; **dare un'~ a** to have a look at.

occhieggia're [ōkkyādjà'rā] *vi* (*apparire qua e là*) to peep (out).

occhiel'lo [ōkkyel'lō] *sm* buttonhole; (*asola*) eyelet.

oc'chio [ok'kyō] *sm* eye; **~!** careful!, watch out!; **a ~ nudo** with the naked eye; **a quattr'~i** privately, in private; **avere ~ to** have a good eye; **chiudere un ~ (su)** (*fig*) to

turn a blind eye (to), shut one's eyes (to); **costare un ~ della testa** to cost a fortune; **dare all'~ o nell'~ a qn** to catch sb's eye; **fare l'~ a qc** to get used to sth; **tenere d'~ qn** to keep an eye on sb; **vedere di buon/mal ~ qc** to look favourably/unfavourably on sth.

occhioli'no [ōkkyōlē'nō] *sm*: **fare l'~ a qn** to wink at sb.

occidenta'le [ōchēdàntà'lā] *ag* western ♦ *sm/f* Westerner.

occiden'te [ōchēden'tā] *sm* west; (*POL*): **l'O~** the West; **a ~** in the west.

occi'pite [ōchē'pētā] *sm* back of the head, occiput (*ANAT*).

occlu'dere *vt* to block.

occlusio'ne *sf* blockage, obstruction.

occlu'so, a *pp di* **occludere.**

occorren'te *ag* necessary ♦ *sm* all that is necessary.

occorren'za [ōkkōrren'tsà] *sf* necessity, need; **all'~** in case of need.

occor'rere *vt* to be needed, be required ♦ *vb impers*: **occorre farlo** it must be done; **occorre che tu parta** you must leave, you'll have to leave; **mi occorrono i soldi** I need the money.

occor'so, a *pp di* **occorrere.**

occultamen'to *sm* concealment.

occulta're *vt* to hide, conceal.

occul'to, a *ag* hidden, concealed; (*scienze, forze*) occult.

occupan'te *sm/f* (*di casa*) occupier, occupant; **~ abusivo** squatter.

occupa're *vt* to occupy; (*manodopera*) to employ; (*ingombrare*) to occupy, take up; **~rsi** *vr* to occupy o.s., keep o.s. busy; (*impiegarsi*) to get a job; **~rsi di** (*interessarsi*) to take an interest in; (*prendersi cura di*) to look after, take care of.

occupa'to, a *ag* (*MIL, POL*) occupied; (*persona: affaccendato*) busy; (*posto, sedia*) taken; (*toilette, TEL*) engaged.

occupaziona'le [ōkkōōpàttsyōnà'lā] *ag* employment *cpd*, of employment.

occupazio'ne [ōkkōōpàttsyō'nā] *sf* occupation; (*impiego, lavoro*) job; (*ECON*) employment.

Ocea'nia [ōchāà'nyà] *sf*: **l'~** Oceania.

oce'ano [ōche'ánō] *sm* ocean.

o'cra *sf* ochre.

OC'SE *sigla f* (= *Organizzazione per la Cooperazione e lo Sviluppo Economico*) OECD (= *Organization for Economic Cooperation and Development*).

ocula're *ag* ocular, eye *cpd*; **testimone ~** eye witness.

oculatez'za [ōkōōlàtāt'tsà] *sf* caution; shrewdness.

ocula'to, a *ag* (*attento*) cautious, prudent; (*accorto*) shrewd.

oculi'sta, i, e *sm/f* eye specialist, oculist.

od cong vedi **o**.

o'de sf ode.

o'de etc vb vedi **udire**.

odia're vt to hate, detest.

odier'no, a ag today's, of today; (attuale) present; **in data ~a** (formale) today.

o'dio sm hatred; **avere in ~ qc/qn** to hate o detest sth/sb.

odio'so, a ag hateful, odious; **rendersi ~ (a)** to make o.s. unpopular (with).

o'do etc vb vedi **udire**.

odontoia'tra, i, e sm/f dentist, dental surgeon.

odontoiatri'a sf dentistry.

odontotec'nico, ci sm dental technician.

odora're vt (annusare) to smell; (profumare) to perfume, scent ♦ vi: **~ (di)** to smell (of).

odora'to sm sense of smell.

odo're sm smell; **gli ~i** smpl (CUC) (aromatic) herbs; **sentire ~ di qc** to smell sth; **morire in ~ di santità** (REL) to die in the odor (US) o odour (Brit) of sanctity.

odoro'so, a ag sweet-smelling.

offen'dere vt to offend; (violare) to break, violate; (insultare) to insult; (ferire) to hurt; **~rsi** vr (con senso reciproco) to insult one another; (risentirsi): **~rsi (di)** to take offence (at), be offended (by).

offensi'vo, a ag, sf offensive.

offenso're sm offender; (MIL) aggressor.

offeren'te sm (in aste): **al migliore ~** to the highest bidder.

offer'to, a pp di **offrire** ♦ sf offer; (donazione, anche REL) offering; (in gara d'appalto) tender; (in aste) bid; (ECON) supply; **fare un'~a** to make an offer; (per appalto) to tender; (ad un'asta) to bid; **~a pubblica d'acquisto (OPA)** takeover bid; **~a pubblica di vendita (OPV)** public offer for sale; **~a reale** tender; **"~e d'impiego"** (STAMPA) "help wanted" (US), "situations vacant" (Brit).

offe'so, a pp di **offendere** ♦ ag offended; (fisicamente) hurt, injured ♦ sm/f offended party ♦ sf insult, affront; (MIL) attack; (DIR) offense (US), offence (Brit); **essere ~ con qn** to be annoyed with sb; **parte ~a** (DIR) plaintiff.

offici'na [ōffēchē'nà] sf workshop.

offri're vt to offer; **~rsi** vr (proporsi) to offer (o.s.), volunteer; (occasione) to present itself; (esporsi): **~rsi a** to expose o.s. to; **ti offro da bere** I'll buy you a drink; **"offresi posto di segretaria"** "secretarial vacancy", "secretary wanted"; **"segretaria offresi"** "secretary seeks employment".

offusca're vt to obscure, darken; (fig: intelletto) to dim, cloud; (: fama) to obscure, overshadow; **~rsi** vr to grow dark; to cloud, grow dim; to be obscured.

oftal'mico, a, ci, che ag ophthalmic.

oggettività [ōdjāttēvētá'] sf objectivity.

oggetti'vo, a [ōdjāttē'vō] ag objective.

ogget'to [ōdjet'tō] sm object; (materia, argomento) subject (matter); (in lettere commerciali): **~ ... re ...;** **essere ~ di** (critiche, controversia) to be the subject of; (odio, pietà etc) to be the object of; **essere ~ di scherno** to be a laughing stock; **in ~ a quanto detto** (in lettere) as regards the matter mentioned above; **~i preziosi** valuables, articles of value; **~i smarriti** lost and found sg (US), lost property sg (Brit).

og'gi [od'jē] av, sm today; **~ stesso** today, this very day; **~ come ~** at present, as things stand; **dall' ~ al domani** from one day to the next; **a tutt'~** up till now, till today; **le spese a tutt'~ sono ...** expenses to date are ...; **~ a otto** a week today.

oggigior'no [ōdjējōr'nō] av nowadays.

ogi'va [ōjē'và] sf ogive, pointed arch.

o'gni [ōn'yē] det every, each; (tutti) all; (con valore distributivo) every; **~ uomo è mortale** all men are mortal; **viene ~ due giorni** he comes every two days; **~ cosa** everything; **ad ~ costo** at all costs, at any price; **in ~ luogo** everywhere; **~ tanto** every so often; **~ volta che** every time you.

Ognissan'ti [ōnyēssàn'tē] sm All Saints' Day.

ognu'no [ōnyōō'nō] pronome everyone, everybody.

o'hi escl oh!; (esprimente dolore) ow!

ohimè escl oh dear!

O'IL sigla f (= Organizzazione Internazionale del Lavoro) ILO.

OL abbr (= onde lunghe) LW.

Olan'da sf: **l'~** Holland.

olande'se ag Dutch ♦ sm (LING) Dutch ♦ sm/f Dutchman/woman; **gli O~i** the Dutch.

olean'dro sm oleander.

olea'to, a ag: **carta ~a** wax paper (US), greaseproof paper (Brit).

oleodot'to sm oil pipeline.

oleo'so, a ag oily; (che contiene olio) oil cpd.

olfat'to sm sense of smell.

olia're vt to oil.

oliato're sm oil can, oiler.

olie'ra sf oil cruet.

olimpi'adi sfpl Olympic Games.

olim'pico, a, ci, che ag Olympic.

o'lio sm oil; (PITTURA): **un (quadro a) ~** an oil painting; **sott'~** (CUC) in oil; **~ di fegato di merluzzo** cod liver oil; **~ d'oliva** olive oil; **~ santo** holy oil; **~ di semi** vegetable oil; **~ solare** suntan oil.

oli'va sf olive.

olivas'tro, a ag olive(-colored) (US), olive(-coloured) (Brit); (carnagione) sallow.

olive'to sm olive grove.

oli'vo sm olive tree.

ol'mo *sm* elm.

oloca'usto *sm* holocaust.

OLP *sigla f* (= *Organizzazione per la Liberazione della Palestina*) PLO.

oltraggia're |ōltràdjá'rā| *vt* to offend, insult.

oltrag'gio |ōltràd'jō| *sm* offense (*US*), offence (*Brit*), insult; (*DIR*): ~ **al pudore** indecent behavior; ~ **alla corte** contempt of court.

oltraggio'so, a |ōltràdjō'sō| *ag* offensive.

oltral'pe *av* beyond the Alps.

oltran'za |ōltràn'tsà| *sf*: **a** ~ to the last, to the bitter end; **sciopero ad** ~ all-out strike.

oltranzi'smo |ōltràntsēz'mō| *sm* (*POL*) extremism.

oltranzi'sta, i, e |ōltràntsē'stà| *sm/f* (*POL*) extremist.

ol'tre *av* (*più in là*) further; (*di più: aspettare*) longer, more ♦ *prep* (*di là da*) beyond, over, on the other side of; (*più di*) more than, over; (*in aggiunta a*) besides; (*eccetto*): ~ **a** except, apart from; ~ **a tutto** on top of all that.

oltrecorti'na *av* behind the Iron Curtain; **paesi d'**~ Iron Curtain countries.

oltrema'nica *av* across the Channel.

oltrema're *av* overseas.

oltremo'do *av* extremely, greatly.

oltreoce'ano |ōltràōche'ànō| *av* overseas ♦ *sm*: **paesi d'**~ overseas countries.

oltrepassa're *vt* to go beyond, exceed.

OM *abbr* (= *onde medie*) MW; (*MIL*) = *ospedale militare*.

omag'gio |ōmád'jō| *sm* (*dono*) gift; (*segno di rispetto*) homage, tribute; ~**i** *smpl* (*complimenti*) respects; **in** ~ (*copia, biglietto*) complimentary; **rendere** ~ **a** to pay homage *o* tribute to; **presentare i propri** ~**i a qn** (*formale*) to pay one's respects to sb.

O'man *sm*: **l'**~ Oman.

ombelica'le *ag* umbilical.

ombeli'co, chi *sm* navel.

om'bra *sf* (*zona non assolata, fantasma*) shade; (*sagoma scura*) shadow ♦ *ag inv*: **bandiera** ~ flag of convenience; **governo** ~ (*POL*) shadow cabinet; **sedere all'**~ to sit in the shade; **nell'**~ (*tramare, agire*) secretly; **restare nell'**~ (*fig: persona*) to remain in obscurity; **senza** ~ **di dubbio** without the shadow of a doubt.

ombreggia're |ōmbrádjá'rā| *vt* to shade.

ombrel'lo *sm* umbrella; ~ **da sole** parasol, sunshade.

ombrello'ne *sm* beach umbrella.

ombret'to *sm* eyeshadow.

ombro'so, a *ag* shady, shaded; (*cavallo*) nervous, skittish; (*persona*) touchy, easily offended.

omelet'te |ōmɘlet'| *sf inv* omelet(te).

omeli'a *sf* (*REL*) homily, sermon.

omeopati'a *sf* homeopathy.

omeopa'tico, a, ci, che *ag* homeopathic ♦ *sm* homeopath.

omertà *sf* conspiracy of silence.

omes'so, a *pp di* **omettere**.

omet'tere *vt* to omit, leave out; ~ **di fare** to omit *o* fail to do.

omici'da, i, e |ōmēchē'dà| *ag* homicidal, murderous ♦ *sm/f* murderer/murderess.

omici'dio |ōmēchē'dyō| *sm* murder; ~ **colposo** (*DIR*) culpable homicide; ~ **premeditato** (*DIR*) murder.

omi'si *etc vb vedi* **omettere**.

omissio'ne *sf* omission; **reato d'**~ criminal negligence; ~ **di atti d'ufficio** negligence (*by a public employee*); ~ **di denuncia** failure to report a crime; ~ **di soccorso** (*DIR*) failure to stop and give assistance.

omogeneizza'to |ōmōjànāēddzà'tō| *sm* baby food.

omoge'neo, a |ōmōje'nàō| *ag* homogeneous.

omologa're *vt* (*DIR*) to approve, recognize; (*ratificare*) to ratify.

omologazio'ne |ōmōlōgàttsyō'nā| *sf* approval; ratification.

omo'logo, a, ghi, ghe *ag* homologous, corresponding.

omo'nimo, a *sm/f* namesake ♦ *sm* (*LING*) homonym.

omosessua'le *ag, sm/f* homosexual.

O.M.S. *sigla f vedi* **Organizzazione Mondiale della Sanità**.

On. *abbr* (*POL*) = **onorevole**.

on'cia, ce |ōn'chà| *sf* ounce.

on'da *sf* wave; **mettere** *o* **mandare in** ~ (*RADIO, TV*) to broadcast; **andare in** ~ (*RADIO, TV*) to go on the air; ~**e corte/medie/lunghe** short/medium/long wave *sg*; **l'**~ **verde** (*AUT*) synchronized traffic lights *pl*.

onda'ta *sf* wave, billow; (*fig*) wave, surge; **a** ~**e** in waves; ~ **di caldo** heatwave; ~ **di freddo** cold spell *o* snap.

on'de *cong* (*affinché: con il congiuntivo*) so that, in order that; (*: con l'infinito*) so as to, in order to.

ondeggia're |ōndàdjá'rā| *vi* (*acqua*) to ripple; (*muoversi sulle onde: barca*) to rock, roll; (*fig: muoversi come le onde, barcollare*) to sway; (*: essere incerto*) to waver.

ondo'so, a *ag* (*moto*) of the waves.

ondula'to, a *ag* (*capelli*) wavy; (*terreno*) undulating; **cartone** ~ corrugated paper; **lamiera** ~**a** sheet of corrugated iron.

ondulato'rio, a *ag* undulating; (*FISICA*) undulatory, wave *cpd*.

ondulazio'ne |ōndōōláttsyō'nā| *sf* undulation; (*acconciatura*) wave.

onera'to, a *ag*: ~ **di** burdened with, loaded with.

o'nere *sm* burden; ~ **finanziario** financial charge; ~**i fiscali** taxes.

onero'so, a *ag* (*fig*) heavy, onerous.

onestà *sf* honesty.

onestamen'te *av* honestly; fairly; virtuously; (*in verità*) honestly, frankly.

one'sto, a *ag* (*probo, retto*) honest; (*giusto*) fair; (*casto*) chaste, virtuous.

o'nice [o'nĕchă] *sf* onyx.

oni'rico, a, ci, che *ag* dreamlike, dream *cpd*.

onnipoten'te *ag* omnipotent.

onnipresen'te *ag* omnipresent; (*scherzoso*) ubiquitous.

onniscien'te [ŏnnĕshcn'tā] *ag* omniscient.

onniveggen'te [ŏnnĕvādjcn'tā] *ag* all-seeing.

onoma'stico, ci *sm* name day.

onoran'ze [ŏnŏràn'tsā] *sfpl* honors (*US*), honours (*Brit*).

onora're *vt* to honor (*US*), honour (*Brit*); (*far onore a*) to do credit to; **~rsi** *vr*: **~rsi di qc/ di fare** to feel hono(u)red by sth/to do.

onora'rio, a *ag* honorary ♦ *sm* fee.

ono're *sm* honor (*US*), honour (*Brit*); **in ~ di** in hono(u)r of; **fare gli ~i di casa** to play host (*o* hostess); **fare ~ a** to hono(u)r; (*pranzo*) to do justice to; (*famiglia*) to be a credit to; **farsi ~** to distinguish o.s.; **posto d'~** place of hono(u)r; **a onor del vero** ... to tell the truth ....

onore'vole *ag* honorable (*US*), honourable (*Brit*) ♦ *sm/f* (*POL*) ≈ Congressman/woman (*US*), ≈ Member of Parliament (*Brit*).

onorificen'za [ŏnŏrēfēchen'tsá] *sf* honor (*US*), honour (*Brit*); decoration.

onori'fico, a, ci, che *ag* honorary.

on'ta *sf* shame, disgrace; **ad ~ di** despite, notwithstanding.

onta'no *sm* alder.

O.'N.U. *sigla f* (= *Organizzazione delle Nazioni Unite*) UN, UNO.

OO.PP. *abbr vedi* **opere pubbliche.**

O'PA *sigla f vedi* **offerta pubblica d'acquisto.**

opa'co, a, chi, che *ag* (*vetro*) opaque; (*metallo*) dull, matt.

opa'le *sm o f* opal.

o'pera *sf* (*gen*) work; (*azione rilevante*) action, deed, work; (*MUS*) work; opus; (: *melodramma*) opera; (: *teatro*) opera house; (*ente*) institution, organization; **per ~ sua** thanks to him; **fare ~ di persuasione presso qn** to try to convince sb; **mettersi/essere all'~** to get down to/be at work; **~ d'arte** work of art; **~ buffa** comic opera; **~ lirica** (grand) opera; **~ pia** religious charity; **~e pubbliche (OO.PP.)** public works; **~e di restauro/di scavo** restoration/excavation work *sg*.

opera'io, a *ag* working-class; workers'; (*ZOOL: ape, formica*) worker *cpd* ♦ *sm/f* worker; **classe ~a** working class; **~ di fabbrica** factory worker; **~ a giornata** day laborer; **~ specializzato o qualificato** skilled laborer; **~ non specializzato** semi-skilled laborer.

opera're *vt* to carry out, make; (*MED*) to operate on ♦ *vi* to operate, work; (*rimedio*) to act, work; (*MED*) to operate; **~rsi** *vr* to occur, take place; (*MED*) to have an operation; **~rsi d'appendicite** to have one's appendix out; **~ qn d'urgenza** to perform an emergency operation on sb.

operati'vo, a *ag* operative, operating; **piano ~** (*MIL*) plan of operations.

opera'to *sm* (*comportamento*) actions *pl*.

operato're, tri'ce *sm/f* operator; (*TV, CINEMA*) cameraman; **aperto solo agli ~i** (*COMM*) open to the trade only; **~ di borsa** dealer on the stock exchange; **~ economico** agent, broker; **~ del suono** sound recordist; **~ turistico** tour operator.

operato'rio, a *ag* (*MED*) operating.

operazio'ne [ŏpàràttsyŏ'nă] *sf* operation.

operet'ta *sf* (*MUS*) operetta, light opera.

operosità *sf* industry.

opero'so, a *ag* industrious, hard-working.

opifi'cio [ŏpĕfĕ'chō] *sm* factory, works *pl*.

opina'bile *ag* (*discutibile*) debatable, questionable; **è ~** it is a matter of opinion.

opinio'ne *sf* opinion; **avere il coraggio delle proprie ~i** to have the courage of one's convictions; **l'~ pubblica** public opinion.

op là *escl* (*per far saltare*) hup!; (*a bimbo che è caduto*) upsy-daisy!

op'pio *sm* opium.

oppio'mane *sm/f* opium addict.

opponen'te *ag* opposing ♦ *sm/f* opponent.

oppon'go *etc vb vedi* **opporre.**

oppor're *vt* to oppose; **opporsi** *vr*: **opporsi (a qc)** to oppose (sth); to object (to sth); **~ resistenza/un rifiuto** to offer resistance/to refuse.

opportuni'sta, i, e *sm/f* opportunist.

opportunità *sf inv* opportunity; (*convenienza*) opportuneness, timeliness.

opportu'no, a *ag* timely, opportune; (*giusto*) right, appropriate; **a tempo ~** at the right *o* the appropriate time.

oppo'si *etc vb vedi* **opporre.**

opposito're, tri'ce *sm/f* opposer, opponent.

opposizio'ne [ŏppŏzēttsyŏ'nă] *sf* opposition; (*DIR*) objection; **essere in netta ~** (*idee, opinioni*) to clash, be in complete opposition; **fare ~ a qn/qc** to oppose sb/sth.

oppo'sto, a *pp di* **opporre** ♦ *ag* opposite; (*opinioni*) conflicting ♦ *sm* opposite, contrary; **all'~** on the contrary.

oppressio'ne *sf* oppression.

oppressi'vo, a *ag* oppressive.

oppres'so, a *pp di* **opprimere.**

oppresso're *sm* oppressor.

opprimen'te *ag* (*caldo, noia*) oppressive; (*persona*) tiresome; (: *deprimente*) depressing.

oppri'mere vt (premere, gravare) to weigh down; (estenuare: sog: caldo) to suffocate, oppress; (tiranneggiare: popolo) to oppress.

oppugna're [ŏppōōnyà'rā] vt (fig) to refute.

oppu're cong or (else).

opta're vi: ~ **per** (scegliere) to opt for, decide upon; (BORSA) to take (out) an option on.

op'timum sm inv optimum.

opulen'to, a ag (ricco) rich, wealthy, affluent; (: arredamento etc) opulent.

opulen'za [ŏpōōlen'tsá] sf (vedi ag) richness, wealth, affluence; opulence.

opu'scolo sm booklet, pamphlet.

OPV sigla f vedi **offerta pubblica di vendita**.

opziona'le [ŏptsyŏnà'lā] ag optional.

opzio'ne [ŏptsyŏ'nā] sf option.

OR sigla = Oristano.

o'ra sf (60 minuti) hour; (momento) time; **che ~ è?, che ~e sono?** what time is it?; **domani a quest'~** this time tomorrow; **non veder l'~ di fare** to long to do, look forward to doing; **fare le ~e piccole** to stay up till the early hours (of the morning); **è ~ di partire** it's time to go; **di buon'~** early; **alla buon'~!** at last!; **~ legale** o **estiva** daylight saving time; **~ locale** local time; **~ di pranzo** lunchtime; **~ di punta** (AUT) rush hour ♦ av (adesso) now; (poco fa): **è uscito proprio ~** he's just gone out; (tra poco) presently, in a minute; (correlativo): **~ ... ~** now ... now; **d'~ in avanti** o **poi** from now on; **or ~** just now, a moment ago; **~ come ~** right now, at present; **10 anni or sono** 10 years ago.

ora'colo sm oracle.

o'rafo sm goldsmith.

ora'le ag, sm oral.

oralmen'te av orally.

orama'i av = ormai.

ora'rio, a ag hourly; (fuso, segnale) time cpd; (velocità) per hour ♦ sm timetable, schedule; (di visite etc) hours pl, time(s pl); **~ di apertura/chiusura** opening/closing time; **~ di apertura degli sportelli** bank opening hours; **~ elastico** o **flessibile** (INDUSTRIA) flexitime; **~ ferroviario** railway timetable; **~ di lavoro/d'ufficio** working/office hours.

ora'ta sf sea bream.

orato're, tri'ce sm/f speaker; orator.

orato'rio, a ag oratorical ♦ sm (REL) oratory; (MUS) oratorio ♦ sf (arte) oratory.

orazio'ne [ŏráttsyŏ'nā] sf (REL) prayer; (discorso) speech, oration.

orbe'ne cong so, well (then).

or'bita sf (ASTR, FISICA) orbit; (ANAT) (eye-) socket.

orbita're vi to orbit.

Or'cadi sfpl: **le (isole) ~** the Orkney Islands, the Orkneys.

orches'tra [ŏrkes'trá] sf orchestra.

orchestra'le [ŏrkástrá'lā] ag orchestral ♦ sm/f orchestra player.

orchestra're [ŏrkástrá'rā] vt to orchestrate; (fig) to stage-manage.

orchide'a [ŏrkēde'á] sf orchid.

or'cio [ŏr'chŏ] sm jar.

or'co, chi sm ogre.

or'da sf horde.

ordi'gno [ŏrdēn'yŏ] sm: **~ esplosivo** explosive device.

ordina'le ag, sm ordinal.

ordinamen'to sm order, arrangement; (regolamento) regulations pl, rules pl; **~ scolastico/giuridico** education/legal system.

ordinan'za [ŏrdēnán'tsá] sf (DIR, MIL) order; (AMM: decreto) decree; (persona: MIL) orderly, batman; **d'~** (MIL) regulation cpd; **ufficiale d'~** orderly; **~ municipale** by(e)-law.

ordina're vt (mettere in ordine) to arrange, organize; (COMM) to order; (prescrivere: medicina) to prescribe; (comandare): **~ a qn di fare qc** to order o command sb to do sth; (REL) to ordain.

ordina'rio, a ag (comune) ordinary; (grossolano) coarse, common ♦ sm ordinary; (di università) full professor.

ordinati'vo, a ag regulating, governing ♦ sm (COMM) order.

ordina'to, a ag tidy, orderly.

ordinazio'ne [ŏrdēnáttsyŏ'nā] sf (COMM) order; (REL) ordination; **fare un'~ di qc** to put in an order for sth, order sth; **eseguire qc su ~** to make sth to order.

or'dine sm order; (carattere): **d'~ pratico** of a practical nature; **all'~** (COMM: assegno) to order; **di prim'~** first-class; **fino a nuovo ~** until further notice; **essere in ~** (documenti) to be in order; (persona, stanza) to be tidy; **mettere in ~** to put in order, tidy (up); **richiamare all'~** to call to order; **le forze dell'~** the forces of law and order; **~ d'acquisto** purchase order; **l'~ degli avvocati** ≈ the Bar; **~ del giorno** (di seduta) agenda; (MIL) order of the day; **l'~ dei medici** ≈ the Medical Association; **~ di pagamento** automatic payment (US), standing order (Brit); **l'~ pubblico** law and order; **~i (sacri)** (REL) holy orders.

ordi're vt (fig) to plot, scheme.

ordi'to sm (di tessuto) warp.

orecchia'bile [ŏrākkyà'bēlā] ag (canzone) catchy.

orecchi'no [ŏrākkē'nŏ] sm earring.

orec'chio [ŏrāk'kyŏ], pl(f) **orec'chie** sm (ANAT) ear; **avere ~** to have a good ear (for music); **venire all'~ di qn** to come to sb's attention; **fare ~e da mercante (a)** to turn a deaf ear (to).

orecchio'ni [ŏrākkyŏ'nē] smpl (MED) mumps

sg.

ore'fice [ōrā'fēchā] *sm* goldsmith; jeweler (*US*), jeweller (*Brit*).

oreficeri'a [ōrāfēchārē'á] *sf* (*arte*) goldsmith's art; (*negozio*) jewelry store (*US*), jeweller's (shop) (*Brit*).

or'fano, a *ag* orphan(ed) ♦ *sm/f* orphan; ~ **di padre/madre** fatherless/motherless.

orfanotro'fio *sm* orphanage.

organet'to *sm* barrel organ; (*fam*: *armonica a bocca*) mouth organ; (: *fisarmonica*) accordion.

orga'nico, a, ci, che *ag* organic ♦ *sm* personnel, staff.

organigram'ma, i *sm* organization chart; (*INFORM*) computer flow chart.

organi'smo *sm* (*BIOL*) organism; (*ANAT, AMM*) body, organism.

organi'sta, i, e *sm/f* organist.

organizza're [ōrgánēddzá'rā] *vt* to organize; ~**rsi** *vr* to get organized.

organizzati'vo, a [ōrgánēddzátē'vō] *ag* organizational.

organizzato're, tri'ce [ōrgánēddzátō'rā] *ag* organizing ♦ *sm/f* organizer.

organizzazio'ne [ōrgánēddzáttsyō'nā] *sf* (*azione*) organizing, arranging; (*risultato*) organization; **O~ Mondiale della Sanità (O.M.S.)** World Health Organization (WHO).

or'gano *sm* organ; (*di congegno*) part; (*portavoce*) spokesman/woman, mouthpiece; ~**i di trasmissione** (*TECN*) transmission (unit) *sg*.

orga'smo *sm* (*FISIOL*) orgasm; (*fig*) agitation, anxiety.

or'gia, ge [or'já] *sf* orgy.

orgo'glio [ōrgōl'yō] *sm* pride.

orgoglio'so, a [ōrgōlyō'sō] *ag* proud.

orienta'bile *ag* adjustable.

orienta'le *ag* (*paese, regione*) eastern; (*tappeti, lingua, civiltà*) oriental.

orientamen'to *sm* positioning; orientation; direction; **senso di** ~ sense of direction; **perdere l'**~ to lose one's bearings; ~ **professionale** careers guidance.

orienta're *vt* (*situare*) to position; (*carta, bussola*) to orientate; (*fig*) to direct; ~**rsi** *vr* to find one's bearings; (*fig*: *tendere*) to tend, lean; (: *indirizzarsi*): ~**rsi verso** to take up, go in for.

orientati'vo, a *ag* indicative, for guidance; **a scopo** ~ for guidance.

orien'te *sm* east; **l'O**~ the East, the Orient; **il Medio/l'Estremo O**~ the Middle/Far East; **a** ~ in the east.

orifi'cio [ōrēfē'chō], **orifi'zio** [ōrēfēt'tsyō] *sm* (*apertura*) opening; (: *di tubo*) mouth; (*ANAT*) orifice.

ori'gano *sm* oregano.

origina'le [ōrējēná'lā] *ag* original; (*bizzarro*)

eccentric ♦ *sm* original.

originalità [ōrējēnálētá'] *sf* originality; eccentricity.

origina're [ōrējēná'rā] *vt* to bring about, produce ♦ *vi*: ~ **da** to arise *o* spring from.

origina'rio, a [ōrējēná'ryō] *ag* original; **essere** ~ **di** to be a native of; (*animale, pianta*) to be indigenous to, be native to.

ori'gine [ōrē'jēnā] *sf* origin; **all'**~ originally; **d'**~ **inglese** of English origin; **avere** ~ **da** to originate from; **dare** ~ **a** to give rise to.

origlia're [ōrēlyá'rā] *vi*: ~ **(a)** to eavesdrop (on).

ori'na *sf* urine.

orina'le *sm* chamberpot.

orina're *vi* to urinate ♦ *vt* to pass.

orinato'io *sm* (public) urinal.

oriun'do, a *ag*: **essere** ~ **di Milano** *etc* to be of Milanese *etc* extraction *o* origin ♦ *sm/f* person of foreign extraction *o* origin.

orizzonta'le [ōrēddzōntá'lā] *ag* horizontal.

orizzon'te [ōrēddzōn'tā] *sm* horizon.

ORL *sigla f* (*MED*: = *otorinolaringoiatria*) ENT.

orla're *vt* to hem.

orlatu'ra *sf* (*azione*) hemming *q*; (*orlo*) hem.

or'lo *sm* edge, border; (*di recipiente*) rim, brim; (*di vestito etc*) hem; **pieno fino all'**~ full to the brim, brimful; **sull'**~ **della pazzia/della rovina** on the brink *o* verge of madness/ruin; ~ **a giorno** hemstitch.

or'ma *sf* (*di persona*) footprint; (*di animale*) track; (*impronta, traccia*) mark, trace; **seguire** *o* **calcare le** ~**e di qn** to follow in sb's footsteps.

orma'i *av* by now, by this time; (*adesso*) now; (*quasi*) almost, nearly.

ormeggia're [ōrmādjá'rā] *vt*, ~**rsi** *vr* (*NAUT*) to moor.

ormeg'gio [ōrmād'jō] *sm* (*atto*) mooring *q*; (*luogo*) moorings *pl*; **posto d'**~ berth.

ormo'ne *sm* hormone.

ornamenta'le *ag* ornamental, decorative.

ornamen'to *sm* ornament, decoration.

orna're *vt* to adorn, decorate; ~**rsi** *vr*: ~**rsi (di)** to deck o.s. (out) (with).

orna'to, a *ag* ornate.

ornitologi'a [ōrnētōlōjē'á] *sf* ornithology.

ornito'logo, a, gi, ghe *sm/f* ornithologist.

o'ro *sm* gold; **d'**~, **in** ~ gold *cpd*; **d'**~ (*colore, occasione*) golden; (*persona*) marvelous (*US*), marvellous (*Brit*); **un affare d'**~ a real bargain; **prendere qc per** ~ **colato** to take sth as gospel (truth); ~ **zecchino** pure gold.

orologeri'a [ōrōlōjārē'á] *sf* watchmaking *q*; watchmaker's (shop); clockmaker's (shop); **bomba a** ~ time bomb.

orologia'io [ōrōlōjá'yō] *sm* watchmaker; clockmaker.

orolo'gio [ōrōlo'jō] *sm* clock; (*da tasca, da*

polso) watch; ~ **da polso** wristwatch; ~ **al quarzo** quartz watch; ~ **a sveglia** alarm clock.

oro'scopo *sm* horoscope.

orren'do, a *ag* (*spaventoso*) horrible, awful; (*bruttissimo*) hideous.

orri'bile *ag* horrible.

or'rido, a *ag* fearful, horrid.

orripilan'te *ag* hair-raising, horrifying.

orro're *sm* horror; **avere in** ~ **qn/qc** to loathe *o* detest sb/sth; **mi fanno** ~ I loathe *o* detest them.

orsacchiot'to [ōrsákkyot'tō] *sm* teddy bear.

or'so *sm* bear; ~ **bruno/bianco** brown/polar bear.

orsù *escl* come now!

ortag'gio [ōrtád'jō] *sm* vegetable.

orten'sia *sf* hydrangea.

orti'ca, che *sf* (stinging) nettle.

ortica'ria *sf* nettle rash.

orticoltu'ra *sf* horticulture.

or'to *sm* vegetable garden, kitchen garden; (*AGR*) truck farm (*US*), market garden (*Brit*); ~ **botanico** botanical garden(s *pl*).

ortodos'so, a *ag* orthodox.

ortofrutti'colo, a *ag* fruit and vegetable *cpd*.

ortogona'le *ag* perpendicular.

ortografi'a *sf* spelling.

ortola'no, a *sm/f* (*venditore*) produce dealer (*US*), greengrocer (*Brit*).

ortopedi'a *sf* orthopedics *sg* (*US*), orthopaedics *sg* (*Brit*).

ortope'dico, a, ci, che *ag* orthopedic (*US*), orthopaedic (*Brit*) ♦ *sm* orthopedist (*US*), orthopaedic specialist (*Brit*).

orzaio'lo [ōrdzáyo'lō] *sm* (*MED*) stye.

orza'ta [ōrdzá'tà] *sf* barley water.

or'zo [or'dzō] *sm* barley.

O'SA *sigla f* (= *Organizzazione degli Stati Americani*) OAS (= *Organization of American States*).

osa're *vt, vi* to dare; ~ **fare** to dare (to) do; **come osi?** how dare you?

oscenità [ōshānētà'] *sf inv* obscenity.

osce'no, a [ōshe'nō] *ag* obscene; (*ripugnante*) ghastly.

oscilla're [ōshēllà'rā] *vi* (*pendolo*) to swing; (*dondolare: al vento etc*) to rock; (*variare*) to fluctuate; (*TECN*) to oscillate; (*fig*): ~ **fra** to waver between.

oscillazio'ne [ōshēllàttsyō'nā] *sf* oscillation; (*di prezzi, temperatura*) fluctuation.

oscuramen'to *sm* darkening; obscuring; (*in tempo di guerra*) blackout.

oscura're *vt* to darken, obscure; (*fig*) to obscure; ~**rsi** *vr* (*cielo*) to darken, cloud over; (*persona*): **si oscurò in volto** his face clouded over.

oscurità *sf* (*vedi ag*) darkness; obscurity; gloominess.

oscu'ro, a *ag* dark; (*fig*: *incomprensibile*) obscure; (: *umile*: *vita*, *natali*) humble, obscure; (: *triste*: *pensiero*) gloomy, sombre ♦ *sm*: **all'**~ in the dark; **tenere qn all'**~ **di qc** to keep sb in the dark about sth.

O'slo *sf* Oslo.

ospeda'le *sm* hospital.

ospedalie'ro, a *ag* hospital *cpd*.

ospita'le *ag* hospitable.

ospitalità *sf* hospitality.

ospita're *vt* to give hospitality to; (*sog*: *albergo*) to accommodate.

o'spite *sm/f* (*persona che ospita*) host/hostess; (*persona ospitata*) guest.

ospi'zio [ōspēt'tsyō] *sm* (*per vecchi etc*) home.

os'sa *sfpl vedi* **osso**.

ossatu'ra *sf* (*ANAT*) skeletal structure, frame; (*TECN*, *fig*) framework.

os'seo, a *ag* bony; (*tessuto etc*) bone *cpd*.

ossequen'te *ag*: ~ **alla legge** law-abiding.

osse'quio *sm* deference, respect; ~**i** *smpl* (*saluto*) respects, regards; **porgere i propri** ~**i a qn** (*formale*) to pay one's respects to sb; ~**i alla signora!** (give my) regards to your wife!

ossequio'so, a *ag* obsequious.

osservan'za [ōssārván'tsà] *sf* observance.

osserva're *vt* to observe, watch; (*esaminare*) to examine; (*notare, rilevare*) to notice, observe; (*DIR: la legge*) to observe, respect; (*mantenere: silenzio*) to keep, observe; **far** ~ **qc a qn** to point sth out to sb.

osservato're, tri'ce *ag* observant, perceptive ♦ *sm/f* observer.

osservato'rio *sm* (*ASTR*) observatory; (*MIL*) observation post.

osservazio'ne [ōssārvàttsyō'nā] *sf* observation; (*di legge etc*) observance; (*considerazione critica*) observation, remark; (*rimprovero*) reproof; **in** ~ under observation; **fare un'**~ to make a remark; to raise an objection; **fare un'**~ **a qn** to criticize sb.

ossessiona're *vt* to obsess, haunt; (*tormentare*) to torment, harass.

ossessio'ne *sf* obsession; (*seccatura*) nuisance.

ossessi'vo, a *ag* obsessive, haunting; troublesome.

osses'so, a *ag* (*spiritato*) possessed.

ossi'a *cong* that is, to be precise.

ossibu'chi [ōssēbōō'kē] *smpl di* **ossobuco**.

ossida're *vt*, ~**rsi** *vr* to oxidize.

ossidazio'ne [ōssēdàttsyō'nā] *sf* oxidization, oxidation.

os'sido *sm* oxide; ~ **di carbonio** carbon monoxide.

ossigena're [ōssējānà'rā] *vt* to oxygenate; (*decolorare*) to bleach; **acqua ossigenata** hydrogen peroxide.

ossi'geno [ōssē'jānō] *sm* oxygen.

os'so *sm* (*pl* (*f*) **ossa** *nel senso* ANAT) bone; **d'~** (*bottone etc*) of bone, bone *cpd*; **~a rotte** to be dead *o* dog tired; **bagnato fino all'~** soaked to the skin; **essere ridotto all'~** (*fig*: *magro*) to be just skin and bone; (: *senza soldi*) to be in dire straits; **rompersi l'~ del collo** to break one's neck; **rimetterci l'~ del collo** (*fig*) to ruin o.s., lose everything; **un ~ duro** (*persona, impresa*) a tough number; **~ di seppia** cuttlebone.

ossobu'co, *pl* **ossibu'chi** *sm* (CUC) marrowbone; (: *piatto*) *stew made with knuckle of veal in tomato sauce*.

ossu'to, a *ag* bony.

ostacola're *vt* to block, obstruct.

osta'colo *sm* obstacle; (EQUITAZIONE) hurdle, jump; **essere di ~ a qn/qc** (*fig*) to stand in the way of sb/sth.

ostag'gio [ōstád'jō] *sm* hostage.

o'ste, ostes'sa *sm/f* innkeeper.

osteggia're [ōstādjá'rā] *vt* to oppose, be opposed to.

ostel'lo *sm*: **~ della gioventù** youth hostel.

ostenso'rio *sm* (REL) monstrance.

ostenta're *vt* to make a show of, flaunt.

ostentazio'ne [ōstāntáttsyō'nā] *sf* ostentation, show.

osteri'a *sf* inn.

ostes'sa *sf vedi* **oste**.

oste'trico, a, ci, che *ag* obstetric ♦ *sm* obstetrician ♦ *sf* midwife.

o'stia *sf* (REL) host; (*per medicinali*) wafer.

o'stico, a, ci, che *ag* difficult, tough.

osti'le *ag* hostile.

ostilità *sf* hostility ♦ *sfpl* (MIL) hostilities.

ostinar'si *vr* to insist, dig one's heels in; **~ a fare** to persist (obstinately) in doing.

ostina'to, a *ag* (*caparbio*) obstinate; (*tenace*) persistent, determined.

ostinazio'ne [ōstēnáttsyō'nā] *sf* obstinacy; persistence.

ostraci'smo [ōstráchēz'mō] *sm* ostracism.

os'trica, che *sf* oyster.

ostrui're *vt* to obstruct, block.

ostruzio'ne [ōstrōōttsyō'nā] *sf* obstruction, blockage.

ostruzioni'smo [ōstrōōttsyōnēz'mō] *sm* (POL) obstructionism; (SPORT) obstruction; **fare dell'~ a** (*progetto, legge*) to obstruct; **~ sindacale** slowdown (US), work-to-rule (*Brit*).

oti'te *sf* ear infection.

otori'no(laringoi'atra), i, e *sm/f* ear, nose and throat specialist.

o'tre *sm* (*recipiente*) goatskin.

ott. *abbr* (= *ottobre*) Oct.

ottagona'le *ag* octagonal.

otta'gono *sm* octagon.

otta'no *sm* octane; **numero di ~i** octane rating.

ottan'ta *num* eighty.

ottanten'ne *ag* eighty-year-old ♦ *sm/f* octogenarian.

ottante'simo, a *num* eightieth.

ottanti'na *sf*: **una ~ (di)** about eighty.

otta'vo, a *num* eighth ♦ *sf* octave.

ottemperan'za [ōttāmpārán'tsá] *sf*: **in ~ a** (AMM) in accordance with, in compliance with.

ottempera're *vi*: **~ a** to comply with, obey.

ottenebra're *vt* to darken; (*fig*) to cloud.

ottene're *vt* to obtain, get; (*risultato*) to achieve, obtain.

ot'tico, a, ci, che *ag* (*della vista: nervo*) optic; (*dell'ottica*) optical ♦ *sm* optician ♦ *sf* (*scienza*) optics *sg*; (FOT: *lenti, prismi etc*) optics *pl*.

ottima'le *ag* optimal, optimum.

ottimamen'te *av* excellently, very well.

ottimi'smo *sm* optimism.

ottimi'sta, i, e *sm/f* optimist.

ot'timo, a *ag* excellent, very good.

ot'to *num* eight.

otto'bre *sm* October; *per fraseologia vedi* **luglio**.

ottobri'no, a *ag* October *cpd*.

ottocente'sco, a, schi, sche [ōttōchāntā'skō] *ag* nineteenth-century.

ottocen'to [ōttōchcn'tō] *num* eight hundred ♦ *sm*: **l'O~** the nineteenth century.

ottomi'la *num* eight thousand.

otto'ne *sm* brass; **gli ~i** (MUS) the brass.

ottuagena'rio, a [ōttōōájānà'ryō] *ag, sm/f* octogenarian.

ottun'dere *vt* (*fig*) to dull.

ottura're *vt* to close (up); (*dente*) to fill.

otturato're *sm* (FOT) shutter; (*nelle armi*) breechblock.

otturazio'ne [ōttōōrāttsyō'nā] *sf* closing (up); (*dentaria*) filling.

ottu'so, a *pp di* **ottundere** ♦ *ag* (MAT, *fig*) obtuse; (*suono*) dull.

ova'ia *sf*, **ova'io** *sm* (ANAT) ovary.

ova'le *ag, sm* oval.

ovat'ta *sf* cotton wool; (*per imbottire*) padding, wadding.

ovatta're *vt* (*imbottire*) to pad; (*fig*: *smorzare*) to muffle.

ovazio'ne [ōvàttsyō'nā] *sf* ovation.

o'vest *sm* west; **a ~ (di)** west (of); **verso ~** westward(s).

ovi'le *sm* pen, enclosure; **tornare all'~** (*fig*) to return to the fold.

ovi'no, a *ag* sheep *cpd*, ovine.

O.'V.N.I. *sigla m* (= *oggetto volante non identificato*) UFO.

ovulazio'ne [ōvōōláttsyō'nā] *sf* ovulation.

o'vulo *sm* (FISIOL) ovum.

ovun'que *av* = **dovunque**.

ovve'ro *cong* (*ossia*) that is, to be precise; (*oppure*) or (else).

ovvia're *vi*: ~ **a** to obviate.
ov'vio, a *ag* obvious.
ozia're |ōttsyà'rā| *vi* to laze around.
o'zio |ot'tsyō| *sm* idleness; (*tempo libero*) leisure; **ore d'~** leisure time; **stare in** ~ to be idle.
ozio'so, a |ōttsyō'sō| *ag* idle.
ozo'no |ōddzo'nō| *sm* ozone.

P

P, p |pē| *sf o m inv* (*lettera*) P, p; **P come Padova** ≈ P for Peter.
P *abbr* (= *peso*) wt; (= *posteggio*) P.
p *abbr* (= *pagina*) p.
PA *sigla* = *Palermo*.
P.A. *abbr* = **pubblica amministrazione.**
pacatez'za |pàkátāt'tsá| *sf* quietness, calmness.
paca'to, a *ag* quiet, calm.
pac'ca, che *sf* slap.
pacchet'to |pàkkāt'tō| *sm* packet; ~ **applicativo** (*INFORM*) applications package; ~ **azionario** (*FINANZA*) shareholding; ~ **software** (*INFORM*) software package; ~ **turistico** package tour.
pacchia'no, a |pàkkyà'nō| *ag* (*colori*) garish; (*abiti, arredamento*) vulgar, garish.
pac'co, chi *sm* parcel; (*involto*) bundle; ~ **postale** parcel.
paccotti'glia |pàkkōttēl'yà| *sf* trash, junk.
pa'ce |pà'chā| *sf* peace; **darsi** ~ to resign o.s.; **fare (la)** ~ **con qn** to make it up with sb.
pachista'no, a |pàkēstà'nō| *ag, sm/f* Pakistani.
pacifica're |pàchēčkà'rā| *vt* (*riconciliare*) to reconcile, make peace between; (*mettere in pace*) to pacify.
paci'fico, a, ci, che |pàchē'fēkō| *ag* (*persona*) peaceable; (*vita*) peaceful; (*fig: indiscusso*) indisputable; (: *ovvio*) obvious, clear ♦ *sm*: **il P~, l'Oceano P~** the Pacific (Ocean).
pacifi'smo |pàchēfēz'mō| *sm* pacifism.
pacifi'sta, i, e |pàchēfē'stá| *sm/f* pacifist.
pada'no, a *ag* of the Po; **la pianura ~a** the Lombardy plain.
padel'la *sf* frying pan; (*per infermi*) bedpan.
padiglio'ne |pàdēlyō'nā| *sm* pavilion.
Pa'dova *sf* Padua.
padova'no, a *ag* of (o from) Padua.
pa'dre *sm* father; ~**i** *smpl* (*antenati*) forefathers.
Padreter'no *sm*: **il** ~ God the Father.
padri'no *sm* godfather.

padrona'le *ag* (*scala, entrata*) main, principal; **casa** ~ country house.
padronan'za |pàdrōnán'tsá| *sf* command, mastery.
padrona'to *sm*: **il** ~ the ruling class.
padro'ne, a *sm/f* master/mistress; (*proprietario*) owner; (*datore di lavoro*) employer; **essere** ~ **di sé** to be in control of o.s.; ~**/a di casa** master/mistress of the house; (*per gli inquilini*) landlord/lady.
padroneggia're |pàdrōnādjá'rā| *vt* (*fig: sentimenti*) to master, control; (: *materia*) to master, know thoroughly; ~**rsi** *vr* to control o.s.
paesag'gio |pààzàd'jō| *sm* landscape.
paesaggi'sta, i, e |pààzàdjē'stá| *sm/f* (*pittore*) landscape painter.
paesa'no, a *ag* country *cpd* ♦ *sm/f* villager; countryman/woman.
pae'se *sm* (*nazione*) country, nation; (*terra*) country, land; (*villaggio*) village; ~ **di provenienza** country of origin; **i P~i Bassi** the Netherlands.
paffu'to, a *ag* chubby, plump.
pa'ga, ghe *sf* pay, wages *pl*; **giorno di** ~ pay day.
paga'bile *ag* payable; ~ **alla consegna/a vista** payable on delivery/on demand.
paga'ia *sf* paddle.
pagamen'to *sm* payment; ~ **anticipato** payment in advance; ~ **alla consegna** payment on delivery; ~ **all'ordine** cash with order.
paga'no, a *ag, sm/f* pagan.
paga're *vt* to pay; (*acquisto, fig: colpa*) to pay for; (*contraccambiare*) to repay, pay back ♦ *vi* to pay; **quanto l'ha pagato?** how much did you pay for it?; ~ **con carta di credito** to pay by credit card; ~ **in contanti** to pay cash; ~ **di persona** (*fig*) to suffer the consequences; **l'ho pagata cara** (*fig*) I paid dearly for it.
pagel'la |pàjcl'là| *sf* (*INS*) report card (*US*), school report (*Brit*).
pag'gio |pàd'jō| *sm* page(boy).
pagherò |pàgàro'| *vb vedi* **pagare** ♦ *sm inv* IOU; ~ **cambiario** promissory note.
pa'gina |pà'jēnà| *sf* page.
pa'glia |pàl'yà| *sf* straw; **avere la coda di** ~ (*fig*) to have a guilty conscience; **fuoco di** ~ (*fig*) flash in the pan.
pagliaccet'to |pàlyàchāt'tō| *sm* (*per bambini*) rompers *pl*.
pagliac'cio |pàlyàch'chō| *sm* clown.
paglia'io |pàlyà'yō| *sm* haystack.
paglieric'cio |pàlyārēch'chō| *sm* straw mattress.
pagliet'ta |pàlyāt'tá| *sf* (*cappello per uomo*) (straw) boater; (*per tegami etc*) steel wool.
pagliuz'za |pàlyōōt'tsá| *sf* (blade of) straw; (*d'oro etc*) tiny particle, speck.

pagnot'ta |pányot'tá| *sf* round loaf.

pago'da *sf* pagoda.

paillet'te |pàyct'| *sf inv* sequin.

pa'io, *pl(f)* **pa'ia** *sm* pair; **un ~ di occhiali** a pair of glasses; **un ~ di** (*alcuni*) a couple of; **è un altro ~ di maniche** (*fig*) that's another kettle of fish.

pa'io *etc vb vedi* **parere**.

paio'lo, paiuo'lo *sm* (copper) pot.

Pa'kistan *sm*: **il ~** Pakistan.

pakista'no, a *ag, sm/f* = **pachistano**.

pal. *abbr* = **palude**.

pa'la *sf* shovel; (*di remo, ventilatore, elica*) blade; (*di ruota*) paddle.

palandra'na *sf* (*scherzoso: abito lungo e largo*) tent.

pala'to *sm* palate.

palaz'zo |pálàt'tsō| *sm* (*reggia*) palace; (*edificio*) building; **~ di giustizia** courthouse; **~ dello sport** sports stadium.

palchet'to |pálkàt'tō| *sm* shelf.

pal'co, chi *sm* (*TEATRO*) box; (*tavolato*) platform, stand; (*ripiano*) layer.

palcosce'nico, ci |pálkōshe'nēkō| *sm* (*TEATRO*) stage.

palermita'no, a *ag* of (*o* from) Palermo ♦ *sm/f* person from Palermo.

Paler'mo *sf* Palermo.

palesa're *vt* to reveal, disclose; **~rsi** *vr* to reveal *o* show o.s.

pale'se *ag* clear, evident.

Palesti'na *sf*: **la ~** Palestine.

palestine'se *ag, sm/f* Palestinian.

pales'tra *sf* gymnasium; (*esercizio atletico*) exercise, training; (*fig*) training ground, school.

palet'ta *sf* spade; (*per il focolare*) shovel; (*del capostazione*) signalling disc.

palet'to *sm* stake, peg; (*spranga*) bolt.

palinse'sto *sm* (*STORIA*) palimpsest; (*TV, RADIO*) program (*US*) *o* programme (*Brit*) schedule.

pa'lio *sm* (*gara*): **il P~** horserace run at Siena; **mettere qc in ~** to offer sth as a prize.

palissan'dro *sm* rosewood.

palizza'ta |pálēttsá'tá| *sf* palisade.

pal'la *sf* ball; (*pallottola*) bullet; **prendere la ~ al balzo** (*fig*) to seize one's opportunity.

pallacanes'tro *sm* basketball.

pallanuo'to *sm* water polo.

pallavo'lo *sm* volleyball.

palleggia're |pállādjà'rā| *vi* (*CALCIO*) to practice (*US*) *o* practise (*Brit*) with the ball.

palliati'vo *sm* palliative; (*fig*) stopgap measure.

pal'lido, a *ag* pale.

palli'na *sf* (*bilia*) marble.

palli'no *sm* (*BILIARDO*) cue ball; (*BOCCE*) jack; (*proiettile*) pellet; (*pois*) dot; **bianco a ~i blu** white with blue dots; **avere il ~ di**

(*fig*) to be crazy about.

pallonci'no |pállōnchē'nō| *sm* balloon; (*lampioncino*) Chinese lantern.

pallo'ne *sm* (*palla*) ball; (*CALCIO*) football; (*aerostato*) balloon; **gioco del ~** ball game.

pallo're *sm* pallor, paleness.

pallot'tola *sf* pellet; (*proiettile*) bullet.

pal'ma *sf* (*ANAT*) = **palmo**; (*BOT*) palm; **~ da datteri** date palm.

palma'to, a *ag* (*ZOOL: piede*) webbed; (*BOT*) palmate.

palmi'pede *ag* web-footed.

palmi'zio |pálmēt'tsyō| *sm* (*palma*) palm tree; (*ramo*) palm.

pal'mo *sm* (*ANAT*) palm; **essere alto un ~** (*fig*) to be tiny; **restare con un ~ di naso** (*fig*) to be badly disappointed.

pa'lo *sm* (*legno appuntito*) stake; (*sostegno*) pole; **fare da o il ~** (*fig*) to act as look-out; **saltare di ~ in frasca** (*fig*) to jump from one topic to another.

palomba'ro *sm* diver.

palom'bo *sm* (*pesce*) dogfish.

palpa're *vt* to feel, finger.

pal'pebra *sf* eyelid.

palpita're *vi* (*cuore, polso*) to beat; (: *più forte*) to pound, throb; (*fremere*) to quiver.

palpitazio'ne |pálpētáttsyō'nà| *sf* palpitation.

pal'pito *sm* (*del cuore*) beat; (*fig: d'amore etc*) throb.

paltò *sm inv* overcoat.

palu'de *sf* marsh, swamp.

paludo'so, a *ag* marshy, swampy.

palus'tre *ag* marsh *cpd*, swamp *cpd*.

pam'pino *sm* vine leaf.

panace'a |pánàche'à| *sf* panacea.

Pa'nama *sf* Panama; **il canale di ~** the Panama Canal.

panamen'se *ag, sm/f* Panamanian.

pan'ca, che *sf* bench.

pancet'ta |pánchàt'tá| *sf* (*CUC*) bacon.

panchet'to |pánkàt'tō| *sm* stool; footstool.

panchi'na |pánkē'nà| *sf* garden seat; (*di giardino pubblico*) (park) bench.

pan'cia, ce |pán'chá| *sf* belly, stomach; **mettere o fare ~** to be getting a paunch; **avere mal di ~** to have stomachache *o* a sore stomach.

pancie'ra |pánche'rá| *sf* corset.

panciol'le |pánchol'lá| *av*: **stare in ~** to lounge around.

panciot'to |pánchot'tō| *sm* waistcoat.

pan'creas *sm inv* pancreas.

pan'da *sm inv* panda.

pandemo'nio *sm* pandemonium.

pando'ro *sm type of sponge cake eaten at Christmas.*

pa'ne *sm* bread; (*pagnotta*) loaf (of bread); (*forma*): **un ~ di burro/cera** *etc* a pat of butter/bar of wax *etc*; **guadagnarsi il ~** to earn one's living; **dire ~ al ~, vino al vino** (*fig*) to call a spade a spade; **rendere pan per focaccia** (*fig*) to give tit for tat; **~ casereccio** homemade bread; **~ a cassetta** sliced bread; **~ integrale** wholewheat (*US*) *o* wholemeal (*Brit*) bread; **~ di segale** rye bread; **pan di Spagna** sponge cake; **~ tostato** toast.

panetteri'a *sf* (*forno*) bakery; (*negozio*) baker's (shop), bakery.

panettie're, a *sm/f* baker.

panetto'ne *sm a kind of spiced brioche with sultanas, eaten at Christmas.*

panfor'te *sm* Sienese nougat-type delicacy.

pangratta'to *sm* breadcrumbs *pl*.

pa'nico, a, ci, che *ag, sm*; **essere in preda al ~** to be panic-stricken; **lasciarsi prendere dal ~** to panic.

panie're *sm* basket.

panifi'cio [pánēfē'chō] *sm* (*forno*) bakery; (*negozio*) baker's (shop), bakery.

pani'no *sm* roll; **~ imbottito** sandwich.

paninote'ca, che *sf* sandwich bar.

pan'na *sf* (*CUC*) cream; (*AUT*) = **panne; ~ di cucina** cooking cream; **~ montata** whipped cream.

pan'ne [pán] *sf inv* (*AUT*) breakdown; **essere in ~** to have broken down.

pannel'lo *sm* panel; **~ di controllo** control panel.

pan'no *sm* cloth; **~i** *smpl* (*abiti*) clothes; **mettiti nei miei ~i** (*fig*) put yourself in my shoes.

pannoc'chia [pánnok'kyá] *sf* (*di mais etc*) ear.

pannoli'no *sm* (*per bambini*) diaper (*US*), nappy (*Brit*).

panora'ma, i *sm* panorama.

panora'mico, a, ci, che *ag* panoramic; **strada ~a** scenic route.

pantalo'ni *smpl* pants (*US*), trousers (*Brit*), pair *sg* of pants *o* trousers.

panta'no *sm* bog.

pante'ra *sf* panther.

panto'fola *sf* slipper.

pantomi'ma *sf* pantomime.

panza'na [pántsá'ná] *sf* fib, tall story.

paonaz'zo, a [páōnát'tsō] *ag* purple.

pa'pa, i *sm* pope.

papà *sm inv* dad(dy); **figlio di ~** spoilt young man.

papa'le *ag* papal.

papa'to *sm* papacy.

papa'vero *sm* poppy.

pa'pero, a *sm/f* (*ZOOL*) gosling ♦ *sf* (*fig*) slip of the tongue, blunder.

papillon' [pápēyôn'] *sm inv* bow tie.

papi'ro *sm* papyrus.

pap'pa *sf* baby cereal.

pappagal'lo *sm* parrot; (*fig: uomo*) Romeo, wolf.

pappagor'gia, ge [páppágor'já] *sf* double chin.

pappa're *vt* (*fam: anche: ~rsi*) to gobble up.

par. *abbr* (= *paragrafo*) par.

pà'ra *sf*: **suole di ~** crepe soles.

parà *abbr m inv* (= *paracadutista*) parachutist.

para'bola *sf* (*MAT*) parabola; (*REL*) parable.

parabrez'za [párábrād'dzá] *sm inv* (*AUT*) windshield (*US*), windscreen (*Brit*).

pàracaduta're *vt, ~rsi* *vr* to parachute.

paracadu'te *sm inv* parachute.

paracaduti'smo *sm* parachuting.

paracaduti'sta, i, e *sm/f* parachutist; (*MIL*) paratrooper.

paracar'ro *sm* curbstone (*US*), kerbstone (*Brit*).

paradi'so *sm* paradise.

paradossa'le *ag* paradoxical.

parados'so *sm* paradox.

parafan'go, ghi *sm* fender (*US*), mudguard (*Brit*).

paraffi'na *sf* paraffin, paraffin wax.

parafrasa're *vt* to paraphrase.

para'frasi *sf inv* paraphrase.

paraful'mine *sm* lightning rod.

parag'gi [párád'jē] *smpl*: **nei ~** in the vicinity, in the neighborhood (*US*) *o* neighbourhood (*Brit*).

paragona're *vt*: **~ con/a** to compare with/to.

parago'ne *sm* comparison; (*esempio analogo*) analogy, parallel; **reggere al ~** to stand comparison.

para'grafo *sm* paragraph.

paraguaia'no, a *ag, sm/f* Paraguayan.

Paraguay' [párágwá'ē] *sm*: **il ~** Paraguay.

para'lisi *sf inv* paralysis.

parali'tico, a, ci, che *ag, sm/f* paralytic.

paralizza're [párálēddzá'rā] *vt* to paralyze.

parallelamen'te *av* in parallel.

paralle'lo, a *ag* parallel ♦ *sm* (*GEO*) parallel; (*comparazione*): **fare un ~ tra** to draw a parallel between ♦ *sf* parallel (line); **~e** *sfpl* (*attrezzo ginnico*) parallel bars.

paralu'me *sm* lampshade.

parame'dico, a, ci, che *ag* paramedical.

paramen'ti *smpl* (*REL*) vestments.

para'metro *sm* parameter.

paramilita're *ag* paramilitary.

paran'co, chi *sm* hoist.

parano'ia *sf* paranoia.

parano'ico, a, ci, che *ag, sm/f* paranoid.

paranorma'le *ag* paranormal.

paraoc'chi [páráok'kē] *smpl* blinders (*US*), blinkers (*Brit*).

parapet'to *sm* parapet.

parapi'glia [párápēl'yá] *sm* commotion, uproar.

parapsicologi'a [párápsēkōlōjē'á] *sf* parapsychology.

para're *vt* (*addobbare*) to adorn, deck; (*pro-*

teggere) to shield, protect; (*scansare: colpo*) to parry; (*CALCIO*) to save ♦ *vi*: **dove vuole andare a ~?** what are you driving at?; **~rsi** *vr* (*presentarsi*) to appear, present o.s.

parascola'stico, a, ci, che *ag* (*attività*) extra-curricular.

paraso'le *sm inv* parasol, sunshade.

parassi'ta, i *sm* parasite.

parassita'rio, a *ag* parasitic.

parastata'le *ag* state-controlled.

parasta'to *sm* *employees in the state-controlled sector.*

para'ta *sf* (*SPORT*) save; (*MIL*) review, parade.

para'ti *smpl* hangings *pl;* **carta da ~** wallpaper.

parati'a *sf* (*di nave*) bulkhead.

paraur'ti *sm inv* (*AUT*) bumper.

paraven'to *sm* folding screen; **fare da ~ a qn** (*fig*) to shield sb.

parcel'la [pàrchcl'là] *sf* fee.

parcheggia're [pàrkàdjà'rà] *vt* to park.

parcheg'gio [pàrkàd'jō] *sm* parking *q;* (*luogo*) parking lot (*US*), car park (*Brit*); (*singolo posto*) parking space.

parchi'metro [pàrkē'màtrō] *sm* parking meter.

par'co, chi *sm* park; (*spazio per deposito*) depot; (*complesso di veicoli*) fleet.

par'co, a, chi, che *ag*: **~ (in)** (*sobrio*) moderate (in); (*avaro*) sparing (with).

parec'chio, a [pàràk'kyō] *det* quite a lot of; (*tempo*) quite a lot of, a long; **~i(e)** *det pl* quite a lot of, several ♦ *pronome* quite a lot, quite a bit; (*tempo*) quite a while, a long time; **~i(e)** *pronome pl* quite a lot, several ♦ *av* (*con ag*) quite, rather; (*con vb*) quite a lot, quite a bit.

pareggia're [pàràdjà'rà] *vt* to make equal; (*terreno*) to level, make level; (*bilancio, conti*) to balance ♦ *vi* (*SPORT*) to draw.

pareg'gio [pàràd'jō] *sm* (*ECON*) balance; (*SPORT*) draw.

parenta'do *sm* relatives *pl,* relations *pl.*

paren'te *sm/f* relative, relation.

parente'la *sf* (*vincolo di sangue, fig*) relationship; (*insieme dei parenti*) relations *pl,* relatives *pl.*

paren'tesi *sf* (*segno grafico*) bracket, parenthesis; (*frase incisa*) parenthesis; (*digressione*) parenthesis, digression; **tra ~** in parentheses; (*fig*) incidentally.

pare're *sm* (*opinione*) opinion; (*consiglio*) advice, opinion; **a mio ~** in my opinion ♦ *vi* to seem, appear ♦ *vb impers:* **pare che** it seems *o* appears that, they say that; **mi pare che** it seems to me that; **mi pare di si/no** I think so/don't think so; **fai come ti pare** do as you like; **che ti pare del mio libro?** what do you think of my book?

pare'te *sf* wall.

pa'ri *ag inv* (*uguale*) equal, same; (*in giochi*) equal; drawn, tied; (*MAT*) even ♦ *sm inv* (*POL: di Gran Bretagna*) peer ♦ *sm/f inv* peer, equal; **copiato ~ ~** copied word for word; **siamo ~** (*fig*) we are even; **alla ~** on the same level; (*BORSA*) at par; **ragazza alla ~ au pair** (girl); **mettersi alla ~ con** to place o.s. on the same level as; **mettersi in ~ con** to catch up with; **andare di ~ passo con qn** to keep pace with sb.

parifica're *vt* (*scuola*) to recognize officially.

parifica'to, a *ag*: **scuola ~a** *officially recognized private school.*

Pari'gi [pàrē'jē] *sf* Paris.

parigi'no, a [pàrējē'nō] *ag, sm/f* Parisian.

pari'glia [pàrēl'yà] *sf* pair; **rendere la ~** to give tit for tat.

parità *sf* parity, equality; (*SPORT*) draw, tie.

parite'tico, a, ci, che *ag*: **commissione ~a** joint committee; **rapporto ~** equal relationship.

parlamenta're *ag* parliamentary ♦ *sm/f* ≈ Congressman/woman (*US*), ≈ Member of Parliament (*Brit*) ♦ *vi* to negotiate, parley.

parlamen'to *sm* parliament.

parlanti'na *sf* (*fam*) talkativeness; **avere una buona ~** to have the gift of the gab.

parla're *vi* to speak, talk; (*confidare cose segrete*) to talk ♦ *vt* to speak; **~ (a qn) di** to speak *o* talk (to sb) about; **~ chiaro** to speak one's mind; **~ male di qn/qc** to speak ill of sb/sth; **~ del più e del meno** to talk of this and that; **ne ho sentito ~** I have heard it mentioned; **non parliamone più** let's just forget about it; **i dati parlano** (*fig*) the facts speak for themselves.

parla'ta *sf* (*dialetto*) dialect.

parlato're, tri'ce *sm/f* speaker.

parlato'rio *sm* (*di carcere etc*) visiting room; (*REL*) parlor (*US*), parlour (*Brit*).

parlotta're *vi* to mutter.

parmigia'no, a [pàrmējà'nō] *ag* Parma *cpd,* of (*o* from) Parma ♦ *sm* (*grana*) Parmesan (cheese); **alla ~a** (*CUC*) with Parmesan cheese.

parodi'a *sf* parody.

paro'la *sf* word; (*facoltà*) speech; **~e** *sfpl* (*chiacchiere*) talk *sg;* **chiedere la ~** to ask permission to speak; **dare la ~ a qn** to call on sb to speak; **dare la propria ~ a qn** to give sb one's word; **mantenere la ~** to keep one's word; **mettere una buona ~ per qn** to put in a good word for sb; **passare dalle ~e ai fatti** to get down to business; **prendere la ~** to take the floor; **rimanere senza ~e** to be speechless; **rimangiarsi la ~** to go back on one's word; **non ho ~e per ringraziarla** I don't know how to thank you; **rivolgere la ~ a qn** to speak to sb; **non è detta l'ultima ~** that's not the end of the\ matter; **è una**

persona di ~ he is a man of his word; **in** ~**e povere** in plain English; ~ **d'onore** word of honour; ~ **d'ordine** (*MIL*) password; ~**e incrociate** crossword (puzzle) *sg*.

parolac'cia, ce [párōlách'chá] *sf* bad word, swearword.

parossi'smo *sm* paroxysm.

parquet' [párke'] *sm* parquet (flooring).

parrò *etc vb vedi* **parere**.

parroc'chia [párrok'kyá] *sf* parish; (*chiesa*) parish church.

parrocchia'no, a [párrōkkyá'nō] *sm/f* parishioner.

par'roco, ci *sm* parish priest.

parruc'ca, che *sf* wig.

parrucchie're, a [párrōōkkye'rā] *sm/f* hairdresser ♦ *sm* barber.

parrucco'ne *sm* (*peg*) old fogey.

parsimo'nia *sf* frugality, thrift.

parsimonio'so, a *ag* frugal, thrifty.

par'so, a *pp di* **parere**.

par'te *sf* part; (*lato*) side; (*quota spettante a ciascuno*) share; (*direzione*) direction; (*POL*) party; faction; (*DIR*) party; **a** ~ *ag* separate ♦ *av* separately; **scherzi a** ~ joking aside; **a** ~ **ciò** apart from that; **inviare a** ~ (*campioni etc*) to send under separate cover; **da** ~ (*in disparte*) to one side, aside; **mettere/prendere da** ~ to put/take aside; **d'altra** ~ on the other hand; **da** ~ **di** (*per conto di*) on behalf of; **da** ~ **mia** as far as I'm concerned, as for me; **da** ~ **di madre** on his (*o her etc*) mother's side; **essere dalla** ~ **della ragione** to be in the right; **da** ~ **a** ~ right through; **da qualche** ~ somewhere; **da nessuna** ~ nowhere; **da questa** ~ (*in questa direzione*) this way; **da ogni** ~ on all sides, everywhere; (*moto da luogo*) from all sides; **fare** ~ **di qc** to belong to sth; **prendere** ~ **a qc** to take part in sth; **prendere le** ~**i di qn** to take sb's side; **mettere qn a** ~ **di qc** to inform sb of sth; **costituirsi** ~ **civile contro qn** (*DIR*) to associate in an action with the public prosecutor against sb; **la** ~ **lesa** (*DIR*) the injured party; **le** ~**i in causa** the parties concerned.

partecipan'te [pártāchēpán'tā] *sm/f*: ~ (**a**) (*a riunione, dibattito*) participant (in); (*a gara sportiva*) competitor (in); (*a concorso*) entrant (to).

partecipa're [pártāchēpá'rā] *vi*: ~ **a** to take part in, participate in; (*utili etc*) to share in; (*spese etc*) to contribute to; (*dolore, successo di qn*) to share (in) ♦ *vt*: ~ **le nozze** (**a**) to announce one's wedding (to).

partecipazio'ne [pártāchēpáttsyō'nā] *sf* participation; sharing; (*ECON*) interest; ~ **a banda armata** (*DIR*) belonging to an armed gang; ~ **di maggioranza/minoranza** controlling/minority interest; ~ **agli utili** profit-sharing; ~**i di nozze** *wedding announcement*

card; **ministro delle P**~**i statali** *minister responsible for companies in which the state has a financial interest.*

parte'cipe [pártā'chēpā] *ag* participating; **essere** ~ **di** to take part in, participate in; (*gioia, dolore*) to share (in); (*consapevole*) to be aware of.

parteggia're [pártādjá'rā] *vi*: ~ **per** to side with, be on the side of.

parten'za [párten'tsá] *sf* departure; (*SPORT*) start; **essere in** ~ to be about to leave, be leaving; **passeggeri in** ~ **per** passengers traveling to; **siamo tornati al punto di** ~ (*fig*) we are back where we started; **falsa** ~ (*anche fig*) false start.

particel'la [pártēchel'lá] *sf* particle.

partici'pio [pártēchē'pyō] *sm* participle.

particola're *ag* (*specifico*) particular; (*proprio*) personal, private; (*speciale*) special, particular; (*caratteristico*) distinctive; (*fuori dal comune*) peculiar ♦ *sm* detail, particular; **in** ~ in particular, particularly; **entrare nei** ~**i** to go into details.

particolareggia'to, a [pártēkōlárādjá'tō] *ag* (extremely) detailed.

particolarità *sf inv* (*carattere eccezionale*) peculiarity; (*dettaglio*) particularity, detail; (*caratteristica*) characteristic, feature.

partigia'no, a [pártējá'nō] *ag* partisan ♦ *sm* (*fautore*) supporter, champion; (*MIL*) partisan.

parti're *vi* to go, leave; (*allontanarsi*) to go (*o drive etc*) away *o* off; (*petardo, colpo*) to go off; (*fig: avere inizio, SPORT*) to start; **sono partita da Roma alle 7** I left Rome at 7; **il volo parte da Ciampino** the flight leaves from Ciampino; **a** ~ **da** from; **la seconda a** ~ **da destra** the second from the right; ~ **in quarta** to drive off at top speed; (*fig*) to be very enthusiastic.

parti'ta *sf* (*COMM*) lot, consignment; (*ECON: registrazione*) entry, item; (*CARTE, SPORT: gioco*) game; (: *competizione*) match, game; ~ **di caccia** hunting party; ~ **IVA** VAT account; ~ **semplice/doppia** (*COMM*) single-/double-entry book-keeping.

parti'to *sm* (*POL*) party; (*decisione*) decision, resolution; (*persona da maritare*) match; **per** ~ **preso** on principle; **mettere la testa a** ~ to settle down.

partitu'ra *sf* (*MUS*) score.

par'to *sm* (*MED*) labor (*US*), labour (*Brit*); **sala** ~ labo(u)r room; **morire di** ~ to die in childbirth.

partorien'te *sf* woman in labor (*US*) *o* labour (*Brit*).

partori're *vt* to give birth to; (*fig*) to produce.

parven'za [párven'tsá] *sf* semblance.

par'vi *etc vb vedi* **parere**.

parzia'le [pártsyá'lā] *ag* (*limitato*) partial;

(*non obiettivo*) biased, partial.

parzialità |pårtsyälētä'| *sf*: ~ (**a favore di**) partiality (for), bias (towards); ~ (**contro**) bias (against).

pa'scere |påsh'shārä| *vi* to graze ♦ *vt* (*brucare*) to graze on; (*far pascolare*) to graze, pasture.

pasciu'to, a |påshōō'tō| *pp di* **pascere** ♦ *ag*: **ben** ~ plump.

pascola're *vt, vi* to graze.

pa'scolo *sm* pasture.

Pa'squa *sf* Easter; **isola di** ~ Easter Island.

pasqua'le *ag* Easter *cpd*.

pasquet'ta *sf* Easter Monday.

passa'bile *ag* fairly good, passable.

passag'gio |påssåd'jō| *sm* passing *q*, passage; (*traversata*) crossing *q*, passage; (*luogo, prezzo della traversata, brano di libro etc*) passage; (*su veicolo altrui*) ride, lift (*Brit*); (*SPORT*) pass; **di** ~ (*persona*) passing through; ~ **pedonale/a livello** pedestrian/grade (*US*) o level (*Brit*) crossing; ~ **di proprietà** transfer of ownership.

passamaneri'a *sf* braid, trimming.

passamonta'gna |påssåmōntån'yå| *sm inv* balaclava.

passan'te *smf* passer-by ♦ *sm* loop.

passapor'to *sm* passport.

passa're *vi* (*andare*) to go; (*veicolo, pedone*) to pass (by), go by; (*fare una breve sosta: postino etc*) to come, call; (: *amico: per fare una visita*) to call o drop in; (*sole, aria, luce*) to get through; (*trascorrere: giorni, tempo*) to pass, go by; (*fig: proposta di legge*) to be passed; (: *dolore*) to pass, go away; (*CARTE*) to pass ♦ *vt* (*attraversare*) to cross; (*trasmettere: messaggio*): ~ **qc a qn** to pass sth on to sb; (*dare*): ~ **qc a qn** to pass sth to sb, give sb sth; (*trascorrere: tempo*) to spend; (*superare: esame*) to pass; (*triturare: verdura*) to strain; (*approvare*) to pass, approve; (*oltrepassare, sorpassare: anche fig*) to go beyond, pass; (*fig: subire*) to go through; ~ **da ... a** to pass from ... to; ~ **di padre in figlio** to be handed down o to pass from father to son; ~ **per** (*anche fig*) to go through; ~ **per stupido/un genio** to be taken for a fool/a genius; ~ **sopra** (*anche fig*) to pass over; ~ **attraverso** (*anche fig*) to go through; ~ **ad altro** to change the subject; (*in una riunione*) to discuss the next item; ~ **in banca/ufficio** to call (in) at the bank/office; ~ **alla storia** to pass into history; ~ **a un esame** to go up (to the next grade (*US*) o class (*Brit*)) after an exam; ~ **di moda** to go out of fashion; ~ **a prendere qc/qn** to call and pick sth/sb up; **le passo il Signor X** (*al telefono*) here is Mr X, I'm putting you through to Mr X; **farsi** ~ **per** to pass o.s. off as, pretend to be; **lasciar** ~ **qn/qc** to let sb/

sth through; **col** ~ **degli anni** (*riferito al presente*) as time goes by; (*riferito al passato*) as time passed o went by; **il peggio è passato** the worst is over; **30 anni e passa** well over 30 years ago; ~ **una mano di vernice su qc** to give sth a coat of paint; **passarsela: come te la passi?** how are you getting on o along?

passa'ta *sf*: **dare una** ~ **di vernice a qc** to give sth a coat of paint; **dare una** ~ **al giornale** to have a look at the paper, skim through the paper.

passatem'po *sm* pastime, hobby.

passa'to, a *ag* (*scorso*) last; (*finito: gloria, generazioni*) past; (*usanze*) out of date; (*sfiorito*) faded ♦ *sm* past; (*LING*) past (tense); **l'anno** ~ last year; **nel corso degli anni** ~**i** over the past years; **nei tempi** ~**i** in the past; **sono le 8** ~**e** it's past o after 8 o'clock; **è acqua** ~**a** (*fig*) it's over and done with; ~ **prossimo** (*LING*) present perfect; ~ **remoto** (*LING*) past historic; ~ **di verdura** (*CUC*) vegetable purée.

passatut'to *sm inv*, **passaverdu'ra** *sm inv* vegetable mill.

passegge'ro, a |påssådje'rō| *ag* passing ♦ *smf* passenger.

passeggia're |påssådjå'rä| *vi* to go for a walk; (*in veicolo*) to go for a drive.

passeggia'ta |påssådjå'tä| *sf* walk; drive; (*luogo*) promenade; **fare una** ~ to go for a walk (o drive).

passeggi'no |påssådjē'nō| *sm* stroller (*US*), pushchair (*Brit*).

passeg'gio |påssåd'jō| *sm* walk, stroll; (*luogo*) promenade; **andare a** ~ to go for a walk o a stroll.

passerel'la *sf* footbridge; (*di nave, aereo*) gangway; (*pedana*) catwalk.

pas'sero *sm* sparrow.

passi'bile *ag*: ~ **di** liable to.

passiona'le *ag* (*temperamento*) passionate; **delitto** ~ crime of passion.

passio'ne *sf* passion.

passività *sf* (*qualità*) passivity, passiveness; (*COMM*) liability.

passi'vo, a *ag* passive ♦ *sm* (*LING*) passive; (*ECON*) debit; (: *complesso dei debiti*) liabilities *pl*.

pas'so *sm* step; (*andatura*) pace; (*rumore*) (foot)step; (*orma*) footprint; (*passaggio, fig: brano*) passage; (*valico*) pass; **a** ~ **d'uomo** at walking pace; (*AUT*) dead slow; ~ (**a**) ~ step by step; **fare due** o **quattro** ~**i** to go for a walk o a stroll; **andare al** ~ **coi tempi** to keep up with the times; **di questo** ~ (*fig*) at this rate; **fare i primi** ~**i** (*anche fig*) to take one's first steps; **fare il gran** ~ (*fig*) to take the plunge; **fare un** ~ **falso** (*fig*) to make the wrong move; **tornare sui propri** ~**i** to retrace one's steps; "~ **carraio**" "vehicle entrance — keep clear".

pa'sta *sf* (*CUC*) dough; (: *impasto per dolce*) pastry; (: *anche*: ~ **alimentare**) pasta; (*massa molle di materia*) paste; (*fig: indole*) nature; ~**e** *sfpl* (*pasticcini*) pastries; ~ **in brodo** noodle soup; ~ **sfoglia** puff paste (*US*) *o* pastry.

pastasciut'ta [pàstàshōōt'tà] *sf* pasta.

pasteggia're [pàstàdjá'rà] *vi*: ~ **a vino/ champagne** to have wine/champagne with one's meal.

pastel'la *sf* batter.

pastel'lo *sm* pastel.

pastet'ta *sf* (*CUC*) = **pastella**.

pastic'ca, che *sf* = **pastiglia**.

pasticceri'a [pàstēchārē'à] *sf* (*pasticcini*) pastries *pl*, cakes *pl*; (*negozio*) cake shop; (*arte*) confectionery.

pasticcia're [pàstēchà'rà] *vt* to mess up, make a mess of ♦ *vi* to make a mess.

pasticce're, a [pàstēche'rà] *sm/f* pastrycook; confectioner.

pasticci'no [pàstēchē'nō] *sm* petit four.

pastic'cio [pàstēch'chō] *sm* (*CUC*) pie; (*lavoro disordinato, imbroglio*) mess; **trovarsi nei ~i** to get into trouble.

pastifi'cio [pàstēfē'chō] *sm* pasta factory.

pasti'glia [pàstēl'yà] *sf* pastille, lozenge.

pasti'na *sf small pasta shapes used in soup.*

pastina'ca, che *sf* parsnip.

pa'sto *sm* meal; **vino da** ~ table wine.

pasto'ia *sf* (*fig*): ~ **burocratica** red tape.

pastora'le *ag* pastoral.

pasto're *sm* shepherd; (*REL*) pastor, minister; (*anche*: **cane** ~) sheepdog; ~ **scozzese** (*ZOOL*) collie; ~ **tedesco** (*ZOOL*) German shepherd (dog).

pastori'zia [pàstōrēt'tsyá] *sf* sheep-rearing, sheep farming.

pastorizza're [pàstōrēddzà'rà] *vt* to pasteurize.

pasto'so, a *ag* doughy; pasty; (*fig*: *voce, colore*) mellow, soft.

pastra'no *sm* greatcoat.

pastu'ra *sf* pasture.

patac'ca, che *sf* (*distintivo*) medal, decoration; (*fig*: *macchia*) grease spot, grease mark.

pata'ta *sf* potato; ~**e fritte** French fries, chips (*Brit*).

patati'ne *sfpl* (*potato*) chips (*US*) *o* crisps (*Brit*).

patatrac' *sm* (*crollo: anche fig*) crash.

pâté [pàtā'] *sm inv* pâté; ~ **di fegato d'oca** pâté de foie gras.

patel'la *sf* (*ZOOL*) limpet.

pate'ma, i *sm* anxiety, worry.

patenta'to, a *ag* (*munito di patente*) licensed, certified; (*fig scherzoso: qualificato*) utter, thorough.

paten'te *sf* license (*US*), licence (*Brit*); (*anche*: ~ **di guida**) driver's license (*US*), driving licence (*Brit*).

patenti'no *sm* temporary license (*US*) *o* licence (*Brit*).

paternità *sf* paternity, fatherhood.

pater'no, a *ag* (*affetto, consigli*) fatherly; (*casa, autorità*) paternal.

pate'tico, a, ci, che *ag* pathetic; (*commovente*) moving, touching.

pat'hos [pà'tōs] *sm* pathos.

pati'bolo *sm* gallows *sg*, scaffold.

patimen'to *sm* suffering.

pa'tina *sf* (*su rame etc*) patina; (*sulla lingua*) fur, coating.

pati're *vt, vi* to suffer.

pati'to, a *sm/f* enthusiast, fan, lover.

patologi'a [pàtōlōjē'à] *sf* pathology.

patolo'gico, a, ci, che [pàtōlo'jēkō] *ag* pathological.

pato'logo, a, gi, ghe *sm/f* pathologist.

pa'tria *sf* homeland; **amor di** ~ patriotism.

patriar'ca, chi *sm* patriarch.

patri'gno [pàtrēn'yō] *sm* stepfather.

patrimo'nio *sm* estate, property; (*fig*) heritage; **mi è costato un** ~ (*fig*) it cost me a fortune, I paid a fortune for it; ~ **spirituale/ culturale** spiritual/cultural heritage; ~ **ereditario** (*fig*) hereditary characteristics *pl*; ~ **pubblico** public property.

pa'trio, a, ii, ie *ag* (*di patria*) native *cpd*, of one's country; (*DIR*): ~**a potestà** parental authority; **amor** ~ love of one's country.

patrio'ta, i, e *sm/f* patriot.

patriot'tico, a, ci, che *ag* patriotic.

patriotti'smo *sm* patriotism.

patrocina're [pàtrōchēnà'rà] *vt* (*DIR: difendere*) to defend; (*sostenere*) to sponsor, support.

patroci'nio [pàtrōchē'nyō] *sm* defense (*US*), defence (*Brit*); support, sponsorship.

patrona'to *sm* patronage; (*istituzione benefica*) charitable institution *o* society.

patro'no *sm* (*REL*) patron saint; (*socio di patronato*) patron; (*DIR*) counsel.

pat'ta *sf* flap; (*dei pantaloni*) fly.

patteggia're [pàttādjá'rà] *vt, vi* to negotiate.

pattinag'gio [pàttēnàd'jō] *sm* skating.

pattina're *vi* to skate; ~ **sul ghiaccio** to ice-skate.

pattinato're, tri'ce *sm/f* skater.

pat'tino *sm* skate; (*di slitta*) runner; (*AER*) skid; (*TECN*) sliding block; ~**i (da ghiaccio)** (ice) skates; ~**i a rotelle** roller skates.

patti'no *sm* (*barca*) *kind of pedalo with oars.*

pat'to *sm* (*accordo*) pact, agreement; (*condizione*) term, condition; **a** ~ **che** on condition that; **a nessun** ~ under no circumstances; **venire** *o* **scendere a** ~**i (con)** to come to an agreement (with).

pattu'glia |pàttōōl'yà| *sf* (*MIL*) patrol.
pattuglia're |pàttōōlyà'rā| *vt* to patrol.
pattui're *vt* to reach an agreement on.
pattumie'ra *sf* ashcan (*US*), (dust)bin (*Brit*).
pau'ra *sf* fear; **aver ~ di/di fare/che** to be
frightened *o* afraid of/of doing/that; **far ~ a** to
frighten; **per ~ di/che** for fear of/that; **ho ~
di si/no** I am afraid so/not.
pauro'so, a *ag* (*che fa paura*) frightening;
(*che ha paura*) fearful, timorous.
pa'usa *sf* (*sosta*) break; (*nel parlare, MUS*)
pause.
paventa'to, a *ag* much-feared.
pave'se *ag* of (*o* from) Pavia.
pa'vido, a (*letterario*) fearful.
pavimenta're *vt* (*stanza*) to floor; (*strada*) to
pave.
pavimentazio'ne |pàvēmāntàttsyō'nā| *sf* floor-
ing; paving.
pavimen'to *sm* floor.
pavo'ne *sm* peacock.
pavoneggiar'si |pàvōnàdjàr'sē| *vr* to strut
about, show off.
pazienta're |pàttsyāntà'rā| *vi* to be patient.
pazien'te |pàttsyen'tā| *ag*, *sm/f* patient.
pazien'za |pàttsyen'tsà| *sf* patience; **perdere la
~** to lose (one's) patience.
pazzamen'te |pàttsàmān'tā| *av* madly; **essere
~ innamorato** to be madly in love.
pazze'sco, a, schi, sche |pàttsà'skō| *ag* mad,
crazy.
pazzi'a |pàttsē'à| *sf* (*MED*) madness, insanity;
(*di azione, decisione*) madness, folly; **è stata
una ~!** it was sheer madness!
paz'zo, a |pàt'tsō| *ag* (*MED*) mad, insane;
(*strano*) wild, mad ♦ *sm/f* madman/woman;
~ di (*gioia, amore etc*) mad *o* crazy with; **~
per qc/qn** mad *o* crazy about sth/sb; **essere
~ da legare** to be raving mad *o* a raving lunatic.
PC *sigla* = Piacenza.
P.C. *abbr* = **polizza di carico**.
p.c. *abbr* = *per condoglianze*; *per conoscenza*.
PCI *sigla m* = *Partito Comunista Italiano*.
PCUS *sigla m* = *Partito Comunista dell'Unione Sovietica*.
PD *sigla* = Padova.
P.D. *abbr* = **partita doppia**.
PE *sigla* = Pescara.
pec'ca, che *sf* defect, flaw, fault.
peccamino'so, a *ag* sinful.
pecca're *vi* to sin; (*fig*) to err.
pecca'to *sm* sin; **è un ~ che** it's a pity that;
che ~! what a shame *o* pity!; **un ~ di gioventù** (*fig*) a youthful error *o* indiscretion.
peccato're, tri'ce *sm/f* sinner.
pecchèrò *etc* |pàkkāro'| *vb vedi* **peccare**.
pe'ce |pā'chā| *sf* pitch.
pechine'se |pākēnā'sā| *ag*, *sm/f* Pekin(g)ese
(*inv*) ♦ *sm* (*anche: cane ~*) Pekin(g)ese *inv*,

Peke.
Pechi'no |pākē'nō| *sf* Beijing, Peking.
pe'cora *sf* sheep; **~ nera** (*fig*) black sheep.
pecora'io *sm* shepherd.
pecorel'la *sf* lamb; **la ~ smarrita** the lost
sheep; **cielo a ~e** (*fig: nuvole*) mackerel sky.
pecori'no *sm* sheep's milk cheese.
pecula'to *sm* (*DIR*) embezzlement.
peculia're *ag*: **~ di** peculiar to.
pecunia'rio, a *ag* financial, money *cpd*.
pedag'gio |pādàd'jō| *sm* toll.
pedagogi'a |pādàgōjē'à| *sf* pedagogy, educa-
tional methods *pl*.
pedago'gico, a, ci, che |pādàgo'jēkō| *ag* peda-
gogic(al).
pedala're *vi* to pedal; (*andare in bicicletta*) to
cycle.
peda'le *sm* pedal.
peda'na *sf* footboard; (*SPORT: nel salto*)
springboard; (: *nella scherma*) piste.
pedan'te *ag* pedantic ♦ *sm/f* pedant.
peda'ta *sf* (*impronta*) footprint; (*colpo*) kick;
prendere a ~e qn/qc to kick sb/sth.
pedera'sta, i *sm* pederast.
pedes'tre *ag* prosaic, pedestrian.
pedia'tra, i, e *sm/f* pediatrician (*US*), paedia-
trician (*Brit*).
pediatri'a *sf* pediatrics *sg* (*US*), paediatrics *sg*
(*Brit*).
pedicu're *sm/f inv* podiatrist (*US*), chiropodist
(*Brit*).
pedilu'vio *sm* footbath.
pedi'na *sf* (*della dama*) draftsman (*US*),
draughtsman (*Brit*); (*fig*) pawn.
pedina're *vt* to shadow, tail.
pedona'le *ag* pedestrian.
pedo'ne, a *sm/f* pedestrian ♦ *sm* (*SCACCHI*)
pawn.
peg'gio |ped'jō| *av*, *ag inv* worse ♦ *sm o f*: **il *o*
la ~** the worst; **cambiare in ~** to get *o* become worse; **alla ~** at worst, if the worst
comes to the worst; **tirare avanti alla meno
~** to get along as best one can; **avere la ~** to
come off worse, get the worst of it.
peggioramen'to |pādjōràmān'tō| *sm* worsen-
ing.
peggiora're |pādjōrà'rā| *vt* to make worse,
worsen ♦ *vi* to grow worse, worsen.
peggiorati'vo, a |pādjōràtē'vō| *ag* pejorative.
peggio're |pādjō'rā| *ag* (*comparativo*) worse;
(*superlativo*) worst ♦ *sm/f*: **il(la) ~** the worst
(person); **nel ~ dei casi** if the worst comes
to the worst.
pe'gno |pān'yō| *sm* (*DIR*) security, pledge;
(*nei giochi di società*) forfeit; (*fig*) pledge, token; **dare in ~ qc** to pawn sth; **in ~ d'amicizia** as a token of friendship; **banco dei ~i**
pawnshop.
pela'me *sm* (*di animale*) coat, fur.
pelapata'te *sm inv* potato peeler.

pela're vt (spennare) to pluck; (spellare) to skin; (sbucciare) to peel; (fig) to make pay through the nose; ~rsi vr to go bald.

pela'to, a ag (sbucciato) peeled; (calvo) bald; (pomodori) ~i peeled tomatoes.

pella'me sm skins pl, hides pl.

pel'le sf skin; (di animale) skin, hide; (cuoio) leather; **essere ~ ed ossa** to be skin and bone; **avere la ~ d'oca** to have goose pimples o goose flesh; **avere i nervi a fior di ~** to be edgy; **non stare più nella ~ dalla gioia** to be beside o.s. with delight; **lasciarci la ~** to lose one's life; **amici per la ~** firm o close friends.

pellegrinag'gio [pāllāgrēnàd'jō] sm pilgrimage.

pellegri'no, a sm/f pilgrim.

pelleros'sa, pelliros'sa, pl **pelliros'se** sm/f Red Indian.

pelletteri'a sf (articoli) leather goods pl; (negozio) leather goods shop.

pellica'no sm pelican.

pellicceri'a [pāllēchārē'à] sf (negozio) furrier's (shop); (quantità di pellicce) furs pl.

pellic'cia, ce [pāllēch'chá] sf (mantello di animale) coat, fur; (indumento) fur coat.

pelliccia'io [pāllēcchá'yō] sm furrier.

pelli'cola sf (membrana sottile) film, layer; (FOT, CINEMA) film.

pelliros'sa sm/f = **pellerossa**.

pe'lo sm hair; (pelame) coat, hair; (pelliccia) fur; (di tappeto) pile; (di liquido) surface; **per un ~: per un ~ non ho perduto il treno** I very nearly missed the train; **c'è mancato un ~ che affogasse** he narrowly escaped drowning; **cercare il ~ nell'uovo** (fig) to split hairs; **non aver ~i sulla lingua** (fig) to speak one's mind.

pelo'so, a ag hairy.

pel'tro sm pewter.

pelu'che [pɔlüsh'] sm plush; **giocattoli di ~** soft toys.

pelu'ria sf down.

pe'na sf (DIR) sentence; (punizione) punishment; (sofferenza) sadness q, sorrow; (fatica) trouble q, effort; (difficoltà) difficulty; **far ~** to be pitiful; **mi fai ~** I feel sorry for you; **essere o stare in ~ (per qc/qn)** to worry o be anxious (about sth/sb); **prendersi o darsi la ~ di fare** to go to the trouble of doing; **vale la ~ farlo** it's worth doing, it's worth it; **non ne vale la ~** it's not worth the effort, it's not worth it; **~ di morte** death sentence; **~ pecuniaria** fine.

pena'le ag penal ♦ sf (anche: **clausola ~**) penalty clause; **causa ~** criminal trial; **diritto ~** criminal law; **pagare la ~** to pay the penalty.

penali'sta, i, e sm/f (avvocato) criminal lawyer.

penalità sf inv penalty.

penalizza're [pānálēddzà'rā] vt (SPORT) to penalize.

pena're vi (patire) to suffer; (faticare) to struggle.

penden'te ag hanging; leaning ♦ sm (ciondolo) pendant; (orecchino) drop earring.

penden'za [pānden'tsá] sf slope, slant; (grado d'inclinazione) gradient; (ECON) outstanding account.

pen'dere vi (essere appeso): **~ da** to hang from; (essere inclinato) to lean; (fig: incombere): **~ su** to hang over.

pendi'o, ii sm slope, slant; (luogo in pendenza) slope.

pen'dola sf pendulum clock.

pendola're ag pendulum cpd, pendular ♦ sm/f commuter.

pendolari'smo sm commuting.

pen'dolo sm (peso) pendulum; (anche: **orologio a ~**) pendulum clock.

pe'ne sm penis.

penetran'te ag piercing, penetrating.

penetra're vi to come o get in ♦ vt to penetrate; **~ in** to enter; (sog: proiettile) to penetrate; (: acqua, aria) to go o come into.

penicilli'na [pānēchēllē'ná] sf penicillin.

peninsula're ag peninsular; **l'Italia ~** mainland Italy.

peni'sola sf peninsula.

peniten'te sm/f penitent.

peniten'za [pānēten'tsá] sf penitence; (punizione) penance.

penitenzia'rio [pānētántsyá'ryō] sm prison.

pen'na sf (di uccello) feather; (per scrivere) pen; **~e** sfpl (CUC) quills (type of pasta); **~ a feltro/stilografica/a sfera** felt-tip/fountain/ballpoint pen.

pennac'chio [pānnák'kyō] sm (ornamento) plume; **un ~ di fumo** (fig) a plume o spiral of smoke.

pennarel'lo sm felt(-tip) pen.

pennella're vi to paint.

pennel'lo sm brush; (per dipingere) (paint)brush; **a ~** (perfettamente) to perfection, perfectly; **~ per la barba** shaving brush.

Penni'ni smpl: **i ~** the Pennines.

penni'no sm nib.

penno'ne sm (NAUT) yard; (stendardo) banner, standard.

penom'bra sf half-light, dim light.

peno'so, a ag painful, distressing; (faticoso) tiring, laborious.

pensa're vi to think ♦ vt to think; (inventare, escogitare) to think out; **~ a** to think of; (amico, vacanze) to think of o about; (problema) to think about; **~ di fare qc** to think of doing sth; **~ bene/male di qn** to think well/badly of sb, have a good/bad opinion of sb;

penso di sì I think so; **penso di no** I don't think so; **a pensarci bene** ... on second thought (US) o thoughts (Brit) ...; **non voglio nemmeno pensarci** I don't even want to think about it; **ci penso io** I'll see to o take care of it.

pensa'ta sf (trovata) idea, thought.

pensato're, tri'ce sm/f thinker.

pensieri'no sm (dono) little gift; (pensiero): **ci farò un ~** I'll think about it.

pensie'ro sm thought; (modo di pensare, dottrina) thinking q; (preoccupazione) worry, care, trouble; **darsi ~ per qc** to worry about sth; **stare in ~ per qn** to be worried about sb; **un ~ gentile** (anche fig: dono etc) a kind thought.

pensiero'so, a ag thoughtful.

pen'sile ag hanging.

pensionamen'to sm retirement; **~ anticipato** early retirement.

pensionan'te sm/f (presso una famiglia) lodger; (di albergo) guest.

pensiona'to, a sm/f pensioner ♦ sm (istituto) hostel.

pensio'ne sf (al prestatore di lavoro) pension; (vitto e alloggio) board and lodging; (albergo) boarding house; **andare in ~** to retire; **mezza ~** half board; **~ completa** full board; **~ d'invalidità** disablement pension; **~ per la vecchiaia** old-age pension.

pensioni'stico, a, ci, che ag pension cpd.

penso'so, a ag thoughtful, pensive, lost in thought.

penta'gono sm pentagon.

pentaparti'to sm (POL) five-party coalition government.

Penteco'ste sf Pentecost, Whit Sunday (Brit).

pentimen'to sm repentance, contrition.

pentir'si vr: **~ di** to repent of; (rammaricarsi) to regret, be sorry for.

pentiti'smo sm confessions from terrorists and members of organized crime rackets.

penti'to, a sm/f ≈ supergrass (Brit), terrorist/criminal who turns police informer.

pen'tola sf pot; **~ a pressione** pressure cooker.

penul'timo, a ag next to last, penultimate.

penu'ria sf shortage.

penzola're [pāndzōlá'rā] vi to dangle, hang loosely.

penzolo'ni [pāndzōlō'nē] av dangling, hanging down; **stare ~** to dangle, hang down.

pepa'to, a ag (condito con pepe) peppery, hot; (fig: pungente) sharp.

pe'pe sm pepper; **~ macinato/in grani** ground/whole pepper.

peperona'ta sf stewed peppers, tomatoes and onions.

peperonci'no [pāpārōnchē'nō] sm chilli pepper.

pepero'ne sm: **~ (rosso)** red pepper, capsicum; **~ (verde)** green pepper, capsicum; **rosso come un ~** fire-engine red (US), as red as a beetroot (Brit); **~i ripieni** stuffed peppers.

pepi'ta sf nugget.

per prep for; (moto attraverso luogo) through; (mezzo, modo) by; (causa) because of, owing to ♦ cong: **~ fare** (so as) to do, in order to do; **~ aver fatto** for having done; **partire ~ l'Inghilterra** to leave for England; **proseguire ~ Londra** to go on to London; **sedere ~ terra** to sit on the ground; **~ lettera/ferrovia** by letter/rail; **~ tutta l'estate** all through the summer, throughout the summer, all summer long; **~ abitudine** out of habit, from habit; **assentarsi ~ malattia** to be off because of o through o owing to illness; **giorno ~ giorno** day by day; **uno ~ uno** one by one; **uno ~ volta** one at a time; **~ persona** per person; **moltiplicare/dividere 9 ~ 3** to multiply/divide 9 by 3; **~ cento** per cent; **~ poco che sia** however little it may be, little though it may be.

pe'ra sf pear.

peral'tro av moreover, what's more.

perbac'co escl by Jove!

perbe'ne ag inv respectable, decent ♦ av (con cura) properly, well.

perbeni'smo sm (so-called) respectability.

percentua'le [pārchāntōōá'lā] sf percentage; (commissione) commission.

percepi're [pārchāpē'rā] vt (sentire) to perceive; (ricevere) to receive.

percetti'bile [pārchāttē'bēlā] ag perceptible.

percezio'ne [pārchāttsyō'nā] sf perception.

perché [pārkā'] av why ♦ cong (causale) because; (finale) in order that, so that; (consecutivo): **è troppo forte ~ si possa batterlo** he's too strong to be beaten ♦ sm inv (motivo) reason; **non c'è un vero ~** there's no real reason for it; **i ~ sono tanti** there are many reasons for it.

perciò [pārcho'] cong so, for this (o that) reason.

percor'rere vt (luogo) to go all over; (: paese) to travel up and down, go all over; (distanza) to cover.

percorri'bile ag (strada) which can be followed.

percor'so, a pp di **percorrere** ♦ sm (tragitto) journey; (tratto) route.

percos'so, a pp di **percuotere** ♦ sf blow.

percuo'tere vt to hit, strike.

percussio'ne sf percussion; **strumenti a ~** (MUS) percussion instruments.

perden'te ag losing ♦ sm/f loser.

per'dere vt to lose; (lasciarsi sfuggire) to miss; (sprecare: tempo, denaro) to waste; (mandare in rovina: persona) to ruin ♦ vi to lose; (*serbatoio etc*) to leak; ~**rsi** *vr* (*smarrirsi*) to get lost; (*svanire*) to disappear, vanish; **saper** ~ to be a good loser; **lascia** ~**!** forget it!, never mind!; **non ho niente da** ~ (*fig*) I've got nothing to lose; **è un'occasione da non** ~ it's a marvellous opportunity; (*affare*) it's a great bargain; **è fatica persa** it's a waste of effort; ~ **al gioco** to lose money gambling; ~ **di vista** qn (*anche fig*) to lose sight of sb; ~**rsi di vista** to lose sight of each other; (*fig*) to lose touch; ~**rsi alla vista** to disappear from sight; ~**rsi in chiacchiere** to waste time talking.

perdifia'to: a ~ *av* (*correre*) at breathtaking speed; (*gridare*) at the top of one's voice.

perdigior'no [pārdējŏr'nō] *sm/f inv* idler, waster.

per'dita *sf* loss; (*spreco*) waste; (*fuoriuscita*) leak; **siamo in** ~ (*COMM*) we are running at a loss; **a** ~ **d'occhio** as far as the eye can see.

perditem'po *sm/f inv* waster, idler.

perdizio'ne [pārdēttsyō'nā] *sf* (*REL*) perdition, damnation; **luogo di** ~ place of ill repute.

perdona're *vt* to pardon, forgive; (*scusare*) to excuse, pardon; **per farsi** ~ in order to be forgiven; **perdona la domanda** ... if you don't mind my asking ...; **vogliate** ~ **il (mio) ritardo** my apologies for being late; **un male che non perdona** an incurable disease.

perdo'no *sm* forgiveness; (*DIR*) pardon; **chiedere** ~ **a** qn (**per**) to ask for sb's forgiveness (for); (*scusarsi*) to apologize to sb (for).

perdura're *vi* to go on, last; (*perseverare*) to persist.

perdutamen'te *av* desperately, passionately.

perdu'to, a *pp di* **perdere** ♦ *ag* (*gen*) lost; **sentirsi** *o* **vedersi** ~ (*fig*) to realize the hopelessness of one's position; **una donna** ~**a** (*fig*) a fallen woman.

peregrina're *vi* to wander, roam.

peren'ne *ag* eternal, perpetual, perennial; (*BOT*) perennial.

perento'rio, a *ag* peremptory; (*definitivo*) final.

perfettamen'te *av* perfectly; **sai** ~ **che** ... you know perfectly well that ....

perfet'to, a *ag* perfect ♦ *sm* (*LING*) perfect (tense).

perfezionamen'to [pārfāttsyōnàmān'tō] *sm*: ~ **(di)** improvement (in), perfection (of); **corso di** ~ proficiency course.

perfeziona're [pārfāttsyōnà'rā] *vt* to improve, perfect; ~**rsi** *vr* to improve.

perfezio'ne [pārfāttsyō'nā] *sf* perfection.

perfezioni'smo [pārfāttsyōnēz'mō] *sm* perfectionism.

perfezioni'sta, i, e [pārfāttsyōnē'stà] *sm/f* perfectionist.

perfi'dia *sf* perfidy.

per'fido, a *ag* perfidious, treacherous.

perfi'no *av* even.

perfora're *vt* to pierce; (*MED*) to perforate; (*banda, schede*) to punch; (*trivellare*) to drill.

perforato're, tri'ce *sm/f* punch-card operator ♦ *sm* (*utensile*) punch; (*INFORM*): ~ **di schede** card punch ♦ *sf* (*TECN*) boring *o* drilling machine; (*INFORM*) card punch.

perforazio'ne [pārfōràttsyō'nā] *sf* piercing; perforation; punching; drilling.

pergame'na *sf* parchment.

pericolan'te *ag* precarious.

peri'colo *sm* danger; **essere fuori** ~ to be out of danger; (*MED*) to be off the danger list; **mettere in** ~ to endanger, put in danger.

pericolo'so, a *ag* dangerous.

periferi'a *sf* periphery; (*di città*) outskirts *pl*.

perife'rico, a, ci, che *ag* (*ANAT, INFORM*) peripheral; (*zona*) outlying.

peri'frasi *sf inv* circumlocution.

peri'metro *sm* perimeter.

perio'dico, a, ci, che *ag* periodic(al); (*MAT*) recurring ♦ *sm* periodical.

peri'odo *sm* period; ~ **contabile** accounting period; ~ **di prova** trial period.

peripezi'e [pārēpàttsē'ā] *sfpl* ups and downs, vicissitudes.

pe'riplo *sm* circumnavigation.

peri're *vi* to perish, die.

perisco'pio *sm* periscope.

peri'to, a *ag* expert, skilled ♦ *sm/f* expert; (*agronomo, navale*) surveyor; **un** ~ **chimico** a qualified chemist.

peritoni'te *sf* peritonitis.

peri'zia [pārēt'tsyà] *sf* (*abilità*) ability; (*giudizio tecnico*) expert opinion; expert's report; ~ **psichiatrica** psychiatrist's report.

pe'rla *sf* pearl.

perli'na *sf* bead.

perlome'no *av* (*almeno*) at least.

perlopiù *av* (*quasi sempre*) in most cases, usually.

perlustra're *vt* to patrol.

perlustrazio'ne [pārlōōsträttsyō'nā] *sf* patrol, reconnaissance; **andare in** ~ to go on patrol.

permalo'so, a *ag* touchy.

permanen'te *ag* permanent ♦ *sf* permanent wave, perm.

permanen'za [pārmánen'tsà] *sf* permanence; (*soggiorno*) stay; **buona** ~**!** enjoy your stay!

permane're *vi* to remain.

perman'go, perma'si *etc vb vedi* **permanere**.

permea'bile *ag* permeable.

permea're *vt* to permeate.

permes'so, a *pp di* **permettere** ♦ *sm* (*autorizzazione*) permission, leave; (*dato a militare, impiegato*) leave; (*licenza*) license (*US*), licence (*Brit*), permit; (*MIL: foglio*) pass; ~**?, è** ~**?** (*posso entrare?*) may I come in?; *(posso passare?)* excuse me; ~ **di lavo-ro** work permit; ~ **di pesca** fishing license *(US) o* permit *(Brit)*.

permet'tere *vt* to allow, permit; ~ **a qn qc/ di fare qc** to allow sb sth/to do sth; ~**rsi** *vr*: ~**rsi qc/di fare qc** *(concedersi)* to allow o.s. sth/to do sth; *(avere la possibilità)* to afford sth/to do sth; **permettete che mi presenti** let me introduce myself, may I introduce myself?; **mi sia permesso di sottolineare che ...** may I take the liberty of pointing out that ....

permi'si *etc vb vedi* **permettere.**

permissi'vo, a *ag* permissive.

per'muta *sf (DIR)* transfer; *(COMM)* trade-in; **accettare qc in** ~ to take sth as a trade-in; **valore di** ~ *(di macchina etc)* trade-in value.

pernac'chia [pārnák'kyà] *sf (fam)*: **fare una** ~ to blow a raspberry.

perni'ce [pārnē'chā] *sf* partridge.

pernicio'so, a [pārnēchō'sō] *ag* pernicious.

per'no *sm* pivot.

pernotta're *vi* to spend the night, stay overnight.

pe'ro *sm* pear tree.

però *cong (ma)* but; *(tuttavia)* however, nevertheless.

perora're *vt (DIR, fig)*: ~ **la causa di qn** to plead sb's case.

perpendicola're *ag, sf* perpendicular.

perpendi'colo *sm*: **a** ~ perpendicularly.

perpetra're *vt* to perpetrate.

perpetua're *vt* to perpetuate.

perpe'tuo, a *ag* perpetual.

perplessità *sf inv* perplexity.

perples'so, a *ag* perplexed, puzzled.

perquisi're *vt* to search.

perquisizio'ne [pārkwēzèttsyō'nā] *sf* (police) search; **mandato di** ~ search warrant.

per'se *etc vb vedi* **perdere.**

persecuto're *sm* persecutor.

persecuzio'ne [pārsākōōttsyō'nā] *sf* persecution.

persegui'bile *ag (DIR)*: **essere** ~ **per legge** to be liable to prosecution.

persegui're *vt* to pursue; *(DIR)* to prosecute.

perseguita're *vt* to persecute.

perseveran'te *ag* persevering.

perseveran'za [pārsāvàrán'tsà] *sf* perseverance.

persevera're *vi* to persevere.

per'si *etc vb vedi* **perdere.**

Per'sia *sf*: **la** ~ Persia.

persia'no, a *ag, sm/f* Persian ♦ *sf* louvered shutter; ~**a avvolgibile** roller blind.

per'sico, a, ci, che *ag*: **il golfo P**~ the Persian Gulf; **pesce** ~ perch.

persi'no *av* = **perfino.**

persisten'te *ag* persistent.

persisten'za [pārsēsten'tsà] *sf* persistence.

persi'stere *vi* to persist; ~ **a fare** to persist in doing.

persisti'to, a *pp di* **persistere.**

per'so, a *pp di* **perdere** ♦ *ag (smarrito: anche fig)* lost; *(sprecato)* wasted; **fare qc a tempo** ~ to do sth in one's spare time; ~ **per** ~ I've *(o* we've *etc)* got nothing further to lose.

perso'na *sf* person; *(qualcuno)*: **una** ~ someone, somebody, *espressione interrogativa +* anyone *o* anybody; ~**e** *sfpl* people *pl*; **non c'è** ~ **che ...** there's nobody who ..., there isn't anybody who ...; **in** ~, **di** ~ in person; **per interposta** ~ through an intermediary *o* a third party; ~ **giuridica** *(DIR)* legal person.

personag'gio [pārsōnàd'jō] *sm (persona ragguardevole)* personality, figure; *(tipo)* character, individual; *(LETTERATURA)* character.

persona'le *ag* personal ♦ *sm* staff, personnel; *(figura fisica)* build ♦ *sf (mostra)* one-man *(o* one-woman) exhibition.

personalità *sf inv* personality.

personalizza'to, a [pārsōnàlēddzá'tō] *ag* personalized.

personalmen'te *av* personally.

personifica're *vt* to personify; to embody.

perspica'ce [pārspēkà'chā] *ag* shrewd, discerning.

perspica'cia [pārspēkà'chà] *sf* perspicacity, shrewdness.

persua'dere *vt*: ~ **qn (di qc/a fare)** to persuade sb (of sth/to do).

persuasio'ne *sf* persuasion.

persuasi'vo, a *ag* persuasive.

persua'so, a *pp di* **persuadere.**

pertan'to *cong (quindi)* so, therefore.

per'tica, che *sf* pole.

pertina'ce [pārtēnà'chā] *ag* determined, persistent.

pertinen'te *ag*: ~ **(a)** relevant (to), pertinent (to).

pertinen'za [pārtēnen'tsà] *sf (attinenza)* pertinence, relevance; *(competenza)*: **essere di** ~ **di qn** to be sb's business.

pertos'se *sf* whooping cough.

pertu'gio [pārtōō'jō] *sm* hole, opening.

perturba're *vt* to disrupt; *(persona)* to disturb, perturb.

perturbazio'ne [pārtōōrbàttsyō'nā] *sf* disruption; disturbance.

Perù *sm*: **il** ~ Peru.

perugi'no, a [pārōōjē'nō] *ag* of *(o* from) Perugia.

peruvia'no, a *ag, sm/f* Peruvian.

perva'dere *vt* to pervade.

perva'so, a *pp di* **pervadere.**

perveni're *vi*: ~ **a** to reach, arrive at, come to; *(venire in possesso)*: **gli pervenne una fortuna** he inherited a fortune; **far** ~ **qc a** to have sth sent to.

pervenu'to, a *pp di* **pervenire.**
perversio'ne *sf* perversion.
perversità *sf* perversity.
perver'so, a *ag* perverted.
perverti're *vt* to pervert.
pervica'ce [pārvēká'chá] *ag* stubborn, obstinate.
pervica'cia [pārvēká'chá] *sf* stubbornness, obstinacy.
p.es. *abbr* (= *per esempio*) e.g.
pe'sa *sf* weighing *q*; weighbridge.
pesan'te *ag* heavy; (*fig: noioso*) dull, boring.
pesantez'za [pāsántát'tsá] *sf* (*anche fig*) heaviness; **avere ~ di stomaco** to feel bloated.
pesaperso'ne *ag inv*: (**bilancia**) **~** (weighing) scales *pl*; (*automatica*) weighing machine.
pesa're *vt* to weigh ♦ *vi* (*avere un peso*) to weigh; (*essere pesante*) to be heavy; (*fig*) to carry weight; **~ su** (*fig*) to lie heavy on; to influence; to hang over; **mi pesa sgridarlo** I find it hard to scold him; **tutta la responsabilità pesa su di lui** all the responsibility rests on his shoulders; **è una situazione che mi pesa** it's a difficult situation for me; **il suo parere pesa molto** his opinion counts for a lot; **~ le parole** to weigh one's words.
pe'sca *sf* (*pl* **pesche**: *frutto*) peach; (*il pescare*) fishing; **andare a ~** to go fishing; **~ di beneficenza** (*lotteria*) raffle; **~ con la lenza** angling; **~ subacquea** underwater fishing.
pescag'gio [pāskád'jō] *sm* (*NAUT*) draft (*US*), draught (*Brit*).
pesca're *vt* (*pesce*) to fish for; to catch; (*qc nell'acqua*) to fish out; (*fig: trovare*) to get hold of, find.
pescato're *sm* fisherman; (*con lenza*) angler.
pe'sce [pāsh'shā] *sm* fish *gen inv*; **P~i** (*dello zodiaco*) Pisces; **essere dei P~i** to be Pisces; **non saper che ~i prendere** (*fig*) not to know which way to turn; **~ d'aprile!** April Fool!; **~ martello** hammerhead; **~ rosso** goldfish; **~ spada** swordfish.
pesceca'ne [pāshākā'nā] *sm* shark.
pescherec'cio [pāskārāch'chō] *sm* fishing boat.
pescheri'a [pāskārē'á] *sf* fishmonger's (shop), fish market (*US*).
pescherò *etc* [pāskāro'] *vb vedi* **pescare.**
peschie'ra [pāskye'rá] *sf* fishpond.
pesciven'dolo, a [pāshēvān'dōlō] *sm/f* fishmonger, fish merchant (*US*).
pe'sco, schi *sm* peach tree.
pesco'so, a *ag* teeming with fish.
pe'so *sm* weight; (*SPORT*) shot; **dar ~ a qc** to attach importance to sth; **essere di ~ a qn** (*fig*) to be a burden to sb; **rubare sul ~** to give short weight; **lo portarono via di ~** they carried him away bodily; **avere due ~i e due misure** (*fig*) to have double standards; **~ lordo/netto** gross/net weight; **~ piuma/**

mosca/gallo/medio/massimo (*PUGILATO*) feather/fly/bantam/middle/heavyweight.
pessimi'smo *sm* pessimism.
pessimi'sta, i, e *ag* pessimistic ♦ *sm/f* pessimist.
pes'simo, a *ag* very bad, awful; **di ~a qualità** of very poor quality.
pesta're *vt* to tread on, trample on; (*sale, pepe*) to grind; (*uva, aglio*) to crush; (*fig: picchiare*): **~ qn** to beat sb up; **~ i piedi** to stamp one's feet; **~ i piedi a qn** (*anche fig*) to tread on sb's toes.
pe'ste *sf* plague; (*persona*) nuisance, pest.
pestel'lo *sm* pestle.
pesti'fero, a *ag* (*anche fig*) pestilential, pestiferous; (*odore*) noxious.
pestilen'za [pāstēlen'tsá] *sf* pestilence; (*fetore*) stench.
pe'sto, a *ag*: **c'è buio ~** it's pitch dark ♦ *sm* (*CUC*) sauce made with basil, garlic, cheese and oil; **occhio ~** black eye.
pe'talo *sm* (*BOT*) petal.
petar'do *sm* firecracker, banger (*Brit*).
petizio'ne [pātēttsyō'nā] *sf* petition; **fare una ~ a** to petition.
pe'to *sm* (*fam!*) fart (!).
petrolchi'mica [pātrōlkē'mēká] *sf* petrochemical industry.
petrolie'ra *sf* (*nave*) oil tanker.
petrolie're *sm* (*industriale*) oilman; (*tecnico*) worker in the oil industry.
petrolie'ro, a *ag* oil *cpd*.
petroli'fero, a *ag* oil *cpd*.
petro'lio *sm* oil, petroleum; (*per lampada, fornello*) kerosene, paraffin (*Brit*); **lume a ~** oil *o* kerosene *o* paraffin (*Brit*) lamp; **~ grezzo** crude oil.
pettegola're *vi* to gossip.
pettegolez'zo [pāttāgōlād'dzō] *sm* gossip *q*; **fare ~i** to gossip.
pette'golo, a *ag* gossipy ♦ *sm/f* gossip.
pettina're *vt* to comb (the hair of); **~rsi** *vr* to comb one's hair.
pettinatu'ra *sf* (*acconciatura*) hairstyle.
pet'tine *sm* comb; (*ZOOL*) scallop.
pettiros'so *sm* robin.
pet'to *sm* chest; (*seno*) breast, bust; (*CUC: di carne bovina*) brisket; (: *di pollo etc*) breast; **prendere qn/qc di ~** to face up to sb/sth; **a doppio ~** (*abito*) double-breasted.
pettora'le *ag* pectoral.
pettoru'to, a *ag* broad-chested; full-breasted.
petulan'te *ag* insolent.
pez'za [pet'tsá] *sf* piece of cloth; (*toppa*) patch; (*cencio*) rag, cloth; (*AMM*): **~ d'appoggio** *o* **giustificativa** voucher; **trattare qn come una ~ da piedi** to treat sb like a doormat.
pezza'to, a [pāttsá'tō] *ag* piebald.
pezzen'te [pāttsen'tā] *sm/f* beggar.

pez'zo [pɛt'tsō] *sm* (*gen*) piece; (*brandello*, *frammento*) piece, bit; (*di macchina*, *arnese etc*) part; (*STAMPA*) article; (*di tempo*): **aspettare un ~** to wait quite a while *o* some time; **andare a ~i** to break into pieces; **essere a ~i** (*oggetto*) to be in pieces *o* bits; (*fig*: *persona*) to be shattered; **un bel ~ d'uomo** a fine figure of a man; **abito a due ~i** two-piece suit; **essere tutto d'un ~** (*fig*) to be a man (*o* woman) of integrity; **~ di cronaca** (*STAMPA*) report; **~ grosso** (*fig*) bigwig; **~ di ricambio** spare part.

P.F. *abbr* = **per favore; prossimo futuro.**

PG *sigla* = **Perugia.**

P.G. *abbr* = **procuratore generale.**

PI *sigla* = **Pisa.**

P.I. *abbr* = **Pubblica Istruzione.**

piac'cio *etc* [pyàch'chō] *vb vedi* **piacere.**

piacen'te [pyàchen'tà] *ag* attractive, pleasant.

piace're [pyàchā'rā] *vi* to please; ♦ *sm* pleasure; (*favore*) favor (*US*), favour (*Brit*); **una ragazza che piace** (*piacevole*) a likeable girl; (*attraente*) an attractive girl; **~ a: mi piace** I like it; **quei ragazzi non mi piacciono** I don't like those boys; **gli piacerebbe andare al cinema** he would like to go to the cinema; **il suo discorso è piaciuto molto** his speech was well received; **"~!"** (*nelle presentazioni*) "pleased to meet you!"; **con ~** certainly, with pleasure; **per ~** please; **fare un ~ a qn** to do sb a favor; **mi fa ~ per lui** I am pleased for him; **mi farebbe ~ rivederlo** I would like to see him again.

piace'vole [pyàchā'vōlā] *ag* pleasant, agreeable.

piacimen'to [pyàchēmān'tō] *sm*: **a ~** (*a volontà*) as much as one likes, at will; **lo farà a suo ~** he'll do it when it suits him.

piaciu'to, a [pyàchōō'tō] *pp di* **piacere.**

piac'qui *etc vb vedi* **piacere.**

pia'ga, ghe *sf* (*lesione*) sore; (*ferita: anche fig*) wound; (*fig: flagello*) scourge, curse; (: *persona*) pest, nuisance.

piagniste'o [pyànyēste'ō] *sm* whining, whimpering.

piagnucola're [pyànyōōkōlà'rā] *vi* to whimper.

piagnucoli'o, ii [pyànyōōkōlē'ō] *sm* whimpering.

piagnucolo'so, a [pyànyōōkōlō'sō] *ag* whiny, whimpering, moaning.

pial'la *sf* (*arnese*) plane.

pialla're *vt* to plane.

piallatri'ce [pyàllàtrē'chā] *sf* planing machine.

pia'na *sf* stretch of level ground; (*più esteso*) plain.

pianeggian'te [pyànādjàn'tā] *ag* flat, level.

pianerot'tolo *sm* landing.

piane'ta *sm* (*ASTR*) planet.

pian'gere [pyàn'jārā] *vi* to cry, weep; (*occhi*) to water ♦ *vt* to cry, weep; (*lamentare*) to

bewail, lament; **~ la morte di qn** to mourn sb's death.

pianifica're *vt* to plan.

pianificazio'ne [pyànēfēkàttsyō'nā] *sf* (*ECON*) planning; **~ aziendale** corporate planning.

piani'sta, i, e *sm/f* pianist.

pia'no, a *ag* (*piatto*) flat, level; (*MAT*) plane; (*facile*) straightforward, simple; (*chiaro*) clear, plain ♦ *av* (*adagio*) slowly; (*a bassa voce*) softly; (*con cautela*) slowly, carefully ♦ *sm* (*MAT*) plane; (*GEO*) plain; (*livello*) level, plane; (*di edificio*) floor; (*programma*) plan; (*MUS*) piano; **pian ~** very slowly; (*poco a poco*) little by little; **una casa di 3 ~i** a 3-storied (*US*) *o* 3-storey (*Brit*) house; **al ~ di sopra/di sotto** on the floor above/below; **all'ultimo ~** on the top floor; **al ~ terra** on the ground floor; **in primo/secondo ~** (*FOT. CINEMA etc*) in the foreground/background; **fare un primo ~** (*FOT. CINEMA*) to take a close-up; **di primo ~** (*fig*) prominent, high-ranking; **un fattore di secondo ~** a secondary *o* minor factor; **passare in secondo ~** to become less important; **mettere tutto sullo stesso ~** to lump everything together, give equal importance to everything; **tutto secondo i ~i** all according to plan; **~ di lavoro** (*superficie*) worktop; (*programma*) work plan; **~ regolatore** (*URBANISTICA*) city planning (*US*), town-planning scheme (*Brit*); **~ stradale** road surface.

pianofor'te *sm* piano, pianoforte.

pianoter'ra *sm inv* = **piano terra.**

pian'si *etc vb vedi* **piangere.**

pian'ta *sf* (*BOT*) plant; (*ANAT: anche:* **~ del piede**) sole (of the foot); (*grafico*) plan; (*cartina topografica*) map; **ufficio a ~ aperta** open-plan office; **in ~ stabile** on the permanent staff; **~ stradale** street map, street plan.

piantagio'ne [pyàntàjō'nā] *sf* plantation.

piantagra'ne *sm/f inv* troublemaker.

pianta're *vt* to plant; (*conficcare*) to drive *o* hammer in; (*tenda*) to put up, pitch; (*fig: lasciare*) to leave, desert; **~rsi** *vr*: **~rsi davanti a qn** to plant o.s. in front of sb; **~ qn in asso** to leave sb in the lurch; **~ grane** (*fig*) to cause trouble; **piantala!** (*fam*) cut it out!

pianta'to, a *ag*: **ben ~** (*persona*) well-built.

piantato're *sm* planter.

pianterre'no *sm* ground floor.

pian'to, a *pp di* **piangere** ♦ *sm* tears *pl*, crying.

piantona're *vt* to guard, watch over.

pianto'ne *sm* (*vigilante*) sentry, guard; (*soldato*) orderly; (*AUT*) steering column.

pianu'ra *sf* plain.

pias'tra *sf* plate; (*di pietra*) slab; (*di fornello*) hotplate; **panino alla ~** ≈ toasted sandwich;

~ di registrazione tape deck.
piastrel'la *sf* tile.
piastrella're *vt* to tile.
piastri'na *sf* (*ANAT*) platelet; (*MIL*) name tag (*US*), identity disc (*Brit*).
piattafor'ma *sf* (*anche fig*) platform; **~ continentale** (*GEO*) continental shelf; **~ girevole** (*TECN*) turntable; **~ di lancio** (*MIL*) launching pad *o* platform; **~ rivendicativa** *document prepared by the unions in an industry which sets out their claims*.
piattel'lo *sm* clay pigeon; **tiro al ~** trapshooting.
piatti'no *sm* (*di tazza*) saucer.
piat'to, a *ag* flat; (*fig: scialbo*) dull ♦ *sm* (*recipiente, vivanda*) dish; (*portata*) course; (*parte piana*) flat (part); **~i** *smpl* (*MUS*) cymbals; **un ~ di minestra** a bowl of soup; **~ fondo** soup dish; **~ forte** main course; **~ del giorno** dish of the day, plat du jour; **~ del giradischi** turntable; **~i già pronti** (*CUC*) ready-cooked dishes.
piaz'za [pyàt'tsá] *sf* square; (*COMM*) market; (*letto, lenzuolo*): **a una ~** single; **a due ~e** double; **far ~ pulita** to make a clean sweep; **mettere in ~** (*fig: rendere pubblico*) to make public; **scendere in ~** (*fig*) to take to the streets, demonstrate; **~ d'armi** (*MIL*) parade ground.
piazzafor'te [pyáttsáfôr'tá], *pl* **piazzefor'ti** *sf* (*MIL*) stronghold.
piazza'le [pyàttsá'lá] *sm* (large) square.
piazzamen'to [pyàttsámán'tô] *sm* (*SPORT*) place, placing.
piazza're [pyàttsá'rá] *vt* to place; (*COMM*) to market, sell; **~rsi** *vr* (*SPORT*) to be placed; **~rsi bene** to finish with the leaders *o* in a good position.
piazzi'sta, i [pyàttsē'stá] *sm* (*COMM*) commercial traveler.
piazzo'la [pyàttso'lá] *sf* (*AUT*) (roadside) stopping place, lay-by (*Brit*).
pic'ca, che *sf* pike; **~che** *sfpl* (*CARTE*) spades; **rispondere ~che a qn** (*fig*) to give sb a flat refusal.
piccan'te *ag* hot, pungent; (*fig*) racy.
piccar'si *vr*: **~ di fare** to pride o.s. on one's ability to do; **~ per qc** to take offense (*US*) *o* offence (*Brit*) at sth.
picchettag'gio [pēkkáttád'jô] *sm* picketing.
picchetta're [pēkkáttá'rá] *vt* to picket.
picchet'to [pēkkát'tô] *sm* (*MIL, di scioperanti*) picket.
picchia're [pēkkyá'rá] *vt* (*persona: colpire*) to hit, strike; (: *prendere a botte*) to beat (up); (*battere*) to beat; (*sbattere*) to bang ♦ *vi* (*bussare*) to knock; (: *con forza*) to bang; (*colpire*) to hit, strike; (*sole*) to beat down.
picchia'ta [pēkkyá'tá] *sf* knock; bang; blow; (*percosse*) beating, thrashing; (*AER*) dive;

scendere in ~ to (nose-)dive.
picchietta're [pēkkyàttá'rá] *vt* (*punteggiare*) to spot, dot; (*colpire*) to tap.
pic'chio [pēk'kyô] *sm* woodpecker.
picci'no, a [pēchē'nô] *ag* tiny, very small.
piccio'lo [pēcho'lô] *sm* (*BOT*) stalk.
picciona'ia [pēchōná'yà] *sf* pigeon-loft; (*TEATRO*): **la ~** the gallery.
piccio'ne [pēchô'nā] *sm* pigeon; **pigliare due ~i con una fava** (*fig*) to kill two birds with one stone.
pic'co, chi *sm* peak; **a ~** vertically; **colare a ~** (*NAUT, fig*) to sink.
piccolez'za [pēkkōlát'tsá] *sf* (*dimensione*) smallness; (*fig: grettezza*) meanness, pettiness; (: *inezia*) trifle.
pic'colo, a *ag* small; (*oggetto, mano, di età: bambino*) small, little (*dav sostantivo*); (*di breve durata: viaggio*) short; (*fig*) mean, petty ♦ *sm/f* child, little one ♦ *sm*: **nel mio ~** in my own small way; **~i** *smpl* (*di animale*) young *pl*; **in ~** in miniature; **la ~a borghesia** the lower middle classes; (*peg*) the petty bourgeoisie.
picco'ne *sm* pickax (*US*), pick(-axe) (*Brit*).
piccoz'za [pēkkot'tsá] *sf* ice ax (*US*), ice-axe (*Brit*).
picnic' *sm inv* picnic; **fare un ~** to have a picnic.
pidoc'chio [pēdok'kyô] *sm* louse.
pidocchio'so, a [pēdōkkyō'sô] *ag* (*infestato*) lousy; (*fig: taccagno*) mean, stingy, tight.
piè *sm inv*: **a ogni ~ sospinto** (*fig*) at every step; **saltare a ~ pari** (*omettere*) to skip; **a ~ di pagina** at the foot of the page; **note a ~ di pagina** footnotes.
pie'de *sm* foot; (*di mobile*) leg; **in ~i** standing; **a ~i** on foot; **a ~i nudi** barefoot; **su due ~i** (*fig*) at once; **mettere qc in ~i** (*azienda etc*) to set sth up; **prendere ~** (*fig*) to gain ground, catch on; **puntare i ~i** (*fig*) to dig one's heels in; **sentirsi mancare la terra sotto i ~i** to feel lost; **non sta in ~i** (*persona*) he can't stand; (*fig: scusa etc*) it doesn't hold water; **tenere in ~i** (*persona*) to keep on his (*o* her) feet; (*fig: ditta etc*) to keep going; **a ~ libero** (*DIR*) on bail; **sul ~ di guerra** (*MIL*) ready for action; **~ di porco** crowbar.
piedistal'lo, piedestal'lo *sm* pedestal.
pie'ga, ghe *sf* (*piegatura, GEO*) fold; (*di gonna*) pleat; (*di pantaloni*) crease; (*grinza*) wrinkle, crease; **prendere una brutta** *o* **cattiva ~** (*fig: persona*) to get into bad ways; (: *situazione*) to take a turn for the worse; **non fa una ~** (*fig: ragionamento*) it's faultless; **non ha fatto una ~** (*fig: persona*) he didn't bat an eye(- lash) (*US*) *o* an eye(lid) (*Brit*).
piegamen'to *sm* folding; bending; **~ sulle gambe** (*GINNASTICA*) kneebend.

piega're *vt* to fold; (*braccia, gambe, testa*) to bend ♦ *vi* to bend; ~**rsi** *vr* to bend; (*fig*): ~**rsi (a)** to yield (to), submit (to).

piegatu'ra *sf* folding *q*; bending *q*; fold; bend.

piegherò *etc* |pyāgāro'| *vb vedi* **piegare**.

pieghetta're |pyāgāttà'rā| *vt* to pleat.

pieghe'vole |pyāgā'vōlā| *ag* pliable, flexible; (*porta*) folding; (*fig*) yielding, docile.

Piemon'te *sm*: **il** ~ Piedmont.

piemonte'se *ag*, *sm/f* Piedmontese.

pie'na *sf vedi* **pieno**.

pienez'za |pyānāt'tsà| *sf* fullness.

pie'no, a *ag* full; (*muro, mattone*) solid ♦ *sm* (*colmo*) height, peak; (*carico*) full load ♦ *sf* (*di fiume*) flood, spate; (*gran folla*) crowd, throng; ~ **di** full of; **a** ~**e mani** abundantly; **a tempo** ~ full-time; **a** ~**i voti** (*eleggere*) unanimously; **laurearsi a** ~**i voti** *to graduate with full marks*; **in** ~ **giorno** in broad daylight; **in** ~ **inverno** in the depths of winter; **in** ~**a notte** in the middle of the night; **in** ~**a stagione** at the height of the season; **in** ~ (*completamente: sbagliare*) completely; (*colpire, centrare*) bang *o* right in the middle; **avere** ~**i poteri** to have full powers; **nel** ~ **possesso delle sue facoltà** in full possession of his faculties; **fare il** ~ **(di benzina)** to fill up (with gasoline).

pietà *sf* pity; (*REL*) piety; **senza** ~ (*agire*) ruthlessly; (*persona*) pitiless, ruthless; **avere** ~ **di** (*compassione*) to pity, feel sorry for; (*misericordia*) to have pity *o* mercy on; **far** ~ to arouse pity; (*peg*) to be terrible.

pietan'za |pyētán'tsà| *sf* dish, course.

pieto'so, a *ag* (*compassionevole*) pitying, compassionate; (*che desta pietà*) pitiful.

pie'tra *sf* stone; **mettiamoci una** ~ **sopra** (*fig*) let bygones be bygones; ~ **preziosa** precious stone, gem; ~ **dello scandalo** (*fig*) cause of scandal.

pietra'ia *sf* (*terreno*) stony ground.

pietrifica're *vt* to petrify; (*fig*) to transfix, paralyze.

pietri'sco, schi *sm* crushed stone, road metal (*Brit*).

pie've *sf* parish church.

pif'fero *sm* (*MUS*) pipe.

pigia'ma |pĭjá'mà| *sm* pajamas *pl* (*US*), pyjamas *pl* (*Brit*).

pi'gia pi'gia |pē'já'pējá| *sm* crowd, press.

pigia're |pējá'rā| *vt* to press.

pigiatri'ce |pējátrē'chā| *sf* (*macchina*) wine press.

pigio'ne |pējō'nā| *sf* rent.

piglia're |pēlyá'rā| *vt* to take, grab; (*afferrare*) to catch.

pi'glio |pēl'yō| *sm* look, expression.

pigmen'to *sm* pigment.

pigme'o, a *sm/f* pygmy.

pi'gna |pēn'yà| *sf* pine cone.

pignoleri'a |pēnyōlārē'à| *sf* fastidiousness, fussiness.

pigno'lo, a |pēnyo'lō| *ag* pernickety.

pignora're |pēnyōrá'rā| *vt* (*DIR*) to distrain.

pigola're *vi* to cheep, chirp.

pigoli'o *sm* cheeping, chirping.

pigri'zia |pēgrēt'tsyà| *sf* laziness.

pi'gro, a *ag* lazy; (*fig: ottuso*) slow, dull.

PIL *sigla m vedi* **prodotto interno lordo**.

pi'la *sf* (*catasta, di ponte*) pile; (*ELETTR*) battery; (*fam: torcia*) flashlight, torch (*Brit*); **a** ~, **a** ~**e** battery-operated.

pilas'tro *sm* pillar.

pil'lola *sf* pill; **prendere la** ~ (*contraccettivo*) to be on the pill.

pilo'ne *sm* (*di ponte*) pier; (*di linea elettrica*) pylon.

pilo'ta, i, e *sm/f* pilot; (*AUT*) driver ♦ *ag inv* pilot *cpd*; ~ **automatico** automatic pilot.

pilotag'gio |pēlōtád'jō| *sm*: **cabina di** ~ flight deck.

pilota're *vt* to pilot; to drive.

pilucca're *vt* to nibble at.

pimen'to *sm* pimento, allspice.

pimpan'te *ag* lively, full of beans.

pinacote'ca, che *sf* art gallery.

pine'ta *sf* pinewood.

ping-pong' |pingpong'| *sm* table tennis.

pin'gue *ag* fat, corpulent.

pingue'dine *sf* corpulence.

pingui'no *sm* (*ZOOL*) penguin.

pin'na *sf* fin; (*di pinguino, spatola di gomma*) flipper.

pinna'colo *sm* pinnacle.

pi'no *sm* pine (tree).

pino'lo *sm* pine kernel.

pin'ta *sf* pint.

pin'za |pēn'tsà| *sf* pliers *pl*; (*MED*) forceps *pl*; (*ZOOL*) pincer.

pinzette |pēntsāt'tā| *sfpl* tweezers.

pi'o, a, pi'i, pi'e *ag* pious; (*opere, istituzione*) charitable, charity *cpd*.

pioggerel'la |pyōdjārel'là| *sf* drizzle.

piog'gia, ge |pyod'jà| *sf* rain; (*fig: di regali, fiori*) shower; (*di insulti*) hail; **sotto la** ~ in the rain; ~ **acida** acid rain.

pio'lo *sm* peg; (*di scala*) rung.

piomba're *vi* to fall heavily; (*gettarsi con impeto*): ~ **su** to fall upon, assail ♦ *vt* (*dente*) to fill.

piombatu'ra *sf* (*di dente*) filling.

piombi'no *sm* (*sigillo*) (lead) seal; (*del filo a piombo*) plummet; (*PESCA*) sinker.

piom'bo *sm* (*CHIM*) lead; (*sigillo*) (lead) seal; (*proiettile*) (lead) shot; **a** ~ (*cadere*) straight down; (*muro etc*) plumb; **andare con i piedi di** ~ (*fig*) to tread carefully.

pionie're, a *sm/f* pioneer.

piop'po *sm* poplar.

piova'no, a *ag*: **acqua** ~**a** rainwater.

pio've·re *vb impers* to rain ♦ *vi* (*fig: scendere dall'alto*) to rain down; (*: affluire in gran numero*): ~ **in** to pour into; **non ci piove sopra** (*fig*) there's no doubt about it.

piovigginà're [pyōvēdjēnà'rā] *vb impers* to drizzle.

piovosità *sf* rainfall.

piovo'so, a *ag* rainy.

pio'vra *sf* octopus.

piov've *etc vb vedi* **piovere**.

pi'pa *sf* pipe.

pipì *sf* (*fam*): **fare** ~ to go wee (wee).

pipistrel'lo *sm* (*ZOOL*) bat.

pira'mide *sf* pyramid.

pira'ta, i *sm* pirate; ~ **della strada** hit-and-run driver.

Pirenè'i *smpl*: **i** ~ the Pyrenees.

pi'rico, a, ci, che *ag*: **polvere** ~**a** gunpowder.

pirì'te *sf* pyrite.

piroet'ta *sf* pirouette.

piro'filo, a *ag* heat-resistant ♦ *sf* heat-resistant glass; (*tegame*) oven proof dish.

piro'ga, ghe *sf* dug-out canoe.

piro'mane *sm/f* arsonist.

piro'scafo *sm* steamer, steamship.

pisa'no, a *ag* Pisan.

piscià're [pēshà'rā] *vi* (*fam!*) to piss (!), pee (!).

pisci'na [pēshē'nà] *sf* (swimming) pool.

pisel'lo *sm* pea.

pisoli'no *sm* nap; **fare un** ~ to have a nap.

pi'sta *sf* (*traccia*) track, trail; (*di stadio*) track; (*di pattinaggio*) rink; (*da sci*) run; (*AER*) runway; (*di circo*) ring; ~ **da ballo** dance floor; ~ **ciclabile** cycle track; ~ **di lancio** launch(ing) pad; ~ **di rullaggio** (*AER*) taxiway; ~ **di volo** (*AER*) runway.

pistac'chio [pēstàk'kyō] *sm* pistachio (tree); pistachio (nut).

pistil'lo *sm* (*BOT*) pistil.

pisto'la *sf* pistol, gun; ~ **a spruzzo** spray gun; ~ **a tamburo** revolver.

pisto'ne *sm* piston.

pitoc'co, chi *sm* skinflint, miser.

pito'ne *sm* python.

pitto're, tri'ce *sm/f* painter.

pittore'sco, a, schi, sche *ag* picturesque.

pitto'rico, a, ci, che *ag* of painting, pictorial.

pittu'ra *sf* painting; ~ **fresca** wet paint.

pittura're *vt* to paint.

più *av* more; (*in frasi comparative*) more, *aggettivo corto* + ...er; (*in frasi superlative*) most, *aggettivo corto* + ...est; (*negativo*): **non** ... ~ no more, *espressione negativa* + any more; no longer; (*di temperatura*) above zero; (*MAT*) plus ♦ *prep* plus, besides ♦ *ag inv* more; (*parecchi*) several ♦ *sm inv* (*la parte maggiore*): **il** ~ the most; (*MAT*) plus (sign); **i** ~ the majority; ~ **che/di** more than; ~ **che altro** above all; ~ **che mai** more than ever; ~ **grande che** bigger than; ~ **di 10 persone/te** more than 10 people/you; **il** ~ **intelligente/grande** the most intelligent/the biggest; **di** ~ more; **e per di** ~ (*inoltre*) and what's more, moreover; **3 ore/litri di** ~ **che** 3 hours/liters more than; **una volta di** ~ once more; **3 chili in** ~ 3 kilos more, 3 extra kilos; **a** ~ **non posso** as much as possible; **al** ~ **presto** as soon as possible; **al** ~ **tardi** at the latest; ~ **o meno** more or less; **né** ~ **né meno** no more, no less; **non lavora** ~ he doesn't work any more, he no longer works; **non ce n'è** ~ there isn't any left; **non c'è** ~ **nessuno** there's no one left; **non c'è** ~ **niente da fare** there's nothing more to be done; **si fa sempre** ~ **difficile** it is getting more and more difficult; **chi** ~ **chi meno hanno tutti contribuito** everybody made a contribution of some sort; **il** ~ **delle volte** more often than not, generally; **tutt'al** ~, **al** ~ if the worst comes to the worst.

piucheperfet'to [pyōōkkàpàrfet'tō] *sm* (*LING*) pluperfect, past perfect.

piu'ma *sf* feather; ~**e** *sfpl* down *sg*; (*piumaggio*) plumage *sg*, feathers.

piumag'gio [pyōōmàd'jō] *sm* plumage, feathers *pl*.

piumi'no *sm* (eider)down; (*per letto*) eiderdown; (*: tipo danese*) down comforter (*US*), duvet (*Brit*); (*giacca*) down (*US*) o quilted (*Brit*) jacket (*with goose-feather padding*); (*per cipria*) powder puff; (*per spolverare*) feather duster.

piutto'sto *av* rather; ~ **che** (*anziché*) rather than.

pivel'lo, a *sm/f* greenhorn.

piz'za [pēt'tsà] *sf* (*CUC*) pizza; (*CINEMA*) reel.

pizzerì'a [pēttsārē'à] *sf* place where pizzas are made, sold or eaten.

pizzica'gnolo, a [pēttsēkàn'yōlō] *sm/f* specialist grocer.

pizzica're [pēttsēkà'rā] *vt* (*stringere*) to nip, pinch; (*pungere*) to sting; to bite; (*MUS*) to pluck ♦ *vi* (*prudere*) to itch, be itchy; (*cibo*) to be hot o spicy.

pizzicherì'a [pēttsēkàrē'à] *sf* delicatessen (shop).

piz'zico, chi [pēt'tsēkō] *sm* (*pizzicotto*) pinch, nip; (*piccola quantità*) pinch, dash; (*d'insetto*) sting; bite.

pizzicot'to [pēttsēkot'tō] *sm* pinch, nip.

piz'zo [pēt'tsō] *sm* (*merletto*) lace; (*barbetta*) goatee beard.

placa're *vt* to placate, soothe; ~**rsi** *vr* to calm down.

plac'ca, che *sf* plate; (*con iscrizione*) plaque; (*anche*: ~ **dentaria**) (dental) plaque.

placca're *vt* to plate; **placcato in oro/argento** gold-/silver-plated.

placen'ta [plàchen'tà] *sf* placenta.

placidità [pláchēdētà'] *sf* calm, peacefulness.
pla'cido, a [plà'chēdō] *ag* placid, calm.
plafonie'ra *sf* ceiling light.
plagia're [plàjà'rā] *vt* (*copiare*) to plagiarize; (*DIR: influenzare*) to coerce.
pla'gio [plà'jō] *sm* plagiarism; (*DIR*) duress.
plaid [pled] *sm inv* lap robe (*US*), (travelling) rug (*Brit*).
plana're *vi* (*AER*) to glide.
plan'cia, ce [plàn'chá] *sf* (*NAUT*) bridge; (*AUT: cruscotto*) dashboard.
plan'cton *sm inv* plankton.
planeta'rio, a *ag* planetary ♦ *sm* (*locale*) planetarium.
pla'sma *sm* plasma.
plasma're *vt* to mold (*US*), mould (*Brit*), shape.
pla'stico, a, ci, che *ag* plastic ♦ *sm* (*rappresentazione*) relief model; (*esplosivo*): **bomba al ~** plastic bomb ♦ *sf* (*arte*) plastic arts *pl*; (*MED*) plastic surgery; (*sostanza*) plastic; **in materiale ~** plastic.
plastili'na ® *sf* plasticine ®.
pla'tano *sm* plane tree.
plate'a *sf* (*TEATRO*) orchestra (*US*), stalls *pl* (*Brit*).
platea'le *ag* (*gesto, atteggiamento*) theatrical.
platealmen'te *av* theatrically.
pla'tino *sm* platinum.
plato'nico, a, ci, che *ag* platonic.
plaudi're *vi*: **~ a** to applaud.
plausi'bile *ag* plausible.
pla'uso *sm* (*fig*) approval.
pleba'glia [plābàl'yà] *sf* (*peg*) rabble, mob.
ple'be *sf* common people.
plebe'o, a *ag* plebeian; (*volgare*) coarse, common.
plebisci'to [plābēshē'tō] *sm* plebiscite.
plena'rio, a *ag* plenary.
plenilu'nio *sm* full moon.
plet'tro *sm* plectrum.
pleuri'te *sf* pleurisy.
PLI *sigla m* (*POL*) = *Partito Liberale Italiano*.
pli'co, chi *sm* (*pacco*) parcel; **in ~ a parte** (*COMM*) under separate cover.
ploto'ne *sm* (*MIL*) platoon; **~ d'esecuzione** firing squad.
plum'beo, a *ag* leaden.
plura'le *ag, sm* plural.
plurali'smo *sm* pluralism.
pluralità *sf* plurality; (*maggioranza*) majority.
plusvalen'za [plōōzvàlen'tsà] *sf* capital gain.
plusvalo're *sm* (*ECON*) surplus.
pluto'nio *sm* plutonium.
pluvia'le *ag* rain *cpd*.
pluvio'metro *sm* rain gauge.
P.M. *abbr* (*POL*) = **Pubblico Ministero**; (= *Polizia Militare*) MP (= *Military Police*).
pm *abbr* = *peso molecolare*.

PN *sigla* = *Pordenone*.
pneuma'tico, a, ci, che *ag* inflatable; (*TECN*) pneumatic ♦ *sm* (*AUT*) tire (*US*), tyre (*Brit*).
PNL *sigla m vedi* **prodotto nazionale lordo**.
Po *sm*: **il ~** the Po.
po' *av, sm vedi* **poco**.
P.O. *abbr* = **posta ordinaria**.
pochez'za [pōkàt'tsà] *sf* insufficiency, shortage; (*fig: meschinità*) meanness, smallness.
po'co, a, chi, che *ag* (*quantità*) little, *negazione* + (*very*) much; (*numero*) few, *negazione* + (*very*) many ♦ *av* little, *espressione negativa* + much; (*con ag*) *espressione negativa* + very ♦ *pronome* (*very*) little; **~chi(che)** *pronome pl* few ♦ *sm*: **il ~ che guadagna** ... what little he earns ...; **con ~a spesa** for a small outlay; **a ~ prezzo** at a low price, cheap; **è un tipo di ~che parole** he's a man of few words; **un po'** a little, a bit; **sono un po' stanco** I'm a bit tired; **un po' di soldi/pane** a little money/bread; **sta ~ bene** he's not very well; **~ prima/dopo** shortly before/afterwards; **~ fa** a short time ago; **a ~ a ~** little by little; **fra ~ o un po'** in a little while; **a dir ~** to say the least; **è una cosa da ~** it's nothing, it's of no importance.
pode're *sm* (*AGR*) farm.
podero'so, a *ag* powerful.
podestà *sm inv* (*nel fascismo*) podestà, mayor.
po'dio *sm* dais, platform; (*MUS*) podium.
podi'smo *sm* (*SPORT: marcia*) walking; (: *corsa*) running.
podi'sta, i, e *sm/f* walker; runner.
poe'ma, i *sm* poem.
poesi'a *sf* (*arte*) poetry; (*componimento*) poem.
poe'ta, es'sa *sm/f* poet/poetess.
poeta're *vi* to write poetry.
poe'tico, a, ci, che *ag* poetic(al).
poggia're [pōdjà'rā] *vt* to lean, rest; (*posare*) to lay, place.
poggiate'sta [pōdjàte'stà] *sm inv* (*AUT*) headrest.
pog'gio [pod'jō] *sm* hillock, knoll.
po'i *av* then; (*alla fine*) finally, at last ♦ *sm*: **pensare al ~** to think of the future; **e ~** (*inoltre*) and besides; **questa ~ (è bella)** (*ironico*) that's a good one!; **d'ora in ~** from now on; **da domani in ~** from tomorrow onwards.
poiché [pōēkà'] *cong* since, as.
po'ker *sm* poker.
polac'co, a, chi, che *ag* Polish ♦ *sm/f* Pole.
pola're *ag* polar.
pol'ca, che *sf* polka.
pole'mico, a, ci, che *ag* polemic(al), controversial ♦ *sf* controversy; **fare ~che** to be contentious.
polemizza're [pōlāmēddzà'rā] *vi*: **~ (su qc)** to

argue (about sth).

polen'ta *sf* (*CUC*) sort of thick porridge made with corn meal.

polento'ne, a *sm/f* slowpoke (*US*), slowcoach (*Brit*).

polesa'no, a *ag* of (*o* from) Polesine (*area between the Po and the Adige*).

POLFER' *abbr f* = Polizia Ferroviaria.

po'li... *prefisso* poly,...

poliambulato'rio *sm* (*MED*) health clinic.

policli'nico, ci *sm* general hospital, polyclinic.

polie'stere *sm* polyester.

poligami'a *sf* polygamy.

poli'gono *sm* polygon; ~ **di tiro** rifle range.

Poline'sia *sf*: **la** ~ Polynesia.

polinesia'no, a *ag, sm/f* Polynesian.

po'lio(mie'lite) *sf* polio(myelitis).

po'lipo *sm* polyp.

polistiro'lo *sm* polystyrene.

politec'nico, ci *sm* postgraduate technical college.

poli'tica, che *sf vedi* politico.

politican'te *sm/f* (*peg*) petty politician.

politicizza're [pōlētēchēddzà'rā] *vt* to politicize.

poli'tico, a, ci, che *ag* political ♦ *sm/f* politician ♦ *sf* politics *sg*; (*linea di condotta*) policy; **elezioni** ~**che** congressional (*US*) *o* parliamentary (*Brit*) election(s); **uomo** ~ politician; **darsi alla** ~**a** to go into politics; **fare** ~**a** (*militante*) to be a political activist; (*come professione*) to be in politics; **la** ~**a del governo** the government's policies; ~**a aziendale** company policy; ~**a estera** foreign policy; ~**a dei prezzi** prices policy; ~**a dei redditi** incomes policy.

polivalen'te *ag* multi-purpose.

polizi'a [pōlēttsē'à] *sf* police; ~ **giudiziaria** ≈ Federal Bureau of Investigation (FBI) (*US*), Criminal Investigation Department (CID) (*Brit*); ~ **sanitaria/tributaria** health/tax inspectorate; (~ **stradale** traffic police.

polizie'sco, a, schi, sche [pōlēttsyā'skō] *ag* police *cpd*; (*film, romanzo*) detective *cpd*.

poliziot'to [pōlēttsyot'tō] *sm* policeman; **cane** ~ police dog; **donna** ~ policewoman.

po'lizza [po'lēttsà] *sf* (*COMM*) bill; ~ **di assicurazione** insurance policy; ~ **di carico** bill of lading.

polla'io *sm* henhouse.

pollaio'lo, a *sm/f* poultryman, poulterer (*Brit*).

polla'me *sm* poultry.

pollas'tro *sm* (*ZOOL*) cockerel.

pol'lice [pol'lēchā] *sm* thumb; (*unità di misura*) inch.

pol'line *sm* pollen.

polliven'dolo, a *sm/f* poultryman, poulterer (*Brit*).

pol'lo *sm* chicken; **far ridere i** ~**i** (*situazione,*

persona) to be utterly ridiculous.

polmona're *ag* lung *cpd*, pulmonary.

polmo'ne *sm* lung.

polmoni'te *sf* pneumonia.

po'lo *sm* (*GEO, FISICA*) pole; (*gioco*) polo; **il P~ sud/nord** the South/North Pole.

Polo'nia *sf*: **la** ~ Poland.

pol'pa *sf* flesh, pulp; (*carne*) lean meat.

polpac'cio [pōlpàch'chō] *sm* (*ANAT*) calf.

polpastrel'lo *sm* fingertip.

polpet'ta *sf* (*CUC*) meatball.

polpetto'ne *sm* (*CUC*) meatloaf.

pol'po *sm* octopus.

polpo'so, a *ag* fleshy.

polsi'no *sm* cuff.

pol'so *sm* (*ANAT*) wrist; (*pulsazione*) pulse; (*fig: forza*) drive, vigor (*US*), vigour (*Brit*); **avere** ~ (*fig*) to be strong; **un uomo di** ~ a man of nerve.

polti'glia [pōltēl'yà] *sf* (*composto*) mash, mush; (*di fango e neve*) slush.

poltri're *vi* to laze about.

poltro'na *sf* armchair; (*TEATRO: posto*) the orchestra (*US*) *o* seat in the front stalls (*Brit*).

poltronci'na [pōltrōnchē'nà] *sf* (*TEATRO*) the orchestra (*US*) *o* seat in the back stalls (*Brit*).

poltro'ne *ag* lazy, slothful.

pol'vere *sf* dust; (*anche*: ~ **da sparo**) (gun)powder; (*sostanza ridotta minutissima*) powder, dust; **caffè in** ~ instant coffee; **latte in** ~ dried *o* powdered milk; **sapone in** ~ powdered soap (*US*), soap powder (*Brit*); ~ **di ferro** iron filings *pl*; ~ **d'oro** gold dust; ~ **pirica** *o* **da sparo** gunpowder.

polverie'ra *sf* powder magazine.

polveri'na *sf* (*gen, MED*) powder; (*gergo*: *cocaina*) snow.

polverizza're [pōlvārēddzà'rā] *vt* to pulverize; (*nebulizzare*) to atomize; (*fig*) to crush, pulverize; (: *record*) to smash.

polvero'ne *sm* thick cloud of dust.

polvero'so, a *ag* dusty.

poma'ta *sf* ointment, cream.

pomel'lo *sm* knob.

pomeridia'no, a *ag* afternoon *cpd*; **nelle ore** ~**e** in the afternoon.

pomerig'gio [pōmārēd'jō] *sm* afternoon; **nel primo/tardo** ~ in the early/late afternoon.

po'mice [pō'mēchā] *sf* pumice.

pomicia're [pōmēchá'rā] *vi* (*fam: sbaciucchiarsi*) to neck.

po'mo *sm* (*mela*) apple; (*ornamentale*) knob; (*di sella*) pommel; ~ **d'Adamo** (*ANAT*) Adam's apple.

pomodo'ro *sm* tomato.

pom'pa *sf* (*sfarzo*) pomp (and ceremony); ~ **antincendio** fire hose; ~ **di benzina** gas (*US*) *o* petrol (*Brit*) pump; (*distributore*) filling station; **(impresa di)** ~**e funebri** mortician's (*US*), funeral parlour *sg*, undertaker's *sg*.

pompa're *vt* to pump; (*trarre*) to pump out; (*gonfiare d'aria*) to pump up.

pompeia'no, a *ag* of (*o* from) Pompei.

pompel'mo *sm* grapefruit.

pompie're *sm* fireman.

pompo'so, a *ag* pompous.

pondera're *vt* to ponder over, consider carefully.

pondero'so, a *ag* (*anche fig*) weighty.

ponen'te *sm* west.

pon'go, po'ni *etc vb vedi* **porre.**

pon'te *sm* bridge; (*di nave*) deck; (*: anche:* ~ **di comando**) bridge; (*impalcatura*) scaffold; **vivere sotto i** ~**i** to be a tramp; **fare il** ~ (*fig*) to take the extra day off (*between 2 public holidays*); **governo** ~ interim government; ~ **aereo** airlift; ~ **di barche** (*MIL*) pontoon bridge; ~ **di coperta** (*NAUT*) upper deck; ~ **levatoio** drawbridge; ~ **radio** radio link; ~ **sospeso** suspension bridge.

ponte'fice [pōntā'fēchā] *sm* (*REL*) pontiff.

ponticel'lo [pōntēchel'lō] *sm* (*di occhiali, MUS*) bridge.

pontifica're *vi* (*anche fig*) to pontificate.

pontifica'to *sm* pontificate.

pontifi'cio, a, ci, cie [pōntēfē'chō] *ag* papal; **Stato P**~ Papal State.

ponti'le *sm* jetty.

po'peline [po'pālēn] *sm* poplin.

popola'no, a *ag* popular, of the people ♦ *sm/f* man/woman of the people.

popola're *ag* popular; (*quartiere, clientela*) working-class ♦ *vt* (*rendere abitato*) to populate; ~**rsi** *vr* to fill with people, get crowded; **manifestazione** ~ mass demonstration; **repubblica** ~ people's republic.

popolarità *sf* popularity.

popolazio'ne [pōpōlāttsyō'nā] *sf* population.

po'polo *sm* people.

popolo'so, a *ag* densely populated.

popo'ne *sm* melon.

pop'pa *sf* (*di nave*) stern; (*mammella*) breast; **a** ~ aft, astern.

poppan'te *sm/f* unweaned infant; (*fig: inesperto*) whippersnapper.

poppa're *vt* to suck.

poppa'ta *sf* (*allattamento*) feed.

poppato'io *sm* (*feeding*) bottle.

populi'sta, i, e *ag* populist.

porca'io *sm* (*anche fig*) pigsty.

porcella'na [pōrchāllā'nā] *sf* porcelain, china; (*oggetto*) piece of porcelain.

porcelli'no, a [pōrchāllē'nō] *sm/f* piglet; ~ **d'India** guinea pig.

porcheri'a [pōrkārē'á] *sf* filth, muck; (*fig: oscenità*) obscenity; (*: azione disonesta*) dirty trick; (*: cosa mal fatta*) rubbish.

porchet'ta [pōrkāt'tá] *sf* roast sucking pig.

porci'le [pōrchē'lā] *sm* pigsty.

porci'no, a [pōrchē'nō] *ag* of pigs, pork *cpd* ♦ *sm* (*fungo*) *type of edible mushroom.*

por'co, ci *sm* pig; (*carne*) pork.

porcospi'no *sm* porcupine.

por'gere [por'jārā] *vt* to hand, give; (*tendere*) to hold out.

pornografi'a *sf* pornography.

pornogra'fico, a, ci, che *ag* pornographic.

po'ro *sm* pore.

poro'so, a *ag* porous.

por'pora *sf* purple.

por're *vt* (*mettere*) to put; (*collocare*) to place; (*posare*) to lay (down), put (down); (*fig: supporre*): **poniamo (il caso) che ...** let's suppose that ...; **porsi** *vr* (*mettersi*): **porsi a sedere/in cammino** to sit down/set off; ~ **le basi di** (*fig*) to lay the foundations of, establish; ~ **una domanda a qn** to ask sb a question, put a question to sb; ~ **la propria fiducia in qn** to place one's trust in sb; ~ **fine** *o* **termine a qc** to put an end *o* a stop to sth; **posto che ...** supposing that ..., on the assumption that ...; **porsi in salvo** to save o.s.

por'ro *sm* (*BOT*) leek; (*MED*) wart.

por'si *etc vb vedi* **porgere.**

por'ta *sf* door; (*SPORT*) goal; (*INFORM*) port; ~**e** *sfpl* (*di città*) gates; **mettere qn alla** ~ to throw sb out; **sbattere** *o* **chiudere la** ~ **in faccia a qn** (*anche fig*) to slam the door in sb's face; **trovare tutte le** ~**e chiuse** (*fig*) to find the way barred; **a** ~**e chiuse** (*DIR*) in closed session; **l'inverno è alle** ~**e** (*fig*) winter is upon us; **vendita** ~ **a** ~ door-to-door selling; ~ **di servizio** service entrance; ~ **di sicurezza** emergency exit; ~ **stagna** watertight door.

portabaga'gli [pōrtábágál'yē] *sm inv* (*facchino*) porter; (*AUT, FERR*) luggage rack.

portabandie'ra *sm inv* standard bearer.

portabor'se *sm inv* (*peg*) lackey.

portace'nere [pōrtáchā'nārā] *sm inv* ashtray.

portachia'vi [pōrtákyá'vē] *sm inv* keyring.

portaci'pria [pōrtáchēp'ryá] *sm inv* powder compact.

portae'rei *sf inv* (*nave*) aircraft carrier ♦ *sm inv* (*aereo*) aircraft transporter.

portafines'tra, *pl* **portefines'tre** *sf* French door (*US*) *o* window (*Brit*).

portafo'glio [pōrtáfol'yō] *sm* (*busta*) wallet; (*cartella*) briefcase; (*POL, BORSA*) portfolio; ~ **titoli** investment portfolio.

portafortu'na *sm inv* lucky charm; mascot.

portagio'ie [pōrtájo'yá] *sm inv,* **portagioiel'li** [pōrtájōyel'lē] *sm inv* jewelry (*US*) *o* jewellery (*Brit*) box.

porta'le *sm* portal.

portalet'tere *sm/f inv* mailman/woman (*US*),

postman/woman (*Brit*).
portamen'to *sm* carriage, bearing.
portamone'te *sm inv* coin purse (*US*), purse (*Brit*).
portan'te *ag* (*muro etc*) supporting, load-bearing.
portanti'na *sf* sedan chair; (*per ammalati*) stretcher.
portaombrel'li *sm inv* umbrella stand.
portapac'chi |pŏrtápák'kč| *sm inv* (*di moto, bicicletta*) luggage rack.
porta're *vt* (*sostenere, sorreggere*: *peso, bambino, pacco*) to carry; (*indossare*: *abito, occhiali*) to wear; (: *capelli lunghi*) to have; (*avere*: *nome, titolo*) to have, bear; (*recare*): ~ **qc a qn** to take (*o* bring) sth to sb; (*fig*: *sentimenti*) to bear; **~rsi** *vr* (*recarsi*) to go; ~ **avanti** (*discorso, idea*) to pursue; ~ **via** to take away; (*rubare*) to take; ~ **i bambini a spasso** to take the children for a walk; ~ **fortuna** to bring good luck; ~ **qc alla bocca** to lift *o* put sth to one's lips; **porta bene i suoi anni** he's wearing well; **dove porta questa strada?** where does this road lead?, where does this road take you?; **il documento porta la tua firma** the document has *o* bears your signature; **non gli porto rancore** I don't bear him a grudge; **la polizia si è portata sul luogo del disastro** the police went to the scene of the disaster.
portarivi'ste *sm inv* magazine rack.
portasapo'ne *sm inv* soap dish.
portasigaret'te *sm inv* cigarette case.
portaspil'li *sm inv* pincushion.
porta'ta *sf* (*vivanda*) course; (*AUT*) carrying (*o* loading) capacity; (*di arma*) range; (*volume d'acqua*) (rate of) flow; (*fig*: *limite*) scope, capability; (: *importanza*) impact, import; **alla ~ di tutti** (*conoscenza*) within everybody's capabilities; (*prezzo*) within everybody's means; **a/fuori ~ (di)** within/out of reach (of); **a ~ di mano** within (arm's) reach; **di grande ~** of great importance.
porta'tile *ag* portable.
porta'to, a *ag* (*incline*): ~ **a** inclined *o* apt to.
portato're, tri'ce *sm/f* (*anche* COMM) bearer; (*MED*) carrier; **pagabile al ~** payable to the bearer.
portatovaglio'lo |pŏrtàtŏvályo'lŏ| *sm* napkin ring.
portauo'vo *sm inv* eggcup.
portavo'ce |pŏrtàvŏ'chà| *sm/f inv* spokesman/woman.
portel'lo *sm* (*di portone*) door; (*NAUT*) hatch.
porten'to *sm* wonder, marvel.
portento'so, a *ag* wonderful, marvelous (*US*), marvellous (*Brit*).
portica'to *sm* portico.
por'tico, ci *sm* portico; (*riparo*) lean-to.
portie'ra *sf* (*AUT*) door.

portie're *sm* (*portinaio*) concierge, caretaker; (*di hotel*) porter; (*nel calcio*) goalkeeper.
portina'io, a *sm/f* concierge, caretaker.
portineri'a *sf* caretaker's lodge.
por'to, a *pp di* **porgere** ♦ *sm* (*NAUT*) harbor (*US*), harbour (*Brit*), port; (*spesa di trasporto*) carriage ♦ *sm inv* port (wine); **andare** *o* **giungere in ~** (*fig*) to come to a successful conclusion; **condurre qc in ~** to bring sth to a successful conclusion; ~ **d'armi** gun license (*US*) *o* licence (*Brit*); ~ **fluviale** river port; ~ **franco** free port; ~ **marittimo** seaport; ~ **militare** naval base; ~ **pagato** carriage paid, post free *o* paid; ~ **di scalo** port of call.
Portogal'lo *sm*: **il ~** Portugal.
portoghe'se |pŏrtŏgã'sà| *ag*, *sm/f*, *sm* Portuguese *inv*.
porto'ne *sm* main entrance, main door.
portorica'no, a *ag*, *sm/f* Puerto Rican.
Portori'co *sf* Puerto Rico.
portua'le *ag* harbor *cpd* (*US*), harbour *cpd* (*Brit*), port *cpd* ♦ *sm* dock worker.
porzio'ne |pŏrtsyŏ'nä| *sf* portion, share; (*di cibo*) portion, helping.
po'sa *sf* (*FOT*) exposure; (*atteggiamento, di modello*) pose; (*riposo*): **lavorare senza ~** to work without a break; **mettersi in ~** to pose; **teatro di ~** photographic studio.
posace'nere |pŏsàchã'nàrà| *sm inv* ashtray.
posa're *vt* to put (down), lay (down) ♦ *vi* (*ponte, edificio, teoria*): ~ **su** to rest on; (*FOT, atteggiarsi*) to pose; **~rsi** *vr* (*ape, aereo*) to land; (*uccello*) to alight; (*sguardo*) to settle.
posa'ta *sf* piece of cutlery; **~e** *sfpl* cutlery *sg*.
posatez'za |pŏsàtãt'tsà| *sf* (*di persona*) composure; (*di discorso*) balanced nature.
posa'to, a *ag* steady; (*discorso*) balanced.
poscrit'to *sm* postscript.
po'si *etc vb vedi* **porre**.
positi'vo, a *ag* positive.
posizio'ne |pŏzčttsyŏ'nä| *sf* position; **farsi una ~** to make one's way in the world; **prendere ~** (*fig*) to take a stand; **luci di ~** (*AUT*) parking lights (*US*), sidelights (*Brit*).
posologi'a, gi'e |pŏzŏlŏjč'à| *sf* dosage, directions *pl* for use.
pospor're *vt* to place after; (*differire*) to postpone, defer.
pospo'sto, a *pp di* **posporre**.
possede're *vt* to own, possess; (*qualità, virtù*) to have, possess; (*conoscere a fondo*: *lingua etc*) to have a thorough knowledge of; (*sog*: *ira etc*) to possess.
possedimen'to *sm* possession.
possen'te *ag* strong, powerful.
possessi'vo, a *ag* possessive.
posses'so *sm* possession; **essere in ~ di qc** to be in possession of sth; **prendere ~ di qc**

to take possession of sth; **entrare in** ~ **dell'eredità** to come into one's inheritance.

possesso're *sm* owner.

possi'bile *ag* possible ♦ *sm*: **fare tutto il** ~ to do everything possible; **nei limiti del** ~ as far as possible; **al più tardi** ~ as late as possible; **vieni prima** ~ come as soon as possible.

possibili'sta, i, e *ag*: **essere** ~ to keep an open mind.

possibilità *sf inv* possibility ♦ *sfpl (mezzi)* means; **aver la** ~ **di fare** to be in a position to do; to have the opportunity to do; **nei limiti delle nostre** ~ in so far as we can.

possibilmen'te *av* if possible.

possiden'te *sm/f* landowner.

possie'do *etc vb vedi* **possedere**.

pos'so *etc vb vedi* **potere**.

post ... *prefisso* post ....

po'sta *sf (servizio)* postal service; *(corrispondenza)* mail, post *(Brit)*; *(ufficio postale)* post office; *(nei giochi d'azzardo)* stake; *(CACCIA)* blind *(US)*, hide *(Brit)*; ~**e** *sfpl (amministrazione)* post office; **fare la** ~ **a qn** *(fig)* to lie in wait for sb; **la** ~ **in gioco è troppo alta** *(fig)* there's too much at stake; **a bella** ~ *(apposta)* on purpose; **piccola** ~ *(su giornale)* letters to the editor, letters page; ~ **aerea** airmail; ~ **elettronica** electronic mail; ~ **ordinaria** ≈ second-class mail; **P~e e Telecomunicazioni (PP.TT.)** *postal and telecommunications service*; **ministro delle P~e e Telecomunicazioni** Postmaster General.

postagi'ro [pŏstájē'rŏ] *sm* post office check *(US)* o cheque *(Brit)*.

posta'le *ag* postal, post office *cpd* ♦ *sm (treno)* mail train; *(nave)* mail boat; *(furgone)* mail truck *(US)* o van *(Brit)*; **timbro** ~ postmark.

postazio'ne [pŏstáttsyŏ'nä] *sf (MIL)* emplacement.

postbel'lico, a, ci, che *ag* postwar.

posteggia're [pŏstädjä'rä] *vt, vi* to park.

posteggiato're, tri'ce [pŏstädjátŏ'rä] *sm/f* parking-lot attendant *(US)*, car-park attendant *(Brit)*.

posteg'gio [pŏstäd'jŏ] *sm* parking lot *(US)*, car park *(Brit)*; *(di taxi)* stand *(US)*, rank *(Brit)*.

postelegrafo'nico, a, ci, che *ag* postal and telecommunications *cpd*.

po'steri *smpl* posterity *sg*; **i nostri** ~ our descendants.

posterio're *ag (dietro)* back; *(dopo)* later ♦ *sm (fam: sedere)* behind.

posterio'ri: a ~ *ag inv* after the event *(dopo sostantivo)* ♦ *av* looking back.

posterità *sf* posterity.

postic'cio, a, ci, ce [pŏstēch'chŏ] *ag* false ♦ *sm* hairpiece.

posticipa're [pŏstēchēpä'rä] *vt* to defer, postpone.

postil'la *sf* marginal note.

posti'no *sm* mailman *(US)*, postman *(Brit)*.

po'sto, a *pp di* **porre** ♦ *sm (sito, posizione)* place; *(impiego)* job; *(spazio libero)* room, space; *(di parcheggio)* space; *(sedile: al teatro, in treno etc)* seat; *(MIL)* post; **a** ~ *(in ordine)* in place, tidy; *(fig)* settled; (: *persona)* reliable; **mettere a** ~ *(riordinare)* to tidy (up), put in order; *(faccende: sistemare)* to straighten out; **prender** ~ to take a seat; **al** ~ **di** in place of; **sul** ~ on the spot; ~ **di blocco** roadblock; ~ **di lavoro** job; ~ **di polizia** police station; ~ **telefonico pubblico (P.T.P.)** public telephone; ~ **di villeggiatura** tourist spot; ~**i in piedi** *(TEATRO, in autobus)* standing room.

postopera to'rio, a *ag (MED)* postoperative.

postri'bolo *sm* brothel.

postscrip'tum *sm inv* postscript.

po'stumo, a *ag* posthumous; *(tardivo)* belated; ~**i** *smpl (conseguenze)* after-effects, consequences.

pota'bile *ag* drinkable; **acqua** ~ drinking water.

pota're *vt* to prune.

potas'sio *sm* potassium.

potatu'ra *sf* pruning.

poten'te *ag (nazione)* strong, powerful; *(veleno, farmaco)* potent, strong.

poten'za [pŏten'tsä] *sf* power; *(forza)* strength; **all'ennesima** ~ to the nth degree; **le Grandi P~e** the Great Powers; ~ **militare** military might o strength.

potenzia'le [pŏtäntsyä'lä] *ag, sm* potential.

potenziamen'to [pŏtäntsyämän'tŏ] *sm* development.

potenzia're [pŏtäntsyä'rä] *vt* to develop.

pote're *vb + infinito* can; *(sog: persona)* can, to be able to; *(autorizzazione)* can, may; *(possibilità, ipotesi)* may ♦ *vb impers*: **può darsi** perhaps; **può darsi che** perhaps, it may be that ♦ *sm* power; **avresti potuto dirmelo!** you could o might have told me!; **non ne posso più!** I can't take any more!; **essere al** ~ *(POL)* to be in power o in office; ~ **d'acquisto** purchasing power; ~ **esecutivo** executive power.

potestà *sf (potere)* power; *(DIR)* authority.

potrò *etc vb vedi* **potere**.

poverac'cio, a, ci, ce [pŏvärách'chŏ] *sm/f* poor devil.

po'vero, a *ag* poor; *(disadorno)* plain, bare ♦ *sm/f* poor man/woman; **i** ~**i** the poor; ~ **di** lacking in, having little; **minerale** ~ **di ferro** ore with a low iron content; **paese** ~ **di risorse** country short of o lacking in resources.

povertà *sf* poverty.

pozio'ne [pŏttsyŏ'nä] *sf* potion.

poz'za [pōt'tsà] *sf* pool.

pozzan'ghera [pōttsán'gàrà] *sf* puddle.

poz'zo [pōt'tsō] *sm* well; (*cava: di carbone*) pit; (*di miniera*) shaft; ~ **nero** cesspool; ~ **petrolifero** oil well.

pp. *abbr* (= *pagine*) pp.

p.p. *abbr* (= *per procura*) pp.

PP.SS. *abbr* = **partecipazioni statali.**

PP.TT. *abbr* = **Poste e Telecomunicazioni**; *vedi* **posta.**

PR *sigla* = *Parma* ♦ *sigla m* (*POL*) = *Partito Radicale.*

P.R. *abbr* = **piano regolatore; procuratore della Repubblica.**

Pra'ga *sf* Prague.

pragma'tico, a, ci, che *ag* pragmatic.

pramma'tica *sf* custom; **essere di** ~ to be customary.

pranza're [pràndzá'rà] *vi* to dine, have dinner; to lunch, have lunch.

pran'zo [pràn'dzō] *sm* dinner; (*a mezzogiorno*) lunch.

pras'si *sf* usual procedure.

pra'tica, che *sf* practice; (*esperienza*) experience; (*conoscenza*) knowledge, familiarity; (*tirocinio*) training, practice; (*AMM: affare*) matter, case; (: *incartamento*) file, dossier; **in** ~ (*praticamente*) in practice; **mettere in** ~ to put into practice; **fare le** ~**che per** (*AMM*) to do the paperwork for; ~ **restrittiva** restrictive practice; ~**che illecite** dishonest practices.

pratica'bile *ag* (*progetto*) practicable, feasible; (*luogo*) passable, practicable.

praticamen'te *av* (*in modo pratico*) in a practical way, practically; (*quasi*) practically, almost.

pratican'te *sm/f* apprentice, trainee; (*REL*) (regular) churchgoer.

pratica're *vt* to practice (*US*), practise (*Brit*); (*SPORT: tennis etc*) to play; (: *nuoto, scherma etc*) to go in for; (*eseguire: apertura, buco*) to make; ~ **uno sconto** to give a discount.

praticità [prátēchētá'] *sf* practicality, practicalness; **per** ~ for practicality's sake.

pra'tico, a, ci, che *ag* practical; ~ **di** (*esperto*) experienced *o* skilled in; (*familiare*) familiar with; **all'atto** ~ in practice; **è** ~ **del mestiere** he knows his trade; **mi è più** ~ **venire di pomeriggio** it's more convenient for me to come in the afternoon.

pra'to *sm* meadow; (*di giardino*) lawn.

preallar'me *sm* warning (signal).

prealpi'no, a *ag* of the Pre-Alps.

pream'bolo *sm* preamble; **senza tanti** ~**i** without beating around the bush.

preannuncia're [pràànnōōnchà'rà], **preannunzia're** [pràànnōōntsyá'rà] *vt* to give advance notice of.

preavvisa're *vt* to give advance notice of.

preavvi'so *sm* notice; **telefonata con** ~ personal *o* person to person call.

prebel'lico, a, ci, che *ag* prewar *cpd.*

precaria'to *sm* temporary employment.

precarietà *sf* precariousness.

preca'rio, a *ag* precarious; (*INS*) temporary, without tenure.

precauziona'le [prākáōōttsyōná'lā] *ag* precautionary.

precauzio'ne [prākáōōttsyō'nā] *sf* caution, care; (*misura*) precaution; **prendere** ~**i** to take precautions.

preceden'te [prāchāden'tā] *ag* previous ♦ *sm* precedent; **il discorso/film** ~ the previous *o* preceding speech/movie; **senza** ~**i** unprecedented; ~**i penali** (*DIR*) criminal record *sg.*

preceden'za [prāchāden'tsà] *sf* priority, precedence; (*AUT*) right of way; **dare** ~ **assoluta a qc** to give sth top priority.

prece'dere [prāche'dārā] *vt* to precede, go (*o* come) before.

precet'to [prāchet'tō] *sm* precept; (*MIL*) call-up notice.

precetto're [prāchāttō'rā] *sm* (private) tutor.

precipita're [prāchēpētá'rā] *vi* (*cadere*) to fall headlong; (*fig: situazione*) to get out of control ♦ *vt* (*gettare dall'alto in basso*) to hurl, fling; (*fig: affrettare*) to rush; ~**rsi** *vr* (*gettarsi*) to hurl *o* fling o.s.; (*affrettarsi*) to rush.

precipita'to, a [prāchēpētá'tō] *ag* hasty ♦ *sm* (*CHIM*) precipitate.

precipitazio'ne [prāchēpētáttsyō'nā] *sf* (*METEOR*) precipitation; (*fig*) haste.

precipito'so, a [prāchēpētō'sō] *ag* (*caduta, fuga*) headlong; (*fig: avventato*) rash, reckless; (: *affrettato*) hasty, rushed.

precipi'zio [prāchēpēt'tsyō] *sm* precipice; **a** ~ (*fig: correre*) headlong.

preci'puo, a [prāchē'pōōō] *ag* principal, main.

precisamen'te [prāchēzámān'tā] *av* (*gen*) precisely; (*con esattezza*) exactly.

precisa're [prāchēzà'rà] *vt* to state, specify; (*spiegare*) to explain (in detail); **vi preciseremo la data in seguito** we'll let you know the exact date later; **tengo a** ~ **che** ... I must point out that ....

precisazio'ne [prāchēzáttsyō'nā] *sf* clarification.

precisio'ne [prāchēzyō'nā] *sf* precision; accuracy; **strumenti di** ~ precision instruments.

preci'so, a [prāchē'zō] *ag* (*esatto*) precise; (*accurato*) accurate, precise; (*deciso: idea*) precise, definite; (*uguale*): **2 vestiti** ~**i** 2 dresses exactly the same; **sono le 9** ~**e** it's exactly 9 o'clock.

preclu'dere *vt* to block, obstruct.

preclu'so, a *pp di* **precludere.**

preco'ce [prāko'chā] *ag* early; (*bambino*) precocious; (*vecchiaia*) premature.

precocità [prăkŏchĕtá'] *sf* (*di morte*) untimeliness; (*di bambino*) precociousness.

preconcet'to, a [prăkŏnchet'tŏ] *ag* preconceived ♦ *sm* preconceived idea, prejudice.

precor'rere *vt* to anticipate; ~ **i tempi** to be ahead of one's time.

precorrito're, tri'ce *sm/f* precursor, forerunner.

precor'so, a *pp di* **precorrere**.

precurso're *sm* forerunner, precursor.

pre'da *sf* (*bottino*) booty; (*animale, fig*) prey; **essere ~ di** to fall prey to; **essere in ~ a** to be prey to.

preda're *vt* to plunder.

predato're *sm* predator.

predecesso're, a [prădăchăssŏ'rā] *sm/f* predecessor.

predel'la *sf* platform, dais; altar-step.

predestina're *vt* to predestine.

predestinazio'ne [prădăstĕnáttsyŏ'nă] *sf* predestination.

predet'to, a *pp di* **predire** ♦ *ag* aforesaid, aforementioned.

pre'dica, che *sf* sermon; (*fig*) lecture, talking-to.

predica're *vt, vi* to preach.

predicati'vo, a *ag* predicative.

predica'to *sm* (*LING*) predicate.

predilet'to, a *pp di* **prediligere** ♦ *ag, sm/f* favorite (*US*), favourite (*Brit*).

predilezio'ne [prădĕlăttsyŏ'nă] *sf* fondness, partiality; **avere una ~ per qc/qn** to be partial to sth/fond of sb.

predili'gere [prădĕlĕ'jārā] *vt* to prefer, have a preference for.

predi're *vt* to foretell, predict.

predispor're *vt* to get ready, prepare; ~ **qn a qc** to predispose sb to sth.

predisposizio'ne [prădĕspŏzĕttsyŏ'nă] *sf* (*MED*) predisposition; (*attitudine*) bent, aptitude; **avere ~ alla musica** to have a bent for music.

predispo'sto, a *pp di* **predisporre**.

predizio'ne [prădĕttsyŏ'nă] *sf* prediction.

predominan'te *ag* predominant.

predomina're *vi* (*prevalere*) to predominate; (*eccellere*) to excel.

predomi'nio *sm* predominance; supremacy.

preesisten'te *ag* pre-existent.

preesi'stere *vi* to pre-exist.

preesisti'to, a *pp di* **preesistere**.

prefabbrica'to, a *ag* (*EDIL*) prefabricated.

prefazio'ne [prăfăttsyŏ'nă] *sf* preface, foreword.

preferen'za [prăfăren'tsá] *sf* preference; **a ~ di** rather than; **di ~** preferably, by preference; **non ho ~e** I have no preferences either way, I don't mind.

preferenzia'le [prăfărăntsyá'lă] *ag* prefer-

ential; **corsia ~** (*AUT*) bus and taxi lane.

preferi'bile *ag*: ~ **(a)** preferable (to), better (than); **sarebbe ~ andarsene** it would be better to go.

preferibilmen'te *av* preferably.

preferi're *vt* to prefer, like better; ~ **il caffè al tè** to prefer coffee to tea, like coffee better than tea.

prefet'to *sm* prefect.

prefettu'ra *sf* prefecture.

prefig'gersi [prăfĕd'jārsĕ] *vr*: ~**rsi uno scopo** to set o.s. a goal.

prefigura're *vt* (*simboleggiare*) to foreshadow; (*prevedere*) to foresee.

prefis'so, a *pp di* **prefiggersi** ♦ *sm* (*LING*) prefix; (*TEL*) area (*US*) *o* dialling (*Brit*) code.

Preg. *abbr* = **pregiatissimo**.

prega're *vi* to pray ♦ *vt* (*REL*) to pray to; (*implorare*) to beg; (*chiedere*): ~ **qn di fare** to ask sb to do; **farsi ~** to need coaxing *o* persuading.

prege'vole [prăjā'vŏlă] *ag* valuable.

pregherò *etc* [prăgăro'] *vb vedi* **pregare**.

preghie'ra [prăgyĕ'rá] *sf* (*REL*) prayer; (*domanda*) request.

pregiar'si [prăjár'sĕ] *vr*: **mi pregio di farle sapere che** ... I am pleased to inform you that ....

pregiatis'simo, a [prăjátĕs'sĕmŏ] *ag* (*in lettere*): ~ **Signor G. Agnelli** G. Agnelli Esquire.

pregia'to, a [prăjá'tŏ] *ag* (*opera*) valuable; (*tessuto*) fine; (*valuta*) strong; **vino ~** vintage wine.

pre'gio [pre'jŏ] *sm* (*stima*) esteem, regard; (*qualità*) (good) quality, merit; (*valore*) value, worth; **il ~ di questo sistema è** ... the merit of this system is ...; **oggetto di ~** valuable object.

pregiudica're [prăjōōdĕká'rā] *vt* to prejudice, harm, be detrimental to.

pregiudica'to, a [prăjōōdĕká'tŏ] *sm/f* (*DIR*) previous offender.

pregiudi'zio [prăjōōdĕt'tsyŏ] *sm* (*idea errata*) prejudice; (*danno*) harm *q*.

pre'gno, a [prăn'yŏ] *ag* (*saturo*): ~ **di** full of, saturated with.

pre'go *escl* (*a chi ringrazia*) don't mention it!; (*invitando qn ad accomodarsi*) please sit down!; (*invitando qn ad andare prima*) after you!

pregusta're *vt* to look forward to.

preisto'ria *sf* prehistory.

preisto'rico, a, ci, che *ag* prehistoric.

prela'to *sm* prelate.

prelavag'gio [prălăvăd'jŏ] *sm* pre-wash.

prelazio'ne [prălăttsyŏ'nă] *sf* (*DIR*) preemption; **avere il diritto di ~ su qc** to have the first option on sth.

prelevamen'to *sm* (*BANCA*) withdrawal; (*di merce*) picking up, collection.

preleva're *vt* (*denaro*) to withdraw; (*campione*) to take; (*merce*) to pick up, collect; (*sog: polizia*) to take, capture.

preliba'to, a *ag* delicious.

prelie'vo *sm* (*BANCA*) withdrawal; (*MED*): **fare un ~ (di)** to take a sample (of).

prelimina're *ag* preliminary; **~i** *smpl* preliminary talks; preliminaries.

prelu'dere *vi*: **~ a** (*preannunciare: crisi, guerra, temporale*) to herald, be a sign of; (*introdurre: dibattito etc*) to introduce, be a prelude to.

prelu'dio *sm* prelude.

prelu'so, a *pp di* preludere.

pré-maman' [prămămầṅ] *sm inv* maternity dress.

prematrimonia'le *ag* premarital.

prematu'ro, a *ag* premature.

premedita're *vt* to premeditate, plan.

premeditazio'ne [prămădētáttsyō'nā] *sf* (*DIR*) premeditation; **con ~** *ag* premeditated ♦ *av* with intent.

pre'mere *vt* to press ♦ *vi*: **~ su** to press down on; (*fig*) to put pressure on; **~ a** (*fig: importare*) to matter to; **~ il grilletto** to pull the trigger.

premes'so, a *pp di* **premettere** ♦ *sf* introductory statement, introduction; **mancano le ~e per una buona riuscita** we lack the basis for a successful outcome.

premet'tere *vt* to put before; (*dire prima*) to start by saying, state first; **premetto che ... I** must say first of all that ...; **premesso che ...** given that ...; **ciò premesso ...** that having been said ....

premia're *vt* to give a prize to; (*fig: merito, onestà*) to reward.

premiazio'ne [prămyáttsyō'nā] *sf* prize-giving.

preminen'te *ag* pre-eminent.

pre'mio *sm* prize; (*ricompensa*) reward; (*COMM*) premium; (*AMM: indennità*) bonus; **in ~ per** as a prize (*o* reward) for; **~ d'ingaggio** (*SPORT*) signing-on fee; **~ di produzione** productivity bonus.

premi'si *etc vb vedi* **premettere**.

premonito're, tri'ce *ag* premonitory.

premonizio'ne [prămōnēttsyō'nā] *sf* premonition.

premunir'si *vr*: **~ di** to provide o.s. with; **~ contro** to protect o.s. from, guard o.s. against.

premu'ra *sf* (*fretta*) haste, hurry; (*riguardo*) attention, care; **aver ~** to be in a hurry; **far ~ a qn** to hurry sb; **usare ogni ~ nei riguardi di qn, circondare qn di ~e** to be very attentive to sb.

premuro'so, a *ag* thoughtful, considerate.

prenata'le *ag* antenatal.

pren'dere *vt* to take; (*andare a prendere*) to get, fetch; (*ottenere*) to get; (*guadagnare*) to get, earn; (*catturare: ladro, pesce*) to catch; (*collaboratore, dipendente*) to take on; (*passeggero*) to pick up; (*chiedere: somma, prezzo*) to charge, ask; (*trattare: persona*) to handle ♦ *vi* (*colla, cemento*) to set; (*pianta*) to take; (*fuoco: nel camino*) to catch; (*voltare*): **~ a destra** to turn (to the) right; **~rsi** *vr* (*azzuffarsi*): **~rsi a pugni** to come to blows; **prende qualcosa?** (*da bere, da mangiare*) would you like something to eat (*o* drink)?; **prendo un caffè** I'll have a coffee; **~ a fare qc** to start doing sth; **~ qn/qc per** (*scambiare*) to take sb/sth for; **~ l'abitudine di** to get into the habit of; **~ fuoco** to catch fire; **~ le generalità di qn** to take down sb's particulars; **~ nota di** to take note of; **~ parte a** to take part in; **~rsi cura di qn/qc** to look after sb/sth; **~rsi un impegno** to take on a commitment; **prendersela** (*adirarsi*) to get annoyed; (*preoccuparsi*) to get upset, worry.

prendiso'le *sm inv* sundress.

prenota're *vt* to book, reserve.

prenotazio'ne [prănōtáttsyō'nā] *sf* booking, reservation.

preoccupan'te *ag* worrying.

preoccupa're *vt* to worry; **~rsi** *vr*: **~rsi di qn/qc** to worry about sb/sth; **~rsi per qn** to be anxious for sb.

preoccupazio'ne [prāōkkōōpáttsyō'nā] *sf* worry, anxiety.

preordina'to, a *ag* preordained.

prepara're *vt* to prepare; (*esame, concorso*) to prepare for; **~rsi** *vr* (*vestirsi*) to get ready; **~rsi a qc/a fare** to get ready *o* prepare (o.s.) for sth/to do; **~ da mangiare** to prepare a meal.

prepara'to, a *ag* (*gen*) prepared; (*pronto*) ready ♦ *sm* (*prodotto*) preparation.

preparato'rio, a *ag* preparatory.

preparazio'ne [prăpárăttsyō'nā] *sf* preparation; **non ha la necessaria ~ per svolgere questo lavoro** he lacks the qualifications necessary for the job.

prepensionamen'to *sm* early retirement.

preponderan'te *ag* predominant.

prepor're *vt* to place before; (*fig*) to prefer.

preposizio'ne [prăpōzēttsyō'nā] *sf* (*LING*) preposition.

prepo'sto, a *pp di* **preporre**.

prepoten'te *ag* (*persona*) domineering, arrogant; (*bisogno, desiderio*) overwhelming, pressing ♦ *sm/f* bully.

prepoten'za [prăpōten'tsà] *sf* arrogance; (*comportamento*) arrogant behavior (*US*) *o* behaviour (*Brit*).

prepu'zio [prăpōōt'tsyō] *sm* (*ANAT*) foreskin.

prerogati'va *sf* prerogative.

pre'sa *sf* taking *q*; catching *q*; *(di città)* capture; *(indurimento: di cemento)* setting; *(appiglio, SPORT)* hold; *(di acqua, gas)* (supply) point; *(ELETTR)*: ~ **(di corrente)** outlet *(US)*, socket *(Brit)*; (: *al muro)* point; *(piccola quantità: di sale etc)* pinch; *(CARTE)* trick; **far** ~ *(colla)* to set; **ha fatto** ~ **sul pubblico** *(fig)* it caught the public's imagination; **a** ~ **rapida** *(cemento)* quick-setting; **di forte** ~ *(fig)* with wide appeal; **essere alle** ~**e con qc** *(fig)* to be struggling with sth; **macchina da** ~ *(CINEMA)* movie camera *(US)*, cine camera *(Brit)*; ~ **d'aria** air inlet; ~ **diretta** *(AUT)* direct drive; ~ **in giro** joke; ~ **di posizione** stand.

presa'gio [prazá'jō] *sm* omen.
presagi're [prazájē'rā] *vt* to foresee.
presala'rio *sm* *(INS)* grant.
pre'sbite *ag* long-sighted.
presbiteria'no, a *ag*, *sm/f* Presbyterian.
presbite'rio *sm* presbytery.
prescin'dere [prāshēn'dārā] *vi*: ~ **da** to leave out of consideration; **a** ~ **da** apart from.
prescis'so, a [prāshēs'sō] *pp di* **prescindere**.
prescola'stico, a [prāshēs'sō] *ag, ci, che* *ag* pre-school *cpd*.
prescrit'to, a *pp di* **prescrivere**.
prescri'vere *vt* to prescribe.
prescrizio'ne [prāskrēttsyō'nā] *sf* *(MED, DIR)* prescription; *(norma)* rule, regulation.
pre'se *etc vb vedi* **prendere**.
presenta're *vt* to present; *(far conoscere)*: ~ **qn (a)** to introduce sb (to); *(AMM: inoltrare)* to submit; ~**rsi** *vr* *(recarsi, farsi vedere)* to present o.s., appear; *(farsi conoscere)* to introduce o.s.; *(occasione)* to arise; ~ **qc in un'esposizione** to show *o* display sth at an exhibition; ~ **qn in società** to introduce sb into society; ~**rsi come candidato** *(POL)* to run *(US) o* stand *(Brit)* as a candidate; ~**rsi bene/male** to have a good/poor appearance; **la situazione si presenta difficile** things aren't looking too good, things look a bit tricky.
presentazio'ne [prāzāntáttsyō'nā] *sf* presentation; introduction.
presentimen'to *sm* premonition.
presen'te *ag* present; *(questo)* this ♦ *sm* present ♦ *sf* *(lettera)*: **con la** ~ **vi comunico ...** this is to inform you that ... ♦ *sm/f* person present; **i** ~**i** those present; **aver** ~ **qc/qn** to remember sth/sb; **essere** ~ **a una riunione** to be present at *o* attend a meeting; **tener** ~ **qn/qc** to keep sb/sth in mind; **esclusi i** ~**i** present company excepted.
presen'za [prāzen'tsá] *sf* presence; *(aspetto esteriore)* appearance; **in** ~ **di** in (the) presence of; **di bella** ~ of good appearance; ~ **di spirito** presence of mind.
presenzia're [prāzāntsyá'rā] *vi*: ~ **a** to be present at, attend.

prese'pio, prese'pe *sm* crib.
preserva're *vt* to protect.
preservati'vo *sm* condom.
pre'si *etc vb vedi* **prendere**.
pre'side *sm/f* *(INS)* principal *(US)*, head (teacher) *(Brit)*; *(di facoltà universitaria)* dean.
presiden'te *sm* *(POL)* president; *(di assemblea, COMM)* chairman; **il P**~ **della Camera** *(POL)* ≈ the Speaker; **P**~ **del Consiglio (dei Ministri)** Prime Minister.
presidentes'sa *sf* president; *(moglie)* president's wife; *(di assemblea, COMM)* chairwoman.
presiden'za [prāsēden'tsá] *sf* presidency; office of president; chairmanship; **assumere la** ~ to become president; to take the chair; **essere alla** ~ to be president *(o* chairman); **candidato alla** ~ presidential candidate; candidate for the chairmanship.
presidenzia'le [prāsēdentsyá'lā] *ag* presidential.
presidia're *vt* to garrison.
presi'dio *sm* garrison.
presie'dere *vt* to preside over ♦ *vi*: ~ **a** to direct, be in charge of.
pre'so, a *pp di* **prendere**.
pres'sa *sb* *(TECN)* press.
pressan'te *ag* *(bisogno, richiesta)* urgent, pressing.
pressappo'co *av* about, roughly, approximately.
pressio'ne *sf* pressure; **far** ~ **su qn** to put pressure on sb; **subire forti** ~**i** to be under strong pressure; ~ **sanguigna** blood pressure.
pres'so *av* *(vicino)* nearby, close at hand ♦ *prep* *(vicino a)* near; *(accanto a)* beside, next to; *(in casa di)*: ~ **qn** at sb's home; *(nelle lettere)* care of *(abbr* c/o); *(alle dipendenza di)*: **lavora** ~ **di noi** he works for *o* with us ♦ *smpl*: **nei** ~**i di** near, in the vicinity of; **ha avuto grande successo** ~ **i giovani** it has been a hit with young people.
pressoché [prāssōkā'] *av* nearly, almost.
pressurizza're [prāssōōrēddzá'rā] *vt* to pressurize.
prestabili're *vt* to arrange beforehand, arrange in advance.
prestano'me *sm/f inv* *(peg)* figurehead.
prestan'te *ag* good-looking.
prestan'za [prāstán'tsá] *sf* (robust) good looks *pl*.
presta're *vt*: ~ **(qc a qn)** to lend (sb sth *o* sth to sb); ~**rsi** *vr* *(offrirsi)*: ~**rsi a fare** to offer to do; *(essere adatto)*: ~**rsi a** to lend itself to, be suitable for; ~ **aiuto** to lend a hand; ~ **ascolto** *o* **orecchio** to listen; ~ **attenzione** to pay attention; ~ **fede a qc/qn** to give credence to sth/sb; ~ **giuramento** to take an

oath; **la frase si presta a molteplici interpretazioni** the phrase lends itself to numerous interpretations.

prestazio'ne [prāstāttsyō'nā] *sf* (*TECN*, *SPORT*) performance; **~i** *sfpl* (*di persona: servizi*) services.

prestigiato're, tri'ce [prāstējātō'rā] *sm/f* conjurer.

presti'gio [prāstē'jō] *sm* (*potere*) prestige; (*illusione*): **gioco di ~** conjuring trick.

prestigio'so, a [prāstējō'sō] *ag* prestigious.

pre'stito *sm* lending *q*; loan; **dar in ~** to lend; **prendere in ~** to borrow; **~ bancario** bank loan; **~ pubblico** public borrowing.

pre'sto *av* (*tra poco*) soon; (*in fretta*) quickly; (*di buon'ora*) early; **a ~** see you soon; **~ o tardi** sooner or later; **fare ~ a fare qc** to hurry up and do sth; (*non costare fatica*) to have no trouble doing sth; **si fa ~ a criticare** it's easy to criticize; **è ancora ~ per decidere** it's still too early o too soon to decide.

presu'mere *vt* to presume, assume.

presumi'bile *ag* (*dati, risultati*) likely.

presun'si *etc vb vedi* **presumere**.

presun'to, a *pp di* **presumere** ♦ *ag*: **il ~ colpevole** the alleged culprit.

presuntuo'so, a *ag* presumptuous.

presunzio'ne [prāzōōntsyō'nā] *sf* presumption.

presuppor're *vt* to suppose; to presuppose.

presuppo'sto, a *pp di* **presupporre** ♦ *sm* (*premessa*) supposition, premise; **partendo dal ~ che ...** assuming that ...; **mancano i ~i necessari** the necessary conditions are lacking.

pre'te *sm* priest.

pretenden'te *sm/f* pretender ♦ *sm* (*corteggiatore*) suitor.

preten'dere *vt* (*esigere*) to demand, require; (*sostenere*): **~ che** to claim that; **pretende di aver sempre ragione** he thinks he's always right.

pretenzio'so, a [prātāntsyō'sō] *ag* pretentious.

preterintenziona'le [prātārēntāntsyōnā'lā] *ag* (*DIR*): **omicidio ~** manslaughter.

prete'so, a *pp di* **pretendere** ♦ *sf* (*esigenza*) claim, demand; (*presunzione, sfarzo*) pretentiousness; **avanzare una ~a** to put forward a claim o demand; **senza ~e** unpretentious ♦ *av* unpretentiously.

prete'sto *sm* pretext, excuse; **con il ~ di** on the pretext of.

pretestuo'so, a *ag* (*data, motivo*) used as an excuse.

preto're *sm* magistrate.

pretu'ra *sf* (*DIR: sede*) circuit o superior court (*US*), magistrate's court (*Brit*); (*: magistratura*) magistracy.

prevalen'te *ag* prevailing.

prevalentemen'te *av* mainly, for the most part.

prevalen'za [prāvālen'tsā] *sf* predominance.

prevale're *vi* to prevail.

preval'so, a *pp di* **prevalere**.

prevarica're *vi* (*abusare del potere*) to abuse one's power.

prevaricazio'ne [prāvārēkāttsyō'nā] *sf* (*abuso di potere*) abuse of power.

prevede're *vt* (*indovinare*) to foresee; (*presagire*) to foretell; (*considerare*) to make provision for; **nulla lasciava ~ che ...** there was nothing to suggest o to make one think that ...; **come previsto** as expected; **spese previste** anticipated expenditure; **previsto per martedi** scheduled for Tuesday.

preve'dibile *ag* predictable; **non era assolutamente ~ che ...** no one could have foreseen that ....

prevedibilmen'te *av* as one would expect.

preveni're *vt* (*anticipare: obiezione*) to forestall; (*: domanda*) to anticipate; (*evitare*) to avoid, prevent; (*avvertire*): **~ qn (di)** to warn sb (of); to inform sb (of).

preventiva're *vt* (*COMM*) to estimate.

preventi'vo, a *ag* preventive ♦ *sm* (*COMM*) estimate; **fare un ~** to give an estimate; **bilancio ~** budget; **carcere ~** custody (*pending trial*).

prevenu'to, a *ag* (*mal disposto*): **~ (contro qc/qn)** prejudiced (against sth/sb).

prevenzio'ne [prāvāntsyō'nā] *sf* prevention; (*preconcetto*) prejudice.

previden'te *ag* showing foresight; prudent.

previden'za [prāvēden'tsā] *sf* foresight; **istituto di ~** provident institution; **~ sociale** welfare (*US*), social security (*Brit*).

previ'di *etc vb vedi* **prevedere**.

pre'vio, a *ag* (*COMM*): **~ avviso** upon notice; **~ pagamento** upon payment.

previsio'ne *sf* forecast, prediction; **~i meteorologiche** o **del tempo** weather forecast *sg*.

previ'sto, a *pp di* **prevedere** ♦ *sm*: **più/meno del ~** more/less than expected; **prima del ~** earlier than expected.

prezio'so, a [prāttsyō'sō] *ag* precious; (*aiuto, consiglio*) invaluable ♦ *sm* jewel; valuable.

prezze'molo [prāttsā'mōlō] *sm* parsley.

prez'zo [pret'tsō] *sm* price; **a ~ di costo** at cost; **tirare sul ~** to bargain, haggle; **il ~ pattuito è 1.000.000 di lire** the agreed price is 1,000,000 lire; **~ d'acquisto/di vendita** buying/selling price; **~ di fabbrica** factory price; **~ di mercato** market price; **~ scontato** reduced price; **~ unitario** unit price.

PRI *sigla m* (*POL*) = *Partito Repubblicano Italiano*.

prigio'ne [prējō'nā] *sf* prison.

prigioni'a [prējōnē'ā] *sf* imprisonment.

prigionie'ro, a [prējōnyē'rō] *ag* captive ♦ *sm/f* prisoner.

pri'ma *sf vedi* **primo** ♦ *av* before; *(in antici-po)* in advance, beforehand; *(per l'addietro)* at one time, formerly; *(più presto)* sooner, earlier; *(in primo luogo)* first ♦ *cong*: ~ **di fare/che parta** before doing/he leaves; ~ **di** *prep* before; ~ **o poi** sooner or later; **due giorni** ~ two days before *o* earlier; ~ **d'ora** before now.

prima'rio, a *ag* primary; *(principale)* chief, leading, primary ♦ *sm/f (medico)* head physician, chief physician.

prima'te *sm (REL. ZOOL)* primate.

primati'sta, i, e *sm/f (SPORT)* record holder.

prima'to *sm* supremacy; *(SPORT)* record.

primave'ra *sf* spring.

primaveri'le *ag* spring *cpd.*

primeggia're [prēmādjá'rā] *vi* to excel, be one of the best.

primiti'vo, a *ag (gen)* primitive; *(significato)* original.

primi'zie [prēmēt'tsyā] *sfpl* early produce *sg.*

pri'mo, a *ag* first; *(fig)* initial; basic; prime ♦ *sm/f* first (one) ♦ *sm (CUC)* first course; *(in date)*: **il** ~ **luglio** the first of July ♦ *sf (TEA-TRO)* first night; *(CINEMA)* première; *(AUT)* first (gear); **le** ~**e ore del mattino** the early hours of the morning; **di** ~**a mattina** early in the morning; **in** ~**a pagina** *(STAMPA)* on the front page; **ai** ~**i freddi** at the first sign of cold weather; **ai** ~**i di maggio** at the beginning of May; **i** ~**i del Novecento** the early twentieth century; **viaggiare in** ~**a** to travel first-class; **per** ~**a cosa** firstly; **in** ~ **luogo** first of all, in the first place; **di prim'ordine** *o* ~**a qualità** first-class, first-rate; **in un** ~ **tempo** *o* **momento** at first; ~**a donna** leading lady; *(di opera lirica)* prima donna.

primoge'nito, a [prēmōje'nētō] *ag, sm/f* firstborn.

primor'di *smpl* beginnings.

primordia'le *ag* primordial.

pri'mula *sf* primrose.

principa'le [prēnchēpá'lā] *ag* main, principal ♦ *sm* manager, boss; **sede** ~ head office.

principalmen'te [prēnchēpálmān'tā] *av* mainly, principally.

principa'to [prēnchēpá'tō] *sm* principality.

prin'cipe [prēn'chēpā] *sm* prince; ~ **ereditario** crown prince.

principe'sco, a, schi, sche [prēnchēpā'skō] *ag (anche fig)* princely.

principes'sa [prēnchēpās'sá] *sf* princess.

principian'te [prēnchēpyán'tā] *sm/f* beginner.

principia're [prēnchēpyá'rā] *vt, vi* to start, begin.

princi'pio [prēnchē'pyō] *sm (inizio)* beginning, start; *(origine)* origin, cause; *(concetto, norma)* principle; **al** *o* **in** ~ at first; **fin dal** ~ right from the start; **per** ~ on principle; **una questione di** ~ a matter of principle; **una**

---

persona di sani ~**i morali** a person of sound moral principles; ~ **attivo** active ingredient.

prio're *sm (REL)* prior.

prio'ri: a ~ *ag inv* prior; **a priori** ♦ *av* at first glance; initially; a priori.

priorità *sf* priority; **avere la** ~ **(su)** to have priority (over).

priorita'rio, a *ag* having priority, of utmost importance.

pri'sma, i *sm* prism.

priva're *vt*: ~ **qn di** to deprive sb of; ~**rsi** *vr*: ~**rsi di** to go *o* do without.

privati'va *sf (ECON)* monopoly.

priva'to, a *ag* private ♦ *sm/f (anche:* ~ **citta-dino)** private citizen; **in** ~ in private; **diritto** ~ *(DIR)* civil law; **ritirarsi a vita** ~**a** to withdraw from public life; **"non vendiamo a** ~**i"** "wholesale only".

privazio'ne [prēvàttsyō'nā] *sf* privation, hardship.

privilegia're [prēvēlājá'rā] *vt* to favor *(US)*, favour *(Brit)*.

privilegia'to, a [prēvēlājá'tō] *ag (individuo, classe)* privileged; *(trattamento, COMM:* credito*)* preferential; **azioni** ~**e** preferred stock *(US)*, preference shares *(Brit)*.

privile'gio [prēvēle'jō] *sm* privilege; **avere il** ~ **di fare** to have the privilege of doing, be privileged to do.

pri'vo, a *ag*: ~ **di** without, lacking.

pro *prep* for, on behalf of ♦ *sm inv (utilità)* advantage, benefit; **a che** ~? what's the use?; **il** ~ **e il contro** the pros and cons.

proba'bile *ag* probable, likely.

probabilità *sf inv* probability; **con molta** ~ very probably, in all probability.

probabilmen'te *av* probably.

proban'te *ag* convincing.

proble'ma, i *sm* problem.

problema'tico, a, ci, che *ag* problematic; *(in-certo)* doubtful ♦ *sf* problems *pl.*

probo'scide [prōbosh'shēdā] *sf (di elefante)* trunk.

procaccia're [prōkáchá'rā] *vt* to get, obtain.

procacciato're [prōkáchátō'rā] *sm* : ~ **d'affari** sales executive.

proca'ce [prōká'chā] *ag (donna, aspetto)* provocative.

proce'dere [prōche'dārā] *vi* to proceed; *(comportarsi)* to behave; *(iniziare)*: ~ **a** to start; ~ **contro** *(DIR)* to start legal proceedings against; ~ **oltre** to go on ahead; **prima di** ~ **oltre** before going any further; **gli affari procedono bene** business is going well; **biso-gna** ~ **con cautela** we have to proceed cautiously; **non luogo a** ~ *(DIR)* nonsuit.

procedimen'to [prōchādēmān'tō] *sm (modo di condurre)* procedure; *(di avvenimenti)* course; *(TECN)* process; ~ **penale** *(DIR)* criminal proceedings *pl.*

procedu'ra [prŏchādōō'rá] *sf* (*DIR*) procedure.

processa're [prŏchăssá'rā] *vt* (*DIR*) to try.

processio'ne [prŏchăssyŏ'nā] *sf* procession.

proces'so [prŏches'sŏ] *sm* (*DIR*) trial; proceedings *pl*; (*metodo*) process; **essere sotto** ~ to be on trial; **mettere sotto** ~ (*anche fig*) to put on trial; ~ **di fabbricazione** manufacturing process.

processua'le [prŏchăssōōá'lā] *ag* (*DIR*): **atti** ~**i** records of a trial; **spese** ~**i** legal costs.

Proc. Gen. *abbr* = **procuratore generale**.

procin'to [prŏchēn'tŏ] *sm*: **in** ~ **di fare** about to do, on the point of doing.

procla'ma, i *sm* proclamation.

proclama're *vt* to proclaim.

proclamazio'ne [prŏklámáttsyŏ'nā] *sf* proclamation, declaration.

procrastina're *vt* (*data*) to postpone; (*pagamento*) to defer.

procrea're *vt* to procreate.

procu'ra *sf* (*DIR*) proxy, power of attorney; (*ufficio*) attorney's office; **per** ~ by proxy; **la P**~ **della Repubblica** the Public Prosecutor's Office.

procura're *vt*: ~ **qc a qn** (*fornire*) to get *o* obtain sth for sb; (*causare: noie etc*) to bring *o* give sb sth.

procurato're, tri'ce *sm/f* (*DIR*) ≈ lawyer; (*: chi ha la procura*) holder of power of attorney; ~ **generale** (*in corte d'appello*) public prosecutor; (*in corte di cassazione*) Attorney General; ~ **legale** ≈ lawyer, solicitor (*Brit*); ~ **della Repubblica** (*in corte d'assise, tribunale*) public prosecutor.

prodiga're *vt* to be lavish with; ~**rsi** *vr*: ~**rsi per qn** to do all one can for sb.

prodi'gio [prŏdē'jŏ] *sm* marvel, wonder; (*persona*) prodigy.

prodigio'so, a [prŏdējŏ'sŏ] *ag* prodigious; phenomenal.

pro'digo, a, ghi, ghe *ag* lavish, extravagant.

prodot'to, a *pp di* **produrre** ♦ *sm* product; ~ **di base** primary product; ~ **finale** end product; ~ **interno lordo (PIL)** gross domestic product (GDP); ~ **nazionale lordo (PNL)** gross national product (GNP); ~**i agricoli** farm produce *sg*; ~**i di bellezza** cosmetics; ~**i chimici** chemicals.

produ'co *etc vb vedi* **produrre**.

produr're *vt* to produce.

produs'si *etc vb vedi* **produrre**.

produttività *sf* productivity.

produtti'vo, a *ag* productive.

produtto're, tri'ce *ag* producing *cpd* ♦ *sm/f* producer; **paese** ~ **di petrolio** oil-producing country.

produzio'ne [prŏdōōttsyŏ'nā] *sf* production; (*rendimento*) output; ~ **in serie** mass production.

proe'mio *sm* introduction, preface.

Prof. *abbr* (= *professore*) Prof.

profana're *vt* to desecrate.

profa'no, a *ag* (*mondano*) secular, profane; (*sacrilego*) profane.

proferi're *vt* to utter.

professa're *vt* to profess; (*medicina etc*) to practice (*US*), practise (*Brit*).

professiona'le *ag* professional; **scuola** ~ training college.

professio'ne *sf* profession; **di** ~ professional, by profession; **libera** ~ profession.

professioni'sta, i, e *sm/f* professional.

professo're, es'sa *sm/f* (*INS*) teacher; (*: di università*) lecturer; (*: titolare di cattedra*) professor; ~ **d'orchestra** member of an orchestra.

profe'ta, i *sm* prophet.

profe'tico, a, ci, che *ag* prophetic.

profetizza're [prŏfātĕddzá'rā] *vt* to prophesy.

profezi'a [prŏfāttsē'á] *sf* prophecy.

profi'cuo, a *ag* useful, profitable.

profila're *vt* to outline; (*ornare: vestito*) to edge; ~**rsi** *vr* to stand out, be silhouetted; to loom up.

profilas'si *sf* (*MED*) preventive treatment, prophylaxis.

profilat'tico, a, ci, che *ag* prophylactic ♦ *sm* (*anticoncezionale*) condom.

profi'lo *sm* profile; (*breve descrizione*) sketch, outline; **di** ~ in profile.

profitta're *vi*: ~ **di** (*trarre profitto*) to profit by; (*approfittare*) to take advantage of.

profit'to *sm* advantage, profit, benefit; (*fig: progresso*) progress; (*COMM*) profit; **ricavare un** ~ **da** to make a profit from *o* out of; **vendere con** ~ to sell at a profit; **conto** ~**i e perdite** profit and loss account.

profon'dere *vt* (*lodi*) to lavish; (*denaro*) to squander; ~**rsi** *vr*: ~**rsi in** to be profuse in.

profondità *sf inv* depth.

profon'do, a *ag* deep; (*rancore, meditazione*) profound ♦ *sm* depth(s *pl*), bottom; ~ **8 metri** 8 meters deep.

profor'ma *ag* routine *cpd* ♦ *sm inv* formality ♦ *av*: **fare qc** ~ to do sth as a formality.

pro'fugo, a, ghi, ghe *sm/f* refugee.

profuma're *vt* to perfume ♦ *vi* to be fragrant; ~**rsi** *vr* to put on perfume *o* scent.

profumatamen'te *av*: **pagare qc** ~ to pay through the nose for sth.

profuma'to, a *ag* (*fiore, aria*) fragrant; (*fazzoletto, saponetta*) scented; (*pelle*) sweet-smelling; (*persona*) wearing perfume.

profumeri'a *sf* perfumery; (*negozio*) perfume shop.

profu'mo *sm* (*prodotto*) perfume, scent; (*fragranza*) scent, fragrance.

profusio'ne *sf* profusion; **a** ~ in plenty.

profu'so, a *pp di* **profondere**.

progenito're, tri'ce [prŏjānĕtŏ'rā] *sm/f*

ancestor.

progetta're [prōjāttá'rā] *vt* to plan; (*TECN*: *edificio*) to plan, design; ~ **di fare qc** to plan to do sth.

progettazio'ne [prōjāttáttsyō'nā] *sf* planning; **in corso di** ~ at the planning stage.

progetti'sta, i, e [prōjāttē'stá] *sm/f* designer.

proget'to [prōjct'tō] *sm* plan; (*idea*) plan, project; **avere in** ~ **di fare qc** to be planning to do sth; ~ **di legge** (*POL*) bill.

pro'gnosi [prōn'yōzē] *sf* (*MED*) prognosis; **essere in** ~ **riservata** to be on the critical list.

program'ma, i *sm* program (*US*), programme (*Brit*); (*TV, RADIO*) program(me)s *pl*; (*INS*) syllabus, curriculum; (*INFORM*) program; **avere in** ~ **di fare qc** to be planning to do sth; ~ **applicativo** (*INFORM*) application program.

programma're *vt* (*TV, RADIO*) to put on; (*INFORM*) to program; (*ECON*) to plan.

programmato're, tri'ce *sm/f* (*INFORM*) computer programer (*US*) *o* programmer (*Brit*).

programmazio'ne [prōgrámmáttsyō'nā] *sf* programing (*US*), programming (*Brit*); planning.

progredi're *vi* to progress, make progress.

progressio'ne *sf* progression.

progressi'sta, i, e *ag, sm/f* progressive.

progressivamen'te *av* progressively.

progressi'vo, a *ag* progressive.

progres'so *sm* progress *q*; **fare** ~**i** to make progress.

proibi're *vt* to forbid, prohibit; ~ **a qn di fare qc** (*vietare*) to forbid sb to do sth; (*impedire*) to prevent sb from doing sth.

proibiti'vo, a *ag* prohibitive.

proibi'to, a *ag* forbidden; "**è** ~ **l'accesso**" "no admittance"; "**è** ~ **fumare**" "no smoking".

proibizio'ne [prōēbēttsyō'nā] *sf* prohibition.

proietta're *vt* (*gen, GEOM, CINEMA*) to project; (: *presentare*) to show, screen; (*luce, ombra*) to throw, cast, project.

proiet'tile *sm* projectile, bullet (*o* shell *etc*).

proietto're *sm* (*CINEMA*) projector; (*AUT*) headlamp; (*MIL*) searchlight.

proiezio'ne [prōyāttsyō'nā] *sf* (*CINEMA*) projection; showing.

pro'le *sf* children *pl*, offspring.

proletaria'to *sm* proletariat.

proleta'rio, a *ag, sm/f* proletarian.

prolifera're *vi* (*fig*) to proliferate.

proli'fico, a, ci, che *ag* prolific.

prolis'so, a *ag* verbose.

pro'logo, ghi *sm* prologue.

prolun'ga, ghe *sf* (*di cavo elettrico etc*) extension.

prolungamen'to *sm* (*gen*) extension; (*di*

strada) continuation.

prolunga're *vt* (*discorso, attesa*) to prolong; (*linea, termine*) to extend.

promemo'ria *sm inv* memorandum.

promes'sa *sf* promise; **fare/mantenere una** ~ to make/keep a promise.

promes'so, a *pp di* **promettere**.

prometten'te *ag* promising.

promet'tere *vt* to promise ♦ *vi* to be *o* look promising; ~ **a qn di fare** to promise sb that one will do.

prominen'te *ag* prominent.

prominen'za [prōmēncn'tsá] *sf* prominence.

promiscuità *sf* promiscuousness.

promi'scuo, a *ag*: **matrimonio** ~ mixed marriage; **nome** ~ (*LING*) common-gender noun.

promi'si *etc vb vedi* **promettere**.

promonto'rio *sm* promontory, headland.

promos'so, a *pp di* **promuovere**.

promoto're, tri'ce *sm/f* promoter, organizer.

promoziona'le [prōmōttsyōná'lā] *ag* promotional; "**vendita** ~" "special offer".

promozio'ne [prōmōttsyō'nā] *sf* promotion; ~ **delle vendite** sales promotion.

promulga're *vt* to promulgate.

promulgazio'ne [prōmōōlgáttsyō'nā] *sf* promulgation.

promuo'vere *vt* to promote.

pronipo'te *sm/f* (*di nonni*) great-grandchild, great-grandson/granddaughter; (*di zii*) great-nephew/niece; ~**i** *smpl* (*discendenti*) descendants.

prono'me *sm* (*LING*) pronoun.

pronomina'le *ag* pronominal.

pronostica're *vt* to foretell, predict.

prono'stico, ci *sm* forecast.

prontez'za [prōntāt'tsá] *sf* readiness; quickness, promptness; ~ **di riflessi** quick reflexes; ~ **di spirito/mente** readiness of wit/mind.

pron'to, a *ag* ready; (*rapido*) fast, quick, prompt; ~! (*TEL*) hello!; **essere** ~ **a fare qc** to be ready to do sth; ~ **all'ira** quick-tempered; **a** ~**a cassa** (*COMM*) collect (*US*) *o* cash (*Brit*) on delivery; ~**a consegna** (*COMM*) prompt delivery; ~ **soccorso** first aid.

prontua'rio *sm* manual, handbook.

pronun'cia [prōnōōn'chá] *sf* pronunciation.

pronuncia're [prōnōōnchá'rā] *vt* (*parola, sentenza*) to pronounce; (*dire*) to utter; (*discorso*) to deliver; ~**rsi** *vr* to declare one's opinion; ~**rsi a favore di/contro** to pronounce o.s. in favor of/against; **non mi pronuncio** I'm not prepared to comment.

pronuncia'to, a [prōnōōnchá'tō] *ag* (*spiccato*) pronounced, marked; (*sporgente*) prominent.

pronun'zia *etc* [prōnōōn'tsyá] = **pronuncia** *etc*.

propagan'da *sf* propaganda.

propaganda're *vt* (*idea*) to propagandize; (*prodotto*, *invenzione*) to push, plug (*fam*).

propaga're *vt* (*notizia*, *malattia*) to spread; (*REL*, *BIOL*) to propagate; **~rsi** *vr* to spread; to propagate; (*FISICA*) to be propagated.

propede'utico, a, ci, che *ag* (*corso*, *trattato*) introductory.

propen'dere *vi*: **~ per** to favor (*US*), favour (*Brit*).

propensio'ne *sf* inclination, propensity; **avere ~ a credere che** ... to be inclined to think that ....

propen'so, a *pp di* **propendere ♦** *ag*: **essere ~ a qc** to be in favor (*US*) *o* favour (*Brit*) of sth; **essere ~ a fare qc** to be inclined to do sth.

propina're *vt* to administer.

propi'zio, a [prŏpĕt'tsyŏ] *ag* favorable (*US*), favourable (*Brit*).

propor're *vt* (*suggerire*): **~ qc (a qn)** to suggest sth (to sb); (*candidato*) to put forward; (*legge*, *brindisi*) to propose; **~ di fare** to suggest *o* propose doing; **proporsi di fare** to propose *o* intend to do; **proporsi una meta** to set o.s. a goal.

proporziona'le [prŏpŏrtsyŏnả'lā] *ag* proportional.

proporziona'to, a [prŏpŏrtsyŏnả'tŏ] *ag*: **~ a** proportionate to, proportional to; **ben ~** well-proportioned.

proporzio'ne [prŏpŏrtsyŏ'nā] *sf* proportion; **in ~ a** in proportion to.

propo'sito *sm* (*intenzione*) intention, aim; (*argomento*) subject, matter; **a ~ di** regarding, with regard to; **a questo ~** on this subject; **di ~** (*apposta*) deliberately, on purpose; **a ~** by the way; **capitare a ~** (*cosa*, *persona*) to turn up at the right time.

proposizio'ne [prŏpŏzĕttsyŏ'nā] *sf* (*LING*) clause; (: *periodo*) sentence.

propo'sto, a *pp di* **proporre ♦** *sf* proposal; (*suggerimento*) suggestion; **fare una ~a** to put forward a proposal; to make a suggestion; **~a di legge** (*POL*) bill.

propriamen'te *av* (*correttamente*) properly, correctly; (*in modo specifico*) specifically; **~ detto** in the strict sense of the word.

proprietà *sf inv* (*ciò che si possiede*) property *gen q*, estate; (*caratteristica*) property; (*correttezza*) correctness; **essere di ~ di qn** to belong to sb; **~ edilizia** (developed) property; **~ privata** private property.

proprieta'rio *sm/f* owner; (*di albergo etc*) proprietor, owner; (*per l'inquilino*) landlord/lady; **~ terriero** landowner.

pro'prio, a *ag* (*possessivo*) own; (: *impersonale*) one's; (*esatto*) exact, correct, proper; (*senso*, *significato*) literal; (*LING*: *nome*) proper; (*particolare*): **~ di** characteristic of,

peculiar to **♦** *av* (*precisamente*) just, exactly; (*davvero*) really; (*affatto*): **non** ... **~** not ... at all **♦** *sm* (*COMM*): **mettersi in ~** to start one's own business; **l'ha visto con i (suoi) ~i occhi** he saw it with his own eyes.

propugna're [prŏpōōnyả'rā] *vt* to support.

propulsio'ne *sf* propulsion; **a ~ atomica** atomic-powered.

propulso're *sm* (*TECN*) propeller.

pro'ra *sf* (*NAUT*) bow(s *pl*), prow.

pro'roga, ghe *sf* extension; postponement.

proroga're *vt* to extend; (*differire*) to postpone, defer.

prorom'pere *vi* to burst out.

prorot'to, a *pp di* **prorompere**.

prorup'pi *etc vb vedi* **prorompere**.

pro'sa *sf* prose; (*TEATRO*): **la stagione della ~** the theater season; **attore di ~** theater actor; **compagnia di ~** theatrical company.

prosa'ico, a, ci, che *ag* (*fig*) prosaic, mundane.

prosci'ogliere [prŏshol'yārā] *vt* to release; (*DIR*) to acquit.

proscioglimen'to [prŏsholyĕmān'tŏ] *sm* acquittal.

prosciol'to, a [prŏshol'tŏ] *pp di* **prosciogliere**.

prosciuga're [prŏshōōgả'rā] *vt* (*terreni*) to drain, reclaim; **~rsi** *vr* to dry up.

prosciut'to [prŏshōōt'tŏ] *sm* ham.

proscrit'to, a *pp di* **proscrivere ♦** *sm/f* exile; outlaw.

proscri'vere *vt* to exile, banish.

prosecuzio'ne [prŏsākōōttsyŏ'nā] *sf* continuation.

proseguimen'to *sm* continuation; **buon ~!** all the best!; (*a chi viaggia*) enjoy the rest of your journey!

prosegui're *vt* to carry on with, continue **♦** *vi* to carry on, go on.

prose'lito *sm* (*REL*, *POL*) convert.

prospera're *vi* to thrive.

prosperità *sf* prosperity.

pro'spero, a *ag* (*fiorente*) flourishing, thriving, prosperous.

prospero'so, a *ag* (*robusto*) hale and hearty; (: *ragazza*) buxom.

prospetta're *vt* (*esporre*) to point out, show; (*ipotesi*) to advance; (*affare*) to outline; **~rsi** *vr* to look, appear.

prospetti'va *sf* (*ARTE*) perspective; (*veduta*) view; (*fig*: *previsione*, *possibilità*) prospect.

prospet'to *sm* (*DISEGNO*) elevation; (*veduta*) view, prospect; (*facciata*) façade, front; (*tabella*) table; (*sommario*) summary.

prospicien'te [prŏspĕchen'tā] *ag*: **~ qc** facing *o* overlooking sth.

prossimamen'te *av* soon.

prossimità *sf* nearness, proximity; **in ~ di** near (to), close to; **in ~ delle feste natalizie** as Christmas approaches.

pros'simo, a *ag* (*vicino*): ~ **a** near (to), close to; (*che viene subito dopo*) next; (*parente*) close ♦ *sm* neighbor (*US*), neighbour (*Brit*), fellow man; **nei ~i giorni** in the next few days; **in un ~ futuro** in the near future; ~ **venturo (pv)** (*AMM*): **venerdì ~ venturo** next Friday.

pro'stata *sf* prostate (gland).

prostitu'ta *sf* prostitute.

prostituzio'ne [prōstētōōttsyō'nä] *sf* prostitution.

prostra're *vt* (*fig*) to exhaust, wear out; **~rsi** *vr* (*fig*) to humble o.s.; **prostrato dal dolore** overcome o prostrate with grief.

prostrazio'ne [prōstráttsyō'nä] *sf* prostration.

protagoni'sta, i, e *sm/f* protagonist.

proteg'gere [prōted'järä] *vt* to protect.

prote'ico, a, ci, che *ag* protein *cpd*; **altamente ~** high in protein.

protei'na *sf* protein.

proten'dere *vt* to stretch out.

prote'so, a *pp di* **protendere**.

prote'sta *sf* protest.

protestan'te *ag, sm/f* Protestant.

protesta're *vt, vi* to protest; **~rsi** *vr*: **~rsi innocente** *etc* to protest one's innocence o that one is innocent *etc*.

prote'sto *sm* (*DIR*) protest; **mandare una cambiale in ~** to dishonor (*US*) o dishonour (*Brit*) a bill.

protetti'vo, a *ag* protective.

protet'to, a *pp di* **proteggere**.

protettora'to *sm* protectorate.

protetto're, tri'ce *sm/f* protector; (*sostenitore*) patron ♦ *ag* (*REL*): **santo ~** patron saint; **società ~trice dei consumatori** consumer protection society.

protezio'ne [prōtáttsyō'nä] *sf* protection; (*patrocinio*) patronage; **misure di ~** protective measures; **~ civile** civil defense (*US*) o defence (*Brit*).

protezioni'smo [prōtáttsyōnēz'mō] *sm* protectionism.

protocolla're *vt* to register ♦ *ag* formal; of protocol.

protocol'lo *sm* protocol; (*registro*) register of documents ♦ *ag inv*: **foglio ~** foolscap; **numero di ~** reference number.

proto'ne *sm* proton.

proto'tipo *sm* prototype.

protrar're *vt* (*prolungare*) to prolong; **protrarsi** *vr* to go on, continue.

protrat'to, a *pp di* **protrarre**.

protuberan'za [prōtōōbärán'tsä] *sf* protuberance, bulge.

Prov. *abbr* (= *provincia*) Prov.

pro'va *sf* (*esperimento, cimento*) test, trial; (*tentativo*) attempt, try; (*MAT, testimonianza etc*) proof *q*; (*DIR*) evidence *q*, proof *q*; (*INS*) exam, test; (*TEATRO*) rehearsal; (*di abito*)

fitting; **a ~ di** (*in testimonianza di*) as proof of; **a ~ di fuoco** fireproof; **assumere in ~** (*per lavoro*) to employ on a trial basis; **essere in ~** (*persona: per lavoro*) to be on trial; **mettere alla ~** to put to the test; **giro di ~** test o trial run; **fino a ~ contraria** until (it's) proved otherwise; **~ a carico/a discarico** (*DIR*) evidence for the prosecution/for the defense; **~ documentale** (*DIR*) documentary evidence; **~ generale** (*TEATRO*) dress rehearsal; **~ testimoniale** (*DIR*) testimonial evidence.

prova're *vt* (*sperimentare*) to test; (*tentare*) to try, attempt; (*assaggiare*) to try, taste; (*sperimentare in sé*) to experience; (*sentire*) to feel; (*cimentare*) to put to the test; (*dimostrare*) to prove; (*abito*) to try on; **~rsi** *vr*: **~rsi (a fare)** to try o attempt (to do); **~ a fare** to try o attempt to do.

provenien'za [prōvänyen'tsä] *sf* origin, source.

proveni're *vi*: **~ da** to come from.

proven'ti *smpl* revenue *sg*.

provenu'to, a *pp di* **provenire**.

Proven'za [prōvän'tsä] *sf*: **la ~** Provence.

provenza'le [prōvántsä'lä] *ag* Provençal.

prover'bio *sm* proverb.

provet'ta *sf* test tube; **bambino in ~** test-tube baby.

provet'to, a *ag* skilled, experienced.

provin'cia, ce o **cie** [prōvēn'chä] *sf* province.

provincia'le [prōvēnchä'lä] *ag* provincial; (**strada**) ~ highway (*US*), main road (*Brit*).

provi'no *sm* (*CINEMA*) screen test; (*campione*) specimen.

provocan'te *ag* (*attraente*) provocative.

provoca're *vt* (*causare*) to cause, bring about; (*eccitare: riso, pietà*) to arouse; (*irritare, sfidare*) to provoke.

provocato're, tri'ce *sm/f* agitator ♦ *ag*: **agente ~** agent provocateur.

provocato'rio, a *ag* provocative.

provocazio'ne [prōvōkáttsyō'nä] *sf* provocation.

provvede're *vi* (*disporre*): **~ (a)** to provide (for); (*prendere un provvedimento*) to take steps, act ♦ *vt*: **~ qc a qn** to supply sth to sb; **~rsi** *vr*: **~rsi di** to provide o.s. with.

provvedimen'to *sm* measure; (*di previdenza*) precaution; **~ disciplinare** disciplinary measure.

provveditora'to *sm* (*AMM*): **~ agli studi** divisional education offices *pl* (*Brit*).

provvedito're *sm* (*AMM*): **~ agli studi** divisional superintendent of education.

provviden'za [prōvvēden'tsä] *sf*: **la ~** providence.

provvidenzia'le [prōvvēdäntsyä'lä] *ag* providential.

provvigio'ne [prōvvējō'nä] *sf* (*COMM*) commission; **lavoro/stipendio a ~** job/salary on a commission basis.

provviso'rio, a *ag* temporary; *(governo)* temporary, provisional.

provvi'sto, a *pp di* **provvedere** ♦ *sf* provision, supply; **fare** ~**e** to take in supplies.

pru'a *sf* (*NAUT*) = **prora.**

pruden'te *ag* cautious, prudent; *(assennato)* sensible, wise.

pruden'za [prōōden'tsá] *sf* prudence, caution; wisdom; **per** ~ as a precaution, to be on the safe side.

pru'dere *vi* to itch, be itchy.

pru'gna [prōōn'yá] *sf* plum; ~ **secca** prune.

prurigino'so, a [prōōrējēnō'sō] *ag* itchy.

pruri'to *sm* itchiness *q*; itch.

PS *sigla* = Pesaro.

P.S. *abbr* (= *postscriptum*) P.S.; (*COMM*) = **partita semplice** ♦ *sigla f vedi* **Pubblica Sicurezza.**

PSDI *sigla m* (*POL*) = *Partito Socialista Democratico Italiano.*

pseudo'nimo *sm* pseudonym.

PSI *sigla m* (*POL*) = *Partito Socialista Italiano.*

psicana'lisi *sf* psychoanalysis.

psicanali'sta, i, e *sm/f* psychoanalyst.

psicanalizza're [psēkánálēddzá'rá] *vt* to psychoanalyse.

psi'che [psē'ká] *sf* psyche.

psichede'lico, a, ci, che [psēkáde'lēkō] *ag* psychedelic.

psichia'tra, i, e [psēkyá'trá] *sm/f* psychiatrist.

psichiatri'a [psēkyátrē'á] *sf* psychiatry.

psichia'trico, a, ci, che [psēkyá'trēkō] *ag* (*caso*) psychiatric; (*reparto, ospedale*) psychiatric, mental.

psi'chico, a, ci, che [psē'kēkō] *ag* psychological.

psicofar'maco, ci *sm* (*MED*) *drug used in treatment of mental conditions.*

psicologi'a [psēkōlōjē'á] *sf* psychology.

psicolo'gico, a, ci, che [psēkōlō'jēkō] *ag* psychological.

psico'logo, a, gi, ghe *sm/f* psychologist.

psicopa'tico, a, ci, che *ag* psychopathic ♦ *sm/f* psychopath.

psico'si *sf inv* (*MED*) psychosis; (*fig*) obsessive fear.

psicosoma'tico, a, ci, che *ag* psychosomatic.

PT *sigla* = Pistoia.

Pt. *abbr* (*GEO*: = *punta*) Pt.

P.T. *abbr* (= *Posta e Telegrafi*) ≈ PO (= *Post Office*); (*FISCO*) = **polizia tributaria.**

P.T.P. *abbr vedi* **posto telefonico pubblico.**

pubblica're *vt* to publish.

pubblicazio'ne [pōōbblēkáttsyō'ná] *sf* publication; ~ **periodica** periodical; ~**i** (**matrimoniali**) *sfpl* (marriage) banns.

pubblici'sta, i, e [pōōbblēchē'stá] *sm/f* (*STAMPA*) freelance journalist.

pubblicità [pōōbblēchētá'] *sf* (*diffusione*) publicity; (*attività*) advertising; (*annunci nei giornali*) advertisements *pl*; **fare** ~ **a qc** to advertise sth.

pubblicita'rio, a [pōōbblēchētá'ryō] *ag* advertising *cpd*; (*trovata, film*) publicity *cpd* ♦ *sm* advertising agent; **annuncio** *o* **avviso** ~ advertisement.

pub'blico, a, ci, che *ag* public; (*statale: scuola etc*) state *cpd* ♦ *sm* public; (*spettatori*) audience; **in** ~ in public; **la** ~**a amministrazione** public administration; **un** ~ **esercizio** a catering (*o* hotel *o* entertainment) business; ~ **funzionario** civil servant; **Ministero della P**~**a Istruzione** ≈ Department of Health, Education and Welfare (*US*), ≈ Department of Education and Science (*Brit*); **P**~ **Ministero** Public Prosecutor's Office; **la P**~**a Sicurezza (P.S.)** the police.

pu'be *sm* (*ANAT*) pubis.

pubertà *sf* puberty.

pu'dico, a, ci, che *ag* modest.

pudo're *sm* modesty.

puericultu'ra *sf* infant care.

pueri'le *ag* childish.

puer'pera *sf woman who has just given birth.*

pugila'to [pōōjēlá'tō] *sm* boxing.

pu'gile [pōō'jēlá] *sm* boxer.

puglie'se [pōōlyá'sá] *ag* of (*o* from) Puglia.

pugnala're [pōōnyàlá'rá] *vt* to stab.

pugna'le [pōōnyá'lá] *sm* dagger.

pu'gno [pōōn'yō] *sm* fist; (*colpo*) punch; (*quantità*) fistful; **avere qn in** ~ to have sb in the palm of one's hand; **tenere la situazione in** ~ to have control of the situation; **scrivere qc di proprio** ~ to write sth in one's own hand.

pul'ce [pōōl'chá] *sf* flea.

pulci'no [pōōlchē'nō] *sm* chick.

pule'dro, a *sm/f* colt/filly.

puleg'gia, ge [pōōlád'já] *sf* pulley.

puli're *vt* to clean; (*lucidare*) to polish; **far** ~ **qc** to have sth cleaned; ~ **a secco** to dry-clean.

puli'to, a *ag* (*anche fig*) clean; (*ordinato*) neat, tidy ♦ *sf* quick clean; **avere la coscienza** ~**a** to have a clear conscience.

pulitu'ra *sf* cleaning; ~ **a secco** dry cleaning.

pulizi'a [pōōlēttsē'á] *sf* (*atto*) cleaning; (*condizione*) cleanness; **fare le** ~**e** to do the cleaning, do the housework.

pul'lman *sm inv* bus.

pullo'ver *sm inv* pullover, jumper.

pullula're *vi* to swarm, teem.

pulmi'no *sm* minibus.

pul'pito *sm* pulpit.

pulsan'te *sm* (push-)button.

pulsa're *vi* to pulsate, beat.

pulsazio'ne [pōōlsáttsyō'ná] *sf* beat.

pulvi'scolo *sm* fine dust.

pu'ma *sm inv* puma.

pungen'te [poonjen'tā] *ag* prickly; stinging; (*anche fig*) biting.

pun'gere [poon'jārā] *vt* to prick; (*sog: insetto, ortica*) to sting; (: *freddo*) to bite; ~ **qn sul vivo** (*fig*) to cut sb to the quick.

pungiglio'ne [poonjēlyo'nā] *sm* sting.

pungola're *vt* to goad.

puni're *vt* to punish.

puniti'vo, a *ag* punitive.

punizio'ne [poonēttsyo'nā] *sf* punishment; (*SPORT*) penalty.

pun'si *etc vb vedi* **pungere**.

pun'ta *sf* point; (*parte terminale*) tip, end; (*di monte*) peak; (*di costa*) promontory; (*minima parte*) touch, trace; **in ~ di piedi** on tiptoe; **ore di ~** peak hours; **uomo di ~** (*SPORT, POL*) front-rank *o* leading man.

punta're *vt* (*piedi a terra, gomiti sul tavolo*) to plant; (*dirigere: pistola*) to point; (*scommettere*): ~ **su** to bet on ♦ *vi* (*mirare*): ~ **a** to aim at; (*avviarsi*): ~ **su** to head *o* make for; (*fig: contare*): ~ **su** to count *o* rely on.

puntaspil'li *sm inv* = **portaspilli**.

punta'ta *sf* (*gita*) short trip; (*scommessa*) bet; (*parte di opera*) installment (*US*), instalment (*Brit*); **farò una ~ a Parigi** I'll pay a flying visit to Paris; **romanzo a ~e** serial.

punteggia're [poontādjā'rā] *vt* to punctuate.

punteggiatu'ra [poontādjāto'rá] *sf* punctuation.

punteg'gio [poontād'jo] *sm* score.

puntella're *vt* to support.

puntel'lo *sm* prop, support.

punteruo'lo *sm* (*TECN*) punch; (: *per stoffa*) bodkin.

punti'glio [poontēl'yo] *sm* obstinacy, stubbornness.

puntiglio'so, a [poontēlyo'so] *ag* punctilious.

punti'na *sf*: ~ **da disegno** thumb tack (*US*), drawing pin (*Brit*); ~**e** *sfpl* (*AUT*) points.

punti'no *sm* dot; **fare qc a** ~ to do sth properly; **arrivare a** ~ to arrive just at the right moment; **cotto a** ~ cooked to perfection; **mettere i** ~**i sulle "i"** (*fig*) to dot the i's and cross the t's.

pun'to, a *pp di* **pungere** ♦ *sm* (*segno, macchiolina*) dot; (*LING*) full stop; (*MAT, momento, di punteggio, fig: argomento*) point; (*posto*) spot; (*a scuola*) mark; (*nel cucire, nella maglia, MED*) stitch ♦ *av*: **non ...** ~ not ... at all; **due** ~**i** *sm inv* (*LING*) colon; **ad un certo** ~ at a certain point; **fino ad un certo** ~ (*fig*) to a certain extent; **sul ~ di fare** (just) about to do; **fare il** ~ (*NAUT*) to take a bearing; **fare il** ~ **della situazione** (*analisi*) to take stock of the situation; (*riassunto*) to sum up the situation; **alle 6 in** ~ at 6 o'clock sharp *o* on the dot; **essere a**

buon ~ to have reached a satisfactory stage; **mettere a** ~ to adjust; (*motore*) to tune; (*cannocchiale*) to focus; (*fig*) to settle; **venire al** ~ to come to the point; **vestito di tutto** ~ all dressed up; **di** ~ **in bianco** point-blank; ~ **d'arrivo** arrival point; ~ **cardinale** point of the compass, cardinal point; ~ **debole** weak point; ~ **esclamativo/interrogativo** exclamation/question mark; ~ **d'incontro** meeting place, meeting point; ~ **morto** standstill; (*comedone*) ~ **nero** blackhead; ~ **nevralgico** (*anche fig*) nerve center; ~ **di partenza** (*anche fig*) starting point; ~ **di riferimento** landmark; (*fig*) point of reference; ~ **di vendita** retail outlet; ~ **e virgola** semicolon; ~ **di vista** (*fig*) point of view; ~**i di sospensione** suspension points.

puntua'le *ag* punctual.

puntualità *sf* punctuality.

puntualizza're [poontoóálēddzá'rā] *vt* to make clear.

puntualmen'te *av* (*gen*) on time; (*ironico: al solito*) as usual.

puntu'ra *sf* (*di ago*) prick; (*di insetto*) sting, bite; (*MED*) puncture; (: *iniezione*) injection; (*dolore*) sharp pain.

punzecchia're [poontsākkyá'rā] *vt* to prick; (*fig*) to tease.

punzona're [poontsoná'rā] *vt* (*TECN*) to stamp.

punzo'ne [poontso'nā] *sm* (*per metalli*) stamp, die.

può, puoi *vb vedi* **potere**.

pu'pa *sf* doll.

pupaz'zo [poopát'tso] *sm* puppet.

pupil'lo, a *sm/f* (*DIR*) ward; (*prediletto*) favorite (*US*), favourite (*Brit*), pet ♦ *sf* (*ANAT*) pupil.

purché [poorkā'] *cong* provided that, on condition that.

pu're *cong* (*tuttavia*) and yet, nevertheless; (*anche se*) even if ♦ *av* (*anche*) too, also; **pur di** (*al fine di*) just to; **faccia** ~! go ahead!, please do!

purè *sm*, **pure'a** *sf* (*CUC*) purée; (: *di patate*) mashed potatoes.

purez'za [poorāt'tsá] *sf* purity.

pur'ga, ghe *sf* (*MED*) purging *q*; purge; (*POL*) purge.

purgan'te *sm* (*MED*) purgative, purge.

purga're *vt* (*MED, POL*) to purge; (*pulire*) to clean.

purgato'rio *sm* purgatory.

purifica're *vt* to purify; (*metallo*) to refine.

purificazio'ne [poorēfēkáttsyo'nā] *sf* purification; refinement.

purita'no, a *ag, sm/f* puritan.

pu'ro, a *ag* pure; (*acqua*) clear, limpid; (*vino*) undiluted; **di razza** ~**a** thoroughbred; **per** ~ **caso** by sheer chance, purely by

chance.
purosan'gue *sm/f inv* thoroughbred.
purtrop'po *av* unfortunately.
pus *sm* pus.
pusilla'nime *ag* cowardly.
pu'stola *sf* pimple.
putaca'so *av* just supposing, suppose.
putife'rio *sm* rumpus, row.
putrefa're *vi* to putrefy, rot.
putrefat'to, a *pp di* **putrefare**.
putrefazio'ne [pootrāfáttsyō'nā] *sf* putrefaction.
pu'trido, a *ag* putrid, rotten.
putta'na *sf* (*fam!*) whore (*!*).
put'to *sm* cupid.
puz'za [poot'tsá] *sf* = **puzzo**.
puzza're [poottsá'rā] *vi* to stink; **la faccenda puzza (d'imbroglio)** the whole business stinks.
puz'zo [poot'tsō] *sm* stink, foul smell.
puz'zola [poot'tsōlá] *sf* polecat.
puzzolen'te [poottsōlen'tā] *ag* stinking.
PV *sigla* = *Pavia.*
pv *abbr vedi* **prossimo venturo**.
PZ *sigla* = *Potenza.*

Q

Q, q [koo] *sf o m inv* (*lettera*) Q, q; **Q come Quarto** ≈ Q for Queen.
q *abbr* (= *quintale*) q.
Qatar' [kátár'] *sm*: **il ~** Qatar.
Q.G. *abbr* = **quartiere generale**.
Q.I. *abbr vedi* **quoziente d'intelligenza**.
qua *av* here; **in ~** (*verso questa parte*) this way; **~ dentro/sotto** *etc* in/under here *etc*; **da un anno in ~** for a year now; **da quando in ~?** since when?; **per di ~** (*passare*) this way; **al di ~ di** (*fiume, strada*) on this side of; *vedi* **questo**.
quac'chero, a [kwák'kārō] *sm/f* Quaker.
quader'no *sm* notebook; (*per scuola*) exercise book.
quadran'golo *sm* quadrangle.
quadran'te *sm* quadrant; (*di orologio*) face.
quadra're *vi* (*bilancio*) to balance, tally; (*fig: corrispondere*): **~ (con)** to correspond (with) ♦ *vt* (*MAT*) to square; **far ~ il bilancio** to balance the books; **non mi quadra** I don't like it.
quadra'to, a *ag* square; (*fig: equilibrato*) level-headed, sensible; (: *peg*) square ♦ *sm* (*MAT*) square; (*PUGILATO*) ring; **5 al ~** 5 squared.
quadretta'to, a *ag* (*foglio*) squared; (*tessuto*) checked.
quadret'to *sm*: **a ~i** (*tessuto*) checked; (*foglio*) squared.
quadrienna'le *ag* (*che dura 4 anni*) four-year *cpd*; (*che avviene ogni 4 anni*) four-yearly.
quadrifo'glio [kwādrēfol'yō] *sm* four-leaf clover.
quadrimes'tre *sm* (*periodo*) four-month period; (*INS*) term.
qua'dro *sm* (*pittura*) painting, picture; (*quadrato*) square; (*tabella*) table, chart; (*TECN*) board, panel; (*TEATRO*) scene; (*fig: scena, spettacolo*) sight; (: *descrizione*) outline, description; **~i** *smpl* (*POL*) party organizers; (*COMM*) managerial staff; (*MIL*) cadres; (*CARTE*) diamonds; **a ~i** (*disegno*) checked; **fare un ~ della situazione** to outline the situation; **~ clinico** (*MED*) case history; **~ di comando** control panel; **~i intermedi** middle management *sg*.
quadru'pede *sm* quadruped.
quadruplica're *vt* to quadruple.
qua'druplo, a *ag, sm* quadruple.
quaggiù [kwādjoo'] *av* down here.
qua'glia [kwál'yá] *sf* quail.
qual'che [kwál'kā] *det* some; (*alcuni*) a few; (*in espressioni interrogative*) any; (*uno*): **c'è ~ medico?** is there a doctor?; **ho comprato ~ libro** I've bought some *o* a few books; **ha ~ sigaretta?** have you any cigarettes?; **una persona di ~ rilievo** a person of some importance; **~ cosa** = **qualcosa**; **in ~ modo** somehow; **~ volta** sometimes.
qualchedu'no [kwálkādoo'nō] *pronome* = **qualcuno**.
qualco'sa *pronome* something; (*in espressioni interrogative*) anything; **qualcos'altro** something else; anything else; **~ di nuovo** something new; anything new; **~ da mangiare** something to eat; anything to eat; **c'è ~ che non va?** is there something *o* anything wrong?
qualcu'no *pronome* (*persona*) someone, somebody; (: *in espressioni interrogative*) anyone, anybody; (*alcuni*) some; **~ è favorevole a noi** some are on our side; **qualcun altro** someone *o* somebody else; anyone *o* anybody else.
qua'le *det* what; (*discriminativo*) which; (*come*) as ♦ *pronome* (*interrogativo*) which; (*relativo*): **il(la) ~** (*persona: soggetto*) who; (: *oggetto, con preposizione*) whom; (*cosa*) which; (*possessivo*): **la signora della ~ ammiriamo la bellezza** the lady whose beauty we admire ♦ *av* (*in qualità di*) as; **~ disgrazia!** what a misfortune!; **in un certo qual modo** in some way or other, somehow or other; **per la qual cosa** for which reason;

accetterò ~i che siano le condizioni I'll accept whatever the conditions; a tutti coloro i ~i fossero interessati ... to whom it may concern ...; ~ legale della signora as the lady's lawyer.

quali'fica, che sf qualification; (titolo) title.

qualifica're vt to qualify; (definire): ~ qn/qc come to describe sb/sth as; ~rsi vr (anche SPORT) to qualify; ~rsi a un concorso to pass a competitive exam.

qualificati'vo, a ag qualifying.

qualifica'to, a ag (dotato di qualifica) qualified; (esperto, abile) skilled; non mi ritengo ~ per questo lavoro I don't think I'm qualified for this job; è un medico molto ~ he is a very distinguished doctor.

qualificazio'ne [kwálčfčkáttsyō'nä] sf qualification; gara di ~ (SPORT) qualifying event.

qualità sf inv quality; di ottima o prima ~ top quality; in ~ di in one's capacity as; in ~ di amica as a friend; articoli di ogni ~ all sorts of goods; controllo (di) ~ quality control; prodotto di ~ quality product.

qualitati'vo, a ag qualitative.

qualo'ra cong in case, if.

qualsi'asi, qualun'que det inv any; (quale che sia) whatever; (discriminativo) whichever; (posposto: mediocre) poor, indifferent; ordinary; mettiti un vestito ~ put on any old dress; ~ cosa anything; ~ cosa accada whatever happens; a ~ costo at any cost, whatever the cost; l'uomo ~ the man in the street; ~ persona anyone, anybody.

qualunqui'sta, i, e sm/f person indifferent to politics.

quan'do cong, av when; ~ sarò ricco when I'm rich; da ~ (dacché) since; (interrogativo): da ~ sei qui? how long have you been here?; di ~ in ~ from time to time; quand'anche even if.

quantifica're vt to quantify.

quantità sf inv quantity; (gran numero): una ~ di a great deal of; a lot of; in grande ~ in large quantities.

quantitati'vo, a ag quantitative ♦ sm (COMM: di merce) amount, quantity.

quan'to, a det (interrogativo: quantità) how much; (: numero) how many; (esclamativo) what a lot of, how much (o many); (relativo) as much ... as; as many ... as ♦ pronome (interrogativo) how much; how many; (: tempo) how long; (relativo) as much as; as many as; ~i(e) pronome pl (persone) all those who ♦ av (interrogativo: con ag, av) how; (: con vb) how much; (esclamativo: con ag, av) how; (: con vb) how much, what a lot; (con valore relativo) as much as; ho ~ denaro mi occorre I have as much money as I need; studierò ~ posso I'll study as much as o all I can; ~i ne abbiamo oggi? what is

the date today?; ~i anni hai? how old are you?; ~ costa?, quant'è? how much does it cost?, how much is it?; in ~ (in qualità di) as; (poiché) since, as; (in) ~ a as for; a ~ dice lui according to him; per ~ sia brava, fa degli errori however good she may be, she makes mistakes; per ~ io sappia as far as I know; ~ prima as soon as possible; ~ tempo? how long?, how much time?; ~ più ... tanto meno the more ... the less; ~ più ... tanto più the more ... the more; saranno scelti ~i hanno fatto la richiesta in tempo all those whose applications arrived in time will be selected; in risposta a ~ esposto nella sua lettera ... in answer to the points raised in your letter ....

quantun'que cong although, though.

quaran'ta num forty.

quarante'na sf quarantine.

quaranten'ne ag, sm/f forty-year-old.

quaranten'nio sm (period of) forty years.

quarante'simo, a num fortieth.

quaranti'na sf: una ~ (di) about forty.

quarantot'to sm inv forty-eight; fare un ~ (fam) to raise hell.

quare'sima sf: la ~ Lent.

quar'ta sf vedi quarto.

quartet'to sm quartet(te).

quartie're sm district, area; (MIL) quarters pl; ~ generale (Q.G.) headquarters pl (HQ); ~ residenziale residential area o district; i ~i alti the rich districts.

quar'to, a ag fourth ♦ sm fourth; (quarta parte) quarter ♦ sf (AUT) fourth (gear); (INS: elementare) fourth year of grade school; (: superiore) seventh year of high school; un ~ di vino a quarter-liter (US) o quarter-litre (Brit) bottle of wine; le 6 e un ~ a quarter after (US) o past (Brit) 6; ~ d'ora quarter of an hour; tre ~i d'ora three quarters of an hour; le otto e tre ~i, le nove meno un ~ (a) quarter of (US) o to nine; passare un brutto ~ d'ora (fig) to have a bad o nasty time of it; ~i di finale (SPORT) quarterfinals.

quar'zo [kwár'tsō] sm quartz.

qua'si av almost, nearly ♦ cong (anche: ~ che) as if; (non) ... ~ mai hardly ever; ~ ~ me ne andrei I've half a mind to leave.

quassù av up here.

quat'to, a ag crouched, squatting; (silenzioso) silent; ~ ~ very quietly; stealthily.

quattordicen'ne [kwáttŏrdčchen'nä] ag, sm/f fourteen-year-old.

quattor'dici [kwáttŏr'dčchē] num fourteen.

quattri'ni smpl money sg, cash sg.

quat'tro num four; in ~ e quattr'otto in less than no time; dirne ~ a qn to give sb a piece of one's mind; fare il diavolo a ~ to kick up a ruckus (US) o rumpus (Brit); fare ~ chiac-

chiere to have a chat; **farsi in ~ per qn** to go out of one's way for sb, put o.s. out for sb.

quattroc'chi [kwàttrok'kē] *sm inv* (*fig fam*: *persona con occhiali*) four-eyes; **a ~** *av* (*tra 2 persone*) face to face; (*privatamente*) in private.

quattrocente'sco, a, schi, sche [kwàttrōchāntā'skō] *ag* fifteenth-century.

quattrocen'to [kwàttrōchen'tō] *num* four hundred ♦ *sm*: **il Q~** the fifteenth century.

quattromi'la *num* four thousand.

quel'lo, a *det* (*dav sm* **quel** + *C*, **quell'** + *V*, **quello** + *s impura, gn, pn, ps, x, z*; *pl* **quei** + *C*, **quegli** + *V o s impura, gn, pn, ps, x, z*; *dav sf* **quella** + *C*, **quell'** + *V*; *pl* **quelle**) that; those *pl* ♦ *pronome* that (one); those (ones) *pl*; (*ciò*) that; **~(a) che** the one who; **~i(e) che** those who; **ho fatto ~ che potevo** I did what I could; **~(a) ... lì o là** *det* that; **quell'uomo lì** that man; **~(a) lo o là** *pronome* that one; **~ bianco** the white one; **da ~ che ho sentito** from what I've heard; **in quel di Milano** in the Milan area *o* region.

quer'cia, ce [kwer'chá] *sf* oak (tree); (*legno*) oak.

quere'la *sf* (*DIR*) (legal) action.

querela're *vt* to bring an action against.

quesi'to *sm* question, query; problem.

que'sti *pronome* (*poetico*) this person.

questiona'rio *sm* questionnaire.

questio'ne *sf* problem, question; (*controversia*) issue; (*litigio*) quarrel; **in ~** in question; **il caso in ~** the matter at hand; **la persona in ~** the person involved; **non voglio essere chiamato in ~** I don't want to be dragged into the argument; **fuor di ~** out of the question; **è ~ di tempo** it's a matter *o* question of time.

que'sto, a *det* this; these *pl* ♦ *pronome* this (one); those (ones) *pl*; (*ciò*) this; **~(a) ... qui** *o* **qua** *det* this; **~ ragazzo qui** this boy; **~(a) qui** *o* **qua** *pronome* this one; **io prendo ~ cappotto, tu prendi quello** I'll take this coat, you take that one; **preferisce ~i o quelli?** do you prefer these (ones) or those (ones)?; **vengono Paolo e Mario: ~ da Roma, quello da Palermo** Paolo and Mario are coming: the latter from Rome, the former from Palermo; **quest'oggi** today; **e con ~?** so what?; **e con ~ se n'è andato** and with that he left; **con tutto ~** in spite of this, despite all this; **~ è quanto** that's all.

questo're *sm* ≈ police commissioner (*US*), ≈ chief constable (*Brit*).

que'stua *sf* collection (of alms).

questu'ra *sf* police headquarters *pl*.

questuri'no *sm* (*fam*: *poliziotto*) cop.

qui *av* here; **da** *o* **di ~** from here; **di ~ in avanti** from now on; **di ~ a poco/una settimana** in a little while/a week's time; **~**

dentro/sopra/vicino in/up/near here; *vedi* **questo**.

quiescen'za [kwyāshen'tsá] *sf* (*AMM*): **porre qn in ~** to retire sb.

quietan'za [kwyātán'tsá] *sf* receipt.

quieta're *vt* to calm, soothe.

quie'te *sf* quiet, quietness; calmness; stillness; peace; **turbare la ~ pubblica** (*DIR*) to disturb the peace.

quie'to, a *ag* quiet; (*notte*) calm, still; (*mare*) calm; **l'ho fatto per il ~ vivere** I did it for a quiet life.

quin'di *av* then ♦ *cong* therefore, so.

quindicen'ne [kwēndēchen'nā] *ag*, *sm/f* fifteen-year-old.

quin'dici [kwēn'dēchē] *num* fifteen; **~ giorni** two weeks, a fortnight (*Brit*).

quindici'na [kwēndēchē'ná] *sf* (*serie*): **una ~ (di)** about fifteen; **fra una ~ di giorni** in two weeks.

quindicina'le [kwēndēchēná'lā] *ag* semimonthly (*US*), fortnightly (*Brit*) ♦ *sm* (*rivista*) semimonthly (*US*), fortnightly magazine (*Brit*).

quinquenna'le *ag* (*che dura 5 anni*) five-year *cpd*; (*che avviene ogni 5 anni*) five-yearly.

quinquen'nio *sm* period of five years.

quinta *sf vedi* **quinto**.

quinta'le *sm* quintal (*100 kg*).

quintet'to *sm* quintet (te).

quin'to, a *num* fifth ♦ *sf* (*AUT*) fifth (gear); (*INS*: *elementare*) fifth year of primary school; (: *superiore*) final year of secondary school; (*TEATRO*) wing; **un ~ della popolazione** a fifth of the population; **tre ~i** three fifths; **in ~a pagina** on the fifth page, on page five.

qui pro quo *sm inv* misunderstanding.

Qu'ito *sf* Quito.

quiz [kwēdz] *sm inv* (*domanda*) question; (*anche*: **gioco a ~**) quiz game.

quo'rum *sm* quorum.

quo'ta *sf* (*parte*) quota, share; (*AER*) height, altitude; (*IPPICA*) odds *pl*; **prendere/perdere ~** (*AER*) to gain/lose height *o* altitude; **~ imponibile** taxable income; **~ d'iscrizione** (*INS*) enrolment fee; (*ad una gara*) entry fee; (*ad un club*) membership fee; **~ di mercato** market share.

quota're *vt* (*BORSA*) to quote; (*valutare*: *anche fig*) to value; **è un pittore molto quotato** he is rated highly as a painter.

quotazio'ne [kwōtáttsyō'nā] *sf* quotation.

quotidianamen'te *av* daily, every day.

quotidia'no, a *ag* daily; (*banale*) everyday ♦ *sm* (*giornale*) daily (paper).

quozien'te [kwōttsyen'tā] *sm* (*MAT*) quotient; **~ di crescita zero** zero growth rate; **~ d'intelligenza (Q.I.)** intelligence quotient (IQ).

R

R, r |er'rā] *sf o m (lettera)* R, r; **R come Roma**
≈ R for Roger.

R *abbr (POSTA)* = **raccomandata**; *(FERR)* =
rapido.

RA *sigla* = *Ravenna*.

rabar'baro *sm* rhubarb.

Rabat' *sf* Rabat.

rabbercia're [ràbbārchà'rā] *vt (anche fig)* to
patch up.

rab'bia *sf (ira)* anger, rage; *(accanimento,
furia)* fury; *(MED: idrofobia)* rabies *sg*.

rabbi'no *sm* rabbi.

rabbio'so, a *ag* angry, furious; *(facile all'ira)*
quick-tempered; *(forze, acqua etc)* furious,
raging; *(MED)* rabid, mad.

rabboni're *vt*, ~**rsi** *vr* to calm down.

rabbrividi're *vi* to shudder, shiver.

rabbuiar'si *vr* to grow dark.

rabdoman'te *sm* water diviner.

racc. *abbr (POSTA)* = **raccomandata**.

raccapezzar'si [ràkkàpàttsàr'sē] *vr*: **non** ~ to
be at a loss.

raccapriccian'te [ràkkàprēchàn'tā] *ag* horrifying.

raccapric'cio [ràkkàprēch'chō] *sm* horror.

raccattapal'le *sm inv (SPORT)* ballboy.

raccatta're *vt* to pick up.

racchet'ta [ràkkāt'tá] *sf (per tennis)* racket;
(per ping-pong) paddle *(US)*, bat *(Brit)*; ~
da neve snowshoe; ~ **da sci** ski pole.

rac'chio, a [ràk'kyō] *ag (fam)* ugly.

racchiu'dere [ràkkyōō'dārā] *vt* to contain.

racchiu'so, a [ràkkyōō'sō] *pp di* **racchiudere**.

racco'gliere [ràkkol'yārā] *vt* to collect;
(raccattare) to pick up; *(frutti, fiori)* to pick,
pluck; *(AGR)* to harvest; *(approvazione, voti)*
to win; *(profughi)* to take in; *(vele)* to furl;
(capelli) to put up; ~**rsi** *vr* to gather; *(fig)* to
gather one's thoughts, to meditate; **non ha
raccolto** *(allusione)* he didn't take the hint;
(frecciata) he took no notice of it; ~ **i frutti
del proprio lavoro** *(fig)* to reap the benefits
of one's work; ~ **le idèe** *(fig)* to gather one's
thoughts.

raccoglimen'to [ràkkōlyēmān'tō] *sm* meditation.

raccoglito're [ràkkōlyētō'rā] *sm (cartella)*
folder, binder; ~ **a fogli mobili** loose-leaf
binder.

raccol'to, a *pp di* **raccogliere** ♦ *ag (persona:*

pensoso) thoughtful; *(luogo: appartato)* secluded, quiet ♦ *sm (AGR)* crop, harvest ♦ *sf*
collecting *q*; collection; *(AGR)* harvesting *q*,
gathering *q*; harvest, crop; **fare la** ~**a di qc**
to collect sth; **chiamare a** ~**a** to gather together.

raccomanda'bile *ag* (highly) commendable;
è un tipo poco ~ he is not to be trusted.

raccomanda're *vt* to recommend; *(affidare)*
to entrust; ~**rsi** *vr*: ~**rsi a qn** to commend
o.s. to sb; ~ **a qn di fare qc** to recommend
that sb does sth; ~ **a qn di non fare qc** to
tell *o* warn sb not to do sth; ~ **qn a qn/alle
cure di qn** to entrust sb to sb/to sb's care; **mi
raccomando!** don't forget!

raccomanda'to, a *ag (lettera, pacco)*
certified *(US)*, recorded-delivery *(Brit)*;
(candidato) recommended ♦ *sm/f*: **essere
un(a)** ~**(a) di ferro** to have friends in high
places ♦ *sf (anche:* **lettera** ~**a)** certified *(US)*
o recorded-delivery *(Brit)* letter; ~**a con ricevuta di ritorno (Rrr)** certified letter with return notice *(US)*, recorded-delivery letter
with advice of receipt *(Brit)*.

raccomandazio'ne [ràkkōmàndáttsyō'nā] *sf*
recommendation; **lettera di** ~ letter of introduction.

raccomoda're *vt (riparare)* to repair, mend.

racconta're *vt*: ~ **(a qn)** *(dire)* to tell (sb);
(narrare) to relate (to sb), tell (sb) about; **a
me non la racconti** don't try and kid me;
cosa mi racconti di nuovo? what's new?

raccon'to *sm* telling *q*, relating *q*; *(fatto
raccontato)* story, tale; *(genere letterario)*
short story; ~**i per bambini** children's stories.

raccorcia're [ràkkōrchà'rā] *vt* to shorten.

raccorda're *vt* to link up, join.

raccor'do *sm (TECN: giunzione)* connection,
joint; *(AUT: di autostrada)* entrance *(o exit)*
ramp *(US)*,˙ slip road *(Brit)*; ~ **anulare**
(AUT) beltway *(US)*, ring road *(Brit)*.

rachi'tico, a, ci, che [ràkē'tēkō] *ag* suffering
from rickets; *(fig)* scraggy, scrawny.

rachiti'smo [ràkētēz'mō] *sm (MED)* rickets *sg*.

racimola're [ràchēmōlà'rā] *vt (fig)* to scrape
together, glean.

ra'da *sf (natural)* harbor *(US) o* harbour
(Brit).

ra'dar *sm inv* radar.

raddolci're [ràddōlchē'rā] *vt (persona, carattere)* to soften; ~**rsi** *vr (tempo)* to grow
milder; *(persona)* to soften, mellow.

raddoppiamen'to *sm* doubling.

raddoppia're *vt, vi* to double.

raddop'pio *sm (gen)* doubling; *(BILIARDO)*
double; *(EQUITAZIONE)* gallop.

raddrizza're [ràddrēttsà'rā] *vt* to straighten;
(fig: correggere) to put straight, correct.

ra'dere *vt (barba)* to shave off; *(mento)* to

shave; (*fig: rasentare*) to graze; to skim; ~**rsi** *vr* to shave (o.s.); ~ **al suolo** to raze to the ground.

radia'le *ag* radial.

radian'te *ag* (*calore, energia*) radiant.

radia're *vt* to strike off.

radiato're *sm* radiator.

radiazio'ne [ràdyàttsyō'nā] *sf* (*FISICA*) radiation; (*cancellazione*) striking off.

radica'le *ag* radical ♦ *sm* (*LING*) root; (*MAT, POL*) radical.

radica'to, a *ag* (*pregiudizio, credenza*) deepseated, deeply-rooted.

radic'chio [ràdēk'kyō] *sm variety of chicory.*

radi'ce [ràdē'chā] *sf* root; **segno di** ~ (*MAT*) radical sign; **colpire alla** ~ (*fig*) to strike at the root; **mettere** ~**i** (*idee, odio etc*) to take root; (*persona*) to put down roots; ~ **quadrata** (*MAT*) square root.

ra'dio *sf inv* radio ♦ *sm* (*CHIM*) radium; **trasmettere per** ~ to broadcast; **stazione/ponte** ~ radio station/link; ~ **ricevente/trasmittente** receiver/transmitter.

radioabbona'to, a *sm/f* radio subscriber.

radioamato're, tri'ce *sm/f* amateur radio operator, ham (*fam*).

radioascoltato're, tri'ce *sm/f* (*radio*) listener.

radioattività *sf* radioactivity.

radioatti'vo, a *ag* radioactive.

radiocomanda're *vt* to operate by remote control.

radiocomanda'to, a *ag* remote-controlled.

radiocoman'do *sm* remote control.

radiocomunicazio'ne [ràdyōkōmōōnēkàttsyō'nā] *sf* radio message.

radiocro'naca, che *sf* radio commentary.

radiocroni'sta, i, e *sm/f* radio commentator.

radiodiffusio'ne *sf* (*radio*) broadcasting.

radiofo'nico, a, ci, che *ag* radio *cpd*.

radiografa're *vt* to X-ray.

radiografi'a *sf* radiography; (*foto*) X-ray photograph.

radioli'na *sf* transistor (radio).

radiologi'a [ràdyōlōjē'à] *sf* radiology.

radio'logo, a, gi, ghe *sm/f* radiologist.

radioriceven'te [ràdyōrēchàven'tā] *sf* (*anche*: **apparecchio** ~) receiver.

radio'so, a *ag* radiant.

radiostazio'ne [ràdyōstàttsyō'nā] *sf* radio station.

radiosve'glia [ràdyōzvāl'yà] *sf* clock radio.

radiotec'nico, a, ci, che *ag* radio engineering *cpd* ♦ *sm* radio engineer.

radiotelegrafi'sta, i, e *sm/f* radiotelegrapher.

radioterapi'a *sf* radiotherapy.

radiotrasmitten'te *ag* (*radio*) broadcasting *cpd* ♦ *sf* (*radio*) broadcasting station.

ra'do, a *ag* (*capelli*) sparse, thin; (*visite*) infrequent; **di** ~ rarely; **non di** ~ not uncommonly.

raduna're *vt*, ~**rsi** *vr* to gather, assemble.

raduna'ta *sf* (*MIL*) muster.

radu'no *sm* gathering, meeting.

radu'ra *sf* clearing.

ra'fano *sm* horseradish.

raffazzona're [ràffàttsōnà'rā] *vt* to patch up.

raffer'mo, a *ag* stale.

raf'fica, che *sf* (*METEOR*) gust (of wind); ~ **di colpi** (*di fucile*) burst of gunfire.

raffigura're *vt* to represent.

raffina're *vt* to refine.

raffinatez'za [ràffēnàtàt'tsà] *sf* refinement.

raffina'to, a *ag* refined.

raffineri'a *sf* refinery.

rafforza're [ràffōrtsà'rā] *vt* to reinforce.

rafforzati'vo, a [ràffōrtsàtē'vō] *ag* (*LING*) intensifying ♦ *sm* (*LING*) intensifier.

raffreddamen'to *sm* cooling.

raffredda're *vt* to cool; (*fig*) to dampen, have a cooling effect on; ~**rsi** *vr* to grow cool *o* cold; (*prendere un raffreddore*) to catch a cold; (*fig*) to cool (off).

raffredda'to, a *ag* (*MED*): **essere** ~ to have a cold.

raffreddo're *sm* (*MED*) cold.

raffronta're *vt* to compare.

raffron'to *sm* comparison.

ra'fia *sf* (*fibra*) raffia.

raganel'la *sf* (*ZOOL*) tree frog.

ragaz'zo, a [ràgàt'tsō] *sm/f* boy/girl; (*fam: fidanzato*) boyfriend/girlfriend; **nome da** ~**a** maiden name; ~**a madre** unmarried mother; ~**a squillo** call girl.

raggela're [ràdjàlà'rā] *vt, vi*, ~**rsi** *vr* to freeze.

raggian'te [ràdjàn'tā] *ag* radiant, shining; ~ **di gioia** beaming *o* radiant with joy.

raggie'ra [ràdje'rà] *sf* (*di ruota*) spokes *pl*; **a** ~ with a sunburst pattern.

rag'gio [ràd'jō] *sm* (*di sole etc*) ray; (*MAT, distanza*) radius; (*di ruota etc*) spoke; **nel** ~ **di 20 km** within a radius of 20 km *o* a 20-km radius; **a largo** ~ (*esplorazione, incursione*) wide-ranging; ~ **d'azione** range; ~ **laser** laser beam; ~**i X** X-rays.

raggira're [ràdjērà'rā] *vt* to take in, trick.

raggi'ro [ràdjē'rō] *sm* trick.

raggiun'gere [ràdjōōn'jàrā] *vt* to reach; (*persona: riprendere*) to catch up (with); (*bersaglio*) to hit; (*fig: meta*) to achieve; ~ **il proprio scopo** to reach one's goal, achieve one's aim; ~ **un accordo** to come to *o* reach an agreement.

raggiun'to, a [ràdjōōn'tō] *pp di* **raggiungere**.

raggomitolar'si *vr* to curl up.

raggranella're *vt* to scrape together.

raggrinza're [ràggrēntsà'rā] *vt, vi* (*anche*: ~**rsi**) to wrinkle.

raggruma're *vt*, ~**rsi** *vr* (*sangue, latte*) to clot.

raggruppamen'to *sm* (*azione*) grouping;

(gruppo) group; (: *MIL*) unit.

raggruppa're *vt* to group (together).

ragguaglia're [ràggwàlyà'rà] *vt* (*paragonare*) to compare; (*informare*) to inform.

raggua'glio [ràggwàl'yō] *sm* comparison; (*informazione, relazione*) piece of information.

ragguarde'vole *ag* (*degno di riguardo*) distinguished, notable; (*notevole: somma*) considerable.

ra'gia [rà'jà] *sf*: **acqua** ~ turpentine.

ragionamen'to [ràjōnàmàn'tō] *sm* reasoning *q*; argument.

ragiona're [ràjōnà'rà] *vi* (*usare la ragione*) to reason; (*discorrere*): ~ **(di)** to argue (about); **cerca di** ~ try and be reasonable.

ragio'ne [ràjō'nà] *sf* reason; (*dimostrazione, prova*) argument, reason; (*diritto*) right; **aver** ~ to be right; **aver** ~ **di qn** to get the better of sb; **dare** ~ **a qn** (*sog: persona*) to side with sb; (: *fatto*) to prove sb right; **farsi una** ~ **di qc** to accept sth, come to terms with sth; **in** ~ **di** at the rate of; **a** *o* **con** ~ rightly, justly; **perdere la** ~ to become insane; (*fig*) to take leave of one's senses; **a ragion veduta** after due consideration; **per** ~**i di famiglia** for family reasons; ~ **di scambio** terms of trade; ~ **sociale** (*COMM*) corporate name; **ragion di stato** reason of State.

ragioneri'a [ràjōnàrē'à] *sf* accountancy; (*ufficio*) accounts department.

ragione'vole [ràjōnà'vōlà] *ag* reasonable.

ragionie're, a [ràjōnye'rà] *sm/f* accountant.

raglia're [ràlyà'rà] *vi* to bray.

ragnate'la [rànyàtà'là] *sf* cobweb, spider's web.

ra'gno [ràn'yō] *sm* spider; **non cavare un** ~ **dal buco** (*fig*) to draw a blank.

ragù *sm inv* (*CUC*) meat sauce (*for pasta*).

RAI-TV [ràētēvōō'] *sigla f* = *Radio televisione italiana*.

rallegramen'ti *smpl* congratulations.

rallegra're *vt* to cheer up; ~**rsi** *vr* to cheer up; (*provare allegrezza*) to rejoice; ~**rsi con qn** to congratulate sb.

rallentamen'to *sm* slowing down; slackening.

rallenta're *vt, vi* to slow down; ~ **il passo** to slacken one's pace.

rallentato're *sm* (*CINEMA*) slow-motion camera; **al** ~ (*anche fig*) in slow motion.

ramanzi'na [ràmàndzē'nà] *sf* lecture, telling-off.

rama're *vt* (*superficie*) to copper, coat with copper; (*AGR: vite*) to spray with copper sulphate.

ramar'ro *sm* green lizard.

rama'to, a *ag* (*oggetto: rivestito di rame*) copper-coated, coppered; (*capelli, barba*) copper *cpd*.

ra'me *sm* (*CHIM*) copper; **di** ~ copper *cpd*;

incisione su ~ copperplate.

ramifica're *vi* (*BOT*) to put out branches; ~**rsi** *vr* (*diramarsi*) to branch out; (*MED: tumore, vene*) to ramify; ~**rsi in** (*biforcarsi*) to branch into.

ramificazio'ne [ràmēfēkàttsyō'nà] *sf* ramification.

ramin'go, a, ghi, ghe *ag* (*poetico*): **andare** ~ to go wandering, wander.

rami'no *sm* (*CARTE*) rummy.

rammaricar'si *vr*: ~ **(di)** (*rincrescersi*) to be sorry (about), regret; (*lamentarsi*) to complain (about).

ramma'rico, chi *sm* regret.

rammenda're *vt* to mend; (*calza*) to darn.

rammen'do *sm* mending *q*; darning *q*; mend; darn.

rammenta're *vt* to remember, recall; ~**rsi** *vr*: ~**rsi (di qc)** to remember (sth); ~ **qc a qn** to remind sb of sth.

rammolli're *vt* to soften ♦ *vi* (*anche:* ~**rsi**) to go soft.

rammolli'to, a *ag* weak ♦ *sm/f* weakling.

ra'mo *sm* branch; (*di commercio*) field; **non è il mio** ~ it's not my field *o* line.

ramoscel'lo [ràmōshcl'lō] *sm* twig.

ram'pa *sf* flight (of stairs); ~ **di lancio** launching pad.

rampican'te *ag* (*BOT*) climbing.

rampi'no *sm* (*gancio*) hook; (*NAUT*) grapnel.

rampol'lo *sm* (*di acqua*) spring; (*BOT: germoglio*) shoot; (*fig: discendente*) descendant.

rampo'ne *sm* harpoon; (*ALPINISMO*) crampon.

ra'na *sf* frog; ~ **pescatrice** angler fish.

ran'cido, a [ràn'chēdō] *ag* rancid.

ran'cio [ràn'chō] *sm* (*MIL*) mess; **ora del** ~ mess time.

ranco're *sm* rancor (*US*), rancour (*Brit*), resentment; **portare** ~ **a qn, provare** ~ **per** *o* **verso qn** to bear sb a grudge.

randa'gio, a, gi, gie *o* **ge** [ràndà'jō] *ag* (*gatto, cane*) stray.

randel'lo *sm* club, cudgel.

ran'go, ghi *sm* (*grado*) rank; (*condizione sociale*) station, social standing; **persone di** ~ **inferiore** people of lower standing; **uscire dai** ~**ghi** to fall out; (*fig*) to step out of line.

Rangun' *sf* Rangoon.

rannicchiar'si [rànnēkkyàr'sē] *vr* to crouch, huddle.

rannuvolar'si *vr* to cloud over, become overcast.

ranoc'chio [rànok'kyō] *sm* (edible) frog.

rantola're *vi* to wheeze.

rantoli'o *sm* (*il respiro affannoso*) wheezing; (: *di agonizzante*) death rattle.

ran'tolo *sm* wheeze; death rattle.

ranun'colo *sm* (*BOT*) buttercup.

ra'pa *sf* (*BOT*) turnip.

rapa'ce [ràpà'chā] *ag* (*animale*) predatory; (*fig*) rapacious, grasping ♦ *sm* bird of prey.

rapa're *vt* (*capelli*) to crop, cut very short.

ra'pida *sf vedi* **rapido**.

rapidamen'te *av* quickly, rapidly.

rapidità *sf* speed.

ra'pido, a *ag* fast; (*esame, occhiata*) quick, rapid ♦ *sm* (*FERR*) express (train) ♦ *sf* (*di fiume*) rapid.

rapimen'to *sm* kidnapping; (*fig*) rapture.

rapi'na *sf* robbery; ~ **in banca** bank robbery; ~ **a mano armata** armed robbery.

rapina're *vt* to rob.

rapinato're, tri'ce *sm/f* robber.

rapi're *vt* (*cose*) to steal; (*persone*) to kidnap; (*fig*) to enrapture, delight.

rapi'to, a *ag* (*persona*) kidnapped; (*fig: in estasi*): **ascoltare** ~ **qn** to be captivated by sb's words ♦ *sm/f* kidnapped person.

rapito're, tri'ce *sm/f* kidnapper.

rappacifica're [ràppàchēfēkà'rā] *vt* (*riconciliare*) to reconcile; ~**rsi** *vr* (*uso reciproco*) to be reconciled, make it up (*fam*).

rappacificazio'ne [ràppàchēfēkàttsyō'nā] *sf* reconciliation.

rappezza're [ràppāttsà'rā] *vt* to patch.

rapporta're *vt* (*confrontare*) to compare; (*riprodurre*) to reproduce.

rappor'to *sm* (*resoconto*) report; (*legame*) relationship; (*MAT, TECN*) ratio; ~**i** *smpl* (*fra persone, paesi*) relations; **in** ~ **a quanto è successo** with regard to *o* in relation to what happened; **fare** ~ **a qn su qc** to report sth to sb; **andare a** ~ **da qn** to report to sb; **chiamare qn a** ~ (*MIL*) to summon sb; **essere in buoni/cattivi** ~**i con qn** to be on good/bad terms with sb; ~ **d'affari,** ~ **di lavoro** business relations; ~ **di compressione** (*TECN*) pressure ratio; ~ **coniugale** marital relationship; ~ **di trasmissione** (*TECN*) gear; ~**i sessuali** sexual intercourse *sg*.

rappren'dersi *vr* to coagulate, clot; (*latte*) to curdle.

rappresa'glia [ràppràsàl'yà] *sf* reprisal, retaliation.

rappresentan'te *sm/f* representative; ~ **di commercio** sales representative, sales rep (*fam*); ~ **sindacale** union delegate *o* representative.

rappresentan'za [ràppràzàntàn'tsà] *sf* delegation, deputation; (*COMM: ufficio, sede*) agency; **in** ~ **di qn** on behalf of sb; **spese di** ~ entertainment expenses; **macchina di** ~ official car; **avere la** ~ **di** to be the agent for; ~ **esclusiva** sole agency; **avere la** ~ **esclusiva** to be sole agent.

rappresenta're *vt* to represent; (*TEATRO*) to perform; **farsi** ~ **dal proprio legale** to be represented by one's lawyer.

rappresentati'vo, a *ag* representative ♦ *sf* (*di partito, sindacale*) representative group; (*SPORT: squadra*) representative (team).

rappresentazio'ne [ràppràzàntàttsyō'nā] *sf* representation; performing *q*; (*spettacolo*) performance; **prima** ~ **assoluta** world première.

rappre'so, a *pp di* **rapprendere**.

rapsodi'a *sf* rhapsody.

rap'tus *sm inv:* ~ **di follia** fit of madness.

raramen'te *av* seldom, rarely.

rarefa're *vt,* ~**rsi** *vr* to rarefy.

rarefat'to, a *pp di* **rarefare** ♦ *ag* rarefied.

rarefazio'ne [ràràfàttsyō'nā] *sf* rarefaction.

rarità *sf inv* rarity.

ra'ro, a *ag* rare.

rasa're *vt* (*barba etc*) to shave off; (*siepi, erba*) to trim, cut; ~**rsi** *vr* to shave (o.s.).

rasa'to, a *ag* (*erba*) trimmed, cut; (*tessuto*) smooth; **avere la barba** ~**a** to be clean-shaven.

rasatu'ra *sf* shave.

raschiamen'to [ràskyàmàn'tō] *sm* (*MED*) curettage; ~ **uterino** D and C.

raschia're [ràskyà'rā] *vt* to scrape; (*macchia, fango*) to scrape off ♦ *vi* to clear one's throat.

rasenta're *vt* (*andar rasente*) to keep close to; (*sfiorare*) to skim along (*o* over); (*fig*) to border on.

rasen'te *prep:* ~ (**a**) close to, very near.

ra'so, a *pp di* **radere** ♦ *ag* (*barba*) shaved; (*capelli*) cropped; (*con misure di capacità*) level; (*pieno: bicchiere*) full to the brim ♦ *sm* (*tessuto*) satin; ~ **terra** close to the ground; **volare** ~ **terra** to hedgehop; **un cucchiaio** ~ a level spoonful.

raso'io *sm* razor; ~ **elettrico** electric shaver *o* razor.

ra'spo *sm* (*di uva*) grape stalk.

rasse'gna [ràssān'yà] *sf* (*MIL*) inspection, review; (*esame*) inspection; (*resoconto*) review, survey; (*pubblicazione letteraria etc*) review; (*mostra*) exhibition, show; **passare in** ~ (*MIL, fig*) to review.

rassegna're [ràssānyà'rā] *vt:* ~ **le dimissioni** to resign, hand in one's resignation; ~**rsi** *vr* (*accettare*): ~**rsi (a qc/a fare)** to resign o.s. (to sth/to doing).

rassegnazio'ne [ràssānyàttsyō'nā] *sf* resignation.

rasserena're *vt* (*persona*) to cheer up; ~**rsi** *vr* (*tempo*) to clear up.

rassetta're *vt* to tidy, put in order; (*aggiustare*) to repair, mend.

rassicuran'te *ag* reassuring.

rassicura're *vt* to reassure; ~**rsi** *vr* to take heart, recover one's confidence.

rassicurazio'ne [ràssēkōōràttsyō'nā] *sf* reassurance.

rassoda're *vt* to harden, stiffen; (*fig*) to

strengthen, consolidate.

rassomiglian'za |ràssōmēlyàn'tsà| *sf* resemblance.

rassomiglia're |ràssōmēlyá'rā| *vi*: ~ **a** to resemble, look like.

rastrellamen'to *sm* (*MIL, di polizia*) (thorough) search.

rastrella're *vt* to rake; (*fig: perlustrare*) to comb.

rastrellie'ra *sf* rack; (*per piatti*) dish rack.

rastrel'lo *sm* rake.

ra'ta *sf* (*quota*) installment (*US*), instalment; **pagare a ~e** to pay by instal(l)ments *o* on hire purchase (*Brit*); **comprare/vendere a ~e** to buy/sell on the installment plan (*US*) *o* on hire purchase (*Brit*).

ratea'le *ag*: **pagamento** ~ payment by instal(l)ments; **vendita** ~ installment plan (*US*), hire purchase (*Brit*).

ratea're, rateizza're |rátāēddzà'rā| *vt* to divide into instal(l)ments.

rateazio'ne |rátāàttsyō'nā| *sf* division into instal(l)ments.

ra'teo *sm* (*COMM*) accrual.

rati'fica, che *sf* ratification.

ratifica're *vt* (*DIR*) to ratify.

rat'to *sm* (*DIR*) abduction; (*ZOOL*) rat.

rattoppa're *vt* to patch.

rattop'po *sm* patching *q*; patch.

rattrappi're *vt* to make stiff; **~rsi** *vr* to be stiff.

rattrista're *vt* to sadden; **~rsi** *vr* to become sad.

rauce'dine |ràōōche'dēnā| *sf* hoarseness.

ra'uco, a, chi, che *ag* hoarse.

ravanel'lo *sm* radish.

ravenna'te *ag* of (*o* from) Ravenna.

ravio'li *smpl* ravioli *sg.*

ravveder'si *vr* to mend one's ways.

ravvia're *vt* (*capelli*) to tidy; **~rsi i capelli** to tidy one's hair.

ravvicinamen'to |ràvvēchēnàmān'tō| *sm* (*tra persone*) reconciliation; (*POL*: *tra paesi etc*) rapprochement.

ravvicina're |ràvvēchēnà'rā| *vt* (*avvicinare*): ~ **qc a** to bring sth nearer to; (*oggetti*) to bring closer together; (*fig: persone*) to reconcile, bring together; **~rsi** *vr* to be reconciled.

ravvisa're *vt* to recognize.

ravviva're *vt* to revive; (*fig*) to brighten up, enliven; **~rsi** *vr* to revive; to brighten up.

Rawalpin'di |ràvàlpēn'dē| *sf* Rawalpindi.

razioci'nio |ràtsyōchē'nyō| *sm* reasoning *q*; reason; (*buon senso*) common sense.

raziona'le |ràtsyōnà'lā| *ag* rational.

razionalità |ràttsyōnálētá'| *sf* rationality; (*buon senso*) common sense.

razionamen'to |ràttsyōnàmān'tō| *sm* rationing.

raziona're |ràttsyōnà'rā| *vt* to ration.

razio'ne |ràttsyō'nā| *sf* ration; (*porzione*) portion, share.

raz'za |ràt'tsà| *sf* race; (*ZOOL*) breed; (*discendenza, stirpe*) stock, race; (*sorta*) sort, kind.

razzi'a |ràttsē'à| *sf* raid, foray.

razzia'le |ràttsyà'lā| *ag* racial.

razzi'smo |ràttsēz'mō| *sm* racism, racialism.

razzi'sta, i, e |ràttsē'stà| *ag, sm/f* racist, racialist.

raz'zo |ràd'dzō| *sm* rocket; ~ **di segnalazione** flare; ~ **vettore** vector rocket.

razzola're |ràttsōlà'rā| *vi* (*galline*) to scratch about.

RC *sigla* = *Reggio Calabria.*

RDT *sigla f vedi* **Repubblica Democratica Tedesca.**

RE *sigla* = *Reggio Emilia.*

re *sm inv* (*sovrano*) king; (*MUS*) D; (: *solfeggiando la scala*) re.

reagen'te |rāàjen'tà| *sm* reagent.

reagi're |rāàjē'rā| *vi* to react.

rea'le *ag* real; (*di, da re*) royal ♦ *sm*: **il ~** reality; **i R~i** the Royal family.

reali'smo *sm* realism.

reali'sta, i, e *sm/f* realist; (*POL*) royalist.

reali'stico, a, ci, che *ag* realistic.

realizza're |rāàlēddzà'rā| *vt* (*progetto etc*) to realize, carry out; (*sogno, desiderio*) to realize, fulfil; (*scopo*) to achieve; (*COMM: titoli etc*) to realize; (*CALCIO etc*) to score; **~rsi** *vr* to be realized.

realizzazio'ne |rāàlēddzàttsyō'nā| *sf* realization; fulfilment; achievement; ~ **scenica** stage production.

realiz'zo |rāàlēd'dzō| *sm* (*conversione in denaro*) conversion into cash; (*vendita forzata*) clearance sale.

realmen'te *av* really, actually.

realtà *sf inv* reality; **in** ~ (*in effetti*) in fact; (*a dire il vero*) really.

rea'me *sm* kingdom, realm; (*fig*) realm.

rea'to *sm* offense (*US*), offence (*Brit*).

reatto're *sm* (*FISICA*) reactor; (*AER: aereo*) jet; (: *motore*) jet engine.

reaziona'rio, a |rāàttsyōnà'ryō| *ag, sm/f* (*POL*) reactionary.

reazio'ne |rāàttsyō'nā| *sf* reaction; **motore/aereo a** ~ jet engine/plane; **forze della** ~ reactionary forces; ~ **a catena** (*anche fig*) chain reaction.

reb'bio *sm* prong.

re'bus *sm inv* rebus; (*fig*) puzzle; enigma.

recapita're *vt* to deliver.

reca'pito *sm* (*indirizzo*) address; (*consegna*) delivery; **ha un ~ telefonico?** do you have a telephone number where you can be reached?; ~ **a domicilio** home delivery (service).

reca're *vt* (*portare*) to bring; (*avere su di sé*) to carry, bear; (*cagionare*) to cause, bring; ~**rsi** *vr* to go; ~ **danno a qn** to harm sb, cause harm to sb.

rece'dere [rāche'dārā] *vi* to withdraw.

recensio'ne [rāchānsyō'nā] *sf* review.

recensi're [rāchānse'rā] *vt* to review.

recenso're, a [rāchānsō'rā] *sm/f* reviewer.

recen'te [rāchen'tā] *ag* recent; **di** ~ recently; **più** ~ latest, most recent.

recentemen'te [rāchāntāmān'tā] *av* recently.

recepi're [rāchāpē'rā] *vt* to understand, take in.

recessio'ne [rāchāssyō'nā] *sf* (*ECON*) recession.

reces'so [rāches'sō] *sm* (*azione*) recession, receding; (*DIR*) withdrawal; (*luogo*) recess.

recherò *etc* [rākāro'] *vb vedi* **recare**.

reci'dere [rāchē'dārā] *vt* to cut off, chop off.

recidi'vo, a [rāchēdē'vō] *sm/f* (*DIR*) second (*o* habitual) offender, recidivist.

recinta're [rāchēntā'rā] *vt* to enclose, fence off.

recin'to [rāchen'tō] *sm* enclosure; (*ciò che recinge*) fence; surrounding wall.

recinzio'ne [rāchēntsyō'nā] *sf* (*azione*) enclosure, fencing-off; (*recinto: di legno*) fence; (: *di mattoni*) wall; (: *reticolato*) wire fencing; (: *a sbarre*) railings *pl*.

recipien'te [rāchēpyen'tā] *sm* container.

reci'proco, a, ci, che [rāchē'prōkō] *ag* reciprocal.

reci'so, a [rāchē'zō] *pp di* **recidere**.

re'cita [re'chētá] *sf* performance.

re'cital [re'chētál] *sm inv* recital.

recita're [rāchētā'rā] *vt* (*poesia, lezione*) to recite; (*dramma*) to perform; (*ruolo*) to play *o* act (the part of).

recitazio'ne [rāchētāttsyō'nā] *sf* recitation; (*di attore*) acting; **scuola di** ~ drama school.

reclama're *vi* to complain ♦ *vt* (*richiedere*) to demand.

récla'me [rāklám'] *sf inv* advertising *q*; advertisement, advert (*Brit*), ad (*fam*).

reclamizza're [rāklāmēddzá'rā] *vt* to advertise.

recla'mo *sm* complaint; **sporgere** ~ **a** to complain to, make a complaint to.

reclina'bile *ag* (*sedile*) reclining.

reclina're *vt* (*capo*) to bow, lower; (*sedile*) to tilt.

reclusio'ne *sf* (*DIR*) imprisonment.

reclu'so, a *sm/f* prisoner.

re'cluta *sf* recruit.

reclutamen'to *sm* recruitment.

recluta're *vt* to recruit.

recon'dito, a *ag* secluded; (*fig*) secret, hidden.

re'cord *ag inv* record *cpd* ♦ *sm inv* record; **in tempo** ~, **a tempo di** ~ in record time; **detenere il** ~ **di** to hold the record for; ~ **mondiale** world record.

recrimina're *vi*: ~ (**su qc**) to complain (about sth).

recriminazio'ne [rākrēmēnáttsyō'nā] *sf* recrimination.

recrudescen'za [rākrōōdāshen'tsá] *sf* fresh outbreak.

recupera're *etc* = **ricuperare** *etc*.

redargui're *vt* to rebuke.

redas'si *etc vb vedi* **redigere**.

redat'to, a *pp di* **redigere**.

redatto're, tri'ce *sm/f* (*STAMPA*) editor; (: *di articolo*) writer; (*di dizionario etc*) compiler; ~ **capo** chief editor.

redazio'ne [rādāttsyō'nā] *sf* editing; writing; (*sede*) editorial office(s); (*personale*) editorial staff; (*versione*) version.

redditi'zio, a [rāddētēt'tsyō] *ag* profitable.

red'dito *sm* income; (*dello Stato*) revenue; (*di un capitale*) yield; ~ **complessivo** gross income; ~ **disponibile** disposable income; ~ **fisso** fixed income; ~ **imponibile/non imponibile** taxable/non-taxable income; ~ **da lavoro** earned income; ~ **nazionale** national income; ~ **pubblico** public revenue.

reden'si *etc vb vedi* **redimere**.

reden'to, a *pp di* **redimere**.

redento're *sm*: **il R**~ the Redeemer.

redenzio'ne [rādāntsyō'nā] *sf* redemption.

redi'gere [rādē'jārā] *vt* to write; (*contratto*) to draw up.

redi'mere *vt* to deliver; (*REL*) to redeem.

re'dini *sfpl* reins.

redivi'vo, a *ag* returned to life, reborn.

re'duce [rā'dōōchā] *ag* (*gen*): ~ **da** returning from, back from ♦ *sm/f* survivor; (*veterano*) veteran; **essere** ~ **da** (*esame, colloquio*) to have been through; (*malattia*) to be just over.

re'fe *sm* thread.

referen'dum *sm inv* referendum.

referen'za [rāfāren'tsá] *sf* reference.

refer'to *sm* medical report.

refetto'rio *sm* refectory.

refezio'ne [rāfēttsyō'nā] *sf* (*INS*) school meal.

refratta'rio, a *ag* refractory; (*fig*): **essere** ~ **alla matematica** to have no aptitude for mathematics.

refrigeran'te [rāfrējārán'tā] *ag* (*TECN*) cooling, refrigerating; (*bevanda*) refreshing ♦ *sm* (*CHIM: fluido*) coolant; (*TECN: apparecchio*) refrigerator.

refrigera're [rāfrējārá'rā] *vt* to refrigerate; (*rinfrescare*) to cool, refresh.

refrigerazio'ne [rāfrējārāttsyō'nā] *sf* refrigeration; (*TECN*) cooling; ~ **ad acqua** (*AUT*) water-cooling.

refrige'rio [rāfrēje'ryō] *sm*: **trovare** ~ to find somewhere cool.

refurti'va *sf* stolen goods *pl*.

Reg. *abbr* (= *reggimento*) Regt; (*AMM*) = **re-**

golamento.

regala're *vt* to give (as a present), make a present of.

rega'le *ag* regal.

rega'lo *sm* gift, present ♦ *ag inv:* **confezione ~** gift pack; **fare un ~ a qn** to give sb a present; "**articoli da ~**" "gifts".

rega'ta *sf* regatta.

reggen'te [rādjen'tā] *ag (proposizione)* main; *(sovrano)* reigning ♦ *sm/f* regent; **principe ~** prince regent.

reggen'za [rādjen'tsà] *sf* regency.

reg'gere [red'jārā] *vt (tenere)* to hold; *(sostenere)* to support, bear, hold up; *(portare)* to carry, bear; *(resistere)* to withstand; *(dirigere: impresa)* to manage, run; *(governare)* to rule, govern; *(LING)* to take, be followed by ♦ *vi (resistere):* **~ a** to stand up to, hold out against; *(sopportare):* **~ a** to stand; *(durare)* to last; *(fig: teoria etc)* to hold water; **~rsi** *vr (stare ritto)* to stand; *(fig: dominarsi)* to control o.s.; **~rsi sulle gambe** *o* **in piedi** to stand up.

reg'gia, ge [red'jà] *sf* royal palace.

reggical'ze [rādjekàl'tsā] *sm inv* garter (US) *o* suspender (Brit) belt.

reggimen'to [rādjēmān'tō] *sm (MIL)* regiment.

reggipet'to [rādjēpet'tō] *sm*, **reggise'no** [rādjē'sānō] *sm* bra.

regi'a, gi'e [rājē'à] *sf (TV, CINEMA etc)* direction.

regi'me [rājē'mā] *sm (POL)* regime; *(DIR: aureo, patrimoniale etc)* system; *(MED)* diet; *(TECN)* (engine) speed; **~ di giri** *(di motore)* revs *pl* per minute; **~ vegetariano** vegetarian diet.

regi'na [rājē'nà] *sf* queen.

re'gio, a, gi, gie [re'jō] *ag* royal.

regiona'le [rājōnà'lā] *ag* regional.

regio'ne [rājō'nā] *sf (gen)* region; *(territorio)* region, area.

regi'sta, i, e [rājē'stà] *sm/f (TV, CINEMA etc)* director.

registra're [rājēstrà'rā] *vt (AMM)* to register; *(COMM)* to enter; *(notare)* to report, note; *(canzone, conversazione, sog: strumento di misura)* to record; *(mettere a punto)* to adjust, regulate; **~ i bagagli** *(AER)* to check in one's luggage; **~ i freni** *(TECN)* to adjust the brakes.

registrato're [rājēstràtō'rā] *sm (strumento)* recorder, register; *(magnetofono)* tape recorder; **~ di cassa** cash register; **~ a cassette** cassette recorder; **~ di volo** *(AER)* flight recorder, black box *(fam)*.

registrazio'ne [rājēstràttsyō'nā] *sf* registration; entry; reporting; recording; adjustment; **~ bagagli** *(AER)* check-in.

regis'tro [rājēs'trō] *sm (libro)* register; *(DIR:*

registry; *(MUS, TECN)* register; *(COMM):* **~ (di cassa)** ledger; **ufficio del ~** registrar's office; **~ di bordo** logbook; **~i contabili** (account) books.

regnan'te [rānyàn'tā] *ag* reigning, ruling ♦ *sm/f* ruler.

regna're [rānyà'rā] *vi* to reign, rule; *(fig)* to reign.

re'gno [rān'yō] *sm* kingdom; *(periodo)* reign; *(fig)* realm; **il ~ animale/vegetale** the animal/vegetable kingdom; **il R~ Unito** the United Kingdom.

re'gola *sf* rule; **a ~ d'arte** duly; perfectly; **essere in ~** *(dipendente)* to be a registered employee; *(fig: essere pulito)* to be clean; **fare le cose in ~** to do things properly; **avere le carte in ~** *(gen)* to have one's papers in order; *(fig: essere adatto)* to be the right person; **per tua (norma e) ~** for your information; **un'eccezione alla ~** an exception to the rule.

regola'bile *ag* adjustable.

regolamenta're *ag (distanza, velocità)* regulation *cpd*, proper; *(disposizione)* statutory ♦ *vt (gen)* to control; **entro il tempo ~** within the time allowed, within the prescribed time.

regolamen'to *sm (complesso di norme)* regulations *pl; (di debito)* settlement; **~ di conti** *(fig)* settling of scores.

regola're *ag* regular; *(velocità)* steady; *(superficie)* even; *(passo)* steady, even; *(in regola: documento)* in order ♦ *vt* to regulate, control; *(apparecchio)* to adjust, regulate; *(questione, conto, debito)* to settle; **~rsi** *vr (moderarsi):* **~rsi nel bere/nello spendere** to control one's drinking/spending; *(comportarsi)* to behave, act; **presentare ~ domanda** to apply through the proper channels; **~ i conti** *(fig)* to settle old scores.

regolarità *sf inv* regularity; steadiness; evenness; *(nel pagare)* punctuality.

regolarizza're [rāgōlàrēddzà'rā] *vt (posizione)* to regularize; *(debito)* to settle.

regola'ta *sf:* **darsi una ~** to pull o.s. together.

regolatez'za [rāgōlàtāt'tsà] *sf (ordine)* orderliness; *(moderazione)* moderation.

regola'to, a *ag (ordinato)* orderly; *(moderato)* moderate.

regolato're *sm (TECN)* regulator; **~ di frequenza/di volume** frequency/volume control.

re'golo *sm* ruler; **~ calcolatore** slide rule.

regredi're *vi* to regress.

regressio'ne *sf* regression.

regres'so *sm (fig: declino)* decline.

reiet'to, a *sm/f* outcast.

reincarnazio'ne [rāēnkàrnáttsyō'nā] *sf* reincarnation.

reintegra're *vt (produzione)* to restore; *(energie)* to recover; *(dipendente)* to reinstate.

reintegrazio'ne [rāēntāgràttsyō'nā] *sf* (*di produzione*) restoration; (*di dipendente*) reinstatement.

relativamen'te *av* relatively.

relatività *sf* relativity.

relati'vo, a *ag* relative; (*attinente*) relevant; (*rispettivo*) respective; ~ **a** (*che concerne*) relating to, concerning; (*proporzionato*) in proportion to.

relato're, tri'ce *sm/f* (*gen*) spokesman/woman; (*INS: di tesi*) supervisor.

relax' *sm* relaxation.

relazio'ne [rālàttsyō'nā] *sf* (*fra cose, persone*) relation(ship); (*resoconto*) report, account; ~**i** *sfpl* (*conoscenze*) connections; **essere in** ~ to be connected; **mettere in** ~ (*fatti, elementi*) to make the connection between; **in** ~ **a quanto detto prima** with regard to what has already been said; **essere in buone** ~**i con qn** to be on good terms with sb; **fare una** ~ to make a report, give an account; ~**i pubbliche (RP)** public relations (PR).

relega're *vt* to banish; (*fig*) to relegate.

religio'ne [rālējō'nā] *sf* religion.

religio'so, a [rālējō'sō] *ag* religious ♦ *sm/f* monk/nun.

reli'quia *sf* relic.

relit'to *sm* wreck; (*fig*) down-and-out.

rema'inder [rēmā'ēndə] *sm inv* (*libro*) remainder.

rema're *vi* to row.

reminiscen'ze [rāmēnēshcn'tsā] *sfpl* reminiscences.

remissio'ne *sf* remission; (*deferenza*) submissiveness, compliance; ~ **del debito** remission of debt; ~ **di querela** (*DIR*) withdrawal of an action.

remissività *sf* submissiveness.

remissi'vo, a *ag* submissive, compliant.

re'mo *sm* oar.

re'mora *sf* (*poetico: indugio*) hesitation.

remo'to, a *ag* remote.

remunera're *etc* = **rimunerare** *etc*.

re'na *sf* sand.

rena'le *ag* kidney *cpd*.

ren'dere *vt* (*ridare*) to return, give back; (: *saluto etc*) to return; (*produrre*) to yield, bring in; (*esprimere, tradurre*) to render; (*far diventare*): ~ **qc possibile** to make sth possible ♦ *vi* (*fruttare: ditta*) to be profitable; (: *investimento, campo*) to yield, be productive; ~ **grazie a qn** to thank sb; ~ **omaggio a qn** to honour sb; ~ **un servizio a qn** to do sb a service; ~ **una testimonianza** to give evidence; ~ **la visita** to pay a return visit; **non so se rendo l'idea** I don't know whether I'm making myself clear; ~**rsi utile** to make o.s. useful; ~**rsi conto di qc** to realize sth.

rendicon'to *sm* (*rapporto*) report, account; (*AMM, COMM*) statement of account.

rendimen'to *sm* (*reddito*) yield; (*di manodopera, TECN*) efficiency; (*capacità di produrre*) output; (*di studenti*) performance.

ren'dita *sf* (*di individuo*) private *o* unearned income; (*COMM*) revenue; ~ **annua** annuity; ~ **vitalizia** life annuity.

re'ne *sm* kidney.

re'ni *sfpl* back *sg*.

reniten'te *ag* reluctant, unwilling; ~ **ai consigli di qn** unwilling to follow sb's advice; **essere** ~ **alla leva** (*MIL*) to fail to report for military service.

ren'na *sf* reindeer *inv*.

Re'no *sm*: **il** ~ the Rhine.

re'o, a *sm/f* (*DIR*) offender.

repar'to *sm* department, section; (*MIL*) detachment; ~ **acquisti** purchasing office.

repellen'te *ag* repulsive; (*CHIM: insettifugo*): **liquido** ~ (liquid) repellant.

repenta'glio [rāpàntàl'yō] *sm*: **mettere a** ~ to jeopardize, risk.

repenti'no, a *ag* sudden, unexpected.

reperi'bile *ag* available.

reperi're *vt* to find, trace.

reper'to *sm* (*ARCHEOLOGIA*) find; (*MED*) report; (*anche*: ~ **giudiziario**) exhibit.

reperto'rio *sm* (*TEATRO*) repertory; (*elenco*) index, (alphabetical) list.

re'plica, che *sf* repetition; reply, answer; (*obiezione*) objection; (*TEATRO, CINEMA*) repeat performance; (*copia*) replica.

replica're *vt* (*ripetere*) to repeat; (*rispondere*) to answer, reply.

repressio'ne *sf* repression.

repressi'vo, a *ag* repressive.

repres'so, a *pp di* **reprimere**.

repri'mere *vt* to suppress, repress.

repub'blica, che *sf* republic; **la R**~ **Democratica Tedesca (RDT)** the German Democratic Republic (GDR); **la R**~ **Federale Tedesca (RFT)** the Federal Republic of Germany (FRG).

repubblica'no, a *ag, sm/f* republican.

reputa're *vt* to consider, judge.

reputazio'ne [rāpōōtàttsyō'nā] *sf* reputation; **farsi una cattiva** ~ to get o.s. a bad name.

re'quie *sf* rest; **dare** ~ **a qn** to give sb some peace; **senza** ~ unceasingly.

requisi're *vt* to requisition.

requisi'to *sm* requirement; **avere i** ~**i necessari per un lavoro** to have the necessary qualifications for a job.

requisito'ria *sf* (*DIR*) closing speech (for the prosecution).

requisizio'ne [rākwēzēttsyō'nā] *sf* requisition.

re'sa *sf* (*l'arrendersi*) surrender; (*restituzione, rendimento*) return; ~ **dei conti** rendering of accounts; (*fig*) day of reckoning.

rescin'dere [rāshēn'dārā] *vt* (*DIR*) to rescind, annul.

rescis'so, a |răshĕs'sō| *pp di* **rescindere.**
re'si *etc vb vedi* **rendere.**
residen'te *ag* resident.
residen'za |răsēdĕn'tsà| *sf* residence.
residenzia'le |răsēdăntsyà'lā| *ag* residential.
residua'le *ag* residual.
resi'duo, a *ag* residual, remaining ♦ *sm* remainder; (*CHIM*) residue; **~i industriali** industrial waste *sg.*
re'sina *sf* resin.
resisten'te *ag* (*che resiste*): **~ a** resistant to; (*forte*) strong; (*duraturo*) long-lasting, durable; **~ all'acqua** waterproof; **~ al caldo** heat-resistant; **~ al fuoco** fireproof; **~ al gelo** frost-resistant.
resisten'za |răsēstĕn'tsà| *sf* (*gen, ELETTR*) resistance; (*di persona: fisica*) stamina, endurance; (*: mentale*) endurance, resistance; **opporre ~ (a)** to offer *o* put up resistance (to); (*decisione, scelta*) to show opposition (to).
resi'stere *vi* to resist; **~ a** (*assalto, tentazioni*) to resist; (*dolore, sog: pianta*) to withstand; (*non patir danno*) to be resistant to.
resisti'to, a *pp di* **resistere.**
re'so, a *pp di* **rendere.**
resocon'to *sm* report, account.
respingen'te |răspĕnjĕn'tā| *sm* (*FERR*) buffer.
respin'gere |răspĕn'jārā| *vt* to drive back, repel; (*rifiutare: pacco, lettera*) to return; (*: invito*) to refuse; (*: proposta*) to reject, turn down; (*INS: bocciare*) to fail.
respin'to, a *pp di* **respingere.**
respira're *vi* to breathe; (*fig*) to get one's breath; to breathe again ♦ *vt* to breathe (in), inhale.
respirato're *sm* respirator.
respirato'rio, a *ag* respiratory.
respirazio'ne |răspēràttsyō'nā| *sf* breathing; **~ artificiale** artificial respiration; **~ bocca a bocca** mouth-to-mouth resuscitation.
respi'ro *sm* breathing *q*; (*singolo atto*) breath; (*fig*) respite, rest; **mandare un ~ di sollievo** to give a sigh of relief; **trattenere il ~** to hold one's breath; **lavorare senza ~** to work non-stop; **di ampio ~** (*opera, lavoro*) far-reaching.
responsa'bile *ag* responsible ♦ *sm/f* person responsible; (*capo*) person in charge; **~ di** responsible for; (*DIR*) liable for.
responsabilità *sf inv* responsibility; (*legale*) liability; **assumere la ~ di** to take on the responsibility for; **affidare a qn la ~ di qc** to make sb responsible for sth; **~ patrimoniale** debt liability; **~ penale** criminal liability.
responsabilizza're |răspōnsàbēlēddzà'rā| *vt*: **~ qn** to make sb feel responsible.
respon'so *sm* answer; (*DIR*) verdict.
res'sa *sf* crowd, throng.
res'si *etc vb vedi* **reggere.**

resta're *vi* (*rimanere*) to remain, stay; (*diventare*): **~ orfano/cieco** to become *o* be left an orphan/become blind; (*trovarsi*): **~ sorpreso** to be surprised; (*avanzare*) to be left, remain; **~ d'accordo** to agree; **non resta più niente** there's nothing left; **restano pochi giorni** there are only a few days left; **che resti tra di noi** this is just between ourselves; **~ in buoni rapporti** to remain on good terms; **~ senza parole** to be left speechless.
restaura're *vt* to restore.
restaurato're, tri'ce *sm/f* restorer.
restaurazio'ne |răstàōōràttsyō'nā| *sf* (*POL*) restoration.
resta'uro *sm* (*di edifici etc*) restoration; **in ~** under repair; **sotto ~** (*dipinto*) being restored; **chiuso per ~i** closed for repairs.
resti'o, a, ti'i, ti'e *ag* restive; (*persona*): **~ a** reluctant to.
restitui're *vt* to return, give back; (*energie, forze*) to restore.
restituzio'ne |răstētōōttsyō'nā| *sf* return; (*di soldi*) repayment.
re'sto *sm* remainder, rest; (*denaro*) change; (*MAT*) remainder; **~i** *smpl* leftovers; (*di città*) remains; **del ~** moreover, besides; **~i mortali** (mortal) remains.
restrin'gere |răstrēn'jārā| *vt* to reduce; (*vestito*) to take in; (*stoffa*) to shrink; (*fig*) to restrict, limit; **~rsi** *vr* (*strada*) to narrow; (*stoffa*) to shrink.
restritti'vo, a *ag* restrictive.
restrizio'ne |răstrēttsyō'nā| *sf* restriction.
resurrezio'ne |răsōōrràttsyō'nā| *sf* = **risurrezione.**
resuscita're |răsōōshētà'rā| *vt, vi* = **risuscitare.**
reta'ta *sf* (*PESCA*) haul, catch; **fare una ~ di** (*fig: persone*) to round up.
re'te *sf* net; (*di recinzione*) wire netting; (*AUT, FERR, di spionaggio etc*) network; (*fig*) trap, snare; **segnare una ~** (*CALCIO*) to score a goal; **~ ferroviaria/stradale/di distribuzione** railway/road/distribution network; **~ del letto** box spring (*US*), (sprung) bed base (*Brit*); **~ da pesca** fishing net; **~ (televisiva)** (*sistema*) network; (*canale*) channel.
reticen'te |rātēchen'tā| *ag* reticent.
reticen'za |rātēchen'tsà| *sf* reticence.
reticola'to *sm* grid; (*rete metallica*) wire netting; (*di filo spinato*) barbed wire fence.
re'tina *sf* (*ANAT*) retina.
reto'rico, a, ci, che *ag* rhetorical ♦ *sf* rhetoric.
retribui're *vt* to pay; (*premiare*) to reward; **un lavoro mal retribuito** a poorly-paid job.
retributi'vo, a *ag* pay *cpd.*
retribuzio'ne |rātrēbōōttsyō'nā| *sf* payment; reward.
retri'vo, a *ag* (*fig*) reactionary.
re'tro *sm inv* back ♦ *av* (*dietro*): **vedi ~** see

over(leaf).

retroattività *sf* retroactivity.

retroatti'vo, a *ag* (*DIR*: *legge*) retroactive; (*AMM*: *salario*) backdated.

retrobotte'ga, ghe *sf* back shop.

retroce'dere [rãtrōche'dãrã] *vi* to withdraw ♦ *vt* (*CALCIO*) to relegate; (*MIL*) to degrade; (*AMM*) to demote.

retrocessio'ne [rãtrōchãssyō'nã] *sf* (*di impiegato*) demotion.

retroces'so, a [rãtrōches'sō] *pp di* **retrocedere**.

retrodata're *vt* (*AMM*) to backdate.

retro'grado, a *ag* (*fig*) reactionary, backward-looking.

retroguar'dia *sf* (*anche fig*) rearguard.

retromar'cia [rãtrōmãr'chã] *sf* (*AUT*) reverse; (: *dispositivo*) reverse gear.

retrosce'na [rãtrōshe'nã] *sm inv* (*TEATRO*) backstage; ~ *smpl* (*fig*) behind-the-scenes activity *sg*.

retrospetti'vo, a *ag* retrospective ♦ *sf* (*ARTE*) retrospective exhibition.

retrostan'te *ag*: ~ (**a**) at the back (of).

retroter'ra *sm* hinterland.

retrovi'a *sf* (*MIL*) zone behind the front; **mandare nelle** ~**e** to send to the rear.

retroviso're *sm* (*AUT*) (rear-view) mirror.

ret'ta *sf* (*MAT*) straight line; (*di convitto*) charge for bed and board; (*fig*: *ascolto*): **dar** ~ **a** to listen to, pay attention to.

rettangola're *ag* rectangular.

rettan'golo, a *ag* right-angled ♦ *sm* rectangle.

retti'fica, che *sf* rectification, correction.

rettifica're *vt* (*curva*) to straighten; (*fig*) to rectify, correct.

ret'tile *sm* reptile.

rettili'neo, a *ag* rectilinear.

rettitu'dine *sf* rectitude, uprightness.

ret'to, a *pp di* **reggere** ♦ *ag* straight; (*MAT*): **angolo** ~ right angle; (*onesto*) honest, upright; (*giusto, esatto*) correct, proper, right.

retto're *sm* (*REL*) rector; (*di università*) ≈ chancellor.

reumati'smo *sm* rheumatism.

Rev. *abbr* (= *Reverendo*) Rev(d).

reveren'do, a *ag*: **il** ~ **padre Belli** the Reverend Father Belli.

reveren'te *ag* = **riverente**.

reveren'za [rãvãren'tsã] *sf* = **riverenza**.

reversi'bile *ag* reversible.

revisiona're *vt* (*conti*) to audit; (*TECN*) to overhaul, service; (*DIR*: *processo*) to review; (*componimento*) to revise.

revisio'ne *sf* auditing *q*; audit; servicing *q*; overhaul; review; revision; ~ **di bilancio** audit; ~ **di bozze** proofreading; ~ **contabile interna** internal audit.

reviso're *sm*: ~ **di conti/bozze** auditor/ proofreader.

re'voca *sf* revocation.

revoca're *vt* to revoke.

revol'ver *sm inv* revolver.

revolvera'ta *sf* revolver shot.

Rey'kjavik [rã'ēkyávēk] *sf* Reykjavik.

RFT *sigla f vedi* **Repubblica Federale Tedesca**.

riab'bia *etc vb vedi* **riavere**.

riabilita're *vt* to rehabilitate; (*fig*) to restore to favor (*US*) *o* favour (*Brit*).

riabilitazio'ne [rēábēlētãttsyō'nã] *sf* rehabilitation.

riaccen'dere [rēãchen'dãrã] *vt* (*sigaretta, fuoco, gas*) to light again; (*luce, radio, TV*) to switch on again; (*fig*: *sentimenti, interesse*) to rekindle, revive; ~**rsi** *vr* (*fuoco*) to catch fire again; (*luce, radio, TV*) to come back on again; (*fig*: *sentimenti*) to revive, be rekindled.

riacce'so, a [rēãchã'sō] *pp di* **riaccendere**.

riacquista're *vt* (*gen*) to buy again; (*ciò che si era venduto*) to buy back; (*fig*: *buonumore, sangue freddo, libertà*) to regain; ~ **la salute** to recover (one's health); ~ **le forze** to regain one's strength.

Riad' *sf* Riyadh.

riaddormenta're *vt* to put to sleep again; ~**rsi** *vr* to fall asleep again.

rialza're [rēãltsã'rã] *vt* to raise, lift; (*alzare di più*) to heighten, raise; (*aumentare*: *prezzi*) to increase, raise ♦ *vi* (*prezzi*) to rise, increase.

rialzi'sta, i [rēãltsē'stã] *sm* (*BORSA*) bull.

rial'zo [rēãl'tsō] *sm* (*di prezzi*) increase, rise; (*sporgenza*) rise; **giocare al** ~ (*BORSA*) to bull.

rianda're *vi*: ~ (**in**), ~ (**a**) to go back (to), return (to).

rianima're *vt* (*MED*) to resuscitate; (*fig*: *rallegrare*) to cheer up; (: *dar coraggio*) to give heart to; ~**rsi** *vr* to recover consciousness; to cheer up; to take heart.

rianimazio'ne [rēãnēmãttsyō'nã] *sf* (*MED*) resuscitation; **centro di** ~ intensive care unit.

riaper'to, a *pp di* **riaprire**.

riapertu'ra *sf* reopening.

riappari're *vi* to reappear.

riappar'so, a *pp di* **riapparire**.

riappen'dere *vt* to rehang; (*TEL*) to hang up.

riapri're *vt*, ~**rsi** *vr* to reopen, open again.

riar'mo *sm* (*MIL*) rearmament.

riar'so, a *ag* (*terreno*) arid; (*gola*) parched; (*labbra*) dry.

riasset'to *sm* (*di stanza etc*) rearrangement; (*ordinamento*) reorganization.

riassu'mere *vt* (*riprendere*) to resume; (*impiegare di nuovo*) to re-employ; (*sintetizzare*) to summarize.

riassun'to, a *pp di* **riassumere** ♦ *sm* summary.

riattacca're *vt* (*attaccare di nuovo*): ~ (**a**)

(*manifesto, francobollo*) to stick back (on); (*bottone*) to sew back (on); (*quadro, chiavi*) to hang back up (on); ~ **(il telefono** *o* **il ricevitore)** to hang up (the receiver).

riave're *vt* to have again; (*avere indietro*) to get back; (*riacquistare*) to recover; **~rsi** *vr* to recover; (*da svenimento, stordimento*) to come round.

ribadi're *vt* (*fig*) to confirm.

ribal'ta *sf* (*sportello*) flap; (*TEATRO*: *proscenio*) front of the stage; (: *apparecchio d'illuminazione*) footlights *pl*; (*fig*) limelight; **tornare alla ~** (*personaggio*) to make a comeback; (*problema*) to come up again.

ribalta'bile *ag* (*sedile*) tip-up.

ribalta're *vt, vi* (*anche:* **~rsi**) to turn over, tip over.

ribassa're *vt* to lower, bring down ♦ *vi* to come down, fall.

ribassi'sta, i *sm* (*BORSA*) bear.

ribas'so *sm* reduction, fall; **essere in ~** (*azioni, prezzi*) to be down; (*fig*: *popolarità*) to be on the decline; **giocare al ~** (*BORSA*) to bear.

ribat'tere *vt* (*battere di nuovo*) to beat again; (*con macchina da scrivere*) to type again; (*palla*) to return; (*confutare*) to refute; **~ che** to retort that.

ribattezza're [rēbáttāddzà'rā] *vt* to rename.

ribellar'si *vr*: **~ (a)** to rebel (against).

ribel'le *ag* (*soldati*) rebel; (*ragazzo*) rebellious ♦ *sm/f* rebel.

ribellio'ne *sf* rebellion.

ri'bes *sm inv* currant; **.~ nero** blackcurrant; **~ rosso** redcurrant.

ribolli're *vi* (*fermentare*) to ferment; (*fare bolle*) to bubble, boil; (*fig*) to seethe.

ribrez'zo [rēbrād'dzō] *sm* disgust, loathing; **far ~ a** to disgust.

ributtan'te *ag* disgusting, revolting.

ricaccia're [rēkáchá'rā] *vt* (*respingere*) to drive back; **~ qn fuori** to throw sb out.

ricade're *vi* to fall again; (*scendere a terra, fig*: *nel peccato etc*) to fall back; (*vestiti, capelli etc*) to hang (down); (*riversarsi: fatiche, colpe*): **~ su** to fall on.

ricadu'ta *sf* (*MED*) relapse.

ricalca're *vt* (*disegni*) to trace; (*fig*) to follow faithfully.

ricalcitra're [rēkálchētrá'rā] *vi* (*cavalli, asini, muli*) to kick.

ricama're *vt* to embroider.

ricambia're *vt* to change again; (*contraccambiare*) to return.

ricam'bio *sm* exchange, return; (*FISIOL*) metabolism; **~i** *smpl*, **pezzi di ~** replacement parts; **~ della manodopera** labor turnover.

rica'mo *sm* embroidery; **senza ~i** (*fig*) without frills.

ricapitola're *vt* to recapitulate, sum up.

ricapitolazio'ne [rēkápētōláttsyō'nā] *sf*

recapitulation, summary.

ricarica're *vt* (*arma, macchina fotografica*) to reload; (*penna*) to refill; (*orologio, giocattolo*) to rewind; (*ELETTR*) to recharge.

ricatta're *vt* to blackmail.

ricattato're, tri'ce *sm/f* blackmailer.

ricat'to *sm* blackmail; **fare un ~ a qn** to blackmail sb; **subire un ~** to be blackmailed.

ricava're *vt* (*estrarre*) to draw out, extract; (*ottenere*) to obtain, gain.

ricava'to *sm* (*di vendite*) proceeds *pl*.

rica'vo *sm* proceeds *pl*; (*CONTABILITÀ*) revenue.

ricchez'za [rēkkāt'tsá] *sf* wealth; (*fig*) richness; **~e** *sfpl* (*beni*) wealth *sg*, riches; **~e naturali** natural resources.

ric'cio, a [rēch'chō] *ag* curly ♦ *sm* (*ZOOL*) hedgehog; (: *anche:* **~ di mare**) sea urchin.

ric'ciolo [rēch'chōlō] *sm* curl.

ricciu'to, a [rēchōō'tō] *ag* curly.

ric'co, a, chi, che *ag* rich; (*persona, paese*) rich, wealthy ♦ *sm/f* rich man/woman; **i ~chi** the rich; **~ di** (*idee, illustrazioni etc*) full of; (*risorse, fauna etc*) rich in.

ricer'ca, che [rēchār'ká] *sf* search; (*indagine*) investigation, inquiry; (*studio*): **la ~** research; **una ~** piece of research; **mettersi alla ~ di** to go in search of, look *o* search *o* hunt for; **essere alla ~ di** to be searching for, be looking for; **~ di mercato** market research; **~ operativa** operational research.

ricerca're [rēchārká'rā] *vt* (*motivi, cause*) to look for, try to determine; (*successo, piacere*) to pursue; (*onore, gloria*) to seek.

ricercatez'za [rēchārkátāt'tsá] *sf* (*raffinatezza*) refinement; (: *peg*) affectation.

ricerca'to, a [rēchārká'tō] *ag* (*apprezzato*) much sought-after; (*affettato*) studied, affected ♦ *sm/f* (*POLIZIA*) wanted man/woman.

ricercato're, tri'ce [rēchārkátō'rā] *sm/f* (*INS*) researcher.

ricet'ta [rēchet'tá] *sf* (*MED*) prescription; (*CUC*) recipe; (*fig*: *antidoto*): **~ contro** remedy for.

ricetta'colo [rēchāttá'kōlō] *sm* (*peg*: *luogo malfamato*) den.

ricetta'rio [rēchāttá'ryō] *sm* (*MED*) prescription pad; (*CULIN*) recipe book.

ricettato're, tri'ce [rēchāttátō'rā] *sm/f* (*DIR*) receiver (of stolen goods).

ricettazio'ne [rēchāttáttsyō'nā] *sf* (*DIR*) receiving (stolen goods).

ricetti'vo, a [rēchāttē'vō] *ag* receptive.

riceven'te [rēchāven'tá] *ag* (*RADIO, TV*) receiving ♦ *sm/f* (*COMM*) receiver.

rice'vere [rēchá'vārá] *vt* to receive; (*stipendio, lettera*) to get, receive; (*accogliere: ospite*) to welcome; (*vedere: cliente, rappresentante etc*) to see; **"confermiamo di aver ricevuto**

tale merce" (*COMM*) "we acknowledge receipt of these goods".

ricevimen'to [rēchāvēmān'tō] *sm* receiving *q*; (*trattenimento*) reception; **al ~ della merce** on receipt of the goods.

ricevito're [rēchāvētō'rā] *sm* (*TECN*) receiver; **~ delle imposte** tax collector.

ricevitori'a [rēchāvētōrē'à] *sf* (*FISCO*): **~ (delle imposte)** Internal Revenue (*US*) *or* Inland Revenue (*Brit*) Office; **~ del lotto** lottery office.

ricevu'ta [rēchāvōō'tà] *sf* receipt; **accusare ~ di qc** (*COMM*) to acknowledge receipt of sth; **~ fiscale** official receipt (for tax purposes); **~ di ritorno** (*POSTA*) return notice (*US*), advice of receipt (*Brit*); **~ di versamento** receipt of payment.

ricezio'ne [rēchāttsyō'nā] *sf* (*RADIO*, *TV*) reception.

richiama're [rēkyàmá'rā] *vt* (*chiamare indietro*, *ritelefonare*) to call back; (*ambasciatore*, *truppe*) to recall; (*rimproverare*) to reprimand; (*attirare*) to attract, draw; **~rsi** *vr*: **~rsi a** (*riferirsi a*) to refer to; **~ qn all'ordine** to call sb to order; **desidero ~ la vostra attenzione su ...** I would like to draw your attention to ....

richia'mo [rēkyà'mō] *sm* call; recall; reprimand; attraction.

richieden'te [rēkyāden'tā] *sm/f* applicant.

richie'dere [rēkye'dārā] *vt* to ask again for; (*chiedere indietro*): **~ qc** to ask for sth back; (*chiedere: per sapere*) to ask; (: *per avere*) to ask for; (*AMM*: *documenti*) to apply for; (*esigere*) to need, require; **essere molto richiesto** to be in great demand.

richie'sto, a [rēkye'stō] *pp di* **richiedere** ♦ *sf* (*domanda*) request; (*AMM*) application, request; (*esigenza*) demand, request; **a ~a** on request.

ricicla're [rēchēklà'rā] *vt* (*vetro*, *carta*, *bottiglie*) to recycle; (*fig: personale*) to retrain.

ri'cino [rē'chēnō] *sm*: **olio di ~** castor oil.

ricognito're [rēkōnyētō'rā] *sm* (*AER*) reconnaissance aircraft.

ricognizio'ne [rēkōnyēttsyō'nā] *sf* (*MIL*) reconnaissance; (*DIR*) recognition, acknowledgement.

ricollega're *vt* (*collegare nuovamente*: *gen*) to join again, link again; (*connettere*: *fatti*): **~ (a, con)** to connect (with); **~rsi** *vr*: **~rsi a** (*sog: fatti: connettersi*) to be connected to; (: *persona: riferirsi*) to refer to.

ricol'mo, a *ag*: **~ (di)** (*bicchiere*) full to the brim (with); (*stanza*) full (of).

ricomincia're [rēkōmēnchá'rā] *vt*, *vi* to start again, begin again; **~ a fare qc** to begin doing *o* to do sth again, start doing *o* to do sth again.

ricompen'sa *sf* reward.

ricompensa're *vt* to reward.

ricompo'rsi *vr* to compose o.s., regain one's composure.

ricompo'sto, a *pp di* **ricomporsi**.

riconcilia're [rēkōnchēlyà'rā] *vt* to reconcile; **~rsi** *vr* to be reconciled.

riconciliazio'ne [rēkōnchēlēàttsyō'nā] *sf* reconciliation.

ricondot'to, a *pp di* **ricondurre**.

ricondur're *vt* to bring (*o* take) back.

riconfer'ma *sf* reconfirmation.

riconferma're *vt* to reconfirm.

riconoscen'te [rēkōnōshen'tā] *ag* grateful.

riconoscen'za [rēkōnōshen'tsà] *sf* gratitude.

ricono'scere [rēkōnōsh'shārā] *vt* to recognize; (*DIR*: *figlio*, *debito*) to acknowledge; (*ammettere: errore*) to admit, acknowledge; **~ qn colpevole** to find sb guilty.

riconoscimen'to [rēkōnōshēmān'tō] *sm* recognition; acknowledgement; (*identificazione*) identification; **come ~ dei servizi resi** in recognition of services rendered; **documento di ~** means of identification; **segno di ~** distinguishing mark.

riconosciu'to, a [rēkōnōshōō'tō] *pp di* **riconoscere**.

riconquista're *vt* (*MIL*) to reconquer; (*libertà*, *stima*) to win back.

ricoper'to, a *pp di* **ricoprire**.

ricopia're *vt* to copy.

ricopri're *vt* to re-cover; (*coprire*) to cover; (*occupare: carica*) to hold.

ricorda're *vt* to remember, recall; (*richiamare alla memoria*): **~ qc a qn** to remind sb of sth; **~rsi** *vr*: **~rsi (di)** to remember; **~rsi di qc/di aver fatto** to remember sth/having done.

ricor'do *sm* memory; (*regalo*) keepsake, souvenir; (*di viaggio*) souvenir; **~i** *smpl* (*memorie*) memoirs.

ricorren'te *ag* recurrent, recurring.

ricorren'za [rēkōrren'tsà] *sf* recurrence; (*festività*) anniversary.

ricor'rere *vi* (*ripetersi*) to recur; **~ a** (*rivolgersi*) to turn to; (: *DIR*) to appeal to; (*servirsi di*) to have recourse to; **~ in appello** to lodge an appeal.

ricor'so, a *pp di* **ricorrere** ♦ *sm* recurrence; (*DIR*) appeal; **far ~ a = ricorrere a**.

ricostituen'te *ag* (*MED*): **cura ~** tonic treatment ♦ *sm* (*MED*) tonic.

ricostitui're *vt* (*società*) to build up again; (*governo*, *partito*) to re-form; **~rsi** *vr* (*gruppo etc*) to re-form.

ricostrui're *vt* (*casa*) to rebuild; (*fatti*) to reconstruct.

ricostruzio'ne [rēkōstrōōttsyō'nā] *sf* rebuilding *q*; reconstruction.

ricot'ta *sf* soft *white unsalted cheese made*

from sheep's milk.

ricovera're *vt* to give shelter to; ~ **qn in ospedale** to admit sb to hospital.

ricovera'to, a *sm/f* patient.

rico'vero *sm* shelter, refuge; (*MIL*) shelter; (*MED*) admission (to hospital); ~ **antiaereo** air-raid shelter.

ricrea're *vt* to recreate; (*rinvigorire*) to restore; (*fig: distrarre*) to amuse.

ricreati'vo, a *ag* recreational.

ricreazio'ne [rēkräāttsyō'nā] *sf* recreation, entertainment; (*INS*) recess (*US*), break (*Brit*).

ricre'dersi *vr* to change one's mind.

ricupera're *vt* (*rientrare in possesso di*) to recover, get back; (*tempo perduto*) to make up for; (*NAUT*) to salvage; (: *naufraghi*) to rescue; (*delinquente*) to rehabilitate; ~ **lo svantaggio** (*SPORT*) to close the gap.

ricu'pero *sm* (*gen*) recovery; (*di relitto etc*) salvaging; **capacità di** ~ resilience.

ricusa're *vt* to refuse.

ridacchia're [rēdàkkyà'rā] *vi* to snigger.

rida're *vt* to return, give back.

rid'da *sf* (*di ammiratori etc*) swarm; (*di pensieri*) jumble.

riden'te *ag* (*occhi, volto*) smiling; (*paesaggio*) delightful.

ri'dere *vi* to laugh; (*deridere, beffare*): ~ **di** to laugh at, make fun of; **non c'è niente da** ~, **c'è poco da** ~ it's not a laughing matter.

ridesta're *vt* (*fig: ricordi, passioni*) to reawaken.

ridet'to, a *pp di* **ridire**.

ridicolag'gine [rēdēkōlàd'jēnā] *sf* (*di situazione*) absurdity; (*cosa detta o fatta*) nonsense *q.*

ridicolizza're [rēdēkōlēddzà'rā] *vt* to ridicule.

ridi'colo, a *ag* ridiculous, absurd ♦ *sm*: **cadere nel** ~ to become ridiculous; **rendersi** ~ to make a fool of o.s.

ridimensionamen'to *sm* reorganization; (*di fatto storico*) reappraisal.

ridimensiona're *vt* to reorganize; (*fig*) to see in the right perspective.

ridi're *vt* to repeat; (*criticare*) to find fault with; to object to; **trova sempre qualcosa da** ~ he always manages to find fault.

ridondan'te *ag* redundant.

ridos'so *sm*: **a** ~ **di** (*dietro*) behind; (*contro*) against.

ridot'to, a *pp di* **ridurre**.

ridu'co *etc vb vedi* **ridurre**.

ridur're *vt* (*anche CHIM, MAT*) to reduce; (*prezzo, spese*) to cut, reduce; (*accorciare: opera letteraria*) to abridge; (: *RADIO, TV*) to adapt; **ridursi** *vr* (*diminuirsi*) to be reduced, shrink; **ridursi a** to be reduced to; **ridursi a pelle e ossa** to be reduced to skin and bone.

ridus'si *etc vb vedi* **ridurre**.

ridutto're *sm* (*TECN, CHIM, ELETTR*) reducer.

riduzio'ne [rēdōōttsyō'nā] *sf* reduction; abridgement; adaptation.

rieb'bi *etc vb vedi* **riavere**.

rieduca're *vt* (*persona, arto*) to re-educate; (*malato*) to rehabilitate.

rieducazio'ne [rēädōōkàttsyō'nā] *sf* re-education; rehabilitation; **centro di** ~ rehabilitation center.

rieleg'gere [rēālēd'jārā] *vt* to re-elect.

rielet'to, a *pp di* **rieleggere**.

riempimen'to *sm* filling (up).

riempi're *vt* to fill (up); (*modulo*) to fill in *o* out; **~rsi** *vr* to fill (up); (*mangiare troppo*) to stuff o.s.; ~ **qc di** to fill sth (up) with.

riempiti'vo, a *ag* filling ♦ *sm* (*anche fig*) filler.

rientran'za [rēäntràn'tsà] *sf* recess; indentation.

rientra're *vi* (*entrare di nuovo*) to go (*o* come) back in; (*tornare*) to return; (*fare una rientranza*) to go in, curve inwards; to be indented; (*riguardare*): ~ **in** to be included among, form part of; ~ **(a casa)** to get back home; **non rientriamo nelle spese** we are not within our budget.

rien'tro *sm* (*ritorno*) return; (*di astronave*) re-entry.

riepiloga're *vt* to summarize ♦ *vi* to recapitulate.

riepi'logo, ghi *sm* recapitulation; **fare un** ~ **di qc** to summarize sth.

riesa'me *sm* re-examination.

riesamina're *vt* to re-examine.

rie'sco *etc vb vedi* **riuscire**.

ries'sere *vi*: **ci risiamo!** (*fam*) we're back to this again!

rievoca're *vt* (*passato*) to recall; (*commemorare: figura, meriti*) to commemorate.

rifacimen'to [rēfàchēmān'tō] *sm* (*di film*) remake; (*di opera letteraria*) rehashing.

rifa're *vt* to do again; (*ricostruire*) to make again; (*nodo*) to tie again, do up again; (*imitare*) to imitate, copy; **~rsi** *vr* (*risarcirsi*): **~rsi di** to make up for; (*vendicarsi*): **~rsi di qc su qn** to get one's own back on sb for sth; (*riferirsi*): **~rsi a** (*periodo, fenomeno storico*) to go back to; ~ **il letto** to make the bed; **~rsi una vita** to make a new life for o.s.

rifat'to, a *pp di* **rifare**.

riferimen'to *sm* reference; **in** *o* **con** ~ **a** with reference to; **far** ~ **a** to refer to.

riferi're *vt* (*riportare*) to report; (*ascrivere*): ~ **qc a** to attribute sth to ♦ *vi* to do a report; **~rsi** *vr*: **~rsi a** to refer to; **riferirò** I'll pass on the message.

rifila're *vt* (*tagliare a filo*) to trim; (*fam: affibbiare*): ~ **qc a qn** to palm sth off on sb.

rifini're *vt* to finish off, put the finishing touches to.

rifinitu'ra *sf* finishing touch; **~e** *sfpl* (*di mo-*

bile, auto) finish *sg*.

rifiuta're *vt* to refuse; ~ **di fare** to refuse to do.

rifiu'to *sm* refusal; ~**i** *smpl* (*spazzatura*) rubbish *sg*, refuse *sg*.

riflessio'ne *sf* (*FISICA*) reflection; (*il pensare*) thought, reflection; (*osservazione*) remark.

riflessi'vo, a *ag* (*persona*) thoughtful, reflective; (*LING*) reflexive.

rifles'so, a *pp di* **riflettere** ♦ *sm* (*di luce, su specchio*) reflection; (*FISIOL*) reflex; (*su capelli*) light; (*fig*) effect; **di** *o* **per** ~ indirectly; **avere i** ~**i pronti** to have quick reflexes.

riflet'tere *vt* to reflect ♦ *vi* to think; ~**rsi** *vr* to be reflected; (*ripercuotersi*): ~**rsi su** to have repercussions on; ~ **su** to think over.

rifletto're *sm* reflector; (*proiettore*) floodlight; (: *MIL*) searchlight.

riflus'so *sm* flowing back; (*della marea*) ebb; **un'epoca di** ~ an era of nostalgia.

rifocillar'si |rēfōchēllàr'sē| *vr* (*poetico*) to take refreshment.

rifon'dere *vt* (*rimborsare*) to refund, repay; ~ **le spese a qn** to refund sb's expenses; ~ **i danni a qn** to compensate sb for damages.

rifor'ma *sf* reform; (*MIL*) declaration of unfitness for service; discharge (*on health grounds*); **la R**~ (*REL*) the Reformation.

riforma're *vt* to re-form; (*cambiare, innovare*) to reform; (*MIL: recluta*) to declare unfit for service; (: *soldato*) to invalid out, discharge.

riformato're, tri'ce *ag* reforming ♦ *sm/f* reformer.

riformato'rio *sm* (*DIR*) reformatory (*US*), community home (*Brit*).

riformi'sta, i e *ag, sm/f* reformist.

rifornimen'to *sm* supplying, providing; restocking; (*di carburante*) refuelling; ~**i** *smpl* supplies, provisions; **fare** ~ **di** (*viveri*) to stock up with; (*benzina*) to fill up with; **posto di** ~ gas (*US*) *o* filling station.

riforni're *vt* (*provvedere*): ~ **di** to supply *o* provide with; (*fornire di nuovo: casa etc*) to restock.

rifran'gere |rēfràn'jārā| *vt* to refract.

rifrat'to, a *pp di* **rifrangere**.

rifrazio'ne |rēfràttsyō'nā| *sf* refraction.

rifuggi're |rēfōōdjē'rā| *vi* to escape again; (*fig*): ~ **da** to shun.

rifugiar'si |rēfōōjàr'sē| *vr* to take refuge.

rifugia'to, a |rēfōōjà'tō| *sm/f* refugee.

rifu'gio |rēfōō'jō| *sm* refuge, shelter; (*in montagna*) shelter; ~ **antiaereo** air-raid shelter.

rifu'so, a *pp di* **rifondere**.

ri'ga, ghe *sf* line; (*striscia*) stripe; (*di persone, cose*) line, row; (*regolo*) ruler; (*scrininatura*) part (*US*), parting (*Brit*); **mettersi in** ~ to line up; **a** ~**ghe** (*foglio*) lined; (*vestito*)

striped; **buttare giù due** ~**ghe** (*note*) to jot down a few notes; **mandami due** ~**ghe appena arrivi** drop me a line as soon as you arrive.

riga'gnolo |rēgàn'yōlō| *sm* rivulet.

riga're *vt* (*foglio*) to rule ♦ *vi*: ~ **diritto** (*fig*) to toe the line.

rigato'ni *smpl* (*CUC*) short, ridged pasta shapes.

rigattie're *sm* junk dealer.

rigatu'ra *sf* (*di pagina, quaderno*) lining, ruling; (*di fucile*) rifling.

rigenera're |rējānàrà'rā| *vt* (*gen, TECN*) to regenerate; (*forze*) to restore; (*gomma*) to retread; ~**rsi** *vr* (*gen*) to regenerate; (*ramo, tumore*) to regenerate, grow again; **gomma rigenerata** retread.

rigenerazio'ne |rējānàràttsyō'nā| *sf* regeneration.

rigetta're |rējàttà'rā| *vt* (*gettare indietro*) to throw back; (*fig: respingere*) to reject; (*vomitare*) to bring *o* throw up.

riget'to |rējct'tō| *sm* (*anche MED*) rejection.

righel'lo |rēgcl'lō| *sm* ruler.

righerò *etc* |rēgàro'| *vb vedi* **rigare**.

rigidez'za |rējēdàt'tsà|, **rigidità** |rējēdētà'| *sf* rigidity; stiffness; severity; strictness.

ri'gido, a |rē'jēdō| *ag* rigid, stiff; (*membra etc: indurite*) stiff; (*METEOR*) harsh, severe; (*fig*) strict.

rigira're |rējērà'rā| *vt* to turn; ~**rsi** *vr* to turn round; (*nel letto*) to turn over; ~ **qc tra le mani** to turn sth over in one's hands; ~ **il discorso** to change the subject.

ri'go, ghi *sm* line; (*MUS*) staff, stave.

rigoglio'so, a |rēgōlyō'sō| *ag* (*pianta*) luxuriant; (*fig: commercio, sviluppo*) thriving.

rigonfiamen'to *sm* (*ANAT*) swelling; (*su legno, intonaco etc*) bulge.

rigon'fio, a *ag* swollen; (*grembiule, sporta*): ~ **di** bulging with.

rigo're *sm* (*METEOR*) harshness, rigors *pl* (*US*), rigours *pl* (*Brit*); (*fig*) severity, strictness; (*anche*: **calcio di** ~) penalty; **di** ~ compulsory; "**è di** ~ **l'abito da sera**" "evening dress"; **area di** ~ (*CALCIO*) penalty box (*Brit*); **a rigor di termini** strictly speaking.

rigorosità *sf* strictness; rigor (*US*), rigour (*Brit*).

rigoro'so, a *ag* (*severo: persona, ordine*) strict; (*preciso*) rigorous.

rigoverna're *vt* to wash (up).

riguarda're *vt* to look at again; (*considerare*) to regard, consider; (*concernere*) to regard, concern; ~**rsi** *vr* (*aver cura di sé*) to look after o.s.; **per quel che mi riguarda** as far as I'm concerned; **sono affari che non ti riguardano** it's none of your business.

riguar'do *sm* (*attenzione*) care; (*considerazione*) regard, respect; ~ **a** concerning, with regard to; **per ~ a** out of respect for; **ospite/persona di ~** very important guest/person; **non aver ~i nell'agire/nel parlare** to act/speak freely.

riguardo'so, a *ag* (*rispettoso*) respectful; (*premuroso*) considerate, thoughtful.

rigurgita're [rēgoōrjĕtà'rā] *vi* (*liquido*): **~ da** to gush out from; (*recipiente: traboccare*): **~ di** to overflow with.

rigur'gito [rēgoōr'jĕtō] *sm* (*MED*) regurgitation; (*fig: ritorno, risveglio*) revival.

rilancia're [rēlánchá'rā] *vt* (*lanciare di nuovo: gen*) to throw again; (: *moda*) to bring back; (: *prodotto*) to re-launch; **~ un'offerta** (*asta*) to make a higher bid.

rilan'cio [rēlàn'chō] *sm* (*CARTE, di offerta*) raising.

rilascia're [rēláshá'rā] *vt* (*rimettere in libertà*) to release; (*AMM: documenti*) to issue; (*intervista*) to give; **~ delle dichiarazioni** to make a statement.

rila'scio [rēlásh'shō] *sm* release; issue.

rilassamen'to *sm* (*gen, MED*) relaxation.

rilassa're *vt* to relax; **~rsi** *vr* to relax; (*fig: disciplina*) to become slack.

rilassatez'za *sf* (*fig: di costumi, disciplina*) laxity.

rilassa'to, a *ag* (*persona, muscoli*) relaxed; (*disciplina, costumi*) lax.

rilega're *vt* (*libro*) to bind.

rilegatu'ra *sf* binding.

rileg'gere [rēled'jārā] *vt* to reread, read again; (*rivedere*) to read over.

rilen'to: a ~ *av* slowly.

rilet'to, a *pp di* **rileggere.**

rilevamen'to *sm* (*topografico, statistico*) survey; (*NAUT*) bearing.

rilevan'te *ag* considerable; important.

rilevan'za [rēlāvàn'tsá] *sf* importance.

rileva're *vt* (*ricavare*) to find; (*notare*) to notice; (*mettere in evidenza*) to point out; (*venire a conoscere: notizia*) to learn; (*raccogliere: dati*) to gather, collect; (*TOPOGRAFIA*) to survey; (*MIL*) to relieve; (*COMM*) to take over.

rilevazio'ne [rēlāvàttsyō'nā] *sf* survey.

rilie'vo *sm* (*ARTE, GEO*) relief; (*fig: rilevanza*) importance; (*osservazione*) point, remark; (*TOPOGRAFIA*) survey; **dar ~ a o mettere in ~ qc** (*fig*) to bring sth out, highlight sth; **di poco/nessun ~** (*fig*) of little/no importance; **un personaggio di ~** an important person.

riluttan'te *ag* reluctant.

riluttan'za [rēloōttàn'tsá] *sf* reluctance.

ri'ma *sf* rhyme; (*verso*) verse; **far ~ con** to rhyme with; **rispondere a qn per le ~e** to give sb tit for tat.

rimanda're *vt* to send again; (*restituire, rinviare*) to send back, return; (*differire*): **~**

qc (a) to postpone sth *o* put sth off (till); (*fare riferimento*): **~ qn a** to refer sb to; **essere rimandato** (*INS*) to have to retake one's final exam.

riman'do *sm* (*rinvio*) return; (*dilazione*) postponement; (*riferimento*) cross-reference.

rimaneggia're [rēmánādjà'rā] *vt* (*testo*) to reshape, recast; (*POL*) to reshuffle.

rimanen'te *ag* remaining ♦ *sm* rest, remainder; **i ~i** (*persone*) the rest of them, the others.

rimanen'za [rēmánen'tsá] *sf* rest, remainder; **~e** *sfpl* (*COMM*) unsold stock *sg*.

rimane're *vi* (*restare*) to remain, stay; (*avanzare*) to be left, remain; (*restare stupito*) to be amazed; (*restare, mancare*): **rimangono poche settimane a Pasqua** there are only a few weeks left till Easter; (*diventare*): **~ vedovo** to be left a widower; (*trovarsi*): **~ confuso/sorpreso** to be confused/surprised; **rimane da vedere se** it remains to be seen whether.

rimangia're [rēmánjà'rā] *vt* to eat again; **~rsi la parola/una promessa** (*fig*) to go back on one's word/one's promise.

riman'go *etc vb vedi* **rimanere.**

rima're *vt, vi* to rhyme.

rimargina're [rēmárjĕná'rā] *vt, vi* (*anche: ~rsi*) to heal.

rima'sto, a *pp di* **rimanere.**

rimasu'gli [rēmásoōl'yĕ] *smpl* leftovers.

rimbalza're [rēmbáltsá'rā] *vi* to bounce back, rebound; (*proiettile*) to ricochet.

rimbal'zo [rēmbál'tsō] *sm* rebound; ricochet.

rimbambi're *vi* to be in one's dotage; (*rincretinire*) to grow foolish.

rimbambi'to, a *ag* senile, gaga (*fam*); **un vecchio ~** a doddering old man.

rimbecca're *vt* (*persona*) to answer back; (*offesa*) to return.

rimbecilli're [rēmbāchĕllē'rā] *vi*, **~rsi** *vr* to become stupid.

rimbocca're *vt* (*orlo*) to turn up; (*coperta*) to tuck in; (*maniche, pantaloni*) to turn *o* roll up.

rimbomba're *vi* to resound.

rimborsa're *vt* to pay back, repay; **~ qc a qn** to reimburse sb for sth.

rimbor'so *sm* repayment; (*di spese, biglietto*) refund; **~ d'imposta** tax rebate.

rimboschimen'to [rēmbōskĕmān'tō] *sm* reafforestation.

rimboschi're [rēmbōskē'rā] *vt* to reafforest.

rimbrotta're *vt* to reproach.

rimbrot'to *sm* reproach.

rimedia're *vi*: **~ a** to remedy ♦ *vt* (*fam: procurarsi*) to get *o* scrape together; **~ da vivere** to scrape a living.

rime'dio *sm* (*medicina*) medicine; (*cura, fig*) remedy, cure; **porre ~ a qc** to remedy sth;

non c'è ~ there's no way out, there's nothing to be done about it.

rimescola're *vt* to mix well, stir well; (*carte*) to shuffle; **sentirsi** ~ **il sangue** (*per rabbia*) to feel one's blood boil.

rimes'sa *sf* (*locale: per veicoli*) garage; (: *per aerei*) hangar; (*COMM: di merce*) consignment; (: *di denaro*) remittance; (*TENNIS*) return; (*CALCIO: anche:* ~ **in gioco**) throw-in.

rimes'so, a *pp di* **rimettere**.

rimesta're *vt* (*mescolare*) to mix well, stir well; (*fig: passato*) to drag up again.

rimet'tere *vt* (*mettere di nuovo*) to put back; (*indossare di nuovo*): ~ **qc** to put sth back on, put sth on again; (*restituire*) to return, give back; (*affidare*) to entrust; (: *decisione*) to refer; (*condonare*) to remit; (*COMM: merci*) to deliver; (: *denaro*) to remit; (*vomitare*) to bring up; (*perdere: anche:* **rimetterci**) to lose; ~**rsi** *vr*: ~**rsi a** (*affidarsi*) to trust; ~ **a nuovo** (*casa etc*) to do over (*US*) *o* up (*Brit*); **rimetterci di tasca propria** to be out of pocket; ~**rsi al bello** (*tempo*) to clear up; ~**rsi in cammino** to set off again; ~**rsi al lavoro** to start working again; ~**rsi in salute** to get better, recover one's health.

rimi'si *etc vb vedi* **rimettere**.

rim'mel ® *sm inv* mascara.

rimodernamen'to *sm* modernization.

rimoderna're *vt* to modernize.

rimon'ta *sf* (*SPORT, gen*) recovery.

rimonta're *vt* (*meccanismo*) to reassemble; (*tenda*) to put up again ♦ *vi* (*salire di nuovo*): ~ **in** (*macchina, treno*) to get back into; (*SPORT*) to close the gap.

rimorchia're [rēmŏrkyà'rā] *vt* to tow; (*fig: ragazza*) to pick up.

rimorchiato're [rēmŏrkyàtō'rā] *sm* (*NAUT*) tug(boat).

rimor'chio [rēmor'kyō] *sm* tow; (*veicolo*) trailer; **andare a** ~ to be towed; **prendere a** ~ to tow; **cavo da** ~ towrope; **autocarro con** ~ semi(trailer) (*US*), articulated lorry (*Brit*).

rimor'so *sm* remorse; **avere il** ~ **di aver fatto qc** to deeply regret having done sth.

rimos'so, a *pp di* **rimuovere**.

rimostran'za [rēmŏstràn'tsà] *sf* protest, complaint; **fare le proprie** ~**e a qn** to remonstrate with sb.

rimozio'ne [rēmŏttsyō'nā] *sf* removal; (*da un impiego*) dismissal; (*PSIC*) repression; "~ **forzata**" "illegally parked vehicles will be removed at owner's expense".

rimpasta're *vt* (*POL: ministero*) to reshuffle.

rimpa'sto *sm* (*POL*) reshuffle; ~ **ministeriale** cabinet reshuffle.

rimpatria're *vi* to return home ♦ *vt* to repatriate.

rimpa'trio *sm* repatriation.

rimpian'gere [rēmpyàn'jārā] *vt* to regret; (*persona*) to miss; ~ **di (non) aver fatto qc** to regret (not) having done sth.

rimpian'to, a *pp di* **rimpiangere** ♦ *sm* regret.

rimpiatti'no *sm* hide-and-seek.

rimpiazza're [rēmpyàttsà'rā] *vt* to replace.

rimpiccioli're [rēmpēchōlē'rā] *vt* to make smaller ♦ *vi* (*anche:* ~**rsi**) to become smaller.

rimpinza're [rēmpēntsà'rā] *vt*: ~ **di** to cram *o* stuff with.

rimprovera're *vt* to rebuke, reprimand.

rimpro'vero *sm* rebuke, reprimand; **di** ~ (*tono, occhiata*) reproachful; (*parole*) of reproach.

rimugina're [rēmōōjēnà'rā] *vt* (*fig*) to turn over in one's mind.

rimunera're *vt* (*retribuire*) to remunerate; (*ricompensare: sacrificio etc*) to reward; **un lavoro ben rimunerato** a well-paid job.

rimunerati'vo, a *ag* (*lavoro, attività*) remunerative, profitable.

rimunerazio'ne [rēmōōnàràttsyō'nā] *sf* remuneration; (*premio*) reward.

rimuo'vere *vt* to remove; (*destituire*) to dismiss; (*fig: distogliere*) to dissuade.

rinascimenta'le [rēnàshēmàntà'lā] *ag* Renaissance *cpd*, of the Renaissance.

Rinascimen'to [rēnàshēmàn'tō] *sm*: **il** ~ the Renaissance.

rina'scita [rēnàsh'shētà] *sf* rebirth, revival.

rincalza're [rēnkàltsà'rā] *vt* (*palo, albero*) to support, prop up; (*lenzuola*) to tuck in.

rincal'zo [rēnkàl'tsō] *sm* support, prop; (*rinforzo*) reinforcement; (*SPORT*) reserve (player); ~**i** *smpl* (*MIL*) reserves.

rincara're *vt* to increase the price of ♦ *vi* to go up, become more expensive; ~ **la dose** (*fig*) to pile it on.

rinca'ro *sm*: ~ **(di)** (*prezzi, costo della vita*) increase (in); (*prodotto*) increase in the price (of).

rincasa're *vi* to go home.

rinchiu'dere [rēnkyōō'dàrā] *vt* to shut (*o* lock) up; ~**rsi** *vr*: ~**rsi in** to shut o.s. up in; ~**rsi in se stesso** to withdraw into o.s.

rinchiu'so, a [rēnkyōō'sō] *pp di* **rinchiudere**.

rincitrullir'si [rēnchētrōōllèr'sē] *vr* to grow foolish.

rincor'rere *vt* to chase, run after.

rincor'so, a *pp di* **rincorrere** ♦ *sf* short run.

rincre'scere [rēnkràsh'shàrā] *vb impers*: **mi rincresce che/di non poter fare** I'm sorry that/I can't do, I regret that/being unable to do.

rincrescimen'to [rēnkràshēmàn'tō] *sm* regret.

rincresciu'to, a [rēnkràshōō'tō] *pp di* **rincrescere**.

rincula're *vi* to draw back; (*arma*) to recoil.

rinfaccia're [rēnfàchà'rā] *vt* (*fig*): ~ **qc a qn**

to throw sth in sb's face.

rinfocola're vt (fig: odio, passioni) to re-kindle; (: risentimento, rabbia) to stir up.

rinforza're [rēnfŏrtsá'rā] vt to reinforce, strengthen ♦ vi (anche: ~rsi) to grow stronger.

rinfor'zo [rēnfor'tsō] sm: **mettere un** ~ **a** to strengthen; ~**i** smpl (MIL) reinforcements; **di** ~ (asse, sbarra) strengthening; (esercito) supporting; (personale) extra, additional.

rinfranca're vt to encourage, reassure.

rinfrescan'te ag (bibita) refreshing.

rinfresca're vt (atmosfera, temperatura) to cool (down); (abito, pareti) to freshen up ♦ vi (tempo) to grow cooler; ~**rsi** vr (ristorarsi) to refresh o.s.; (lavarsi) to freshen up; ~ **la memoria a qn** to refresh sb's memory.

rinfre'sco, schi sm (festa) party; ~**schi** smpl (cibi e bevande) refreshments.

rinfu'sa sf: **alla** ~ in confusion, higgledy-piggledy.

ringhia're [rēngyá'rā] vi to growl, snarl.

ringhie'ra [rēngye'rá] sf railing; (delle scale) banister(s pl).

rin'ghio [rēn'gyō] sm growl, snarl.

ringhio'so, a [rēngyō'sō] ag growling, snarl-ing.

ringiovani're [rēnjōvánē'rā] vt (sog: vestito, acconciatura etc): ~ **qn** to make sb look younger; (: vacanze etc) to rejuvenate ♦ vi (anche: ~rsi) to become (o look) younger.

ringraziamen'to [rēngráttsyámán'tō] sm thanks pl; **lettera/biglietto di** ~ thank you letter/card.

ringrazia're [rēngráttsyá'rā] vt to thank; ~ **qn di qc** to thank sb for sth; ~ **qn per aver fatto qc** to thank sb for doing sth.

rinnega're vt (fede) to renounce; (figlio) to disown, repudiate.

rinnega'to, a sm/f renegade.

rinnovamen'to sm renewal; (economico) re-vival.

rinnova're vt to renew; (ripetere) to repeat, renew; ~**rsi** vr (fenomeno) to be repeated, recur.

rinno'vo sm (di contratto) renewal; "**chiuso per** ~ (**dei**) **locali**" (negozio) "closed for alterations".

rinoceron'te [rēnōchárōn'tā] sm rhinoceros.

rinoma'to, a ag renowned, celebrated.

rinsalda're vt to strengthen.

rinsavi're vi to come to one's senses.

rinsecchi'to, a [rēnsákkē'tō] ag (vecchio, albero) thin, gaunt.

rintanar'si vr (animale) to go into its den; (persona: nascondersi) to hide.

rintocca're vi (campana) to toll; (orologio) to strike.

rintoc'co, chi sm toll.

rintraccia're [rēntráchá'rā] vt to track down;

(persona scomparsa, documento) to trace.

rintrona're vi to boom, roar ♦ vt (assordare) to deafen; (stordire) to stun.

rintuzza're [rēntŏōttsá'rā] vt (fig: sentimento) to check, repress; (: accusa) to refute.

rinun'cia [rēnōōn'chá] sf renunciation; ~ **a** (carica) resignation from; (eredità) re-linquishment of; ~ **agli atti del giudizio** (DIR) abandonment of a claim.

rinuncia're [rēnōōnchá'rā] vi: ~ **a** to give up, renounce; ~ **a fare qc** to give up doing sth.

rinunciata'rio, a [rēnōōnchátá'ryō] ag defeat-ist.

rinun'zia etc [rēnōōn'tsyá] = **rinuncia** etc.

rinvasa're vt to repot.

rinvenimen'to sm (ritrovamento) recovery; (scoperta) discovery; (METALLURGIA) tem-pering.

rinveni're vt to find, recover; (scoprire) to discover, find out ♦ vi (riprendere i sensi) to come round; (riprendere l'aspetto naturale) to revive.

rinvenu'to, a pp di **rinvenire**.

rinverdi're vi (bosco, ramo) to become green again.

rinvia're vt (rimandare indietro) to send back, return; (differire): ~ **qc (a)** to postpone sth o put sth off (till); (: seduta) to adjourn sth (till); (fare un rimando): ~ **qn a** to refer sb to; ~ **a giudizio** (DIR) to commit for trial.

rinvigori're vt to strengthen.

rinvi'o, vi'i sm (rimando) return; (differi-mento) postponement; (: di seduta) adjourn-ment; (in un testo) cross-reference.

riò etc vb vedi **riavere**.

Ri'o de Jane'iro [rē'ōdájá'nāērō] sf Rio de Ja-neiro.

riona'le ag (mercato, cinema) local, district cpd.

rio'ne sm district, quarter.

riordinamen'to sm (di ente, azienda) reor-ganization.

riordina're vt (rimettere in ordine) to tidy; (riorganizzare) to reorganize.

riorganizza're [rēōrgánēddzá'rā] vt to reorgan-ize.

riorganizzazio'ne [rēōrgánēddzáttsyō'nā] sf re-organization.

ripaga're vt to repay.

ripara're vt (proteggere) to protect, defend; (correggere: male, torto) to make up for; (: errore) to put right; (aggiustare) to repair ♦ vi (mettere rimedio): ~ **a** to make up for; ~**rsi** vr (rifugiarsi) to take refuge o shelter.

ripara'to, a ag (posto) sheltered.

riparazio'ne [rēpáráttsyō'nā] sf (di un torto) reparation; (di guasto, scarpe) repairing q; repair; (risarcimento) compensation; (INS): **fare** o **dare un esame di** ~ to retake a test.

ripa'ro sm (protezione) shelter, protection;

(*rimedio*) remedy; **al ~ da** (*sole, vento*) sheltered from; **mettersi al ~** to take shelter; **correre ai ~i** (*fig*) to take remedial action.

riparti're *vt* (*dividere*) to divide up; (*distribuire*) to share out, distribute ♦ *vi* to leave again; (*motore*) to start again.

ripartizio'ne [rēpártēttsyō'nä] *sf* division; sharing out, distribution; (*AMM*: *dipartimento*) department.

ripassa're *vi* to come (*o* go) back ♦ *vt* (*scritto, lezione*) to go over (again).

ripas'so *sm* (*di lezione*) review (*US*), revision (*Brit*).

ripensamen'to *sm* second thoughts *pl*, change of mind; **avere un ~** to have second thoughts, change one's mind.

ripensa're *vi* to think; (*cambiare idea*) to change one's mind; (*tornare col pensiero*): **~ a** to recall; **a ripensarci** ... on thinking it over ....

ripercor'rere *vt* (*itinerario*) to travel over again; (*strada*) to go along again; (*fig*: *ricordi, passato*) to go back over.

ripercor'so, a *pp di* **ripercorrere.**

ripercos'so, a *pp di* **ripercuotersi.**

ripercuo'tersi *vr*: **~ su** (*fig*) to have repercussions on.

ripercussio'ne *sf* (*fig*): **avere una ~** *o* **delle ~i su** to have repercussions on.

ripesca're *vt* (*pesce*) to catch again; (*persona, cosa*) to fish out; (*fig*: *ritrovare*) to dig out.

ripeten'te *sm/f* repeater (*US*), student repeating the year.

ripe'tere *vt* to repeat; (*ripassare*) to go over.

ripetito're *sm* (*RADIO, TV*) relay.

ripetizio'ne [rēpātēttsyō'nä] *sf* repetition; (*di lezione*) review (*US*), revision (*Brit*); **~i** *sfpl* (*INS*) private tutoring *o* coaching *sg*; **fucile a ~** repeating rifle.

ripetutamen'te *av* repeatedly, again and again.

ripia'no *sm* (*GEO*) terrace; (*di mobile*) shelf.

ripic'ca *sf*: **per ~** out of spite.

ri'pido, a *ag* steep.

ripiegamen'to *sm* (*MIL*) retreat.

ripiega're *vt* to refold; (*piegare più volte*) to fold (up) ♦ *vi* (*MIL*) to retreat, fall back; (*fig*: *accontentarsi*): **~ su** to make do with; **~rsi** *vr* to bend.

ripie'go, ghi *sm* expedient; **una soluzione di ~** a makeshift solution.

ripie'no, a *ag* full; (*CUC*) stuffed; (: *panino*) filled ♦ *sm* (*CUC*) stuffing.

ripo'ne, ripon'go *etc vb vedi* **riporre.**

ripor're *vt* (*porre al suo posto*) to put back, replace; (*mettere via*) to put away; (*fiducia, speranza*): **~ qc in qn** to place *o* put sth in sb.

riporta're *vt* (*portare indietro*) to bring (*o* take) back; (*riferire*) to report; (*citare*) to quote; (*ricevere*) to receive, get; (*vittoria*) to gain; (*successo*) to have; (*MAT*) to carry; (*COMM*) to carry forward; **~rsi** *vr*: **~rsi a** (*anche fig*) to go back to; (*riferirsi a*) to refer to; **~ danni** to suffer damage; **ha riportato gravi ferite** he was seriously injured.

ripor'to *sm* amount carried over; amount carried forward.

riposan'te *ag* (*gen*) restful; (*musica, colore*) soothing.

riposa're *vt* (*bicchiere, valigia*) to put down; (*dare sollievo*) to rest ♦ *vi* to rest; **~rsi** *vr* to rest; **qui riposa** ... (*su tomba*) here lies ....

riposa'to, a *ag* (*viso, aspetto*) rested; (*mente*) fresh.

ripo'si *etc vb vedi* **riporre.**

ripo'so *sm* rest; (*MIL*): **~!** at ease!; **a ~** (*in pensione*) retired; **giorno di ~** day off; "**oggi ~**" (*CINEMA, TEATRO*) "no performance today"; (*ristorante*) "closed today".

riposti'glio [rēpōstēl'yō] *sm* storage closet (*US*), lumber room (*Brit*).

ripo'sto, a *pp di* **riporre** ♦ *ag* (*fig*: *senso, significato*) hidden.

ripren'dere *vt* (*prigioniero, fortezza*) to recapture; (*prendere indietro*) to take back; (*ricominciare: lavoro*) to resume; (*andare a prendere*) to fetch, come back for; (*assumere di nuovo: impiegati*) to take on again, reemploy; (*rimproverare*) to tell off; (*restringere: abito*) to take in; (*CINEMA*) to shoot; **~rsi** *vr* to recover; (*correggersi*) to correct o.s.; **~ a fare qc** to start doing sth again; **~ il cammino** to set off again; **~ i sensi** to recover consciousness; **~ sonno** to go back to sleep.

ripresenta're *vt* (*certificato*) to submit again; (*domanda*) to put forward again; (*persona*) to introduce again; **~rsi** *vr* (*ritornare: persona*) to come back; (: *occasione*) to arise again; **~rsi a** (*esame*) to retake; (*concorso*) to enter again; **~rsi come candidato** (*POL*) to run again (as a candidate).

ripre'so, a *pp di* **riprendere** ♦ *sf* recapture; resumption; (*economica, da malattia, emozione*) recovery; (*AUT*) acceleration *q*; (*TEATRO, CINEMA*) rerun; (*CINEMA*: *presa*) shooting *q*; shot; (*SPORT*) second half; (: *PUGILATO*) round; **a più ~e** on several occasions, several times.

ripristina're *vt* to restore.

ripri'stino *sm* (*gen*) restoration; (*di tradizioni*) revival.

riprodot'to, a *pp di* **riprodurre.**

riprodur're *vt* to reproduce; **riprodursi** *vr* (*BIOL*) to reproduce; (*riformarsi*) to form again.

riproduttiv'vo, a *ag* reproductive.

riprodutto're, tri'ce *ag* (*organo*) reproductive ♦ *sm*: ~ **acustico** pick-up; ~ **a cassetta** cassette player.

riproduzio'ne [rĕprōdōōttsyō'nā] *sf* reproduction; ~ **vietata** all rights reserved.

ripromes'so, a *pp di* **ripromettersi**.

ripromet'tersi *vt* (*aspettarsi*): ~ **qc da** to expect sth from; (*intendere*): ~ **di fare qc** to intend to do sth.

ripropor're *vt*: **riproporsi di fare qc** to intend to do sth.

ripropo'sto, a *pp di* **riproporre**.

ripro'va *sf* confirmation; **a ~ di** as confirmation of.

riprova're *vt* (*provare di nuovo*: *gen*) to try again; (: *vestito*) to try on again; (: *sensazione*) to experience again ♦ *vi* (*tentare*): ~ **(a fare qc)** to try (to do sth) again; **riproverò più tardi** I'll try again later.

riprove'vole *ag* reprehensible.

ripudia're *vt* to repudiate, disown.

ripu'dio *sm* repudiation, disowning.

ripugnan'te [rĕpōōnyán'tā] *ag* disgusting, repulsive.

ripugnan'za [rĕpōōnyán'tsà] *sf* repugnance, disgust.

ripugna're [rĕpōōnyá'rā] *vi*: ~ **a qn** to repel o disgust sb.

ripuli're *vt* to clean up; (*sog*: *ladri*) to clean out; (*perfezionare*) to polish, refine.

ripulsio'ne *sf* (*FISICA, fig*) repulsion.

riqua'dro *sm* square; (*ARCHIT*) panel.

risac'ca, che *sf* backwash.

risa'ia *sf* (rice) paddy.

risali're *vi* (*ritornare in su*) to go back up; ~ **a** (*ritornare con la mente*) to go back to; (*datare da*) to date back to, go back to.

risali'ta *sf*: **mezzi di ~** (*SCI*) ski lifts.

risalta're *vi* (*fig*: *distinguersi*) to stand out; (*ARCHIT*) to project, jut out.

risal'to *sm* prominence; (*sporgenza*) projection; **mettere** o **porre in ~ qc** to make sth stand out.

risanamen'to *sm* (*economico*) improvement; (*bonifica*) reclamation; ~ **del bilancio** reorganization of the budget; ~ **edilizio** building improvement.

risana're *vt* (*guarire*) to heal, cure; (*palude*) to reclaim; (*economia*) to improve; (*bilancio*) to reorganize.

risape're *vt*: ~ **qc** to come to know of sth.

risapu'to, a *ag*: **è ~ che** ... everyone knows that ..., it's common knowledge that ....

risarcimen'to [rĕsárchēmān'tō] *sm*: ~ **(di)** compensation (for); **aver diritto al ~ dei danni** to be entitled to damages.

risarci're [rĕsárchē'rā] *vt* (*cose*) to pay compensation for; (*persona*): ~ **qn di qc** to compensate sb for sth; ~ **i danni a qn** to pay sb damages.

risa'ta *sf* laugh.

riscaldamen'to *sm* heating; ~ **centrale** central heating.

riscalda're *vt* (*scaldare*) to heat; (: *mani, persona*) to warm; (*minestra*) to reheat; ~**rsi** *vr* to warm up.

riscatta're *vt* (*prigioniero*) to ransom, pay a ransom for; (*DIR*) to redeem; ~**rsi** *vr* (*da disonore*) to redeem o.s.

riscat'to *sm* ransom; redemption.

rischiara're [rĕskyárá'rā] *vt* (*illuminare*) to light up; (*colore*) to make lighter; ~**rsi** *vr* (*tempo*) to clear up; (*cielo*) to clear; (*fig*: *volto*) to brighten up; ~**rsi la voce** to clear one's throat.

rischia're [rĕskyá'rā] *vt* to risk ♦ *vi*: ~ **di fare qc** to risk o run the risk of doing sth.

ris'chio [rēs'kyō] *sm* risk; **a proprio ~ e pericolo** at one's own risk; **correre il ~ di fare qc** to run the risk of doing sth; ~ **del mestiere** occupational hazard.

rischio'so, a [rĕskyō'sō] *ag* risky, dangerous.

risciacqua're [rĕshákkwá'rā] *vt* to rinse.

risciac'quo [rĕshák'kwō] *sm* rinse.

riscontra're *vt* (*confrontare*: *due cose*) to compare; (*esaminare*) to check, verify; (*rilevare*) to find.

riscon'tro *sm* comparison; check, verification; (*AMM*: *lettera di risposta*) reply; **mettere a ~** to compare; **in attesa di un vostro cortese ~** we look forward to your reply.

riscoper'to, a *pp di* **riscoprire**.

riscopri're *vt* to rediscover.

riscossio'ne *sf* collection.

riscos'so, a *pp di* **riscuotere** ♦ *sf* (*riconquista*) recovery, reconquest.

riscuo'tere *vt* (*ritirare una somma dovuta*) to collect; (: *stipendio*) to draw, collect; (*fig*: *successo etc*) to win, earn; ~**rsi** *vr*: ~**rsi (da)** to shake o.s. (out of), rouse o.s. (from); ~ **un assegno** to cash a check.

ri'se *etc vb vedi* **ridere**.

risentimen'to *sm* resentment.

risenti're *vt* to hear again; (*provare*) to feel ♦ *vi*: ~ **di** to feel (o show) the effects of; ~**rsi** *vr*: ~**rsi di** o **per** to take offense (*US*) o offence (*Brit*) at, resent.

risenti'to, a *ag* resentful.

riser'bo *sm* reserve.

riser'va *sf* reserve; (*di caccia, pesca*) preserve; (*restrizione, di indigeni*) reservation; **fare ~ di** (*cibo*) to get in a supply of; **tenere di ~** to keep in reserve; **con le dovute ~e** with certain reservations; **ha accettato con la ~ di potersi ritirare** he accepted with the proviso that he could pull out.

riserva're *vt* (*tenere in serbo*) to keep, put aside; (*prenotare*) to book, reserve; ~**rsi** *vr*: ~**rsi di fare qc** to intend to do sth; ~**rsi il diritto di fare qc** to reserve the right to do sth.

riservatez'za [rēsārvàtāt'tsá] *sf* reserve.

riserva'to, a *ag* (*prenotato*, *fig*: *persona*) reserved; (*confidenziale*) confidential; (*lettera*, *informazione*) confidential.

ri'si *etc vb vedi* **ridere.**

risi'bile *ag* laughable.

risie'dere *vi*: ~ **a** *o* **in** to reside in.

ri'sma *sf* (*di carta*) ream; (*fig*) kind, sort.

ri'so, a *pp di* **ridere** ♦ *sm* (*pianta*) rice; (*pl(f)* ~**a**: *il ridere*): **un** ~ a laugh; **il** ~ laughter; **uno scoppio di** ~**a** a burst of laughter.

risoli'no *sm* snicker.

risolleva're *vt* (*sollevare di nuovo*: *testa*) to raise again, lift up again; (*fig*: *questione*) to raise again, bring up again; (: *morale*) to raise; ~**rsi** *vr* (*da terra*) to rise again; (*fig*: *da malattia*) to recover; ~ **le sorti di qc** to improve the chances of sth.

risol'si *etc vb vedi* **risolvere.**

risol'to, a *pp di* **risolvere.**

risolutez'za [rēsōloōtát'tsá] *sf* determination.

risoluti'vo, a *ag* (*determinante*) decisive; (*che risolve*): **arrivare ad una formula** ~**a** to come up with a formula to resolve a situation.

risolu'to, a *ag* determined, resolute.

risoluzio'ne [rēsōloōōtsyō'nā] *sf* solving *q*; (*MAT*) solution; (*decisione*, *di immagine*) resolution; (*DIR*: *di contratto*) annulment, cancellation.

risol'vere *vt* (*difficoltà*, *controversia*) to resolve; (*problema*) to solve; (*decidere*): ~ **di fare** to resolve to do; ~**rsi** *vr* (*decidersi*): ~**rsi a fare** to make up one's mind to do; (*andare a finire*): ~**rsi in** to end up, turn out; ~**rsi in nulla** to come to nothing.

risolvi'bile *ag* solvable.

risonan'za [rēsōnán'tsá] *sf* resonance; **aver vasta** ~ (*fig*: *fatto etc*) to be known far and wide.

risona're *vt*, *vi* = **risuonare.**

risor'gere [rēsōr'jārá] *vi* to rise again.

risorgimenta'le [rēsōrjēmāntá'lā] *ag* of the Risorgimento.

risorgimen'to [rēsōrjēmān'tō] *sm* revival; **il R**~ (*STORIA*) the Risorgimento.

risor'sa *sf* expedient, resort; ~**e** *sfpl* (*naturali*, *finanziarie etc*) resources; **persona piena di** ~**e** resourceful person.

risor'si *etc vb vedi* **risorgere.**

risor'to, a *pp di* **risorgere.**

risot'to *sm* (*CUC*) risotto.

risparmia're *vt* to save; (*non uccidere*) to spare ♦ *vi* to save; ~ **qc a qn** to spare sb sth; ~ **fatica/fiato** to save one's energy/breath; **risparmiati il disturbo** *o* **la fatica** (*anche ironico*) save yourself the trouble.

risparmiato're, tri'ce *sm/f* saver.

rispar'mio *sm* saving *q*; (*denaro*) savings *pl*.

rispecchia're [rēspākkyá'rā] *vt* to reflect; ~**rsi** *vr* to be reflected.

rispedi're *vt* to send back; ~ **qc a qn** to send sth back to sb.

rispetta'bile *ag* respectable; (*considerevole*: *somma*) sizeable, considerable.

rispetta're *vt* to respect; (*legge*) to obey, comply with, abide by; (*promessa*) to keep; **farsi** ~ to command respect; ~ **le distanze** to keep one's distance; ~ **i tempi** to keep to schedule; **ogni medico che si rispetti** every self-respecting doctor.

rispettabilità *sf* respectability.

rispettivamen'te *av* respectively.

rispetti'vo, a *ag* respective.

rispet'to *sm* respect; ~**i** *smpl* (*saluti*) respects, regards; ~ **a** (*in paragone a*) compared to; (*in relazione a*) as regards, as for; ~ (**di** *o* **per**) (*norme*, *leggi*) observance (of), compliance (with); **portare** ~ **a qn/qc** to have *o* feel respect for sb/sth; **mancare di** ~ **a qn** to be disrespectful to sb; **con** ~ **parlando** with respect, if you will excuse my saying so; (**porga**) **i miei** ~**i alla signora** (give) my regards to your wife.

rispetto'so, a *ag* respectful.

risplenden'te *ag* (*giornata*, *sole*) bright, shining; (*occhi*) sparkling.

risplen'dere *vi* to shine.

risponden'te *ag*: ~ **a** in keeping *o* conformity with.

risponden'za [rēspōnden'tsá] *sf* correspondence.

rispon'dere *vi* to answer, reply; (*freni*) to respond; ~ **a** (*domanda*) to answer, reply to; (*persona*) to answer; (*invito*) to reply to; (*provocazione*, *sog*: *veicolo*, *apparecchio*) to respond to; (*corrispondere a*) to correspond to; (: *speranze*, *bisogno*) to answer; ~ **a qn di qc** (*essere responsabile*) to be answerable to sb for sth.

risposar'si *vr* to get married again, remarry.

rispo'sto, a *pp di* **rispondere** ♦ *sf* answer, reply; **in** ~**a a** in reply to; **dare una** ~**a** to give an answer; **diamo** ~**a alla vostra lettera del** ... in reply to your letter of ....

ris'sa *sf* brawl.

risso'so, a *ag* quarrelsome.

rist. *abbr* = **ristampa.**

ristabili're *vt* to re-establish, restore; (*persona*: *sog*: *riposo etc*) to restore to health; ~**rsi** *vr* to recover.

ristagna're [rēstànyà'rā] *vi* (*acqua*) to become stagnant; (*sangue*) to cease flowing; (*fig*: *industria*) to stagnate.

rista'gno [rēstán'yō] *sm* stagnation; **c'è un** ~ **delle vendite** business is slack.

ristam'pa *sf* reprinting *q*; reprint.

ristampa're *vt* to reprint.

ristoran'te *sm* restaurant.

ristorar'si *vr* to have something to eat and

(riposarsi) to rest, have a rest.

ristorato're, tri'ce *ag* refreshing, reviving ♦ *sm (gestore di ristorante)* restaurateur.

risto'ro *sm (bevanda, cibo)* refreshment; **posto di ~** *(FERR)* buffet, snack bar; **servizio di ~** *(FERR)* refreshments *pl*.

ristrettez'za [rēstrāttāt'tsá] *sf (strettezza)* narrowness; *(fig: scarsezza)* scarcity, lack; *(: meschinità)* meanness; **~e** *sfpl (povertà)* poverty *sg*.

ristret'to, a *pp di* **restringere** ♦ *ag (racchiuso)* enclosed, hemmed in; *(angusto)* narrow; *(limitato)*: **~ (a)** restricted *o* limited (to); *(CUC: brodo)* thick; *(: caffè)* extra strong.

ristruttura're *vt (azienda)* to reorganize; *(edificio)* to restore; *(appartamento)* to alter.

ristrutturazio'ne [rēstrōōttōōrāttsyō'nā] *sf* reorganization; restoration; alteration.

risucchia're [rēsōōkkyá'rā] *vt* to suck in.

risuc'chio [rēsōōk'kyō] *sm (di acqua)* undertow, pull; *(di aria)* suction.

risulta're *vi (dimostrarsi)* to prove (to be), turn out (to be); *(riuscire)*: **~ vincitore** to emerge as the winner; **~ da** *(provenire)* to result from, be the result of; **mi risulta che ... I** understand that ..., as far as I know ...; **(ne) risulta che ...** it follows that ...; **non mi risulta** not as far as I know.

risulta'to *sm* result.

risuona're *vi (rimbombare)* to resound.

risurrezio'ne [rēsōōrrāttsyō'nā] *sf (REL)* resurrection.

risuscita're [rēsōōshētā'rā] *vt* to resuscitate, restore to life; *(fig)* to revive, bring back ♦ *vi* to rise (from the dead).

risveglia're [rēzvālyá'rā] *vt (gen)* to wake up, waken; *(fig: interesse)* to stir up, arouse; *(: curiosità)* to arouse; *(fig: dall'inerzia etc)*: **~ qn (da)** to rouse sb (from); **~rsi** *vr* to wake up, awaken; *(fig: interesse, curiosità)* to be aroused.

risve'glio [rēzvāl'yō] *sm* waking up; *(fig)* revival.

risvol'to *sm (di giacca)* lapel; *(di pantaloni)* cuff *(US)*, turn-up *(Brit)*; *(di manica)* cuff; *(di tasca)* flap; *(di libro)* inside flap; *(fig)* implication.

ritaglia're [rētályá'rā] *vt (tagliar via)* to cut out.

rita'glio [rētál'yō] *sm (di giornale)* cutting, clipping; *(di stoffa etc)* scrap; **nei ~i di tempo** in one's spare time.

ritarda're *vi (persona, treno)* to be late; *(orologio)* to be slow ♦ *vt (rallentare)* to slow down; *(impedire)* to delay, hold up; *(differire)* to postpone, delay; **~ il pagamento** to defer payment.

ritardata'rio, a *sm/f* latecomer.

ritarda'to, a *ag (PSIC)* retarded.

ritar'do *sm* delay; *(di persona aspettata)* late-

ness *q*; *(fig: mentale)* backwardness; **in ~** late.

rite'gno [rētān'yō] *sm* restraint.

ritempra're *vt (forze, spirito)* to restore.

ritene're *vt (trattenere)* to hold back; *(: somma)* to deduct; *(giudicare)* to consider, believe.

riten'go, riten'ni *etc vb vedi* **ritenere.**

ritenta're *vt* to try again, make another attempt at.

ritenu'ta *sf (sul salario)* deduction; **~ d'acconto** advance deduction of tax; **~ alla fonte** *(FISCO)* taxation at source.

riterrò, ritie'ne *etc vb vedi* **ritenere.**

ritira're *vt* to withdraw; *(POL: richiamare)* to recall; *(andare a prendere: pacco etc)* to collect, pick up; **~rsi** *vr* to withdraw; *(da un'attività)* to retire; *(stoffa)* to shrink; *(marea)* to recede; **gli hanno ritirato la patente** they took away his license; **~rsi a vita privata** to withdraw from public life.

ritira'ta *sf (MIL)* retreat; *(latrina)* lavatory.

ritira'to, a *ag* secluded; **fare vita ~a** to live in seclusion.

riti'ro *sm (di truppe, candidati, soldi)* withdrawal; *(di pacchi)* collection; *(di passaporto)* confiscation; *(da attività)* retirement; *(luogo appartato)* retreat.

ritma'to, a *ag* rhythmic(al).

rit'mico, a, ci, che *ag* rhythmic(al).

rit'mo *sm* rhythm; *(fig)* rate; *(: della vita)* pace, tempo; **al ~ di** at a speed *o* rate of; **ballare al ~ di valzer** to waltz.

ri'to *sm* rite; **di ~** usual, customary.

ritocca're *vt (disegno, fotografia)* to touch up; *(testo)* to alter.

ritoc'co, chi *sm* touching up *q*; alteration.

ritor'cere [rētor'chārā] *vt (filato)* to twist; *(fig: accusa, insulto)* to throw back; **~rsi** *vr (tornare a danno di)*: **~rsi contro** to turn against.

ritorna're *vi* to return, go *(o come)* back; *(ripresentarsi)* to recur; *(ridiventare)*: **~ ricco** to become rich again ♦ *vt (restituire)* to return, give back.

ritornel'lo *sm* refrain.

ritor'no *sm* return; **durante il (viaggio di) ~** on the return trip, on the way back; **al ~** *(tornando)* on the way back; **essere di ~** to be back; **far ~** to return; **avere un ~ di fiamma** *(AUT)* to backfire; *(fig: persona)* to be back in love again.

ritorsio'ne *sf (rappresaglia)* retaliation.

ritor'to, a *pp di* **ritorcere** ♦ *ag (cotone, corda)* twisted.

ritrar're *vt (trarre indietro, via)* to withdraw; *(distogliere: sguardo)* to turn away; *(rappresentare)* to portray, depict; *(ricavare)* to get, obtain; **ritrarsi** *vr* to move back.

ritratta're *vt (disdire)* to retract, take back;

(*trattare nuovamente*) to deal with again.

ritrattazio'ne [rētráttáttsyō'nā] *sf* withdrawal.

ritratti'sta, i, e *sm/f* portrait painter.

ritrat'to, a *pp di* **ritrarre** ♦ *sm* portrait.

ritrosi'a *sf* (*riluttanza*) reluctance, unwillingness; (*timidezza*) shyness.

ritro'so, a *ag* (*restio*): ~ **(a)** reluctant (to); (*schivo*) shy; **andare a** ~ to go backwards.

ritrovamen'to *sm* (*di cadavere, oggetto smarrito etc*) finding; (*oggetto ritrovato*) find.

ritrova're *vt* to find; (*salute*) to regain; (*persona*) to find; to meet again; ~**rsi** *vr* (*essere, capitare*) to find o.s.; (*raccapezzarsi*) to find one's way; (*con senso reciproco*) to meet (again).

ritrova'to *sm* discovery.

ritro'vo *sm* meeting place; ~ **notturno** night club.

rit'to, a *ag* (*in piedi*) standing, on one's feet; (*levato in alto*) erect, raised; (: *capelli*) standing on end; (*posto verticalmente*) upright.

ritua'le *ag, sm* ritual.

riunio'ne *sf* (*adunanza*) meeting; (*riconciliazione*) reunion; **essere in** ~ to be at a meeting.

riuni're *vt* (*ricongiungere*) to join (together); (*riconciliare*) to reunite, bring together (again); ~**rsi** *vr* (*adunarsi*) to meet; (*tornare a stare insieme*) to be reunited; **siamo qui riuniti per festeggiare il vostro anniversario** we are gathered here to celebrate your anniversary.

riusci're [rēōōshē'rā] *vi* (*uscire di nuovo*) to go out again, go back out; (*aver esito: fatti, azioni*) to go, turn out; (*aver successo*) to succeed, be successful; (*essere, apparire*) to be, prove; (*raggiungere il fine*) to manage, succeed; ~ **a fare qc** to manage *o* be able to do sth; **questo mi riesce nuovo** this is new to me.

riusci'ta [rēōōshē'tà] *sf* (*esito*) result, outcome; (*buon esito*) success.

riutilizza're [rēōōtēlēddzá'rā] *vt* to use again, reuse.

ri'va *sf* (*di fiume*) bank; (*di lago, mare*) shore; **in** ~ **al mare** on the (sea) shore.

riva'le *ag* rival *cpd* ♦ *sm/f* rival; **non avere** ~**i** (*anche fig*) to be unrivalled.

rivaleggia're [rēvālādjá'rā] *vi* to compete, vie.

rivalità *sf* rivalry.

rival'sa *sf* (*rivincita*) revenge; (*risarcimento*) compensation; **prendersi una** ~ **su qn** to take revenge on sb.

rivaluta're *vt* (*ECON*) to revalue.

rivalutazio'ne [rēválōōtáttsyō'nā] *sf* (*ECON*) revaluation; (*fig*) reevaluation.

rivanga're *vt* (*ricordi etc*) to dig up (again).

rivede're *vt* to see again; (*ripassare*) to revise; (*verificare*) to check.

rivedrò *etc vb vedi* **rivedere**.

rivela're *vt* to reveal; (*divulgare*) to reveal, disclose; (*dare indizio*) to reveal, show; ~**rsi** *vr* (*manifestarsi*) to be revealed; ~**rsi onesto** *etc* to prove to be honest *etc*.

rivelato're, tri'ce *ag* revealing ♦ *sm* (*TECN*) detector; (*FOT*) developer.

rivelazio'ne [rēvāláttsyō'nā] *sf* revelation.

riven'dere *vt* (*vendere: di nuovo*) to resell, sell again; (: *al dettaglio*) to retail, sell retail.

rivendica're *vt* to claim, demand.

rivendicazio'ne [rēvāndēkáttsyō'nā] *sf* claim; ~**i salariali** wage claims.

riven'dita *sf* (*bottega*) retailer's (shop); ~ **di tabacchi** tobacconist's (shop).

rivendito're, tri'ce *sm/f* retailer; ~ **autorizzato** authorized dealer.

riverbera're *vt* to reflect.

river'bero *sm* (*di luce, calore*) reflection; (*di suono*) reverberation.

riveren'te *ag* reverent, respectful.

riveren'za [rēvāren'tsà] *sf* reverence; (*inchino*) bow; curtsey.

riveri're *vt* (*rispettare*) to revere; (*salutare*) to pay one's respects to.

riversa're *vt* (*anche fig*) to pour; ~**rsi** *vr* (*fig: persone*) to pour out.

rivestimen'to *sm* covering; coating.

rivesti're *vt* to dress again; (*ricoprire*) to cover; (: *con vernice*) to coat; (*fig: carica*) to hold; ~**rsi** *vr* to get dressed again; to change (one's clothes); ~ **di piastrelle** to tile.

rivi'di *etc vb vedi* **rivedere**.

rivie'ra *sf* coast; **la** ~ **italiana** the Italian Riviera.

rivin'cita [rēvēn'chētà] *sf* (*SPORT*) return match; (*fig*) revenge; **prendersi la** ~ **(su qn)** to take *o* get one's revenge (on sb).

rivissu'to, a *pp di* **rivivere**.

rivi'sta *sf* review; (*periodico*) magazine, review; (*TEATRO*) revue; variety show.

rivi'sto, a *pp di* **rivedere**.

rivitalizza're [rēvētálēddzá'rā] *vt* to revitalize.

rivi'vere *vi* (*riacquistare forza*) to come alive again; (*tornare in uso*) to be revived ♦ *vt* to relive.

ri'vo *sm* stream.

rivol'gere [rēvol'jārā] *vt* (*attenzione, sguardo*) to turn, direct; (*parole*) to address; ~**rsi** *vr* to turn round; (*fig: dirigersi per informazioni*): ~**rsi a** to go and see, go and speak to; ~ **un'accusa/una critica a qn** to accuse/criticize sb; ~**rsi all'ufficio competente** to go to the proper authorities.

rivolgimen'to [rēvōljēmān'tō] *sm* upheaval.

rivol'si *etc vb vedi* **rivolgere**.

rivol'ta *sf* revolt, rebellion.

rivoltan'te *ag* revolting, disgusting.

rivolta're *vt* to turn over; (*con l'interno*

all'esterno) to turn inside out; (*disgustare*: *stomaco*) to upset, turn; (: *fig*) to revolt, disgust; **~rsi** *vr* (*ribellarsi*): **~rsi (a)** to rebel (against).

rivoltel'la *sf* revolver.

rivol'to, a *pp di* **rivolgere**.

rivolto'so, a *ag* rebellious ♦ *sm/f* rebel.

rivoluziona're [rēvōlōottsyōnà'rā] *vt* to revolutionize.

rivoluziona'rio, a [rēvōlōottsyōnà'ryō] *ag, sm/f* revolutionary.

rivoluzio'ne [rēvōlōottsyō'nā] *sf* revolution.

rizza're [rēttsà'rā] *vt* to raise, erect; **~rsi** *vr* to stand up; (*capelli*) to stand on end; **~rsi in piedi** to stand up, get to one's feet.

RNA *sigla m* RNA (= *ribonucleic acid*).

RO *sigla* = *Rovigo*.

ro'ba *sf* stuff, things *pl*; (*possessi, beni*) belongings *pl*, things *pl*, possessions *pl*; **~ da mangiare** things to eat, food; **~ da matti!** it's sheer madness *o* lunacy!

robivec'chi [rōbĕvek'kē] *sm/f inv* junk dealer.

ro'bot *sm inv* robot.

robo'tica *sf* robotics *sg*.

robustez'za [rōbōostāt'tsà] *sf* (*di persona, pianta*) robustness, sturdiness; (*di edificio, ponte*) soundness.

robu'sto, a *ag* robust, sturdy; (*solido: catena*) strong; (: *edificio, ponte*) sound, solid; (*vino*) full-bodied.

roc'ca, che *sf* fortress.

roccafor'te *sf* stronghold.

rocchet'to [rōkkāt'tō] *sm* reel, spool.

roc'cia, ce [roch'chà] *sf* rock; **fare ~** (*SPORT*) to go rock climbing.

rocciato're, tri'ce [rōchàtō'rā] *sm/f* rock climber.

roccio'so, a [rōchō'sō] *ag* rocky; **le Montagne R~e** the Rocky Mountains.

ro'co, a, chi, che *ag* hoarse.

rodag'gio [rōdàd'jō] *sm* breaking (*US*) *o* running (*Brit*) in; **in ~** breaking *o* running in; **periodo di ~** (*fig*) period of adjustment.

Ro'dano *sm*: **il ~** the Rhone.

roda're *vt* (*AUT, TECN*) to break (*US*) *o* run (*Brit*) in.

rode'o *sm* rodeo.

ro'dere *vt* to gnaw (at); (*distruggere poco a poco*) to eat into.

Ro'di *sf* Rhodes.

rodito're *sm* (*ZOOL*) rodent.

rododen'dro *sm* rhododendron.

ro'gito [ro'jētō] *sm* (*DIR*) (notary's) deed.

ro'gna [ron'yà] *sf* (*MED*) scabies *sg*; (*di animale*) mange; (*fig*) bother, nuisance.

rogno'ne [rōnyō'nā] *sm* (*CUC*) kidney.

rogno'so, a [rōnyō'sō] *ag* (*persona*) scabby; (*animale*) mangy; (*fig*) troublesome.

ro'go, ghi *sm* (*per cadaveri*) (funeral) pyre; (*supplizio*): **il ~** the stake.

rolla're *vi* (*NAUT, AER*) to roll.

rolli'o *sm* roll(ing).

Ro'ma *sf* Rome.

romagno'lo, a [rōmányo'lō] *ag* of (*o* from) Romagna.

romane'sco, a, schi, sche *ag* Roman ♦ *sm* Roman dialect.

Romani'a *sf*: **la ~** Romania.

roma'nico, a, ci, che *ag* Romanesque.

roma'no, a *ag, sm/f* Roman.

romanticheri'a [rōmántēkārē'à] *sf* sentimentality.

romantici'smo [rōmántēchēz'mō] *sm* romanticism.

roman'tico, a, ci, che *ag* romantic.

roman'za [rōmàn'dzà] *sf* (*MUS, LETTERATURA*) romance.

romanza're [rōmándzà'rā] *vt* to romanticize.

romanze'sco, a, schi, sche [rōmándzà'skō] *ag* (*stile, personaggi*) fictional; (*fig*) storybook *cpd*.

romanzie're [rōmándzye'rā] *sm* novelist.

roman'zo, a [rōmàn'dzō] *ag* (*LING*) romance *cpd* ♦ *sm* (*medievale*) romance; (*moderno*) novel; **~ d'amore** love story; **~ d'appendice** serial (story); **~ cavalleresco** tale of chivalry; **~ poliziesco**, **~ giallo** detective story; **~ rosa** romantic novel.

romba're *vi* to rumble, thunder, roar.

rom'bo *sm* rumble, thunder, roar; (*MAT*) rhombus; (*ZOOL*) turbot.

rome'no, a *ag, sm/f, sm* = **rumeno**.

rom'pere *vt* to break; (*conversazione, fidanzamento*) to break off ♦ *vi* to break; **~rsi** *vr* to break; **mi rompe le scatole** (*fam*) he (*o* she) is a pain in the neck; **~rsi un braccio** to break an arm.

rompica'po *sm* worry, headache; (*indovinello*) puzzle; (*in enigmistica*) brain-teaser.

rompicol'lo *sm* daredevil.

rompighiac'cio [rōmpēgyách'chō] *sm* (*NAUT*) icebreaker.

rompisca'tole *sm/f inv* (*fam*) pest, pain in the neck.

ron'da *sf* (*MIL*) rounds *pl*, patrol.

rondel'la *sf* (*TECN*) washer.

ron'dine *sf* (*ZOOL*) swallow.

rondo'ne *sm* (*ZOOL*) swift.

ronfa're *vi* (*russare*) to snore.

ronza're [rōndzà'rā] *vi* to buzz, hum.

ronzi'no [rōndzē'nō] *sm* (*peg: cavallo*) nag.

ronzi'o, ii [rōndzē'ō] *sm* buzzing, humming.

ro'sa *sf* rose; (*fig: gruppo*): **~ dei candidati** list of candidates ♦ *ag inv, sm* pink.

rosa'io *sm* (*pianta*) rosebush, rose tree; (*giardino*) rose garden.

rosa'rio *sm* (*REL*) rosary.

rosa'to, a *ag* pink, rosy ♦ *sm* (*vino*) rosé (wine).

rose'o, a *ag* (*anche fig*) rosy.

rose'to sm rose garden.
roset'ta sf (diamante) rose-cut diamond; (rondella) washer.
ro'si vb vedi **rodere.**
rosicchia're |rŏsĕkkyả'rā| vt to gnaw (at); (mangiucchiare) to nibble (at).
rosmari'no sm rosemary.
ro'so, a pp di **rodere.**
rosola're vt (CUC) to brown.
rosoli'a sf (MED) German measles sg, rubella.
roso'ne sm rosette; (vetrata) rose window.
ro'spo sm (ZOOL) toad; **mandar giù** o **ingoiare un** o **il ~** (fig) to swallow a bitter pill; **sputa il ~!** out with it!
rosset'to sm (per labbra) lipstick; (per guance) rouge.
rossic'cio, a, ci, ce |rŏssĕch'chŏ| ag reddish.
ros'so, a ag, sm, sm/f red; **diventare ~ (per la vergogna)** to blush o go red (with o for shame); **il mar R~** the Red Sea; **~ d'uovo** egg yolk.
rosso're sm flush, blush.
rosticceri'a |rŏstĕchārč'ả| sf shop selling roast meat and other cooked food.
ros'tro sm rostrum; (becco) beak.
rota'bile ag (percorribile): **strada ~** roadway; (FERR): **materiale ~** rolling stock.
rota'ia sf rut, track; (FERR) rail.
rota're vt, vi to rotate.
rotati'vo, a ag rotating, rotation cpd.
rotazio'ne |rŏtáttsyŏ'nā| sf rotation.
rotea're vt, vi to whirl; **~ gli occhi** to roll one's eyes.
rotel'la sf small wheel; (di mobile) castor.
rotocalc'co, chi sm (TIP) rotogravure; (rivista) illustrated magazine.
rotola're vt, vi to roll; **~rsi** vr to roll (about).
rotoli'o sm rolling.
ro'tolo sm (di carta, stoffa) roll; (di corda) coil; **andare a ~i** (fig) to go to rack and ruin; **mandare a ~i** (fig) to ruin.
roton'do, a ag round ♦ sf rotunda.
roto're sm rotor.
rot'ta sf (AER, NAUT) course, route; (MIL) rout; **a ~ di collo** at breakneck speed; **essere in ~ con qn** to be on bad terms with sb; **fare ~ su** o **per** o **verso** to head for o towards; **cambiare ~** (anche fig) to change course; **in ~ di collisione** on a collision course; **ufficiale di ~** navigator, navigating officer.
rotta'me sm fragment, scrap, broken bit; **~i** smpl (di nave, aereo etc) wreckage sg; **~i di ferro** scrap iron sg.
rot'to, a pp di **rompere** ♦ ag broken; (calzoni) torn, split; (persona: pratico, resistente): **~ a** accustomed o inured to ♦ sm: **per il ~ della cuffia** by the skin of one's teeth; **~i** smpl: **20.000 lire e ~i** 20,000-odd lire.
rottu'ra sf (azione) breaking q; (di rapporti)

breaking off; (MED) fracture, break.
roulot'te |rōolot'| sf inv caravan.
roven'te ag red-hot.
ro'vere sm oak.
rove'scia |rŏvesh'shá| sf: **alla ~** upside-down; inside-out; **oggi mi va tutto alla ~** everything is going wrong (for me) today.
rovescia're |rŏvāshả'rā| vt (versare in giù) to pour; (: accidentalmente) to spill; (capovolgere) to turn upside down; (gettare a terra) to knock down; (: fig: governo) to overthrow; (piegare all'indietro: testa) to throw back; **~rsi** vr (sedia, macchina) to overturn; (barca) to capsize; (liquido) to spill; (fig: situazione) to be reversed.
rove'scio, sci |rŏvcsh'shŏ| sm other side, wrong side; (della mano) back; (di moneta) reverse; (pioggia) sudden downpour; (fig) setback; (MAGLIA: anche: **punto ~**) purl (stitch); (TENNIS) backhand (stroke); **a ~** (sottosopra) upside-down; (con l'esterno all'interno) inside-out; **capire qc a ~** to misunderstand sth; **~ di fortuna** setback.
rovi'na sf ruin; **~e** sfpl ruins; **andare in ~** (andare a pezzi) to collapse; (fig) to go to rack and ruin; **mandare qc/qn in ~** to ruin sth/sb.
rovina're vi to collapse, fall down ♦ vt (far cadere giù: casa) to demolish; (danneggiare, fig) to ruin.
rovina'to, a ag ruined, damaged; (fig: persona) ruined.
rovino'so, a ag ruinous.
rovista're vt (casa) to ransack; (tasche) to rummage in (o through).
ro'vo sm (BOT) blackberry bush, bramble bush.
rozzez'za |rŏddzăt'tsả| sf roughness, coarseness.
roz'zo, a |rŏd'dzŏ| ag rough, coarse.
RP sigla fpl vedi **relazioni pubbliche.**
R.R. abbr (POSTA) = **ricevuta di ritorno.**
Rrr abbr (POSTA) = **raccomandata con ricevuta di ritorno.**
RSVP abbr (= répondez s'il vous plaît) RSVP.
ru'ba sf: **andare a ~** to sell like hot cakes.
rubacuo'ri sm inv ladykiller.
ruba're vt to steal; **~ qc a qn** to steal sth from sb.
rubicon'do, a ag ruddy.
rubinet'to sm faucet (US), tap (Brit).
rubi'no sm ruby.
rubiz'zo, a |rōobĕt'tsŏ| ag lively, sprightly.
ru'blo sm ruble.
rubri'ca, che sf (di giornale: colonna) column; (: pagina) page; (quadernetto) index book; (: per indirizzi) address book.
ru'de ag tough, rough.
ru'dere sm (rovina) ruins pl.
rudimenta'le ag rudimentary, basic.

rudimen'ti *smpl* rudiments; basic principles.
ruffia'no *sm* pimp.
ru'ga, ghe *sf* wrinkle.
rug'gine |rōōd'jēnā| *sf* rust.
ruggi're |rōōdjē'rā| *vi* to roar.
ruggi'to |rōōdjē'tō| *sm* roar.
rugia'da |rōōjà'dà| *sf* dew.
rugo'so, a *ag* wrinkled; (*scabro: superficie etc*) rough.
rulla're *vi* (*tamburo, nave*) to roll; (*aereo*) to taxi.
rulli'no *sm* (*FOT*) roll of film, spool.
rulli'o, ii *sm* (*di tamburi*) roll.
rul'lo *sm* (*di tamburi*) roll; (*arnese cilindrico, TIP*) roller; ~ **compressore** steam roller; ~ **di pellicola** roll of film.
rum *sm* rum.
rume'no, a *ag, sm/f, sm* Romanian.
ruminan'te *sm* (*ZOOL*) ruminant.
rumina're *vt* (*ZOOL*) to ruminate; (*fig*) to ruminate on *o* over, chew over.
rumo're *sm*: **un** ~ a noise, a sound; **il** ~ noise; **fare** ~ to make a noise; **un** ~ **di passi** the sound of footsteps; **la notizia ha fatto molto** ~ (*fig*) the news aroused great interest.
rumoreggia're |rōōmōrādjá'rā| *vi* (*tuono etc*) to rumble; (*fig: folla*) to clamor (*US*), clamour (*Brit*).
rumoro'so, a *ag* noisy.
ruo'lo *sm* (*TEATRO, fig*) role, part; (*elenco*) roll, register, list; **di** ~ permanent, on the permanent staff; **professore di** ~ (*INS*) ≈ teacher with tenure; **fuori** ~ (*personale, insegnante*) temporary.
ruo'ta *sf* wheel; **a** ~ (*forma*) circular; ~ **anteriore/posteriore** front/back wheel; **andare a** ~ **libera** to freewheel; **parlare a** ~ **libera** (*fig*) to speak freely; ~ **di scorta** spare tire (*US*) *o* wheel (*Brit*).
ruota're *vt, vi* = **rotare.**
ru'pe *sf* cliff, rock.
rupes'tre *ag* rocky.
rup'pi *etc* *vb vedi* **rompere.**
rura'le *ag* rural, country *cpd*.
ruscel'lo |rōōshel'lō| *sm* stream.
ru'spa *sf* excavator.
ruspan'te *ag* (*pollo*) free-range.
russa're *vi* to snore.
Rus'sia *sf*: **la** ~ Russia.
rus'so, a *ag, sm/f, sm* Russian.
ru'stico, a, ci, che *ag* country *cpd*, rural; (*arredamento*) rustic; (*fig*) rough, unrefined ♦ *sm* (*fabbricato: per attrezzi*) shed; (*per abitazione*) hired hand's house (*US*), farm labourer's cottage (*Brit*).
ru'ta *sf* (*BOT*) rue.
rutta're *vi* to belch.
rut'to *sm* belch.
ru'vido, a *ag* rough, coarse.

ruzzola're |rōōttsōlá'rā| *vi* to tumble down.
ruzzolo'ni |rōōttsōlō'nē| *av*: **cadere** ~ to tumble down; **fare le scale** ~ to tumble down the stairs.

S

S, s |es'sā| *sf o m* (*lettera*) S, s; **S come Savona** ≈ S for Sugar.
s *abbr* (= *secondo*) sec.
S. *abbr* (= *sud*) S; (= *santo*) St.
SA *sigla* = *Salerno* ♦ *abbr vedi* **società anonima.**
sa *vb vedi* **sapere.**
sab. *abbr* (= *sabato*) Sat.
sa'bato *sm* Saturday; *per fraseologia vedi* **martedì.**
sab'bia *sf* sand; ~**e mobili** quicksand(s *pl*).
sabbiatu'ra *sf* (*MED*) sand bath; (*TECN*) sand-blasting; **fare le** ~**e** to take sand baths.
sabbio'so, a *ag* sandy.
sabotag'gio |sábōtád'jō| *sm* sabotage.
sabota're *vt* to sabotage.
sabotato're, tri'ce *sm/f* saboteur.
sac'ca, che *sf* bag; (*bisaccia*) haversack; (*insenatura*) inlet; ~ **d'aria** air pocket; ~ **da viaggio** travelling bag.
saccari'na *sf* saccharin(e).
saccen'te |sáchen'tā| *sm/f* know-it-all (*US*), know-all (*Brit*).
saccheggia're |sákkādjá'rā| *vt* to sack, plunder.
saccheg'gio |sákkād'jō| *sm* sack(ing).
sacchet'to |sákkāt'tō| *sm* (small) bag; (small) sack; ~ **di carta/di plastica** paper/plastic bag.
sac'co, chi *sm* bag; (*per carbone etc*) sack; (*ANAT, BIOL*) sac; (*tela*) sacking; (*saccheggio*) sack(ing); (*fig: grande quantità*): **un** ~ **di** lots of, heaps of; **cogliere** *o* **prendere qn con le mani nel** ~ to catch sb redhanded; **vuotare il** ~ to confess, spill the beans; **mettere qn nel** ~ to cheat sb; **colazione** *f* **al** ~ packed lunch; ~ **a pelo** sleeping bag; ~ **per i rifiuti** garbage bag (*US*), bin bag (*Brit*).
sacerdo'te |sáchārdo'tā| *sm* priest.
sacerdo'zio |sáchārdot'tsyō| *sm* priesthood.
sacramen'to *sm* sacrament.
sacra'rio *sm* memorial chapel.
sacresta'no *sm* = **sagrestano.**
sacresti'a *sf* = **sagrestia.**
sacrifica're *vt* to sacrifice; ~**rsi** *vr* to sacrifice

o.s.; (*privarsi di qc*) to make sacrifices.
sacrifi'cio [sákrēfē'chō] *sm* sacrifice.
sacrile'gio [sákrēle'jō] *sm* sacrilege.
sacri'lego, a, ghi, ghe *ag* (*REL*) sacrilegious.
sa'cro, a *ag* sacred.
sacrosan'to, a *ag* sacrosanct.
sa'dico, a, ci, che *ag* sadistic ♦ *sm/f* sadist.
sadi'smo *sm* sadism.
saet'ta *sf* arrow; (*fulmine*: *anche fig*) thunderbolt.
safa'ri *sm inv* safari.
saga'ce [ságá'chā] *ag* shrewd, sagacious.
saga'cia [ságá'chá] *sf* sagacity, shrewdness.
saggez'za [sádjāt'tsá] *sf* wisdom.
saggia're [sádjá'rā] *vt* (*metalli*) to assay; (*fig*) to test.
sag'gio, a, gi, ge [sád'jō] *ag* wise ♦ *sm* (*persona*) sage; (*operazione sperimentale*) test; (: *dell'oro*) assay; (*fig*: *prova*) proof; (*campione indicativo*) sample; (*scritto*: *letterario*) essay; (: *INS*) written test; **dare ~ di** to give proof of; **in ~ as** a sample.
saggi'stica [sádjē'stēká] *sf* ≈ non-fiction.
Sagitta'rio [sájēttá'ryō] *sm* Sagittarius; **essere del ~** to be Sagittarius.
sa'goma *sf* (*profilo*) outline, profile; (*forma*) form, shape; (*TECN*) template; (*bersaglio*) target; (*fig*: *persona*) character.
sa'gra *sf* festival.
sagra'to *sm* churchyard.
sagresta'no *sm* sacristan; sexton.
sagresti'a *sf* sacristy; (*culto protestante*) vestry.
Saha'ra [sáá'rá] *sm*: **il (Deserto del) ~** the Sahara (Desert).
saharia'na [sááryá'ná] *sf* bush jacket.
sa'i *vb vedi* **sapere.**
Saigon' *sf* Saigon.
sa'la *sf* hall; (*stanza*) room; **~ d'aspetto** waiting room; **~ da ballo** ballroom; **~ (dei) comandi** control room; **~ per concerti** concert hall; **~ per conferenze** (*INS*) lecture hall; (*in aziende*) conference room; **~ da gioco** gaming room; **~ macchine** (*NAUT*) engine room; **~ operatoria** (*MED*) operating room (*US*) *o* theatre (*Brit*); **~ da pranzo** dining room; **~ per ricevimenti** banquet (*US*) *o* banqueting (*Brit*) hall; **~ delle udienze** (*DIR*) courtroom.
sala'ce [sálá'chā] *ag* (*spinto, piccante*) salacious, saucy; (*mordace*) cutting, biting.
salaman'dra *sf* salamander.
sala'me *sm* salami *q*, salami sausage.
salamo'ia *sf* (*CUC*) brine.
sala're *vt* to salt.
salaria'le *ag* wage *cpd*, pay *cpd*; **aumento ~** wage *o* pay raise (*US*) *o* increase (*Brit*).
salaria'to, a *sm/f* wage-earner.
sala'rio *sm* pay, wages *pl*; **~ base** basic wage; **~ minimo garantito** minimum wage.

salassa're *vt* (*MED*) to bleed.
salas'so *sm* (*MED*) bleeding, bloodletting; (*fig*: *forte spesa*) drain.
salati'no *sm* cracker, salted biscuit.
sala'to, a *ag* (*sapore*) salty; (*CUC*) salted, salt *cpd*; (*fig*: *discorso etc*) biting, sharp; (: *prezzi*) steep, stiff.
salda're *vt* (*congiungere*) to join, bind; (*parti metalliche*) to solder; (: *con saldatura autogena*) to weld; (*conto*) to settle, pay.
saldato're *sm* (*operaio*) solderer; welder; (*utensile*) soldering iron.
saldatri'ce [sáldátrē'chā] *sf* (*macchina*) welder, welding machine; **~ ad arco** arc welder.
saldatu'ra *sf* soldering; welding; (*punto saldato*) soldered joint; weld; **~ autogena** welding; **~ dolce** soft soldering.
saldez'za [sáldāt'tsá] *sf* firmness, strength.
sal'do, a *ag* (*resistente, forte*) strong, firm; (*fermo*) firm, steady, stable; (*fig*) firm, steadfast ♦ *sm* (*svendita*) sale; (*di conto*) settlement; (*ECON*) balance; **pagare a ~** to pay in full; **~ attivo** credit; **~ passivo** deficit; **~ da riportare** balance carried forward.
sa'le *sm* salt; (*fig*) wit; **~i** *smpl* (*Med*: *da annusare*) smelling salts; **sotto ~** salted; **restare di ~** (*fig*) to be dumbfounded; **ha poco ~ in zucca** he doesn't have much sense; **~ da cucina, ~ grosso** cooking salt; **~ da tavola, ~ fino** table salt; **~i da bagno** bath salts; **~i minerali** mineral salts; **~i e tabacchi** tobacconist's (shop).
salgem'ma [sáljem'má] *sm* rock salt.
sal'go *etc vb vedi* **salire.**
sa'lice [sá'lēchā] *sm* willow; **~ piangente** weeping willow.
salien'te *ag* (*fig*) salient, main.
salie'ra *sf* salt cellar.
sali'no, a *ag* saline ♦ *sf* saltworks *sg*.
sali're *vi* to go (*o* come) up; (*aereo etc*) to climb, go up; (*passeggero*) to get on; (*sentiero, prezzi, livello*) to go up, rise ♦ *vt* (*scale, gradini*) to go (*o* come) up; **~ su** to climb (up); **~ sul treno/sull'autobus** to board the train/the bus; **~ in macchina** to get into the car; **~ a cavallo** to mount; **~ al potere** to rise to power; **~ al trono** to ascend the throne; **~ alle stelle** (*prezzi*) to rocket.
saliscen'di [sálēshān'dē] *sm inv* latch.
sali'ta *sf* climb, ascent; (*erta*) hill, slope; **in ~** *ag, av* uphill.
sali'va *sf* saliva.
sal'ma *sf* corpse.
salmas'tro, a *ag* (*acqua*) salt *cpd*; (*sapore*) salty ♦ *sm* (*sapore*) salty taste; (*odore*) salty smell.
sal'mo *sm* psalm.
salmo'ne *sm* salmon.

salmonel'la *sf* salmonella.

Salomo'ne: **le isole ~** *sfpl* the Solomon Islands.

salo'ne *sm* (*stanza*) sitting room, lounge; (*in albergo*) lounge; (*di ricevimento*) reception room; (*su nave*) lounge, saloon; (*mostra*) show, exhibition; (*negozio: di parrucchiere*) hairdresser's (salon); **~ dell'automobile** motor show; **~ di bellezza** beauty salon.

salottie'ro, a *ag* mundane.

salot'to *sm* lounge, sitting room; (*mobilio*) lounge suite.

salpa're *vi* (*NAUT*) to set sail; (*anche: ~ l'ancora*) to weigh anchor.

sal'sa *sf* (*CUC*) sauce; **in tutte le ~e** (*fig*) in all kinds of ways; **~ di pomodoro** tomato sauce.

salse'dine *sf* (*del mare, vento*) saltiness; (*incrostazione*) (dried) salt.

salsic'cia, ce [sàlsēch'chà] *sf* pork sausage.

salsie'ra *sf* gravy boat.

salta're *vi* to jump, leap; (*esplodere*) to blow up, explode; (: *valvola*) to blow; (*venir via*) to pop off; (*non aver luogo: corso etc*) to be cancelled ♦ *vt* to jump (over), leap (over); (*fig: pranzo, capitolo*) to skip, miss (out); (*CUC*) to sauté; **far ~** to blow up; (*serratura: forzare*) to break; **far ~ il banco** (*GIOCO*) to break the bank; **farsi ~ le cervella** to blow one's brains out; **ma che ti salta in mente?** what are you thinking of?; **~ da un argomento all'altro** to jump from one subject to another; **~ addosso a qn** (*aggredire*) to attack sb; **~ fuori** to jump out, leap out; (*venire trovato*) to turn up; **~ fuori con** (*frase, commento*) to come out with; **~ giù da qc** to jump off sth, jump down from sth.

saltella're *vi* to skip; to hop.

saltel'lo *sm* hop, little jump.

saltimban'co, chi *sm* acrobat.

sal'to *sm* jump; (*SPORT*) jumping; (*dislivello*) drop; **fare un ~** to jump, leap; **fare un ~ da qn** to pop over to sb's (place); **~ in alto/lungo** high/long jump; **~ con l'asta** pole vaulting; **~ mortale** somersault; **un ~ di qualità** (*miglioramento*) significant improvement.

saltua'rio, a *ag* occasional, irregular.

salu'bre *ag* healthy, salubrious.

salumeri'a *sf* delicatessen.

salu'mi *smpl* salted pork meats.

salumie're, a *sm/f* ≈ delicatessen owner.

salumifi'cio [sàlōōmēfē'chō] *sm* cured pork meat factory.

saluta're *ag* healthy; (*fig*) salutary, beneficial ♦ *vt* (*per dire buon giorno, fig*) to greet; (*per dire addio*) to say goodbye to; (*MIL*) to salute; **mi saluti sua moglie** my regards to your wife.

salu'te *sf* health; **~!** (*a chi starnutisce*) bless you!; (*nei brindisi*) cheers!; **bere alla ~ di qn** to drink (to) sb's health; **la ~ pubblica** public welfare; **godere di buona ~** to be healthy, enjoy good health.

salu'to *sm* (*gesto*) wave; (*parola*) greeting; (*MIL*) salute; **gli ha tolto il ~** he no longer says hello to him; **cari ~i, tanti ~i** best regards; **vogliate gradire i nostri più distinti ~i** yours faithfully; **i miei ~i alla sua signora** my regards to your wife.

sal'va *sf* salvo.

salvacondot'to *sm* (*MIL*) safe-conduct.

salvadana'io *sm* moneybox, piggy bank.

salvadore'gno, a [sàlvádōrān'yō] *ag*, *sm/f* Salvadorean.

salvagen'te [sàlvájen'tā] *sm* (*NAUT*) lifebuoy; (*pl inv: stradale*) traffic island; **~ a ciambella** lifebelt; **~ a giubbotto** life preserver (*US*), lifejacket (*Brit*).

salvaguarda're *vt* to safeguard.

salvaguar'dia *sf* safeguard; **a ~ di** for the safeguard of.

salva're *vt* to save; (*trarre da un pericolo*) to rescue; (*proteggere*) to protect; **~rsi** *vr* to save o.s.; to escape; **~ la vita a qn** to save sb's life; **~ le apparenze** to keep up appearances.

salvatag'gio [sàlvàtád'jō] *sm* rescue.

salvato're, tri'ce *sm/f* savior (*US*), saviour (*Brit*).

salvazio'ne [sàlvàttsyō'nā] *sf* (*REL*) salvation.

sal've *escl* (*fam*) hi!

salvez'za [sàlvāt'tsà] *sf* salvation; (*sicurezza*) safety.

sal'via *sf* (*BOT*) sage.

salviet'ta *sf* napkin.

sal'vo, a *ag* safe, unhurt, unharmed; (*fuori pericolo*) safe, out of danger ♦ *sm*: **in ~** safe ♦ *prep* (*eccetto*) except; **~ che** *cong* (*a meno che*) unless; (*eccetto che*) except (that); **mettere qc in ~** to put sth in a safe place; **mettersi in ~** to reach safety; **portare qn in ~** to lead sb to safety; **~ contrordini** barring instructions to the contrary; **~ errori e omissioni** errors and omissions excepted; **~ imprevisti** barring accidents.

sambu'co *sm* elder (tree).

sana're *vt* to heal, cure; (*economia*) to fix.

sanato'rio *sm* sanitarium (*US*), sanatorium (*Brit*).

sanci're [sànchē'rà] *vt* to sanction.

san'dalo *sm* (*BOT*) sandalwood; (*calzatura*) sandal.

san'gue *sm* blood; **farsi cattivo ~** to fret, get worked up; **all'ultimo ~** (*duello, lotta*) to the death; **non corre buon ~ tra di loro** there's bad blood between them; **buon ~ non mente!** it runs in the family!; **~ freddo** (*fig*) sang-froid, calm; **a ~ freddo** in cold blood.

sangui'gno, a [sàngwēn'yō] *ag* blood *cpd*;

(*colore*) blood-red.

sanguinan'te *ag* bleeding.

sanguina're *vi* to bleed.

sanguina'rio, a *ag* bloodthirsty.

sanguino'so, a *ag* bloody.

sanguisu'ga, ghe *sf* leech.

sanità *sf* health; (*salubrità*) healthiness; **Ministero della S~** Department of Health; **~ mentale** sanity; **~ pubblica** public health.

sanita'rio, a *ag* health *cpd*; (*condizioni*) sanitary ♦ *sm* (*AMM*) doctor; **Ufficiale S~** Health Officer; (**impianti**) **~i** *smpl* bathroom *o* sanitary fittings.

San Mari'no *sf*: **la Repubblica di ~** the Republic of San Marino.

san'no *vb vedi* **sapere**.

sa'no, a *ag* healthy; (*denti, costituzione*) healthy, sound; (*integro*) whole, unbroken; (*fig: politica, consigli*) sound; **~ di mente** sane; **di ~a pianta** completely, entirely; **~ e salvo** safe and sound.

Santia'go *sf*: **~ (del Cile)** Santiago (de Chile).

santifica're *vt* to sanctify; (*feste*) to observe.

santi'no *sm* holy picture.

santis'simo, a *ag*: **il S~ Sacramento** the Holy Sacrament; **il Padre S~** (*papa*) the Holy Father.

santità *sf* sanctity; holiness; **Sua/Vostra ~** (*titolo di papa*) His/Your Holiness.

san'to, a *ag* holy; (*fig*) saintly; (*seguito da nome proprio: dav sm* san + C, **sant'** + V, **santo** + *s impura, gn, pn, ps, x, z*; *dav sf* **santa** + C, **sant'** + V) saint ♦ *sm/f* saint; **parole ~e!** very true!; **tutto il ~ giorno** the whole blessed day, all day long; **non c'è ~ che tenga!** that's no excuse!; **la S~a Sede** the Holy See.

santo'ne *sm* holy man.

santua'rio *sm* sanctuary.

sanziona're [sàntsyònà'rà] *vt* to sanction.

sanzio'ne [sàntsyò'nà] *sf* sanction; (*penale, civile*) sanction, penalty; **~i economiche** economic sanctions.

sape're *vt* to know; (*essere capace di*): **so nuotare** I know how to swim, I can swim ♦ *vi*: **~ di** (*aver sapore*) to taste of; (*aver odore*) to smell of ♦ *sm* knowledge; **far ~ qc a qn** to inform sb about sth, let sb know sth; **venire a ~ qc (da qn)** to find out *o* hear about sth (from sb); **non ne vuole più ~ di lei** he doesn't want to have anything more to do with her; **mi sa che non sia vero** I don't think that's true.

sapien'te *ag* (*dotto*) learned; (*che rivela abilità*) masterly ♦ *sm/f* scholar.

sapien'ne, a *sm/f* (*peg*) know-it-all (*US*), know-all (*Brit*).

sapien'za [sàpyen'tsà] *sf* wisdom.

sapo'ne *sm* soap; **~ da barba** shaving soap;

~ da bucato laundry (*US*) *o* washing (*Brit*) soap; **~ liquido** liquid soap; **~ in scaglie** soapflakes *pl*.

saponet'ta *sf* cake *o* bar *o* tablet of soap.

sapo're *sm* taste, flavor (*US*), flavour (*Brit*).

sapori'to, a *ag* tasty; (*fig: arguto*) witty; (: *piccante*) racy.

sappia'mo *vb vedi* **sapere**.

saprò *etc vb vedi* **sapere**.

saputel'lo, a *sm/f* know-it-all (*US*), know-all (*Brit*).

sarà *etc vb vedi* **essere**.

saraban'da *sf* (*fig*) uproar.

saracine'sca, sche [sàràchènà'skà] *sf* (*serranda*) roller shutter.

sarca'smo *sm* sarcasm *q*; sarcastic remark.

sarca'stico, a, ci, che *ag* sarcastic.

sarchia're [sàrkyà'rà] *vt* (*AGR*) to hoe.

sarco'fago, gi *o* **ghi** *sm* sarcophagus.

Sarde'gna [sàrdàn'yà] *sf*: **la ~** Sardinia.

sardi'na *sf* sardine.

sar'do, a *ag, sm/f* Sardinian.

sardo'nico, a, ci, che *ag* sardonic.

sare'i *etc vb vedi* **essere**.

sar'ta *sf vedi* **sarto**.

sar'tia *sf* (*NAUT*) stay.

sartia'me *sm* (*NAUT*) stays *pl*.

sar'to, a *sm/f* tailor/dressmaker; **~ d'alta moda** couturier.

sartori'a *sf* tailor's (shop); dressmaker's (shop); (*casa di moda*) fashion house; (*arte*) couture.

sassa'ta *sf* blow with a stone; **tirare una ~ contro** *o* **a qc/qn** to throw a stone at sth/sb.

sas'so *sm* stone; (*ciottolo*) pebble; (*masso*) rock; **restare** *o* **rimanere di ~** to be dumbfounded.

sassofoni'sta, i, e *sm/f* saxophonist.

sasso'fono *sm* saxophone.

sasso'ne *ag, sm/f, sm* Saxon.

sasso'so, a *ag* stony; pebbly.

Sa'tana *sm* Satan.

sata'nico, a, ci, che *ag* satanic, fiendish.

satel'lite *sm, ag* satellite.

sa'tira *sf* satire.

satireggia're [sàtèràdjà'rà] *vt* to satirize ♦ *vi* (*fare della satira*) to be satirical; (*scrivere satire*) to write satires.

sati'rico, a, ci, che *ag* satiric(al).

satol'lo, a *ag* full, replete.

satura're *vt* to saturate.

saturazio'ne [sàtòòràttsyò'nà] *sf* saturation.

sa'turo, a *ag* saturated; (*fig*): **~ di** full of; **~ d'acqua** (*terreno*) waterlogged.

SA'UB *sigla f* (= *Struttura Amministrativa Unificata di Base*) state welfare system.

sa'una *sf* sauna; **fare la ~** to have *o* take a sauna.

sava'na *sf* savannah.

sa'vio, a *ag* wise, sensible ♦ *sm* wise man.

Savo'ia *sf*: **la** ~ Savoy.

savoiar'do, a *ag* of Savoy, Savoyard ♦ *sm* (*biscotto*) sponge finger.

sazia're |sàttsyà'rā| *vt* to satisfy, satiate; ~**rsi** *vr* (*riempirsi di cibo*): ~**rsi (di)** to eat one's fill (of); (*fig*): ~**rsi di** to grow tired *o* weary of.

sazietà |sàttsyātà'| *sf* satiety, satiation.

sa'zio, a |sàt'tsyō| *ag*: ~ **(di)** sated (with), full (of); (*fig*: *stufo*) fed up (with), sick (of).

sbadatag'gine |zbàdàtàd'jēnā| *sf* (*sventatez-za*) carelessness; (*azione*) oversight.

sbada'to, a *ag* careless, inattentive.

sbadiglia're |zbàdēlyà'rā| *vi* to yawn.

sbadi'glio |zbàdēl'yō| *sm* yawn; **fare uno** ~ to yawn.

sba'fo *sm*: **a** ~ at somebody else's expense.

sbaglia're |zbàlyà'rā| *vt* to make a mistake in, get wrong ♦ *vi* (*fare errori*) to make a mistake (*o* mistakes), be mistaken; (*ingannarsi*) to be wrong; (*operare in modo non giusto*) to err; ~**rsi** *vr* to make a mistake, be mistaken, be wrong; ~ **la mira/strada** to miss one's aim/take the wrong road; **scusi, ho sbagliato numero** (*TEL*) sorry, I've got the wrong number; **non c'è da** ~**rsi** there can be no mistake.

sbaglia'to, a |zbàlyà'tō| *ag* (*gen*) wrong; (*compito*) full of mistakes; (*conclusione*) erroneous.

sba'glio |zbàl'yō| *sm* mistake, error; (*morale*) error; **fare uno** ~ to make a mistake.

sbalestra'to, a *ag* (*persona: scombussolato*) unsettled.

sballa're *vt* (*merce*) to unpack ♦ *vi* (*nel fare un conto*) to overestimate; (*DROGA*: *gergo*) to get high.

sballa'to, a *ag* (*calcolo*) wrong; (*fam: ragionamento, persona*) screwy.

sbal'lo *sm* (*DROGA*: *gergo*) trip.

sballotta're *vt* to toss (around).

sbalordi're *vt* to stun, amaze ♦ *vi* to be stunned, be amazed.

sbalorditi'vo, a *ag* amazing; (*prezzo*) incredible, absurd.

sbalza're |zbàltsà'rā| *vt* to throw, hurl; (*fig*: *da una carica*) to remove, dismiss ♦ *vi* (*balzare*) to bounce; (*saltare*) to leap, bound.

sbal'zo |zbàl'tsō| *sm* (*spostamento improvviso*) jolt, jerk; **a** ~**i** jerkily; (*fig*) in fits and starts; **uno** ~ **di temperatura** a sudden change in temperature.

sbanca're *vt* (*nei giochi*) to break the bank at (*o* of); (*fig*) to ruin, bankrupt.

sbandamen'to *sm* (*NAUT*) list; (*AUT*) skid; (*fig*: *di persona*) confusion; **ha avuto un periodo di** ~ he went off the rails for a bit.

sbanda're *vi* (*NAUT*) to list; (*AUT*) to skid; ~**rsi** *vr* (*folla*) to disperse; (*truppe*) to scatter; (*fig*: *famiglia*) to break up.

sbanda'ta *sf* (*AUT*) skid; (*NAUT*) list; **prendere una** ~ **per qn** (*fig*) to fall for sb.

sbanda'to, a *sm/f* mixed-up person.

sbandiera're *vt* (*bandiera*) to wave; (*fig*) to parade, show off.

sban'do *sm*: **essere allo** ~ to drift.

sbaracca're *vt* (*libri, piatti etc*) to clear (up).

sbaraglia're |zbàràlyà'rā| *vt* (*MIL*) to rout; (*in gare sportive etc*) to beat, defeat.

sbara'glio |zbàràl'yō| *sm*: **gettarsi allo** ~ (*soldato*) to throw o.s. into the fray; (*fig*) to risk everything.

sbarazzar'si |zbàràttsàr'sē| *vr*: ~ **di** to get rid of, rid o.s. of.

sbarazzi'no, a |zbàràttsē'nō| *ag* impish, cheeky.

sbarba're *vt*, ~**rsi** *vr* to shave.

sbarbatel'lo *sm* novice, greenhorn.

sbarca're *vt* (*passeggeri*) to disembark; (*merci*) to unload ♦ *vi* to disembark.

sbar'co *sm* disembarkation; unloading; (*MIL*) landing.

sbar'ra *sf* bar; (*di passaggio a livello*) barrier; (*DIR*): **mettere/presentarsi alla** ~ to bring/appear before the court.

sbarramen'to *sm* (*stradale*) barrier; (*diga*) dam, barrage; (*MIL*) barrage.

sbarra're *vt* (*bloccare*) to block, bar; (*cancellare: assegno*) to endorse "for deposit only" (*US*), cross (*Brit*); ~ **il passo** to bar the way; ~ **gli occhi** to open one's eyes wide.

sbarra'to, a *ag* (*porta*) barred; (*passaggio*) blocked, barred; (*strada*) blocked, obstructed; (*occhi*) staring; (*assegno*) endorsed "for deposit only" (*US*), crossed (*Brit*).

sbat'tere *vt* (*porta*) to bang; (*tappeti, ali, CUC*) to beat; (*urtare*) to knock, hit ♦ *vi* (*porta, finestra*) to bang; (*agitarsi: ali, vele etc*) to flap; ~ **qn fuori/in galera** to throw sb out/into prison; **me ne sbatto!** (*fam*) I don't give a damn!

sbattu'to, a *ag* (*viso, aria*) dejected, worn out; (*uovo*) beaten.

sbava're *vi* to dribble; (*colore*) to smear, smudge.

sbavatu'ra *sf* (*di persone*) dribbling; (*di lumache*) slime; (*di rossetto, vernice*) smear.

sbellicar'si *vr*: ~ **dalle risa** to split one's sides laughing.

sbe'rla *sf* slap.

sberlef'fo *sm*: **fare uno** ~ **a qn** to make a face at sb.

sbiadi're *vi* (*anche*: ~**rsi**), *vt* to fade.

sbiadi'to, a *ag* faded; (*fig*) colorless (*US*), colourless (*Brit*), dull.

sbianca're *vt* to whiten; (*tessuto*) to bleach ♦ *vi* (*impallidire*) to grow pale *o* white.

sbie'co, a, chi, che *ag* (*storto*) squint, askew; **di** ~: **guardare qn di** ~ (*fig*) to look askance at sb; **tagliare una stoffa di** ~ to cut material on the bias.

sbigotti're *vt* to dismay, stun ♦ *vi* (*anche:* ~**rsi**) to be dismayed.

sbilancia're [zbēlānchá'rā] *vt* to throw off balance; ~**rsi** *vr* (*perdere l'equilibrio*) to overbalance, lose one's balance; (*fig: compromettersi*) to compromise o.s.

sbilen'co, a, chi, che *ag* (*persona*) crooked, misshapen; (*fig: idea, ragionamento*) twisted.

sbircia're [zbērchá'rā] *vt* to cast sidelong glances at, eye.

sbircia'ta [zbērchá'tá] *sf*: **dare una** ~ **a qc** to glance at sth, have a look at sth.

sbir'ro *sm* (*peg*) cop.

sbizzarrir'si [zbēddzárrēr'sē] *vr* to indulge one's whims.

sblocca're *vt* to unblock, free; (*freno*) to release; (*prezzi, affitti*) to free from controls; ~**rsi** *vr* (*gen*) to become unblocked; (*passaggio, strada*) to clear, become unblocked; **la situazione si è sbloccata** things are moving again.

sbocca're *vi*: ~ **in** (*fiume*) to flow into; (*strada*) to lead into; (*persona*) to come (out) into; (*fig: concludersi*) to end (up) in.

sbocca'to, a *ag* (*persona*) foul-mouthed; (*linguaggio*) foul.

sboccia're [zbōchá'rā] *vi* (*fiore*) to bloom, open (out).

sboc'co, chi *sm* (*di fiume*) mouth; (*di strada*) end; (*di tubazione, COMM*) outlet; (*uscita: anche fig*) way out; **una strada senza** ~ **a** dead end; **siamo in una situazione senza** ~**chi** there's no way out of this for us.

sbocconcella're [zbōkkōnchāllá'rā] *vt*: ~ **(qc)** to nibble (at sth).

sbollenta're *vt* (*CUC*) to parboil.

sbolli're *vi* (*fig*) to cool down, calm down.

sbor'nia *sf* (*fam*): **prendersi una** ~ to get plastered.

sborsa're *vt* (*denaro*) to pay out.

sbotta're *vi*: ~ **in una risata/per la collera** to burst out laughing/explode with anger.

sbottona're *vt* to unbutton, undo.

sbraca'to, a *ag* slovenly.

sbracciar'si [zbrácchár'sē] *vr* to wave (one's arms about).

sbraccia'to, a [zbrácchá'tō] *ag* (*camicia*) sleeveless; (*persona*) bare-armed.

sbraita're *vi* to yell, bawl.

sbrana're *vt* to tear to pieces.

sbriciola're [zbrēchōlá'rā] *vt*, ~**rsi** *vr* to crumble.

sbriga're *vt* to deal with, get through; (*cliente*) to attend to, deal with; ~**rsi** *vr* to hurry (up).

sbrigati'vo, a *ag* (*persona, modo*) quick, expeditious; (*giudizio*) hasty.

sbrinamen'to *sm* defrosting.

sbrina're *vt* to defrost.

sbrindella'to, a *ag* tattered, in tatters.

sbrodola're *vt* to stain, dirty.

sbronzar'si [zbrōntsár'sē] *vr* (*fam*) to get sozzled.

sbron'zo, a [zbrōn'tsō] (*fam*) *ag* sozzled ♦ *sf*: **prendersi una** ~**a** to get sozzled.

sbruffo'ne, a *sm/f* boaster, braggart.

sbuca're *vi* (*apparire*) to pop out (o up).

sbuccia're [zbōōchá'rā] *vt* (*arancia, patata*) to peel; (*piselli*) to shell; ~**rsi un ginocchio** to graze one's knee.

sbucherò *etc* [zbōōkáro'] *vb vedi* **sbucare**.

sbudellar'si *vr*: ~ **dalle risa** to split one's sides laughing.

sbuffa're *vi* (*persona, cavallo*) to snort; (*: ansimare*) to puff, pant; (*treno*) to puff.

sbuf'fo *sm* (*di aria, fumo, vapore*) puff; **maniche a** ~ puff(ed) sleeves.

sc. *abbr* (*TEATRO*: = *scena*) sc.

S.C. *abbr* = **stato civile; Suprema Corte (di Cassazione).**

scab'bia *sf* (*MED*) scabies *sg*.

sca'bro, a *ag* rough, harsh; (*fig*) concise, terse.

scabro'so, a *ag* (*fig: difficile*) difficult, thorny; (*: imbarazzante*) embarrassing; (*: sconcio*) indecent.

scacchie'ra [skákkye'rá] *sf* chessboard.

scacchiere [skákkye'rā] *sm* (*MIL*) sector; **S**~ (*in Gran Bretagna*) Exchequer.

scacciacia'ni [skácháká'nē] *sm o f inv* pistol with blanks.

scacciapensie'ri [skáchápānsye'rē] *sm inv* (*MUS*) jew's-harp.

scaccia're [skáchá'rā] *vt* to chase away *o* out, drive away *o* out; ~ **qn di casa** to turn sb out of the house.

scac'co, chi *sm* (*pezzo del gioco*) chessman; (*quadretto di scacchiera*) square; (*fig*) setback, reverse; ~**chi** *smpl* (*gioco*) chess *sg*; **a** ~**chi** (*tessuto*) check(ed); **subire uno** ~ (*fig: sconfitta*) to suffer a setback.

scaccomat'to *sm* checkmate; **dare** ~ **a qn** (*anche fig*) to checkmate sb.

scad'di *etc vb vedi* **scadere**.

scaden'te *ag* shoddy, of poor quality.

scaden'za [skáden'tsá] *sf* (*di cambiale, contratto*) maturity; (*di passaporto*) expiry date; **a breve/lunga** ~ short-/long-term; **data di** ~ expiry date; **a termine** fixed deadline.

scade're *vi* (*contratto etc*) to expire; (*debito*) to fall due; (*valore, forze, peso*) to decline, go down.

scafan'dro *sm* (*di palombaro*) diving suit; (*di astronauta*) spacesuit.

scaffalatu'ra *sf* shelving, shelves *pl*.

scaffa'le *sm* shelf; (*mobile*) set of shelves.

sca'fo *sm* (*NAUT, AER*) hull.

scagiona're [skájōná'rā] *vt* to exonerate, free from blame.

sca'glia [skål'yå] *sf* (*ZOOL*) scale; (*scheggia*) chip, flake.

scaglia're [skålyå'rå] *vt* (*lanciare: anche fig*) to hurl, fling; **~rsi** *vr*: **~rsi su** *o* **contro** to hurl *o* fling o.s. at; (*fig*) to rail at.

scaglionamen'to [skålyōnåmån'tō] *sm* (*MIL*) arrangement in echelons.

scagliona're [skålyōnå'rå] *vt* (*pagamenti*) to space out, spread out; (*MIL*) to echelon.

scaglio'ne [skålyō'nå] *sm* (*MIL*) echelon; (*GEO*) terrace; **a ~i** in groups.

scagnoz'zo [skånyot'tsō] *sm* (*peg*) lackey.

sca'la *sf* (*a gradini etc*) staircase, stairs *pl*; (*a pioli, di corda*) ladder; (*MUS, GEO, di colori, valori, fig*) scale; **~e** *sfpl* (*scalinata*) stairs; **su larga** *o* **vasta ~** on a large scale; **su piccola ~, su ~ ridotta** on a small scale; **su ~ nazionale/mondiale** on a national/worldwide scale; **in ~ di 1 a 100.000** on a scale of 1 cm to 1 km; **riproduzione in ~** reproduction to scale; **~ a chiocciola** spiral staircase; **~ a libretto** stepladder; **~ di misure** system of weights and measures; **~ mobile** escalator; (*ECON*) sliding scale; **~ mobile (dei salari)** index-linked pay scale; **~ di sicurezza** (*antincendio*) fire escape.

scala're *vt* (*ALPINISMO, muro*) to climb, scale; (*debito*) to scale down, reduce; **questa somma vi viene scalata dal prezzo originale** this sum is deducted from the original price.

scala'ta *sf* scaling *q*, climbing *q*; (*arrampicata, fig*) climb; **dare la ~ a** (*fig*) to make a bid for.

scalato're, tri'ce *sm/f* climber.

scalcagna'to, a [skålkånyå'tō] *ag* (*logoro*) worn; (*persona*) shabby.

scalcia're [skålchå'rå] *vi* to kick.

scalcia'to, a [skålchēnå'tō] *ag* (*fig peg*) shabby.

scaldaba'gno [skåldåbån'yō] *sm* water heater.

scalda're *vt* to heat; **~rsi** *vr* to warm up, heat up; (*al fuoco, al sole*) to warm o.s.; (*fig*) to get excited; **~ la sedia** (*fig*) to twiddle one's thumbs.

scaldavivan'de *sm inv* dish warmer.

scaldi'no *sm* (*per mani*) hand-warmer; (*per piedi*) foot-warmer; (*per letto*) bedwarmer.

scalfi're *vt* to scratch.

scalfittu'ra *sf* scratch.

scalina'ta *sf* staircase.

scali'no *sm* (*anche fig*) step; (*di scala a pioli*) rung.

scalma'na *sf* (hot) flush.

scalmanar'si *vr* (*affaticarsi*) to rush about, rush around; (*agitarsi, darsi da fare*) to get all hot and bothered; (*arrabbiarsi*) to get excited, get steamed up.

scalmana'to, a *sm/f* hothead.

sca'lo *sm* (*NAUT*) slipway; (*: porto d'approdo*) port of call; (*AER*) stopover; **fare ~ (a)** (*NAUT*) to call (at), put in (at); (*AER*) to land (at), make a stop (at); **volo senza ~** non-stop flight; **~ merci** (*FERR*) freight yard.

scalo'gna [skålōn'yå] *sf* (*fam*) bad luck.

scalogna'to, a [skålōnyå'tō] *ag* (*fam*) unlucky.

scaloppi'na *sf* (*CUC*) escalope.

scalpel'lo *sm* chisel.

scalpita're *vi* (*cavallo*) to paw the ground; (*persona*) to stamp one's feet.

scalpo're *sm* noise, row; **far ~** (*notizia*) to cause a sensation *o* a stir.

scal'tro, a *ag* cunning, shrewd.

scalza're [skåltså'rå] *vt* (*albero*) to bare the roots of; (*muro, fig: autorità*) to undermine.

scal'zo, a [skål'tsō] *ag* barefoot.

scambia're *vt* to exchange; (*confondere*): **~ qn/qc per** to take *o* mistake sb/sth for; **mi hanno scambiato il cappello** they've given me the wrong hat.

scambie'vole *ag* mutual, reciprocal.

scam'bio *sm* exchange; (*COMM*) trade; (*FERR*) switch (*US*), points *pl* (*Brit*); **fare (uno) ~** to make a swap; **libero ~** free trade; **~i con l'estero** foreign trade.

scamoscia'to, a [skåmōshå'tō] *ag* suede.

scampagna'ta [skåmpånyå'tå] *sf* trip to the country.

scampana're *vi* to peal.

scampa're *vt* (*salvare*) to rescue, save; (*evitare: morte, prigione*) to escape ♦ *vi*: **~ (a qc)** to survive (sth), escape (sth); **scamparla bella** to have a narrow escape.

scam'po *sm* (*salvezza*) escape; (*ZOOL*) prawn; **cercare ~ nella fuga** to seek safety in flight; **non c'è (via di) ~** there's no way out.

scam'polo *sm* remnant.

scanalatu'ra *sf* (*incavo*) channel, groove.

scandaglia're [skåndålyå'rå] *vt* (*NAUT*) to sound; (*fig*) to sound out; to probe.

scandali'stico, a, ci, che *ag* (*settimanale etc*) sensational.

scandalizza're [skåndålēddzå'rå] *vt* to shock, scandalize; **~rsi** *vr* to be shocked.

scan'dalo *sm* scandal; **dare ~** to cause a scandal.

scandalo'so, a *ag* scandalous, shocking.

Scandina'via *sf*: **la ~** Scandinavia.

scandina'vo, a *ag, sm/f* Scandinavian.

scandi're *vt* (*versi*) to scan; (*parole*) to articulate, pronounce distinctly; **~ il tempo** (*MUS*) to beat time.

scanna're *vt* (*animale*) to butcher, slaughter; (*persona*) to cut *o* slit the throat of.

scan'no *sm* seat, bench.

scansafati'che [skånsåfåtē'kå] *sm/f inv* idler, loafer.

scansa're *vt* (*rimuovere*) to move (aside), shift; (*schivare: schiaffo*) to dodge; (*sfuggire*) to avoid; **~rsi** *vr* to move aside.

scansi'a *sf* shelves *pl*; (*per libri*) bookcase.

scan'so *sm*: **a ~ di** in order to avoid, as a precaution against; **a ~ di equivoci** to avoid (any) misunderstanding.

scantina'to *sm* basement.

scantona're *vi* to turn the corner; (*svignarsela*) to sneak off.

scanzona'to, a [skántsōná'tō] *ag* easy-going.

scapaccio'ne [skápáchō'nā] *sm* clout, slap.

scapestra'to, a *ag* dissolute.

sca'pito *sm* (*perdita*) loss; (*danno*) damage, detriment; **a ~ di** to the detriment of.

sca'pola *sf* shoulder blade.

sca'polo *sm* bachelor.

scappamen'to *sm* (*AUT*) exhaust.

scappa're *vi* (*fuggire*) to escape; (*andare via in fretta*) to rush off; **~ di prigione** to escape from prison; **~ di mano** (*oggetto*) to slip out of one's hands; **~ di mente a qn** to slip sb's mind; **lasciarsi ~** (*occasione, affare*) to miss, let go by; (*dettaglio*) to overlook; (*parola*) to let slip; (*prigioniero*) to let escape; **mi scappò detto** I let it slip.

scappa'ta *sf* quick visit *o* call.

scappatel'la *sf* escapade.

scappato'ia *sf* way out.

scarabe'o *sm* beetle.

scarabocchia're [skárábōkkyà'rā] *vt* to scribble, scrawl.

scaraboc'chio [skárábok'kyō] *sm* scribble, scrawl.

scarafag'gio [skáráfád'jō] *sm* cockroach.

scaramanzi'a [skáràmántsē'á] *sf*: **per ~ for** luck.

scaramuc'cia, ce [skáràmōōch'chá] *sf* skirmish.

scaraventa're *vt* to fling, hurl.

scarcera're [skárchārá'rā] *vt* to release (from prison).

scarcerazio'ne [skárcháráttsyō'nā] *sf* release (from prison).

scardina're *vt* to take off its hinges.

sca'rica, che *sf* (*di più armi*) volley of shots; (*di sassi, pugni*) hail, shower; (*ELETTR*) discharge; **~ di mitra** burst of machine-gun fire.

scarica're *vt* (*merci, camion etc*) to unload; (*passeggeri*) to set down; (*arma*) to unload; (: *sparare, ELETTR*) to discharge; (*sog: corso d'acqua*) to empty, pour; (*fig: liberare da un peso*) to unburden, relieve; **~rsi** *vr* (*orologio*) to run *o* wind down; (*batteria, accumulatore*) to go dead; (*fig: rilassarsi*) to unwind; (: *sfogarsi*) to let off steam; **~ le proprie responsabilità su qn** to unload one's responsibilities onto sb; **~ la colpa addosso a qn** to blame sb; **il fulmine si scaricò su un albero** the lightning struck a tree.

scaricato're *sm* loader; (*di porto*) docker.

sca'rico, a, chi, che *ag* unloaded; (*orologio*) run down; (*batteria, accumulatore*) dead, flat (*Brit*) ♦ *sm* (*di merci, materiali*) unloading;

(*di immondizie*) dumping, tipping (*Brit*); (: *luogo*) garbage (*US*) *o* rubbish (*Brit*) dump; (*TECN: deflusso*) draining; (: *dispositivo*) drain; (*AUT*) exhaust; **~ del lavandino** drain.

scarlatti'na *sf* scarlet fever.

scarlat'to, a *ag* scarlet.

scar'no, a *ag* thin, bony.

scar'pa *sf* shoe; **fare le ~e a qn** (*fig*) to double-cross sb; **~e da ginnastica** gym shoes; **~e coi tacchi (alti)** high-heeled shoes; **~e col tacco basso** low-heeled shoes; **~e senza tacco** flat shoes; **~e da tennis** tennis shoes.

scarpa'ta *sf* escarpment.

scarpie'ra *sf* shoe rack.

scarpo'ne *sm* boot; **~i da montagna** climbing boots; **~i da sci** ski-boots.

scarrozza're [skárrōttsá'rā] *vt* to drive around.

scarseggia're [skársādjá'rā] *vi* to be scarce; **~ di** to be short of, lack.

scarsez'za [skársát'tsá] *sf* scarcity, lack.

scar'so, a *ag* (*insufficiente*) insufficient, meager (*US*), meagre (*Brit*); (*povero: annata*) poor, lean; (*INS: voto*) poor; **~ di** lacking in; **3 chili ~i** just under 3 kilos, barely 3 kilos.

scartabella're *vt* to skim through, glance through.

scartafac'cio [skártáfách'chō] *sm* notebook.

scartamen'to *sm* (*FERR*) gauge; **~ normale/ridotto** standard/narrow gauge.

scarta're *vt* (*pacco*) to unwrap; (*idea*) to reject; (*MIL*) to declare unfit for military service; (*carte da gioco*) to discard; (*CALCIO*) to dodge (past) ♦ *vi* to swerve.

scar'to *sm* (*cosa scartata, anche COMM*) reject; (*di veicolo*) swerve; (*differenza*) gap, difference; **~ salariale** wage differential.

scartof'fie *sfpl* (*peg*) papers *pl*.

scassa're *vt* (*fam: rompere*) to wreck.

scassina're *vt* to break, force.

scas'so *sm vedi* **furto.**

scatena're *vt* (*fig*) to incite, stir up; **~rsi** *vr* (*temporale*) to break; (*rivolta*) to break out; (*persona: infuriarsi*) to rage.

scatena'to, a *ag* wild.

sca'tola *sf* box; (*di latta*) can, tin (*Brit*); **cibi in ~** canned foods; **una ~ di cioccolatini** a box of chocolates; **comprare qc a ~ chiusa** to buy sth sight unseen; **~ cranica** cranium.

scattan'te *ag* quick off the mark; (*agile*) agile.

scatta're *vt* (*fotografia*) to take ♦ *vi* (*congegno, molla etc*) to be released; (*balzare*) to spring up; (*SPORT*) to put on a spurt; (*fig: per l'ira*) to fly into a rage; (*legge, provvedimento*) to come into effect; **~ in piedi** to spring to one's feet; **far ~** to release.

scat'to *sm* (*dispositivo*) release; (: *di arma da fuoco*) trigger mechanism; (*rumore*) click; (*balzo*) jump, start; (*SPORT*) spurt; (*fig*: *di ira etc*) fit; (: *di stipendio*) increment; **di** ~ suddenly; **serratura a** ~ spring lock.

scaturi're *vi* to gush, spring.

scavalca're *vt* (*ostacolo*) to pass (*o* climb) over; (*fig*) to get ahead of, overtake.

scava're *vt* (*terreno*) to dig; (*legno*) to hollow out; (*pozzo, galleria*) to bore; (*città sepolta etc*) to excavate.

scavatri'ce |skàvàtrē'chā| *sf* (*macchina*) excavator.

scavezzacol'lo |skàvàttsàkol'lō| *sm* daredevil.

sca'vo *sm* excavating *q*; excavation.

scazzotta're |skàttsōttà'rā| *vt* (*fam*) to beat up, give a thrashing to.

sce'gliere |shāl'yārā| *vt* (*gen*) to choose; (*candidato, prodotto*) to choose, select; ~ **di fare** to choose to do.

sceic'co, chi |shāēk'kō| *sm* sheik.

scel'go *etc* |shāl'gō| *vb vedi* **scegliere**.

scellera'to, a |shāllàrà'tō| *ag* wicked, evil.

scelli'no |shāllē'nō| *sm* shilling.

scel'to, a |shāl'tō| *pp di* **scegliere** ♦ *ag* (*gruppo*) carefully selected; (*frutta, verdura*) choice, top quality; (*MIL*: *specializzato*) crack *cpd*, highly skilled ♦ *sf* choice; (*selezione*) selection, choice; **frutta o formaggi a** ~**a** choice of fruit or cheese; **fare una** ~**a** to make a choice, choose; **non avere** ~**a** to have no choice *o* option; **di prima** ~**a** top grade *o* quality.

scema're |shāmà'rā| *vt, vi* to diminish.

scemen'za |shāmen'tsà| *sf* stupidity *q*; stupid thing (to do *o* say).

sce'mo, a |shā'mō| *ag* stupid, silly.

scem'pio |shām'pyō| *sm* slaughter, massacre; (*fig*) ruin; **far** ~ **di** (*fig*) to play havoc with, ruin.

sce'na |shē'nà| *sf* (*gen*) scene; (*palcoscenico*) stage; **le** ~**e** (*fig*: *teatro*) the stage; **andare in** ~ to be staged *o* put on *o* performed; **mettere in** ~ to stage; **uscire di** ~ to leave the stage; (*fig*) to leave the scene; **fare una** ~ (*fig*) to make a scene; **ha fatto** ~ **muta** (*fig*) he didn't open his mouth.

scena'rio |shānà'ryō| *sm* scenery; (*di film*) scenario.

scena'ta |shānà'tà| *sf* row, scene.

scen'dere |shān'dārā| *vi* to go (*o* come) down; (*strada, sole*) to go down; (*notte*) to fall; (*passeggero: fermarsi*) to get out; (*fig*: *temperatura, prezzi*) to fall, drop ♦ *vt* (*scale, pendio*) to go (*o* come) down; ~ **dalle scale** to go (*o* come) down the stairs; ~ **dal treno** to get off *o* out of the train; ~ **dalla macchi-na** to get out of the car; ~ **da cavallo** to dismount, get off one's horse; ~ **ad un albergo** to put up *o* stay at a hotel.

sceneggia'to |shānādjà'tō| *sm* television drama.

sceneggiato're, tri'ce |shānādjàtō'rā| *sm/f* script-writer.

sceneggiatu'ra |shānādjàtōō'rà| *sf* (*TEATRO*) scenario; (*CINEMA*) screenplay, scenario.

sce'nico, a, ci, che |shc'nēkō| *ag* stage *cpd*.

scenografi'a |shānōgràfē'à| *sf* (*TEATRO*) stage design; (*CINEMA*) set design; (*elementi scenici*) scenery.

sceno'grafo, a |shāno'gràfō| *sm/f* set designer.

scerif'fo |shārēf'fō| *sm* sheriff.

scervellar'si |shārvāllàr'sē| *vr*: ~ **(su qc)** to rack one's brains (over sth).

scervella'to, a |shārvāllà'tō| *ag* featherbrained, scatterbrained.

sce'so, a |shà'sō| *pp di* **scendere**.

scettici'smo |shāttēchēz'mō| *sm* skepticism (*US*), scepticism (*Brit*).

scet'tico, a, ci, che |shct'tēkō| *ag* skeptical (*US*), sceptical (*Brit*).

scet'tro |shct'trō| *sm* scepter (*US*), sceptre (*Brit*).

sche'da |skc'dà| *sf* (index) card; ~ **a circuito stampato** printed-circuit board; ~ **elettorale** ballot (*US*), ballot paper (*Brit*); ~ **perforata** punch card.

scheda're |skādà'rā| *vt* (*dati*) to file; (*libri*) to catalogue; (*registrare: anche POLIZIA*) to put on one's files.

scheda'rio |skādà'ryō| *sm* file; (*mobile*) filing cabinet.

scheda'to, a |skādà'tō| *ag* with a (police) record ♦ *sm/f* person with a (police) record.

schedi'na |skādē'nà| *sf* ≈ lottery ticket.

scheg'gia, ge |skād'jà| *sf* splinter, sliver.

sche'letro |skc'lātrō| *sm* skeleton.

sche'ma, i |skc'mà| *sm* (*diagramma*) diagram, sketch; (*progetto, abbozzo*) outline, plan; **ribellarsi agli** ~**i** to rebel against traditional values; **secondo gli** ~**i tradizionali** in accordance with traditional values.

schema'tico, a, ci, che |skāmà'tēkō| *ag* schematic.

schematizza're |skāmàtēddzà'rā| *vt* to schematize.

scher'ma |skār'mà| *sf* fencing.

scherma'glia |skārmàl'yà| *sf* (*fig*) skirmish.

schermir'si |skārmēr'sē| *vr* to defend o.s., protect o.s.

scher'mo |skār'mō| *sm* shield, screen; (*CINEMA, TV*) screen.

schermografi'a |skārmōgràfē'à| *sf* X-rays *pl*.

scherni're |skārnē'rā| *vt* to mock, sneer at.

scher'no |skār'nō| *sm* mockery, derision; **farsi** ~ **di** to sneer at; **essere oggetto di** ~ to be a laughing stock.

scherza're |skārtsà'rā| *vi* to joke.

scher'zo |skār'tsō| *sm* joke; (*tiro*) trick; (*MUS*) scherzo; **è uno** ~**!** (*una cosa facile*) it's child's play!, it's easy!; **per** ~ for a joke *o* a laugh; **fare un brutto ~ a qn** to play a nasty trick on sb; **~i a parte** seriously, joking apart.

scherzo'so, a [skărtsō'sō] *ag* (*tono, gesto*) playful; (*osservazione*) facetious; **è un tipo ~** he likes a joke.

schiacciano'ci [skyàchánō'chē] *sm inv* nutcracker.

schiaccian'te [skyàchán'tā] *ag* overwhelming.

schiaccia're [skyàchá'rā] *vt* (*dito*) to crush; (*noci*) to crack; **~ un pisolino** to have a nap.

schiaffeggia're [skyàffädjá'rā] *vt* to slap.

schiaf'fo [skyàf'fō] *sm* slap; **prendere qn a ~i** to slap sb's face; **uno ~ morale** a slap in the face, a rebuff.

schiamazza're [skyàmáttsá'rā] *vi* to squawk, cackle.

schiamaz'zo [skyàmát'tsō] *sm* (*fig: chiasso*) din, racket.

schianta're [skyàntá'rā] *vt* to break, tear apart; **~rsi** *vr* to break (up), shatter; **~rsi al suolo** (*aereo*) to crash (to the ground).

schian'to [skyàn'tō] *sm* (*rumore*) crash; tearing sound; **è uno ~!** (*fam*) it's (*o* he's *o* she's) terrific!; **di ~** all of a sudden.

schiari're [skyàrē'rā] *vt* to lighten, make lighter ♦ *vi* (*anche:* **~rsi**) to grow lighter; (*tornar sereno*) to clear, brighten up; **~rsi la voce** to clear one's throat.

schiari'ta [skyàrē'tá] *sf* (*METEOR*) bright spell; (*fig*) improvement, turn for the better.

schiatta're [skyàttá'rā] *vi* to burst; **~ d'invidia** to be green with envy; **~ di rabbia** to be beside o.s. with rage.

schiavitù [skyàvētōō'] *sf* slavery.

schiavizza're [skyàvēddzá'rā] *vt* to enslave.

schia'vo, a [skyà'vō] *sm/f* slave.

schie'na [skyc'nà] *sf* (*ANAT*) back.

schiena'le [skyänà'lā] *sm* (*di sedia*) back.

schie'ra [skyc'rà] *sf* (*MIL*) rank; (*gruppo*) group, band.

schieramen'to [skyàrámàn'tō] *sm* (*MIL. SPORT*) formation; (*fig*) alliance.

schiera're [skyārà'rā] *vt* (*esercito*) to line up, draw up, marshal; **~rsi** *vr* to line up; (*fig*): **~rsi con** *o* **dalla parte di/contro qn** to side with/oppose sb.

schiet'to, a [skyct'tō] *ag* (*puro*) pure; (*fig*) frank, straightforward.

schifa're [skēfà'rā] *vt* to disgust.

schifez'za [skēfát'tsá] *sf*: **essere una ~** (*cibo, bibita etc*) to be disgusting; (*film, libro*) to be dreadful.

schifilto'so, a [skēfēltō'sō] *ag* fussy, difficult.

schi'fo [skē'fō] *sm* disgust; **fare ~** (*essere fatto male, dare pessimi risultati*) to be awful; **mi fa ~** it makes me sick, it's disgusting; **quel libro è uno ~** that book's rotten.

schifo'so, a [skēfō'sō] *ag* disgusting, revolting; (*molto scadente*) rotten, lousy.

schiocca're [skyōkká'rā] *vt* (*frusta*) to crack; (*dita*) to snap; (*lingua*) to click; **~ le labbra** to smack one's lips.

schioppetta'ta [skyōppàttá'tà] *sf* gunshot.

schiop'po [skyop'pō] *sm* rifle, gun.

schiu'dere [skyōō'dārā] *vt*, **~rsi** *vr* to open.

schiu'ma [skyōō'mà] *sf* foam; (*di sapone*) lather; (*di latte*) froth.

schiuma're [skyōōmà'rā] *vt* to skim ♦ *vi* to foam.

schiu'so, a [skyōō'sō] *pp* di **schiudere**.

schiva're [skēvà'rā] *vt* to dodge, avoid.

schi'vo, a [skē'vō] *ag* (*ritroso*) stand-offish, reserved; (*timido*) shy.

schizofreni'a [skēddzōfrānē'á] *sf* schizophrenia.

schizofre'nico, a, ci, che [skēddzōfrc'nēkō] *ag* schizophrenic.

schizza're [skēttsá'rā] *vt* (*spruzzare*) to spurt, squirt; (*sporcare*) to splash, spatter; (*fig: abbozzare*) to sketch ♦ *vi* to spurt, squirt; (*saltar fuori*) to dart up (*o* off *etc*); **~ via** (*animale, persona*) to dart away; (*macchina, moto*) to accelerate away.

schizzino'so, a [skēttsēnō'sō] *ag* fussy, finicky.

schiz'zo [skēt'tsō] *sm* (*di liquido*) spurt; splash, spatter; (*abbozzo*) sketch.

sci [shē] *sm inv* (*attrezzo*) ski; (*attività*) skiing; **~ di fondo** cross-country skiing, ski touring (*US*); **~ nautico** water-skiing.

sci'a, *pl* sci'e [shē'à] *sf* (*di imbarcazione*) wake; (*di profumo*) trail.

scià [shá] *sm inv* shah.

scia'bola [shà'bōlà] *sf* saber (*US*), sabre (*Brit*).

sciacal'lo [shàkàl'lō] *sm* jackal; (*fig peg: profittatore*) shark, profiteer; (: *ladro*) looter.

sciacqua're [shàkkwà'rā] *vt* to rinse.

sciagu'ra [shàgōō'rà] *sf* disaster, calamity.

sciagura'to, a [shàgōōrà'tō] *ag* unfortunate; (*malvagio*) wicked.

scialacqua're [shàlàkkwà'rā] *vt* to squander.

sciala're [shàlà'rā] *vi* to throw one's money around.

scial'bo, a [shàl'bō] *ag* pale, dull; (*fig*) dull.

scial'le [shàl'lā] *sm* shawl.

scia'lo [shà'lō] *sm* squandering, waste.

scialup'pa [shàlōōp'pà] *sf* (*NAUT*) sloop; (*anche:* **~ di salvataggio**) lifeboat.

sciama're [shàmà'rā] *vi* to swarm.

scia'me [shà'mā] *sm* swarm.

scianca'to, a [shànkà'tō] *ag* lame; (*mobile*) rickety.

scia're [shēà'rā] *vi* to ski; **andare a ~** to go skiing.

sciar'pa [shàr'pá] *sf* scarf; (*fascia*) sash.

scia'tore, tri'ce [shēàtō'rā] *sm/f* skier.

sciattez'za [shàttàt'tsá] *sf* slovenliness.

sciat'to, a [shát'tō] *ag* (*persona: nell'aspetto*) slovenly, unkempt; (: *nel lavoro*) sloppy, careless.

sci'bile |shē'bēlā| *sm* knowledge.

scienti'fico, a, ci, che |shāntē'fĕkō| *ag* scientific; **la (polizia)** ~a the forensic department.

scien'za |shen'tsà| *sf* science; (*sapere*) knowledge; ~**e** *sfpl* (*INS*) science *sg*; ~**e naturali** natural sciences; ~**e politiche** political science *sg*.

scienzia'to, a |shāntsyá'tō| *sm/f* scientist.

Scilly' |shēl'lē|: **le isole** ~ *sfpl* the Scilly Isles.

scim'mia |shĕm'myà| *sf* monkey.

scimmiotta're |shĕmmyòttà'rā| *vt* to ape, mimic.

scimpanzé |shĕmpàntsā'| *sm inv* chimpanzee.

scimuni'to, a |shĕmōōnē'tō| *ag* silly, idiotic.

scin'dere |shēn'dārā| *vt*, ~**rsi** *vr* to split (up).

scintil'la |shēntēl'là| *sf* spark.

scintilla're |shēntēllà'rā| *vi* to spark; (*acqua, occhi*) to sparkle.

scintilli'o |shēntēllē'ō| *sm* sparkling.

sciocca're |shŏkkà'rā| *vt* to shock.

sciocchez'za |shŏkkāt'tsà| *sf* stupidity *q*; stupid *o* foolish thing; **dire** ~**e** to talk nonsense.

scioc'co, a, chi, che |shok'kō| *ag* stupid, foolish.

scio'gliere |shol'yārā| *vt* (*nodo*) to untie; (*capelli*) to loosen; (*persona, animale*) to untie, release; (*fig: persona*): ~ **da** to release from; (*neve*) to melt; (*nell'acqua: zucchero etc*) to dissolve; (*fig: mistero*) to solve; (*porre fine a: contratto*) to cancel; (: *società, matrimonio*) to dissolve; (: *riunione*) to bring to an end; ~**rsi** *vr* to loosen, come untied; to melt; to dissolve; (*assemblea, corteo, duo*) to break up; ~ **i muscoli** to limber up; ~ **il ghiaccio** (*fig*) to break the ice; ~ **le vele** (*NAUT*) to set sail; ~**rsi dai legami** (*fig*) to free o.s. from all ties.

sciol'go *etc* |shol'gō| *vb vedi* **sciogliere**.

scioltez'za |shōltāt'tsà| *sf* agility; suppleness; ease.

sciol'to, a |shol'tō| *pp di* **sciogliere** ♦ *ag* loose; (*agile*) agile, nimble; (*disinvolto*) free and easy; **essere** ~ **nei movimenti** to be supple; **versi** ~**i** (*POESIA*) blank verse.

scioperan'te |shōpārán'tā| *sm/f* striker.

sciopera're |shōpàrà'rā| *vi* to strike, go on strike.

scio'pero |sho'pārō| *sm* strike; **fare** ~ to strike; **entrare in** ~ to go on *o* come out on strike; ~ **bianco** slowdown (*US*), work-to-rule (*Brit*); ~ **della fame** hunger strike; ~ **selvaggio** wildcat strike; ~ **a singhiozzo** on-off strike; ~ **di solidarietà** sympathy strike.

sciorina're |shōrēnà'rā| *vt* (*ostentare*) to show off, display.

sciovi'a |shēōvē'à| *sf* ski lift.

sciovini'smo |shōvēnēz'mō| *sm* chauvinism.

sciovini'sta, i, e |shōvēnē'stà| *sm/f* chauvinist.

scipi'to, a |shēpē'tō| *ag* insipid.

scippa're |shēppà'rā| *vt*: ~ **qn** to snatch sb's bag.

scippato're |shēppátō'rā| *sm* purse-snatcher (*US*), bag-snatcher (*Brit*).

scip'po |shēp'pō| *sm* purse-snatching (*US*), bag-snatching (*Brit*).

sciroc'co |shĕrok'kō| *sm* sirocco.

scirop'po |shĕrop'pō| *sm* syrup; ~ **per la tosse** cough syrup, cough mixture.

sci'sma, i |shēz'mà| *sm* (*REL*) schism.

scissio'ne |shēssyō'nà| *sf* (*anche fig*) split, division; (*FISICA*) fission.

scis'so, a |shēs'sō| *pp di* **scindere**.

sciupa're |shōōpà'rā| *vt* (*abito, libro, appetito*) to spoil, ruin; (*tempo, denaro*) to waste; ~**rsi** *vr* to get spoilt *o* ruined; (*rovinarsi la salute*) to ruin one's health.

scivola're |shēvōlà'rā| *vi* to slide *o* glide along; (*involontariamente*) to slip, slide.

sci'volo |shē'vōlō| *sm* slide; (*TECN*) chute.

scivolo'so, a |shēvōlō'sō| *ag* slippery.

sclero'si |shēro'sē| *sf* sclerosis.

scocca're *vt* (*freccia*) to shoot ♦ *vi* (*guizzare*) to shoot up; (*battere: ora*) to strike.

scoccherò *etc* |skōkkàro'| *vb vedi* **scoccare**.

scoccia're |skōchà'rā| *vt* to bother, annoy; ~**rsi** *vr* to be bothered *o* annoyed.

scocciato're, tri'ce |skōchátō'rā| *sm/f* nuisance, pest (*fam*).

scocciatu'ra |skōchátōō'rà| *sf* nuisance, bore.

scodel'la *sf* bowl.

scodinzola're |skōdēntsōlà'rā| *vi* to wag its tail.

scoglie'ra |skōlye'rà| *sf* reef; (*rupe*) cliff.

sco'glio |skol'yō| *sm* (*al mare*) rock; (*fig: ostacolo*) difficulty, stumbling block.

scoglio'so, a |skōlyō'sō| *ag* rocky.

scoiat'tolo *sm* squirrel.

scolapa'sta *sm inv* colander.

scola're *ag*: **età** ~ school age ♦ *vt* to drain ♦ *vi* to drip.

scolare'sca *sf* schoolchildren *pl*, pupils *pl*.

scola'ro, a *sm/f* pupil, schoolboy/girl.

scola'stico, a, ci, che *ag* (*gen*) scholastic; (*libro, anno, divisa*) school *cpd*.

scolla're *vt* (*staccare*) to unstick; ~**rsi** *vr* to come unstuck.

scolla'to, a *ag* (*vestito*) low-cut, low-necked; (*donna*) wearing a low-cut dress (*o* blouse *etc*).

scollatu'ra *sf* neckline.

sco'lo *sm* drainage; (*sbocco*) drain; (*acqua*) waste water; **canale di** ~ drain; **tubo di** ~ drainpipe.

scolori're *vt* to fade; to discolor (*US*), discolour (*Brit*) ♦ *vi* (*anche*: ~**rsi**) to fade; to become discolo(u)red; (*impallidire*) to turn pale.

scolpi're *vt* to carve, sculpt.

scombina're *vt* to mess up, upset.
scombina'to, a *ag* confused, muddled.
scombussola're *vt* to upset.
scommes'so, a *pp di* **scommettere** ♦ *sf* bet, wager; **fare una** ~**a** to bet.
scommet'tere *vt, vi* to bet.
scomoda're *vt* to trouble, bother, disturb; *(fig: nome famoso)* to involve, drag in; ~**rsi** *vr* to put o.s. out; ~**rsi a fare** to go to the bother *o* trouble of doing.
scomodità *sf inv (di sedia, letto etc)* discomfort; *(di orario, sistemazione etc)* inconvenience.
sco'modo, a *ag* uncomfortable; *(sistemazione, posto)* awkward, inconvenient.
scompagina're [skōmpájĕná'rā] *vt* to upset, throw into disorder.
scompari're *vi (sparire)* to disappear, vanish; *(fig)* to be insignificant.
scompar'so, a *pp di* **scomparire** ♦ *sf* disappearance; *(fig: morte)* passing away, death.
scompartimen'to *sm (FERR)* compartment; *(sezione)* division.
scompar'to *sm* compartment, division.
scompen'so *sm* imbalance, lack of balance.
scompiglia're [skōmpēlyá'rā] *vt (cassetto, capelli)* to mess up, disarrange; *(fig: piani)* to upset.
scompi'glio [skōmpēl'yō] *sm* mess, confusion.
scompor're *vt (parola, numero)* to break up; *(CHIM)* to decompose; **scomporsi** *vr (CHIM)* to decompose; *(fig)* to get upset, lose one's composure; **senza scomporsi** unperturbed.
scompo'sto, a *pp di* **scomporre** ♦ *ag (gesto)* unseemly; *(capelli)* ruffled, dishevelled.
scomu'nica, che *sf* excommunication.
scomunica're *vt* to excommunicate.
sconcertan'te [skōnchártán'tā] *ag* disconcerting.
sconcerta're [skōnchártá'rā] *vt* to disconcert, bewilder.
scon'cio, a, ci, ce [skōn'chō] *ag (osceno)* indecent, obscene ♦ *sm (cosa riprovevole, mal fatta)* disgrace.
sconclusiona'to, a *ag* incoherent, illogical.
sconfessa're *vt* to renounce, disavow; to repudiate.
sconfig'gere [skōnfēd'jārā] *vt* to defeat, overcome.
sconfina're *vi* to cross the border; *(in proprietà privata)* to trespass; *(fig)*: ~ **da** to stray *o* digress from.
sconfina'to, a *ag* boundless, unlimited.
sconfit'ta, a *pp di* **sconfiggere** ♦ *sf* defeat.
sconfortan'te, a *ag* discouraging, disheartening.
sconforta're *vt* to discourage, dishearten; ~**rsi** *vr* to become discouraged, become disheartened, lose heart.

sconfor'to *sm* despondency.
scongela're [skōnjālá'rā] *vt* to defrost.
scongiura're [skōnjōōrá'rā] *vt (implorare)* to beseech, implore; *(eludere: pericolo)* to ward off, avert.
scongiu'ro [skōnjōō'rō] *sm (esorcismo)* exorcism; **fare gli** ~**i** to knock on wood *(US)*, touch wood *(Brit)*.
sconnes'so, a *ag (fig: discorso)* incoherent, rambling.
sconosciu'to, a [skōnōshōō'tō] *ag* unknown; new, strange ♦ *sm/f* stranger, unknown person.
sconquassa're *vt* to shatter, smash.
sconquas'so *sm (danno)* damage; *(fig)* confusion.
sconsidera'to, a *ag* thoughtless, rash.
sconsiglia're [skōnsēlyá'rā] *vt*: ~ **qc a qn** to advise sb against sth; ~ **qn dal fare qc** to advise sb not to do *o* against doing sth.
sconsola'to, a *ag* disconsolate.
sconta're *vt (COMM: detrarre)* to deduct; *(: debito)* to pay off; *(: cambiale)* to discount; *(pena)* to serve; *(colpa, errori)* to pay for, suffer for.
sconta'to, a *ag (previsto)* foreseen, taken for granted; *(prezzo, merce)* discounted, at a discount; **dare per** ~ **che** to take it for granted that.
scontenta're *vt* to displease, dissatisfy.
scontentez'za [skōntántāt'tsà] *sf* displeasure, dissatisfaction.
scontven'to, a *ag*: ~ **(di)** discontented *o* dissatisfied (with) ♦ *sm* discontent, dissatisfaction.
scon'to *sm* discount; **fare** *o* **concedere uno** ~ to give a discount; **uno** ~ **del 10%** a 10% discount.
scontrar'si *vr (treni etc)* to crash, collide; *(venire ad uno scontro, fig)* to clash; ~ **con** to crash into; collide with.
scontri'no *sm* ticket.
scon'tro *sm (MIL, fig)* clash; *(di veicoli)* crash, collision; ~ **a fuoco** shoot-out.
scontro'so, a *ag* sullen, surly; *(permaloso)* touchy.
sconvenien'te *ag* unseemly, improper.
sconvolgen'te [skōnvōljen'tā] *ag (notizia, brutta esperienza)* upsetting, disturbing; *(bellezza)* amazing; *(passione)* overwhelming.
sconvol'gere [skōnvol'jārā] *vt* to throw into confusion, upset; *(turbare)* to shake, disturb, upset.
sconvol'to, a *pp di* **sconvolgere** ♦ *ag (persona)* distraught, very upset.
sco'pa *sf* broom; *(CARTE) Italian card game.*
scopa're *vt* to sweep; *(fam!)* to screw *(!)*.
scoperchia're [skōpárkyá'rā] *vt (pentola, vaso)* to take the lid off, uncover; *(casa)* to take the roof off.
scoper'to, a *pp di* **scoprire** ♦ *ag* uncovered;

(*capo*) uncovered, bare; (*macchina*) open; (*MIL*) exposed, without cover; (*conto*) overdrawn ♦ *sf* discovery ♦ *sm*: **allo** ~ (*dormire etc*) out in the open; **assegno** ~ rubber check (*US fam*), uncovered cheque (*Brit*); **avere un conto** ~ to be overdrawn.

sco'po *sm* aim, purpose; **a che** ~? what for?; **adatto allo** ~ fit for its purpose; **allo** ~ **di fare qc** in order to do sth; **a** ~ **di lucro** for gain *o* money; **senza** ~ (*fare, cercare*) pointlessly.

scoppia're *vi* (*spaccarsi*) to burst; (*esplodere*) to explode; (*fig*) to break out; ~ **in pianto** *o* **a piangere** to burst out crying; ~ **dalle risa** *o* **dal ridere** to split one's sides laughing; ~ **dal caldo** to be boiling; ~ **di salute** to be the picture of health.

scoppietta're *vi* to crackle.

scop'pio *sm* explosion; (*di tuono, arma etc*) crash, bang; (*di pneumatico*) bang; (*fig: di guerra*) outbreak; **a** ~ **ritardato** delayed-action; **reazione a** ~ **ritardato** delayed *o* slow reaction; **uno** ~ **di risa** a burst of laughter; **uno** ~ **di collera** an explosion of anger.

scopri're *vt* to discover; (*liberare da ciò che copre*) to uncover; (: *monumento*) to unveil; ~**rsi** *vr* to put on lighter clothes; (*fig*) to give o.s. away.

scoprito're, tri'ce *sm/f* discoverer.

scoraggia're [skŏràdjà'rā] *vt* to discourage; ~**rsi** *vr* to become discouraged, lose heart.

scorbu'tico, a, ci, che *ag* (*fig*) cantankerous.

scorciato'ia [skŏrchàtō'yà] *sf* short cut.

scor'cio [skŏr'chō] *sm* (*ARTE*) foreshortening; (*di secolo, periodo*) end, close; ~ **panoramico** vista.

scorda're *vt* to forget; ~**rsi** *vr*: ~**rsi di qc/di fare** to forget sth/to do.

scoreg'gia [skŏràd'jà] (*fam!*) *sf* fart (!).

scoreggia're [skŏràdjà'rā] (*fam!*) *vi* to fart (!).

scor'gere [skor'jàrā] *vt* to make out, distinguish, see.

scori'a *sf* (*di metalli*) slag; (*vulcanica*) scoria; ~**e radioattive** (*FISICA*) radioactive waste *sg*.

scor'no *sm* ignominy, disgrace.

scorpaccia'ta [skŏrpàchà'tà] *sf*: **fare una** ~ (**di**) to stuff o.s. (with), eat one's fill (of).

scorpio'ne *sm* scorpion; (*dello zodiaco*): **S**~ Scorpio; **essere dello S**~ to be Scorpio.

scorrazza're [skŏrràttsà'rā] *vi* to run about.

scor'rere *vt* (*giornale, lettera*) to run *o* skim through ♦ *vi* (*liquido, fiume*) to run, flow; (*fune*) to run; (*cassetto, porta*) to slide easily; (*tempo*) to pass (by).

scorreri'a *sf* raid, incursion.

scorrettez'za [skŏrràttàt'tsà] *sf* incorrectness; lack of politeness, rudeness; unfairness; **commettere una** ~ (*essere sleale*) to be un-

fair.

scorret'to, a *ag* (*sbagliato*) incorrect; (*sgarbato*) impolite; (*sconveniente*) improper; (*sleale*) unfair; (*gioco*) foul.

scorre'vole *ag* (*porta*) sliding; (*fig: stile*) fluent, flowing.

scorriban'da *sf* (*MIL*) raid; (*escursione*) trip, excursion.

scor'si etc *vb vedi* **scorgere**.

scor'so, a *pp di* **scorrere** ♦ *ag* last ♦ *sf* quick look, glance; **lo** ~ **mese** last month.

scorso'io, a *ag*: **nodo** ~ noose.

scor'ta *sf* (*di personalità, convoglio*) escort; (*provvista*) supply, stock; **sotto la** ~ **di due agenti** escorted by two policemen; **fare** ~ **di** to stock up with, get in a supply of; **di** ~ (*materiali*) spare; **ruota di** ~ spare tire (*US*) *o* wheel (*Brit*).

scorta're *vt* to escort.

scorte'se *ag* discourteous, rude.

scortesi'a *sf* discourtesy, rudeness; (*azione*) discourtesy.

scortica're *vt* to skin.

scor'to, a *pp di* **scorgere**.

scor'za [skor'dzà] *sf* (*di albero*) bark; (*di agrumi*) peel, skin.

scosce'so, a [skōshà'sō] *ag* steep.

scos'so, a *pp di* **scuotere** ♦ *ag* (*turbato*) shaken, upset ♦ *sf* jerk, jolt, shake; (*ELETTR, fig*) shock; **prendere la** ~**a** to get an electric shock; ~**a di terremoto** earth tremor.

scosso'ne *sm*: **dare uno** ~ **a qn** to give sb a shake; **procedere a** ~**i** to jolt *o* jerk along.

scostan'te *ag* (*fig*) unpleasant.

scosta're *vt* to move (away), shift; ~**rsi** *vr* to move away.

scostuma'to, a *ag* immoral, dissolute.

scottan'te *ag* (*fig: urgente*) pressing; (: *delicato*) delicate.

scotta're *vt* (*ustionare*) to burn; (: *con liquido bollente*) to scald ♦ *vi* to burn; (*caffè*) to be too hot.

scottatu'ra *sf* burn; scald.

scot'to, a *ag* overcooked ♦ *sm* (*fig*): **pagare lo** ~ (**di**) to pay the penalty (for).

scova're *vt* to drive out, flush out; (*fig*) to discover.

Sco'zia [skot'tsyà] *sf*: **la** ~ Scotland.

scozze'se [skŏttsà'sà] *ag* Scottish ♦ *sm/f* Scot.

screanza'to, a [skrààntsà'tō] *ag* ill-mannered ♦ *sm/f* boor.

scredita're *vt* to discredit.

screma're *vt* to skim.

screma'to, a *ag* skimmed.

screpola're *vt*, ~**rsi** *vr* to crack.

screpolatu'ra *sf* cracking *q*; crack.

screzia'to, a [skràttsyà'tō] *ag* streaked.

scre'zio [skret'tsyō] *sm* disagreement.

scribacchi'no [skrēbàkkē'nō] *sm* (*peg: impiegato*) penpusher; (: *scrittore*) hack.

scricchiola're [skrĕkkyōlá'rā] *vi* to creak, squeak.

scricchioli'o [skrĕkkyōlē'ō] *sm* creaking.

scric'ciolo [skrĕch'chōlō] *sm* wren.

scri'gno [skrĕn'yō] *sm* casket.

scriminatu'ra *sf* part (*US*), parting (*Brit*).

scris'si *etc vb vedi* **scrivere**.

scrit'to, a *pp di* **scrivere** ♦ *ag* written ♦ *sm* writing; (*lettera*) letter, note ♦ *sf* inscription; ~**i** *smpl* (*letterari etc*) work(s), writings; **per o in** ~ in writing.

scritto'io *sm* writing desk.

scritto're, tri'ce *sm/f* writer.

scrittu'ra *sf* writing; (*COMM*) entry; (*contratto*) contract; (*REL*): **la Sacra S~** the Scriptures *pl*; ~**e** *sfpl* (*COMM*) accounts, books.

scrittura're *vt* (*TEATRO, CINEMA*) to sign up, engage; (*COMM*) to enter.

scrivani'a *sf* desk.

scriva'no *sm* (*amanuense*) scribe; (*impiegato*) clerk.

scriven'te *sm/f* writer.

scri've re *vt* to write; **come si scrive?** how is it spelled?, how do you write it?; ~ **qc a qn** to write sth to sb; ~ **qc a macchina** to type sth; ~ **a penna/matita** to write in pen/pencil; ~ **qc maiuscolo/minuscolo** to write sth in capital/small letters.

scrocca're *vt* (*fam*) to scrounge, cadge.

scrocco'ne, a *sm/f* scrounger.

scro'fa *sf* (*ZOOL*) sow.

scrolla're *vt* to shake; ~**rsi** *vr* (*anche fig*) to give o.s. a shake; ~ **le spalle/il capo** to shrug one's shoulders/shake one's head; ~**rsi qc di dosso** (*anche fig*) to shake sth off.

scrolla'ta *sf* shake; ~ **di spalle** shrug (of one's shoulders).

scroscian'te [skrōshàn'tā] *ag* (*pioggia*) pouring; (*fig: applausi*) thunderous.

scroscia're [skrōshá'rā] *vi* (*pioggia*) to pour down, pelt down; (*torrente, fig: applausi*) to thunder, roar.

scro'scio [skrosh'shō] *sm* pelting; thunder, roar; (*di applausi*) burst.

scrosta're *vt* (*intonaco*) to scrape off, strip; ~**rsi** *vr* to peel off, flake off.

scru'polo *sm* scruple; (*meticolosità*) care, conscientiousness; **essere senza** ~**i** to be unscrupulous.

scrupolo'so, a *ag* scrupulous; conscientious.

scruta're *vt* to scrutinize; (*intenzioni, causa*) to examine, scrutinize.

scrutina're *vt* (*voti*) to count.

scruti'nio *sm* (*votazione*) ballot; (*insieme delle operazioni*) poll; (*INS*) (*meeting for*) assignment of marks at end of a term or year.

scuci're [skōōchē'rā] *vt* (*orlo etc*) to unpick, undo; ~**rsi** *vr* to come unstitched.

scuderi'a *sf* stable.

scudet'to *sm* (*SPORT*) (championship) shield; (*distintivo*) badge.

scudi'scio [skōōdĕsh'shō] *sm* (riding) crop, (riding) whip.

scu'do *sm* shield; **farsi** ~ **di** *o* **con qc** to shield o.s. with sth; ~ **aereo/missilistico** air/missile defense (*US*) *o* defence (*Brit*); ~ **termico** heat shield.

sculaccia're [skōōlàchà'rā] *vt* to spank.

sculaccio'ne [skōōlàchō'nā] *sm* spanking.

sculto're, tri'ce *sm/f* sculptor.

scultu'ra *sf* sculpture.

scuo'la *sf* school; ~ **elementare** grade (*US*) *o* primary (*Brit*) school; ~ **guida** driver's education school (*US*), driving school (*Brit*); ~ **materna** nursery school; ~ **dell'obbligo** compulsory education; ~ **privata/pubblica** private/state school; ~**e serali** evening classes, night school *sg*; ~ **tecnica** technical college.

scuo'tere *vt* to shake; ~**rsi** *vr* to jump, be startled; (*fig: muoversi*) to rouse o.s., stir o.s.; (: *turbarsi*) to be shaken.

scu're *sf* ax, (*US*) axe (*Brit*).

scuri're *vt* to darken, make darker.

scu'ro, a *ag* dark; (*fig: espressione*) grim ♦ *sm* darkness; dark color (*US*) *o* colour (*Brit*); (*imposta*) (window) shutter; **verde/rosso** *etc* ~ dark green/red *etc*.

scurri'le *ag* scurrilous.

scu'sa *sf* excuse; ~**e** *sfpl* apology *sg*, apologies; **chiedere** ~ **a qn (per)** to apologize to sb (for); **chiedo** ~ I'm sorry; (*disturbando etc*) excuse me; **vi prego di accettare le mie** ~**e** please accept my apologies.

scusa're *vt* to excuse; ~**rsi** *vr*: ~**rsi (di)** to apologize (for); (**mi) scusi** I'm sorry; (*per richiamare l'attenzione*) excuse me.

S.C.V. *sigla* = *Stato della Città del Vaticano*.

sdebitar'si *vt*: ~**rsi (con qn di** *o* **per qc)** (*anche fig*) to repay (sb for sth).

sdegna're [zdānyà'rā] *vt* to scorn, despise; ~**rsi** *vr* (*adirarsi*) to get angry.

sdegna'to, a [zdānyà'tō] *ag* indignant, angry.

sde'gno [zdān'yō] *sm* scorn, disdain.

sdegno'so, a [zdānyō'sō] *ag* scornful, disdainful.

sdilinquir'si *vr* (*illanguidirsi*) to become sentimental.

sdogana're *vt* (*COMM*) to clear through customs.

sdolcina'to, a [zdōlchēnà'tō] *ag* mawkish, oversentimental.

sdoppiamen'to *sm* (*CHIM: di composto*) splitting; (*PSIC*): ~ **della personalità** split personality.

sdoppia're *vt* (*dividere*) to divide *o* split in two.

sdraiar'si *vr* to stretch out, lie down.

sdra'io *sm*: **sedia a** ~ deck chair.

sdrammatizza're |zdrámmátĕddzà'rā| *vt* to play down, minimize.

sdrucciola're |zdrōōchŏlà'rā| *vi* to slip, slide.

sdrucciole'vole |zdrōōchŏlā'vōlā| *ag* slippery.

sdruci'to, a |zdrōōchĕ'tō| *ag* (*strappato*) torn; (*logoro*) threadbare.

se *pronome vedi* **si** ♦ *cong* if; (*in frasi interrogative indirette*) if, whether; **non so** ~ **scrivere o telefonare** I don't known whether *o* if I should write or phone; ~ **mai** if, if ever; (*caso mai*) in case; ~ **solo** *o* **solamente** if only; ~ **fossi in te** if I were you; ~ **no** otherwise, or else; ~ **non** (*anzi*) if not; (*tranne*) except; ~ **non altro** 'if nothing else, at least; **come** ~ as if.

S.E. *abbr* (= *sud-est*) SE; (= *Sua Eccellenza*) HE.

sé *pronome* (*gen*) oneself; (*esso, essa, lui, lei, loro*) itself; himself; herself; themselves; ~ **stesso(a)** *pronome* oneself; itself; himself; herself; ~ **stessi(e)** *pronome pl* themselves; **di per** ~ **non è un problema** it's no problem in itself; **parlare tra** ~ **e** ~ to talk to oneself; **va da** ~ **che ...** it goes without saying that ..., it's obvious that ...., it stands to reason that ...; **è un caso a** ~ *o* **a** ~ **stante** it's a special case.

sebbe'ne *cong* although, though.

se'bo *sm* sebum.

sec. *abbr* (= *secolo*) c.

sec'ca *sf vedi* **secco**.

secca're *vt* to dry; (*prosciugare*) to dry up; (*fig: importunare*) to annoy, bother ♦ *vi* to dry; to dry up; ~**rsi** *vr* to dry; to dry up; (*fig*) to grow annoyed; **si è seccato molto** he was very annoyed.

secca'to, a *ag* (*fig: infastidito*) bothered, annoyed; (: *stufo*) fed up.

seccato're, tri'ce *sm/f* nuisance, bother.

seccatu'ra *sf* (*fig*) bother *q*, trouble *q*.

seccherò *etc* |sākkāro'| *vb vedi* **seccare**.

sec'chia |sāk'kyà| *sf* bucket, pail.

secchiel'lo |sākkyĕl'lō| *sm* (*per bambini*) pail, bucket.

sec'chio |sāk'kyō| *sm* bucket, pail; ~ **della spazzatura** *o* **delle immondizie** garbage can (*US*), dustbin (*Brit*).

sec'co, a, chi, che *ag* dry; (*fichi, pesce*) dried; (*foglie, ramo*) withered; (*magro: persona*) thin, skinny; (*fig: risposta, modo di fare*) curt, abrupt; (: *colpo*) clean, sharp ♦ *sm* (*siccità*) drought ♦ *sf* (*del mare*) shallows *pl*; **restarci** ~ (*fig: morire sul colpo*) to drop dead; **avere la gola** ~**a** to feel dry, be parched; **lavare a** ~ to dry-clean; **tirare a** ~ (*barca*) to beach.

secente'sco, a, schi, sche |sāchāntà'skō| *ag* = **seicentesco**.

secer'nere |sāchĕr'nārā| *vt* to secrete.

secola're *ag* age-old, centuries-old; (*laico, mondano*) secular.

se'colo *sm* century; (*epoca*) age.

secon'da *sf vedi* **secondo**.

secondariamen'te *av* secondly.

seconda'rio, a *ag* secondary; **scuola/ istruzione** ~**a** secondary school/education.

secondi'no *sm* prison officer.

secon'do, a *ag* second ♦ *sm* second; (*di pranzo*) main course ♦ *sf* (*AUT*) second (gear); (*FERR*) second class ♦ *prep* according to; (*nel modo prescritto*) in accordance with; ~ **me** in my opinion, to my mind; ~ **la legge/quanto si era deciso** in accordance with the law/the decision taken; **di** ~**a classe** second-class; **di** ~**a mano** second-hand; **viaggiare in** ~**a** to travel second-class; **comandante** *m* **in** ~**a** second-in-command; **a** ~**a di** *prep* according to; in accordance with.

secondoge'nito, a |sākōndōjc'nĕtō| *sm/f* second-born.

secrezio'ne |sākrāttsyō'nā| *sf* secretion.

se'dano *sm* celery.

seda're *vt* (*dolore*) to soothe; (*rivolta*) to put down, suppress.

sedati'vo, a *ag, sm* sedative.

se'de *sf* (*luogo di residenza*) (place of) residence; (*di ditta: principale*) head office; (: *secondaria*) branch (office); (*di organizzazione*) headquarters *pl*; (*di governo, parlamento*) seat; (*REL*) see; **in** ~ **di** (*in occasione di*) during; **in altra** ~ on another occasion; **in** ~ **legislativa** in legislative sitting; **prendere** ~ to take up residence; **un'azienda con diverse** ~**i in città** a firm with several branches in the city; ~ **centrale** head office; ~ **sociale** registered office.

sedenta'rio, a *ag* sedentary.

sede're *vi* to sit, be seated; ~**rsi** *vr* to sit down ♦ *sm* (*deretano*) bottom; **posto a** ~ seat.

se'dia *sf* chair; ~ **elettrica** electric chair; ~ **a rotelle** wheelchair.

sedicen'ne |sādĕchen'nā| *ag, sm/f* sixteen-year-old.

sedicen'te |sādĕchcn'tā| *ag* self-styled.

sedice'simo, a |sādĕche'zĕmō| *num* sixteenth.

se'dici |sā'dĕchĕ| *num* sixteen.

sedi'le *sm* seat; (*panchina*) bench.

sedimen'to *sm* sediment.

sedizio'ne |sādĕttsyō'nā| *sf* revolt, rebellion.

sedizio'so, a |sādĕttsyō'sō| *ag* seditious.

sedot'to, a *pp di* **sedurre**.

seducen'te |sādōōchĕn'tā| *ag* seductive; (*proposta*) very attractive.

sedur're *vt* to seduce.

sedu'ta *sf* session, sitting; (*riunione*) meeting; **essere in** ~ to be in session, be sitting; ~ **stante** (*fig*) immediately; ~ **spiritica** seance.

sedutto're, tri'ce *sm/f* seducer/seductress.

seduzio'ne [sādo͞ottsyō'nā] *sf* seduction; (*fascino*) charm, appeal.

SEeO *abbr* (= *salvo errori e omissioni*) E & OE.

se'ga, ghe *sf* saw; ~ **circolare** circular saw; ~ **a mano** handsaw.

se'gale *sf* rye.

sega're *vt* to saw; (*recidere*) to saw off.

segatu'ra *sf* (*residuo*) sawdust.

seg'gio [sed'jō] *sm* seat; ~ **elettorale** polling station.

seg'giola [sed'jōlà] *sf* chair.

seggioli'no [sādjōlē'nō] *sm* seat; (*per bambini*) child's chair; ~ **di sicurezza** (*AUT*) (child's) car seat.

seggiolo'ne [sādjōlō'nā] *sm* (*per bambini*) highchair.

seggiovi'a [sādjōvē'à] *sf* chairlift.

segheri'a [sāgārē'à] *sf* sawmill.

segherò *etc* [sāgāro'] *vb vedi* **segare**.

seghetta'to, a [sāgāttà'tō] *ag* serrated.

seghet'to [sāgāt'tō] *sm* hacksaw.

segmen'to *sm* segment.

segnala're [sānyálá'rā] *vt* (*essere segno di*) to indicate, be a sign of; (*avvertire*) to signal; (*menzionare*) to indicate; (: *fatto, risultato, aumento*) to report; (: *errore, dettaglio*) to point out; (*AUT*) to signal, indicate; ~**rsi** *vr* (*distinguersi*) to distinguish o.s.; ~ **qn a qn** (*per lavoro etc*) to bring sb to sb's attention.

segnalazio'ne [sānyálàttsyō'nā] *sf* (*azione*) signalling; (*segnale*) signal; (*annuncio*) report; (*raccomandazione*) recommendation.

segna'le [sānyà'lā] *sm* signal; (*cartello*): ~ **stradale** road sign; ~ **acustico** acoustic *o* sound signal; ~ **d'allarme** alarm; (*FERR*) alarm cord; ~ **di linea libera** (*TEL*) dial (*US*) *o* dialling (*Brit*) tone; ~ **luminoso** light signal; ~ **di occupato** (*TEL*) busy signal (*US*), engaged tone (*Brit*); ~ **orario** (*RADIO*) time signal.

segnale'tica [sānyàle'tēkà] *sf* signalling, signposting; ~ **stradale** road signs *pl*.

segnali'bro [sānyálē'brō] *sm* bookmark.

segnapun'ti [sānyàpo͞on'tē] *sm/f inv* scorer, scorekeeper.

segna're [sānyà'rā] *vt* to mark; (*prendere nota*) to note; (*indicare*) to indicate, mark; (*SPORT: goal*) to score; ~**rsi** *vr* (*REL*) to make the sign of the cross, cross o.s.

se'gno [sān'yō] *sm* sign; (*impronta, contrassegno*) mark; (*bersaglio*) target; **fare** ~ **di si/no** to nod (one's head)/shake one's head; **fare** ~ **a qn di fermarsi** to motion (to) sb to stop; **cogliere** *o* **colpire nel** ~ (*fig*) to hit the mark; **in** *o* **come** ~ **d'amicizia** as a mark *o* token of friendship; "~**i particolari**" (*su documento etc*) "distinguishing marks".

segrega're *vt* to segregate, isolate.

segregazio'ne [sāgrāgàttsyō'nā] *sf* segrega-

tion.

segre'ta *sf vedi* **segreto**.

segreta'rio, a *sm/f* secretary; ~ **comunale** town clerk; ~ **del partito** party leader; ~ **di Stato** Secretary of State.

segreteri'a *sf* (*di ditta, scuola*) (secretary's) office; (*d'organizzazione internazionale*) secretariat; (*POL etc: carica*) office of Secretary; ~ **telefonica** answering service.

segretez'za [sāgrātāt'tsà] *sf* secrecy; **notizie della massima** ~ confidential information; **in tutta** ~ in secret; (*confidenzialmente*) in confidence.

segre'to, a *ag* secret ♦ *sm* secret ♦ *sf* dungeon; **in** ~ in secret, secretly; **il** ~ **professionale** professional secrecy; **un** ~ **professionale** a professional secret.

segua'ce [sāgwà'chā] *sm/f* follower, disciple.

seguen'te *ag* following, next; **nel modo** ~ as follows, in the following way.

segu'gio [sāgo͞o'jō] *sm* hound, hunting dog; (*fig*) private eye, sleuth.

segui're *vt* to follow; (*frequentare: corso*) to attend ♦ *vi* to follow; (*continuare: testo*) to continue; ~ **i consigli di qn** to follow *o* to take sb's advice; ~ **gli avvenimenti di attualità** to follow *o* keep up with current events; **come segue** as follows; **"segue"** "to be continued".

seguita're *vt* to continue, carry on with ♦ *vi* to continue, carry on.

se'guito *sm* (*scorta*) suite, retinue; (*discepoli*) followers *pl*; (*serie*) sequence, series *sg*; (*continuazione*) continuation; (*conseguenza*) result; **di** ~ at a stretch, on end; **in** ~ later on; **in** ~ **a, a** ~ **di** following; (*a causa di*) as a result of, owing to; **essere al** ~ **di qn** to be among sb's suite, be one of sb's retinue; **non aver** ~ (*conseguenze*) to have no repercussions; **facciamo** ~ **alla lettera del** ... further to *o* in answer to your letter of ....

se'i *vb vedi* **essere** ♦ *num* six.

Seicel'le [sāēchel'lā] *sfpl*: **le** ~ the Seychelles.

seicente'sco, a, schi, sche [sāēchāntà'skō] *ag* seventeenth-century.

seicen'to [sāēchen'tō] *num* six hundred ♦ *sm*: **il S**~ the seventeenth century.

seimi'la *num* six thousand.

sel'ce [sāl'chā] *sf* flint, flintstone.

selcia'to [sālchá'tō] *sm* cobbled surface.

seletti'vo, a *ag* selective.

seletto're *sm* (*TECN*) selector.

seleziona're [sālāttsyōnà'rā] *vt* to select.

selezio'ne [sālāttsyō'nā] *sf* selection; **fare una** ~ to make a selection *o* choice.

sel'la *sf* saddle.

sella're *vt* to saddle.

selli'no *sm* saddle.

seltz *sm inv* soda (water).

sel'va *sf* (*bosco*) wood; (*foresta*) forest.

selvaggi'na [sālvádjē'ná] *sf (animali)* game.
selvag'gio, a, gi, ge [sālvád'jō] *ag* wild; *(tribù)* savage, uncivilized; *(fig)* savage, brutal ♦ *sm/f* savage.
selva'tico, a, ci, che *ag* wild.
S.Em. *abbr* (= *Sua Eminenza*) HE.
sema'foro *sm (AUT)* traffic lights *pl.*
sembian'za [sāmbyán'tsá] *sf (poetico: aspetto)* appearance; **~e** *pl (lineamenti)* features; *(fig: falsa apparenza)* semblance.
sembra're *vi* to seem ♦ *vb impers:* **sembra che** it seems that; **mi sembra che** it seems to me that; *(penso che)* I think (that); **~ di essere** to seem to be; **non mi sembra vero!** I can't believe it!
se'me *sm* seed; *(sperma)* semen; *(CARTE)* suit.
semen'te *sf* seed.
semestra'le *ag (che dura 6 mesi)* six-month *cpd*; *(che avviene ogni 6 mesi)* six-monthly.
semes'tre *sm* half-year, six-month period.
se'mi... *prefisso* semi....
semicer'chio [sāmēchār'kyō] *sm* semicircle.
semiconduttо're *sm* semiconductor.
semidetenzio'ne [sāmēdātántsyō'nā] *sf custodial sentence whereby individual must spend a minimum of 10 hours per day in prison.*
semifina'le *sf* semifinal.
semifred'do, a *ag (CUC)* chilled ♦ *sm* ice-cream cake.
semilibertà *sf custodial sentence which allows prisoner to study or work outside prison for part of the day.*
se'mina *sf (AGR)* sowing.
semina're *vt* to sow.
semina'rio *sm* seminar; *(REL)* seminary.
semina'to *sm:* **uscire dal ~** *(fig)* to wander off the point.
seminterra'to *sm* basement; *(appartamento)* basement apartment.
semio'logo, a, gi, ghe *sm/f* semiologist.
semi'tico, a, ci, che *ag* semitic.
semma'i = **se mai.**
se'mola *sf* bran; **~ di grano duro** durum wheat.
semola'to *ag:* **zucchero ~** powdered *(US)* o caster *(Brit)* sugar.
semoli'no *sm* semolina.
sem'plice [sām'plēchā] *ag* simple; *(di un solo elemento)* single; **è una ~ formalità** it's a mere formality.
semplicemen'te [sāmplēchāmān'tā] *av* simply.
semplici'stico, a, ci, che [sāmplēchē'stēkō] *ag* simplistic.
semplicità [sāmplēchētá'] *sf* simplicity.
semplifica're *vt* to simplify.
semplificazio'ne [sāmplēfēkáttsyō'nā] *sf* simplification; **fare una ~ di** to simplify.
sem'pre *av* always; *(ancora)* still; **posso ~**

tentare I can always *o* still try; **da ~** always; **per ~** forever; **una volta per ~** once and for all; **~ che** *cong* provided (that); **~ più** more and more; **~ meno** less and less; **va ~ meglio** things are getting better and better; **è ~ meglio che niente** it's better than nothing; **è (pur) ~ tuo fratello** he is still your brother (however); **c'è ~ la possibilità che** ... there's still a chance that ..., there's always the possibility that ....
semprever'de *ag, sm o f (BOT)* evergreen.
Sen. *abbr* (= *senatore*) Sen.
se'nape *sf (CUC)* mustard.
sena'to *sm* senate.
senato're, tri'ce *sm/f* senator.
Se'negal *sm:* **il ~** Senegal.
senegale'se *ag, sm/f* Senegalese *inv.*
sene'se *ag* of (*o* from) Siena.
seni'le *ag* senile.
Sen'na *sf:* **la ~** the Seine.
sen'no *sm* judgment, (common) sense; **col ~ di poi** with hindsight.
sennò *av* = **se no.**
se'no *sm (ANAT: petto, mammella)* breast; (: *grembo, fig)* womb; (: *cavità)* sinus; *(GEO)* inlet, creek; *(MAT)* sine; **in ~ al partito/all'organizzazione** within the party/the organization.
sensa'le *sm (COMM)* agent.
sensatez'za [sānsátāt'tsá] *sf* good sense, good judgment.
sensa'to, a *ag* sensible.
sensaziona'le [sānsáttsyōná'lā] *ag* sensational.
sensazio'ne [sānsáttsyō'nā] *sf* feeling, sensation; **fare ~** to cause a sensation, create a stir; **avere la ~ che** to have a feeling that.
sensi'bile *ag* sensitive; *(ai sensi)* perceptible; *(rilevante, notevole)* appreciable, noticeable; **~ a** sensitive to.
sensibilità *sf* sensitivity.
sensibilizza're [sānsēbēlēddzá'rā] *vt (fig)* to make aware, awaken.
sen'so *sm (FISIOL, istinto)* sense; *(impressione, sensazione)* feeling, sensation; *(significato)* meaning, sense; *(direzione)* direction; **~i** *smpl (coscienza)* consciousness *sg*; *(sensualità)* senses; **perdere/riprendere i ~i** to lose/regain consciousness; **avere ~ pratico** to be practical; **avere un sesto ~** to have a sixth sense; **fare ~ a** *(ripugnare)* to disgust, repel; **ciò non ha ~** that doesn't make sense; **senza o privo di ~** meaningless; **nel ~ che** in the sense that; **nel vero ~ della parola** in the true sense of the word; **nel ~ della lunghezza** lengthwise, lengthways; **nel ~ della larghezza** widthwise; **ho dato disposizioni in quel ~** I've given instructions to that end *o* effect; **~ comune** common sense; **~ del dovere** sense of duty; **in ~ opposto** in the opposite direction; **in ~ orario/antiorario**

clockwise/anticlockwise; ~ **dell'umorismo** sense of humor; **a ~ unico** one-way; **"~ vietato"** (*AUT*) "no entry".

sensua'le *ag* sensual; sensuous.

sensualità *sf* sensuality; sensuousness.

senten'za [sānten'tså] *sf* (*DIR*) sentence; (*massima*) maxim.

sentenzia're [sāntāntsyá'rā] *vi* (*DIR*) to pass judgment.

sentie'ro *sm* path.

sentimenta'le *ag* sentimental; (*vita, avventura*) love *cpd.*

sentimen'to *sm* feeling.

sentinel'la *sf* sentry.

senti're *vt* (*percepire al tatto, fig*) to feel; (*udire*) to hear; (*ascoltare*) to listen to; (*odore*) to smell; (*avvertire con il gusto, assaggiare*) to taste ♦ *vi:* ~ **di** (*avere sapore*) to taste of; (*avere odore*) to smell of; **~rsi** *vr* (*uso reciproco*) to be in touch; **~rsi bene/male** to feel well/unwell *o* ill; **~rsi di fare qc** (*essere disposto*) to feel like doing sth; **~ la mancanza di qn** to miss sb; **ho sentito dire che ...** I have heard that ...; **a ~ lui ...** to hear him talk ...; **fatti ~** keep in touch; **intendo ~ il mio legale/il parere di un medico** I'm going to consult my lawyer/a doctor.

sentitamen'te *av* sincerely; **ringraziare ~ to** thank sincerely.

senti'to, a *ag* (*sincero*) sincere, warm; **per ~ dire** by hearsay.

sento're *sm* rumor (*US*), rumour (*Brit*), talk; **aver ~ di qc** to hear about sth.

sen'za [sɛn'tså] *prep, cong* without; **~ dir nulla** without saying a word; **~ dire che ...** not to mention the fact that ...; **~ contare che ...** without considering that ...; **fare ~ qc** to do without sth; **~ di me** without me; **~ che io lo sapessi** without me *o* my knowing; **~ amici** friendless; **senz'altro** of course, certainly; **~ dubbio** no doubt; **~ scrupoli** unscrupulous.

senzatet'to [sāntsåtãt'tō] *sm/f inv* homeless person; **i ~** the homeless.

separa're *vt* to separate; (*dividere*) to divide; (*tenere distinto*) to distinguish; **~rsi** *vr* (*coniugi*) to separate, part; (*amici*) to part; **~rsi da** (*coniuge*) to separate *o* part from; (*amico, socio*) to part company with; (*oggetto*) to part with.

separatamen'te *av* separately.

separa'to, a *ag* (*letti, conto etc*) separate; (*coniugi*) separated.

separazio'ne [sāpárāttsyō'nā] *sf* separation; **~ dei beni** division of property.

séparé [sāpárā'] *sm inv* screen.

sepol'cro *sm* sepulcher (*US*), sepulchre (*Brit*).

sepol'to, a *pp di* **seppellire.**

sepoltu'ra *sf* burial; **dare ~ a qn** to bury sb.

seppelli're *vt* to bury.

sep'pi *etc vb vedi* **sapere.**

sep'pia *sf* cuttlefish ♦ *ag inv* sepia.

seppu're *cong* even if.

seque'la *sf* (*di avvenimenti*) series, sequence; (*di offese, ingiurie*) string.

sequen'za [sākwān'tså] *sf* sequence.

sequenzia'le [sākwāntsyá'lā] *ag* sequential.

sequestra're *vt* (*DIR*) to impound; (*rapire*) to kidnap; (*costringere in un luogo*) to keep, confine.

seques'tro *sm* (*DIR*) impoundment; **~ di persona** kidnapping.

sequo'ia *sf* sequoia.

se'ra *sf* evening; **di ~** in the evening; **domani ~** tomorrow evening, tomorrow night; **questa ~** this evening, tonight.

sera'le *ag* evening *cpd*; **scuola ~** evening classes *pl*, night school.

sera'ta *sf* evening; (*ricevimento*) party.

serba're *vt* to keep; (*mettere da parte*) to put aside; **~ rancore/odio verso qn** to bear sb a grudge/hate sb.

serbato'io *sm* tank; (*cisterna*) cistern.

ser'bo *ag* Serbian ♦ *sm/f* Serbian, Serb ♦ *sm* (*LING*) Serbian; (*il serbare*): **mettere/tenere** *o* **avere in ~ qc** to put/keep sth aside.

serbocroa'to, a *ag, sm* Serbo-Croatian.

serena'ta *sf* (*MUS*) serenade.

serenità *sf* serenity.

sere'no, a *ag* (*tempo, cielo*) clear; (*fig*) serene, calm ♦ *sm* (*tempo*) good weather; **un fulmine a ciel ~** (*fig*) a bolt from the blue.

serg. *abbr* (= *sergente*) Sgt.

sergen'te [sārjen'tā] *sm* (*MIL*) sergeant.

se'rie *sf inv* (*successione*) series *inv*; (*gruppo, collezione: di chiavi etc*) set; (*SPORT*) division; league; (*COMM*): **modello di ~/fuori ~** standard/custom-built model; **in ~** in quick succession; (*COMM*) mass *cpd*; **tutta una ~ di problemi** a whole string *o* series of problems.

serietà *sf* seriousness; reliability.

se'rio, a *ag* serious; (*impiegato*) responsible, reliable; (*ditta, cliente*) reliable, dependable; **sul ~** (*davvero*) really, truly; (*seriamente*) seriously, in earnest; **dico sul ~** I'm serious; **faccio sul ~** I mean it; **prendere qc/qn sul ~** to take sth/sb seriously.

sermo'ne *sm* sermon.

ser'pe *sf* snake; (*fig peg*) viper.

serpeggia're [sārpādjá'rā] *vi* to wind; (*fig*) to spread.

serpen'te *sm* snake; **~ a sonagli** rattlesnake.

ser'ra *sf* greenhouse; hothouse; (*GEO*) sierra.

serrama'nico *sm*: **coltello a ~** jack-knife.

serran'da *sf* roller shutter.

serra're *vt* to close, shut; (*a chiave*) to lock; (*stringere*) to tighten; (*premere: nemico*) to close in on; **~ i pugni/i denti** to clench one's fists/teeth; ~ **le file** to close ranks.

serra'ta *sf* (*INDUSTRIA*) lockout.

serra'to, a *ag* (*veloce*): **a ritmo** ~ quickly, fast.

serratu'ra *sf* lock.

ser'va *sf vedi* **servo**.

servi'gio [sãrvẽ'jõ] *sm* favor (*US*), favour (*Brit*), service.

servi're *vt* to serve; (*clienti: al ristorante*) to wait on; (: *al negozio*) to serve, attend to; (*fig: giovare*) to aid, help; (*CARTE*) to deal ♦ *vi* (*TENNIS*) to serve; (*essere utile*): ~ **a qn** to be of use to sb; ~ **a qc/a fare** (*utensile etc*) to be used for sth/for doing; ~ **(a qn) da** to serve as (for sb); **~rsi** *vr* (*usare*): **~rsi di** to use; (*prendere: cibo*): **~rsi (di)** to help o.s. (*to*); (*essere cliente abituale*): **~rsi da** to be a regular customer at, go to; **non mi serve più** I don't need it any more; **non serve che lei vada** you don't need to go.

servitù *sf* servitude; slavery; (*personale di servizio*) servants *pl*, domestic staff.

servizie'vole [sãrvẽttsyã'võlã] *ag* obliging, willing to help.

servi'zio [sãrvẽt'tsyõ] *sm* service; (*al ristorante: sul conto*) service (charge); (*STAMPA, TV, RADIO*) report; (*da tè, caffè etc*) set, service; **~i** *smpl* (*di casa*) kitchen and bathroom; (*ECON*) services; **essere di** ~ to be on duty; **fuori** ~ (*telefono etc*) out of order; ~ **compreso/escluso** service included/not included; **entrata di** ~ service *o* tradesman's (*Brit*) entrance; **casa con doppi ~i** house with two bathrooms; ~ **assistenza clienti** after-sales service; ~ **in diretta** (*TV, RADIO*) live coverage; ~ **fotografico** (*STAMPA*) photo feature; ~ **militare** military service; ~ **d'ordine** (*POLIZIA*) police patrol; (*di manifestanti*) team of stewards (*responsible for crowd control*); **~i segreti** secret service *sg;* **~i di sicurezza** security forces.

ser'vo, a *sm/f* servant.

servofre'no *sm* (*AUT*) servo brake.

servoster'zo [sãrvõster'tsõ] *sm* (*AUT*) power steering.

se'samo *sm* (*BOT*) sesame.

sessan'ta *num* sixty.

sessanten'ne *ag, sm/f* sixty-year-old.

sessante'simo, a *num* sixtieth.

sessanti'na *sf:* **una** ~ **(di)** about sixty.

sessio'ne *sf* session.

ses'so *sm* sex; **il** ~ **debole/forte** the weaker/stronger sex.

sessua'le *ag* sexual, sex *cpd*.

sessualità *sf* sexuality.

sessuo'logo, a, gi, ghe *sm/f* sexologist, sex specialist.

sestan'te *sm* sextant.

se'sto, a *num* sixth ♦ *sm:* **rimettere in** ~ (*aggiustare*) to put back in order; (*fig: perso-*

na) to put back on his (*o* her) feet; **rimettersi in** ~ (*riprendersi*) to recover, get well; (*riassettarsi*) to tidy o.s. up.

se'ta *sf* silk.

setaccia're [sãtàchà'rã] *vt* (*farina etc*) to sift, sieve; (*fig: zona*) to search, comb.

setac'cio [sãtàch'chõ] *sm* sieve; **passare al** ~ (*fig*) to search, comb.

se'te *sf* thirst; **avere** ~ to be thirsty; ~ **di potere** thirst for power.

setifi'cio [sãtẽfẽ'chõ] *sm* silk factory.

se'tola *sf* bristle.

sett. *abbr* (= *settembre*) Sept. .

set'ta *sf* sect.

settan'ta *num* seventy.

settanten'ne *ag, sm/f* seventy-year-old.

settante'simo, a *num* seventieth.

settanti'na *sf:* **una** ~ **(di)** about seventy.

set'te *num* seven.

settecente'sco, a, schi, sche [sãttãchãntã'skõ] *ag* eighteenth-century.

settecen'to [sãttãchen'tõ] *num* seven hundred ♦ *sm:* **il S~** the eighteenth century.

settem'bre *sm* September; *per fraseologia vedi* **luglio**.

settemi'la *num* seven thousand.

settentriona'le *ag* northern ♦ *sm/f* northerner.

settentrio'ne *sm* north.

set'tico, a, ci, che *ag* (*MED*) septic.

settima'na *sf* week; **la** ~ **scorsa/prossima** last/next week; **a metà** ~ in the middle of the week.

settimana'le *ag, sm* weekly.

set'timo, a *num* seventh.

setto're *sm* sector; ~ **privato/pubblico** private/public sector; ~ **terziario** service industries *pl*.

Seul' *sf* Seoul.

severità *sf* severity.

seve'ro, a *ag* severe.

sevizia're [sãvẽttsyà'rã] *vt* to torture.

sevi'zie [sãvẽt'tsyã] *sfpl* torture *sg*.

sez. *abbr* = **sezione**.

seziona're [sãttsyõnà'rã] *vt* to divide into sections; (*MED*) to dissect.

sezio'ne [sãttsyõ'nã] *sf* section; (*MED*) dissection.

sfaccenda'to, a [sfàchãndã'tõ] *ag* idle.

sfaccettatu'ra [sfàchãttàtõõ'rã] *sf* (*azione*) faceting; (*parte sfaccettata, fig*) facet.

sfacchina're [sfàkkẽnã'rã] *vi* (*fam*) to toil, drudge.

sfacchina'ta [sfàkkẽnã'tã] *sf* (*fam*) chore, drudgery *q*.

sfacciatag'gine [sfàchàtàd'jẽnã] *sf* insolence, cheek.

sfaccia'to, a [sfàchà'tõ] *ag* (*maleducato*) cheeky, impudent; (*vistoso*) gaudy.

sface'lo [sfàchẽ'lõ] *sm* (*fig*) ruin, collapse.

sfaldar'si vr to flake (off).

sfalsa're vt to offset.

sfama're vt (nutrire) to feed; (soddisfare la fame): ~ **qn** to satisfy sb's hunger; ~**rsi** vr to satisfy one's hunger, fill o.s. up.

sfarfalli'o sm (CINEMA, TV) flickering.

sfar'zo [sfàr'tsō] sm pomp, splendor (US), splendour (Brit).

sfarzo'so, a [sfàrtsō'sō] ag splendid, magnificent.

sfasamen'to sm (ELETTR) phase displacement; (fig) confusion, bewilderment.

sfasa'to, a ag (ELETTR, motore) out of phase; (fig: persona) confused, bewildered.

sfascia're [sfàshà'rā] vt (ferita) to unbandage; (distruggere: porta) to smash, shatter; ~**rsi** vr (rompersi) to smash, shatter.

sfata're vt (leggenda) to explode.

sfatica'to, a sm/f idler, loafer.

sfat'to, a ag (letto) unmade; (orlo etc) undone; (gelato, neve) melted; (frutta) overripe; (riso, pasta etc) overdone, overcooked; (fam: persona, corpo) flabby.

sfavilla're vi to spark, send out sparks; (risplendere) to sparkle.

sfavo're sm disfavor (US), disfavour (Brit), disapproval.

sfavore'vole ag unfavorable (US), unfavourable (Brit).

sfegata'to, a ag fanatical.

sfe'ra sf sphere.

sfe'rico, a, ci, che ag spherical.

sferra're vt (fig: colpo) to land, deal; (: attacco) to launch.

sferzan'te [sfārtsàn'tā] ag (critiche, parole) stinging.

sferza're [sfārtsà'rā] vt to whip; (fig) to lash out at.

sfianca're vt to wear out, exhaust; ~**rsi** vr to exhaust o.s., wear o.s. out.

sfiata're vi to allow air (o gas etc) to escape.

sfiatato'io sm blowhole; (TECN) vent.

sfibran'te ag exhausting, energy-sapping.

sfibra're vt (indebolire) to exhaust, enervate.

sfibra'to, a ag exhausted, worn out.

sfi'da sf challenge.

sfidan'te ag challenging ♦ sm/f challenger.

sfida're vt to challenge; (fig) to defy, brave; ~ **qn a fare qc** to challenge sb to do sth; ~ **un pericolo** to brave a danger; **sfido che** ... I dare say (that) ....

sfidu'cia [sfēdōō'chà] sf distrust, mistrust; **avere** ~ **in** qn/qc to distrust sb/sth.

sfigura're vt (persona) to disfigure; (quadro, statua) to deface ♦ vi (far cattiva figura) to make a bad impression.

sfilaccia're [sfēlàchà'rā] vt, vi, ~**rsi** vr to fray.

sfila're vt (ago) to unthread; (abito, scarpe) to slip off ♦ vi (truppe) to march past, parade; (manifestanti) to march; ~**rsi** vr

(perle etc) to come unstrung; (orlo, tessuto) to fray; (calza) to run, ladder.

sfila'ta sf (MIL) parade; (di manifestanti) march; ~ **di moda** fashion show.

sfil'za [sfēl'tsà] sf (di case) row; (di errori) series inv.

sfin'ge [sfēn'jā] sf sphinx.

sfinimen'to sm exhaustion.

sfini'to, a ag exhausted.

sfiora're vt to brush (against); (argomento) to touch upon; ~ **la velocità di 150 km/h** to touch 150 km/h.

sfiori're vi to wither, fade.

sfit'to, a ag vacant, empty.

sfoca'to, a ag (FOT) out of focus.

sfocia're [sfōchà'rā] vi: ~ **in** to flow into; (fig: malcontento) to develop into.

sfodera'to, a ag (vestito) unlined.

sfoga're vt to vent, pour out; ~**rsi** vr (sfogare la propria rabbia) to give vent to one's anger; (confidarsi): ~**rsi (con)** to pour out one's feelings (to); **non sfogarti su di me!** don't take your bad temper out on me!

sfoggia're [sfōdjà'rā] vt, vi to show off.

sfog'gio [sfod'jō] sm show, display; **fare** ~ **di** to show off, display.

sfogherò etc [sfōgàro'] vb vedi **sfogare**.

sfo'glia [sfol'yà] sf sheet of pasta dough; **pasta** ~ (CUC) puff pastry.

sfoglia're [sfōlyà'rā] vt (libro) to leaf through.

sfo'go, ghi sm outlet; (eruzione cutanea) rash; (fig) outburst; **dare** ~ **a** (fig) to give vent to.

sfolgoran'te ag (luce) blazing; (fig: vittoria) brilliant.

sfolgora're vi to blaze.

sfollagen'te [sfōllàjēn'tā] sm inv billy club (US), truncheon (Brit).

sfolla're vt to empty, clear ♦ vi to disperse; ~ **da** (città) to evacuate.

sfolla'to, a ag evacuated ♦ sm/f evacuee.

sfolti're vt, ~**rsi** vr to thin (out).

sfonda're vt (porta) to break down; (scarpe) to wear a hole in; (cesto, scatola) to burst, knock the bottom out of; (MIL) to break through ♦ vi (riuscire) to make a name for o.s.

sfonda'to, a ag (scarpe) worn out; (scatola) burst; (sedia) broken, damaged; **essere ricco** ~ to be rolling in it.

sfon'do sm background.

sforma're vt to put out of shape, knock out of shape; ~**rsi** vr to lose shape, get out of shape.

sforma'to, a ag (che ha perso forma) shapeless ♦ sm (CUC) type of soufflé.

sforna're vt (pane) to take out of the oven; (fig) to churn out.

sforni'to, a ag: ~ **di** lacking in, without; (negozio) out of.

sfortu'na *sf* misfortune, ill luck *q*; **avere ~** to be unlucky; **che ~!** how unfortunate!

sfortuna'to, a *ag* unlucky; (*impresa, film*) unsuccessful.

sforza're [sfōrtsá'rā] *vt* to force; (*voce, occhi*) to strain; **~rsi** *vr*: **~rsi di** *o a o* **per fare to** try hard to do.

sfor'zo [sfor'tsō] *sm* effort; (*tensione eccessiva, TECN*) strain; **fare uno ~** to make an effort; **essere sotto ~** (*motore, macchina, fig: persona*) to be under stress.

sfot'tere *vt* (*fam*) to tease.

sfracella're [sfráchāllá'rā] *vt*, **~rsi** *vr* to smash.

sfratta're *vt* to evict.

sfrat'to *sm* eviction; **dare lo ~ a qn** to give sb notice to quit.

sfreccia're [sfrāchá'rā] *vi* to shoot *o* flash past.

sfrega're *vt* (*strofinare*) to rub; (*graffiare*) to scratch; **~rsi le mani** to rub one's hands; **~ un fiammifero** to strike a match.

sfregia're [sfrājá'rā] *vt* to slash, gash; (*persona*) to disfigure; (*quadro*) to deface.

sfre'gio [sfrā'jō] *sm* gash; scar; (*fig*) insult.

sfrena'to, a *ag* (*fig*) unrestrained, unbridled.

sfronda're *vt* (*albero*) to prune, thin out; (*fig: discorso, scritto*) to prune (down).

sfrontatez'za [sfrōntátāt'tsá] *sf* impudence, cheek.

sfronta'to, a *ag* impudent, cheeky.

sfruttamen'to *sm* exploitation.

sfrutta're *vt* (*terreno*) to overwork, exhaust; (*miniera*) to exploit, work; (*fig: operai, occasione, potere*) to exploit.

sfruttato're, tri'ce *sm/f* exploiter.

sfuggen'te [sfōōdjen'tā] *ag* (*fig: sguardo*) elusive; (*mento*) receding.

sfuggi're [sfōōdjē'rā] *vi* to escape; **~ a** (*custode*) to escape (from); (*morte*) to escape; **~ a qn** (*dettaglio, nome*) to escape sb; **~ di mano a qn** to slip out of sb's hand (*o* hands); **lasciarsi ~ un'occasione** to let an opportunity go by; **~ al controllo** (*macchina*) to go out of control; (*situazione*) to be no longer under control.

sfuggi'ta [sfōōdjē'tá] *sf*: **di ~** (*rapidamente, in fretta*) in passing.

sfuma're *vt* (*colori, contorni*) to soften, shade off ♦ *vi* to shade (off), fade; (*fig: svanire*) to vanish, disappear; (*: speranze*) to come to nothing.

sfumatu'ra *sf* shading off *q*; (*tonalità*) shade, tone; (*fig*) touch, hint.

sfuria'ta *sf* (*scatto di collera*) fit of anger; (*rimprovero*) sharp rebuke.

sfu'so, a *ag* (*caramelle etc*) loose, unpacked; (*vino*) unbottled; (*birra*) draft (*US*), draught (*Brit*).

sg. *abbr* = **seguente**.

S.G. *abbr* = **Sua Grazia**.

sgabel'lo *sm* stool.

sgabuzzi'no [zgábōōddzē'nō] *sm* storage closet (*US*), lumber room (*Brit*).

sgambetta're *vi* to kick one's legs about.

sgambet'to *sm*: **far lo ~ a qn** to trip sb up; (*fig*) to oust sb.

sganasciar'si [zgánáshár'sē] *vr*: **~ dalle risa** to roar with laughter.

sgancia're [zgánchá'rā] *vt* to unhook; (*chiusura*) to unfasten, undo; (*FERR*) to uncouple; (*bombe: da aereo*) to release, drop; (*fig: fam: soldi*) to fork out; **~rsi** *vr* to come unhooked; to come unfastened, come undone; to uncouple; (*fig*): **~rsi (da)** to get away (from).

sganghera'to, a [zgángārá'tō] *ag* (*porta*) off its hinges; (*auto*) ramshackle; (*riso*) wild, boisterous.

sgarba'to, a *ag* rude, impolite.

sgar'bo *sm*: **fare uno ~ a qn** to be rude to sb.

sgargian'te [zgárján'tā] *ag* gaudy, showy.

sgarra're *vi* (*persona*) to step out of line; (*orologio: essere avanti*) to gain; (*: essere indietro*) to lose.

sgar'ro *sm* inaccuracy.

sgattaiola're *vi* to sneak away *o* off.

sgela're [zjālá'rā] *vi*, *vt* to thaw.

sghem'bo, a [zgām'bō] *ag* (*obliquo*) slanting; (*storto*) crooked.

sghignazza're [zgēnyáttsá'rā] *vi* to laugh scornfully.

sghignazza'ta [zgēnyáttsá'tá] *sf* scornful laugh.

sgobba're *vi* (*fam: scolaro*) to cram, (*: operaio*) to toil.

sgoccila're [zgōchōlá'rā] *vt* (*vuotare*) to drain (to the last drop) ♦ *vi* (*acqua*) to drip; (*recipiente*) to drain.

sgoc'cioli [zgōch'chōlē] *smpl*: **essere agli ~** (*lavoro, provviste etc*) to be nearly finished; (*periodo*) to be nearly over; **siamo agli ~** we've nearly finished, the end is in sight.

sgolar'si *vr* to talk (*o* shout *o* sing) o.s. hoarse.

sgomb(e)ra're *vt* to clear; (*andarsene da: stanza*) to vacate; (*evacuare*) to evacuate.

sgom'bro, a *ag*: **~ (di)** clear (of), free (from) ♦ *sm* (*ZOOL*) mackerel; (*anche:* **sgombero**) clearing; vacating; evacuation; (*: trasloco*) removal.

sgomenta're *vt* to dismay; **~rsi** *vr* to be dismayed.

sgomen'to, a *ag* dismayed ♦ *sm* dismay, consternation.

sgomina're *vt* (*nemico*) to rout; (*avversario*) to defeat; (*fig: epidemia*) to overcome.

sgonfia're *vt* to let down, deflate; **~rsi** *vr* to go down.

sgon'fio, a *ag* (*pneumatico, pallone*) flat.

sgor'bio *sm* blot; scribble.

sgorga're *vi* to gush (out...

sgozza're [zgōttsà'rā] *vt* t[o] cut the throat of.

sgrade'vole *ag* unpleasa[nt], disagreeable.

sgradi'to, a *ag* unpleasa[nt], unwelcome.

sgraffigna're [zgràffēnyi...] *vt* (*fam*) to pinch, swipe.

sgrammatica'to, a *ag* [g]rammatical.

sgrana're *vt* (*piselli*) [to]...; ~ gli occhi to open one's eyes wide.

sgranchir'si [zgrànkēr...] *vr* to stretch; ~ le gambe to stretch on[e']s... [le]gs.

sgranocchia're [zgr...ya'rā] *vt* to munch.

sgrassa're *vt* to re[m...]he grease from.

sgra'vio *sm*: ~ fis[cale] contributivo tax relief.

sgrazia'to, a [z...à'tō] *ag* clumsy, ungainly.

sgretola're *vt* t[o]... to crumble; ~rsi *vr* to crumble.

sgrida're *vt* to...

sgrida'ta *sf* s[cold]e, vulgar.

sguaia'to, a...w, unsheathe.

sguaina're [...'rā] *vt* to crumple (up),

sgualci're... crease. [...]) slut.

sgualdri'[na] (*occhiata*) look, glance;

sguar'd[o]...k (in one's eye); dare uno (*espre...* se at sth, cast a glance *o* an ~ a ...are *o* sollevare lo ~ to raise eye *o*... up; cercare qc/qn con lo ~ one...d for sth/sb.

to ...*m/f* scullery boy/maid.

...*u* [zgwàttsà'rā] *vi* (*nell'acqua*) to ...gu[...]: (*nella melma*) to wallow; ~ sp...e rolling in money.

...na're [zgwēntsàlyà'rā] *vt* to let off the s[t]eam; ...*g: persona*): ~ qn dietro a qn to ...sb.

...re [zgōōshà'rā] *vt* to shell ♦ *vi* (*sfuggi-* ...*mano*) to slip; ~ via to slip *o* slink

...poo [shàm'pō] *sm inv* shampoo.

...k [shok] *sm inv* shock.

...gla = Siena.

...pronome (*dav lo, la, li, le, ne diventa* se) (*riflessivo*) oneself, *m* himself, *f* herself, *soggetto non umano* itself; *pl* themselves; (*reciproco*) one another, each other; (*passivante*): lo ~ ripara facilmente it is easily repaired; (*possessivo*): lavarsi le mani to wash one's hands; (*impersonale*): ~ vede che è felice one *o* you can see that he's happy; (*noi*): tra poco ~ parte we're leaving soon; (*la gente*): ~ dice che they *o* people say that; mi ~ dice che ... I am told that ... ♦ *sm* (*MUS*) B; (: *solfeggiando la scala*) ti.

sì *av* yes ♦ *sm*: non mi aspettavo un ~ I didn't expect him (*o* her *etc*) to say yes; per me è ~ I should think so, I expect so; sa-

ranno stati ~ e no in 20 there must have been about 20 of them; uno ~ e uno no every other one; un giorno ~ e uno no every other day; dire di ~ to say yes; spero/penso di ~ I hope/think so; fece di ~ col capo he nodded (his head); e ~ che ... and to think that ....

si'a *cong*: ~ ... ~ (*o* ... *o*): ~ che lavori, ~ che non lavori whether he works or not; (*tanto ... quanto*): verranno ~ Luigi ~ suo fratello both Luigi and his brother will be coming.

si'a *etc vb vedi* essere.

SIAE *sigla f* = Società Italiana Autori ed Editori.

Siam' *sm*: il ~ Siam.

siame'se *ag, sm/f* siamese *inv*.

sia'mo *vb vedi* essere.

Sibe'ria *sf*: la ~ Siberia.

sibila're *vi* to hiss; (*fischiare*) to whistle.

si'bilo *sm* hiss; whistle.

sica'rio *sm* hired killer.

sicché [sēkkā'] *cong* (*perciò*) so (that), therefore; (*e quindi*) (and) so.

siccità [sēchētà'] *sf* drought.

sicco'me *cong* since, as.

Sici'lia [sēchē'lyà] *sf*: la ~ Sicily.

sicilia'no, a [sēchēlyà'nō] *ag, sm/f* Sicilian.

sicomo'ro *sm* sycamore.

si'culo, a *ag, sm/f* Sicilian.

sicu'ra *sf* (*di arma, spilla*) safety catch; (*di portiera*) safety lock.

sicurez'za [sēkōōrāt'tsà] *sf* safety; security; confidence; certainty; di ~ safety *cpd*; la ~ stradale road safety; avere la ~ di qc to be sure *o* certain of sth; lo so con ~ I am quite certain; ha risposto con molta ~ he answered very confidently.

sicu'ro, a *ag* safe; (*ben difeso*) secure; (*fiducioso*) confident; (*certo*) sure, certain; (*notizia, amico*) reliable; (*esperto*) skilled ♦ *av* (*anche*: di ~) certainly ♦ *sm*: andare sul ~ to play safe; essere/mettere al ~ to be safe/ put in a safe place; ~ di sé self-confident, sure of o.s.; sentirsi ~ to feel safe *o* secure; essere ~ di/che to be sure of/that; da fonte ~a from reliable sources.

siderurgi'a [sēdārōōrjē'à] *sf* iron and steel industry.

siderur'gico, a, ci, che [sēdārōōr'jēkō] *ag* iron and steel *cpd*.

si'dro *sm* hard cider (*US*), cider (*Brit*).

sie'do *etc vb vedi* sedere.

sie'pe *sf* hedge.

sie'ro *sm* (*MED*) serum; ~ antivipera snake bite serum; ~ del latte whey.

sieropositi'vo, a *ag* HIV positive.

sier'ra *sf* (*GEO*) sierra.

Sier'ra Leo'ne *sf*: la ~ Sierra Leone.

sie'sta *sf* siesta, (afternoon) nap.

sie'te *vb vedi* **essere.**
sifi'lide *sf* syphilis.
sifo'ne *sm* siphon.
Sig. *abbr* (= *signore*) Mr.
sigaret'ta *sf* cigarette.
si'garo *sm* cigar.
Sigg. *abbr* (= *signori*) Messrs.
sigilla're [sējēllá'rā] *vt* to seal.
sigil'lo [sējēl'lō] *sm* seal.
si'gla *sf* (*iniziali*) initials *pl*; (*abbreviazione*) acronym, abbreviation; ~ **automobilistica** *abbreviation of province on vehicle number plate*; ~ **musicale** signature tune.
sigla're *vt* to initial.
Sig.na *abbr* (= *signorina*) Miss.
significa're [sēnyēfēká'rā] *vt* to mean; **cosa significa?** what does this mean?
significati'vo, a [sēnyēfēkátē'vō] *ag* significant.
significa'to [sēnyēfēká'tō] *sm* meaning.
signo'ra [sēnyō'rà] *sf* lady; **la ~ X** Mrs [mi'siz] X; **buon giorno S~/Signore/Signorina** good morning; (*deferente*) good morning Madam/ Sir/Madam; (*quando si conosce il nome*) good morning Mrs/Mr/Miss X; **Gentile S~/ Signore/Signorina** (*in una lettera*) Dear Madam/Sir/Madam; **Gentile** (*o* **Cara**) **S~ Rossi** Dear Mrs Rossi; **Gentile S~ Anna Rossi** (*sulle buste*) Mrs Anna Rossi; **il signor Rossi e ~** Mr and Mrs Rossi **~e e e signori** ladies and gentlemen; **le presento la mia ~** may I introduce my wife?
signo're [sēnyō'rā] *sm* gentleman; (*padrone*) lord, master; (*REL*): **il S~** the Lord; **il signor X** Mr [mi'stûr] X; **signor Presidente** Mr Chairman; **Gentile** (*o* **Caro**) **Signor Rossi** (*in lettere*) Dear Mr Rossi; **Gentile Signor Paolo Rossi** (*sulle buste*) Mr Paolo Rossi; **i ~i Bianchi** (*coniugi*) Mr and Mrs Bianchi; *vedi anche* **signora.**
signori'a [sēnyōrē'á] *sf* (*STORIA*) seignory, signoria; **S~ Vostra (S.V.)** (*AMM*) you.
signori'le [sēnyōrē'lā] *ag* refined.
signorilità [sēnyōrēlētá'] *sf* (*raffinatezza*) refinement; (*eleganza*) elegance.
signori'na [sēnyōrē'nà] *sf* young lady; **la ~ X** Miss X; **Gentile** (*o* **Cara**) **S~ Rossi** (*in lettere*) Dear Miss Rossi; **Gentile S~ Anna Rossi** (*sulle buste*) Miss Anna Rossi; *vedi anche* **signora.**
signori'no [sēnyōrē'nō] *sm* young master.
Sig.ra *abbr* (= *signora*) Mrs.
silenziato're [sēlāntsyátō'rā] *sm* silencer.
silen'zio [sēlen'tsyō] *sm* silence; **fare ~** to be quiet, stop talking; **far passare qc sotto ~** to keep quiet about sth, hush sth up.
silenzio'so, a [sēlāntsyō'sō] *ag* silent, quiet.
si'lice [sē'lēchā] *sf* silica.
sili'cio [sēlē'chō] *sm* silicon; **piastrina di ~** silicon chip.

sil'laba *sf* syllable.
silura're *vt* to tor
mando) to oust.
silu'ro *sm* torpedo.
simbio'si (*BIOL*) symbiosis.
simboleggia're [s ōlādjá'rā] *vt* to symbolize.
simbo'lico, a, ci, ch symbolic(al).
simboli'smo *sm* syr   ism.
sim'bolo *sm* symbol.
simila're *ag* similar.
si'mile *ag* (*analogo*) s
un uomo ~ such a : (*di questo tipo*): *sm* (*persona*) fellow   man like this ♦ books; ~ **a** similar t **libri ~i** such **niente di ~** I've nev   **ho mai visto** that; **è insegnante o d** anything like teacher or something lik   **a di ~** he's a e **~i** they sell vases an   **vendono vasi suoi ~i** one's fellow men;   like that; **i**
similitu'dine *sf* (*LING*) simers.
simmetri'a *sf* symmetry.
simme'trico, a, ci, che *ag* sy
simpati'a *sf* (*qualità*) pleas al). *zione*) liking; **avere ~ per qn** inclina- a liking for sb; **con ~** (*su l* have much affection.   with
simpa'tico, a, ci, che *ag* (*p* pleasant, likeable; (*casa, alber* ice, pleasant.   e,
simpatizzan'te [sēmpátēddzàn sympathizer.
simpatizza're [sēmpátēddzá'rā] *vi:* take a liking to.
simpo'sio *sm* symposium.
simula're *vt* to fake, simulate; (simulate.
simulazio'ne [sēmōōláttsyō'nā] *sf* shar simulation.
simulta'neo, a *ag* simultaneous.
sin. *abbr* (= *sinistra*) L.
sinago'ga, ghe *sf* synagogue.
sinceramen'te [sēnchàrámàn'tā] *av* (g sincerely; (*francamente*) honestly, sincerel
sincerar'si [sēnchàrár'sē] *vr:* ~ (**di qc**) make sure (of sth).
sincerità [sēnchàrētá'] *sf* sincerity.
since'ro, a [sēnchà'rō] *ag* (*genuino*) sincere; (*onesto*) genuine.
sin'cope *sf* syncopation; (*MED*) blackout.
sincro'nico, a, ci, che *ag* synchronic.
sincronizza're [sēnkrōnēddzá'rā] *vt* to synchronize.
sindaca'le *ag* (trade-)union *cpd*.
sindacali'sta, i, e *sm/f* trade unionist.
sindaca're *vt* (*controllare*) to inspect; (*fig:* *criticare*) to criticize.
sindaca'to *sm* (*di lavoratori*) (trade) union; ~ **dei datori di lavoro** employers' association.

sin'daco, ci *sm* mayor.
sin'drome *sf* (*MED*) syndrome.
sinfoni'a *sf* (*MUS*) symphony.
sinfo'nico, a, ci, che *ag* symphonic; (*orchestra*) symphony *cpd*.
singale'se *ag, sm/f, sm* Sin(g)halese *inv*.
Singapo're *sf* Singapore.
singhiozza're [sēngyōttsà'rā] *vi* to sob; to hiccup.
singhioz'zo [sēngyōt'tsō] *sm* (*di pianto*) sob; (*MED*) hiccup; **avere il ~** to have the hiccups; **a ~** (*fig*) by fits and starts.
singola're *ag* (*insolito*) remarkable, singular; (*LING*) singular ♦ *sm* (*LING*) singular; (*TENNIS*): **~ maschile/femminile** men's/women's singles.
singolarmen'te *av* (*separatamente*) individually, one at a time; (*in modo strano*) strangely, peculiarly, oddly.
sin'golo, a *ag* single, individual ♦ *sm* (*persona*) individual; (*TENNIS*) = **singolare**; **ogni ~ individuo** each individual; **camera ~a** single room.
sinistra'to, a *ag* damaged ♦ *sm/f* disaster victim; **zona ~a** disaster area.
sinis'tro, a *ag* left, left-hand; (*fig*) sinister ♦ *sm* (*incidente*) accident ♦ *sf* (*POL*) left (wing); **a ~a** on the left; (*direzione*) to the left; **a ~a di** to the left of; **di ~a** left-wing; **tenere la ~a** to keep to the left; **guida a ~a** left-hand drive.
si'no *prep* = **fino**.
sino'nimo, a *ag* synonymous ♦ *sm* synonym; **~ di** synonymous with.
sintas'si *sf* syntax.
sintat'tico, a, ci, che *ag* syntactic.
sin'tesi *sf* synthesis; (*riassunto*) summary, synopsis; **in ~** in brief, in short.
sinte'tico, a, ci, che *ag* synthetic; (*conciso*) brief, concise.
sintetizza're [sēntātēddzà'rā] *vt* to synthesize; (*riassumere*) to summarize.
sintetizzato're [sēntātēddzátō'rā] *sm* (*MUS*) synthesizer; **~ di voce** voice synthesizer.
sintoma'tico, a, ci, che *ag* symptomatic.
sin'tomo *sm* symptom.
sintoni'a *sf* (*RADIO*) tuning; **essere in ~ con qn** (*fig*) to be on the same wavelength as sb.
sintonizza're [sēntōnēddzà'rā] *vt* to tune (in); **~rsi** *vr*: **~rsi su** to tune in to.
sintonizzato're [sēntōnēddzátō'rā] *sm* tuner.
sinuo'so, a *ag* (*strada*) winding.
sinusi'te *sf* sinusitis.
SIP *sigla f* (= *Società Italiana per l'esercizio telefonico*) *Italian telephone company*.
sipa'rio *sm* (*TEATRO*) curtain.
sire'na *sf* (*apparecchio*) siren; (*nella mitologia, fig*) siren, mermaid; **~ d'allarme** (*per incendio*) fire alarm; (*per furto*) burglar alarm.

Si'ria *sf*: **la ~** Syria.
siria'no, a *ag, sm/f* Syrian.
sirin'ga, ghe *sf* syringe.
si'sma, i *sm* earthquake.
SI'SMI *sigla m* (= *Servizio per l'Informazione e la Sicurezza Militari*) *military security service*.
si'smico, a, ci, che *ag* seismic; (*zona*) earthquake *cpd*.
sismo'grafo *sm* seismograph.
sissigno're [sēssēnyō'rā] *av* (*a un superiore*) yes, sir; (*enfatico*) yes indeed, of course.
siste'ma, i *sm* system; (*metodo*) method, way; **trovare il ~ per fare qc** to find a way to do sth; **~ decimale/metrico** decimal/metric system; **~ operativo** (*INFORM*) operating system; **~ solare** solar system; **~ di vita** way of life.
sistema're *vt* (*mettere a posto*) to tidy, put in order; (*risolvere: questione*) to sort out, settle; (*procurare un lavoro a*) to find a job for; (*dare un alloggio a*) to settle, find accommodations (*US*) *o* accommodation (*Brit*) for; **~rsi** *vr* (*problema*) to be settled; (*persona: trovare alloggio*) to find accommodation(s); (: *trovarsi un lavoro*) to find a job; **ti sistemo io!** I'll soon sort you out!; **~ qn in un albergo** to fix sb up with a hotel.
sistema'tico, a, ci, che *ag* systematic.
sistemazio'ne [sēstāmàttsyō'nā] *sf* arrangement, order; settlement; employment; accommodations (*US*), accommodation (*Brit*).
si'to, a *ag* (*AMM*) situated ♦ *sm* (*letterario*) place.
situa're *vt* to site, situate.
situa'to, a *ag*: **~ a/su** situated at/on.
situazio'ne [sētōōàttsyō'nā] *sf* situation; **vista la sua ~ familiare** given your family situation *o* circumstances; **nella sua ~** in your position *o* situation; **mi trovo in una ~ critica** I'm in a very difficult situation *o* position.
ska'i ® *sm* Leatherette ®.
slaccia're [zlàchá'rā] *vt* to undo, unfasten.
slanciar'si [zlànchár'sē] *vr* to dash, fling o.s.
slancia'to, a [zlànchá'tō] *ag* slender.
slan'cio [zlàn'chō] *sm* dash, leap; (*fig*) surge; **in uno ~ d'affetto** in a burst *o* rush of affection; **di ~** impetuously.
slava'to, a *ag* faded, washed out; (*fig: viso, occhi*) pale, colorless (*US*) colourless (*Brit*).
slavi'na *sf* snowslide.
sla'vo, a *ag* Slav(onic), Slavic.
slea'le *ag* disloyal; (*concorrenza etc*) unfair.
slealtà *sf* disloyalty; unfairness.
slega're *vt* to untie.
slit'ta *sf* sled (*US*), sledge (*Brit*); (*trainata*) sleigh.
slittamen'to *sm* slipping; skidding; postponement; **~ salariale** wage drift.
slitta're *vi* to slip, slide; (*AUT*) to skid;

(incontro, conferenza) to be put off, be postponed.

s.l.m. *abbr* (= *sul livello del mare*) a.s.l.

sloga're *vt* (*MED*) to dislocate; (: *caviglia, polso*) to sprain.

slogatu'ra *sf* dislocation; sprain.

sloggia're |zlōdjà'rā| *vt* (*inquilino*) to turn out; (*nemico*) to drive out, dislodge ♦ *vi* to move out.

S.M. *abbr* (*MIL*) = **Stato Maggiore**; (= *Sua Maestà*) HM.

smacchia're |zmàkkyà'rā| *vt* to remove stains from.

smacchiato're |zmàkkyàtō'rā| *sm* stain remover.

smac'co, chi *sm* humiliating defeat.

smaglian'te |zmàlyàn'tā| *ag* brilliant, dazzling.

smaglia're |zmàlyà'rā| *vt*, **~rsi** *vr* (*calza*) to run (*US*), ladder (*Brit*).

smagliatu'ra |zmàlyàtōō'rà| *sf* (*su maglia, calza*) run, ladder (*Brit*); (*MED*: *sulla pelle*) stretch mark.

smagri'to, a *ag*: essere ~ to have lost a lot of weight.

smalizia'to, a |smàlēttsyà'tō| *ag* shrewd, cunning.

smalta're *vt* to enamel; (*ceramica*) to glaze; (*unghie*) to varnish.

smalti're *vt* (*merce*) to sell off; (*rifiuti*) to dispose of; (*cibo*) to digest; (*peso*) to lose; (*rabbia*) to get over; ~ **la sbornia** to sober up.

smal'to *sm* (*anche di denti*) enamel; (*per ceramica*) glaze; ~ **per unghie** nail polish.

smanceri'e |zmànchārē'à| *sfpl* mawkishness *sg*.

sma'nia *sf* agitation, restlessness; (*fig*): ~ **di** thirst for, craving for; **avere la** ~ **addosso** to have the fidgets; **avere la** ~ **di fare** to long *o* yearn to do.

smania're *vi* (*agitarsi*) to be restless *o* agitated; (*fig*): ~ **di fare** to long *o* yearn to do.

smantellamen'to *sm* dismantling.

smantella're *vt* to dismantle.

smargias'so |zmàrjàs'sō| *sm* show-off.

smarrimen'to *sm* loss; (*fig*) bewilderment; dismay.

smarri're *vt* to lose; (*non riuscire a trovare*) to mislay; **~rsi** *vr* (*perdersi*) to lose one's way, get lost; (: *oggetto*) to go astray.

smarri'to, a *ag* (*oggetto*) lost; (*fig*: *confuso*: *persona*) bewildered, nonplussed; (: *sguardo*) bewildered; **ufficio oggetti ~i** lost and found (*US*), lost property office (*Brit*).

smaschera're |zmàskārā'rā| *vt* to unmask.

SME *abbr* = **Stato Maggiore Esercito** ♦ *sigla m* (= *Sistema Monetario Europeo*) EMS (= *European Monetary System*).

smembra're *vt* (*gruppo, partito etc*) to split; **~rsi** *vr* to split up.

smemora'to, a *ag* forgetful.

smenti're *vt* (*negare*) to deny; (*testimonianza*) to refute; (*reputazione*) to give the lie to; **~rsi** *vr* to be inconsistent.

smenti'ta *sf* denial; refutation.

smeral'do *sm, ag inv* emerald.

smercia're |zmàrchà'rā| *vt* (*COMM*) to sell; (: *svendere*) to sell off.

smer'cio |zmcr'chō| *sm* sale; **avere poco/ molto** ~ to have poor/good sales.

smeriglia're |zmārēlyà'tō| *ag*: **carta** ~**a** emery paper; **vetro** ~ frosted glass.

smeri'glio |zmārēl'yō| *sm* emery.

smes'so, a *pp di* **smettere** ♦ *ag*: **abiti** *mpl* ~**i** cast-offs.

smet'tere *vt* to stop; (*vestiti*) to stop wearing ♦ *vi* to stop, cease; ~ **di fare** to stop doing.

smidolla'to, a *ag* spineless ♦ *sm/f* spineless person.

smilitarizzazio'ne |zmēlētàrēddzàttsyō'nā| *sf* demilitarization.

smil'zo, a |zmēl'tsō| *ag* thin, lean.

sminui're *vt* to diminish, lessen; (*fig*) to belittle; ~ **l'importanza di qc** to play sth down.

sminuzza're |zmēnōōttsà'rā| *vt* to break into small pieces; to crumble.

smi'si *etc vb vedi* **smettere**.

smistamen'to *sm* (*di posta*) sorting; (*FERR*) shunting.

smista're *vt* (*pacchi etc*) to sort; (*FERR*) to shunt.

smisura'to, a *ag* boundless, immeasurable; (*grandissimo*) immense, enormous.

smitizza're |zmētēddzà'rā| *vt* to debunk.

smobilita're *vt* to demobilize.

smobiliz'zo |zmōbēlēd'dzō| *sm* (*COMM*) disinvestment.

smoda'to, a *ag* excessive, unrestrained.

smodera'to, a *ag* immoderate.

smo'king |smō'king| *sm inv* tuxedo.

smonta're *vt* (*mobile, macchina etc*) to take to pieces, dismantle; (*fig*: *scoraggiare*) to dishearten ♦ *vi* (*scendere*: *da cavallo*) to dismount; (: *da treno*) to get off; (*terminare il lavoro*) to stop (work); **~rsi** *vr* to lose heart; to lose one's enthusiasm.

smor'fia *sf* grimace; (*atteggiamento lezioso*) simpering; **fare ~e** to make faces; to simper.

smorfio'so, a *ag* simpering.

smor'to, a *ag* (*viso*) pale, wan; (*colore*) dull.

smorza're |zmōrtsà'rā| *vt* (*suoni*) to deaden; (*colori*) to tone down; (*luce*) to dim; (*sete*) to quench; (*entusiasmo*) to dampen; **~rsi** *vr* (*suono, luce*) to fade; (*entusiasmo*) to dampen.

smos'so, a *pp di* **smuovere**.

smottamen'to *sm* landslide.

smun'to, a *ag* haggard, pinched.

smuo'vere *vt* to move, shift; (*fig*: *commuovere*) to move; (: *dall'inerzia*) to rouse, stir;

~**rsi** *vr* to move, shift.

smussa're *vt* (*angolo*) to round off, smooth; (*lama etc*) to blunt; ~**rsi** *vr* to become blunt.

s.n. *abbr* = *senza numero.*

snatura'to, a *ag* inhuman, heartless.

snazionalizza're [znáttsyōnálēddzá'rā] *vt* to denationalize.

snellimen'to *sm* (*di traffico*) speeding up; (*di procedura*) streamlining.

snelli're *vt* (*persona*) to make slim; (*traffico*) to speed up; (*procedura*) to streamline; ~**rsi** *vr* (*persona*) to (get) slim; (*traffico*) to speed up.

snel'lo, a *ag* (*agile*) agile; (*svelto*) slender, slim.

snervan'te *ag* (*attesa, lavoro*) exasperating.

snerva're *vt* to enervate, wear out; ~**rsi** *vr* to become enervated.

snida're *vt* to drive out, flush out.

snobba're *vt* to snub.

snobi'smo *sm* snobbery.

snocciola're [znōchōlá'rā] *vt* (*frutta*) to stone; (*fig: orazioni*) to rattle off; (*: verità*) to blab; (*: fam: soldi*) to shell out.

snoda'bile *ag* (*lampada*) adjustable; (*tubo, braccio*) hinged; **rasoio con testina** ~ swivel-head razor.

snoda're *vt* to untie, undo; (*rendere agile, mobile*) to loosen; ~**rsi** *vr* to come loose; (*articolarsi*) to bend; (*strada, fiume*) to wind.

SO *sigla* = *Sondrio.*

so *vb vedi* **sapere.**

S.O. *abbr* (= *sudovest*) SW.

soa've *ag* (*voce, maniera*) gentle; (*volto*) delicate, sweet; (*musica*) soft, sweet; (*profumo*) delicate.

soavità *sf* gentleness; delicacy; sweetness; softness.

sobbalza're [sōbbáltsá'rā] *vi* to jolt, jerk; (*trasalire*) to jump, start.

sobbal'zo [sōbbál'tsō] *sm* jerk, jolt; jump, start.

sobbarcar'si *vr:* ~ **a** to take on, undertake.

sobbor'go, ghi *sm* suburb.

sobilla're *vt* to stir up, incite.

so'brio, a *ag* sober.

Soc. *abbr* (= *società*) Soc.

socchiu'dere [sōkkyōō'dārā] *vt* (*porta*) to leave ajar; (*occhi*) to half-close.

socchiu'so, a [sōkkyōō'sō] *pp di* **socchiudere** ♦ *ag* (*porta, finestra*) ajar; (*occhi*) half-closed.

soccom'bere *vi* to succumb, give way.

soccor'rere *vt* to help, assist.

soccorrito're, tri'ce *sm/f* rescuer.

soccor'so, a *pp di* **soccorrere** ♦ *sm* help, aid, assistance; ~**i** *smpl* relief *sg*, aid *sg*; **presta-re** ~ **a qn** to help *o* assist sb; **venire in** ~ **di qn** to help sb, come to sb's aid; **operazioni di** ~ rescue operations; ~ **stradale** road (*US*) *o*

breakdown (*Brit*) service.

socialdemocra'tico, a, ci, che [sōchál-dāmōkrá'tēkō] *sm/f* Social Democrat.

socia'le [sōchá'lā] *ag* social; (*di associazione*) club *cpd*, association *cpd.*

sociali'smo [sōchálēz'mō] *sm* socialism.

sociali'sta, i, e [sōchálē'stá] *ag, sm/f* socialist.

socializza're [sōchálēddzá'rā] *vi* to socialize.

società [sōchátá'] *sf inv* society; (*sportiva*) club; (*COMM*) company; **in** ~ **con qn** in partnership with sb; **mettersi in** ~ **con qn** to go into business with sb; **l'alta** ~ high society; ~ **anonima (SA)** ≈ incorporated (*US*) *o* limited (*Brit*) company; ~ **per azioni (S.p.A.)** joint-stock company; ~ **di comodo** shell company; ~ **fiduciaria** trust company; ~ **di mutuo soccorso** benefit society (*US*), friendly society (*Brit*); ~ **a responsabilità limitata (S.r.l.)** *type of limited liability company.*

socie'vole [sōchā'vōlā] *ag* sociable.

socievolez'za [sōchāvōlát'tsá] *sf* sociableness.

so'cio [so'chō] *sm* (*DIR, COMM*) partner; (*membro di associazione*) member.

sociologi'a [sōchōlōjē'á] *sf* sociology.

socio'logo, a, gi, ghe [sōcho'lōgō] *sm/f* sociologist.

so'da *sf* (*CHIM*) soda; (*acqua gassata*) soda (water).

sodali'zio [sōdálēt'tsyō] *sm* association, society.

soddisfacen'te [sōddēsfáchen'tā] *ag* satisfactory.

soddisfa're *vt, vi:* ~ **a** to satisfy; (*impegno*) to fulfil; (*debito*) to pay off; (*richiesta*) to meet, comply with; (*offesa*) to make amends for.

soddisfat'to, a *pp di* **soddisfare** ♦ *ag* satisfied, pleased; **essere** ~ **di** to be satisfied *o* pleased with.

soddisfazio'ne [sōddēsfáttsyō'nā] *sf* satisfaction.

so'dio *sm* (*CHIM*) sodium.

so'do, a *ag* firm, hard ♦ *sm:* **venire al** ~ to come to the point ♦ *av* (*picchiare, lavorare*) hard; **dormire** ~ to sleep soundly.

sofà *sm inv* sofa.

sofferen'za [sōffāren'tsá] *sf* suffering; (*COMM*): **in** ~ unpaid.

soffer'to, a *pp di* **soffrire** ♦ *ag* (*vittoria*) hard-fought; (*distacco, decisione*) painful.

soffia're *vt* to blow; (*notizia, segreto*) to whisper ♦ *vi* to blow; (*sbuffare*) to puff (and blow); ~**rsi il naso** to blow one's nose; ~ **qc/qn a qn** (*fig*) to pinch *o* steal sth/sb from sb; ~ **via qc** to blow sth away.

soffia'ta *sf* (*fam*) tip-off; **fare una** ~ **alla polizia** to tip off the police.

sof'fice [sof'fēchā] *ag* soft.

soffiet'to *sm* (*MUS, per fuoco*) bellows *pl;*

porta a ~ folding door.
sof'fio sm (di vento) breath; (di fumo) puff; (MED) murmur.
soffio'ne sm (BOT) dandelion.
soffit'ta sf attic.
soffit'to sm ceiling.
soffocan'te ag suffocating, stifling.
soffoca're vi (anche: ~rsi) to suffocate, choke ♦ vt to suffocate, choke; (fig) to stifle, suppress.
soffocazio'ne [sŏffŏkåttsyŏ'nā] sf suffocation.
soffrig'gere [sŏffrēd'jārā] vt to fry lightly.
soffri're vt to suffer, endure; (sopportare) to bear, stand ♦ vi to suffer; to be in pain; ~ (di) qc (MED) to suffer from sth.
soffrit'to, a pp di **soffriggere** ♦ sm (CUC) fried mixture of herbs, bacon and onions.
Sofi'a sf (GEO) Sofia.
sofistica're vt (vino, cibo) to adulterate.
sofistica'to, a ag sophisticated; (vino) adulterated.
sofisticazio'ne [sŏfēstēkåttsyŏ'nā] sf adulteration.
sof'tware [sof'tweə] sm: ~ **applicativo** applications package.
soggetti'vo, a [sŏdjāttē'vŏ] ag subjective.
sogget'to, a [sŏdjet'tŏ] ag: ~ **a** (sottomesso) subject to; (esposto: a variazioni, danni etc) subject o liable to ♦ sm subject; ~ **a tassa** taxable; **recitare a** ~ (TEATRO) to improvise.
soggezio'ne [sŏdjāttsyŏ'nā] sf subjection; (timidezza) awe; **avere** ~ **di qn** to be ill at ease in sb's presence.
sogghigna're [sŏggēnyà'rā] vi to sneer.
sogghi'gno [sŏggēn'yŏ] sm sneer.
soggiace're [sŏdjáchà'rā] vi: ~ **a** to be subjected to.
soggioga're [sŏdjŏgà'rā] vt to subdue, subjugate.
soggiorna're [sŏdjŏrnà'rā] vi to stay.
soggior'no [sŏdjŏr'nŏ] sm (invernale, marino) stay; (stanza) living room.
soggiun'gere [sŏdjōōn'jārā] vt to add.
soggiun'to, a [sŏdjōōn'tŏ] pp di **soggiungere**.
so'glia [sol'yà] sf doorstep; (anche fig) threshold.
so'gliola [sol'yŏlà] sf (ZOOL) sole.
sognan'te [sŏnyán'tā] ag dreamy.
sogna're [sŏnyà'rā] vt, vi to dream; ~ **a occhi aperti** to daydream.
sognato're, tri'ce [sŏnyátŏ'rā] sm/f dreamer.
so'gno [sŏn'yŏ] sm dream.
so'ia sf (BOT) soy.
sol sm (MUS) G; (: solfeggiando la scala) so(h).
sola'io sm (soffitta) attic.
solamen'te av only, just.
sola're ag solar, sun cpd.
solca're vt (terreno, fig: mari) to plow (US) plough (Brit).

sol'co, chi sm (scavo, fig: ruga) furrow; (incavo) rut, track; (di disco) groove; (scia) wake.
solda'to sm soldier; ~ **di leva** conscript; ~ **semplice** private.
sol'do sm (fig): **non avere un** ~ to be penniless; **non vale un** ~ it's not worth a penny; ~**i** smpl (denaro) money sg.
so'le sm sun; (luce) sun(light); (tempo assolato) sun(shine); **prendere il** ~ to sunbathe.
soleggia'to, a [sŏlādjà'tŏ] ag sunny.
solen'ne ag solemn.
solennità sf solemnity; (festività) holiday, feast day.
sole're vt: ~ **fare qc** to be in the habit of doing sth ♦ vb impers: **come suole accadere** as is usually the case, as usually happens; **come si suol dire** as they say.
soler'te ag diligent.
soler'zia [sŏler'tsyà] sf diligence.
solet'ta sf (per scarpe) insole.
solfa'to sm sulfate (US), sulphate (Brit).
solfo'rico, a, ci, che ag sulfuric (US), sulphuric (Brit); **acido** ~ sulfuric o sulphuric acid.
solfu'ro sm sulfur (US), sulphur (Brit).
solida'le ag in agreement; **essere** ~ **con qn** (essere d'accordo) to be in agreement with sb; (appoggiare) to be behind sb.
solidarietà sf solidarity.
solidifica're vt, vi (anche: ~rsi) to solidify.
solidità sf solidity.
so'lido, a ag solid; (forte, robusto) sturdy, solid; (fig: ditta) sound, solid ♦ sm (MAT) solid.
solilo'quio sm soliloquy.
soli'sta, i, e ag solo ♦ sm/f soloist.
solitamen'te av usually, as a rule.
solita'rio, a ag (senza compagnia) solitary, lonely; (solo, isolato) solitary, lone; (deserto) lonely ♦ sm (gioiello, gioco) solitaire.
so'lito, a ag usual; **essere** ~ **fare** to be in the habit of doing; **di** ~ usually; **più tardi del** ~ later than usual; **come al** ~ as usual; **siamo alle** ~**e!** (fam) here we go again!
solitu'dine sf solitude.
sollazza're [sŏllàttsà'rā] vt to entertain; ~**rsi** vr to amuse o.s.
sollaz'zo [sŏllàt'tsŏ] sm amusement.
sollecita're [sŏllāchētà'rā] vt (lavoro) to speed up; (persona) to urge on; (chiedere con insistenza) to press for, request urgently; (stimolare): ~ **qn a fare** to urge sb to do; (TECN) to stress.
sollecitazio'ne [sŏllāchētàttsyŏ'nā] sf entreaty, request; (fig) incentive; (TECN) stress; **lettera di** ~ (COMM) reminder.
solle'cito, a [sŏllà'chētŏ] ag prompt, quick ♦ sm (COMM) reminder; ~ **di pagamento** payment reminder.
sollecitu'dine [sŏllāchētōō'dēnā] sf promptness, speed.

solletica're vt to tickle.

solle'tico sm tickling; **soffrire il ~** to be ticklish.

sollevamen'to sm raising; lifting; (ribellione) revolt; **~ pesi** (sport) weight-lifting.

solleva're vt to lift, raise; (fig: persona: alleggerire): **~ (da)** to relieve (of); (: dar conforto) to comfort, relieve; (: questione) to raise; (: far insorgere) to stir (to revolt); **~rsi** vr to rise; (fig: riprendersi) to recover; (: ribellarsi) to rise up; **~rsi da terra** (persona) to get up from the ground; (aereo) to take off; **sentirsi sollevato** to feel relieved.

sollie'vo sm relief; (conforto) comfort; **con mio grande ~** to my great relief.

so'lo, a ag alone; (in senso spirituale: isolato) lonely; (unico): **un ~ libro** only one book, a single book; (con ag numerale): **veniamo noi tre ~i** just o only the three of us are coming ♦ av (soltanto) only, just; **~ che** cong but; **è il ~ proprietario** he's the sole proprietor; **l'incontrò due ~e volte** he only met him twice; **non ~ ... ma anche** not only ... but also; **fare qc da ~** to do sth (all) by oneself; **vive (da) ~** he lives on his own; **possiamo vederci da ~i?** can I see you in private?

solsti'zio [sōlstēt'tsyō] sm solstice.

soltan'to av only.

solu'bile ag (sostanza) soluble; **caffè ~** instant coffee.

soluzio'ne [sōlōōt'tsyō'nā] sf solution; **senza ~ di continuità** uninterruptedly.

solven'te ag, sm solvent; **~ per unghie** nail polish remover; **~ per vernici** paint remover.

solven'za [sōlven'tsà] sf (COMM) solvency.

so'ma sf load, burden; **bestia da ~** beast of burden.

Soma'lia sf: **la ~** Somalia.

so'malo, a ag, sm/f, sm Somali.

soma'ro sm ass, donkey.

soma'tico, a, ci, che ag somatic.

somiglian'za [sōmēlyàn'tsà] sf resemblance.

somiglia're [sōmēlyà'rā] vi: **~ a** to be like, resemble; (nell'aspetto fisico) to look like; **~rsi** vr to be like (o look) alike.

som'ma sf (MAT) sum; (di denaro) sum (of money); (complesso di varie cose) whole amount, sum total; **tirare le ~e** (fig) to sum up; **tirate le ~e** (fig) all things considered.

somma're vt to add up; (aggiungere) to add; **tutto sommato** all things considered.

somma'rio, a ag (racconto, indagine) brief; (giustizia) summary ♦ sm summary.

sommer'gere [sōmmer'jārā] vt to submerge.

sommergi'bile [sōmmärjē'bēlā] sm submarine.

sommer'so, a pp di **sommergere**.

sommes'so, a ag (voce) soft, subdued.

somministra're vt to give, administer.

sommità sf inv summit, top; (fig) height.

som'mo, a ag highest; (rispetto) highest, greatest; (poeta, artista) great, outstanding ♦ sm (fig) height; **per ~i capi** in short, in brief.

sommos'sa sf uprising.

sommozzato're [sōmmōttsátō'rā] sm (deepsea) diver; (MIL) frogman.

sona'glio [sōnàl'yō] sm (di mucche etc) bell; (per bambini) rattle.

sonan'te ag: **denaro** o **moneta ~** (ready) cash.

sona're etc = **suonare** etc.

son'da sf (MED. METEOR. AER) probe; (MINERALOGIA) drill ♦ ag inv: **pallone** m **~** weather balloon.

sondag'gio [sōndàd'jō] sm sounding; probe; boring, drilling; (indagine) survey; **~ d'opinioni** opinion poll.

sonda're vt (NAUT) to sound; (atmosfera, piaga) to probe; (MINERALOGIA) to bore, drill; (fig: opinione etc) to survey, poll.

sonet'to sm sonnet.

sonnam'bulo, a smf sleepwalker.

sonnecchia're [sōnnàkkyà'rā] vi to doze, nod.

sonnelli'no sm nap.

sonni'fero sm sleeping drug (o pill).

son'no sm sleep; **aver ~** to be sleepy; **prendere ~** to fall asleep.

sonnolen'to, a ag sleepy, drowsy; (movimenti) sluggish.

sonnolen'za [sōnnōlen'tsà] sf sleepiness, drowsiness.

so'no vb vedi **essere**.

sono'ro, a ag (ambiente) resonant; (voce) sonorous, ringing; (onde, film) sound cpd ♦ sm: **il ~** (CINEMA) the talkies pl.

sontuo'so, a ag sumptuous.

sopi're vt (fig: dolore, tensione) to soothe.

sopo're sm drowsiness.

sopori'fero, a ag soporific.

sopperi're vi: **~ a** to provide for; **~ alla mancanza di qc** to make up for the lack of sth.

soppesa're vt to weigh in one's hand(s), feel the weight of; (fig) to weigh up.

soppianta're vt to supplant.

soppiat'to av: **di ~** secretly; furtively.

sopporta'bile ag tolerable, bearable.

sopporta're vt (reggere) to support; (subire: perdita, spese) to bear, sustain; (soffrire: dolore) to bear, endure; (sog: cosa: freddo) to withstand; (: persona: freddo, vino) to take; (tollerare) to put up with, tolerate.

sopportazio'ne [sōppōrtáttsyō'nā] sf patience; **avere spirito di ~, avere capacità di ~** to be tolerant.

soppressio'ne sf aboliton; withdrawal; suppression; deletion; elimination, liquidation.

soppres'so, a pp di **sopprimere**.

soppri'mere vt (carica, privilegi etc) to abolish, do away with; (servizio) to withdraw;

(pubblicazione) to suppress; *(parola, frase)* to delete; *(uccidere)* to eliminate, liquidate.

so'pra *prep (gen)* on; *(al di sopra di, più in alto di)* above; over; *(riguardo a)* on, about ♦ *av* on top; *(attaccato, scritto)* on it; *(al di sopra)* above; *(al piano superiore)* upstairs; **donne ~ i 30 anni** women over 30 (years of age); **100 metri ~ il livello del mare** 100 meters above sea level; **5 gradi ~ lo zero** 5 degrees above zero; **abito di ~** I live upstairs; **essere al di ~ di ogni sospetto** to be above suspicion; **per i motivi ~ illustrati** for the above-mentioned reasons, for the reasons shown above; **dormirci ~** *(fig)* to sleep on it; **passar ~ a qc** *(anche fig)* to pass over sth.

sopra'bito *sm* overcoat.

sopraccenna'to, a [sōpráchānnä'tō] *ag* above-mentioned.

sopracci'glio [sōpràchēl'yō], *pl(f)* **sopracci'glia** *sm* eyebrow.

sopraccoper'ta *sf (di letto)* bedspread; *(di libro)* jacket.

sopraddet'to, a *ag* aforesaid.

sopraffa're *vt* to overcome, overwhelm.

sopraffat'to, a *pp di* **sopraffare**.

sopraffazio'ne [sōpráffáttsyō'nä] *sf* overwhelming, overpowering.

sopraffi'no, a *ag (pranzo, vino)* excellent; *(fig)* masterly.

sopraggiun'gere [sōprádjōōn'järä] *vi (giungere all'improvviso)* to arrive (unexpectedly); *(accadere)* to occur (unexpectedly).

sopraggiun'to, a [sōprádjōōn'tō] *pp di* **sopraggiungere**.

sopralluo'go, ghi *sm (di esperti)* inspection; *(di polizia)* on-the-spot investigation.

soprammo'bile *sm* ornament.

soprannatura'le *ag* supernatural.

sopranno'me *sm* nickname.

soprannomina're *vt* to nickname.

soprannu'mero *av:* **in ~** in excess.

sopra'no, a *sm/f (persona)* soprano ♦ *sm (voce)* soprano.

soprappensie'ro *av* lost in thought.

soprappiù *sm* surplus, extra; **in ~** extra, surplus; *(per giunta)* besides, in addition.

soprassal'to *sm:* **di ~** with a start, with a jump.

soprassede're *vi:* **~ a** to delay, put off.

soprattas'sa *sf* surtax.

soprattut'to *av (anzitutto)* above all; *(specialmente)* especially.

sopravvaluta're *vt (persona, capacità)* to overestimate.

sopravveni're *vi* to arrive, appear; *(fatto)* to occur.

sopravven'to *sm:* **avere/prendere il ~ su qn** to have/get the upper hand over sb.

sopravvissu'to, a *pp di* **sopravvivere** ♦ *sm/f* survivor.

sopravviven'za [sōprävvēven'tsä] *sf* survival.

sopravvi'vere *vi* to survive; *(continuare a vivere):* **~ (in)** to live on (in); **~ a** *(incidente etc)* to survive; *(persona)* to outlive.

sopreleva'ta *sf (di strada, ferrovia)* elevated section.

soprintenden'te *sm/f* supervisor; *(statale: di belle arti etc)* curator.

soprintenden'za [sōprēntänden'tsä] *sf* supervision; *(ente):* **~ alle Belle Arti** government department responsible for monuments and artistic treasures.

soprinten'dere *vi:* **~ a** to superintend, supervise.

soprinte'so, a *pp di* **soprintendere**.

sopru'so *sm* abuse of power; **subire un ~** to be abused.

soqqua'dro *sm:* **mettere a ~** to turn upside-down.

sorbet'to *sm* sorbet.

sorbi're *vt* to sip; *(fig)* to put up with.

sor'cio [sōr'chō] *sm* mouse.

sor'dido, a *ag* sordid; *(fig: gretto)* stingy.

sordi'na *sf:* **in ~** softly; *(fig)* on the sly.

sordità *sf* deafness.

sor'do, a *ag* deaf; *(rumore)* muffled; *(dolore)* dull; *(lotta)* silent, hidden; *(odio, rancore)* veiled ♦ *sm/f* deaf person.

sordomu'to, a *ag* deaf-and-dumb ♦ *sm/f* deaf-mute.

sorel'la *sf* sister.

sorellas'tra *sf* stepsister.

sorgen'te [sōrjen'tä] *sf (acqua che sgorga)* spring; *(di fiume, FISICA, fig)* source; **acqua di ~** spring water; **~ di calore** source of heat; **~ termale** thermal spring.

sor'gere [sōr'järä] *vi* to rise; *(scaturire)* to spring, rise; *(fig: difficoltà)* to arise ♦ *sm:* **al ~ del sole** at sunrise.

soria'no, a *ag, sm/f* tabby.

sormonta're *vt (fig)* to overcome, surmount.

sornio'ne, a *ag* sly.

sorpassa're *vt (AUT)* to overtake; *(fig)* to surpass; *(: eccedere)* to exceed, go beyond; **~ in altezza** to be higher than; *(persona)* to be taller than.

sorpassa'to, a *ag (metodo, moda)* outmoded, old-fashioned; *(macchina)* obsolete.

sorpas'so *sm (AUT)* overtaking.

sorprenden'te *ag* surprising; *(eccezionale, inaspettato)* astonishing, amazing.

sorpren'dere *vt (cogliere: in flagrante etc)* to catch; *(stupire)* to surprise; **~rsi** *vr:* **~rsi (di)** to be surprised (at).

sorpre'so, a *pp di* **sorprendere** ♦ *sf* surprise; **fare una ~a a qn** to give sb a surprise; **prendere qn di ~a** to take sb by surprise *o* unawares.

sorreg'gere [sōrred'järä] *vt* to support, hold up; *(fig)* to sustain.

sorret'to, a *pp di* **sorreggere.**
sorri'dere *vi* to smile.
sorri'so, a *pp di* **sorridere** ♦ *sm* smile.
sorsa'ta *sf* gulp; **bere a** ~**e** to gulp.
sorseggia're |sōrsādjà'rā| *vt* to sip.
sor'si *etc vb vedi* **sorgere.**
sor'so *sm* sip; **d'un** ~, **in un** ~ **solo** at one gulp.
sor'ta *sf* sort, kind; **di** ~ whatever, of any kind, at all; **ogni** ~ **di** all sorts of; **di ogni** ~ of every kind.
sor'te *sf* (*fato*) fate, destiny; (*evento fortuito*) chance; **tirare a** ~ to draw lots; **tentare la** ~ to try one's luck.
sorteggia're |sōrtādjà'rā| *vt* to draw for.
sorteg'gio |sōrtād'jō| *sm* draw.
sortile'gio |sōrtēlc'jō| *sm* witchcraft *q*; (*incantesimo*) spell; **fare un** ~ **a qn** to cast a spell on sb.
sorti're *vr* (*ottenere*) to produce.
sorti'ta *sf* (*MIL*) sortie.
sor'to, a *pp di* **sorgere.**
sorveglian'te |sōrvālyán'tā| *sm/f* (*di carcere*) guard; (*di fabbrica etc*) supervisor.
sorveglian'za |sōrvālyán'tsā| *sf* watch; supervision; (*POLIZIA, MIL*) surveillance.
sorveglia're |sōrvālyá'rā| *vt* (*bambino, bagagli, prigioniero*) to watch, keep an eye on; (*malato*) to watch over; (*territorio, casa*) to watch *o* keep watch over; (*lavori*) to supervise.
sorvola're *vt* (*territorio*) to fly over ♦ *vi*: ~ **su** (*fig*) to skim over.
S.O.S. *sigla m* mayday, SOS.
so'sia *sm inv* double.
sospen'dere *vt* (*appendere*) to hang (up); (*interrompere, privare di una carica*) to suspend; (*rimandare*) to defer; ~ **un quadro al muro/un lampadario al soffitto** to hang a picture on the wall/a chandelier from the ceiling; ~ **qn dal suo incarico** to suspend sb from office.
sospensio'ne *sf* (*anche CHIM, AUT*) suspension; deferment; ~ **condizionale della pena** (*DIR*) suspended sentence.
sospe'so, a *pp di* **sospendere** ♦ *ag* (*appeso*): ~ **a** hanging on (*o* from); (*treno, autobus*) cancelled; **in** ~ in abeyance; (*conto*) outstanding; **tenere in** ~ (*fig*) to keep in suspense; **col fiato** ~ with bated breath.
sospetta're *vt* to suspect ♦ *vi*: ~ **di** to suspect; (*diffidare*) to be suspicious of.
sospet'to, a *ag* suspicious ♦ *sm* suspicion; **destare** ~**i** to arouse suspicion.
sospetto'so, a *ag* suspicious.
sospin'gere |sōspēn'jārā| *vt* to drive, push.
sospin'to, a *pp di* **sospingere.**
sospira're *vi* to sigh ♦ *vt* to long for, yearn for.
sospi'ro *sm* sigh; ~ **di sollievo** sigh of relief.

so'sta *sf* (*fermata*) stop, halt; (*pausa*) pause, break; **senza** ~ non-stop, without a break.
sostantiva'to, a *ag* (*LING*): **aggettivo** ~ adjective used as a noun.
sostanti'vo *sm* noun, substantive.
sostan'za |sōstàn'tsā| *sf* substance; ~**e** *sfpl* (*ricchezze*) wealth *sg*, possessions; **in** ~ in short, to sum up; **la** ~ **del discorso** the essence of the speech.
sostanzia'le |sōstántsyá'lā| *ag* substantial.
sostanzio'so, a |sōstántsyō'sō| *ag* (*cibo*) nourishing, substantial.
sosta're *vi* (*fermarsi*) to stop (for a while), stay; (*fare una pausa*) to take a break.
soste'gno |sōstān'yō| *sm* support; **a** ~ **di** in support of; **muro di** ~ supporting wall.
sostene're *vt* to support; (*prendere su di sé*) to take on, bear; (*resistere*) to withstand, stand up to; (*affermare*): ~ **che** to maintain that; ~**rsi** *vr* to hold o.s. up, support o.s.; (*fig*) to keep up one's strength; ~ **qn** (*moralmente*) to be a support to sb; (*difendere*) to stand up for sb, take sb's part; ~ **gli esami** to sit exams; ~ **il confronto** to bear *o* stand comparison.
sosteni'bile *ag* (*tesi*) tenable; (*spese*) bearable.
sostenito're, tri'ce *sm/f* supporter.
sostentamen'to *sm* maintenance, support; **mezzi di** ~ means of support.
sostenu'to, a *ag* (*stile*) elevated; (*velocità, ritmo*) sustained; (*prezzo*) high ♦ *sm/f*: **fare il(la)** ~**(a)** to be standoffish, keep one's distance.
sostitui're *vt* (*mettere al posto di*): ~ **qn/qc a** to substitute sb/sth for; (*prendere il posto di*) to replace, take the place of.
sostituti'vo, a *ag* (*AMM*: *documento, certificato*) equivalent.
sostitu'to, a *sm/f* substitute; ~ **procuratore della Repubblica** (*DIR*) deputy public prosecutor.
sostituzio'ne |sōstētōōttsyō'nā| *sf* substitution; **in** ~ **di** as a substitute for, in place of.
sottace'ti |sōttàchā'tē| *smpl* pickles.
sotta'na *sf* (*sottoveste*) underskirt; (*gonna*) skirt; (*REL*) soutane, cassock.
sottec'chi |sōttāk'kē| *av*: **guardare di** ~ to steal a glance at.
sotterfu'gio |sōttārfōō'jō| *sm* subterfuge.
sotterra'neo, a *ag* underground ♦ *sm* cellar.
sotterra're *vt* to bury.
sottigliez'za |sōttēlyāt'tsā| *sf* thinness; slimness; (*fig*: *acutezza*) subtlety; shrewdness; ~**e** *sfpl* (*pedanteria*) quibbles.
sotti'le *ag* thin; (*figura, caviglia*) thin, slim, slender; (*fine*: *polvere, capelli*) fine; (*fig*: *leggero*) light; (: *vista*) sharp, keen; (: *olfatto*) fine, discriminating; (: *mente*) subtle; shrewd ♦ *sm*: **non andare per il** ~

not to mince matters.

sottilizza're [sōttēlēddzá'rā] *vi* to split hairs.

sottinten'dere *vt* (*intendere qc non espresso*) to understand; (*implicare*) to imply; **lasciare ~ che** to let it be understood that.

sottinte'so, a *pp di* **sottintendere ♦** *sm* allusion; **parlare senza ~i** to speak plainly.

sot'to *prep* (*gen*) under; (*più in basso di*) below **♦** *av* underneath, beneath; below; (*al piano inferiore*): **(al piano) di ~** downstairs; **~ il monte** at the foot of the mountain; **~ la pioggia/il sole** in the rain/sun(shine); **tutti quelli ~ i 18 anni** all those under 18 (years of age); **~ il livello del mare** below sea level; **~ il chilo** under *o* less than a kilo; **ha 5 impiegati ~ di sé** he has 5 employees under him; **siamo ~ Natale/Pasqua** it's nearly Christmas/Easter; **~ un certo punto di vista** in a sense; **~ forma di** in the form of; **~ falso nome** under a false name; **~ terra** underground; **~ voce** in a low voice; **chiuso ~ vuoto** vacuum packed.

sottoban'co *av* (*di nascosto*: *vendere, comprare*) under the counter; (*agire*) in an underhand way.

sottobicchie're [sōttōbĕkkye'rā] *sm* mat, coaster.

sottobo'sco, schi *sm* undergrowth *q*.

sottobrac'cio [sōttōbrách'chō] *av* by the arm; **prendere qn ~** to take sb by the arm; **camminare ~ a qn** to walk arm in arm with sb.

sottochia've [sōttōkyá'vā] *av* under lock and key.

sottocoper'ta *av* (*NAUT*) below deck.

sottoco'sto *av* below cost (price).

sottocuta'neo, a *ag* subcutaneous.

sottoespo're, a *ag* (*fotografia, pellicola*) underexposed.

sottofon'do *sm* background; **~ musicale** background music.

sottogam'ba *av*: **prendere qc ~** not to take sth seriously.

sottogon'na *sf* underskirt.

sottogover'no *sm* political patronage.

sottogrup'po *sm* subgroup; (*di partito*) faction.

sottolinea're *vt* to underline; (*fig*) to emphasize, stress.

sott'o'lio *av, ag inv* in oil.

sottoma'no *av* (*a portata di mano*) within reach, to hand; (*di nascosto*) secretly.

sottomari'no, a *ag* (*flora*) submarine; (*cavo, navigazione*) underwater **♦** *sm* (*NAUT*) submarine.

sottomes'so, a *pp di* **sottomettere ♦** *ag* submissive.

sottomet'tere *vt* to subdue, subjugate; **~rsi** *vr* to submit.

sottomissio'ne *sf* submission.

sottopassag'gio [sōttōpássád'jō] *sm* (*AUT*) underpass; (*pedonale*) subway, underpass.

sottopor're *vt* (*costringere*) to subject; (*fig*: *presentare*) to submit; **sottoporsi** *vr* to submit; **sottoporsi a** (*subire*) to undergo.

sottopo'sto, a *pp di* **sottoporre**.

sottoprodot'to *sm* by-product.

sottoproduzio'ne [sōttōprōdōōttsyō'nā] *sf* underproduction.

sottoproletaria'to *sm*: **il ~** the underprivileged class.

sottor'dine *av*: **passare in ~** to become of minor importance.

sottosca'la *sm inv* (*ripostiglio*) closet under the stairs; (*stanza*) room under the stairs.

sottoscrit'to, a *pp di* **sottoscrivere ♦** *sm/f*: **io ~, il ~** the undersigned.

sottoscri'vere *vt* to sign **♦** *vi*: **~ a** to subscribe to.

sottoscrizio'ne [sōttōskrēttsyō'nā] *sf* signing; subscription.

sottosegreta'rio *sm*: **S~ di Stato** Assistant Secretary of State (*US*), Under-Secretary of State (*Brit*).

sottoso'pra *av* upside-down.

sottostan'te *ag* (*piani*) lower; **nella valle ~** in the valley below.

sottosta're *vi*: **~ a** (*assoggettarsi a*) to submit to; (: *richieste*) to give in to; (*subire*: *prova*) to undergo.

sottosuo'lo *sm* subsoil.

sottosviluppa'to, a *ag* underdeveloped.

sottosvilup'po *sm* underdevelopment.

sottotenen'te *sm* (*MIL*) second lieutenant.

sottoter'ra *av* underground.

sottotet'to *sm* attic.

sottoti'tolo *sm* subtitle.

sottovaluta're *vt* (*persona, prova*) to underestimate, underrate.

sottoven'to *av* (*NAUT*) leeward(s) **♦** *ag inv* (*lato*) leeward, lee.

sottove'ste *sf* underskirt.

sottovo'ce [sōttōvō'chā] *av* in a low voice.

sottovuo'to *av*: **confezionare ~** to vacuum-pack **♦** *ag*: **confezione** *f* **~** vacuum pack.

sottrar're *vt* (*MAT*) to subtract, take away; **sottrarsi** *vr*: **sottrarsi a** (*sfuggire*) to escape; (*evitare*) to avoid; **~ qn/qc a** (*togliere*) to remove sb/sth from; (*salvare*) to save *o* rescue sb/sth from; **~ qc a qn** (*rubare*) to steal sth from sb; **sottratte le spese** once expenses have been deducted.

sottrat'to, a *pp di* **sottrarre**.

sottrazio'ne [sōttráttsyō'nā] *sf* (*MAT*) subtraction; (*furto*) removal.

sottuffícia'le [sōttōōffēchá'lā] *sm* (*MIL*) non-commissioned officer; (*NAUT*) petty officer.

soven'te *av* often.

soverchia're [sōvárkyá'rā] *vt* to overpower, overwhelm.

soverchieri'a [sōvārkyārc̄'à] *sf* (*prepotenza*) abuse (of power).

sovie'tico, a, ci, che *ag* Soviet ♦ *sm/f* Soviet citizen.

sovrabbondan'te *ag* overabundant.

sovrabbondan'za [sōvràbbōndán'tsà] *sf* overabundance; **in** ~ in excess.

sovraccarica're *vt* to overload.

sovracca'rico, a, chi, che *ag*: ~ **(di)** overloaded (with) ♦ *sm* excess load; ~ **di lavoro** extra work.

sovraesposizio'ne [sōvráàspōzēttsyō'nā] *sf* (*FOT*) overexposure.

sovraffolla'to, a *ag* overcrowded.

sovraimmagazzina're [sōvràc̄mmàgáddzē-nà'rā] *vt* to overstock.

sovranità *sf* sovereignty; (*fig*: *superiorità*) supremacy.

sovrannatura'le *ag* = **soprannaturale.**

sovra'no, a *ag* sovereign; (*fig*: *sommo*) supreme ♦ *sm/f* sovereign, monarch.

sovrappopolazio'ne [sōvràppōpōláttsyō'nā] *sf* overpopulation.

sovrappor're *vt* to place on top of, put on top of; (*FOT. GEOM*) to superimpose; **sovrapporsi** *vr* (*fig*: *aggiungersi*) to be added; (*FOT*) to be superimposed.

sovrapposizio'ne [sōvràppōsēttsyō'nā] *sf* superimposition.

sovrappo'sto, a *pp di* **sovrapporre.**

sovrapproduzio'ne [sōvràpprōdōōttsyō'nā] *sf* overproduction.

sovrasta're *vi*: ~ **a,** *vt* (*vallata, fiume*) to overhang; (*fig*) to hang over, threaten.

sovrastruttu'ra *sf* superstructure.

sovreccita're [sōvràchētà'rā] *vt* to overexcite.

sovrimpressio'ne *sf* (*FOT, CINEMA*) double exposure; **immagini in** ~ superimposed images.

sovrintenden'te *etc* = **soprintendente** *etc*.

sovruma'no, a *ag* superhuman.

sovveni're *vi* (*venire in mente*): ~ **a** to occur to.

sovvenziona're [sōvvāntsyōnà'rā] *vt* to subsidize.

sovvenzio'ne [sōvvāntsyō'nā] *sf* subsidy, grant.

sovversi'vo, a *ag* subversive.

sovvertimen'to *sm* subversion, undermining.

sovverti're *vt* (*POL*: *ordine, stato*) to subvert, undermine.

soz'zo, a [sōt'tsō] *ag* filthy, dirty.

SP *sigla* = **La Spezia.**

S.P. *abbr* = **strada provinciale;** *vedi* **provinciale.**

S.p.A. *abbr vedi* **società per azioni.**

spacca're *vt* to split, break; (*legna*) to chop; ~**rsi** *vr* to split, break.

spaccatu'ra *sf* split.

spaccherò [spàkkàro'] *etc vb vedi* **spaccare.**

spaccia're [spàchà'rā] *vt* (*vendere*) to sell (off); (*mettere in circolazione*) to circulate; (*droga*) to peddle, push; ~**rsi** *vr*: ~**rsi per** (*farsi credere*) to pass o.s. off as, pretend to be.

spaccia'to, a [spàchà'tō] *ag* (*fam*: *malato, fuggiasco*): **essere** ~ to be done for.

spacciato're, tri'ce [spàchàtō'rā] *sm/f* (*di droga*) pusher; (*di denaro falso*) dealer.

spac'cio [spàch'chō] *sm* (*di merce rubata, droga*): ~ **(di)** trafficking (in); (*di denaro falso*): ~ **(di)** passing (of); (*vendita*) sale; (*bottega*) shop.

spac'co, chi *sm* (*fenditura*) split, crack; (*strappo*) tear; (*di gonna*) slit.

spacco'ne *sm/f* boaster, braggart.

spa'da *sf* sword.

spadroneggia're [spàdrōnādjà'rā] *vi* to swagger.

spaesa'to, a *ag* disorientated, lost.

spaghetta'ta [spágàttà'tà] *sf* spaghetti meal.

spaghet'ti [spágàt'tē] *smpl* (*CUC*) spaghetti *sg*.

Spa'gna [spán'yà] *sf*: **la** ~ Spain.

spagno'lo, a [spányo'lō] *ag* Spanish ♦ *sm/f* Spaniard ♦ *sm* (*LING*) Spanish; **gli S~i** the Spanish.

spa'go, ghi *sm* string, twine; **dare** ~ **a qn** (*fig*) to let sb have his (*o* her) way.

spaia'to, a *ag* (*calza, guanto*) odd.

spalanca're *vt*, ~**rsi** *vr* to open wide.

spala're *vt* to shovel.

spal'la *sf* shoulder; (*fig*: *TEATRO*) stooge; ~**e** *sfpl* (*dorso*) back; **di** ~**e** from behind; **seduto alle mie** ~**e** sitting behind me; **prendere/colpire qn alle** ~**e** to take/hit sb from behind; **mettere qn con le** ~**e al muro** (*fig*) to put sb with his (*o* her) back to the wall; **vivere alle** ~**e di qn** (*fig*) to live off sb.

spalleggia're [spàllādjà'rā] *vt* to back up, support.

spallet'ta *sf* (*parapetto*) parapet.

spallie'ra *sf* (*di sedia etc*) back; (*di letto*: *da capo*) head(board); (: *da piedi*) foot(board); (*GINNASTICA*) wall bars *pl*.

spalli'na *sf* (*MIL*) epaulette; (*di sottoveste, maglietta*) strap; **senza** ~**e** strapless.

spalma're *vt* to spread.

spal'ti *smpl* (*di stadio*) terraces (*Brit*), ≈ bleachers (*US*).

span'dere *vt* to spread; (*versare*) to pour (out); ~**rsi** *vr* to spread; ~ **lacrime** to shed tears.

span'to, a *pp di* **spandere.**

spara're *vt* to fire ♦ *vi* (*far fuoco*) to fire; (*tirare*) to shoot; ~ **a qn/qc** to shoot sb/sth, fire at sb/sth.

spara'to *sm* (*di camicia*) dicky.

sparato're *sm* gunman.

sparato'ria *sf* exchange of shots.

sparecchia're [spárākkyà'rā] *vt*: ~ **(la tavola)**

to clear the table.

spareg'gio |spárád'jō| *sm* (*SPORT*) play-off.

spar'gere |spár'jārā| *vt* (*sparpagliare*) to scatter; (*versare: vino*) to spill; (: *lacrime, sangue*) to shed; (*diffondere*) to spread; (*emanare*) to give off (*o* out); ~**rsi** *vr* (*voce, notizia*) to spread; (*persone*) to scatter; **si è sparsa una voce sul suo conto** there is a rumor going round about him.

spargimen'to |spárjēmän'tō| *sm* scattering; spilling; shedding; ~ **di sangue** bloodshed.

spari're *vi* to disappear, vanish; ~ **dalla circolazione** (*fig fam*) to lie low, keep a low profile.

sparizio'ne |spárēttsyō'nā| *sf* disappearance.

sparla're *vi*: ~ **di** to run down, speak ill of.

spa'ro *sm* shot.

sparpaglia're |spárpályá'rā| *vt*, ~**rsi** *vr* to scatter.

spar'so, a *pp di* **spargere** ♦ *ag* scattered; (*sciolto*) loose; **in ordine** ~ (*MIL*) in open order.

spartiac'que *sm* (*GEO*) watershed.

spartine've *sm inv* snowplow (*US*), snowplough (*Brit*).

sparti're *vt* (*eredità, bottino*) to share out; (*avversari*) to separate.

sparti'to *sm* (*MUS*) score.

spartitraf'fico *sm inv* (*AUT*) median (strip) (*US*), central reservation (*Brit*).

spartizio'ne |spártēttsyō'nā| *sf* division.

sparu'to, a *ag* (*viso etc*) haggard.

sparvie'ro *sm* (*ZOOL*) sparrowhawk.

spasiman'te *sm* suitor.

spasima're *vi* to be in agony; ~ **di fare** (*fig*) to yearn to do; ~ **per qn** to be madly in love with sb.

spa'simo *sm* pang.

spa'smo *sm* (*MED*) spasm.

spasmo'dico, a, ci, che *ag* (*angoscioso*) agonizing; (*MED*) spasmodic.

spassar'sela *vi* to enjoy o.s., have a good time.

spassiona'to, a *ag* dispassionate, impartial.

spas'so *sm* (*divertimento*) amusement, enjoyment; **andare a** ~ to go out for a walk; **essere a** ~ (*fig*) to be out of work; **mandare qn a** ~ (*fig*) to fire sb.

spasso'so, a *ag* amusing, entertaining.

spa'stico, a, ci, che *ag*, *sm/f* spastic.

spa'tola *sf* spatula.

spaurac'chio |spáōōrák'kyō| *sm* scarecrow.

spauri're *vt* to frighten, terrify.

spavalderi'a *sf* boldness, arrogance.

spaval'do, a *ag* arrogant, bold.

spaventapas'seri *sm inv* scarecrow.

spaventa're *vt* to frighten, scare; ~**rsi** *vr* to become frightened, become scared.

spaven'to *sm* fear, fright; **far** ~ **a qn** to give sb a fright.

spavento'so, a *ag* frightening, terrible; (*fig fam*) tremendous, fantastic.

spazia'le |spáttsyá'lā| *ag* (*volo, nave, tuta*) space *cpd*; (*ARCHIT, GEOM*) spatial.

spaziatu'ra |spáttsyátōō'rá| *sf* (*TIP*) spacing.

spazienti're |spáttsyäntē'rā| *vi* (*anche*: ~**rsi**) to lose one's patience.

spa'zio |spát'tsyō| *sm* space; (*posto*) room, space; **fare** ~ **per qc/qn** to make room for sth/sb; **nello** ~ **di un'ora** within an hour, in the space of an hour; **dare** ~ **a** (*fig*) to make room for; ~ **aereo** airspace.

spazio'so, a |spáttsyō'sō| *ag* spacious.

spazzacami'no |spáttsákámē'nō| *sm* chimney sweep.

spazzane've |spáttsáná'vā| *sm inv* (*spartineve, SCI*) snowplow (*US*), snowplough (*Brit*).

spazza're |spáttsá'rā| *vt* to sweep; (*foglie etc*) to sweep up; (*cacciare*) to sweep away.

spazzatu'ra |spáttsátōō'rá| *sf* sweepings *pl*; (*immondizia*) trash (*US*), rubbish.

spazzi'no |spáttsē'nō| *sm* street sweeper.

spaz'zola |spát'tsólá| *sf* brush; **capelli a** ~ crew cut *sg*; ~ **per abiti** clothesbrush; ~ **da capelli** hairbrush.

spazzola're |spáttsōlá'rā| *vt* to brush.

spazzoli'no |spáttsōlē'nō| *sm* (small) brush; ~ **da denti** toothbrush.

specchiar'si |späkkyár'sē| *vr* to look at o.s. in a mirror; (*riflettersi*) to be mirrored, be reflected.

specchie'ra |späkkye'rá| *sf* large mirror; (*mobile*) dressing table.

specchiet'to |späkkyát'tō| *sm* (*tabella*) table, chart; ~ **da borsetta** pocket mirror; ~ **retrovisore** (*AUT*) rear-view mirror.

spec'chio |spck'kyō| *sm* mirror; (*tabella*) table, chart; **uno** ~ **d'acqua** a sheet of water.

specia'le |spáchá'lā| *ag* special; **in special modo** especially; **inviato** ~ (*RADIO, TV, STAMPA*) special correspondent; **offerta** ~ special offer; **poteri/leggi** ~**i** (*POL*) emergency powers/legislation.

speciali'sta, i, e |spáchálē'stá| *sm/f* specialist.

speciali'stico, a, ci, che |spáchálē'stēkō| *ag* (*conoscenza, preparazione*) specialized.

specialità |spáchálētá'| *sf inv* speciality; (*branca di studio*) special field, speciality.

specializza're |spáchálēddzá'rā| *vt* (*industria*) to make more specialized; ~**rsi** *vr*: ~**rsi (in)** to specialize (in).

specializza'to, a |spáchálēddzá'tō| *ag* (*manodopera*) skilled; **operaio non** ~ semiskilled worker; **essere** ~ **in** to be a specialist in.

specializzazio'ne |spáchálēddzáttsyō'nā| *sf* specialization; **prendere la** ~ **in** to specialize in.

specialmen'te |spáchálmän'tā| *av* especially, particularly.

spe'cie |spe'chā| *sf inv* (*BIOL, BOT, ZOOL*) species *inv*; (*tipo*) kind, sort ♦ *av* especially, particularly; **una ~ di** a kind of; **fare ~ a qn** to surprise sb; **la ~ umana** mankind.

speci'fica, che |spāchē'fēká| *sf* specification.

specifica're |spāchēfēká'rā| *vt* to specify, state.

speci'fico, a, ci, che |spāchē'fēkō| *ag* specific.

specula're *vi*: **~ su** (*COMM*) to speculate in; (*sfruttare*) to exploit; (*meditare*) to speculate on.

speculato're, tri'ce *sm/f* (*COMM*) speculator.

speculazio'ne |spākōōlàttsyō'nā| *sf* speculation.

spedi're *vt* to send; (*COMM*) to dispatch, forward; **~ per posta** to mail (*US*), post (*Brit*); **~ per mare** to ship.

speditamen'te *av* quickly; **camminare ~** to walk at a brisk pace.

spedi'to, a *ag* (*gen*) quick; **con passo ~** at a brisk pace.

spedizio'ne |spādēttsyō'nā| *sf* sending; (*collo*) consignment; (*scientifica etc*) expedition; (*COMM*) forwarding; shipping; **fare una ~** to send a consignment; **agenzia di ~** forwarding agency; **spese di ~** postal charges; (*COMM*) forwarding charges.

spedizionie're |spādēttsyōnye'rā| *sm* forwarding agent, shipping agent.

spe'gnere |spen'yārā| *vt* (*fuoco, sigaretta*) to put out, extinguish; (*apparecchio elettrico*) to turn *o* switch off; (*gas*) to turn off; (*fig: suoni, passioni*) to stifle; (*debito*) to extinguish; **~rsi** *vr* to go out; to go off; (*morire*) to pass away.

speleologi'a |spālāōlōjē'á| *sf* (*studio*) speleology; (*pratica*) spelunking (*US*), potholing (*Brit*).

speleo'logo, a, gi, ghe *sm/f* spelunker (*US*), potholer (*Brit*).

spella're *vt* (*scuoiare*) to skin; (*scorticare*) to graze; **~rsi** *vr* to peel.

spen'dere *vt* to spend; **~ una buona parola per qn** (*fig*) to put in a good word for sb.

spen'go *etc vb vedi* **spegnere.**

spenna're *vt* to pluck.

spen'si *etc vb vedi* **spegnere.**

spensieratez'za |spānsyárátàt'tsá| *sf* carefreeness, lightheartedness.

spensiera'to, a *ag* carefree.

spen'to, a *pp di* **spegnere** ♦ *ag* (*suono*) muffled; (*colore*) dull; (*sigaretta*) out; (*civiltà, vulcano*) extinct.

speran'za |spāràn'tsá| *sf* hope; **nella ~ di rivederti** hoping to see *o* in the hope of seeing you again; **pieno di ~e** hopeful; **senza ~** (*situazione*) hopeless; (*amare*) without hope.

speranzo'so, a |spāràntsō'sō| *ag* hopeful.

spera're *vt* to hope for ♦ *vi*: **~ in** to trust in; **~ che/di fare** to hope that/to do; **lo spero, spero di sì** I hope so; **tutto fa ~ per il me-**

glio everything leads one to hope for the best.

sperdu'to, a *ag* (*isolato*) out-of-the-way; (*persona: smarrita, a disagio*) lost.

spergiu'ro, a |spárjōō'rō| *sm/f* perjurer ♦ *sm* perjury.

spericola'to, a *ag* fearless, daring; (*guidatore*) reckless.

sperimenta'le *ag* experimental; **fare qc in via ~** to try sth out.

sperimenta're *vt* to experiment with, test; (*fig*) to test, put to the test.

sperimentazio'ne |spārēmàntàttsyō'nā| *sf* experimentation.

sper'ma, i *sm* (*BIOL*) sperm.

spermatozo'o, i |spārmátōddzo'ō| *sm* spermatozoon.

spero'ne *sm* spur.

sperpera're *vt* to squander.

sper'pero *sm* (*di denaro*) squandering, waste; (*di cibo, materiali*) waste.

spe'sa *sf* (*soldi spesi*) expense; (*costo*) cost; (*acquisto*) purchase; (*fam: acquisto del cibo quotidiano*) shopping; **~e** *sfpl* expenses; (*COMM*) costs; charges; **ridurre le ~e** (*gen*) to cut down; (*COMM*) to reduce expenditure; **fare la ~** to do the shopping; **fare le ~e di qc** (*fig*) to pay the price for sth; **a ~e di** (*a carico di*) at the expense of; **con la modica ~ di un milione di lire** for the modest sum *o* outlay of one million lire; **~ pubblica** public expenditure; **~e accessorie** incidental expenses; **~e generali** overhead (*US*) *o* overheads (*Brit*); **~e di gestione** operating expenses; **~e d'impianto** initial outlay; **~e legali** legal costs; **~e di manutenzione, ~e di mantenimento** maintenance costs; **~e postali** postage *sg*; **~e di sbarco e sdoganamento** landing charges; **~e di trasporto** handling charge; **~e di viaggio** traveling (*US*) expenses.

spesa're *vt*: **viaggio tutto spesato** expense-paid journey (*US*), all-expenses-paid trip (*Brit*).

spe'so, a *pp di* **spendere.**

spes'so, a *ag* (*fitto*) thick; (*frequente*) frequent ♦ *av* often; **~e volte** frequently, often.

spesso're *sm* thickness; **ha uno ~ di 20 cm** it is 20 cm thick.

Spett. *abbr vedi* **spettabile.**

spetta'bile *ag* (*abbr*: **Spett.**: *in lettere*): **~ ditta X** Messrs X and Co; **avvertiamo la ~ clientela ...** we inform our customers ....

spettacola're *ag* spectacular.

spetta'colo *sm* (*rappresentazione*) performance, show; (*vista, scena*) sight; **dare ~ di sé** to make an exhibition *o* a spectacle of o.s.

spettacolo'so, a *ag* spectacular.

spettan'za |spāttàn'tsá| *sf* (*competenza*) concern; **non è di mia ~** it's no concern of mine.

spetta're vi: ~ **a** (decisione) to be up to; (stipendio) to be due to; **spetta a lei decidere** it's up to you to decide.

spettato're, tri'ce sm/f (CINEMA, TEATRO) member of the audience; (di avvenimento) onlooker, witness.

spettegola're vi to gossip.

spettina're vt: ~ **qn** to ruffle sb's hair; ~**rsi** vr to get one's hair messed up.

spettra'le ag spectral, ghostly.

spet'tro sm (fantasma) specter (US), spectre (Brit); (FISICA) spectrum.

spe'zie [spet'tsyā] sfpl (CUC) spices.

spezza're [spāttsá'rā] vt (rompere) to break; (fig: interrompere) to break up; ~**rsi** vr to break.

spezzati'no [spāttsátē'nō] sm (CUC) stew.

spezza'to, a [spāttsá'tō] ag (unghia, ramo, braccio) broken ♦ sm (abito maschile) color-coordinated sports coat and pants (US) o jacket and trousers (Brit); **fare orario** ~ to work a split shift.

spezzetta're [spāttsāttá'rā] vt to break up (o chop) into small pieces.

spezzi'no, a [spāttsē'nō] ag of (o from) La Spezia.

spezzo'ne [spāttsō'nā] sm (CINEMA) clip.

spi'a sf spy; (confidente della polizia) informer; (ELETTR) warning light; indicator (US); (fessura) peephole; (fig: sintomo) sign, indication; ~ **dell'olio** (AUT) oil warning light.

spiacen'te [spyáchen'tā] ag sorry; **essere** ~ **di qc/di fare qc** to be sorry about sth/for doing sth; **siamo** ~**i di doverVi annunciare che ...** we regret to announce that ....

spiace'vole [spyáchā'vōlā] ag unpleasant, disagreeable.

spiag'gia, ge [spyád'já] sf beach.

spiana're vt (terreno) to level, make level; (edificio) to raze to the ground; (pasta) to roll out; (rendere liscio) to smooth (out).

spia'no sm: **a tutto** ~ (lavorare) non-stop, without a break; (spendere) lavishly.

spianta'to, a ag penniless, ruined.

spia're vt to spy on; (occasione etc) to watch o wait for.

spia'ta sf tip-off.

spiattella're vt (fam: verità, segreto) to blurt out.

spiaz'zo [spyát'tsō] sm open space; (radura) clearing.

spicca're vt (assegno, mandato di cattura) to issue ♦ vi (risaltare) to stand out; ~ **il volo** to fly off; (fig) to spread one's wings; ~ **un balzo** to jump, leap.

spicca'to, a ag (marcato) marked, strong; (notevole) remarkable.

spiccherò etc [spēkkāro'] vb vedi **spiccare**.

spic'chio [spēk'kyō] sm (di agrumi) segment; (di aglio) clove; (parte) piece, slice.

spicciar'si [spēchár'sē] vr to hurry up.

spicciola'ta [spēchōlá'tá] av: **alla** ~ in dribs and drabs, a few at a time.

spic'ciolo, a [spēch'chōlō] ag: **moneta** ~**a**, ~**i** smpl (small) change.

spic'co, chi sm: **fare** ~ to stand out; **di** ~ outstanding, prominent; (tema) main, principal.

spiedi'no sm (utensile) skewer; (cibo) kebab.

spie'do sm (CUC) spit; **pollo allo** ~ spit-roasted chicken.

spiegamen'to sm (MIL): ~ **di forze** deployment of forces.

spiega're vt (far capire) to explain; (tovaglia) to unfold; (vele) to unfurl; ~**rsi** vr to explain o.s., make o.s. clear; ~ **qc a qn** to explain sth to sb; **il problema si spiega** one can understand the problem; **non mi spiego come ...** I can't understand how ....

spiegazio'ne [spyāgáttsyō'nā] sf explanation; **avere una** ~ **con qn** to have it out with sb.

spiegazza're [spyāgáttsá'rā] vt to crease, crumple.

spiegherò etc [spyāgāro'] vb vedi **spiegare**.

spieta'to, a ag ruthless, pitiless.

spiffera're vt (fam) to blurt out, blab.

spif'fero sm draft (US), draught (Brit).

spi'ga, ghe sf (BOT) ear.

spiglia'to, a [spēlyá'tō] ag self-possessed, self-confident.

spigola're vt (anche fig) to glean.

spi'golo sm corner; (GEOM) edge.

spigolo'so, a ag (mobile) angular; (persona, carattere) difficult.

spil'la sf brooch; (da cravatta, cappello) pin.

spilla're vt (vino, fig) to tap; ~ **denaro/ notizie a qn** to tap sb for money/information.

spil'lo sm pin; (spilla) brooch; **tacco a** ~ spike (US) o stiletto heel; ~ **di sicurezza** o **da balia** safety pin; ~ **di sicurezza** (MIL) (safety) pin.

spilorceri'a [spēlōrchārē'á] sf meanness, stinginess.

spilor'cio, a, ci, ce [spēlōr'chō] ag mean, stingy.

spilungo'ne sm/f beanpole.

spi'na sf (BOT) thorn; (ZOOL) spine, prickle; (di pesce) bone; (ELETTR) plug; (di botte) bunghole; **birra alla** ~ draft beer; **stare sulle** ~**e** (fig) to be on tenterhooks; ~ **dorsale** (ANAT) backbone.

spina'cio [spēná'chō] sm spinach q; (CUC): ~**i** spinach sg.

spina'le ag (ANAT) spinal.

spina'to, a ag (fornito di spine): **filo** ~ barbed wire; (tessuto) herringbone cpd.

spinel'lo sm (DROGA: gergo) joint.

spin'gere [spēn'jārā] vt to push; (condurre: anche fig) to drive; (stimolare): ~ **qn a fare**

to urge o press sb to do; **~rsi** vr (inoltrarsi) to push on, carry on; **~rsi troppo lontano** (anche fig) to go too far.

spi'no sm (BOT) thorn bush.

spino'so, a ag thorny, prickly.

spin'si etc vb vedi **spingere**.

spintero'geno [spĕntāro'jänō] sm (AUT) coil ignition.

spin'to, a pp di **spingere** ♦ sf (urto) push; (FISICA) thrust; (fig: stimolo) incentive, spur; (: appoggio) string-pulling q; **dare una ~a a qn** (fig) to pull strings for sb.

spinto'ne sm push, shove.

spionag'gio [spĕōnád'jō] sm espionage, spying.

spionci'no [spĕōnchē'nō] sm peephole.

spioni'stico, a, ci, che ag (organizzazione) spy cpd; **rete ~a** spy ring.

spio'vere vi (scorrere) to flow down; (ricadere) to hang down, fall.

spi'ra sf coil.

spira'glio [spĕrál'yō] sm (fessura) chink, narrow opening; (raggio di luce, fig) glimmer, gleam.

spira'le sf spiral; (contraccettivo) coil; **a ~** spiral(-shaped); **~ inflazionistica** inflationary spiral.

spira're vi (vento) to blow; (morire) to expire, pass away.

spirita'to, a ag possessed; (fig: persona, espressione) wild.

spiriti'smo sm spiritualism.

spi'rito sm (REL, CHIM, disposizione d'animo, di legge etc, fantasma) spirit; (pensieri, intelletto) mind; (arguzia) wit; (umorismo) humor (US), humour (Brit), wit; **in buone condizioni di ~** in the right frame of mind; **è una persona di ~** he has a sense of humor; **battuta di ~** joke; **~ di classe** class consciousness; **non ha ~ di parte** he never takes sides; **lo S~** Santo the Holy Spirit o Ghost.

spiritosag'gine [spĕrĕtōsád'jĕnā] sf witticism; (peg) wisecrack.

spirito'so, a ag witty.

spiritua'le ag spiritual.

splenden'te ag (giornata) bright, sunny; (occhi) shining; (pavimento) shining, gleaming.

splen'dere vi to shine.

splen'dido, a ag splendid; (splendente) shining; (sfarzoso) magnificent, splendid.

splendo're sm splendor (US), splendour (Brit); (luce intensa) brilliance, brightness.

spodesta're vt to deprive of power; (sovrano) to depose.

spo'glia [spol'yá] sf vedi **spoglio**.

spoglia're [spōlyá'rā] vt (svestire) to undress; (privare, fig: depredare): **~ qn di qc** to deprive sb of sth; (togliere ornamenti: anche fig): **~ qn/qc di** to strip sb/sth of; **~rsi** vr to

undress, strip; **~rsi di** (ricchezze etc) to deprive o.s. of, give up; (pregiudizi) to rid o.s. of.

spogliarel'lo [spōlyárèl'lō] sm striptease.

spogliato'io [spōlyátō'yō] sm dressing room; (di scuola etc) cloakroom; (SPORT) locker room.

spo'glio, a [spol'yō] ag (pianta, terreno) bare; (privo): **~ di** stripped of; lacking in, without ♦ sm (di voti) counting ♦ sf (ZOOL) skin, hide; (: di rettile) slough; **~e** sfpl (salma) remains; (preda) spoils, booty sg.

spo'la sf shuttle; (bobina) spool; **fare la ~ (fra)** to go to and fro o shuttle (between).

spolet'ta sf (CUCITO: bobina) spool; (di bomba) fuse.

spolpa're vt to strip the flesh off.

spolvera're vt (anche CUC) to dust; (con spazzola) to brush; (con battipanni) to beat; (fig: mangiare) to polish off ♦ vi to dust.

spon'da sf (di fiume) bank; (di mare, lago) shore; (bordo) edge.

sponsorizza're [spōnsōrĕddzá'rā] vt to sponsor.

sponsorizzazio'ne [spōnsōrĕddzáttsyō'nā] sf sponsorship.

sponta'neo, a ag spontaneous; (persona) unaffected, natural; **di sua ~a volontà** of his own free will.

spopola're vt to depopulate ♦ vi (attirare folla) to draw the crowds; **~rsi** vr to become depopulated.

spora'dico, a, ci, che ag sporadic.

sporcaccio'ne, a [spōrkáchō'nā] sm/f (peg) pig, filthy person.

sporca're vt to dirty, make dirty; (fig) to sully, soil; **~rsi** vr to get dirty.

sporci'zia [spōrchēt'tsyá] sf (stato) dirtiness; (sudiciume) dirt, filth; (fig: cosa oscena) obscenity.

spor'co, a, chi, che ag dirty, filthy; **avere la coscienza ~a** to have a guilty conscience.

sporgen'za [spōrjen'tsá] sf projection.

spor'gere [spor'jārā] vt to put out, stretch out ♦ vi (venire in fuori) to stick out; **~rsi** vr to lean out; **~ querela contro qn** (DIR) to take legal action against sb.

spor'si etc vb vedi **sporgere**.

sport sm inv sport.

spor'ta sf shopping bag.

sportel'lo sm (di treno, auto etc) door; (di banca, ufficio) window, counter; **~ automatico** (BANCA) cash dispenser.

sporti'vo, a ag (gara, giornale) sports cpd; (persona) sporty; (abito) casual; (spirito, atteggiamento) sporting ♦ sm/f sportsman/woman; **campo ~** playing field; **giacca ~a** sportjacket (US), sports jacket (Brit).

spor'to, a pp di **sporgere**.

spo'sa sf bride; (moglie) wife; **abito o vestito**

da ~ wedding dress.

sposali'zio [spōzàlēt'tsyō] *sm* wedding.

sposa're *vt* to marry; (*fig: idea, fede*) to espouse; ~**rsi** *vr* to get married, marry; ~**rsi con qn** to marry sb, get married to sb.

sposa'to, a *ag* married.

spo'so *sm* (bride)groom; (*marito*) husband; **gli** ~**i** the newlyweds.

spossan'te *ag* exhausting.

spossatez'za [spōssàtāt'tsá] *sf* exhaustion.

spossa'to, a *ag* exhausted, weary.

spostamen'to *sm* movement, change of position.

sposta're *vt* to move, shift; (*cambiare: orario*) to change; ~**rsi** *vr* to move; **hanno spostato la partenza di qualche giorno** they postponed *o* put off their departure by a few days.

spran'ga, ghe *sf* (*sbarra*) bar; (*catenaccio*) bolt.

spranga're *vt* to bar; to bolt.

spraz'zo [sprát'tsō] *sm* (*di sole etc*) flash; (*fig: di gioia etc*) burst.

spreca're *vt* to waste; ~**rsi** *vr* (*persona*) to waste one's energy.

spre'co, chi *sm* waste.

sprege'vole [sprājā'vōlā] *ag* contemptible, despicable.

spre'gio [spre'jō] *sm* scorn, disdain.

spregiudica'to, a [sprājōōdēkà'tō] *ag* unprejudiced, unbiased; (*peg*) unscrupulous.

spre'mere *vt* to squeeze; ~**rsi le meningi** (*fig*) to rack one's brains.

spremu'ta *sf* fresh fruit juice; ~ **d'arancia** fresh orange juice.

sprezzan'te [sprāttsán'tā] *ag* scornful, contemptuous.

sprez'zo [spret'tsō] *sm* contempt, scorn, disdain.

sprigiona're [sprējōná'rā] *vt* to give off, emit; ~**rsi** *vr* to emanate; (*uscire con impeto*) to burst out.

sprizza're [sprēttsá'rā] *vt, vi* to spurt; ~ **gioia/salute** to be bursting with joy/health.

sprofonda're *vi* to sink; (*casa*) to collapse; (*suolo*) to give way, subside; ~**rsi** *vr*: ~**rsi in** (*poltrona*) to sink into; (*fig*) to become immersed *o* absorbed in.

sproloquia're *vi* to ramble on.

sprolo'quio *sm* rambling speech.

sprona're *vt* to spur (on).

spro'ne *sm* (*sperone, fig*) spur.

sproporziona'to, a [sprōpōrtsyōná'tō] *ag* disproportionate, out of all proportion.

sproporzio'ne [sprōpōrtsyō'nā] *sf* disproportion.

sproposita'to, a *ag* (*lettera, discorso*) full of mistakes; (*fig: costo*) excessive, enormous.

spropo'sito *sm* blunder; **a** ~ at the wrong time; (*rispondere, parlare*) irrelevantly.

sprovvedu'to, a *ag* inexperienced, naïve.

sprovvi'sto, a *ag* (*mancante*): ~ **di** lacking in, without; **ne siamo** ~**i** (*negozio*) we are out of it (*o* them); **alla** ~**a** unawares.

spruzza're [sprōōttsá'rā] *vt* (*a nebulizzazione*) to spray; (*aspergere*) to sprinkle; (*inzaccherare*) to splash.

spruzzato're [sprōōttsátō'rā] *sm* (*per profumi*) spray, atomizer; (*per biancheria*) sprinkler, spray.

spruz'zo [sprōōt'tsō] *sm* spray; splash; **verniciatura a** ~ spray painting.

spudoratez'za [spōōdōrátāt'tsá] *sf* shamelessness.

spudora'to, a *ag* shameless.

spu'gna [spōōn'yá] *sf* (*ZOOL*) sponge; (*tessuto*) towelling.

spugno'so, a [spōōnyō'sō] *ag* spongy.

spulcia're [spōōlchá'rā] *vt* (*animali*) to rid of fleas; (*fig: testo, compito*) to examine thoroughly.

spu'ma *sf* (*schiuma*) foam; (*bibita*) fizzy drink.

spuman'te *sm* sparkling wine.

spumeggian'te [spōōmádjàn'tā] *ag* (*vino, fig*) sparkling; (*birra, mare*) foaming.

spumo'ne *sm* (*CUC*) mousse.

spunta're *sm*: **allo** ~ **del sole** at sunrise; **allo** ~ **del giorno** at daybreak ♦ *vt* (*coltello*) to break the point of; (*capelli*) to trim; (*elenco*) to check off (*US*), tick off (*Brit*) ♦ *vi* (*uscire: germogli*) to sprout; (: *capelli*) to begin to grow; (: *denti*) to come through; (*apparire*) to appear (suddenly); ~**rsi** *vr* to become blunt, lose its point; **spuntarla** (*fig*) to make it, win through.

spunti'no *sm* snack.

spun'to *sm* (*TEATRO, MUS*) cue; (*fig*) starting point; **dare lo** ~ **a** to give rise to; **prendere** ~ **da qc** to take sth as one's starting point.

spurga're *vt* (*fogna*) to clean, clear; ~**rsi** *vr* (*MED*) to expectorate.

sputa're *vt* to spit out; (*fig*) to belch (out) ♦ *vi* to spit.

spu'to *sm* spittle *q*, spit *q*.

sputtana're *vt* (*fam*) to bad-mouth.

squa'dra *sf* (*strumento*) square; (*set*) (*gruppo*) team, squad; (*di operai*) gang, squad; (*MIL*) squad; (: *AER, NAUT*) squadron; (*SPORT*) team; **lavoro a** ~**e** teamwork; ~ **mobile/del buon costume** (*POLIZIA*) flying/vice squad.

squadra're *vt* to square, make square; (*osservare*) to look at closely.

squadri'glia [skwàdrēl'yá] *sf* (*AER*) flight; (*NAUT*) squadron.

squadro'ne *sm* squadron.

squagliar'si [skwályár'sē] *vr* to melt; (*fig*) to sneak off.

squali'fica, che *sf* disqualification.

squalifica're *vt* to disqualify.

squal'lido, a *ag* wretched, bleak.

squallo're *sm* wretchedness, bleakness.

squa'lo *sm* shark.

squa'ma *sf* scale.

squama're *vt* to scale; ~**rsi** *vr* to flake *o* peel (off).

squarciago'la [skwárchágō'là]: **a** ~ *av* at the top of one's voice.

squarcia're [skwárchà'rā] *vt* (*muro, corpo*) to rip open; (*tessuto*) to rip; (*fig: tenebre, silenzio*) to split; (: *nuvole*) to pierce.

squar'cio [skwàr'chō] *sm* (*ferita*) gash; (*in lenzuolo, abito*) rip; (*in un muro*) breach; (*in una nave*) hole; (*brano*) passage, excerpt; **uno** ~ **di sole** a burst of sunlight.

squarta're *vt* to quarter, cut up; (*cadavere*) to dismember.

squattrina'to, a *ag* penniless ♦ *sm/f* pauper.

squilibra're *vt* to unbalance.

squilibra'to, a *ag* (*PSIC*) unbalanced ♦ *sm/f* deranged person.

squili'brio *sm* (*differenza, sbilancio*) imbalance; (*PSIC*) derangement.

squillan'te *ag* (*suono*) shrill, sharp; (*voce*) shrill.

squilla're *vi* (*campanello, telefono*) to ring; (*tromba*) to blare.

squil'lo *sm* ring, ringing *q*; blare ♦ *sf inv* (*anche*: **ragazza** ~) call girl.

squisi'to, a *ag* exquisite; (*cibo*) delicious; (*persona*) delightful.

squitti're *vi* (*uccello*) to squawk; (*topo*) to squeak.

SR *sigla* = *Siracusa*.

sradica're *vt* to uproot; (*fig*) to eradicate.

sragiona're [zrájōná'rā] *vi* to talk nonsense, rave.

sregolatez'za [zrāgōlátāt'tsá] *sf* (*nel mangiare, bere*) lack of moderation; (*di vita*) dissoluteness, dissipation.

sregola'to, a *ag* (*senza ordine*: *vita*) disorderly; (*smodato*) immoderate; (*dissoluto*) dissolute.

Sri Lan'ka [srēlán'kà] *sm*: **il** ~ Sri Lanka.

srotola're *vt*, ~**rsi** *vr* to unroll.

SS *sigla* = *Sassari*.

S.S. *abbr* (*REL*) = *Sua Santità*; *Santa Sede*; *santi, santissimo*; (*AUT*) = **strada statale**; *vedi* **statale**.

sta *etc vb vedi* **stare**.

stab'bio *sm* (*recinto*) pen, fold; (*di maiali*) pigsty; (*letame*) manure.

sta'bile *ag* stable, steady; (*tempo*: *non variabile*) settled; (*TEATRO*: *compagnia*) resident ♦ *sm* (*edificio*) building; **teatro** ~ civic theatre.

stabilimen'to *sm* (*edificio*) establishment;

(*fabbrica*) plant, factory; ~ **balneare** bathing establishment; ~ **tessile** textile mill.

stabili're *vt* to establish; (*fissare*: *prezzi, data*) to fix; (*decidere*) to decide; ~**rsi** *vr* (*prendere dimora*) to settle; **resta stabilito che** ... it is agreed that ....

stabilità *sf* stability.

stabilizza're [stábēlēddzá'rā] *vt* to stabilize.

stabilizzato're [stábēlēddzātō'rā] *sm* stabilizer.

stabilizzazio'ne [stábēlēddzáttsyō'nā] *sf* stabilization.

staccanovi'sta, i, e *sm/f* (*ironico*) eager beaver.

stacca're *vt* (*levare*) to detach, remove; (*separare*: *anche fig*) to separate, divide; (*strappare*) to tear off (*o* out); (*scandire*: *parole*) to pronounce clearly; (*SPORT*) to leave behind; ~**rsi** *vr* (*bottone etc*) to come off; (*scostarsi*): ~**rsi (da)** to move away (from); (*fig*: *separarsi*): ~**rsi da** to leave; **non** ~ **gli occhi da qn** not to take one's eyes off sb; ~ **la televisione/il telefono** to disconnect the television/the phone; ~ **un assegno** to write a check.

staccio'na'ta [stáchōná'tá] *sf* (*gen*) fence; (*IPPICA*) hurdle.

stac'co, chi *sm* (*intervallo*) gap; (: *tra due scene*) break; (*differenza*) difference; (*SPORT*: *nel salto*) takeoff.

stade'ra *sf* lever scales *pl*.

sta'dio *sm* (*SPORT*) stadium; (*periodo, fase*) phase, stage.

staf'fa *sf* (*di sella*, *TECN*) stirrup; **perdere le** ~**e** (*fig*) to fly off the handle.

staffet'ta *sf* (*messo*) dispatch rider; (*SPORT*) relay race.

stagflazio'ne [stágflàttsyō'nā] *sf* (*ECON*) stagflation.

stagiona'le [stájōná'lā] *ag* seasonal ♦ *sm/f* seasonal worker.

stagiona're [stájōná'rā] *vt* (*legno*) to season; (*formaggi, vino*) to mature.

stagiona'to, a [stájōná'tō] *ag* (*vedi vb*) seasoned; matured; (*scherzoso*: *attempato*) getting on in years.

stagio'ne [stájō'nā] *sf* season; **alta/bassa** ~ high/low season.

stagliar'si [stályàr'sē] *vr* to stand out, be silhouetted.

stagnan'te [stányàn'tā] *ag* stagnant.

stagna're [stányá'rā] *vt* (*vaso, tegame*) to tinplate; (*barca, botte*) to make watertight; (*sangue*) to stop ♦ *vi* to stagnate.

stagni'no [stányē'nō] *sm* tinsmith.

sta'gno, a [stán'yō] *ag* (*a tenuta d'acqua*) watertight; (*a tenuta d'aria*) airtight ♦ *sm* (*acquitrino*) pond; (*CHIM*) tin.

stagno'la [stányo'là] *sf* tinfoil.

stalagmi'te *sf* stalagmite.

stalatti'te *sf* stalactite.
stal'la *sf* (*per bovini*) cowshed; (*per cavalli*) stable.
stallie're *sm* groom, stableboy.
stal'lo *sm* stall, seat; (*SCACCHI*) stalemate; (*AER*) stall; **situazione di ~** (*fig*) stalemate.
stallo'ne *sm* stallion.
stama'ni, stamatti'na *av* this morning.
stambec'co, chi *sm* ibex.
stamber'ga, ghe *sf* hovel.
stam'pa *sf* (*TIP, FOT*: *tecnica*) printing; (*impressione, copia fotografica*) print; (*insieme di quotidiani, giornalisti etc*): **la ~** the press; **andare in ~** to go to press; **mandare in ~** to pass for press; **errore di ~** printing error; **prova di ~** print sample; **libertà di ~** freedom of the press; **"~e** "printed matter".
stampan'te *sf* (*INFORM*) printer; **~ seriale/ termica** serial/thermal printer.
stampa're *vt* to print; (*pubblicare*) to publish; (*coniare*) to strike, coin; (*imprimere*: *anche fig*) to impress.
stampatel'lo *sm* block letters *pl*.
stampa'to, a *ag* printed ♦ *sm* (*opuscolo*) leaflet; (*modulo*) form; **~i** *smpl* printed matter *sg*.
stampel'la *sf* crutch.
stampiglia're [stámpēlyá'rā] *vt* to stamp.
stampigliatu'ra [stámpēlyátōō'rá] *sf* (*atto*) stamping; (*marchio*) stamp.
stam'po *sm* mould (*US*), mould (*Brit*); (*fig: indole*) type, kind, sort.
stana're *vt* to drive out.
stanca're *vt* to tire, make tired; (*annoiare*) to bore; (*infastidire*) to annoy; **~rsi** *vr* to get tired, tire o.s. out; **~rsi (di)** (*stufarsi*) to grow weary (of), grow tired (of).
stanchez'za [stánkāt'tsá] *sf* tiredness, fatigue.
stan'co, a, chi, che *ag* tired; **~ di** tired of, fed up with.
standardizza're [stándárdēddzá'rā] *vt* to standardize.
standi'sta, i, e *sm/f* (*in una fiera etc*) person responsible for a stand.
stan'ga, ghe *sf* bar; (*di carro*) shaft.
stanga'ta *sf* (*colpo: anche fig*) blow; (*cattivo risultato*) poor result; (*CALCIO*) shot.
stanghet'ta [stángāt'tá] *sf* (*di occhiali*) leg; (*MUS, di scrittura*) bar.
stan'no *vb vedi* stare.
stanot'te *av* tonight; (*notte passata*) last night.
stan'te *prep* owing to, because of; **a sé ~** (*appartamento, casa*) independent, separate.
stanti'o, a, ti'i, ti'e *ag* stale; (*burro*) rancid; (*fig*) old.
stantuf'fo *sm* piston.
stan'za [stán'tsá] *sf* room; (*POESIA*) stanza; **essere di ~ a** (*MIL*) to be stationed in; **~ da bagno** bathroom; **~ da letto** bedroom.

stanziamen'to [stántsyámān'tō] *sm* allocation.
stanzia're [stántsyá'rā] *vt* to allocate.
stanzi'no [stántsē'nō] *sm* (*ripostiglio*) storeroom; (*spogliatoio*) locker room (*US*), changing room (*Brit*).
stappa're *vt* to uncork; (*tappo a corona*) to uncap.
sta're *vi* (*restare in un luogo*) to stay, remain; (*abitare*) to stay, live; (*essere situato*) to be, be situated; (*anche*: **~ in piedi**) to stand; (*essere, trovarsi*) to be; (*dipendere*): **se stesse in me** if it were up to me, if it depended on me; (*seguito da gerundio*): **sta studiando** he's studying; **~ per fare qc** to be about to do sth; **starci** (*esserci spazio*): **nel baule non ci sta più niente** there's no more room in the trunk; (*accettare*): **ci stai?** is that okay with you?; **~ a** (*attenersi a*) to follow, stick to; (*seguito dall'infinito*): **~ a sentire** to listen; **staremo a vedere** let's wait and see; **stiamo a discutere** we're talking; (*toccare a*): **sta a te giocare** it's your turn to play; **sta a te decidere** it's up to you to decide; **~ a qn** (*abiti etc*) to fit sb; **queste scarpe mi stanno strette** these shoes are tight for me; **il rosso ti sta bene** red suits you; **come sta?** how are you?; **io sto bene/ male** I'm very well/not very well; **~ fermo** to keep o stay still; **~ seduto** to sit, be sitting; **~ zitto** to keep quiet; **stando così le cose** given the situation; **stando a ciò che dice lui** according to him o to his version.
starnazza're [stárnáttsá'rā] *vi* to squawk.
starnuti're *vi* to sneeze.
starnu'to *sm* sneeze.
stase'ra *av* this evening, tonight.
sta'si *sf* (*MED, fig*) stasis.
stata'le *ag* state *cpd*, government *cpd* ♦ *sm/f* state employee; (*nell'amministrazione*) ≈ civil servant; **bilancio ~** national budget; **strada ~** ≈ state highway (*US*), trunk road (*Brit*).
statalizza're [státálēddzá'rā] *vt* to nationalize, put under state control.
sta'tico, a, ci, che *ag* (*ELETTR, fig*) static.
stati'sta, i *sm* statesman.
stati'stico, a, ci, che *ag* statistical ♦ *sf* statistic; (*scienza*) statistics *sg*; **fare una ~a** to carry out a statistical examination.
sta'to, a *pp di* essere, stare ♦ *sm* (*condizione*) state, condition; (*POL*) state; (*DIR*) status; **essere in ~ d'accusa** (*DIR*) to be committed for trial; **essere in ~ d'arresto** (*DIR*) to be under arrest; **essere in ~ interessante** to be pregnant; **~ d'assedio/d'emergenza** state of siege/emergency; **~ civile** (*AMM*) marital status; **~ di famiglia** (*AMM*) *certificate giving details of a household and its dependents*; **~ maggiore** (*MIL*) general staff; **~ patrimoniale** (*COMM*) statement of assets and liabilities;

gli S~i Uniti (d'America) the United States (of America).

sta'tua *sf* statue.

statuniten'se *ag* United States *cpd*, of the United States.

statu'ra *sf* (*ANAT*) height; (*fig*) stature; **essere alto/basso di** ~ to be tall/short *o* small.

statu'to *sm* (*DIR*) statute; **regione a** ~ **speciale** *Italian region with political autonomy in certain matters*; ~ **della società** (*COMM*) articles *pl* of association.

stavol'ta *av* this time.

stazionamen'to [stàttsyōnàmān'tō] *sm* (*AUT*) parking; (: *sosta*) waiting; **freno di** ~ handbrake.

staziona're [stàttsyōnà'rā] *vi* (*veicoli*) to be parked.

staziona'rio, a [stàttsyōnà'ryō] *ag* stationary; (*fig*) unchanged.

stazio'ne [stàttsyō'nā] *sf* station; (*balneare, invernale etc*) resort; ~ **degli autobus** bus station; ~ **balneare** seaside resort; ~ **climatica** health resort; ~ **ferroviaria** railroad (*US*) *o* railway (*Brit*) station; ~ **invernale** winter sports resort; ~ **di lavoro** work station; ~ **di polizia** police station (*in small town*); ~ **di servizio** service *o* filling station; ~ **termale** spa.

staz'za [stàt'tsà] *sf* tonnage.

st. civ. *abbr* = **stato civile.**

stec'ca, che *sf* stick; (*di ombrello*) rib; (*di sigarette*) carton; (*MED*) splint; (*stonatura*): **fare una** ~ to sing (*o* play) a wrong note.

stecca'to *sm* fence.

stecchi'to, a [stākkē'tō] *ag* dried up; (*persona*) skinny; **lasciar** ~ **qn** (*fig*) to leave sb flabbergasted; **morto** ~ stone dead.

stel'la *sf* star; ~ **alpina** (*BOT*) edelweiss; ~ **cadente** *o* **filante** shooting star; ~ **di mare** (*ZOOL*) starfish.

stella'to, a *ag* (*cielo, notte*) starry.

ste'lo *sm* stem; (*asta*) rod; **lampada a** ~ floor lamp.

stem'ma, i *sm* coat of arms.

stem'mo *vb vedi* **stare.**

stempera're *vt* (*calce, colore*) to dissolve.

stempia'to, a *ag* with a receding hairline.

stempiatu'ra *sf* receding hairline.

stendar'do *sm* standard.

sten'dere *vt* (*braccia, gambe*) to stretch (out); (*tovaglia*) to spread (out); (*bucato*) to hang out; (*mettere a giacere*) to lay (down); (*spalmare*: *colore*) to spread; (*mettere per iscritto*) to draw up; ~**rsi** *vr* (*coricarsi*) to stretch out, lie down; (*estendersi*) to extend, stretch.

stendibiancheri'a [stāndēbyànkārē'à] *sm inv* clotheshorse.

stendito'io *sm* (*locale*) drying room; (*stendibiancheria*) clotheshorse.

stenodattilografi'a *sf* stenography (*US*), shorthand typing (*Brit*).

stenodattilo'grafo, a *sm/f* stenographer (*US*), shorthand typist (*Brit*).

stenografa're *vt* to take down in shorthand.

stenografi'a *sf* shorthand.

steno'grafo, a *sm/f* stenographer.

stenta're *vi*: ~ **a fare** to find it hard to do, have difficulty doing.

stenta'to, a *ag* (*compito, stile*) labored (*US*), laboured (*Brit*); (*sorriso*) forced.

sten'to *sm* (*fatica*) difficulty; ~**i** *smpl* (*privazioni*) hardship *sg*, privation *sg*; **a** ~ *av* with difficulty, barely.

step'pa *sf* steppe.

ster'co *sm* dung.

stereofoni'a *sf* stereophony.

ste'reo('fonico, a, ci, che) *ag* stereo(phonic).

stereotipa'to, a *ag* stereotyped.

stereo'tipo *sm* stereotype; **pensare per** ~**i** to think in clichés.

ste'rile *ag* sterile; (*terra*) barren; (*fig*) futile, fruitless.

sterilità *sf* sterility.

sterilizza're [stārēlēddzà'rā] *vt* to sterilize.

sterilizzazio'ne [stārēlēddzàttsyō'nā] *sf* sterilization.

sterli'na *sf* pound (sterling).

stermina're *vt* to exterminate, wipe out.

stermina'to, a *ag* immense, endless.

stermi'nio *sm* extermination, destruction; **campo di** ~ death camp.

ster'no *sm* (*ANAT*) breastbone.

sterpa'glia [stārpál'yà] *sf* brushwood.

ster'po *sm* dry twig.

sterra're *vt* to excavate.

sterza're [stārtsà'rā] *vt, vi* (*AUT*) to steer.

ster'zo [ster'tsō] *sm* steering; (*volante*) steering wheel.

ste'so, a *pp di* **stendere.**

stes'si *etc vb vedi* **stare.**

stes'so, a *ag* same; (*rafforzativo: in persona, proprio*): **il re** ~ the king himself *o* in person ♦ *pronome*: **lo(la)** ~**(a)** the same (one); **quello** ~ **giorno** that very day; **i suoi** ~**i avversari lo ammirano** even his enemies admire him; **fa lo** ~ it doesn't matter; **parto lo** ~ I'm going all the same; **per me è lo** ~ it's all the same to me, it doesn't matter to me; *vedi* **io, tu** *etc*.

stesu'ra *sf* (*azione*) drafting *q*, drawing up *q*; (*documento*) draft.

stetosco'pio *sm* stethoscope.

stet'ti *etc vb vedi* **stare.**

sti'a *sf* hutch.

sti'a *etc vb vedi* **stare.**

stig'ma, i *sm* stigma.

stig'mate *sfpl* (*REL*) stigmata.

stila're *vt* to draw up, draft.

sti'le *sm* style; (*classe*) style, class; (*SPORT*):

~ **libero** freestyle; **mobili in** ~ period furniture; **in grande** ~ in great style; **è proprio nel suo** ~ (*fig*) it's just like him.

stili'smo *sm* concern for style.

stili'sta, i, e *sm/f* designer.

stili'stico, a, ci, che *ag* stylistic.

stilizza'to, a [stēlēddzà'tō] *ag* stylized.

stilla're *vi* (*trasudare*) to ooze; (*gocciolare*) to drip.

stillici'dio [stēllēchē'dyō] *sm* (*fig*) continual pestering (*o* moaning *etc*).

stilogra'fica, che *sf* (*anche*: **penna** ~) fountain pen.

Stim. *abbr* = **stimata.**

sti'ma *sf* esteem; valuation; assessment, estimate; **avere** ~ **di qn** to have respect for sb; **godere della** ~ **di qn** to enjoy sb's respect; **fare la** ~ **di qc** to estimate the value of sth.

stima're *vt* (*persona*) to esteem, hold in high regard; (*terreno, casa etc*) to value; (*stabilire in misura approssimativa*) to estimate, assess; (*ritenere*): ~ **che** to consider that; **~rsi fortunato** to consider o.s. (to be) lucky.

Stim.ma *abbr* = **stimatissima.**

stimolan'te *ag* stimulating ♦ *sm* (*MED*) stimulant.

stimola're *vt* to stimulate; (*incitare*): ~ **qn (a fare)** to spur sb on (to do).

stimolazio'ne [stēmōlàttsyō'nā] *sf* stimulation.

sti'molo *sm* (*anche fig*) stimulus.

stin'co, chi *sm* shin; shinbone.

stin'gere [stēn'jārā] *vt, vi* (*anche*: **~rsi**) to fade.

stin'to, a *pp di* **stingere.**

stipa're *vt* to cram, pack; **~rsi** *vr* (*accalcarsi*) to crowd, throng.

stipendia're *vt* (*pagare*) to pay (a salary to).

stipendia'to, a *ag* salaried ♦ *sm/f* salaried worker.

stipen'dio *sm* salary.

sti'pite *sm* (*di porta, finestra*) jamb.

stipula're *vt* (*redigere*) to draw up.

stipulazio'ne [stēpōōlàttsyō'nā] *sf* (*di contratto*: *stesura*) drafting; (: *firma*) signing.

stiracchia're [stēràkkyà'rā] *vt* (*fig*: *significato di una parola*) to stretch, force; **~rsi** *vr* (*persona*) to stretch.

stiramen'to *sm* (*MED*) sprain.

stira're *vt* (*abito*) to iron; (*distendere*) to stretch; (*strappare*: *muscolo*) to strain; **~rsi** *vr* (*fam*) to stretch (o.s.).

stiratu'ra *sf* ironing.

stir'pe *sf* birth, stock; descendants *pl*.

stitichez'za [stētēkàt'tsà] *sf* constipation.

sti'tico, a, ci, che *ag* constipated.

sti'va *sf* (*di nave*) hold.

stiva'le *sm* boot.

stivalet'to *sm* ankle boot.

stiva're *vt* to stow, load.

stiz'za [stēt'tsà] *sf* anger, vexation.

stizzi're [stēttsē'rā] *vt* to irritate ♦ *vi*, **~rsi** *vr* to become irritated, become vexed.

stizzo'so, a [stēttsō'sō] *ag* (*persona*) quick-tempered, irascible; (*risposta*) angry.

stoccafis'so *sm* stockfish, dried cod.

Stoccar'da *sf* Stuttgart.

stocca'ta *sf* (*colpo*) stab, thrust; (*fig*) gibe, cutting remark.

Stoccol'ma *sf* Stockholm.

stof'fa *sf* material, fabric; (*fig*): **aver la** ~ **di** to have the makings of; **avere della** ~ to have what it takes.

stoici'smo [stōēchēz'mō] *sm* stoicism.

sto'ico, a, ci, che *ag* stoic(al).

stoi'no *sm* doormat.

sto'la *sf* stole.

stoltez'za [stōltàt'tsà] *sf* stupidity; (*azione*) foolish action.

stol'to, a *ag* stupid, foolish.

sto'maco, chi *sm* stomach; **dare di** ~ to vomit, be sick.

stona're *vt* to sing (*o* play) out of tune ♦ *vi* to be out of tune, sing (*o* play) out of tune; (*fig*) to be out of place, jar; (: *colori*) to clash.

stona'to, a *ag* (*persona*) off-key; (*strumento*) off-key, out of tune.

stonatu'ra *sf* (*suono*) false note.

stop *sm inv* (*TELEGRAFIA*) stop; (*AUT*: *cartello*) stop sign; (: *fanalino d'arresto*) stoplight.

stop'pa *sf* tow.

stop'pia *sf* (*AGR*) stubble.

stoppi'no *sm* (*di candela*) wick; (*miccia*) fuse.

stor'cere [stor'chārā] *vt* to twist; **~rsi** *vr* to writhe, twist; ~ **il naso** (*fig*) to turn up one's nose; **~rsi la caviglia** to twist one's ankle.

stordimen'to *sm* (*gen*) dizziness; (*da droga*) stupefaction.

stordi're *vt* (*intontire*) to stun, daze; **~rsi** *vr*: **~rsi col bere** to dull one's senses with drink.

stordi'to, a *ag* stunned; (*sventato*) scatter-brained, heedless.

sto'ria *sf* (*scienza, avvenimenti*) history; (*racconto, bugia*) story; (*faccenda, questione*) business *q*; (*pretesto*) excuse, pretext; **~e** *sfpl* (*smancerie*) fuss *sg*; **passare alla** ~ to go down in history; **non ha fatto ~e** he didn't make a fuss.

storicità [stōrēchētà'] *sf* historical authenticity.

sto'rico, a, ci, che *ag* historic(al) ♦ *sm/f* historian.

storiografi'a *sf* historiography.

storio'ne *sm* (*ZOOL*) sturgeon.

stormi're *vi* to rustle.

stor'mo *sm* (*di uccelli*) flock.

storna're *vt* (*COMM*) to transfer.

stornel'lo *sm* kind of folk song.

stor'no *sm* starling.

storpia're *vt* to cripple, maim; (*fig*: *parole*)

to mangle; (: *significato*) to twist.

storpiatu'ra *sf* (*fig*: *di parola*) twisting, distortion.

stor'pio, a *ag* crippled, maimed.

stor'si *etc vb vedi* **storcere**.

stor'to, a *pp di* **storcere** ♦ *ag* (*chiodo*) twisted, bent; (*gamba, quadro*) crooked; (*fig: ragionamento*) false, wrong ♦ *sf* (*distorsione*) sprain, twist; (*recipiente*) retort ♦ *av*: **guardare** ~ **qn** (*fig*) to look askance at sb; **andar** ~ to go wrong.

stovi'glie [stōvēl'yā] *sfpl* dishes *pl*, crockery.

str. *abbr* (*GEO*) = **stretto**.

stra'bico, a, ci, che *ag* squint-eyed; (*occhi*) squint.

strabilian'te *ag* astonishing, amazing.

strabilia're *vi* to astonish, amaze.

strabi'smo *sm* squinting.

strabuzza're [stràbōōddzà'rā] *vt*: ~ **gli occhi** to open one's eyes wide.

straca'rico, a, chi, che *ag* overloaded.

stracchi'no [stràkkē'nō] *sm* *type of soft cheese*.

straccia're [stràchà'rā] *vt* to tear.

strac'cio, a, ci, ce [stràch'chō] *ag*: **carta** ~**a** waste paper ♦ *sm* rag; (*per pulire*) cloth, dust cloth (*US*), duster (*Brit*).

straccio'ne, a [stràchō'nā] *sm/f* ragamuffin.

stracciven'dolo [stràchēvàn'dōlō] *sm* ragman.

strac'co, a, chi, che *ag*: ~ (**morto**) exhausted, dead tired.

stracot'to, a *ag* overcooked ♦ *sm* (*CUC*) beef stew.

stra'da *sf* road; (*di città*) street; (*cammino, via, fig*) way; ~ **facendo** on the way; **tre ore di** ~ (**a piedi**)/(**in macchina**) three hours' walk/drive; **essere sulla buona** ~ (*nella vita*) to be on the right road *o* path; (*con indagine etc*) to be on the right track; **essere fuori** ~ (*fig*) to be on the wrong track; **fare** ~ **a qn** to show sb the way; **fare** *o* **farsi** ~ (*fig: persona*) to get on in life; **portare qn sulla cattiva** ~ to lead sb astray; **donna di** ~ (*fig peg*) streetwalker; **ragazzo di** ~ (*fig peg*) street urchin; ~ **ferrata** railroad (*US*), railway (*Brit*); ~ **principale** main road; ~ **senza uscita** dead end, cul-de-sac.

strada'le *ag* road *cpd*; (*polizia, regolamento*) traffic *cpd*.

strada'rio *sm* street guide.

stradi'no *sm* road worker.

strafalcio'ne [stràfàlchō'nā] *sm* blunder, howler.

strafa're *vi* to overdo it.

strafat'to, a *pp di* **strafare**.

strafo'ro: di ~ *av* (*di nascosto*) on the sly.

strafotten'te *ag*: **è** ~ he doesn't give a damn, he couldn't care less.

strafotten'za [stràfōtten'tsà] *sf* arrogance.

stra'ge [strà'jā] *sf* massacre, slaughter.

stragran'de *ag*: **la** ~ **maggioranza** the overwhelming majority.

stralcia're [stràlchà'rā] *vt* to remove.

stral'cio [stràl'chō] *sm* (*COMM*): **vendere in** ~ to sell off (at bargain prices) ♦ *ag inv*: **legge** ~ abridged version of an act.

straluna'to, a *ag* (*occhi*) rolling; (*persona*) beside o.s., very upset.

stramazza're [stràmàttsà'rā] *vi* to fall heavily.

stramberi'a *sf* eccentricity.

stram'bo, a *ag* strange, queer.

strampala'to, a *ag* odd, eccentric.

stranez'za [strànāt'tsà] *sf* strangeness.

strangola're *vt* to strangle; ~**rsi** *vr* to choke.

stranie'ro, a *ag* foreign ♦ *sm/f* foreigner.

strani'to, a *ag* dazed.

stra'no, a *ag* strange, odd.

straordina'rio, a *ag* extraordinary; (*treno etc*) special ♦ *sm* (*lavoro*) overtime.

strapazza're [stràpàttsà'rā] *vt* to ill-treat; ~**rsi** *vr* to tire o.s. out, overdo things.

strapaz'zo [stràpàt'tsō] *sm* strain, fatigue; **da** ~ (*fig*) third-rate.

strapie'no, a *ag* full to overflowing.

strapiom'bo *sm* overhanging rock; **a** ~ overhanging.

strapote're *sm* excessive power.

strappala'crime *ag inv* (*fam*): **romanzo** (*o* **film** *etc*) ~ tear-jerker.

strappa're *vt* (*gen*) to tear, rip; (*pagina etc*) to tear off, tear out; (*sradicare*) to pull up; (*togliere*): ~ **qc a qn** to snatch sth from sb; (*fig*) to wrest sth from sb; ~**rsi** *vr* (*lacerarsi*) to rip, tear; (*rompersi*) to break; ~**rsi un muscolo** to tear a muscle.

strap'po *sm* (*strattone*) pull, tug; (*lacerazione*) tear, rip; (*fig fam: passaggio*) ride (*US*), lift (*Brit*); **fare uno** ~ **alla regola** to make an exception to the rule; ~ **muscolare** torn muscle.

strapunti'no *sm* jump *o* foldaway seat.

straripa're *vi* to overflow.

Strasbur'go *sf* Strasbourg.

strascica're [stràshēkà'rā] *vt* to trail; (*piedi*) to drag; ~ **le parole** to drawl.

stra'scico, chi [stràsh'shēkō] *sm* (*di abito*) train; (*conseguenza*) after-effect.

stratagem'ma, i [stràtàjem'mà] *sm* stratagem.

strate'ga, ghi *sm* strategist.

strategi'a, gi'e [stràtàjē'à] *sf* strategy.

strate'gico, a, ci, che [stràte'jēkō] *ag* strategic.

stra'to *sm* layer; (*rivestimento*) coat, coating; (*GEO, fig*) stratum; (*METEOR*) stratus.

stratosfe'ra *sf* stratosphere.

stratto'ne *sm* tug, jerk; **dare uno** ~ **a qc** to tug *o* jerk sth, give sth a tug *o* jerk.

stravacca'to, a *ag* sprawling.

stravagan'te *ag* odd, eccentric.

stravagan'za [stràvàgàn'tsà] *sf* eccentricity.

stravec'chio, a [stråvek'kyō] *ag* very old.
stravede're *vi*: ~ **per qn** to dote on sb.
stravi'sto, a *pp di* **stravedere**.
stravi'zio [stråvēt'tsyo] *sm* excess.
stravol'gere [stråvol'jārā] *vt (volto)* to contort; *(fig: animo)* to trouble deeply; (: *verità*) to twist, distort.
stravol'to, a *pp di* **stravolgere** ♦ *ag (persona: per stanchezza etc)* in a terrible state; (: *per sofferenza)* distraught.
strazian'te [stråttsyàn'tā] *ag (scena)* harrowing; *(urlo)* bloodcurdling; *(dolore)* excruciating.
strazia're [stråttsyà'rā] *vt* to torture, torment.
stra'zio [stråt'tsyō] *sm* torture; *(fig: cosa fatta male)*: **essere uno ~** to be appalling; **fare ~ di** *(corpo, vittima)* to mutilate.
stre'ga, ghe *sf* witch.
strega're *vt* to bewitch.
strego'ne *sm (mago)* wizard; *(di tribù)* witch doctor.
stregoneri'a *sf (pratica)* witchcraft; **fare una ~** to cast a spell.
stre'gua *sf*: **alla ~ di** by the same standard as.
strema're *vt* to exhaust.
stre'mo *sm*: **essere allo ~** to be at the end of one's tether.
stren'na *sf*: **~ natalizia** *(regalo)* Christmas present; *(libro) book published for the Christmas market*.
stre'nuo, a *ag* brave, courageous.
strepita're *vi* to yell and shout.
stre'pito *sm (di voci, folla)* clamor *(US)*, clamour *(Brit)*; *(di catene)* clanking, rattling.
strepito'so, a *ag* clamorous, deafening; *(fig: successo)* resounding.
stressan'te *ag* stressful.
stressa're *vt* to put under stress.
stressa'to, a *ag* under stress.
stret'ta *sf vedi* **stretto**.
strettamen'te *av* tightly; *(rigorosamente)* strictly.
strettez'za [stråttāt'tså] *sf* narrowness; **~e** *sfpl (povertà)* poverty *sg*, straitened circumstances.
stret'to, a *pp di* **stringere** ♦ *ag (corridoio, limiti)* narrow; *(gonna, scarpe, nodo, curva)* tight; *(intimo: parente, amico)* close; *(rigoroso: osservanza)* strict; *(preciso: significato)* precise, exact ♦ *sm (braccio di mare)* strait ♦ *sf (di mano)* grasp; *(finanziaria)* squeeze; *(fig: dolore, turbamento)* pang; **a denti ~i** with clenched teeth; **lo ~ necessario** the bare minimum; **una ~a di mano** a handshake; **essere alle ~e** to have one's back to the wall.
stretto'ia *sf* bottleneck; *(fig)* tricky situation.

stria'to, a *ag* streaked.
striatu'ra *sf (atto)* streaking; *(effetto)* streaks *pl*.
stricni'na *sf* strychnine.
stri'da *sfpl* screaming *sg*.
striden'te *ag* strident.
stri'dere *vi (porta)* to squeak; *(animale)* to screech, shriek; *(colori)* to clash.
stri'do, pl(f) strida *sm* screech, shriek.
strido're *sm* screeching, shrieking.
stri'dulo, a *ag* shrill.
stri'glia [strēl'yà] *sf* currycomb.
striglia're [strēlyà'rā] *vt (cavallo)* to curry.
striglia'ta [strēlyà'tá] *sf (di cavallo)* currying; *(fig)*: **dare una ~ a qn** to give sb a scolding.
strilla're *vt, vi* to scream, shriek.
stril'lo *sm* scream, shriek.
strillo'ne *sm* newspaper seller.
striminzi'to, a [strēmēntsē'tō] *ag (misero)* shabby; *(molto magro)* skinny.
strimpella're *vt (MUS)* to strum.
strin'ga, ghe *sf* lace.
stringa're *vt (fig: discorso)* to condense.
stringa'to, a *ag (fig)* concise.
strin'gere [strēn'jārā] *vt (avvicinare due cose)* to press (together), squeeze (together); *(tenere stretto)* to hold tight, clasp, clutch; *(pugno, mascella, denti)* to clench; *(labbra)* to compress; *(avvitare)* to tighten; *(abito)* to take in; *(sog: scarpe)* to pinch, be tight for; *(fig: concludere: patto)* to make; (: *accelerare: passo)* to quicken ♦ *vi (incalzare)* to be pressing; **~rsi** *vr (accostarsi)*: **~rsi a** to press o.s. up against; **~ la mano a qn** to shake sb's hand; **~ gli occhi** to screw up one's eyes; **~ amicizia con qn** to make friends with sb; **stringi stringi** in conclusion; **il tempo stringe** time is short.
strin'si *etc vb vedi* **stringere**.
stri'scia, sce [strēsh'shá] *sf (di carta, tessuto etc)* strip; *(riga)* stripe; **~sce (pedonali)** pedestrian crossing *sg*; **a ~sce** striped.
striscian'te [strēshàn'tā] *ag (fig peg)* unctuous; *(ECON: inflazione)* creeping.
striscia're [strēshà'rā] *vt (piedi)* to drag; *(muro, macchina)* to graze ♦ *vi* to crawl, creep.
stri'scio [strēsh'shō] *sm* graze; *(MED)* smear; **colpire di ~** to graze.
striscio'ne [strēshō'nā] *sm* banner.
stritola're *vt* to grind.
strizza're [strēttsà'rā] *vt (arancia)* to squeeze; *(panni)* to wring (out); **~ l'occhio** to wink.
strizza'ta [strēttsà'tá] *sf*: **dare una ~ a qc** to give sth a wring; **una ~ d'occhio** a wink.
stro'fa *sf*, **stro'fe** *sf inv* strophe.
strofinac'cio [strōfēnàch'chō] *sm* cloth, dust cloth *(US)*, duster *(Brit)*; *(per piatti)* dishcloth; *(per pavimenti)* scrubbing rag *(US)*, floorcloth *(Brit)*.

strofina're *vt* to rub.
stronca're *vt* to break off; (*fig: ribellione*) to suppress, put down; (*: film, libro*) to tear to pieces.
stron'zo [strōn'tsō] *sm* (*sterco*) turd; (*fig fam!: persona*) shit (*!*).
stropiccia're [strōpĕchá'rā] *vt* to rub.
strozza're [strōttsá'rā] *vt* (*soffocare*) to choke, strangle; **~rsi** *vr* to choke.
strozzatu'ra [strōttsátōō'rá] *sf* (*restringimento*) narrowing; (*di strada etc*) bottleneck.
strozzi'no, a [strōttsē'nō] *sm/f* (*usuraio*) usurer; (*fig*) shark.
strucca're *vt* to remove make-up from; **~rsi** *vr* to remove one's make-up.
strug'gere [strōōd'jārā] *vt* (*fig*) to consume; **~rsi** *vr* (*fig*): **~rsi di** to be consumed with.
struggimen'to [strōōdjēmān'tō] *sm* (*desiderio*) yearning.
strumenta'le *ag* (*MUS*) instrumental.
strumentalizza're [strōōmāntálēddzà'rā] *vt* to exploit, use to one's own ends.
strumentazio'ne [strōōmāntáttsyō'nā] *sf* (*MUS*) orchestration; (*TECN*) instrumentation.
strumen'to *sm* (*arnese, fig*) instrument, tool; (*MUS*) instrument; **~ a corda** *o* **ad arco/a fiato** string(ed)/wind instrument.
strus'si *etc vb vedi* **struggere**.
strut'to *sm* lard.
struttu'ra *sf* structure.
struttura're *vt* to structure.
struz'zo [strōōt'tsō] *sm* ostrich; **fare lo ~, fare la politica dello ~** to bury one's head in the sand.
stucca're *vt* (*muro*) to plaster; (*vetro*) to putty; (*decorare con stucchi*) to stucco.
stuccato're, tri'ce *sm/f* plasterer; (*artista*) stucco worker.
stucche'vole [stōōkkā'vōlā] *ag* nauseating; (*fig*) tedious, boring.
stuc'co, chi *sm* plaster; (*da vetri*) putty; (*ornamentale*) stucco; **rimanere di ~** (*fig*) to be dumbfounded.
studen'te, es'sa *sm/f* student; (*scolaro*) pupil, schoolboy/girl.
studente'sco, a, schi, sche *ag* student *cpd*.
studia're *vt* to study; **~rsi** *vr* (*sforzarsi*): **~rsi di fare** to try *o* endeavor (*US*) *o* endeavour (*Brit*) to do.
studia'to, a *ag* (*modi, sorriso*) affected.
stu'dio *sm* studying; (*ricerca, saggio, stanza*) study; (*di professionista*) office; (*di artista,* CINEMA, TV, RADIO) studio; (*di medico*) office (*US*), surgery (*Brit*); **~i** *smpl* (*INS*) studies; **alla fine degli ~i** at the end of one's course (of studies); **secondo recenti ~i, appare che ...** recent research indicates that ...; **la proposta è allo ~** the proposal is under consideration; **~ legale** lawyer's office.
studio'so, a *ag* studious, hardworking ♦ *sm/f*

scholar.
stu'fa *sf* stove; **~ elettrica** electric fire *o* heater; **~ a legna/carbone** wood-burning/coal stove.
stufa're *vt* (*CUC*) to stew; (*fig fam*) to bore.
stufa'to *sm* (*CUC*) stew.
stu'fo, a *ag* (*fam*): **essere ~ di** to be fed up with, be sick and tired of.
stuo'ia *sf* mat.
stuo'lo *sm* crowd, host.
stupefacen'te [stōōpāfáchen'tā] *ag* stunning, astounding ♦ *sm* drug, narcotic.
stupefa're *vt* to stun, astound.
stupefat'to, a *pp di* **stupefare**.
stupefazio'ne [stōōpāfáttsyō'nā] *sf* astonishment.
stupen'do, a *ag* marvellous, wonderful.
stupidag'gine [stōōpēdàd'jēnā] *sf* stupid thing (to do *o* say).
stupidità *sf* stupidity.
stu'pido, a *ag* stupid.
stupi're *vt* to amaze, stun ♦ *vi* (*anche:* **~rsi**): **~ (di)** to be amazed (at), be stunned (by); **non c'è da ~rsi** that's not surprising.
stupo're *sm* amazement, astonishment.
stupra're *vt* to rape.
stuprato're *sm* rapist.
stu'pro *sm* rape.
stura're *vt* (*lavandino*) to clear.
stuzzicaden'ti [stōōttsēkáden'tē] *sm* toothpick.
stuzzican'te [stōōttsēkán'tā] *ag* (*gen*) stimulating; (*appetitoso*) appetizing.
stuzzica're [stōōttsēká'rā] *vt* (*ferita etc*) to poke (at), prod (at); (*fig*) to tease; (*: appetito*) to whet; (*: curiosità*) to stimulate; **~ i denti** to pick one's teeth.
su *prep* (*su* + *il* = **sul**, *su* + *lo* = **sullo**, *su* + *l'* = **sull'**, *su* + *la* = **sulla**, *su* + *i* = **sui**, *su* + *gli* = **sugli**, *su* + *le* = **sulle**) on; (*moto a luogo*) on, on to; (*addosso, sopra*) over; (*intorno a, riguardo a*) about, on; (*approssimazione: circa*) about, around ♦ *av* up; (*sopra*) (up) above; (*al piano superiore*) upstairs ♦ *escl* come on!; **è sulla destra** it's on the right; **100 metri sul livello del mare** 100 meters above sea level; **fecero rotta ~ Palermo** they set out towards Palermo; **sul vestito indossava un golf rosso** she was wearing a red sweater over her dress; **una ragazza sui 17 anni** a girl of about 17 (years of age); **in 3 casi ~ 10** in 3 cases out of 10; **spedire qc ~ richiesta** to send sth on request; **sta sulle sue** he keeps to himself; **dai 20 anni in ~** from the age of 20 onwards; **prezzi dalle mille lire in ~** prices from 1000 lire (upwards); **andare ~ e giù** to go up and down.
su'a *vedi* **suo**.
suaden'te *ag* persuasive.
sub *sm/f inv* skin-diver.
subac'queo, a *ag* underwater ♦ *sm* skin-

subaffitta're vt to sublet.

subaffit'to sm (contratto) sublet.

subalter'no, a ag, sm subordinate; (MIL) subaltern.

subappalta're vt to subcontract.

subappal'to sm subcontract.

subbu'glio [sōōbbōōl'yō] sm confusion, turmoil; **essere/mettere in** ~ to be in/throw into a turmoil.

subcon'scio, a [sōōbkon'shō], **subcoscien'te** [sōōbkōshen'tà] ag, sm subconscious.

sub'dolo, a ag underhand, sneaky.

subentra're vi: ~ **a qn in qc** to take over sth from sb; **sono subentrati altri problemi** other problems arose.

subi're vt to suffer, endure.

subissa're vt (fig): ~ **di** to overwhelm with, load with.

subita'neo, a ag sudden.

su'bito av immediately, at once, straight away.

subli'me ag sublime.

subloca're vt to sublease.

sublocazio'ne [sōōblōkáttsyō'nà] sf sublease.

subnorma'le ag subnormal ♦ sm/f mentally handicapped person.

subodora're vt (insidia etc) to smell, suspect.

subordina're vt to subordinate.

subordina'to, a ag subordinate; (dipendente): ~ **a** dependent on, subject to.

subordinazio'ne [sōōbōrdēnáttsyō'nà] sf subordination.

subor'dine sm: **in** ~ secondarily.

subur'ba'no, a ag suburban.

succeda'neo [sōōchádà'nàō] sm substitute.

succe'dere [sōōche'dàrà] vi (prendere il posto di qn): ~ **a** to succeed; (venire dopo): ~ **a** to follow; (accadere) to happen; ~**rsi** vr to follow each other; ~ **al trono** to succeed to the throne; **sono cose che succedono** these things happen.

successio'ne [sōōchàssyō'nà] sf succession; **tassa di** ~ inheritance tax (US), death duty (Brit).

successivamen'te [sōōchàssēvámàn'tà] av subsequently.

successi'vo, a [sōōchàssē'vō] ag successive; **il giorno** ~ the following day; **in un momento** ~ subsequently.

succes'so, a [sōōches·sō] pp di **succedere** ♦ sm (esito) outcome; (buona riuscita) success; **di** ~ (libro, personaggio) successful; **avere** ~ (persona) to be successful; (idea) to be well received.

successo're [sōōchàssō'rà] sm successor.

succhia're [sōōkkyà'rà] vt to suck (up).

succhiot'to [sōōkkyot'tō] sm pacifier (US), dummy (Brit).

succin'to, a [sōōchēn'tō] ag (discorso)

succinct; (abito) brief.

suc'co, chi sm juice; (fig) essence, gist; ~ **di frutta/pomodoro** fruit/tomato juice.

succo'so, a ag juicy; (fig) pithy.

suc'cube sm/f victim; **essere** ~ **di qn** to be dominated by sb.

succulen'to, a ag succulent.

succursa'le sf branch (office).

sud sm south ♦ ag inv south; (regione) southern; **verso** ~ south, southwards; **l'Italia del S**~ Southern Italy; **l'America del S**~ South America.

Suda'frica sm: **il** ~ South Africa.

sudafrica'no, a ag, sm/f South African.

Sudame'rica sm: **il** ~ South America.

sudamerica'no, a ag, sm/f South American.

Sudan' sm: **il** ~ (the) Sudan.

sudane'se ag, sm/f Sudanese inv.

suda're vi to perspire, sweat; ~ **freddo** to come out in a cold sweat.

suda'to, a ag (persona, mani) sweaty; (fig: denaro) hard-earned ♦ sf (anche fig) sweat; **una vittoria** ~**a** a hard-won victory; **ho fatto una bella** ~**a per finirlo in tempo** it was a real sweat to get it finished in time.

suddet'to, a ag above-mentioned.

suddidan'za [sōōddétàn'tsà] sf subjection; (cittadinanza) citizenship.

suddi'to, a sm/f subject.

suddivi'dere vt to subdivide.

suddivisio'ne sf subdivision.

suddivi'so, a pp di **suddividere**.

sudest' sm south-east; **vento di** ~ south-easterly wind; **il** ~ **asiatico** Southeast Asia.

sudiceri'a [sōōdēchàrē'à] sf (qualità) filthiness, dirtiness; (cosa sporca) dirty thing.

su'dicio, a, ci, ce [sōō'dēchō] ag dirty, filthy.

sudiciu'me [sōōdēchōō'mà] sm dirt, filth.

sudo're sm perspiration, sweat.

sudo'vest sm south-west; **vento di** ~ south-westerly wind.

su'e vedi **suo**.

Su'ez [sōō'àz] sm: **il Canale di** ~ the Suez Canal.

sufficien'te [sōōffēchen'tà] ag enough, sufficient; (borioso) self-important; (INS) satisfactory.

sufficien'za [sōōffēchen'tsà] sf (INS) passing grade (US), pass mark (Brit); **con un'aria di** ~ (fig) with a condescending air; **a** ~ enough; **ne ho avuto a** ~! I've had enough of this!

suffis'so sm (LING) suffix.

suffraga're vt to support.

suffra'gio [sōōffrà'jō] sm (voto) vote; ~ **universale** universal suffrage.

suggella're [sōōdjàllà'rà] vt (fig) to seal.

suggerimen'to [sōōdjàrēmàn'tō] sm suggestion; (consiglio) piece of advice, advice q; **dietro suo** ~ on his advice.

suggeri're [sōōdjārē'rā] *vt* (*risposta*) to tell; (*consigliare*) to advise; (*proporre*) to suggest; (*TEATRO*) to prompt; ~ **a qn di fare qc** to suggest to sb that he (*o* she) do sth.

suggerito're, tri'ce [sōōdjārētō'rā] *sm/f* (*TEATRO*) prompter.

suggestiona're [sōōdjāstyōna'rā] *vt* to influence.

suggestio'ne [sōōdjāstyō'nā] *sf* (*PSIC*) suggestion; (*istigazione*) instigation.

suggesti'vo, a [sōōdjāstē'vō] *ag* (*paesaggio*) evocative; (*teoria*) interesting, attractive.

su'ghero [sōō'gārō] *sm* cork.

su'gli [sōōl'yē] *prep* + *det vedi* **su**.

su'go, ghi *sm* (*succo*) juice; (*di carne*) gravy; (*condimento*) sauce; (*fig*) gist, essence.

sugo'so, a *ag* (*frutto*) juicy; (*fig: articolo etc*) pithy.

su'i *prep* + *det vedi* **su**.

suici'da, i, e [sōōēchē'dā] *ag* suicidal ♦ *sm/f* suicide.

suicidar'si [sōōēchēdār'sē] *vr* to commit suicide.

suici'dio [sōōēchē'dyō] *sm* suicide.

sui'no, a *ag:* **carne** ~**a** pork ♦ *sm* pig; ~**i** *smpl* swine *pl*.

sul, sull', sul'la, sul'le, sul'lo *prep* + *det vedi* **su**.

sultani'na *sf:* **(uva)** ~ sultana.

sulta'no, a *sm/f* sultan/sultana.

Suma'tra *sf* Sumatra.

sunnomina'to, a *ag* aforesaid *cpd*.

sun'to *sm* summary.

su'o, su'a, su'e, suo'i *det:* **il** ~, **la sua** *etc* (*di lui*) his; (*di lei*) her; (*di esso*) its; (*con valore indefinito*) one's, his/her; (*forma di cortesia: anche:* **S**~) your ♦ *pronome:* **il** ~, **la sua** *etc* his; hers; yours ♦ *sm:* **ha speso del** ~ he (*o* she *etc*) spent his (*o* her *etc*) own money ♦ *sf:* **la** ~**a** (*opinione*) his (*o* her *etc*) view; **i suoi** (*parenti*) his (*o* her *etc*) family; **un** ~ **amico** a friend of his (*o* hers *etc*); **è dalla** ~**a** he's on his (*o* her *etc*) side; **anche lui ha avuto le** ~**e** (*disavventure*) he's had his problems too.

suo'cero, a [swo'chārō] *sm/f* father/mother-in-law; **i** ~**i** *smpl* father- and mother-in-law.

suo'i *vedi* **suo**.

suo'la *sf* (*di scarpa*) sole.

suo'lo *sm* (*terreno*) ground; (*terra*) soil.

suona're *vt* (*MUS*) to play; (*campana*) to ring; (*ore*) to strike; (*clacson, allarme*) to sound ♦ *vi* to play; (*telefono, campana*) to ring; (*ore*) to strike; (*clacson, fig: parole*) to sound.

suona'to, a *ag* (*compiuto*): **ha cinquant'anni** ~**i** he is well over fifty.

suonato're, tri'ce *sm/f* player; ~ **ambulante** street musician.

suoneri'a *sf* alarm.

suo'no *sm* sound.

suo'ra *sf* (*REL*) nun; **Suor Maria** Sister Maria.

su'per *ag inv:* **(benzina)** ~ ≈ premium (*US*), four-star (petrol) (*Brit*).

superamen'to *sm* (*di ostacolo*) overcoming; (*di montagna*) crossing.

supera're *vt* (*oltrepassare: limite*) to exceed, surpass; (*attraversare: fiume*) to cross; (*sorpassare: veicolo*) to overtake; (*fig: essere più bravo di*) to surpass, outdo; (*: difficoltà*) to overcome; (*: esame*) to get through; ~ **qn in altezza/peso** to be taller/ heavier than sb; **ha superato la cinquantina** he's over fifty (years of age); ~ **i limiti di velocità** to exceed the speed limit; **stavolta ha superato se stesso** this time he has surpassed himself.

supera'to, a *ag* outmoded.

super'bia *sf* pride.

super'bo, a *ag* proud; (*fig*) magnificent, superb.

superficia'le [sōōpārfēchá'lā] *ag* superficial.

superficialità [sōōpārfēchálētā'] *sf* superficiality.

superfi'cie, ci [sōōpārfē'chā] *sf* surface; **tornare in** ~ (*a galla*) to return to the surface; (*fig: problemi etc*) to resurface; ~ **alare** (*AER*) wing area; ~ **velica** (*NAUT*) sail area.

super'fluo, a *ag* superfluous.

superio'ra *sf* (*REL: anche:* **madre** ~) mother superior.

superio're *ag* (*piano, arto, classi*) upper; (*più elevato: temperatura, livello*): ~ **(a)** higher (than); (*migliore*): ~ **(a)** superior (to) ♦ *sfpl:* **le** ~**i** (*INS*) ≈ senior high (school) (*US*), senior comprehensive school (*Brit*); **il corso** ~ **di un fiume** the upper reaches of a river.

superiorità *sf* superiority.

superlati'vo, a *ag, sm* superlative.

superlavo'ro *sm* overwork.

supermerca'to *sm* supermarket.

superpoten'za [sōōpārpōtān'tsá] *sf* (*POL*) superpower.

superso'nico, a, ci, che *ag* supersonic.

super'stite *ag* surviving ♦ *sm/f* survivor.

superstizio'ne [sōōpārstēttsyō'nā] *sf* superstition.

superstizio'so, a [sōōpārstēttsyō'sō] *ag* superstitious.

superstra'da *sf* ≈ expressway.

supervisio'ne *sf* supervision.

superviso're *sm* supervisor.

supi'no, a *ag* supine; **accettazione** ~**a** (*fig*) blind acceptance.

suppellet'tile *sf* furnishings *pl*.

suppergiù [sōōppārjōō'] *av* more or less, roughly.

suppl. *abbr* (= *supplemento*) supp(l).

supplementa're *ag* extra; (*treno*) relief *cpd*; (*entrate*) additional.

supplemen'to sm supplement.

supplen'te ag temporary; (insegnante) substitute cpd (US), supply cpd (Brit) ♦ sm/f temporary member of staff; substitute teacher.

supplen'za [sōōpplen'tsá] sf: **fare ~ to** do substitute (US) o supply (Brit) teaching.

suppleti'vo, a ag (gen) supplementary; (sessione d'esami) extra.

sup'plica, che sf (preghiera) plea; (domanda scritta) petition, request.

supplica're vt to implore, beseech.

suppliche'vole [sōōpplēkā'vōlā] ag imploring.

suppli're vi: **~ a** to make up for, compensate for.

suppli'zio [sōōpplēt'tsyō] sm torture.

suppon'go, suppo'ni etc vb vedi **supporre**.

suppor're vt to suppose; **supponiamo che ...** let's o just suppose that ....

suppor'to sm (sostegno) support.

supposizio'ne [sōōppōzēttsyō'nā] sf supposition.

suppo'sta sf (MED) suppository.

suppo'sto, a pp di **supporre**.

suppura're vi to suppurate.

supremazi'a [sōōprāmáttsē'á] sf supremacy.

supre'mo, a ag supreme; **S~a Corte (di Cassazione)** Supreme Court.

surclassa're vt to outclass.

surgela're [sōōrjālá'rā] vt to (deep-)freeze.

surgela'to, a [sōōrjālá'tō] ag frozen ♦ smpl: **i ~i** frozen food sg.

surmena'ge [sürmənàzh'] sm (fisico) overwork; (mentale) mental strain; (SPORT) overtraining.

surplus' sm inv (ECON) surplus; **~ di mano-dopera** overmanning.

surrea'le ag surrealistic.

surriscaldamen'to sm (gen, TECN) overheating.

surriscalda're vt to overheat.

surroga'to sm substitute.

suscetti'bile [sōōshāttē'bēlā] ag (sensibile) touchy, sensitive; (soggetto): **~ di miglioramento** that can be improved, open to improvement.

suscettibilità [sōōshāttēbēlētá'] sf touchiness; **urtare la ~ di qn** to hurt sb's feelings.

suscita're [sōōshētá'rā] vt to provoke, arouse.

susi'na sf plum.

susi'no sm plum (tree).

sussegui're vt to follow; **~rsi** vr to follow one another.

sussidia'rio, a ag subsidiary; (treno) relief cpd; (fermata) extra.

sussi'dio sm subsidy; (aiuto) aid; **~i didattici/audiovisivi** teaching/audiovisual aids; **~ di disoccupazione** unemployment benefits (US) o benefit (Brit); **~ per malattia**

sickness benefit.

sussie'go sm haughtiness; **con aria di ~** haughtily.

sussisten'za [sōōssēsten'tsá] sf subsistence.

sussi'stere vi to exist; (essere fondato) to be valid o sound.

sussulta're vi to shudder.

sussul'to sm start.

sussurra're vt, vi to whisper, murmur; **si sussurra che ...** it's rumored (US) o rumoured (Brit) that ....

sussur'ro sm whisper, murmur.

sutu'ra sf (MED) suture.

sutura're vt to stitch up, suture.

suvvi'a escl come on!

SV sigla = Savona.

S.V. abbr vedi **Signoria Vostra**.

svaga're vt (divertire) to amuse; (distrarre): **~ qn** to take sb's mind off things; **~rsi** vr to amuse o.s.; to take one's mind off things.

sva'go, ghi sm (riposo) relaxation; (ricreazione) amusement; (passatempo) pastime.

svaligia're [zválējá'rā] vt to rob, burglarize (US), burgle (Brit).

svaligiato're, tri'ce [zválējátō'rā] sm/f (di banca) robber; (di casa) burglar.

svaluta're vt (ECON) to devalue; (fig) to belittle; **~rsi** vr (ECON) to be devalued.

svalutazio'ne [zválōōtáttsyō'nā] sf devaluation.

svampi'to, a ag absent-minded ♦ sm/f absent-minded person.

svani're vi to disappear, vanish.

svani'to, a ag (fig: persona) absent-minded.

svantaggia'to, a [zvántádjá'tō] ag at a disadvantage.

svantag'gio [zvántád'jō] sm disadvantage; (inconveniente) drawback, disadvantage; **tornerà a suo ~** it will work against you.

svantaggio'so, a [zvántádjō'sō] ag disadvantageous; **è un'offerta ~a per me** it's not in my interest to accept this offer; **è un prezzo ~** it is not an attractive price.

svapora're vi to evaporate.

svapora'to, a ag (bibita) flat.

svaria'to, a ag (vario, diverso) varied; (numeroso) various.

sva'stica, che sf swastika.

svede'se ag Swedish ♦ sm/f Swede ♦ sm (LING) Swedish.

sve'glia [zvāl'yá] sf waking up; (orologio) alarm (clock); **suonare la ~** (MIL) to sound the reveille; **~ telefonica** alarm call.

sveglia're [zvālyá'rā] vt to wake up; (fig) to awaken, arouse; **~rsi** vr to wake up; (fig) to be revived, reawaken.

sve'glio, a [zvāl'yō] ag awake; (fig) alert, quick-witted.

svela're vt to reveal.

sveltez'za [zvāltāt'tsá] sf (gen) speed;

(mentale) quick-wittedness.

svelti're *vt* *(gen)* to speed up; *(procedura)* to streamline.

svel'to, a *ag* *(passo)* quick; *(mente)* quick, alert; *(linea)* slim, slender; **alla ~a** quickly.

sven'dere *vt* to sell off, clear.

sven'dita *sf* *(COMM)* (clearance) sale.

svene'vole *ag* mawkish.

sven'go *etc* *vb* *vedi* **svenire.**

svenimen'to *sm* fainting fit, faint.

sveni're *vi* to faint.

sventa're *vt* to foil, thwart.

sventatez'za [zvāntátāt'tsá] *sf* *(distrazione)* absent-mindedness; *(mancanza di prudenza)* rashness.

sventa'to, a *ag* *(distratto)* scatterbrained; *(imprudente)* rash.

sventola're *vt, vi* to wave, flutter.

sventra're *vt* to disembowel.

sventu'ra *sf* misfortune.

sventura'to, a *ag* unlucky, unfortunate.

svenu'to, a *pp di* **svenire.**

svergogna're [zvārgōnyá'rā] *vt* to shame.

svergogna'to, a [zvārgōnyà'tō] *ag* shameless ♦ *sm/f* shameless person.

sverna're *vi* to spend the winter.

sverrò *etc* *vb* *vedi* **svenire.**

svesti're *vt* to undress; **~rsi** *vr* to get undressed.

Sve'zia [zvet'tsyá] *sf:* **la ~** Sweden.

svezza're [zvāttsà'rā] *vt* to wean.

svia're *vt* to divert; *(fig)* to lead astray; **~rsi** *vr* to go astray.

svicola're *vi* to slip down an alley; *(fig)* to sneak off.

svignar'sela [zvēnyàr'sālá] *vr* to slip away, sneak off.

svilimen'to *sm* debasement.

svili're *vt* to debase.

sviluppa're *vt,* **~rsi** *vr* to develop.

svilup'po *sm* development; *(di industria)* expansion; **in via di ~** in the process of development; **paesi in via di ~** developing countries.

svincola're *vt* to free, release; *(merce)* to clear.

svin'colo *sm* *(COMM)* clearance; *(stradale)* expressway *(US)* *o* motorway *(Brit)* intersection.

sviscera're [zvēshārá'rā] *vt* *(fig: argomento)* to examine in depth.

sviscera'to, a [zvēshārà'tō] *ag* *(amore, odio)* passionate.

svi'sta *sf* oversight.

svita're *vt* to unscrew.

Sviz'zera [zvēt'tsárá] *sf:* **la ~** Switzerland.

sviz'zero, a [zvēt'tsárō] *ag, sm/f* Swiss.

svogliatez'za [zvōlyátàt'tsá] *sf* listlessness; indolence.

svoglia'to, a [zvōlyà'tō] *ag* listless; *(pigro)* lazy, indolent.

svolazza're [zvōlàttsá'rā] *vi* to flutter.

svol'gere [zvol'jārā] *vt* to unwind; *(srotolare)* to unroll; *(fig: argomento)* to develop; *(: piano, programma)* to carry out; **~rsi** *vr* to unwind; to unroll; *(fig: aver luogo)* to take place; *(: procedere)* to go on; **tutto si è svolto secondo i piani** everything went according to plan.

svolgimen'to [zvōljēmān'tō] *sm* development; carrying out; *(andamento)* course.

svol'si *etc* *vb* *vedi* **svolgere.**

svol'ta *sf* *(atto)* turning *q*; *(curva)* turn, bend; *(fig)* turning-point; **essere ad una ~ nella propria vita** to be at a crossroads in one's life.

svolta're *vi* to turn.

svol'to, a *pp di* **svolgere.**

svuota're *vt* to empty (out).

Swa'ziland [swád'zēländ] *sm:* **lo ~** Swaziland.

Sydney' [sēd'nāē] *sf* Sydney.

T

T, t [tē] *sf o m inv* *(lettera)* T, t; **T come Taranto** ≈ T for Tommy.

T *abbr* = **tabaccheria.**

t *abbr* = **tara; tonnellata.**

TA *sigla* = *Taranto.*

tabacca'io, a *sm/f* tobacconist.

tabaccheri'a [tábákkārē'á] *sf* tobacconist's (shop).

tabacchie'ra [tábákkye'rà] *sf* snuffbox.

tabac'co, chi *sm* tobacco.

tabel'la *sf* *(tavola)* table; *(elenco)* list; **~ di marcia** schedule; **~ dei prezzi** price list.

tabello'ne *sm* *(per pubblicità)* billboard; *(per informazioni)* bulletin board *(: in stazione)* timetable board.

taberna'colo *sm* tabernacle.

tabù *ag, sm inv* taboo.

ta'bula ra'sa *sf* tabula rasa; **fare ~** *(fig)* to make a clean sweep.

tabula're *vt* to tabulate.

tabula'to *sm* *(INFORM)* printout.

tabulato're *sm* tabulator.

TAC *sigla f* *(MED:* = *Tomografia Assiale Computerizzata)* CAT.

tac'ca, che *sf* notch, nick; **di mezza ~** *(fig)* mediocre.

taccagneri'a [tàkkànyārē'á] *sf* meanness, stinginess.

tacca'gno, a [tàkkán'yō] *ag* mean, stingy.

taccheg'gio [tàkkàd'jō] *sm* shoplifting.

tacchi'no [tàkkē'nō] *sm* turkey.

tac'cia, ce [tàch'chà] *sf* bad reputation.

taccia're [tàchá'rā] *vt*: ~ **qn di** (*vigliaccheria* ▸ *etc*) to accuse sb of.

tac'cio *etc* [tàch'chō] *vb vedi* **tacere**.

tac'co, chi *sm* heel.

taccui'no *sm* notebook.

tace're [tàchà'rā] *vi* to be silent *o* quiet; (*smettere di parlare*) to fall silent ♦ *vt* to keep to oneself, say nothing about; **far ~ qn** to make sb be quiet; (*fig*) to silence sb; **mettere a ~ qc** to hush sth up.

tachi'metro [tàkē'màtrō] *sm* speedometer.

ta'cito, a [tà'chētō] *ag* silent; (*sottinteso*) tacit, unspoken.

tacitur'no, a [tàchētōōr'nō] *ag* taciturn.

taciu'to, a [tàchōō'tō] *pp di* **tacere**.

tac'qui *etc vb vedi* **tacere**.

tafa'no *sm* horsefly.

tafferu'glio [tàffàrōōl'yō] *sm* brawl, scuffle.

taffettà *sm* taffeta.

ta'glia [tàl'yà] *sf* (*statura*) height; (*misura*) size; (*riscatto*) ransom; (*ricompensa*) reward; **~e forti** (*ABBIGLIAMENTO*) outsize.

tagliabos'chi [tàlyàbo'skē] *sm inv* woodcutter.

tagliacar'te [tàlyàkàr'tā] *sm inv* paperknife.

tagliale'gna [tàlyàlàn'yà] *sm inv* woodcutter.

taglian'do [tàlyàn'dō] *sm* coupon.

taglia're [tàlyà'rā] *vt* to cut; (*recidere, interrompere*) to cut off; (*intersecare*) to cut across, intersect; (*carne*) to carve; (*vini*) to blend ♦ *vi* to cut; (*prendere una scorciatoia*) to take a short-cut; **~ la strada a qn** to cut across in front of sb; **~ corto** (*fig*) to cut short.

tagliatel'le [tàlyàtel'lā] *sfpl* tagliatelle *pl*.

taglia'to, a [tàlyà'tō] *ag*: **essere ~ per qc** (*fig*) to be cut out for sth.

tagliatri'ce [tàlyàtrē'chà] *sf* (*TECN*) cutter.

tagliaun'ghie [tàlyàōōn'gyà] *sm inv* nail clippers *pl*.

taglieggia're [tàlyàdjà'rā] *vt* to exact a tribute from.

taglien'te [tàlyen'tā] *ag* sharp.

taglie're [tàlye'rā] *sm* chopping board; (*per il pane*) bread board.

ta'glio [tàl'yō] *sm* cutting *q*; cut; (*parte tagliente*) cutting edge; (*di abito*) cut; (*di stoffa: lunghezza*) length; (*di vini*) blending; **di ~** on edge, edgeways; **banconote di piccolo/grosso ~** notes of small/large denomination.

taglio'la [tàlyo'là] *sf* trap, snare.

taglio'ne [tàlyō'nā] *sm*: **la legge del ~** the concept of an eye for an eye and a tooth for a tooth.

tagliuzza're [tàlyōōttsà'rā] *vt* to cut into small pieces.

Tahi'ti [tàē'tē] *sf* Tahiti.

tailande'se *ag, sm/f, sm* Thai.

Tailan'dia *sf*: **la ~** Thailand.

taille'ur [tàyēēr'] *sm inv* lady's suit.

Taiwan' [tàēwàn'] *sm*: **il ~** Taiwan.

ta'lamo *sm* (*poetico*) marriage bed.

tal'co *sm* talcum powder.

ta'le *det* such; (*intensivo*): **un ~/~i** ... such (a)/such ... ♦ *pronome* (*questa, quella persona già menzionata*) the one, the person; (*indefinito*): **un(una) ~** someone; **il ~ giorno alla ~ ora** on such and such a day at such and such a time; **~ quale: il tuo vestito è ~ quale il mio** your dress is just *o* exactly like mine; **quel/quella ~** that person, that man/woman; **il tal dei ~i** what's-his-name.

talen'to *sm* talent.

talisma'no *sm* talisman.

tallona're *vt* to pursue; **~ il pallone** (*CALCIO, RUGBY*) to heel the ball.

tallonci'no [tàllōnchē'nō] *sm* stub; **~ del prezzo** (*di medicinali*) tear-off tag.

tallo'ne *sm* heel.

talmen'te *av* so.

talo'ra *av* = **talvolta**.

tal'pa *sf* (*ZOOL*) mole.

talvol'ta *av* sometimes, at times.

tamburel'lo *sm* tambourine.

tamburi'no *sm* drummer boy.

tambu'ro *sm* drum; **freni a ~** drum brakes; **pistola a ~** revolver; **a ~ battente** (*fig*) immediately, at once.

Tami'gi [tàmē'jē] *sm*: **il ~** the Thames.

tamponamen'to *sm* (*AUT*) collision; **~ a catena** pile-up.

tampona're *vt* (*otturare*) to plug; (*urtare: macchina*) to crash *o* ram into.

tampo'ne *sm* (*MED*) wad, pad; (*per timbri*) ink-pad; (*respingente*) buffer; **~ assorbente** tampon.

ta'na *sf* lair, den; (*fig*) den, hideout.

tan'fo *sm* (*di muffa*) musty smell; (*puzza*) stench.

tangen'te [tànjen'tà] *ag* (*MAT*): **~ a** tangential to ♦ *sf* tangent; (*quota*) share; (*denaro estorto*) rake-off (*fam*), cut.

tangenzia'le [tànjàntsyà'là] *sf* (*strada*) bypass.

Tan'geri [tàn'jàrē] *sf* Tangiers.

tangi'bile [tànjē'bēlà] *ag* tangible.

tan'go, ghi *sm* tango.

ta'nica, che *sf* jerry can.

tanni'no *sm* tannin.

tanti'no: un ~ *av* a little, a bit.

tan'to, a *det* (*pane, acqua, soldi*) so much; (*persone, libri*) so many ♦ *pronome* so much (*o* many) ♦ *av* (*con ag, av*) so; (*con vb*) so much, such a lot; (: *così a lungo*) so long; **due volte ~** twice as much; **~ ... quanto:** **ho ~i libri quanti (ne hanno) loro** I have as many books as they have *o* as them; **conosco ~ Carlo quanto suo padre** I know both Carlo

and his father; **è ~ bella quanto buona** she
is as beautiful as she is good; **~ più ... ~ più**
the more ... the more; **~ ... da** so ... as; **un
~: costa un ~ al metro** it costs so much per
metre; **guardare con ~ d'occhi** to gaze
wide-eyed at; **~ per cambiare** just for a
change; **una volta ~** just once; **~ è inutile**
in any case it's useless; **~ .vale che ...** you
may *o* might as well ...; **di ~ in ~, ogni ~**
every so often.

Tanzani'a [tándzánč'à] *sf*: **la ~** Tanzania.

tapio'ca *sf* tapioca.

tap'pa *sf* (*luogo di sosta, fermata*) stop, halt;
(*parte di un percorso*) stage, leg; (*SPORT*)
lap; **a ~e** in stages; **bruciare le ~e** (*fig*) to
be a whizz kid.

tappabu'chi [táppáboo'kē] *sm inv* stopgap;
fare da ~ to act as a stopgap.

tappa're *vt* to plug, stop up; (*bottiglia*) to
cork.

tapparel'la *sf* roller shutter.

tappe'to *sm* carpet; (*anche:* **tappetino**) rug;
(*di tavolo*) cloth; (*SPORT*): **andare al ~** to go
down for the count; **mettere sul ~** (*fig*) to
bring up for discussion.

tappezza're [táppättsà'rā] *vt* (*con carta*) to paper; (*rivestire*): **~ qc (di)** to cover sth
(with).

tappezzeri'a [táppättsārč'à] *sf* (*arredamento*)
soft furnishings *pl*; (*carta da parati*) wall
covering; (*di automobile*) upholstery; **far da
~** (*fig*) to be a wallflower.

tappezzie're [táppättsyc'rā] *sm* upholsterer.

tap'po *sm* stopper; (*in sughero*) cork; **~ a corona** bottle top; **~ a vite** screw top.

TAR *sigla m* = *Tribunale Amministrativo Regionale.*

ta'ra *sf* (*peso*) tare; (*MED*) hereditary defect;
(*difetto*) flaw.

taran'tola *sf* tarantula.

tara're *vt* (*COMM*) to tare; (*TECN*) to calibrate.

tara'to, a *ag* (*COMM*) tared; (*MED*) with a
hereditary defect.

taratu'ra *sf* (*COMM*) taring; (*TECN*) calibra-
tion.

tarchia'to, a [tárkyá'tō] *ag* stocky, thickset.

tarda're *vi* to be late ♦ *vt* to delay; **~ a fare**
to delay doing.

tar'di *av* late; **più ~** later (on); **al più ~** at
the latest; **sul ~** (*verso sera*) late in the day;
far ~ to be late; (*restare alzato*) to stay up
late.

tardi'vo, a *ag* (*primavera*) late; (*rimedio*) belated, tardy; (*fig: bambino*) retarded.

tar'do, a *ag* (*lento, fig: ottuso*) slow; (*tempo:
avanzato*) late.

tardo'na *sf* (*peg*): **essere una ~** to be mutton
dressed as lamb.

tar'ga, ghe *sf* plate; (*AUT*) license (*US*) *o*

number (*Brit*) plate.

targa're *vt* (*AUT*) to register.

tariff'fa *sf* (*gen*) rate, tariff; (*di trasporti*)
fare; (*elenco*) price list; tariff; **la ~ in vigore** the going rate; **~ normale/ridotta**
standard/reduced rate; (*su mezzi di trasporto*) full/concessionary fare; **~ salariale**
wage rate; **~ unica** flat rate; **~e doganali**
customs rates *o* tariff; **~e postali/telefoniche**
postal/telephone charges.

tariffa'rio, ii *ag*: **aumento ~** increase in
charges *o* rates ♦ *sm* tariff, table of charges.

tar'lo *sm* woodworm.

tar'ma *sf* moth.

tarmici'da, i [tármēchč'dá] *ag, sm* moth-killer.

taroc'co, chi *sm* tarot card; **~chi** *smpl* (*gioco*) tarot *sg*.

tarpa're *vt* (*fig*): **~ le ali a qn** to clip sb's
wings.

tartaglia're [tártályá'rā] *vi* to stutter,
stammer.

tar'taro, a *ag, sm* (*in tutti i sensi*) tartar.

tartaru'ga, ghe *sf* tortoise; (*di mare*) turtle;
(*materiale*) tortoiseshell.

tartassa're *vt* (*fam*): **~ qn** to give sb the
works; **~ qn a un esame** to give sb a grill-
ing at an exam.

tarti'na *sf* canapé.

tartu'fo *sm* (*BOT*) truffle.

ta'sca, sche *sf* pocket; **da ~** pocket *cpd*; **fare i
conti in ~ a qn** (*fig*) to meddle in sb's
affairs.

tasca'bile *ag* (*libro*) pocket *cpd*.

tascapa'ne *sm* haversack.

taschi'no [táskē'nō] *sm* breast pocket.

Tasma'nia *sf*: **la ~** Tasmania.

tas'sa *sf* (*imposta*) tax; (*doganale*) duty; (*per
iscrizione: a scuola etc*) fee; **~ di
circolazione/di soggiorno** road/tourist tax.

tassa'metro *sm* taximeter.

tassa're *vt* to tax; to levy a duty on.

tassati'vo, a *ag* peremptory.

tassazio'ne [tássáttsyō'nā] *sf* taxation;
soggetto a ~ taxable.

tassel'lo *sm* (*di legno, pietra*) plug;
(*assaggio*) wedge.

tassi *sm inv* = **taxi**.

tassi'sta, i, e *sm/f* taxi driver.

tas'so *sm* (*di natalità, d'interesse etc*) rate;
(*BOT*) yew; (*ZOOL*) badger; **~ di cambio/
d'interesse** rate of exchange/interest; **~ di
crescita** growth rate.

tasta're *vt* to feel; **~ il terreno** (*fig*) to see
how the land lies.

tastie'ra *sf* keyboard.

tastieri'no *sm*: **~ numerico** numeric keypad.

ta'sto *sm* key; (*tatto*) touch, feel; **toccare un
~ delicato** (*fig*) to touch on a delicate subject; **toccare il ~ giusto** (*fig*) to strike the
right note; **~ funzione** (*INFORM*) function

key; ~ **delle maiuscole** (*su macchina da scrivere etc*) shift key.

tasto'ni *av*: **procedere (a)** ~ to grope one's way forward.

ta'ta *sf* (*linguaggio infantile*) nanny.

tat'tico, a, ci, che *ag* tactical ♦ *sf* tactics *pl*.

tat'to *sm* (*senso*) touch; (*fig*) tact; **duro al** ~ hard to the touch; **aver** ~ to be tactful, have tact.

tatuag'gio [tátōōád'jō] *sm* tattooing; (*disegno*) tattoo.

tatua're *vt* to tattoo.

taver'na *sf* (*osteria*) tavern.

ta'vola *sf* table; (*asse*) plank, board; (*lastra*) tablet; (*quadro*) panel (painting); (*illustrazione*) plate; ~ **calda** snack bar; ~ **pieghevole** folding table.

tavola'ta *sf* company at table.

tavola'to *sm* boarding; (*pavimento*) wooden floor.

tavolet'ta *sf* tablet, bar; **a** ~ (*AUT*) flat out.

tavoli'no *sm* small table; (*scrivania*) desk; ~ **da tè/gioco** coffee/card table; **mettersi a** ~ to get down to work; **decidere qc a** ~ (*fig*) to decide sth on a theoretical level.

ta'volo *sm* table; ~ **da disegno** drafting table (*US*), drawing board (*Brit*); ~ **da lavoro** desk; (*TECN*) workbench; ~ **operatorio** (*MED*) operating table.

tavoloz'za [tàvōlot'tsá] *sf* (*ARTE*) palette.

ta'xi *sm inv* taxi.

taz'za [tàt'tsá] *sf* cup; ~ **da caffè/tè** coffee/tea cup; **una** ~ **di caffè/tè** a cup of coffee/tea.

tazzi'na [táttsē'ná] *sf* coffee cup.

TBC *abbr f* (= *tubercolosi*) TB.

TCI *sigla m* = *Touring Club Italiano*.

TE *sigla* = *Teramo*.

te *pronome* (*soggetto: in forme comparative, oggetto*) you.

tè *sm inv* tea; (*trattenimento*) tea party.

teatra'le *ag* theatrical.

tea'tro *sm* theater (*US*), theatre (*Brit*); ~ **comico** comedy; ~ **di posa** movie (*US*) *o* film (*Brit*) studio.

tec'nico, a, ci, che *ag* technical ♦ *sm/f* technician ♦ *sf* technique; (*tecnologia*) technology.

tecnologi'a [tàknōlōjē'á] *sf* technology; **alta** ~ high technology, hi-tech.

tecnolo'gico, a, ci, che [tàknōlo'jēkō] *ag* technological.

tede'sco, a, schi, sche *ag, sm/f, sm* German; ~ **orientale/occidentale** East/West German.

tedia're *vt* (*infastidire*) to bother, annoy; (*annoiare*) to bore.

te'dio *sm* tedium, boredom.

tedio'so, a *ag* tedious, boring.

tega'me *sm* (*CUC*) pan; **al** ~ fried.

te'glia [tāl'yà] *sf* (*CUC: per dolci*) cake pan (*US*), (baking) tin (*Brit*); (: *per arrosti*) (roasting) pan (*US*) *o* tin (*Brit*).

te'gola *sf* tile.

Tehran' *sf* Tehran.

teie'ra *sf* teapot.

tel. *abbr* (= *telefono*) tel.

te'la *sf* (*tessuto*) cloth; (*per vele, quadri*) canvas; (*dipinto*) canvas, painting; **di** ~ (*calzoni*) (heavy) cotton *cpd*; (*scarpe, borsa*) canvas *cpd*; ~ **cerata** oilcloth; ~ **di ragno** spider's web.

tela'io *sm* (*apparecchio*) loom; (*struttura*) frame.

Tel Aviv' *sf* Tel Aviv.

teleabbona'to *sm* television license holder.

teleca'mera *sf* television camera.

telecomanda're *vt* to operate by remote control.

telecoman'do *sm* remote control; (*dispositivo*) remote-control device.

telecomunicazio'ni [tālākōmōōnēkáttsyō'nē] *sfpl* telecommunications.

telecro'naca, che *sf* television report.

telecroni'sta, i, e *sm/f* (*television*) commentator.

telefe'rica, che *sf* cableway.

telefilm' *sm inv* television film.

telefona're *vi* to telephone, ring; (*fare una chiamata*) to make a phone call ♦ *vt* to telephone; ~ **a qn** to telephone sb, phone *o* ring *o* call sb (up).

telefona'ta *sf* (telephone) call; ~ **urbana/interurbana** local/long-distance call; ~ **a carico del destinatario** collect (*US*) *o* reverse charge (*Brit*) call; ~ **con preavviso** person-to-person call.

telefonicamen'te *av* by (tele)phone.

telefo'nico, a, ci, che *ag* (tele)phone *cpd*.

telefoni'sta, i, e *sm/f* telephone operator; (*d'impresa*) switchboard operator.

tele'fono *sm* telephone; **avere il** ~ to be on the (tele)phone; ~ **a gettoni** ≈ pay phone; ~ **interno** internal phone; ~ **pubblico** public phone.

telegiorna'le [tālājōrná'lā] *sm* television news (program).

telegrafa're *vt, vi* to telegraph, cable.

telegrafi'a *sf* telegraphy.

telegra'fico, a, ci, che *ag* telegraph *cpd*, telegraphic.

telegrafi'sta, i, e *sm/f* telegraphist, telegraph operator.

tele'grafo *sm* telegraph; (*ufficio*) telegraph office.

telegram'ma, i *sm* telegram.

telema'tica *sf* data transmission; data communications.

teleobietti'vo *sm* telephoto lens *sg*.

telepati'a *sf* telepathy.

telescher'mo [tālāsker'mō] *sm* television screen.

telesco'pio *sm* telescope.

telescriven'te *sf* teletypewriter (*US*), tele-printer (*Brit*).

teleseletti'vo, a *ag*: **prefisso** ~ area code (*US*), dialling code (*Brit*).

teleselezio'ne [tālāsālāttsyō'nā] *sf* direct dialling.

telespettato're, tri'ce *sm/f* (television) viewer.

teleta'xe ® [tālātáks'] *sm inv* telephone meter.

televi'deo *sm* videotext service.

televisio'ne *sf* television.

televiso're *sm* television set.

te'lex *sm inv* telex.

te'lo *sm* length of cloth.

telo'ne *sm* (*per merci etc*) tarpaulin; (*sipario*) drop curtain.

te'ma, i *sm* theme; (*INS*) essay, composition.

tema'tica *sf* basic themes *pl*.

temera'rio, a *ag* rash, reckless.

teme're *vt* to fear, be afraid of; (*essere sensibile a: freddo, calore*) to be sensitive to ♦ *vi* to be afraid; (*essere preoccupato*): ~ **per** to worry about, fear for; ~ **di/che** to be afraid of/that.

temperamati'te *sm inv* pencil sharpener.

temperamen'to *sm* temperament.

temperan'te *ag* moderate.

tempera're *vt* (*aguzzare*) to sharpen; (*fig*) to moderate, control, temper.

tempera'to, a *ag* moderate, temperate; (*clima*) temperate.

temperatu'ra *sf* temperature; ~ **ambiente** room temperature.

temperi'no *sm* penknife.

tempe'sta *sf* storm; ~ **di sabbia/neve** sand/snowstorm.

tempesta're *vt* (*percuotere*): ~ **qn di colpi** to rain blows on sb; (*bombardare*): ~ **qn di domande** to bombard sb with questions; (*ornare*) to stud.

tempestività *sf* timeliness.

tempesti'vo, a *ag* timely.

tempesto'so, a *ag* stormy.

tem'pia *sf* (*ANAT*) temple.

tem'pio *sm* (*edificio*) temple.

tempi'smo *sm* sense of timing.

tempi'stiche [tāmpē'stēkā] *sfpl* (*COMM*) time and motion.

tem'po *sm* (*METEOR*) weather; (*cronologico*) time; (*epoca*) time, times *pl*; (*di film, gioco: parte*) part; (*MUS*) time; (: *battuta*) beat; (*LING*) tense; **un** ~ once; **da** ~ for a long time now; ~ **fa** some time ago; **poco** ~ **dopo** not long after; **a** ~ **e luogo** at the right time and place; **ogni cosa a suo** ~ we'll (*o* you'll *etc*) deal with it in due course; **al** ~ **stesso** *o* **a un** ~ at the same time; **per** ~ early; **per qualche** ~ for a while; **trovare il** ~ **di fare qc** to find the time to do sth; **aver fatto il proprio** ~ to have had its (*o* his *etc*)

day; **primo/secondo** ~ (*TEATRO*) first/second part; (*SPORT*) first/second half; **rispettare i** ~**i** to keep to the timetable; **stringere i** ~**i** to speed things up; **con i** ~**i che corrono** these days; **in questi ultimi** ~**i** of late; **ai miei** ~**i** in my day; ~ **di cottura** cooking time; **in** ~ **utile** in due time *o* course; ~**i di esecuzione** (*COMM*) time scale *sg*; ~**i di lavorazione** (*COMM*) throughput time *sg*; ~**i morti** (*COMM*) downtime *sg*, idle time *sg*.

tempora'le *ag* temporal ♦ *sm* (*METEOR*) (thunder)storm.

temporale'sco, a, schi, sche *ag* stormy.

tempora'neo, a *ag* temporary.

temporeggia're [tāmpōrādjá'rā] *vi* to play for time, temporize.

tem'pra *sf* (*TECN*: *atto*) tempering, hardening; (: *effetto*) temper; (*fig*: *costituzione fisica*) constitution; (: *intellettuale*) temperament.

tempra're *vt* to temper.

tena'ce [tānà'chā] *ag* strong, tough; (*fig*) tenacious.

tena'cia [tānà'chà] *sf* tenacity.

tena'glie [tānàl'yā] *sfpl* pincers *pl*.

ten'da *sf* (*riparo*) awning; (*di finestra*) curtain; (*per campeggio etc*) tent.

tendag'gio [tāndád'jō] *sm* drapes *pl* (*US*), curtains *pl*.

tenden'za [tānden'tsà] *sf* tendency; (*orientamento*) trend; **avere** ~ **a** *o* **per qc** to have a bent for sth; ~ **al rialzo/ribasso** (*BORSA*) upward/downward trend.

tendenziosità [tāndāntsyōsētá'] *sf* tendentiousness.

tendenzio'so, a [tāndāntsyō'sō] *ag* tendentious, bias(s)ed.

ten'dere *vt* (*allungare al massimo*) to stretch, draw tight; (*porgere: mano*) to hold out; (*fig*: *trappola*) to lay, set ♦ *vi*: ~ **a qc/a fare** to tend towards sth/to do; **tutti i nostri sforzi sono tesi a** ... all our efforts are geared towards ...; ~ **l'orecchio** to prick up one's ears; **il tempo tende al caldo** the weather is getting hot; **un blu che tende al verde** a greenish blue.

tendi'na *sf* curtain.

ten'dine *sm* tendon, sinew.

tendo'ne *sm* (*da circo*) big top.

tendo'poli *sf inv* (large) camp.

te'nebre *sfpl* darkness *sg*.

tenebro'so, a *ag* dark, gloomy.

tenen'te *sm* lieutenant.

tene're *vt* to hold; (*conservare, mantenere*) to keep; (*ritenere, considerare*) to consider; (*spazio: occupare*) to take up, occupy; (*seguire: strada*) to keep to; (*dare: lezione, conferenza*) to give ♦ *vi* to hold; (*colori*) to be fast; (*dare importanza*): ~ **a** to care about; ~ **a fare** to want to do, be keen to do; ~**rsi**

vr (*stare in una determinata posizione*) to stand; (*stimarsi*) to consider o.s.; (*aggrapparsi*): ~**rsi a** to hold on to; (*attenersi*): ~**rsi a** to stick to; ~ **in gran conto** *o* **considerazione qn** to have a high regard for sb, think highly of sb; ~ **conto di qc** to take sth into consideration; ~ **presente qc** to bear sth in mind; **non ci sono scuse che tengano** I'll take no excuses; ~**rsi per la mano** (*uso reciproco*) to hold hands; ~**rsi in piedi** to stay on one's feet.

tenerez'za [tānārāt'tsà] *sf* tenderness.

te'nero, a *ag* tender; (*pietra, cera, colore*) soft; (*fig*) tender, loving ♦ *sm*: **tra quei due c'è del** ~ there's a romance budding between those two.

ten'go *etc vb vedi* **tenere.**

te'nia *sf* tapeworm.

ten'ni *etc vb vedi* **tenere.**

ten'nis *sm* tennis; ~ **da tavolo** table tennis.

tenni'sta, i, e *sm/f* tennis player.

teno're *sm* (*tono*) tone; (*MUS*) tenor; ~ **di vita** way of life; (*livello*) standard of living.

tensio'ne *sf* tension; **ad alta** ~ (*ELETTR*) high-voltage *cpd*, high-tension *cpd*.

tenta'colo *sm* tentacle.

tenta're *vt* (*indurre*) to tempt; (*provare*): ~ **qc/di fare** to attempt *o* try sth/to do; ~ **la sorte** to try one's luck.

tentati'vo *sm* attempt.

tentazio'ne [tāntáttsyō'nā] *sf* temptation; **aver la** ~ **di fare** to be tempted to do.

tentennamen'to *sm* (*fig*) hesitation, wavering; **dopo molti** ~**i** after much hesitation.

tentenna're *vi* to shake, be unsteady; (*fig*) to hesitate, waver ♦ *vt*: ~ **il capo** to shake one's head.

tento'ni *av*: **andare a** ~ (*anche fig*) to grope one's way.

te'nue *ag* (*sottile*) fine; (*colore*) soft; (*fig*) slender, slight.

tenu'ta *sf* (*capacità*) capacity; (*divisa*) uniform; (*abito*) dress; (*AGR*) estate; **a** ~ **d'aria** airtight; ~ **di strada** roadholding power; **in** ~ **da lavoro** in one's working clothes; **in** ~ **da sci** in a skiing outfit.

teologi'a [tāōlōjē'à] *sf* theology.

teolo'gico, a, ci, che [tāōlo'jēkō] *ag* theological.

teo'logo, gi *sm* theologian.

teore'ma, i *sm* theorem.

teori'a *sf* theory; **in** ~ in theory, theoretically.

teo'rico, a, ci, che *ag* theoretic(al) ♦ *sm* theorist, theoretician; **a livello** ~, **in linea** ~**a** theoretically.

teorizza're [tāōrĕddzà'rā] *vt* to theorize.

te'pido, a *ag* = **tiepido.**

tepo're *sm* warmth.

tep'pa *sf* mob, hooligans *pl*.

teppa'glia [tāppàl'yà] *sf* hooligans *pl*.

teppi'smo *sm* hooliganism.

teppi'sta, i *sm* hooligan.

terape'utico, a, ci, che *ag* therapeutic.

terapi'a *sf* therapy.

terapi'sta, i, e *sm/f* therapist.

tergicristal'lo [tārjĕkrĕstál'lō] *sm* windshield (*US*) *o* windscreen (*Brit*) wiper.

tergiversa're [tārjĕvārsà'rā] *vi* to shilly-shally.

ter'go *sm*: **a** ~ behind; **vedi a** ~ please turn over.

te'rital ® *sm inv* Terylene ®.

terma'le *ag* thermal.

ter'me *sfpl* thermal baths.

ter'mico, a, ci, che *ag* thermal; **centrale** ~**a** thermal power station.

termina'le *ag* (*fase, parte*) final; (*MED*) terminal ♦ *sm* terminal; **tratto** ~ (*di fiume*) lower reaches *pl*.

termina're *vt* to end; (*lavoro*) to finish ♦ *vi* to end.

terminazio'ne [tārmĕnàttsyō'nā] *sf* (*fine*) end; (*LING*) ending; ~**i nervose** (*ANAT*) nerve endings.

ter'mine *sm* term; (*fine, estremità*) end; (*di territorio*) boundary, limit; **fissare un** ~ to set a deadline; **portare a** ~ **qc** to bring sth to a conclusion; **contratto a** ~ (*COMM*) forward contract; **a breve/lungo** ~ short-/long-term; **ai** ~**i di legge** by law; **in altri** ~**i** in other words; **parlare senza mezzi** ~**i** to talk frankly, not to mince one's words.

terminologi'a [tārmĕnōlōjē'à] *sf* terminology.

ter'mite *sf* termite.

termocoper'ta *sf* electric blanket.

termo'metro *sm* thermometer.

termonuclea're *ag* thermonuclear.

ter'mos *sm inv* = **thermos.**

termosifo'ne *sm* radiator; (**riscaldamento a**) ~ central heating.

termo'stato *sm* thermostat.

ter'na *sf* set of three; (*lista di tre nomi*) list of three candidates.

ter'no *sm* (*al lotto etc*) (set of) three winning numbers; **vincere un** ~ **al lotto** (*fig*) to hit the jackpot.

ter'ra *sf* (*gen, ELETTR*) earth; (*sostanza*) soil, earth; (*opposto al mare*) land *q*; (*regione, paese*) land; (*argilla*) clay; ~**e** *sfpl* (*possedimento*) lands, land *sg*; **a o per** ~ (*stato*) on the ground (*o floor*); (*moto*) to the ground, down; **mettere a** ~ (*ELETTR*) to ground (*US*), earth (*Brit*); **essere a** ~ (*fig: depresso*) to be at rock bottom; **via** ~ (*viaggiare*) by land, overland; **strada in** ~ battuta dirt road; ~ **di nessuno** no man's land; **la T**~ **Santa** the Holy Land; ~ **di Siena** sienna; ~ ~ (*fig: persona, argomento*) prosaic, pedestrian.

terracot'ta *sf* terracotta; **vasellame di** ~ earthenware.

terrafer'ma *sf* dry land, terra firma; *(continente)* mainland.

terra'glia [tārrál'yá] *sf* pottery; ~**e** *pl (oggetti)* crockery *sg*, earthenware *sg*.

Terrano'va *sf*: **la** ~ Newfoundland.

terrapie'no *sm* embankment, bank.

terraz'za [tārrát'tsá] *sf*, **terraz'zo** [tārrát'tsō] *sm* terrace.

terremota'to, a *ag (zona)* devastated by an earthquake ♦ *sm/f* earthquake victim.

terremo'to *sm* earthquake.

terre'no, a *ag (vita, beni)* earthly ♦ *sm (suolo, fig)* ground; *(COMM)* land *q*, plot (of land); site; *(SPORT, MIL)* field; **perdere** ~ *(anche fig)* to lose ground; **un** ~ **montuoso** a mountainous terrain; ~ **alluvionale** *(GEO)* alluvial soil.

ter'reo, a *ag (viso, colorito)* wan.

terres'tre *ag (superficie)* of the earth, earth's; *(di terra: battaglia, animale)* land *cpd*; *(REL)* earthly, worldly.

terri'bile *ag* terrible, dreadful.

terric'cio [tārrēch'chō] *sm* soil.

terrie'ro, a *ag*: **proprietà** ~**a** landed property; **proprietario** ~ landowner.

terrifican'te *ag* terrifying.

terri'na *sf (zuppiera)* tureen.

territoria'le *ag* territorial.

territo'rio *sm* territory.

terro'ne, a *sm/f derogatory term used by Northern Italians to describe Southern Italians.*

terro're *sm* terror; **avere il** ~ **di qc** to be terrified of sth.

terrori'smo *sm* terrorism.

terrori'sta, i, e *sm/f* terrorist.

terrorizza're [tārrōrēddzá'rá] *vt* to terrorize.

ter'so, a *ag* clear.

terzet'to [tārtsát'tō] *sm (MUS)* trio, terzetto; *(di persone)* trio.

terzia'rio, a [tārtsya'ryō] *ag (GEO, ECON)* tertiary.

terzi'no [tārtsē'nō] *sm (CALCIO)* fullback, back.

ter'zo, a [ter'tsō] *ag* third ♦ *sm (frazione)* third; *(DIR)* third party ♦ *sf (gen)* third; *(AUT)* third (gear); *(di trasporti)* third class; *(INS: elementare) 3rd year at grade school*; *(: media) third year at high school*; *(: superiore) sixth year at high school*; ~**i** *smpl (altri)* others, other people; **agire per conto di** ~**i** to act on behalf of a third party; **assicurazione contro** ~**i** liability insurance *(US)*, third-party insurance *(Brit)*; **la** ~**a età** old age; **il** ~ **mondo** the Third World; **di terzor'dine** third rate; **la** ~**a pagina** *(STAMPA)* the Arts page.

te'sa *sf* brim; **a larghe** ~**e** wide-brimmed.

tes'chio [tes'kyō] *sm* skull.

te'si *sf inv* thesis; ~ **di laurea** degree thesis.

te'si *etc vb vedi* **tendere**.

te'so, a *pp di* **tendere** ♦ *ag (tirato)* taut, tight; *(fig)* tense.

tesoreri'a *sf* treasury.

tesorie're *sm* treasurer.

teso'ro *sm* treasure; **il Ministero del T~** the Treasury; **far** ~ **dei consigli di qn** to take sb's advice to heart.

tes'sera *sf (documento)* card; *(di abbonato)* commutation *(US)* o season *(Brit)* ticket; *(di giornalista)* pass; **ha la** ~ **del partito** he's a party member.

tessera're *vt (iscrivere)* to give a membership card to.

tessera'to, a *sm/f (di società sportiva etc)* (fully paid-up) member; *(POL)* (card-carrying) member.

tes'sere *vt* to weave; ~ **le lodi di qn** *(fig)* to sing sb's praises.

tes'sile *ag*, *sm* textile.

tessito're, tri'ce *sm/f* weaver.

tessitu'ra *sf* weaving.

tessu'to *sm* fabric, material; *(BIOL)* tissue; *(fig)* web.

te'sta *sf* head; *(di cose: estremità, parte anteriore)* head, front; **5.000 lire a** ~ 5,000 lire apiece o a head o per person; **a** ~ **alta** with one's head held high; **a** ~ **bassa** *(correre)* headlong; *(con aria dimessa)* with head bowed; **di** ~ *ag (vettura etc)* front; **dare alla** ~ to go to one's head; **fare di** ~ **propria** to go one's own way; **in** ~ *(SPORT)* in the lead; **essere in** ~ **alla classifica** *(corridore)* to be number one; *(squadra)* to be at the top of the league table; *(disco)* to be top of the charts, be number one; **essere alla** ~ **di qc** *(società)* to be the head of; *(esercito)* to be at the head of; **tenere** ~ **a qn** *(nemico etc)* to stand up to sb; **una** ~ **d'aglio** a bulb of garlic; ~ **o croce?** heads or tails?; **avere la** ~ **dura** to be stubborn; ~ **di serie** *(TENNIS)* seed, seeded player.

te'sta-co'da *sm inv (AUT)* spin.

testamenta'rio, a *ag (DIR)* testamentary; **le sue disposizioni** ~**e** the provisions of his will.

testamen'to *sm (atto)* will, testament; **l'Antico/il Nuovo T~** *(REL)* the Old/New Testament.

testardag'gine [tāstárdád'jēnā] *sf* stubbornness, obstinacy.

testar'do, a *ag* stubborn, pig-headed.

testa're *vt* to test.

testa'ta *sf (parte anteriore)* head; *(intestazione)* heading; **missile a** ~ **nucleare** missile with a nuclear warhead.

te'ste *sm/f* witness.

testi'colo *sm* testicle.

testie'ra *sf (del letto)* headboard; *(di cavallo)* headpiece.

testimo'ne *sm/f (DIR)* witness; **fare da** ~ **alle**

nozze di qn to be a witness at sb's wedding; ~ oculare eye witness.

testimonian'za [tāstēmōnyán'tsá] *sf* (*atto*) deposition; (*effetto*) evidence; (*fig*: *prova*) proof; **accusare qn di falsa ~** to accuse sb of perjury; **rilasciare una ~** to give evidence.

testimonia're *vt* to testify; (*fig*) to bear witness to, testify to ♦ *vi* to give evidence, testify; ~ **il vero** to tell the truth; ~ **il falso** to perjure o.s.

testi'na *sf* (*di giradischi, registratore*) head.

te'sto *sm* text; **fare ~** (*opera, autore*) to be authoritative; (*fig*: *dichiarazione*) to carry weight.

testua'le *ag* textual; **le sue parole ~i** his (*o* her) actual words.

testug'gine [tāstōōd'jēnā] *sf* tortoise; (*di mare*) turtle.

te'tano *sm* (*MED*) tetanus.

te'tro, a *ag* gloomy.

tet'ta *sf* (*fam*) boob, tit.

tettarel'la *sf* teat.

tet'to *sm* roof; **abbandonare il ~ coniugale** to desert one's family; ~ **a cupola** dome.

tetto'ia *sf* roofing; canopy.

Te'vere *sm*: **il ~** the Tiber.

TG, Tg *abbr m* = **telegiornale**.

ther'mos ® [ter'mōs] *sm inv* Thermos ® bottle (*US*) *o* flask (*Brit*).

thril'ler [thrē'lə], **thril'ling** [thrē'lēng] *sm inv* thriller.

ti *pronome* (*dav lo, la, li, le, ne diventa* **te**) (*oggetto*) you; (*complemento di termine*) (to) you; (*riflessivo*) yourself; ~ **aiuto?** can I give you a hand?; **te lo ha dato?** did he give it to you?; ~ **sei lavato?** have you washed?

tia'ra *sf* (*REL*) tiara.

Ti'bet *sm*: **il ~** Tibet.

tibeta'no, a *ag, sm/f* Tibetan.

ti'bia *sf* tibia, shinbone.

tic *sm inv* tic, (nervous) twitch; (*fig*) mannerism.

ticchetti'o [tēkkāttē'ō] *sm* (*di macchina da scrivere*) clatter; (*di orologio*) ticking; (*della pioggia*) patter.

tic'chio [tēk'kyō] *sm* (*ghiribizzo*) whim; (*tic*) tic, (nervous) twitch.

tic'ket *sm inv* (*MED*) prescription charge (*Brit*).

tie'ne *etc vb vedi* **tenere**.

tie'pido, a *ag* lukewarm, tepid.

tifa're *vi*: ~ **per** to be a fan of; (*parteggiare*) to side with.

ti'fo *sm* (*MED*) typhus; (*fig*): **fare il ~ per** to be a fan of.

tifoide'a *sf* typhoid.

tifo'ne *sm* typhoon.

tifo'so, a *sm/f* (*SPORT etc*) fan.

tight [tá'ēt] *sm inv* morning suit.

ti'glio [tēl'yō] *sm* lime (tree), linden (tree).

ti'gna [tēn'yá] *sf* (*MED*) ringworm.

tigra'to, a *ag* striped.

ti'gre *sf* tiger.

tilt *sm*: **andare in ~** (*fig*) to go haywire.

timbal'lo *sm* (*strumento*) kettledrum; (*CUC*) timbale.

timbra're *vt* to stamp; (*annullare*: *francobolli*) to postmark; ~ **il cartellino** to clock in.

tim'bro *sm* stamp; (*MUS*) timbre, tone.

timidez'za [tēmēdāt'tsá] *sf* shyness, timidity.

ti'mido, a *ag* shy, timid.

ti'mo *sm* thyme.

timo'ne *sm* (*NAUT*) rudder.

timonie're *sm* helmsman.

timora'to, a *ag* conscientious; ~ **di Dio** Godfearing.

timo're *sm* (*paura*) fear; (*rispetto*) awe; **avere ~ di qc/qn** (*paura*) to be afraid of sth/sb.

timoro'so, a *ag* timid, timorous.

tim'pano *sm* (*ANAT*) eardrum; (*MUS*): ~**i** kettledrums, timpani.

tinel'lo *sm* small dining room.

tin'gere [tēn'jārā] *vt* to dye.

ti'no *sm* vat.

tinoz'za [tēnot'tsá] *sf* tub.

tin'si *etc vb vedi* **tingere**.

tin'ta *sf* (*materia colorante*) dye; (*colore*) color (*US*), colour (*Brit*), shade.

tintarel'la *sf* (*fam*) (sun)tan.

tintinna're *vi* to tinkle.

tintin'nio *sm* tinkling.

tin'to, a *pp di* **tingere**.

tintori'a *sf* (*officina*) dyeworks *sg*; (*lavasecco*) dry cleaner's (shop).

tintu'ra *sf* (*operazione*) dyeing; (*colorante*) dye; ~ **di iodio** tincture of iodine.

ti'pico, a, ci, che *ag* typical.

ti'po *sm* type; (*genere*) kind, type; (*fam*) chap, fellow; **vestiti di tutti i ~i** all kinds of clothes; **sul ~ di questo** of this sort; **sei un bel ~!** you're a fine one!

tipografi'a *sf* typography.

tipogra'fico, a, ci, che *ag* typographic(al).

tipo'grafo *sm* typographer.

ti'ra e mol'la *sm inv* tug-of-war.

tirag'gio [tērád'jō] *sm* (*di camino etc*) draft (*US*), draught (*Brit*).

Tira'na *sf* Tirana.

tiranneggia're [tērānnādjá'rā] *vt* to tyrannize.

tiranni'a *sf* tyranny.

tiran'no, a *ag* tyrannical ♦ *sm* tyrant.

tiran'te *sm* (*NAUT, di tenda etc*) guy; (*EDIL*) brace.

tirapie'di *sm/f inv* hanger-on.

tira're *vt* (*gen*) to pull; (*estrarre*): ~ **qc da** to take *o* pull sth out of; to get sth out of; to extract sth from; (*chiudere*: *tenda etc*) to draw, pull; (*tracciare, disegnare*) to draw, trace; (*lanciare*: *sasso, palla*) to throw; (*stampare*) to print; (*pistola, freccia*) to fire

♦ *vi* (*pipa, camino*) to draw; (*vento*) to blow; (*abito*) to be tight; (*fare fuoco*) to fire; (*fare del tiro, CALCIO*) to shoot; ~ **qn da parte** to take *o* draw sb aside; ~ **un sospiro (di sollievo)** to heave a sigh (of relief); ~ **a indovinare** to take a guess; ~ **sul prezzo** to bargain; ~ **avanti** *vi* to struggle on ♦ *vt* (*famiglia*) to provide for; (*ditta*) to look after; ~ **fuori** to take out, pull out; ~ **giù** to pull down; ~ **su** to pull up; (*capelli*) to put up; (*fig: bambino*) to bring up; ~**rsi indietro** to move back; (*fig*) to back out; ~**rsi su** to pull o.s. up; (*fig*) to cheer o.s. up.

tirato're *sm* gunman; **un buon** ~ a good shot; ~ **scelto** marksman.

tiratu'ra *sf* (*azione*) printing; (*di libro*) (print) run; (*di giornale*) circulation.

tirchieri'a [tĕrkyārḗ'à] *sf* meanness, stinginess.

tir'chio, a [tĕr'kyō] *ag* mean, stingy.

tirite'ra *sf* drivel, hot air.

ti'ro *sm* shooting *q*; firing *q*; (*colpo, sparo*) shot; (*di palla: lancio*) throwing *q*; throw; (*fig*) trick; **essere a** ~ to be in range; **giocare un brutto** ~ *o* **un** ~**mancino a qn** to play a dirty trick on s.b.; **cavallo da** ~ draft (*US*) *o* draught (*Brit*) horse; ~ **a segno** target shooting; (*luogo*) shooting range.

tirocinan'te [tĕrōchēnán'tā] *ag, sm/f* apprentice (*cpd*); trainee (*cpd*).

tiroci'nio [tĕrōchē'nyō] *sm* apprenticeship; (*professionale*) training.

tiro'ide *sf* thyroid (gland).

tirole'se *ag, sm/f* Tyrolean, Tyrolese *inv*.

Tiro'lo *sm*: **il** ~ the Tyrol.

tirren'nico, a, ci, che *ag* Tyrrhenian.

Tirre'no *sm*: **il (mar)** ~ the Tyrrhenian Sea.

tisa'na *sf* herb tea.

ti'si *sf* (*MED*) consumption.

ti'sico, a, ci, che *ag* (*MED*) consumptive; (*fig: gracile*) frail ♦ *sm/f* consumptive (person).

tita'nico, a, ci, che *ag* gigantic, enormous.

tita'no *sm* (*MITOLOGIA, fig*) titan.

titola're *ag* appointed; (*sovrano*) titular ♦ *sm/f* incumbent; (*proprietario*) owner; (*CALCIO*) regular player.

titola'to, a *ag* (*persona*) titled.

ti'tolo *sm* title; (*di giornale*) headline; (*diploma*) qualification; (*COMM*) security; (*: azione*) share; **a che** ~**?** for what reason?; **a** ~ **di amicizia** out of friendship; **a** ~ **di cronaca** for your information; **a** ~ **di premio** as a prize; ~ **di credito** share; ~ **obbligazionario** bond; ~ **al portatore** bearer bond; ~ **di proprietà** title deed; ~**i di stato** government securities; ~**i di testa** (*CINEMA*) credits.

tituban'te *ag* hesitant, irresolute.

tivù *sf inv* (*fam*) TV.

ti'zio, a [tĕt'tsyō] *sm/f* fellow, chap.

tizzo'ne [tĕttsō'nā] *sm* brand.

T.M.G. *abbr* (= *tempo medio di Greenwich*)

GMT.

TN *sigla* = *Trento*.

TNT *sigla m* (= *trinitrotoluolo*) TNT.

TO *sigla* = *Torino*.

toast [tōst] *sm inv* toasted sandwich.

toccan'te *ag* touching.

tocca're *vt* to touch; (*tastare*) to feel; (*fig: riguardare*) to concern; (*: commuovere*) to touch, move; (*: pungere*) to hurt, wound; (*: far cenno a: argomento*) to touch on, mention ♦ *vi*: ~ **a** (*accadere*) to happen to; (*spettare*) to be up to; **tocca a te difenderci** it's up to you to defend us; **a chi tocca?** whose turn is it?; **mi toccò pagare** I had to pay; ~ **il fondo** (*in acqua*) to touch the bottom; (*fig*) to touch rock bottom; ~ **con mano** (*fig*) to find out for o.s.; ~ **qn sul vivo** to cut sb to the quick.

toccasa'na *sm inv* cure-all, panacea.

tocche'rò *etc* [tōkkāro'] *vb vedi* **toccare**.

toc'co, chi *sm* touch; (*ARTE*) stroke, touch.

to'ga, ghe *sf* toga; (*di magistrato, professore*) gown.

to'gliere [tol'yārā] *vt* (*rimuovere*) to take away (*o* off), remove; (*riprendere, non concedere più*) to take away, remove; (*MAT*) to take away, subtract; (*liberare*) to free; ~ **qc a qn** to take sth (away) from sb; **ciò non toglie che** ... nevertheless ..., be that as it may ...; ~**rsi il cappello** to take off one's hat.

To'go *sm*: **il** ~ Togo.

toilette [twålet'] *sf inv* (*gabinetto*) toilet; (*cosmesi*) make-up; (*abbigliamento*) gown, dress; (*mobile*) dressing table; **fare** ~ to get made up, make o.s. beautiful.

Tok'yo *sf* Tokyo.

tolet'ta *sf* = **toilette**.

tol'go *etc vb vedi* **togliere**.

tolleran'te *ag* tolerant.

tolleran'za [tōllārán'tsá] *sf* tolerance; **casa di** ~ brothel.

tollera're *vt* to tolerate; **non tollero repliche** I won't stand for objections; **non sono tollerati i ritardi** lateness will not be tolerated.

Tolo'sa *sf* Toulouse.

tol'si *etc vb vedi* **togliere**.

tol'to, a *pp di* **togliere**.

toma'ia *sf* (*di scarpa*) upper.

tom'ba *sf* tomb.

tomba'le *ag*: **pietra** ~ tombstone, gravestone.

tombi'no *sm* manhole cover.

tom'bola *sf* (*gioco*) tombola; (*ruzzolone*) tumble.

to'mo *sm* volume.

to'naca, che *sf* (*REL*) habit.

tona're *vi* = **tuonare**.

ton'do, a *ag* round.

ton'fo *sm* splash; (*rumore sordo*) thud; (*caduta*): **fare un** ~ to take a tumble.

to'nico, a, ci, che *ag* tonic ♦ *sm* tonic;

(*cosmetico*) toner.

tonifican'te *ag* invigorating, bracing.

tonifica're *vt* (*muscoli, pelle*) to tone up; (*irrobustire*) to invigorate, brace.

tonna'ra *sf* tuna-fishing nets *pl*.

tonnellag'gio [tōnnāllád'jō] *sm* (*NAUT*) tonnage.

tonnella'ta *sf* ton.

ton'no *sm* tuna (fish).

to'no *sm* (*gen, MUS*) tone; (*di colore*) shade, tone; **rispondere a ~** (*a proposito*) to answer to the point; (*nello stesso modo*) to answer in kind; (*per le rime*) to answer back.

tonsil'la *sf* tonsil.

tonsilli'te *sf* tonsillitis.

tonsu'ra *sf* tonsure.

ton'to, a *ag* dull, stupid ♦ *sm/f* blockhead, dunce; **fare il finto ~** to play dumb.

topa'ia *sf* (*di topo*) mousehole; (*di ratto*) rat's nest; (*fig: casa etc*) hovel, dump.

topa'zio [tōpát'tsyō] *sm* topaz.

topici'da, i [tōpēchē'dá] *sm* rat poison.

to'pless [to'plēs] *sm inv* topless bathing costume.

to'po *sm* mouse; **~ d'albergo** (*fig*) hotel thief; **~ di biblioteca** (*fig*) bookworm.

topografi'a *sf* topography.

top'pa *sf* (*serratura*) keyhole; (*pezza*) patch.

tora'ce [tōrá'chā] *sm* chest.

tor'ba *sf* peat.

tor'bido, a *ag* (*liquido*) cloudy; (: *fiume*) muddy; (*fig*) dark; troubled ♦ *sm*: **pescare nel ~** (*fig*) to fish in troubled waters.

tor'cere [tor'chārā] *vt* to twist; (*biancheria*) to wring (out); **~rsi** *vr* to twist, writhe; **dare del filo da ~ a qn** to make life o things difficult for sb.

torchia're [tōrkyá'rā] *vt* to press.

tor'chio [tor'kyō] *sm* press; **mettere qn sotto il ~** (*fig fam: interrogare*) to grill sb; **~ tipografico** printing press.

tor'cia, ce [tor'chá] *sf* torch; **~ elettrica** flashlight (*US*), torch (*Brit*).

torcicol'lo [tōrchēkol'lō] *sm* stiff neck.

tor'do *sm* thrush.

tore'ro *sm* bullfighter, toreador.

torine'se *ag* of (o from) Turin ♦ *sm/f* person from Turin.

Tori'no *sf* Turin.

tormen'ta *sf* snowstorm.

tormenta're *vt* to torment; **~rsi** *vr* to fret, worry o.s.

tormen'to *sm* torment.

tornacon'to *sm* advantage, benefit.

torna'do *sm* tornado.

tornan'te *sm* hairpin curve (*US*) o bend (*Brit*).

torna're *vi* to return, go (o come) back; (*ridiventare: anche fig*) to become (again); (*riuscire giusto, esatto: conto*) to work out; (*ri-*

sultare) to turn out (to be), prove (to be); **~ al punto di partenza** to start again; **~ a casa** to go (o come) home; **i conti tornano** the accounts balance; **~ utile** to prove o turn out (to be) useful.

tornaso'le *sm inv* litmus.

torne'o *sm* tournament.

tor'nio *sm* lathe.

torni're *vt* (*TECN*) to turn (on a lathe); (*fig*) to shape, polish.

torni'to, a *ag* (*gambe, caviglie*) well-shaped.

to'ro *sm* bull; (*dello zodiaco*): **T~** Taurus; **essere del T~** to be Taurus.

torpe'dine *sf* torpedo.

torpedinie'ra *sf* torpedo boat.

torpo're *sm* torpor.

tor're *sf* tower; (*SCACCHI*) rook, castle; **~ di controllo** (*AER*) control tower.

torrefazio'ne [tōrrāfáttsyō'nā] *sf* roasting.

torreggia're [tōrrādjá'rā] *vi*: **~ (su)** to tower (over).

torren'te *sm* torrent.

torrenti'zio, a [tōrrāntēt'tsyō] *ag* torrential.

torrenzia'le [tōrrāntsyá'lā] *ag* torrential.

torret'ta *sf* turret.

tor'rido, a *ag* torrid.

torrio'ne *sm* keep.

torro'ne *sm* nougat.

tor'si *etc vb vedi* **torcere.**

torsio'ne *sf* twisting; (*TECN*) torsion.

tor'so *sm* torso, trunk; (*ARTE*) torso; **a ~ nudo** bare-chested.

tor'solo *sm* (*di cavolo etc*) stump; (*di frutta*) core.

tor'ta *sf* cake.

tortie'ra *sf* cake pan (*US*), cake tin (*Brit*).

tor'to, a *pp di* **torcere** ♦ *ag* (*ritorto*) twisted; (*storto*) twisted, crooked ♦ *sm* (*ingiustizia*) wrong; (*colpa*) fault; **a ~** wrongly; **a ~ o a ragione** rightly or wrongly; **aver ~** to be wrong; **fare un ~ a qn** to wrong sb; **essere/passare dalla parte del ~** to be/put o.s. in the wrong; **lui non ha tutti i ~i** there's something in what he says.

tor'tora *sf* turtle dove.

tortuo'so, a *ag* (*strada*) twisting; (*fig*) tortuous.

tortu'ra *sf* torture.

tortura're *vt* to torture.

tor'vo, a *ag* menacing, grim.

tosaer'ba *sm o f inv* (lawn)mower.

tosa're *vt* (*pecora*) to shear; (*cane*) to clip; (*siepe*) to clip, trim.

tosatu'ra *sf* (*di pecore*) shearing; (*di cani*) clipping; (*di siepi*) trimming, clipping.

Tosca'na *sf*: **la ~** Tuscany.

tosca'no, a *ag, sm/f* Tuscan ♦ *sm* (*anche*: **sigaro ~**) *strong Italian cigar.*

tos'se *sf* cough.

tossicità [tōssēchētá'] *sf* toxicity.

tos'sico, a, ci, che *ag* toxic.
tossicodipenden'te *sm/f* drug addict.
tossicodipenden'za [tōssēkōdēpānden'tsá] *sf* drug addiction.
tossico'mane *sm/f* drug addict.
tossicomani'a *sf* drug addiction.
tossi'na *sf* toxin.
tossi're *vi* to cough.
tostapa'ne *sm inv* toaster.
tosta're *vt* to toast; *(caffè)* to roast.
tostatu'ra *sf* *(di pane)* toasting; *(di caffè)* roasting.
to'sto, a *ag*: **faccia** ~a cheek ♦ *av* at once, immediately; ~ **che** as soon as.
tota'le *ag, sm* total.
totalità *sf*: **la** ~ **di** all of, the total amount (*o* number) of; the whole + *sg.*
totalita'rio, a *ag* totalitarian; *(totale)* complete, total; **adesione** ~a complete support.
totalitari'smo *sm* (*POL*) totalitarianism.
totalizza're [tōtálēddzà'rā] *vt* to total; (*SPORT*: *punti*) to score.
totalizzato're [tōtálēddzàtō'rā] *sm* (*TECN*) totalizator; (*IPPICA*) totalizator, tote (*fam*).
totocal'cio [tōtōkál'chō] *sm* gambling pool betting on football results.
tournée' [tōōrnā'] *sf* tour; **essere in** ~ to be on tour.
tova'glia [tōvál'yá] *sf* tablecloth.
tovaglio'lo [tōvályo'lō] *sm* napkin.
toz'zo, a [tot'tsō] *ag* squat ♦ *sm*: ~ **di pane** crust of bread.
TP *sigla* = *Trapani.*
TR *sigla* = *Terni.*
Tr *abbr* (*COMM*) = **tratta.**
tra *prep* *(di due persone, cose)* between; *(di più persone, cose)* among(st); *(tempo: entro)* within, in; **prendere qn** ~ **le braccia** to take sb in one's arms; **litigano** ~ **(di) loro** they're fighting amongst themselves; ~ **5 giorni** in 5 days' time; ~ **breve** *o* **poco** soon; ~ **sé e sé** *(parlare etc)* to oneself; **sia detto** ~ **noi ...** between you and me ...; ~ **una cosa e l'altra** what with one thing and another.
traballan'te *ag* shaky.
traballa're *vi* to stagger, totter.
trabic'colo *sm* (*peg*: *auto*) jalopy.
trabocca're *vi* to overflow.
trabocchet'to [trábōkkāt'tō] *sm* (*fig*) trap ♦ *ag inv* trap cpd; **domanda** ~ trick question.
tracagnot'to, a [trákányot'tō] *ag* dumpy ♦ *sm/f* dumpy person.
tracanna're *vt* to gulp down.
trac'cia, ce [trách'chá] *sf* *(segno, striscia)* trail, track; *(orma)* tracks *pl*; *(residuo, testimonianza)* trace, sign; *(abbozzo)* outline; **essere sulle** ~**ce di qn** to be on sb's trail.
traccia're [tráchá'rā] *vt* to trace, mark (out); *(disegnare)* to draw; *(fig: abbozzare)* to outline; ~ **un quadro della situazione** to outline

the situation.
traccia'to [tráchá'tō] *sm* *(grafico)* layout, plan; ~ **di gara** (*SPORT*) race route.
trache'a [tráke'á] *sf* windpipe, trachea.
tracol'la *sf* shoulder strap; **portare qc a** ~ to carry sth over one's shoulder; **borsa a** ~ shoulder bag.
tracol'lo *sm* *(fig)* collapse, ruin; ~ **finanziario** crash; **avere un** ~ (*MED*) to have a setback; (*COMM*) to collapse.
tracotan'te *ag* overbearing, arrogant.
tracotan'za [trákōtán'tsá] *sf* arrogance.
trad. *abbr* = **traduzione.**
tradimen'to *sm* betrayal; (*DIR*, *MIL*) treason; **a** ~ by surprise; **alto** ~ high treason.
tradi're *vt* to betray; *(coniuge)* to be unfaithful to; *(doveri: mancare)* to fail in; *(rivelare)* to give away, reveal; **ha tradito le attese di tutti** he let everyone down.
tradito're, tri'ce *sm/f* traitor.
tradiziona'le [trádēttsyōná'lā] *ag* traditional.
tradizio'ne [trádēttsyō'nā] *sf* tradition.
tradot'to, a *pp di* **tradurre** ♦ *sf* (*MIL*) troop train.
tradur're *vt* to translate; *(spiegare)* to render, convey; (*DIR*): ~ **qn in carcere/tribunale** to take sb to prison/court; ~ **in cifre** to put into figures; ~ **in atto** *(fig)* to put into effect.
tradutto're, tri'ce *sm/f* translator.
traduzio'ne [trádōōttsyō'nā] *sf* translation; (*DIR*) transfer.
tra'e *vb vedi* **trarre.**
traen'te *sm/f* (*ECON*) drawer.
trafela'to, a *ag* out of breath.
traffican'te *sm/f* dealer; *(peg)* trafficker.
traffica're *vi* *(commerciare)*: ~ **(in)** to trade (in), deal (in); *(affaccendarsi)* to busy o.s. ♦ *vt* *(peg)* to traffic in.
traffica'to, a *ag* *(strada, zona)* busy.
traf'fico, ci *sm* traffic; *(commercio)* trade, traffic; ~ **aereo/ferroviario** air/rail traffic; ~ **di droga** drug trafficking; ~ **stradale** traffic.
trafig'gere [tráfēd'jārā] *vt* to run through, stab; *(fig)* to pierce.
trafi'la *sf* procedure.
trafilet'to *sm* *(di giornale)* short article.
trafit'to, a *pp di* **trafiggere.**
trafora're *vt* to bore, drill.
trafo'ro *sm* *(azione)* boring, drilling; *(galleria)* tunnel.
trafuga're *vt* to purloin.
trage'dia [tráje'dyá] *sf* tragedy.
trag'go *etc vb vedi* **trarre.**
traghetta're [trágāttá'rā] *vt* to ferry.
traghet'to [trágāt'tō] *sm* crossing; *(barca)* ferry(boat).
tragicità [trájēchētá'] *sf* tragedy.
tra'gico, a, ci, che [trá'jēkō] *ag* tragic ♦ *sm* *(autore)* tragedian; **prendere tutto sul** ~ *(fig)* to take everything far too seriously.

tragico'mico, a, ci, che [tràjĕko'mēkō] *ag* tragicomic.

tragit'to [tràjĕt'tō] *sm* (*passaggio*) crossing; (*viaggio*) journey.

traguar'do *sm* (SPORT) finishing line; (*fig*) goal, aim.

tra'i *etc vb vedi* **trarre.**

traietto'ria *sf* trajectory.

traina're *vt* to drag, haul; (*rimorchiare*) to tow.

tra'ino *sm* (*carro*) wagon; (*slitta*) sledge; (*carico*) load.

tralascia're [tràlàshá'rā] *vt* (*studi*) to neglect; (*dettagli*) to leave out, omit.

tral'cio [tràl'chō] *sm* (BOT) shoot.

tralic'cio [tràlēch'chō] *sm* (*tela*) ticking; (*struttura*) trellis; (ELETTR) pylon.

tram *sm inv* streetcar (US), tram (Brit).

tra'ma *sf* (*filo*) weft, woof; (*fig*: argomento, maneggio)) plot.

tramanda're *vt* to pass on, hand down.

trama're *vt* (*fig*) to scheme, plot.

trambu'sto *sm* turmoil.

tramesti'o *sm* bustle.

tramezzi'no [tràmàddzē'nō] *sm* sandwich.

tramez'zo [tràmed'dzō] *sm* partition.

tra'mite *prep* through ♦ *sm* means *pl*; **agire/ fare da** ~ to act as/be a go-between.

tramonta'na *sf* (METEOR) north wind.

tramonta're *vi* to set, go down.

tramon'to *sm* setting; (*del sole*) sunset.

tramorti're *vi* to faint ♦ *vt* to stun.

trampoli'no *sm* (*per tuffi*) springboard, diving board; (*per lo sci*) ski-jump.

tram'polo *sm* stilt.

tramuta're *vt*: ~ **in** to change into, turn into.

tran'cia, ce [tràn'chà] *sf* slice; (*cesoia*) shearing machine.

trancia're [trànchá'rā] *vt* (TECN) to shear.

tran'cio [tràn'chō] *sm* slice.

tranel'lo *sm* trap; **tendere un** ~ **a qn** to set a trap for sb; **cadere in un** ~ to fall into a trap.

trangugia're [tràngoōjá'rā] *vt* to gulp down.

tran'ne *prep* except (for), but (for); ~ **che** *cong* unless; **tutti i giorni** ~ **il venerdì** every day except *o* with the exception of Friday.

tranquillan'te *sm* (MED) tranquillizer.

tranquillità *sf* calm, stillness; quietness; peace of mind.

tranquillizza're [trànkwēllēddzà'rā] *vt* to reassure.

tranquil'lo, a *ag* calm, quiet; (*bambino, scolaro*) quiet; (*sereno*) with one's mind at rest; **sta'** ~ don't worry.

transatlan'tico, a, ci, che *ag* transatlantic ♦ *sm* transatlantic liner.

transat'to, a *pp di* **transigere.**

transazio'ne [trànsàttsyō'nā] *sf* (DIR) settlement; (COMM) transaction, deal.

transen'na *sf* barrier.

transet'to *sm* transept.

transiberia'no, a *ag* trans-Siberian.

transi'gere [trànsē'jārā] *vi* (DIR) to reach a settlement; (*venire a patti*) to compromise, come to an agreement.

transi'stor *sm inv*, **transisto're** *sm* transistor.

transita'bile *ag* passable.

transita're *vi* to pass.

transiti'vo, a *ag* transitive.

tran'sito *sm* transit; **di** ~ (*merci*) in transit; (*stazione*) transit *cpd*; **"divieto di** ~**"** "no entry"; **"** ~ **interrotto"** "road closed".

transito'rio, a *ag* transitory, transient; (*provvisorio*) provisional.

transizio'ne [trànsēttsyō'nā] *sf* transition.

tran tran' *sm* routine; **il solito** ~ the same old routine.

tranvi'a *sf* streetcar line (US), tramway (Brit).

tranvia'rio, a *ag* streetcar *cpd* (US), tram *cpd* (Brit); **linea** ~**a** streetcar line, tramline.

tranvie're *sm* (*conducente*) streetcar driver (US), tram driver (Brit); (*bigliettaio*) streetcar *o* tram conductor.

trapana're *vt* (TECN) to drill.

tra'pano *sm* (*utensile*) drill; (: MED) trepan.

trapassa're *vt* to pierce.

trapassa'to *sm* (LING) past perfect.

trapas'so *sm* passage; ~ **di proprietà** (*di case*) conveyancing; (*di auto etc*) legal transfer.

trapela're *vi* to leak, drip; (*fig*) to leak out.

trape'zio [tràpet'tsyō] *sm* (MAT) trapezium; (*attrezzo ginnico*) trapeze.

trapezi'sta, i, e [tràpàttsē'stà] *sm/f* trapeze artist.

trapianta're *vt* to transplant.

trapian'to *sm* transplanting; (MED) transplant.

trap'pola *sf* trap.

trapun'ta *sf* quilt.

trar're *vt* to draw, pull; (*prendere, tirare fuori*) to take (out), draw; (*derivare*) to obtain; ~ **beneficio** *o* **profitto da qc** to benefit from sth; ~ **le conclusioni** to draw one's own conclusions; ~ **esempio da qn** to follow sb's example; ~ **guadagno** to make a profit; ~ **qn d'impaccio** to get sb out of an awkward situation; ~ **origine da qc** to have its origins *o* originate in sth; ~ **in salvo** to rescue.

trasali're *vi* to start, jump.

trasanda'to, a *ag* shabby.

trasborda're *vt* to transfer; (NAUT) to tran(s)ship ♦ *vi* (NAUT) to change ship; (AER) to change plane; (FERR) to change (trains).

trascendenta'le [tràshāndāntá'lā] *ag* transcendental.

trascen'dere [tràshān'dārā] *vt* (FILOSOFIA,

REL) to transcend; (*fig: superare*) to surpass, go beyond.

trasce'so, a [tràshā'sō] *pp di* **trascendere**.

trascina're [tràshēná'rā] *vt* to drag; ~**rsi** *vr* to drag o.s. along; (*fig*) to drag on.

trascor'rere *vt* (*tempo*) to spend, pass ♦ *vi* to pass.

trascor'so, a *pp di* **trascorrere** ♦ *ag* past ♦ *sm* mistake.

trascrit'to, a *pp di* **trascrivere**.

trascri'vere *vt* to transcribe.

trascrizio'ne [tràskrēttsyō'nā] *sf* transcription.

trascura're *vt* to neglect; (*non considerare*) to disregard.

trascuratez'za [tràskōōrátāt'tsá] *sf* carelessness, negligence.

trascura'to, a *ag* (*casa*) neglected; (*persona*) careless, negligent.

trasecola'to, a *ag* astounded, amazed.

trasferimen'to *sm* transfer; (*trasloco*) removal, move.

trasferi're *vt* to transfer; ~**rsi** *vr* to move.

trasfer'ta *sf* transfer; (*indennità*) traveling expenses *pl*; (*SPORT*) away game.

trasfigura're *vt* to transfigure.

trasforma're *vt* to transform, change.

trasformato're *sm* transformer.

trasformazio'ne [tràsfōrmáttsyō'nā] *sf* transformation.

trasfusio'ne *sf* (*MED*) transfusion.

trasgredi're *vt* to break, infringe; (*ordini*) to disobey.

trasgressio'ne *sf* breaking, infringement; disobeying.

trasgresso're, trasgreditri'ce [tràzgrádē'trēchā] *sm/f* (*DIR*) transgressor.

trasla'to, a *ag* metaphorical, figurative.

trasloca're *vt* to move, transfer; ~**rsi** *vr* to move.

traslo'co, chi *sm* removal.

trasmes'so, a *pp di* **trasmettere**.

trasmet'tere *vt* (*passare*): ~ **qc a qn** to pass sth on to sb; (*mandare*) to send; (*TECN, TEL, MED*) to transmit; (*TV, RADIO*) to broadcast.

trasmettito're *sm* transmitter.

trasmissio'ne *sf* (*gen*, *FISICA*, *TECN*) transmission; (*passaggio*) transmission, passing on; (*TV, RADIO*) broadcast.

trasmitten'te *sf* transmitting *o* broadcasting station.

trasogna'to, a [tràsōnyá'tō] *ag* dreamy.

trasparen'te *ag* transparent.

trasparen'za [tràspáren'tsá] *sf* transparency; **guardare qc in** ~ to look at sth against the light.

traspari're *vi* to show (through).

traspar'so, a *pp di* **trasparire**.

traspira're *vi* to perspire; (*fig*) to come to light, leak out.

traspirazio'ne [tràspēráttsyō'nā] *sf* perspiration.

traspor're *vt* to transpose.

trasporta're *vt* to carry, move; (*merce*) to transport, convey; **lasciarsi** ~ (**da qc**) (*fig*) to let o.s. be carried away (by sth).

traspor'to *sm* transport; (*fig*) rapture, passion; **con** ~ passionately; **compagnia di** ~ carriers *pl*; (*per strada*) haulers *pl* (*US*), hauliers *pl* (*Brit*); **mezzi di** ~ means of transport; **nave/aereo da** ~ transport ship/aircraft *inv*; ~ (**funebre**) funeral procession; ~ **marittimo/aereo** sea/air transport; ~ **stradale** (road) haulage; **i** ~**i pubblici** public transport.

traspo'sto, a *pp di* **trasporre**.

tras'si *etc vb vedi* **trarre**.

trastulla're *vt* to amuse; ~**rsi** *vr* to amuse o.s.

trastul'lo *sm* game.

trasuda're *vi* (*filtrare*) to ooze; (*sudare*) to sweat ♦ *vt* to ooze with.

trasversa'le *ag* (*taglio*, *sbarra*) cross(-); (*retta*) transverse; **via** ~ side street.

trasvola're *vt* to fly over.

trat'ta *sf* (*ECON*) draft; (*di persone*): **la** ~ **delle bianche** the white slave trade; ~ **documentaria** documentary bill of exchange.

trattamen'to *sm* treatment; (*servizio*) service; **ricevere un buon** ~ (*cliente*) to get good service; ~ **di fine rapporto** (*COMM*) severance pay.

tratta're *vt* (*gen*) to treat; (*commerciare*) to deal in; (*svolgere: argomento*) to discuss, deal with; (*negoziare*) to negotiate ♦ *vi*: ~ **di** to deal with; ~ **con** (*persona*) to deal with; **si tratta di ...** it's about ...; **si tratterebbe solo di poche ore** it would just be a matter of a few hours.

trattati've *sfpl* negotiations; **essere in** ~ **con qn** to negotiate with sb.

tratta'to *sm* (*testo*) treatise; (*accordo*) treaty; ~ **commerciale** trade agreement; ~ **di pace** peace treaty.

trattazio'ne [tràttáttsyō'nā] *sf* treatment.

tratteggia're [tràttādjá'rā] *vt* (*disegnare: a tratti*) to sketch, outline; (: *col tratteggio*) to hatch.

tratteg'gio [tràttād'jō] *sm* hatching.

trattene're *vt* (*far rimanere: persona*) to detain; (*tenere, frenare, reprimere*) to hold back, keep back; (*astenersi dal consegnare*) to hold, keep; (*detrarre: somma*) to deduct; ~**rsi** *vr* (*astenersi*) to restrain o.s., stop o.s.; (*soffermarsi*) to stay, remain; **sono stato trattenuto in ufficio** I was delayed at the office.

trattenimen'to *sm* entertainment; (*festa*) party.

trattenu'ta *sf* deduction.

tratti'no *sm* dash; (*in parole composte*)

hyphen.

trat'to, a *pp di* **trarre** ♦ *sm* (*di penna, matita*) stroke; (*parte*) part, piece; (*di strada*) stretch; (*di mare, cielo*) expanse; (*di tempo*) period (of time); ~**i** *smpl* (*caratteristiche*) features; (*modo di fare*) ways, manners; **a un ~, d'un ~** suddenly.

tratto're *sm* tractor.

trattori'a *sf* (small) restaurant.

tra'uma, i *sm* trauma; ~ **cranico** concussion.

trauma'tico, a, ci, che *ag* traumatic.

traumatizza're [tràōōmàtēddzà'rā] *vt* (*MED*) to traumatize; (*fig: impressionare*) to shock.

trava'glio [tràvàl'yō] *sm* (*angoscia*) pain, suffering; (*MED*) pains *pl*; ~ **di parto** labor pains.

travasa're *vt* to pour; (*vino*) to decant.

trava'so *sm* pouring; decanting.

travatu'ra *sf* beams *pl*.

tra've *sf* beam.

traveg'gole *sfpl*: **avere le ~** to be seeing things.

traver'sa *sf* (*trave*) crosspiece; (*via*) side-street; (*FERR*) (railroad) tie (*US*), sleeper (*Brit*); (*CALCIO*) crossbar.

traversa're *vt* to cross.

traversa'ta *sf* crossing; (*AER*) flight, trip.

traversi'e *sfpl* mishaps, misfortunes.

traversi'na *sf* (*FERR*) (railroad) tie (*US*), sleeper (*Brit*).

traver'so, a *ag* oblique; **di ~** *ag* askew ♦ *av* sideways; **andare di ~** (*cibo*) to go down the wrong way; **messo di ~** sideways on; **guardare di ~** to look askance at; **via ~a** side road; **ottenere qc per vie ~e** (*fig*) to obtain sth in an underhand way.

travestimen'to *sm* disguise.

travesti're *vt* to disguise; ~**rsi** *vr* to disguise o.s.

travesti'to *sm* transvestite.

travia're *vt* (*fig*) to lead astray.

travisa're *vt* (*fig*) to distort, misrepresent.

travolgen'te [tràvōljen'tā] *ag* overwhelming.

travol'gere [tràvol'jàrā] *vt* to sweep away, carry away; (*fig*) to overwhelm.

travol'to, a *pp di* **travolgere**.

trazio'ne [tràttsyō'nā] *sf* traction; ~ **anteriore/posteriore** (*AUT*) front-wheel/rear-wheel drive.

tre *num* three.

treal'beri *sm inv* (*NAUT*) three-master.

treb'bia *sf* (*AGR: operazione*) threshing; (*: stagione*) threshing season.

trebbia're *vt* to thresh.

trebbiatri'ce [tràbbyàtrē'chā] *sf* threshing machine.

trec'cia, ce [tràch'chá] *sf* plait, braid; **lavorato a ~ce** (*pullover etc*) cable-knit.

trecente'sco, a, schi, sche [tràchàntà'skō] *ag* fourteenth-century.

trecen'to [tràchen'tō] *num* three hundred ♦ *sm*: **il T~** the fourteenth century.

tredicen'ne [trādēchen'nā] *ag, sm/f* thirteen-year-old.

tredice'simo, a [trādēche'zēmō] *num* thirteenth ♦ *sf Christmas bonus of a month's pay.*

tre'dici [trā'dēchē] *num* thirteen ♦ *sm inv*: **fare ~** (*TOTOCALCIO*) ≈ to win the (football) lottery.

tre'gua *sf* truce; (*fig*) respite; **senza ~** nonstop, without stopping, uninterruptedly.

treman'te *ag* trembling, shaking.

trema're *vi* to tremble, shake; ~ **di** (*freddo etc*) to shiver o tremble with; (*paura, rabbia*) to shake o tremble with.

tremarel'la *sf* shivers *pl*.

tremen'do, a *ag* terrible, awful.

trementi'na *sf* turpentine.

tremi'la *num* three thousand.

tre'mito *sm* trembling *q*; shaking *q*; shivering *q*.

tremola're *vi* to tremble; (*luce*) to flicker; (*foglie*) to quiver.

tremo're *sm* tremor.

tre'no *sm* train; (*AUT*): ~ **di gomme** set of tires; ~ **locale/diretto/espresso** local/fast/express train; ~ **merci** freight train; ~ **rapido** express (train) (*for which supplement must be paid*); ~ **straordinario** special train; ~ **viaggiatori** passenger train.

tren'ta *num* thirty ♦ *sm inv* (*INS*): ~ **e lode** full marks plus distinction o cum laude.

trenten'ne *ag, sm/f* thirty-year-old.

trenten'nio *sm* period of thirty years.

trente'simo, a *num* thirtieth.

trenti'na *sf*: **una ~ (di)** thirty or so, about thirty.

trepidan'te *ag* anxious.

trepida're *vi* to be anxious; ~ **per qn** to be anxious about sb.

tre'pido, a *ag* anxious.

treppie'de *sm* tripod; (*CUC*) trivet.

trequar'ti *sm inv* three-quarter-length coat.

tre'sca, sche *sf* (*fig*) intrigue; (*: relazione amorosa*) affair.

tre'spolo *sm* trestle.

trevigia'no, a [trāvējá'nō] *ag* of (o from) Treviso.

triangola're *ag* triangular.

trian'golo *sm* triangle.

tribola're *vi* (*patire*) to suffer; (*fare fatica*) to have a lot of trouble.

tribolazio'ne [trēbōlàttsyō'nā] *sf* suffering, tribulation.

tribor'do *sm* (*NAUT*) starboard.

tribù *sf inv* tribe.

tribu'na *sf* (*podio*) platform; (*in aule etc*) gallery; (*di stadio*) stand; ~ **della stampa/riservata al pubblico** press/public gallery.

tribuna'le *sm* court; **presentarsi** *o* **comparire in** ~ to appear in court; ~ **militare** military tribunal; ~ **supremo** supreme court.

tributa're *vt* to bestow; ~ **gli onori dovuti a qn** to pay tribute to sb.

tributa'rio, a *ag* (*imposta*) fiscal, tax *cpd*; (*GEO*): **essere** ~ **di** to be a tributary of.

tribu'to *sm* tax; (*fig*) tribute.

triche'co, chi [triĕke'kō] *sm* (*ZOOL*) walrus.

trici'clo [trēchē'klō] *sm* tricycle.

tricolo're *ag* three-colored (*US*), three-coloured (*Brit*) ♦ *sm* tricolo(u)r; (*bandiera italiana*) Italian flag.

triden'te *sm* trident.

trienna'le *ag* (*che dura 3 anni*) three-year *cpd*; (*che avviene ogni 3 anni*) three-yearly.

trien'nio *sm* period of three years.·

triesti'no, a *ag* of (*o* from) Trieste.

trifa'se *ag* (*ELETTR*) three-phase.

trifo'glio [trēfol'yō] *sm* clover.

trifola'to, a *ag* (*CUC*) cooked in oil, garlic and parsley.

tri'glia [trēl'yà] *sf* red mullet.

trigonometri'a *sf* trigonometry.

trilla're *vi* (*MUS*) to trill.

trimes'tre *sm* period of three months; (*INS*) quarter (*US*), term; (*COMM*) quarter.

trimoto're *sm* (*AER*) three-engined plane.

tri'na *sf* lace.

trince'a [trēnche'à] *sf* trench.

trincera're [trēnchàrà'rà] *vt* to entrench.

trincia're [trēnchà'rà] *vt* to cut up.

Tri'nidad *sm*: ~ **e Tobago** Trinidad and Tobago.

Trinità *sf* (*REL*) Trinity.

tri'o, *pl* tri'i *sm* trio.

trionfa'le *ag* triumphal, triumphant.

trionfan'te *ag* triumphant.

trionfa're *vi* to triumph, win; ~ **su** to triumph over, overcome.

trion'fo *sm* triumph.

triplica're *vt* to triple.

tri'plice [trē'plēchā] *ag* triple; **in** ~ **copia** in triplicate.

tri'plo, a *ag* triple, treble ♦ *sm*: **il** ~ **(di)** three times as much (as); **la spesa è** ~**a** it costs three times as much.

tri'pode *sm* tripod.

Tri'poli *sf* Tripoli.

trip'pa *sf* (*CUC*) tripe.

tripu'dio *sm* triumph, jubilation; (*fig: di colori*) galaxy.

tris *sm inv* (*CARTE*): ~ **d'assi/di re** *etc* three aces/kings *etc*.

tri'ste *ag* sad; (*luogo*) dreary, gloomy.

tristez'za [trēstàt'tsà] *sf* sadness; gloominess.

tri'sto, a *ag* (*cattivo*) wicked, evil; (*meschino*) sorry, poor.

tritacar'ne *sm inv* meat grinder (*US*), mincer.

tritaghi'accio [trētàgyàch'chō] *sm inv* ice crusher.

trita're *vt* to grind (*US*), mince.

tritatut'to *sm inv* food grinder (*US*), mincer.

tri'to, a *ag* (*tritato*) ground (*US*), minced; ~ **e ritrito** (*idee, argomenti, frasi*) trite, hackneyed.

trito'lo *sm* trinitrotoluene.

trit'tico, ci *sm* (*ARTE*) triptych.

tritura're *vt* to grind.

trivel'la *sf* drill.

trivella're *vt* to drill.

trivellazio'ne [trēvàllàttsyō'nà] *sf* drilling; **torre di** ~ derrick.

trivia'le *ag* vulgar, low.

trivialità *sf inv* (*volgarità*) coarseness, crudeness; (: *osservazione*) coarse *o* crude remark.

trofe'o *sm* trophy.

tro'golo *sm* (*per maiali*) trough.

tro'ia *sf* (*ZOOL*) sow; (*fig peg*) whore.

trom'ba *sf* (*MUS*) trumpet; (*AUT*) horn; ~ **d'aria** whirlwind; ~ **delle scale** stairwell.

trombetti'sta, i, e *sm/f* trumpeter, trumpet (player).

trombo'ne *sm* trombone.

trombo'si *sf* thrombosis.

tronca're *vt* to cut off; (*spezzare*) to break off.

tron'co, a, chi, che *ag* cut off; broken off; (*LING*) truncated ♦ *sm* (*BOT, ANAT*) trunk; (*fig: tratto*) section; (: *pezzo: di lancia*) stump; **licenziare qn in** ~ (*fig*) to fire sb on the spot.

troneggia're [trōnàdjà'rà] *vi:* ~ **(su)** to tower (over).

tron'fio, a *ag* conceited.

tro'no *sm* throne.

tropica'le *ag* tropical.

tro'pico, ci *sm* tropic; ~ **del Cancro/ Capricorno** Tropic of Cancer/Capricorn; **i** ~**ci** the tropics.

trop'po, a *det, pronome* (*quantità*) too much; (*numero*) too many ♦ *av* (*con vb*) too much; (*con ag, av*) too; **di** ~: **qualche tazza di** ~ a few cups too many, a few extra cups; **3000 lire di** ~ 3000 lire too much; **essere di** ~ to be in the way; ~ **buono da parte tua!** (*anche ironico*) you're too kind!

tro'ta *sf* trout.

trotta're *vi* to trot.

trotterella're *vi* to trot along; (*bambino*) to toddle.

trot'to *sm* trot.

trot'tola *sf* spinning top.

trova're *vt* to find; (*giudicare*): **trovo che** I find *o* think that; ~**rsi** *vr* (*reciproco: incontrarsi*) to meet; (*essere, stare*) to be; (*arrivare, capitare*) to find o.s.; **andare a** ~ **qn** to go and see sb; ~ **qn colpevole** to find sb guilty; **trovo giusto/sbagliato che** ... I think/don't think it's right that ...; ~**rsi bene/male** (*in un luogo, con qn*) to get on well/badly; ~**rsi d'accordo con qn** to be in agreement with sb.

trova'ta *sf* good idea; ~ **pubblicitaria** advertising gimmick.

trovatel'lo, a *sm/f* foundling.

trucca're *vt* (*falsare*) to fake; (*attore etc*) to make up; (*travestire*) to disguise; (*SPORT*) to fix; (*AUT*) to soup up; ~**rsi** *vr* to make up (one's face).

truccato're, tri'ce *sm/f* (*CINEMA, TEATRO*) make-up artist.

truc'co, chi *sm* trick; (*cosmesi*) make-up; **i** ~**chi del mestiere** the tricks of the trade.

tru'ce [troō'chā] *ag* fierce.

trucida're [troōchĕdá'rā] *vt* to slaughter.

tru'ciolo [troō'chōlō] *sm* shaving.

truf'fa *sf* fraud, swindle.

truffa're *vt* to swindle, cheat.

truffato're, tri'ce *sm/f* swindler, cheat.

trup'pa *sf* troop.

TS *sigla* = *Trieste*.

tu *pronome* you; ~ **stesso(a)** you yourself; **dare del** ~ **a qn** to address sb as "tu"; **tro-varsi a** ~ **per** ~ **con qn** to find o.s. face to face with sb.

tu'a *vedi* **tuo**.

tu'ba *sf* (*MUS*) tuba; (*cappello*) top hat.

tuba're *vi* to coo.

tubatu'ra *sf*, **tubazio'ne** [toōbáttsyō'nā] *sf* piping *q*, pipes *pl*.

tubercolo'si *sf* tuberculosis.

tubet'to *sm* tube.

tubi'no *sm* (*cappello*) derby (*US*), bowler (*Brit*); (*abito da donna*) sheath dress.

tu'bo *sm* tube; (*per conduttore*) pipe; ~ **dige-rente** (*ANAT*) alimentary canal, digestive tract; ~ **di scappamento** (*AUT*) exhaust pipe.

tubola're *ag* tubular ♦ *sm* tubeless tire (*US*) *o* tyre (*Brit*).

tu'e *vedi* **tuo**.

tuffa're *vt* to plunge; (*intingere*) to dip; ~**rsi** *vr* to plunge, dive.

tuffato're, tri'ce *sm/f* (*SPORT*) diver.

tuf'fo *sm* dive; (*breve bagno*) dip.

tugu'rio *sm* hovel.

tulipa'no *sm* tulip.

tumefar'si *vr* (*MED*) to swell.

tu'mido, a *ag* swollen.

tumo're *sm* (*MED*) tumor (*US*), tumour (*Brit*).

tumulazio'ne [toōmoōláttsyō'nā] *sf* burial.

tumul'to *sm* uproar, commotion; (*sommossa*) riot; (*fig*) turmoil.

tumultuo'so, a *ag* rowdy, unruly; (*fig*) turbu-lent, stormy.

tungste'no *sm* tungsten.

tu'nica, che *sf* tunic.

Tu'nisi *sf* Tunis.

Tunisi'a *sf*: **la** ~ Tunisia.

tunisi'no, a *ag*, *sm/f* Tunisian.

tun'nel *sm inv* tunnel.

tu'o, tu'a, tuo'i, tu'e *det*: **il** ~, **la tua** *etc* your ♦ *pronome*: **il** ~, **la tua** *etc* yours ♦ *sm*: **hai speso del** ~? did you spend your own money? ♦ *sf*: **la** ~**a** (*opinione*) your view; **i tuoi** (*genitori, famiglia*) your family; **una** ~**a amica** a friend of yours; **è dalla** ~**a** he is on your side; **alla** ~**a!** (*brindisi*) your health!; **ne hai fatta una delle** ~**e!** (*sciocchezze*) you've done it again!

tuona're *vi* to thunder; **tuona** it is thundering, there's some thunder.

tuo'no *sm* thunder.

tuor'lo *sm* yolk.

turac'ciolo [toōrách'chōlō] *sm* cap, top; (*di sughero*) cork.

tura're *vt* to stop, plug; (*con sughero*) to cork; ~**rsi il naso** to hold one's nose.

tur'ba *sf* (*folla*) crowd, throng; (: *peg*) mob; ~**e** *sfpl* disorder(s); **soffrire di** ~**e psichiche** to suffer from a mental disorder.

turbamen'to *sm* disturbance; (*di animo*) anxiety, agitation.

turban'te *sm* turban.

turba're *vt* to disturb, trouble; ~ **la quiete pubblica** (*DIR*) to disturb the peace.

turbi'na *sf* turbine.

turbina're *vi* to whirl.

tur'bine *sm* whirlwind; ~ **di neve** swirl of snow; ~ **di polvere/sabbia** dust/sandstorm.

turbino'so, a *ag* (*vento, danza etc*) whirling.

turbolen'to, a *ag* turbulent; (*ragazzo*) boisterous, unruly.

turbolen'za [toōrbōlen'tsá] *sf* turbulence.

turboreatto're *sm* turbojet engine.

turche'se [toōrkā'sā] *ag*, *sm*, *sf* turquoise.

Turchi'a [toōrkē'á] *sf*: **la** ~ Turkey.

turchi'no, a [toōrkē'nō] *ag* deep blue.

tur'co, a, chi, che *ag* Turkish ♦ *sm/f* Turk/Turkish woman ♦ *sm* (*LING*) Turkish; **parlare** ~ (*fig*) to talk double Dutch.

tur'gido, a [toōr'jēdō] *ag* swollen.

turi'smo *sm* tourism.

turi'sta, i, e *sm/f* tourist.

turi'stico, a, ci, che *ag* tourist *cpd*.

turni'sta, i, e *sm/f* shift worker.

tur'no *sm* turn; (*di lavoro*) shift; **di** ~ (*solda-to, medico, custode*) on duty; **a** ~ (*ri-spondere*) in turn; (*lavorare*) in shifts; **fare a** ~ **a fare qc** to take turns to do sth; **è il suo** ~ it's your (*o his etc*) turn.

tur'pe *ag* filthy, vile.

turpilo'quio *sm* obscene language.

tu'ta *sf* overalls *pl*; (*SPORT*) tracksuit; ~ **mi-metica** (*MIL*) camouflage clothing; ~ **spazia-le** spacesuit; ~ **subacquea** wetsuit.

tute'la *sf* (*DIR*: *di minore*) guardianship; (:

protezione) protection; (*difesa*) defense (*US*), defence (*Brit*); ~ **dell'ambiente** environmental protection; ~ **del consumatore** consumer protection.

tutela're *vt* to protect, defend ♦ *ag* (*DIR*): **giudice** ~ *judge with responsibility for guardianship cases.*

tuto're, tri'ce *sm/f* (*DIR*) guardian.

tuttavi'a *cong* nevertheless, yet.

tut'to, a *det* all ♦ *pronome* everything, all; ~**i(e)** *pronome pl* all (of them); (*ognuno*) everyone ♦ *av* (*completamente*) completely, quite ♦ *sm* whole; (*l'intero*): **il** ~ all of it, the whole lot; ~ **il libro** all the book, the whole of the book; ~**a la sera** all evening, the whole evening; ~**a una bottiglia** a whole bottle; ~**i i ragazzi** all the boys; ~**e le sere** every evening; ~**i e due** both *o* each of us (*o* them); ~**i e cinque** all five of us (*o* them); **a** ~**a velocità** at full *o* top speed; **famoso in** ~ **il mondo** world-famous, famous the world over; ~**e le volte che** every time (that); **a tutt'oggi** so far, up till now; **questo è** ~, **ecco** ~ that's all; ~ **compreso** inclusive, all-in (*Brit*); ~ **considerato** all things considered; **in** ~ in all; **in** ~ **e per** ~ (*completamente*) entirely, completely; **con** ~ **che** (*malgrado*) although; **del** ~ competely; ... **che è** ~ **dire** ... and that's saying a lot; **tutt'altro** on the contrary; (*affatto*) not at all; **tutt'altro che felice** anything but happy; **tutt'al più** at (the) most; (*al più tardi*) at the latest; **tutt'al più possiamo prendere un treno** if the worst comes to the worst we can catch a train; **tutt'intorno** all around.

tuttofa're *ag inv*: **domestica** ~ general maid; **ragazzo** ~ office boy ♦ *sm/f inv* handyman/ woman.

tutto'ra *av* still.

tutù *sm inv* tutu, ballet skirt.

TV [těvōo'] *sf inv* (= *televisione*) TV ♦ *sigla* = *Treviso.*

U

U, u [ōo] *sf o m inv* (*lettera*) U, u; **U come Udine** ≈ U for Uncle; **inversione ad U** U-turn.

ubbi'a *sf* (*letterario*) irrational fear.

ubbidien'te *ag* obedient.

ubbidien'za [ōobbědyen'tsä] *sf* obedience.

ubbidi're *vi* to obey; ~ **a** to obey; (*sog: veicolo, macchina*) to respond to.

ubicazio'ne [ōobēkàttsyō'nä] *sf* site, location.

ubiquità *sf*: **non ho il dono dell'**~ I can't be everywhere at once.

ubriaca're *vt*: ~ **qn** to get sb drunk; (*sog: alcool*) to make sb drunk; (*fig*) to make sb's head spin *o* reel; ~**rsi** *vr* to get drunk; ~**rsi di** (*fig*) to become intoxicated with.

ubriachez'za [ōobrēàkàt'tsä] *sf* drunkenness.

ubria'co, a, chi, che *ag, sm/f* drunk.

ubriaco'ne *sm* drunkard.

uccellagio'ne [ōochāllàjō'nä] *sf* bird catching.

uccellato're [ōochāllàtō'rä] *sm* bird catcher.

uccellie'ra [ōochāllyc'rä] *sf* aviary.

uccelli'no [ōochāllē'nō] *sm* baby bird, chick.

uccel'lo [ōochel'lō] *sm* bird.

ucci'dere [ōochē'dārä] *vt* to kill; ~**rsi** *vr* (*suicidarsi*) to kill o.s.; (*perdere la vita*) to be killed.

uccisio'ne [ōochēzyō'nä] *sf* killing.

ucci'so, a [ōochē'zō] *pp di* **uccidere.**

ucciso're [ōochēzō'rä] *sm* killer.

UD *sigla* = *Udine.*

udi'bile *ag* audible.

udien'za [ōodyen'tsä] *sf* audience; (*DIR*) hearing; **dare** ~ **(a)** to grant an audience (to); ~ **a porte chiuse** hearing in camera.

udi're *vt* to hear.

uditi'vo, a *ag* auditory.

udi'to *sm* (sense of) hearing.

udito're, tri'ce *sm/f* listener; (*INS*) auditor (*US*), unregistered student (*attending lectures*) (*Brit*).

udito'rio *sm* (*persone*) audience.

U.E. *abbr* = *uso esterno.*

UEFA *sigla f* UEFA (= *Union of European Football Associations*).

uf'fa *escl* tut!

uffcia'le [ōoffēchá'lä] *ag* official ♦ *sm* (*AMM*) official, officer; (*MIL*) officer; **pubblico** ~ public official; ~ **giudiziario** clerk of the court; ~ **di marina** naval officer; ~ **sanitario** health inspector; ~ **di stato civile** registrar.

ufficializza're [ōoffēchálēddzà'rä] *vt* to make official.

uffi'cio [ōoffē'chō] *sm* (*gen*) office; (*dovere*) duty; (*mansione*) task, function, job; (*agenzia*) agency, bureau; (*REL*) service; **d'**~ *ag* office *cpd*; official ♦ *av* officially; **provvedere d'**~ to act officially; **convocare d'**~ (*DIR*) to summons; **difensore** *o* **avvocato d'**~ (*DIR*) court-appointed counsel for the defense; ~ **brevetti** patent office; ~ **di collocamento** employment office; ~ **informazioni** information bureau; ~ **oggetti smarriti** lost and found (*US*), lost property office (*Brit*); ~ **postale** post office; ~ **vendite/del personale** sales/personnel department.

uffcio'so, a [ōoffēchō'sō] *ag* unofficial.

U'FO *sm inv* UFO.

u'fo: a ~ *av* free, for nothing.

Ugan'da *sf*: **l'~** Uganda.

ug'gia |ōōd'jà| *sf* (*noia*) boredom; (*fastidio*) bore; **avere/prendere qn in ~** to dislike/take a dislike to sb.

uggio'so, a |ōōdjō'sō| *ag* tiresome; (*tempo*) dull.

u'gola *sf* uvula.

uguaglian'za |ōōgwàlyàn'tsà| *sf* equality.

uguaglia're |ōōgwàlyà'rà| *vt* to make equal; (*essere uguale*) to equal, be equal to; (*livellare*) to level; **~rsi** *vr*: **~rsi a** *o* **con qn** (*paragonarsi*) to compare o.s. to sb.

ugua'le *ag* equal; (*identico*) identical, the same; (*uniforme*) level, even ♦ *av*: **costano ~** they cost the same; **sono bravi ~** they're equally good.

ugualmen'te *av* equally; (*lo stesso*) all the same.

U.I. *abbr* = *uso interno*.

UIL *sigla f* (= *Unione Italiana del Lavoro*) trade union federation.

ul'cera |ōōl'chàrà| *sf* ulcer.

ulcerazio'ne |ōōlchàràttsyō'nà| *sf* ulceration.

uli'va *etc* = *oliva etc*.

ulterio're *ag* further.

ultimamen'te *av* lately, of late.

ultima're *vt* to finish, complete.

ultima'tum *sm inv* ultimatum.

ultimis'sime *sfpl* latest news *sg*.

ul'timo, a *ag* (*finale*) last; (*estremo*) farthest, utmost; (*recente: notizia, moda*) latest; (*fig: sommo, fondamentale*) ultimate ♦ *sm/f* last (one); **fino all'~** to the last, until the end; **da ~, in ~** in the end; **per ~** (*entrare, arrivare*) last; **abitare all'~ piano** to live on the top floor; **in ~a pagina** (*di giornale*) on the back page; **negli ~i tempi** recently; **all'~ momento** at the last minute; **... la vostra lettera del 7 aprile ~ scorso** ... your letter of April 7th last; **in ~a analisi** in the final *o* last analysis; **in ~ luogo** finally.

ultrasinis'tra *sf* (*POL*) extreme left.

ultrasuo'no *sm* ultrasound.

ultraviolet'to, a *ag* ultraviolet.

ulula're *vi* to howl.

ulula'to *sm* howling *q*; howl.

umanamen'te *av* (*con umanità*) humanely; (*nei limiti delle capacità umane*) humanly.

umane'simo *sm* humanism.

umanità *sf* humanity.

umanita'rio, a *ag* humanitarian.

umanizza're |ōōmànèddzà'rà| *vt* to humanize.

uma'no, a *ag* human; (*comprensivo*) humane.

umbili'co *sm* = **ombelico**.

um'bro, a *ag* of (*o* from) Umbria.

umetta're *vt* to dampen, moisten.

umidic'cio, a, ce |ōōmèdèch'chō| *ag* (*terreno*) damp; (*mano*) moist, clammy.

umidifica're *vt* to humidify.

umidificato're *sm* humidifier.

umidità *sf* dampness; moistness; humidity.

u'mido, a *ag* damp; (*mano, occhi*) moist; (*clima*) humid ♦ *sm* dampness, damp; **carne in ~ stew.**

u'mile *ag* humble.

umilian'te *ag* humiliating.

umilia're *vt* to humiliate; **~rsi** *vr* to humble o.s.

umiliazio'ne |ōōmèlyàttsyō'nà| *sf* humiliation.

umiltà *sf* humility, humbleness.

umo're *sm* (*disposizione d'animo*) mood; (*carattere*) temper; **di buon/cattivo ~** in a good/bad mood.

umori'smo *sm* humor (*US*), humour (*Brit*); **avere il senso dell'~** to have a sense of humo(u)r.

umori'sta, i, e *sm/f* humorist.

umori'stico, a, ci, che *ag* humorous, funny.

un, un', una *vedi* **uno.**

una'nime *ag* unanimous.

unanimità *sf* unanimity; **all'~** unanimously.

u'na tan'tum *ag* one time (*US*) *o* one-off (*Brit*) *cpd* ♦ *sf* (*imposta*) one time (*US*) *o* one-off (*Brit*) tax.

uncina'to, a |ōōnchènà'tō| *ag* (*amo*) barbed; (*ferro*) hooked; **croce ~a** swastika.

uncinet'to |ōōnchènàt'tō| *sm* crochet hook.

unci'no |ōōnchē'nō| *sm* hook.

undicen'ne |ōōndēchen'nà| *ag*, *sm/f* eleven-year-old.

undice'simo, a |ōōndēche'zēmō| *num* eleventh.

un'dici |ōōn'dēchē| *num* eleven.

un'gere |ōōn'jàrà| *vt* to grease, oil; (*REL*) to anoint; (*fig*) to flatter, butter up; **~rsi** *vr* (*sporcarsi*) to get covered in grease; **~rsi con la crema** to put on cream.

unghere'se |ōōngàrà'sà| *ag*, *sm/f*, *sm* Hungarian.

Ungheri'a |ōōngàrē'à| *sf*: **l'~** Hungary.

un'ghia |ōōn'gyà| *sf* (*ANAT*) nail; (*di animale*) claw; (*di rapace*) talon; (*di cavallo*) hoof; **pagare sull'~** (*fig*) to pay on the nail

unghia'ta |ōōngyà'tà| *sf* (*graffio*) scratch.

unguen'to *sm* ointment.

u'nico, a, ci, che *ag* (*solo*) only; (*ineguagliabile*) unique; (*singolo: binario*) single; **è figlio ~** he's an only child; **atto ~** (*TEATRO*) one-act play; **agente ~** (*COMM*) sole agent.

unicor'no *sm* unicorn.

unifica're *vt* to unite, unify; (*sistemi*) to standardize.

unificazio'ne |ōōnēfēkàttsyō'nà| *sf* unification; standardization.

uniforma're *vt* (*terreno, superficie*) to level; **~rsi** *vr*: **~rsi a** to conform to; **~ qc a** to adjust *o* relate sth to.

unifor'me *ag* uniform; (*superficie*) even ♦ *sf* (*divisa*) uniform; **alta ~** dress uniform.

uniformità *sf* uniformity; evenness.
unilatera'le *ag* one-sided; (*DIR, POL*) unilateral.
unio'ne *sf* union; (*fig: concordia*) unity, harmony; **l'U~ Sovietica** the Soviet Union.
uni're *vt* to unite; (*congiungere*) to join, connect; (*: ingredienti, colori*) to combine; (*in matrimonio*) to unite, join together; **~rsi** *vr* to unite; (*in matrimonio*) to be joined together; **~ qc a** to unite sth with; to join *o* connect sth with; to combine sth with; **~rsi a** (*gruppo, società*) to join.
uni'sono *sm*: **all'~** in unison.
unità *sf inv* (*unione, concordia*) unity; (*MAT, MIL, COMM, di misura*) unit; **~ centrale (di elaborazione)** (*INFORM*) central processing unit; **~ disco** (*INFORM*) disk drive; **~ monetaria** monetary unit.
unita'rio, a *ag* unitary; **prezzo ~** price per unit.
uni'to, a *ag* (*paese*) united; (*amici, famiglia*) close; **in tinta ~a** plain, self-colored (*US*), self-coloured (*Brit*).
universa'le *ag* universal; general.
universalità *sf* universality.
universalmen'te *av* universally.
università *sf inv* university.
universita'rio, a *ag* university *cpd* ♦ *sm/f* (*studente*) university student; (*insegnante*) academic.
univer'so *sm* universe.
uni'voco, a, ci, che *ag* unambiguous.
u'no, a *det, num* (*dav sm* **un** + *C, V,* **uno** + *s impura, gn, pn, ps, x, z; dav sf* **un'** + *V,* **una** + *C*) *det* a, an + *vocale* ♦ *num* one ♦ *pronome* (*un tale*) someone, somebody; (*con valore impersonale*) one, you ♦ *sf*: **è l'~a** it's one o'clock; **facciamo metà per ~** let's go halves; **a ~ a ~** one by one.
un'si *etc vb vedi* **ungere.**
un'to, a *pp di* **ungere** ♦ *ag* greasy, oily ♦ *sm* grease.
untuo'so, a *ag* greasy, oily.
unzio'ne [ōōntsyō'nä] *sf*: **l'Estrema U~** (*REL*) Extreme Unction.
uo'mo, *pl* **uo'mini** *sm* man; **da ~** (*abito, scarpe*) men's, for men; **a memoria d'~** since the world began; **a passo d'~** at walking pace; **~ d'affari** businessman; **~ d'azione** man of action; **~ di fiducia** right-hand man; **~ di mondo** man of the world; **~ di paglia** stooge; **~ rana** frogman; **l'~ della strada** the man on (*US*) *o* in (*Brit*) the street.
uo'po *sm*: **all'~** if necessary.
uo'vo, *pl(f)* **uo'va** *sm* egg; **cercare il pelo nell'~** (*fig*) to split hairs; **~ affogato** *o* **in camicia** poached egg; **~ bazzotto/sodo** soft-/hard-boiled egg; **~ alla coque** boiled egg; **~ di Pasqua** Easter egg; **~ al tegame** *o* **all'occhio di bue** fried egg; **uova strapazzate**

scrambled eggs.
uraga'no *sm* hurricane.
Ura'li *smpl*: **gli ~, i Monti ~** the Urals; the Ural Mountains.
ura'nio *sm* uranium.
urbane'simo *sm* urbanization.
urbani'sta, i, e *sm/f* city (*US*) *o* town (*Brit*) planner.
urbani'stica *sf* city (*US*) *o* town (*Brit*) planning.
urbanità *sf* urbanity.
urba'no, a *ag* urban, city *cpd*, town *cpd*; (*TEL: chiamata*) local; (*fig*) urbane.
urgen'te [ōōrjen'tä] *ag* urgent.
urgen'za [ōōrjen'tsä] *sf* urgency; **in caso d'~** in (case of) an emergency; **d'~** *ag* emergency ♦ *av* urgently, as a matter of urgency; **non c'è ~** there's no hurry; **questo lavoro va fatto con ~** this work is urgent.
ur'gere [ōōr'jārā] *vi* to be needed urgently.
uri'na *etc* = **orina** *etc.*
urla're *vi* (*persona*) to scream, yell; (*animale, vento*) to howl ♦ *vt* to scream, yell.
ur'lo, *pl(m)* **ur'li,** *pl(f)* **ur'la** *sm* scream, yell; howl.
ur'na *sf* urn; (*elettorale*) ballot box; **andare alle ~e** to go to the polls.
urrà *escl* hurrah!
U.R.S.S. *sigla f* (= *Unione delle Repubbliche Socialiste Sovietiche*): **l'~** the USSR.
urta're *vt* to bump into, knock against; (*fig: irritare*) to annoy ♦ *vi*: **~ contro** *o* **in** to bump into, knock against; (*fig: imbattersi*) to come up against; **~rsi** *vr* (*reciproco: scontrarsi*) to collide; (*: fig*) to clash; (*irritarsi*) to get annoyed.
ur'to *sm* (*colpo*) knock, bump; (*scontro*) crash, collision; (*fig*) clash; **terapia d'~** (*MED*) shock treatment.
uruguaia'no, a *ag, sm/f* Uruguayan.
Uruguay' *sm*: **l'~** Uruguay.
u.s. *abbr* = **ultimo scorso.**
U'SA *smpl*: **gli ~** the USA.
usan'za [ōōzán'tsä] *sf* custom; (*moda*) fashion.
usa're *vt* to use, employ ♦ *vi* (*essere di moda*) to be fashionable; (*servirsi*): **~ di** to use; (*: diritto*) to exercise; (*essere solito*): **~ fare** to be in the habit of doing, be accustomed to doing ♦ *vb impers*: **qui usa così** it's the custom round here; **~ la massima cura nel fare qc** to exercise great care when doing sth.
usa'to, a *ag* used; (*consumato*) worn; (*di seconda mano*) used, second-hand ♦ *sm* second-hand goods *pl.*
uscen'te [ōōshen'tä] *ag* (*AMM*) outgoing.
uscie're [ōōshe'rä] *sm* usher.
u'scio [ōō'shō] *sm* door.
usci're [ōōshē'rä] *vi* (*gen*) to come out; (*partire, andare a passeggio, a uno spettacolo etc*)

to go out; (*essere sorteggiato: numero*) to come up; ~ **da** (*gen*) to leave; (*posto*) to go (*o come*) out of, leave; (*solco, vasca etc*) to come out of; (*muro*) to stick out of; (*competenza etc*) to be outside; (*infanzia, adolescenza*) to leave behind; (*famiglia nobile etc*) to come from; ~ **da** *o* **di casa** to go out; (*fig*) to leave home; ~ **in automobile** to go out in the car, go for a drive; ~ **di strada** (*AUT*) to go off *o* leave the road.

usci'ta [ōōshē'tá] *sf* (*passaggio, varco*) exit, way out; (*per divertimento*) outing; (*ECON: somma*) expenditure; (*fig: battuta*) witty remark; **"vietata l'~"** "no exit"; ~ **di sicurezza** emergency exit.

usigno'lo [ōōzēnyo'lō] *sm* nightingale.

U.S.L. [ōōzl] *sigla f* (= *unità sanitaria locale*) local health centre.

u'so *sm* (*utilizzazione*) use; (*esercizio*) practise (*US*), practice (*Brit*); (*abitudine*) custom; **fare** ~ **di qc** to use sth; **con l'~** with practice; **a** ~ **di** for (the use of); **d'~** (*corrente*) in use; **fuori** ~ out of use; **essere in** ~ to be in common *o* current use.

ustiona're *vt* to burn; ~**rsi** *vr* to burn o.s.

ustio'ne *sf* burn.

usua'le *ag* common, everyday.

usufrui're *vi*: ~ **di** (*giovarsi di*) to take advantage of, make use of.

usufrut'to *sm* (*DIR*) usufruct.

usu'ra *sf* usury; (*logoramento*) wear (and tear).

usura'io *sm* usurer.

usurpa're *vt* to usurp.

usurpato're, tri'ce *sm/f* usurper.

utensi'le *sm* tool, implement ♦ *ag*: **macchina** ~ machine tool; ~**i da cucina** kitchen utensils.

utensileri'a *sf* (*utensili*) tools *pl*; (*reparto*) tool room.

uten'te *sm/f* user; (*di gas etc*) consumer; (*del telefono*) customer; ~ **finale** end user.

u'tero *sm* uterus, womb.

u'tile *ag* useful ♦ *sm* (*vantaggio*) advantage, benefit; (*ECON: profitto*) profit; **rendersi** ~ to be helpful; **in tempo** ~ **per** in time for; **unire l'~ al dilettevole** to combine business with pleasure; **partecipare agli** ~**i** (*ECON*) to share in the profits.

utilità *sf* usefulness *q*; use; (*vantaggio*) benefit; **essere di grande** ~ to be very useful.

utilita'rio, a *ag* utilitarian ♦ *sf* (*AUT*) economy car.

utilizza're [ōōtēlēddzá'rā] *vt* to use, make use of, utilize.

utilizzazio'ne [ōōtēlēddzáttsyō'nā] *sf* utilization, use.

utiliz'zo [ōōtēlēd'dzō] *sm* (*AMM*) utilization; (*BANCA: di credito*) availment.

utilmen'te *av* usefully, profitably.

utopi'a *sf* utopia; **è pura** ~ that's sheer utopianism.

utopi'stico, a, ci, che *ag* utopian.

UVA *abbr* = *ultravioletto prossimo*.

u'va *sf* grapes *pl*; ~ **passa** raisins *pl*; ~ **spina** gooseberry.

uvet'ta *sf* raisins *pl*.

V

V, v [vē, vōō] *sf o m inv* (*lettera*) V, v; **V come Venezia** ≈ V for Victor.

V *abbr* (= *volt*) V.

v. *abbr* (= *vedi, verso, versetto*) v.

VA *sigla* = *Varese*.

va, va' *vb vedi* **andare**.

vacan'te *ag* vacant.

vacan'za [vákán'tsá] *sf* (*l'essere vacante*) vacancy; (*riposo, ferie*) vacation (*US*), holiday(s *pl*) (*Brit*); (*giorno di permesso*) day off, holiday; ~**e** *sfpl* (*periodo di ferie*) vacation *sg*, holidays; **essere/andare in** ~ to be/ go on vacation *o* holiday; **far** ~ to take a vacation (*US*), have a holiday (*Brit*); ~**e estive** summer vacation *o* holiday(s).

vac'ca, che *sf* cow.

vaccina're [váchēná'rā] *vt* to vaccinate; **farsi** ~ to have a vaccination, get vaccinated.

vaccinazio'ne [váchēnáttsyō'nā] *sf* vaccination.

vacci'no [váchē'nō] *sm* (*MED*) vaccine.

vacillan'te [váchēllán'tá] *ag* (*edificio, vecchio*) shaky, unsteady; (*fiamma*) flickering; (*salute, memoria*) shaky, failing.

vacilla're [váchēllá'rā] *vi* to sway; (*fiamma*) to flicker; (*fig: memoria, coraggio*) to be failing, falter.

va'cuo, a *ag* (*fig*) empty, vacuous ♦ *sm* vacuum.

va'do *etc vb vedi* **andare**.

vagabondag'gio [vágábōndád'jō] *sm* wandering, roaming; (*DIR*) vagrancy.

vagabonda're *vi* to roam, wander.

vagabon'do, a *smf* tramp, vagrant; (*fannullone*) idler, loafer.

vaga're *vi* to wander.

vagheggia're [vágēdjá'rā] *vt* to long for, dream of.

vaghe'rò *etc* [vágáro'] *vb vedi* **vagare**.

vaghez'za [vágāt'tsá] *sf* vagueness.

vagi'na [vájē'ná] *sf* vagina.

vagi're [vájē'rā] *vi* to whimper.

vagi'to [vájē'tō] *sm* cry, wailing.

va'glia [vàl'yà] *sm inv* money order; ~ **cambiario** promissory note; ~ **postale** postal order.

vaglia're [vàlyà'rā] *vt* to sift; *(fig)* to weigh up.

va'glio [vàl'yō] *sm* sieve; **passare al** ~ *(fig)* to examine closely.

va'go, a, ghi, ghe *ag* vague.

vago'ne *sm (FERR: per passeggeri)* car *(US)*, carriage *(Brit)*; (: *per merci)* truck, wagon; ~ **letto** sleeper, sleeping car; ~ **ristorante** dining car.

va'i *vb vedi* **andare**.

vaio'lo *sm* smallpox.

val. *abbr* = **valuta**.

valan'ga, ghe *sf* avalanche.

valen'te *ag* able, talented.

vale're *vi (avere forza, potenza)* to have influence; *(essere valido)* to be valid; *(avere vigore, autorità)* to hold, apply; *(essere capace: poeta, studente)* to be good, be able ♦ *vt (prezzo, sforzo)* to be worth; *(corrispondere)* to correspond to; *(procurare)*: ~ **qc a qn** to earn sb sth; ~**rsi** *vr:* ~**rsi di** to make use of, take advantage of; **far** ~ *(autorità etc)* to assert; **far** ~ **le proprie ragioni** to make o.s. heard; **farsi** ~ to make o.s. appreciated *o* respected; **vale a dire** that is to say; ~ **la pena** to be worth the effort *o* worth it; **l'uno vale l'altro** the one is as good as the other, they amount to the same thing; **non vale niente** it's worthless; ~**rsi dei consigli di qn** to take sb's advice, act upon sb's advice.

vale'vole *ag* valid.

val'go *etc vb vedi* **valere**.

valica're *vt* to cross.

va'lico, chi *sm (passo)* pass.

validità *sf* validity.

va'lido, a *ag* valid; *(rimedio)* effective; *(persona)* worthwhile; **essere di** ~ **aiuto a qn** to be a great help to sb.

valigeri'a [vàlējārē'à] *sf (assortimento)* leather goods *pl*; *(fabbrica)* leather goods factory; *(negozio)* leather goods shop.

vali'gia, gie *o* **ge** [vàlē'jà] *sf* (suit)case; **fare le** ~**gie** to pack (up); ~ **diplomatica** diplomatic bag.

valla'ta *sf* valley.

val'le *sf* valley; **a** ~ *(di fiume)* downstream; **scendere a** ~ to go downhill.

vallet'to *sm* valet.

valligia'no, a [vàllējà'nō] *sm/f* inhabitant of a valley.

valo're *sm (gen, COMM)* value; *(merito)* merit, worth; *(coraggio)* valor *(US)*, valour *(Brit)*, courage; *(FINANZA: titolo)* security; ~**i** *smpl (oggetti preziosi)* valuables; **crescere/diminuire di** ~ to go up/down in value, gain/lose in value; **è di gran** ~ it's worth a lot, it's very valuable; **privo di** ~ worthless; ~ **contabile** book value; ~ **effetti-**

vo real value; ~ **nominale** *o* **facciale** nominal value; ~ **di realizzo** break-up value; ~ **di riscatto** surrender value; ~**i bollati** (revenue) stamps.

valorizza're [vàlōrēddzà'rā] *vt (terreno)* to develop; *(fig)* to make the most of.

valoro'so, a *ag* courageous.

val'so, a *pp di* **valere**.

valu'ta *sf* currency, money; *(BANCA)*: ~ **15 gennaio** interest to run from January 15th; ~ **estera** foreign currency.

valuta're *vt (casa, gioiello, fig)* to value; *(stabilire: peso, entrate, fig)* to estimate.

valuta'rio, a *ag (FINANZA: norme)* currency *cpd*.

valutazio'ne [vàlōōtàttsyō'nā] *sf* valuation; estimate.

val'va *sf (ZOOL, BOT)* valve.

val'vola *sf (TECN, ANAT)* valve; *(ELETTR)* fuse; ~ **a farfalla del carburatore** *(AUT)* butterfly valve *(US)*, throttle *(Brit)*; ~ **di sicurezza** safety valve.

val'zer [vàl'tsàr] *sm inv* waltz.

vampa'ta *sf (di fiamma)* blaze; *(di calore)* blast; (: *al viso)* flush.

vampi'ro *sm* vampire.

vanaglo'ria *sf* boastfulness.

vanda'lico, a, ci, che *ag* vandal *cpd*; **atto** ~ act of vandalism.

vandali'smo *sm* vandalism.

van'dalo *sm* vandal.

vaneggiamen'to [vànādjàmān'tō] *sm* raving, delirium.

vaneggia're [vànàdjà'rā] *vi* to rave.

vane'sio, a *ag* vain, conceited.

van'ga, ghe *sf* spade.

vanga're *vt* to dig.

vange'lo [vànje'lō] *sm* gospel.

vanifica're *vt* to nullify.

vani'glia [vànēl'yà] *sf* vanilla.

vanità *sf* vanity; *(di promessa)* emptiness; *(di sforzo)* futility.

vanito'so, a *ag* vain, conceited.

van'no *vb vedi* **andare**.

va'no, a *ag* vain ♦ *sm (spazio)* space; *(apertura)* opening; *(stanza)* room; **il** ~ **della porta** the doorway; **il** ~ **portabagagli** *(AUT)* the trunk *(US)*, the boot *(Brit)*.

vantag'gio [vàntàd'jō] *sm* advantage; **trarre** ~ **da qc** to benefit from sth; **essere/portarsi in** ~ *(SPORT)* to be in/take the lead.

vantaggio'so, a [vàntàdjō'sō] *ag* advantageous, favorable *(US)*, favourable *(Brit)*.

vanta're *vt* to praise, speak highly of; ~**rsi** *vr:* ~**rsi (di/di aver fatto)** to boast *o* brag (about/about having done).

vanteri'a *sf* boasting.

van'to *sm* boasting; *(merito)* virtue, merit; *(gloria)* pride.

van'vera *sf:* **a** ~ haphazardly; **parlare a** ~ to

talk nonsense.

vapo're *sm* vapor (*US*), vapour (*Brit*); (*anche:* ~ **acqueo**) steam; (*nave*) steamer; **a** ~ (*turbina etc*) steam *cpd*; **al** ~ · (*CUC*) steamed.

vaporet'to *sm* steamer.

vaporie'ra *sf* (*FERR*) steam engine.

vaporizza're [vȧpōrēddzȧ'rā] *vt* to vaporize.

vaporizzato're [vȧpōrēddzȧtō'rā] *sm* spray.

vaporizzazio'ne [vȧpōrēddzȧttsyō'nā] *sf* vaporization.

vaporo'so, a *ag* (*tessuto*) filmy; (*capelli*) soft and full.

vara're *vt* (*NAUT, fig*) to launch; (*DIR*) to pass.

varca're *vt* to cross.

var'co, chi *sm* passage; **aprirsi un** ~ **tra la folla** to push one's way through the crowd.

varechi'na [vȧrākē'nȧ] *sf* bleach.

varia'bile *ag* variable; (*tempo, umore*) changeable, variable ♦ *sf* (*MAT*) variable.

varian'te *sf* (*gen*) variation, change; (*LING*) variant; (*SPORT*) alternative route.

varia're *vt, vi* to vary; ~ **di opinione** to change one's mind.

variazio'ne [vȧryȧttsyō'nā] *sf* variation, change; (*MUS*) variation; **una** ~ **di programma** a change of plan.

vari'ce [vȧrē'chā] *sf* varicose vein.

varicel'la [vȧrēchȧl'lȧ] *sf* chickenpox.

varico'so, a *ag* varicose.

variega'to, a *ag* variegated.

varietà *sf inv* variety ♦ *sm inv* variety show.

va'rio, a *ag* varied; (*parecchi: col sostantivo al pl*) various; (*mutevole: umore*) changeable; ~**e** *sfpl:* ~**e ed eventuali** (*nell'ordine del giorno*) any other business.

variopin'to, a *ag* multicolored (*US*), multicoloured (*Brit*).

va'ro *sm* (*NAUT, fig*) launch; (*di leggi*) passing.

varrò *etc vb vedi* **valere.**

Varsa'via *sf* Warsaw.

vasa'io *sm* potter.

va'sca, sche *sf* basin; (*anche:* ~ **da bagno**) bathtub, bath.

vascel'lo [vȧshcl'lō] *sm* (*NAUT*) vessel, ship.

vaschet'ta [vȧskāt'tȧ] *sf* (*per gelato*) tub; (*per sviluppare fotografie*) dish.

vaseli'na *sf* vaseline.

vasella'me *sm* (*stoviglie*) crockery; (: *di porcellana*) china; ~ **d'oro/d'argento** gold/silver plate.

va'so *sm* (*recipiente*) pot; (: *barattolo*) jar; (: *decorativo*) vase; (*ANAT*) vessel; ~ **da fiori** vase; (*per piante*) flowerpot.

vasso'io *sm* tray.

vastità *sf* vastness.

va'sto, a *ag* vast, immense; **di** ~**e proporzioni** (*incendio*) huge; (*fenomeno, rivolta*) wide-

spread; **su** ~**a scala** on a vast *o* huge scale.

Vatica'no *sm:* **il** ~ the Vatican; **la Città del** ~ the Vatican City.

VC *sigla* = *Vercelli.*

VE *sigla* = *Venezia* ♦ *abbr* = *Vostra Eccellenza.*

ve *pronome, av vedi* **vi.**

vecchia'ia [vākkyȧ'yȧ] *sf* old age.

vec'chio, a [vck'kyō] *ag* old ♦ *sm/f* old man/woman; **i** ~**i** the old; **è un mio** ~ **amico** he's an old friend of mine; **è un uomo** ~ **stile** *o* **stampo** he's an old-fashioned man; **è** ~ **del mestiere** he's an old hand at the job.

ve'ce [vā'chā] *sf:* **in** ~ **di** in the place of, for; **fare le** ~**i di qn** to take sb's place; **firma del padre** *o* **di chi ne fa le** ~**i** signature of the parent or guardian.

vede're *vt, vi* to see; ~**rsi** *vr* to meet, see one another; ~ **di fare qc** to see (to it) that sth is done, make sure that sth is done; **avere a che** ~ **con** to have to do with; **far** ~ **qc a qn** to show sb sth; **farsi** ~ to show o.s.; (*farsi vivo*) to show one's face; **farsi** ~ **da un medico** to go and see a doctor; **modo di** ~ outlook, view of things; **vedi pagina 8** (*rimando*) see page 8; **è da** ~ **se ...** it remains to be seen whether ...; **non vedo la ragione di farlo** I can't see any reason to do it; **si era visto costretto a ...** he found himself forced to ...; **non (ci) si vede** (*è buio etc*) you can't see a thing; **ci vediamo domani!** see you tomorrow!; **non lo posso** ~ (*fig*) I can't stand him.

vedet'ta *sf* (*sentinella, posto*) look-out; (*NAUT*) patrol boat.

vedet'te [vȧdct'] *sf inv* (*attrice*) star.

ve'dovo, a *sm/f* widower/widow; **rimaner** ~ to be widowed.

vedrò *etc vb vedi* **vedere.**

vedu'ta *sf* view; **di larghe** *o* **ampie** ~**e** broadminded; **di** ~**e limitate** narrow-minded.

veemen'te *ag* (*discorso, azione*) vehement; (*assalto*) vigorous; (*passione*) overwhelming.

veemen'za [vāāmcn'tsȧ] *sf* vehemence; **con** ~ vehemently.

vegeta'le [vājȧtȧ'lā] *ag, sm* vegetable.

vegeta're [vājȧtȧ'rā] *vi* (*fig*) to vegetate.

vegetaria'no, a [vājȧtȧryȧ'nō] *ag, sm/f* vegetarian.

vegetazio'ne [vājȧtȧttsyō'nā] *sf* vegetation.

ve'geto, a [vc'jȧtō] *ag* (*pianta*) thriving; (*persona*) strong, vigorous.

veggen'te [vādjcn'tā] *sm/f* (*indovino*) clairvoyant.

ve'glia [vāl'yȧ] *sf* (*sorveglianza*) watch; (*trattenimento*) evening gathering; **tra la** ~ **e il sonno** half awake; **fare la** ~ **a un malato** to watch over a sick person; ~ **funebre** wake.

veglia're [vālyȧ'rā] *vi* to stay *o* sit up; (*stare*

vigile) to watch; to keep watch ♦ *vt* (*malato, morto*) to watch over, sit up with.

veglio'ne [vālyō'nā] *sm* ball, dance.

vei'colo *sm* vehicle; ~ **spaziale** spacecraft *inv*.

ve'la *sf* (*NAUT*: *tela*) sail; (*sport*) sailing; **tutto va a gonfie** ~**e** (*fig*) everything is going perfectly.

vela're *vt* to veil; ~**rsi** *vr* (*occhi, luna*) to mist over; (*voce*) to become husky; ~**rsi il viso** to cover one's face (with a veil).

vela'to, a *ag* veiled.

velatu'ra *sf* (*NAUT*) sails *pl*.

veleggia're [vālādjá'rā] *vi* to sail; (*AER*) to glide.

vele'no *sm* poison.

veleno'so, a *ag* poisonous.

velet'ta *sf* (*di cappello*) veil.

velie'ro *sm* sailing ship.

veli'na *sf* (*anche:* **carta** ~: *per imballare*) tissue paper; (: *per copie*) flimsy paper; (*copia*) carbon copy.

veli'sta, i, e *sm/f* yachtsman/woman.

veli'volo *sm* aircraft.

velleità *sf inv* vain ambition, vain desire.

velleita'rio, a *ag* unrealistic.

vel'lo *sm* fleece.

velluta'to, a *ag* (*stoffa, pesca, colore*) velvety; (*voce*) mellow.

vellu'to *sm* velvet; ~ **a coste** cord.

ve'lo *sm* veil; (*tessuto*) voile.

velo'ce [vālō'chā] *ag* fast, quick ♦ *av* fast, quickly.

veloci'sta, i, e [vālōchē'stá] *sm/f* (*SPORT*) sprinter.

velocità [vālōchētá'] *sf* speed; **a forte** ~ at high speed; ~ **di crociera** cruising speed.

velo'dromo *sm* velodrome.

ven. *abbr* (*REL*) = **venerabile**; (= *venerdì*) Fri.

ve'na *sf* (*gen*) vein; (*filone*) vein, seam; (*fig*: *ispirazione*) inspiration; (: *umore*) mood; **essere in** ~ **di qc** to be in the mood for sth.

vena'le *ag* (*prezzo, valore*) market *cpd*; (*fig*) venal; mercenary.

venalità *sf* venality.

vena'to, a *ag* (*marmo*) veined, streaked; (*legno*) grained.

venato'rio, a *ag* hunting; **la stagione** ~**a** the hunting season.

venatu'ra *sf* (*di marmo*) vein, streak; (*di legno*) grain.

vendem'mia *sf* (*raccolta*) grape harvest; (*quantità d'uva*) grape crop, grapes *pl*; (*vino ottenuto*) vintage.

vendemmia're *vt* to harvest ♦ *vi* to harvest the grapes.

ven'dere *vt* to sell; ~ **all'ingrosso/al dettaglio** *o* **minuto** to sell wholesale/retail; ~ **all'asta** to auction, sell by auction; "**vendesi**"

"for sale".

vendet'ta *sf* revenge.

vendica're *vt* to avenge; ~**rsi** *vr*: ~**rsi (di)** to avenge o.s. (for); (*per rancore*) to take one's revenge (for); ~**rsi su qn** to revenge o.s. on sb.

vendicati'vo, a *ag* vindictive.

ven'dita *sf* sale; **la** ~ (*attività*) selling; (*smercio*) sales *pl*; **in** ~ on sale; **mettere in** ~ to put on sale; **in** ~ **presso** on sale at; **contratto di** ~ sales agreement; **reparto** ~**e** sales department; ~ **all'asta** sale by auction; ~ **al dettaglio** *o* **minuto** retail; ~ **all'ingrosso** wholesale.

vendito're, tri'ce *sm/f* seller, vendor; (*gestore di negozio*) trader, dealer.

vene'fico, a, ci, che *ag* poisonous.

venera'bile *ag*, **veneran'do, a** *ag* venerable.

venera're *vt* to venerate.

venerazio'ne [vānārāttsyō'nā] *sf* veneration.

venerdì *sm inv* Friday; **V**~ **Santo** Good Friday; *per fraseologia vedi* **martedì**.

Ve'nere *sm, ag* Venus.

vene'reo, a *ag* venereal.

ve'neto, a *ag* (*o* from) the Veneto.

ve'neto-giulia'no, a [ve'nātōjōōlyá'nō] *ag* (*o* from) Venezia-Giulia.

Vene'zia [vānet'tsyá] *sf* Venice.

venezia'no, a [vānāttsyá'nō] *ag*, *sm/f* Venetian.

Venezue'la [vānāttsōōā'lá] *sm*: **il** ~ Venezuela.

venezuela'no, a [vānāttsōōālá'nō] *ag*, *sm/f* Venezuelan.

ven'go *etc vb vedi* **venire**.

venia'le *ag* venial.

veni're *vi* to come; (*riuscire*: *dolce, fotografia*) to turn out; (*come ausiliare*: *essere*): **viene ammirato da tutti** he is admired by everyone; ~ **da** to come from; **quanto viene?** how much does it cost?; **far** ~ (*mandare a chiamare*) to send for; (*medico*) to call, send for; ~ **a capo di qc** to unravel sth, sort sth out; ~ **al dunque** *o* **nocciolo** *o* **fatto** to come to the point; ~ **fuori** to come out; ~ **giù** to come down; ~ **meno** (*svenire*) to faint; ~ **meno a qc** not to fulfill sth; ~ **su** to come up; ~ **via** to come away; ~ **a sapere qc** to learn sth; ~ **a trovare qn** to come and see sb; **negli anni a** ~ in the years to come, in future; **è venuto il momento di** ... the time has come to ....

ven'ni *etc vb vedi* **venire**.

venta'glio [vāntál'yō] *sm* fan.

venta'ta *sf* gust (of wind).

ventenna'le *ag* (*che dura 20 anni*) twenty-year *cpd*; (*che ricorre ogni 20 anni*) which takes place every twenty years.

venten'ne *ag*, *sm/f* twenty-year-old.

venten'nio *sm* period of twenty years; **il** ~ **fascista** the Fascist period.

vente'simo, a *num* twentieth.

ven'ti *num* twenty.
ventila're *vt* (*stanza*) to air, ventilate; (*fig: idea, proposta*) to air.
ventila'to, a *ag* (*camera, zona*) airy; **poco ~** airless.
ventilato're *sm* fan; (*su parete, finestra*) ventilator, fan.
ventilazio'ne [vāntēláttsyō'nā] *sf* ventilation.
venti'na *sf*: **una ~ (di)** around twenty, twenty or so.
ventiquattr'o're *sfpl* (*periodo*) twenty-four hours ♦ *sf inv* (*SPORT*) twenty-four-hour race; (*valigetta*) overnight case.
ventiset'te *num* twenty-seven; **il ~** (*giorno di paga*) (monthly) pay day.
ventitré *num* twenty-three ♦ *sfpl*: **portava il cappello sulle ~** he wore his hat cocked on his head.
ven'to *sm* wind; **c'è ~** it's windy; **un colpo di ~** a gust of wind; **contro ~** against the wind; **~ contrario** (*NAUT*) headwind.
ven'tola *sf* (*AUT, TECN*) fan.
vento'sa *sf* (*ZOOL*) sucker; (*di gomma*) suction pad.
vento'so, a *ag* windy.
ventot'to *num* twenty-eight.
ven'tre *sm* stomach.
ventri'loquo *sm* ventriloquist.
ventu'no *num* twenty-one.
ventu'ra *sf*: **andare alla ~** to trust to luck; **soldato di ~** mercenary.
ventu'ro, a *ag* next, coming.
venu'to, a *pp di* **venire** ♦ *sm/f*: **il(la) primo(a) ~(a)** the first person who comes along ♦ *sf* coming, arrival.
ver. *abbr* = **versamento.**
ve'ra *sf* wedding ring.
vera'ce [vārá'chā] *ag* (*testimone*) truthful; (*testimonianza*) accurate; (*cibi*) real, genuine.
veramen'te *av* really.
veran'da *sf* veranda(h).
verba'le *ag* verbal ♦ *sm* (*di riunione*) minutes *pl*; **accordo ~** verbal agreement; **mettere a ~** to place in the minutes *o* on record.
ver'bo *sm* (*LING*) verb; (*parola*) word; (*REL*): **il V~** the Word.
verbo'so, a *ag* verbose, wordy.
verdas'tro, a *ag* greenish.
ver'de *ag, sm* green; **essere al ~** (*fig*) to be broke; **~ bottiglia/oliva** *ag inv* bottle/olive green; **i V~i** (*POL*) the Greens.
verdeggian'te [vārdādján'tā] *ag* green, verdant.
verdera'me *sm* verdigris.
verdet'to *sm* verdict.
verdu'ra *sf* vegetables *pl*.
verecon'dia *sf* modesty.
verecon'do, a *ag* modest.
ver'ga, ghe *sf* rod.

verga'to a *ag* (*foglio*) ruled.
vergina'le [vārjēná'lā] *ag* virginal.
ver'gine [vār'jēnā] *sf* virgin; (*dello zodiaco*): **V~** Virgo ♦ *ag* virgin; (*ragazza*): **essere ~** to be a virgin; **essere della V~** (*dello zodiaco*) to be Virgo; **pura lana ~** virgin wool (*US*), pure new wool (*Brit*); **olio ~ d'oliva** virgin olive oil.
verginità [vārjēnētá'] *sf* virginity.
vergo'gna [vārgōn'yá] *sf* shame; (*timidezza*) shyness, embarrassment.
vergognar'si [vārgōnyár'sē] *vr*: **~ (di)** to be *o* feel ashamed (of); to be shy (about), be embarrassed (about).
vergogno'so, a [vārgōnyō'sō] *ag* ashamed; (*timido*) shy, embarrassed; (*causa di vergogna: azione*) shameful.
veridicità [vārēdēchētá'] *sf* truthfulness.
veri'dico, a, ci, che *ag* truthful.
veri'fica, che *sf* checking *q*; check; **fare una ~ di** (*freni, testimonianza, firma*) to check; **~ contabile** (*FINANZA*) audit.
verifica're *vt* (*controllare*) to check; (*confermare*) to confirm, bear out; (*FINANZA*) to audit.
verità *sf inv* truth; **a dire la ~, per la ~** truth to tell, actually.
veritie'ro, a *ag* (*che dice la verità*) truthful; (*conforme a verità*) true.
ver'me *sm* worm.
vermicel'li [vārmēchel'lē] *smpl* vermicelli *sg*.
vermi'glio [vārmēl'yō] *sm* vermilion, scarlet.
ver'mut *sm inv* vermouth.
verna'colo *sm* vernacular.
verni'ce [vārnē'chā] *sf* (*colorazione*) paint; (*trasparente*) varnish; (*pelle*) patent leather; **"~ fresca"** "wet paint".
vernicia're [vārnēchá'rā] *vt* to paint; to varnish.
verniciatu'ra [vārnēchátōō'rá] *sf* painting; varnishing.
ve'ro, a *ag* (*veridico: fatti, testimonianza*) true; (*autentico*) real ♦ *sm* (*verità*) truth; (*realtà*) (real) life; **un ~ e proprio delinquente** a real criminal, an out and out criminal; **tant'è ~ che ...** so much so that ...; **a onor del ~, a dire il ~** to tell the truth.
verone'se *ag* of (*o* from) Verona.
verosi'mile *ag* likely, probable.
verrò *etc vb vedi* **venire**.
verru'ca, che *sf* wart.
versamen'to *sm* (*pagamento*) payment; (*deposito di denaro*) deposit.
versan'te *sm* slopes *pl*, side.
versa're *vt* (*fare uscire: vino, farina*) to pour (out); (*spargere: lacrime, sangue*) to shed; (*rovesciare*) to spill; (*ECON*) to pay; (: *depositare*) to deposit, pay in ♦ *vi*: **~ in gravi difficoltà** to find o.s. with serious problems; **~rsi** *vr* (*rovesciarsi*) to spill; (*fiume, folla*):

~rsi (in) to pour (into).
versati'le *ag* versatile.
versatilità *sf* versatility.
versa'to, a *ag*: **~ in** to be (well-)versed in.
verset'to *sm* (*REL*) verse.
versio'ne *sf* version; (*traduzione*) translation.
ver'so *sm* (*di poesia*) verse, line; (*di animale, uccello, venditore ambulante*) cry; (*direzione*) direction; (*modo*) way; (*di foglio di carta*) verso; (*di moneta*) reverse; **~i** *smpl* (*poesia*) verse *sg*; **per un ~ o per l'altro** one way or another; **prendere qn/qc per il ~ giusto** to approach sb/sth the right way; **rifare il ~ a qn** (*imitare*) to mimic sb; **non c'è ~ di persuaderlo** there's no way of persuading him, he can't be persuaded ♦ *prep* (*in direzione di*) toward(s); (*nei pressi di*) near, around (about); (*in senso temporale*) about, around; (*nei confronti di*) for; **~ di me** towards me; **~ l'alto** upwards; **~ il basso** downwards; **~ sera** towards evening.
ver'tebra *sf* vertebra.
vertebra'le *ag* vertebral; **colonna ~** spinal column, spine.
vertebra'to, a *ag, sm* vertebrate.
verten'za [vārten'tsà] *sf* (*lite*) lawsuit, case; (*sindacale*) dispute.
ver'tere *vi*: **~ su** to deal with, be about.
vertica'le *ag, sf* vertical.
ver'tice [ver'tēchā] *sm* summit, top; (*MAT*) vertex; **conferenza al ~** (*POL*) summit conference.
verti'gine [vārtē'jēnā] *sf* dizziness *q*; dizzy spell; (*MED*) vertigo; **avere le ~i** to feel dizzy.
vertigino'so, a [vārtējēnō'sō] *ag* (*altezza*) dizzy; (*fig*) breathtakingly high (*o* deep *etc*).
ver'za [vār'dzà] *sf* Savoy cabbage.
vesci'ca, che [vāshē'kà] *sf* (*ANAT*) bladder; (*MED*) blister.
vescovi'le *ag* episcopal.
ve'scovo *sm* bishop.
ve'spa *sf* wasp; (®: *veicolo*) (motor) scooter.
vespa'io *sm* wasps' nest; **suscitare un ~** (*fig*) to stir up a hornets' nest.
vespasia'no *sm* urinal.
ves'pro *sm* (*REL*) vespers *pl*.
vessa're *vt* to oppress.
vessazio'ne [vāssáttsyō'nā] *sf* oppression.
vessil'lo *sm* standard; (*bandiera*) flag.
vesta'glia [vāstál'yà] *sf* robe (*US*), dressing gown.
ve'ste *sf* garment; (*rivestimento*) covering; (*qualità, facoltà*) capacity; **~i** *sfpl* clothes, clothing *sg*; **in ~ ufficiale** (*fig*) in an official capacity; **in ~ di** in the guise of, as; **~ da camera** robe (*US*), dressing gown; **~ editoriale** layout.
vestia'rio *sm* wardrobe, clothes *pl*; **capo di ~** article of clothing, garment.

vesti'bolo *sm* (entrance) hall.
vesti'gia [vāstē'jà] *sfpl* (*tracce*) vestiges, traces; (*rovine*) ruins, remains.
vesti're *vt* (*bambino, malato*) to dress; (*avere indosso*) to have on, wear; **~rsi** *vr* to dress, get dressed; **~rsi da** (*negozio, sarto*) to buy *o* get one's clothes at.
vesti'to, a *ag* dressed ♦ *sm* garment; (*da donna*) dress; (*da uomo*) suit; **~i** *smpl* (*indumenti*) clothes; **~ di bianco** dressed in white.
Vesu'vio *sm*: **il ~** Vesuvius.
vetera'no, a *ag, sm/f* veteran.
veterina'rio, a *ag* veterinary ♦ *sm* veterinarian (*US*), veterinary surgeon (*Brit*), vet ♦ *sf* veterinary medicine.
ve'to *sm inv* veto; **porre il ~ a qc** to veto sth.
vetra'io *sm* glassmaker; (*per finestre*) glazier.
vetra'to, a *ag* (*porta, finestra*) glazed; (*che contiene vetro*) glass *cpd* ♦ *sf* glass door (*o* window); (*di chiesa*) stained glass window; **carta ~a** sandpaper.
vetreri'a *sf* (*stabilimento*) glassworks *sg*; (*oggetti di vetro*) glassware.
vetri'na *sf* (*di negozio*) (shop) window; (*armadio*) display cabinet.
vetrini'sta, i, e *sm/f* window dresser.
vetri'no *sm* slide.
vetrio'lo *sm* vitriol.
ve'tro *sm* glass; (*per finestra, porta*) pane (of glass); **~ blindato** bulletproof glass; **~ infrangibile** shatterproof glass; **~ di sicurezza** safety glass; **i ~i di Murano** Murano glassware *sg*.
vetro'so, a *ag* vitreous.
vet'ta *sf* peak, summit, top.
vetto're *sm* (*MAT, FISICA*) vector; (*chi trasporta*) carrier.
vettova'glie [vāttōvál'yā] *sfpl* supplies.
vettu'ra *sf* (*carrozza*) carriage; (*FERR*) car (*US*), carriage (*Brit*); (*auto*) automobile (*US*), car (*Brit*); **~ di piazza** hackney carriage.
vetturi'no *sm* coach driver, coachman.
vezzeggia're [vāttsādjá'rā] *vt* to fondle, caress.
vezzeggiati'vo [vāttsādjátē'vō] *sm* (*LING*) term of endearment.
vez'zo [vāt'tsō] *sm* habit; **~i** *smpl* (*smancerie*) affected ways; (*leggiadria*) charms.
vezzo'so, a [vāttsō'sō] *ag* (*grazioso*) charming, pretty; (*lezioso*) affected.
V.F. *abbr* = **vigili del fuoco**.
V.G. *abbr* = *Vostra Grazia*.
VI *sigla* = *Vicenza*.
vi (*dav lo, la, li, le, ne diventa* **ve**) *pronome* (*oggetto*) you; (*complemento di termine*) (to) you; (*riflessivo*) yourselves; (*reciproco*) each other ♦ *av* (*lì*) there; (*qui*) here; (*per questo/quel luogo*) through here/there; **~ è/ sono** there is/are.
vi'a *sf* (*gen*) way; (*strada*) street; (*sentiero,*

pista) path, track; (*AMM*: *procedimento*) channels *pl* ♦ *prep* (*passando per*) via, by way of ♦ *av* away ♦ *escl* go away!; (*suvvia*) come on!; (*SPORT*) go! ♦ *sm* (*SPORT*) starting signal; **per** ~ **di** (*a causa di*) because of, on account of; **in** *o* **per** ~ on the way; **in** ~ **di guarigione** (*fig*) on the road to recovery; **per** ~ **aerea** by air; (*lettere*) by airmail; ~ **satellite** by satellite; **andare/essere** ~ to go/ be away; ~ ~ (*pian piano*) gradually; ~ ~ **che** (*a mano a mano*) as; **e** ~ **dicendo, e** ~ **di questo passo** and so on (and so forth); **dare il** ~ (*SPORT*) to give the starting signal; **dare il** ~ **a un progetto** to give the green light to a project; **hanno dato il** ~ **ai lavori** they've begun *o* started work; **in** ~ **amichevole** in a friendly manner; **comporre una disputa in** ~ **amichevole** (*DIR*) to settle a dispute out of court; **in** ~ **eccezionale** as an exception; **in** ~ **privata** *o* **confidenziale** (*dire etc*) in confidence; **in** ~ **provvisoria** provisionally; **V**~ **lattea** (*ASTR*) Milky Way; ~ **di mezzo** middle course; **non c'è** ~ **di scampo** *o* **d'uscita** there's no way out; ~**e di comunicazione** communication routes.

viabilità *sf* (*di strada*) practicability; (*rete stradale*) roads *pl*, road network.

viadot'to *sm* viaduct.

viaggia're [věǎdjá'rā] *vi* to travel; **le merci viaggiano via mare** the goods go *o* are sent by sea.

viaggiato're, tri'ce [věǎdjàtō'rā] *ag* traveling (*US*), travelling (*Brit*) ♦ *sm* traveler (*US*), traveller (*Brit*); (*passeggero*) passenger.

viag'gio [věǎd'jō] *sm* travel(ling); (*tragitto*) journey, trip; **buon** ~! have a good trip!; ~ **d'affari** business trip; ~ **di nozze** honeymoon; ~ **organizzato** package tour.

via'le *sm* avenue.

viandan'te *sm/f* vagrant.

via'tico, ci *sm* (*REL*) viaticum; (*fig*) encouragement.

viava'i *sm* coming and going, bustle.

vibra're *vi* to vibrate; (*agitarsi*): ~ (**di**) to quiver (with).

vibrazio'ne [věbrȧttsyō'nā] *sf* vibration.

vica'rio *sm* (*apostolico etc*) vicar.

vi'ce [vē'chā] *sm/f* deputy ♦ *prefisso* vice.

vicecon'sole [věchākon'sōlā] *sm* vice-consul.

vicediretto're, tri'ce [věchādērǎttō'rā] *sm/f* assistant manager/manageress; (*di giornale etc*) deputy editor.

vicen'da [věchen'dá] *sf* event; ~**e** *sfpl* (*sorte*) fortunes; **a** ~ in turn; **con alterne** ~**e** with mixed fortunes.

vicende'vole [věchāndā'vōlā] *ag* mutual, reciprocal.

vicenti'no, a [věchāntē'nō] *ag* of (*o* from) Vicenza.

vicepresiden'te [věchāprāsēden'tā] *sm* vice-president, vice-chairman.

vicever'sa [věchāvcr'sȧ] *av* vice versa; **da Roma a Pisa e** ~ from Rome to Pisa and back.

vichin'go, a, ghi, ghe [věkēn'gō] *ag, sm/f* Viking.

vicinan'za [věchēnȧn'tsȧ] *sf* nearness, closeness; ~**e** *sfpl* (*paraggi*) neighborhood (*US*), neighbourhood (*Brit*), vicinity.

vicina'to [věchēnȧ'tō] *sm* neighborhood (*US*), neighbourhood (*Brit*); (*vicini*) neighbo(u)rs *pl*.

vici'no, a [věchē'nō] *ag* (*gen*) near; (*nello spazio*) near, nearby; (*accanto*) next; (*nel tempo*) near, close at hand ♦ *sm/f* neighbor (*US*), neighbour (*Brit*) ♦ *av* near, close; **da** ~ (*guardare*) close up; (*esaminare, seguire*) closely; (*conoscere*) well, intimately; ~ **a** *prep* near (to), close to; (*accanto a*) beside; **mi sono stati molto** ~**i** (*fig*) they were very supportive towards me; ~ **di casa** neighbo(u)r.

vicissitu'dini [věchēssētōō'dēnē] *sfpl* trials and tribulations.

vi'colo *sm* alley; ~ **cieco** blind alley.

vi'deo *sm inv* (*TV*: *schermo*) screen.

videocasset'ta *sf* videocassette.

videogio'co, chi [vědāōjo'kō] *sm* video game.

videoregistrato're [vědāōrājēstrȧtō'rā] *sm* (*apparecchio*) video (recorder).

videotermina'le *sm* visual display unit.

vi'di *etc vb vedi* **vedere**.

vidima're *vt* (*AMM*) to authenticate.

vidimazio'ne [vědēmȧttsyō'nā] *sf* (*AMM*) authentication.

Vien'na *sf* Vienna.

vienne'se *ag, sm/f* Viennese *inv*.

vieta're *vt* to forbid; (*AMM*) to prohibit; (*libro*) to ban; ~ **a qn di fare** to forbid sb to do; to prohibit sb from doing.

vieta'to, a *ag* (*vedi vb*) forbidden; prohibited; banned; **"~ fumare/l'ingresso"** "no smoking/admittance"; ~ **ai minori di 14/18 anni** prohibited to children under 14/18; **"senso ~"** (*AUT*) "no entry"; **"sosta ~a"** (*AUT*) "no parking".

Vietnam' *sm*: **il** ~ Vietnam.

vietnami'ta, i, e *ag, sm/f, sm* Vietnamese *inv*.

vie'to, a *ag* worthless.

vigen'te [vējen'tā] *ag* in force.

vi'gere [vē'jārā] *vi* (*difettivo*: *si usa solo alla terza persona*) to be in force; **in casa mia vige l'abitudine di ...** at home we are in the habit of ....

vigilan'te [vējēlȧn'tā] *ag* vigilant, watchful.

vigilan'za [vējēlȧn'tsȧ] *sf* vigilance; (*sorveglianza*: *di operai, alunni*) supervision; (: *di sospetti, criminali*) surveillance; ~ **notturna** night-watchman service.

vigila're [vējēlȧ'rā] *vt* to watch over, keep an

eye on; ~ **che** to make sure that, see to it that.

vigila'to, a [vējēlå'tō] smf (DIR) person under police surveillance.

vigilatri'ce [vējēlåtrē'chā] sf: ~ **d'infanzia** nursery-school teacher; ~ **scolastica** school health officer.

vi'gile [vē'jēlā] ag watchful ♦ sm (anche: ~ **urbano**) policeman (in towns); ~ **del fuoco** fireman.

vigiles'sa [vējēlās'så] sf (traffic) policewoman.

vigi'lia [vējē'lyå] sf (giorno antecedente) eve; **la** ~ **di Natale** Christmas Eve.

vigliaccheri'a [vēlyåkkārē'å] sf cowardice.

vigliac'co, a, chi, che [vēlyåk'kō] ag cowardly ♦ smf coward.

vi'gna [vēn'yå] sf, **vigne'to** [vēnyā'tō] sm vineyard.

vignet'ta [vēnyāt'tå] sf cartoon.

vigo'gna [vēgōn'yå] sf vicuña.

vigo're sm vigor (US), vigour (Brit); (DIR): **essere/entrare in** ~ to be in/come into force; **non è più in** ~ it is no longer in force, it no longer applies.

vigoro'so, a ag vigorous.

vi'le ag (spregevole) low, mean, base; (codardo) cowardly.

vilipen'dere vt to despise, scorn.

vilipen'dio sm contempt, scorn.

vilipe'so, a pp di **vilipendere**.

vil'la sf villa.

villag'gio [vēllåd'jō] sm village; ~ **turistico** holiday village.

villani'a sf rudeness, lack of manners; **fare** (o **dire**) **una** ~ **a qn** to be rude to sb.

villa'no, a ag rude, ill-mannered ♦ smf boor.

villeggian'te [vēllādjån'tā] smf vacationer (US), holiday-maker (Brit).

villeggia're [vēllādjå'rā] vi to vacation (US), spend one's holiday (Brit).

villeggiatu'ra [vēllādjåtōō'rå] sf vacation (US), holiday(s pl) (Brit); **luogo di** ~ (holiday) resort.

villet'ta sf, **villi'no** sm small house (with a garden), cottage.

villo'so, a ag hairy.

viltà sf cowardice q; (gesto) cowardly act.

vi'mine sm wicker; **mobili di** ~**i** wicker furniture sg.

vina'io sm wine merchant.

vin'cere [vēn'chārā] vt (in guerra, al gioco, a una gara) to defeat, beat; (premio, guerra, partita) to win; (fig) to overcome, conquer ♦ vi to win; ~ **qn in** (abilità, bellezza) to surpass sb in.

vin'cita [vēn'chētå] sf win; (denaro vinto) winnings pl.

vincito're, tri'ce [vēnchētō'rā] smf winner; (MIL) victor.

vincolan'te ag binding.

vincola're vt to bind; (COMM: denaro) to tie up.

vincola'to, a ag: **deposito** ~ (COMM) fixed deposit.

vin'colo sm (fig) bond, tie; (DIR) obligation.

vini'colo, a ag wine cpd; **regione** ~**a** wine-producing area.

vinificazio'ne [vēnēfēkåttsyō'nā] sf wine-making.

vi'no sm wine; ~ **bianco/rosso** white/red wine.

vin'si etc vb vedi **vincere**.

vin'to, a pp di **vincere** ♦ ag: **darla** ~**a a qn** to let sb have his (o her) way; **darsi per** ~ to give up, give in.

vio'la sf (BOT) violet; (MUS) viola ♦ ag, sm inv (colore) purple.

viola're vt (chiesa) to desecrate, violate; (giuramento, legge) to violate.

violazio'ne [vēōlåttsyō'nā] sf desecration; violation; ~ **di domicilio** (DIR) breaking and entering.

violenta're vt to use violence on; (donna) to rape.

violen'to, a ag violent.

violen'za [vēōlen'tså] sf violence; ~ **carnale** rape.

violet'to, a ag, sm (colore) violet ♦ sf (BOT) violet.

violini'sta, i, e smf violinist.

violi'no sm violin.

violoncelli'sta, i, e [vēōlōnchållē'stå] smf cellist, cello player.

violoncel'lo [vēōlōnchel'lō] sm cello.

viot'tolo sm path, trail.

VIP smf inv VIP.

vi'pera sf viper, adder.

virag'gio [vēråd'jō] sm (NAUT, AER) turn; (FOT) toning.

vira'le ag viral.

vira're vi (NAUT) to come about; (AER) to turn; (FOT) to tone; ~ **di bordo** to change course.

vira'ta sf coming about; turning; change of course.

vir'gola sf (LING) comma; (MAT) decimal point.

virgolet'te sfpl quotation marks.

viri'le ag (proprio dell'uomo) masculine; (non puerile, da uomo) manly, virile.

virilità sf masculinity; manliness; (sessuale) virility.

virtù sf inv virtue; **in** o **per** ~ **di** by virtue of, by.

virtua'le ag virtual.

virtuo'so, a ag virtuous ♦ smf (MUS etc) virtuoso.

virulen'to, a ag virulent.

vi'rus sm inv virus.

visagi'sta, i, e [vēzåjē'stå] smf beautician.

viscera'le [vēshārá'lā] *ag* (*MED*) visceral; (*fig*) profound, deep-rooted.

vi'scere [vēsh'shārā] *sm* (*ANAT*) internal organ ♦ *sfpl* (*di animale*) entrails *pl*; (*fig*) depths *pl*, bowels *pl*.

vis'chio [vēs'kyō] *sm* (*BOT*) mistletoe; (*pania*) birdlime.

vischio'so, a [vēskyō'sō] *ag* sticky.

viscidità [vēshēdētá'] *sf* sliminess.

vi'scido, a [vēsh'shēdō] *ag* slimy.

viscon'te, es'sa *sm/f* viscount/viscountess.

viscosità *sf* viscosity.

visco'so, a *ag* viscous.

visi'bile *ag* visible.

visibi'lio *sm*: **andare in** ~ to go into raptures.

visibilità *sf* visibility.

visie'ra *sf* (*di elmo*) visor; (*di berretto*) peak.

visiona're *vt* (*gen*) to look at, examine; (*CINEMA*) to screen.

visiona'rio, a *ag*, *sm/f* visionary.

visio'ne *sf* vision; **prendere** ~ **di qc** to examine sth, look sth over; **prima/seconda** ~ (*CINEMA*) first/second showing.

vi'sita *sf* visit; (*MED*) call; (*: esame*) examination; **far** ~ **a qn, andare in** ~ **da qn** to visit sb, pay sb a visit; **in** ~ **ufficiale in Italia** on an official visit to Italy; **orario di** ~**e** (*ospedale*) visiting hours; ~ **di controllo** (*MED*) checkup; ~ **a domicilio** house call; ~ **guidata** guided tour; ~ **sanitaria** sanitary inspection.

visita're *vt* to visit; (*MED*) to call on; (*: esaminare*) to examine.

visitato're, tri'ce *sm/f* visitor.

visi'vo, a *ag* visual.

vi'so *sm* face; **fare buon** ~ **a cattivo gioco** to make the best of things.

viso'ne *sm* mink.

viso're *sm* (*FOT*) viewer.

vi'spo, a *ag* quick, lively.

vis'si *etc vb vedi* **vivere**.

vissu'to, a *pp di* **vivere** ♦ *ag* (*aria, modo di fare*) experienced.

vi'sta *sf* (*facoltà*) (eye)sight; (*fatto di vedere*) **la** ~ **di** the sight of; (*veduta*) view; **con** ~ **sul lago** with a view over the lake; **sparare a** ~ to shoot on sight; **pagabile a** ~ payable on demand; **in** ~ in sight; **avere in** ~ **qc** to have sth in view; **mettersi in** ~ to draw attention to o.s.; (*peg*) to show off; **perdere qn di** ~ to lose sight of sb; (*fig*) to lose touch with sb; **far** ~ **di fare** to pretend to do; **a** ~ **d'occhio** as far as the eye can see; (*fig*) before one's very eyes.

vista're *vt* to approve; (*AMM*: *passaporto*) to visa.

vi'sto, a *pp di* **vedere** ♦ *sm* visa; ~ **che** *cong* seeing (that); ~ **d'ingresso/di transito** entry/transit visa; ~ **permanente/di soggiorno** permanent/tourist visa.

visto'so, a *ag* gaudy, garish; (*ingente*) considerable.

visua'le *ag* visual.

visualizza're [vēzōōálēddzá'rā] *vt* to visualize.

visualizzato're [vēzōōálēddzàtō'rā] *sm* (*INFORM*) visual display unit, VDU.

visualizzazio'ne [vēzōōálēddzàttsyō'nā] *sf* (*INFORM*) display.

vi'ta *sf* life; (*ANAT*) waist; **essere in** ~ to be alive; **pieno di** ~ full of life; **a** ~ for life; **membro a** ~ life member.

vita'le *ag* vital.

vitalità *sf* vitality.

vitali'zio, a [vētálēt'tsyō] *ag* life *cpd* ♦ *sm* life annuity.

vitami'na *sf* vitamin.

vi'te *sf* (*BOT*) vine; (*TECN*) screw; **giro di** ~ (*anche fig*) turn of the screw.

vitel'lo *sm* (*ZOOL*) calf; (*carne*) veal; (*pelle*) calfskin.

vitic'cio [vētēch'chō] *sm* (*BOT*) tendril.

viticolto're *sm* wine grower.

viticoltu'ra *sf* wine growing.

vi'treo, a *ag* vitreous; (*occhio, sguardo*) glassy.

vit'tima *sf* victim.

vittimi'smo *sm* self-pity.

vit'to *sm* food; (*in un albergo etc*) board; ~ **e alloggio** room and board.

vitto'ria *sf* victory.

vittoria'no, a *ag* Victorian.

vittorio'so, a *ag* victorious.

vitupera're *vt* to rail at *o* against.

viuz'za [vēōōt'tsá] *sf* (*in città*) alley.

vi'va *escl*: ~ **il re!** long live the king!

vivacchia're [vēvàkkyá'rā] *vi* to scrape a living.

viva'ce [vēvá'chā] *ag* (*vivo, animato*) lively; (*: mente*) lively, sharp; (*colore*) bright.

vivacità [vēvàchētá'] *sf* liveliness; brightness.

vivacizza're [vēvàchēddzá'rā] *vt* to liven up.

viva'io *sm* (*di pesci*) hatchery; (*AGR*) nursery.

vivamen'te *av* (*commuoversi*) deeply, profoundly; (*ringraziare etc*) sincerely, warmly.

vivan'da *sf* food; (*piatto*) dish.

viven'te *ag* living, alive; **i** ~**i** the living.

vi'vere *vi* to live ♦ *vt* to live; (*passare: brutto momento*) to live through, go through; (*sentire: gioie, pene di qn*) to share ♦ *sm* life; (*anche*: **modo di** ~) way of life; ~**i** *smpl* food *sg*, provisions; ~ **di** to live on.

vive'ur [vēvēr'] *sm inv* pleasure-seeker.

vi'vido, a *ag* (*colore*) vivid, bright.

vivifica're *vt* to enliven, give life to; (*piante etc*) to revive.

vivisezio'ne [vēvēsàttsyō'nā] *sf* vivisection.

vi'vo, a *ag* (*vivente*) alive, living; (*fig*) lively; (*: colore*) bright, brilliant ♦ *sm*: **entrare nel** ~ **di una questione** to get to the heart of a matter; **i ~i** the living; **esperimenti su animali ~i** experiments on live *o* living animals; **~ e vegeto** hale and hearty; **farsi ~** (*fig*) to show one's face; to keep in touch; **con ~ rammarico** with deep regret; **congratulazioni vivissime** heartiest congratulations; **con i più ~i ringraziamenti** with deepest *o* warmest thanks; **ritrarre dal ~** to paint from life; **pungere qn nel ~** (*fig*) to cut sb to the quick.

vivrò *etc vb vedi* **vivere**.

vizia're [vēttsyà'rā] *vt* (*bambino*) to spoil; (*corrompere moralmente*) to corrupt; (*DIR*) to invalidate.

vizia'to, a [vēttsyà'tō] *ag* spoilt; (*aria, acqua*) polluted; (*DIR*) invalid, invalidated.

vi'zio [vēt'tsyō] *sm* (*morale*) vice; (*cattiva abitudine*) bad habit; (*imperfezione*) flaw, defect; (*errore*) fault, mistake; **~ di forma** legal flaw *o* irregularity; **~ procedurale** procedural error.

vizio'so, a [vēttsyō'sō] *ag* depraved; (*inesatto*) incorrect, wrong; **circolo ~** vicious circle.

V.le *abbr* = **viale**.

vocabola'rio *sm* (*dizionario*) dictionary; (*lessico*) vocabulary.

voca'bolo *sm* word.

voca'le *ag* vocal ♦ *sf* vowel.

vocazio'ne [vōkáttsyō'nā] *sf* vocation; (*fig*) natural bent.

vo'ce [vō'chā] *sf* voice; (*diceria*) rumor (*US*), rumour (*Brit*); (*di un elenco, in bilancio*) item; (*di dizionario*) entry; **parlare a alta/ bassa ~** to speak in a loud/low *o* soft voice; **fare la ~ grossa** to raise one's voice; **dar ~ a qc** to voice sth, give voice to sth; **a gran ~** in a loud voice, loudly; **te lo dico a ~** I'll tell you when I see you; **a una ~** unanimously; **aver ~ in capitolo** (*fig*) to have a say in the matter; **~i di corridoio** rumors.

vocia're [vōchà'rā] *vi* to shout, yell.

vociferan'te [vōchēfàràn'tā] *ag* noisy.

voci'o [vōchē'ō] *sm* shouting.

vod'ka *sf inv* vodka.

vo'ga *sf* (*NAUT*) rowing; (*usanza*): **essere in ~** to be in fashion *o* in vogue.

voga're *vi* to row.

vogato're, tri'ce *sm/f* oarsman/woman ♦ *sm* rowing machine.

vogherò *etc* [vōgàro'] *vb vedi* **vogare**.

vo'glia [vol'yà] *sf* desire, wish; (*macchia*) birthmark; **aver ~ di qc/di fare** to feel like sth/like doing; (*più forte*) to want sth/to do; **di buona ~** willingly.

vo'glio *etc* [vol'yō] *vb vedi* **volere**.

voglio'so, a [vōlyō'sō] *ag* (*sguardo etc*) longing; (*più forte*) full of desire.

vo'i *pronome* you; **~ stessi(e)** you yourselves.

voial'tri *pronome* you.

vol. *abbr* (= *volume*) vol.

vola'no *sm* (*SPORT*) shuttlecock; (*TECN*) flywheel.

volant' [volàn'] *sm inv* frill.

volan'te *ag* flying ♦ *sm* (steering) wheel ♦ *sf* (*POLIZIA*: *anche*: **squadra ~**) flying squad.

volantinag'gio [vōlántēnàd'jō] *sm* leafleting.

volanti'no *sm* leaflet.

vola're *vi* (*uccello, aereo, fig*) to fly; (*cappello*) to blow away *o* off, fly away *o* off; **~ via** to fly away *o* off.

vola'ta *sf* flight; (*d'uccelli*) flock, flight; (*corsa*) rush; (*SPORT*) final sprint; **passare di ~ da qn** to drop in on sb briefly.

vola'tile *ag* (*CHIM*) volatile ♦ *sm* (*ZOOL*) bird.

volatilizzar'si [vōlátēlēddzàr'sē] *vr* (*CHIM*) to volatilize; (*fig*) to vanish, disappear.

volen'te *ag*: **verrai ~ o nolente** you'll come whether you like it or not.

volentero'so, a *ag* willing, keen.

volentie'ri *av* willingly; **"~"** "with pleasure", "I'd be glad to".

vole're *sm* will; **~i** *smpl* wishes; **contro il ~ di** against the wishes of; **per ~ del padre** in obedience to his father's will *o* wishes ♦ *vt* to want; (*esigere, richiedere*) to demand, require; **vuole un po' di formaggio?** would you like some cheese?; **voglio una risposta da voi** I want an answer from you; **che lei lo voglia o no** whether you like it or not; **come vuole** as you like; **voler fare qc** to want to do sth; **volevo parlartene** I meant to talk to you about it; **vuole *o* vorrebbe essere così gentile da ...?** would you be so kind as to ...?; **~ che qn faccia** to want sb to do; **vorrei questo** I would like this; **~rci** (*essere necessario*): **quanto ci vuole per andare da Roma a Firenze?** how long does it take to go from Rome to Florence?; **ci vogliono 4 metri di stoffa** 4 meters of material are required, you will need 4 meters of material; **è quel che ci vuole** it's just what is needed; **~ bene a qn** to love sb; **~ male a qn** to dislike sb; **volerne a qn** to bear sb a grudge; **~ dire (che)** to mean (that); **voglio dire ...** (*per correggersi*) I mean ...; **volevo ben dire!** I thought as much!; **senza ~** without meaning to, unintentionally; **la tradizione vuole che ...** custom requires that ...; **la leggenda vuole che ...** legend has it that ...; **te la sei voluta** you asked for it.

volga're *ag* vulgar.

volgarità *sf* vulgarity.

volgarizza're [vōlgàrēddzà'rā] *vt* to popularize.

volgarmen'te *av* (*in modo volgare*) vulgarly, coarsely; (*del popolo*) commonly, popularly.

vol'gere [vol'jārā] *vt* to turn ♦ *vi* to turn; (*tendere*): **~ a**: **il tempo volge al brutto/al bello** the weather is breaking/is setting fair; **un rosso che volge al viola** a red verging on purple; **~rsi** *vr* to turn; **~ al peggio** to take a turn for the worse; **~ al termine** to draw to an end.

vol'go *sm* common people.

volie'ra *sf* aviary.

voliti'vo, a *ag* strong-willed.

vol'li *etc vb vedi* **volere.**

vo'lo *sm* flight; **ci sono due ore di ~ da Londra a Milano** it's a two-hour flight between London and Milan; **al ~: colpire qc al ~** to hit sth as it flies past; **prendere al ~** (*autobus, treno*) to catch at the last possible moment; (*palla*) to catch as it flies past; (*occasione*) to seize; **capire al ~** to understand immediately; **veduta a ~ d'uccello** bird's-eye view; **~ di linea** scheduled flight.

volontà *sf inv* will; **a ~** (*mangiare, bere*) as much as one likes; **buona/cattiva ~** goodwill/lack of goodwill; **le sue ultime ~** (*testamento*) his last will and testament *sg*.

volontariamen'te *av* voluntarily.

volontaria'to *sm* (*MIL*) voluntary service; (*lavoro*) voluntary work.

volonta'rio, a *ag* voluntary ♦ *sm* (*MIL*) volunteer.

vol'pe *sf* fox.

volpi'no, a *ag* (*pelo, coda*) fox's; (*aspetto, astuzia*) fox-like ♦ *sm* (*cane*) Pomeranian.

volpo'ne, a *sm/f* (*fig*) old fox.

vol'si *etc vb vedi* **volgere.**

volt *sm inv* (*ELETTR*) volt.

vol'ta *sf* (*momento, circostanza*) time; (*turno, giro*) turn; (*curva*) turn, bend; (*ARCHIT*) vault; (*direzione*): **partire alla ~ di** to set off for; **a mia** (*o* **tua** *etc*) **~** in turn; **una ~** once; **una ~ sola** only once; **c'era una ~** once upon a time there was; **le cose di una ~** the things of the past; **due ~e** twice; **tre ~e** three times; **una cosa per ~** one thing at a time; **una ~ o l'altra** one of these days; **una ~ per tutte** once and for all; **una ~ tanto** just for once; **lo facciamo un'altra ~** we'll do it another time *o* some other time; **a ~e** at times, sometimes; **di ~ in ~** from time to time; **una ~ che** (*temporale*) once; (*causale*) since; **3 ~e 4** 3 times 4; **ti ha dato di ~ il cervello?** have you gone out of your mind?

voltafac'cia [voltafàch'chà] *sm inv* (*fig*) volteface.

voltag'gio [voltàd'jō] *sm* (*ELETTR*) voltage.

volta're *vt* to turn; (*girare: moneta*) to turn over; (*rigirare*) to turn round ♦ *vi* to turn; **~rsi** *vr* to turn; to turn over; to turn round.

voltasto'maco *sm* nausea; (*fig*) disgust.

volteggia're [voltedjà'rà] *vi* (*volare*) to circle; (*in equitazione*) to do trick riding; (*in ginnastica*) to vault.

vol'to, a *pp di* **volgere** ♦ *ag* (*inteso a*): **il mio discorso è ~ a spiegare ...** in my speech I intend to explain ... ♦ *sm* face.

volu'bile *ag* changeable, fickle.

volu'me *sm* volume.

volumino'so, a *ag* voluminous, bulky.

volu'ta *sf* (*gen*) spiral; (*ARCHIT*) volute.

voluttà *sf* sensual pleasure *o* delight.

voluttuo'so, a *ag* voluptuous.

vomita're *vt, vi* to vomit.

vo'mito *sm* vomit; **ho il ~** I feel sick.

von'gola *sf* clam.

vora'ce [vōrá'chā] *ag* voracious, greedy.

voracità [vōráchētá'] *sf* voracity, voraciousness.

vora'gine [vōrà'jēnā] *sf* abyss, chasm.

vorrò *etc vb vedi* **volere.**

vor'tice [vor'tēchā] *sm* whirl, vortex; (*fig*) whirl.

vortico'so, a *ag* whirling.

vos'tro, a *det*: **il(la) ~(a)** *etc* your ♦ *pronome*: **il(la) ~(a)** *etc* yours ♦ *sm*: **avete speso del ~?** did you spend your own money? ♦ *sf*: **la ~a** (*opinione*) your view; **i ~i** (*famiglia*) your family; **un ~ amico** a friend of yours; **è dei ~i, è dalla ~a** he's on your side; **l'ultima ~a** (*COMM: lettera*) your most recent letter; **alla ~a!** (*brindisi*) here's to you!, your health!

votan'te *sm/f* voter.

vota're *vi* to vote ♦ *vt* (*sottoporre a votazione*) to take a vote on; (*approvare*) to vote for; (*REL*): **~ qc a** to dedicate sth to; **~rsi** *vr*: to devote o.s. to.

votazio'ne [vōtáttsyō'nā] *sf* vote, voting; **~i** *sfpl* (*POL*) votes; (*INS*) marks.

vo'to *sm* (*POL*) vote; (*INS*) mark (*Brit*), grade (*US*); (*REL*) vow; (: *offerta*) votive offering; **aver ~i belli/brutti** (*INS*) to get good/bad marks *o* grades; **prendere i ~i** to take one's vows; **~ di fiducia** vote of confidence.

V.P. *abbr* (= *vicepresidente*) VP.

VR *sigla* = *Verona*.

v.r. *abbr* (= *vedi retro*) PTO.

V.S. *abbr* = *Vostra Santità*, *Vostra Signoria*.

vs. *abbr* (= *vostro*) yr.

v.s. *abbr* = *vedi sopra*.

VT *sigla* = *Viterbo*.

V.U. *abbr* = *vigile urbano*.

vulca'nico, a, ci, che *ag* volcanic.

vulcanizzazio'ne [vōōlkánēddzáttsyō'nā] *sf* vulcanization.

vulca'no *sm* volcano.

vulnera'bile *ag* vulnerable.

vulnerabilità *sf* vulnerability.

vuo'i, vuo'le *vb vedi* **volere.**

vuota're *vt, ~rsi* *vr* to empty.

vuo'to, a *ag* empty; (*fig: privo*): **~ di** (*senso etc*) devoid of ♦ *sm* empty space, gap; (*spazio in bianco*) blank; (*FISICA*) vacuum; (*fig: mancanza*) gap, void; **a mani ~e** emptyhanded; **assegno a ~** bad check (*US*), dud cheque (*Brit*); **~ d'aria** air pocket; **"~ a perdere"** ''no deposit''; **"~ a rendere"** ''re-

turnable bottle".
v.v. *abbr* (= *vostro*) yr.

W

W, w [dop'pyōvōō] *sf o m inv* (*lettera*) W, w;
  W come Washington ≈ W for William.
W *abbr'* = **viva, evviva.**
wa'fer [và'fār] *sm inv* (*CUC, ELETTR*) wafer.
wagon-lit' [vàgônlē'] *sm inv* (*FERR*) sleeping
  car.
wa'ter clo'set [wo:'tə'klozit] *sm inv* toilet,
  lavatory.
watt [vàt] *sm inv* (*ELETTR*) watt.
watto'ra [vàttō'rà] *sm inv* (*ELETTR*) watt-hour.
WC *sm inv* restroom (*US*), WC (*Brit*).
we'ekend [wē:'kānd] *sm inv* weekend.
we'stern [we'stārn] *ag* (*CINEMA*) cowboy *cpd*
  ♦ *sm inv* western, cowboy film; ∼ **all'italiana**
  spaghetti western.
whis'ky [wē'skē] *sm inv* whiskey.
würstel' [vür'stəl] *sm inv* frankfurter.

X

X, x [ēks] *sf o m inv* (*lettera*) X, x; **X come**
  Xeres ≈ X for Xmas.
xenofobi'a [ksānōfōbē'à] *sf* xenophobia.
xeno'fobo, a [ksāno'fōbō] *ag* xenophobic ♦
  sm/f xenophobe.
xe'res [kse'rās] *sm inv* sherry.
xeroco'pia [ksārōko'pyà] *sf* xerox ®, photocopy.
xerocopia're [ksārōkōpyà'rā] *vt* to photocopy.
xilo'fono [ksēlo'fōnō] *sm* xylophone.

Y

Y, y [ēp'sēlōn] *sf o m inv* (*lettera*) Y, ý; **Y**
  come Yacht ≈ Y for Yoke.
yacht [yot] *sm inv* yacht.
yan'kee [yang'kē] *sm/f inv* Yank, Yankee.
Y.C.I. *abbr* = *Yacht Club d'Italia.*
Ye'men [yā'mān] *sm*: **lo** ∼ Yemen.
yid'dish [yē'dēsh] *ag inv, sm inv* Yiddish.
yo'ga [yo'gà] *ag inv, sm* yoga (*cpd*).
yo'ghurt [yo'gōōrt] *sm inv* yog(h)ourt.

Z

Z, z [dze'tà] *sf o m inv* (*lettera*) Z, z; **Z come**
  Zara ≈ Z for Zebra.
zabaio'ne [dzàbàyō'nā] *sm dessert made of*
  egg yolks, sugar and marsala.
zaffa'ta [tsàffá'tá] *sf* (*tanfo*) stench.
zaffera'no [dzàffārà'nō] *sm* saffron.
zaffi'ro [dzàffē'rō] *sm* sapphire.
za'gara [dzà'gàrà] *sf* orange blossom.
za'ino [dzà'ēnō] *sm* rucksack.
Zai're [dzàē'rà] *sm*: **lo** ∼ Zaire.
Zam'bia [dzàm'byà] *sm*: **lo** ∼ Zambia.
zam'pa [tsàm'pà] *sf* (*di animale: gamba*) leg;
  (: *piede*) paw; **a quattro** ∼**e** on all fours; ∼
  di gallina (*calligrafia*) scrawl; (*rughe*
  crow's feet.
zampa'ta [tsàmpá'tà] *sf* (*di cane, gatto*) blo
  with a paw.
zampetta're [tsàmpàttà'rā] *vi* to scamper.
zampilla're [tsàmpēllà'rā] *vi* to gush, spurt.
zampil'lo [tsàmpēl'lō] *sm* gush, spurt.
zampi'no [tsàmpē'nō] *sm* paw; **qui c'è sot**
  suo ∼ (*fig*) he's had a hand in this.
zampo'gna [tsàmpōn'yà] *sf instrument si*
  to bagpipes.
zan'na [tsàn'nà] *sf* (*di elefante*) tusk
  carnivori) fang.
zanza'ra [dzàndzà'rà] *sf* mosquito.
zanzarie'ra [dzàndzàrye'rà] *sf* mosquito
zap'pa [tsàp'pà] *sf* hoe.
zappa're [tsàppá'rā] *vt* to hoe.
zappato're [tsáppàtō'rā] *sm* (*AGR*) ho
zappatu'ra [tsàppàtōō'rà] *sf* (*AGR*) ho
zar, zari'na [tsàr, tsàrē'nà] *sm/f* tsar/ts
zat'tera [dzàt'tàrà] *sf* raft.
zavor'ra [dzàvor'rà] *sf* ballast.
zaz'zera [tsàt'tsàrà] *sf* shock of hair
ze'bra [dze'brà] *sf* zebra; ∼**e** *sfpl* (
  walk *sg* (*US*), zebra crossing *sg* (
zebra'to, a [dzàbrà'tō] *ag* with bla
  stripes; **strisce** ∼**e, attrave**
  (*AUT*) crosswalk (*US*), zebra cr
zec'ca, che [tsāk'ká] *sf* (*ZOOL*)

di monete) mint.

zecchi'no [tsākkē'nō] *sm* gold coin; **oro** ~ pure gold.

zelan'te [dzālán'tā] *ag* zealous.

ze'lo [dze'lō] *sm* zeal.

ze'nit [dze'nēt] *sm* zenith.

zen'zero [dzān'dzārō] *sm* ginger.

zep'pa [tsāp'pá] *sf* wedge.

zep'po, a [tsāp'pō] *ag:* ~ **di** crammed o packed with.

zerbi'no [dzārbē'nō] *sm* doormat.

ze'ro [dze'rō] *sm* zero, nought; **vincere per tre a** ~ *(SPORT)* to win three-nothing, win three-nil (*Brit*).

ze'ta [dze'tá] *sm o f* zed, (the letter) z.

zi'a [tsē'á] *sf* aunt.

zibelli'no [dzēbāllē'nō] *sm* sable.

ziga'no, a [tsēgá'nō] *ag, sm/f* gypsy.

zi'gomo [dzē'gōmō] *sm* cheekbone.

zigrina're [dzēgrēná'rā] *vt (gen)* to knurl; *(pellame)* to grain; *(monete)* to mill.

gzag' [dzēgdzág'] *sm inv* zigzag; **andare a** ~ ɔ zigzag.

ɪbab'we [tsēmbá'bwā] *sm:* **lo** ~ Zimbabwe.

ɪel'lo [dzēmbel'lō] *sm (oggetto di burle)* ʰing-stock.

[dzēn'kō] *sm* zinc.

ʳ'sco, a, schi, sche** [dzēngárā'skō] *ag* ɔpd.

a [dzēn'gárō] *sm/f* gipsy.

pl **zi'i** *sm* uncle; **zii** *smpl (zio e zia)* aunt.

ʳl'lá] *sf* spinster; *(peg)* old maid.

'rā] *vt* to silence, hush *o* shut up ♦

ɔ] *ag* quiet, silent; **sta'** ~! be

á'nyá] *sf (BOT)* darnel; *(fig)* o **seminare** ~ to sow dis-

sm (calzatura) clog; (*di* (*ARCHIT*) plinth; (*di pa-* *US*), skirting (board) ase.

ag zodiac *cpd*; **segno**

ɔdiac.

n (sulfur) *(US)* o

sulphur (*Brit*).

ɪp.

'i depressione

(*METEOR*) trough of low pressure; ~ **pedonale** pedestrian mall *(US)* o precinct *(Brit)*; ~ **verde** (*di abitato*) green area.

zon'zo [dzōn'dzō]: **a** ~ *av:* **andare a** ~ to wander about, stroll about.

zo'o [dzo'ō] *sm inv* zoo.

zoologi'a [dzōōlōjē'á] *sf* zoology.

zoolo'gico, a, ci, che [dzōōlo'jēkō] *ag* zoological.

zoo'logo, a, gi, ghe [dzōo'lōgō] *sm/f* zoologist.

zoosafa'ri [dzōōsáfá'rē] *sm inv* safari park.

zootec'nico, a, ci, che [dzōōtek'nēkō] *ag* zootechnical; **il patrimonio** ~ **di un paese** a country's livestock resources.

zoppica're [tsōppēká'rā] *vi* to limp; *(fig: mobile)* to be shaky, rickety.

zop'po, a [tsop'pō] *ag* lame; *(fig: mobile)* shaky, rickety.

zotico'ne [dzōtēkō'nā] *sm* lout.

zua'va [dzōōá'vá] *sf:* **pantaloni** *mpl* **alla** ~ knickerbockers.

zuc'ca, che [tsōōk'ká] *sf (BOT)* vegetable marrow *(US)*, marrow *(Brit)*; pumpkin; *(scherzoso)* head.

zucchera're [tsōōkkārá'rā] *vt* to put sugar in.

zucchera'to, a [tsōōkkārá'tō] *ag* sweet, sweetened.

zuccherie'ra [tsōōkkārye'rá] *sf* sugar bowl.

zuccherifi'cio [tsōōkkārēfē'chō] *sm* sugar refinery.

zuccheri'no, a [tsōōkkārē'nō] *ag* sugary, sweet.

zuc'chero [tsōōk'kārō] *sm* sugar; ~ **di canna** cane sugar; ~ **caramellato** caramel; ~ **filato** cotton candy *(US)*, candy floss *(Brit)*; ~ **a velo** confectioner's sugar *(US)*, icing sugar *(Brit)*.

zucchero'so, a [tsōōkkārō'sō] *ag* sugary.

zucchi'na [tsōōkkē'ná] *sf,* **zucchi'no** [tsōōk'kēnō] *sm* zucchini *(US)*, courgette *(Brit)*.

zuccot'to [tsōōkkot'tō] *sm* ice-cream sponge.

zuf'fa [tsōōf'fá] *sf* brawl.

zufola're [tsōōfōlá'rā] *vt, vi* to whistle.

zup'pa [tsōōp'pá] *sf* soup; *(fig)* mixture, muddle; ~ **inglese** *(CUC)* dessert made with sponge cake, custard and chocolate, ≈ trifle *(Brit)*.

zuppie'ra [tsōōppye'rá] *sf* soup tureen.

zup'po, a [tsōōp'pō] *ag:* ~ **(di)** drenched (with), soaked (with).

Zuri'go [dzōōrē'gō] *sf* Zurich.

ENGLISH-ITALIAN
INGLESE-ITALIANO *inglese-italiano*

A

A, a [ā] *n* (*letter*) A, a *f or m inv*; (*SCOL*: *mark*) ≈ 10 (*ottimo*); (*MUS*): **A** la *m*; **A for Able** ≈ A come Ancona; **A road** *n* (*Brit AUT*) ≈ strada statale; **A shares** *npl* (*Brit STOCK EXCHANGE*) azioni *fpl* senza diritto di voto.

a, an [ā, ə, an, ən] *indefinite article* un (uno + *s impure, gn, pn, ps, x, z*), *f* una (un' + *vowel*); ~ **mirror** uno specchio; **an apple** una mela; **I haven't got** ~ **car** non ho la macchina; **he's** ~ **doctor** è medico, fa il medico; **3** ~ **day/week** 3 al giorno/la *or* alla settimana; **10 km an hour** 10 km all'ora.

a. *abbr* = **acre.**

AA *n abbr* (*US*: = *Associate in/of Arts*) titolo di studio; (= *Alcoholics Anonymous*) A.A. *f* (= *Anonima Alcolisti*); (*MIL*) = **anti-aircraft**; (*Brit*: = *Automobile Association*) ≈ A.C.I. *m* (= *Automobile Club d'Italia*).

AAA [trip'əlā] *n abbr* (= *American Automobile Association*) ≈ A.C.I. *m* (= *Automobile Club d'Italia*); (*Brit*) = *Amateur Athletics Association*.

AAUP *n abbr* (= *American Association of University Professors*) *associazione dei professori universitari.*

AB *abbr see* **able-bodied seaman**; (*Canada*) = *Alberta.*

ABA *n abbr* (= *American Bankers Association*) *gruppo bancario*; (= *American Bar Association*) *associazione di legali.*

aback [əbak'] *ad*: **to be taken** ~ essere sbalordito(a).

abacus, *pl* **abaci** [ab'əkəs, -saɪ] *n* pallottoliere *m*, abaco.

abandon [əban'dən] *vt* abbandonare ♦ *n* abbandono; **to** ~ **ship** abbandonare la nave.

abandoned [əban'dənd] *a* (*child, house etc*) abbandonato(a); (*unrestrained: manner*) disinvolto(a).

abase [əbās'] *vt*: **to** ~ **o.s. (so far as to do)** umiliarsi *or* abbassarsi (al punto di fare).

abashed [əbasht'] *a* imbarazzato(a).

abate [əbāt'] *vi* calmarsi.

abatement [əbāt'mənt] *n* (*of pollution, noise*) soppressione *f*, eliminazione *f*; **noise** ~ **society** associazione *f* per la lotta contro i rumori.

abattoir [abətwâr'] *n* (*Brit*) mattatoio.

abbey [ab'ē] *n* abbazia, badia.

abbot [ab'ət] *n* abate *m*.

abbreviate [əbrē'vēāt] *vt* abbreviare.

abbreviation [əbrēvēā'shən] *n* abbreviazione *f*.

ABC [ābēsē'] *n abbr* (= *American Broadcasting Company*) *rete televisiva americana.*

abdicate [ab'dikāt] *vt* abdicare a ♦ *vi* abdicare.

abdication [abdikā'shən] *n* abdicazione *f*.

abdomen [ab'dəmən] *n* addome *m*.

abdominal [abdâm'ənəl] *a* addominale.

abduct [abdukt'] *vt* rapire.

abduction [abduk'shən] *n* rapimento.

aberration [abərā'shən] *n* aberrazione *f*.

abet [əbet'] *vt see* **aid.**

abeyance [əbā'əns] *n*: **in** ~ in sospeso.

abhor [abhôr'] *vt* aborrire.

abhorrent [abhôr'ənt] *a* odioso(a).

abide [əbīd'] *vt* sopportare.

abide by *vt fus* conformarsi a.

ability [əbil'itē] *n* abilità *f inv*; **to the best of my** ~ con il massimo impegno.

abject [ab'jekt] *a* (*poverty*) abietto(a); (*apology*) umiliante; (*coward*) indegno(a), vile.

ablaze [əblāz']· *a* in fiamme; ~ **with light** risplendente di luce.

able [ā'bəl] *a* capace; **to be** ~ **to do sth** essere capace di fare qc, poter fare qc.

able-bodied [ā'bəlbâd'ēd] *a* robusto(a).

able-bodied seaman (AB) *n* marinaio scelto.

ably [ā'blē] *ad* abilmente.

ABM *n abbr* (= *anti-ballistic missile*) ABM *m*.

abnormal [abnôr'məl] *a* anormale.

abnormality [abnôrmal'ətē] *n* (*condition*) anormalità; (*instance*) anomalia.

aboard [əbôrd'] *ad* a bordo ♦ *prep* a bordo di; ~ **the train** in *or* sul treno.

abode [əbōd'] *n* (*old*) dimora; (*LAW*) domicilio, dimora; **of no fixed** ~ senza fissa dimora.

abolish [əbâl'ish] *vt* abolire.

abolition [abəlish'ən] *n* abolizione *f*.

abominable [əbâm'inəbəl] *a* abominevole.

aborigine [abərij'ənē] *n* aborigeno/a.

abort [əbôrt'] *vt* (*MED, fig*) abortire; (*COMPUT*) interrompere l'esecuzione di.

abortion [əbôr'shən] *n* aborto; **to have an** ~ avere un aborto, abortire.

abortive [əbôr'tiv] *a* abortivo(a).

abound [əbound'] *vi* abbondare; **to** ~ **in** abbondare di.

about [əbout'] *prep* intorno a, riguardo a ♦ *ad* circa; (*here and there*) qua e là; **do some-**

thing ~ it! fai qualcosa!; **it takes ~ 10 hours** ci vogliono circa 10 ore; **at ~ 2 o'clock** verso le due; **it's just ~ finished** è quasi finito; **it's ~ here** è qui dintorno; **to walk ~ the town** camminare per la città; **they left all their things lying ~** hanno lasciato tutta la loro roba in giro; **to be ~ to: he was ~ to cry** stava per piangere; **I'm not ~ to do all that for nothing** non ho intenzione di fare tutto questo per niente; **what** or **how ~ doing this?** che ne pensa di fare questo?

about-face [əbout'fās] n (US MIL) dietro front m inv.

about-turn [əbout'tûrn] n (Brit) = **about-face**.

above [əbuv'] ad, prep sopra; **mentioned ~** suddetto; **costing ~ $10** più caro di 10 dollari; **he's not ~ a bit of blackmail** non rifuggirebbe dal ricatto; **~ all** soprattutto.

aboveboard [əbuv'bôrd] a aperto(a); onesto(a).

abrasion [əbrā'zhən] n abrasione f.

abrasive [əbrā'siv] a abrasivo(a).

abreast [əbrest'] ad di fianco; **3 ~** per 3 di fronte; **to keep ~ of** tenersi aggiornato su.

abridge [əbrij'] vt ridurre.

abroad [əbrôd'] ad all'estero; **there is a rumor ~ that ...** (fig) si sente dire in giro che ..., circola la voce che ....

abrupt [əbrupt'] a (steep) erto(a); (sudden) improvviso(a); (gruff, blunt) brusco(a).

abscess [ab'ses] n ascesso.

abscond [abskånd'] vi scappare.

absence [ab'səns] n assenza; **in the ~ of** (person) in assenza di; (thing) in mancanza di.

absent [ab'sənt] a assente; **to be ~ without leave (AWOL)** (MIL etc) essere assente ingiustificato.

absentee [absəntē'] n assente m/f.

absentee ballot n voto per posta.

absenteeism [absəntē'izəm] n assenteismo.

absent-minded [ab'səntmīn'did] a distratto(a).

absent-mindedness [ab'səntmīn'didnis] n distrazione f.

absolute [ab'səlōōt] a assoluto(a).

absolutely [absəlōōt'lē] ad assolutamente.

absolve [abzålv'] vt: **to ~ sb (from)** (sin etc) assolvere qn (da); **to ~ sb from** (oath) sciogliere qn da.

absorb [absôrb'] vt assorbire; **to be ~ed in a book** essere immerso(a) in un libro.

absorbent [absôr'bənt] a assorbente.

absorbent cotton n (US) cotone m idrofilo.

absorbing [absôr'bing] a avvincente, molto interessante.

absorption [absôrp'shən] n assorbimento.

abstain [abstān'] vi: **to ~ (from)** astenersi (da).

abstemious [abstē'mēəs] a astemio(a).

abstention [absten'shən] n astensione f.

abstinence [ab'stənəns] n astinenza.

abstract [ab'strakt] a astratto(a) ♦ n (summary) riassunto ♦ vt [əbstrakt'] estrarre.

absurd [absûrd'] a assurdo(a).

absurdity [absûr'dətē] n assurdità f inv.

Abu Dhabi [áb'ōō dã'bē] n Abu Dhabi f.

abundance [əbun'dəns] n abbondanza.

abundant [əbun'dənt] a abbondante.

abuse n [əbyōōs'] abuso; (insults) ingiurie fpl ♦ vt [əbyōōz'] abusare di; **open to ~** che si presta ad abusi.

abusive [əbyōō'siv] a ingiurioso(a).

abysmal [əbiz'məl] a spaventoso(a).

abyss [əbis'] n abisso.

AC n abbr (US) = athletic club ♦ abbr = **alternating current**.

a/c abbr (BANKING etc: = account, account current) c.

academic [akədem'ik] a accademico(a); (pej: issue) puramente formale ♦ n universitario/a.

academic year n anno accademico.

academy [əkad'əmē] n (learned body) accademia; (school) scuola privata; **military/naval ~** scuola militare/navale; **~ of music** conservatorio.

accede [aksēd'] vi: **to ~ to** (request) accedere a; (throne) ascendere a.

accelerate [aksel'ərāt] vt, vi accelerare.

acceleration [akselərā'shən] n accelerazione f.

accelerator [aksel'ərātûr] n acceleratore m.

accent [ak'sent] n accento.

accentuate [aksen'chōōāt] vt (syllable) accentuare; (need, difference etc) accentuare, mettere in risalto or in evidenza.

accept [aksept'] vt accettare.

acceptable [aksep'təbəl] a accettabile.

acceptance [aksep'təns] n accettazione f; **to meet with general ~** incontrare il favore or il consenso generale.

access [ak'ses] n accesso ♦ vt (COMPUT) accedere a; **to have ~ to** avere accesso a; **the burglars gained ~ through a window** i ladri sono riusciti a penetrare da or attraverso una finestra.

accessible [akses'əbəl] a accessibile.

accession [aksesh'ən] n (addition) aggiunta; (to library) accessione f, acquisto; (of king) ascesa or salita al trono.

accessory [akses'ûrē] n accessorio; **toilet accessories** npl (Brit) articoli mpl da toilette.

access road n strada d'accesso; (to freeway) raccordo di entrata.

access time n (COMPUT) tempo di accesso.

accident [ak'sidənt] n incidente m; (chance) caso; **to meet with** or **to have an ~** avere un incidente; **~s at work** infortuni mpl sul lavoro; **by ~** per caso.

accidental [aksiden'təl] a accidentale.

accidentally [aksiden'təlē] ad per caso.

accident insurance n assicurazione f contro gli infortuni.

accident-prone [ak'sidəntprōn'] *a*: **he's very ~** è un vero passaguai.

acclaim [əklām'] *vt* acclamare ♦ *n* acclamazione *f*.

acclamation [akləmā'shən] *n* (*approval*) acclamazione *f*; (*applause*) applauso.

acclimate [əklī'mit] *vt* (*US*): **to become ~d** acclimatarsi.

acclimatize [əklī'mətīz] *vt* (*Brit*) = **acclimate**.

accolade [akəlād'] *n* encomio.

accommodate [əkâm'ədāt] *vt* alloggiare; (*oblige*, *help*) favorire; **this car ~s 4 people comfortably** quest'auto può trasportare comodamente 4 persone.

accommodating [əkâm'ədāting] *a* compiacente.

accommodations, (*Brit*) **accommodation** [əkâmədā'shən(z)] *n*(*pl*) alloggio.

accompaniment [əkum'pənimənt] *n* accompagnamento.

accompanist [əkum'pənist] *n* (*MUS*) accompagnatore/trice.

accompany [əkum'pənē] *vt* accompagnare.

accomplice [əkâm'plis] *n* complice *m/f*.

accomplish [əkâm'plish] *vt* compiere; (*achieve*) ottenere.

accomplished [əkâm'plisht] *a* (*person*) esperto(a).

accomplishment [əkâm'plishmənt] *n* compimento; (*thing achieved*) risultato; **~s** *npl* (*skills*) doti *fpl*.

accord [əkôrd'] *n* accordo ♦ *vt* accordare; **of his own ~** di propria iniziativa; **with one ~** all'unanimità, di comune accordo.

accordance [əkôr'dəns] *n*: **in ~ with** in conformità con.

according [əkôr'ding]: **~ to** *prep* secondo; **it went ~ to plan** è andata secondo il previsto.

accordingly [əkôr'dinglē] *ad* in conformità.

accordion [əkôr'dēən] *n* fisarmonica.

accost [əkôst'] *vt* avvicinare.

account [əkount'] *n* (*COMM*) conto; (*report*) descrizione *f*; **~s** *npl* (*COMM*) conti; **to keep an ~ of** tenere nota di; **to bring sb to ~ for sth/for having done sth** chiedere a qn di render conto di qc/per aver fatto qc; **by all ~s** a quanto si dice; **of little ~** di poca importanza; **on ~** in acconto; **to buy sth on ~** comprare qc a credito; **on no ~** per nessun motivo; **on ~ of** a causa di; **to take into ~, take ~ of** tener conto di.

account for *vt fus* (*explain*) spiegare; giustificare; **all the children were ~ed for** nessun bambino mancava all'appello.

accountability [əkountəbil'ətē] *n* responsabilità.

accountable [əkoun'təbəl] *a* responsabile.

accountancy [əkoun'tənsē] *n* ragioneria.

accountant [əkoun'tənt] *n* ragioniere/a.

accounting [əkoun'ting] *n* contabilità.

accounting period *n* esercizio finanziario,

periodo contabile.

account number *n* numero di conto.

account payable *n* conto passivo.

account receivable *n* conto da esigere.

accredited [əkred'itid] *a* accreditato(a).

accretion [əkrē'shən] *n* accrescimento.

accrue [əkrōō'] *vi* (*mount up*) aumentare; **to ~ to** derivare a; **~d charges** ratei *mpl* passivi; **~d interest** interesse *m* maturato.

actt. *n abbr* = **account**; **accountant**.

accumulate [əkyōōm'yəlāt] *vt* accumulare ♦ *vi* accumularsi.

accumulation [əkyōōmyəlā'shən] *n* accumulazione *f*.

accuracy [ak'yûrəsē] *n* precisione *f*.

accurate [ak'yûrit] *a* preciso(a).

accurately [ak'yûritlē] *ad* precisamente.

accusation [akyōōzā'shən] *n* accusa.

accusative [əkyōō'zətiv] *n* (*LING*) accusativo.

accuse [əkyōōz'] *vt* accusare.

accused [əkyōōzd'] *n* accusato/a.

accustom [əkus'təm] *vt* abituare; **to ~ o.s. to sth** abituarsi a qc.

accustomed [əkus'təmd] *a* (*usual*) abituale; **~ to** abituato(a) a.

AC/DC *abbr* (= *alternating current/direct current*) c.a./c.c.

ACE [ās] *n abbr* = *American Council on Education*.

ace [ās] *n* asso; **within an ~ of** a un pelo da.

Ace bandage ® *n* (*US*) fascia elastica.

acerbic [əsûr'bik] *a* (*also fig*) acido(a).

acetate [as'itāt] *n* acetato.

ache [āk] *n* male *m*, dolore *m* ♦ *vi* (*be sore*) far male, dolere; (*yearn*): **to ~ to do sth** morire dalla voglia di fare qc; **I've got a stomach~** *or* (*Brit*) **stomach ~** ho mal di stomaco; **my head ~s** mi fa male la testa; **I'm aching all over** mi duole dappertutto.

achieve [əchēv'] *vt* (*aim*) raggiungere; (*victory*, *success*) ottenere; (*task*) compiere.

achievement [əchēv'mənt] *n* compimento; successo.

acid [as'id] *a* acido(a) ♦ *n* acido.

acidity [əsid'itē] *n* acidità.

acid rain *n* pioggia acida.

acknowledge [aknâl'ij] *vt* riconoscere; (*letter: also*: **~ receipt of**) accusare ricevuta di.

acknowledgement [aknâl'ijmənt] *n* riconoscimento; (*of letter*) conferma; **~s** (*in book*) ringraziamenti *mpl*.

ACLU *n abbr* (= *American Civil Liberties Union*) unione americana per le libertà civili.

acme [ak'mē] *n* culmine *m*, acme *m*.

acne [ak'nē] *n* acne *f*.

acorn [ā'kôrn] *n* ghianda.

acoustic [əkōōs'tik] *a* acustico(a); *see also* **acoustics**.

acoustic coupler [əkōōs'tik kup'lûr] *n* (*COMPUT*) accoppiatore *m* acustico.

acoustics [əkōōs'tiks] n, npl acustica.

acoustic screen n schermo acustico.

acquaint [əkwānt'] vt: **to ~ sb with sth** far sapere qc a qn; **to be ~ed with** (person) conoscere.

acquaintance [əkwān'təns] n conoscenza; (person) conoscente m/f; **to make sb's ~** fare la conoscenza di qn.

acquiesce [akwēes'] vi (agree): **to ~ (in)** acconsentire (a).

acquire [əkwī'ûr] vt acquistare.

acquired [əkwī'ûrd] a acquisito(a); **it's an ~ taste** è una cosa che si impara ad apprezzare.

acquisition [akwizish'ən] n acquisto.

acquisitive [əkwiz'ətiv] a a cui piace accumulare le cose.

acquit [əkwit'] vt assolvere; **to ~ o.s. well** comportarsi bene.

acquittal [əkwit'əl] n assoluzione f.

acre [ā'kûr] n acro (= 4047 m²).

acreage [ā'kûrij] n superficie f in acri.

acrid [ak'rid] a (smell) acre, pungente; (fig) pungente.

acrimonious [akrəmō'nēəs] a astioso(a).

acrobat [ak'rəbat] n acrobata m/f.

acrobatic [akrəbat'ik] a acrobatico(a).

acrobatics [akrəbat'iks] n acrobatica ♦ npl acrobazie fpl.

Acropolis [əkrăp'əlis] n: **the ~** l'Acropoli f.

across [əkrôs'] prep (on the other side) dall'altra parte di; (crosswise) attraverso ♦ ad dall'altra parte; in larghezza; **to walk ~ (the road)** attraversare (la strada); **to take sb ~ the road** far attraversare la strada a qn; **~ from** di fronte a; **the lake is 12 km ~** il lago ha una larghezza di 12 km or è largo 12 km; **to get sth ~ to sb** far capire qc a qn.

acrylic [əkril'ik] a acrilico(a) ♦ n acrilico.

ACT n abbr (= American College Test) esame di ammissione a college.

act [akt] n atto; (in music-hall etc) numero; (LAW) decreto ♦ vi agire; (THEATER) recitare; (pretend) fingere ♦ vt (part) recitare; **to catch sb in the ~** cogliere qn in flagrante or sul fatto; **it's only an ~** è tutta scena, è solo una messinscena; **~ of God** (LAW) calamità f inv naturale; **to ~ Hamlet** (Brit) recitare la parte di Amleto; **to ~ the fool** fare lo stupido; **to ~ as** agire da; **it ~s as a deterrent** serve da deterrente; **~ing in my capacity as chairman, I ...** in qualità di presidente, io ....

act on vt: **to ~ on sth** agire in base a qc.

act out vt (event) ricostruire; (fantasies) dare forma concreta a.

act up vi (cause trouble) fare i capricci.

acting [ak'ting] a che fa le funzioni di ♦ n (of actor) recitazione f; (activity): **to do some ~** fare del teatro (or del cinema); **he is the ~ manager** fa le veci del direttore.

action [ak'shən] n azione f; (MIL) combatti-

mento; (LAW) processo; **to take ~** agire; **to put a plan into ~** realizzare un piano; **out of ~** fuori combattimento; (machine etc) fuori servizio; **killed in ~** (MIL) ucciso in combattimento; **to bring an ~ against sb** (LAW) intentare causa contro qn.

action replay n (Brit TV) replay m inv.

activate [ak'təvāt] vt (mechanism) fare funzionare; (CHEM, PHYSICS) rendere attivo(a).

active [ak'tiv] a attivo(a); **to play an ~ part in** partecipare attivamente a.

active duty (AD) n (US MIL): **to be on ~** prestar servizio in zona di operazioni.

actively [ak'tivlē] ad attivamente.

active partner n (COMM) socio effettivo.

active service n (Brit MIL) = **active duty**.

activist [ak'tivist] n attivista m/f.

activity [aktiv'ətē] n attività f inv.

actor [ak'tûr] n attore m.

actress [ak'tris] n attrice f.

actual [ak'chōōəl] a reale, vero(a).

actually [ak'chōōəlē] ad veramente; (even) addirittura.

actuary [ak'chōōärē] n attuario/a.

actuate [ak'chōōāt] vt attivare.

acuity [əkyōō'itē] n acutezza.

acumen [əkyōō'mən] n acume m; **business ~** fiuto negli affari.

acupuncture [ak'yōōpungkchûr] n agopuntura.

acute [əkyōōt'] a acuto(a).

AD ad abbr (= Anno Domini) d. C. ♦ n abbr (US MIL) see **active duty**.

ad [ad] n abbr = **advertisement**.

adamant [ad'əmənt] a irremovibile.

Adam's apple [ad'əms ap'əl] n pomo di Adamo.

adapt [ədapt'] vt adattare ♦ vi: **to ~ (to)** adattarsi (a).

adaptability [ədaptəbil'ətē] n adattabilità.

adaptable [ədap'təbəl] a (device) adattabile; (person) che sa adattarsi.

adaptation [adəptā'shən] n adattamento.

adapter, adaptor [ədap'tûr] n (ELEC) adattatore m.

ADC n abbr (MIL) = **aide-de-camp**; (US: = Aid to Dependent Children) sussidio per figli a carico.

add [ad] vt aggiungere; (figures) addizionare ♦ vi: **to ~ to** (increase) aumentare.

add on vt aggiungere.

add up vt (figures) addizionare ♦ vi (fig): **it doesn't ~ up** non ha senso; **it doesn't ~ up to much** non è un granché.

adder [ad'ûr] n vipera.

addict [ad'ikt] n tossicomane m/f; (fig) fanatico/a; **heroin ~** eroinomane m/f; **drug ~** tossicodipendente m/f, tossicomane m/f.

addicted [ədik'tid] a: **to be ~ to** (drink etc) essere dedito(a) a; (fig: football etc) essere tifoso(a) di.

addiction [ədik'shən] n (MED) tossicomania.

adding machine |ad'ing məshēn'| *n* addizionatrice *f*.

Addis Ababa |ad'is âb'əbá| *n* Addis Abeba *f*.

addition |ədish'ən| *n* addizione *f*; **in** ~ inoltre; **in** ~ **to** oltre.

additional |ədish'ənəl| *a* supplementare.

additive |ad'ətiv| *n* additivo.

address |ədrĕs'| *n* (*gen*, *COMPUT*) indirizzo; (*talk*) discorso ♦ *vt* indirizzare; (*speak to*) fare un discorso a; **form of** ~ (*gen*) formula di cortesia; (*in letters*) formula d'indirizzo *or* di intestazione; **to** ~ **o.s. to sth** indirizzare le proprie energie verso qc; **absolute/relative** ~ (*COMPUT*) indirizzo assoluto/relativo.

Aden |ã'dən| *n*: **the Gulf of** ~ il golfo di Aden.

adenoids |ad'ənoidz| *npl* adenoidi *fpl*.

adept |ədept'| *a*: ~ **at** esperto(a) in.

adequate |ad'əkwit| *a* (*description*, *reward*) adeguato(a); (*amount*) sufficiente; **to feel** ~ **to a task** sentirsi all'altezza di un compito.

adequately |ad'əkwitlē| *ad* adeguatamente; sufficientemente.

adhere |adhēr'| *vi*: **to** ~ **to** aderire a; (*fig*: *rule*, *decision*) seguire.

adhesion |adhē'zhən| *n* adesione *f*.

adhesive |adhē'siv| *a* adesivo(a) ♦ *n* adesivo; ~ **tape** (*US*: *MED*) cerotto adesivo; (*Brit*: *for parcels etc*) nastro adesivo.

ad hoc |ad hák'| *a* (*decision*) ad hoc *inv*; (*committee*) apposito(a).

ad infinitum |ad infənī'təm| *ad* all'infinito.

adjacent |əjā'sənt| *a* adiacente; ~ **to** accanto a.

adjective |aj'iktiv| *n* aggettivo.

adjoin |əjoin'| *vt* essere contiguo(a) *or* attiguo(a) a.

adjoining |əjoi'ning| *a* accanto *inv*, adiacente ♦ *prep* accanto a.

adjourn |əjûrn'| *vt* rimandare, aggiornare; (*US*: *end*) sospendere ♦ *vi* sospendere la seduta; (*PARLIAMENT*) sospendere i lavori; (*go*) spostarsi; **to** ~ **a meeting till the following week** aggiornare *or* rinviare un incontro alla settimana seguente.

adjournment |əjûrn'mənt| *n* rinvio, aggiornamento; sospensione *f*.

Adjt *abbr* (*MIL*) = **adjutant**.

adjudicate |əjōō'dikāt| *vt* (*contest*) giudicare; (*claim*) decidere su.

adjudication |əjōōdikā'shən| *n* decisione *f*.

adjust |əjust'| *vt* aggiustare; (*COMM*) rettificare ♦ *vi*: **to** ~ (**to**) adattarsi (a).

adjustable |əjust'əbəl| *a* regolabile.

adjuster |əjust'ûr| *n see* **loss adjuster**.

adjustment |əjust'mənt| *n* adattamento; (*of prices*, *wages*) adeguamento.

adjutant |aj'ətənt| *n* aiutante *m*.

ad-lib |adlib'| *vt*, *vi* improvvisare ♦ *n* improvvisazione *f* ♦ *ad*: **ad lib** a piacere, a volontà.

adman |ad'man| *n* (*col*) pubblicitario/a.

admin |ad'min| *n* *abbr* (*col*) = **administration**.

administer |admin'istûr| *vt* amministrare; (*justice*) somministrare.

administration |administrā'shən| *n* amministrazione *f*; **the A**~ (*US*) il Governo.

administrative |admin'istrātiv| *a* amministrativo(a).

administrator |admin'istrātûr| *n* amministratore/trice.

admirable |ad'mûrəbəl| *a* ammirevole.

admiral |ad'mûrəl| *n* ammiraglio.

Admiralty |ad'mûrəltē| *n* (*Brit*: *also*: ~ **Board**) Ministero della Marina.

admiration |admərā'shən| *n* ammirazione *f*.

admire |admī'ûr| *vt* ammirare.

admirer |admī'ərûr| *n* ammiratore/trice.

admission |admish'ən| *n* ammissione *f*; (*to exhibition*, *night club etc*) ingresso; (*confession*) confessione *f*; **by his own** ~ per sua ammissione; **"**~ **free"**, **"free** ~**"** "ingresso gratuito".

admit |admit'| *vt* ammettere; far entrare; (*agree*) riconoscere; **"children not** ~**ted"** "vietato l'ingresso ai bambini"; **this ticket** ~**s two** questo biglietto è valido per due persone; **I must** ~ **that** ... devo ammettere *or* confessare che ....

admit of *vt fus* lasciare adito a.

admit to *vt fus* riconoscere.

admittance |admit'əns| *n* ingresso; **"no** ~**"** "vietato l'ingresso".

admittedly |admit'idlē| *ad* bisogna pur riconoscere (che).

admonish |admán'ish| *vt* ammonire.

ad nauseam |ad nô'zēəm| *ad* fino alla nausea, a non finire.

ado |ədōō'| *n*: **without further** ~ senza più indugi.

adolescence |adəlĕs'əns| *n* adolescenza.

adolescent |adəlĕs'ənt| *a*, *n* adolescente (*m/f*).

adopt |ədápt'| *vt* adottare.

adopted |ədáp'tid| *a* adottivo(a).

adoption |ədáp'shən| *n* adozione *f*.

adore |ədôr'| *vt* adorare.

adoringly |ədôr'inglē| *ad* con adorazione.

adorn |ədôrn'| *vt* ornare.

adornment |ədôrn'mənt| *n* ornamento.

ADP *n abbr see* **automatic data processing**.

adrenalin |ədrĕn'əlin| *n* adrenalina; **it gets the** ~ **going** ti dà una carica.

Adriatic (Sea) |ādrēat'ik (sē')| *n* Adriatico.

adrift |ədrift'| *ad* alla deriva; **to come** ~ (*boat*) andare alla deriva; (*wire*, *rope etc*) essersi staccato(a) *or* sciolto(a).

adroit |ədroit'| *a* abile, destro(a).

adult |ədult'| *n* adulto/a.

adult education *n* scuola per adulti.

adulterate |ədul'tûrāt| *vt* adulterare.

adultery |ədul'tûrē| *n* adulterio.

adulthood |ədult'hōōd| *n* età adulta.

advance |advans'| *n* avanzamento; (*money*)

anticipo ♦ *vt* avanzare; (*date, money*) anticipare ♦ *vi* avanzare; **in ~** in anticipo; **to
make ~s to sb** (*gen*) fare degli approcci a
qn; (*amorously*) fare delle avances a qn.

advanced [advanst'] *a* avanzato(a); (*SCOL:
studies*) superiore; **~ in years** avanti negli
anni.

advancement [advans'mənt] *n* avanzamento.

advance notice *n* preavviso.

advantage [advan'tij] *n* (*also TENNIS*)
vantaggio; **to take ~ of** approfittarsi di; **it's
to our ~** è nel nostro interesse, torna a nostro vantaggio.

advantageous [advəntā'jəs] *a* vantaggioso(a).

advent [ad'vent] *n* avvento; **A~** (*REL*)
Avvento.

Advent calendar *n* calendario dell'Avvento.

adventure [adven'chûr] *n* avventura.

adventurous [adven'chûrəs] *a* avventuroso(a).

adverb [ad'vûrb] *n* avverbio.

adversary [ad'vûrsärē] *n* avversario/a.

adverse [advûrs'] *a* avverso(a); **in ~ circumstances** nelle avversità; **~ to** contrario(a) a.

adversity [advûr'sitē] *n* avversità.

advert [ad'vûrt] *n* *abbr* (*Brit*) = **advertisement**.

advertise [ad'vûrtīz] *vi* (*vt*) fare pubblicità *or*
réclame (a); fare un'inserzione (per vende-
re); **to ~ for** (*staff*) cercare tramite
annuncio.

advertisement [advûrtīz'mənt] *n* (*COMM*) réclame *f inv*, pubblicità *f inv*; (*in classified
ads*) inserzione *f*.

advertiser [ad'vûrtīzûr] *n* azienda che reclamizza un prodotto; (*in newspaper*) inserzioni-
sta *m/f*.

advertising [ad'vûrtīzing] *n* pubblicità.

advertising agency *n* agenzia pubblicitaria
or di pubblicità.

advertising campaign *n* campagna pubblicitaria.

advice [advīs'] *n* consigli *mpl*; (*notification*)
avviso; **piece of ~** consiglio; **to ask (sb) for
~** chiedere il consiglio (di qn), chiedere un
consiglio (a qn); **legal ~** consulenza legale.

advice slip *n* avviso di spedizione.

advisable [advī'zəbəl] *a* consigliabile.

advise [advīz'] *vt* consigliare; **to ~ sb of sth**
informare qn di qc; **to ~ sb against sth/
against doing sth** sconsigliare qc a qn/a qn
di fare qc; **you will be well/ill ~d to go** fareste bene/male ad andare.

advisedly [advī'zidlē] *ad* (*deliberately*) deliberatamente.

adviser [advī'zûr] *n* consigliere/a; (*in business*)
consulente *m/f*, consigliere/a.

advisory [advī'zûrē] *a* consultivo(a); **in an ~
capacity** in veste di consulente.

advocate [ad'vəkāt] *n* (*upholder*) sostenitore/
trice ♦ *vt* propugnare; **to be an ~ of** essere
a favore di.

advt. *abbr* = **advertisement**.

AEA *n* *abbr* (*Brit*: = *Atomic Energy Authority*) *ente di controllo sulla ricerca e lo sviluppo dell'energia atomica.*

AEC *n* *abbr* (*US*: = *Atomic Energy
Commission*) *ente di controllo sulla ricerca e
lo sviluppo dell'energia atomica.*

Aegean (Sea) [ējē'ən (sē')] *n* (*mare m*) Egeo.

aegis [ē'jis] *n*: **under the ~ of** sotto gli auspici
di.

aeon [ē'ən] *n* (*Brit*) = **eon**.

aerial [är'ēəl] *n* antenna ♦ *a* aereo(a).

aerie [är'ē] *n* (*US*) nido (d'aquila).

aerobatics [ärəbat'iks] *npl* acrobazia aerea *sg*;
(*stunts*) acrobazie *fpl* aeree.

aerobics [ärō'biks] *n* aerobica.

aerodrome [är'ədrōm] *n* (*Brit*) aerodromo.

aerodynamic [ärōdīnam'ik] *a* aero-
dinamico(a).

aerogramme [är'əgram] *n* aerogramma *m*.

aeronautics [ärənô'tiks] *n* aeronautica.

aeroplane [är'əplān] *n* (*Brit*) aeroplano.

aerosol [är'əsôl] *n* aerosol *m inv*.

aerospace industry [är'əspās in'dəstrē] *n*
industria aerospaziale.

aesthetic [esthet'ik] *a* (*Brit*) = **esthetic**.

afar [əfâr'] *ad* lontano; **from ~** da lontano.

AFB *n* *abbr* (*US*) = *Air Force Base*.

AFDC *n* *abbr* (*US*: = *Aid to Families with Dependent Children*) ≈ A.F. (= *assegni familiari*).

affable [af'əbəl] *a* affabile.

affair [əfâr'] *n* affare *m*; (*also:* **love ~**) relazione *f* amorosa; **~s** (*business*) affari; **the
Watergate ~** il caso Watergate.

affect [əfekt'] *vt* toccare; (*feign*) fingere.

affectation [afektā'shən] *n* affettazione *f*.

affected [əfek'tid] *a* affettato(a).

affection [əfek'shən] *n* affezione *f*.

affectionate [əfek'shənit] *a* affettuoso(a).

affectionately [əfek'shənitlē] *ad* affettuosamente.

affidavit [afidā'vit] *n* (*LAW*) affidavit *m inv*.

affiliated [əfil'ēātid] *a* affiliato(a); **~ company**
filiale *f*.

affinity [əfin'ətē] *n* affinità *f inv*.

affirm [əfûrm'] *vt* affermare, asserire.

affirmation [afûrmā'shən] *n* affermazione *f*.

affirmative [əfûr'mətiv] *a* affermativo(a) ♦ *n*:
in the ~ affermativamente.

affix [əfiks'] *vt* apporre; attaccare.

afflict [əflikt'] *vt* affliggere.

affliction [əflik'shən] *n* afflizione *f*.

affluence [af'lōōəns] *n* ricchezza.

affluent [af'lōōənt] *a* ricco(a); **the ~ society**
la società del benessere.

afford [əfôrd'] *vt* permettersi; (*provide*) fornire; **I can't ~ the time** non ho veramente il
tempo; **can we ~ a car?** possiamo
permetterci un'automobile?

affront [əfrunt'] *n* affronto.

affronted [əfrun'tid] *a* insultato(a).

Afghan [af'gan] *a, n* afgano(a).

Afghanistan [afgan'istan] *n* Afganistan *m*.

afield [əfēld'] *ad*: **far** ~ lontano.

AFL-CIO *n abbr* (= *American Federation of Labor and Congress of Industrial Organizations*) *confederazione sindacale*.

afloat [əflōt'] *a, ad* a galla.

afoot [əfŏŏt'] *ad*: **there is something** ~ si sta preparando qualcosa.

aforementioned [əfôr'menshənd] *a* suddetto(a).

aforesaid [əfôr'sed] *a* suddetto(a), predetto(a).

afraid [əfrād'] *a* impaurito(a); **to be** ~ **of** aver paura di; **to be** ~ **of doing** *or* **to do** aver paura di fare; **I am** ~ **that I'll be late** mi dispiace, ma farò tardi; **I'm** ~ **so!** ho paura di sì!, temo proprio di sì!; **I'm** ~ **not** no, mi dispiace, purtroppo no.

afresh [əfresh'] *ad* di nuovo.

Africa [af'rikə] *n* Africa.

African [af'rikən] *a, n* africano(a).

Afrikaans [afrikâns'] *n* afrikaans *m*.

Afrikaner [afrikä'nûr] *n* africander *m inv*.

Afro-American [af'rōəmär'ikən] *a* afroamericano(a).

AFT *n abbr* (= *American Federation of Teachers*) *sindacato degli insegnanti*.

aft [aft] *ad* a poppa, verso poppa.

after [af'tûr] *prep, ad* dopo; ~ **dinner** dopo cena; **the day** ~ **tomorrow** dopodomani; **what/who are you** ~? che/chi cerca?; **the police are** ~ **him** è ricercato dalla polizia; ~ **you!** prima lei!, dopo di lei!; ~ **all** dopo tutto; **quarter/half** ~ **four** le quattro e un quarto/e mezzo; **ten/twenty** ~ **four** le quattro e dieci/venti.

aftercare [af'tûrkär] *n* (*MED*) assistenza medica post-degenza.

after-effects [af'tûrifekts] *npl* conseguenze *fpl*; (*of illness*) postumi *mpl*.

afterlife [af'tûrlīf] *n* vita dell'al di là.

aftermath [af'tûrmath] *n* conseguenze *fpl*; **in the** ~ **of** nel periodo dopo.

afternoon [aftûrnōōn'] *n* pomeriggio; **good** ~! buon giorno!

after-sales service [af'tûrsālz sûr'vis] *n* (*Brit*) servizio assistenza clienti.

after-shave (lotion) [af'tûrshāv (lō'shən)] *n* dopobarba *m inv*.

aftershock [af'tûrshák] *n* scossa di assestamento.

afterthought [af'tûrthôt] *n*: **as an** ~ come aggiunta.

afterwards [af'tûrwûrdz] *ad* dopo.

again [əgen'] *ad* di nuovo; **to begin/see** ~ ricominciare/rivedere; **he opened it** ~ l'ha aperto di nuovo, l'ha riaperto; **not** ... ~ non ... più; ~ **and** ~ ripetutamente; **now and** ~ di tanto in tanto, a volte.

against [əgenst'] *prep* contro; ~ **a blue background** su uno sfondo azzurro; **leaning** ~ **the desk** appoggiato alla scrivania; **(over)** ~ in confronto a, contro.

age [āj] *n* età *f inv* ♦ *vt, vi* invecchiare; **what** ~ **is he?** quanti anni ha?; **he is 20 years of** ~ ha 20 anni; **under** ~ minorenne; **to come of** ~ diventare maggiorenne; **it's been** ~s **since** ... sono secoli che ....

aged [ājd] *a*: ~ **10** di 10 anni; **the** ~ [ā'jid] *npl* (*elderly*) gli anziani.

age group *n* generazione *f*; **the 40 to 50** ~ le persone fra i 40 e i 50 anni.

ageless [āj'lis] *a* senza età.

age limit *n* limite *m* d'età.

agency [ā'jənsē] *n* agenzia; **through** *or* **by the** ~ **of** grazie a.

agenda [əjen'də] *n* ordine *m* del giorno; **on the** ~ all'ordine del giorno.

agent [ā'jənt] *n* agente *m*.

aggravate [ag'rəvāt] *vt* aggravare, peggiorare; (*annoy*) esasperare.

aggravation [agrəvā'shən] *n* peggioramento; esasperazione *f*.

aggregate [ag'rəgit] *n* aggregato; **on** ~ (*SPORT*) con punteggio complessivo.

aggression [əgresh'ən] *n* aggressione *f*.

aggressive [əgres'iv] *a* aggressivo(a).

aggressiveness [əgres'ivnis] *n* aggressività.

aggrieved [əgrēvd'] *a* addolorato(a).

aghast [əgast'] *a* sbigottito(a).

agile [aj'əl] *a* agile.

agitate [aj'ətāt] *vt* turbare; agitare ♦ *vi*: **to** ~ **for** agitarsi per.

agitator [aj'itātûr] *n* agitatore/trice.

AGM *n abbr* (*Brit*) *see* **annual general meeting**.

agnostic [agnás'tik] *a, n* agnostico(a).

ago [əgō'] *ad*: **2 days** ~ 2 giorni fa; **not long** ~ poco tempo fa; **as long** ~ **as 1960** già nel 1960; **how long** ~? quanto tempo fa?

agog [əgàg'] *a*: **(all)** ~ **(for)** ansioso(a) (di), impaziente (di).

agonize [ag'ənīz] *vi*: **to** ~ **(over)** angosciarsi (per).

agonizing [ag'ənīzing] *a* straziante.

agony [ag'ənē] *n* agonia; **I was in** ~ avevo dei dolori atroci.

agony column *n* posta del cuore.

agree [əgrē'] *vt* (*price*) pattuire ♦ *vi*: **to** ~ **(with)** essere d'accordo (con); (*LING*) concordare (con); **to** ~ **to sth/to do sth** accettare qc/di fare qc; **to** ~ **that** (*admit*) ammettere che; **to** ~ **on sth** accordarsi su qc; **it was** ~**d that** ... è stato deciso di comune accordo che ...; **garlic doesn't** ~ **with me** l'aglio non mi va.

agreeable [əgrē'əbəl] *a* gradevole; (*willing*) disposto(a); **are you** ~ **to this?** è d'accordo con questo?

agreed [əgrēd'] *a* (*time, place*) stabilito(a); **to be** ~ essere d'accordo.

agreement [əgrē'mənt] *n* accordo; **in** ~ d'accordo; **by mutual** ~ di comune accordo.
agricultural [agrəkul'chûrəl] *a* agricolo(a).
agriculture [ag'rəkulchûr] *n* agricoltura.
aground [əground'] *ad*: **to run** ~ arenarsi.
agt. *n abbr* = **agent.**
ahead [əhed'] *ad* avanti; davanti; ~ **of** davanti a; *(fig: schedule etc)* in anticipo su; ~ **of time** in anticipo; **go** ~! avanti!; **go right** *or* **straight** ~ tiri diritto; **they were (right)** ~ **of us** erano (proprio) davanti a noi.
AI *n abbr* = *Amnesty International*; *(COMPUT)* *see* **artificial intelligence.**
AID *n abbr* = *artificial insemination by donor*; *(US: = Agency for International Development)* A.I.D. *f*.
aid [ād] *n* aiuto ♦ *vt* aiutare; **with the** ~ **of** con l'aiuto di; **in** ~ **of** a favore di; **to** ~ **and abet** *(LAW)* essere complice di.
aide [ād] *n (person)* aiutante *m*.
aide-de-camp (ADC) [ād'dəkamp] *n* (*MIL*) aiutante *m* di campo.
AIDS [ādz] *n abbr* (= *acquired immune deficiency syndrome*) A.I.D.S. *f*.
AIH *n abbr* = *artificial insemination by husband*.
ailing [ā'ling] *a* sofferente; *(fig: economy, industry etc)* in difficoltà.
ailment [āl'mənt] *n* indisposizione *f*.
aim [ām] *vt*: **to** ~ **sth at** *(gun)* mirare qc a, puntare qc a; *(camera, remark)* rivolgere qc a; *(missile)* lanciare qc contro; *(blow etc)* tirare qc a ♦ *vi (also:* **to take** ~) prendere la mira ♦ *n* mira; **to** ~ **at** mirare a; **to** ~ **to do** aver l'intenzione di fare.
aimless [ām'lis] *a* senza scopo.
aimlessly [ām'lislē] *ad* senza scopo.
ain't [ānt] *(col)* = **am not; aren't; isn't.**
air [âr] *n* aria ♦ *vt (room, bed)* arieggiare; *(clothes)* far prendere aria a; *(idea, grievance)* esprimere pubblicamente, manifestare; *(views)* far conoscere ♦ *cpd (currents)* d'aria; *(attack)* aereo(a); **by** ~ *(travel)* in aereo; **to be on the** ~ *(RADIO, TV: station)* trasmettere; *(: program)* essere in onda.
air base *n* base *f* aerea.
air bed *n* materassino.
airborne [âr'bôrn] *a (plane)* in volo; *(troops)* aerotrasportato(a); **as soon as the plane was** ~ appena l'aereo ebbe decollato.
air cargo *n* carico trasportato per via aerea.
air-conditioned [âr'kəndishənd] *a* con *or* ad aria condizionata.
air conditioning *n* condizionamento d'aria.
air-cooled [âr'kōōld] *a* raffreddato(a) ad aria.
aircraft [âr'kraft] *n (pl inv)* apparecchio.
aircraft carrier *n* portaerei *f inv*.
air cushion *n* cuscino gonfiabile; *(TECH)* cuscino d'aria.
airdrome [âr'drōm] *n (US)* aerodromo.
airfield [âr'fēld] *n* campo d'aviazione.

Air Force *n* aviazione *f* militare.
air freight *n* spedizione *f* di merci per via aerea; *(goods)* carico spedito per via aerea.
air gun *n* fucile *m* ad aria compressa.
air hostess *n (Brit)* hostess *f inv*.
airily [âr'ilē] *ad* con disinvoltura.
airing [âr'ing] *n*: **to give an** ~ **to** *(linen)* far prendere aria a; *(room)* arieggiare; *(fig: ideas etc)* ventilare.
air letter *n* aerogramma *m*.
airlift [âr'lift] *n* ponte *m* aereo.
airline [âr'līn] *n* linea aerea.
airliner [âr'līnûr] *n* aereo di linea.
airlock [âr'lâk] *n* cassa d'aria.
air mail *n* posta aerea; **by** ~ per via *or* posta aerea.
air mattress *n* materassino gonfiabile.
airplane [âr'plān] *n (US)* aeroplano.
airport [âr'pôrt] *n* aeroporto.
air raid *n* incursione *f* aerea.
airsick [âr'sik] *a*: **to be** ~ soffrire di mal d'aereo.
airspace [âr'spās] *n* spazio aereo.
airstrip [âr'strip] *n* pista d'atterraggio.
air terminal *n (Brit)* air-terminal *m inv*.
airtight [âr'tīt] *a* ermetico(a).
air traffic control *n* controllo del traffico aereo.
air traffic controller *n* controllore *m* del traffico aereo.
air waybill [âr' wā'bil] *n (COMM)* bolletta di trasporto aereo.
airy [âr'ē] *a* arioso(a); *(manners)* noncurante.
aisle [īl] *n (of church)* navata laterale; navata centrale; *(of plane)* corridoio; *(US: of bus)* passaggio.
ajar [əjâr'] *a* socchiuso(a).
AK *abbr (US MAIL)* = *Alaska*.
aka *abbr* (= *also known as*) alias.
akin [əkin'] *prep* simile a.
AL *abbr (US MAIL)* = *Alabama*.
ALA *n abbr* = *American Library Association*.
Ala. *abbr (US)* = *Alabama*.
à la carte [lə lâ kârt'] *ad* alla carta.
alacrity [əlak'ritē] *n*: **with** ~ con prontezza.
alarm [əlârm'] *n* allarme *m* ♦ *vt* allarmare.
alarm clock *n* sveglia.
alarming [əlâr'ming] *a* allarmante, preoccupante.
alarmist [əlâr'mist] *n* allarmista *m/f*.
Alas. *abbr (US)* = *Alaska*.
alas [əlas'] *excl* ohimè!, ahimè!
Alaska [əlas'kə] *n* Alasca.
Albania [albā'nēə] *n* Albania.
Albanian [albā'nēən] *a* albanese ♦ *n* albanese *m/f*; *(LING)* albanese *m*.
albeit [ôlbē'it] *cj* sebbene + *sub*, benché + *sub*.
album [al'bəm] *n* album *m inv*; *(L.P.)* 33 giri *m inv*, L.P. *m inv*.
albumen [albyōō'mən] *n* albume *m*.
alchemy [al'kəmē] *n* alchimia.

alcohol [al'kəhól] *n* alcool *m*.
alcoholic [alkəhól'ik] *a* alcolico(a) ♦ *n* alcolizzato/a.
alcoholism [al'kəhəlizəm] *n* alcolismo.
alcove [al'kōv] *n* alcova.
ald. *abbr* = **alderman**.
alderman [ôl'dûrmən] *n* consigliere *m* comunale.
ale [āl] *n* birra.
alert [əlûrt'] *a* vivo(a); (*watchful*) vigile ♦ *n* allarme *m* ♦ *vt*: **to ~ sb (to sth)** avvisare qn (di qc), avvertire qn (di qc); **to ~ sb to the dangers of sth** mettere qn in guardia contro qc; **on the ~** all'erta.
Aleutian Islands [əlōō'shən ī'ləndz] *npl* isole *fpl* Aleutine.
Alexandria [aligzan'drēə] *n* Alessandria (d'Egitto).
alfresco [alfres'kō] *a, ad* all'aperto.
algebra [al'jəbrə] *n* algebra.
Algeria [aljē'rēə] *n* Algeria.
Algerian [aljə'rēən] *a, n* algerino(a).
Algiers [aljērz'] *n* Algeri *f*.
algorithm [al'gəriŧhəm] *n* algoritmo.
alias [ā'lēəs] *ad* alias ♦ *n* pseudonimo, falso nome *m*.
alibi [al'əbī] *n* alibi *m inv*.
alien [āl'yən] *n* straniero/a ♦ *a*: **~ (to)** estraneo(a) (a).
alienate [āl'yənāt] *vt* alienare.
alienation [ālyənā'shən] *n* alienazione *f*.
alight [əlīt'] *a* acceso(a) ♦ *vi* scendere; (*bird*) posarsi.
align [əlīn'] *vt* allineare.
alignment [əlīn'mənt] *n* allineamento; **out of ~ (with)** non allineato (con).
alike [əlīk'] *a* simile ♦ *ad* allo stesso modo; **to look ~** assomigliarsi; **winter and summer ~** sia d'estate che d'inverno.
alimony [al'əmōnē] *n* (*payment*) alimenti *mpl*.
alive [əlīv'] *a* vivo(a); (*active*) attivo(a); **~ with** pieno(a) di; **~ to** conscio(a) di.
alkali [al'kəlī] *n* alcali *m inv*.
all [ôl] *a* tutto(a), tutti(e) *pl* ♦ *pronoun* tutto *m*; (*pl*) tutti(e) ♦ *ad* tutto; **~ wrong/alone** tutto sbagliato/solo; **~ the time/his life** tutto il tempo/tutta la sua vita; **~ five** tutti e cinque; **~ five girls** tutt'e cinque le ragazze; **~ of them** tutti(e); **~ of it** tutto; **~ of us went** ci siamo andati tutti; **~ day** tutto il giorno; **is that ~?** non c'è altro?; (*in shop*) basta così?; **for ~ their efforts** nonostante tutti i loro sforzi; **it's not as hard** *etc* **as ~ that** non è mica così duro *etc*; **at ~ : not at ~** (*in answer to question*) per niente, (niente) affatto; (*in answer to thanks*) prego!, s'immagini!, si figuri!; **I'm not at ~ tired** non sono affatto *or* per niente stanco; **anything at ~ will do** andrà bene qualsiasi cosa; **~ but** quasi; **to be/feel ~ in** (*col*) essere/sentirsi sfinito *or* distrutto; **~ in ~** tutto sommato; **~ out** *ad*: **to go ~ out** mettercela tutta.
all-around [ôl'əround] *a* completo(a).
allay [əlā'] *vt* (*fears*) dissipare.
all clear *n* (*MIL*) cessato allarme *m inv*; (*fig*) okay *m*.
allegation [aləgā'shən] *n* asserzione *f*.
allege [əlej'] *vt* asserire; **he is ~d to have said ...** avrebbe detto che ...
alleged [əlejd'] *a* presunto(a).
allegedly [əlej'idlē] *ad* secondo quanto si asserisce.
allegiance [əlē'jəns] *n* fedeltà.
allegory [al'əgôrē] *n* allegoria.
all-embracing [ôl'embräs'ing] *a* universale.
allergic [əlûr'jik] *a*: **~ to** allergico(a) a.
allergy [al'ûrjē] *n* allergia.
alleviate [əlē'vēāt] *vt* alleviare.
alley [al'ē] *n* vicolo; (*in garden*) vialetto.
alliance [əlī'əns] *n* alleanza.
allied [əlīd'] *a* alleato(a).
alligator [al'əgātûr] *n* alligatore *m*.
all-important [ôl'impôr'tənt] *a* importantissimo(a).
all-inclusive [ôl'inklōō'siv] *a* (*also ad: charge*) tutto compreso.
all-in wrestling [ôl'in res'ling] *n* (*Brit*) lotta americana.
alliteration [əlitərā'shən] *n* allitterazione *f*.
all-night [ôl'nīt] *a* aperto(a) (*or* che dura) tutta la notte.
allocate [al'əkāt] *vt* (*share out*) distribuire; (*duties, sum, time*): **to ~ sth to** assegnare qc a; **to ~ sth for** stanziare qc per.
allocation [aləkā'shən] *n*: **~ (of money)** stanziamento.
allot [əlât'] *vt* (*share out*) spartire; **to ~ sth to** (*time*) dare qc a; (*duties*) assegnare qc a; **in the ~ted time** nel tempo fissato *or* prestabilito.
allotment [əlât'mənt] *n* (*share*) spartizione *f*; (*Brit: garden*) lotto di terra.
all-out [ôl'out'] *a* (*effort etc*) totale ♦ *ad*: **to go all out for** mettercela tutta per.
allow [əlou'] *vt* (*practice, behavior*) permettere; (*sum to spend etc*) accordare; (*sum, time estimated*) dare; (*concede*): **to ~ that** ammettere che; **to ~ sb to do** permettere a qn di fare; **he is ~ed to (do it)** lo può fare; **smoking is not ~ed** è vietato fumare, non è permesso fumare; **we must ~ 3 days for the journey** dobbiamo calcolare 3 giorni per il viaggio.
allow for *vt fus* tener conto di.
allowance [əlou'əns] *n* (*money received*) assegno; (*for travelling, accommodation*) indennità *f inv*; (*TAX*) detrazione *f* di imposta; **to make ~(s) for** tener conto di; (*person*) scusare.
alloy [al'oi] *n* lega.
all right *ad* (*feel, work*) bene; (*as answer*) va

bene.

all-rounder |ôlroun'dûr| *n* (*Brit*): **to be a good** ~ essere bravo(a) in tutto.

allspice |ôl'spîs| *n* pepe *m* della Giamaica.

all-time |ôl'tîm| *a* (*record*) assoluto(a).

allude |əlōod'| *vi*: **to** ~ **to** alludere a.

alluring |əlōo'ring| *a* seducente.

allusion |əlōo'zhən| *n* allusione *f*.

alluvium |əlōo'vēəm| *n* materiale *m* alluvionale.

ally *n* |al'ī| alleato ♦ *vt* |əlī'|: **to** ~ **o.s. with** allearsi con.

almighty |ôlmī'tē| *a* onnipotente.

almond |â'mənd| *n* mandorla.

almost |ôl'mōst| *ad* quasi; **he** ~ **fell** per poco non è caduto.

alms |âmz| *n* elemosina.

aloft |əlôft'| *ad* in alto; (*NAUT*) sull'alberatura.

alone |əlōn'| *a*, *ad* solo(a); **to leave sb** ~ lasciare qn in pace; **to leave sth** ~ lasciare stare qc; **let** ~ ... figuriamoci poi ..., tanto meno ....

along |əlông'| *prep* lungo ♦ *ad*: **is he coming** ~**?** viene con noi?; **he was hopping/limping** ~ veniva saltellando/zoppicando; ~ **with** insieme con.

alongside |əlông'sîd| *prep* accanto a; lungo ♦ *ad* accanto; (*NAUT*) sottobordo; **we brought our boat** ~ (*of a pier/shore etc*) abbiamo accostato la barca (al molo/alla riva *etc*).

aloof |əlōof'| *a* distaccato(a) ♦ *ad* a distanza, in disparte; **to stand** ~ tenersi a distanza *or* in disparte.

aloofness |əlōof'nis| *n* distacco, riserbo.

aloud |əloud'| *ad* ad alta voce.

alphabet |al'fəbet| *n* alfabeto.

alphabetical |alfəbet'ikəl| *a* alfabetico(a); **in** ~ **order** in ordine alfabetico.

alphanumeric |alfənōomär'ik| *a* alfanumerico(a).

alpine |al'pīn| *a* alpino(a); ~ **hut** rifugio alpino; ~ **pasture** pascolo alpestre; ~ **skiing** sci alpino.

Alps |alps| *npl*: **the** ~ le Alpi.

already |ôlred'ē| *ad* già.

alright |ôlrīt'| *ad* = **all right**.

Alsatian |alsā'shən| *n* (*Brit*: *dog*) pastore *m* tedesco, (cane *m*) lupo.

also |ôl'sō| *ad* anche.

Alta. *abbr* (*Canada*) = *Alberta*.

altar |ôl'tûr| *n* altare *m*.

alter |ôl'tûr| *vt*, *vi* alterare.

alteration |ôltərā'shən| *n* modificazione *f*, alterazione *f*; ~**s** (*SEWING*, *ARCHIT*) modifiche *fpl*; **timetable subject to** ~ orario soggetto a variazioni.

alternate *a* |ôl'tûrnit| alterno(a) ♦ *vi* |ôl'tərnāt| alternare; **on** ~ **days** ogni due giorni.

alternately |ôl'tûrnitlē| *ad* alternatamente.

alternating current |ôl'tûrnāting kûr'ənt| *n* corrente *f* alternata.

alternative |ôltûr'nətiv| *a* (*solutions*) alternativo(a); (*solution*) altro(a) ♦ *n* (*choice*) alternativa; (*other possibility*) altra possibilità.

alternatively |ôltûr'nətivlē| *ad* altrimenti, come alternativa.

alternator |ôl'tûrnātûr| *n* (*AUT*) alternatore *m*.

although |ôlthō'| *cj* benché + *sub*, sebbene + *sub*.

altitude |al'tətōod| *n* altitudine *f*.

alto |al'tō| *n* contralto.

altogether |ôltəgeth'ûr| *ad* del tutto, completamente; (*on the whole*) tutto considerato; (*in all*) in tutto; **how much is that** ~**?** quant'è in tutto?

altruistic |altrōōis'tik| *a* altruistico(a).

aluminium |alōōmin'ēəm| (*Brit*) = **aluminum**.

aluminum |əlōō'mənəm| *n* (*US*) alluminio.

aluminum foil *n* carta stagnola.

alumnus |əlum'nəs| *n* (*US*) *ex-studente di un collegio, università etc*.

always |ôl'wāz| *ad* sempre.

AM *abbr* (= *amplitude modulation*) AM.

am |am| *vb see* **be**.

a.m. *ad abbr* (= *ante meridiem*) della mattina.

AMA *n abbr* = *American Medical Assocation*.

amalgam |əmal'gəm| *n* amalgama *m*.

amalgamate |əmal'gəmāt| *vt* amalgamare ♦ *vi* amalgamarsi.

amalgamation |əmalgəmā'shən| *n* amalgamazione *f*; (*COMM*) fusione *f*.

amass |əmas'| *vt* ammassare.

amateur |am'əchûr| *n* dilettante *m/f* ♦ *a* (*SPORT*) dilettante; ~ **dramatics** *n* filodrammatica.

amateurish |aməchōō'rish| *a* (*pej*) da dilettante.

amaze |əmāz'| *vt* stupire; **to be** ~**d (at)** essere sbalordito(a) (da).

amazement |əmāz'mənt| *n* stupore *m*.

amazing |əmā'zing| *a* sorprendente, sbalorditivo(a); (*bargain*, *offer*) sensazionale.

amazingly |əmā'zinglē| *ad* incredibilmente, sbalorditivamente.

Amazon |am'əzän| *n* (*MYTHOLOGY*) Amazzone *f*; (*river*): **the** ~ il Rio delle Amazzoni ♦ *cpd* (*basin*, *jungle*) amazzonico(a).

Amazonian |aməzō'nēən| *a* amazzonico(a).

ambassador |ambas'ədûr| *n* ambasciatore/trice.

amber |am'bûr| *n* ambra; **at** ~ (*Brit AUT*) giallo.

ambidextrous |ambidek'strəs| *a* ambidestro(a).

ambience |am'bēəns| *n* ambiente *m*.

ambiguity |ambəgyōo'itē| *n* ambiguità *f inv*.

ambiguous |ambig'yōoəs| *a* ambiguo(a).

ambition |ambish'ən| *n* ambizione *f*; **to achieve one's** ~ realizzare le proprie aspirazioni *or* ambizioni.

ambitious |ambish'əs| *a* ambizioso(a).

ambivalent [ambiv'ələnt] *a* ambivalente.

amble [am'bəl] *vi* (*gen*: **to ~ along**) camminare tranquillamente.

ambulance [am'byələns] *n* ambulanza.

ambush [am'bŏosh] *n* imboscata ♦ *vt* fare un'imboscata a.

ameba [əmē'bə] *n* (*US*) = **amoeba**.

ameliorate [əmēl'yərāt] *vt* migliorare.

amen [ā'men'] *excl* così sia, amen.

amenable [əmē'nəbəl] *a*: ~ **to** (*advice etc*) ben disposto(a) a.

amend [əmend'] *vt* (*law*) emendare; (*text*) correggere ♦ *vi* emendarsi; **to make ~s** fare ammenda.

amendment [əmend'mənt] *n* emendamento; correzione *f*.

amenities [əmen'itēz] *npl* attrezzature *fpl* ricreative e culturali.

amenity [əmen'itē] *n* amenità *f inv*.

America [əmär'ikə] *n* America.

American [əmär'ikən] *a*, *n* americano(a).

americanize [əmär'ikənīz] *vt* americanizzare.

Amerindian [amərin'dēən] *a*, *n* indiano(a) d'America.

amethyst [am'ithist] *n* ametista.

Amex [am'eks] *n abbr* = *American Stock Exchange*.

amiable [ā'mēəbəl] *a* amabile, gentile.

amicable [am'ikəbəl] *a* amichevole.

amid(st) [əmid(st)'] *prep* fra, tra, in mezzo a.

amiss [əmis'] *a*, *ad*: **there's something ~** c'è qualcosa che non va bene; **don't take it ~** non avertene a male.

ammo [am'ō] *n abbr* (*col*) = **ammunition**.

ammonia [əmōn'yə] *n* ammoniaca.

ammunition [amyənish'ən] *n* munizioni *fpl*; (*fig*) arma.

ammunition dump *n* deposito di munizioni.

amnesia [amnē'zhə] *n* amnesia.

amnesty [am'nistē] *n* amnistia; **to grant an ~ to** concedere l'amnistia a, amnistiare.

amoeba [əmē'bə] *n* ameba.

amok [əmuk'] *ad*: **to run ~** diventare pazzo(a) furioso(a).

among(st) [əmung(st)'] *prep* fra, tra, in mezzo a.

amoral [āmôr'əl] *a* amorale.

amorous [am'ûrəs] *a* amoroso(a).

amorphous [əmôr'fəs] *a* amorfo(a).

amortization [amûrtəzā'shən] *n* (*COMM*) ammortamento.

amount [əmount'] *n* (*sum of money*) somma; (*of bill etc*) importo; (*quantity*) quantità *f inv* ♦ *vi*: **to ~ to** (*total*) ammontare a; (*be same as*) essere come; **this ~s to a refusal** questo equivale a un rifiuto.

amp(ere) [am'pēr] *n* ampere *m inv*; **a 13 ~ plug** una spina con fusibile da 13 ampere.

ampersand [am'pûrsand] *n e f* commerciale.

amphibian [amfib'ēən] *n* anfibio.

amphibious [amfib'ēəs] *a* anfibio(a).

amphitheater, (*Brit*) **amphitheatre** [am'fəthēətûr] *n* anfiteatro.

ample [am'pəl] *a* ampio(a); spazioso(a); (*enough*): **this is ~** questo è più che sufficiente; **to have ~ time/room** avere assai tempo/posto.

amplifier [am'pləfiûr] *n* amplificatore *m*.

amplify [am'pləfī] *vt* amplificare.

amply [am'plē] *ad* ampiamente.

ampule, (*Brit*) **ampoule** [am'pyōol] *n* (*MED*) fiala.

amputate [am'pyŏotāt] *vt* amputare.

Amsterdam [am'stûrdam] *n* Amsterdam *f*.

amt *abbr* = **amount**.

amuck [əmuk'] *ad* = **amok**.

amuse [əmyŏoz'] *vt* divertire; **to ~ o.s. with sth/by doing sth** divertirsi con qc/a fare qc; **to be ~d at** essere divertito da; **he was not ~d** non l'ha trovato divertente.

amusement [əmyŏoz'mənt] *n* divertimento; **much to my ~** con mio grande spasso.

amusement arcade *n* sala giochi (*solo con macchinette a gettoni*).

amusement park *n* luna park *m inv*.

amusing [əmyŏo'zing] *a* divertente.

an [an, ən] *indefinite article see* **a**.

ANA *n abbr* = *American Newspaper Association*; *American Nurses Association*.

anachronism [ənak'rənizəm] *n* anacronismo.

anaemia [ənē'mēə] *etc* (*Brit*) = **anemia** *etc*.

anaesthetic [anisthet'ik] *a*, *n* (*Brit*) = **anesthetic**.

anaesthetist [ənēs'thətist] *n* (*Brit*) anestesista *m/f*.

anagram [an'əgram] *n* anagramma *m*.

analgesic [anəljē'zik] *a* analgesico(a) ♦ *n* analgesico.

analog(ue) [an'əlôg] *a* (*watch*, *computer*) analogico(a).

analogy [ənal'əjē] *n* analogia; **to draw an ~ between** fare un'analogia tra.

analyse [an'əlīz] *vt* (*Brit*) = **analyze**.

analysis, *pl* **analyses** [ənal'isis, -sēz] *n* analisi *f inv*; **in the last ~** in ultima analisi.

analyst [an'əlist] *n* (*political ~ etc*) analista *m/f*; (*US*) (psic)analista *m/f*.

analytic(al) [anəlit'ik(əl)] *a* analitico(a).

analyze [an'əlīz] *vt* (*US*) analizzare.

anarchist [an'ûrkist] *a*, *n* anarchico(a).

anarchy [an'ûrkē] *n* anarchia.

anathema [ənath'əmə] *n*: **it is ~ to him** non ne vuol neanche sentir parlare.

anatomical [anətâm'ikəl] *a* anatomico(a).

anatomy [ənat'əmē] *n* anatomia.

ANC *n abbr* = *African National Congress*.

ancestor [an'sestûr] *n* antenato/a.

ancestral [anses'trəl] *a* avito(a).

ancestry [an'sestrē] *n* antenati *mpl*; ascendenza.

anchor [ang'kûr] *n* ancora ♦ *vi* (*also*: **to drop ~**) gettare l'ancora ♦ *vt* ancorare; **to weigh**

~ salpare *or* levare l'ancora.

anchorage [ang'kûrij] *n* ancoraggio.

anchovy [an'chōvē] *n* acciuga.

ancient [ān'shənt] *a* antico(a); (*fig*) anziano(a); ~ **monument** monumento storico.

ancillary [an'səlärē] *a* ausiliario(a).

and [and] *cj* e (*often* ed *before vowel*); ~ **so on** e così via; **try** ~ **do it** prova a farlo; **come** ~ **sit here** vieni a sedere qui; **better** ~ **better** sempre meglio; **more** ~ **more** sempre di più.

Andes [an'dēz] *npl*: **the** ~ le Ande.

Andorra [andôr'ə] *n* Andorra.

anecdote [an'ikdōt] *n* aneddoto.

anemia [ənē'mēə] *n* (*US*) anemia.

anemic [ənē'mik] *a* (*US*) anemico(a).

anemone [ənem'ənē] *n* (*BOT*) anemone *m*; (*sea* ~) anemone *m* di mare, attinia.

anesthesiologist [an'isthēzēâl'əjist] *n* (*US*) anestesista *m/f*.

anesthetic [anisthet'ik] (*US*) *a* anestetico(a) ♦ *n* anestetico; **local/general** ~ anestesia locale/totale; **under the** ~ sotto anestesia.

anew [ənōō'] *ad* di nuovo.

angel [ān'jəl] *n* angelo.

anger [ang'gûr] *n* rabbia ♦ *vt* arrabbiare.

angina [anji'nə] *n* angina pectoris.

angle [ang'gəl] *n* angolo ♦ *vi*: **to** ~ **for** (*fig*) cercare di avere; **from their** ~ dal loro punto di vista.

angler [ang'glûr] *n* pescatore *m* con la lenza.

Anglican [ang'glikən] *a*, *n* anglicano(a).

anglicize [ang'gləsīz] *vt* anglicizzare.

angling [ang'gling] *n* pesca con la lenza.

Anglo- [an'glō] *prefix* anglo...; ~**Italian** *a*, *n* italobritannico(a).

Anglo-Saxon [an'glōsak'sən] *a*, *n* anglosassone (*m/f*).

Angola [anggō'lə] *n* Angola.

Angolan [anggō'lən] *a*, *n* angolano(a).

angrily [ang'grilē] *ad* con rabbia.

angry [ang'grē] *a* arrabbiato(a), furioso(a); **to be** ~ **with sb/at sth** essere in collera con qn/per qc; **to get** ~ arrabbiarsi; **to make sb** ~ fare arrabbiare qn.

anguish [ang'gwish] *n* angoscia.

angular [ang'gyəlûr] *a* angolare.

animal [an'əməl] *a*, *n* animale (*m*).

animal spirits *npl* vivacità.

animate *vt* [an'əmāt] animare ♦ *a* [an'əmit] animato(a).

animated [an'əmātid] *a* animato(a).

animosity [anəmâs'ətē] *n* animosità.

aniseed [an'isēd] *n* semi *mpl* di anice.

Ankara [ang'kûrə] *n* Ankara.

ankle [ang'kəl] *n* caviglia.

ankle socks *npl* calzini *mpl*.

annex *n* [an'eks] (*also*: *Brit*: **annexe**) edificio annesso ♦ *vt* [əneks'] annettere.

annexation [anəksā'shən] *n* annessione *f*.

annihilate [ənī'əlāt] *vt* annientare.

anniversary [anəvûr'sûrē] *n* anniversario.

anniversary dinner *n* cena commemorativa.

annotate [an'ōtāt] *vt* annotare.

announce [ənouns'] *vt* annunciare; **he** ~**d that he wasn't going** ha dichiarato che non (ci) sarebbe andato.

announcement [ənouns'mənt] *n* annuncio; (*letter*, *card*) partecipazione *f*; **I'd like to make an** ~ ho una comunicazione da fare.

announcer [ənoun'sûr] *n* (*RADIO*, *TV*: *between programs*) annunciatore/trice; (: *in a program*) presentatore/trice.

annoy [ənoi'] *vt* dare fastidio a; **to be** ~**ed (at sth/with sb)** essere seccato *or* irritato (per qc/con qn); **don't get** ~**ed!** non irritarti!

annoyance [ənoi'əns] *n* fastidio; (*cause of* ~) noia.

annoying [ənoi'ing] *a* irritante, seccante.

annual [an'yōōəl] *a* annuale ♦ *n* (*BOT*) pianta annua; (*book*) annuario.

annual general meeting (AGM) *n* (*Brit*) assemblea generale.

annually [an'yōōəlē] *ad* annualmente.

annual report *n* relazione *f* annuale.

annuity [ənōō'itē] *n* annualità *f* *inv*; **life** ~ vitalizio.

annul [ənul'] *vt* annullare; (*law*) rescindere.

annulment [ənul'mənt] *n* annullamento; rescissione *f*.

annum [an'əm] *n see* **per annum**.

Annunciation [ənunsēā'shən] *n* Annunciazione *f*.

anode [an'ōd] *n* anodo.

anoint [ənoint'] *vt* ungere.

anomalous [ənâm'ələs] *a* anomalo(a).

anomaly [ənâm'əlē] *n* anomalia.

anon. [ənân'] *abbr* = **anonymous**.

anonymity [anənim'itē] *n* anonimato.

anonymous [ənân'əməs] *a* anonimo(a); **to remain** ~ mantenere l'anonimato.

anorak [än'əråk] *n* giacca a vento.

anorexia [anərek'sēə] *n* (*also*: ~ **nervosa**) anoressia.

another [ənuth'ûr] *a*: ~ **book** (*one more*) un altro libro, ancora un libro; (*a different one*) un altro libro ♦ *pronoun* un altro(un'altra), ancora uno(a); ~ **drink?** ancora qualcosa da bere?; **in** ~ **5 years** fra altri 5 anni; **some actor or** ~ un certo attore; *see also* **one**.

ANSI *n abbr* (= *American National Standards Institute*) *associazione per la normalizzazione*.

answer [an'sûr] *n* risposta; soluzione *f* ♦ *vi* rispondere ♦ *vt* (*reply to*) rispondere a; (*problem*) risolvere; (*prayer*) esaudire; **in** ~ **to your letter** in risposta alla sua lettera; **to** ~ **the phone** rispondere (al telefono); **to** ~ **the bell** rispondere al campanello; **to** ~ **the door** aprire la porta.

answer back *vi* ribattere.

answer for *vt fus* essere responsabile di.

answer to *vt fus* (*description*) corrispondere a.

answerable [an'sûrəbəl] *a*: ~ **(to sb/for sth)** responsabile (verso qn/di qc); **I am ~ to no one** non devo rispondere a nessuno.

answering machine [an'sûring məshēn'] *n* segreteria (telefonica) automatica.

ant [ant] *n* formìca.

ANTA *n abbr* = *American National Theater and Academy*.

antagonism [antag'ənizəm] *n* antagonismo.

antagonist [antag'ənist] *n* antagonista *m/f*.

antagonistic [antagənis'tik] *a* antagonistico(a).

antagonize [antag'ənīz] *vt* provocare l'ostilità di.

Antarctic [antârk'tik] *n*: **the** ~ l'Antartide *f* ♦ *a* antartico(a).

Antarctica [antârk'tikə] *n* Antartide *f*.

Antarctic Circle *n* Circolo polare antartico.

Antarctic Ocean *n* Oceano antartico.

ante [an'tē] *n* (*CARDS*, *fig*): **to up the** ~ alzare la posta in palio.

ante... *prefix* anti..., ante..., pre....

anteater [ant'ētûr] *n* formichiere *m*.

antecedent [antisē'dənt] *n* antecedente *m*, precedente *m*.

antechamber [an'tēchâmbûr] *n* anticamera.

antelope [an'təlōp] *n* antilope *f*.

antenatal [antēnā'təl] *a* (*Brit*) = **prenatal**.

antenna, *pl* **antennae** [anten'ə, *pl* -nī] *n* antenna.

anthem [an'thəm] *n* antifona; **national** ~ inno nazionale.

anthill [ant·hil'] *n* formicaio.

anthology [anthâl'əjē] *n* antologia.

anthropologist [anthrəpâl'əjist] *n* antropologo/a.

anthropology [anthrəpâl'əjē] *n* antropologia.

anti- [an'tī] *prefix* anti....

antiaircraft [antiär'kraft] *a* antiaereo(a).

antiaircraft defense *n* difesa antiaerea.

antiballistic [antēbəlis'tik] *a* antibalistico(a).

antibiotic [antēbīât'ik] *a* antibiotico(a) ♦ *n* antibiotico.

antibody [an'tēbâdē] *n* anticorpo.

anticipate [antis'əpāt] *vt* prevedere; pregustare; (*wishes, request*) prevenire; **as** ~**d** come previsto; **this is worse than I** ~**d** è peggio di quel che immaginavo *or* pensavo.

anticipation [antisəpā'shən] *n* anticipazione *f*; (*expectation*) aspettative *fpl*; **thanking you in** ~ vi ringrazio in anticipo.

anticlimax [antēklī'maks] *n*: **it was an** ~ fu una completa delusione.

anticlockwise [antēklâk'wīz] *a* (*Brit*) in senso antiorario.

antics [an'tiks] *npl* buffonerie *fpl*.

anticyclone [antēsī'klōn] *n* anticiclone *m*.

antidote [an'tidōt] *n* antidoto.

antifreeze [an'tēfrēz] *n* anticongelante *m*.

antihistamine [antēhis'təmēn] *n* antistaminico.

Antilles [antil'ēz] *npl*: **the** ~ le Antille.

antipathy [antip'əthē] *n* antipatia.

Antipodean [antipədē'ən] *a* degli Antipodi.

Antipodes [antip'ədēz] *npl*: **the** ~ gli Antipodi.

antiquarian [antəkwär'ēən] *a*: ~ **bookshop** libreria antiquaria ♦ *n* antiquario/a.

antiquated [an'təkwātid] *a* antiquato(a).

antique [antēk'] *n* antichità *f inv* ♦ *a* antico(a).

antique dealer *n* antiquario/a.

antique shop *n* negozio d'antichità.

antiquity [antik'witē] *n* antichità *f inv*.

anti-semitic [antīsəmit'ik] *a* antisemitico(a), antisemita.

anti-semitism [antīsem'ətizəm] *n* antisemitismo.

antiseptic [antēsep'tik] *a* antisettico(a) ♦ *n* antisettico.

antisocial [antēsō'shəl] *a* asociale; (*against society*) antisociale.

antitank [antētangk'] *a* anticarro *inv*.

antithesis, *pl* **antitheses** [antith'əsis, *pl* -sēz] *n* antitesi *f inv*; (*contrast*) carattere *m* antitetico.

antitrust [antētrust'] *a* (*COMM*): ~ **legislation** legislazione *f* antitrust *inv*.

antlers [ant'lûrz] *npl* palchi *mpl*.

Antwerp [ant'wûrp] *n* Anversa.

anus [ā'nəs] *n* ano.

anvil [an'vil] *n* incudine *f*.

anxiety [angzī'ətē] *n* ansia; (*keenness*): ~ **to do** smania di fare.

anxious [angk'shəs] *a* ansioso(a), inquieto(a); (*keen*): ~ **to do/that** impaziente di fare/che + *sub*; **I'm very** ~ **about you** sono molto preoccupato *or* in pensiero per te.

anxiously [angk'shəslē] *ad* ansiosamente, con ansia.

any [en'ē] *a* (*in negative and interrogative sentences* = *some*) del, dell', dello, dei, degli, della, delle; alcuno(a); qualche; nessuno(a); (*no matter which*) non importa che; (*each and every*) tutto(a), ogni; **I haven't** ~ **bread/books** non ho pane/libri; **have you** ~ **money?** hai (dei) soldi?, hai qualche soldo?; **without** ~ **difficulty** senza (nessuna *or* alcuna) difficoltà; **come (at)** ~ **time** vieni a qualsiasi ora; **at** ~ **moment** da un momento all'altro; ~ **day now** da un giorno all'altro; **in** ~ **case** in ogni caso; **at** ~ **rate** ad ogni modo ♦ *pronoun* uno(a) qualsiasi; (*anybody*) chiunque; (*in negative and interrogative sentences*): **I haven't** ~ non ne ho; **have you got** ~**?** ne hai?; **can** ~ **of you sing?** c'è qualcuno che sa cantare? ♦ *ad* (*in negative sentences*) per niente; (*in interrogative and conditional constructions*) un po'; **I can't hear him** ~ **more** non lo sento più; **are you feeling** ~ **better?** ti senti un po' meglio?; **do you**

want ~ more soup? vuoi ancora della mine- stra?

anybody [en'ĕbâdē] *pronoun* qualsiasi perso- na; (*in interrogative sentences*) qualcuno; (*in negative sentences*): **I don't see ~** non vedo nessuno.

anyhow [en'ĕhou] *ad* in qualsiasi modo; (*haphazard*) come capita; **I shall go ~** ci an- drò lo stesso *or* comunque.

anyone [en'ĕwun] *pronoun* = **anybody.**

anyplace [en'ĕplās] *pronoun* (*US col*) = **any- where.**

anything [en'ĕthing] *pronoun* qualsiasi cosa; (*in interrogative sentences*) qualcosa; (*in negative sentences*) non ... niente, non ... nul- la; **~ else?** (*in shop*) basta (così)?

anytime [en'ĕtĭm] *ad* in qualunque momento; quando vuole.

anyway [en'ĕwā] *ad* in *or* ad ogni modo.

anywhere [en'ĕhwär] *ad* da qualsiasi parte; (*in interrogative sentences*) da qualche parte; **I don't see him ~** non lo vedo da nessuna parte; **~ in the world** dovunque nel mondo.

Anzac [an'zak] *n abbr* (= *Australia-New Zealand Army Corps*) A.N.Z.A.C. *m*; (*soldier*) soldato dell'A.N.Z.A.C.

apart [əpârt'] *ad* (*to one side*) a parte; (*sepa- rately*) separatamente; **with one's legs ~** con le gambe divaricate; **10 miles/a long way ~** a 10 miglia di distanza/molto lontani l'uno dall'altro; **they are living ~** sono sepa- rati; **~ from** *prep* a parte, eccetto.

apartheid [əpârt'hĭt] *n* apartheid *f.*

apartment [əpârt'mənt] *n* appartamento.

apartment block *or* **building** *or* **house** *n* stabile *m*, caseggiato.

apathetic [apəthet'ik] *a* apatico(a).

apathy [ap'əthē] *n* apatia.

APB *n abbr* (*US*: = *all points bulletin*: *police expression*) espressione della polizia che significa "*trovate e arrestate il sospetto*".

ape [āp] *n* scimmia ♦ *vt* scimmiottare.

Apennines [ap'ənĭnz] *npl*: **the ~** gli Apennini.

aperitif [əpārĕtēf'] *n* aperitivo.

aperture [ap'ûrchûr] *n* apertura.

APEX [ā'peks] *n abbr* (*AVIAT*: = *advance purchase excursion*) APEX *m inv.*

apex [ā'peks] *n* apice *m.*

aphid [ā'fid] *n* afide *f.*

aphrodisiac [afrədiz'ēak] *a* afrodisiaco(a) ♦ *n* afrodisiaco.

API *n abbr* = *American Press Institute.*

apiece [əpēs'] *ad* ciascuno(a).

aplomb [əplâm'] *n* disinvoltura.

APO *n abbr* (*US*: = *Army Post Office*) ufficio postale dell'esercito.

apocalypse [əpâk'əlips] *n* apocalisse *f.*

apolitical [āpəlit'ikəl] *a* apolitico(a).

apologetic [əpâləjet'ik] *a* (*tone, letter*) di scu- sa; **to be very ~ about** scusarsi moltissimo

di.

apologetically [əpâləjet'iklē] *ad* per scusarsi.

apologize [əpâl'əjīz] *vi*: **to ~ (for sth to sb)** scusarsi (di qc a qn), chiedere scusa (a qn per qc).

apology [əpâl'əjē] *n* scuse *fpl*; **please accept my apologies** la prego di accettare le mie scuse.

apoplectic [apəplek'tik] *a* (*MED*) apopletti- co(a); **~ with rage** (*col*) livido(a) per la rabbia.

apoplexy [ap'əpleksē] *n* apoplessia.

apostle [əpâs'əl] *n* apostolo.

apostrophe [əpâs'trəfē] *n* (*sign*) apostrofo.

Appalachian Mountains [apəlā'chēən moun'tənz] *npl*: **the ~** i Monti Appalachi.

appall, (*Brit*) **appal** [əpôl] *vt* atterrire; sgo- mentare.

appalling [əpôl'ing] *a* spaventoso(a); **she's an ~ cook** è un disastro come cuoca.

apparatus [apərat'əs] *n* apparato.

apparel [əpar'əl] *n* (*US*) abbigliamento, confe- zioni *fpl.*

apparent [əpär'ənt] *a* evidente.

apparently [əpar'əntlē] *ad* evidentemente, a quanto pare.

apparition [apərish'ən] *n* apparizione *f.*

appeal [əpēl'] *vi* (*LAW*) appellarsi alla legge ♦ *n* (*LAW*) appello; (*request*) richiesta; (*charm*) attrattiva; **to ~ for** chiedere (con insistenza); **to ~ to** (*subj: person*) appellarsi a; (: *thing*) piacere a; **to ~ to sb for mercy** chiedere pietà a qn; **it doesn't ~ to me** mi dice poco; **right of ~** diritto d'appello.

appealing [əpē'ling] *a* (*moving*) commovente; (*attractive*) attraente.

appear [əpēr'] *vi* apparire; (*LAW*) comparire; (*publication*) essere pubblicato(a); (*seem*) sembrare; **it would ~ that** sembra che; **to ~ in Hamlet** recitare nell'Amleto; **to ~ on TV** presentarsi in televisione.

appearance [əpē'rəns] *n* apparizione *f*; (*look, aspect*) aspetto; **to put in** *or* **make an ~** fare atto di presenza; **by order of ~** (*THEATER*) in ordine di apparizione; **to keep up ~s** salvare le apparenze; **to all ~s** a giudicar dalle apparenze.

appease [əpēz'] *vt* calmare, appagare.

appeasement [əpēz'mənt] *n* (*POL*) appease- ment *m inv.*

appellate court [əpel'it kôrt] *n* (*US*) corte d'appello.

append [əpend'] *vt* (*COMPUT*) aggiungere in coda.

appendage [əpen'dij] *n* aggiunta.

appendicitis [əpendisī'tis] *n* appendicite *f.*

appendix, *pl* **appendices** [əpen'diks, -sēz] *n* appendice *f*; **to have one's ~ out** operarsi *or* farsi operare di appendicite.

appetite [ap'itīt] *n* appetito; **that walk has given me an ~** la passeggiata mi ha messo appetito.

appetizer |ap'itizûr| *n* (*food*) stuzzichino; (*drink*) aperitivo.

appetizing |ap'itizing| *a* appetitoso(a).

applaud |əplôd'| *vt, vi* applaudire.

applause |əplôz'| *n* applauso.

apple |ap'əl| *n* mela; (*also*: ~ **tree**) melo; **the ~ of one's eye** la pupilla dei propri occhi.

apple turnover *n* sfogliatella alle mele.

appliance |əplī'əns| *n* apparecchio; **electrical ~s** elettrodomestici *mpl*.

applicable |ap'likəbəl| *a* applicabile; **to be ~ to** essere valido per; **the law is ~ from January** la legge entrerà in vigore in gennaio.

applicant |ap'likənt| *n* candidato/a; (*ADMIN*: *for benefit etc*) chi ha fatto domanda *or* richiesta.

application |aplikā'shən| *n* applicazione *f*; (*for a job, a grant etc*) domanda; **on ~** su richiesta.

application form *n* modulo di domanda.

application program *n* (*COMPUT*) programma applicativo.

applications package *n* (*COMPUT*) software *m inv* applicativo.

applied |əplīd'| *a* applicato(a); **~ arts** (*Brit*) arti *fpl* applicate.

apply |əplī'| *vt*: **to ~ (to)** (*paint, ointment*) dare (a); (*theory, technique*) applicare (a) ♦ *vi*: **to ~ to** (*ask*) rivolgersi a; (*be suitable for, relevant to*) riguardare, riferirsi a; **to ~ (for)** (*permit, grant, job*) fare domanda (per); **to ~ the brakes** frenare; **to ~ o.s. to** dedicarsi a.

appoint |əpoint'| *vt* nominare.

appointee |əpointē'| *n* incaricato/a.

appointment |əpoint'mənt| *n* nomina; (*arrangement to meet*) appuntamento; **by ~** su *or* per appuntamento; **to make an ~ with sb** prendere un appuntamento con qn.

appointment book *n* agenda.

apportion |əpôr'shən| *vt* attribuire.

appraisal |əprā'zəl| *n* valutazione *f*.

appraise |əprāz'| *vt* (*value*) valutare, fare una stima di; (*situation etc*) fare il bilancio di.

appreciable |əprē'shēəbəl| *a* apprezzabile.

appreciate |əprē'shēāt| *vt* (*like*) apprezzare; (*be grateful for*) essere riconoscente di; (*be aware of*) rendersi conto di ♦ *vi* (*COMM*) aumentare; **I ~d your help** ti sono grato per l'aiuto.

appreciation |əprēshēā'shən| *n* apprezzamento; (*FINANCE*) aumento del valore.

appreciative |əprē'shətiv| *a* (*person*) sensibile; (*comment*) elogiativo(a).

apprehend |aprihend'| *vt* (*arrest*) arrestare; (*understand*) comprendere.

apprehension |aprihen'shən| *n* (*fear*) inquietudine *f*.

apprehensive |aprihen'siv| *a* apprensivo(a).

apprentice |əpren'tis| *n* apprendista *m/f* ♦ *vt*: **to be ~d to** lavorare come apprendista presso.

apprenticeship |əpren'tisship| *n* apprendistato; **to serve one's ~** fare il proprio apprendistato *or* tirocinio.

approach |əprōch'| *vi* avvicinarsi ♦ *vt* (*come near*) avvicinarsi a; (*ask, apply to*) rivolgersi a; (*subject, passer-by*) avvicinare ♦ *n* approccio; accesso; (*to problem*) modo di affrontare; **to ~ sb about sth** rivolgersi a qn per qc.

approachable |əprō'chəbəl| *a* accessibile.

approbation |aprəbā'shən| *n* approvazione *f*, benestare *m*.

appropriate *vt* |əprōp'rēāt| (*take*) appropriarsi di ♦ *a* |əprōp'rēit| appropriato(a); adatto(a); **it would not be ~ for me to comment** non sta a me fare dei commenti.

appropriately |əprōp'rēitlē| *ad* in modo appropriato.

appropriation |əprōprēā'shən| *n* stanziamento.

approval |əprōō'vəl| *n* approvazione *f*; **on ~** (*COMM*) in prova, in esame; **to meet with sb's ~** soddisfare qn, essere di gradimento di qn.

approve |əprōōv'| *vt, vi* approvare.

approve of *vt fus* approvare.

approvingly |əprōō'vinglē| *ad* in approvazione.

approx. *abbr* = **approximately**.

approximate *a* |əprāk'səmit| approssimativo(a) ♦ *vt* |əprāk'səmāt| essere un'approssimazione di, avvicinarsi a.

approximately |əprāk'səmitlē| *ad* circa.

approximation |əprāksəmā'shən| *n* approssimazione *f*.

appt. *n abbr* (*US*) = **appointment**.

apr *n abbr* (= *annual percentage rate*) tasso di percentuale annuo.

Apr. *abbr* (= *April*) apr.

apricot |ap'rikât| *n* albicocca.

April |āp'rəl| *n* aprile *m*; ~ **fool!** pesce d'aprile!; *for phrases see also* **July**.

April Fool's Day *n* il primo d'aprile.

apron |ā'prən| *n* grembiule *m*; (*AVIAT*) area di stazionamento.

apse |aps| *n* (*ARCHIT*) abside *f*.

apt |apt| *a* (*suitable*) adatto(a); (*able*) capace; (*likely*): **to be ~ to do** avere tendenza a fare.

Apt. *abbr* = **apartment**.

aptitude |ap'tətōōd| *n* abilità *f inv*.

aptitude test *n* test *m inv* attitudinale.

aptly |apt'lē| *ad* appropriatamente, in modo adatto.

aqualung |ak'wəlung| *n* autorespiratore *m*.

aquarium |əkwär'ēəm| *n* acquario.

Aquarius |əkwär'ēəs| *n* Acquario; **to be ~** essere dell'Acquario.

aquatic |əkwat'ik| *a* acquatico(a).

aqueduct |ak'widukt| *n* acquedotto.

passare

AR *abbr* (*US MAIL*) = *Arkansas.*
Arab [ar'əb] *a, n* arabo(a).
Arabia [ərā'bēə] *n* Arabia.
Arabian [ərā'bēən] *a* arabo(a).
Arabian Desert *n* deserto arabico.
Arabian Sea *n* mare *m* arabico.
Arabic [ar'əbik] *a* arabico(a) ♦ *n* arabo.
Arabic numerals *npl* numeri arabi *mpl*, numerazione *f* araba.
arable [ar'əbəl] *a* arabile.
arbiter [âr'bitûr] *n* arbitro.
arbitrary [âr'biträrē] *a* arbitrario(a).
arbitrate [âr'bitrāt] *vi* arbitrare.
arbitration [ârbitrā'shən] *n* (*LAW*) arbitrato; (*INDUSTRY*) arbitraggio.
arbitrator [âr'bitrātûr] *n* arbitro.
ARC *n abbr* (= *American Red Cross*) C.R.I. *f* (= *Croce Rossa Italiana*).
arc [ârk] *n* arco.
arcade [ârkād'] *n* portico; (*passage with shops*) galleria.
arch [ârch] *n* arco; (*of foot*) arco plantare ♦ *vt* inarcare ♦ *prefix*: ~(-) grande (*before n*); per eccellenza.
archaeology [ârkēál'əjē] *etc* = **archeology** *etc*.
archaic [ârkā'ik] *a* arcaico(a).
archangel [ârkān'jəl] *n* arcangelo.
archbishop [ârchbish'əp] *n* arcivescovo.
arched [ârcht] *a* arcuato(a), ad arco.
archenemy [ârch'en'əmē] *n* arcinemico/a.
archeological [ârkēəláj'ikəl] *a* archeologico(a).
archeologist [ârkēál'əjist] *n* archeologo/a.
archeology [ârkēál'əjē] *n* archeologia.
archer [âr'chûr] *n* arciere *m*.
archery [âr'chûrē] *n* tiro all'arco.
archetypal [âr'kitīpəl] *a* tipico(a).
archetype [âr'kitīp] *n* archetipo.
archipelago [ârkəpel'əgō] *n* arcipelago.
architect [âr'kitekt] *n* architetto.
architectural [âr'kitekchûrəl] *a* architettonico(a).
architecture [âr'kitekchûr] *n* architettura.
archive file *n* (*COMPUT*) file *m inv* di archivio.
archives [âr'kīvz] *npl* archivi *mpl*.
archivist [âr'kəvist] *n* archivista *m/f*.
archway [ârch'wā] *n* arco.
Arctic [ârk'tik] *a* artico(a) ♦ *n*: **the** ~ l'Artico.
Arctic Circle *n* Circolo polare artico.
Arctic Ocean *n* Oceano artico.
ARD *n abbr* (*US MED*) = *acute respiratory disease.*
ardent [âr'dənt] *a* ardente.
ardor, (*Brit*) **ardour** [âr'dûr] *n* ardore *m*.
arduous [âr'jōōəs] *a* arduo(a).
are [âr] *vb see* **be**.
area [är'ēə] *n* (*GEOM*) area; (*zone*) zona; (: *smaller*) settore *m*; **dining** ~ zona pranzo; **the Boston** ~ la zona di Boston.

area code *n* (*TEL*) prefisso.
arena [ərē'nə] *n* arena.
aren't [ârnt] = **are not**.
Argentina [ârjəntē'nə] *n* Argentina.
Argentine [âr'jentēn] *a, n* argentino(a).
Argentinian [ârjəntin'ēən] *a, n* argentino(a).
arguable [âr'gyōōəbəl] *a* discutibile; **it is** ~ **whether** ... è una cosa discutibile se ... + *sub.*
arguably [âr'gyōōəblē] *ad*: **it is** ~ ... si può sostenere che sia ....
argue [âr'gyōō] *vi* (*quarrel*) litigare; (*reason*) ragionare ♦ *vt* (*debate: case, matter*) dibattere; **to** ~ **that** sostenere che; **to** ~ **about sth** (**with sb**) litigare per *or* a proposito di qc (con qn).
argument [âr'gyəmənt] *n* (*reasons*) argomento; (*quarrel*) lite *f*; (*debate*) discussione *f*; ~ **for/against** argomento a *or* in favore di/contro.
argumentative [ârgyəmen'tətiv] *a* litigioso(a).
aria [âr'ēə] *n* aria.
arid [ar'id] *a* arido(a).
aridity [ərid'itē] *n* aridità.
Aries [âr'ēz] *n* Ariete *m*; **to be** ~ essere dell'Ariete.
arise, *pt* **arose,** *pp* **arisen** [ərīz', ərōz', əriz'ən] *vi* alzarsi; (*opportunity, problem*) presentarsi; **to** ~ **from** risultare da; **should the need** ~ dovesse presentarsi la necessità, in caso di necessità.
aristocracy [aristák'rəsē] *n* aristocrazia.
aristocrat [əris'təkrat] *n* aristocratico/a.
aristocratic [əristəkrat'ik] *a* aristocratico(a).
arithmetic [ərith'mətik] *n* aritmetica.
arithmetical [arithmet'ikəl] *a* aritmetico(a).
Ariz. *abbr* (*US*) = *Arizona.*
Ark. *abbr* (*US*) = *Arkansas.*
ark [ârk] *n*: **Noah's A**~ l'arca di Noè.
arm [ârm] *n* braccio; (*MIL: branch*) arma ♦ *vt* armare; ~ **in** ~ a braccetto; *see also* **arms**.
armaments [âr'məmənts] *npl* (*weapons*) armamenti *mpl*.
armband [ârm'band] *n* bracciale *m*.
armchair [ârm'chär] *n* poltrona.
armed [ârmd] *a* armato(a).
armed forces *npl* forze *fpl* armate.
armed robbery *n* rapina a mano armata.
Armenia [ârmē'nēə] *n* Armenia.
Armenian [ârmē'nēən] *a* armeno(a) ♦ *n* armeno/a; (*LING*) armeno.
armful [ârm'fəl] *n* bracciata.
armistice [âr'mistis] *n* armistizio.
armor, [âr'mûr] *n* (*US*) armatura; (*also*: ~-**plating**) corazza, blindatura; (*MIL: tanks*) mezzi *mpl* blindati.
armored car [âr'mûrd kâr'] *n* autoblinda *f inv*.
armory [âr'mûrē] *n* arsenale *m*.
armour [âr'mûr] *etc* (*Brit*) = **armor** *etc*.
armpit [ârm'pit] *n* ascella.
armrest [ârm'rest] *n* bracciolo.

Quello è molto stupido

arms [ârmz] *npl* (*weapons*) armi *fpl*; (*HERALDRY*) stemma *m*.
arms control *n* controllo degli armamenti.
arms race *n* corsa agli armamenti.
army [âr'mē] *n* esercito.
aroma [ərō'mə] *n* aroma.
aromatic [arəmat'ik] *a* aromatico(a).
arose [ərōz'] *pt of* **arise**.
around [əround'] *ad* attorno, intorno ♦ *prep* intorno a; (*fig: about*): ~ $5/3 o'clock circa 5 dollari/le 3; **is he ~?** è in giro?; **all ~** tutt'attorno; **the long way ~** il giro più lungo; **it's just ~ the corner** (*also fig*) è dietro l'angolo; **to ask sb ~** invitare qn (a casa propria); **I'll be ~ at 6 o'clock** ci sarò alle 6; **to go ~** fare il giro; **to go ~ to sb's (house)** andare da qn; **to go ~ an obstacle** aggirare un ostacolo; **go ~ the back** passi da dietro; **to go ~ a house** visitare una casa; **enough to go ~** abbastanza per tutti; **she arrived ~ (about) noon** è arrivata intorno a mezzogiorno; **~ the clock** 24 ore su 24.
arouse [ərouz'] *vt* (*sleeper*) svegliare; (*curiosity, passions*) suscitare.
arrange [ərānj'] *vt* sistemare; (*program*) preparare ♦ *vi*: **we have ~d for a taxi to pick you up** la faremo venire a prendere da un taxi; **it was ~d that ...** è stato deciso *or* stabilito che ...; **to ~ to do sth** mettersi d'accordo per fare qc.
arrangement [ərānj'mənt] *n* sistemazione *f*; (*plans etc*): **~s** progetti *mpl*, piani *mpl*; **by ~** su richiesta; **to come to an ~ (with sb)** venire ad un accordo (con qn), mettersi d'accordo *or* accordarsi (con qn); **I'll make ~s for you to be met** darò disposizioni *or* istruzioni perché ci sia qualcuno ad incontrarla.
array [ərā'] *n* fila; (*COMPUT*) array *m inv*, insieme *mpl*.
arrears [ərērz'] *npl* arretrati *mpl*; **to be in ~ with one's rent** essere in arretrato con l'affitto.
arrest [ərest'] *vt* arrestare; (*sb's attention*) attirare ♦ *n* arresto; **under ~** in arresto.
arresting [əres'ting] *a* (*fig*) che colpisce.
arrival [ərī'vəl] *n* arrivo; (*person*) arrivato/a; **new ~** nuovo venuto.
arrive [ərīv'] *vi* arrivare.
  arrive at *vt fus* arrivare a.
arrogance [ar'əgəns] *n* arroganza.
arrogant [ar'əgənt] *a* arrogante.
arrow [ar'ō] *n* freccia.
arse [ârs] *n* (*Brit col*!) culo(!).
arsenal [âr'sənəl] *n* arsenale *m*.
arsenic [âr'sənik] *n* arsenico.
arson [âr'sən] *n* incendio doloso.
art [ârt] *n* arte *f*; (*craft*) mestiere *m*; **work of ~** opera d'arte; *see also* **arts**.
artefact [âr'təfakt] *n* (*Brit*) = **artifact**.
arterial [ârtē'rēəl] *a* (*ANAT*) arterioso(a);

(*road etc*) di grande comunicazione; **~ roads** le (grandi *or* principali) arterie.
artery [âr'tûrē] *n* arteria.
artful [ârt'fəl] *a* furbo(a).
art gallery *n* galleria d'arte.
arthritis [ârthrī'tis] *n* artrite *f*.
artichoke [âr'tichōk] *n* carciofo; **Jerusalem ~** topinambur *m inv*.
article [âr'tikəl] *n* articolo; **~s** *npl* (*Brit LAW: training*) contratto di tirocinio; **~s of clothing** indumenti *mpl*.
articles of association *npl* (*COMM*) statuto sociale.
articulate *a* [ârtik'yəlit] (*person*) che si esprime forbitamente; (*speech*) articolato(a) ♦ *vi* [ârtik'yəlāt] articolare.
articulated lorry [ârtik'yəlātid lôr'ē] *n* (*Brit*) autotreno.
artifact [âr'təfakt] *n* (*US*) manufatto.
artifice [âr'təfis] *n* (*cunning*) abilità, destrezza; (*trick*) artificio.
artificial [ârtəfish'əl] *a* artificiale.
artificial insemination [ârtəfish'əl insemənā'shən] *n* fecondazione *f* artificiale.
artificial intelligence (AI) *n* intelligenza artificiale (IA).
artificial respiration *n* respirazione *f* artificiale.
artillery [ârtil'ûrē] *n* artiglieria.
artisan [âr'tizən] *n* artigiano/a.
artist [âr'tist] *n* artista *m/f*.
artistic [ârtis'tik] *a* artistico(a).
artistry [âr'tistrē] *n* arte *f*.
artless [ârt'lis] *a* semplice, ingenuo(a).
arts [ârts] *npl* (*SCOL*) lettere *fpl*.
art school *n* scuola d'arte.
ARV *n abbr* (= *American Revised Version*) traduzione della Bibbia.
AS *n abbr* (*US SCOL*: = *Associate in/of Sciences*) titolo di studio ♦ *abbr* (*US MAIL*) = *American Samoa*.
as [az] *cj* (*cause*) siccome, poiché; (*time: moment*) come, quando; (: *duration*) mentre; (*manner*) come ♦ *prep* (*in the capacity of*) da; **~ big ~** tanto grande quanto; **twice ~ big ~** due volte più grande che; **big ~ it is** grande com'è; **much ~ I like them**, ... per quanto mi siano simpatici, ...; **~ the years went by** col passare degli anni; **~ she said** come lei ha detto; **he gave it to me ~ a present** me lo ha regalato; **~ if** *or* **though** come se + *sub*; **~ for** *or* **to** quanto a; **~ or so long ~** *cj* finché; purché; **~ much (~)** tanto(a) (... quanto(a)); **~ many (~)** tanti(e) (... quanti(e)); **~ soon ~** *cj* appena; **~ soon ~ possible** prima possibile; **~ such** *ad* come tale; **~ well** *ad* anche; **~ well ~** *cj* come pure; *see also* **so, such**.
ASA *n abbr* (= *American Standards Association*) associazione per la normalizzazione.
a.s.a.p. *abbr* (= *as soon as possible*) prima

possibile.
asbestos [asbes'təs] *n* asbesto, amianto.
ascend [əsend'] *vt* salire.
ascendancy [əsen'dənsē] *n* ascendente *m*.
ascendant [əsen'dənt] *n*: **to be in the** ~ essere in auge.
ascension [əsen'shən] *n*: **the A~** (REL) l'Ascensione *f*.
Ascension Island *n* isola dell'Ascensione.
ascent [əsent'] *n* salita.
ascertain [asûrtān'] *vt* accertare.
ascetic [əset'ik] *a* ascetico(a).
asceticism [əset'isizəm] *n* ascetismo.
ASCII [as'kē] *n abbr* (= *American Standard Code for Information Interchange*) ASCII *m*.
ascribe [əskrīb'] *vt*: **to** ~ **sth to** attribuire qc a.
ASCU *n abbr* (US) = *Association of State Colleges and Universities*.
ASE *n abbr* = *American Stock Exchange*.
ash [ash] *n* (*dust*) cenere *f*; ~ (**tree**) frassino.
ashamed [əshāmd'] *a* vergognoso(a); **to be** ~ **of** vergognarsi di; **to be** ~ (**of o.s.**) **for having done** vergognarsi di aver fatto.
ashcan [ash'kan] *n* (US) pattumiera.
ashen [ash'ən] *a* (*pale*) livido(a).
ashore [əshôr'] *ad* a terra; **to go** ~ sbarcare.
ashtray [ash'trā] *n* portacenere *m*.
Ash Wednesday *n* Mercoledì *m inv* delle Ceneri.
Asia [ā'zhə] *n* Asia.
Asia Minor *n* Asia minore.
Asian [ā'zhən] *a*, *n* asiatico(a).
Asiatic [āzhēat'ik] *a* asiatico(a).
aside [əsīd'] *ad* da parte ♦ *n* a parte *m*; **to take sb** ~ prendere qn da parte; ~ **from** (*as well as*) oltre a; (*except for*) a parte.
ask [ask] *vt* (*request*) chiedere; (*question*) domandare; (*invite*) invitare; **to** ~ **about sth** informarsi su *or* di qc; **to** ~ **sb sth/sb to do sth** chiedere qc a qn/a qn di fare qc; **to** ~ **sb about sth** chiedere a qn di qc; **to** ~ (**sb**) **a question** fare una domanda (a qn); **to** ~ **sb the time** chiedere l'ora a qn; **to** ~ **sb out to dinner** invitare qn a mangiare fuori; **you should** ~ **at the information desk** dovreste rivolgersi all'ufficio informazioni.
ask about *vt fus* chiedere di.
ask for *vt fus* chiedere; **it's just** ~**ing for trouble** *or* **for it** è proprio (come) andarsele a cercare.
askance [əskans'] *ad*: **to look** ~ **at sb** guardare qn di traverso.
askew [əskyōō'] *ad* di traverso, storto.
asking price [as'king prīs] *n* prezzo di partenza.
asleep [əslēp'] *a* addormentato(a); **to be** ~ dormire; **to fall** ~ addormentarsi.
asp [asp] *n* cobra *m inv* egiziano.
asparagus [əspar'əgəs] *n* asparagi *mpl*.
asparagus tips *npl* punte *fpl* d'asparagi.

ASPCA *n abbr* (= *American Society for the Prevention of Cruelty to Animals*) ≈ E.N.P.A. *m* (*Ente Nazionale per la Protezione degli Animali*).
aspect [as'pekt] *n* aspetto.
aspersions [əspûr'zhənz] *npl*: **to cast** ~ **on** diffamare.
asphalt [as'fôlt] *n* asfalto.
asphyxiate [asfik'sēāt] *vt* asfissiare.
asphyxiation [asfiksēā'shən] *n* asfissia.
aspiration [aspərā'shən] *n* aspirazione *f*.
aspire [əspī'ûr] *vi*: **to** ~ **to** aspirare a.
aspirin [as'pûrin] *n* aspirina.
ass [as] *n* asino; (*US col!*) culo(!); **kiss my** ~! (*US col!*) va' a farti fottere! (*!*).
assail [əsāl'] *vt* assalire.
assailant [əsā'lənt] *n* assalitore *m*.
assassin [əsas'in] *n* assassino.
assassinate [əsas'ənāt] *vt* assassinare.
assassination [əsasinā'shən] *n* assassinio.
assault [əsôlt'] *n* (MIL) assalto; (*gen: attack*) aggressione *f*; (LAW): ~ (**and battery**) minacce e vie di fatto *fpl* ♦ *vt* assaltare; aggredire; (*sexually*) violentare.
assemble [əsem'bəl] *vt* riunire; (TECH) montare ♦ *vi* riunirsi.
assembly [əsem'blē] *n* (*meeting*) assemblea; (*construction*) montaggio.
assembly language *n* (COMPUT) linguaggio assemblativo.
assembly line *n* catena di montaggio.
assent [əsent'] *n* assenso, consenso ♦ *vi* assentire; **to** ~ (**to sth**) approvare (qc).
assert [əsûrt'] *vt* asserire; (*insist on*) far valere; **to** ~ **o.s.** farsi valere.
assertion [əsûr'shən] *n* asserzione *f*.
assertive [əsûr'tiv] *a* che sa imporsi.
assess [əses'] *vt* valutare.
assessment [əses'mənt] *n* valutazione *f*; (*judgment*): ~ (**of**) giudizio (su).
assessor [əses'ûr] *n* perito; funzionario del fisco.
asset [as'et] *n* vantaggio; (*person*) elemento prezioso; ~**s** *npl* (COMM) beni *mpl*; disponibilità *fpl*; attivo.
asset-stripping [as'etstriping] *n* (COMM) acquisto di una società in fallimento con lo scopo di rivenderne le attività.
assiduous [əsij'ōōəs] *a* assiduo(a).
assign [əsīn'] *vt*: **to** ~ (**to**) (*task*) assegnare (a); (*resources*) riservare (a); (*cause, meaning*) attribuire (a); **to** ~ **a date to sth** fissare la data di qc.
assignment [əsīn'mənt] *n* compito.
assimilate [əsim'əlāt] *vt* assimilare.
assimilation [əsimilā'shən] *n* assimilazione *f*.
assist [əsist'] *vt* assistere, aiutare.
assistance [əsis'təns] *n* assistenza, aiuto.
assistant [əsis'tənt] *n* assistente *m/f*; (Brit: *also*: **shop** ~) commesso/a.
assistant manager *n* vicedirettore *m*.

assizes [əsī'ziz] *npl* assise *fpl*.

associate [əsō'shēit] *a* associato(a); (*member*) aggiunto(a) ♦ *n* collega *m/f*; (*in business*) socio/a ♦ *vb* [əsō'shēāt] *vt* associare ♦ *vi*: to ~ **with sb** frequentare qn.

associated company *n* società collegata.

associate director *n* amministratore *m* aggiunto.

association [əsōsēā'shən] *n* associazione *f*; **in** ~ **with** in collaborazione con.

association football *n* (*Brit*) (gioco del) calcio.

assorted [əsôr'tid] *a* assortito(a); **in** ~ **sizes** in diverse taglie.

assortment [əsôrt'mənt] *n* assortimento.

Asst. *abbr* = **assistant**.

assuage [əswāj'] *vt* alleviare.

assume [əsōōm'] *vt* supporre; (*responsibilities etc*) assumere; (*attitude, name*) prendere.

assumed name [əsōōmd' nām] *n* nome *m* falso.

assumption [əsump'shən] *n* supposizione *f*, ipotesi *f inv*; **on the** ~ **that** ... partendo dal presupposto che ....

assurance [əshōōr'əns] *n* assicurazione *f*; (*self-confidence*) fiducia in se stesso; **I can give you no** ~**s** non posso assicurarle *or* garantirle niente.

assure [əshōōr'] *vt* assicurare.

AST *abbr* (*US*: = *Atlantic Standard Time*) ora invernale di Nuova Scozia.

asterisk [as'tûrisk] *n* asterisco.

astern [əstûrn'] *ad* a poppa.

asteroid [as'təroid] *n* asteroide *m*.

asthma [az'mə] *n* asma.

asthmatic [azmat'ik] *a, n* asmatico(a).

astigmatism [əstig'mətizəm] *n* astigmatismo.

astir [əstûr'] *ad* in piedi; (*excited*) in fermento.

ASTM *n abbr* (= *American Society for Testing Materials*) società americana per il controllo di materiali.

astonish [əstân'ish] *vt* stupire.

astonishing [əstân'ishing] *a* sorprendente, stupefacente; **I find it** ~ **that** ... mi stupisce che ....

astonishingly [əstân'ishinglē] *ad* straordinariamente, incredibilmente.

astonishment [əstân'ishmənt] *n* stupore *m*; **to my** ~ con mia gran meraviglia, con mio grande stupore.

astound [əstound'] *vt* sbalordire.

astray [əstrā'] *ad*: **to go** ~ smarrirsi; (*fig*) traviarsi; **to go** ~ **in one's calculations** sbagliare i calcoli.

astride [əstrīd'] *ad* a cavalcioni ♦ *prep* a cavalcioni di.

astringent [əstrin'jənt] *a, n* astringente (*m*).

astrologer [əstrâl'əjûr] *n* astrologo/a.

astrology [əstrâl'əjē] *n* astrologia.

astronaut [as'trənôt] *n* astronauta *m/f*.

astronomer [əstrân'əmûr] *n* astronomo/a.

astronomical [astrənâm'ikəl] *a* astronomico(a).

astronomy [əstrân'əmē] *n* astronomia.

astrophysics [astrōfiz'iks] *n* astrofisica.

astute [əstōōt'] *a* astuto(a).

asunder [əsun'dûr] *ad*: **to tear** ~ strappare.

ASV *n abbr* (= *American Standard Version*) traduzione della Bibbia.

asylum [əsī'ləm] *n* asilo; (*insane* ~) manicomio; **to seek political** ~ chiedere asilo politico.

asymmetric(al) [āsəmet'rik(əl)] *a* asimmetrico(a).

at [at] *prep* a; (*because of: following surprised, annoyed etc*) di; con; ~ **the top** in cima; ~ **Paolo's** da Paolo; ~ **the baker's** dal panettiere; ~ **times** talvolta; ~ **4 o'clock** alle quattro; ~ **night** di notte; ~ **$1 a kilo** a 1 dollaro al chilo; **two** ~ **a time** due alla *or* per volta; ~ **full speed** a tutta velocità.

ate [āt] *pt of* **eat**.

atheism [ā'thēizəm] *n* ateismo.

atheist [ā'thēist] *n* ateo/a.

Athenian [əthē'nēən] *a, n* ateniese (*m/f*).

Athens [ath'ənz] *n* Atene *f*.

athlete [ath'lēt] *n* atleta *m/f*.

athletic [athlet'ik] *a* atletico(a).

athletics [athlet'iks] *n* atletica.

Atlantic [atlan'tik] *a* atlantico(a) ♦ *n*: **the** ~ **(Ocean)** l'Atlantico, l'Oceano Atlantico.

atlas [at'ləs] *n* atlante *m*.

Atlas Mountains *npl*: **the** ~ i Monti dell'Atlante.

A.T.M. *abbr* (= *automated teller machine*) cassa automatica prelievi, sportello automatico.

atmosphere [at'məsfēr] *n* atmosfera; (*air*) aria.

atmospheric [atməsfēr'ik] *a* atmosferico(a).

atmospherics [atməsfär'iks] *npl* (*RADIO*) scariche *fpl*.

atoll [at'ôl] *n* atollo.

atom [at'əm] *n* atomo.

atomic [ətâm'ik] *a* atomico(a).

atom(ic) bomb *n* bomba atomica.

atomizer [at'əmīzûr] *n* atomizzatore *m*.

atone [ətōn'] *vi*: **to** ~ **for** espiare.

atonement [ətōn'mənt] *n* espiazione *f*.

ATP *n abbr* = *Association of Tennis Professionals*.

atrocious [ətrō'shəs] *a* atroce, pessimo(a).

atrocity [ətrâs'itē] *n* atrocità *f inv*.

atrophy [at'rəfē] *n* atrofia ♦ *vi* atrofizzarsi.

attach [ətach'] *vt* attaccare; (*document, letter*) allegare; (*MIL: troops*) assegnare; **to be** ~**ed to sb/sth** (*to like*) essere affezionato(a) a qn/qc; **the** ~**ed letter** la lettera acclusa *or* allegata.

attaché [atashā'] *n* addetto.

attaché case *n* valigetta per documenti.

attachment [ətach'mənt] *n* (*tool*) accessorio;

(love): ~ **(to)** affetto (per).

attack |ətak'| vt attaccare; (task etc) iniziare; (problem) affrontare ♦ n attacco; (also: **heart** ~) infarto.

attacker |ətak'ûr| n aggressore m, assalitore/trice.

attain |ətān'| vt (also: **to** ~ **to**) arrivare a, raggiungere.

attainments |ətān'mənts| npl cognizioni fpl.

attempt |ətempt'| n tentativo ♦ vt tentare; ~**ed murder** (LAW) tentato omicidio; **to make an** ~ **on sb's life** attentare alla vita di qn; **he made no** ~ **to help** non ha (neanche) tentato or cercato di aiutare.

attend |ətend'| vt frequentare; (meeting, talk) andare a; (patient) assistere. **attend to** vt fus (needs, affairs etc) prendersi cura di; (customer) occuparsi di.

attendance |əten'dəns| n (being present) presenza; (people present) gente f presente.

attendant |əten'dənt| n custode m/f; persona di servizio ♦ a concomitante.

attention |əten'shən| n attenzione f; ~**s** premure fpl, attenzioni fpl; ~**!** (MIL) attenti!; **at** ~ (MIL) sull'attenti; **for the** ~ **of** (ADMIN) per l'attenzione di; **it has come to my** ~ **that** ... sono venuto a conoscenza (del fatto) che ....

attentive |əten'tiv| a attento(a); (kind) premuroso(a).

attentively |əten'tivlē| ad attentamente.

attenuate |əten'yōōāt| vt attenuare ♦ vi attenuarsi.

attest |ətest'| vi: **to** ~ **to** attestare.

attic |at'ik| n soffitta.

attire |ətīûr'| n abbigliamento.

attitude |at'ətōōd| n (behavior) atteggiamento; (posture) posa; (view): ~ **(to)** punto di vista (nei confronti di).

attorney |ətûr'nē| n (US: lawyer) avvocato; (having proxy) mandatario; **power of** ~ procura.

Attorney General n (US) Ministro della Giustizia; (Brit) Procuratore m Generale.

attract |ətrakt'| vt attirare.

attraction |ətrak'shən| n (gen pl: pleasant things) attrattiva; (PHYSICS, fig: towards sth) attrazione f.

attractive |ətrak'tiv| a attraente; (idea, offer, price) allettante, interessante.

attribute n |at'rəbyōōt| attributo ♦ vt |ətrib'yōōt|: **to** ~ **sth to** attribuire qc a.

attrition |ətrish'ən| n: **war of** ~ guerra di logoramento.

atty n abbr (US) = **attorney**.

Atty Gen abbr = **Attorney General**.

ATV n abbr (MIL etc) = all terrain vehicle.

aubergine |ō'bûrzhēn| n melanzana.

auburn |ô'bûrn| a tizianesco(a).

auction |ôk'shən| n (also: **sale by** ~) asta ♦ vt (also: **to sell by** ~) vendere all'asta; (also:

to put up for ~) mettere all'asta.

auctioneer |ôkshənēr'| n banditore m.

auction room n sala dell'asta.

aud. n abbr = **audit**; **auditor**.

audacious |ôdā'shəs| a (bold) audace; (impudent) sfrontato(a).

audacity |ôdas'itē| n audacia.

audible |ôd'əbəl| a udibile.

audience |ôd'ēəns| n (people) pubblico; spettatori mpl; ascoltatori mpl; (interview) udienza.

audiovisual |ôd'ēōvizh'ōōəl| a audiovisivo(a); ~ **aids** sussidi mpl audiovisivi.

audit |ôd'it| n revisione f, verifica ♦ vt rivedere, verificare.

audition |ôdish'ən| n (THEATER) audizione f; (CINEMA) provino ♦ vi fare un'audizione (or un provino).

auditor |ô'ditûr| n revisore m; (US SCOL) uditore/trice.

auditorium |ôditôr'ēəm| n auditorio.

Aug. abbr (= August) ago., ag.

augment |ôgment'| vt, vi aumentare.

augur |ô'gûr| vt (be a sign of) predire ♦ vi: **it** ~**s well** promette bene.

August |ôg'əst| n agosto; for phrases see also **July**.

august |ôgust'| a augusto(a).

aunt |ant| n zia.

auntie, aunty |an'tē| n zietta.

au pair |ô pär'| n (also: ~ **girl**) (ragazza f) alla pari inv.

aura |ôr'ə| n aura.

auspices |ôs'pisiz| npl: **under the** ~ **of** sotto gli auspici di.

auspicious |ôspish'əs| a propizio(a).

austere |ôstēr'| a austero(a).

austerity |ôstār'itē| n austerità f inv.

Australasia |ôstrəlā'zhə| n Australasia.

Australia |ôstrāl'yə| n Australia.

Australian |ôstrāl'yən| a, n australiano(a).

Austria |ôs'trēə| n Austria.

Austrian |ôs'trēən| a, n austriaco(a).

authentic |ôthen'tik| a autentico(a).

authenticate |ôthen'tikāt| vt autenticare.

authenticity |ôthəntis'itē| n autenticità.

author |ô'thûr| n autore/trice.

authoritarian |əthôritār'ēən| a autoritario(a).

authoritative |əthôr'itātiv| a (account etc) autorevole; (manner) autoritario(a).

authority |əthôr'itē| n autorità f inv; (permission) autorizzazione f; **the authorities** npl le autorità; **to have** ~ **to do sth** avere l'autorizzazione a fare o il diritto di fare qc.

authorization |ôthûrəzā'shən| n autorizzazione f.

authorize |ô'thərīz| vt autorizzare.

authorized capital |ô'thərīzd kap'itəl| n capitale m nominale.

authorship |ô'thûrship| n paternità (letteraria etc).

autistic [ôtis'tik] a autistico(a).
autobiography [ôtəbiâg'rəfē] n autobiografia.
autocratic [ôtəkrat'ik] a autocratico(a).
autograph [ô'təgraf] n autografo ♦ vt firmare.
automat [ô'təmat] n (US) tavola calda fornita esclusivamente di distributori automatici.
automated [ô'təmātid] a automatizzato(a).
automatic [ôtəmat'ik] a automatico(a) ♦ n (gun) arma automatica; (car) automobile f con cambio automatico; (washing machine) lavatrice f automatica.
automatically [ôtəmat'iklē] ad automaticamente.
automatic data processing (ADP) n elaborazione f automatica dei dati (EAD).
automation [ôtəmā'shən] n automazione f.
automaton, pl **automata** [ôtâm'ətân, -tə] n automa m.
automobile [ôtəməbēl'] n (US) automobile f.
autonomous [ôtân'əməs] a autonomo(a).
autonomy [ôtân'əmē] n autonomia.
autopsy [ô'tâpsē] n autopsia.
autumn [ô'təm] n autunno.
auxiliary [ôgzil'yûrē] a ausiliario(a) ♦ n ausiliare m/f.
AV n abbr (= Authorized Version) traduzione inglese della Bibbia ♦ abbr = **audiovisual.**
Av. abbr = **avenue.**
avail [əvāl'] vt: **to ~ o.s. of** servirsi di; approfittarsi di ♦ n: **to no ~** inutilmente.
availability [əvāləbil'ətē] n disponibilità.
available [əvā'ləbəl] a disponibile; **every ~ means** tutti i mezzi disponibili; **to make sth ~ to sb** mettere qc a disposizione di qn; **is the manager ~?** è libero il direttore?
avalanche [av'əlanch] n valanga.
avant-garde [avântgârd'] a d'avanguardia.
avarice [av'ûris] n avarizia.
avaricious [avərish'əs] a avaro(a).
avdp. abbr (= avoirdupoids) sistema ponderale anglosassone basato su libbra, oncia e multipli.
Ave. abbr = **avenue.**
avenge [əvenj'] vt vendicare.
avenue [av'ənōō] n viale m.
average [av'ûrij] n media ♦ a medio(a) ♦ vt (also: **~ out at**) aggirarsi in media su, essere in media di; **on (the) ~** in media; **above/below (the) ~** sopra/sotto la media.
averse [əvûrs'] a: **to be ~ to sth/doing** essere contrario(a) a qc/a fare; **I wouldn't be ~ to a drink** non avrei nulla in contrario a bere qualcosa.
aversion [əvûr'zhən] n avversione f.
avert [əvûrt'] vt evitare, prevenire; (one's eyes) distogliere.
aviary [ā'vēærē] n voliera, uccelliera.
aviation [āvēā'shən] n aviazione f.
avid [av'id] a avido(a).
avidly [av'idlē] ad avidamente.
avocado [avəkâd'ō] n avocado m inv.

avoid [əvoid'] vt evitare.
avoidable [əvoid'əbəl] a evitabile.
avoidance [əvoid'əns] n l'evitare m.
avowed [əvoud'] a dichiarato(a).
AVP n abbr (US) = assistant vice-president.
AWACS [ā'waks] n abbr (= airborne warning and control system) sistema di allarme e controllo in volo.
await [əwāt'] vt aspettare; **~ing attention** (COMM: letter) in attesa di risposta; (: order) in attesa di essere evaso; **long ~ed** tanto atteso(a).
awake [əwāk'] a sveglio(a) ♦ vb (pt **awoke** [əwōk'], pp **awaked** or **awoken** [əwō'kən]) vt svegliare ♦ vi svegliarsi; **~ to** consapevole di.
awakening [əwā'kəning] n risveglio.
award [əwôrd'] n premio; (LAW) decreto ♦ vt assegnare; (LAW: damages) decretare.
aware [əwär'] a: **~ of** (conscious) conscio(a) di; (informed) informato(a) di; **to become ~ of** accorgersi di; **politically/socially ~** politicamente/socialmente preparato; **I am fully ~ that ...** mi rendo perfettamente conto che ....
awareness [əwär'nis] n consapevolezza; coscienza; **to develop people's ~ (of)** sensibilizzare la gente (a).
awash [əwâsh'] a: **~ (with)** inondato(a) (da).
away [əwā'] a, ad via; lontano(a); **two kilometers ~** a due chilometri di distanza; **two hours ~ by car** a due ore di distanza in macchina; **the vacation was two weeks ~** mancavano due settimane alle vacanze; **~ from** lontano da; **he's ~ for a week** è andato via per una settimana; **he's ~ in Milan** è (andato) a Milano; **to take ~** vt portare via; **he was working/pedalling etc ~** la particella indica la continuità e l'energia dell'azione: lavorava/pedalava etc più che poteva; **to fade/wither** etc **~** la particella rinforza l'idea della diminuzione.
away game n (SPORT) partita fuori casa.
awe [ô] n timore m.
awe-inspiring [ô'inspīûring] a imponente.
awesome [ô'səm] a imponente.
awestruck [ô'struk] a sgomento(a).
awful [ô'fəl] a terribile; **an ~ lot of** (people, cars, dogs) un numero incredibile di; (jam, flowers) una quantità incredibile di.
awfully [ô'fəlē] ad (very) terribilmente.
awhile [əhwīl'] ad (per) un po'.
awkward [ôk'wûrd] a (clumsy) goffo(a); (inconvenient) scomodo(a); (embarrassing) imbarazzante; (difficult) delicato(a), difficile.
awkwardness [ôk'wûrdnis] n goffaggine f; scomodità; imbarazzo; delicatezza, difficoltà.
awl [ôl] n punteruolo.
awning [ô'ning] n (of tent) veranda; (of shop, hotel etc) tenda.
awoke [əwōk'] pt of **awake.**

awoken |əwō'kən| *pp of* **awake**.
AWOL |ā'wôl| *abbr* (*MIL etc*) = **absent without leave**.
awry |ərī'| *ad* di traverso ♦ *a* storto(a); **to go ~** andare a monte.
ax, (*Brit*) **axe** |aks| *n* scure *f* ♦ *vt* (*project etc*) abolire; (*jobs*) sopprimere; **to have an ~ to grind** (*fig*) fare i propri interessi *or* il proprio tornaconto.
axiom |ak'sēəm| *n* assioma *m*.
axiomatic |aksēəmat'ik| *a* assiomatico(a).
axis, *pl* **axes** |ak'sis, *pl* -sēz| *n* asse *m*.
axle |ak'səl| *n* (*also*: **~-tree**) asse *m*.
ay(e) |ī| *excl* (*yes*) sì.
AYH *n abbr* = *American Youth Hostels*.
AZ *abbr* (*US MAIL*) = *Arizona*.
azalea |əzāl'yə| *n* azalea.
Azores |əzôrz'| *npl*: **the ~** le Azzorre.
Aztec |az'tek| *a, n* azteco(a).
azure |azh'ûr| *a* azzurro(a).

B

B, b *n* (*letter*) B, b *f or m inv*; (*SCOL*: *mark*) ≈ 8 (*buono*); (*MUS*): **B** si *m*; **B for Baker** ≈ B come Bologna; **B road** *n* (*Brit AUT*) ≈ strada secondaria.
b. *abbr* = **born**.
BA *n abbr* (*SCOL*) *see* **Bachelor of Arts**.
babble |bab'əl| *vi* cianciare; mormorare ♦ *n* ciance *fpl*; mormorio.
baboon |baboon'| *n* babbuino.
baby |bā'bē| *n* bambino/a.
baby buggy |bā'bē bug'ē| *n* carrozzina.
baby carriage *n* (*US*) carrozzina.
baby grand *n* (*also*: **~ piano**) pianoforte *m* a mezza coda.
babyhood |bā'bēhood| *n* prima infanzia.
babyish |bā'bēish| *a* infantile.
baby-minder |bā'bēmīndûr| *n* (*Brit*) bambinaia (*che tiene i bambini mentre la madre lavora*).
baby-sit |bā'bēsit| *vi* fare il (*or* la) babysitter.
baby-sitter |bā'bēsitûr| *n* baby-sitter *m/f inv*.
bachelor |bach'əlûr| *n* scapolo; **B~ of Arts/ Science (BA/BSc)** ≈ laureato/a in lettere/ scienze; **B~ of Arts/Science degree (BA/ BSc)** *n* ≈ laurea in lettere/scienze.
bachelorhood |bach'əlûrhood| *n* celibato.
bachelor party *n* (*US*) festa di addio al celibato.
back |bak| *n* (*of person, horse*) dorso, schiena; (*of hand*) dorso; (*of house, car*) didietro; (*of train*) coda; (*of chair*) schienale *m*; (*of page*) rovescio; (*SOCCER*) difensore *m*; **~ to front** all'incontrario; **to have one's ~ to the wall** (*fig*) essere *or* trovarsi con le spalle al muro ♦ *vt* (*financially*) finanziare; (*candidate: also*: **~ up**) appoggiare; (*horse: at races*) puntare su; (*car*) guidare a marcia indietro ♦ *vi* indietreggiare; (*car etc*) fare marcia indietro ♦ *a* (*in compounds*) posteriore, di dietro; arretrato(a); **~ seats/wheels** (*AUT*) sedili *mpl*/ruote *fpl* posteriori; **~ payments/rent** arretrati *mpl*; **~ garden/ room** giardino/stanza sul retro (della casa); **to take a ~ seat** (*fig*) restare in secondo piano ♦ *ad* (*not forward*) indietro; (*returned*): **he's ~** è tornato; **when will you be ~?** quando torni?; **he ran ~** tornò indietro di corsa; (*restitution*): **throw the ball ~** ritira la palla; **can I have it ~?** posso riaverlo?; (*again*): **he called ~** ha richiamato.
back down *vi* (*fig*) fare marcia indietro.
back on to *vt fus*: **the house ~s on to the golf course** il retro della casa dà sul campo da golf.
back out *vi* (*of promise*) tirarsi indietro.
back up *vt* (*support*) appoggiare, sostenere; (*COMPUT*) fare una copia di riserva di.
backache |bak'āk| *n* mal *m* di schiena.
backbencher |bak'benchûr| *n* (*Brit*) *membro del Parlamento senza potere amministrativo*.
backbiting |bak'bīting| *n* maldicenza.
backbone |bak'bōn| *n* spina dorsale; **the ~ of the organization** l'anima dell'organizzazione.
back burner *n*: **to put sth on the ~** accantonare qc per il momento.
backcomb |bak'kōm| *vt* (*Brit*) cotonare.
backdate |bakdāt'| *vt* (*letter*) retrodatare; **~d pay raise** aumento retroattivo.
backdrop |bak'dráp| *n* scena di sfondo.
backer |bak'ûr| *n* sostenitore/trice; (*COMM*) fautore *m*.
backfire |bak'fîûr| *vi* (*AUT*) dar ritorni di fiamma; (*plans*) fallire.
backgammon |bak'gamən| *n* tavola reale.
background |bak'ground| *n* sfondo; (*of events, COMPUT*) background *m inv*; (*basic knowledge*) base *f*; (*experience*) esperienza ♦ *cpd* (*noise, music*) di fondo; **~ reading** letture *fpl* sull'argomento; **family ~** ambiente *m* familiare.
backhand |bak'hand| *n* (*TENNIS: also*: **~ stroke**) rovescio.
backhanded |bak'handid| *a* (*fig*) ambiguo(a).
backhander |bak'handûr| *n* (*Brit: bribe*) bustarella.
backing |bak'ing| *n* (*COMM*) finanziamento; (*MUS*) accompagnamento; (*fig*) appoggio.
backlash |bak'lash| *n* contraccolpo, ripercussione *f*.
backlog |bak'lóg| *n*: **~ of work** lavoro arretrato.
back number *n* (*of magazine etc*) numero

arretrato.

backpack [bak'pak] *n* zaino.

backpacker [bak'pakûr] *n chi viaggia con zaino e sacco a pelo.*

back pay *n* arretrato di paga.

backpedal [bak'pedəl] *vi* pedalare all'indietro; *(fig)* far marcia indietro.

backside [bak'sīd] *n (col)* sedere *m.*

backslash [bak'slash] *n* backslash *m inv,* barra obliqua inversa.

backslide [bak'slīd] *vi* ricadere.

backspace [bak'spās] *vi (in typing)* battere il tasto di ritorno.

backstage [bak'stāj'] *ad* nel retroscena.

back street *n* vicolo.

back-street [bak'strēt] *a:* ~ **abortionist** praticante *m/f* di aborti clandestini.

backstroke [bak'strōk] *n* nuoto sul dorso.

backtalk [bak'tôk] *n (col)* impertinenza.

backtrack [bak'trak] *vi* = **backpedal.**

backup [bak'up] *a (train, plane)* supplementare; *(COMPUT)* di riserva ♦ *n (support)* appoggio, sostegno; *(COMPUT: also:* ~ **file)** file *m inv* di riserva.

backup lights [bak'up līts] *npl (US AUT)* luci *fpl* per la retromarcia.

backward [bak'wûrd] *a (movement)* indietro *inv; (person)* tardivo(a); *(country)* arretrato(a); ~ **and forward movement** movimento avanti e indietro.

backwards [bak'wûrdz] *ad* indietro; *(fall, walk)* all'indietro; **to know sth** ~ **and forwards** *or (Brit)* ~ *(col)* sapere qc a menadito.

backwater [bak'wôtûr] *n (fig)* posto morto.

back yard *n* cortile *m* sul retro.

bacon [bā'kən] *n* pancetta.

bacteria [baktē'rēə] *npl* batteri *mpl.*

bacteriology [baktērēâl'əjē] *n* batteriologia.

bad [bad] *a* cattivo(a); *(child)* cattivello(a); *(meat, food)* andato(a) a male; **his** ~ **leg** la sua gamba malata; **to go** ~ *(meat, food)* andare a male; **to have a** ~ **time of it** passarsela male; **I feel** ~ **about it** *(guilty)* mi sento un po' in colpa; ~ **debt** credito difficile da recuperare; ~ **faith** malafede *f.*

bade [bad] *pt of* **bid.**

bad feeling [bad fē'ling] *n* rancore *m.*

badge [baj] *n* insegna; *(of policeman)* stemma *m; (stick-on)* adesivo.

badger [baj'ûr] *n* tasso ♦ *vt* tormentare.

badly [bad'lē] *ad (work, dress etc)* male; **things are going** ~ le cose vanno male; ~ **wounded** gravemente ferito; **he needs it** ~ ne ha gran bisogno; ~ **off** *a* povero(a).

bad-mannered [badman'ûrd] *a* maleducato(a), sgarbato(a).

badminton [bad'mintən] *n* badminton *m.*

bad-mouth [bad'mouth'] *vt (US: criticize)* criticare.

bad-smelling [bad'sme'ling] *a* puzzolente.

bad-tempered [bad'tem'pûrd] *a* irritabile; *(in bad mood)* di malumore.

baffle [baf'əl] *vt (puzzle)* confondere.

baffling [baf'ling] *a* sconcertante.

bag [bag] *n* sacco; *(handbag etc)* borsa; *(of hunter)* carniere *m;* bottino ♦ *vt (col: take)* mettersi in tasca; prendersi; ~**s of** *(col: lots of)* un sacco di; **to pack one's** ~**s** fare le valigie; ~**s under the eyes** borse sotto gli occhi.

bagful [bag'fəl] *n* sacco (pieno).

baggage [bag'ij] *n* bagagli *mpl.*

baggage car *n (US)* bagagliaio.

baggage check *n* controllo bagaglio.

baggage claim *n* ritiro bagagli.

baggy [bag'ē] *a* largo(a), sformato(a).

Baghdad [bag'dad] *n* Bagdad *f.*

bagpipes [bag'pīps] *npl* cornamusa.

bag-snatcher [bag'snachûr] *n (Brit)* scippatore/trice.

Bahamas [bəhâm'əz] *npl:* **the** ~ le isole Bahama.

Bahrain [bârân'] *n* Bahrein *m.*

bail [bāl] *n* cauzione *f* ♦ *vt (prisoner: gen: to grant* ~ **to)** concedere la libertà provvisoria su cauzione a; *(also:* ~ **out:** *water)* vuotare; *(: boat)* aggottare; **to be released on** ~ essere rilasciato(a) su cauzione.

bail out *vt (prisoner)* ottenere la libertà provvisoria su cauzione di; *(fig)* tirare fuori dai guai; *(NAUT: water)* vuotare; *(: boat)* aggottare ♦ *vi (of a plane)* gettarsi col paracadute.

bailiff [bā'lif] *n* usciere *m;* fattore *m.*

bait [bāt] *n* esca ♦ *vt (hook)* innescare; *(trap)* munire di esca; *(fig)* tormentare.

bake [bāk] *vt* cuocere al forno ♦ *vi* cuocersi al forno.

baked beans *npl* fagioli *mpl* all'uccelletto.

baker [bā'kûr] *n* fornaio/a, panettiere/a.

bakery [bā'kûrē] *n* panetteria.

baking [bā'king] *n* cottura (al forno).

baking powder *n* lievito in polvere.

baking pan, *(Brit)* **baking tin** *n* stampo, tortiera.

baking sheet *n* teglia.

balaclava [bələklâv'a] *n (also:* ~ **helmet)** passamontagna *m inv.*

balance [bal'əns] *n* equilibrio; *(COMM: sum)* bilancio; *(scales)* bilancia ♦ *vt* tenere in equilibrio; *(pros and cons)* soppesare; *(budget)* far quadrare; *(account)* pareggiare; *(compensate)* contrappesare; ~ **of trade/payments** bilancia commerciale/dei pagamenti; ~ **brought forward** saldo riportato; ~ **carried forward** saldo da riportare; **to** ~ **the books** fare il bilancio.

balanced [bal'ənst] *a (personality, diet)* equilibrato(a).

balance sheet *n* bilancio.

balcony [bal'kənē] *n* balcone *m;* **first balcony**

(*US*) prima galleria.
bald [bôld] *a* calvo(a).
baldness [bôld'nis] *n* calvizie *f*.
bale [bāl] *n* balla.
  bale out (*Brit*) *vt* (*NAUT*: *water*) vuotare; (: *boat*) aggottare ♦ *vi* (*of a plane*) gettarsi col paracadute.
Balearic [balēār'ik] *a*: **the ~ Islands** le (isole) Baleari.
baleful [bāl'fəl] *a* funesto(a).
balk [bôk] *vi*: **to ~ (at)** tirarsi indietro (davanti a); (*horse*) recalcitrare (davanti a).
Balkan [bôl'kən] *a* balcanico(a) ♦ *n*: **the ~s** i Balcani.
ball [bôl] *n* palla; (*football*) pallone *m*; (*for golf*) pallina; (*dance*) ballo; **to play ~ (with sb)** giocare a palla (con qn); (*fig*) stare al gioco (di qn); **to be on the ~** (*fig: competent*) essere in gamba; (: *alert*) stare all'erta; **to start the ~ rolling** (*fig*) fare la prima mossa; **the ~ is in your court** (*fig*) a lei la prossima mossa; *see also* **balls**.
ballad [bal'əd] *n* ballata.
ballast [bal'əst] *n* zavorra.
ball bearing *n* cuscinetto a sfere.
ball cock *n* galleggiante *m*.
ballerina [balərē'nə] *n* ballerina.
ballet [balā'] *n* balletto.
ballet dancer *n* ballerino/a.
ballistic [bəlis'tik] *a* balistico(a).
ballistics [bəlis'tiks] *n* balistica.
balloon [bəlōōn'] *n* pallone *m*; (*in comic strip*) fumetto ♦ *vi* gonfiarsi.
balloonist [bəlōō'nist] *n* aeronauta *m/f*.
ballot [bal'ət] *n* scrutinio; (*US*: ~ *paper*) scheda.
ballot box *n* urna (per le schede).
ballot paper *n* scheda.
ballpark [bôl'pârk] *n* (*US*) stadio di baseball.
ballpark figure *n* (*col*) cifra approssimativa.
ball-point (pen) [bôl'point (pen')] *n* penna a sfera.
ballroom [bôl'rōōm] *n* sala da ballo.
balls [bôlz] *npl* (*col!*) coglioni *mpl* (!).
balm [bâm] *n* balsamo.
balmy [bâ'mē] *a* (*breeze*, *air*) balsamico(a); (*Brit col*) = **barmy**.
balsam [bôl'səm] *n* balsamo.
balsa (wood) [bôl'sə (wōōd)] *n* (legno di) balsa.
Baltic [bôl'tik] *a*, *n*: **the ~ (Sea)** il (mar) Baltico.
balustrade [bal'əstrād] *n* balaustrata.
bamboo [bambōō'] *n* bambù *m*.
bamboozle [bambōō'zəl] *vt* (*col*) infinocchiare.
ban [ban] *n* interdizione *f* ♦ *vt* interdire.
banal [bənal'] *a* banale.
banana [bənan'ə] *n* banana.
band [band] *n* banda; (*at a dance*) orchestra; (*MIL*) fanfara.

band together *vi* collegarsi.
bandage [ban'dij] *n* benda.
Band-Aid [band'ād] *n* ® (*US*) cerotto.
bandit [ban'dit] *n* bandito.
bandstand [band'stand] *n* palco dell'orchestra.
bandwagon [band'wagən] *n*: **to jump on the ~** (*fig*) seguire la corrente.
bandy [ban'dē] *vt* (*jokes*, *insults*) scambiare.
  bandy about *vt* far circolare.
bandy-legged [ban'dēlegid] *a* dalle gambe storte.
bane [bān] *n*: **it** (*or* **he** *etc*) **is the ~ of my life** è la mia rovina.
bang [bang] *n* botta; (*of door*) lo sbattere; (*blow*) colpo ♦ *vt* battere (violentemente); (*door*) sbattere ♦ *vi* scoppiare; sbattere; **to ~ at the door** picchiare alla porta; **to ~ into sth** sbattere contro qc; *see also* **bangs**.
banger [bang'ûr] *n* (*Brit*: *car*: *also*: **old ~**) macinino; (*Brit col*: *sausage*) salsiccia; (*firework*) mortaretto.
Bangkok [bang'kâk] *n* Bangkok *f*.
Bangladesh [banggladesh'] *n* Bangladesh *m*.
bangle [bang'gəl] *n* braccialetto.
bangs [bangz] *npl* (*US*: *hair*) frangia, frangetta.
banish [ban'ish] *vt* bandire.
banister(s) [ban'istûr(z)] *n(pl)* ringhiera.
banjo, **~es** *or* **~s** [ban'jō] *n* banjo *m inv*.
bank [bangk] *n* (*for money*) banca, banco; (*of river*, *lake*) riva, sponda; (*of earth*) banco ♦ *vi* (*AVIAT*) inclinarsi in virata; (*COMM*): **they ~ with Pitt's** sono clienti di Pitt's.
  bank on *vt fus* contare su.
bank account *n* conto in banca.
bank card *n* carta *f* assegni *inv*.
bank charges *npl* spese *fpl* bancarie.
bank draft *n* assegno circolare *or* bancario.
banker [bangk'ûr] *n* banchiere *m*; **~'s order** (*Brit*) ordine *m* di banca.
Bank holiday *n* (*Brit*) giorno di festa (*in cui le banche sono chiuse*).
banking [bangk'ing] *n* attività bancaria; professione *f* di banchiere.
banking hours *npl* orario di sportello.
bank loan *n* prestito bancario.
bank manager *n* direttore *m* di banca.
bank note *n* banconota.
bank rate *n* tasso bancario.
bankrupt [bangk'rupt] *a*, *n* fallito(a); **to go ~** fallire.
bankruptcy [bangk'ruptsē] *n* fallimento.
bank statement *n* estratto conto.
banner [ban'ûr] *n* bandiera.
bannister(s) *n(pl)* = **banister(s)**.
banns [banz] *npl* pubblicazioni *fpl* di matrimonio.
banquet [bang'kwit] *n* banchetto.
bantamweight [ban'təmwāt] *n* peso gallo.
banter [ban'tûr] *n* scherzi *mpl* bonari.
BAOR *n abbr* = *British Army of the Rhine*.

baptism [bap'tizəm] *n* battesimo.
Baptist [bap'tist] *a, n* battista *(m/f)*.
baptize [baptīz'] *vt* battezzare.
bar [bár] *n* barra; *(of window etc)* sbarra; *(of chocolate)* tavoletta; *(fig)* ostacolo; restrizione *f*; *(place)* bar *m inv*; *(counter)* banco; *(MUS)* battuta ♦ *vt (road, window)* sbarrare; *(person)* escludere; *(activity)* interdire; ~ **of soap** saponetta; **the B~** *(LAW)* l'Ordine *m* degli avvocati; **behind ~s** *(prisoner)* dietro le sbarre; ~ **none** senza eccezione.
Barbados [bárbā'dōs] *n* Barbados *fpl*.
barbaric [bárbar'ik], **barbarous** [bār'bərəs] *a* barbaro(a); barbarico(a).
barbecue [bár'bəkyōō] *n* barbecue *m inv*.
barbed wire [bárbd wīûr] *n* filo spinato.
barber [bár'bûr] *n* barbiere *m*.
barbiturate [bárbich'ûrit] *n* barbiturico.
Barcelona [bársəlō'nə] *n* Barcellona.
bar chart *n* diagramma *m* di frequenza.
bar code *n* codice *m* a barre.
bare [bär] *a* nudo(a) ♦ *vt* scoprire, denudare; *(teeth)* mostrare; **the ~ essentials** lo stretto necessario.
bareback [bär'bak] *ad* senza sella.
barefaced [bär'fāst] *a* sfacciato(a).
barefoot [bär'fōōt] *a, ad* scalzo(a).
bareheaded [bär'hedid] *a, ad* a capo scoperto.
barely [bär'lē] *ad* appena.
Barents Sea [bär'ənts sē] *n*: **the ~** il mar di Barents.
bargain [bár'gin] *n (transaction)* contratto; *(good buy)* affare *m* ♦ *vi (haggle)* tirare sul prezzo; *(trade)* contrattare; **into the ~** per giunta.
   bargain for *vt fus (col)*: **to ~ for sth** aspettarsi qc; **he got more than he ~ed for** gli è andata peggio di quel che si aspettasse.
bargaining [bár'gining] *n* contrattazione *f*.
barge [bárj] *n* chiatta.
   barge in *vi (walk in)* piombare dentro; *(interrupt talk)* intromettersi a sproposito.
   barge into *vt fus* urtare contro.
baritone [bar'itōn] *n* baritono.
barium meal [bar'ēəm mēl'] *n* (pasto di) bario.
bark [bárk] *n (of tree)* corteccia; *(of dog)* abbaio ♦ *vi* abbaiare.
barley [bár'lē] *n* orzo.
barley sugar *n* zucchero d'orzo.
barmaid [bár'mād] *n* cameriera al banco.
barman [bár'mən] *n* barista *m*.
barn [bárn] *n* granaio; *(for animals)* stalla.
barnacle [bár'nəkəl] *n* cirripede *m*.
barometer [bəräm'itûr] *n* barometro.
baron [bar'ən] *n* barone *m*; *(fig)* magnate *m*; **the oil ~s** i magnati del petrolio; **the press ~s** i baroni della stampa.
baroness [bar'ənis] *n* baronessa.
baronet [bar'ənit] *n* baronetto.
barracks [bar'əks] *npl* caserma.

barrage [bərázh'] *n (MIL)* sbarramento; **a ~ of questions** una raffica di *or* un fuoco di fila di domande.
barrel [bar'əl] *n* barile *m*; *(of gun)* canna.
barrel organ *n* organetto a cilindro.
barren [bar'ən] *a* sterile; *(soil)* arido(a).
barrette [bəret'] *n (US)* forcina.
barricade [bar'əkād] *n* barricata ♦ *vt* barricare.
barrier [bar'ēûr] *n* barriera; *(Brit: also:* **crash ~)** guardrail *m inv*.
barring [bár'ing] *prep* salvo.
barrister [bar'istûr] *n (Brit)* avvocato/essa *(con diritto di parlare davanti a tutte le corti)*.
barrow [bar'ō] *n (cart)* carriola.
barstool [bár'stōōl] *n* sgabello.
bartender [bár'tendûr] *n (US)* barista *m*.
barter [bár'tûr] *n* baratto ♦ *vt*: **to ~ sth for** barattare qc con.
base [bās] *n* base *f* ♦ *a* vile ♦ *vt*: **to ~ sth on** basare qc su; **to ~ at** *(troops)* mettere di stanza a; **coffee-~d** a base di caffè; **a Paris-~d firm** una ditta con sede centrale a Parigi; **I'm ~d in London** sono di base *or* ho base a Londra.
baseball [bās'bôl] *n* baseball *m*.
baseboard [bās'bôrd] *n (US)* zoccolo, battiscopa *m inv*.
base camp *n* campo *m* base *inv*.
Basel [báz'əl] *n* = **Basle**.
basement [bās'mənt] *n* seminterrato; *(of shop)* sotterraneo.
base pay *n (US)* stipendio base *(inv)*.
base rate *n* tasso di base.
bases [bā'siz] *npl of* **base**; ♦ [bā'sēz] *npl of* **basis**.
bash [bash] *vt (col)* picchiare ♦ *n*: **I'll have a ~ (at it)** *(Brit col)* ci proverò; **~ed in** *a* sfondato(a).
   bash up *vt (col: car)* sfasciare; (*: Brit: person)* riempire di *or* prendere a botte.
bashful [bash'fəl] *a* timido(a).
bashing [bash'ing] *n*: **Paki-~** atti *mpl* di violenza contro i pachistani.
BASIC [bā'sik] *n (COMPUT)* BASIC *m*.
basic [bā'sik] *a (principles, precautions, rules)* elementare; *(salary)* base *inv (after n)*.
basically [bā'siklē] *ad* fondamentalmente, sostanzialmente.
basic rate *n (of tax)* aliquota minima.
basil [baz'əl] *n* basilico.
basin [bā'sin] *n (vessel, also GEO)* bacino; *(also:* **wash~)** lavabo; *(Brit: for food)* terrina.
basis, *pl* **bases** [bā'sis, -sēz] *n* base *f*; **on the ~ of what you've said** in base alle sue asserzioni.
bask [bask] *vi*: **to ~ in the sun** crogiolarsi al sole.
basket [bas'kit] *n* cesta; *(smaller)* cestino;

(*with handle*) paniere *m*.

basketball [bas'kitbôl] *n* pallacanestro *f*.

basketball player *n* cestista *m/f*.

Basle [baz'əl] *n* Basilea.

Basque [bask] *a*, *n* basco(a).

bass [bās] *n* (*MUS*) basso.

bass clef [bās klef] *n* chiave *f* di basso.

bassoon [basōōn'] *n* fagotto.

bastard [bas'tûrd] *n* bastardo/a; (*col!*) stronzo (*!*).

baste [bāst] *vt* (*CULIN*) ungere con grasso; (*SEWING*) imbastire.

bastion [bas'chən] *n* bastione *m*; (*fig*) baluardo.

bat [bat] *n* pipistrello; (*for baseball etc*) mazza; (*Brit: for table tennis*) racchetta ♦ *vt*: **he didn't ~ an eyelid** non battè ciglio; **to take off like a ~ out of hell** (*col*) sparire come un fulmine.

batch [bach] *n* (*of bread*) infornata; (*of papers*) cumulo; (*of applicants, letters*) gruppo; (*of work*) sezione *f*; (*of goods*) partita, lotto.

batch processing *n* (*COMPUT*) elaborazione *f* a blocchi.

bated [bā'tid] *a*: **with ~ breath** col fiato sospeso.

bath [bath, *pl* bathz] *n* bagno; (*bathtub*) vasca da bagno ♦ *vt* far fare il bagno a; **to have a ~** fare un bagno; *see also* **baths**.

bathe [bāth] *vi* fare il bagno ♦ *vt* bagnare; (*wound etc*) lavare.

bather [bāth'ûr] *n* bagnante *m/f*.

bathing [bā'thing] *n* bagni *mpl*.

bathing cap *n* cuffia da bagno.

bathing suit *n* costume *m* da bagno.

bathmat [bath'mat] *n* tappetino da bagno.

bathrobe [bath'rōb] *n* accappatoio.

bathroom [bath'rōōm] *n* stanza da bagno.

baths [bathz] *npl* bagni *mpl* pubblici.

bath towel [bath' toul] *n* asciugamano da bagno.

bathtub [bath'tub] *n* (vasca da) bagno.

baton [batân'] *n* bastone *m*; (*MUS*) bacchetta.

battalion [bətal'yən] *n* battaglione *m*.

batten [bat'ən] *n* (*CARPENTRY*) assicella, correntino; (*for flooring*) tavola per pavimenti; (*NAUT*) serretta; (*: on sail*) stecca.

batten down *vt* (*NAUT*): **to ~ down the hatches** chiudere i boccaporti.

batter [bat'ûr] *vt* battere ♦ *n* pastetta.

battered [bat'ûrd] *a* (*hat*) sformato(a); (*pan*) ammaccato(a); **~ wife/baby** consorte *f*/ bambino(a) maltrattato(a).

battering ram [bat'ûring ram] *n* ariete *m*.

battery [bat'ûrē] *n* batteria; (*of torch*) pila.

battery charger *n* caricabatterie *m inv*.

battery farming *n* allevamento intensivo.

battle [bat'əl] *n* battaglia ♦ *vi* battagliare, lottare; **to fight a losing ~** (*fig*) battersi per una causa persa; **that's half the ~** (*col*) è già una mezza vittoria.

battle dress *n* uniforme *f* da combattimento.

battlefield [bat'əlfēld] *n* campo di battaglia.

battlements [bat'əlmənts] *npl* bastioni *mpl*.

battleship [bat'əlship] *n* nave *f* da guerra.

bauble [bô'bəl] *n* ninnolo.

baud [bôd] *n* (*COMPUT*) baud *m inv*.

baulk [bôk] *vi* (*Brit*) = **balk**.

bauxite [bôk'sīt] *n* bauxite *f*.

Bavaria [bəvär'ēə] *n* Bavaria.

Bavarian [bəvär'ēən] *a*, *n* bavarese (*m/f*).

bawdy [bô'dē] *a* piccante.

bawl [bôl] *vi* urlare.

bawl out *vt fus* dare una lavata di capo a.

bay [bā] *n* (*of sea*) baia; (*Brit: for parking*) piazzola di sosta; (*loading*) piazzale *m* di (sosta e) carico; **to hold sb at ~** tenere qn a bada.

bay leaf *n* foglia d'alloro.

bayonet [bā'ənet] *n* baionetta.

bay tree *n* alloro.

bay window *n* bovindo.

bazaar [bəzâr'] *n* bazar *m inv*; vendita di beneficenza.

bazooka [bəzōō'kə] *n* bazooka *m inv*.

B & B [bē and bē] *n abbr see* **bed and breakfast**.

BBA *n abbr* (*US*: = *Bachelor of Business Administration*) titolo di studio.

BBB *n abbr* (*US*: = *Better Business Bureau*) organismo per la difesa dei consumatori.

BBC *n abbr* (= *British Broadcasting Corporation*) rete nazionale di radiotelevisione in Gran Bretagna.

BC *n abbr* (*US*: = *Bachelor of Commerce*) titolo di studio ♦ *ad abbr* (= *before Christ*) a.C. ♦ *abbr* (*Canada*) = *British Columbia*.

BCG *n abbr* (= *Bacillus Calmette-Guérin*) vaccino antitubercolare.

BD *n abbr* (= *Bachelor of Divinity*) titolo di studio.

B/D *abbr* = **bank draft**.

BDS *n abbr* (= *Bachelor of Dental Surgery*) titolo di studio.

be, *pt* **was, were**, *pp* **been** [bē, wôz, wûr, bin] *vi* essere; **how are you?** come sta?; **I am warm** ho caldo; **it is cold** fa freddo; **how much is it?** quanto costa?; **it's 8 o'clock** sono le 8; **it's only me** sono solo io; **he is four (years old)** ha quattro anni; **2 and 2 are 4** 2 più 2 fa 4; **where have you been?** dov'è stato?; **dov'è andato?**; **what are you doing?** che fa?, che sta facendo?; **if I were you ...** se fossi in lei ...; **am I to understand that ...?** devo dedurre che ...?; **I've been waiting for her for 2 hours** l'aspetto da 2 ore; **he was to have come yesterday** sarebbe dovuto venire ieri; **to ~ killed** essere *or* venire ucciso; **he is nowhere to ~ found** non lo si trova da nessuna parte; **the car is to ~ sold** abbiamo (*or* hanno *etc*) intenzione di vendere la macchina.

B/E *abbr* = **bill of exchange.**

beach [bēch] *n* spiaggia ♦ *vt* tirare in secco.

beach buggy [bēch' bug'ē] *n* dune buggy *f inv*.

beachcomber [bēch'kōmûr] *n* vagabondo (che s'aggira sulla spiaggia).

beachwear [bēch'wär] *n* articoli *mpl* da spiaggia.

beacon [bē'kən] *n* (*lighthouse*) faro; (*marker*) segnale *m;* (*radio* ~) radiofaro.

bead [bēd] *n* perlina; (*of dew, sweat*) goccia; ~s (*necklace*) collana.

beady [bē'dē] *a:* ~ **eyes** occhi *mpl* piccoli e penetranti.

beagle [bē'gəl] *n* cane *m* da lepre.

beak [bēk] *n* becco; (*col: nose*) nasone *m*.

beaker [bē'kûr] *n* coppa.

beam [bēm] *n* trave *f;* (*of light*) raggio; (*RADIO*) fascio (d'onde) ♦ *vi* brillare ♦ *vt* (*smile*): **to** ~ **at sb** rivolgere un radioso sorriso a qn; **to drive on high** *or* (*Brit*) **full** ~ guidare con gli abbaglianti accesi.

beaming [bē'ming] *a* (*sun, smile*) raggiante.

bean [bēn] *n* fagiolo; (*of coffee*) chicco.

bean sprouts *npl* germogli *mpl* di soia.

bear [bär] *n* orso; (*STOCK EXCHANGE*) ribassista *m/f* ♦ *vb* (*pt* **bore,** *pp* **borne** [bôr, bôrn]) *vt* (*gen*) portare; (*produce: fruit*) produrre, dare; (*: traces, signs*) mostrare; (*COMM: interest*) fruttare; (*endure*) sopportare ♦ *vi:* **to** ~ **right/left** piegare a destra/sinistra; **to** ~ **the responsibility of** assumersi la responsabilità di; **to** ~ **comparison with** reggere al paragone con; **I can't** ~ **him** non lo posso soffrire *or* sopportare; **to bring pressure to** ~ **on sb** fare pressione su qn.
bear out *vt* (*theory, suspicion*) confermare, convalidare.
bear up *vi* farsi coraggio; **he bore up well under the strain** ha sopportato bene lo stress.
bear with *vt fus* (*sb's moods, temper*) sopportare (con pazienza); ~ **with me a minute** solo un attimo, prego.

bearable [bär'əbəl] *a* sopportabile.

beard [bērd] *n* barba.

bearded [bērd'id] *a* barbuto(a).

bearer [bär'ûr] *n* portatore *m;* (*of passport*) titolare *m/f*.

bearing [bär'ing] *n* portamento; (*connection*) rapporto; (**ball**) ~s *npl* cuscinetti *mpl* a sfere; **to take a** ~ fare un rilevamento; **to find one's** ~s orientarsi.

beast [bēst] *n* bestia.

beastly [bēst'lē] *a* meschino(a); (*weather*) da cani.

beat [bēt] *n* colpo; (*of heart*) battito; (*MUS*) tempo; battuta; (*of policeman*) giro ♦ *vt* (*pt* **beat,** *pp* **beaten**) battere; (*CULIN*) sbattere, frullare ♦ *a* (*US col: tired*) sfinito(a), a pezzi; **off the** ~**en track** fuori mano; **to** ~ **around the bush** menare il cane per l'aia; **to** ~ **time**

battere il tempo; **that** ~**s everything!** (*col*) questo è il colmo!
beat down *vt* (*door*) abbattere, buttare giù; (*price*) far abbassare; (*seller*) far scendere ♦ *vi* (*rain*) scrosciare; (*sun*) picchiare.
beat off *vt* respingere.
beat up *vt* (*col: person*) picchiare; (*eggs*) sbattere.

beater [bē'tûr] *n* (*for eggs, cream*) frullino.

beating [bē'ting] *n* botte *fpl;* (*defeat*) batosta; **to take a** ~ prendere una (bella) batosta.

beat-up [bēt'up] *a* (*col*) scassato(a).

beautician [byōōtish'ən] *n* estetista *m/f*.

beautiful [byōō'təfəl] *a* bello(a).

beautifully [byōō'təfəlē] *ad* splendidamente.

beautify [byōō'təfī] *vt* abbellire.

beauty [byōō'tē] *n* bellezza; (*concept*) bello; **the** ~ **of it is that** ... il bello è che ....

beauty contest *n* concorso di bellezza.

beauty queen *n* miss *f inv*, reginetta di bellezza.

beauty salon *n* istituto di bellezza.

beauty spot *n* neo; (*Brit: TOURISM*) luogo pittoresco.

beaver [bē'vûr] *n* castoro.

becalmed [bikâmd'] *a* in bonaccia.

became [bikām'] *pt of* **become.**

because [bikôz'] *cj* perché; ~ **of** *prep* a causa di.

beck [bek] *n:* **to be at sb's** ~ **and call** essere a completa disposizione di qn.

beckon [bek'ən] *vt* (*also:* ~ **to**) chiamare con un cenno.

become [bikum'] *vt* (*irg: like* **come**) diventare; **to** ~ **fat/thin** ingrassarsi/dimagrire; **to** ~ **angry** arrabbiarsi; **it became known that** ... si è venuto a sapere che ...; **what has** ~ **of him?** che gli è successo?

becoming [bikum'ing] *a* (*behavior*) che si conviene; (*clothes*) grazioso(a).

BEd *n abbr* (= *Bachelor of Education*) laurea con abilitazione all'insegnamento.

bed [bed] *n* letto; (*of flowers*) aiuola; (*of coal, clay*) strato; (*of sea, lake*) fondo; **to go to** ~ andare a letto.
bed down *vi* sistemarsi (per dormire).

bed and breakfast (B & B) *n* (*terms*) camera con colazione; (*place*) ≈ pensione *f* familiare.

bedbug [bed'bug] *n* cimice *f*.

bedclothes [bed'klōz] *npl* coperte e lenzuola *fpl*.

bedcover [bed'kuvûr] *n* copriletto.

bedding [bed'ing] *n* coperte e lenzuola *fpl*.

bedevil [bidev'əl] *vt* (*person*) tormentare; (*plans*) ostacolare continuamente.

bedfellow [bed'felō] *n:* **they are strange** ~**s** (*fig*) fanno una coppia ben strana.

bedlam [bed'ləm] *n* baraonda.

bedpan [bed'pan] *n* padella.

bedpost |bed'pōst| *n* colonnina del letto.
bedraggled |bidrag'əld| *a* fradicio(a).
bedridden |bed'ridən| *a* costretto(a) a letto.
bedrock |bed'râk| *n* (GEO) basamento; (*fig*) fatti *mpl* di base.
bedroom |bed'rōōm| *n* camera da letto.
Beds |bedz| *abbr* (*Brit*) = *Bedfordshire*.
bedside |bed'sīd| *n*: **at sb's ~** al capezzale di qn.
bedside lamp *n* lampada da comodino.
bedsit(ter) |bed'sit(ûr)| *n* (*Brit*) monolocale *m*.
bedspread |bed'spred| *n* copriletto.
bedtime |bed'tīm| *n*: **it's ~** è ora di andare a letto.
bee |bē| *n* ape *f*; **to have a ~ in one's bonnet (about sth)** avere la fissazione (di qc).
beech |bēch| *n* faggio.
beef |bēf| *n* manzo.
beef up *vt* (col) rinforzare.
beefburger |bēf'bûrgûr| *n* hamburger *m inv*.
beefeater |bēf'ētûr| *n* *guardia della Torre di Londra*.
beehive |bē'hīv| *n* alveare *m*.
beeline |bē'līn| *n*: **to make a ~ for** buttarsi a capo fitto verso.
been |bin| *pp of* **be**.
beeper |bēp'ûr| *n* (*of doctor etc*) cicalino.
beer |bēr| *n* birra.
beer can *n* lattina di birra.
beet |bēt| *n* (*US*) barbabietola.
beetle |bēt'əl| *n* scarafaggio; coleottero.
beetroot |bēt'rōōt| *n* (*Brit*) = **beet**.
befall |bifôl'| *vi(vt)* (*irg: like* **fall**) accadere (a).
befit |bifit'| *vt* addirsi a.
before |bifôr'| *prep* (*in time*) prima di; (*in space*) davanti a ♦ *cj* prima che + *sub*; prima di ♦ *ad* prima; **~ going** prima di andare; **~ she goes** prima che vada; **the week ~** la settimana prima; **I've seen it ~** l'ho già visto; **I've never seen it ~** è la prima volta che lo vedo.
beforehand |bifôr'hand| *ad* in anticipo.
befriend |bifrend'| *vt* assistere; mostrarsi amico a.
befuddled |bifud'əld| *a* confuso(a).
beg |beg| *vi* chiedere l'elemosina ♦ *vt* chiedere in elemosina; (*favor*) chiedere; (*entreat*) pregare; **I ~ your pardon** (*apologizing*) mi scusi; (*not hearing*) scusi?; **this ~s the question of ...** questo presuppone che sia già risolto il problema di ....
began |bigan'| *pt of* **begin**.
beggar |beg'ûr| *n* (*also:* **~man, ~woman**) mendicante *m/f*.
begin, *pt* **began**, *pp* **begun** |bigin', bigan', bigun'| *vt, vi* cominciare; **to ~ doing** *or* **to do sth** incominciare *or* iniziare a fare qc; **I can't ~ to thank you** non so proprio come ringraziarla; **to ~ with, I'd like to know ...** tanto per cominciare vorrei sapere ...; **~ning from**

Monday a partire da lunedì.
beginner |bigin'ûr| *n* principiante *m/f*.
beginner's slope *n* (SKI) pista per principianti.
beginning |bigin'ing| *n* inizio, principio; **right from the ~** fin dall'inizio.
begrudge |bigruj'| *vt*: **to ~ sb sth** dare qc a qn a malincuore; invidiare qn per qc.
beguile |bigīl'| *vt* (*enchant*) incantare.
beguiling |bigī'ling| *a* (*charming*) allettante; (*deluding*) ingannevole.
begun |bigun'| *pp of* **begin**.
behalf |bihaf'| *n*: **in ~ of**, (*Brit*) **on ~ of** per conto di; a nome di.
behave |bihāv'| *vi* comportarsi; (*well: also:* **~ o.s.**) comportarsi bene.
behavior, (*Brit*) **behaviour** |bihāv'yûr| *n* comportamento, condotta.
behead |bihed'| *vt* decapitare.
beheld |biheld'| *pt, pp of* **behold**.
behind |bihīnd'| *prep* dietro; (*followed by pronoun*) dietro di; (*time*) in ritardo con ♦ *ad* dietro; in ritardo ♦ *n* didietro; **we're ~ them in technology** siamo più indietro *or* più arretrati di loro nella tecnica; **~ the scenes** dietro le quinte; **to be ~ (schedule) with sth** essere indietro con qc; (*payments*) essere in arretrato con qc; **to leave sth ~** dimenticare di prendere qc.
behold |bihōld'| *vt* (*irg: like* **hold**) vedere, scorgere.
beige |bāzh| *a* beige *inv*.
Beijing |bājing'| *n* Pechino *f*.
being |bē'ing| *n* essere *m*; **to come into ~** cominciare ad esistere.
Beirut |bārōōt'| *n* Beirut *f*.
belated |bilā'tid| *a* tardo(a).
belch |belch| *vi* ruttare ♦ *vt* (*gen:* **~ out:** *smoke etc*) eruttare.
beleaguered |bilē'gûrd| *a* (*city*) assediato(a); (*army*) accerchiato(a); (*fig*) assillato(a).
Belfast |bel'fast| *n* Belfast *f*.
belfry |bel'frē| *n* campanile *m*.
Belgian |bel'jən| *a, n* belga (*m/f*).
Belgium |bel'jəm| *n* Belgio.
Belgrade |belgrād'| *n* Belgrado *f*.
belie |bilī'| *vt* smentire; (*give false impression of*) nascondere.
belief |bilēf'| *n* (*opinion*) opinione *f*, convinzione *f*; (*trust, faith*) fede *f*; (*acceptance as true*) credenza; **in the ~ that** nella convinzione che; **it's beyond ~** è incredibile.
believe |bilēv'| *vt, vi* credere; **to ~ in** (*God*) credere in; (*ghosts*) credere a; (*method*) avere fiducia in; **I don't ~ in corporal punishment** sono contrario alle punizioni corporali; **he is ~d to be abroad** si pensa (che) sia all'estero.
believer |bilēv'ûr| *n* (REL) credente *m/f*; (*in idea, activity*): **to be a ~ in** credere in.
belittle |bilit'əl| *vt* sminuire.

Belize [bəlēz'] n Belize m.

bell [bel] n campana; (small, on door, electric) campanello; **that rings a ~** (fig) mi ricorda qualcosa.

bell-bottoms [bel'bâtəmz] npl calzoni mpl a zampa d'elefante.

bellboy [bel'boi] n (Brit) = bellhop.

bellhop [bel'hâp] n (US) ragazzo d'albergo, fattorino d'albergo.

belligerent [bəlij'ûrənt] a (at war) belligerante; (fig) bellicoso(a).

bellow [bel'ō] vi muggire; (cry) urlare (a squarciagola) ♦ vt (orders) urlare (a squarciagola).

bellows [bel'ōz] npl soffietto.

belly [bel'ē] n pancia.

bellyache [bel'ēāk] n mal m di pancia ♦ vi (col) mugugnare.

bellybutton [bel'ēbutən] n ombelico.

belong [bilông'] vi: **to ~ to** appartenere a; (club etc) essere socio di; **this book ~s here** questo libro va qui.

belongings [bilông'ingz] npl cose fpl, roba; **personal ~** effetti mpl personali.

beloved [biluv'id] a adorato(a).

below [bilō'] prep sotto, al di sotto di ♦ ad sotto, di sotto; giù; **see ~** vedi sotto or oltre; **temperatures ~ normal** temperature al di sotto del normale.

belt [belt] n cintura; (TECH) cinghia ♦ vt (thrash) picchiare; **industrial ~** zona industriale.

belt out vt (song) cantare a squarciagola.

belt up vi (Brit col) chiudere la boccaccia.

beltway [belt'wā] n (US AUT) circonvallazione f; (: freeway) autostrada.

bemoan [bimōn'] vt lamentare.

bemused [bimyōōzd'] a perplesso(a), stupito(a).

bench [bench] n panca; (in workshop) banco; **the B~** (LAW) la Corte.

bench mark n banco di prova.

bend [bend] vb (pt, pp **bent** [bent]) vt curvare; (leg, arm) piegare ♦ vi curvarsi; piegarsi ♦ n (Brit: in road) curva; (in pipe, river) gomito.

bend down vi chinarsi.

bend over vi piegarsi.

bends [bendz] npl (MED) embolia.

beneath [binēth'] prep sotto, al di sotto di; (unworthy of) indegno(a) di ♦ ad sotto, di sotto.

benefactor [ben'əfaktûr] n benefattore m.

benefactress [ben'əfaktris] n benefattrice f.

beneficial [benəfish'əl] a che fa bene; **~ to** che giova a.

beneficiary [benəfish'ēārē] n (LAW) beneficiario/a.

benefit [ben'əfit] n beneficio, vantaggio; (allowance of money) indennità f inv ♦ vt far bene a ♦ vi: **he'll ~ from it** ne trarrà beneficio or profitto.

benefit performance n spettacolo di beneficenza.

benefit society n (US) società f inv di mutuo soccorso.

Benelux [ben'əluks] n Benelux m.

benevolent [bənev'ələnt] a benevolo(a).

BEng n abbr (= Bachelor of Engineering) laurea in ingegneria.

benign [binīn'] a benevolo(a); (MED) benigno(a).

bent [bent] pt, pp of **bend** ♦ n inclinazione f ♦ a (wire, pipe) piegato(a), storto(a); (col: dishonest) losco(a); **to be ~ on** essere deciso(a) a.

bequeath [bikwēth'] vt lasciare in eredità.

bequest [bikwest'] n lascito.

bereaved [birēvd'] a in lutto ♦ npl: **the ~** i familiari in lutto.

bereavement [birēv'mənt] n lutto.

beret [bərā'] n berretto.

Bering Sea [bar'ing sē] n: **the ~** il mar di Bering.

Berks abbr (Brit) = Berkshire.

Berlin [bûrlin'] n Berlino f; **East/West ~** Berlino est/ovest.

berm [bûrm] n (US AUT) corsia d'emergenza.

Bermuda [bûrmōō'də] n le Bermude.

Bermuda shorts npl bermuda mpl.

Bern [bûrn] n Berna f.

berry [bär'ē] n bacca.

berserk [bûrsûrk'] a: **to go ~** montare su tutte le furie.

berth [bûrth] n (bed) cuccetta; (for ship) ormeggio ♦ vi (in harbour) entrare in porto; (at anchor) gettare l'ancora; **to give sb a wide ~** (fig) tenersi alla larga da qn.

beseech, pt, pp **besought** [bisēch', bisôt'] vt implorare.

beset, pt, pp **beset** [biset'] vt assalire ♦ a: **a policy ~ with dangers** una politica irta or piena di pericoli.

besetting [biset'ing] a: **his ~ sin** il suo più grande difetto.

beside [bisīd'] prep accanto a; (compared with) rispetto a, in confronto a; **to be ~ o.s. (with anger)** essere fuori di sé; **that's ~ the point** non c'entra.

besides [bisīdz'] ad inoltre, per di più ♦ prep oltre a; (except) a parte.

besiege [bisēj'] vt (town) assediare; (fig) tempestare.

besotted [bisât'id] a: **~ with** infatuato(a) di.

besought [bisôt'] pt, pp of **beseech**.

bespectacled [bispek'təkəld] a occhialuto(a).

best [best] a migliore ♦ ad meglio; **the ~ thing to do is ...** la cosa migliore da fare or fare è ...; **the ~ part of** (quantity) la maggior parte di; **at ~** tutt'al più; **to make the ~ of sth** cavare il meglio possibile da qc; **to do one's ~** fare del proprio meglio;

to the ~ of my knowledge per quel che ne so; to the ~ of my ability al massimo delle mie capacità; he's not exactly patient at the ~ of times non è mai molto paziente.

best man *n* testimone *m* dello sposo.

bestow |bǐstō'| *vt*: to ~ sth on sb conferire qc a qn.

best seller *n* bestseller *m inv*.

bet |bĕt| *n* scommessa ♦ *vt, vi* (*pt, pp* **bet** *or* **betted**) scommettere; **it's a safe ~** (*fig*) è molto probabile.

Bethlehem |bĕth'lēəm| *n* Betlemme *f*.

betray |bǐtrā'| *vt* tradire.

betrayal |bǐtrā'əl| *n* tradimento.

better |bĕt'ûr| *a* migliore ♦ *ad* meglio ♦ *vt* migliorare ♦ *n*: **to get the ~ of** avere la meglio su; **you had ~ do it** è meglio che lo faccia; **he thought ~ of it** cambiò idea; **to get ~** migliorare; **a change for the ~** un cambiamento in meglio; **that's ~!** così va meglio!; **I had ~ go** dovrei andare; **~ off** *a* più ricco(a); (*fig*): **you'd be ~ off this way** starebbe meglio così.

betting |bĕt'ing| *n* scommesse *fpl*.

betting shop *n* (*Brit*) ufficio dell'allibratore.

between |bǐtwēn'| *prep* tra ♦ *ad* in mezzo, nel mezzo; **the road ~ here and Chicago** la strada da qui a Chicago; **we only had $5 ~ us** fra tutti e due avevamo solo 5 dollari.

bevel |bĕv'əl| *n* (*also*: **~(led) edge**) profilo smussato.

beverage |bĕv'ûrij| *n* bevanda.

bevy |bĕv'ē| *n*: **a ~ of** una banda di.

bewail |bǐwāl'| *vt* lamentare.

beware |bǐwär'| *vt, vi*: **to ~ (of)** stare attento(a) (a).

bewildered |bǐwil'dûrd| *a* sconcertato(a), confuso(a).

bewildering |bǐwil'dûring| *a* sconcertante, sbalorditivo(a).

bewitching |bǐwich'ing| *a* affascinante.

beyond |bēǎnd'| *prep* (*in space*) oltre; (*exceeding*) al di sopra di ♦ *ad* di là; **~ doubt** senza dubbio; **~ repair** irreparabile.

b/f *abbr see* **brought forward.**

BFPO *n abbr* (= *British Forces Post Office*) recapito delle truppe britanniche all'estero.

bhp *n abbr* (*AUT*: = *brake horsepower*) c.v. (= *cavallo vapore*).

bi... *prefix* bi....

biannual |bīan'yōōəl| *a* semestrale.

bias |bī'əs| *n* (*prejudice*) pregiudizio; (*preference*) preferenza.

bias(s)ed |bī'əst| *a* parziale; **to be ~ against** essere prevenuto(a) contro.

bib |bib| *n* bavaglino.

Bible |bī'bəl| *n* Bibbia.

bibliography |biblēǎg'rəfē| *n* bibliografia.

bicarbonate of soda |bīkâr'bənit əv sō'də| *n* bicarbonato (di sodio).

bicentenary |bīsĕn'tənärē|, **bicentennial** |bi-

sĕntĕn'ēəl| *n* bicentenario.

biceps |bī'sĕps| *n* bicipite *m*.

bicker |bik'ûr| *vi* bisticciare.

bicycle |bī'sikəl| *n* bicicletta.

bicycle path *n* sentiero ciclabile.

bicycle pump *n* pompa della bicicletta.

bicycle track *n* sentiero ciclabile.

bid |bid| *n* offerta; (*attempt*) tentativo ♦ *vb* (*pt* **bade** |bad| *or* **bid**, *pp* **bidden** |bid'ən| *or* **bid**) *vi* fare un'offerta ♦ *vt* fare un'offerta di; **to ~ sb good day** dire buon giorno a qn.

bidder |bid'ûr| *n*: **the highest ~** il maggior offerente.

bidding |bid'ing| *n* offerte *fpl*.

bide |bīd| *vt*: **to ~ one's time** aspettare il momento giusto.

bidet |bēdā'| *n* bidè *m inv*.

bidirectional |bīdirĕk'shənəl| *a* bidirezionale.

biennial |bīĕn'ēəl| *a* biennale ♦ *n* (pianta) biennale *f*.

bier |bēr| *n* bara.

bifocals |bīfō'kəlz| *npl* occhiali *mpl* bifocali.

big |big| *a* grande; grosso(a); **my ~ brother** mio fratello maggiore; **to do things in a ~ way** fare le cose in grande.

bigamy |big'əmē| *n* bigamia.

big dipper |big dip'ûr| *n* (*Brit*) montagne *fpl* russe, otto *m inv* volante.

big end *n* (*Brit AUT*) testa di biella.

bigheaded |big'hĕdid| *a* presuntuoso(a).

big-hearted |big'hârtid| *a* generoso(a).

bigot |big'ət| *n* persona gretta.

bigoted |big'ətid| *a* gretto(a).

bigotry |big'ətrē| *n* grettezza.

big toe *n* alluce *m*.

big top *n* tendone *m* del circo.

big wheel *n* (*Brit*: *at fair*) ruota (panoramica).

bigwig |big'wig| *n* (*col*) pezzo grosso.

bike |bīk| *n* bici *f inv*.

bike rack *n* (*US*) portabiciclette *m inv*.

bikeway |bīk'wā| *n* (*US*) sentiero ciclabile.

bikini |bǐkē'nē| *n* bikini *m inv*.

bilateral |bīlat'ûrəl| *a* bilaterale.

bile |bīl| *n* bile *f*.

bilingual |bīling'gwəl| *a* bilingue.

bilious |bil'yəs| *a* biliare; (*fig*) bilioso(a).

bill |bil| *n* (*in hotel, restaurant*) conto; (*COMM*) fattura; (*for gas, electricity*) bolletta, conto; (*POL*) atto; (*US: bank note*) banconota; (*notice*) avviso; (*THEATER*): **on the ~** in cartellone; (*of bird*) becco ♦ *vt* mandare il conto a; **may I have the ~ please?** posso avere il conto per piacere?; **"post no ~s"** "divieto di affissione"; **to fit** *or* **fill the ~** (*fig*) fare al caso; **~ of exchange** cambiale *f*, tratta; **~ of lading** polizza di carico; **~ of sale** atto di vendita.

billboard |bil'bôrd| *n* tabellone *m*.

billet |bil'it| *n* alloggio ♦ *vt* (*troops etc*) alloggiare.

billfold [bil'fōld] *n* (*US*) portafoglio.
billiards [bil'yûrdz] *n* biliardo.
billion [bil'yən] *n* (*US*) miliardo; (*Brit*) bilione *m*.
billionaire [bilyənär'] *n* multimiliardario/a.
billow [bil'ō] *n* (*of smoke*) nuvola; (*of sail*) rigonfiamento ♦ *vi* (*smoke*) alzarsi in volute; (*sail*) gonfiarsi.
bills payable (B/P, b.p.) *npl* effetti *mpl* passivi.
bills receivable (B/R, b.r.) *npl* effetti *mpl* attivi.
billy [bil'ē] *n* (*US*) sfollagente *m inv*.
billy goat [bil'ē gōt] *n* caprone *m*, becco.
bin [bin] *n* bidone *m*; (*Brit*: *also*: **dust~**) pattumiera; (: *also*: **litter ~**) cestino.
binary [bī'nûrē] *a* binario(a).
bind, *pt, pp* **bound** [bīnd, bound] *vt* legare; (*oblige*) obbligare.
   bind over *vt* (*LAW*) dare la condizionale a.
   bind up *vt* (*wound*) fasciare, bendare; **to be bound up in** (*work, research etc*) essere completamente assorbito da; **to be bound up with** (*person*) dedicarsi completamente a.
binder [bīn'dûr] *n* (*file*) classificatore *m*.
binding [bīn'ding] *n* (*of book*) legatura ♦ *a* (*contract*) vincolante.
binge [binj] *n* (*col*): **to go on a ~** fare baldoria.
bingo [bing'gō] *n* gioco simile alla tombola.
binoculars [bənák'yəlûrz] *npl* binocolo.
biochemistry [bīōkem'istrē] *n* biochimica.
biodegradable [bīōdigrā'dəbəl] *a* biodegradabile.
biographer [bīág'rəfûr] *n* biografo/a.
biographic(al) [bīəgraf'ik(əl)] *a* biografico(a).
biography [bīág'rəfē] *n* biografia.
biological [bīəlâj'ikəl] *a* biologico(a).
biologist [bīál'əjist] *n* biologo/a.
biology [bīál'əjē] *n* biologia.
biophysics [bīōfiz'iks] *n* biofisica.
biopsy [bī'ápsē] *n* biopsia.
biorhythm [bī'ōriṭḥəm] *n* bioritmo.
biotechnology [bīōteknál'əjē] *n* biotecnologia.
birch [bûrch] *n* betulla.
bird [bûrd] *n* uccello; (*Brit col*: *girl*) bambola.
bird's-eye view [bûrdz'ī vyōō'] *n* vista panoramica.
bird watcher *n* ornitologo/a dilettante.
Biro [bē'rō] ® *n* (*Brit*) biro ® *f inv*.
birth [bûrth] *n* nascita; **to give ~ to** dare alla luce; (*fig*) dare inizio a.
birth certificate *n* certificato di nascita.
birth control *n* controllo delle nascite; contraccezione *f*.
birthday [bûrth'dā] *n* compleanno.
birthmark [bûrth'márk] *n* voglia.
birthplace [bûrth'plās] *n* luogo di nascita.
birth rate [bûrth' rāt] *n* indice *m* di natalità.
Biscay [bis'kā] *n*: **the Bay of ~** il golfo di Biscaglia.

biscuit [bis'kit] *n* (*US*) panino al latte; (*Brit*) biscotto.
bisect [bīsekt'] *vt* tagliare in due (parti); (*MATH*) bisecare.
bishop [bish'əp] *n* vescovo; (*CHESS*) alfiere *m*.
bison [bī'sən] *n* bisonte *m*.
bit [bit] *pt of* **bite** ♦ *n* pezzo; (*of tool*) punta; (*of horse*) morso; (*COMPUT*) bit *m inv*; (*US*: *coin*) ottavo di dollaro; **a ~ of** un po' di; **a ~ mad/dangerous** un po' matto/pericoloso; **~ by ~** a poco a poco; **to do one's ~** fare la propria parte; **to come to ~s** (*break*) andare a pezzi; **bring all your ~s and pieces** porta tutte le tue cose.
bitch [bich] *n* (*dog*) cagna; (*col!*) puttana (!).
bite [bīt] *vt, vi* (*pt* **bit** [bit] , *pp* **bitten** [bit'ən]) mordere ♦ *n* morso; (*insect ~*) puntura; (*mouthful*) boccone *m*; **let's have a ~ (to eat)** mangiamo un boccone; **to ~ one's nails** mangiarsi le unghie.
biting [bī'ting] *a* pungente.
bit part *n* (*THEATER*) particina.
bitten [bit'ən] *pp of* **bite.**
bitter [bit'ûr] *a* amaro(a); (*wind, criticism*) pungente; (*icy*: *weather*) gelido(a) ♦ *n* (*Brit*: *beer*) birra amara; **to the ~ end** a oltranza.
bitterly [bit'ûrlē] *ad* (*disappoint, complain, weep*) amaramente; (*oppose, criticise*) aspramente; (*jealous*) profondamente; **it's ~ cold** fa un freddo gelido.
bitterness [bit'ûrnis] *n* amarezza; gusto amaro.
bittersweet [bit'ûrswēt] *a* agrodolce.
bitty [bit'ē] *a* (*US*: *tiny*) minuscolo(a); (*Brit col*) frammentario(a).
bitumen [bitōō'mən] *n* bitume *m*.
bivouac [biv'ōōak] *n* bivacco.
bizarre [bizár'] *a* bizzarro(a).
bk *abbr* = **bank; book.**
BL *n abbr* (= *Bachelor of Law(s)*, *Bachelor of Letters*) titolo di studio.
b/l *abbr* = **bill of lading.**
blab [blab] *vi* parlare troppo ♦ *vt* (*also*: **~ out**) spifferare.
black [blak] *a* nero(a) ♦ *n* nero; (*person*): **B~** negro/a ♦ *vt* (*Brit INDUSTRY*) boicottare; **~ coffee** caffè *m inv* nero; **to give sb a ~ eye** fare un occhio nero a qn; **in the ~** (*in credit*) in attivo; **there it is in ~ and white** (*fig*) eccolo nero su bianco; **~ and blue** *a* tutto(a) pesto(a).
   black out *vi* (*faint*) svenire.
black belt *n* (*SPORT*) cintura nera; (*US*: *area*): **the ~** *zona abitata principalmente da negri*.
blackberry [blak'bärē] *n* mora.
blackbird [blak'bûrd] *n* merlo.
blackboard [blak'bôrd] *n* lavagna.
black box *n* (*AVIAT*) scatola nera.
blackcurrant [blakkur'ənt] *n* ribes *m inv*.
black economy *n* (*Brit*) economia

sommersa.

blacken [blak'ən] *vt* annerire.

Black Forest *n*: **the ~** la Foresta Nera.

blackhead [blak'hed] *n* punto nero, comedone *m*.

black ice *n* strato trasparente di ghiaccio.

blackjack [blak'jak] *n* (*CARDS*) ventuno; (*US*: *billy*) manganello.

blackleg [blak'leg] *n* (*Brit*) crumiro.

blacklist [blak'list] *n* lista nera ♦ *vt* mettere sulla lista nera.

blackmail [blak'māl] *n* ricatto ♦ *vt* ricattare.

blackmailer [blak'mālûr] *n* ricattatore/trice.

black market *n* mercato nero.

blackout [blak'out] *n* oscuramento; (*fainting*) svenimento; (*TV*) interruzione *f* delle trasmissioni.

Black Sea *n*: **the ~** il mar Nero.

black sheep *n* pecora nera.

blacksmith [blak'smith] *n* fabbro ferraio.

black spot *n* (*Brit AUT*) luogo famigerato per gli incidenti.

bladder [blad'ûr] *n* vescica.

blade [blād] *n* lama; (*of oar*) pala; **~ of grass** filo d'erba.

blame [blām] *n* colpa ♦ *vt*: **to ~ sb/sth for sth** dare la colpa di qc a qn/qc; **who's to ~?** chi è colpevole?; **I'm not to ~** non è colpa mia.

blameless [blām'lis] *a* irreprensibile.

blanch [blanch] *vi* (*person*) sbiancare in viso ♦ *vt* (*CULIN*) scottare.

bland [bland] *a* mite; (*taste*) blando(a).

blank [blangk] *a* bianco(a); (*look*) distratto(a) ♦ *n* spazio vuoto; (*cartridge*) cartuccia a salve; **to draw a ~** (*fig*) non aver nessun risultato.

blank check *n* assegno in bianco; **to give sb a ~ to do** (*fig*) dare carta bianca a qn per fare.

blanket [blang'kit] *n* coperta ♦ *a* (*statement*, *agreement*) globale.

blare [blār] *vi* strombettare; (*radio*) suonare a tutto volume.

blasé [bläzā'] *a* blasé *inv.*

blasphemous [blas'fəməs] *a* blasfemo(a).

blasphemy [blas'fəmē] *n* bestemmia.

blast [blast] *n* (*of wind*) raffica; (*of air, steam*) getto; (*bomb ~*) esplosione *f* ♦ *vt* far saltare ♦ *excl* (*Brit col*) mannaggia!; **(at) full ~** a tutta forza.

blast off *vi* (*SPACE*) essere lanciato(a).

blast-off [blast'ôf] *n* (*SPACE*) lancio.

blatant [blā'tənt] *a* flagrante.

blatantly [blā'təntlē] *ad*: **it's ~ obvious** è lampante.

blaze [blāz] *n* (*fire*) incendio; (*glow: of fire, sun etc*) bagliore *m*; (*fig*) vampata ♦ *vi* (*fire*) ardere, fiammeggiare; (*fig*) infiammarsi ♦ *vt*: **to ~ a trail** (*fig*) tracciare una via nuova; **in a ~ of publicity** circondato da grande pub-

blicità.

blazer [blā'zûr] *n* blazer *m inv.*

bleach [blēch] *n* (*also*: **household ~**) varechina ♦ *vt* (*material*) candeggiare.

bleached [blēcht] *a* (*hair*) decolorato(a).

bleachers [blē'chûrz] *npl* (*US*) posti *mpl* di gradinata.

bleak [blēk] *a* (*prospect, future*) tetro(a); (*landscape*) desolato(a); (*weather*) gelido(a); (*smile*) pallido(a).

bleary-eyed [blē'rēīd] *a* dagli occhi offuscati.

bleat [blēt] *vi* belare.

bleed, *pt*, *pp* **bled** [blēd, bled] *vt* dissanguare; (*brakes, radiator*) spurgare ♦ *vi* sanguinare; **my nose is ~ing** mi viene fuori sangue dal naso.

bleeper [blē'pûr] *n* (*Brit*) = **beeper**.

blemish [blem'ish] *n* macchia.

blend [blend] *n* miscela ♦ *vt* mescolare ♦ *vi* (*colors etc*) armonizzare.

blender [blen'dûr] *n* (*CULIN*) frullatore *m*.

bless, *pt*, *pp* **blessed** or **blest** [bles, blest] *vt* benedire; **~ you!** (*sneezing*) salute!; **to be ~ed with** godere di.

blessed [bles'id] *a* (*REL: holy*) benedetto(a); (*happy*) beato(a); **every ~ day** tutti i santi giorni.

blessing [bles'ing] *n* benedizione *f*; fortuna; **to count one's ~s** ringraziare Iddio, ritenersi fortunato; **it was a ~ in disguise** in fondo è stato un bene.

blest [blest] *pt*, *pp of* **bless**.

blew [bloo] *pt of* **blow**.

blight [blīt] *n* (*of plants*) golpe *f* ♦ *vt* (*hopes etc*) deludere; (*life*) rovinare.

blind [blīnd] *a* cieco(a) ♦ *n* (*for window*) avvolgibile *m*; (*Venetian ~*) veneziana ♦ *vt* accecare; **to turn a ~ eye (on or to)** chiudere un occhio (su).

blind alley *n* vicolo cieco.

blind corner *n* svolta cieca.

blinders [blīn'dûrz] *npl* (*US*) paraocchi *mpl*.

blindfold [blīnd'fōld] *n* benda ♦ *a*, *ad* bendato(a) ♦ *vt* bendare gli occhi a.

blindly [blīnd'lē] *ad* ciecamente.

blindness [blīnd'nis] *n* cecità.

blind spot *n* (*AUT etc*) punto cieco; (*fig*) punto debole.

blink [blingk] *vi* battere gli occhi; (*light*) lampeggiare ♦ *n*: **to be on the ~** (*col*) essere scassato(a).

blinkers [blingk'ûrz] *npl* (*Brit*) = **blinders**.

bliss [blis] *n* estasi *f*.

blissful [blis'fəl] *a* (*event, day*) stupendo(a), meraviglioso(a); (*smile*) beato(a); **in ~ ignorance** nella (più) beata ignoranza.

blissfully [blis'fəlē] *a* (*sigh, smile*) beatamente; **~ happy** magnificamente felice.

blister [blis'tûr] *n* (*on skin*) vescica; (*on paintwork*) bolla ♦ *vi* (*paint*) coprirsi di bolle.

blithe [blīth] *a* gioioso(a), allegro(a).

blithely [blĭth'lē] *ad* allegramente.
blithering [blĭth'ûring] *a* (*col*): **this ~ idiot** questa razza d'idiota.
BLit(t) *n abbr* (= *Bachelor of Literature*) titolo di studio.
blitz [blĭts] *n* blitz *m*; **to have a ~ on sth** (*fig*) prendere d'assalto qc.
blizzard [blĭz'ûrd] *n* bufera di neve.
BLM *n abbr* (*US*: = *Bureau of Land Management*) ≈ il demanio.
bloated [blō'tĭd] *a* gonfio(a).
blob [blŏb] *n* (*drop*) goccia; (*stain, spot*) macchia.
bloc [blŏk] *n* (*POL*) blocco.
block [blŏk] *n* (*gen, COMPUT*) blocco; (*in pipes*) ingombro; (*toy*) cubo; (*of buildings*) isolato; **~ of flats** (*Brit*) caseggiato ♦ *vt* (*gen, COMPUT*) bloccare; **3 ~s from here** a 3 isolati di distanza da qui; **mental ~** blocco mentale.
  block up *vt* bloccare; (*pipe*) ingorgare, intasare.
blockade [blŏkād'] *n* blocco ♦ *vt* assediare.
blockage [blŏk'ĭj] *n* ostacolo.
block and tackle *n* (*TECH*) paranco.
block booking *n* prenotazione *f* in blocco.
blockbuster [blŏk'bustûr] *n* libro *or* film *etc* sensazionale.
block capitals *npl* (*Brit*) stampatello.
blockhead [blŏk'hed] *n* testa di legno.
block letters *npl* stampatello.
block release *n* (*Brit*) *periodo pagato concesso al tirocinante per effettuare studi superiori.*
block vote *n* (*Brit*) voto per delega.
bloke [blōk] *n* (*Brit col*) tizio.
blond [blŏnd] *n* (*man*) biondo ♦ *a* biondo(a).
blonde [blŏnd] *n* (*woman*) bionda ♦ *a* biondo(a).
blood [blud] *n* sangue *m*; **new ~** (*fig*) nuova linfa.
bloodcurdling [blud'kûrdling] *a* raccapricciante, da far gelare il sangue.
blood donor *n* donatore/trice di sangue.
blood group *n* gruppo sanguigno.
bloodhound [blud'hound] *n* segugio.
bloodless [blud'lĭs] *a* (*pale*) smorto(a), esangue; (*coup*) senza spargimento di sangue.
bloodletting [blud'letĭng] *n* (*MED*) salasso; (*fig*) spargimento di sangue.
blood poisoning *n* setticemia.
blood pressure *n* pressione *f* sanguigna; **to have high/low ~** avere la pressione alta/bassa.
blood sausage *n* (*US*) sanguinaccio.
bloodshed [blud'shed] *n* spargimento di sangue.
bloodshot [blud'shŏt] *a*: **~ eyes** occhi iniettati di sangue.
bloodstained [blud'stānd] *a* macchiato(a) di sangue.
bloodstream [blud'strēm] *n* flusso del sangue.
blood test *n* analisi *f inv* del sangue.
bloodthirsty [blud'thûrstē] *a* assetato(a) di sangue.
blood transfusion *n* trasfusione *f* di sangue.
blood vessel *n* vaso sanguigno.
bloody [blud'ē] *a* sanguinoso(a); (*Brit col!*): **this ~ ...** questo maledetto ...; **a ~ awful day** (*col!*) una giornata di merda (*!*); **~ good** (*col!*) maledettamente buono.
bloody-minded [blud'ēmĭn'dĭd] *a* (*Brit col*) indisponente.
bloom [bloom] *n* fiore *m* ♦ *vi* essere in fiore.
blossom [blŏs'əm] *n* fiore *m*; (*with pl sense*) fiori *mpl* ♦ *vi* essere in fiore; **to ~ into** (*fig*) diventare.
blot [blŏt] *n* macchia ♦ *vt* macchiare; **to be a ~ on the landscape** rovinare il paesaggio.
  blot out *vt* (*memories*) cancellare; (*view*) nascondere; (*nation, city*) annientare.
blotchy [blŏch'ē] *a* (*complexion*) coperto(a) di macchie.
blotter [blŏt'ûr] *n* tampone *m* (di carta assorbente).
blotting paper [blŏt'ĭng pā'pûr] *n* carta assorbente.
blouse [blous] *n* camicetta.
blow [blō] *n* colpo ♦ *vb* (*pt* **blew**, *pp* **blown** [blōō, blōn]) *vi* soffiare ♦ *vt* (*fuse*) far saltare; **to come to ~s** venire alle mani; **to ~ one's nose** soffiarsi il naso; **to ~ a whistle** fischiare.
  blow away *vi* volare via ♦ *vt* portare via.
  blow down *vt* abbattere.
  blow off *vt* far volare via; **to ~ off course** far uscire di rotta.
  blow out *vi* scoppiare.
  blow over *vi* calmarsi.
  blow up *vi* saltare in aria ♦ *vt* far saltare in aria; (*tyre*) gonfiare; (*PHOT*) ingrandire.
blow-dry [blō'drī] *n* (*hairstyle*) messa in piega a föhn ♦ *vt* asciugare con il föhn.
blowfly [blō'flī] *n* (*US*) moscone *m*.
blown [blōn] *pp* of **blow**.
blowout [blō'out] *n* (*of tire*) scoppio; (*col: big meal*) abbuffata.
blowtorch [blō'tôrch] *n* lampada a benzina per saldare.
BLS *n abbr* (*US*) = *Bureau of Labor Statistics*.
BLT *n abbr* = *bacon, lettuce and tomato* (*sandwich*).
blubber [blub'ûr] *n* grasso di balena ♦ *vi* (*pej*) piangere forte.
bludgeon [bluj'ən] *vt* prendere a randellate.
blue [bloo] *a* azzurro(a), celeste; (*darker*) blu *inv*; **~ film/joke** film/barzelletta pornografico(a); (**only**) **once in a ~ moon** a ogni morte di papa; **out of the ~** (*fig*) all'improvviso; *see also* **blues**.
blue baby *n* neonato cianotico.

bluebell [bloō'bɛl] *n* giacinto di bosco.
blueberry [bloō'bäre] *n* (*US*) mirtillo.
bluebottle [bloō'bátəl] *n* moscone *m*.
blue cheese *n formaggio tipo gorgonzola*.
blue-chip [bloō'chip'] *a*: ~ **investment** investimento sicuro.
blue-collar worker [bloō'kâl'ûr wûr'kûr] *n* operaio/a.
blue jeans *npl* blue-jeans *mpl*.
blueprint [bloō'print] *n* cianografia; (*fig*): ~ **(for)** formula (di).
blues [bloōz] *npl*: **the** ~ (*MUS*) il blues; **to have the** ~ (*col*: *feeling*) essere a terra.
bluff [bluf] *vi* bluffare ♦ *n* bluff *m inv*; (*promontory*) promontorio scosceso ♦ *a* (*person*) brusco(a); **to call sb's** ~ mettere alla prova il bluff di qn.
blunder [blun'dûr] *n* abbaglio ♦ *vi* prendere un abbaglio; **to** ~ **into sb/sth** andare a sbattere contro qn/qc.
blunt [blunt] *a* (*edge*) smussato(a); (*point*) spuntato(a); (*knife*) che non taglia; (*person*) brusco(a) ♦ *vt* smussare; spuntare; **this pencil is** ~ questa matita non ha più la punta; ~ **instrument** (*LAW*) corpo contundente.
bluntly [blunt'le] *ad* (*speak*) senza mezzi termini.
bluntness [blunt'nis] *n* (*of person*) brutale franchezza.
blur [blûr] *n* cosa offuscata ♦ *vt* offuscare.
blurb [blûrb] *n* trafiletto pubblicitario.
blurred [blûrd] *a* (*photo*) mosso(a); (*TV*) sfuocato(a).
blurt out *vt* lasciarsi sfuggire.
blush [blush] *vi* arrossire ♦ *n* rossore *m*.
blusher [blush'ûr] *n* fard *m inv*.
bluster [blus'tûr] *n* spacconate *fpl*; (*threats*) vuote minacce *fpl* ♦ *vi* fare lo spaccone; minacciare a vuoto.
blustering [blus'tûring] *a* (*tone etc*) da spaccone.
blustery [blus'tûre] *a* (*weather*) burrascoso(a).
Blvd *abbr* = **boulevard**.
BM *n abbr* (*SCOL*: = *Bachelor of Medicine*) titolo di studio.
BMA *n abbr* = *British Medical Association*.
BMus *n abbr* (= *Bachelor of Music*) titolo di studio.
BO *n abbr* (*col* = *body odor*) odori *mpl* sgradevoli (del corpo); (*US*) = **box office**.
boar [bôr] *n* cinghiale *m*.
board [bôrd] *n* tavola; (*on wall*) tabellone *m*; (*for chess etc*) scacchiera; (*committee*) consiglio, comitato; (*in firm*) consiglio d'amministrazione; (*NAUT, AVIAT*): **on** ~ a bordo ♦ *vt* (*ship*) salire a bordo di; (*train*) salire su; **full** ~ (*Brit*) pensione *f* completa; **half** ~ (*Brit*) mezza pensione; ~ **and lodging** vitto e alloggio; **above** ~ (*fig*) regolare; **across the** ~ (*fig: ad*) per tutte le categorie;

(: *a*) generale; **to go by the** ~ venir messo(a) da parte.
board up *vt* (*door*) chiudere con assi.
boarder [bôr'dûr] *n* pensionante *m/f*; (*SCOL*) convittore/trice.
board game *n* gioco da tavolo.
boardinghouse [bôr'dinghous] *n* pensione *f*.
boarding pass [bôr'ding pas] *n* (*AVIAT, NAUT*) carta d'imbarco.
boarding school [bôr'ding skoōl] *n* collegio.
board meeting *n* riunione *f* di consiglio.
board room *n* sala del consiglio.
boardwalk [bôrd'wôk] *n* (*US*) passeggiata a mare.
boast [bôst] *vi*: **to** ~ **(about *or* of)** vantarsi (di) ♦ *vt* vantare ♦ *n* vanteria; vanto.
boastful [bôst'fəl] *a* vanaglorioso(a).
boastfulness [bôst'fəlnis] *n* vanagloria.
boat [bôt] *n* nave *f*; (*small*) barca; **to go by** ~ andare in barca *or* in nave; **we're all in the same** ~ (*fig*) siamo tutti nella stessa barca.
boater [bô'tûr] *n* (*hat*) paglietta.
boating [bô'ting] *n* canottaggio.
boatswain [bô'sən] *n* nostromo.
bob [bâb] *vi* (*boat, cork on water: also*: ~ **up and down**) andare su e giù ♦ *n* (*Brit col*) = **shilling**.
bob up *vi* saltare fuori.
bobbin [bâb'in] *n* bobina; (*of sewing machine*) rocchetto.
bobby [bâb'e] *n* (*Brit col*) ≈ poliziotto.
bobby pin [bâb'e pin] *n* (*US*) forcina.
bobsled [bâb'sled] *n* (*US*) bob *m inv*.
bobsleigh [bâb'slā] *n* (*Brit*) = **bobsled**.
bode [bôd] *vi*: **to** ~ **well/ill (for)** essere di buon/cattivo auspicio (per).
bodice [bâd'is] *n* corsetto.
bodily [bâd'əle] *a* (*comfort, needs*) materiale; (*pain*) fisico(a) ♦ *ad* (*carry*) in braccio; (*lift*) di peso.
body [bâd'e] *n* corpo; (*of car*) carrozzeria; (*of plane*) fusoliera; (*organization*) associazione *f*, organizzazione *f*; (*quantity*) quantità *f inv*; (*of speech, document*) parte *f* principale; (*also*: ~ **stocking**) calzamaglia intera; **in a** ~ in massa; **ruling** ~ direttivo; **a wine with** ~ un vino corposo.
body-building [bâd'ebil'ding] *n* culturismo.
bodyguard [bâd'egârd] *n* guardia del corpo.
body repairs *npl* (*AUT*) lavori *mpl* di carrozzeria.
bodywork [bâd'ewûrk] *n* carrozzeria.
boffin [bâf'in] *n* (*Brit*) scienziato.
bog [bâg] *n* palude *f* ♦ *vt*: **to get ~ged down** (*fig*) impantanarsi.
bogey [bô'ge] *n* (*worry*) spauracchio; (*also*: ~ **man**) *n* *m inv*.
boggle [bâg'əl] *vi*: **the mind ~s** è incredibile.
Bogotà [bôgətâ'] *n* Bogotà *f*.
bogus [bô'gəs] *a* falso(a); finto(a).

Bohemia |bōhē'mēə| *n* Boemia.
Bohemian |bōhē'mēən| *a*, *n* boemo(a).
boil |boil| *vt*, *vi* bollire ♦ *n* (*MED*) foruncolo; **to come to a** *or* (*Brit*) **the** ~ raggiungere l'ebollizione; **to bring to a** *or* (*Brit*) **the** ~ portare a ebollizione; ~**ed egg** uovo alla coque; ~**ed potatoes** patate *fpl* bollite *or* lesse. **boil down** *vi* (*fig*): **to** ~ **down to** ridursi a. **boil over** *vi* traboccare (bollendo).
boiler |boi'lûr| *n* caldaia.
boiler suit *n* (*Brit*) tuta.
boiling |boi'ling| *a* bollente; **I'm** ~ (**hot**) (*col*) sto morendo di caldo.
boiling point *n* punto di ebollizione.
boisterous |bois'tûrəs| *a* chiassoso(a).
bold |bōld| *a* audace; (*child*) impudente; (*outline*) chiaro(a); (*color*) deciso(a).
boldness |bōld'nis| *n* audacia; impudenza.
bold type *n* (*TYP*) neretto, grassetto.
Bolivia |bōliv'ēə| *n* Bolivia.
Bolivian |bōliv'ēən| *a*, *n* boliviano(a).
bollard |bâl'ûrd| *n* (*NAUT*) bitta; (*Brit AUT*) colonnina luminosa.
bolster |bōl'stûr| *n* capezzale *m*.
bolster up *vt* sostenere.
bolt |bōlt| *n* chiavistello; (*with nut*) bullone *m* ♦ *ad*: ~ **upright** diritto(a) come un fuso ♦ *vt* serrare; (*food*) mangiare in fretta ♦ *vi* scappare via; **a** ~ **from the blue** (*fig*) un fulmine a ciel sereno.
bomb |bâm| *n* bomba ♦ *vt* bombardare.
bombard |bâmbârd'| *vt* bombardare.
bombardment |bâmbârd'mənt| *n* bombardamento.
bombastic |bâmbas'tik| *a* ampolloso(a).
bomb disposal *n*: ~ **expert** artificiere *m*; ~ **unit** corpo degli artificieri.
bomber |bâm'ûr| *n* bombardiere *m*; (*terrorist*) dinamitardo/a.
bombing |bâm'ing| *n* bombardamento.
bombshell |bâm'shcl| *n* (*fig*) notizia bomba.
bomb site *n* luogo bombardato.
bona fide |bō'nə fīd'| *a* sincero(a); (*offer*) onesto(a).
bonanza |bənan'zə| *n* cuccagna.
bond |bând| *n* legame *m*; (*binding promise, FINANCE*) obbligazione *f*; **in** ~ (*of goods*) in attesa di sdoganamento.
bondage |bân'dij| *n* schiavitù *f*.
bonded warehouse |bân'did wär'hous| *n* magazzino doganale.
bone |bōn| *n* osso; (*of fish*) spina, lisca ♦ *vt* disossare; togliere le spine a.
bone up on *vt* sgobbare su.
bone china *n* porcellana fine.
bone-dry |bōn'drī'| *a* asciuttissimo(a).
bone idle *a*: **to be** ~ essere un(a) fannullone(a).
boner |bō'nûr| *n* (*US*) gaffe *f inv*.
bonfire |bân'fīûr| *n* falò *m inv*.
Bonn |bân| *n* Bonn *f*.

bonnet |bân'it| *n* cuffia; (*Brit*: *of car*) cofano.
bonny |bân'ē| *a* (*esp Scottish*) bello(a), carino(a).
bonus |bō'nəs| *n* premio; (*on wages*) gratifica.
bony |bō'nē| *a* (*thin*: *person*) ossuto(a), angoloso(a); (*arm, face, MED*: *tissue*) osseo(a); (*meat*) pieno(a) di ossi; (*fish*) pieno(a) di spine.
boo |bōō| *excl* ba! ♦ *vt* fischiare ♦ *n* fischio.
boob |bōōb| *n* (*col*: *breast*) tetta; (: *Brit*: *mistake*) gaffe *f inv*.
boo-boo |bōō'bōō| *n* (*US*) gaffe *f inv*.
booby prize |bōō'bē prīz| *n* premio per il peggior contendente.
booby trap |bōō'bē trap| *n* trabocchetto; (*bomb*) congegno che esplode al contatto.
booby-trapped |bōō'bētrapt| *a*: **a** ~ **car** una macchina con dell'esplosivo a bordo.
book |bōōk| *n* libro; (*of stamps etc*) blocchetto ♦ *vt* (*ticket, seat, room*) prenotare; (*driver*) multare; (*football player*) ammonire; ~**s** *npl* (*COMM*) conti *mpl*; **to keep the** ~**s** (*COMM*) tenere la contabilità; **by the** ~ secondo le regole; **to throw the** ~ **at sb** incriminare qn seriamente *or* con tutte le aggravanti.
book in *vi* (*Brit*: *at hotel*) prendere una camera.
book up *vt* riservare, prenotare; **the hotel is** ~**ed up** l'albergo è al completo; **all seats are** ~**ed up** è tutto esaurito.
bookable |bōōk'əbəl| *a*: **seats are** ~ si possono prenotare i posti.
bookcase |bōōk'kās| *n* scaffale *m*.
book ends *npl* reggilibri *mpl*.
booking |bōōk'ing| *n* (*Brit*) prenotazione *f*.
booking office |bōōk'ing ôf'is| *n* (*Brit*) biglietteria.
book-keeping |bōōkkē'ping| *n* contabilità.
booklet |bōōk'lit| *n* opuscolo, libretto.
bookmaker |bōōk'mākûr| *n* allibratore *m*.
bookseller |bōōk'sclûr| *n* libraio.
bookshop |bōōk'shâp| *n* libreria.
bookstall |bōōk'stôl| *n* (*Brit*) bancarella di libri.
bookstore |bōōk'stôr| *n* libreria.
book token *n* (*Brit*) buono *m* libri *inv*.
book value *n* valore *m* contabile.
boom |bōōm| *n* (*noise*) rimbombo; (*busy period*) boom *m inv* ♦ *vi* rimbombare; andare a gonfie vele.
boomerang |bōō'mərang| *n* boomerang *m inv* ♦ *vi* (*fig*) avere effetto contrario; **to** ~ **on sb** (*fig*) ritorcersi contro qn.
boom town *n* città *f inv* in rapidissima espansione.
boon |bōōn| *n* vantaggio.
boorish |bōō'rish| *a* maleducato(a).
boost |bōōst| *n* spinta ♦ *vt* spingere; (*increase*: *sales, production*) incentivare; **to give a** ~ **to** (*morale*) tirar su; **it gave a** ~ **to his confidence** è stata per lui un'iniezione

di fiducia.

booster [bōōs'tûr] *n* (*ELEC*) amplificatore *m*; (*TV*) amplificatore *m* di segnale; (*also*: ~ **rocket**) razzo vettore; (*MED*) richiamo.

booster seat *n* (*Brit AUT*: *for children*) seggiolino di sicurezza.

boot [bōōt] *n* stivale *m*; (*ankle* ~) stivaletto; (*for hiking*) scarpone *m* da montagna; (*for football etc*) scarpa; (*US*: *also*: **Denver** ~) morsetto *m* bloccaruota *inv*; (*Brit*: *of car*) portabagagli *m inv* ♦ *vt* (*COMPUT*) inizializzare; **to** ~ (*in addition*) per giunta, in più; **to give sb the** ~ (*col*) mettere qn alla porta.

booth [bōōth] *n* (*at fair*) baraccone *m*; (*of cinema, telephone etc*) cabina; (*also*: **voting** ~) cabina (elettorale).

bootleg [bōōt'leg] *a* di contrabbando; ~ **record** registrazione *f* pirata *inv*.

bootlicker [bōōt'likûr] *n* (*col*) leccapiedi *m/f inv*.

booty [bōō'tē] *n* bottino.

booze [bōōz] (*col*) *n* alcool *m* ♦ *vi* trincare.

boozer [bōōz'ûr] *n* (*col*: *person*) beone *m*.

border [bôr'dûr] *n* orlo; margine *m*; (*of a country*) frontiera; **the B~** *la frontiera tra l'Inghilterra e la Scozia*; **the B~s** *la zona di confine tra l'Inghilterra e la Scozia*.

border on *vt fus* confinare con.

borderline [bôr'dûrlīn] *n* (*fig*) linea di demarcazione ♦ *a*: ~ **case** caso limite.

bore [bôr] *pt of* **bear** ♦ *vt* (*hole*) perforare; (*person*) annoiare ♦ *n* (*of gun*) calibro; **he's ~d to tears** *or* ~**d to death** *or* ~**d stiff** è annoiato a morte, si annoia da morire.

boredom [bôr'dəm] *n* noia.

boring [bôr'ing] *a* noioso(a).

born [bôrn] *a*: **to be** ~ nascere; **I was** ~ **in 1960** sono nato nel 1960; ~ **blind** cieco dalla nascita; **a** ~ **comedian** un comico nato.

borne [bôrn] *pp of* **bear**.

Borneo [bôr'nēō] *n* Borneo.

borough [bur'ə] *n* comune *m*.

borrow [bâr'ō] *vt*: **to** ~ **sth (from sb)** prendere in prestito qc (da qn); **may I** ~ **your car?** può prestarmi la macchina?

borrower [bâr'ōûr] *n* (*gen*) chi prende a prestito; (*ECON*) mutuatario/a.

borrowing [bâr'ōing] *n* prestito.

bosom [bōōz'əm] *n* petto; (*fig*) seno.

bosom friend *n* amico/a del cuore.

boss [bôs] *n* capo ♦ *vt* (*also*: ~ **around**) comandare a bacchetta; **stop** ~**ing everyone around!** smettila di dare ordini a tutti!

bossy [bôs'ē] *a* prepotente.

bosun [bō'sən] *n* nostromo.

botanical [bətan'ikəl] *a* botanico(a).

botanist [bât'ənist] *n* botanico/a.

botany [bât'ənē] *n* botanica.

botch [bâch] *vt* fare un pasticcio di.

both [bōth] *a* entrambi(e), tutt'e due ♦ *pro-*

noun: ~ (**of them**) entrambi(e); ~ **of us went, we** ~ **went** ci siamo andati tutt'e due ♦ *ad*: **they sell** ~ **meat and poultry** vendono insieme la carne ed il pollame.

bother [bâth'ûr] *vt* (*worry*) preoccupare; (*annoy*) infastidire ♦ *vi* (*gen*: ~ **o.s.**) preoccuparsi ♦ *n*: **it is a** ~ **to have to do** è una seccatura dover fare ♦ *excl* uffa!, accidenti!; **to** ~ **doing sth** darsi la pena di fare qc; **I'm sorry to** ~ **you** mi dispiace disturbarla; **please don't** ~ non si scomodi; **it's no** ~ non c'è problema.

Botswana [bâchwân'ə] *n* Botswana *m*.

bottle [bât'əl] *n* bottiglia; (*of perfume, shampoo etc*) flacone *m*; (*baby's*) biberon *m inv* ♦ *vt* imbottigliare; ~ **of wine/milk** bottiglia di vino/latte; **wine/milk** ~ bottiglia da vino/del latte.

bottle up *vt* contenere.

bottle-fed [bât'əlfed] *a* allattato(a) artificialmente.

bottleneck [bât'əlnek] *n* ingorgo.

bottle opener *n* apribottiglie *m inv*.

bottom [bât'əm] *n* fondo; (*of mountain, tree, hill*) piedi *mpl*; (*buttocks*) sedere *m* ♦ *a* più basso(a); ultimo(a); **at the** ~ **of** in fondo a; **to get to the** ~ **of sth** (*fig*) andare al fondo di *or* in fondo a qc.

bottom line *n* (*fig*): **the** ~ **is** ... la conclusione è ....

bottomless [bât'əmlis] *a* senza fondo.

bough [bou] *n* ramo.

bought [bôt] *pt, pp of* **buy**.

bouillon cube [bōōl'yən kyōōb] *n* (*US CULIN*) dado.

boulder [bōl'dûr] *n* masso (tondeggiante).

boulevard [vōōl'əvârd] *n* viale *m*.

bounce [bouns] *vi* (*ball*) rimbalzare; (*check*) essere restituito(a) ♦ *vt* far rimbalzare ♦ *n* (*rebound*) rimbalzo; **to** ~ **in** entrare di slancio *or* con foga; **he's got plenty of** ~ (*fig*) è molto esuberante.

bouncer [boun'sûr] *n* buttafuori *m inv*.

bound [bound] *pt, pp of* **bind** ♦ *n* (*gen pl*) limite *m*; (*leap*) salto ♦ *vi* (*leap*) saltare; (*limit*) delimitare ♦ *a*: **to be** ~ **to do sth** (*obliged*) essere costretto(a) a fare qc; **he's** ~ **to fail** (*likely*) è certo di fallire; ~ **for** diretto(a) a; **out of** ~**s** il cui accesso è vietato.

boundary [boun'dûrē] *n* confine *m*.

boundless [bound'lis] *a* illimitato(a).

bountiful [boun'təfəl] *a* (*person*) munifico(a); (*God*) misericordioso(a); (*supply*) abbondante.

bounty [boun'tē] *n* (*generosity*) liberalità, munificenza; (*reward*) taglia.

bounty hunter *n* cacciatore *m* di taglie.

bouquet [bōōkā'] *n* bouquet *m inv*.

bourbon [bûr'bən] *n* (*US*: *also*: ~ **whiskey**) bourbon *m inv*.

bourgeois [bōōr'zhwâ] *a, n* borghese (*m/f*).

bout [bout] *n* periodo; (*of malaria etc*) attacco; (*BOXING etc*) incontro.

boutique [bōōtēk'] *n* boutique *f inv*.

bow *n* [bō] nodo; (*weapon*) arco; (*MUS*) archetto; (*NAUT*: *also*: ~**s**) prua; [bou] (*with body*) inchino ♦ *vi* [bou] inchinarsi; (*yield*): **to** ~ **to** *or* **before** sottomettersi a; **to** ~ **to the inevitable** rassegnarsi all'inevitabile.

bowels [bou'əlz] *npl* intestini *mpl*; (*fig*) viscere *fpl*.

bowl [bōl] *n* (*for eating*) scodella; (*for washing*) bacino; (*ball*) boccia; (*of pipe*) fornello; (*US*: *stadium*) stadio ♦ *vi* (*CRICKET*) servire (la palla); *see also* **bowls**.

bowl over *vt* (*fig*) sconcertare.

bow-legged [bō'legid] *a* dalle gambe storte.

bowler [bō'lûr] *n* giocatore *m* di bocce; (*CRICKET*) giocatore che serve la palla; (*Brit*: *also*: ~ **hat**) bombetta.

bowling [bō'ling] *n* (*game*) gioco delle bocce; bowling *m*.

bowling alley *n* pista da bowling.

bowling green *n* campo di bocce.

bowls [bōlz] *n* (*Brit*) gioco delle bocce.

bow tie [bō tī] *n* cravatta a farfalla.

box [báks] *n* scatola; (*also*: **cardboard** ~) (scatola di) cartone *m*; (*crate*; *also for money*) cassetta; (*THEATER*) palco; (*Brit AUT*) area d'incrocio ♦ *vi* fare pugilato ♦ *vt* mettere in (una) scatola; (*SPORT*) combattere contro.

boxcar [báks'kâr] *n* (*US RAIL*) vagone *m* (merci).

boxer [bâk'sûr] *n* (*person*) pugile *m*; (*dog*) boxer *m inv*.

boxing [bâk'sing] *n* (*SPORT*) pugilato.

Boxing Day *n* (*Brit*) Santo Stefano.

boxing gloves *npl* guantoni *mpl* da pugile.

boxing ring *n* ring *m inv*.

box number *n* (*Brit*: *for advertisements*) casella.

box office *n* biglietteria.

boy [boi] *n* ragazzo; (*small*) bambino; (*son*) figlio; (*servant*) servo.

boycott [boi'kât] *n* boicottaggio ♦ *vt* boicottare.

boyfriend [boi'frend] *n* ragazzo.

boyish [boi'ish] *a* di *or* da ragazzo.

Bp *abbr* = **bishop**.

BPOE *n abbr* (*US*: *Benevolent and Protective Order of Elks*) organizzazione filantropica.

BR *abbr see* **British Rail**.

bra [brâ] *n* reggipetto, reggiseno.

brace [brās] *n* sostegno; (*on teeth*) apparecchio correttore; (*tool*) trapano; (*TYP*: *also*: *Brit*: ~ **bracket**) graffa ♦ *vt* rinforzare, sostenere; **to** ~ **o.s.** (*fig*) farsi coraggio; *see also* **braces**.

bracelet [brās'lit] *n* braccialetto.

braces [brā'siz] *npl* (*US*: *on teeth*) apparecchio correttore; (*Brit*) bretelle *fpl*.

bracing [brā'sing] *a* invigorante.

bracken [brak'ən] *n* felce *f*.

bracket [brak'it] *n* (*TECH*) mensola; (*group*) gruppo; (*TYP*) parentesi *f inv* ♦ *vt* mettere fra parentesi; (*fig*: *also*: ~ **together**) mettere insieme; **in** ~**s** tra parentesi; **round** ~**s** (*Brit*) parentesi tonde; **square** ~**s** parentesi quadre; **income** ~ fascia di reddito.

brackish [brak'ish] *a* (*water*) salmastro(a).

brag [brag] *vi* vantarsi.

braid [brād] *n* (*trimming*) passamano; (*of hair*) treccia.

Braille [brāl] *n* braille *m*.

brain [brān] *n* cervello; ~**s** *npl* cervella *fpl*; **he's got** ~**s** è intelligente.

brainchild [brān'chīld] *n* creatura, creazione *f*.

brainless [brān'lis] *a* deficiente, stupido(a).

brainstorm [brān'stôrm] *n* (*fig*) attacco di pazzia; (*US*: *brain wave*) lampo di genio.

brainwash [brān'wâsh] *vt* fare un lavaggio di cervello a.

brain wave [brān' wāv] *n* lampo di genio.

brainy [brā'nē] *a* intelligente.

braise [brāz] *vt* brasare.

brake [brāk] *n* (*on vehicle*) freno ♦ *vt*, *vi* frenare.

brake light *n* (fanalino dello) stop *m inv*.

brake pedal *n* pedale *m* del freno.

bramble [bram'bəl] *n* rovo; (*fruit*) mora.

bran [bran] *n* crusca.

branch [branch] *n* ramo; (*COMM*) succursale *f*, filiale *f* ♦ *vi* diramarsi.

branch out *vi*: **to** ~ **out into** intraprendere una nuova attività nel ramo di.

branch line *n* (*RAIL*) linea secondaria.

branch manager *n* direttore *m* di filiale.

brand [brand] *n* marca ♦ *vt* (*cattle*) marcare (a ferro rovente); (*fig*: *pej*): **to** ~ **sb a communist** *etc* definire qn come comunista *etc*.

brandish [bran'dish] *vt* brandire.

brand name *n* marca.

brand-new [brand'nōō'] *a* nuovo(a) di zecca.

brandy [bran'dē] *n* brandy *m inv*.

brash [brash] *a* sfacciato(a).

Brasilia [brəzil'ēə] *n* Brasilia.

brass [bras] *n* ottone *m*; **the** ~ (*MUS*) gli ottoni.

brass band *n* fanfara.

brassière [brəzēr'] *n* reggipetto, reggiseno.

brass knuckles *npl* tirapugni *m inv*.

brass tacks *npl*: **to get down to** ~ (*col*) venire al sodo.

brat [brat] *n* (*pej*) marmocchio, monello/a.

bravado [brəvâ'dō] *n* spavalderia.

brave [brāv] *a* coraggioso(a) ♦ *n* guerriero *m* pellerossa *inv* ♦ *vt* affrontare.

bravery [brā'vûrē] *n* coraggio.

bravo [brâ'vō] *excl* bravo!, bene!

brawl [brôl] *n* rissa ♦ *vi* azzuffarsi.

brawn [brôn] *n* muscolo; (*Brit*: *meat*) carne *f*

di testa di maiale.

brawny [brô'nē] *a* muscoloso(a).

bray [brā] *n* raglio ♦ *vi* ragliare.

brazen [brā'zən] *a* svergognato(a) ♦ *vt*: **to ~ it out** fare lo sfacciato.

brazier [brā'zhûr] *n* braciere *m*.

Brazil [brəzil'] *n* Brasile *m*.

Brazilian [brəzil'ēən] *a*, *n* brasiliano(a).

Brazil nut *n* noce *f* del Brasile.

breach [brēch] *vt* aprire una breccia in ♦ *n* (*gap*) breccia, varco; (*estrangement*) rottura; (*of duty*) abuso; (*breaking*): **~ of contract** rottura di contratto; **~ of the peace** violazione *f* dell'ordine pubblico; **~ of trust** abuso di fiducia.

bread [bred] *n* pane *m*; (*col: money*) grana; **to earn one's daily ~** guadagnarsi il pane; **to know which side one's ~ is buttered on** saper fare i propri interessi; **~ and butter** *n* pane e burro; (*fig*) mezzi *mpl* di sussistenza.

breadbin [bred'bin] *n* (*Brit*) cassetta *f* portapane *inv*.

breadboard [bred'bôrd] *n* tagliere *m* (*per il pane*); (*COMPUT*) pannello per esperimenti.

breadbox [bred'bâks] *n* (*US*) cassetta *f* portapane *inv*.

breadcrumbs [bred'krumz] *npl* briciole *fpl*; (*CULIN*) pangrattato.

breadline [bred'līn] *n*: **to be on the ~** avere appena denaro per vivere.

breadth [bredth] *n* larghezza.

breadwinner [bred'winûr] *n* chi guadagna il pane per tutta la famiglia.

break [brāk] *vb* (*pt* **broke** , *pp* **broken** [brōk, brō'kən]) *vt* rompere; (*law*) violare; (*promise*) mancare a ♦ *vi* rompersi; (*weather*) cambiare ♦ *n* (*gap*) breccia; (*fracture*) rottura; (*rest, also SCOL*) intervallo; (: *short*) pausa; (*chance*) possibilità *f inv*; (*vacation*) vacanza; **to ~ one's leg** *etc* rompersi la gamba *etc*; **to ~ a record** battere un primato; **to ~ the news to sb** comunicare per primo la notizia a qn; **to ~ with sb** (*fig*) rompere con qn; **to ~ even** *vi* coprire le spese; **to ~ free** *or* **loose** liberarsi; **without a ~** senza una pausa; **to have** *or* **take a ~** (*few minutes*) fare una pausa; (*vacation*) prendere un po' di riposo; **a lucky ~** un colpo di fortuna.

break down *vt* (*figures, data*) analizzare; (*door etc*) buttare giù, abbattere; (*resistance*) stroncare ♦ *vi* crollare; (*MED*) avere un esaurimento (nervoso); (*AUT*) guastarsi.

break in *vt* (*horse etc*) domare; (*US: car*) rodare, fare il rodaggio di ♦ *vi* (*burglar*) fare irruzione.

break into *vt fus* (*house*) fare irruzione in.

break off *vi* (*speaker*) interrompersi; (*branch*) troncarsi ♦ *vt* (*talks, engagement*) rompere.

break open *vt* (*door etc*) sfondare.

break out *vi* evadere; **to ~ out in spots**

coprirsi di macchie.

break through *vi*: **the sun broke through** il sole ha fatto capolino tra le nuvole ♦ *vt* (*defences, barrier*) sfondare, penetrare in; (*crowd*) aprirsi un varco in *or* tra, aprirsi un passaggio in *or* tra.

break up *vi* (*partnership*) sciogliersi; (*friends*) separarsi ♦ *vt* fare in pezzi, spaccare; (*fight etc*) interrompere, far cessare; (*marriage*) finire.

breakable [brā'kəbəl] *a* fragile; **~s** *npl* oggetti *mpl* fragili.

breakage [brā'kij] *n* rottura; **to pay for ~s** pagare i danni.

breakaway [brā'kəwā] *a* (*group etc*) scissionista, dissidente.

break-dancing [brāk'dansing] *n* breakdance *f*.

breakdown [brāk'doun] *n* (*AUT*) guasto; (*in communications*) interruzione *f*; (*MED: also*: **nervous ~**) esaurimento nervoso; (*of payments etc*) resoconto.

breakdown service *n* (*Brit*) servizio riparazioni.

breakdown van *n* (*Brit*) carro *m* attrezzi *inv*.

breaker [brā'kûr] *n* frangente *m*.

breakeven [brākē'vən] *cpd*: **~ chart** *n* diagramma *m* del punto di rottura *or* pareggio; **~ point** *n* punto di rottura *or* pareggio.

breakfast [brek'fəst] *n* colazione *f*.

breakfast cereal *n* fiocchi *mpl* d'avena *or* di mais *etc*.

break-in [brāk'in] *n* irruzione *f*.

breaking point [brā'king point] *n* punto di rottura.

breakthrough [brāk'thrōō] *n* (*MIL*) breccia; (*fig*) passo avanti.

break-up [brāk'up] *n* (*of partnership, marriage*) rottura.

break-up value *n* (*COMM*) valore *m* di realizzo.

breakwater [brāk'wôtûr] *n* frangiflutti *m inv*.

breast [brest] *n* (*of woman*) seno; (*chest*) petto.

breast-feed [brest'fēd] *vt, vi* (*irg: like* **feed**) allattare (al seno).

breast pocket *n* taschino.

breast-stroke *n* nuoto a rana.

breath [breth] *n* fiato; **out of ~** senza fiato; **to go out for a ~ of air** andare a prendere una boccata d'aria.

Breathalyzer [breth'əlīzûr] *n* ® alcoltest *m inv*.

breathe [brēth] *vt, vi* respirare; **I won't ~ a word about it** non fiaterò.

breathe in *vi* inspirare ♦ *vt* respirare.

breathe out *vt, vi* espirare.

breather [brē'thûr] *n* attimo di respiro.

breathing [brē'thing] *n* respiro, respirazione *f*.

breathing space *n* (*fig*) attimo di respiro.

breathless [breth'lis] *a* senza fiato; (*with ex-*

citement) con il fiato sospeso.
breathtaking [breth'tāking] *a* sbalorditivo(a).
breed [brēd] *vb* (*pt, pp* **bred** [bred]) *vt* allevare; (*fig: hate, suspicion*) generare, provocare ♦ *vi* riprodursi ♦ *n* razza, varietà *f inv*.
breeder [brē'dûr] *n* (*PHYSICS: also:* ~ **reactor**) reattore *m* autofertilizzante.
breeding [brē'ding] *n* riproduzione *f*; allevamento.
breeze [brēz] *n* brezza.
breeze block *n* (*Brit*) = **cinder block**.
breezy [brē'zē] *a* arioso(a); allegro(a).
Breton [bret'an] *a, n* brettone (*m/f*).
brevity [brev'itē] *n* brevità.
brew [brōō] *vt* (*tea*) fare un infuso di; (*beer*) fare; (*plot*) tramare ♦ *vi* (*tea*) essere in infusione; (*beer*) essere in fermentazione; (*fig*) bollire in pentola.
brewer [brōō'ûr] *n* birraio.
brewery [brōō'ûrē] *n* fabbrica di birra.
briar [brī'ûr] *n* (*thorny bush*) rovo; (*wild rose*) rosa selvatica.
bribe [brīb] *n* bustarella ♦ *vt* comprare; **to** ~ **sb to do sth** pagare qn sottobanco perché faccia qc.
bribery [brī'bûrē] *n* corruzione *f*.
bric-a-brac [brik'abrak] *n* bric-a-brac *m*.
brick [brik] *n* mattone *m*.
bricklayer [brik'lāûr] *n* muratore *m*.
brickwork [brik'wûrk] *n* muratura in mattoni.
brickyard [brik'yârd] *n* fabbrica di mattoni.
bridal [brīd'al] *a* nuziale; ~ **party** corteo nuziale.
bride [brīd] *n* sposa.
bridegroom [brīd'grōōm] *n* sposo.
bridesmaid [brīdz'mād] *n* damigella d'onore.
bridge [brij] *n* ponte *m*; (*NAUT*) ponte di comando; (*of nose*) dorso; (*CARDS, DENTISTRY*) bridge *m inv* ♦ *vt* (*river*) fare un ponte sopra; (*gap*) colmare.
bridge loan, (*Brit*) **bridging loan** [brij'ing lōn] *n* anticipazione *f* sul mutuo.
bridle [brīd'al] *n* briglia ♦ *vt* tenere a freno; (*horse*) mettere la briglia a ♦ *vi* (*in anger etc*) adombrarsi, adontarsi.
bridle path *n* sentiero (per cavalli).
brief [brēf] *a* breve ♦ *n* (*LAW*) comparsa ♦ *vt* (*MIL etc*) dare istruzioni a; **in** ~ ... in breve ..., a farla breve ...; **to** ~ **sb (about sth)** mettere qn al corrente (di qc); *see also* **briefs**.
briefcase [brēf'kās] *n* cartella.
briefing [brē'fing] *n* istruzioni *fpl*.
briefly [brēf'lē] *ad* (*speak, visit*) brevemente; (*glimpse*) di sfuggita.
briefness [brēf'nis] *n* brevità.
briefs [brēfs] *npl* mutande *fpl*.
Brig. *abbr* = **brigadier**.
brigade [brigād'] *n* (*MIL*) brigata.
brigadier [brigadi'ûr] *n* generale *m* di brigata.
bright [brīt] *a* luminoso(a); (*person*) sve-

glio(a); (*color*) vivace; **to look on the** ~ **side** vedere il lato positivo delle cose.
brighten [brīt'an] (*also:* ~ **up**) *vt* (*room*) rendere luminoso(a); rallegrare ♦ *vi* schiarirsi; (*person*) rallegrarsi.
brightly [brīt'lē] *ad* (*shine*) vivamente, intensamente; (*smile*) radiosamente; (*talk*) con animazione.
brilliance [bril'yans] *n* splendore *m*; (*fig: of person*) genialità, talento.
brilliant [bril'yant] *a* brillante; (*sunshine*) sfolgorante.
brim [brim] *n* orlo.
brimful [brim'fōōl'] *a* pieno(a) *or* colmo(a) fino all'orlo; (*fig*) pieno(a).
brine [brīn] *n* acqua salmastra; (*CULIN*) salamoia.
bring, *pt, pp* **brought** [bring, brôt] *vt* portare; **to** ~ **sth to an end** mettere fine a qc; **I can't** ~ **myself to fire him** non so risolvermi a licenziarlo.
bring about *vt* causare.
bring around *vt* (*US: unconscious person*) far rinvenire.
bring back *vt* riportare.
bring down *vt* (*lower*) far scendere; (*shoot down*) abbattere; (*government*) far cadere.
bring forward *vt* portare avanti; (*in time*) anticipare; (*BOOK-KEEPING*) riportare.
bring in *vt* (*person*) fare entrare; (*object*) portare; (*POL: bill*) presentare; (: *legislation*) introdurre; (*LAW: verdict*) emettere; (*produce: income*) rendere.
bring off *vt* (*task, plan*) portare a compimento; (*deal*) concludere.
bring out *vt* (*meaning*) mettere in evidenza; (*new product*) lanciare; (*book*) pubblicare, fare uscire.
bring round *or* **to** *vt* (*Brit*) = **bring around**.
bring up *vt* allevare; (*question*) introdurre.
brink [bringk] *n* orlo; **on the** ~ **of doing sth** sul punto di fare qc; **she was on the** ~ **of tears** era lì lì per piangere.
brisk [brisk] *a* (*person, tone*) spiccio(a), sbrigativo(a); (: *abrupt*) brusco(a); (*wind*) fresco(a); (*trade etc*) vivace, attivo(a); **to go for a** ~ **walk** fare una camminata di buon passo; **business is** ~ gli affari vanno bene.
bristle [bris'al] *n* setola ♦ *vi* rizzarsi; **bristling with** irto(a) di.
bristly [bris'lē] *a* (*chin*) ispido(a); (*beard, hair*) irsuto(a), setoloso(a).
Brit [brit] *n abbr* (*col:* = *British person*) britannico/a.
Britain [brit'in] *n* Gran Bretagna.
British [brit'ish] *a* britannico(a); **the** ~ *npl* i Britannici; **the** ~ **Isles** *npl* le Isole Britanniche.
British Rail (BR) *n compagnia ferroviaria britannica,* ≈ Ferrovie *fpl* dello Stato (F.S.).

Briton |brit'ən| *n* britannico/a.

Brittany |brit'ənē| *n* Bretagna.

brittle |brit'əl| *a* fragile.

Br(o) *abbr* (*REL*) = **brother**.

broach |brōch| *vt* (*subject*) affrontare.

broad |brôd| *a* largo(a); (*distinction*) generale; (*accent*) spiccato(a) ♦ *n* (*US col*) bellona; ~ **hint** allusione *f* esplicita; **in ~ daylight** in pieno giorno; **the ~ outlines** le grandi linee.

broad bean *n* fava.

broadcast |brôd'kast| *n* trasmissione *f* ♦ *vb* (*pt, pp* **broadcast**) *vt* trasmettere per radio (*or* per televisione) ♦ *vi* fare una trasmissione.

broadcasting |brôd'kasting| *n* radiodiffusione *f*; televisione *f*.

broadcasting station *n* stazione *f* trasmittente.

broaden |brôd'ən| *vt* allargare ♦ *vi* allargarsi.

broadly |brôd'lē| *ad* (*fig*) in generale.

broad-minded |brôd'mīn'did| *a* di mente aperta.

broccoli |brāk'əlē| *n* (*BOT*) broccolo; (*CULIN*) broccoli *mpl*.

brochure |brōshōōr'| *n* dépliant *m inv*.

brogue |brōg| *n* (*shoe*) scarpa rozza in cuoio; (*accent*) accento irlandese.

broil |broil| *vt* cuocere a fuoco vivo.

broke |brōk| *pt of* **break** ♦ *a* (*col*) squattrinato(a); **to go ~** fare fallimento.

broken |brō'kən| *pp of* **break** ♦ *a* (*gen*) rotto(a); (*stick, promise, vow*) spezzato(a); (*marriage*) fallito(a); **he comes from a ~ home** i suoi sono divisi; **in ~ French/English** in un francese/inglese stentato.

broken-down |brō'kəndoun'| *a* (*car*) in panne, rotto(a); (*machine*) guasto(a), fuori uso; (*house*) abbandonato(a), in rovina.

brokenhearted |brō'kənhâr'tid| *a*: **to be ~** avere il cuore spezzato.

broker |brō'kûr| *n* agente *m*.

brokerage |brō'kûrij| *n* (*COMM*) commissione *f* di intermediazione.

brolly |brál'ē| *n* (*Brit col*) ombrello.

bronchitis |brāngkī'tis| *n* bronchite *f*.

bronze |brānz| *n* bronzo.

bronzed |brānzd| *a* abbronzato(a).

brooch |brōch| *n* spilla.

brood |brōōd| *n* covata ♦ *vi* (*hen*) covare; (*person*) rimuginare.

broody |brōō'dē| *a* (*fig*) cupo(a) e taciturno(a).

brook |brōōk| *n* ruscello.

broom |brōōm| *n* scopa.

broomstick |brōōm'stik| *n* manico di scopa.

Bros. *abbr* (*COMM*: = *brothers*) F.lli (= *Fratelli*).

broth |brôth| *n* brodo.

brothel |bráth'əl| *n* bordello.

brother |bruth'ûr| *n* fratello.

brotherhood |bruth'ûrhōōd| *n* fratellanza;

confraternità *f inv*.

brother-in-law |bruth'ûrinlô| *n* cognato.

brotherly |bruth'ûrlē| *a* fraterno(a).

brought |brôt| *pt, pp of* **bring**.

brought forward (b/f) *a* (*COMM*) riportato(a).

brow |brou| *n* fronte *f*; (*rare, gen*: **eye~**) sopracciglio; (*of hill*) cima.

browbeat |brou'bēt| *vt* intimidire.

brown |broun| *a* bruno(a), marrone; (*hair*) castano(a) ♦ *n* (*color*) color *m* bruno *or* marrone ♦ *vt* (*CULIN*) rosolare; **to go ~** (*person*) abbronzarsi; (*leaves*) ingiallire.

brown bread *n* pane *m* integrale, pane nero.

brownie |brou'nē| *n* giovane esploratrice *f*; (*US*: *cake*) dolcetto di cioccolato e frutta secca.

brownnose(r) |broun'nōz'(ûr)| *n* (*US col*) leccapiedi *m/f inv*.

brown paper *n* carta da pacchi *or* da imballaggio.

brown rice *n* riso greggio.

brown sugar *n* zucchero greggio.

browse |brouz| *vi* (*animal*) brucare; (*in bookshop etc*) curiosare ♦ *n*: **to have a ~ (around)** dare un'occhiata (in giro); **to ~ through a book** sfogliare un libro.

bruise |brōōz| *n* ammaccatura; (*on person*) livido ♦ *vt* ammaccare; (*leg etc*) farsi un livido a; (*fig*: *feelings*) urtare ♦ *vi* (*fruit*) ammaccarsi.

brunch |brunch| *n* ricca colazione consumata in tarda mattinata.

brunette |brōōnet'| *n* bruna.

brunt |brunt| *n*: **the ~ of** (*attack, criticism etc*) il peso maggiore di.

brush |brush| *n* spazzola; (*quarrel*) schermaglia ♦ *vt* spazzolare; (*gen*: ~ **past**, ~ **against**) sfiorare; **to have a ~ with sb** (*verbally*) avere uno scontro con qn; (*physically*) venire a diverbio *or* alle mani con qn; **to have a ~ with the police** avere delle noie con la polizia.

brush aside *vt* scostare.

brush up *vt* (*knowledge*) rinfrescare.

brushed |brusht| *a* (*TECH*: *steel, chrome etc*) sabbiato(a); (*nylon, denim etc*) pettinato(a).

brush-off |brush'ôf| *n*: **to give sb the ~** dare il ben servito a qn.

brushwood |brush'wōōd| *n* macchia.

brusque |brusk| *a* (*person, manner*) brusco(a); (*tone*) secco(a).

Brussels |brus'əlz| *n* Bruxelles *f*.

Brussels sprout *n* cavolo di Bruxelles.

brutal |brōōt'əl| *a* brutale.

brutality |brōōtal'itē| *n* brutalità.

brute |brōōt| *n* bestia; **by ~ force** con la forza, a viva forza.

brutish |brōō'tish| *a* da bruto.

BS *n abbr* (*US*: = *Bachelor of Science*) titolo di studio.

bs *abbr* = **bill of sale.**
BSc *n abbr see* **Bachelor of Science.**
BSI *n abbr* (= *British Standards Institution*) associazione per la normalizzazione.
BST *abbr* (= *British Summer Time*) *ora legale*.
btu *n abbr* (= *British thermal unit*) Btu *m* (= *1054.2 joules*).
bubble [bub'əl] *n* bolla ♦ *vi* ribollire; (*sparkle, fig*) essere effervescente.
bubble bath *n* bagno *m* schiuma *inv*.
Bucharest [bōō'kûrest] *n* Bucarest *f*.
buck [buk] *n* maschio (*di camoscio, caprone, coniglio etc*); (*US col*) dollaro ♦ *vi* sgroppare; **to pass the ~ (to sb)** scaricare (su di qn) la propria responsabilità.
buck up *vi* (*cheer up*) rianimarsi ♦ *vt*: **to ~ one's ideas up** mettere la testa a partito.
bucket [buk'it] *n* secchio.
buckle [buk'əl] *n* fibbia ♦ *vt* affibbiare; (*warp*) deformare.
buckle down *vi* mettersi sotto.
buckle up *vi* (*AUT*) allacciare la cintura di sicurezza.
Bucks *abbr* (*Brit*) = *Buckinghamshire.*
bud [bud] *n* gemma; (*of flower*) boccio ♦ *vi* germogliare; (*flower*) sbocciare.
Budapest [bōō'dəpest] *n* Budapest *f*.
Buddha [bōō'də] *n* Budda *m*.
Buddhism [bōō'dizəm] *n* buddismo.
Buddhist [bōō'dist] *a*, *n* buddista (*m/f*).
budding [bud'ing] *a* (*flower*) in boccio; (*poet etc*) in erba.
buddy [bud'ē] *n* (*US*) compagno.
budge [buj] *vt* scostare ♦ *vi* spostarsi.
budgerigar [buj'ûrēgâr] *n* (*Brit*) pappagallino.
budget [buj'it] *n* bilancio preventivo ♦ *vi*: **to ~ for sth** fare il bilancio per qc; **I'm on a tight ~** devo contare la lira; **she works out her ~ every month** fa il preventivo delle spese ogni mese.
budgie [buj'ē] *n* (*Brit*) = **budgerigar.**
Buenos Aires [bwā'nəs ī'riz] *n* Buenos Aires *f*.
buff [buf] *a* color camoscio *inv* ♦ *n* (*enthusiast*) appassionato/a.
buffalo, *pl* **~** *or* **~es** [buf'əlō] *n* (*US*) bisonte *m*; bufalo.
buffer [buf'ûr] *n* respingente *m*; (*COMPUT*) memoria tampone, buffer *m inv*.
buffering [buf'ûring] *n* (*COMPUT*) bufferizzazione *f*, memorizzazione *f* transitoria.
buffer state *n* stato cuscinetto.
buffet *n* [bōōfā'] (*food, bar*) buffet *m inv* ♦ *vt* [buf'it] schiaffeggiare; scuotere; urtare.
buffet car [bōōfā' kâr] *n* (*Brit RAIL*) ≈ servizio ristoro.
buffet lunch [bōōfā' lunch] *n* pranzo in piedi.
buffoon [bufōōn'] *n* buffone *m*.
bug [bug] *n* (*insect*) cimice *f*; (: *gen*) insetto; (*fig: germ*) virus *m inv*; (*spy device*) microfono spia; (*COMPUT*) bug *m inv*, errore *m* nel

programma ♦ *vt* mettere sotto controllo; (*room*) installare microfoni spia in; (*annoy*) scocciare; **I've got the travel ~** (*fig*) mi è presa la mania dei viaggi.
bugbear [bug'bär] *n* spauracchio.
bugle [byōō'gəl] *n* tromba.
build [bild] *n* (*of person*) corporatura ♦ *vt* (*pt, pp* **built** [bilt]) costruire.
build on *vt fus* (*fig*) prendere il via da.
build up *vt* (*establish: business*) costruire; (: *reputation*) fare, consolidare; (*increase: production*) allargare, incrementare; **don't ~ your hopes up too soon** non sperarci troppo.
builder [bil'dûr] *n* costruttore *m*.
building [bil'ding] *n* costruzione *f*; edificio; (*also:* **~ trade**) edilizia.
building contractor *n* costruttore *m*, imprenditore *m* (edile).
building industry *n* industria edilizia.
building site *n* cantiere *m* di costruzione.
building society *n* (*Brit*) società *f inv* immobiliare.
building trade *n* = **building industry.**
build-up [bild'up] *n* (*of gas etc*) accumulo; (*publicity*): **to give sb/sth a good ~** fare buona pubblicità a qn/qc.
built [bilt] *pt, pp of* **build**; **well-~** robusto(a).
built-in [bilt'in'] *a* (*closet*) a muro; (*device*) incorporato(a).
built-up area [bilt'up är'ēə] *n* abitato.
bulb [bulb] *n* (*BOT*) bulbo; (*ELEC*) lampadina.
bulbous [bul'bəs] *a* bulboso(a).
Bulgaria [bulgär'ēə] *n* Bulgaria.
Bulgarian [bulgär'ēən] *a* bulgaro(a) ♦ *n* bulgaro/a; (*LING*) bulgaro.
bulge [bulj] *n* rigonfiamento; (*in birth rate, sales*) punta ♦ *vi* essere protuberante *or* rigonfio(a); **to be bulging with** essere pieno(a) *or* zeppo(a) di.
bulk [bulk] *n* massa, volume *m*; **the ~ of** il grosso di; **(to buy) in ~** (comprare) in grande quantità.
bulk buying [bulk bī'ing] *n* acquisto di merce in grande quantità.
bulkhead [bulk'hed] *n* paratia.
bulky [bul'kē] *a* grosso(a); voluminoso(a).
bull [bōōl] *n* toro; (*STOCK EXCHANGE*) rialzista *m/f*; (*REL*) bolla (papale).
bulldog [bōōl'dôg] *n* bulldog *m inv*.
bulldoze [bōōl'dōz] *vt* aprire *or* spianare col bulldozer; **I was ~d into doing it** (*fig col*) mi ci hanno costretto con la prepotenza.
bulldozer [bōōl'dōzûr] *n* bulldozer *m inv*.
bullet [bōōl'it] *n* pallottola.
bulletin [bōōl'itən] *n* bollettino.
bulletin board *n* tabellone *m* per affissi; (*COMPUT*) bulletin board *m inv*.
bullet-proof [bōōl'itprōōf] *a* a prova di proiettile; **~ vest** giubbotto antiproiettile.
bullfight [bōōl'fit] *n* corrida.
bullfighter [bōōl'fitûr] *n* torero.

bullfighting [boŏl'fīting] *n* tauromachia.

bullhorn [boŏl'hôrn] *n* (*US*) portavoce *m inv*.

bullion [boŏl'yən] *n* oro *or* argento in lingotti.

bullock [boŏl'ək] *n* giovenco.

bullring [boŏl'ring] *n* arena (per corride).

bull's-eye [boŏlz'ī] *n* centro del bersaglio.

bully [boŏl'ē] *n* prepotente *m* ♦ *vt* angariare; (*frighten*) intimidire.

bullying [boŏl'ēing] *n* prepotenze *fpl*.

bum [bum] *n* (*col*: *backside*) culo; (*tramp*) vagabondo/a; (*US*: *idler*) fannullone/a.

bum around *vi* (*col*) fare il vagabondo.

bumblebee [bum'bəlbē] *n* (*ZOOL*) bombo.

bumf [bumf] *n* (*Brit col*: *forms etc*) scartoffie *fpl*.

bump [bump] *n* (*blow*) colpo; (*jolt*) scossa; (*noise*) botto; (*on road etc*) protuberanza; (*on head*) bernoccolo ♦ *vt* battere; (*car*) urtare, sbattere.

bump along *vi* procedere sobbalzando.

bump into *vt fus* scontrarsi con; (*col*: *meet*) imbattersi in, incontrare per caso.

bumper [bum'pûr] *n* paraurti *m inv* ♦ *a*: ~ **harvest** raccolto eccezionale.

bumper cars *npl* autoscontri *mpl*.

bumptious [bump'shəs] *a* presuntuoso(a).

bumpy [bum'pē] *a* (*road*) dissestato(a); (*journey*, *flight*) movimentato(a).

bun [bun] *n* focaccia; (*of hair*) crocchia.

bunch [bunch] *n* (*of flowers*, *keys*) mazzo; (*of bananas*) ciuffo; (*of people*) gruppo; ~ **of grapes** grappolo d'uva.

bundle [bun'dəl] *n* fascio ♦ *vt* (*also*: ~ **up**) legare in un fascio; (*put*): **to** ~ **sth/sb into** spingere qc/qn in.

bundle off *vt* (*person*) mandare via in gran fretta.

bundle out *vt* far uscire (senza tante cerimonie).

bung [bung] *n* tappo ♦ *vt* (*Brit*: *throw*: *also*: ~ **into**) buttare; (*also*: ~ **up**: *pipe*, *hole*) tappare, otturare.

bungalow [bung'gəlō] *n* bungalow *m inv*.

bungle [bung'gəl] *vt* abborracciare.

bunion [bun'yən] *n* callo (al piede).

bunk [bungk] *n* cuccetta.

bunk beds *npl* letti *mpl* a castello.

bunker [bung'kûr] *n* (*coal store*) ripostiglio per il carbone; (*MIL*, *GOLF*) bunker *m inv*.

bunny [bun'ē] *n* (*also*: ~ **rabbit**) coniglietto.

bunny girl *n* coniglietta.

bunny hill *n* (*US SKI*) pista per principianti.

bunting [bun'ting] *n* pavesi *mpl*, bandierine *fpl*.

buoy [boŏ'ē] *n* boa.

buoy up *vt* tenere a galla; (*fig*) sostenere.

buoyancy [boi'ənsē] *n* (*of ship*) galleggiabilità.

buoyant [boi'ənt] *a* galleggiante; (*fig*) vivace; (*COMM*: *market*) sostenuto(a); (*prices*, *currency*) stabile.

burden [bûr'dən] *n* carico, fardello ♦ *vt* caricare; (*oppress*) opprimere; **to be a** ~ **to sb** essere di peso a qn.

bureau, *pl* ~**x** [byoŏr'ō, -z] *n* (*US*: *chest of drawers*) cassettone *m*; (*Brit*: *writing desk*) scrivania; (*office*) ufficio, agenzia.

bureaucracy [byoŏrák'rəsē] *n* burocrazia.

bureaucrat [byoŏr'əkrat] *n* burocrate *m/f*.

bureaucratic [byoŏrəkrat'ik] *a* burocratico(a).

burgeon [bûr'jən] *vi* svilupparsi rapidamente.

burglar [bûr'glûr] *n* scassinatore *m*.

burglar alarm *n* antifurto *m inv*.

burglarize [bûr'glərīz] *vt* (*US*) svaligiare.

burglary [bûr'glûrē] *n* furto con scasso.

burgle [bûr'gəl] *vt* svaligiare.

Burgundy [bûr'gəndē] *n* Borgogna.

burial [bär'ēəl] *n* sepoltura.

burial ground *n* cimitero.

burly [bûr'lē] *a* robusto(a).

Burma [bûr'mə] *n* Birmania.

Burmese [bûrmēz'] *a* birmano(a) ♦ *n* (*pl inv*) birmano/a; (*LING*) birmano.

burn [bûrn] *vt*, *vi* (*pt*, *pp* **burned** *or* **burnt** [bûrnt]) bruciare ♦ *n* bruciatura, scottatura; (*MED*) ustione *f*; **I've** ~**ed myself!** mi sono bruciato!; **the cigarette** ~**ed a hole in her dress** si è fatta un buco nel vestito con la sigaretta.

burn down *vt* distruggere col fuoco.

burn out *vt* (*subj*: *writer etc*): **to** ~ **o.s. out** esaurirsi.

burner [bûr'nûr] *n* fornello.

burning [bûr'ning] *a* (*building*, *forest*) in fiamme; (*issue*, *question*) scottante.

burnish [bûr'nish] *vt* brunire.

burnt [bûrnt] *pt*, *pp* *of* **burn**.

burp [bûrp] (*col*) *n* rutto ♦ *vi* ruttare.

burrow [bûr'ō] *n* tana ♦ *vt* scavare.

bursar [bûr'sûr] *n* economo/a; (*Brit*: *student*) borsista *m/f*.

bursary [bûr'sûrē] *n* (*Brit*) borsa di studio.

burst [bûrst] *vb* (*pt*, *pp* **burst**) *vt* far scoppiare *or* esplodere ♦ *vi* esplodere; (*tyre*) scoppiare ♦ *n* scoppio; (*also*: ~ **pipe**) rottura nel tubo, perdita; ~ **of energy/laughter** scoppio d'energia/di risa; **a** ~ **of applause** uno scroscio d'applausi; **a** ~ **of speed** uno scatto (di velocità); ~ **blood vessel** rottura di un vaso sanguigno; **the river has** ~ **its banks** il fiume ha rotto gli argini o ha straripato; **to** ~ **into flames/tears** scoppiare in fiamme/lacrime; **to be** ~**ing with** essere pronto a scoppiare di; **to** ~ **out laughing** scoppiare a ridere; **to** ~ **open** aprirsi improvvisamente; (*door*) spalancarsi.

burst into *vt fus* (*room etc*) irrompere in.

burst out of *vt fus* precipitarsi fuori da.

bury [bär'ē] *vt* seppellire; **to** ~ **one's face in one's hands** nascondere la faccia tra le mani; **to** ~ **one's head in the sand** (*fig*) fare (la politica dello) struzzo; **to** ~ **the hatchet**

(fig) seppellire l'ascia di guerra.
bus, ~**es** [bus, bus'iz] *n* autobus *m inv.*
bush [boosh] *n* cespuglio; *(scrub land)* macchia.
bushel [boosh'əl] *n* staio.
bushy [boosh'ē] *a (plant, tail, beard)* folto(a); *(eyebrows)* irsuto(a).
busily [biz'ilē] *ad* con impegno, alacremente.
business [biz'nis] *n (matter)* affare *m*; *(trading)* affari *mpl*; *(firm)* azienda; *(job, duty)* lavoro; **to be away on** ~ essere andato via per affari; **I'm here on** ~ sono qui per affari; **to do** ~ **with sb** fare affari con qn; **he's in the insurance** ~ lavora nel campo delle assicurazioni; **it's none of my** ~ questo non mi riguarda; **he means** ~ non scherza.
business address *n* indirizzo di lavoro *or* d'ufficio.
business card *n* biglietto da visita della ditta.
business hours *npl* orario d'ufficio.
businesslike [biz'nislīk] *a* serio(a); efficiente.
businessman [biz'nisman] *n* uomo d'affari.
business suit *n* completo da uomo.
business trip *n* viaggio d'affari.
businesswoman [biz'niswoomən] *n* donna d'affari.
busker [bus'kûr] *n (Brit)* suonatore/trice ambulante.
bus lane *n* corsia riservata agli autobus.
bus shelter *n* pensilina *(alla fermata dell'autobus).*
bus station *n* stazione *f* delle autolinee, autostazione *f.*
bus stop *n* fermata d'autobus.
bust [bust] *n (ART)* busto; *(bosom)* seno ♦ *a (broken)* rotto(a) ♦ *vt (col: POLICE: arrest)* pizzicare, beccare; **to go** ~ fallire.
bustle [bus'əl] *n* movimento, attività ♦ *vi* darsi da fare.
bustling [bus'ling] *a (person)* indaffarato(a); *(town)* animato(a).
bust-up [bust'up] *n (Brit col)* lite *f.*
busy [biz'ē] *a* occupato(a); *(shop, street)* molto frequentato(a) ♦ *vt:* **to** ~ **o.s.** darsi da fare; **he's a** ~ **man** *(normally)* è un uomo molto occupato; *(temporarily)* ha molto da fare, è molto occupato.
busybody [biz'ēbâdē] *n* ficcanaso *m/f inv.*
busy signal *n (US)* segnale *m* di occupato.
but [but] *cj* ma ♦ *prep* eccetto, tranne; **no one** ~ **him** solo lui; **nothing** ~ null'altro che; ~ **for** senza, se non fosse per; **all** ~ **finished** quasi finito; **anything** ~ **finished** tutt'altro che finito.
butane [byoo'tān] *n (also:* ~ **gas)** butano.
butcher [booch'ûr] *n* macellaio ♦ *vt* macellare; ~**'s (shop)** macelleria.
butler [but'lûr] *n* maggiordomo.
butt [but] *n (cask)* grossa botte *f*; *(thick end)* estremità *f inv* più grossa; *(of gun)* calcio; *(of cigarette)* mozzicone *m*; *(US col)* culo;

(Brit fig: target) oggetto ♦ *vt* cozzare.
butt in *vi (interrupt)* interrompere.
butter [but'ûr] *n* burro ♦ *vt* imburrare.
buttercup [but'ûrkup] *n* ranuncolo.
butter dish *n* burriera.
butterfingers [but'ûrfinggûrz] *n (col)* mani *fpl* di ricotta.
butterfly [but'ûrflī] *n* farfalla; *(SWIMMING: also:* ~ **stroke)** (nuoto a) farfalla.
buttocks [but'əks] *npl* natiche *fpl.*
button [but'ən] *n* bottone *m* ♦ *vt (also:* ~ **up)** abbottonare ♦ *vi* abbottonarsi.
buttonhole [but'ənhōl] *n* asola, occhiello ♦ *vt (person)* attaccar bottone a.
buttress [but'tris] *n* contrafforte *m.*
buxom [buk'səm] *a* formoso(a).
buy [bī] *vt (pt, pp* **bought** [bôt])* comprare, acquistare ♦ *n:* **a good/bad** ~ un buon/cattivo acquisto *or* affare; **to** ~ **sb sth/sth from sb** comprare qc per qn/qc da qn; **to** ~ **sb a drink** offrire da bere a qn.
buy back *vt* riprendersi, prendersi indietro.
buy in *vt (Brit: goods)* far provvista di.
buy into *vt fus (COMM)* acquistare delle azioni di.
buy off *vt (col: bribe)* comprare.
buy out *vt (business)* rilevare.
buy up *vt* accaparrare.
buyer [bī'ûr] *n* compratore/trice; ~**'s market** mercato favorevole ai compratori.
buzz [buz] *n* ronzio; *(col: phone call)* colpo di telefono ♦ *vi* ronzare ♦ *vt (call on intercom)* chiamare al citofono; *(: with buzzer)* chiamare col cicalino; *(AVIAT: plane, building)* passare rasente; **my head is** ~**ing** mi gira la testa.
buzzard [buz'ûrd] *n* poiana.
buzzer [buz'ûr] *n* cicalino.
buzz word *n (col)* termine *m* in voga.
by [bī] *prep* da; *(beside)* accanto a; vicino a, presso; *(before)* ~ **4 o'clock** entro le 4 ♦ *ad see* **pass, go** *etc*; **surrounded** ~ **enemies** circondato(a) da nemici; **a painting** ~ **Picasso** un quadro di Picasso; ~ **bus/car** in autobus/macchina; **paid** ~ **the hour** pagato(a) a ore; **to increase** *etc* ~ **the hour** aumentare di ora in ora; **to pay** ~ **check** pagare con (un) assegno; ~ **the kilo/meter** a chili/metri; **a room 3 meters** ~ **4** una stanza di 3 metri per 4; **it missed me** ~ **inches** mi ha mancato per un millimetro; ~ **saving hard, he ...** risparmiando molto, lui ...; **(all)** ~ **oneself** tutto(a) solo(a); ~ **the way** a proposito; ~ **and large** nell'insieme; ~ **and** ~ di qui a poco *or* presto.
bye(-bye) [bī'(-bī')] *excl* ciao!, arrivederci!
by(e)-law [bī'lô] *n* legge *f* locale.
by-election [bī'ilekshən] *n* elezione *f* straordinaria.
bygone [bī'gôn] *a* passato(a) ♦ *n:* **let** ~**s be** ~**s** mettiamoci una pietra sopra.

bypass [bĭ'pas] *n* circonvallazione *f*; (*MED*) by-pass *m inv* ♦ *vt* fare una deviazione intorno a.

by-product [bĭ'prâdǝkt] *n* sottoprodotto; (*fig*) conseguenza secondaria.

bystander [bĭ'standûr] *n* spettatore/trice.

byte [bīt] *n* (*COMPUT*) byte *m inv*.

byway [bĭ'wā] *n* strada secondaria.

byword [bĭ'wûrd] *n*: **to be a ~ for** essere sinonimo di.

by-your-leave [bĭyo͞orlēv'] *n*: **without so much as a ~** senza nemmeno chiedere il permesso.

C

C, c [sē] *n* (*letter*) C, c *f or m inv*; (*SCOL*: *grade*) ≈ 6 (*sufficiente*); (*MUS*): **C** do; **~ for Charlie** ≈ C come Como.

C *abbr* (= *Celsius, centigrade*) C.

c. *abbr* (= *century*) sec.; (= *circa*) c; (*US etc*) = cent(s).

CA *abbr* = **Central America**; (*US MAIL*) = *California* ♦ *n abbr* = **chartered accountant**.

ca. *abbr* (= *circa*) ca.

c/a *abbr* = **capital account; credit account; current account.**

CAA *n abbr* (*US*: = *Civil Aeronautics Authority*, *Brit*: = *Civil Aviation Authority*) organismo di controllo e di sviluppo dell'aviazione civile.

cab [kab] *n* taxi *m inv*; (*of train, truck*) cabina; (*horsedrawn*) carrozza.

cabaret [kabǝrā'] *n* cabaret *m inv*.

cabbage [kab'ij] *n* cavolo.

cabin [kab'in] *n* capanna; (*on ship*) cabina.

cabin cruiser *n* cabinato.

cabinet [kab'ǝnit] *n* (*POL*) consiglio dei ministri; (*furniture*) armadietto; (*also*: **display** **~**) vetrinetta; **cocktail ~** (*Brit*) mobile *m* bar *inv*.

cabinet-maker [kab'ǝnitmākûr] *n* stipettaio.

cabinet minister *n* ministro (*membro del Consiglio*).

cable [kā'bǝl] *n* cavo; fune *f*; (*TEL*) cablogramma *m* ♦ *vt* telegrafare.

cable car *n* funivia.

cablegram [kā'bǝlgram] *n* cablogramma *m*.

cable railway *n* funicolare *f*.

cable television *n* televisione *f* via cavo.

caboose [kǝbo͞os'] *n* (*US RAIL*) vagone *m* di servizio.

cache [kash] *n* nascondiglio; **a ~ of food** *etc* un deposito segreto di viveri *etc*.

cackle [kak'ǝl] *vi* schiamazzare.

cactus, ** *pl* **cacti [kak'tǝs, -tī] *n* cactus *m inv*.

CAD *n abbr* (= *computer-aided design*) progettazione *f* con l'ausilio dell'elaboratore.

caddie [kad'ē] *n* caddie *m inv*.

cadet [kǝdet'] *n* (*MIL*) cadetto; **police ~** allievo poliziotto.

cadge [kaj] *vt* (*col*) scroccare; **to ~ a meal** **(off sb)** scroccare un pranzo (a qn).

cadre [kâd'rǝ] *n* quadro.

Caesarean [sizär'ēǝn] *a* (*Brit*) = **Cesarean**.

CAF *abbr* (= *cost and freight*) Caf *m*.

café [kafā'] *n* caffè *m inv*.

cafeteria [kafitē'rēǝ] *n* self-service *m inv*.

caffein(e) [ka'fēn] *n* caffeina.

cage [kāj] *n* gabbia ♦ *vt* mettere in gabbia.

cagey [kā'jē] *a* (*col*) chiuso(a); guardingo(a).

cagoule [kǝgo͞ol'] *n* (*Brit*) K-way ® *m inv*.

CAI *n abbr* (= *computer-aided instruction*) istruzione *f* assistita dall'elaboratore.

Cairo [kī'rō] *n* il Cairo.

cajole [kǝjōl'] *vt* allettare.

cake [kāk] *n* torta; **~ of soap** saponetta; **it's a piece of ~** (*col*) è una cosa da nulla; **he wants to have his ~ and eat it too** (*fig*) vuole la botte piena e la moglie ubriaca.

caked [kākt] *a*: **~ with** incrostato(a) di.

cake pan *n* (*US*) stampo, tortiera.

Cal. *abbr* (*US*) = *California*.

calamitous [kǝlam'itǝs] *a* disastroso(a).

calamity [kǝlam'itē] *n* calamità *f inv*.

calcium [kal'sēǝm] *n* calcio.

calculate [kal'kyǝlāt] *vt* calcolare; (*estimate*: *chances, effect*) valutare.

calculate on *vt fus*: **to ~ on sth/on doing sth** contare su qc/di fare qc.

calculated [kal'kyǝlātid] *a* calcolato(a), intenzionale; **a ~ risk** un rischio calcolato.

calculating [kal'kyǝlāting] *a* calcolatore(trice).

calculation [kalkyǝlā'shǝn] *n* calcolo.

calculator [kal'kyǝlātûr] *n* calcolatrice *f*.

calculus [kal'kyǝlǝs] *n* calcolo; **integral/differential ~** calcolo integrale/differenziale.

calendar [kal'ǝndûr] *n* calendario.

calendar month *n* mese *m* (secondo il calendario).

calendar year *n* anno civile.

calf, ** *pl* **calves [kaf, kavz] *n* (*of cow*) vitello; (*of other animals*) piccolo; (*also*: **~skin**) (pelle *f* di) vitello; (*ANAT*) polpaccio.

caliber [kal'ǝbûr] *n* (*US*) calibro.

calibrate [kal'ǝbrāt] *vt* (*gun etc*) calibrare; (*scale of measuring instrument*) tarare.

calibre [kal'ǝbûr] *n* (*Brit*) = **caliber**.

calico [kal'ikō] *n* tela grezza, cotone *m* grezzo; (*US*) cotonina stampata.

Calif. *abbr* (*US*) = *California*.

California [kalǝfôrn'yǝ] *n* California.

calipers [kal'ǝpûrz] *npl* (*US MED*) gambale *m*; (: *MATH*) calibro.

call [kôl] *vt* (*gen, also TEL*) chiamare;

(*announce*: *flight*) annunciare; (*meeting, strike*) indire, proclamare; ♦ *vi* chiamare; (*visit*: *also*: ~ **in**) passare ♦ *n* (*shout*) grido, urlo; visita; (*summons*: *for flight etc*) chiamata; (*fig*: *lure*) richiamo; (*also*: **telephone** ~) telefonata; **to be on** ~ essere a disposizione; **to make a** ~ telefonare, fare una telefonata; **please give me a** ~ **at 7** per piacere mi chiami alle 7; **to pay a** ~ **on sb** fare (una) visita a qn; **there's not much** ~ **for these items** non c'è molta richiesta di questi articoli; **she's** ~**ed Jane** si chiama Jane; **who is** ~**ing?** (*TEL*) chi parla?; **New York** ~**ing** (*RADIO*) qui New York.

call at *vt fus* (*subj*: *ship*) fare scalo a; (*: train*) fermarsi a.

call back *vi* (*return*) ritornare; (*TEL*) ritelefonare, richiamare ♦ *vt* (*TEL*) ritelefonare a, richiamare.

call for *vt fus* (*demand*: *action etc*) richiedere; (*collect*: *person*) passare a prendere; (*: goods*) ritirare.

call in *vt* (*doctor, expert, police*) chiamare, far venire.

call off *vt* (*meeting, race*) disdire; (*deal*) cancellare; (*dog*) richiamare; **the strike was** ~**ed off** lo sciopero è stato revocato.

call on *vt fus* (*visit*) passare da; (*request*): **to** ~ **on sb to do** chiedere a qn di fare.

call out *vi* urlare ♦ *vt* (*doctor, police, troops*) chiamare.

call up *vt* (*MIL*) richiamare.

callbox |kôl'bâks| *n* (*Brit*) cabina telefonica.

caller |kôl'ûr| *n* persona che chiama; visitatore/trice; **hold the line,** ~**!** (*TEL*) rimanga in linea, signore (*or* signora)!

call girl *n* ragazza *f* squillo *inv*.

call-in |kôl'in| *n* (*US RADIO, TV*) trasmissione radiofonica o televisiva con intervento telefonico degli ascoltatori.

calling |kôl'ing| *n* vocazione *f*.

calling card *n* (*US*) biglietto da visita.

callipers |kal'əpûrz| *npl* (*Brit*) = **calipers**.

callous |kal'əs| *a* indurito(a), insensibile.

callousness |kal'əsnis| *n* insensibilità.

callow |kal'ō| *a* immaturo(a).

calm |kâm| *a* calmo(a) ♦ *n* calma ♦ *vt* calmare.

calm down *vi* calmarsi ♦ *vt* calmare.

calmly |kâm'lē| *ad* con calma.

calmness |kâm'nis| *n* calma.

Calor gas |kā'lûr gas| ® *n* (*Brit*) butano.

calorie |kal'ûrē| *n* caloria; **low-**~ **product** prodotto a basso contenuto di calorie.

calve |kav| *vi* figliare.

calves |kavz| *npl of* **calf**.

CAM *n abbr* (= *computer-aided manufacturing*) fabbricazione *f* con l'ausilio dell'elaboratore.

camber |kam'bûr| *n* (*of road*) bombatura.

Cambodia |kambō'dēə| *n* Cambogia.

Cambodian |kambō'dēən| *a, n* cambogiano(a).

Cambs *abbr* (*Brit*) = *Cambridgeshire*.

camcorder |kam'kôrdûr| *n* videocamera.

came |kām| *pt of* **come**.

camel |kam'əl| *n* cammello.

cameo |kam'ēō| *n* cammeo.

camera |kam'ûrə| *n* macchina fotografica; (*CINEMA, TV*) telecamera; (*also*: **cine**~, **movie** ~) cinepresa.

cameraman |kam'ûrəman| *n* cameraman *m inv*.

Cameroon, Cameroun |kamərōōn'| *n* Camerun *m*.

camouflage |kam'əflâzh| *n* camuffamento; (*MIL*) mimetizzazione *f* ♦ *vt* camuffare; mimetizzare.

camp |kamp| *n* campeggio; (*MIL*) campo ♦ *vi* campeggiare; accamparsi; **to go** ~**ing** andare in campeggio.

campaign |kampān'| *n* (*MIL, POL etc*) campagna ♦ *vi*: **to** ~ **(for/against)** (*also fig*) fare una campagna (per/contro).

campaigner |kampān'ûr| *n*: ~ **for** fautore/trice di; ~ **against** oppositore/trice di.

camp bed *n* brandina.

camper |kam'pûr| *n* campeggiatore/trice; (*vehicle*) camper *m inv*.

camping |kam'ping| *n* campeggio.

camp(ing) site *n* campeggio.

campus |kam'pəs| *n* campus *m inv*.

camshaft |kam'shaft| *n* albero a camme.

can |kan| *auxiliary vb see next headword* ♦ *n* (*of milk*) scatola (*of oil*) bidone *m*; (*of water*) tanica; (*of fruit, soup etc*) scatola ♦ *vt* mettere in scatola; **to carry the** ~ (*Brit col*) prendere la colpa.

can |kan| *n, vt see previous headword* ♦ *auxiliary vb* (*gen*) potere; (*know how to*) sapere; **I** ~ **speak French** so parlare francese; **I** ~ **swim** *etc* so nuotare *etc*; **I** ~**'t see you** non ti vedo; ~ **you hear me?** mi senti?; **could I have a word with you?** potrei parlarti un attimo?; **he could be in the library** può darsi che sia in biblioteca; **they could have forgotten** potrebbero essersene dimenticati.

Canada |kan'ədə| *n* Canada *m*.

Canadian |kanā'dēən| *a, n* canadese (*m/f*).

canal |kənal'| *n* canale *m*.

canary |kənär'ē| *n* canarino.

Canary Islands, Canaries |kənär'ēz| *npl*: **the** ~ le (isole) Canarie.

Canberra |kan'bərə| *n* Camberra.

cancel |kan'səl| *vt* annullare; (*train*) sopprimere; (*cross out*) cancellare.

cancel out *vt* (*MATH*) semplificare; (*fig*) annullare; **they** ~ **each other out** (*also fig*) si annullano a vicenda.

cancellation |kansəlā'shən| *n* annullamento; soppressione *f*; cancellazione *f*; (*TOURISM*) prenotazione *f* annullata.

cancer [kan'sûr] *n* cancro; **C~** (*sign*) Cancro; **to be C~** essere del Cancro.
cancerous [kan'sûrəs] *a* canceroso(a).
cancer patient *n* malato/a di cancro.
cancer research *n* ricerca sul cancro.
C and F *abbr* (= *cost and freight*) Caf *m*.
candid [kan'did] *a* onesto(a).
candidacy [kan'didəsē] *n* candidatura.
candidate [kan'didāt] *n* candidato/a.
candied [kan'dēd] *a* candito(a); **~ apple** (*US*) mela caramellata.
candle [kan'dəl] *n* candela.
candlelight [kan'dəllīt] *n*: **by ~** a lume di candela.
candlestick [kan'dəlstik] *n* (*also*: **candle holder**) bugia; (*bigger, ornate*) candeliere *m*.
candor, (*Brit*) **candour** [kan'dûr] *n* sincerità.
candy [kan'dē] *n* zucchero candito; (*US*) caramella; caramelle *fpl*.
candy-floss [kan'dēflôs] *n* (*Brit*) zucchero filato.
candy store *n* (*US*) ≈ pasticceria.
cane [kān] *n* canna; (*for baskets, chairs etc*) bambù *m*; (*SCOL*) verga; (*for walking*) bastone *m* (da passeggio) ♦ *vt* (*Brit SCOL*) punire a colpi di verga.
canine [kā'nīn] *a* canino(a).
canister [kan'istûr] *n* barattolo.
cannabis [kan'əbis] *n* canapa indiana.
canned [kand] *a* (*food*) in scatola; (*col: recorded*: *music*) registrato(a); (*US col: worker*) licenziato(a); (*Brit col: drunk*) sbronzo(a).
cannibal [kan'əbəl] *n* cannibale *m/f*.
cannibalism [kan'əbəlizəm] *n* cannibalismo.
cannon, *pl* **~** *or* **~s** [kan'ən] *n* (*gun*) cannone *m*.
cannonball [kan'ənbôl] *n* palla di cannone.
cannon fodder *n* carne *f* da macello.
cannot [kan'ât] = **can not**.
canny [kan'ē] *a* furbo(a).
canoe [kənōō'] *n* canoa; (*SPORT*) canotto.
canoeing [kənōō'ing] *n* (*sport*) canottaggio.
canoeist [kənōō'ist] *n* canottiere *m*.
canon [kan'ən] *n* (*clergyman*) canonico; (*standard*) canone *m*.
canonize [kan'ənīz] *vt* canonizzare.
can opener [kan' ō'pənûr] *n* apriscatole *m inv*.
canopy [kan'əpē] *n* baldacchino.
cant [kant] *n* gergo ♦ *vt* inclinare ♦ *vi* inclinarsi.
can't [kant] = **can not**.
cantankerous [kantang'kûrəs] *a* stizzoso(a).
canteen [kantēn'] *n* mensa; (*Brit: of cutlery*) portaposate *m inv*.
canter [kan'tûr] *n* piccolo galoppo ♦ *vi* andare al piccolo galoppo.
cantilever [kan'təlevûr] *n* trave *f* a sbalzo.
canvas [kan'vəs] *n* tela; **under ~** (*camping*) sotto la tenda; (*NAUT*) sotto la vela.

canvass [kan'vəs] *vt* (*COMM*: *district*) fare un'indagine di mercato in; (: *citizens, opinions*) fare un sondaggio di; (*POL*: *district*) fare un giro elettorale di; (: *person*) fare propaganda elettorale a.
canvasser [kan'vəsûr] *n* (*COMM*) agente *m* viaggiatore, piazzista *m*; (*POL*) propagandista *m/f* (elettorale).
canvassing [kan'vəsing] *n* sollecitazione *f*.
canyon [kan'yən] *n* canyon *m inv*.
CAP *n abbr* (*Brit*: = *Common Agricultural Policy*) PAC *f*.
cap [kap] *n* (*also SOCCER*) berretto; (*of pen*) coperchio; (*of bottle*) tappo; (*for swimming*) cuffia; (*Brit: contraceptive: also*: **Dutch ~**) diaframma *m* ♦ *vt* tappare; (*outdo*) superare; **~ped with** ricoperto(a) di; **and to ~ it all, he ...** (*Brit*) e per completare l'opera, lui ...
capability [kāpəbil'ətē] *n* capacità *f inv*, abilità *f inv*.
capable [kā'pəbəl] *a* capace; **~ of** capace di; suscettibile di.
capacious [kəpā'shəs] *a* capace.
capacity [kəpas'itē] *n* capacità *f inv*; (*of lift etc*) capienza; **in his ~ as** nella sua qualità di; **to work at full ~** lavorare al massimo delle proprie capacità; **this work is beyond my ~** questo lavoro supera le mie possibilità; **filled to ~** pieno zeppo; **in an advisory ~** a titolo consultativo.
cape [kāp] *n* (*garment*) cappa; (*GEO*) capo.
Cape of Good Hope *n* Capo di Buona Speranza.
caper [kā'pûr] *n* (*CULIN*: *also*: **~s**) cappero; (*leap*) saltello; (*escapade*) birichinata.
Cape Town *n* Città del Capo.
capita [kap'itə] *see* **per capita**.
capital [kap'itəl] *n* (*also*: **~ city**) capitale *f*; (*money*) capitale *m*; (*also*: **~ letter**) (lettera) maiuscola.
capital account *n* conto capitale.
capital allowance *n* ammortamento fiscale.
capital assets *npl* capitale *m* fisso.
capital expenditure *n* spese *fpl* in capitale.
capital gains tax *n* imposta sulla plusvalenza.
capital goods *n* beni *mpl* d'investimento, beni *mpl* capitali.
capital-intensive [kap'itəlinten'siv] *a* ad alta intensità di capitale.
capitalism [kap'itəlizəm] *n* capitalismo.
capitalist [kap'itəlist] *a*, *n* capitalista (*m/f*).
capitalize [kap'itəlīz] *vt* (*provide with capital*) capitalizzare.
capitalize on *vt fus* (*fig*) trarre vantaggio da.
capital punishment *n* pena capitale.
capitulate [kəpich'ōōlāt] *vi* capitolare.
capitulation [kəpichōōlā'shən] *n* capitolazione *f*.

capricious |kəprish'əs| *a* capriccioso(a).
Capricorn |kap'rikôrn| *n* Capricorno; **to be** ~ essere del Capricorno.
caps |kaps| *abbr* = **capital letters.**
capsize |kap'sīz| *vt* capovolgere ♦ *vi* capovolgersi.
capstan |kap'stən| *n* argano.
capsule |kap'səl| *n* capsula.
Capt. *abbr* (= *captain*) Cap.
captain |kap'tin| *n* capitano ♦ *vt* capitanare.
caption |kap'shən| *n* leggenda.
captivate |kap'təvāt| *vt* avvincere.
captive |kap'tiv| *a, n* prigioniero(a).
captivity |kaptiv'ətē| *n* prigionia; **in** ~ (*animal*) in cattività.
captor |kap'tûr| *n* (*lawful*) chi ha catturato; (*unlawful*) rapitore *m.*
capture |kap'chûr| *vt* catturare, prendere; (*attention*) attirare ♦ *n* cattura; (*data* ~) registrazione *f or* rilevazione *f* di dati.
car |kâr| *n* macchina, automobile *f*; (*US RAIL*) carrozza; **by** ~ in macchina.
Caracas |kərak'əs| *n* Caracas *f.*
carafe |kəraf'| *n* caraffa.
carafe wine *n* (*in restaurant*) ≈ vino sfuso.
caramel |kar'əməl| *n* caramello.
carat |kar'ət| *n* carato; **18** ~ **gold** oro a 18 carati.
caravan |kar'əvan| *n* (*Brit: camper*) roulotte *f inv.*
caravan site *n* (*Brit*) campeggio per roulotte.
caraway |kar'əwā| *n*: ~ **seed** seme *m* di cumino.
carbohydrates |kârbōhī'drāts| *npl* (*foods*) carboidrati *mpl.*
carbolic acid |kârbâl'ik as'id| *n* acido fenico, fenolo.
carbon |kâr'bən| *n* carbonio.
carbonated |kâr'bənātid| *a* (*drink*) gassato(a).
carbon copy *n* copia *f* carbone *inv.*
carbon dioxide |kâr'bən dīāk'sīd| *n* diossido di carbonio.
carbon paper *n* carta carbone.
carbon ribbon *n* nastro carbonato.
carburetor, (*Brit*) **carburettor** |kâr'bərātûr| *n* carburatore *m.*
carcass |kâr'kəs| *n* carcassa.
carcinogenic |kârsinəjen'ik| *a* cancerogeno(a).
card |kârd| *n* carta; (*thin cardboard*) cartoncino; (*visiting* ~ *etc*) biglietto; (*membership* ~) tessera; (*Christmas* ~ *etc*) cartolina; **to play** ~**s** giocare a carte.
cardamom |kâr'dəməm| *n* cardamomo.
cardboard |kârd'bôrd| *n* cartone *m.*
cardboard box *n* (scatola di) cartone *m.*
card-carrying member |kârd'karēing mem'bûr| *n* tesserato/a.
card game *n* gioco di carte.
cardiac |kâr'dēak| *a* cardiaco(a).
cardigan |kâr'digən| *n* cardigan *m inv.*
cardinal |kâr'dənəl| *a, n* cardinale (*m*).

card index *n* schedario.
Cards *abbr* (*Brit*) = *Cardiganshire.*
cardsharp |kârd'shârp| *n* baro.
CARE *n abbr* = *Cooperative for American Relief Everywhere.*
care |kâr| *n* cura, attenzione *f*; (*worry*) preoccupazione *f* ♦ *vi*: **to** ~ **about** interessarsi di; **would you** ~ **to/for ...?** le piacerebbe **...?**; **I wouldn't** ~ **to do it** non lo vorrei fare; **in sb's** ~ alle cure di qn; **to take** ~ fare attenzione; **to take** ~ **of** curarsi di; (*details, arrangements*) occuparsi di; **I don't** ~ non me ne importa; **I could** ~ **less,** (*Brit*) **I couldn't** ~ **less** non me ne importa un bel niente; ~ **of (c/o)** (*on letter*) presso; **"handle with** ~**" "fragile"; the child has been taken into** ~ il bambino è stato preso in custodia.
care for *vt fus* aver cura di; (*like*) voler bene a.
careen |kərēn'| *vi* (*ship*) sbandare ♦ *vt* carenare.
career |kərēr'| *n* carriera; (*occupation*) professione *f* ♦ *vi* (*also:* ~ **along**) andare di (gran) carriera.
career counselor *n* (*US*) consulente *m/f* d'orientamento professionale.
career girl *n* donna dedita alla carriera.
careers officer *n* (*Brit*) = **career counselor.**
carefree |kâr'frē| *a* sgombro(a) di preoccupazioni.
careful |kâr'fəl| *a* attento(a); (*cautious*) cauto(a); **(be)** ~**!** attenzione!; **he's very** ~ **with his money** bada molto alle spese.
carefully |kâr'fəlē| *ad* con cura; cautamente.
careless |kâr'lis| *a* negligente; (*remark*) privo(a) di tatto.
carelessly |kâr'lislē| *ad* negligentemente; senza tatto; (*without thinking*) distrattamente.
carelessness |kâr'lisnis| *n* negligenza; mancanza di tatto.
caress |kəres'| *n* carezza ♦ *vt* accarezzare.
caretaker |kâr'tākûr| *n* custode *m.*
caretaker government *n* governo *m* ponte *inv.*
car ferry *n* traghetto.
cargo, ~**es** |kâr'gō| *n* carico.
cargo boat *n* cargo.
cargo plane *n* aereo di linea da carico.
car hire *n* (*Brit*) autonoleggio.
Caribbean |karəbē'ən| *a* caraibico(a); **the** ~ **(Sea)** il Mar dei Caraibi.
caricature |kar'əkəchûr| *n* caricatura.
caring |kâr'ing| *a* (*person*) premuroso(a); (*society, organization*) umanitario(a).
carnage |kâr'nij| *n* carneficina.
carnal |kâr'nəl| *a* carnale.
carnation |kârnā'shən| *n* garofano.
carnival |kâr'nəvəl| *n* (*public celebration*) carnevale *m*; (*US*) luna park *m inv.*

carnivorous [kârnĭv'ûrəs] *a* carnivoro(a).

carol [kar'əl] *n*: (Christmas) ~ canto di Natale.

carouse [kərouz'] *vi* far baldoria.

carousel [karəsel'] *n* (*US*) giostra.

carp [kârp] *n* (*fish*) carpa.

carp at *vt fus* trovare a ridire su.

car park *n* (*Brit*) parcheggio.

carpenter [kâr'pəntûr] *n* carpentiere *m*.

carpentry [kâr'pəntrē] *n* carpenteria.

carpet [kâr'pit] *n* tappeto ♦ *vt* coprire con tappeto.

carpet slippers *npl* pantofole *fpl*.

carpet sweeper [kâr'pit swē'pûr] *n* scopatappeti *m inv*.

car phone *n* radiotelefono (per macchina).

car rental *n* (*US*) autonoleggio.

carriage [kar'ij] *n* vettura; (*of goods*) trasporto; (*of typewriter*) carrello; (*bearing*) portamento; ~ **forward** porto assegnato; ~ **free** franco di porto; ~ **paid** porto pagato.

carriage return *n* (*on typewriter etc*) leva (*or tasto*) del ritorno a capo.

carriageway [kar'ijwā] *n* (*Brit: part of road*) carreggiata.

carrier [kar'ēûr] *n* (*of disease*) portatore/trice; (*COMM*) impresa di trasporti; (*NAUT*) portaerei *f inv*.

carrier bag *n* (*Brit*) sacchetto.

carrier pigeon *n* colombo viaggiatore.

carrion [kar'ēən] *n* carogna.

carrot [kar'ət] *n* carota.

carry [kar'ē] *vt* (*subj: person*) portare; (: *vehicle*) trasportare; (*a motion, bill*) far passare; (*involve: responsibilities etc*) comportare; (*COMM: goods*) tenere; (: *interest*) avere; (*MATH: figure*) riportare ♦ *vi* (*sound*) farsi sentire; **this loan carries 10% interest** questo prestito è sulla base di un interesse del 10%; **to be carried away** (*fig*) farsi trascinare.

carry forward *vt* (*MATH, COMM*) riportare.

carry on *vi*: **to ~ on with sth/doing** continuare qc/a fare ♦ *vt* mandare avanti.

carry out *vt* (*orders*) eseguire; (*investigation*) svolgere; (*accomplish etc: plan*) realizzare; (*perform, implement*: *idea, threat*) mettere in pratica.

carryall [kar'ēôl] *n* (*US*) borsone *m*.

carrycot [kar'ēkât] *n* (*Brit*) culla portabile.

carry-on [kar'ēân] *n* (*col: fuss*) casino, confusione *f*.

cart [kârt] *n* carro; (*US: for shopping*) carrello ♦ *vt* (*col*) trascinare, scarrozzare.

carte blanche [kârt' blânsh'] *n*: **to give sb ~** dare carta bianca a qn.

cartel [kârtel'] *n* (*COMM*) cartello.

cartilage [kâr'təlij] *n* cartilagine *f*.

cartographer [kârtâg'rəfûr] *n* cartografo/a.

cartography [kârtâg'rəfē] *n* cartografia.

carton [kâr'tən] *n* (*box*) scatola di cartone; (*of yogurt*) cartone *m*; (*of cigarettes*) stecca.

cartoon [kârtōōn'] *n* (*in newspaper etc*) vignetta; (*CINEMA, TV*) cartone *m* animato; (*ART*) cartone.

cartoonist [kârtōō'nist] *n* vignettista *m/f*; cartonista *m/f*.

cartridge [kâr'trij] *n* (*for gun, pen*) cartuccia; (*for camera*) caricatore *m*; (*music tape*) cassetta; (*of record player*) testina.

cartwheel [kârt'hwēl] *n*: **to turn a ~** (*SPORT etc*) fare la ruota.

carve [kârv] *vt* (*meat*) trinciare; (*wood, stone*) intagliare.

carve up *vt* (*meat*) tagliare; (*fig: country*) suddividere.

carving [kâr'ving] *n* (*in wood etc*) scultura.

carving knife *n* trinciante *m*.

car wash *n* lavaggio auto.

Casablanca [kasəblang'kə] *n* Casablanca.

cascade [kaskād'] *n* cascata ♦ *vi* scendere a cascata.

case [kās] *n* caso; (*LAW*) causa, processo; (*box*) scatola; (*also:* **suit**~) valigia; (*TYP*): **lower/upper** ~ (carattere *m*) minuscolo/maiuscolo; **to have a good ~** avere pretese legittime; **there's a strong ~ for reform** ci sono validi argomenti a favore della riforma; **in ~ of** in caso di; **in ~ he** caso mai lui; **just in ~** in caso di bisogno.

case-hardened [kās'hâr'dənd] *a* indurito(a) dall'esperienza.

case history *n* (*MED*) cartella clinica.

case study *n* studio di un caso.

cash [kash] *n* (*coins, notes*) soldi *mpl*, denaro; (*col: money*) quattrini *mpl* ♦ *vt* incassare; **to pay (in)** ~ pagare in contanti; **to be short of** ~ essere a corto di soldi; ~ **on delivery** (**COD**) (*COMM*) pagamento all'ordinazione/alla consegna.

cash in *vt* (*insurance policy etc*) riscuotere, riconvertire.

cash in on *vt fus*: **to ~ in on sth** sfruttare qc.

cash account *n* conto *m* cassa *inv*.

cash-and-carry [kash'ənkar'ē] *n* cash and carry *m inv*.

cashbook [kash'bŏŏk] *n* giornale *m* di cassa.

cash box *n* cassetta per il denaro spicciolo.

cash card *n* carta per prelievi automatici.

cash desk *n* (*Brit*) cassa.

cash discount *n* sconto per contanti.

cash dispenser *n* sportello automatico.

cashew [kash'ōō] *n* (*also:* ~ **nut**) anacardio.

cash flow *n* cash-flow *m inv*, liquidità *f inv*.

cashier [kashi'ûr] *n* cassiere/a ♦ *vt* (*esp MIL*) destituire.

cashmere [kazh'mēr] *n* cachemire *m*.

cash payment *n* pagamento in contanti.

cash price *n* prezzo per contanti.

cash register *n* registratore *m* di cassa.

cash sale *n* vendita per contanti.

casing [kā'sing] *n* rivestimento.

casino [kəsē'nō] *n* casinò *m inv*.
cask [kask] *n* botte *f*.
casket [kas'kit] *n* cofanetto; *(US: coffin)* bara.
Caspian Sea [kas'pēən sē] *n*: **the** ~ il mar Caspio.
casserole [kas'ərōl] *n* casseruola; *(food)*: **chicken** ~ pollo in casseruola.
cassette [kəset'] *n* cassetta.
cassette deck *n* piastra di registrazione.
cassette player *n* riproduttore *m* a cassette.
cassette recorder *n* registratore *m* a cassette.
cast [kast] *vt (pt, pp* **cast)** *(throw)* gettare; *(shed)* perdere; spogliarsi di; *(metal)* gettare, fondere ♦ *n (THEATER)* complesso di attori; *(mold)* forma; *(also:* **plaster** ~) ingessatura; *(THEATER):* **to** ~ **sb as Hamlet** scegliere qn per la parte di Amleto; **to** ~ **one's vote** votare, dare il voto.
cast aside *vt (reject)* mettere da parte.
cast off *vi (NAUT)* salpare; *(KNITTING)* diminuire, calare ♦ *vt + adv (NAUT)* disormeggiare; *(KNITTING)* diminuire, calare.
cast on *vt (KNITTING)* avviare ♦ *vi* avviare (le maglie).
castanets [kastənets'] *npl* castagnette *fpl*.
castaway [kas'təwā] *n* naufrago/a.
caste [kast] *n* casta.
caster sugar [kas'tûr shōog'ûr] *n (Brit)* zucchero semolato.
casting vote [kas'ting vōt] *n (Brit)* voto decisivo.
cast iron *n* ghisa ♦ *a:* **cast-iron** *(fig: will, alibi)* di ferro, d'acciaio.
castle [kas'əl] *n* castello; *(fortified)* rocca.
castor [kas'tûr] *n (wheel)* rotella.
castor oil *n* olio di ricino.
castrate [kas'trāt] *vt* castrare.
casual [kazh'ōōəl] *a (by chance)* casuale, fortuito(a); *(irregular: work etc)* avventizio(a); *(unconcerned)* noncurante, indifferente; ~ **wear** casual *m*.
casual labor *n* manodopera avventizia.
casually [kazh'ōōəlē] *ad* con disinvoltura; *(by chance)* casualmente.
casualty [kazh'ōōəltē] *n* ferito/a; *(dead)* morto/a, vittima; **heavy casualties** *npl* grosse perdite *fpl*.
cat [kat] *n* gatto.
catacombs [kat'əkōmz] *npl* catacombe *fpl*.
catalog, *(Brit)* **catalogue** [kat'əlôg] *n* catalogo ♦ *vt* catalogare.
catalyst [kat'əlist] *n* catalizzatore *m*.
catalytic converter [katelit'ik kânvûrt'ûr] *n (AUT)* marmitta catalitica.
catapult [kat'əpult] *n* catapulta; fionda.
cataract [kat'ərakt] *n (also MED)* cateratta.
catarrh [kətâr'] *n* catarro.
catastrophe [kətas'trəfē] *n* catastrofe *f*.
catastrophic [katəstrâf'ik] *a* catastrofico(a).
catcall [kat'kôl] *n (at meeting etc)* fischio.

catch [kach] *vb (pt, pp* **caught** [kôt]) *vt (train, thief, cold)* acchiappare; *(ball)* afferrare; *(person: by surprise)* sorprendere; *(understand)* comprendere; *(get entangled)* impigliare ♦ *vi (fire)* prendere ♦ *n (fish etc caught)* retata, presa; *(trick)* inganno; *(TECH)* gancio; **to** ~ **sb's attention** *or* **eye** attirare l'attenzione di qn; **to** ~ **fire** prendere fuoco; **to** ~ **sight of** scorgere.
catch on *vi (become popular)* affermarsi, far presa; *(understand):* **to** ~ **on (to sth)** capire (qc).
catch out *vt (Brit fig: with trick question)* cogliere in fallo.
catch up *vi* mettersi in pari ♦ *vt (also:* ~ **up with)** raggiungere.
catching [kach'ing] *a (MED)* contagioso(a).
catchment area [kach'mənt är'ēə] *n (Brit SCOL)* circoscrizione *f* scolare; *(GEO)* bacino pluviale.
catch phrase *n* slogan *m inv*; frase *f* fatta.
catch-22 [kach'twentētōō'] *n*: **it's a** ~ **situation** non c'è via d'uscita.
catchy [kach'ē] *a* orecchiabile.
cat door *n (US)* gattaiola.
catechism [kat'əkizəm] *n* catechismo.
categoric(al) [katəgôr'ik(əl)] *a* categorico(a).
categorize [kat'əgərīz] *vt* categorizzare.
category [kat'əgôrē] *n* categoria.
cater [kā'tûr] *vi (gen:* ~ **for)** provvedere da mangiare (per).
cater to *vt fus (needs)* provvedere a; *(: readers, consumers)* incontrare i gusti di.
caterer [kā'tûrûr] *n* fornitore *m*.
catering [kā'tûring] *n* approvvigionamento.
catering trade *n* settore *m* ristoranti.
caterpillar [kat'ûrpilûr] *n (ZOOL)* bruco ♦ *cpd (vehicle)* cingolato(a); ~ **track** cingolo.
cathedral [kəthē'drəl] *n* cattedrale *f*, duomo.
cathode [kath'ōd] *n* catodo.
cathode ray tube [kath'ōd rā' tōōb] *n* tubo a raggi catodici.
catholic [kath'əlik] *a* universale; aperto(a); eclettico(a); **C~** *a, n (REL)* cattolico(a).
cat's-eye [kats'ī'] *n (Brit AUT)* catarifrangente *m*.
catsup [kat'səp] *n (US)* ketchup *m inv*.
cattle [kat'əl] *npl* bestiame *m*, bestie *fpl*.
catty [kat'ē] *a* maligno(a), dispettoso(a).
CATV *n abbr (US:* = *community antenna television)* sistema televisivo via cavo a pagamento per zone non servite dalla rete nazionale.
Caucasian [kôkā'zhən] *a, n* caucasico(a).
Caucasus [kôk'əsəs] *n* Caucaso.
caucus [kô'kəs] *n (US Pol)* (riunione *f* del) comitato elettorale; *(Brit POL: group)* comitato di dirigenti.
caught [kôt] *pt, pp of* **catch.**
cauliflower [kô'ləflouûr] *n* cavolfiore *m*.
cause [kôz] *n* causa ♦ *vt* causare; **there is no**

~ **for concern** non c'è ragione di preoccuparsi; **to** ~ **sb to do sth** far fare qc a qn; **to** ~ **sth to be done** far fare qc.

causeway [kòz'wā] *n* strada rialzata.

caustic [kòs'tik] *a* caustico(a).

caution [kò'shən] *n* prudenza; *(warning)* avvertimento ♦ *vt* ammonire.

cautious [kò'shəs] *a* cauto(a), prudente.

cautiously [kò'shəslē] *ad* prudentemente.

cautiousness [kò'shəsnes] *n* cautela.

cavalier [kavəliúr'] *n* *(knight)* cavaliere *m* ♦ *a* *(pej: offhand)* brusco(a).

cavalry [kav'əlrē] *n* cavalleria.

cave [kāv] *n* caverna, grotta ♦ *vi*: **to go caving** fare speleologia.

cave in *vi* *(roof etc)* crollare.

caveman [kāv'mən] *n* uomo delle caverne.

cavern [kav'ûrn] *n* caverna.

caviar(e) [kav'ēâr] *n* caviale *m*.

cavity [kav'itē] *n* cavità *f inv.*

cavity wall insulation *n* isolamento per pareti a intercapedine.

cavort [kəvòrt'] *vi* far capriole.

cayenne (pepper) [kīen' (pep'úr)] *n* pepe *m* di Caienna.

CB *n abbr* (= *Citizens' Band (Radio)*) C.B. *m*; ~ **radio (set)** baracchino.

CBC *n abbr* = *Canadian Broadcasting Corporation.*

CBI *n abbr* (= *Confederation of British Industry*) ≈ CONFINDUSTRIA (= *Confederazione Generale dell'Industria Italiana*).

CBS *n abbr* (US) = *Columbia Broadcasting System.*

cc *abbr* (= *cubic centimeter*) cc; *(on letter etc)* = **carbon copy.**

CCA *n abbr* (US: = *Circuit Court of Appeals*) corte *f* d'appello itinerante.

CCC *n abbr* (US: = *Commodity Credit Corporation*) organismo per la stabilizzazione dei prezzi dei prodotti agricoli.

CCU *n abbr* (US: = *coronary care unit*) unità coronarica.

CD *n abbr* (= *compact disk*) compact disk *m inv*; *(MIL: US)* = *Civil Defense*, (: *Brit*) = *Civil Defence (Corps)* ♦ *abbr* (= *Corps Diplomatique*) C.D.

CDC *n abbr* (US) = *center for disease control.*

Cdr. *abbr* (= *commander*) Com.

CDV *n abbr* = *compact disc video.*

CDW *n abbr see* **collision damage waiver.**

cease [sēs] *vt, vi* cessare.

ceasefire [sēs'fīûr'] *n* cessate il fuoco *m inv.*

ceaseless [sēs'lis] *a* incessante, continuo(a).

CED *n abbr* (US) = *Committee for Economic Development.*

cedar [sē'dûr] *n* cedro.

cede [sēd] *vt* cedere.

CEEB *n abbr* (US: = *College Entrance Examination Board*) commissione *f* per l'esame di ammissione al college.

ceiling [sē'ling] *n* soffitto; *(fig: upper limit)* tetto, limite *m* massimo.

celebrate [sel'əbrāt] *vt, vi* celebrare.

celebrated [sel'əbrātid] *a* celebre.

celebration [sclabrā'shən] *n* celebrazione *f.*

celebrity [səleb'ritē] *n* celebrità *f inv.*

celeriac [səlär'ēak] *n* sedano *m* rapa *inv.*

celery [sel'ûrē] *n* sedano.

celestial [səles'chəl] *a* celeste.

celibacy [sel'əbasē] *n* celibato.

cell [sel] *n* cella; *(BIOL)* cellula; *(ELEC)* elemento (di batteria).

cellar [sel'ûr] *n* sottosuolo, cantina.

cellophane [sel'əfān] ® *n* cellophane ® *m.*

cellular [sel'yəlûr] *a* cellulare.

celluloid [sel'yəloid] *n* celluloide *f.*

cellulose [sel'yəlōs] *n* cellulosa.

Celsius [sel'sēəs] *a* Celsius *inv.*

Celt [selt, kelt] *n* celta *m/f.*

Celtic [sel'tik, kel'tik] *a* celtico(a) ♦ *n* *(LING)* celtico.

cement [siment'] *n* cemento ♦ *vt* cementare.

cement mixer *n* betoniera.

cemetery [sem'itārē] *n* cimitero.

cenotaph [sen'ətaf] *n* cenotafio.

censor [sen'sûr] *n* censore *m* ♦ *vt* censurare.

censorship [sen'sûrship] *n* censura.

censure [sen'shûr] *vt* censurare.

census [sen'səs] *n* censimento.

cent [sent] *n* (*US: coin*) centesimo (= *1:100 di un dollaro*); *see also* **percent.**

centenary [sen'tənārē], **centennial** [senten'ēəl] *n* centenario.

center [sen'tûr] (US) *n* centro ♦ *vt* *(concentrate)*: **to** ~ **(on)** concentrare su.

centerfold [sen'tûrfōld] *n* *(PRESS)* poster *m* (all'interno di rivista).

center forward *n* *(SPORT)* centroavanti *m inv.*

center half *n* *(SPORT)* centromediano.

centerpiece [sen'tûrpēs] *n* centrotavola *m*; *(fig)* punto centrale.

centigrade [sen'tigrād] *a* centigrado(a).

centiliter, *(Brit)* **centilitre** [sen'tələtūr] *n* centilitro.

centimeter, *(Brit)* **centimetre** [sen'təmētūr] *n* centimetro.

centipede [sen'təpēd] *n* centopiedi *m inv.*

central [sen'trəl] *a* centrale.

Central African Republic *n* Repubblica centrafricana.

Central America *n* America centrale.

central heating *n* riscaldamento centrale.

centralize [sen'trəlīz] *vt* accentrare.

central processing unit (CPU) *n* *(COMPUT)* unità *f inv* centrale di elaborazione.

central reservation *n* *(Brit AUT)* banchina *f* spartitraffico *inv.*

centre [sen'tûr] *etc* *(Brit)* = **center** *etc.*

centrifugal [sentrif'əgəl] *a* centrifugo(a).

centrifuge [sen'trəfyōōj] *n* centrifuga.

century [sen'chûrē] *n* secolo; **in the twentieth** ~ nel ventesimo secolo.

CEO *n abbr* (*US*) *see* **chief executive officer.**

ceramic [sǝram'ik] *a* ceramico(a).

cereal [sēr'ēǝl] *n* cereale *m.*

cerebral [sär'ǝbrǝl] *a* cerebrale.

ceremonial [särǝmō'nēǝl] *n* cerimoniale *m*; (*rite*) rito.

ceremony [sär'ǝmōnē] *n* cerimonia; **to stand on** ~ fare complimenti.

cert [sûrt] *n* (*Brit col*): **it's a dead** ~ non c'è alcun dubbio.

certain [sûr'tǝn] *a* certo(a); **to make** ~ **of** assicurarsi di; **for** ~ per certo, di sicuro.

certainly [sûr'tǝnlē] *ad* certamente, certo.

certainty [sûr'tǝntē] *n* certezza.

certificate [sǝrtif'ǝkit] *n* certificato; diploma *m.*

certified letter [sûr'tǝfīd let'ûr] *n* (*US*) lettera raccomandata.

certified public accountant (CPA) *n* (*US*) ≈ commercialista *m/f.*

certify [sûr'tǝfī] *vt* certificare ♦ *vi*: **to** ~ **to** attestare a.

cervical [sûr'vikǝl] *a*: ~ **cancer** cancro della cervice, tumore *m* al collo dell'utero; ~ **smear** Pap-test *m inv.*

cervix [sûr'viks] *n* cervice *f.*

Cesarean [sizär'ēǝn] *a* (*US*): ~ **(section)** (taglio) cesareo.

cessation [sesā'shǝn] *n* cessazione *f*; arresto.

cesspit [ses'pit] *n* pozzo nero.

CET *abbr* (= *Central European Time*) *fuso orario.*

Ceylon [silän'] *n* Ceylon *f.*

cf. *abbr* (= *compare*) cfr.

c/f *abbr* (*COMM*) = *carried forward.*

C.F. *abbr* = *cost and freight.*

cfc *n abbr* (= *chlorofluorocarbon*) cfc *m inv.*

C.F.I. *abbr* = *cost, freight and insurance.*

CG *n abbr* (*US*) = **coastguard.**

cg *abbr* (= *centigram*) cg.

ch *abbr* (*Brit*) = **central heating.**

ch. *abbr* (= *chapter*) cap.

Chad [chad] *n* Chad *m.*

chafe [chāf] *vt* fregare, irritare ♦ *vi* (*fig*): **to** ~ **against** scontrarsi con.

chaffinch [chaf'inch] *n* fringuello.

chagrin [shǝgrin'] *n* disappunto, dispiacere *m.*

chain [chān] *n* catena ♦ *vt* (*also*: ~ **up**) incatenare.

chain reaction *n* reazione *f* a catena.

chain-smoke [chān'smōk] *vi* fumare una sigaretta dopo l'altra.

chain store *n* negozio a catena.

chair [chär] *n* sedia; (*armchair*) poltrona; (*of university*) cattedra ♦ *vt* (*meeting*) presiedere; **the** ~ (*US: electric* ~) la sedia elettrica.

chairlift [chär'lift] *n* seggiovia.

chairman [chär'mǝn] *n* presidente *m.*

chairperson [chär'pûrsǝn] *n* presidente/essa.

chairwoman [chär'wo͞omǝn] *n* presidentessa.

chalet [shalā'] *n* chalet *m inv.*

chalice [chal'is] *n* calice *m.*

chalk [chôk] *n* gesso.

chalk up *vt* scrivere col gesso; (*fig*: *success*) ottenere; (: *victory*) riportare.

challenge [chal'inj] *n* sfida ♦ *vt* sfidare; (*statement*, *right*) mettere in dubbio; **to** ~ **sb to a fight/game** sfidare qn a battersi/ad una partita; **to** ~ **sb to do** sfidare qn a fare.

challenger [chal'injûr] *n* (*SPORT*) sfidante *m/f.*

challenging [chal'injing] *a* sfidante; (*remark*, *look*) provocatorio(a).

chamber [chām'bûr] *n* camera; ~ **of commerce** camera di commercio.

chambermaid [chām'bûrmād] *n* cameriera.

chamber music *n* musica da camera.

chamber pot *n* vaso da notte.

chameleon [kǝmē'lēǝn] *n* camaleonte *m.*

chamois [sham'ē] *n* camoscio.

chamois leather [sham'ē leth'ûr] *n* pelle *f* di camoscio.

champagne [shampān'] *n* champagne *m inv.*

champion [cham'pēǝn] *n* campione/essa; (*of cause*) difensore *m* ♦ *vt* difendere, lottare per.

championship [cham'pēǝnship] *n* campionato.

chance [chans] *n* caso; (*opportunity*) occasione *f*; (*likelihood*) possibilità *f inv* ♦ *vt*: **to** ~ **it** rischiare, provarci ♦ *a* fortuito(a); **there is little** ~ **of his coming** è molto improbabile che venga; **to take a** ~ rischiare; **by** ~ per caso; **it's the** ~ **of a lifetime** è un'occasione unica; **the** ~**s are that** ... probabilmente ..., è probabile che ... + *sub*; **to** ~ **to do sth** (*formal*: *happen*) fare per caso qc.

chance (up)on *vt fus* (*person*) incontrare per caso, imbattersi in; (*thing*) trovare per caso.

chancel [chan'sǝl] *n* coro.

chancellor [chan'sǝlûr] *n* cancelliere *m*; (*of university*) rettore *m* (onorario); **C**~ **of the Exchequer** (*Brit*) Cancelliere *m* dello Scacchiere.

chandelier [shandǝliûr'] *n* lampadario.

change [chānj] *vt* cambiare; (*transform*): **to** ~ **sb into** trasformare qn in ♦ *vi* cambiarsi; (*be transformed*): **to** ~ **into** trasformarsi in ♦ *n* cambiamento; (*money*) resto; **to** ~ **one's mind** cambiare idea; **to** ~ **gear** (*AUT*) cambiare (marcia); **she** ~**d into an old skirt** si è cambiata e ha messo una vecchia gonna; **a** ~ **of clothes** un cambio (di vestiti); **for a** ~ tanto per cambiare; **small** ~ spiccioli *mpl*, moneta; **keep the** ~ tenga il resto; **can you give me** ~ **for $1?** mi può cambiare un dollaro?

changeable [chān'jǝbǝl] *a* (*weather*) variabile; (*person*) mutevole.

change machine *n* distributore *m* automatico di monete.

changeover [chănj'ōvûr] *n* cambiamento, passaggio.

changing [chān'jing] *a* che cambia; (*colors*) cangiante.

changing room *n* (*Brit*: *in shop*) camerino; (: *SPORT*) spogliatoio.

channel [chan'əl] *n* canale *m*; (*of river, sea*) alveo ♦ *vt* canalizzare; (*fig*: *interest, energies*): **to ~ into** concentrare su, indirizzare verso; **through the usual ~s** per le solite vie; **the (English) C~** la Manica; **green/red ~** (*CUSTOMS*) uscita "niente da dichiarare"/"merci da dichiarare".

Channel Islands *npl*: **the ~** le Isole Normanne.

chant [chant] *n* canto; salmodia; (*of crowd*) slogan *m inv* ♦ *vt* cantare; salmodiare; **the demonstrators ~ed their disapproval** i dimostranti lanciavano slogan di protesta.

chaos [kā'âs] *n* caos *m*.

chaotic [kāât'ik] *a* caotico(a).

chap [chap] *n* (*Brit col*: *man*) tipo ♦ *vt* (*skin*) screpolare; **old ~** vecchio mio.

chapel [chap'əl] *n* cappella.

chaperone [shap'ərōn] *n* accompagnatore/trice ♦ *vt* accompagnare.

chaplain [chap'lin] *n* cappellano.

chapped [chapt] *a* (*skin, lips*) screpolato(a).

chapter [chap'tûr] *n* capitolo.

char [chár] *vt* (*burn*) carbonizzare ♦ *vi* (*Brit*: *cleaner*) lavorare come domestica (a ore) ♦ *n* (*Brit*) = **charlady**.

character [kar'iktûr] *n* (*gen*, *COMPUT*) carattere *m*; (*in novel, film*) personaggio; (*eccentric*) originale *m*; **a person of good ~** una persona a modo.

character code *n* (*COMPUT*) codice *m* di carattere.

characteristic [kariktəris'tik] *a* caratteristico(a) ♦ *n* caratteristica; **~ of** tipico(a) di.

characterize [kar'iktərīz] *vt* caratterizzare; (*describe*): **to ~ (as)** descrivere (come).

charade [shərād'] *n* sciarada.

charcoal [chár'kōl] *n* carbone *m* di legna.

charge [chárj] *n* accusa; (*cost*) prezzo; (*of gun, battery*, *MIL*: *attack*) carica ♦ *vt* (*gun, battery*, *MIL*: *enemy*) caricare; (*customer*) fare pagare a; (*sum*) fare pagare; (*LAW*): **to ~ sb (with)** accusare qn (di) ♦ *vi* (*gen with*: *up, along etc*) lanciarsi; **~s** *npl*: **bank ~s** commissioni *fpl* bancarie; **labor ~s** costi *mpl* del lavoro; **to ~ in/out** precipitarsi dentro/fuori; **to ~ up/down** lanciarsi su/giù per; **is there a ~?** c'è da pagare?; **there's no ~** non c'è niente da pagare; **extra ~** supplemento; **to take ~ of** incaricarsi di; **to be in ~ of** essere responsabile per; **to have ~ of sb** aver cura di qn; **how much do you ~ for this repair?** quanto chiede per la riparazione?; **to ~ an expense (up) to sb** addebitare una spesa a qn; **~ it to my account** lo metta

or addebiti sul mio conto.

charge account *n* conto.

charge card *n* carta di credito commerciale.

chargé d'affaires [shârzhā' dâfärz'] *n* incaricato d'affari.

chargehand [chârj'hand] *n* (*Brit*) caposquadra *m/f*.

charger [chár'jûr] *n* (*also*: **battery ~**) caricabatterie *m inv*; (*old*: *warhorse*) destriero.

chariot [char'ēət] *n* carro.

charitable [char'itəbəl] *a* caritatevole.

charity [char'itē] *n* carità; (*organization*) opera pia.

charlady [chár'lādē] *n* (*Brit*) domestica a ore.

charlatan [shâr'lətən] *n* ciarlatano.

charm [chârm] *n* fascino; (*on bracelet*) ciondolo ♦ *vt* affascinare, incantare.

charm bracelet *n* braccialetto con ciondoli.

charming [chár'ming] *a* affascinante.

chart [chârt] *n* tabella; grafico; (*map*) carta nautica; (*weather ~*) carta del tempo ♦ *vt* fare una carta nautica di; (*sales, progress*) tracciare il grafico di; **to be on** *or* (*Brit*) **in the ~s** (*record, pop group*) essere in classifica.

charter [chár'tûr] *vt* (*plane*) noleggiare ♦ *n* (*document*) carta; **on ~** a nolo.

chartered accountant (CA) [chár'tûrd əkoun'tənt] *n* ragioniere/a professionista.

charter flight *n* volo *m* charter *inv*.

charwoman [chár'wōomən] *n* = **charlady**.

chase [chās] *vt* inseguire; (*also*: **~ away**) cacciare ♦ *n* caccia.

chase down *vt* (*US*: *person*) scovare; (: *information*) scoprire, raccogliere.

chase up *vt* (*Brit*) = **chase down**.

chasm [kaz'əm] *n* abisso.

chassis [shas'ē] *n* telaio.

chastened [chā'sənd] *a* abbattuto(a), provato(a).

chastening [chā'səning] *a* che fa riflettere.

chastise [chastīz'] *vt* punire, castigare.

chastity [chas'titē] *n* castità.

chat [chat] *vi* (*also*: **have a ~**) chiacchierare ♦ *n* chiacchierata.

chat up *vt* (*Brit col*: *girl*) abbordare.

chat show *n* (*Brit*) talk show *m inv*, conversazione *f* televisiva.

chattel [chat'əl] *n* see **goods**.

chatter [chat'ûr] *vi* (*person*) ciarlare ♦ *n* ciarle *fpl*; **her teeth were ~ing** batteva i denti.

chatterbox [chat'ûrbâks] *n* chiacchierone/a.

chatty [chat'ē] *a* (*style*) familiare; (*person*) chiacchierino(a).

chauffeur [shō'fûr] *n* autista *m*.

chauvinism [shō'vənizəm] *n* (*also*: **male ~**) maschilismo; (*nationalism*) sciovinismo.

chauvinist [shō'vənist] *n* (*also*: **male ~**) maschilista *m*; (*nationalist*) sciovinista *m/f*.

chauvinistic [shōvənis'tik] *a* sciovinistico(a).

ChE *abbr* = *chemical engineer*.

cheap [chēp] *a* a buon mercato; *(reduced: fare, ticket)* ridotto(a); *(joke)* grossolano(a); *(poor quality)* di cattiva qualità ♦ *ad* a buon mercato; ~**er** meno caro; ~ **money** denaro a basso tasso di interesse.

cheapen [chē'pən] *vt* ribassare; *(fig)* avvilire.

cheaply [chēp'lē] *ad* a buon prezzo, a buon mercato.

cheat [chēt] *vi* imbrogliare; *(at school)* copiare ♦ *vt* ingannare; *(rob)* defraudare ♦ *n* imbroglione *m*; copione *m*; *(trick)* inganno; **he's been** ~**ing on his wife** ha tradito sua moglie.

cheating [chē'ting] *n* imbrogliare *m*; copiare *m*.

check [chek] *vt* verificare; *(passport, ticket)* controllare; *(halt)* fermare; *(restrain)* contenere ♦ *vi* *(official etc)* informarsi ♦ *n* verifica; controllo; *(curb)* freno; *(bill)* conto; *(pattern: gen pl)* quadretti *mpl*; *(US)* assegno ♦ *a* *(also:* ~**ed**: *pattern, cloth)* a scacchi, a quadretti; **to** ~ **with sb** chiedere a qn; **to keep a** ~ **on sb/sth** controllare qn/qc, fare attenzione a qn/qc; **to pay by** ~ pagare per assegno *or* con assegno.

check in *vi* *(in hotel)* registrare; *(at airport)* presentarsi all'accettazione ♦ *vt* *(luggage)* depositare.

check off *vt* segnare.

check out *vi* *(from hotel)* saldare il conto ♦ *vt* *(luggage)* ritirare; *(investigate: story)* controllare, verificare; *(: person)* prendere informazioni su.

check up *vi*: **to** ~ **up (on sth)** investigare (qc); **to** ~ **up on sb** informarsi sul conto di qn.

checkbook [chek'bŏŏk] *n* libretto degli assegni.

checkerboard [chek'ərbôrd] *n* *(US)* scacchiera.

checkered [chek'ûrd] *a* *(US: fig)* movimentato(a).

checkers [chek'ûrz] *n* *(US)* dama.

check guarantee card *n* carta *f* assegni *inv*.

check-in [chek'in] *n* *(also:* ~ **desk**: *at airport)* check-in *m inv*, accettazione *f* (bagagli *inv*).

checking account [chek'ing əkount'] *n* *(US)* conto corrente.

checklist [chek'list] *n* lista di controllo.

checkmate [chek'māt] *n* scaccomatto.

checkout [chek'out] *n* *(in supermarket)* cassa.

checkpoint [chek'point] *n* posto di blocco.

checkroom [chek'rŏŏm] *n* *(US: for coats etc)* guardaroba *m inv*; *(: for luggage)* deposito *m* bagagli *inv*.

checkup [chek'up] *n* *(MED)* controllo medico.

cheek [chēk] *n* guancia; *(impudence)* faccia tosta.

cheekbone [chēk'bōn] *n* zigomo.

cheeky [chē'kē] *a* sfacciato(a).

cheep [chēp] *n* *(of bird)* pigolio ♦ *vi* pigolare.

cheer [chēr] *vt* applaudire; *(gladden)* rallegrare ♦ *vi* applaudire ♦ *n* *(gen pl)* applausi *mpl*; evviva *mpl*; ~**s!** salute!

cheer on *vt* *(person etc)* incitare.

cheer up *vi* rallegrarsi, farsi animo ♦ *vt* rallegrare.

cheerful [chēr'fəl] *a* allegro(a).

cheerfulness [chēr'fəlnis] *n* allegria.

cheerio [chēr'ēō] *excl* *(Brit)* ciao!

cheerless [chēr'lis] *a* triste.

cheese [chēz] *n* formaggio.

cheeseboard [chēz'bôrd] *n* piatto del *(or* per il) formaggio.

cheesecake [chēz'kāk] *n* specie di torta di ricotta, a volte con frutta.

cheetah [chē'tə] *n* ghepardo.

chef [shef] *n* capocuoco.

chemical [kem'ikəl] *a* chimico(a) ♦ *n* prodotto chimico.

chemical engineering *n* ingegneria chimica.

chemist [kem'ist] *n* *(Brit: pharmacist)* farmacista *m/f*; *(scientist)* chimico/a; ~**'s shop** *n* *(Brit)* farmacia.

chemistry [kem'istrē] *n* chimica.

cheque [chek] *etc* *(Brit)* = **check** *etc*.

cheque card *n* *(Brit)* carta *f* assegni *inv*.

chequered [chek'ûrd] *a* *(Brit)* = **checkered**.

cherish [chär'ish] *vt* aver caro; *(hope etc)* nutrire.

cheroot [shərŏŏt'] *n* sigaro spuntato.

cherry [chär'ē] *n* ciliegia.

Ches *abbr* *(Brit)* = *Cheshire*.

chess [ches] *n* scacchi *mpl*.

chessboard [ches'bôrd] *n* scacchiera.

chessman [ches'man] *n* pezzo degli scacchi.

chessplayer [ches'plâùr] *n* scacchista *m/f*.

chest [chest] *n* petto; *(box)* cassa; **to get sth off one's** ~ *(col)* sputare il rospo; ~ **of drawers** cassettone *m*.

chest measurement *n* giro *m* torace *inv*.

chestnut [ches'nut] *n* castagna; *(also:* ~ *tree)* castagno ♦ *a* castano(a).

chew [chŏŏ] *vt* masticare.

chewing gum [chŏŏ'ing gum] *n* chewing gum *m*.

chic [shēk] *a* elegante.

chick [chik] *n* pulcino; *(col)* pollastrella.

chicken [chik'ən] *n* pollo; *(col: coward)* coniglio.

chicken out *vi* *(col)* avere fifa; **to** ~ **out of sth** tirarsi indietro da qc per fifa *or* paura.

chicken feed *n* *(fig)* miseria.

chickenpox [chik'ənpâks] *n* varicella.

chickpea [chik'pē] *n* cece *m*.

chicory [chik'ûrē] *n* cicoria.

chide [chīd] *vt* rimproverare.

chief [chēf] *n* capo ♦ *a* principale; **C**~ **of Staff** *(MIL)* Capo di Stato Maggiore.

chief constable *n* *(Brit)* ≈ questore *m*.

chief executive officer, *(Brit)* **chief executive** *n* direttore *m* generale.

chiefly [chēf'lē] *ad* per lo più, soprattutto.
chiffon [shifân'] *n* chiffon *m inv*.
chilblain [chil'blān] *n* gelone *m*.
child, *pl* ~**ren** [chīld, chīl'drən] *n* bambino/a.
childbirth [chīld'bûrth] *n* parto.
childhood [chīld'hood] *n* infanzia.
childish [chīl'dish] *a* puerile.
childless [chīld'lis] *a* senza figli.
childlike [chīld'līk] *a* fanciullesco(a).
child minder *n* (*Brit*) bambinaia.
children [chil'drən] *npl of* **child**.
Chile [chil'ē] *n* Cile *m*.
Chilean [chēl'āən] *a*, *n* cileno(a).
chili, (*Brit*) **chilli** [chil'ē] *n* peperoncino.
chill [chil] *n* freddo; (*MED*) infreddatura ♦ *a* freddo(a), gelido(a) ♦ *vt* raffreddare; (*CULIN*) mettere in fresco; "serve ~ed" "servire fresco".
chilly [chil'ē] *a* freddo(a), fresco(a); (*sensitive to cold*) freddoloso(a); **to feel** ~ sentirsi infreddolito(a).
chime [chīm] *n* carillon *m inv* ♦ *vi* suonare, scampanare.
chimney [chim'nē] *n* camino.
chimney sweep *n* spazzacamino.
chimpanzee [chimpanzē'] *n* scimpanzé *m inv*.
chin [chin] *n* mento.
China [chī'nə] *n* Cina.
china [chī'nə] *n* porcellana.
Chinese [chīnēz'] *a* cinese ♦ *n* (*pl inv*) cinese *m/f*; (*LING*) cinese *m*.
chink [chingk] *n* (*opening*) fessura; (*noise*) tintinnio.
chip [chip] *n* (*gen pl:* US: *also:* **potato** ~) patatina; (: *Brit CULIN*) patatina fritta; (*of wood, glass, stone*) scheggia; (*in gambling*) fiche *f inv*; (*COMPUT*: *micro*~) chip *m inv* ♦ *vt* (*cup, plate*) scheggiare; **when the** ~**s are down** (*fig*) al momento critico.
    chip in *vi* (*col: contribute*) contribuire; (*: interrupt*) intromettersi.
chipboard [chip'bôrd] *n* (*Brit*) agglomerato.
chipmunk [chip'mungk] *n* tamia *m* striato.
chiropodist [kirâp'ədist] *n* (*Brit*) pedicure *m/f inv*.
chiropody [kirâp'ədē] *n* (*Brit*) mestiere *m* di callista.
chirp [chûrp] *n* cinguettio; (*of crickets*) cri cri *m* ♦ *vi* cinguettare.
chirpy [chûr'pē] *a* (*col*) frizzante.
chisel [chiz'əl] *n* cesello.
chit [chit] *n* biglietto.
chitchat [chit'chat] *n* (*col*) chiacchiere *fpl*.
chivalrous [shiv'əlrəs] *a* cavalleresco(a).
chivalry [shiv'əlrē] *n* cavalleria; cortesia.
chives [chīvz] *npl* erba cipollina.
chloride [klôr'īd] *n* cloruro.
chlorinate [klôr'ənāt] *vt* clorare.
chlorine [klôr'ēn] *n* cloro.
chock [châk] *n* zeppa.
chock-a-block [châk'əblâk'], **chockfull**

[châk'fool] *a* pieno(a) zeppo(a).
chocolate [chôk'əlit] *n* (*substance*) cioccolato, cioccolata; (*drink*) cioccolata; (*a sweet*) cioccolatino.
choice [chois] *n* scelta ♦ *a* scelto(a); **a wide** ~ un'ampia scelta; **I did it by** *or* **from** ~ l'ho fatto di mia volontà *or* per mia scelta.
choir [kwī'ûr] *n* coro.
choirboy [kwiûr'boi] *n* corista *m* fanciullo.
choke [chōk] *vi* soffocare ♦ *vt* soffocare; (*block*) ingombrare ♦ *n* (*AUT*) valvola dell'aria.
cholera [kâl'ûrə] *n* colera *m*.
cholesterol [kəles'tərôl] *n* colesterolo.
choose, *pt* **chose**, *pp* **chosen** [chōoz, chōz, chō'zən] *vt* scegliere; **to** ~ **to do** decidere di fare; preferire fare; **to** ~ **between** scegliere tra; **to** ~ **from** scegliere da *or* tra.
choosy [chōo'zē] *a*: (**to be**) ~ (fare lo(la)) schizzinoso(a).
chop [châp] *vt* (*wood*) spaccare; (*CULIN: also:* ~ **up**) tritare ♦ *n* colpo netto; (*CULIN*) costoletta; **to get the** ~ (*Brit col: project*) essere bocciato(a); (*: person: be sacked*) essere licenziato(a); *see also* **chops**.
    chop down *vt* (*tree*) abbattere.
choppy [châp'ē] *a* (*sea*) mosso(a).
chops [châps] *npl* (*jaws*) mascelle *fpl*.
chopsticks [châp'stiks] *npl* bastoncini *mpl* cinesi.
choral [kôr'əl] *a* corale.
chord [kôrd] *n* (*MUS*) accordo.
chore [chôr] *n* faccenda; **household** ~**s** faccende *fpl* domestiche.
choreographer [kôrēâg'rəfûr] *n* coreografo/a.
chorister [kôr'istûr] *n* corista *m/f*.
chortle [chôr'təl] *vi* ridacchiare.
chorus [kôr'əs] *n* coro; (*repeated part of song, also fig*) ritornello.
chose [chōz] *pt of* **choose**.
chosen [chō'zən] *pp of* **choose**.
chowder [chou'dûr] *n* zuppa di pesce.
Christ [krīst] *n* Cristo.
christen [kris'ən] *vt* battezzare.
christening [kris'əning] *n* battesimo.
Christian [kris'chən] *a*, *n* cristiano(a).
Christianity [krischēan'itē] *n* cristianesimo.
Christian name *n* nome *m* di battesimo.
Christmas [kris'məs] *n* Natale *m*; **happy** *or* **merry** ~! Buon Natale!
Christmas card *n* cartolina di Natale.
Christmas Day *n* il giorno di Natale.
Christmas Eve *n* la vigilia di Natale.
Christmas Island *n* isola di Christmas.
Christmas tree *n* albero di Natale.
chrome [krōm] *n* = **chromium**.
chromium [krō'mēəm] *n* cromo; (*also:* ~ **plating**) cromatura.
chromosome [krō'məsōm] *n* cromosoma *m*.
chronic [krân'ik] *a* cronico(a); (*fig: liar, smoker*) incallito(a).

chronicle |krân'ikəl| *n* cronaca.

chronological |krânəlâj'ikəl| *a* cronologico(a).

chrysanthemum |krisan'thəməm| *n* crisantemo.

chubby |chub'ē| *a* paffuto(a).

chuck |chuk| *vt* buttare, gettare; **to ~ (up** *or* **in)** (*Brit: job, person*) piantare.

chuck out *vt* buttar fuori.

chuckle |chuk'əl| *vi* ridere sommessamente.

chug |chug| *vi* (*also*: **~ along**: *train*) muoversi sbuffando.

chum |chum| *n* compagno/a

chump |chump| *n* (*col*) idiota *m/f*.

chunk |chungk| *n* pezzo; (*of bread*) tocco.

chunky |chung'kē| *a* (*furniture etc*) basso(a) e largo(a); (*person*) ben piantato(a); (*knitwear*) di lana grossa.

church |chûrch| *n* chiesa; **the C~ of England** la Chiesa anglicana.

churchyard |chûrch'yârd| *n* sagrato.

churlish |chûr'lish| *a* rozzo(a), sgarbato(a).

churn |chûrn| *n* (*for butter*) zangola; (*also*: **milk ~**) bidone *m*.

churn out *vt* sfornare.

chute |shōōt| *n* cascata; (*also*: **garbage ~**) canale *m* di scarico; (*Brit: children's slide*) scivolo.

chutney |chut'nē| *n* salsa piccante (di frutta, zucchero e spezie).

CIA *n abbr* (*US*: = *Central Intelligence Agency*) C.I.A. *f*.

CID *n abbr* (*Brit*) *see* **Criminal Investigation Department**.

cider |sī'dûr| *n* sidro.

CIF *abbr* (= *cost, insurance and freight*) C.I.F. *m*.

cigar |sigâr'| *n* sigaro.

cigarette |sigərct'| *n* sigaretta.

cigarette butt *n* (*US*) mozzicone *m*.

cigarette case *n* portasigarette *m inv*.

cigarette end *n* (*Brit*) mozzicone *m*.

cigarette holder *n* bocchino.

C in C *abbr see* **commander in chief**.

cinch |sinch| *n* (*col*): **it's a ~** è presto fatto; (*sure thing*) è una cosa sicura.

cinder |sin'dûr| *n* cenere *f*.

cinder block |sin'dûr blâk| *n* (*US*) *mattone composto di scorie di coke*.

Cinderella |sindərcl'ə| *n* Cenerentola.

cine-camera |sin'ēkam'ûrə| *n* (*Brit*) cinepresa.

cine-film |sin'ēfilm| *n* (*Brit*) pellicola.

cinema |sin'əmə| *n* cinema *m inv*.

cinnamon |sin'əmən| *n* cannella.

cipher |sī'fûr| *n* cifra; (*fig: faceless employee etc*) persona di nessun conto; **in ~** in codice.

circa |sûr'kə| *prep* circa.

circle |sûr'kəl| *n* cerchio; (*of friends etc*) circolo; (*in cinema*) galleria ♦ *vi* girare in circolo ♦ *vt* (*surround*) circondare; (*move around*) girare intorno a.

circuit |sûr'kit| *n* circuito.

circuit board *n* (*COMPUT*) tavola dei circuiti.

circuit court *n* (*US*) ≈ corte *f* d'assise.

circuitous |sûrkyōō'itəs| *a* indiretto(a).

circular |sûr'kyəlûr| *a* circolare ♦ *n* (*letter*) circolare *f*; (*as advertisement*) volantino pubblicitario.

circulate |sûr'kyəlāt| *vi* circolare; (*person: socially*) girare e andare un po' da tutti ♦ *vt* far circolare.

circulating capital *n* (*COMM*) capitale *m* d'esercizio.

circulation |sûrkyəlā'shən| *n* circolazione *f*; (*of newspaper*) tiratura.

circumcise |sûr'kəmsīz| *vt* circoncidere.

circumference |sûrkum'fûrəns| *n* circonferenza.

circumflex |sûr'kəmflcks| *n* (*also*: **~ accent**) accento circonflesso.

circumscribe |sûrkəmskrīb'| *vt* circoscrivere; (*fig: limit*) limitare.

circumspect |sûr'kəmspckt| *a* circospetto(a).

circumstances |sûr'kəmstansiz| *npl* circostanze *fpl*; (*financial condition*) condizioni *fpl* finanziarie; **under the ~s** date le circostanze; **under no ~s** per nessun motivo.

circumstantial |sûrkəmstan'shəl| *a* (*report, statement*) circostanziato(a), dettagliato(a); **~ evidence** prova indiretta.

circumvent |sûrkəmvcnt'| *vt* (*rule etc*) aggirare.

circus |sûr'kəs| *n* circo; (*also*: **C~**: *in place names*) piazza (di forma circolare).

cistern |sis'tûrn| *n* cisterna; (*Brit: in toilet*) serbatoio d'acqua.

citation |sītā'shən| *n* citazione *f*.

cite |sit| *vt* citare.

citizen |sit'əzən| *n* (*POL*) cittadino/a; (*resident*): **the ~s of this town** gli abitanti di questa città.

citizenship |sit'əzənship| *n* cittadinanza.

citric |sit'rik| *a*: **~ acid** acido citrico.

citrus fruit |sit'rəs frōōt| *n* agrume *m*.

city |sit'ē| *n* città *f inv*.

city center *n* centro della città.

city hall *n* (*US*) autorità *fpl* municipali.

city plan *n* pianta della città.

city planner *n* (*US*) urbanista *m/f*.

city planning *n* (*US*) urbanistica.

civic |siv'ik| *a* civico(a).

civil |siv'əl| *a* civile; (*polite*) educato(a), gentile.

civil disobedience *n* disubbidienza civile.

civil engineer *n* ingegnere *m* civile.

civil engineering *n* ingegneria civile.

civilian |sivil'yən| *a, n* borghese (*m/f*).

civilization |sivələzā'shən| *n* civiltà *f inv*.

civilized |siv'əlīzd| *a* civilizzato(a); (*fig*) cortese.

civil law *n* codice *m* civile; (*study*) diritto civile.

civil rights *npl* diritti *mpl* civili.

civil servant n impiegato/a statale.
Civil Service n amministrazione f statale.
civil war n guerra civile.
cl abbr (= centiliter) cl.
clad [klad] a: ~ **(in)** vestito(a) (di).
claim [klām] vt (rights etc) rivendicare; (damages) richiedere; (assert) sostenere, pretendere ♦ vi (for insurance) fare una domanda d'indennizzo ♦ n rivendicazione f; pretesa; (right) diritto; **to ~ that/to be** sostenere che/di essere; **(insurance)** ~ domanda d'indennizzo; **to put in a ~ for sth** fare una richiesta di qc.
claimant [klā'mənt] n (ADMIN, LAW) richiedente m/f.
claim form n (gen) modulo di richiesta; (for expenses) modulo di rimborso spese.
clairvoyant [klärvoi'ənt] n chiaroveggente m/f.
clam [klam] n vongola.
    clam up vi (col) azzittirsi.
clamber [klam'bûr] vi arrampicarsi.
clammy [klam'ē] a (weather) caldo(a) umido(a); (hands) viscido(a).
clamor, (Brit) **clamour** [klam'ûr] n (noise) clamore m; (protest) protesta ♦ vi: **to ~ for sth** chiedere a gran voce qc.
clamp [klamp] n pinza; morsa ♦ vt ammorsare.
    clamp down vt fus (fig): **to ~ down (on)** dare un giro di vite (a).
clan [klan] n clan m inv.
clandestine [klandes'tin] a clandestino(a).
clang [klang] n fragore m, suono metallico.
clansman [klanz'mən] n membro di un clan.
clap [klap] vi applaudire ♦ vt: **to ~ one's hands** battere le mani ♦ n: **a ~ of thunder** un tuono.
clapping [klap'ing] n applausi mpl.
claret [klar'it] n vino di Bordeaux.
clarification [klarəfəkā'shən] n (fig) chiarificazione f, chiarimento.
clarify [klar'əfī] vt chiarificare, chiarire.
clarinet [klarənet'] n clarinetto.
clarity [klar'itē] n chiarezza.
clash [klash] n frastuono; (fig) scontro ♦ vi (MIL, fig: have an argument) scontrarsi; (colors) stridere; (dates, events) coincidere.
clasp [klasp] n fermaglio, fibbia ♦ vt stringere.
class [klas] n classe f; (group, category) tipo, categoria ♦ vt classificare.
class-conscious [klas'kản'shəs] a che ha coscienza di classe.
class consciousness n coscienza di classe.
classic [klas'ik] a classico(a) ♦ n classico.
classical [klas'ikəl] a classico(a).
classics [klas'iks] npl (SCOL) studi mpl umanistici.
classification [klasəfəkā'shən] n classificazione f.
classified [klas'əfīd] a (information) segreto(a), riservato(a); ~ **ads** annunci economi-

ci.
classify [klas'əfī] vt classificare.
classmate [klas'māt] n compagno/a di classe.
classroom [klas'rōōm] n aula.
clatter [klat'ûr] n acciottolio; scalpitio ♦ vi acciottolare; scalpitare.
clause [klôz] n clausola; (LING) proposizione f.
claustrophobia [klôstrəfō'bēə] n claustrofobia.
claw [klô] n tenaglia; (of bird of prey) artiglio; (of lobster) pinza ♦ vt graffiare; afferrare.
clay [klā] n argilla.
clean [klēn] a pulito(a); (clear, smooth) netto(a) ♦ vt pulire ♦ ad: **he ~ forgot** si è completamente dimenticato; **to come ~** (col: admit guilt) confessare; **to have a ~ driving record** non aver mai preso contravvenzioni; **to ~ one's teeth** (Brit) lavarsi i denti.
    clean off vt togliere.
    clean out vt ripulire.
    clean up vi far pulizia ♦ vt (also fig) ripulire; (fig: make profit): **to ~ up on** fare una barca di soldi con.
clean-cut [klēn'kut'] a (man) curato(a); (situation etc) ben definito(a).
cleaner [klē'nûr] n (person) uomo/donna delle pulizie; (also: **dry ~**) tintore/a; (product) smacchiatore m.
cleaning [klē'ning] n pulizia.
cleaning lady or **woman** n donna delle pulizie.
cleanliness [klen'lēnis] n pulizia.
cleanly [klēn'lē] ad in modo netto.
cleanse [klenz] vt pulire; purificare.
cleanser [klen'zûr] n detergente m; (cosmetic) latte m detergente.
clean-shaven [klēn'shā'vən] a sbarbato(a).
cleansing department [klen'zing dipárt'mənt] n (Brit) nettezza urbana.
clean-up [klēn'up] n pulizia.
clear [kli'ûr] a chiaro(a); (road, way) libero(a); (profit, majority) netto(a) ♦ vt sgombrare; liberare; (site, woodland) spianare; (COMM: goods) liquidare; (LAW: suspect) discolpare; (obstacle) superare; (check) fare la compensazione di ♦ vi (weather) rasserenarsi; (fog) andarsene ♦ ad: ~ **of** distante da ♦ n: **to be in the ~** (out of debt) essere in attivo; (out of suspicion) essere a posto; (out of danger) essere fuori pericolo; **to ~ the table** sparecchiare (la tavola); **to ~ one's throat** schiarirsi la gola; **to ~ a profit** avere un profitto netto; **to make o.s. ~** spiegarsi bene; **to make it ~ to sb that ...** far capire a qn che ...; **I have a ~ day tomorrow** (Brit) non ho impegni domani; **to keep ~ of sb/sth** tenersi lontano da qn/qc, stare alla larga da qn/qc.
    clear off vi (Brit col) = clear out.
    clear out vi (US col: leave) svignarsela.
    clear up vi schiarirsi ♦ vt mettere in ordi-

ne; (*mystery*) risolvere.

clearance [klē'rəns] *n* (*removal*) sgombro; (*free space*) spazio; (*permission*) autorizzazione *f*, permesso.

clearance sale *n* vendita di liquidazione.

clear-cut [kli'ûrkut'] *a* ben delineato(a), distinto(a).

clearing [klē'ring] *n* radura; (*Brit BANKING*) clearing *m*.

clearing bank *n* (*Brit*) *banca che fa uso della camera di compensazione.*

clearing house *n* (*COMM*) camera di compensazione.

clearly [kli'ûrlē] *ad* chiaramente.

clearway [klēr'wā] *n* (*Brit*) strada con divieto di sosta.

cleavage [klē'vij] *n* (*of woman*) scollatura.

cleaver [klē'vûr] *n* mannaia.

clef [klef] *n* (*MUS*) chiave *f*.

cleft [kleft] *n* (*in rock*) crepa, fenditura.

clemency [klem'ənsē] *n* clemenza.

clement [klem'ənt] *a* (*weather*) mite, clemente.

clench [klench] *vt* stringere.

clergy [klûr'jē] *n* clero.

clergyman [klûr'jēmən] *n* ecclesiastico.

clerical [klär'ikəl] *a* d'impiegato; (*REL*) clericale.

clerk [klûrk, (*Brit*) klärk] *n* impiegato/a; (*US: salesman/woman*) commesso/a; **C~ of the Court** (*LAW*) cancelliere *m*.

clever [klev'ûr] *a* (*mentally*) intelligente; (*deft, skilful*) abile; (*device, arrangement*) ingegnoso(a).

clew [kloo] *n* (*US*) = **clue.**

cliché [klēshā'] *n* cliché *m inv.*

click [klik] *vi* scattare ♦ *vt:* **to ~ one's tongue** schioccare la lingua; **to ~ one's heels** battere i tacchi.

client [klī'ənt] *n* cliente *m/f.*

clientele [klīəntel'] *n* clientela.

cliff [klif] *n* scogliera scoscesa, rupe *f.*

cliffhanger [klif'hangûr] *n* (*TV, fig*) episodio (*or* situazione *etc*) ricco(a) di suspense.

climactic [klīmak'tik] *a* culminante.

climate [klī'mit] *n* clima *m.*

climax [klī'maks] *n* culmine *m*; (*of play etc*) momento più emozionante; (*sexual ~*) orgasmo.

climb [klīm] *vi* salire; (*clamber*) arrampicarsi; (*plane*) prendere quota ♦ *vt* salire; (*CLIMBING*) scalare ♦ *n* salita; arrampicata, scalata; **to ~ over a wall** scavalcare un muro.

climb down *vi* scendere; (*Brit fig*) far marcia indietro.

climbdown [klīm'doun] *n* (*Brit*) ritirata.

climber [klī'mûr] *n* (*also*: **rock ~**) rocciatore/trice; alpinista *m/f.*

climbing [klī'ming] *n* (*also*: **rock ~**) alpinismo.

clinch [klinch] *vt* (*deal*) concludere.

cling, *pt, pp* **clung** [kling, klung] *vi:* **to ~ (to)** tenersi stretto(a) (a); (*of clothes*) aderire strettamente (a).

clinic [klin'ik] *n* clinica; (*session*) seduta; serie *f* di sedute.

clinical [klin'ikəl] *a* clinico(a); (*fig*) freddo(a), distaccato(a).

clink [klingk] *vi* tintinnare.

clip [klip] *n* (*for hair*) forcina; (*also*: **paper ~**) graffetta; (*clamp*) fermafogli *m inv*; (*holding hose etc*) anello d'attacco ♦ *vt* (*also*: **~ together**: *papers*) attaccare insieme; (*hair, nails*) tagliare; (*hedge*) tosare.

clippers [klip'ûrz] *npl* macchinetta per capelli; (*also*: **nail ~**) forbicine *fpl* per le unghie.

clipping [klip'ing] *n* (*from newspaper*) ritaglio.

clique [klēk] *n* cricca.

cloak [klōk] *n* mantello ♦ *vt* avvolgere.

cloakroom [klōk'rōōm] *n* (*for coats etc*) guardaroba *m inv*; (*Brit:* W.C.) gabinetti *mpl.*

clock [kläk] *n* orologio; (*of taxi*) tassametro; **around the ~** ventiquattr'ore su ventiquattro; **to sleep around the ~** dormire un giorno intero; **to work against the ~** lavorare in gara col tempo; **30,000 on the ~** (*Brit AUT*) 30.000 sul contachilometri.

clock in, clock on *vi* timbrare il cartellino (all'entrata).

clock off, clock out *vi* timbrare il cartellino (all'uscita).

clock up *vt* (*miles, hours etc*) fare.

clockwise [kläk'wīz] *ad* in senso orario.

clockwork [kläk'wûrk] *n* movimento *or* meccanismo a orologeria ♦ *a* (*toy, train*) a molla.

clod [kläd] *n* (*col: idiot*) scemo/a.

clog [kläg] *n* zoccolo ♦ *vt* intasare ♦ *vi* intasarsi, bloccarsi.

cloister [klois'tûr] *n* chiostro.

clone [klōn] *n* clone *m.*

close [klōs] *a, ad and derivatives a* vicino(a); (*writing, texture*) fitto(a); (*watch*) stretto(a); (*examination*) attento(a); (*weather*) afoso(a) ♦ *ad* vicino, dappresso; **~ to** *prep* vicino a; **~ by, ~ at hand** qui (*or* lì) vicino; **how ~ is Boston to New York?** quanto dista Boston da New York?; **a ~ friend** un amico intimo; **to have a ~ shave** (*fig*) scamparla bella; **at ~ quarters** da vicino ♦ *vb, n and derivatives* [klōz] *vt* chiudere; (*bargain, deal*) concludere ♦ *vi* (*shop etc*) chiudere; (*lid, door etc*) chiudersi; (*end*) finire ♦ *n* (*end*) fine *f*; **to bring sth to a ~** terminare qc.

close down *vt* chiudere (definitivamente) ♦ *vi* cessare (definitivamente).

close in *vi* (*hunters*) stringersi attorno; (*evening, night, fog*) calare; **to ~ in on sb** accerchiare qn; **the days are closing in** le giornate si accorciano.

close off vt (area) chiudere.

closed [klōzd] a chiuso(a).

closed-circuit [klōzdsûr'kit] a: ~ **television** televisione f a circuito chiuso.

closed shop n azienda o fabbrica che impiega solo aderenti ai sindacati.

close-knit [klōs'nit'] a (family, community) molto unito(a).

closely [klōs'lē] ad (examine, watch) da vicino; **we are ~ related** siamo parenti stretti; **a ~ guarded secret** un assoluto segreto.

closet [klâz'it] n armadio.

close-up [klōs'up] n primo piano.

closing [klō'zing] a (stages, remarks) conclusivo(a), finale; ~ **price** (STOCK EXCHANGE) prezzo di chiusura.

closure [klō'zhûr] n chiusura.

clot [klât] n (also: **blood** ~) coagulo; (Brit: col: idiot) scemo/a ♦ vi coagularsi.

cloth [klôth] n (material) tessuto, stoffa; (Brit: also: **tea~**) strofinaccio; (also: **table~**) tovaglia.

clothe [klōth] vt vestire.

clothes [klōz] npl abiti mpl, vestiti mpl; **to put one's ~ on** vestirsi; **to take one's ~ off** togliersi i vestiti, svestirsi.

clothes brush n spazzola per abiti.

clothes line n corda (per stendere il bucato).

clothes pin, (Brit) **clothes peg** n molletta.

clothing [klō'thing] n = **clothes**.

clotted cream [klât'id krēm] n (Brit) panna rappresa.

cloud [kloud] n nuvola; (of dust, smoke, gas) nube f ♦ vt (liquid) intorbidire; **to ~ the issue** distogliere dal problema; **every ~ has a silver lining** (proverb) non tutto il male vien per nuocere.

cloud over vi rannuvolarsi; (fig) offuscarsi.

cloudburst [kloud'bûrst] n acquazzone m.

cloudland [kloud'land] n (US) mondo dei sogni.

cloud-cuckoo-land [kloudkōō'kōōland] n (Brit) = **cloudland**.

cloudy [klou'dē] a nuvoloso(a); (liquid) torbido(a).

clout [klout] n (blow) colpo; (fig) influenza ♦ vt dare un colpo a.

clove [klōv] n chiodo di garofano; ~ **of garlic** spicchio d'aglio.

clover [klō'vûr] n trifoglio.

cloverleaf [klō'vûrlēf] n foglia di trifoglio; (AUT) raccordo (a quadrifoglio).

clown [kloun] n pagliaccio ♦ vi (also: ~ **around**, (Brit) ~ **about**) fare il pagliaccio.

cloying [kloi'ing] a (taste, smell) nauseabondo(a).

CLU n abbr (US: = Chartered Life Underwriter) qualifica professionale di assicuratore sulla vita.

club [klub] n (society) club m inv, circolo; (weapon, GOLF) mazza ♦ vt bastonare ♦ vi:

to ~ together associarsi; **~s** npl (CARDS) fiori mpl.

club car n (US RAIL) carrozza or vagone m ristorante.

clubhouse [klub'hous] n sede f del circolo.

cluck [kluk] vi chiocciare.

clue [klōō] n indizio; (in crosswords) definizione f; **I haven't a ~** non ho la minima idea.

clued in [klōōd in] a (US col) (ben) informato(a).

clued up [klōōd up] a (Brit) = **clued in**.

clump [klump] n: ~ **of trees** folto d'alberi.

clumsy [klum'zē] a (person) goffo(a), maldestro(a); (object) malfatto(a), mal costruito(a).

clung [klung] pt, pp of **cling**.

clunker [klunk'ûr] n (US: pej) macinino.

cluster [klus'tûr] n gruppo ♦ vi raggrupparsi.

clutch [kluch] n (grip, grasp) presa, stretta; (AUT) frizione f ♦ vt afferrare, stringere forte; **to ~ at** aggrapparsi a.

clutter [klut'ûr] vt (also: ~ **up**) ingombrare ♦ n confusione f, disordine m.

CM abbr (US MAIL) = North Marianna Islands.

cm abbr (= centimeter) cm.

CND n abbr = Campaign for Nuclear Disarmament.

CO n abbr (= commanding officer) Com. ♦ abbr (US MAIL) = Colorado.

Co. abbr = county; (= company) C., C.ia.

c/o abbr (= care of) c/o.

coach [kōch] n (SPORT) allenatore/trice; (Brit: bus) pullman m inv; (: horse-drawn, of train) carrozza ♦ vt allenare.

coach trip n (Brit) viaggio in pullman.

coagulate [kōag'yəlāt] vt coagulare ♦ vi coagularsi.

coal [kōl] n carbone m.

coalfield [kōl'fēld] n bacino carbonifero.

coalition [kōəlish'ən] n coalizione f.

coalman [kōl'mən] n = **coal merchant**.

coal merchant [kōl' mûrchənt] n negoziante m di carbone.

coal mine n miniera di carbone.

coal miner n minatore m.

coal mining n estrazione f del carbone.

coarse [kôrs] a (salt, sand etc) grosso(a); (cloth, person) rozzo(a); (vulgar: character, laugh) volgare.

coast [kōst] n costa ♦ vi (with cycle etc) scendere a ruota libera.

coastal [kōs'təl] a costiero(a).

coaster [kōs'tûr] n (for glass) sottobicchiere m; (Brit NAUT) nave f da cabotaggio.

coastguard [kōst'gârd] n guardia costiera.

coastline [kōst'līn] n linea costiera.

coat [kōt] n cappotto; (of animal) pelo; (of paint) mano f ♦ vt coprire; ~ **of arms** n stemma m.

coated [kō'tid] a (US): **to have a ~ tongue**

avere la lingua bianca.
coat hanger *n* attaccapanni *m inv*.
coating [kō'ting] *n* rivestimento.
co-author [kōōth'ûr] *n* coautore/trice.
coax [kōks] *vt* indurre (con moine).
cob [kâb] *n see* **corn**.
cobbler [kâb'lûr] *n* calzolaio.
cobble(stone)s [kâb'əl(stōn)z] *npl* ciottoli *mpl*.
COBOL [kō'bōl] *n* COBOL *m*.
cobra [kōb'rə] *n* cobra *m inv*.
cobweb [kâb'web] *n* ragnatela.
cocaine [kōkān'] *n* cocaina.
cock [kâk] *n* (*rooster*) gallo; (*male bird*) maschio ♦ *vt* (*gun*) armare; **to ~ one's ears** (*fig*) drizzare le orecchie.
cock-a-hoop [kâkəhōōp'] *a* euforico(a).
cockerel [kâk'ûrəl] *n* galletto.
cockeyed [kâk'īd] *a* (*fig*) storto(a); strampalato(a).
cockle [kâk'əl] *n* cardio.
cockney [kâk'nē] *n* cockney *m/f inv* (*abitante dei quartieri popolari dell'East End di Londra*).
cockpit [kâk'pit] *n* abitacolo.
cockroach [kâk'rōch] *n* blatta.
cocktail [kâk'tāl] *n* cocktail *m inv*; **shrimp ~**, (*Brit*) **prawn ~** cocktail di gamberetti.
cocktail cabinet *n* (*Brit*) mobile *m* bar *inv*.
cocktail party *n* cocktail *m inv*.
cocktail shaker [kâk'tāl shā'kûr] *n* shaker *m inv*.
cocoa [kō'kō] *n* cacao.
coconut [kō'kənut] *n* noce *f* di cocco.
cocoon [kəkōōn'] *n* bozzolo.
COD *abbr see* **cash on delivery, collect on delivery.**
cod [kâd] *n* merluzzo.
code [kōd] *n* codice *m*; **~ of behavior** regole *fpl* di condotta; **~ of practice** codice professionale.
codeine [kō'dēn] *n* codeina.
codicil [kâd'isəl] *n* codicillo.
codify [kâd'əfī] *vt* codificare.
cod-liver oil [kâd'livûr oil'] *n* olio di fegato di merluzzo.
co-driver [kōdrī'vûr] *n* (*in race*) copilota *m*; (*of truck*) secondo autista *m*.
co-ed [kōed'] *a abbr* = **coeducational** ♦ *n abbr* (*US: female student*) studentessa presso un'università mista; (*Brit: school*) scuola mista.
coeducational [kōejōōkā'shənəl] *a* misto(a).
coerce [kōûrs'] *vt* costringere.
coercion [kōûr'shən] *n* coercizione *f*.
coexistence [kōigzis'təns] *n* coesistenza.
C. of C. *n abbr* = **chamber of commerce.**
C of E *abbr* = **Church of England.**
coffee [kôf'ē] *n* caffè *m inv*; **~ with cream** caffellatte *m*.
coffee bar *n* (*Brit*) caffè *m inv*.

coffee bean *n* grano *or* chicco di caffè.
coffee break *n* pausa per il caffè.
coffeecake [kôf'ēkāk] *n* (*US*) panino dolce all'uva.
coffee cup *n* tazzina da caffè.
coffeepot [kôf'ēpât] *n* caffettiera.
coffee table *n* tavolino da tè.
coffin [kôf'in] *n* bara.
cog [kâg] *n* dente *m*.
cogent [kō'jənt] *a* convincente.
cognac [kōn'yak] *n* cognac *m inv*.
cogwheel [kâg'hwēl] *n* ruota dentata.
cohabit [kōhab'it] *vi* (*formal*): **to ~ (with sb)** coabitare (con qn).
coherent [kōhē'rənt] *a* coerente.
cohesion [kōhē'zhən] *n* coesione *f*.
cohesive [kōhē'siv] *a* (*fig*) unificante, coesivo(a).
coil [koil] *n* rotolo; (*one loop*) anello; (*AUT, ELEC*) bobina; (*contraceptive*) spirale *f*; (*of smoke*) filo ♦ *vt* avvolgere.
coin [koin] *n* moneta ♦ *vt* (*word*) coniare.
coinage [koi'nij] *n* sistema *m* monetario.
coincide [kōinsīd'] *vi* coincidere.
coincidence [kōin'sidəns] *n* combinazione *f*.
coin-operated [koinâp'ərātid] *a* (*machine*) (che funziona) a monete.
coin purse *n* (*US*) borsellino.
Coke [kōk] ® *n* (*Coca-Cola*) coca *f inv*.
coke [kōk] *n* coke *m*.
Col. *abbr* = **colonel**; (*US*) = *Colorado*.
COLA *n abbr* (*US*: = *cost-of-living adjustment*) ≈ scala mobile.
colander [kâl'əndûr] *n* colino.
cold [kōld] *a* freddo(a) ♦ *n* freddo; (*MED*) raffreddore *m*; **it's ~** fa freddo; **to be ~** aver freddo; **to catch ~** prendere freddo; **to catch a ~** prendere un raffreddore; **in ~ blood** a sangue freddo; **to have ~ feet** avere i piedi freddi; (*fig*) aver la fifa; **to give sb the ~ shoulder** ignorare qn.
cold-blooded [kōld'blud'id] *a* (*ZOOL*) a sangue freddo.
cold cream *n* crema emolliente.
coldly [kōld'lē] *ad* freddamente.
cold sore *n* erpete *m*.
coleslaw [kōl'slô] *n* insalata di cavolo bianco.
colic [kâl'ik] *n* colica.
collaborate [kəlab'ərāt] *vi* collaborare.
collaboration [kəlabərā'shən] *n* collaborazione *f*.
collaborator [kəlab'ərātûr] *n* collaboratore/trice.
collage [kəlâzh'] *n* (*ART*) collage *m inv*.
collagen [kâl'əjən] *n* collageno.
collapse [kəlaps'] *vi* (*gen*) crollare; (*government*) cadere; (*MED*) avere un collasso; (*plans*) fallire ♦ *n* crollo; caduta; collasso; fallimento.
collapsible [kəlaps'əbəl] *a* pieghevole.
collar [kâl'ûr] *n* (*of coat, shirt*) colletto; (*for*

dog) collare *m*; (*TECH*) anello, fascetta ♦ *vt* (*col: person, object*) beccare.

collarbone [kâl'ûrbōn] *n* clavicola.

collate [kəlāt'] *vt* collazionare.

collateral [kəlat'ûrəl] *n* garanzia.

collation [kəlā'shən] *n* collazione *f*.

colleague [kâl'ēg] *n* collega *m/f*.

collect [kəlekt'] *vt* (*gen*) raccogliere; (*as a hobby*) fare collezione di; (*Brit: call for*) prendere; (*money owed, pension*) riscuotere; (*donations, subscriptions*) fare una colletta di ♦ *vi* (*people*) adunarsi, riunirsi; (*rubbish etc*) ammucchiarsi ♦ *ad* (*US TEL*): **to call** ~ fare una chiamata a carico del destinatario; **to** ~ **one's thoughts** raccogliere le idee; ~ **on delivery (COD)** (*US COMM*) pagamento alla consegna.

collect call *n* (*US TEL*) telefonata con addebito al ricevente.

collected [kəlek'tid] *a*: ~ **works** opere *fpl* raccolte.

collection [kəlek'shən] *n* collezione *f*; raccolta; (*for money*) colletta; (*MAIL*) levata.

collective [kəlek'tiv] *a* collettivo(a) ♦ *n* collettivo.

collective bargaining *n* trattative *fpl* (sindacali) collettive.

collector [kəlek'tûr] *n* collezionista *m/f*; (*of taxes*) esattore *m*; ~**'s item** *or* **piece** pezzo da collezionista.

college [kâl'ij] *n* (*Brit, US SCOL*) college *m inv*; (*of technology, agriculture etc*) istituto superiore; (*body*) collegio; ~ **of education** ≈ facoltà *f inv* di Magistero.

collide [kəlīd'] *vi*: **to** ~ (**with**) scontrarsi (con).

collie [kâl'ē] *n* (*dog*) collie *m inv*.

colliery [kâl'yûrē] *n* (*Brit*) miniera di carbone.

collision [kəlizh'ən] *n* collisione *f*, scontro; **to be on a** ~ **course** (*also fig*) essere in rotta di collisione.

collision damage waiver (CDW) *n* (*Brit INSURANCE*) *copertura per i danni alla vettura.*

colloquial [kəlō'kwēəl] *a* familiare.

collusion [kəlōō'zhən] *n* collusione *f*; **in** ~ **with** in accordo segreto con.

Colo. *abbr* (*US*) = *Colorado*.

Cologne [kəlōn'] *n* Colonia.

cologne [kəlōn'] *n* (*also*: **eau de** ~) acqua di colonia.

Colombia [kəlum'bēə] *n* Colombia.

Colombian [kəlum'bēən] *a, n* colombiano(a).

colon [kō'lən] *n* (*sign*) due punti *mpl*; (*MED*) colon *m inv*.

colonel [kûr'nəl] *n* colonnello.

colonial [kəlō'nēəl] *a* coloniale.

colonize [kâl'ənīz] *vt* colonizzare.

colony [kâl'ənē] *n* colonia.

color [kul'ûr] (*US*) *n* colore *m* ♦ *vt* colorare;

(*tint, dye*) tingere; (*fig: affect*) influenzare ♦ *vi* arrossire ♦ *cpd* (*film, photograph, television*) a colori; ~**s** *npl* (*of party, club*) emblemi *mpl*.

Colorado beetle [kâlərád'ō bē'təl] *n* dorifora.

color bar *n* discriminazione *f* razziale (*in locali etc*).

color-blind [kul'ûrblīnd] *a* daltonico(a).

colored [kul'ûrd] *a* colorato(a); (*photo*) a colori ♦ *n*: ~**s** gente *f* di colore.

color film *n* (*for camera*) pellicola a colori.

colorful [kul'ûrfəl] *a* pieno(a) di colore, a vivaci colori; (*personality*) colorato(a).

coloring [kul'ûring] *n* colorazione *f*; (*complexion*) colorito.

color scheme *n* combinazione *f* di colori.

color television *n* televisione *f* a colori.

colossal [kəlâs'əl] *a* colossale.

colour [kul'ûr] *etc* (*Brit*) = **color** *etc*.

colt [kōlt] *n* puledro.

column [kâl'əm] *n* colonna; (*fashion* ~, *sports* ~ *etc*) rubrica; **the editorial** ~ l'articolo di fondo.

columnist [kâl'əmist] *n* articolista *m/f*.

coma [kō'mə] *n* coma *m inv*.

comb [kōm] *n* pettine *m* ♦ *vt* (*hair*) pettinare; (*area*) battere a tappeto.

combat *n* [kâm'bat] combattimento ♦ *vt* [kəmbat'] combattere, lottare contro.

combination [kâmbənā'shən] *n* combinazione *f*.

combination lock *n* serratura a combinazione.

combine *vb* [kəmbīn'] *vt* combinare; (*one quality with another*): **to** ~ **sth with sth** unire qc a qc ♦ *vi* unirsi; (*CHEM*) combinarsi ♦ *n* [kâm'bīn] lega; (*ECON*) associazione *f*; **a** ~**d effort** uno sforzo collettivo.

combine (harvester) *n* mietitrebbia.

combo [kâm'bō] *n* (*JAZZ etc*) gruppo.

combustible [kəmbus'təbəl] *a* combustibile.

combustion [kəmbus'chən] *n* combustione *f*.

come, *pt* **came**, *pp* **come** [kum, kām] *vi* venire; (*arrive*) venire, arrivare; ~ **with me** vieni con me; **we've just** ~ **from Paris** siamo appena arrivati da Parigi; **nothing came of it** non è saltato fuori niente; **to** ~ **into sight** *or* **view** apparire; **to** ~ **to** (*decision etc*) raggiungere; **to** ~ **undone/loose** slacciarsi/allentarsi; **coming!** vengo!; **if it** ~**s to it** nella peggiore delle ipotesi.

come about *vi* succedere.

come across *vt fus* trovare per caso; **to** ~ **across well/badly** fare una buona/cattiva impressione.

come along *vi* (*pupil, work*) fare progressi; ~ **along!** avanti!, andiamo!, forza!

come apart *vi* andare in pezzi; (*become detached*) staccarsi.

come around *vi* (*after faint, operation*) riprendere conoscenza, rinvenire.

come away vi venire via; (become detached) staccarsi.

come back vi ritornare; (reply: col): **can I ~ back to you on that one?** possiamo riparlarne più tardi?

come by vt fus (acquire) ottenere; procurarsi.

come down vi scendere; (prices) calare; (buildings) essere demolito(a).

come forward vi farsi avanti; presentarsi.

come from vt fus venire da; provenire da.

come in vi entrare.

come in for vt fus (criticism etc) ricevere.

come into vt fus (money) ereditare.

come off vi (button) staccarsi; (stain) andar via; (attempt) riuscire.

come on vi (lights, electricity) accendersi; (pupil, undertaking) fare progressi; **~ on!** avanti!, andiamo!, forza!

come out vi uscire; (strike) entrare in sciopero.

come over vt fus: **I don't know what's ~ over him!** non so cosa gli sia successo!

come round vi (Brit) = **come around.**

come through vi (survive) sopravvivere, farcela; **the call came through** ci hanno passato la telefonata.

come to vi rinvenire ♦ vt (add up to: amount): **how much does it ~ to?** quanto costa?, quanto viene?

come under vt fus (heading) trovarsi sotto; (influence) cadere sotto, subire.

come up vi venire su.

come up against vt fus (resistance, difficulties) urtare contro.

come up to vt fus arrivare (fino) a; **the film didn't ~ up to our expectations** il film ci ha delusi.

come up with vt fus: **he came up with an idea** venne fuori con un'idea.

come upon vt fus trovare per caso.

comeback [kum'bak] n (THEATER etc) ritorno; (reaction) reazione f; (response) risultato, risposta.

COMECON n abbr (= Council for Mutual Economic Aid) COMECON m.

comedian [kəmē'dēən] n comico.

comedienne [kəmēdēen'] n attrice f comica.

comedown [kum'doun] n rovescio.

comedy [kâm'idē] n commedia.

comet [kâm'it] n cometa.

comeuppance [kumup'əns] n: **to get one's ~** ricevere ciò che si merita.

comfort [kum'fûrt] n comodità f inv, benessere m; (solace) consolazione f, conforto ♦ vt consolare, confortare; see also **comforts.**

comfortable [kumf'təbəl] a comodo(a); (income, majority) più che sufficiente; **I don't feel very ~ about it** non mi sento molto tranquillo.

comfortably [kum'fûrtəblē] ad (sit) comoda-

mente; (live) bene.

comforter [kum'fûrtûr] n (US) trapunta.

comforts [kum'fûrts] npl comforts mpl, comodità fpl.

comfort station n (US) gabinetti mpl.

comic [kâm'ik] a comico(a) ♦ n comico; (magazine) giornaletto.

comical [kâm'ikəl] a divertente, buffo(a).

comic strip n fumetto.

coming [kum'ing] n arrivo ♦ a (next) prossimo(a); (future) futuro(a); **in the ~ weeks** nelle prossime settimane.

coming(s) and going(s) n(pl) andirivieni m inv.

Comintern [kâm'intûrn] n KOMINTERN m.

comma [kâm'ə] n virgola.

command [kəmand'] n ordine m, comando; (MIL: authority) comando; (mastery) padronanza; (COMPUT) command m inv, comando ♦ vt comandare; **to ~ sb to do** ordinare a qn di fare; **to have/take ~ of** avere/prendere il comando di; **to have at one's ~** (money, resources etc) avere a propria disposizione.

commandeer [kâməndēr'] vt requisire.

commander [kəman'dûr] n capo; (MIL) comandante m.

commander in chief (C in C) n (MIL) comandante m in capo.

commanding [kəman'ding] a (appearance) imponente; (voice, tone) autorevole; (lead, position) dominante.

commanding officer n comandante m.

commandment [kəmand'mənt] n (REL) comandamento.

command module n (SPACE) modulo di comando.

commando [kəman'dō] n commando m inv; membro di un commando.

commemorate [kəmem'ərāt] vt commemorare.

commemoration [kəmemərā'shən] n commemorazione f.

commemorative [kəmem'ərātiv] a commemorativo(a).

commence [kəmens'] vt, vi cominciare.

commend [kəmend'] vt lodare; raccomandare.

commendable [kəmend'əbəl] a lodevole.

commendation [kâməndā'shən] n lode f; raccomandazione f; (for bravery etc) encomio.

commensurate [kəmen'sərit] a: **~ with** proporzionato(a) a.

comment [kâm'ent] n commento ♦ vi: **to ~ (on)** fare commenti (su); **to ~ that** osservare che; **"no ~"** "niente da dire".

commentary [kâm'əntärē] n commentario; (SPORT) radiocronaca; telecronaca.

commentator [kâm'əntātûr] n commentatore/trice; (SPORT) radiocronista m/f; telecronista m/f.

commerce [kâm'ûrs] n commercio.
commercial [kəmûr'shəl] a commerciale ♦ n (TV: also: ~ **break**) pubblicità f inv.
commercial bank n banca commerciale.
commercialism [kəmûr'shəlizəm] n affarismo.
commercialize [kəmûr'shəlīz] vt commercializzare.
commercial television n televisione f commerciale.
commercial vehicle n veicolo commerciale.
commiserate [kəmiz'ərāt] vi: **to** ~ **with** condolersi con.
commission [kəmish'ən] n commissione f; (for salesman) commissione, provvigione f ♦ vt (MIL) nominare (al comando); (work of art) commissionare; **I get 10%** ~ ricevo il 10% sulle vendite; **out of** ~ (NAUT) in disarmo; (machine) fuori uso; **to** ~ **sb to do sth** incaricare qn di fare qc; **to** ~ **sth from sb** (painting etc) commissionare qc a qn.
commissionaire [kəmishənär'] n (Brit: at shop, cinema etc) portiere m in livrea.
commissioner [kəmish'ənûr] n commissionario; (POLICE) questore m.
commit [kəmit'] vt (act) commettere; (to sb's care) affidare; **to** ~ **o.s.** (**to do**) impegnarsi (a fare); **to** ~ **suicide** suicidarsi; **to** ~ **sb for trial** rinviare qn a giudizio.
commitment [kəmit'mənt] n impegno.
committed [kəmit'id] a (writer) impegnato(a); (Christian) convinto(a).
committee [kəmit'ē] n comitato; **to be on a** ~ far parte di un comitato or di una commissione.
committee meeting n riunione f di comitato or di commissione.
commodity [kəmâd'itē] n prodotto, articolo; (food) derrata.
commodity exchange n borsa f merci inv.
common [kâm'ən] a comune; (pej) volgare; (usual) normale ♦ n terreno comune; **in** ~ in comune; **in** ~ **use** di uso comune; **it's** ~ **knowledge that** è di dominio pubblico che; **to the** ~ **good** nell'interesse generale, per il bene comune; see also **Commons**.
commoner [kâm'ənûr] n cittadino/a (non nobile).
common ground n (fig) terreno comune.
common law n diritto consuetudinario.
common-law [kâm'ənlô'] a: ~ **wife** convivente f more uxorio.
commonly [kâm'ənlē] ad comunemente, usualmente.
Common Market n Mercato Comune.
commonplace [kâm'ənplās] a banale, ordinario(a).
common room n (Brit) sala di riunione; (SCOL) sala dei professori.
Commons [kâm'ənz] npl (Brit POL): **the** (**House of**) ~ la Camera dei Comuni.
commons [kâm'ənz] n sg (US) refettorio.

common sense n buon senso.
common stock n (US) azioni fpl ordinarie.
Commonwealth [kâm'ənwelth] n: **the** ~ il Commonwealth.
commotion [kəmō'shən] n confusione f, tumulto.
communal [kəmyōō'nəl] a (life) comunale; (for common use) pubblico(a).
commune n [kâm'yōōn] (group) comune f ♦ vi [kəmyōōn']: **to** ~ **with** mettersi in comunione con.
communicate [kəmyōō'nikāt] vt comunicare, trasmettere ♦ vi: **to** ~ (**with**) comunicare (con).
communication [kəmyōōnikā'shən] n comunicazione f.
communication cord n (Brit) segnale m d'allarme.
communications network n rete f delle comunicazioni.
communications satellite n satellite m per telecomunicazioni.
communicative [kəmyōō'nikātiv] a (gen) loquace.
communion [kəmyōōn'yən] n (also: **Holy C**~) comunione f.
communiqué [kəmyōōnēkā'] n comunicato.
communism [kâm'yənizəm] n comunismo.
communist [kâm'yənist] a, n comunista (m/f).
community [kəmyōō'nitē] n comunità f inv.
community center n circolo ricreativo.
community chest n (US) fondo di beneficenza.
community health center n centro sociosanitario.
community home n (Brit) riformatorio.
community spirit n spirito civico.
commutation ticket [kâmyətā'shən tik'it] n (US) biglietto di abbonamento.
commute [kəmyōōt'] vi fare il pendolare ♦ vt (LAW) commutare.
commuter [kəmyōōt'ûr] n pendolare m/f.
compact [kâm'pakt] a compatto(a) ♦ n (also: **powder** ~) portacipria m inv.
compact disc n compact disk m inv.
companion [kəmpan'yən] n compagno/a.
companionship [kəmpan'yənship] n compagnia.
companionway [kəmpan'yənwā] n (NAUT) scala.
company [kum'pənē] n (also COMM, MIL, THEATER) compagnia; **he's good** ~ è di buona compagnia; **we have** ~ abbiamo ospiti; **to keep sb** ~ tenere compagnia a qn; **to part** ~ **with** separarsi da; **Smith and C**~ Smith e soci.
company car n macchina (di proprietà) della ditta.
company director n amministratore m, consigliere m di amministrazione.
company secretary n (Brit COMM)

segretario/a generale.

comparable [kâm'pûrəbəl] *a* comparabile.

comparative [kəmpar'ətiv] *a (freedom, cost)* relativo(a); *(adjective, adverb etc)* comparativo(a); *(literature)* comparato(a).

comparatively [kəmpar'ətivlē] *ad* relativamente.

compare [kəmpär'] *vt*: **to ~ sth/sb with/to** confrontare qc/qn con/a ♦ *vi*: **to ~ (with)** reggere il confronto (con); **~d with** *or* **to** a paragone di, rispetto a; **how do the prices ~?** che differenza di prezzo c'è?

comparison [kəmpar'isən] *n* confronto; **in ~ (with)** a confronto (di).

compartment [kəmpärt'mənt] *n* compartimento; *(RAIL)* scompartimento.

compass [kum'pəs] *n* bussola; **(a pair of) ~es** *(MATH)* compasso; **within the ~ of** entro i limiti di.

compassion [kəmpash'ən] *n* compassione *f*.

compassionate [kəmpash'ənit] *a* compassionevole; **on ~ grounds** per motivi personali.

compatibility [kəmpatəbil'ətē] *n* compatibilità.

compatible [kəmpat'əbəl] *a* compatibile.

compel [kəmpel'] *vt* costringere, obbligare.

compelling [kəmpel'ing] *a (fig: argument)* irresistibile.

compendium [kəmpen'dēəm] *n* compendio.

compensate [kâm'pənsāt] *vt* risarcire ♦ *vi*: **to ~ for** compensare.

compensation [kâmpənsā'shən] *n* compensazione *f*; *(money)* risarcimento.

compere [kâmpär'] *n (Brit)* presentatore/trice.

compete [kəmpēt'] *vi (take part)* concorrere; *(vie)*: **to ~ (with)** fare concorrenza (a).

competence [kâm'pitəns] *n* competenza.

competent [kâm'pitənt] *a* competente.

competition [kâmpitish'ən] *n* gara, concorso; *(SPORT)* gara; *(ECON)* concorrenza; **in ~ with** in concorrenza con.

competitive [kəmpet'ətiv] *a (sports)* agonistico(a); *(person)* che ha spirito di competizione; *(ECON)* concorrenziale.

competitive examination *n* concorso.

competitor [kəmpet'itûr] *n* concorrente *m/f*.

compile [kəmpīl'] *vt* compilare.

complacency [kəmplā'sənsē] *n* compiacenza di sé.

complacent [kəmplā'sənt] *a* compiaciuto(a) di sé.

complain [kəmplān'] *vi*: **to ~ (about)** lagnarsi (di); *(in shop etc)* reclamare (per).

complain of *vt fus (MED)* accusare.

complaint [kəmplānt'] *n* lamento; reclamo; *(MED)* malattia.

complement *n* [kâm'pləmənt] complemento; *(especially of ship's crew etc)* effettivo ♦ *vt* [kâm'pləment] *(enhance)* accompagnarsi bene a.

complementary [kâmpləmən'tûrē] *a* comple-

mentare.

complete [kəmplēt'] *a* completo(a) ♦ *vt* completare; *(a form)* riempire; **it's a ~ disaster** è un vero disastro.

completely [kəmplēt'lē] *ad* completamente.

completion [kəmplē'shən] *n* completamento; **to be nearing ~** essere in fase di completamento; **on ~ of contract** alla firma del contratto.

complex [kəmpleks'] *a* complesso(a) ♦ *n (PSYCH, buildings etc)* complesso.

complexion [kəmplek'shən] *n (of face)* carnagione *f*; *(of event etc)* aspetto.

complexity [kəmplek'sitē] *n* complessità *f inv*.

compliance [kəmplī'əns] *n* acquiescenza; **in ~ with** *(orders, wishes etc)* in conformità con.

compliant [kəmplī'ənt] *a* acquiescente, arrendevole.

complicate [kâm'pləkāt] *vt* complicare.

complicated [kâm'pləkātid] *a* complicato(a).

complication [kâmpləkā'shən] *n* complicazione *f*.

compliment *n* [kâm'pləmənt] complimento ♦ *vt* [kâm'pləment] fare un complimento a; **~s** *npl* complimenti *mpl*; rispetti *mpl*; **to pay sb a ~** fare un complimento a qn; **to ~ sb (on sth/on doing sth)** congratularsi *or* complimentarsi con qn (per qc/per aver fatto qc).

complimentary [kâmpləmen'tûrē] *a* complimentoso(a), elogiativo(a); *(free)* in omaggio.

complimentary ticket *n* biglietto d'omaggio.

compliments slip *n* cartoncino della società.

comply [kəmplī'] *vi*: **to ~ with** assentire a; conformarsi a.

component [kəmpō'nənt] *a, n* componente *(m)*.

compose [kəmpōz'] *vt* comporre; **to ~ o.s.** ricomporsi; **~d of** composto(a) di.

composed [kəmpōzd'] *a* calmo(a).

composer [kəmpō'zûr] *n (MUS)* compositore/trice.

composite [kəmpáz'it] *a* composito(a); *(MATH)* composto(a).

composition [kâmpəzish'ən] *n* composizione *f*.

compost [kâm'pōst] *n* composta, concime *m*.

composure [kəmpō'zhûr] *n* calma.

compound *n* [kâm'pound] *(CHEM, LING)* composto; *(enclosure)* recinto ♦ *a* composto(a) ♦ *vt* [kəmpound'] *(fig: problem, difficulty)* peggiorare.

compound fracture *n* frattura esposta.

compound interest *n* interesse *m* composto.

comprehend [kâmprihend'] *vt* comprendere, capire.

comprehension [kâmprihen'shən] *n* comprensione *f*.

comprehensive [kâmprihen'siv] *a* comprensivo(a).

comprehensive insurance policy *n* polizza multi-rischio *inv*.

comprehensive (school) *n (Brit)* scuola

secondaria aperta a tutti.

compress *vt* [kəmpres'] comprimere ♦ *n* [kâm'pres] (*MED*) compressa.

compression [kəmpresh'ən] *n* compressione *f*.

comprise [kəmprīz'] *vt* (*also*: **be** ~**d of**) comprendere.

compromise [kâm'prəmīz] *n* compromesso ♦ *vt* compromettere ♦ *vi* venire a un compromesso ♦ *cpd* (*decision, solution*) di compromesso.

compulsion [kəmpul'shən] *n* costrizione *f*; **under** ~ sotto pressioni.

compulsive [kəmpul'siv] *a* (*PSYCH*) incontrollabile; **he's a** ~ **smoker** non riesce a controllarsi nel fumare.

compulsory [kəmpul'sûrē] *a* obbligatorio(a).

compulsory purchase *n* (*Brit*) espropriazione *f*.

compunction [kəmpungk'shən] *n* scrupolo; **to have no** ~ **about doing sth** non farsi scrupoli a fare qc.

computer [kəmpyōō'tûr] *n* computer *m inv*, elaboratore *m* elettronico.

computerization [kəmpyōōtərīzā'shun] *n* computerizzazione *f*.

computerize [kəmpyōō'tərīz] *vt* computerizzare.

computer language *n* linguaggio *m* macchina *inv*.

computer peripheral *n* unità periferica.

computer program *n* programma *m* di computer.

computer program(m)er *n* programmatore/trice.

computer program(m)ing *n* programmazione *f* di computer.

computer science *n* informatica.

computer scientist *n* informatico/a.

computer virus *n* virus *m inv* del computer.

computing [kəmpyōō'ting] *n* informatica.

comrade [kâm'rad] *n* compagno/a.

comradeship [kâm'rədship] *n* cameratismo.

comsat [kâm'sat] *n abbr* = **communications satellite.**

con [kân] *vt* (*col*) truffare ♦ *n* truffa; **to** ~ **sb into doing sth** indurre qn a fare qc con raggiri.

concave [kânkāv'] *a* concavo(a).

conceal [kənsēl'] *vt* nascondere.

concede [kənsēd'] *vt* concedere ♦ *vi* fare una concessione.

conceit [kənsēt'] *n* presunzione *f*, vanità.

conceited [kənsē'tid] *a* presuntuoso(a), vanitoso(a).

conceivable [kənsēv'əbəl] *a* concepibile; **it is** ~ **that** ... può anche darsi che ....

conceivably [kənsēv'əblē] *ad*: **he may** ~ **be right** può anche darsi che abbia ragione.

conceive [kənsēv'] *vt* concepire ♦ *vi* concepire un bambino; **to** ~ **of sth/of doing sth** immaginare qc/di fare qc.

concentrate [kân'səntrāt] *vi* concentrarsi ♦ *vt* concentrare.

concentration [kânsəntrā'shən] *n* concentrazione *f*.

concentration camp *n* campo di concentramento.

concentric [kənsen'trik] *a* concentrico(a).

concept [kân'sept] *n* concetto.

conception [kənsep'shən] *n* concezione *f*; (*idea*) idea, concetto.

concern [kənsûrn'] *n* affare *m*; (*COMM*) azienda, ditta; (*anxiety*) preoccupazione *f* ♦ *vt* riguardare; **to be** ~**ed** (**about**) preoccuparsi (di); **to be** ~**ed with** occuparsi di; **as far as I am** ~**ed** per quanto mi riguarda; "**to whom it may** ~" "a tutti gli interessati"; **the department** ~**ed** (*under discussion*) l'ufficio in questione; (*relevant*) l'ufficio competente.

concerning [kənsûr'ning] *prep* riguardo a, circa.

concert [kân'sûrt] *n* concerto; **in** ~ di concerto.

concerted [kənsûr'tid] *a* concertato(a).

concert hall *n* sala da concerti.

concertina [kânsûrtē'nə] *n* piccola fisarmonica ♦ *vi* ridursi come una fisarmonica.

concertmaster [kân'sûrtmastûr] *n* (*US*) primo violino.

concerto [kənchär'tō] *n* concerto.

concession [kənsesh'ən] *n* concessione *f*.

concessionaire [kənseshənär'] *n* concessionario.

concessionary [kənsesh'ənârē] *a* (*ticket, fare*) a prezzo ridotto.

conciliation [kənsilēā'shən] *n* conciliazione *f*.

conciliatory [kənsil'ēətôrē] *a* conciliativo(a).

concise [kənsīs'] *a* conciso(a).

conclave [kân'klāv] *n* riunione *f* segreta; (*REL*) conclave *m*.

conclude [kənklōōd'] *vt* concludere ♦ *vi* (*speaker*) concludere; (*events*): **to** ~ (**with**) concludersi (con).

conclusion [kənklōō'zhən] *n* conclusione *f*; **to come to the** ~ **that** ... concludere che ..., arrivare alla conclusione che ....

conclusive [kənklōō'siv] *a* conclusivo(a).

concoct [kənkâkt'] *vt* inventare.

concoction [kənkâk'shən] *n* (*food, drink*) miscuglio.

concord [kân'kôrd] *n* (*harmony*) armonia, concordia; (*treaty*) accordo.

concourse [kân'kôrs] *n* (*hall*) atrio.

concrete [kân'krēt] *n* calcestruzzo ♦ *a* concreto(a); (*CONSTR*) di calcestruzzo.

concrete mixer *n* betoniera.

concur [kənkûr'] *vi* concordare.

concurrently [kənkûr'əntlē] *ad* simultaneamente.

concussion [kənkush'ən] *n* (*MED*) commozione *f* cerebrale.

condemn [kəndɛm'] vt condannare.
condemnation [kándɛmnā'shən] n condanna.
condensation [kándɛnsā'shən] n condensazione f.
condense [kəndɛns'] vi condensarsi ♦ vt condensare.
condensed milk [kəndɛnst' milk'] n latte m condensato.
condescend [kándisɛnd'] vi condiscendere; **to ~ to do sth** degnarsi di fare qc.
condescending [kándisɛn'ding] a condiscendente.
condition [kəndish'ən] n condizione f; (disease) malattia ♦ vt condizionare, regolare; **in good/poor ~** in buone/cattive condizioni; **to have a heart ~** soffrire di (mal di) cuore; **weather ~s** condizioni meteorologiche; **on ~ that** a condizione che + sub, a condizione di.
conditional [kəndish'ənəl] a condizionale; **to be ~ upon** dipendere da.
conditioner [kəndish'ənûr] n (for hair) balsamo.
condolences [kəndō'lənsiz] npl condoglianze fpl.
condom [kán'dəm] n preservativo.
condo(minium) [kán'dō(min'čəm)] n (US) condominio.
condone [kəndōn'] vt condonare.
conducive [kəndōō'siv] a: **~ to** favorevole a.
conduct n [kán'dukt] condotta ♦ vt [kəndukt'] condurre; (manage) dirigere; amministrare; (MUS) dirigere; **to ~ o.s.** comportarsi.
conductor [kənduk'tûr] n (of orchestra) direttore m d'orchestra; (on bus) bigliettaio; (US RAIL) controllore m; (ELEC) conduttore m.
conductress [kənduk'tris] n (on bus) bigliettaia.
conduit [kán'dōōwit] n condotto; tubo.
cone [kōn] n cono; (BOT) pigna.
confectioner [kənfɛk'shənûr] n: **~'s (shop)** ≈ pasticceria.
confectioners' sugar n (US) zucchero a velo.
confectionery [kənfɛk'shənärē] n dolciumi mpl.
confederate [kənfɛd'ûrit] a confederato(a) ♦ n (pej) complice m/f; (US HISTORY) confederato.
confederation [kənfɛdərā'shən] n confederazione f.
confer [kənfûr'] vt: **to ~ sth on** conferire qc a ♦ vi conferire; **to ~ (with sb about sth)** consultarsi (con qn su qc).
conference [kán'fûrəns] n congresso; **to be in ~** essere in riunione.
conference room n sala f conferenze inv.
confess [kənfɛs'] vt confessare, ammettere ♦ vi confessarsi.
confession [kənfɛsh'ən] n confessione f.
confessional [kənfɛsh'ənəl] n confessionale m.

confessor [kənfɛs'ûr] n confessore m.
confetti [kənfɛt'ē] n coriandoli mpl.
confide [kənfīd'] vi: **to ~ in** confidarsi con.
confidence [kán'fidəns] n confidenza; (trust) fiducia; (also: **self-~**) sicurezza di sé; **to tell sb sth in strict ~** dire qc a qn in via strettamente confidenziale; **to have (every) ~ that** ... essere assolutamente certo(a) che ...; **motion of no ~** mozione f di sfiducia.
confidence game n truffa.
confident [kán'fidənt] a sicuro(a); (also: **self-~**) sicuro(a) di sé.
confidential [kánfidɛn'shəl] a riservato(a); (secretary) particolare.
confidentiality [kánfidɛnshēal'itē] n riservatezza, carattere m confidenziale.
configuration [kənfigyərā'shən] n (COMPUT) configurazione f.
confine [kənfīn'] vt limitare; (shut up) rinchiudere; **to ~ o.s. to doing sth** limitarsi a fare qc; see also **confines**.
confined [kənfīnd'] a (space) ristretto(a).
confinement [kənfīn'mənt] n prigionia; (MIL) consegna; (MED) parto.
confines [kán'fīnz] npl confini mpl.
confirm [kənfûrm'] vt confermare; (REL) cresimare.
confirmation [kánfûrmā'shən] n conferma; cresima.
confirmed [kənfûrmd'] a inveterato(a).
confiscate [kán'fiskāt] vt confiscare.
confiscation [kánfiskā'shən] n confisca.
conflagration [kánfləgrā'shən] n conflagrazione f.
conflict n [kán'flikt] conflitto ♦ vi [kənflikt'] essere in conflitto.
conflicting [kənflik'ting] a contrastante; (reports, evidence, opinions) contraddittorio(a).
conform [kənfôrm'] vi: **to ~ (to)** conformarsi (a).
conformist [kənfôr'mist] n conformista m/f.
confound [kənfound'] vt confondere; (amaze) sconcertare.
confounded [kənfoun'did] a maledetto(a).
confront [kənfrunt'] vt confrontare; (enemy, danger) affrontare.
confrontation [kánfrəntā'shən] n scontro.
confuse [kənfyōōz'] vt imbrogliare; (one thing with another) confondere.
confused [kənfyōōzd'] a confuso(a); **to get ~** confondersi.
confusing [kənfyōō'zing] a che fa confondere.
confusion [kənfyōō'zhən] n confusione f.
congeal [kənjēl'] vi (blood) congelarsi.
congenial [kənjēn'yəl] a (person) simpatico(a); (place, work, company) piacevole.
congenital [kənjɛn'itəl] a congenito(a).
conger eel [káng'gûr ēl] n grongo.
congested [kənjɛs'tid] a congestionato(a); (telephone lines) sovraccarico(a).
congestion [kənjɛs'chən] n congestione f.

conglomerate [kənglâm'ûrit] *n* (*COMM*) conglomerato.

conglomeration [kənglâmərā'shən] *n* conglomerazione *f*.

Congo [kâng'gō] *n* (*state*) Congo.

congratulate [kəngrach'ōōlāt] *vt*: **to ~ sb (on)** congratularsi con qn (per *or* di).

congratulations [kəngrachōōlā'shənz] *npl*: **~ (on)** congratulazioni *fpl* (per) ♦ *excl* congratulazioni!, rallegramenti!

congregate [kâng'grəgāt] *vi* congregarsi, riunirsi.

congregation [kânggrəgā'shən] *n* congregazione *f*.

congress [kâng'gris] *n* congresso.

congressman [kâng'grismən] *n* (*US*) membro del Congresso.

congresswoman [kâng'griswōōmən] *n* (*US*) (donna) membro del Congresso.

conical [kân'ikəl] *a* conico(a).

conifer [kō'nifûr] *n* conifero.

coniferous [kōnif'ûrəs] *a* (*forest*) di conifere.

conjecture [kənjek'chûr] *n* congettura ♦ *vt*, *vi* congetturare.

conjugal [kân'jəgəl] *a* coniugale.

conjugate [kân'jəgāt] *vt* coniugare.

conjugation [kânjəgā'shən] *n* coniugazione *f*.

conjunction [kənjungk'shən] *n* congiunzione *f*; **in ~ with** in accordo con, insieme con.

conjunctivitis [kənjungktəvī'tis] *n* congiuntivite *f*.

conjure [kân'jûr] *vi* fare giochi di prestigio.

conjure up *vt* (*ghost*, *spirit*) evocare; (*memories*) rievocare.

conjurer [kân'jûrûr] *n* prestigiatore/trice, prestidigitatore/trice.

conjuring trick [kân'jûring trik] *n* gioco di prestigio.

conker [kâng'kûr] *n* (*Brit*) castagna (d'ippocastano).

conk out [kângk out] *vi* (*col*) andare in panne.

con man *n* truffatore *m*.

Conn. *abbr* (*US*) = *Connecticut*.

connect [kənekt'] *vt* connettere, collegare; (*ELEC*) collegare; (*fig*) associare ♦ *vi* (*train*): **to ~ with** essere in coincidenza con; **to be ~ed with** aver rapporti con; essere imparentato(a) con; **I am trying to ~ you** (*TEL*) sto cercando di darle la linea.

connection [kənek'shən] *n* relazione *f*, rapporto; (*ELEC*) connessione *f*; (*TEL*) collegamento; (*train etc*) coincidenza; **in ~ with** con riferimento a, a proposito di; **what is the ~ between them?** in che modo sono legati?; **business ~s** rapporti d'affari; **to miss/get one's ~** (*train etc*) perdere/prendere la coincidenza.

connexion [kənek'shən] *n* (*Brit*) = **connection**.

conning tower [kân'ing tou'ûr] *n* torretta di comando.

connive [kənīv'] *vi*: **to ~ at** essere connivente in.

connoisseur [kânisûr'] *n* conoscitore/trice.

connotation [kânətā'shən] *n* connotazione *f*.

connubial [kənōō'bēəl] *a* coniugale.

conquer [kâng'kûr] *vt* conquistare; (*feelings*) vincere.

conqueror [kâng'kûrûr] *n* conquistatore *m*.

conquest [kân'kwest] *n* conquista.

cons [kânz] *npl see* **pro, convenience**.

conscience [kân'shəns] *n* coscienza; **in all ~** onestamente, in coscienza.

conscientious [kânshēen'shəs] *a* coscienzioso(a).

conscientious objector *n* obiettore *m* di coscienza.

conscious [kân'shəs] *a* consapevole; (*MED*) conscio(a); (*deliberate*: *insult*, *error*) intenzionale, voluto(a); **to become ~ of sth/that** rendersi conto di qc/che.

consciousness [kân'shəsnis] *n* consapevolezza; (*MED*) coscienza; **to lose/regain ~** perdere/riprendere coscienza.

conscript [kân'skript] *n* (*Brit*) coscritto.

conscription [kənskrip'shən] *n* coscrizione *f*.

consecrate [kân'səkrāt] *vt* consacrare.

consecutive [kənsek'yətiv] *a* consecutivo(a); **on 3 ~ occasions** 3 volte di fila.

consensus [kənsen'səs] *n* consenso; **the ~ of opinion** l'opinione *f* unanime *or* comune.

consent [kənsent'] *n* consenso ♦ *vi*: **to ~ (to)** acconsentire (a); **age of ~** età legale (per avere rapporti sessuali); **by common ~** di comune accordo.

consequence [kân'səkwens] *n* conseguenza, risultato; importanza; **in ~** di conseguenza.

consequently [kân'səkwentlē] *ad* di conseguenza, dunque.

conservation [kânsûrvā'shən] *n* conservazione *f*; (*also*: **nature ~**) tutela dell'ambiente; **energy ~** risparmio energetico.

conservationist [kânsûrvā'shənist] *n* fautore/trice della tutela dell'ambiente.

conservative [kənsûr'vətiv] *a* conservatore(trice); (*cautious*) cauto(a); **C~** *a*, *n* (*Brit POL*) conservatore(trice).

conservatory [kənsûr'vətôrē] *n* (*greenhouse*) serra.

conserve *vt* [kənsûrv'] conservare ♦ *n* [kân'sûrv] conserva.

consider [kənsid'ûr] *vt* considerare; (*take into account*) tener conto di; **to ~ doing sth** considerare la possibilità di fare qc; **all things ~ed** tutto sommato *or* considerato; **~ yourself lucky** puoi dirti fortunato.

considerable [kənsid'ûrəbəl] *a* considerevole, notevole.

considerably [kənsid'ûrəblē] *ad* notevolmente, decisamente.

considerate [kənsid'ûrit] *a* premuroso(a).

consideration [kənsidərā'shən] *n* considerazione *f*; (*reward*) rimunerazione *f*; **out of ~ for** per riguardo a; **under ~** in esame; **my first ~ is my family** il mio primo pensiero è per la mia famiglia.

considering [kənsid'ùring] *prep* in considerazione di; **~ (that)** se si considera (che).

consign [kənsīn'] *vt* consegnare; (*send: goods*) spedire.

consignee [kânsīnē'] *n* consegnatario/a, destinatario/a.

consignment [kənsīn'mənt] *n* consegna; spedizione *f*.

consignment note *n* (*Brit COMM*) nota di spedizione.

consignor [kənsī'nûr] *n* mittente *m/f*.

consist [kənsist'] *vi*: **to ~ of** constare di, essere composto(a) di.

consistency [kənsis'tənsē] *n* consistenza; (*fig*) coerenza.

consistent [kənsis'tənt] *a* coerente; (*constant*) costante; **~ with** compatibile con.

consolation [kânsəlā'shən] *n* consolazione *f*.

console *vt* [kənsōl'] consolare ♦ *n* [kân'sōl] quadro di comando.

consolidate [kənsâl'idāt] *vt* consolidare.

consommé [kânsəmā'] *n* consommé *m inv*, brodo ristretto.

consonant [kân'sənənt] *n* consonante *f*.

consort *n* [kən'sôrt] consorte *m/f*; **prince ~** principe *m* consorte ♦ *vi* [kənsôrt'] (*often pej*): **to ~ with sb** frequentare qn.

consortium [kənsôr'shēəm] *n* consorzio.

conspicuous [kənspik'yōōəs] *a* cospicuo(a); **to make o.s. ~** farsi notare.

conspiracy [kənspir'əsē] *n* congiura, cospirazione *f*.

conspiratorial [kənspirətôr'ēəl] *a* cospiratorio(a).

conspire [kənspī'ûr] *vi* congiurare, cospirare.

constable [kân'stəbəl] *n* (*Brit: also:* **police ~**) ≈ poliziotto, agente *m* di polizia.

constabulary [kənstab'yəlärē] *n* forze *fpl* dell'ordine.

constant [kân'stənt] *a* costante; continuo(a).

constantly [kân'stəntlē] *ad* costantemente; continuamente.

constellation [kânstəlā'shən] *n* costellazione *f*.

consternation [kânstûrnā'shən] *n* costernazione *f*.

constipated [kân'stəpātid] *a* stitico(a).

constipation [kânstəpā'shən] *n* stitichezza.

constituency [kənstich'ōōənsē] *n* collegio elettorale; (*people*) elettori *mpl* (del collegio).

constituency party *n* sezione *f* locale (del partito).

constituent [kənstich'ōōənt] *n* elettore/trice; (*part*) elemento componente.

constitute [kân'stitōōt] *vt* costituire.

constitution [kânstitōō'shən] *n* costituzione *f*.

constitutional [kânstitōō'shənəl] *a* costituzio-

nale.

constrain [kənstrān'] *vt* costringere.

constrained [kənstrānd'] *a* costretto(a).

constraint [kənstrānt'] *n* (*restraint*) limitazione *f*, costrizione *f*; (*embarrassment*) imbarazzo, soggezione *f*.

constrict [kənstrikt'] *vt* comprimere; opprimere.

construct [kənstrukt'] *vt* costruire.

construction [kənstruk'shən] *n* costruzione *f*; (*fig: interpretation*) interpretazione *f*; **under ~** in costruzione.

construction industry *n* edilizia, industria edile.

constructive [kənstruk'tiv] *a* costruttivo(a).

construe [kənstrōō'] *vt* interpretare.

consul [kân'səl] *n* console *m*.

consulate [kân'səlit] *n* consolato.

consult [kənsult'] *vt*: **to ~ sb (about sth)** consultare qn (su *or* riguardo a qc).

consultancy [kənsul'tənsē] *n* consulenza.

consultancy fee *n* onorario di consulenza.

consultant [kənsul'tənt] *n* (*MED*) consulente *m* medico; (*other specialist*) consulente ♦ *cpd*: **~ engineer** *n* ingegnere *m* consulente; **~ pediatrician** *n* specialista *m/f* in pediatria; **legal/management ~** consulente legale/gestionale.

consultation [kânsəltā'shən] *n* consultazione *f*; (*MED, LAW*) consulto; **in ~ with** consultandosi con.

consulting room [kənsul'ting rōōm] *n* ambulatorio.

consume [kənsōōm'] *vt* consumare.

consumer [kənsōō'mûr] *n* consumatore/trice; (*of electricity, gas etc*) utente *m/f*.

consumer credit *n* credito al consumatore.

consumer durables *npl* prodotti *mpl* di consumo durevole.

consumer goods *npl* beni *mpl* di consumo.

consumerism [kənsōō'mərizəm] *n* (*consumer protection*) tutela del consumatore; (*ECON*) consumismo.

consumer society *n* società dei consumi.

consummate [kân'səmāt] *vt* consumare.

consumption [kənsump'shən] *n* consumo; (*MED*) consunzione *f*; **not fit for human ~** non commestibile.

cont. *abbr* (= *continued*) segue.

contact [kân'takt] *n* contatto; (*person*) conoscenza ♦ *vt* mettersi in contatto con; **to be in ~ with sb/sth** essere in contatto con qn/qc; **business ~s** contatti *mpl* d'affari.

contact lenses *npl* lenti *fpl* a contatto.

contagious [kəntā'jəs] *a* contagioso(a).

contain [kəntān'] *vt* contenere; **to ~ o.s.** contenersi.

container [kəntā'nûr] *n* recipiente *m*; (*for shipping etc*) container *m*.

containerize [kəntā'nərīz] *vt* mettere in container.

contaminate [kəntam'ənāt] vt contaminare.

contamination [kəntamənā'shən] n contaminazione f.

cont'd abbr (= continued) segue.

contemplate [kân'təmplāt] vt contemplare; (consider) pensare a (or di).

contemplation [kântəmplā'shən] n contemplazione f.

contemporary [kəntem'pərärē] a contemporaneo(a); (design) moderno(a) ♦ n contemporaneo/a; (of the same age) coetaneo/a.

contempt [kəntempt'] n disprezzo; ~ **of court** (LAW) oltraggio alla Corte.

contemptible [kəntemp'təbəl] a spregevole, vergognoso(a).

contemptuous [kəntemp'chōōəs] a sdegnoso(a).

contend [kəntend'] vt: **to** ~ **that** sostenere che ♦ vi: **to** ~ **with** lottare contro; **he has a lot to** ~ **with** ha un sacco di guai.

contender [kəntend'ûr] n contendente m/f; concorrente m/f.

content a [kəntent'] contento(a), soddisfatto(a) ♦ vt contentare, soddisfare ♦ n [kân'tent] contenuto; ~**s** npl contenuto; (of barrel etc: capacity) capacità f inv; **(table of)** ~**s** indice m; **to be** ~ **with** essere contento di; **to** ~ **o.s. with sth/with doing sth** accontentarsi di qc/di fare qc.

contented [kəntent'tid] a contento(a), soddisfatto(a).

contentedly [kənten'tidlē] ad con soddisfazione.

contention [kənten'shən] n contesa; (assertion) tesi f inv; **bone of** ~ pomo della discordia.

contentious [kənten'shəs] a polemico(a).

contentment [kəntent'mənt] n contentezza.

contest n [kân'test] lotta; (competition) gara, concorso ♦ vt [kəntest'] contestare; (LAW) impugnare; (compete for) contendere.

contestant [kəntes'tənt] n concorrente m/f; (in fight) avversario/a.

context [kân'tekst] n contesto; **in/out of** ~ nel/fuori dal contesto.

continent [kân'tənənt] n continente m; **the C**~ l'Europa continentale; **on the C**~ in Europa.

continental [kântənen'təl] a continentale ♦ n abitante m/f dell'Europa continentale.

continental breakfast n colazione f all'europea.

continental quilt n (Brit) piumino.

contingency [kəntin'jənsē] n eventualità f inv.

contingency plan n misura d'emergenza.

contingent [kəntin'jənt] n contingenza ♦ a: **to be** ~ **upon** dipendere da.

continual [kəntin'yōōəl] a continuo(a).

continually [kəntin'yōōəlē] ad di continuo.

continuation [kəntinyōōā'shən] n continuazione f; (after interruption) ripresa; (of story) seguito.

continue [kəntin'yōō] vi continuare ♦ vt continuare; (start again) riprendere; **to be** ~**d** (story) continua; ~**d on page 10** segue or continua a pagina 10.

continuity [kântənōō'itē] n continuità; (CINEMA) (ordine m della) sceneggiatura.

continuous [kəntin'yōōəs] a continuo(a), ininterrotto(a); ~ **performance** (CINEMA) spettacolo continuato.

continuously [kəntin'yōōəslē] ad (repeatedly) continuamente; (uninterruptedly) ininterrottamente.

contort [kəntôrt'] vt contorcere.

contortion [kəntôr'shən] n contorcimento; (of acrobat) contorsione f.

contortionist [kəntôr'shənist] n contorsionista m/f.

contour [kân'tōōr] n contorno, profilo; (also: ~ **line**) curva di livello.

contraband [kân'trəband] n contrabbando ♦ a di contrabbando.

contraception [kântrəsep'shən] n contraccezione f.

contraceptive [kântrəsep'tiv] a contraccettivo(a) ♦ n contraccettivo.

contract n [kân'trakt] contratto ♦ cpd (price, date) del contratto; (work) a contratto ♦ vi [kəntrakt'] (COMM): **to** ~ **to do sth** fare un contratto per fare qc; (become smaller) contrarre; **to be under** ~ **to do sth** aver stipulato un contratto per fare qc; ~ **of employment** contratto di lavoro.

contraction [kəntrak'shən] n contrazione f.

contractor [kân'traktûr] n imprenditore m.

contractual [kəntrak'chōōəl] a contrattuale.

contradict [kântrədikt'] vt contraddire.

contradiction [kântrədik'shən] n contraddizione f; **to be in** ~ **with** discordare con.

contradictory [kântrədik'tûrē] a contraddittorio(a).

contralto [kəntral'tō] n contralto.

contraption [kəntrap'shən] n (pej) aggeggio.

contrary [kân'trärē] a contrario(a); (unfavorable) avverso(a), contrario(a); (perverse) bisbetico(a) ♦ n contrario; **on the** ~ al contrario; **unless you hear to the** ~ a meno che non si disdica; ~ **to what we thought** a differenza di or contrariamente a quanto pensavamo.

contrast n [kân'trast] contrasto ♦ vt [kəntrast'] mettere in contrasto; **in** ~ **to** or **with** a differenza di, contrariamente a.

contrasting [kəntras'ting] a contrastante, di contrasto.

contravene [kântrəvēn'] vt contravvenire.

contravention [kântrəven'shən] n: ~ **(of)** contravvenzione f (a), infrazione f (di).

contribute [kəntrib'yōōt] vi contribuire ♦ vt: **to** ~ **$10/an article to** dare 10 dollari/un articolo a; **to** ~ **to** contribuire a; (newspaper) scrivere per; (discussion) partecipare a.

contribution [kântrəbyōō'shən] n contribuzione f.

contributor [kəntrib'yətûr] n (to newspaper) collaboratore/trice.

contributory [kəntrib'yətôrē] a (cause) che contribuisce; **it was a ~ factor in** ... quello ha contribuito a ....

contributory pension plan n sistema di pensionamento finanziato congiuntamente dai contributi del lavoratore e del datore di lavoro.

contrite [kəntrīt'] a contrito(a).

contrivance [kəntrī'vəns] n congegno; espediente m.

contrive [kəntrīv'] vt inventare; escogitare ♦ vi: **to ~ to do** fare in modo di fare.

control [kəntrōl'] vt dominare; (firm, operation etc) dirigere; (check) controllare; (disease, fire) arginare, limitare ♦ n controllo; **~s** npl comandi mpl; **to take ~ of** assumere il controllo di; **to be in ~ of** aver autorità su; essere responsabile di; controllare; **to ~ o.s.** controllarsi; **everything is under ~** tutto è sotto controllo; **the car went out of ~** la macchina non rispondeva ai comandi; **circumstances beyond our ~** circostanze fpl che non dipendono da noi.

control key n (COMPUT) tasto di controllo.

controller [kəntrō'lûr] n controllore m.

controlling interest n (COMM) maggioranza delle azioni.

control panel n (on aircraft, ship, TV etc) quadro dei comandi.

control point n punto di controllo.

control room n (NAUT, MIL) sala di comando; (RADIO, TV) sala di regia.

control tower n (AVIAT) torre f di controllo.

control unit n (COMPUT) unità f inv di controllo.

controversial [kântrəvûr'shəl] a controverso(a), polemico(a).

controversy [kân'trəvûrsē] n controversia, polemica.

conurbation [kânûrbā'shən] n conurbazione f.

convalesce [kânvəles'] vi rimettersi in salute.

convalescence [kânvəles'əns] n convalescenza.

convalescent [kânvəles'ənt] a, n convalescente (m/f).

convector [kənvek'tûr] n convettore m.

convene [kənvēn'] vt convocare; (meeting) organizzare ♦ vi convenire, adunarsi.

convenience [kənvēn'yəns] n comodità f inv; **at your ~** a suo comodo; **at your earliest ~** (COMM) appena possibile; **all modern ~s** tutte le comodità moderne.

convenience foods npl cibi mpl di veloce preparazione.

convenient [kənvēn'yənt] a conveniente, comodo(a); **if it is ~ to you** se per lei va bene, se non la incomoda.

conveniently [kənvēn'yəntlē] ad (happen) a proposito; (situated) in un posto comodo.

convent [kân'vent] n convento.

convention [kənven'shən] n convenzione f; (meeting) convegno.

conventional [kənven'shənəl] a convenzionale.

convent school n scuola retta da suore.

converge [kənvûrj'] vi convergere.

conversant [kənvûr'sənt] a: **to be ~ with** essere al corrente di; essere pratico(a) di.

conversation [kânvûrsā'shən] n conversazione f.

conversational [kânvûrsā'shənəl] a non formale; (COMPUT) conversazionale; **~ Italian** l'italiano parlato.

conversationalist [kânvûrsāsh'nəlist] n conversatore/trice.

converse n [kân'vûrs] contrario, opposto ♦ vi [kənvûrs']: **to ~ (with sb about sth)** conversare (con qn su qc).

conversely [kənvûrs'lē] ad al contrario, per contro.

conversion [kənvûr'zhən] n conversione f; (Brit: of house) trasformazione f, rimodernamento.

conversion table n tavola di equivalenze.

convert vt [kənvûrt'] (REL, COMM) convertire; (alter) trasformare ♦ n [kân'vûrt] convertito/a.

convertible [kənvûr'təbəl] n macchina decappottabile.

convex [kânveks'] a convesso(a).

convey [kənvā'] vt trasportare; (thanks) comunicare; (idea) dare.

conveyance [kənvā'əns] n (of goods) trasporto; (vehicle) mezzo di trasporto.

conveyancing [kənvā'ənsing] n (LAW) redazione f di transazioni di proprietà.

conveyor belt [kənvā'ûr belt] n nastro trasportatore.

convict vt [kənvikt'] dichiarare colpevole ♦ n [kân'vikt] carcerato/a.

conviction [kənvik'shən] n condanna; (belief) convinzione f.

convince [kənvins'] vt: **to ~ sb (of sth/that)** convincere qn (di qc/che), persuadere qn (di qc/che).

convincing [kənvin'sing] a convincente.

convincingly [kənvin'singlē] ad in modo convincente.

convivial [kənviv'ēəl] a allegro(a).

convoluted [kân'vəlōōtid] a (shape) attorcigliato(a), avvolto(a); (argument) involuto(a).

convoy [kân'voi] n convoglio.

convulse [kənvuls'] vt sconvolgere; **to be ~d with laughter** contorcersi dalle risa.

convulsion [kənvul'shən] n convulsione f.

coo [kōō] vi tubare.

cook [kōōk] vt cucinare, cuocere; (meal) preparare ♦ vi cuocere; (person) cucinare ♦ n cuoco/a.

cook up *vt* (*col: excuse, story*) improvvisare, inventare.

cookbook |kŏŏk'bŏŏk| *n* libro di cucina.

cooker |kŏŏk'ûr| *n* fornello, cucina.

cookery |kŏŏk'ûrē| *n* cucina.

cookery book *n* (*Brit*) = **cookbook**.

cookie |kŏŏk'ē| *n* (*US*) biscotto.

cooking |kŏŏk'ing| *n* cucina ♦ *cpd* (*apples, chocolate*) da cuocere; (*utensils, salt, foil*) da cucina.

cookout |kŏŏk'out| *n* (*US*) pranzo (cucinato) all'aperto.

cool |kŏŏl| *a* fresco(a); (*not afraid*) calmo(a); (*unfriendly*) freddo(a); (*impertinent*) sfacciato(a) ♦ *vt* raffreddare, rinfrescare ♦ *vi* raffreddarsi, rinfrescarsi; **it's** ~ (*weather*) fa fresco; **to keep sth** ~ *or* **in a** ~ **place** tenere qc in fresco.

cool down *vi* raffreddarsi; (*fig: person, situation*) calmarsi.

cool box *n* (*Brit*) = **cooler**.

cooler |kŏŏl'ûr| *n* (*US*) borsa termica.

cooling tower |kŏŏl'ing tou'ûr| *n* torre *f* di raffreddamento.

coolly |kŏŏl'lē| *ad* (*calmly*) con calma, tranquillamente; (*audaciously*) come se niente fosse; (*unenthusiastically*) freddamente.

coolness |kŏŏl'nis| *n* freschezza; sangue *m* freddo, calma.

coop |kŏŏp| *n* stia ♦ *vt*: **to** ~ **up** (*fig*) rinchiudere.

co-op |kŏ'âp| *n abbr* (= *cooperative* (*society*)) coop *f*.

cooperate |kŏâp'ərāt| *vi* cooperare, collaborare.

cooperation |kŏâpərā'shən| *n* cooperazione *f*, collaborazione *f*.

cooperative |kŏâp'rətiv| *a* cooperativo(a) ♦ *n* cooperativa.

co-opt |kŏâpt'| *vt*: **to** ~ **sb into sth** cooptare qn per qc.

coordinate *vt* |kŏŏr'dənāt| coordinare ♦ *n* |kŏŏr'dənit| (*MATH*) coordinata; **~s** *npl* (*clothes*) coordinati *mpl*.

coordination |kŏŏrdənā'shən| *n* coordinazione *f*.

coot |kŏŏt| *n* folaga.

co-ownership |kŏŏ'nûrship| *n* comproprietà.

cop |kâp| *n* (*col*) sbirro.

cope |kŏp| *vi* farcela; **to** ~ **with** (*problems*) far fronte a.

Copenhagen |kŏpənhā'gən| *n* Copenhagen *f*.

copier |kâp'ēûr| *n* (*also:* **photo~**) (foto)copiatrice *f*.

copilot |kŏ'pīlət| *n* secondo pilota *m*.

copious |kŏ'pēəs| *a* copioso(a), abbondante.

copper |kâp'ûr| *n* rame *m*; (*col: policeman*) sbirro; **~s** *npl* spiccioli *mpl*.

copse |kâps| *n* bosco ceduo.

copulate |kâp'yəlāt| *vi* accoppiarsi.

copy |kâp'ē| *n* copia; (*book etc*) esemplare *m*; (*material: for printing*) materiale *m*, testo ♦ *vt* (*gen*, *COMPUT*) copiare; (*imitate*) imitare; **to make good** ~ (*fig*) fare notizia.

copy out *vt* ricopiare, trascrivere.

copycat |kâp'ēkat| *n* (*pej*) copione *m*.

copyright |kâp'ērīt| *n* diritto d'autore; ~ **reserved** tutti i diritti riservati.

copy typist *n* dattilografo/a.

copywriter |kâp'ērītûr| *n* redattore *m* pubblicitario.

coral |kôr'əl| *n* corallo.

coral reef *n* barriera corallina.

Coral Sea *n*: **the** ~ il mar dei Coralli.

cord |kôrd| *n* corda; (*US ELEC*) filo; (*fabric*) velluto a coste; **~s** *npl* (*pants*) calzoni *mpl* (di velluto) a coste.

cordial |kôr'jəl| *a, n* cordiale (*m*).

cordless |kôrd'lis| *a* senza cavo.

cordon |kôr'dən| *n* cordone *m*.

cordon off *vt* fare cordone intorno a.

corduroy |kôr'dəroi| *n* fustagno.

CORE *n abbr* (*US*) = *Congress of Racial Equality*.

core |kôr| *n* (*of fruit*) torsolo; (*TECH*) centro; (*of earth, nuclear reactor*) nucleo; (*of problem etc*) cuore *m*, nocciolo ♦ *vt* estrarre il torsolo da; **rotten to the** ~ marcio fino al midollo.

Corfu |kôr'fŏŏ| *n* Corfù *f*.

coriander |kôrēan'dûr| *n* coriandolo.

cork |kôrk| *n* sughero; (*of bottle*) tappo.

corked |kôrkt| *a* (*Brit*) = **corky**.

corkscrew |kôrk'skrŏŏ| *n* cavatappi *m inv*.

corky |kôrk'ē| *a* (*US: wine*) che sa di tappo.

corm |kôrm| *n* cormo.

cormorant |kôr'mûrənt| *n* cormorano.

Corn *abbr* (*Brit*) = *Cornwall*.

corn |kôrn| *n* (*US: maize*) granturco; (*Brit: wheat*) grano; (*on foot*) callo; ~ **on the cob** (*CULIN*) pannocchia cotta.

cornea |kôr'nēə| *n* cornea.

corned beef |kôrnd bēf| *n* carne *f* di manzo in scatola.

corner |kôr'nûr| *n* angolo; (*AUT*) curva; (*SOCCER: also:* ~ **kick**) corner *m inv*, calcio d'angolo ♦ *vt* intrappolare; mettere con le spalle al muro; (*COMM: market*) accaparrare ♦ *vi* prendere una curva; **to cut ~s** (*fig*) prendere una scorciatoia.

corner flag *n* (*SOCCER*) bandierina d'angolo.

corner kick *n* (*SOCCER*) calcio d'angolo.

cornerstone |kôr'nûrstōn| *n* pietra angolare.

cornet |kôrnet'| *n* (*MUS*) cornetta; (*Brit: of ice-cream*) cono.

cornflakes |kôrn'flāks| *npl* fiocchi *mpl* di granturco.

cornflour |kôrn'flouûr| *n* (*Brit*) ≈ fecola di patate.

cornice |kôr'nis| *n* cornicione *m*; cornice *f*.

corn oil *n* olio di mais.

cornstarch [kôrn'stârch] *n* (*US*) ≈ fecola di patate.

cornucopia [kôrnəkō'pēə] *n* grande abbondanza.

corny [kôr'nē] *a* (*col*) trito(a).

corollary [kôr'əlārē] *n* corollario.

coronary [kôr'ənārē] *n*: ~ (**thrombosis**) trombosi *f* coronaria.

coronation [kôrənā'shən] *n* incoronazione *f*.

coroner [kôr'ənûr] *n* magistrato incaricato di indagare la causa la causa di morte in circostanze sospette.

coronet [kôr'ənit] *n* diadema *m*.

Corp. *abbr* = **corporation**.

corporal [kôr'pûrəl] *n* caporalmaggiore *m* ♦ *a*: ~ **punishment** pena corporale.

corporate [kôr'pərit] *a* comune; (*COMM*) costituito(a) (in corporazione).

corporate identity, corporate image *n* (*of organization*) immagine *f* di marca.

corporation [kôrpərā'shən] *n* (*of town*) consiglio comunale; (*COMM*) ente *m*.

corporation tax *n* ≈ imposta societaria.

corps [kôr], *pl* **corps** [kôrz] *n* corpo; **press** ~ ufficio *m* stampa *inv*.

corpse [kôrps] *n* cadavere *m*.

corpuscle [kôr'pəsəl] *n* corpuscolo.

corral [kəral'] *n* recinto.

correct [kərekt'] *a* (*accurate*) corretto(a), esatto(a); (*proper*) corretto(a) ♦ *vt* correggere; **you are** ~ ha ragione.

correction [kərek'shən] *n* correzione *f*.

correlate [kôr'əlāt] *vt* mettere in correlazione ♦ *vi*: **to** ~ **with** essere in rapporto con.

correlation [kôrəlā'shən] *n* correlazione *f*.

correspond [kôrəspând'] *vi* corrispondere.

correspondence [kôrəspân'dəns] *n* corrispondenza.

correspondence column *n* (*PRESS*) rubrica delle lettere (al direttore).

correspondence course *n* corso per corrispondenza.

correspondent [kôrəspán'dənt] *n* corrispondente *m/f*.

corridor [kôr'idûr] *n* corridoio.

corroborate [kəráb'ərāt] *vt* corroborare, confermare.

corrode [kərōd'] *vt* corrodere ♦ *vi* corrodersi.

corrosion [kərō'zhən] *n* corrosione *f*.

corrosive [kərō'siv] *a* corrosivo(a).

corrugated [kôr'əgātid] *a* increspato(a); ondulato(a).

corrugated iron *n* lamiera di ferro ondulata.

corrupt [kərupt'] *a* corrotto(a) ♦ *vt* corrompere; ~ **practices** (*dishonesty, bribery*) pratiche *fpl* illecite.

corruption [kərup'shən] *n* corruzione *f*.

corset [kôr'sit] *n* busto.

Corsica [kôr'sikə] *n* Corsica.

Corsican [kôr'sikən] *a, n* corso(a).

cortège [kôrtezh'] *n* corteo.

cortisone [kôr'tisōn] *n* cortisone *m*.

coruscating [kôr'əskāting] *a* scintillante.

c.o.s. *abbr* (= *cash on shipment*) pagamento alla spedizione.

cosh [kâsh] *n* (*Brit*) randello (corto).

cosignatory [kōsig'nətôrē] *n* cofirmatario/a.

cosiness [kō'zēnis] *n* (*Brit*) = **coziness**.

cosmetic [kâzmet'ik] *n* cosmetico ♦ *a* (*preparation*) cosmetico(a); (*surgery*) estetico(a); (*fig: reforms*) ornamentale.

cosmic [kâz'mik] *a* cosmico(a).

cosmonaut [kâz'mənôt] *n* cosmonauta *m/f*.

cosmopolitan [kâzməpâl'itən] *a* cosmopolita.

cosmos [kâz'məs] *n* cosmo.

cosset [kâs'it] *vt* vezzeggiare.

cost [kôst] *n* costo ♦ *vb* (*pt, pp* **cost**) *vi* costare ♦ *vt* stabilire il prezzo di; ~**s** *npl* (*LAW*) spese *fpl*; **it** ~**s $5/too much** costa 5 dollari/ troppo; **it** ~ **him his life/job** gli costò la vita/ il suo lavoro; **how much does it** ~? quanto costa?, quanto viene?; **what will it** ~ **to have it repaired?** quanto costerà farlo riparare?; ~ **of living** costo della vita; **at all** ~**s** a ogni costo.

cost accountant *n* analizzatore *m* dei costi.

co-star [kō'stâr] *n* attore/trice della stessa importanza del protagonista.

Costa Rica [kâs'tə rē'kə] *n* Costa Rica.

cost center *n* centro di costo.

cost control *n* controllo dei costi.

cost-effective [kôstifek'tiv] *a* (*gen*) conveniente, economico(a); (*COMM*) redditizio(a), conveniente.

cost-effectiveness [kôstifek'tivnis] *n* convenienza.

costing [kôs'ting] *n* (determinazione *f* dei) costi *mpl*.

costly [kôst'lē] *a* costoso(a), caro(a).

cost-of-living [kôstəvliv'ing] *a*: ~ **allowance** indennità *f inv* di contingenza; ~ **index** indice *m* della scala mobile.

cost price *n* (*Brit*) prezzo all'ingrosso.

costume [kâs'tōōm] *n* costume *m*; (*lady's suit*) tailleur *m inv*; (*Brit: also:* **swimming** ~) costume da bagno.

costume ball *n* ballo in maschera.

costume jewelry *n* bigiotteria.

cosy [kō'zē] *a* (*Brit*) = **cozy**.

cot [kât] *n* (*US: folding bed*) brandina; (*Brit: child's*) lettino.

cottage [kât'ij] *n* cottage *m inv*.

cottage cheese *n* fiocchi *mpl* di latte magro.

cottage industry *n* industria artigianale basata sul lavoro a cottimo.

cottage pie *n* (*Brit*) piatto a base di carne macinata in sugo e purè di patate.

cotton [kât'ən] *n* cotone *m*; (*US MED*) cotone idrofilo; ~ **dress** *etc* vestito *etc* di cotone.

cotton on *vi* (*col*): **to** ~ **on (to sth)** afferrare (qc).

cotton candy n (US) zucchero filato.
cotton wool n (Brit) cotone m idrofilo.
couch [kouch] n sofà m inv; (in doctor's office) lettino ♦ vt esprimere.
couchette [kōōshet'] n cuccetta.
cough [kôf] vi tossire ♦ n tosse f.
cough drop n pasticca per la tosse.
cough syrup n sciroppo per la tosse.
could [kōōd] pt of **can**.
couldn't [kōōd'ənt] = **could not**.
council [koun'səl] n consiglio; **city** or **town** ~ consiglio comunale; **C~ of Europe** Consiglio d'Europa.
council estate n (Brit) quartiere m di case popolari.
council house n (Brit) casa popolare.
councilor [koun'sələr], (Brit) **councillor** n consigliere/a.
counsel [koun'səl] n avvocato; consultazione f ♦ vt: **to ~ sth/sb to do sth** consigliare qc/a qn di fare qc; **~ for the defense/the prosecution** avvocato difensore/di parte civile.
counselor, (Brit) **counsellor** [koun'sələr] n consigliere/a; (US: lawyer) avvocato/essa.
count [kount] vt, vi contare ♦ n conto; (nobleman) conte m; **to ~ (up) to 10** contare fino a 10; **to ~ the cost of** calcolare il costo di; **not ~ing the children** senza contare i bambini; **10 ~ing him** 10 compreso lui; **~ yourself lucky** considerati fortunato; **it ~s for very little** non conta molto, non ha molta importanza; **to keep ~ of sth** tenere il conto di qc.
  count on vt fus contare su; **to ~ on doing sth** contare di fare qc.
  count up vt addizionare.
countdown [kount'doun] n conto alla rovescia.
countenance [koun'tənəns] n volto, aspetto ♦ vt approvare.
counter [koun'tûr] n banco; (position: in post office, bank) sportello; (in game) gettone m; (TECH) contatore m ♦ vt opporsi a; (blow) parare ♦ ad: **~ to** contro; **in opposizione a**; **to buy under the ~** (fig) comperare sottobanco; **to ~ sth with sth/by doing sth** rispondere a qc con qc/facendo qc.
counteract [kountûrakt'] vt agire in opposizione a; (poison etc) annullare gli effetti di.
counterattack n [koun'tûratak] contrattacco ♦ vi [kountərətak'] contrattaccare.
counterbalance [kountûrbal'əns] vt contrappesare.
counterclockwise [kountûrklâk'wīz] ad in senso antiorario.
counterespionage [kountûres'pēənâzh] n controspionaggio.
counterfeit [koun'tûrfit] n contraffazione f, falso ♦ vt contraffare, falsificare ♦ a falso(a).
counterfoil [koun'tûrfoil] n matrice f.
counterintelligence [kountûrintel'ijəns] n =

counterespionage.
countermand [kountûrmand'] vt annullare.
countermeasure [koun'tûrmezhûr] n contromisura.
counteroffensive [kountûrəfen'siv] n controffensiva.
counterpane [koun'tûrpān] n copriletto m inv.
counterpart [koun'tûrpârt] n (of document etc) copia; (of person) corrispondente m/f.
counterproductive [kountûrprəduk'tiv] a controproducente.
counterproposal [koun'tûrprəpōzəl] n controproposta.
countersign [koun'tûrsīn] vt controfirmare.
countersink [koun'tûrsingk] vt (hole) svasare.
countess [koun'tis] n contessa.
countless [kount'lis] a innumerevole.
countrified [kun'trəfīd] a rustico(a), campagnolo(a).
country [kun'trē] n paese m; (native land) patria; (as opposed to town) campagna; (region) regione f; **in the ~** in campagna; **mountainous ~** territorio montagnoso.
country-and-western (music) [kuntrēənwes'tûrn (myōō'zik)] n musica country e western, country m.
country dancing n (Brit) danza popolare.
country house n villa in campagna.
countryman [kun'trēmən] n (national) compatriota m; (rural) contadino.
countryside [kun'trēsīd] n campagna.
country-wide [kun'trēwīd] a diffuso(a) in tutto il paese ♦ ad in tutto il paese.
county [koun'tē] n contea.
county seat n capoluogo.
coup, ~s [kōō] n (also: ~ d'état) colpo di Stato; (triumph) bel colpo.
coupé [kōōpā'] n coupé m inv.
couple [kup'əl] n coppia ♦ vt (carriages) agganciare; (TECH) accoppiare; (ideas, names) associare; **a ~ of** un paio di.
couplet [kup'lit] n distico.
coupling [kup'ling] n (RAIL) agganciamento.
coupon [kōō'pân] n (voucher) buono; (COMM) coupon m inv.
courage [kûr'ij] n coraggio.
courageous [kərā'jəs] a coraggioso(a).
courgette [kōōrzhet'] n (Brit) zucchina.
courier [kûr'ēûr] n corriere m; (for tourists) guida.
course [kôrs] n corso; (of ship) rotta; (for golf) campo; (part of meal) piatto; **first ~** primo piatto; **of ~** ad senz'altro, naturalmente; **(no) of ~ not!** certo che no!, no di certo!; **in the ~ of the next few days** nel corso dei prossimi giorni; **in due ~** a tempo debito; **~ (of action)** modo d'agire; **the best ~ would be to ...** la cosa migliore sarebbe ...; **we have no other ~ but to ...** non possiamo far altro che ...; **~ of lectures** corso di lezioni; **a ~ of treatment** (MED) una

cura.

court [kôrt] *n* corte *f*; (*TENNIS*) campo ♦ *vt* (*woman*) fare la corte a; (*fig: favor, popularity*) cercare di conquistare; (: *death, disaster*) sfiorare, rasentare; **out of** ~ (*LAW: settle*) in via amichevole; **to take to** ~ citare in tribunale; ~ **of appeal** corte d'appello.

courteous [kûr'tēəs] *a* cortese.

courtesan [kôr'tizən] *n* cortigiana.

courtesy [kûr'tisē] *n* cortesia; **by** ~ **of** per gentile concessione di.

courtesy bus *n* autobus *m inv* gratuito (*di hotel, aeroporto etc*).

courtesy light *n* (*AUT*) luce *f* interna.

courthouse [kôrt'hous] *n* (*US*) palazzo di giustizia.

courtier [kôr'tēûr] *n* cortigiano/a.

court-martial, *pl* **courts-martial** [kôrt'mâr'shəl] *n* corte *f* marziale.

courtroom [kôrt'rōōm] *n* tribunale *m*.

court shoe *n* (*Brit*) scarpa *f* décolleté *inv*.

courtyard [kôrt'yârd] *n* cortile *m*.

cousin [kuz'in] *n* cugino/a.

cove [kōv] *n* piccola baia.

covenant [kuv'ənənt] *n* accordo.

Coventry [kuv'intrē] *n*: **to send sb to** ~ (*fig*) dare l'ostracismo a qn.

cover [kuv'ûr] *vt* (*gen*) coprire; (*distance*) coprire, percorrere; (*PRESS: report on*) fare un servizio su ♦ *n* (*of pan*) coperchio; (*over furniture*) fodera; (*of book*) copertina; (*shelter*) riparo; (*COMM, INSURANCE*) copertura; **to take** ~ mettersi al coperto; **under** ~ al riparo; **under** ~ **of darkness** protetto dall'oscurità; **under separate** ~ (*COMM*) a parte, in plico separato; **$10 will** ~ **everything** 10 dollari saranno sufficienti.

cover up *vt* (*child, object*): **to** ~ **up (with)** coprire (di); (*fig: hide: truth, facts*) nascondere ♦ *vi*: **to** ~ **up for sb** (*fig*) coprire qn.

coverage [kuv'ûrij] *n* (*INSURANCE*) copertura; (*PRESS, TV, RADIO*): **to give full** ~ **to** fare un ampio servizio su.

coveralls [kuv'ûrôlz] *npl* (*US*) tuta.

cover charge *n* coperto.

covering [kuv'ûring] *n* copertura.

cover letter, (*Brit*) **covering letter** *n* lettera d'accompagnamento.

cover note *n* (*INSURANCE*) polizza (di assicurazione) provvisoria.

cover price *n* prezzo di copertina.

covert [kō'vûrt] *a* nascosto(a); (*glance*) di sottecchi, furtivo(a).

cover-up [kuv'ûrup] *n* occultamento (di informazioni).

covet [kuv'it] *vt* bramare.

cow [kou] *n* vacca ♦ *cpd* femmina ♦ *vt* intimidire; ~ **elephant** *n* elefantessa.

coward [kou'ûrd] *n* vigliacco/a.

cowardice [kou'ûrdis] *n* vigliaccheria.

cowardly [kou'ûrdlē] *a* vigliacco(a).

cowboy [kou'boi] *n* cow-boy *m inv*.

cower [kou'ûr] *vi* acquattarsi.

cowshed [kou'shed] *n* stalla.

cowslip [kou'slip] *n* (*BOT*) primula (odorata).

coxswain [kâk'sin] *n* (*abbr*: **cox**) timoniere *m*.

coy [koi] *a* falsamente timido(a).

coyote [kīōt'ē] *n* coyote *m inv*.

coziness [kō'zēnis] *n* (*US*) intimità.

cozy [kō'zē] *a* (*US*) intimo(a); (*room, atmosphere*) accogliente.

CP *n abbr* (= *Communist Party*) P.C. *m*.

cp. *abbr* (= *compare*) cfr.

c/p *abbr* (*Brit*) = **carriage paid**.

CPA *n abbr* (*US*) *see* **certified public accountant**.

CPI *n abbr* (*US*: = *Consumer Price Index*) indice dei prezzi al consumo.

Cpl. *abbr* = **corporal**.

CP/M *n abbr* (= *Control Program for Microcomputers*) CP/M *m*.

c.p.s. *abbr* (= *characters per second*) c.p.s.

CPU *n abbr see* **central processing unit**.

cr. *abbr* = **credit**; **creditor**.

crab [krab] *n* granchio.

crab apple *n* mela selvatica.

crack [krak] *n* (*split, slit*) fessura, crepa; incrinatura; (*noise*) schiocco; (: *of gun*) scoppio; (*joke*) battuta; (*col: attempt*): **to have a** ~ **at sth** tentare qc; (*DRUGS*) crack *m inv* ♦ *vt* spaccare; incrinare; (*whip*) schioccare; (*nut*) schiacciare; (*case, mystery: solve*) risolvere; (*code*) decifrare ♦ *cpd* (*athlete*) di prim'ordine; **to** ~ **jokes** (*col*) dire battute, scherzare; **to get** ~**ing** (*col*) darsi una mossa.

crack down on *vt fus* prendere serie misure contro, porre freno a.

crack up *vi* crollare.

crackdown [krak'doun] *n* repressione *f*.

cracked [krakt] *a* (*col*) matto(a).

cracker [krak'ûr] *n* cracker *m inv*; (*firework*) petardo; (*Christmas* ~) mortaretto natalizio (con sorpresa).

crackle [krak'əl] *vi* crepitare.

crackling [krak'ling] *n* crepitio; (*on radio, telephone*) disturbo; (*of pork*) cotenna croccante (del maiale).

cradle [krā'dəl] *n* culla ♦ *vt* (*child*) tenere fra le braccia; (*object*) reggere tra le braccia.

craft [kraft] *n* mestiere *m*; (*cunning*) astuzia; (*boat*) naviglio.

craftsman [krafts'mən] *n* artigiano.

craftsmanship [krafts'mənship] *n* abilità.

crafty [kraf'tē] *a* furbo(a), astuto(a).

crag [krag] *n* roccia.

cram [kram] *vt* (*fill*): **to** ~ **sth with** riempire qc di; (*put*): **to** ~ **sth into** stipare qc in.

cramming [kram'ing] *n* (*fig: pej*) sgobbare *m*.

cramp [kramp] *n* crampo ♦ *vt* soffocare, impedire.

cramped [krampt] *a* ristretto(a).

crampon [kram'pân] n (CLIMBING) rampone m.

cranberry [kran'bärē] n mirtillo.

crane [krān] n gru f inv ♦ vt, vi: **to ~ forward, to ~ one's neck** allungare il collo.

cranium, pl **crania** [krā'nēəm, krā'nēə] n cranio.

crank [krangk] n manovella; (person) persona stramba.

crankshaft [krangk'shaft] n albero a gomiti.

cranky [krang'kē] a eccentrico(a); (bad-tempered): **to be ~** avere i nervi.

cranny [kran'ē] n see **nook.**

crap [krap] n (col!) fesserie fpl; **to ~** cacare (!).

crash [krash] n fragore m; (of car) incidente m; (of plane) caduta; (of business) fallimento; (STOCK EXCHANGE) crollo ♦ vt fracassare ♦ vi (plane) fracassarsi; (car) avere un incidente; (two cars) scontrarsi; (fig) fallire, andare in rovina; **to ~ into** scontrarsi con; **he ~ed the car into a wall** andò a sbattere contro un muro con la macchina.

crash barrier n (Brit AUT) guardrail m inv.

crash course n corso intensivo.

crash helmet n casco.

crash landing n atterraggio di fortuna.

crass [kras] a crasso(a).

crate [krāt] n gabbia.

crater [krā'tûr] n cratere m.

cravat(e) [krəvat'] n fazzoletto da collo.

crave [krāv] vi: **to ~ for** desiderare ardentemente.

craving [krā'ving] n: **~ (for)** (for food, cigarettes etc) (gran) voglia (di).

crawfish [krô'fish] n (US) = **crayfish.**

crawl [krôl] vi strisciare carponi; (child) andare a gattoni; (vehicle) avanzare lentamente ♦ n (SWIMMING) crawl m; **to ~ to sb** (col: suck up) arruffianarsi qn.

crayfish [krā'fish] n (pl inv) gambero (d'acqua dolce).

crayon [krā'ân] n matita colorata.

craze [krāz] n mania.

crazed [krāzd] a (look, person) folle, pazzo(a); (pottery, glaze) incrinato(a).

crazy [krā'zē] a matto(a); **to go ~** uscir di senno, impazzire; **to be ~ about sb** (col: keen) essere pazzo di qn; **to be ~ about sth** andare matto per qc.

crazy paving n (Brit) lastricato a mosaico irregolare.

CRC n abbr (US: = Civil Rights Commission) commissione f per i diritti civili.

creak [krēk] vi cigolare, scricchiolare.

cream [krēm] n crema; (fresh) panna ♦ a (color) color crema inv; **whipped ~** panna montata.

cream cake n torta alla panna.

cream cheese n formaggio fresco.

creamery [krē'mûrē] n (shop) latteria; (facto-

ry) caseificio.

creamy [krē'mē] a cremoso(a).

crease [krēs] n grinza; (deliberate) piega ♦ vt sgualcire ♦ vi sgualcirsi.

crease-resistant [krēsrizis'tənt] a ingualcibile.

create [krēat'] vt creare; (fuss, noise) fare.

creation [krēā'shən] n creazione f.

creative [krēā'tiv] a creativo(a).

creativity [krēātiv'ətē] n creatività.

creator [krēā'tûr] n creatore/trice.

creature [krē'chûr] n creatura.

crèche, creche [kresh'] n (Brit) asilo infantile.

credence [krēd'əns] n credenza, fede f.

credentials [kriden'shəlz] npl (papers) credenziali fpl; (letters of reference) referenze fpl.

credibility [kredəbil'ətē] n credibilità.

credible [kred'əbəl] a credibile; (witness, source) attendibile.

credit [kred'it] n credito; onore m; (SCOL: esp US) certificato del compimento di una parte del corso universitario ♦ vt (COMM) accreditare; (believe: also: **give ~ to**) credere, prestar fede a; **to ~ $5 to sb** accreditare 5 dollari a qn; **to ~ sb with sth** (fig) attribuire qc a qn; **on ~** a credito; **to one's ~** a proprio onore; **to take the ~ for** farsi il merito di; **to be in ~** (person) essere creditore(trice); (bank account) essere coperto(a); **he's a ~ to his family** fa onore alla sua famiglia; see also **credits.**

creditable [kred'itəbəl] a che fa onore, degno(a) di lode.

credit account n conto di credito.

credit agency n (Brit) agenzia di analisi di credito.

credit balance n saldo attivo.

credit bureau n (US) agenzia di analisi di credito.

credit card n carta di credito.

credit control n controllo dei crediti.

credit facilities npl agevolazioni fpl creditizie.

credit limit n limite m di credito.

credit note n (Brit) nota di credito.

creditor [kred'itûr] n creditore/trice.

credits [kred'its] npl (CINEMA) titoli mpl.

credit transfer n bancogiro, postagiro.

creditworthy [kred'itwûrthē] a autorizzabile al credito.

credulity [krədōō'litē] n credulità.

creed [krēd] n credo; dottrina.

creek [krēk] n insenatura; (US) piccolo fiume m.

creel [krēl] n cestino per il pesce; (also: **lobster ~**) nassa.

creep [krēp] vi (pt, pp **crept** [krept]) avanzare furtivamente (or pian piano); (plant) arrampicarsi ♦ n (col): **he's a ~** è un tipo viscido; **it gives me the ~s** (col) mi fa venire la pelle d'oca; **to ~ up on sb** avvicinarsi quatto quatto a qn; (*fig: old age etc*) cogliere qn alla sprovvista.

creeper [krē'pûr] *n* pianta rampicante.

creepers [krē'pûrz] *npl* (*US: rompers*) tutina.

creepy [krē'pē] *a* (*frightening*) che fa accapponare la pelle.

creepy-crawly [krē'pēkról'ē] *n* (*col*) bestiolina, insetto.

cremate [krē'māt] *vt* cremare.

cremation [krimā'shən] *n* cremazione *f*.

crematorium, *pl* **crematoria** [krĕmətôr'ēəm, -ēə] *n* forno crematorio.

creosote [krē'əsōt] *n* creosoto.

crêpe [krāp] *n* crespo.

crêpe bandage *n* (*Brit*) fascia elastica.

crêpe paper *n* carta crespa.

crêpe sole *n* suola di para.

crept [krɛpt] *pt, pp of* **creep.**

crescendo [krishen'dō] *n* crescendo.

crescent [kres'ənt] *n* (*shape*) mezzaluna; (*street*) strada semicircolare.

cress [krɛs] *n* crescione *m.*

crest [krɛst] *n* cresta; (*of helmet*) pennacchiera; (*of coat of arms*) cimiero.

crestfallen [krɛst'fôlən] *a* mortificato(a).

Crete [krēt] *n* Creta.

crevasse [krəvas'] *n* crepaccio.

crevice [krev'is] *n* fessura, crepa.

crew [krōō] *n* equipaggio; (*CINEMA*) troupe *f inv;* (*gang*) banda, compagnia.

crew cut [crōō' kut] *n:* **to have a ~** avere i capelli a spazzola.

crew neck [krōō' nek] *n* girocollo.

crib [krib] *n* culla; (*REL*) presepio ♦ *vt* (*col*) copiare.

cribbage [krib'ij] *n tipo di gioco di carte.*

crick [krik] *n* crampo; **~ in the neck** torcicollo.

cricket [krik'it] *n* (*insect*) grillo; (*game*) cricket *m.*

cricketer [krik'itûr] *n* giocatore *m* di cricket.

crime [krīm] *n* (*in general*) criminalità; (*instance*) crimine *m*, delitto.

crime wave *n* ondata di criminalità.

criminal [krim'ənəl] *a, n* criminale (*m/f*); **C~ Investigation Department (CID)** (*Brit*) ≈ polizia giudiziaria.

crimp [krimp] *vt* arricciare.

crimson [krim'zən] *a* color cremisi *inv.*

cringe [krinj] *vi* acquattarsi; (*fig*) essere servile.

crinkle [kring'kəl] *vt* arricciare, increspare.

cripple [krip'əl] *n* zoppo/a ♦ *vt* azzoppare; (*ship, plane*) avariare; (*production, exports*) rovinare; **~d with arthritis** sciancato(a) per l'artrite.

crippling [krip'ling] *a* (*taxes, debts*) esorbitante; (*disease*) molto debilitante.

crisis, *pl* **crises** [krī'sis, -sēz] *n* crisi *f inv.*

crisp [krisp] *a* croccante; (*fig*) frizzante; vivace; deciso(a).

crisps [krisps] *npl* (*Brit*) patatine *fpl* fritte.

crisscross [kris'krôs] *a* incrociato(a) ♦ *vt* incrociarsi.

criterion, *pl* **criteria** [krītēr'ēən, -ēə] *n* criterio.

critic [krit'ik] *n* critico/a.

critical [krit'ikəl] *a* critico(a); **to be ~ of sb/ sth** criticare qn/qc, essere critico verso qn/qc.

critically [krit'iklē] *ad* criticamente; **~ ill** gravemente malato.

criticism [krit'isizəm] *n* critica.

criticize [krit'əsīz] *vt* criticare.

critique [kritēk'] *n* critica, saggio critico.

croak [krōk] *vi* gracchiare.

crochet [krōshā'] *n* lavoro all'uncinetto.

crock [krák] *n* coccio; (*col: person: also:* **old ~**) rottame *m*; (*: car etc*) caffettiera, rottame *m.*

crockery [krák'ûrē] *n* vasellame *m*; (*plates, cups etc*) stoviglie *fpl.*

crocodile [krák'ədīl] *n* coccodrillo.

crocus [krō'kəs] *n* croco.

croft [krôft] *n* (*Brit*) piccolo podere *m.*

crone [krōn] *n* strega.

crony [krō'nē] *n* (*col*) amicone/a.

crook [krŏŏk] *n* truffatore *m*; (*of shepherd*) bastone *m.*

crooked [krŏŏk'id] *a* curvo(a), storto(a); (*person, action*) disonesto(a).

crop [krâp] *n* raccolto; (*produce*) coltivazione *f*; (*of bird*) gozzo, ingluvie *f* ♦ *vt* (*cut: hair*) tagliare, rapare; (*subj: animals: grass*) brucare.

crop up *vi* presentarsi.

crop spraying [krâp sprā'ing] *n* spruzzatura di antiparassitari.

croquet [krōkā'] *n* croquet *m.*

croquette [krōket'] *n* crocchetta.

cross [krôs] *n* croce *f*; (*BIOL*) incrocio ♦ *vt* (*street etc*) attraversare; (*arms, legs, BIOL*) incrociare; (*thwart: person, plan*) contrastare, ostacolare; (*Brit: check*) sbarrare ♦ *vi:* **the boat ~es from ... to ...** la barca fa la traversata da ... a ... ♦ *a* di cattivo umore; **to ~ o.s.** fare il segno della croce, segnarsi; **we have a ~ed line** (*Brit: on telephone*) c'è un'interferenza; **they've got their wires ~ed** (*fig*) si sono fraintesi; **to be/get ~ with sb (about sth)** essere arrabbiato(a)/arrabbiarsi con qn (per qc).

cross out *vt* cancellare.

cross over *vi* attraversare.

crossbar [krôs'bâr] *n* traversa.

crossbreed [krôs'brēd] *n* incrocio.

cross-Channel ferry [krôs'chanəl fär'ē] *n* traghetto che attraversa la Manica.

cross-check [krôs'chck] *n* controprova ♦ *vi* fare una controprova.

crosscountry (race) [krôskun'trē (rās')] *n* cross-country *m inv.*

cross-examination [krôs'igzamənā'shən] *n* (*LAW*) interrogatorio in contraddittorio.

cross-examine [krôs'igzam'in] *vt* (*LAW*) interrogare in contraddittorio.

cross-eyed [krôs'īd] *a* strabico(a).

crossfire [krôs'fîûr] *n* fuoco incrociato.

crossing [krôs'ing] *n* incrocio; (*sea-passage*) traversata; (*also:* **pedestrian** ~) passaggio pedonale.

cross-purposes [krôs'pûr'pəsiz] *npl*: **to be at** ~ **with sb** (*misunderstand*) fraintendere qn; **to talk at** ~ fraintendersi.

cross-reference [krôs'ref'ûrəns] *n* rinvio, rimando.

crossroads [krôs'rōdz] *n* incrocio.

cross section *n* (*BIOL*) sezione *f* trasversale; (*in population*) settore *m* rappresentativo.

crosswalk [krôs'wôk] *n* (*US*) strisce *fpl* pedonali, passaggio pedonale.

crosswind [krôs'wind] *n* vento di traverso.

crosswise [krôs'wīz] *ad* di traverso.

crossword [krôs'wûrd] *n* cruciverba *m inv*.

crotch [krâch] *n* (*ANAT*) inforcatura; (*of garment*) pattina.

crotchet [krâch'it] *n* (*MUS*) semiminima.

crotchety [krâch'ətē] *a* (*person*) burbero(a).

crouch [krouch] *vi* acquattarsi; rannicchiarsi.

croup [krōōp] *n* (*MED*) crup *m*.

crouton [krōō'tân] *n* crostino.

crow [krō] *n* (*bird*) cornacchia; (*of cock*) canto del gallo ♦ *vi* (*cock*) cantare; (*fig*) vantarsi; cantar vittoria.

crowbar [krō'bâr] *n* piede *m* di porco.

crowd [kroud] *n* folla ♦ *vt* affollare, stipare ♦ *vi* affollarsi; ~**s of people** un sacco di gente.

crowded [krou'did] *a* affollato(a); ~ **with** stipato(a) di.

crowd scene *n* (*CINEMA, THEATER*) scena di massa.

crown [kroun] *n* corona; (*of head*) calotta cranica; (*of hat*) cocuzzolo; (*of hill*) cima ♦ *vt* incoronare; (*tooth*) incapsulare; **and to** ~ **it (all) off** ... (*fig*) e per giunta ..., e come se non bastasse ....

crown court *n* (*Brit*) ≈ corte *f* d'assise.

crowning [krou'ning] *a* (*achievement, glory*) supremo(a).

crown jewels *npl* gioielli *mpl* della Corona.

crown prince *n* principe *m* ereditario.

crow's-feet [krōz'fēt] *npl* zampe *fpl* di gallina.

crow's-nest [krōz'nest] *n* (*on sailing-ship*) coffa.

crucial [krōō'shəl] *a* cruciale, decisivo(a); ~ **to** essenziale per.

crucifix [krōō'səfiks] *n* crocifisso.

crucifixion [krōōsəfik'shən] *n* crocifissione *f*.

crucify [krōō'səfī] *vt* crocifiggere, mettere in croce; (*fig*) distruggere, fare a pezzi.

crude [krōōd] *a* (*materials*) greggio(a); non raffinato(a); (*fig: basic*) crudo(a), primitivo(a); (*: vulgar*) rozzo(a), grossolano(a).

crude (oil) *n* (petrolio) greggio.

cruel [krōō'əl] *a* crudele.

cruelty [krōō'əltē] *n* crudeltà *f inv*.

cruet [krōō'it] *n* ampolla.

cruise [krōōz] *n* crociera ♦ *vi* andare a velocità di crociera; (*taxi*) circolare.

cruise missile *n* missile *m* cruise *inv*.

cruiser [krōō'zûr] *n* incrociatore *m*.

cruising speed [krōō'zing spēd] *n* velocità *f inv* di crociera.

crumb [krum] *n* briciola.

crumble [krum'bəl] *vt* sbriciolare ♦ *vi* sbriciolarsi; (*plaster etc*) sgrettolarsi; (*land, earth*) franare; (*building, fig*) crollare.

crumbly [krum'blē] *a* friabile.

crummy [krum'ē] *a* (*col: cheap*) di infima categoria; (*: depressed*) giù *inv*.

crumpet [krum'pit] *n* specie di frittella.

crumple [krum'pəl] *vt* raggrinzare, spiegazzare.

crunch [krunch] *vt* sgranocchiare; (*underfoot*) scricchiolare ♦ *n* (*fig*) punto *or* momento cruciale.

crunchy [krun'chē] *a* croccante.

crusade [krōōsād'] *n* crociata ♦ *vi* (*fig*): **to** ~ **for/against** fare una crociata per/contro.

crusader [krōōsā'dûr] *n* crociato; (*fig*): ~ **(for)** sostenitore/trice (di).

crush [krush] *n* folla; (*love*): **to have a** ~ **on sb** avere una cotta per qn ♦ *vt* schiacciare; (*crumple*) sgualcire; (*grind, break up*: *garlic, ice*) tritare; (*: grapes*) pigiare.

crushing [krush'ing] *a* schiacciante.

crust [krust] *n* crosta.

crustacean [krustā'shən] *n* crostaceo.

crusty [krus'tē] *a* (*loaf*) croccante.

crutch [kruch] *n* (*MED*) gruccia; (*support*) sostegno; (*also:* **crotch**) pattina.

crux [kruks] *n* nodo.

cry [krī] *vi* piangere; (*shout: also:* ~ **out**) urlare ♦ *vi* urlo, grido; (*of animal*) verso; **to** ~ **for help** gridare aiuto; **what are you** ~**ing about?** perché piangi?; **she had a good** ~ si è fatta un bel pianto; **it's a far** ~ **from** ... (*fig*) è tutt'un'altra cosa da ....

cry off *vi* (*Brit*) ritirarsi.

crying [krī'ing] *a* (*fig*) palese; urgente.

crypt [kript] *n* cripta.

cryptic [krip'tik] *a* ermetico(a).

crystal [kris'təl] *n* cristallo.

crystal-clear [kris'təlkli'ûr] *a* cristallino(a); (*fig*) chiaro(a) (come il sole).

crystallize [kris'təlīz] *vi* cristallizzarsi ♦ *vt* (*fig*) concretizzare, concretare; ~**d fruits** (*Brit*) frutta candita.

CSA *n abbr* = *Confederate States of America*.

CS gas [sē'es gas'] *n* (*Brit*) tipo di gas lacrimogeno.

CST *abbr* (*US*: = *central standard time*) fuso orario.

CT *abbr* (*US MAIL*) = *Connecticut*.

Ct. *abbr* (*US*) = *Connecticut*.

ct *abbr* = **carat**.

cu. *abbr* = **cubic.**
cub [kub] *n* cucciolo; (*also:* ~ **scout**) lupetto.
Cuba [kyōō'bə] *n* Cuba.
Cuban [kyōō'bən] *a, n* cubano(a).
cubbyhole [kub'ēhōl] *n* angolino.
cube [kyōōb] *n* cubo ♦ *vt* (*MATH*) elevare al cubo.
cube root *n* radice *f* cubica.
cubic [kyōō'bik] *a* cubico(a); ~ **meter** *etc* metro *etc* cubo; ~ **capacity** (*AUT*) cilindrata.
cubicle [kyōō'bikəl] *n* scompartimento separato; cabina.
cuckoo [kōō'kōō] *n* cucù *m inv*.
cuckoo clock *n* orologio a cucù.
cucumber [kyōō'kumbûr] *n* cetriolo.
cud [kud] *n*: **to chew the** ~ ruminare.
cuddle [kud'əl] *vt* abbracciare, coccolare ♦ *vi* abbracciarsi.
cuddly [kud'lē] *a* da coccolare.
cudgel [kuj'əl] *n* randello ♦ *vt*: **to** ~ **one's brains** scervellarsi, spremere le meningi.
cue [kyōō] *n* stecca; (*THEATER etc*) segnale *m*.
cuff [kuf] *n* (*of shirt, coat etc*) polsino; (*US: on pants*) risvolto; (*blow*) schiaffo ♦ *vt* dare uno schiaffo a; **off the** ~ *ad* improvvisando.
cuff link *n* gemello.
cu. ft. *abbr* = *cubic feet.*
cu. in. *abbr* = *cubic inches.*
cuisine [kwizēn'] *n* cucina.
cul-de-sac [kul'dəsak'] *n* vicolo cieco.
culinary [kyōō'lənārē] *a* culinario(a).
cull [kul] *vt* (*kill selectively: animals*) selezionare e abbattere.
culminate [kul'mənāt] *vi*: **to** ~ **in** culminare con.
culmination [kulmənā'shən] *n* culmine *m*.
culottes [kyōōläts'] *npl* gonna *f* pantalone *inv*.
culpable [kul'pəbəl] *a* colpevole.
culprit [kul'prit] *n* colpevole *m/f*.
cult [kult] *n* culto.
cult figure *n* idolo.
cultivate [kul'təvāt] *vt* (*also fig*) coltivare.
cultivation [kultəvā'shən] *n* coltivazione *f*.
cultural [kul'chûrəl] *a* culturale.
culture [kul'chûr] *n* (*also fig*) cultura.
cultured [kul'chûrd] *a* colto(a).
cumbersome [kum'bûrsəm] *a* ingombrante.
cumin [kyōōm'in] *n* (*spice*) cumino.
cumulative [kyōōm'yələtiv] *a* cumulativo(a).
cunning [kun'ing] *n* astuzia, furberia ♦ *a* astuto(a), furbo(a); (*clever: device, idea*) ingegnoso(a).
cup [kup] *n* tazza; (*prize*) coppa; **a** ~ **of tea** una tazza di tè.
cupboard [kub'ûrd] *n* armadio.
Cupid [kyōō'pid] *n* Cupido; (*figurine*): **c**~ cupido.
cupidity [kyōōpid'itē] *n* cupidigia.
cupola [kyōō'pələ] *n* cupola.
cup-tie [kup'tī] *n* (*Brit FOOTBALL*) partita di coppa.

curable [kyōō'rəbəl] *a* curabile.
curate [kyōō'rit] *n* cappellano.
curator [kyōōrā'tûr] *n* direttore *m* (*di museo etc*).
curb [kûrb] *vt* tenere a freno; (*expenditure*) limitare ♦ *n* freno; (*US*) orlo del marciapiede.
curd cheese [kûrd chēz] *n* cagliata.
curdle [kûr'dəl] *vi* cagliare.
curds [kûrdz] *npl* latte *m* cagliato.
cure [kyōōr] *vt* guarire; (*CULIN*) trattare; affumicare; essiccare ♦ *n* rimedio; **to be** ~**d of sth** essere guarito(a) da qc.
cure-all [kyōōr'ôl] *n* (*also fig*) panacea, toccasana *m inv*.
curfew [kûr'fyōō] *n* coprifuoco.
curio [kyōō'rēō] *n* curiosità *f inv*.
curiosity [kyōōrēās'ətē] *n* curiosità.
curious [kyōō'rēəs] *a* curioso(a); **I'm** ~ **about him** m'incuriosisce.
curiously [kyōō'rēəslē] *ad* con curiosità; (*strangely*) stranamente; ~ **enough,** ... per quanto possa sembrare strano, ...
curl [kûrl] *n* riccio; (*of smoke etc*) anello ♦ *vt* ondulare; (*tightly*) arricciare ♦ *vi* arricciarsi.
curl up *vi* avvolgersi a spirale; rannicchiarsi.
curler [kûr'lûr] *n* bigodino; (*SPORT*) giocatore/trice di curling.
curlew [kûr'lōō] *n* chiurlo.
curling [kûr'ling] *n* (*SPORT*) curling *m*.
curling irons [kûr'ling i'ûrnz] *npl* (*US: for hair*) arricciacapelli *m inv*.
curling tongs [kûr'ling tôngz] *npl* (*Brit*) = **curling irons.**
curly [kûr'lē] *a* ricciuto(a).
currant [kûr'ənt] *n* uva passa.
currency [kûr'ənsē] *n* moneta; **foreign** ~ divisa estera; **to gain** ~ (*fig*) acquistare larga diffusione.
current [kûr'ənt] *a* corrente; (*tendency, price, event*) attuale ♦ *n* corrente *f*; **in** ~ **use** in uso corrente, d'uso comune; **the** ~ **issue of a magazine** l'ultimo numero di una rivista; **direct/alternating** ~ (*ELEC*) corrente continua/alternata.
current account *n* (*Brit*) conto corrente.
current affairs *npl* attualità *fpl*.
current assets *npl* (*COMM*) attivo realizzabile e disponibile.
current liabilities *npl* (*COMM*) passività *fpl* correnti.
currently [kûr'əntlē] *ad* attualmente.
curriculum, *pl* ~**s** *or* **curricula** [kərik'yələm, -lə] *n* curriculum *m inv*.
curriculum vitae (CV) [kərik'yələm vē'tī] *n* curriculum vitae *m inv*.
curry [kûr'ē] *n* curry *m inv* ♦ *vt*: **to** ~ **favor with** cercare di attirarsi i favori di; **chicken** ~ pollo al curry.
curry powder *n* curry *m*.
curse [kûrs] *vt* maledire ♦ *vi* bestemmiare ♦ *n*

maledizione *f*; bestemmia.

cursor [kûr'sûr] *n* (*COMPUT*) cursore *m*.

cursory [kûr'sûrē] *a* superficiale.

curt [kûrt] *a* secco(a).

curtail [kûrtāl'] *vt* (*visit etc*) accorciare; (*expenses etc*) ridurre, decurtare.

curtain [kûr'tən] *n* tenda; (*THEATER*) sipario; **to draw the ~s** (*together*) chiudere *or* tirare le tende; (*apart*) aprire le tende.

curtain call *n* (*THEATER*) chinata alla ribalta.

curts(e)y [kûrt'sē] *n* inchino, riverenza ♦ *vi* fare un inchino *or* una riverenza.

curvature [kûr'vəchûr] *n* curvatura.

curve [kûrv] *n* curva ♦ *vt* curvare ♦ *vi* curvarsi; (*road*) fare una curva.

curved [kûrvd] *a* curvo(a).

cushion [koosh'ən] *n* cuscino ♦ *vt* (*shock*) fare da cuscinetto a.

cushy [koosh'ē] *a* (*col*): **a ~ job** un lavoro di tutto riposo.

custard [kus'tûrd] *n* (*for pouring*) crema.

custodian [kustō'dēən] *n* custode *m/f*; (*Brit*: *of museum etc*) soprintendente *m/f*.

custody [kus'tədē] *n* (*of child*) custodia; (*for offenders*) arresto; **to take sb into ~** mettere qn in detenzione preventiva; **in the ~ of** alla custodia di.

custom [kus'təm] *n* costume *m*, usanza; (*LAW*) consuetudine *f*; (*COMM*) clientela; *see also* **customs**.

customary [kus'təmärē] *a* consueto(a); **it is ~ to do** è consuetudine fare.

custom-built [kus'təmbilt'] *a see* **custom-made**.

customer [kus'təmûr] *n* cliente *m/f*; **he's a tough ~** (*col*) è un tipo incontentabile.

customer profile *n* profilo del cliente.

customer service *n* servizio assistenza clienti.

customized [kus'təmīzd] *a* personalizzato(a); (*car*) fuoriserie *inv*.

custom-made [kus'təmmād'] *a* (*clothes*) fatto(a) su misura; (*other goods*: *also*: **custom-built**) fatto(a) su ordinazione.

customs [kus'təmz] *npl* dogana; **to go through (the)** ~ passare la dogana.

Customs and Excise *n* (*Brit*) Ufficio Dazi e Dogana.

customs duty *n* dazio doganale.

customs officer *n* doganiere *m*.

cut [kut] *vb* (*pt*, *pp* **cut**) *vt* tagliare; (*shape*, *make*) intagliare; (*reduce*) ridurre; (*col*: *avoid*: *class*, *lecture*, *appointment*) saltare ♦ *vi* tagliare; (*intersect*) tagliarsi ♦ *n* taglio; (*in salary etc*) riduzione *f*; **cold ~s** *npl* affettati *mpl*; **power ~** mancanza di corrente elettrica; **to ~ one's finger** tagliarsi un dito; **to get one's hair ~** farsi tagliare i capelli; **to ~ a tooth** mettere un dente; **to ~ sb/sth short** interrompere qn/qc.

cut back *vt* (*plants*) tagliare; (*production*,

expenditure) ridurre.

cut down *vt* (*tree*) abbattere; (*consumption*, *expenses*) ridurre; **to ~ sb down to size** (*fig*) sgonfiare *or* ridimensionare qn.

cut down on *vt fus* ridurre.

cut in *vi* (*interrupt conversation*): **to ~ in (on)** intromettersi . (in); (*AUT*) tagliare la strada (a).

cut off *vt* tagliare; (*fig*) isolare; **we've been ~ off** (*TEL*) è caduta la linea.

cut out *vt* tagliare; (*picture*) ritagliare.

cut up *vt* (*gen*) tagliare; (*chop*: *food*) sminuzzare.

cut-and-dried [kutəndrīd'] *a* (*also*: **cut-and-dry**) assodato(a).

cutaway [kut'əwā] *a, n:* ~ **(drawing)** spaccato.

cutback [kut'bak] *n* riduzione *f*.

cute [kyoot] *a* grazioso(a); (*clever*) astuto(a).

cut glass *n* cristallo.

cuticle [kyoo'tikəl] *n* (*on nail*) pellicina, cuticola.

cutlery [kut'lûrē] *n* posate *fpl*.

cutlet [kut'lit] *n* costoletta.

cutoff [kut'ôf] *n* (*also*: ~ **point**) limite *m*.

cutoff switch *n* interruttore *m*.

cutout [kut'out] *n* (*switch*) interruttore *m*; (*paper*, *cardboard figure*) ritaglio.

cut-price [kut'prīs] *a* (*Brit*) = **cut-rate**.

cut-rate [kut'rāt] *a* (*US*) a prezzo ridotto.

cutthroat [kut'thrōt] *n* assassino ♦ *a:* ~ **competition** concorrenza spietata.

cutting [kut'ing] *a* tagliente; (*fig*) pungente ♦ *n* (*Brit*: *PRESS*) ritaglio (di giornale); (: *RAIL*) trincea; (*CINEMA*) montaggio.

cuttlefish [kut'əlfish] *n* seppia.

CV *n abbr see* **curriculum vitae**.

C & W *n abbr* = **country and western (music)**.

cwo *abbr* = **cash with order**.

cwt. *abbr* = **hundredweight**.

cyanide [sī'ənīd] *n* cianuro.

cybernetics [sībûrnet'iks] *n* cibernetica.

cyclamen [sik'ləmən] *n* ciclamino.

cycle [sī'kəl] *n* ciclo; (*bicycle*) bicicletta ♦ *vi* andare in bicicletta.

cycle race *n* gara *or* corsa ciclistica.

cycle rack *n* (*Brit*) portabiciclette *m inv*.

cycling [sīk'ling] *n* ciclismo.

cyclist [sīk'list] *n* ciclista *m/f*.

cyclone [sīk'lōn] *n* ciclone *m*.

cygnet [sig'nit] *n* cigno giovane.

cylinder [sil'indûr] *n* cilindro.

cylinder capacity *n* cilindrata.

cylinder head *n* testata.

cylinder head gasket *n* guarnizione *f* della testata del cilindro.

cymbals [sim'bəlz] *npl* cembali *mpl*.

cynic [sin'ik] *n* cinico/a.

cynical [sin'ikəl] *a* cinico(a).

cynicism [sin'əsizəm] *n* cinismo.
CYO *n abbr* (*US*) = *Catholic Youth Organization.*
cypress [sī'pris] *n* cipresso.
Cypriot [sip'rēət] *a, n* cipriota (*m/f*).
Cyprus [sīp'rəs] *n* Cipro.
cyst [sist] *n* cisti *f inv.*
cystitis [sistī'tis] *n* cistite *f.*
CZ *n abbr* (*US*: = *Canal Zone*) *zona del Canale di Panama.*
czar [zär] *n* zar *m inv.*
Czech [chek] *a* ceco(a) ♦ *n* ceco/a; (*LING*) ceco.
Czechoslovak [chekəslō'vak] *a, n* = **Czechoslovakian.**
Czechoslovakia [chekəsləvâk'ēə] *n* Cecoslovacchia.
Czechoslovakian [chekəsləvâk'ēən] *a, n* cecoslovacco(a).

D

D, d [dē] *n* (*letter*) D, d *f or m inv*; (*MUS*): **D** re *m*; **D for Dog** ≈ D come Domodossola.
D *abbr* (*US POL*) = **democrat(ic).**
d. *abbr* = *died.*
DA *n abbr* (*US*) *see* **district attorney.**
dab [dab] *vt* (*eyes, wound*) tamponare; (*paint, cream*) applicare (con leggeri colpetti); **a ~ of paint** un colpetto di vernice.
dabble [dab'əl] *vi*: **to ~ in** occuparsi (da dilettante) di.
Dacca [dak'ə] *n* Dacca *f.*
dachshund [dâks'ŏŏnd] *n* bassotto.
dad [dad], **daddy** [dad'ē] *n* babbo, papà *m inv.*
daddy-long-legs [dadēlông'legz] *n* tipula, zanzarone *m.*
daffodil [daf'ədil] *n* trombone *m*, giunchiglia.
daft [daft] *a* sciocco(a); **to be ~ about sb** perdere la testa per qn; **to be ~ about sth** andare pazzo per qc.
dagger [dag'ûr] *n* pugnale *m.*
dahlia [dāl'yə] *n* dalia.
daily [dā'lē] *a* quotidiano(a), giornaliero(a) ♦ *n* quotidiano; (*Brit: domestic help*) donna di servizio ♦ *ad* tutti i giorni; **twice ~** due volte al giorno.
dainty [dān'tē] *a* delicato(a), grazioso(a).
dairy [där'ē] *n* (*shop*) latteria; (*on farm*) caseificio ♦ *cpd* caseario(a).
dairy cow *n* mucca da latte.
dairy farm *n* caseificio.
dairy produce *n* latticini *mpl.*

dais [dā'is] *n* pedana, palco.
daisy [dā'zē] *n* margherita.
daisy wheel *n* (*on printer*) margherita.
daisy-wheel printer *n* stampante *f* a margherita.
Dakar [dâkâr'] *n* Dakar *f.*
dale [dāl] *n* valle *f.*
dally [dal'ē] *vi* trastullarsi.
dalmatian [dalmā'shən] *n* (*dog*) dalmata *m.*
dam [dam] *n* diga; (*reservoir*) bacino artificiale ♦ *vt* sbarrare; costruire dighe su.
damage [dam'ij] *n* danno, danni *mpl*; (*fig*) danno ♦ *vt* danneggiare; (*fig*) recar danno a; **~ to property** danni materiali.
damages [dam'ijiz] *npl* (*LAW*) danni *mpl*; **to pay $5000 in ~** pagare 5000 dollari di indennizzo.
damaging [dam'ijing] *a*: **~ (to)** nocivo(a) (a).
Damascus [dəmas'kəs] *n* Damasco *f.*
dame [dām] *n* (*title*) donna; (*THEATER*) vecchia signora (*ruolo comico di donna recitato da un uomo*).
damn [dam] *vt* condannare; (*curse*) maledire ♦ *n* (*col*): **I don't give a ~** non me ne importa un fico ♦ *a* (*col*): **this ~ ...** questo maledetto ...; **~ (it)!** accidenti!
damnable [dam'nəbəl] *a* (*col: behavior*) vergognoso(a); (*: weather*) schifoso(a).
damnation [damnā'shən] *n* (*REL*) dannazione *f* ♦ *excl* (*col*) dannazione!, diavolo!
damning [dam'ing] *a* (*evidence*) schiacciante.
damp [damp] *a* umido(a) ♦ *n* umidità, umido ♦ *vt* (*also:* **~en**) (*cloth, rag*) inumidire, bagnare; (*enthusiasm etc*) spegnere.
dampcourse [damp'kôrs] *n* strato *m* isolante antiumido *inv.*
damper [dam'pûr] *n* (*MUS*) sordina; (*of fire*) valvola di tiraggio; **to put a ~ on sth** (*fig: atmosphere*) gelare; (*: enthusiasm*) far sbollire.
dampness [damp'nis] *n* umidità, umido.
damson [dam'zən] *n* susina damaschina.
dance [dans] *n* danza, ballo; (*ball*) ballo ♦ *vi* ballare; **to ~ about** saltellare.
dance hall *n* dancing *m inv*, sala da ballo.
dancer [dan'sûr] *n* danzatore/trice; (*professional*) ballerino/a.
dancing [dan'sing] *n* danza, ballo.
D and C *n abbr* (*MED*: = *dilation and curettage*) raschiamento.
dandelion [dan'dəlīən] *n* dente *m* di leone.
dandruff [dan'drəf] *n* forfora.
dandy [dan'dē] *n* dandy *m inv*, elegantone *m* ♦ *a* (*US col*) fantastico(a).
Dane [dān] *n* danese *m/f.*
danger [dān'jûr] *n* pericolo; **there is a ~ of fire** c'è pericolo di incendio; **in ~** in pericolo; **out of ~** fuori pericolo; **he was in ~ of falling** rischiava di cadere.
danger list *n* (*Brit MED*): **on the ~ list** in prognosi riservata.

dangerous [dān'jûrəs] *a* pericoloso(a).

dangerously [dān'jûrəslē] *ad*: ~ **ill** in pericolo di vita.

danger zone *n* area di pericolo.

dangle [dang'gəl] *vt* dondolare; (*fig*) far balenare ♦ *vi* pendolare.

Danish [dā'nish] *a* danese ♦ *n* (*LING*) danese *m*.

Danish pastry *n* dolce *m* di pasta sfoglia.

dank [dangk] *a* freddo(a) e umido(a).

Danube [dan'yōōb] *n*: **the** ~ il Danubio.

dapper [dap'ûr] *a* lindo(a).

Dardanelles [dârdənelz'] *npl* Dardanelli *mpl*.

dare [dār] *vt*: **to** ~ **sb to do** sfidare qn a fare ♦ *vi*: **to** ~ (**to**) **do sth** osare fare qc; **I** ~**n't tell him** (*Brit*) non oso dirglielo; **I** ~ **say he'll turn up** immagino che spunterà.

daredevil [dār'devəl] *n* scavezzacollo *m/f*.

Dar es Salaam [dâr es səlâm'] *n* Dar-es-Salaam *f*.

daring [dār'ing] *a* audace, ardito(a).

dark [dârk] *a* (*night, room*) buio(a), scuro(a); (*color, complexion*) scuro(a); (*fig*) cupo(a), tetro(a), nero(a) ♦ *n*: **in the** ~ al buio; **it is/ is getting** ~ è/si sta facendo buio; **in the** ~ **about** (*fig*) all'oscuro di; **after** ~ a notte fatta.

dark chocolate *n* cioccolata amara.

darken [dâr'kən] *vt* (*room*) oscurare; (*photo, painting*) far scuro(a) ♦ *vi* oscurarsi; imbrunirsi.

dark glasses *npl* occhiali *mpl* scuri.

darkly [dârk'lē] *ad* (*gloomily*) cupamente, con aria cupa; (*in a sinister way*) minacciosamente.

darkness [dârk'nis] *n* oscurità, buio.

darkroom [dârk'rōōm] *n* camera oscura.

darling [dâr'ling] *a* caro(a) ♦ *n* tesoro.

darn [dârn] *vt* rammendare.

dart [dârt] *n* freccetta ♦ *vi*: **to** ~ **towards** (*also*: **make a** ~ **towards**) precipitarsi verso; **to** ~ **along** passare come un razzo; **to** ~ **away** guizzare via; *see also* **darts**.

dartboard [dârt'bôrd] *n* bersaglio (per freccette).

darts [dârts] *n* tiro al bersaglio (con freccette).

dash [dash] *n* (*sign*) lineetta; (*small quantity*: *of liquid*) goccio, goccino; (: *of soda*) spruzzo ♦ *vt* (*missile*) gettare; (*hopes*) infrangere ♦ *vi*: **to** ~ **towards** (*also*: **make a** ~ **towards**) precipitarsi verso.

dash away *vi* scappare via.

dashboard [dash'bôrd] *n* cruscotto.

dashing [dash'ing] *a* ardito(a).

dastardly [das'tûrdlē] *a* vile.

data [dā'tə] *npl* dati *mpl*.

database [dā'təbās] *n* database *m*, base *f* di dati.

data capture *n* registrazione *f* or rilevazione *f* di dati.

data processing *n* elaborazione *f* (elettronica) dei dati.

data transmission *n* trasmissione *f* di dati.

date [dāt] *n* data; (*appointment*) appuntamento; (*fruit*) dattero ♦ *vt* datare; (*col: girl etc*) uscire con; **what's the** ~ **today?** quanti ne abbiamo oggi?; ~ **of birth** data di nascita; **closing** ~ scadenza, termine *m*; **to** ~ *ad* fino a oggi; **out of** ~ scaduto(a); (*old-fashioned*) passato(a) di moda; **up to** ~ moderno(a); aggiornato(a); **to bring up to** ~ (*correspondence, information*) aggiornare; (*method*) modernizzare; (*person*) aggiornare, mettere al corrente; ~**d the 13th** datato il 13; **thank you for your letter** ~**d July 5th** la ringrazio per la sua lettera in data 5 luglio.

dated [dā'tid] *a* passato(a) di moda.

dateline [dāt'līn] *n* linea del cambiamento di data.

date stamp *n* timbro datario.

daub [dôb] *vt* imbrattare.

daughter [dôt'ûr] *n* figlia.

daughter-in-law [dô'tûrinlô] *n* nuora.

daunt [dônt] *vt* intimidire.

daunting [dôn'ting] *a* non invidiabile.

dauntless [dônt'lis] *a* intrepido(a).

dawdle [dôd'əl] *vi* bighellonare; **to** ~ **over one's work** gingillarsi con il lavoro.

dawn [dôn] *n* alba ♦ *vi* (*day*) spuntare; (*fig*) venire in mente; **at** ~ all'alba; **from** ~ **to dusk** dall'alba al tramonto; **it** ~**ed on him that** ... gli è venuto in mente che ....

day [dā] *n* giorno; (*as duration*) giornata; (*period of time, age*) tempo, epoca; **the** ~ **before** il giorno avanti *or* prima; **the** ~ **after, the following** ~ il giorno dopo, il giorno seguente; **the** ~ **before yesterday** l'altroieri; **the** ~ **after tomorrow** dopodomani; (**on**) **that** ~ quel giorno; (**on**) **the** ~ **that** ... il giorno che *or* in cui ...; **to work an 8-hour** ~ avere una giornata lavorativa di 8 ore; **by** ~ di giorno; ~ **by** ~ giorno per giorno; **paid by the** ~ pagato(a) a giornata; **these** ~**s, in the present** ~ di questi tempi, oggigiorno.

daybreak [dā'brāk] *n* spuntar *m* del giorno.

day-care center [dā'kär sen'tûr] *n* asilo infantile.

daydream [dā'drēm] *n* sogno a occhi aperti ♦ *vi* sognare a occhi aperti.

daylight [dā'līt] *n* luce *f* del giorno.

Daylight Saving Time (*US*) ora legale.

day nursery *n* asilo infantile.

day release *n* (*Brit*): **to be on** ~ *avere un giorno di congedo alla settimana per formazione professionale*.

day return (ticket) *n* (*Brit*) biglietto giornaliero di andata e ritorno.

day shift *n* turno di giorno.

day student *n* (*at school*) alunno/a esterno/a.

daytime [dā'tīm] *n* giorno.

day-to-day [dātōōdā'] *a* (*routine*) quotidiano(a); (*expenses*) giornaliero(a); **on a ~ basis** a giornata.

day trip *n* gita (di un giorno).

day-tripper [dā'tripûr] *n* (*Brit*) gitante *m/f*.

daze [dāz] *vt* (*subj: drug*) inebetire; (: *blow*) stordire ♦ *n*: **in a ~** inebetito(a); stordito(a).

dazzle [daz'əl] *vt* abbagliare.

dazzling [daz'ling] *a* (*light*) abbagliante; (*color*) violento(a); (*smile*) smagliante.

dB *abbr* (= *decibel*) db.

DC *abbr* (*US MAIL*) = *District of Columbia*; (*ELEC*: = *direct current*) c.c.

DD *n abbr* (= *Doctor of Divinity*) titolo di studio.

D/D *abbr* = **demand draft**; (*Brit*) = **direct debit**.

D-day [dē'dā] *n* giorno dello sbarco alleato in Normandia.

DDS *n abbr* (*US*: = *Doctor of Dental Science*; *Doctor of Dental Surgery*) titoli di studio.

DDT *n abbr* (= *dichlorodiphenyltrichloroethane*) D.D.T. *m*.

DE *abbr* (*US MAIL*) = *Delaware*.

DEA *n abbr* (*US*: = *Drug Enforcement Administration*) ≈ squadra narcotici.

deacon [dē'kən] *n* diacono.

dead [ded] *a* morto(a); (*numb*) intirizzito(a); (*battery*) scarico(a) ♦ *ad* assolutamente, perfettamente; **the ~** *npl* i morti; **he was shot ~** fu colpito a morte; **~ on time** in perfetto orario; **~ tired** stanco(a) morto(a); **to stop ~** fermarsi in tronco; **the line has gone ~** (*TEL*) è caduta la linea.

deaden [ded'ən] *vt* (*blow, sound*) ammortire; (*make numb*) intirizzire.

dead end *n* vicolo cieco.

dead-end [dedend'] *a*: **a ~ job** un lavoro senza sbocchi.

dead heat *n* (*SPORT*): **to finish in a ~** finire alla pari.

dead-letter office [ded'let'ûr ôf'is] *n* ufficio della posta in giacenza.

deadline [ded'līn] *n* scadenza; **to work to a ~** avere una scadenza.

deadlock [ded'lâk] *n* punto morto.

dead loss [ded' lôs] *n* (*col*): **to be a ~** (*person, thing*) non valere niente.

deadly [ded'lē] *a* mortale; (*weapon, poison*) micidiale ♦ *ad*: **~ dull** di una noia micidiale.

deadpan [ded'pan] *a* a faccia impassibile.

Dead Sea *n*: **the ~** il mar Morto.

dead season *n* (*TOURISM*) stagione *f* morta.

deaf [def] *a* sordo(a); **to turn a ~ ear to sth** fare orecchi da mercante a qc.

deaf-and-dumb [def'əndum'] *a* (*person*) sordomuto(a); (*alphabet*) dei sordomuti.

deafen [def'ən] *vt* assordare.

deafening [def'əning] *a* fragoroso(a), assordante.

deaf-mute [def'myo͞ot'] *n* sordomuto/a.

deafness [def'nis] *n* sordità.

deal [dēl] *n* accordo; (*business ~*) affare *m* ♦ *vt* (*pt, pp* **dealt** [delt]) (*blow, cards*) dare; **to strike a ~ with sb** fare un affare con qn; **it's a ~!** (*col*) affare fatto!; **he got a bad/fair ~ from them** l'hanno trattato male/bene; **a good ~ of, a great ~ of** molto(a).

deal in *vt fus* (*COMM*) occuparsi di.

deal with *vt fus* (*COMM*) fare affari con, trattare con; (*handle*) occuparsi di; (*be about: book etc*) trattare di.

dealer [dē'lûr] *n* commerciante *m/f*.

dealership [dē'lûrship] *n* rivenditore *m*.

dealings [dē'lingz] *npl* rapporti *mpl*; (*in goods, shares*) transazioni *fpl*.

dealt [delt] *pt, pp of* **deal**.

dean [dēn] *n* (*REL*) decano; (*SCOL*) preside *m* di facoltà (*or* di collegio).

dear [dēr] *a* caro(a) ♦ *n*: **my ~** caro mio/cara mia; **~ me!** Dio mio!; **D~ Sir/Madam** (*in letter*) Egregio Signore/Egregia Signora; **D~ Mr/Mrs X** Gentile Signor/Signora X.

dearly [dēr'lē] *ad* (*love*) moltissimo; (*pay*) a caro prezzo.

dearth [dûrth] *n* scarsità, carestia.

death [deth] *n* morte *f*; (*ADMIN*) decesso.

deathbed [deth'bed] *n* letto di morte.

death certificate *n* atto di decesso.

deathly [deth'lē] *a* di morte ♦ *ad* come un cadavere.

death penalty *n* pena di morte.

death rate *n* indice *m* di mortalità.

death sentence *n* condanna a morte.

deathtrap [deth'trap] *n* trappola mortale.

debacle [dəbâk'əl] *n* (*defeat*) disfatta; (*collapse*) sfacelo.

debar [dibâr'] *vt*: **to ~ sb from a club** *etc* escludere qn da un club *etc*; **to ~ sb from doing** vietare a qn di fare.

debase [dibās'] *vt* (*currency*) adulterare; (*person*) degradare.

debatable [dibā'təbəl] *a* discutibile; **it is ~ whether ...** è in dubbio se ....

debate [dibāt'] *n* dibattito ♦ *vt* dibattere, discutere ♦ *vi* (*consider*): **to ~ whether** riflettere se.

debauchery [debô'chûrē] *n* dissolutezza.

debenture [diben'chûr] *n* (*COMM*) obbligazione *f*.

debilitate [dibil'ətāt] *vt* debilitare.

debit [deb'it] *n* debito ♦ *vt*: **to ~ a sum to sb** *or* **to sb's account** addebitare una somma a qn.

debit balance *n* saldo debitore.

debit note *n* nota di addebito.

debonair [debənār'] *a* gioviale e disinvolto(a).

debrief [dēbrēf'] *vt* chiamare a rapporto (a operazione ultimata).

debriefing [dēbrēf'ing] *n* rapporto.

debris [dəbrē'] *n* detriti *mpl*.

debt [det] *n* debito; **to be in ~** essere indebitato(a); **~s of $5000** debiti per 5000 dollari;

bad ~ debito insoluto.
debt collector *n* agente *m* di recupero crediti.
debtor [det'ûr] *n* debitore/trice.
debug [dēbug'] *vt* (*COMPUT*) localizzare e rimuovere errori in.
debunk [dibungk'] *vt* (*col: theory*) demistificare; (: *claim*) smentire; (: *person, institution*) screditare.
debut [dābyōō'] *n* debutto.
debutante [debyōōtânt'] *n* debuttante *f*.
Dec. *abbr* (= *December*) dic.
decade [dek'ād] *n* decennio.
decadence [dek'ədəns] *n* decadenza.
decadent [dek'ədənt] *a* decadente.
decaffeinated [dēkaf'ənātid] *a* decaffeinato(a).
decamp [dikamp'] *vi* (*col*) filarsela, levare le tende.
decant [dikant'] *vt* (*wine*) travasare.
decanter [dikan'tûr] *n* caraffa.
decarbonize [dēkár'bənīz] *vt* (*AUT*) decarburare.
decay [dikā'] *n* decadimento; imputridimento; (*fig*) rovina; (*also*: **tooth** ~) carie *f* ♦ *vi* (*rot*) imputridire; (*fig*) andare in rovina.
decease [disēs'] *n* decesso.
deceased [disēst'] *n*: **the** ~ il(la) defunto(a).
deceit [disēt'] *n* inganno.
deceitful [disēt'fəl] *a* ingannevole, perfido(a).
deceive [disēv'] *vt* ingannare; **to** ~ **o.s.** illudersi, ingannarsi.
decelerate [dēsel'ərāt] *vt, vi* rallentare.
December [disem'bûr] *n* dicembre *m*; *for phrases see also* **July**.
decency [dē'sənsē] *n* decenza.
decent [dē'sənt] *a* decente; **they were very** ~ **about it** si sono comportati da signori riguardo a ciò.
decently [dē'səntlē] *ad* (*respectably*) decentemente, convenientemente; (*kindly*) gentilmente.
decentralization [dēsentrəlizā'shən] *n* decentramento.
decentralize [dēsen'trəlīz] *vt* decentrare.
deception [disep'shən] *n* inganno.
deceptive [disep'tiv] *a* ingannevole.
decibel [des'əbəl] *n* decibel *m inv*.
decide [disīd'] *vt* (*person*) far prendere una decisione a; (*question, argument*) risolvere, decidere ♦ *vi* decidere, decidersi; **to** ~ **to do/that** decidere di fare/che; **to** ~ **on** decidere per; **to** ~ **against doing sth** decidere di non fare qc.
decided [disī'did] *a* (*resolute*) deciso(a); (*clear, definite*) netto(a), chiaro(a).
decidedly [disī'didlē] *ad* indubbiamente; decisamente.
deciding [disī'ding] *a* decisivo(a).
deciduous [disij'ōōəs] *a* deciduo(a).
decimal [des'əməl] *a, n* decimale (*m*); **to 3** ~

places al terzo decimale.
decimalize [des'əməlīz] *vt* convertire al sistema metrico decimale.
decimal point *n* ≈ virgola.
decimate [des'əmāt] *vt* decimare.
decipher [disī'fûr] *vt* decifrare.
decision [disizh'ən] *n* decisione *f*; **to make a** ~ prendere una decisione.
decisive [disī'siv] *a* (*victory, factor*) decisivo(a); (*influence*) determinante; (*manner, person*) risoluto(a), deciso(a); (*reply*) deciso(a), categorico(a).
deck [dek] *n* (*NAUT*) ponte *m*; (*of cards*) mazzo; (*of bus*): **top** ~ imperiale *m*; **to go up on** ~ salire in coperta; **below** ~ sotto coperta; **cassette** ~ piastra (di registrazione); **record** ~ piatto (giradischi).
deck chair *n* sedia a sdraio.
deck hand *n* marinaio.
declaration [deklərā'shən] *n* dichiarazione *f*.
declare [diklär'] *vt* dichiarare.
declassify [dēklas'əfī] *vt* rendere accessibile al pubblico.
decline [diklīn'] *n* (*decay*) declino; (*lessening*) ribasso ♦ *vt* declinare; rifiutare ♦ *vi* declinare; diminuire; ~ **in living standards** abbassamento del tenore di vita; **to** ~ **to do sth** rifiutar(si) di fare qc.
declutch [dēkluch'] *vi* (*Brit*) premere la frizione.
decode [dēkōd'] *vt* decifrare.
decoder [dēkō'dûr] *n* decodificatore *m*.
decompose [dēkəmpōz'] *vi* decomporre.
decomposition [dēkâmpəzish'ən] *n* decomposizione *f*.
decompression [dēkəmpresh'ən] *n* decompressione *f*.
decompression chamber *n* camera di decompressione.
decongestant [dēkənjes'tənt] *n* decongestionante *m*.
decontaminate [dēkəntam'ənāt] *vt* decontaminare.
decontrol [dēkəntrōl'] *vt* (*Brit: trade*) liberalizzare; (: *prices*) togliere il controllo governativo a.
decor [dākôr'] *n* decorazione *f*.
decorate [dek'ərāt] *vt* (*adorn, give a medal to*) decorare; (*paint and paper*) pitturare e tappezzare.
decoration [dekərā'shən] *n* decorazione *f*.
decorative [dek'ûrətiv] *a* decorativo(a).
decorator [dek'ərātûr] *n* decoratore/trice.
decorum [dikôr'əm] *n* decoro.
decoy [dē'koi] *n* zimbello; **they used him as a** ~ **for the enemy** l'hanno usato come esca per il nemico.
decrease *n* [dē'krēs] diminuzione *f* ♦ *vt, vi* [dikrēs'] diminuire; **to be on the** ~ essere in diminuzione.
decreasing [dikrēs'ing] *a* sempre meno *inv*.

decree [dikrē'] *n* decreto ♦ *vt*: **to ~ (that)** decretare (che + *sub*); **~ absolute** sentenza di divorzio definitiva; **~ nisi** [-nī'sī] sentenza provvisoria di divorzio.

decrepit [dikrep'it] *a* decrepito(a); (*building*) cadente.

decry [dikrī'] *vt* condannare, deplorare.

dedicate [ded'ikāt] *vt* consacrare; (*book etc*) dedicare.

dedicated [ded'ikātid] *a* coscienzioso(a); (*COMPUT*) specializzato(a), dedicato(a).

dedication [dedikā'shən] *n* (*devotion*) dedizione *f*; (*in book*) dedica.

deduce [didōōs'] *vt* dedurre.

deduct [didukt'] *vt*: **to ~ sth** (**from**) dedurre qc (da); (*from wage etc*) trattenere qc (da).

deduction [diduk'shən] *n* (*deducting*) deduzione *f*; (*from wage etc*) trattenuta; (*deducing*) deduzione *f*, conclusione *f*.

deed [dēd] *n* azione *f*, atto; (*LAW*) atto; **~ of covenant** atto di donazione.

deem [dēm] *vt* (*formal*) giudicare, ritenere; **to ~ it wise to do** ritenere prudente fare.

deep [dēp] *a* profondo(a) ♦ *ad*: **~ in snow** affondato(a) nella neve; **spectators stood 20 ~** c'erano 20 file di spettatori; **knee-~ in water** in acqua fino alle ginocchia; **4 meters ~** profondo(a) 4 metri; **he took a ~ breath** fece un respiro profondo.

deepen [dē'pən] *vt* (*hole*) approfondire ♦ *vi* approfondirsi; (*darkness*) farsi più intenso(a).

deep-freeze [dēp'frēz'] *n* congelatore *m* ♦ *vt* congelare.

deep-fry [dēp'frī'] *vt* friggere in olio abbondante.

deep (fat) fryer [dēp (fat) frī'ûr] *n* friggitrice *f*.

deeply [dēp'lē] *ad* profondamente; **to regret sth ~** rammaricarsi sinceramente di qc.

deep-rooted [dēp'rōo'tid] *a* (*prejudice*) profondamente radicato(a); (*affection*) profondo(a); (*habit*) inveterato(a).

deep-sea diver [dēp'sē' di'vûr] *n* palombaro.

deep-sea diving *n* immersione *f* in alto mare.

deep-sea fishing *n* pesca d'alto mare.

deep-seated [dēp'sē'tid] *a* (*beliefs*) radicato(a).

deep-set [dēp'set] *a* (*eyes*) infossato(a).

deer [dēr] *n* (*pl inv*): **the ~** i cervidi (*ZOOL*); (**red**) **~** cervo; (**fallow**) **~** daino; (**roe**) **~** capriolo.

deerskin [dēr'skin] *n* pelle *f* di daino.

deerstalker [dēr'stôkûr] *n* berretto da cacciatore.

deface [difās'] *vt* imbrattare.

defamation [defəmā'shən] *n* diffamazione *f*.

defamatory [difam'ətôrē] *a* diffamatorio(a).

default [difôlt'] *vi* (*LAW*) essere contumace; (*gen*) essere inadempiente ♦ *n* (*COMPUT*:

also: **~ value**) default *m inv*; **by ~** (*LAW*) in contumacia; (*SPORT*) per abbandono; **to ~ on a debt** non onorare un debito.

defaulter [difôlt'ûr] *n* (*on debt*) inadempiente *m/f*.

default option *n* (*COMPUT*) opzione *f* di default.

defeat [difēt'] *n* sconfitta ♦ *vt* (*team, opponents*) sconfiggere; (*fig: plans, efforts*) frustrare.

defeatism [difē'tizəm] *n* disfattismo.

defeatist [difē'tist] *a, n* disfattista (*m/f*).

defect *n* [dē'fekt] difetto ♦ *vi* [difekt']: **to ~ to the enemy/the West** passare al nemico/all'Ovest; **physical ~** difetto fisico; **mental ~** anomalia mentale.

defective [difek'tiv] *a* difettoso(a).

defector [difek'tûr] *n* rifugiato(a) politico(a).

defence [difens'] *etc* (*Brit*) = **defense** *etc*; **the Ministry of D~** il Ministero della Difesa.

defend [difend'] *vt* difendere; (*decision, action*) giustificare; (*opinion*) sostenere.

defendant [difen'dənt] *n* imputato/a.

defender [difen'dûr] *n* difensore/a.

defending champion [difen'ding cham'pēən] *n* (*SPORT*) campione/essa in carica.

defending counsel [difen'ding koun'səl] *n* (*Brit LAW*) avvocato difensore.

defense [difens'] *n* (*US*) difesa; **in ~ of** in difesa di; **the Department of D~** il Ministero della Difesa.

defense counsel *n* (*US LAW*) avvocato difensore.

defenseless [difens'lis] *a* senza difesa.

defensive [difen'siv] *a* difensivo(a) ♦ *n* difensiva; **on the ~** sulla difensiva.

defer [difûr'] *vt* (*postpone*) differire, rinviare ♦ *vi* (*submit*): **to ~ to sb/sth** rimettersi a qn/qc.

deference [def'ûrəns] *n* deferenza; riguardo; **out of** *or* **in ~ to** per riguardo a.

defiance [difī'əns] *n* sfida; **in ~ of** a dispetto di.

defiant [difī'ənt] *a* (*attitude*) di sfida; (*person*) ribelle.

defiantly [difī'əntlē] *ad* con aria di sfida.

deficiency [difish'ənsē] *n* deficienza; carenza; (*COMM*) ammanco.

deficiency disease *n* malattia da carenza.

deficient [difish'ənt] *a* deficiente; insufficiente; **to be ~ in** mancare di.

deficit [def'isit] *n* disavanzo.

defile [difīl'] *vt* contaminare ♦ *vi* sfilare ♦ *n* gola, stretta.

define [difīn'] *vt* (*gen, COMPUT*) definire.

definite [def'ənit] *a* (*fixed*) definito(a), preciso(a); (*clear, obvious*) ben definito(a), esatto(a); (*LING*) determinativo(a); **he was ~ about it** ne era sicuro.

definitely [def'ənitlē] *ad* indubbiamente.

definition [defənish'ən] *n* definizione *f*.

definitive [difin'ətiv] *a* definitivo(a).

deflate [diflāt'] *vt* sgonfiare; (*ECON*) deflazionare; (*pompous person*) fare abbassare la cresta a.

deflation [diflā'shən] *n* (*ECON*) deflazione *f*.

deflationary [diflā'shənärē] *a* (*ECON*) deflazionistico(a).

deflect [diflekt'] *vt* deflettere, deviare.

defog [dēfôg'] *vt* (*US AUT*) sbrinare.

defogger [dēfôg'ûr] *n* (*US AUT*) sbrinatore *m*.

deforestation [dēfôristā'shən] *n* disboscamento.

deform [difôrm'] *vt* deformare.

deformed [difôrmd'] *a* deforme.

deformity [difôr'mitē] *n* deformità *f inv*.

defraud [difrôd'] *vt*: **to ~ (of)** defraudare (di).

defray [difrā'] *vt*: **to ~ sb's expenses** sostenere le spese di qn.

defrost [difrôst'] *vt* (*fridge*) disgelare; (*frozen food*) scongelare.

deft [deft] *a* svelto(a), destro(a).

defunct [difungkt'] *a* defunto(a).

defuse [dēfyōoz'] *vt* disinnescare; (*fig*) distendere.

defy [difī'] *vt* sfidare; (*efforts etc*) resistere a; (*refuse to obey*) rifiutare di obbedire a.

degenerate *vi* [dijen'ûrāt] degenerare ♦ *a* [dijen'ûrit] degenere.

degradation [degrədā'shən] *n* degradazione *f*.

degrade [digrād'] *vt* degradare.

degrading [digrā'ding] *a* degradante.

degree [digrē'] *n* grado; (*SCOL*) laurea (universitaria); **10 ~s below freezing** 10 gradi sotto zero; **a (first) ~ in math** una laurea in matematica; **a considerable ~ of risk** una grossa percentuale di rischio; **by ~s** (*gradually*) gradualmente, a poco a poco; **to some ~, to a certain ~** fino a un certo punto, in certa misura.

dehydrated [dēhī'drātid] *a* disidratato(a); (*milk, eggs*) in polvere.

dehydration [dēhīdrā'shən] *n* disidratazione *f*.

de-ice [dēīs'] *vt* (*windshield*) disgelare.

de-icer [dēī'sûr] *n* sbrinatore *m*.

deign [dān] *vi*: **to ~ to do** degnarsi di fare.

deity [dē'itē] *n* divinità *f inv*; dio/dea.

dejected [dijek'tid] *a* abbattuto(a), avvilito(a).

dejection [dijek'shən] *n* abbattimento, avvilimento.

Del. *abbr* (*US*) = *Delaware*.

del. *abbr* = **delete**.

delay [dilā'] *vt* (*journey, operation*) ritardare, rinviare; (*travelers, trains*) ritardare; (*payment*) differire ♦ *n* ritardo; **without ~** senza ritardo.

delayed-action [dilād'ak'shən] *a* a azione ritardata.

delectable [dilek'təbəl] *a* delizioso(a).

delegate *n* [del'əgit] delegato/a ♦ *vt* [del'əgāt] delegare; **to ~ sth to sb/sb to do sth** delegare qc a qn/qn a fare qc.

delegation [deləgā'shən] *n* delegazione *f*; (*of work etc*) delega.

delete [dilēt'] *vt* (*gen*, *COMPUT*) cancellare.

Delhi [del'ē] *n* Delhi *f*.

deliberate *a* [dilib'ûrit] (*intentional*) intenzionale; (*slow*) misurato(a) ♦ *vi* [dilib'ûrāt] deliberare, riflettere.

deliberately [dilib'ûritlē] *ad* (*on purpose*) deliberatamente.

deliberation [dilibərā'shən] *n* (*consideration*) riflessione *f*; (*discussion*) discussione *f*, deliberazione *f*.

delicacy [del'əkəsē] *n* delicatezza.

delicate [del'əkit] *a* delicato(a).

delicately [del'əkitlē] *ad* (*gen*) delicatamente; (*act, express*) con delicatezza.

delicatessen [deləkətes'ən] *n* ≈ salumeria.

delicious [dilish'əs] *a* delizioso(a), squisito(a).

delight [dilīt'] *n* delizia, gran piacere *m* ♦ *vt* dilettare; **it is a ~ to the eyes** è un piacere guardarlo; **to take ~ in** divertirsi a; **to be the ~ of** essere la gioia di.

delighted [dilī'tid] *a*: **~ (at** *or* **with sth)** contentissimo(a) (di qc), felice (di qc); **to be ~ to do sth/that** essere felice di fare qc/che + *sub*; **I'd be ~** con grande piacere.

delightful [dilīt'fəl] *a* (*person*, *place*, *meal*) delizioso(a); (*smile*, *manner*) incantevole.

delimit [dilim'it] *vt* delimitare.

delineate [dilin'ēāt] *vt* delineare.

delinquency [diling'kwənsē] *n* delinquenza.

delinquent [diling'kwint] *a*, *n* delinquente (*m/f*).

delirious [dilēr'ēəs] *a* (*MED*, *fig*) delirante, in delirio; **to be ~** delirare; (*fig*) farneticare.

delirium [dilēr'ēəm] *n* delirio.

deliver [diliv'ûr] *vt* (*mail*) distribuire; (*goods*) consegnare; (*speech*) pronunciare; (*free*) liberare; (*MED*) far partorire; **to ~ a message** fare un'ambasciata; **to ~ the goods** (*fig*) partorire.

deliverance [diliv'ûrəns] *n* liberazione *f*.

delivery [diliv'ûrē] *n* distribuzione *f*; consegna; (*of speaker*) dizione *f*; (*MED*) parto; **to take ~ of** prendere in consegna.

delivery slip *n* bolla di consegna.

delivery truck, (*Brit*) **delivery van** *n* furgoncino (per le consegne).

delouse [dēlous'] *vt* spidocchiare.

delta [del'tə] *n* delta *m*.

delude [dilōod'] *vt* deludere, illudere.

deluge [del'yōoj] *n* diluvio ♦ *vt* (*fig*): **to ~ (with)** subissare (di), inondare (di).

delusion [dilōo'zhən] *n* illusione *f*.

de luxe [dəluks'] *a* di lusso.

delve [delv] *vi*: **to ~ into** frugare in; (*subject*) far ricerche in.

Dem. *abbr* (*US POL*) = **democrat(ic)**.

demagogue [dem'əgôg] *n* demagogo.

demand [dimand'] *vt* richiedere ♦ *n* richiesta; (*ECON*) domanda; **to ~ sth (from** *or* **of sb)**

pretendere qc (da qn), esigere qc (da qn); **in**
~ ricercato(a), richiesto(a); **on** ~ a richiesta.

demand draft *n* (*COMM*) tratta a vista.
demanding [dimand'ing] *a* (*boss*) esigente;
(*work*) impegnativo(a).
demarcation [dēmârkā'shən] *n* demarcazione
f.
demarcation dispute *n* (*INDUSTRY*) controversia settoriale (*or* di categoria).
demean [dimēn'] *vt:* **to** ~ **o.s.** umiliarsi.
demeanor, (*Brit*) **demeanour** [dimē'nûr] *n*
comportamento; contegno.
demented [dimen'tid] *a* demente, impazzi-
to(a).
demilitarized zone [dēmil'itərīzd zōn] *n* zona
smilitarizzata.
demise [dimīz'] *n* decesso.
demist [dēmist'] *vt* (*Brit AUT*) sbrinare.
demister [dimis'tûr] *n* (*Brit AUT*) sbrinatore
m.
demo [dem'ō] *n abbr* (*col*) = **demonstration.**
demobilize [dēmō'bəlīz] *vt* smobilitare.
democracy [dimâk'rəsē] *n* democrazia.
democrat [dem'əkrat] *n* (*also: POL:* **D~**)
democratico/a.
democratic [deməkrat'ik] *a* democratico(a).
demography [dimâg'rəfē] *n* demografia.
demolish [dimál'ish] *vt* demolire.
demolition [deməlish'ən] *n* demolizione *f.*
demon [dē'mən] *n* (*also fig*) demonio ♦ *cpd:* **a**
~ **squash player** un mago dello squash; **a** ~
driver un guidatore folle.
demonstrate [dem'ənstrāt] *vt* dimostrare, provare ♦ *vi:* **to** ~ **(for/against)** dimostrare
(per/contro), manifestare (per/contro).
demonstration [demənstrā'shən] *n* dimostrazione *f;* (*POL*) manifestazione *f,* dimostrazione; **to hold a** ~ (*POL*) tenere una manifestazione, fare una dimostrazione.
demonstrative [dimán'strətiv] *a* dimostrati-
vo(a).
demonstrator [dem'ənstrātûr] *n* (*POL*) dimostrante *m/f;* (*COMM*: *sales person*)
dimostratore/trice; (: *car, computer etc*) modello per dimostrazione.
demoralize [dimôr'əlīz] *vt* demoralizzare.
demote [dimōt'] *vt* far retrocedere.
demotion [dimō'shən] *n* retrocessione *f,* degradazione *f.*
demur [dimûr'] *vi* (*formal*): **to** ~ **(at)** sollevare obiezioni (a *or* su) ♦ *n:* **without** ~ senza
obiezioni.
demure [dimyoōr'] *a* contegnoso(a).
demurrage [dimûr'ij] *n* diritti *mpl* di imma-
gazzinaggio; spese *fpl* di controstallia.
den [den] *n* tana, covo.
denationalization [dēnashnəlizā'shən] *n* dena-
zionalizzazione *f.*
denationalize [dēnash'nəlīz] *vt* snazio-
nalizzare.

denial [dinī'əl] *n* diniego; rifiuto.
denier [den'yûr] *n* denaro (*di filati, calze*).
denigrate [den'əgrāt] *vt* denigrare.
denim [den'əm] *n* tessuto di cotone ritorto; *see
also* **denims.**
denim jacket *n* giubbotto di jeans.
denims [den'əmz] *npl* blue jeans *mpl.*
denizen [den'izən] *n* (*inhabitant*) abitante *m/f;*
(*foreigner*) straniero(a) naturalizzato(a).
Denmark [den'mârk] *n* Danimarca.
denomination [dinâmənā'shən] *n* (*money*) valore *m;* (*REL*) confessione *f.*
denominator [dinâm'ənātûr] *n* denominatore
m.
denote [dinōt'] *vt* denotare.
denounce [dinouns'] *vt* denunciare.
dense [dens] *a* fitto(a); (*stupid*) ottuso(a),
duro(a).
densely [dens'lē] *ad:* ~ **wooded** fittamente bo-
scoso(a); ~ **populated** densamente popola-
to(a).
density [den'sitē] *n* densità *f inv;* **single/
double** ~ **disk** (*COMPUT*) disco a singola/
doppia densità di registrazione.
dent [dent] *n* ammaccatura ♦ *vt* (*also:* **make a**
~ **in**) ammaccare; (*fig*) intaccare.
dental [den'təl] *a* dentale.
dental surgeon *n* medico/a dentista.
dentist [den'tist] *n* dentista *m/f;* ~**'s office** *or*
(*Brit*) **surgery** gabinetto dentistico.
dentistry [den'tistrē] *n* odontoiatria.
denture(s) [den'chûr(z)] *n(pl)* dentiera.
denunciation [dinunsēā'shən] *n* denuncia.
deny [dinī'] *vt* negare; (*refuse*) rifiutare; **he
denies having said it** nega di averlo detto.
deodorant [dēō'dûrənt] *n* deodorante *m.*
depart [dipârt'] *vi* partire; **to** ~ **from** (*leave*)
allontanarsi da, partire da; (*fig*) deviare da.
department [dipârt'mənt] *n* (*COMM*) reparto;
(*SCOL*) sezione *f,* dipartimento; (*POL*) ministero; **D~ of State** (*US*) Dipartimento di Stato; **that's not my** ~ (*also fig*) questo non è di
mia competenza.
departmental [dēpârtmen'təl] *a* (*dispute*)
settoriale; (*meeting*) di sezione; ~ **manager**
caporeparto *m/f.*
department store *n* grande magazzino.
departure [dipâr'chûr] *n* partenza; (*fig*): ~
from deviazione *f* da; **a new** ~ una novità.
departure lounge *n* sala d'attesa.
depend [dipend'] *vi:* **to** ~ **(up)on** dipendere
da; (*rely on*) contare su; (*be dependent on*)
dipendere (economicamente) da, essere a ca-
rico di; **it** ~**s** dipende; ~**ing on the result** ...
a seconda del risultato ....
dependable [dipen'dəbəl] *a* fidato(a); (*car
etc*) affidabile.
dependant [dipen'dənt] *n* persona a carico.
dependence [dipen'dəns] *n* dipendenza.
dependent [dipen'dənt] *a:* **to be** ~ **(on)** (*gen*)
dipendere (da); (*child, relative*) essere a ca-

rico (di) ♦ n = **dependant.**
depict [dipikt'] vt (in picture) dipingere; (in words) descrivere.
depilatory [dipil'ətôrē] n (also: ~ **cream**) crema depilatoria.
deplane [dēplān'] vi sbarcare.
depleted [diplēt'id] a diminuito(a).
deplorable [diplôr'əbəl] a deplorevole, lamentevole.
deplore [diplôr'] vt deplorare.
deploy [diploi'] vt dispiegare.
depopulate [dipáp'yəlāt] vt spopolare.
depopulation [dipápyəlā'shən] n spopolamento.
deport [dipôrt'] vt deportare; espellere.
deportation [dēpôrtā'shən] n deportazione f.
deportation order n foglio di via obbligatorio.
deportment [dipôrt'mənt] n portamento.
depose [dipōz'] vt deporre.
deposit [dipáz'it] n (COMM, GEO) deposito; (of ore, oil) giacimento; (CHEM) sedimento; (part payment) acconto; (for rented goods etc) cauzione f ♦ vt depositare; dare in acconto; (luggage etc) mettere or lasciare in deposito; **to put down a ~ of** $50 versare una caparra di 50 dollari.
deposit account n conto vincolato.
depositor [dipáz'itûr] n depositante m/f.
depository [dipáz'itôrē] n (person) depositario/a; (place) deposito.
depot [dē'pō] n deposito.
depraved [diprāvd'] a depravato(a).
depravity [diprav'itē] n depravazione f.
deprecate [dep'rəkāt] vt deprecare.
deprecating [dep'rəkāting] a (disapproving) di biasimo; (apologetic): **a ~ smile** un sorriso di scusa.
depreciate [diprē'shēāt] vt svalutare ♦ vi svalutarsi.
depreciation [diprēshēā'shən] n svalutazione f.
depress [dipres'] vt deprimere; (press down) premere.
depressant [dipres'ənt] n (MED) sedativo.
depressed [diprest'] a (person) depresso(a), abbattuto(a); (area) depresso(a); (COMM: market, trade) stagnante, in ribasso; **to get ~** deprimersi.
depressing [dipres'ing] a deprimente.
depression [dipresh'ən] n depressione f.
deprivation [deprəvā'shən] n privazione f; (state) indigenza; (PSYCH) carenza affettiva.
deprive [diprīv'] vt: **to ~ sb of** privare qn di.
deprived [diprīvd'] a disgraziato(a).
dept. abbr = **department.**
depth [depth] n profondità f inv; **at a ~ of 3 meters** a una profondità di 3 metri, a 3 metri di profondità; **in the ~s of** nel profondo di; nel cuore di; **in the ~s of winter** in pieno inverno; **to study sth in ~** studiare qc in profondità; **to be out of one's ~** (swimmer)

essere dove non si tocca; (fig) non sentirsi all'altezza della situazione.
depth charge n carica di profondità.
deputation [depyətā'shən] n deputazione f, delegazione f.
deputize [dep'yətīz] vi: **to ~ for** svolgere le funzioni di.
deputy [dep'yətē] n (replacement) supplente m/f; (second in command) vice m/f ♦ cpd: ~ **chairman** vicepresidente m; ~ **head** (SCOL) vicepreside m/f; ~ **leader** (Brit POL) sottosegretario.
derail [dirāl'] vt far deragliare; **to be ~ed** deragliare.
derailment [dirāl'mənt] n deragliamento.
deranged [dirānjd'] a: **to be (mentally) ~** essere pazzo(a).
derby (hat) [dûr'bē (hat')] n (US) bombetta.
Derbys abbr (Brit) = Derbyshire.
deregulate [dēreg'yəlāt] vt eliminare la regolamentazione di.
deregulation [dēregyəlā'shən] n eliminazione f della regolamentazione.
derelict [där'əlikt] a abbandonato(a).
deride [dirid'] vt deridere.
derision [dirizh'ən] n derisione f.
derisive [dirī'siv] a di derisione.
derisory [dirī'sûrē] a (sum) irrisorio(a).
derivation [därəvā'shən] n derivazione f.
derivative [diriv'ətiv] n derivato ♦ a derivato(a).
derive [dirīv'] vt: **to ~ sth from** derivare qc da; trarre qc da ♦ vi: **to ~ from** derivare da.
dermatitis [dûrmətī'tis] n dermatite f.
dermatology [dûrmətàl'əjē] n dermatologia.
derogatory [diràg'ətôrē] a denigratorio(a).
derrick [där'ik] n gru f inv; (for oil) derrick m inv.
derv [dûrv] n (Brit) gasolio.
DES n abbr (Brit: = Department of Education and Science) ≈ ministero della Pubblica Istruzione.
desalination [dēsalənā'shən] n desalinizzazione f, dissalazione f.
descend [disend'] vt, vi discendere, scendere; **to ~ from** discendere da; **in ~ing order of importance** in ordine decrescente d'importanza.
descend on vt fus (subj: enemy, angry person) assalire, piombare su; (: misfortune) arrivare addosso a; (: fig: gloom, silence) scendere su; **visitors ~ed (up)on us** ci sono arrivate visite tra capo e collo.
descendant [disen'dənt] n discendente m/f.
descent [disent'] n discesa; (origin) discendenza, famiglia.
describe [diskrīb'] vt descrivere.
description [diskrip'shən] n descrizione f; (sort) genere m, specie f; **of every ~** di ogni genere e specie.
descriptive [diskrip'tiv] a descrittivo(a).

desecrate [des'əkrāt] *vt* profanare.
desert *n* [dez'ûrt] deserto ♦ *vb* [dizûrt'] *vt* lasciare, abbandonare ♦ *vi* (*MIL*) disertare; *see also* **deserts**.
deserter [dizûr'tûr] *n* disertore *m*.
desertion [dizûr'shən] *n* diserzione *f*.
desert island [dez'ûrt ī'lənd] *n* isola deserta.
deserts [dizûrts'] *npl*: **to get one's just ~** avere ciò che si merita.
deserve [dizûrv'] *vt* meritare.
deservedly [dizûr'vidlē] *ad* meritatamente, giustamente.
deserving [dizûr'ving] *a* (*person*) meritevole, degno(a); (*cause*) meritorio(a).
desiccated [des'əkātid] *a* essiccato(a).
design [dizīn'] *n* (*sketch*) disegno; (: *of dress, car*) modello; (*layout, shape*) linea; (*pattern*) fantasia; (*COMM*) disegno tecnico; (*intention*) intenzione *f* ♦ *vt* disegnare; progettare; **to have ~s on** aver mire su; **well-~ed** ben concepito(a); **industrial ~** disegno industriale.
designate *vt* [dez'ignāt] designare ♦ *a* [dez'ignit] designato(a).
designation [dezignā'shən] *n* designazione *f*.
designer [dizī'nûr] *n* (*TECH*) disegnatore/trice, progettista *m/f*; (*of furniture*) designer *m/f inv*; (*fashion ~*) disegnatore/trice di moda; (*of theater sets*) scenografo/a.
desirability [dizīûrəbil'ətē] *n* desiderabilità; vantaggio.
desirable [dizī'ûrəbəl] *a* desiderabile; **it is ~ that** è opportuno chè + *sub*.
desire [dizī'ûr] *n* desiderio, voglia ♦ *vt* desiderare, volere; **to ~ sth/to do sth/that** desiderare qc/di fare qc/che + *sub*.
desirous [dizī'ûrəs] *a*: **~ of** desideroso(a) di.
desk [desk] *n* (*in office*) scrivania; (*for pupil*) banco; (*Brit: in store, restaurant*) cassa; (*in hotel*) ricevimento; (*at airport*) accettazione *f*.
desk job *n* lavoro d'ufficio.
desktop publishing [desk'tâp pub'lishing] *n* editoria individuale.
desolate [des'əlit] *a* desolato(a).
desolation [desəlā'shən] *n* desolazione *f*.
despair [dispār'] *n* disperazione *f* ♦ *vi*: **to ~ of** disperare di; **in ~** disperato(a).
despatch [dispach'] *n*, *vt* = **dispatch**.
desperate [des'pûrit] *a* disperato(a); (*measures*) estremo(a); (*fugitive*) capace di tutto; **we are getting ~** siamo sull'orlo della disperazione.
desperately [des'pûritlē] *ad* disperatamente; (*very*) terribilmente, estremamente; **~ ill** in pericolo di vita.
desperation [despərā'shən] *n* disperazione *f*; **in ~** per disperazione.
despicable [des'pikəbəl] *a* disprezzabile.
despise [dispīz'] *vt* disprezzare, sdegnare.
despite [dispīt'] *prep* malgrado, a dispetto di, nonostante.
despondent [dispân'dənt] *a* abbattuto(a), scoraggiato(a).
despot [des'pət] *n* despota *m*.
dessert [dizûrt'] *n* dolce *m*; frutta.
dessertspoon [dizûrt'spoon] *n* cucchiaio da dolci.
destabilize [dēstā'bəlīz] *vt* privare di stabilità; (*fig*) destabilizzare.
destination [destənā'shən] *n* destinazione *f*.
destine [des'tin] *vt* destinare.
destined [des'tind] *a*: **to be ~ to do sth** essere destinato(a) a fare qc; **~ for New York** diretto a New York, con destinazione New York.
destiny [des'tənē] *n* destino.
destitute [des'titoot] *a* indigente, bisognoso(a); **~ of** privo(a) di.
destroy [distroi'] *vt* distruggere.
destroyer [distroi'ûr] *n* (*NAUT*) cacciatorpediniere *m*.
destruction [distruk'shən] *n* distruzione *f*.
destructive [distruk'tiv] *a* distruttivo(a).
desultory [des'əltôrē] *a* (*reading*) disordinato(a); (*conversation*) sconnesso(a); (*contact*) saltuario(a), irregolare.
detach [ditach'] *vt* staccare, distaccare.
detachable [ditach'əbəl] *a* staccabile.
detached [ditacht'] *a* (*attitude*) distante.
detached house *n* (*Brit*) villa.
detachment [ditach'mənt] *n* (*MIL*) distaccamento; (*fig*) distacco.
detail [ditāl'] *n* particolare *m*, dettaglio; (*MIL*) piccolo distaccamento ♦ *vt* dettagliare, particolareggiare; (*MIL*): **to ~ sb (for)** assegnare qn (a); **in ~** nei particolari; **to go into ~(s)** scendere nei particolari.
detailed [ditāld'] *a* particolareggiato(a).
detain [ditān'] *vt* trattenere; (*in captivity*) detenere.
detainee [dētānē'] *n* detenuto/a.
detect [ditekt'] *vt* scoprire, scorgere; (*MED, POLICE, RADAR etc*) individuare.
detection [ditek'shən] *n* scoperta; individuazione *f*; **crime ~** indagini *fpl* criminali; **to escape ~** (*criminal*) eludere le ricerche; (*mistake*) passare inosservato(a).
detective [ditek'tiv] *n* investigatore/trice; **private ~** investigatore *m* privato.
detective story *n* giallo.
detector [ditek'tûr] *n* rivelatore *m*.
détente [dātânt'] *n* distensione *f*.
detention [diten'chən] *n* detenzione *f*; (*SCOL*) permanenza forzata per punizione.
deter [ditûr'] *vt* dissuadere.
detergent [ditûr'jənt] *n* detersivo.
deteriorate [ditē'rēərāt] *vi* deteriorarsi.
deterioration [ditērēərā'shən] *n* deterioramento.
determination [ditûrmənā'shən] *n* determinazione *f*.

determine [ditûr'min] *vt* determinare; **to ~ to do sth** decidere di fare qc.

determined [ditûr'mind] *a* (*person*) risoluto(a), deciso(a); **to be ~ to do sth** essere determinato *or* deciso a fare qc; **a ~ effort** uno sforzo di volontà.

deterrence [ditûr'əns] *n* deterrenza.

deterrent [ditûr'ənt] *n* deterrente *m*; **to act as a ~** fungere da deterrente.

detest [ditest'] *vt* detestare.

detestable [dites'təbəl] *a* detestabile, abominevole.

detonate [det'ənāt] *vi* detonare ♦ *vt* far detonare.

detonator [det'ənātûr] *n* detonatore *m*.

detour [dē'tōōr] *n* deviazione *f*.

detract [ditrakt'] *vt*: **to ~ from** detrarre da.

detractor [ditrak'tûr] *n* detrattore/trice.

detriment [det'rəmənt] *n*: **to the ~ of** a detrimento di; **without ~ to** senza danno a.

detrimental [detrəmen'təl] *a*: **~ to** dannoso(a) a, nocivo(a) a.

deuce [dōōs] *n* (*TENNIS*) quaranta pari *m inv*.

devaluation [dēvalyōōā'shən] *n* svalutazione *f*.

devalue [dēval'yōō] *vt* svalutare.

devastate [dev'əstāt] *vt* devastare; **he was ~d by the news** la notizia fu per lui un colpo terribile.

devastating [dev'əstāting] *a* devastatore(trice).

devastation [devəstā'shən] *n* devastazione *f*.

develop [divel'əp] *vt* sviluppare; (*habit*) prendere (gradualmente) ♦ *vi* svilupparsi; (*facts, symptoms*: *appear*) manifestarsi, rivelarsi; **to ~ a taste for sth** imparare a gustare qc; **to ~ into** diventare.

developer [divel'əpûr] *n* (*PHOT*) sviluppatore *m*; **property ~** costruttore *m* (edile).

developing country *n* paese *m* in via di sviluppo.

development [divel'əpmənt] *n* sviluppo.

development area *n* area di sviluppo industriale.

deviant [dē'vēənt] *a* deviante.

deviate [dē'vēāt] *vi*: **to ~ (from)** deviare (da).

deviation [dēvēā'shən] *n* deviazione *f*.

device [divīs'] *n* (*apparatus*) congegno; (*explosive ~*) ordigno esplosivo.

devil [dev'əl] *n* diavolo; demonio.

devilish [dev'əlish] *a* diabolico(a).

devil-may-care [dev'əlmākär'] *a* impudente.

devious [dē'vēəs] *a* (*means*) indiretto(a), tortuoso(a); (*person*) subdolo(a).

devise [divīz'] *vt* escogitare, concepire.

devoid [divoid'] *a*: **~ of** privo(a) di.

devolution [devəlōō'shən] *n* (*POL*) decentramento.

devolve [divälv'] *vi*: **to ~ (up)on** ricadere su.

devote [divōt'] *vt*: **to ~ sth to** dedicare qc a.

devoted [divōt'id] *a* devoto(a); **to be ~ to** essere molto attaccato(a) a.

devotee [devōtē'] *n* (*REL*) adepto/a; (*MUS, SPORT*) appassionato/a.

devotion [divō'shən] *n* devozione *f*, attaccamento; (*REL*) atto di devozione, preghiera.

devour [divou'ûr] *vt* divorare.

devout [divout'] *a* pio(a), devoto(a).

dew [dōō] *n* rugiada.

dexterity [dekstär'itē] *n* destrezza.

dext(e)rous [dek'strəs] *a* (*skillful*) destro(a), abile; (*movement*) agile.

dg *abbr* (= *decigram*) dg.

diabetes [dīəbē'tis] *n* diabete *m*.

diabetic [dīəbet'ik] *a* diabetico(a); (*chocolate, jam*) per diabetici ♦ *n* diabetico/a.

diabolical [dīəbâl'ikəl] *a* diabolico(a); (*col*: *dreadful*) infernale, atroce.

diaeresis [dīär'əsis] *n* dieresi *f inv*.

diagnose [dīəgnōs'] *vt* diagnosticare.

diagnosis, *pl* **diagnoses** [dīəgnō'sis, dīəgnō'sēz] *n* diagnosi *f inv*.

diagonal [dīag'ənəl] *a*, *n* diagonale (*f*).

diagram [dī'əgram] *n* diagramma *m*.

dial [dīl] *n* quadrante *m*; (*on telephone*) disco combinatore ♦ *vt* (*number*) fare; **to ~ a wrong number** sbagliare numero; **can I ~ Chicago direct?** si può chiamare Chicago in teleselezione?

dial. *abbr* = **dialect**.

dial code *n* (*US*) prefisso.

dialect [dī'əlekt] *n* dialetto.

dialling code [dī'ling kōd] *n* (*Brit*) prefisso.

dialling tone [dī'ling tōn] *n* (*Brit*) segnale *m* di linea libera.

dialogue [dī'əlôg] *n* dialogo.

dial tone *n* (*US*) segnale *m* di linea libera.

dialysis [dīal'isis] *n* dialisi *f*.

diameter [dīam'itûr] *n* diametro.

diametrically [dīəmet'riklē] *ad*: **~ opposed (to)** diametralmente opposto(a) a).

diamond [dī'mənd] *n* diamante *m*; (*shape*) rombo; **~s** *npl* (*CARDS*) quadri *mpl*.

diamond ring *n* anello di brillanti; (*with one diamond*) anello con brillante.

diaper [dī'pûr] *n* (*US*) pannolino.

diaper liner *n* (*US*) foglietino igienico.

diaphragm [dī'əfram] *n* diaframma *m*.

diarrhea, (*Brit*) **diarrhoea** [dīərē'ə] *n* diarrea.

diary [dī'ûrē] *n* (*daily account*) diario; (*book*) agenda; **to keep a ~** tenere un diario.

diatribe [dī'ətrīb] *n* diatriba.

dice [dīs] *n* (*pl inv*) dado ♦ *vt* (*CULIN*) tagliare a dadini.

dicey [dī'sē] *a* (*col*): **it's a bit ~** è un po' un rischio.

dichotomy [dīkât'əmē] *n* dicotomia.

Dictaphone [dik'təfōn] ® *n* dittafono.

dictate *vt* [diktāt'] dettare ♦ *vi*: **to ~ to** (*person*) dare ordini a, dettar legge a ♦ *n* [dik'tāt] dettame *m*; **I won't be ~d to** non ricevo ordini.

dictation [diktā'shən] *n* dettato; (*to secretary*

etc) dettatura; **at ~ speed** a velocità di dettatura.

dictator [dik'tātûr] *n* dittatore *m*.

dictatorship [dik'tātûrship] *n* dittatura.

diction [dik'shən] *n* dizione *f*.

dictionary [dik'shənārē] *n* dizionario.

did [did] *pt of* **do**.

didactic [dīdak'tik] *a* didattico(a).

didn't [did'ənt] = **did not**.

die [dī] *n* (*pl*: **dies**) conio; matrice *f*; stampo ♦ *vi* morire; **to be dying** star morendo; **to be dying for sth/to do sth** morire dalla voglia di qc/di fare qc; **to ~ (of** *or* **from)** morire (di).
die away *vi* spegnersi a poco a poco.
die down *vi* abbassarsi.
die out *vi* estinguersi.

diehard [dī'hârd] *n* reazionario/a.

dieresis [dīår'əsis] *n* dieresi *f inv*.

diesel [dē'zəl] *n* diesel *m*.

diesel engine *n* motore *m* diesel *inv*.

diesel fuel, diesel oil *n* gasolio (per motori diesel).

diet [dī'ət] *n* alimentazione *f*; (*restricted food*) dieta ♦ *vi* (*also*: **be on a ~**) stare a dieta; **to live on a ~ of** nutrirsi di.

dietician [dīətish'ən] *n* dietologo/a.

differ [dif'ûr] *vi*: **to ~ from sth** differire da qc; essere diverso(a) da qc; **to ~ from sb over sth** essere in disaccordo con qn su qc.

difference [dif'ûrəns] *n* differenza; (*quarrel*) screzio; **it makes no ~ to me** per me è lo stesso; **to settle one's ~s** risolvere la situazione.

different [dif'ûrənt] *a* diverso(a).

differential [difərən'chəl] *n* (*AUT. wages*) differenziale *m*.

differentiate [difərən'chēāt] *vi* differenziarsi; **to ~ between** discriminare fra, fare differenza fra.

differently [dif'ûrəntlē] *ad* diversamente.

difficult [dif'əkult] *a* difficile; **~ to understand** difficile da capire.

difficulty [dif'əkultē] *n* difficoltà *f inv*; **to have difficulties with** (*police, landlord etc*) avere noie con; **to be in ~** essere *or* trovarsi in difficoltà.

diffidence [dif'idəns] *n* mancanza di sicurezza.

diffident [dif'idənt] *a* sfiduciato(a).

diffuse *a* [difyōōs'] diffuso(a) ♦ *vt* [difyōōz'] diffondere, emanare.

dig [dig] *vb* (*pt, pp* **dug** [dug]) *vt* (*hole*) scavare; (*garden*) vangare ♦ *vi* scavare ♦ *n* (*prod*) gomitata; (*fig*) frecciata; (*ARCHEOLOGY*) scavo, scavi *mpl*; **to ~ into** (*snow, soil*) scavare; **to ~ into one's pockets for sth** frugarsi le tasche cercando qc; **to ~ one's nails into** conficcare le unghie in; *see also* **digs**.
dig in *vi* (*col: eat*) attaccare a mangiare; (*also*: **~ o.s. in**: *MIL*) trincerarsi; (: *fig*) insediarsi, installarsi ♦ *vt* (*compost*) interra-

re; (*knife, claw*) affondare; **to ~ in one's heels** (*fig*) impuntarsi.
dig out *vt* (*survivors, car from snow*) tirar fuori (scavando), estrarre (scavando).
dig up *vt* scavare; (*tree etc*) sradicare.

digest [dī'jest] *vt* digerire.

digestible [dijes'təbəl] *a* digeribile.

digestion [dijes'chən] *n* digestione *f*.

digestive [dijes'tiv] *a* digestivo(a); **~ system** apparato digerente.

digit [dij'it] *n* cifra; (*finger*) dito.

digital [dij'itəl] *a* digitale.

dignified [dig'nəfīd] *a* dignitoso(a).

dignitary [dig'nitārē] *n* dignitario.

dignity [dig'nitē] *n* dignità.

digress [digres'] *vi*: **to ~ from** divagare da.

digression [digresh'ən] *n* digressione *f*.

digs [digz] *npl* (*Brit col*) camera ammobiliata.

dike [dīk] *n* diga; (*channel*) canale *m* di scolo; (*causeway*) sentiero rialzato.

dilapidated [dilap'ədātid] *a* cadente.

dilate [dīlāt'] *vt* dilatare ♦ *vi* dilatarsi.

dilatory [dil'ətôrē] *a* dilatorio(a).

dilemma [dilem'ə] *n* dilemma *m*; **to be in a ~** essere di fronte a un dilemma.

diligent [dil'ijənt] *a* diligente.

dill [dil] *n* aneto.

dilly-dally [dil'ēdalē] *vi* gingillarsi.

dilute [dilōōt'] *vt* diluire; (*with water*) annacquare ♦ *a* diluito(a).

dim [dim] *a* (*light, eyesight*) debole; (*memory, outline*) vago(a); (*stupid*) ottuso(a) ♦ *vt* (*light*: *also*: *US AUT*) abbassare; **to take a ~ view of sth** non vedere di buon occhio qc.

dime [dīm] *n* (*US*) = *10 cents*.

dimension [dimen'chən] *n* dimensione *f*.

diminish [dimin'ish] *vt, vi* diminuire.

diminished [dimin'isht] *a*: **~ responsibility** (*LAW*) incapacità d'intendere e di volere.

diminutive [dimin'yətiv] *a* minuscolo(a) ♦ *n* (*LING*) diminutivo.

dimly [dim'lē] *ad* debolmente; indistintamente.

dimmers [dim'ûrz] *npl* (*US AUT*) anabbaglianti *mpl*; (: *parking lights*) luci *fpl* di posizione.

dimple [dim'pəl] *n* fossetta.

dim-witted [dim'witid] *a* (*col*) sciocco(a), stupido(a).

din [din] *n* chiasso, fracasso ♦ *vt*: **to ~ sth into sb** (*col*) ficcare qc in testa a qn.

dine [dīn] *vi* pranzare.

diner [dīn'ûr] *n* (*person: in restaurant*) cliente *m*; (*US: eating place*) tavola calda; (*RAIL*) carrozza *or* vagone *m* ristorante.

dinghy [ding'ē] *n* battello pneumatico; (*also*: **sailing ~**) dinghy *m inv*.

dingy [din'jē] *a* grigio(a).

dining area [dīn'ing ār'ēə] *n* zona pranzo *inv*.

dining car [dīn'ing kâr] *n* vagone *m* ristorante.

dining room [dīn'ing rōōm] *n* sala da pranzo.

dinner [din'ûr] *n* pranzo; (*evening meal*) cena; (*public*) banchetto; **~'s ready!** a tavola!

dinner jacket n smoking m inv.
dinner party n cena.
dinner service n servizio da tavola.
dinner time n ora di pranzo (or cena).
dinosaur |dī'nəsôr| n dinosauro.
dint |dint| n: **by ~ of (doing) sth** a forza di (fare) qc.
diocese |dī'əsēs| n diocesi f inv.
dioxide |dīăk'sīd| n biossido.
dioxin |dīăk'sin| n diossina.
dip |dip| n (slope) discesa; (in sea) bagno ♦ vt immergere, bagnare; (Brit AUT: lights) abbassare ♦ vi (road) essere in pendenza; (bird, plane) abbassarsi.
diphtheria |dipthē'rēə| n difterite f.
diphthong |dif'thông| n dittongo.
diploma |diplō'mə| n diploma m.
diplomacy |diplō'məsē| n diplomazia.
diplomat |dip'ləmat| n diplomatico.
diplomatic |dipləmat'ik| a diplomatico(a); **to break off ~ relations** rompere le relazioni diplomatiche.
diplomatic corps n corpo diplomatico.
dipstick |dip'stik| n (AUT) indicatore m di livello dell'olio.
dip switch n (Brit AUT) levetta dei fari.
dire |dī'ûr| a terribile; estremo(a).
direct |direkt'| a diretto(a); (manner, person) franco(a), esplicito(a) ♦ vt dirigere; **to ~ sb to do sth** dare direttive a qn di fare qc; **can you ~ me to ...?** mi può indicare la strada per ...?
direct cost n (COMM) costo diretto.
direct current n (ELEC) corrente f continua.
direct debit n (Brit BANKING) addebito effettuato per ordine di un cliente di banca.
direct dialing n (TEL) ≈ teleselezione f.
direct hit n (MIL) colpo diretto.
direction |direk'shən| n direzione f; (of play, film, programme) regia; **~s** npl (advice) chiarimenti mpl; (instructions: to a place) indicazioni fpl; **~s for use** istruzioni fpl; **to ask for ~s** chiedere la strada; **sense of ~** senso dell'orientamento; **in the ~ of** in direzione di.
directive |direk'tiv| n direttiva, ordine m; **a government ~** una disposizione governativa.
directly |direkt'lē| ad (in straight line) direttamente; (at once) subito.
direct mail n pubblicità diretta.
direct mailshot n (Brit) materiale m pubblicitario ad approccio diretto.
directness |direkt'nis| n (of person, speech) franchezza.
director |direk'tûr| n direttore/trice; amministratore/trice; (THEATER, CINEMA, TV) regista m/f; **D~ of Public Prosecutions (DPP)** (Brit) ≈ Procuratore m della Repubblica.
directory |direk'tûrē| n elenco; (street ~) stradario; (trade ~) repertorio del commercio;

(COMPUT) directory m inv.
directory assistance, (Brit) **directory enquiries** n (TEL) servizio informazioni, informazioni fpl elenco abbonati.
dirt |dûrt| n sporcizia; immondizia; **to treat sb like ~** trattare qn come uno straccio.
dirt-cheap |dûrt'chēp| a da due soldi.
dirt road n strada non asfaltata.
dirty |dûr'tē| a sporco(a) ♦ vt sporcare; **~ story** storia oscena; **~ trick** brutto scherzo.
disability |disəbil'ətē| n invalidità f inv; (LAW) incapacità f inv.
disability allowance n pensione f d'invalidità.
disable |disā'bəl| vt (subj: illness, accident) rendere invalido(a); (tank, gun) mettere fuori uso.
disabled |disā'bəld| a invalido(a); (maimed) mutilato(a); (through illness, old age) inabile.
disadvantage |disədvan'tij| n svantaggio.
disadvantaged |disədvan'tijd| a (person) svantaggiato(a).
disadvantageous |disadvəntā'jəs| a svantaggioso(a).
disaffected |disəfek'tid| a: **~ (to or towards)** scontento(a) di, insoddisfatto(a) di.
disaffection |disəfek'shən| n malcontento, insoddisfazione f.
disagree |disəgrē'| vi (differ) discordare; (be against, think otherwise): **to ~ (with)** essere in disaccordo (con), dissentire (da); **I ~ with you** non sono d'accordo con lei; **garlic ~s with me** l'aglio non mi va.
disagreeable |disəgrē'əbəl| a sgradevole; (person) antipatico(a).
disagreement |disəgrē'mənt| n disaccordo; (quarrel) disputa m; **to have a ~ with sb** litigare con qn.
disallow |disəlou'| vt respingere.
disappear |disəpiür'| vi scomparire.
disappearance |disəpi'ûrəns| n scomparsa.
disappoint |disəpoint'| vt deludere.
disappointed |disəpoin'tid| a deluso(a).
disappointing |disəpoin'ting| a deludente.
disappointment |disəpoint'mənt| n delusione f.
disapproval |disəprōō'vəl| n disapprovazione f.
disapprove |disəprōōv'| vi: **to ~ of** disapprovare.
disapproving |disəprōō'ving| a di disapprovazione.
disarm |disârm'| vt disarmare.
disarmament |disâr'məmənt| n disarmo.
disarming |disârm'ing| a (smile) disarmante.
disarray |disərā'| n: **in ~** (troops) in rotta; (thoughts) confuso(a); (clothes) in disordine; **to throw into ~** buttare all'aria.
disaster |dizas'tûr| n disastro.
disaster area n zona disastrata.
disastrous |dizas'trəs| a disastroso(a).

disband [disband'] vt sbandare; (MIL) congedare ◊ vi sciogliersi.

disbelief [disbilēf'] n incredulità; **in** ~ incredulo(a).

disbelieve [disbilēv'] vt (person, story) non ·credere a, mettere in dubbio; **I don't** ~ **you** vorrei poterle credere.

disc [disk] n (Brit) disco.

disc. abbr (COMM) = **discount.**

discard [diskârd'] vt (old things) scartare; (fig) abbandonare.

disc brake [disk brāk] n freno a disco.

discern [disûrn'] vt discernere, distinguere.

discernible [disûr'nəbəl] a percepibile.

discerning [disûr'ning] a perspicace.

discharge vt [dischârj'] (duties) compiere; (settle: debt) pagare, estinguere; (ELEC, waste etc) scaricare; (MED) emettere; (patient) dimettere; (employee) licenziare; (soldier) congedare; (defendant) liberare ◊ n [dis'chârj] (ELEC) scarica; (MED, of gas, chemicals) emissione f; (vaginal ~) perdite fpl (bianche); (dismissal) licenziamento; congedo; liberazione f; **to** ~ **one's gun** fare fuoco.

discharged bankrupt [dischârjd' bang'rupt] n (Brit) fallito cui il tribunale ha concesso la riabilitazione.

disciple [disī'pəl] n discepolo.

disciplinary [dis'əplənärē] a disciplinare; **to take** ~ **action against sb** prendere un provvedimento disciplinare contro qn.

discipline [dis'əplin] n disciplina ◊ vt disciplinare; (punish) punire; **to** ~ **o.s. to do sth** imporsi di fare qc.

disc jockey (DJ) n disc jockey m inv.

disclaim [disklām'] vt negare, smentire.

disclaimer [disklām'ûr] n smentita; **to issue a** ~ pubblicare una smentita.

disclose [disklōz'] vt rivelare, svelare.

disclosure [disklō'zhûr] n rivelazione f.

disco [dis'kō] n abbr = **discothèque.**

discolor [diskul'ûr] (US) vt scolorire; (sth white) ingiallire ◊ vi sbiadire, scolorirsi; (sth white) ingiallire.

discoloration [diskulərā'shən] n scolorimento.

discolored [diskul'ûrd] a scolorito(a); ingiallito(a).

discolour [diskul'ûr] etc (Brit) = **discolor** etc.

discomfort [diskum'fûrt] n disagio; (lack of comfort) scomodità f inv.

disconcert [diskənsûrt'] vt sconcertare.

disconnect [diskənekt'] vt sconnettere, staccare; (ELEC, RADIO) staccare; (gas, water) chiudere.

disconnected [diskənekt'id] a (speech, thought) sconnesso(a).

disconsolate [diskən'səlit] a sconsolato(a).

discontent [diskəntent'] n scontentezza.

discontented [diskəntent'id] a scontento(a).

discontinue [diskəntin'yōō] vt smettere, cessare; "~d" (COMM) "sospeso".

discord [dis'kôrd] n disaccordo; (MUS) dissonanza.

discordant [diskôr'dənt] a discordante; dissonante.

discothèque [dis'kōtek] n discoteca.

discount n [dis'kount] sconto ◊ vt [diskount'] scontare; (report etc) non badare a; **at a** ~ con uno sconto; **to give sb a** ~ **on sth** fare uno sconto a qn su qc; ~ **for cash** sconto m cassa inv.

discount house n (FINANCE) casa di sconto, discount house f inv; (COMM: also: **discount store**) discount m inv.

discount rate n tasso di sconto.

discourage [diskûr'ij] vt scoraggiare; (dissuade, deter) tentare di dissuadere.

discouragement [diskûr'ijmənt] n (dissuasion) disapprovazione f; (depression) scoraggiamento; **to act as a** ~ **to** ostacolare.

discouraging [diskûr'ijing] a scoraggiante.

discourteous [diskûr'tēəs] a scortese.

discover [diskuv'ûr] vt scoprire.

discovery [diskuv'ûrē] n scoperta.

discredit [diskred'it] vt screditare; mettere in dubbio ◊ n discredito.

discreet [diskrēt'] a discreto(a).

discreetly [diskrēt'lē] ad con discrezione.

discrepancy [diskrep'ənsē] n discrepanza.

discretion [diskresh'ən] n discrezione f; **use your own** ~ giudichi lei.

discretionary [diskresh'ənärē] a (powers) discrezionale.

discriminate [diskrim'ənāt] vi: **to** ~ **between** distinguere tra; **to** ~ **against** discriminare contro.

discriminating [diskrim'ənāting] a (ear, taste) fine, giudizioso(a); (person) esigente; (tax, duty) discriminante.

discrimination [diskrimənā'shən] n discriminazione f; (judgement) discernimento; **racial/sexual** ~ discriminazione razziale/sessuale.

discus [dis'kəs] n disco.

discuss [diskus'] vt discutere; (debate) dibattere.

discussion [diskush'ən] n discussione f; **under** ~ in discussione.

disdain [disdān'] n disdegno.

disease [dizēz'] n malattia.

diseased [dizēzd'] a malato(a).

disembark [disembârk'] vt, vi = **deplane.**

disembarkation [disembârkā'shən] n sbarco.

disembodied [disembâd'ēd] a disincarnato(a).

disembowel [disembou'əl] vt sbudellare, sventrare.

disenchanted [disenchan'tid] a disincantato(a); ~ **(with)** deluso(a) (da).

disenfranchise [disenfran'chīz] vt privare del diritto di voto; (COMM) revocare una condizione di privilegio commerciale a.

disengage [disengāj'] vt disimpegnare;

(*TECH*) distaccare; (*AUT*) disinnestare.

disengagement [disengāj'mənt] *n* (*POL*) disimpegno.

disentangle [disentang'gəl] *vt* sbrogliare.

disfavor, (*Brit*) **disfavour** [disfā'vûr] *n* sfavore *m*; disgrazia.

disfigure [disfig'yûr] *vt* sfigurare.

disgorge [disgôrj'] *vt* (*subj: river*) riversare.

disgrace [disgrās'] *n* vergogna; (*disfavor*) disgrazia ♦ *vt* disonorare, far cadere in disgrazia.

disgraceful [disgrās'fəl] *a* scandaloso(a), vergognoso(a).

disgruntled [disgrun'təld] *a* scontento(a), di cattivo umore.

disguise [disgīz'] *n* travestimento ♦ *vt* travestire; (*voice*) contraffare; (*feelings etc*) mascherare; **to ~ o.s.** as travestirsi da; **in ~** travestito(a); **there's no disguising the fact that** ... non si può nascondere (il fatto) che ....

disgust [disgust'] *n* disgusto, nausea ♦ *vt* disgustare, far schifo a.

disgusting [disgus'ting] *a* disgustoso(a).

dish [dish] *n* (*Brit*) piatto; **to do** *or* **wash the ~es** fare i piatti.

dish out *vt* (*food*) servire; (*advice*) elargire; (*money*) tirare fuori; (*exam papers*) distribuire.

dish up *vt* (*food*) servire; (*facts, statistics*) presentare.

dishcloth [dish'klôth] *n* strofinaccio dei piatti.

dishearten [dis·hâr'tən] *vt* scoraggiare.

disheveled, (*Brit*) **dishevelled** [dishev'əld] *a* arruffato(a); scapigliato(a).

dishonest [disân'ist] *a* disonesto(a).

dishonesty [disân'istē] *n* disonestà.

dishonor [disân'ûr] *n* (*US*) disonore *m*.

dishonorable [disân'ûrəbəl] *a* disonorevole.

dishonour [disân'ûr] *etc* (*Brit*) = **dishonor** *etc*.

dish soap *n* (*US*) detersivo liquido (per stoviglie).

dishtowel [dish'touəl] *n* strofinaccio dei piatti.

dishwasher [dish'wâshûr] *n* lavastoviglie *f inv*; (*person*) sguattero/a.

dishwashing liquid [dish'wâshing lik'wid] *n* detersivo liquido (per stoviglie).

disillusion [disiloo'zhən] *vt* disilludere, disingannare ♦ *n* disillusione *f*; **to become ~ed (with)** perdere le illusioni (su).

disillusionment [disiloo'zhənmənt] *n* disillusione *f*.

disincentive [disinsen'tiv] *n*: **to act as a ~ (to)** agire da freno (su); **to be a ~ to** scoraggiare.

disinclined [disinklīnd'] *a*: **to be ~ to do sth** essere poco propenso(a) a fare qc.

disinfect [disinfekt'] *vt* disinfettare.

disinfectant [disinfek'tənt] *n* disinfettante *m*.

disinflation [disinflā'shən] *n* disinflazione *f*.

disinherit [disinhär'it] *vt* diseredare.

disintegrate [disin'təgrāt] *vi* disintegrarsi.

disinterested [disin'tristid] *a* disinteressato(a).

disjointed [disjoint'id] *a* sconnesso(a).

disk [disk] *n* (*gen, COMPUT*) disco; **single-/ double-sided ~** disco *m* monofaccia *inv*/a doppia faccia.

disk drive *n* disk drive *m inv*, unità *f inv* a dischi magnetici.

disk operating system (DOS) *n* sistema *m* operativo a disco.

diskette [disket'] *n* (*COMPUT*) dischetto.

dislike [dislīk'] *n* antipatia, avversione *f* ♦ *vt*: **he ~s it** non gli piace; **I ~ the idea** l'idea non mi va; **to take a ~ to sb/sth** prendere in antipatia qn/qc.

dislocate [dis'lōkāt] *vt* (*MED*) slogare; (*fig*) disorganizzare; **he ~d his shoulder** si è lussato una spalla.

dislodge [dislâj'] *vt* rimuovere, staccare; (*enemy*) sloggiare.

disloyal [disloi'əl] *a* sleale.

dismal [diz'məl] *a* triste, cupo(a).

dismantle [disman'təl] *vt* smantellare, smontare; (*fort, warship*) disarmare.

dismast [dismast'] *vt* disalberare.

dismay [dismā'] *n* costernazione *f* ♦ *vt* sgomentare; **much to my ~** con mio gran stupore.

dismiss [dismis'] *vt* congedare; (*employee*) licenziare; (*idea*) scacciare; (*LAW*) respingere ♦ *vi* (*MIL*) rompere i ranghi.

dismissal [dismis'əl] *n* congedo; licenziamento.

dismount [dismount'] *vi* scendere ♦ *vt* (*rider*) disarcionare.

disobedience [disəbē'dēəns] *n* disubbidienza.

disobedient [disəbē'dēənt] *a* disubbidiente.

disobey [disəbā'] *vt* disubbidire; (*rule*) trasgredire.

disorder [disôr'dûr] *n* disordine *m*; (*rioting*) tumulto; (*MED*) disturbo; **civil ~** disordini *mpl* interni.

disorderly [disôr'dûrlē] *a* disordinato(a); tumultuoso(a).

disorderly conduct *n* (*LAW*) comportamento atto a turbare l'ordine pubblico.

disorganize [disôr'gənīz] *vt* disorganizzare.

disorganized [disôr'gənīzd] *a* (*person, life*) disorganizzato(a); (*system, meeting*) male organizzato(a).

disorientated [disô'rēintātid] *a* disorientato(a).

disown [disōn'] *vt* ripudiare.

disparaging [dispar'ijing] *a* spregiativo(a), sprezzante; **to be ~ about sb/sth** denigrare qn/qc.

disparate [dis'pûrit] *a* disparato(a).

disparity [dispar'itē] *n* disparità *f inv*.

dispassionate [dispash'ənit] *a* calmo(a), freddo(a); imparziale.

dispatch [dispach'] *vt* spedire, inviare; (*deal*

with: *business*) sbrigare ♦ *n* spedizione *f*, invio; (*MIL*, *PRESS*) dispaccio.
dispatch department *n* reparto spedizioni.
dispatch rider *n* (*MIL*) corriere *m*, portaordini *m inv*.
dispel [dispel'] *vt* dissipare, scacciare.
dispensary [dispen'sûrē] *n* farmacia; (*in chemist's*) dispensario.
dispense [dispens'] *vt* distribuire, amministrare; (*medicine*) preparare e dare; **to ~ sb from** dispensare qn da.
  dispense with *vt fus* fare a meno di; (*make unnecessary*) rendere superfluo(a).
dispenser [dispen'sûr] *n* (*container*) distributore *m*.
dispensing chemist *n* (*Brit*) farmacista *m/f*.
dispersal [dispûr'səl] *n* dispersione *f*.
disperse [dispûrs'] *vt* disperdere; (*knowledge*) disseminare ♦ *vi* disperdersi.
dispirited [dispir'itid] *a* scoraggiato(a), abbattuto(a).
displace [displās'] *vt* spostare.
displaced person *n* (*POL*) profugo/a.
displacement [displās'mənt] *n* spostamento.
display [displā'] *n* mostra; esposizione *f*; (*of feeling etc*) manifestazione *f*; (*military ~*) parata (militare); (*computer ~*) display *m inv*; (*pej*) ostentazione *f* ♦ *vt* mostrare; (*goods*) esporre; (*results*) affiggere; (*departure times*) indicare; **on ~** (*gen*) in mostra; (*goods*) in vetrina.
display advertising *n* pubblicità tabellare.
displease [displēz'] *vt* dispiacere a, scontentare; **~d with** scontento(a) di.
displeasure [displezh'ûr] *n* dispiacere *m*.
disposable [dispō'zəbəl] *a* (*pack etc*) a perdere; (*income*) disponibile; **~ diaper** (*US*) pannolino di carta.
disposal [dispō'zəl] *n* (*of rubbish*) evacuazione *f*; distruzione *f*; (*of property etc*: *by selling*) vendita; (: *by giving away*) cessione *f*; **at one's ~** alla sua disposizione; **to put sth at sb's ~** mettere qc a disposizione di qn.
dispose [dispōz'] *vt* disporre.
  dispose of *vt fus* (*time, money*) disporre di; (*COMM*: *sell*) vendere; (*unwanted goods*) sbarazzarsi di; (*problem*) eliminare.
disposed [dispōzd'] *a*: **~ to do** disposto(a) a fare.
disposition [dispəzish'ən] *n* disposizione *f*; (*temperament*) carattere *m*.
dispossess [dispəzes'] *vt*: **to ~ sb (of)** spossessare qn (di).
disproportion [disprəpôr'shən] *n* sproporzione *f*.
disproportionate [disprəpôr'shənit] *a* sproporzionato(a).
disprove [disprōōv'] *vt* confutare.
dispute [dispyōōt'] *n* disputa; (*also*: **industrial ~**) controversia (sindacale) ♦ *vt* contestare; (*matter*) discutere; (*victory*) disputare; **to**

be in *or* **under ~** (*matter*) essere in discussione; (*territory*) essere oggetto di contesa.
disqualification [diskwâləfəkā'shən] *n* squalifica; **~ (from driving)** (*Brit*) ritiro della patente.
disqualify [diskwâl'əfī] *vt* (*SPORT*) squalificare; **to ~ sb from sth/from doing** rendere qn incapace a qc/a fare; squalificare qn da qc/da fare; **to ~ sb from driving** (*Brit*) ritirare la patente a qn.
disquiet [diskwī'it] *n* inquietudine *f*.
disquieting [diskwī'iting] *a* inquietante, allarmante.
disregard [disrigârd'] *vt* non far caso a, non badare a ♦ *n* (*indifference*): **~ (for)** (*feelings*) insensibilità (a), indifferenza (verso); (*danger*) noncuranza (di); (*money*) disprezzo (di).
disrepair [disripār'] *n* cattivo stato; **to fall into ~** (*building*) andare in rovina; (*street*) deteriorarsi.
disreputable [disrep'yətəbəl] *a* (*person*) di cattiva fama; (*area*) malfamato(a), poco raccomandabile.
disrepute [disripyōōt'] *n* disonore *m*, vergogna; **to bring into ~** rovinare la reputazione di.
disrespectful [disrispekt'fəl] *a* che manca di rispetto.
disrupt [disrupt'] *vt* (*meeting, lesson*) disturbare, interrompere; (*public transport*) creare scompiglio in; (*plans*) scombussolare.
disruption [disrup'shən] *n* disordine *m*; interruzione *f*.
disruptive [disrup'tiv] *a* (*influence*) negativo(a), deleterio(a); (*strike action*) paralizzante.
dissatisfaction [dissatisfak'shən] *n* scontentezza, insoddisfazione *f*.
dissatisfied [dissat'isfīd] *a*: **~ (with)** scontento(a) *or* insoddisfatto(a) (di).
dissect [disekt'] *vt* sezionare; (*fig*) sviscerare.
disseminate [disem'ənāt] *vt* disseminare.
dissent [disent'] *n* dissenso.
dissenter [disen'tûr] *n* (*REL*, *POL etc*) dissidente *m/f*.
dissertation [disûrtā'shən] *n* (*SCOL*) tesi *f inv*, dissertazione *f*.
disservice [dissûr'vis] *n*: **to do sb a ~** fare un cattivo servizio a qn.
dissident [dis'idənt] *a* dissidente; (*speech, voice*) di dissenso ♦ *n* dissidente *m/f*.
dissimilar [disim'ilûr] *a*: **~ (to)** dissimile *or* diverso(a) (da).
dissipate [dis'əpāt] *vt* dissipare.
dissipated [dis'əpātid] *a* dissipato(a).
dissociate [disō'shēāt] *vt* dissociare; **to ~ o.s. from** dichiarare di non avere niente a che fare con.
dissolute [dis'əlōōt] *a* dissoluto(a), licenzio-

so(a).

dissolve [dizălv'] vt dissolvere, sciogliere; (COMM, POL, marriage) sciogliere ♦ vi dissolversi, sciogliersi; (fig) svanire.

dissuade [diswād'] vt: **to ~ sb (from)** dissuadere qn (da).

distaff side [dis'taf sīd'] n ramo femminile di una famiglia.

distance [dis'təns] n distanza; **in the ~** in lontananza; **what's the ~ to Chicago?** quanto dista Chicago?; **it's within walking ~** ci si arriva a piedi; **at a ~ of 2 meters** a 2 metri di distanza.

distant [dis'tənt] a lontano(a), distante; (manner) riservato(a), freddo(a).

distaste [distāst'] n ripugnanza.

distasteful [distāst'fəl] a ripugnante, sgradevole.

Dist. Atty. abbr (US) = **district attorney**.

distemper [distem'pûr] n (paint) tempera; (of dogs) cimurro.

distend [distend'] vt dilatare ♦ vi dilatarsi.

distended [distend'id] a (stomach) dilatato(a).

distill, (Brit) **distil** [distil'] vt distillare.

distillery [distil'ûrē] n distilleria.

distinct [distingkt'] a distinto(a); (preference, progress) definito(a); **as ~ from** a differenza di.

distinction [distingk'shən] n distinzione f; (in exam) lode f; **to draw a ~ between** fare distinzione tra; **a writer of ~** uno scrittore di notevoli qualità.

distinctive [distingk'tiv] a distintivo(a).

distinctly [distingkt'lē] ad distintamente; (remember) chiaramente; (unhappy, better) decisamente.

distinguish [disting'gwish] vt distinguere; discernere ♦ vi: **to ~ (between)** distinguere (tra); **to ~ o.s.** distinguersi.

distinguished [disting'gwisht] a (eminent) eminente; (career) brillante; (refined) distinto(a), signorile.

distinguishing [disting'gwishing] a (feature) distinto(a), caratteristico(a).

distort [distôrt'] vt (also fig) distorcere; (account, news) falsare; (TECH) deformare.

distortion [distôr'shən] n (gen) distorsione f; (of truth etc) alterazione f; (of facts) travisamento; (TECH) deformazione f.

distr. n abbr = **distribution; distributor**.

distract [distrakt'] vt distrarre.

distracted [distrak'tid] a distratto(a).

distraction [distrak'shən] n distrazione f; **to drive sb to ~** spingere qn alla pazzia.

distraught [distrôt'] a stravolto(a).

distress [distres'] n angoscia; (pain) dolore m ♦ vt affliggere; **in ~** (ship etc) in pericolo, in difficoltà.

distressing [distres'ing] a doloroso(a), penoso(a).

distress signal n segnale m di pericolo.

distribute [distrib'yōot] vt distribuire.

distribution [distrəbyōo'shən] n distribuzione f.

distribution cost n costo di distribuzione.

distributor [distrib'yətûr] n distributore m; (COMM) concessionario.

district [dis'trikt] n (of country) regione f; (of town) quartiere m; (ADMIN) distretto.

district attorney (DA) n (US) ≈ sostituto procuratore m della Repubblica.

district council n (Brit) consiglio comunale.

district nurse n (Brit) infermiera di quartiere.

distrust [distrust'] n diffidenza, sfiducia ♦ vt non aver fiducia in.

distrustful [distrust'fəl] a diffidente.

disturb [distûrb'] vt disturbare; (inconvenience) scomodare; **sorry to ~ you** scusi se la disturbo.

disturbance [distûr'bəns] n disturbo; (political etc) tumulto; (by drunks etc) disordini mpl; **~ of the peace** disturbo della quiete pubblica; **to cause a ~** provocare disordini.

disturbed [distûrbd'] a turbato(a); **to be emotionally ~** avere problemi emotivi; **to be mentally ~** essere malato(a) di mente.

disturbing [distûrb'ing] a sconvolgente.

disuse [disyōos'] n: **to fall into ~** cadere in disuso.

disused [disyōozd'] a abbandonato(a).

ditch [dich] n fossa ♦ vt (col) piantare in asso.

dither [dith'ûr] vi vacillare.

ditto [dit'ō] ad idem.

div. n abbr = **dividend**.

divan [divan'] n divano.

divan bed n divano letto inv.

dive [dīv] n tuffo; (of submarine) immersione f; (AVIAT) picchiata; (pej) buco ♦ vi tuffarsi.

diver [dī'vûr] n tuffatore/trice; (deep-sea ~) palombaro.

diverge [divûrj'] vi divergere.

divergent [divûr'jənt] a divergente.

diverse [divûrs'] a vario(a).

diversification [divûrsəfəkā'shən] n diversificazione f.

diversify [divûr'səfī] vt diversificare.

diversion [divûr'zhən] n (distraction) divertimento; (Brit AUT) deviazione f.

diversity [divûr'sitē] n diversità f inv, varietà f inv.

divert [divûrt'] vt (traffic, river) deviare; (train, plane) dirottare; (amuse) divertire.

divest [divest'] vt: **to ~ sb of** spogliare qn di.

divide [divid'] vt dividere; (separate) separare ♦ vi dividersi; **to ~ (between or among)** dividere (tra), ripartire (tra); **40 ~d by 5** 40 diviso 5.

divide out vt: **to ~ out (between or among)** (candy etc) distribuire (tra); (tasks) distribuire or ripartire (tra).

divided [divid'id] a (country) diviso(a); (opinions) discordi.

divided highway n (US) strada a doppia carreggiata.

divided skirt n (Brit) gonna f pantalone inv.

dividend [div'idend] n dividendo.

dividend cover n rapporto dividendo profitti.

dividers [divī'dûrz] npl compasso a punte fisse.

divine [divīn'] a divino(a) ♦ vt (future) divinare, predire; (truth) indovinare; (water, metal) individuare tramite radioestesia.

diving [dīv'ing] n tuffo.

diving board [dīv'ing bôrd] n trampolino.

diving suit n scafandro.

divinity [divin'ətē] n divinità f inv; teologia.

division [divizh'ən] n divisione f; separazione f; (Brit SOCCER) serie f inv; ~ **of labor** divisione f del lavoro.

divisive [divī'siv] a che è causa di discordia.

divorce [divôrs'] n divorzio ♦ vt divorziare da.

divorced [divôrst'] a divorziato(a).

divorcee [divôrsē'] n divorziato/a.

divulge [divulj'] vt divulgare, rivelare.

D.I.Y. a, n abbr (Brit) see **do-it-yourself**.

dizziness [diz'ēnis] n vertigini fpl.

dizzy [diz'ē] a (height) vertiginoso(a); **to make sb ~** far girare la testa a qn; **to feel ~** avere il capogiro; **I feel ~** mi gira la testa, ho il capogiro.

DJ n abbr see **disc jockey**.

Djakarta [jəkâr'tə] n Djakarta.

DJIA n abbr (US STOCK EXCHANGE: = Dow-Jones Industrial Average) indice m Dow-Jones.

dl abbr (= deciliter) dl.

DLit(t) n abbr = Doctor of Literature; Doctor of Letters.

DLO n abbr = **dead-letter office**.

dm abbr (= decimeter) dm.

DMus n abbr = Doctor of Music.

DMZ n abbr (= demilitarized zone) zona smilitarizzata.

DNA n abbr (= deoxyribonucleic acid) DNA m.

do [dōō] vt, vi (pt did [did], pp done [dun]) fare ♦ n (col: party) festa; (: formal gathering) occasione f; **he didn't laugh** non ha riso; ~ **you want any?** ne vuole?; ~ **you speak English?** parla inglese?; **he laughed, didn't he?** lui ha riso, vero?; ~ **they?** ah sì?, vero?; **who broke it? - I did** chi l'ha rotto? - sono stato io; ~ **you agree? - I** ~ è d'accordo? - sì; **you speak better than I** ~ parla meglio di me; **so does he** anche lui; **DO come!** dai, vieni!; **I DO wish I could** ... magari potessi ...; **but I DO like it!** mi piace proprio!; **I'll** ~ **all I can** farò tutto il possibile; **how** ~ **you like your steak done?** come preferisce la bistecca?; **well done** ben cotto; **what can I** ~ **for you?** (in store) desidera?; **to** ~ **one's nails** farsi le unghie; **to** ~ **one's teeth** pulirsi i denti; **to** ~ **one's hair** pettinarsi; **will it** ~? andrà bene?; **he's ~ing**

well/badly at school va bene/male a scuola; **that'll** ~! (in annoyance) ora basta!; **to** ~ **sb out of sth** fregare qc a qn; **to make** ~ **(with)** arrangiarsi (con); **to** ~ **without sth** fare a meno di qc; **what did he** ~ **with the cat?** che ne ha fatto del gatto?; **what has that got to** ~ **with it?** che c'entra?

do away with vt fus abolire; (kill) far fuori.

do up vt abbottonare; allacciare; (house etc) rimettere a nuovo; **to** ~ **o.s. up** farsi bello(a).

do with vt fus (with can, could: need) avere bisogno di; **I could** ~ **with some help/a drink** un aiuto/un bicchierino non guasterebbe; **it could** ~ **with a wash** una lavata non gli farebbe male.

do. abbr = **ditto**.

DOA abbr (= dead on arrival) morto(a) durante il trasporto.

d.o.b. abbr = **date of birth**.

docile [dâs'əl] a docile.

dock [dâk] n bacino; (wharf) molo; (LAW) banco degli imputati ♦ vi entrare in bacino ♦ vt (pay etc) decurtare.

dock dues npl diritti mpl di banchina.

docker [dâk'ûr] n scaricatore m.

docket [dâk'it] n (on parcel etc) etichetta, cartellino.

dockyard [dâk'yârd] n cantiere m navale.

doctor [dâk'tûr] n medico, dottore/essa; (Ph.D. etc) dottore/essa ♦ vt (interfere with: food, drink) adulterare; (: text, document) alterare, manipolare; ~'s **office** or (Brit) **surgery** gabinetto medico, ambulatorio; **D~ of Philosophy (PhD)** dottorato di ricerca; (person) titolare m/f di un dottorato di ricerca.

doctorate [dâk'tûrit] n ≈ dottorato di ricerca.

doctrine [dâk'trin] n dottrina.

document n [dâk'yəmənt] documento ♦ vt [dâk'yəment] documentare.

documentary [dâkyəmen'tûrē] a documentario(a); (evidence) documentato(a) ♦ n documentario.

documentation [dâkyəməntā'shən] n documentazione f.

DOD n abbr (US) = **Department of Defense**; see **defense**.

doddering [dâd'ûring] a traballante.

Dodecanese Islands [dōdckənēs' i'ləndz] npl Isole fpl del Dodecanneso.

dodge [dâj] n trucco; schivata ♦ vt schivare, eludere ♦ vi scansarsi; (SPORT) fare una schivata; **to** ~ **out of the way** scansarsi; **to** ~ **through the traffic** destreggiarsi nel traffico.

dodgems [dâj'əmz] npl autoscontri mpl.

DOE n abbr (US) = **Department of Energy**; (Brit) = **Department of the Environment**; see **energy**; **environment**.

doe [dō] n (deer) femmina di daino; (rabbit)

coniglia.

does [duz] *see* **do**.

doesn't [duz'nt] = **does not**.

dog [dôg] *n* cane *m* ♦ *vt* (*follow closely*) pedinare; (*fig: memory etc*) perseguitare; **to go
to the** ~**s** (*person*) ridursi male, lasciarsi
andare; (*nation etc*) andare in malora.

dog biscuits *npl* biscotti *mpl* per cani.

dog collar *n* collare *m* di cane; (*fig*) collari-
no.

dog-eared [dôg'ērd] *a* (*book*) con orecchie.

dog food *n* cibo per cani.

dogged [dôg'id] *a* ostinato(a), tenace.

dogma [dôg'mə] *n* dogma *m*.

dogmatic [dôgmat'ik] *a* dogmatico(a).

do-gooder [dōōgōōd'ûr] *n* (*col pej*): **to be a**
~ fare il filantropo.

dogsbody [dôgz'bàdē] *n* (*Brit*) factotum *m
inv*.

dog tag *n* piastrina.

doing [dōō'ing] *n*: **this is your** ~ è opera tua,
sei stato tu.

doings [dōō'ingz] *npl* attività *fpl*.

do-it-yourself (DIY) [dōō'ityōōrself'] *n* il far
da sé.

do-it-yourselfer [dōō'ityōōrself'ûr] *n* (*US*)
entusiasta *m/f* del fai da te.

doldrums [dōl'drəmz] *npl* (*fig*): **to be in the**
~ essere giù; (*business*) attraversare un momento difficile.

dole [dōl] *n* sussidio di disoccupazione; **to be
on the** ~ vivere del sussidio.

  dole out *vt* distribuire.

doleful [dōl'fəl] *a* triste, doloroso(a).

doll [dâl] *n* bambola.

  doll up *vt*: **to** ~ **o.s. up** farsi bello(a).

dollar [dâl'ûr] *n* dollaro.

dollar area *n* area del dollaro.

dolphin [dâl'fin] *n* delfino.

domain [dōmān'] *n* dominio; (*fig*) campo, sfera.

dome [dōm] *n* cupola.

domestic [dəmes'tik] *a* (*duty, happiness, animal*) domestico(a); (*policy, affairs, flights*)
nazionale; (*news*) dall'interno.

domesticated [dəmes'tikātid] *a* addomestica-
to(a); (*person*) casalingo(a).

domesticity [dōmestis'itē] *n* vita di famiglia.

domestic servant *n* domestico/a.

domicile [dâm'isīl] *n* domicilio.

dominant [dâm'ənənt] *a* dominante.

dominate [dâm'ənāt] *vt* dominare.

domination [dâmənā'shən] *n* dominazione *f*.

domineering [dâmənēr'ing] *a* dispotico(a), au-
toritario(a).

Dominican Republic [dəmin'əkən ripub'lik] *n*
Repubblica Dominicana.

dominion [dəmin'yən] *n* dominio; sovranità;
(*Brit POL*) dominion *m inv*.

domino, ~**es** [dâm'ənō] *n* domino; ~**es** *n*
(*game*) gioco del domino.

don [dân] *n* (*Brit*) docente *m/f* universitario(a)
♦ *vt* indossare.

donate [dō'nāt] *vt* donare.

donation [dōnā'shən] *n* donazione *f*.

done [dun] *pp of* **do**.

donkey [dâng'kē] *n* asino.

donkey-work [dâng'kēwûrk] *n* (*Brit col*) lavoro ingrato.

donor [dō'nûr] *n* donatore/trice.

don't [dōnt] *vb* = **do not**.

donut [dō'nut] *n* (*US*) bombolone *m*.

doodle [dōōd'əl] *n* scarabocchio ♦ *vi* scarabocchiare.

doom [dōōm] *n* destino; rovina ♦ *vt*: **to be**
~**ed** (**to failure**) essere predestinato(a) (a
fallire).

doomsday [dōōmz'dā] *n* il giorno del Giudizio.

door [dôr] *n* porta; (*of vehicle*) sportello,
portiera; **from** ~ **to** ~ di porta in porta.

doorbell [dôr'bel] *n* campanello.

door handle *n* maniglia.

doorman [dôr'man] *n* (*in hotel*) portiere *m* in
livrea; (*in apartment building*) portinaio.

doormat [dôr'mat] *n* stuoia della porta.

doorstep [dôr'step] *n* gradino della porta.

door-to-door [dôr'tədôr'] *a*: ~ **selling** vendita
porta a porta.

doorway [dôr'wā] *n* porta; **in the** ~ nel vano
della porta.

dope [dōp] *n* (*col: drugs*) roba; (: *information*) dati *mpl*; (: *idiot*) scemo/a ♦ *vt* (*horse
etc*) drogare.

dopey [dō'pē] *a* (*col*) inebetito(a).

dormant [dôr'mənt] *a* inattivo(a); (*fig*) latente.

dormer [dôr'mûr] *n* (*also*: ~ **window**) abbai-
no.

dormice [dôr'mīs] *npl of* **dormouse**.

dormitory [dôr'mitôrē] *n* dormitorio; (*US: for
students*) casa dello studente.

dormouse, *pl* **dormice** [dôr'mous, -mīs] *n* ghiro.

Dors *abbr* (*Brit*) = **Dorset**.

DOS [dōs] *n abbr see* **disk operating system**.

dosage [dō'sij] *n* (*on medicine bottle*) posolo-
gia.

dose [dōs] *n* dose *f*; (*Brit: bout*) attacco ♦ *vt*:
to ~ **sb with sth** somministrare qc a qn; **a**
~ **of flu** una bella influenza.

doss house [dâs' hous] *n* (*Brit*) asilo
notturno.

dossier [dâs'ēā] *n* dossier *m inv*.

DOT *n abbr* (*US*) = **Department of Transportation**; *see* **transportation**.

dot [dât] *n* punto; macchiolina ♦ *vt*: ~**ted with**
punteggiato(a) di; **on the** ~ in punto.

dot command *n* (*COMPUT*) dot command *m
inv*.

dote [dōt]: **to** ~ **on** *vt fus* essere infatuato(a)
di.

dot-matrix printer [dâtmāt'riks prin'tûr] *n*

stampante *f* a matrice a punti.
dotted line [dât'id līn'] *n* linea punteggiata; **to sign on the** ~ firmare (nell'apposito spazio); (*fig*) accettare.
dotty [dât'ē] *a* (*col*) strambo(a).
double [dub'əl] *a* doppio(a) ♦ *ad* (*fold*) in due, doppio; (*twice*): **to cost** ~ (**sth**) costare il doppio (di qc) ♦ *n* sosia *m inv*; (*CINEMA*) controfigura ♦ *vt* raddoppiare; (*fold*) piegare doppio *or* in due ♦ *vi* raddoppiarsi; **spelled with a** ~ "**l**" scritto con due elle *or* con doppia elle; **on the** ~ a passo di corsa; **to** ~ **as** (*have two uses etc*) funzionare *or* servire anche da; *see also* **doubles**.
double back *vi* (*person*) tornare sui propri passi.
double up *vi* (*bend over*) piegarsi in due; (*share room*) dividere la stanza.
double bass *n* contrabbasso.
double bed *n* letto matrimoniale.
double bend *n* (*Brit*) doppia curva.
double-breasted [dub'əlbres'tid] *a* a doppio petto.
double-check [dub'əlchek'] *vt, vi* ricontrollare.
double-clutch [dub'əlkluch'] *vi* (*US*) fare la doppietta.
double cream *n* (*Brit*) doppia panna.
doublecross [dub'əlkrôs'] *vt* fare il doppio gioco con.
doubledecker [dubəldek'ûr] *n* autobus *m inv* a due piani.
double-declutch [dub'əldēkluch'] *vi* fare la doppietta.
double exposure *n* (*PHOT*) sovrimpressione *f*.
double glazing [dub'əl glāz'ing] *n* (*Brit*) doppi vetri *mpl*.
double-page [dub'əlpāj] *a*: ~ **spread** pubblicità a doppia pagina.
double parking *n* parcheggio in doppia fila.
double room *n* camera per due.
doubles [dub'əlz] *n* (*TENNIS*) doppio.
double time *n* tariffa doppia per lavoro straordinario.
doubly [dub'lē] *ad* doppiamente.
doubt [dout] *n* dubbio ♦ *vt* dubitare di; **to** ~ **that** dubitare che + *sub*; **without (a)** ~ senza dubbio; **beyond** ~ fuor di dubbio; **I** ~ **it very much** ho i miei dubbi, nutro seri dubbi in proposito.
doubtful [dout'fəl] *a* dubbioso(a), incerto(a); (*person*) equivoco(a); **to be** ~ **about sth** avere dei dubbi su qc, non essere convinto di qc; **I'm a bit** ~ non ne sono sicuro.
doubtless [dout'lis] *ad* indubbiamente.
dough [dō] *n* pasta, impasto; (*col: money*) grana.
doughnut [dō'nut] *n* bombolone *m*.
dour [dōōr] *a* arcigno(a).
douse [dous] *vt* (*with water*) infradiciare;

(*flames*) spegnere.
dove [duv] *n* colombo/a.
Dover [dō'vûr] *n* Dover *f*.
dovetail [duv'tāl] *n*: ~ **joint** incastro a coda di rondine ♦ *vi* (*fig*) combaciare.
dowager [dou'əjûr] *n* vedova titolata.
dowdy [dou'dē] *a* trasandato(a); malvestito(a).
Dow-Jones average [dou'jōnz' av'ûrij] *n* (*US*) indice *m* Dow-Jones.
down [doun] *n* (*fluff*) piumino; (*hill*) collina, colle *m* ♦ *ad* giù, di sotto ♦ *prep* giù per ♦ *vt* (*col: drink*) scolarsi; ~ **there** laggiù, là in fondo; ~ **here** quaggiù; **I'll be** ~ **in a minute** scendo tra un minuto; **the price of meat is** ~ il prezzo della carne è sceso; **I've got it** ~ **in my diary** ce l'ho sulla mia agenda; **to pay $2** ~ dare 2 dollari in acconto *or* di anticipo; **I've been** ~ **with flu** sono stato a letto con l'influenza; **England is two goals** ~ l'Inghilterra sta perdendo per due goal; **to** ~ **tools** (*Brit*) incrociare le braccia; ~ **with X!** abbasso X!
down-and-out [doun'ənout] *n* (*tramp*) barbone *m*.
down-at-heel(s) [dounat·hēl(z)'] *a* scalcagnato(a); (*fig*) trasandato(a).
downbeat [doun'bēt] *n* (*MUS*) tempo in battere ♦ *a* (*col*) volutamente distaccato(a).
downcast [doun'kast] *a* abbattuto(a).
downer [dou'nûr] *n* (*col: drug*) farmaco depressivo; **to be on a** ~ (*depressed*) essere giù.
downfall [doun'fôl] *n* caduta; rovina.
downgrade [doun'grād] *vt* (*job, hotel*) declassare; (*employee*) degradare.
downhearted [doun'hâr'tid] *a* scoraggiato(a).
downhill [doun'hil'] *ad* verso il basso ♦ *n* (*SKI: also*: ~ **race**) discesa libera; **to go** ~ andare in discesa; (*business*) andare a rotoli.
Downing Street [dou'ning strēt] *n* (*Brit*): **10** ~ **residenza del primo ministro.**
download [doun'lōd] *vt* (*COMPUT*) trasferire (*per esempio da un grosso calcolatore ad un microcalcolatore*).
down-market [dounmâr'kit] *a* (*Brit*) rivolto(a) ad una fascia di mercato inferiore.
down payment *n* acconto.
downplay [doun'plā] *vt* (*US*) minimizzare.
downpour [doun'pôr] *n* scroscio di pioggia.
downright [doun'rīt] *a* franco(a); (*refusal*) assoluto(a).
Down's Syndrome [dounz' sin'drōm] *n* (*MED*) sindrome *f* di Down.
downstairs [doun'stärz'] *ad* di sotto; al piano inferiore; **to come** ~, **go** ~ scendere giù.
downstream [doun'strēm'] *ad* a valle.
downtime [doun'tīm] *n* (*COMM*) tempi *mpl* morti.
down-to-earth [dountōōûrth'] *a* pratico(a).
downtown [doun'toun'] *ad* in città ♦ *a* (*US*):

~ **Chicago** il centro di Chicago.
downtrodden [doun'trådən] *a* oppresso(a).
down under *ad* agli antipodi.
downward [doun'wûrd] *a* in giù, in discesa; **a**
~ **trend** una diminuzione progressiva.
downward(s) *ad* in giù, in discesa.
dowry [dou'rē] *n* dote *f*.
doz. *abbr* = **dozen**.
doze [dōz] *vi* sonnecchiare.
doze off *vi* appisolarsi.
dozen [duz'ən] *n* dozzina; **a** ~ **books** una
dozzina di libri; **80c a** ~ 80 centesimi la
dozzina; ~**s of times** centinaia *or* migliaia di
volte.
DPh, DPhil *n abbr* (= *Doctor of Philosophy*) ≈
dottorato di ricerca.
DPP *n abbr* (*Brit*) *see* **Director of Public
Prosecutions.**
DPT *n abbr* (*MED*: = *diphtheria, pertussis,
tetanus*) *vaccino*.
DPW *n abbr* (*US*: = *Department of Public
Works*) ≈ Ministero dei Lavori Pubblici.
Dr, Dr. *abbr* (= *doctor*) Dr, Dott./Dott.ssa.
dr *abbr* (*COMM*) = **debtor.**
Dr. *abbr* (*in street names*) = **drive.**
drab [drab] *a* tetro(a), grigio(a).
draft [draft] *n* abbozzo; (*COMM*) tratta; (*US
MIL*) contingente *m*; (: *call-up*) leva; (: *of
air*) corrente *f* d'aria; (: *NAUT*) pescaggio ♦
vt abbozzare; (*document, report*) stendere
(in versione preliminare); **on** ~ (*beer*) alla
spina.
draftee [draftē'] *n* (*US MIL*) coscritto.
draftsman [drafts'mən] *n* (*US*) disegnatore *m*.
draftsmanship [drafts'mənship] *n* (*US*) disegno tecnico; (: *skill*) arte *f* del disegno.
drag [drag] *vt* trascinare; (*river*) dragare ♦ *vi*
trascinarsi ♦ *n* (*AVIAT, NAUT*) resistenza (aerodinamica); (*col: person*) nioso/a; (: *task*)
noia; (*women's clothing*): **in** ~ travestito (da
donna).
drag away *vt*: **to** ~ **away (from)** tirare via
(da).
drag on *vi* tirar avanti lentamente.
dragnet [drag'net] *n* giacchio; (*fig*) rastrella-
mento.
dragon [drag'ən] *n* drago.
dragonfly [drag'ənflī] *n* libellula.
dragoon [drəgōōn'] *n* (*cavalryman*) dragone
m ♦ *vt*: **to** ~ **sb into doing sth** (*Brit*) costringere qn a fare qc.
drain [drān] *n* canale *m* di scolo; (*for sewage*)
fogna; (*on resources*) salasso ♦ *vt* (*land,
marshes*) prosciugare; (*vegetables*) scolare;
(*reservoir etc*) vuotare ♦ *vi* (*water*) defluire;
to feel ~**ed** sentirsi svuotato(a), sentirsi
sfinito(a).
drainage [drā'nij] *n* prosciugamento; fognatu-
ra.
drainboard [drān'bôrd] *n* (*US*) piano del lavello.

draining board [drā'ning bôrd] *n* (*Brit*) =
drainboard.
drainpipe [drān'pīp] *n* tubo di scarico.
drake [drāk] *n* maschio dell'anatra.
dram [dram] *n* bicchierino (di whisky *etc*).
drama [drâm'ə] *n* (*art*) dramma *m*, teatro;
(*play*) commedia; (*event*) dramma.
dramatic [drəmat'ik] *a* drammatico(a).
dramatically [drəmat'iklē] *ad* in modo spetta-
colare.
dramatist [dram'ətist] *n* drammaturgo/a.
dramatize [dram'ətīz] *vt* (*events etc*) drammatizzare; (*adapt: novel: for TV*) ridurre *or*
adattare per la televisione; (: *for cinema*) ridurre *or* adattare per lo schermo.
drank [drangk] *pt of* **drink.**
drape [drāp] *vt* drappeggiare; *see also* **drapes.**
drapes [drāps] *npl* (*US*) tende *fpl*.
drastic [dras'tik] *a* drastico(a).
drastically [dras'tiklē] *ad* drasticamente.
draught [draft] *n* (*Brit*) corrente *f* d'aria;
(*NAUT*) pescaggio; **on** ~ (*beer*) alla spina.
draughtboard [draft'bôrd] *n* (*Brit*) scacchiera.
draughts [drafts] *n* (*Brit*) (gioco della) dama.
draughtsman [drafts'mən] *etc* (*Brit*) = **draftsman** *etc*.
draw [drô] *vb* (*pt* **drew**, *pp* **drawn** [drōō,
drôn]) *vt* tirare; (*attract*) attirare; (*picture*)
disegnare; (*line, circle*) tracciare; (*money*)
ritirare; (*formulate: conclusion*) trarre, ricavare; (: *comparison, distinction*): **to** ~
(**between**) fare (tra) ♦ *vi* (*SPORT*) pareggiare
♦ *n* (*SPORT*) pareggio; (*in lottery*) estrazione
f; (*attraction*) attrazione *f*; **to** ~ **to a close**
avvicinarsi alla conclusione; **to** ~ **near** *vi*
avvicinarsi.
draw back *vi*: **to** ~ **back (from)** indietreggiare (di fronte a), tirarsi indietro (di
fronte a).
draw in *vi* (*Brit: train*) entrare in stazione;
(*car*) accostarsi.
draw on *vt* (*resources*) attingere a; (*imagination, person*) far ricorso a.
draw out *vi* (*lengthen*) allungarsi ♦ *vt*
(*money*) ritirare.
draw up *vi* (*stop*) arrestarsi, fermarsi ♦ *vt*
(*document*) compilare; (*plans*) formulare.
drawback [drô'bak] *n* svantaggio, inconveniente *m*.
drawbridge [drô'brij] *n* ponte *m* levatoio.
drawee [drôē'] *n* trattario.
drawer [drôr] *n* cassetto; [drô'ûr] (*of check*)
riscuotitore/trice.
drawing [drô'ing] *n* disegno.
drawing board *n* tavola da disegno.
drawing pin *n* (*Brit*) puntina da disegno.
drawing room *n* salotto.
drawl [drôl] *n* pronuncia strascicata.
drawn [drôn] *pp of* **draw** ♦ *a* (*haggard: with
tiredness*) tirato(a); (: *with pain*) con-

tratto(a) (dal dolore).

drawstring [drô'string] *n* laccio (*per stringere maglie, sacche etc*).

dread [dred] *n* terrore *m* ♦ *vt* tremare all'idea di.

dreadful [dred'fəl] *a* terribile; **I feel ~!** (*ill*) mi sento uno straccio!; (*ashamed*) vorrei scomparire (dalla vergogna)!

dream [drēm] *n* sogno ♦ *vt, vi* (*pt, pp* **dreamed** *or* **dreamt** [dremt]) sognare; **to have a ~ about sb/sth** fare un sogno su qn/qc; **sweet ~s!** sogni d'oro!

dream up *vt* (*reason, excuse*) inventare; (*plan, idea*) escogitare.

dreamer [drē'mûr] *n* sognatore/trice.

dreamt [dremt] *pt, pp of* **dream.**

dreamy [drē'mē] *a* (*look, voice*) sognante; (*person*) distratto(a), sognatore(trice).

dreary [drēr'ē] *a* tetro(a); monotono(a).

dredge [drej] *vt* dragare.

dredge up *vt* tirare alla superficie; (*fig: unpleasant facts*) rivangare.

dredger [drej'ûr] *n* draga; (*for sugar*) spargizucchero *m inv.*

dregs [dregz] *npl* feccia.

drench [drench] *vt* inzuppare; **~ed to the skin** bagnato(a) fino all'osso, bagnato(a) fradicio(a).

dress [dres] *n* vestito; (*clothing*) abbigliamento ♦ *vt* vestire; (*wound*) fasciare; (*food*) condire; preparare; (*shop window*) allestire ♦ *vi* vestirsi; **to ~ o.s., to get ~ed** vestirsi; **she ~es very well** veste molto bene.

dress up *vi* vestirsi a festa; (*in fancy dress*) vestirsi in costume.

dress circle *n* prima galleria.

dress designer *n* disegnatore/trice di moda.

dresser [dres'ûr] *n* (*THEATER*) assistente *m/f* del camerino; (*also:* **window ~**) vetrinista *m/f*; (*furniture*) credenza.

dressing [dres'ing] *n* (*MED*) benda; (*CULIN*) condimento.

dressing gown *n* (*Brit*) vestaglia.

dressing room *n* (*THEATER*) camerino; (*SPORT*) spogliatoio.

dressing table *n* toilette *f inv.*

dressmaker [dres'mākûr] *n* sarta.

dressmaking [dres'māking] *n* sartoria; confezioni *fpl* per donna.

dress rehearsal *n* prova generale.

dress shirt *n* camicia da sera.

dressy [dres'ē] *a* (*col*) elegante.

drew [drōō] *pt of* **draw.**

dribble [drib'əl] *vi* gocciolare; (*baby*) sbavare; (*BASKETBALL*) dribblare ♦ *vt* dribblare.

dried [drīd] *a* (*fruit, beans*) secco(a); (*eggs, milk*) in polvere.

drier [drī'ûr] *n* = **dryer.**

drift [drift] *n* (*of current etc*) direzione *f*; forza; (*of sand, snow*) cumulo; (*general meaning*) senso ♦ *vi* (*boat*) essere trasporta-to(a) dalla corrente; (*sand, snow*) ammucchiarsi; **to catch sb's ~** capire dove qn vuole arrivare; **to let things ~** lasciare che le cose vadano come vogliono; **to ~ apart** (*friends*) perdersi di vista; (*lovers*) allontanarsi l'uno dall'altro.

drifter [drif'tûr] *n* persona che fa una vita da zingaro.

driftwood [drift'wŏŏd] *n* resti *mpl* della mareggiata.

drill [dril] *n* trapano; (*MIL*) esercitazione *f* ♦ *vt* trapanare; (*soldiers*) esercitare, addestrare; (*pupils: in grammar*) fare esercitare ♦ *vi* (*for oil*) fare trivellazioni.

drilling [dril'ing] *n* (*for oil*) trivellazione *f*.

drilling rig *n* (*on land*) torre *f* di perforazione; (*at sea*) piattaforma (per trivellazioni subacquee).

drily [drī'lē] *ad* = **dryly.**

drink [dringk] *n* bevanda, bibita ♦ *vt, vi* (*pt* **drank,** *pp* **drunk** [drangk, drungk]) bere; **to have a ~** bere qualcosa; **a ~ of water** un bicchier d'acqua; **would you like something to ~?** vuole qualcosa da bere?; **we had ~s before lunch** abbiamo preso l'aperitivo.

drink in *vt* (*subj: person: fresh air*) aspirare; (: *story*) ascoltare avidamente; (: *sight*) ammirare, bersi con gli occhi.

drinkable [dring'kəbəl] *a* (*not poisonous*) potabile; (*palatable*) bevibile.

drinker [dring'kûr] *n* bevitore/trice.

drinking [dring'king] *n* (*drunkenness*) il bere, alcoolismo.

drinking fountain *n* fontanella.

drinking water *n* acqua potabile.

drip [drip] *n* goccia; (~*ping*) sgocciolio; (*Brit MED*) fleboclisi *f inv*; (*col: spineless person*) lavativo ♦ *vi* gocciolare; (*washing*) sgocciolare; (*wall*) trasudare.

drip-dry [drip'drī] *a* (*shirt*) che non si stira.

drip-feed [drip'fēd] *vt* (*Brit*) alimentare mediante fleboclisi.

dripping [drip'ing] *n* (*CULIN*) grasso d'arrosto ♦ *a*: **~ wet** fradicio(a).

drive [drīv] *n* passeggiata *or* giro in macchina; (*also:* **~way**) viale *m* d'accesso; (*energy*) energia; (*PSYCH*) impulso; bisogno; (*push*) sforzo eccezionale; campagna; (*SPORT*) drive *m inv*; (*TECH*) trasmissione *f*; (*COMPUT: also:* **disk ~**) disk drive *m inv*, unità *f inv* a dischi magnetici ♦ *vb* (*pt* **drove,** *pp* **driven** [drōv, driv'ən]) *vt* (*vehicle*) guidare; (*nail*) piantare; (*push*) cacciare, spingere; (*TECH: motor*) azionare; far funzionare ♦ *vi* (*AUT: at controls*) guidare; (: *travel*) andare in macchina; **to go for a ~** andare a fare un giro in macchina; **it's 3 hours' ~ from Chicago** è a 3 ore di macchina da Chicago; **left-/right-hand ~** (*AUT*) guida a sinistra/destra; **front-/rear-wheel ~** (*AUT*) trazione *f* anteriore/posteriore; **to ~ sb to (do) sth** spingere qn a (fare) qc; **he ~s a taxi** fa il tassista; **to ~ at 50 km an hour** guidare or andare a 50 km all'ora.

drive at vt fus (fig: intend, mean) mirare a, voler dire.

drive on vi proseguire, andare (più) avanti ♦ vt (incite, encourage) sospingere, spingere.

drive-in [drīv'in] a, n (esp US) drive-in (m inv).

drive-in window n (US) sportello di drive-in.

drivel [driv'əl] n (col: nonsense) ciance fpl.

driven [driv'ən] pp of **drive**.

driver [drī'vûr] n conducente m/f; (of taxi) tassista m; (of bus) autista m.

driver's license n (US) patente f di guida.

driveway [drīv'wā] n viale m d'accesso.

driving [drī'ving] a: **~ rain** pioggia sferzante ♦ n guida.

driving belt n cinghia di trasmissione.

driving force n forza trainante.

driving instructor n istruttore/trice di scuola guida.

driving lesson n lezione f di guida.

driving licence n (Brit) patente f di guida.

driving school n scuola f guida inv.

driving test n esame m di guida.

drizzle [driz'əl] n pioggerella ♦ vi piovigginare.

droll [drōl] a buffo(a).

dromedary [drām'idârē] n dromedario.

drone [drōn] n ronzio; (male bee) fuco ♦ vi (bee, aircraft, engine) ronzare; (also: ~ on: person) continuare a parlare (in modo monotono); (: voice) continuare a ronzare.

drool [drōōl] vi sbavare; **to ~ over sb/sth** (fig) andare in estasi per qn/qc.

droop [drōōp] vi abbassarsi; languire.

drop [drāp] n goccia; (fall: in price) calo, ribasso; (: in salary) riduzione f, taglio; (also: **parachute ~**) lancio; (steep incline) salto ♦ vt lasciar cadere; (voice, eyes, price) abbassare; (set down from car) far scendere ♦ vi cascare; (decrease: wind, temperature, price, voice) calare; (numbers, attendance) diminuire; **~s** npl (MED) gocce fpl; **cough ~s** pastiglie fpl per la tosse; **a ~ of 10%** un calo del 10%; **to ~ sb a line** mandare due righe a qn; **to ~ anchor** gettare l'ancora.

drop in vi (col: visit): **to ~ in (on)** fare un salto (da), passare (da).

drop off vi (sleep) addormentarsi ♦ vt: **to ~ sb off** far scendere qn.

drop out vi (withdraw) ritirarsi; (student etc) smettere di studiare.

droplet [drāp'lit] n gocciolina.

dropout [drāp'out] n (from society/university) chi ha abbandonato (la società/gli studi).

dropper [drāp'ûr] n (MED etc) contagocce m inv.

droppings [drāp'ingz] npl sterco.

dross [drôs] n scoria; scarto.

drought [drout] n siccità f inv.

drove [drōv] pt of **drive** ♦ n: **~s of people** una moltitudine di persone.

drown [droun] vt affogare; (also: ~ **out**: sound) coprire ♦ vi affogare.

drowse [drouz] vi sonnecchiare.

drowsy [drou'zē] a sonnolento(a), assonnato(a).

drudge [druj] n (person) uomo/donna di fatica; (job) faticaccia.

drudgery [druj'ûrē] n fatica improba; **housework is sheer ~** le faccende domestiche sono alienanti.

drug [drug] n farmaco; (narcotic) droga ♦ vt drogare; **he's on ~s** si droga; (MED) segue una cura.

drug addict n tossicomane m/f.

druggist [drug'ist] n (US) farmacista m/f.

drug peddler n spacciatore/trice di droga.

drugstore [drug'stôr] n negozio di generi vari e di articoli di farmacia.

drum [drum] n tamburo; (for oil, petrol) fusto ♦ vt: **to ~ one's fingers on the table** tamburellare con le dita sulla tavola; **~s** npl (MUS) batteria.

drum up vt (enthusiasm, support) conquistarsi.

drummer [drum'ûr] n batterista m/f.

drum roll n rullio di tamburi.

drumstick [drum'stik] n (MUS) bacchetta; (chicken leg) coscia di pollo.

drunk [drungk] pp of **drink** ♦ a ubriaco(a); ebbro(a) ♦ n ubriacone/a; **to get ~** ubriacarsi, prendere una sbornia.

drunkard [drung'kûrd] n ubriacone/a.

drunken [drung'kən] a ubriaco(a); da ubriaco; **~ driving** guida in stato di ebbrezza.

drunkenness [drung'kənnis] n ubriachezza; ebbrezza.

dry [drī] a secco(a); (day, clothes, fig: humor) asciutto(a); (uninteresting: lecture, subject) poco avvincente ♦ vt seccare; (clothes, hair, hands) asciugare ♦ vi asciugarsi; **on ~ land** sulla terraferma; **to ~ one's hands/hair/eyes** asciugarsi le mani/i capelli/gli occhi.

dry up vi seccarsi; (source of supply) esaurirsi; (fig: imagination etc) inaridirsi; (fall silent: speaker) azzittirsi.

dry-clean [drī'klēn'] vt pulire or lavare a secco.

dry-cleaner's [drī'klē'nûrz] n lavasecco m inv.

dry-cleaning [drī'klē'ning] n pulitura a secco.

dry dock n (NAUT) bacino di carenaggio.

dryer [drī'ûr] n (for hair) fôhn m inv, asciugacapelli m inv; (for clothes) asciugabiancheria m inv.

dry goods npl (COMM) tessuti mpl e mercerie fpl.

dry goods store n (US) negozio di stoffe.

dry ice n ghiaccio secco.

dryly [drī'lē] ad con fare asciutto.

dryness [drī'nis] n secchezza; (of ground) aridità.

dry rot *n* fungo del legno.

dry run *n* (*fig*) prova.

dry ski slope *n* pista artificiale.

DSc *n abbr* (= *Doctor of Science*) *titolo di studio.*

DSS *n abbr* (*Brit*) = **Department of Social Security**; *see* **social security.**

DST *abbr* (*US*) = **Daylight Saving Time.**

DT *n abbr* (*COMPUT*) = **data transmission.**

DTI *n abbr* (*Brit*) = **Department of Trade and Industry**; *see* **trade.**

DT's *n abbr* (*col*) = *delirium tremens.*

dual [dōō'əl] *a* doppio(a).

dual carriageway *n* (*Brit*) strada a doppia carreggiata.

dual-control [dōō'əlkəntrōl'] *a* con doppi comandi.

dual nationality *n* doppia nazionalità.

dual-purpose [dōō'əlpûr'pəs] *a* a doppio uso.

dubbed [dubd] *a* (*CINEMA*) doppiato(a); (*nicknamed*) soprannominato(a).

dubious [dōō'bēəs] *a* dubbio(a); (*character, manner*) ambiguo(a), equivoco(a); **I'm very** ~ **about it** ho i miei dubbi in proposito.

Dublin [dub'lin] *n* Dublino *f.*

Dubliner [dub'linûr] *n* dublinese *m/f.*

duchess [duch'is] *n* duchessa.

duck [duk] *n* anatra ♦ *vi* abbassare la testa ♦ *vt* spingere sotto (acqua).

duckling [duk'ling] *n* anatroccolo.

duct [dukt] *n* condotto; (*ANAT*) canale *m.*

dud [dud] *n* (*shell*) proiettile *m* che fa cilecca; (*object, tool*): **it's a** ~ è inutile, non funziona ♦ *a* (*Brit: check*) a vuoto; (*note, coin*) falso(a).

dude [dōōd] *n* (*US col*) tizio.

due [dōō] *a* dovuto(a); (*expected*) atteso(a); (*fitting*) giusto(a) ♦ *n* dovuto ♦ *ad*: ~ **north** diritto verso nord; ~**s** *npl* (*for club, union*) quota; (*in harbor*) diritti *mpl* di porto; **in** ~ **course** a tempo debito; finalmente; ~ **to** dovuto a; a causa di; **the rent's** ~ **on the 30th** l'affitto scade il 30; **the train is** ~ **at 8** il treno è atteso per le 8; **she is** ~ **back tomorrow** dovrebbe essere di ritorno domani; **I am** ~ **6 days' leave** mi spettano 6 giorni di ferie.

due date *n* data di scadenza.

duel [dōō'əl] *n* duello.

duet [dōōet'] *n* duetto.

duff [duf] *a* (*Brit col*) barboso(a).

duffelbag, duffle bag [duf'əlbag] *n* sacca da viaggio di tela.

duffelcoat, duffle coat [duf'əlkōt] *n* montgomery *m inv.*

duffer [duf'ûr] *n* (*col*) schiappa.

dug [dug] *pt, pp of* **dig.**

duke [dōōk] *n* duca *m.*

dull [dul] *a* (*boring*) noioso(a); (*slow-witted*) ottuso(a); (*sound, pain*) sordo(a); (*weather, day*) fosco(a), scuro(a); (*blade*) smussato(a)

♦ *vt* (*pain, grief*) attutire; (*mind, senses*) intorpidire.

duly [dōō'lē] *ad* (*on time*) a tempo debito; (*as expected*) debitamente.

dumb [dum] *a* muto(a); (*stupid*) stupido(a); **to be struck** ~ (*fig*) ammutolire, restare senza parole.

dumbbell [dum'bel] *n* (*SPORT*) manubrio, peso; (*US col: idiot*) scemo/a.

dumbfounded [dumfound'id] *a* stupito(a), stordito(a).

dummy [dum'ē] *n* (*tailor's model*) manichino; (*SPORT*) finto; (*Brit: for baby*) tettarella ♦ *a* falso(a), finto(a).

dummy run *n* giro di prova.

dump [dump] *n* mucchio di rifiuti; (*place*) luogo di scarico; (*MIL*) deposito; (*COMPUT*) scaricamento, dump *m inv* ♦ *vt* (*put down*) scaricare; mettere giù; (*get rid of*) buttar via; (*COMM: goods*) svendere; (*COMPUT*) scaricare; **to be (down) in the** ~**s** (*col*) essere giù di corda.

dumping [dum'ping] *n* (*ECON*) dumping *m*; (*of rubbish*): **"no** ~**"** "vietato lo scarico".

dumpling [dump'ling] *n specie di gnocco.*

dumpy [dump'ē] *a* tracagnotto(a).

dunce [duns] *n* asino.

dune [dōōn] *n* duna.

dung [dung] *n* concime *m.*

dungarees [dunggərēz'] *npl* tuta.

dungeon [dun'jən] *n* prigione *f* sotterranea.

dunk [dungk] *vt* inzuppare.

duo [dōō'ō] *n* (*gen, MUS*) duo *m inv.*

duodenal [dōōədē'nəl] *a* (*ulcer*) duodenale.

duodenum [dōōədē'nəm] *n* duodeno.

dupe [dōōp] *vt* gabbare, ingannare.

duplex [dōō'pleks] *n* (*US: also:* ~ **apartment**) appartamento su due piani.

duplicate *n* [dōō'plikit] doppio; (*copy of letter etc*) duplicato ♦ *vt* [dōō'plikāt] raddoppiare; (*on machine*) ciclostilare ♦ *a* (*copy*) conforme, esattamente uguale; **in** ~ in duplice copia; ~ **key** duplicato (della chiave).

duplicating machine [dōō'plikāting məshēn'], **duplicator** [dōō'plikātûr] *n* duplicatore *m.*

duplicity [dōōplis'ətē] *n* doppiezza, duplicità.

Dur *abbr* (*Brit*) = *Durham.*

durability [dōōrəbil'ətē] *n* durevolezza; resistenza.

durable [dōōr'əbəl] *a* durevole; (*clothes, metal*) resistente.

duration [dōōrā'shən] *n* durata.

duress [dōōres'] *n*: **under** ~ sotto costrizione.

Durex [dōō'reks] *n* ® (*Brit*) preservativo.

during [dōōr'ing] *prep* durante, nel corso di.

dusk [dusk] *n* crepuscolo.

dusky [dus'kē] *a* scuro(a).

dust [dust] *n* polvere *f* ♦ *vt* (*furniture*) spolverare; (*cake etc*): **to** ~ **with** cospargere con.

dust off *vt* rispolverare.

dustbin [dust'bin] *n* (*Brit*) pattumiera.

duster [dus'tûr] *n* straccio per la polvere.
dust jacket *n* sopraccoperta.
dustman [dust'man] *n* (*Brit*) netturbino.
dustpan [dust'pan] *n* pattumiera.
dusty [dus'tē] *a* polveroso(a).
Dutch [duch] *a* olandese ♦ *n* (*LING*) olandese *m* ♦ *ad*: **to go** ~ *or* **d**~ fare alla romana; **the** ~ gli Olandesi.
Dutch auction *n* asta all'olandese.
Dutchman [duch'man], **Dutchwoman** [duch'woomən] *n* olandese *m/f*.
dutiable [dōō'tēəbəl] *a* soggetto(a) a dazio.
dutiful [dōō'tifəl] *a* (*child*) rispettoso(a); (*husband*) premuroso(a); (*employee*) coscienzioso(a).
duty [dōō'tē] *n* dovere *m*; (*tax*) dazio, tassa; **duties** *npl* mansioni *fpl*; **on** ~ di servizio; (*MED*: *in hospital*) di guardia; **off** ~ libero(a), fuori servizio; **to make it one's** ~ **to do sth** assumersi l'obbligo di fare qc; **to pay** ~ **on sth** pagare il dazio su qc.
duty-free [dōō'tēfrē'] *a* esente da dazio; ~ **shop** duty free *m inv*.
duty officer *n* (*MIL etc*) ufficiale *m* di servizio.
duvet [dōō'vā] *n* piumino, piumone *m*.
DV *abbr* (= *Deo volente*) D.V.
DVM *n abbr* (*US*: = *Doctor of Veterinary Medicine*) titolo di studio.
dwarf [dwôrf] *n* nano/a ♦ *vt* far apparire piccolo.
dwell, *pt*, *pp* **dwelt** [dwel, dwelt] *vi* dimorare.
dwell on *vt fus* indugiare su.
dweller [dwel'ûr] *n* abitante *m/f*; **city** ~ cittadino/a.
dwelling [dwel'ing] *n* dimora.
dwelt [dwelt] *pt*, *pp of* **dwell**.
dwindle [dwin'dəl] *vi* diminuire, decrescere.
dwindling [dwin'dling] *a* (*strength, interest*) che si affievolisce; (*resources, supplies*) in diminuzione.
dye [dī] *n* colore *m*; (*chemical*) colorante *m*, tintura ♦ *vt* tingere; **hair** ~ tinta per capelli.
dyestuffs [dī'stufs] *npl* coloranti *mpl*.
dying [dī'ing] *a* morente, moribondo(a).
dyke [dīk] *n* = **dike**.
dynamic [dīnam'ik] *a* dinamico(a).
dynamics [dīnam'iks] *n or npl* dinamica.
dynamite [dī'nəmīt] *n* dinamite *f* ♦ *vt* far saltare con la dinamite.
dynamo [dī'nəmō] *n* dinamo *f inv*.
dynasty [dī'nəstē] *n* dinastia.
dysentery [dis'əntärē] *n* dissenteria.
dyslexia [dislek'sēə] *n* dislessia.
dyslexic [dislek'sik] *a*, *n* dislessico(a).
dyspepsia [dispep'shə] *n* dispepsia.
dystrophy [dis'trəfē] *n* distrofia; **muscular** ~ distrofia muscolare.

E

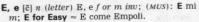

E, e [ē] *n* (*letter*) E, e *f or m inv*; (*MUS*): **E** mi *m*; **E for Easy** ≈ E come Empoli.
E *abbr* (= *east*) E.
E111 *n abbr* (*Brit*) (*also*: **form** ~) E111 (*modulo CEE per rimborso spese mediche*).
ea. *abbr* = **each**.
E.A. *n abbr* (*US*) = *educational age*.
each [ēch] *a* ogni, ciascuno(a) ♦ *pronoun* ciascuno(a), ognuno(a); ~ **one** ognuno(a); ~ **other** si (*or* ci *etc*); **they hate** ~ **other** si odiano (l'un l'altro); **you are jealous of** ~ **other** siete gelosi l'uno dell'altro; ~ **day** ogni giorno; **they have 2 books** ~ hanno 2 libri ciascuno; **they cost $5** ~ costano 5 dollari l'uno; ~ **of us** ciascuno *or* ognuno di noi.
eager [ē'gûr] *a* impaziente; desideroso(a); ardente; (*keen*: *pupil*) appassionato(a), attento(a); **to be** ~ **to do sth** non veder l'ora di fare qc; essere desideroso di fare qc; **to be** ~ **for** essere desideroso di, aver gran voglia di.
eagle [ē'gəl] *n* aquila.
E and OE *abbr* (= *errors and omissions excepted*) S.E.O.
ear [ēr] *n* orecchio; (*of corn*) pannocchia; **up to the** ~**s in debt** nei debiti fino al collo.
earache [ēr'āk] *n* mal *m* d'orecchi.
eardrum [ēr'drum] *n* timpano.
earl [ûrl] *n* conte *m*.
earlier [ûr'lēûr] *a* (*date etc*) anteriore; (*edition etc*) precedente, anteriore ♦ *ad* prima; **I can't come any** ~ non posso venire prima.
early [ûr'lē] *ad* presto, di buon'ora; (*ahead of time*) in anticipo ♦ *a* precoce; anticipato(a); che si fa vedere di buon'ora; (*man*) primitivo(a); (*Christians, settlers*) primo(a); ~ **in the morning/afternoon** nelle prime ore del mattino/del pomeriggio; **you're** ~! sei in anticipo!; **have an** ~ **night/start** vada a letto/parta presto; **in the** ~ *or* ~ **in the spring/19th century** all'inizio della primavera/dell'Ottocento; **she's in her** ~ **forties** ha appena passato la quarantina; **at your earliest convenience** (*COMM*) non appena possibile.
early retirement *n* ritiro anticipato.
early warning system *n* sistema *m* del preallarme.
earmark [ēr'mârk] *vt*: **to** ~ **sth for** destinare qc a.
earn [ûrn] *vt* guadagnare; (*rest, reward*) meri-

tare; (COMM: yield) maturare; **to** ~ **one's living** guadagnarsi da vivere; **this** ~**ed him much praise, he** ~**ed much praise for this** si è attirato grandi lodi per questo.

earned income [ûrnd' in'kum] n reddito da lavoro.

earnest [ûr'nist] a serio(a) ♦ n (also: ~ **money**) caparra; **in** ~ ad sul serio.

earnings [ûr'ningz] npl guadagni mpl; (of company etc) proventi mpl; (salary) stipendio.

ear, nose and throat specialist n otorino-laringoiatra m/f.

earphones [ēr'fōnz] npl cuffia.

earplugs [ēr'plugz] npl tappi mpl per le orecchie.

earring [ēr'ring] n orecchino.

earshot [ēr'shât] n: **out of/within** ~ fuori portata/a portata d'orecchio.

earth [ûrth] n (gen, also Brit ELEC) terra; (of fox etc) tana ♦ vt (Brit ELEC) mettere a terra.

earthenware [ûr'thənwär] n terracotta; stoviglie fpl di terracotta ♦ a di terracotta.

earthly [ûrth'lē] a terreno(a); ~ **paradise** paradiso terrestre; **there is no** ~ **reason to think** ... non vi è ragione di pensare ....

earthquake [ûrth'kwāk] n terremoto.

earth tremor n scossa sismica.

earthworks [ûrth'wûrks] npl lavori mpl di sterro.

earthworm [ûrth'wûrm] n lombrico.

earthy [ûr'thē] a (fig) grossolano(a).

earwax [ēr'waks] n cerume m.

earwig [ēr'wig] n forbicina.

ease [ēz] n agio, comodo ♦ vt (soothe) calmare; (loosen) allentare ♦ vi (situation) allentarsi, distendersi; **life of** ~ vita comoda; **with** ~ senza difficoltà; **at** ~ a proprio agio; (MIL) a riposo; **to feel at** ~**/ill at** ~ sentirsi a proprio agio/a disagio; **to** ~ **sth out/in** tirare fuori/infilare qc con delicatezza; facilitare l'uscita/l'entrata di qc.

ease off, ease up vi diminuire; (slow down) rallentarsi; (fig) rilassarsi.

easel [ē'zəl] n cavalletto.

easily [ē'zilē] ad facilmente.

easiness [ē'zēnis] n facilità, semplicità; (of manners) disinvoltura.

east [ēst] n est m ♦ a dell'est ♦ ad a oriente; **the E**~ l'Oriente m; (POL) i Paesi dell'Est.

Easter [ēs'tûr] n Pasqua ♦ a (vacation) pasquale, di Pasqua.

Easter egg n uovo di Pasqua.

Easter Island n isola di Pasqua.

easterly [ēs'tûrlē] a dall'est, d'oriente.

Easter Monday n Pasquetta.

eastern [ēs'tûrn] a orientale, d'oriente; **E**~ **Europe** l'Europa orientale; **the E**~ **bloc** (POL) i Paesi dell'Est.

Easter Sunday n domenica di Pasqua.

East Germany n Germania dell'Est.

eastward(s) [ēst'wûrdz] ad verso est, verso levante.

easy [ē'zē] a facile; (manner) disinvolto(a); (carefree: life) agiato(a), tranquillo(a) ♦ ad: **to take it** or **things** ~ prendersela con calma; **I'm** ~ (col) non ho problemi; **easier said than done** tra il dire e il fare c'è di mezzo il mare; **payment on** ~ **terms** (COMM) facilitazioni fpl di pagamento.

easy chair n poltrona.

easy-going [ē'zēgō'ing] a accomodante.

eat, pt **ate**, pp **eaten** [ēt, āt, ē'tən] vt mangiare.

eat away vt (subj: sea) erodere; (: acid) corrodere.

eat away at, eat into vt fus rodere.

eat out vi mangiare fuori.

eat up vt (meal etc) finire di mangiare; **it** ~**s up electricity** consuma un sacco di corrente.

eatable [ē'təbəl] a mangiabile; (safe to eat) commestibile.

eaten [ē'tən] pp of **eat**.

eau de Cologne [ō' də kəlōn'] n acqua di colonia.

eaves [ēvz] npl gronda.

eavesdrop [ēvz'drâp] vi: **to** ~ **(on a conversation)** origliare (una conversazione).

ebb [eb] n riflusso ♦ vi rifluire; (fig: also: ~ **away**) declinare; ~ **and flow** flusso e riflusso; **to be at a low** ~ (fig: person, spirits) avere il morale a terra; (: business) andar male.

ebb tide n marea discendente.

ebony [eb'ənē] n ebano.

ebullient [ibul'yənt] a esuberante.

eccentric [iksen'trik] a, n eccentrico(a).

ecclesiastic [iklēzēas'tik] n ecclesiastico.

ecclesiastic(al) [iklēzēas'tik(əl)] a ecclesiastico(a).

ECG n abbr see **electrocardiogram**.

ECGD n abbr (= Export Credits Guarantee Department) servizio di garanzia finanziaria per l'esportazione.

echo, ~**es** [ek'ō] n eco m or f ♦ vt ripetere; fare eco a ♦ vi echeggiare; dare un eco.

éclair [iklär'] n = bignè m inv.

eclipse [iklips'] n eclissi f inv ♦ vt eclissare.

ECM n abbr (US: = European Common Market) MEC m.

ecologist [ikâl'əjist] n ecologo/a.

ecology [ikâl'əjē] n ecologia.

economic [ēkənâm'ik] a economico(a); (profitable: price) vantaggioso(a); (business) che rende.

economical [ēkənâm'ikəl] a economico(a); (person) economo(a).

economically [ēkənâm'iklē] ad con economia; (regarding economics) dal punto di vista economico.

economics [ēkənâm'iks] n economia ♦ npl aspetto or lato economico.

economist [ikân'əmist] n economista m/f.

economize [ikân'əmīz] vi risparmiare, fare economia.

economy [ikân'əmē] n economia; **economies of scale** (COMM) economie fpl di scala.

economy class n (AVIAT etc) classe f turistica.

economy size n confezione f economica.

ecosystem [ek'ōsistəm] n ecosistema m.

ECSC n abbr (= European Coal & Steel Community) C.E.C.A. f (= Comunità Europea del Carbone e dell'Acciaio).

ecstasy [ek'stəsē] n estasi f inv; **to go into ecstasies over** andare in estasi davanti a.

ecstatic [ekstat'ik] a estatico(a), in estasi.

ECT n abbr see **electroconvulsive therapy**.

ECU n abbr (= European Currency Unit) ECU m inv.

Ecuador [ek'wədôr] n Ecuador m.

ecumenical [ekyōōmen'ikəl] a ecumenico(a).

eczema [ek'səmə] n eczema m.

eddy [ed'ē] n mulinello.

edge [ej] n margine m; (of table, plate, cup) orlo; (of knife etc) taglio ♦ vt bordare ♦ vi: **to ~ away from** sgattaiolare da; **to ~ past** passar rasente; **to ~ forward** avanzare a poco a poco; **on ~** (fig) = **edgy**; **to have the ~ on** essere in vantaggio su.

edgeways [ej'wāz] ad di fianco; **he couldn't get a word in ~** non riuscì a dire una parola.

edging [ej'ing] n bordo.

edgy [ej'ē] a nervoso(a).

edible [ed'əbəl] a commestibile; (meal) mangiabile.

edict [ē'dikt] n editto.

edifice [ed'əfis] n edificio.

edifying [ed'əfīing] a edificante.

Edinburgh [ed'ənbûrə] n Edimburgo f.

edit [ed'it] vt curare; (newspaper, magazine) dirigere; (COMPUT) correggere e modificare, editare.

edition [idish'ən] n edizione f.

editor [ed'itûr] n (in newspaper) redattore/trice; redattore/trice capo; (of sb's work) curatore/trice; (film ~) responsabile m/f del montaggio.

editorial [editôr'ēəl] a redazionale, editoriale ♦ n editoriale m; **the ~ staff** la redazione.

EDP n abbr see **electronic data processing**.

EDT abbr (US: = Eastern Daylight Time) ora legale di New York.

educate [ej'ōōkāt] vt istruire; educare.

education [ejōōkā'shən] n (teaching) insegnamento; istruzione f; (knowledge, culture) cultura; (SCOL: subject etc) pedagogia; **elementary** or (Brit) **primary/secondary ~** scuola primaria/secondaria.

educational [ejōōkā'shənəl] a pedagogico(a);

scolastico(a); istruttivo(a); **~ technology** tecnologie fpl applicate alla didattica.

Edwardian [edwôr'dēən] a edoardiano(a).

EE abbr = **electrical engineer**.

EEC n abbr (= European Economic Community) C.E.E. f (= Comunità Economica Europea).

EEG n abbr see **electroencephalogram**.

eel [ēl] n anguilla.

EENT n abbr (US MED) = eye, ear, nose and throat.

EEOC n abbr (US) = **Equal Employment Opportunity Commission**.

eerie [ē'rē] a che fa accapponare la pelle.

EET abbr (= Eastern European Time) fuso orario.

effect [ifekt'] n effetto ♦ vt effettuare; **to take ~** (law) entrare in vigore; (drug) fare effetto; **to have an ~ on sb/sth** avere or produrre un effetto su qn/qc; **to put into ~** (plan) attuare; **in ~** effettivamente; **his letter is to the ~ that** ... il contenuto della sua lettera è che ...; see also **effects**.

effective [ifek'tiv] a efficace; (striking: display, outfit) che fa colpo; **~ date** data d'entrata in vigore; **to become ~** (LAW) entrare in vigore.

effectively [ifek'tivlē] ad (efficiently) efficacemente; (strikingly) ad effetto; (in reality) di fatto; (in effect) in effetti.

effectiveness [ifek'tivnis] n efficacia.

effects [ifekts'] npl (THEATER) effetti mpl scenici; (property) effetti mpl.

effeminate [ifem'ənit] a effeminato(a).

effervescent [efûrves'ənt] a effervescente.

efficacy [ef'ikəsē] n efficacia.

efficiency [ifish'ənsē] n efficienza; rendimento effettivo.

efficiency apartment n (US) miniappartamento.

efficient [ifish'ənt] a efficiente; (remedy, product, system) efficace; (machine, car) che ha un buon rendimento.

efficiently [ifish'əntlē] ad efficientemente; efficacemente.

effigy [ef'ijē] n effigie f.

effluent [ef'lōōənt] n effluente m.

effort [ef'ûrt] n sforzo; **to make an ~ to do sth** sforzarsi di fare qc.

effortless [ef'ûrtlis] a senza sforzo, facile.

effrontery [ifrun'tûrē] n sfrontatezza.

effusive [ifyōō'siv] a (person) espansivo(a); (welcome, letter) caloroso(a); (thanks, apologies) interminabile.

EFL n abbr (SCOL) = English as a foreign language.

EFT n abbr (US: = electronic funds transfer) trasferimento elettronico di fondi.

EFTA [ef'tə] n abbr (= European Free Trade Association) E.F.T.A. f.

e.g. ad abbr (= exempli gratia: for example)

p.es.

egalitarian [igalitär'ēən] *a* egualitario(a).

egg [eg] *n* uovo.

egg on *vt* incitare.

eggcup [eg'kup] *n* portauovo *m inv*.

eggplant [eg'plant] *n* (*esp US*) melanzana.

eggshell [eg'shel] *n* guscio d'uovo ♦ *a* (*color*) guscio d'uovo *inv*.

egg white *n* albume *m*, bianco d'uovo.

egg yolk *n* tuorlo, rosso (d'uovo).

ego [ē'gō] *n* ego *m inv*.

egoism [ē'gōizəm] *n* egoismo.

egoist [ē'gōist] *n* egoista *m/f*.

egotism [ē'gətizəm] *n* egotismo.

egotist [ē'gətist] *n* egotista *m/f*.

Egypt [ē'jipt] *n* Egitto.

Egyptian [ijip'shən] *a*, *n* egiziano(a).

eiderdown [ī'dûrdoun] *n* piumino.

eight [āt] *num* otto.

eighteen [ā'tēn'] *num* diciotto.

eighth [ātth] *num* ottavo(a).

eighth note *n* (*US MUS*) croma.

eighty [ā'tē] *num* ottanta.

Eire [är'ə] *n* Repubblica d'Irlanda.

either [ē'thûr] *a* l'uno(a) o l'altro(a); (*both*, *each*) ciascuno(a); **on ~ side** su ciascun lato ♦ *pronoun*: **~** (**of them**) (o) l'uno(a) o l'altro(a); **I don't like ~** non mi piace né l'uno né l'altro ♦ *ad* neanche; **no, I don't ~** no, neanch'io ♦ *cj*: **~ good or bad** o buono o cattivo; **I haven't seen ~ one or the other** non ho visto né l'uno né l'altro.

ejaculation [ijakyəlā'shən] *n* (*PHYSIOL*) eiaculazione *f*.

eject [ijekt'] *vt* espellere; lanciare ♦ *vi* (*pilot*) catapultarsi.

ejector seat [ijek'tûr sēt] *n* sedile *m* eiettabile.

eke [ēk]: **to ~ out** *vt* far durare; aumentare.

EKG *n abbr* (*US*) = **electrocardiogram**.

el [cl] *n abbr* (*US col*) *see* **elevated railroad**.

elaborate *a* [ilab'ûrit] elaborato(a), minuzioso(a) ♦ *vb* [ilab'ərāt] *vt* elaborare ♦ *vi* entrare in dettagli.

elapse [ilaps'] *vi* trascorrere, passare.

elastic [ilas'tik] *a* elastico(a) ♦ *n* elastico.

elastic band *n* (*Brit*) elastico.

elasticity [ilastis'itē] *n* elasticità.

elated [ilā'tid] *a* pieno(a) di gioia.

elation [ilā'shən] *n* gioia.

elbow [el'bō] *n* gomito ♦ *vt* : **to ~ one's way through the crowd** farsi largo tra la folla a gomitate.

elbowroom [el'bōrōōm] *n* spazio.

elder [el'dûr] *a* maggiore, più vecchio(a) ♦ *n* (*tree*) sambuco; **one's ~s** i più anziani.

elderly [el'dûrlē] *a* anziano(a) ♦ *npl*: **the ~** gli anziani.

eldest [el'dist] *a*, *n*: **the ~** (**child**) il(la) maggiore (dei bambini).

elect [ilekt'] *vt* eleggere; (*choose*): **to ~ to do** decidere di fare ♦ *a*: **the president ~** il pre-

sidente designato.

election [ilek'shən] *n* elezione *f*; **to hold an ~** indire un'elezione.

election campaign *n* campagna elettorale.

electioneering [ilekshənē'ring] *n* propaganda elettorale.

elective [ilek'tiv] *n* (*SCOL*) materia facoltativa.

elector [ilek'tûr] *n* elettore/trice.

electoral [ilek'tûrəl] *a* elettorale.

electoral college *n* collegio elettorale.

electoral roll *n* (*Brit*) registro elettorale.

electorate [ilek'tûrit] *n* elettorato.

electric [ilek'trik] *a* elettrico(a).

electrical [ilek'trikəl] *a* elettrico(a).

electrical engineer *n* ingegnere *m* elettrotecnico.

electrical failure *n* guasto all'impianto elettrico.

electric blanket *n* coperta elettrica.

electric chair *n* sedia elettrica.

electric current *n* corrente *f* elettrica.

electrician [ilektrish'ən] *n* elettricista *m*.

electricity [ilektris'ətē] *n* elettricità; **to switch on/off the ~** attaccare/staccare la corrente.

electric light *n* luce *f* elettrica.

electric shock *n* scossa (elettrica).

electric stove *n* cucina elettrica.

electrify [ilek'trəfī] *vt* (*RAIL*) elettrificare; (*audience*) elettrizzare.

electro... *prefix* elettro....

electrocardiogram (**ECG**) [ilektrōkär'dēəgram] *n* elettrocardiogramma *m*.

electroconvulsive therapy (**ECT**) [ilek'trōkənvul'siv thär'əpē] *n* elettroshockterapia.

electrocute [ilek'trəkyōōt] *vt* fulminare.

electrode [ilek'trōd] *n* elettrodo.

electroencephalogram (**EEG**) [ilektrōensef'ələgram] *n* (*MED*) elettroencefalogramma *m* (EEG).

electrolysis [ilektrâl'isis] *n* elettrolisi *f*.

electromagnetic [ilektrōmagnet'ik] *n* elettromagnetico(a).

electron [ilek'trân] *n* elettrone *m*.

electronic [ilektrân'ik] *a* elettronico(a); *see also* **electronics**.

electronic data processing (**EDP**) *n* elaborazione *f* elettronica di dati.

electronic mail *n* posta elettronica.

electronics [ilektrân'iks] *n* elettronica.

electron microscope *n* microscopio elettronico.

electroplated [ilek'trəplātid] *a* galvanizzato(a).

electrotherapy [ilektrōthär'əpē] *n* elettroterapia.

elegance [el'əgəns] *n* eleganza.

elegant [el'əgənt] *a* elegante.

element [el'əmənt] *n* elemento; (*of heater*, *kettle etc*) resistenza.

elementary [climen'tûrē] *a* elementare.

elephant [el'əfənt] *n* elefante/essa.
elevate [el'əvāt] *vt* elevare.
elevated railroad (el) *n* (*US*) (ferrovia) soprelevata.
elevation [eləvā'shən] *n* elevazione *f*; (*height*) altitudine *f*.
elevator [el'əvātûr] *n* elevatore *m*; (*US: lift*) ascensore *m*.
eleven [ilev'ən] *num* undici.
elevenses [ilev'ənziz] *npl* (*Brit*) caffè *m* a metà mattina.
eleventh [ilev'ənth] *a* undicesimo(a); **at the ~ hour** (*fig*) all'ultimo minuto.
elf, *pl* **elves** [elf, elvz] *n* elfo.
elicit [ilis'it] *vt*: **to ~ (from)** trarre (da), cavare fuori (da); **to ~ sth (from sb)** strappare qc (a qn).
eligible [el'ijəbəl] *a* eleggibile; (*for membership*) che ha i requisiti; **to be ~ for a pension** essere pensionabile.
eliminate [əlim'ənāt] *vt* eliminare.
elimination [əlimənā'shən] *n* eliminazione *f*; **by process of ~** per eliminazione.
élite [ilēt'] *n* élite *f inv*.
elitist [ilē'tist] *a* (*pej*) elitario(a).
elixir [ilik'sûr] *n* elisir *m inv*.
Elizabethan [ilizəbē'thən] *n* elisabettiano(a).
ellipse [ilips'] *n* ellisse *f*.
elliptical [ilip'tikəl] *a* ellittico(a).
elm [elm] *n* olmo.
elocution [eləkyōō'shən] *n* elocuzione *f*.
elongated [ilông'gātid] *a* allungato(a).
elope [ilōp'] *vi* (*lovers*) scappare.
elopement [ilōp'mənt] *n* fuga romantica.
eloquence [el'əkwəns] *n* eloquenza.
eloquent [el'əkwənt] *a* eloquente.
else [els] *ad* altro; **something ~** qualcos'altro; **somewhere ~** altrove; **everywhere ~** in qualsiasi altro luogo; **where ~?** in quale altro luogo?; **little ~** poco altro; **everyone ~** tutti gli altri; **nothing ~** nient'altro; **or ~** (*otherwise*) altrimenti; **is there anything ~ I can do?** posso fare qualcos'altro?
elsewhere [els'hwär] *ad* altrove.
ELT *n abbr* (*SCOL*) = *English Language Teaching*.
elucidate [ilōō'sidāt] *vt* delucidare.
elude [ilōōd'] *vt* eludere.
elusive [ilōō'siv] *a* elusivo(a); (*answer*) evasivo(a); **he is very ~** è proprio inafferrabile *or* irraggiungibile.
elves [elvz] *npl of* **elf**.
emaciated [imā'shēātid] *a* emaciato(a).
emanate [em'ənāt] *vi*: **to ~ from** emanare da.
emancipate [iman'səpāt] *vt* emancipare.
emancipation [imansəpā'shən] *n* emancipazione *f*.
emasculate [imas'kyəlāt] *vt* (*fig*) rendere impotente.
embalm [embâm'] *vt* imbalsamare.
embankment [embangk'mənt] *n* (*of road,*

railway) massicciata; (*riverside*) argine *m*; (*dike*) diga.
embargo [embâr'gō] *n* (*pl* ~**es**: *COMM, NAUT*) embargo ♦ *vt* mettere l'embargo su; **to put an ~ on sth** mettere l'embargo su qc.
embark [embârk'] *vi*: **to ~ (on)** imbarcarsi (su) ♦ *vt* imbarcare; **to ~ on** (*fig*) imbarcarsi in; (*journey*) intraprendere.
embarkation [embârkā'shən] *n* imbarco.
embarkation card *n* carta d'imbarco.
embarrass [embar'əs] *vt* imbarazzare; **to be ~ed** essere imbarazzato(a).
embarrassing [embar'əsing] *a* imbarazzante.
embarrassment [embar'əsmənt] *n* imbarazzo.
embassy [em'bəsē] *n* ambasciata; **the Italian E~** l'ambasciata d'Italia.
embed [embed'] *vt* conficcare; incastrare.
embellish [embel'ish] *vt* abbellire; **to ~ (with)** (*fig: story, truth*) infiorare (con).
embers [em'bûrz] *npl* braci *fpl*.
embezzle [embez'əl] *vt* appropriarsi indebitamente di.
embezzlement [embez'əlmənt] *n* appropriazione *f* indebita, malversazione *f*.
embezzler [embez'lûr] *n* malversatore/trice.
embitter [embit'ûr] *vt* amareggiare; inasprire.
emblem [em'bləm] *n* emblema *m*.
embodiment [embâd'ēmənt] *n* personificazione *f*, incarnazione *f*.
embody [embâd'ē] *vt* (*features*) racchiudere, comprendere; (*ideas*) dar forma concreta a, esprimere.
embolden [embōl'dən] *vt* incitare.
embolism [em'bəlizəm] *n* embolia.
embossed [embôst'] *a* in rilievo; goffrato(a); **~ with ...** con in rilievo ....
embrace [embrās'] *vt* abbracciare; (*include*) comprendere ♦ *vi* abbracciarsi ♦ *n* abbraccio.
embroider [embroi'dûr] *vt* ricamare; (*fig: story*) abbellire.
embroidery [embroi'dûrē] *n* ricamo.
embroil [embroil'] *vt*: **to become ~ed (in sth)** restare invischiato(a) (in qc).
embryo [em'brēō] *n* (*also fig*) embrione *m*.
emcee [em'sē'] *n* (*US col*) presentatore/trice.
emend [imend'] *vt* (*text*) correggere, emendare.
emerald [em'ûrəld] *n* smeraldo.
emerge [imûrj'] *vi* apparire, sorgere; **it ~s that** (*Brit*) risulta che.
emergence [imûr'jəns] *n* apparizione *f*; (*of nation*) nascita.
emergency [imûr'jənsē] *n* emergenza; **in an ~** in caso di emergenza; **to declare a state of ~** dichiarare lo stato di emergenza.
emergency exit *n* uscita di sicurezza.
emergency flasher [imûr'jənsē flash'ûr] *n* (*US AUT*) luci *fpl* di emergenza.
emergency landing *n* atterraggio forzato.
emergency lane *n* (*US AUT*) corsia d'emergenza.

emergency road service *n* (*US*) servizio riparazioni.

emergency service *n* servizio di pronto intervento.

emergency stop *n* (*AUT*) frenata improvvisa.

emergent [imûr'jənt] *a*: ~ **nation** paese *m* in via di sviluppo.

emery board [em'ûrē bōrd] *n* limetta di carta smerigliata.

emery paper [em'ûrē pāpûr] *n* carta smerigliata.

emetic [imet'ik] *n* emetico.

emigrant [em'əgrənt] *n* emigrante *m/f*.

emigrate [em'əgrāt] *vi* emigrare.

emigration [eməgrā'shən] *n* emigrazione *f*.

émigré [emigrā'] *n* emigrato/a.

eminence [em'ənəns] *n* eminenza.

eminent [em'ənənt] *a* eminente.

eminently [em'ənəntlē] *ad* assolutamente, perfettamente.

emirate [emē'rit] *n* emirato.

emission [imish'ən] *n* emissione *f*.

emit [imit'] *vt* emettere.

emolument [imâl'yəmənt] *n* (*often pl: formal*) emolumento.

emotion [imō'shən] *n* emozione *f*; (*love, jealousy etc*) sentimento.

emotional [imō'shənəl] *a* (*person*) emotivo(a); (*scene*) commovente; (*tone, speech*) carico(a) d'emozione.

emotionally [imō'shənəlē] *ad* (*behave, be involved*) sentimentalmente; (*speak*) con emozione; ~ **disturbed** con turbe emotive.

emotive [imō'tiv] *a* emotivo(a); ~ **power** capacità di commuovere.

empathy [em'pəthē] *n* immedesimazione *f*; **to feel** ~ **with sb** immedesimarsi con i sentimenti di qn.

emperor [em'pûrûr] *n* imperatore *m*.

emphasis, *pl* **-ases** [em'fəsis, -fəsez] *n* enfasi *f inv*; importanza; **to lay** *or* **place** ~ **on sth** (*fig*) mettere in risalto *or* in evidenza qc; **the** ~ **is on sport** si dà molta importanza allo sport.

emphasize [em'fəsīz] *vt* (*word, point*) sottolineare; (*feature*) mettere in evidenza.

emphatic [əmfat'ik] *a* (*strong*) vigoroso(a); (*unambiguous, clear*) netto(a); categorico(a).

emphatically [əmfat'iklē] *ad* vigorosamente, nettamente.

emphysema [emfisē'mə] *n* (*MED*) enfisema *m*.

empire [em'pīûr] *n* impero.

empirical [empir'ikəl] *a* empirico(a).

employ [emploi'] *vt* (*make use of: thing, method, person*) impiegare, servirsi di; (*give job to*) dare lavoro a, impiegare; **he's ~ed in a bank** lavora in banca.

employee [emploi'ē] *n* impiegato/a.

employer [emploi'ûr] *n* principale *m/f*, datore *m* di lavoro.

employment [emploi'mənt] *n* impiego; **to find** ~ trovare impiego *or* lavoro; **without** ~ disoccupato(a); **place of** ~ posto di lavoro.

employment agency *n* agenzia di collocamento.

empower [empou'ûr] *vt*: **to** ~ **sb to do** concedere autorità a qn di fare.

empress [em'pris] *n* imperatrice *f*.

emptiness [emp'tēnis] *n* vuoto.

empty [emp'tē] *a* vuoto(a); (*street, area*) deserto(a); (*threat, promise*) vano(a) ♦ *n* (*bottle*) vuoto ♦ *vt* vuotare ♦ *vi* vuotarsi; (*liquid*) scaricarsi; **on an** ~ **stomach** a stomaco vuoto; **to** ~ **into** (*river*) gettarsi in.

empty-handed [emp'tēhan'did] *a* a mani vuote.

empty-headed [emp'tēhed'id] *a* sciocco(a).

EMT *n abbr* = *emergency medical technician*.

emulate [em'yəlāt] *vt* emulare.

emulsion [imul'shən] *n* emulsione *f*; (*also:* ~ **paint**) colore *m* a tempera.

enable [enā'bəl] *vt*: **to** ~ **sb to do** permettere a qn di fare.

enact [enakt'] *vt* (*law*) emanare; (*play, scene*) rappresentare.

enamel [inam'əl] *n* smalto.

enamel paint *n* vernice *f* a smalto.

enamored, (*Brit*) **enamoured** [enam'ûrd] *a*: ~ **of** innamorato(a) di.

encampment [enkamp'mənt] *n* accampamento.

encased [enkāst'] *a*: ~ **in** racchiuso(a) in; rivestito(a) di.

enchant [enchant'] *vt* incantare; (*subj: magic spell*) catturare.

enchanting [enchan'ting] *a* incantevole, affascinante.

encircle [ensûr'kəl] *vt* accerchiare.

enc(l). *abbr* (*on letters etc*: = *enclosed, enclosure*) all., alleg.

enclose [enklōz'] *vt* (*land*) circondare, recingere; (*letter etc*): **to** ~ (**with**) allegare (con); **please find ~d** trovi qui accluso.

enclosure [enklō'zhûr] *n* recinto; (*COMM*) allegato.

encoder [enkō'dûr] *n* (*COMPUT*) codificatore *m*.

encompass [enkum'pəs] *vt* comprendere.

encore [âng'kôr] *excl, n* bis (*m inv*).

encounter [enkoun'tûr] *n* incontro ♦ *vt* incontrare.

encourage [enkûr'ij] *vt* incoraggiare; (*industry, growth etc*) favorire; **to** ~ **sb to do sth** incoraggiare qn a fare qc.

encouragement [enkûr'ijmənt] *n* incoraggiamento.

encouraging [enkûr'ijing] *a* incoraggiante.

encroach [enkrōch'] *vi*: **to** ~ (**up**)**on** (*rights*) usurpare; (*time*) abusare di; (*land*) oltrepassare i limiti di.

encrusted [enkrus'tid] *a*: ~ **with** incrostato(a)

di.

encumbered [ɛnkum'bûrd] *a*: **to be ~ (with)** essere carico(a) di.

encyclopedia [ɛnsīkləpē'dēə] *n* enciclopedia.

end [ɛnd] *n* fine *f*; (*aim*) fine *m*; (*of table*) bordo estremo; (*of line, rope etc*) estremità *f inv*; (*of pointed object*) punta; (*of town*) parte *f* ♦ *vt* finire; (*also*: **bring to an ~, put an ~ to**) mettere fine a ♦ *vi* finire; **from ~ to ~** da un'estremità all'altra; **to come to an ~** arrivare alla fine, finire; **to be at an ~** essere finito; **in the ~** alla fine; **at the ~ of the street** in fondo alla strada; **at the ~ of the day** (*Brit fig*) in fin dei conti; **on ~** (*object*) ritto(a); **to stand on ~** (*hair*) rizzarsi; **for 5 hours on ~** per 5 ore di fila; **for hours on ~** per ore e ore; **to this ~, with this ~ in view** a questo fine; **to ~ (with)** concludere (con).

end up *vi*: **to ~ up in** finire in.

endanger [ɛndān'jûr] *vt* mettere in pericolo; **an ~ed species** una specie in via di estinzione.

endear [ɛndēr'] *vt*: **to ~ o.s. to sb** accattivarsi le simpatie di qn.

endearing [ɛndēr'ing] *a* accattivante.

endearment [ɛndēr'mənt] *n*: **to whisper ~s** sussurrare tenerezze; **term of ~** vezzeggiativo, parola affettuosa.

endeavor, endeavour [ɛndev'ûr] *n* sforzo, tentativo ♦ *vi*: **to ~ to do** cercare *or* sforzarsi di fare.

endemic [ɛndem'ik] *a* endemico(a).

ending [ɛn'ding] *n* fine *f*, conclusione *f*; (*LING*) desinenza.

endive [ɛn'dīv] *n* (*curly*) indivia (riccia); (*smooth, flat*) indivia belga.

endless [ɛnd'lis] *a* senza fine; (*patience, resources*) infinito(a); (*possibilities*) illimitato(a).

endorse [ɛndôrs'] *vt* (*check*) girare; (*approve*) approvare, appoggiare.

endorsee [ɛndôrsē'] *n* giratario/a.

endorsement [ɛndôrs'mənt] *n* (*approval*) approvazione *f*; (*signature*) firma; (*Brit: on driver's license*) contravvenzione registrata sulla patente.

endorser [ɛndôrs'ûr] *n* girante *m/f*.

endow [ɛndou'] *vt* (*prize*) istituire; (*hospital*) fondare; (*provide with money*) devolvere denaro a; (*equip*): **to ~ with** fornire di, dotare di.

endowment [ɛndou'mənt] *n* istituzione *f*, fondazione *f*; (*amount*) donazione *f*.

endowment insurance *n* assicurazione *f* mista.

end product *n* (*INDUSTRY*) prodotto finito; (*fig*) risultato.

end result *n* risultato finale.

endurable [ɛndoo'rəbəl] *a* sopportabile.

endurance [ɛndoo'rəns] *n* resistenza; pa-

zienza.

endurance test *n* prova di resistenza.

endure [ɛndoor'] *vt* sopportare, resistere a ♦ *vi* durare.

end user *n* (*COMPUT*) consumatore(trice) effettivo(a).

enema [ɛn'əmə] *n* (*MED*) clistere *m*.

enemy [ɛn'əmē] *a, n* nemico(a); **to make an ~ of sb** inimicarsi qn.

energetic [ɛnûrjet'ik] *a* energico(a); attivo(a).

energy [ɛn'ûrjē] *n* energia; **Department of E~** Ministero dell'Energia.

energy crisis *n* crisi *f* energetica.

energy-saving [ɛn'ûrjēsāving] *a* (*policy*) del risparmio energetico; (*device*) che risparmia energia.

enervating [ɛn'ûrvāting] *a* debilitante.

enforce [ɛnfôrs'] *vt* (*LAW*) applicare, far osservare.

enforced [ɛnfôrst'] *a* forzato(a).

enfranchise [ɛnfran'chīz] *vt* (*give vote to*) concedere il diritto di voto a; (*set free*) affrancare.

engage [ɛngāj'] *vt* (*hire*) assumere; (*lawyer*) incaricare; (*attention, interest*) assorbire; (*MIL*) attaccare; (*TECH*): **to ~ gear/the clutch** (*Brit*) innestare la marcia/la frizione ♦ *vi* (*TECH*) ingranare; **to ~ in** impegnarsi in; **he is ~d in research/a survey** si occupa di ricerca/di un'inchiesta; **to ~ sb in conversation** attaccare conversazione con qn.

engaged [ɛngājd'] *a* (*betrothed*) fidanzato(a); (*Brit: busy, in use*) occupato(a); **to get ~** fidanzarsi.

engaged tone *n* (*Brit TEL*) segnale *m* di occupato.

engagement [ɛngāj'mənt] *n* impegno, obbligo; appuntamento; (*to marry*) fidanzamento; (*MIL*) combattimento; **I have a previous ~** ho già un impegno.

engagement ring *n* anello di fidanzamento.

engaging [ɛngā'jing] *a* attraente.

engender [ɛnjen'dûr] *vt* produrre, causare.

engine [ɛn'jən] *n* (*AUT*) motore *m*; (*RAIL*) locomotiva.

engine driver *n* (*Brit: of train*) macchinista *m*.

engineer [ɛnjənēr'] *n* ingegnere *m*; (*US RAIL*) macchinista *m*; (*Brit: for domestic appliances*) tecnico; **civil/mechanical ~** ingegnere civile/meccanico.

engineering [ɛnjənēr'ing] *n* ingegneria ♦ *cpd* (*works, factory, worker etc*) metalmeccanico(a).

engine failure *n* guasto al motore.

engine trouble *n* panne *f*.

England [ing'glənd] *n* Inghilterra.

English [ing'glish] *a* inglese ♦ *n* (*LING*) inglese *m*; **the ~** *npl* gli Inglesi ♦ **to be an ~ speaker** essere anglofono(a).

English Channel *n*: the ~ il Canale della Manica.
English horn *n* (*US*) corno inglese.
Englishman [ing'glishmən], **Englishwoman** [ing'glishwo͞omən] *n* inglese *m/f*.
English-speaking [ing'glishpē'king] *a* di lingua inglese.
engrave [engrāv'] *vt* incidere.
engraving [engrā'ving] *n* incisione *f*.
engrossed [engrōst'] *a*: ~ **in** assorbito(a) da, preso(a) da.
engulf [engulf'] *vt* inghiottire.
enhance [enhans'] *vt* accrescere; (*position, reputation*) migliorare.
enigma [ənig'mə] *n* enigma *m*.
enigmatic [enigmat'ik] *a* enigmatico(a).
enjoy [enjoi'] *vt* godere; (*have: success, fortune*) avere; (*have benefit of: health*) godere (di); **I ~ dancing** mi piace ballare; **to ~ o.s.** godersela, divertirsi.
enjoyable [enjoi'əbəl] *a* piacevole.
enjoyment [enjoi'mənt] *n* piacere *m*, godimento.
enlarge [enlârj'] *vt* ingrandire ♦ *vi*: **to ~ on** (*subject*) dilungarsi su.
enlarged [enlârjd'] *a* (*edition*) ampliato(a); (*MED: organ, gland*) ingrossato(a).
enlargement [enlârj'mənt] *n* (*PHOT*) ingrandimento.
enlighten [enlīt'ən] *vt* illuminare; dare chiarimenti a.
enlightened [enlīt'ənd] *a* illuminato(a).
enlightening [enlīt'əning] *a* istruttivo(a).
enlightenment [enlīt'ənmənt] *n* progresso culturale; chiarimenti *mpl*; (*HISTORY*): **the E~** l'Illuminismo.
enlist [enlist'] *vt* arruolare; (*support*) procurare ♦ *vi* arruolarsi; **~ed man** (*US MIL*) soldato semplice.
enliven [enlī'vən] *vt* (*people*) rallegrare; (*events*) ravvivare.
enmity [en'mitē] *n* inimicizia.
ennoble [ennō'bəl] *vt* nobilitare; (*with title*) conferire un titolo nobiliare a.
enormity [inôr'mitē] *n* enormità *f inv*.
enormous [inôr'məs] *a* enorme.
enormously [inôr'məslē] *ad* enormemente.
enough [inuf'] *a, n*: ~ **time/books** assai tempo/libri; **have you got ~?** ne ha abbastanza *or* a sufficienza? ♦ *ad*: **big ~** abbastanza grande; **he has not worked ~** non ha lavorato abbastanza; **~!** basta!; **it's hot ~ (as it is)!** fa abbastanza caldo così!; **will $5 be ~?** bastano 5 dollari?; **that's ~** basta; **I've had ~!** non ne posso più!; **he was kind ~ to lend me the money** è stato così gentile da prestarmi i soldi; **... which, funnily ~ ...** che, strano a dirsi.
enquire [enkwī'ûr] *vt, vi* = **inquire**.
enrage [enrāj'] *vt* fare arrabbiare.
enrich [enrich'] *vt* arricchire.

enroll, (*Brit*) **enrol** [enrōl'] *vt* iscrivere; (*at university*) immatricolare ♦ *vi* iscriversi.
enrollment [enrōl'mənt] *n* iscrizione *f*.
en route [ôn ro͞ot'] *ad*: ~ **for/from/to** in viaggio per/da/a.
ensconced [enskânst'] *a*: ~ **in** ben sistemato(a) in.
ensemble [ânsâm'bəl] *n* (*MUS*) ensemble *m inv*.
enshrine [enshrīn'] *vt* conservare come una reliquia.
ensign [en'sən] *n* (*NAUT*) bandiera.
enslave [enslāv'] *vt* fare schiavo.
ensue [enso͞o'] *vi* seguire, risultare.
ensure [ensho͞or'] *vt* assicurare; garantire; **to ~ that** assicurarsi che.
ENT *n abbr* (*MED*: = *Ear, Nose & Throat*) O.R.L.
entail [entāl'] *vt* comportare.
entangle [entang'gəl] *vt* (*thread etc*) impigliare; **to become ~d in sth** (*fig*) rimanere impegolato in qc.
enter [en'tûr] *vt* (*gen*) entrare in; (*club*) associarsi a; (*profession*) intraprendere; (*army*) arruolarsi in; (*competition*) partecipare a; (*sb for a competition*) iscrivere; (*write down*) registrare; (*COMPUT: data*) introdurre, inserire ♦ *vi* entrare.
enter for *vt fus* iscriversi a.
enter into *vt fus* (*explanation*) cominciare a dare; (*debate*) partecipare a; (*agreement*) concludere; (*negotiations*) prendere parte a.
enter (up)on *vt fus* cominciare.
enteritis [entərī'tis] *n* enterite *f*.
enterprise [en'tûrprīz] *n* (*undertaking, company*) impresa; (*spirit*) iniziativa.
enterprising [en'tûrprīzing] *a* intraprendente.
entertain [entûrtān'] *vt* divertire; (*invite*) ricevere; (*idea, plan*) nutrire.
entertainer [entûrtān'ûr] *n* comico/a.
entertaining [entûrtā'ning] *a* divertente ♦ *n*: **to do a lot of ~** avere molti ospiti.
entertainment [entûrtān'mənt] *n* (*amusement*) divertimento; (*show*) spettacolo.
entertainment allowance *n* spese *fpl* di rappresentanza.
enthralled [enthrôld'] *a* affascinato(a).
enthralling [enthrôl'ing] *a* avvincente.
enthuse [entho͞oz'] *vi*: **to ~ (about** *or* **over)** entusiasmarsi (per).
enthusiasm [entho͞o'zēəzəm] *n* entusiasmo.
enthusiast [entho͞o'zēast] *n* entusiasta *m/f*; **a jazz** *etc* ~ un appassionato di jazz *etc*.
enthusiastic [entho͞ozēas'tik] *a* entusiasta, entusiastico(a); **to be ~ about sth/sb** essere appassionato di qc/entusiasta di qn.
entice [entīs'] *vt* allettare, sedurre.
enticing [entī'sing] *a* allettante.
entire [entī'ûr] *a* intero(a).
entirely [entīûr'lē] *ad* completamente, interamente.

entirety [entīr'tē] *n*: **in its ~** nel suo complesso.

entitle [entīt'əl] *vt* (*give right*): **to ~ sb to** sth/to do dare diritto a qn a qc/a fare.

entitled [entīt'əld] *a* (*book*) che si intitola; **to be ~ to sth/to do sth** avere diritto a qc/a fare qc.

entity [en'titē] *n* entità *f inv*.

entrails [en'trālz] *npl* interiora *fpl*.

entrance *n* [en'trəns] entrata, ingresso; (*of person*) entrata ♦ *vt* [entrans'] incantare, rapire; **to gain ~ to** (*university etc*) essere ammesso a.

entrance examination *n* (*to school*) esame *m* di ammissione.

entrance fee *n* tassa d'iscrizione; (*to museum etc*) prezzo d'ingresso.

entrance ramp *n* (*US AUT*) rampa di accesso.

entrancing [entrans'ing] *a* incantevole.

entrant [en'trənt] *n* partecipante *m/f*; concorrente *m/f*; (*Brit*: *in exam*) candidato/a.

entreat [entrēt'] *vt* supplicare.

entreaty [entrē'tē] *n* supplica, preghiera.

entrée [ântrā'] *n* (*CULIN*) prima portata.

entrenched [entrencht'] *a* radicato(a).

entrepreneur [ântrəprənûr'] *n* imprenditore *m*.

entrepreneurial [ântrəprənûr'ēəl] *a* imprenditoriale.

entrust [entrust'] *vt*: **to ~ sth to** affidare qc a.

entry [en'trē] *n* entrata; (*way in*) entrata, ingresso; (*in dictionary*) voce *f*; (*in diary, ship's log*) annotazione *f*; (*in account book, ledger, list*) registrazione *f*; **"no ~"** "vietato l'ingresso"; (*AUT*) "divieto di accesso"; **single/double ~ book-keeping** partita semplice/doppia.

entry form *n* modulo d'iscrizione.

entry phone *n* (*Brit*) citofono.

entwine [entwīn'] *vt* intrecciare.

enumerate [inōō'mûrāt] *vt* enumerare.

enunciate [inun'sēāt] *vt* enunciare; pronunciare.

envelop [envel'əp] *vt* avvolgere, avviluppare.

envelope [en'vəlōp] *n* busta.

enviable [en'vēəbəl] *a* invidiabile.

envious [en'vēəs] *a* invidioso(a).

environment [envī'rənmənt] *n* ambiente *m*; **Department of the E~** (*Brit*) ≈ Ministero dell'Ambiente.

environmental [envīrənmen'təl] *a* ecologico(a); ambientale; **~ studies** (*in school etc*) ecologia.

Environmental Protection Agency (EPA) *n* (*US*) ≈ Ministero dell'Ambiente.

environment-friendly [envī'rənməntfrend'lē] *a* che non danneggia l'ambiente.

envisage [enviz'ij] *vt* immaginare; prevedere.

envision [envizh'ən] *vt* concepire, prevedere.

envoy [en'voi] *n* inviato/a.

envy [en'vē] *n* invidia ♦ *vt* invidiare; **to ~ sb sth** invidiare qn per qc.

enzyme [en'zīm] *n* enzima *m*.

eon [ē'ân] *n* (*US*) eternità *f inv*.

EPA *n abbr* (*US*) *see* **Environmental Protection Agency**.

ephemeral [ifem'ûrəl] *a* effimero(a).

epic [ep'ik] *n* poema *m* epico ♦ *a* epico(a).

epicenter, (*Brit*) **epicentre** [ep'isentûr] *n* epicentro.

epidemic [epidem'ik] *n* epidemia.

epilepsy [ep'əlepsē] *n* epilessia.

epileptic [epəlep'tik] *a*, *n* epilettico(a).

epilogue [ep'əlôg] *n* epilogo.

Epiphany [ēpif'ənē] *n* Epifania.

episcopal [ipis'kəpəl] *a* episcopale.

episode [ep'isōd] *n* episodio.

epistle [ipis'əl] *n* epistola.

epitaph [ep'itaf] *n* epitaffio.

epithet [ep'əthet] *n* epiteto.

epitome [ipit'əmē] *n* epitome *f*; quintessenza.

epitomize [ipit'əmīz] *vt* (*fig*) incarnare.

epoch [ep'ək] *n* epoca.

epoch-making [ep'əkmāking] *a* che fa epoca.

eponymous [epân'əməs] *a* dello stesso nome.

equable [ek'wəbəl] *a* uniforme; (*climate*) costante; (*character*) equilibrato(a).

equal [ē'kwəl] *a*, *n* uguale (*m/f*) ♦ *vt* uguagliare; **~ to** (*task*) all'altezza di.

Equal Employment Opportunity Commission, (*Brit*) **Equal Opportunities Commission** *n* commissione contro discriminazioni sessuali o razziali nel mondo del lavoro.

equality [ikwâl'itē] *n* uguaglianza.

equalize [ē'kwəlīz] *vt*, *vi* pareggiare.

equalizer [ē'kwəlīzûr] *n* punto del pareggio.

equally [ē'kwəlē] *ad* ugualmente; **they are ~ clever** sono intelligenti allo stesso modo.

equal(s) sign [ē'kwəl(z) sīn] *n* segno d'uguaglianza.

equanimity [ēkwənim'itē] *n* serenità.

equate [ikwāt'] *vt*: **to ~ sth with** considerare qc uguale a; (*compare*) paragonare qc con; **to ~ A to B** mettere in equazione A e B.

equation [ikwā'zhən] *n* (*MATH*) equazione *f*.

equator [ikwā'tûr] *n* equatore *m*.

Equatorial Guinea [ēkwətôr'ēəl gin'ē] *n* Guinea Equatoriale.

equestrian [ikwes'trēən] *a* equestre ♦ *n* cavaliere/amazzone.

equilibrium [ēkwəlib'rēəm] *n* equilibrio.

equinox [ē'kwənâks] *n* equinozio.

equip [ikwip'] *vt* equipaggiare, attrezzare; **to ~ sb/sth with** fornire qn/qc di; **~ped with** (*machinery etc*) dotato(a) di; **he is well ~ped for the job** ha i requisiti necessari per quel lavoro.

equipment [ikwip'mənt] *n* attrezzatura; (*elec-*

trical etc) apparecchiatura.
equitable [ɛk'witəbəl] *a* equo(a), giusto(a).
equities [ɛk'witēz] *npl* (*Brit COMM*) azioni *fpl* ordinarie.
equity [ɛk'witē] *n* equità.
equity capital *n* capitale *m* azionario.
equivalent [ikwiv'ələnt] *a, n* equivalente (*m*); **to be ~ to** equivalere a.
equivocal [ikwiv'əkəl] *a* equivoco(a); (*open to suspicion*) dubbio(a).
equivocate [ikwiv'əkāt] *vi* esprimersi in modo equivoco.
equivocation [ikwivəkā'shən] *n* parole *fpl* equivoche.
ER *abbr* (*Brit*) = *Elizabeth Regina*.
ERA *n abbr* (*US POL*) = *Equal Rights Amendment*.
era [ē'rə] *n* era, età *f inv*.
eradicate [irad'ikāt] *vt* sradicare.
erase [irās'] *vt* cancellare.
eraser [irā'sûr] *n* gomma.
erect [irɛkt'] *a* eretto(a) ♦ *vt* costruire; (*monument, tent*) alzare.
erection [irɛk'shən] *n* (*also PHYSIOL*) erezione *f*; (*of building*) costruzione *f*; (*of machinery*) montaggio.
ergonomics [ûrgənâm'iks] *n* ergonomia.
ERISA *n abbr* (*US*: = *Employee Retirement Income Security Act*) *legge relativa al pensionamento statale.*
ermine [ûr'min] *n* ermellino.
erode [irōd'] *vt* erodere; (*metal*) corrodere.
erosion [irō'zhən] *n* erosione *f*.
erotic [irât'ik] *a* erotico(a).
eroticism [irât'isizəm] *n* erotismo.
err [ûr] *vi* errare; (*REL*) peccare.
errand [är'ənd] *n* commissione *f*; **to run ~s** fare commissioni; **~ of mercy** atto di carità.
errand boy *n* fattorino.
erratic [irat'ik] *a* imprevedibile; (*person, mood*) incostante.
erroneous [irō'nēəs] *a* erroneo(a).
error [är'ûr] *n* errore *m; typing/spelling ~** errore di battitura/di ortografia; **in ~** per errore; **~s and omissions excepted** salvo errori ed omissioni.
error message *n* (*COMPUT*) messaggio di errore.
erstwhile [ûrst'hwīl] *ad* allora, un tempo ♦ *a* di allora.
erudite [är'yōōdīt] *a* erudito(a).
erupt [irupt'] *vi* erompere; (*volcano*) mettersi (*or* essere) in eruzione.
eruption [irup'shən] *n* eruzione *f*; (*of anger, violence*) esplosione *f*.
ESA *n abbr* (= *European Space Agency*) ESA *f*.
escalate [ɛs'kəlāt] *vi* intensificarsi; (*costs*) salire.
escalation [ɛskəlā'shən] *n* escalation *f*; (*of prices*) aumento.

escalation clause [ɛskəlā'shən klôz] *n* clausola di revisione.
escalator [ɛs'kəlātûr] *n* scala mobile.
escapade [ɛs'kəpād] *n* scappatella; avventura.
escape [ɛskāp'] *n* evasione *f*; fuga; (*of gas etc*) fuga, fuoriuscita ♦ *vi* fuggire; (*from jail*) evadere, scappare; (*fig*) sfuggire; (*leak*) uscire ♦ *vt* sfuggire a; **to ~ from sb** sfuggire a qn; **to ~ to** (*another place*) fuggire in; (*freedom, safety*) fuggire verso; **to ~ notice** passare inosservato(a).
escape artist *n* mago della fuga.
escape clause *n* clausola scappatoia.
escape hatch *n* (*in submarine, space rocket*) portello di sicurezza.
escape key *n* (*COMPUT*) tasto di escape, tasto per cambio di codice.
escape route *n* percorso della fuga.
escapism [ɛskā'pizəm] *n* evasione *f* (dalla realtà).
escapist [ɛskā'pist] *a* d'evasione ♦ *n* persona che cerca di evadere dalla realtà.
escapologist [ɛskəpâl'əjist] *n* (*Brit*) = **escape artist**.
escarpment [ɛskârp'mənt] *n* scarpata.
eschew [ɛschōō'] *vt* evitare.
escort *n* [ɛs'kôrt] scorta; (*to dance etc*): **her ~** il suo cavaliere; **his ~** la sua dama ♦ *vt* [ɛskôrt'] scortare; accompagnare.
escort agency *n* agenzia di hostess.
Eskimo [ɛs'kəmō] *a* eschimese ♦ *n* eschimese *m/f*; (*LING*) eschimese *m*.
ESL *n abbr* (*SCOL*) = *English as a Second Language*.
esophagus [isâf'əgəs] *n* (*US*) esofago.
esoteric [ɛsətär'ik] *a* esoterico(a).
ESP *n abbr see* **extrasensory perception**.
esp. *abbr* (= *especially*) spec.
especially [ɛspesh'əlē] *ad* specialmente; (*above all*) soprattutto; (*specifically*) espressamente; (*particularly*) particolarmente.
espionage [ɛs'pēənâzh] *n* spionaggio.
esplanade [ɛs'plənâd] *n* lungomare *m*.
espouse [ɛspouz'] *vt* abbracciare.
Esquire [ɛs'kwiûr] *n* (*Brit*: *abbr* **Esq.**): **J. Brown, ~** Signor J. Brown.
essay [ɛs'ā] *n* (*SCOL*) composizione *f*; (*LITERATURE*) saggio.
essence [ɛs'əns] *n* essenza; **in ~** in sostanza; **speed is of the ~** la velocità è di estrema importanza.
essential [əsen'chəl] *a* essenziale; (*basic*) fondamentale ♦ *n* elemento essenziale; **it is ~ that** è essenziale che + *sub*.
essentially [əsen'chəlē] *ad* essenzialmente.
EST *abbr* (*US*: = *Eastern Standard Time*) *fuso orario*.
est. *abbr* = *established*; *estimate(d)*.
establish [əstab'lish] *vt* stabilire; (*business*) mettere su; (*one's power etc*) confermare;

(*prove*: *fact, identity, sb's innocence*) dimostrare.

establishment [əstab'lishmənt] n stabilimento; (*business*) azienda; **the E~** la classe dirigente; l'establishment m; **a teaching ~** un istituto d'istruzione.

estate [əstāt'] n proprietà f *inv*; (*LAW*) beni mpl, patrimonio; (*Brit*: *also*: **housing ~**) complesso edilizio.

estate agent n (*Brit*) agente m immobiliare.

estate car n (*Brit*) giardiniera.

esteem [əstēm'] n stima ♦ vt considerare; stimare; **I hold him in high ~** gode di tutta la mia stima.

esthetic [esthet'ik] a (*US*) estetico(a).

estimate n [es'təmit] stima; (*COMM*) preventivo ♦ vb [est'əmāt] vt stimare, valutare; **to give sb an ~ of** fare a qn una valutazione approssimativa (*or* un preventivo) di; **at a rough ~** approssimativamente.

estimation [estəmā'shən] n stima; opinione f; **in my ~** a mio giudizio, a mio avviso.

estimator [es'təmātûr] n perito stimatore.

Estonia [estō'nēə] n Estonia.

estranged [estrānjd'] a separato(a).

estrangement [estrānj'mənt] n alienazione f.

estrogen [es'trəjən] n (*US*) estrogeno.

estuary [es'chōōārē] n estuario.

ETA n abbr (= *estimated time of arrival*) ora di arrivo prevista.

et al. [et âl] abbr (= *et alii*: *and others*) ed altri.

etc. abbr (= *et cetera*) ecc., etc.

etch [ech] vt incidere all'acquaforte.

etching [ech'ing] n acquaforte f.

ETD n abbr (= *estimated time of departure*) ora di partenza prevista.

eternal [itûr'nəl] a eterno(a).

eternity [itûr'nitē] n eternità.

ether [ē'thûr] n etere m.

ethereal [ithēr'ēəl] a etereo(a).

ethical [eth'ikəl] a etico(a), morale.

ethics [eth'iks] n etica ♦ npl morale f.

Ethiopia [ēthēō'pēə] n Etiopia.

Ethiopian [ēthēō'pēən] a, n etiope (m/f).

ethnic [eth'nik] a etnico(a).

ethnology [ethnāl'əjē] n etnologia.

ethos [ē'thâs] n (*of culture, group*) norma di vita.

etiquette [et'əkit] n etichetta.

ETV n abbr (*US*) = *Educational Television*.

etymology [etəmāl'əjē] n etimologia.

eucalyptus [yōōkəlip'təs] n eucalipto.

eulogy [yōō'ləjē] n elogio.

euphemism [yōō'fəmizəm] n eufemismo.

euphemistic [yōōfəmis'tik] a eufemistico(a).

euphoria [yōōfôr'ēə] n euforia.

Eurasia [yōōrā'zhə] n Eurasia.

Eurasian [yōōrā'zhən] a, n eurasiano(a).

Euratom [yōōrat'əm] n abbr (= *European Atomic Energy Community*) EURATOM f.

Euro... *prefix* euro....

Eurocheque [yōō'rōchek] n (*Brit*) eurochèque m *inv*.

Eurocrat [yōō'rəkrat] n eurocrate m/f.

Eurodollar [yōō'rōdâlûr] n eurodollaro.

Europe [yōō'rəp] n Europa.

European [yōōrəpē'ən] a, n europeo(a).

European Court of Justice n Corte f di Giustizia della Comunità Europea.

euthanasia [yōōthənā'zhə] n eutanasia.

evacuate [ivak'yōōāt] vt evacuare.

evacuation [ivakyōōā'shən] n evacuazione f.

evade [ivād'] vt eludere; (*duties etc*) sottrarsi a.

evaluate [ival'yōōāt] vt valutare.

evangelist [ivan'jəlist] n evangelista m.

evangelize [ivan'jəliz] vt evangelizzare.

evaporate [ivap'ərāt] vi evaporare ♦ vt far evaporare.

evaporated milk [ivap'ərātid milk'] n latte m concentrato.

evaporation [ivapərā'shən] n evaporazione f.

evasion [ivā'zhən] n evasione f.

evasive [ivā'siv] a evasivo(a).

eve [ēv] n: **on the ~ of** alla vigilia di.

even [ē'vən] a regolare; (*number*) pari *inv* ♦ ad anche, perfino; **~ if, ~ though** anche se; **~ more** ancora di più; **he loves her ~ more** la ama ancora di più; **~ faster** ancora più veloce; **~ so** ciò nonostante; **not ~ ...** nemmeno ...; **to break ~** finire in pari or alla pari; **to get ~ with sb** dare la pari a qn.

even out vi pareggiare.

evening [ēv'ning] n sera; (*as duration, event*) serata; **in the ~** la sera; **this ~** stasera, questa sera; **tomorrow/yesterday ~** domani/ieri sera.

evening class n corso serale.

evening dress n (*woman's*) abito da sera; **in ~** (*man*) in abito scuro; (*woman*) in abito lungo.

evenly [ē'vənlē] ad (*distribute, space, spread*) uniformemente; (*divide*) in parti uguali.

evensong [ē'vənsông] n ≈ vespro.

event [ivent'] n avvenimento; (*SPORT*) gara; **in the ~ of** in caso di; **in any ~** in ogni caso; **in the ~** in realtà, di fatto; **in the course of ~s** nel corso degli eventi.

eventful [ivent'fəl] a denso(a) di eventi.

eventual [iven'chōōəl] a finale.

eventuality [ivenchōōal'itē] n possibilità f *inv*, eventualità f *inv*.

eventually [iven'chōōəlē] ad finalmente.

ever [ev'ûr] ad mai; (*at all times*) sempre; **for ~** per sempre; **the best ~** il migliore che ci sia mai stato; **hardly ~** non ... quasi mai; **did you ~ meet him?** l'ha mai incontrato?; **have you ~ been there?** c'è mai stato?; **~ so pretty** così bello(a); **thank you ~ so much** grazie mille; **yours ~** (*Brit: in letters*) sempre tuo; **~ since** ad da allora ♦ cj sin da quando.

Everest [ev'ûrist] *n* (*also*: **Mount** ~) Everest *m*.

evergreen [ev'ûrgrēn] *n* sempreverde *m*.

everlasting [evûrlas'ting] *a* eterno(a).

every [ev'rē] *a* ogni; ~ **day** tutti i giorni, ogni giorno; ~ **other/third day** ogni due/tre giorni; ~ **other car** una macchina su due; ~ **now and then** ogni tanto, di quando in quando; **I have** ~ **confidence in him** ho piena fiducia in lui.

everybody [ev'rēbâdē] *pronoun* ognuno, tutti *pl*; ~ **else** tutti gli altri; ~ **knows about it** lo sanno tutti.

everyday [ev'rēdā] *a* quotidiano(a); di ogni giorno; (*use, occurrence, experience*) comune; (*expression*) di uso corrente.

everyone [ev'rēwun] = **everybody**.

everything [ev'rēthing] *pronoun* tutto, ogni cosa; ~ **is ready** è tutto pronto; **he did** ~ **possible** ha fatto tutto il possibile.

everywhere [ev'rēhwär] *ad* in ogni luogo, dappertutto; (*wherever*) ovunque; ~ **you go you meet ...** ovunque si vada si trova ....

evict [ivikt'] *vt* sfrattare.

eviction [ivik'shən] *n* sfratto.

eviction notice *n* avviso di sfratto.

evidence [ev'idəns] *n* (*proof*) prova; (*of witness*) testimonianza; (*sign*): **to show** ~ **of** dare segni di; **to give** ~ deporre; **in** ~ (*obvious*) in evidenza; in vista.

evident [ev'idənt] *a* evidente.

evidently [ev'idəntlē] *ad* evidentemente.

evil [ē'vəl] *a* cattivo(a), maligno(a) ♦ *n* male *m*.

evince [ivins'] *vt* manifestare.

evocative [ivâk'ətiv] *a* evocativo(a).

evoke [ivōk'] *vt* evocare; (*admiration*) suscitare.

evolution [evəlōō'shən] *n* evoluzione *f*.

evolve [ivâlv'] *vt* elaborare ♦ *vi* svilupparsi, evolversi.

ewe [yōō] *n* pecora.

ex- [eks] *prefix* ex; (*out of*): **the price** ~**works** il prezzo franco fabbrica.

exacerbate [igzas'ûrbāt] *vt* (*pain*) aggravare; (*fig*: *relations, situation*) esacerbare, esasperare.

exact [igzakt'] *a* esatto(a) ♦ *vt*: **to** ~ **sth (from)** estorcere qc (da); esigere qc (da).

exacting [igzak'ting] *a* esigente; (*work*) faticoso(a).

exactitude [igzakt'ətōōd] *n* esattezza, precisione *f*.

exactly [igzakt'lē] *ad* esattamente; ~**!** esatto!

exaggerate [igzaj'ərāt] *vt, vi* esagerare.

exaggeration [igzajərā'shən] *n* esagerazione *f*.

exalt [igzôlt'] *vt* esaltare; elevare.

exalted [igzôl'tid] *a* (*rank, person*) elevato(a); (*elated*) esaltato(a).

exam [igzam'] *n abbr* (*SCOL*) = **examination**.

examination [igzamənā'shən] *n* (*SCOL*) esame *m*; (*MED*) controllo; **to take an** ~ sostenere *or* dare un esame; **the matter is under** ~ la questione è all'esame.

examine [igzam'in] *vt* esaminare; (*SCOL*: *orally, LAW*: *person*) interrogare; (*inspect*: *machine, premises*) ispezionare; (*luggage, passport*) controllare; (*MED*) visitare.

examiner [igzam'inûr] *n* esaminatore/trice.

example [igzam'pəl] *n* esempio; **for** ~ ad *or* per esempio; **to set a good/bad** ~ dare il buon/cattivo esempio.

exasperate [igzas'pərāt] *vt* esasperare; ~**d by** (*or* **at** *or* **with**) esasperato da.

exasperating [igzas'pərāting] *a* esasperante.

exasperation [igzaspərā'shən] *n* esasperazione *f*.

excavate [eks'kəvāt] *vt* scavare.

excavation [eks'kəvā'shən] *n* escavazione *f*.

excavator [eks'kəvātûr] *n* scavatore *m*, scavatrice *f*.

exceed [iksēd'] *vt* superare; (*one's powers, time limit*) oltrepassare.

exceedingly [iksē'dinglē] *ad* eccessivamente.

excel [iksel'] *vi* eccellere ♦ *vt* sorpassare.

excellence [ek'sələns] *n* eccellenza.

Excellency [ek'selənsē] *n*: **His** ~ Sua Eccellenza.

excellent [ek'sələnt] *a* eccellente.

except [iksept'] *prep* (*also*: ~ **for**, ~**ing**) salvo, all'infuori di, eccetto ♦ *vt* escludere; ~ **if/when** salvo se/quando; ~ **that** salvo che.

exception [iksep'shən] *n* eccezione *f*; **to take** ~ **to** trovare a ridire su; **with the** ~ **of** ad eccezione di.

exceptional [iksep'shənəl] *a* eccezionale.

excerpt [ek'sûrpt] *n* estratto.

excess [ekses'] *n* eccesso; **in** ~ **of** al di sopra di.

excess baggage *n* bagaglio in eccedenza.

excess fare *n* supplemento.

excessive [ikses'iv] *a* eccessivo(a).

excess supply *n* eccesso di offerta.

exchange [ikschānj'] *n* scambio; (*also*: **telephone** ~) centralino ♦ *vt*: **to** ~ **(for)** scambiare (con); **in** ~ **for** in cambio di; **foreign** ~ (*COMM*) cambio.

exchange control *n* controllo sui cambi.

exchange market *n* mercato dei cambi.

exchange rate *n* tasso di cambio.

Exchequer [eks'chekûr] *n*: **the** ~ (*Brit*) lo Scacchiere, ≈ il ministero delle Finanze.

excisable [iksī'zəbəl] *a* soggetto a dazio.

excise *n* [ek'sīz] imposta, dazio ♦ *vt* [iksīz'] recidere.

excise duties *npl* dazi *mpl*.

excitable [iksī'təbəl] *a* eccitabile.

excite [iksīt'] *vt* eccitare; **to get** ~**d** eccitarsi.

excitement [iksīt'mənt] *n* eccitazione *f*; agitazione *f*.

exciting [iksī'ting] *a* avventuroso(a); (*movie*,

book) appassionante.
excl. *abbr* (= *excluding, exclusive (of)*) escl.
exclaim [iksklām'] *vi* esclamare.
exclamation [ckskləmā'shən] *n* esclamazione *f.*
exclamation mark *n* punto esclamativo.
exclude [iksklōōd'] *vt* escludere.
excluding [iksklōō'ding] *prep:* ~ **VAT** IVA esclusa.
exclusion [iksklōō'zhən] *n* esclusione *f; to the* ~ *of* escludendo.
exclusion clause *n* clausola di esclusione.
exclusive [iksklōō'siv] *a* esclusivo(a); (*club*) selettivo(a); (*district*) snob *inv* ♦ *ad* (*COMM*) non compreso; ~ *of VAT* IVA esclusa; ~ *of postage* spese postali escluse; ~ *of service* servizio escluso; *from 1st to 15th March* ~ dal 1° al 15 marzo esclusi; ~ *rights npl* (*COMM*) diritti *mpl* esclusivi.
exclusively [iksklōō'sivlē] *ad* esclusivamente.
excommunicate [ckskəmyōō'nəkāt] *vt* scomunicare.
excrement [eks'krəmənt] *n* escremento.
excruciating [ikskrōō'shēāting] *a* straziante, atroce.
excursion [ikskûr'zhən] *n* escursione *f,* gita.
excursion ticket *n* biglietto a tariffa escursionistica.
excusable [ikskyōō'zəbəl] *a* scusabile.
excuse *n* [ekskyōōs'] scusa ♦ *vt* [ikskyōōz'] scusare; (*justify*) giustificare; *to make* ~s *for sb* trovare giustificazioni per qn; *to* ~ *sb from* (*activity*) dispensare qn da; ~ *me!* mi scusi!; *now if you will* ~ *me,* ... ora, mi scusi ma ...; *to* ~ *o.s. (for (doing) sth)* giustificarsi (per (aver fatto) qc).
ex-directory [cksdirek'tûrē] *a* (*Brit*): ~ **(phone) number** numero non compreso nell'elenco telefonico.
exec. [igzek'] *n abbr* = **executive.**
execrable [ek'səkrəbəl] *a* (*gen*) pessimo(a); (*manners*) esecrabile.
execute [ek'səkyōōt] *vt* (*prisoner*) giustiziare; (*plan etc*) eseguire.
execution [eksəkyōō'shən] *n* esecuzione *f.*
executioner [eksəkyōō'shənûr] *n* boia *m inv.*
executive [igzek'yətiv] *n* (*COMM*) dirigente *m;* (*POL*) esecutivo ♦ *a* esecutivo(a); (*secretary*) di direzione; (*offices, suite*) della direzione; (*car, plane*) dirigenziale; (*position, job, duties*) direttivo(a).
executive director *n* amministratore/trice.
executor [igzek'yətûr] *n* esecutore(trice) testamentario(a).
exemplary [igzem'plûrē] *a* esemplare.
exemplify [igzem'pləfi] *vt* esemplificare.
exempt [igzempt'] *a:* ~ **(from)** (*person: from tax*) esentato(a) (da); (: *from military service etc*) esonerato(a) (da); (*goods*) esente (da) ♦ *vt:* **to** ~ **sb from** esentare qn da.

exemption [igzemp'shən] *n* esenzione *f.*
exercise [ek'sûrsiz] *n* esercizio ♦ *vt* esercitare; (*dog*) portar fuori ♦ *vi* fare del movimento *or* moto.
exercise book *n* (*Brit*) quaderno.
exert [igzûrt'] *vt* esercitare; (*strength, force*) impiegare; **to** ~ **o.s.** sforzarsi.
exertion [igzûr'shən] *n* sforzo.
ex gratia [eks grā'tēə] *a:* ~ **payment** gratifica.
exhale [eks·hāl'] *vt, vi* espirare.
exhaust [igzôst'] *n* (*also:* ~ **fumes**) scappamento; (*also:* ~ **pipe**) tubo di scappamento ♦ *vt* esaurire; **to** ~ **o.s.** sfiancarsi.
exhausted [igzôs'tid] *a* esaurito(a).
exhausting [igzôs'ting] *a* estenuante.
exhaustion [igzôs'chən] *n* esaurimento; **nervous** ~ sovraffaticamento mentale.
exhaustive [igzôs'tiv] *a* esauriente.
exhibit [igzib'it] *n* (*ART*) oggetto esposto; (*LAW*) documento *or* oggetto esibito ♦ *vt* esporre; (*courage, skill*) dimostrare.
exhibition [cksəbish'ən] *n* mostra, esposizione *f;* (*of rudeness etc*) spettacolo; **to make an** ~ **of o.s.** dare spettacolo di sé.
exhibitionist [cksəbish'ənist] *n* esibizionista *m/f.*
exhibitor [igzib'ətûr] *n* espositore/trice.
exhilarating [igzil'ərāting] *a* esilarante; stimolante.
exhilaration [igzilərā'shən] *n* esaltazione *f,* ebbrezza.
exhort [igzôrt'] *vt* esortare.
exile [eg'zīl] *n* esilio; (*person*) esiliato/a ♦ *vt* esiliare; **in** ~ in esilio.
exist [igzist'] *vi* esistere.
existence [igzis'təns] *n* esistenza; **to be in** ~ esistere.
existentialism [egzisten'chəlizəm] *n* esistenzialismo.
existing [igzis'ting] *a* (*laws, regime*) attuale.
exit [eg'zit] *n* uscita ♦ *vi* (*COMPUT. THEATER*) uscire.
exit poll *n* (*POL*) sondaggio elettorale a votazioni effettuate.
exit ramp *n* (*US AUT*) rampa di uscita.
exit visa *n* visto d'uscita.
exodus [ek'sədəs] *n* esodo.
ex officio [cks əfish'ēō] *a, ad* d'ufficio.
exonerate [igzán'ərāt] *vt:* **to** ~ **from** discolpare da.
exorbitant [igzôr'bətənt] *a* (*price*) esorbitante; (*demands*) spropositato(a).
exorcize [ek'sôrsīz] *vt* esorcizzare.
exotic [igzát'ik] *a* esotico(a).
exp. *abbr* = *expenses; expired; export; express.*
expand [ikspand'] *vt* (*chest, economy etc*) sviluppare; (*market, operations*) espandere; (*influence*) estendere; (*horizons*) allargare ♦ *vi* svilupparsi; (*also gas*) espandersi; (*metal*) dilatarsi; **to** ~ **on** (*notes, story etc*) amplia-

re.

expanse [ikspans'] *n* distesa, estensione *f*.

expansion [ikspan'chən] *n* (*gen*) espansione *f*; (*of town, economy*) sviluppo; (*of metal*) dilatazione *f*.

expansionism [ikspan'chənizəm] *n* espansionismo.

expansionist [ikspan'chənist] *a* espansionistico(a).

expatriate *n* [ckspā'trēit] espatriato/a ♦ *vt* [ckspā'trēāt] espatriare.

expect [ikspckt'] *vt* (*anticipate*) prevedere, aspettarsi, prevedere *or* aspettarsi che + *sub*; (*count on*) contare su; (*hope for*) sperare; (*require*) richiedere, esigere; (*suppose*) supporre; (*await, also baby*) aspettare ♦ *vi*: **to be ~ing** essere in stato interessante; **to ~ sb to do** aspettarsi che qn faccia; **to ~ to do sth** pensare *or* contare di fare qc; **as ~ed** come previsto; **I ~ so** credo di sì.

expectancy [ikspck'tənsē] *n* attesa; **life ~** probabilità *fpl* di vita.

expectant [ikspck'tənt] *a* pieno(a) di aspettative.

expectantly [ikspck'təntlē] *ad* (*look, listen*) con un'aria d'attesa.

expectant mother *n* gestante *f*.

expectation [ckspcktā'shən] *n* aspettativa; speranza; **in ~ of** in previsione di; **against** *or* **contrary to all ~(s)** contro ogni aspettativa; **to come** *or* **live up to sb's ~s** rispondere alle attese di qn.

expedience [ikspē'dēəns] *n* convenienza; **for the sake of ~** per una questione di comodità.

expediency [ikspē'dēənsē] *n* = **expedience.**

expedient [ikspē'dēənt] *a* conveniente; vantaggioso(a) ♦ *n* espediente *m*.

expedite [ck'spidit] *vt* sbrigare; facilitare.

expedition [ckspidish'ən] *n* spedizione *f*.

expeditionary force [ckspədish'ənärē fôrs] *n* corpo di spedizione.

expeditious [ckspidish'əs] *a* sollecito(a), rapido(a).

expel [ikspcl'] *vt* espellere.

expend [ikspcnd'] *vt* spendere; (*use up*) consumare.

expendable [ikspcn'dəbəl] *a* sacrificabile.

expenditure [ikspcn'dichŭr] *n* spesa; (*of time, effort*) dispendio.

expense [ikspcns'] *n* spesa; (*high cost*) costo; **~s** *npl* (*COMM*) spese *fpl*, indennità *fpl*; **to go to the ~ of** sobbarcarsi la spesa di; **at great ~** con grande impiego di mezzi; **at the ~ of** a spese di.

expense account *n* conto *m* spese *inv*.

expensive [ikspcn'siv] *a* caro(a), costoso(a); **she has ~ tastes** le piacciono le cose costose.

experience [ikspēr'ēəns] *n* esperienza ♦ *vt* (*pleasure*) provare; (*hardship*) soffrire; **to learn by ~** imparare per esperienza.

experienced [ikspēr'ēənst] *a* che ha esperienza.

experiment *n* [ikspär'əmənt] esperimento, esperienza ♦ *vi* [ikspcr'əmcnt] fare esperimenti; **to perform** *or* **carry out an ~** fare un esperimento; **as an ~** a titolo di esperimento; **to ~ with a new vaccine** sperimentare un nuovo vaccino.

experimental [ikspärəmcn'təl] *a* sperimentale; **at the ~ stage** in via di sperimentazione.

expert [ck'spûrt] *a, n* esperto(a); **~ witness** (*LAW*) esperto/a; **~ in** *or* **at doing sth** esperto nel fare qc; **an ~ on sth** un esperto di qc.

expertise [ckspûrtēz'] *n* competenza.

expiration [ckspərā'shən] *n* scadenza.

expire [ikspī'ûr] *vi* (*period of time, license*) (*Brit*) scadere.

expiry [ikspiûr'ē] *n* (*Brit*) scadenza.

explain [iksplān'] *vt* spiegare.

explain away *vt* dar ragione di.

explanation [cksplənā'shən] *n* spiegazione *f*; **to find an ~ for sth** trovare la spiegazione di qc.

explanatory [iksplan'ətôrē] *a* esplicativo(a).

explicit [iksplis'it] *a* esplicito(a); (*definite*) netto(a).

explode [iksplōd'] *vi* esplodere ♦ *vt* (*fig: theory*) demolire; **to ~ a myth** distruggere un mito.

exploit *n* [cks'ploit] impresa ♦ *vt* [iksploit'] sfruttare.

exploitation [cksploitā'shən] *n* sfruttamento.

exploration [cksplərā'shən] *n* esplorazione *f*.

exploratory [iksplôr'ətôrē] *a* (*fig: talks*) esplorativo(a); **~ operation** (*MED*) intervento d'esplorazione.

explore [iksplôr'] *vt* esplorare; (*possibilities*) esaminare.

explorer [iksplôr'ûr] *n* esploratore/trice.

explosion [iksplō'zhən] *n* esplosione *f*.

explosive [iksplō'siv] *a* esplosivo(a) ♦ *n* esplosivo.

exponent [ikspō'ncnt] *n* esponente *m/f*.

export *vt* [ikspôrt'] esportare ♦ *n* [cks'pôrt] esportazione *f*; articolo di esportazione ♦ *cpd* d'esportazione.

exportation [ckspôrtā'shən] *n* esportazione *f*.

exporter [ckspôr'tûr] *n* esportatore *m*.

export license *n* licenza d'esportazione.

expose [ikspōz'] *vt* esporre; (*unmask*) smascherare; **to ~ o.s.** (*LAW*) oltraggiare il pudore.

exposed [ikspōzd'] *a* (*land, house*) esposto(a); (*ELEC: wire*) scoperto(a); (*pipe, beam*) a vista.

exposition [ckspəzish'ən] *n* esposizione *f*.

exposure [ikspō'zhûr] *n* esposizione *f*; (*PHOT*) posa; (*MED*) assideramento; **to die of ~** morire assiderato(a).

exposure meter *n* esposimetro.

expound [ikspound'] *vt* esporre; (*theory, text*) spiegare.

express [ikspres'] *a* (*definite*) chiaro(a), espresso(a); (*Brit: letter etc*) espresso *inv* ♦ *n* (*train*) espresso ♦ *ad*: **to send sth ~** spedire qc per espresso ♦ *vt* esprimere; **to ~ o.s.** esprimersi.

expression [ikspresh'ən] *n* espressione *f*.

expressionism [ikspresh'ənizəm] *n* espressionismo.

expressive [ikspres'iv] *a* espressivo(a).

expressly [ikspres'lē] *ad* espressamente.

expressway [ikspres'wā] *n* autostrada che attraversa la città.

expropriate [eksprōp'rēāt] *vt* espropriare.

expulsion [ikspul'shən] *n* espulsione *f*.

exquisite [ekskwiz'it] *a* squisito(a).

ex-serviceman [ekssûr'vismən] *n* (*Brit*) ex combattente *m*.

ext. *abbr* (*TEL*: = *extension*) int. (= *interno*).

extemporize [ikstem'pəriz] *vi* improvvisare.

extend [ikstend'] *vt* (*visit*) protrarre; (*road, deadline*) prolungare; (*building*) ampliare; (*offer*) offrire, porgere; (*COMM: credit*) accordare ♦ *vi* (*land*) estendersi.

extension [iksten'chən] *n* (*of road, term*) prolungamento; (*of contract, deadline*) proroga; (*building*) annesso; (*to wire, table*) prolunga; (*telephone*) interno; (: *in private house*) apparecchio supplementare; **~ 3718** (*TEL*) interno 3718.

extension cord *n* (*ELEC*) prolunga.

extensive [iksten'siv] *a* esteso(a), ampio(a); (*damage*) su larga scala; (*alterations*) notevole; (*inquiries*) esauriente; (*use*) grande.

extensively [iksten'sivlē] *ad* (*altered, damaged etc*) radicalmente; **he's traveled ~** ha viaggiato molto.

extent [ikstent'] *n* estensione *f*; (*of knowledge, activities, power*) portata; (*degree: of damage, loss*) proporzioni *fpl*; **to some ~** fino a un certo punto; **to a certain/large ~** in certa/larga misura; **to what ~?** fino a che punto?; **to such an ~ that** ... a tal punto che ....

extenuating [iksten'yōōāting] *a*: **~ circumstances** attenuanti *fpl*.

exterior [ikstēr'ēûr] *a* esteriore, esterno(a) ♦ *n* esteriore *m*, esterno; aspetto (esteriore).

exterminate [ikstûr'mənāt] *vt* sterminare.

extermination [ikstûrmənā'shən] *n* sterminio.

extern [eks'tûrn] *n* (*US*) medico esterno.

external [ikstûr'nəl] *a* esterno(a), esteriore ♦ *n*: **the ~s** le apparenze; **for ~ use only** (*MED*) solo per uso esterno; **~ affairs** (*POL*) affari *mpl* esteri.

externally [ikstûr'nəlē] *ad* esternamente.

extinct [ikstingkt'] *a* estinto(a).

extinction [ikstingk'shən] *n* estinzione *f*.

extinguish [iksting'gwish] *vt* estinguere.

extinguisher [iksting'gwishûr] *n* estintore *m*.

extoll, (*Brit*) **extol** [ikstōl'] *vt* (*merits, virtues*) magnificare; (*person*) celebrare.

extort [ikstôrt'] *vt*: **to ~ sth (from)** estorcere qc (da).

extortion [ikstôr'shən] *n* estorsione *f*.

extortionate [ikstôr'shənit] *a* esorbitante.

extra [eks'trə] *a* extra *inv*, supplementare ♦ *ad* (*in addition*) di più ♦ *n* supplemento; (*THEATER*) comparso; **wine will cost ~** il vino è extra; **~ large sizes** taglie *fpl* forti.

extra... *prefix* extra....

extract *vt* [ikstrakt'] estrarre; (*money, promise*) strappare ♦ *n* [eks'trakt] estratto; (*passage*) brano.

extraction [ikstrak'shən] *n* estrazione *f*; (*descent*) origine *f*.

extracurricular [ekstrəkərik'yəlûr] *a* (*SCOL*) parascolastico(a).

extradite [eks'trədīt] *vt* estradare.

extradition [ekstrədish'ən] *n* estradizione *f*.

extramarital [ekstrəmar'itəl] *a* extraconiugale.

extramural [ekstrəmyōōr'əl] *a* fuori dell'università.

extraneous [ikstrā'nēəs] *a*: **~ to** estraneo(a) a.

extraordinary [ikstrôr'dənärē] *a* straordinario(a); **the ~ thing is that** ... la cosa strana è che ....

extraordinary general meeting *n* assemblea straordinaria.

extrapolation [ikstrapəlā'shən] *n* estrapolazione *f*.

extrasensory perception (ESP) [ekstrəsen'sûrē pûrsep'shən] *n* percezione *f* extrasensoriale.

extra time *n* (*Brit SOCCER*) tempo supplementare.

extravagance [ikstrav'əgəns] *n* (*excessive spending*) sperpero; (*thing bought*) stravaganza.

extravagant [ikstrav'əgənt] *a* stravagante; (*in spending: person*) prodigo(a); (: *tastes*) dispendioso(a).

extreme [ikstrēm'] *a* estremo(a) ♦ *n* estremo; **~s of temperature** eccessivi sbalzi *mpl* di temperatura; **the ~ left/right** (*POL*) l'estrema sinistra/destra.

extremely [ikstrēm'lē] *ad* estremamente.

extremist [ikstrē'mist] *a, n* estremista (*m/f*).

extremity [ikstrem'itē] *n* estremità *f inv*.

extricate [eks'trikāt] *vt*: **to ~ sth (from)** districare qc (da).

extrovert [ek'strōvûrt] *n* estroverso/a.

exuberance [igzōō'bûrəns] *n* esuberanza.

exuberant [igzōō'bûrənt] *a* esuberante.

exude [igzōōd'] *vt* trasudare; (*fig*) emanare.

exult [igzult'] *vi* esultare, gioire.

exultant [igzul'tənt] *a* (*person, smile*) esultante; (*shout, expression*) di giubilo.

exultation [egzultā'shən] *n* giubilo; **in ~** per la gioia.

eye [ī] *n* occhio; (*of needle*) cruna ♦ *vt* osservare; **to keep an ~ on** tenere d'occhio; **in the public ~** esposto(a) al pubblico; **as far as the ~ can see** a perdita d'occhio; **to have an ~ for sth** avere occhio per qc; **there's more to this than meets the ~** non è così semplice come sembra.

eyeball [ī'bôl] *n* globo dell'occhio.

eyebath [ī'bath] *n* (*Brit*) occhino.

eyebrow [ī'brou] *n* sopracciglio.

eyebrow pencil *n* matita per le sopracciglia.

eye-catching [ī'kaching] *a* che colpisce l'occhio.

eyecup [ī'kup] *n* (*US*) occhino.

eyedrops [ī'drâps] *npl* gocce *fpl* oculari, collirio.

eyeglass [ī'glas] *n* monocolo.

eyelash [ī'lash] *n* ciglio.

eyelet [ī'lit] *n* occhiello.

eye-level [ī'levəl] *a* all'altezza degli occhi.

eyelid [ī'lid] *n* palpebra.

eyeliner [ī'līnûr] *n* eye-liner *m inv*.

eye-opener [ī'ōpənûr] *n* rivelazione *f*.

eyeshadow [ī'shadō] *n* ombretto.

eyesight [ī'sīt] *n* vista.

eyesore [ī'sôr] *n* pugno nell'occhio.

eyestrain [ī'strān] *n*: **to get ~** stancarsi gli occhi.

eye test *n* controllo della vista.

eyetooth, *pl* -teeth [ī'tōōth, -tēth] *n* canino superiore; **to give one's eyeteeth for sth/to do sth** (*fig*) dare non so che cosa per qc/per fare qc.

eyewash [ī'wâsh] *n* collirio; (*fig*) sciocchezze *fpl*.

eyewitness [ī'witnis] *n* testimone *m/f* oculare.

eyrie [är'ē] *n* (*Brit*) nido (d'aquila).

F

F, f [ef] *n* (*letter*) F, f *f or m inv*; (*MUS*): F fa *m*; **F for Fox** ≈ F come Firenze.

F. *abbr* (= *Fahrenheit*) F.

FA *n abbr* (*Brit*) = *Football Association*.

FAA *n abbr* (*US*) = *Federal Aviation Administration*.

fable [fā'bəl] *n* favola.

fabric [fab'rik] *n* stoffa, tessuto; (*ARCHIT*) struttura.

fabrrricate [fab'rikāt] *vt* fabbricare.

fabrication [fabrikā'shən] *n* fabbricazione *f*.

fabric ribbon *n* (*for typewriter*) dattilonastro di tessuto.

fabulous [fab'yələs] *a* favoloso(a); (*col*: *su-*

per) favoloso(a), fantastico(a).

façade [fəsâd'] *n* facciata; (*fig*) apparenza.

face [fās] *n* faccia, viso, volto; (*expression*) faccia; (*grimace*) smorfia; (*of clock*) quadrante *m*; (*of building*) facciata; (*side, surface*) faccia; (*of mountain, cliff*) parete *f*; (*in mine*) fronte *f* ♦ *vt* fronteggiare; (*fig*) affrontare; **~ down** (*person*) bocconi; (*object*) a faccia in giù; **to lose/save ~** perdere/salvare la faccia; **to make a ~** fare una smorfia; **in the ~ of** (*difficulties etc*) di fronte a; **on the ~ of it** a prima vista; **to ~ the fact that ...** riconoscere *or* ammettere che ....

face up to *vt fus* affrontare, far fronte a.

facecloth [fās'klôth] *n* guanto di spugna.

face cream *n* crema per il viso.

faceless [fās'lis] *a* anonimo(a).

face lift *n* lifting *m inv*; (*of façade etc*) ripulita.

face powder *n* cipria.

face-saving [fās'sāving] *a* che salva la faccia.

facet [fas'it] *n* faccetta, sfaccettatura; (*fig*) sfaccettatura.

facetious [fəsē'shəs] *a* faceto(a).

face-to-face [fās'təfās'] *ad* faccia a faccia.

face value *n* (*of coin*) valore *m* facciale *or* nominale; **to take sth at ~** (*fig*) giudicare qc dalle apparenze.

facia [fā'shēə] *n* = **fascia**.

facial [fā'shəl] *a* facciale ♦ *n* trattamento del viso.

facile [fas'əl] *a* facile; superficiale.

facilitate [fəsil'ətāt] *vt* facilitare.

facility [fəsil'ətē] *n* facilità; **facilities** *npl* attrezzature *fpl*; **credit facilities** facilitazioni *fpl* di credito.

facing [fā'sing] *n* (*of wall etc*) rivestimento; (*SEWING*) paramontura.

facsimile [faksim'əlē] *n* facsimile *m inv*.

facsimile machine *n* facsimile *m inv*.

fact [fakt] *n* fatto; **in ~** infatti; **to know for a ~ that ...** sapere per certo che ...; **the ~ (of the matter) is that ...** la verità è che ...; **the ~s of life** (*sex*) i fatti riguardanti la vita sessuale; (*fig*) le realtà della vita.

fact-finding [fakt'finding] *a*: **a ~ tour/mission** un viaggio/una missione d'inchiesta.

faction [fak'shən] *n* fazione *f*.

factor [fak'tûr] *n* fattore *m*; (*COMM*: *company*) organizzazione specializzata nell'incasso di crediti per conto terzi; (: *agent*) agente *m* depositario ♦ *vi* incassare crediti per conto terzi; **human ~** elemento umano; **safety ~** coefficiente *m* di sicurezza.

factory [fak'tûrē] *n* fabbrica, stabilimento.

factory farming *n* (*Brit*) allevamento su scala industriale.

factory ship *n* nave *f* fattoria *inv*.

factual [fak'chōōəl] *a* che si attiene ai fatti.

faculty [fak'əltē] *n* facoltà *f inv*; (*US: teaching*

staff) corpo insegnante.

fad [fad] *n* mania; capriccio.

fade [fād] *vi* sbiadire, sbiadirsi; (*light, sound, hope*) attenuarsi, affievolirsi; (*flower*) appassire.

fade in *vt* (*picture*) aprire in dissolvenza; (*sound*) aumentare gradualmente d'intensità.

fade out *vt* (*picture*) chiudere in dissolvenza; (*sound*) diminuire gradualmente d'intensità.

faeces [fē'sēz] *npl* (*Brit*) feci *fpl.*

fag [fag] *n* (*US col: homosexual*) frocio; (*Brit col: cigarette*) cicca; (: *chore*) sfacchinata.

fag end *n* (*Brit col*) mozzicone *m.*

fail [fāl] *vt* (*exam*) non superare; (*candidate*) bocciare; (*subj: courage, memory*) mancare a ♦ *vi* fallire; (*student*) essere respinto(a); (*supplies*) mancare; (*eyesight, health, light*: *also*: **be ~ing**) venire a mancare; (*brakes*) non funzionare; **to ~ to do sth** (*neglect*) mancare di fare qc; (*be unable*) non riuscire a fare qc; **without ~** senza fallo; certamente.

failing [fā'ling] *n* difetto ♦ *prep* in mancanza di; **~ that** se questo non è possibile.

failsafe [fāl'sāf] *a* (*device etc*) di sicurezza.

failure [fāl'yûr] *n* fallimento; (*person*) fallito/a; (*mechanical etc*) guasto; (*in exam*) insuccesso, bocciatura; (*of crops*) perdita; **his ~ to come** il fatto che non sia venuto; **it was a complete ~** è stato un vero fiasco.

faint [fānt] *a* debole; (*recollection*) vago(a); (*mark*) indistinto(a); (*smell, breeze, trace*) leggero(a) ♦ *vi* svenire; **to feel ~** sentirsi svenire.

faint-hearted [fānthâr'tid] *a* pusillanime.

faintly [fānt'lē] *ad* debolmente; vagamente.

faintness [fānt'nis] *n* debolezza.

fair [fär] *a* (*person, decision*) giusto(a), equo(a); (*hair etc*) biondo(a); (*skin, complexion*) bianco(a); (*weather*) bello(a), clemente; (*good enough*) assai buono(a); (*sizeable*) bello(a) ♦ *ad*: **to play ~** giocare correttamente ♦ *n* fiera; (*Brit: carnival*) luna park *m inv*; (*also*: **trade ~**) fiera campionaria; **it's not ~!** non è giusto!; **a ~ amount of** un bel po' di.

fairground [fär'ground] *n* luna park *m inv.*

fair-haired [fär'härd] *a* (*person*) biondo(a).

fairly [fär'lē] *ad* equamente; (*quite*) abbastanza.

fairness [fär'nis] *n* equità, giustizia; **in all ~** per essere giusti, a dire il vero.

fair play *n* correttezza.

fairy [fär'ē] *n* fata.

fairy godmother *n* fata buona.

fairy tale *n* fiaba.

faith [fāth] *n* fede *f*; (*trust*) fiducia; (*sect*) religione *f*, fede *f*; **to have ~ in sb/sth** avere fiducia in qn/qc.

faithful [fāth'fəl] *a* fedele.

faithfully [fāth'fəlē] *ad* fedelmente; **yours ~** (*Brit: in letters*) distinti saluti.

faith healer [fāth' hē'lûr] *n* guaritore/trice.

fake [fāk] *n* imitazione *f*; (*picture*) falso; (*person*) impostore/a ♦ *a* falso(a) ♦ *vt* (*accounts*) falsificare; (*illness*) fingere; (*painting*) contraffare; **his illness is a ~** fa finta di essere malato.

falcon [fal'kən] *n* falco, falcone *m.*

Falkland Islands [fôlk'lənd ī'ləndz] *npl*: **the ~** le isole Falkland.

fall [fôl] *n* caduta; (*decrease*) diminuzione *f*, calo; (*in temperature*) abbassamento; (*in price*) ribasso; (*US: autumn*) autunno ♦ *vi* (*pt* **fell**, *pp* **fallen** [fel, fôlən]) cadere; (*temperature, price*) abbassare; **a ~ of snow** (*Brit*) una nevicata; **to ~ in love (with sb/sth)** innamorarsi (di qn/qc); **to ~ short of** (*sb's expectations*) non corrispondere a; **to ~ flat** *vi* (*on one's face*) cadere bocconi; (*joke*) fare cilecca; (*plan*) fallire; *see also* **falls.**

fall apart *vi* cadere a pezzi.

fall back *vi* indietreggiare; (*MIL*) ritirarsi.

fall back on *vt fus* ripiegare su; **to have sth to ~ back on** avere qc di riserva.

fall behind *vi* rimanere indietro; (*fig: with payments*) essere in arretrato.

fall down *vi* (*person*) cadere; (*building, hopes*) crollare.

fall for *vt fus* (*person*) prendere una cotta per; **to ~ for a trick** (*or* **a story** *etc*) cascarci.

fall in *vi* crollare; (*MIL*) mettersi in riga.

fall in with *vt fus* (*sb's plans etc*) trovarsi d'accordo con.

fall off *vi* cadere; (*diminish*) diminuire, abbassarsi.

fall out *vi* (*friends etc*) litigare.

fall over *vi* cadere.

fall through *vi* (*plan, project*) fallire.

fallacy [fal'əsē] *n* errore *m.*

fallback [fôl'bak] *a*: **~ position** posizione *f* di ripiego.

fallen [fôl'ən] *pp of* **fall.**

fallible [fal'əbəl] *a* fallibile.

falling [fôl'ing] *a*: **~ market** (*COMM*) mercato in ribasso.

falling-off [fôl'ing-ôf'] *n* calo.

fallopian tube [fələ'pēən tōōb] *n* (*ANAT*) tuba di Falloppio.

fallout [fôl'out] *n* fall-out *m.*

fallout shelter *n* rifugio antiatomico.

fallow [fal'ō] *a* incolto(a); a maggese.

falls [fôlz] *npl* (*waterfall*) cascate *fpl.*

false [fôls] *a* falso(a); **under ~ pretenses** con l'inganno.

false alarm *n* falso allarme *m.*

falsehood [fôls'hŏŏd] *n* menzogna.

falsely [fôls'lē] *ad* (*accuse*) a torto.

false teeth *npl* denti *mpl* finti.

falsify [fôl'səfī] vt falsificare; (figures) alterare.

falter [fôl'túr] vi esitare, vacillare.

fame [fām] n fama, celebrità.

familiar [fəmil'yúr] a familiare; (common) comune; (close) intimo(a); **to be ~ with** (subject) conoscere; **to make o.s. ~ with** familiarizzarsi con; **to be on ~ terms with** essere in confidenza con.

familiarity [fəmilēar'ətē] n familiarità; intimità.

familiarize [fəmil'yərīz] vt: **to ~ sb with sth** far conoscere qc a qn.

family [fam'lē] n famiglia.

family allowance n assegni mpl familiari.

family business n impresa familiare.

family doctor n medico di famiglia.

family life n vita familiare.

family planning clinic n consultorio familiare.

family tree n albergo genealogico.

famine [fam'in] n carestia.

famished [fam'isht] a affamato(a); **I'm ~!** (col) ho una fame da lupo!

famous [fā'məs] a famoso(a).

famously [fā'məslē] ad (get on) a meraviglia.

fan [fan] n (folding) ventaglio; (machine) ventilatore m; (person) ammiratore/trice; (SPORT) tifoso/a ♦ vt far vento a; (fire, quarrel) alimentare.

fan out vi spargersi (a ventaglio).

fanatic [fənat'ik] n fanatico/a.

fanatical [fənat'ikəl] a fanatico(a).

fan belt n cinghia del ventilatore.

fancied [fan'sēd] a immaginario(a).

fanciful [fan'sifəl] a fantasioso(a); (object) di fantasia.

fancy [fan'sē] n immaginazione f, fantasia; (whim) capriccio ♦ a (house, car) di lusso; (price) esorbitante ♦ cpd (di) fantasia inv ♦ vt (feel like, want) aver voglia di; (imagine) immaginare, credere; **to take a ~ to** incapricciarsi di; **it took** or **caught my ~** mi è piaciuto; **when the ~ takes him** quando ne ha voglia; **to ~ that** immaginare che; **he fancies her** (Brit) gli piace.

fancy dress n costume m (per maschera).

fancy-dress ball n (Brit) ballo in maschera.

fancy goods npl articoli mpl di ogni genere.

fanfare [fan'fâr] n fanfara.

fanfold paper [fan'fōld pā'pûr] n carta a moduli continui.

fang [fang] n zanna; (of snake) dente m.

fan heater n (Brit) stufa ad aria calda.

fanlight [fan'līt] n lunetta.

fantasize [fan'təsīz] vi fantasticare, sognare.

fantastic [fantas'tik] a fantastico(a).

fantasy [fan'təsē] n fantasia, immaginazione f; fantasticheria; chimera.

FAO n abbr (= Food and Agriculture Organization) FAO f.

far [fâr] a: **the ~ side/end** l'altra parte/l'altro capo; **the ~ left/right** (POL) l'estrema sinistra/destra ♦ ad lontano; **is it ~ to New York?** è lontana New York?; **it's not ~ (from here)** non è lontano (da qui); **~ away, ~ off** lontano, distante; **~ better** assai migliore; **~ from** lontano da; **by ~** di gran lunga; **as ~ back as the 13th century** già nel duecento; **go as ~ as the farm** vada fino alla fattoria; **as ~ as I know** per quel che so; **as ~ as possible** nei limiti del possibile; **how ~ have you got with your work?** dov'è arrivato con il suo lavoro?

faraway [fâr'əwā] a lontano(a); (voice, look) assente.

farce [fârs] n farsa.

farcical [fâr'sikəl] a farsesco(a).

fare [fär] n (on trains, buses) tariffa; (in taxi) prezzo della corsa; (food) vitto, cibo ♦ vi passarsela.

Far East n: **the ~** l'Estremo Oriente m.

farewell [fâr'wel'] excl, n addio ♦ cpd [fâr'wel] (party etc) d'addio.

far-fetched [fâr'fecht'] a (explanation) stiracchiato(a), forzato(a); (idea, scheme, story) inverosimile.

farm [fârm] n fattoria, podere m ♦ vt coltivare.

farm out vt (work) dare in consegna.

farmer [fâr'mûr] n coltivatore/trice; agricoltore/trice.

farmhand [fârm'hand] n bracciante m agricolo.

farmhouse [fârm'hous] n fattoria.

farming [fâr'ming] n agricoltura; **intensive ~** coltura intensiva; **sheep ~** allevamento di pecore.

farm laborer n = **farmhand**.

farmland [fârm'land] n terreno da coltivare.

farm produce n prodotti mpl agricoli.

farm worker n = **farmhand**.

farmyard [fârm'yârd] n aia.

Faroe Islands [fərō' i'ləndz], **Faroes** [fərōz'] npl: **the ~** le isole Faeroer.

far-reaching [fâr'rē'ching] a di vasta portata.

farsighted [fâr'sī'tid] a presbite; (fig) lungimirante.

fart [fârt] (col!) n scoreggia(!) ♦ vi scoreggiare (!).

farther [fâr'thûr] ad più lontano ♦ a più lontano(a).

farthest [fâr'thist] superlative of **far**.

FAS abbr (= free alongside ship) franco banchina nave.

fascia [fā'shēə] n (AUT) cruscotto.

fascinate [fas'ənāt] vt affascinare.

fascinating [fas'ənāting] a affascinante.

fascination [fasənā'shən] n fascino.

fascism [fash'izəm] n fascismo.

fascist [fash'ist] a, n fascista (m/f).

fashion [fash'ən] n moda; (manner) maniera, modo ♦ vt foggiare, formare; **in ~** alla moda; **out of** ~ passato(a) di moda; **after a** ~ (*finish, manage etc*) così così; **in the Greek** ~ alla greca.

fashionable [fash'ənəbəl] *a* alla moda, di moda; (*writer*) di grido.

fashion designer *n* disegnatore/trice di moda.

fashion show *n* sfilata di moda.

fast [fast] *a* rapido(a), svelto(a), veloce; (*clock*): **to be** ~ andare avanti; (*dye, color*) solido(a) ♦ *ad* rapidamente; (*stuck, held*) saldamente ♦ *n* digiuno ♦ *vi* digiunare; ~ **asleep** profondamente addormentato; **as** ~ **as I can** più in fretta possibile; **my watch is 5 minutes** ~ il mio orologio va avanti di 5 minuti.

fasten [fas'ən] *vt* chiudere, fissare; (*coat*) abbottonare, allacciare ♦ *vi* chiudersi, fissarsi; abbottonarsi, allacciarsi.

fasten (up)on *vt fus* (*idea*) cogliere al volo.

fastener [fas'ənûr], **fastening** [fas'əning] *n* fermaglio, chiusura; (*Brit*: *zip* ~) chiusura lampo.

fast food *n* fast food *m inv*.

fastidious [fastid'ēəs] *a* esigente, difficile.

fast lane *n* (*AUT*) ≈ corsia di sorpasso.

fat [fat] *a* grasso(a) ♦ *n* grasso; **to live off the** ~ **of the land** vivere nel lusso, avere ogni ben di Dio.

fatal [fāt'əl] *a* fatale; mortale; disastroso(a).

fatalism [fāt'əlizəm] *n* fatalismo.

fatality [fātal'itē] *n* (*road death etc*) morto/a, vittima.

fatally [fāt'əlē] *ad* a morte.

fate [fāt] *n* destino; (*of person*) sorte *f*; **to meet one's** ~ trovare la morte.

fated [fā'tid] *a* (*governed by fate*) destinato(a); (*person, project etc*) destinato(a) a finire male.

fateful [fāt'fəl] *a* fatidico(a).

father [fá'thûr] *n* padre *m*.

Father Christmas *n* (*Brit*) Babbo Natale.

fatherhood [fá'thûrhōod] *n* paternità.

father-in-law [fá'thûrinló] *n* suocero.

fatherland [fá'thûrland] *n* patria.

fatherly [fá'thûrlē] *a* paterno(a).

fathom [fath'əm] *n* braccio (= *1828 mm*) ♦ *vt* (*mystery*) penetrare, sondare.

fatigue [fətēg'] *n* stanchezza; (*MIL*) corvé *f*; **metal** ~ fatica del metallo.

fatness [fat'nis] *n* grassezza.

fatten [fat'ən] *vt, vi* ingrassare; **chocolate is** ~**ing** la cioccolata fa ingrassare.

fatty [fat'ē] *a* (*food*) grasso(a) ♦ *n* (*col*) ciccione/a.

fatuous [fach'ōōəs] *a* fatuo(a).

faucet [fó'sit] *n* (*US*) rubinetto.

fault [fólt] *n* colpa; (*TENNIS*) fallo; (*defect*) difetto; (*GEO*) faglia ♦ *vt* criticare; **it's my** ~ è colpa mia; **to find** ~ **with** trovare da ridire su; **at** ~ in fallo; **generous to a** ~ eccessiva-

mente generoso.

faultless [fólt'lis] *a* perfetto(a); senza difetto; impeccabile.

faulty [fól'tē] *a* difettoso(a).

fauna [fón'ə] *n* fauna.

faux pas [fō pâ'] *n* gaffe *f inv*.

favor [fā'vûr] (*US*) *n* favore *m* ♦ *vt* (*proposition*) favorire, essere favorevole a; (*pupil etc*) favorire; (*team, horse*) dare per vincente; **to do sb a** ~ fare un favore *or* una cortesia a qn; **in** ~ **of** in favore di; **to be in** ~ **of sth/of doing sth** essere favorevole a qc/a fare qc; **to find** ~ **with sb** (*subj: person*) entrare nelle buone grazie di qn; (: *suggestion*) avere l'approvazione di qn.

favorable [fā'vûrəbəl] *a* favorevole.

favorably [fā'vûrəblē] *ad* favorevolmente.

favorite [fā'vûrit] *a*, *n* favorito(a).

favoritism [fā'vûritizəm] *n* favoritismo.

favour [fā'vûr] *etc* (*Brit*) = **favor** *etc*.

fawn [fón] *n* daino ♦ *a* (*also*: ~**-colored**) marrone chiaro *inv* ♦ *vi*: **to** ~ (**up**)**on** adulare servilmente.

fax [faks] *n* (*document, machine*) facsimile *m inv* ♦ *vt* teletrasmettere, spedire in facsimile.

fazed [fāzd] *a* (*col*) scombussolato(a).

FBI *n abbr* (*US*: = *Federal Bureau of Investigation*) FBI *f*.

FCA *n abbr* (*US*) = *Farm Credit Administration*.

FCC *n abbr* (*US*) = *Federal Communications Commission*.

FCO *n abbr* (*Brit*: = *Foreign and Commonwealth Office*) ≈ Ufficio affari esteri.

FD *n abbr* (*US*) = **fire department**.

FDA *n abbr* (*US*) = *Food and Drug Administration*.

FDIC *n abbr* (*US*) = *Federal Deposit Insurance Corporation*.

fear [fēr] *n* paura, timore *m* ♦ *vt* aver paura di, temere ♦ *vi*: **to** ~ **for** temere per, essere in ansia per; ~ **of heights** vertigini *fpl*; **for** ~ **of** per paura di; **to** ~ **that** avere paura di (*or* che + *sub*), temere di (*or* che + *sub*).

fearful [fēr'fəl] *a* pauroso(a); (*sight, noise*) terribile, spaventoso(a); (*frightened*): **to be** ~ **of** temere.

fearfully [fēr'fəlē] *ad* (*timidly*) timorosamente; (*col*: *very*) terribilmente, spaventosamente.

fearless [fēr'lis] *a* intrepido(a), senza paura.

fearsome [fēr'səm] *a* (*opponent*) formidabile, terribile; (*sight*) terrificante.

feasibility [fēzəbil'ətē] *n* praticabilità.

feasibility study *n* studio delle possibilità di realizzazione.

feasible [fē'zəbəl] *a* possibile, realizzabile.

feast [fēst] *n* festa, banchetto; (*REL*: *also*: ~ **day**) festa ♦ *vi* banchettare; **to** ~ **on** godersi, gustare.

feat [fēt] *n* impresa, fatto insigne.

feather [feth'ûr] *n* penna ♦ *cpd* (*mattress, bed,*

pillow) di piume ♦ *vt*: **to ~ one's nest** (*fig*) arricchirsi.

featherweight [feth'ûrwāt] *n* peso *m* piuma *inv*.

feature [fē'chûr] *n* caratteristica; (*article*) articolo ♦ *vt* (*subj*: *film*) avere come protagonista ♦ *vi* figurare; **~s** *npl* (*of face*) fisionomia; **a** (**special**) **~ on sth/sb** un servizio speciale su qc/qn; **it ~d prominently in ...** ha avuto un posto di prima importanza in ....

feature film *n* film *m inv* principale.

featureless [fē'chûrlis] *a* anonimo(a), senza caratteri distinti.

Feb. *abbr* (= *February*) feb.

February [feb'yəwārē] *n* febbraio; *for phrases see also* **July.**

feces [fē'sēz] *npl* (*US*) feci *fpl*.

feckless [fek'lis] *a* irresponsabile, incosciente.

Fed [fed] *abbr* (*US*) = **federal; federation.**

fed [fed] *pt, pp of* **feed; to be ~ up** essere stufo(a).

Fed. *n abbr* (*US col*) = **Federal Reserve Board.**

federal [fed'ûrəl] *a* federale.

Federal Republic of Germany (FRG) *n* Repubblica Federale Tedesca (RFT).

Federal Reserve Board (Fed.) *n* (*US*) *organo di controllo del sistema bancario statunitense.*

Federal Trade Commission (FTC) *n* (*US*) *organismo di protezione contro le pratiche commerciali abusive.*

federation [fedərā'shən] *n* federazione *f*.

fedora [fədôr'ə] *n* (*US*) cappello floscio di feltro.

fee [fē] *n* pagamento; (*of doctor, lawyer*) onorario; (*for examination*) tassa d'esame; **school ~s** tasse *fpl* scolastiche; **entrance ~,** **membership ~** quota d'iscrizione; **for a small ~** per una somma modesta.

feeble [fē'bəl] *a* debole.

feeble-minded [fē'bəlmīndid] *a* deficiente.

feed [fēd] *n* (*of baby*) pappa ♦ *vt* (*pt, pp* **fed** [fed]) nutrire; (*horse etc*) dare da mangiare a; (*fire, machine*) alimentare ♦ *vi* (*baby, animal*) mangiare; **to ~ material into sth** introdurre materiale in qc; **to ~ data/information into sth** inserire dati/informazioni in qc.

feed back *vt* (*results*) riferire.

feed on *vt fus* nutrirsi di.

feedback [fēd'bak] *n* feed-back *m*; (*from person*) reazioni *fpl*.

feeder [fē'dûr] *n* (*bib*) bavaglino.

feeding bottle [fē'ding bát'əl] *n* (*Brit*) biberon *m inv*.

feel [fēl] *n* sensazione *f*; (*sense of touch*) tatto; (*of substance*) consistenza ♦ *vt* (*pt, pp* **felt** [felt]) toccare; palpare; tastare; (*cold, pain, anger*) sentire; (*grief*) provare; (*think, believe*): **to ~ (that)** pensare che; **I ~ that**

you ought to do it penso che dovreste farlo; **to ~ hungry/cold** aver fame/freddo; **to ~ lonely/better** sentirsi solo/meglio; **I don't ~ well** non mi sento bene; **to ~ sorry for** dispiacersi per; **it ~s soft** è morbido al tatto; **it ~s colder out here** sembra più freddo qui fuori; **it ~s like velvet** sembra velluto (al tatto); **to ~ like** (*want*) aver voglia di; **to ~ around for** cercare a tastoni; **to ~ around in one's pocket for** frugarsi in tasca per cercare; **I'm still ~ing my way** (*fig*) sto ancora tastando il terreno; **to get the ~ of sth** (*fig*) abituarsi a qc.

feeler [fē'lûr] *n* (*of insect*) antenna; **to put out ~s** (*fig*) fare un sondaggio.

feeling [fē'ling] *n* sensazione *f*; sentimento; (*impression*) senso, impressione *f*; **to hurt sb's ~s** offendere qn; **what are your ~s about the matter?** che cosa ne pensa?; **my ~ is that ...** ho l'impressione che ...; **I got the ~ that ...** ho avuto l'impressione che ...; **~s ran high about it** la cosa aveva provocato grande eccitazione.

feet [fēt] *npl of* **foot.**

feign [fān] *vt* fingere, simulare.

felicitous [filis'itəs] *a* felice.

fell [fel] *pt of* **fall** ♦ *vt* (*tree*) abbattere; (*person*) atterrare ♦ *a*: **with one ~ blow** con un colpo terribile; **in one ~ swoop** in un colpo solo.

fellow [fel'ō] *n* individuo, tipo; (*comrade*) compagno; (*of learned society*) membro; (*of university*) ≈ docente *m/f* ♦ *cpd*: **their ~ prisoners/students** i loro compagni di prigione/studio.

fellow citizen *n* concittadino/a.

fellow countryman *n* compatriota *m*.

fellow feeling *n* simpatia.

fellow men *npl* simili *mpl*.

fellowship [fel'ōship] *n* associazione *f*; compagnia; (*SCOL*) specie di borsa di studio universitaria.

fellow traveler *n* compagno/a di viaggio; (*POL*) simpatizzante *m/f*.

fell-walking [fel'wôking] *n* (*Brit*) passeggiate *fpl* in montagna.

felon [fel'ən] *n* (*LAW*) criminale *m/f*.

felony [fel'ənē] *n* (*LAW*) reato, crimine *m*.

felt [felt] *pt, pp of* **feel** ♦ *n* feltro.

felt-tip pen [felt'tip pen'] *n* pennarello.

female [fē'māl] *n* (*ZOOL*) femmina; (*pej*: *woman*) donna, femmina ♦ *a* femminile; (*BIOL, ELEC*) femmina *inv*; **male and ~ students** studenti e studentesse.

female impersonator *n* (*THEATER*) *attore comico che fa parti da donna.*

feminine [fem'ənin] *a, n* femminile (*m*).

femininity [femənin'ətē] *n* femminilità.

feminism [fem'ənizəm] *n* femminismo.

feminist [fem'ənist] *n* femminista *m/f*.

fence [fens] *n* recinto; (*SPORT*) ostacolo; (*col*:

person) ricettatore/trice ♦ *vt* (*also:* ~ **in**) recingere ♦ *vi* schermire; **to sit on the** ~ (*fig*) rimanere neutrale.

fencing [fen'sing] *n* (*SPORT*) scherma.

fend [fend] *vi:* **to** ~ **for o.s.** arrangiarsi.

fend off *vt* (*attack*, *attacker*) respingere, difendersi da; (*blow*) parare; (*awkward question*) eludere.

fender [fen'dûr] *n* (*of fireplace*) parafuoco; (*US AUT*) parafango; ala.

fennel [fen'əl] *n* finocchio.

FEPC *n abbr* (*US*) = *Fair Employment Practices Committee*.

FERC *n abbr* (*US:* = *Federal Energy Regulatory Commission*) *agenzia federale indipendente per la regolamentazione dell'elettricità.*

ferment *vi* [fərment'] fermentare ♦ *n* [fûr'ment] agitazione *f*, eccitazione *f*.

fermentation [fûrmentā'shən] *n* fermentazione *f*.

fern [fûrn] *n* felce *f*.

ferocious [fərō'shəs] *a* feroce.

ferocity [fərâs'itē] *n* ferocità.

ferret [fär'it] *n* furetto.

ferret around *vi* frugare.

ferret out *vt* (*person*) scovare, scoprire; (*secret*, *truth*) scoprire.

ferris wheel [fer'is wēl] *n* (*at fair*) montagne *fpl* russe, otto *m inv* volante.

ferry [fär'ē] *n* (*small*) traghetto; (*large:* also: ~**boat**) nave *f* traghetto *inv* ♦ *vt* traghettare; **to** ~ **sth/sb across** *or* **over** traghettare qc/qn da una parte all'altra.

ferryman [fär'ēmən] *n* traghettatore *m*.

fertile [fûr'təl] *a* fertile; (*BIOL*) fecondo(a); ~ **period** periodo di fecondità.

fertility [fûrtil'ətē] *n* fertilità; fecondità.

fertility drug *n* farmaco fecondativo.

fertilize [fûr'təliz] *vt* fertilizzare; fecondare.

fertilizer [fûr'təlīzûr] *n* fertilizzante *m*.

fervent [fûr'vənt] *a* ardente, fervente.

fervor, (*Brit*) **fervour** [fûr'vûr] *n* fervore *m*, ardore *m*.

fester [fes'tûr] *vi* suppurare.

festival [fes'təvəl] *n* (*REL*) festa; (*ART, MUS*) festival *m inv*.

festive [fes'tiv] *a* di festa; **the** ~ **season** (*Brit:* *Christmas*) il periodo delle feste.

festivities [festiv'itēz] *npl* festeggiamenti *mpl*.

festoon [festoon'] *vt:* **to** ~ **with** ornare di; decorare con.

FET *n abbr* (*US:* = *Federal Excise Tax*) *tipo di imposta indiretta.*

fetal [fēt'l] *a* (*US*) fetale.

fetch [fech] *vt* andare a prendere; (*sell for*) essere venduto(a) per.

fetching [fech'ing] *a* attraente.

fête [fet] *n* festa.

fetid [fet'id] *a* fetido(a).

fetish [fet'ish] *n* feticcio.

fetter [fet'ûr] *vt* (*person*) incatenare; (*horse*) legare; (*fig*) ostacolare.

fetters [fet'ûrz] *npl* catene *fpl*.

fettle [fet'əl] *n* (*Brit*): **in fine** ~ in gran forma.

fetus [fē'təs] *n* (*US*) feto.

feud [fyood] *n* contesa, lotta ♦ *vi* essere in lotta; **a family** ~ una lite in famiglia.

feudal [fyood'əl] *a* feudale.

feudalism [fyoo'dəlizəm] *n* feudalesimo.

fever [fē'vûr] *n* febbre *f*; **he has a** ~ ha la febbre.

feverish [fē'vûrish] *a* (*also fig*) febbrile; (*person*) febbricitante.

few [fyoo] *a* pochi(e) ♦ *pronoun* alcuni(e); ~ **succeed** pochi ci riescono; **they were** ~ erano pochi; **a** ~ ... qualche ...; **I know a** ~ ne conosco alcuni; **a good** ~, **quite a** ~ parecchi; **in the next** ~ **days** nei prossimi giorni; **in the past** ~ **days** negli ultimi giorni, in questi ultimi giorni; **every** ~ **days/months** ogni due o tre giorni/mesi; **a** ~ **more days** qualche altro giorno.

fewer [fyoo'ûr] *a* meno *inv*; meno numerosi(e) ♦ *pronoun* meno; **they are** ~ **now** adesso ce ne sono di meno.

fewest [fyoo'ist] *a* il minor numero di.

FFA *n abbr* = *Future Farmers of America*.

FHA *n abbr* (*US*) = *Federal Housing Administration.*

fiancé [fēânsā'] *n* fidanzato.

fiancée [fēânsā'] *n* fidanzata.

fiasco [fēas'kō] *n* fiasco.

fib [fib] *n* piccola bugia.

fiber, (*Brit*) **fibre** [fī'bûr] *n* fibra.

fiberboard, (*Brit*) **fibreboard** [fī'bûrbôrd] *n* pannello di fibre.

fiberglass, (*Brit*) **fibreglass** [fī'bûrglas] *n* fibra di vetro.

fibrositis [fibrəsī'tis] *n* cellulite *f*.

FIC *n abbr* (*US*) = *Federal Information Centers.*

FICA *n abbr* (*US*) = *Federal Insurance Contributions Act.*

fickle [fik'əl] *a* incostante, capriccioso(a).

fiction [fik'shən] *n* narrativa; (*sth made up*) finzione *f*.

fictional [fik'shənəl] *a* immaginario(a).

fictionalize [fik'shənəliz] *vt* romanzare.

fictitious [fiktish'əs] *a* fittizio(a).

fiddle [fid'əl] *n* (*MUS*) violino; (*cheating*) imbroglio; truffa ♦ *vt* (*accounts*) falsificare, falsare; **to work a** ~ (*Brit*) fare un imbroglio.

fiddle with *vt fus* gingillarsi con.

fiddler [fid'lûr] *n* violinista *m/f*.

fiddly [fid'lē] *a* (*task*) da certosino; (*object*) complesso(a).

fidelity [fidel'itē] *n* fedeltà; (*accuracy*) esattezza.

fidget [fij'it] *vi* agitarsi.

fidgety [fij'itē] *a* agitato(a).

fiduciary [fidoo'shēārē] *n* fiduciario.

field [fēld] *n* (*gen, COMPUT*) campo; **to lead the ~** (*SPORT, COMM*) essere in testa, essere al primo posto; **to have a ~ day** (*fig*) divertirsi, spassarsela.

field glasses *npl* binocolo (da campagna).

field marshal (FM) *n* feldmaresciallo.

fieldwork [fēld'wûrk] *n* ricerche *fpl* esterne; (*ARCHEOLOGY, GEO*) lavoro sul campo.

fiend [fēnd] *n* demonio.

fiendish [fēn'dish] *a* demoniaco(a).

fierce [fērs] *a* (*look, fighting*) fiero(a); (*wind*) furioso(a); (*attack*) feroce; (*enemy*) acerrimo(a).

fiery [fī'ûrē] *a* ardente; infocato(a).

FIFA [fē'fa] *n abbr* (= *Fédération Internationale de Football Association*) F.I.F.A. *f.*

fifteen [fif'tēn'] *num* quindici.

fifth [fifth] *num* quinto(a).

fiftieth [fif'tēith] *num* cinquantesimo(a).

fifty [fif'tē] *num* cinquanta.

fifty-fifty [fif'tēfif'tē] *a, ad*: **to go ~ with sb** fare a metà con qn; **we have a ~ chance of success** abbiamo una probabilità su due di successo.

fig [fig] *n* fico.

fight [fīt] *n* zuffa, rissa; (*MIL*) battaglia, combattimento; (*against cancer etc*) lotta ♦ *vb* (*pt, pp* **fought** [fôt]) *vt* combattere; (*cancer, alcoholism*) lottare contro, combattere; (*LAW: case*) difendere ♦ *vi* battersi, combattere; (*quarrel*): **to ~ (with sb)** litigare (con qn); (*fig*): **to ~ (for/against)** lottare (per/contro).

fight back *vi* difendersi; (*SPORT, after illness*) riprendersi ♦ *vt* (*tears*) ricacciare.

fight down *vt* (*anger, anxiety*) vincere; (*urge*) reprimere.

fight off *vt* (*attack, attacker*) respingere; (*disease, sleep, urge*) lottare contro.

fight out *vt*: **to ~ it out** risolvere la questione a pugni.

fighter [fī'tûr] *n* combattente *m*; (*plane*) aeroplano da caccia.

fighter-bomber [fī'tûrbâm'ûr] *n* cacciabombardiere *m*.

fighter pilot *n* pilota *m* di caccia.

fighting [fī'ting] *n* combattimento; (*in streets*) scontri *mpl*.

figment [fig'mənt] *n*: **a ~ of the imagination** un parto della fantasia.

figurative [fig'yûrətiv] *a* figurato(a).

figure [fig'yûr] *n* (*DRAWING, GEOM, person*) figura; (*number, cipher*) cifra; (*body, outline*) forma ♦ *vi* (*appear*) figurare; (*US: make sense*) spiegarsi, essere logico(a) ♦ *vt* (*US: think, calculate*) pensare, immaginare; **public ~** personaggio pubblico; **~ of speech** figura retorica.

figure on *vt fus* (*US*) contare su.

figure out *vt* riuscire a capire; calcolare.

figurehead [fig'yûrhed] *n* (*NAUT*) polena; (*pej*) prestanome *m/f inv.*

figure skating *n* pattinaggio artistico.

Fiji (Islands) [fē'jē i'ləndz] *n(pl)* le (isole) Figi.

filament [fil'əmənt] *n* filamento.

filch [filch] *vt* (*col: steal*) grattare.

file [fīl] *n* (*tool*) lima; (*for nails*) limetta; (*dossier*) incartamento; (*in cabinet*) scheda; (*folder*) cartellina; (*for loose leaf*) raccoglitore *m*; (*row*) fila; (*COMPUT*) archivio, file *m inv* ♦ *vt* (*nails, wood*) limare; (*papers*) archiviare; (*LAW: claim*) presentare ♦ *vi*: **to ~ in/out** entrare/uscire in fila; **to ~ past** marciare in fila davanti a; **to ~ a suit against sb** intentare causa contro qn.

file name *n* (*COMPUT*) nome *m* del file.

filibuster [fil'əbustûr] (*esp US POL*) *n* (*also:* **~er**) ostruzionista *m/f* ♦ *vi* fare ostruzionismo.

filing [fī'ling] *n* archiviare *m; see also* **filings**.

filing cabinet *n* casellario.

filing clerk *n* archivista *m/f*.

filings [fī'lingz] *npl* limatura.

Filipino [filəpē'nō] *n* filippino/a; (*LING*) tagal *m.*

fill [fil] *vt* riempire; (*tooth*) otturare; (*job*) coprire; (*supply: order, requirements, need*) soddisfare ♦ *n*: **to eat one's ~** mangiare a sazietà; **we've already ~ed that vacancy** abbiamo già assunto qualcuno per quel posto.

fill in *vt* (*hole*) riempire; (*form*) compilare; (*details, report*) completare ♦ *vi*: **to ~ in for sb** sostituire qn; **to ~ sb in on sth** (*col*) mettere qn al corrente di qc.

fill out *vt* (*form, receipt*) riempire.

fill up *vt* riempire ♦ *vi* (*AUT*) fare il pieno; **~ it up, please** (*AUT*) mi faccia il pieno, per piacere.

fillet [filā'] *n* filetto.

fillet steak *n* bistecca di filetto.

filling [fil'ing] *n* (*CULIN*) impasto, ripieno; (*for tooth*) otturazione *f.*

filling station *n* stazione *f* di rifornimento.

fillip [fil'əp] *n* incentivo, stimolo.

filly [fil'ē] *n* puledra.

film [film] *n* (*CINEMA*) film *m inv*; (*PHOT*) pellicola; (*thin layer*) velo ♦ *vt* (*scene*) filmare.

film script *n* copione *m.*

film star *n* divo/a dello schermo.

filmstrip [film'strip] *n* filmina.

film studio *n* studio cinematografico.

filter [fil'tûr] *n* filtro ♦ *vt* filtrare.

filter in, filter through *vi* (*news*) trapelare.

filter coffee *n* caffè *m* da passare al filtro.

filter lane *n* (*Brit AUT*) corsia di svincolo.

filter tip *n* filtro.

filter-tipped [fil'tûrtipt] *a* col filtro.

filth [filth] *n* sporcizia; (*fig*) oscenità.

filthy [fil'thē] *a* lordo(a), sozzo(a); (*language*)

osceno(a).

fin. *abbr* = **finance**.

fin |fin| *n* (*of fish*) pinna.

final |fĭ'nəl| *a* finale, ultimo(a); definitivo(a) ♦ *n* (*SPORT*) finale *f*; **~s** *npl* (*SCOL*) esami *mpl* finali; **~ demand** ingiunzione *f* di pagamento.

finale |final'ē| *n* finale *m*.

finalist |fĭ'nəlist| *n* (*SPORT*) finalista *m/f*.

finality |fĭnal'itē| *n* irrevocabilità; **with an air of ~** con risolutezza.

finalize |fĭ'nəliz| *vt* mettere a punto.

finally |fĭ'nəlē| *ad* (*lastly*) alla fine; (*eventually*) finalmente; (*once and for all*) definitivamente.

finance *n* |fĭ'nans| finanza; (*funds*) fondi *mpl*, capitale *m* ♦ *vt* |finans'| finanziare; **~s** *npl* finanze *fpl*.

financial |finan'chəl| *a* finanziario(a); **~ statement** estratto conto finanziario.

financially |fĭnan'chəlē| *ad* finanziariamente.

financial year *n* anno finanziario, esercizio finanziario.

financier |fĭnansiûr'| *n* finanziatore *m*.

find |fīnd| *vt* (*pt, pp* **found** |found|) trovare; (*lost object*) ritrovare ♦ *n* trovata, scoperta; **to ~** (*some*) **difficulty in doing sth** trovare delle difficoltà nel fare qc; **to ~ sb guilty** (*LAW*) giudicare qn colpevole.

find out *vt* informarsi di; (*truth, secret*) scoprire; (*person*) cogliere in fallo ♦ *vi*: **to ~ out about** informarsi su; (*by chance*) venire a sapere.

findings |fīn'dingz| *npl* (*LAW*) sentenza, conclusioni *fpl*; (*of report*) conclusioni *fpl*.

fine |fīn| *a* bello(a); ottimo(a); (*thin, subtle*) fine ♦ *ad* (*well*) molto bene; (*small*) finemente ♦ *n* (*LAW*) multa ♦ *vt* (*LAW*) multare; **he's ~** sta bene; **the weather is ~** il tempo è bello; **you're doing ~** te la cavi benissimo; **to cut it ~** (*of time, money*) farcela per un pelo.

fine arts *npl* belle arti *fpl*.

finely |fīn'lē| *ad* (*splendidly*) in modo stupendo; (*chop*) finemente; (*adjust*) con precisione.

finery |fĭ'nûrē| *n* abiti *mpl* eleganti.

finesse |fines'| *n* finezza.

fine-tooth comb |fīn'tōōth kōm| *n*: **to go through sth with a ~** (*fig*) passare qc al setaccio.

finger |fing'gûr| *n* dito ♦ *vt* toccare, tastare.

fingernail |fing'gûrnāl| *n* unghia.

fingerprint |fing'gûrprint| *n* impronta digitale ♦ *vt* (*person*) prendere le impronte digitali di.

fingerstall |fing'gûrstôl| *n* (*Brit*) ditale *m*.

fingertip |fing'gûrtip| *n* punta del dito; **to have sth at one's ~s** (*fig*) avere qc sulla punta delle dita.

finicky |fin'ikē| *a* esigente, pignolo(a); minuzioso(a).

finish |fin'ish| *n* fine *f*; (*SPORT*: *place*) tra-

guardo; (*polish etc*) finitura ♦ *vt* finire; (*use up*) esaurire ♦ *vi* finire; (*session*) terminare; **to ~ doing sth** finire di fare qc; **to ~ first/second** (*SPORT*) arrivare primo/secondo; **she's ~ed with him** ha chiuso con lui.

finish off *vt* compiere; (*kill*) uccidere.

finish up *vi*, *vt* finire.

finished |fin'isht| *a* (*product*) finito(a); (*performance*) perfetto(a); (*col*: *tired*) sfinito(a).

finish line *n* linea d'arrivo.

finishing school |fin'ishing skōōl| *n* scuola privata di perfezionamento (*per signorine*).

finishing touches |fin'ishing tuch'əz| *npl* ultimi ritocchi *mpl*.

finite |fī'nīt| *a* limitato(a); (*verb*) finito(a).

Finland |fin'lənd| *n* Finlandia.

Finn |fin| *n* finlandese *m/f*.

Finnish |fin'ish| *a* finlandese ♦ *n* (*LING*) finlandese *m*.

fiord |fyôrd| *n* fiordo.

fir |fûr| *n* abete *m*.

fire |fī'ûr| *n* fuoco; incendio ♦ *vt* (*discharge*): **to ~ a gun** scaricare un fucile; (*fig*) infiammare; (*dismiss*) licenziare ♦ *vi* sparare, far fuoco; **on ~** in fiamme; **insured against ~** assicurato contro gli incendi; **electric/gas ~** (*Brit*) stufa elettrica/a gas; **to set ~ to sth, set sth on ~** dar fuoco a qc, incendiare qc; **to be/come under ~** (**from**) essere/finire sotto il fuoco *or* il tiro (di).

fire alarm *n* allarme *m* d'incendio.

firearm |fĭûr'ärm| *n* arma da fuoco.

fire brigade *n* (*Brit*) = **fire department**.

fire chief *n* comandante *m* dei vigili del fuoco.

fire department *n* (*US*) (corpo dei) pompieri *mpl*.

fire drill *n* esercitazione *f* antincendio.

fire engine *n* autopompa.

fire escape *n* scala di sicurezza.

fire extinguisher *n* estintore *m*.

fire hazard *n*: **that's a ~** comporta rischi in caso d'incendio.

fire hydrant *n* idrante *m*.

fire insurance *n* assicurazione *f* contro gli incendi.

fireman |fĭûr'mən| *n* pompiere *m*.

fireplace |fĭûr'plās| *n* focolare *m*.

fireplug |fĭûr'plug| *n* (*US*) idrante *m*.

fire practice *n* = **fire drill**.

fireproof |fĭûr'prōōf| *a* resistente al fuoco.

fire regulations *npl* norme *fpl* antincendio.

fire screen *n* parafuoco.

fireside |fĭûr'sīd| *n* angolo del focolare.

fire station *n* caserma dei pompieri.

firewood |fĭûr'wōōd| *n* legna.

firework |fĭûr'wûrk| *n* fuoco d'artificio.

firing |fĭûr'ing| *n* (*MIL*) spari *mpl*, tiro.

firing line *n* linea del fuoco; **to be in the ~** (*fig*) essere sotto tiro.

firing squad *n* plotone *m* d'esecuzione.

firm |fûrm| *a* fermo(a); (*offer, decision*) definitivo(a) ♦ *n* ditta, azienda; **to be a ~ believer in sth** credere fermamente in qc.

firmly [fûrm'lē] *ad* fermamente.

firmness [fûrm'nis] *n* fermezza.

first [fûrst] *a* primo(a) ♦ *ad* (*before others*) il primo, la prima; (*before other things*) per primo; (*for the first time*) per la prima volta; (*when listing reasons etc*) per prima cosa ♦ *n* (*person: in race*) primo/a; (*AUT*) prima; **at ~** dapprima, all'inizio; **~ of all** prima di tutto; **in the ~ place** prima di tutto, in primo luogo; **I'll do it ~ thing tomorrow** lo farò per prima cosa domani; **from the (very) ~** fin dall'inizio, fin dal primo momento; **the ~ of January** il primo (di) gennaio.

first aid *n* pronto soccorso.

first-aid kit [fûrst'ād' kit] *n* cassetta pronto soccorso.

first-class [fûrst'klas'] *a* di prima classe.

first-class mail *n ≈* espresso.

first-hand [fûrst'hand'] *a* di prima mano; diretto(a).

first lady *n* (*US*) moglie *f* del presidente.

firstly [fûrst'lē] *ad* in primo luogo.

first name *n* prenome *m*.

first night *n* (*THEATER*) prima.

first-rate [fûrst'rāt'] *a* di prima qualità, ottimo(a).

fir tree *n* abete *m*.

fiscal [fis'kəl] *a* fiscale; **~ year** anno fiscale.

fish [fish] *n* (*pl inv*) pesce *m* ♦ *vt, vi* pescare; **to ~ a river** pescare in un fiume; **to go ~ing** andare a pesca.

fish out *vt* (*from water*) ripescare; (*from box etc*) tirare fuori.

fishbone [fish'bōn] *n* lisca, spina.

fisherman [fish'ûrmən] *n* pescatore *m*.

fishery [fish'ûrē] *n* zona da pesca.

fish factory *n* (*Brit*) fabbrica per la lavorazione del pesce.

fish farm *n* vivaio.

fish fingers *npl* (*Brit*) = **fish sticks**.

fish hook *n* amo.

fishing boat [fish'ing bōt] *n* barca da pesca.

fishing industry *n* industria della pesca.

fishing line *n* lenza.

fishing net *n* rete *f* da pesca.

fishing rod *n* canna da pesca.

fishing tackle *n* attrezzatura da pesca.

fish market *n* mercato del pesce.

fishmonger [fish'munggûr] *n* pescivendolo; **~'s (shop)** pescheria.

fish slice *n* (*Brit*) posata per servire il pesce.

fish sticks *npl* (*US*) bastoncini *mpl* di pesce (surgelati).

fishy [fish'ē] *a* (*fig*) sospetto(a).

fission [fish'ən] *n* fissione *f*; **atomic/nuclear ~** fissione atomica/nucleare.

fissure [fish'ûr] *n* fessura.

fist [fist] *n* pugno.

fistfight [fist'fīt] *n* scazzottata.

fit [fit] *a* (*MED, SPORT*) in forma; (*proper*) adatto(a), appropriato(a); conveniente ♦ *vt* (*subj: clothes*) stare bene a; (*match: facts etc*) concordare con; (*: description*) corrispondere a; (*adjust*) aggiustare; (*put in, attach*) mettere; installare; (*equip*) fornire, equipaggiare ♦ *vi* (*clothes*) stare bene; (*parts*) andare bene, adattarsi; (*in space, gap*) entrare ♦ *n* (*MED*) attacco; **~ to** in grado di; **~ for** adatto(a) a; degno(a) di; **to keep ~** tenersi in forma; **~ for work** (*after illness*) in grado di riprendere il lavoro; **do as you think** *or* **see ~** faccia come meglio crede; **this dress is a tight/good ~** questo vestito è stretto/sta bene; **~ of anger/enthusiasm** accesso d'ira/d'entusiasmo; **to have a ~** (*MED*) avere un attacco di convulsioni; (*col*) andare su tutte le furie; **by ~s and starts** a sbalzi.

fit in *vi* accordarsi; adattarsi ♦ *vt* (*object*) far entrare; (*fig: appointment, visitor*) trovare il tempo per; **to ~ in with sb's plans** adattarsi ai progetti di qn.

fit out *vt* equipaggiare.

fitful [fit'fəl] *a* saltuario(a).

fitment [fit'mənt] *n* (*Brit*) componibile *m*.

fitness [fit'nis] *n* (*MED*) forma fisica; (*of remark*) appropriatezza.

fitted [fit'id] *a*: **~ carpet** moquette *f inv*; **~ kitchen** (*Brit*) cucina componibile.

fitter [fit'ûr] *n* aggiustatore *m or* montatore *m* meccanico; (*DRESSMAKING*) sarto/a.

fitting [fit'ing] *a* appropriato(a) ♦ *n* (*of dress*) prova; (*of piece of equipment*) montaggio, aggiustaggio; *see also* **fittings**.

fitting room *n* (*in shop*) camerino.

fittings [fit'ingz] *npl* impianti *mpl*.

five [fīv] *num* cinque.

five-day week [fīv'dā wēk'] *n* settimana di 5 giorni (lavorativi).

fiver [fī'vûr] *n* (*col: US*) biglietto da cinque dollari.

fix [fiks] *vt* fissare; (*mend*) riparare; (*make ready: meal, drink*) preparare; (*US: castrate: cat etc*) castrare ♦ *n*: **to be in a ~** essere nei guai.

fix up *vt* (*arrange: date, meeting*) fissare, stabilire; **to ~ sb up with sth** procurare qc a qn.

fixation [fiksā'shən] *n* (*PSYCH, fig*) fissazione *f*, ossessione *f*.

fixed [fikst] *a* (*prices etc*) fisso(a); **there's a ~ charge** c'è una quota fissa; **how are you ~ for money?** (*col*) a soldi come stai?

fixed assets *npl* beni *mpl* patrimoniali.

fixture [fiks'chûr] *n* impianto (fisso); (*SPORT*) incontro (del calendario sportivo).

fizz [fiz] *vi* frizzare.

fizzle [fiz'əl] *vi* frizzare; (*also: ~ out: enthusiasm, interest*) smorzarsi, svanire; (*: plan*) fallire.

fizzy [fiz'ē] *a* frizzante; gassato(a).

fjord [fyôrd] *n* = **fiord.**

FL *abbr* (*US MAIL*) = *Florida*.

Fla. *abbr* (*US*) = *Florida*.

flabbergasted [flab'ûrgastid] *a* sbalordito(a).

flabby [flab'ē] *a* flaccido(a).

flag [flag] *n* bandiera; (*also:* ~**stone**) pietra da lastricare ♦ *vi* stancarsi; affievolirsi; ~ **of convenience** bandiera di convenienza.

flag down *vt* fare segno (di fermarsi) a.

flagon [flag'ən] *n* bottiglione *m*.

flagpole [flag'pōl] *n* albero.

flagrant [flā'grənt] *a* flagrante.

flag stop *n* (*US: for bus*) fermata facoltativa, fermata a richiesta.

flair [flär] *n* (*for business etc*) fiuto; (*for languages etc*) facilità.

flak [flak] *n* (*MIL*) fuoco d'artiglieria; (*col: criticism*) critiche *fpl*.

flake [flāk] *n* (*of rust, paint*) scaglia; (*of snow, soap powder*) fiocco ♦ *vi* (*also:* ~ **off**) sfaldarsi.

flaky [flā'kē] *a* (*paintwork*) scrostato(a); (*skin*) squamoso(a); ~ **pastry** (*Brit CULIN*) pasta sfoglia.

flamboyant [flamboi'ənt] *a* sgargiante.

flame [flām] *n* fiamma; **old** ~ (*col*) vecchia fiamma.

flamingo [fləming'gō] *n* fenicottero, fiammingo.

flammable [flam'əbəl] *a* infiammabile.

flan [flan] *n* flan *m inv*.

Flanders [flan'dûrz] *n* Fiandre *fpl*.

flange [flanj] *n* flangia; (*on wheel*) suola.

flank [flangk] *n* fianco.

flannel [flan'əl] *n* (*Brit: also:* **face** ~) guanto di spugna; (*fabric*) flanella; ~**s** *npl* (*Brit*) pantaloni *mpl* di flanella.

flannelette [flanəlet'] *n* flanella di cotone.

flap [flap] *n* (*of pocket*) patta; (*of envelope*) lembo; (*AVIAT*) flap *m inv* ♦ *vt* (*wings*) battere ♦ *vi* (*sail, flag*) sbattere; (*col: also:* **be in a** ~) essere in agitazione.

flapjack [flap'jak] *n* (*US*) frittella; (*Brit: biscuit*) biscotto di avena.

flare [flär] *n* razzo; (*in skirt etc*) svasatura.

flare up *vi* andare in fiamme; (*fig: person*) infiammarsi di rabbia; (: *revolt*) scoppiare.

flared [flärd] *a* (*pants*) svasato(a).

flash [flash] *n* vampata; (*also:* **news** ~) notizia *f* lampo *inv*; (*PHOT*) flash *m inv*; (*US: torch*) torcia elettrica, lampadina tascabile ♦ *vt* accendere e spegnere; (*send: message*) trasmettere; (*flaunt*) ostentare ♦ *vi* brillare; (*light on ambulance, eyes etc*) lampeggiare; **in a** ~ in un lampo; ~ **of inspiration** lampo di genio; **to** ~ **one's headlights** lampeggiare; **he** ~**ed by** *or* **past** ci passò davanti come un lampo.

flashback [flash'bak] *n* flashback *m inv*.

flashbulb [flash'bulb] *n* flash *m inv*.

flash card *n* (*SCOL*) scheda didattica.

flashcube [flash'kyōōb] *n* cubo *m* flash *inv*.

flashlight [flash'līt] *n* (*torch*) lampadina tascabile.

flash point *n* punto di infiammabilità; (*fig*) livello critico.

flashy [flash'ē] *a* (*pej*) vistoso(a).

flask [flask] *n* fiasco; (*CHEM*) beuta; (*also:* **vacuum** ~) thermos ® *m inv*.

flat [flat] *a* piatto(a); (*tire*) sgonfio(a), a terra; (*battery*) scarico(a); (*denial*) netto(a); (*MUS*) bemolle *inv*; (: *voice*) stonato(a); (: *instrument*) scordato(a) ♦ *n* (*Brit: apartment*) appartamento; (*MUS*) bemolle *m*; (*AUT*) pneumatico sgonfio ♦ *ad*: **(to work)** ~ **out** (*lavorare*) a più non posso; ~ **rate of pay** tariffa unica di pagamento.

flat-footed [flat'fōōtid] *a*: **to be** ~ avere i piedi piatti.

flatly [flat'lē] *ad* categoricamente, nettamente.

flatmate [flat'māt] *n* (*Brit*): **he's my** ~ divide l'appartamento con me.

flatness [flat'nis] *n* (*of land*) assenza di rilievi.

flatten [flat'ən] *vt* (*also:* ~ **out**) appiattire; (*house, city*) abbattere, radere al suolo.

flatter [flat'ûr] *vt* lusingare; (*show to advantage*) donare a.

flatterer [flat'ûrûr] *n* adulatore/trice.

flattering [flat'ûring] *a* lusinghiero(a); (*clothes etc*) che dona, che abbellisce.

flattery [flat'ûrē] *n* adulazione *f*.

flatulence [flach'ələns] *n* flatulenza.

flaunt [flônt] *vt* fare mostra di.

flavor [flā'vûr] (*US*) *n* gusto, sapore *m* ♦ *vt* insaporire, aggiungere sapore a; **vanilla-~ed** al gusto di vaniglia.

flavoring [flā'vûring] *n* essenza (artificiale).

flavour [flā'vûr] *etc* (*Brit*) = **flavor** *etc*.

flaw [flô] *n* difetto.

flawless [flô'lis] *a* senza difetti.

flax [flaks] *n* lino.

flaxen [flaks'ən] *a* biondo(a).

flea [flē] *n* pulce *f*.

flea market *n* mercato delle pulci.

fleck [flek] *n* (*of mud, paint, color*) macchiolina; (*of dust*) granello ♦ *vt* (*with blood, mud etc*) macchiettare; **brown ~ed with white** marrone screziato di bianco.

fled [fled] *pt, pp* of **flee**.

fledg(e)ling [flej'ling] *n* uccellino.

flee, *pt, pp* **fled** [flē, fled] *vt* fuggire da ♦ *vi* fuggire, scappare.

fleece [flēs] *n* vello ♦ *vt* (*col*) pelare.

fleecy [flē'sē] *a* (*blanket*) soffice; (*cloud*) come ovatta.

fleet [flēt] *n* flotta; (*of trucks etc*) convoglio; (*of cars*) parco.

fleeting [flē'ting] *a* fugace, fuggitivo(a); (*visit*) volante.

Flemish [flem'ish] *a* fiammingo(a) ♦ *n* (*LING*)

fiammingo; **the** ~ *npl* i Fiamminghi.
flesh |flɛsh| *n* carne *f*; (*of fruit*) polpa.
flesh wound *n* ferita superficiale.
flew |flōō| *pt of* **fly.**
flex |flɛks| *n* filo (flessibile) ♦ *vt* flettere; (*muscles*) contrarre.
flexibility |flɛksəbil'ətē| *n* flessibilità.
flexible |flɛk'səbəl| *a* flessibile.
flick |flik| *n* colpetto.
 flick through *vt fus* sfogliare.
flicker |flik'ûr| *vi* tremolare ♦ *n* tremolio; **a** ~ **of light** un breve bagliore.
flick knife *n* (*Brit*) coltello a serramanico.
flier |flī'ûr| *n* aviatore *m*.
flight |flīt| *n* volo; (*escape*) fuga; (*also:* ~ **of steps**) scalinata; **to take** ~ darsi alla fuga; **to put to** ~ mettere in fuga.
flight attendant *n* steward *m*, hostess *f inv*.
flight crew *n* equipaggio.
flight deck *n* (*AVIAT*) cabina di controllo; (*NAUT*) ponte *m* di comando.
flight recorder *n* registratore *m* di volo.
flimsy |flim'zē| *a* (*fabric*) inconsistente; (*excuse*) meschino(a).
flinch |flinch| *vi* ritirarsi; **to** ~ **from** tirarsi indietro di fronte a.
fling, *pt*, *pp* **flung** |fling, flung| *vt* lanciare, gettare ♦ *n* (*love affair*) avventura.
flint |flint| *n* selce *f*; (*in lighter*) pietrina.
flip |flip| *n* colpetto ♦ *vt* dare un colpetto a; (*US: flapjack*) far saltare (in aria) ♦ *vi:* **to** ~ **for sth** (*US*) fare a testa e croce per qc.
 flip through *vt fus* (*book, records*) dare una scorsa a.
flippant |flip'ənt| *a* senza rispetto, irriverente.
flipper |flip'ûr| *n* pinna.
flip side *n* (*of record*) retro.
flirt |flûrt| *vi* flirtare ♦ *n* civetta.
flirtation |flûrtā'shən| *n* flirt *m inv*.
flit |flit| *vi* svolazzare.
float |flōt| *n* galleggiante *m*; (*in procession*) carro; (*sum of money*) somma ♦ *vi* galleggiare; (*bather*) fare il morto; (*COMM: currency*) fluttuare ♦ *vt* far galleggiare; (*loan, business*) lanciare; **to** ~ **an idea** ventilare un'idea.
floating |flō'ting| *a* a galla; ~ **vote** voto oscillante; ~ **voter** elettore *m* indeciso.
flock |flåk| *n* gregge *m*; (*of people*) folla; (*of birds*) stormo.
floe |flō| *n* (*also:* **ice** ~) banchisa.
flog |flåg| *vt* flagellare.
flood |flud| *n* alluvione *m*; (*of words, tears etc*) diluvio ♦ *vt* inondare, allagare; (*AUT: carburetor*) ingolfare; **in** ~ in piena; **to** ~ **the market** (*COMM*) inondare il mercato.
flooding |flud'ing| *n* inondazione *f*.
floodlight |flud'līt| *n* riflettore *m* ♦ *vt* illuminare a giorno.
floodlit |flud'lit| *pt*, *pp of* **floodlight** ♦ *a* illuminato(a) a giorno.

flood tide *n* alta marea, marea crescente.
floor |flôr| *n* pavimento; (*storey*) piano; (*of sea, valley*) fondo; (*fig: at meeting*): **the** ~ il pubblico ♦ *vt* pavimentare; (*knock down*) atterrare; (*baffle*) confondere; (*silence*) far tacere; **on the** ~ sul pavimento, per terra; **first** ~, (*Brit*) **ground** ~ pianterreno; **second** ~, (*Brit*) **first** ~ primo piano; **top** ~ ultimo piano; **to have the** ~ (*speaker*) prendere la parola.
floorboard |flôr'bôrd| *n* tavellone *m* di legno.
flooring |flôr'ing| *n* (*floor*) pavimento; (*material*) materiale *m* per pavimentazioni.
floor lamp *n* (*US*) lampada a stelo.
floor show *n* spettacolo di varietà.
floorwalker |flôr'wôkûr| *n* (*esp US*) ispettore *m* di reparto.
flop |flåp| *n* fiasco ♦ *vi* (*fail*) far fiasco.
flophouse |flåp'hous| *n* (*US*) asilo notturno.
floppy |flåp'ē| *a* floscio(a), molle ♦ *n* (*COMPUT*) = **floppy disk**; ~ **hat** cappello floscio.
floppy disk *n* floppy disk *m inv*.
flora |flôr'ə| *n* flora.
floral |flôr'əl| *a* floreale.
Florence |flår'əns| *n* Firenze *f*.
Florentine |flôr'əntēn| *a* fiorentino(a).
florid |flôr'id| *a* (*complexion*) florido(a); (*style*) fiorito(a).
florist |flôr'ist| *n* fioraio/a; **at the** ~**'s (shop)** dal fioraio.
flotation |flōtā'shən| *n* (*COMM*) lancio.
flounce |flouns| *n* balzo.
 flounce out *vi* uscire stizzito(a).
flounder |floun'dûr| *vi* annaspare ♦ *n* (*ZOOL*) passera di mare.
flour |flou'ûr| *n* farina.
flourish |flûr'ish| *vi* fiorire ♦ *vt* brandire ♦ *n* abbellimento; svolazzo; (*of trumpets*) fanfara.
flourishing |flûr'ishing| *a* prosperoso(a), fiorente.
flout |flout| *vt* (*order*) contravvenire a; (*convention*) sfidare.
flow |flō| *n* flusso; circolazione *f*; (*of river, also ELEC*) corrente *f* ♦ *vi* fluire; (*traffic, blood in veins*) circolare; (*hair*) scendere.
flow chart *n* schema *m* di flusso.
flow diagram *n* organigramma *m*.
flower |flou'ûr| *n* fiore *m* ♦ *vi* fiorire; **in** ~ in fiore.
flower bed *n* aiuola.
flowerpot |flou'ûrpåt| *n* vaso da fiori.
flowery |flou'ûrē| *a* fiorito(a).
flown |flōn| *pp of* **fly.**
flu |flōō| *n* influenza.
fluctuate |fluk'chōōāt| *vi* fluttuare, oscillare.
fluctuation |flukchōōā'shən| *n* fluttuazione *f*, oscillazione *f*.
flue |flōō| *n* canna fumaria.
fluency |flōō'ənsē| *n* facilità, scioltezza; **his** ~

in English la sua scioltezza nel parlare l'inglese.

fluent [flōō'ənt] *a* (*speech*) facile, sciolto(a); **he's a ~ speaker/reader** si esprime/legge senza difficoltà; **he speaks ~ Italian, he's ~ in Italian** parla l'italiano correntemente.

fluently [flōō'əntlē] *ad* con facilità; correntemente.

fluff [fluf] *n* lanugine *f*.

fluffy [fluf'ē] *a* lanuginoso(a).

fluid [flōō'id] *a* fluido(a) ♦ *n* fluido; (*in diet*) liquido.

fluid ounce *n* (*Brit*) = 0.028 l; 0.05 pints.

fluke [flōōk] *n* (*col*) colpo di fortuna.

flummox [flum'əks] *vt* rendere perplesso(a).

flung [flung] *pt, pp of* **fling**.

flunky [flung'kē] *n* tirapiedi *m/f inv*.

fluorescent [flōōəres'ənt] *a* fluorescente.

fluoride [flōō'ərīd] *n* fluoruro.

fluorine [flōō'ərēn] *n* fluoro.

flurry [flûr'ē] *n* (*of snow*) tempesta; **a ~ of activity/excitement** una febbre di attività/un'improvvisa agitazione.

flush [flush] *n* rossore *m*; (*fig*) ebbrezza ♦ *vt* ripulire con un getto d'acqua; (*also:* **~ out:** *birds*) far alzare in volo; (: *animals, fig: criminal*) stanare ♦ *vi* arrossire ♦ *a:* **~ with** a livello di, pari a; **~ against** aderente a; **to ~ the toilet** tirare l'acqua.

flushed [flusht] *a* tutto(a) rosso(a).

fluster [flus'tûr] *n* agitazione *f*.

flustered [flus'tûrd] *a* sconvolto(a).

flute [flōōt] *n* flauto.

flutter [flut'ûr] *n* agitazione *f*; (*of wings*) frullio ♦ *vi* (*bird*) battere le ali.

flux [fluks] *n:* **in a state of ~** in continuo mutamento.

fly [flī] *n* (*insect*) mosca; (*on pants: also:* **flies**) bracchetta ♦ *vb* (*pt* **flew**, *pp* **flown** [flōō, flōn]) *vt* pilotare; (*passengers, cargo*) trasportare (in aereo); (*distances*) percorrere ♦ *vi* volare; (*passengers*) andare in aereo; (*escape*) fuggire; (*flag*) sventolare; **to ~ open** spalancarsi all'improvviso; **to ~ off the handle** perdere le staffe, uscire dai gangheri.

fly away *vi* volar via.

fly in *vi* (*plane*) arrivare; (*person*) arrivare in aereo.

fly off *vi* volare via.

fly out *vi* (*plane*) partire; (*person*) partire in aereo.

fly-fishing [flī'fishing] *n* pesca con la mosca.

flying [flī'ing] *n* (*activity*) aviazione *f*; (*action*) volo ♦ *a:* **~ visit** visita volante; **with ~ colors** con risultati brillanti; **he doesn't like ~** non gli piace viaggiare in aereo.

flying buttress *n* arco rampante.

flying saucer *n* disco volante.

flying squad *n* volante *f*.

flying start *n:* **to get off to a ~** partire come

un razzo.

flyleaf [flī'lēf] *n* risguardo.

flyover [flī'ōvûr] *n* (*Brit: bridge*) cavalcavia *m inv*; (*US: flypast*) parata aerea.

flypast [flī'past] *n* parata aerea.

flysheet [flī'shēt] *n* (*for tent*) sopratetto.

flywheel [flī'hwēl] *n* volano.

FM *abbr see* **frequency modulation**; (*Brit MIL*) *see* **Field Marshal**.

FMB *n abbr* (*US*) = *Federal Maritime Board*.

FMCS *n abbr* (*US*: = *Federal Mediation and Conciliation Services*) organismo di conciliazione in caso di conflitti sul lavoro.

foal [fōl] *n* puledro.

foam [fōm] *n* schiuma ♦ *vi* schiumare.

foam rubber *n* gommapiuma ®.

FOB *abbr* (= *free on board*) franco a bordo.

fob [fäb] *vt:* **to ~ sb off with** appioppare qn con; sbarazzarsi di qn con ♦ *n* (*also:* **watch ~:** *chain*) catena per orologio; (: *band of cloth*) nastro per orologio.

foc *abbr* = **free of charge**.

focal [fō'kəl] *a* focale.

focal point *n* punto focale.

focus [fō'kəs] *n* (*pl* **~es**) fuoco; (*of interest*) centro ♦ *vt* (*field glasses etc*) mettere a fuoco; (*light rays*) far convergere ♦ *vi:* **to ~ on** (*with camera*) mettere a fuoco; (*person*) fissare lo sguardo su; **in ~** a fuoco; **out of ~** sfocato(a).

fodder [fäd'ûr] *n* foraggio.

FOE *n abbr* (*US:* = *Fraternal Order of Eagles*) organizzazione filantropica; (= *Friends of the Earth*) Amici *mpl* della Terra.

foe [fō] *n* nemico.

foetus [fē'təs] *etc* (*Brit*) = **fetus** *etc*.

fog [fôg] *n* nebbia.

fog up *vi* (*windows*) appannarsi.

fogbound [fôg'bound] *a* fermo(a) a causa della nebbia.

foggy [fôg'ē] *a* nebbioso(a); **it's ~** c'è nebbia.

fog light *n* (*AUT*) faro *m* antinebbia *inv*.

foible [foi'bəl] *n* debolezza, punto debole.

foil [foil] *vt* confondere, frustrare ♦ *n* lamina di metallo; (*also:* **tin~**) foglio di alluminio; (*FENCING*) fioretto; **to act as a ~ to** (*fig*) far risaltare.

foist [foist] *vt:* **to ~ sth on sb** rifilare qc a qn.

fold [fōld] *n* (*bend, crease*) piega; (*AGR*) ovile *m*; (*fig*) gregge *m* ♦ *vt* piegare; **to ~ one's arms** incrociare le braccia.

fold up *vi* (*map etc*) piegarsi; (*business*) crollare ♦ *vt* (*map etc*) piegare, ripiegare.

folder [fōl'dûr] *n* (*for papers*) cartella; cartellina; (*binder*) raccoglitore *m*.

folding [fōl'ding] *a* (*chair, bed*) pieghevole.

foliage [fō'lēij] *n* fogliame *m*.

folk [fōk] *npl* gente *f* ♦ *cpd* popolare; **~s** *npl* famiglia.

folklore [fōk'lôr] *n* folclore *m*.

folk music *n* musica folk *inv*.

folk singer n cantante m/f folk inv.

folksong [fōk'sông] n canto popolare.

follow [fâl'ō] vt seguire ♦ vi seguire; (result) conseguire, risultare; **to ~ sb's advice** seguire il consiglio di qn; **I don't quite ~ you** non ti capisco or seguo affatto; **to ~ in sb's footsteps** seguire le orme di qn; **it ~s that ...** ne consegue che ...; **he ~ed suit** lui ha fatto lo stesso.

follow on vi (continue): **to ~ on from** seguire.

follow out vt (implement: idea, plan) eseguire, portare a termine.

follow through vt = follow out.

follow up vt (victory) sfruttare; (letter, offer) fare seguito a; (case) seguire.

follower [fâl'ōûr] n seguace m/f, discepolo/a.

following [fâl'ōing] a seguente, successivo(a) ♦ n seguito, discepoli mpl.

follow-up [fâl'ōup] n seguito.

folly [fâl'ē] n pazzia, follia.

fond [fând] a (memory, look) tenero(a), affettuoso(a); **to be ~ of** volere bene a; **she's ~ of swimming** le piace nuotare.

fondle [fân'dəl] vt accarezzare.

fondly [fând'lē] ad (lovingly) affettuosamente; (naïvely): **he ~ believed that ...** ha avuto l'ingenuità di credere che ....

fondness [fând'nis] n affetto; **~ (for sth)** predilezione f (per qc).

font [fânt] n (REL) fonte m (battesimale); (TYP) stile m di carattere.

food [fōōd] n cibo.

food mixer n frullatore m.

food poisoning n intossicazione f alimentare.

food processor [fōōd prâs'esûr] n tritatutto m inv elettrico.

foodstuffs [fōōd'stufs] npl generi fpl alimentari.

fool [fōōl] n sciocco/a; (HISTORY: of king) buffone m; (Brit CULIN) frullato ♦ vt ingannare ♦ vi (gen: ~ around) fare lo sciocco; **to make a ~ of sb** prendere in giro qn; **to make a ~ of o.s.** coprirsi di ridicolo; **you can't ~ me** non mi inganna.

fool around vi (waste time) perdere tempo.

foolhardy [fōōl'hârdē] a avventato(a).

foolish [fōō'lish] a scemo(a), stupido(a); imprudente.

foolishly [fōō'lishlē] ad stupidamente.

foolishness [fōō'lishnis] n stupidità.

foolproof [fōōl'prōōf] a (plan etc) sicurissimo(a).

foolscap [fōōlz'kap] n carta protocollo.

foot [fōōt] n (pl **feet** [fēt]) piede m; (measure) piede (= 304 mm; 12 inches); (of animal) zampa; (of page, stairs etc) fondo ♦ vt (bill) pagare; **on ~** a piedi; **to put one's ~ down** (AUT) schiacciare l'accelleratore; (say no) imporsi; **to find one's feet** ambientarsi.

footage [fōōt'ij] n (CINEMA: length) ≈ metraggio; (: material) sequenza.

foot and mouth (disease) [fōōt' ənmouth' (dizēz')] n afta epizootica.

football [fōōt'bôl] n pallone m; (sport: US) football m americano; (: Brit) calcio.

footballer [fōōt'bôlûr] n (Brit) = **football player.**

football field n campo di calcio.

football game n partita di calcio.

football player n (US) giocatore m di football americano; (Brit) calciatore m.

footbrake [fōōt'brāk] n freno a pedale.

footbridge [fōōt'brij] n passerella.

foothills [fōōt'hilz] npl contrafforti fpl.

foothold [fōōt'hōld] n punto d'appoggio.

footing [fōōt'ing] n (fig) posizione f; **to lose one's ~** mettere un piede in fallo; **on an equal ~** in condizioni di parità.

footlights [fōōt'līts] npl luci fpl della ribalta.

footman [fōōt'mən] n lacchè m inv.

footnote [fōōt'nōt] n nota (a piè di pagina).

footpath [fōōt'path] n sentiero; (in street) marciapiede m.

footprint [fōōt'print] n orma, impronta.

footrest [fōōt'rest] n poggiapiedi m inv.

footsore [fōōt'sôr] a coi piedi doloranti or dolenti.

footstep [fōōt'step] n passo.

footwear [fōōt'weûr] n calzatura.

FOR abbr (= free on rail) franco vagone.

for [fôr] prep per ♦ cj poiché; (in spite of): **~ all that** malgrado ciò; **the train ~ Chicago** il treno per Chicago; **it's time ~ lunch** è ora di pranzo; **what ~?** perché?; **what's this button ~?** a cosa serve questo bottone?; **~ all his money/he says ...** nonostante or malgrado tutto il suo denaro/quel che dice ...; **I haven't seen him ~ a week** è una settimana che non lo vedo, non lo vedo da una settimana; **I'll be away ~ 3 weeks** starò via 3 settimane; **he was away ~ 2 years** è stato via per 2 anni; **he went down ~ the paper** è sceso a prendere il giornale; **I sold it ~ $5** l'ho venduto per 5 dollari; **the campaign ~ ...** la campagna a favore di or per ...; **~ sale** da vendere; **there's nothing ~ it but to jump** (Brit) non c'è altro da fare che saltare

forage [fôr'ij] vi foraggiare.

forage cap n (Brit) bustina.

foray [fôr'ā] n incursione f.

forbad(e) [fûrbād'] pt of forbid.

forbearing [fôrbär'ing] a paziente, tollerante.

forbid, pt **forbad(e)**, pp **forbidden** [fûrbid', fûrbād', fûrbid'ən] vt vietare, interdire; **to ~ sb to do sth** proibire a qn di fare qc.

forbidden [fûrbid'ən] a vietato(a).

forbidding [fûrbid'ing] a arcigno(a), d'aspetto minaccioso.

force [fôrs] n forza ♦ vt forzare; (obtain by ~: smile, confession) strappare; **the Armed F~s** npl (Brit) le forze armate; **in ~** (in large *numbers*) in gran numero; (*law*) in vigore; **to come into** ~ entrare in vigore; **a** ~ **5 wind** un vento forza 5; **to join** ~**s** unire le forze; **the sales** ~ (*COMM*) l'effettivo dei rappresentanti; **to** ~ **sb to do sth** costringere qn a fare qc.

force back *vt* (*crowd*, *enemy*) respingere; (*tears*) ingoiare.

force down *vt* (*food*) sforzarsi di mangiare.

forced |fôrst| *a* forzato(a).

force-feed |fôrs'fēd| *vt* sottoporre ad alimentazione forzata.

forceful |fôrs'fəl| *a* forte, vigoroso(a).

forceps |fôr'səps| *npl* forcipe *m*.

forcibly |fôr'səblē| *ad* con la forza; (*vigorously*) vigorosamente.

ford |fôrd| *n* guado ♦ *vt* guadare.

fore |fôr| *n*: **to the** ~ in prima linea; **to come to the** ~ mettersi in evidenza.

forearm |fôr'ärm| *n* avambraccio.

forebear |fôr'bcûr| *n* antenato.

foreboding |fôrbō'ding| *n* presagio di male.

forecast |fôr'kast| *n* previsione *f*; (*weather* ~) previsioni *fpl* del tempo ♦ *vt* (*irg*: *like* **cast**) prevedere.

foreclose |fôrklōz'| *vt* (*LAW*: *also*: ~ **on**) sequestrare l'immobile ipotecato di.

foreclosure |fôrklō'zhûr| *n* sequestro di immobile ipotecato.

forecourt |fôr'kôrt| *n* (*of garage*) corte *f* esterna.

forefathers |fôr'fáꞇhûrz| *npl* antenati *mpl*, avi *mpl*.

forefinger |fôr'finggûr| *n* (dito) indice *m*.

forefront |fôr'frunt| *n*: **in the** ~ **of** all'avanguardia di.

forego |fôrgō'| *vt* = **forgo**.

foregoing |fôrgō'ing| *a* precedente.

foregone |fôrgôn'| *pp of* **forego** ♦ *a*: **it's a** ~ **conclusion** è una conclusione scontata.

foreground |fôr'ground| *n* primo piano ♦ *cpd* (*COMPUT*) foreground *inv*, di primo piano.

forehand |fôr'hand| *n* (*TENNIS*) diritto.

forehead |fôr'hcd| *n* fronte *f*.

foreign |fôr'in| *a* straniero(a); (*trade*) estero(a).

foreign body *n* corpo estraneo.

foreign currency *n* valuta estera.

foreigner |fôr'ənûr| *n* straniero/a.

foreign exchange *n* cambio di valuta; (*currency*) valuta estera.

foreign exchange market *n* mercato delle valute.

foreign exchange rate *n* cambio.

foreign investment *n* investimento all'estero.

foreign minister *n* ministro degli Affari esteri.

Foreign Office (FO) *n* (*Brit*) Ministero degli Esteri.

foreign secretary *n* (*Brit*) ministro degli Affari esteri.

foreleg |fôr'lcg| *n* zampa anteriore.

foreman |fôr'mən| *n* caposquadra *m*; (*LAW*: *of jury*) portavoce *m* della giuria.

foremost |fôr'mōst| *a* principale; più in vista ♦ *ad*: **first and** ~ innanzitutto.

forename |fôr'nām| *n* nome *m* di battesimo.

forensic |fərcn'sik| *a*: ~ **medicine** medicina legale; ~ **expert** esperto della (polizia) scientifica.

forerunner |fôr'runûr| *n* precursore *m*.

foresee |fôrsē'|, *pt* **foresaw**, *pp* **foreseen** |fôrsē'|, fôrsô'|, fôrsēn'| *vt* prevedere.

foreseeable |fôrsē'əbəl| *a* prevedibile.

foreseen |fôrsēn'| *pp of* **foresee**.

foreshadow |fôrshad'ō| *vt* presagire, far prevedere.

foreshorten |fôrshôr'tən| *vt* (*figure*, *scene*) rappresentare in scorcio.

foresight |fôr'sīt| *n* previdenza.

foreskin |fôr'skin| *n* (*ANAT*) prepuzio.

forest |fôr'ist| *n* foresta.

forestall |fôrstôl'| *vt* prevenire.

forestry |fôr'istrē| *n* silvicoltura.

foretaste |fôr'tāst| *n* pregustazione *f*.

foretell |fôrtcl'|, *pt*, *pp* **foretold** |fôrtcl'|, fôrtōld'| *vt* predire.

forethought |fôr'thôt| *n* previdenza.

foretold |fôrtōld'| *pt*, *pp of* **foretell**.

forever |fôrcv'ûr| *ad* per sempre; (*fig*) sempre, di continuo.

forewarn |fôrwôrn'| *vt* avvisare in precedenza.

forewent |fôrwent'| *pt of* **forego**.

foreword |fôr'wûrd| *n* prefazione *f*.

forfeit |fôr'fit| *n* ammenda, pena ♦ *vt* perdere; (*one's happiness*, *health*) giocarsi.

forgave |fûrgāv'| *pt of* **forgive**.

forge |fôrj| *n* fucina ♦ *vt* falsificare; (*signature*) contraffare, falsificare; (*wrought iron*) fucinare, foggiare.

forge ahead *vi* tirare avanti.

forger |fôr'jûr| *n* contraffattore *m*.

forgery |fôr'jûrē| *n* falso; (*activity*) contraffazione *f*.

forget, *pt* **forgot**, *pp* **forgotten** |fûrget'|, fûrgât', fûrgât'ən| *vt*, *vi* dimenticare.

forgetful |fûrget'fəl| *a* di corta memoria; ~ **of** dimentico(a) di.

forgetfulness |fûrget'fəlnis| *n* smemoratezza; (*oblivion*) oblio.

forget-me-not |fûrget'mēnât| *n* nontiscordardimé *m inv*.

forgive, *pt* **forgave**, *pp* **forgiven** |fûrgiv'|, fûrgāv'|, fûrgiv'ən| *vt* perdonare; **to** ~ **sb for sth/for doing sth** perdonare qc a qn/a qn di aver fatto qc.

forgiveness |fûrgiv'nis| *n* perdono.

forgiving |fûrgiv'ing| *a* indulgente.

forgo, *pt* **forwent**, *pp* **forgone** |fôrgō'|, fôrwent'|, fôrgôn'| *vt* rinunciare a.

forgot [fûrgât'] *pt of* **forget**.

forgotten [fûrgât'ən] *pp of* **forget**.

fork [fôrk] *n* (*for eating*) forchetta; (*for gardening*) forca; (*of roads*) bivio; (*of railways*) inforcazione *f* ♦ *vi* (*road*) biforcarsi.

fork out (*col*: *pay*) *vt* sborsare ♦ *vi* pagare.

forked [fôrkt] *a* (*lightning*) a zigzag.

forklift truck [fôrk'lift truk'] *n* carrello elevatore.

forlorn [fôrlôrn'] *a* (*person*) sconsolato(a); (*deserted*: *cottage*) abbandonato(a); (*desperate*: *attempt*) disperato(a).

form [fôrm] *n* forma; (*Brit SCOL*) classe *f*; (*questionnaire*) modulo ♦ *vt* formare; (*circle, queue etc*) fare; **in the ~ of** a forma di, sotto forma di; **to be in good ~** (*SPORT, fig*) essere in forma; **in top ~** in gran forma; **to ~ part of sth** far parte di qc.

formal [fôr'məl] *a* (*offer, receipt*) vero(a) e proprio(a); (*person*) cerimonioso(a); (*occasion, dinner*) formale, ufficiale; (*ART, PHILOSOPHY*) formale; **~ dress** abito da cerimonia; (*evening dress*) abito da sera.

formality [fôrmal'itē] *n* formalità *f inv*.

formalize [fôr'məlīz] *vt* rendere ufficiale.

formally   [fôr'məlē]   *ad*   ufficialmente; formalmente; cerimoniosamente; **to be ~ invited** ricevere un invito ufficiale.

format [fôr'mat] *n* formato ♦ *vt* (*COMPUT*) formattare.

formation-[fôrmā'shən] *n* formazione *f*.

formative [fôr'mətiv] *a*: **~ years** anni *mpl* formativi.

former [fôr'mûr] *a* vecchio(a) (*before n*), ex *inv* (*before n*); **the ~ president** l'ex presidente; **the ~ ... the latter** quello ... questo.

formerly [fôr'mûrlē] *ad* in passato.

form feed *n* (*on printer*) alimentazione *f* modulo.

formidable [fôr'midəbəl] *a* formidabile.

formula [fôr'myələ] *n* formula; **F~ One** (*AUT*) formula uno.

formulate [fôr'myəlāt] *vt* formulare.

fornicate [fôr'nikāt] *vi* fornicare.

forsake, *pt* **forsook,** *pp* **forsaken** [fôrsāk', fôrsōōk, fôrsā'kən] *vt* abbandonare.

fort [fôrt] *n* forte *m*; **to hold the ~** (*fig*) prendere le redini (della situazione).

forte [fôr'tā] *n* forte *m*.

forth [fôrth] *ad* in avanti; **to go back and ~** andare avanti e indietro; **and so ~** e così via.

forthcoming [fôrth'kum'ing] *a* prossimo(a); (*character*) aperto(a), comunicativo(a).

forthright [fôrth'rīt] *a* franco(a), schietto(a).

forthwith [fôrthwith'] *ad* immediatamente, subito.

fortieth [fôr'tēith] *num* quarantesimo(a).

fortification [fôrtəfəkā'shən] *n* fortificazione *f*.

fortified wine [fôr'təfīd wīn'] *n* vino ad alta gradazione alcolica.

fortify [fôr'təfī] *vt* fortificare.

fortitude [fôr'tətōōd] *n* forza d'animo.

fortnight [fôrt'nīt] *n* (*Brit*) quindici giorni *mpl*, due settimane *fpl*; **it's a ~ since ...** sono due settimane da quando ....

fortnightly [fôrt'nītlē] (*Brit*) *a* bimensile ♦ *ad* ogni quindici giorni.

FORTRAN [fôr'tran] *n* FORTRAN *m*.

fortress [fôr'tris] *n* fortezza, rocca.

fortuitous [fôrtōō'itəs] *a* fortuito(a).

fortunate [fôr'chənit] *a* fortunato(a); **he is ~ to have ...** ha la fortuna di avere ...; **it is ~ that** è una fortuna che + *sub*.

fortunately [fôr'chənitlē] *ad* fortunatamente.

fortune [fôr'chən] *n* fortuna; **to make a ~** farsi una fortuna.

fortuneteller [fôr'chəntelûr] *n* indovino/a.

forty [fôr'tē] *num* quaranta.

forum [fôr'əm] *n* foro; (*fig*) luogo di pubblica discussione.

forward [fôr'wûrd] *a* (*movement, position*) in avanti; (*not shy*) sfacciato(a); (*COMM*: *delivery, sales, exchange*) a termine ♦ *n* (*SPORT*) avanti *m inv* ♦ *vt* (*letter*) inoltrare; (*parcel, goods*) spedire; (*fig*) promuovere, appoggiare; **to move ~** avanzare; **"please ~"** "si prega di inoltrare".

forward(s) [fôr'wûrd(z)] *ad* avanti.

forwent [fôrwent'] *pt of* **forgo**.

fossil [fâs'əl] *a, n* fossile (*m*); **~ fuel** combustibile *m* fossile.

foster [fôs'tûr] *vt* incoraggiare, nutrire; (*child*) avere in affidamento.

foster brother *n* fratellastro.

foster child *n* bambino(a) preso(a) in affidamento.

foster mother *n* madre *f* affidataria.

fought [fôt] *pt, pp of* **fight**.

foul [foul] *a* (*smell, food*) cattivo(a); (*weather*) brutto(a), orribile; (*language*) osceno(a); (*deed*) infame ♦ *n* (*SPORT*) fallo ♦ *vt* sporcare; (*player*) commettere un fallo su; (*entangle*: *anchor, propeller*) impigliarsi in.

foul play *n* (*SPORT*) gioco scorretto; **~ is not suspected** si è scartata l'ipotesi del delitto (*or* dell'attentato *etc*).

found [found] *pt, pp of* **find** ♦ *vt* (*establish*) fondare.

foundation [foundā'shən] *n* (*act*) fondazione *f*; (*base*) base *f*; (*also*: **~ cream**) fondo tinta; **~s** *npl* (*of building*) fondamenta *fpl*; **to lay the ~s** gettare le fondamenta.

foundation stone *n* prima pietra.

founder [foun'dûr] *n* fondatore/trice ♦ *vi* affondare.

founding [foun'ding] *a*: **~ fathers** (*US*) padri *mpl* fondatori; **~ member** socio fondatore.

foundry [foun'drē] *n* fonderia.

fount [fount] *n* fonte *f*; (*Brit TYP*) stile *m* di

carattere.
fountain [foun'tin] *n* fontana.
fountain pen *n* penna stilografica.
four [fôr] *num* quattro; **on all ~s** a carponi.
four-poster [fôr'pōs'tûr] *n* (*also*: ~ **bed**) letto a quattro colonne.
foursome [fôr'səm] *n* partita a quattro; uscita in quattro.
fourteen [fôr'tēn'] *num* quattordici.
fourth [fôrth] *num* quarto(a) ♦ *n* (*AUT*: *also*: ~ **gear**) quarta.
four-wheel drive [fôr'hwēl drĭv] *n* (*AUT*): **with ~** con quattro ruote motrici.
fowl [foul] *n* pollame *m*; volatile *m*.
fox [fâks] *n* volpe *f* ♦ *vt* confondere.
fox fur *n* volpe *f*, pelliccia di volpe.
foxglove [fâks'gluv] *n* (*BOT*) digitale *f*.
fox hunting *n* caccia alla volpe.
foyer [foi'ûr] *n* atrio; (*THEATER*) ridotto.
FP *n abbr* (*US*) = **fireplug**; (*Brit*) = *former pupil*.
Fr. *abbr* (*REL*) = **father; friar**.
fr. *abbr* (= *franc*) fr.
fracas [frā'kəs] *n* rissa, lite *f*.
fraction [frak'shən] *n* frazione *f*.
fractionally [frak'shənəlē] *ad* un tantino, minimamente.
fractious [frak'shəs] *a* irritabile.
fracture [frak'chûr] *n* frattura ♦ *vt* fratturare.
fragile [fraj'əl] *a* fragile.
fragment [frag'mənt] *n* frammento.
fragmentary [frag'məntärē] *a* frammentario(a).
fragrance [frā'grəns] *n* fragranza, profumo.
fragrant [frā'grənt] *a* fragrante, profumato(a).
frail [frāl] *a* debole, delicato(a).
frame [frām] *n* (*of building*) armatura; (*of human, animal*) ossatura, corpo; (*of picture*) cornice *f*; (*of door, window*) telaio; (*of spectacles*: *also*: ~**s**) montatura ♦ *vt* (*picture*) incorniciare; **to ~ sb** (*col*) incastrare qn; ~ **of mind** stato d'animo.
framework [frām'wûrk] *n* struttura.
France [frans] *n* Francia.
franchise [fran'chīz] *n* (*POL*) diritto di voto; (*COMM*) concessione *f*.
franchisee [franchīzē'] *n* concessionaria.
franchiser [fran'chīzûr] *n* concedente *m*.
frank [frangk] *a* franco(a), aperto(a) ♦ *vt* (*Brit letter*) affrancare.
Frankfurt [frangk'fûrt] *n* Francoforte *f*.
frankfurter [frangk'fûrtûr] *n* würstel *m inv*.
frankly [frangk'lē] *ad* francamente, sinceramente.
frankness [frangk'nis] *n* franchezza.
frantic [fran'tik] *a* (*activity, pace*) frenetico(a); (*desperate: need, desire*) pazzo(a), sfrenato(a); (: *search*) affannoso(a); (*person*) fuori di sé.
frantically [fran'tiklē] *ad* freneticamente; affannosamente.

fraternal [frətûr'nəl] *a* fraterno(a).
fraternity [frətûr'nitē] *n* (*club*) associazione *f*; (*spirit*) fratellanza.
fraternize [frat'ûrnīz] *vi* fraternizzare.
fraud [frôd] *n* truffa; (*LAW*) frode *f*; (*person*) impostore/a.
fraudulent [frô'jələnt] *a* fraudolento(a).
fraught [frôt] *a* (*tense*) teso(a); ~ **with** pieno(a) di, intriso(a) da.
fray [frā] *n* baruffa ♦ *vt* logorare ♦ *vi* logorarsi; **to return to the** ~ tornare nella mischia; **tempers were getting** ~**ed** cominciavano ad innervosirsi; **her nerves were** ~**ed** aveva i nervi a pezzi.
FRB *n abbr* (*US*) = **Federal Reserve Board**.
freak [frēk] *n* fenomeno, mostro; (*col: enthusiast*) fanatico/a ♦ *a* (*storm, conditions*) anormale; (*victory*) inatteso(a).
freak out *vi* (*col*) andare fuori di testa.
freakish [frēk'ish] *a* (*result, appearance*) strano(a), bizzarro(a); (*weather*) anormale.
freckle [frek'əl] *n* lentiggine *f*.
free [frē] *a* libero(a); (*gratis*) gratuito(a); (*liberal*) generoso(a) ♦ *vt* (*prisoner, jammed person*) liberare; (*jammed object*) districare; ~ (**of charge**) gratuitamente; **admission** ~ entrata libera; **to give sb a** ~ **hand** dare carta bianca a qn; ~ **and easy** rilassato.
-free *suffix*: **additive**~ senza additivi; **tax**~ esentasse.
freebie [frē'bē] *n* (*col*): **it's a** ~ è in omaggio.
freedom [frē'dəm] *n* libertà.
freedom fighter *n* combattente *m/f* per la libertà.
free enterprise *n* liberalismo economico.
free-for-all [frē'fûrôl'] *n* parapiglia *m* generale.
free gift *n* regalo, omaggio.
freehold [frē'hōld] *n* (*Brit*) proprietà assoluta.
free kick *n* (*SPORT*) calcio libero.
freelance [frē'lans] *a* indipendente; ~ **work** collaborazione *f* esterna.
freeloader [frē'lōdûr] *n* (*pej*) scroccone/a.
freely [frē'lē] *ad* liberamente; (*liberally*) liberalmente.
freemason [frē'māsən] *n* massone *m*.
freemasonry [frē'māsənrē] *n* massoneria.
free-range [frē'rānj] *a* (*eggs*) di gallina ruspante.
free sample *n* campione *m* gratuito.
free speech *n* libertà di parola.
freestyle [frē'stīl] *n* (*in swimming*) stile *m* libero.
freestyle wrestling [frē'stīl res'ling] *n* (*US*) lotta americana.
free trade *n* libero scambio.
freeway [frē'wā] *n* (*US*) superstrada.
freewheel [frē'hwēl] *vi* andare a ruota libera.
freewheeling [frē'hwē'ling] *a* a ruota libera.
free will *n* libero arbitrio; **of one's own** ~ di spontanea volontà.

freeze [frēz] *vb* (*pt* **froze**, *pp* **frozen** [frōz, frō'zən]) *vi* gelare ♦ *vt* gelare; (*food*) congelare; (*prices, salaries*) bloccare ♦ *n* gelo; blocco.
freeze over *vi* (*lake, river*) ghiacciarsi; (*windows, windshield*) coprirsi di ghiaccio.
freeze up *vi* gelarsi.
freeze-dried [frēz'drīd'] *a* liofilizzato(a).
freezer [frē'zûr] *n* congelatore *m*.
freezing [frē'zing] *a*: **I'm ~** mi sto congelando ♦ *n* (*also*: ~ **point**) punto di congelamento; **3 degrees below ~** 3 gradi sotto zero.
freight [frāt] *n* (*goods*) merce *f*, merci *fpl*; (*money charged*) spese *fpl* di trasporto; ~ **forward** spese a carico del destinatario; ~ **inward** spese di trasporto sulla merce in entrata.
freight car *n* (*US*) carro *m* merci *inv*.
freighter [frā'tûr] *n* (*NAUT*) nave *f* da carico.
freight forwarder [frāt' fôr'wûrdûr] *n* spedizioniere *m*.
freight train *n* (*US*) treno *m* merci *inv*.
French [french] *a* francese ♦ *n* (*LING*) francese *m*; **the** ~ *npl* i Francesi.
French bean *n* (*Brit*) fagiolino.
French Canadian *a, n* franco-canadese (*m/f*).
French dressing *n* (*CULIN*) condimento per insalata.
French fries [french' frīz] *npl* patate *fpl* fritte.
French Guiana [french gēan'ə] *n* Guiana francese.
Frenchman [french'mən] *n* francese *m*.
French Riviera *n*: **the** ~ la Costa Azzurra.
French window *n* portafinestra.
Frenchwoman [french'wõõmən] *n* francese *f*.
frenetic [frənet'ik] *a* frenetico(a).
frenzy [fren'zē] *n* frenesia.
frequency [frē'kwənsē] *n* frequenza.
frequency modulation (FM) *n* modulazione *f* di frequenza (F.M.).
frequent *a* [frē'kwint] frequente ♦ *vt* [frikwent'] frequentare.
frequently [frē'kwintlē] *ad* frequentemente, spesso.
fresco [fres'kō] *n* affresco.
fresh [fresh] *a* fresco(a); (*new*) nuovo(a); (*cheeky*) sfacciato(a); **to make a ~ start** cominciare da capo.
freshen [fresh'ən] *vi* (*wind, air*) rinfrescare.
freshen up *vi* rinfrescarsi.
freshener [fresh'ənûr] *n*: **skin ~** tonico rinfrescante; **air ~** deodorante *m* per ambienti.
fresher [fresh'ûr] *n* (*Brit SCOL*: *col*) = **freshman**.
freshly [fresh'lē] *ad* di recente, di fresco.
freshman [fresh'mən] *n* (*SCOL*) matricola.
freshness [fresh'nis] *n* freschezza.
freshwater [fresh'wôtûr] *a* (*fish*) d'acqua dolce.
fret [fret] *vi* agitarsi, affliggersi.
fretful [fret'fəl] *a* (*child*) irritabile.

Freudian [froi'dēən] *a* freudiano(a); ~ **slip** lapsus *m inv* freudiano.
FRG *n abbr see* **Federal Republic of Germany**.
Fri. *abbr* (= *Friday*) ven.
friar [frī'ûr] *n* frate *m*.
friction [frik'shən] *n* frizione *f*, attrito.
friction feed *n* (*on printer*) trascinamento ad attrito.
Friday [frī'dā] *n* venerdì *m inv*; *for phrases see also* **Tuesday**.
fridge [frij] *n* (*Brit*) frigo, frigorifero.
fried [frīd] *pt, pp of* **fry** ♦ *a* fritto(a); ~ **egg** uovo fritto.
friend [frend] *n* amico/a; **to make ~s with** fare amicizia con.
friendliness [frend'lēnis] *n* amichevolezza.
friendly [frend'lē] *a* amichevole ♦ *n* (*also*: ~ **match**) partita amichevole; **to be ~ with** essere amico di; **to be ~ to** essere cordiale con.
friendly society *n* (*Brit*) società *f inv* di mutuo soccorso.
friendship [frend'ship] *n* amicizia.
frieze [frēz] *n* fregio.
frigate [frig'it] *n* (*NAUT*: *modern*) fregata.
fright [frīt] *n* paura, spavento; **to take ~** spaventarsi; **she looks a ~!** guarda com'è conciata!
frighten [frīt'ən] *vt* spaventare, far paura a.
frighten away, frighten off *vt* (*birds, children etc*) scacciare (facendogli paura).
frightened [frīt'ənd] *a*: **to be ~ (of)** avere paura (di).
frightening [frīt'ning] *a* spaventoso(a), pauroso(a).
frightful [frīt'fəl] *a* orribile.
frightfully [frīt'fəlē] *ad* terribilmente; **I'm ~ sorry** (*Brit*) mi dispiace moltissimo.
frigid [frij'id] *a* (*woman*) frigido(a).
frigidity [frijid'itē] *n* frigidità.
frill [fril] *n* balza; **without ~s** (*fig*) senza fronzoli.
fringe [frinj] *n* (*edge: of forest etc*) margine *m*; (*Brit*) frangia; (*fig*): **on the ~** al margine.
fringe benefits *npl* vantaggi *mpl*.
fringe theatre *n* (*Brit*) teatro d'avanguardia.
frisk [frisk] *vt* perquisire.
frisky [fris'kē] *a* vivace, vispo(a).
fritter [frit'ûr] *n* frittella.
fritter away *vt* sprecare.
frivolity [frəvāl'itē] *n* frivolezza.
frivolous [friv'ələs] *a* frivolo(a).
frizzy [friz'ē] *a* crespo(a).
fro [frō] *ad*: **to and ~** avanti e indietro.
frock [fräk] *n* vestito.
frog [frôg] *n* rana; **to have a ~ in one's throat** avere la voce rauca.
frogman [frôg'man] *n* uomo *m* rana *inv*.
frogmarch [frôg'märch] *vt* (*Brit*): **to ~ sb in/out** portar qn dentro/fuori con la forza.

frolic [frâl'ik] *vi* sgambettare.

from [frum] *prep* da; ~ **a dollar/January** da un dollaro in su/gennaio in poi; **(as)** ~ **Friday** da *or* a partire da venerdì; ~ **what he says** a quanto dice; **where is he** ~? da dove viene?, di dov'è?; **where has he come** ~? da dove arriva?; **a telephone call** ~ **Mr. Smith** una telefonata dal Signor Smith; **prices range** ~ **$10 to $50** i prezzi vanno dai 10 ai 50 dollari.

frond [frând] *n* fronda.

front [frunt] *n* (*of house, dress*) davanti *m inv*; (*of train*) testa; (*of book*) copertina; (*promenade*: *also*: **sea** ~) lungomare *m*; (*MIL. POL. METEOR*) fronte *m*; (*fig*: *appearances*) fronte *f* ♦ *a* primo(a); anteriore, davanti *inv* ♦ *vi*: **to** ~ **onto sth** dare su qc, guardare verso qc; **in** ~ **(of)** davanti (a).

frontage [frun'tij] *n* facciata.

frontal [frun'təl] *a* frontale.

front bench *n* (*Brit POL*) banco dei ministri dell'opposizione.

front desk *n* (*in hotel*) reception *f inv*; (*at doctor's*) accettazione *f*.

front door *n* porta d'entrata; (*of car*) sportello anteriore.

frontier [fruntēûr'] *n* frontiera.

frontispiece [frun'tispēs] *n* frontespizio.

front page *n* prima pagina.

front room *n* salotto.

front runner *n* (*fig*) favorito/a.

front-wheel drive [frunt'hwēl drīv] *n* trasmissione *f* anteriore.

frost [frôst] *n* gelo; (*also*: **hoar**~) brina ♦ *vt* (*US*: *cake*) glassare.

frostbite [frôst'bīt] *n* congelamento.

frosted [frôs'tid] *a* (*glass*) smerigliato(a); (*US*: *cake*) glassato(a).

frosting [frôs'ting] *n* (*US*: *on cake*) glassa.

frosty [frôs'tē] *a* (*window*) coperto(a) di ghiaccio; (*welcome*) gelido(a).

froth [frôth] *n* spuma; schiuma.

frown [froun] *n* cipiglio ♦ *vi* acciglirsi.

frown on *vt fus* (*fig*) disapprovare.

froze [frōz] *pt of* **freeze**.

frozen [frō'zən] *pp of* **freeze** ♦ *a* (*food*) congelato(a); (*COMM*: *assets*) bloccato(a).

FRS *n abbr* (*US*: = *Federal Reserve System*) *sistema bancario degli Stati Uniti*.

frugal [frōō'gəl] *a* frugale; (*person*) economo(a).

fruit [frōōt] *n* (*pl inv*) frutto; (*collectively*) frutta.

fruiterer [frōōt'ərûr] *n* (*Brit*) fruttivendolo; **at the** ~**'s (shop)** dal fruttivendolo.

fruitful [frōōt'fəl] *a* fruttuoso(a); (*plant*) fruttifero(a); (*soil*) fertile.

fruition [frōōish'ən] *n*: **to come to** ~ realizzarsi.

fruit juice *n* succo di frutta.

fruitless [frōōt'lis] *a* (*fig*) vano(a), inutile.

fruit machine *n* (*Brit*) macchina *f* mangiasoldi *inv*.

fruit salad *n* macedonia.

frump [frump] *n*: **to feel a** ~ sentirsi infagottato(a).

frustrate [frus'trāt] *vt* frustrare.

frustrated [frus'trātid] *a* frustrato(a).

frustrating [frus'trāting] *a* (*job*) frustrante; (*day*) disastroso(a).

frustration [frustrā'shən] *n* frustrazione *f*.

fry, *pt, pp* **fried** [frī, frīd] *vt* friggere ♦ *npl*: **the small** ~ i pesci piccoli.

frying pan [frī'ing pan] *n* padella.

FSLIC *n abbr* (*US*) = *Federal Savings and Loan Insurance Corporation*.

FT *n abbr* (*Brit*: = *Financial Times*) *giornale finanziario*; **the** ~ **index** l'indice FT.

ft. *abbr* = **foot, feet**.

FTC *n abbr* (*US*) *see* **Federal Trade Commission**.

fuchsia [fyōō'shə] *n* fucsia.

fuck [fuk] *vt, vi* (*col!*) fottere (*!*); ~ **off!** vaffanculo! (*!*).

fuddled [fud'əld] *a* (*muddled*) confuso(a); (*col*: *tipsy*) brillo(a).

fuddy-duddy [fud'ēdudē] *n* (*pej*) parruccone *m*.

fudge [fuj] *n* (*CULIN*) specie di caramella a base di latte, burro e zucchero ♦ *vt* (*issue, problem*) evitare.

fuel [fyōō'əl] *n* (*for heating*) combustibile *m*; (*for propelling*) carburante *m* ♦ *vt* (*furnace etc*) alimentare; (*aircraft, ship etc*) rifornire di carburante.

fuel oil *n* nafta.

fuel pump *n* (*AUT*) pompa del carburante.

fuel tank *n* deposito *m* nafta *inv*; (*on vehicle*) serbatoio (della benzina).

fug [fug] *n* (*Brit*) aria viziata.

fugitive [fyōō'jətiv] *n* fuggitivo/a, profugo/a; (*from prison*) evaso/a.

fulfill, (*Brit*) **fulfil** [fōōlfil'] *vt* (*function*) compiere; (*order*) eseguire; (*wish, desire*) soddisfare, appagare.

fulfilled [fōōlfild'] *a* (*person*) realizzato(a), soddisfatto(a).

fulfilment [fōōlfil'mənt] *n* (*of wishes*) soddisfazione *f*, appagamento.

full [fōōl] *a* pieno(a); (*details, skirt*) ampio(a); (*price*) intero(a) ♦ *ad*: **to know** ~ **well that** sapere benissimo che; ~ **(up)** (*hotel etc*) al completo; **I'm** ~ **(up)** sono pieno; **a** ~ **two hours** due ore intere; **at** ~ **speed** a tutta velocità; **in** ~ per intero; **to pay in** ~ pagare tutto; ~ **name** nome *m* e cognome *m*; ~ **employment** piena occupazione; ~ **fare** tariffa completa.

fullback [fōōl'bak] *n* (*RUGBY, SOCCER*) terzino.

full-blooded [fōōl'blud'id] *a* (*vigorous*: *attack*) energico(a); (*virile*: *male*) virile.

full-cream [fōōl'krēm] *a*: ~ **milk** (*Brit*) latte

m intero.

full-fledged |fŏŏl'flejd'| *a* (*US*: *bird*) adulto(a); (: *fig*: *teacher*, *member etc*) a tutti gli effetti.

full-grown |fŏŏl'grōn'| *a* maturo(a).

full-length |fŏŏl'lengkth'| *a* (*portrait*) in piedi; (*film*) a lungometraggio.

full moon *n* luna piena.

full-scale |fŏŏl'skāl'| *a* (*plan*, *model*) in grandezza naturale; (*search*, *retreat*) su vasta scala.

full-sized |fŏŏl'sīzd| *a* (*portrait etc*) a grandezza naturale.

full stop *n* (*Brit*) punto.

full-time |fŏŏl'tīm| *a*, *ad* (*work*) a tempo pieno ♦ *n* (*Brit SPORT*) fine *f* partita.

fully |fŏŏl'ē| *ad* interamente, pienamente, completamente; (*at least*): ~ **as big** (*Brit*) almeno così grosso.

fully-fledged |fŏŏl'ēflejd'| *a* (*Brit*) = **fullfledged.**

fulsome |fŏŏl'səm| *a* (*pej: praise*) esagerato(a), eccessivo(a); (: *manner*) insincero.

fumble |fum'bəl| *vi* brancolare, andare a tentoni ♦ *vt* (*ball*) lasciarsi sfuggire.

fumble with *vt fus* trafficare.

fume |fyōom| *vi* essere furioso(a); ~**s** *npl* esalazioni *fpl*, vapori *mpl*.

fumigate |fyōo'məgāt| *vt* suffumicare.

fun |fun| *n* divertimento, spasso; **to have** ~ divertirsi; **for** ~ per scherzo; **it's not much** ~ non è molto divertente; **to make** ~ **of** prendersi gioco di.

function |fungk'shən| *n* funzione *f*; cerimonia, ricevimento ♦ *vi* funzionare; **to** ~ **as** fungere da, funzionare da.

functional |fungk'shənəl| *a* funzionale.

function key *n* (*COMPUT*) tasto di funzioni.

fund |fund| *n* fondo, cassa; (*source*) fondo; (*store*) riserva; ~**s** *npl* (*money*) fondi *mpl*.

fundamental |fundəmen'təl| *a* fondamentale; ~**s** *npl* basi *fpl*.

fundamentalist |fundəmen'təlist| *n* fondamentalista *m/f*.

fundamentally |fundəmen'təlē| *ad* essenzialmente, fondamentalmente.

fund-raising |fund'rāzing| *n* raccolta di fondi.

funeral |fyōo'nûrəl| *n* funerale *m*.

funeral director *n* impresario di pompe funebri.

funeral home, (*Brit*) **funeral parlour** *n* impresa di pompe funebri.

funeral service *n* ufficio funebre.

funereal |fyōonē'rēəl| *a* funereo(a), lugubre.

funfair |fun'fär| *n* (*Brit*) luna park *m inv*.

fungus, *pl* **fungi** |fung'gəs, -ji| *n* fungo; (*mold*) muffa.

funicular |fyōonik'yəlûr| *a* (*also:* ~ **railway**) funicolare *f*.

funnel |fun'əl| *n* imbuto; (*of ship*) ciminiera.

funnily |fun'ilē| *ad* in modo divertente; (*oddly*) stranamente.

funny |fun'ē| *a* divertente, buffo(a); (*strange*) strano(a), bizzarro(a).

funny bone *n* osso cubitale.

fur |fûr| *n* pelo; pelliccia; pelle *f*; (*Brit: in kettle etc*) deposito calcare.

fur coat *n* pelliccia.

furious |fyōor'ēəs| *a* furioso(a); (*effort*) accanito(a); (*argument*) violento(a).

furiously |fyōor'ēəslē| *ad* furiosamente; accanitamente.

furl |fûrl| *vt* (*sail*) piegare.

furlong |fûr'lông| *n* = 201.17 *m* (*termine ippico*).

furlough |fûr'lō| *n* (*US*) congedo, permesso.

furnace |fûr'nis| *n* fornace *f*.

furnish |fûr'nish| *vt* ammobiliare; (*supply*) fornire; ~**ed apartment** *or* (*Brit*) **flat** appartamento ammobiliato.

furnishings |fûr'nishingz| *npl* mobili *mpl*, mobilia.

furniture |fûr'nichûr| *n* mobili *mpl*; **piece of** ~ mobile *m*.

furniture mover *n* (*US*) addetto ai traslochi.

furore |fyōor'ôr| *n* (*protests*) scalpore *m*; (*enthusiasm*) entusiasmo.

furrier |fûr'ēûr| *n* pellicciaio/a.

furrow |fûr'ō| *n* solco ♦ *vt* (*forehead*) segnare di rughe.

furry |fûr'ē| *a* (*animal*) peloso(a); (*toy*) di peluche.

further |fûr'thûr| *a* supplementare, altro(a); nuovo(a); più lontano(a) ♦ *ad* più lontano; (*more*) di più; (*moreover*) inoltre ♦ *vt* favorire, promuovere; **until** ~ **notice** fino a nuovo avviso; **how much** ~ **is it?** quanto manca *or* dista?; ~ **to your letter of** ... (*Brit COMM*) con riferimento alla vostra lettera del ...; **to** ~ **one's interests** fare i propri interessi.

further education *n* istruzione *f* superiore.

furthermore |fûr'thûrmôr| *ad* inoltre, per di più.

furthermost |fûr'thûrmōst| *a* più lontano(a).

furthest |fûr'thist| *superlative of* **far.**

furtive |fûr'tiv| *a* furtivo(a).

furtively |fûr'tivlē| *ad* furtivamente.

fury |fyōor'ē| *n* furore *m*.

fuse |fyōoz| *n* fusibile *m*; (*Brit: for bomb etc*) miccia, spoletta ♦ *vt* fondere; (*Brit: ELEC*): **to** ~ **the lights** far saltare i fusibili ♦ *vi* fondersi; **a** ~ **has blown** è saltato un fusibile.

fuse box *n* cassetta dei fusibili.

fuselage |fyōo'səlázh| *n* fusoliera.

fuse wire *n* filo (di fusibile).

fusillade |fyōos'əläd| *n* scarica di fucileria; (*fig*) fuoco di fila, serie *f inv* incalzante.

fusion |fyōo'zhən| *n* fusione *f*.

fuss |fus| *n* chiasso, trambusto, confusione *f*; (*complaining*) storie *fpl* ♦ *vt* (*person*) infastidire, scocciare ♦ *vi* agitarsi; **to make a** ~

fare delle storie.

fuss over *vt fus* (*person*) circondare di premure.

fussy [fus'ē] *a* (*person*) puntiglioso(a), esigente; che fa le storie; (*dress*) carico(a) di fronzoli; (*style*) elaborato(a); **I'm not ~** (*col*) per me è lo stesso.

futile [fyōō'təl] *a* futile.

futility [fyōōtil'ətē] *n* futilità.

future [fyōō'chûr] *a* futuro(a) ♦ *n* futuro, avvenire *m*; (*LING*) futuro; **in the ~** in futuro; **in the near ~** in un prossimo futuro; **in the immediate ~** nell'immediato futuro.

futures [fyōō'chûrz] *npl* (*COMM*) operazioni *fpl* a termine.

futuristic [fyōōchəris'tik] *a* futuristico(a).

fuze [fyōōz] *n* (*US: for bomb etc*) miccia, spoletta ♦ *vt, vi* = **fuse**.

fuzzy [fuz'ē] *a* (*PHOT*) indistinto(a), sfocato(a); (*hair*) crespo(a).

fwd. *abbr* = **forward**.

fwy *abbr* (*US*) = **freeway**.

FY *abbr* = **fiscal year**.

FYI *abbr* = *for your information*.

G

G, g [jē] *n* (*letter*) G, g *f or m inv*; (*MUS*): **G** sol *m*; **G for George** ≈ G come Genova.

G [jē] *n abbr* (*US CINEMA*: = *general audience*) per tutti; (*Brit SCOL*: mark: = *good*) ≈ buono.

g *abbr* (= *gram*; *gravity*) g.

GA *abbr* (*US MAIL*) = Georgia.

gab [gab] *n* (*col*): **to have the gift of ~** or (*Brit*) **the ~** avere lo scilinguagnolo sciolto.

gabble [gab'əl] *vi* borbottare; farfugliare.

gaberdine [gab'ûrdēn] *n* gabardine *m inv*.

gable [gā'bəl] *n* frontone *m*.

Gabon [gā'bân'] *n* Gabon *m*.

gad about [gad əbout'] *vi* (*col*) svolazzare (qua e là).

gadget [gaj'it] *n* aggeggio.

Gaelic [gā'lik] *a* gaelico(a) ♦ *n* (*language*) gaelico.

gaffe [gaf] *n* gaffe *f inv*.

gag [gag] *n* bavaglio; (*joke*) facezia, scherzo ♦ *vt* imbavagliare.

gaga [gâ'gâ] *a*: **to go ~** rimbambirsi.

gage [gāj] (*US*) *n, vt* = **gauge**.

gaiety [gā'ətē] *n* gaiezza.

gaily [gā'lē] *ad* allegramente.

gain [gān] *n* guadagno, profitto ♦ *vt* guadagnare ♦ *vi* (*watch*) andare avanti; **to ~ in/by**

aumentare di/con; **to ~ 3 lbs (in weight)** aumentare di 3 libbre; **to ~ ground** guadagnare terreno.

gain (up)on *vt fus* accorciare le distanze da, riprendere.

gainful [gān'fəl] *a* profittevole, lucrativo(a).

gainsay [gānsā'] *vt irg* (*like* **say**) contraddire; negare.

gait [gāt] *n* andatura.

gal. *abbr* (*Brit*) = **gallon**.

gala [gā'lə] *n* gala; **swimming ~** manifestazione *f* di nuoto.

Galapagos Islands [gələ'pəgōs i'ləndz] *npl*: **the ~** le isole Galapagos.

galaxy [gal'əksē] *n* galassia.

gale [gāl] *n* vento forte; burrasca; **~ force 10** vento forza 10.

gall [gôl] *n* (*ANAT*) bile *f*; (*fig: impudence*) fegato, faccia ♦ *vt* urtare (i nervi a).

gall. *abbr* = **gallon**.

gallant [gal'ənt] *a* valoroso(a); [gəlânt'] (*towards ladies*) galante, cortese.

gallantry [gal'əntrē] *n* valore *m* militare; galanteria, cortesia.

gall bladder [gôl' bladûr] *n* cistifellea.

galleon [gal'ēən] *n* galeone *m*.

gallery [gal'ûrē] *n* galleria; loggia; (*for spectators*) tribuna; (*in theater*) loggione *m*, balconata; (*also:* **art ~**: *government-owned*) museo; (: *private*) galleria.

galley [gal'ē] *n* (*ship's kitchen*) cambusa; (*ship*) galea; (*also:* **~ proof**) bozza in colonna.

Gallic [gal'ik] *a* gallico(a); (*French*) francese.

galling [gô'ling] *a* irritante.

gallon [gal'ən] *n* gallone *m* (*US = 3.785 l*; *Brit:* = *4.543 l*; *8 pints*).

gallop [gal'əp] *n* galoppo ♦ *vi* galoppare; **~ing inflation** inflazione *f* galoppante.

gallows [gal'ōz] *n* forca.

gallstone [gôl'stōn] *n* calcolo biliare.

galore [gəlôr'] *ad* a iosa, a profusione.

galvanize [gal'vəniz] *vt* galvanizzare; **to ~ sb into action** (*fig*) galvanizzare qn, spronare qn all'azione.

Gambia [gam'bēə] *n* Gambia *m*.

gambit [gam'bit] *n* (*fig*): (**opening**) **~** prima mossa.

gamble [gam'bəl] *n* azzardo, rischio calcolato ♦ *vt, vi* giocare; **to ~ on** (*fig*) giocare su; **to ~ on the Stock Exchange** giocare in Borsa.

gambler [gam'blûr] *n* giocatore/trice d'azzardo.

gambling [gam'bling] *n* gioco d'azzardo.

gambol [gam'bəl] *vi* saltellare.

game [gām] *n* gioco; (*event*) partita; (*HUNTING*) selvaggina ♦ *a* coraggioso(a); (*ready*): **to be ~ (for sth/to do)** essere pronto(a) (a qc/a fare); **~s** *npl* (*SCOL*) attività *fpl* sportive; **big ~** selvaggina grossa.

game bird *n* uccello selvatico.

gamekeeper [gām'kēpûr] *n* guardacaccia *m*

inv.
gamely [gām'lē] *ad* coraggiosamente.
game reserve *n* riserva di caccia.
gamesmanship [gāmz'mənship] *n* abilità.
gammon [gam'ən] *n* (*bacon*) quarto di maiale; (*ham*) prosciutto affumicato.
gamut [gam'ət] *n* gamma.
gang [gang] *n* banda, squadra ♦ *vi*: **to ~ up on sb** far combutta contro qn.
Ganges [gan'jēz] *n*: **the ~** il Gange.
gangling [gang'gling] *a* allampanato(a).
gangplank [gang'plangk] *n* passerella.
gangrene [gang'grēn] *n* cancrena.
gangster [gang'stûr] *n* gangster *m inv.*
gangway [gang'wā] *n* passerella; (*Brit*: *of bus*) passaggio.
gantry [gan'trē] *n* (*for crane*, *railway signal*) cavalletto; (*for rocket*) torre *f* di lancio.
GAO *n abbr* (*US*: = *General Accounting Office*) ≈ Corte *fr* dei Conti.
gaol [jāl] *n*, *vt* (*Brit*) = **jail.**
gap [gap] *n* buco; (*in time*) intervallo; (*fig*) lacuna; vuoto.
gape [gāp] *vi* restare a bocca aperta.
gaping [gā'ping] *a* (*hole*) squarciato(a).
garage [gərázh'] *n* garage *m inv.*
garb [gârb] *n* abiti *mpl*, veste *f.*
garbage [gâr'bij] *n* immondizie *fpl*, rifiuti *mpl*; (*fig*: *movie*, *book*) porcheria, robaccia; (: *nonsense*) fesserie *fpl.*
garbage can *n* (*US*) bidone *m* della spazzatura.
garbage disposal unit *n* tritarifiuti *m inv.*
garbage dump *n* (*US*) luogo di scarico.
garbageman [gâr'bijmən] *n* (*US*) netturbino.
garbage truck *n* (*US*) carro della nettezza urbana *or* delle immondizie.
garbled [gâr'bəld] *a* deformato(a); ingarbugliato(a).
garden [gâr'dən] *n* giardino ♦ *vi* lavorare nel giardino; **~s** *npl* (*public*) giardini pubblici; (*private*) parco.
garden center *n* vivaio.
gardener [gârd'nûr] *n* giardiniere/a.
gardening [gâr'dəning] *n* giardinaggio.
gargle [gâr'gəl] *vi* fare gargarismi ♦ *n* gargarismo.
gargoyle [gâr'goil] *n* gargouille *f inv.*
garish [gär'ish] *a* vistoso(a).
garland [gâr'lənd] *n* ghirlanda; corona.
garlic [gâr'lik] *n* aglio.
garment [gâr'mənt] *n* indumento.
garner [gâr'nûr] *vt* ammucchiare, raccogliere.
garnish [gâr'nish] *vt* guarnire.
garret [gar'it] *n* soffitta.
garrison [gar'isən] *n* guarnigione *f* ♦ *vt* guarnire.
garrison cap *n* (*US*) bustina.
garrulous [gar'ələs] *a* ciarliero(a), loquace.
garter [gâr'tûr] *n* giarrettiera; (*US*: *suspender*) gancio (di reggicalze).

garter belt *n* (*US*) reggicalze *m inv.*
gas [gas] *n* gas *m inv*; (*used as anesthetic*) etere *m*; (*US*: *gasoline*) benzina ♦ *vt* asfissiare con il gas; (*MIL*) gasare.
gas can *n* (*US*) tanica per benzina.
gas cylinder *n* bombola del gas.
gaseous [gas'ēəs] *a* gassoso(a).
gash [gash] *n* sfregio ♦ *vt* sfregiare.
gasket [gas'kit] *n* (*AUT*) guarnizione *f.*
gas mask *n* maschera *f* antigas *inv.*
gas meter *n* contatore *m* del gas.
gas(oline) [gas(əlēn')] *n* (*US*) benzina.
gasp [gasp] *vi* ansare, boccheggiare; (*in surprise*) restare senza fiato.
gasp out *vt* dire affannosamente.
gas pedal *n* (*US*) acceleratore *m.*
gas-permeable [gaspûr'mēəbəl] *a* (*contact lenses*) permeabile ai gas.
gas pump *n* (*US*: *in car*, *at garage*) pompa di benzina.
gas ring *n* fornello a gas.
gas station *n* (*US*) distributore *m* di benzina.
gas stove *n* cucina a gas.
gassy [gas'ē] *a* gassoso(a).
gas tank *n* (*US AUT*) serbatoio (di benzina).
gas tap *n* (*on cooker*) manopola del gas; (*on pipe*) rubinetto del gas.
gastric [gas'trik] *a* gastrico(a).
gastric ulcer *n* ulcera gastrica.
gastroenteritis [gastrōentərī'tis] *n* gastroenterite *f.*
gastronomy [gastrân'əmē] *n* gastronomia.
gasworks [gas'wûrks] *n or npl* impianto di produzione del gas.
gate [gāt] *n* cancello; (*of castle*, *town*) porta; (*at airport*) uscita; (*at grade crossing*) barriera.
gateau, *pl* **~x** [gatō, -z'] *n* (*Brit*) torta.
gate-crash [gāt'krash] *vt* partecipare senza invito a.
gate-crasher [gāt'krashûr] *n* intruso(a), ospite *m/f* non invitato(a).
gateway [gāt'wā] *n* porta.
gather [gath'ûr] *vt* (*flowers*, *fruit*) cogliere; (*pick up*) raccogliere; (*assemble*) radunare; raccogliere; (*understand*) capire ♦ *vi* (*assemble*) radunarsi; (*dust*) accumularsi; (*clouds*) addensarsi; **to ~ speed** acquistare velocità; **to ~ (from/that)** comprendere (da/che), dedurre (da/che); **as far as I can ~** da quel che ho potuto capire.
gathering [gath'ûring] *n* adunanza.
GATT [gat] *n abbr* (= *General Agreement on Tariffs and Trade*) G.A.T.T. *m.*
gauche [gōsh] *a* goffo(a), maldestro(a).
gaudy [gô'dē] *a* vistoso(a).
gauge [gāj] *n* (*standard measure*) calibro; (*RAIL*) scartamento; (*instrument*) indicatore *m* ♦ *vt* misurare; (*fig*: *sb's capabilities*, *character*) valutare, stimare; **to ~ the right moment** calcolare il momento giusto; **gas ~,**

(Brit) **petrol** ~ indicatore *m or* spia della benzina.

gaunt [gônt] *a* scarno(a); *(grim, desolate)* desolato(a).

gauntlet [gônt'lit] *n (fig)*: **to run the ~ through an angry crowd** passare sotto il fuoco di una folla ostile; **to throw down the ~** gettare il guanto.

gauze [gôz] *n* garza.

gave [gāv] *pt of* **give**.

gawky [gó'kē] *a* goffo(a), sgraziato(a).

gawp [gôp] *vi:* **to ~ at** guardare a bocca aperta.

gay [gā] *a (person)* gaio(a), allegro(a); *(color)* vivace, vivo(a); *(col)* omosessuale.

gaze [gāz] *n* sguardo fisso ♦ *vi:* **to ~ at** guardare fisso.

gazelle [gəzel'] *n* gazzella.

gazette [gəzet'] *n (newspaper)* gazzetta; *(official publication)* gazzetta ufficiale.

gazetteer [gazitēr'] *n (book)* dizionario dei nomi geografici; *(section of book)* indice *m* dei nomi geografici.

GB *abbr* (= *Great Britain*) GB.

GCE *n abbr (Brit: = General Certificate of Education)* ≈ diploma *m* di maturità.

GCSE *n abbr (Brit: = General Certificate of Secondary Education) diploma di istruzione secondaria conseguito a 16 anni in Inghilterra e Galles*.

Gdns. *abbr* = *Gardens*.

GDP *n abbr* = **gross domestic product**.

GDR *n abbr see* **German Democratic Republic**.

gear [gēr] *n* attrezzi *mpl*, equipaggiamento; *(belongings)* roba; *(TECH)* ingranaggio; *(AUT)* marcia ♦ *vt (fig: adapt)* adattare; **high** *or (Brit)* **top/low/bottom** ~ quarta *(or* quinta)/ seconda/prima; **in** ~ in marcia; **out of** ~ in folle; **our service is** ~ed **to meet the needs of the disabled** la nostra organizzazione risponde espressamente alle esigenze degli handicappati.

    gear up *vi:* **to** ~ **up (to do)** prepararsi (a fare).

gear box *(Brit) n* scatola del cambio.

gear shift, *(Brit)* **gear lever** *n* leva del cambio.

GED *n abbr (US SCOL)* = *general educational development*.

geese [gēs] *npl of* **goose**.

Geiger counter [gī'gûr koun'tûr] *n* geiger *m inv*.

gel [jel] *n* gel *m inv*.

gelatin(e) [jel'ətin] *n* gelatina.

gelignite [jel'ignīt] *n* nitroglicerina.

gem [jem] *n* gemma.

Gemini [jem'ənī] *n* Gemelli *mpl*; **to be** ~ essere dei Gemelli.

gen [jen] *n (Brit col)*: **to give sb the** ~ **on sth** mettere qn al corrente di qc.

Gen. *abbr (MIL: = General)* Gen.

gender [jen'dûr] *n* genere *m*.

gene [jēn] *n (BIOL)* gene *m*.

genealogy [jēnēal'əjē] *n* genealogia.

general [jen'ûrəl] *n* generale *m* ♦ *a* generale; **in** ~ in genere; **the** ~ **public** il grande pubblico.

general anesthetic *n* anestesia totale.

general delivery *n (US)* fermo posta *m*.

general election *n* elezioni *fpl* generali.

generalization [jenûrələzā'shən] *n* generalizzazione *f*.

generalize [jen'ûrəlīz] *vi* generalizzare.

generally [jen'ûrəlē] *ad* generalmente.

general manager *n* direttore *m* generale.

general practitioner (GP) *n* medico generico; **who's your GP?** qual'è il suo medico di fiducia?

general strike *n* sciopero generale.

generate [jen'ərāt] *vt* generare.

generation [jenərā'shən] *n* generazione *f; (of electricity etc)* produzione *f*.

generator [jen'ərātûr] *n* generatore *m*.

generic [jənär'ik] *a* generico(a).

generosity [jenərás'ətē] *n* generosità.

generous [jen'ûrəs] *a* generoso(a); *(copious)* abbondante.

genesis [jen'əsis] *n* genesi *f*.

genetic [jinet'ik] *a* genetico(a); ~ **engineering** selezione *f* genetica.

genetics [jənet'iks] *n* genetica.

Geneva [jənē'və] *n* Ginevra; **Lake** ~ il lago di Ginevra.

genial [jē'nēəl] *a* geniale, cordiale.

genitals [jen'itəlz] *npl* genitali *mpl*.

genitive [jen'ətiv] *n* genitivo.

genius [jēn'yəs] *n* genio.

Genoa [jen'ōə] *n* Genova.

genocide [jen'əsīd] *n* genocidio.

Genoese [jenōēz'] *a, n (pl inv)* genovese *(m/ f)*.

genteel [jentēl'] *a* raffinato(a), distinto(a).

gentle [jen'təl] *a* delicato(a); *(person)* dolce.

gentleman [jen'təlmən] *n* signore *m; (well-bred man)* gentiluomo; ~'s **agreement** impegno sulla parola.

gentlemanly [jen'təlmənlē] *a* da gentiluomo.

gentleness [jen'təlnis] *n* delicatezza; dolcezza.

gently [jen'tlē] *ad* delicatamente.

gentry [jen'trē] *n* nobiltà minore.

genuine [jen'yōōin] *a* autentico(a); sincero(a).

genuinely [jen'yōōinlē] *ad* genuinamente.

geographer [jēåg'rəfûr] *n* geografo/a.

geographic(al) [jēəgraf'ik(əl)] *a* geografico(a).

geography [jēåg'rəfē] *n* geografia.

geological [jēəlåj'ikəl] *a* geologico(a).

geologist [jēål'əjist] *n* geologo/a.

geology [jēål'əjē] *n* geologia.

geometric(al) [jēəmet'rik(əl)] *a* geometrico(a).

geometry [jēåm'ətrē] *n* geometria.

geranium [jərā'nēəm] *n* geranio.

geriatric [järēat'rik] *a* geriatrico(a).

germ [jûrm] *n* (*MED*) microbo; (*BIOL*, *fig*) germe *m*.

German [jûr'mən] *a* tedesco(a) ♦ *n* tedesco/a; (*LING*) tedesco.

German Democratic Republic (GDR) *n* Repubblica Democratica Tedesca (R.D.T.).

German measles *n* rosolia.

German shepherd *n* (*US*: *dog*) pastore *m* tedesco, (cane *m*) lupo.

Germany [jûr'mənē] *n* Germania.

germination [jûrmənā'shən] *n* germinazione *f*.

germ warfare *n* guerra batteriologica.

gerrymandering [jär'ēmandûring] *n* manipolazione *f* dei distretti elettorali.

gestation [jestā'shən] *n* gestazione *f*.

gesticulate [jestik'yəlāt] *vi* gesticolare.

gesture [jes'chûr] *n* gesto; **as a ~ of friendship** in segno d'amicizia.

get, *pt*, *pp* **got,** (*US*) *pp* **gotten** [get, gât, gât'ən] *vt* (*obtain*) avere, ottenere; (*receive*) ricevere; (*find*) trovare; (*buy*) comprare; (*catch*) acchiappare; (*fetch*) andare a prendere; (*take, move*) portare; (*understand*) comprendere, capire; (*have*): **to ~ got** avere; (*become*): **to ~ rich/old** arricchirsi/invecchiare; (*col*: *annoy*): **he really ~s me** mi dà proprio sui nervi ♦ *vi* (*go*): **to ~ to** (*place*) andare a; arrivare a; pervenire a; (*modal auxiliary vb*): **you've got to do it** deve farlo; **he got across the bridge/under the fence** ha attraversato il ponte/è passato sotto il recinto; **to ~ sth for sb** prendere *or* procurare qc a qn; **~ me Mr Jones, please** (*TEL*) mi passi il signor Jones, per favore; **can I ~ you a drink?** ti posso offrire da bere?; **to ~ ready/washed/shaved** *etc* prepararsi/lavarsi/farsi la barba *etc*; **to ~ sth done** (*do*) fare qc; (*have done*) far fare qc; **to ~ sth/sb ready** preparare qc/qn; **to ~ one's hair cut** farsi tagliare i capelli; **to ~ sb to do sth** far fare qc a qn; **to ~ sth through/out of** far passare qc per/uscire qc da; **let's ~ going** *or* **started!** muoviamoci!

get about *vi* muoversi; (*news*) diffondersi.

get across *vt*: **to ~ across (to)** (*message, meaning*) comunicare (a) ♦ *vi*: **to ~ across to** (*subj*: *speaker*) comunicare con.

get along *vi* (*depart*) andarsene; (*agree*) andare d'accordo; (*manage*) = **to get by**; **how are you ~ting along?** come va (la vita)?

get around *vi*: **to ~ around to doing sth** trovare il tempo di fare qc ♦ *vt fus* aggirare; (*fig*: *person*) rigirare.

get at *vt fus* (*attack*) prendersela con; (*reach*) raggiungere, arrivare a; **what are you ~ting at?** dove vuoi arrivare?

get away *vi* partire, andarsene; (*escape*) scappare.

get away with *vt fus* cavarsela con; farla

franca con; **he'll never ~ away with it!** non riuscirà a farla franca!

get back *vi* (*return*) ritornare, tornare ♦ *vt* riottenere, riavere; **to ~ back to** (*start again*) ritornare a; (*contact again*) rimettersi in contatto con.

get back at *vt fus* (*col*): **to ~ back at sb (for sth)** rendere pan per focaccia a qn (per qc).

get by *vi* (*pass*) passare; (*manage*) farcela; **I can ~ by in Dutch** mi arrango in olandese.

get down *vi*, *vt fus* scendere ♦ *vt* far scendere; (*depress*) buttare giù.

get down to *vt fus* (*work*) mettersi a; **to ~ down to business** venire al dunque.

get in *vi* entrare; (*train*) arrivare; (*arrive home*) ritornare, tornare ♦ *vt* (*bring in*: *harvest*) raccogliere; (*: coal, shopping, supplies*) fare provvista di; (*insert*) far entrare, infilare.

get into *vt fus* entrare in; (*vehicle*) salire in, montare in; **to ~ into bed** mettersi a letto; **to ~ into a rage** incavolarsi.

get off *vi* (*from train etc*) scendere; (*depart*: *person, car*) andare via; (*escape*) cavarsela ♦ *vt* (*remove*: *clothes, stain*) levare; (*send off*) spedire; (*have as leave*: *day, time*): **we got 2 days off** abbiamo avuto 2 giorni liberi ♦ *vt fus* (*train, bus*) scendere da; **to ~ off to a good start** (*fig*) cominciare bene.

get on *vi* (*at exam etc*) andare; (*agree*): **to ~ on (with)** andare d'accordo (con) ♦ *vt fus* montare in; (*horse*) montare su.

get on to *vt fus* (*Brit col*: *contact*: *on phone etc*) contattare, rintracciare; (*: deal with*) occuparsi di.

get out *vi* uscire; (*of vehicle*) scendere; (*news etc*) venirsi a sapere, spargersi ♦ *vt* tirar fuori, far uscire; **to ~ out (of)** (*money from bank etc*) ritirare (da).

get out of *vt fus* uscire da; (*duty etc*) evitare ♦ *vt* (*extract*: *confession, words*) tirare fuori di bocca a; (*gain from*: *pleasure, benefit*) trarre da.

get over *vt fus* (*illness*) riaversi da; (*communicate*: *idea etc*) comunicare, passare; **let's ~ it over (with)** togliamoci il pensiero.

get round *vi*, *vt fus* = **get around**.

get through *vi* (*TEL*) avere la linea ♦ *vt fus* (*finish*: *work*) sbrigare; (*: book*) finire.

get through to *vt fus* (*TEL*) parlare a.

get together *vi* riunirsi ♦ *vt* raccogliere; (*people*) adunare.

get up *vi* (*rise*) alzarsi ♦ *vt fus* salire su per; **to ~ up enthusiasm for sth** entusiasmarsi per qc.

get up to *vt fus* (*reach*) raggiungere; (*Brit*: *prank etc*) fare.

getaway |gct'əwā| n fuga.

getaway car n macchina per la fuga.

get-together |gct'təgcthûr| n (piccola) riunione f; (party) festicciola.

getup |gct'up| n (col: outfit) tenuta.

get-well card |gctwcl' kârd| n cartolina di auguri di pronta guarigione.

geyser |gī'zûr| n (GEO) geyser m inv.

Ghana |gân'ə| n Ghana m.

Ghanaian |gənā'čən| a, n ganaense (m/f).

ghastly |gast'lē| a orribile, orrendo(a).

gherkin |gûr'kin| n cetriolino.

ghetto |gct'ō| n ghetto.

ghost |gōst| n fantasma m, spettro ♦ vt (book) fare lo scrittore ombra per.

ghostly |gōst'lē| a spettrale.

ghostwriter |gōst'rītûr| n scrittore/trice ombra inv.

ghoul |gōōl| n vampiro che si nutre di cadaveri.

ghoulish |gōōl'ish| a (tastes etc) macabro(a).

GHQ n abbr (MIL: = general headquarters) ≈ comando di Stato maggiore.

GI n abbr (US col: = government issue) G.I. m, soldato americano.

giant |jī'ənt| n gigante/essa ♦ a gigante, enorme; ~ **(size) packet** confezione f gigante.

gibber |jib'ûr| vi (monkey) squittire confusamente; (idiot) farfugliare.

gibberish |jib'ûrish| n parole fpl senza senso.

gibe |jīb| n frecciata ♦ vi: **to** ~ **at** lanciare frecciate a.

giblets |jib'lits| npl frattaglie fpl.

Gibraltar |jibrôl'tûr| n Gibilterra.

giddiness |gid'ēnis| n vertigine f.

giddy |gid'ē| a (dizzy): **to be** ~ aver le vertigini; (height) vertiginoso(a); **I feel** ~ mi gira la testa.

gift |gift| n regalo; (donation, ability) dono; (COMM: also: **free** ~) omaggio; **to have a** ~ **for sth** (talent) avere il dono di qc.

gift certificate n (US) buono (d')acquisto.

gifted |gif'tid| a dotato(a).

gift token n (Brit) buono (d')acquisto.

gig |gig| n (col: of musician) serata.

gigantic |jīgan'tik| a gigantesco(a).

giggle |gig'əl| vi ridere scioccamente ♦ n risolino (sciocco).

GIGO |gig'ō| abbr (COMPUT: col: = garbage in, garbage out) qualità di input = qualità di output.

gild |gild| vt dorare.

gill |jil| n (measure) = 0.25 pints (US = 0.118 l; Brit = 0.148 l).

gills |gilz| npl (of fish) branchie fpl.

gilt |gilt| n doratura ♦ a dorato(a).

gilt-edged |gilt'cjd| a (stocks, securities) della massima sicurezza.

gimlet |gim'lit| n succhiello.

gimmick |gim'ik| n trucco; **sales** ~ trovata commerciale.

gin |jin| n (liquor) gin m inv.

ginger |jin'jûr| n zenzero.

ginger up vt scuotere; animare.

ginger ale, ginger beer n bibita gassosa allo zenzero.

gingerbread |jin'jûrbrcd| n pan m di zenzero.

ginger group n (Brit) gruppo di pressione.

ginger-haired |jin'jûrhärd| a rossiccio(a).

gingerly |jin'jûrlē| ad cautamente.

gingham |ging'əm| n percalle m a righe (or quadretti).

gipsy |jip'sē| n = **gypsy**.

giraffe |jəraf'| n giraffa.

girder |gûr'dûr| n trave f.

girdle |gûr'dəl| n (corset) guaina.

girl |gûrl| n ragazza; (young unmarried woman) signorina; (daughter) figlia, figliola; **a little** ~ una bambina.

girl Friday n impiegato tuttofare inv.

girlfriend |gûrl'frcnd| n (of girl) amica; (of boy) ragazza.

girlish |gûr'lish| a da ragazza.

Girl Scout n (US) Giovane Esploratrice f.

Giro |jī'rō| n: **the National** ~ (Brit) ≈ la or il Bancoposta.

giro |jī'rō| n (Brit: bank ~) versamento bancario; (: post office ~) postagiro.

girth |gûrth| n circonferenza; (of horse) cinghia.

gist |jist| n succo.

give |giv| n (of fabric) elasticità ♦ vb (pt **gave**, pp **given** |gāv, giv'ən|) vt dare ♦ vi cedere; **to** ~ **sb sth**, ~ **sth to sb** dare qc a qn; **to** ~ **a cry/sigh** emettere un grido/sospiro; **how much did you** ~ **for it?** quanto (l')hai pagato?; **12 o'clock,** ~ **or take a few minutes** mezzogiorno, minuto più minuto meno; **to** ~ **way** vi cedere; (Brit AUT) dare la precedenza.

give away vt dare via; (give free) fare dono di; (betray) tradire; (disclose) rivelare; (bride) condurre all'altare.

give back vt rendere.

give in vi cedere ♦ vt consegnare.

give off vt emettere.

give out vt distribuire; annunciare ♦ vi (be exhausted: supplies) esaurirsi, venir meno; (fail: engine) fermarsi; (: strength) mancare.

give up vi rinunciare ♦ vt rinunciare a; **to** ~ **up smoking** smettere di fumare; **to** ~ **o.s. up** arrendersi.

give-and-take |giv'əntāk'| n (col) elasticità (da ambo le parti), concessioni fpl reciproche.

giveaway |giv'əwā| n (col): **her expression was a** ~ le si leggeva tutto in volto; **the exam was a** ~! l'esame è stato uno scherzo! ♦ cpd: ~ **prices** prezzi stracciati.

given |giv'ən| pp of **give** ♦ a (fixed: time, amount) dato(a), determinato(a) ♦ cj: ~

(that) ... dato che ...; ~ **the circumstances** ... date le circostanze ....

glacial [glā'shəl] a glaciale.

glacier [glä'shûr] n ghiacciaio.

glad [glad] a lieto(a), contento(a); **to be ~ about sth/that** essere contento or lieto di qc/ che + sub; **I was ~ of his help** gli sono stato grato del suo aiuto.

gladden [glad'ən] vt rallegrare, allietare.

glade [glād] n radura.

gladioli [gladēō'lē] npl gladioli mpl.

gladly [glad'lē] ad volentieri.

glamorous [glam'ûrəs] a (gen) favoloso(a); (person) affascinante, seducente; (occasion) brillante, elegante.

glamour [glam'ûr] n fascino.

glance [glans] n occhiata, sguardo ♦ vi: **to ~ at** dare un'occhiata a.

glance off vt fus (bullet) rimbalzare su.

glancing [glan'sing] a (blow) che colpisce di striscio.

gland [gland] n ghiandola.

glandular [glan'jəlûr] a: ~ **fever** (Brit) mononucleosi f.

glare [glär] n riverbero, luce f abbagliante; (look) sguardo furioso ♦ vi abbagliare; **to ~ at** guardare male.

glaring [glär'ing] a (mistake) madornale.

glass [glas] n (substance) vetro; (tumbler) bicchiere m; (also: **looking ~**) specchio; see also **glasses**.

glass-blowing [glas'blōing] n soffiatura del vetro.

glasses [glas'iz] npl (spectacles) occhiali mpl.

glass fiber n fibra di vetro.

glasshouse [glas'·hous] n (Brit) serra.

glassware [glas'wär] n vetrame m.

glassy [glas'ē] a (eyes) vitreo(a).

glaze [glāz] vt (door) fornire di vetri; (pottery) smaltare; (CULIN) glassare ♦ n smalto; glassa.

glazed [glāzd] a (eye) vitreo(a); (tiles, pottery) smaltato(a).

glazier [glā'zhûr] n vetraio.

gleam [glēm] n barlume m; raggio ♦ vi luccicare; **a ~ of hope** un barlume di speranza.

gleaming [glē'ming] a lucente.

glean [glēn] vt (information) racimolare.

glee [glē] n allegrezza, gioia.

gleeful [glē'fəl] a allegro(a), gioioso(a).

glen [glen] n valletta.

glib [glib] a dalla parola facile; facile.

glide [glīd] vi scivolare; (AVIAT, birds) planare ♦ n scivolata; planata.

glider [glī'dûr] n (AVIAT) aliante m.

gliding [glī'ding] n (AVIAT) volo a vela.

glimmer [glim'ûr] vi luccicare ♦ n barlume m.

glimpse [glimps] n impressione f fugace ♦ vt vedere di sfuggita; **to catch a ~ of** vedere di sfuggita.

glint [glint] n luccichio ♦ vi luccicare.

glisten [glis'ən] vi luccicare.

glitter [glit'ûr] vi scintillare ♦ n scintillio.

glitz [glits] n (col) vistosità, chiassosità.

gloat [glōt] vi: **to ~ (over)** gongolare di piacere (per).

global [glō'bəl] a globale; (world-wide) mondiale.

globe [glōb] n globo, sfera.

globetrotter [glōb'trâtûr] n giramondo m/f inv.

globule [glâb'yōōl] n (ANAT) globulo; (of water etc) gocciolina.

gloom [glōōm] n oscurità, buio; (sadness) tristezza, malinconia.

gloomy [glōō'mē] a fosco(a), triste; **to feel ~** sentirsi giù or depresso.

glorification [glôrəfəkā'shən] n glorificazione f.

glorify [glôr'əfī] vt glorificare; celebrare, esaltare.

glorious [glôr'ēəs] a glorioso(a); magnifico(a).

glory [glôr'ē] n gloria; splendore m ♦ vi: **to ~ in** gloriarsi di or in.

glory hole n (Brit col) ripostiglio.

Glos abbr (Brit) = Gloucestershire.

gloss [glôs] n (shine) lucentezza; (also: ~ **paint**) vernice f a olio.

gloss over vt fus scivolare su.

glossary [glâs'ûrē] n glossario.

glossy [glâs'ē] a lucente ♦ n (also: ~ **magazine**) rivista di lusso.

glove [gluv] n guanto.

glove compartment n (AUT) vano portaoggetti.

glow [glō] vi ardere; (face) essere luminoso(a) ♦ n bagliore m; (of face) colorito acceso.

glower [glou'ûr] vi: **to ~ (at sb)** guardare (qn) in cagnesco.

glowing [glō'ing] a (fire) ardente; (complexion) luminoso(a); (fig: report, description etc) entusiasta.

glow-worm [glō'wûrm] n lucciola.

glucose [glōō'kōs] n glucosio.

glue [glōō] n colla ♦ vt incollare.

glue-sniffing [glōō'snifing] n sniffare m (colla).

glum [glum] a abbattuto(a).

glut [glut] n eccesso ♦ vt saziare; (market) saturare.

glutinous [glōōt'ənəs] a colloso(a), appiccicoso(a).

glutton [glut'ən] n ghiottone/a; **a ~ for work** un(a) patito(a) del lavoro.

gluttonous [glut'ənəs] a ghiotto(a), goloso(a).

gluttony [glut'ənē] n ghiottoneria; (sin) gola.

glycerin(e) [glis'ûrin] n glicerina.

gm abbr = **gram**.

GMAT n abbr (US: = Graduate Management Admissions Test) esame di ammissione all'ultimo biennio di scuola superiore.

GMT abbr (= Greenwich Mean Time) T.M.G.

gnarled [nârld] *a* nodoso(a).

gnash [nash] *vt*: **to ~ one's teeth** digrignare i denti.

gnat [nat] *n* moscerino.

gnaw [nó] *vt* rodere.

gnome [nōm] *n* gnomo.

GNP *n abbr* = **gross national product.**

go [gō] *vb* (*pt* **went,** *pp* **gone** [went, gón]) *vi* andare; (*depart*) partire, andarsene; (*work*) funzionare; (*break etc*) cedere; (*be sold*): **to ~ for $10** essere venduto per 10 dollari; (*fit, suit*): **to ~ with** andare bene con; (*become*): **to ~ pale** diventare pallido(a); **to ~ moldy** ammuffire ♦ *n* (*pl* **~es**): **to have a ~ (at)** provare; **to be on the ~** essere in moto; **whose ~ is it?** a chi tocca?; **to ~ by car/on foot** andare in macchina/a piedi; **he's ~ing to do** sta per fare; **to ~ for a walk** andare a fare una passeggiata; **to ~ dancing/shopping** andare a ballare/fare la spesa; **to ~ looking for sb/sth** andare in cerca di qn/qc; **to ~ to sleep** addormentarsi; **to ~ and see sb, to ~ to see sb** andare a trovare qn; **how is it ~ing?** come va (la vita)?; **how did it ~?** com'è andato?; **to ~ round the back/by the shop** passare da dietro/davanti al negozio; **my voice has gone** m'è andata via la voce; **the cake is all gone** il dolce è finito tutto; **I'll take whatever is ~ing** (*Brit*) prendo quello che c'è; **... to ~** (*US: food*) ... da portar via; **the money will ~ towards our vacation** questi soldi li mettiamo per la vacanza.

go about *vt fus*: **how do I ~ about this?** qual'è la prassi per questo? ♦ *vi* (*Brit*) = **go around**; **to ~ about one's business** occuparsi delle proprie faccende.

go after *vt fus* (*pursue*) correr dietro a, rincorrere; (*job, record etc*) mirare a.

go against *vt fus* (*be unfavorable to*) essere contro; (*be contrary to*) andare contro.

go ahead *vi* andare avanti; **~ ahead!** faccia pure!

go along *vi* andare, avanzare ♦ *vt fus* percorrere; **to ~ along with** (*accompany*) andare con, accompagnare; (*agree with*: *idea*) sottoscrivere, appoggiare.

go around *vi* (*circulate*: *news, rumor*) circolare; (*revolve*) girare; (*visit*): **to ~ around (to sb's)** passare (da qn); (*make a detour*): **to ~ around (by)** passare (per); (*suffice*) bastare (per tutti).

go away *vi* partire, andarsene.

go back *vi* tornare, ritornare; (*go again*) andare di nuovo.

go back on *vt fus* (*promise*) non mantenere.

go by *vi* (*years, time*) scorrere ♦ *vt fus* attenersi a, seguire (alla lettera); prestar fede a.

go down *vi* scendere; (*ship*) affondare;

(*sun*) tramontare ♦ *vt fus* scendere; **that should ~ down well with him** dovrebbe incontrare la sua approvazione.

go for *vt fus* (*fetch*) andare a prendere; (*like*) andar matto(a) per; (*attack*) attaccare; saltare addosso a.

go in *vi* entrare.

go in for *vt fus* (*competition*) iscriversi a; (*be interested in*) interessarsi di.

go into *vt fus* entrare in; (*investigate*) indagare, esaminare; (*embark on*) lanciarsi in.

go off *vi* partire, andar via; (*food*) guastarsi; (*explode*) esplodere, scoppiare; (*lights etc*) spegnersi; (*event*) passare ♦ *vt fus*: **I've gone off chocolate** la cioccolata non mi piace più; **the gun went off** il fucile si scaricò; **the party went off well** la festa è andata *or* è riuscita bene; **to ~ off to sleep** addormentarsi.

go on *vi* continuare; (*happen*) succedere; (*lights*) accendersi ♦ *vt fus* (*be guided by*: *evidence etc*) basarsi su, fondarsi su; **to ~ on doing** continuare a fare; **what's ~ing on here?** che succede *or* che sta succedendo qui?

go on at *vt fus* (*nag*) assillare.

go on with *vt fus* continuare, proseguire.

go out *vi* uscire; (*fire, light*) spegnersi; (*ebb: tide*) calare; **to ~ out with sb** uscire con qn.

go over *vi* (*ship*) ribaltarsi ♦ *vt fus* (*check*) esaminare; **to ~ over sth in one's mind** pensare bene a qc.

go round *vi* (*Brit*) = **go around.**

go through *vt fus* (*town etc*) attraversare; (*search through*) frugare in; (*examine*: *list, book*) leggere da capo a fondo; (*perform*) fare.

go through with *vt fus* (*plan, crime*) mettere in atto, eseguire; **I couldn't ~ through with it** non sono riuscito ad andare fino in fondo.

go under *vi* (*sink*: *ship*) affondare, colare a picco; (: *person*) andare sotto; (*fig: business, firm*) fallire.

go up *vi* salire ♦ *vt fus* salire su per; **to ~ up in flames** andare in fiamme.

go without *vt fus* fare a meno di.

goad [gōd] *vt* spronare.

go-ahead [gō'əhed] *a* intraprendente ♦ *n*: **to give sb/sth the ~** dare l'okay a qn/qc.

goal [gōl] *n* (*SPORT*) gol *m*, rete *f*; (: *place*) porta; (*fig: aim*) fine *m*, scopo.

goalkeeper [gōl'kēpúr] *n* portiere *m*.

goalpost [gōl'lpōst] *n* palo (della porta).

goat [gōt] *n* capra.

gobble [gâb'əl] *vt* (*also*: **~ down, ~ up**) ingoiare.

gobbledygook [gâb'əldēgōōk] *n* parole *fpl* senza senso.

go-between [gō'bitwēn] *n* intermediario/a.

Gobi Desert [gō'bē dez'úrt] *n*: **the ~** il Deserto dei Gobi.

goblet [gáb'lit] *n* calice *m*, coppa.

goblin [gáb'lin] *n* folletto.

go-cart [gō'kárt] *n* go-kart *m inv* ♦ *cpd*: ~ **racing** *n* kartismo.

god [gád] *n* dio; **G~** Dio.

godchild [gád'chīld] *n* figlioccio/a.

goddamn [gád'dam'] *a* (*US col!*): **this** ~ ... questo maledetto ....

goddaughter [gád'dôtûr] *n* figlioccia.

goddess [gád'is] *n* dea.

godfather [gád'fáthûr] *n* padrino.

godforsaken [gád'fûrsā'kən] *a* desolato(a), sperduto(a).

godmother [gád'muthûr] *n* madrina.

godparents [gád'pärənts] *npl*: **the** ~ il padrino e la madrina.

godsend [gád'send] *n* dono del cielo.

godson [gád'sun] *n* figlioccio.

goes [gōz] *vb see* **go**.

gofer [gō'fûr] *n* (*US col*) factotum *m inv*.

go-getter [gō'get'ûr] *n* arrivista *m/f*.

goggle [gág'əl] *vi*: **to** ~ **(at)** stare con gli occhi incollati *or* appiccicati (a *or* addosso a).

goggles [gág'əlz] *npl* occhiali *mpl* (di protezione).

going [gō'ing] *n* (*conditions*) andare *m*, stato del terreno ♦ *a*: **the** ~ **rate** la tariffa in vigore; **a** ~ **concern** un'azienda avviata; **it was slow** ~ si andava a rilento.

goings-on [gō'ingzân'] *npl* (*col*) fatti *mpl* strani, cose *fpl* strane.

go-kart [gō'kárt] *n* = **go-cart**.

gold [gōld] *n* oro ♦ *a* d'oro; (*reserves*) aureo(a).

golden [gōl'dən] *a* (*made of gold*) d'oro; (*gold in color*) dorato(a).

golden age *n* età d'oro.

golden rule *n* regola principale.

goldfish [gōld'fish] *n* pesce *m* dorato *or* rosso.

gold leaf *n* lamina d'oro.

gold medal *n* (*SPORT*) medaglia d'oro.

gold mine *n* miniera d'oro.

gold-plated [gōldplā'tid] *a* placcato(a) oro *inv*.

goldsmith [gōld'smith] *n* orefice *m*, orafo.

gold standard *n* tallone *m* aureo.

golf [gálf] *n* golf *m*.

golf ball *n* pallina da golf.

golf club *n* circolo di golf; (*stick*) bastone *m or* mazza da golf.

golf course *n* campo di golf.

golfer [gál'fûr] *n* giocatore/trice di golf.

gondola [gán'dələ] *n* gondola.

gondolier [gándəliûr'] *n* gondoliere *m*.

gone [gòn] *pp of* **go**.

gong [gòng] *n* gong *m inv*.

good [gōod] *a* buono(a); (*kind*) buono(a), gentile; (*child*) bravo(a) ♦ *n* bene *m*; ~! bene!, ottimo!; **to be** ~ **at** essere bravo(a) in; **it's** ~ **for you** fa bene; **it's a** ~ **thing you were there** meno male che c'era; **she is** ~

with children/her hands ci sa fare coi bambini/è abile nei lavori manuali; **to feel** ~ sentirsi bene; **it's** ~ **to see you** che piacere vederla; **he's up to no** ~ ne sta combinando qualcuna; **it's no** ~ **complaining** brontolare non serve a niente; **for the common** ~ nell'interesse generale, per il bene comune; **for** ~ (*for ever*) per sempre, definitivamente; **would you be** ~ **enough to ...?** avrebbe la gentilezza di ...?; **that's very** ~ **of you** è molto gentile da parte sua; **is this any** ~? (*will it do?*) va bene questo?; (*what's it like?*) com'è?; **a** ~ **deal (of)** molto(a), una buona quantità (di); **a** ~ **many** molti(e); ~ **morning!** buon giorno!; ~ **afternoon/evening!** buona sera!; ~ **night!** buona notte!; *see also* **goods**.

goodbye [gōodbī'] *excl* arrivederci!; **to say** ~ **to** (*person*) salutare.

good faith *n* buona fede.

good-for-nothing [gōod'fərnuth'ing] *n* buono/a a nulla, vagabondo/a.

Good Friday *n* Venerdì Santo.

good-humored [gōod'hyōo'mûrd] *a* (*person*) di buon umore; (*remark, joke*) bonario(a).

good-looking [gōod'lōok'ing] *a* bello(a).

good-natured [gōod'nā'chûrd] *a* (*person*) affabile; (*discussion*) amichevole, cordiale.

goodness [gōod'nis] *n* (*of person*) bontà; **for** ~ **sake!** per amor di Dio!; ~ **gracious!** santo cielo!, mamma mia!

goods [gōodz] *npl* (*COMM etc*) merci *fpl*, articoli *mpl*; ~ **and chattels** beni *mpl* e effetti *mpl*.

goods train *n* (*Brit*) treno *m* merci *inv*.

goodwill [gōod'wil'] *n* amicizia, benevolenza; (*COMM*) avviamento.

goody-goody [gōod'ēgōod'ē] *n* (*pej*) santarellino/a.

goof [gōof] *vi* (*US col*) prendere un abbaglio.

goose, *pl* **geese** [gōos, gēs] *n* oca.

gooseberry [gōos'bärē] *n* uva spina; **to play** ~ (*Brit*) tenere la candela.

gooseflesh [gōos'flesh] *n* pelle *f* d'oca.

goosepimples [gōos'pim'pəlz] *npl* pelle *f* d'oca.

goose step *n* (*MIL*) passo dell'oca.

GOP *n abbr* (*US POL*: *col*: = *Grand Old Party*) partito repubblicano.

gore [gôr] *vt* incornare ♦ *n* sangue *m* (coagulato).

gorge [gôrj] *n* gola ♦ *vt*: **to** ~ **o.s. (on)** ingozzarsi (di).

gorgeous [gôr'jəs] *a* magnifico(a).

gorilla [gôril'ə] *n* gorilla *m inv*.

gorse [gôrs] *n* ginestrone *m*.

gory [gôr'ē] *a* sanguinoso(a).

go-slow [gō'slō'] *n* (*Brit*) rallentamento dei lavori (*per agitazione sindacale*).

gospel [gás'pəl] *n* vangelo.

gossamer [gás'əmûr] *n* (*cobweb*) fili *mpl* della

Madonna *or* di ragnatela; *(light fabric)* stoffa sottilissima.

gossip [gàs'əp] *n* chiacchiere *fpl*; pettegolezzi *mpl*; *(person)* pettegolo/a ♦ *vi* chiacchierare; *(maliciously)* pettegolare; **a piece of** ~ un pettegolezzo.

gossip column *n* cronaca mondana.

got [gàt] *pt*, *pp of* **get**.

Gothic [gàth'ik] *a* gotico(a).

gotten [gàt'ən] *(US) pp of* **get**.

gouge [gouj] *vt (also:* ~ **out**: *hole etc)* scavare; (: *initials)* scolpire; (: *sb's eyes)* cavare.

gourd [gôrd] *n* zucca.

gourmet [gŏŏrmā'] *n* buongustaio/a.

gout [gout] *n* gotta.

govern [guv'ûrn] *vt* governare; *(LING)* reggere.

governess [guv'ûrnis] *n* governante *f*.

governing [guv'ûrning] *a (POL)* al potere, al governo; ~ **body** consiglio di amministrazione.

government [guv'ûrnmənt] *n* governo; *(Brit: ministers)* ministero ♦ *cpd* statale; **local** ~ amministrazione *f* locale.

governmental [guvûrnmen'təl] *a* governativo(a).

government housing *n (US)* alloggi *mpl* popolari.

government stock *n* titoli *mpl* di stato.

governor [guv'ûrnûr] *n (of state, bank)* governatore *m*; *(of school, hospital)* amministratore *m*; *(Brit: of prison)* direttore/trice.

Govt *abbr* = **government**.

gown [goun] *n* vestito lungo; *(of teacher, judge)* toga.

GP *n abbr (MED) see* **general practitioner**.

GPO *n abbr (US:* = *Government Printing Office)* ≈ Poligrafici dello Stato.

gr. *abbr (COMM)* = **gross**.

grab [grab] *vt* afferrare, arraffare; *(property, power)* impadronirsi di ♦ *vi:* **to** ~ **at** tentare disperatamente di afferrare.

grace [grās] *n* grazia; *(graciousness)* garbo, cortesia ♦ *vt* onorare; **5 days'** ~ dilazione *f* di 5 giorni; **to say** ~ dire il benedicite; **with a good/bad** ~ volentieri/malvolentieri; **his sense of humor is his saving** ~ il suo senso dell'umorismo è quello che lo salva.

graceful [grās'fəl] *a* elegante, aggraziato(a).

gracious [grā'shəs] *a* grazioso(a); misericordioso(a) ♦ *excl:* **(good)** ~**!** madonna (mia)!

gradation [grādā'shən] *n* gradazione *f*.

grade [grād] *n (COMM)* qualità *f inv*; classe *f*; categoria; *(in hierarchy)* grado; *(US SCOL)* voto; classe; *(gradient)* pendenza, gradiente *m* ♦ *vt* classificare; ordinare; graduare; **to make the** ~ *(fig)* farcela.

grade crossing *n (US)* passaggio a livello.

grade school *n (US)* scuola elementare *or* primaria.

gradient [grā'dēənt] *n* pendenza, gradiente *m*.

gradual [graj'ŏŏəl] *a* graduale.

gradually [graj'ŏŏəlē] *ad* man mano, a poco a poco.

graduate *n* [graj'ŏŏit] laureato/a; *(US SCOL)* diplomato/a, licenziato/a ♦ *vi* [graj'ŏŏāt] laurearsi.

graduated pension [graj'ŏŏātid pen'shən] *n* pensione calcolata sugli ultimi stipendi.

graduation [grajŏŏā'shən] *n* cerimonia del conferimento della laurea; *(US SCOL)* consegna dei diplomi.

graffiti [grəfē'tē] *npl* graffiti *mpl*.

graft [graft] *n (AGR, MED)* innesto ♦ *vt* innestare; **hard** ~ *(col)* duro lavoro.

grain [grān] *n (no pl: cereals)* cereali *mpl*; *(US)* grano; *(of sand)* granello; *(of wood)* venatura; **it goes against the** ~ *(fig)* va contro la mia *(or* la sua *etc)* natura.

gram [gram] *n* grammo.

grammar [gram'ûr] *n* grammatica.

grammatical [grəmat'ikəl] *a* grammaticale.

gramme [gram] *n (Brit)* = **gram**.

granary [grā'nûrē] *n* granaio.

grand [grand] *a* grande, magnifico(a); grandioso(a) ♦ *n (col: thousand)* mille dollari *mpl (or* sterline *fpl)*.

grandchild, *pl* **-children** [gran'chīld, -chil'drən] *n* nipote *m*.

granddad [gran'dad] *n (col)* nonno.

granddaughter [gran'dôtûr] *n* nipote *f*.

grandeur [gran'jûr] *n (of style, house)* splendore *m*; *(of occasion, scenery etc)* grandiosità, maestà.

grandfather [gran'fâthûr] *n* nonno.

grandiose [gran'dēōs] *a* grandioso(a); *(pej)* pomposo(a).

grand jury *n (US)* giuria *(formata da 12 a 23 membri)*.

grandma [gran'mâ] *n (col)* nonna.

grandmother [gran'muthûr] *n* nonna.

grandpa [gran'pâ] *n (col)* = **granddad**.

grandparent [gran'pârənt] *n* nonno/a.

grand piano *n* pianoforte *m* a coda.

Grand Prix [grand prē'] *n (AUT)* Gran Premio, Grand Prix *m inv*.

grandson [gran'sun] *n* nipote *m*.

grandstand [gran'stand] *n (SPORT)* tribuna.

grand total *n* somma complessiva.

granite [gran'it] *n* granito.

granny [gran'ē] *n (col)* nonna.

grant [grant] *vt* accordare; *(a request)* accogliere; *(admit)* ammettere, concedere ♦ *n (SCOL)* borsa; *(ADMIN)* sussidio, sovvenzione *f*; **to take sth for** ~**ed** dare qc per scontato.

granulated [gran'yəlātid] *a:* ~ **sugar** zucchero cristallizzato.

granule [gran'yŏŏl] *n* granello.

grape [grāp] *n* chicco d'uva, acino; **a bunch of** ~**s** un grappolo d'uva.

grapefruit [grāp'frŏŏt] *n* pompelmo.

grapevine [grāp'vīn] n vite f; **I heard it on the** ~ (fig) me l'ha detto l'uccellino.

graph [graf] n grafico.

graphic [graf'ik] a grafico(a); (vivid) vivido(a); see also **graphics**.

graphic designer n grafico/a.

graphics [graf'iks] n (art, process) grafica; (pl: drawings) illustrazioni fpl.

graphite [graf'īt] n grafite f.

graph paper n carta millimetrata.

grapple [grap'əl] vi: **to** ~ **with** essere alle prese con.

grappling iron [grap'ling ī'ûrn] n (NAUT) grappino.

grasp [grasp] vt afferrare ♦ n (grip) presa; (fig) potere m; comprensione f; **to have sth within one's** ~ avere qc a portata di mano; **to have a good** ~ **of** (subject) avere una buona padronanza di.

grasp at vt fus (rope etc) afferrarsi a, aggrapparsi a; (fig: opportunity) non farsi sfuggire, approfittare di.

grasping [gras'ping] a avido(a).

grass [gras] n erba; (pasture) pascolo, prato; (Brit col: informer) informatore/trice; (: exterrorist) pentito/a.

grasshopper [gras'hâpûr] n cavalletta.

grassland [gras'land] n prateria.

grass roots npl (fig) base f.

grass snake n natrice f.

grassy [gras'ē] a erboso(a).

grate [grāt] n graticola (del focolare) ♦ vi cigolare, stridere ♦ vt (CULIN) grattugiare.

grateful [grāt'fəl] a grato(a), riconoscente.

gratefully [grāt'fəlē] ad con gratitudine.

grater [grā'tûr] n grattugia.

gratification [gratəfəkā'shən] n soddisfazione f.

gratify [grat'əfī] vt appagare; (whim) soddisfare.

gratifying [grat'əfīing] a gradito(a); soddisfacente.

grating [grā'ting] n (iron bars) grata ♦ a (noise) stridente, stridulo(a).

gratitude [grat'ətood] n gratitudine f.

gratuitous [grətoo'itəs] a gratuito(a).

gratuity [grətoo'itē] n mancia.

grave [grāv] n tomba ♦ a grave, serio(a).

gravedigger [grāv'digûr] n becchino.

gravel [grav'əl] n ghiaia.

gravely [grāv'lē] ad gravemente, solennemente; ~ **ill** in pericolo di vita.

gravestone [grāv'stōn] n pietra tombale.

graveyard [grāv'yârd] n cimitero.

gravitate [grav'ətāt] vi gravitare.

gravity [grav'itē] n (all senses) gravità.

gravy [grā'vē] n intingolo della carne; salsa.

gravy boat n salsiera.

gravy train n: **the** ~ (col) l'albero della cuccagna.

gray [grā] a (US) grigio(a); **to go** ~ diventar grigio.

gray-haired [grā'hârd] a dai capelli grigi.

grayhound [grā'hound] n levriere m.

graze [grāz] vi pascolare, pascere ♦ vt (touch lightly) sfiorare; (scrape) escoriare ♦ n (MED) escoriazione f.

grazing [grā'zing] n pascolo.

grease [grēs] n (fat) grasso; (lubricant) lubrificante m ♦ vt ingrassare; lubrificare; **to** ~ **the skids** (US: fig) spianare la strada.

grease gun n ingrassatore m.

greasepaint [grēs'pānt] n cerone m.

greaseproof paper [grēs'prōof pā'pûr] n (Brit) carta oleata.

greasy [grē'sē] a grasso(a); untuoso(a); (hands, clothes) unto(a); (Brit: road, surface) scivoloso(a).

great [grāt] a grande; (pain, heat) forte, intenso(a); (col) magnifico(a), meraviglioso(a); **they're** ~ **friends** sono grandi amici; **the** ~ **thing is that** ... il bello è che ...; **it was** ~! è stato fantastico!; **we had a** ~ **time** ci siamo divertiti un mondo.

Great Barrier Reef n: **the** ~ la Grande Barriera Corallina.

Great Britain n Gran Bretagna.

great-grandchild, pl **-children** [grāt'gran'chīld, -chil'drən] n pronipote m/f.

great-grandfather [grāt'gran'fâthûr] n bisnonno.

great-grandmother [grāt'gran'muthûr] n bisnonna.

Great Lakes npl: **the** ~ i Grandi Laghi.

greatly [grāt'lē] ad molto.

greatness [grāt'nis] n grandezza.

Grecian [grē'shən] a greco(a).

Greece [grēs] n Grecia.

greed [grēd] n (also: ~iness) avarizia; (for food) golosità, ghiottoneria.

greedily [grē'dilē] ad avidamente; golosamente.

greedy [grē'dē] a avido(a); goloso(a), ghiotto(a).

Greek [grēk] a greco(a) ♦ n greco/a; (LING) greco; **ancient/modern** ~ greco antico/moderno.

green [grēn] a verde; (inexperienced) inesperto(a), ingenuo(a); (POL) verde ♦ n verde m; (stretch of grass) prato; (also: **village** ~) ≈ piazza del paese; ~**s** npl (vegetables) verdura; (of golf course) green m inv; **the G~s** i Verdi; **to have a** ~ **thumb** or (Brit) ~ **fingers** (fig) avere il pollice verde.

greenback [grēn'bak] n (US col: dollar bill) (banconota da un) dollaro.

green bean n fagiolino.

greenbelt [grēn'belt] n (round town) cintura di verde.

green card n (US: work permit) permesso di lavoro; (Brit AUT) carta verde.

greenery [grē'nûrē] n verde m.

greenfly [grēn'flī] n (Brit) afide f.

greengage [grēn'gāj] *n* susina Regina Claudia.
greengrocer [grēn'grōsûr] *n* (*Brit*) fruttivendolo/a, erbivendolo/a.
greenhouse [grēn'hous] *n* serra.
greenhouse effect *n* effetto serra.
greenish [grē'nish] *a* verdastro(a).
Greenland [grēn'lənd] *n* Groenlandia.
Greenlander [grēn'ləndûr] *n* groenlandese *m/f*.
green pepper *n* peperone *m* verde.
green pound *n* (*ECON*) sterlina verde.
greet [grēt] *vt* salutare.
greeting [grē'ting] *n* saluto; **Christmas/ birthday** ~**s** auguri *mpl* di Natale/di compleanno; **Season's** ~**s** Buone Feste.
greeting(s) card *n* cartolina d'auguri.
gregarious [grigär'ēəs] *a* gregario(a); socievole.
grenade [grinād'] *n* (*also:* **hand** ~) granata.
grew [grōō] *pt of* **grow**.
grey [grā] *etc* (*Brit*) = **gray** *etc.*
grid [grid] *n* grata; (*ELEC*) rete *f*; (*US AUT*) area d'incrocio.
griddle [grid'əl] *n* piastra.
gridiron [grid'îûrn] *n* graticola.
grief [grēf] *n* dolore *m*; **to come to** ~ (*plan*) naufragare; (*person*) finire male.
grievance [grē'vəns] *n* doglianza, lagnanza; (*cause for complaint*) motivo di risentimento.
grieve [grēv] *vi* addolorarsi, soffrire ♦ *vt* addolorare; **to** ~ **for sb** compiangere qn; (*dead person*) piangere qn.
grievous bodily harm (GBH) [grēv'əs bâd'lē hârm] *n* (*LAW*) aggressione *f*.
grill [gril] *n* (*on cooker*) griglia ♦ *vt* cuocere ai ferri; (*question*) interrogare senza sosta; ~**ed meat** carne *f* ai ferri or alla griglia.
grille [gril] *n* grata; (*AUT*) griglia.
grill(room) [gril'(rōōm)] *n* rosticceria.
grim [grim] *a* sinistro(a); brutto(a).
grimace [grim'əs] *n* smorfia ♦ *vi* fare smorfie.
grime [grīm] *n* sudiciume *m*.
grimy [grīm'ē] *a* sudicio(a).
grin [grin] *n* sorriso smagliante ♦ *vi*: **to** ~ **(at)** sorridere (a), fare un gran sorriso (a).
grind [grīnd] *vb* (*pt, pp* **ground** [ground]) *vt* macinare; (*US: meat*) tritare, macinare; (*make sharp*) arrotare; (*polish: gem, lens*) molare ♦ *vi* (*car gears*) grattare ♦ *n* (*work*) sgobbata; **to** ~ **one's teeth** digrignare i denti; **to** ~ **to a halt** (*vehicle*) arrestarsi con uno stridio di freni; (*fig: talks, scheme*) insabbiarsi; (: *work, production*) cessare del tutto; **the daily** ~ (*col*) il trantran quotidiano.
grinder [grīn'dûr] *n* (*machine: for coffee*) macinino; (: *for meat*) tritacarne *m inv*.
grindstone [grīnd'stōn] *n*: **to keep one's nose to the** ~ darci sotto.
grip [grip] *n* presa; (*carryall*) borsa da viaggio ♦ *vt* afferrare; **to come to** ~**s with** affrontare; cercare di risolvere; **to** ~ **the road**

(*tires*) far presa sulla strada; (*car*) tenere bene la strada; **to lose one's** ~ perdere *or* allentare la presa; (*fig*) perdere la grinta.
gripe [grīp] *n* (*MED*) colica; (*col: complaint*) lagna ♦ *vi* (*col*) brontolare.
gripping [grip'ing] *a* avvincente.
grisly [griz'lē] *a* macabro(a), orrido(a).
grist [grist] *n* (*fig*): **it's (all)** ~ **to the mill** tutto aiuta.
gristle [gris'əl] *n* cartilagine *f*.
grit [grit] *n* ghiaia; (*courage*) fegato ♦ *vt* (*road*) coprire di sabbia; **to** ~ **one's teeth** stringere i denti; **I've got a piece of** ~ **in my eye** ho un bruscolino nell'occhio.
grits [grits] *npl* (*US*) macinato grosso (di avena *etc*).
grizzly [griz'lē] *n* (*also:* ~ **bear**) orso grigio, grizzly *m inv*.
groan [grōn] *n* gemito ♦ *vi* gemere.
grocer [grō'sûr] *n* negoziante *m* di generi alimentari; ~**'s (shop)** negozio di alimentari.
groceries [grō'sûrēz] *npl* provviste *fpl*.
grocery [grō'sûrē] *n* (*also:* ~ **store**) (negozio di) alimentari.
grog [grâg] *n* grog *m inv*.
groggy [grâg'ē] *a* barcollante.
groin [groin] *n* inguine *m*.
groom [grōōm] *n* palafreniere *m*; (*also:* **bride**~) sposo ♦ *vt* (*horse*) strigliare; (*fig*): **to** ~ **sb for** avviare qn a.
groove [grōōv] *n* scanalatura, solco.
grope [grōp] *vi* andare a tentoni; **to** ~ **for sth** cercare qc a tastoni.
grosgrain [grō'grān] *n* gros-grain *m inv*.
gross [grōs] *a* grossolano(a); (*COMM*) lordo(a) ♦ *n* (*pl inv*) (*twelve dozen*) grossa ♦ *vt* (*COMM*) incassare, avere un incasso lordo di.
gross domestic product (GDP) *n* prodotto interno lordo (P.I.L.).
grossly [grōs'lē] *ad* (*greatly*) molto.
gross national product (GNP) *n* prodotto nazionale lordo (P.N.L.).
grotesque [grōtesk'] *a* grottesco(a).
grotto [grât'ō] *n* grotta.
grouch [grouch] (*col*) *vi* brontolare ♦ *n* (*person*) brontolone/a.
ground [ground] *pt, pp of* **grind** ♦ *a* (*coffee etc*) macinato(a) ♦ *n* suolo, terra; (*land*) terreno; (*SPORT*) campo; (*reason: gen pl*) ragione *f*; (*US: also:* ~ **wire**) (presa a) terra ♦ *vt* (*plane*) tenere a terra; (*US ELEC*) mettere la presa a terra a ♦ *vi* (*ship*) arenarsi; ~**s** *npl* (*of coffee etc*) fondi *mpl*; (*gardens etc*) terreno, giardini *mpl*; **on/to the** ~ per/a terra; **below** ~ sottoterra; **common** ~ terreno comune; **to gain/lose** ~ guadagnare/ perdere terreno; **he covered a lot of** ~ **in his lecture** ha toccato molti argomenti nel corso della conferenza.
ground cloth *n* (*US*) telone *m* impermeabile.
ground control *n* (*AVIAT, SPACE*) base *f* di

controllo.

ground floor *n* pianterreno.

grounding [groun'ding] *n* (*in education*) basi *fpl*.

groundless [ground'lis] *a* infondato(a).

ground meat *n* (*US*) carne *f* tritta *or* macinata.

groundnut [ground'nut] *n* (*Brit*) arachide *f*.

ground rent *n* (*Brit*) canone *m* di affitto di un terreno.

groundsheet [ground'shēt] *n* (*Brit*) = **ground cloth**.

groundskeeper [groundz'kēpûr] *n* (*US SPORT*) custode *m* (di campo sportivo).

groundsman [groundz'mən] *n* (*Brit*) = **groundskeeper**.

ground staff *n* personale *m* di terra.

groundswell [ground'swel] *n* maremoto; (*fig*) movimento.

ground-to-ground [ground'təground'] *a*: ~ **missile** missile *m* terra-terra.

groundwork [ground'wûrk] *n* preparazione *f*.

group [grōōp] *n* gruppo; (*MUS*: *pop* ~) complesso, gruppo ♦ *vt* raggruppare ♦ *vi* raggrupparsi.

grouse [grous] *n* (*pl inv*) (*bird*) tetraone *m* ♦ *vi* (*complain*) brontolare.

grove [grōv] *n* boschetto.

grovel [gruv'əl] *vi* (*fig*): **to ~ (before)** strisciare (di fronte a).

grow, *pt* **grew**, *pp* **grown** [grō, grōō, grōn] *vi* crescere; (*increase*) aumentare; (*become*): **to ~ rich/weak** arricchirsi/indebolirsi ♦ *vt* coltivare, far crescere; **to ~ tired of waiting** stancarsi di aspettare.

grow apart *vi* (*fig*) estraniarsi.

grow away from *vt fus* (*fig*) allontanarsi da, staccarsi da.

grow on *vt fus*: **that painting is ~ing on me** quel quadro più lo guardo più mi piace.

grow out of *vt fus* (*clothes*) diventare troppo grande per indossare; (*habit*) perdere (col tempo); **he'll ~ out of it** gli passerà.

grow up *vi* farsi grande, crescere.

grower [grō'ûr] *n* coltivatore/trice.

growing [grō'ing] *a* (*fear*, *amount*) crescente; **~ pains** (*also fig*) problemi *mpl* di crescita.

growl [groul] *vi* ringhiare.

grown [grōn] *pp of* **grow** ♦ *a* adulto(a), maturo(a).

grown-up [grōn'up'] *n* adulto/a, grande *m/f*.

growth [grōth] *n* crescita, sviluppo; (*what has grown*) crescita; (*MED*) escrescenza, tumore *m*.

growth rate *n* tasso di crescita.

grub [grub] *n* larva; (*col*: *food*) roba (da mangiare).

grubby [grub'ē] *a* sporco(a).

grudge [gruj] *n* rancore *m* ♦ *vt*: **to ~ sb sth** dare qc a qn di malavoglia; invidiare qc a qn; **to bear sb a ~ (for)** serbar rancore a qn

(per).

grudgingly [gruj'inglē] *ad* di malavoglia, di malincuore.

grueling, (*Brit*) **gruelling** [grōō'əling] *a* estenuante.

gruesome [grōō'səm] *a* orribile.

gruff [gruf] *a* rozzo(a).

grumble [grum'bəl] *vi* brontolare, lagnarsi.

grumpy [grum'pē] *a* stizzito(a).

grunt [grunt] *vi* grugnire ♦ *n* grugnito.

GSA *n abbr* (*US*: = *General Services Administration*) *agenzia indipendente per la gestione di proprietà federali, costruzioni etc*.

G-string [jē'string] *n* (*garment*) tanga *m inv*.

GSUSA *n abbr* = *Girl Scouts of the United States of America*.

GT *abbr* (*AUT*: = *gran turismo*) GT.

GU *abbr* (*US MAIL*) = *Guam*.

guarantee [garəntē'] *n* garanzia ♦ *vt* garantire; **he can't ~ (that) he'll come** non può garantire che verrà.

guarantor [garəntôr] *n* garante *m/f*.

guard [gárd] *n* guardia; (*protection*) riparo, protezione *f*; (*BOXING*) difesa; (*one man*) guardia, sentinella; (*in prison*) guardia carceraria; (*Brit RAIL*) capotreno; (*safety device*: *on machine*) schermo protettivo; (*also*: **fire** ~) parafuoco ♦ *vt* fare la guardia a; **to ~ (against** *or* **from)** proteggere (da), salvaguardare (da); **to be on one's ~** (*fig*) stare in guardia.

guard against *vi*: **to ~ against doing sth** guardarsi dal fare qc.

guard dog *n* cane *m* da guardia.

guarded [gár'did] *a* (*fig*) cauto(a), guardingo(a).

guardian [gár'dēən] *n* custode *m*; (*of minor*) tutore/trice.

guard's van *n* (*Brit RAIL*) vagone *m* di servizio.

Guatemala [gwâtəmâl'ə] *n* Guatemala *m*.

guerrilla [gəril'ə] *n* guerrigliero.

guerrilla warfare *n* guerriglia.

guess [ges] *vi* indovinare ♦ *vt* indovinare; (*US*) credere, pensare ♦ *n* congettura; **to take** *or* **have a ~** cercare di indovinare; **my ~ is that ...** suppongo che ...; **to keep sb ~ing** tenere qn in sospeso *or* sulla corda; **I ~ you're right** mi sa che hai ragione.

guesstimate [ges'təmit] *n* (*col*) stima approssimativa.

guesswork [ges'wûrk] *n*: **I got the answer by ~** ho azzeccato la risposta.

guest [gest] *n* ospite *m/f*; (*in hotel*) cliente *m/f*; **be my ~** (*col*) fai come (se fossi) a casa tua.

guestbook [gest'bōōk] *n* libro d'oro.

guesthouse [gest'hous] *n* pensione *f*.

guest room *n* camera degli ospiti.

guffaw [gufô'] *n* risata sonora ♦ *vi* scoppiare di una risata sonora.

guidance [gīd'əns] *n* guida, direzione *f*; **marriage/vocational** ~ consulenza matrimoniale/per l'avviamento professionale.

guide [gīd] *n* (*person, book etc*) guida; (*also*: **girl** ~) giovane esploratrice *f* ♦ *vt* guidare; **to be** ~**d by sb/sth** farsi *or* lasciarsi guidare da qn/qc.

guidebook [gīd'book] *n* guida.

guided missile [gī'did mis'əl] *n* missile *m* telecomandato.

guide dog *n* (*Brit*) cane *m* guida *inv*.

guided tour [gīd'id tour] *n* gita accompagnata.

guidelines [gīd'līnz] *npl* (*fig*) indicazioni *fpl*, linee *fpl* direttive.

guild [gild] *n* arte *f*, corporazione *f*; associazione *f*.

guile [gīl] *n* astuzia.

guileless [gīl'lis] *a* candido(a).

guillotine [gil'ətēn] *n* ghigliottina.

guilt [gilt] *n* colpevolezza.

guilty [gil'tē] *a* colpevole; **to feel** ~ (**about**) sentirsi in colpa (per); **to plead** ~/**not** ~ dichiararsi colpevole/innocente.

Guinea [gin'ē] *n*: **Republic of** ~ Repubblica di Guinea.

guinea pig *n* cavia.

guise [gīz] *n* maschera.

guitar [gitár'] *n* chitarra.

guitarist [gitár'ist] *n* chitarrista *m/f*.

gulch [gulch] *n* (*US*) burrone *m*.

gulf [gulf] *n* golfo; (*abyss*) abisso; **the (Persian) G**~ il Golfo Persico.

Gulf States *npl*: **the** ~ i paesi del Golfo Persico.

Gulf Stream *n*: **the** ~ la corrente del Golfo.

gull [gul] *n* gabbiano.

gullet [gul'it] *n* gola.

gullibility [guləbil'ətē] *n* semplicioneria.

gullible [gul'əbəl] *a* credulo(a).

gully [gul'ē] *n* burrone *m*; gola; canale *m*.

gulp [gulp] *vi* deglutire; (*from emotion*) avere il nodo in gola ♦ *vt* (*also*: ~ **down**) tracannare, inghiottire ♦ *n* (*of liquid*) sorso; (*of food*) boccone *m*; **at one** ~ in un sorso, d'un fiato.

gum [gum] *n* (*ANAT*) gengiva; (*glue*) colla; (*sweet*) gelatina di frutta; (*also*: **chewing-**~) chewing-gum *m* ♦ *vt* incollare.

gum up *vt*: **to** ~ **up the works** (*col*) mettere il bastone tra le ruote.

gumboil [gum'boil] *n* ascesso (dentario).

gumboots [gum'boots] *npl* (*Brit*) stivali *mpl* di gomma.

gun [gun] *n* fucile *m*; (*small*) pistola, rivoltella; (*rifle*) carabina; (*shotgun*) fucile da caccia; (*cannon*) cannone *m* ♦ *vt* (*also*: ~ **down**) abbattere a colpi di pistola *or* fucile; **to stick to one's** ~**s** (*fig*) tener duro.

gunboat [gun'bōt] *n* cannoniera.

gun dog *n* cane *m* da caccia.

gunfire [gun'fīur] *n* spari *mpl*.

gung-ho [gung'hō'] *a* (*col*) stupidamente entusiasta.

gunk [gungk] *n* porcherie *fpl*.

gunman [gun'mən] *n* bandito armato.

gunner [gun'ûr] *n* artigliere *m*.

gunpoint [gun'point] *n*: **at** ~ sotto minaccia di fucile.

gunpowder [gun'poudûr] *n* polvere *f* da sparo.

gunrunner [gun'runûr] *n* contrabbandiere d'armi.

gunrunning [gun'runing] *n* contrabbando d'armi.

gunshot [gun'shât] *n* sparo; **within** ~ a portata di fucile.

gunsmith [gun'smith] *n* armaiolo.

gurgle [gûr'gəl] *n* gorgoglio ♦ *vi* gorgogliare.

guru [goo'roo] *n* guru *m inv*.

gush [gush] *n* fiotto, getto ♦ *vi* sgorgare; (*fig*) abbandonarsi ad effusioni.

gusset [gus'it] *n* gherone *m*; (*in tights, pants*) rinforzo.

gust [gust] *n* (*of wind*) raffica; (*of smoke*) buffata.

gusto [gus'tō] *n* entusiasmo.

gut [gut] *n* intestino, budello; (*MUS etc*) minugia; ~**s** *npl* (*col: innards*) budella *fpl*; (: *of animals*) interiora *fpl*; (*courage*) fegato ♦ *vt* (*poultry, fish*) levare le interiora a, sventrare; (*building*) svuotare; (: *subj: fire*) divorare l'interno di; **to hate sb's** ~**s** odiare qn a morte.

gut reaction *n* reazione *f* istintiva.

gutter [gut'ûr] *n* (*of roof*) grondaia; (*in street*) cunetta.

guttural [gut'ûrəl] *a* gutturale.

guy [gī] *n* (*also*: ~**rope**) cavo *or* corda di fissaggio; (*col: man*) tipo, elemento; (*figure*) effigie di Guy Fawkes.

Guyana [gēân'ə] *n* Guayana *f*.

guzzle [guz'əl] *vi* gozzovigliare ♦ *vt* trangugiare.

gym [jim] *n* (*also*: **gymnasium**) palestra; (*also*: **gymnastics**) ginnastica.

gymkhana [jimkâ'nə] *n* gimkana.

gymnasium [jimnâ'zēəm] *n* palestra.

gymnast [jim'nast] *n* ginnasta *m/f*.

gymnastics [jimnas'tiks] *n*, *npl* ginnastica.

gym shoes *npl* scarpe *fpl* da ginnastica.

gym slip *n* (*Brit*) grembiule *m* da scuola (*per ragazze*).

gynecologist, (*Brit*) **gynaecologist** [gīnəkâl'əjist] *n* ginecologo/a.

gynecology, (*Brit*) **gynaecology** [gīnəkâl'əjē] *n* ginecologia.

gypsy [jip'sē] *n* zingaro/a ♦ *a* degli zingari.

gyrate [jī'rāt] *vi* girare.

gyroscope [jī'rəskōp] *n* giroscopio.

H

H, h [āch] *n* (*letter*) H, h *f or m inv*; **H for How** ≈ H come hotel.
habeas corpus [hā'bēəs kôr'pəs] *n* (*LAW*) habeas corpus *m inv*.
haberdashery [hab'ûrdashûrē] *n* (*US*) camiceria; (*Brit: notions*) merceria.
habit [hab'it] *n* abitudine *f*; (*costume*) abito; (*REL*) tonaca; **to get out of/into the ~ of doing sth** perdere/prendere l'abitudine di fare qc.
habitable [hab'itəbəl] *a* abitabile.
habitat [hab'itat] *n* habitat *m inv*.
habitation [habitā'shən] *n* abitazione *f*.
habitual [həbich'ōōəl] *a* abituale; (*drinker, liar*) inveterato(a).
habitually [həbich'ōōəlē] *ad* abitualmente, di solito.
hack [hak] *vt* tagliare, fare a pezzi ♦ *n* (*cut*) taglio; (*blow*) colpo; (*old horse*) ronzino; (*pej: writer*) negro.
hacker [hak'ûr] *n* (*COMPUT*) pirata *m* informatico.
hackles [hak'əlz] *npl*: **to make sb's ~ rise** (*fig*) rendere qn furioso.
hackney cab [hak'nē kab] *n* carrozza a nolo.
hackneyed [hak'nēd] *a* comune, trito(a).
had [had] *pt, pp of* **have**.
haddock [had'ək] *n* eglefino.
hadn't [had'ənt] = **had not**.
haematology [hēmətål'əjē] *n* (*Brit*) ematologia.
haemoglobin [hē'məglōbin] *n* (*Brit*) emoglobina.
haemophilia [hēməfil'ēə] *n* (*Brit*) emofilia.
haemorrhage [hem'ûrij] *n* (*Brit*) emorragia.
haemorrhoids [hem'əroidz] *npl* (*Brit*) emorroidi *fpl*.
hag [hag] *n* (*ugly*) befana; (*nasty*) megera; (*witch*) strega.
haggard [hag'ûrd] *a* smunto(a).
haggis [hag'is] *n* (*Scottish*) insaccato a base di frattaglie di pecora e avena.
haggle [hag'əl] *vi*: **to ~ (over)** contrattare (su); (*argue*) discutere (su).
haggling [hag'ling] *n* contrattazioni *fpl*.
Hague [hāg] *n*: **The ~** L'Aia.
hail [hāl] *n* grandine *f* ♦ *vt* (*call*) chiamare; (*greet*) salutare ♦ *vi* grandinare; **to ~ (as)** acclamare (come); **he ~s from Scotland** viene dalla Scozia.
hailstone [hāl'stōn] *n* chicco di grandine.

hailstorm [hāl'stôrm] *n* grandinata.
hair [hār] *n* capelli *mpl*; (*single hair*: *on head*) capello; (: *on body*) pelo; **to do one's ~** pettinarsi.
hairbrush [hār'brush] *n* spazzola per capelli.
haircut [hār'kut] *n* taglio di capelli; **I need a ~** devo tagliarmi i capelli.
hairdo [hār'dōō] *n* acconciatura, pettinatura.
hairdresser [hār'dresûr] *n* parrucchiere/a.
hair dryer [hārdrī'ûr] *n* asciugacapelli *m inv*.
-haired [-hārd] *suffix*: **fair/long~** dai capelli biondi/lunghi.
hair gel *n* fissatore *m*.
hairgrip [hār'grip] *n* (*Brit*) forcina.
hairline [hār'līn] *n* attaccatura dei capelli.
hairline fracture *n* incrinatura.
hairnet [hār'net] *n* retina (per capelli).
hair oil *n* brillantina.
hairpiece [hār'pēs] *n* toupet *m inv*.
hairpin [hār'pin] *n* forcina.
hairpin curve, (*Brit*) **hairpin bend** *n* tornante *m*.
hair-raising [hār'rāzing] *a* orripilante.
hair remover *n* crema depilatoria.
hair spray *n* lacca per capelli.
hairstyle [hār'stīl] *n* pettinatura, acconciatura.
hairy [hār'ē] *a* irsuto(a); peloso(a); (*col: frightening*) spaventoso(a).
Haiti [hā'tē] *n* Haiti *f*.
hake, *pl* **~** *or* **~s** [hāk] *n* nasello.
halcyon [hal'sēən] *a* sereno(a).
hale [hāl] *a*: **~ and hearty** che scoppia di salute.
half [haf] *n* (*pl* **halves** [havz]) mezzo, metà *f inv*; (*SPORT*: *of match*) tempo; (: *of ground*) metà campo ♦ *a* mezzo(a) ♦ *ad* a mezzo, a metà; **~ an hour** mezz'ora; **~ a dozen** mezza dozzina; **~ a pound** mezza libbra; **two and a ~** due e mezzo; **a week and a ~** una settimana e mezza; **~ (of it)** la metà; **~ (of)** la metà di; **~ the amount of** la metà di; **to cut sth in ~** tagliare qc in due; **~ empty/closed** mezzo vuoto/chiuso, semivuoto/semichiuso; **~ after 3** le 3 e mezza; **to go halves (with sb)** fare a metà (con qn).
halfback [haf'bak] *n* (*SPORT*) mediano.
half-baked [haf'bākt'] *a* (*fig col: idea, scheme*) mal combinato(a), che non sta in piedi.
half-breed [haf'brēd] *n* = **half-caste**.
half brother *n* fratellastro.
half-caste [haf'kast] *n* meticcio/a.
halfhearted [haf'här'tid] *a* tiepido(a).
half-hour [haf'our'] *n* mezz'ora.
half-mast [haf'mast'] *n*: **at ~** (*flag*) a mezz'asta.
half note *n* (*US MUS*) minima.
halfpenny [hā'pənē] *n* mezzo penny *m inv*.
half-price [haf'prīs'] *a* a metà prezzo ♦ *ad* (*also*: **at ~**) a metà prezzo.

half term n (*Brit SCOL*) vacanza a or di metà trimestre.

half-time [haf'tĭm'] n (*SPORT*) intervallo.

halfway [haf'wā'] ad a metà strada; **to meet sb ~** (*fig*) arrivare a un compromesso con qn.

half-yearly [haf'yĕr'lē] ad semestralmente, ogni sei mesi ♦ a semestrale.

halibut [hal'əbət] n (*pl inv*) ippoglosso.

halitosis [halitō'sis] n alitosi f.

hall [hôl] n sala, salone m; (*entrance way*) entrata; (*corridor*) corridoio; (*mansion*) grande villa, maniero; **~ of residence** n (*Brit*) casa dello studente.

hallmark [hôl'mârk] n marchio di garanzia; (*fig*) caratteristica.

hallo [həlō'] excl = **hello**.

Hallowe'en [haləwēn'] n vigilia d'Ognissanti.

hallucination [həlōōsənā'shən] n allucinazione f.

hallway [hôl'wā] n ingresso; corridoio.

halo [hā'lō] n (*of saint etc*) aureola; (*of sun*) alone m.

halt [hôlt] n fermata ♦ vt fermare ♦ vi fermarsi; **to call a ~ (to sth)** (*fig*) mettere or porre fine (a qc).

halter [hôl'tûr] n (*for horse*) cavezza.

halterneck [hôl'tûrnɛk] a allacciato(a) dietro il collo.

halve [hav] vt (*apple etc*) dividere a metà; (*expense*) ridurre di metà.

halves [havz] npl of **half**.

ham [ham] n prosciutto; (*col: also*: **radio ~**) radioamatore/trice; (*also*: **~ actor**) attore/trice senza talento.

Hamburg [ham'bûrg] n Amburgo f.

hamburger [ham'bûrgûr] n hamburger m inv.

ham-handed [ham'handid] a maldestro(a).

hamlet [ham'lit] n paesetto.

hammer [ham'ûr] n martello ♦ vt martellare; (*fig*) sconfiggere duramente ♦ vi (*at door*) picchiare; **to ~ a point home to sb** cacciare un'idea in testa a qn.

hammer out vt (*metal*) spianare (a martellate); (*fig: solution, agreement*) mettere a punto.

hammock [ham'ək] n amaca.

hamper [ham'pûr] vt impedire ♦ n cesta.

hamster [ham'stûr] n criceto.

hamstring [ham'string] n (*ANAT*) tendine m del ginocchio.

hand [hand] n mano f; (*of clock*) lancetta; (*handwriting*) scrittura; (*at cards*) mano; (: *game*) partita; (*worker*) operaio/a; (*measurement: of horse*) ≈ dieci centimetri ♦ vt dare, passare; **to give sb a ~** dare una mano a qn; **at ~** a portata di mano; **in ~** a disposizione; (*work*) in corso; **we have the matter in ~** ci stiamo occupando della cosa; **we have the situation in ~** abbiamo la situazione sotto controllo; **to be on ~** (*person*)

essere disponibile; (*emergency services*) essere pronto(a) a intervenire; **to ~** (*information etc*) a portata di mano; **to force sb's ~** forzare la mano a qn; **to have a free ~** avere carta bianca; **to have in one's ~** (*also fig*) avere in mano or in pugno; **on the one ~ ..., on the other ~** da un lato ..., dall'altro.

hand down vt passare giù; (*US: sentence, verdict*) emettere; (*tradition, heirloom*) tramandare.

hand in vt consegnare.

hand out vt (*leaflets*) distribuire; (*advice*) elargire.

hand over vt passare; cedere.

hand round vt (*distribute: chocolates etc*) far girare; (*subj: hostess*) offrire; (*Brit: information, papers*) far passare.

handbag [hand'bag] n borsetta.

handball [hand'bôl] n pallamano f.

hand basin n lavandino.

handbook [hand'bŏŏk] n manuale m.

handbrake [hand'brāk] n freno a mano.

handcuffs [hand'kufs] npl manette fpl.

handful [hand'fŏŏl] n manciata, pugno.

handicap [han'dēkap] n handicap m inv ♦ vt handicappare; **to be mentally ~ped** essere un handicappato mentale; **to be physically ~ped** essere handicappato.

handicraft [han'dēkraft] n lavoro d'artigiano.

handiwork [han'dēwûrk] n lavorazione f a mano; **this looks like his ~** (*pej*) qui c'è il suo zampino.

handkerchief [hang'kûrchif] n fazzoletto.

handle [han'dəl] n (*of door etc*) maniglia; (*of cup etc*) ansa; (*of knife etc*) impugnatura; (*of saucepan*) manico; (*for winding*) manovella ♦ vt toccare, maneggiare; manovrare; (*deal with*) occuparsi di; (*treat: people*) trattare; **"~ with care"** "fragile".

handlebar(s) [han'dəlbâr(z)] n(*pl*) manubrio.

handling charges [hand'ling chârjəz] npl commissione f per la prestazione; (*for goods*) spese fpl di trasporto; (*BANKING*) spese fpl bancarie.

hand lotion n crema per le mani.

hand luggage n bagagli mpl a mano.

handmade [hand'mād'] a fatto(a) a mano; (*biscuits etc*) fatto(a) in casa.

handout [hand'out] n (*leaflet*) volantino; (*press ~*) comunicato stampa.

hand-picked [hand'pikt'] a (*produce*) scelto(a), selezionato(a); (*staff etc*) scelto(a).

handrail [hand'rāl] n (*on staircase etc*) corrimano.

handshake [hand'shāk] n stretta di mano; (*COMPUT*) colloquio.

handsome [han'səm] a bello(a); (*reward*) generoso(a); (*profit, fortune*) considerevole.

hands-on [handz'ân'] a: **~ experience** esperienza diretta.

handstand [hand'stand] *n*: **to do a** ~ fare la verticale.

hand-to-mouth [hand'təmouth'] *a* (*existence*) precario(a).

handwriting [hand'rīting] *n* scrittura.

handwritten [hand'ritən] *a* scritto(a) a mano, manoscritto(a).

handy [han'dē] *a* (*person*) bravo(a); (*close at hand*) a portata di mano; (*convenient*) comodo(a); (*useful: machine etc*) pratico(a), utile; **to come in** ~ servire.

handyman [han'dēman] *n* tuttofare *m inv*; **tools for the** ~ arnesi per il fatelo-da-voi.

hang, *pt*, *pp* **hung** [hang, hung] *vt* appendere; (*criminal*: *pt*, *pp* **hanged**) impiccare ♦ *vi* pendere; (*hair*) scendere; (*drapery*) cadere; **to get the** ~ **of** (**doing**) **sth** (*col*) cominciare a capire (come si fa) qc.

hang around *vi* bighellonare, ciondolare.

hang back *vi* (*hesitate*): **to** ~ **back** (**from doing**) essere riluttante (a fare).

hang on *vi* (*wait*) aspettare ♦ *vt fus* (*depend on: decision etc*) dipendere da; **to** ~ **on to** (*keep hold of*) aggrapparsi a, attaccarsi a; (*keep*) tenere.

hang out *vt* (*washing*) stendere (fuori); (*col: live*) abitare ♦ *vi* penzolare, pendere.

hang together *vi* (*argument etc*) stare in piedi.

hang up *vi* (*TEL*) riattaccare ♦ *vt* appendere; **to** ~ **up on sb** (*TEL*) metter giù il ricevitore a qn.

hangar [hang'ûr] *n* hangar *m inv*.

hangdog [hang'dôg] *a* (*guilty*: *look*, *expression*) da cane bastonato.

hanger [hang'ûr] *n* gruccia.

hanger-on [hang'ûrân'] *n* parassita *m*.

hang gliding [hang' glīding] *n* volo col deltaplano.

hanging [hang'ing] *n* (*execution*) impiccagione *f*.

hangman [hang'mən] *n* boia *m*, carnefice *m*.

hangover [hang'ōvûr] *n* (*after drinking*) postumi *mpl* di sbornia.

hang-up [hang'up] *n* complesso.

hank [hangk] *n* matassa.

hanker [hang'kûr] *vi*: **to** ~ **after** bramare.

hankie, hanky [hang'kē] *n abbr* = **handkerchief**.

hanky-panky [hang'kēpang'kē] *n* (*col*): **there's some** ~ **going on here** qui c'è del losco.

Hants *abbr* (*Brit*) = *Hampshire*.

haphazard [hap'haz'ûrd] *a* a casaccio, alla carlona.

hapless [hap'lis] *a* disgraziato(a); (*unfortunate*) sventurato(a).

happen [hap'ən] *vi* accadere, succedere; **she** ~**ed to be free** per caso era libera; **if anything** ~**ed to him** se dovesse succedergli

qualcosa; **as it** ~**s** guarda caso; **what's** ~**ing?** cosa succede?, cosa sta succedendo?

happen (up)on *vt fus* capitare su.

happening [hap'əning] *n* avvenimento.

happily [hap'ilē] *ad* felicemente; fortunatamente.

happiness [hap'ēnis] *n* felicità, contentezza.

happy [hap'ē] *a* felice, contento(a); ~ **with** (*arrangements etc*) soddisfatto(a) di; **yes, I'd be** ~ **to** (certo,) con piacere, (ben) volentieri; ~ **birthday!** buon compleanno!; ~ **Christmas/New Year!** buon natale/anno!

happy-go-lucky [hap'ēgōluk'ē] *a* spensierato(a).

harangue [hərang'] *vt* arringare.

harass [həras'] *vt* molestare.

harassed [hərast'] *a* assillato(a).

harassment [həras'mənt] *n* molestia.

harbor [hâr'bûr] (*US*) *n* porto ♦ *vt* dare rifugio a; (*retain: grudge etc*) covare, nutrire.

harbor dues *npl* diritti *mpl* portuali.

harbor master *n* capitano di porto.

harbour [hâr'bûr] *etc* (*Brit*) = **harbor** *etc*.

hard [hârd] *a* duro(a) ♦ *ad* (*work*) sodo; (*think, try*) bene; **to look** ~ **at** guardare fissamente; esaminare attentamente; **to drink** ~ bere forte; ~ **luck!** peccato!; **no** ~ **feelings!** senza rancore!; **to be** ~ **of hearing** essere duro(a) d'orecchio; **to be** ~ **on sb** essere severo con qn; **I find it** ~ **to believe that** ... stento *or* faccio fatica a credere che ... + *sub*.

hard-and-fast [hârd'ənfast'] *a* ferreo(a).

hardback [hârd'bak] *n* libro rilegato.

hardboard [hârd'bôrd] *n* legno precompresso.

hard-boiled egg [hârd'boild' eg] *n* uovo sodo.

hard cash *n* denaro in contanti.

hard copy *n* (*COMPUT*) hard copy *f inv*, terminale *m* di stampa.

hard-core [hârd'kôr'] *a* (*pornography*) hard-core *inv*; (*supporters*) irriducibile.

hard court *n* (*TENNIS*) campo in terra battuta.

hard disk *n* (*COMPUT*) hard disk *m inv*, disco rigido.

harden [hâr'dən] *vt* indurire; (*steel*) temprare; (*fig*: *determination*) rafforzare ♦ *vi* (*substance*) indurirsi.

hardened [hâr'dənd] *a* (*criminal*) incallito(a); **to be** ~ **to sth** essere (diventato) insensibile a qc.

hard-headed [hârd'hed'id] *a* pratico(a).

hard-hearted [hârd'hâr'tid] *a* che non si lascia commuovere, dal cuore duro.

hard labor *n* lavori forzati *mpl*.

hardliner [hârdlī'nûr] *n* fautore/trice della linea dura.

hardly [hârd'lē] *ad* (*scarcely*) appena, a mala pena; **it's** ~ **the case** non è proprio il caso; ~ **anyone/anywhere** quasi nessuno/da nessuna parte; **I can** ~ **believe it** stento a crederci.

hardness [hârd'nis] n durezza.

hard sell n (COMM) intensa campagna promozionale.

hardship [hârd'ship] n avversità f inv; privazioni fpl.

hard shoulder n (Brit AUT) corsia d'emergenza.

hard up a (col) al verde.

hardware [hârd'wär] n ferramenta fpl; (COMPUT) hardware m.

hardware dealer n (US) negoziante m in ferramenta.

hardware store n (negozio di) ferramenta fpl.

hard-wearing [hârd'wär'ing] a resistente, robusto(a).

hard-working [hârd'wûr'king] a lavoratore(trice).

hardy [hâr'dē] a robusto(a); (plant) resistente al gelo.

hare [hâr] n lepre f.

harebrained [hâr'brānd] a folle; scervellato(a).

harelip [hâr'lip] n (MED) labbro leporino.

harem [hâr'əm] n harem m inv.

hark back [hârk bak] vi: **to ~ to** (former days) rievocare; (earlier occasion) ritornare a or su.

harm [hârm] n male m; (wrong) danno ♦ vt (person) fare male a; (thing) danneggiare; **to mean no ~** non avere l'intenzione d'offendere; **out of ~'s way** al sicuro; **there's no ~ in trying** tentar non nuoce.

harmful [hârm'fəl] a dannoso(a).

harmless [hârm'lis] a innocuo(a); inoffensivo(a).

harmonic [hârmân'ik] a armonico(a).

harmonica [hârmân'ikə] n armonica.

harmonics [hârmân'iks] npl armonia.

harmonious [hârmō'nēəs] a armonioso(a).

harmonium [hârmō'nēəm] n armonium m inv.

harmonize [hâr'mənīz] vt, vi armonizzare.

harmony [hâr'mənē] n armonia.

harness [hâr'nis] n bardatura, finimenti mpl ♦ vt (horse) bardare; (resources) sfruttare.

harp [hârp] n arpa ♦ vi: **to ~ on about** insistere tediosamente su.

harpist [hâr'pist] n arpista m/f.

harpoon [hârpōōn'] n arpione m.

harpsichord [hârp'sikôrd] n clavicembalo.

harrow [har'ō] n (AGR) erpice m.

harrowing [har'ōing] a straziante.

harry [har'ē] vt (MIL) saccheggiare; (person) assillare.

harsh [hârsh] a (hard) duro(a); (severe) severo(a); (unpleasant: sound) rauco(a); (: color) chiassoso(a); violento(a).

harshly [hârsh'lē] ad duramente; severamente.

harshness [hârsh'nis] n durezza; severità.

harvest [hâr'vist] n raccolto, (of grapes) vendemmia ♦ vt fare il raccolto di, raccogliere; vendemmiare ♦ vi fare il raccolto; vendemmiare.

harvester [hâr'vistûr] n (machine) mietitrice f; (also: **combine ~**) mietitrebbia; (person) mietitore/trice.

has [haz] see **have**.

has-been [haz'bin] n (col: person): **he's/she's a ~** ha fatto il suo tempo.

hash [hash] n (CULIN) specie di spezzatino fatto con carne già cotta; (fig: mess) pasticcio ♦ n abbr (col) = **hashish**.

hashish [hash'ēsh] n hascisc m.

hasn't [haz'ənt] = **has not**.

hassle [has'əl] n (col) sacco di problemi.

haste [hāst] n fretta.

hasten [hā'sən] vt affrettare ♦ vi affrettarsi; **I ~ to add that** ... mi preme di aggiungere che ....

hastily [hās'tilē] ad in fretta, precipitosamente.

hasty [hās'tē] a affrettato(a), precipitoso(a).

hat [hat] n cappello.

hatbox [hat'bâks] n cappelliera.

hatch [hach] n (NAUT: also: **~way**) boccaporto ♦ vi schiudersi ♦ vt covare; (fig: scheme, plot) elaborare, mettere a punto.

hatchback [hach'bak] n (AUT) tre (or cinque) porte f inv.

hatchet [hach'it] n accetta.

hate [hāt] vt odiare, detestare ♦ n odio; **to ~ to do** or **doing** detestare fare; **I ~ to trouble you, but** ... mi dispiace disturbarla, ma ....

hateful [hāt'fəl] a odioso(a), detestabile.

hatred [hā'trid] n odio.

hat trick n (SPORT, also fig): **to get a ~** segnare tre punti consecutivi (or vincere per tre volte consecutive).

haughty [hô'tē] a altero(a), arrogante.

haul [hôl] vt trascinare, tirare ♦ n (of fish) pescata; (of stolen goods etc) bottino.

haulage [hô'lij] n trasporto; autotrasporto.

haulage contractor n (company) impresa di trasporti; (person) autotrasportatore m.

hauler [hô'lûr] n autotrasportatore m.

haulier [hôl'ēûr] n (Brit) = **hauler**.

haunch [hônch] n anca.

haunt [hônt] vt (subj: fear) pervadere; (: person) frequentare ♦ n rifugio; **a ghost ~s this house** questa casa è abitata da un fantasma.

haunted [hôn'tid] a (castle etc) abitato(a) dai fantasmi or dagli spiriti; (look) ossessionato(a), tormentato(a).

haunting [hôn'ting] a (sight, music) ossessionante, che perseguita.

Havana [həvan'ə] n l'Avana.

have [hav] pt, pp **had** [hav, had] vt avere; (meal, shower) fare ♦ auxiliary vb avere; **to ~ eaten** aver mangiato; **to ~ arrived** essere arrivato(a); **to ~ breakfast** far colazione; **to ~ lunch** pranzare; **to ~ dinner** cenare; **I'll ~**

a coffee prendo un caffè; **to ~ an operation** avere *or* subire un'operazione; **to ~ a party** dare una festa; **to ~ sth done** far fare qc; **he had a suit made** si fece fare un abito; **let me ~ a try** fammi *or* lasciami provare; **she has to do it** lo deve fare; **I had better leave** è meglio che io vada; **I won't ~ it** questo non mi va affatto; **he's been had** (*col*) c'è cascato dentro; *see also* **haves**.

have in *vt*: **to ~ it in for sb** (*col*) avercela con qn.

have on *vt* (*garment*) avere addosso; (*be busy with*) avere da fare; **I don't ~ any money on me** non ho soldi addosso; **~ you anything on tomorrow?** (*Brit*) ha qualcosa in programma per domani?; **to ~ sb on** (*Brit col*) prendere in giro qn.

have out *vt*: **to ~ it out with sb** mettere le cose in chiaro con qn.

haven [hā'vən] *n* porto; (*fig*) rifugio.

haversack [hav'ûrsak] *n* zaino.

haves [havz] *npl* (*col*): **the ~ and the have-nots** gli abbienti e i non abbienti.

havoc [hav'ək] *n* caos *m*.

Hawaii [həwī'yē] *n* le Hawaii.

Hawaiian [həwī'ən] *a* hawaiano(a) ♦ *n* hawaiano/a; (*LING*) lingua hawaiana.

hawk [hók] *n* falco ♦ *vt* (*goods for sale*) vendere per strada.

hawker [hô'kûr] *n* venditore *m* ambulante.

hawthorn [hô'thôrn] *n* biancospino.

hay [hā] *n* fieno.

hay fever *n* febbre *f* da fieno.

haystack [hā'stak] *n* pagliaio.

haywire [hā'wīûr] *a* (*col*): **to go ~** perdere la testa; impazzire.

hazard [haz'ûrd] *n* (*chance*) azzardo; (*risk*) pericolo, rischio ♦ *vt* (*one's life*) rischiare, mettere a repentaglio; (*remark*) azzardare; **to be a health/fire ~** essere pericoloso per la salute/in caso d'incendio; **to ~ a guess** tirare a indovinare.

hazardous [haz'ûrdəs] *a* pericoloso(a), rischioso(a).

hazardous pay *n* (*US*) indennità di rischio.

hazard warning lights *npl* (*Brit AUT*) luci *fpl* di emergenza.

haze [hāz] *n* foschia.

hazel [hā'zəl] *n* (*tree*) nocciolo ♦ *a* (*eyes*) (color) nocciola *inv*.

hazelnut [hā'zəlnut] *n* nocciola.

hazy [hā'zē] *a* fosco(a); (*idea*) vago(a); (*photograph*) indistinto(a).

H-bomb [āch'bám] *n* bomba H.

h & c *abbr* (*Brit*) = *hot and cold* (*water*).

HE *abbr* = *high explosive*; (*REL, DIPLOMACY*: = *His* (*or Her*) *Excellency*) S.E.

he [hē] *pronoun* lui, egli; **it is ~ who ...** è lui che ...; **here ~ is** eccolo; **~-bear** *etc* orso *etc* maschio.

head [hed] *n* testa, capo; (*leader*) capo; (*on*

tape recorder, computer etc) testina ♦ *vt* (*list*) essere in testa a; (*group*) essere a capo di; **~s** (*or tails*) testa (*o* croce), pari (*o* dispari); **~ first** a capofitto; **~ over heels in love** pazzamente innamorato(a); **$10 a** *or* **per ~** 10 dollari a testa; **to sit at the ~ of the table** sedersi a capotavola; **to have a ~ for business** essere tagliato per gli affari; **to have no ~ for heights** soffrire di vertigini; **to lose/keep one's ~** perdere/non perdere la testa; **to come to a ~** (*fig: situation etc*) precipitare.

head for *vt fus* dirigersi verso.

head off *vt* (*threat, danger*) sventare.

headache [hed'āk] *n* mal *m* di testa; **to have a ~** aver mal di testa.

headcheese [hed'chēz] *n* (*US*) soppressata.

head cold *n* raffreddore *m* di testa.

headdress [hed'dres] *n* (*of Indian etc*) copricapo; (*of bride*) acconciatura.

header [hed'ûr] *n* (*Brit col*: *SOCCER*) colpo di testa; (: *fall*) caduta di testa.

headhunter [hed'huntûr] *n* cacciatore *m* di teste.

heading [hed'ing] *n* titolo; intestazione *f*.

headlamp [hed'lamp] *n* (*Brit*) = **headlight**.

headland [hed'land] *n* promontorio.

headlight [hed'līt] *n* fanale *m*.

headline [hed'līn] *n* titolo; **to make the ~s** far titolo.

headlong [hed'lông] *ad* (*fall*) a capofitto; (*rush*) precipitosamente.

headmaster [hed'mas'tûr] *n* (*Brit*) preside *m*.

headmistress [hed'mis'tris] *n* (*Brit*) preside *f*.

head office *n* sede *f* (centrale).

head-on [hed'ân'] *a* (*collision*) frontale.

headphones [hed'fōnz] *npl* cuffia.

headquarters (HQ) [hed'kwôrtûrz] *npl* ufficio centrale; (*MIL*) quartiere *m* generale.

headrest [hed'rest] *n* poggiacapo.

headroom [hed'rōom] *n* (*in car*) altezza dell'abitacolo; (*under bridge*) altezza limite.

headscarf [hed'skârf] *n* foulard *m inv*.

headset [hed'set] *n* = **headphones**.

headstone [hed'stōn] *n* (*on grave*) lapide *f*, pietra tombale.

headstrong [hed'strông] *a* testardo(a).

head waiter *n* capocameriere *m*.

headway [hed'wā] *n*: **to make ~** fare progressi *or* passi avanti.

headwind [hed'wind] *n* controvento.

heady [hed'ē] *a* che dà alla testa; inebriante.

heal [hēl] *vt, vi* guarire.

health [helth] *n* salute *f*; **Department of H~** ≈ Ministero della Sanità.

health benefit *n* (*US*) indennità di malattia.

health centre *n* (*Brit*) poliambulatorio.

health food(s) *n*(*pl*) alimenti *mpl* integrali.

health food store *n* negozio di alimenti dietetici e macrobiotici.

health hazard *n* pericolo per la salute.

Health Service n: the ~ (Brit) ≈ il Servizio Sanitario Statale.

healthy [hɛl'thē] a (person) in buona salute; (climate) salubre; (food) salutare; (attitude etc) sano(a); (economy) florido(a); (bank balance) solido(a).

heap [hēp] n mucchio ♦ vt ammucchiare; ~s (of) (col: lots) un sacco (di), un mucchio (di); **to ~ favors/praise/gifts** etc **on sb** ricolmare qn di favori/lodi/regali etc.

hear, pt, pp **heard** [hēr, hûrd] vt sentire; (news) ascoltare; (lecture) assistere a; (LAW: case) esaminare ♦ vi sentire; **to ~ about** sentire parlare di; (have news of) avere notizie di; **did you ~ about the move?** ha sentito del trasloco?; **to ~ from sb** ricevere notizie da qn.

hear out vt ascoltare senza interrompere.

hearing [hē'ring] n (sense) udito; (of witnesses) audizione f; (of a case) udienza; **to give sb a ~** dare ascolto a qn.

hearing aid n apparecchio acustico.

hearsay [hēr'sā] n dicerie fpl, chiacchiere fpl; **by ~** ad per sentito dire.

hearse [hûrs] n carro funebre.

heart [hârt] n cuore m; ~s npl (CARDS) cuori mpl; **at ~** in fondo; **by ~** (learn, know) a memoria; **to take ~** farsi coraggio or animo; **to lose ~** perdere coraggio, scoraggiarsi; **to have a weak ~** avere il cuore debole; **to set one's ~ on sth/on doing sth** tenere molto a qc/a fare qc; **the ~ of the matter** il nocciolo della questione.

heart attack n attacco di cuore.

heartbeat [hârt'bēt] n battito del cuore.

heartbreak [hârt'brāk] n immenso dolore m.

heartbreaking [hârt'brāking] a straziante.

heartbroken [hârt'brōkən] a affranto(a); **to be ~** avere il cuore spezzato.

heartburn [hârt'bûrn] n bruciore m di stomaco.

-hearted [hârt'id] suffix: **a kind~ person** una persona molto gentile.

heartening [hâr'təning] a incoraggiante.

heart failure n (MED) arresto cardiaco.

heartfelt [hârt'felt] a sincero(a).

hearth [hârth] n focolare m.

heartily [hâr'təlē] ad (laugh) di cuore; (eat) di buon appetito; (agree) in pieno, completamente; **to be ~ sick of** (Brit) essere veramente stufo di, essere arcistufo di.

heartland [hârt'land] n zona centrale; **Italy's industrial ~** il cuore dell'industria italiana.

heartless [hârt'lis] a senza cuore, insensibile; crudele.

heart-to-heart [hârt'təhârt'] a, ad a cuore aperto.

heart transplant n trapianto del cuore.

heartwarming [hârt'wôrming] a confortante, che scalda il cuore.

hearty [hâr'tē] a caloroso(a); robusto(a),

sano(a); vigoroso(a).

heat [hēt] n calore m; (fig) ardore m; fuoco; (SPORT: also: **qualifying ~**) prova eliminatoria; (ZOOL): **in** or (Brit) **on ~** in calore ♦ vt scaldare.

heat up vi (liquids) scaldarsi; (room) riscaldarsi ♦ vt riscaldare.

heated [hē'tid] a riscaldato(a); (fig) appassionato(a); acceso(a), eccitato(a).

heater [hē'tûr] n stufa; radiatore m.

heath [hēth] n (Brit) landa.

heathen [hē'thən] a, n pagano(a).

heather [heth'ûr] n erica.

heating [hē'ting] n riscaldamento.

heat-resistant [hēt'rizistənt] a termoresistente.

heatstroke [hēt'strōk] n colpo di sole.

heat wave n ondata di caldo.

heave [hēv] vt sollevare (con forza) ♦ vi sollevarsi ♦ n (push) grande spinta; **to ~ a sigh** emettere or mandare un sospiro.

heave to (pt, pp **hove** [hōv]) vi (NAUT) mettersi in cappa.

heaven [hev'ən] n paradiso, cielo; **~ forbid!** Dio ce ne guardi!; **for ~'s sake!** (pleading) per amor del cielo!, per carità!; (protesting) santo cielo!, in nome del cielo!; **thank ~!** grazie al cielo!; **to be in seventh ~** essere al settimo cielo.

heavenly [hev'ənlē] a divino(a), celeste.

heavily [hev'ilē] ad pesantemente; (drink, smoke) molto.

heavy [hev'ē] a pesante; (sea) grosso(a); (rain) forte; (drinker, smoker) gran (before noun); **it's ~ going** è una gran fatica; **~ industry** industria pesante.

heavy cream n (US) doppia panna.

heavy-duty [hev'ēdōō'tē] a molto resistente.

heavy goods vehicle (HGV) n (Brit) veicolo per trasporti pesanti.

heavy-handed [hev'ēhan'did] a (clumsy, tactless) pesante.

heavy-set [hev'ēset] a (US) tarchiato(a), tozzo(a).

heavyweight [hev'ēwāt] n (SPORT) peso massimo.

Hebrew [hē'brōō] a ebreo(a) ♦ n (LING) ebraico.

heckle [hek'əl] vt interpellare e dare noia a (un oratore).

heckler [hek'lûr] n agitatore/trice.

hectic [hek'tik] a movimentato(a); (busy) frenetico(a).

hector [hek'tûr] vt usare le maniere forti con.

he'd [hēd] = he would; he had.

hedge [hej] n siepe f ♦ vi essere elusivo(a); **as a ~ against inflation** per cautelarsi contro l'inflazione; **to ~ one's bets** (fig) coprirsi dai rischi.

hedge in vt recintare con una siepe.

hedgehog [hej'hâg] n riccio.

hedgerow [hej'rō] *n* siepe *f.*

hedonism [hēd'ənizəm] *n* edonismo.

heed [hēd] *vt* (*also:* **take ~ of**) badare a, far conto di ♦ *n:* **to pay (no) ~ to, to take (no) ~ of** (non) ascoltare, (non) tener conto di.

heedless [hēd'lis] *a* sbadato(a).

heel [hēl] *n* (*ANAT*) calcagno; (*of shoe*) tacco ♦ *vt* (*shoe*) rifare i tacchi a; **to bring to ~** addomesticare; **to take to one's ~s** (*col*) darsela a gambe, alzare i tacchi; **down at the ~(s)** (*US*) scalcagnato(a); (*fig*) trasandato(a).

hefty [hef'tē] *a* (*person*) solido(a); (*parcel*) pesante; (*piece, price*) grosso(a).

heifer [hef'ûr] *n* giovenca.

height [hit] *n* altezza; (*high ground*) altura; (*fig: of glory*) apice *m*; (: *of stupidity*) colmo; **what ~ are you?** quanto sei alto?; **of average ~** di statura media; **to be afraid of ~s** soffrire di vertigini; **it's the ~ of fashion** è l'ultimo grido della moda.

heighten [hit'ən] *vt* innalzare; (*fig*) accrescere.

heinous [hā'nəs] *a* nefando(a), atroce.

heir [är] *n* erede *m.*

heir apparent *n* erede *m/f* legittimo(a).

heiress [är'is] *n* erede *f.*

heirloom [är'lōōm] *n* mobile *m* (*or* gioiello *or* quadro) di famiglia.

heist [hist] *n* (*US col*) rapina.

held [held] *pt, pp of* **hold.**

helicopter [hel'əkâptûr] *n* elicottero.

heliport [hel'əpôrt] *n* eliporto.

helium [hē'lēəm] *n* elio.

hell [hel] *n* inferno; **a ~ of a ...** (*col*) un(a) maledetto(a) ...; **oh ~!** (*col*) porca miseria!, accidenti!

he'll [hēl] = **he will, he shall.**

hellish [hel'ish] *a* infernale.

hello [helō'] *excl* buon giorno!; ciao! (*to sb one addresses as "tu"*); (*surprise*) ma guarda!

helm [helm] *n* (*NAUT*) timone *m.*

helmet [hel'mit] *n* casco.

helmsman [helmz'mən] *n* timoniere *m.*

help [help] *n* aiuto; (*charwoman*) donna di servizio; (*assistant etc*) impiegato/a ♦ *vt* aiutare; **~!** aiuto!; **with the ~ of** con l'aiuto di; **to be of ~ to sb** essere di aiuto *or* essere utile a qn; "**~ wanted**" (*US*) "domande di impiego"; **to ~ sb (to) do sth** aiutare qn a far qc; **can I ~ you?** (*in store*) desidera?; **~ yourself (to bread)** si serva (del pane); **I can't ~ saying** non posso evitare di dire; **he can't ~ it** non ci può far niente.

helper [hel'pûr] *n* aiutante *m/f,* assistente *m/f.*

helpful [help'fəl] *a* di grande aiuto; (*useful*) utile.

helping [hel'ping] *n* porzione *f.*

helpless [help'lis] *a* impotente; debole; (*baby*) indifeso(a).

helplessly [help'islē] *ad* (*watch*) senza poter fare nulla.

Helsinki [hel'singkē] *n* Helsinki *f.*

helter-skelter [hel'tûrskel'tûr] *n* (*Brit: in funfair*) scivolo (a spirale).

hem [hem] *n* orlo ♦ *vt* fare l'orlo a.

hem in *vt* cingere; **to feel ~med in** (*fig*) sentirsi soffocare.

he-man [hē'man] *n* (*col*) fusto.

hematology [hēmətâl'əjē] *n* (*US*) ematologia.

hemisphere [hem'isfēr] *n* emisfero.

hemlock [hem'lâk] *n* cicuta.

hemoglobin [hē'məglōbin] *n* (*US*) emoglobina.

hemophilia [hēməfil'ēə] *n* (*US*) emofilia.

hemorrhage [hem'ûrij] *n* (*US*) emorragia.

hemorrhoids [hem'əroidz] *npl* (*US*) emmorroidi.

hemp [hemp] *n* canapa.

hen [hen] *n* gallina; (*female bird*) femmina.

hence [hens] *ad* (*therefore*) dunque; **2 years ~** di qui a 2 anni.

henceforth [hens'fôrth] *ad* d'ora in poi.

henchman [hench'mən] *n* (*pej*) caudatario.

henna [hen'ə] *n* henna.

hen party *n* (*col*) festa di sole donne.

henpecked [hen'pekt] *a* dominato dalla moglie.

hepatitis [hepətī'tis] *n* epatite *f.*

her [hûr] *pronoun* (*direct*) la, l' + *vowel;* (*indirect*) le; (*stressed, after prep*) lei; *see note at* **she** ♦ *a* il(la) suo(a), i(le) suoi(sue); **I see ~ la vedo; give ~ a book** le dia un libro; **after ~** dopo (di) lei.

herald [här'əld] *n* araldo ♦ *vt* annunciare.

heraldic [hiral'dik] *a* araldico(a).

heraldry [här'əldrē] *n* araldica.

herb [ûrb] *n* erba; **~s** *npl* (*CULIN*) erbette *fpl.*

herbaceous [hûrbā'shəs] *a* erbaceo(a).

herbal [hûr'bəl] *a* di erbe; **~ tea** tisana.

herbicide [hûr'bisīd] *n* erbicida *m.*

herd [hûrd] *n* mandria; (*of wild animals, swine*) branco ♦ *vt* (*drive, gather: animals*) guidare; (: *people*) radunare; **~ed together** ammassati (come bestie).

here [hēr] *ad* qui, qua ♦ *excl* ehi!; **~!** (*at roll call*) presente!; **~ is, ~ are** ecco; **~'s my sister** ecco mia sorella; **~ she is** eccola; **~ she comes** eccola che viene; **come ~!** vieni qui!; **~ and there** qua e là.

hereabouts [hē'rəbouts] *ad* da queste parti.

hereafter [hēraf'tûr] *ad* in futuro; dopo questo ♦ *n:* **the ~** l'al di là *m.*

hereby [hērbī'] *ad* (*in letter*) con la presente.

hereditary [hered'itärē] *a* ereditario(a).

heredity [hered'itē] *n* eredità.

heresy [här'isē] *n* eresia.

heretic [här'itik] *n* eretico/a.

heretical [həret'ikəl] *a* eretico(a).

herewith [hērwith'] *ad* qui accluso.

heritage [här'itij] *n* eredità; (*fig*) retaggio; **our national ~** il nostro patrimonio nazionale.

hermetically [hûrmet'iklē] *ad* ermeticamente; ~ **sealed** ermeticamente chiuso.

hermit [hûr'mit] *n* eremita *m*.

hernia [hûr'nēə] *n* ernia.

hero, ~**es** [hē'rō] *n* eroe *m*.

heroic [hirō'ik] *a* eroico(a).

heroin [här'ōin] *n* eroina (*droga*).

heroin addict *n* eroinomane *m/f*.

heroine [här'ōin] *n* eroina (*donna*).

heroism [här'ōizəm] *n* eroismo.

heron [här'ən] *n* airone *m*.

hero worship *n* divismo.

herring [här'ing] *n* aringa.

hers [hûrz] *pronoun* il(la) suo(a), i(le) suoi(sue); **a friend of** ~ un suo amico; **this is** ~ questo è (il) suo.

herself [hûrself'] *pronoun* (*reflexive*) si; (*emphatic*) lei stessa; (*after prep*) se stessa, sé.

Herts *abbr* (*Brit*) = Hertfordshire.

he's [hēz] = **he is; he has.**

hesitant [hez'ətənt] *a* esitante, indeciso(a); **to be** ~ **about doing sth** esitare a fare qc.

hesitate [hez'ətāt] *vi*: **to** ~ **(about/to do)** esitare (su/a fare); **don't** ~ **to ask (me)** non aver timore *or* paura di chiedermelo.

hesitation [hezətā'shən] *n* esitazione *f*; **I have no** ~ **in saying (that)** ... non esito a dire che ....

hessian [hesh'ən] *n* tela di canapa.

heterogeneous [hetûrəjē'nēəs] *a* eterogeneo(a).

heterosexual [hetûrəsek'shōōəl] *a, n* eterosessuale (*m/f*).

het up [het up] *a* agitato(a).

hew [hyōō] *vt* tagliare (con l'accetta).

hex [heks] (*US*) *n* stregoneria ♦ *vt* stregare.

hexagon [hek'səgàn] *n* esagono.

hexagonal [heksag'ənəl] *a* esagonale.

hey [hā] *excl* ehi!

heyday [hā'dā] *n*: **the** ~ **of** i bei giorni di, l'età d'oro di.

HF *n abbr* (= *high frequency*) AF.

HGV *n abbr* (*Brit*) *see* **heavy goods vehicle.**

HI *abbr* (*US MAIL*) = Hawaii.

hi [hī] *excl* ciao!

hiatus [hīā'təs] *n* vuoto; (*LING*) iato.

hibernate [hī'bûrnāt] *vi* ibernare.

hibernation [hībûrnā'shən] *n* letargo, ibernazione *f*.

hiccough, hiccup [hik'up] *vi* singhiozzare ♦ *n* singhiozzo; **to have (the)** ~**s** avere il singhiozzo.

hick [hik] *n* (*US*) bifolco/a.

hid [hid] *pt of* **hide.**

hidden [hid'ən] *pp of* **hide** ♦ *a* nascosto(a); **there are no** ~ **extras** è veramente tutto compreso nel prezzo.

hide [hīd] *n* (*skin*) pelle *f* ♦ *vb* (*pt* **hid**, *pp* **hidden** [hid, hid'ən]) *vt*: **to** ~ **sth (from sb)** nascondere qc (a qn) ♦ *vi*: **to** ~ **(from sb)**

nascondersi (da qn).

hide-and-seek [hīd'ənsēk'] *n* rimpiattino.

hideaway [hīd'əwā] *n* nascondiglio.

hideous [hid'ēəs] *a* laido(a); orribile.

hide-out [hīd'out] *n* nascondiglio.

hiding [hī'ding] *n* (*beating*) bastonata; **to be in** ~ (*concealed*) tenersi nascosto(a).

hiding place *n* nascondiglio.

hierarchy [hī'ərárkē] *n* gerarchia.

hieroglyphic [hīûrəglif'ik] *a* geroglifico(a); ~**s** *npl* geroglifici *mpl*.

hi-fi [hī'fī'] *a, n abbr* (= *high fidelity*) hi-fi (*m*) *inv*.

higgledy-piggledy [hig'əldēpig'əldē] *ad* alla rinfusa.

high [hī] *a* alto(a); (*speed, respect, number*) grande; (*wind*) forte; (*Brit CULIN: meat, game*) frollato(a); (: *spoilt*) andato(a) a male; (*col: on drugs*) fatto(a); (: *on drink*) su di giri ♦ *ad* alto, in alto ♦ *n*: **exports have reached a new** ~ le esportazioni hanno toccato un nuovo record; **20m** ~ alto(a) 20m; **to pay a** ~ **price for sth** pagare (molto) caro qc.

highball [hī'bôl] *n* (*US: drink*) whisky (*or* brandy) e soda con ghiaccio.

highboy [hī'boi] *n* (*US*) cassettone *m*.

highbrow [hī'brou] *a, n* intellettuale (*m/f*).

highchair [hī'chär] *n* seggiolone *m*.

high-class [hī'klas'] *a* (*neighborhood*) elegante; (*hotel*) di prim'ordine; (*person*) di gran classe; (*food*) raffinato(a).

high court *n* (*LAW*) corte *f* suprema.

higher [hī'ûr] *a* (*form of life, study etc*) superiore ♦ *ad* più in alto, più in su.

higher education *n* istruzione *f* superiore, istruzione universitaria.

high finance *n* alta finanza.

high-flier [hī'flī'ûr] *n* uno/a che ha delle mire ambiziose.

high-flying [hī'flī'ing] *a* (*fig*) ambizioso(a).

high-handed [hī'han'did] *a* prepotente.

high-heeled [hī'hēld] *a* a tacchi alti.

highjack [hī'jak] *vt, n* = **hijack.**

high jump *n* (*SPORT*) salto in alto.

highlands [hī'ləndz] *npl* zona montuosa.

high-level [hī'ləvəl] *a* (*talks etc*, *COMPUT*) ad alto livello.

highlight [hī'līt] *n* (*fig: of event*) momento culminante ♦ *vt* mettere in evidenza; ~**s** *npl* (*in hair*) colpi *mpl* di sole.

highlighter [hī'lītûr] *n* (*pen*) evidenziatore *m*.

highly [hī'lē] *ad* molto; ~ **paid** pagato molto bene; **to speak** ~ **of** parlare molto bene di.

highly-strung [hī'lēstrung'] *a* (*Brit*) = **high-strung.**

High Mass *n* messa cantata *or* solenne.

highness [hī'nis] *n* altezza; **Her H**~ Sua Altezza.

high-pitched [hī'picht'] *a* acuto(a).

high-powered [hī'pou'ûrd] *a* (*engine*) molto

potente, ad alta potenza; (*fig: person*) di prestigio.

high-pressure [hī'presh'ûr] *a* ad alta pressione; (*fig*) aggressivo(a).

high-rise block [hī'rīz'blâk] *n* palazzone *m*.

high school *n* (*US*) istituto superiore d'istruzione; (*Brit*) scuola secondaria.

high season *n* alta stagione.

high spirits *npl* buonumore *m*, euforia; **to be in** ~ essere euforico(a).

high street *n* (*Brit*) strada principale.

high-strung [hī'strung'] *a* (*US*) teso(a) di nervi, eccitabile.

highway [hī'wā] *n* strada maestra.

Highway Code *n* (*Brit*) codice *m* della strada.

highwayman [hī'wāmən] *n* bandito.

hijack [hī'jak] *vt* dirottare ♦ *n* dirottamento; (*also*: ~**ing**) pirateria aerea.

hijacker [hī'jakûr] *n* dirottatore/trice.

hike [hīk] *vi* fare un'escursione a piedi ♦ *n* escursione *f* a piedi; (*col: in prices etc*) aumento ♦ *vt* (*col*) aumentare.

hiker [hī'kûr] *n* escursionista *m/f*.

hiking [hī'king] *n* escursioni *fpl* a piedi.

hilarious [hilār'ēəs] *a* che fa schiantare dal ridere.

hilarity [hilar'itē] *n* ilarità.

hill [hil] *n* collina, colle *m*; (*fairly high*) montagna; (*on road*) salita.

hillbilly [hil'bilē] *n* (*US*) montanaro/a dal sud degli Stati Uniti; (*pej*) zotico/a.

hillock [hil'ək] *n* collinetta, poggio.

hillside [hil'sīd] *n* fianco della collina.

hill start *n* (*AUT*) partenza in salita.

hilly [hil'ē] *a* collinoso(a); montagnoso(a).

hilt [hilt] *n* (*of sword*) elsa; **to the** ~ (*fig: support*) fino in fondo.

him [him] *pronoun* (*direct*) lo, l' + *vowel*; (*indirect*) gli; (*stressed, after prep*) lui; **I see** ~ lo vedo; **give** ~ **a book** gli dia un libro; **after** ~ dopo (di) lui.

Himalayas [himəlā'əz] *npl*: **the** ~ l'Himalaia *m*.

himself [himself'] *pronoun* (*reflexive*) si; (*emphatic*) lui stesso; (*after prep*) se stesso, sé.

hind [hīnd] *a* posteriore ♦ *n* cerva.

hinder [hin'dûr] *vt* ostacolare; (*delay*) tardare; (*prevent*): **to** ~ **sb from doing** impedire a qn di fare.

hindquarters [hīnd'kwôrtûrz] *npl* (*ZOOL*) posteriore *m*.

hindrance [hin'drəns] *n* ostacolo, impedimento.

hindsight [hīnd'sīt] *n* senno di poi; **with the benefit of** ~ con il senno di poi.

Hindu [hin'dōō] *n* indù *m/f inv*.

hinge [hinj] *n* cardine *m* ♦ *vi* (*fig*): **to** ~ **on** dipendere da.

hint [hint] *n* accenno, allusione *f*; (*advice*) consiglio ♦ *vt*: **to** ~ **that** lasciar capire che ♦

vi: **to** ~ **at** accennare a; **to drop a** ~ lasciar capire; **give me a** ~ (*clue*) dammi almeno un'idea, dammi un'indicazione.

hip [hip] *n* anca, fianco; (*BOT*) frutto della rosa canina.

hip flask *n* fiaschetta da liquore tascabile.

hippie [hip'ē] *n* hippy *m/f inv*.

hip pocket *n* tasca posteriore dei calzoni.

hippopotamus, *pl* ~**es** *or* **hippopotami** [hipəpât'əməs, -pât'əmī] *n* ippopotamo.

hippy [hip'ē] *n* = **hippie**.

hire [hīûr] *vt* (*worker*) assumere, dare lavoro a; (*Brit: car, equipment*) noleggiare ♦ *n* nolo, noleggio; **for** ~ da nolo; (*taxi*) libero(a); **on** ~ a nolo.

hire out *vt* noleggiare, dare a nolo *or* noleggio, affittare.

hire(d) car *n* (*Brit*) macchina a nolo.

hire purchase (HP) *n* (*Brit*) acquisto (*or* vendita) rateale; **to buy sth on** ~ comprare qc a rate.

his [hiz] *a, pronoun* il(la) suo(sua), i(le) suoi(sue); **this is** ~ questo è (il) suo.

hiss [his] *vi* fischiare; (*cat, snake*) sibilare ♦ *n* fischio; sibilo.

histogram [his'təgram] *n* istogramma *m*.

historian [histôr'ēən] *n* storico/a.

historic(al) [histôr'ik(əl)] *a* storico(a).

history [his'tûrē] *n* storia; **there's a long** ~ **of that illness in his family** ci sono molti precedenti (della malattia) nella sua famiglia.

histrionics [histrēân'iks] *n* istrionismo.

hit [hit] *vt* (*pt, pp* **hit**) colpire, picchiare; (*knock against*) battere; (*reach: target*) raggiungere; (*collide with: car*) urtare contro; (*fig: affect*) colpire; (*find: problem*) incontrare ♦ *n* colpo; (*success, song*) successo; **to** ~ **the road** (*col*) mettersi in cammino; **to** ~ **it off with sb** andare molto d'accordo con qn.

hit back *vi*: **to** ~ **back at sb** restituire il colpo a qn.

hit out at *vt fus* sferrare dei colpi contro; (*fig*) attaccare.

hit (up)on *vt fus* (*answer*) imbroccare, azzeccare; (*solution*) trovare (per caso).

hit-and-run driver [hit'ənrun' drī'vûr] *n* pirata *m* della strada.

hitch [hich] *vt* (*fasten*) attaccare; (*also*: ~ **up**) tirare su ♦ *n* (*difficulty*) intoppo, difficoltà *f inv*; **technical** ~ difficoltà tecnica; **to** ~ **a ride** *or* (*Brit*) **lift** fare l'autostop.

hitch up *vt* (*horse, cart*) attaccare.

hitchhike [hich'hīk] *vi* fare l'autostop.

hitchhiker [hich'hīkûr] *n* autostoppista *m/f*.

hi-tech [hī'tek'] *n* alta tecnologia ♦ *a* di alta tecnologia.

hitherto [hith'ûrtōō] *ad* finora.

hit man *n* sicario.

hit-or-miss [hit'ərmis'] *a*: **it's** ~ **whether** ... è in dubbio se ....

hit parade n hit-parade f.

hive [hīv] n alveare m; **the shop was a ~ of activity** (fig) c'era una grande attività nel negozio.

hive off vt (col) separare.

hl abbr (= hectoliter) hl.

HM abbr (= His (or Her) Majesty) S.M. (= Sua Maestà).

HMG abbr (Brit) = His (or Her) Majesty's Government.

HMO n abbr (US: = health maintenance organization) organo per la salvaguardia della salute pubblica.

HMS abbr (Brit) = His (or Her) Majesty's Ship.

hoard [hôrd] n (of food) provviste fpl; (of money) gruzzolo ♦ vt ammassare.

hoarding [hôr'ding] n (Brit) tabellone m per affissioni.

hoarfrost [hôr'frâst] n brina.

hoarse [hôrs] a rauco(a).

hoax [hōks] n scherzo; falso allarme.

hob [hâb] n piastra (con fornelli).

hobble [hâb'əl] vi zoppicare.

hobby [hâb'ē] n hobby m inv, passatempo.

hobbyhorse [hâb'ēhôrs] n cavallo a dondolo; (fig) chiodo fisso.

hobnob [hâb'nâb] vi: **to ~ (with)** mescolarsi (con).

hobo [hō'bō] n (US) vagabondo.

hock [hâk] n (of animal, CULIN) garretto; (Brit: wine) vino del Reno; (col): **to be in ~** avere debiti.

hockey [hâk'ē] n hockey m.

hocus-pocus [hō'kəspō'kəs] n (trickery) trucco; (words: of magician) abracadabra m inv; (: jargon) parolone fpl.

hodgepodge [hâj'pâj] n pot-pourri m.

hoe [hō] n zappa ♦ vt (ground) zappare.

hog [hôg] n maiale m ♦ vt (fig) arraffare; **to go the whole ~** farlo fino in fondo.

hoist [hoist] n paranco ♦ vt issare.

hold [hōld] vb (pt, pp **held** [held]) vt tenere; (contain) contenere; (keep back) trattenere; (believe) mantenere; considerare; (possess) avere, possedere; detenere ♦ vi (withstand pressure) tenere; (be valid) essere valido(a) ♦ n presa; (fig) potere m; (NAUT) stiva; **~ the line!** (TEL) resti in linea!; **to ~ office** (POL) essere in carica; **to ~ sb responsible for sth** considerare or ritenere qn responsabile di qc; **to ~ one's own** (fig) difendersi bene; **he ~s the view that ...** è del parere che ...; **to ~ firm** or **fast** resistere bene, tenere; **to catch** or **get (a) ~ of** afferrare; **to get ~ of** (fig) trovare; **to get ~ of o.s.** trattenersi.

hold back vt trattenere; (secret) tenere celato(a); **to ~ sb back from doing sth** impedire a qn di fare qc.

hold down vt (person) tenere a terra;

(job) tenere.

hold forth vi fare or tenere una concione.

hold off vt tener lontano ♦ vi (rain): **if the rain ~s off** se continua a non piovere.

hold on vi tener fermo; (wait) aspettare; **~ on!** (TEL) resti in linea!

hold on to vt fus tenersi stretto(a) a; (keep) conservare.

hold out vt offrire ♦ vi (resist): **to ~ out (against)** resistere (a).

hold over vt (meeting etc) rimandare, rinviare.

hold up vt (raise) alzare; (support) sostenere; (delay) ritardare; (traffic) rallentare; (rob: bank) assaltare.

holdall [hōld'ôl] n (Brit) borsone m.

holder [hōl'dûr] n (of ticket, title) possessore/posseditrice; (of office etc) incaricato/a; (of passport, post) titolare; (of record) detentore/trice.

holding [hōl'ding] n (share) azioni fpl, titoli mpl; (farm) podere m, tenuta.

holding company n holding f inv.

holdup [hōld'up] n (robbery) rapina a mano armata; (delay) ritardo; (in traffic) blocco.

hole [hōl] n buco, buca ♦ vt bucare; **~ in the heart** (MED) morbo blu; **to pick ~s in** (fig) trovare da ridire su.

hole up vi nascondersi, rifugiarsi.

holiday [hâl'idā] n (day off) giorno di vacanza; (public) giorno festivo; (Brit) vacanza; (: from work) ferie fpl; **to be on ~** (Brit) essere in vacanza; **tomorrow is a ~** domani è festa.

holiday camp n (Brit: for children) colonia (di villeggiatura); (also: **holiday centre**) ≈ villaggio (di vacanze).

holiday-maker [hâl'idāmākûr] n (Brit) villeggiante m/f.

holiday pay n (Brit) stipendio delle ferie.

holiday resort n (Brit) luogo di villeggiatura.

holiday season n (US) periodo natalizio; (Brit) stagione f delle vacanze.

holiness [hō'lēnis] n santità.

Holland [hâl'ənd] n Olanda.

hollow [hâl'ō] a cavo(a), vuoto(a); (fig) falso(a); vano(a) ♦ n cavità f inv; (in land) valletta, depressione f.

hollow out vt scavare.

holly [hâl'ē] n agrifoglio.

hollyhock [hâl'ēhâk] n malvone m.

holocaust [hâl'əkôst] n olocausto.

holster [hōl'stûr] n fondina (di pistola).

holy [hō'lē] a santo(a); (bread) benedetto(a), consacrato(a); (ground) consacrato(a); **the H~ Father** il Santo Padre.

Holy Communion n la Santa Comunione.

Holy Ghost, Holy Spirit n Spirito Santo.

Holy Land n: **the ~** la Terra Santa.

holy orders npl ordini mpl (sacri).

homage [hâm'ij] *n* omaggio; **to pay ~ to** rendere omaggio a.

home [hōm] *n* casa; (*country*) patria; (*institution*) casa, ricovero ♦ *cpd* (*life*) familiare; (*cooking etc*) casalingo(a); (*ECON, POL*) nazionale, interno(a); (*SPORT: team*) di casa; (: *match, win*) in casa ♦ *ad* a casa; in patria; (*right in: nail etc*) fino in fondo; **at ~** a casa; **to go** (*or* **come**) **~** tornare a casa (*or* in patria); **it's near my ~** è vicino a casa mia; **make yourself at ~** si metta a suo agio. **home in on** *vt fus* (*missiles*) dirigersi (automaticamente) verso.

home address *n* indirizzo di casa.

home-brew [hōm'brōō'] *n* birra *or* vino fatto(a) in casa.

homecoming [hōm'kuming] *n* ritorno.

home computer *n* home computer *m inv*.

home economics *n* economia domestica.

home furnishings [hōm fûr'nishingz] *npl* (*curtains etc*) tessuti *mpl* d'arredo.

home-grown [hōm'grōn'] *a* nostrano(a), di produzione locale.

homeland [hōm'land] *n* patria.

homeless [hōm'lis] *a* senza tetto; spatriato(a); **the ~** *npl* i senzatetto.

home loan *n* prestito con garanzia immobiliare.

homely [hōm'lē] *a* semplice, alla buona; accogliente.

homemade [hōm'mād'] *a* casalingo(a).

Home Office *n* (*Brit*) ministero degli Interni.

homeopath [hō'mēəpath] *n* omeopatico.

homeopathic [hōmēəpath'ik] *a* omeopatico(a).

homeopathy [hōmēāp'əthē] *n* (*US*) omeopatia.

home rule *n* autogoverno.

Home Secretary *n* (*Brit*) ministro degli Interni.

homesick [hōm'sik] *a*: **to be ~** avere la nostalgia.

homestead [hōm'sted] *n* fattoria e terreni.

home town *n* città *f inv* natale.

homeward [hōm'wûrd] *a* (*journey*) di ritorno.

homeward(s) [hōm'wûrd(z)] *ad* verso casa.

homework [hōm'wûrk] *n* compiti *mpl* (per casa).

homicidal [hâmisīd'əl] *a* omicida.

homicide [hâm'isīd] *n* (*US*) omicidio.

homily [hâm'ilē] *n* omelia.

homing [hō'ming] *a* (*device, missile*) autocercante; **~ pigeon** piccione *m* viaggiatore.

homoeopathy [hōmēāp'əthē] *etc* (*Brit*) = **homeopathy** *etc*.

homogeneous [hōməjē'nēəs] *a* omogeneo(a).

homogenize [həmâj'ənīz] *vt* omogenizzare.

homosexual [hōməsek'shōōəl] *a, n* omosessuale (*m/f*).

Hon. *abbr* = **honorable; honorary.**

Honduras [hundōō'rəs] *n* Honduras *m*.

hone [hōn] *vt* (*sharpen*) affilare; (*fig*) affinare.

honest [ân'ist] *a* onesto(a); sincero(a); **to be quite ~ with you** ... se devo dirle la verità ....

honestly [ân'istlē] *ad* onestamente; sinceramente.

honesty [ân'istē] *n* onestà.

honey [hun'ē] *n* miele *m*; (*US col*) tesoro, amore *m*.

honeycomb [hun'ēkōm] *n* favo ♦ *vt* (*fig*): **~ed with tunnels** *etc* pieno(a) di gallerie *etc*.

honeymoon [hun'ēmōōn] *n* luna di miele, viaggio di nozze.

honeysuckle [hun'ēsukəl] *n* caprifoglio.

Hong Kong [hâng' kông'] *n* Hong Kong *f*.

honk [hângk] *n* (*AUT*) colpo di clacson ♦ *vi* (*US*) suonare il clacson.

Honolulu [hânəlōō'lōō] *n* Honolulu *f*.

honor [ân'ûr] (*US*) *vt* onorare ♦ *n* onore *m*; **in ~ of** in onore di.

honorable [ân'ûrəbəl] *a* onorevole.

honorary [ân'ərärē] *a* onorario(a); (*duty, title*) onorifico(a).

honor-bound [ân'ûrbound'] *a*: **to be ~ to do** dover fare per una questione di onore.

honors degree *n* (*SCOL*) *laurea specializzata.*

honour [ân'ûr] *etc* (*Brit*) = **honor** *etc.*

Hons. *abbr* (*SCOL*) = **honors degree.**

hood [hōōd] *n* cappuccio; (*US AUT*) cofano; (*Brit AUT*) capote *f*; (*col*) malvivente *m/f*.

hooded [hōōd'id] *a* (*robber*) mascherato(a).

hoodlum [hōōd'ləm] *n* malvivente *m/f*.

hoodwink [hōōd'wingk] *vt* infinocchiare.

hoof, *pl* **~s** *or* **hooves** [hōōf, hōōvz] *n* zoccolo.

hoof and mouth (disease) *n* (*US*) afta epizootica.

hook [hōōk] *n* gancio; (*for fishing*) amo ♦ *vt* uncinare; (*dress*) agganciare; **to be ~ed on** (*col*) essere fanatico di; **~s and eyes** gancetti; **by ~ or by crook** in un modo o nell'altro.

hook up *vt* (*RADIO, TV etc*) allacciare, collegare.

hooker [hōōk'ûr] *n* (*col: pej*) puttana.

hooky [hōōk'ē] *n*: **to play ~** marinare la scuola.

hooligan [hōō'ligən] *n* giovinastro, teppista *m*.

hooliganism [hōō'ligənizəm] *n* teppismo.

hoop [hōōp] *n* cerchio.

hoot [hōōt] *vi* (*owl*) gufare; (*Brit AUT*) suonare il clacson ♦ *n* colpo di clacson; **to ~ with laughter** farsi una gran risata.

hooter [hōō'tûr] *n* (*NAUT, at factory*) sirena; (*Brit: AUT*) clacson *m inv*.

hoover [hōō'vûr] ® *n* (*Brit*) aspirapolvere *m inv* ♦ *vt* pulire con l'aspirapolvere.

hooves [hōōvz] *npl of* **hoof.**

hop [hâp] *vi* saltellare, saltare; (*on one foot*) saltare su una gamba ♦ *n* salto; *see also*

hops.

hope |hōp| vt, vi sperare ♦ n speranza; **I ~ so/not** spero di sì/no.

hopeful |hōp'fəl| a (person) pieno(a) di speranza; (situation) promettente; **I'm ~ that she'll manage to come** ho buone speranze che venga.

hopefully |hōp'fəlē| ad con speranza; **~ he will recover** speriamo che si riprenda.

hopeless |hōp'lis| a senza speranza, disperato(a); (useless) inutile.

hopelessly |hōp'lislē| ad (live etc) senza speranza; (involved, complicated) spaventosamente; (late) disperatamente, irrimediabilmente; **I'm ~ confused/lost** sono completamente confuso/perso.

hopper |háp'ûr| n (chute) tramoggia.

hops |háps| npl luppoli mpl.

horde |hôrd| n orda.

horizon |hərī'zən| n orizzonte m.

horizontal |hôrizán'təl| a orizzontale.

hormone |hôr'mōn| n ormone m.

horn |hôrn| n corno; (AUT) clacson m inv.

horned |hôrnd| a (animal) cornuto(a).

hornet |hôr'nit| n calabrone m.

horny |hôr'nē| a corneo(a); (hands) calloso(a); (col: aroused) arrapato(a).

horoscope |hôr'əskōp| n oroscopo.

horrendous |hôren'dəs| n orrendo(a).

horrible |hôr'əbəl| a orribile, tremendo(a).

horrid |hôr'id| a orrido(a); (person) antipatico(a).

horrific |hôrif'ik| a (accident) spaventoso(a); (film) orripilante.

horrify |hôr'əfī| vt lasciare inorridito(a).

horrifying |hôr'əfiing| a terrificante.

horror |hôr'ûr| n orrore m.

horror movie n film m inv dell'orrore.

horror-struck |hôr'ûrstruk|, **horror-stricken** |hôr'ûrstrikən| a inorridito(a).

hors d'œuvre |ôr dûrv'| n antipasto.

horse |hôrs| n cavallo.

horseback |hôrs'bak|: **on ~** a, ad a cavallo; **to go ~ riding** andare a cavallo.

horsebox |hôrs'bâks| n (Brit) = **horse trailer.**

horse chestnut n ippocastano.

horse-drawn |hôrs'drôn| a tirato(a) da cavallo.

horsefly |hôrs'flī| n tafano, mosca cavallina.

horseman |hôrs'mən| n cavaliere m.

horsemanship |hôrs'mənship| n equitazione f.

horseplay |hôrs'plā| n giochi mpl scatenati.

horsepower (hp) |hôrs'pouûr| n cavallo (vapore) (c/v).

horse racing n ippica.

horseradish |hôrs'radish| n rafano.

horseshoe |hôrs'shōō| n ferro di cavallo.

horse show n concorso ippico, gare fpl ippiche.

horse-trading |hôrs'trāding| n mercanteggiamento.

horse trailer n (US) carro or furgone m per cavalli.

horse trials npl = **horse show.**

horsewhip |hôrs'hwip| vt frustare.

horsewoman |hôrs'wōōmən| n amazzone f.

horsey |hôr'sē| a (col: person) che adora i cavalli; (appearance) cavallino(a), da cavallo.

horticulture |hôr'təkulchûr| n orticoltura.

hose |hōz| n (also: **~pipe**) tubo; (also: **garden ~**) tubo per annaffiare.

hose down vt lavare con un getto d'acqua.

hosiery |hō'zhûrē| n (in store) (reparto di) calze fpl e calzini mpl.

hospice |hás'pis| n ricovero, ospizio.

hospitable |hás'pit'əbəl| a ospitale.

hospital |hás'pitəl| n ospedale m; **in the ~,** (Brit) **in ~** all'ospedale.

hospitality |háspətal'itē| n ospitalità.

hospitalize |hás'pitəlīz| vt ricoverare (in or all'ospedale).

host |hōst| n ospite m; (TV, RADIO) presentatore/trice; (REL) ostia; (large number): **a ~ of** una schiera di ♦ vt (TV program, games) presentare.

hostage |hás'tij| n ostaggio/a.

host country n paese m ospite, paese che ospita.

hostel |hás'təl| n ostello; (for students, nurses etc) pensionato; (for homeless people) ospizio, ricovero; (also: **youth ~**) ostello della gioventù.

hostelling |hás'təling| n: **to go (youth) ~** passare le vacanze negli ostelli della gioventù.

hostess |hōs'tis| n ospite f; (AVIAT) hostess f inv; (in nightclub) entraineuse f inv.

hostile |hás'təl| a ostile.

hostility |hástil'ətē| n ostilità f inv.

hot |hát| a caldo(a); (as opposed to only warm) molto caldo(a); (spicy) piccante; (fig) accanito(a); ardente; violento(a), focoso(a); **to be ~** (person) aver caldo; (thing) essere caldo(a); (METEOR) far caldo.

hot up (Brit col) vi (situation) farsi più teso(a); (party) scaldarsi ♦ vt (pace) affrettare; (engine) truccare.

hot-air balloon |hátâr' bəlōōn'| n mongolfiera.

hotbed |hát'bed| n (fig) focolaio.

hotchpotch |hách'pách| n (Brit) = **hodgepodge.**

hot dog n hot dog m inv.

hotel |hōtel'| n albergo.

hotelier |ōtelyā'| n albergatore/trice.

hotel industry n industria alberghiera.

hotel room n camera d'albergo.

hotfoot |hát'fōōt| ad di gran carriera.

hotheaded |hát'hedid| a focoso(a), eccitabile.

hothouse |hát'hous| n serra.

hot line |hát līn| n (POL) telefono rosso.

hotly |hát'lē| ad violentemente.

hotplate |hát'plāt| n fornello; piastra ri-

scaldante.
hotpot [hât'pât] *n* (*Brit CULIN*) stufato.
hot seat *n* (*fig*) posto che scotta.
hot spot *n* (*fig*) zona calda.
hot spring *n* sorgente *f* termale.
hot-tempered [hât'tem'pûrd] *a* irascibile.
hot-water bottle [hâtwôt'ûr bâtəl] *n* borsa dell'acqua calda.
hound [hound] *vt* perseguitare ♦ *n* segugio; **the ~s** la muta.
hour [ou'ûr] *n* ora; **at 30 miles an ~** a 30 miglia all'ora; **lunch ~** intervallo di pranzo; **to pay sb by the ~** pagare qn a ore.
hourly [ouȓ'lē] *a* (ad) ogni ora; (*rate*) orario(a) ♦ *ad* ogni ora; **~ paid** *a* pagato(a) a ore.
house *n* [hous] (*pl* ~**s** [hou'ziz]) (*also*: *firm*) casa; (*POL*) camera; (*THEATER*) sala; pubblico; spettacolo ♦ *vt* [houz] (*person*) ospitare; **at** (*or* **to**) **my ~** a casa mia; **the H~** (**of Representatives**) (*US*) ≈ la Camera dei Deputati; **the H~** (**of Commons**) (*Brit*) la Camera dei Comuni; **on the ~** (*fig*) offerto(a) dalla casa.
house arrest *n* arresti *mpl* domiciliari.
houseboat [hous'bōt] *n* house boat *f inv*.
housebound [hous'bound] *a* confinato(a) in casa.
housebreaking [hous'brāking] *n* furto con scasso.
housebroken [hous'brōkən] *a* (*US*: *animal*) che non sporca in casa.
housecoat [hous'kōt] *n* vestaglia.
household [hous'hōld] *n* famiglia, casa.
householder [hous'hōldûr] *n* padrone/a di casa; (*head of house*) capofamiglia *m/f*.
household name *n* nome *m* che tutti conoscono.
house hunting *n*: **to go ~** mettersi a cercar casa.
housekeeper [hous'kēpûr] *n* governante *f*.
housekeeping [hous'kēping] *n* (*work*) governo della casa; (*also*: **~ money**) soldi *mpl* per le spese di casa; (*COMPUT*) ausilio.
houseman [hous'mən] *n* (*Brit MED*) ≈ interno.
house plant *n* pianta da appartamento.
house-proud [hous'proud] *a* che è maniaco(a) della pulizia.
house-to-house [houstəhous'] *a* (*collection*) di porta in porta; (*search*) casa per casa.
house-trained [hous'trānd] *a* (*Brit*) = **housebroken**.
house-warming party [hous'wôrming pâr'tē] *n* festa per inaugurare la casa nuova.
housewife [hous'wīf] *n* massaia, casalinga.
housework [hous'wûrk] *n* faccende *fpl* domestiche.
housing [hou'zing] *n* alloggio ♦ *cpd* (*problem*, *shortage*) degli alloggi.
housing association *n* cooperativa edilizia.

housing conditions *npl* condizioni *fpl* di abitazione.
housing development, (*Brit*) **housing estate** *n* zona residenziale con case popolari e/o private.
hovel [huv'əl] *n* casupola.
hover [huv'ûr] *vi* (*bird*) librarsi; (*helicopter*) volare a punto fisso; **to ~ around sb** aggirarsi intorno a qn.
hovercraft [huv'ûrkraft] *n* hovercraft *m inv*.
hoverport [huv'ûrpôrt] *n* porto per hovercraft.
how [hou] *ad* come; **~ are you?** come sta?; **~ do you do?** piacere!, molto lieto!; **~ far is it to ...?** quanto è lontano ...?; **~ long have you been here?** da quanto tempo sta qui?; **~ lovely!** che bello!; **~ many?** quanti(e)?; **~ much?** quanto(a)?; **~ many people/much milk?** quante persone/quanto latte?; **~ old are you?** quanti anni ha?; **~'s life?** (*col*) come va (la vita)?; **~ about a drink?** che ne diresti di andare a bere qualcosa?; **~ is it that ...?** com'è che ... + *sub*?
however [houev'ûr] *ad* in qualsiasi modo *or* maniera che; (+ *adjective*) per quanto + *sub*; (*in questions*) come ♦ *cj* comunque, però.
howitzer [hou'itsûr] *n* (*MIL*) obice *m*.
howl [houl] *n* ululato ♦ *vi* ululare.
howler [hou'lûr] *n* marronata.
HP *n abbr* (*Brit*) *see* **hire purchase**.
hp *abbr* (*AUT*) *see* **horsepower**.
HQ *n abbr* (= *headquarters*) Q.G.
HR *n abbr* (*US*) = **House of Representatives**.
HRH *abbr* (= *His* (*or Her*) *Royal Highness*) S.A.R.
hr(s) *abbr* (= *hour(s)*) h.
HS *abbr* (*US*) = **high school**.
HST *abbr* (*US*: = *Hawaiian Standard Time*) fuso orario.
HT *abbr* (= *high tension*) A.T.
hub [hub] *n* (*of wheel*) mozzo; (*fig*) fulcro.
hubbub [hub'ub] *n* baccano.
hubcap [hub'kap] *n* (*AUT*) coprimozzo.
HUD *n abbr* (*US*: = *Department of Housing and Urban Development*) dipartimento del governo federale per la gestione dei programmi di sviluppo urbanistico.
huddle [hud'əl] *vi*: **to ~ together** rannicchiarsi l'uno contro l'altro.
hue [hyōō] *n* tinta; **~ and cry** *n* clamore *m*.
huff [huf] *n*: **in a ~** stizzito(a); **to get into a ~** mettere il broncio.
hug [hug] *vt* abbracciare; (*shore, curb*) stringere ♦ *n* abbraccio, stretta; **to give sb a ~** abbracciare qn.
huge [hyōōj] *a* enorme, immenso(a).
hulk [hulk] *n* carcassa.
hulking [hul'king] *a*: **~ (great)** grosso(a) e goffo(a).
hull [hul] *n* (*of ship*) scafo.
hullabaloo [huləbəlōō'] *n* (*col*: *noise*) fra-

casso.

hullo [həlō'] *excl* = **hello**.

hum [hum] *vt* (*tune*) canticchiare ♦ *vi* canticchiare; (*insect, plane, tool*) ronzare ♦ *n* (*also* ELEC) ronzio; (*of traffic, machines*) rumore *m*; (*of voices etc*) mormorio, brusio.

human [hyōō'mən] *a* umano(a) ♦ *n* (*also*: ~ **being**) essere *m* umano.

humane [hyōōmān'] *a* umanitário(a).

humanism [hyōō'mənizəm] *n* umanesimo.

humanitarian [hyōōmanitär'ēən] *a* umanitario(a).

humanity [hyōōman'itē] *n* umanità; **the humanities** gli studi umanistici.

humanly [hyōō'mənlē] *ad* umanamente.

humanoid [hyōō'mənoid] *a* che sembra umano(a) ♦ *n* umanoide *m/f*.

humble [hum'bəl] *a* umile, modesto(a) ♦ *vt* umiliare.

humbly [hum'blē] *ad* umilmente, modestamente.

humbug [hum'bug] *n* inganno; sciocchezze *fpl*; (*Brit: candy*) caramella alla menta.

humdrum [hum'drum] *a* monotono(a), tedioso(a).

humid [hyōō'mid] *a* umido(a).

humidifier [hyōōmid'əfiûr] *n* umidificatore *m*.

humidity [hyōōmid'ətē] *n* umidità.

humiliate [hyōōmil'ēāt] *vt* umiliare.

humiliation [hyōōmilēā'shən] *n* umiliazione *f*.

humility [hyōōmil'ətē] *n* umiltà.

humor [hyōō'mûr] (*US*) *n* umore *m* ♦ *vt* (*person*) compiacere; (*sb's whims*) assecondare; **sense of** ~ senso dell'umorismo; **to be in a good/bad** ~ essere di buon/cattivo umore.

humorist [hyōō'mûrist] *n* umorista *m/f*.

humorless [hyōō'mûrlis] *a* privo(a) di umorismo.

humorous [hyōō'mûrəs] *a* umoristico(a); (*person*) buffo(a).

humour [hyōō'mûr] *etc* (*Brit*) = **humor** *etc*.

hump [hump] *n* gobba.

humpback [hump'bak] *n* schiena d'asino.

humus [hyōō'məs] *n* humus *m*.

hunch [hunch] *n* gobba; (*premonition*) intuizione *f*; **I have a** ~ **that** ho la vaga impressione che.

hunchback [hunch'bak] *n* gobbo/a.

hunched [huncht] *a* incurvato(a).

hundred [hun'drid] *num* cento; **about a** ~ **people** un centinaio di persone; **~s of people** centinaia *fpl* di persone; **I'm a** ~ **percent sure** sono sicuro al cento per cento.

hundredweight [hun'dridwāt] *n* (*US*) = 45.3 *kg*; 100 *lb*; (*Brit*) = 50.8 *kg*; 112 *lb*.

hung [hung] *pt, pp of* **hang**.

Hungarian [hunggär'ēən] *a* ungherese ♦ *n* ungherese *m/f*; (LING) ungherese *m*.

Hungary [hung'gûrē] *n* Ungheria.

hunger [hung'gûr] *n* fame *f* ♦ *vi*: **to** ~ **for** desiderare ardentemente.

hunger strike *n* sciopero della fame.

hungrily [hung'grilē] *ad* voracemente; (*fig*) avidamente.

hungry [hung'grē] *a* affamato(a); **to be** ~ aver fame; ~ **for** (*fig*) assetato di.

hung up *a* (*col*) complessato(a).

hunk [hungk] *n* bel pezzo.

hunt [hunt] *vt* (*seek*) cercare; (SPORT) cacciare ♦ *vi* andare a caccia ♦ *n* caccia.

   hunt down *vt* scovare.

hunter [hun'tûr] *n* cacciatore *m*; (*Brit: horse*) cavallo da caccia.

hunting [hun'ting] *n* caccia.

hurdle [hûr'dəl] *n* (SPORT, *fig*) ostacolo.

hurl [hûrl] *vt* lanciare con violenza.

hurrah, [hərä'] **hurray** [hərā'] *excl* urra!, evviva!

hurricane [hûr'əkān] *n* uragano.

hurried [hûr'ēd] *a* affrettato(a); (*work*) fatto(a) in fretta.

hurriedly [hûr'ēdlē] *ad* in fretta.

hurry [hûr'ē] *n* fretta ♦ *vi* affrettarsi ♦ *vt* (*person*) affrettare; (*work*) far in fretta; **to be in a** ~ aver fretta; **to do sth in a** ~ fare qc in fretta; **to** ~ **in/out** entrare/uscire in fretta; **to** ~ **back/home** affrettarsi a tornare indietro/a casa.

   hurry along *vi* camminare in fretta.

   hurry away, hurry off *vi* andarsene in fretta.

   hurry up *vi* sbrigarsi.

hurt [hûrt] *vb* (*pt, pp* **hurt**) *vt* (*cause pain to*) far male a; (*injure, fig*) ferire; (*business, interests etc*) colpire, danneggiare ♦ *vi* far male ♦ *a* ferito(a); **I** ~ **my arm** mi sono fatto male al braccio; **where does it** ~? dove ti fa male?

hurtful [hûrt'fəl] *a* (*remark*) che ferisce.

hurtle [hûr'təl] *vt* scagliare ♦ *vi*: **to** ~ **past/down** passare/scendere a razzo.

husband [huz'bənd] *n* marito.

hush [hush] *n* silenzio, calma ♦ *vt* zittire; **~!** zitto(a)!

   hush up *vt* (*fact*) cercare di far passare sotto silenzio.

hush-hush [hush'hush] *a* (*col*) segretissimo(a).

husk [husk] *n* (*of wheat*) cartoccio; (*of rice, maize*) buccia.

husky [hus'kē] *a* roco(a) ♦ *n* cane *m* eschimese.

hustings [hus'tingz] *npl* (*Brit* POL) comizi *mpl* elettorali.

hustle [hus'əl] *vt* spingere, incalzare ♦ *n* pigia pigia *m inv*; ~ **and bustle** trambusto.

hut [hut] *n* rifugio; (*shed*) ripostiglio.

hutch [huch] *n* gabbia.

hyacinth [hī'əsinth] *n* giacinto.

hybrid [hī'brid] *a* ibrido(a) ♦ *n* ibrido.

hydrant [hī'drənt] *n* (*also*: **fire ~**) idrante *m*.

hydraulic [hīdrô'lik] *a* idraulico(a).
hydraulics [hīdrô'liks] *n* idraulica.
hydrochloric [hīdrəklôr'ik] *a*: ~ **acid** acido cloridrico.
hydroelectric [hīdrōilek'trik] *a* idroelettrico(a).
hydrofoil [hī'drəfoil] *n* aliscafo.
hydrogen [hī'drəjən] *n* idrogeno.
hydrogen bomb *n* bomba all'idrogeno.
hydrophobia [hīdrəfō'bēə] *n* idrofobia.
hydroplane [hī'drəplān] *n* idrovolante *m*.
hyena [hīē'nə] *n* iena.
hygiene [hī'jēn] *n* igiene *f*.
hygienic [hījēen'ik] *a* igienico(a).
hymn [him] *n* inno; cantica.
hype [hīp] *n* (*col*) clamorosa pubblicità.
hyperactive [hīpūrak'tiv] *a* iperattivo(a).
hypermarket [hī'pūrmärkit] *n* (*Brit*) ipermercato.
hypertension [hīpûrten'chən] *n* (*MED*) ipertensione *f*.
hyphen [hī'fən] *n* trattino.
hypnosis [hipnō'sis] *n* ipnosi *f*.
hypnotic [hipnât'ik] *a* ipnotico(a).
hypnotism [hip'nətizəm] *n* ipnotismo.
hypnotist [hip'nətist] *n* ipnotizzatore/trice.
hypnotize [hip'nətīz] *vt* ipnotizzare.
hypoallergenic [hīpōalûrjen'ik] *a* ipoallergico(a).
hypochondriac [hīpəkân'drēak] *n* ipocondriaco/a.
hypocrisy [hipâk'rəsē] *n* ipocrisia.
hypocrite [hip'əkrit] *n* ipocrita *m/f*.
hypocritical [hipəkrit'ikəl] *a* ipocrita.
hypodermic [hīpədûr'mik] *a* ipodermico(a) ♦ *n* (*syringe*) siringa ipodermica.
hypothermia [hīpəthûr'mēə] *n* ipotermia.
hypothesis, *pl* **hypotheses** [hīpâth'əsis, -'əsēz] *n* ipotesi *f inv*.
hypothetical [hīpəthet'ikəl] *a* ipotetico(a).
hysterectomy [histərek'təmē] *n* isterectomia.
hysteria [histē'rēə] *n* isteria.
hysterical [histär'ikəl] *a* isterico(a); **to become** ~ avere una crisi isterica.
hysterics [histär'iks] *npl* accesso di isteria; (*laughter*) attacco di riso; **to have** ~ avere una crisi isterica.
Hz *abbr* (= *hertz*) Hz.

I

I, i [ī] *n* (*letter*) I, i *f or m inv*; **I for Item** ≈ I come Imola.
I *pronoun* io ♦ *abbr* (= *island, isle*) Is.; (US) =

interstate (highway).
IA *abbr* (*US MAIL*) = *Iowa*.
IAEA *n abbr* = **International Atomic Energy Agency.**
IBA *n abbr* (*Brit*: = *Independent Broadcasting Authority*) organo di controllo sulle reti televisive.
Iberian [ībēr'ēən] *a* iberico(a).
Iberian Peninsula *n*: **the** ~ la Penisola iberica.
IBEW *n abbr* (*US*: = *International Brotherhood of Electrical Workers*) associazione internazionale degli elettrotecnici.
ib(id). *abbr* (= *ibidem*: *from the same source*) ibid.
i/c *abbr* (*Brit*) = **in charge.**
ICC *n abbr* (*US*: = *Interstate Commerce Commission*) commissione per il commercio tra gli stati degli USA; (= *International Chamber of Commerce*) C.C.I. *f*.
ice [īs] *n* ghiaccio; (*on road*) gelo ♦ *vt* (*cake*) glassare; (*drink*) mettere in fresco ♦ *vi* (*also*: ~ **over**) ghiacciare; (*also*: ~ **up**) gelare; **to keep sth on** ~ (*fig*: *plan*, *project*) mettere da parte (per il momento), accantonare.
Ice Age *n* era glaciale.
ice ax, (*Brit*) **ice axe** *n* piccozza da ghiaccio.
iceberg [īs'bûrg] *n* iceberg *m inv*; **tip of the** ~ (*also fig*) punta dell'iceberg.
icebox [īs'bâks] *n* (*US*) frigorifero; (*Brit*) reparto ghiaccio; (*insulated box*) frigo portatile.
icebreaker [īs'brākûr] *n* rompighiaccio *m inv*.
ice bucket *n* secchiello del ghiaccio.
ice-cold [īs'kōld'] *a* gelato(a).
ice cream *n* gelato.
ice-cream soda [īs'krēm sō'də] *n* (gelato) affogato al seltz.
ice cube *n* cubetto di ghiaccio.
iced [īst] *a* (*drink*) ghiacciato(a); (*coffee*, *tea*) freddo(a); (*cake*) glassato(a).
ice hockey *n* hockey *m* su ghiaccio.
Iceland [īs'lənd] *n* Islanda.
Icelander [īs'landûr] *n* islandese *m/f*.
Icelandic [īslan'dik] *a* islandese ♦ *n* (*LING*) islandese *m*.
ice lolly [īs lâl'ē] *n* (*Brit*) ghiacciolo.
ice pick *n* piccone *m* per ghiaccio.
ice rink *n* pista di pattinaggio.
ice-skate [īs'skāt] *n* pattino da ghiaccio ♦ *vi* pattinare sul ghiaccio.
ice-skating [īs'skāting] *n* pattinaggio sul ghiaccio.
icicle [ī'sikəl] *n* ghiacciolo.
icing [ī'sing] *n* (*AVIAT etc*) patina di ghiaccio; (*CULIN*) glassa.
icing sugar *n* (*Brit*) zucchero a velo.
ICJ *n abbr see* **International Court of Justice.**
icon [ī'kân] *n* icona; (*COMPUT*) immagine *f*.
ICR *n abbr* (*US*) = *Institute for Cancer Re-*

search.

ICU *n abbr see* **intensive care unit.**

icy [ī'sē] *a* ghiacciatò(a); (*weather, temperature*) gelido(a).

ID *abbr* (*US MAIL*) = *Idaho.*

I'd [īd] = **I would; I had.**

ID card *n* carta d'identità.

Ida. *abbr* (*US*) = *Idaho.*

idea [īdē'ə] *n* idea; **good** ~! buon'idea!; **to have an** ~ **that** ... aver l'impressione che ...; **I haven't the least** ~ non ne ho la minima idea.

ideal [īdē'əl] *a, n* ideale (*m*).

idealist [īdē'əlist] *n* idealista *m/f.*

ideally [īdē'əlē] *ad* perfettamente, assolutamente; ~ **the book should have** ... l'ideale sarebbe che il libro avesse ....

identical [īden'tikəl] *a* identico(a).

identification [īdentəfəkā'shən] *n* identificazione *f*; **means of** ~ carta d'identità.

identify [īden'təfī] *vt* identificare ♦ *vi*: **to** ~ **with** identificarsi con.

Identikit [īden'təkit] ® *n* (*Brit*): ~ **(picture)** identikit *m inv.*

identity [īden'titē] *n* identità *f inv.*

identity card *n* (*Brit*) carta d'identità.

identity parade *n* (*Brit*) confronto all'americana.

ideological [īdēəlâj'ikəl] *a* ideologico(a).

ideology [īdēâl'əjē] *n* ideologia.

idiocy [id'ēəsē] *n* idiozia.

idiom [id'ēəm] *n* idioma *m*; (*phrase*) espressione *f* idiomatica.

idiomatic [īdēəmat'ik] *a* idiomatico(a).

idiosyncrasy [īdēəsing'krəsē] *n* idiosincrasia.

idiot [id'ēət] *n* idiota *m/f.*

idiotic [īdēát'ik] *a* idiota.

idle [ī'dəl] *a* inattivo(a); (*lazy*) pigro(a), ozioso(a); (*unemployed*) disoccupato(a); (*question, pleasures*) ozioso(a) ♦ *vi* (*engine*) girare al minimo; **to lie** ~ stare fermo, non funzionare.

    idle away *vt* (*time*) sprecare, buttar via.

idleness [ī'dəlnis] *n* ozio; pigrizia.

idler [īd'lûr] *n* ozioso/a, fannullone/a.

idle time *n* tempi *mpl* morti.

idol [ī'dəl] *n* idolo.

idolize [ī'dəlīz] *vt* idoleggiare.

idyllic [idil'ik] *a* idillico(a).

i.e. *abbr* (= *id est: that is*) cioè.

if [if] *cj* se ♦ *n*: **there are a lot of** ~**s and buts** ci sono molti se e ma; **I'd be pleased** ~ **you could do it** sarei molto contento se potesse farlo; ~ **necessary** se (è) necessario; ~ **only he were here** se solo fosse qui; ~ **only to show him my gratitude** se non altro per esprimergli la mia gratitudine.

igloo [ig'lōō] *n* igloo *m inv.*

ignite [ignīt'] *vt* accendere ♦ *vi* accendersi.

ignition [ignish'ən] *n* (*AUT*) accensione *f*; **to switch on/off the** ~ accendere/spegnere il

motore.

ignition key *n* (*AUT*) chiave *f* dell'accensione.

ignoble [ignō'bəl] *a* ignobile.

ignominious [ignəmin'ēəs] *a* vergognoso(a), ignominioso(a).

ignoramus [ignərā'məs] *n* ignorante *m/f.*

ignorance [ig'nûrəns] *n* ignoranza; **to keep sb in** ~ **of sth** tenere qn all'oscuro di qc.

ignorant [ig'nûrənt] *a* ignorante; **to be** ~ **of** (*subject*) essere ignorante in; (*events*) essere ignaro(a) di.

ignore [ignôr'] *vt* non tener conto di; (*person, fact*) ignorare.

ikon [ī'kán] *n* = **icon.**

IL *abbr* (*US MAIL*) = *Illinois.*

ILA *n abbr* (*US*: = *International Longshoremen's Association*) *associazione internazionale degli scaricatori di porto.*

ILGWU *n abbr* (*US*: = *International Ladies' Garment Workers Union*) *sindacato internazionale dei lavoratori nell'abbigliamento femminile.*

Ill. *abbr* (*US*) = *Illinois.*

ill [il] *a* (*sick*) malato(a); (*bad*) cattivo(a) ♦ *n* male *m*; **to take** *or* **be taken** ~ ammalarsi; **to feel** ~ star male; **to speak/think** ~ **of sb** parlar/pensar male di qn.

I'll [īl] = **I will, I shall.**

ill-advised [il'advīzd'] *a* (*decision*) poco giudizioso(a); (*person*) mal consigliato(a).

ill-at-ease [il'ətēz'] *a* a disagio.

ill-considered [il'kənsid'ûrd] *a* (*plan*) avventato(a).

ill-disposed [il'dispōzd'] *a*: **to be** ~ **towards sb/sth** essere maldisposto(a) verso qn/qc *or* nei riguardi di qn/qc.

illegal [ilē'gəl] *a* illegale.

illegally [ilē'gəlē] *ad* illegalmente.

illegible [ilej'əbəl] *a* illeggibile.

illegitimate [ilijit'əmit] *a* illegittimo(a).

ill-fated [il'fā'tid] *a* nefasto(a).

ill-favored, (*Brit*) **ill-favoured** [il'fā'vûrd] *a* sgraziato(a), brutto(a).

ill feeling *n* (*Brit*) rancore *m.*

ill-gotten [il'gât'ən] *a*: ~ **gains** maltolto.

illicit [ilis'it] *a* illecito(a).

ill-informed [il'infôrmd'] *a* (*judgement, speech*) pieno(a) di inesattezze; (*person*) male informato(a).

illiterate [ilit'ûrit] *a* analfabeta, illetterato(a); (*letter*) scorretto(a).

ill-mannered [il'man'ûrd] *a* maleducato(a), sgarbato(a).

illness [il'nis] *n* malattia.

illogical [ilâj'ikəl] *a* illogico(a).

ill-suited [il'sōō'tid] *a* (*couple*) mal assortito(a); **he is** ~ **to the job** è inadatto a quel lavoro.

ill-timed [il'tīmd] *a* intempestivo(a), inopportuno(a).

ill-treat [il'trēt] vt maltrattare.

ill-treatment [il'trēt'mənt] n maltrattamenti mpl.

illuminate [ilōō'mənāt] vt illuminare; **~d sign** insegna luminosa.

illuminating [ilōō'mənāting] a chiarificatore(trice).

illumination [ilōōmənā'shən] n illuminazione f.

illusion [ilōō'zhən] n illusione f; **to be under the ~ that** avere l'impressione che.

illusive [ilōō'siv], **illusory** [ilōō'sûrē] a illusorio(a).

illustrate [il'əstrāt] vt illustrare.

illustration [iləstrā'shən] n illustrazione f.

illustrator [il'əstrātûr] n illustratore/trice.

illustrious [ilus'trēəs] a illustre.

ill will n cattiva volontà.

ILO n abbr (= International Labour Organization) OIL f.

ILWU n abbr (US: = International Longshoremen's and Warehousemen's Union) sindacato internazionale degli scaricatori di porto e magazzinieri.

I'm [īm] = **I am.**

image [im'ij] n immagine f; (public face) immagine (pubblica).

imagery [im'ijrē] n immagini fpl.

imaginable [imaj'ənəbəl] a immaginabile, che si possa immaginare.

imaginary [imaj'ənārē] a immaginario(a).

imagination [imajənā'shən] n immaginazione f, fantasia.

imaginative [imaj'ənətiv] a immaginoso(a).

imagine [imaj'in] vt immaginare.

imbalance [imbal'əns] n squilibrio.

imbecile [im'bəsil] n imbecille m/f.

imbue [imbyōō'] vt: **to ~ sth with** impregnare qc di.

IMF n abbr see **International Monetary Fund.**

imitate [im'ətāt] vt imitare.

imitation [imətā'shən] n imitazione f.

imitator [im'ətātūr] n imitatore/trice.

immaculate [imak'yəlit] a immacolato(a); (dress, appearance) impeccabile.

immaterial [imətē'rēəl] a immateriale, indifferente; **it is ~ whether** poco importa se or che + sub.

immature [imətōōr'] a immaturo(a).

immaturity [imətōō'ritē] n immaturità, mancanza di maturità.

immeasurable [imezh'úrəbəl] a incommensurabile.

immediacy [imē'dēəsē] n immediatezza.

immediate [imē'dēit] a immediato(a).

immediately [imē'dēitlē] ad (at once) subito, immediatamente; **~ next to** proprio accanto a.

immense [imens'] a immenso(a); enorme.

immensity [imen'sitē] n (of size, difference) enormità; (of problem etc) vastità.

immerse [imûrs'] vt immergere.

immersion heater [imûr'zhən hē'tûr] n scaldaacqua m inv a immersione.

immigrant [im'əgrənt] n immigrante m/f; (already established) immigrato/a.

immigration [iməgrā'shən] n immigrazione f.

immigration authorities npl ufficio stranieri.

immigration laws npl leggi fpl relative all'immigrazione.

imminent [im'ənənt] a imminente.

immobile [imō'bəl] a immobile.

immobilize [imō'bəlīz] vt immobilizzare.

immoderate [imâd'ûrit] a (person) smodato(a), sregolato(a); (opinion, reaction, demand) eccessivo(a).

immodest [imâd'ist] a (indecent) indecente, impudico(a); (boasting) presuntuoso(a).

immoral [imôr'əl] a immorale.

immorality [iməral'itē] n immoralità.

immortal [imôr'təl] a, n immortale (m/f).

immortalize [imôr'təlīz] vt rendere immortale.

immovable [imōō'vəbəl] a (object) non movibile; (person) irremovibile.

immune [imyōōn'] a: **~ (to)** immune (da).

immunity [imyōō'nitē] n (also fig: of diplomat) immunità; **diplomatic ~** immunità diplomatica.

immunization [imyōōnəzā'shən] n immunizzazione f.

immunize [im'yənīz] vt immunizzare.

imp [imp] n folletto, diavoletto; (child) diavoletto.

impact [im'pakt] n impatto.

impair [impār'] vt danneggiare.

impale [impāl'] vt impalare.

impart [impârt'] vt (make known) comunicare; (bestow) impartire.

impartial [impâr'shəl] a imparziale.

impartiality [impârshēal'itē] n imparzialità.

impassable [impas'əbəl] a insuperabile; (road) impraticabile.

impasse [im'pas] n impasse f inv.

impassioned [impash'ənd] a appassionato(a).

impassive [impas'iv] a impassibile.

impatience [impā'shəns] n impazienza.

impatient [impā'shənt] a impaziente; **to get** or **grow ~** perdere la pazienza.

impeach [impēch'] vt accusare, attaccare; (public official) mettere sotto accusa.

impeachment [impēch'mənt] n (LAW) imputazione f.

impeccable [impek'əbəl] a impeccabile.

impecunious [impəkyōō'nēəs] a povero(a).

impede [impēd'] vt impedire.

impediment [impəd'əmənt] n impedimento; (also: **speech ~**) difetto di pronuncia.

impel [impel'] vt (force): **to ~ sb (to do sth)** costringere or obbligare qn (a fare qc).

impending [impen'ding] a imminente.

impenetrable [impen'itrəbəl] a impenetrabile.

imperative [impār'ətiv] a imperativo(a); necessario(a), urgente; (voice) imperioso(a) ♦ n (LING) imperativo.

imperceptible [impûrsep'təbəl] a impercettibile.

imperfect [impûr'fikt] a imperfetto(a); (goods etc) difettoso(a) ♦ n (LING: also: ~ tense) imperfetto.

imperfection [impûrfek'shən] n imperfezione f; (flaw) difetto.

imperial [impēr'ēəl] a imperiale; (measure) legale.

imperialism [impēr'ēəlizəm] n imperialismo.

imperil [impär'əl] vt mettere in pericolo.

imperious [impēr'ēəs] a imperioso(a).

impersonal [impûr'sənəl] a impersonale.

impersonate [impûr'sənāt] vt impersonare; (THEATER) imitare.

impersonation [impûrsənā'shən] n (LAW) usurpazione f d'identità; (THEATER) imitazione f.

impersonator [impûr'sənātûr] n (gen, THEATER) imitatore/trice.

impertinence [impûr'tənəns] n impertinenza.

impertinent [impûr'tənənt] a impertinente.

imperturbable [impûrtûr'bəbəl] a imperturbabile.

impervious [impûr'vēəs] a impermeabile; (fig): ~ to insensibile a; impassibile di fronte a.

impetuous [impech'ōōəs] a impetuoso(a), precipitoso(a).

impetus [im'pitəs] n impeto.

impinge [impinj'] : to ~ on vt fus (person) colpire; (rights) ledere.

impish [imp'ish] a malizioso(a), birichino(a).

implacable [implak'əbəl] a implacabile.

implant [implant'] vt (MED) innestare; (fig: idea, principle) inculcare.

implausible [implô'zəbəl] a non plausibile.

implement n [im'pləmənt] attrezzo; (for cooking) utensile m ♦ vt [im'pləment] effettuare.

implicate [im'plikāt] vt implicare.

implication [implikā'shən] n implicazione f; by ~ implicitamente.

implicit [implis'it] a implicito(a); (complete) completo(a).

implicitly [implis'itlē] ad implicitamente.

implore [implôr'] vt implorare.

imply [impli'] vt insinuare; suggerire.

impolite [impəlīt'] a scortese.

imponderable [impân'dûrəbəl] a imponderabile.

import vt [impôrt'] importare ♦ n [im'pôrt] (COMM) importazione f; (meaning) significato, senso ♦ cpd (duty, license etc) d'importazione.

importance [impôr'təns] n importanza; to be of great/little ~ importare molto/poco, essere molto/poco importante.

important [impôr'tənt] a importante; it's not ~ non ha importanza; it is ~ that è

importante che + sub.

importantly [impôr'təntlē] ad (pej) con (un'aria d')importanza; but, more ~, ... ma, quel che più conta or importa, ...

importation [impôrtā'shən] n importazione f.

imported [impôr'tid] a importato(a).

importer [impôr'tûr] n importatore/trice.

impose [impōz'] vt imporre ♦ vi: to ~ on sb sfruttare la bontà di qn.

imposing [impō'zing] a imponente.

imposition [impəzish'ən] n imposizione f; to be an ~ on (person) abusare della gentilezza di.

impossibility [impâsəbil'itē] n impossibilità.

impossible [impâs'əbəl] a impossibile; it is ~ for me to leave now mi è impossibile venir via adesso.

impostor [impâs'tûr] n impostore/a.

impotence [im'pətəns] n impotenza.

impotent [im'pətənt] a impotente.

impound [impound'] vt confiscare.

impoverished [impâv'ûrisht] a impoverito(a).

impracticable [imprak'tikəbəl] a impraticabile.

impractical [imprak'tikəl] a non pratico(a).

imprecise [imprisīs'] a impreciso(a).

impregnable [impreg'nəbəl] a (fortress) inespugnabile; (fig) inoppugnabile; irrefutabile.

impregnate [impreg'nāt] vt impregnare; (fertilize) fecondare.

impresario [imprəsâr'ēō] n impresario.

impress [impres'] vt impressionare; (mark) imprimere, stampare; to ~ sth on sb far capire qc a qn.

impression [impresh'ən] n impressione f; to be under the ~ that avere l'impressione che; to make a good/bad ~ on sb fare una buona/cattiva impressione a or su qn.

impressionable [impresh'ənəbəl] a impressionabile.

impressionist [impresh'ənist] n impressionista m/f.

impressive [impres'iv] a impressionante.

imprint [im'print] n (PUBLISHING) sigla editoriale.

imprinted [imprin'tid] a: ~ on impresso(a) in.

imprison [impriz'ən] vt imprigionare.

imprisonment [impriz'ənmənt] n imprigionamento.

improbable [imprâb'əbəl] a improbabile; (excuse) inverosimile.

impromptu [imprâmp'tōō] a improvvisato(a) ♦ ad improvvisando, così su due piedi.

improper [imprâp'ûr] a scorretto(a); (unsuitable) inadatto(a), improprio(a); sconveniente, indecente.

impropriety [imprəprī'ətē] n sconvenienza; (of expression) improprietà.

improve [improov'] vt migliorare ♦ vi migliorare; (pupil etc) fare progressi.

improve (up)on vt fus (offer) aumentare.

improvement [imprōōv'mənt] *n* miglioramento; progresso; **to make ~s to** migliorare, apportare dei miglioramenti a.

improvisation [imprəvəzā'shən] *n* improvvisazione *f*.

improvise [im'prəvīz] *vt, vi* improvvisare.

imprudence [imprōōd'əns] *n* imprudenza.

imprudent [imprōōd'ənt] *a* imprudente.

impudence [im'pyōōdəns] *n* impudenza.

impudent [im'pyədənt] *a* impudente, sfacciato(a).

impugn [impyōōn'] *vt* impugnare.

impulse [im'puls] *n* impulso; **to act on ~** agire d'impulso *or* impulsivamente.

impulse buying [im'puls bī'ing] *n* tendenza ad acquistare sull'impulso del momento.

impulsive [impul'siv] *a* impulsivo(a).

impunity [impyōō'nitē] *n*: **with ~** impunemente.

impure [impyōōr'] *a* impuro(a).

impurity [impyōōr'itē] *n* impurità *f inv*.

IN *abbr* (*US MAIL*) = Indiana.

in [in] *prep* in; (*with time: during, within*): **~ May/2 days** in maggio/2 giorni; (: *after*): **~ 2 weeks** entro 2 settimane; (*with town*) a; (*with country*): **it's ~ France/the United States** è in Francia/negli Stati Uniti ♦ *ad* entro, dentro; (*fashionable*) alla moda; **is he ~?** lui c'è?; **~ town/the country** in città/ campagna; **~ the sun** al sole; **~ the rain** sotto la pioggia; **~ 1986** nel 1986; **~ spring/ fall** in primavera/autunno; **~ the morning** di *or* alla mattina, la mattina, nella mattinata; **~ here/there** qui/lì dentro; **~ French** in francese; **~ writing** per iscritto; **one man ~ 10** un uomo su 10; **once ~ a hundred years** una volta ogni cento anni; **~ hundreds** a centinaia; **the best pupil ~ the class** il migliore alunno della classe; **a rise ~ prices** un aumento dei prezzi; **~ saying this** nel dire questo; **dressed ~ green/a skirt/pants** vestito di verde/con una gonna/con i calzoni; **to be ~ insurance** lavorare nelle assicurazioni; **to be ~ publishing** essere nell'editoria; **~ that** dal momento che, visto che; **their party is ~** il loro partito è al potere; **to ask sb ~** invitare qn a entrare; **to run/limp** *etc* **~** entrare correndo/zoppicando *etc*; **the ~s and outs of** i dettagli di.

in., ins *abbr* = **inch(es)**.

inability [inəbil'ətē] *n* inabilità, incapacità; **~ to pay** impossibilità di pagare.

inaccessible [inakses'əbəl] *a* inaccessibile.

inaccuracy [inak'yûrəsē] *n* inaccuratezza; inesattezza; imprecisione *f*.

inaccurate [inak'yûrit] *a* inaccurato(a); (*figures*) inesatto(a); (*translation*) impreciso(a).

inaction [inak'shən] *n* inazione *f*.

inactivity [inaktiv'itē] *n* inattività.

inadequacy [inad'əkwəsē] *n* insufficienza.

inadequate [inad'əkwit] *a* insufficiente.

inadmissible [inədmis'əbəl] *a* inammissibile.

inadvertent [inədvûr'tənt] *a* involontario(a).

inadvertently [inədvûr'təntlē] *ad* senza volerlo.

inadvisable [inədvī'zəbəl] *a* sconsigliabile.

inane [inān'] *a* vacuo(a), stupido(a).

inanimate [inan'əmit] *a* inanimato(a).

inapplicable [inap'likəbəl] *a* inapplicabile.

inappropriate [inəprō'prēit] *a* disadatto(a); (*word, expression*) improprio(a).

inapt [inapt'] *a* maldestro(a); fuori luogo.

inaptitude [inap'tətōōd] *n* improprietà.

inarticulate [inârtik'yəlit] *a* (*person*) che si esprime male; (*speech*) inarticolato(a).

inasmuch as [inəzmuch' az] *ad* in quanto che; (*seeing that*) poiché.

inattention [inəten'chən] *n* mancanza di attenzione.

inattentive [inəten'tiv] *a* disattento(a), distratto(a); negligente.

inaudible [inô'dəbəl] *a* che non si riesce a sentire.

inaugural [inô'gyûrəl] *a* inaugurale.

inaugurate [inô'gyərāt] *vt* inaugurare; (*president, official*) insediare.

inauguration [inôgyərā'shən] *n* inaugurazione *f*; insediamento in carica.

inauspicious [inôspish'əs] *a* poco propizio(a).

in-between [in'bitwēn'] *a* fra i (*or* le) due.

inborn [in'bôrn'] *a* (*feeling*) innato(a); (*defect*) congenito(a).

inbred [in'bred] *a* innato(a); (*family*) connaturato(a).

inbreeding [in'brēding] *n* incrocio ripetuto di animali consanguinei; unioni *fpl* fra consanguinei.

Inc. *abbr see* **incorporated**.

Inca [ing'kə] *a* (*also: ~n*) inca *inv* ♦ *n* inca *m/f inv*.

incalculable [inkal'kyələbəl] *a* incalcolabile.

incapability [inkāpəbil'ətē] *n* incapacità.

incapable [inkā'pəbəl] *a:* **~ (of doing sth)** incapace (di fare qc).

incapacitate [inkəpas'ətāt] *vt:* **to ~ sb from doing** rendere qn incapace di fare.

incapacitated [inkəpas'ətātid] *a* (*LAW*) inabilitato(a).

incapacity [inkəpas'itē] *n* incapacità.

incarcerate [inkâr'sûrit] *vt* imprigionare.

incarnate *a* [inkâr'nit] incarnato(a) ♦ *vt* [inkâr'nāt] incarnare.

incarnation [inkârnā'shən] *n* incarnazione *f*.

incendiary [insen'dēârē] *a* incendiario(a) ♦ *n* (*bomb*) bomba incendiaria.

incense *n* [in'sens] incenso ♦ *vt* [insens'] (*anger*) infuriare.

incense burner *n* incensiere *m*.

incentive [insen'tiv] *n* incentivo.

incentive plan *n* piano di incentivazione.

inception [insep'shən] *n* inizio, principio.

incessant [inses'ənt] *a* incessante.

incessantly [inses'əntlē] *ad* di continuo, senza sosta.

incest [in'sest] *n* incesto.

inch [inch] *n* pollice *m* (= 25 *mm*; 12 *in a foot*); **within an ~ of** a un pelo da; **he wouldn't give an ~** (*fig*) non ha ceduto di un millimetro.

inch forward *vi* avanzare pian piano.

incidence [in'sidəns] *n* incidenza.

incident [in'sidənt] *n* incidente *m*; (*in book*) episodio.

incidental [insiden'təl] *a* accessorio(a), d'accompagnamento; (*unplanned*) incidentale; **~ to** marginale a; **~ expenses** *npl* spese *fpl* accessorie.

incidentally [insiden'təlē] *ad* (*by the way*) a proposito.

incidental music *n* sottofondo (musicale), musica di sottofondo.

incinerate [insin'ərāt] *vt* incenerire.

incinerator [insin'ərātûr] *n* inceneritore *m*.

incipient [insip'ēənt] *a* incipiente.

incision [insizh'ən] *n* incisione *f*.

incisive [insī'siv] *a* incisivo(a); tagliante; acuto(a).

incisor [insī'zûr] *n* incisivo.

incite [insīt'] *vt* incitare.

incl. *abbr* = **including, inclusive (of)**.

inclement [inklem'ənt] *a* inclemente.

inclination [inklənā'shən] *n* inclinazione *f*.

incline *n* [in'klīn] pendenza, pendio ♦ *vb* [inklīn'] *vt* inclinare ♦ *vi*: **to ~ to** tendere a; **to be ~d to do** tendere a fare; essere propenso(a) a fare; **to be well ~d towards sb** essere ben disposto(a) verso qn.

include [inklōōd'] *vt* includere, comprendere; **the tip is/is not ~d** la mancia è compresa/esclusa.

including [inklōōd'ing] *prep* compreso(a), incluso(a); **~ tip** mancia compresa, compresa la mancia.

inclusion [inklōō'zhən] *n* inclusione *f*.

inclusive [inklōō'siv] *a* incluso(a), compreso(a); **$50, ~ of all surcharges** 50 dollari, incluse tutte le soprattasse.

inclusive terms *npl* (*Brit*) prezzo tutto compreso.

incognito [inkâgnē'tō] *ad* in incognito.

incoherent [inkōhē'rənt] *a* incoerente.

income [in'kum] *n* reddito; **gross/net ~** reddito lordo/netto; **~ and expenditure account** conto entrate ed uscite.

income tax *n* imposta sul reddito.

income tax auditor, (*Brit*) **income tax inspector** *n* ispettore *m* delle imposte dirette.

income tax return *n* dichiarazione *f* annuale dei redditi.

incoming [in'kuming] *a* (*passengers*) in arrivo; (*government, tenant*) subentrante; **~ tide** marea montante.

incommunicado [inkəmyōōnəkä'dō] *a*: **to**

hold sb ~ tenere qn in segregazione.

incomparable [inkâm'pûrəbəl] *a* incomparabile.

incompatible [inkəmpat'əbəl] *a* incompatibile.

incompetence [inkâm'pitəns] *n* incompetenza, incapacità.

incompetent [inkâm'pitənt] *a* incompetente, incapace.

incomplete [inkəmplēt'] *a* incompleto(a).

incomprehensible [inkâmprihen'səbəl] *a* incomprensibile.

inconceivable [inkənsē'vəbəl] *a* inimmaginabile.

inconclusive [inkənklōō'siv] *a* improduttivo(a); (*argument*) poco convincente.

incongruous [inkâng'grōōəs] *a* poco appropriato(a); (*remark, act*) incongruo(a).

inconsequential [inkânsəkwen'chəl] *a* senza importanza.

inconsiderable [inkənsid'ûrəbəl] *a*: **not ~** non trascurabile.

inconsiderate [inkənsid'ûrit] *a* sconsiderato(a).

inconsistency [inkənsis'tənsē] *n* (*of actions etc*) incongruenza; (*of work*) irregolarità; (*of statement etc*) contraddizione *f*.

inconsistent [inkənsis'tənt] *a* incoerente; poco logico(a); contraddittorio(a); **~ with** in contraddizione con.

inconsolable [inkənsō'ləbəl] *a* inconsolabile.

inconspicuous [inkənspik'yōōəs] *a* incospicuo(a); (*color*) poco appariscente; (*dress*) dimesso(a); **to make o.s. ~** cercare di passare inosservato(a).

inconstant [inkân'stənt] *a* incostante; mutevole.

incontinence [inkân'tənəns] *n* incontinenza.

incontinent [inkân'tənənt] *a* incontinente.

incontrovertible [inkântrəvûr'təbəl] *a* incontrovertibile.

inconvenience [inkənvēn'yəns] *n* inconveniente *m*; (*trouble*) disturbo ♦ *vt* disturbare; **to put sb to great ~** creare degli inconvenienti a qn; **don't ~ yourself** non si disturbi.

inconvenient [inkənvēn'yənt] *a* scomodo(a); **that time is very ~ for me** quell'ora mi è molto scomoda, non è un'ora adatta per me.

incorporate [inkôr'pûrāt] *vt* incorporare; (*contain*) contenere.

incorporated [inkôr'pərātid] *a*: **~ company** (*US*: *abbr* **Inc.**) società *f* *inv* registrata.

incorrect [inkərekt'] *a* scorretto(a); (*statement*) impreciso(a).

incorrigible [inkôr'ijəbəl] *a* incorreggibile.

incorruptible [inkərup'təbəl] *a* incorruttibile.

increase *n* [in'krēs] aumento ♦ *vi* [inkrēs'] aumentare; **to be on the ~** essere in aumento; **an ~ of $5/10%** un aumento di 5 dollari/del 10%.

increasing [inkrēs'ing] *a* (*number*) crescente.

increasingly [inkrēs'inglē] *ad* sempre più.

incredible [inkred'əbəl] a incredibile.

incredulous [inkrej'ələs] a incredulo(a).

increment [in'krəmənt] n aumento, incremento.

incriminate [inkrim'ənāt] vt compromettere.

incriminating [inkrim'ənāting] a incriminante.

incubate [in'kyəbāt] vt (eggs) covare ♦ vi (egg) essere in incubazione; (disease) avere un'incubazione.

incubation [inkyəbā'shən] n incubazione f.

incubation period n (periodo di) incubazione f.

incubator [in'kyəbātûr] n incubatrice f.

inculcate [in'kulkāt] vt: **to ~ sth in sb** inculcare qc a qn, instillare qc a qn.

incumbent [inkum'bənt] a: **it is ~ on him to do ...** è suo dovere fare ... ♦ n titolare m/f.

incur [inkûr'] vt (expenses) incorrere; (debt) contrarre; (loss) subire; (anger, risk) esporsi a.

incurable [inkyŏŏr'əbəl] a incurabile.

incursion [inkûr'zhən] n incursione f.

Ind. abbr (US) = Indiana.

indebted [indet'id] a: **to be ~ to sb (for)** essere obbligato(a) verso qn (per).

indecency [indē'sənsē] n indecenza.

indecent [indē'sənt] a indecente.

indecent assault n (Brit) aggressione f a scopo di violenza sessuale.

indecent exposure n atti mpl osceni in luogo pubblico.

indecipherable [indisi'fûrəbəl] a indecifrabile.

indecision [indisizh'ən] n indecisione f.

indecisive [indisī'siv] a indeciso(a); (discussion) non decisivo(a).

indeed [indēd'] ad infatti; veramente; **yes ~!** certamente!

indefatigable [indifat'əgəbəl] a infaticabile, instancabile.

indefensible [indifen'səbəl] a (conduct) ingiustificabile.

indefinable [indifī'nəbəl] a indefinibile.

indefinite [indef'ənit] a indefinito(a); (answer) vago(a); (period, number) indeterminato(a).

indefinitely [indef'ənitlē] ad (wait) indefinitamente.

indelible [indel'əbəl] a indelebile.

indelicate [indel'əkit] a (tactless) indelicato(a), privo(a) di tatto; (not polite) sconveniente.

indemnify [indem'nəfī] vt indennizzare.

indemnity [indem'nitē] n (insurance) assicurazione f; (compensation) indennità, indennizzo.

indent [indent'] vt (TYP: text) far rientrare dal margine.

indentation [indentā'shən] n dentellatura; (TYP) rientranza; (dent) tacca.

indented [inden'tid] a (TYP) rientrante.

independence [indipen'dəns] n indipendenza.

independent [indipen'dənt] a indipendente.

independently [indipen'dəntlē] ad indi-

pendentemente; separatamente; **~ of** indipendentemente da.

indescribable [indiskrī'bəbəl] a indescrivibile.

indestructible [indistruk'təbəl] a indistruttibile.

indeterminate [inditûr'mənit] a indeterminato(a).

index [in'deks] n (pl ~es: in book) indice m; (: in library etc) catalogo; (pl **indices** [in'disēz]: ratio, sign) indice m.

index card n scheda.

indexed [in'dekst] a legato(a) al costo della vita.

index finger n (dito) indice m.

index-linked [in'dekslingkt'] a (Brit) = **indexed**.

India [in'dēə] n India.

India ink n inchiostro di china.

Indian [in'dēən] a, n indiano(a).

Indian Ocean n: **the ~** l'Oceano Indiano.

Indian Summer n (fig) estate f di San Martino.

India paper n carta d'India, carta bibbia.

indicate [in'dikāt] vt indicare ♦ vi (Brit AUT): **to ~ left/right** mettere la freccia a sinistra/a destra.

indication [indikā'shən] n indicazione f, segno.

indicative [indik'ətiv] a indicativo(a) ♦ n (LING) indicativo; **to be ~ of sth** essere indicativo(a) or un indice di qc.

indicator [in'dikātûr] n (sign) segno; (Brit AUT) indicatore m di direzione, freccia.

indices [in'disēz] npl of **index**.

indict [indīt'] vt accusare.

indictable [indīt'əbəl] a passibile di pena; **~ offense** atto che costituisce reato.

indictment [indīt'mənt] n accusa.

indifference [indif'ûrəns] n indifferenza.

indifferent [indif'ûrənt] a indifferente; (poor) mediocre.

indigenous [indij'ənəs] a indigeno(a).

indigestible [indijes'təbəl] a indigeribile.

indigestion [indijes'chən] n indigestione f.

indignant [indig'nənt] a: **~ (at sth/with sb)** indignato(a) (per qc/contro qn).

indignation [indignā'shən] n indignazione f.

indignity [indig'nitē] n umiliazione f.

indigo [in'dəgō] a, n indaco (inv).

indirect [indirekt'] a indiretto(a).

indirectly [indirekt'lē] ad indirettamente.

indiscreet [indiskrēt'] a indiscreto(a); (rash) imprudente.

indiscretion [indiskresh'ən] n indiscrezione f; imprudenza.

indiscriminate [indiskrim'ənit] a (person) che non sa discernere; (admiration) cieco(a); (killings) indiscriminato(a).

indispensable [indispen'səbəl] a indispensabile.

indisposed [indispōzd'] a (unwell) indisposto(a).

indisposition |indispəzish'ən| n (illness) indisposizione f.

indisputable |indispyōō'təbəl| a incontestabile, indiscutibile.

indistinct |indistingkt'| a indistinto(a); (memory, noise) vago(a).

indistinguishable |indisting'gwishəbəl| a indistinguibile.

individual |indəvij'ōōəl| n individuo ♦ a individuale; (characteristic) particolare, originale.

individualist |indəvij'ōōəlist| n individualista m/f.

individuality |indəvijōōal'itē| n individualità.

individually |indəvij'ōōəlē| ad singolarmente, uno(a) per uno(a).

indivisible |indəviz'əbəl| a indivisibile.

Indo-China |in'dōchī'nə| n Indocina.

indoctrinate |indâk'trənāt| vt indottrinare.

indoctrination |indâktrənā'shən| n indottrinamento.

indolent |in'dələnt| a indolente.

Indonesia |indənē'zhə| n Indonesia.

Indonesian |indənē'zhən| a, n indonesiano(a).

indoor |in'dôr| a da interno; (plant) d'appartamento; (swimming pool) coperto(a); (sport, games) fatto(a) al coperto.

indoors |indôrz'| ad all'interno; (at home) in casa.

indubitable |indōō'bitəbəl| a indubitabile.

induce |indōōs'| vt persuadere; (bring about) provocare; **to ~ sb to do sth** persuadere qn a fare qc.

inducement |indōōs'mənt| n incitamento; (incentive) stimolo, incentivo.

induct |indukt'| vt insediare; (fig) iniziare.

induction |induk'shən| n (MED: of birth) parto indotto.

induction course n (Brit) corso di avviamento.

indulge |indulj'| vt (whim) compiacere, soddisfare; (child) viziare ♦ vi: **to ~ in sth** concedersi qc; abbandonarsi a qc.

indulgence |indul'jəns| n lusso (che uno si permette); (leniency) indulgenza.

indulgent |indul'jənt| a indulgente.

industrial |indus'trēəl| a industriale; (injury) sul lavoro; (dispute) di lavoro.

industrial action n (Brit) azione f rivendicativa.

industrial estate n (Brit) zona industriale.

industrialist |indus'trēəlist| n industriale m.

industrialize |indus'trēəlīz| vt industrializzare.

industrial park n (US) zona industriale.

industrial relations npl relazioni fpl industriali.

industrial tribunal n (Brit) ≈ Tribunale m Amministrativo Regionale.

industrial unrest n (Brit) agitazione f (sindacale).

industrious |indus'trēəs| a industrioso(a), assiduo(a).

industry |in'dəstrē| n industria; (diligence) operosità.

inebriated |inēb'rēātid| a ubriaco(a).

inedible |incd'əbəl| a immangiabile; non commestibile.

ineffective |inifck'tiv| a inefficace.

ineffectual |incfck'chōōəl| a inefficace; incompetente.

inefficiency |inifish'ənsē| n inefficienza.

inefficient |inifish'ənt| a inefficiente.

inelegant |incl'əgənt| a poco elegante.

ineligible |incl'ijəbəl| a (candidate) ineleggibile; **to be ~ for sth** non avere il diritto a qc.

inept |incpt'| a inetto(a).

ineptitude |incp'tətōōd| n inettitudine f, stupidità.

inequality |inikwâl'itē| n ineguaglianza.

inequitable |inck'witəbəl| a iniquo(a).

ineradicable |inirad'ikəbəl| a inestirpabile.

inert |inûrt'| a inerte.

inertia |inûr'shə| n inerzia.

inertia-reel seat belt |inûr'shərēl sēt belt| n cintura di sicurezza con arrotolatore.

inescapable |inəskā'pəbəl| a inevitabile.

inessential |inisen'chəl| a non essenziale.

inestimable |ines'təməbəl| a inestimabile, incalcolabile.

inevitable |inev'itəbəl| a inevitabile.

inevitably |inev'itəblē| ad inevitabilmente; **as ~ happens** ... come immancabilmente succede ....

inexact |in'igzakt'| a inesatto(a).

inexcusable |inikskyōō'zəbəl| a imperdonabile.

inexhaustible |inigzôs'təbəl| a inesauribile; (person) instancabile.

inexorable |inck'sûrəbəl| a inesorabile.

inexpensive |inikspen'siv| a poco costoso(a).

inexperience |inikspēr'ēəns| n inesperienza.

inexperienced |inikspēr'ēənst| a inesperto(a), senza esperienza; **to be ~ in sth** essere poco pratico di qc.

inexplicable |ineks'plikəbəl| a inesplicabile.

inexpressible |inikspres'əbəl| a inesprimibile.

inextricable |ineks'trikəbəl| a inestricabile.

infallibility |infaləbil'ətē| n infallibilità.

infallible |infal'əbəl| a infallibile.

infamous |in'fəməs| a infame.

infamy |in'fəmē| n infamia.

infancy |in'fənsē| n infanzia.

infant |in'fənt| n bambino/a.

infantile |in'fəntīl| a infantile.

infant mortality n mortalità infantile.

infantry |in'fəntrē| n fanteria.

infantryman |in'fəntrēmən| n fante m.

infant school n (Brit) scuola elementare (per bambini dall'età di 5 a 7 anni).

infatuated |infach'ōōātid| a: **~ with** infatuato(a) di; **to become ~ (with sb)** infatuarsi (di qn).

infatuation |infachōōā'shən| n infatuazione f.

infect |infekt'| vt infettare; **~ed with** (illness)

affetto(a) da; **to become** ~ed (*wound*) infettarsi.

infection [infek'shən] *n* infezione *f*.

infectious [infek'shəs] *a* (*disease*) infettivo(a), contagioso(a); (*person, laughter*) contagioso(a).

infer [infûr'] *vt*: **to** ~ **(from)** dedurre (da), concludere (da).

inference [in'fûrəns] *n* deduzione *f*, conclusione *f*.

inferior [infē'rēûr] *a* inferiore; (*goods*) di qualità scadente ♦ *n* inferiore *m/f*; (*in rank*) subalterno/a; **to feel** ~ sentirsi inferiore.

inferiority [infērēôr'itē] *n* inferiorità.

inferiority complex *n* complesso di inferiorità.

infernal [infûr'nəl] *a* infernale.

inferno [infûr'nō] *n* inferno.

infertile [infûr'təl] *a* sterile.

infertility [infûrtil'ətē] *n* sterilità.

infested [infes'tid] *a*: ~ **(with)** infestato(a) (di).

infidelity [infidel'itē] *n* infedeltà.

infighting [in'fīting] *n* lotte *fpl* intestine.

infiltrate [infil'trāt] *vt* (*troops etc*) far penetrare; (*enemy line etc*) infiltrare ♦ *vi* infiltrarsi.

infinite [in'fənit] *a* infinito(a); **an** ~ **amount of time/money** un'illimitata quantità di tempo/denaro.

infinitely [in'fənitlē] *ad* infinitamente.

infinitesimal [infinites'əməl] *a* infinitesimale.

infinitive [infin'ətiv] *n* infinito.

infinity [infin'ətē] *n* infinità; (*also MATH*) infinito.

infirm [infûrm'] *a* infermo(a).

infirmary [infûr'mûrē] *n* ospedale *m*; (*in school, factory*) infermeria.

infirmity [infûr'mitē] *n* infermità *f inv*.

inflamed [inflāmd'] *a* infiammato(a).

inflammable [inflam'əbəl] *a* infiammabile.

inflammation [infləmā'shən] *n* infiammazione *f*.

inflammatory [inflam'ətôrē] *a* (*speech*) incendiario(a).

inflatable [inflā'təbəl] *a* gonfiabile.

inflate [inflāt'] *vt* (*tire, balloon*) gonfiare; (*fig*) esagerare; gonfiare; **to** ~ **the currency** far ricorso all'inflazione.

inflated [inflā'tid] *a* (*style*) gonfio(a); (*value*) esagerato(a).

inflation [inflā'shən] *n* (*ECON*) inflazione *f*.

inflationary [inflā'shənârē] *a* inflazionistico(a).

inflection [inflek'shən] *n* inflessione *f*; (*ending*) desinenza.

inflexible [inflek'səbəl] *a* inflessibile, rigido(a).

inflict [inflikt'] *vt*: **to** ~ **on** infliggere a.

infliction [inflik'shən] *n* inflizione *f*; afflizione *f*.

in-flight [in'flīt] *a* a bordo.

inflow [in'flō] *n* afflusso.

influence [in'flooəns] *n* influenza ♦ *vt* influenzare; **under the** ~ **of** sotto l'influenza di; **under**

the ~ **of alcohol** sotto l'influenza *or* l'effetto dell'alcool.

influential [inflooen'chəl] *a* influente.

influenza [inflooen'zə] *n* (*MED*) influenza.

influx [in'fluks] *n* afflusso.

inform [infôrm'] *vt*: **to** ~ **sb (of)** informare qn (di) ♦ *vi*: **to** ~ **on sb** denunciare qn; **to** ~ **sb about** mettere qn al corrente di.

informal [infôr'məl] *a* (*person, manner*) alla buona, semplice; (*visit, discussion*) informale; (*announcement, invitation*) non ufficiale; "**dress** ~" "non è richiesto l'abito scuro"; ~ **language** linguaggio colloquiale.

informality [infôrmal'itē] *n* semplicità, informalità; carattere *m* non ufficiale.

informally [infôr'məlē] *ad* senza cerimonie; (*invite*) in modo non ufficiale.

informant [infôr'mənt] *n* informatore/trice.

informatics [infôrmat'iks] *n* informatica.

information [infûrmā'shən] *n* informazioni *fpl*; particolari *mpl*; **to get** ~ **on** informarsi su; **a piece of** ~ un'informazione; **for your** ~ a titolo d'informazione, per sua informazione.

information bureau *n* ufficio *m* informazioni *inv*.

information desk *n* banco delle informazioni.

information processing *n* elaborazione *f* delle informazioni.

information retrieval *n* ricupero delle informazioni.

information technology (IT) *n* informatica.

informative [infôr'ətiv] *a* istruttivo(a).

informed [infôrmd'] *a* (*observer*) (ben) informato(a); **an** ~ **guess** un'ipotesi fondata.

informer [infôr'mûr] *n* informatore/trice.

infra dig [in'frə dig] *a abbr* (*col*: = *infra dignitatem: beneath one's dignity*) indecoroso(a).

infra-red [in'frəred] *a* infrarosso(a).

infrastructure [in'frəstruk'chûr] *n* infrastruttura.

infrequent [infrē'kwint] *a* infrequente, raro(a).

infringe [infrinj'] *vt* infrangere ♦ *vi*: **to** ~ **on** calpestare.

infringement [infrinj'mənt] *n*: ~ **(of)** infrazione *f* (di).

infuriate [infyoor'ēāt] *vt* rendere furioso(a).

infuriating [infyoor'ēāting] *a* molto irritante.

infuse [infyooz'] *vt* (*with courage, enthusiasm*): **to** ~ **sb with sth** infondere qc a qn, riempire qn di qc.

infusion [infyoo'zhən] *n* (*tea etc*) infuso, infusione *f*.

ingenious [injēn'yəs] *a* ingegnoso(a).

ingenuity [injənoo'itē] *n* ingegnosità.

ingenuous [injen'yooəs] *a* ingenuo(a).

ingot [ing'gət] *n* lingotto.

ingrained [ingrānd'] *a* radicato(a).

ingratiate [ingrā'shēāt] *vt*: **to** ~ **o.s. with sb** ingraziarsi qn.

ingratiating [ingrā'shēāting] *a* (*smile, speech*) suadente, cattivante; (*person*) compiacente.

ingratitude [ingrat'ətōōd] n ingratitudine f.
ingredient [ingrē'dēənt] n ingrediente m; elemento.
ingrowing [in'grōing] a: ~ **(toe)nail** unghia incarnita.
ingrown [in'grōn] a = **ingrowing**.
inhabit [inhab'it] vt abitare.
inhabitable [inhab'itəbəl] a abitabile.
inhabitant [inhab'ətənt] n abitante m/f.
inhale [inhāl'] vt inalare ♦ vi (in smoking) aspirare.
inherent [inhär'ent] a: ~ **(in** or **to)** inerente (a).
inherently [inhär'entlē] ad (easy, difficult) di per sé, di per se stesso(a); ~ **lazy** pigro di natura.
inherit [inhär'it] vt ereditare.
inheritance [inhär'itəns] n eredità.
inheritance tax n imposta or tassa di successione.
inhibit [inhib'it] vt (PSYCH) inibire; **to ~ sb from doing** impedire a qn di fare.
inhibited [inhib'itid] a (person) inibito(a).
inhibiting [inhib'iting] a che inibisce.
inhibition [inibish'ən] n inibizione f.
inhospitable [inhâspit'əbəl] a inospitale.
inhuman [inhyōō'mən] a inumano(a), disumano(a).
inhumane [inhyōōmān'] a inumano(a), disumano(a).
inimitable [inim'itəbəl] a inimitabile.
iniquity [inik'witē] n iniquità f inv.
initial [inish'əl] a iniziale ♦ n iniziale f ♦ vt siglare; ~**s** npl iniziali fpl; (as signature) sigla.
initialize [inish'əlīz] vt (COMPUT) inizializzare.
initially [inish'əlē] ad inizialmente, all'inizio.
initiate [inish'ēāt] vt (start) avviare; intraprendere; iniziare; (person) iniziare; **to ~ sb into sth** iniziare qn a qc; **to ~ proceedings against sb** (LAW) intentare causa a or contro qn.
initiation [inishēā'shən] n iniziazione f.
initiative [inish'ēətiv] n iniziativa; **to take the ~** prendere l'iniziativa.
inject [injekt'] vt (liquid) iniettare; (person) fare una puntura a; (fig: money): **to ~ into** immettere in.
injection [injek'shən] n (Brit) iniezione f, puntura; **to have an ~** farsi fare un'iniezione or una puntura.
injudicious [injōōdish'əs] a poco saggio(a).
injunction [injungk'shən] n (LAW) ingiunzione f, intimazione f.
injure [in'jûr] vt ferire; (wrong) fare male or torto a; (damage: reputation etc) nuocere a; (feelings) offendere; **to ~ o.s.** farsi male.
injured [in'jûrd] a (person, leg etc) ferito(a); (tone, feelings) offeso(a); ~ **party** (LAW) parte f lesa.
injurious [injōōr'ēəs] a: ~ **(to)** nocivo(a) (a),

pregiudizievole (per).
injury [in'jûrē] n ferita; (wrong) torto; **to escape without ~** rimanere illeso.
injury time n (SPORT) tempo di ricupero.
injustice [injus'tis] n ingiustizia; **you do me an ~** mi fa un torto, è ingiusto verso di me.
ink [ingk] n inchiostro.
ink-jet printer [ingk'jet prin'tûr] n stampante f a getto d'inchiostro.
inkling [ingk'ling] n sentore m, vaga idea.
inkpad [ingk'pad] n tampone m, cuscinetto per timbri.
inky [ing'kē] a macchiato(a) or sporco(a) d'inchiostro.
inlaid [in'lād] a incrostato(a); (table etc) intarsiato(a).
inland a [in'lənd] interno(a) ♦ ad [in'land] all'interno; ~ **waterways** canali e fiumi mpl navigabili.
Inland Revenue n (Brit) Fisco.
in-laws [in'lôz] npl suoceri mpl; famiglia del marito (or della moglie).
inlet [in'let] n (GEO) insenatura, baia.
inlet pipe n (TECH) tubo d'immissione.
inmate [in'māt] n (in prison) carcerato/a; (in asylum) ricoverato/a.
inmost [in'mōst] a più profondo(a), più intimo(a).
inn [in] n locanda.
innards [in'ûrdz] npl (col) interiora fpl, budella fpl.
innate [ināt'] a innato(a).
inner [in'ûr] a interno(a), interiore.
inner city n centro di una zona urbana.
innermost [in'ûrmōst] a = **inmost**.
inner tube n camera d'aria.
innings [in'ingz] n (SPORT) turno di battuta.
innocence [in'əsəns] n innocenza.
innocent [in'əsənt] a innocente.
innocuous [inâk'yōōəs] a innocuo(a).
innovation [inəvā'shən] n innovazione f.
innuendo, ~**es** [inyōōen'dō] n insinuazione f.
innumerable [inōō'mûrəbəl] a innumerevole.
inoculate [inâk'yəlāt] vt: **to ~ sb with sth/against sth** inoculare qc a qn/qn contro qc.
inoculation [inâkyəlā'shən] n inoculazione f.
inoffensive [inəfen'siv] a inoffensivo(a), innocuo(a).
inopportune [inâpûrtōōn'] a inopportuno(a).
inordinate [inôr'dənit] a eccessivo(a).
inordinately [inôr'dənitlē] ad smoderatamente.
inorganic [inôrgan'ik] a inorganico(a).
inpatient [in'pāshənt] n ricoverato/a.
input [in'pōōt] n (ELEC) energia, potenza; (of machine) alimentazione f; (of computer) input m ♦ vt (COMPUT) inserire, introdurre.
inquest [in'kwest] n inchiesta.
inquire [inkwīûr'] vi informarsi ♦ vt domandare, informarsi di or su; **to ~ about** informarsi di or su, chiedere informazioni su;

to ~ **when/where/whether** informarsi di quando/su dove/se.

inquire after vt fus (person) chiedere di; (sb's health) informarsi di.

inquire into vt fus indagare su, fare delle indagini or ricerche su.

inquiring [inkwīŭr'ing] a (mind) inquisitivo(a).

inquiry [inkwī'ŭr'ē] n domanda; (LAW) indagine f, investigazione f; **to hold an ~ into sth** fare un'inchiesta su qc.

inquiry desk n (Brit) banco delle informazioni.

inquiry office n (Brit) ufficio m informazioni inv.

inquisition [inkwizish'ən] n inquisizione f, inchiesta; (REL): **the I~** l'Inquisizione.

inquisitive [inkwiz'ətiv] a curioso(a).

inroads [in'rōdz] npl: **to make ~ into** (savings, supplies) intaccare (seriamente).

insane [insān'] a matto(a), pazzo(a); (MED) alienato(a).

insanitary [insan'itärē] a insalubre.

insanity [insan'itē] n follia; (MED) alienazione f mentale.

insatiable [insā'shəbəl] a insaziabile.

inscribe [inskrīb'] vt iscrivere; (book etc): **to ~ (to sb)** dedicare (a qn).

inscription [inskrip'shən] n iscrizione f; (in book) dedica.

inscrutable [inskrōō'təbəl] a imperscrutabile.

inseam [in'sēm] n (US): **~ measurement** lunghezza interna.

insect [in'sekt] n insetto.

insect bite n puntura or morsicatura di insetto.

insecticide [insek'tisīd] n insetticida m.

insect repellent n insettifugo.

insecure [insikyōōr'] a malsicuro(a); (person) insicuro(a).

insecurity [insikyōōr'itē] n mancanza di sicurezza.

insensible [insen'səbəl] a insensibile; (unconscious) privo(a) di sensi.

insensitive [insen'sətiv] a insensibile.

insensitivity [insensətiv'itē] n mancanza di sensibilità.

inseparable [insep'ûrəbəl] a inseparabile.

insert vt [insûrt'] inserire, introdurre ♦ n [in'sûrt] inserto.

insertion [insûr'shən] n inserzione f.

in-service [in'sûr'vis] a (course, training) dopo l'assunzione.

inshore [in'shôr] a costiero(a) ♦ ad presso la riva; verso la riva.

inside [in'sīd'] n interno, parte f interiore; (of road: US, in Europe etc) destra; (: Brit) sinistra ♦ a interno(a), interiore ♦ ad dentro, all'interno ♦ prep dentro, all'interno di; (of time): **~ 10 minutes** entro 10 minuti; **~s** npl (col) ventre m; **~ out** ad alla rovescia; **to turn sth ~ out** rivoltare qc; **to know sth ~**

out conoscere qc a fondo; **~ information** informazioni fpl riservate; **~ story** storia segreta.

inside forward n (SPORT) mezzala, interno.

inside lane n (AUT) corsia di marcia.

inside leg measurement n (Brit) lunghezza interna.

insider [insī'dûr] n uno(a) che ha le mani in pasta.

insider dealing n (STOCK EXCHANGE) insider dealing m.

insidious [insid'ēəs] a insidioso(a).

insight [in'sīt] n acume m, perspicacia; (glimpse, idea) percezione f; **to gain** or get **an ~ into sth** potersi render conto di qc.

insignia [insig'nēə] npl insegne fpl.

insignificant [insignif'ikənt] a insignificante.

insincere [insinsēr'] a insincero(a).

insincerity [insinsār'itē] n falsità, insincerità.

insinuate [insin'yōōāt] vt insinuare.

insinuation [insinyōōā'shən] n insinuazione f.

insipid [insip'id] a insipido(a), insulso(a).

insist [insist'] vi insistere; **to ~ on doing** insistere per fare; **to ~ that** insistere perché + sub; (claim) sostenere che.

insistence [insis'təns] n insistenza.

insistent [insis'tənt] a insistente.

insole [in'sōl] n soletta; (fixed part of shoe) tramezza.

insolence [in'sələns] n insolenza.

insolent [in'sələnt] a insolente.

insoluble [insâl'yəbəl] a insolubile.

insolvency [insâl'vənsē] n insolvenza.

insolvent [insâl'vənt] a insolvente.

insomnia [insâm'nēə] n insonnia.

insomniac [insâm'nēak] n chi soffre di insonnia.

inspect [inspekt'] vt ispezionare; (Brit: ticket) controllare.

inspection [inspek'shən] n ispezione f; controllo.

inspector [inspek'tûr] n ispettore/trice; controllore m.

inspiration [inspərā'shən] n ispirazione f.

inspire [inspīr'] vt ispirare.

inspired [inspīûrd'] a (writer, book etc) ispirato(a); **in an ~ moment** in un momento d'ispirazione.

inspiring [inspīûr'ing] a stimolante.

inst. abbr (Brit COMM: = instant) c.m. (corrente mese).

instability [instəbil'ətē] n instabilità.

install [instôl'] vt installare.

installation [instəlā'shən] n installazione f.

installment, (Brit) **instalment** [instôl'mənt] n rata; (of TV serial etc) puntata; **to pay in ~s** pagare a rate.

installment plan n (US) acquisto a rate.

instance [in'stəns] n esempio, caso; **for ~** per or ad esempio; **in that ~** in quel caso; **in the first ~** in primo luogo.

instant [in'stənt] n istante m, attimo ♦ a immediato(a); urgente; (coffee, food) in polvere.

instantaneous [instəntā'nēəs] a istantaneo(a).

instantly [in'stəntlē] ad immediatamente, subito.

instant replay n (US TV) replay m inv.

instead [insted'] ad invece; ~ **of** invece di; ~ **of sb** al posto di qn.

instep [in'step] n collo del piede; (of shoe) collo della scarpa.

instigate [in'stəgāt] vt (rebellion, strike, crime) istigare a; (new ideas etc) promuovere.

instigation [instəgā'shən] n istigazione f; **at sb's** ~ per or in seguito al suggerimento di qn.

instil(l) [instil'] vt: **to** ~ **(into)** inculcare (in).

instinct [in'stingkt] n istinto.

instinctive [instingk'tiv] a istintivo(a).

instinctively [instingk'tivlē] ad per istinto.

institute [in'stitōōt] n istituto ♦ vt istituire, stabilire; (inquiry) avviare; (proceedings) iniziare.

institution [institōō'shən] n istituzione f; istituto (d'istruzione); istituto (psichiatrico).

institutional [institōō'shənəl] a istituzionale; ~ **care** assistenza medica presso un istituto.

instruct [instrukt'] vt istruire; **to** ~ **sb in sth** insegnare qc a qn; **to** ~ **sb to do** dare ordini a qn di fare.

instruction [instruk'shən] n istruzione f; ~**s (for use)** istruzioni per l'uso.

instruction book n libretto di istruzioni.

instructive [instruk'tiv] a istruttivo(a).

instructor [instruk'tûr] n istruttore/trice; (for skiing) maestro/a; (US: at university) professore/essa, docente m/f.

instrument [in'strəmənt] n strumento.

instrumental [instrəmen'təl] a (MUS) strumentale; **to be** ~ **in sth/in doing sth** avere un ruolo importante in qc/nel fare qc.

instrumentalist [instrəmen'təlist] n strumentista m/f.

instrument panel n quadro m portastrumenti inv.

insubordinate [insəbôr'dənit] a insubordinato(a).

insubordination [insəbôrdənā'shən] n insubordinazione f.

insufferable [insuf'ûrəbəl] a insopportabile.

insufficient [insəfish'ənt] a insufficiente.

insufficiently [insəfish'əntlē] ad in modo insufficiente.

insular [in'səlûr] a insulare; (person) di mente ristretta.

insulate [in'səlāt] vt isolare.

insulating tape [in'səlāting tāp] n nastro isolante.

insulation [insəlā'shən] n isolamento.

insulin [in'səlin] n insulina.

insult n [in'sult] insulto, affronto ♦ vt [insult'] insultare.

insulting [insul'ting] a offensivo(a), ingiurioso(a).

insuperable [insōō'pûrəbəl] a insormontabile, insuperabile.

insurance [inshûr'əns] n assicurazione f; **fire/life** ~ assicurazione contro gli incendi/sulla vita; **to take out** ~ **(against)** fare un'assicurazione (contro), assicurarsi (contro).

insurance agent n agente m d'assicurazioni.

insurance broker n broker m inv d'assicurazioni.

insurance policy n polizza d'assicurazione.

insurance premium n premio assicurativo.

insure [inshōōr'] vt assicurare; **to** ~ **sb** or **sb's life** assicurare qn sulla vita; **to be** ~**d for $5000** essere assicurato per 5000 dollari.

insured [inshōōrd'] n: **the** ~ l'assicurato/a.

insurer [inshōō'rûr] n assicuratore/trice.

insurgent [insûr'jənt] a ribelle ♦ n insorto/a, rivoltoso/a.

insurmountable [insûrmoun'təbəl] a insormontabile.

insurrection [insərek'shən] n insurrezione f.

intact [intakt'] a intatto(a).

intake [in'tāk] n (TECH) immissione f; (of food) consumo; (of pupils etc) afflusso.

intangible [intan'jəbəl] a intangibile.

integral [in'təgrəl] a integrale; (part) integrante.

integrate [in'təgrāt] vt integrare.

integrated circuit [in'təgrātid sûr'kit] n (COMPUT) circuito integrato.

integration [intəgrā'shən] n integrazione f; **racial** ~ integrazione razziale.

integrity [integ'ritē] n integrità.

intellect [in'təlekt] n intelletto.

intellectual [intəlek'chōōəl] a, n intellettuale (m/f).

intelligence [intel'ijəns] n intelligenza; (MIL etc) informazioni fpl.

intelligence quotient (IQ) n quoziente m d'intelligenza (Q.I.).

Intelligence Service n servizio segreto.

intelligence test n test m inv d'intelligenza.

intelligent [intel'ijənt] a intelligente.

intelligible [intel'ijəbəl] a intelligibile.

intemperate [intem'pûrit] a immoderato(a); (drinking too much) intemperante nel bere.

intend [intend'] vt (gift etc): **to** ~ **sth for** destinare qc a; **to** ~ **to do** aver l'intenzione di fare.

intended [inten'did] a (insult) intenzionale; (effect) voluto(a); (journey, route) progettato(a).

intense [intens'] a intenso(a); (person) di forti sentimenti.

intensely [intens'lē] ad intensamente; profondamente.

intensify [inten'səfī] vt intensificare.

intensity [inten'sitē] *n* intensità.
intensive [inten'siv] *a* intensivo(a).
intensive care *n* terapia intensiva; ~ **unit (ICU)** *n* reparto terapia intensiva.
intent [intent'] *n* intenzione *f* ♦ *a*: ~ **(on)** intento(a) (a), immerso(a) (in); **to all ~s and purposes** a tutti gli effetti; **to be** ~ **on doing sth** essere deciso a fare qc.
intention [inten'chən] *n* intenzione *f*.
intentional [inten'chənəl] *a* intenzionale, deliberato(a).
intentionally [inten'chənəlē] *ad* apposta.
intently [intent'lē] *ad* attentamente.
inter [intûr'] *vt* sotterrare.
interact [intûrakt'] *vi* agire reciprocamente, interagire.
interaction [intûrak'shən] *n* azione *f* reciproca, interazione *f*.
interactive [intûrak'tiv] *a* interattivo(a).
intercede [intûrsēd'] *vi*: **to** ~ **(with sb/on behalf of sb)** intercedere (presso qn/a favore di qn).
intercept [in'tûrsept] *vt* intercettare; (*person*) fermare.
interception [intûrsep'shən] *n* intercettamento.
interchange *n* [in'tûrchānj] (*exchange*) scambio; (*on freeway*) incrocio pluridirezionale ♦ *vt* [intərchānj'] scambiare; sostituire l'uno(a) per l'altro(a).
interchangeable [intûrchān'jəbəl] *a* intercambiabile.
intercity [in'tûrsitē] *a*: ~ **(train)** ≈ (treno) rapido.
intercom [in'tûrkâm] *n* interfono.
interconnect [intûrkənckt'] *vi* (*rooms*) essere in comunicazione.
intercontinental [intûrkântənən'təl] *a* intercontinentale.
intercourse [in'tûrkôrs] *n* rapporti *mpl*; (*sexual* ~) rapporti sessuali.
interdependent [intûrdipen'dənt] *a* interdipendente.
interest [in'trist] *n* interesse *m*; (*COMM*: *stake, share*) interessi *mpl* ♦ *vt* interessare; **compound/simple** ~ interesse composto/semplice; **business** ~**s** attività *fpl* commerciali; **American** ~**s in the Middle East** gli interessi (commerciali) americani nel Medio Oriente.
interested [in'tristid] *a* interessato(a); **to be** ~ **in** interessarsi di.
interest-free [in'tristfrē] *a* senza interesse.
interesting [in'tristing] *a* interessante.
interest rate *n* tasso di interesse.
interface [in'tûrfās] *n* (*COMPUT*) interfaccia.
interfere [intûrfēr'] *vi*: **to** ~ **(in)** (*quarrel, other people's business*) immischiarsi (in); **to** ~ **with** (*object*) toccare; (*plans*) ostacolare; (*duty*) interferire con.
interference [intûrfēr'əns] *n* interferenza.
interfering [intûrfēr'ing] *a* invadente.

interim [in'tûrim] *a* provvisorio(a) ♦ *n*: **in the** ~ nel frattempo; ~ **dividend** (*COMM*) acconto di dividendo.
interior [intē'rēûr] *n* interno; (*of country*) entroterra ♦ *a* interiore, interno(a).
interior decorator, interior designer *n* decoratore/trice (d'interni).
interjection [intûrjek'shən] *n* interiezione *f*.
interlock [intûrlâk'] *vi* ingranarsi ♦ *vt* ingranare.
interloper [intûrlō'pûr] *n* intruso/a.
interlude [in'tûrlōōd] *n* intervallo; (*THEATER*) intermezzo.
intermarry [intûrmar'ē] *vi* imparentarsi per mezzo di matrimonio; sposarsi tra parenti.
intermediary [intûrmē'dēârē] *n* intermediario/a.
intermediate [intûrmē'dēit] *a* intermedio(a); (*SCOL*: *course, level*) medio(a).
interminable [intûr'mənəbəl] *a* interminabile.
intermission [intûrmish'ən] *n* pausa; (*THEATER, CINEMA*) intermissione *f*, intervallo.
intermittent [intûrmit'ənt] *a* intermittente.
intermittently [intûrmit'əntlē] *ad* a intermittenza.
intern *vt* [in'tûrn'] internare ♦ *n* [in'tûrn] (*US*) medico interno.
internal [intûr'nəl] *a* interno(a); ~ **injuries** lesioni *fpl* interne.
internally [intûr'nəlē] *ad* all'interno; "**not to be taken** ~" "per uso esterno".
Internal Revenue (Service) (IRS) *n* (*US*) Fisco.
international [intûrnash'ənəl] *a* internazionale ♦ *n* (*Brit SPORT*) partita internazionale.
International Atomic Energy Agency (IAEA) *n* Agenzia Internazionale per l'Energia Atomica (IAEA).
International Court of Justice (ICJ) *n* Corte *f* Internazionale di Giustizia.
international date line *n* linea del cambiamento di data.
internationally [intûrnash'ənəlē] *ad* a livello internazionale.
International Monetary Fund (IMF) *n* Fondo monetario internazionale (F.M.I.).
internecine [intûrnē'sīn] *a* sanguinoso(a).
internee [intûrnē'] *n* internato/a.
internment [intûrn'mənt] *n* internamento.
interplay [in'tûrplā] *n* azione e reazione *f*.
Interpol [in'tûrpōl] *n* Interpol *f*.
interpret [intûr'prit] *vt* interpretare ♦ *vi* fare da interprete.
interpretation [intûrpritā'shən] *n* interpretazione *f*.
interpreter [intûr'pritûr] *n* interprete *m/f*.
interpreting [intûr'priting] *n* (*profession*) interpretariato.
interrelated [intərilā'tid] *a* correlato(a).
interrogate [intär'əgāt] *vt* interrogare.
interrogation [intärəgā'shən] *n* interrogazione

f; (*of suspect etc*) interrogatorio.
interrogative [intərág'ətiv] *a* interrogativo(a)
♦ *n* (*LING*) interrogativo.
interrogator [intär'əgātûr] *n* interrogante *m/f*.
interrupt [intərupt'] *vt* interrompere.
interruption [intərup'shən] *n* interruzione *f*.
intersect [intûrsekt'] *vt* intersecare ♦ *vi*
(*roads*) intersecarsi.
intersection [intûrsek'shən] *n* intersezione *f*;
(*of roads*) incrocio.
intersperse [intûrspûrs'] *vt*: **to ~ with** co-
stellare di.
interstate (highway) [in'tûrstāt (hī'wā)] *n*
(*US*) autostrada.
intertwine [intûrtwīn'] *vt* intrecciare ♦ *vi* in-
trecciarsi.
interval [in'tûrvəl] *n* intervallo; (*Brit SCOL*) ricreazione *f*, intervallo; **bright ~s** (*in
weather*) schiarite *fpl*; **at ~s** a intervalli.
intervene [intûrvēn'] *vi* (*time*) intercorrere;
(*event, person*) intervenire.
intervention [intûrven'chən] *n* intervento.
interview [in'tûrvyōō] *n* (*RADIO. TV etc*)
intervista; (*for job*) colloquio ♦ *vt* intervista-
re; avere un colloquio con.
interviewer [in'tûrvyōōûr] *n* intervistatore/
trice.
intestate [intes'tāt] *a* intestato(a).
intestinal [intes'tənəl] *a* intestinale.
intestine [intes'tin] *n* intestino; **large/small ~**
intestino crasso/tenue.
intimacy [in'təməsē] *n* intimità.
intimate *a* [in'təmit] intimo(a); (*knowledge*)
profondo(a) ♦ *vt* [in'təmāt] lasciar capire.
intimately [in'təmitlē] *ad* intimamente.
intimation [intəmā'shən] *n* annuncio.
intimidate [intim'idāt] *vt* intimidire, intimori-
re.
intimidation [intimidā'shən] *n* intimidazione *f*.
into [in'tōō] *prep* dentro, in; **come ~ the
house** vieni dentro la casa; **~ pieces** a pezzi;
~ Italian in italiano; **to change pounds ~
dollars** cambiare delle sterline in dollari.
intolerable [intâl'ûrəbəl] *a* intollerabile.
intolerance [intâl'ûrəns] *n* intolleranza.
intolerant [intâl'ûrənt] *a*: **~ (of)** intollerante
(di).
intonation [intōnā'shən] *n* intonazione *f*.
intoxicate [intâk'sikāt] *vt* inebriare.
intoxicated [intâk'sikātid] *a* inebriato(a).
intoxication [intâksikā'shən] *n* ebbrezza.
intractable [intrak'təbəl] *a* intrattabile;
(*illness*) difficile da curare; (*problem*) insolubile.
intransigence [intran'sijəns] *n* intransigenza.
intransigent [intran'sijənt] *a* intransigente.
intransitive [intran'sətiv] *a* intransitivo(a).
intra-uterine device (IUD) [intrəyōō'turin di-
vīs'] *n* dispositivo intrauterino (IUD).
intravenous [intrəvē'nəs] *a* endovenoso(a).
in-tray [in'trā] *n* raccoglitore *m* per le carte in

arrivo.
intrepid [intrep'id] *a* intrepido(a).
intricacy [in'trəkəsē] *n* complessità *f inv*.
intricate [in'trəkit] *a* intricato(a), complica-
to(a).
intrigue [intrēg'] *n* intrigo ♦ *vt* affascinare ♦ *vi*
complottare, tramare.
intriguing [intrē'ging] *a* affascinante.
intrinsic [intrin'sik] *a* intrinseco(a).
introduce [intrədōōs'] *vt* introdurre; **to ~ sb
(to sb)** presentare qn (a qn); **to ~ sb to**
(*pastime, technique*) iniziare qn a; **may I ~
...?** permette che le presenti ...?
introduction [intrəduk'shən] *n* introduzione *f*;
(*of person*) presentazione *f*; **a letter of ~** una
lettera di presentazione.
introductory [intrəduk'tûrē] *a* introduttivo(a);
an ~ offer un'offerta di lancio; **~ remarks**
osservazioni *fpl* preliminari.
introspection [intrəspek'shən] *n* introspezione
f.
introspective [intrəspek'tiv] *a* introspettivo(a).
introvert [in'trəvûrt] *a, n* introverso(a).
intrude [intrōōd'] *vi* (*person*) intromettersi; **to
~ on** (*person*) importunare; **~ on** *or* **into**
(*conversation*) intromettersi in; **am I intrud-
ing?** disturbo?
intruder [intrōō'dûr] *n* intruso/a.
intrusion [intrōō'zhən] *n* intrusione *f*.
intrusive [intrōō'siv] *a* importuno(a).
intuition [intōōish'ən] *n* intuizione *f*.
intuitive [intōō'ətiv] *a* intuitivo(a); dotato(a)
di intuito.
Inuit [in'ōōwit] *n, a* Innuit *inv*, eschimese (*m/f*)
(del Nord America e Groenlandia).
inundate [in'undāt] *vt*: **to ~ with** inondare di.
inure [inyōōr'] *vt*: **to ~ (to)** assuefare (a).
invade [invād'] *vt* invadere.
invader [invā'dûr] *n* invasore *m*.
invalid *n* [in'vəlid] malato/a; (*with disability*)
invalido/a ♦ *a* [inva'lid] (*not valid*) invali-
do(a), non valido(a).
invalidate [inval'idāt] *vt* invalidare.
invalid chair *n* (*Brit*) sedia a rotelle.
invaluable [inval'yōōəbəl] *a* prezioso(a); inestimabile.
invariable [invär'ēəbəl] *a* costante, invariabile.
invariably [invär'ēablē] *ad* invariabilmente;
she is ~ late è immancabilmente in ritardo.
invasion [invā'zhən] *n* invasione *f*.
invective [invek'tiv] *n* invettiva.
inveigle [invē'gəl] *vt*: **to ~ sb into (doing) sth**
circuire qn per (fargli fare) qc.
invent [invent'] *vt* inventare.
invention [inven'chən] *n* invenzione *f*.
inventive [inven'tiv] *a* inventivo(a).
inventiveness [inven'tivnis] *n* inventiva.
inventor [inven'tûr] *n* inventore *m*.
inventory [in'vəntôrē] *n* inventario.
inventory control *n* (*COMM*) controllo delle
giacenze.

inverse [invûrs'] a inverso(a) ♦ n inverso, contrario; **in ~ proportion (to)** in modo inversamente proporzionale (a).

inversely [invûrs'lē] ad inversamente.

invert [invûrt'] vt invertire; (object) rovesciare.

invertebrate [invûr'təbrit] n invertebrato.

inverted commas [invûr'tid kâm'əz] npl (Brit) virgolette fpl.

invest [invest'] vt investire; (fig: time, effort) impiegare; (endow): **to ~ sb with sth** investire qn di qc ♦ vi fare investimenti; **to ~ in** investire in, fare (degli) investimenti in; (acquire) comprarsi.

investigate [inves'təgāt] vt investigare, indagare; (crime) fare indagini su.

investigation [inves'təgāshən] n investigazione f; (of crime) indagine f.

investigative [inves'təgātiv] a: **~ journalism** giornalismo investigativo.

investigator [inves'təgātûr] n investigatore/trice; **a private ~** un investigatore privato, un detective.

investiture [inves'tichûr] n investitura.

investment [invest'mənt] n investimento.

investment income n reddito da investimenti.

investment trust n fondo comune di investimento.

investor [inves'tûr] n investitore/trice; (shareholder) azionista m/f.

inveterate [invet'ûrit] a inveterato(a).

invidious [invid'ēəs] a odioso(a); (task) spiacevole.

invigilator [invij'əlātûr] n (Brit) chi sorveglia agli esami.

invigorating [invig'ərāting] a stimolante; vivificante.

invincible [invin'səbəl] a invincibile.

inviolate [invī'əlit] a inviolato(a).

invisible [inviz'əbəl] a invisibile.

invisible ink n inchiostro simpatico.

invisible mending n rammendo invisibile.

invitation [invitā'shən] n invito; **by ~ only** esclusivamente su or per invito; **at sb's ~** dietro invito di qn.

invite [invīt'] vt invitare; (opinions etc) sollecitare; (trouble) provocare; **to ~ sb (to do)** invitare qn (a fare); **to ~ sb to dinner** invitare qn a cena.

invite out vt invitare fuori.

invite over vt invitare (a casa).

inviting [invī'ting] a invitante, attraente.

invoice [in'vois] n fattura ♦ vt fatturare; **to ~ sb for goods** inviare a qn la fattura per le or delle merci.

invoke [invōk'] vt invocare.

involuntary [invâl'əntārē] a involontario(a).

involve [invâlv'] vt (entail) richiedere, comportare; (associate): **to ~ sb (in)** implicare qn (in); coinvolgere qn (in); **to involve**

o.s. in sth (politics etc) impegnarsi in qc.

involved [invâlvd'] a involuto(a), complesso(a); **to feel ~** sentirsi coinvolto(a); **to become ~ with sb** (socially) legarsi a qn; (emotionally) legarsi sentimentalmente a qn.

involvement [invâlv'mənt] n implicazione f; coinvolgimento; impegno; partecipazione f.

invulnerable [invul'nûrəbəl] a invulnerabile.

inward [in'wûrd] a (movement) verso l'interno; (thought, feeling) interiore, intimo(a); see also **inward(s)**.

inwardly [in'wûrdlē] ad (feel, think etc) nell'intimo, entro di sé.

inward(s) [in'wûrd(z)] ad verso l'interno.

I/O abbr (COMPUT: = input/output) I/O.

IOC n abbr (= International Olympic Committee) CIO m (= Comitato Internazionale Olimpico).

iodine [ī'ədīn] n iodio.

IOM abbr (Brit) = Isle of Man.

ion [ī'ən] n ione m.

Ionian Sea [īō'nēən sē] n: **the ~** il mare Ionio.

iota [īō'tə] n (fig) briciolo.

IOU n abbr (= I owe you) pagherò m inv.

IOW abbr (Brit) = Isle of Wight.

IPA n abbr (= International Phonetic Alphabet) I.P.A. m.

IQ n abbr = **intelligence quotient**.

IRA n abbr (US) = individual retirement account; (= Irish Republican Army) I.R.A. f.

Iran [iran'] n Iran m.

Iranian [irā'nēən] a iraniano(a) ♦ n iraniano/a; (LING) iranico.

Iraq [irak'] n Iraq m.

Iraqi [irâk'ē] a iracheno(a) ♦ n iracheno/a; (LING) iracheno.

irascible [iras'əbəl] a irascibile.

irate [irāt'] a irato(a).

Ireland [īûr'lənd] n Irlanda; **Republic of ~** Repubblica d'Irlanda, Eire f.

iris, ~es [ī'ris, -ēz] n iride f; (BOT) giaggiolo, iride.

Irish [ī'rish] a irlandese ♦ npl: **the ~** gli Irlandesi.

Irishman [ī'rishmən] n irlandese m.

Irish Sea n: **the ~** il mar d'Irlanda.

Irishwoman [ī'rishwŏomən] n irlandese f.

irk [ûrk] vt seccare.

irksome [ûrk'səm] a seccante.

IRO n abbr (US: = International Refugee Organization) O.I.R. f (= Organizzazione Internazionale per i Rifugiati).

iron [ī'ûrn] n ferro; (for clothes) ferro da stiro ♦ a di or in ferro ♦ vt (clothes) stirare; see also **irons**.

iron out vt (crease) appianare; (fig) spianare; far sparire.

Iron Curtain n: **the ~** la cortina di ferro.

iron foundry n fonderia.

ironic(al) [irân'ik(əl)] a ironico(a).

ironically [īrân'iklē] *ad* ironicamente.
ironing [ī'ûrning] *n* (*act*) stirare *m*; (*clothes*) roba da stirare.
ironing board *n* asse *f* da stiro.
iron lung *n* (*MED*) polmone *m* d'acciaio.
ironmonger [ī'ûrnmunggûr] *n* (*Brit*) negoziante *m* in ferramenta; **~'s** (**shop**) *n* negozio di ferramenta.
iron ore [ī'ûrn ôr] *n* minerale *m* di ferro.
irons [ī'ûrnz] *npl* (*chains*) catene *fpl*.
ironworks [ī'ûrnwûrks] *n* ferriera.
irony [ī'rənē] *n* ironia.
irrational [irash'ənəl] *a* irrazionale; irragionevole; illogico(a).
irreconcilable [irek'ənsīləbəl] *a* irreconciliabile; (*opinion*): **~ with** inconciliabile con.
irredeemable [iridē'məbəl] *a* (*COMM*) irredimibile.
irrefutable [irifyōō'təbəl] *a* irrefutabile.
irregular [ireg'yəlûr] *a* irregolare.
irregularity [iregyəlar'itē] *n* irregolarità *f inv*.
irrelevance [irel'əvəns] *n* inappropriatezza.
irrelevant [irel'əvənt] *a* non pertinente.
irreligious [irilij'əs] *a* irreligioso(a).
irreparable [irep'ûrəbəl] *a* irreparabile.
irreplaceable [iriplā'səbəl] *a* insostituibile.
irrepressible [iripres'əbəl] *a* irrefrenabile.
irreproachable [iriprō'chəbəl] *a* irreprensibile.
irresistible [irizis'təbəl] *a* irresistibile.
irresolute [irez'əlōōt] *a* irresoluto(a), indeciso(a).
irrespective [irispek'tiv]: **~ of** *prep* senza riguardo a.
irresponsible [irispân'səbəl] *a* irresponsabile.
irretrievable [iritrē'vəbəl] *a* (*object*) irrecuperabile; (*loss, damage*) irreparabile.
irreverent [irev'ûrənt] *a* irriverente.
irrevocable [irev'əkəbəl] *a* irrevocabile.
irrigate [ir'igāt] *vt* irrigare.
irrigation [irigā'shən] *n* irrigazione *f*.
irritable [ir'itəbəl] *a* irritabile.
irritant [ir'ətənt] *n* sostanza irritante.
irritate [ir'ətāt] *vt* irritare.
irritation [iritā'shən] *n* irritazione *f*.
IRS *n abbr* (*US*) *see* **Internal Revenue Service**.
is [iz] *vb see* **be**.
ISBN *n abbr* (= *International Standard Book Number*) I.S.B.N. *m*.
Islam [iz'lâm] *n* Islam *m*.
island [ī'lənd] *n* isola; (*also:* **traffic ~**) salvagente *m*.
islander [ī'ləndûr] *n* isolano/a.
isle [īl] *n* isola.
isn't [iz'ənt] = **is not**.
isolate [ī'səlāt] *vt* isolare.
isolated [ī'səlātid] *a* isolato(a).
isolation [īsəlā'shən] *n* isolamento.
isolationism [īsəlā'shənizəm] *n* isolazionismo.
isotope [ī'sətōp] *n* isotopo.
Israel [iz'rāəl] *n* Israele *m*.
Israeli [izrā'lē] *a, n* israeliano(a).

issue [ish'ōō] *n* questione *f*, problema *m*; (*outcome*) esito, risultato; (*of bank notes etc*) emissione *f*; (*of newspaper etc*) numero; (*offspring*) discendenza ♦ *vt* (*rations, equipment*) distribuire; (*orders*) dare; (*book*) pubblicare; (*bank notes, checks, stamps*) emettere ♦ *vi*: **to ~ (from)** uscire (da), venir fuori (da); **at ~ in gioco**, in discussione; **to avoid the ~** evitare la discussione; **to take ~ with sb (over sth)** prendere posizione contro qn (riguardo a qc); **to confuse** *or* **obscure the ~** confondere le cose; **to make an ~ of sth** fare un problema di qc; **to ~ sth to sb, ~ sb with sth** consegnare qc a qn.
Istanbul [istambōōl'] *n* Istanbul *f*.
isthmus [is'məs] *n* istmo.
IT *n abbr see* **information technology**.
it [it] *pronoun* (*subject*) esso(a); (*direct object*) lo(la), l'; (*indirect object*) gli(le); **of ~**, **from ~**, **about ~**, **out of ~** *etc* ne; **in ~**, **to ~**, **at ~** *etc* ci; **above ~**, **over ~** (al) di sopra; **below ~**, **under ~** (al) di sotto; **in front of/ behind ~** lì davanti/dietro; **who is ~?** chi è?; **~'s me** sono io; **what is ~?** cosa c'è?; **where is ~?** dov'è?; **~'s Friday tomorrow** domani è venerdì; **~'s raining** piove; **~'s 6 o'clock** sono le 6; **~'s 2 hours on the train** sono *or* ci vogliono 2 ore di treno; **I've come from ~** vengo da lì; **it's on ~** è lì sopra; **he's proud of ~** ne è fiero; **he agreed to ~** ha acconsentito.
Italian [ital'yən] *a* italiano(a) ♦ *n* italiano/a; (*LING*) italiano; **the ~s** gli Italiani.
italic [ital'ik] *a* corsivo(a); **~s** *npl* corsivo.
Italy [it'əlē] *n* Italia.
itch [ich] *n* prurito ♦ *vi* (*person*) avere il prurito; (*part of body*) prudere; **to be ~ing to do** non veder l'ora di fare.
itchy [ich'ē] *a* che prude; **my back is ~** ho prurito alla schiena.
it'd [it'əd] = **it would**; **it had**.
item [ī'təm] *n* articolo; (*on agenda*) punto; (*in program*) numero; (*also:* **news ~**) notizia; **~s of clothing** capi *mpl* di abbigliamento.
itemize [ī'təmīz] *vt* specificare, dettagliare.
itinerant [itin'ûrənt] *a* ambulante.
itinerary [ītin'ərārē] *n* itinerario.
it'll [it'əl] = **it will**; **it shall**.
its [its] *a, pronoun* il(la) suo(a), i(le) suoi(sue).
it's [its] = **it is**; **it has**.
itself [itself'] *pronoun* (*emphatic*) esso(a) stesso(a); (*reflexive*) si.
ITV *n abbr* (*Brit:* = *Independent Television*) rete televisiva indipendente.
IUD *n abbr* = **intra-uterine device**.
I.V. *n abbr* (*US:* = *intravenous*) fleboclisi *f inv*.
I've [īv] = **I have**.
ivory [ī'vûrē] *n* avorio.
Ivory Coast *n* Costa d'Avorio.
ivory tower *n* torre *f* d'avorio.

ivy [ĭ'vē] *n* edera.
Ivy League *n* (*US*) *insieme delle grandi uni-*
  versità del Nord-Est degli Stati Uniti.

J

J, j [jā] *n* (*letter*) J, j *f or m inv*; **J for Jig** ≈ J
  come jersey.
JA *n abbr see* **judge advocate.**
J/A *abbr see* **joint account.**
jab [jab] *vt*: **to ~ sth into** affondare *or* piantare qc dentro ♦ *vi*: **to ~ at** dare colpi a ♦ *n*
  colpo; (*MED: col*) puntura.
jabber [jab'ûr] *vt, vi* borbottare.
jack [jak] *n* (*AUT*) cricco; (*BOWLS*) boccino,
  pallino; (*CARDS*) fante *m*.
  jack in *vt* (*col*) mollare.
  jack up *vt* sollevare sul cricco; (*raise:
  prices etc*) alzare.
jackal [jak'əl] *n* sciacallo.
jackass [jak'as] *n* (*also fig*) asino, somaro.
jackdaw [jak'dô] *n* taccola.
jacket [jak'it] *n* giacca; (*of book*) copertura.
jack-in-the-box [jak'intḫəbâks] *n* scatola a
  sorpresa (con pupazzo a molla).
jackknife [jak'nīf] *vi*: **the truck ~d** l'autotreno
  si è piegato su se stesso.
jack-of-all-trades [jak'əvôltrādz'] *n* uno che fa
  un po' di tutto.
jack plug *n* (*Brit*) jack plug *f inv*.
jackpot [jak'pât] *n* primo premio (in denaro).
jacuzzi [jəkōō'zē] ⓇⒸ *n* vasca per idro-
  massaggio Jacuzzi ⓇⒸ.
jade [jād] *n* (*stone*) giada.
jaded [jā'did] *a* sfinito(a), spossato(a).
JAG *n abbr see* **Judge Advocate General.**
jagged [jag'id] *a* sboconcellato(a); (*cliffs etc*)
  frastagliato(a).
jaguar [jag'wâr] *n* giaguaro.
jail [jāl] *n* prigione *f* ♦ *vt* mandare in prigione.
jailbird [jāl'bûrd] *n* avanzo di galera.
jailbreak [jāl'brāk] *n* evasione *f*.
jailer [jā'lûr] *n* custode *m* del carcere.
jalopy [jəlâp'ē] *n* (*col*) macinino.
jam [jam] *n* marmellata; (*of shoppers etc*)
  ressa; (*also:* **traffic ~**) ingorgo ♦ *vt* (*passage
  etc*) ingombrare, ostacolare; (*mechanism,
  drawer etc*) bloccare; (*RADIO*) disturbare
  con interferenze ♦ *vi* (*mechanism, sliding
  part*) incepparsi, bloccarsi; (*gun*) incepparsi;
  to get sb out of a ~ tirare qn fuori dai pasticci; **to ~ sth into** forzare qc dentro; infilare qc a forza dentro; **the telephone lines are
  ~med** le linee sono sovraccariche.

Jamaica [jəmā'kə] *n* Giamaica.
Jamaican [jəmā'kən] *a, n* giamaicano(a).
jamb [jam] *n* stipite *m*.
jam-packed [jam'pakt'] *a*: **~ (with)** pieno(a)
  zeppo(a) (di), strapieno(a) (di).
jam session *n* improvvisazione *f* jazzistica.
Jan. *abbr* (= *January*) gen., genn.
jangle [jang'gəl] *vi* risuonare; (*bracelet*)
  tintinnare.
janitor [jan'itûr] *n* (*caretaker*) portiere *m*;
  (*SCOL*) bidello.
January [jan'yōōwärē] *n* gennaio; *for phrases
  see also* **July.**
Japan [jəpan'] *n* Giappone *m*.
Japanese [japənēz'] *a* giapponese ♦ *n* (*pl inv*)
  giapponese *m/f*; (*LING*) giapponese *m*.
jar [jâr] *n* (*container*) barattolo, vasetto ♦ *vi*
  (*sound*) stridere; (*colors etc*) stonare ♦ *vt*
  (*shake*) scuotere.
jargon [jâr'gən] *n* gergo.
jarring [jâr'ing] *a* (*sound, color*) stonato(a).
Jas. *abbr* = *James.*
jasmin(e) [jaz'min] *n* gelsomino.
jaundice [jôn'dis] *n* itterizia.
jaundiced [jôn'dist] *a* (*fig*) invidioso(a) e criti-
  co(a).
jaunt [jônt] *n* gita.
jaunty [jôn'tē] *a* vivace; disinvolto(a), spiglia-
  to(a).
Java [jâv'ə] *n* Giava.
javelin [jav'lin] *n* giavellotto.
jaw [jô] *n* mascella; **~s** (*TECH: of vice etc*)
  morsa.
jawbone [jô'bōn] *n* mandibola.
jay [jā] *n* ghiandaia.
jaywalker [jā'wôkûr] *n* pedone(a) indisciplina-
  to(a).
jazz [jaz] *n* jazz *m*.
  jazz up *vt* rendere vivace.
jazz band *n* banda *f* jazz *inv*.
jazzy [jaz'ē] *a* vistoso(a), chiassoso(a).
JCC *n abbr* (*US*) = *Junior Chamber of
  Commerce.*
JCS *n abbr* (*US*) = *Joint Chiefs of Staff.*
JD *n abbr* (*US:* = *Doctor of Laws*) *titolo di
  studio*; (: = *Justice Department*) *ministero
  della Giustizia.*
jealous [jel'əs] *a* geloso(a).
jealously [jel'əslē] *ad* (*enviously*) con gelosia;
  (*watchfully*) gelosamente.
jealousy [jel'əsē] *n* gelosia.
jeans [jēnz] *npl* (blue-)jeans *mpl*.
jeep [jēp] *n* jeep *m inv*.
jeer [jēr] *vi*: **to ~ (at)** fischiare; beffeggiare;
  see also **jeers.**
jeering [jē'ring] *a* (*crowd*) che urla e fischia ♦
  n fischi *mpl*; parole *fpl* di scherno.
jeers [jērz] *npl* fischi *mpl*.
jelly [jel'ē] *n* gelatina.
jellyfish [jel'ēfish] *n* medusa.
jeopardize [jep'ûrdīz] *vt* mettere in pericolo.

jeopardy |jɛp'ûrdē| *n*: **in** ~ in pericolo.

jerk |jûrk| *n* sobbalzo, scossa; sussulto; (*col*) povero scemo ♦ *vt* dare una scossa a ♦ *vi* (*vehicles*) sobbalzare.

jerkin |jûr'kin| *n* giubbotto.

jerky |jûr'kē| *a* a scatti; a sobbalzi.

jerry-built |jär'ōbilt| *a* fatto(a) di cartapesta.

jerry can |jär'ē kan| *n* tanica.

jersey |jûr'zē| *n* maglia, jersey *m*.

Jerusalem |jərōō'sələm| *n* Gerusalemme *f*.

jest |jɛst| *n* scherzo; **in** ~ per scherzo.

jester |jɛs'tûr| *n* (*HISTORY*) buffone *m*.

Jesus |jē'səs| *n* Gesù *m*; ~ **Christ** Gesù Cristo.

jet |jɛt| *n* (*of gas, liquid*) getto; (*AUT*) spruzzatore *m*; (*AVIAT*) aviogetto.

jet-black |jɛt'blak'| *a* nero(a) come l'ebano, corvino(a).

jet engine *n* motore *m* a reazione.

jet lag *n* (problemi *mpl* dovuti allo) sbalzo dei fusi orari.

jetsam |jɛt'səm| *n* relitti *mpl* di mare.

jettison |jɛt'əsən| *vt* gettare in mare.

jetty |jɛt'ē| *n* molo.

Jew |jōō| *n* ebreo.

jewel |jōō'əl| *n* gioiello.

jeweler, (*Brit*) **jeweller** |jōō'əlûr| *n* orefice *m*, gioielliere/a.

jewelry, (*Brit*) **jewellery** |jōō'əlrē| *n* gioielli *mpl*; ~ **store** *n* (*US*) oreficeria, gioielleria.

Jewess |jōō'is| *n* ebrea.

Jewish |jōō'ish| *a* ebreo(a), ebraico(a).

JFK *n abbr* (*US*) = *John Fitzgerald Kennedy International Airport*.

jib |jib| *n* (*NAUT*) fiocco; (*of crane*) braccio ♦ *vi* (*horse*) impennarsi; **to** ~ **at doing sth** essere restio a fare qc.

jibe |jīb| *n* beffa.

jiffy |jif'ē| *n* (*col*): **in a** ~ in un batter d'occhio.

jig |jig| *n* (*dance, tune*) giga.

jigsaw |jig'sô| *n* (*tool*) sega da traforo; (*also*: ~ **puzzle**) puzzle *m inv*.

jilt |jilt| *vt* piantare in asso.

jingle |jing'gəl| *n* (*advert*) sigla pubblicitaria ♦ *vi* tintinnare, scampanellare.

jingoism |jing'gōizəm| *n* sciovinismo.

jinx |jingks| *n* (*col*) iettatura; (*person*) iettatore/trice.

jitters |jit'ûrz| *npl* (*col*): **to get the** ~ aver fifa.

jittery |jit'ûrē| *a* (*col*) nervoso(a), agitato(a).

jiujitsu |jōōjit'sōō| *n* jujitsu *m*.

job |jâb| *n* lavoro; (*employment*) impiego, posto; **a part-time/full-time** ~ un lavoro a mezza giornata/a tempo pieno; **that's not my** ~ non è compito mio; **he's only doing his** ~ non fa che il suo dovere; **it's a good** ~ **that** ... meno male che ...; **just the** ~! proprio quello che ci vuole!

jobber |jâb'ûr| *n* (*Brit STOCK EXCHANGE*) intermediario tra agenti di cambio.

jobbing |jâb'ing| *a* (*Brit*: *workman*) a ore, a giornata.

Jobcentre |jâb'sɛntûr| *n* (*Brit*) ufficio di collocamento.

job creation scheme *n* (*Brit*) progetto per la creazione di nuovi posti di lavoro.

job description *n* caratteristiche *fpl* (di un lavoro).

jobless |jâb'lis| *a* senza lavoro, disoccupato(a).

job lot *n* partita di articoli disparati.

job satisfaction *n* soddisfazione *f* nel lavoro.

job security *n* sicurezza del posto di lavoro.

job specification *n* caratteristiche *fpl* (di un lavoro).

jockey |jâk'ē| *n* fantino, jockey *m inv* ♦ *vi*: **to** ~ **for position** manovrare per una posizione di vantaggio.

jocular |jâk'yəlûr| *a* gioviale; scherzoso(a).

jog |jâg| *vt* urtare ♦ *vi* (*SPORT*) fare footing, fare jogging; **to** ~ **along** trottare; (*fig*) andare avanti piano piano; **to** ~ **sb's memory** stimolare la memoria di qn.

jogger |jâg'ûr| *n* persona che fa footing *or* jogging.

jogging |jâg'ing| *n* footing *m*, jogging *m*.

john |jân| *n* (*US col*) W.C. *m inv*, cesso.

join |join| *vt* unire, congiungere; (*become member of*) iscriversi a; (*meet*) raggiungere; riunirsi a ♦ *vi* (*roads, rivers*) confluire ♦ *n* giuntura; **to** ~ **forces (with)** allearsi (con *or* a); (*fig*) mettersi insieme (a); **will you** ~ **us for dinner?** viene a cena con noi?; **I'll** ~ **you later** vi raggiungo più tardi.

join in *vt fus* unirsi a, prendere parte a, partecipare a ♦ *vi* partecipare.

join up *vi* arruolarsi.

joiner |join'ûr| *n* falegname *m*.

joinery |join'ûrē| *n* falegnameria.

joint |joint| *n* (*TECH*) giuntura; giunto; (*ANAT*) articolazione *f*, giuntura; (*CULIN*) arrosto; (*col*: *place*) locale *m* ♦ *a* comune; (*responsibility*) collettivo(a); (*committee*) misto(a).

joint account (J/A) *n* (*at bank etc*) conto in comune.

jointly |joint'lē| *ad* in comune, insieme.

joint ownership *n* comproprietà.

joint-stock company |joint'stâk' kum'pənē| *n* società *f inv* per azioni.

joint venture *n* associazione *f* in partecipazione.

joist |joist| *n* trave *f*.

joke |jōk| *n* scherzo; (*funny story*) barzelletta ♦ *vi* scherzare; **to play a** ~ **on** fare uno scherzo a.

joker |jō'kûr| *n* buffone/a, burlone/a; (*CARDS*) matta, jolly *m inv*.

joking |jō'king| *n* scherzi *mpl*.

jollity |jâl'itē| *n* allegria.

jolly |jâl'ē| *a* allegro(a), gioioso(a) ♦ *ad* (*Brit col*) veramente, proprio; ~ **good!** (*Brit*) benissimo!

jolt [jōlt] n scossa, sobbalzo ♦ vt urtare.
Jordan [jôr'dun] n (country) Giordania; (river) Giordano.
Jordanian [jôrdā'nēən] a, n giordano(a).
joss stick [jâs stik] n bastoncino d'incenso.
jostle [jâs'əl] vt spingere coi gomiti ♦ vi farsi spazio coi gomiti.
jot [jât] n: **not one** ~ nemmeno un po'.
jot down vt annotare in fretta, buttare giù.
jotter [jât'ûr] n (Brit) quaderno; blocco.
journal [jûr'nəl] n (newspaper) giornale m; (periodical) rivista; (diary) diario.
journalese [jûrnəlēz'] n (pej) stile m giornalistico.
journalism [jûr'nəlizəm] n giornalismo.
journalist [jûr'nəlist] n giornalista m/f.
journey [jûr'nē] n viaggio; (distance covered) tragitto; **a 5-hour** ~ un viaggio or un tragitto di 5 ore.
jovial [jō'vēəl] a gioviale, allegro(a).
jowl [joul] n mandibola; guancia.
joy [joi] n gioia.
joyful [joi'fəl], **joyous** [joi'əs] a gioioso(a), allegro(a).
joy ride n gita in automobile (specialmente rubata).
joystick [joi'stik] n (AVIAT) barra di comando; (COMPUT) joystick m inv.
JP n abbr see **Justice of the Peace.**
Jr. abbr = **junior.**
JTPA n abbr (US: = Job Training Partnership Act) piano governativo di parziale sovvenzione per l'addestramento sul lavoro di apprendisti.
jubilant [jōō'bələnt] a giubilante; trionfante.
jubilation [jōōbəlā'shən] n giubilo.
jubilee [jōō'bəlē] n giubileo; **silver** ~ venticinquesimo anniversario.
judge [juj] n giudice m/f ♦ vt giudicare; (consider) ritenere; (estimate: weight, size etc) calcolare, valutare ♦ vi: **judging** or **to** ~ **by his expression** as far as I can ~ a mio giudizio; **I** ~**d it necessary to inform him** ho ritenuto necessario informarlo.
judge advocate (JA) n (MIL) magistrato militare.
Judge Advocate General (JAG) n (MIL) consigliere principale in materia di diritto militare.
judg(e)ment [juj'mənt] n giudizio; (punishment) punizione f; **in my** ~ a mio giudizio; **to pass** ~ **(on)** (LAW) pronunciare un giudizio (su); (fig) dare giudizi affrettati (su).
judicial [jōōdish'əl] a giudiziale, giudiziario(a).
judiciary [jōōdish'ēärē] n magistratura.
judicious [jōōdish'əs] a giudizioso(a).
judo [jōō'dō] n judo.
jug [jug] n brocca, bricco.
juggernaut [jug'ûrnôt] n (Brit: huge truck)

bestione m.
juggle [jug'əl] vi fare giochi di destrezza.
juggler [jug'lûr] n giocoliere/a.
Jugoslav [yōō'gōslâv] a, n = **Yugoslav.**
jugular [jug'yəlûr] a: ~ **(vein)** vena giugulare.
juice [jōōs] n succo; (of meat) sugo; **we've run out of** ~ (col: gas) siamo rimasti a secco.
juicy [jōō'sē] a succoso(a).
jukebox [jōōk'bâks] n juke-box m inv.
Jul. abbr (= July) lug., lu.
July [julī'] n luglio; **the first of** ~ il primo luglio; **(on) the eleventh of** ~ l'undici luglio; **in the month of** ~ nel mese di luglio; **at the beginning/end of** ~ all'inizio/alla fine di luglio; **in the middle of** ~ a metà luglio; **during** ~ durante (il mese di) luglio; **in** ~ **of next year** a luglio dell'anno prossimo; **each** or **every** ~ ogni anno a luglio; ~ **was wet this year** ha piovuto molto a luglio quest'anno.
jumble [jum'bəl] n miscuglio ♦ vt (also: ~ **up,** ~ **together)** mischiare, mettere alla rinfusa.
jumble sale n (Brit) vendita di oggetti per beneficenza.
jumbo [jum'bō] a: ~ **jet** jumbo-jet m inv; ~ **size** formato gigante.
jump [jump] vi saltare, balzare; (start) sobbalzare; (increase) rincarare ♦ vt saltare ♦ n salto, balzo; sobbalzo; (fence) ostacolo.
jump about vi fare salti, saltellare.
jump at vt fus (fig) cogliere or afferrare al volo; **he** ~**ed at the offer** si affrettò ad accettare l'offerta.
jump down vi saltare giù.
jump up vi saltare in piedi.
jumped-up [jumpt'up] a (Brit pej) presuntuoso(a).
jumper [jum'pûr] n (US: pinafore dress) scamiciato; (Brit: pullover) maglia; (SPORT) saltatore/trice.
jumper cables, (Brit) **jump leads** npl cavi mpl per batteria.
jump rope n (US) corda per saltare.
jump suit n tuta.
jumpy [jum'pē] a nervoso(a), agitato(a).
Jun. abbr (= June) giu.
Jun., Junr abbr = **junior.**
junction [jungk'shən] n (of railroad) nodo ferroviario; (Brit: of roads) incrocio.
juncture [jungk'chûr] n: **at this** ~ in questa congiuntura.
June [jōōn] n giugno; for phrases see also **July.**
jungle [jung'gəl] n giungla.
junior [jōōn'yûr] a, n: **he's** ~ **to me (by 2 years), he's my** ~ **(by 2 years)** è più giovane di me (di 2 anni); **he's** ~ **to me** (seniority) è al di sotto di me, ho più anzianità di lui.
junior executive n giovane dirigente m.
junior high school n (US) scuola media (da

12 a 15 anni).

junior minister *n* (*Brit POL*) ministro che *non fa parte del Cabinet.*

junior partner *n* socio meno anziano.

junior school *n* (*Brit*) scuola elementare (*da 8 a 11 anni*).

junior sizes *npl* (*COMM*) taglie *fpl* per ragazzi.

juniper [jōō'nəpûr] *n*: ~ **berry** bacca di ginepro.

junk [jungk] *n* (*rubbish*) chincaglia; (*ship*) giunca ♦ *vt* disfarsi di.

junk dealer *n* rigattiere *m.*

junket [jung'kit] *n* (*CULIN*) giuncata; (*Brit col*: *also*: ~**ing**): **to go on a** ~, **go** ~**ing** fare bisboccia.

junk foods *npl* porcherie *fpl.*

junkie [jung'kē] *n* (*col*) drogato/a.

junk room *n* ripostiglio.

junk store *n* chincaglieria.

junkyard [jungk'yârd] *n* deposito di rottami; (*for cars*) cimitero delle macchine.

junta [hōōn'tə] *n* giunta.

Jupiter [jōō'pitûr] *n* (*planet*) Giove *m.*

jurisdiction [jōōrisdik'shən] *n* giurisdizione *f*; **it falls** *or* **comes within/outside our** ~ è/non è di nostra competenza.

jurisprudence [jōōrisprōōd'əns] *n* giurisprudenza.

juror [jōō'rûr] *n* giurato/a.

jury [jōō'rē] *n* giuria.

jury box *n* banco della giuria.

juryman [jōōr'ēmən] *n* = **juror.**

just [just] *a* giusto(a) ♦ *ad*: **he's** ~ **done it/left** lo ha appena fatto/è appena partito; ~ **as I expected** proprio come me lo aspettavo; ~ **right** proprio giusto; ~ **2 o'clock** le 2 precise; **we were** ~ **going** stavamo uscendo; **I was** ~ **about to phone** stavo proprio per telefonare; ~ **as he was leaving** proprio mentre se ne stava andando; **it was** ~ **before/enough/ here** era poco prima/appena assai/proprio qui; **it's** ~ **me** sono solo io; **it's** ~ **a mistake** non è che uno sbaglio; ~ **missed/caught** appena perso/preso; ~ **listen to this!** senta un po' questo!; ~ **ask someone the way** basta che tu chieda la strada a qualcuno; **it's** ~ **as good** è altrettanto buono; **it's** ~ **as well you didn't go** per fortuna non ci sei andato; **not** ~ **now** non proprio adesso; ~ **a minute!**, ~ **one moment!** un attimo!

justice [jus'tis] *n* giustizia; **this photo doesn't do you** ~ questa foto non ti fa giustizia.

Justice of the Peace (JP) *n* giudice *m* conciliatore.

justifiable [jus'tifiəbəl] *a* giustificabile.

justifiably [jus'təfiəblē] *ad* legittimamente, con ragione.

justification [justəfəkā'shən] *n* giustificazione *f*; (*TYP*) giustezza.

justify [jus'təfī] *vt* giustificare; (*TYP etc*) alli-

neare, giustificare; **to be justified in doing sth** avere ragione di fare qc.

justly [just'lē] *ad* giustamente.

justness [just'nis] *n* giustezza.

jut [jut] *vi* (*also*: ~ **out**) sporgersi.

jute [jōōt] *n* iuta.

juvenile [jōō'vənəl] *a* giovane, giovanile; (*court*) dei minorenni; (*books*) per ragazzi ♦ *n* giovane *m/f*, minorenne *m/f.*

juvenile delinquency *n* delinquenza minorile.

juvenile delinquent *n* delinquente *m/f* minorenne.

juxtapose [jukstəpōz'] *vt* giustapporre.

juxtaposition [jukstəpəzish'ən] *n* giustapposizione *f.*

K

K, k [kā] *n* (*letter*) K, k *f or m inv*; **K for King** ≈ K come Kursaal.

K [kā] *n abbr* (= *one thousand*) mille ♦ *abbr* (= *kilobyte*) K.

kaftan [kaf'tən] *n* caffettano.

Kalahari Desert [kâləhâr'ē dez'ûrt] *n* Deserto di Calahari.

kale [kāl] *n* cavolo verde.

kaleidoscope [kəlī'dəskōp] *n* caleidoscopio.

Kampala [kâmpâl'ə] *n* Kampala *f.*

Kampuchea [kampōōchē'ə] *n* Kampuchea *f.*

kangaroo [kanggərōō'] *n* canguro.

Kans. *abbr* (*US*) = *Kansas.*

kaput [kəpōōt'] *a* (*col*) kaputt *inv.*

karate [kərâ'tē] *n* karate *m.*

Kashmir [kazh'mēr] *n* Kashmir *m.*

kd *abbr* (*US*: = *knocked down*) da montare.

kebab [kəbâb'] *n* spiedino.

keel [kēl] *n* chiglia; **on an even** ~ (*fig*) in uno stato normale.

    keel over *vi* (*NAUT*) capovolgersi; (*person*) crollare.

keen [kēn] *a* (*interest, desire*) vivo(a); (*eye, intelligence*) acuto(a); (*competition*) serrato(a); (*edge*) affilato(a); (*eager*) entusiasta; **to be** ~ **on doing sth** avere una gran voglia di fare qc; **to be** ~ **on sth** essere appassionato(a) di qc; **to be** ~ **on sb** avere un debole per qn; **I'm not** ~ **on going** non mi va di andare.

keenly [kēn'lē] *ad* (*enthusiastically*) con entusiasmo; (*acutely*) vivamente; in modo penetrante.

keenness [kēn'nis] *n* (*eagerness*) entusiasmo.

keep [kēp] *vb* (*pt, pp* **kept** [kept]) *vt* tenere;

(*hold back*) trattenere; (*feed: one's family etc*) mantenere, sostentare; (*a promise*) mantenere; (*chickens, bees, pigs etc*) allevare ♦ *vi* (*food*) mantenersi; (*remain: in a certain state or place*) restare ♦ *n* (*of castle*) maschio; (*food etc*): **enough for his ~** abbastanza per vitto e alloggio; **to ~ doing sth** continuare a fare qc; fare qc di continuo; **to ~ sb from doing/sth from happening** impedire a qn di fare/che qc succeda; **to ~ sb busy/a place tidy** tenere qn occupato(a)/un luogo in ordine; **to ~ sb waiting** far aspettare qn; **to ~ an appointment** andare ad un appuntamento; **to ~ a record** *or* **note of sth** prendere nota di qc; **to ~ sth to o.s.** tenere qc per sé; **to ~ sth (back) from sb** celare qc a qn; **to ~ time** (*clock*) andar bene; **~ the change** tenga il resto; *see also* **keeps.**

keep away *vt*: **to ~ sth/sb away from sb** tenere qc/qn lontano da qn ♦ *vi*: **to ~ away (from)** stare lontano (da).

keep back *vt* (*crowds, tears, money*) trattenere ♦ *vi* tenersi indietro.

keep down *vt* (*control: prices, spending*) contenere, ridurre; (*retain: food*) trattenere, ritenere ♦ *vi* tenersi giù, stare giù.

keep in *vt* (*invalid, child*) tenere a casa ♦ *vi* (*col*): **to ~ in with sb** tenersi buono qn.

keep off *vt* (*dog, person*) tenere lontano da ♦ *vi* stare alla larga; **~ your hands off!** non toccare!, giù le mani!; **"~ off the grass"** "non calpestare l'erba".

keep on *vi* continuare; **to ~ on doing** continuare a fare.

keep out *vt* tener fuori ♦ *vi* restare fuori; **"~ out"** "vietato l'accesso".

keep up *vi* mantenersi ♦ *vt* continuare, mantenere; **to ~ up with** tener dietro a, andare di pari passo con; (*work etc*) farcela a seguire; **to ~ up with sb** (*in race etc*) mantenersi al passo con qn.

keeper [kē'pûr] *n* custode *m/f*, guardiano/a.

keep-fit [kēp'fit'] *n* (*Brit*) ginnastica.

keeping [kē'ping] *n* (*care*) custodia; **in ~ with** in armonia con; in accordo con.

keeps [kēps] *n*: **for ~** (*col*) per sempre.

keepsake [kēp'sāk] *n* ricordo.

keg [keg] *n* barilotto.

Ken. *abbr* (*US*) = *Kentucky*.

kennel [ken'əl] *n* canile *m*.

Kenya [ken'yə] *n* Kenia *m*.

Kenyan [ken'yən] *a*, *n* Keniano(a), Keniota (*m/f*).

kept [kept] *pt, pp of* **keep.**

kerb [kûrb] *n* (*Brit*) orlo del marciapiede.

kernel [kûr'nəl] *n* nocciolo.

kerosene [kär'əsēn] *n* cherosene *m*.

ketchup [kech'əp] *n* ketchup *m inv*.

kettle [ket'əl] *n* bollitore *m*.

kettle drum *n* timpano.

key [kē] *n* (*gen, MUS*) chiave *f*; (*of piano,*

typewriter) tasto; (*on map*) leg(g)enda ♦ *cpd* (*vital: position, industry etc*) chiave *inv*.

key in *vt* (*text*) introdurre da tastiera.

keyboard [kē'bôrd] *n* tastiera ♦ *vt* (*text*) comporre su tastiera.

keyed up [kēd up] *a*: **to be ~** essere agitato(a).

keyhole [kē'hōl] *n* buco della serratura.

keynote [kē'nōt] *n* (*MUS*) tonica; (*fig*) nota dominante.

keypad [kē'pad] *n* tastierino numerico.

key ring *n* portachiavi *m inv*.

keystroke [kē'strōk] *n* battuta (di un tasto).

kg *abbr* (= *kilogram*) Kg.

KGB *n abbr* KGB *m*.

khaki [kak'ē] *a*, *n* cachi (*m*).

kibbutz [kiboōts'] *n* kibbutz *m inv*.

kick [kik] *vt* calciare, dare calci a ♦ *vi* (*horse*) tirar calci ♦ *n* calcio; (*of rifle*) contraccolpo; (*thrill*): **he does it for ~s** lo fa giusto per il piacere di farlo.

kick around *vi* (*col*) essere in giro.

kick off *vi* (*SPORT*) dare il primo calcio.

kickoff [kik'ôf] *n* (*SPORT*) calcio d'inizio.

kick-start [kik'stárt] *n* (*Brit: also: ~er*) pedale *m* d'avviamento.

kid [kid] *n* ragazzino/a; (*animal, leather*) capretto ♦ *vi* (*col*) scherzare ♦ *vt* (*col*) prendere in giro.

kidnap [kid'nap] *vt* rapire, sequestrare.

kidnap(p)er [kid'napûr] *n* rapitore/trice.

kidnap(p)ing [kid'naping] *n* sequestro (di persona).

kidney [kid'nē] *n* (*ANAT*) rene *m*; (*CULIN*) rognone *m*.

kidney bean *n* fagiolo borlotto.

kidney machine *n* rene *m* artificiale.

Kilimanjaro [kiləmənjár'ō] *n*: **Mount ~** il monte Kilimangiaro.

kill [kil] *vt* uccidere, ammazzare; (*fig*) sopprimere; soppraffare; ammazzare ♦ *n* uccisione *f*; **to ~ time** ammazzare il tempo.

kill off *vt* sterminare; (*fig*) eliminare, soffocare.

killer [kil'ûr] *n* uccisore *m*, killer *m inv*; assassino/a.

killing [kil'ing] *n* assassinio; (*massacre*) strage *f*; (*col*): **to make a ~** fare un bel colpo.

killjoy [kil'joi] *n* guastafeste *m/f inv*.

kiln [kiln] *n* forno.

kilo [kē'lō] *n abbr* (= *kilogram*) chilo.

kilobyte [kil'əbīt] *n* kilobyte *m inv*.

kilogram, (Brit) kilogramme [kil'əgram] *n* chilogrammo.

kilometer, (Brit) kilometre [kil'əmētûr] *n* chilometro.

kilowatt [kil'əwât] *n* chilowatt *m inv*.

kilt [kilt] *n* gonnellino scozzese.

kilter [kil'tûr] *n*: **out of ~** fuori fase.

kimono [kimō'nō] *n* chimono.

kin [kin] *n see* **next of kin, kith.**

kind [kīnd] *a* gentile, buono(a) ♦ *n* sorta, specie *f*; (*species*) genere *m*; **to be two of a ~** essere molto simili; **would you be ~ enough to ...?, would you be so ~ as to ...?** sarebbe così gentile da ...?; **it's very ~ of you (to do)** è molto gentile da parte sua (di fare); **in ~** (*COMM*) in natura; (*fig*): **to repay sb in ~** ripagare qn della stessa moneta.

kindergarten [kin'dûrgârtən] *n* giardino d'infanzia.

kind-hearted [kīnd'hâr'tid] *a* di buon cuore.

kindle [kin'dəl] *vt* accendere, infiammare.

kindling [kind'ling] *n* frasche *fpl*, ramoscelli *mpl*.

kindly [kīnd'lē] *a* pieno(a) di bontà, benevolo(a) ♦ *ad* con bontà, gentilmente; **will you ~ ... vuole ... per favore; **he didn't take it ~** se l'è presa a male.

kindness [kīnd'nis] *n* bontà, gentilezza.

kindred [kin'drid] *a* imparentato(a); **~ spirit** spirito affine.

kinetic [kinet'ik] *a* cinetico(a).

king [king] *n* re *m inv*.

kingdom [king'dəm] *n* regno, reame *m*.

kingfisher [king'fishûr] *n* martin *m inv* pescatore.

kingpin [king'pin] *n* (*TECH*, *fig*) perno.

king-size(d) [king'sīz(d)] *a* super *inv*; gigante; (*cigarette*) extra lungo(a).

kink [kingk] *n* (*of rope*) attorcigliamento; (*in hair*) ondina; (*fig*) aberrazione *f*.

kinky [king'kē] *a* (*fig*) eccentrico(a); dai gusti particolari.

kinship [kin'ship] *n* parentela.

kinsman [kinz'mən] *n* parente *m*.

kinswoman [kinz'wo͞omən] *n* parente *f*.

kiosk [kēăsk'] *n* edicola, chiosco; (*Brit*: *also*: **telephone ~**) cabina (telefonica); (: *newspaper ~*) edicola.

kipper [kip'ûr] *n* aringa affumicata.

kiss [kis] *n* bacio ♦ *vt* baciare; **to ~ (each other)** baciarsi; **to ~ sb goodbye** congedarsi da qn con un bacio; **~ of life** (*Brit*) respirazione *f* bocca a bocca.

kit [kit] *n* equipaggiamento, corredo; (*set of tools etc*) attrezzi *mpl*; (*for assembly*) scatola di montaggio; **tool ~** cassetta *or* borsa degli attrezzi.

  kit out *vt* (*Brit*) attrezzare, equipaggiare.

kitbag [kit'bag] *n* zaino; sacco militare.

kitchen [kich'ən] *n* cucina.

kitchen garden *n* orto.

kitchen sink *n* acquaio.

kitchen unit *n* (*Brit*) elemento da cucina.

kitchenware [kich'ənwär] *n* stoviglie *fpl*; utensili *mpl* da cucina.

kite [kīt] *n* (*toy*) aquilone *m*; (*ZOOL*) nibbio.

kith [kith] *n*: **~ and kin** amici e parenti *mpl*.

kitten [kit'ən] *n* gattino/a, micino/a.

kitty [kit'ē] *n* (*money*) fondo comune.

KKK *n abbr* (*US*) = *Ku Klux Klan*.

Kleenex [klē'neks] ® *n* fazzolettino di carta.

kleptomaniac [kleptəmā'nēak] *n* cleptomane *m/f*.

km *abbr* (= *kilometer*) km.

km/h *abbr* (= *kilometers per hour*) km/h.

knack [nak] *n*: **to have a ~ (for doing)** avere una pratica (per fare); **to have the ~ of** avere l'abilità di; **there's a ~ to doing this** c'è un trucco per fare questo.

knapsack [nap'sak] *n* zaino, sacco da montagna.

knave [nāv] *n* (*CARDS*) fante *m*.

knead [nēd] *vt* impastare.

knee [nē] *n* ginocchio.

kneecap [nē'kap] *n* rotula.

knee-deep [nē'dēp] *a*: **the water was ~** l'acqua ci arrivava alle ginocchia.

kneel [nēl] *vi* (*pt*, *pp* **knelt** [nelt]) inginocchiarsi.

kneepad [nē'pad] *n* ginocchiera.

knell [nel] *n* rintocco.

knelt [nelt] *pt*, *pp of* **kneel**.

knew [no͞o] *pt of* **know**.

knickers [nik'ûrz] *npl* (*Brit*) mutandine *fpl*.

knick-knack [nik'nak] *n* ninnolo.

knife [nīf] *n* (*pl* **knives**) coltello ♦ *vt* accoltellare, dare una coltellata a; **~, fork and spoon** coperto.

knight [nīt] *n* cavaliere *m*; (*CHESS*) cavallo.

knighthood [nīt'ho͝od] *n* cavalleria; (*title*): **to get a ~** essere fatto cavaliere.

knit [nit] *vt* fare a maglia; (*fig*): **to ~ together** unire ♦ *vi* lavorare a maglia; (*broken bones*) saldarsi.

knitted [nit'id] *a* lavorato(a) a maglia.

knitting [nit'ing] *n* lavoro a maglia.

knitting machine *n* macchina per maglieria.

knitting needle *n* ferro (da calza).

knitting pattern *n* modello (per maglia).

knitwear [nit'wär] *n* maglieria.

knives [nīvz] *npl of* **knife**.

knob [nâb] *n* bottone *m*; manopola; (*Brit*): **~ of butter** una noce di burro.

knobby [nâb'ē] *a* (*US*: *wood*, *surface*) nodoso(a); (: *knee*) ossuto(a).

knobbly [nâb'lē] *a* (*Brit*) = **knobby**.

knock [nak] *vt* (*strike*) colpire; urtare; (*fig*: *col*) criticare ♦ *vi* (*engine*) battere; (*at door etc*): **to ~ at/on** bussare a ♦ *n* bussata; colpo, botta; **he ~ed at the door** ha bussato alla porta; **to ~ a nail into sth** conficcare un chiodo in qc.

  knock down *vt* abbattere; (*pedestrian*) investire; (*price*) abbassare.

  knock off *vi* (*col*: *finish*) smettere (di lavorare) ♦ *vt* (*strike off*) far cadere; (*col*: *steal*) sgraffignare, grattare; **to ~ off $10** fare uno sconto di 10 dollari.

  knock out *vt* stendere; (*BOXING*) mettere K.O., mettere fuori combattimento.

  knock over *vt* (*object*) far cadere; (*pe-*

destrian) investire.

knockdown |nåk'doun| a (*price*) fortemente scontato(a); ~ **furniture** (*US*) mobili scomponibili.

knocker |nåk'ûr| n (*on door*) battente *m*.

knock-for-knock |nåk'fûrnåk'| a (*Brit*): ~ **agreement** *accordo fra compagnie di assicurazione per il risarcimento dei rispettivi clienti*.

knocking |nåk'ing| n colpi *mpl*.

knock-kneed |nåk'nēd| a che ha le gambe ad x.

knock-on effect |nåk'ån ifckt'| n: **to have a ~ on sth** travolgere completamente qc.

knockout |nåk'out| n (*BOXING*) knock out *m inv*.

knot |nåt| n nodo ♦ *vt* annodare; **to tie a ~** fare un nodo.

knotty |nåt'ē| a (*fig*) spinoso(a).

know |nō| *vt* (*pt* **knew,** *pp* **known** |nōō, nōn|) sapere; (*person, author, place*) conoscere ♦ *vi* sapere; **to ~ that ...** sapere che ...; **to ~ how to do** sapere fare; **to get to ~ sth** venire a sapere qc; **I ~ nothing about it** non ne so niente; **I don't ~ him** non lo conosco; **to ~ right from wrong** distinguere il bene dal male; **as far as I ~ ...** che io sappia ..., per quanto io ne sappia ...; **yes, I ~** sì, lo so; **I don't ~** non lo so.

know-all |nō'ôl| n (*Brit pej*) = **know-it-all**.

know-how |nō'hou| n tecnica; pratica.

knowing |nō'ing| a (*look etc*) d'intesa.

knowingly |nō'inglē| ad consapevolmente; di complicità.

know-it-all |nō'itôl| n (*US pej*) sapientone/a.

knowledge |nål'ij| n consapevolezza; (*learning*) conoscenza, sapere *m*; **to have no ~ of** ignorare, non sapere; **not to my ~** che io sappia, no; **to have a working ~ of Italian** avere una conoscenza pratica dell'italiano; **without my ~** a mia insaputa; **it is common ~ that ...** è risaputo che ...; **it has come to my ~ that ...** sono venuto a sapere che ....

knowledgeable |nål'ijəbəl| a ben informato(a).

known |nōn| *pp of* **know** ♦ a (*thief, facts*) noto(a); (*expert*) riconosciuto(a).

knuckle |nuk'əl| n nocca.

knuckle under *vi* (*col*) cedere.

knuckle-duster |nuk'əldustûr| n tirapugni *m inv*.

knucklehead |nuk'clhcd| n (*US*) sciocco/a.

KO abbr (= *knock out*) n K.O. *m* ♦ *vt* mettere K.O.

koala |kōål'ə| n (*also:* **~ bear**) koala *m inv*.

kook |kōōk| n (*US col*) svitato/a.

Koran |kôrán'| n Corano.

Korea |kôrē'ə| n Corea; **North/South ~** Corea del Nord/Sud.

Korean |kôrē'ən| a, n coreano(a).

kosher |kō'shûr| a kasher *inv*.

kowtow |kou'tou| *vi*: **to ~ to sb** mostrarsi ossequioso(a) verso qn.

Kremlin |krem'lin| n: **the ~** il Cremlino.

KS abbr (*US MAIL*) = *Kansas*.

Kuala Lumpur |kōōå'lə lōōm'pōōr| n Kuala Lumpur *f*.

kudos |kyōō'dōs| n gloria, fama.

Kuwait |kōōwāt'| n Kuwait *m*.

Kuwaiti |kōōåt'ē| a, n kuwaitiano(a).

kw abbr (= *kilowatt*) kw.

KY abbr (*US MAIL*) = *Kentucky*.

L

L, l |(c)l| n (*letter*) L, l *f or m inv*; **L for Love** ≈ L come Livorno.

L abbr (= *lake*) l; (= *large*) taglia grande; (= *left*) sin.; (*Brit AUT*) = **learner**.

l abbr (= *liter*) l.

LA n abbr (*US*) = *Los Angeles* ♦ abbr (*US MAIL*) = *Louisiana*.

Lab. abbr (*Canada*) = *Labrador*.

lab |lab| n abbr (= *laboratory*) laboratorio.

label |lā'bəl| n etichetta, cartellino; (*brand: of record*) casa ♦ *vt* etichettare; classificare.

labor |lā'bûr| (*US*) n (*task*) lavoro; (*workmen*) manodopera; (*MED*) travaglio del parto, doglie *fpl* ♦ *vi*: **to ~ (at)** lavorare duro(a); **to be in ~** (*MED*) avere le doglie.

laboratory |lab'rətôrē| n laboratorio.

labor camp n campo dei lavori forzati.

labor cost n costo del lavoro.

Labor Day n (*US*) festa del lavoro.

labor dispute n conflitto tra lavoratori e datori di lavoro.

labored |lā'bûrd| a (*breathing*) affaticato(a), affannoso(a); (*style*) elaborato(a), pesante.

laborer |lā'bûrûr| n manovale *m*; (*on farm*) lavoratore *m* agricolo.

labor force n manodopera.

labor-intensive |lā'bûrintcnsiv| a che assorbe molta manodopera.

laborious |ləbôr'ēəs| a laborioso(a).

labor market n mercato del lavoro.

labor pains *npl* doglie *fpl*.

labor relations *npl* relazioni *fpl* industriali.

labor-saving |lā'bûrsā'ving| a che fa risparmiare fatica or lavoro.

labor union n (*US*) sindacato.

labor unrest n agitazioni *fpl* degli operai.

Labour |lā'bûr| n (*Brit POL*: *also:* **the ~ Party**) il partito laburista, i laburisti.

labour |lā'bûr| *etc* (*Brit*) = **labor** *etc*.

labyrinth |lab'ûrinth| n labirinto.

lace [lās] *n* merletto, pizzo; (*of shoe etc*) laccio ♦ *vt* (*shoe*) allacciare; (*drink: fortify with spirits*) correggere.

lacemaking [lās'māking] *n* fabbricazione *f* dei pizzi *or* dei merletti.

laceration [lasərā'shən] *n* lacerazione *f*.

lace-up [lās'up] *a* (*shoes etc*) con i lacci, con le stringhe.

lack [lak] *n* mancanza, scarsità ♦ *vt* mancare di; **through** *or* **for** ~ **of** per mancanza di; **to be** ~**ing** mancare; **to be** ~**ing in** mancare di.

lackadaisical [lakədā'zikəl] *a* disinteressato(a), noncurante.

lackey [lak'ē] *n* (*also fig*) lacchè *m inv*.

lackluster, (*Brit*) **lacklustre** [lak'lustûr] *a* (*surface*) opaco(a); (*style*) scialbo(a); (*eyes*) spento(a).

laconic [ləkân'ik] *a* laconico(a).

lacquer [lak'ûr] *n* lacca; **hair** ~ lacca per (i) capelli.

lacy [lā'sē] *a* (*like lace*) che sembra un pizzo.

lad [lad] *n* ragazzo, giovanotto; (*Brit: in stable etc*) mozzo *or* garzone *m* di stalla.

ladder [lad'ûr] *n* scala; (*Brit: in tights*) smagliatura ♦ *vt* (*Brit*) smagliare ♦ *vi* (*Brit*) smagliarsi.

laden [lad'ən] *a*: ~ (**with**) carico(a) *or* caricato(a) (di); **fully** ~ (*truck*, *ship*) a pieno carico.

ladle [lā'dəl] *n* mestolo.

lady [lā'dē] *n* signora; **L**~ **Smith** lady Smith; **the ladies' (toilets)** i gabinetti per signore; **a** ~ **doctor** una dottoressa.

ladybird [lā'dēbûrd] *n* (*Brit*) = **ladybug**.

ladybug [lā'debug] *n* (*US*) coccinella.

lady-in-waiting [lā'dēinwā'ting] *n* dama di compagnia.

ladykiller [lā'dēkilûr] *n* dongiovanni *m inv*.

ladylike [lā'dēlīk] *a* da signora, distinto(a).

ladyship [lā'dēship] *n*: **your L**~ signora contessa *etc*.

lag [lag] *n* = **time** ~ ♦ *vi* (*also:* ~ **behind**) trascinarsi ♦ *vt* (*pipes*) rivestire di materiale isolante.

lager [lâ'gûr] *n* lager *m inv*.

lagging [lag'ing] *n* rivestimento di materiale isolante.

lagoon [ləgōōn'] *n* laguna.

Lagos [lâg'ōs] *n* Lagos *f*.

laid [lād] *pt*, *pp of* **lay**.

laid-back [lād'bak'] *a* (*col*) rilassato(a).

lain [lān] *pp of* **lie**.

lair [lär] *n* covo, tana.

laissez-faire [lesāfär'] *n* liberismo.

laity [lā'itē] *n* laici *mpl*.

lake [lāk] *n* lago.

lamb [lam] *n* agnello.

lamb chop *n* cotoletta d'agnello.

lambskin [lam'skin] *n* (pelle *f* d')agnello.

lambswool [lamz'wŏōl] *n* lamb's wool *m*.

lame [lām] *a* zoppo(a); ~ **duck** (*fig: person*) persona inetta; (*: firm*) azienda traballante.

lamely [lām'lē] *ad* (*fig*) in modo poco convincente.

lament [ləment'] *n* lamento ♦ *vt* lamentare, piangere.

lamentable [ləmen'təbəl] *a* doloroso(a); deplorevole.

laminated [lam'ənātid] *a* laminato(a).

lamp [lamp] *n* lampada.

lamplight [lamp'līt] *n*: **by** ~ a lume della lampada.

lampoon [lampōōn'] *n* satira.

lamppost [lamp'pōst] *n* lampione *m*.

lampshade [lamp'shād] *n* paralume *m*.

lance [lans] *n* lancia ♦ *vt* (*MED*) incidere.

lance corporal *n* (*Brit*) caporale *m*.

lancet [lan'sit] *n* (*MED*) bisturi *m inv*.

Lancs [langks] *abbr* (*Brit*) = *Lancashire*.

land [land] *n* (*as opposed to sea*) terra (ferma); (*country*) paese *m*; (*soil*) terreno; (*estate*) terreni *mpl*, terre *fpl* ♦ *vi* (*from ship*) sbarcare; (*AVIAT*) atterrare; (*fig: fall*) cadere ♦ *vt* (*obtain*) acchiappare; (*passengers*) sbarcare; (*goods*) scaricare; **to go/travel by** ~ andare/viaggiare per via di terra; **to own** ~ possedere dei terreni, avere delle proprietà (terriere); **to** ~ **on one's feet** cadere in piedi; (*fig: to be lucky*) cascar bene.

land up *vi* andare a finire.

landing [lan'ding] *n* (*from ship*) sbarco; (*AVIAT*) atterraggio; (*of staircase*) pianerottolo.

landing card *n* carta di sbarco.

landing craft *n* mezzo da sbarco.

landing gear *n* (*AVIAT*) carrello d'atterraggio.

landing stage *n* (*Brit*) pontile *m* da sbarco.

landing strip *n* pista d'atterraggio.

landlady [land'lādē] *n* padrona *or* proprietaria di casa.

landlocked [land'lâkt] *a* senza sbocco sul mare.

landlord [land'lôrd] *n* padrone *m or* proprietario di casa; (*of pub etc*) oste *m*.

landlubber [land'lubûr] *n* marinaio d'acqua dolce.

landmark [land'mârk] *n* punto di riferimento; (*fig*) pietra miliare.

landowner [land'ōnûr] *n* proprietario(a) terriero(a).

landscape [land'skāp] *n* paesaggio.

landscape architect, **landscape gardener** *n* paesaggista *m/f*.

landscape painting *n* (*ART*) paesaggistica.

landslide [land'slīd] *n* (*GEO*) frana; (*fig: POL*) valanga.

lane [lān] *n* (*in country*) viottolo; (*in town*) stradetta; (*AUT, in race*) corsia; **shipping** ~ rotta (marittima).

language [lang'gwij] *n* lingua; (*way one speaks*) linguaggio; **bad** ~ linguaggio volgare.

language laboratory *n* laboratorio linguistico.

languid [lang'gwid] *a* languente; languido(a).

languish [lang'gwish] *vi* languire.

lank [langk] *a* (*hair*) liscio(a) e opaco(a).

lanky [lang'kē] *a* allampanato(a).

lanolin(e) [lən'əlin] *n* lanolina.

lantern [lan'tûrn] *n* lanterna.

Laos [lâ'ōs] *n* Laos *m*.

lap [lap] *n* (*of track*) giro; (*of body*): **in** or **on one's** ~ in grembo ♦ *vt* (*also*: ~ **up**) papparsi, leccare ♦ *vi* (*waves*) sciabordare.

lap up *vt* (*fig*: *compliments, attention*) bearsi di.

La Paz [lâ pâs'] *n* La Paz *f*.

lapdog [lap'dôg] *n* cane *m* da grembo.

lapel [ləpel'] *n* risvolto.

Lapland [lap'lənd] *n* Lapponia.

Lapp [lap] *a* lappone ♦ *n* lappone *m/f*; (*LING*) lappone *m*.

lapse [laps] *n* lapsus *m inv*; (*longer*) caduta; (*fault*) mancanza; (*in behaviour*) scorrettezza ♦ *vi* (*law, act*) cadere; (*ticket, passport*) scadere; **to** ~ **into bad habits** pigliare cattive abitudini; ~ **of time** spazio di tempo; **a** ~ **of memory** un vuoto di memoria.

laptop [lap'tâp] *n* (*also*: ~ **computer**) computer *m inv* portatile.

larceny [lâr'sənē] *n* furto.

lard [lârd] *n* lardo.

larder [lâr'dûr] *n* dispensa.

large [lârj] *a* grande; (*person, animal*) grosso(a) ♦ *ad*: **by and** ~ generalmente; **at** ~ (*free*) in libertà; (*generally*) in generale; **nell'insieme; to make** ~**r** ingrandire; **a** ~ **number of people** molta gente; **on a** ~ **scale** su vasta scala.

largely [lârj'lē] *ad* in gran parte.

large-scale [lârj'skāl] *a* (*map, drawing etc*) in grande scala; (*reforms, business activities*) su vasta scala.

lark [lârk] *n* (*bird*) allodola; (*joke*) scherzo, gioco.

lark about *vi* fare lo stupido.

larva, *pl* **larvae** [lâr'va, -vā] *n* larva.

laryngitis [larənjī'tis] *n* laringite *f*.

larynx [lar'ingks] *n* laringe *f*.

lascivious [ləsiv'ēəs] *a* lascivo(a).

laser [lā'zûr] *n* laser *m*.

laser beam [lā'zûr bēm] *n* raggio *m* laser *inv*.

laser printer *n* stampante *f* laser *inv*.

lash [lash] *n* frustata; (*also*: **eye**~) ciglio ♦ *vt* frustare; (*tie*) legare.

lash down *vt* assicurare (con corde) ♦ *vi* (*rain*) scrosciare.

lash out *vi*: **to** ~ **out (at** or **against sb/sth)** attaccare violentemente (qn/qc); **to** ~ **out (on sth)** (*col*: *spend*) spendere un sacco di

soldi (per qc).

lashing [lash'ing] *n* (*beating*) frustata, sferzata.

lass [las] *n* ragazza.

lasso [las'ō] *n* laccio ♦ *vt* acchiappare con il laccio.

last [last] *a* ultimo(a); (*week, month, year*) scorso(a), passato(a) ♦ *ad* per ultimo ♦ *vi* durare; ~ **week** la settimana scorsa; ~ **night** ieri sera, la notte scorsa; **at** ~ finalmente, alla fine; **next to (the)** ~, ~ **but one** penultimo(a); **the** ~ **time** l'ultima volta; **it** ~**s (for) 2 hours** dura 2 ore.

last-ditch [last'dich'] *a* ultimo(a) e disperato(a).

lasting [las'ting] *a* durevole.

lastly [last'lē] *ad* infine, per finire, per ultimo.

last-minute [last'min'it] *a* fatto(a) (*or* preso(a) *etc*) all'ultimo momento.

latch [lach] *n* serratura a scatto.

latch on to *vt fus* (*cling to*: *person*) attaccarsi a, appiccicarsi a; (: *idea*) afferrare, capire.

latchkey [lach'kē] *n* chiave *f* di casa.

late [lāt] *a* (*not on time*) in ritardo; (*far on in day etc*) tardi *inv*; tardo(a); (*recent*) recente, ultimo(a); (*former*) ex; (*dead*) defunto(a) ♦ *ad* tardi; (*behind time, schedule*) in ritardo; **to be (10 minutes)** ~ essere in ritardo (di 10 minuti); **to work** ~ lavorare fino a tardi; ~ **in life** in età avanzata; **of** ~ di recente; **in the** ~ **afternoon** nel tardo pomeriggio; **in** ~ **May** verso la fine di maggio; **the** ~ **Mr X** il defunto Signor X.

latecomer [lāt'kumûr] *n* ritardatario/a.

lately [lāt'lē] *ad* recentemente.

lateness [lāt'nis] *n* (*of person*) ritardo; (*of event*) tardezza, ora tarda.

latent [lā'tənt] *a* latente; ~ **defect** vizio occulto.

later [lā'tûr] *a* (*date etc*) posteriore; (*version etc*) successivo(a) ♦ *ad* più tardi; ~ **on to-day** oggi più tardi.

lateral [lat'ûrəl] *a* laterale.

latest [lā'tist] *a* ultimo(a), più recente; **at the** ~ al più tardi; **the** ~ **news** le ultime notizie.

latex [lā'teks] *n* latice *m*.

lath, *pl* ~**s** [lath, laths] *n* assicella.

lathe [lāth] *n* tornio.

lather [lath'ûr] *n* schiuma di sapone ♦ *vt* insaponare ♦ *vi* far schiuma.

Latin [lat'in] *n* latino ♦ *a* latino(a).

Latin America *n* America Latina.

Latin American *a* sudamericano(a).

latitude [lat'ətōōd] *n* latitudine *f*; (*fig*: *freedom*) libertà d'azione.

latrine [lətrēn'] *n* latrina.

latter [lat'ûr] *a* secondo(a); più recente ♦ *n*: **the** ~ quest'ultimo, il secondo.

latterly [lat'ûrlē] *ad* recentemente, negli ultimi tempi.

lattice [lat'is] *n* traliccio; graticolato.
lattice window [lat'is win'dō] *n* finestra con vetrata a losanghe.
Latvia [lat'vēə] *n* Lettonia.
laudable [lô'dəbəl] *a* lodevole.
laudatory [lô'dətôrē] *a* elogiativo(a).
laugh [laf] *n* risata ♦ *vi* ridere.
　laugh at *vt fus* (*misfortune etc*) ridere di; **I ~ed at his joke** la sua barzelletta mi fece ridere.
　laugh off *vt* prendere alla leggera.
laughable [laf'əbəl] *a* ridicolo(a).
laughing [laf'ing] *a* (*face*) ridente; **this is no ~ matter** non è una cosa da ridere.
laughing gas *n* gas *m* esilarante.
laughing stock *n*: **the ~ of** lo zimbello di.
laughter [laf'tûr] *n* riso; risate *fpl*.
launch [lônch] *n* (*of rocket, product etc*) lancio; (*of new ship*) varo; (*boat*) scialuppa; (*also:* **motor ~**) lancia ♦ *vt* (*rocket, product*) lanciare; (*ship, plan*) varare.
　launch out *vi*: **to ~ out (into)** lanciarsi (in).
launching [lôn'ching] *n* lancio; varo.
launch(ing) pad *n* rampa di lancio.
launder [lôn'dûr] *vt* lavare e stirare.
launderette [lôndəret'] *n* (*Brit*) = **laundromat**.
laundromat [lôn'drəmat] *n* (*US*) lavanderia (automatica).
laundry [lôn'drē] *n* lavanderia; (*clothes*) biancheria; **to do the ~** fare il bucato.
laureate [lôr'rēit] *a see* **poet laureate**.
laurel [lôr'əl] *n* lauro, alloro; **to rest on one's ~s** riposare *or* dormire sugli allori.
Lausanne [lōzan'] *n* Losanna.
lava [lâv'ə] *n* lava.
lavatory [lav'ətôrē] *n* gabinetto.
lavender [lav'əndûr] *n* lavanda.
lavish [lav'ish] *a* abbondante; sontuoso(a); (*giving freely*): **~ with** prodigo(a) di, largo(a) in ♦ *vt*: **to ~ sth on sb/sth** profondere qc a qn/qc.
lavishly [lav'ishlē] *ad* (*give, spend*) generosamente; (*furnished*) sontuosamente, lussuosamente.
law [lô] *n* legge *f*; **against the ~** contro la legge; **to study ~** studiare diritto; **civil/criminal ~** diritto civile/penale.
law-abiding [lô'əbīding] *a* ubbidiente alla legge.
law and order *n* l'ordine *m* pubblico.
lawbreaker [lô'brākûr] *n* violatore/trice della legge.
law court *n* tribunale *m*, corte *f* di giustizia.
lawful [lô'fəl] *a* legale.
lawfully [lô'fəlē] *ad* legalmente.
lawless [lô'lis] *a* senza legge; illegale.
lawmaker [lô'mākûr] *n* legislatore *m*.
lawn [lôn] *n* tappeto erboso.
lawnmower [lôn'mōûr] *n* tosaerba *m or f inv*.

lawn tennis *n* tennis *m* su prato.
law school *n* facoltà *f inv* di legge.
law student [lô' stōōd'ənt] *n* studente/essa di legge.
lawsuit [lô'sōōt] *n* processo, causa; **to bring a ~ against** intentare causa a.
lawyer [lô'yûr] *n* (*consultant, with company*) giurista *m/f*; (*for sales, wills etc*) ≈ notaio; (*partner, in court*) ≈ avvocato/essa.
lax [laks] *a* (*conduct*) rilassato(a); (*person: careless*) negligente; (: *on discipline*) permissivo(a).
laxative [lak'sətiv] *n* lassativo.
laxity [lak'sitē] *n* rilassatezza; negligenza.
lay [lā] *pt of* **lie** ♦ *a* laico(a); secolare ♦ *vt* (*pt, pp* **laid** [lād]) posare, mettere; (*eggs*) fare; (*trap*) tendere; (*plans*) fare, elaborare; **to ~ the table** (*Brit*) apparecchiare la tavola; **to ~ the facts/one's proposals before sb** presentare i fatti/delle proposte a qn; **to get laid** (*col!*) scopare (!); essere scopato(a) (!).
　lay aside, lay by *vt* mettere da parte.
　lay down *vt* mettere giù; **to ~ down the law** (*fig*) dettar legge.
　lay in *vt* fare una scorta di.
　lay into *vt fus* (*col: attack, scold*) aggredire.
　lay off *vt* (*workers*) licenziare.
　lay on *vt* (*water, gas*) installare, mettere; (*provide: meal etc*) fornire; (*paint*) applicare.
　lay out *vt* (*design*) progettare; (*display*) presentare; (*spend*) sborsare.
　lay up *vt* (*to store*) accumulare; (*ship*) mettere in disarmo; (*subj: illness*) costringere a letto.
layabout [lā'əbout] *n* (*Brit*) sfaccendato/a, fannullone/a.
lay-by [lā'bī] *n* (*Brit*) piazzola (di sosta).
lay days *npl* (*NAUT*) stallie *fpl*.
layer [lā'ûr] *n* strato.
layette [lāet'] *n* corredino (per neonato).
layman [lā'mən] *n* laico; profano.
layoff [lā'ôf] *n* sospensione *f*, licenziamento.
layout [lā'out] *n* lay-out *m inv*, disposizione *f*; (*PRESS*) impaginazione *f*.
layover [lā'ōvûr] *n* (*US*) scalo.
laze [lāz] *vi* oziare.
laziness [lā'zēnis] *n* pigrizia.
lazy [lā'zē] *a* pigro(a).
LB *abbr* (*Canada*) = Labrador.
lb. *abbr* (= *libra: pound*) lb.
LC *n abbr* (*US*) = Library of Congress.
lc *abbr* (*TYP*: = *lower case*) minuscolo.
L/C *abbr* = **letter of credit**.
LCD *n abbr see* **liquid crystal display**.
LDS *n abbr* (= *Latter-day Saint(s)*) Chiesa di Gesù Cristo dei Santi degli Ultimi Giorni.
lead [lēd] *n* (*front position*) posizione *f* di testa; (*distance, time ahead*) vantaggio; (*clue*) indizio; (*ELEC*) filo (elettrico); (*for dog*)

guinzaglio; (*THEATER*) parte *f* principale; (*metal*) piombo; (*in pencil*) mina ♦ *vb* (*pt, pp* **led** [led]) *vt* menare, guidare, condurre; (*induce*) indurre; (*be leader of*) essere a capo di; (: *orchestra*: *US*) dirigere; (: *Brit*) essere il primo violino di; (*SPORT*) essere in testa a ♦ *vi* condurre, essere in testa; **to be in the** ~ (*SPORT*) essere in testa; **to take the** ~ (*SPORT*) passare in testa; (*fig*) prendere l'iniziativa; **to** ~ **to** menare a; condurre a; portare a; **to** ~ **astray** sviare; **to** ~ **sb to believe that** ... far credere a qn che ...; **to** ~ **sb to do sth** portare qn a fare qc.

lead away *vt* condurre via.

lead back *vt* riportare, ricondurre.

lead off *vt* portare ♦ *vi* partire da.

lead on *vt* (*tease*) tenere sulla corda.

lead on to *vt* (*induce*) portare a.

lead up to *vt fus* portare a; (*fig*) preparare la strada per.

leaded [led'id] *a* (*gas*) con piombo; ~ **windows** vetrate *fpl* (artistiche).

leaden [led'ən] *a* di piombo.

leader [lē'dûr] *n* capo; leader *m inv*; (*of orchestra*: *US*) direttore *m* d'orchestra; (: *Brit*) primo violino; (*Brit: in newspaper*) editoriale *m*; **they are ~s in their field** (*fig*) sono all'avanguardia nel loro campo.

leadership [lē'dûrship] *n* direzione *f*; **under the** ~ **of** ... sotto la direzione *or* guida di ...; **qualities of** ~ qualità *fpl* di un capo.

lead-free [ledfrē'] *a* senza piombo.

leading [lē'ding] *a* primo(a); principale; **a** ~ **question** una domanda tendenziosa; ~ **role** ruolo principale.

leading lady *n* (*THEATER*) prima attrice.

leading light *n* (*person*) personaggio di primo piano.

leading man *n* (*THEATER*) primo attore.

lead pencil [led pen'səl] *n* matita con la mina di grafite.

lead poisoning [led' poi'zəning] *n* saturnismo.

lead time *n* (*COMM*) tempo di consegna.

lead weight [led wāt] *n* piombino, piombo.

leaf [lēf] *n* (*pl* **leaves**) foglia; (*of table*) ribalta; **to turn over a new** ~ (*fig*) cambiar vita; **to take a** ~ **out of sb's book** (*fig*) prendere esempio da qn.

leaf through *vt* (*book*) sfogliare.

leaflet [lēf'lit] *n* dépliant *m inv*; (*POL, REL*) volantino.

leafy [lē'fē] *a* ricco(a) di foglie.

league [lēg] *n* lega; (*SPORT*) campionato; **to be in** ~ **with** essere in lega con.

leak [lēk] *n* (*out*) fuga; (*in*) infiltrazione *f*; (*fig: of information*) fuga di notizie ♦ *vi* (*roof, bucket*) perdere; (*liquid*) uscire; (*shoes*) lasciar passare l'acqua ♦ *vt* (*liquid*) spandere; (*information*) divulgare.

leak out *vi* uscire; (*information*) trapelare.

leakage [lē'kij] *n* (*of water, gas etc*) perdita.

leaky [lē'kē] *a* (*pipe, bucket, roof*) che perde; (*shoe*) che lascia passare l'acqua; (*boat*) che fa acqua.

lean [lēn] *a* magro(a) ♦ *n* (*of meat*) carne *f* magra ♦ *vb* (*pt, pp* **leaned** *or* **leant** [lent]) *vt*: **to** ~ **sth on** appoggiare qc su ♦ *vi* (*slope*) pendere; (*rest*): **to** ~ **against** appoggiarsi contro; essere appoggiato(a) a; **to** ~ **on** appoggiarsi a.

lean back *vi* sporgersi indietro.

lean forward *vi* sporgersi in avanti.

lean out *vi*: **to** ~ **out (of)** sporgersi (da).

lean over *vi* inclinarsi.

leaning [lē'ning] *n*: ~ **(towards)** propensione *f* (per) ♦ *a* inclinato(a), pendente; **the** ~ **Tower of Pisa** la torre (pendente) di Pisa.

leant [lent] *pt, pp of* **lean**.

lean-to [lēn'tōō] *n* (*roof*) tettoia; (*building*) edificio con tetto appoggiato ad altro edificio.

leap [lēp] *n* salto, balzo ♦ *vi* (*pt, pp* **leaped** *or* **leapt** [lept]) saltare, balzare; **to** ~ **at an offer** afferrare al volo una proposta.

leap up *vi* (*person*) alzarsi d'un balzo, balzare su.

leapfrog [lēp'frâg] *n* gioco della cavallina ♦ *vi*: **to** ~ **over sb/sth** saltare (alla cavallina) qn/qc.

leapt [lept] *pt, pp of* **leap**.

leap year *n* anno bisestile.

learn, *pt, pp* **learned** *or* **learnt** [lûrn, -t] *vt, vi* imparare; **to** ~ **how to do sth** imparare a fare qc; **to** ~ **that** ... apprendere che ...; **to** ~ **about sth** (*SCOL*) studiare qc; (*hear*) apprendere qc; **we were sorry to** ~ **that it was closing down** la notizia della chiusura ci ha fatto dispiacere.

learned [lûr'nid] *a* erudito(a), dotto(a).

learner [lûr'nûr] *n* principiante *m/f*; apprendista *m/f*.

learning [lûr'ning] *n* erudizione *f*, sapienza.

learnt [lûrnt] *pt, pp of* **learn**.

lease [lēs] *n* contratto d'affitto ♦ *vt* affittare; **on** ~ in affitto.

lease back *vt* (*Brit*) effettuare un lease-back *inv*.

leaseback [lēs'bak] *n* (*Brit*) lease-back *m inv*.

leasehold [lēs'hōld] *n* (*contract*) contratto di affitto (*a lungo termine con responsabilità simili a quelle di un proprietario*) ♦ *a* in affitto.

leash [lēsh] *n* guinzaglio.

least [lēst] *a*: **the** ~ + *noun* il(la) più piccolo(a), il(la) minimo(a); (*smallest amount of*) il(la) meno ♦ *ad*: **the** ~ + *adjective*: **the** ~ **beautiful girl** la ragazza meno bella; **the** ~ **expensive** il(la) meno caro(a); **I have the** ~ **money** ho meno denaro di tutti; **at** ~ almeno; **not in the** ~ affatto, per nulla.

leather [leth'ûr] *n* (*soft*) pelle *f*; (*hard*) cuoio ♦ *cpd* di *or* in pelle; di cuoio; ~ **goods** pelletteria, pelletterie *fpl*.

leave [lēv] *vb* (*pt, pp* **left** [left]) *vt* lasciare;

(*go away from*) partire da ♦ *vi* partire, andarsene ♦ *n* (*time off*) congedo; (*MIL.*, *also*: *consent*) licenza; **to be left** rimanere; **there's some milk left over** c'è rimasto del latte; **to take one's ~ of** congedarsi di; **he's already left for the airport** è già uscito per andare all'aeroporto; **to ~ school** finire la scuola; **~ it to me!** ci penso io!, lascia fare a me!; **on ~ in** congedo; **on ~ of absence** in permesso; (*public employee*) in congedo; (*MIL*) in licenza.

leave behind *vt* (*also fig*) lasciare indietro; (*forget*) dimenticare.

leave off *vt* non mettere.

leave on *vt* lasciare su; (*light*, *stove*) lasciare acceso(a).

leave out *vt* omettere, tralasciare.

leaves [lēvz] *npl of* **leaf**.

leavetaking [lēv'tāking] *n* commiato, addio.

Lebanese [lcbənēz'] *a*, *n* (*pl inv*) libanese (*m/f*).

Lebanon [lcb'ənən] *n* Libano.

lecherous [lcch'ûrəs] *a* lascivo(a), lubrico(a).

lectern [lck'tûrn] *n* leggio.

lecture [lck'chûr] *n* conferenza; (*SCOL*) lezione *f* ♦ *vi* fare conferenze; fare lezioni; (*reprove*) rimproverare, fare una ramanzina a; **to ~ on** fare una conferenza su; **to give a ~ (on)** fare una conferenza (su); fare lezione (su).

lecture hall *n* aula magna.

lecturer [lck'chûrûr] *n* (*speaker*) conferenziere/a; (*Brit*: *at university*) professore/essa, docente *m/f*.

LED *n abbr* (*ELEC*: = *light-emitting diode*) diodo a emissione luminosa.

led [lcd] *pt*, *pp of* **lead**.

ledge [lcj] *n* (*of window*) davanzale *m*; (*on wall etc*) sporgenza; (*of mountain*) cornice *f*, cengia.

ledger [lcj'ûr] *n* libro maestro, registro.

lee [lē] *n* lato sottovento; **in the ~ of** a ridosso di, al riparo di.

leech [lēch] *n* sanguisuga.

leek [lēk] *n* porro.

leer [lēr] *vi*: **to ~ at sb** gettare uno sguardo voglioso (*or* maligno) su qn.

leeward [lē'wûrd] *a* sottovento *inv* ♦ *n* lato sottovento; **to ~** sottovento.

leeway [lē'wā] *n* (*fig*): **to have some ~** avere una certa libertà di agire.

left [lcft] *pt*, *pp of* **leave** ♦ *a* sinistro(a) ♦ *ad* a sinistra ♦ *n* sinistra; **on the ~**, **to the ~** a sinistra; **the L~** (*POL*) la sinistra.

left-hand drive [lcft'hand drīv] *n* guida a sinistra.

left-handed [lcft'han'did] *a* mancino(a); **~ scissors** forbici *fpl* per mancini.

left-hand side [lcft'hand' sīd] *n* lato *or* fianco sinistro.

leftist [lcf'tist] *a* (*POL*) di sinistra.

left-luggage (office) [lcftlug'ij ôf'is] *n* deposi-

to *m* bagagli *inv*.

leftovers [lcft'ōvûrz] *npl* avanzi *mpl*, resti *mpl*.

left wing *n* (*MIL. SPORT*) ala sinistra; (*POL*) sinistra ♦ *a*: **left-wing** (*POL*) di sinistra.

left-winger [lcft'wingûr] *n* (*POL*) uno/a di sinistra; (*SPORT*) ala sinistra.

leg [lcg] *n* gamba; (*of animal*) zampa; (*of furniture*) piede *m*; (*CULIN*: *of chicken*) coscia; (*of journey*) tappa; **lst/2nd ~ of** (*SPORT*) partita di andata/ritorno; **~ of lamb** (*CULIN*) cosciotto d'agnello; **to stretch one's ~s** sgranchirsi le gambe.

legacy [lcg'əsē] *n* eredità *f inv*; (*fig*) retaggio.

legal [lē'gəl] *a* legale; **to take ~ action** *or* **proceedings against sb** intentare un'azione legale contro qn, far causa a qn.

legal adviser *n* consulente *m/f* legale.

legal holiday *n* (*US*) giorno festivo, festa nazionale.

legality [lēgal'itē] *n* legalità.

legalize [lē'gəlīz] *vt* legalizzare.

legally [lē'gəlē] *ad* legalmente; **~ binding** legalmente vincolante.

legal tender *n* moneta legale.

legation [ligā'shən] *n* legazione *f*.

legend [lcj'ənd] *n* leggenda.

legendary [lcj'əndārē] *a* leggendario(a).

-legged [lcg'id] *suffix*: **two~** a due gambe (*or* zampe), bipede.

leggings [lcg'ingz] *npl* ghette *fpl*.

legibility [lcjəbil'ətē] *n* leggibilità.

legible [lcj'əbəl] *a* leggibile.

legibly [lcj'əblē] *ad* in modo leggibile.

legion [lē'jən] *n* legione *f*.

legionnaire [lējənär'] *n* legionario; **~s' disease** morbo del legionario.

legislate [lcj'islāt] *vi* legiferare.

legislation [lcjislā'shən] *n* legislazione *f*; **a piece of ~** una legge.

legislative [lcj'islātiv] *a* legislativo(a).

legislator [lcj'islātûr] *n* legislatore/trice.

legislature [lcj'islāchûr] *n* corpo legislativo.

legitimacy [lijit'əməsē] *n* legittimità.

legitimate [lijit'əmit] *a* legittimo(a).

legitimize [lijit'əmīz] *vt* (*gen*) legalizzare, rendere legale; (*child*) legittimare.

legroom [lcg'rōōm] *n* spazio per le gambe.

leg warmers *npl* scaldamuscoli *inv*.

Leics *abbr* (*Brit*) = *Leicestershire*.

leisure [lē'zhûr] *n* agio, tempo libero; ricreazioni *fpl*; **at ~** all'agio; a proprio comodo.

leisurely [lē'zhûrlē] *a* tranquillo(a); fatto(a) con comodo *or* senza fretta.

leisure suit *n* tuta (da ginnastica).

lemon [lcm'ən] *n* limone *m*.

lemonade [lcmənād'] *n* limonata.

lemon cheese, **lemon curd** *n* crema di limone (*che si spalma sul pane etc*).

lemon juice *n* succo di limone.

lemon juicer [lcm'ən jōō'sûr] *n* spremiagrumi *m inv*.

lemon tea *n* tè *m inv* al limone.

lend, *pt*, *pp* **lent** [lɛnd, lɛnt] *vt*: **to ~ sth (to sb)** prestare qc (a qn); **to ~ a hand** dare una mano.

lender [lɛn'dûr] *n* prestatore/trice.

lending library [lɛn'ding lī'brärē] *n* biblioteca circolante.

length [lɛngkth] *n* lunghezza; (*section: of road, pipe etc*) pezzo, tratto; **~ of time** periodo (di tempo); **what ~ is it?** quant'è lungo?; **it is 2 meters in ~** è lungo 2 metri; **to fall full ~** cadere lungo disteso; **at ~** (*at last*) finalmente, alla fine; (*lengthily*) a lungo; **to go to any ~(s) to do sth** fare qualsiasi cosa pur di *or* per fare qc.

lengthen [lɛngk'thən] *vt* allungare, prolungare ♦ *vi* allungarsi.

lengthwise [lɛngth'wīz] *ad* per il lungo.

lengthy [lɛngk'thē] *a* molto lungo(a).

leniency [lē'nēənsē] *n* indulgenza, clemenza.

lenient [lē'nēənt] *a* indulgente, clemente.

leniently [lē'nēəntlē] *ad* con indulgenza.

lens [lɛnz] *n* lente *f*; (*of camera*) obiettivo.

Lent [lɛnt] *n* Quaresima.

lent [lɛnt] *pt*, *pp of* **lend**.

lentil [lɛn'təl] *n* lenticchia.

Leo [lē'ō] *n* Leone *m*; **to be ~** essere del Leone.

leopard [lɛp'ûrd] *n* leopardo.

leotard [lē'ətârd] *n* calzamaglia.

leper [lɛp'ûr] *n* lebbroso/a.

leper colony *n* lebbrosario.

leprosy [lɛp'rəsē] *n* lebbra.

lesbian [lɛz'bēən] *n* lesbica ♦ *a* lesbico(a).

lesion [lē'zhən] *n* (*MED*) lesione *f*.

Lesotho [lisō̄'tō̄] *n* Lesotho *m*.

less [lɛs] *a, pronoun, ad* meno; **~ than you/ever** meno di lei/che mai; **~ than half** meno della metà; **~ and ~** sempre meno; **the ~ he works** ... meno lavora ...; **~ than $1/a kilo/3 meters** meno di un dollaro/un chilo/3 metri; **~ 5%** meno il 5%.

lessee [lɛsē'] *n* affittuario/a, locatario/a.

lessen [lɛs'ən] *vi* diminuire, attenuarsi ♦ *vt* diminuire, ridurre.

lesser [lɛs'ûr] *a* minore, più piccolo(a); **to a ~ extent** *or* **degree** in grado *or* misura minore.

lesson [lɛs'ən] *n* lezione *f*; **an English ~** una lezione di inglese; **to give ~s in** dare *or* impartire lezioni di; **it taught him a ~** (*fig*) gli è servito di lezione.

lessor [lɛs'ôr] *n* locatore/trice.

lest [lɛst] *cj* per paura di + *infinitive*, per paura che + *sub*.

let, *pt*, *pp* **let** [lɛt] *vt* lasciare; (*Brit: lease*) dare in affitto; **to ~ sb do sth** lasciar fare qc a qn, lasciare che qn faccia qc; **to ~ sb know sth** far sapere qc a qn; **to ~ sb have sth** dare qc a qn; **he ~ me go** mi ha lasciato andare; **~ the water boil and** ... fate bollire l'acqua e ...; **~'s go** andiamo; **~ him come**

lo lasci venire; **"to ~"** (*Brit*) "affittasi".

let down *vt* (*lower*) abbassare; (*dress*) allungare; (*hair*) sciogliere; (*disappoint*) deludere; (*Brit: tire*) sgonfiare.

let go *vi* mollare ♦ *vt* mollare; (*allow to go*) lasciare andare.

let in *vt* lasciare entrare; (*visitor etc*) far entrare; **what have you ~ yourself in for?** in che guai *or* pasticci sei andato a cacciarti?

let off *vt* (*allow to go*) lasciare andare; (*firework etc*) far partire; (*smell etc*) emettere; (*subj: taxi driver, bus driver*) far scendere; **to ~ off steam** (*fig col*) sfogarsi, scaricarsi.

let on *vi* (*col*): **to ~ on that** ... lasciar capire che ....

let out *vt* lasciare uscire; (*dress*) allargare; (*scream*) emettere; (*rent out*) affittare, dare in affitto.

let up *vi* diminuire.

letdown [lɛt'doun] *n* (*disappointment*) delusione *f*.

lethal [lē'thəl] *a* letale, mortale.

lethargic [ləthâr'jik] *a* letargico(a).

lethargy [lɛth'ûrjē] *n* letargia.

letter [lɛt'ûr] *n* lettera; **~s** *npl* (*LITERATURE*) lettere; **small/capital ~** lettera minuscola/ maiuscola; **~ of credit** lettera di credito; **documentary ~ of credit** lettera di credito documentata.

letter bomb *n* lettera esplosiva.

letterbox [lɛt'ûrbâks] *n* (*Brit*) buca delle lettere.

letterhead [lɛt'ûrhɛd] *n* intestazione *f*.

lettering [lɛt'ûring] *n* iscrizione *f*; caratteri *mpl*.

letter-opener [lɛt'ûrōpənûr] *n* tagliacarte *m inv*.

letterpress [lɛt'ûrprɛs] *n* (*method*) rilievografia.

letter quality *n* (*of printer*) qualità di stampa.

letters patent *npl* brevetto di invenzione.

lettuce [lɛt'is] *n* lattuga, insalata.

letup [lɛt'up] *n* (*col*) interruzione *f*.

leukemia, (*Brit*) **leukaemia** [lōōkē'mēə] *n* leucemia.

level [lɛv'əl] *a* piatto(a), piano(a); orizzontale ♦ *n* livello; (*also: spirit ~*) livella (a bolla d'aria) ♦ *vt* livellare, spianare; (*gun*) puntare (verso); (*accusation*): **to ~ (against)** lanciare (a *or* contro) ♦ *vi* (*col*): **to ~ with sb** esser franco(a) con qn; **to be ~ with** essere alla pari di; **a ~ spoonful** (*CULIN*) un cucchiaio raso; **to draw ~ with** (*team*) mettersi alla pari di; (*runner, car*) affiancarsi a; **A ~s** *npl* (*Brit*) ≈ esami *mpl* di maturità; **O ~s** *npl* (*Brit*) esami fatti in Inghilterra all'età di 16 anni; **on the ~** piatto(a); (*fig*) onesto(a).

level off, level out *vi* (*prices etc*) stabilizzarsi; (ground) diventare pianeggiante; (aircraft) volare in quota.

level crossing n (Brit) passaggio a livello.

levelheaded [lev'əlhed'id] a equilibrato(a).

leveling, (Brit) **levelling** [lev'əling] a (process, effect) di livellamento.

lever [lev'ûr] n leva ♦ vt: **to ~ up/out** sollevare/estrarre con una leva.

leverage [lev'ûrij] n: ~ **(on** or **with)** ascendente m (su).

levity [lev'itē] n leggerezza, frivolità.

levy [lev'ē] n tassa, imposta ♦ vt imporre.

lewd [lōōd] a osceno(a), lascivo(a).

LF abbr (= low frequency) BF (= bassa frequenza).

LI abbr (US) = Long Island.

liabilities [līəbil'ətēz] npl debiti mpl; (on balance sheet) passivo.

liability [līəbil'ətē] n responsabilità f inv; (handicap) peso.

liability insurance n (US) assicurazione f contro terzi.

liable [lī'əbəl] a (subject): ~ **to** soggetto(a) a; passibile di; (responsible): ~ **(for)** responsabile (di); (likely): ~ **to do** propenso(a) a fare; **to be** ~ **to a fine** essere passibile di multa.

liaise [lēāz'] vi: **to** ~ **(with)** mantenere i contatti (con).

liaison [lēā'zán] n relazione f; (MIL) collegamento.

liar [lī'ûr] n bugiardo/a.

libel [lī'bəl] n libello, diffamazione f ♦ vt diffamare.

libelous, (Brit) **libellous** [lī'bələs] a diffamatorio(a).

liberal [lib'ûrəl] a liberale; (generous): **to be** ~ **with** distribuire liberalmente ♦ n (POL): **L~** liberale m/f.

liberality [libəral'itē] n (generosity) generosità, liberalità.

liberalize [lib'ûrəlīz] vt liberalizzare.

liberal-minded [lib'ûrəlmīn'did] a tollerante.

liberate [lib'ərāt] vt liberare.

liberation [libərā'shən] n liberazione f.

Liberia [lībē'rēə] n Liberia.

Liberian [lībē'rēən] a, n liberiano(a).

liberty [lib'ûrtē] n libertà f inv; **at** ~ **to do** libero(a) di fare; **to take the** ~ **of** prendersi la libertà di, permettersi di.

libido [libē'dō] n libido f.

Libra [lēb'rə] n Bilancia; **to be** ~ essere della Bilancia.

librarian [lībrär'ēən] n bibliotecario/a.

library [lī'brärē] n biblioteca.

library book n libro della biblioteca.

libretto [libret'ō] n libretto.

Libya [lib'ēə] n Libia.

Libyan [lib'ēən] a, n libico(a).

lice [līs] npl of **louse.**

licence [lī'səns] n (Brit) = **license.**

license [lī'səns] n (US) autorizzazione f, permesso; (COMM) licenza; (RADIO, TV) canone m, abbonamento; (also: **driver's** ~, (Brit) **driving** ~) patente f di guida; (excessive freedom) licenza; **import** ~ licenza di importazione; **produced under** ~ prodotto su licenza ♦ vt dare una licenza a; (car) pagare la tassa di circolazione or il bollo di.

licensed [lī'sənst] a (for alcohol) che ha la licenza di vendere bibite alcoliche.

license plate n (esp US AUT) targa (automobilistica).

licentious [līsen'chəs] a licenzioso(a).

lichen [lī'kən] n lichene m.

lick [lik] vt leccare; (col: defeat) suonarle a, stracciare ♦ n leccata; **a** ~ **of paint** una passata di vernice.

licorice [lik'ûris] n (US) liquirizia.

lid [lid] n coperchio; **to take the** ~ **off sth** (fig) smascherare qc.

lido [lē'dō] n piscina all'aperto; (part of the beach) lido, stabilimento balneare.

lie [lī] n bugia, menzogna ♦ vi mentire, dire bugie; (pt **lay,** pp **lain** [lā, lān]) (rest) giacere, star disteso(a); (in grave) giacere, riposare; (of object: be situated) trovarsi, essere; **to tell** ~**s** raccontare or dire bugie; **to** ~ **low** (fig) latitare.

lie around vi (things) essere in giro; (person) bighellonare.

lie back vi stendersi.

lie down vi stendersi, sdraiarsi.

lie up vi (hide) nascondersi.

Liechtenstein [lēch'tenstīn] n Liechtenstein m.

lie detector n macchina della verità.

lieu [lōō] n: **in** ~ **of** invece di, al posto di.

Lieut. abbr (= lieutenant) Ten.

lieutenant [lōōten'ənt, (Brit) leften'ənt] n tenente m.

lieutenant colonel n tenente colonnello.

life [līf] n (pl **lives**) vita ♦ cpd di vita; della vita; **a** ~ **vita; country/city** ~ vita di campagna/di città; **to be sent to prison for** ~ essere condannato all'ergastolo; **true to** ~ fedele alla realtà; **to paint from** ~ dipingere dal vero.

life annuity n rendita vitalizia.

life belt n salvagente m.

lifeblood [līf'blud] n (fig) linfa vitale.

lifeboat [līf'bōt] n scialuppa di salvataggio.

life buoy n salvagente m.

life expectancy n durata media della vita.

lifeguard [līf'gárd] n bagnino.

life imprisonment n ergastolo.

life insurance n assicurazione f sulla vita.

life jacket n giubbotto di salvataggio.

lifeless [līf'lis] a senza vita.

lifelike [līf'līk] a che sembra vero(a); rassomigliante.

lifeline [līf'līn] n cavo di salvataggio.

lifelong [lĭf'lông] *a* per tutta la vita.
life preserver [lĭf prĕzûrv'ûr] *n* (*US*) salvagente *m*; giubbotto di salvataggio.
life raft *n* zattera di salvataggio.
lifesaver [lĭf'sāvûr] *n* bagnino.
life sentence *n* (condanna all')ergastolo.
life-sized [lĭf'sīzd] *a* a grandezza naturale.
life span *n* (durata della) vita.
life style *n* stile *m* di vita.
life support system *n* (*MED*) respiratore *m* automatico.
lifetime [lĭf'tīm] *n*: **in his ~** durante la sua vita; **in a ~** nell'arco della vita; in tutta la vita; **the chance of a ~** un'occasione unica.
lift [lĭft] *vt* sollevare, levare; (*steal*) prendere, rubare ♦ *vi* (*fog*) alzarsi ♦ *n* (*Brit*: *elevator*) ascensore *m*; **to give sb a ~** (*Brit*) dare un passaggio a qn.
lift off *vt* togliere ♦ *vi* (*rocket*) partire; (*helicopter*) decollare.
lift out *vt* tirar fuori; (*troops, evacuees etc*) far evacuare per mezzo di elicotteri (*or* aerei).
lift up *vt* sollevare, alzare.
lift-off [lĭft'ôf] *n* decollo.
ligament [lĭg'əmənt] *n* legamento.
light [lĭt] *n* luce *f*, lume *m*; (*daylight*) luce *f*, giorno; (*lamp*) lampada; (*AUT*: *taillight*) luce *f* di posizione; (: *headlight*) fanale *m*; (*for cigarette etc*): **have you got a ~?** ha da accendere? ♦ *vt* (*pt, pp* **lighted** *or* **lit** [lĭt]) (*candle, cigarette, fire*) accendere; (*room*) illuminare ♦ *a* (*room, color*) chiaro(a); (*not heavy, also fig*) leggero(a) ♦ *ad* (*travel*) con poco bagaglio; **~s** *npl* (*AUT*: *traffic* **~s**) semaforo; **in the ~ of** alla luce di; **to turn the ~ on/off** accendere/spegnere la luce; **to come to ~** venire in luce; **to cast** *or* **shed** *or* **throw ~ on** gettare luce su; **to make ~ of sth** (*fig*) prendere alla leggera qc, non dar peso a qc.
light up *vi* illuminarsi ♦ *vt* illuminare.
light bulb *n* lampadina.
lighten [lī'tən] *vi* schiarirsi ♦ *vt* (*give light to*) illuminare; (*make lighter*) schiarire; (*make less heavy*) alleggerire.
lighter [lī'tûr] *n* (*also*: **cigarette ~**) accendino; (*boat*) chiatta.
lighter fluid *n* gas *m inv* liquido per accendini.
light-fingered [līt'fĭng'gûrd] *a* lesto(a) di mano.
light-headed [līt'hed'id] *a* stordito(a).
lighthearted [līt'hâr'tid] *a* gioioso(a), gaio(a).
lighthouse [līt'hous] *n* faro.
lighting [lī'tĭng] *n* illuminazione *f*.
lightly [līt'lē] *ad* leggermente; **to get off ~** cavarsela a buon mercato.
light meter *n* (*PHOT*) esposimetro.
lightness [līt'nis] *n* chiarezza; (*in weight*) leggerezza.

lightning [līt'nĭng] *n* lampo, fulmine *m*; **a flash of ~** un lampo, un fulmine.
lightning rod, (*Brit*) **lightning conductor** *n* parafulmine *m*.
lightning strike *n* (*Brit*) sciopero *m* lampo *inv*.
light pen *n* penna luminosa.
lightship [līt'shĭp] *n* battello *m* faro *inv*.
lightweight [līt'wāt] *a* (*suit*) leggero(a); (*boxer*) peso leggero *inv*.
light-year [līt'yēr] *n* anno *m* luce *inv*.
Ligurian [lĭgyōōr'ēən] *a, n* ligure (*m/f*).
like [līk] *vt* (*person*) volere bene a; (*activity, object, food*): **I ~ swimming/that book/chocolate** mi piace nuotare/quel libro/il cioccolato ♦ *prep* come ♦ *a* simile, uguale ♦ *n*: **the ~** uno(a) uguale; **his ~s and dislikes** i suoi gusti; **I would ~, I'd ~** mi piacerebbe, vorrei; **would you ~ a coffee?** gradirebbe un caffè?; **if you ~** se vuoi; **to be/look ~ sb/sth** somigliare a qn/qc; **what's he ~?** che tipo è?, com'è?; **what's the weather ~?** che tempo fa?; **that's just ~ him** è proprio da lui; **something ~ that** qualcosa del genere; **I feel ~ a drink** avrei voglia di bere qualcosa; **there's nothing ~ ...** non c'è niente di meglio di *or* niente come ....
likeable [lī'kəbəl] *a* simpatico(a).
likelihood [līk'lēhŏŏd] *n* probabilità; **in all ~** con ogni probabilità, molto probabilmente.
likely [līk'lē] *a* probabile; plausibile; **he's ~ to leave** probabilmente partirà, è probabile che parta; **not ~!** (*col*) neanche per sogno!
like-minded [līk'mīn'did] *a* che pensa allo stesso modo.
liken [lī'kən] *vt*: **to ~ sth to** paragonare qc a.
likeness [līk'nis] *n* (*similarity*) somiglianza.
likewise [līk'wīz] *ad* similmente, nello stesso modo.
liking [lī'kĭng] *n*: **~ (for)** simpatia (per); debole *m* (per); **to be to sb's ~** essere di gusto *or* gradimento di qn; **to take a ~ to sb** prendere qn in simpatia.
lilac [lī'lək] *n* lilla *m inv* ♦ *a* lilla *inv*.
lilt [lĭlt] *n* cadenza.
lilting [lĭl'tĭng] *a* melodioso(a).
lily [lĭl'ē] *n* giglio; **~ of the valley** mughetto.
Lima [lē'mə] *n* Lima.
limb [lĭm] *n* membro; **to be out on a ~** (*fig*) sentirsi spaesato *or* tagliato fuori.
limber [lĭm'bûr]: **to ~ up** *vi* riscaldarsi i muscoli.
limbo [lĭm'bō] *n*: **to be in ~** (*fig*) essere lasciato(a) nel dimenticatoio.
lime [līm] *n* (*tree*) tiglio; (*fruit*) limetta; (*GEO*) calce *f*.
lime juice *n* succo di limetta.
limelight [līm'lĭt] *n*: **in the ~** (*fig*) alla ribalta, in vista.
limerick [lĭm'ûrik] *n* poesiola umoristica di 5 versi.

limestone [līm'stōn] n pietra calcarea; (GEO) calcare m.

limit [lim'it] n limite m' ♦ vt limitare; **weight/speed** ~ limite di peso/di velocità; **within ~s** entro certi limiti.

limitation [limitā'shən] n limitazione f, limite m.

limited [lim'itid] a limitato(a), ristretto(a); ~ **edition** edizione f a bassa tiratura.

limited (liability) company (Ltd) n (Brit) ≈ società f inv a responsabilità limitata (S.r.l.).

limitless [lim'itlis] a illimitato(a).

limousine [lim'əzēn] n limousine f inv.

limp [limp] n: **to have a** ~ zoppicare ♦ vi zoppicare ♦ a floscio(a), flaccido(a).

limpet [lim'pit] n patella.

limpid [lim'pid] a (poet) limpido(a).

linchpin [linch'pin] n acciarino, bietta; (fig) perno.

Lincs [lingks] abbr (Brit) = Lincolnshire.

line [līn] n (gen, COMM) linea; (rope) corda; (wire) filo; (of poem) verso; (row, series) fila, riga; coda ♦ vt (clothes): **to** ~ **(with)** foderare (di); (box): **to** ~ **(with)** rivestire or foderare (di); (subj: trees, crowd) fiancheggiare; **to cut in** ~ (US) passare avanti; **in his** ~ **of business** nel suo ramo (di affari); **on the right** ~**s** sulla buona strada; **a new** ~ **in cosmetics** una nuova linea di cosmetici; **hold the** ~ **please** (Brit TEL) resti in linea per cortesia; **to be in** ~ **for sth** (fig) essere in lista per qc; **in** ~ **with** d'accordo con, in linea con; **to bring sth into** ~ **with sth** mettere qc al passo con qc; **to draw the** ~ **at (doing) sth** (fig) rifiutarsi di fare qc; **to take the** ~ **that** ... essere del parere che ....

line up vi allinearsi, mettersi in fila ♦ vt mettere in fila; **to have sth** ~**d up** avere qc in programma; **to have sb** ~**d up** avere qn in mente.

linear [lin'ûr] a lineare.

lined [līnd] a (paper) a righe, rigato(a); (face) rugoso(a); (clothes) foderato(a).

line feed n (COMPUT) avanzamento di una interlinea.

linen [lin'ən] n biancheria, panni mpl; (cloth) tela di lino.

line printer n stampatrice f per righe.

liner [lī'nûr] n nave f di linea; **trash can** ~ sacchetto per la pattumiera.

linesman [līnz'mən] n guardalinee m inv, segnalinee m inv.

lineup [līn'up] n allineamento, fila; (also: **police** ~) confronto all'americana; (SPORT) formazione f di gioco.

linger [ling'gûr] vi attardarsi; indugiare; (smell, tradition) persistere.

lingerie [lán'jərā] n biancheria intima (femminile).

lingering [ling'gûring] a lungo(a); persistente;

(death) lento(a).

lingo, ~es [ling'gō] n (pej) gergo.

linguist [ling'gwist] n linguista m/f; poliglotta m/f.

linguistic [linggwis'tik] a linguistico(a).

linguistics [linggwis'tiks] n linguistica.

lining [lī'ning] n fodera; (TECH) rivestimento (interno); (of brake) guarnizione f.

link [lingk] n (of a chain) anello; (connection) legame m, collegamento ♦ vt collegare, unire, congiungere; **rail** ~ collegamento ferroviario; see also **links**.

link up vt collegare, unire ♦ vi riunirsi; associarsi.

links [lingks] npl pista or terreno da golf.

linkup [lingk'up] n legame m; (of roads) nodo; (of spaceships) aggancio; (RADIO, TV) collegamento.

linoleum [linō'lēəm] n linoleum m inv.

linseed oil [lin'sēd oil] n olio di semi di lino.

lint [lint] n garza.

lintel [lin'təl] n architrave f.

lion [lī'ən] n leone m.

lion cub n leoncino.

lioness [lī'ənis] n leonessa.

lip [lip] n labbro; (of cup etc) orlo; (insolence) sfacciataggine f.

lip-read [lip'rēd] vi leggere sulle labbra.

lip salve [lip' sav] n burro di cacao.

lip service n: **to pay** ~ **to sth** essere favorevole a qc solo a parole.

lipstick [lip'stik] n rossetto.

liquefy [lik'wəfī] vt liquefare ♦ vi liquefarsi.

liqueur [lik'ûr] n liquore m.

liquid [lik'wid] n liquido ♦ a liquido(a).

liquid assets npl attività fpl liquide, crediti mpl liquidi.

liquidate [lik'widāt] vt liquidare.

liquidation [likwidā'shən] n liquidazione f; **to go into** ~ andare in liquidazione.

liquidator [lik'widātûr] n liquidatore m.

liquid crystal display (LCD) n visualizzazione f a cristalli liquidi.

liquidity [likwid'itē] n (COMM) liquidità.

liquidize [lik'widīz] vt (Brit CULIN) passare al frullatore.

liquidizer [lik'widīzûr] n (Brit CULIN) frullatore m (a brocca).

Liquid Paper n ® (US) liquido correttore.

liquor [lik'ûr] n alcool m.

liquorice [lik'ûris] n (Brit) liquirizia.

liquor store n (US) spaccio di bevande alcoliche.

Lisbon [liz'bən] n Lisbona.

lisp [lisp] n difetto nel pronunciare le sibilanti.

lissom [lis'əm] a leggiadro(a).

list [list] n lista, elenco; (of ship) sbandamento ♦ vt (write down) mettere in lista; fare una lista di; (enumerate) elencare; (COMPUT) stampare (un prospetto di) ♦ vi (ship) sbandare; **shopping** ~ lista or nota della spe-

sa.
listed company *n* società quotata in Borsa.
listen [lis'ən] *vi* ascoltare; **to ~ to** ascoltare.
listener [lis'ənûr] *n* ascoltatore/trice.
listing [lis'ting] *n* (*COMPUT*) lista stampata.
listless [list'lis] *a* svogliato(a); apatico(a).
listlessly [list'lislē] *ad* svogliatamente; apatica-
mente.
list price *n* prezzo di listino.
lit [lit] *pt, pp of* **light.**
litany [lit'ənē] *n* litania.
liter [lē'tûr] *n* (*US*) litro.
literacy [lit'ûrəsē] *n* il sapere leggere e scrivere.
literacy campaign *n* lotta contro l'analfabeti-
smo.
literal [lit'ûrəl] *a* letterale.
literally [lit'ûrəlē] *ad* alla lettera, lette-
ralmente.
literary [lit'ərärē] *a* letterario(a).
literate [lit'ûrit] *a* che sa leggere e scrivere.
literature [lit'ûrəchûr] *n* letteratura;
(*brochures etc*) materiale *m.*
lithe [līth] *a* agile, snello(a).
lithography [lithâg'rəfē] *n* litografia.
Lithuania [lithōōā'nēə] *n* Lituania.
litigate [lit'əgāt] *vt* muovere causa a ♦ *vi* litigare.
litigation [litəgā'shən] *n* causa.
litmus [lit'məs] *n*: **~ paper** cartina di tornaso-
le.
litre [lē'tûr] *n* (*Brit*) = **liter.**
litter [lit'ûr] *n* (*rubbish*) rifiuti *mpl*; (*young
animals*) figliata ♦ *vt* sparpagliare; lasciare
rifiuti in; **~ed with** coperto(a) di.
litter bin *n* (*Brit*) cestino per rifiuti.
litterbug [lit'ûrbug] *n persona che butta per
terra le cartacce o i rifiuti.*
little [lit'əl] *a* (*small*) piccolo(a); (*not much*)
poco(a) ♦ *ad* poco; **a ~** un po' (di); **a ~ milk**
un po' di latte; **with ~ difficulty** senza fatica
or difficoltà; **~ by ~** a poco a poco; **as ~ as
possible** il meno possibile; **for a ~ while** per
un po'; **to make ~ of** dare poca importanza
a; **~ finger** mignolo.
liturgy [lit'ûrjē] *n* liturgia.
live *vi* [liv] vivere; (*reside*) vivere, abitare ♦ *a*
[līv] (*animal*) vivo(a); (*issue*) scottante,
d'attualità; (*wire*) sotto tensione; (*broadcast*)
diretto(a); (*ammunition: not blank*) cari-
co(a); (*unexploded*) inesploso(a); **to ~ in
Chicago** abitare a Chicago; **to ~ together** vivere insieme, convivere.
live down *vt* far dimenticare (alla gente).
live in *vi* essere interno(a); avere vitto e
alloggio.
live off *vi* (*land, fish etc*) vivere di; (*pej:
parents etc*) vivere alle spalle *or* a spese di.
live on *vt fus* (*food*) vivere di ♦ *vi* sopravvivere, continuare a vivere; **to ~ on $50 a
week** vivere con 50 dollari la settimana.

live out *vt*: **to ~ out one's days** *or* life trascorrere gli ultimi anni ♦ *vi* (*Brit: students*)
essere esterno(a).
live up *vt*: **to ~ it up** (*col*) fare la bella
vita.
live up to *vt fus* tener fede a, non venir
meno a.
livelihood [līv'lēhŏŏd] *n* mezzi *mpl* di sostentamento.
liveliness [līv'lēnis] *n* vivacità.
lively [līv'lē] *a* vivace, vivo(a).
liven up [līv'ən up] *vt* (*room etc*) ravvivare;
(*discussion, evening*) animare.
liver [liv'ûr] *n* fegato.
liverish [liv'ûrish] *a* che soffre di mal di fegato; (*fig*) scontroso(a).
livery [liv'ûrē] *n* livrea.
lives [līvz] *npl of* **life.**
livestock [līv'stàk] *n* bestiame *m.*
livid [liv'id] *a* livido(a); (*furious*) livido(a) di
rabbia, furibondo(a).
living [liv'ing] *a* vivo(a), vivente ♦ *n*: **to earn**
or **make a ~** guadagnarsi la vita; **cost of ~**
costo della vita, carovita *m*; **within ~
memory** a memoria d'uomo.
living conditions *npl* condizioni *fpl* di vita.
living expenses *npl* spese *fpl* di mantenimento.
living room *n* soggiorno.
living standards *npl* tenore *m* di vita.
living wage *n* salario sufficiente per vivere.
lizard [liz'ûrd] *n* lucertola.
llama [lâm'ə] *n* lama *m inv.*
LLB *n abbr* (= *Bachelor of Laws*) *titolo di studio.*
LLD *n abbr* (= *Doctor of Laws*) *titolo di studio.*
load [lōd] *n* (*weight*) peso; (*ELEC, TECH, thing
carried*) carico ♦ *vt*: **to ~ (with)** (*truck,
ship*) caricare (di); (*gun, camera*) caricare
(con); **a ~ of, ~s of** (*fig*) un sacco di; **to ~
a program** (*COMPUT*) caricare un programma.
loaded [lō'did] *a* (*dice*) falsato(a); (*question,
word*) capzioso(a); (*col: rich*) pieno(a) di
soldi.
loading dock [lō'ding dàk] *n* (*US*) piazzola di
carico.
loaf [lōf] *n* (*pl* **loaves**) pane *m*, pagnotta ♦ *vi*
(*also:* **~ about, ~ around**) bighellonare.
loafer [lō'fûr] *n* sfaccendato/a, fannullone/a.
loam [lōm] *n* terra di marna.
loan [lōn] *n* prestito ♦ *vt* dare in prestito; **on
~** in prestito.
loan account *n* conto dei prestiti.
loan capital *n* capitale *m* di prestito.
loath [lōth] *a*: **to be ~ to do** essere restio(a)
a fare.
loathe [lōth] *vt* detestare, aborrire.
loathing [lō'thing] *n* aborrimento, disgusto.
loathsome [lōth'səm] *a* (*gen*) ripugnante;
(*person*) detestabile, odioso(a).

loaves [lōvz] *npl of* **loaf**.
lob [lâb] *vt* (*ball*) lanciare.
lobby [lâb'ē] *n* atrio, vestibolo; (*POL: pressure group*) gruppo di pressione ♦ *vt* fare pressione su.
lobbyist [lâb'ēist] *n* appartenente *m/f* ad un gruppo di pressione.
lobe [lōb] *n* lobo.
lobster [lâb'stûr] *n* aragosta.
lobster pot *n* nassa per aragoste.
local [lō'kəl] *a* locale ♦ *n*: **the ~s** *npl* la gente della zona; (*Brit: pub*) ≈ bar *m inv* all'angolo.
local anesthetic *n* anestesia locale.
local authority *n* (*Brit*) autorità locale.
local call *n* (*TEL*) telefonata urbana.
local government *n* amministrazione *f* locale.
locality [lōkal'itē] *n* località *f inv*; (*position*) posto, luogo.
localize [lō'kəlīz] *vt* localizzare.
locally [lō'kəlē] *ad* da queste parti; nel vicinato.
locate [lō'kāt] *vt* (*find*) trovare; (*situate*) collocare.
location [lōkā'shən] *n* posizione *f*; **on ~** (*CINEMA*) all'esterno.
loch [lâk] *n* (*Brit*) lago.
lock [lâk] *n* (*of door, box*) serratura; (*of canal*) chiusa; (*of hair*) ciocca, riccio ♦ *vt* (*with key*) chiudere a chiave; (*immobilize*) bloccare ♦ *vi* (*door etc*) chiudersi; (*wheels*) bloccarsi, incepparsi; **~ stock and barrel** (*fig*) in blocco.
lock away *vt* (*valuables*) tenere (rinchiuso(a)) al sicuro; (*criminal*) metter dentro.
lock out *vt* chiudere fuori; **to ~ workers out** fare una serrata.
lock up *vi* chiudere tutto (a chiave).
locker [lâk'ûr] *n* armadietto.
locker room *n* (*US SPORT*) spogliatoio.
locket [lâk'it] *n* medaglione *m*.
lockjaw [lâk'jô] *n* tetano.
lockout [lâk'out] *n* (*INDUSTRY*) serrata.
locksmith [lâk'smith] *n* magnano.
lockup [lâk'up] *n* (*prison*) prigione *f*; (*cell*) guardina.
locomotive [lōkəmō'tiv] *n* locomotiva.
locum tenens [lō'kəm tē'nenz] *n* (*MED*) medico sostituto.
locust [lō'kəst] *n* locusta.
lodge [lâj] *n* casetta, portineria; (*FREEMASONRY*) loggia ♦ *vi* (*person*): **to ~ (with)** essere a pensione (presso *or* da) ♦ *vt* (*appeal etc*) presentare, fare; **to ~ a complaint** presentare un reclamo; **to ~ (itself) in/between** piantarsi dentro/fra.
lodger [lâj'ûr] *n* affittuario/a; (*with room and meals*) pensionante *m/f*.
lodging [lâj'ing] *n* alloggio; *see also* **board**; **lodgings**.

lodgings [lâj'ingz] *npl* camera d'affitto; camera ammobiliata.
loft [lôft] *n* soffitta; (*AGR*) granaio; (*US*) appartamento ricavato da solaio (*or* granaio *etc*).
lofty [lôf'tē] *a* alto(a); (*haughty*) altezzoso(a); (*sentiments, aims*) nobile.
log [lôg] *n* (*of wood*) ceppo; (*book*) = **logbook** ♦ *n abbr* (= *logarithm*) log ♦ *vt* registrare.
log in, log on *vi* (*COMPUT*) aprire una sessione (*con codice di riconoscimento*).
log off, log out *vi* (*COMPUT*) terminare una sessione.
logarithm [lôg'ərithəm] *n* logaritmo.
logbook [lôg'bŏŏk] *n* (*NAUT, AVIAT*) diario di bordo; (*AUT*) libretto di circolazione; (*of truck driver*) registro di viaggio; (*of events, movement of goods etc*) registro.
log cabin *n* capanna di tronchi.
log fire *n* fuoco di legna.
loggerheads [lôg'ûrhedz] *npl*: **at ~ (with)** ai ferri corti (con).
logic [lâj'ik] *n* logica.
logical [lâj'ikəl] *a* logico(a).
logically [lâj'iklē] *ad* logicamente.
logistics [lōjis'tiks] *n* logistica.
logo [lō'gō] *n* logo *m inv*.
loin [loin] *n* (*CULIN*) lombata; **~s** *npl* reni *fpl*.
loincloth [loin'kloth] *n* perizoma *m*.
loiter [loi'tûr] *vi* attardarsi; **to ~ (about)** indugiare, bighellonare.
loll [lâl] *vi* (*also*: **~ about**) essere stravaccato(a).
lollipop [lâl'ēpâp] *n* lecca lecca *m inv*.
Lombardy [lâm'bârdē] *n* Lombardia.
London [lun'dən] *n* Londra.
Londoner [lun'dənûr] *n* londinese *m/f*.
lone [lōn] *a* solitario(a).
loneliness [lōn'lēnis] *n* solitudine *f*, isolamento.
lonely [lōn'lē] *a* solitario(a); (*place*) isolato(a); **to feel ~** sentirsi solo(a).
loner [lō'nûr] *n* solitario/a.
lonesome [lōn'səm] *a* solitario(a).
long [lông] *a* lungo(a) ♦ *ad* a lungo, per molto tempo ♦ *n*: **the ~ and the short of it is that** ... (*fig*) a farla breve ... ♦ *vi*: **to ~ for sth/to do** desiderare qc/di fare; non veder l'ora di aver qc/di fare; **he had ~ understood that** ... aveva capito da molto tempo che ...; **how ~ is this river/course?** quanto è lungo questo fiume/corso?; **6 meters ~** lungo 6 metri; **6 months ~** che dura 6 mesi, di 6 mesi; **all night ~** tutta la notte; **he no ~er comes** non viene più; **~ before** molto tempo prima; **before ~** (+ *future*) presto, fra poco; (+ *past*) poco tempo dopo; **~ ago** molto tempo fa; **don't be ~!** faccia presto!; **I won't be ~** non ne avrò per molto; **at ~ last** finalmente; **in the ~ run** alla fin fine; **so** *or* **as ~ as** sempre che + *sub*.

long-distance [lông'dis'təns] *a* (*race*) di fondo; (*call*) interurbano(a).

long-haired [lông'härd] *a* (*person*) dai capelli lunghi; (*animal*) dal pelo lungo.

longhand [lông'hand] *n* scrittura normale.

longing [lông'ing] *n* desiderio, voglia, brama ♦ *a* di desiderio; pieno(a) di nostalgia.

longingly [lông'inglē] *ad* con desiderio (*or* nostalgia).

longitude [lân'jətōōd] *n* longitudine *f*.

long johns [lông jânz] *npl* mutande *fpl* lunghe.

long jump *n* salto in lungo.

long-lost [lông'lôst] *a* perduto(a) da tempo.

long-playing [lông'plā'ing] *a*: ~ **record (LP)** (disco) 33 giri *m inv*.

long-range [lông'rānj] *a* a lunga portata; (*weather forecast*) a lungo termine.

longshoreman [lông'shôrmən] *n* (*US*) scaricatore *m* (di porto), portuale *m*.

longsighted [lông'sītid] *a* presbite; (*fig*) lungimirante.

long-standing [lông'stan'ding] *a* di vecchia data.

long-suffering [lông'suf'ûring] *a* estremamente paziente; infinitamente tollerante.

long-term [lông'tûrm'] *a* a lungo termine.

long wave *n* (*RADIO*) onde *fpl* lunghe.

long-winded [lông'win'did] *a* prolisso(a), interminabile.

loo [lōō] *n* (*Brit col*) W.C. *m inv*, cesso.

loofah [lōō'fə] *n* luffa.

look [lōōk] *vi* guardare; (*seem*) sembrare, parere; (*building etc*): **to ~ south/on to the sea** dare a sud/sul mare ♦ *n* sguardo; (*appearance*) aspetto, aria; ~**s** *npl* aspetto; bellezza; **to ~ like** assomigliare a; **to have a ~ at sth** dare un'occhiata a qc; **to have a ~ for sth** cercare qc; **to ~ ahead** guardare avanti; **it ~s about 4 meters long** sarà lungo un 4 metri; **it ~s all right to me** a me pare che vada bene.

look after *vt fus* occuparsi di, prendersi cura di; (*keep an eye on*) guardare, badare a.

look around *vi* guardarsi intorno; (*turn*) girarsi, voltarsi; (*in shops*) dare un'occhiata; **to ~ around for sth** guardarsi intorno cercando qc.

look at *vt fus* guardare.

look back *vi*: **to ~ back at sth/sb** voltarsi a guardare qc/qn; **to ~ back on** (*event, period*) ripensare a.

look down on *vt fus* (*fig*) guardare dall'alto, disprezzare.

look for *vt fus* cercare.

look forward to *vt fus* non veder l'ora di; **I'm not ~ing forward to it** non ne ho nessuna voglia; **~ing forward to hearing from you** (*in letter*) aspettando tue notizie.

look in *vi*: **to ~ in on sb** (*visit*) fare un salto da qn.

look into *vt fus* (*matter, possibility*) esaminare.

look on *vi* fare da spettatore.

look out *vi* (*beware*): **to ~ out (for)** stare in guardia (per).

look out for *vt fus* cercare; (*watch out for*): **to ~ out for sb/sth** guardare se arriva qn/qc.

look over *vt* (*essay*) dare un'occhiata a, riguardare; (*town, building*) vedere; (*person*) esaminare.

look round *vi* (*Brit*) = **look around**.

look through *vt fus* (*papers, book*) scorrere; (*telescope*) guardare attraverso.

look to *vt fus* stare attento(a) a; (*rely on*) contare su.

look up *vi* alzare gli occhi; (*improve*) migliorare ♦ *vt* (*word*) cercare; (*friend*) andare a trovare.

look up to *vt fus* avere rispetto per.

lookout [lōōk'out] *n* posto d'osservazione; guardia; **to be on the ~ (for)** stare in guardia (per).

look-up table [lōōk'up tā'bəl] *n* (*COMPUT*) tabella di consultazione.

LOOM *n abbr* (*US*: = *Loyal Order of Moose*) organizzazione filantropica.

loom [lōōm] *n* telaio ♦ *vi* sorgere; (*fig*) minacciare.

loony [lōō'nē] *a, n* (*col*) pazzo(a).

loop [lōōp] *n* cappio; (*COMPUT*) anello.

loophole [lōōp'hōl] *n* via d'uscita; scappatoia.

loose [lōōs] *a* (*knot*) sciolto(a); (*screw*) allentato(a); (*stone*) cadente; (*clothes*) ampio(a), largo(a); (*animal*) in libertà, scappato(a); (*life, morals*) dissoluto(a); (*discipline*) allentato(a); (*thinking*) poco rigoroso(a), vago(a) ♦ *vt* (*untie*) sciogliere; (*slacken*) allentare; (*free*) liberare; ~ **connection** (*ELEC*) contatto difettoso; **to be at ~ ends** *or* (*Brit*) **at a ~ end** (*fig*) non saper che fare; **to tie up ~ ends** (*fig*) avere ancora qualcosa da sistemare.

loose change *n* spiccioli *mpl*, moneta.

loose-fitting [lōōs'fit'ing] *a* ampio(a).

loose-leaf [lōōs'lēf] *a*: ~ **binder** *or* **folder** raccoglitore *m*.

loosely [lōōs'lē] *ad* lentamente; approssimativamente.

loosen [lōō'sən] *vt* sciogliere.

loosen up *vi* (*before game*) sciogliere i muscoli, scaldarsi; (*col: relax*) rilassarsi.

loot [lōōt] *n* bottino ♦ *vt* saccheggiare.

looter [lōō'tûr] *n* saccheggiatore/trice.

looting [lōō'ting] *n* saccheggio.

lop [lâp] *vt* (*also*: ~ **off**) tagliare via, recidere.

lopsided [lâp'sī'did] *a* non equilibrato(a), asimmetrico(a).

lord [lôrd] *n* signore *m*; **L~ Smith** lord Smith; **the L~** (*REL*) il Signore; **the (House of) L~s** (*Brit*) la Camera dei Lord.

lordly [lôrd'lē] *a* nobile, maestoso(a); (*arrogant*) altero(a).

lore [lôr] *n* tradizioni *fpl*.

lorry [lôr'ē] *n* (*Brit*) camion *m inv*.

lorry driver *n* (*Brit*) camionista *m/f*.

lose, *pt, pp* **lost** [lōōz, lôst] *vt* perdere; (*pursuers*) distanziare ♦ *vi* perdere; **to ~ (time)** (*clock*) ritardare; **to ~ no time (in doing sth)** non perdere tempo (a fare qc); **to get lost** (*person*) perdersi, smarrirsi; (*object*) andare perso *or* perduto.

loser [lōō'zûr] *n* perdente *m/f*; **to be a good/bad ~** saper/non saper perdere.

loss [lós] *n* perdita; **to cut one's ~es** rimetterci il meno possibile; **to make a ~** subire una perdita; **to sell sth at a ~** vendere qc in perdita; **to be at a ~** essere perplesso(a); **to be at a ~ to explain sth** non saper come fare a spiegare qc.

loss adjuster *n* (*INSURANCE*) responsabile *m/f* della valutazione dei danni.

loss leader *n* (*COMM*) articolo a prezzo ridottissimo per attirare la clientela.

lost [lôst] *pt, pp of* **lose** ♦ *a* perduto(a); **~ in thought** immerso *or* perso nei propri pensieri; **~ and found property** *n* (*US*) oggetti *mpl* smarriti; **~ and found** *n* (*US*) ufficio oggetti smarriti.

lost property *n* (*Brit*) oggetti *mpl* smarriti; **~ office** *or* **department** ufficio oggetti smarriti.

lot [lât] *n* (*at auctions*) lotto; (*US: plot of land*) lotto; (*destiny*) destino, sorte *f*; **the ~** tutto(a) quanto(a); tutti(e) quanti(e); **a ~ molto; a ~ of** una gran quantità di, un sacco di; **~s of** molto(a); **to draw ~s (for sth)** tirare a sorte (per qc).

lotion [lō'shən] *n* lozione *f*.

lottery [lât'ûrē] *n* lotteria.

loud [loud] *a* forte, alto(a); (*gaudy*) vistoso(a), sgargiante ♦ *ad* (*speak etc*) forte; **out ~** ad alta voce.

loudly [loud'lē] *ad* fortemente, ad alta voce.

loudspeaker [loud'spēkûr] *n* altoparlante *m*.

lounge [lounj] *n* (*of hotel*) salone *m*; (*of airport*) sala d'attesa ♦ *vi* oziare; starsene colle mani in mano.

lounge bar *n* bar *m inv* con servizio a tavolino.

lounge suit *n* (*Brit*) completo da uomo.

louse [lous] *n* (*pl* **lice**) pidocchio.

louse up *vt* (*col*) rovinare.

lousy [lou'zē] *a* (*fig*) orrendo(a), schifoso(a).

lout [lout] *n* zoticone *m*.

louver, (*Brit*) **louvre** [lōō'vûr] *a* (*door, window*) con apertura a gelosia.

lovable [luv'əbəl] *a* simpatico(a), carino(a); amabile.

love [luv] *n* amore *m* ♦ *vt* amare; voler bene a; **to ~ to do: I ~ to do** mi piace fare; **I'd ~ to come** mi piacerebbe molto venire; **to be in ~ with** essere innamorato(a) di; **to fall in ~ with** innamorarsi di; **to make ~** fare l'amore; **~ at first sight** amore a prima vista, colpo di fulmine; **to send one's ~ to sb** mandare i propri saluti a qn; **~ from Anne, ~, Anne** con affetto, Anne; **"15 ~"** (*TENNIS*) "15 a zero".

love affair *n* relazione *f*.

love letter *n* lettera d'amore.

love life *n* vita sentimentale.

lovely [luv'lē] *a* bello(a); (*delicious: smell, meal*) buono(a); **we had a ~ time** ci siamo divertiti molto.

lover [luv'ûr] *n* amante *m/f*; (*amateur*): **a ~ of** un(un')amante di; un(un')appassionato(a) di.

lovesick [luv'sik] *a* malato(a) d'amore.

lovesong [luv'sông] *n* canzone *f* d'amore.

loving [luv'ing] *a* affettuoso(a), amoroso(a), tenero(a).

low [lō] *a* basso(a) ♦ *ad* in basso ♦ *n* (*METEOR*) depressione *f* ♦ *vi* (*cow*) muggire; **to feel ~** sentirsi giù; **he's very ~** (*ill*) è molto debole; **to reach a new** *or* **an all-time ~** toccare il livello più basso *or* il minimo; **to turn (down) ~** *vt* abbassare.

lowbrow [lō'brou] *a* (*person*) senza pretese intellettuali.

low-calorie [lō'kal'ûrē] *a* a basso contenuto calorico.

low-cut [lō'kut'] *a* (*dress*) scollato(a).

lowdown [lō'doun] *a* (*mean*) ignobile ♦ *n* (*col*): **he gave me the ~ on it** mi ha messo al corrente dei fatti.

lower [lō'ûr] *a, ad comparative of* **low** ♦ *vt* (*gen*) calare; (*reduce: price*) abbassare, ridurre; (*resistance*) indebolire; (*US AUT: lights*) abbassare ♦ *vi* [lou'ûr] (*person*): **to ~ (at sb)** dare un'occhiataccia (a qn); (*sky*) minacciare.

low-fat [lō'fat'] *a* magro(a).

low-key [lō'kē'] *a* moderato(a); (*operation*) condotto(a) con discrezione.

lowland [lō'lənd] *n* bassopiano, pianura.

low-level [lō'ləvəl] *a* a basso livello; (*flying*) a bassa quota.

lowly [lō'lē] *a* umile, modesto(a).

low-lying [lō'lī'ing] *a* a basso livello.

low-paid [lō'pād'] *a* mal pagato(a).

loyal [loi'əl] *a* fedele, leale.

loyalist [loi'əlist] *n* lealista *m/f*.

loyalty [loi'əltē] *n* fedeltà, lealtà.

lozenge [lâz'inj] *n* (*MED*) pastiglia; (*GEOM*) losanga.

LP *n abbr* (= *long-playing record*) LP *m*.

L-plates [el plāts] *npl* (*Brit*) cartelli sui veicoli dei guidatori principianti.

LPN *n abbr* (*US:* = *Licensed Practical Nurse*) ≈ infermiera diplomata.

LSAT *n abbr* (*US*) = *Law School Admissions Test*.

LSD *n abbr* (= *lysergic acid diethylamide*) L.S.D. *m*.

LSE *n abbr* = *London School of Economics*.

LST *abbr* (= *local standard time*) ora locale.

LT *abbr* (*ELEC*: = *low tension*) B.T.

Lt. *abbr* (= *lieutenant*) Ten.

Ltd *abbr* (*Brit COMM*) = **limited**.

lubricant [lōōb'rikənt] *n* lubrificante *m*.

lubricate [lōōb'rikāt] *vt* lubrificare.

lucid [lōō'sid] *a* lucido(a).

lucidity [lōōsid'itē] *n* lucidità.

luck [luk] *n* fortuna, sorte *f*; **bad** ~ sfortuna, mala sorte; **good** ~ (buona) fortuna; **to be in** ~ essere fortunato(a); **to be out of** ~ essere sfortunato(a).

luckily [luk'ilē] *ad* fortunatamente, per fortuna.

lucky [luk'ē] *a* fortunato(a); (*number etc*) che porta fortuna.

lucrative [lōō'krətiv] *a* lucrativo(a), lucroso(a), profittevole.

ludicrous [lōō'dəkrəs] *a* ridicolo(a), assurdo(a).

luffa [luf'ə] *n* (*US*) luffa.

lug [lug] *vt* trascinare.

luggage [lug'ij] *n* bagagli *mpl*.

luggage car *n* (*US RAIL*) bagagliaio.

luggage rack *n* portabagagli *m inv*.

lugubrious [lōōgōō'brēəs] *a* lugubre.

lukewarm [lōōk'wôrm'] *a* tiepido(a).

lull [lul] *n* intervallo di calma ♦ *vt* (*child*) cullare; (*person, fear*) acquietare, calmare.

lullaby [lul'əbī] *n* ninnananna.

lumbago [lumbā'gō] *n* lombaggine *f*.

lumber [lum'bûr] *n* roba vecchia; (*wood*) legname *m* ♦ *vt* (*Brit col*): **to** ~ **sb with sth/sb** affibbiare *or* rifilare qc/qn a qn ♦ *vi* (*also*: ~ **along**) muoversi pesantemente.

lumberjack [lum'bûrjak] *n* boscaiolo.

lumberyard [lum'bûryârd] *n* segheria.

luminous [lōō'minəs] *a* luminoso(a).

lump [lump] *n* pezzo; (*in sauce*) grumo; (*swelling*) gonfiore *m* ♦ *vt* (*also*: ~ **together**) riunire, mettere insieme.

lump sum *n* somma globale.

lumpy [lum'pē] *a* (*sauce*) grumoso(a).

lunacy [lōō'nəsē] *n* demenza, follia, pazzia.

lunar [lōō'nûr] *a* lunare.

lunatic [lōō'nətik] *a*, *n* pazzo(a), matto(a).

lunatic asylum *n* manicomio.

lunch [lunch] *n* pranzo, colazione *f*; **to invite sb to** *or* **for** ~ invitare qn a pranzo *or* a colazione.

lunch break *n* intervallo del pranzo.

luncheon [lun'chən] *n* pranzo.

luncheon meat *n* ≈ mortadella.

lunch hour *n* = **lunch break**.

lunchtime [lunch'tīm] *n* ora di pranzo.

lung [lung] *n* polmone *m*.

lung cancer *n* cancro del polmone.

lunge [lunj] *vi* (*also*: ~ **forward**) fare un balzo in avanti; **to** ~ **at sb** balzare su qn.

lupin [lōō'pin] *n* lupino.

lurch [lûrch] *vi* vacillare, barcollare ♦ *n* scatto improvviso; **to leave sb in the** ~ piantare in asso qn.

lure [lōōr] *n* richiamo; lusinga ♦ *vt* attirare (con l'inganno).

lurid [lōō'rid] *a* sgargiante; (*details etc*) impressionante.

lurk [lûrk] *vi* stare in agguato.

luscious [lush'əs] *a* succulento(a); delizioso(a).

lush [lush] *a* lussureggiante.

lust [lust] *n* lussuria; cupidigia; desiderio; (*fig*): ~ **for** sete *f* di.

lust after *vt fus* bramare, desiderare.

luster [lus'tûr] *n* (*US*) lustro, splendore *m*.

lustful [lust'fəl] *a* lascivo(a), voglioso(a).

lustre [lus'tûr] *n* (*Brit*) = **luster**.

lusty [lus'tē] *a* vigoroso(a), robusto(a).

lute [lōōt] *n* liuto.

Luxembourg [luk'səmbûrg] *n* (*state*) Lussemburgo *m*; (*city*) Lussemburgo *f*.

luxuriant [lōōgzhōōr'cənt] *a* lussureggiante.

luxurious [lōōgzhōōr'ēəs] *a* sontuoso(a), di lusso.

luxury [luk'shûrē] *n* lusso ♦ *cpd* di lusso.

LW *abbr* (*RADIO*: = *long wave*) O.L.

lying [lī'ing] *n* bugie *fpl*, menzogne *fpl* ♦ *a* (*statement, story*) falso(a); (*person*) bugiardo(a).

lynch [linch] *vt* linciare.

lynx [lingks] *n* lince *f*.

Lyons [lī'ənz] *n* Lione *f*.

lyre [lī'ûr] *n* lira.

lyric [lir'ik] *a* lirico(a); ~**s** *npl* (*of song*) parole *fpl*.

lyrical [lir'ikəl] *a* lirico(a).

lyricism [lir'əsizəm] *n* lirismo.

M

M, m [em] *n* (*letter*) M, m *f or m inv*; **M for Mike** ≈ M come Milano.

M [em] *n abbr* (*Brit*: = *motorway*): **the M8** ≈ l'A8 ♦ *abbr* (= *medium*) taglia media.

m *abbr* (= *meter*) m; = **mile**; **million**.

MA *n abbr* (*SCOL*) *see* **Master of Arts**; (*US*) = *military academy* ♦ (*US MAIL*) = *Massachusetts*.

mac [mak] *n* (*Brit*) impermeabile *m*.

macabre [məkâ'brə] *a* macabro(a).

macaroni [makərō'nē] *n* maccheroni *mpl*.

macaroon [makərōōn'] *n* amaretto (*biscotto*).

mace [mās] *n* mazza; (*spice*) macis *m or f*.

machinations |makənā'shənz| *npl* macchinazioni *fpl*, intrighi *mpl*.

machine |məshēn'| *n* macchina ♦ *vt* (*dress etc*) cucire a macchina; (*TECH*) lavorare (a macchina).

machine code *n* (*COMPUT*) codice *m* di macchina, codice assoluto.

machine gun *n* mitragliatrice *f*.

machine language *n* (*COMPUT*) linguaggio *m* macchina *inv*.

machine-readable |məshēn'rē'dəbəl| *a* (*COMPUT*) leggibile dalla macchina.

machinery |məshē'nūrē| *n* macchinario, macchine *fpl*; (*fig*) macchina.

machine shop *n* officina meccanica.

machine tool *n* macchina utensile.

machine washable *a* lavabile in lavatrice.

machinist |məshē'nist| *n* macchinista *m/f*.

macho |mách'ō| *a* macho *inv*.

mackerel |mak'ûrəl| *n* (*pl inv*) sgombro.

mackintosh |mak'intâsh| *n* (*Brit*) impermeabile *m*.

macro... |mak'rō| *prefix* macro....

macroeconomics |makrōēkənám'iks| *n* macroeconomia.

mad |mad| *a* (*Brit*) matto(a), pazzo(a); (*foolish*) sciocco(a); (*angry*) furioso(a); **to go ~** impazzire, diventar matto; **~ (at** *or* **with sb)** furibondo(a) (con qn); **to be ~ (keen) about** *or* **on sth** (*col*) andar pazzo *or* matto per qc.

madam |mad'əm| *n* signora; **M~ Chairman** Signora Presidentessa.

madden |mad'ən| *vt* fare infuriare.

maddening |mad'əning| *a* esasperante.

made |mād| *pt, pp* *of* **make**.

Madeira |mədē'rə| *n* (*GEO*) Madera; (*wine*) madera *m*.

made-to-measure |mād'təmezh'ûr| *a* (*Brit*) = **made-to-order**.

made-to-order |mād'tōōôr'dûr| *a* (*US*) fatto(a) su misura.

madly |mad'lē| *ad* follemente; (*love*) alla follia.

madman |mad'man| *n* pazzo, alienato.

madness |mad'nis| *n* pazzia.

Madrid |mədrid'| *n* Madrid *f*.

Mafia |mâf'ēə| *n* mafia *f*.

magazine |magəzēn'| *n* (*PRESS*) rivista; (*MIL: store*) magazzino, deposito; (*of firearm*) caricatore *m*.

maggot |mag'ət| *n* baco, verme *m*.

magic |maj'ik| *n* magia ♦ *a* magico(a).

magical |maj'ikəl| *a* magico(a).

magician |məjish'ən| *n* mago/a.

magistrate |maj'istrāt| *n* magistrato; giudice *m/f*.

magnanimous |magnan'əməs| *a* magnanimo(a).

magnate |mag'nāt| *n* magnate *m*.

magnesium |magnē'zēəm| *n* magnesio.

magnet |mag'nit| *n* magnete *m*, calamita.

magnetic |magnet'ik| *a* magnetico(a).

magnetic disk *n* (*COMPUT*) disco magnetico.

magnetic tape *n* nastro magnetico.

magnetism |mag'nitizəm| *n* magnetismo.

magnification |magnəfəkā'shən| *n* ingrandimento.

magnificence |magnif'isəns| *n* magnificenza.

magnificent |magnif'əsənt| *a* magnifico(a).

magnify |mag'nəfī| *vt* ingrandire.

magnifying glass |mag'nəfīing glas| *n* lente *f* d'ingrandimento.

magnitude |mag'nətōōd| *n* grandezza; importanza.

magnolia |magnōl'yə| *n* magnolia.

magpie |mag'pī| *n* gazza.

mahogany |məhâg'ənē| *n* mogano ♦ *cpd* di *or* in mogano.

maid |mād| *n* domestica; (*in hotel*) cameriera; **old ~** (*pej*) vecchia zitella.

maiden |mād'ən| *n* fanciulla ♦ *a* (*aunt etc*) nubile; (*speech, voyage*) inaugurale.

maiden name *n* nome *m* nubile *or* da ragazza.

mail |māl| *n* posta ♦ *vt* spedire (per posta); **by ~** per posta; **by return ~** a stretto giro di posta.

mailbag |māl'bag| *n* (*US*) sacco postale, sacco della posta.

mailbox |māl'bâks| *n* (*US*) cassetta delle lettere; (*COMPUT*) mailbox *f inv*.

mailing |mā'ling| *n* (*US*) incarico.

mailing list |mā'ling list| *n* elenco d'indirizzi.

mailman |māl'man| *n* (*US*) portalettere *m inv*, postino.

mail order *n* vendita (*or* acquisto) per corrispondenza ♦ **mail-order** *cpd*: **~ house** *or* **firm** ditta di vendita per corrispondenza.

mailshot |māl'shât| *n* (*Brit*) mailing *m inv*.

mail train *n* treno postale.

mail truck *n* (*US: AUT*) furgone *m* postale; (*: RAIL*) vagone *m* postale.

mail van *n* (*Brit AUT*) = **mail truck**.

maim |mām| *vt* mutilare.

main |mān| *a* principale ♦ *n* (*pipe*) conduttura principale; **the ~s** (*ELEC*) la linea principale; **~s operated** *a* (*Brit*) che funziona a elettricità; **in the ~** nel complesso, nell'insieme.

main course *n* (*CULIN*) piatto principale, piatto forte.

mainframe |mān'frām| *n* (*also:* **~ computer**) mainframe *m inv*.

mainland |mān'lənd| *n* continente *m*.

mainline |mān'līn| *a* (*RAIL*) della linea principale ♦ *vb* (*drugs slang*) *vt* bucarsi di ♦ *vi* bucarsi.

main line *n* (*RAIL*) linea principale.

mainly |mān'lē| *ad* principalmente, soprattutto.

main road *n* strada principale.

mainstay |mān'stā| *n* (*fig*) sostegno principale.

mainstream |mān'strēm| *n* (*fig*) corrente *f*

principale.

maintain [mān'tān'] *vt* mantenere; *(affirm)* sostenere; **to ~ that ...** sostenere che ....

maintenance [mān'tənəns] *n* manutenzione *f*; *(alimony)* alimenti *mpl.*

maintenance contract *n* contratto di manutenzione.

maintenance order *n* *(LAW)* obbligo degli alimenti.

maisonette [māzənet'] *n* *(Brit)* appartamento a due piani.

maize [māz] *n* granturco, mais *m.*

Maj. *abbr* *(MIL)* = **major.**

majestic [məjes'tik] *a* maestoso(a).

majesty [maj'istē] *n* maestà *f inv.*

major [mā'jûr] *n* *(MIL)* maggiore *m* ♦ *a* *(greater, MUS)* maggiore; *(in importance)* principale, importante ♦ *vi* *(US SCOL)*: **to ~ (in)** specializzarsi (in); **a ~ operation** *(MED)* una grossa operazione.

Majorca [məyôr'kə] *n* Maiorca.

major general *n* *(MIL)* generale *m* di divisione.

majority [məjôr'itē] *n* maggioranza ♦ *cpd* *(verdict)* maggioritario(a).

majority holding *n* *(COMM)*: **to have a ~** essere maggiore azionista.

make [māk] *vt* *(pt, pp* **made** [mād])* fare; *(manufacture)* fare, fabbricare; *(cause to be)*: **to ~ sb sad** *etc* rendere qn triste *etc*; *(force)*: **to ~ sb do sth** costringere qn a fare qc, far fare qc a qn; *(equal)*: **2 and 2 ~ 4** 2 più 2 fa 4 ♦ *n* fabbricazione *f*; *(brand)* marca; **to ~ it** *(in time etc)* arrivare; **what time do you ~ it?** che ora fai?; **to ~ good** *vi* *(succeed)* aver successo ♦ *vt* *(deficit)* colmare; *(losses)* compensare; **to ~ do with** arrangiarsi con.

make for *vt fus* *(place)* avviarsi verso.

make off *vi* svignarsela.

make out *vt* *(write out)* scrivere; *(understand)* capire; *(see)* distinguere; *(: numbers)* decifrare; *(claim, imply)*: **to ~ out (that)** voler far credere (che); **to ~ out a case for sth** presentare delle valide ragioni in favore di qc.

make over *vt* *(assign)*: **to ~ over (to)** passare (a), trasferire (a).

make up *vt* *(invent)* inventare; *(parcel)* fare ♦ *vi* conciliarsi; *(with cosmetics)* truccarsi; **to be made up of** essere composto di *or* formato da.

make up for *vt fus* compensare; ricuperare.

make-believe [māk'bilēv] *n*: **a world of ~** un mondo di favole; **it's just ~** è tutta un'invenzione.

maker [mā'kûr] *n* fabbricante *m*; creatore/trice, autore/trice.

makeshift [māk'shift] *a* improvvisato(a).

make-up [māk'up] *n* trucco.

make-up bag *n* borsa del trucco.

make-up remover *n* struccatore *m.*

making [mā'king] *n* *(fig)*: **in the ~** in formazione; **he has the ~s of an actor** ha la stoffa dell'attore.

maladjusted [maləjus'tid] *a* disadattato(a).

maladroit [malədroit'] *a* maldestro(a).

malaise [malāz'] *n* malessere *m.*

malaria [məlär'ēə] *n* malaria.

Malawi [mə'lâwē] *n* Malawi *m.*

Malay [məlā'] *a* malese ♦ *n* malese *m/f*; *(LING)* malese *m.*

Malaya [məlā'yə] *n* Malesia.

Malayan [məlā'yən] *a, n* = **Malay.**

Malaysia [məlā'zhə] *n* Malaysia.

Malaysian [məlā'zhən] *a, n* malaysiano(a).

Maldives [mal'dīvz] *npl*: **the ~** le (isole) Maldive.

male [māl] *n* *(BIO, ELEC)* maschio ♦ *a* *(gen, sex)* maschile; *(animal, child)* maschio(a); **~ and female students** studenti e studentesse.

male chauvinist *n* maschilista *m.*

male nurse *n* infermiere *m.*

malevolence [məlev'ələns] *n* malevolenza.

malevolent [məlev'ələnt] *a* malevolo(a).

malfunction [malfungk'shən] *n* funzione *f* difettosa.

malice [mal'is] *n* malevolenza.

malicious [məlish'əs] *a* malevolo(a); *(LAW)* doloso(a).

malign [məlīn'] *vt* malignare su; calunniare.

malignant [məlig'nənt] *a* *(MED)* maligno(a).

malingerer [məling'gûrûr] *n* scansafatiche *m/f inv.*

mall [môl] *n* *(also:* **shopping ~)** centro commerciale.

malleable [mal'ēəbəl] *a* malleabile.

mallet [mal'it] *n* maglio.

malnutrition [malnōōtrish'ən] *n* denutrizione *f.*

malpractice [malprak'tis] *n* prevaricazione *f*; negligenza.

malt [môlt] *n* malto ♦ *cpd* *(whisky)* di malto.

Malta [môl'tə] *n* Malta.

Maltese [môltēz'] *a, n* *(pl inv)* maltese *(m/f)*; *(LING)* maltese *m.*

maltreat [maltrēt'] *vt* maltrattare.

mammal [mam'əl] *n* mammifero.

mammoth [mam'əth] *n* mammut *m inv* ♦ *a* enorme, gigantesco(a).

Man. *abbr* *(Canada)* = Manitoba.

man [man] *n* *(pl* **men** [men])* uomo; *(CHESS)* pezzo; *(DRAUGHTS)* pedina ♦ *vt* fornire d'uomini; stare a; essere di servizio a.

manacles [man'əkəlz] *npl* manette *fpl.*

manage [man'ij] *vi* farcela ♦ *vt* *(be in charge of)* occuparsi di; *(store, restaurant)* gestire; **to ~ without sth/sb** fare a meno di qc/qn; **to ~ to do sth** riuscire a far qc.

manageable [man'ijəbəl] *a* maneggevole; *(task etc)* fattibile.

management [man'ijmənt] *n* amministrazione *f*, direzione *f*; gestione *f*; (*persons: of business, firm*) dirigenti *mpl*; (: *of hotel, store, theater*) direzione *f*; **"under new ~"** "sotto nuova gestione".

management accounting *n* contabilità di gestione.

management consultant *n* consulente *m/f* aziendale.

manager [man'ijûr] *n* direttore *m*; (*of store, restaurant*) gerente *m*; (*of artist*) manager *m inv*; **sales ~** direttore *m* delle vendite.

manageress [man'ijûris] *n* direttrice *f*; gerente *f*.

managerial [manijē'rēəl] *a* dirigenziale.

managing director (MD) [man'ijing dirɛk'tûr] *n* amministratore *m* delegato.

mandarin [man'dərin] *n* (*person, fruit*) mandarino.

mandate [man'dāt] *n* mandato.

mandatory [man'dətôrē] *a* obbligatorio(a); ingiuntivo(a).

mandolin(e) [man'dəlin] *n* mandolino.

mane [mān] *n* criniera.

maneuver [mənōō'vûr] (*US*) *vt* manovrare ♦ *vi* far manovrare ♦ *n* manovra; **to ~ sb into doing sth** costringere abilmente qn a fare qc.

maneuverable [mənōō'vrəbəl] *a* (*US*) facile da manovrare; (*car*) maneggevole.

manful [man'fəl] *a* coraggioso(a), valoroso(a).

manfully [man'fəlē] *ad* valorosamente.

manganese [mang'gənēz] *n* manganese *m*.

mangle [mang'gəl] *vt* straziare; mutilare ♦ *n* strizzatoio.

mango, ~es [mang'gō] *n* mango.

mangrove [mang'grōv] *n* mangrovia.

mangy [mān'jē] *a* rognoso(a).

manhandle [man'handəl] *vt* (*treat roughly*) malmenare; (*move by hand: goods*) spostare a mano.

manhole [man'hōl] *n* botola stradale.

manhood [man'hŏŏd] *n* età virile; virilità.

man-hour [man'ouûr] *n* ora di lavoro.

manhunt [man'hunt] *n* caccia all'uomo.

mania [mā'nēə] *n* mania.

maniac [mā'nēak] *n* maniaco/a.

manic [man'ik] *a* maniacale.

manic-depressive [man'ikdiprɛs'iv] *a* maniaco-depressivo(a) ♦ *n* persona affetta da mania depressiva.

manicure [man'əkyŏŏr] *n* manicure *f inv*.

manicure set *n* trousse *f inv* della manicure.

manifest [man'əfɛst] *vt* manifestare ♦ *a* manifesto(a), palese ♦ *n* (*AVIAT, NAUT*) manifesto.

manifestation [manəfɛstā'shən] *n* manifestazione *f*.

manifesto [manəfɛs'tō] *n* manifesto.

manifold [man'əfōld] *a* molteplice ♦ *n* (*AUT etc*): **exhaust ~** collettore *m* di scarico.

Manila [mənil'ə] *n* Manila.

manil(l)a [mənil'ə] *a* (*paper, envelope*) manilla *inv*.

manipulate [mənip'yəlāt] *vt* (*tool*) maneggiare; (*controls*) azionare; (*limb, facts*) manipolare.

manipulation [mənipyəlā'shən] *n* maneggiare *m*; capacità di azionare; manipolazione *f*.

mankind [man'kīnd'] *n* umanità, genere *m* umano.

manliness [man'lēnis] *n* virilità.

manly [man'lē] *a* virile; coraggioso(a).

man-made [man'mād] *a* sintetico(a); artificiale.

manna [man'ə] *n* manna.

mannequin [man'əkin] *n* (*dummy*) manichino; (*fashion model*) indossatrice *f*.

manner [man'ûr] *n* maniera, modo; **~s** *npl* maniere *fpl*; **(good) ~s** buona educazione *f*, buone maniere; **bad ~s** maleducazione *f*; **all ~ of** ogni sorta di.

mannerism [man'ərizəm] *n* vezzo, tic *m inv*.

mannerly [man'ûrlē] *a* educato(a), civile.

manoeuvre [mənōō'vûr] *etc* (*Brit*) = **maneuver** *etc*.

manor [man'ûr] *n* (*also*: **~ house**) maniero.

manpower [man'pouûr] *n* manodopera.

manservant, *pl* **menservants** [man'sûrvənt, men'sûrvənts] *n* domestico.

mansion [man'chən] *n* casa signorile.

manslaughter [man'slôtûr] *n* omicidio preterintenzionale.

mantelpiece [man'təlpēs] *n* mensola del caminetto.

mantle [man'təl] *n* mantello.

man-to-man [man'təman'] *a, ad* da uomo a uomo.

Mantua [man'chŏŏwə] *n* Mantova.

manual [man'yŏŏəl] *a, n* manuale (*m*).

manual worker *n* manovale *m*.

manufacture [manyəfak'chûr] *vt* fabbricare ♦ *n* fabbricazione *f*, manifattura.

manufactured goods [manyəfak'chûrd gŏŏdz] *npl* manufatti *mpl*.

manufacturer [manyəfak'chûrûr] *n* fabbricante *m*.

manufacturing industries [manyəfak'chûring in'dəstrēz] *npl* industrie *fpl* manifatturiere.

manure [mənŏŏr'] *n* concime *m*.

manuscript [man'yəskript] *n* manoscritto.

many [men'ē] *a* molti(e) ♦ *pronoun* molti(e), un gran numero; **a great ~** moltissimi(e), un gran numero (di); **~ a** ... molti(e) ..., più di un(a) ...; **too ~ difficulties** troppe difficoltà; **twice as ~** due volte tanto; **how ~?** quanti(e)?

map [map] *n* carta (geografica) ♦ *vt* fare una carta di.

map out *vt* tracciare un piano di; (*fig: career, vacation, essay*) pianificare.

maple [mā'pəl] *n* acero.

mar [mâr] *vt* sciupare.

Mar. *abbr* (= *March*) mar.

marathon [mar'əthán] *n* maratona ♦ *a*: **a ~ session** una seduta fiume.
marathon runner *n* maratoneta *m/f*.
marauder [mərôd'ûr] *n* saccheggiatore *m*; predatore *m*.
marble [mâr'bəl] *n* marmo; (*toy*) pallina, bilia; ~**s** *n* (*game*) palline, bilie.
marble mason *n* (*US*) lapidario.
March [mârch] *n* marzo; *for phrases see also* **July.**
march [mârch] *vi* marciare; sfilare ♦ *n* marcia; (*demonstration*) dimostrazione *f*; **to ~ into a room** entrare a passo deciso in una stanza.
marcher [mâr'chûr] *n* dimostrante *m/f*.
marching [mâr'ching] *n*: **to give sb his ~ orders** (*fig*) dare il benservito a qn.
march-past [mârch'past] *n* sfilata.
mare [mär] *n* giumenta.
marg. [mârj] *n abbr* (*col*) = **margarine.**
margarine [mâr'jûrin] *n* margarina.
margin [mâr'jin] *n* margine *m*.
marginal [mâr'jinəl] *a* marginale; ~ **seat** (*POL*) *seggio elettorale ottenuto con una stretta maggioranza.*
marginally [mâr'jinəlē] *ad* (*bigger*, *better*) lievemente, di poco; (*different*) un po'.
marigold [mar'əgōld] *n* calendola.
marijuana [marəwâ'nə] *n* marijuana.
marina [mərē'nə] *n* marina.
marinade *n* [mar'ənād] marinata ♦ *vt* [marənād'] = **marinate.**
marinate [mar'ənāt] *vt* marinare.
marine [mərēn'] *a* (*animal*, *plant*) marino(a); (*forces*, *engineering*) marittimo(a) ♦ *n* fante *m* di marina; (*US*) marine *m inv*.
marine insurance *n* assicurazione *f* marittima.
marital [mar'itəl] *a* maritale, coniugale; ~ **status** stato coniugale.
maritime [mar'itīm] *a* marittimo(a).
maritime law *n* diritto marittimo.
marjoram [mâr'jûrəm] *n* maggiorana.
mark [mârk] *n* segno; (*stain*) macchia; (*of skid etc*) traccia; (*Brit SCOL*) voto; (*SPORT*) bersaglio; (*currency*) marco; (*Brit TECH*) **M~ 2/3** 1a/2a serie *f* ♦ *vt* segnare; (*stain*) macchiare; (*Brit SCOL*) dare un voto a; correggere; (*SPORT*: *player*) marcare; **punctuation ~s** segni di punteggiatura; **to be quick off the ~ (in doing)** (*fig*) non perdere tempo (per fare); **up to the ~** (*in efficiency*) all'altezza; **to ~ time** segnare il passo.
mark down *vt* (*reduce*: *prices*, *goods*) ribassare, ridurre.
mark off *vt* (*tick off*) spuntare, cancellare.
mark out *vt* delimitare.
mark up *vt* (*price*) aumentare.
marked [mârkt] *a* spiccato(a), chiaro(a).
markedly [mâr'kidlē] *ad* visibilmente, note-

volmente.
marker [mâr'kûr] *n* (*sign*) segno; (*bookmark*) segnalibro.
market [mâr'kit] *n* mercato ♦ *vt* (*COMM*) mettere in vendita; (*promote*) lanciare sul mercato; **to play the ~** giocare *or* speculare in borsa; **to be on the ~** essere (messo) in vendita *or* in commercio; **open ~** mercato libero.
marketable [mâr'kitəbəl] *a* commercializzabile.
market analysis *n* analisi *f* di mercato.
market day *n* giorno di mercato.
market demand *n* domanda del mercato.
market forces *npl* forze *fpl* di mercato.
market garden *n* (*Brit*) orto industriale.
marketing [mâr'kiting] *n* marketing *m*.
marketplace [mâr'kitplâs] *n* (piazza del) mercato; (*world of trade*) piazza, mercato.
market price *n* prezzo di mercato.
market research *n* indagine *f or* ricerca di mercato.
market value *n* valore *m* di mercato.
marking [mâr'king] *n* (*on animal*) marcatura di colore; (*on road*) segnaletica orizzontale.
marksman [mârks'mən] *n* tiratore *m* scelto.
marksmanship [mârks'mənship] *n* abilità nel tiro.
markup [mârk'up] *n* (*COMM*: *margin*) margine *m* di vendita; (: *increase*) aumento.
marmalade [mâr'məlād] *n* marmellata d'arance.
maroon [mərōōn'] *vt* (*fig*): **to be ~ed (in** *or* **at)** essere abbandonato(a) (in) ♦ *a* bordeaux *inv*.
marquee [mârkē'] *n* padiglione *m*.
marquess, marquis [mâr'kwis] *n* marchese *m*.
Marrakech, Marrakesh [mâr'əkesh] *n* Marrakesh *f*.
marriage [mar'ij] *n* matrimonio.
marriage bureau *n* agenzia matrimoniale.
marriage certificate *n* certificato di matrimonio.
marriage counseling, (*Brit*) **marriage guidance** *n* consulenza matrimoniale.
married [mar'ēd] *a* sposato(a); (*life*, *love*) coniugale, matrimoniale.
marrow [mar'ō] *n* midollo; (*vegetable*) zucca.
marry [mar'ē] *vt* sposare, sposarsi con; (*subj*: *father*, *priest etc*) dare in matrimonio ♦ *vi* (*also*: **get married**) sposarsi.
Mars [mârz] *n* (*planet*) Marte *m*.
Marseilles [mârsā'] *n* Marsiglia.
marsh [mârsh] *n* palude *f*.
marshal [mâr'shəl] *n* maresciallo; (*US*: *fire* ~) capo; (: *police* ~) capitano ♦ *vt* adunare.
marshalling yard [mâr'shəling yârd] *n* (*Brit*) scalo smistamento.
marshmallow [mârsh'melō] *n* (*BOT*) altea; (*sweet*) caramella soffice e gommosa.
marshy [mâr'shē] *a* paludoso(a).

marsupial [mârsōō'pēəl] *a, n* marsupiale (*m*).
martial [mâr'shəl] *a* marziale.
martial law *n* legge *f* marziale.
Martian [mâr'shən] *n* marziano/a.
martin [mâr'tən] *n* (*also:* **house** ~) balestruccio.
martyr [mâr'tûr] *n* martire *m/f* ♦ *vt* martirizzare.
martyrdom [mâr'tûrdəm] *n* martirio.
marvel [mâr'vəl] *n* meraviglia ♦ *vi:* **to** ~ **(at)** meravigliarsi (di).
marvelous, (*Brit*) **marvellous** [mâr'vələs] *a* meraviglioso(a).
Marxism [mârk'sizəm] *n* marxismo.
Marxist [mâr'ksist] *a, n* marxista (*m/f*).
marzipan [mâr'zəpan] *n* marzapane *m.*
mascara [maskar'ə] *n* mascara *m inv.*
mascot [mas'kət] *n* mascotte *f inv.*
masculine [mas'kyəlin] *a* maschile ♦ *n* genere *m* maschile.
masculinity [maskyəlin'itē] *n* mascolinità.
MASH [mash] *n abbr* (*US MIL:* = *mobile army surgical hospital*) *ospedale di campo di unità mobile dell'esercito.*
mash [mash] *vt* (*CULIN*) passare, schiacciare.
mashed [masht] *a:* ~ **potatoes** purè *m* di patate.
mask [mask] *n* (*gen, ELEC*) maschera ♦ *vt* mascherare.
masochism [mas'əkizəm] *n* masochismo.
masochist [mas'əkist] *n* masochista *m/f.*
mason [mā'sən] *n* (*also:* **stone**~) scalpellino; (*also:* **free**~) massone *m.*
masonic [məsân'ik] *a* massonico(a).
masonry [mā'sənrē] *n* muratura.
masquerade [maskərād'] *n* ballo in maschera; (*fig*) mascherata ♦ *vi:* **to** ~ **as** farsi passare per.
Mass. *abbr* (*US*) = *Massachusetts.*
mass [mas] *n* moltitudine *f*, massa; (*PHYSICS*) massa; (*REL*) messa ♦ *vi* ammassarsi; **the** ~**es** le masse; **to go to** ~ andare a *or* alla messa.
massacre [mas'əkûr] *n* massacro ♦ *vt* massacrare.
massage [məsâzh'] *n* massaggio ♦ *vt* massaggiare.
masseur [masûr'] *n* massaggiatore *m.*
masseuse [məsōōs'] *n* massaggiatrice *f.*
massive [mas'iv] *a* enorme, massiccio(a).
mass market *n* mercato di massa.
mass media [mas mē'dēə] *npl* mass media *mpl.*
mass meeting *n* (*of everyone concerned*) riunione *f* generale; (*huge*) adunata popolare.
mass-produce [mas'prədōōs'] *vt* produrre in serie.
mass production *n* produzione *f* in serie.
mast [mast] *n* albero; (*RADIO, TV*) pilone *m* (a traliccio).
master [mas'tûr] *n* padrone *m;* (*ART etc,*

teacher: in primary school) maestro; (: *in secondary school*) professore *m;* (*title for boys*): **M~** **X** Signorino X ♦ *vt* domare; (*learn*) imparare a fondo; (*understand*) conoscere a fondo; **M~ of Arts/Science (MA/ MSc)** *n* (*detentore di*) *titolo accademico in lettere/scienze superiore alla laurea;* **M~'s degree** *n titolo accademico superiore alla laurea;* ~ **of ceremonies (MC)** *n* maestro di cerimonie.
master disk *n* (*COMPUT*) disco master *inv,* disco principale.
masterful [mas'tûrfəl] *a* autoritario(a), imperioso(a).
master key *n* chiave *f* maestra.
masterly [mas'tûrlē] *a* magistrale.
mastermind [mas'tûrmīnd] *n* mente *f* superiore ♦ *vt* essere il cervello di.
masterpiece [mas'tûrpēs] *n* capolavoro.
master plan *n* piano generale.
masterstroke [mas'tûrstrōk] *n* colpo maestro.
mastery [mas'tûrē] *n* dominio; padronanza.
mastiff [mas'tif] *n* mastino inglese.
masturbate [mas'tûrbāt] *vi* masturbare.
masturbation [mastûrbā'shən] *n* masturbazione *f.*
mat [mat] *n* stuoia; (*also:* **door**~) stoino, zerbino ♦ *a* = **matt.**
match [mach] *n* fiammifero; (*game*) partita, incontro; (*fig*) uguale *m/f;* matrimonio; partito ♦ *vt* intonare; (*go well with*) andare benissimo con; (*equal*) uguagliare ♦ *vi* intonarsi; **to be a good** ~ andare bene.
match up *vt* intonare.
matchbox [mach'bâks] *n* scatola per fiammiferi.
matching [mach'ing] *a* ben assortito(a).
matchless [mach'lis] *a* senza pari.
mate [māt] *n* (*animal*) compagno/a; (*in merchant navy*) secondo; (*Brit: colleague*) compagno/a di lavoro; (: *col: friend*) amico/a ♦ *vi* accoppiarsi *vt* accoppiare.
material [mətē'rēəl] *n* (*substance*) materiale *m,* materia; (*cloth*) stoffa ♦ *a* materiale; (*important*) essenziale; ~**s** *npl* (*equipment etc*) materiali *mpl;* occorrente *m.*
materialistic [mətērēəlis'tik] *a* materialistico(a).
materialize [mətēr'ēəlīz] *vi* materializzarsi, realizzarsi.
materially [mətēr'ēəlē] *ad* dal punto di vista materiale; sostanzialmente.
maternal [mətûr'nəl] *a* materno(a).
maternity [mətûr'nitē] *n* maternità ♦ *cpd* di maternità; (*clothes*) pre-maman *inv.*
maternity benefit *n* sussidio di maternità.
maternity hospital *n* ≈ clinica ostetrica.
math. [math] *n abbr* (*US*) = **mathematics.**
mathematical [mathəmat'ikəl] *a* matematico(a).
mathematician [mathəmətish'ən] *n* mate-

matico/a.

mathematics [mathəmat'iks] *n* matematica.

maths [maths] *n abbr* (*Brit*) = **mathematics**.

matinée [matənā'] *n* matinée *f inv.*

mating [mā'ting] *n* accoppiamento.

mating call *n* chiamata all'accoppiamento.

mating season *n* stagione *f* degli amori.

matriarchal [mātrēâr'kəl] *a* matriarcale.

matrices [māt'risēz] *npl of* **matrix**.

matriculation [mətrikyəlā'shən] *n* immatricolazione *f.*

matrimonial [matrəmō'nēəl] *a* matrimoniale, coniugale.

matrimony [mat'rəmōnē] *n* matrimonio.

matrix, *pl* matrices [mā'triks, māt'risēz] *n* matrice *f.*

matron [mā'trən] *n* (*in hospital*) capoinfermiera; (*in school*) infermiera.

matronly [mā'trənlē] *a* da matrona.

matt [mat] *a* opaco(a).

matted [mat'id] *a* ingarbugliato(a).

matter [mat'ûr] *n* questione *f*; (*PHYSICS*) materia, sostanza; (*content*) contenuto; (*MED*: *pus*) pus *m* ♦ *vi* importare; **it doesn't ~** non importa; (*I don't mind*) non fa niente; **what's the ~?** che cosa c'è?; **no ~ what** qualsiasi cosa accada; **that's another ~** quello è un altro affare; **as a ~ of course** come cosa naturale; **as a ~ of fact** in verità; **it's a ~ of habit** è una questione di abitudine; **printed ~** stampe *fpl*; **reading ~** qualcosa da leggere.

matter-of-fact [mat'ûrəvfakt'] *a* prosaico(a).

matting [mat'ing] *n* stuoia.

mattress [mat'ris] *n* materasso.

mature [mətōōr'] *a* maturo(a); (*cheese*) stagionato(a) ♦ *vi* maturare; stagionare; (*COMM*) scadere.

maturity [mətōō'ritē] *n* maturità.

maudlin [môd'lin] *a* lacrimoso(a).

maul [môl] *vt* lacerare.

Mauritania [môritā'nēə] *n* Mauritania.

Mauritius [môrish'ēəs] *n* Maurizio.

mausoleum [môsəlē'əm] *n* mausoleo.

mauve [mōv] *a* malva *inv.*

maverick [mav'ûrik] *n* (*fig*) chi sta fuori del branco.

mawkish [môk'ish] *a* sdolcinato(a); insipido(a).

max. *abbr* = **maximum.**

maxim [mak'sim] *n* massima.

maxima [mak'səmə] *npl of* **maximum**.

maximize [mak'səmīz] *vt* (*profits etc*) massimizzare; (*chances*) aumentare al massimo.

maximum [mak'səməm] *a* massimo(a) ♦ *n* (*pl* **maxima** [mak'səmə]) massimo.

May [mā] *n* maggio; *for phrases see also* **July.**

may [mā] *vi* (*conditional*: **might**) (*indicating possibility*): **he ~ come** può darsi che venga; (*be allowed to*): **~ I smoke?** posso fumare?; **~ I sit here?** le dispiace se mi siedo qua?;

(*wishes*): **~ God bless you!** Dio la benedica!; **he might be there** può darsi che ci sia; **he might come** potrebbe venire, può anche darsi che venga; **I might as well go** potrei anche andarmene; **you might like to try** forse le piacerebbe provare.

maybe [mā'bē] *ad* forse, può darsi; **~ he'll ...** può darsi che lui ...+*sub*, forse lui ...; **~ not** forse no, può darsi di no.

mayday [mā'dā] *n* S.O.S. *m.*

May Day *n* il primo maggio.

mayhem [mā'hem] *n* cagnara.

mayonnaise [māənāz'] *n* maionese *f.*

mayor [mā'ûr] *n* sindaco.

mayoress [mā'ûris] *n* sindaco (*donna*); moglie *f* del sindaco.

maypole [mā'pōl] *n* palo ornato di fiori attorno a cui si danza durante la festa di maggio.

maze [māz] *n* labirinto, dedalo.

MB *abbr* (*COMPUT*) = megabyte; (*Canada*) = Manitoba.

MBA *n abbr* (= *Master of Business Administration*) titolo di studio.

MBBS, MBChB *n abbr* (*Brit*: = *Bachelor of Medicine and Surgery*) titolo di studio.

MC *n abbr* (*US*: = *Member of Congress*) membro del Congresso; *see* **master of ceremonies**.

MCAT *n abbr* (*US*: = *Medical College Admissions Test*) esame di ammissione a studi superiori di medicina.

MCP *n abbr* (*Brit col*: = *male chauvinist pig*) sporco maschilista *m.*

MD *n abbr* (*US MAIL*) = Maryland ♦ (= *Doctor of Medicine*) titolo di studio; (*COMM*) *see* **managing director**.

ME *abbr* (*US MAIL*) = Maine ♦ *n abbr* (*US*) = medical examiner; (*MED*) = myalgic encephalomyelitis.

me [mē] *pronoun* mi, m' + *vowel*; (*stressed, after prep*) me; **it's ~** sono io; **it's for ~** è per me.

meadow [med'ō] *n* prato.

meager (*Brit*) **meagre** [mē'gûr] *a* magro(a).

meal [mēl] *n* pasto; (*flour*) farina; **to go out for a ~** mangiare fuori.

meal ticket *n* (*US*) buono *m* pasto *inv.*

mealtime [mēl'tim] *n* l'ora di mangiare.

mealy-mouthed [mē'lēmouthd] *a* che parla attraverso eufemismi.

mean [mēn] *a* (*with money*) avaro(a), gretto(a); (*unkind*) meschino(a), maligno(a); (*US*: *vicious*: *animal*) cattivo(a); (: *person*) perfido(a); (*average*) medio(a) ♦ *vt* (*pt, pp* **meant** [ment]) (*signify*) significare, voler dire; (*intend*): **to ~ to do** aver l'intenzione di fare ♦ *n* mezzo; (*MATH*) media; **to be meant for** essere destinato(a) a; **do you ~ it?** dice sul serio?; **what do you ~?** che cosa vuol dire?; *see also* **means.**

meander [mēan'dûr] *vi* far meandri; (*fig*) divagare.

meaning [mē'ning] *n* significato, senso.

meaningful [mē'ningfəl] *a* significativo(a); (*relationship*) valido(a).

meaningless [mē'ninglis] *a* senza senso.

meanness [mēn'nis] *n* avarizia; meschinità.

means [mēnz] *npl* mezzi *mpl*; **by ~ of** per mezzo di; (*person*) a mezzo di; **by all ~** ma certo, prego.

means test *n* (*Brit ADMIN*) accertamento dei redditi (*per una persona che ha chiesto un aiuto finanziario*).

meant [ment] *pt*, *pp of* **mean**.

meantime [mēn'tīm] *ad* (*also*: **in the ~**) nel frattempo.

meanwhile [mēn'wīl] *ad* nel frattempo.

measles [mē'zəlz] *n* morbillo.

measly [mēz'lē] *a* (*col*) miserabile.

measurable [mezh'ûrəbəl] *a* misurabile.

measure [mezh'ûr] *vt*, *vi* misurare ♦ *n* misura; (*ruler*) metro; **a liter ~** una misura da un litro; **some ~ of success** un certo successo; **to take ~s to do sth** prendere provvedimenti per fare qc.

measure up *vi*: **to ~ up (to)** dimostrarsi *or* essere all'altezza (di).

measured [mezh'ûrd] *a* misurato(a).

measurement [mezh'ûrmənt] *n* (*act*) misurazione *f*; (*measure*) misura; **chest/hip ~** petto/fianchi; **to take sb's ~s** prendere le misure di qn.

meat [mēt] *n* carne *f*; **cold ~s** (*Brit*) affettati *mpl*; **crab ~** polpa di granchio.

meatball [mēt'bôl] *n* polpetta di carne.

meat pie *n* torta salata in pasta frolla con ripieno di carne.

meaty [mē'tē] *a* che sa di carne; (*fig*) sostanzioso(a).

Mecca [mek'ə] *n* La Mecca; (*fig*): **a ~ (for)** la Mecca (di).

mechanic [məkan'ik] *n* meccanico; *see also* **mechanics**.

mechanical [məkan'ikəl] *a* meccanico(a).

mechanical engineering *n* (*science*) ingegneria meccanica; (*industry*) costruzioni *fpl* meccaniche.

mechanical pencil *n* (*US*) matita a mina.

mechanics [məkan'iks] *n* meccanica ♦ *npl* meccanismo.

mechanism [mek'ənizəm] *n* meccanismo.

mechanization [mekənizā'shən] *n* meccanizzazione *f*.

MEd *n* abbr (= *Master of Education*) titolo di studio.

medal [med'əl] *n* medaglia.

medallion [mədal'yən] *n* medaglione *m*.

medalist, (*Brit*) **medallist** [med'əlist] *n* (*SPORT*) vincitore/trice di medaglia.

meddle [med'əl] *vi*: **to ~ in** immischiarsi in, mettere le mani in; **to ~ with** toccare.

meddlesome [med'əlsəm], **meddling**

[med'ling] *a* (*interfering*) che mette il naso dappertutto; (*touching things*) che tocca tutto.

media [mē'dēə] *npl* (*PRESS, RADIO, TV*) media *mpl*; (*means*) *pl of* **medium**.

mediaeval [mēdēē'vəl] *a* = **medieval**.

median [mē'dēən] *n* (*US*: *also*: **~ strip**) banchina *f* spartitraffico *inv*.

media research *n* sondaggio tra gli utenti dei mass media.

mediate [mē'dēāt] *vi* interporsi; fare da mediatore/trice.

mediation [mēdēā'shən] *n* mediazione *f*.

mediator [mē'dēātûr] *n* mediatore/trice.

Medicaid [med'əkād] *n* (*US*) assistenza *medica ai poveri*.

medical [med'ikəl] *a* medico(a); **~ (examination)** visita medica.

medical certificate *n* certificato medico.

medical examiner (ME) *n* (*US*) *medico incaricato di indagare la causa di morte in circostanze sospette*.

medical student *n* studente/essa di medicina.

Medicare [med'əkär] *n* (*US*) *assistenza medica agli anziani*.

medicated [med'ikātid] *a* medicato(a).

medication [medikā'shən] *n* (*drugs etc*) medicinali *mpl*, farmaci *mpl*.

medicinal [mədis'ənəl] *a* medicinale.

medicine [med'isin] *n* medicina.

medicine chest *n* armadietto farmaceutico.

medicine man *n* stregone *m*.

medieval [mēdēē'vəl] *a* medievale.

mediocre [mē'dēōkûr] *a* mediocre.

mediocrity [mēdēäk'ritē] *n* mediocrità.

meditate [med'ətāt] *vi*: **to ~ (on)** meditare (su).

meditation [meditā'shən] *n* meditazione *f*.

Mediterranean [meditərā'nēən] *a* mediterraneo(a); **the ~ (Sea)** il (mare) Mediterraneo.

medium [mē'dēəm] *a* medio(a) ♦ *n* (*pl* **media**: *means*) mezzo; (*pl* **mediums**: *person*) medium *m inv*; **the happy ~** una giusta via di mezzo; *see also* **media**.

medium-sized [mē'dēəmsīzd] *a* (*can etc*) di grandezza media; (*clothes*) di taglia media.

medium wave *n* (*RADIO*) onde *fpl* medie.

medley [med'lē] *n* selezione *f*.

meek [mēk] *a* dolce, umile.

meet *pt*, *pp* **met** [mēt, met] *vt* incontrare; (*for the first time*) fare la conoscenza di; (*fig*) affrontare; far fronte a; soddisfare; raggiungere ♦ *vi* incontrarsi; (*in session*) riunirsi; (*join*: *objects*) unirsi ♦ *n* (*US SPORT*) raduno (sportivo); (*Brit HUNTING*) raduno (dei partecipanti alla caccia alla volpe); **I'll ~ you at the station** verrò a prenderla alla stazione; **pleased to ~ you!** lieto di conoscerla!, piacere!

meet up *vi*: **to ~ up with sb** incontrare

qn.

meet with *vt fus* incontrare; **he met with an accident** ha avuto un incidente.

meeting [mē'ting] *n* incontro; (*session: of club etc*) riunione *f*; (*interview*) intervista; (*formal*) colloquio; (*SPORT: rally*) raduno; **she's at a** ~ (*COMM*) è in riunione; **to call a** ~ convocare una riunione.

meeting place *n* luogo d'incontro.

megabyte [meg'əbīt] *n* megabyte *m inv.*

megalomaniac [megəlōmā'nēak] *n* megalomane *m/f.*

megaphone [meg'əfōn] *n* megafono.

melancholy [mel'ənkâlē] *n* malinconia ♦ *a* malinconico(a).

mellow [mel'ō] *a* (*wine, sound*) ricco(a); (*person, light*) dolce; (*color*) caldo(a); (*fruit*) maturo(a) ♦ *vi* (*person*) addolcirsi.

melodious [məlō'dēəs] *a* melodioso(a).

melodrama [mel'ədrâmə] *n* melodramma *m.*

melodramatic [melədrəmat'ik] *a* melodrammatico(a).

melody [mel'ədē] *n* melodia.

melon [mel'ən] *n* melone *m.*

melt [melt] *vi* (*gen*) sciogliersi, struggersi; (*metals*) fondersi; (*fig*) intenerirsi ♦ *vt* sciogliere, struggere; fondere; (*person*) commuovere; ~**ed butter** burro fuso.

melt away *vi* sciogliersi completamente.

melt down *vt* fondere.

meltdown [melt'doun] *n* melt-down *m inv.*

melting point [melt'ing point] *n* punto di fusione.

melting pot [melt'ing pât] *n* (*fig*) crogiolo; **to be in the** ~ essere ancora in discussione.

member [mem'bûr] *n* membro; (*of club*) socio/a, iscritto/a; (*of political party*) iscritto/a; ~ **country/state** *n* paese *m*/stato membro; **M~ of Congress (MC)** *n* (*US*) membro del Congresso; **M~ of the House of Representatives (MHR)** *n* (*US*) membro della Camera dei Rappresentanti; **M~ of Parliament (MP)** *n* (*Brit*) deputato; **M~ of the European Parliament (MEP)** *n* eurodeputato.

membership [mem'bûrship] *n* iscrizione *f*; (*numero d'*)iscritti *mpl*, membri *mpl.*

membership card *n* tessera (di iscrizione).

membrane [mem'brān] *n* membrana.

memento [məmen'tō] *n* ricordo, souvenir *m inv.*

memo [mem'ō] *n* appunto; (*COMM etc*) comunicazione *f* di servizio.

memoir [mem'wâr] *n* memoria; ~**s** *npl* memorie *fpl*, ricordi *mpl.*

memo pad *n* blocchetto per appunti.

memorable [mem'ûrəbəl] *a* memorabile.

memorandum, *pl* **memoranda** [meməran'dəm, -də] *n* appunto; (*COMM etc*) comunicazione *f* di servizio; (*DIPLOMACY*) memorandum *m inv.*

memorial [məmô'rēəl] *n* monumento commemorativo ♦ *a* commemorativo(a).

memorize [mem'ərīz] *vt* imparare a memoria.

memory [mem'ûrē] *n* (*gen*, *COMPUT*) memoria; (*recollection*) ricordo; **in** ~ **of** in memoria di; **to have a good/bad** ~ aver buona/cattiva memoria; **loss of** ~ amnesia.

men [men] *npl of* **man.**

menace [men'is] *n* minaccia; (*col: nuisance*) peste *f* ♦ *vt* minacciare; **a public** ~ un pericolo pubblico.

menacing [men'ising] *a* minaccioso(a).

menagerie [mənaj'ûrē] *n* serraglio.

mend [mend] *vt* aggiustare, riparare; (*darn*) rammendare ♦ *n* rammendo; **on the** ~ in via di guarigione.

mending [mend'ing] *n* rammendo; (*items to be mended*) roba da rammendare.

menial [mē'nēəl] *a* da servo, domestico(a); umile.

meningitis [meninjī'tis] *n* meningite *f.*

menopause [men'əpôz] *n* menopausa.

menservants [men'sûrvənts] *npl of* **manservant.**

menstruate [men'strōōāt] *vi* mestruare.

menstruation [menstrōōā'shən] *n* mestruazione *f.*

mental [men'təl] *a* mentale; ~ **illness** malattia mentale.

mentality [mental'itē] *n* mentalità *f inv.*

mentally [men'təlē] *ad*: **to be** ~ **handicapped** essere minorato psichico.

menthol [men'thôl] *n* mentolo.

mention [men'chən] *n* menzione *f* ♦ *vt* menzionare, far menzione di; **don't** ~ **it!** non c'è di che!, prego!; **I need hardly** ~ **that** ... inutile dire che ...; **not to** ~, **without** ~**ing** per non parlare di, senza contare.

mentor [men'tûr] *n* mentore *m.*

menu [men'yōō] *n* (*set* ~, *COMPUT*) menù *m inv*; (*printed*) carta.

menu-driven [men'yōōdriv'ən] *a* (*COMPUT*) guidato(a) da menù.

meow [mēou'] *vi* miagolare.

MEP *n abbr see* **Member of the European Parliament.**

mercantile [mûr'kəntil] *a* mercantile; (*law*) commerciale.

mercenary [mûr'sənerē] *a* venale ♦ *n* mercenario.

merchandise [mûr'chəndīs] *n* merci *fpl* ♦ *vt* commercializzare.

merchandiser [mûr'chəndīzûr] *n* merchandiser *m inv.*

merchant [mûr'chənt] *n* (*trader*) commerciante *m*; (*storekeeper*) negoziante *m*; **timber/wine** ~ negoziante di legno/vino.

merchant bank *n* (*Brit*) banca d'affari.

merchantman [mûr'chəntmən] *n* mercantile *m.*

merchant marine, (*Brit*) **merchant navy** *n* marina mercantile.

merciful [mûr'sifəl] *a* pietoso(a), clemente.

mercifully [mûr'sifəlē] *ad* con clemenza; (*fortunately*) per fortuna.

merciless [mûr'silis] *a* spietato(a).

mercurial [mûrkyōō'rēəl] *a* (*unpredictable*) volubile.

mercury [mûrk'yûrē] *n* mercurio.

mercy [mûr'sē] *n* pietà; (*REL*) misericordia; **to have ~ on sb** aver pietà di qn; **at the ~ of** alla mercè di.

mercy killing *n* eutanasia.

mere [mēr] *a* semplice; **by a ~ chance** per mero caso.

merely [mēr'lē] *ad* semplicemente, non ... che.

merge [mûrj] *vt* unire; (*COMPUT*: *files*, *text*) fondere ♦ *vi* fondersi, unirsi; (*COMM*) fondersi.

merger [mûr'jûr] *n* (*COMM*) fusione *f*.

meridian [mərid'ēən] *n* meridiano.

meringue [mərang'] *n* meringa.

merit [mär'it] *n* merito, valore *m* ♦ *vt* meritare.

meritocracy [märiták'rəsē] *n* meritocrazia.

mermaid [mûr'mād] *n* sirena.

merriment [mär'imənt] *n* gaiezza, allegria.

merry [mär'ē] *a* gaio(a), allegro(a); **M~ Christmas!** Buon Natale!

merry-go-round [mär'ēgōround] *n* carosello.

mesh [mesh] *n* maglia; rete *f* ♦ *vi* (*gears*) ingranarsi; **wire ~** rete *f* metallica.

mesmerize [mez'mərīz] *vt* ipnotizzare; affascinare.

mess [mes] *n* confusione *f*, disordine *m*; (*fig*) pasticcio; (*MIL*) mensa; **to be (in) a ~** (*house*, *room*) essere in disordine (*or* molto sporco); (*fig*: *marriage*, *life*) essere un caos; **to be/get o.s. in a ~** (*fig*) essere/cacciarsi in un pasticcio.

mess about *vi* (*Brit*) = **mess around**.

mess around *vi* (*col*) trastullarsi.

mess around with *vt fus* (*col*) gingillarsi con; (*plans*) fare un pasticcio di.

mess up *vt* sporcare; fare un pasticcio di; rovinare.

message [mes'ij] *n* messaggio; **to get the ~** (*fig col*) capire l'antifona.

message switching *n* (*COMPUT*) smistamento messaggi.

messenger [mes'injûr] *n* messaggero/a.

Messiah [misī'ə] *n* Messia *m*.

Messrs, Messrs. [mes'ûrz] *abbr* (*on letters*: = *messieurs*) Spett.

messy [mes'ē] *a* sporco(a); disordinato(a); (*confused*: *situation etc*) ingarbugliato(a).

Met [met] *n abbr* (*US*) = *Metropolitan Opera*.

met [met] *pt*, *pp of* **meet** ♦ *a abbr* (*Brit*: = *meteorological*): **the M~ Office** l'Ufficio Meteorologico.

metabolism [mətab'əlizəm] *n* metabolismo.

metal [met'əl] *n* metallo ♦ *vt* massicciare.

metallic [mital'ik] *a* metallico(a).

metallurgy [met'əlûrjē] *n* metallurgia.

metalwork [met'əlwûrk] *n* (*craft*) lavorazione *f* del metallo.

metamorphosis, *pl* **-phoses** [metəmôr'fəsis, -sēz] *n* metamorfosi *f inv*.

metaphor [met'əfôr] *n* metafora.

metaphysics [metəfiz'iks] *n* metafisica.

mete [mēt]: **to ~ out** *vt fus* infliggere.

meteor [mē'tēôr] *n* meteora.

meteoric [mētēôr'ik] *a* (*fig*) fulmineo(a).

meteorite [mē'tēərīt] *n* meteorite *m*.

meteorological [mētēûrəlâj'ikəl] *a* meteorologico(a).

meteorology [mētēərâl'əjē] *n* meteorologia.

meter [mē'tûr] *n* (*instrument*) contatore *m*; (*parking ~*) parchimetro; (*US*: *measurement*) metro.

methane [meth'ān] *n* metano.

method [meth'əd] *n* metodo; **~ of payment** modo *or* modalità *f inv* di pagamento.

methodical [məthâd'ikəl] *a* metodico(a).

Methodist [meth'ədist] *a*, *n* metodista (*m/f*).

methylated spirit(s) [meth'əlātid spir'it(s)] *n* (*Brit*: *also*: **meths**) alcool *m* denaturato.

meticulous [mətik'yələs] *a* meticoloso(a).

metre [mē'tûr] *n* (*Brit*: *measurement*) metro.

metric [met'rik] *a* metrico(a); **to go ~** adottare il sistema metrico decimale.

metrical [met'rikəl] *a* metrico(a).

metrication [metrikā'shən] *n* conversione *f* al sistema metrico.

metric system *n* sistema *m* metrico decimale.

metric ton *n* tonnellata.

metronome [met'rənōm] *n* metronomo.

metropolis [mitrâp'əlis] *n* metropoli *f inv*.

metropolitan [metrəpâl'itən] *a* metropolitano(a).

Metropolitan Police *n* (*Brit*): **the ~** la polizia di Londra.

mettle [met'əl] *n* coraggio.

mew [myōō] *vi* (*cat*) miagolare.

mews [myōōz] *n* (*Brit*): **~ flat** appartamentino ricavato da una vecchia scuderia.

Mexican [mek'səkən] *a*, *n* messicano(a).

Mexico [mek'səkō] *n* Messico.

Mexico City *n* Città del Messico.

mezzanine [mez'ənēn] *n* mezzanino.

MFA *n abbr* (*US*: = *Master of Fine Arts*) titolo di studio.

mfr *abbr* = **manufacture; manufacturer.**

mg *abbr* (= *milligram*) mg.

Mgr *abbr* (= *Monseigneur, Monsignor*) mons.; (*COMM*) = **manager.**

MHR *n abbr* (*US*) *see* **Member of the House of Representatives.**

MHz *abbr* (= *megahertz*) MHz.

MI *abbr* (*US MAIL*) = *Michigan.*

MI5 *n abbr* (*Brit*: = *Military Intelligence 5*) agenzia di controspionaggio.

MI6 *n abbr* (*Brit*: = *Military Intelligence 6*)

agenzia di spionaggio.
MIA *abbr* = **missing in action.**
mice [mīs] *npl of* **mouse.**
Mich. *abbr (US)* = *Michigan.*
microbe [mī'krōb] *n* microbio.
microbiology [mīkrōbiâl'əjē] *n* microbiologia.
microchip [mī'krəchip] *n* microcircuito integrato, chip *m inv.*
microcomputer [mīkrōkəmpyōō'tûr] *n* microcomputer *m inv.*
microcosm [mī'krəkâzəm] *n* microcosmo.
microeconomics [mīkrōēkənâm'iks] *n* microeconomia.
microfiche [mī'krōfēsh] *n* microfiche *f inv.*
microfilm [mī'krəfilm] *n* microfilm *m inv* ♦ *vt* microfilmare.
micrometer [mīkrâm'itûr] *n* micrometro, palmer *m inv.*
microphone [mī'krəfōn] *n* microfono.
microprocessor [mīkrōprâs'esûr] *n* microprocessore *m.*
microscope [mī'krəskōp] *n* microscopio; **under the** ~ al microscopio.
microscopic [mī'krəskâp'ik] *a* microscopico(a).
microwave [mī'krōwâv] *n* (*also:* ~ **oven**) forno a microonde.
mid [mid] *a:* ~ **May** metà maggio; ~ **afternoon** metà pomeriggio; **in** ~ **air** a mezz'aria; **he's in his** ~ **thirties** avrà circa trentacinque anni.
midday [mid'dā] *n* mezzogiorno.
middle [mid'əl] *n* mezzo; centro; (*waist*) vita ♦ *a* di mezzo; **I'm in the** ~ **of reading it** sto proprio leggendolo ora; **in the** ~ **of the night** nel mezzo della notte.
middle age *n* mezza età.
middle-aged [mid'əlājd'] *a* di mezza età.
Middle Ages *npl:* **the** ~ il Medioevo.
middle class *a* (*also:* **middle-class**) ≈ borghese ♦ *n:* **the** ~(**es**) ≈ la borghesia.
Middle East *n:* **the** ~ il Medio Oriente.
middleman [mid'əlman] *n* intermediario; agente *m* rivenditore.
middle management *n* quadri *mpl* intermedi.
middle name *n* secondo nome *m.*
middle-of-the-road [mid'ələvthərōd'] *a* moderato(a).
middleweight [mid'əlwāt] *n* (*BOXING*) peso medio.
middling [mid'ling] *a* medio(a).
Middx. *abbr (Brit)* = *Middlesex.*
midge [mij] *n* moscerino.
midget [mij'it] *n* nano/a.
midnight [mid'nīt] *n* mezzanotte *f;* **at** ~ a mezzanotte.
midriff [mid'rif] *n* diaframma *m.*
midst [midst] *n:* **in the** ~ **of** in mezzo a.
midsummer [mid'sum'ûr] *n* mezza *or* piena estate *f.*

midway [mid'wā] *a, ad:* ~ (**between**) a mezza strada (fra).
midweek [mid'wēk] *ad, a* a metà settimana.
midwife, *pl* **midwives** [mid'wīf, -wivz] *n* levatrice *f.*
midwifery [mid'wīfûrē] *n* ostetrica.
midwinter [mid'win'tûr] *n* pieno inverno.
might [mīt] *vb see* **may** ♦ *n* potere *m,* forza.
mighty [mī'tē] *a* forte, potente ♦ *ad (col)* molto.
migraine [mī'grān] *n* emicrania.
migrant [mī'grənt] *n* (*bird, animal*) migratore *m;* (*person*) migrante *m/f;* nomade *m/f* ♦ *a* migratore(trice); nomade; (*worker*) emigrato(a).
migrate [mī'grāt] *vi* migrare.
migration [mīgrā'shən] *n* migrazione *f.*
mike [mīk] *n abbr* (= *microphone*) microfono.
Milan [milan'] *n* Milano *f.*
mild [mīld] *a* mite; (*person, voice*) dolce; (*flavor*) delicato(a); (*illness*) leggero(a) ♦ *n* birra leggera.
mildew [mil'dōō] *n* muffa.
mildly [mīld'lē] *ad* mitemente; dolcemente; delicatamente; leggeramente; **to put it** ~ a dire poco.
mildness [mīld'nis] *n* mitezza; dolcezza; delicatezza; non gravità.
mile [mīl] *n* miglio; **to do 20** ~**s per gallon** ≈ usare 14 litri per cento chilometri.
mileage [mī'lij] *n* distanza in miglia, ≈ chilometraggio.
mileage allowance *n* rimborso per miglio.
mileometer [mīlâm'itûr] *n* (*Brit*) = **milometer.**
milestone [mīl'stōn] *n* pietra miliare.
milieu [mēlyōō'] *n* ambiente *m.*
militant [mil'ətənt] *a, n* militante (*m/f*).
militarism [mil'itərizəm] *n* militarismo.
militaristic [militəris'tik] *a* militaristico(a).
military [mil'itärē] *a* militare ♦ *n:* **the** ~ i militari, l'esercito.
militate [mil'ətāt] *vi:* **to** ~ **against** essere d'ostacolo a.
militia [milish'ə] *n* milizia.
milk [milk] *n* latte *m* ♦ *vt* (*cow*) mungere; (*fig*) sfruttare.
milk chocolate *n* cioccolato al latte.
milk float *n* (*Brit*) = **milk truck.**
milking [mil'king] *n* mungitura.
milkman [milk'man] *n* lattaio.
milk shake *n* frappé *m inv.*
milk tooth *n* dente *m* di latte.
milk truck *n* (*US*) furgone *m* del lattaio.
milky [mil'kē] *a* lattiginoso(a); (*color*) latteo(a).
Milky Way *n* Via Lattea.
mill [mil] *n* mulino; (*small: for coffee, pepper etc*) macinino; (*factory*) fabbrica; (*spinning* ~) filatura ♦ *vt* macinare ♦ *vi* (*also:* ~ **about**) formicolare.

millennium, *pl* ~**s** *or* **millennia** |milɛn'čəm, -čə| *n* millennio.
miller |mil'ûr| *n* mugnaio.
millet |mil'it| *n* miglio.
milli... |mil'i| *prefix* milli ....
milligram(me) |mil'əgram| *n* milligrammo.
milliliter, (*Brit*) **millilitre** |mil'əlētûr| *n* millilitro.
millimeter, (*Brit*) **millimetre** |mil'əmētûr| *n* millimetro.
milliner |mil'inûr| *n* modista.
millinery |mil'ənärē| *n* modisteria.
million |mil'yən| *n* milione *m*.
millionaire |milyənär'| *n* milionario, ≈ miliardario.
millipede |mil'əpēd| *n* millepiedi *m inv*.
millstone |mil'stōn| *n* macina.
millwheel |mil'wēl| *n* ruota di mulino.
milometer |mī'lōmētûr| *n* (*Brit*) ≈ contachilometri *m inv*.
mime |mīm| *n* mimo ♦ *vt*, *vi* mimare.
mimic |mim'ik| *n* imitatore/trice ♦ *vt* (*subj: comedian*) imitare; (: *animal*, *person*) scimmiottare.
mimicry |mim'ikrē| *n* imitazioni *fpl*; (*ZOOL*) mimetismo.
Min. *abbr* (*Brit* POL: = *ministry*) Min.
min. *abbr* (= *minute*, *minimum*) min.
minaret |minəret'| *n* minareto.
mince |mins| *vt* tritare, macinare ♦ *vi* (*in walking*) camminare a passettini ♦ *n* (*Brit* CULIN) carne *f* tritata *or* macinata; **he does not** ~ (**his**) **words** parla chiaro e tondo.
mincemeat |mins'mēt| *n* frutta secca tritata per uso in pasticceria.
mince pie *n* (*Brit*) specie di torta con frutta secca.
mincer |min'sûr| *n* (*Brit*) tritacarne *m inv*.
mincing |min'sing| *a* lezioso(a).
mind |mīnd| *n* mente *f* ♦ *vt* (*attend to*, *look after*) badare a, occuparsi di; (*be careful*) fare attenzione a, stare attento(a) a; (*object to*): **I don't** ~ **the noise** il rumore non mi dà alcun fastidio; **do you** ~ **if ...?** le dispiace se ...?; **I don't** ~ non m'importa; ~ **you,** ... sì, però si deve dire che ...; **never** ~ non importa, non fa niente; **it is on my** ~ mi preoccupa; **to change one's** ~ cambiare idea; **to be in** *or* **of two** ~**s about sth** essere incerto su qc; **to my** ~ secondo me, a mio parere; **to be out of one's** ~ essere uscito(a) di mente; **to keep sth in** ~ non dimenticare qc; **to bear sth in** ~ tener presente qc; **to have sb/sth in** ~ avere in mente qn/qc; **to have in** ~ **to do** aver l'intenzione di fare; **it went right out of my** ~ mi è completamente passato di mente, me ne sono completamente dimenticato; **to bring** *or* **call sth to** ~ riportare *or* richiamare qc alla mente; **to make up one's** ~ decidersi.
minded |mīn'did| *a*: **fair**~ imparziale; **an in-**

dustrially~ **nation** una nazione orientata verso l'industria.
minder |mīn'dûr| *n* (*child* ~) bambinaia; (*bodyguard*) guardia del corpo.
mindful |mīnd'fəl| *a*: ~ **of** attento(a) a; memore di.
mindless |mīnd'lis| *a* idiota; (*violence*, *crime*) insensato(a).
mine |mīn| *pronoun* il(la) mio(a), *pl* i(le) miei(mie); **this book is** ~ questo libro è mio ♦ *n* miniera; (*explosive*) mina ♦ *vt* (*coal*) estrarre; (*ship*, *beach*) minare.
mine detector *n* rivelatore *m* di mine.
minefield |mīn'fēld| *n* campo minato.
miner |mīn'ûr| *n* minatore *m*.
mineral |min'ûrəl| *a* minerale ♦ *n* minerale *m*; ~**s** *npl* (*Brit*: *soft drinks*) bevande *fpl* gasate.
mineralogy |minərál'əjē| *n* mineralogia.
mineral water *n* acqua minerale.
minesweeper |mīn'swēpûr| *n* dragamine *m inv*.
mingle |ming'gəl| *vt* mescolare, mischiare ♦ *vi*: **to** ~ **with** mescolarsi a, mischiarsi con.
mingy |min'jē| *a* (*col*: *amount*) misero(a); (: *person*) spilorcio(a).
miniature |min'ēəchûr| *a* in miniatura ♦ *n* miniatura.
miniature golf *n* minigolf *m inv*.
minibus |min'ēbus| *n* minibus *m inv*.
minicab |min'ēkab| *n* (*Brit*) ≈ taxi *m inv*.
minicomputer |min'ēkəmpyōōtûr| *n* minicomputer *m inv*.
minim |min'əm| *n* (*MUS*) minima.
minima |min'əmə| *npl of* **minimum**.
minimal |min'əməl| *a* minimo(a).
minimize |min'əmīz| *vt* minimizzare.
minimum |min'əməm| *n* (*pl* **minima** |min'əmə|) minimo ♦ *a* minimo(a); **to reduce to a** ~ ridurre al minimo; ~ **wage** salario minimo garantito.
minimum lending rate (MLR) *n* (*Brit*) ≈ tasso ufficiale di sconto (T.U.S.).
mining |mī'ning| *n* industria mineraria ♦ *a* minerario(a); di minatori.
minion |min'yən| *n* (*pej*) caudatario; favorito/a.
miniskirt |min'ēskûrt| *n* minigonna.
minister |min'istûr| *n* (*Brit* POL) ministro; (*REL*) pastore *m* ♦ *vi*: **to** ~ **to sb** assistere qn; **to** ~ **to sb's needs** provvedere ai bisogni di qn.
ministerial |ministēr'ēəl| *a* (*Brit* POL) ministeriale.
ministry |min'istrē| *n* (*Brit* POL) ministero; (*REL*): **to go into the** ~ diventare pastore.
mink |mingk| *n* visone *m*.
mink coat *n* pelliccia di visone.
Minn. *abbr* (*US*) = Minnesota.
minnow |min'ō| *n* pesciolino d'acqua dolce.
minor |mī'nûr| *a* minore, di poca importanza; (*MUS*) minore ♦ *n* (*LAW*) minorenne *m/f*; (*US*

SCOL) materia complementare.

Minorca [minôr'kə] *n* Minorca.

minority [minôr'itē] *n* minoranza; **to be in a** ~ essere in minoranza.

minster [min'stûr] *n* cattedrale *f* (*annessa a monastero*).

minstrel [min'strəl] *n* giullare *m*, menestrello.

mint [mint] *n* (*plant*) menta; (*sweet*) pasticca di menta ♦ *vt* (*coins*) battere; **the (US) M**~, (*Brit*) **the (Royal) M**~ la Zecca; **in** ~ **condition** come nuovo(a) di zecca.

mint sauce *n* salsa di menta.

minuet [minyōōet'] *n* minuetto.

minus [mī'nəs] *n* (*also:* ~ **sign**) segno meno ♦ *prep* meno.

minute *a* [mīnōōt'] minuscolo(a); (*detail*) minuzioso(a) ♦ *n* [min'it] minuto; (*official record*) processo verbale, resoconto sommario; ~**s** *npl* verbale *m*, verbali *mpl*; **it is 5** ~**s past 3** sono le 3 e 5 (minuti); **wait a** ~! (aspetta) un momento!; **at the last** ~ all'ultimo momento; **up to the** ~ ultimissimo; modernissimo; **in** ~ **detail** minuziosamente.

minute book *n* libro dei verbali.

minute hand *n* lancetta dei minuti.

minutely [mīnōōt'lē] *ad* (*by a small amount*) di poco; (*in detail*) minuziosamente.

miracle [mir'əkəl] *n* miracolo.

miraculous [mirak'yələs] *a* miracoloso(a).

mirage [mirâzh'] *n* miraggio.

mire [mī'ûr] *n* pantano, melma.

mirror [mir'ûr] *n* specchio ♦ *vt* rispecchiare, riflettere.

mirror image *n* immagine *f* speculare.

mirth [mûrth] *n* gaiezza.

misadventure [misədven'chûr] *n* disavventura; **death by** ~ (*Brit*) morte *f* accidentale.

misanthropist [misan'thrəpist] *n* misantropo/a.

misapply [misəplī'] *vt* impiegare male.

misapprehension [misaprihen'chən] *n* malinteso.

misappropriate [misəprō'prēāt] *vt* appropriarsi indebitamente di.

misappropriation [misəprōprēā'shən] *n* appropriazione *f* indebita.

misbehave [misbihāv'] *vi* comportarsi male.

misbehavior, (*Brit*) **misbehaviour** [misbihāv'yûr] *n* comportamento scorretto.

misc. *abbr* = **miscellaneous.**

miscalculate [miskal'kyəlāt] *vt* calcolare male.

miscalculation [miskalkyəlā'shən] *n* errore *m* di calcolo.

miscarriage [miskar'ij] *n* (*MED*) aborto spontaneo; ~ **of justice** errore *m* giudiziario.

miscarry [miskar'ē] *vi* (*MED*) abortire; (*fail: plans*) andare a monte, fallire.

miscellaneous [misəlā'nēəs] *a* (*items*) vario(a); (*selection*) misto(a); ~ **expenses** spese varie.

miscellany [mis'əlānē] *n* raccolta.

mischance [mischans'] *n*: **by (some)** ~ per

sfortuna.

mischief [mis'chif] *n* (*naughtiness*) birichineria; (*harm*) male *m*, danno; (*maliciousness*) malizia.

mischievous [mis'chəvəs] *a* (*naughty*) birichino(a); (*harmful*) dannoso(a).

misconception [miskənsep'shən] *n* idea sbagliata.

misconduct [miskân'dukt] *n* cattiva condotta; **professional** ~ reato professionale.

misconstrue [miskənstrōō'] *vt* interpretare male.

miscount [miskount'] *vt, vi* contare male.

misdeed [misdēd'] *n* (*old*) misfatto.

misdemeanor, (*Brit*) **misdemeanour** [misdimē'nûr] *n* misfatto; infrazione *f*.

misdirect [misdirekt'] *vt* mal indirizzare.

miser [mī'zûr] *n* avaro.

miserable [miz'ûrəbəl] *a* infelice; (*wretched*) miserabile; (*weather*) deprimente; **to feel** ~ sentirsi avvilito *or* giù di morale.

miserably [miz'ûrəblē] *ad* (*fail, live, pay*) miseramente; (*smile, answer*) tristemente.

miserly [mī'zûrlē] *a* avaro(a).

misery [miz'ûrē] *n* (*unhappiness*) tristezza; (*pain*) sofferenza; (*wretchedness*) miseria.

misfire [misfīr'] *vi* far cilecca; (*car engine*) perdere colpi.

misfit [mis'fit] *n* (*person*) spostato/a.

misfortune [misfôr'chən] *n* sfortuna.

misgiving(s) [misgiv'ing(z)] *n(pl)* dubbi *mpl*, sospetti *mpl*; **to have** ~**s about sth** essere diffidente *or* avere dei dubbi per quanto riguarda qc.

misguided [misgī'did] *a* sbagliato(a); poco giudizioso(a).

mishandle [mis·han'dəl] *vt* (*treat roughly*) maltrattare; (*mismanage*) trattare male.

mishap [mis'hap] *n* disgrazia.

mishear [mis·hiûr'] *vt, vi irg* capire male.

mishmash [mish'mash] *n* (*col*) minestrone *m*, guazzabuglio.

misinform [misinfôrm'] *vt* informare male.

misinterpret [misintûr'prit] *vt* interpretare male.

misinterpretation [misintûrpritā'shən] *n* errata interpretazione *f*.

misjudge [misjuj'] *vt* giudicare male.

mislay [mislā'] *vt irg* smarrire.

mislead [mislēd'] *vt irg* sviare.

misleading [mislē'ding] *a* ingannevole.

misled [misled'] *pt, pp of* **mislead.**

mismanage [misman'ij] *vt* gestire male; trattare male.

mismanagement [misman'ijmənt] *n* cattiva amministrazione *f*.

misnomer [misnō'mûr] *n* termine *m* sbagliato *or* improprio.

misogynist [misâj'ənist] *n* misogino.

misplace [misplās'] *vt* smarrire; collocare fuori posto; **to be** ~**d** (*trust etc*) essere malripososto(a).

misprint [mis'print] *n* errore *m* di stampa.

mispronounce [m_isprənouns'] *vt* pronunziare male.

misquote [miskwōt'] *vt* citare erroneamente.

misread [misrēd'] *vt irg* leggere male.

misrepresent [misreprizent'] *vt* travisare.

Miss. *abbr* (*US*) = *Mississippi.*

Miss [mis] *n* Signorina; **Dear ~ Smith** Cara Signorina; (*more formal*) Gentile Signorina.

miss [mis] *vt* (*fail to get*) perdere; (*appointment, class*) mancare a; (*escape, avoid*) evitare; (*notice loss of: money etc*) accorgersi di non avere più; (*regret the absence of*): **I ~ him/it** sento la sua mancanza, lui/esso mi manca ♦ *vi* mancare ♦ *n* (*shot*) colpo mancato; (*fig*): **that was a near ~** c'è mancato poco; **the bus just ~ed the wall** l'autobus per un pelo non è andato a finire contro il muro; **you're ~ing the point** non capisce.

miss out *vt* (*Brit*) omettere.

miss out on *vt fus* (*fun, party*) perdersi; (*chance, bargain*) lasciarsi sfuggire.

missal [mis'əl] *n* messale *m.*

misshapen [mis·shā'pən] *a* deforme.

missile [mis'əl] *n* (*AVIAT*) missile *m*; (*object thrown*) proiettile *m.*

missile base *n* base *f* missilistica.

missile launcher *n* lancia-missili *m inv.*

missing [mis'ing] *a* perso(a), smarrito(a); **to go ~** sparire; **~ person** scomparso/a, disperso/a; **~ in action** (*MIL*) disperso/a.

mission [mish'ən] *n* missione *f*; **on a ~ to sb** in missione da qn.

missionary [mish'ənärē] *n* missionario/a.

misspell [misspel'] *vt* (*irg: like* **spell**) sbagliare l'ortografia di.

misspent [misspent'] *a*: **his ~ youth** la sua gioventù sciupata.

mist [mist] *n* nebbia, foschia ♦ *vi* (*also: ~ over, ~ up*) annebbiarsi; (*Brit: windows*) appannarsi.

mistake [mistāk'] *n* sbaglio, errore *m* ♦ *vt* (*irg: like* **take**) sbagliarsi di; fraintendere; **to ~ for** prendere per; **by ~** per sbaglio; **to make a ~** (*in writing, calculating etc*) fare uno sbaglio or un errore; **to make a ~ about sb/sth** sbagliarsi sul conto di qn/su qc.

mistaken [mistā'kən] *pp of* **mistake** ♦ *a* (*idea etc*) sbagliato(a); **to be ~** sbagliarsi.

mistaken identity *n* errore *m* di persona.

mistakenly [mistā'kənlē] *ad* per errore.

mister [mis'tûr] *n* (*col*) signore *m; see* **Mr.**

mistletoe [mis'əltō] *n* vischio.

mistook [mistōōk'] *pt of* **mistake.**

mistranslation [mistranzlā'shən] *n* traduzione *f* errata.

mistreat [mistrēt'] *vt* maltrattare.

mistress [mis'tris] *n* padrona; (*lover*) amante *f*; (*Brit SCOL*) insegnante *f.*

mistrust [mistrust'] *vt* diffidare di ♦ *n*: **~ (of)** diffidenza (nei confronti di).

mistrustful [mistrust'fəl] *a*: **~ (of)** diffidente (nei confronti di).

misty [mis'tē] *a* nebbioso(a), brumoso(a).

misty-eyed [mis'tēid'] *a* trasognato(a).

misunderstand [misundûrstand'] *vt, vi irg* capire male, fraintendere.

misunderstanding [misundûrstan'ding] *n* malinteso, equivoco.

misunderstood [misundûrstōōd'] *pt, pp of* **misunderstand.**

misuse *n* [misyōōs'] cattivo uso; (*of power*) abuso ♦ *vt* [misyōōz'] far cattivo uso di; abusare di.

MIT *n abbr* (*US*) = *Massachusetts Institute of Technology.*

mite [mīt] *n* (*small quantity*) briciolo.

miter [mī'tûr] *n* (*US*) mitra; (*CARPENTRY*) giunto ad angolo retto.

mitigate [mit'əgāt] *vt* mitigare; (*suffering*) alleviare; **mitigating circumstances** circostanze *fpl* attenuanti.

mitigation [mitəgā'shən] *n* mitigazione *f*; alleviamento.

mitre [mī'tûr] *n* (*Brit*) = **miter.**

mitt(en) [mit'(ən)] *n* mezzo guanto; manopola.

mix [miks] *vt* mescolare ♦ *vi* mescolarsi ♦ *n* mescolanza; preparato; **to ~ sth with sth** mischiare qc a qc; **to ~ business with pleasure** unire l'utile al dilettevole; **cake ~** preparato per torta.

mix in *vt* (*eggs etc*) incorporare.

mix up *vt* mescolare; (*confuse*) confondere; **to be ~ed up in sth** essere coinvolto in qc.

mixed [mikst] *a* misto(a).

mixed doubles *npl* (*SPORT*) doppio misto.

mixed economy *n* economia mista.

mixed grill *n* (*Brit*) misto alla griglia.

mixed-up [mikst'up] *a* (*confused*) confuso(a).

mixer [mik'sûr] *n* (*for food: electric*) frullatore *m*; (*: hand*) frullino; (*person*): **he is a good ~** è molto socievole.

mixture [miks'chûr] *n* mescolanza; (*blend: of tobacco etc*) miscela; (*MED*) sciroppo.

mix-up [miks'up] *n* confusione *f.*

MK *abbr* (*Brit TECH*) = **mark.**

mk *abbr* = **mark** (*currency*).

mkt *abbr* = **market.**

MLitt *n abbr* (= *Master of Literature, Master of Letters*) titolo di studio.

MLR *n abbr* (*Brit*) *see* **minimum lending rate.**

mm *abbr* (= *millimeter*) mm.

MN *abbr* (*US MAIL*) = *Minnesota*; (*Brit*) = **Merchant Navy.**

MO *n abbr* = *medical officer*; (*US col*: = *modus operandi*) modo d'agire ♦ *abbr* (*US MAIL*) = *Missouri.*

mo *abbr* (= *month*) m.

m.o. *abbr* = **money order.**

moan [mōn] *n* gemito ♦ *vi* gemere; (*col: com-*

plain): **to ~ (about)** lamentarsi (di).
moaning [mō'ning] *n* gemiti *mpl*.
moat [mōt] *n* fossato.
mob [mâb] *n* folla; (*disorderly*) calca; (*pej*): **the ~** la plebaglia ♦ *vt* accalcarsi intorno a.
mobile [mō'bəl] *a* mobile ♦ *n* (*ART*) mobile *m inv*.
mobile home *n* grande roulotte *f inv* (*utilizzata come domicilio*).
mobility [mōbil'ətē] *n* mobilità; (*of applicant*) disponibilità a viaggiare.
mobilize [mō'bəlīz] *vt* mobilitare ♦ *vi* mobilitarsi.
moccasin [mâk'əsin] *n* mocassino.
mock [mâk] *vt* deridere, burlarsi di ♦ *a* falso(a).
mockery [mâk'ûrē] *n* derisione *f*; **to make a ~ of** rendere ridicolo.
mocking [mâk'ing] *a* derisorio(a).
mockingbird [mâk'ingbûrd] *n* mimo (*uccello*).
mock-up [mâk'up] *n* modello dimostrativo; abbozzo.
MOD *n abbr* (*Brit*) = **Ministry of Defence**; *see* **defence**.
mod cons [mâd kânz] *npl abbr* (*Brit*) *see* **modern conveniences**.
mode [mōd] *n* modo; (*of transport*) mezzo; (*COMPUT*) modalità *f inv*.
model [mâd'əl] *n* modello; (*person: for fashion*) indossatore/trice; (*: for artist*) modello/a ♦ *vt* modellare ♦ *vi* fare l'indossatore (*or* l'indossatrice) ♦ *a* (*small-scale: railway etc*) in miniatura; (*child, factory*) modello *inv*; **to ~ clothes** presentare degli abiti; **to ~ sb/sth on** modellare qn/qc su.
model apartment *n* (*US*) *modello di appartamento aperto al pubblico*.
modelling clay [mâd'əling klā] *n* plastilina ®.
modem [mō'dem] *n* modem *m inv*.
moderate [mâd'ûrit] *a* moderato(a) ♦ *n* (*POL*) moderato/a ♦ *vb* [mâd'ərāt] *vi* moderarsi, placarsi ♦ *vt* moderare.
moderately [mâd'ûritlē] *ad* (*act*) con moderazione; (*expensive, difficult*) non troppo; (*pleased, happy*) abbastanza, discretamente; **~ priced** a prezzo modico.
moderation [mâdərā'shən] *n* moderazione *f*, misura; **in ~** in quantità moderata, con moderazione.
modern [mâd'ûrn] *a* moderno(a); **~ conveniences** comodità *fpl* moderne; **~ languages** lingue *fpl* moderne.
modernization [mâdûrnəzā'shən] *n* rimodernamento, modernizzazione *f*.
modernize [mâd'ûrnīz] *vt* modernizzare.
modest [mâd'ist] *a* modesto(a).
modesty [mâd'istē] *n* modestia.
modicum [mâd'əkəm] *n*: **a ~ of** un minimo di.
modification [mâdəfəkā'shən] *n* modificazione *f*; **to make ~s** fare *or* apportare delle modifiche.

modify [mâd'əfī] *vt* modificare.
modular [mâj'ələr] *a* (*filing, unit*) modulare.
modulate [mâj'əlāt] *vt* modulare.
modulation [mâjəlā'shən] *n* modulazione *f*.
module [mâj'ōōl] *n* modulo.
Mogadishu [mâgədish'ōō] *n* Mogadiscio *f*.
mogul [mō'gəl] *n* (*fig*) magnate *m*, pezzo grosso; (*SKI*) cunetta.
mohair [mō'här] *n* mohair *m*.
Mohammed [mōham'id] *n* Maometto.
moist [moist] *a* umido(a).
moisten [mois'ən] *vt* inumidire.
moisture [mois'chûr] *n* umidità; (*on glass*) goccioline *fpl* di vapore.
moisturize [mois'chərīz] *vt* (*skin*) idratare.
moisturizer [mois'chərīzûr] *n* idratante *f*.
molar [mō'lûr] *n* molare *m*.
molasses [məlas'iz] *n* molassa.
mold [mōld] (*US*) *n* forma, stampo; (*mildew*) muffa ♦ *vt* formare; (*fig*) foggiare.
molder [mōl'dûr] *vi* (*decay*) ammuffire.
molding [mōl'ding] *n* (*ARCHIT*) modanatura.
moldy [mōl'dē] *a* ammuffito(a).
mole [mōl] *n* (*animal*) talpa; (*spot*) neo.
molecule [mâl'əkyōōl] *n* molecola.
molehill [mōl'hil] *n* cumulo di terra sulla tana di una talpa.
molest [məlest'] *vt* molestare.
mollusk, (*Brit*) **mollusc** [mâl'əsk] *n* mollusco.
mollycoddle [mâl'ēkâdəl] *vt* coccolare, vezzeggiare.
molt [mōlt] *vi* (*US*) far la muta.
molten [mōl'tən] *a* fuso(a).
mom [mâm] *n* (*US*) mamma.
moment [mō'mənt] *n* momento, istante *m*; importanza; **at the ~** al momento, in questo momento; **for the ~** per il momento, per ora; **in a ~** tra un momento; **"one ~ please"** (*TEL*) "attenda, prego".
momentarily [mōməntäri'lē] *ad* per un momento; (*US: very soon*) da un momento all'altro.
momentary [mō'məntärē] *a* momentaneo(a), passeggero(a).
momentous [mōmen'təs] *a* di grande importanza.
momentum [mōmen'təm] *n* velocità acquisita, slancio; (*PHYSICS*) momento; **to gather ~** aumentare di velocità; (*fig*) prendere *or* guadagnare terreno.
mommy [mâm'ē] *n* (*US*) mamma.
Mon. *abbr* (= *Monday*) lun.
Monaco [mân'əkō] *n* Monaco *f*.
monarch [mân'ûrk] *n* monarca *m*.
monarchist [mân'ûrkist] *n* monarchico/a.
monarchy [mân'ûrkē] *n* monarchia.
monastery [mân'əstärē] *n* monastero.
monastic [mənas'tik] *a* monastico(a).
Monday [mun'dā] *n* lunedì *m inv*; *for phrases see also* **Tuesday**.
Monegasque [mânāgask'] *a*, *n* monegasco(a).

monetarist [mân'itärist] *n* monetarista *m/f*.
monetary [mân'itärē] *a* monetario(a).
money [mun'ē] *n* denaro, soldi *mpl*; **to make**
~ (*person*) fare (i) soldi; (*business*) rendere;
I've got no ~ left non ho più neanche una
lira.
moneyed [mun'ēd] *a* ricco(a).
moneylender [mun'ēlendûr] *n* prestatore *m* di
denaro.
moneymaking [mun'ēmāking] *a* che rende
(bene *or* molto), lucrativo(a).
money market *n* mercato monetario.
money order *n* vaglia *m inv*.
money-spinner [mun'ēspinûr] *n* (*col*) miniera
d'oro (*fig*).
money supply *n* liquidità monetaria.
Mongol [mâng'gəl] *n* mongolo/a; (*LING*)
mongolo.
mongol [mâng'gəl] *a*, *n* (*MED*) mongoloide
(*m/f*).
Mongolia [mânggō'lēə] *n* Mongolia.
Mongolian [mânggō'lēən] *a* mongolico(a) ♦ *n*
mongolo/a; (*LING*) mongolo.
mongoose [mâng'gōōs] *n* mangusta.
mongrel [mung'grəl] *n* (*dog*) cane *m* bastardo.
monitor [mân'itûr] *n* (*US SCOL*) chi sorveglia
agli esami; (*Brit SCOL*) capoclasse *m/f*; (*TV*,
COMPUT) monitor *m inv* ♦ *vt* controllare;
(*foreign station*) ascoltare le trasmissioni di.
monk [mungk] *n* monaco.
monkey [mung'kē] *n* scimmia.
monkey business *n* (*col*) scherzi *mpl*.
monkey nut *n* (*Brit*) nocciolina americana.
monkey wrench *n* chiave *f* a rullino.
mono [mân'ō] *a* mono *inv*; (*broadcast*) in
mono.
mono... *prefix* mono....
monochrome [mân'əkrōm] *a* monocromo(a).
monocle [mân'əkəl] *n* monocolo.
monogram [mân'əgram] *n* monogramma *m*.
monolith [mân'əlith] *n* monolito.
monologue [mân'əlòg] *n* monologo.
mononucleosis [mânōnōōklēō'sis] *n* (*US*) mononucleosi *f*.
monoplane [mân'əplān] *n* monoplano.
monopolize [mənâp'əlīz] *vt* monopolizzare.
monopoly [mənâp'əlē] *n* monopolio; **Mo-
nopolies and Mergers Commission** (*Brit*)
commissione *f* antimonopoli.
monorail [mân'ərāl] *n* monorotaia.
monosodium glutamate (MSG) [mânə-
sō'dēəm glōō'təmāt] *n* glutammato di sodio.
monosyllabic [mânəsilab'ik] *a* monosil-
labico(a); (*person*) che parla a monosillabi.
monosyllable [mân'əsiləbəl] *n* monosillabo.
monotone [mân'ətōn] *n* pronunzia (*or* voce *f*)
monotona; **to speak in a** ~ parlare con voce
monotona.
monotonous [mənât'ənəs] *a* monotono(a).
monotony [mənât'ənē] *n* monotonia.
monoxide [mənâk'sīd] *n*: **carbon** ~ ossido di

carbonio.
monsoon [mânsōōn'] *n* monsone *m*.
monster [mân'stûr] *n* mostro.
monstrosity [mânstrâs'ətē] *n* mostruosità *f*
inv.
monstrous [mân'strəs] *a* mostruoso(a).
Mont. *abbr* (*US*) = *Montana*.
montage [mântâzh'] *n* montaggio.
Mont Blanc [mânt blangk'] *n* Monte *m* Bianco.
month [munth] *n* mese *m*; **300 dollars a** ~ 300
dollari al mese; **every** ~ (*happen*) tutti i
mesi; (*pay*) mensilmente, ogni mese.
monthly [munth'lē] *a* mensile ♦ *ad* al mese;
ogni mese ♦ *n* (*magazine*) rivista mensile;
twice ~ due volte al mese.
monument [mân'yəmənt] *n* monumento.
monumental [mânyəmen'təl] *a* monumentale;
(*fig*) colossale.
moo [mōō] *vi* muggire, mugghiare.
mood [mōōd] *n* umore *m*; **to be in a good/
bad** ~ essere di buon/cattivo umore; **to be in
the** ~ **for** essere disposto(a) a, aver voglia
di.
moody [mōō'dē] *a* (*variable*) capriccioso(a),
lunatico(a); (*sullen*) imbronciato(a).
moon [mōōn] *n* luna.
moonbeam [mōōn'bēm] *n* raggio di luna.
moon landing *n* allunaggio.
moonlight [mōōn'līt] *n* chiaro di luna ♦ *vi* fare
del lavoro nero.
moonlighting [mōōn'līting] *n* lavoro nero.
moonlit [mōōn'lit] *a* illuminato(a) dalla luna;
a ~ **night** una notte rischiarata dalla luna.
moonshot [mōōn'shât] *n* lancio sulla luna.
moonstruck [mōōn'struk] *a* lunatico(a).
Moor [mōōr] *n* moro/a.
moor [mōōr] *n* brughiera ♦ *vt* (*ship*) ormeggiare ♦ *vi* ormeggiarsi.
moorings [mōōr'ingz] *npl* (*chains*) ormeggi
mpl; (*place*) ormeggio.
Moorish [mōō'rish] *a* moresco(a).
moorland [mōōr'land] *n* brughiera.
moose [mōōs] *n* (*pl inv*) alce *m*.
moot [mōōt] *vt* sollevare ♦ *a*: ~ **point** punto
discutibile.
mop [mâp] *n* lavapavimenti *m inv*; (*also*: ~ **of
hair**) zazzera ♦ *vt* lavare con lo straccio; **to
~ one's brow** asciugarsi la fronte.
mop up *vt* asciugare con uno straccio.
mope [mōp] *vi* fare il broncio.
mope around *vi* trascinarsi *or* aggirarsi
con aria avvilita.
moped [mō'ped] *n* ciclomotore *m*.
moral [môr'əl] *a* morale ♦ *n* morale *f*; **~s** *npl*
moralità.
morale [məral'] *n* morale *m*.
morality [məral'itē] *n* moralità.
moralize [môr'əlīz] *vi*: **to** ~ (**about**) fare il (*or*
la) moralista (riguardo), moraleggiare (ri-
guardo).
morally [môr'əlē] *ad* moralmente.

morass [mǝras'] *n* palude *f*, pantano.
moratorium [môrǝtôr'ēǝm] *n* moratoria.
morbid [môr'bid] *a* morboso(a).
more [môr] *a* più ♦ *ad* più, di più; ~ **people** più gente; **I want** ~ ne voglio ancora *or* di più; **is there any** ~**?** ce n'è ancora?; ~ **dangerous than** più pericoloso di (*or* che); ~ **or less** più o meno; ~ **than ever** più che mai; **many/much** ~ molti/molto di più; ~ **and** ~ sempre di più; **and what's** ~ ... e per di più ...; **once** ~ ancora (una volta), un'altra volta; **no** ~, **not any** ~ non ... più.
moreover [môrō'vûr] *ad* inoltre, di più.
morgue [môrg] *n* obitorio.
MORI [mō'rē] *n abbr* (*Brit*: = *Market & Opinion Research Institute*) *istituto di sondaggio.*
moribund [môr'ǝbund] *a* moribondo(a).
morning [môr'ning] *n* mattina, mattino; (*duration*) mattinata; **in the** ~ la mattina; **this** ~ stamattina; **7 o'clock in the** ~ le 7 di *or* della mattina.
morning sickness *n* nausee *fpl* mattutine.
Moroccan [mǝrâk'ǝn] *a*, *n* marocchino(a).
Morocco [mǝrâk'ō] *n* Marocco.
moron [môr'ân] *n* deficiente *m/f*.
moronic [mǝrân'ik] *a* deficiente.
morose [mǝrōs'] *a* cupo(a), tetro(a).
morphine [môr'fēn] *n* morfina.
Morse [môrs] *n* (*also:* ~ **code**) alfabeto Morse.
morsel [môr'sǝl] *n* boccone *m*.
mortal [môr'tǝl] *a*, *n* mortale (*m*).
mortality [môrtal'itē] *n* mortalità.
mortality rate *n* tasso di mortalità.
mortar [môr'tûr] *n* (*CONSTR*) malta; (*dish*) mortaio.
mortgage [môr'gij] *n* ipoteca; (*in house buying*) mutuo ipotecario ♦ *vt* ipotecare; **to take out a** ~ contrarre un mutuo (*or* un'ipoteca).
mortgage company *n* (*US*) società *f inv* immobiliare.
mortgagee [môrgǝjē'] *n* creditore *m* ipotecario.
mortgagor [môr'gǝjûr] *n* debitore *m* ipotecario.
mortician [môrtish'ǝn] *n* (*US*) impresario di pompe funebri.
mortified [môr'tǝfīd] *a* umiliato(a).
mortise lock [môr'tis lâk] *n* serratura incastrata.
mortuary [môr'chōōârē] *n* camera mortuaria; (*Brit*) obitorio.
mosaic [mōzā'ik] *n* mosaico.
Moscow [mâs'kou] *n* Mosca.
Moslem [mâz'lǝm] *a*, *n* = **Muslim**.
mosque [mâsk] *n* moschea.
mosquito, ~es [mǝskē'tō] *n* zanzara.
mosquito net *n* zanzariera.
moss [môs] *n* muschio.
mossy [môs'ē] *a* muscoso(a).

most [mōst] *a* la maggior parte di; il più di ♦ *pronoun* la maggior parte ♦ *ad* più; (*work, sleep etc*) di più; (*very*) molto, estremamente; **the** ~ (*also:* + *adjective*) il(la) più; ~ **fish** la maggior parte dei pesci; ~ **of** la maggior parte di; ~ **of them** quasi tutti; **at the** (**very**) ~ al massimo; **to make the** ~ **of** trarre il massimo vantaggio da.
mostly [mōst'lē] *ad* per lo più.
MOT *n abbr* (*Brit*: = *Ministry of Transport*): **the** ~ (**test**) *revisione obbligatoria dei autoveicoli.*
motel [mōtel'] *n* motel *m inv*.
moth [môth] *n* farfalla notturna; tarma.
mothball [môth'bôl] *n* pallina di naftalina.
moth-eaten [môth'ētǝn] *a* tarmato(a).
mother [muth'ûr] *n* madre *f* ♦ *vt* (*care for*) fare da madre a.
mother board *n* (*COMPUT*) scheda madre.
motherhood [muth'ûrhōōd] *n* maternità.
mother-in-law [muth'ûrinlô] *n* suocera.
motherly [muth'ûrlē] *a* materno(a).
mother-of-pearl [muth'ûrǝvpûrl'] *n* madreperla.
mother's help *n* bambinaia.
mother-to-be [muth'ûrtǝbē'] *n* futura mamma.
mother tongue *n* madrelingua.
mothproof [môth'prōōf] *a* antitarmico(a).
motif [mōtēf'] *n* motivo.
motion [mō'shǝn] *n* movimento, moto; (*gesture*) gesto; (*at meeting*) mozione *f*; (*Brit: also:* **bowel** ~) evacuazione *f* ♦ *vt*, *vi*: **to** ~ (**to**) **sb to do** fare cenno a qn di fare; **to be in** ~ (*vehicle*) essere in moto; **to set in** ~ avviare; **to go through the** ~**s of doing sth** (*fig*) fare qc pro forma.
motionless [mō'shǝnlis] *a* immobile.
motion picture *n* film *m inv*.
motivate [mō'tǝvat] *vt* (*act, decision*) dare origine a, motivare; (*person*) spingere.
motivated [mō'tǝvatid] *a* motivato(a).
motivation [mōtǝvā'shǝn] *n* motivazione *f*.
motive [mō'tiv] *n* motivo ♦ *a* motore(trice); **from the best** ~**s** con le migliori intenzioni.
motley [mât'lē] *a* eterogeneo(a), molto vario(a).
motor [mō'tûr] *n* motore *m*; (*Brit col: vehicle*) macchina ♦ *a* motore(trice).
motorbike [mō'tûrbīk] *n* moto *f inv*.
motorboat [mō'tûrbōt] *n* motoscafo.
motorcar [mō'tûrkâr] *n* automobile *f*.
motorcoach [mō'tûrkōch] *n* (*Brit*) pullman *m inv*.
motorcycle [mō'tûrsī'kǝl] *n* motocicletta.
motorcyclist [mō'tûrsīklist] *n* motociclista *m/f*.
motor home *n* (*US*) camper *m inv*.
motoring [mō'tûring] *n* (*Brit*) turismo automobilistico ♦ *a* (*accident*) d'auto, automobilistico(a); (*offense*) di guida; ~ **vacation** vacanza in macchina.

motorist |mō'tûrist| *n* automobilista *m/f.*
motorize |mō'tərīz| *vt* motorizzare.
motor oil *n* olio lubrificante.
motor racing *n* (*Brit*) corse *fpl* automobilistiche.
motor scooter *n* motorscooter *m inv.*
motor vehicle *n* autoveicolo.
motorway |mō'tûrwā| *n* (*Brit*) autostrada.
mottled |mât'əld| *a* chiazzato(a), marezzato(a).
motto, ~es |mât'ō| *n* motto.
mould |mōld| *etc* (*Brit*) = **mold** *etc.*
moult |mōlt| *vi* (*Brit*) = **molt**.
mound |mound| *n* rialzo, collinetta.
mount |mount| *n* monte *m*, montagna; (*horse*) cavalcatura; (*for jewel etc*) montatura ♦ *vt* montare; (*horse*) montare a; (*exhibition*) organizzare; (*attack*) sferrare, condurre; (*picture, stamp*) sistemare ♦ *vi* salire; (*get on a horse*) montare a cavallo; (*also:* ~ **up**) aumentare.
mountain |moun'tən| *n* montagna ♦ *cpd* di montagna; **to make a ~ out of a molehill** fare di una mosca un elefante.
mountaineer |mountənēr'| *n* alpinista *m/f.*
mountaineering |mountənē'ring| *n* alpinismo; **to go ~** fare dell'alpinismo.
mountainous |moun'tənəs| *a* montagnoso(a).
mountain rescue team *n* ≈ squadra di soccorso alpino.
mountainside |moun'tənsīd| *n* fianco della montagna.
mounted |moun'tid| *a* a cavallo.
mourn |môrn| *vt* piangere, lamentare ♦ *vi*: **to ~ (for sb)** piangere (la morte di qn).
mourner |môr'nûr| *n* parente *m/f* (*or* amico/a) del defunto.
mournful |môrn'fəl| *a* triste, lugubre.
mourning |môr'ning| *n* lutto ♦ *cpd* (*dress*) da lutto; **in ~** in lutto.
mouse, *pl* **mice** |mous, mīs| *n* topo; (*COMPUT*) mouse *m inv.*
mousetrap |mous'trap| *n* trappola per i topi.
mousse |mōōs| *n* mousse *f inv.*
moustache |məstash'| *n* (*Brit*) = **mustache**.
mousy |mou'sē| *a* (*person*) timido(a); (*hair*) né chiaro(a) né scuro(a).
mouth, ~s |mouth, mouthz| *n* bocca; (*of river*) bocca, foce *f*; (*opening*) orifizio.
mouthful |mouth'fōōl| *n* boccata.
mouth organ *n* armonica.
mouthpiece |mouth'pēs| *n* (*MUS*) bocchino; (*TEL*) microfono; (*of breathing apparatus*) boccaglio; (*person*) portavoce *m/f.*
mouth-to-mouth |mouth'təmouth'| *a*: **~ resuscitation** respirazione *f* bocca a bocca.
mouthwash |mouth'wôsh| *n* collutorio.
mouth-watering |mouth'wôtûring| *a* che fa venire l'acquolina in bocca.
movable |mōō'vəbəl| *a* mobile.
move |mōōv| *n* (*movement*) movimento; (*in*

game) mossa; (: *turn to play*) turno; (*change of house*) trasloco ♦ *vt* muovere, spostare; (*emotionally*) commuovere; (*POL: resolution etc*) proporre ♦ *vi* (*gen*) muoversi, spostarsi; (*traffic*) circolare; (*also: Brit:* ~ **house**) cambiar casa, traslocare; **to ~ towards** andare verso; **to ~ sb to do sth** indurre *or* spingere qn a fare qc; **to get a ~ on** affrettarsi, sbrigarsi; **to be ~d** (*emotionally*) essere commosso(a).
move along *vi* muoversi avanti.
move around *vi* (*fidget*) agitarsi; (*travel*) viaggiare.
move away *vi* allontanarsi, andarsene.
move back *vi* indietreggiare; (*return*) ritornare.
move forward *vi* avanzare ♦ *vt* avanzare, spostare in avanti; (*people*) far avanzare.
move in *vi* (*to a house*) entrare (*in una nuova casa*).
move off *vi* partire.
move on *vi* riprendere la strada ♦ *vt* (*onlookers*) far circolare.
move out *vi* (*of house*) sgombrare.
move over *vi* spostarsi.
move up *vi* avanzare.
movement |mōōv'mənt| *n* (*gen*) movimento; (*gesture*) gesto; (*of stars, water, physical*) moto; ~ (**of the bowels**) (*MED*) evacuazione *f.*
mover |mōō'vûr| *n* proponente *m/f*; (*furniture ~*) addetto ai traslochi.
movie |mōō'vē| *n* film *m inv*; **the ~s** il cinema.
movie camera *n* cinepresa.
moviegoer |mōō'vēgōūr| *n* frequentatore/trice di cinema.
movie projector *n* (*US*) cinepresa.
movie theatre *n* (*US*) cinema *m inv.*
moving |mōō'ving| *a* mobile; (*causing emotion*) commovente; (*instigating*) animatore(trice).
moving van *n* (*US*) furgone *m* per traslochi.
mow, *pt* **mowed**, *pp* **mowed** *or* **mown** |mō, mōd, mōn| *vt* falciare; (*grass*) tagliare.
mow down *vt* falciare.
mower |mō'ûr| *n* (*also:* **lawn ~**) tagliaerba *m inv.*
mown |mōn| *pp* of **mow**.
Mozambique |mōzambēk'| *n* Mozambico.
MP *n abbr* = *Military Police*; (*Canada*) = *Mounted Police*; *see* **Member of Parliament**.
mpg *n abbr* = *miles per gallon* (30 *mpg* = 9.4 *l. per 100 km*).
mph *n abbr* = *miles per hour* (60 *mph* = 96 *km/h*).
MPhil *n abbr* (*US:* = *Master of Philosophy*) titolo di studio.
Mr, Mr. |mis'tûr| *n*: ~ **X** Signor X, Sig. X.
Mrs, Mrs. |mis'iz| *n*: ~ **X** Signora X, Sig.ra X.
MS *n abbr* (*US:* = *Master of Science*) titolo di

studio; (= *manuscript*) ms; (*MED*) = **multiple sclerosis** ♦ *abbr* (*US MAIL*) = Mississippi.

Ms, Ms. [miz] *n* (= *Miss or Mrs*): ~ **X** ≈ Signora X, Sig.ra X.

MSA *n abbr* (*US*: = *Master of Science in Agriculture*) titolo di studio.

MSc *n abbr see* **Master of Science.**

MSG *abbr see* **monosodium glutamate.**

MST *abbr* (*US*: = *Mountain Standard Time*) ora invernale delle Montagne Rocciose.

MSW *n abbr* (*US*: = *Master of Social Work*) titolo di studio.

MT *n abbr* (*US MAIL*) = *Montana* ♦ = *machine translation*.

Mt *abbr* (*GEO*: = *mount*) M.

much [much] *a* molto(a) ♦ *ad*, *n or pronoun* molto; ~ **milk** molto latte; **how** ~ **is it?** quanto costa?; **it's not** ~ non è tanto; **too** ~ troppo; **so** ~ così (tanto); **I like it very/so** ~ mi piace moltissimo/così tanto; **thank you very** ~ molte grazie; ~ **to my amazement** con mio grande stupore.

muck [muk] *n* (*mud*) fango; (*dirt*) sporcizia.

muck about *or* **around** *vi* (*Brit*) = **mess around.**

muck in *vi* (*Brit col*) mettersi insieme.

muck out *vt* (*stable*) pulire.

muck up *vt* (*col: dirty*) sporcare; (: *spoil*) rovinare.

muckraking [muk'rāk'ing] *n* (*fig col*) caccia agli scandali ♦ *a* scandalistico(a).

mucky [muk'ē] *a* (*dirty*) sporco(a), lordo(a).

mucus [myōō'kəs] *n* muco.

mud [mud] *n* fango.

muddle [mud'əl] *n* confusione *f*, disordine *m*; pasticcio ♦ *vt* (*also*: ~ **up**) mettere sottosopra; confondere; **to be in a** ~ (*person*) non riuscire a raccapezzarsi; **to get in a** ~ (*while explaining etc*) imbrogliarsi.

muddle along *vi* andare avanti a casaccio.

muddle through *vi* cavarsela alla meno peggio.

muddle-headed [mud'əlhedid] *a* (*person*) confusionario(a).

muddy [mud'ē] *a* fangoso(a).

mud flats *npl* distesa fangosa.

mudguard [mud'gârd] *n* parafango.

mudpack [mud'pak] *n* maschera di fango.

mudslinging [mud'slinging] *n* (*fig*) infangamento.

muff [muf] *n* manicotto ♦ *vt* (*shot, catch etc*) mancare, sbagliare; **to** ~ **it** sbagliare tutto.

muffin [muf'in] *n* specie di pasticcino soffice da tè.

muffle [muf'əl] *vt* (*sound*) smorzare, attutire; (*against cold*) imbacuccare.

muffled [muf'əld] *a* smorzato(a), attutito(a).

muffler [muf'lûr] *n* (*scarf*) sciarpa (pesante); (*US AUT*) marmitta; (*on motorbike*) silenziatore *m*.

mufti [muf'tē] *n*: **in** ~ in borghese.

mug [mug] *n* (*cup*) tazzone *m*; (*for beer*) boccale *m*; (*col: face*) muso; (: *fool*) scemo/a ♦ *vt* (*assault*) assalire.

mug up *vt* (*Brit col: also*: ~ **up on**) studiare bene.

mugger [mug'ûr] *n* aggressore *m*.

mugging [mug'ing] *n* aggressione *f* (a scopo di rapina).

muggy [mug'ē] *a* afoso(a).

mulatto, ~es [məlât'ō] *n* mulatto/a.

mulberry [mul'bärē] *n* (*fruit*) mora (di gelso); (*tree*) gelso, moro.

mule [myōōl] *n* mulo.

mull [mul]: **to** ~ **over** *vt* rimuginare.

mulled [muld] *a*: ~ **wine** vino caldo.

multi.. [mul'ti] *prefix* multi....

multi-access [multēak'ses] *a* (*COMPUT*) ad accesso multiplo.

multicolored, (*Brit*) **multicoloured** [mul'tikulûrd] *a* multicolore, variopinto(a).

multifarious [multəfär'ēəs] *a* molteplice, svariato(a).

multilateral [multilat'ûrəl] *a* (*POL*) multilaterale.

multi-level [multēlev'əl] *a* (*US: building, car park*) a più piani.

multimillionaire [multēmilyənär'] *n* multimiliardario/a.

multinational [multənash'ənəl] *a, n* multinazionale (*f*).

multiple [mul'təpəl] *a* multiplo(a); molteplice ♦ *n* multiplo; (*Brit: also*: ~ **store**) grande magazzino che fa parte di una catena.

multiple choice *n* esercizi *mpl* a scelta multipla.

multiple crash *n* serie *f inv* di incidenti a catena.

multiple sclerosis [mul'təpəl sklirō'sis] *n* sclerosi *f* a placche.

multiplication [multəpləkā'shən] *n* moltiplicazione *f*.

multiplication table *n* tavola pitagorica.

multiplicity [multəplis'ətē] *n* molteplicità.

multiply [mul'təplī] *vt* moltiplicare ♦ *vi* moltiplicarsi.

multiracial [multērā'shəl] *a* multirazziale.

multistorey [multēstôr'ē] *a* (*Brit*) = **multilevel.**

multitude [mul'tətōōd] *n* moltitudine *f*.

mum [mum] (*Brit*) *n* mamma ♦ *a*: **to keep** ~ non aprire bocca; ~**'s the word!** acqua in bocca!

mumble [mum'bəl] *vt, vi* borbottare.

mummify [mum'əfī] *vt* mummificare.

mummy [mum'ē] *n* (*Brit: mother*) mamma; (*embalmed*) mummia.

mumps [mumps] *n* orecchioni *mpl*.

munch [munch] *vt, vi* sgranocchiare.

mundane [mundān'] *a* terra a terra *inv*.

Munich [myōō'nik] *n* Monaco *f* (di Baviera).

municipal [myōōnis'əpəl] *a* municipale.
municipality [myōōnisəpal'itē] *n* municipio.
munitions [myōōnish'ənz] *npl* munizioni *fpl*.
mural [myōōr'əl] *n* dipinto murale.
murder [mûr'dûr] *n* assassinio, omicidio ♦ *vt* assassinare; **to commit** ~ commettere un omicidio.
murderer [mûr'dûrûr] *n* omicida *m*, assassino.
murderess [mûr'dûris] *n* omicida *f*, assassina.
murderous [mûr'dûrəs] *a* micidiale.
murk [mûrk] *n* oscurità, buio.
murky [mûr'kē] *a* tenebroso(a), buio(a).
murmur [mûr'mûr] *n* mormorio ♦ *vt, vi* mormorare; **heart** ~ (*MED*) soffio al cuore.
MusB(ac) *n abbr* (= *Bachelor of Music*) titolo di studio.
muscle [mus'əl] *n* muscolo.
  muscle in *vi* immischiarsi.
muscular [mus'kyələr] *a* muscolare; (*person, arm*) muscoloso(a).
MusD(oc) *n abbr* (= *Doctor of Music*) titolo di studio.
muse [myōōz] *vi* meditare, sognare ♦ *n* musa.
museum [myōōzē'əm] *n* museo.
mush [mush] *n* pappa.
mushroom [mush'rōōm] *n* fungo ♦ *vi* (*fig*) svilupparsi rapidamente.
music [myōō'zik] *n* musica.
musical [myōō'zikəl] *a* musicale ♦ *n* (*show*) commedia musicale.
musical instrument *n* strumento musicale.
music box *n* carillon *m inv*.
music hall *n* teatro di varietà.
musician [myōōzish'ən] *n* musicista *m/f*.
music stand *n* leggio.
musk [musk] *n* muschio.
musket [mus'kit] *n* moschetto.
muskrat [musk'rat] *n* topo muschiato.
musk rose *n* (*BOT*) rosa muschiata.
Muslim [muz'lim] *a, n* musulmano(a).
muslin [muz'lin] *n* mussola.
musquash [mus'kwâsh] *n* (*fur*) rat musqué *m inv*.
mussel [mus'əl] *n* cozza.
must [must] *auxiliary vb* (*obligation*): **I** ~ **do it** devo farlo; (*probability*): **he** ~ **be there by now** dovrebbe essere arrivato ormai; **I** ~ **have made a mistake** devo essermi sbagliato ♦ *n*: **this program/trip is a** ~ è un programma/viaggio da non perdersi.
mustache [məstash'] *n* (*US*) baffi *mpl*.
mustard [mus'tûrd] *n* senape *f*, mostarda.
mustard gas *n* iprite *f*.
muster [mus'tûr] *vt* radunare; (*also*: ~ **up**: *strength, courage*) fare appello a.
mustiness [mus'tēnis] *n* odor di muffa *or* di stantio.
mustn't [mus'ənt] = **must not**.
musty [mus'tē] *a* che sa di muffa *or* di rinchiuso.
mutant [myōō'tənt] *a, n* mutante (*m*).

mutate [myōō'tāt] *vi* subire una mutazione.
mutation [myōōtā'shən] *n* mutazione *f*.
mute [myōōt] *a, n* muto(a).
muted [myōō'tid] *a* (*noise*) attutito(a), smorzato(a); (*criticism*) attenuato(a); (*MUS*) in sordina; (: *trumpet*) con sordina.
mutilate [myōō'təlāt] *vt* mutilare.
mutilation [myōōtəlā'shən] *n* mutilazione *f*.
mutinous [myōō'tənəs] *a* (*troops*) ammutinato(a); (*attitude*) ribelle.
mutiny [myōō'tənē] *n* ammutinamento ♦ *vi* ammutinarsi.
mutter [mut'ûr] *vt, vi* borbottare, brontolare.
mutton [mut'ən] *n* carne *f* di montone.
mutual [myōō'chōōəl] *a* mutuo(a), reciproco(a).
mutual fund *n* (*US COMM*) fondo d'investimento.
mutually [myōō'chōōəlē] *ad* reciprocamente.
muzzle [muz'əl] *n* muso; (*protective device*) museruola; (*of gun*) bocca ♦ *vt* mettere la museruola a.
MV *abbr* (= *motor vessel*) M/N, m/n.
MVP *n abbr* (*US SPORT*: = *most valuable player*) titolo ottenuto da sportivo.
MW *abbr* (*RADIO*: = *medium wave*) O.M.
my [mī] *a* il(la) mio(a), *pl* i(le) miei(mie).
myopic [mīăp'ik] *a* miope.
myriad [mir'ēəd] *n* miriade *f*.
myself [mīself'] *pronoun* (*reflexive*) mi; (*emphatic*) io stesso(a); (*after prep*) me.
mysterious [mistēr'ēəs] *a* misterioso(a).
mystery [mis'tûrē] *n* mistero.
mystery story *n* racconto del mistero.
mystic [mis'tik] *a, n* mistico(a).
mystical [mis'tikəl] *a* mistico(a).
mystify [mis'təfī] *vt* mistificare; (*puzzle*) confondere.
mystique [mistēk'] *n* fascino.
myth [mith] *n* mito.
mythical [mith'ikəl] *a* mitico(a).
mythological [mithəlâj'ikəl] *a* mitologico(a).
mythology [mithâl'əjē] *n* mitologia.

N

N, n [en] *n* (*letter*) N, n *f or m inv*; **N for Nan** ≈ N come Napoli.
N *abbr* (= *north*) N.
NA *n abbr* (*US*: = *Narcotics Anonymous*) associazione in aiuto dei tossicodipendenti; (*US*) = *National Academy*.
n/a *abbr* (= *not applicable*) non pertinente; (*COMM etc*) = *no account*.

NAACP n abbr (US) = National Association for the Advancement of Colored People.

nab [nab] vt (col) beccare, acchiappare.

NACU n abbr (US) = National Association of Colleges and Universities.

nadir [nā'dûr] n (ASTR) nadir m; (fig) punto più basso.

nag [nag] n (pej: horse) ronzino; (person) brontolone/a ♦ vt tormentare ♦ vi brontolare in continuazione.

nagging [nag'ing] a (doubt, pain) persistente ♦ n brontolii mpl, osservazioni fpl continue.

nail [nāl] n (human) unghia; (metal) chiodo ♦ vt inchiodare; **to ~ sb down to a date/price** costringere qn a un appuntamento/ad accettare un prezzo; **to pay cash on the ~** (Brit) pagare a tamburo battente.

nailbrush [nāl'brush] n spazzolino da or per unghie.

nailfile [nāl'fīl] n lima da or per unghie.

nail polish n smalto da or per unghie.

nail polish remover n acetone m, solvente m.

nail scissors npl forbici fpl da or per unghie.

nail varnish n (Brit) = nail polish.

Nairobi [nīrō'bē] n Nairobi f.

naïve [nīēv'] a ingenuo(a).

naïveté, naivety [nīēvtā'] n ingenuità f inv.

naked [nā'kid] a nudo(a); **with the ~ eye** a occhio nudo.

nakedness [nā'kidnis] n nudità.

NAM n abbr (US) = National Association of Manufacturers.

name [nām] n nome m; (reputation) nome, reputazione f ♦ vt (baby etc) chiamare; (person, object) identificare; (price, date) fissare; **by ~** di nome; **she knows them all by ~** li conosce tutti per nome; **in the ~ of** in nome di; **what's your ~?** come si chiama?; **my ~ is Peter** mi chiamo Peter; **to take sb's ~ and address** prendere nome e indirizzo di qn; **to make a ~ for o.s.** farsi un nome; **to get (o.s.) a bad ~** farsi una cattiva fama or una brutta reputazione; **to call sb ~s** insultare qn.

name dropping n menzionare qn o qc per fare bella figura.

nameless [nām'lis] a senza nome.

namely [nām'lē] ad cioè.

nameplate [nām'plāt] n (on door etc) targa.

namesake [nām'sāk] n omonimo.

nanny [nan'ē] n bambinaia.

nanny goat n capra.

nap [nap] n (sleep) pisolino; (of cloth) peluria ♦ vi: **to be caught ~ping** essere preso alla sprovvista; **to have a ~** schiacciare un pisolino.

NAPA n abbr (US: = National Association of Performing Artists) associazione nazionale degli artisti di palcoscenico.

napalm [nā'pâm] n napalm m.

nape [nāp] n: **~ of the neck** nuca.

napkin [nap'kin] n tovagliolo; (Brit: for baby) pannolino.

Naples [nā'pəlz] n Napoli f.

Napoleonic [nəpōlēán'ik] a napoleonico(a).

nappy [nap'ē] n (Brit) pannolino.

narcissistic [nârsisis'tik] a narcisistico(a).

narcissus, pl **narcissi** [nârsis'əs, nârsis'ī] n narciso.

narcotic [nârkât'ik] n (MED) narcotico; **~s** npl (drugs) narcotici mpl, stupefacenti mpl.

nark [nârk] vt (Brit col) scocciare.

narrate [nar'āt] vt raccontare, narrare.

narration [narā'shən] n narrazione f.

narrative [nar'ətiv] n narrativa ♦ a narrativo(a).

narrator [nar'ātûr] n narratore/trice.

narrow [nar'ō] a stretto(a); (resources, means) limitato(a), modesto(a); (fig): **to take a ~ view of** avere una visione limitata di ♦ vi restringersi; **to have a ~ escape** farcela per un pelo; **to ~ sth down to** ridurre qc a.

narrow gauge a (RAIL) a scartamento ridotto.

narrowly [nar'ōlē] ad: **Maria ~ escaped drowning** per un pelo Maria non è affogata; **he ~ missed hitting the cyclist** per poco non ha investito la ciclista.

narrow-minded [nar'ōmīn'did] a meschino(a).

NAS n abbr (US) = National Academy of Sciences.

NASA [nas'ə] n abbr (US: = National Aeronautics and Space Administration) N.A.S.A. f.

nasal [nā'zəl] a nasale.

Nassau [nas'ô] n Nassau f.

nastily [nas'tilē] ad con cattiveria.

nastiness [nas'tēnis] n (of person, remark) cattiveria; (: spitefulness) malignità.

nasturtium [nəstûr'shəm] n cappuccina, nasturzio (indiano).

nasty [nas'tē] a (person, remark) cattivo(a); (: spiteful) maligno(a); (smell, wound, situation) brutto(a); **to turn ~** (situation) mettersi male; (weather) guastarsi; (person) incattivirsi; **it's a ~ business** è una brutta faccenda, è un brutto affare.

nation [nā'shən] n nazione f.

national [nash'ənəl] a nazionale ♦ n cittadino/a.

national anthem n inno nazionale.

national debt n debito pubblico.

national dress n costume m nazionale.

National Forest Service n (US) ≈ Corpo Forestale dello Stato.

National Guard n (US) milizia nazionale (volontaria, in ogni stato).

National Health Service (NHS) n (Brit) servizio nazionale di assistenza sanitaria, ≈ S.A.U.B. f.

National Insurance n (Brit) ≈ Previdenza

Sociale.

nationalism |nash'ənəlizəm| *n* nazionalismo.

nationalist |nash'nəlist| *a, n* nazionalista (*m/f*).

nationality |nashənal'ətē| *n* nazionalità *f inv*.

nationalization |nashnələzā'shən| *n* nazionalizzazione *f*.

nationalize |nash'nəlīz| *vt* nazionalizzare.

nationally |nash'nəlē| *ad* a livello nazionale.

national park *n* parco nazionale.

national press *n* stampa a diffusione nazionale.

National Security Council *n* (*US*) consiglio nazionale di sicurezza.

national service *n* (*MIL*) servizio militare.

National Weather Service *n* (*US*) l'Ufficio Meteorologico.

nationwide |nā'shənwīd'| *a* diffuso(a) in tutto il paese ♦ *ad* in tutto il paese.

native |nā'tiv| *n* abitante *m/f* del paese; (*in colonies*) indigeno/a ♦ *a* indigeno(a); (*country*) natio(a); (*ability*) innato(a); **a ~ of Russia** un nativo della Russia; **a ~ speaker of French** una persona di madrelingua francese; **~ language** madrelingua.

Nativity |nətiv'ətē| *n* (*REL*): **the ~** la Natività.

NATO |nā'tō| *n abbr* (= *North Atlantic Treaty Organization*) N.A.T.O. *f*.

natter |nat'ûr| (*Brit col*) *vi* chiacchierare ♦ *n* chiacchierata.

natural |nach'ûrəl| *a* naturale; (*ability*) innato(a); (*manner*) semplice; **death from ~ causes** (*LAW*) morte *f* per cause naturali.

natural childbirth *n* parto indolore.

natural gas *n* gas *m* metano.

naturalist |nach'ûrəlist| *n* naturalista *m/f*.

naturalization |nachûrələzā'shən| *n* naturalizzazione *f*; acclimatazione *f*.

naturalize |nach'ûrəlīz| *vt*: **to be ~d** (*person*) naturalizzarsi; **to become ~d** (*animal, plant*) acclimatarsi.

naturally |nach'ûrəlē| *ad* naturalmente; (*by nature: gifted*) di natura.

naturalness |nach'ûrəlnis| *n* naturalezza.

natural resources *npl* risorse *fpl* naturali.

natural wastage *n* (*INDUSTRY*) diminuzione *f* di manodopera (*per pensionamento, decesso etc*).

nature |nā'chûr| *n* natura; (*character*) natura, indole *f*; **by ~** di natura; **documents of a confidential ~** documenti *mpl* di natura privata.

-natured |nā'chûrd| *suffix*: **ill~** maldisposto(a).

nature reserve *n* (*Brit*) parco naturale.

nature trail *n* percorso tracciato in parchi nazionali *etc* con scopi educativi.

naturist |nā'chûrist| *n* naturista *m/f*, nudista *m/f*.

naught |nôt| *n* = **nought**.

naughtiness |nôt'ēnis| *n* cattiveria.

naughty |nôt'ē| *a* (*child*) birichino(a), catti-

vello(a); (*story, film*) spinto(a).

nausea |nô'zēə| *n* (*MED*) nausea; (*fig: disgust*) schifo.

nauseate |nô'zēāt| *vt* nauseare; far schifo a.

nauseating |nô'zēāting| *a* nauseante; (*fig*) disgustoso(a).

nauseous |nô'shəs| *a* nauseabondo(a); (*feeling sick*): **to be ~** avere la nausea.

nautical |nô'tikəl| *a* nautico(a).

nautical mile *n* miglio nautico *or* marino.

naval |nā'vəl| *a* navale.

naval officer *n* ufficiale *m* di marina.

nave |nāv| *n* navata centrale.

navel |nā'vəl| *n* ombelico.

navigable |nav'əgəbəl| *a* navigabile.

navigate |nav'əgāt| *vt* percorrere navigando ♦ *vi* navigare; (*AUT*) fare da navigatore.

navigation |navəgā'shən| *n* navigazione *f*.

navigator |nav'əgātûr| *n* (*NAUT, AVIAT*) ufficiale *m* di rotta; (*explorer*) navigatore *m*; (*AUT*) copilota *m/f*.

navvy |nav'ē| *n* (*Brit*) manovale *m*.

navy |nā'vē| *n* marina; **Department of the N~** (*US*) Ministero della Marina.

navy (blue) *a* blu scuro *inv*.

Nazareth |naz'ûrith| *n* Nazareth *f*.

Nazi |nât'sē| *a, n* nazista (*m/f*).

NB *abbr* (= *nota bene*) N.B.; (*Canada*) = *New Brunswick*.

NBA *n abbr* (*US*: = *National Basketball Association*) ≈ F.I.P. *f* (= *Federazione Italiana Pallacanestro*); = *National Boxing Association*.

NBC *n abbr* (*US*: = *National Broadcasting Company*) compagnia nazionale di radiodiffusione.

NBS *n abbr* (*US*: = *National Bureau of Standards*) ufficio per la normalizzazione.

NC *abbr* (*COMM etc*: = *no charge*) gratis; (*US MAIL*) = *North Carolina*.

NCC *n abbr* (*US*) = *National Council of Churches*.

NCO *n abbr see* **noncommissioned**.

ND *abbr* (*US MAIL*) = *North Dakota*.

N.Dak. *abbr* (*US*) = *North Dakota*.

NE *abbr* (*US MAIL*) = *Nebraska*; *New England*.

NEA *n abbr* (*US*) = *National Education Association*.

neap |nēp| *n* (*also*: **~ tide**) marea di quadratura.

Neapolitan |nēəpál'ətən| *a, n* napoletano(a).

near |nēr| *a* vicino(a); (*relation*) prossimo(a) ♦ *ad* vicino ♦ *prep* (*also*: **~ to**) vicino a, presso; (*time*) verso ♦ *vt* avvicinarsi a; **to come ~** avvicinarsi; **~ here/there** qui/lì vicino; **£25,000 or ~est offer** (*Brit*) 25.000 sterline trattabili; **in the ~ future** in un prossimo futuro; **the building is ~ing completion** il palazzo è quasi terminato *or* ultimato.

nearby |nēr'bī'| *a* vicino(a) ♦ *ad* vicino.

Near East n: **the ~** il Medio Oriente.
nearer [nē'rûr] a più vicino(a) ♦ ad più vicino.
nearly [nēr'lē] ad quasi; **not ~** non ... affatto;
I **~ lost it** per poco non lo perdevo; **she was
~ crying** era lì lì per piangere.
near miss n: **that was a ~** c'è mancato poco.
nearness [nēr'nis] n vicinanza.
nearside [nēr'sīd] n (right-hand drive) lato sinistro; (left-hand drive) lato destro ♦ a sini-
stro(a); destro(a).
near-sighted [nēr'sītid] a miope.
neat [nēt] a (person, room) ordinato(a);
(work) pulito(a); (solution, plan) ben indovina-
to(a), azzeccato(a); (US col) magnifico(a),
meraviglioso(a); (spirits) liscio(a).
neatly [nēt'lē] ad con ordine; (skillfully)
abilmente.
neatness [nēt'nis] n (tidiness) ordine m;
(skillfulness) abilità.
Nebr. abbr (US) = Nebraska.
nebulous [neb'yələs] a nebuloso(a); (fig)
vago(a).
necessarily [nesəsär'ilē] ad necessariamente;
not ~ non è detto, non necessariamente.
necessary [nes'isärē] a necessario(a); **if ~** se
necessario.
necessitate [nəses'ətāt] vt rendere necessa-
rio(a).
necessity [nəses'itē] n necessità f inv; **in case
of ~** in caso di necessità.
neck [nek] n collo; (of garment) colletto ♦ vi
(col) pomiciare, sbaciucchiarsi; **~ and ~** testa a testa; **to stick one's ~ out** (col) rischiare (forte).
necklace [nek'lis] n collana.
neckline [nek'līn] n scollatura.
necktie [nek'tī] n (esp US) cravatta.
nectar [nek'tûr] n nettare m.
nectarine [nektərēn'] n nocepesca.
née [nā] a: **~ Scott** nata Scott.
need [nēd] n bisogno ♦ vt aver bisogno di; I **~
to do it** lo devo fare, bisogna che io lo
faccia; **you don't ~ to go** non deve andare,
non c'è bisogno che lei vada; **a signature is
~ed** occorre or ci vuole una firma; **to be in
~ of, have ~ of** aver bisogno di; **$10 will
meet my immediate ~s** 10 dollari mi baste-
ranno per le necessità più urgenti; **in case of
~** in caso di bisogno or necessità; **there's no
~ for ...** non c'è bisogno or non occorre che
...; **there's no ~ to do ...** non occorre fare
...; **the ~s of industry** le esigenze dell'industria.
needle [nē'dəl] n ago; (on record player)
puntina ♦ vt punzecchiare.
needless [nēd'lis] a inutile; **~ to say, ...** inutile dire che ....
needlessly [nēd'lislē] ad inutilmente.
needlework [nēd'əlwûrk] n cucito.
needn't [nēd'ənt] = need not.
needy [nē'dē] a bisognoso(a).

negation [nigā'shən] n negazione f.
negative [neg'ətiv] n (PHOT) negativa, negativo; (ELEC) polo negativo; (LING) negazione f
♦ a negativo(a); **to answer in the ~** rispondere negativamente or di no.
neglect [niglekt'] vt trascurare ♦ n (of person,
duty) negligenza; **state of ~** stato di
abbandono; **to ~ to do sth** trascurare or tralasciare di fare qc.
neglected [niglek'tid] a trascurato(a).
neglectful [niglekt'fəl] a (gen) negligente; **to
be ~ of sb/sth** trascurare qn/qc.
negligee [neg'lazhā] n négligé m inv.
negligence [neg'lijəns] n negligenza.
negligent [neg'lijənt] a negligente.
negligently [neg'lijəntlē] ad con negligenza.
negligible [neg'lijəbəl] a insignificante, trascurabile.
negotiable [nigō'shəbəl] a negoziabile;
(check) trasferibile; (road) transitabile.
negotiate [nigō'shēāt] vi negoziare ♦ vt
(COMM) negoziare; (obstacle) superare;
(curve in road) prendere; **to ~ with sb for
sth** trattare con qn per ottenere qc.
negotiation [nigōshēā'shən] n trattativa;
(POL) negoziato; **to enter into ~s with sb**
entrare in trattative (or intavolare i negozia-
ti) con qn.
negotiator [nigō'shēātûr] n negoziatore/trice.
Negress [nēg'ris] n negra.
Negro [nēg'rō] a, n (pl **~es**) negro(a).
neigh [nā] vi nitrire.
neighbor [nā'bûr] n (US) vicino/a.
neighborhood [nā'bûrhōōd] n vicinato.
neighboring [nā'bûring] a vicino(a).
neighborly [nā'bûrlē] a: **he is a ~ person** è
un buon vicino.
neighbour [nā'bûr] etc (Brit) = **neighbor** etc.
neither [nē'thûr] a, pronoun né l'uno(a) né l'al-
tro(a), nessuno(a) dei(delle) due ♦ cj neanche, nemmeno, neppure ♦ ad: **~ good nor
bad** né buono né cattivo; I **didn't move and
~ did Claude** io non mi mossi e nemmeno
Claude; **... ~ did I refuse ...**, ma non ho
nemmeno rifiutato.
neo... [nē'ō] prefix neo....
neolithic [nēəlith'ik] a neolitico(a).
neologism [nēâl'əjizəm] n neologismo.
neon [nē'án] n neon m.
neon light n luce f al neon.
neon sign n insegna al neon.
Nepal [nəpôl'] n Nepal m.
nephew [nef'yōō] n nipote m.
nepotism [nep'ətizəm] n nepotismo.
nerve [nûrv] n nervo; (fig) coraggio; (impudence) faccia tosta; **he gets on my ~s** mi dà
ai nervi, mi fa venire i nervi; **a fit of ~s** una
crisi di nervi; **to lose one's ~** (self-
confidence) perdere fiducia in se stesso; I **lost
my ~** (courage) mi è mancato il coraggio.
nerve center n (ANAT) centro nervoso; (fig)

cervello, centro vitale.
nerve gas *n* gas *m* nervino.
nerve-racking [nûrv'raking] *a* che spezza i nervi.
nervous [nûr'vəs] *a* nervoso(a).
nervous breakdown *n* esaurimento nervoso.
nervously [nûr'vəslē] *ad* nervosamente.
nervousness [nûr'vəsnis] *n* nervosismo.
nest [nest] *n* nido; ~ **of tables** tavolini *mpl* cicogna *inv*.
nest egg *n* (*fig*) gruzzolo.
nestle [nes'əl] *vi* accoccolarsi.
nestling [nest'ling] *n* uccellino di nido.
NET *n abbr* (*US*) = *National Educational Television*.
net [net] *n* rete *f*; (*fabric*) tulle *m* ♦ *a* netto(a) ♦ *vt* (*subj: person*) ricavare un utile netto di; (*deal, sale*) dare un utile netto di; ~ **of tax** netto, al netto di tasse; **he earns $10,000** ~ **per year** guadagna 10.000 dollari netti all'anno.
netball [net'bôl] *n* specie di pallacanestro.
net curtains *npl* (*Brit*) tende *fpl* di tulle.
Netherlands [neth'ûrləndz] *npl*: **the** ~ i Paesi Bassi.
net profit *n* utile *m* netto.
nett [net] *a* = **net**.
netting [net'ing] *n* (*for fence etc*) reticolato; (*fabric*) tulle *m*.
nettle [net'əl] *n* ortica.
network [net'wûrk] *n* rete *f* ♦ *vt* (*RADIO, TV*) trasmettere simultaneamente; (*COMPUT*) collegare in network.
neuralgia [nōōral'jə] *n* nevralgia.
neurosis, *pl* neuroses [nōōrō'sis, -sēz] *n* nevrosi *f inv*.
neurotic [nōōrât'ik] *a, n* nevrotico(a).
neuter [nōō'tûr] *a* neutro(a) ♦ *n* neutro ♦ *vt* (*cat etc*) castrare.
neutral [nōō'trəl] *a* neutro(a); (*person, nation*) neutrale ♦ *n* (*AUT*): **in** ~ in folle.
neutrality [nōōtral'itē] *n* neutralità.
neutralize [nōō'trəlīz] *vt* neutralizzare.
neutron bomb [nōō'trân bâm] *n* bomba al neutrone.
Nev. *abbr* (*US*) = *Nevada*.
never [nev'ûr] *ad* (non...) mai; ~ **again** mai più; **I'll** ~ **go there again** non ci vado più; ~ **in my life** mai in vita mia; *see also* **mind**.
never-ending [nev'ûren'ding] *a* interminabile.
nevertheless [nevûrthəles'] *ad* tuttavia, ciò nonostante, ciò nondimeno.
new [nōō] *a* nuovo(a); (*brand new*) nuovo(a) di zecca; **as good as** ~ come nuovo.
newborn [nōō'bôrn] *a* neonato(a).
newcomer [nōō'kumûr] *n* nuovo(a) venuto(a).
newfangled [nōō'fang'gəld] *a* (*pej*) stramoderno(a).
newfound [nōō'found] *a* nuovo(a).
Newfoundland [nōō'fəndland] *n* Terranova.
New Guinea [nōō gin'ē] *n* Nuova Guinea.

newly [nōō'lē] *ad* di recente.
newlyweds [nōō'lēwedz] *npl* sposini *mpl*, sposi *mpl* novelli.
new moon *n* luna nuova.
newness [nōō'nis] *n* novità.
news [nōōz] *n* notizie *fpl*; (*RADIO*) giornale *m* radio; (*TV*) telegiornale *m*; **a piece of** ~ una notizia; **good/bad** ~ buone/cattive notizie; **financial** ~ (*PRESS*) pagina economica e finanziaria; (*RADIO, TV*) notiziario economico.
news agency *n* agenzia di stampa.
newsagent [nōōz'ājənt] *n* (*Brit*) giornalaio.
news bulletin *n* (*RADIO, TV*) notiziario.
newscaster [nōōz'kastûr] *n* (*RADIO, TV*) annunciatore/trice.
newsdealer [nōōz'dēlûr] *n* (*US*) giornalaio.
newsflash [nōōz'flash] *n* notizia *f* lampo *inv*.
newsletter [nōōz'letûr] *n* bollettino (*di ditta, associazione*).
newspaper [nōōz'pāpûr] *n* giornale *m*; **daily** ~ quotidiano; **weekly** ~ settimanale *m*.
newsprint [nōōz'print] *n* carta da giornale.
newsreader [nōōz'rēdûr] *n* (*Brit*) = **newscaster**.
newsreel [nōōz'rēl] *n* cinegiornale *m*.
newsroom [nōōz'rōōm] *n* (*PRESS*) redazione *f*; (*RADIO, TV*) studio.
news stand *n* edicola.
newt [nōōt] *n* tritone *m*.
New Year *n* Anno Nuovo; **Happy** ~**!** Buon Anno!; **to wish sb a happy** ~ augurare Buon Anno a qn.
New Year's Day *n* il Capodanno.
New Year's Eve *n* la vigilia di Capodanno.
New York [nōō yôrk] *n* New York *f*, Nuova York *f*; (*also*: ~ **State**) stato di New York.
New Zealand [nōō zē'lənd] *n* Nuova Zelanda ♦ *a* neozelandese.
New Zealander [nōō zē'ləndûr] *n* neozelandese *m/f*.
next [nekst] *a* prossimo(a) ♦ *ad* accanto; (*in time*) dopo; ~ **to** *prep* accanto a; ~ **to nothing** quasi niente; ~ **time** *ad* la prossima volta; ~ **week** la settimana prossima; **the** ~ **week** la settimana dopo *or* seguente; **the week after** ~ fra due settimane; **the** ~ **day** il giorno dopo, l'indomani; ~ **year** l'anno prossimo *or* venturo; "**turn to the** ~ **page**" "vedi pagina seguente"; **who's** ~**?** a chi tocca?; **when do we meet** ~**?** quando ci rincontriamo?
next door *ad* accanto.
next of kin *n* parente *m/f* prossimo(a).
NF *n abbr* (*Canada*) = **Newfoundland** ♦ *abbr* (*Brit POL*: = *National Front*) *partito di estrema destra*.
NFL *n abbr* (*US*) = *National Football League*.
Nfld. *abbr* (*Canada*) = *Newfoundland*.
NG *abbr* (*US*) = **National Guard**.
NGO *n abbr* (*US*) = *non-governmental organi-*

zation.

NH *abbr* (*US* MAIL) = *New Hampshire*.

NHL *n abbr* (*US*: = *National Hockey League*) ≈ F.I.H.P. *f* (= *Federazione Italiana Hockey e Pattinaggio*).

NHS *n abbr* (*Brit*) *see* **National Health Service**.

NI *abbr* = **Northern Ireland**; (*Brit*) = **National Insurance**.

Niagara Falls [nīag'rə fôlz] *n* cascate *fpl* del Niagara.

nib [nib] *n* (*of pen*) pennino.

nibble [nib'əl] *vt* mordicchiare.

Nicaragua [nikərâg'wə] *n* Nicaragua *m*.

Nicaraguan [nikərâg'wən] *a*, *n* nicaraguense (*m/f*).

Nice [nēs] *n* Nizza.

nice [nīs] *a* (*vacation, trip*) piacevole; (*apartment, picture*) bello(a); (*person*) simpatico(a), gentile; (*taste, smell, meal*) buono(a); (*distinction, point*) sottile.

nice-looking [nīs'lōōk'ing] *a* bello(a).

nicely [nīs'lē] *ad* bene; **that will do ~** andrà benissimo.

niceties [nī'sətēz] *npl* finezze *fpl*.

niche [nich] *n* (ARCHIT) nicchia.

nick [nik] *n* tacca ♦ *vt* intaccare; tagliare; (*Brit: col: steal*) rubare; (: *arrest*) beccare; **in the ~ of time** appena in tempo; **to ~ o.s.** farsi un taglietto.

nickel [nik'əl] *n* nichel *m*; (*US*) *moneta da cinque centesimi di dollaro*.

nickname [nik'nām] *n* soprannome *m* ♦ *vt* soprannominare.

Nicosia [nikōsē'ə] *n* Nicosia.

nicotine [nik'ətēn] *n* nicotina.

niece [nēs] *n* nipote *f*.

nifty [nif'tē] *a* (*col: car, jacket*) chic *inv*; (: *gadget, tool*) ingegnoso(a).

Niger [nī'jûr] *n* Niger *m*.

Nigeria [nījē'rēə] *n* Nigeria.

Nigerian [nījē'rēən] *a*, *n* nigeriano(a).

niggardly [nig'ûrdlē] *a* (*person*) tirchio(a), spilorcio(a); (*allowance, amount*) misero(a).

nigger [nig'ûr] *n* (*col!: highly offensive*) negro/a.

niggle [nig'əl] *vt* assillare ♦ *vi* fare il(la) pignolo(a).

niggling [nig'ling] *a* pignolo(a); (*detail*) insignificante; (*doubt, pain*) persistente.

night [nīt] *n* notte *f*; (*evening*) sera; **at ~** la notte; la sera; **by ~** di notte; **in the ~**, **during the ~** durante la notte; **the ~ before last** l'altro ieri notte; l'altro ieri sera.

nightcap [nīt'kap] *n* bicchierino prima di andare a letto.

nightclub [nīt'klub] *n* locale *m* notturno.

nightdress [nīt'dres] *n* camicia da notte.

nightfall [nīt'fôl] *n* crepuscolo.

nightgown [nīt'goun] *n* camicia da notte.

nightie [nīt'tē] *n* (*Brit*) camicia da notte.

nightingale [nī'təngāl] *n* usignolo.

nightlife [nīt'līf] *n* vita notturna.

nightly [nīt'lē] *a* di ogni notte *or* sera; (*by night*) notturno(a) ♦ *ad* ogni notte *or* sera.

nightmare [nīt'mâr] *n* incubo.

night owl *n* (*fig*) nottambulo/a.

night porter *n* portiere *m* di notte.

night safe *n* cassa continua.

night school *n* scuola serale.

nightshade [nīt'shād] *n*: **deadly ~** (BOT) belladonna.

night shift *n* turno di notte.

nightstick [nīt'stik] *n* (*US*) sfollagente *m inv*.

night-time [nīt'tīm] *n* notte *f*.

night watchman *n* guardiano notturno.

NIH *n abbr* (*US*) = *National Institutes of Health*.

nihilism [nē'əlizəm] *n* nichilismo.

nil [nil] *n* nulla *m*; zero.

Nile [nīl] *n*: **the ~** il Nilo.

nimble [nim'bəl] *a* agile.

nine [nīn] *num* nove.

nineteen [nīn'tēn'] *num* diciannove.

ninety [nīn'tē] *num* novanta.

ninth [nīnth] *num* nono(a).

nip [nip] *vt* pizzicare ♦ *vi* (*Brit col*): **to ~ out/down/up** fare un salto fuori/giù/di sopra ♦ *n* (*pinch*) pizzico; (*drink*) goccio, bicchierino.

nipple [nip'əl] *n* (ANAT) capezzolo.

nippy [nip'ē] *a* (*weather*) pungente; (*Brit: car, person*) svelto(a).

nit [nit] *n* (*of louse*) lendine *m*; (*col: idiot*) cretino/a, scemo/a.

nitpick [nit'pik] *vi* (*col*) cercare il pelo nell'uovo.

nitrogen [nī'trəjən] *n* azoto.

nitroglycerin(e) [nītrəglis'ûrin] *n* nitroglicerina.

nitty-gritty [nit'ēgrit'ē] *n* (*col*): **to get down to the ~** venire al sodo.

nitwit [nit'wit] *n* (*col*) scemo/a.

NJ *abbr* (*US* MAIL) = *New Jersey*.

NLF *n abbr* (= *National Liberation Front*) ≈ F.L.N. *m*.

NLQ *abbr* (= *near letter quality*) qualità quasi di corrispondenza.

NLRB *n abbr* (*US*: = *National Labor Relations Board*) organismo per la tutela dei lavoratori.

NM *abbr* (*US* MAIL) = *New Mexico*.

N. Mex. *abbr* (*US*) = *New Mexico*.

no [nō] *a* nessuno(a), non; **I have ~ money** non ho soldi; **there is ~ reason to believe ...** non c'è nessuna ragione per credere ...; **I have ~ books** non ho libri ♦ *ad* non; **I have ~ more wine** non ho più vino ♦ *excl*, *n* no (*m inv*); **"~ entry"** "vietata l'entrata"; **I won't take ~ for an answer** non accetterò un rifiuto; **"~ dogs"** "vietato l'accesso ai cani".

no. *abbr* (= *number*) n.

nobble [nâb'əl] *vt* (*Brit col: bribe: person*)

comprare, corrompere; (: *person to speak to, criminal*) bloccare, beccare; (: *RACING: horse, dog*) drogare.

Nobel prize [nō'bɛl prīz'] *n* premio Nobel.

nobility [nōbil'ətē] *n* nobiltà.

noble [nō'bəl] *a*, *n* nobile (*m*).

nobleman [nō'bəlmən] *n* nobile *m*, nobiluomo.

nobly [nō'blē] *ad* (*selflessly*) generosamente.

nobody [nō'bâdē] *pronoun* nessuno.

no-claims bonus [nō'klāmz bō'nəs] *n* (*Brit*) = **no-claims discount**.

no-claims discount [nō'klāmz' dis'kount] *n* (*US*) bonus malus *m inv*.

nocturnal [nâktûr'nəl] *a* notturno(a).

nod [nâd] *vi* accennare col capo, fare un cenno; (*sleep*) sonnecchiare ♦ *vt*: **to ~ one's head** fare di sì col capo ♦ *n* cenno; **they ~ded their agreement** accennarono di sì (col capo).

nod off *vi* assopirsi.

no fault agreement *n* (*US*) *accordo fra compagnie di assicurazione per il risarcimento dei rispettivi clienti*.

noise [noiz] *n* rumore *m*; (*din*, *racket*) chiasso.

noiseless [noiz'lis] *a* silenzioso(a).

noisily [noi'zilē] *ad* rumorosamente.

noisy [noi'zē] *a* (*street*, *car*) rumoroso(a); (*person*) chiassoso(a).

nomad [nō'mad] *n* nomade *m/f*.

nomadic [nōmad'ik] *a* nomade.

no man's land *n* terra di nessuno.

nominal [nâm'ənəl] *a* nominale.

nominate [nâm'ənāt] *vt* (*propose*) proporre come candidato; (*elect*) nominare.

nomination [nâmənā'shən] *n* nomina; candidatura.

nominee [nâmənē'] *n* persona nominata; candidato/a.

non... [nân] *prefix* non....

nonalcoholic [nânalkəhôl'ik] *a* analcolico(a).

nonbreakable [nânbrā'kəbəl] *a* infrangibile.

nonce word [nâns wûrd] *n* parola coniata per l'occasione.

nonchalant [nânshəlânt'] *a* incurante, indifferente.

noncommissioned [nânkəmish'ənd] *a*: **~ officer (NCO)** sottufficiale *m*.

noncommittal [nânkəmit'əl] *a* evasivo(a).

nonconformist [nânkənfôr'mist] *n* anticonformista *m/f*; (*Brit REL*) dissidente *m/f* ♦ *a* anticonformista.

noncontributory [nânkəntrib'yətôrē] *a*: **~ pension plan** *or* (*Brit*) **scheme** *sistema di pensionamento con i contributi interamente a carico del datore di lavoro*.

noncooperation [nânkōəpərā'shən] *n* non cooperazione *f*, non collaborazione *f*.

nondescript [nân'diskript] *a* qualunque *inv*.

none [nun] *pronoun* (*not one thing*) niente; (*not one person*) nessuno(a); **~ of you** nessu-

no(a) di voi; **I have ~** non ne ho nemmeno uno; **I have ~ left** non ne ho più; **~ at all** proprio niente; (*not one*) nemmeno uno; **he's ~ the worse for it** non ne ha risentito.

nonentity [nânen'titē] *n* persona insignificante.

nonessential [nânəsen'chəl] *a* non essenziale ♦ *n*: **~s** superfluo, cose *fpl* superflue.

nonetheless [nun'thəles'] *ad* nondimeno.

nonexecutive [nânigzek'yətiv] *a*: **~ director** direttore *m* senza potere esecutivo.

nonexistent [nânigzis'tənt] *a* inesistente.

nonfiction [nânfik'shən] *n* saggistica.

nonflammable [nânflam'əbəl] *a* ininfiammabile.

nonintervention [nânintûrven'chən] *n* non intervento.

non obst. *abbr* (= *non obstante*: *notwithstanding*) nonostante.

nonpayment [nânpā'mənt] *n* mancato pagamento.

nonplussed [nânplust'] *a* sconcertato(a).

nonprofit-making [nânpráf'itmāking] *a* senza scopo di lucro.

nonsense [nân'sens] *n* sciocchezze *fpl*; **~!** che sciocchezze!, che assurdità!; **it is ~ to say that** ... è un'assurdità *or* non ha senso dire che ....

nonskid [nânskid'] *a* antisdrucciolo(a).

nonsmoker [nânsmō'kûr] *n* non fumatore/trice.

nonstick [nânstik'] *a* antiaderente, antiadesivo(a).

nonstop [nân'stâp'] *a* continuo(a); (*train*, *bus*) direttissimo(a) ♦ *ad* senza sosta.

nontaxable [nântak'səbəl] *a*: **~ income** reddito non imponibile.

nonvolatile [nânvâl'ətəl] *a*: **~ memory** (*COMPUT*) memoria permanente.

nonvoting [nânvō'ting] *a*: **~ shares** azioni *fpl* senza diritto di voto.

nonwhite [nânwīt'] *a* di colore ♦ *n* persona di colore.

noodles [nōō'dəlz] *npl* taglierini *mpl*.

nook [nōōk] *n*: **~s and crannies** angoli *mpl*.

noon [nōōn] *n* mezzogiorno.

no one *pronoun* = **nobody**.

noose [nōōs] *n* nodo scorsoio, cappio; (*hangman's*) cappio.

nor [nôr] *cj* = **neither** ♦ *ad see* **neither**.

Norf *abbr* (*Brit*) = *Norfolk*.

norm [nôrm] *n* norma.

normal [nôr'məl] *a* normale ♦ *n*: **to return to ~** tornare alla normalità.

normality [nôrmal'itē] *n* normalità.

normally [nôr'məlē] *ad* normalmente.

Normandy [nôr'məndē] *n* Normandia.

north [nôrth] *n* nord *m*, settentrione *m* ♦ *a* nord *inv*, del nord, settentrionale ♦ *ad* verso nord.

North Africa *n* Africa del Nord.

North African *a*, *n* nordafricano(a).

North America *n* America del Nord.
North American *a, n* nordamericano(a).
Northants [nôrthants'] *abbr* (*Brit*) = *Northamptonshire*.
northbound [nôrth'bound'] *a* (*traffic*) diretto(a) a nord; (*carriageway*) nord *inv.*
Northd *abbr* (*Brit*) = *Northumberland*.
northeast [nôrthēst'] *n* nord-est *m.*
northerly [nôr'thûrlē] *a* (*wind*) del nord; (*direction*) verso nord.
northern [nôr'thûrn] *a* del nord, settentrionale.
Northern Ireland *n* Irlanda del Nord.
North Pole *n*: the ~ il Polo Nord.
North Sea *n*: the ~ il mare del Nord.
North Sea oil *n* petrolio del mare del Nord.
northward(s) [nôrth'wûrdz] *ad* verso nord.
northwest [nôrth'west] *n* nord-ovest *m.*
Norway [nôr'wā] *n* Norvegia.
Norwegian [nôrwē'jən] *a* norvegese ♦ *n* norvegese *m/f*; (*LING*) norvegese *m.*
nos. *abbr* (= *numbers*) nn.
nose [nōz] *n* naso; (*of animal*) muso ♦ *vi* (*also*: ~ **one's way**) avanzare cautamente; **to pay through the** ~ (**for sth**) (*col*) pagare (qc) un occhio della testa.
nose around *vi* aggirarsi.
nosebleed [nōz'blēd] *n* emorragia nasale.
nose dive *n* picchiata.
nose drops *npl* gocce *fpl* per il naso.
nosey [nō'zē] *a* curioso(a).
nostalgia [nəstal'jə] *n* nostalgia.
nostalgic [nəstal'jik] *a* nostalgico(a).
nostril [nâs'trəl] *n* narice *f*; (*of horse*) frogia.
nosy [nō'zē] *a* = **nosey.**
not [nât] *ad* non; ~ **at all** niente affatto; (*after thanks*) prego, s'immagini; **you must** ~ *or* **mustn't do this** non deve fare questo; **he isn't** ... egli non è ...; **I hope** ~ spero di no.
notable [nō'təbəl] *a* notevole.
notably [nō'təblē] *ad* notevolmente; (*in particular*) in particolare.
notary [nō'tûrē] *n* (*also*: ~ **public**) notaio.
notation [nōtā'shən] *n* notazione *f.*
notch [nâch] *n* tacca ♦ *vt* (*score, victory*) marcare, segnare.
note [nōt] *n* nota; (*letter, banknote*) biglietto ♦ *vt* prendere nota di; **to take** ~ **of** prendere nota di; **to take** ~**s** prendere appunti; **to compare** ~**s** (*fig*) scambiarsi le impressioni; **of** ~ eminente, importante; **just a quick** ~ **to let you know** ... ti scrivo solo due righe per informarti ....
notebook [nōt'book] *n* taccuino; (*for shorthand*) bloc-notes *m inv.*
note-case [nōt'kās] *n* (*Brit*) portafoglio.
noted [nō'tid] *a* celebre.
notepad [nōt'pad] *n* bloc-notes *m inv*, bloc-chetto.
notepaper [nōt'pāpûr] *n* carta da lettere.
noteworthy [nōt'wûrthē] *a* degno(a) di nota, importante.

nothing [nuth'ing] *n* nulla *m*, niente *m*; **he does** ~ non fa niente; ~ **new** niente di nuovo; **for** ~ (*free*) per niente; ~ **at all** proprio niente.
notice [nō'tis] *n* avviso; (*of leaving*) preavviso; (*Brit: review: of play etc*) critica, recensione *f* ♦ *vt* notare, accorgersi di; **to take** ~ **of** fare attenzione a; **to bring sth to sb's** ~ (*Brit*) far notare qc a qn; **to give sb** ~ **of** sth avvisare qn di qc; **to give** ~, **hand in one's** ~ (*subj: employee*) licenziarsi; **without** ~ senza preavviso; **at short** ~ con un breve preavviso; **until further** ~ fino a nuovo avviso; **advance** ~ preavviso; **to escape** *or* **avoid** ~ passare inosservato; **it has come to my** ~ **that** ... sono venuto a sapere che ....
noticeable [nō'tisəbəl] *a* evidente.
notice board *n* (*Brit*) tabellone *m* per affissi.
notification [nōtəfəkā'shən] *n* annuncio; notifica; denuncia.
notify [nō'təfī] *vt*: **to** ~ **sth to sb** notificare qc a qn; **to** ~ **sb of sth** avvisare qn di qc; (*police*) denunciare qc a qn.
notion [nō'shən] *n* idea; (*concept*) nozione *f.*
notions [nō'shənz] *npl* (*US*) merceria.
notoriety [nōtərī'ətē] *n* notorietà.
notorious [nōtôr'ēəs] *a* famigerato(a).
notoriously [nōtôr'ēəslē] *ad* notoriamente.
Notts [nâts] *abbr* (*Brit*) = *Nottinghamshire*.
notwithstanding [nâtwithstan'ding] *ad* nondimeno ♦ *prep* nonostante, malgrado.
nougat [nōō'gət] *n* torrone *m.*
nought [nôt] *n* zero.
noun [noun] *n* nome *m*, sostantivo.
nourish [nûr'ish] *vt* nutrire.
nourishing [nûr'ishing] *a* nutriente.
nourishment [nûr'ishmənt] *n* nutrimento.
Nov. *abbr* (= *November*) nov.
Nova Scotia [nō'və skō'shə] *n* Nuova Scozia.
novel [nâv'əl] *n* romanzo ♦ *a* nuovo(a).
novelist [nâv'əlist] *n* romanziere/a.
novelty [nâv'əltē] *n* novità *f inv.*
November [nōvem'bûr] *n* novembre *m*; *for phrases see also* **July.**
novice [nâv'is] *n* principiante *m/f*; (*REL*) novizio/a.
NOW [nou] *n abbr* (*US*: = *National Organization for Women*) ≈ U.D.I. *f* (= *Unione Donne Italiane*).
now [nou] *ad* ora, adesso; ♦ *cj*: ~ (**that**) adesso che, ora che; **right** ~ subito; **by** ~ ormai; **just** ~: **that's the fashion just** ~ è la moda del momento; **I saw her right** ~ l'ho vista proprio adesso; **I'll read it right** ~ lo leggo subito; ~ **and then,** ~ **and again** ogni tanto; **from** ~ **on** da ora in poi; **in 3 days from** ~ fra 3 giorni; **between** ~ **and Monday** da qui a lunedì, entro lunedì; **that's all for** ~ per ora basta.
nowadays [nou'ədāz] *ad* oggidì.
nowhere [nō'wär] *ad* in nessun luogo, da

nessuna parte; ~ **else** in nessun altro posto.

noxious [nãk'shɔs] a nocivo(a).

nozzle [nãz'əl] n (of hose etc) boccaglio.

NP n abbr = **notary public.**

NS abbr (Canada) = **Nova Scotia.**

NSC n abbr (US) = **National Security Council.**

NSF n abbr (US) = National Science Foundation.

NSW abbr (Australia) = New South Wales.

NT n abbr (= New Testament) N.T.

nth [enth] a: **for the** ~ **time** (col) per l'ennesima volta.

nuance [noō'ãnts] n sfumatura.

nubile [noō'bil] a nubile; (attractive) giovane e desiderabile.

nuclear [noō'klēûr] a nucleare; (warfare) atomico(a).

nuclear disarmament n disarmo nucleare.

nucleus, pl **nuclei** [noō'klēəs, noō'klēī] n nucleo.

nude [noōd] a nudo(a) ♦ n (ART) nudo; **in the** ~ tutto(a) nudo(a).

nudge [nuj] vt dare una gomitata a.

nudist [noō'dist] n nudista m/f.

nudist colony n colonia di nudisti.

nudity [noō'ditē] n nudità.

nugget [nug'it] n pepita.

nuisance [noō'səns] n: **it's a** ~ è una seccatura; **he's a** ~ lui dà fastidio; **what a** ~! che seccatura!

nuke [noōk] vt (attack) sferrare un attacco nucleare contro; (destroy) distruggere con armi nucleari.

null [nul] a: ~ **and void** nullo(a).

nullify [nul'əfī] vt annullare.

numb [num] a intorpidito(a) ♦ vt intorpidire; ~ **with** (fear) paralizzato(a) da; (grief) impietrito(a) da; ~ **with cold** intirizzito(a) (dal freddo).

number [num'bûr] n numero ♦ vt numerare; (include) contare; **a** ~ **of** un certo numero di; **telephone** ~ numero di telefono; **wrong** ~ (TEL) numero sbagliato; **the staff** ~s **20** gli impiegati sono in 20.

numbered account [num'bûrd əkount'] n (in bank) conto numerato.

number plate n (Brit AUT) targa.

Number Ten n (Brit: = 10 Downing Street) residenza del Primo Ministro del Regno Unito.

numbness [num'nis] n intorpidimento; (due to cold) intirizzimento.

numeral [noō'mûrəl] n numero, cifra.

numerical [noōmär'ikəl] a numerico(a).

numerous [noō'mûrəs] a numeroso(a).

nun [nun] n suora, monaca.

nuptial [nup'shəl] a nuziale.

nurse [nûrs] n infermiere/a; (also: ~**maid**) bambinaia ♦ vt (patient, cold) curare; (hope) nutrire; (baby: US) allattare, dare il latte a;

(: Brit) cullare.

nursery [nûr'sûrē] n (room) camera dei bambini; (institution) asilo; (for plants) vivaio.

nursery rhyme n filastrocca.

nursery school n scuola materna.

nursery slope n (Brit SKI) pista per principianti.

nursing [nûrs'ing] n (profession) professione f di infermiere (or di infermiera) ♦ a (mother) che allatta.

nursing home n casa di cura.

nurture [nûr'chûr] vt allevare; nutrire.

nut [nut] n (of metal) dado; (fruit) noce f (or nocciola or mandorla etc) ♦ a (chocolate etc) alla nocciola etc.

nutcase [nut'kãs] n (Brit col) mattarello/a.

nutcracker [nut'krakûr] n schiaccianoci m inv.

nutmeg [nut'meg] n noce f moscata.

nutrient [noō'trēənt] a nutriente ♦ n sostanza nutritiva.

nutrition [noōtrish'ən] n nutrizione f.

nutritionist [noōtrish'ənist] n nutrizionista m/f.

nutritious [noōtrish'əs] a nutriente.

nuts [nuts] a (col) matto(a) ♦ excl al diavolo!

nutshell [nut'shel] n guscio di noce; **in a** ~ in poche parole.

nuzzle [nuz'əl] vi: **to** ~ **up to** strofinare il muso contro.

NV abbr (US MAIL) = Nevada.

NWT abbr (Canada) = Northwest Territories.

NY abbr (US MAIL) = New York.

NYC abbr (US MAIL) = New York City.

nylon [nī'lân] n nailon m; ~**s** npl calze fpl di nailon.

nymph [nimf] n ninfa.

nymphomaniac [nimfəmā'nēak] a, n ninfomane (f).

NYSE abbr (US) = New York Stock Exchange.

NZ abbr = **New Zealand.**

O

O, o [ō] n (letter) O, o f or m inv; (US SCOL: = outstanding) ≈ ottimo; (number: TEL etc) zero; **O for Oboe** ≈ O come Otranto.

oaf [ōf] n zoticone m.

oak [ōk] n quercia ♦ cpd di quercia.

OAP n abbr (Brit) see **old-age pensioner.**

oar [ôr] n remo; **to put** or **shove one's** ~ **in** (fig col) intromettersi.

oarlock [ôr'lák] n (US) scalmo.

oarsman [ôrz'mən], **oarswoman** [ôrz'woōmən]

n rematore/trice.

OAS *n abbr* (= *Organization of American States*) O.S.A. *f* (= *Organizzazione degli Stati Americani*).

oasis, *pl* **oases** [ōā'sis, -sēz] *n* oasi *f inv.*

oath [ōth] *n* giuramento; (*swear word*) bestemmia; **to take the ~** giurare; **under** *or* (*Brit*) **on ~** sotto giuramento.

oatmeal [ōt'mēl] *n* fiocchi d'avena.

oats [ōts] *npl* avena.

OAU *n abbr* (= *Organization of African Unity*) O.A.U. *f.*

obdurate [âb'dyərit] *a* testardo(a); incallito(a); ostinato(a), irremovibile.

obedience [ōbē'dēəns] *n* ubbidienza; **in ~ to** conformemente a.

obedient [ōbē'dēənt] *a* ubbidiente; **to be ~ to sb/sth** ubbidire a qn/qc.

obelisk [âb'əlisk] *n* obelisco.

obesity [ōbē'sitē] *n* obesità.

obey [ōbā'] *vt* ubbidire a; (*instructions, regulations*) osservare ♦ *vi* ubbidire.

obituary [ōbich'ōōārē] *n* necrologia.

object *n* [âb'jikt] oggetto; (*purpose*) scopo, intento; (*LING*) complemento oggetto ♦ *vi* [əbjekt']: **to ~ to** (*attitude*) disapprovare; (*proposal*) protestare contro, sollevare delle obiezioni contro; **I ~!** mi oppongo!; **he ~ed that ...** obiettò che ...; **do you ~ to my smoking?** la disturba se fumo?; **what's the ~ of doing that?** a che serve farlo?; **expense is no ~** non si bada a spese.

objection [əbjek'shən] *n* obiezione *f*; (*drawback*) inconveniente *m*; **if you have no ~** se non ha obiezioni; **to make** *or* **raise an ~** sollevare un'obiezione.

objectionable [əbjek'shənəbəl] *a* antipatico(a); (*smell*) sgradevole; (*language*) scostumato(a).

objective [əbjek'tiv] *n* obiettivo ♦ *a* obiettivo(a).

objectivity [âbjektiv'ətē] *n* obiettività.

object lesson *n*: **~ (in)** dimostrazione *f* (di).

objector [əbjek'tûr] *n* oppositore/trice.

obligation [âbləgā'shən] *n* obbligo, dovere *m*; (*debt*) obbligo (di riconoscenza); **"without ~"** "senza impegno"; **to be under an ~ to sb/to do sth** essere in dovere verso qn/di fare qc.

obligatory [əblig'ətôrē] *a* obbligatorio(a).

oblige [əblīj'] *vt* (*force*): **to ~ sb to do** costringere qn a fare; (*do a favor*) fare una cortesia a; **to be ~d to sb for sth** essere grato a qn per qc; **anything to ~!** (*col*) questo e altro!

obliging [əblī'jing] *a* servizievole, compiacente.

oblique [əblēk'] *a* obliquo(a); (*allusion*) indiretto(a) ♦ *n* (*Brit TYP*): **~ (stroke)** barra.

obliterate [əblit'ərāt] *vt* cancellare.

oblivion [əbliv'ēən] *n* oblio.

oblivious [əbliv'ēəs] *a*: **~ of** incurante di;

inconscio(a) di.

oblong [âb'lông] *a* oblungo(a) ♦ *n* rettangolo.

obnoxious [əbnâk'shəs] *a* odioso(a); (*smell*) disgustoso(a), ripugnante.

o.b.o. *abbr* (*US*: = *or best offer*: *in classified ads*) o al miglior offerente.

oboe [ō'bō] *n* oboe *m*.

obscene [əbsēn'] *a* osceno(a).

obscenity [əbsen'itē] *n* oscenità *f inv.*

obscure [əbskyōōr'] *a* oscuro(a) ♦ *vt* oscurare; (*hide*: *sun*) nascondere.

obscurity [əbskyōōr'itē] *n* oscurità; (*obscure point*) punto oscuro; (*lack of fame*) anonimato.

obsequious [əbsē'kwēəs] *a* ossequioso(a).

observable [əbzûr'vəbəl] *a* osservabile; (*appreciable*) notevole.

observance [əbzûr'vəns] *n* osservanza; **religious ~s** pratiche *fpl* religiose.

observant [əbzûr'vənt] *a* attento(a).

observation [âbzûrvā'shən] *n* osservazione *f*; (*by police etc*) sorveglianza.

observation post *n* (*MIL*) osservatorio.

observatory [əbzûr'vətôrē] *n* osservatorio.

observe [əbzûrv'] *vt* osservare.

observer [əbzûr'vûr] *n* osservatore/trice.

obsess [əbses'] *vt* ossessionare; **to be ~ed by** *or* **with sb/sth** essere ossessionato da qn/qc.

obsession [əbsesh'ən] *n* ossessione *f.*

obsessive [əbses'iv] *a* ossessivo(a).

obsolescence [âbsəles'əns] *n* obsolescenza; **built-in** *or* **planned ~** (*COMM*) obsolescenza programmata.

obsolescent [âbsəles'ənt] *a* obsolescente.

obsolete [âbsəlēt'] *a* obsoleto(a); (*word*) desueto(a).

obstacle [âb'stəkəl] *n* ostacolo.

obstacle race *n* corsa agli ostacoli.

obstetrics [əbstet'riks] *n* ostetrica.

obstinacy [âb'stənəsē] *n* ostinatezza.

obstinate [âb'stənit] *a* ostinato(a).

obstreperous [əbstrep'ûrəs] *a* turbolento(a).

obstruct [əbstrukt'] *vt* (*block*) ostruire, ostacolare; (*halt*) fermare; (*hinder*) impedire.

obstruction [əbstruk'shən] *n* ostruzione *f*; ostacolo.

obstructive [əbstruk'tiv] *a* ostruttivo(a); che crea impedimenti.

obtain [əbtān'] *vt* ottenere ♦ *vi* essere in uso; **to ~ sth (for o.s.)** procurarsi qc.

obtainable [əbtān'əbəl] *a* ottenibile.

obtrusive [əbtrōō'siv] *a* (*person*) importuno(a); (*smell*) invadente; (*building etc*) imponente e invadente.

obtuse [əbtōōs'] *a* ottuso(a).

obverse [âb'vûrs] *n* opposto, inverso.

obviate [âb'vēāt] *vt* ovviare a, evitare.

obvious [âb'vēəs] *a* ovvio(a), evidente.

obviously [âb'vēəslē] *ad* ovviamente; **~!** certo!; **~ not!** certo che no!; **he was ~ not drunk** si vedeva che non era ubriaco; **he was**

apparel
appareil

not ~ **drunk** non si vedeva che era ubriaco.

OCAS *n abbr* = *Organization of Central American States*.

occasion [əkā'zhən] *n* occasione *f*; (*event*) avvenimento ♦ *vt* cagionare; **on that** ~ in quell'occasione, quella volta; **to rise to the** ~ mostrarsi all'altezza della situazione.

occasional [əkā'zhənəl] *a* occasionale; (*work etc*) avventizio(a); **I smoke an** ~ **cigarette** ogni tanto fumo una sigaretta.

occasionally [əkā'zhənəlē] *ad* ogni tanto; **very** ~ molto raramente.

occasional table *n* tavolino.

occult [əkult'] *a* occulto(a) ♦ *n*: **the** ~ l'occulto.

occupancy [âk'yəpənsē] *n* occupazione *f*.

occupant [âk'yəpənt] *n* occupante *m/f*; (*of boat, car etc*) persona a bordo.

occupation [âkyəpā'shən] *n* occupazione *f*; (*job*) mestiere *m*, professione *f*; **unfit for** ~ (*house*) inabitabile.

occupational [âkyəpā'shənəl] *a* (*disease*) professionale; (*hazard*) del mestiere; ~ **accident** infortunio sul lavoro.

occupational pension plan *n* sistema pensionistico programmato dal datore di lavoro.

occupational therapy *n* ergoterapia.

occupied [âk'yəpīd] *a* (*busy, in use*) occupato(a).

occupier [âk'yəpīûr] *n* occupante *m/f*.

occupy [âk'yəpī] *vt* occupare; **to** ~ **o.s. by doing** occuparsi a fare; **to be occupied with sth/in doing sth** essere preso da qc/occupato a fare qc.

occur [əkûr'] *vi* accadere; (*difficulty, opportunity*) capitare; (*phenomenon, error*) trovarsi; **to** ~ **to sb** venire in mente a qn.

occurrence [əkûr'əns] *n* caso, fatto; presenza.

ocean [ō'shən] *n* oceano; ~**s of** (*col*) un sacco di.

ocean bed *n* fondale *m* oceanico.

oceangoing [ō'shəngōing] *a* d'alto mare.

Oceania [ōshēan'ēə] *n* Oceania.

ocean liner *n* transatlantico.

ocher, (*Brit*) **ochre** [ō'kûr] *a* ocra *inv*.

o'clock [əklâk'] *ad*: **it is one** ~ è l'una; **it is 5** ~ sono le 5.

OCR *n abbr see* **optical character reader**; **optical character recognition**.

Oct. *abbr* (= *October*) ott.

octagonal [âktag'ənəl] *a* ottagonale.

octane [âk'tān] *n* ottano; **high-**~ **gas** *or* (*Brit*) **petrol** benzina ad alto numero di ottani.

octave [âk'tiv] *n* ottavo.

October [âktō'bûr] *n* ottobre *m*; *for phrases see also* **July**.

octogenarian [âktəjənâr'ēən] *n* ottuagenario/a.

octopus [âk'təpəs] *n* polpo, piovra.

odd [âd] *a* (*strange*) strano(a), bizzarro(a); (*number*) dispari *inv*; (*left over*) in più; (*not*

of a set) spaiato(a); **60-**~ 60 e oltre; **at** ~ **times** di tanto in tanto; **the** ~ **one out** l'eccezione *f*.

oddball [âd'bôl] *n* (*col*) eccentrico/a.

oddity [âd'itē] *n* bizzarria; (*person*) originale *m/f*.

odd-job man [âd'jâb' man] *n* tuttofare *m inv*.

odd jobs *npl* lavori *mpl* occasionali.

oddly [âd'lē] *ad* stranamente.

odds [âdz] *npl* (*in betting*) quota; **the** ~ **are against his coming** c'è poca probabilità che venga; **it makes no** ~ non importa; **at** ~ in contesa; **to succeed against all the** ~ riuscire contro ogni aspettativa; ~ **and ends** avanzi *mpl*.

ode [ōd] *n* ode *f*.

odious [ō'dēəs] *a* odioso(a), ripugnante.

odometer [ōdâm'itûr] *n* odometro.

odor [ō'dûr] *n* (*US*) odore *m*.

odorless [ō'dûrlis] *a* inodoro(a).

odour [ō'dûr] *etc* (*Brit*) = **odor** *etc*.

OECD *n abbr* (= *Organization for Economic Cooperation and Development*) O.C.S.E. *f* (= *Organizzazione per la Cooperazione e lo Sviluppo Economico*).

oesophagus [isâf'əgəs] *n* (*Brit*) esofago.

oestrogen [es'trəjən] *n* (*Brit*) estrogeno.

of [uv, âv] *prep* di; **a friend** ~ **ours** un nostro amico; **3** ~ **them went** 3 di loro sono andati; **the 4th** ~ **July** il 4 luglio; **a boy** ~ **10** un ragazzo di 10 anni; **made** ~ **wood** (fatto) di *or* in legno; **a kilo** ~ **flour** un chilo di farina; **that was very kind** ~ **you** è stato molto carino da parte sua; **a quarter** ~ **4** (*US*) le 4 meno un quarto.

off [ôf] *a*, *ad* (*engine*) spento(a); (*tap*) chiuso(a); (*Brit: food*) andato(a) a male; (*absent*) assente; (*cancelled*) sospeso(a) ♦ *prep* a poca distanza di; **to be** ~ (*to leave*) partire, andarsene; **to be** ~ **sick** essere assente per malattia; **a day** ~ un giorno di vacanza; **to have an** ~ **day** non essere in forma; **to be well/badly** ~ essere/non essere benestante; **to be** ~ **in one's calculations** essersi sbagliato nei calcoli; **he had his coat** ~ si era tolto il cappotto; **the lid was** ~ non c'era il coperchio; **10%** ~ (*COMM*) con uno sconto di 10%; **5 km** ~ **(the road)** a 5 km (dalla strada); ~ **the coast** al largo della costa; **a house** ~ **the main road** una casa fuori della strada maestra; **it's a long way** ~ è molto lontano; **I'm** ~ **meat** la carne non mi va più; non mangio più la carne; **on the** ~ **chance** a caso; ~ **and on, on and** ~ di tanto in tanto; **that's a bit** ~, **isn't it?** (*fig col*) non è molto carino, vero?

offal [ôf'əl] *n* (*CULIN*) frattaglie *fpl*.

offbeat [ôf'bēt'] *a* eccentrico(a).

off-center [ôf'sen'tûr] *a* storto(a), fuori centro.

off-color [ôf'kôl'ûr] *a* (*ill*) malato(a), indisposto(a); **to feel** ~ sentirsi poco bene.

offence [əfɛns'] *n* (*Brit*) = **offense**.
offend [əfɛnd'] *vt* (*person*) offendere ♦ *vi*: **to ~ against** (*law*, *rule*) trasgredire.
offender [əfɛn'dûr] *n* delinquente *m/f*; (*against regulations*) contravventore/trice.
offense [əfɛns'] *n* (*US LAW*) contravvenzione *f*; (: *more serious*) reato; **to give ~ to** offendere; **to take ~ at** offendersi per; **to commit an ~** commettere un reato.
offensive [əfɛn'siv] *a* offensivo(a); (*smell etc*) sgradevole, ripugnante ♦ *n* (*MIL*) offensiva.
offer [ôf'ûr] *n* offerta, proposta ♦ *vt* offrire; **"on ~"** (*Brit COMM*) "in offerta speciale"; **to make an ~ for sth** fare un'offerta per qc; **to ~ sth to sb, ~ sb sth** offrire qc a qn; **to ~ to do sth** offrirsi di fare qc.
offering [ôf'ûring] *n* offerta.
offhand [ôf'hand'] *a* disinvolto(a), noncurante ♦ *ad* all'improvviso; **I can't tell you ~** non posso dirglielo su due piedi.
office [ôf'is] *n* (*place*) ufficio; (*position*) carica; **doctor's ~** (*US*) ambulatorio; **to take ~** entrare in carica; **through his good ~s** con il suo prezioso aiuto.
office automation *n* automazione *f* d'ufficio, burotica.
office bearer *n* (*Brit*) = **office holder**.
office building, (*Brit*) **office block** *n* complesso di uffici.
office boy *n* garzone *m*.
office holder *n* (*US: of club etc*) membro dell'amministrazione.
office hours *npl* orario d'ufficio; (*US MED*) orario di visite.
office manager *n* capoufficio *m/f*.
officer [ôf'isûr] *n* (*MIL etc*) ufficiale *m*; (*of organization*) funzionario; (*of club etc*) membro dell'amministrazione; (*also:* **police ~**) agente *m* di polizia.
office work *n* lavoro d'ufficio.
office worker *n* impiegato/a d'ufficio.
official [əfish'əl] *a* (*authorized*) ufficiale ♦ *n* ufficiale *m*; (*civil servant*) impiegato/a statale; funzionario.
officialdom [əfish'əldəm] *n* burocrazia.
officially [əfish'əlē] *ad* ufficialmente.
officiate [əfish'ēāt] *vi* (*REL*) ufficiare; **to ~ as Mayor** esplicare le funzioni di sindaco; **to ~ at a marriage** celebrare un matrimonio.
officious [əfish'əs] *a* invadente.
offing [ôf'ing] *n*: **in the ~** (*fig*) in vista.
off-key [ôfkē'] *a* stonato(a) ♦ *ad* fuori tono.
off-licence [ôf'līsəns] *n* (*Brit*) spaccio di bevande alcoliche.
off-limits [ôf'lim'its] *a* (*esp US*) in cui vige il divieto d'accesso.
off line *a*, *ad* (*COMPUT*) off line *inv*, fuori linea; (: *switched off*) spento(a).
off-load [ôf'lōd'] *vt* scaricare.
off-peak [ôf'pēk'] *a* (*ticket etc*) a tariffa ridotta; (*time*) non di punta.

off-putting [ôf'pŏŏt'ing] *a* (*Brit*) un po' scostante.
off-ramp [ôf'ramp] *n* (*US AUT*) rampa di uscita.
off-season [ôf'sēzən] *a*, *ad* fuori stagione.
offset *vt irg* [ôfsɛt'] (*counteract*) controbilanciare, compensare ♦ *n* [ôf'sɛt] (*also:* **~ printing**) offset *m*.
offshoot [ôf'shŏŏt] *n* (*fig*) diramazione *f*.
offshore [ôf'shôr'] *a* (*breeze*) di terra; (*island*) vicino alla costa; (*fishing*) costiero(a); **~ oilfield** giacimento petrolifero in mare aperto.
offside *a* [ôf'sīd'] (*SPORT*) fuori gioco; (*AUT: with right-hand drive*) destro(a); (: *with left-hand drive*) sinistro(a) ♦ *n* destra; sinistra.
offspring [ôf'spring] *n* prole *f*, discendenza.
offstage [ôf'stāj'] *ad* dietro le quinte.
off-the-cuff [ôf'thəkuf'] *ad* improvvisando.
off-the-job [ôf'thəjâb'] *a*: **~ training** addestramento fuori sede.
off-the-peg [ôf'thəpɛg'] *ad* (*Brit*) = **off-the-rack**.
off-the-rack [ôf'thərak'] *ad* (*US*) prêt-à-porter.
off-the-wall [ôf'thəwôl'] *a* un po' pazzo(a).
off-white [ôf'wīt] *a* bianco sporco *inv*.
off-year election [ôf'yēr ilɛk'shən] *n* (*US*) elezione *f* straordinaria.
often [ôf'ən] *ad* spesso; **how ~ do you go?** quanto spesso ci va?; **as ~ as not** quasi sempre.
ogle [ō'gəl] *vt* occhieggiare.
ogre [ō'gûr] *n* orco.
OH *abbr* (*US MAIL*) = Ohio.
oh [ō] *excl* oh!
OHMS *abbr* (*Brit*) = On His (or Her) Majesty's Service.
oil [oil] *n* olio; (*petroleum*) petrolio; (*for central heating*) nafta ♦ *vt* (*machine*) lubrificare.
oilcan [oil'kan] *n* oliatore *m* a mano; (*for storing*) latta da olio.
oil change *n* cambio dell'olio.
oilfield [oil'fēld] *n* giacimento petrolifero.
oil filter *n* (*AUT*) filtro dell'olio.
oil-fired [oil'fiûrd] *a* a nafta.
oil gauge *n* indicatore *m* del livello dell'olio.
oil industry *n* industria del petrolio.
oil level *n* livello dell'olio.
oil painting *n* quadro a olio.
oil pan *n* (*US AUT*) coppa dell'olio.
oil refinery *n* raffineria di petrolio.
oil rig *n* derrick *m inv*; (*at sea*) piattaforma per trivellazioni subacquee.
oilskins [oil'skinz] *npl* (*Brit*) indumenti *mpl* di tela cerata.
oil slick *n* chiazza d'olio.
oil tanker *n* petroliera.
oil well *n* pozzo petrolifero.
oily [oi'lē] *a* unto(a), oleoso(a); (*food*) untuoso(a).
ointment [oint'mənt] *n* unguento.

OJT *n abbr* (*US*: = *on-the-job training*) addestramento in sede.

OK *abbr* (*US MAIL*) = *Oklahoma*.

O.K., okay |ōkā'| *excl* d'accordo! ♦ *vt* approvare ♦ *n*: **to give sth one's** ~ approvare qc ♦ *a*: **is it** ~?, **are you** ~? tutto bene?; **it's** ~ **with** *or* **by me** per me va bene; **are you** ~ **for money?** sei a posto coi soldi?

Okla. *abbr* (*US*) = *Oklahoma*.

old |ōld| *a* vecchio(a); (*ancient*) antico(a), vecchio(a); (*person*) vecchio(a), anziano(a); **how** ~ **are you?** quanti anni ha?; **he's 10 years** ~ ha 10 anni; ~**er brother/sister** fratello/sorella maggiore; **any** ~ **thing will do** va bene qualsiasi cosa.

old age *n* vecchiaia.

old-age pensioner (OAP) |ōld'āj pɛn'chənûr| *n* (*Brit*) pensionato/a.

old-fashioned |ōld'fash'ənd| *a* antiquato(a), fuori moda; (*person*) all'antica.

old folks' home *n* ricovero per anziani.

old maid *n* zitella.

old-time |ōld'tīm| *a* di una volta.

old-timer |ōld'tī'mûr| *n* veterano/a.

old wives' tale *n* vecchia superstizione *f*.

olive |âl'iv| *n* (*fruit*) oliva; (*tree*) olivo ♦ *a* (*also*: ~**-green**) verde oliva *inv*.

olive oil *n* olio d'oliva.

Olympic |ōlim'pik| *a* olimpico(a); **the** ~ **Games, the** ~**s** i giochi olimpici, le Olimpiadi.

O & M *abbr* = *organization and method*.

Oman |ō'mán| *n* Oman *m*.

OMB *n abbr* (*US*: = *Office of Management and Budget*) servizio di consulenza al Presidente in materia di bilancio.

omelet(te) |âm'lit| *n* omelette *f inv*; **ham/ cheese** ~ omelette al prosciutto/al formaggio.

omen |ō'mən| *n* presagio, augurio.

ominous |âm'ənəs| *a* minaccioso(a); (*event*) di malaugurio.

omission |ōmish'ən| *n* omissione *f*.

omit |ōmit'| *vt* omettere; **to** ~ **to do sth** tralasciare *or* trascurare di fare qc.

omnivorous |âmniv'ûrəs| *a* onnivoro(a).

ON *abbr* (*Canada*) = *Ontario*.

on |ân| *prep* su; (*on top of*) sopra ♦ *a, ad* (*machine*) in moto; (*light, radio*) acceso(a); (*tap*) aperto(a); **is the meeting still** ~? avrà sempre luogo la riunione?; la riunione è ancora in corso?; **when is this movie** ~? quando c'è questo film?; ~ **the train** in treno; ~ **the wall** sul *or* al muro; ~ **television** alla televisione; ~ **the Continent** nell'Europa continentale; **a book** ~ **physics** un libro di *or* sulla fisica; ~ **learning this** imparando questo; ~ **arrival** all'arrivo; ~ **the left** sulla *or* a sinistra; ~ **Friday** venerdì; ~ **Fridays** di *or* il venerdì; **to be** ~ **vacation** *or* (*Brit*) ~ **holiday** essere in vacanza; **I don't have any money** ~ **me** non ho soldi con me; **he's** ~

$6000 a year guadagna 6000 dollari all'anno; **this round's** ~ **me** questo giro lo offro io; **put your coat** ~ mettiti il cappotto; **to walk** *etc* ~ continuare a camminare *etc*; **from that day** ~ da quel giorno in poi; **my father's always** ~ **(at) me to get a job** (*col*) mio padre mi sta sempre addosso perché trovi un lavoro; **that's not** ~! (*not acceptable*) non si fa così!; (*not possible*) non se ne parla neanche!; ~ **and off** ogni tanto.

once |wuns| *ad* una volta ♦ *cj* non appena, quando; ~ **he had left/it was done** dopo che se n'era andato/fu fatto; **at** ~ subito; (*simultaneously*) a un tempo; **all at** ~ (tutto) ad un tratto; ~ **a week** una volta alla settimana; ~ **more** ancora una volta; **I knew him** ~ un tempo *or* in passato lo conoscevo; ~ **and for all** una volta per sempre; ~ **upon a time there was** ... c'era una volta ....

oncoming |ân'kuming| *a* (*traffic*) che viene in senso opposto.

one |wun| *a, num* un(uno) *m*, una(un') *f* ♦ *pronoun* uno(a); (*impersonal*) si; **this** ~ questo(a) qui; **that** ~ quello(a) là; **the** ~ **book which** ... l'unico libro che ...; ~ **by** ~ a uno(a) a uno(a); ~ **never knows** non si sa mai; **to express** ~**'s opinion** esprimere la propria opinione; ~ **another** l'un(a) l'altro(a); **it's** ~ **(o'clock)** è l'una; **which** ~ **do you want?** quale vuole?; **to be** ~ **up on sb** essere avvantaggiato rispetto a qn; **to be at** ~ **(with sb)** andare d'accordo (con qn).

one-armed bandit |wun'ârmd ban'dit| *n* slot-machine *f inv*.

one-day excursion |wun'dā ikskûr'zhən| *n* (*US*) biglietto giornaliero di andata e ritorno.

one-man |wun'man| *a* (*business*) diretto(a) *etc* da un solo uomo.

one-man band *n* suonatore ambulante con vari strumenti.

one-off |wun'ôf| (*Brit col*) *n, a* = **one-shot**.

one-piece |wun'pēs| *a* (*bathing suit*) intero(a).

onerous |ân'ûrəs| *a* (*task, duty*) gravoso(a); (*responsibility*) pesante.

oneself |wunself'| *pronoun* si; (*after prep*) sé, se stesso(a); **to do sth (by)** ~ fare qc da sé.

one-shot |wun'shât| *n* (*US col*) fatto eccezionale ♦ *a* eccezionale.

one-sided |wun'sīdid| *a* (*decision, view*) unilaterale; (*judgement, account*) parziale; (*game, contest*) impari *inv*.

one-time |wun'tīm| *a* ex *inv*.

one-to-one |wun'təwun'| *a* (*relationship*) univoco(a).

one-upmanship |wunup'mənship| *n*: **the art of** ~ l'arte *f* di primeggiare.

one-way |wun'wā'| *a* (*street, traffic*) a senso unico.

one-way ticket *n* biglietto di (sola) andata.

ongoing |ân'gōing| *a* in corso; in attuazione.

onion |un'yən| *n* cipolla.

on line *a* (*COMPUT*) on line *inv*, in linea; (: *switched on*) acceso(a).

onlooker [ân'lōōkûr] *n* spettatore/trice.

only [ōn'lē] *ad* solo, soltanto ♦ *a* solo(a), unico(a) ♦ *cj* solo che, ma; **an ~ child** un figlio unico; **not ~** non solo; **I ~ took one** ne ho preso soltanto uno, non ne ho preso che uno; **I saw her ~ yesterday** l'ho vista appena ieri; **I'd be ~ too pleased to help** sarei proprio felice di essere d'aiuto; **I would come, ~ I'm very busy** verrei volentieri, solo che sono molto occupato.

ono *abbr* (*Brit*) = **or nearest offer;** *see* **near.**

on-ramp [ân'ramp] *n* (*US AUT*) rampa di accesso.

onset [ân'set] *n* inizio; (*of winter*) arrivo.

onshore [ân'shôr'] *a* (*wind*) di mare.

onslaught [ân'slôt] *n* attacco, assalto.

Ont. *abbr* (*Canada*) = Ontario.

on-the-job [ânthəjáb'] *a:* **~ training** addestramento in sede.

onto [ân'tōō] *prep* su, sopra.

onus [ō'nəs] *n* onere *m*, peso; **the ~ is upon him to prove it** sta a lui dimostrarlo.

onward(s) [ân'wûrdz] *ad* (*move*) in avanti; **from this time ~** d'ora in poi.

onyx [ân'iks] *n* onice *f*.

ooze [ōōz] *vi* stillare.

opacity [ōpas'itē] *n* opacità.

opal [ō'pəl] *n* opale *m or f*.

opaque [ōpāk'] *a* opaco(a).

OPEC [ō'pek] *n abbr* (= *Organization of Petroleum-Exporting Countries*) O.P.E.C. *f*.

open [ō'pən] *a* aperto(a); (*road*) libero(a); (*meeting*) pubblico(a); (*admiration*) evidente, franco(a); (*question*) insoluto(a); (*enemy*) dichiarato(a) ♦ *vt* aprire ♦ *vi* (*eyes, door, debate*) aprirsi; (*flower*) sbocciare; (*store, bank, museum*) aprire; (*book etc: commence*) cominciare; **in the ~ (air)** all'aperto; **the ~ sea** il mare aperto, l'alto mare; **~ ground** (*among trees*) radura; (*waste ground*) terreno non edificato; **to have an ~ mind (on sth)** non avere ancora deciso (su qc).

open on to *vt fus* (*subj: room, door*) dare su.

open out *vt* aprire ♦ *vi* aprirsi.

open up *vt* aprire; (*blocked road*) sgombrare ♦ *vi* aprirsi.

open-air [ō'pənār'] *a* all'aperto.

open-and-shut [ō'pənənshut'] *a:* **~ case** caso indubbio.

open day *n* (*Brit*) giornata di apertura al pubblico.

open-ended [ō'pənen'did] *a* (*fig*) aperto(a), senza limiti.

opener [ō'pənûr] *n* (*also:* **can ~**) apriscatole *m inv*.

open-faced sandwich [ō'pənfāst' sand'wich] *n* (*US*) canapè *m inv*.

open-heart [ō'pənhârt] *a:* **~ surgery** chirurgia a cuore aperto.

opening [ō'pəning] *n* apertura; (*opportunity*) occasione *f*, opportunità *f inv*; sbocco; (*job*) posto vacante.

opening night *n* (*THEATER*) prima.

openly [ō'pənlē] *ad* apertamente.

open-minded [ō'pənmîn'did] *a* che ha la mente aperta.

open-necked [ō'pənnekt'] *a* col collo slacciato.

openness [ō'pənnis] *n* (*frankness*) franchezza, sincerità.

open-plan [ō'pənplan'] *a* senza pareti divisorie.

open sandwich *n* (*Brit*) canapè *m inv*.

open shop *n* fabbrica o ditta dove sono accolti anche operai non iscritti ai sindacati.

opera [âp'rə] *n* opera.

opera glasses *npl* binocolo da teatro.

opera house *n* opera.

opera singer *n* cantante *m/f* d'opera *or* lirico(a).

operate [âp'ərāt] *vt* (*machine*) azionare, far funzionare; (*system*) usare ♦ *vi* funzionare; (*drug, person*) agire; **to ~ on sb (for)** (*MED*) operare qn (di).

operatic [âpərat'ik] *a* dell'opera, lirico(a).

operating [âp'ərāting] *a* (*COMM: costs etc*) di gestione; (*MED*) operatorio(a).

operating room *n* (*US MED*) sala operatoria.

operating system *n* (*COMPUT*) sistema *m* operativo.

operating theatre *n* (*Brit MED*) sala operatoria.

operation [âpərā'shən] *n* operazione *f*; **to be in ~** (*machine*) essere in azione *or* funzionamento; (*system*) essere in vigore; **to have an ~ (for)** (*MED*) essere operato(a) (di).

operational [âpərā'shənəl] *a* operativo(a); (*COMM*) di gestione, d'esercizio; (*ready for use or action*) in attività, in funzione; **when the service is fully ~** quando il servizio sarà completamente in funzione.

operative [âp'ûrətiv] *a* (*measure*) operativo(a) ♦ *n* (*in factory*) operaio/a; **the ~ word** la parola chiave.

operator [âp'ərātûr] *n* (*of machine*) operatore/trice; (*TEL*) centralinista *m/f*.

operetta [âpəret'ə] *n* operetta.

ophthalmologist [âfthalmâl'əjist] *n* oftalmologo/a.

opinion [əpin'yən] *n* opinione *f*, parere *m*; **in my ~** secondo me, a mio avviso; **to seek a second ~** (*MED etc*) consultarsi con un altro medico *etc*.

opinionated [əpin'yənātid] *a* dogmatico(a).

opinion poll *n* sondaggio di opinioni.

opium [ō'pēəm] *n* oppio.

opponent [əpō'nənt] *n* avversario/a.

opportune [âpûrtōōn'] *a* opportuno(a).

opportunist [âpûrtōō'nist] *n* opportunista *m/f*.

opportunity [âpûrtyōō'nitē] *n* opportunità *f inv*, occasione *f*; **to take the ~ to do** *or* **of doing** cogliere l'occasione per fare.

oppose [əpōz'] *vt* opporsi a; **~d to** contrario(a) a; **as ~d to** in contrasto con.

opposing [əpōz'ing] *a* opposto(a); *(team)* avversario(a).

opposite [âp'əzit] *a* opposto(a); *(house etc)* di fronte ♦ *ad* di fronte, dirimpetto ♦ *prep* di fronte a ♦ *n* opposto, contrario; *(of word)* contrario; **"see ~ page"** "vedere pagina a fronte".

opposite number *n* controparte *f*, corrispondente *m/f*.

opposite sex *n*: **the ~** l'altro sesso.

opposition [âpəzish'ən] *n* opposizione *f*.

oppress [əpres'] *vt* opprimere.

oppression [əpresh'ən] *n* oppressione *f*.

oppressive [əpres'iv] *a* oppressivo(a).

opprobrium [əprō'brēəm] *n* *(formal)* obbrobrio.

opt [âpt] *vi*: **to ~ for** optare per; **to ~ to do** scegliere di fare; **to ~ out of** ritirarsi da.

optical [âp'tikəl] *a* ottico(a).

optical character reader/recognition (OCR) *n* lettore *m* ottico/lettura ottica di caratteri.

optical fiber *n* fibra ottica.

optician [âptish'ən] *n* ottico.

optics [âp'tiks] *n* ottica.

optimism [âp'təmizəm] *n* ottimismo.

optimist [âp'təmist] *n* ottimista *m/f*.

optimistic [âptəmis'tik] *a* ottimistico(a).

optimum [âp'təməm] *a* ottimale.

option [âp'shən] *n* scelta; *(SCOL)* materia facoltativa; *(COMM)* opzione *f*; **~s** *npl* optional *m inv*; **to keep one's ~s open** *(fig)* non impegnarsi; **I have no ~** non ho scelta.

optional [âp'shənəl] *a* facoltativo(a); *(COMM)* a scelta; **~ extra** *(Brit)* optional *m inv*.

opulence [âp'yələns] *n* opulenza.

opulent [âp'yələnt] *a* opulento(a).

OR *abbr (US MAIL)* = Oregon.

or [ôr] *cj* o, oppure; *(with negative)*: **he hasn't seen ~ heard anything** non ha visto né sentito niente; **~ else** se no, altrimenti; oppure.

oracle [ôr'əkəl] *n* oracolo.

oral [ôr'əl] *a* orale ♦ *n* esame *m* orale.

orange [ôr'inj] *n* *(fruit)* arancia ♦ *a* arancione.

orangeade [ôrinjād'] *n* aranciata.

orange juice *n* succo di arancia.

oration [ôrā'shən] *n* orazione *f*.

orator [ôr'ətûr] *n* oratore/trice.

oratorio [ôrətôr'ēō] *n* oratorio.

orb [ôrb] *n* orbe *m*.

orbit [ôr'bit] *n* orbita ♦ *vt* orbitare intorno a; **to be in/go into ~ (around)** essere/entrare in orbita (attorno a).

orchard [ôr'chûrd] *n* frutteto; **apple ~** meleto.

orchestra [ôr'kistrə] *n* orchestra; *(US: seat-*ing)* platea.

orchestral [ôrkes'trəl] *a* orchestrale; *(concert)* sinfonico(a).

orchestrate [ôr'kistrāt] *vt* *(MUS, fig)* orchestrare.

orchid [ôr'kid] *n* orchidea.

ordain [ôrdān'] *vt* *(REL)* ordinare; *(decide)* decretare.

ordeal [ôrdēl'] *n* prova, travaglio.

order [ôr'dûr] *n* ordine *m*; *(COMM)* ordinazione *f* ♦ *vt* ordinare; **to ~ sb to do** ordinare a qn di fare; **in ~** in ordine; *(of document)* in regola; **in ~ of size** in ordine di grandezza; **in ~ to do** per fare; **in ~ that** affinché +*sub*; **a machine in working ~** una macchina che funziona bene; **to be out of ~** *(machine, toilets)* essere guasto(a); *(telephone)* essere fuori servizio; **to place an ~ for sth with sb** ordinare qc a qn; **to the ~ of** *(BANKING)* all'ordine di; **to be under ~s to do sth** avere l'ordine di fare qc; **a point of ~** una questione di procedura; **to be on ~** essere stato ordinato; **made to ~** fatto su commissione; **the lower ~s** *(pej)* i ceti inferiori.

order book *n* copiacommissioni *m inv*.

order form *n* modulo d'ordinazione.

orderly [ôr'dûrlē] *n* *(MIL)* attendente *m* ♦ *a* *(room)* in ordine; *(mind)* metodico(a); *(person)* ordinato(a), metodico(a).

order number *n* numero di ordinazione.

ordinal [ôr'dənəl] *a* *(number)* ordinale.

ordinary [ôr'dənärē] *a* normale, comune; *(pej)* mediocre ♦ *n*: **out of the ~** diverso dal solito, fuori dell'ordinario.

ordinary shares *npl* *(Brit)* azioni *fpl* ordinarie.

ordination [ôrdənā'shən] *n* ordinazione *f*.

ordnance [ôrd'nəns] *n* *(MIL: unit)* (reparto di) sussistenza.

Ore. *abbr (US)* = Oregon.

ore [ôr] *n* minerale *m* grezzo.

Oreg. *abbr (US)* = Oregon.

organ [ôr'gən] *n* organo.

organic [ôrgan'ik] *a* organico(a).

organism [ôr'gənizəm] *n* organismo.

organist [ôr'gənist] *n* organista *m/f*.

organization [ôrgənəzā'shən] *n* organizzazione *f*.

organization chart *n* organigramma *m*.

organize [ôr'gənīz] *vt* organizzare; **to get ~d** organizzarsi.

organized labor *n* manodopera organizzata.

organizer [ôr'gənīzûr] *n* organizzatore/trice.

orgasm [ôr'gazəm] *n* orgasmo.

orgy [ôr'jē] *n* orgia.

Orient [ôr'ēənt] *n*: **the ~** l'Oriente *m*.

oriental [ôrēen'təl] *a, n* orientale *(m/f)*.

orientate [ôr'ēentāt] *vt* orientare.

orifice [ôr'əfis] *n* orifizio.

origin [ôr'ijin] *n* origine *f*; **country of ~** paese *m* d'origine.

original [ərij'ənəl] *a* originale; (*earliest*) originario(a) ♦ *n* originale *m*.
originality [ərijənal'itē] *n* originalità.
originally [ərij'ənəlē] *ad* (*at first*) all'inizio.
originate [ərij'ənāt] *vi*: **to ~ from** venire da, essere originario(a) di; (*suggestion*) provenire da; **to ~ in** nascere in; (*custom*) avere origine in.
originator [ərij'inātûr] *n* iniziatore/trice.
ornament [ôr'nəmənt] *n* ornamento; (*trinket*) ninnolo.
ornamental [ôrnəmen'təl] *a* ornamentale.
ornamentation [ôrnəməntā'shən] *n* decorazione *f*, ornamento.
ornate [ôrnāt'] *a* molto ornato(a).
ornithologist [ôrnəthâl'əjist] *n* ornitologo/a.
ornithology [ôrnəthâl'əjē] *n* ornitologia.
orphan [ôr'fən] *n* orfano/a ♦ *vt*: **to be ~ed** diventare orfano.
orphanage [ôr'fənij] *n* orfanotrofio.
orthodox [ôr'thədâks] *a* ortodosso(a).
orthopedic, (*Brit*) **orthopaedic** [ôrthəpē'dik] *a* ortopedico(a).
O/S *abbr* = **out of stock.**
oscillate [âs'əlāt] *vi* oscillare.
OSHA *n abbr* (*US*: = *Occupational Safety and Health Administration*) Amministrazione per la sicurezza e la salute sul lavoro.
Oslo [âz'lō] *n* Oslo *f*.
ostensible [âsten'səbəl] *a* preteso(a); apparente.
ostensibly [âsten'səblē] *ad* all'apparenza.
ostentation [âstentā'shən] *n* ostentazione *f*.
ostentatious [âstentā'shəs] *a* pretenzioso(a); ostentato(a).
osteopath [âs'tēəpath] *n* specialista *m/f* di osteopatia.
ostracize [âs'trəsīz] *vt* dare l'ostracismo a.
ostrich [ôs'trich] *n* struzzo.
OT *abbr* (= *Old Testament*) V.T.
OTB *n abbr* (*US*: = *off-track betting*) puntate effettuate fuori dagli ippodromi.
OTE *abbr* (*Brit*: = *on-target earnings*) stipendio compreso le commissioni.
other [uth'ûr] *a* altro(a) ♦ *pronoun*: **the ~** l'altro(a); **the ~s** gli altri; **the ~ day** l'altro giorno; **some ~ people still have to arrive** (alcuni) altri devono ancora arrivare; **some actor or ~** (*Brit*) un certo attore; **somebody or ~** qualcuno; **~ than** altro che; a parte; **the car was none ~ than Roberta's** la macchina era proprio di Roberta.
otherwise [uth'ûrwīz] *ad*, *cj* altrimenti; **an ~ good piece of work** un lavoro comunque buono.
OTT *abbr* (*col*) = **over the top;** *see* **top.**
otter [ât'ûr] *n* lontra.
ouch [ouch] *excl* ohi!, ahi!
ought, *pt* **ought** [ôt] *auxiliary vb*: **I ~ to do it** dovrei farlo; **this ~ to have been corrected** questo avrebbe dovuto essere corretto; **he ~**

to win dovrebbe vincere; **you ~ to go and see it** dovreste andare a vederlo, fareste bene ad andarlo a vedere.
ounce [ouns] *n* oncia (= *28.35 g*; *16 in a pound*).
our [ou'ûr] *a* il(la) nostro(a), *pl* i(le) nostri(e).
ours [ou'ûrz] *pronoun* il(la) nostro(a), *pl* i(le) nostri(e).
ourselves [ouûrselvz'] *pronoun pl* (*reflexive*) ci; (*after preposition*) noi; (*emphatic*) noi stessi(e); **we did it (all) by ~** l'abbiamo fatto (tutto) da soli.
oust [oust] *vt* cacciare, espellere.
out [out] *ad* fuori; (*published, not at home etc*) uscito(a); (*light, fire*) spento(a); (*on strike*) in sciopero; **~ here** qui fuori; **~ there** là fuori; **he's ~** è uscito; (*unconscious*) ha perso conoscenza; **to be ~ in one's calculations** (*Brit*) essersi sbagliato nei calcoli; **to run/back** *etc* **~** uscire di corsa/a marcia indietro *etc*; **to be ~ and around** *or* (*Brit*) **about again** essere di nuovo in piedi; **the journey ~** l'andata; **the boat was 10 km ~** la barca era a 10 km dalla costa; **before the week was ~** entro la fine della settimana; **he's ~ for all he can get** sta cercando di trarne il massimo profitto; **~ of** (*outside*) fuori di; (*because of: anger etc*) per; (*from among*): **~ of 10** su 10; (*without*): **~ of gas** senza benzina, a corto di benzina; **made ~ of wood** (fatto) di *or* in legno; **it's ~ of stock** (*COMM*) non è disponibile.
outage [ou'tij] *n* (*esp US: power failure*) interruzione *f or* mancanza di corrente elettrica.
out-and-out [out'əndout'] *a* vero(a) e proprio(a).
outback [out'bak] *n* zona isolata; (*in Australia*) interno, entroterra.
outbid [out'bid'] *pt, pp* **outbid** [outbid'] *vt* fare un'offerta più alta di.
outboard [out'bôrd] *n*: **~ (motor)** (motore *m*) fuoribordo.
outbreak [out'brāk] *n* scoppio; epidemia.
outbuilding [out'bilding] *n* dipendenza.
outburst [out'bûrst] *n* scoppio.
outcast [out'kast] *n* esule *m/f*; (*socially*) paria *m inv*.
outclass [outklas'] *vt* surclassare.
outcome [out'kum] *n* esito, risultato.
outcrop [out'krâp] *n* affioramento.
outcry [out'krī] *n* protesta, clamore *m*.
outdated [outdā'tid] *a* (*custom, clothes*) fuori moda; (*idea*) sorpassato(a).
outdistance [outdis'təns] *vt* distanziare.
outdo [outdoo'] *vt irg* sorpassare; **to ~ o.s.** (*US*) superare se stesso.
outdoor [out'dôr] *a* all'aperto.
outdoors [outdôrz'] *ad* fuori; all'aria aperta.
outer [out'ûr] *a* esteriore; **~ suburbs** estrema periferia.

outer space n spazio cosmico.

outfit [out'fit] n equipaggiamento; (*clothes*) abito; (*col: organization*) organizzazione f.

outfitter [out'fitûr] n: **"(gent's) ~s"** "confezioni da uomo".

outgoing [out'gōing] a (*president, tenant*) uscente; (*means of transport*) in partenza; (*character*) socievole.

outgoings [out'gōingz] npl (*Brit: expenses*) spese fpl.

outgrow [outgrō'] vt irg (*clothes*) diventare troppo grande per.

outhouse [out'hous] n (*US*) toilette f inv esterna; (*Brit*) costruzione f annessa.

outing [ou'ting] n gita; escursione f.

outlandish [outlan'dish] a strano(a).

outlast [outlast'] vt sopravvivere a.

outlaw [out'lô] n fuorilegge m/f ♦ vt (*person*) mettere fuori della legge; (*practice*) proscrivere.

outlay [out'lā] n spesa.

outlet [out'let] n (*for liquid etc*) sbocco, scarico; (*for emotion*) sfogo; (*for goods*) sbocco, mercato; (*also:* **retail ~**) punto di vendita; (*US ELEC*) presa di corrente.

outline [out'līn] n contorno, profilo; (*summary*) abbozzo, grandi linee fpl.

outlive [outliv'] vt sopravvivere a.

outlook [out'lōok] n prospettiva, vista.

outlying [out'lïing] a periferico(a).

outmaneuver, (*Brit*) **outmanœuvre** [outmənōō'vûr] vt (*rival etc*) superare in strategia.

outmoded [outmō'did] a passato(a) di moda; antiquato(a).

outnumber [outnum'bûr] vt superare in numero.

out-of-date [outəvdāt'] a (*passport, ticket*) scaduto(a); (*theory, idea*) sorpassato(a), superato(a); (*custom*) antiquato(a); (*clothes*) fuori moda.

out-of-the-way [outəvthəwā'] a (*remote*) fuori mano; (*unusual*) originale, insolito(a).

outpatient [out'pāshənt] n paziente m/f esterno(a).

outpost [out'pōst] n avamposto.

output [out'pōot] n produzione f; (*COMPUT*) output m inv ♦ vt emettere.

outrage [out'rāj] n oltraggio; scandalo ♦ vt oltraggiare.

outrageous [outrā'jəs] a oltraggioso(a); scandaloso(a).

outrider [out'rīdûr] n (*on motorcycle*) battistrada m inv.

outright ad [outrīt'] completamente; schiettamente; apertamente; sul colpo ♦ a [out'rīt] completo(a); schietto(a) e netto(a).

outrun [outrun'] vt irg superare (nella corsa).

outset [out'set] n inizio.

outshine [outshīn'] vt irg (*fig*) eclissare.

outside [out'sīd'] n esterno, esteriore m ♦ a esterno(a), esteriore; (*remote, unlikely*): **an ~ chance** una vaga possibilità ♦ ad fuori, all'esterno ♦ prep fuori di, all'esterno di; **at the ~** (*fig*) al massimo; **~ left/right** n (*SOCCER*) ala sinistra/destra.

outside broadcast n (*RADIO, TV*) trasmissione f in esterno.

outside line n (*TEL*) linea esterna.

outsider [outsī'dûr] n (*in race etc*) outsider m inv; (*stranger*) straniero/a.

outsize [out'sīz] a (*Brit*) = **oversize**.

outskirts [out'skûrts] npl sobborghi mpl.

outsmart [outsmärt'] vt superare in astuzia.

outspoken [out'spō'kən] a molto franco(a).

outspread [out'spred] a (*wings*) aperto(a), spiegato(a).

outstanding [outstan'ding] a eccezionale, di rilievo; (*unfinished*) non completo(a); non evaso(a); non regolato(a); **your account is still ~** deve ancora saldare il conto.

outstretched [outstrecht'] a (*hand*) teso(a); (*body*) disteso(a).

outstrip [outstrip'] vt (*also fig*) superare.

out-tray [out'trā] n raccoglitore m per le carte da spedire.

outvote [outvōt'] vt: **to ~ sb (by)** avere la maggioranza rispetto a qn (per); **to ~ sth (by)** respingere qc (per).

outward [out'wûrd] a (*sign, appearances*) esteriore; (*journey*) d'andata.

outwardly [out'wûrdlē] ad esteriormente; in apparenza.

outweigh [outwā'] vt avere maggior peso di.

outwit [outwit'] vt superare in astuzia.

oval [ō'vəl] a, n ovale (m).

ovary [ō'vûrē] n ovaia.

ovation [ōvā'shən] n ovazione f.

oven [uv'ən] n forno.

ovenproof [uv'ənprōof] a da forno.

oven-ready [uv'ənred'ē] a pronto(a) da infornare.

ovenware [uv'ənwär] n vasellame m da mettere in forno.

over [ō'vûr] ad al di sopra; (*excessively*) molto, troppo ♦ a (*or ad*) (*finished*) finito(a), terminato(a); (*too much*) troppo; (*remaining*) che avanza ♦ prep su; sopra; (*above*) al di sopra di; (*on the other side of*) di là di; (*more than*) più di; (*during*) durante; **~ here** qui; **~ there** là; **all ~** (*everywhere*) dappertutto; (*finished*) tutto(a) finito(a); **~ and ~ (again)** più e più volte; **~ and above** oltre (a); **to ask sb ~** invitare qn (a passare); **the world ~** in tutto il mondo.

over... prefix: **~abundant** sovrabbondante.

overact [ōvûrakt'] vi (*THEATER*) esagerare or strafare la propria parte.

overall a, n [ō'vûrôl] a totale ♦ n (*Brit*) grembiule m ♦ ad [ōvûrôl'] nell'insieme, complessivamente; **~s** npl (*Brit*) tuta (da lavoro).

overanxious [ōvûrangk'shəs] a troppo ansioso(a).

overawe [ōvûrô'] vt intimidire.

overbalance [ōvûrbal'əns] vi perdere l'equilibrio.

overbearing [ōvûrbär'ing] a imperioso(a), prepotente.

overboard [ō'vûrbôrd] ad (NAUT) fuori bordo, in mare; **to go ~ for sth** (fig) impazzire per qc.

overbook [ō'vûrbŏŏk'] vt sovrapprenotare.

overcapitalize [ōvûrkap'itəlīz] vt sovraccapitalizzare.

overcast [ō'vûrkast] a coperto(a).

overcharge [ōvûrchârj'] vt: **to ~ sb for sth** far pagare troppo caro a qn per qc.

overcoat [ō'vûrkōt] n soprabito, cappotto.

overcome [ōvûrkum'] vt irg superare; sopraffare; **~ with grief** sopraffatto(a) dal dolore.

overconfident [ōvûrkân'fidənt] a troppo sicuro(a) (di sé), presuntuoso(a).

overcrowded [ōvûrkrou'did] a sovraffollato(a).

overcrowding [ōvûrkrou'ding] n sovraffollamento; (in bus) calca.

overdo [ōvûrdōō'] vt irg esagerare; (overcook) cuocere troppo; **to ~ it, to ~ things** (work too hard) lavorare troppo.

overdose [ō'vûrdōs] n dose f eccessiva.

overdraft [ō'vûrdraft] n scoperto (di conto).

overdrawn [ōvûrdrôn'] a (account) scoperto(a).

overdrive [ō'vûrdrīv] n (AUT) overdrive m inv.

overdue [ōvûrdōō'] a in ritardo; (recognition) tardivo(a); (bill) insoluto(a); **that change was long ~** quel cambiamento ci voleva da tempo.

overestimate [ōvûrɛs'təmāt] vt sopravvalutare.

overexcited [ōvûriksī'tid] a sovraeccitato(a).

overexertion [ōvûrigzûr'shən] n logorio (fisico).

overexpose [ōvûrikspōz'] vt (PHOT) sovraesporre.

overflow vi [ōvûrflō'] traboccare ♦ n [ō'vûrflō] eccesso; (also: **~ pipe**) troppopieno.

overfly [ōvûrflī'] vt irg sorvolare.

overgenerous [ōvûrjɛn'ûrəs] a troppo generoso(a).

overgrown [ōvûrgrōn'] a (garden) ricoperto(a) di vegetazione; **he's just an ~ schoolboy** è proprio un bambinone.

overhang [ōvûrhang'] vt irg sporgere da ♦ vi sporgere.

overhaul vt [ōvûrhôl'] revisionare ♦ n [ō'vûrhôl] revisione f.

overhead [ō'vûrhed] ad di sopra ♦ a aereo(a); (lighting) verticale ♦ n [ō'vûrhed] (US) spese fpl generali.

overheads [ō'vûrhedz] npl (Brit) spese fpl generali.

overhear [ōvûrhiûr'] vt irg sentire (per caso).

overheat [ōvûrhēt'] vi surriscaldarsi.

overjoyed [ōvûrjoid'] a pazzo(a) di gioia.

overkill [ō'vûrkil] n (fig) strafare m.

overland [ō'vûrland] a, ad per via di terra.

overlap vi [ōvûrlap'] sovrapporsi ♦ n [ō'vûrlap] sovrapposizione f.

overleaf [ō'vûrlēf] ad a tergo.

overload [ōvûrlōd'] vt sovraccaricare.

overlook [ōvûrlŏŏk'] vt (have view of) dare su; (miss) trascurare; (forgive) passare sopra a.

overlord [ō'vûrlôrd] n capo supremo.

overmanning [ōvûrman'ing] n eccedenza di manodopera.

overnight ad [ōvûrnīt'] (happen) durante la notte; (fig) tutto ad un tratto ♦ a [ō'vûrnīt] di notte; fulmineo(a); **he stayed there ~** ci ha passato la notte; **if you travel ~ ...** se viaggia di notte ...; **he'll be away ~** passerà la notte fuori.

overnight bag n ventiquattr'ore f inv.

overpass [ō'vûrpas] n cavalcavia m inv.

overpay [ōvûrpā'] vt: **to ~ sb by $50** pagare 50 dollari in più a qn.

overpower [ōvûrpou'ûr] vt sopraffare.

overpowering [ōvûrpou'ûring] a irresistibile; (heat, stench) soffocante.

overproduction [ōvûrprəduk'shən] n sovrapproduzione f.

overrate [ōvərrāt'] vt sopravvalutare.

overreach [ōvərēch'] vt: **to ~ o.s.** volere strafare.

overreact [ōvərēakt'] vi reagire in modo esagerato.

override [ōvərīd'] vt (irg: like **ride**) (order, objection) passar sopra a; (decision) annullare.

overriding [ōvərīd'ing] a preponderante.

overrule [ōvərōōl'] vt (decision) annullare; (claim) respingere.

overrun [ō'vərun] vt irg (MIL: country etc) invadere; (time limit etc) superare, andare al di là di ♦ vi protrarsi; **the town is ~ with tourists** la città è invasa dai turisti.

overseas ad [ō'vûrsēz'] oltremare; (abroad) all'estero ♦ a [ō'vûrsēz] (trade) estero(a); (visitor) straniero(a).

overseer [ō'vûrsēûr] n (in factory) caposquadra m.

overshadow [ōvûrshad'ō] vt (fig) eclissare.

overshoot [ōvûrshōōt'] vt irg superare.

oversight [ō'vûrsīt] n omissione f, svista; **due to an ~** per una svista.

oversimplify [ōvûrsim'pləfī] vt rendere troppo semplice.

oversize [ō'vûrsīz] a (US) enorme; (clothes) per taglie forti.

oversleep [ōvûrslēp'] vi irg dormire troppo a lungo.

overspend [ōvûrspend'] *vi irg* spendere troppo; **we have overspent by 5000 dollars** abbiamo speso 5000 dollari di troppo.

overspill [ō'vûrspil] *n* eccedenza di popolazione.

overstaffed [ō'vûrstaft] *a*: **to be** ~ avere troppo personale.

overstate [ōvûrstāt'] *vt* esagerare.

overstatement [ōvûrstāt'mənt] *n* esagerazione *f*.

overstay [ōvûrstā'] *vt*: **to** ~ **one's welcome** diventare un ospite sgradito.

overstep [ōvûrstep'] *vt*: **to** ~ **the mark** superare ogni limite.

overstock [ōvûrstâk'] *vt* sovrapprovvigionare, sovraimmagazzinare.

overstrike *n* [ō'vûrstrīk] (*on printer*) sovrapposizione *f* (di caratteri) ♦ *vt irg* [ōvûrstrīk'] sovrapporre.

overt [ōvûrt'] *a* palese.

overtake [ōvûrtāk'] *vt irg* (*Brit*) sorpassare.

overtaking [ōvûrtā'king] *n* (*Brit AUT*) sorpasso.

overtax [ōvûrtaks'] *vt* (*ECON*) imporre tasse eccessive a, tassare eccessivamente; (*fig*: *strength, patience*) mettere alla prova, abusare di; **to** ~ **o.s.** chiedere troppo alle proprie forze.

overthrow [ōvûrthrō'] *vt irg* (*government*) rovesciare.

overtime [ō'vûrtīm] *n* (lavoro) straordinario; (*US SPORT*) tempo supplementare; **to do** *or* **work** ~ fare lo straordinario.

overtime ban *n* rifiuto sindacale a fare gli straordinari.

overtone [ō'vûrtōn] *n* (*also*: ~**s**) sfumatura.

overture [ō'vûrchûr] *n* (*MUS*) ouverture *f inv*; (*fig*) approccio.

overturn [ōvûrtûrn'] *vt* rovesciare ♦ *vi* rovesciarsi.

overweight [ōvûrwāt'] *a* (*person*) troppo grasso(a); (*luggage*) troppo pesante.

overwhelm [ōvûrwelm'] *vt* sopraffare; sommergere; schiacciare.

overwhelming [ōvûrwel'ming] *a* (*victory, defeat*) schiacciante; (*desire*) irresistibile; **one's** ~ **impression is of heat** l'impressione dominante è quella di caldo.

overwhelmingly [ōvûrwel'minglē] *ad* in massa.

overwork [ōvûrwûrk'] *vt* far lavorare troppo ♦ *vi* lavorare troppo, strapazzarsi.

overwrite [ōvərit'] *vt* (*COMPUT*) ricoprire.

overwrought [ō'vərôt'] *a* molto agitato(a).

ovulation [âvyəlā'shən] *n* ovulazione *f*.

owe [ō] *vt* dovere; **to** ~ **sb sth, to** ~ **sth to sb** dovere qc a qn.

owing to [ō'ing tōō] *prep* a causa di.

owl [oul] *n* gufo.

own [ōn] *a* proprio(a) ♦ *vt* possedere ♦ *vi* (*Brit*): **to** ~ **to sth** ammettere qc; **to** ~ **to**
having done sth ammettere di aver fatto qc; **a room of my** ~ la mia propria camera; **on one's** ~ tutto(a) solo(a); **can I have it for my (very)** ~? posso averlo tutto per me?; **to come into one's** ~ mostrare le proprie qualità.

own up *vi* confessare.

own brand *n* (*COMM*) etichetta propria.

owner [ō'nûr] *n* proprietario/a.

owner-occupier [ō'nûrâk'yəpīûr] *n* (*Brit*) *proprietario/a della casa in cui abita.*

ownership [ō'nûrship] *n* possesso; **it's under new** ~ ha un nuovo proprietario.

ox, *pl* **oxen** [âks, âk'sən] *n* bue *m*.

Oxfam [âks'fam] *n abbr* (*Brit*: = *Oxford Committee for Famine Relief*) *organizzazione per aiuti al terzo mondo.*

oxide [âk'sīd] *n* ossido.

oxtail [âks'tāl] *n*: ~ **soup** minestra di coda di bue.

oxyacetylene [âksēəset'əlin] *a* (*Brit*) ossiacetilenico(a); ~ **burner**, ~ **lamp** cannello ossiacetilenico.

oxygen [âk'sijən] *n* ossigeno.

oxygen mask *n* maschera ad ossigeno.

oxygen tent *n* tenda ad ossigeno.

oyster [ois'tûr] *n* ostrica.

oz. *abbr* = **ounce**.

ozone [ō'zōn] *n* ozono.

ozone-friendly [ō'zōnfrend'lē] *a* che non danneggia l'ozono.

ozone layer *n* strato di ozono.

P

P, p [pē] *n* (*letter*) P, p *f or m inv*; **P for Peter** ≈ P come Padova.

P *abbr* = **president; prince.**

p *abbr* (= *page*) p; (*Brit*) = **penny, pence.**

PA *n abbr* (*US MAIL*) = *Pennsylvania* ♦ *abbr see* **personal assistant; public address system.**

pa [pâ] *n* (*col*) papà *m inv*, babbo.

p.a. *abbr* = **per annum.**

PAC *n abbr* (*US*) = *political action committee.*

pace [pās] *n* passo; (*speed*) passo; velocità ♦ *vi*: **to** ~ **up and down** camminare su e giù; **to keep** ~ **with** camminare di pari passo a; (*events*) tenersi al corrente di; **to put sb through his** ~**s** (*fig*) mettere qn alla prova; **to set the** ~ (*running*) fare l'andatura; (*fig*) dare il la *or* il tono.

pacemaker [pās'mākûr] *n* (*MED*) pacemaker *m inv*, stimolatore *m* cardiaco; (*SPORT*) chi fa l'andatura.

pacific [pəsif'ik] *a* pacifico(a) ♦ *n*: **the P~ (Ocean)** il Pacifico, l'Oceano Pacifico.

pacification [pasəfəkā'shən] *n* pacificazione *f*.

pacifier [pas'əfīûr] *n* (*US*) succhiotto, ciuccio (*col*).

pacifist [pas'əfist] *n* pacifista *m/f*.

pacify [pas'əfī] *vt* pacificare; (*soothe*) calmare.

pack [pak] *n* (*packet*) pacco; (*COMM*) confezione *f*; (*of cigarettes*) pacchetto; (*of goods*) balla; (*of hounds*) muta; (*of wolves*) branco; (*of thieves etc*) banda; (*of cards*) mazzo ♦ *vt* (*goods*) impaccare, imballare; (*in suitcase etc*) mettere; (*box*) riempire; (*cram*) stipare, pigiare; (*press down*) tamponare; turare; (*COMPUT*) comprimere, impaccare ♦ *vi*: **to ~ (one's bags)** fare la valigia; **to send sb ~ing** (*col*) spedire via qn.

pack in (*Brit col*) *vi* (*watch, car*) guastarsi ♦ *vt* mollare, piantare.

pack off *vt* (*person*) spedire.

pack up *vt* (*belongings, clothes*) mettere in una valigia; (*goods, presents*) imballare ♦ *vi* (*Brit col: machine*) guastarsi; (: *person*) far fagotto.

package [pak'ij] *n* pacco; balla; (*also*: ~ **deal**) pacchetto; forfait *m inv* ♦ *vt* impaccare; (*COMM: goods*) confezionare.

package bomb *n* (*US*) pacchetto esplosivo.

package holiday *n* (*Brit*) vacanza organizzata.

package tour *n* viaggio organizzato.

packaging [pak'ijing] *n* confezione *f*, imballo.

packed [pakt] *a* (*crowded*) affollato(a); ~ **lunch** (*Brit*) pranzo al sacco.

packer [pak'ûr] *n* (*person*) imballatore/trice.

packet [pak'it] *n* pacchetto.

packet switching [pak'it swich'ing] *n* (*COMPUT*) commutazione *f* di pacchetto.

pack ice [pak īs] *n* banchisa.

packing [pak'ing] *n* imballaggio.

packing case *n* cassa da imballaggio.

pact [pakt] *n* patto, accordo; trattato.

pad [pad] *n* blocco; (*for inking*) tampone *m*; (*col: apartment*) appartamento ♦ *vt* imbottire ♦ *vi*: **to ~ about/in** *etc* camminare/entrare *etc* a passi felpati.

padding [pad'ing] *n* imbottitura; (*fig*) riempitivo.

paddle [pad'əl] *n* (*oar*) pagaia; (*US: for table tennis*) racchetta ♦ *vi* sguazzare ♦ *vt* (*boat*) fare andare a colpi di pagaia.

paddle steamer *n* battello a ruote.

paddling pool [pad'ling pōōl] *n* (*Brit*) piscina per bambini.

paddock [pad'ək] *n* recinto; paddock *m inv*.

paddy [pad'ē] *n* (*US: also*: **rice ~**) risaia.

padlock [pad'lâk] *n* lucchetto ♦ *vt* chiudere con il lucchetto.

Padua [paj'ōōə] *n* Padova.

paediatrics [pēdēat'riks] *etc* (*Brit*) = **pediat-**

---

rics *etc*.

pagan [pā'gən] *a, n* pagano(a).

page [pāj] *n* pagina; (*also*: *Brit*: ~ **boy**) fattorino; (: *at wedding*) paggio ♦ *vt* (*in hotel etc*) (*far*) chiamare.

pageant [paj'ənt] *n* spettacolo storico; grande cerimonia.

pageantry [paj'əntrē] *n* pompa.

page break *n* interruzione *f* di pagina.

pager [pā'jûr] *n* cicalino.

paginate [paj'ənāt] *vt* impaginare.

pagination [pajənā'shən] *n* impaginazione *f*.

pagoda [pəgō'də] *n* pagoda.

paid [pād] *pt, pp* of **pay** ♦ *a* (*work, official*) rimunerato(a).

paid-up [pād'up] *a* (*member*) che ha pagato la sua quota; (*share*) interamente pagato(a); ~ **capital** capitale *m* interamente versato.

pail [pāl] *n* secchio.

pain [pān] *n* dolore *m*; **to be in ~** soffrire, aver male; **to have a ~ in** aver male *or* un dolore a; **to take ~s to do** mettercela tutta per fare; **on ~ of death** sotto pena di morte.

pained [pānd] *a* addolorato(a), afflitto(a).

painful [pān'fəl] *a* doloroso(a), che fa male; (*difficult*) difficile, penoso(a).

painfully [pān'fəlē] *ad* (*fig: very*) fin troppo.

painkiller [pān'kilûr] *n* antalgico, antidolorifico.

painless [pān'lis] *a* indolore.

painstaking [pānz'tāking] *a* sollecito(a).

paint [pānt] *n* (*for house etc*) tinta, vernice *f*; (*ART*) colore *m* ♦ *vt* (*ART, walls*) dipingere; (*door etc*) verniciare; **a can of ~** un barattolo di tinta *or* vernice; **to ~ the door blue** verniciare la porta di azzurro; **to ~ in oils** dipingere a olio.

paintbox [pānt'bâks] *n* scatola di colori.

paintbrush [pānt'brush] *n* pennello.

painter [pānt'ûr] *n* (*artist*) pittore *m*; (*decorator*) imbianchino.

painting [pān'ting] *n* (*activity: of artist*) pittura; (: *of decorator*) imbiancatura; verniciatura; (*picture*) dipinto, quadro.

paint stripper *n* prodotto sverniciante.

paintwork [pānt'wûrk] *n* (*Brit*) tinta; (: *of car*) vernice *f*.

pair [pär] *n* (*of shoes, gloves etc*) paio; (*of people*) coppia; duo *m inv*; **a ~ of scissors/ pants** un paio di forbici/pantaloni.

pair off *vi*: **to ~ off (with sb)** fare coppia (con qn).

pajamas [pəjâm'əz] *npl* (*US*) pigiama *m*; **a pair of ~** un pigiama.

Pakistan [pak'istan] *n* Pakistan *m*.

Pakistani [pak'əstan'ē] *a, n* pakistano(a).

PAL [pal] *n abbr* (*TV*: = *phase alternation line*) PAL *m*.

pal [pal] *n* (*col*) amico/a, compagno/a.

palace [pal'is] *n* palazzo.

palatable [pal'ətəbəl] *a* gustoso(a).

palate [pal'it] *n* palato.

palatial [pəlā'shəl] *a* sontuoso(a), sfarzoso(a).
palaver [pəlav'ûr] *n* chiacchiere *fpl*; storie *fpl*.
pale [pāl] *a* pallido(a) ♦ *vi* impallidire ♦ *n*: **to be beyond the** ~ aver oltrepassato ogni limite; **to grow** *or* **turn** ~ (*person*) diventare pallido(a), impallidire; **to** ~ **into insignificance (beside)** perdere d'importanza (nei confronti di); ~ **blue** azzurro *or* blu pallido *inv.*
paleness [pāl'nis] *n* pallore *m*.
Palestine [pal'istīn] *n* Palestina.
Palestinian [palistin'ēən] *a*, *n* palestinese (*m/f*).
palette [pal'it] *n* tavolozza.
paling [pā'ling] *n* (*stake*) palo; (*fence*) palizzata.
palisade [palisād'] *n* palizzata.
pall [pôl] *n* (*of smoke*) cappa ♦ *vi*: **to** ~ (**on**) diventare noioso(a) (a).
pallet [pal'it] *n* (*for goods*) paletta.
pallid [pal'id] *a* pallido(a), smorto(a).
pallor [pal'ûr] *n* pallore *m*.
pally [pal'ē] *a* (*col*) amichevole.
palm [pâm] *n* (*ANAT*) palma, palmo; (*also*: ~ **tree**) palma ♦ *vt*: **to** ~ **sth off on sb** (*col*) rifilare qc a qn.
palmist [pâm'ist] *n* chiromante *m/f*.
Palm Sunday *n* Domenica delle Palme.
palpable [pal'pəbəl] *a* palpabile.
palpitation [palpitā'shən] *n* palpitazione *f*; **to have** ~**s** avere le palpitazioni.
paltry [pôl'trē] *a* derisorio(a); insignificante.
pamper [pam'pûr] *vt* viziare, accarezzare.
pamphlet [pam'flit] *n* dépliant *m inv*; (*political etc*) volantino, manifestino.
pan [pan] *n* (*also*: **sauce**~) casseruola; (*also*: **frying** ~) padella ♦ *vi* (*CINEMA*) fare una panoramica ♦ *vt* (*col*: *criticize*) stroncare, distruggere; **to** ~ **for gold** (lavare le sabbie aurifere per) cercare l'oro.
panacea [panəsē'ə] *n* panacea.
panache [pənash'] *n* stile *m*.
Panama [pan'əmâ] *n* Panama *m*.
Panama Canal *n* canale *m* di Panama.
Panamanian [panəmā'nēən] *a*, *n* panamense (*m/f*).
pancake [pan'kāk] *n* frittella.
Pancake Day *n* (*Brit*) martedì *m* grasso.
pancreas [pan'krēəs] *n* pancreas *m inv.*
panda [pan'də] *n* panda *m inv.*
pandemonium [pandəmō'nēəm] *n* pandemonio.
pander [pan'dûr] *vi*: **to** ~ **to** lusingare; concedere tutto a.
pane [pān] *n* vetro.
panel [pan'əl] *n* (*of wood, cloth etc*) pannello; (*RADIO, TV*) giuria.
panel game *n* quiz *m inv* a squadre.
paneling, (*Brit*) **panelling** [pan'əling] *n* rivestimento a pannelli.
panelist, (*Brit*) **panellist** [pan'əlist] *n* parteci-

pante *m/f* (al quiz, alla tavola rotonda *etc*).
pang [pang] *n*: **to feel** ~**s of remorse** essere torturato(a) dal rimorso; ~**s of hunger** spasimi *mpl* della fame; ~**s of conscience** morsi *mpl* di coscienza.
panic [pan'ik] *n* panico ♦ *vi* perdere il sangue freddo.
panicky [pan'ikē] *a* (*person*) pauroso(a).
panic-stricken [pan'ikstrikən] *a* (*person*) preso(a) dal panico, in preda al panico; (*look*) terrorizzato(a).
pannier [pan'yûr] *n* (*on animal*) bisaccia; (*on bicycle*) borsa.
panorama [panəram'ə] *n* panorama *m*.
panoramic [panəram'ik] *a* panoramico(a).
pansy [pan'zē] *n* (*BOT*) viola del pensiero, pensée *f inv*; (*col*) femminuccia.
pant [pant] *vi* ansare.
panther [pan'thûr] *n* pantera.
panties [pan'tēz] *npl* slip *m*, mutandine *fpl*.
pantomime [pan'təmīm] *n* pantomima; (*Brit*: *at Christmas*) spettacolo natalizio (*sulla falsariga delle favole per bambini*).
pantry [pan'trē] *n* dispensa.
pants [pants] *npl* (*trousers*) pantaloni *mpl*; (*Brit*) mutande *fpl*, slip *m*.
pants press *n* (*US*) stirapantaloni *m inv.*
pantsuit [pant'sōōt] *n* completo *m or* tailleur *m inv* pantalone *m*.
pantyhose [pan'tēhōz] *n* (*US*) collant *m inv.*
papacy [pā'pəsē] *n* papato.
papal [pā'pəl] *a* papale, pontificio(a).
paper [pā'pûr] *n* carta; (*also*: **wall**~) carta da parati, tappezzeria; (*also*: **news**~) giornale *m*; (*study, article*) saggio; (*exam*) prova scritta ♦ *a* di carta ♦ *vt* tappezzare; **a piece of** ~ (*odd bit*) un pezzo di carta; (*sheet*) un foglio (di carta); **to put sth down on** ~ mettere qc per iscritto; *see also* **papers**.
paper advance *n* (*on printer*) avanzamento della carta.
paperback [pā'pûrbak] *n* tascabile *m*; edizione *f* economica ♦ *a*: ~ **edition** edizione *f* tascabile.
paper bag *n* sacchetto di carta.
paperboy [pā'pûrboi] *n* (*selling*) strillone *m*; (*delivering*) ragazzo che recapita i giornali.
paper clip *n* graffetta, clip *f inv.*
paper handkerchief *n* (*Brit*) fazzolettino di carta.
paper mill *n* cartiera.
paper money *n* cartamoneta, moneta cartacea.
paper profit *n* utile *m* teorico.
papers [pā'pûrz] *npl* (*also*: **identity** ~) carte *fpl*, documenti *mpl.*
paperweight [pā'pûrwāt] *n* fermacarte *m inv.*
paperwork [pā'pûrwûrk] *n* lavoro amministrativo.
papier-mâché [pā'pûrməshā] *n* cartapesta.
paprika [paprē'kə] *n* paprica.

par |pâr| *n* parità, pari *f*; (*GOLF*) norma; **on a ~ with** alla pari con; **at/above/below ~** (*COMM*) alla/sopra la/sotto la pari; **above/below ~** (*gen*, *GOLF*) al di sopra/al di sotto della norma; **to feel below** *or* **under** *or* **not up to ~** non sentirsi in forma.

parable |par'əbəl| *n* parabola (*REL*).

parabola |pərab'ələ| *n* parabola (*MATH*).

parachute |par'əshōōt| *n* paracadute *m inv* ♦ *vi* scendere col paracadute.

parachute jump *n* lancio col paracadute.

parachutist |par'əshōōtist| *n* paracadutista *m/ f.*

parade |pərād'| *n* parata; (*inspection*) rivista, rassegna ♦ *vt* (*fig*) fare sfoggio di ♦ *vi* sfilare in parata.

parade ground *n* piazza d'armi.

paradise |par'ədīs| *n* paradiso.

paradox |par'ədāks| *n* paradosso.

paradoxical |parədâk'sikəl| *a* paradossale.

paradoxically |parədâk'siklē| *ad* paradossalmente.

paraffin |par'əfin| *n* (*Brit*): **~ (oil)** paraffina; **liquid ~** olio di paraffina.

paragon |par'əgân| *n* modello di perfezione *or* di virtù.

paragraph |par'əgraf| *n* paragrafo; **to begin a new ~** andare a capo.

Paraguay |par'əgwā| *n* Paraguay *m*.

Paraguayan |parəgwā'ən| *a*, *n* paraguaiano(a).

parakeet |par'əkēt| *n* (*US*) pappagallino.

parallel |par'əlel| *a* (*also COMPUT*) parallelo(a); (*fig*) analogo(a) ♦ *n* (*line*) parallela; (*fig*, *GEO*) parallelo; **~ (with** *or* **to)** parallelo(a) (a).

paralysis, *pl* **paralyses** |pəral'isis, -sēz| *n* paralisi *f inv*.

paralytic |parəlit'ik| *a* paralitico(a).

paralyze |par'əlīz| *vt* paralizzare.

paramedic |parəmed'ik| *n* (*US*) paramedico(a).

parameter |pəram'itûr| *n* parametro.

paramilitary |parəmil'itärē| *a* paramilitare.

paramount |par'əmount| *a*: **of ~ importance** di capitale importanza.

paranoia |parənoi'ə| *n* paranoia.

paranoid |par'ənoid| *a* paranoico(a).

paranormal |parənôr'məl| *a* paranormale.

paraphernalia |parəfûrnāl'yə| *n* attrezzi *mpl*, roba.

paraphrase |par'əfrāz| *vt* parafrasare.

paraplegic |parəplē'jik| *n* paraplegico(a).

parapsychology |parəsīkâl'əjē| *n* parapsicologia.

parasite |par'əsīt| *n* parassita *m*.

parasol |par'əsôl| *n* parasole *m inv*.

paratrooper |par'ətrōōpûr| *n* paracadutista *m* (*soldato*).

parcel |pâr'səl| *n* pacco, pacchetto ♦ *vt* impaccare.

parcel out *vt* spartire.

parcel bomb *n* (*Brit*) pacchetto esplosivo.

parcel post *n* servizio pacchi.

parch |pârch| *vt* riardere.

parched |pârcht| *a* (*person*) assetato(a).

parchment |pârch'mənt| *n* pergamena.

pardon |pâr'dən| *n* perdono; grazia ♦ *vt* perdonare; (*LAW*) graziare; **~! scusi!**; **~ me!** mi scusi!; **I beg your ~!** scusi!; **~ me?**, (*Brit*) **(I beg your) ~?** prego?

pare |pār| *vt* (*Brit*: *nails*) tagliarsi; (: *fruit etc*) sbucciare, pelare.

parent |pār'ənt| *n* padre *m* (*or* madre *f*); **~s** *npl* genitori *mpl*.

parentage |pār'əntij| *n* natali *mpl*; **of unknown ~** di genitori sconosciuti.

parental |pɔren'təl| *a* dei genitori.

parent company *n* società madre *f inv*.

parenthesis, *pl* **parentheses** |pɔren'thəsis, -sēz| *n* parentesi *f inv*; **in parentheses** fra parentesi.

parenthood |pār'ənt-hōōd| *n* paternità *or* maternità.

parenting |pār'ənting| *n* mestiere *m* di genitore.

Paris |par'is| *n* Parigi *f*.

parish |par'ish| *n* parrocchia; (*civil*) ≈ municipio ♦ *a* parrocchiale.

parish council *n* (*Brit*) ≈ consiglio comunale.

parishioner |pərish'ənûr| *n* parrocchiano/a.

Parisian |pərizh'ən| *a*, *n* parigino(a).

parity |par'itē| *n* parità.

park |pârk| *n* parco; (*public*) giardino pubblico ♦ *vt*, *vi* parcheggiare.

parka |pâr'ka| *n* eskimo.

parking |pâr'king| *n* parcheggio; **"no ~"** "sosta vietata".

parking lights *npl* luci *fpl* di posizione.

parking lot *n* (*US*) posteggio, parcheggio.

parking meter *n* parchimetro.

parking offence *n* (*Brit*) = **parking violation.**

parking place *n* posto di parcheggio.

parking ticket *n* multa per sosta vietata.

parking violation *n* (*US*) infrazione *f* al divieto di sosta.

parkway |pârk'wā| *n* (*US*) viale *m*.

parlance |pâr'ləns| *n*: **in common/modern ~** nel gergo *or* linguaggio comune/moderno.

parliament |pâr'ləmənt| *n* parlamento.

parliamentary |pârləmen'tûrē| *a* parlamentare.

parlor, (*Brit*) **parlour** |pâr'lûr| *n* salotto.

parlous |pâr'ləs| *a* periglioso(a).

Parmesan |pâr'məzan| *n* (*also*: **~ cheese**) parmigiano.

parochial |pərō'kēəl| *a* parrocchiale; (*pej*) provinciale.

parody |par'ədē| *n* parodia.

parole |pərōl'| *n*: **on ~** in libertà per buona condotta.

paroxysm |par'ɔksizəm| n (*MED*) parossismo; (*of anger, laughter, coughing*) convulso; (*of grief*) attacco.

parquet |pârkā'| n: ~ **floor(ing)** parquet m.

parrot |par'ət| n pappagallo.

parrot fashion ad (*Brit*) in modo pappagallesco.

parry |par'ē| vt parare.

parsimonious |pârsəmō'nēəs| a parsimonioso(a).

parsley |pârz'lē| n prezzemolo.

parsnip |pârs'nip| n pastinaca.

parson |pâr'sən| n prete m; (*Church of England*) parroco.

part |pârt| n parte f; (*of machine*) pezzo; (*THEATER etc*) parte, ruolo; (*US: in hair*) scriminatura; (*MUS*) voce f; parte ♦ a in parte ♦ ad = **partly** ♦ vt separare ♦ vi (*people*) separarsi; (*roads*) dividersi; **to take ~ in** prendere parte a; **to take sb's ~** parteggiare per qn, prendere le parti di qn; **on his ~** da parte sua; **for my ~** per parte mia; **for the most ~** in generale; nella maggior parte dei casi; **for the better ~ of the day** per la maggior parte della giornata; **to be ~ and parcel of** essere parte integrante di; **~ of speech** (*LING*) parte del discorso.

part with vt fus separarsi da; rinunciare a.

partake |pârtāk'| vi irg (*formal*): **to ~ of sth** consumare qc, prendere qc.

part exchange n (*Brit*): **in ~** in pagamento parziale.

partial |pâr'shəl| a parziale; **to be ~ to** avere un debole per.

partially |pâr'shəlē| ad in parte, parzialmente.

participant |pârtis'əpənt| n: ~ **(in)** partecipante m/f (a).

participate |pârtis'əpāt| vi: **to ~ (in)** prendere parte (a), partecipare (a).

participation |pârtisəpā'shən| n partecipazione f.

participle |pâr'tisipəl| n participio.

particle |pâr'tikəl| n particella.

particleboard |pâr'tikəlbôrd| n (*US*) agglomerato.

particular |pûrtik'yəlûr| a particolare; speciale; (*fussy*) difficile; meticoloso(a); **~s** npl particolari mpl, dettagli mpl; (*information*) informazioni fpl; **in ~** in particolare, particolarmente; **to be very ~ about** essere molto pignolo(a) su; **I'm not ~** per me va bene tutto.

particularly |pûrtik'yəlûrlē| ad particolarmente; in particolare.

parting |pâr'ting| n separazione f; (*Brit: in hair*) scriminatura ♦ a d'addio; ~ **shot** (*fig*) battuta finale.

partisan |pâr'tizən| n partigiano/a ♦ a partigiano(a); di parte.

partition |pârtish'ən| n (*POL*) partizione f;

(*wall*) tramezzo.

partly |pârt'lē| ad parzialmente; in parte.

partner |pârt'nûr| n (*COMM*) socio/a; (*SPORT*) compagno/a; (*at dance*) cavaliere/dama.

partnership |pârt'nûrship| n associazione f; (*COMM*) società f inv; **to go into ~ (with)**, **form a ~ (with)** mettersi in società (con), associarsi (a).

part payment n acconto.

partridge |pâr'trij| n pernice f.

part-time |pârt'tīm| a, ad a orario ridotto, part-time (*inv*).

part-timer |pârttī'mûr| n (*also:* **part-time worker**) lavoratore/trice part-time.

party |pâr'tē| n (*POL*) partito; (*team*) squadra; gruppo; (*LAW*) parte f; (*celebration*) ricevimento; serata; festa; **dinner ~** cena; **to give** or **throw a ~** dare una festa or un party; **to be a ~ to a crime** essere coinvolto in un reato.

party line n (*POL*) linea del partito; (*TEL*) duplex m inv.

par value n (*of share, bond*) valore m nominale.

pass |pas| vt (*gen*) passare; (*place*) passare davanti a; (*exam*) passare, superare; (*candidate*) promuovere; (*overtake, surpass*) sorpassare, superare; (*approve*) approvare ♦ vi passare; (*SCOL*) essere promosso/a ♦ n (*permit*) lasciapassare m inv; permesso; (*in mountains*) passo, gola; (*SPORT*) passaggio; (*SCOL*): **to get a ~** prendere la sufficienza; **to ~ for** passare per; **could you ~ the vegetables around?** potrebbe far passare i contorni?; **to make a ~ at sb** (*col*) fare delle proposte or delle avances a qn.

pass away vi morire.

pass by vi passare ♦ vt trascurare.

pass down vt (*customs, inheritance*) tramandare, trasmettere.

pass on vi (*die*) spegnersi, mancare ♦ vt (*hand on*): **to ~ on (to)** (*news, information, object*) passare (a); (*cold, illness*) attaccare (a); (*benefits*) trasmettere (a); (*price rises*) riversare (su).

pass out vi svenire.

pass over vi (*die*) spirare ♦ vt lasciare da parte.

pass up vt (*opportunity*) lasciarsi sfuggire, perdere.

passable |pas'əbəl| a (*road*) praticabile; (*work*) accettabile.

passage |pas'ij| n (*gen*) passaggio; (*also:* **~way**) corridoio; (*in book*) brano, passo; (*by boat*) traversata.

passbook |pas'bo͞ok| n libretto di risparmio.

passenger |pas'injûr| n passeggero/a.

passer-by |pasûrbī'| n passante m/f.

passing |pas'ing| a (*fig*) fuggevole; **to mention sth in ~** accennare a qc di sfuggita.

passing place n (*AUT*) piazzola (di sosta).

passion [pash'ən] n passione f; amore m; **to have a ~ for sth** aver la passione di or per qc.

passionate [pash'ənit] a appassionato(a).

passive [pas'iv] a (also LING) passivo(a).

passkey [pas'kē] n passe-partout m inv.

Passover [pas'ōvûr] n Pasqua ebraica.

passport [pas'pôrt] n passaporto.

passport control n controllo m passaporti inv.

password [pas'wûrd] n parola d'ordine.

past [past] prep (further than) oltre, di là di; dopo; (later than) dopo ♦ ad: **to run ~** passare di corsa; **to walk ~** passare ♦ a passato(a); (president etc) ex inv ♦ n passato; **quarter/half ~ four** le quattro e un quarto/e mezzo; **ten/twenty ~ four** le quattro e dieci/venti; **he's ~ forty** ha più di quarant'anni; **it's ~ midnight** è mezzanotte passata; **for the ~ few days** da qualche giorno; in questi ultimi giorni; **for the ~ 3 days** negli ultimi 3 giorni; **in the ~** in or nel passato; (LING) al passato; **I'm ~ caring** non me ne importa più nulla; **to be ~ one's prime** essere finito(a).

pasta [pás'ta] n pasta.

paste [pāst] n (glue) colla; (CULIN) pâté m inv; pasta ♦ vt collare; **tomato ~** concentrato di pomodoro.

pastel [pastel'] a pastello inv.

pasteurized [pas'chərīzd] a pastorizzato(a).

pastille [pastēl'] n pastiglia.

pastime [pas'tīm] n passatempo.

pastor [pas'tûr] n pastore m.

pastoral [pas'tûrəl] a pastorale.

pastry [pās'trē] n pasta.

pastry shop n (US) pasticceria.

pasture [pas'chûr] n pascolo.

pasty a [pās'tē] pastoso(a); (complexion) pallido(a) ♦ n [pas'tē] pasticcio di carne.

pat [pat] vt accarezzare, dare un colpetto (affettuoso) a ♦ n: **a ~ of butter** un panetto di burro; **to give sb/o.s. a ~ on the back** (fig) congratularsi or compiacersi con qn/se stesso; **he has it down ~** lo conosce or sa a menadito.

patch [pach] n (of material) toppa; (spot) macchia; (of land) pezzo ♦ vt (clothes) rattoppare.

patch up vt rappezzare.

patchwork [pach'wûrk] n patchwork m.

patchy [pach'ē] a irregolare.

pate [pāt] n: **a bald ~** una testa pelata.

pâté [pátā'] n pâté m inv.

patent [pat'ənt] n brevetto ♦ vt brevettare ♦ a patente, manifesto(a).

patent leather n cuoio verniciato.

patently [pat'əntlē] ad palesemente.

patent medicine n specialità f inv medicinale.

patent office n ufficio brevetti.

paternal [pətûr'nəl] a paterno(a).

paternity [pətûr'nitē] n paternità.

paternity suit n (LAW) causa di riconoscimento della paternità.

path [path] n sentiero, viottolo; viale m; (fig) via, strada; (of planet, missile) traiettoria.

pathetic [pəthet'ik] a (pitiful) patetico(a); (very bad) penoso(a).

pathological [pathəlâj'ikəl] a patologico(a).

pathologist [pəthâl'əjist] n patologo/a.

pathology [pəthâl'əjē] n patologia.

pathos [pā'thâs] n pathos m.

pathway [path'wā] n sentiero, viottolo.

patience [pā'shəns] n pazienza; (Brit CARDS) solitario; **to lose one's ~** spazientirsi.

patient [pā'shənt] n paziente m/f; malato/a ♦ a paziente; **to be ~ with sb** essere paziente or aver pazienza con qn.

patiently [pā'shəntlē] ad pazientemente.

patio [pat'ēō] n terrazza.

patriot [pā'trēət] n patriota m/f.

patriotic [pātrēāt'ik] a patriottico(a).

patriotism [pā'trēətizəm] n patriottismo.

patrol [pətrōl'] n pattuglia ♦ vt pattugliare; **to be on ~** fare la ronda; essere in ricognizione; essere in perlustrazione.

patrol boat n guardacoste m inv.

patrol car n autoradio f inv (della polizia).

patrolman [pətrōl'mən] n (US) poliziotto.

patron [pā'trən] n (in store) cliente m/f; (of charity) benefattore/trice; **~ of the arts** mecenate m/f.

patronage [pā'trənij] n patronato.

patronize [pā'trənīz] vt essere cliente abituale di; (fig) trattare con condiscendenza.

patronizing [pā'trənīzing] a condiscendente.

patron saint n patrono.

patter [pat'ûr] n picchiettio; (sales talk) propaganda di vendita ♦ vi picchiettare.

pattern [pat'ûrn] n modello; (SEWING etc) modello (di carta), cartamodello; (design) disegno, motivo; (sample) campione m; **behavior ~s** tipi mpl di comportamento.

patterned [pat'ûrnd] a a disegni, a motivi; (material) fantasia inv.

paucity [pô'sitē] n scarsità.

paunch [pônch] n pancione m.

pauper [pô'pûr] n indigente m/f; **~'s grave** fossa comune.

pause [pôz] n pausa ♦ vi fare una pausa, arrestarsi; **to ~ for breath** fermarsi un attimo per riprender fiato.

pave [pāv] vt pavimentare; **to ~ the way for** aprire la via a.

pavement [pāv'mənt] n (US) pavimentazione f stradale; (Brit) marciapiede m.

pavilion [pəvil'yən] n padiglione m; tendone m; (SPORT) edificio annesso ad un campo sportivo.

paving [pā'ving] n pavimentazione f.

paving stone n lastra di pietra.

paw [pó] *n* zampa ♦ *vt* dare una zampata a; (*subj: person: pej*) palpare.

pawn [pôn] *n* pegno; (*CHESS*) pedone *m*; (*fig*) pedina ♦ *vt* dare in pegno.

pawnbroker [pôn'brōkûr] *n* prestatore *m* su pegno.

pawnshop [pôn'shâp] *n* monte *m* di pietà.

pay [pā] *n* (*gen*) paga ♦ *vb* (*pt, pp* **paid** [pād]) *vt* pagare; (*be profitable to: also fig*) convenire a ♦ *vi* pagare; (*be profitable*) rendere; **to ~ attention (to)** fare attenzione (a); **I paid $5 for that record** quel disco l'ho pagato 5 dollari; **how much did you ~ for it?** quanto l'ha pagato?; **to ~ one's way** pagare la propria parte; (*company*) coprire le spese; **to ~ dividends** (*fig*) dare buoni frutti.

pay back *vt* rimborsare.

pay for *vt fus* pagare.

pay in *vt* versare.

pay off *vt* (*debts*) saldare; (*creditor*) pagare; (*mortgage*) estinguere; (*workers*) licenziare ♦ *vi* (*scheme*) funzionare; (*patience*) dare dei frutti; **to ~ sth off in installments** pagare qc a rate.

pay out *vt* (*money*) sborsare, tirar fuori; (*rope*) far allentare.

pay up *vt* saldare.

payable [pā'əbəl] *a* pagabile; **to make a check ~ to sb** intestare un assegno a (nome di) qn.

pay day *n* giorno di paga.

PAYE *n abbr* (*Brit:* = *pay as you earn*) pagamento di imposte tramite ritenute alla fonte.

payee [pāē'] *n* beneficiario/a.

pay envelope *n* (*US*) busta *f* paga *inv*.

paying [pā'ing] *a:* **~ guest** ospite *m/f* pagante, pensionante *m/f*.

payload [pā'lōd] *n* carico utile.

payment [pā'mənt] *n* pagamento; **advance ~** (*part sum*) anticipo, acconto; (*total sum*) pagamento anticipato; **deferred ~, ~ by installments** pagamento dilazionato *or* a rate; **in ~ for, in ~ of** in pagamento di; **on ~ of $5** dietro pagamento di 5 dollari.

pay packet *n* (*Brit*) busta *f* paga *inv*.

pay phone *n* cabina telefonica.

payroll [pā'rōl] *n* ruolo (organico); **to be on a firm's ~** far parte del personale di una ditta.

pay slip *n* (*Brit*) foglio *m* paga *inv*.

pay station *n* (*US*) cabina telefonica.

PBS *n abbr* (*US:* = *Public Broadcasting Service*) *servizio che collabora alla realizzazione di programmi per la rete televisiva nazionale*.

PBX *n abbr* (*US:* = *private branch* (*telephone*) *exchange*) *centralino telefonico interno*.

PC *n abbr see* **personal computer**; (*Brit*) *see* **police constable**.

pc *abbr* = **percent**; (= *postcard*) C.P.

p/c *abbr* = **petty cash**.

PCB *n abbr see* **printed circuit board**.

pcm *abbr* = *per calendar month*. ·

PD *n abbr* (*US*) = **police department**.

pd *abbr* = **paid**.

PDQ *abbr* (*col*) = *pretty damn quick*.

PDT *abbr* (*US:* = *Pacific Daylight Time*) *ora legale del Pacifico*.

PE *n abbr* (= *physical education*) ed. fisica.

pea [pē] *n* pisello.

peace [pēs] *n* pace *f*; (*calm*) calma, tranquillità; **to be at ~ with sb/sth** essere in pace con qn/qc; **to keep the ~** (*subj: policeman*) mantenere l'ordine pubblico; (*: citizen*) rispettare l'ordine pubblico.

peaceable [pē'səbəl] *a* pacifico(a).

Peace Corps *n* (*US*) *servizio volontario in paesi sottosviluppati*.

peaceful [pēs'fəl] *a* pacifico(a), calmo(a).

peacekeeping [pēs'kēping] *n* mantenimento della pace.

peace offering *n* (*fig*) dono in segno di riconciliazione.

peach [pēch] *n* pesca.

peacock [pē'kâk] *n* pavone *m*.

peak [pēk] *n* (*of mountain*) cima, vetta; (*mountain itself*) picco; (*fig*) massimo; (*: of career*) acme *f*.

peaked [pēk'id] *a* (*US col*) sbattuto(a).

peak-hour [pēk'ouûr] *a* (*traffic etc*) delle ore di punta.

peak hours *npl* ore *fpl* di punta.

peak period *n* periodo di punta.

peaky [pē'kē] *a* (*Brit col*) = **peaked**.

peal [pēl] *n* (*of bells*) scampanio, carillon *m inv*; **~s of laughter** scoppi *mpl* di risa.

peanut [pē'nut] *n* arachide *f*, nocciolina americana.

peanut butter *n* burro di arachidi.

peanut oil *n* (*US*) olio d'arachide.

pear [pär] *n* pera.

pearl [pûrl] *n* perla.

peasant [pez'ənt] *n* contadino/a.

peat [pēt] *n* torba.

pebble [peb'əl] *n* ciottolo.

peck [pek] *vt* (*also:* **~ at**) beccare; (*: food*) mangiucchiare ♦ *n* colpo di becco; (*kiss*) bacetto.

pecking order [pek'ing ôrdûr] *n* (*fig*) ordine *m* gerarchico.

peckish [pek'ish] *a* (*Brit col*): **I feel ~** ho un languorino.

peculiar [pikyōōl'yûr] *a* strano(a), bizzarro(a); (*particular: importance, qualities*) particolare; **~ to** tipico(a) di, caratteristico(a) di.

peculiarity [pikyōōlēar'itē] *n* peculiarità *f inv*; (*oddity*) bizzarria.

pecuniary [pikyōō'nēârē] *a* pecuniario(a).

pedal [ped'əl] *n* pedale *m* ♦ *vi* pedalare.

pedal bin *n* (*Brit*) pattumiera a pedale.

pedantic [pədan'tik] *a* pedantesco(a).

peddle [ped'əl] *vt* (*goods*) andare in giro a vendere; (*drugs*) spacciare; (*gossip*) mettere in giro.

peddler [ped'lûr] *n* venditore *m* ambulante.
pedestal [ped'istəl] *n* piedestallo.
pedestrian [pədes'trēən] *n* pedone/a ♦ *a* pedonale; (*fig*) prosaico(a), pedestre.
pedestrian crossing *n* passaggio pedonale.
pedestrian precinct *n* (*Brit*) zona pedonale.
pediatrician [pēdēətrish'ən] *n* (*US*) pediatra *m/f*.
pediatrics [pēdēat'riks] *n* (*US*) pediatria.
pedigree [ped'əgrē] *n* stirpe *f*; (*of animal*) pedigree *m inv* ♦ *cpd* (*animal*) di razza.
pedlar [ped'lûr] *n* (*Brit*) = **peddler**.
pee [pē] *vi* (*col*) pisciare.
peek [pēk] *vi* guardare furtivamente.
peel [pēl] *n* buccia; (*of orange, lemon*) scorza ♦ *vt* sbucciare ♦ *vi* (*paint etc*) staccarsi.
   peel back *vt* togliere, levare.
peeler [pē'lûr] *n*: **potato ~** sbucciapatate *m inv*.
peelings [pē'lingz] *npl* bucce *fpl*.
peep [pēp] *n* (*sound*) pigolio; (*Brit: look*) sguardo furtivo, sbirciata ♦ *vi* (*Brit*) guardare furtivamente.
   peep out *vi* (*Brit*) mostrarsi furtivamente.
peephole [pēp'hōl] *n* spioncino.
peer [pēr] *vi*: **to ~ at** scrutare ♦ *n* (*noble*) pari *m inv*; (*equal*) pari *m/f inv*, uguale *m/f*.
peerage [pē'rij] *n* dignità di pari; pari *mpl*.
peerless [pēr'lis] *a* impareggiabile, senza pari.
peeved [pēvd] *a* stizzito(a).
peevish [pē'vish] *a* stizzoso(a).
peg [peg] *n* (*tent ~*) picchetto; (*for coat etc*) attaccapanni *m inv*; (*Brit: also*: **clothes ~**) molletta ♦ *vt* (*clothes*) appendere con le mollette; (*fig: prices, wages*) fissare, stabilizzare.
PEI *abbr* (*Canada*) = *Prince Edward Island*.
pejorative [pijôr'ətiv] *a* peggiorativo(a).
Pekin [pē'kin], **Peking** [pē'king'] *n* Pechino *f*.
pekin(g)ese [pēkənēz'] *n* pechinese *m*.
pelican [pel'ikən] *n* pellicano.
pelican crossing *n* (*Brit AUT*) attraversamento pedonale con semaforo a controllo manuale.
pellet [pel'it] *n* pallottola, pallina.
pell-mell [pel'mel'] *ad* disordinatamente, alla rinfusa.
pelmet [pel'mit] *n* mantovana; cassonetto.
pelt [pelt] *vt*: **to ~ sb (with)** bombardare qn (con) ♦ *vi* (*rain*) piovere a dirotto ♦ *n* pelle *f*.
pelvis [pel'vis] *n* pelvi *f inv*, bacino.
pen [pen] *n* penna; (*for sheep*) recinto; (*US col: prison*) galera; **to put ~ to paper** prendere la penna in mano.
penal [pē'nəl] *a* penale.
penalize [pē'nəliz] *vt* punire; (*SPORT*) penalizzare; (*fig*) svantaggiare.
penal servitude [pē'nəl sûr'vətōōd] *n* lavori *mpl* forzati.
penalty [pen'əltē] *n* penalità *f inv*; sanzione *f* penale; (*fine*) ammenda; (*SPORT*) penalizza-

zione *f*; (*SOCCER*: *also*: **~ kick**) calcio di rigore.
penalty clause *n* penale *f*.
penalty kick *n* (*SOCCER*) calcio di rigore.
penance [pen'əns] *n* penitenza.
pence [pens] *npl* (*Brit*) *of* **penny**.
penchant [pen'chənt] *n* debole *m*.
pencil [pen'səl] *n* matita ♦ *vt* (*also*: **~ in**) scrivere a matita.
pencil case *n* astuccio per matite.
pencil sharpener *n* temperamatite *m inv*.
pendant [pen'dənt] *n* pendaglio.
pending [pen'ding] *prep* in attesa di ♦ *a* in sospeso.
pendulum [pen'jələm] *n* pendolo.
penetrate [pen'itrāt] *vt* penetrare.
penetrating [pen'itrāting] *a* penetrante.
penetration [penitrā'shən] *n* penetrazione *f*.
pen friend *n* corrispondente *m/f*.
penguin [pen'gwin] *n* pinguino.
penicillin [penisil'in] *n* penicillina.
peninsula [pənin'sələ] *n* penisola.
penis [pē'nis] *n* pene *m*.
penitence [pen'itəns] *n* penitenza.
penitent [pen'itənt] *a* penitente.
penitentiary [peniten'chûrē] *n* (*US*) carcere *m*.
penknife [pen'nīf] *n* temperino.
Penn., Penna. *abbr* (*US*) = *Pennsylvania*.
pen name *n* pseudonimo.
pennant [pen'ənt] *n* banderuola.
penniless [pen'ēlis] *a* senza un soldo.
Pennines [pen'īnz] *npl*: **the ~** i Pennini.
penny, *pl* **pennies** *or* **pence** [pen'ē, pen'ēz, pens] *n* penny *m* (*pl* **pence**); (*US*) centesimo.
pen pal *n* corrispondente *m/f*.
pension [pen'chən] *n* pensione *f*.
   pension off *vt* mandare in pensione.
pensionable [pen'chənəbəl] *a* che ha diritto a una pensione.
pensioner [pen'chənûr] *n* (*Brit*) pensionato/a.
pension fund *n* fondo pensioni.
pensive [pen'siv] *a* pensoso(a).
pentagon [pen'təgân] *n* pentagono.
Pentecost [pen'təkôst] *n* Pentecoste *f*.
penthouse [pent'hous] *n* appartamento (di lusso) nell'attico.
pent-up [pent'up'] *a* (*feelings*) represso(a).
penultimate [pinul'təmit] *a* penultimo(a).
penury [pen'yûrē] *n* indigenza.
people [pē'pəl] *npl* gente *f*; persone *fpl*; (*citizens*) popolo *m*; (*nation, race*) popolo ♦ *vt* popolare; **old ~** i vecchi; **young ~** i giovani; **~ at large** il grande pubblico; **a man of the ~** un uomo del popolo; **4/several ~ came** 4/parecchie persone sono venute; **the room was full of ~** la stanza era piena di gente; **~ say that ...** si dice *or* la gente dice che ....
pep [pep] *n* (*col*) dinamismo.
   pep up *vt* vivacizzare; (*food*) rendere più gustoso(a).

pepper |pep'ûr| n pepe m; (vegetable) peperone m ♦ vt pepare.
peppermill |pep'ûrmil| n macinapepe m inv.
peppermint |pep'ûrmint| n (plant) menta peperita; (sweet) pasticca di menta.
pepper shaker |pep'ûr shā'kûr|, (Brit) **pepperpot** |pep'ûrpât| n pepaiola.
pep talk n (col) discorso di incoraggiamento.
per |pûr| prep per; a; ~ hour all'ora; ~ kilo etc il chilo etc; ~ day al giorno; ~ week alla settimana; ~ person a testa, a or per persona; as ~ your instructions secondo le vostre istruzioni.
per annum ad all'anno.
per capita a, ad pro capite.
perceive |pûrsēv'| vt percepire; (notice) accorgersi di.
percent, (Brit) **per cent** |pûr'sent| ad per cento; **a 20 ~ discount** uno sconto del 20 per cento.
percentage |pûrsen'tij| n percentuale f; **on a ~ basis** a percentuale.
perceptible |pûrsep'təbəl| a percettibile.
perception |pûrsep'shən| n percezione f; sensibilità; perspicacia.
perceptive |pûrsep'tiv| a percettivo(a); perspicace.
perch |pûrch| n (fish) pesce m persico; (for bird) sostegno, ramo ♦ vi appollaiarsi.
percolate |pûr'kəlāt| vt filtrare.
percolator |pûr'kəlātûr| n caffettiera a pressione; caffettiera elettrica.
percussion |pûrkush'ən| n percussione f; (MUS) strumenti mpl a percussione.
peremptory |pəremp'tûrē| a perentorio(a).
perennial |pəren'ēəl| a perenne ♦ n pianta perenne.
perfect a, n |pûr'fikt| a perfetto(a) ♦ n (also: ~ tense) perfetto, passato prossimo ♦ vt |pərfekt'| perfezionare; mettere a punto; **he's a ~ stranger to me** mi è completamente sconosciuto.
perfection |pûrfek'shən| n perfezione f.
perfectionist |pûrfek'shənist| n perfezionista m/f.
perfectly |pûr'fiktlē| ad perfettamente; **I'm ~ happy with the situation** sono completamente soddisfatta della situazione; **you know ~ well** sa benissimo.
perforate |pûr'fûrāt| vt perforare.
perforated ulcer |pûr'fûrātid ul'sûr| n (MED) ulcera perforata.
perforation |pûrfûrā'shən| n perforazione f; (line of holes) dentellatura.
perform |pûrfôrm'| vt (carry out) eseguire, fare; (symphony etc) suonare; (play, ballet) dare; (opera) fare ♦ vi suonare; recitare.
performance |pûrfôr'məns| n esecuzione f; (at theater etc) rappresentazione f, spettacolo; (of an artist) interpretazione f; (of player etc) performance f; (of car, engine) presta-

zione f.
performer |pûrfôr'mûr| n artista m/f.
performing |pûrfôr'ming| a (animal) ammaestrato(a).
perfume n |pûr'fyōōm| profumo ♦ vt |pərfyōōm'| profumare.
perfunctory |pûrfungk'tûrē| a superficiale, per la forma.
perhaps |pûrhaps'| ad forse; ~ **he'll come** forse verrà, può darsi che venga; ~ **so/not** forse sì/no, può darsi di sì/di no.
peril |pär'əl| n pericolo.
perilous |pär'ələs| a pericoloso(a).
perilously |pär'ələslē| ad: **they came ~ close to being caught** sono stati a un pelo dall'esser presi.
perimeter |pərim'itûr| n perimetro.
perimeter wall n muro di cinta.
period |pēr'ēəd| n periodo; (HISTORY) epoca; (SCOL) lezione f; (punctuation) punto; (US FOOTBALL) tempo; (MED) mestruazioni fpl ♦ a (costume, furniture) d'epoca; **for a ~ of three weeks** per un periodo di or per la durata di tre settimane; **the vacation ~** il periodo delle vacanze.
periodic |pērēād'ik| a periodico(a).
periodical |pērēād'ikəl| a periodico(a) ♦ n periodico.
periodically |pērēād'iklē| ad periodicamente.
peripatetic |päripətet'ik| a (salesman) ambulante; (teacher) peripatetico(a).
peripheral |pərif'ûrəl| a periferico(a) ♦ n (COMPUT) unità f inv periferica.
periphery |pərif'ûrē| n periferia.
periscope |pär'iskōp| n periscopio.
perish |pär'ish| vi perire, morire; (decay) deteriorarsi.
perishable |pär'ishəbəl| a deperibile.
perishables |pär'ishəbəlz| npl merci fpl deperibili.
peritonitis |pär'itəni'tis| n peritonite f.
perjure |pûr'jûr| vt: **to ~ o.s.** spergiurare.
perjury |pûr'jûrē| n (LAW: in court) falso giuramento; (breach of oath) spergiuro.
perk |pûrk| n vantaggio.
perk up vi (cheer up) rianimarsi.
perky |pûr'kē| a (cheerful) vivace, allegro(a).
perm |pûrm| n (for hair) permanente f ♦ vt: **to have one's hair ~ed** farsi fare la permanente.
permanence |pûr'mənəns| n permanenza.
permanent |pûr'mənənt| a permanente; (job, position) fisso(a); (dye, ink) indelebile; ~ **address** residenza fissa; **I'm not ~ here** non sono fisso qui.
permanently |pûr'mənəntlē| ad definitivamente.
permeable |pûr'mēəbəl| a permeabile.
permeate |pûr'mēāt| vi penetrare ♦ vt permeare.
permissible |pûrmis'əbəl| a permissibile,

ammissibile.

permission [pûrmish'ən] n permesso; **to give sb ~ to do sth** dare a qn il permesso di fare qc.

permissive [pûrmis'iv] a tollerante; **the ~ society** la società permissiva.

permit n [pûr'mit] permesso; (entrance pass) lasciapassare m ♦ vt, vi [pərmit'] permettere; **to ~ sb to do** permettere a qn di fare, dare il permesso a qn di fare; **weather ~ting** tempo permettendo.

permutation [pûrmyətā'shən] n permutazione f.

pernicious [pûrnish'əs] a pernicioso(a), nocivo(a).

pernickety [pûrnik'ətē] a (Brit) = **persnickety**.

perpendicular [pûrpəndik'yəlûr] a, n perpendicolare (f).

perpetrate [pûr'pitrāt] vt perpetrare, commettere.

perpetual [pûrpech'ōōəl] a perpetuo(a).

perpetuate [pûrpech'ōōāt] vt perpetuare.

perpetuity [pûrpətōō'itē] n: **in ~** in perpetuo.

perplex [pûrplcks'] vt lasciare perplesso(a).

perplexing [pûrplek'sing] a che lascia perplesso(a).

perquisites [pûr'kwizits] npl (also: **perks**) benefici mpl collaterali.

persecute [pûr'səkyōōt] vt perseguitare.

persecution [pûrsəkyōō'shən] n persecuzione f.

perseverance [pûrsəvēr'əns] n perseveranza.

persevere [pûrsəvēr'] vi perseverare.

Persia [pûr'zhə] n Persia.

Persian [pûr'zhən] a persiano(a) ♦ n (LING) persiano; **the (~) Gulf** il Golfo Persico.

persist [pûrsist'] vi: **to ~ (in doing)** persistere (nel fare); ostinarsi (a fare).

persistence [pûrsis'təns] n persistenza; ostinazione f.

persistent [pûrsis'tənt] a persistente; ostinato(a); (lateness, rain) continuo(a).

persnickety [pûrsnik'ətē] a (US col: person) pignolo(a); (: task) da certosino.

person [pûr'sən] n persona; **in ~** di or in persona, personalmente; **on** or **about one's ~** (weapon) su di sé; (money) con sé; **a ~ to ~ call** (TEL) una chiamata con preavviso.

personable [pûr'sənəbəl] a di bell'aspetto.

personal [pûr'sənəl] a personale; individuale; **~ belongings, ~ effects** oggetti mpl d'uso personale; **a ~ interview** un incontro privato.

personal allowance n (Brit TAX) quota del reddito non imponibile.

personal assistant (PA) n (Brit) segretaria personale.

personal call n (TEL) chiamata con preavviso.

personal column n messaggi mpl personali.

personal computer (PC) n personal compu-

ter m inv.

personal details npl dati mpl personali.

personality [pûrsənal'itē] n personalità f inv.

personally [pûr'sənəlē] ad personalmente.

personal organizer n agenda.

personal property n beni mpl personali.

personify [pûrsân'əfī] vt personificare.

personnel [pûrsənel'] n personale m.

personnel department n ufficio del personale.

personnel manager n direttore/trice del personale.

perspective [pûrspek'tiv] n prospettiva; **to get sth into ~** ridimensionare qc.

Perspex [pûr'speks] ® n (Brit) tipo di resina termoplastica.

perspicacity [pûrspəka'sitē] n perspicacia.

perspiration [pûrspərā'shən] n traspirazione f, sudore m.

perspire [pûrspiûr'] vi traspirare.

persuade [pûrswād'] vt: **to ~ sb to do sth** persuadere qn a fare qc; **to ~ sb of sth/that** persuadere qn di qc/che.

persuasion [pûrswā'zhən] n persuasione f; (creed) convinzione f, credo.

persuasive [pûrswā'siv] a persuasivo(a).

pert [pûrt] a (bold) sfacciato(a), impertinente; (hat) spiritoso(a).

pertaining [pûrtān'ing]: **~ to** prep che riguarda.

pertinent [pûr'tənənt] a pertinente.

perturb [pûrtûrb'] vt turbare.

perturbing [pûrtûrb'ing] a inquietante.

Peru [pərōō'] n Perù m.

perusal [pərōō'zəl] n attenta lettura.

Peruvian [pərōō'vēən] a, n peruviano(a).

pervade [pûrvād'] vt pervadere.

pervasive [pûrvā'siv] a (smell) penetrante; (influence) dilagante; (gloom, feelings) diffuso(a).

perverse [pûrvûrs'] a perverso(a).

perversion [pûrvûr'zhən] n pervertimento, perversione f.

perversity [pûrvûr'sitē] n perversità.

pervert n [pûr'vûrt] pervertito/a ♦ vt [pûrvûrt'] pervertire.

pessimism [pes'əmizəm] n pessimismo.

pessimist [pes'əmist] n pessimista m/f.

pessimistic [pesəmis'tik] a pessimistico(a).

pest [pest] n animale m (or insetto) pestifero; (fig) peste f.

pest control n disinfestazione f.

pester [pcs'tûr] vt tormentare, molestare.

pesticide [pcs'tisīd] n pesticida m.

pestilent [pcs'tələnt], **pestilential** [pcstəlcn'shəl] a (col: exasperating) pestifero(a).

pestle [pcs'əl] n pestello.

pet [pct] n animale m domestico; (favorite) favorito/a ♦ vt accarezzare ♦ vi (col) fare il petting; **~ lion** etc leone m etc ammaestrato.

petal [pct'əl] n petalo.

peter [pē'tûr]: **to ~ out** *vi* esaurirsi; estinguersi.
petite [pətēt'] *a* piccolo(a) e aggraziato(a).
petition [pətish'ən] *n* petizione *f* ♦ *vi* richiedere; **to ~ for divorce** presentare un'istanza di divorzio.
pet name *n* (*Brit*) nomignolo.
petrified [pet'rəfīd] *a* (*fig*) morto(a) di paura.
petrify [pet'rəfī] *vt* pietrificare; (*fig*) terrorizzare.
petrochemical [petrōkem'ikəl] *a* petrolchimico(a).
petrodollars [petrōdâl'ûrz] *npl* petrodollari *mpl*.
petrol [pet'rəl] *n* (*Brit*) benzina.
petrol can *n* (*Brit*) tanica per benzina.
petrol engine *n* (*Brit*) motore *m* a benzina.
petroleum [pətrō'lēəm] *n* petrolio.
petroleum jelly *n* vaselina.
petrol pump *n* (*Brit*: *in car*, *at garage*) pompa di benzina.
petrol station *n* (*Brit*) stazione *f* di rifornimento.
petrol tank *n* (*Brit*) serbatoio della benzina.
petticoat [pet'ēkōt] *n* sottana.
pettifogging [pet'ēfâging] *a* cavilloso(a).
pettiness [pet'ēnis] *n* meschinità.
petty [pet'ē] *a* (*mean*) meschino(a); (*unimportant*) insignificante.
petty cash *n* piccola cassa.
petty officer *n* sottufficiale *m* di marina.
petulant [pech'ələnt] *a* irritabile.
pew [pyōō] *n* panca (di chiesa).
pewter [pyōō'tûr] *n* peltro.
Pfc *abbr* (*US MIL*) = *private first class.*
PG *n abbr* (*CINEMA*: = *parental guidance*) consenso dei genitori richiesto.
PGA *n abbr* (= *Professional Golfers Association*) associazione dei giocatori di golf professionisti.
PH *n abbr* (*US MIL*: = *Purple Heart*) decorazione per ferite riportate in guerra.
p&h *abbr* (*US*: = *postage and handling*) affrancatura e trasporto.
PHA *n abbr* (*US*: = *Public Housing Administration*) amministrazione per l'edilizia pubblica.
phallic [fal'ik] *a* fallico(a).
phantom [fan'təm] *n* fantasma *m*.
Pharaoh [fār'ō] *n* faraone *m*.
pharmaceutical [fârməsōō'tikəl] *a* farmaceutico(a) ♦ *n*: **~s** prodotti *mpl* farmaceutici.
pharmacist [fâr'məsist] *n* farmacista *m/f*.
pharmacy [fâr'məsē] *n* farmacia.
phase [fāz] *n* fase *f*, periodo ♦ *vt*: **to ~ sth in/out** introdurre/eliminare qc progressivamente.
PhD *n abbr* = **Doctor of Philosophy.**
pheasant [fez'ənt] *n* fagiano.
phenomenon, *pl* **phenomena** [finâm'ənân, -ənə] *n* fenomeno.

phew [fyōō] *excl* uff!
phial [fī'əl] *n* fiala.
philanderer [filan'dûrûr] *n* donnaiolo.
philanthropic [filənthrâp'ik] *a* filantropico(a).
philanthropist [filan'thrəpist] *n* filantropo.
philatelist [filat'əlist] *n* filatelico/a.
philately [filat'əlē] *n* filatelia.
Philippines [fil'ipēnz] *npl* (*also:* **Philippine Islands**): **the ~** le Filippine.
philosopher [filâs'əfûr] *n* filosofo/a.
philosophical [filâsâf'ikəl] *a* filosofico(a).
philosophy [filâs'əfē] *n* filosofia.
phlegm [flem] *n* flemma.
phlegmatic [flegmat'ik] *a* flemmatico(a).
phobia [fō'bēə] *n* fobia.
phone [fōn] *n* telefono ♦ *vt* telefonare a ♦ *vi* telefonare; **to be on the ~** avere il telefono; (*be calling*) essere al telefono.
phone back *vt*, *vi* richiamare.
phone book *n* guida del telefono, elenco telefonico.
phone booth, (*Brit*) **phone box** *n* cabina telefonica.
phone call *n* telefonata.
phone-in [fōn'in] *n* (*Brit RADIO,* *TV*) trasmissione radiofonica o televisiva con intervento telefonico degli ascoltatori.
phonetics [fənet'iks] *n* fonetica.
phoney [fō'nē] *a* falso(a), fasullo(a) ♦ *n* (*person*) ciarlatano.
phonograph [fō'nəgraf] *n* (*US*) giradischi *m* inv.
phony [fō'nē] *a*, *n* = **phoney**.
phosphate [fâs'fāt] *n* fosfato.
phosphorus [fâs'fûrəs] *n* fosforo.
photo [fō'tō] *n* foto *f* inv.
photo... *prefix* foto....
photocopier [fō'təkâpēûr] *n* fotocopiatrice *f*.
photocopy [fō'təkâpē] *n* fotocopia ♦ *vt* fotocopiare.
photoelectric [fōtōilek'trik] *a*: **~ cell** cellula fotoelettrica.
photogenic [fōtəjen'ik] *a* fotogenico(a).
photograph [fō'təgraf] *n* fotografia ♦ *vt* fotografare; **to take a ~ of sb** fare una fotografia a *or* fotografare qn.
photographer [fətâg'rəfûr] *n* fotografo.
photographic [fōtəgraf'ik] *a* fotografico(a).
photography [fətâg'rəfē] *n* fotografia.
photostat [fō'təstat] ® *n* fotocopia.
photosynthesis [fōtəsin'thəsis] *n* fotosintesi *f*.
phrase [frāz] *n* espressione *f*; (*LING*) locuzione *f*; (*MUS*) frase *f* ♦ *vt* esprimere; (*letter*) redigere.
phrase book *n* vocabolarietto.
physical [fiz'ikəl] *a* fisico(a) ♦ *n* visita medica; **~ examination** visita medica; **~ education** educazione *f* fisica; **~ exercises** ginnastica.
physically [fiz'iklē] *ad* fisicamente.
physician [fizish'ən] *n* medico.
physicist [fiz'əsist] *n* fisico.

physics [fiz'iks] *n* fisica.
physiological [fizēəláj'ikəl] *a* fisiologico(a).
physiology [fizēál'əjē] *n* fisiologia.
physiotherapist [fizēōthär'əpist] *n* fisioterapista *m/f*.
physiotherapy [fizēōthär'əpē] *n* fisioterapia.
physique [fizēk'] *n* fisico.
pianist [pēan'ist] *n* pianista *m/f*.
piano [pēan'ō] *n* pianoforte *m*.
piano accordion *n* (*Brit*) fisarmonica (a tastiera).
piccolo [pik'əlō] *n* ottavino.
pick [pik] *n* (*tool*) piccone *m* ♦ *vt* scegliere; (*gather*) cogliere; (*scab, spot*) grattarsi ♦ *vi*: **to ~ and choose** scegliere con cura; **take your ~** scelga; **the ~ of** il fior fiore di; **to ~ one's nose** mettersi le dita nel naso; **to ~ one's teeth** stuzzicarsi i denti; **to ~ sb's brains** farsi dare dei suggerimenti da qn; **to ~ pockets** borseggiare; **to ~ a fight with sb** attaccar rissa con qn; **to ~ one's way through** attraversare stando ben attento a dove mettere i piedi.
pick off *vt* (*kill*) abbattere.
pick on *vt fus* (*person*) avercela con.
pick out *vt* scegliere; (*distinguish*) distinguere.
pick up *vi* (*improve*) migliorarsi ♦ *vt* raccogliere; (*collect*) passare a prendere; (*AUT: give lift to*) far salire; (*learn*) imparare; (*RADIO, TV, TEL*) captare; **to ~ o.s. up** rialzarsi; **to ~ up where one left off** riprendere dal punto in cui ci si era fermati; **to ~ up speed** acquistare velocità.
pickax, (*Brit*) **pickaxe** [pik'aks] *n* piccone *m*.
picket [pik'it] *n* (*in strike*) scioperante *m/f* che fa parte di un picchetto; picchetto ♦ *vt* picchettare.
picket line *n* cordone *m* degli scioperanti.
pickings [pik'ingz] *npl* (*pilferings*): **there are good ~ to be had here** qui ci sono buone possibilità di intascare qualcosa sottobanco.
pickle [pik'əl] *n* (*also:* **~s:** *as condiment*) sottaceti *mpl*; (*fig*): **in a ~** nei pasticci ♦ *vt* mettere sottaceto; mettere in salamoia.
pick-me-up [pik'mēup] *n* tiramisù *m inv*.
pickpocket [pik'päkit] *n* borsaiolo.
pickup [pik'up] *n* (*on record player*) pick-up *m inv*; (*small truck: also:* **~ truck**) camioncino.
picnic [pik'nik] *n* picnic *m inv* ♦ *vi* fare un picnic.
picnicker [pik'nikûr] *n* chi partecipa a un picnic.
pictorial [piktôr'ēəl] *a* illustrato(a).
picture [pik'chûr] *n* quadro; (*painting*) pittura; (*photograph*) foto(grafia); (*drawing*) disegno; (*TV*) immagine *f*; (*film*) film *m inv* ♦ *vt* raffigurarsi; **the ~s** (*Brit*) il cinema; **to take a ~ of sb/sth** fare una foto a qn/di qc; **we get a good ~ here** (*TV*) la ricezione qui è buona; **the overall ~** il quadro generale; **to**

put sb in the ~ mettere qn al corrente.
picture book *n* libro illustrato.
picturesque [pikchəresk'] *a* pittoresco(a).
picture window *n* finestra panoramica.
piddling [pid'ling] *a* (*col*) insignificante.
pidgin English [pij'in ing'glish] *n* inglese semplificato misto ad elementi indigeni.
pie [pī] *n* torta; (*of meat*) pasticcio.
piebald [pī'bôld] *a* pezzato(a).
piece [pēs] *n* pezzo; (*of land*) appezzamento; (*CHECKERS etc*) pedina; (*item*): **a ~ of furniture/advice** un mobile/consiglio ♦ *vt*: **to ~ together** mettere insieme; **in ~s** (*broken*) in pezzi; (*not yet assembled*) smontato(a); **to take to ~s** smontare; **~ by ~** poco alla volta; **a 10¢ ~** una moneta da 10 centesimi; **a six-~ band** un complesso di sei strumentisti; **in one ~** (*object*) intatto; **to get back all in one ~** (*person*) tornare a casa incolume *or* sano e salvo; **to say one's ~** dire la propria.
piecemeal [pēs'mēl] *ad* pezzo a pezzo, a spizzico.
piece rate *n* tariffa a cottimo.
piecework [pēs'wûrk] *n* (lavoro a) cottimo.
pie chart *n* grafico a torta.
pie crust pastry *n* (*US*) pasta frolla.
Piedmont [pēd'mänt] *n* Piemonte *m*.
pier [pēr] *n* molo; (*of bridge etc*) pila.
pierce [pērs] *vt* trafiggere; **to have one's ears ~d** farsi fare i buchi per gli orecchini.
piercing [pēr'sing] *a* (*cry*) acuto(a).
piety [pī'ətē] *n* pietà, devozione *f*.
piffling [pif'ling] *a* insignificante.
pig [pig] *n* maiale *m*, porco.
pigeon [pij'ən] *n* piccione *m*.
pigeonhole [pij'ənhōl] *n* casella ♦ *vt* classificare.
pigeon-toed [pij'əntōd] *a* che cammina con i piedi in dentro.
piggy bank [pig'ē bangk] *n* salvadanaio.
pigheaded [pig'hedid] *a* caparbio(a), cocciuto(a).
piglet [pig'lit] *n* porcellino.
pigment [pig'mənt] *n* pigmento.
pigmentation [pigmäntā'shən] *n* pigmentazione *f*.
pigmy [pig'mē] *n* = **pygmy**.
pigskin [pig'skin] *n* cinghiale *m*.
pigsty [pig'stī] *n* porcile *m*.
pigtail [pig'tāl] *n* treccina.
pike [pīk] *n* (*spear*) picca; (*fish*) luccio.
pilchard [pil'chûrd] *n* specie di sardina.
pile [pīl] *n* (*pillar, of books*) pila; (*heap*) mucchio; (*of carpet*) pelo ♦ *vb* (*also:* **~ up**) *vt* ammucchiare ♦ *vi* ammucchiarsi; **in a ~** ammucchiato; *see also* **piles**.
pile on *vt*: **to ~ it on** (*col*) esagerare, drammatizzare.
piles [pīlz] *npl* (*MED*) emorroidi *fpl*.
pileup [pīl'up] *n* (*AUT*) tamponamento a cate-

na.

pilfer [pil'fûr] vt rubacchiare ♦ vi fare dei furtarelli.

pilfering [pil'fûring] n rubacchiare m.

pilgrim [pil'grim] n pellegrino/a.

pilgrimage [pil'grəmij] n pellegrinaggio.

pill [pil] n pillola; **to be on the ~** prendere la pillola.

pillage [pil'ij] vt saccheggiare.

pillar [pil'ûr] n colonna.

pillar box n (Brit) cassetta delle lettere (a colonnina).

pillion [pil'yən] n (of motor cycle) sellino posteriore; **to ride ~** viaggiare dietro.

pillory [pil'ûrē] n berlina ♦ vt mettere alla berlina.

pillow [pil'ō] n guanciale m.

pillowcase [pil'ōkās], **pillowslip** [pil'ōslip] n federa.

pilot [pī'lət] n pilota m/f ♦ cpd (plan etc) pilota inv ♦ vt pilotare.

pilot boat n pilotina.

pilot light n fiammella di sicurezza.

pimento [pimen'tō] n peperoncino.

pimp [pimp] n mezzano.

pimple [pim'pəl] n foruncolo.

pimply [pim'plē] a foruncoloso(a).

pin [pin] n spillo; (TECH) perno; (US: also: **clothes ~**) molletta; (Brit: drawing **~**) puntina da disegno; (Brit ELEC: of plug) spinotto ♦ vt attaccare con uno spillo; **~s and needles** formicolio; **to ~ sb against/to** inchiodare qn contro/a; **to ~ sth on sb** (fig) addossare la colpa di qc a qn.

pin down vt (fig): **to ~ sb down** obbligare qn a pronunziarsi; **there's something strange here but I can't quite ~ it down** c'è qualcosa di strano qua ma non riesco a capire cos'è.

pinafore [pin'əfôr] n grembiule m (senza maniche).

pinafore dress n (Brit) scamiciato.

pinball [pin'bôl] n flipper m inv.

pincers [pin'sûrz] npl pinzette fpl.

pinch [pinch] n pizzicotto, pizzico ♦ vt pizzicare; (col: steal) grattare ♦ vi (shoe) stringere; **at a ~** in caso di bisogno; **to feel the ~** (fig) trovarsi nelle ristrettezze.

pinched [pincht] a (drawn) dai lineamenti tirati; (short): **~ for money/space** a corto di soldi/di spazio; **~ with cold** raggrinzito dal freddo.

pincushion [pin'kōōshən] n puntaspilli m inv.

pine [pīn] n (also: **~ tree**) pino ♦ vi: **to ~ for** struggersi dal desiderio di.

pine away vi languire.

pineapple [pīn'apəl] n ananas m inv.

pine nut n pinolo.

ping [ping] n (noise) tintinnio.

ping-pong [ping'pông] ® n ping-pong ® m.

pink [pingk] a rosa inv ♦ n (color) rosa m inv;

(BOT) garofano.

pinking shears [ping'king shirz] n forbici fpl a zigzag.

pin money n denaro per le piccole spese.

pinnacle [pin'əkəl] n pinnacolo.

pinpoint [pin'point] vt indicare con precisione.

pinstripe [pin'strīp] n stoffa gessata; (also: **~ suit**) gessato.

pint [pīnt] n pinta (US = 0.47 l; Brit = 0.57 l).

pinup [pin'up] n pin-up girl f inv.

pinwheel [pin'wēl] n (US) girandola.

pioneer [pīənēr'] n pioniere/a ♦ vt essere un pioniere in.

pious [pī'əs] a pio(a).

pip [pip] n (seed) seme m; (Brit: time signal on radio) segnale m orario.

pipe [pīp] n tubo; (for smoking) pipa; (MUS) piffero ♦ vt portare per mezzo di tubazione; **~s** npl (also: **bag~s**) cornamusa (scozzese).

pipe down vi (col) calmarsi.

pipe cleaner n scovolino.

piped music [pīpt myōō'zik] n musica di sottofondo.

pipe dream n vana speranza.

pipeline [pīp'līn] n conduttura; (for oil) oleodotto; (for natural gas) metanodotto; **it is in the ~** (fig) è in arrivo.

piper [pī'pûr] n piffero; suonatore/trice di cornamusa.

pipe tobacco n tabacco da pipa.

piping [pī'ping] ad: **~ hot** bollente.

piquant [pē'kənt] a (sauce) piccante; (conversation) stimolante.

pique [pēk] n picca.

piracy [pī'rəsē] n pirateria.

pirate [pī'rət] n pirata m ♦ vt (record, video, book) riprodurre abusivamente.

pirate radio (station) n radio pirata f inv.

pirouette [pirōōet'] n piroetta ♦ vi piroettare.

Pisces [pī'sēz] n Pesci mpl; **to be ~** essere dei Pesci.

piss [pis] vi (col!) pisciare; **~ off!** vaffanculo! (!).

pissed [pist] a (Brit col: drunk) ubriaco(a) fradicio(a).

pistol [pis'təl] n pistola.

piston [pis'tən] n pistone m.

pit [pit] n buca, fossa; (also: **coal ~**) miniera; (also: **orchestra ~**) orchestra; (US: of fruit) nocciolo ♦ vt (US: fruit) snocciolare; **to ~ sb against sb** opporre qn a qn; **~s** npl (AUT) box m; **to ~ o.s. against** opporsi a.

pitapat [pit'əpat] ad: **to go ~** (heart) palpitare, battere forte; (rain) picchiettare.

pitch [pich] n (throw) lancia; (MUS) tono; (of voice) altezza; (fig: degree) grado, punto; (also: **sales ~**) discorso di vendita, imbonimento; (Brit SPORT) campo; (NAUT) beccheggio; (tar) pece f ♦ vt (throw) lanciare ♦ vi (fall) cascare; (NAUT) beccheggiare; **to ~ a tent** piantare una tenda; **at this ~** a questo ritmo.

pitch-black [pich'blak'] *a* nero(a) come la pece.

pitched battle [picht bat'əl] *n* battaglia campale.

pitcher [pich'ûr] *n* brocca.

pitchfork [pich'fôrk] *n* forcone *m*.

piteous [pit'ēəs] *a* pietoso(a).

pitfall [pit'fôl] *n* trappola.

pith [pith] *n* (*of plant*) midollo; (*of orange*) parte *f* interna della scorza; (*fig*) essenza, succo; vigore *m*.

pithy [pith'ē] *a* conciso(a); vigoroso(a).

pitiable [pit'ēəbəl] *a* pietoso(a).

pitiful [pit'ifəl] *a* (*touching*) pietoso(a); (*contemptible*) miserabile.

pitifully [pit'ifəlē] *ad* pietosamente; **it's ~ obvious** è penosamente chiaro.

pitiless [pit'ilis] *a* spietato(a).

pittance [pit'əns] *n* miseria, magro salario.

pitted [pit'id] *a*: **~ with** (*potholes*) pieno(a) di; (*chickenpox*) butterato(a) da.

pity [pit'ē] *n* pietà ♦ *vt* aver pietà di, compatire, commiserare; **to have** *or* **take ~ on sb** aver pietà di qn; **it is a ~ that you can't come** è un peccato che non possa venire; **what a ~!** che peccato!

pitying [pit'ēing] *a* compassionevole.

pivot [piv'ət] *n* perno ♦ *vi* imperniarsi.

pixel [pik'səl] *n* (*COMPUT*) pixel *m inv*.

pixie [pik'sē] *n* folletto.

pizza [pēt'sə] *n* pizza.

P&L *abbr* (= *profit and loss*) P.P.

placard [plak'ârd] *n* affisso.

placate [plā'kāt] *vt* placare, calmare.

placatory [plā'kətôrē] *a* conciliante.

place [plās] *n* posto, luogo; (*proper position, rank, seat*) posto; (*house*) casa, alloggio; (*home*): **at/to his ~** a casa sua; (*in street names*): **Laurel P~** via dei Lauri ♦ *vt* (*object*) posare, mettere; (*identify*) riconoscere; (*goods*) piazzare; **to take ~** aver luogo; succedere; **out of ~** (*not suitable*) inopportuno(a); **I feel rather out of ~ here** qui mi sento un po' fuori posto; **in the first ~** in primo luogo; **to change ~s with sb** scambiare il posto con qn; **to put sb in his ~** (*fig*) mettere a posto qn, mettere qn al suo posto; **from ~ to ~** da un posto all'altro; **all over the ~** dappertutto; **he's going ~s** (*fig col*) si sta facendo strada; **it is not my ~ to do it** non sta a me farlo; **how are you ~d next week?** com'è messo la settimana prossima?; **to ~ an order with sb (for)** (*COMM*) fare un'ordinazione a qn (di).

placebo [pləsē'bō] *n* placebo *m inv*.

place mat *n* sottopiatto; (*in linen etc*) tovaglietta.

placement [plās'mənt] *n* collocamento; (*job*) lavoro.

place name *n* toponimo.

placenta [pləsen'tə] *n* placenta.

placid [plas'id] *a* placido(a), calmo(a).

placidity [pləsid'itē] *n* placidità.

plagiarism [plā'jərizəm] *n* plagio.

plagiarist [plā'jûrist] *n* plagiario/a.

plagiarize [plā'jərīz] *vt* plagiare.

plague [plāg] *n* peste *f* ♦ *vt* tormentare; **to ~ sb with questions** assillare qn di domande.

plaice [plās] *n* (*pl inv*) pianuzza.

plaid [plad] *n* plaid *m inv*.

plain [plān] *a* (*clear*) chiaro(a), palese; (*simple*) semplice; (*frank*) franco(a), aperto(a); (*not handsome*) bruttino(a); (*without seasoning etc*) scondito(a); naturale; (*in one color*) tinta unita *inv* ♦ *ad* francamente, chiaramente ♦ *n* pianura; **to make sth ~ to sb** far capire chiaramente qc a qn; **in ~ clothes** (*police*) in borghese.

plain chocolate *n* cioccolato fondente.

plainly [plān'lē] *ad* chiaramente; (*frankly*) francamente.

plainness [plān'nis] *n* semplicità.

plaintiff [plān'tif] *n* attore/trice.

plaintive [plān'tiv] *a* (*voice, song*) lamentoso(a); (*look*) struggente.

plait [plat] *n* treccia ♦ *vt* intrecciare; **to ~ one's hair** farsi una treccia (*or* le trecce).

plan [plan] *n* pianta; (*scheme*) progetto, piano ♦ *vt* (*think in advance*) progettare; (*prepare*) organizzare; (*intend*) avere in progetto ♦ *vi*: **to ~ (for)** far piani *or* progetti (per); **to ~ to do** progettare di fare, avere l'intenzione di fare; **how long do you ~ to stay?** quanto conta di restare?

plane [plān] *n* (*AVIAT*) aereo; (*tree*) platano; (*tool*) pialla; (*ART, MATH etc*) piano ♦ *a* piano(a), piatto(a) ♦ *vt* (*with tool*) piallare.

planet [plan'it] *n* pianeta *m*.

planetarium [planitär'ēəm] *n* planetario.

plank [plangk] *n* tavola, asse *f*.

plankton [plangk'tən] *n* plancton *m*.

planner [plan'ûr] *n* pianificatore/trice; (*chart*) calendario; **city** *or* (*Brit*) **town ~** urbanista *m/f*.

planning [plan'ing] *n* progettazione *f*; (*POL, ECON*) pianificazione *f*; **family ~** pianificazione delle nascite.

plant [plant] *n* pianta; (*machinery*) impianto; (*factory*) fabbrica ♦ *vt* piantare; (*bomb*) mettere.

plantation [plantā'shən] *n* piantagione *f*.

plant pot *n* (*Brit*) vaso (di fiori).

plaque [plak] *n* placca.

plasma [plaz'mə] *n* plasma *m*.

plaster [plas'tûr] *n* intonaco; (*also*: **~ of Paris**) gesso; (*Brit: also*: **sticking ~**) cerotto ♦ *vt* intonacare; ingessare; (*cover*): **to ~ with** coprire di; (*col: mud etc*) impiastricciare; **in ~** (*Brit: leg etc*) ingessato(a).

plaster cast *n* (*MED*) ingessatura, gesso; (*model, statue*) modello in gesso.

plastered |plas'tûrd| *a* (*col*) ubriaco(a) fradicio(a).

plasterer |plas'tərûr| *n* intonacatore *m*.

plastic |plas'tik| *n* plastica ♦ *a* (*made of plastic*) di *or* in plastica; (*flexible*) plastico(a), malleabile; (*art*) plastico(a).

plastic bag *n* sacchetto di plastica.

plastic surgery *n* chirurgia plastica.

plate |plāt| *n* (*dish*) piatto; (*sheet of metal*) lamiera; (*PHOT*) lastra; (*TYP*) cliché *m inv*; (*in book*) tavola; (*on door*) targa, targhetta; (*AUT*: *license* ~) targa; (*dishes*): **gold** ~ vasellame *m* d'oro; **silver** ~ argenteria.

plateau, ~s *or* ~x |platō', -z| *n* altipiano.

plateful |plāt'fəl| *n* piatto.

plate glass *n* vetro piano.

platen |plat'ən| *n* (*on typewriter*, *printer*) rullo.

platform |plat'fôrm| *n* (*stage*, *at meeting*) palco; (*Brit*: *on bus*) piattaforma; (*RAIL*) marciapiede *m*; **the train leaves from** ~ **7** il treno parte dal binario 7.

platinum |plat'ənəm| *n* platino.

platitude |plat'ətōōd| *n* luogo comune.

platoon |plətōōn'| *n* plotone *m*.

platter |plat'ûr| *n* piatto.

plaudits |plô'dits| *npl* plauso.

plausible |plô'zəbəl| *a* plausibile, credibile; (*person*) convincente.

play |plā| *n* gioco; (*THEATER*) commedia ♦ *vt* (*game*) giocare a; (*team*, *opponent*) giocare contro; (*instrument*, *piece of music*) suonare; (*play*, *part*) interpretare ♦ *vi* giocare; suonare; recitare; **to bring** *or* **call into** ~ (*plan*) mettere in azione; (*emotions*) esprimere; ~ **on words** gioco di parole; **to** ~ **a trick on sb** fare uno scherzo a qn; **they're** ~**ing soldiers** stanno giocando ai soldati; **to** ~ **for time** (*fig*) cercare di guadagnar tempo; **to** ~ **into sb's hands** (*fig*) fare il gioco di qn.

play along *vi*: **to** ~ **along with** (*fig*: *person*) stare al gioco di; (*: plan*, *idea*) fingere di assecondare.

play around *vi* (*person*) divertirsi; **to** ~ **around with** (*fiddle with*) giocherellare con; (*idea*) accarezzare.

play back *vt* riascoltare, risentire.

play down *vt* minimizzare.

play on *vt fus* (*sb's feelings*, *credulity*) giocare su; **to** ~ **on sb's nerves** dare sui nervi a qn.

play up *vi* (*Brit*: *cause trouble*) fare i capricci.

playact |plā'akt| *vi* fare la commedia.

playboy |plā'boi| *n* playboy *m inv*.

played-out |plād'out| *a* spossato(a).

player |plā'ûr| *n* giocatore/trice; (*THEATER*) attore/trice; (*MUS*) musicista *m/f*.

playful |plā'fəl| *a* gioioso(a).

playgoer |plā'gōûr| *n* assiduo(a) frequentatore(trice) di teatri.

playground |plā'ground| *n* (*in school*) cortile *m* per la ricreazione; (*in park*) parco *m* giochi *inv*.

playgroup |plā'grōōp| *n* giardino d'infanzia.

playing card |plā'ing kârd| *n* carta da gioco.

playing field *n* campo sportivo.

playmate |plā'māt| *n* compagno/a di gioco.

play-off |plā'ôf| *n* (*SPORT*) bella.

playpen |plā'pen| *n* box *m inv*.

playroom |plā'rōōm| *n* stanza dei giochi.

plaything |plā'thing| *n* giocattolo.

playtime |plā'tīm| *n* (*SCOL*) ricreazione *f*.

playwright |plā'rit| *n* drammaturgo/a.

plc *abbr* (*Brit*) *see* **public limited company**.

plea |plē| *n* (*request*) preghiera, domanda; (*excuse*) scusa; (*LAW*) (argomento di) difesa.

plead |plēd| *vt* patrocinare; (*give as excuse*) addurre a pretesto ♦ *vi* (*LAW*) perorare la causa; (*beg*): **to** ~ **with sb** implorare qn; **to** ~ **for sth** implorare qc; **to** ~ **guilty/not guilty** (*defendant*) dichiararsi colpevole/innocente.

pleasant |plez'ənt| *a* piacevole, gradevole.

pleasantly |plez'əntlē| *ad* piacevolmente.

pleasantness |plez'əntnis| *n* (*of person*) amabilità; (*of place*) amenità.

pleasantry |plez'əntrē| *n* (*joke*) scherzo; (*polite remark*): **to exchange pleasantries** scambiarsi i convenevoli.

please |plēz| *vt* piacere a ♦ *vi* (*think fit*): **do as you** ~ faccia come le pare; ~**!** per piacere!; **my bill,** ~ il conto, per piacere; ~ **yourself!** come ti (*or* le) pare!; ~ **don't cry!** ti prego, non piangere!

pleased |plēzd| *a* (*happy*) felice, lieto(a); ~ (**with**) (*satisfied*) contento(a) (di); **we are** ~ **to inform you that** ... abbiamo il piacere di informarla che ...; ~ **to meet you!** piacere!

pleasing |plē'zing| *a* piacevole, che fa piacere.

pleasurable |plezh'ûrəbəl| *a* molto piacevole, molto gradevole.

pleasure |plezh'ûr| *n* piacere *m*; **with** ~ con piacere, volentieri; "**it's a** ~**"** "prego"; **is this trip for business or** ~**?** è un viaggio d'affari o di piacere?

pleasure steamer *n* vapore *m* da diporto.

pleat |plēt| *n* piega.

plebiscite |pleb'isīt| *n* plebiscito.

plebs |plebs| *npl* (*pej*) plebe *f*.

plectrum |plek'trəm| *n* plettro.

pledge |plej| *n* pegno; (*promise*) promessa ♦ *vt* impegnare; promettere; **to** ~ **support for sb** impegnarsi a sostenere qn; **to** ~ **sb to secrecy** far promettere a qn di mantenere il segreto.

plenary |plē'nûrē| *a* plenario(a); **in** ~ **session** in seduta plenaria.

plentiful |plen'tifəl| *a* abbondante, copioso(a).

plenty |plen'tē| *n* abbondanza; ~ **of** tanto(a), molto(a); un'abbondanza di; **we've got** ~ **of**

time to get there abbiamo un sacco di tempo per arrivarci.

pleurisy [plŏŏr'isē] *n* pleurite *f*.

Plexiglas [plek'səglas] ® *n* (*US*) plexiglas ® *m*.

pliable [plī'əbəl] *a* flessibile; (*person*) malleabile.

pliers [plī'ûrz] *npl* pinza.

plight [plīt] *n* situazione *f* critica.

plimsolls [plim'səlz] *npl* (*Brit*) scarpe *fpl* da tennis.

plinth [plinth] *n* plinto; piedistallo.

PLO *n abbr* (= *Palestine Liberation Organization*) O.L.P. *f*.

plod [plâd] *vi* camminare a stento; (*fig*) sgobbare.

plodder [plâd'ûr] *n* sgobbone *m*.

plodding [plâd'ing] *a* lento(a) e pesante.

plonk [plângk] *n* (*Brit col*: *wine*) vino da poco.

plot [plât] *n* congiura, cospirazione *f*; (*of story, play*) trama; (*of land*) lotto ♦ *vt* (*mark out*) fare la pianta di; rilevare; (: *diagram etc*) tracciare; (*conspire*) congiurare, cospirare ♦ *vi* congiurare.

plotter [plât'ûr] *n* cospiratore/trice; (*COMPUT*) plotter *m inv*, tracciatore *m* di curve.

plough [plou] *etc* (*Brit*) = **plow** *etc*.

plow [plou] (*US*) *n* aratro ♦ *vt* (*earth*) arare.
    plow back *vt* (*COMM*) reinvestire.
    plow through *vt fus* (*snow etc*) procedere a fatica in.

plowing [plou'ing] *n* aratura.

plowman [plou'mən] *n* aratore *m*.

ploy [ploi] *n* stratagemma *m*.

pluck [pluk] *vt* (*fruit*) cogliere; (*musical instrument*) pizzicare; (*bird*) spennare ♦ *n* coraggio, fegato; **to ~ one's eyebrows** depilarsi le sopracciglia; **to ~ up courage** farsi coraggio.

plucky [pluk'ē] *a* coraggioso(a).

plug [plug] *n* tappo; (*ELEC*) spina; (*AUT*: *also*: **spark ~**) candela ♦ *vt* (*hole*) tappare; (*col*: *advertise*) spingere; **to give sb/sth a ~** fare pubblicità a qn/qc.
    plug in (*ELEC*) *vi* inserire la spina ♦ *vt* attaccare a una presa.

plughole [plug'hōl] *n* (*Brit*) scarico.

plum [plum] *n* (*fruit*) susina ♦ *cpd*: **~ job** (*col*) impiego ottimo or favoloso.

plumage [plōō'mij] *n* piume *fpl*, piumaggio.

plumb [plum] *a* verticale ♦ *n* piombo ♦ *ad* (*exactly*) esattamente ♦ *vt* sondare.
    plumb in *vt* (*washing machine*) collegare all'impianto idraulico.

plumber [plum'ûr] *n* idraulico.

plumbing [plum'ing] *n* (*trade*) lavoro di idraulico; (*piping*) tubature *fpl*.

plumbline [plum'līn] *n* filo a piombo.

plume [plōōm] *n* piuma, penna; (*decorative*) pennacchio.

plummet [plum'it] *vi* cadere a piombo.

plump [plump] *a* grassoccio(a) ♦ *vt*: **to ~ sth (down) on** lasciar cadere qc di peso su.
    plump up *vt* sprimacciare.

plunder [plun'dûr] *n* saccheggio ♦ *vt* saccheggiare.

plunge [plunj] *n* tuffo ♦ *vt* immergere ♦ *vi* (*dive*) tuffarsi; (*fall*) cadere, precipitare; **to take the ~** (*fig*) saltare il fosso; **to ~ a room into darkness** far piombare una stanza nel buio.

plunger [plun'jûr] *n* (*for blocked sink*) sturalavandini *m inv*.

plunging [plun'jing] *a* (*neckline*) profondo(a).

pluperfect [plōōpûr'fikt] *n* piuccheperfetto.

plural [plōōr'əl] *a*, *n* plurale (*m*).

plus [plus] *n* (*also*: **~ sign**) segno più ♦ *prep* più ♦ *a* (*MATH*, *ELEC*) positivo(a); **ten/ twenty ~** più di dieci/venti; **it's a ~** (*fig*) è un vantaggio.

plus fours *npl* calzoni *mpl* alla zuava.

plush [plush] *a* lussuoso(a) ♦ *n* felpa.

plutonium [plōōtō'nēəm] *n* plutonio.

ply [plī] *n* (*of wool*) capo; (*of wood*) strato ♦ *vt* (*tool*) maneggiare; (*a trade*) esercitare ♦ *vi* (*ship*) fare il servizio; **three ~ (wool)** lana a tre capi; **to ~ sb with drink** dare da bere continuamente a qn.

plywood [plī'wŏŏd] *n* legno compensato.

PM *n abbr see* **prime minister**.

p.m. *ad abbr* (= *post meridiem*) del pomeriggio.

pneumatic [nōōmat'ik] *a* pneumatico(a); **~ drill** martello pneumatico.

pneumonia [nyōōmōn'yə] *n* polmonite *f*.

PO *n abbr* (= *Post Office*) ≈ P.T. (= *Poste e Telegrafi*) ♦ *abbr* (*NAUT*) = **petty officer**.

po *abbr* = **postal order**.

poach [pōch] *vt* (*cook*) affogare; (*steal*) cacciare (*or* pescare) di frodo ♦ *vi* fare il bracconiere.

poached [pōcht] *a* (*egg*) affogato(a).

poacher [pō'chûr] *n* bracconiere *m*.

poaching [pō'ching] *n* caccia (*or* pesca) di frodo.

PO Box *n abbr see* **Post Office Box**.

pocket [pâk'it] *n* tasca ♦ *vt* intascare; **air ~** vuoto d'aria.

pocketbook [pâk'itbŏŏk] *n* (*US*: *handbag*) busta; (*wallet*) portafoglio; (*notebook*) taccuino.

pocket knife *n* temperino.

pocket money *n* paghetta, settimana.

pockmarked [pâk'mârkt] *a* (*face*) butterato(a).

pod [pâd] *n* guscio ♦ *vt* sgusciare.

podgy [pâj'ē] *a* grassoccio(a).

podiatrist [pədī'ətrist] *n* (*US*) callista *m/f*, pedicure *m/f*.

podiatry [pədī'ətrē] *n* (*US*) mestiere *m* di callista.

podium [pō'dēəm] *n* podio.

POE n abbr = port of embarkation; port of entry.

poem |pō'əm| n poesia.

poet |pō'it| n poeta/essa.

poetic |pōet'ik| a poetico(a).

poet laureate |pō'it lô'rēit| n (Brit) poeta m laureato (nominato dalla Corte Reale).

poetry |pō'itrē| n poesia.

poignant |poin'yənt| a struggente.

point |point| n (gen) punto; (tip: of needle etc) punta; (Brit ELEC: also: **power ~**) presa (di corrente); (in time) punto, momento; (SCOL) voto; (main idea, important part) nocciolo; (also: **decimal ~**): **2 ~ 3 (2.3)** 2 virgola 3 (2,3) ♦ vt (show) indicare; (gun etc): **to ~ sth at** puntare qc contro ♦ vi mostrare a dito; **~s** npl (AUT) puntine fpl; (RAIL) scambio; **to ~ to** indicare; (fig) dimostrare; **to make a ~** fare un'osservazione; **to get the ~** capire; **to come to the ~** venire al fatto; **when it comes to the ~** quando si arriva al dunque; **to be on the ~ of doing sth** essere sul punto di or stare (proprio) per fare qc; **to be beside the ~** non entrarci; **to make a ~ of doing sth** non mancare di fare qc; **there's no ~ (in doing)** è inutile (fare); **in ~ of fact** a dire il vero; **that's the whole ~!** precisamente!, sta tutto lì!; **you've got a ~ there!** giusto!, ha ragione!; **the train stops at Boston and all ~s south** il treno ferma a Boston e in tutte le stazioni a sud di Boston; **good ~s** vantaggi mpl; (of person) qualità fpl; **~ of departure** (also fig) punto di partenza; **~ of order** mozione f d'ordine; **~ of sale** (COMM) punto di vendita; **~ of view** punto di vista.

point out vt far notare.

point-blank |point'blangk'| ad (also: **at ~ range**) a bruciapelo; (fig) categoricamente.

pointed |poin'tid| a (shape) aguzzo(a), appuntito(a); (remark) specifico(a).

pointedly |poin'tidlē| ad in maniera inequivocabile.

pointer |poin'tûr| n (stick) bacchetta; (needle) lancetta; (clue) indizio; (advice) consiglio; (dog) pointer m, cane m da punta.

pointless |point'lis| a inutile, vano(a).

poise |poiz| n (balance) equilibrio; (of head, body) portamento; (calmness) calma ♦ vt tenere in equilibrio; **to be ~d for** (fig) essere pronto(a) a.

poison |poi'zən| n veleno ♦ vt avvelenare.

poisoning |poi'zəning| n avvelenamento.

poisonous |poi'zənəs| a velenoso(a); (fumes) venefico(a), tossico(a); (ideas, literature) pernicioso(a); (rumors, individual) perfido(a).

poke |pōk| vt (fire) attizzare; (jab with finger, stick etc) punzecchiare; (put): **to ~ sth in(to)** spingere qc dentro ♦ n (jab) colpetto; (with elbow) gomitata; **to ~ one's head out**

of the window mettere la testa fuori dalla finestra; **to ~ fun at sb** prendere in giro qn.

poke around vi frugare.

poker |pō'kûr| n attizzatoio; (CARDS) poker m.

poker-faced |pō'kûrfāst'| a dal viso impassibile.

poky |pō'kē| a piccolo(a) e stretto(a).

Poland |pō'lənd| n Polonia.

polar |pō'lûr| a polare.

polar bear n orso bianco.

polarize |pō'lərīz| vt polarizzare.

Pole |pōl| n polacco/a.

pole |pōl| n (of wood) palo; (ELEC, GEO) polo.

pole bean n (US) fagiolino.

polecat |pōl'kat| n puzzola; (US: skunk) moffetta.

Pol. Econ. n abbr = political economy.

polemic |pəlem'ik| n polemica.

pole star n stella polare.

pole vault n salto con l'asta.

police |pəlēs'| n polizia ♦ vt mantenere l'ordine in; (streets, city, frontier) presidiare; **a large number of ~ were hurt** molti poliziotti sono rimasti feriti.

police captain n (US) commissario (capo).

police car n macchina della polizia.

police constable (PC) n (Brit) agente m di polizia.

police department n (US) dipartimento di polizia.

police force n corpo di polizia, polizia.

policeman |pəlēs'mən| n poliziotto, agente m di polizia; (US: also: **traffic ~**) addetto al controllo del traffico e del parcheggio.

police officer n = **police constable**.

police record n: **to have a ~** avere precedenti penali.

police state n stato di polizia.

police station n posto di polizia.

policewoman |pəlēs'wŏŏmən| n donna f poliziotto inv.

policy |pâl'isē| n politica; (of newspaper, company) linea di condotta, prassi f inv; (also: **insurance ~**) polizza (d'assicurazione); **to take out a ~** (INSURANCE) stipulare una polizza di assicurazione.

policy holder n assicurato/a.

polio |pō'lēō| n polio f.

Polish |pō'lish| a polacco(a) ♦ n (LING) polacco.

polish |pâl'ish| n (for shoes) lucido; (for floor) cera; (for nails) smalto; (shine) lucentezza, lustro; (fig: refinement) raffinatezza ♦ vt lucidare; (fig: improve) raffinare.

polish off vt (work) sbrigare; (food) mangiarsi.

polished |pâl'isht| a (fig) raffinato(a).

polite |pəlīt'| a cortese; **it's not ~ to do that** non è educato or buona educazione fare questo.

politely |pəlīt'lē| ad cortesemente.

politeness [pəlīt'nis] *n* cortesia.
politic [pâl'itik] *a* diplomatico(a).
political [pəlit'ikəl] *a* politico(a).
political asylum *n* asilo politico.
politically [pəlit'iklē] *ad* politicamente.
politician [pâlitish'ən] *n* politico.
politics [pâl'itiks] *n* politica ♦ *npl* idee *fpl* politiche.
polka [pōl'kə] *n* polca.
polka dot *n* pois *m inv.*
poll [pōl] *n* scrutinio; (*votes cast*) voti *mpl*; (*also*: **opinion ~**) sondaggio (d'opinioni) ♦ *vt* ottenere; **to go to the ~s** (*voters*) andare alle urne; (*government*) indire le elezioni.
pollen [pâl'ən] *n* polline *m.*
pollen count *n* tasso di polline nell'aria.
pollination [pâlənā'shən] *n* impollinazione *f.*
polling [pō'ling] *n* (*Brit POL*) votazione *f*, votazioni *fpl*; (*TEL*) interrogazione *f* ciclica.
pollute [pəlōōt'] *vt* inquinare.
pollution [pəlōō'shən] *n* inquinamento.
polo [pō'lō] *n* polo.
polo neck *n* collo alto; (*also*: **~ sweater**) dolcevita ♦ *a* a collo alto.
poly [pâl'ē] *n abbr* = **polytechnic.**
polyester [pâlēes'tûr] *n* poliestere *m.*
polygamy [pəlig'əmē] *n* poligamia.
Polynesia [pâlinē'zhə] *n* Polinesia.
Polynesian [pâlənē'zhən] *a, n* polinesiano(a).
polyp [pâl'ip] *n* (*MED*) polipo.
polystyrene [pâlēstī'rēn] *n* polistirolo.
polytechnic [pâlētek'nik] *n* (*college*) istituto superiore ad indirizzo tecnologico.
polythene [pâl'əthēn] *n* politene *m.*
polythene bag *n* sacco di plastica.
polyurethane [pâlēyōōr'əthān] *n* poliuretano.
pomegranate [pâm'əgranit] *n* melagrana.
pommel [pum'əl] *n* pomo ♦ *vt* = **pummel.**
pomp [pâmp] *n* pompa, fasto.
pompom [pâm'pâm], **pompon** [pâm'pân] *n* pompon *m inv.*
pompous [pâm'pəs] *a* pomposo(a); (*person*) pieno(a) di boria.
pond [pând] *n* stagno; (*in park*) laghetto.
ponder [pân'dûr] *vi* riflettere, meditare ♦ *vt* ponderare, riflettere su.
ponderous [pân'dûrəs] *a* ponderoso(a), pesante.
pong [pông] (*Brit col*) *n* puzzo ♦ *vi* puzzare.
pontiff [pân'tif] *n* pontefice *m.*
pontificate [pântif'ikāt] *vi* (*fig*): **to ~ (about)** pontificare (su).
pontoon [pântōōn'] *n* pontone *m*; (*CARDS*) ventuno.
pony [pō'nē] *n* pony *m inv.*
ponytail [pō'nētāl] *n* coda di cavallo.
pony trekking [pō'nē trek'ing] *n* (*Brit*) escursione *f* a cavallo.
poodle [pōō'dəl] *n* barboncino, barbone *m.*
pooh-pooh [pōōpōō'] *vt* deridere.
pool [pōōl] *n* (*of rain*) pozza; (*pond*) stagno;

(*artificial*) vasca; (*also*: **swimming ~**) piscina; (*sth shared*) fondo comune; (*COMM: consortium*) pool *m inv*; (*US: monopoly trust*) trust *m inv*; (*billiards*) specie di biliardo a buca ♦ *vt* mettere in comune; **secretary ~**, (*Brit*) **typing ~** servizio comune di dattilografia; **to do the (football) ~s** (*Brit*) ≈ fare la schedina, giocare al totocalcio.
pooped [pōōpt] *a* (*US col: tired*) sfinito(a), a pezzi.
poor [pōōr] *a* povero(a); (*mediocre*) mediocre, cattivo(a) ♦ *npl*: **the ~** i poveri.
poorly [pōōr'lē] *ad* poveramente; (*badly*) male ♦ *a* indisposto(a), malato(a).
pop [pâp] *n* (*noise*) schiocco; (*MUS*) musica pop; (*US col: father*) babbo; (*col: drink*) bevanda gasata ♦ *vt* (*put*) mettere (in fretta) ♦ *vi* scoppiare; (*cork*) schioccare; **she ~ped her head out** (*of the window*) sporse fuori la testa.
pop in *vi* passare.
pop out *vi* fare un salto fuori.
pop up *vi* apparire, sorgere.
pop concert *n* concerto *m* pop *inv.*
popcorn [pâp'kôrn] *n* pop-corn *m.*
pope [pōp] *n* papa *m.*
poplar [pâp'lûr] *n* pioppo.
poplin [pâp'lin] *n* popeline *f.*
poppy [pâp'ē] *n* papavero.
poppycock [pâp'ēkâk] *n* (*col*) scempiaggini *fpl.*
Popsicle [pâp'sikəl] ® *n* (*US*) ghiacciolo.
populace [pâp'yələs] *n* popolo.
popular [pâp'yəlûr] *a* popolare; (*fashionable*) in voga; **to be ~ (with)** (*person*) essere benvoluto(a) *or* ben visto(a) (da); (*decision*) essere gradito(a) (a); **a ~ song** una canzone di successo.
popularity [pâpyəlar'itē] *n* popolarità.
popularize [pâp'yələrīz] *vt* divulgare; (*science*) volgarizzare.
populate [pâp'yəlāt] *vt* popolare.
population [pâpyəlā'shən] *n* popolazione *f.*
population explosion *n* forte espansione *f* demografica.
populous [pâp'yələs] *a* popolato(a).
porcelain [pôr'səlin] *n* porcellana.
porch [pôrch] *n* veranda.
porcupine [pôr'kyəpīn] *n* porcospino.
pore [pôr] *n* poro ♦ *vi*: **to ~ over** essere immerso(a) in.
pork [pôrk] *n* carne *f* di maiale.
pork chop *n* braciola *or* costoletta di maiale.
pornographic [pôrnəgraf'ik] *a* pornografico(a).
pornography [pôrnâ'grəfē] *n* pornografia.
porous [pôr'əs] *a* poroso(a).
porpoise [pôr'pəs] *n* focena.
porridge [pôr'ij] *n* porridge *m.*
port [pôrt] *n* porto; (*opening in ship*) portello; (*NAUT: left side*) babordo; (*COMPUT*) porta;

(*wine*) porto; **to** ~ (*NAUT*) a babordo; ~ **of call** (porto di) scalo.

portable [pôr'təbəl] *a* portatile.

portal [pôr'təl] *n* portale *m*.

portcullis [pôrtkul'is] *n* saracinesca.

portent [pôr'tent] *n* presagio.

porter [pôr'tûr] *n* (*US RAIL*) addetto ai vagoni letto; (*for luggage*) facchino, portabagagli *m inv*; (*doorkeeper*) portiere *m*, portinaio.

portfolio [pôrtfō'lēō] *n* (*POL*: *office*; *ECON*) portafoglio; (*of artist*) raccolta dei propri lavori.

porthole [pôrt'hōl] *n* oblò *m inv*.

portico [pôr'tikō] *n* portico.

portion [pôr'shən] *n* porzione *f*.

portly [pôrt'lē] *a* corpulento(a).

portrait [pôr'trit] *n* ritratto.

portray [pôrtrā'] *vt* fare il ritratto di; (*character on stage*) rappresentare; (*in writing*) ritrarre.

portrayal [pôrtrā'əl] *n* ritratto; rappresentazione *f*.

Portugal [pôr'chəgəl] *n* Portogallo.

Portuguese [pôrchəgēz'] *a* portoghese ♦ *n* (*pl inv*) portoghese *m/f*; (*LING*) portoghese *m*.

Portuguese man-of-war [pôrchəgēz' manəvwôr'] *n* (*jellyfish*) medusa.

pose [pōz] *n* posa ♦ *vi* posare; (*pretend*): **to** ~ **as** atteggiarsi a, posare a ♦ *vt* porre; **to strike a** ~ mettersi in posa.

poser [pō'zûr] *n* domanda difficile; (*person*) = **poseur.**

poseur [pōzir'] *n* (*pej*) persona affettata.

posh [pásh] *a* (*col*) elegante; (*family*) per bene ♦ *ad* (*col*): **to talk** ~ parlare in modo snob.

position [pəzish'ən] *n* posizione *f*; (*job*) posto ♦ *vt* mettere in posizione, collocare; **to be in a** ~ **to do sth** essere nella posizione di fare qc.

positive [páz'ətiv] *a* positivo(a); (*certain*) sicuro(a), certo(a); (*definite*) preciso(a); definitivo(a).

posse [pás'ē] *n* (*US*) drappello.

possess [pəzes'] *vt* possedere; **like one** ~**ed** come un ossesso; **what ever** ~**ed you?** cosa ti ha preso?

possession [pəzesh'ən] *n* possesso; (*object*) bene *m*; **to take** ~ **of sth** impossessarsi *or* impadronirsi di qc.

possessive [pəzes'iv] *a* possessivo(a).

possessively [pəzes'ivlē] *ad* in modo possessivo.

possessor [pəzes'úr] *n* possessore/posseditrice.

possibility [pásəbil'ətē] *n* possibilità *f inv*; **he's a** ~ **for the part** è uno dei candidati per la parte.

possible [pás'əbəl] *a* possibile; **it is** ~ **to do it** è possibile farlo; **if** ~ se possibile; **as big as** ~ il più grande possibile; **as far as** ~ nei limiti del possibile.

possibly [pás'əblē] *ad* (*perhaps*) forse; **if you** ~ **can** se le è possibile; **I cannot** ~ **come** proprio non posso venire.

post [pōst] *n* (*Brit*: *mail, letters, delivery*) posta; (: *collection*) levata; (*job, situation*) posto; (*pole*) palo; (*trading* ~) stazione *f* commerciale ♦ *vt* (*Brit*: *send by post*) impostare; (*MIL*) appostare; (*notice*) affiggere; (*Brit*: *appoint*): **to** ~ **to** assegnare a; **by** ~ (*Brit*) per posta; **by return of** ~ (*Brit*) a giro di posta; **to keep sb** ~**ed** tenere qn al corrente.

post... *prefix* post...; ~**-1990** dopo il 1990.

postage [pōs'tij] *n* affrancatura.

postage paid *a* già affrancato(a).

postage stamp *n* francobollo.

postal [pōs'təl] *a* postale.

postal order *n* (*Brit*) vaglia *m inv* postale.

postbag [pōst'bag] *n* (*Brit*) sacco postale, sacco della posta.

postbox [pōst'báks] *n* cassetta delle lettere.

postcard [pōst'kárd] *n* cartolina.

postcode [pōst'kōd] *n* (*Brit*) codice *m* (di avviamento) postale.

postdate [pōst'dāt] *vt* (*check*) postdatare.

poster [pōs'tûr] *n* manifesto, affisso.

posterior [pástēr'ēûr] *n* (*col*) deretano, didietro.

posterity [pástär'itē] *n* posterità.

poster paint *n* tempera.

post exchange (PX) *n* (*US MIL*) spaccio militare.

post-free [pōst'frē'] *a, ad* (*Brit*) franco di porto.

postgraduate [pōstgraj'ōōit] *n* laureato/a che continua gli studi.

posthumous [pás'chəməs] *a* postumo(a).

posthumously [pás'chəməslē] *ad* dopo la mia (*or* sua *etc*) morte.

postman [pōst'mən] *n* postino.

postmark [pōst'márk] *n* bollo *or* timbro postale.

postmaster [pōst'mastûr] *n* direttore *m* di un ufficio postale.

Postmaster General *n* ≈ ministro delle Poste.

postmistress [pōst'mistris] *n* direttrice *f* di un ufficio postale.

postmortem [pōstmôr'təm] *n* autopsia; (*fig*) analisi *f inv* a posteriori.

postnatal [pōstnāt'əl] *a* post-parto *inv*.

post office *n* (*building*) ufficio postale; (*organization*) poste *fpl*.

post office box (PO box) *n* casella postale (C.P.).

postpone [pōstpōn'] *vt* rinviare.

postponement [pōstpōn'mənt] *n* rinvio.

postscript [pōst'skript] *n* poscritto.

postulate [pás'chəlāt] *vt* postulare.

posture [pás'chûr] *n* portamento; (*pose*) posa, atteggiamento ♦ *vi* posare.

post-viral syndrome [pōstvī'rəl sin'drōm] *n* sindrome *f* post-virale.

postwar [pōst'wôr'] *a* del dopoguerra.

posy [pō'zē] *n* mazzetto di fiori.

pot [pát] *n* (*for cooking*) pentola; casseruola; (*for plants, jam*) vaso; (*piece of pottery*) ceramica; (*col: marijuana*) erba ♦ *vt* (*plant*) piantare in vaso; **to go to ~** (*col*) andare in malora; **~s of** (*Brit col*) un sacco di.

potash [pát'ash] *n* potassa.

potassium [pətas'ēəm] *n* potassio.

potato, ~es [pətā'tō] *n* patata.

potato chips, (*Brit*) **potato crisps** *npl* patatine *fpl.*

potato flour *n* fecola di patate.

potato peeler [pətā'tō pē'lûr] *n* sbucciapatate *m inv.*

potbellied [pát'belēd] *a* (*from overeating*) panciuto(a); (*from malnutrition*) dal ventre gonfio.

potency [pōt'ənsē] *n* potenza; (*of drink*) forza.

potent [pōt'ənt] *a* potente, forte.

potentate [pōt'əntāt] *n* potentato.

potential [pəten'chəl] *a* potenziale ♦ *n* possibilità *fpl*; **to have ~** essere promettente.

potentially [pəten'chəlē] *ad* potenzialmente.

pothole [pát'hōl] *n* (*in road*) buca; (*Brit: underground*) marmitta.

potholer [pát'hōlûr] *n* (*Brit*) speleologo/a.

potion [pō'shən] *n* pozione *f.*

potluck [pát'luk] *n*: **to take ~** tentare la sorte.

potpourri [pōpərē'] *n* (*dried petals etc*) miscuglio di petali essiccati profumati; (*fig*) pot-pourri *m inv.*

pot roast *n* brasato.

potshot [pát'shát] *n*: **to take ~s at** tirare a casaccio contro.

potted [pát'id] *a* (*food*) in conserva; (*plant*) in vaso; (*fig: shortened*) condensato(a).

potter [pát'ûr] *n* vasaio ♦ *vi* (*Brit*) = **putter**; **~'s wheel** tornio (da vasaio).

pottery [pát'ûrē] *n* ceramiche *fpl*; **a piece of ~** una ceramica.

potty [pát'ē] *n* (*child's*) vasino.

potty-trained [pát'ētránd] *a* che ha imparato a farla nel vasino.

pouch [pouch] *n* borsa; (*ZOOL*) marsupio.

pouf(fe) [pōōf] *n* (*stool*) pouf *m inv.*

poultice [pōl'tis] *n* impiastro, cataplasma *m.*

poultry [pōl'trē] *n* pollame *m.*

poultry farm *n* azienda avicola.

poultry farmer *n* pollicoltore/trice.

pounce [pouns] *vi*: **to ~ (on)** balzare addosso (a), piombare (su) ♦ *n* balzo.

pound [pound] *n* (*weight* = 453g, 16 ounces) libbra; (*for dogs*) canile *m* municipale; (*Brit: money* = 100 pence) (lira) sterlina ♦ *vt* (*beat*) battere; (*crush*) pestare, polverizzare ♦ *vi* (*beat*) battere, martellare; **half a ~** mezza libbra; **a five-~ note** una banconota da cinque sterline.

pounding [poun'ding] *n*: **to take a ~** (*fig*) prendere una batosta.

pound sterling *n* sterlina.

pour [pôr] *vt* versare ♦ *vi* riversarsi; (*rain*) piovere a dirotto.

pour away, pour off *vt* vuotare.

pour in *vi* (*people*) entrare in fiotto; **to come ~ing in** (*water*) entrare a fiotti; (*letters*) arrivare a valanghe; (*cars, people*) affluire in gran quantità.

pour out *vi* (*people*) riversarsi fuori ♦ *vt* vuotare; versare.

pouring [pôr'ing] *a*: **~ rain** pioggia torrenziale.

pout [pout] *vi* sporgere le labbra; fare il broncio.

poverty [pâv'ûrtē] *n* povertà, miseria.

poverty-stricken [pâv'ûrtēstrikən] *a* molto povero(a), misero(a).

POW *n abbr* = **prisoner of war.**

powder [pou'dûr] *n* polvere *f* ♦ *vt* spolverizzare; (*face*) incipriare; **~ed milk** latte *m* in polvere; **to ~ one's nose** incipriarsi il naso; (*euphemism*) andare alla toilette.

powder compact *n* portacipria *m inv.*

powdered sugar [pou'dûrd shōōg'ûr] *n* (*US*) zucchero semolato.

powder puff *n* piumino della cipria.

powder room *n* toilette *f inv* (per signore).

powdery [pou'dûrē] *a* polveroso(a).

power [pou'ûr] *n* (*strength*) potenza, forza; (*ability, POL: of party, leader*) potere *m*; (*MATH*) potenza; (*ELEC*) corrente *f* ♦ *vt* fornire di energia; azionare; **to be in ~** essere al potere; **to do all in one's ~ to help sb** fare tutto quello che si può per aiutare qn; **the world ~s** le grandi potenze; **mental ~s** capacità *fpl* mentali.

power cut *n* (*Brit*) interruzione *f or* mancanza di corrente.

power-driven [pou'ûrdrivən] *a* a motore; (*ELEC*) elettrico(a).

powered [pou'ûrd] *a*: **~ by** azionato(a) da; **nuclear-~ submarine** sottomarino a propulsione atomica.

power failure *n* guasto alla linea elettrica.

powerful [pou'ûrfəl] *a* potente, forte.

powerhouse [pou'ûrhous] *n* (*fig: person*) persona molto dinamica; **a ~ of ideas** una miniera di idee.

powerless [pou'ûrlis] *a* impotente, senza potere.

power line *n* linea elettrica.

power outage [pou'ûr out'ij] *n* (*US*) interruzione *f or* mancanza di corrente.

power station *n* centrale *f* elettrica.

power steering *n* (*AUT: also:* **power-assisted steering**) servosterzo.

powwow [pou'wou] *n* riunione *f.*

pp *abbr* (= *pages*) pp.; (= *per procurationem*: *by proxy*): **~ J. Smith** per il Signor J. Smith.

p&p *abbr* (*Brit:* = *postage and packing*) affrancatura ed imballaggio.

PPS *n abbr* = *post-scriptum.*

PQ *abbr* (*Canada*) = *Province of Quebec.*

PR *n abbr* (*US MAIL*) = *Puerto Rico* ♦ *abbr see* **proportional representation; public relations.**

Pr. *abbr* = **prince.**

practicability |praktikəbil'ətē| *n* praticabilità.

practicable |prak'tikəbəl| *a* (*scheme*) praticabile.

practical |prak'tikəl| *a* pratico(a).

practicality |praktikal'itē| *n* (*of plan*) fattibilità; (*of person*) senso pratico; **practicalities** dettagli *mpl* pratici.

practical joke *n* beffa.

practically |prak'tiklē| *ad* (*almost*) quasi, praticamente.

practice |prak'tis| *n* pratica; (*of profession*) esercizio; (*at football etc*) allenamento; (*business*) gabinetto; clientela ♦ *vb* (*US*) *vt* (*work at: piano, one's backhand etc*) esercitarsi a; (*train for: skiing, running etc*) allenarsi a; (*a sport, religion*) praticare; (*method*) usare; (*profession*) esercitare ♦ *vi* esercitarsi; (*train*) allenarsi; **in ~** (*in reality*) in pratica; **out of ~** fuori esercizio; **2 hours' piano ~** 2 ore di esercizio al pianoforte; **it's common ~** è d'uso; **to put sth into ~** mettere qc in pratica; **target ~** pratica di tiro; **to ~ for a match** allenarsi per una partita.

practiced |prak'tist| *a* (*person*) esperto(a); (*performance*) da virtuoso(a); (*liar*) matricolato(a); **with a ~ eye** con occhio esperto.

practicing |prak'tising| *a* (*Christian etc*) praticante; (*lawyer*) che esercita la professione; (*homosexual*) attivo(a).

practise |prak'tis| *vb* (*Brit*) = **practice.**

practitioner |praktish'ənŭr| *n* professionista *m/f*; (*MED*) medico.

pragmatic |pragmat'ik| *a* prammatico(a).

Prague |prâg| *n* Praga.

prairie |prär'ē| *n* prateria.

praise |prāz| *n* elogio, lode *f* ♦ *vt* elogiare, lodare.

praiseworthy |prāz'wûrthē| *a* lodevole.

pram |pram| *n* (*Brit*) carrozzina.

prance |prans| *vi* (*horse*) impennarsi.

prank |prangk| *n* burla.

prattle |prat'əl| *vi* cinguettare.

prawn |prôn| *n* gamberetto.

pray |prā| *vi* pregare.

prayer |prär| *n* preghiera.

prayer book *n* libro di preghiere.

pre... |prē| *prefix* pre...; **~-1970** prima del 1970.

preach |prēch| *vt, vi* predicare; **to ~ at sb** fare la predica a qn.

preacher |prē'chŭr| *n* predicatore/trice; (*clergyman*) pastore *m.*

preamble |prē'ambəl| *n* preambolo.

prearranged |prēərānjd'| *a* organizzato(a) in anticipo.

precarious |prikär'ēəs| *a* precario(a).

precaution |prikô'shən| *n* precauzione *f.*

precautionary |prikô'shənärē| *a* (*measure*) precauzionale.

precede |prisēd'| *vt, vi* precedere.

precedence |pres'idəns| *n* precedenza; **to take ~ over** avere la precedenza su.

precedent |pres'idənt| *n* precedente *m*; **to establish** *or* **set a ~** creare un precedente.

preceding |prisē'ding| *a* precedente.

precept |prē'sept| *n* precetto.

precinct |prē'singkt| *n* (*round cathedral*) recinto; (*US: district*) circoscrizione *f*; (*: of policeman*) giro; **~s** *npl* (*neighborhood*) dintorni *mpl*, vicinanze *fpl*; **pedestrian ~** zona pedonale; **shopping ~** (*Brit*) centro commerciale.

precious |presh'əs| *a* prezioso(a) ♦ *ad* (*col*): **~ little/few** ben poco/pochi.

precipice |pres'əpis| *n* precipizio.

precipitate *a* |prisip'itit| (*hasty*) precipitoso(a) ♦ *vt* |prisip'itāt| accelerare.

precipitation |prisipitā'shən| *n* precipitazione *f.*

precipitous |prisip'itəs| *a* (*steep*) erto(a), ripido(a).

précis, *pl* **précis** |prā'sē, -sēz| *n* riassunto.

precise |prisīs'| *a* preciso(a).

precisely |prisīs'lē| *ad* precisamente; **~!** appunto!

precision |prisizh'ən| *n* precisione *f.*

preclude |priklōōd'| *vt* precludere, impedire; **to ~ sb from doing** impedire a qn di fare.

precocious |prikō'shəs| *a* precoce.

preconceived |prēkənsēvd'| *a* (*idea*) preconcetto(a).

preconception |prēkənsep'shən| *n* preconcetto.

precondition |prēkəndish'ən| *n* condizione *f* necessaria.

precursor |prikûr'sûr| *n* precursore *m.*

predate |prēdāt'| *vt* (*precede*) precedere.

predator |pred'ətûr| *n* predatore *m.*

predatory |pred'ətôrē| *a* predatore(trice).

predecessor |pred'isesûr| *n* predecessore/a.

predestination |prēdestinā'shən| *n* predestinazione *f.*

predetermine |prēditûr'min| *vt* predeterminare.

predicament |pridik'əmənt| *n* situazione *f* difficile.

predicate |pred'əkit| *n* (*LING*) predicativo.

predict |pridikt'| *vt* predire.

predictable |pridikt'əbəl| *a* prevedibile.

predictably |pridikt'əblē| *ad* (*behave, react*) in modo prevedibile; **~ she didn't arrive** come era da prevedere, non è arrivata.

prediction |pridik'shən| *n* predizione *f.*

predispose [prēdispōz'] *vt* predisporre.
predominance [pridâm'ənəns] *n* predominanza.
predominant [pridâm'ənənt] *a* predominante.
predominantly [pridâm'ənəntlē] *ad* in maggior parte; soprattutto.
predominate [pridâm'ənāt] *vi* predominare.
preeminent [prēem'ənənt] *a* preminente.
preempt [prēempt'] *vt* acquistare per diritto di prelazione; *(fig)* anticipare.
preemptive [prēemp'tiv] *a*: ~ **strike** azione *f* preventiva.
preen [prēn] *vt*: **to** ~ **itself** *(bird)* lisciarsi le penne; **to** ~ **o.s.** agghindarsi.
prefab [prē'fab'] *n* casa prefabbricata.
prefabricated [prēfab'rikātid] *a* prefabbricato(a).
preface [pref'is] *n* prefazione *f*.
prefect [prē'fekt] *n* (*Brit: in school*) studente/ essa con funzioni disciplinari; (*in Italy*) prefetto.
prefer [prifûr'] *vt* preferire; (*LAW: charges, complaint*) sporgere; (*: action*) intentare; **to** ~ **coffee to tea** preferire il caffè al tè.
preferable [pref'ûrəbəl] *a* preferibile.
preferably [prifûr'əblē] *ad* preferibilmente.
preference [pref'ûrəns] *n* preferenza; **in** ~ **to sth** piuttosto che qc.
preference shares *npl* (*Brit*) = **preferred stock.**
preferential [prefəren'chəl] *a* preferenziale; ~ **treatment** trattamento di favore.
preferred stock [prifûrd' stâk] *npl* (*US*) azioni *fpl* privilegiate.
prefix [prē'fiks] *n* prefisso.
pregnancy [preg'nənsē] *n* gravidanza.
pregnant [preg'nənt] *a* incinta *af*; (*animal*) gravido(a); (*fig: remark, pause*) significativo(a); **3 months** ~ incinta di 3 mesi.
prehistoric [prēhistôr'ik] *a* preistorico(a).
prehistory [prēhis'tûrē] *n* preistoria.
prejudge [prējuj'] *vt* pregiudicare.
prejudice [prej'ədis] *n* pregiudizio; (*harm*) torto, danno ♦ *vt* pregiudicare, ledere; (*bias*): **to** ~ **sb in favor of/against** disporre bene/male qn verso.
prejudiced [prej'ədist] *a* (*person*) pieno(a) di pregiudizi; (*view*) prevenuto(a); **to be** ~ **against sb/sth** essere prevenuto contro qn/qc.
prelate [prel'it] *n* prelato.
preliminaries [prilim'ənârēz] *npl* preliminari *mpl*.
preliminary [prilim'ənärē] *a* preliminare.
prelude [prā'lōōd] *n* preludio.
premarital [prēmar'itəl] *a* prematrimoniale.
premature [prēməchōōr'] *a* prematuro(a); (*arrival*) (molto) anticipato(a); **you are being a little** ~ è un po' troppo precipitoso.
premeditated [primed'ətātid] *a* premeditato(a).
premeditation [primeditā'shən] *n* premedita-

zione *f*.
premenstrual tension [prēmen'strōōəl ten'chən] *n* (*MED*) tensione *f* premestruale.
premier [primyēr'] *a* primo(a) ♦ *n* (*POL*) primo ministro.
première [primyēr'] *n* prima.
premise [prem'is] *n* premessa.
premises [prem'isiz] *npl* locale *m*; **on the** ~ sul posto; **business** ~ locali commerciali.
premium [prē'mēəm] *n* premio; **to be at a** ~ (*fig: housing etc*) essere ricercatissimo; **to sell at a** ~ (*shares*) vendere sopra la pari.
premium bond *n* (*Brit*) obbligazione *f* a premio.
premium deal *n* (*COMM*) offerta speciale.
premium gas(oline) *n* (*US*) super *f*.
premonition [premənish'ən] *n* premonizione *f*.
prenatal [prēnāt'l] *a* (*US*) prenatale.
preoccupation [prēăkyəpā'shən] *n* preoccupazione *f*.
preoccupied [prēăk'yəpīd] *a* preoccupato(a).
prep [prep] *a* *abbr*: ~ **school** = **preparatory school.**
prepackaged [prēpak'ijd] *a* già impacchettato(a).
prepaid [prēpād'] *a* pagato(a) in anticipo; (*envelope*) affrancato(a).
preparation [prepərā'shən] *n* preparazione *f*; ~**s** *npl* (*for trip, war*) preparativi *mpl*; **in** ~ **for sth** in vista di qc.
preparatory [pripar'ətôrē] *a* preparatorio(a); ~ **to sth/to doing sth** prima di qc/di fare qc.
preparatory school *n* (*US*) scuola superiore privata in preparazione al college; (*Brit*) scuola elementare privata.
prepare [pripâr'] *vt* preparare ♦ *vi*: **to** ~ **for** prepararsi a.
prepared [pripärd'] *a*: ~ **for** preparato(a) a; ~ **to** pronto(a) a; **to be** ~ **to help sb** (*willing*) essere disposto or pronto ad aiutare qn.
preponderance [pripân'dûrəns] *n* preponderanza.
preposition [prepəzish'ən] *n* preposizione *f*.
prepossessing [prēpəzes'ing] *a* simpatico(a), attraente.
preposterous [pripâs'tûrəs] *a* assurdo(a).
prerecord [prērikôrd'] *vt* registrare in anticipo; ~**ed broadcast** trasmissione *f* registrata; ~**ed cassette** (*musi*)cassetta.
prerequisite [prirek'wizit] *n* requisito indispensabile.
prerogative [prərâg'ətiv] *n* prerogativa.
presbyterian [prezbitēr'ēən] *a*, *n* presbiteriano(a).
presbytery [prez'bitärē] *n* presbiterio.
preschool [prē'skōōl'] *a* (*age*) prescolastico(a); (*child*) in età prescolastica.
prescribe [priskrīb'] *vt* prescrivere; (*MED*) ordinare.
prescription [priskrip'shən] *n* prescrizione *f*;

(*MED*) ricetta; **to fill a** ~ preparare *or* fare una ricetta.

prescriptive [priskrip'tiv] *a* normativo(a).

presence [prez'əns] *n* presenza; ~ **of mind** presenza di spirito.

present [prez'ənt] *a* presente; (*wife, residence, job*) attuale ♦ *n* regalo; (*also*: ~ **tense**) tempo presente ♦ *vt* [prizent'] presentare; (*give*): **to** ~ **sb with sth** offrire qc a qn; **to be** ~ **at** essere presente a; **those** ~ i presenti; **at** ~ al momento; **to make sb a** ~ **of sth** regalare qc a qn.

presentable [prizen'təbəl] *a* presentabile.

presentation [prezəntā'shən] *n* presentazione *f*; (*gift*) regalo, dono; (*ceremony*) consegna ufficiale; **on** ~ **of the voucher** dietro presentazione del buono.

present-day [prez'əntdā'] *a* attuale, d'oggigiorno.

presenter [prizen'tûr] *n* (*RADIO*, *TV*) presentatore/trice.

presently [prez'əntlē] *ad* (*US: now*) adesso, ora; (*soon*) fra poco, presto; (*at present*) al momento.

preservation [prezûrvā'shən] *n* preservazione *f*, conservazione *f*.

preservative [prizûr'vətiv] *n* conservante *m*.

preserve [prizûrv'] *vt* (*keep safe*) preservare, proteggere; (*maintain*) conservare; (*food*) mettere in conserva ♦ *n* (*for game, fish*) riserva; (*often pl: jam*) marmellata; (: *fruit*) frutta sciroppata.

preshrunk [prē'shrungk'] *a* irrestringibile.

preside [prizīd'] *vi* presiedere.

presidency [prez'idənsē] *n* presidenza; (*US: of company*) direzione *f*.

president [prez'idənt] *n* presidente *m*; (*US: of company*) direttore/trice generale.

presidential [prezidən'chəl] *a* presidenziale.

press [pres] *n* (*tool, machine*) pressa; (*for wine*) torchio; (*newspapers*) stampa; (*crowd*) folla ♦ *vt* (*push*) premere, pigiare; (*doorbell*) suonare; (*squeeze*) spremere; (: *hand*) stringere; (*clothes: iron*) stirare; (*pursue*) incalzare; (*insist*): **to** ~ **sth on sb** far accettare qc da qn; (*urge, entreat*): **to** ~ **sb to do** *or* **into doing sth** fare pressione su qn affinché faccia qc ♦ *vi* premere, accalcarsi; **to go to** ~ (*newspaper*) andare in macchina; **to be in the** ~ (*in the newspapers*) essere sui giornali; **we are** ~**ed for time** ci manca il tempo; **to** ~ **for sth** insistere per avere qc; **to** ~ **sb for an answer** insistere perché qn risponda; **to** ~ **charges against sb** (*LAW*) sporgere una denuncia contro qn.

press on *vi* continuare.

press agency *n* agenzia di stampa.

press clipping *n* ritaglio di giornale.

press conference *n* conferenza stampa.

press cutting *n* (*Brit*) = **press clipping**.

press-gang [pres'gang] *vt*: **to** ~ **sb into doing**

sth costringere qn a viva forza a fare qc.

pressing [pres'ing] *a* urgente ♦ *n* stiratura.

press release *n* comunicato stampa.

press stud *n* (*Brit*) bottone *m* a pressione.

press-up [pres'up] *n* (*Brit*) flessione *f* sulle braccia.

pressure [presh'ûr] *n* pressione *f* ♦ *vt* = **to put** ~ **on**; **high/low** ~ alta/bassa pressione; **to put** ~ **on sb** fare pressione su qn.

pressure cooker *n* pentola a pressione.

pressure gauge *n* manometro.

pressure group *n* gruppo di pressione.

pressurize [presh'ərīz] *vt* pressurizzare; (*fig*): **to** ~ **sb (into doing sth)** fare delle pressioni su qn (per costringerlo a fare qc).

pressurized [presh'ərīzd] *a* pressurizzato(a).

prestige [prestēzh'] *n* prestigio.

prestigious [prestij'əs] *a* prestigioso(a).

presumably [prizōō'məblē] *ad* presumibilmente; ~ **he did it** penso *or* presumo che l'abbia fatto.

presume [prizōōm'] *vt* supporre; **to** ~ **to do** (*dare*) permettersi di fare.

presumption [prizump'shən] *n* presunzione *f*; (*boldness*) audacia.

presumptuous [prizump'chōōəs] *a* presuntuoso(a).

presuppose [prēsəpōz'] *vt* presupporre.

pretax [prē'taks'] *a* al lordo d'imposta.

pretence [pritens'] *n* (*Brit*) = **pretense**.

pretend [pritend'] *vt* (*feign*) fingere ♦ *vi* far finta; (*claim*): **to** ~ **to sth** pretendere a qc; **to** ~ **to do** far finta di fare.

pretense [pritens'] *n* (*US: claim*) pretesa; (: *pretext*) pretesto, scusa; **to make a** ~ **of doing** far finta di fare; **on** *or* **under the** ~ **of doing sth** con il pretesto *or* la scusa di fare qc; **she is devoid of all** ~ non si nasconde dietro false apparenze.

pretension [priten'chən] *n* (*claim*) pretesa; **to have no** ~**s to sth/to being sth** non avere la pretesa di avere qc/di essere qc.

pretentious [priten'chəs] *a* pretenzioso(a).

preterite [pret'ûrit] *n* preterito.

pretext [prē'tekst] *n* pretesto; **on** *or* **under the** ~ **of doing sth** col pretesto di fare qc.

pretty [prit'ē] *a* grazioso(a), carino(a) ♦ *ad* abbastanza, assai.

prevail [privāl'] *vi* (*win, be usual*) prevalere; (*persuade*): **to** ~ **(up)on sb to do** persuadere qn a fare.

prevailing [privā'ling] *a* dominante.

prevalent [prev'ələnt] *a* (*belief*) predominante; (*customs*) diffuso(a); (*fashion*) corrente; (*disease*) comune.

prevarication [privarikā'shən] *n* tergiversazione *f*.

prevent [privent'] *vt* prevenire; **to** ~ **sb from doing** impedire a qn di fare.

preventable [privent'əbəl] *a* evitabile.

preventative [priven'tətiv] *a* preventivo(a).

prevention [priven'chən] *n* prevenzione *f*.
preventive [priven'tiv] *a* preventivo(a).
preview [prē'vyōō] *n* (*of movie*) anteprima.
previous [prē'vēəs] *a* precedente; anteriore; **I have a ~ engagement** ho già (preso) un impegno; **~ to doing** prima di fare.
previously [prē'vēəslē] *ad* prima.
prewar [prē'wôr'] *a* anteguerra *inv*.
prey [prā] *n* preda ♦ *vi:* **to ~ on** far preda di; **it was ~ing on his mind** gli rodeva la mente.
price [prīs] *n* prezzo; (*BETTING: odds*) quotazione *f* ♦ *vt* (*goods*) fissare il prezzo di; valutare; **what is the ~ of ...?** quanto costa ...?; **to go up** *or* **rise in ~** salire *or* aumentare di prezzo; **to put a ~ on sth** valutare *or* stimare qc; **he regained his freedom, but at a ~** ha riconquistato la sua libertà, ma a caro prezzo; **to be ~d out of the market** (*article*) essere così caro da diventare invendibile; (*producer, nation*) non poter sostenere la concorrenza.
price control *n* controllo dei prezzi.
price-cutting [prīs'kuting] *n* riduzione *f* dei prezzi.
priceless [prīs'lis] *a* di valore inestimabile; (*col: amusing*) impagabile, spassosissimo(a).
price list *n* listino (dei) prezzi.
price range *n* gamma di prezzi; **it's within my ~** rientra nelle mie possibilità.
price tag *n* cartellino del prezzo.
price war *n* guerra dei prezzi.
pricey [prī'sē] *a* (*col*) caruccio(a).
prick [prik] *n* puntura ♦ *vt* pungere; **to ~ up one's ears** drizzare gli orecchi.
prickle [prik'əl] *n* (*of plant*) spina; (*sensation*) pizzicore *m*.
prickly [prik'lē] *a* spinoso(a); (*fig: person*) permaloso(a).
prickly heat *n* sudamina.
prickly pear *n* fico d'India.
pride [prīd] *n* orgoglio; superbia ♦ *vt:* **to ~ o.s. on** essere orgoglioso(a) di; vantarsi di; **to take (a) ~ in** tenere molto a; essere orgoglioso di; **to take a ~ in doing** andare orgoglioso di fare.
priest [prēst] *n* prete *m*, sacerdote *m*.
priestess [prēs'tis] *n* sacerdotessa.
priesthood [prēst'hood] *n* sacerdozio.
prig [prig] *n:* **he's a ~** è compiaciuto di se stesso.
prim [prim] *a* pudico(a); contegnoso(a).
prima facie [prē'mə fā'sē] *a:* **to have a ~ case** (*LAW*) presentare una causa in apparenza fondata.
primarily [prīmär'ilē] *ad* principalmente, essenzialmente.
primary [prī'märē] *a* primario(a); (*first in importance*) primo(a); (*US: election*) primarie *fpl*.
primary color *n* colore *m* fondamentale.

primary products *npl* prodotti *mpl* di base.
primary school *n* (*Brit*) scuola elementare.
primate *n* (*REL:* [prī'mit], *ZOOL:* [prī'māt]) primate *m*.
prime [prīm] *a* primario(a), fondamentale; (*excellent*) di prima qualità ♦ *n:* **in the ~ of life** nel fiore della vita ♦ *vt* (*gun*) innescare; (*pump*) adescare; (*fig*) mettere al corrente.
prime minister (PM) *n* primo ministro.
primer [prī'mûr] *n* (*book*) testo elementare; (*paint*) mano *f* preparatoria.
prime time *n* (*RADIO, TV*) fascia di massimo ascolto.
primeval [prīmē'vəl] *a* primitivo(a).
primitive [prim'ətiv] *a* primitivo(a).
primrose [prim'rōz] *n* primavera.
primus (stove) [prī'məs (stōv')] ® *n* (*Brit*) fornello a petrolio.
prince [prins] *n* principe *m*.
prince charming *n* principe *m* azzurro.
princess [prin'sis] *n* principessa.
principal [prin'səpəl] *a* principale ♦ *n* (*US: of school, college etc*) preside *m/f*; (*money*) capitale *m*; (*in play*) protagonista *m/f*.
principality [prinsəpal'itē] *n* principato.
principally [prin'səpəlē] *ad* principalmente.
principle [prin'səpəl] *n* principio; **in ~** in linea di principio; **on ~** per principio.
print [print] *n* (*mark*) impronta; (*letters*) caratteri *mpl*; (*fabric*) tessuto stampato; (*ART, PHOT*) stampa ♦ *vt* imprimere; (*publish*) stampare, pubblicare; (*write in capitals*) scrivere in stampatello; **out of ~** esaurito(a).
print out *vt* (*COMPUT*) stampare.
printed circuit board (PCB) *n* circuito stampato.
printed matter *n* stampe *fpl*.
printer [prin'tûr] *n* tipografo; (*machine*) stampante *m*.
printhead [print'hed] *n* testa di stampa.
printing [prin'ting] *n* stampa.
printing press *n* macchina tipografica.
print-out [print'out] *n* tabulato.
print wheel *n* margherita.
prior [prī'ûr] *a* precedente ♦ *n* (*REL*) priore *m*; **~ to doing** prima di fare; **without ~ notice** senza preavviso; **to have a ~ claim to sth** avere un diritto di precedenza su qc.
priority [prīôr'itē] *n* priorità *f inv*, precedenza; **to have** *or* **take ~ over sth** avere la precedenza su qc.
priory [prī'ərē] *n* monastero.
prise [prīz] *vt* (*Brit*) = **prize**.
prism [priz'əm] *n* prisma *m*.
prison [priz'ən] *n* prigione *f*.
prison camp *n* campo di prigionia.
prisoner [priz'ənûr] *n* prigioniero/a; **to take sb ~** far prigioniero qn; **the ~ at the bar** l'accusato, l'imputato; **~ of war** prigioniero/a di guerra.

prison warden *n* (*US*) direttore/trice di carcere.

prissy |pris'ē| *a* per benino.

pristine |pris'tēn| *a* originario(a); intatto(a); puro(a).

privacy |prī'vəsē| *n* solitudine *f*, intimità.

private |prī'vit| *a* privato(a); personale ♦ *n* soldato semplice; "~" (*on envelope*) "riservata"; **in ~** in privato; **in (his) ~ life** nella vita privata; **he is a very ~ person** è una persona molto riservata; **~ hearing** (*LAW*) udienza a porte chiuse; **to be in ~ practice** essere medico non convenzionato (con la mutua).

private enterprise *n* iniziativa privata.

private eye *n* investigatore *m* privato.

private limited company *n* (*Brit*) società per azioni non quotata in Borsa.

privately |prī'vitlē| *ad* in privato; (*within o.s.*) dentro di sé.

private parts *npl* (*ANAT*) parti *fpl* intime.

private property *n* proprietà privata.

private school *n* scuola privata.

privation |prīvā'shən| *n* (*state*) privazione *f*; (*hardship*) privazioni *fpl*, stenti *mpl*.

privatize |prī'vətiz| *vt* privatizzare.

privet |priv'it| *n* ligustro.

privilege |priv'əlij| *n* privilegio.

privileged |priv'əlijd| *a* privilegiato(a); **to be ~ to do sth** avere il privilegio *or* l'onore di fare qc.

privy |priv'ē| *a*: **to be ~ to** essere al corrente di.

Privy Council *n* (*Brit*) Consiglio della Corona.

Privy Councillor *n* (*Brit*) Consigliere *m* della Corona.

prize |prīz| *n* premio ♦ *a* (*example, idiot*) perfetto(a); (*bull, novel*) premiato(a) ♦ *vt* apprezzare, pregiare; **to ~ open** (*US*) forzare.

prize fight *n* incontro di pugilato tra professionisti.

prize giving *n* premiazione *f*.

prize money *n* soldi *mpl* del premio.

prizewinner |prīz'winûr| *n* premiato/a.

prizewinning |prīz'wining| *a* vincente; (*novel, essay etc*) premiato(a).

PRO *n abbr* = **public relations officer**.

pro |prō| *n* (*SPORT*) professionista *m/f*; **the ~s and cons** il pro e il contro.

pro- |prō| *prefix* (*in favor of*) filo...; **~Soviet** *a* filosovietico(a).

probability |prâbəbil'ətē| *n* probabilità *f inv*; **in all ~** con ogni probabilità.

probable |prâb'əbəl| *a* probabile; **it is ~/ hardly ~ that** ... è probabile/poco probabile che ... + *sub.*

probably |prâb'əblē| *ad* probabilmente.

probate |prō'bāt| *n* (*LAW*) omologazione *f* (di un testamento).

probation |prōbā'shən| *n* (*in employment*) pe-

riodo di prova; (*LAW*) libertà vigilata; (*REL*) probandato; **on ~** (*employee*) in prova; (*LAW*) in libertà vigilata.

probationary |prōbā'shənârē| *a*: **~ period** periodo di prova.

probe |prōb| *n* (*MED, SPACE*) sonda; (*enquiry*) indagine *f*, investigazione *f* ♦ *vt* sondare, esplorare; indagare.

probity |prō'bitē| *n* probità.

problem |prâb'ləm| *n* problema *m*; **to have ~s with the car** avere dei problemi con la macchina; **what's the ~?** che cosa c'è?; **I had no ~ in finding her** non mi è stato difficile trovarla; **no ~!** ma certamente!, non c'è problema!

problematic |prâbləmat'ik| *a* problematico(a).

procedure |prəsē'jûr| *n* (*ADMIN, LAW*) procedura; (*method*) metodo, procedimento.

proceed |prəsēd'| *vi* (*go forward*) avanzare, andare avanti; (*go about it*) procedere; (*continue*): **to ~ (with)** continuare; **to ~ to** andare a; passare a; **to ~ to do** mettersi a fare; **to ~ against sb** (*LAW*) procedere contro qn; **I am not sure how to ~** non so bene come fare.

proceeding |prəsē'ding| *n* procedimento, modo d'agire.

proceedings |prəsē'dingz| *npl* misure *fpl*; (*LAW*) procedimento; (*meeting*) riunione *f*; (*records*) rendiconti *mpl*; atti *mpl*.

proceeds |prō'sēds| *npl* profitto, incasso.

process |prâs'es| *n* processo; (*method*) metodo, sistema *m* ♦ *vt* trattare; (*information*) elaborare ♦ *vi* |prəses'| (*Brit formal: go in procession*) sfilare, procedere in corteo; **we are in the ~ of moving to ...** stiamo per trasferirci a ....

process(ed) cheese |prâs'es(t) chēz'| *n* formaggio fuso.

processing |prâs'esing| *n* trattamento; elaborazione *f*.

procession |prəsesh'ən| *n* processione *f*, corteo; **funeral ~** corteo funebre.

proclaim |prəklām'| *vt* proclamare, dichiarare.

proclamation |prâkləmā'shən| *n* proclamazione *f*.

proclivity |prōkliv'ətē| *n* tendenza, propensione *f*.

procrastination |prōkrastənā'shən| *n* procrastinazione *f*.

procreation |prōkrēā'shən| *n* procreazione *f*.

proctor |prâk'tûr| (*US*) *n* chi sorveglia agli esami ♦ *vt* sorvegliare.

procure |prəkyōōr'| *vt* (*for o.s.*) procurarsi; (*for sb*) procurare.

procurement |prəkyōōr'mənt| *n* approvvigionamento.

prod |prâd| *vt* dare un colpetto a ♦ *n* (*push, jab*) colpetto.

prodigal |prâd'əgəl| *a* prodigo(a).

prodigious |prədij'əs| *a* prodigioso(a).

prodigy [prâd'əjē] *n* prodigio.

produce *n* [prō'dōōs] (*AGR*) prodotto, prodotti *mpl* ♦ *vt* [prədōōs'] produrre; (*to show*) esibire, mostrare; (*proof of identity*) produrre, fornire; (*cause*) cagionare, causare; (*THEATER*) mettere in scena.

producer [prədōō'sûr] *n* (*THEATER*) direttore/trice; (*AGR. CINEMA*) produttore *m*.

product [prâd'əkt] *n* prodotto.

production [prəduk'shən] *n* produzione *f*; (*THEATER*) messa in scena; **to put into** ~ mettere in produzione.

production agreement *n* (*US*) accordo sui tempi di produzione.

production control *n* controllo di produzione.

production line *n* catena di lavorazione.

production manager *n* production manager *m inv*, direttore *m* della produzione.

productive [prəduk'tiv] *a* produttivo(a).

productivity [prâdəktiv'ətē] *n* produttività.

productivity agreement *n* (*Brit*) = **production agreement**.

productivity bonus *n* premio di produzione.

Prof. *abbr* (= *professor*) Prof.

profane [prəfān'] *a* profano(a); (*language*) empio(a).

profess [prəfes'] *vt* professare; **I do not** ~ **to be an expert** non pretendo di essere un esperto.

professed [prəfest'] *a* (*self-declared*) dichiarato(a).

profession [prəfesh'ən] *n* professione *f*; **the** ~**s** le professioni liberali.

professional [prəfesh'ənəl] *n* (*SPORT*) professionista *m/f* ♦ *a* professionale; (*work*) da professionista; **he's a** ~ **man** è un professionista; **to seek** ~ **advice** consultare un esperto.

professionalism [prəfesh'ənəlizəm] *n* professionismo.

professionally [prəfesh'ənəlē] *ad* professionalmente, in modo professionale; (*SPORT*: *play*) come professionista; **I only know him** ~ con lui ho solo rapporti di lavoro.

professor [prəfes'ûr] *n* (*US*: *teacher*) professore/essa; professore *m* (*titolare di una cattedra*).

professorship [prəfes'ûrship] *n* cattedra.

proffer [prâf'ûr] *vt* (*remark*) profferire; (*apologies*) porgere, presentare; (*one's hand*) porgere.

proficiency [prəfish'ənsē] *n* competenza, abilità.

proficient [prəfish'ənt] *a* competente, abile.

profile [prō'fīl] *n* profilo; **to keep a low** ~ (*fig*) cercare di passare inosservato *or* di non farsi notare troppo; **to maintain a high** ~ mettersi in mostra.

profit [prâf'it] *n* profitto; beneficio ♦ *vi*: **to** ~ (**by** *or* **from**) approfittare (di); ~ **and loss**

statement conto perdite e profitti; **to make a** ~ realizzare un profitto; **to sell sth at a** ~ vendere qc con un utile.

profitability [prâfitəbil'ətē] *n* redditività.

profitable [prâf'itəbəl] *a* redditizio(a); (*fig*: *beneficial*) vantaggioso(a); (: *meeting*, *visit*) fruttuoso(a).

profit center *n* centro di profitto.

profiteering [prâfitēr'ing] *n* (*pej*) affarismo.

profit-making [prâf'itmāking] *a* a scopo di lucro.

profit margin *n* margine *m* di profitto.

profit sharing [prâf'it shä'ring] *n* compartecipazione *f* agli utili.

profligate [prâf'ləgit] *a* (*dissolute*: *behavior*) dissipato(a); (: *person*) debosciato(a); (*extravagant*): **he's very** ~ **with his money** è uno che sperpera i suoi soldi.

pro forma [prō fôr'mə] *ad*: ~ **invoice** fattura proforma.

profound [prəfound'] *a* profondo(a).

profuse [prəfyōōs'] *a* infinito(a), abbondante.

profusely [prəfyōōs'lē] *ad* con grande effusione.

profusion [prəfyōō'zhən] *n* profusione *f*, abbondanza.

progeny [prâj'ənē] *n* progenie *f*; discendenti *mpl*.

program [prō'grəm] (*US*) *n* programma *m* ♦ *vt* (*also*: *Brit*: *COMPUT*) programmare.

program(m)er [prō'gramûr] *n* programmatore/trice.

program(m)ing [prō'graming] *n* programmazione *f*.

program(m)ing language *n* linguaggio di programmazione.

programme [prō'gram] *etc* (*Brit*) = **program** *etc*.

progress *n* [prâg'res] progresso ♦ *vi* [prəgres'] (*go forward*) avanzare, procedere; (*in time*) procedere; (*also*: **make** ~) far progressi; **in** ~ in corso.

progression [prəgresh'ən] *n* progressione *f*.

progressive [prəgres'iv] *a* progressivo(a); (*person*) progressista.

progressively [prəgres'ivlē] *ad* progressivamente.

progress report *n* (*MED*) bollettino medico; (*ADMIN*) rendiconto dei lavori.

prohibit [prōhib'it] *vt* proibire, vietare; **to** ~ **sb from doing sth** vietare *or* proibire a qn di fare qc; **"smoking** ~**ed"** "vietato fumare".

prohibition [prōəbish'ən] *n* (*US*) proibizionismo.

prohibitive [prōhib'ətiv] *a* (*price etc*) proibitivo(a).

project *n* [prâj'ekt] (*plan*) piano; (*venture*) progetto; (*SCOL*) studio, ricerca ♦ *vb* [prəjekt'] *vt* proiettare ♦ *vi* (*stick out*) sporgere.

projectile [prəjek'təl] *n* proiettile *m*.

projection [prəjek'shən] *n* proiezione *f*;

sporgenza.

projectionist [prəjek'shənist] *n* (*CINEMA*) proiezionista *m/f*.

projection room *n* (*CINEMA*) cabina *or* sala di proiezione.

projector [prəjek'tûr] *n* proiettore *m*.

proletarian [prōlitär'ēən] *a, n* proletario(a).

proletariat [prōlitär'ēət] *n* proletariato.

proliferate [prōlif'ərāt] *vi* proliferare.

proliferation [prōlifərā'shən] *n* proliferazione *f*.

prolific [prōlif'ik] *a* prolifico(a).

prolog(ue) [prō'lóg] *n* prologo.

prolong [prəlóng'] *vt* prolungare.

prom [prâm] *n abbr* = **promenade**; (*Brit*) **promenade concert**; (*US: ball*) ballo studentesco.

promenade [prâmənād'] *n* (*by sea*) lungomare *m*.

promenade concert *n* (*Brit*) concerto (*con posti in piedi*).

promenade deck *n* (*NAUT*) ponte *m* di passeggiata.

prominence [prâm'ənəns] *n* prominenza; importanza.

prominent [prâm'ənənt] *a* (*standing out*) prominente; (*important*) importante; **he is ~ in the field of** ... è un'autorità nel campo di ....

prominently [prâm'ənəntlē] *ad* (*display, set*) ben in vista; **he figured ~ in the case** ha avuto una parte di primo piano nella faccenda.

promiscuity [prâmiskyōō'itē] *n* (*sexual*) rapporti *mpl* multipli.

promiscuous [prəmis'kyōōəs] *a* (*sexually*) di facili costumi.

promise [prâm'is] *n* promessa ♦ *vt, vi* promettere; **to make sb a ~** fare una promessa a qn; **a young man of ~** un giovane promettente; **to ~ (sb) to do sth** promettere (a qn) di fare qc.

promising [prâm'ising] *a* promettente.

promissory note [prâm'isôrē nōt] *n* pagherò *m inv*.

promontory [prâm'əntôrē] *n* promontorio.

promote [prəmōt'] *vt* promuovere; (*venture, event*) organizzare; (*product*) lanciare, reclamizzare; **the team was ~d to the second division** (*Brit SOCCER*) la squadra è stata promossa in serie B.

promoter [prəmō'tûr] *n* (*of sporting event*) organizzatore/trice; (*of cause etc*) sostenitore/trice.

promotion [prəmō'shən] *n* promozione *f*.

prompt [prâmpt] *a* rapido(a), svelto(a); puntuale; (*reply*) sollecito(a) ♦ *ad* (*punctually*) in punto ♦ *n* (*COMPUT*) guida ♦ *vt* incitare; provocare; (*THEATER*) suggerire a; **at 8 o'clock ~** alle 8 in punto; **to be ~ to do sth** essere sollecito nel fare qc; **to ~ sb to do sth** spingere qn a fare.

prompter [prâmp'tûr] *n* (*THEATER*) suggerito-

re *m*.

promptly [prâmpt'lē] *ad* prontamente; puntualmente.

promptness [prâmpt'nis] *n* prontezza; puntualità.

prone [prōn] *a* (*lying*) prono(a); **~ to** propenso(a) a, incline a; **to be ~ to illness** essere soggetto(a) a malattie; **she is ~ to burst into tears if** ... può facilmente scoppiare in lacrime se ....

prong [próng] *n* rebbio, punta.

pronoun [prō'noun] *n* pronome *m*.

pronounce [prənouns'] *vt* pronunziare ♦ *vi*: **to ~ (up)on** pronunziare su; **they ~d him unfit to drive** lo hanno dichiarato inabile alla guida.

pronounced [prənounst'] *a* (*marked*) spiccato(a).

pronouncement [prənouns'mənt] *n* dichiarazione *f*.

pronunciation [prənunsēā'shən] *n* pronunzia.

proof [prōōf] *n* prova; (*of book*) bozza; (*PHOT*) provino; (*of alcohol*): **35% ~** ≈ 40° in volume ♦ *a*: **~ against** a prova di.

proofreader [prōōf'rēdûr] *n* correttore/trice di bozze.

prop [prâp] *n* sostegno, appoggio ♦ *vt* (*also: ~ up*) sostenere, appoggiare; *(lean)*: **to ~ sth against** appoggiare qc contro *or* a.

Prop. *abbr* (*COMM*) = **proprietor**.

propaganda [prâpəgan'də] *n* propaganda.

propagation [prâpəgā'shən] *n* propagazione *f*.

propel [prəpel'] *vt* spingere (in avanti), muovere.

propeller [prəpel'ûr] *n* elica.

propelling pencil [prəpel'ing pen'səl] *n* (*Brit*) matita a mina.

propensity [prəpen'sitē] *n* tendenza.

proper [prâp'ûr] *a* (*suited, right*) adatto(a), appropriato(a); (*seemly*) decente; (*authentic*) vero(a); (*col: real*) *n* + vero(a) e proprio(a); **to go through the ~ channels** (*ADMIN*) seguire la regolare procedura.

properly [prâp'ûrlē] *ad* decentemente; (*really, thoroughly*) veramente.

proper noun *n* nome *m* proprio.

property [prâp'ûrtē] *n* (*things owned*) beni *mpl*; (*land, building, CHEM etc*) proprietà *f inv*.

property developer *n* (*Brit*) costruttore *m* edile.

property owner *n* proprietario/a.

property tax *n* imposta patrimoniale.

prophecy [prâf'isē] *n* profezia.

prophesy [prâf'isī] *vt* predire, profetizzare.

prophet [prâf'it] *n* profeta *m*.

prophetic [prəfet'ik] *a* profetico(a).

prophylactic [prōfəlak'tik] *n* preservativo.

proportion [prəpôr'shən] *n* proporzione *f*; (*share*) parte *f* ♦ *vt* proporzionare, commisurare; **to be in/out of ~ to** *or* **with sth** essere in proporzione/sproporzionato rispetto a qc; **to see sth in** ~ (*fig*) dare il giusto peso a qc.

proportional [prəpôr'shənəl] *a* proporzionale.

proportional representation (PR) *n* rappresentanza proporzionale.

proportionate [prəpôr'shənit] *a* proporzionato(a).

proposal [prəpō'zəl] *n* proposta; (*plan*) progetto; (*of marriage*) proposta di matrimonio.

propose [prəpōz'] *vt* proporre, suggerire ♦ *vi* fare una proposta di matrimonio; **to ~ to do** proporsi di fare, aver l'intenzione di fare.

proposer [prəpō'zûr] *n* (*of motion*) proponente *m/f*.

proposition [prâpəzish'ən] *n* proposizione *f*; (*proposal*) proposta; **to make sb a** ~ proporre qualcosa a qn.

propound [prəpound'] *vt* proporre, presentare.

proprietary [prəprī'itârē] *a*: ~ **article** prodotto con marchio depositato; ~ **brand** marchio di fabbrica.

proprietor [prəprī'ətûr] *n* proprietario/a.

propriety [prəprī'ətē] *n* (*seemliness*) decoro, rispetto delle convenienze sociali.

propulsion [prəpul'shən] *n* propulsione *f*.

pro rata [prō ra'tə] *ad* in proporzione.

prosaic [prōzā'ik] *a* prosaico(a).

Pros. Atty. *abbr* (*US*) = **prosecuting attorney.**

proscribe [prōskrīb'] *vt* proscrivere.

prose [prōz] *n* prosa; (*Brit*: SCOL: *translation*) traduzione *f* dalla madrelingua.

prosecute [prâs'əkyōōt] *vt* intentare azione contro.

prosecuting attorney *n* (*US*) ≈ procuratore *m*.

prosecution [prâsəkyōō'shən] *n* (LAW) azione *f* giudiziaria; (*accusing side*) accusa.

prosecutor [prâs'əkyōōtûr] *n* (*also*: **public** ~) ≈ procuratore *m* della Repubblica.

prospect *n* [prâs'pekt] prospettiva; (*hope*) speranza ♦ *vb* [prəspekt'] *vt* esplorare ♦ *vi*: **to** ~ **for gold** cercare l'oro; **there is every** ~ **of an early victory** tutto lascia prevedere una rapida vittoria; *see also* **prospects.**

prospecting [prâs'pekting] *n* prospezione *f*.

prospective [prəspek'tiv] *a* (*buyer*) probabile; (*legislation, son-in-law*) futuro(a).

prospector [prâs'pektûr] *n* prospettore *m*; **gold** ~ cercatore *m* d'oro.

prospects [prâs'pekts] *npl* (*for work etc*) prospettive *fpl*.

prospectus [prəspek'təs] *n* prospetto, programma *m*.

prosper [prâs'pûr] *vi* prosperare.

prosperity [prâspär'itē] *n* prosperità.

prosperous [prâs'pûrəs] *a* prospero(a).

prostate [prâs'tāt] *n* (*also*: ~ **gland**) prostata, ghiandola prostatica.

prostitute [prâs'titōōt] *n* prostituta; **male** ~

uomo che si prostituisce.

prostitution [prâstitōō'shən] *n* prostituzione *f*.

prostrate [prâs'trāt] *a* prostrato(a) ♦ *vt*: **to** ~ **o.s.** (*before sb*) prostrarsi.

protagonist [prōtag'ənist] *n* protagonista *m/f*.

protect [prətekt'] *vt* proteggere, salvaguardare.

protection [prətek'shən] *n* protezione *f*; **to be under sb's** ~ essere sotto la protezione di qn.

protectionism [prətek'shənizəm] *n* protezionismo.

protection racket *n* racket *m inv*.

protective [prətek'tiv] *a* protettivo(a); ~ **custody** (LAW) protezione *f*.

protector [prətek'tûr] *n* protettore/trice.

protégé [prō'təzhā] *n* protetto.

protégée [prō'təzhā] *n* protetta.

protein [prō'tēn] *n* proteina.

pro tem [prō tem] *ad abbr* (= *pro tempore*: *for the time being*) pro tempore.

protest *n* [prō'test] protesta ♦ *vt*, *vi* [prətest'] protestare; **to do sth under** ~ fare qc protestando; **to** ~ **against/about** protestare contro/per.

Protestant [prât'istənt] *a*, *n* protestante (*m/f*).

protester, protestor [prətes'tûr] *n* (*in demonstration*) dimostrante *m/f*.

protest march *n* marcia di protesta.

protocol [prō'təkôl] *n* protocollo.

prototype [prō'tətīp] *n* prototipo.

protracted [prōtrak'tid] *a* tirato(a) per le lunghe.

protractor [prōtrak'tûr] *n* (GEOM) goniometro.

protrude [prōtrōōd'] *vi* sporgere.

protuberance [prōtōō'bûrəns] *n* sporgenza.

proud [proud] *a* fiero(a), orgoglioso(a); (*pej*) superbo(a); **to be** ~ **to do sth** essere onorato(a) di fare qc; **to do sb** ~ non far mancare nulla a qn; **to do o.s.** ~ trattarsi bene.

proudly [proud'lē] *ad* con orgoglio, fieramente.

prove [prōōv] *vt* provare, dimostrare ♦ *vi*: **to** ~ **correct** *etc* risultare vero(a) *etc*; **to** ~ **o.s.** mostrare le proprie capacità; **to** ~ **o.s./itself (to be) useful** *etc* mostrarsi *or* rivelarsi utile *etc*; **he was** ~**d right in the end** alla fine i fatti gli hanno dato ragione.

Provence [prâvâns'] *n* Provenza.

proverb [prâv'ûrb] *n* proverbio.

proverbial [prəvûr'bēəl] *a* proverbiale.

provide [prəvīd'] *vt* fornire, provvedere; **to** ~ **sb with sth** fornire *or* provvedere qn di qc; **to be** ~**d with** essere dotato *or* munito di.

provide for *vt fus* provvedere a.

provided [prəvī'did] *cj*: ~ **that** purché + *sub*, a condizione che + *sub*.

Providence [prâv'idəns] *n* Provvidenza.

providing [prəvī'ding] *cj* purché + *sub*, a condizione che + *sub*.

province [prâv'ins] *n* provincia.

provincial [prəvin'chəl] *a* provinciale.

provision [prəvizh'ən] *n* (*supply*) riserva;

(*supplying*) provvista; rifornimento; (*stipula-tion*) condizione *f*; ~s *npl* (*food*) provviste *fpl*; **to make ~ for** (*one's family, future*) pensare a; **there's no ~ for this in the con-tract** il contratto non lo prevede.

provisional [prəvizh'ənəl] *a* provvisorio(a) ♦ *n*: **P~** (*Irish POL*) provisional *m inv*.

provisional licence *n* (*Brit AUT*) ≈ foglio *m* rosa *inv*.

provisionally [prəvizh'ənəlē] *ad* provvisoria-mente; (*appoint*) a titolo provvisorio.

proviso [prəvī'zō] *n* condizione *f*; **with the ~ that** a condizione che + *sub*, a patto che + *sub*.

Provo [prō'vō] *n abbr* (*Irish POL*) = **Provi-sional**.

provocation [právəkā'shən] *n* provocazione *f*.

provocative [prəvåk'ətiv] *a* (*aggressive*) pro-vocatorio(a); (*thought-provoking*) stimolante; (*seductive*) provocante.

provoke [prəvōk'] *vt* provocare; incitare; **to ~ sb to sth/to do** *or* **into doing sth** spingere qn a qc/a fare qc.

provoking [prəvōk'ing] *a* irritante, esaspe-rante.

provost [práv'əst] *n* (*of university*) rettore *m*; (*Scottish*) sindaco.

prow [prou] *n* prua.

prowess [prou'is] *n* prodezza; **his ~ as a foot-ball player** le sue capacità di calciatore.

prowl [proul] *vi* (*also:* ~ **around**) aggirarsi furtivamente; **on the ~** in cerca di preda.

prowler [prou'lûr] *n* tipo sospetto (*che s'aggira con l'intenzione di rubare, aggredire etc*).

proximity [práksim'itē] *n* prossimità.

proxy [prák'sē] *n* procura; **by ~** per procura.

prude [prōōd] *n* puritano/a.

prudence [prōō'dəns] *n* prudenza.

prudent [prōō'dənt] *a* prudente.

prudish [prōō'dish] *a* puritano(a).

prune [prōōn] *n* prugna secca ♦ *vt* potare.

pruning shears [prōōn'ing shirz] *npl* forbici *fpl* per potare.

pry [prī] *vi*: **to ~ into** ficcare il naso in; **to ~ open** (*US*) forzare.

PS *n abbr* (= *postscript*) P.S.

psalm [sâm] *n* salmo.

PSAT *n abbr* (*US*) = *Preliminary Scholastic Aptitude Test*.

pseudo- [sōō'dō] *prefix* pseudo....

pseudonym [sōō'dənim] *n* pseudonimo.

PST *abbr* (*US*: = *Pacific Standard Time*) ora invernale del Pacifico.

psyche [sī'kē] *n* psiche *f*.

psychedelic [sīkədel'ik] *a* psichedelico(a).

psychiatric [sīkēat'rik] *a* psichiatrico(a).

psychiatrist [sikī'ətrist] *n* psichiatra *m/f*.

psychiatry [sikī'ətrē] *n* psichiatria.

psychic [sī'kik] *a* (*also:* ~**al**) psichico(a); (*person*) dotato(a) di qualità telepatiche.

psychoanalysis, *pl* **-lyses** [sīkōənal'isis, -sēz] *n* psicanalisi *f inv*.

psychoanalyst [sīkōan'əlist] *n* psicanalista *m/f*.

psychoanalyze [sīkōan'əlīz] *vt* psicanalizzare.

psychological [sīkəlåj'ikəl] *a* psicologico(a).

psychologist [sīkål'əjist] *n* psicologo/a.

psychology [sīkål'əjē] *n* psicologia.

psychopath [sī'kəpath] *n* psicopatico/a.

psychosis, *pl* **psychoses** [sīkō'sis, -sēz] *n* psi-cosi *f inv*.

psychosomatic [sīkōsōmat'ik] *a* psicosomati-co(a).

psychotherapy [sīkōthär'əpē] *n* psicoterapia.

psychotic [sīkåt'ik] *a, n* psicotico(a).

PT *n abbr* (*Brit*: = *physical training*) ed. fisi-ca.

pt *abbr* (= *pint; point*) pt.

PTA *n abbr* (= *Parent-Teacher Association*) associazione genitori e insegnanti.

PTO *abbr* (= *please turn over*) v.r. (= *vedi retro*).

PTV *n abbr* (*US*) = *pay television, public tele-vision*.

pub [pub] *n* (*Brit*) pub *m inv*.

puberty [pyōō'bûrtē] *n* pubertà.

pubic [pyōō'bik] *a* pubico(a), del pube.

public [pub'lik] *a* pubblico(a) ♦ *n* il pubblico; **in ~** in pubblico; **the general ~** il pubblico; **to make sth ~** render noto *or* di pubblico domi-nio qc; **to be ~ knowledge** essere di dominio pubblico; **to go ~** (*COMM*) emettere le azioni sul mercato.

public address system (PA) *n* impianto di amplificazione.

publican [pub'likən] *n* (*Brit*) gestore *m* (*or* proprietario) di un pub.

publication [publikā'shən] *n* pubblicazione *f*.

public company *n* ≈ società *f inv* per azioni (*costituita tramite pubblica sottoscrizione*).

public convenience *n* (*Brit*) gabinetti *mpl*.

public holiday *n* (*Brit*) giorno festivo, festa nazionale.

public house *n* (*Brit*) pub *m inv*.

public housing unit *n* (*US*) casa popolare.

publicity [publis'ətē] *n* pubblicità.

publicize [pub'ləsīz] *vt* fare (della) pubblicità a, reclamizzare.

public limited company (plc) *n* (*Brit*) ≈ società per azioni a responsabilità limitata (*quotata in Borsa*).

publicly [pub'liklē] *ad* pubblicamente.

public opinion *n* opinione *f* pubblica.

public ownership *n* proprietà pubblica *or* so-ciale; **to be taken into ~** essere statalizza-to(a).

public relations *n* pubbliche relazioni *fpl*.

public relations officer *n* addetto/a alle pub-bliche relazioni.

public school *n* (*US*) scuola statale; (*Brit*) scuola privata.

public sector *n* settore *m* pubblico.

public-spirited [pub'likspir'itid] *a* che ha senso civico.
public transportation, (*Brit*) **public transport** *n* mezzi *mpl* pubblici.
public utility *n* servizio pubblico.
public works *npl* lavori *mpl* pubblici.
publish [pub'lish] *vt* pubblicare.
publisher [pub'lishûr] *n* editore *m*; (*firm*) casa editrice.
publishing [pub'lishing] *n* (*industry*) editoria; (*of a book*) pubblicazione *f*.
publishing company *n* casa *or* società editrice.
puce [pyōōs] *a* color pulce *inv*.
puck [puk] *n* (*ICE HOCKEY*) disco.
pucker [puk'ûr] *vt* corrugare.
pudding [pŏŏd'ing] *n* budino; **rice** ~ budino di riso.
puddle [pud'əl] *n* pozza, pozzanghera.
pudgy [puj'ē] *a* (*US*) grassoccio(a).
puerile [pyōō'ûrəl] *a* puerile.
Puerto Rico [pwär'tō rē'kō] *n* Portorico.
puff [puf] *n* sbuffo; (*also:* **powder** ~) piumino ♦ *vt* (*also:* ~ **out**: *sails, cheeks*) gonfiare ♦ *vi* uscire a sbuffi; (*pant*) ansare; **to** ~ **out smoke** mandar fuori sbuffi di fumo; **to** ~ **one's pipe** tirare sboccate di fumo.
puffed [puft] *a* (*col: out of breath*) senza fiato.
puffin [puf'in] *n* puffino.
puff paste, (*Brit*) **puff pastry** *n* pasta sfoglia.
puffy [puf'ē] *a* gonfio(a).
pugnacious [pugnā'shəs] *a* combattivo(a).
pull [pŏŏl] *n* (*tug*) strattone *m*, tirata; (*of moon, magnet, the sea etc*) attrazione *f*; (*fig*) influenza ♦ *vt* tirare; (*muscle*) strappare, farsi uno strappo a ♦ *vi* tirare; **to give sth a** ~ tirare su qc; **to** ~ **to pieces** fare a pezzi; **to** ~ **one's punches** (*BOXING*) risparmiare l'avversario; **not to** ~ **one's punches** (*fig*) non avere peli sulla lingua; **to** ~ **one's weight** dare il proprio contributo; **to o.s. together** ricomporsi, riprendersi; **to** ~ **sb's leg** prendere in giro qn; **to** ~ **strings (for sb)** muovere qualche pedina (per qn).
pull apart *vt* (*break*) fare a pezzi.
pull around *vt* (*handle roughly: object*) strapazzare; (*: person*) malmenare.
pull down *vt* (*house*) demolire; (*tree*) abbattere.
pull in *vi* (*AUT: at the curb*) accostarsi; (*RAIL*) entrare in stazione.
pull off *vt* (*deal etc*) portare a compimento.
pull out *vi* partire; (*withdraw*) ritirarsi; (*AUT: come out of line*) spostarsi sulla mezzeria ♦ *vt* staccare; far uscire; (*withdraw*) ritirare.
pull over *vi* (*AUT*) accostare.
pull through *vi* farcela.
pull up *vi* (*stop*) fermarsi ♦ *vt* (*uproot*) sradicare; (*stop*) fermare.
pulley [pŏŏl'ē] *n* puleggia, carrucola.

Pullman [pŏŏl'mən] *n* (*US*) vagone *m* letto *inv*, carrozza *f* letto *inv*.
pull-out [pŏŏl'out] *n* inserto ♦ *cpd* staccabile.
pullover [pŏŏl'ōvûr] *n* pullover *m inv*.
pulp [pulp] *n* (*of fruit*) polpa; (*for paper*) pasta per carta; (*magazines, books*) stampa di qualità e di tono scadenti; **to reduce sth to** ~ spappolare qc.
pulpit [pŏŏl'pit] *n* pulpito.
pulsate [pul'sāt] *vi* battere, palpitare.
pulse [puls] *n* polso; **to feel** *or* **take sb's** ~ sentire *or* tastare il polso a qn.
pulses [pul'siz] *npl* (*CULIN*) legumi *mpl*.
pulverize [pul'vərīz] *vt* polverizzare.
puma [pyōō'mə] *n* puma *m inv*.
pumice (stone) [pum'is (stōn')] *n* (*pietra*) pomice *f*.
pummel [pum'əl] *vt* dare pugni a.
pump [pump] *n* pompa; (*shoe*) scarpetta ♦ *vt* pompare; (*fig: col*) far parlare; **to** ~ **sb for information** cercare di strappare delle informazioni a qn.
pump up *vt* gonfiare.
pumpkin [pump'kin] *n* zucca.
pun [pun] *n* gioco di parole.
punch [punch] *n* (*blow*) pugno; (*fig: force*) forza; (*tool*) punzone *m*; (*drink*) ponce *m* ♦ *vt* (*hit*): **to** ~ **sb/sth** dare un pugno a qn/qc; **to** ~ **a hole (in)** fare un buco (in).
punch in *vi* (*US*) timbrare il cartellino (all'entrata).
punch out *vi* (*US*) timbrare il cartellino (all'uscita).
punch-drunk [punch'drungk] *a* (*Brit*) stordito(a).
punch(ed) card [punch(t) kârd] *n* scheda perforata.
punch line *n* (*of joke*) battuta finale.
punch-up [punch'up] *n* (*Brit col*) rissa.
punctual [pungk'chōōəl] *a* puntuale.
punctuality [pungkchōōal'itē] *n* puntualità.
punctually [pungk'chōōəlē] *ad* puntualmente; **it will start** ~ **at 6** comincerà alle 6 precise *or* in punto.
punctuate [pungk'chōōāt] *vt* punteggiare.
punctuation [pungkchōōā'shən] *n* interpunzione *f*, punteggiatura.
punctuation mark *n* segno d'interpunzione.
puncture [pungk'chûr] *n* (*Brit*) foratura ♦ *vt* forare; **to have a** ~ (*AUT*) forare (una gomma).
pundit [pun'dit] *n* sapientone/a.
pungent [pun'jənt] *a* piccante; (*fig*) mordace, caustico(a).
punish [pun'ish] *vt* punire; **to** ~ **sb for sth/for doing sth** punire qn per qc/per aver fatto qc.
punishable [pun'ishəbəl] *a* punibile.
punishing [pun'ishing] *a* (*fig: exhausting*) sfiancante.
punishment [pun'ishmənt] *n* punizione *f*; (*fig col*): **to take a lot of** ~ (*boxer*) incassare

parecchi colpi; (car) essere messo(a) a dura prova.

punk [pungk] n (person: also: ~ **rocker**) punk m/f inv; (music: also: ~ **rock**) musica punk, punk rock m; (US col: hoodlum) teppista m.

punt [punt] n (boat) barchino; (SOCCER) colpo a volo.

puny [pyōo'nē] a gracile.

pup [pup] n cucciolo/a.

pupil [pyōo'pəl] n allievo/a; (ANAT) pupilla.

puppet [pup'it] n burattino.

puppet government n governo fantoccio.

puppy [pup'ē] n cucciolo/a, cagnolino/a.

purchase [pûr'chis] n acquisto, compera; (grip) presa ♦ vt comprare; **to get a ~ on** (grip) trovare un appoggio su.

purchase order n ordine m d'acquisto, ordinazione f.

purchase price n prezzo d'acquisto.

purchaser [pûr'chisûr] n compratore/trice.

purchasing power [pûr'chising pou'ûr] n potere m d'acquisto.

pure [pyŏor] a puro(a); **a ~ wool jumper** un golf di pura lana; **it's laziness ~ and simple** è pura pigrizia.

purebred [pyŏor'bred'] a di razza pura.

purée [pyŏorā'] n purè m inv.

purely [pyŏor'lē] ad puramente.

purge [pûrj] n (MED) purga; (POL) epurazione f ♦ vt purgare; (fig) epurare.

purification [pyŏorəfəkā'shən] n purificazione f.

purify [pyŏor'əfī] vt purificare.

purist [pyŏor'ist] n purista m/f.

puritan [pyŏor'itən] a, n puritano(a).

puritanical [pyŏoritan'ikəl] a puritano(a).

purity [pyŏor'itē] n purità.

purl [pûrl] n punto rovescio ♦ vt lavorare a rovescio.

purloin [pûrloin'] vt rubare.

purple [pûr'pəl] a di porpora; viola inv.

purport [pûr'pôrt] vi: **to ~ to be/do** pretendere di essere/fare.

purpose [pûr'pəs] n intenzione f, scopo; **on ~** apposta, di proposito; **for illustrative ~s** a titolo illustrativo; **for teaching ~s** per l'insegnamento; **for the ~s of this meeting** agli effetti di questa riunione; **to no ~** senza nessun risultato, inutilmente.

purpose-built [pûr'pəsbilt'] a (Brit) costruito(a) allo scopo.

purposeful [pûr'pəsfəl] a deciso(a), risoluto(a).

purposely [pûr'pəslē] ad apposta.

purr [pûr] n fusa fpl ♦ vi fare le fusa.

purse [pûrs] n (US: handbag) borsetta, borsa; (Brit) borsellino ♦ vt contrarre.

purser [pûr'sûr] n (NAUT) commissario di bordo.

purse snatcher [pûrs' snach'ûr] n (US) scippatore m.

pursue [pûrsōo'] vt inseguire; essere alla ricerca di; (inquiry, matter) approfondire.

pursuer [pûrsōo'ûr] n inseguitore/trice.

pursuit [pûrsōot'] n inseguimento; (occupation) occupazione f, attività f inv; **in (the) ~ of sth** alla ricerca di qc; **scientific ~s** ricerche fpl scientifiche.

purveyor [pûrvā'ûr] n fornitore/trice.

pus [pus] n pus m.

push [pōosh] n spinta; (effort) grande sforzo; (drive) energia ♦ vt spingere; (button) premere; **to ~ sth (into)** ficcare qc (in); (fig) fare pubblicità ♦ vi spingere; premere; **to ~ a door open/shut** aprire/chiudere una porta con una spinta or spingendola; **to be ~ed for time/money** essere a corto di tempo/soldi; **she is ~ing 50** (col) va per i 50; **to ~ for** (better pay, conditions etc) fare pressione per ottenere; **"~"** (on door) "spingere"; (on bell) "suonare"; **at a ~** (Brit col) in caso di necessità.

push aside vt scostare.

push in vi introdursi a forza.

push off vi (col) filare.

push on vi (continue) continuare.

push over vt far cadere.

push through vt (measure) far approvare.

push up vt (total, prices) far salire.

push-button [pōosh'butn] a a pulsante.

pushchair [pōosh'chär] n (Brit) passeggino.

pusher [pōosh'ûr] n (also: **drug ~**) spacciatore/trice (di droga).

pushing [pōosh'ing] a (pej) troppo intraprendente.

pushover [pōosh'ōvûr] n (col): **it's a ~** è un lavoro da bambini.

push-up [pōosh'up] n flessione f sulle braccia.

pushy [pōosh'ē] a (pej) troppo intraprendente.

pussycat [pōos'ēkat] n micio.

put, pt, pp **put** [pōot] vt mettere, porre; (say) dire, esprimere; (a question) fare; (estimate) stimare ♦ ad: **to stay ~** non muoversi; **to ~ sb to bed** mettere qn a letto; **to ~ sb in a good/bad mood** mettere qn di buon/cattivo umore; **to ~ sb to a lot of trouble** scomodare qn; **to ~ a lot of time into sth** dedicare molto tempo a qc; **to ~ money on a horse** scommettere su un cavallo; **how shall I ~ it?** come dire?

put about vi (NAUT) virare di bordo ♦ vt (rumor) diffondere.

put across vt (ideas etc) comunicare, far capire.

put aside vt (lay down: book etc) mettere da una parte, posare; (save) mettere da parte; (in store) tenere da parte.

put away vt (clothes, toys etc) mettere via.

put back vt (replace) rimettere (a posto); (Brit: postpone) rinviare (: delay) ritardare; (: set back: watch, clock) mettere indietro; **this will ~ us back 10 years** questo ci farà tornare indietro di 10 anni.

put down *vt* (*box etc*) posare, mettere giù; (*pay*) versare; (*in writing*) mettere per iscritto; (*suppress: revolt etc*) reprimere, sopprimere; (*attribute*) attribuire.

put forward *vt* (*ideas*) avanzare, proporre; (*Brit: date*) anticipare.

put in *vt* (*application, complaint*) presentare.

put in for *vt fus* (*Brit: job*) far domanda per; (: *promotion*) far domanda di.

put off *vt* (*discourage*) dissuadere; (*Brit: postpone*) rimandare, rinviare.

put on *vt* (*clothes, lipstick etc*) mettere; (*play etc*) mettere in scena; (*concert, exhibition etc*) allestire, organizzare; (*food, meal*) servire; (*brake*) mettere; (*assume: accent, manner*) affettare; (*col: tease*): **to ~ sb on** prendere in giro qn; (*Brit: light etc*) accendere; (: *extra bus, train etc*) mettere in servizio; (*inform, indicate*): **to ~ sb on to sb/sth** indicare qn/qc a qn; **to ~ on weight** ingrassare; **to ~ on airs** darsi delle arie.

put out *vt* mettere fuori; (*one's hand*) porgere; (*light etc*) spegnere; (*person: inconvenience*) scomodare; (*dislocate: shoulder, knee*) lussarsi; (: *back*) farsi uno strappo a ♦ *vi* (*NAUT*): **to ~ out to sea** prendere il largo; **to ~ out from New York** partire da New York.

put through *vt* (*caller*) mettere in comunicazione; (*call*) passare; **~ me through to Miss Blair** mi passi la signorina Blair.

put together *vt* mettere insieme, riunire; (*assemble: furniture*) montare; (: *meal*) improvvisare.

put up *vt* (*raise*) sollevare, alzare; (*pin up*) affiggere; (*hang*) appendere; (*build*) costruire, erigere; (*increase*) aumentare; (*accommodate*) alloggiare; (*incite*): **to ~ sb up to doing sth** istigare qn a fare qc; **to ~ sth up for sale** mettere in vendita qc.

put upon *vt fus*: **to be ~ upon** (*imposed on*) farsi mettere sotto i piedi.

put up with *vt fus* sopportare.

putrid [pyōō'trid] *a* putrido(a).

putt [put] *vt* (*ball*) colpire leggermente ♦ *n* colpo leggero.

putter [put'ûr] *n* (*GOLF*) putter *m inv* ♦ *vi* (*US*): **to ~ around** lavoracchiare; **to ~ around the house** sbrigare con calma le faccende di casa.

putting green [put'ing grēn] *n* green *m inv*; campo da putting.

putty [put'ē] *n* stucco.

put-up [pōōt'up] *a*: **~ job** montatura.

puzzle [puz'əl] *n* enigma *m*, mistero; (*jigsaw*) puzzle *m* ♦ *vt* confondere, rendere perplesso(a) ♦ *vi* scervellarsi; **to be ~d about sth** domandarsi il perché di qc; **to ~ over** (*sb's actions*) cercare di capire; (*mystery,*

problem) cercare di risolvere.

puzzling [puz'ling] *a* (*question*) poco chiaro(a); (*attitude, set of instructions*) incomprensibile.

PVC *n abbr* (= *polyvinyl chloride*) P.V.C. *m*.

PVS *n abbr* = **post-viral syndrome**.

Pvt. *abbr* (*US MIL*) = **private**.

PW *n abbr* (*US*) = **prisoner of war**.

pw *abbr* = *per week*.

PX *n abbr* (*US MIL*) *see* **post exchange**.

pygmy [pig'mē] *n* pigmeo/a.

pyjamas [pəjăm'əz] *etc* (*Brit*) = **pajamas** *etc*.

pylon [pī'lân] *n* pilone *m*.

pyramid [pir'əmid] *n* piramide *f*.

Pyrenean [pirənē'ən] *a* pirenaico(a).

Pyrenees [pir'ənēz] *npl*: **the ~** i Pirenei.

python [pī'thân] *n* pitone *m*.

Q

Q, q [kyōō] *n* (*letter*) Q, q *f or m inv*; **Q for Queen** ≈ Q come Quarto.

Qatar [kətâr'] *n* Qatar *m*.

QC *n abbr* (*Brit*: = *Queen's Counsel*) avvocato della Corona.

QED *abbr* (= *quod erat demonstrandum*) qed.

QM *n abbr see* **quartermaster**.

q.t. *n abbr* (*col*: = *quiet*): **on the ~** di nascosto.

qty *abbr* = **quantity**.

quack [kwak] *n* (*of duck*) qua qua *m inv*; (*pej: doctor*) ciarlatano/a.

quad [kwâd] *n abbr* = **quadrangle**; **quadruple**; **quadruplet**.

quadrangle [kwâd'ranggəl] *n* (*MATH*) quadrilatero; (*courtyard: abbr* **quad**) cortile *m*.

quadruped [kwâd'rōōped] *n* quadrupede *m*.

quadruple [kwâdrōō'pəl] *a* quadruplo(a) ♦ *n* quadruplo ♦ *vt* quadruplicare ♦ *vi* quadruplicarsi.

quadruplet [kwâdru'plit] *n* uno/a di quattro gemelli.

quagmire [kwag'mīûr] *n* pantano.

quail [kwāl] *n* (*ZOOL*) quaglia ♦ *vi*: **to ~ at** *or* **before** perdersi d'animo davanti a.

quaint [kwānt] *a* bizzarro(a); (*old-fashioned*) antiquato(a) e pittoresco(a).

quake [kwāk] *vi* tremare ♦ *n abbr* = **earthquake**.

Quaker [kwā'kûr] *n* quacchero/a.

qualification [kwâləfəkā'shən] *n* (*degree etc*) qualifica, titolo; (*ability*) competenza, qualificazione *f*; (*limitation*) riserva, restrizione *f*; **what are your ~s?** quali sono le sue qualifiche?

qualified [kwâl'əfīd] *a* qualificato(a); (*able*) competente, qualificato(a); (*limited*) condizionato(a); ~ **for/to do** qualificato(a) per/per fare; **he's not** ~ **for the job** non ha i requisiti necessari per questo lavoro; **it was a** ~ **success** è stato un successo parziale.

qualify [kwâl'əfī] *vt* abilitare; (*limit: statement*) modificare, precisare ♦ *vi*: **to** ~ **(as)** qualificarsi (come); **to** ~ **(for)** acquistare i requisiti necessari (per); (*SPORT*) qualificarsi (per *or* a); **to** ~ **as an engineer** diventare un perito tecnico.

qualifying [kwâl'əfīing] *a* (*exam*) di ammissione; (*round*) eliminatorio(a).

qualitative [kwâl'itātiv] *a* qualitativo(a).

quality [kwâl'itē] *n* qualità *f inv* ♦ *cpd* di qualità; **of good** ~ di buona qualità; **of poor** ~ scadente.

quality control *n* controllo di qualità.

quality papers *npl* (*Brit*): **the** ~ la stampa d'informazione.

qualm [kwâm] *n* dubbio; scrupolo; **to have ~s about sth** avere degli scrupoli per qc.

quandary [kwân'drē] *n*: **in a** ~ in un dilemma.

quantitative [kwân'titātiv] *a* quantitativo(a).

quantity [kwân'titē] *n* quantità *f inv*; **in** ~ in grande quantità.

quarantine [kwôr'əntēn] *n* quarantena.

quarrel [kwôr'əl] *n* lite *f*, disputa ♦ *vi* litigare; **to have a** ~ **with sb** litigare con qn; **I've no** ~ **with him** non ho niente contro di lui; **I can't** ~ **with that** non ho niente da ridire su questo.

quarrelsome [kwôr'əlsəm] *a* litigioso(a).

quarry [kwôr'ē] *n* (*for stone*) cava; (*animal*) preda ♦ *vt* (*marble etc*) estrarre.

quart [kwôrt] *n* = litro.

quarter [kwôr'tûr] *n* quarto; (*of year*) trimestre *m*; (*district*) quartiere *m*; (*US, Canada*: *25 cents*) quarto di dollaro, 25 centesimi ♦ *vt* dividere in quattro; (*MIL*) alloggiare; **~s** *npl* alloggio; (*MIL*) alloggi *mpl*, quadrato; **to pay by the** ~ pagare trimestralmente; **a** ~ **of an hour** un quarto d'ora; **it's a** ~ **of 3**, (*Brit*) **it's a** ~ **to 3** sono le 3 meno un quarto, manca un quarto alle 3; **it's a** ~ **after 3**, (*Brit*) **it's a** ~ **past 3** sono le 3 e un quarto; **from all** ~**s** da tutte la parti *or* direzioni; **at close ~s** a distanza ravvicinata.

quarter-deck [kwôr'tûrdek] *n* (*NAUT*) cassero.

quarter final *n* quarto di finale.

quarterly [kwôr'tûrlē] *a* trimestrale ♦ *ad* trimestralmente ♦ *n* periodico trimestrale.

quartermaster (QM) [kwôr'tûrmastûr] *n* (*MIL*) furiere *m*.

quarter note *n* (*US*) semiminima.

quartet(te) [kwôrtet'] *n* quartetto.

quarto [kwôr'tō] *a* in quarto *(m)* *inv*.

quartz [kwôrts] *n* quarzo ♦ *cpd* di quarzo; (*watch*, *clock*) al quarzo.

quash [kwâsh] *vt* (*verdict*) annullare.

quasi- [kwā'zī] *prefix* quasi + *noun*; quasi, pressoché + *adjective*.

quaver [kwā'vûr] *n* (*Brit MUS*) croma ♦ *vi* tremolare.

quay [kē] *n* (*also:* ~**side**) banchina.

Que. *abbr* (*Canada*) = Quebec.

queasy [kwē'zē] *a* (*stomach*) delicato(a); **to feel** ~ aver la nausea.

Quebec [kwibek'] *n* Quebec *m*.

queen [kwēn] *n* (*gen*) regina; (*CARDS etc*) regina, donna.

queen mother *n* regina madre.

queer [kwēr] *a* strano(a), curioso(a); (*suspicious*) dubbio(a), sospetto(a); (*sick*): **I feel** ~ mi sento poco bene.

quell [kwel] *vt* domare.

quench [kwench] *vt* (*flames*) spegnere; **to** ~ **one's thirst** dissetarsi.

querulous [kwär'ələs] *a* querulo(a).

query [kwiûr'ē] *n* domanda, questione *f*; (*doubt*) dubbio ♦ *vt* mettere in questione; (*disagree with*, *dispute*) contestare.

quest [kwest] *n* cerca, ricerca.

question [kwes'chən] *n* domanda, questione *f* ♦ *vt* (*person*) interrogare; (*plan*, *idea*) mettere in questione *or* in dubbio; **to ask sb a** ~, **put a** ~ **to sb** fare una domanda a qn; **to bring** *or* **call sth into** ~ mettere in dubbio qc; **the** ~ **is** ... il problema è ...; **it's a** ~ **of doing** si tratta di fare; **there's some** ~ **of doing** c'è chi suggerisce di fare; **beyond** ~ fuori di dubbio; **out of the** ~ fuori discussione, impossibile.

questionable [kwes'chənəbəl] *a* discutibile.

questioner [kwes'chənûr] *n* interrogante *m/f*.

questioning [kwes'chəning] *a* interrogativo(a) ♦ *n* interrogatorio.

question mark *n* punto interrogativo.

questionnaire [kweschənär'] *n* questionario.

queue [kyōō] *n* coda, fila ♦ *vi* fare la coda; **to jump the** ~ passare davanti agli altri (in una coda).

quibble [kwib'əl] *vi* cavillare.

quick [kwik] *a* rapido(a), veloce; (*reply*) pronto(a); (*mind*) pronto(a), acuto(a) ♦ *ad* rapidamente, presto ♦ *n*: **cut to the** ~ (*fig*) toccato(a) sul vivo; **be ~!** fa presto!; **to be** ~ **to act** agire prontamente; **she was** ~ **to see that** ... ha visto subito che ....

quicken [kwik'ən] *vt* accelerare, affrettare; (*rouse*) animare, stimolare ♦ *vi* accelerarsi, affrettarsi.

quicklime [kwik'līm] *n* calce *f* viva.

quickly [kwik'lē] *ad* rapidamente, velocemente; **we must act** ~ dobbiamo agire tempestivamente.

quickness [kwik'nis] *n* rapidità; prontezza; acutezza.

quicksand [kwik'sand] *n* sabbie *fpl* mobili.

quickstep [kwik'step] *n* (*dance*) fox-trot *m inv*.

quick-tempered [kwik'tempûrd] *a* che si arrabbia facilmente.
quick-witted [kwik'wit'id] *a* pronto(a) d'ingegno.
quid [kwid] *n* (*pl inv*) (*Brit col*) sterlina.
quid pro quo [kwid' prō' kwō] *n* contraccambio.
quiet [kwī'it] *a* tranquillo(a), quieto(a); (*reserved*) quieto(a), taciturno(a); (*ceremony*) semplice; (*not noisy: engine*) silenzioso(a); (*not busy: day*) calmo(a), tranquillo(a); (*color*) discreto(a) ♦ *n* tranquillità, calma ♦ *vb* (*US: also:* ~ **down**) *vi* calmarsi, chetarsi ♦ *vt* clamare, chetare; **keep** ~! sta zitto!; **on the** ~ di nascosto; **I'll have a** ~ **word with him** gli dirò due parole in privato; **business is** ~ **at this time of year** questa è la stagione morta.
quieten [kwī'itən] (*Brit: also:* ~ **down**) *vi*, *vt* = **quiet**.
quietly [kwī'itlē] *ad* tranquillamente, calmamente; silenziosamente.
quietness [kwī'itnis] *n* tranquillità, calma; silenzio.
quill [kwil] *n* penna d'oca.
quilt [kwilt] *n* trapunta; **continental** ~ piumino.
quilting [kwil'ting] *n* stoffa per trapunta; trapunto.
quin [kwin] *n abbr* = **quintuplet**.
quince [kwins] *n* (mela) cotogna; (*tree*) cotogno.
quinine [kwī'nīn] *n* chinino.
quintet(te) [kwintet'] *n* quintetto.
quintuplet [kwintu'plit] *n* uno/a di cinque gemelli.
quip [kwip] *n* battuta di spirito.
quire [kwīûr] *n* ventesima parte di una risma.
quirk [kwûrk] *n* ghiribizzo; **by some** ~ **of fate** per un capriccio della sorte.
quit, *pt, pp* **quit** *or* **quitted** [kwit] *vt* lasciare, partire da ♦ *vi* (*give up*) mollare; (*resign*) dimettersi; **to** ~ **doing** smettere di fare; ~ **stalling!** (*US col*) non tirarla per le lunghe!; **notice to** ~ (*Brit*) preavviso (*dato all'inquilino*).
quite [kwīt] *ad* (*rather*) assai; (*entirely*) completamente, del tutto; **I** ~ **understand** capisco perfettamente; ~ **a few of them** non pochi di loro; ~ **(so)!** esatto!; ~ **new** proprio nuovo; **that's not** ~ **right** non è proprio esatto; **she's** ~ **pretty** è piuttosto carina.
Quito [kē'tō] *n* Quito *m*.
quits [kwits] *a*: ~ **(with)** pari (con); **let's call it** ~ adesso siamo pari.
quiver [kwiv'ûr] *vi* tremare, fremere ♦ *n* (*for arrows*) faretra.
quiz [kwiz] *n* (*game*) quiz *m inv*; indovinello ♦ *vt* interrogare.
quizzical [kwiz'ikəl] *a* enigmatico(a).
quoits [kwoits] *npl* gioco degli anelli.

quorum [kwôr'əm] *n* quorum *m*.
quota [kwō'tə] *n* quota.
quotation [kwōtā'shən] *n* citazione *f*; (*Brit: estimate*) preventivo.
quotation marks *npl* virgolette *fpl*.
quote [kwōt] *n* citazione *f*; (*estimate*) preventivo ♦ *vt* (*sentence*) citare; (*price*) dare, indicare, fissare; (*shares*) quotare ♦ *vi*: **to** ~ **from** citare; **to** ~ **for a job** dare un preventivo per un lavoro; ~**s** *npl* (*col*) = **quotation marks**; **in** ~**s** tra virgolette; ~ ... **unquote** (*in dictation*) aprire le virgolette ... chiudere le virgolette.
quotient [kwō'shənt] *n* quoziente *m*.
qv *abbr* (= *quod vide: which see*) v.
qwerty keyboard [kwûr'tē kē'bôrd] *n* (*Brit*) tastiera qwerty *inv*.

R

R, r [âr] *n* (*letter*) R, r *f or m inv*; **R for Roger** ≈ R come Roma.
R *abbr* (= *Réaumur* (*scale*)) R; (= *river*) F; (= *right*) D; (*US CINEMA:* = *restricted*) ≈ vietato; (*US POL*) = **republican**; (*Brit*) = *Rex, Regina*.
RA *n abbr* = **rear admiral**.
RAAF *n abbr* = *Royal Australian Air Force*.
Rabat [râbât'] *n* Rabat *f*.
rabbi [rab'ī] *n* rabbino.
rabbit [rab'it] *n* coniglio.
rabbit hole *n* tana di coniglio.
rabbit hutch *n* conigliera.
rabble [rab'əl] *n* (*pej*) canaglia, plebaglia.
rabid [rab'id] *a* rabbioso(a); (*fig*) fanatico(a).
rabies [rā'bēz] *n* rabbia.
RAC *n abbr* (*Brit*: = *Royal Automobile Club*) ≈ A.C.I. *m* (= *Automobile Club d'Italia*).
raccoon [rakōōn'] *n* procione *m*.
race [rās] *n* razza; (*competition, rush*) corsa ♦ *vt* (*person*) gareggiare (in corsa) con; (*horse*) far correre; (*engine*) imballare ♦ *vi* correre; **the human** ~ la razza umana; **he** ~**d across the road** ha attraversato la strada di corsa; **to** ~ **in/out** *etc* precipitarsi dentro/fuori *etc*.
race car *n* (*US*) macchina da corsa.
race car driver *n* (*US*) corridore *m* automobilista.
racecourse [rās'kôrs] *n* campo di corse, ippodromo.
racehorse [rās'hôrs] *n* cavallo da corsa.
race relations *npl* rapporti razziali.
racetrack [rās'trak] *n* pista.

racial |rā'shəl| *a* razziale.
racial discrimination *n* discriminazione *f* razziale.
racialism |rā'shəlizəm| *n* razzismo.
racialist |rā'shəlist| *a, n* razzista *(m/f)*.
racing |rā'sing| *n* corsa.
racing car *n (Brit)* = **race car.**
racing driver *n (Brit)* = **race car driver.**
racism |rā'sizəm| *n* razzismo.
racist |rā'sist| *a, n (pej)* razzista *(m/f)*.
rack |rak| *n* rastrelliera; *(also:* **luggage ~)** rete *f*, portabagagli *m inv; (also:* **roof ~)** portabagagli ♦ *vt* torturare, tormentare; **magazine ~** portariviste *m inv;* **shoe ~** scarpiera; **toast ~** portatoast *m inv;* **to ~ one's brains** scervellarsi; **to go to ~ and ruin** *(building)* andare in rovina; *(business)* andare in malora *or* a catafascio.
rack up *vt* accumulare.
rack-and-pinion |rak'əndpin'yən| *n (TECH)* rocchetto-cremagliera *m*.
racket |rak'it| *n (for tennis)* racchetta; *(noise)* fracasso, baccano; *(swindle)* imbroglio, truffa; *(organized crime)* racket *m inv*.
racketeer |rakitēr'| *n (US)* trafficante *m/f*.
racoon |rakōōn'| *n* = **raccoon.**
racquet |rak'it| *n* racchetta.
racy |rā'sē| *a* brioso(a); piccante.
radar |rā'dâr| *n* radar *m* ♦ *cpd* radar *inv*.
radar trap *n* controllo della velocità con radar.
radial |rā'dēəl| *a (also:* **~-ply)** radiale.
radiance |rā'dēəns| *n* splendore *m*, radiosità.
radiant |rā'dēənt| *a* raggiante; *(PHYSICS)* radiante.
radiate |rā'dēāt| *vt (heat)* irraggiare, irradiare ♦ *vi (lines)* irradiarsi.
radiation |rādēā'shən| *n* irradiamento; *(radioactive)* radiazione *f*.
radiation sickness *n* malattia da radiazioni.
radiator |rā'dēātûr| *n* radiatore *m*.
radiator cap *n* tappo del radiatore.
radiator grill *n (AUT)* mascherina, calandra.
radical |rad'ikəl| *a* radicale.
radii |rā'dēī| *npl of* **radius.**
radio |rā'dēō| *n* radio *f inv* ♦ *vt (information)* trasmettere per radio; *(one's position)* comunicare via radio; *(person)* chiamare via radio ♦ *vi:* **to ~ to sb** comunicare via radio con qn; **on the ~** alla radio.
radio... *prefix* radio....
radioactive |rādēōak'tiv| *a* radioattivo(a).
radioactivity |rādēōaktiv'ətē| *n* radioattività.
radio announcer *n* annunciatore/trice della radio.
radio-controlled |rā'dēōkəntrōld'| *a* radiocomandato(a), radioguidato(a).
radiographer |rādēāg'rəfûr| *n* radiologo/a *(tecnico)*.
radiography |rādēāg'rəfē| *n* radiografia.
radiologist |rādēāl'əjist| *n* radiologo/a *(medi-*

co).
radiology |rādēāl'əjē| *n* radiologia.
radio station *n* stazione *f* radio *inv*.
radio taxi *n* radiotaxi *m inv*.
radiotelephone |rādēōtel'əfōn| *n* radiotelefono.
radiotherapist |rādēōthār'əpist| *n* radioterapista *m/f*.
radiotherapy |rādēōthār'əpē| *n* radioterapia.
radish |rad'ish| *n* ravanello.
radium |rā'dēəm| *n* radio.
radius, *pl* **radii** |rā'dēəs, rā'dēī| *n* raggio; *(ANAT)* radio; **within a ~ of 50 miles** in un raggio di 50 miglia.
RAF *n abbr (Brit) see* **Royal Air Force.**
raffia |raf'ēə| *n* rafia.
raffish |raf'ish| *a* dal look trasandato.
raffle |raf'əl| *n* lotteria ♦ *vt (object)* mettere in palio.
raft |raft| *n* zattera.
rafter |raf'tûr| *n* trave *f*.
rag |rag| *n* straccio, cencio; *(pej: newspaper)* giornalaccio; *(for charity)* iniziativa studentesca a scopo benefico; **~s** *npl* stracci *mpl*, brandelli *mpl;* **in ~s** stracciato.
rag-and-bone man |ragənbōn' man| *n (Brit)* = **ragman.**
ragbag |rag'bag| *n (fig)* guazzabuglio.
rag doll *n* bambola di pezza.
rage |rāj| *n (fury)* collera, furia ♦ *vi (person)* andare su tutte le furie; *(storm)* infuriare; **it's all the ~** fa furore; **to fly into a ~** andare *or* montare su tutte le furie.
ragged |rag'id| *a (edge)* irregolare; *(cuff)* logoro(a); *(appearance)* pezzente.
raging |rā'jing| *a (all senses)* furioso(a); **in a ~ temper** su tutte le furie.
ragman |rag'man| *n* straccivendolo.
rag trade *n (col):* **the ~** l'abbigliamento.
raid |rād| *n (MIL)* incursione *f; (criminal)* rapina; *(by police)* irruzione *f* ♦ *vt* fare un'incursione in; rapinare; fare irruzione in.
raider |rā'dûr| *n* rapinatore/trice; *(plane)* aeroplano da incursione.
rail |rāl| *n (on stair)* ringhiera; *(on bridge, balcony)* parapetto; *(of ship)* battagliola; *(Brit: for train)* rotaia; **~s** *npl (Brit)* binario, rotaie *fpl;* **by ~** per ferrovia, in treno.
railing(s) |rā'ling(z)| *n(pl)* ringhiere *fpl*.
railroad |rāl'rōd| *n (US)* ferrovia.
railroader |rāl'rōdûr| *n (US)* ferroviere *m*.
railroad line *n* linea ferroviaria.
railroad station *n* stazione *f* ferroviaria.
railway |rāl'wā| *etc (Brit)* = **railroad** *etc*.
railway engine *n (Brit)* locomotiva.
railwayman |rāl'wāmən| *n (Brit)* = **railroader.**
rain |rān| *n* pioggia ♦ *vi* piovere; **in the ~** sotto la pioggia; **it's ~ing** piove; **it's ~ing cats and dogs** piove a catinelle.
rainbow |rān'bō| *n* arcobaleno.
raincoat |rān'kōt| *n* impermeabile *m*.

raindrop [rān'dråp] *n* goccia di pioggia.
rainfall [rān'fôl] *n* pioggia; (*measurement*) piovosità.
rainforest [rān'fôrist] *n* (*also*: **tropical** ~) foresta amazzonica.
rainproof [rān'prōōf] *a* impermeabile.
rainstorm [rān'stôrm] *n* pioggia torrenziale.
rainwater [rān'wôtûr] *n* acqua piovana.
rainy [rā'nē] *a* piovoso(a).
raise [rāz] *n* aumento ♦ *vt* (*lift*) alzare, sollevare; (*build*) erigere; (*increase*) aumentare; (*a protest, doubt, question*) sollevare; (*cattle, family*) allevare; (*crop*) coltivare; (*army, funds*) raccogliere; (*loan*) ottenere; (*end: siege, embargo*) togliere; **to ~ one's voice** alzare la voce; **to ~ sb's hopes** accendere le speranze di qn; **to ~ one's glass to sb/sth** brindare a qn/qc; **to ~ a laugh/a smile** far ridere/sorridere.
raisin [rā'zin] *n* uva secca.
Raj [râj] *n*: **the ~** l'impero britannico (*in India*).
rajah [râ'jə] *n* ragià *m inv*.
rake [rāk] *n* (*tool*) rastrello; (*person*) libertino ♦ *vt* (*garden*) rastrellare; (*with machine gun*) spazzare ♦ *vi*: **to ~ through** (*fig: search*) frugare tra.
rake-off [rāk'ôf] *n* (*col*) parte *f* percentuale, fetta.
rakish [rā'kish] *a* dissoluto(a); disinvolto(a).
rally [ral'ē] *n* (*POL etc*) riunione *f*; (*AUT*) rally *m inv*; (*TENNIS*) scambio ♦ *vt* riunire, radunare ♦ *vi* raccogliersi, radunarsi; (*sick person, STOCK EXCHANGE*) riprendersi.
  rally around *vt fus* raggrupparsi intorno a; venire in aiuto di.
rallying point [ral'ēing point] *n* (*POL, MIL*) punto di riunione, punto di raduno.
RAM [ram] *n abbr* (*COMPUT*: = *random access memory*) RAM *f*.
ram [ram] *n* montone *m*, ariete *m*; (*device*) ariete ♦ *vt* conficcare; (*crash into*) cozzare, sbattere contro; percuotere; speronare.
ramble [ram'bəl] *n* escursione *f* ♦ *vi* (*pej: also*: ~ **on**) divagare.
rambler [ram'blûr] *n* escursionista *m/f*; (*BOT*) rosa rampicante.
rambling [ram'bling] *a* (*speech*) sconnesso(a); (*BOT*) rampicante; (*house*) tutto(a) nicchie e corridoi.
rambunctious [rambungk'shəs] *a* (*US: person*): **to be ~** essere un terremoto.
ramification [raməfəkā'shən] *n* ramificazione *f*.
ramp [ramp] *n* rampa; "~" (*Brit AUT*) "fondo stradale in rifacimento".
rampage [ram'pāj] *n*: **to go on the ~** scatenarsi in modo violento ♦ *vi*: **they went rampaging through the town** si sono scatenati in modo violento per la città.
rampant [ram'pənt] *a* (*disease etc*) che infierisce.

rampart [ram'pârt] *n* bastione *m*.
ramshackle [ram'shakəl] *a* (*house*) cadente; (*car etc*) sgangherato(a).
ran [ran] *pt of* **run**.
ranch [ranch] *n* ranch *m inv*.
rancher [ran'chûr] *n* (*owner*) proprietario di un ranch; (*ranch hand*) cowboy *m inv*.
rancid [ran'sid] *a* rancido(a).
rancor, (*Brit*) **rancour** [rang'kûr] *n* rancore *m*.
random [ran'dəm] *a* fatto(a) *or* detto(a) per caso; (*COMPUT, MATH*) casuale ♦ *n*: **at ~** a casaccio.
random access *n* (*COMPUT*) accesso casuale.
randy [ran'dē] *a* (*col*) arrapato(a); lascivo(a).
rang [rang] *pt of* **ring**.
range [rānj] *n* (*of mountains*) catena; (*of missile, voice*) portata; (*of products*) gamma; (*MIL: also*: **shooting** ~) campo di tiro; (*also*: **kitchen** ~) fornello, cucina economica ♦ *vt* (*place*) disporre, allineare; (*roam*) vagare per ♦ *vi*: **to ~ over** coprire; **to ~ from ... to** andare da ... a; **price ~** gamma di prezzi; **do you have anything else in this price ~?** ha nient'altro su *or* di questo prezzo?; **within (firing) ~** a portata di tiro; **~d left/right** (*text*) allineato(a) a sinistra/destra.
ranger [rān'jûr] *n* guardia forestale.
Rangoon [ranggōōn'] *n* Rangun *f*.
rank [rangk] *n* (*MIL*) grado; (*Brit: also*: **taxi** ~) posteggio di taxi ♦ *vi*: **to ~ among** essere nel numero di ♦ *a* (*smell*) puzzolente; (*hypocrisy, injustice*) vero(a) e proprio(a); **the ~s** (*MIL*) la truppa; **the ~ and file** (*fig*) la gran massa; **to close ~s** (*MIL, fig*) serrare i ranghi; **I ~ him 6th** gli do il sesto posto, lo metto al sesto posto.
rankle [rang'kəl] *vi*: **to ~** (**with sb**) bruciare (a qn).
ransack [ran'sak] *vt* rovistare; (*plunder*) saccheggiare.
ransom [ran'səm] *n* riscatto; **to hold sb to ~** (*fig*) esercitare pressione su qn.
rant [rant] *vi* vociare.
ranting [ran'ting] *n* vociare *m*.
rap [rap] *n* (*noise*) colpetti *mpl*; (*at a door*) bussata ♦ *vt* dare dei colpetti a; bussare a.
rape [rāp] *n* violenza carnale, stupro ♦ *vt* violentare.
rape(seed) oil [rāp'(sēd) oil] *n* olio di ravizzone.
rapid [rap'id] *a* rapido(a).
rapidity [rəpid'itē] *n* rapidità.
rapidly [rap'idlē] *ad* rapidamente.
rapids [rap'idz] *npl* (*GEO*) rapida.
rapist [rā'pist] *n* violentatore *m*.
rapport [rapôr'] *n* rapporto.
rapt [rapt] *a* (*attention*) rapito(a), profondo(a); **to be ~ in contemplation** essere in estatica contemplazione.
rapture [rap'chûr] *n* estasi *f inv*; **to go into ~s over** andare in solluchero per.

rapturous [rap'chûrəs] *a* estatico(a).

rare [rär] *a* raro(a); (*CULIN: steak*) al sangue; **it is ~ to find that ...** capita di rado *or* raramente che ... + *sub*.

rarebit [rär'bit] *n see* **Welsh rarebit**.

rarefied [rär'əfīd] *a* (*air, atmosphere*) rarefatto(a).

rarely [reûr'lē] *ad* raramente.

raring [rär'ing] *a*: **to be ~ to go** (*col*) non veder l'ora di cominciare.

rarity [rär'itē] *n* rarità *f inv*.

rascal [ras'kəl] *n* mascalzone *m*.

rash [rash] *a* imprudente, sconsiderato(a) + *n* (*MED*) eruzione *f*; **to come out in a ~** avere uno sfogo.

rasher [rash'ûr] *n* fetta sottile (di lardo *or* prosciutto).

rasp [rasp] *n* (*tool*) lima + *vt* (*speak: also:* **~ out**) gracchiare.

raspberry [raz'bärē] *n* lampone *m*.

raspberry bush *n* lampone *m* (*pianta*).

rasping [ras'ping] *a* stridulo(a).

rat [rat] *n* ratto.

ratchet [rach'it] *n*: **~ wheel** ruota dentata.

rate [rāt] *n* (*proportion*) tasso, percentuale *f*; (*speed*) velocità *f inv*; (*price*) tariffa + *vt* valutare; stimare; **to ~ sb/sth as** valutare qn/qc come; **to ~ sb/sth among** annoverare qn/qc tra; **to ~ sb/sth highly** stimare molto qn/qc; **at a ~ of 60 kph** alla velocità di 60 km all'ora; **~ of exchange** tasso di cambio; **~ of flow** flusso medio; **~ of growth** tasso di crescita; **~ of return** tasso di rendimento; **pulse ~** frequenza delle pulsazioni; *see also* **rates**.

rates [rāts] *npl* (*Brit*) imposte *fpl* comunali.

rather [rath'ûr] *ad* piuttosto; (*somewhat*) abbastanza; (*to some extent*) un po'; **it's ~ expensive** è piuttosto caro; (*too much*) un po' caro; **there's ~ a lot** (*Brit*) ce n'è parecchio; **I would** *or* **I'd ~ go** preferirei andare; **I had ~ go** farei meglio ad andare; **I'd ~ not leave** preferirei non partire; **or ~** (*more accurately*) anzi, per essere (più) precisi.

ratification [ratəfəkā'shən] *n* ratificazione *f*.

ratify [rat'əfī] *vt* ratificare.

rating [rā'ting] *n* classificazione *f*; punteggio di merito; (*NAUT: category*) classe *f*; (: *sailor: Brit*) marinaio semplice.

ratings [rā'tingz] *npl* (*RADIO, TV*) indice *m* di ascolto.

ratio [rā'shō] *n* proporzione *f*; **in the ~ of 2 to 1** in rapporto di 2 a 1.

ration [rash'ən] *n* razione *f* + *vt* razionare.

rational [rash'ənəl] *a* razionale, ragionevole; (*solution, reasoning*) logico(a).

rationale [rashənal'] *n* fondamento logico; giustificazione *f*.

rationalization [rashənələzā'shən] *n* razionalizzazione *f*.

rationalize [rash'ənəlīz] *vt* razionalizzare.

rationally [rash'ənəlē] *ad* razionalmente; logicamente.

rationing [rash'əning] *n* razionamento.

rat poison *n* veleno per topi.

rat race *n* carrierismo, corsa al successo.

rattan [ratan'] *n* malacca.

rattle [rat'əl] *n* tintinnio; (*louder*) rumore *m* di ferraglia; (*object: of baby*) sonaglino; (: *of sports fan*) raganella + *vi* risuonare, tintinnare; fare un rumore di ferraglia + *vt* agitare; far tintinnare; (*col: disconcert*) sconcertare.

rattlesnake [rat'əlsnāk] *n* serpente *m* a sonagli.

ratty [rat'ē] *a* (*col: US: shabby*) trasandato(a); (: *Brit: annoyed*) incavolato(a).

raucous [rô'kəs] *a* sguaiato(a).

raucously [rô'kəslē] *ad* sguaiatamente.

ravage [rav'ij] *vt* devastare.

ravages [rav'ijiz] *npl* danni *mpl*.

rave [rāv] *vi* (*in anger*) infuriarsi; (*with enthusiasm*) andare in estasi; (*MED*) delirare + *cpd*: **~ review** (*col*) critica entusiastica.

raven [rā'vən] *n* corvo.

ravenous [rav'ənəs] *a* affamato(a).

ravine [rəvēn'] *n* burrone *m*.

raving [rā'ving] *a*: **~ lunatic** pazzo(a) furioso(a).

ravings [rā'vingz] *npl* vaneggiamenti *mpl*.

ravioli [ravēō'lē] *n* ravioli *mpl*.

ravish [rav'ish] *vt* (*delight*) estasiare.

ravishing [rav'ishing] *a* incantevole.

raw [rô] *a* (*uncooked*) crudo(a); (*not processed*) greggio(a); (*sore*) vivo(a); (*inexperienced*) inesperto(a); **to get a ~ deal** (*col: bad bargain*) prendere un bidone; (: *harsh treatment*) venire trattato ingiustamente.

Rawalpindi [râwəlpin'dē] *n* Rawalpindi *f*.

raw material *n* materia prima.

ray [rā] *n* raggio.

rayon [rā'ân] *n* raion *m*.

raze [rāz] *vt* radere, distruggere; (*also:* **~ to the ground**) radere al suolo.

razor [rā'zûr] *n* rasoio.

razor blade *n* lama di rasoio.

razzmatazz [raz'mətaz] *n* (*col*) clamore *m*.

R&B *n abbr* = *rhythm and blues*.

RC *abbr* = **Roman Catholic**.

RCAF *n abbr* = *Royal Canadian Air Force*.

RCMP *n abbr* = *Royal Canadian Mounted Police*.

RCN *n abbr* = *Royal Canadian Navy*.

RD *abbr* (*US MAIL*) = *rural delivery*.

Rd *abbr* = *road*.

R&D *n abbr see* **research and development**.

re [rā] *prep* con riferimento a.

reach [rēch] *n* portata; (*of river etc*) tratto + *vt* raggiungere; arrivare a + *vi* stendersi; (*stretch out hand: also:* **~ down**, **~ over**, **~ across** *etc*) allungare una mano; **out of/within ~** (*object*) fuori/a portata di mano; **within easy ~ (of)** (*place*) a breve distanza

(di), vicino (a); **to ~ sb by phone** contattare qn per telefono; **can I ~ you at your hotel?** posso trovarla al suo albergo?
reach out *vi*: **to ~ out for** stendere la mano per prendere.
react [rēakt'] *vi* reagire.
reaction [rēak'shən] *n* reazione *f*.
reactionary [rēak'shənärē] *a, n* reazionario(a).
reactor [rēak'tûr] *n* reattore *m*.
read, *pt, pp* **read** [rēd, red] *vi* leggere ♦ *vt* leggere; (*understand*) intendere, interpretare; (*study*) studiare; **do you ~ me?** (*TEL*) mi ricevete?; **to take sth as read** (*fig*) dare qc per scontato.
read out *vt* leggere ad alta voce.
read over *vt* rileggere attentamente.
read through *vt* (*quickly*) dare una scorsa a; (*thoroughly*) leggere da cima a fondo.
read up *vt*, **read up on** *vt fus* studiare bene.
readable [rē'dəbəl] *a* leggibile; che si legge volentieri.
reader [rē'dûr] *n* lettore/trice; (*book*) libro di lettura.
readership [rē'dûrship] *n* (*of paper etc*) numero di lettori.
readily [red'əlē] *ad* volentieri; (*easily*) facilmente.
readiness [red'ēnis] *n* prontezza; **in ~** (*prepared*) pronto(a).
reading [rēd'ing] *n* lettura; (*understanding*) interpretazione *f*; (*on instrument*) indicazione *f*.
reading lamp *n* lampada da studio.
reading room *n* sala di lettura.
readjust [rēəjust'] *vt* raggiustare ♦ *vi* (*person*): **to ~ (to)** riadattarsi (a).
ready [red'ē] *a* pronto(a); (*willing*) pronto(a), disposto(a); (*quick*) rapido(a); (*available*) disponibile ♦ *n*: **at the ~** (*MIL*) pronto a sparare; (*fig*) tutto(a) pronto(a); **~ for use** pronto per l'uso; **to be ~ to do sth** essere pronto a fare qc; **to get ~** *vi* prepararsi ♦ *vt* preparare.
ready cash *n* denaro in contanti.
ready-cooked [red'ēkŏŏkt'] *a* già cotto(a).
ready-made [red'ēmād'] *a* prefabbricato(a); (*clothes*) confezionato(a).
ready-to-wear [red'ētəwär'] *a* prêt-à-porter *inv*.
reagent [rēā'jənt] *n*: **chemical ~** reagente *m* chimico.
real [rēl] *a* reale; vero(a) ♦ *ad* (*US col: very*) veramente, proprio; **in ~ terms** in realtà; **in ~ life** nella realtà.
real estate *n* beni *mpl* immobili.
real estate agent *n* (*US*) agente *m* immobiliare.
real estate office *n* (*US*) agenzia immobiliare.
realism [rē'əlizəm] *n* (*also ART*) realismo.

realist [rē'əlist] *n* realista *m/f*.
realistic [rēəlis'tik] *a* realistico(a).
reality [rēal'itē] *n* realtà *f inv*; **in ~** in realtà, in effetti.
realization [rēələzā'shən] *n* (*awareness*) presa di coscienza; (*of hopes, project etc*) realizzazione *f*.
realize [rē'əlīz] *vt* (*understand*) rendersi conto di; (*a project, COMM: asset*) realizzare; **I ~ that ...** mi rendo conto o capisco che ....
really [rē'əlē] *ad* veramente, davvero.
realm [relm] *n* reame *m*, regno.
real time *n* (*COMPUT*) tempo reale.
realtor [rē'əltûr] *n* (*US*) agente *m* immobiliare.
ream [rēm] *n* risma; **~s** (*fig col*) pagine e pagine *fpl*.
reap [rēp] *vt* mietere; (*fig*) raccogliere.
reaper [rē'pûr] *n* (*machine*) mietitrice *f*.
reappear [rēəpi'ûr] *vi* ricomparire, riapparire.
reappearance [rēəpēr'əns] *n* riapparizione *f*.
reapply [rēəplī'] *vi*: **to ~ for** fare un'altra domanda per.
reappraisal [rēəprā'zəl] *n* riesame *m*.
rear [rēr] *a* di dietro; (*AUT: wheel etc*) posteriore ♦ *n* didietro, parte *f* posteriore ♦ *vt* (*cattle, family*) allevare ♦ *vi* (*also*: **~ up**: *animal*) impennarsi.
rear admiral *n* contrammiraglio.
rear-engined [rēr'en'jənd] *a* (*AUT*) con motore posteriore.
rearguard [rēr'gârd] *n* retroguardia.
rearm [rēârm'] *vt, vi* riarmare.
rearmament [rēârm'əmənt] *n* riarmo.
rearrange [rēərānj'] *vt* riordinare.
rear-view mirror [rēr'vyōō' mir'ûr] *n* (*AUT*) specchio retrovisivo.
reason [rē'zən] *n* ragione *f*; (*cause, motive*) ragione, motivo ♦ *vi*: **to ~ with sb** far ragionare qn; **to have ~ to think** avere motivi per pensare; **it stands to ~ that** è ovvio che; **the ~ for/why** la ragione *or* il motivo di/per cui; **with good ~** a ragione; **all the more ~ why you should not sell it** ragione di più per non venderlo.
reasonable [rē'zənəbəl] *a* ragionevole; (*not bad*) accettabile.
reasonably [rē'zənəblē] *ad* ragionevolmente; **one can ~ assume that ...** uno può facilmente supporre che ....
reasoned [rē'zənd] *a* (*argument*) ponderato(a).
reasoning [rē'zəning] *n* ragionamento.
reassemble [rēəsem'bəl] *vt* riunire; (*machine*) rimontare.
reassert [rēəsûrt'] *vt* riaffermare.
reassurance [rēəshŏŏr'əns] *n* rassicurazione *f*.
reassure [rēəshŏŏr'] *vt* rassicurare; **to ~ sb of** rassicurare qn di *or* su.
reassuring [rēəshŏŏr'ing] *a* rassicurante.
reawakening [rēəwā'kəning] *n* risveglio.
rebate [rē'bāt] *n* rimborso.

rebel *n* [reb'əl] ribelle *m/f* ♦ *vi* [ribel'] ribellarsi.

rebellion [ribel'yən] *n* ribellione *f*.

rebellious [ribel'yəs] *a* ribelle.

rebirth [rēbûrth'] *n* rinascita.

rebound *vi* [ribound'] *(ball)* rimbalzare ♦ *n* [rē'bound] rimbalzo.

rebuff [ribuf'] *n* secco rifiuto ♦ *vt* respingere.

rebuild [rēbild'] *vt irg* ricostruire.

rebuke [ribyōōk'] *n* rimprovero ♦ *vt* rimproverare.

rebut [ribut'] *vt* rifiutare.

rebuttal [ribut'əl] *n* rifiuto.

recalcitrant [rikal'sitrənt] *a* recalcitrante.

recall *vt* [rikôl'] *(gen, COMPUT)* richiamare; *(remember)* ricordare, richiamare alla mente ♦ *n* [rē'kôl] richiamo; **beyond ~** irrevocabile.

recant [rikant'] *vi* ritrattarsi; *(REL)* fare abiura.

recap [rē'kap] *n* ricapitolazione *f* ♦ *vt* ricapitolare ♦ *vi* riassumere.

recapture [rēkap'chûr] *vt* riprendere; *(atmosphere)* ricreare.

recd. *abbr* = received.

recede [risēd'] *vi* allontanarsi; ritirarsi; calare.

receding [risē'ding] *a* *(forehead, chin)* sfuggente; **he's got a ~ hairline** è stempiato.

receipt [risēt'] *n* *(document)* ricevuta; **to acknowledge ~ of** accusare ricevuta di; **we are in ~ of** ... abbiamo ricevuto ....

receipts [risēts'] *npl* *(COMM)* introiti *mpl*.

receivable [risē'vəbəl] *a* *(COMM)* esigibile; *(: owed)* dovuto(a).

receive [risēv'] *vt* ricevere; *(guest)* ricevere, accogliere; **"~d with thanks"** *(COMM)* "per quietanza".

receiver [risē'vûr] *n* *(TEL)* ricevitore *m*; *(RADIO)* apparecchio ricevente; *(of stolen goods)* ricettatore/trice; *(LAW)* curatore *m* fallimentare.

recent [rē'sənt] *a* recente; **in ~ years** negli ultimi anni.

recently [rē'səntlē] *ad* recentemente; **as ~ as** ... soltanto ...; **until ~** fino a poco tempo fa.

receptacle [risep'təkəl] *n* recipiente *m*.

reception [risep'shən] *n* *(gen)* ricevimento; *(welcome)* accoglienza; *(TV etc)* ricezione *f*.

reception center *n* centro di raccolta.

reception desk *n* *(in hotel)* reception *f inv*; *(in hospital, at doctor's)* accettazione *f*; *(in large building, offices)* portineria.

receptionist [risep'shənist] *n* receptionist *m/f inv*.

receptive [risep'tiv] *a* ricettivo(a).

recess [rē'ses] *n* *(in room)* alcova; *(POL etc: holiday)* vacanze *fpl*; *(US LAW: short break)* sospensione *f*; *(US SCOL)* intervallo.

recession [risesh'ən] *n* *(ECON)* recessione *f*.

recharge [rēchârj'] *vt* *(battery)* ricaricare.

rechargeable [rēchâr'jəbəl] *a* ricaricabile.

recipe [res'əpē] *n* ricetta.

recipient [risip'ēənt] *n* beneficiario/a; *(of letter)* destinatario/a.

reciprocal [risip'rəkəl] *a* reciproco(a).

reciprocate [risip'rəkāt] *vt* ricambiare, contraccambiare.

recital [risīt'əl] *n* recital *m inv*; concerto (di solista).

recite [risīt'] *vt* *(poem)* recitare.

reckless [rek'lis] *a* *(driver etc)* spericolato(a); *(spender)* incosciente.

recklessly [rek'lislē] *ad* in modo spericolato; da incosciente.

reckon [rek'ən] *vt* *(count)* calcolare; *(consider)* considerare, stimare; *(think)*: **I ~ that** ... penso che ... ♦ *vi* contare, calcolare; **to ~ without sb/sth** non tener conto di qn/qc; **he is somebody to be ~ed with** è uno da non sottovalutare.

reckon on *vt fus* contare su.

reckoning [rek'əning] *n* conto; stima; **the day of ~** il giorno del giudizio.

reclaim [riklām'] *vt* *(land)* bonificare; *(demand back)* richiedere, reclamare.

reclamation [rekləmā'shən] *n* bonifica.

recline [riklīn'] *vi* stare sdraiato(a).

reclining [riklī'ning] *a* *(seat)* ribaltabile.

recluse [rek'lōōs] *n* eremita *m*, recluso/a.

recognition [rekəgnish'ən] *n* riconoscimento; **to gain ~** essere riconosciuto(a); **in ~ of** in or come segno di riconoscimento per; **transformed beyond ~** irriconoscibile.

recognizable [rekəgnī'zəbəl] *a*: **~ (by)** riconoscibile (a or da).

recognize [rek'əgnīz] *vt*: **to ~ (by/as)** riconoscere (a or da/come).

recoil [rikoil'] *vi* *(gun)* rinculare; *(spring)* balzare indietro; *(person)*: **to ~ (from)** indietreggiare (davanti a) ♦ *n* *(of gun)* rinculo.

recollect [rekəlekt'] *vt* ricordare.

recollection [rekəlek'shən] *n* ricordo; **to the best of my ~** per quello che mi ricordo.

recommend [rekəmend'] *vt* raccomandare; *(advise)* consigliare; **she has a lot to ~ her** ha molti elementi a suo favore.

recommendation [rekəmendā'shən] *n* raccomandazione *f*; consiglio.

recommended retail price (RRP) [rekəmen'did rē'tāl prīs] *n* *(Brit)* prezzo raccomandato al dettaglio.

recompense [rek'əmpens] *vt* ricompensare; *(compensate)* risarcire ♦ *n* ricompensa; risarcimento.

reconcilable [rek'ənsīləbəl] *a* conciliabile.

reconcile [rek'ənsīl] *vt* *(two people)* riconciliare; *(two facts)* conciliare, quadrare; **to ~ o.s.** to rassegnarsi a.

reconciliation [rekənsilēā'shən] *n* riconciliazione *f*; conciliazione *f*.

recondite [rek'əndīt] *a* recondito(a).

recondition [rēkəndi'shən] *vt* rimettere a nuovo; rifare.

reconnaissance [rikán'isəns] *n* (*MIL*) ricognizione *f*.

reconnoiter, (*Brit*) **reconnoitre** [rēkənoi'tûr] (*MIL*) *vt* fare una ricognizione di ♦ *vi* fare una ricognizione.

reconsider [rēkənsid'ûr] *vt* riconsiderare.

reconstitute [rēkán'stitōōt] *vt* ricostituire.

reconstruct [rēkənstrukt'] *vt* ricostruire.

reconstruction [rēkənstruk'shən] *n* ricostruzione *f*.

record *n* [rek'ûrd] ricordo, documento; (*of meeting etc*) nota, verbale *m*; (*register*) registro; (*file*) pratica, dossier *m inv*; (*COMPUT*) record *m inv*, registrazione *f*; (*also*: **police** ~) fedina penale sporca; (*MUS*: *disc*) disco; (*SPORT*) record *m inv*, primato ♦ *vt* [rikôrd'] (*set down*) prendere nota di, registrare; (*relate*) raccontare; (*COMPUT. MUS*: *song etc*) registrare; **public** ~**s** archivi *mpl*; **Italy's excellent** ~ i brillanti successi italiani; **in** ~ **time** a tempo di record; **to keep a** ~ **of** tener nota di; **to set the** ~ **straight** mettere le cose in chiaro; **off the** ~ *a* ufficioso(a) ♦ *ad* ufficiosamente; **he is on** ~ **as saying that ...** ha dichiarato pubblicamente che ....

record card *n* (*in file*) scheda.

recorded delivery letter *n* (*Brit MAIL*) lettera raccomandata.

recorder [rikôr'dûr] *n* (*MUS*) flauto diritto.

record holder *n* (*SPORT*) primatista *m/f*.

recording [rikôr'ding] *n* (*MUS*) registrazione *f*.

recording studio *n* studio di registrazione.

record library *n* discoteca.

record player *n* giradischi *m inv*.

recount [rikount'] *vt* raccontare, narrare.

re-count *n* [rē'kount] (*POL*: *of votes*) nuovo conteggio ♦ *vt* [rēkount'] ricontare.

recoup [rikōōp'] *vt* ricuperare; **to** ~ **one's losses** ricuperare le perdite, rifarsi.

recourse [rē'kôrs] *n*: **to have** ~ **to** ricorrere a.

recover [rikuv'ûr] *vt* ricuperare ♦ *vi* (*from illness*) rimettersi (in salute), ristabilirsi; (*country, person*: *from shock*) riprendersi.

re-cover [rēkuv'ûr] *vt* (*chair etc*) ricoprire.

recovery [rikuv'ûrē] *n* ricupero; ristabilimento; ripresa.

re-create [rēkrēāt'] *vt* ricreare.

recreation [rekrēā'shən] *n* ricreazione *f*; svago.

recreational [rekrēā'shənəl] *a* ricreativo(a).

recreational vehicle (RV) *n* (*US*) camper *m inv*.

recreation center *n* centro di ricreazione.

recrimination [rikrimənā'shən] *n* recriminazione *f*.

recruit [rikrōōt'] *n* recluta ♦ *vt* reclutare.

recruiting office [rikrōōt'ing ôf'is] *n* ufficio di reclutamento.

recruitment [rikrōōt'mənt] *n* reclutamento.

rectangle [rek'tanggəl] *n* rettangolo.

rectangular [rektang'gyəlûr] *a* rettangolare.

rectify [rek'təfī] *vt* (*error*) rettificare; (*omission*) riparare.

rector [rek'tûr] *n* (*REL*) parroco (*anglicano*); (*in Scottish universities*) *personalità eletta dagli studenti per rappresentarli.*

rectory [rek'tûrē] *n* presbiterio.

rectum [rek'təm] *n* (*ANAT*) retto.

recuperate [rikōō'pərāt] *vi* ristabilirsi.

recur [rikûr'] *vi* riaccadere; (*idea, opportunity*) riapparire; (*symptoms*) ripresentarsi.

recurrence [rikûr'əns] *n* ripresentarsi *m*; riapparizione *f*.

recurrent [rikûr'ənt] *a* ricorrente, periodico(a).

recurring [rikûr'ing] *a* (*MATH*) periodico(a).

recycle [rēsī'kəl] *vt* (*waste, paper etc*) riciclare.

red [red] *n* rosso; (*POL*: *pej*) rosso/a ♦ *a* rosso(a); **in the** ~ (*account*) scoperto; (*business*) in deficit.

red carpet treatment *n* cerimonia col gran pavese.

Red Cross *n* Croce *f* Rossa.

redcurrant [red'kur'ənt] *n* ribes *m inv*.

redden [red'ən] *vt* arrossare ♦ *vi* arrossire.

reddish [red'ish] *a* rossiccio(a).

redecorate [rēdek'ərāt] *vt* tinteggiare (e tappezzare) di nuovo.

redeem [ridēm'] *vt* (*debt*) riscattare; (*sth in pawn*) ritirare; (*fig, also REL*) redimere.

redeemable [ridē'məbəl] *a* con diritto di riscatto; redimibile.

redeeming [ridē'ming] *a* (*feature*) che salva.

redeploy [rēdiploi'] *vt* (*MIL*) riorganizzare lo schieramento di; (*resources*) riorganizzare.

redeployment [rēdiploi'mənt] *n* riorganizzazione *f*.

redevelop [rēdivel'əp] *vt* ristrutturare.

redevelopment [rēdivel'əpmənt] *n* ristrutturazione *f*.

red-haired [red'härd] *a* dai capelli rossi.

red-handed [red'han'did] *a*: **to be caught** ~ essere preso(a) in flagrante *or* con le mani nel sacco.

redhead [red'hed] *n* rosso/a.

red herring *n* (*fig*) falsa pista.

red-hot [red'hät'] *a* arroventato(a).

redirect [rēdərekt'] *vt* (*mail*) far seguire.

redistribute [rēdistrib'yōōt] *vt* ridistribuire.

red-letter day [red'let'ûr dā] *n* giorno memorabile.

red light *n*: **to go through a** ~ (*AUT*) passare col rosso.

red-light district [red'līt dis'trikt] *n* quartiere *m* luce rossa *inv*.

redness [red'nis] *n* rossore *m*; (*of hair*) rosso.

redo [rēdōō'] *vt irg* rifare.

redolent [red'ələnt] *a*: ~ **of** che sa di; (*fig*) che ricorda.

redouble [rĕdub'əl] *vt*: **to ~ one's efforts** raddoppiare gli sforzi.

redraft [rĕdraft'] *vt* fare una nuova stesura di.

redress [ridres'] *n* riparazione *f* ♦ *vt* riparare; **to ~ the balance** ristabilire l'equilibrio.

Red Sea *n*: **the ~** il mar Rosso.

redskin [red'skin] *n* pellerossa *m/f*.

red tape *n* (*fig*) burocrazia.

reduce [ridōōs'] *vt* ridurre; (*lower*) ridurre, abbassare; **to ~ sth by/to** ridurre qc di/a; **to ~ sb to silence/despair/tears** ridurre qn al silenzio/alla disperazione/in lacrime.

reduced [ridōōst'] *a* (*decreased*) ridotto(a); **at a ~ price** a prezzo ribassato *or* ridotto; **"greatly ~ prices"** "grandi ribassi".

reduction [riduk'shən] *n* riduzione *f*; (*of price*) ribasso; (*discount*) sconto.

redundancy [ridun'dənsē] *n* (*Brit*) licenziamento (per eccesso di personale); **compulsory ~** licenziamento; **voluntary ~** *forma di cassa integrazione volontaria*.

redundancy payment *n* (*Brit*) indennità *f inv* di licenziamento.

redundant [ridun'dənt] *a* (*Brit*: *worker*) licenziato(a); (*detail*, *object*) superfluo(a); **to make ~** (*Brit*) licenziare (per eccesso di personale).

reed [rēd] *n* (*BOT*) canna; (*MUS*: *of clarinet etc*) ancia.

reedy [rē'dē] *a* (*voice*, *instrument*) acuto(a).

reef [rēf] *n* (*at sea*) scogliera; **coral ~** barriera corallina.

reek [rēk] *vi*: **to ~ (of)** puzzare (di).

reel [rēl] *n* bobina, rocchetto; (*TECH*) aspo; (*FISHING*) mulinello; (*CINEMA*) rotolo ♦ *vt* (*TECH*) annaspare; (*also*: **~ up**) avvolgere ♦ *vi* (*sway*) barcollare, vacillare; **my head is ~ing** mi gira la testa.

reel off *vt* snocciolare.

re-election [rēilek'shən] *n* rielezione *f*.

re-enter [rēen'tûr] *vt* rientrare in.

re-entry [rēen'trē] *n* rientro.

re-export *vt* [rēikspôrt'] riesportare ♦ *n* [rēek'spôrt] merce *f* riesportata, riesportazione *f*.

ref [ref] *n abbr* (*col*: = *referee*) arbitro.

ref. *abbr* (*Comm*: = *with reference to*) sogg.

refectory [rifek'tûrē] *n* refettorio.

refer [rifûr'] *vt*: **to ~ sth to** (*dispute*, *decision*) deferire qc a; **to ~ sb to** (*inquirer*: *for information*) indirizzare qn a; (*reader*: *to text*) rimandare qn a; **he ~red me to the manager** mi ha detto di rivolgermi al direttore.

refer to *vt fus* (*allude to*) accennare a; (*apply to*) riferire a; (*consult*) rivolgersi a; **~ring to your letter** (*COMM*) in riferimento alla Vostra lettera.

referee [refərē'] *n* arbitro; (*TENNIS*) giudice *m* di gara; (*Brit*: *for job application*) referenza ♦ *vt* arbitrare.

reference [ref'ûrəns] *n* riferimento; (*mention*) menzione *f*, allusione *f*; (*for job application*: *letter*) referenza; lettera di raccomandazione; (: *person*) referenza; (*in book*) rimando; **with ~ to** riguardo a; (*COMM*: *in letter*) in *or* con riferimento a; **"please quote this ~"** (*COMM*) "si prega di far riferimento al numero di protocollo".

reference book *n* libro di consultazione.

reference number *n* (*COMM*) numero di riferimento.

referendum, *pl* **referenda** [refəren'dəm, -də] *n* referendum *m inv*.

refill *vt* [rēfil'] riempire di nuovo; (*pen*, *lighter etc*) ricaricare ♦ *n* [rē'fil] (*for pen etc*) ricambio.

refine [rifin'] *vt* raffinare.

refined [rifind'] *a* raffinato(a).

refinement [rifin'mənt] *n* (*of person*) raffinatezza.

refinery [rifi'nûrē] *n* raffineria.

refit *n* [rē'fit] (*NAUT*) raddobbo ♦ *vt* [rēfit'] (*ship*) raddobbare.

reflate [riflāt'] *vt* (*economy*) rilanciare.

reflation [riflā'shən] *n* rilancio.

reflationary [riflā'shənärē] *a* nuovamente inflazionario(a).

reflect [riflekt'] *vt* (*light*, *image*) riflettere; (*fig*) rispecchiare ♦ *vi* (*think*) riflettere, considerare.

reflect on *vt fus* (*discredit*) rispecchiarsi su.

reflection [riflek'shən] *n* riflessione *f*; (*image*) riflesso; (*criticism*): **~ on** giudizio su; attacco a; **on ~** pensandoci sopra.

reflector [riflek'tûr] *n* (*also AUT*) catarifrangente *m*.

reflex [rē'fleks] *a* riflesso(a) ♦ *n* riflesso.

reflexive [riflek'siv] *a* (*LING*) riflessivo(a).

reforest [rēfôr'ist] *vt* rimboscare.

reform [rifôrm'] *n* riforma ♦ *vt* riformare.

reformat [rēfôr'mat] *vt* (*COMPUT*) riformattare.

Reformation [refûrmā'shən] *n*: **the ~** la Riforma.

reformatory [rifôr'mətôrē] *n* riformatorio.

reformed [rifôrmd'] *a* cambiato(a) (per il meglio).

reformer [rifôr'mûr] *n* riformatore/trice.

refrain [rifrān'] *vi*: **to ~ from doing** trattenersi dal fare ♦ *n* ritornello.

refresh [rifresh'] *vt* rinfrescare; (*subj*: *food*, *sleep*) ristorare.

refresher course [rifresh'ûr kôrs] *n* corso di aggiornamento.

refreshing [rifresh'ing] *a* (*drink*) rinfrescante; (*sleep*) riposante, ristoratore(trice); (*change etc*) piacevole; (*idea*, *point of view*) originale.

refreshment [rifresh'mənt] *n* (*eating*, *resting etc*) ristoro; **~(s)** rinfreschi *mpl*.

refreshment room n (Brit) posto di ristoro.
refreshment stand n banco rinfreschi.
refrigeration [rifrijərā'shən] n refrigerazione f.
refrigerator [rifrij'ərātûr] n frigorifero.
refuel [rēfyōō'əl] vt rifornire (di carburante) ♦ vi far rifornimento (di carburante).
refuge [ref'yōōj] n rifugio; **to take ~ in** rifugiarsi in.
refugee [refyōōjē'] n rifugiato/a, profugo/a.
refugee camp n campo (di) profughi.
refund n [rē'fund] rimborso ♦ vt [rifund'] rimborsare.
refurbish [rēfûr'bish] vt rimettere a nuovo.
refurnish [rēfûr'nish] vt ammobiliare di nuovo.
refusal [rifyōō'zəl] n rifiuto; **to have first ~ on sth** avere il diritto d'opzione su qc.
refuse n [ref'yōōs] rifiuti mpl ♦ vt, vi [rifyōōz'] rifiutare; **to ~ to do sth** rifiutare or rifiutarsi di fare qc.
refuse collection n (Brit) raccolta di rifiuti.
refuse collector n (Brit) netturbino.
refuse disposal n (Brit) sistema m di scarico dei rifiuti.
refute [rifyōōt'] vt confutare.
regain [rigān'] vt riguadagnare; riacquistare, ricuperare.
regal [rē'gəl] a regale.
regale [rigāl'] vt: **to ~ sb with sth** intrattenere qn con qc.
regalia [rigā'lēə] n insegne fpl reali.
regard [rigârd'] n riguardo, stima ♦ vt considerare, stimare; **to give one's ~s** to porgere i suoi saluti a; **(kind) ~s** cordiali saluti; **as ~s, with ~ to** riguardo a.
regarding [rigâr'ding] prep riguardo a, per quanto riguarda.
regardless [rigârd'lis] ad lo stesso; **~ of** a dispetto di, nonostante.
regatta [rigât'ə] n regata.
regency [rē'jənsē] n reggenza.
regenerate [rējen'ûrāt] vt rigenerare; (feelings, enthusiasm) far rinascere ♦ vi rigenerarsi; rinascere.
regent [rē'jənt] n reggente m.
régime [rāzhēm'] n regime m.
regiment [rej'əmənt] n reggimento ♦ vt irreggimentare.
regimental [rejəmen'təl] a reggimentale.
regimentation [rejəməntā'shən] n irreggimentazione f.
region [rē'jən] n regione f; **in the ~ of** (fig) all'incirca di.
regional [rē'jənəl] a regionale.
regional development n sviluppo regionale.
register [rej'istûr] n registro; (also: **electoral ~**) lista elettorale ♦ vt registrare; (vehicle) immatricolare; (luggage) spedire assicurato(a); (letter) assicurare; (subj: instrument) segnare ♦ vi iscriversi; (at hotel) firmare il registro; (make impression) entrare in testa; **to ~ a protest** fare un esposto; **to ~ for a**

course iscriversi a un corso.
registered [rej'istûrd] a (design) depositato(a); (Brit: letter) assicurato(a); (student, voter) iscritto(a).
registered company n società iscritta al registro.
registered nurse n (US) infermiere(a) diplomato(a).
registered office n (Brit) sede f legale.
registered trademark n marchio depositato.
registrar [rej'istrâr] n ufficiale m di stato civile; segretario.
registration [rejistrā'shən] n (act) registrazione f; iscrizione f; (Brit: AUT: also: **~ number**) numero di targa.
registry [rej'istrē] n ufficio del registro.
registry office [rej'istrē ôfis] n (Brit) anagrafe f; **to get married in a ~** ≈ sposarsi in municipio.
regret [rigret'] n rimpianto, rincrescimento ♦ vt rimpiangere; **I ~ that I/he cannot help** mi rincresce di non poter aiutare/che lui non possa aiutare; **we ~ to inform you that ...** siamo spiacenti di informarla che ....
regretfully [rigret'fəlē] ad con rincrescimento.
regrettable [rigret'əbəl] a deplorevole.
regrettably [rigret'əblē] ad purtroppo, sfortunatamente.
regroup [rēgrōōp'] vt raggruppare ♦ vi raggrupparsi.
regt abbr (= regiment) Reg.
regular [reg'yəlûr] a regolare; (usual) abituale, normale; (listener, reader) fedele; (soldier) dell'esercito regolare; (COMM: size) normale ♦ n (client etc) cliente m/f abituale; **~ (gas)** (US) ≈ benzina normale.
regularity [regyəlar'itē] n regolarità f inv.
regularly [reg'yəlûrlē] ad regolarmente.
regulate [reg'yəlāt] vt regolare.
regulation [regyəlā'shən] n (rule) regola, regolamento; (adjustment) regolazione f ♦ cpd (MIL) di ordinanza.
rehabilitation [rēhəbilətā'shən] n (of offender) riabilitazione f; (of disabled) riadattamento.
rehash [rēhash'] vt (col) rimaneggiare.
rehearsal [rihûr'səl] n prova; **dress ~** prova generale.
rehearse [rihûrs'] vt provare.
rehouse [rēhouz'] vt rialloggiare.
reign [rān] n regno ♦ vi regnare.
reigning [rā'ning] a (monarch) regnante; (champion) attuale.
reimburse [rēimbûrs'] vt rimborsare.
rein [rān] n (for horse) briglia; **to give sb free ~** (fig) lasciare completa libertà a qn.
reincarnation [rēinkârnā'shən] n reincarnazione f.
reindeer [rān'dēr] n (pl inv) renna.
reinforce [rēinfôrs'] vt rinforzare.
reinforced concrete [rēinfôrst' kân'krēt] n cemento armato.

reinforcement [rēinfôrs'mənt] *n* (*action*) rinforzamento; ~s *npl* (*MIL*) rinforzi *mpl*.

reinstate [rēinstāt'] *vt* reintegrare.

reinstatement [rēinstāt'mənt] *n* reintegrazione *f*.

reissue [rēish'ōō] *vt* (*book*) ristampare, ripubblicare; (*film*) distribuire di nuovo.

reiterate [rēit'ərāt] *vt* reiterare, ripetere.

reject *n* [rē'jekt] (*COMM*) scarto ♦ *vt* [rijekt'] rifiutare, respingere; (*COMM*: *goods*) scartare.

rejection [rijek'shən] *n* rifiuto.

rejoice [rijois'] *vi*: **to ~ (at** *or* **over)** provare diletto (in).

rejoinder [rijoin'dûr] *n* (*retort*) replica.

rejuvenate [rijōō'vənāt] *vt* ringiovanire.

rekindle [rēkin'dəl] *vt* riaccendere.

relapse [rilaps'] *n* (*MED*) ricaduta.

relate [rilāt'] *vt* (*tell*) raccontare; (*connect*) collegare ♦ *vi*: **to ~ to** (*refer to*) riferirsi a; (*get on with*) stabilire un rapporto con.

related [rilā'tid] *a* imparentato(a); collegato(a), connesso(a); **~ to** imparentato(a) con; collegato(a) *or* connesso(a) con.

relating [rilā'ting]: **~ to** *prep* che riguarda, rispetto a.

relation [rilā'shən] *n* (*person*) parente *m/f*; (*link*) rapporto, relazione *f*; **in ~ to** con riferimento a; **diplomatic/international ~s** rapporti diplomatici/internazionali; **to bear a ~ to** corrispondere a.

relationship [rilā'shənship] *n* rapporto; (*personal ties*) rapporti *mpl*, relazioni *fpl*; (*also*: **family ~**) legami *mpl* di parentela; (*affair*) relazione *f*; **they have a good ~** vanno molto d'accordo.

relative [rel'ətiv] *n* parente *m/f* ♦ *a* relativo(a); (*respective*) rispettivo(a).

relatively [rel'ətivlē] *ad* relativamente; (*fairly*, *rather*) abbastanza.

relax [rilaks'] *vi* rilasciarsi; (*person: unwind*) rilassarsi ♦ *vt* rilasciare; (*mind*, *person*) rilassare; **~!** (*calm down*) calma!

relaxation [rēlaksā'shən] *n* rilasciamento; rilassamento; (*entertainment*) ricreazione *f*, svago.

relaxed [rilakst'] *a* rilasciato(a); rilassato(a).

relaxing [rilaks'ing] *a* rilassante.

relay *n* [rē'lā] (*SPORT*) corsa a staffetta ♦ *vt* [rēlā'] (*message*) trasmettere.

release [rilēs'] *n* (*from prison*) rilascio; (*from obligation*) liberazione *f*; (*of gas etc*) emissione *f*; (*of movie etc*) distribuzione *f*; (*record*) disco; (*device*) disinnesto ♦ *vt* (*prisoner*) rilasciare; (*from obligation*, *wreckage etc*) liberare; (*book*, *movie*) fare uscire; (*news*) rendere pubblico(a); (*gas etc*) emettere; (*TECH: catch*, *spring etc*) disinnestare; (*let go*) rilasciare; lasciar andare; sciogliere; **to ~ one's grip** mollare la presa; **to ~ the clutch** (*AUT*) staccare la frizione.

relegate [rel'əgāt] *vt* relegare; (*SPORT*): **to be**

~d essere retrocesso(a).

relent [rilent'] *vi* cedere.

relentless [rilent'lis] *a* implacabile.

relevance [rel'əvəns] *n* pertinenza; **~ of sth to sth** rapporto tra qc e qc.

relevant [rel'əvənt] *a* pertinente; (*chapter*) in questione; **~ to** pertinente a.

reliability [rilīəbil'ətē] *n* (*of person*) serietà; (*of machine*) affidabilità.

reliable [rilī'əbəl] *a* (*person*, *firm*) fidato(a), che dà affidamento; (*method*) sicuro(a); (*machine*) affidabile.

reliably [rilī'əblē] *ad*: **to be ~ informed** sapere da fonti sicure.

reliance [rilī'əns] *n*: **~ (on)** dipendenza (da).

reliant [rilī'ənt] *a*: **to be ~ on sth/sb** dipendere da qc/qn.

relic [rel'ik] *n* (*REL*) reliquia; (*of the past*) resto.

relief [rilēf'] *n* (*from pain*, *anxiety*) sollievo; (*help*, *supplies*) soccorsi *mpl*; (*of guard*) cambio; (*ART*, *GEO*) rilievo; **by way of light ~** come diversivo.

relief map *n* carta in rilievo.

relief road *n* (*Brit*) circonvallazione *f*.

relieve [rilēv'] *vt* (*pain*, *patient*) sollevare; (*bring help*) soccorrere; (*take over from: gen*) sostituire; (: *guard*) rilevare; **to ~ sb of sth** (*load*) alleggerire qn di qc; **to ~ sb of his command** (*MIL*) esonerare qn dal comando; **to ~ o.s.** (*euphemism*) fare i propri bisogni.

religion [rilij'ən] *n* religione *f*.

religious [rilij'əs] *a* religioso(a).

reline [rēlīn'] *vt* (*brakes*) sostituire le guarnizioni di.

relinquish [riling'kwish] *vt* abbandonare; (*plan*, *habit*) rinunziare a.

relish [rel'ish] *n* (*CULIN*) condimento; (*enjoyment*) gran piacere *m* ♦ *vt* (*food etc*) godere; **to ~ doing** adorare fare.

relive [rēliv'] *vt* rivivere.

reload [rēlōd'] *vt* ricaricare.

relocate [rēlō'kāt] *vt* (*business*) trasferire ♦ *vi*: **to ~ in** trasferire la propria sede a.

reluctance [riluk'təns] *n* riluttanza.

reluctant [riluk'tənt] *a* riluttante, mal disposto(a); **to be ~ to do sth** essere restio a fare qc.

reluctantly [riluk'təntlē] *ad* di mala voglia, a malincuore.

rely [rilī']: **to ~ on** *vt fus* contare su; (*be dependent*) dipendere da.

remain [rimān'] *vi* restare, rimanere; **to ~ silent** restare in silenzio.

remainder [rimān'dûr] *n* resto; (*COMM*) rimanenza.

remaining [rimā'ning] *a* che rimane.

remains [rimānz'] *npl* resti *mpl*.

remand [rimand'] *n*: **on ~** in detenzione preventiva ♦ *vt*: **to ~ in custody** rinviare in carcere; trattenere a disposizione della legge.

remark [rimârk'] *n* osservazione *f* ♦ *vt* osservare, dire; (*notice*) notare ♦ *vi*: **to ~ on sth** fare dei commenti su qc.

remarkable [rimâr'kəbəl] *a* notevole; eccezionale.

remarry [rēmar'ē] *vi* risposarsi.

remedial [rimē'dēəl] *a* (*tuition, classes*) di riparazione.

remedy [rem'idē] *n*: **~ (for)** rimedio (per) ♦ *vt* rimediare a.

remember [rimem'bûr] *vt* ricordare, ricordarsi di; **I ~ seeing it, I ~ having seen it** (mi) ricordo di averlo visto; **she ~ed to do it** si è ricordata di farlo; **~ me to your wife and children!** saluti sua moglie e i bambini da parte mia!

remembrance [rimem'brəns] *n* memoria; ricordo.

remind [rimīnd'] *vt*: **to ~ sb of sth** ricordare qc a qn; **to ~ sb to do** ricordare a qn di fare; **that ~s me!** a proposito!

reminder [rimīnd'ûr] *n* richiamo; (*note etc*) promemoria *m inv*.

reminisce [remənis'] *vi*: **to ~ (about)** abbandonarsi ai ricordi (di).

reminiscences [remənis'ənsiz] *npl* reminiscenze *fpl*, memorie *fpl*.

reminiscent [remənis'ənt] *a*: **~ of** che fa pensare a, che richiama.

remiss [rimis'] *a* negligente; **it was ~ of me** è stata una negligenza da parte mia.

remission [rimish'ən] *n* remissione *f*; (*of fee*) esonero.

remit [rimit'] *vt* rimettere.

remittance [rimit'əns] *n* rimessa.

remnant [rem'nənt] *n* resto, avanzo; **~s** *npl* (*COMM*) scampoli *mpl*; fine *f* serie.

remonstrate [rimân'strāt] *vi* protestare; **to ~ with sb about sth** fare le proprie rimostranze a qn circa qc.

remorse [rimôrs'] *n* rimorso.

remorseful [rimôrs'fəl] *a* pieno(a) di rimorsi.

remorseless [rimôrs'lis] *a* (*fig*) spietato(a).

remote [rimōt'] *a* remoto(a), lontano(a); (*person*) distaccato(a); **there is a ~ possibility that ...** c'è una vaga possibilità che ... + *sub*.

remote control *n* telecomando.

remote-controlled [rimōt'kəntrōld'] *a* telecomandato(a).

remotely [rimōt'lē] *ad* remotamente; (*slightly*) vagamente.

remoteness [rimōt'nis] *n* lontananza.

remould [rē'mōld] *n* (*Brit*: *tire*) gomma rivestita.

removable [rimōō'vəbəl] *a* (*detachable*) staccabile.

removal [rimōō'vəl] *n* (*taking away*) rimozione *f*; soppressione *f*; (*from office*: *sacking*) destituzione *f*; (*MED*) ablazione *f*; (*Brit*: *from house*) trasloco.

removal man *n* (*Brit*) addetto ai traslochi.

removal van *n* (*Brit*) furgone *m* per traslochi.

remove [rimōōv'] *vt* togliere, rimuovere; (*employee*) destituire; (*stain*) far sparire; (*doubt, abuse*) sopprimere, eliminare; **first cousin once ~d** cugino di secondo grado.

remover [rimōō'vûr] *n* (*for paint*) prodotto sverniciante; (*for varnish*) solvente *m*; **make-up ~** struccatore *m*; **~s** *npl* (*Brit*: *company*) ditta *or* impresa di traslochi.

remunerate [rimyōō'nərāt] *vt* rimunerare.

remuneration [rimyōōnərā'shən] *n* rimunerazione *f*.

Renaissance [ren'isâns] *n*: **the ~** il Rinascimento.

rename [rēnām'] *vt* ribattezzare.

rend, *pt, pp* **rent** [rend, rent] *vt* lacerare.

render [ren'dûr] *vt* rendere; (*CULIN*: *fat*) struggere.

rendering [ren'dûring] *n* (*MUS etc*) interpretazione *f*.

rendezvous [rân'dāvōō] *n* appuntamento; (*place*) luogo d'incontro; (*meeting*) incontro ♦ *vi* ritrovarsi; (*spaceship*) effettuare un rendez-vous.

rendition [rendish'ən] *n* (*MUS*) interpretazione *f*.

renegade [ren'əgād] *n* rinnegato/a.

renew [rinōō'] *vt* rinnovare; (*negotiations*) riprendere.

renewable [rinōō'əbəl] *a* (*lease, contract*) rinnovabile; (*energy, resources*) riutilizzabile.

renewal [rinōō'əl] *n* rinnovamento; ripresa.

renounce [rinouns'] *vt* rinunziare a; (*disown*) ripudiare.

renovate [ren'əvāt] *vt* rinnovare; (*art work*) restaurare.

renovation [renəvā'shən] *n* rinnovamento; restauro.

renown [rinoun'] *n* rinomanza.

renowned [rinound'] *a* rinomato(a).

rent [rent] *pt, pp of* **rend** ♦ *n* affitto ♦ *vt* (*take for rent*) prendere in affitto; (*car, TV*) noleggiare, prendere a noleggio; (*also*: **~ out**) dare in affitto; (*car, TV*) noleggiare, dare a noleggio; **"for ~"** (*US*) "affittasi".

rental [ren'təl] *n* (*cost*: *on TV, telephone*) abbonamento; (: *on car*) nolo, noleggio.

rental car *n* (*US*) macchina a nolo.

renunciation [rinunsēā'shən] *n* rinnegamento; (*self-denial*) rinunzia.

reopen [rēō'pən] *vt* riaprire.

reopening [rēō'pəning] *n* riapertura.

reorder [rēôr'dûr] *vt* ordinare di nuovo; (*rearrange*) riordinare.

reorganize [rēôr'gənīz] *vt* riorganizzare.

Rep *abbr* (*US POL*) = **representative; republican**.

rep |rɛp| *n abbr* (*COMM:* = *representative*) rappresentante *m/f*; (*THEATER:* = *repertory*) teatro di repertorio.

repair |ripär'| *n* riparazione *f* ♦ *vt* riparare; **in good/bad** ~ in buona/cattiva condizione; **under** ~ in riparazione.

repair kit *n* corredo per riparazioni.

repair man *n* riparatore *m.*

repair shop *n* (*AUT etc*) officina.

repartee |rɛpûrtē'| *n* risposta pronta.

repast |ripast'| *n* (*formal*) pranzo.

repatriate |rēpā'trēāt| *vt* rimpatriare.

repay |ripā'| *vt irg* (*money, creditor*) rimborsare, ripagare; (*sb's efforts*) ricompensare.

repayment |ripā'mənt| *n* rimborsamento; ricompensa.

repeal |ripēl'| *n* (*of law*) abrogazione *f*; (*of sentence*) annullamento ♦ *vt* abrogare; annullare.

repeat |ripēt'| *n* (*RADIO, TV*) replica ♦ *vt* ripetere; (*pattern*) riprodurre; (*promise, attack, also COMM: order*) rinnovare ♦ *vi* ripetere.

repeatedly |ripēt'idlē| *ad* ripetutamente, spesso.

repeat order *n* (*COMM*): **to place a** ~ **(for)** rinnovare l'ordinazione (di).

repel |ripel'| *vt* respingere.

repellent |ripel'ənt| *a* repellente ♦ *n*: **insect** ~ prodotto *m* anti-insetti *inv*; **moth** ~ antitarmico.

repent |ripent'| *vi*: **to** ~ **(of)** pentirsi (di).

repentance |ripen'təns| *n* pentimento.

repercussion |rēpûrkush'ən| *n* (*consequence*) ripercussione *f*.

repertoire |rep'ûrtwâr| *n* repertorio.

repertory |rep'ûrtôrē| *n* (*also:* ~ **theater**) teatro di repertorio.

repertory company *n* compagnia di repertorio.

repetition |repitish'ən| *n* ripetizione *f*; (*COMM: of order etc*) rinnovo.

repetitious |repitish'əs| *a* (*speech*) pieno(a) di ripetizioni.

repetitive |ripet'ətiv| *a* (*movement*) che si ripete; (*work*) monotono(a); (*speech*) pieno(a) di ripetizioni.

replace |riplās'| *vt* (*put back*) rimettere a posto; (*take the place of*) sostituire; (*TEL*): **"**~ **the receiver"** "riattaccare".

replacement |riplās'mənt| *n* rimessa; sostituzione *f*; (*person*) sostituto/a.

replacement part *n* pezzo di ricambio.

replay |rē'plā| *n* (*of game*) partita ripetuta; (*of tape, movie*) replay *m inv*.

replenish |riplen'ish| *vt* (*glass*) riempire; (*stock etc*) rifornire.

replete |riplēt'| *a*: ~ **(with)** ripieno(a) (di); (*well-fed*) sazio(a) (di).

replica |rep'ləkə| *n* replica, copia.

reply |riplī'| *n* risposta ♦ *vi* rispondere; **in** ~ **in** risposta.

report |ripôrt'| *n* rapporto; (*PRESS etc*) cronaca; (*Brit: also:* **school** ~) pagella ♦ *vt* riportare; (*PRESS etc*) fare una cronaca su; (*bring to notice: occurrence*) segnalare; (*: person*) denunciare ♦ *vi* (*make a report*) fare un rapporto (*or* una cronaca); (*present o.s.*): **to** ~ **(to sb)** presentarsi (a qn); **to** ~ **(on)** fare un rapporto (su); **it is** ~**ed that** si dice che; **it is** ~**ed from Berlin that** ... ci è stato riferito da Berlino che ....

report card *n* (*US, Scottish*) pagella.

reportedly |ripôr'tidlē| *ad*: **she is** ~ **living in Spain** si dice che vive in Spagna.

reporter |ripôr'tûr| *n* (*PRESS*) cronista *m/f*, reporter *m inv*; (*RADIO*) radiocronista *m/f*; (*TV*) telecronista *m/f*.

repose |ripōz'| *n*: **in** ~ **in** riposo.

repossess |rēpəzes'| *vt* rientrare in possesso di.

reprehensible |reprihen'səbəl| *a* riprensibile.

represent |reprizent'| *vt* rappresentare.

representation |reprizentā'shən| *n* rappresentazione *f*; ~**s** *npl* (*protest*) protesta.

representative |reprizen'tətiv| *n* rappresentativo/a; (*COMM*) rappresentante *m* (di commercio); (*US: POL*) deputato/a ♦ *a*: ~ **(of)** rappresentativo(a) (di).

repress |ripres'| *vt* reprimere.

repression |ripresh'ən| *n* repressione *f*.

repressive |ripres'iv| *a* repressivo(a).

reprieve |riprēv'| *n* (*LAW*) sospensione *f* dell'esecuzione della condanna; (*fig*) dilazione *f* ♦ *vt* sospendere l'esecuzione della condanna a; accordare una dilazione a.

reprimand |rep'rəmand| *n* rimprovero ♦ *vt* rimproverare, redarguire.

reprint *n* |rē'print| ristampa ♦ *vt* |rēprint'| ristampare.

reprisal |riprī'zəl| *n* rappresaglia; **to take** ~**s** fare delle rappresaglie.

reproach |riprōch'| *n* rimprovero ♦ *vt*: **to** ~ **sb with sth** rimproverare qn di qc; **beyond** ~ irreprensibile.

reproachful |riprōch'fəl| *a* di rimprovero.

reproduce |rēprədōōs'| *vt* riprodurre ♦ *vi* riprodursi.

reproduction |rēprəduk'shən| *n* riproduzione *f*.

reproductive |rēprəduk'tiv| *a* riproduttore(trice); riproduttivo(a).

reproof |riprōōf'| *n* riprovazione *f*.

reprove |riprōōv'| *vt* (*action*) disapprovare; (*person*): **to** ~ **(for)** biasimare (per).

reproving |riprōō'ving| *a* di disapprovazione.

reptile |rep'til| *n* rettile *m.*

Repub. *abbr* (*US POL*) = **republican.**

republic |ripub'lik| *n* repubblica.

republican |ripub'likən| *a, n* repubblicano(a).

repudiate |ripyōō'dēāt| *vt* ripudiare.

repugnant |ripug'nənt| *a* ripugnante.

repulse |ripuls'| *vt* respingere.

repulsion [ripul'shən] *n* ripulsione *f*.
repulsive [ripul'siv] *a* ripugnante, ripulsivo(a).
reputable [rep'yətəbəl] *a* di buona reputazione; (*occupation*) rispettabile.
reputation [repyətā'shən] *n* reputazione *f*; **he has a ~ for being awkward** ha la fama di essere un tipo difficile.
repute [ripyōōt'] *n* reputazione *f*.
reputed [ripyōō'tid] *a* reputato(a); **to be ~ to be rich/intelligent** *etc* essere ritenuto(a) ricco(a)/intelligente *etc*.
reputedly [ripyōō'tidlē] *ad* secondo quanto si dice.
request [rikwest'] *n* domanda; (*formal*) richiesta ♦ *vt*: **to ~ (of** *or* **from sb)** chiedere (a qn); **at the ~ of** su richiesta di; **"you are ~ed not to smoke"** "si prega di non fumare".
request stop *n* (*Brit: for bus*) fermata facoltativa *or* a richiesta.
requiem [rek'wēəm] *n* requiem *m or f inv*.
require [rikwīûr'] *vt* (*need: subj: person*) aver bisogno di; (: *thing, situation*) richiedere; (*want*) volere; esigere; (*order*) obbligare; **to ~ sb to do sth/sth of sb** esigere che qn faccia qc/qc da qn; **what qualifications are ~d?** che requisiti ci vogliono?; **~d by law** prescritto dalla legge; **if ~d** in caso di bisogno.
required [rikwīûrd'] *a* richiesto(a).
requirement [rikwīûr'mənt] *n* (*need*) esigenza; (*condition*) requisito; **to meet sb's ~s** soddisfare le esigenze di qn.
requisite [rek'wizit] *n* cosa necessaria ♦ *a* necessario(a); **toilet ~s** (*Brit*) articoli *mpl* da toletta.
requisition [rekwizish'ən] *n*: **~ (for)** richiesta (di) ♦ *vt* (*MIL*) requisire.
reroute [rērout'] *vt* (*train etc*) deviare.
resale [rē'sāl] *n* rivendita.
resale price maintenance (RPM) *n* prezzo minimo di vendita imposto.
rescind [risind'] *vt* annullare; (*law*) abrogare; (*judgement*) rescindere.
rescue [res'kyōō] *n* salvataggio; (*help*) soccorso ♦ *vt* salvare; **to come/go to sb's ~** venire/andare in aiuto a *or* di qn.
rescue party *n* squadra di salvataggio.
rescuer [res'kyōōûr] *n* salvatore/trice.
research [risûrch'] *n* ricerca, ricerche *fpl* ♦ *vt* fare ricerche su ♦ *vi*: **to ~ (into sth)** fare ricerca (su qc); **a piece of ~** un lavoro di ricerca; **~ and development (R&D)** ricerca e sviluppo.
researcher [risûr'chûr] *n* ricercatore/trice.
research work *n* ricerche *fpl*.
resell [rēsel'] *vt irg* rivendere.
resemblance [rizem'bləns] *n* somiglianza; **to bear a strong ~ to** somigliare moltissimo a.
resemble [rizem'bəl] *vt* assomigliare a.
resent [rizent'] *vt* risentirsi di.

resentful [rizent'fəl] *a* pieno(a) di risentimento.
resentment [rizent'mənt] *n* risentimento.
reservation [rezûrvā'shən] *n* (*booking*) prenotazione *f*; (*doubt*) dubbio; (*protected area*) riserva; (*Brit AUT: also:* **central ~**) spartitraffico *m inv*; **to make a ~ (in an hotel/a restaurant/on a plane)** prenotare (una camera/una tavola/un posto); **with ~s** (*doubts*) con le dovute riserve.
reservation desk *n* (*US: in hotel*) reception *f inv*.
reserve [rizûrv'] *n* riserva ♦ *vt* (*seats etc*) prenotare; **~s** *npl* (*MIL*) riserve *fpl*; **in ~** in serbo.
reserve currency *n* valuta di riserva.
reserved [rizûrvd'] *a* (*shy*) riservato(a); (*seat*) prenotato(a).
reserve price *n* (*Brit*) prezzo di riserva, prezzo *m* base *inv*.
reservist [rizûr'vist] *n* (*MIL*) riservista *m*.
reservoir [rez'ûrvwâr] *n* serbatoio; (*artificial lake*) bacino idrico.
reset [rēset'] *vt* (*COMPUT*) azzerare.
reshape [rēshāp'] *vt* (*policy*) ristrutturare.
reshuffle [rēshuf'əl] *n*: **Cabinet ~** (*POL*) rimpasto governativo.
reside [rizīd'] *vi* risiedere.
residence [rez'idəns] *n* residenza; **to take up ~** prendere residenza; **in ~** (*queen etc*) in sede; (*doctor*) fisso.
resident [rez'idənt] *n* (*gen, COMPUT*) residente *m/f*; (*in hotel*) cliente *m/f* fisso(a) ♦ *a* residente.
residential [rezidèn'chəl] *a* di residenza; (*area*) residenziale.
residue [rez'idōō] *n* resto; (*CHEM, PHYSICS*) residuo.
resign [rizīn'] *vt* (*one's post*) dimettersi da ♦ *vi*: **to ~ (from)** dimettersi (da), dare le dimissioni (da); **to ~ o.s. to** rassegnarsi a.
resignation [rezignā'shən] *n* dimissioni *fpl*; rassegnazione *f*; **to tender one's ~** dare le dimissioni.
resigned [rizīnd'] *a* rassegnato(a).
resilience [rizil'yəns] *n* (*of material*) elasticità, resilienza; (*of person*) capacità di recupero.
resilient [rizil'yənt] *a* elastico(a); (*person*) che si riprende facilmente.
resin [rez'in] *n* resina.
resist [rizist'] *vt* resistere a.
resistance [rizis'təns] *n* resistenza.
resistant [rizis'tənt] *a*: **~ (to)** resistente (a).
resolute [rez'əlōōt] *a* risoluto(a).
resolution [rezəlōō'shən] *n* (*resolve*) fermo proposito, risoluzione *f*; (*determination*) risolutezza; (*on screen*) risoluzione *f*; **to make a ~** fare un proposito.
resolve [rizâlv'] *n* risoluzione *f* ♦ *vi* (*decide*): **to ~ to do** decidere di fare ♦ *vt* (*problem*) risolvere.

resolved [rizâlvd'] *a* risoluto(a).

resonance [rez'ənəns] *n* risonanza.

resonant [rez'ənənt] *a* risonante.

resort [rizôrt'] *n* (*town*) stazione *f*; (*place*) località *f inv*; (*recourse*) ricorso ♦ *vi*: **to ~ to** far ricorso a; **seaside/winter sports ~** stazione *f* balneare/di sport invernali; **as a last ~** come ultima risorsa.

resound [rizound'] *vi*: **to ~ (with)** risonare (di).

resounding [rizoun'ding] *a* risonante.

resource [rē'sôrs] *n* risorsa; **~s** *npl* risorse *fpl*; **natural ~s** risorse naturali; **to leave sb to his (or her) own ~s** (*fig*) lasciare che qn si arrangi (per conto suo).

resourceful [risôrs'fəl] *a* pieno(a) di risorse, intraprendente.

resourcefulness [risôrs'fəlnis] *n* intraprendenza.

respect [rispekt'] *n* rispetto; (*point, detail*): **in some ~s** sotto certi aspetti ♦ *vt* rispettare; **~s** *npl* ossequi *mpl*; **to have** *or* **show ~ for** aver rispetto per; **out of ~ for** per rispetto *or* riguardo a; **with ~ to** rispetto a, riguardo a; **in ~ of** quanto a; **in this ~** per questo riguardo; **with (all) due ~ I ...** con rispetto parlando, io ....

respectability [rispektəbil'ətē] *n* rispettabilità.

respectable [rispek'təbəl] *a* rispettabile; (*quite big*: *amount etc*) considerevole; (*quite good*: *player, result etc*) niente male *inv*.

respectful [rispekt'fəl] *a* rispettoso(a).

respective [rispek'tiv] *a* rispettivo(a).

respectively [rispek'tivlē] *ad* rispettivamente.

respiration [respərā'shən] *n* respirazione *f*.

respirator [res'pərātûr] *n* respiratore *m*.

respiratory [res'pûrətôrē] *a* respiratorio(a).

respite [res'pit] *n* respiro, tregua.

resplendent [risplen'dənt] *a* risplendente.

respond [rispând'] *vi* rispondere.

respondent [rispân'dənt] *n* (*LAW*) convenuto/a.

response [rispâns'] *n* risposta; **in ~ to** in risposta a.

responsibility [rispânsəbil'ətē] *n* responsabilità *f inv*; **to take ~ for sth/sb** assumersi *or* prendersi la responsabilità di qc/per qn.

responsible [rispân'səbəl] *a* (*liable*): **~ (for)** responsabile (di); (*trustworthy*) fidato(a); (*job*) di (grande) responsabilità; **to be ~ to sb (for sth)** dover rispondere a qn (di qc).

responsibly [rispân'səblē] *ad* responsabilmente.

responsive [rispân'siv] *a* che reagisce.

rest [rest] *n* riposo; (*stop*) sosta, pausa; (*MUS*) pausa; (*support*) appoggio, sostegno; (*remainder*) resto, avanzi *mpl* ♦ *vi* riposarsi; (*remain*) rimanere, restare; (*be supported*): **to ~ on** appoggiarsi su ♦ *vt* (*lean*): **to ~ sth on/against** appoggiare qc su/contro; **to set sb's mind at ~** tranquillizzare qn; **the ~ of**

them gli altri; **to ~ one's eyes** *or* **gaze on** posare lo sguardo su; **~ assured that ...** stia tranquillo che ...; **it ~s with him to decide** sta a lui decidere.

rest area *n* (*US*) = **rest stop**.

restart [rē'stârt] *vt* (*engine*) rimettere in marcia; (*work*) ricominciare.

restaurant [res'tûrənt] *n* ristorante *m*.

restaurant car *n* (*Brit*) vagone *m* ristorante.

rest cure *n* cura del riposo.

restful [rest'fəl] *a* riposante.

rest home *n* casa di riposo.

restitution [restitōō'shən] *n* (*act*) restituzione *f*; (*reparation*) riparazione *f*.

restive [res'tiv] *a* agitato(a), impaziente; (*horse*) restio(a).

restless [rest'lis] *a* agitato(a), irrequieto(a); **to get ~** spazientirsi.

restlessly [rest'lislē] *ad* in preda all'agitazione.

restock [rēstâk'] *vt* rifornire.

restoration [restərā'shən] *n* restauro; restituzione *f*.

restorative [ristôr'ətiv] *a* corroborante, ristorativo(a) ♦ *n* ricostituente *m*.

restore [ristôr'] *vt* (*building*) restaurare; (*sth stolen*) restituire; (*peace, health*) ristorare.

restorer [ristôr'ûr] *n* (*ART etc*) restauratore/trice.

restrain [ristrān'] *vt* (*feeling*) contenere, frenare; (*person*): **to ~ (from doing)** trattenere (dal fare).

restrained [ristrānd'] *a* (*style*) contenuto(a), sobrio(a); (*manner*) riservato(a).

restraint [ristrānt'] *n* (*restriction*) limitazione *f*; (*moderation*) ritegno; **wage ~** restrizioni *fpl* salariali.

restrict [ristrikt'] *vt* restringere, limitare.

restricted area *n* (*AUT*) zona a velocità limitata.

restriction [ristrik'shən] *n* restrizione *f*, limitazione *f*.

restrictive [ristrik'tiv] *a* restrittivo(a).

restrictive practices *npl* (*INDUSTRY*) pratiche restrittive di produzione.

rest room *n* (*US*) toletta.

rest stop *n* (*US*) piazzola di sosta.

restructure [rēstruk'chûr] *vt* ristrutturare.

result [rizult'] *n* risultato ♦ *vi*: **to ~ in** avere per risultato; **as a ~ (of)** in *or* di conseguenza (a), in seguito (a); **to ~ (from)** essere una conseguenza (di), essere causato(a) (da).

resultant [rizul'tənt] *a* risultante, conseguente.

resume [rēzōōm'] *vt*, *vi* (*work, journey*) riprendere; (*sum up*) riassumere.

résumé [rez'ōōmā] *n* riassunto; (*US: curriculum vitae*) curriculum vitae *m inv*.

resumption [rizump'shən] *n* ripresa.

resurgence [risûr'jəns] *n* rinascita.

resurrection [rezərek'shən] *n* risurrezione *f*.

resuscitate [risus'ətāt] *vt* (*MED*) risuscitare.

resuscitation [risusətā'shən] *n* rianimazione *f.*
retail [rē'tāl] *n* (vendita al) minuto ♦ *cpd* al minuto ♦ *vt* vendere al minuto ♦ *vi*: **to ~ at** essere in vendita al pubblico al prezzo di.
retailer [rē'tālûr] *n* commerciante *m/f* al minuto, dettagliante *m/f.*
retail outlet *n* punto di vendita al dettaglio.
retail price *n* prezzo al minuto.
retail price index *n* indice *m* dei prezzi al consumo.
retain [ritān'] *vt* (*keep*) tenere, serbare.
retainer [ritā'nûr] *n* (*servant*) servitore *m*; (*fee*) onorario.
retaliate [rital'ēāt] *vi*: **to ~ (against)** vendicarsi (di); **to ~ on sb** fare una rappresaglia contro qn.
retaliation [ritalēā'shən] *n* rappresaglie *fpl*; **in ~ for** per vendicarsi di.
retaliatory [rital'ēətôrē] *a* di rappresaglia, di ritorsione.
retarded [ritâr'did] *a* ritardato(a); (*also*: **mentally ~**) tardo(a) (di mente).
retch [rech] *vi* aver conati di vomito.
retentive [riten'tiv] *a* ritentivo(a).
rethink [rēthingk'] *vt* ripensare.
reticence [ret'isəns] *n* reticenza.
reticent [ret'isənt] *a* reticente.
retina [ret'ənə] *n* retina.
retinue [ret'ənōō] *n* seguito, scorta.
retire [ritīûr'] *vi* (*give up work*) andare in pensione; (*withdraw*) ritirarsi, andarsene; (*go to bed*) andare a letto, ritirarsi.
retired [ritīûrd'] *a* (*person*) pensionato(a).
retirement [ritīûr'mənt] *n* pensione *f.*
retirement age *n* età del pensionamento.
retiring [ritīûr'ing] *a* (*person*) riservato(a); (*departing*: *chairman*) uscente.
retort [ritôrt'] *n* (*reply*) rimbecco; (*container*) storta ♦ *vi* rimbeccare.
retrace [rētrās'] *vt* ricostruire; **to ~ one's steps** tornare sui propri passi.
retract [ritrakt'] *vt* (*statement*) ritrattare; (*claws, undercarriage, aerial*) ritrarre, ritirare ♦ *vi* ritrarsi.
retractable [ritrakt'əbəl] *a* retrattile.
retrain [rētrān'] *vt* (*worker*) riaddestrare.
retraining [rētrā'ning] *n* riaddestramento.
retread *vt* [rētred'] (*AUT*: *tire*) rigenerare ♦ *n* [rē'tred] gomma rigenerata.
retreat [ritrēt'] *n* ritirata; (*place*) rifugio ♦ *vi* battere in ritirata; (*flood*) ritirarsi; **to beat a hasty ~** (*fig*) battersela.
retrial [rētrīl'] *n* nuovo processo.
retribution [retrəbyōō'shən] *n* castigo.
retrieval [ritrē'vəl] *n* ricupero.
retrieve [ritrēv'] *vt* (*sth lost*) ricuperare, ritrovare; (*situation, honor*) salvare; (*COMPUT*) ricuperare.
retriever [ritrē'vûr] *n* cane *m* da riporto.
retroactive [retrōak'tiv] *a* retroattivo(a).
retrograde [ret'rəgrād] *a* retrogrado(a).

retrospect [ret'rəspekt] *n*: **in ~** guardando indietro.
retrospective [retrəspek'tiv] *a* retrospettivo(a); (*Brit*: *law*) retroattivo(a) ♦ *n* (*ART*) retrospettiva.
return [ritûrn'] *n* (*going or coming back*) ritorno; (*of sth stolen etc*) restituzione *f*; (*COMM: from land, shares*) profitto, reddito; (: *of merchandise*) resa; (*report*) rapporto; (*reward*): **in ~ (for)** in cambio (di) ♦ *cpd* (*journey, match*) di ritorno; (*Brit*: *ticket*) di andata e ritorno ♦ *vi* tornare, ritornare ♦ *vt* rendere, restituire; (*bring back*) riportare; (*send back*) mandare indietro; (*put back*) rimettere; (*POL: candidate*) eleggere; **~s** *npl* (*COMM*) incassi *mpl*; profitti *mpl*; **by ~ of mail** a stretto giro di posta; **many happy ~s!** auguri!, buon compleanno!
returnable [ritûr'nəbəl] *a*: **~ bottle** vuoto a rendere.
return key *n* (*COMPUT*) tasto di ritorno.
reunion [rēyōōn'yən] *n* riunione *f.*
reunite [rēyōōnīt'] *vt* riunire.
rev [rev] *n abbr* (= *revolution*: *AUT*) giro ♦ *vb* (*also*: **~ up**) *vt* imballare ♦ *vi* imballarsi.
revaluation [rēval'yōōāshən] *n* rivalutazione *f.*
revamp [rēvamp'] *vt* rinnovare, riorganizzare.
Rev(d). *abbr* = **Reverend.**
reveal [rivēl'] *vt* (*make known*) rivelare, svelare; (*display*) rivelare, mostrare.
revealing [rivē'ling] *a* rivelatore(trice); (*dress*) scollato(a).
reveille [rev'əlē] *n* (*MIL*) sveglia.
revel [rev'əl] *vi*: **to ~ in sth/in doing** dilettarsi di qc/a fare.
revelation [revəlā'shən] *n* rivelazione *f.*
revel(l)er [rev'əlûr] *n* festaiolo/a.
revelry [rev'əlrē] *n* baldoria.
revenge [rivenj'] *n* vendetta; (*in game etc*) rivincita ♦ *vt* vendicare; **to take ~** vendicarsi; **to get one's ~ (for sth)** vendicarsi (di qc).
revengeful [rivenj'fəl] *a* vendicatore(trice); vendicativo(a).
revenue [rev'ənōō] *n* reddito.
reverberate [rivûr'bərāt] *vi* (*sound*) rimbombare; (*light*) riverberarsi.
reverberation [rivûrbərā'shən] *n* (*of light, sound*) riverberazione *f.*
revere [rivēr'] *vt* venerare.
reverence [rev'ûrəns] *n* venerazione *f*, riverenza.
Reverend [rev'ûrənd] *a* (*in titles*) reverendo(a).
reverent [rev'ûrənt] *a* riverente.
reverie [rev'ûrē] *n* fantasticheria.
reversal [rivûr'səl] *n* capovolgimento.
reverse [rivûrs'] *n* contrario, opposto; (*back*) rovescio; (*AUT*: *also*: **~ gear**) marcia indietro ♦ *a* (*order*) inverso(a); (*direction*) opposto(a) ♦ *vt* (*turn*) invertire, rivoltare; (*change*) capovolgere, rovesciare; (*LAW*:

judgement) cassare ♦ *vi* (*Brit AUT*) fare marcia indietro; **in** ~ **order** in ordine inverso; **to go into** ~ fare marcia indietro.

reversed charge call *n* (*Brit TEL*) telefonata con addebito al ricevente.

reverse video *n* reverse video *m*.

reversible [rivûr'səbəl] *a* (*garment*) double-face *inv*; (*procedure*) reversibile.

reversing lights [rivûr'sing līts] *npl* (*Brit AUT*) luci *fpl* per la retromarcia.

reversion [rivûr'zhən] *n* ritorno.

revert [rivûrt'] *vi*: **to** ~ **to** tornare a.

review [rivyōō'] *n* rivista; (*of book, movie*) recensione *f* ♦ *vt* passare in rivista; fare la recensione di; (*US: study: subject, notes*) ripassare; **to come under** ~ essere preso in esame.

reviewer [rivyōō'ûr] *n* recensore/a.

revile [rivīl'] *vt* insultare.

revise [rivīz'] *vt* (*manuscript*) rivedere, correggere; (*opinion*) emendare, modificare; (*Brit: study: subject, notes*) ripassare; **~d edition** edizione riveduta.

revision [rivizh'ən] *n* revisione *f*; ripasso; (*revised version*) versione *f* riveduta e corretta.

revitalize [rēvī'təlīz] *vt* ravvivare.

revival [rivī'vəl] *n* ripresa; ristabilimento; (*of faith*) risveglio.

revive [rivīv'] *vt* (*person*) rianimare; (*custom*) far rivivere; (*hope, courage*) ravvivare; (*play, fashion*) riesumare ♦ *vi* (*person*) rianimarsi; (*hope*) ravvivarsi; (*activity*) riprendersi.

revoke [rivōk'] *vt* revocare; (*promise, decision*) rinvenire su.

revolt [rivōlt'] *n* rivolta, ribellione *f* ♦ *vi* rivoltarsi, ribellarsi; **to** ~ **(against sb/sth)** ribellarsi (a qn/qc).

revolting [rivōl'ting] *a* ripugnante.

revolution [revəlōō'shən] *n* rivoluzione *f*; (*of wheel etc*) rivoluzione, giro.

revolutionary [revəlōō'shənärē] *a*, *n* rivoluzionario(a).

revolutionize [revəlōō'shənīz] *vt* rivoluzionare.

revolve [rivâlv'] *vi* girare.

revolver [rivâl'vûr] *n* rivoltella.

revolving [rivâl'ving] *a* girevole.

revolving credit [rivâl'ving kred'it] *n* credito a termine rinnovabile automaticamente.

revolving door *n* porta girevole.

revue [rivyōō'] *n* (*THEATER*) rivista.

revulsion [rivul'shən] *n* ripugnanza.

reward [riwôrd'] *n* ricompensa, premio ♦ *vt*: **to** ~ **(for)** ricompensare (per).

rewarding [riwôrd'ing] *a* (*fig*) soddisfacente; **financially** ~ conveniente dal punto di vista economico.

rewind [rēwīnd'] *vt irg* (*watch*) ricaricare; (*ribbon etc*) riavvolgere.

rewire [rēwīûr'] *vt* (*house*) rifare l'impianto elettrico di.

reword [rēwûrd'] *vt* formulare *or* esprimere con altre parole.

rewrite [rērīt'] *vt irg* riscrivere.

Reykjavik [rā'kyəvik] *n* Reykjavik *f*.

RFD *abbr* (*US MAIL*) = *rural free delivery*.

Rh *abbr* (= *rhesus*) Rh.

rhapsody [rap'sədē] *n* (*MUS*) rapsodia; (*fig*) elogio stravagante.

rhetoric [ret'ûrik] *n* retorica.

rhetorical [ritôr'ikəl] *a* retorico(a).

rheumatic [rōōmat'ik] *a* reumatico(a).

rheumatism [rōō'mətizəm] *n* reumatismo.

rheumatoid arthritis [rōō'mətoid ârthrī'tis] *n* artrite *f* reumatoide.

Rh factor *n* (*MED*) fattore *m* Rh.

Rhine [rīn] *n*: **the** ~ il Reno.

rhinestone [rīn'stōn] *n* diamante *m* falso.

rhinoceros [rīnâs'ûrəs] *n* rinoceronte *m*.

Rhodes [rōdz] *n* Rodi *f*.

Rhodesia [rōdē'zhə] *n* Rhodesia.

Rhodesian [rōdē'zhən] *a*, *n* Rhodesiano(a).

rhododendron [rōdəden'drən] *n* rododendro.

Rhone [rōn] *n*: **the** ~ il Rodano.

rhubarb [rōō'bârb] *n* rabarbaro.

rhyme [rīm] *n* rima; (*verse*) poesia ♦ *vi*: **to** ~ **(with)** fare rima (con); **without** ~ **or reason** senza capo né coda.

rhythm [rith'əm] *n* ritmo.

rhythmic(al) [rith'mik(əl)] *a* ritmico(a).

rhythmically [rith'miklē] *ad* con ritmo.

RI *abbr* (*US MAIL*) = *Rhode Island*.

rib [rib] *n* (*ANAT*) costola ♦ *vt* (*tease*) punzecchiare.

ribald [rib'əld] *a* licenzioso(a), volgare.

ribbed [ribd] *a* (*knitting*) a coste.

ribbon [rib'ən] *n* nastro; **in** ~**s** (*torn*) a brandelli.

rice [rīs] *n* riso.

ricefield [rīs'fēld] *n* risaia.

rich [rich] *a* ricco(a); (*clothes*) sontuoso(a); **the** ~ *npl* i ricchi; ~**es** *npl* ricchezze *fpl*; **to be** ~ **in sth** essere ricco di qc.

richly [rich'lē] *ad* riccamente; (*dressed*) sontuosamente; (*deserved*) pienamente.

richness [rich'nis] *n* ricchezza.

rickets [rik'its] *n* rachitismo.

rickety [rik'ətē] *a* zoppicante.

rickshaw [rik'shô] *n* risciò *m inv*.

ricochet [rikəshā'] *n* rimbalzo ♦ *vi* rimbalzare.

rid [rid], *pt*, *pp* **rid** [rid] *vt*: **to** ~ **sb of** sbarazzare *or* liberare qn di; **to get** ~ **of** sbarazzarsi di.

riddance [rid'əns] *n*: **good** ~! che liberazione!

ridden [rid'ən] *pp* *of* **ride**.

riddle [rid'əl] *n* (*puzzle*) indovinello ♦ *vt*: **to be** ~**d with** essere crivellato(a) di.

ride [rīd] *n* (*on horse*) cavalcata; (*outing*) passeggiata; (*distance covered*) cavalcata; corsa ♦ *vb* (*pt* **rode**, *pp* **ridden** [rōd, ri'dən]) *vi* (*as sport*) cavalcare; (*go somewhere: on horse, bicycle*) andare (a cavallo *or* in bicicletta *etc*); (*journey*: on bicycle, motorcycle, bus) andare, viaggiare ♦ *vt* (*a horse*) montare, cavalcare; **to go for a ~** andare a fare una cavalcata; andare a fare un giro; **can you ~ a bike?** sai andare in bicicletta?; **we rode all day/all the way** abbiamo cavalcato tutto il giorno/per tutto il tragitto; **to ~ a horse/bicycle/camel** montare a cavallo/in bicicletta/in groppa a un cammello; **to ~ at anchor** (*NAUT*) essere alla fonda; **horse ~** cavalcata; **car ~** passeggiata in macchina; **to give sb a ~** dare un passaggio a qn; **to take sb for a ~** (*fig*) prendere in giro qn; fregare qn.

ride out *vt*: **to ~ out the storm** (*fig*) mantenersi a galla.

rider |rī'dûr| *n* cavalcatore/trice; (*jockey*) fantino; (*on bicycle*) ciclista *m/f*; (*on motorcycle*) motociclista *m/f*; (*in document*) clausola addizionale, aggiunta.

ridge |rij| *n* (*of hill*) cresta; (*of roof*) colmo; (*of mountain*) giogo; (*on object*) riga (in rilievo).

ridicule |rid'əkyōōl| *n* ridicolo ♦ *vt* mettere in ridicolo; **to hold sb/sth up to ~** mettere in ridicolo qn/qc.

ridiculous |ridik'yələs| *a* ridicolo(a).

riding |rī'ding| *n* equitazione *f*.

riding school *n* scuola d'equitazione.

rife |rīf| *a* diffuso(a); **to be ~ with** abbondare di.

riffraff |rif'raf| *n* canaglia, gentaglia.

rifle |rī'fəl| *n* carabina ♦ *vt* vuotare.

rifle through *vt fus* frugare.

rifle range *n* campo di tiro; (*at fair*) tiro a segno.

rift |rift| *n* fessura, crepatura; (*fig*: *disagreement*) incrinatura.

rig |rig| *n* (*also*: **oil ~**: *on land*) derrick *m inv*; (: *at sea*) piattaforma di trivellazione ♦ *vt* (*election etc*) truccare.

rig up *vt* allestire.

rigging |rig'ing| *n* (*NAUT*) attrezzatura.

right |rīt| *a* giusto(a); (*suitable*) appropriato(a); (*not left*) destro(a) ♦ *n* (*title, claim*) diritto; (*not left*) destra ♦ *ad* (*answer*) correttamente; (*not on the left*) a destra ♦ *vt* raddrizzare; (*fig*) riparare ♦ *excl* bene!; **the ~ time** l'ora esatta; **to be ~** (*person*) aver ragione; (*answer*) essere giusto(a) *or* corretto(a); **to get sth ~** far giusto qc; **you did the ~ thing** ha fatto bene; **let's get it ~ this time!** cerchiamo di farlo bene stavolta!; **~ now** proprio adesso; subito; **~ away** subito; **~ before/after** subito prima/dopo; **~ off** senza esitare; **to go ~ to the end of sth** andare fino in fondo a qc; **~ against the wall** proprio contro il muro; **~ ahead** sempre diritto; proprio davanti; **~ in the middle** proprio nel mezzo; **by ~s** di diritto; **on the ~**, **to the ~** a destra; **~ and wrong** il bene e il

male; **to have a ~ to sth** aver diritto a qc; **film ~s** diritti di riproduzione cinematografica; **~ of way** diritto di passaggio; (*AUT*) precedenza.

right angle *n* angolo retto.

righteous |rī'chəs| *a* retto(a), virtuoso(a); (*anger*) giusto(a), giustificato(a).

righteousness |rī'chəsnis| *n* rettitudine *f*, virtù *f*.

rightful |rīt'fəl| *a* (*heir*) legittimo(a).

rightfully |rīt'fəlē| *ad* legittimamente.

right-handed |rīt'handid| *a* (*person*) che adopera la mano destra.

right-hand man |rīt'hand' man| *n* braccio destro (*fig*).

right-hand side |rīt'hand' sīd| *n* lato destro.

rightly |rīt'lē| *ad* bene, correttamente; (*with reason*) a ragione; **if I remember ~** se mi ricordo bene.

right-minded |rīt'mīndid| *a* sensato(a).

rights issue *n* (*STOCK EXCHANGE*) emissione *f* di azioni riservate agli azionisti.

right wing *n* (*MIL*, *SPORT*) ala destra; (*POL*) destra ♦ *a*: **right-wing** (*POL*) di destra.

right-winger |rīt'wing'ûr| *n* (*POL*) uno/a di destra; (*SPORT*) ala destra.

rigid |rij'id| *a* rigido(a); (*principle*) rigoroso(a).

rigidity |rijid'itē| *n* rigidità.

rigidly |rij'idlē| *ad* rigidamente.

rigmarole |rig'mərōl| *n* tiritera; commedia.

rigor |rig'ûr| *n* (*US*) rigore *m*.

rigor mortis |rig'ûr môr'tis| *n* rigidità cadaverica.

rigorous |rig'ûrəs| *a* rigoroso(a).

rigorously |rig'ûrəslē| *ad* rigorosamente.

rigour |rig'ûr| *n* (*Brit*) = **rigor**.

rig-out |rig'out| *n* (*Brit col*) tenuta.

rile |rīl| *vt* irritare, seccare.

rim |rim| *n* orlo; (*of spectacles*) montatura; (*of wheel*) cerchione *m*.

rimless |rim'lis| *a* (*spectacles*) senza montatura.

rimmed |rimd| *a* bordato(a); cerchiato(a).

rind |rīnd| *n* (*of bacon*) cotenna; (*of lemon etc*) scorza.

ring |ring| *n* anello; (*also*: **wedding ~**) fede *f*; (*of people, objects*) cerchio; (*of spies*) giro; (*of smoke etc*) spirale *m*; (*arena*) pista, arena; (*for boxing*) ring *m inv*; (*sound of bell*) scampanio; (*telephone call*) colpo di telefono ♦ *vb* (*pt* **rang**, *pp* **rung** |rang, rung|) *vi* (*person, bell, telephone*) suonare; (*also*: **~ out**: *voice, words*) risuonare; (*TEL*) telefonare ♦ *vt* (*Brit TEL*: *also*: **~ up**) telefonare a; **to ~ the bell** suonare il campanello; **to give sb a ~** (*TEL*) dare un colpo di telefono a qn; **that has the ~ of truth about it** questo ha l'aria d'essere vero; **the name doesn't ~ a bell (with me)** questo nome non mi dice niente.

ring back *vt, vi* (*Brit TEL*) richiamare.

ring off *vi* (*Brit TEL*) mettere giù, riattaccare.

ring binder *n* classificatore *m* a anelli.

ring finger *n* anulare *m*.

ringing [ring'ing] *n* (*of bell*) scampanio; (: *louder*) scampanellata; (*of telephone*) squillo; (*in ears*) fischio, ronzio.

ringing tone *n* (*TEL*) segnale *m* di libero.

ringleader [ring'lêdûr] *n* (*of gang*) capobanda *m*.

ringlets [ring'lits] *npl* boccoli *mpl*.

ring road *n* (*Brit*) raccordo anulare.

rink [ringk] *n* (*also:* **ice ~**) pista di pattinaggio; (*for roller-skating*) pista di pattinaggio (a rotelle).

rinse [rins] *n* risciacquatura; (*hair tint*) cachet *m inv* ♦ *vt* sciacquare.

Rio (de Janeiro) [rē'ō (dē zhənär'ō)] *n* Rio de Janeiro *f*.

riot [rī'ət] *n* sommossa, tumulto ♦ *vi* tumultuare; **a ~ of colors** un'orgia di colori; **to run ~** creare disordine.

rioter [rī'ətûr] *n* dimostrante *m/f* (*durante dei disordini*).

riotous [rī'ətəs] *a* tumultuoso(a); che fa crepare dal ridere.

riotously [rī'ətəslē] *ad*: **~ funny** che fa crepare dal ridere.

riot police *n* ≈ la Celere.

RIP *abbr* (= *rest in peace*) R.I.P.

rip [rip] *n* strappo ♦ *vt* strappare ♦ *vi* strapparsi.

  rip up *vt* stracciare.

ripcord [rip'kôrd] *n* cavo di spiegamento.

ripe [rīp] *a* (*fruit*) maturo(a); (*cheese*) stagionato(a).

ripen [rī'pən] *vt* maturare ♦ *vi* maturarsi; stagionarsi.

ripeness [rīp'nis] *n* maturità.

rip-off [rip'ôf] *n* (*col*): **it's a ~!** è un furto!

riposte [ripōst'] *n* risposta per le rime.

ripple [rip'əl] *n* increspamento, ondulazione *f*; mormorio ♦ *vi* incresparsi ♦ *vt* increspare.

rise [rīz] *n* (*slope*) salita, pendio; (*hill*) altura; (*increase: in prices, temperature*) rialzo, aumento; (*fig: to power etc*) ascesa ♦ *vi* (*pt rose, pp risen* [rōz, ri'zən]) alzarsi, levarsi; (*prices*) aumentare; (*waters, river*) crescere; (*sun, wind*) levarsi; (*also:* **~ up:** *rebel*) insorgere; ribellarsi; **to give ~ to** provocare, dare origine a; **to ~ to the occasion** dimostrarsi all'altezza della situazione.

rising [rī'zing] *a* (*increasing: number*) sempre crescente; (*prices*) in aumento; (*tide*) montante; (*sun, moon*) nascente, che sorge ♦ *n* (*uprising*) sommossa.

rising damp *n* (*Brit*) infiltrazioni *fpl* d'umidità.

risk [risk] *n* rischio ♦ *vt* rischiare; **to take** *or* **run the ~ of doing** correre il rischio di fare;

at ~ in pericolo; **at one's own ~** a proprio rischio e pericolo; **fire/health ~** rischio d'incendio/per la salute; **I'll ~ it** ci proverò lo stesso.

risk capital *n* capitale *m* di rischio.

risky [ris'kē] *a* rischioso(a).

risqué [riskā'] *a* (*joke*) spinto(a).

rissole [ris'ôl] *n* crocchetta.

rite [rīt] *n* rito; **last ~s** l'estrema unzione.

ritual [rich'ōōəl] *a, n* rituale (*m*).

rival [rī'vəl] *n* rivale *m/f*; (*in business*) concorrente *m/f* ♦ *a* rivale; che fa concorrenza ♦ *vt* essere in concorrenza con; **to ~ sb/sth in** competere con qn/qc in.

rivalry [rī'vəlrē] *n* rivalità; concorrenza.

river [riv'ûr] *n* fiume *m* ♦ *cpd* (*port, traffic*) fluviale; **up/down ~** a monte/valle.

riverbank [riv'ûrbangk] *n* argine *m*.

riverbed [riv'ûrbed] *n* alveo (fluviale).

riverside [riv'ûrsīd] *n* sponda del fiume.

rivet [riv'it] *n* ribattino, rivetto ♦ *vt* ribadire; (*fig*) concentrare, fissare.

riveting [riv'iting] *a* (*fig*) avvincente.

Riviera [rivēär'ə] *n*: **the (French) ~** la Costa Azzurra; **the Italian ~** la Riviera.

Riyadh [rēyâd'] *n* Riad *f*.

RN *n abbr* (*US*) = **registered nurse**; (*Brit*) = **Royal Navy**.

RNA *n abbr* (= *ribonucleic acid*) R.N.A. *m*.

road [rōd] *n* strada; (*small*) cammino; (*in town*) via; **main ~** strada principale; **major/minor ~** strada con/senza diritto di precedenza; **it takes 4 hours by ~** sono 4 ore di macchina (*or* in camion *etc*); **on the ~ to success** sulla via del successo.

roadblock [rōd'blâk] *n* blocco stradale.

road haulage *n* autotrasporti *mpl*.

road hog *n* pirata *m* della strada.

road map *n* carta stradale.

road safety *n* sicurezza sulle strade.

roadside [rōd'sīd] *n* margine *m* della strada; **by the ~** a lato della strada.

road sign *n* cartello stradale.

roadsweeper [rōd'swēpûr] *n* (*Brit: person*) spazzino.

road transport *n* autotrasporti *mpl*.

road user *n* utente *m/f* della strada.

roadway [rōd'wā] *n* carreggiata.

roadworthy [rōd'wûrthē] *a* in buono stato di marcia.

roam [rōm] *vi* errare, vagabondare ♦ *vt* vagare per.

roar [rôr] *n* ruggito; (*of crowd*) tumulto; (*of thunder, storm*) muggito ♦ *vi* ruggire; tumultuare; muggire; **to ~ with laughter** scoppiare dalle risa.

roaring [rôr'ing] *a*: **a ~ fire** un bel fuoco; **to do a ~ trade** fare affari d'oro; **a ~ success** un successo strepitoso.

roast [rōst] *n* arrosto ♦ *vt* (*meat*) arrostire.

roast beef *n* arrosto di manzo.

rob [râb] *vt* (*person*) rubare; (*bank*) svaligiare; **to ~ sb of sth** derubare qn di qc; (*fig: deprive*) privare qn di qc.

robber [râb'ûr] *n* ladro; (*armed*) rapinatore *m*.

robbery [râb'ûrē] *n* furto; rapina; **it's highway ~** (*US col*) è una rapina!

robe [rōb] *n* (*for ceremony etc*) abito; (*also:* **bath~**) accappatoio ♦ *vt* vestire.

robin [râb'in] *n* pettirosso.

robot [rō'bət] *n* robot *m inv.*

robotics [rōbât'iks] *n* robotica.

robust [rōbust'] *a* robusto(a); (*material*) solido(a).

rock [râk] *n* (*substance*) roccia; (*boulder*) masso; roccia; (*in sea*) scoglio; (*Brit: candy*) zucchero candito ♦ *vt* (*swing gently:* *cradle*) dondolare; (*: child*) cullare; (*shake*) scrollare, far tremare ♦ *vi* dondolarsi; oscillare; **on the ~s** (*drink*) col ghiaccio; (*ship*) sugli scogli; (*marriage etc*) in crisi; **to ~ the boat** (*fig*) piantare grane.

rock and roll *n* rock and roll *m.*

rock-bottom [râk'bât'əm] *n* (*fig*) stremo; **to reach** *or* **touch ~** (*price*) raggiungere il livello più basso; (*person*) toccare il fondo.

rock climber *n* rocciatore/trice, scalatore/trice.

rock climbing *n* roccia.

rocket [râk'it] *n* razzo; (*MIL*) razzo, missile *m* ♦ *vi* (*prices*) salire alle stelle.

rocket launcher [râk'it lônch'ûr] *n* lanciarazzi *m inv.*

rock face *n* parete *f* della roccia.

rock fall *n* caduta di massi.

rock garden *n* giardino roccioso.

rocking chair [râk'ing chär] *n* sedia a dondolo.

rocking horse [râk'ing hôrs] *n* cavallo a dondolo.

rocky [râk'ē] *a* (*hill*) roccioso(a); (*path*) sassoso(a); (*unsteady: table*) traballante.

Rocky Mountains *npl:* **the ~** le Montagne Rocciose.

rod [râd] *n* (*metallic, TECH*) asta; (*wooden*) bacchetta; (*also:* **fishing ~**) canna da pesca.

rode [rōd] *pt of* **ride.**

rodent [rō'dənt] *n* roditore *m.*

rodeo [rō'dēō] *n* rodeo.

roe [rō] *n* (*species: also:* **~ deer**) capriolo; (*of fish: also:* **hard ~**) uova *fpl* di pesce; **soft ~** latte *m* di pesce.

roe deer *n* (*species*) capriolo; (*female deer: pl inv*) capriolo femmina.

rogue [rōg] *n* mascalzone *m.*

roguish [rō'gish] *a* birbantesco(a).

ROI *n abbr* (*US*) = *return on investment.*

role [rōl] *n* ruolo.

roll [rōl] *n* rotolo; (*of banknotes*) mazzo; (*also:* **bread ~**) panino; (*register*) lista; (*sound: of drums etc*) rullo; (*movement: of ship*) rullio ♦ *vt* rotolare; (*also:* **~ up:** *string*) aggomito-

lare; (*also:* **~ out:** *pastry*) stendere ♦ *vi* rotolare; (*wheel*) girare; **cheese ~** panino al formaggio.

roll around *vi* rotolare qua e là; (*person*) rotolarsi.

roll by *vi* (*time*) passare.

roll in *vi* (*mail, cash*) arrivare a bizzeffe.

roll over *vi* rivoltarsi.

roll up *vi* (*col: arrive*) arrivare ♦ *vt* (*carpet, cloth, map*) arrotolare; (*sleeves*) rimboccare; **to ~ o.s. up into a ball** raggomitolarsi.

roll call *n* appello.

roller [rō'lûr] *n* rullo; (*wheel*) rotella.

roller coaster *n* montagne *fpl* russe.

roller skates *npl* pattini *mpl* a rotelle.

rollicking [râl'iking] *a* allegro(a) e chiassoso(a); **to have a ~ time** divertirsi pazzamente.

rolling [rō'ling] *a* (*landscape*) ondulato(a).

rolling mill *n* fabbrica di laminati.

rolling pin *n* matterello.

rolling stock *n* (*RAIL*) materiale *m* rotabile.

ROM [râm] *n abbr* (*COMPUT:* = *read-only memory*) ROM *f.*

romaine lettuce [rōmān' let'is] *n* (*US*) lattuga romana.

Roman [rō'mən] *a, n* romano(a).

Roman Catholic *a, n* cattolico(a).

romance [rōmans'] *n* storia (*or* avventura *or* film *m inv*) romantico(a); (*charm*) poesia; (*love affair*) idillio.

Romanesque [rōmənesk'] *a* romanico(a).

Romania [rōmā'nēə] *n* Romania.

Romanian [rōmā'nēən] *a* romeno(a) ♦ *n* romeno/a; (*LING*) romeno.

Roman numeral *n* numero romano.

romantic [rōman'tik] *a* romantico(a); sentimentale.

romanticism [rōman'tisizəm] *n* romanticismo.

Romany [rōm'ənē] *a* zingaresco(a) ♦ *n* (*person*) zingaro/a; (*LING*) lingua degli zingari.

Rome [rōm] *n* Roma.

romp [râmp] *n* gioco chiassoso ♦ *vi* (*also:* **~ around**) giocare chiassosamente; **to ~ home** (*horse*) vincere senza difficoltà, stravincere.

rompers [râm'pûrz] *npl* pagliaccetto.

rondo [rân'dō] *n* (*MUS*) rondò *m inv.*

roof [rōōf] *n* tetto; (*of tunnel, cave*) volta ♦ *vt* coprire (con un tetto); **~ of the mouth** palato.

roof garden *n* giardino pensile.

roofing [rōō'fing] *n* materiale *m* per copertura.

roof rack *n* (*AUT*) portabagagli *m inv.*

rook [rōōk] *n* (*bird*) corvo nero; (*CHESS*) torre *f* ♦ *vt* (*cheat*) truffare, spennare.

room [rōōm] *n* (*in house*) stanza, camera; (*in school etc*) sala; (*space*) posto, spazio; **~s** *npl* (*lodging*) alloggio; **"~s for rent"**, (*Brit*) **"~s to let"** "si affittano camere"; **is there ~**

for this? c'è spazio per questo?, ci sta anche questo?; **to make ~ for sb** far posto a qn; **there is ~ for improvement** si potrebbe migliorare; **~ and board** (*US*) vitto e alloggio.

rooming house [rōō'ming hous] *n* (*US*) *casa in cui si affittano camere o appartamentini ammobiliati*.

roommate [rōōm'māt] *n* compagno/a di stanza.

room service *n* servizio da camera.

room temperature *n* temperatura ambiente.

roomy [rōō'mē] *a* spazioso(a); (*garment*) ampio(a).

roost [rōōst] *n* appollaiato ♦ *vi* appollaiarsi.

rooster [rōōs'tûr] *n* gallo.

root [rōōt] *n* radice *f* ♦ *vt* (*plant, belief*) far radicare; **to take ~** (*plant*) attecchire, prendere; (*idea*) far presa; **the ~ of the problem is that ...** il problema deriva dal fatto che ....

root about (*Brit*) = **root around.**

root around *vi* (*fig*) frugare.

root for *vt fus* (*col*) fare il tifo per.

root out *vt* estirpare.

rope [rōp] *n* corda, fune *f*; (*NAUT*) cavo ♦ *vt* (*box*) legare; (*climbers*) legare in cordata; **to jump** *or* **skip ~** (*US*) saltare la corda; **to ~ sb in** (*fig*) coinvolgere qn; **to know the ~s** (*fig*) conoscere i trucchi del mestiere; **at the end of one's ~** al limite (della pazienza).

rope ladder *n* scala di corda.

rosary [rō'zûrē] *n* rosario; roseto.

rose [rōz] *pt of* **rise** ♦ *n* rosa; (*also:* **~ bush**) rosaio; (*on watering can*) rosetta ♦ *a* rosa *inv.*

rosé [rōzā'] *n* vino rosato.

rosebed [rōz'bed] *n* roseto.

rosebud [rōz'bud] *n* bocciolo di rosa.

rosebush [rōz'bōōsh] *n* rosaio.

rosemary [rōz'mârē] *n* rosmarino.

rosette [rōzet'] *n* coccarda.

roster [râs'tûr] *n*: **duty ~** ruolino di servizio.

rostrum [râs'trəm] *n* tribuna.

rosy [rō'zē] *a* roseo(a).

rot [rât] *n* (*decay*) putrefazione *f*; (*col: nonsense*) stupidaggini *fpl* ♦ *vt, vi* imputridire, marcire; **dry/wet ~** funghi parassiti del legno; **to stop the ~** (*Brit fig*) salvare la situazione.

rota [rō'tə] *n* (*Brit*) tabella dei turni; **on a ~ basis** a turno.

rotary [rō'tûrē] *a* rotante.

rotate [rō'tāt] *vt* (*revolve*) far girare; (*change round: crops*) avvicendare; (: *jobs*) fare a turno ♦ *vi* (*revolve*) girare.

rotating [rō'tāting] *a* (*movement*) rotante.

rotation [rōtā'shən] *n* rotazione *f*; **in ~** a turno, in rotazione.

rote [rōt] *n*: **to learn sth by ~** imparare qc a memoria.

rotor [rō'tûr] *n* rotore *m*.

rotten [rât'ən] *a* (*decayed*) putrido(a), marcio(a); (: *teeth*) cariato(a); (*dishonest*) corrotto(a); (*col: bad*) brutto(a); (: *action*) vigliacco(a); **to feel ~** (*ill*) sentirsi proprio male.

rotting [rât'ing] *a* in putrefazione.

rotund [rōtund'] *a* grassoccio(a); tondo(a).

rouge [rōōzh] *n* belletto.

rough [ruf] *a* aspro(a); (*person, manner: coarse*) rozzo(a), aspro(a); (: *violent*) brutale; (*district*) malfamato(a); (*weather*) cattivo(a); (*plan*) abbozzato(a); (*guess*) approssimativo(a) ♦ *n* (*GOLF*) macchia; **~ estimate** approssimazione *f*; **to ~ it** far vita dura; **to play ~** far il gioco pesante; **to have a ~ time (of it)** passare un periodaccio; **the sea is ~ today** c'è mare grosso oggi.

rough out *vt* (*draft*) abbozzare.

roughage [ruf'ij] *n* alimenti *mpl* ricchi di cellulosa.

rough-and-ready [ruf'ənred'ē] *a* rudimentale.

rough-and-tumble [ruf'əntum'bəl] *n* zuffa.

roughcast [ruf'kast] *n* intonaco grezzo.

rough draft *n* brutta copia.

roughen [ruf'ən] *vt* (*a surface*) rendere ruvido(a).

roughly [ruf'lē] *ad* (*handle*) rudemente, brutalmente; (*make*) grossolanamente; (*approximately*) approssimativamente; **~ speaking** grosso modo, ad occhio e croce.

roughness [ruf'nis] *n* asprezza; rozzezza; brutalità.

roughshod [ruf'shâd'] *ad*: **to ride ~ over** (*person*) mettere sotto i piedi; (*objection*) passare sopra a.

rough work *n* (*Brit: at school etc*) brutta copia.

roulette [rōōlet'] *n* roulette *f*.

Roumania [rōōmā'nēə] *etc* = **Romania** *etc.*

round [round] *a* rotondo(a) ♦ *n* tondo, cerchio; (*Brit: of toast*) fetta; (*duty: of policeman, milkman etc*) giro; (: *of doctor*) visite *fpl*; (*game: of cards, in competition*) partita; (*BOXING*) round *m inv*; (*of talks*) serie *f inv* ♦ *vt* (*corner*) girare; (*bend*) prendere; (*cape*) doppiare ♦ *prep* intorno a ♦ *ad*: **right ~** tutt'attorno; **all the year ~** tutto l'anno; **in ~ figures** in cifra tonda; **she arrived ~ (about) noon** è arrivata intorno a mezzogiorno; **to go the ~s** (*illness*) diffondersi; (*story*) circolare, passare di bocca in bocca; **the daily ~** (*fig*) la routine quotidiana; **~ of ammunition** cartuccia; **~ of applause** applausi *mpl*; **~ of drinks** giro di bibite; **~ of sandwiches** (*Brit*) sandwich *m inv*; *see also* **around.**

round off *vt* (*speech etc*) finire.

round up *vt* radunare; (*criminals*) fare una retata di; (*prices*) arrotondare.

roundabout [round'əbout] *n* (*at fair*) giostra; (*Brit AUT*) rotatoria ♦ *a* (*route, means*) indiretto(a).

rounded [roun'did] *a* arrotondato(a); (*style*) armonioso(a).

rounders [roun'dûrz] *npl* (*game*) *gioco simile al baseball*.

roundly [round'lē] *ad* (*fig*) chiaro e tondo.

round-shouldered [round'shōldûrd] *a* dalle spalle tonde.

round trip *n* (viaggio di) andata e ritorno.

round trip ticket *n* (*US*) biglietto di andata e ritorno.

roundup [round'up] *n* raduno; (*of criminals*) retata; **a ~ of the latest news** un sommario *or* riepilogo delle ultime notizie.

rouse [rouz] *vt* (*wake up*) svegliare; (*stir up*) destare; provocare; risvegliare.

rousing [rou'zing] *a* (*speech, applause*) entusiastico(a).

rout [rout] *n* (*MIL*) rotta ♦ *vt* mettere in rotta.

route [rōōt] *n* itinerario; (*of bus*) percorso; (*of trade, shipping*) rotta; **"all ~s"** (*AUT*) "tutte le direzioni"; **the best ~ to Chicago** la strada migliore per andare a Chicago; **en ~ for** in viaggio verso; **en ~ from ... to** viaggiando da ... a.

routine [rōōtēn'] *a* (*work*) corrente, abituale; (*procedure*) solito(a) ♦ *n* (*pej*) routine *f*, tran tran *m*; (*THEATER*) numero; (*COMPUT*) sottoprogramma *m*; **daily ~** orario quotidiano; **~ procedure** prassi *f*.

roving [rō'ving] *a* (*life*) itinerante.

roving reporter *n* reporter *m inv* volante.

row [rō] *n* (*line*) riga, fila; (*behind one another: of cars, people*) fila; (*Brit KNITTING*) ferro; [rou] (*dispute*) lite *f*; (*Brit: noise*) baccano, chiasso ♦ *vi* (*in boat*) remare; (*as sport*) vogare; [rou] litigare ♦ *vt* (*boat*) manovrare a remi; **in a ~** (*fig*) di fila; **to make a ~** far baccano; **to have a ~** litigare.

rowboat [rō'bōt] *n* (*US*) barca a remi.

rowdiness [rou'dēnis] *n* baccano; (*fighting*) zuffa.

rowdy [rou'dē] *a* chiassoso(a); turbolento(a) ♦ *n* teppista *m/f*.

rowdyism [rou'dēizəm] *n* teppismo.

rowing [rō'ing] *n* canottaggio.

rowing boat *n* (*Brit*) = **rowboat**.

rowlock [rō'lâk] *n* (*Brit*) scalmo.

royal [roi'əl] *a* reale.

Royal Air Force (RAF) *n* (*Brit*) aeronautica militare britannica.

royal blue *a* blu reale *inv*.

royalist [roi'əlist] *a, n* realista (*m/f*).

Royal Navy (RN) *n* (*Brit*) marina militare britannica.

royalty [roi'əltē] *n* (*royal persons*) (membri *mpl* della) famiglia reale; (*payment: to author*) diritti *mpl* d'autore; (: *to inventor*) diritti di brevetto.

RP *n abbr* (*Brit*: = *received pronunciation*)

pronuncia standard.

RPM *abbr* = **resale price maintenance**.

rpm *abbr* (= *revolutions per minute*) giri/min.

RR *abbr* (*US* = *railroad*) Ferr.

R&R *n abbr* (*US MIL*: = *rest and recreation*) permesso per militari.

RRP *n abbr* (*Brit*) *see* **recommended retail price**.

RSVP *abbr* (= *répondez s'il vous plaît*) R.S.V.P.

Rt Hon. *abbr* (*Brit*: = *Right Honourable*) ≈ On. (= *Onorevole*).

Rt Rev. *abbr* (= *Right Reverend*) Rev.

rub [rub] *n* (*with cloth*) fregata, strofinata; (*on person*) frizione *f*, massaggio ♦ *vt* fregare, strofinare; frizionare; **to ~ sb the wrong way** *or* (*Brit*) **~ sb up the wrong way** lisciare qn contro pelo.

rub down *vt* (*body*) strofinare, frizionare; (*horse*) strigliare.

rub in *vt* (*ointment*) far penetrare (massaggiando *or* frizionando).

rub off *vi* andare via; **to ~ off on** lasciare una traccia su.

rub out (*Brit*) *vt* cancellare ♦ *vi* cancellarsi.

rubber [rub'ûr] *n* (*gen, Brit*: *eraser*) gomma; (*US col*) preservativo.

rubber band *n* elastico.

rubber plant *n* ficus *m inv*.

rubber stamp *n* timbro di gomma.

rubber-stamp [rubûrstamp'] *vt* (*fig*) approvare senza discussione.

rubbery [rub'ûrē] *a* gommoso(a).

rubbing alcohol [rub'ing al'kəhôl] *n* (*US*) alcool denaturato.

rubbish [rub'ish] *n* (*fig: pej*) cose *fpl* senza valore; robaccia; (*nonsense*) sciocchezze *fpl*; (*Brit: from household*) immondizie *fpl*, rifiuti *mpl* ♦ *vt* (*Brit col*) sputtanare; **what you've just said is ~** quello che ha appena detto è una sciocchezza.

rubbish bin *n* (*Brit*) pattumiera.

rubbish dump *n* (*Brit*) luogo di scarico.

rubbishy [rub'ishē] *a* (*Brit col*) scadente, che non vale niente.

rubble [rub'əl] *n* macerie *fpl*; (*smaller*) pietrisco.

ruble [rōō'bəl] *n* rublo.

ruby [rōō'bē] *n* rubino.

RUC *n abbr* (*Brit*: = *Royal Ulster Constabulary*) forza di polizia dell'Irlanda del Nord.

rucksack [ruk'sak] *n* zaino.

rudder [rud'ûr] *n* timone *m*.

ruddy [rud'ē] *a* (*face*) fresco(a).

rude [rōōd] *a* (*impolite: person*) scortese, rozzo(a); (: *word, manners*) grossolano(a), rozzo(a); (*shocking*) indecente; **to be ~ to sb** essere maleducato con qn.

rudely [rōōd'lē] *ad* scortesemente; grossolanamente.

rudeness |rōōd'nis| *n* scortesia; grossolanità.
rudiment |rōō'dəmənt| *n* rudimento.
rudimentary |rōōdəmcn'tûrē| *a* rudimentale.
rueful |rōō'fəl| *a* mesto(a), triste.
ruff |ruf| *n* gorgiera.
ruffian |ruf'ēən| *n* briccone *m*, furfante *m*.
ruffle |ruf'əl| *vt* (*hair*) scompigliare; (*clothes, water*) increspare; (*fig: person*) turbare.
rug |rug| *n* tappeto.
rugby |rug'bē| *n* (*also:* ~ **football**) rugby *m*.
rugged |rug'id| *a* (*landscape*) aspro(a); (*features, determination*) duro(a); (*character*) brusco(a).
ruin |rōō'in| *n* rovina ♦ *vt* rovinare; (*spoil: clothes*) sciupare; ~**s** *npl* rovine *fpl*, ruderi *mpl*; **in** ~**s** in rovina.
ruination |rōōinā'shən| *n* rovina.
ruinous |rōō'inəs| *a* rovinoso(a); (*expenditure*) inverosimile.
rule |rōōl| *n* (*gen*) regola; (*regulation*) regolamento, regola; (*government*) governo; (*dominion etc*): **under British** ~ sotto la sovranità britannica ♦ *vt* (*country*) governare; (*person*) dominare; (*decide*) decidere ♦ *vi* regnare; decidere; (*LAW*) dichiarare; **to** ~ **against/in favor of/on** (*LAW*) pronunciarsi a sfavore di/in favore di/su; **it's against the** ~**s** è contro le regole *or* il regolamento; **by** ~ **of thumb** a lume di naso; **as a** ~ normalmente, di regola; **the** ~**s of the road** ≈ il codice *m* della strada.
  rule out *vt* escludere; **murder cannot be** ~**d out** non si esclude che si tratti di omicidio.
ruled |rōōld| *a* (*paper*) vergato(a).
ruler |rōō'lûr| *n* (*sovereign*) sovrano/a; (*leader*) capo (dello Stato); (*for measuring*) regolo, riga.
ruling |rōō'ling| *a* (*party*) al potere; (*class*) dirigente ♦ *n* (*LAW*) decisione *f*.
rum |rum| *n* rum *m*.
Rumania |rōōmā'nēə| *etc* = **Romania** *etc*.
rumble |rum'bəl| *n* rimbombo; brontolio ♦ *vi* rimbombare; (*stomach, pipe*) brontolare.
rummage |rum'ij| *vi* frugare.
rummage sale *n* (*US*) vendita di oggetti per beneficenza.
rumor, (*Brit*) **rumour** |rōō'mûr| *n* voce *f* ♦ *vt*: **it is** ~**ed that** corre voce che.
rump |rump| *n* (*of animal*) groppa.
rumple |rum'pəl| *vt* (*hair*) arruffare, scompigliare; (*clothes*) spiegazzare, sgualcire.
rump steak *n* bistecca di girello.
rumpus |rum'pəs| *n* (*col*) baccano; (*: quarrel*) rissa; **to kick up a** ~ fare un putiferio.
run |run| *n* corsa; (*trip*) gita (in macchina); (*distance traveled*) percorso, tragitto; (*series*) serie *f inv*; (*THEATER*) periodo di rappresentazione; (*SKI*) pista; (*in tights*) smagliatura ♦ *vb* (*pt* **ran**, *pp* **run** |ran, run|) *vt* (*operate: business*) gestire, dirigere; (*:

competition, course) organizzare; (*: hotel*) gestire; (*: house*) governare; (*COMPUT: program*) eseguire; (*water, bath*) far scorrere; (*force through: rope, pipe*): **to** ~ **sth through** far passare qc attraverso; (*to pass: hand, finger*): **to** ~ **sth over** passare qc su ♦ *vi* correre; (*pass: road etc*) passare; (*work: machine, factory*) funzionare, andare; (*bus, train: operate*) far servizio; (*: travel*) circolare; (*continue: play, contract*) durare; (*slide: drawer; flow: river, bath*) scorrere; (*colors, washing*) stemperarsi; (*in election*) presentarsi come candidato; **to go for a** ~ andare a correre; (*in car*) fare un giro (in macchina); **to break into a** ~ mettersi a correre; **a** ~ **of luck** un periodo di fortuna; **to have the** ~ **of sb's house** essere libero di andare e venire in casa di qn; **there was a** ~ **on** ... c'era una corsa a ...; **in the long** ~ alla lunga; in fin dei conti; **in the short** ~ sulle prime; **on the** ~ in fuga; **to make a** ~ **for it** scappare, tagliare la corda; **I'll** ~ **you to the station** ti porto alla stazione; **to** ~ **a risk** correre un rischio; **to** ~ **a stoplight** (*US*) passare col rosso; **to** ~ **errands** andare a fare commissioni; **the train** ~**s between New York and Boston** il treno collega New York alla stazione Boston; **the bus** ~**s every 20 minutes** c'è un autobus ogni 20 minuti; **it's very cheap to** ~ comporta poche spese; **to** ~ **on gas** *or* (*Brit*) **petrol/on diesel/off batteries** andare a benzina/a diesel/a batterie; **to** ~ **for the bus** fare una corsa per prendere l'autobus; **to** ~ **for president** presentarsi come candidato per la presidenza; **their losses ran into millions** le loro perdite hanno raggiunto i milioni.
run about *vi* (*Brit*) = **run around**.
run across *vt fus* (*find*) trovare per caso.
run around *vi* (*children*) correre qua e là.
run away *vi* fuggire.
run down *vi* (*clock*) scaricarsi ♦ *vt* (*AUT*) investire; (*criticize*) criticare; (*Brit: reduce: production*) ridurre gradualmente; (*: factory, shop*) rallentare l'attività di; **to be** ~ **down** (*battery*) essere scarico(a); (*person*) essere giù (di corda).
run in *vt* (*Brit: car*) rodare, fare il rodaggio di.
run into *vt fus* (*meet: person*) incontrare per caso; (*: trouble*) incontrare, trovare; (*collide with*) andare a sbattere contro; **to** ~ **into debt** trovarsi nei debiti.
run off *vi* fuggire ♦ *vt* (*water*) far defluire; (*copies*) fare.
run out *vi* (*person*) uscire di corsa; (*liquid*) colare; (*lease*) scadere; (*money*) esaurirsi.
run out of *vt fus* rimanere a corto di; **I've** ~ **out of gas** *or* (*Brit*) **petrol** sono rimasto senza benzina.
run over *vt* (*AUT*) investire, mettere sotto ♦

vt fus (*revise*) rivedere.
run through *vt fus* (*instructions*) dare una scorsa a.
run up *vt* (*debt*) lasciar accumulare; **to ~ up against** (*difficulties*) incontrare.
runaway [run'əwā] *a* (*person*) fuggiasco(a); (*horse*) in libertà; (*truck*) fuori controllo; (*inflation*) galoppante.
rundown [run'doun] *n* (*Brit: of industry etc*) riduzione *f* graduale dell'attività di.
rung [rung] *pp of* **ring** ♦ *n* (*of ladder*) piolo.
run-in [run'in] *n* (*col*) scontro.
runner [run'ûr] *n* (*in race*) corridore *m*; (*on sleigh*) pattino; (*for drawer etc, carpet*) guida.
runner bean *n* (*Brit*) fagiolino.
runner-up [runûrup'] *n* secondo(a) arrivato(a).
running [run'ing] *n* corsa; direzione *f*; organizzazione *f*; funzionamento ♦ *a* (*water*) corrente; (*commentary*) simultaneo(a); **6 days ~** 6 giorni di seguito; **to be in/out of the ~ for sth** essere/non essere più in lizza per qc.
running costs *npl* (*of business*) costi *mpl* d'esercizio; (*of car*) spese *fpl* di mantenimento.
running head *n* (*TYP, etc*) testata, titolo corrente.
running mate *n* (*US POL*) candidato alla vicepresidenza.
runny [run'ē] *a* che cola.
run-off [run'ôf] *n* (*in contest, election*) confronto definitivo; (*extra race*) spareggio.
run-of-the-mill [runəv th̩əmil'] *a* solito(a), banale.
runt [runt] *n* (*also pej*) omuncolo; (*ZOOL*) animale *m* più piccolo del normale.
run-through [run'thrōō] *n* prova.
run-up [run'up] *n* (*Brit*): **~ to sth** periodo che precede qc.
runway [run'wā] *n* (*AVIAT*) pista (di decollo).
rupee [rōō'pē] *n* rupia.
rupture [rup'chûr] *n* (*MED*) ernia ♦ *vt*: **to ~ o.s.** farsi venire un'ernia.
rural [rōōr'əl] *a* rurale.
ruse [rōōz] *n* trucco.
rush [rush] *n* corsa precipitosa; (*of crowd*) afflusso; (*hurry*) furia, fretta; (*current*) flusso; (*BOT*) giunco ♦ *vt* mandare *or* spedire velocemente; (*attack: town etc*) prendere d'assalto ♦ *vi* precipitarsi; **is there any ~ for this?** è urgente?; **we've had a ~ of orders** abbiamo avuto una valanga di ordinazioni; **I'm in a ~ (to do)** ho fretta *or* premura (di fare); **gold ~** corsa all'oro; **to ~ sth off** spedire con urgenza qc; **don't ~ me!** non farmi fretta!
rush through *vt* (*meal*) mangiare in fretta; (*book*) dare una scorsa frettolosa a; (*town*) attraversare in fretta; (*COMM: order*)

eseguire d'urgenza ♦ *vt fus* (*work*) sbrigare frettolosamente.
rush hour *n* ora di punta.
rush job *n* (*urgent*) lavoro urgente.
rush matting [rush mat'ing] *n* stuoia.
rusk [rusk] *n* fetta biscottata.
Russia [rush'ə] *n* Russia.
Russian [rush'ən] *a* russo(a) ♦ *n* russo/a; (*LING*) russo.
rust [rust] *n* ruggine *f* ♦ *vi* arrugginirsi.
rustic [rus'tik] *a* rustico(a) ♦ *n* (*pej*) cafone/a.
rustle [rus'əl] *vi* frusciare ♦ *vt* (*paper*) far frusciare; (*US: cattle*) rubare.
rustproof [rust'prōōf] *a* inossidabile.
rustproofing [rust'prōōfing] *n* trattamento antiruggine.
rusty [rus'tē] *a* arrugginito(a).
rut [rut] *n* solco; (*ZOOL*) fregola; **to be in a ~** (*fig*) essersi fossilizzato(a).
rutabaga [rōōtəbā'gə] *n* (*US*) rapa svedese.
ruthless [rōōth'lis] *a* spietato(a).
ruthlessness [rōōth'lisnis] *n* spietatezza.
RV *abbr* (= *revised version*) versione riveduta della *Bibbia Anglicana* ♦ *n abbr* (*US*) *see* **recreational vehicle**.
rye [rī] *n* segale *f*.
rye bread *n* pane *m* di segale.

S

S, s [es] *n* (*letter*) S, s *f or m inv*; (*US SCOL: = satisfactory*) ≈ sufficiente; **S for Sugar** ≈ S come Savona.
S *abbr* (= *saint*) S.; (= *south*) S; (*on clothes*) = *small*.
SA *abbr* = **South Africa; South America**.
Sabbath [sab'əth] *n* (*Jewish*) sabato; (*Christian*) domenica.
sabbatical [səbat'ikəl] *a*: **~ year** anno sabbatico.
sabotage [sab'ətâzh] *n* sabotaggio ♦ *vt* sabotare.
saccharine [sak'ûrin] *n* saccarina.
sachet [sashā'] *n* bustina.
sack [sak] *n* (*bag*) sacco ♦ *vt* (*dismiss*) licenziare, mandare a spasso; (*plunder*) saccheggiare; **to get the ~** (*Brit*) essere mandato a spasso.
sackful [sak'fəl] *n*: **a ~ of** un sacco di.
sacking [sak'ing] *n* tela di sacco; (*Brit: dismissal*) licenziamento.
sacrament [sak'rəmənt] *n* sacramento.
sacred [sā'krid] *a* sacro(a).
sacrifice [sak'rəfīs] *n* sacrificio ♦ *vt* sacrificare;

to make ~s (for sb) fare (dei) sacrifici (per qn).

sacrilege |sak'rəlij| *n* sacrilegio.

sacrosanct |sak'rōsangkt| *a* sacrosanto(a).

sad |sad| *a* triste; (*deplorable*) deplorevole.

sadden |sad'ən| *vt* rattristare.

saddle |sad'əl| *n* sella ♦ *vt* (*horse*) sellare; **to be ~d with sth** (*col*) avere qc sulle spalle.

saddlebag |sad'əlbag| *n* bisaccia; (*on bicycle*) borsa.

sadism |sā'dizəm| *n* sadismo.

sadist |sā'dist| *n* sadico/a.

sadistic |sədis'tik| *a* sadico(a).

sadly |sad'lē| *ad* tristemente; (*regrettably*) sfortunatamente; **~ lacking in** penosamente privo di.

sadness |sad'nis| *n* tristezza.

sae *abbr* (*Brit*) = **stamped addressed envelope**; *see* **stamp**.

safari |səfä'rē| *n* safari *m inv*.

safari park *n* zoosafari *m inv*.

safe |sāf| *a* sicuro(a); (*out of danger*) salvo(a), al sicuro; (*cautious*) prudente ♦ *n* cassaforte *f*; **~ from** al sicuro da; **~ and sound** sano(a) e salvo(a); **~ journey!** buon viaggio!; **(just) to be on the ~ side** per non correre rischi; **to play it ~** giocare sul sicuro; **it is ~ to say that ...** si può affermare con sicurezza che ....

safe-breaker |sāf'brākûr| *n* (*Brit*) = **safe-cracker**.

safe-conduct |sāf'kân'dukt| *n* salvacondotto.

safe-cracker |sāf'krakûr| *n* (*US*) scassinatore *m*.

safe-deposit |sāf'dipâzit| *n* (*vault*) caveau *m inv*; (*box*) cassetta di sicurezza.

safeguard |sāf'gârd| *n* salvaguardia ♦ *vt* salvaguardare.

safekeeping |sāfkē'ping| *n* custodia.

safely |sāf'lē| *ad* sicuramente; sano(a) e salvo(a); prudentemente; **I can ~ say ...** posso tranquillamente asserire ....

safe(r) sex |sāf('ûr) seks| *n* sesso (più) sicuro.

safety |sāf'tē| *n* sicurezza; **~ first!** la prudenza innanzitutto!

safety belt *n* cintura di sicurezza.

safety curtain *n* telone *m*.

safety net *n* rete *f* di protezione.

safety pin *n* spilla di sicurezza.

safety valve *n* valvola di sicurezza.

saffron |saf'rən| *n* zafferano.

sag |sag| *vi* incurvarsi; afflosciarsi.

saga |sâg'ə| *n* saga; (*fig*) odissea.

sage |sāj| *n* (*herb*) salvia; (*man*) saggio.

Sagittarius |sajitär'ēəs| *n* Sagittario; **to be ~** essere del Sagittario.

sago |sā'gō| *n* sagù *m*.

Sahara |səhär'ə| *n*: **the ~ Desert** il Deserto del Sahara.

Sahel |sáhel| *n* Sahel *m*.

said |sed| *pt, pp of* **say**.

Saigon |sīgân'| *n* Saigon *f*.

sail |sāl| *n* (*on boat*) vela; (*trip*): **to go for a ~** (*Brit*) fare un giro in barca a vela ♦ *vt* (*boat*) condurre, governare ♦ *vi* (*travel: ship*) navigare; (: *passenger*) viaggiare per mare; (*set off*) salpare; (*SPORT*) fare della vela; **they ~ed into Genoa** entrarono nel porto di Genova.

sail through *vt fus* (*fig*) superare senza difficoltà ♦ *vi* farcela senza difficoltà.

sailboat |sāl'bōt| *n* (*US*) barca a vela.

sailing |sā'ling| *n* (*sport*) vela; **to go ~** fare della vela.

sailing boat *n* (*Brit*) = **sailboat**.

sailing ship *n* veliero.

sailor |sā'lûr| *n* marinaio.

saint |sānt| *n* santo/a.

saintly |sānt'lē| *a* da santo(a); santo(a).

sake |sāk| *n*: **for the ~ of** per, per amore di; **for pity's ~** per pietà; **for the ~ of argument** tanto per fare un esempio; **art for art's ~** l'arte per l'arte.

salad |sal'əd| *n* insalata; **tomato ~** insalata di pomodori.

salad bowl *n* insalatiera.

salad cream *n* (*Brit*) (tipo di) maionese *f*.

salad dressing *n* condimento per insalata.

salad oil *n* olio da tavola.

salami |səlä'mē| *n* salame *m*.

salaried |sal'ûrēd| *a* stipendiato(a).

salary |sal'ûrē| *n* stipendio.

salary scale *n* scala dei salari.

sale |sāl| *n* vendita; (*at reduced prices*) svendita, liquidazione *f*; **"for ~"** "in vendita"; **on ~** in vendita; **on ~ or return** (*Brit*) da vendere o rimandare; **a liquidation ~** una liquidazione; **~ and lease back** *n* lease back *m inv*.

saleroom |sāl'rōōm| *n* (*Brit*) = **salesroom**.

sales assistant *n* (*Brit*) = **sales clerk**.

sales clerk *n* (*US*) commesso/a.

sales conference *n* riunione *f* marketing e vendite.

sales drive *n* campagna di vendita, sforzo promozionale.

sales force *n* personale *m* addetto alle vendite.

salesman |sālz'mən| *n* commesso; (*representative*) rappresentante *m*.

sales manager *n* direttore *m* commerciale.

salesmanship |sālz'mənship| *n* arte *f* del vendere.

salesroom |sālz'rōōm| *n* (*US*) sala delle aste.

sales slip *n* scontrino di cassa.

sales tax *n* (*US*) imposta sulle vendite.

saleswoman |sālz'wōōmən| *n* commessa.

salient |sā'lēənt| *a* saliente.

saline |sā'lēn| *a* salino(a).

saliva |səlī'və| *n* saliva.

sallow |sal'ō| *a* giallastro(a).

salmon |sam'ən| *n* (*pl inv*) salmone *m*.

salmon trout *n* trota (di mare).
saloon [səlōōn'] *n* (*US*) saloon *m inv*, bar *m inv*; (*Brit* AUT) berlina; (*ship's lounge*) salone *m*.
Salop [sal'əp] *n abbr* (*Brit*) = Shropshire.
SALT [sôlt] *n abbr* (= Strategic Arms Limitation Talks/Treaty) S.A.L.T. *m*.
salt [sôlt] *n* sale *m* ♦ *vt* salare ♦ *cpd* di sale; (CULIN) salato(a); **an old ~** un lupo di mare.
  salt away *vt* ammucchiare, mettere via.
salt cellar *n* (*Brit*) = **salt shaker.**
salt-free [sôlt'frē'] *a* senza sale.
salt shaker [sôlt shā'kûr] *n* (*US*) saliera.
saltwater [sôlt'wôtûr] *a* (*fish etc*) di mare.
salty [sôl'tē] *a* salato(a).
salubrious [səlōō'brēəs] *a* salubre; (*fig: district etc*) raccomandabile.
salutary [sal'yətārē] *a* salutare.
salute [səlōōt'] *n* saluto ♦ *vt* salutare.
salvage [sal'vij] *n* (*saving*) salvataggio; (*things saved*) beni *mpl* salvati *or* recuperati ♦ *vt* salvare, mettere in salvo.
salvage vessel *n* scialuppa di salvataggio.
salvation [salvā'shən] *n* salvezza.
Salvation Army *n* Esercito della Salvezza.
salver [sal'vûr] *n* vassoio.
salvo, ~es [sal'vō] *n* salva.
same [sām] *a* stesso(a), medesimo(a) ♦ *pronoun:* **the ~** lo(la) stesso(a), gli(le) stessi(e); **the ~ book as** lo stesso libro di (*or* che); **on the ~ day** lo stesso giorno; **at the ~ time** allo stesso tempo; **all** *or* **just the ~** tuttavia; **to do the ~** fare la stessa cosa; **to do the ~ as sb** fare come qn; **the ~ again** (*in bar etc*) un altro; **they're one and the ~** (*person/thing*) sono la stessa persona/cosa; **and the ~ to you!** altrettanto a lei!; **~ here!** anch'io!
sample [sam'pəl] *n* campione *m* ♦ *vt* (*food*) assaggiare; (*wine*) degustare; **to take a ~** prelevare un campione; **free ~** campione omaggio.
sanatorium, *pl* **sanatoria** [sanətôr'ēəm, sanətôr'ēə] *n* (*Brit*) = **sanitarium.**
sanctify [sangk'təfī] *vt* santificare.
sanctimonious [sangktəmō'nēəs] *a* bigotto(a), bacchettone(a).
sanction [sangk'shən] *n* sanzione *f* ♦ *vt* sancire, sanzionare; **to impose economic ~s on** *or* **against** adottare sanzioni economiche contro.
sanctity [sangk'titē] *n* santità.
sanctuary [sangk'chōōärē] *n* (*holy place*) santuario; (*refuge*) rifugio; (*for wildlife*) riserva.
sand [sand] *n* sabbia ♦ *vt* cospargere di sabbia; (*also:* **~ down:** *wood etc*) cartavetrare; *see also* **sands.**
sandal [san'dəl] *n* sandalo.
sandbag [sand'bag] *n* sacco di sabbia.
sandblast [sand'blast] *vt* sabbiare.

sandbox [sand'bâks] *n* (*US: for children*) buca di sabbia.
sand castle *n* castello di sabbia.
sand dune *n* duna di sabbia.
sandpaper [sand'pāpûr] *n* carta vetrata.
sandpit [sand'pit] *n* (*Brit*) = **sandbox.**
sands [sandz] *npl* spiaggia.
sandstone [sand'stōn] *n* arenaria.
sandstorm [sand'stôrm] *n* tempesta di sabbia.
sandwich [sand'wich] *n* tramezzino, panino, sandwich *m inv* ♦ *vt* (*also:* **~ in**) infilare; **cheese/ham ~** sandwich al formaggio/prosciutto; **to be ~ed between** essere incastrato(a) fra.
sandwich board *n* cartello pubblicitario (*portato da un uomo sandwich*).
sandwich man *n* uomo *m* sandwich *inv.*
sandy [san'dē] *a* sabbioso(a); (*color*) color sabbia *inv*, biondo(a) rossiccio(a).
sane [sān] *a* (*person*) sano(a) di mente; (*outlook*) sensato(a).
sang [sang] *pt of* **sing.**
sanguine [sang'gwin] *a* ottimista.
sanitarium, *pl* **sanitaria** [sanitär'ēəm, sanitär'ēə] *n* (*US*) sanatorio.
sanitary [san'itärē] *a* (*system, arrangements*) sanitario(a); (*clean*) igienico(a).
sanitary napkin *n* assorbente *m* (igienico).
sanitation [sanitā'shən] *n* (*in house*) impianti *mpl* sanitari; (*in town*) fognature *fpl.*
sanitation department *n* (*US*) nettezza urbana.
sanity [san'itē] *n* sanità mentale; (*common sense*) buon senso.
sank [sangk] *pt of* **sink.**
San Marino [san mərē'nō] *n* San Marino *f.*
Santa Claus [san'tə klôz] *n* Babbo Natale.
Santiago [santēä'gō] *n* (*also:* **~ de Chile**) Santiago (del Cile) *f.*
sap [sap] *n* (*of plants*) linfa ♦ *vt* (*strength*) fiaccare.
sapling [sap'ling] *n* alberello.
sapphire [saf'īûr] *n* zaffiro.
sarcasm [sâr'kazəm] *n* sarcasmo.
sarcastic [sârkas'tik] *a* sarcastico(a); **to be ~** fare del sarcasmo.
sardine [sârdēn'] *n* sardina.
Sardinia [sârdin'ēə] *n* Sardegna.
Sardinian [sârdin'ēən] *a, n* sardo(a).
sardonic [sârdán'ik] *a* sardonico(a).
sari [sâ'rē] *n* sari *m inv.*
sartorial [sârtôr'ēəl] *a* di sartoria.
SAS *n abbr* (*Brit* MIL: = Special Air Service) reparto dell'esercito britannico specializzato in operazioni clandestine.
SASE *n abbr* (*US*) = **self-addressed stamped envelope;** *see* **self-addressed.**
sash [sash] *n* fascia.
sash window *n* finestra a ghigliottina.

Sask. abbr (Canada) = Saskatchewan.
sassy [sas'ē] a (US) sfacciato(a).
SAT n abbr (US: = Scholastic Aptitude Test) test attitudinale per l'ammissione al college.
Sat. abbr (= Saturday) sab.
sat [sat] pt, pp of **sit**.
Satan [sā'tən] n Satana m.
satanic [sətan'ik] a satanico(a).
satchel [sach'əl] n (Brit) cartella.
sated [sā'tid] a soddisfatto(a); sazio(a).
satellite [sat'əlīt] a, n satellite (m).
satellite dish n (TV) antenna parabolica.
satiate [sā'shēāt] vt saziare.
satin [sat'ən] n satin m ♦ a di or in satin; **with a ~ finish** satinato(a).
satire [sat'īûr] n satira.
satirical [sətir'ikəl] a satirico(a).
satirist [sat'ûrist] n (writer etc) scrittore(trice) etc satirico(a); (cartoonist) caricaturista m/f.
satirize [sat'ərīz] vt satireggiare.
satisfaction [satisfak'shən] n soddisfazione f; **has it been done to your ~?** ne è rimasto soddisfatto?
satisfactory [satisfak'tûrē] a soddisfacente.
satisfy [sat'isfī] vt soddisfare; (convince) convincere; **to ~ the requirements** rispondere ai requisiti; **to ~ sb (that)** convincere qn (che), persuadere qn (che); **to ~ o.s. of sth** accertarsi di qc.
satisfying [sat'isfīing] a soddisfacente.
saturate [sach'ûrāt] vt: **to ~ (with)** saturare (di).
saturation [sachərā'shən] n saturazione f.
Saturday [sat'ûrdā] n sabato; for phrases see also **Tuesday**.
sauce [sôs] n salsa; (containing meat, fish) sugo.
saucepan [sôs'pan] n casseruola.
saucer [sô'sûr] n piattino.
saucy [sôs'ē] a impertinente.
Saudi Arabia [sou'dē ərā'bēə] n Arabia Saudita.
Saudi (Arabian) [sou'dē (ərā'bēən)] a, n saudita (m/f).
sauna [sô'nə] n sauna.
saunter [sôn'tûr] vi andare a zonzo, bighellonare.
sausage [sô'sij] n salsiccia; (salami etc) salame m.
sausage roll n rotolo di pasta sfoglia ripieno di salsiccia.
sauté [sôtā'] a (CULIN: potatoes) saltato(a); (: onions) soffritto(a) ♦ vt far saltare; far soffriggere.
savage [sav'ij] a (cruel, fierce) selvaggio(a), feroce; (primitive) primitivo(a) ♦ n selvaggio/a ♦ vt attaccare selvaggiamente.
savagery [sav'ijrē] n crudeltà, ferocia.
save [sāv] vt (person, belongings, COMPUT) salvare; (money) risparmiare, mettere da parte; (time) risparmiare; (food) conserva-

re; (avoid: trouble) evitare ♦ vi (also: ~ **up**) economizzare ♦ n (SPORT) parata ♦ prep salvo, a eccezione di; **it will ~ me an hour** mi farà risparmiare un'ora; **to ~ face** salvare la faccia; **God ~ the Queen!** (Brit) Dio salvi la Regina!
saving [sā'ving] n risparmio ♦ a: **the ~ grace of** l'unica cosa buona di; **~s** npl risparmi mpl; **to make ~s** fare economia.
savings account n libretto di risparmio.
savings and loan association n (US) società f inv immobiliare.
savings bank n cassa di risparmio.
savior, (Brit) saviour [sāv'yûr] n salvatore m.
savor [sā'vûr] (US) n sapore m, gusto ♦ vt gustare.
savory [sā'vûrē] a (US) saporito(a); (dish: not sweet) salato(a).
savour [sā'vûr] etc (Brit) = **savor** etc.
savvy [sav'ē] n (col) arguzia.
saw [sô] pt of **see** ♦ n (tool) sega ♦ vt (pt **sawed**, pp **sawed** or **sawn** [sôn]) segare; **to ~ sth up** fare a pezzi qc con la sega.
sawdust [sô'dust] n segatura.
sawed-off [sôd'ôf] a (US): **~ shotgun** fucile m a canne mozze.
sawmill [sô'mil] n segheria.
sawn [sôn] pp of **saw**.
sawn-off [sôn'ôf] a (Brit) = **sawed-off**.
saxophone [sak'səfōn] n sassofono.
say [sā] n: **to have one's ~** fare sentire il proprio parere; **to have a** or **some ~** avere voce in capitolo ♦ vt (pt, pp **said** [sed]) dire; **could you ~ that again?** potrebbe ripeterlo?; **to ~ yes/no** dire di sì/di no; **she said (that) I was to give you this** ha detto di darle questo; **my watch ~s 3 o'clock** il mio orologio fa le 3; **shall we ~ Tuesday?** facciamo martedì?; **that doesn't ~ much for him** non torna a suo credito; **when all is said and done** a conti fatti; **there is something** or **a lot to be said for it** ha i suoi lati positivi; **that is to ~** cioè, vale a dire; **to ~ nothing of** per non parlare di; **~ that ...** mettiamo or diciamo che ...; **that goes without ~ing** va da sé.
saying [sā'ing] n proverbio, detto.
SBA n abbr (US: = Small Business Administration) organismo ausiliario per piccole imprese.
SC n abbr (US) = **supreme court** ♦ abbr (US MAIL) = South Carolina.
s/c abbr (= self-contained) indipendente.
scab [skab] n crosta; (pej) crumiro/a.
scabby [skab'ē] a crostoso(a).
scaffold [skaf'əld] n impalcatura; (gallows) patibolo.
scaffolding [skaf'əlding] n impalcatura.
scald [skôld] n scottatura ♦ vt scottare.
scalding [skôl'ding] a (also: ~ **hot**) bollente.
scale [skāl] n scala; (of fish) squama ♦ vt

(*mountain*) scalare; **pay** ~ scala dei salari; ~ **of charges** tariffa; **on a large** ~ su vasta scala; **to draw sth to** ~ disegnare qc in scala; **small-~ model** modello in scala ridotta; *see also* **scales**.

scale down *vt* ridurre (proporzionalmente).

scale drawing *n* disegno in scala.

scale model *n* modello in scala.

scales |skālz| *npl* bilancia.

scallion |skal'yən| *n* cipolla; (*US: shallot*) scalogna; (: *leek*) porro.

scallop |skal'əp| *n* pettine *m*.

scalp |skalp| *n* cuoio capelluto ♦ *vt* scotennare.

scalpel |skal'pəl| *n* bisturi *m inv*.

scalper |skal'pûr| *n* (*US col: of tickets*) bagarino.

scamp |skamp| *n* (*col: child*) peste *f*.

scamper |skam'pûr| *vi:* **to** ~ **away**, ~ **off** darsela a gambe.

scampi |skam'pē| *npl* scampi *mpl*.

scan |skan| *vt* scrutare; (*glance at quickly*) scorrere, dare un'occhiata a; (*poetry*) scandire; (*TV*) analizzare; (*RADAR*) esplorare ♦ *n* (*MED*) ecografia.

scandal |skan'dəl| *n* scandalo; (*gossip*) pettegolezzi *mpl*.

scandalize |skan'dəlīz| *vt* scandalizzare.

scandalous |skan'dələs| *a* scandaloso(a).

Scandinavia |skandənā'vēə| *n* Scandinavia.

Scandinavian |skandənā'vēən| *a*, *n* scandinavo(a).

scanner |skan'ûr| *n* (*RADAR*, *MED*) scanner *m inv*.

scant |skant| *a* scarso(a).

scantily |skan'tilē| *ad:* ~ **clad** *or* **dressed** succintamente vestito(a).

scanty |skan'tē| *a* insufficiente; (*swimsuit*) ridotto(a).

scapegoat |skāp'gōt| *n* capro espiatorio.

scar |skär| *n* cicatrice *f* ♦ *vt* sfregiare.

scarce |skärs| *a* scarso(a); (*copy*, *edition*) raro(a).

scarcely |skärs'lē| *ad* appena; ~ **anybody** quasi nessuno; **I can** ~ **believe it** faccio fatica a crederci.

scarcity |skär'sitē| *n* scarsità, mancanza.

scarcity value *n* valore *m* di rarità.

scare |skär| *n* spavento, paura ♦ *vt* spaventare, atterrire; **to** ~ **sb stiff** spaventare a morte qn; **bomb** ~ evacuazione *f* per sospetta presenza di un ordigno esplosivo.

scare away, **scare off** *vt* mettere in fuga.

scarecrow |skär'krō| *n* spaventapasseri *m inv*.

scared |skärd| *a:* **to be** ~ aver paura.

scaremonger |skär'munggûr| *n* allarmista *m/f*.

scarf, *pl* **scarves** |skärf, skärvz| *n* (*long*) sciarpa; (*square*) fazzoletto da testa, foulard *m inv*.

scarlet |skär'lit| *a* scarlatto(a).

scarlet fever *n* scarlattina.

scarves |skärvz| *npl of* **scarf**.

scary |skär'ē| *a* (*col*) che fa paura.

scathing |skā'thing| *a* aspro(a); **to be** ~ **about sth** essere molto critico rispetto a qc.

scatter |skat'ûr| *vt* spargere; (*crowd*) disperdere ♦ *vi* disperdersi.

scatterbrained |skat'ûrbrānd| *a* scervellato(a), sbadato(a).

scattered |skat'ûrd| *a* sparso(a), sparpagliato(a).

scatty |skat'ē| *a* (*col*) scervellato(a), sbadato(a).

scavenge |skav'inj| *vi* (*person*): **to** ~ **(for)** frugare tra i rifiuti (alla ricerca di); (*hyenas etc*) nutrirsi di carogne.

scavenger |skav'injûr| *n* spazzino.

scenario |sinär'ēō| *n* (*THEATER*, *CINEMA*) copione *m*; (*fig*) situazione *f*.

scene |sēn| *n* (*THEATER*, *fig etc*) scena; (*of crime*, *accident*) scena, luogo; (*sight*, *view*) vista, veduta; **behind the ~s** (*also fig*) dietro le quinte; **to appear** *or* **come on the** ~ (*also fig*) entrare in scena; **the political** ~ **in Italy** il quadro politico in Italia; **to make a** ~ (*col: fuss*) fare una scenata.

scenery |sē'nûrē| *n* (*THEATER*) scenario; (*landscape*) panorama *m*.

scenic |sē'nik| *a* scenico(a); panoramico(a).

scent |sent| *n* odore *m*, profumo; (*sense of smell*) olfatto, odorato; (*fig: track*) pista; **to put** *or* **throw sb off the** ~ (*fig*) far perdere le tracce a qn, sviare qn.

scepter |sep'tûr| *n* (*US*) scettro.

sceptic |skep'tik| *etc* (*Brit*) = **skeptic** *etc*.

sceptre |sep'tûr| *n* (*Brit*) = **scepter**.

schedule |skej'ōōl, (*Brit*) shed'yōōl| *n* programma *m*, piano; (*of trains*) orario; (*of prices etc*) lista, tabella ♦ *vt* fissare; **as ~d** come stabilito; **on** ~ in orario; **to be ahead of/behind** ~ essere in anticipo/ritardo sul previsto; **we are working to a very tight** ~ il nostro programma di lavoro è molto intenso; **everything went according to** ~ tutto è andato secondo i piani *or* secondo il previsto.

scheduled |skej'ōōld, (*Brit*) shed'yōōld| *a* (*date*, *time*) fissato(a); (*visit*, *event*) programmato(a); (*train*, *bus*, *stop*) previsto(a) (sull'orario); ~ **flight** volo di linea.

schematic |skēmat'ik| *a* schematico(a).

scheme |skēm| *n* piano, progetto; (*method*) sistema *m*; (*dishonest plan*, *plot*) intrigo, trama; (*arrangement*) disposizione *f*, sistemazione *f* ♦ *vt* progettare; (*plot*) ordire ♦ *vi* fare progetti; (*intrigue*) complottare; **color** ~ combinazione *f* di colori.

scheming |skē'ming| *a* intrigante ♦ *n* intrighi *mpl*, macchinazioni *fpl*.

schism |skiz'əm| *n* scisma *m*.

schizophrenia |skitsəfrē'nēə| *n* schizofrenia.

schizophrenic |skitsəfren'ik| *a*, *n* schizofrenico(a).

scholar |skäl'ûr| *n* erudito/a.

scholarly |skăl'ûrlē| *a* dotto(a), erudito(a).

scholarship |skăl'ûrship| *n* erudizione *f*; (*grant*) borsa di studio.

school |skōōl| *n* scuola; (*in university*) scuola, facoltà *f inv*; (*of fish*) banco ♦ *cpd* scolare, scolastico(a) ♦ *vt* (*animal*) addestrare.

school age *n* età scolare.

school bag *n* cartella.

schoolbook |skōōl'bŏŏk| *n* libro scolastico.

schoolboy |skōōl'boi| *n* scolaro.

schoolchild, *pl* **-children** |skōōl'chīld. -children| *n* scolaro/a.

schooldays |skōōl'dāz| *npl* giorni *mpl* di scuola.

schoolgirl |skōōl'gûrl| *n* scolara.

schooling |skōō'ling| *n* istruzione *f*.

school-leaving age |skōōl'lēving āj| *n* limite *m* d'età della scuola dell'obbligo.

schoolmaster |skōōl'mastûr| *n* (*grade*) maestro; (*high*) insegnante *m*.

schoolmistress |skōōl'mistris| *n* (*grade*) maestra; (*high*) insegnante *f*.

schoolroom |skōōl'rōōm| *n* classe *f*, aula.

schoolteacher |skōōl'tēchûr| *n* insegnante *m/f*, docente *m/f*; (*grade*) maestro/a.

schoolyard |skōōl'yârd| *n* cortile *m* per la ricreazione.

schooner |skōō'nûr| *n* (*ship*) goletta, schooner *m inv*; (*glass*) bicchiere *m* alto da sherry.

sciatica |sīat'ikə| *n* sciatica.

science |sī'əns| *n* scienza; **the ~s** le scienze; (*SCOL*) le materie scientifiche.

science fiction *n* fantascienza.

scientific |sīəntif'ik| *a* scientifico(a).

scientist |sī'əntist| *n* scienziato/a.

sci-fi |sī'fī| *n abbr* (*col*) = **science fiction**.

scintillating |sin'təlāting| *a* scintillante; (*wit, conversation, company*) brillante.

scissors |siz'ûrz| *npl* forbici *fpl*; **a pair of ~** un paio di forbici.

sclerosis |sklirō'sis| *n* sclerosi *f*.

scoff |skâf| *vi*: **to ~ (at)** (*mock*) farsi beffe (di).

scold |skōld| *vt* rimproverare.

scolding |skōld'ing| *n* lavata di capo, sgridata.

scone |skōn| *n* focaccia da tè.

scoop |skōōp| *n* mestolo; (*for ice cream*) cucchiaio dosatore; (*PRESS*) colpo giornalistico, notizia (*n*) esclusiva.

scoop out *vt* scavare.

scoop up *vt* tirare su, sollevare.

scooter |skōō'tûr| *n* (*motorcycle*) motoretta, scooter *m inv*; (*toy*) monopattino.

scope |skōp| *n* (*capacity: of plan, undertaking*) portata; (: *of person*) capacità *fpl*; (*opportunity*) possibilità *fpl*; **to be within the ~ of** rientrare nei limiti di; **it's well within his ~ to ...** è perfettamente in grado di ...; **there is plenty of ~ for improvement** (*Brit*) ci sono notevoli possibilità di miglioramento.

scorch |skôrch| *vt* (*clothes*) strinare, bruciac-

chiare; (*earth, grass*) seccare, bruciare.

scorched earth policy *n* tattica della terra bruciata.

scorcher |skôr'chûr| *n* (*col: hot day*) giornata torrida.

scorching |skôrch'ing| *a* cocente, scottante.

score |skôr| *n* punti *mpl*, punteggio; (*MUS*) partitura, spartito; (*twenty*): **a ~** venti ♦ *vt* (*goal, point*) segnare, fare; (*success*) ottenere; (*cut: leather, wood, card*) incidere ♦ *vi* segnare; (*SOCCER*) fare un goal; (*keep score*) segnare i punti; **on that ~** a questo riguardo; **to have an old ~ to settle with sb** (*fig*) avere un vecchio conto da saldare con qn; **~s of people** (*fig*) un sacco di gente; **to ~ 6 out of 10** prendere 6 su 10.

score out *vt* cancellare con un segno.

scoreboard |skôr'bôrd| *n* tabellone *m* segnapunti.

scorecard |skôr'kârd| *n* cartoncino segnapunti.

scorer |skôr'ûr| *n* marcatore/trice; (*keeping score*) segnapunti *m inv*.

scorn |skôrn| *n* disprezzo ♦ *vt* disprezzare.

scornful |skôrn'fəl| *a* sprezzante.

Scorpio |skôr'pēō| *n* Scorpione *m*; **to be ~** essere dello Scorpione.

scorpion |skôr'pēən| *n* scorpione *m*.

Scot |skât| *n* scozzese *m/f*.

Scotch |skâch| *n* whisky *m* scozzese, scotch *m*.

scotch |skâch| *vt* (*rumor etc*) soffocare.

Scotch tape ® *n* (*US*) scotch ® *m*.

scot-free |skât'frē'| *a* impunito(a); **to get off ~** (*unpunished*) farla franca; (*unhurt*) uscire illeso(a).

Scotland |skât'lənd| *n* Scozia.

Scots |skâts| *a* scozzese.

Scotsman |skâts'mən| *n* scozzese *m*.

Scotswoman |skâts'wŏŏmən| *n* scozzese *f*.

Scottish |skât'ish| *a* scozzese.

scoundrel |skoun'drəl| *n* farabutto/a; (*child*) furfantello/a.

scour |skour| *vt* (*clean*) pulire strofinando; raschiare via; ripulire; (*search*) battere, perlustrare.

scourer |skour'ûr| *n* (*powder*) (detersivo) abrasivo; (*Brit*) = **scouring pad**.

scourge |skûrj| *n* flagello.

scouring pad |skour'ing pad| *n* paglietta.

scout |skout| *n* (*MIL*) esploratore *m*; (*also:* **boy ~**) giovane esploratore, scout *m inv*.

scout around *vi* cercare in giro.

scowl |skoul| *vi* accigliarsi, aggrottare le sopracciglia; **to ~ at** guardare torvo.

scrabble |skrab'əl| *vi* (*claw*): **to ~ (at)** graffiare, grattare; **to ~ about** *or* **around for sth** cercare affannosamente qc ♦ *n*: **S~** ® Scarabeo ®.

scraggy |skrag'ē| *a* scarno(a), molto magro(a).

scram |skram| *vi* (*col*) filare via.

scramble |skram'bəl| *n* arrampicata ♦ *vi*

inerpicarsi; **to ~ out** *etc* uscire *etc* in fretta; **to ~ for** azzuffarsi per; **to go scrambling** (*SPORT*) fare il motocross.

scrambled eggs [skram'bəld egz] *npl* uova *fpl* strapazzate.

scrap [skrap] *n* pezzo, pezzetto; (*fight*) zuffa; (*also*: ~ **iron**) rottami *mpl* di ferro, ferraglia ♦ *vt* demolire; (*fig*) scartare; **~s** *npl* (*waste*) scarti *mpl*; **to sell sth for ~** vendere qc come ferro vecchio.

scrapbook [skrap'book] *n* album *m inv* di ritagli.

scrap dealer *n* commerciante *m* di ferraglia.

scrape [skrāp] *vt, vi* raschiare, grattare ♦ *n*: **to get into a ~** cacciarsi in un guaio.

scrape through *vi* (*succeed*) farcela per un pelo, cavarsela ♦ *vt fus* (*exam*) passare per miracolo, passare per il rotto della cuffia.

scraper [skrā'pûr] *n* raschietto.

scrapheap [skrap'hēp] *n* mucchio di rottami; **to throw sth on the ~** (*fig*) mettere qc nel dimenticatoio.

scrap metal *n* ferraglia.

scrap paper *n* cartaccia.

scrappy [skrap'ē] *a* frammentario(a), sconnesso(a).

scrap yard *n* (*Brit*) deposito di rottami; (: *for cars*) cimitero delle macchine.

scratch [skrach] *n* graffio ♦ *vt* graffiare, rigare ♦ *vi* grattare, graffiare; **to start from ~** cominciare *or* partire da zero; **to be up to ~** essere all'altezza.

scratch pad *n* (*US*) notes *m inv*, blocchetto.

scrawl [skrôl] *n* scarabocchio ♦ *vi* scarabocchiare.

scrawny [skrô'nē] *a* scarno(a), pelle e ossa *inv*.

scream [skrēm] *n* grido, urlo ♦ *vi* urlare, gridare; **to ~ at sb (to do sth)** gridare a qn (di fare qc); **it was a ~** (*fig col*) era da crepar dal ridere; **he's a ~** (*fig col*) è una sagoma, è uno spasso.

scree [skrē] *n* ghiaione *m*.

screech [skrēch] *n* strido; (*of tires, brakes*) stridore *m* ♦ *vi* stridere.

screen [skrēn] *n* schermo; (*fig*) muro, cortina, velo ♦ *vt* schermare, fare schermo a; (*from the wind etc*) riparare; (*movie*) proiettare; (*book*) adattare per lo schermo; (*candidates etc*) passare al vaglio; (*for illness*) sottoporre a controlli medici.

screen editing *n* (*COMPUT*) correzione *f* e modifica su schermo.

screening [skrē'ning] *n* (*MED*) dépistage *m inv*; (*of movie*) proiezione *f*; (*for security*) controlli *mpl* (di sicurezza).

screen memory *n* (*COMPUT*) memoria di schermo.

screenplay [skrēn'plā] *n* sceneggiatura.

screen test *n* provino (cinematografico).

screw [skrōō] *n* vite *f*; (*propeller*) elica ♦ *vt*

avvitare; **to ~ sth to the wall** fissare qc al muro con viti.

screw up *vt* (*paper, material*) spiegazzare; (*col*: *ruin*) mandare a monte; **to ~ up one's face** fare una smorfia.

screwball [skrōō'bôl] *n* (*col*) mattarello/a.

screwdriver [skrōō'drīvûr] *n* cacciavite *m*.

screwy [skrōō'ē] *a* (*col*) svitato(a).

scribble [skrib'əl] *n* scarabocchio ♦ *vt* scribacchiare ♦ *vi* scarabocchiare; **to ~ sth down** scribacchiare qc.

scribe [skrīb] *n* scriba *m*.

script [skript] *n* (*CINEMA etc*) copione *m*; (*in exam*) elaborato *or* compito d'esame; (*writing*) scrittura.

scripted [skrip'tid] *a* (*RADIO, TV*) preparato(a).

Scripture [skrip'chûr] *n* Sacre Scritture *fpl*.

scriptwriter [skript'rītûr] *n* soggettista *m/f*.

scroll [skrōl] *n* rotolo di carta ♦ *vt* (*COMPUT*) scorrere.

scrotum [skrō'təm] *n* scroto.

scrounge [skrounj] *vt* (*col*): **to ~ sth (off or from sb)** scroccare qc (a qn) ♦ *vi*: **to ~ on sb** vivere alle spalle di qn.

scrounger [skrounj'ûr] *n* scroccone/a.

scrub [skrub] *n* (*clean*) strofinata; (*land*) boscaglia ♦ *vt* pulire strofinando; (*reject*) annullare.

scrubbing brush [skrub'ing brush] *n* (*Brit*) = **scrub brush**.

scrub brush *n* spazzolone *m*.

scruff [skruf] *n*: **by the ~ of the neck** per la collottola.

scruffy [skruf'ē] *a* sciatto(a).

scrum(mage) [skrum'(ij)] *n* (*RUGBY*) mischia.

scruple [skrōō'pəl] *n* scrupolo; **to have no ~s about doing sth** non avere scrupoli a fare qc.

scrupulous [skrōō'pyələs] *a* scrupoloso(a).

scrupulously [skrōō'pyələslē] *ad* scrupolosamente; **he tries to be ~ fair/honest** cerca di essere più imparziale/onesto che può.

scrutinize [skrōō'tənīz] *vt* scrutare, esaminare attentamente.

scrutiny [skrōō'tənē] *n* esame *m* accurato; **under the ~ of sb** sotto la sorveglianza di qn.

scuba [skōō'bə] *n* autorespiratore *m*.

scuba diving *n* immersioni *fpl* subacquee.

scuff [skuf] *vt* (*shoes*) consumare strascicando.

scuffle [skuf'əl] *n* baruffa, tafferuglio.

scullery [skul'ûrē] *n* retrocucina *m or f*.

sculptor [skulp'tûr] *n* scultore *m*.

sculpture [skulp'chûr] *n* scultura.

scum [skum] *n* schiuma; (*pej*: *people*) feccia.

scurrilous [skûr'ələs] *a* scurrile, volgare.

scurry [skûr'ē] *vi* sgambare, affrettarsi.

scurvy [skûr'vē] *n* scorbuto.

scuttle [skut'əl] *n* (*NAUT*) portellino; (*also*: **coal ~**) secchio del carbone ♦ *vt* (*ship*) auto-

affondare ♦ *vi* (*scamper*): **to ~ away, ~ off**
darsela a gambe, scappare.

scythe |sīth| *n* falce *f*.

SD *abbr* (*US MAIL*) = *South Dakota*.

S.Dak. *abbr* (*US*) = *South Dakota*.

SDI *n abbr* (= *Strategic Defense Initiative*)
S.D.I. *f*.

SDLP *n abbr* (*Brit POL*) = *Social Democratic
and Labour Party*.

SDP *n abbr* (*Brit POL*) = *Social Democratic
Party*.

sea |sē| *n* mare *m* ♦ *cpd* marino(a), del mare;
(*ship, port*) marittimo(a), di mare; **on the ~**
(*boat*) in mare; (*town*) di mare; **to go by ~**
andare per mare; **by** *or* **beside the ~** (*vacation*) al mare; (*village*) sul mare; **to look
out to ~** guardare il mare; **(out) at ~** al
largo; **heavy** *or* **rough ~(s)** mare grosso *or*
agitato; **a ~ of faces** (*fig*) una marea di
gente.

sea bed *n* fondo marino.

sea bird *n* uccello di mare.

seaboard |sē'bôrd| *n* costa.

sea breeze *n* brezza di mare.

seafarer |sē'fârûr| *n* navigante *m*.

seafaring |sē'fâring| *a* (*community*) marina-
ro(a); (*life*) da marinaio.

seafood |sē'foōd| *n* frutti *mpl* di mare.

sea front *n* lungomare *m*.

seagoing |sē'gōing| *a* (*ship*) d'alto mare.

seagull |sē'gul| *n* gabbiano.

seal |sēl| *n* (*animal*) foca; (*stamp*) sigillo;
(*impression*) impronta del sigillo ♦ *vt* sigillare; (*decide: sb's fate*) segnare; (: *bargain*)
concludere; **~ of approval** beneplacito.

seal off *vt* (*close*) sigillare; (*forbid entry
to*) bloccare l'accesso a.

sea level *n* livello del mare.

sealing wax |sē'ling waks| *n* ceralacca.

sea lion *n* leone *m* marino.

sealskin |sēl'skin| *n* pelle *f* di foca.

seam |sēm| *n* cucitura; (*of coal*) filone *m*; **the
hall was bursting at the ~s** l'aula era piena
zeppa.

seaman |sē'mən| *n* marinaio.

seamanship |sē'mənship| *n* tecnica di naviga-
zione.

seamless |sēm'lis| *a* senza cucitura.

seamy |sē'mē| *a* malfamato(a); squallido(a).

seance |sā'âns| *n* seduta spiritica.

seaplane |sē'plān| *n* idrovolante *m*.

seaport |sē'pôrt| *n* porto di mare.

search |sûrch| *n* (*for person, thing*) ricerca;
(*of drawer, pockets*) esame *m* accurato;
(*LAW: at sb's home*) perquisizione *f* ♦ *vt*
perlustrare, frugare; (*scan, examine*) esaminare minuziosamente; (*COMPUT*) ricercare ♦
vi: **to ~ for** ricercare; **in ~ of** alla ricerca
di; **"~ and replace"** (*COMPUT*) "ricercare e
sostituire".

search through *vt fus* frugare.

searcher |sûr'chûr| *n* chi cerca.

searching |sûr'ching| *a* minuzioso(a); pene-
trante; (*question*) pressante.

searchlight |sûrch'lit| *n* proiettore *m*.

search party *n* squadra di soccorso.

search warrant *n* mandato di perquisizione.

searing |sē'ring| *a* (*heat*) rovente; (*pain*) acu-
to(a).

seashore |sē'shôr| *n* spiaggia; **on the ~** sulla
riva del mare.

seasick |sē'sik| *a* che soffre il mal di mare; **to
be ~** avere il mal di mare.

seaside |sē'sīd| *n* spiaggia; **to go to the ~**
andare al mare.

seaside resort *n* stazione *f* balneare.

season |sē'zən| *n* stagione *f* ♦ *vt* condire, insa-
porire; **to be in/out of ~** essere di/fuori stagione; **the busy ~** (*for shops*) il periodo di
punta; (*for hotels etc*) l'alta stagione; **the
open ~** (*HUNTING*) la stagione della caccia.

seasonal |sē'zənəl| *a* stagionale.

seasoned |sē'zənd| *a* (*wood*) stagionato(a);
(*fig: worker, actor, troops*) con esperienza; **a
~ campaigner** un veterano.

seasoning |sē'zəning| *n* condimento.

season ticket *n* abbonamento.

seat |sēt| *n* sedile *m*; (*in bus, train: place*) po-
sto; (*PARLIAMENT*) seggio; (*center: of
government etc, of infection*) sede *f*;
(*buttocks*) didietro; (*of pants*) fondo ♦ *vt* far
sedere; (*have room for*) avere *or* essere
fornito(a) di posti a sedere per; **are there
any ~s left?** ci sono posti?; **to take one's ~**
prendere posto; **to be ~ed** essere seduto(a);
please be ~ed accomodatevi per favore.

seat belt *n* cintura di sicurezza.

seating arrangements |sē'ting ərānj'məntz|
npl sistemazione *f or* disposizione *f* dei posti.

seating capacity |sē'ting kəpas'itē| *n* posti
mpl a sedere.

SEATO |sē'tō| *n abbr* (= *Southeast Asia Trea-
ty Organization*) SEATO *f*.

sea water *n* acqua di mare.

seaweed |sē'wēd| *n* alghe *fpl*.

seaworthy |sē'wûrthē| *a* atto(a) alla naviga-
zione.

SEC *n abbr* (*US*: = *Securities and Exchange
Commission*) commissione di controllo sulle
operazioni in Borsa.

sec. *abbr \= second*.

secateurs |sek'ətûrz| *npl* (*Brit*) forbici *fpl* per
potare.

secede |sisēd'| *vi*: **to ~ (from)** ritirarsi (da).

secluded |siklōō'did| *a* isolato(a), apparta-
to(a).

seclusion |siklōō'zhən| *n* isolamento.

second |sek'ənd| *num* secondo(a) ♦ *ad* (*in
race etc*) al secondo posto; (*RAIL*) in seconda
♦ *n* (*unit of time*) secondo; (*in series, position*) secondo/a; (*Brit SCOL*) laurea con
punteggio discreto; (*AUT: also*: **~ gear**) se-

conda; (*COMM: imperfect*) scarto ♦ *vt* (*motion*) appoggiare; [sikând'] (*employee*) distaccare; **Charles the S~** Carlo Secondo; **just a ~!** un attimo!; **~ floor** (*US*) primo piano; (*Brit*) secondo piano; **to ask for a ~ opinion** (*MED*) chiedere un altro *or* ulteriore parere; **to have ~ thoughts (about doing sth)** avere dei ripensamenti (quanto a fare qc); **on ~ thought** *or* (*Brit*) **thoughts** a ripensarci, ripensandoci bene.

secondary [sek'əndārē] *a* secondario(a).

secondary picket *n* picchetto di solidarietà.

secondary school *n* scuola secondaria.

second-best [sek'əndbest'] *n* ripiego; **as a ~** in mancanza di meglio.

second-class [sek'əndklas'] *a* di seconda classe ♦ *ad*: **to travel ~** viaggiare in seconda (classe); **to send sth ~** spedire qc per posta ordinaria; **~ citizen** cittadino di second'ordine.

second cousin *n* cugino di secondo grado.

seconder [sek'əndûr] *n* sostenitore/trice.

second hand *n* (*on clock*) lancetta dei secondi.

secondhand [sek'əndhand'] *a* di seconda mano, usato(a) ♦ *ad* (*buy*) di seconda mano; **to hear sth ~** venire a sapere qc da terze persone.

second-in-command [sek'əndinkəmand'] *n* (*MIL*) comandante *m* in seconda; (*ADMIN*) aggiunto.

secondly [sek'əndlē] *ad* in secondo luogo.

second-rate [sek'əndrāt'] *a* scadente.

secrecy [sē'krisē] *n* segretezza.

secret [sē'krit] *a* segreto(a) ♦ *n* segreto; **in ~** in segreto, segretamente; **to keep sth ~ (from sb)** tenere qc segreto (a qn), tenere qc nascosto (a qn); **keep it ~** che rimanga un segreto; **to make no ~ of sth** non far mistero di qc.

secret agent *n* agente *m* segreto.

secretarial [sekritâr'ēəl] *a* (*work*) da segretario/a; (*college, course*) di segretariato.

secretariat [sekritâr'ēət] *n* segretariato.

secretary [sek'ritārē] *n* segretario/a; **S~ of State** (*US POL*) ≈ Ministro degli Esteri; (*Brit POL*): **S~ of State (for)** ministro (di).

secrete [sikrēt'] *vt* (*MED, ANAT, BIOL*) secernere; (*hide*) nascondere.

secretion [sikrē'shən] *n* secrezione *f*.

secretive [sē'kritiv] *a* riservato(a).

secretly [sē'kritlē] *ad* in segreto, segretamente.

sect [sekt] *n* setta.

sectarian [sektâr'ēən] *a* settario(a).

section [sek'shən] *n* sezione *f*; (*of document*) articolo ♦ *vt* sezionare, dividere in sezioni; **the business ~** (*PRESS*) la pagina economica.

sector [sek'tûr] *n* settore *m*.

secular [sek'yəlûr] *a* secolare.

secure [sikyōōr'] *a* (*free from anxiety*) sicuro(a); (*firmly fixed*) assicurato(a), ben fermato(a); (*in safe place*) al sicuro ♦ *vt* (*fix*) fissare, assicurare; (*get*) ottenere, assicurarsi; (*COMM: loan*) garantire; **to make sth ~** fissare bene qc; **to ~ sth for sb** procurare qc per *or* a qn.

secured creditor [sikyōōrd' kred'itûr] *n* creditore *m* privilegiato.

security [sikyōōr'itē] *n* sicurezza; (*for loan*) garanzia; **securities** *npl* (*STOCK EXCHANGE*) titoli *mpl*; **to increase/tighten ~** aumentare/intensificare la sorveglianza; **~ of tenure** garanzia del posto di lavoro, garanzia di titolo *or* di godimento.

security forces *npl* forze *fpl* dell'ordine.

security guard *n* guardia giurata.

security risk *n* rischio per la sicurezza.

secy. *abbr* = **secretary**.

sedan [sidan'] *n* (*US AUT*) berlina.

sedate [sidāt'] *a* posato(a); calmo(a) ♦ *vt* calmare.

sedation [sidā'shən] *n* (*MED*): **to be under ~** essere sotto l'azione di sedativi.

sedative [sed'ətiv] *n* sedativo, calmante *m*.

sedentary [sed'əntārē] *a* sedentario(a).

sediment [sed'əmənt] *n* sedimento.

sedition [sidish'ən] *n* sedizione *f*.

seduce [sidōōs'] *vt* sedurre.

seduction [siduk'shən] *n* seduzione *f*.

seductive [siduk'tiv] *a* seducente.

see [sē] *vb* (*pt* **saw**, *pp* **seen** [sô, sēn]) *vt* vedere; (*accompany*): **to ~ sb to the door** accompagnare qn alla porta ♦ *vi* vedere; (*understand*) capire ♦ *n* sede *f* vescovile; **to ~ that** (*ensure*) badare che + *sub*, fare in modo che + *sub*; **to go and ~ sb** andare a trovare qn; **~ you soon/later/tomorrow!** a presto/più tardi/domani!; **as far as I can ~** da quanto posso vedere; **there was nobody to be ~n** non c'era anima viva; **let me ~** (*show me*) fammi vedere; (*let me think*) vediamo (un po'); **~ for yourself** vai a vedere con i tuoi occhi; **I don't know what she ~s in him** non so che cosa ci trovi in lui.

see about *vt fus* (*deal with*) occuparsi di.

see off *vt* salutare alla partenza.

see through *vt* portare a termine ♦ *vt fus* non lasciarsi ingannare da.

see to *vt fus* occuparsi di.

seed [sēd] *n* seme *m*; (*fig*) germe *m*; (*TENNIS*) testa di serie; **to go to ~** fare seme; (*fig*) scadere.

seedless [sēd'lis] *a* senza semi.

seedling [sēd'ling] *n* piantina di semenzaio.

seedy [sē'dē] *a* (*shabby: person*) sciatto(a); (*: place*) cadente.

seeing [sē'ing] *cj*: **~ (that)** visto che.

seek, *pt, pp* **sought** [sēk, sôt] *vt* cercare; **to ~ advice/help from sb** chiedere consiglio/aiuto a qn.

seek out *vt* (*person*) andare a cercare.

seem |sēm| *vi* sembrare, parere; **there ~s to be** ... sembra che ci sia ...; **it ~s (that)** ... sembra *or* pare che ... + *sub*; **what ~s to be the trouble?** cosa c'è che non va?
seemingly |sē'minglē| *ad* apparentemente.
seen |sēn| *pp of* **see**.
seep |sēp| *vi* filtrare, trapelare.
seer |sēr| *n* profeta/essa, veggente *m/f*.
seersucker |sēr'sukûr| *n* cotone *m* indiano.
seesaw |sē'sô| *n* altalena a bilico.
seethe |sēth̩| *vi* ribollire; **to ~ with anger** fremere di rabbia.
see-through |sē'thrōō| *a* trasparente.
segment |seg'mənt| *n* segmento.
segregate |seg'rəgāt| *vt* segregare, isolare.
segregation |segrəgā'shən| *n* segregazione *f*.
Seine |sān| *n* Senna.
seismic |sīz'mik| *a* sismico(a).
seize |sēz| *vt (grasp)* afferrare; *(take possession of)* impadronirsi di; *(LAW)* sequestrare.
seize up *vi (TECH)* grippare.
seize (up)on *vt fus* ricorrere a.
seizure |sē'zhûr| *n (MED)* attacco; *(LAW)* confisca, sequestro.
seldom |sel'dəm| *ad* raramente.
select |silekt'| *a* scelto(a); *(hotel, restaurant)* chic *inv*; *(club)* esclusivo(a) ♦ *vt* scegliere, selezionare; **a ~ few** pochi eletti *mpl*.
selection |silek'shən| *n* selezione *f*, scelta.
selection committee *n* comitato di selezione.
selective |silek'tiv| *a* selettivo(a).
selector |silek'tûr| *n (person)* selezionatore/trice; *(TECH)* selettore *m*.
self |self| *n (pl* **selves** |selvz|): **the ~** l'io *m* ♦ *prefix* auto....
self-addressed |self'ədrest'| *a*: **~ envelope** busta col proprio nome e indirizzo; **~ stamped envelope (SASE)** *(US)* busta affrancata e con indirizzo.
self-adhesive |self'adhē'siv| *a* autoadesivo(a).
self-assertive |self'əsûr'tiv| *a* autoritario(a).
self-assurance |self'əshōōr'əns| *n* sicurezza di sé.
self-assured |self'əshōōrd'| *a* sicuro(a) di sé.
self-catering |self'kā'tûring| *a (Brit)* in cui ci si cucina da sé; **~ apartment** appartamento (per le vacanze).
self-centered |self'sen'tûrd| *a* egocentrico(a).
self-cleaning |self'klē'ning| *a* autopulente.
self-colored |self'kul'ûrd| *a* monocolore.
self-confessed |self'kənfest'| *a (alcoholic etc)* dichiarato(a).
self-confidence |self'kân'fidəns| *n* sicurezza di sé.
self-conscious |self'kân'chəs| *a* timido(a).
self-contained |self'kəntānd'| *a (Brit: apartment)* indipendente.
self-control |self'kəntrōl'| *n* autocontrollo.
self-defeating |self'difē'ting| *a* futile.
self-defense |self'difens'| *n* autodifesa; *(LAW)* legittima difesa.

self-discipline |self'dis'əplin| *n* autodisciplina.
self-employed |self'imploid'| *a* che lavora in proprio.
self-esteem |self'əstēm'| *n* amor proprio *m*.
self-evident |self'ev'idənt| *a* evidente.
self-explanatory |self'iksplan'ətôrē| *a* ovvio(a).
self-governing |self'guv'ûrning| *a* autonomo(a).
self-help |self'help'| *n* iniziativa individuale.
self-importance |self'impôr'təns| *n* sufficienza.
self-indulgent |self'indul'jənt| *a* indulgente verso se stesso(a).
self-inflicted |self'inflik'tid| *a* autoinflitto(a).
self-interest |self'in'trist| *n* interesse *m* personale.
selfish |sel'fish| *a* egoista.
selfishly |sel'fishlē| *ad* egoisticamente.
selfishness |sel'fishnis| *n* egoismo.
selfless |self'lis| *a* altruista.
selflessly |self'lislē| *ad* altruisticamente.
selflessness |self'flisnis| *n* altruismo.
self-made man |self'mād' man| *n* self-made man *m inv*, uomo che si è fatto da sé.
self-pity |self'pit'ē| *n* autocommiserazione *f*.
self-portrait |self'pôr'trit| *n* autoritratto.
self-possessed |self'pəzest'| *a* controllato(a).
self-preservation |self'prezûrvā'shən| *n* istinto di conservazione.
self-raising |self'rā'zing| *a (Brit)* = **self-rising**.
self-reliant |self'rili'ənt| *a* indipendente.
self-respect |self'rispekt'| *n* rispetto di sé, amor proprio.
self-respecting |self'rispekt'ing| *a* che ha rispetto di sé.
self-righteous |self'rī'chəs| *a* soddisfatto(a) di sé.
self-rising |self'rī'zing| *a (US)*: **~ flour** miscela di farina e lievito.
self-sacrifice |self'sak'rəfīs| *n* abnegazione *f*.
self-same |self'sām| *a* stesso(a).
self-satisfied |self'sat'isfīd| *a* compiaciuto(a) di sé.
self-sealing |self'sēl'ing| *a* autosigillante.
self-service |self'sûr'vis| *n* autoservizio, self-service *m*.
self-styled |self'stīld'| *a* sedicente.
self-sufficient |self'səfish'ənt| *a* autosufficiente.
self-supporting |self'səpôrt'ing| *a* economicamente indipendente.
self-taught |self'tôt'| *a* autodidatta.
self-test |self'test'| *n (COMPUT)* autoverifica.
sell, *pt*, *pp* **sold** |sel, sōld| *vt* vendere ♦ *vi* vendersi; **to ~ at** *or* **for 1000 lire** essere in vendita a 1000 lire; **to ~ sb an idea** *(fig)* far accettare un'idea a qn.
sell off *vt* svendere, liquidare.
sell out *vi*: **to ~ out (to sb/sth)** *(COMM)* vendere (tutto) (a qn/qc) ♦ *vt* esaurire; **the tickets are all sold out** i biglietti sono esauri-

ti.

sell-by date [sel'bī dāt] *n* scadenza.

seller [sel'ûr] *n* venditore/trice; ~'s **market** mercato favorevole ai venditori.

selling price [sel'ing prīs] *n* prezzo di vendita.

sellotape [sel'ɔtāp] ® *n* (*Brit*) nastro adesivo, scotch ® *m*.

sellout [sel'out] *n* (*betrayal*) tradimento; (*of tickets*): **it was a** ~ registrò un tutto esaurito.

selves [selvz] *npl of* **self**.

semantic [siman'tik] *a* semantico(a).

semantics [siman'tiks] *n* semantica.

semaphore [sem'ɔfôr] *n* segnali *mpl* con bandiere; (*RAIL*) semaforo.

semblance [sem'bləns] *n* parvenza, apparenza.

semen [sē'mən] *n* sperma *m*.

semester [simes'tûr] *n* semestre *m*.

semi... [sem'ē] *prefix* semi... ♦ *n*: **semi** = **semidetached (house).**

semiannually [sem'ēan'yōōəlē] *ad* (*US*) semestralmente, ogni sei mesi.

semi-breve [sem'ēbrēv] *n* (*Brit*) = **whole note.**

semicircle [sem'ēsûrkəl] *n* semicerchio.

semicircular [semēsûr'kyəlûr] *a* semicircolare.

semicolon [sem'ēkōlən] *n* punto e virgola.

semiconductor [semēkənduk'tûr] *n* semiconduttore *m*.

semiconscious [semēkân'chəs] *a* parzialmente cosciente.

semidetached (house) [semēditacht' (hous)] *n* (*Brit*) casa gemella.

semifinal [semēfī'nəl] *n* semifinale *f*.

seminal [sem'ənəl] *a* (*fig*) fondamentale.

seminar [sem'ənâr] *n* seminario.

seminary [sem'ənārē] *n* (*REL: for priests*) seminario.

semiprecious [semēpresh'əs] *a* semiprezioso(a).

semiquaver [sem'ēkwāvûr] *n* (*Brit*) = **sixteenth note.**

semiskilled [semēskild'] *a*: ~ **worker** operaio(a) non specializzato(a).

semitone [sem'ētōn] *n* (*MUS*) semitono.

semi(trailer) [sem'ē(trā'lûr)] *n* (*US*) autotreno.

semolina [semələ'nə] *n* semolino.

Sen., sen. *abbr* = **senator; senior.**

senate [sen'it] *n* senato.

senator [sen'ətûr] *n* senatore/trice.

send, *pt, pp* **sent** [send, sent] *vt* mandare; **to** ~ **by mail** spedire per posta; **to** ~ **sb for sth** mandare qn a prendere qc; **to** ~ **word that** ... mandare a dire che ...; **she** ~**s (you) her love** ti saluta affettuosamente; **to** ~ **sb to sleep/into fits of laughter** far addormentare/ scoppiare dal ridere qn; **to** ~ **sth flying** far volare via qc.

send around *vt* (*letter, document etc*) far circolare.

send away *vt* (*letter, goods*) spedire;

(*person*) mandare via.

send away for *vt fus* richiedere per posta, farsi spedire.

send back *vt* rimandare.

send for *vt fus* mandare a chiamare, far venire; (*by mail*) ordinare per posta.

send in *vt* (*report, application, resignation*) presentare.

send off *vt* (*goods*) spedire.

send on *vt* (*Brit: letter*) inoltrare; (: *baggage etc: in advance*) spedire in anticipo.

send out *vt* (*invitation*) diramare; (*emit: light, heat*) mandare, emanare; (: *signals*) emettere.

send round *vt* (*Brit*) = **send around.**

send up *vt* (*person, price*) far salire.

sender [send'ûr] *n* mittente *m/f*.

send-off [send'ôf] *n*: **to give sb a good** ~ festeggiare la partenza di qn.

Senegal [sen'əgâl] *n* Senegal *m*.

Senegalese [senəgəlēz'] *a, n* senegalese (*m/f*).

senile [sē'nīl] *a* senile.

senility [sinil'ətē] *n* senilità *f*.

senior [sēn'yûr] *a* (*older*) più vecchio(a); (*of higher rank*) di grado più elevato ♦ *n* persona più anziana; (*in service*) persona con maggiore anzianità; **P. Jones** ~ P. Jones senior, P. Jones padre.

senior citizen *n* anziano/a.

senior high school *n* (*US*) ≈ liceo.

seniority [sēnyôr'itē] *n* anzianità; (*in rank*) superiorità.

sensation [sensā'shən] *n* sensazione *f*; **to create a** ~ fare scalpore.

sensational [sensā'shənəl] *a* sensazionale; (*marvelous*) eccezionale.

sense [sens] *n* senso; (*feeling*) sensazione *f*, senso; (*meaning*) senso, significato; (*wisdom*) buonsenso ♦ *vt* sentire, percepire; ~**s** *npl* (*sanity*) ragione *f*; **it makes** ~ ha senso; **there is no** ~ **in (doing) that** non ha senso (farlo); ~ **of humor** (senso dell')umorismo; **to come to one's** ~**s** (*regain consciousness*) riprendere i sensi; (*become reasonable*) tornare in sé; **to take leave of one's** ~**s** perdere il lume *or* l'uso della ragione.

senseless [sens'lis] *a* sciocco(a); (*unconscious*) privo(a) di sensi.

sensibilities [sensəbil'ətēz] *npl* sensibilità *fsg*.

sensible [sen'səbəl] *a* sensato(a), ragionevole.

sensitive [sen'sətiv] *a*: ~ **(to)** sensibile (a); **he is very** ~ **about it** è un tasto che è meglio non toccare con lui.

sensitivity [sensətiv'ətē] *n* sensibilità.

sensual [sen'shōōəl] *a* sensuale.

sensuous [sen'shōōəs] *a* sensuale.

sent [sent] *pt, pp of* **send.**

sentence [sen'təns] *n* (*LING*) frase *f*; (*LAW: judgement*) sentenza; (: *punishment*) condanna ♦ *vt*: **to** ~ **sb to death/to 5 years** condannare qn a morte/a 5 anni; **to pass** ~

on sb condannare qn.

sentiment [sɛn'təmənt] *n* sentimento; (*opinion*) opinione *f*.

sentimental [sɛntəmɛn'təl] *a* sentimentale.

sentimentality [sɛntəmental'itē] *n* sentimentalità, sentimentalismo.

sentry [sɛn'trē] *n* sentinella.

sentry duty *n*: **to be on ~** essere di sentinella.

Seoul [sōl] *n* Seul *f*.

separable [sɛp'úrəbəl] *a* separabile.

separate *a* [sɛp'rit] separato(a) ♦ *vb* [sɛp'ərāt] *vt* separare ♦ *vi* separarsi; **~ from** separato da; **under ~ cover** (*COMM*) in plico a parte; **to ~ into** dividere in; *see also* **separates**.

separately [sɛp'ritlē] *ad* separatamente.

separates [sɛp'rits] *npl* (*clothes*) coordinati *mpl*.

separation [sɛpərā'shən] *n* separazione *f*.

Sept. *abbr* (= *September*) sett., set.

September [sɛptem'búr] *n* settembre *m*; *for phrases see also* **July**.

septic [sɛp'tik] *a* settico(a); (*wound*) infettato(a); **to go ~** infettarsi.

septicaemia, (*Brit*) **septicaemia** [sɛptisē'mēə] *n* setticemia.

septic tank *n* fossa settica.

sequel [sē'kwəl] *n* conseguenza; (*of story*) seguito.

sequence [sē'kwins] *n* (*series*) serie *f inv*; (*order*) ordine *m*; **in ~** in ordine, di seguito; **~ of tenses** concordanza dei tempi.

sequential [sikwen'chəl] *a*: **~ access** (*COMPUT*) accesso sequenziale.

sequin [sē'kwin] *n* lustrino, paillette *f inv*.

Serbo-Croat [sûr'bōkrōat] *n* (*LING*) serbocroato.

serenade [särənad'] *n* serenata ♦ *vt* fare la serenata a.

serene [sərēn'] *a* sereno(a), calmo(a).

serenity [sərɛn'itē] *n* serenità, tranquillità.

sergeant [sâr'jənt] *n* sergente *m*; (*POLICE*) brigadiere *m*.

sergeant major *n* maresciallo.

serial [sēr'ēəl] *n* (*PRESS*) romanzo a puntate; (*RADIO, TV*) trasmissione *f* a puntate ♦ *cpd* (*number*) di serie; (*COMPUT*) seriale.

serialize [sēr'ēəlīz] *vt* pubblicare a puntate; trasmettere a puntate.

serial number *n* numero di serie.

series [sēr'ēz] *n* (*pl inv*) serie *f inv*; (*PUBLISHING*) collana.

serious [sēr'ēəs] *a* serio(a), grave; **are you ~ (about it)?** parla sul serio?

seriously [sē'rēəslē] *ad* seriamente; **to take sth/sb ~** prendere qc/qn sul serio.

seriousness [sē'rēəsnis] *n* serietà, gravità.

sermon [sûr'mən] *n* sermone *m*.

serrated [särā'tid] *a* seghettato(a).

serum [sēr'əm] *n* siero.

servant [sûr'vənt] *n* domestico/a.

serve [sûrv] *vt* (*employer etc*) servire, essere a servizio di; (*purpose*) servire a; (*customer, food, meal*) servire; (*apprenticeship*) fare; (*prison term*) scontare ♦ *vi* (*also TENNIS*) servire; (*soldier etc*) prestare servizio; (*be useful*): **to ~ as/for/to do** servire da/per/per fare ♦ *n* (*TENNIS*) servizio; **are you being ~d?** (*Brit*) la stanno servendo?; **to ~ on a committee/jury** far parte di un comitato/una giuria; **it ~s him right** ben gli sta, se l'è meritata; **it ~s my purpose** fa al caso mio, serve al mio scopo.

serve up *vt* (*food*) servire.

service [sûr'vis] *n* servizio; (*AUT: maintenance*) revisione *f*; (*REL*) funzione *f* ♦ *vt* (*car, washing machine*) revisionare; **the Armed S~s** *npl* le forze armate; **to be of ~ to sb, to do sb a ~** essere d'aiuto a qn; **to put one's car in for (a) ~** portare la macchina in officina per una revisione; **dinner ~** servizio da tavola.

serviceable [sûr'visəbəl] *a* pratico(a), utile; (*usable, working*) usabile.

service area *n* (*on freeway*) area di servizio.

service charge *n* (*Brit*) servizio.

service industries *npl* settore *m* terziario.

serviceman [sûr'visman] *n* militare *m*.

service station *n* stazione *f* di servizio.

serviette [sûrvēet'] *n* (*Brit*) tovagliolo.

servile [sûr'vīl] *a* servile.

serving cart [sûr'ving kârt] *n* (*US*) carrello (portavivande).

session [sesh'ən] *n* (*sitting*) seduta, sessione *f*; (*SCOL*) anno scolastico (*or* accademico); **to be in ~** essere in seduta.

set [sɛt] *n* serie *f inv*; (*RADIO, TV*) apparecchio; (*TENNIS*) set *m inv*; (*group of people*) mondo, ambiente *m*; (*CINEMA*) scenario; (*THEATER: stage*) scene *fpl*; (: *scenery*) scenario; (*MATH*) insieme *m*; (*HAIRDRESSING*) messa in piega ♦ *a* (*fixed*) stabilito(a), determinato(a); (*ready*) pronto(a) ♦ *vb* (*pt, pp* set) (*place*) posare, mettere; (*fix*) fissare; (*assign: task, homework*) dare, assegnare; (*adjust*) regolare; (*decide: rules etc*) stabilire, fissare; (*TYP*) comporre ♦ *vi* (*sun*) tramontare; (*jam, jelly*) rapprendersi; (*concrete*) fare presa; **to be ~ on doing** essere deciso a fare; **to be all ~ to do sth** essere pronto fare qc; **to be (dead) ~ against** essere completamente contrario a; **~ in one's ways** abitudinario; **a novel ~ in Rome** un romanzo ambientato a Roma; **to ~ to music** mettere in musica; **to ~ on fire** dare fuoco a; **to ~ free** liberare; **to ~ sth going** mettere in moto qc; **to ~ sail** prendere il mare; **to ~ the table** apparecchiare la tavola; **a ~ phrase** una frase fatta; **a ~ of false teeth** una dentiera; **a ~ of dining-room furniture** una camera da pranzo.

set about *vt fus* (*task*) intraprendere,

mettersi a; **to ~ about doing sth** mettersi a fare qc.

set aside *vt* mettere da parte.

set back *vt* (*progress*) ritardare; **to ~ back (by)** (*in time*) mettere indietro (di); **a house ~ back from the road** una casa a una certa distanza dalla strada.

set in *vi* (*infection*) svilupparsi; (*complications*) intervenire; **the rain has ~ in for the day** ormai pioverà tutto il giorno.

set off *vi* partire ♦ *vt* (*bomb*) far scoppiare; (*cause to start*) mettere in moto; (*show up well*) dare risalto a.

set out *vi* partire; (*aim*): **to ~ out to do** proporsi di fare ♦ *vt* (*arrange*) disporre; (*state*) esporre, presentare.

set up *vt* (*organization*) fondare, costituire; (*record*) stabilire; (*monument*) innalzare.

setback [set'bak] *n* (*hitch*) contrattempo, inconveniente *m*; (*in health*) ricaduta.

set menu *n* menù *m inv* fisso.

set square *n* (*Brit*) squadra.

settee [setē'] *n* divano, sofà *m inv.*

setting [set'ing] *n* ambiente *m*; (*scenery*) sfondo; (*of jewel*) montatura.

settle [set'əl] *vt* (*argument, matter*) appianare; (*problem*) risolvere; (*pay: bill, account*) regolare, saldare; (*MED: calm*) calmare; (*colonize: land*) colonizzare ♦ *vi* (*bird, dust etc*) posarsi; (*sediment*) depositarsi; (*also: ~ down*) sistemarsi, stabilirsi; (*become calmer*) calmarsi; **to ~ to sth** applicarsi a qc; **to ~ for sth** accontentarsi di qc; **to ~ on sth** decidersi per qc; **that's ~d then** allora è deciso; **to ~ one's stomach** calmare il mal di stomaco.

settle in *vi* sistemarsi.

settle up *vi*: **to ~ up with sb** regolare i conti con qn.

settlement [set'əlmənt] *n* (*payment*) pagamento, saldo; (*agreement*) accordo; (*colony*) colonia; (*village etc*) villaggio, comunità *f inv*; **in ~ of our account** (*COMM*) a saldo del nostro conto.

settler [set'lûr] *n* colonizzatore/trice.

setup [set'up] *n* (*arrangement*) sistemazione *f*; (*situation*) situazione *f.*

seven [sev'ən] *num* sette.

seventeen [sev'əntēn'] *num* diciassette.

seventh [sev'ənth] *num* settimo(a).

seventy [sev'əntē] *num* settanta.

sever [sev'ûr] *vt* recidere, tagliare; (*relations*) troncare.

several [sev'ûrəl] *a, pronoun* alcuni(e), diversi(e); **~ of us** alcuni di noi; **~ times** diverse volte.

severance [sev'ûrəns] *n* (*of relations*) rottura.

severance pay *n* indennità di licenziamento.

severe [sivēr'] *a* severo(a); (*serious*) serio(a), grave; (*hard*) duro(a); (*plain*) semplice, sobrio(a).

severely [sivēr'lē] *ad* (*gen*) severamente; (*wounded, ill*) gravemente.

severity [sivär'itē] *n* severità; gravità; (*of weather*) rigore *m.*

sew, *pt* **sewed,** *pp* **sewn** [sō, sōd, sōn] *vt, vi* cucire.

sew up *vt* ricucire; **it is all sewn up** (*fig*) è tutto apposto.

sewage [sōō'ij] *n* acque *fpl* di scolo.

sewer [sōō'ûr] *n* fogna.

sewing [sō'ing] *n* cucito.

sewing machine *n* macchina da cucire.

sewn [sōn] *pp of* **sew.**

sex [seks] *n* sesso; **to have ~ with** avere rapporti sessuali con.

sex act *n* atto sessuale.

sexism [sek'sizəm] *n* sessismo.

sexist [seks'ist] *a* sessista.

sextet [sekstet'] *n* sestetto.

sexual [sek'shōōəl] *a* sessuale; **~ assault** violenza carnale; **~ intercourse** rapporti *mpl* sessuali.

sexy [sek'sē] *a* provocante, sexy *inv.*

Seychelles [sāshel'] *npl*: **the ~** le Seicelle.

SF *n abbr* = **science fiction.**

SG *n abbr* (*US*) = **Surgeon General.**

Sgt. *abbr* (= *sergeant*) serg.

shabbiness [shab'ēnis] *n* trasandatezza; squallore *m*; meschinità.

shabby [shab'ē] *a* trasandato(a); (*building*) squallido(a), malandato(a); (*behavior*) meschino(a).

shack [shak] *n* baracca, capanna.

shackles [shak'əlz] *npl* ferri *mpl*, catene *fpl.*

shade [shād] *n* ombra; (*for lamp*) paralume *m*; (*of color*) tonalità *f inv*; (*US: window ~*) veneziana; (*small quantity*): **a ~ of** un po' or un'ombra di ♦ *vt* ombreggiare, fare ombra a; **~s** *npl* (*sunglasses*) occhiali *mpl* da sole; **in the ~** all'ombra; **a ~ smaller** un tantino più piccolo.

shadow [shad'ō] *n* ombra ♦ *vt* (*follow*) pedinare; **without** or **beyond a ~ of doubt** senz'ombra di dubbio.

shadow cabinet *n* (*Brit POL*) governo *m* ombra *inv.*

shadowy [shad'ōē] *a* ombreggiato(a), ombroso(a); (*dim*) vago(a), indistinto(a).

shady [shā'dē] *a* ombroso(a); (*fig: dishonest*) losco(a), equivoco(a).

shaft [shaft] *n* (*of arrow, spear*) asta; (*AUT, TECH*) albero; (*of mine*) pozzo; (*of elevator*) tromba; (*of light*) raggio; **ventilator ~** condotto di ventilazione.

shaggy [shag'ē] *a* ispido(a).

shake [shāk] *vb* (*pt* **shook,** *pp* **shaken** [shōōk, shāk'ən]) *vt* scuotere; (*bottle, cocktail*) agitare ♦ *vi* tremare ♦ *n* scossa; **to ~ one's head** scuotere la testa; **to ~ hands with sb** stringere or dare la mano a qn.

shake off *vt* scrollare (via); (*fig*) sba-

razzarsi di.
shake up *vt* scuotere.
shake-up [shāk'up] *n* riorganizzazione *f* drasti-ca.
shakily [shā'kilē] *ad* (*reply*) con voce tre-mante; (*walk*) con passo malfermo; (*write*) con mano tremante.
shaky [shā'kē] *a* (*hand, voice*) tremante; (*memory*) labile; (*knowledge*) incerto(a); (*building*) traballante.
shale [shāl] *n* roccia scistosa.
shall [shal] *auxiliary vb:* **I ~ go** andrò.
shallot [shəlăt'] *n* scalogna.
shallow [shal'ō] *a* poco profondo(a); (*fig*) su-perficiale.
sham [sham] *n* finzione *f*, messinscena; (*jew-elry, furniture*) imitazione *f* ♦ *a* finto(a) ♦ *vt* fingere, simulare.
shambles [sham'bəlz] *n* confusione *f*, bara-onda, scompiglio; **the economy is (in) a complete ~** l'economia è nel caos più totale.
shame [shām] *n* vergogna ♦ *vt* far vergognare; **it is a ~ (that/to do)** è un peccato (che + *sub*/fare); **what a ~!** che peccato!; **to put sb/sth to ~** (*fig*) far sfigurare qn/qc.
shamefaced [shām'fāst] *a* vergognoso(a).
shameful [shām'fəl] *a* vergognoso(a).
shameless [shām'lis] *a* sfrontato(a); (*immod-est*) spudorato(a).
shampoo [shampōō'] *n* shampoo *m inv* ♦ *vt* fare lo shampoo a; **~ and set** shampoo e messa in piega.
shamrock [sham'räk] *n* trifoglio (*simbolo na-zionale dell'Irlanda*).
shandy [shan'dē] *n* birra con gassosa.
shan't [shant] = **shall not**.
shanty town [shən'te toun] *n* bidonville *f inv.*
SHAPE [shāp] *n abbr* (= *Supreme Head-quarters Allied Powers, Europe*) supremo quartier generale delle Potenze Alleate in Europa.
shape [shāp] *n* forma ♦ *vt* (*clay, stone*) dar forma a; (*fig: ideas, character*) formare; (: *course of events*) determinare, condizionare; (*statement*) formulare; (*sb's ideas*) condizio-nare ♦ *vi* (*also:* **~ up**: *events*) andare, mettersi; (: *person*) cavarsela; **to take ~** prendere forma; **in the ~ of a heart** a forma di cuore; **to get o.s. into ~** rimettersi in forma; **I can't bear gardening in any ~ or form** detesto il giardinaggio d'ogni genere e specie.
-shaped [shāpt] *suffix:* **heart~** a forma di cuo-re.
shapeless [shāp'lis] *a* senza forma, informe.
shapely [shāp'lē] *a* ben proporzionato(a).
share [shär] *n* (*thing received, contribution*) parte *f*; (*COMM*) azione *f* ♦ *vt* dividere; (*have in common*) condividere, avere in comune; **to ~ out (among** *or* **between)** dividere (tra); **to ~ in** partecipare a.

share capital *n* capitale *m* azionario.
share certificate *n* certificato azionario.
shareholder [shär'hōldûr] *n* azionista *m/f.*
share index *n* listino di Borsa.
shark [shärk] *n* squalo, pescecane *m.*
sharp [shärp] *a* (*razor, knife*) affilato(a); (*point*) acuto(a), acuminato(a); (*nose, chin*) aguzzo(a); (*outline*) netto(a); (*curve, bend*) stretto(a), accentuato(a); (*cold, pain*) pungente; (*voice*) stridulo(a); (*person: quick-witted*) sveglio(a); (: *unscrupulous*) di-sonesto(a); (*MUS*): **C ~** do diesis ♦ *n* (*MUS*) diesis *m inv* ♦ *ad:* **at 2 o'clock ~** alle due in punto; **turn ~ left** giri tutto a sinistra; **to be ~ with sb** rimproverare qn; **look ~!** sbriga-ti!
sharpen [shär'pən] *vt* affilare; (*pencil*) fare la punta a; (*fig*) aguzzare.
sharpener [shär'pənûr] *n* (*also:* **pencil ~**) temperamatite *m inv*; (*also:* **knife ~**) affila-coltelli *m inv.*
sharp-eyed [shärp'īd] *a* dalla vista acuta.
sharply [shärp'lē] *ad* (*abruptly*) bruscamente; (*clearly*) nettamente; (*harshly*) duramente, aspramente.
sharp-tempered [shärp'tempûrd] *a* irascibile.
shatter [shat'ûr] *vt* mandare in frantumi, frantumare; (*fig: upset*) distruggere; (: *ruin*) rovinare ♦ *vi* frantumarsi, andare in pezzi.
shattered [shat'ûrd] *a* (*grief-stricken*) sconvolto(a); (*exhausted*) a pezzi, di-strutto(a).
shatterproof [shat'ûrprōōf] *a* infrangibile.
shave [shāv] *vt* radere, rasare ♦ *vi* radersi, farsi la barba ♦ *n:* **to have a ~** farsi la barba.
shaven [shā'vən] *a* (*head*) rasato(a), tonsura-to(a).
shaver [shā'vûr] *n* (*also:* **electric ~**) rasoio elettrico.
shaving [shā'ving] *n* (*action*) rasatura; **~s** *npl* (*of wood etc*) trucioli *mpl.*
shaving brush *n* pennello da barba.
shaving cream *n* crema da barba.
shaving soap *n* sapone *m* da barba.
shawl [shôl] *n* scialle *m.*
she [shē] *pronoun* ella, lei; **there ~ is** eccola; **~-bear** orsa; **~-elephant** elefantessa; *NB: for ships, countries follow the gender of your translation.*
sheaf, *pl* **sheaves** [shēf, shēvz] *n* covone *m.*
shear [shē'ûr] *vt* (*pt* **~ed**, *pp* **~ed** *or* **shorn** [shē'rd, shôrn]) (*sheep*) tosare.
shear off *vi* (*break off*) spezzarsi.
shears [shē'ûrz] *npl* (*for hedge*) cesoie *fpl.*
sheath [shēth] *n* fodero, guaina; (*contracep-tive*) preservativo.
sheathe [shēth] *vt* rivestire; (*sword*) rinfode-rare.
sheath knife *n* coltello (con fodero).
sheaves [shēvz] *npl of* **sheaf.**

shed |shed| *n* capannone *m* ♦ *vt* (*pt, pp* **shed**) (*leaves, fur etc*) perdere; (*tears*) versare; **to ~ light on** (*problem, mystery*) far luce su.

she'd |shēd| = **she had; she would.**

sheen |shēn| *n* lucentezza.

sheep |shēp| *n* (*pl inv*) pecora.

sheepdog |shēp'dôg| *n* cane *m* da pastore.

sheep farmer *n* allevatore *m* di pecore.

sheepish |shē'pish| *a* vergognoso(a), timido(a).

sheepskin |shēp'skin| *n* pelle *f* di pecora.

sheepskin jacket *n* (giacca di) montone *m*.

sheer |shēr| *a* (*utter*) vero(a) (e proprio(a)); (*steep*) a picco, perpendicolare; (*transparent*) trasparente ♦ *ad* a picco; **by ~ chance** per puro caso.

sheer curtains *npl* (*US*) tende *fpl* di tulle.

sheet |shēt| *n* (*on bed*) lenzuolo; (*of paper*) foglio; (*of glass*) lastra; (*of metal*) foglio, lamina.

sheet feed *n* (*on printer*) alimentazione *f* di fogli.

sheet lightning *n* lampo diffuso.

sheet metal *n* lamiera.

sheet music *n* fogli *mpl* di musica.

sheik(h) |shēk| *n* sceicco.

shelf, *pl* **shelves** |shelf, shelvz| *n* scaffale *m*, mensola.

shelf life *n* (*COMM*) durata di conservazione.

shell |shel| *n* (*on beach*) conchiglia; (*of egg, nut etc*) guscio; (*explosive*) granata; (*of building*) scheletro, struttura ♦ *vt* (*peas*) sgranare; (*MIL*) bombardare, cannoneggiare.

shell out *vi* (*col*): **to ~ out (for)** sganciare soldi (per).

she'll |shēl| = **she will; she shall.**

shellfish |shel'fish| *n* (*pl inv*) (*crab etc*) crostaceo; (*scallop etc*) mollusco; (*pl: as food*) crostacei; molluschi.

shelter |shel'tûr| *n* riparo, rifugio ♦ *vt* riparare, proteggere; (*give lodging to*) dare rifugio *or* asilo a ♦ *vi* ripararsi, mettersi al riparo; **to take ~ (from)** mettersi al riparo (da).

sheltered |shel'tûrd| *a* (*life*) ritirato(a); (*spot*) riparato(a), protetto(a).

shelve |shelv| *vt* (*fig*) accantonare, rimandare.

shelves |shelvz| *npl of* **shelf.**

shelving |shel'ving| *n* scaffalature *fpl*.

shepherd |shep'ûrd| *n* pastore *m* ♦ *vt* (*guide*) guidare.

shepherdess |shep'ûrdis| *n* pastora.

shepherd's pie *n* timballo di carne macinata e purè di patate.

sherbet |shûr'bit| *n* (*US: dessert*) sorbetto; (*Brit: powder*) polvere effervescente al gusto di frutta.

sheriff |shär'if| *n* sceriffo.

sherry |shēr'ē| *n* sherry *m inv*.

she's |shēz| = **she is; she has.**

Shetland |shet'land| *n* (*also:* **the ~s, the ~ Isles**) le (isole) Shetland.

shield |shēld| *n* scudo ♦ *vt*: **to ~ (from)** riparare (da), proteggere (da *or* contro).

shift |shift| *n* (*change*) cambiamento; (*of workers*) turno ♦ *vt* spostare, muovere; (*remove*) rimuovere; (*AUT*) cambiare marcia ♦ *vi* spostarsi, muoversi; **~ in demand** (*COMM*) variazione *f* della domanda; **the wind has ~ed to the south** il vento si è girato e soffia da sud.

shift key *n* (*on typewriter*) tasto delle maiuscole.

shiftless |shift'lis| *a* fannullone(a).

shift work *n* lavoro a squadre; **to do ~** fare i turni.

shifty |shif'tē| *a* ambiguo(a); (*eyes*) sfuggente.

shilling |shil'ing| *n* (*Brit*) scellino (= *12 old pence; 20 in a pound*).

shilly-shally |shil'ēshalē| *vi* tentennare, esitare.

shimmer |shim'ûr| *vi* brillare, luccicare.

shimmering |shim'ûring| *a* (*gen*) luccicante, scintillante; (*haze*) tremolante; (*satin etc*) cangiante.

shin |shin| *n* tibia ♦ *vi*: **to ~ up/down a tree** arrampicarsi in cima a/scivolare giù da un albero.

shindig |shin'dig| *n* (*col*) festa chiassosa.

shine |shīn| *n* splendore *m*, lucentezza ♦ *vb* (*pt, pp* **shone** |shōn|) *vi* (ri)splendere, brillare ♦ *vt* far brillare, far risplendere; (*flashlight*): **to ~ sth on** puntare qc verso.

shingle |shing'gəl| *n* (*on beach*) ciottoli *mpl*; (*on roof*) assicella di copertura.

shingles |shing'gəlz| *n* (*MED*) herpes zoster *m*.

shining |shī'ning| *a* (*surface, hair*) lucente; (*light*) brillante.

shiny |shī'nē| *a* lucente, lucido(a).

ship |ship| *n* nave *f* ♦ *vt* trasportare (via mare); (*send*) spedire (via mare); (*load*) imbarcare, caricare; **on board ~** a bordo.

shipbuilder |ship'bildûr| *n* costruttore *m* navale.

shipbuilding |ship'bilding| *n* costruzione *f* navale.

ship chandler |ship chan'dlûr| *n* fornitore *m* marittimo.

shipment |ship'mənt| *n* carico.

shipowner |ship'ōnûr| *n* armatore *m*.

shipper |ship'ûr| *n* spedizioniere *m* (marittimo).

shipping |ship'ing| *n* (*ships*) naviglio; (*traffic*) navigazione *f*.

shipping agent *n* agente *m* marittimo.

shipping company *n* compagnia di navigazione.

shipping lane *n* rotta (di navigazione).

shipping line *n* = **shipping company.**

shipshape |ship'shāp| *a* in perfetto ordine.

shipwreck |ship'rck| *n* relitto; (*event*) naufragio ♦ *vt*: **to be ~ed** naufragare, fare naufragio.

shipyard [ship'yärd] *n* cantiere *m* navale.

shirk [shûrk] *vt* sottrarsi a, evitare.

shirt [shûrt] *n* (*man's*) camicia; **in ~ sleeves** in maniche di camicia.

shit [shit] *excl* (*col!*) merda(*!*).

shiver [shiv'ûr] *n* brivido ♦ *vi* rabbrividire, tremare.

shoal [shōl] *n* (*Brit: of fish*) banco.

shock [shäk] *n* (*impact*) urto, colpo; (*ELEC*) scossa; (*emotional*) colpo, shock *m inv*; (*MED*) shock ♦ *vt* colpire, scioccare; scandalizzare; **to give sb a ~** far venire un colpo a qn; **to be suffering from ~** essere in stato di shock; **it came as a ~ to hear that ...** è stata una grossa sorpresa sentire che ....

shock absorber [shäk əbsôrb'ûr] *n* ammortizzatore *m*.

shocking [shäk'ing] *a* scioccante, traumatizzante; (*scandalous*) scandaloso(a); (*very bad: weather, handwriting*) orribile; (: *results*) disastroso(a).

shockproof [shäk'prōof] *a* antiurto *inv*.

shock therapy, shock treatment *n* (*MED*) shockterapia.

shod [shäd] *pt, pp of* **shoe.**

shoddy [shäd'ē] *a* scadente.

shoe [shōo] *n* scarpa; (*also: horse~*) ferro di cavallo; (*brake ~*) ganascia (del freno) ♦ *vt* (*pt, pp* **shod** [shäd]) (*horse*) ferrare.

shoe brush *n* spazzola per le scarpe.

shoehorn [shōo'hôrn] *n* calzante *m*.

shoelace [shōo'lās] *n* stringa.

shoemaker [shōo'mākûr] *n* calzolaio.

shoe polish *n* lucido per scarpe.

shoe shop *n* calzoleria.

shoestring [shōo'string] *n* stringa (delle scarpe); **on a ~** (*fig: do sth*) con quattro soldi.

shoetree [shōo'trē] *n* forma per scarpe.

shone [shōn] *pt, pp of* **shine.**

shoo [shōo] *excl* sciò!, via! ♦ *vt* (*also: ~ away, ~ off*) cacciare (via).

shook [shook] *pt of* **shake.**

shoot [shōot] *n* (*on branch, seedling*) germoglio; (*shooting party*) partita di caccia; (*competition*) gara di tiro ♦ *vb* (*pt, pp* **shot** [shät]) *vt* (*person*) sparare a; (*execute*) fucilare; (*movie*) girare; (*game: Brit*) cacciare, andare a caccia di ♦ *vi* (*with gun*): **to ~ (at)** sparare (a), fare fuoco (su); (*with bow*): **to ~ (at)** tirare (su); (*SOCCER*) sparare, tirare (forte); **to ~ past sb** passare vicino a qn come un fulmine; **to ~ in/out** entrare/uscire come una freccia.

  shoot down *vt* (*plane*) abbattere.

  shoot up *vi* (*fig*) salire alle stelle.

shooting [shōo'ting] *n* (*shots*) sparatoria; (*murder*) uccisione *f* (a colpi d'arma da fuoco); (*Brit HUNTING*) caccia; (*CINEMA*) ripresa *fpl*.

shooting range *n* poligono (di tiro), tirassegno.

shooting star *n* stella cadente.

shop [shäp] *n* negozio; (*workshop*) officina ♦ *vi* (*also:* **go ~ping**) fare spese; **repair ~** officina di riparazione; **to talk ~** (*fig*) parlare di lavoro.

  shop around *vi* fare il giro dei negozi.

shop assistant *n* (*Brit*) commesso/a.

shop floor *n* (*fig*) operai *mpl*, maestranze *fpl*.

shopkeeper [shäp'kēpûr] *n* negoziante *m/f*, bottegaio/a.

shoplift [shäp'lift] *vi* taccheggiare.

shoplifter [shäp'liftûr] *n* taccheggiatore/trice.

shoplifting [shäp'lifting] *n* taccheggio.

shopper [shäp'ûr] *n* compratore/trice.

shopping [shäp'ing] *n* (*goods*) spesa, acquisti *mpl.*

shopping bag *n* borsa per la spesa.

shopping cart *n* (*US*) carrello.

shopping center *n* centro commerciale.

shopping mall *n* centro commerciale.

shop-soiled [shäp'soild] *a* (*Brit*) = **shopworn.**

shop steward *n* (*INDUSTRY*) rappresentante *m* sindacale.

shop window *n* vetrina.

shopworn [shäp'wôrn] *a* (*US*) sciupato(a) a forza di stare in vetrina.

shore [shôr] *n* (*of sea*) riva, spiaggia; (*of lake*) riva ♦ *vt*: **to ~ (up)** puntellare; **on ~** a terra.

shore leave *n* (*NAUT*) franchigia.

shorn [shôrn] *pp of* **shear.**

short [shôrt] *a* (*not long*) corto(a); (*soon finished*) breve; (*person*) basso(a); (*curt*) brusco(a), secco(a); (*insufficient*) insufficiente ♦ *n* (*also: ~ film*) cortometraggio; **it is ~ for** è l'abbreviazione *or* il diminutivo di; **a ~ time ago** poco tempo fa; **in the ~ term** nell'immediato futuro; **to be ~ of sth** essere a corto di *or* mancare di qc; **to run ~ of sth** rimanere senza qc; **to be in ~ supply** scarseggiare; **I'm 3 ~** me ne mancano 3; **in ~** in breve; **~ of doing** a meno che non si faccia; **everything ~ of** tutto fuorché; **to cut ~** (*speech, visit*) accorciare, abbreviare; (*person*) interrompere; **to fall ~ of** venire meno a; non soddisfare; **to stop ~** fermarsi di colpo; **to stop ~ of** non arrivare fino a; *see also* **shorts.**

shortage [shôr'tij] *n* scarsezza, carenza.

shortbread [shôrt'bred] *n* biscotto di pasta frolla.

shortchange [shôrt'chänj'] *vt*: **to ~ sb** imbrogliare qn sul resto.

short circuit *n* cortocircuito.

short-circuit [shôrtsûr'kit] *vt* cortocircuitare ♦ *vi* fare cortocircuito.

shortcoming [shôrt'kuming] *n* difetto.

short(crust) pastry [shôrt'(krust) pās'trē] *n* (*Brit*) pasta frolla.

shortcut [shôrt'kut] n scorciatoia.
shorten [shôr'tən] vt accorciare, ridurre.
shortening [shôr'təning] n grasso per pasticceria.
shortfall [shôrt'fôl] n deficienza.
shorthand [shôrt'hand] n stenografia; **to take sth down in** ~ stenografare qc.
shorthand notebook n (Brit) bloc-notes m inv per stenografia.
shorthand typist n (Brit) stenodattilografo/a.
short list n (for job) rosa dei candidati.
short-lived [shôrt'livd'] a effimero(a), di breve durata.
shortly [shôrt'lē] ad fra poco.
shortness [shôrt'nis] n brevità; insufficienza.
shorts [shôrts] npl (also: **a pair of** ~) i calzoncini.
short-sighted [shôrt'sī'tid] a miope; (fig) poco avveduto(a).
short-staffed [shôrt'staft'] a (Brit) a corto di personale.
short story n racconto, novella.
short-tempered [shôrt'tempûrd] a irascibile.
short-term [shôrt'tûrm'] a (effect) di or a breve durata.
short time n (INDUSTRY): **to work** ~, **be on** ~ essere or lavorare a orario ridotto.
shortwave [shôrt'wāv'] n (RADIO) onde fpl corte.
shot [shât] pt, pp of **shoot** ♦ n sparo, colpo; (shotgun pellets) pallottole fpl; (person) tiratore m; (try) prova; (MED) iniezione f; (PHOT) foto f inv; **like a** ~ come un razzo; (very readily) immediatamente; **to fire a** ~ **at sb/sth** sparare un colpo a qn/qc; **to have a** ~ **at sth/doing sth** provarci con qc/a fare qc; **a big** ~ (col) un pezzo grosso, un papavero; **to get** ~ **of sb/sth** (col) sbarazzarsi di qn/qc.
shotgun [shât'gun] n fucile m da caccia.
should [shŏŏd] auxiliary vb: **I** ~ **go now** dovrei andare ora; **he** ~ **be there now** dovrebbe essere arrivato ora; ~ **he phone** ... se telefonasse ....
shoulder [shōl'dûr] n spalla; (Brit: of road): **hard** ~ corsia d'emergenza ♦ vt (fig) addossarsi, prendere sulle proprie spalle; **to look over one's** ~ guardarsi alle spalle; **to rub** ~s **with sb** (fig) essere a contatto con qn; **to give sb the cold** ~ (fig) trattare qn con freddezza.
shoulder bag n borsa a tracolla.
shoulder blade n scapola.
shoulder strap n bretella, spallina.
shouldn't [shŏŏd'ənt] = **should not**.
shout [shout] n urlo, grido ♦ vt gridare ♦ vi urlare, gridare; **to give sb a** ~ chiamare qn gridando.
shout down vt zittire gridando.
shouting [shout'ing] n urli mpl.

shove [shuv] vt spingere; (col: put): **to** ~ **sth in** ficcare qc in ♦ n spintone m; **he** ~**d me out of the way** mi ha spinto da parte.
shove off vi (NAUT) scostarsi.
shovel [shuv'əl] n pala ♦ vt spalare.
show [shō] n (of emotion) dimostrazione f, manifestazione f; (semblance) apparenza; (exhibition) mostra, esposizione f; (THEATER, CINEMA)◦ spettacolo; (COMM, TECH) salone m, fiera ♦ vb (pt ~**ed**, pp **shown** [shōn]) vt far vedere, mostrare; (courage etc) dimostrare, dar prova di; (exhibit) esporre ♦ vi vedersi, essere visibile; **to** ~ **sb to his seat/ to the door** accompagnare qn al suo posto/ alla porta; **to** ~ **a profit/loss** (COMM) registrare un utile/una perdita; **it just goes to** ~ **that** ... il che sta a dimostrare che ...; **to ask for a** ~ **of hands** chiedere che si voti per alzata di mano; **to be on** ~ essere esposto; **it's just for** ~ è solo per far scena; **who's running the** ~ **here?** (col) chi è il padrone qui?
show in vt far entrare.
show off vi (pej) esibirsi, mettersi in mostra ♦ vt (display) mettere in risalto; (pej) mettere in mostra.
show out vt accompagnare alla porta.
show up vi (stand out) essere ben visibile; (col: turn up) farsi vedere ♦ vt mettere in risalto; (unmask) smascherare.
show business n industria dello spettacolo.
showcase [shō'kās] n vetrina, bacheca.
showdown [shō'doun] n prova di forza.
shower [shou'ûr] n (also: ~ **bath**) doccia; (rain) acquazzone m; (of stones etc) pioggia; (US: party) festa (di fidanzamento etc) in cui si fanno regali alla persona festeggiata ♦ vi fare la doccia ♦ vt: **to** ~ **sb with** (gifts, abuse etc) coprire qn di; (missiles) lanciare contro qn una pioggia di; **to have or take a** ~ fare la doccia.
shower cap n cuffia da doccia.
showerproof [shou'ûrprōōf] a impermeabile.
showery [shou'ûrē] a (weather) con piogge intermittenti.
showground [shō'ground] n (Brit) terreno d'esposizione.
showing [shō'ing] n (of movie) proiezione f.
show jumping [shō' jum'ping] n concorso ippico (di salto ad ostacoli).
showman [shō'mən] n (at fair, circus) impresario; (fig) attore m.
showmanship [shō'mənship] n abilità d'impresario.
shown [shōn] pp of **show**.
show-off [shō'ôf] n (col: person) esibizionista m/f.
showpiece [shō'pēs] n (of exhibition) pezzo forte; **that hospital is a** ~ è un ospedale modello.
showroom [shō'rōōm] n sala d'esposizione.

showy [shō'ē] *a* vistoso(a), appariscente.

shrank [shrangk] *pt of* **shrink**.

shrapnel [shrap'nəl] *n* shrapnel *m*.

shred [shred] *n* (*gen pl*) brandello; (*fig: of truth, evidence*) briciolo ♦ *vt* fare a brandelli; (*CULIN*) sminuzzare, tagliuzzare; (*documents*) distruggere, sminuzzare.

shredder [shred'ûr] *n* (*for documents, papers*) distruttore *m* di documenti, sminuzzatrice *f*.

shrew [shrōō] *n* (*ZOOL*) toporagno; (*fig: pej: woman*) strega.

shrewd [shrōōd] *a* astuto(a), scaltro(a).

shrewdness [shrōōd'nis] *n* astuzia.

shriek [shrēk] *n* strillo ♦ *vt, vi* strillare.

shrift [shrift] *n*: **to give sb short ~** sbrigare qn.

shrill [shril] *a* acuto(a), stridulo(a), stridente.

shrimp [shrimp] *n* gamberetto.

shrine [shrīn] *n* reliquario; (*place*) santuario.

shrink [shringk] *vb* (*pt* **shrank**, *pp* **shrunk** [shrangk, shrungk]) *vi* restringersi; (*fig*) ridursi ♦ *vt* (*wool*) far restringere ♦ *n* (*col: pej*) psicanalista *m/f*; **to ~ from doing sth** rifuggire dal fare qc.

shrinkage [shringk'ij] *n* restringimento.

shrink-wrap [shringk'rap] *vt* confezionare con plastica sottile.

shrivel [shriv'əl] (*also: ~ up*) *vt* raggrinzare, avvizzire ♦ *vi* raggrinzirsi, avvizzire.

shroud [shroud] *n* lenzuolo funebre ♦ *vt*: **~ed in mystery** avvolto(a) nel mistero.

Shrove Tuesday [shrōv tōōz'dā] *n* martedì *m* grasso.

shrub [shrub] *n* arbusto.

shrubbery [shrub'ûrē] *n* arbusti *mpl*.

shrug [shrug] *n* scrollata di spalle ♦ *vt, vi*: **to ~ (one's shoulders)** alzare le spalle, fare spallucce.

shrug off *vt* passare sopra a; (*cold, illness*) sbarazzarsi di.

shrunk [shrungk] *pp of* **shrink**.

shrunken [shrung'kən] *a* rattrappito(a).

shudder [shud'ûr] *n* brivido ♦ *vi* rabbrividire.

shuffle [shuf'əl] *vt* (*cards*) mescolare; **to ~ (one's feet)** strascicare i piedi.

shun [shun] *vt* sfuggire, evitare.

shunt [shunt] *vt* (*RAIL: direct*) smistare; (*: divert*) deviare ♦ *vi*: **to ~ (to and fro)** fare la spola.

shunting [shun'ting] *n* (*RAIL*) smistamento.

shush [shush] *excl* zitto(a)!

shut, *pt, pp* **shut** [shut] *vt* chiudere ♦ *vi* chiudersi, chiudere.

shut down *vt, vi* chiudere definitivamente.

shut off *vt* (*stop: power*) staccare; (*: water*) chiudere; (*: engine*) spegnere; (*isolate*) isolare.

shut out *vt* (*person, noise, cold*) non far entrare; (*block: view*) impedire, bloccare; (*: memory*) scacciare.

shut up *vi* (*col: keep quiet*) stare zitto(a) ♦

vt (*close*) chiudere; (*silence*) far tacere.

shutdown [shut'doun] *n* chiusura.

shutter [shut'ûr] *n* imposta; (*PHOT*) otturatore *m*.

shuttle [shut'əl] *n* spola, navetta; (*also: ~ service*) servizio *m* navetta *inv* ♦ *vi* (*subj: vehicle, person*) fare la spola ♦ *vt* (*to and fro: passengers*) portare (avanti e indietro).

shuttlecock [shut'əlkâk] *n* volano.

shy [shī] *a* timido(a) ♦ *vi*: **to ~ away from doing sth** (*fig*) rifuggire dal fare qc; **to fight ~ of** tenersi alla larga da; **to be ~ of doing sth** essere restio a fare qc.

shyness [shī'nis] *n* timidezza.

Siam [sīam'] *n* Siam *m*.

Siamese [sīəmēz'] *a*: **~ cat** gatto siamese; **~ twins** fratelli *mpl* (*or* sorelle *fpl*) siamesi.

Siberia [sībē'rēə] *n* Siberia.

sibling [sib'ling] *n* (*formal*) fratello/sorella.

Sicilian [sisil'yən] *a*, *n* siciliano(a).

Sicily [sis'ilē] *n* Sicilia.

sick [sik] *a* (*ill*) malato(a); (*vomiting*): **to be ~** vomitare; (*humor*) macabro(a); **to feel ~** to one's stomach avere il voltastomaco; **to be ~ of** (*fig*) averne abbastanza di; **a ~ person** un malato; **to be (off) ~** essere assente perché malato; **to fall** *or* **take ~** ammalarsi.

sick bay *n* infermeria.

sick benefit *n* (*US*) indennità di malattia.

sicken [sik'ən] *vt* nauseare.

sickening [sik'əning] *a* (*fig*) disgustoso(a), rivoltante.

sickle [sik'əl] *n* falcetto.

sick leave *n* congedo per malattia.

sickly [sik'lē] *a* malaticcio(a); (*causing nausea*) nauseante.

sickness [sik'nis] *n* malattia; (*vomiting*) vomito.

sickness benefit *n* (*Brit*) = **sick benefit**.

sick pay *n* sussidio per malattia.

sickroom [sik'rōōm] *n* stanza di malato.

side [sīd] *n* (*gen*) lato; (*of person, animal*) fianco; (*of lake*) riva; (*face, surface: gen*) faccia; (*: of paper*) facciata; (*fig: aspect*) aspetto, lato; (*team: SPORT*) squadra; (*: POL etc*) parte *f* ♦ *cpd* (*door, entrance*) laterale ♦ *vi*: **to ~ with sb** parteggiare per qn, prendere le parti di qn; **by the ~ of** a fianco di; (*road*) sul ciglio di; **~ by ~** fianco a fianco; **to take ~s (with)** schierarsi (con); **the right/wrong ~** il dritto/rovescio; **from ~ to ~** da una parte all'altra; **~ of beef** quarto di bue.

sideboard [sīd'bôrd] *n* credenza.

sideburns [sīd'bûrnz] *npl* (*whiskers*) basette *fpl*.

sidecar [sīd'kâr] *n* sidecar *m inv*.

side dish *n* contorno.

side drum *n* (*MUS*) piccolo tamburo.

side effect *n* (*MED*) effetto collaterale.

sidekick [sīd'kik] n (col) compagno/a.
sidelight [sīd'līt] n (AUT) luce f di posizione.
sideline [sīd'līn] n (SPORT) linea laterale; (fig) attività secondaria.
sidelong [sīd'lông] a obliquo(a); **to give a ~ glance at sth** guardare qc con la coda dell'occhio.
side plate n piattino.
side road n strada secondaria.
sidesaddle [sīd'sadəl] ad all'amazzone.
sideshow [sīd'shō] n attrazione f.
sidestep [sīd'step] vt (question) eludere; (problem) scavalcare ♦ vi (BOXING etc) sposarsi di lato.
side street n traversa.
sidetrack [sīd'trak] vt (fig) distrarre.
sidewalk [sīd'wôk] n (US) marciapiede m.
sideways [sīd'wāz] ad (move) di lato, di fianco; (look) con la coda dell'occhio.
siding [sī'ding] n (RAIL) binario di raccordo.
sidle [sī'dəl] vi: **to ~ up (to)** avvicinarsi furtivamente (a).
siege [sēj] n assedio; **to lay ~ to** porre l'assedio a.
siege economy n economia da stato d'assedio.
Sierra Leone [sēar'ə lēōn'] n Sierra Leone f.
sieve [siv] n setaccio ♦ vt setacciare.
sift [sift] vt passare al crivello; (fig) vagliare ♦ vi: **to ~ through** esaminare minuziosamente.
sigh [sī] n sospiro ♦ vi sospirare.
sight [sīt] n (faculty) vista; (spectacle) spettacolo; (on gun) mira ♦ vt avvistare; **in ~** in vista; **out of ~** non visibile; **at first ~** a prima vista; **to catch ~ of sb/sth** scorgere qc/qn; **to lose ~ of sb/sth** perdere di vista qn/qc; **to set one's ~s on sth/on doing sth** mirare a qc/a fare qc; **on ~** a vista; **I know her by ~** la conosco di vista.
sighted [sī'tid] a che ha il dono della vista; **partially ~** parzialmente cieco.
sightseeing [sīt'sēing] n turismo; **to go ~** visitare una località.
sightseer [sīt'sēr] n turista m/f.
sign [sīn] n segno; (with hand etc) segno, gesto; (notice) insegna, cartello; (road ~) segnale m ♦ vt firmare; **as a ~ of** in segno di; **it's a good/bad ~** è buon/brutto segno; **to show ~s/no ~ of doing sth** accennare/non accennare a fare qc; **plus/minus ~** segno del più/meno; **to ~ one's name** firmare, apporre la propria firma.
sign away vt (rights etc) cedere (con una firma).
sign in vi firmare il registro (all'arrivo).
sign off vi (RADIO, TV) chiudere le trasmissioni.
sign on vi (as unemployed) iscriversi sulla lista (dell'ufficio di collocamento); (begin work) prendere servizio; (enroll): **to ~ on for a course** iscriversi a un corso.

sign out vi firmare il registro (alla partenza).
sign over vt: **to ~ sth over to sb** cedere qc con scrittura legale a qn.
sign up (MIL) vt arruolare ♦ vi arruolarsi.
signal [sig'nəl] n segnale m ♦ vt (person) fare segno a; (message) comunicare per mezzo di segnali ♦ vi: **to ~ to sb (to do sth)** far segno a qn (di fare qc); **to ~ a left/right turn** (AUT) segnalare un cambiamento di direzione a sinistra/destra.
signal box n (Brit RAIL) cabina di manovra.
signalman [sig'nəlmən] n (RAIL) deviatore m.
signatory [sig'nətôrē] n firmatario/a.
signature [sig'nəchûr] n firma.
signature tune n sigla musicale.
signet ring [sig'nit ring] n anello con sigillo.
significance [signif'əkəns] n (of remark) significato; (of event) importanza; **that is of no ~** ciò non ha importanza.
significant [signif'ikənt] a (improvement, amount) notevole; (discovery, event) importante; (evidence, smile) significativo(a); **it is ~ that ...** è significativo che ....
significantly [signif'ikəntlē] ad (smile) in modo eloquente; (improve, increase) considerevolmente, decisamente.
signify [sig'nəfī] vt significare.
sign language n linguaggio dei muti.
signpost [sīn'pōst] n cartello indicatore.
silage [sī'lij] n insilato.
silence [sī'ləns] n silenzio ♦ vt far tacere, ridurre al silenzio.
silencer [sī'lənsûr] n (on gun, Brit AUT) silenziatore m.
silent [sī'lənt] a silenzioso(a); (movie) muto(a); **to keep** or **remain ~** tacere, stare zitto(a).
silently [sī'ləntlē] ad silenziosamente, in silenzio.
silent partner n (COMM) socio accomandante.
silhouette [silōōet'] n silhouette f inv ♦ vt: **to be ~d against** stagliarsi contro.
silicon [sil'ikən] n silicio.
silicon chip [sil'ikən chip] n piastrina di silicio.
silicone [sil'əkōn] n silicone m.
silk [silk] n seta ♦ cpd di seta.
silky [sil'kē] a di seta, come la seta.
sill [sil] n (window~) davanzale m; (Brit AUT) predellino.
silly [sil'ē] a stupido(a), sciocco(a); **to do something ~** fare una sciocchezza.
silo [sī'lō] n silo.
silt [silt] n limo.
silver [sil'vûr] n argento; (also: **~ware**) argenteria ♦ cpd d'argento.
silver foil n carta argentata, (carta) stagnola.
silver-plated [sil'vûrplā'tid] a argentato(a).
silversmith [sil'vûrsmith] n argentiere m.
silverware [sil'vûrwär] n argenteria, argento.

silvery |sil'vûrē| *a* (*color*) argenteo(a); (*sound*) argentino(a).

similar |sim'ələr| *a*: ~ **(to)** simile (a).

similarity |siməlar'itē| *n* somiglianza, rassomiglianza.

similarly |sim'əlûrlē| *ad* (*in a similar way*) allo stesso modo; (*as is similar*) così pure.

simile |sim'əlē| *n* similitudine *f*.

simmer |sim'ûr| *vi* cuocere a fuoco lento.

   simmer down *vi* (*fig col*) calmarsi.

simper |sim'pûr| *vi* fare lo(la) smorfioso(a).

simpering |sim'pûring| *a* lezioso(a), smorfioso(a).

simple |sim'pəl| *a* semplice; **the ~ truth** la pura verità.

simple interest *n* (*MATH, COMM*) interesse *m* semplice.

simple-minded |sim'pəlmīn'did| *a* sempliciotto(a).

simpleton |sim'pəltən| *n* semplicione/a, sempliciotto/a.

simplicity |simplis'ətē| *n* semplicità.

simplification |simpləfəkā'shən| *n* semplificazione *f*.

simplify |sim'pləfī| *vt* semplificare.

simply |sim'plē| *ad* semplicemente.

simulate |sim'yəlāt| *vt* fingere, simulare.

simulation |simyəlā'shən| *n* simulazione *f*.

simultaneous |sīməltā'nēəs| *a* simultaneo(a).

simultaneously |sīməltā'nēəslē| *ad* simultaneamente, contemporaneamente.

sin |sin| *n* peccato ♦ *vi* peccare.

Sinai |sī'nī| *n* Sinai *m*.

since |sins| *ad* da allora ♦ *prep* da ♦ *cj* (*time*) da quando; (*because*) poiché, dato che; ~ **then** da allora; ~ **Monday** da lunedì; (*ever*) ~ **I arrived** (fin) da quando sono arrivato.

sincere |sinsēr'| *a* sincero(a).

sincerely |sinsēr'lē| *ad* sinceramente; ~ **yours**, (*Brit*) **yours** ~ (*at end of letter*) distinti saluti.

sincerity |sinsär'itē| *n* sincerità.

sine |sīn| *n* (*MATH*) seno.

sinew |sin'yōō| *n* tendine *m*; ~**s** *npl* (*muscles*) muscoli *mpl*.

sinful |sin'fəl| *a* peccaminoso(a).

sing, *pt* **sang**, *pp* **sung** |sing, sang, sung| *vt, vi* cantare.

Singapore |sing'gəpôr| *n* Singapore *f*.

singe |sinj| *vt* bruciacchiare.

singer |sing'ûr| *n* cantante *m/f*.

Singhalese |singəlēz'| *a* = **Sinhalese**.

singing |sing'ing| *n* (*of person, bird*) canto; (*of kettle, bullet, in ears*) fischio.

single |sing'gəl| *a* solo(a), unico(a); (*unmarried*) celibe; (: *woman*) nubile; (*not double*) semplice ♦ *n* (*Brit: also*: ~ **ticket**) biglietto di (sola) andata; (*record*) 45 giri *m inv*; **not a** ~ **one was left** non ne è rimasto nemmeno uno; **every** ~ **day** tutti i santi giorni; *see also* **singles**.

single out *vt* scegliere; (*distinguish*) distinguere.

single bed *n* letto a una piazza.

single-breasted |sing'gəlbrcs'tid| *a* a un petto.

single file *n*: **in** ~ in fila indiana.

single-handed |sing'gəlhan'did| *ad* senza aiuto, da solo(a).

single-minded |sing'gəlmīn'did| *a* tenace, risoluto(a).

single parent *n* ragazzo padre/ragazza madre; genitore *m* separato.

single room *n* camera singola.

singles |sing'gəlz| *npl* (*US: single people*) single *m/fpl*; (*TENNIS*) singolo.

singly |sing'glē| *ad* separatamente.

singsong |sing'sông| *a* (*tone*) cantilenante.

singular |sing'gyəlûr| *a* (*LING*) singolare; (*unusual*) strano(a), singolare ♦ *n* (*LING*) singolare *m*; **in the feminine** ~ al femminile singolare.

singularly |sing'gyəlûrlē| *ad* stranamente.

Sinhalese |sinhəlēz'| *a* singalese.

sinister |sin'istûr| *a* sinistro(a).

sink |singk| *n* lavandino, acquaio ♦ *vb* (*pt* **sank**, *pp* **sunk** |sangk, sungk|) *vt* (*ship*) (fare) affondare, colare a picco; (*foundations*) scavare; (*piles etc*): **to** ~ **sth into** conficcare qc in ♦ *vi* affondare, andare a fondo; (*ground etc*) cedere, avvallarsi; **he sank into a chair/the mud** sprofondò in una poltrona/nel fango.

sink in *vi* penetrare; **it took a long time to** ~ **in** ci ho (*or* ha *etc*) messo molto a capirlo.

sinking fund |sing'king fund| *n* (*COMM*) fondo d'ammortamento.

sink unit *n* blocco lavello.

sinner |sin'ûr| *n* peccatore/trice.

sinuous |sin'yōōəs| *a* sinuoso(a).

sinus |sī'nəs| *n* (*ANAT*) seno.

sip |sip| *n* sorso ♦ *vt* sorseggiare.

siphon |sī'fən| *n* sifone *m* ♦ *vt* (*funds*) trasferire.

siphon off *vt* travasare (con un sifone).

sir |sûr| *n* signore *m*; **S~ John Smith** Sir John Smith; **yes** ~ sì, signore; **Dear S~** (*in letter*) Egregio signor; (*followed by name*); **Dear S~s** Spettabile ditta.

siren |sī'rən| *n* sirena.

sirloin |sûr'loin| *n* controfiletto.

sirloin steak |sûr'loin stāk| *n* bistecca di controfiletto.

sirocco |sərâk'ō| *n* scirocco.

sisal |sī'səl| *n* sisal *f inv*.

sissy |sis'ē| *n* (*col*) femminuccia.

sister |sis'tûr| *n* sorella; (*nun*) suora; (*Brit: nurse*) infermiera *f* caposala *inv* ♦ *cpd*: ~ **organization** organizzazione *f* affine; ~ **ship** nave *f* gemella.

sister-in-law |sis'tûrinlô| *n* cognata.

sit, *pt, pp* **sat** |sit, sat| *vi* sedere, sedersi; (*assembly*) essere in seduta; (*Brit: dress*

[handwritten notes at bottom:] volere   credere   sedere / vorrei / credei

etc) cadere ♦ *vt* (*exam*) sostenere, dare; **to ~ on a committee** far parte di una commissione.

sit about *vi* (*Brit*) = **sit around.**

sit around *vi* star seduto(a) (senza far nulla).

sit back *vi* (*in seat*) appoggiarsi allo schienale.

sit down *vi* sedersi; **to be ~ting down** essere seduto(a).

sit in *vi*: **to ~ in on a discussion** assistere ad una discussione.

sit up *vi* tirarsi su a sedere; (*not go to bed*) stare alzato(a) fino a tardi.

sitcom [sit'kâm] *n abbr* (*TV*: = *situation comedy*) sceneggiato a episodi (*comico*).

sit-down [sit'doun] *a*: **~ strike** sciopero bianco (con occupazione della fabbrica); **a ~ meal** (*Brit*) un pranzo.

site [sīt] *n* posto; (*also*: **building ~**) cantiere *m* ♦ *vt* situare.

sit-in [sit'in] *n* (*demonstration*) sit-in *m inv.*

siting [sī'ting] *n* ubicazione *f.*

sitter [sit'ûr] *n* (*also*: **baby ~**) babysitter *m/f inv.*

sitting [sit'ing] *n* (*of assembly etc*) seduta; (*Brit*: *in canteen*) turno.

sitting member *n* (*Brit POL*) deputato/a in carica.

sitting room *n* (*Brit*) soggiorno.

situate [sich'ōōāt] *vt* collocare.

situated [sich'ōōātid] *a* situato(a).

situation [sichōōā'shən] *n* situazione *f.*

situation comedy *n* (*TV*) commedia di situazione.

six [siks] *num* sei.

sixteen [siks'tēn'] *num* sedici.

sixteenth note [siks'tēnth' nōt] *n* (*US*) semicroma.

sixth [siksth] *num* sesto(a) ♦ *n*: **the upper/ lower ~** (*Brit SCOL*) l'ultimo/il penultimo anno di scuola superiore.

sixty [siks'tē] *num* sessanta.

size [sīz] *n* dimensioni *fpl*; (*of clothing*) taglia, misura; (*of shoes*) numero; (*glue*) colla; **I take ~ 14 in a dress** ≈ porto la 44 di vestiti; **I'd like the small/large ~** (*of soap powder etc*) vorrei la confezione piccola/grande.

size up *vt* giudicare, farsi un'idea di.

sizeable [sī'zəbəl] *a* considerevole.

sizzle [siz'əl] *vi* sfrigolare.

SK *abbr* (*Canada*) = *Saskatchewan.*

skate [skāt] *n* pattino; (*fish*: *pl inv*) razza ♦ *vi* pattinare.

skate over, skate around *vi* (*problem, issue*) prendere alla leggera, prendere sottogamba.

skateboard [skāt'bôrd] *n* skateboard *m inv.*

skater [skā'tûr] *n* pattinatore/trice.

skating [skā'ting] *n* pattinaggio.

skating rink *n* pista di pattinaggio.

skeleton [skel'itən] *n* scheletro.

skeleton key *n* passe-partout *m inv.*

skeleton staff *n* personale *m* ridotto.

skeptic [skep'tik] *n* (*US*) scettico/a.

skeptical [skep'tikəl] *a* (*US*) scettico(a).

skepticism [skep'tisizəm] *n* (*US*) scetticismo.

sketch [skech] *n* (*drawing*) schizzo, abbozzo; (*THEATER etc*) scenetta comica, sketch *m inv* ♦ *vt* abbozzare, schizzare.

sketch book *n* album *m inv* per schizzi.

sketch pad *n* blocco per schizzi.

sketchy [skech'ē] *a* incompleto(a), lacunoso(a).

skew [skyōō] *n* (*Brit*): **on the ~** di traverso.

skewer [skyōō'ûr] *n* spiedo.

ski [skē] *n* sci *m inv* ♦ *vi* sciare.

ski boot *n* scarpone *m* da sci.

skid [skid] *n* slittamento; (*sideways slip*) sbandamento ♦ *vi* slittare; sbandare; **to go into a ~** slittare; sbandare.

skid mark *n* segno della frenata.

skier [skē'ûr] *n* sciatore/trice.

skiing [skē'ing] *n* sci *m.*

ski instructor *n* maestro/a di sci.

ski jump *n* (*ramp*) trampolino; (*event*) salto con gli sci.

skilful [skil'fəl] *etc* (*Brit*) = **skillful** *etc.*

ski lift *n* sciovia.

skill [skil] *n* abilità *f inv*, capacità *f inv*; (*technique*) tecnica.

skilled [skild] *a* esperto(a); (*worker*) qualificato(a), specializzato(a).

skillet [skil'it] *n* padella.

skillful [skil'fəl] *a* (*US*) abile.

skillfully [skil'fəlē] *ad* abilmente.

skim [skim] *vt* (*milk*) scremare; (*soup*) schiumare; (*glide `over*) sfiorare ♦ *vi*: **to ~ through** (*fig*) scorrere, dare una scorsa a.

skimmed milk [skimd milk] *n* latte *m* scremato.

skimp [skimp] *vi*: **to ~ on,** *vt* (*work*) fare alla carlona; (*cloth etc*) lesinare.

skimpy [skim'pē] *a* misero(a); striminzito(a); frugale.

skin [skin] *n* pelle *f*; (*of fruit, vegetable*) buccia; (*on dessert, paint*) crosta ♦ *vt* (*fruit etc*) sbucciare; (*animal*) scuoiare, spellare; **wet** *or* **soaked to the ~** bagnato fino al midollo.

skin-deep [skin'dēp'] *a* superficiale.

skin diver *n* subacqueo.

skin diving *n* nuoto subacqueo.

skinflint [skin'flint] *n* taccagno/a, tirchio/a.

skin graft *n* innesto epidermico.

skinny [skin'ē] *a* molto magro(a), pelle e ossa *inv.*

skin test *n* prova di reazione cutanea.

skintight [skin'tīt] *a* aderente.

skip [skip] *n* saltello, balzo; (*Brit*: *container*) benna ♦ *vi* saltare; (*with rope*) saltare la corda ♦ *vt* (*pass over*) saltare; **to ~ school**

marinare la scuola.

ski pants *npl* pantaloni *mpl* da sci.

ski pole *n* racchetta (da sci).

skipper [skip'ûr] *n* (*NAUT, SPORT*) capitano.

skipping rope [skip'ing rōp] *n* (*Brit*) corda per saltare.

ski resort *n* località *f inv* sciistica.

skirmish [skûr'mish] *n* scaramuccia.

skirt [skûrt] *n* gonna, sottana ♦ *vt* fiancheggiare, costeggiare.

skirting board [skûr'ting bōrd] *n* (*Brit*) zoccolo.

ski run *n* pista (da sci).

ski suit *n* tuta da sci.

skit [skit] *n* parodia; scenetta satirica.

skittle [skit'əl] *n* birillo; **~s** *n* (*game*) (gioco dei) birilli *mpl*.

skive [skīv] *vi* (*Brit col*) fare il lavativo.

skulk [skulk] *vi* muoversi furtivamente.

skull [skul] *n* cranio, teschio.

skullcap [skul'kap] *n* (*worn by Jews*) zucchetto; (*worn by Pope*) papalina.

skunk [skungk] *n* moffetta.

sky [skī] *n* cielo; **to praise sb to the skies** portare alle stelle qn.

sky-blue [skī'blōō'] *a* azzurro(a), celeste.

sky-high [skī'hī'] *ad* (*throw*) molto in alto; **prices have gone ~** i prezzi sono saliti alle stelle.

skylark [skī'lârk] *n* allodola.

skylight [skī'līt] *n* lucernario.

skyline [skī'līn] *n* (*horizon*) orizzonte *m*; (*of city*) profilo.

skyscraper [skī'skrāpûr] *n* grattacielo.

slab [slab] *n* lastra; (*of wood*) tavola; (*of meat, cheese*) pezzo.

slack [slak] *a* (*loose*) allentato(a); (*slow*) lento(a); (*careless*) negligente; (*COMM: market*) stagnante; (: *demand*) scarso(a); (*period*) morto(a) ♦ *n* (*in rope etc*) parte *f* non tesa; **business is ~** l'attività commerciale è scarsa; *see also* **slacks**.

slacken [slak'ən] (*also*: **~ off**) *vi* rallentare, diminuire ♦ *vt* allentare; (*pressure*) diminuire.

slacks [slaks] *npl* pantaloni *mpl*.

slag [slag] *n* scorie *fpl*.

slag heap *n* ammasso di scorie.

slain [slān] *pp* of **slay**.

slake [slāk] *vt* (*one's thirst*) spegnere.

slalom [slā'ləm] *n* slalom *m*.

slam [slam] *vt* (*door*) sbattere; (*throw*) scaraventare; (*criticize*) stroncare ♦ *vi* sbattere.

slander [slan'dûr] *n* calunnia; (*LAW*) diffamazione *f* ♦ *vt* calunniare; diffamare.

slanderous [slan'dûrəs] *a* calunnioso(a); diffamatorio(a).

slang [slang] *n* gergo, slang *m*.

slant [slant] *n* pendenza, inclinazione *f*; (*fig*) angolazione *f*, punto di vista.

slanted [slan'tid] *a* tendenzioso(a).

slanting [slan'ting] *a* in pendenza, inclinato(a).

slap [slap] *n* manata, pacca; (*on face*) schiaffo ♦ *vt* dare una manata a; schiaffeggiare ♦ *ad* (*directly*) in pieno; **it fell ~ in the middle** cadde proprio nel mezzo.

slapdash [slap'dash] *a* abborracciato(a).

slapstick [slap'stik] *n* (*comedy*) farsa grossolana.

slash [slash] *vt* squarciare; (*face*) sfregiare; (*fig: prices*) ridurre drasticamente, tagliare ♦ *n* (*US TYP*) barra.

slat [slat] *n* (*of wood*) stecca.

slate [slāt] *n* ardesia ♦ *vt* (*fig: criticize*) stroncare, distruggere.

slaughter [slô'tûr] *n* (*of animals*) macellazione *f*; (*of people*) strage *f*, massacro ♦ *vt* macellare; trucidare, massacrare.

slaughterhouse [slô'tûrhous] *n* macello, mattatoio.

Slav [slâv] *a*, *n* slavo(a).

slave [slāv] *n* schiavo/a ♦ *vi* (*also*: **~ away**) lavorare come uno schiavo; **to ~ (away) at sth/at doing sth** ammazzarsi di fatica *or* sgobbare per qc/per fare qc.

slave labor *n* lavoro degli schiavi; (*fig*): **we're just ~ here** siamo solamente sfruttati qui dentro.

slaver [slā'vûr] *vi* (*Brit: dribble*) sbavare.

slavery [slā'vûrē] *n* schiavitù *f*.

Slavic [slâv'ik] *a* slavo(a).

slavish [slā'vish] *a* servile; pedissequo(a).

Slavonic [sləvân'ik] *a* slavo(a).

slay [slā], *pt* **slew**, *pp* **slain** [slā, slōō, slān] *vt* (*formal*) uccidere.

SLD *n abbr* (*Brit POL*) = *Social and Liberal Democratic Party.*

sleazy [slē'zē] *a* trasandato(a).

sled [sled] *n* (*US*) slitta.

sledge [slej] *n* (*Brit*) = **sled.**

sledgehammer [slej'hamûr] *n* martello da fabbro.

sleek [slēk] *a* (*hair, fur*) lucido(a), lucente; (*car, boat*) slanciato(a), affusolato(a).

sleep [slēp] *n* sonno ♦ *vi* (*pt, pp* **slept** [slept]) dormire ♦ *vt*: **we can ~ 4** abbiamo 4 posti letto, possiamo alloggiare 4 persone; **to have a good night's ~** farsi una bella dormita; **to go to ~** addormentarsi; **to ~ lightly** avere il sonno leggero; **to put to ~** (*patient*) far addormentare; (*animal: euphemistic*: *kill*) abbattere; **to ~ with sb** (*euphemistic*: *have sex*) andare a letto con qn.

sleep in *vi* (*lie late*) alzarsi tardi; (*oversleep*) dormire fino a tardi.

sleeper [slē'pûr] *n* (*person*) dormiente *m/f*; (*Brit RAIL*: *on track*) traversina; (: *train*) treno di vagoni letto.

sleepily [slē'pilē] *ad* con aria assonnata.

sleeping [slē'ping] *a* addormentato(a).

sleeping bag *n* sacco a pelo.

sleeping car *n* vagone *m* letto *inv*, carrozza *f*

letto *inv*.
sleeping partner *n* (*Brit COMM*) = **silent partner**.
sleeping pill *n* sonnifero.
sleepless [slēp'lis] *a* (*person*) insonne; **a ~ night** una notte in bianco.
sleeplessness [slēp'lisnis] *n* insonnia.
sleepwalker [slēp'wôkûr] *n* sonnambulo/a.
sleepy [slē'pē] *a* assonnato(a), sonnolento(a); (*fig*) addormentato(a); **to be** *or* **feel ~** avere sonno.
sleet [slēt] *n* nevischio.
sleeve [slēv] *n* manica; (*of record*) copertina.
sleeveless [slēv'lis] *a* (*garment*) senza maniche.
sleigh [slā] *n* slitta.
sleight [slīt] *n*: **~ of hand** gioco di destrezza.
slender [slen'dûr] *a* snello(a), sottile; (*not enough*) scarso(a), esiguo(a).
slept [slept] *pt*, *pp of* **sleep**.
sleuth [slōōth] *n* (*col*) segugio.
slew [slōō] *vi* (*Brit*) = **slue** ♦ *pt of* **slay**.
slice [slīs] *n* fetta ♦ *vt* affettare, tagliare a fette; **~d bread** pane *m* a cassetta.
slick [slik] *a* (*clever*) brillante; (*insincere*) untuoso(a), falso(a) ♦ *n* (*also*: **oil ~**) chiazza di petrolio.
slid [slid] *pt*, *pp of* **slide**.
slide [slīd] *n* (*in playground*) scivolo; (*PHOT*) diapositiva; (*microscope ~*) vetrino; (*Brit*: *also*: **hair ~**) fermaglio (per capelli); (*in prices*) caduta ♦ *vb* (*pt*, *pp* **slid** [slid]) *vt* far scivolare ♦ *vi* scivolare; **to let things ~** (*fig*) lasciare andare tutto, trascurare tutto.
slide projector *n* proiettore *m* per diapositive.
slide rule *n* regolo calcolatore.
sliding [slī'ding] *a* (*door*) scorrevole; **~ roof** (*AUT*) capotte *f inv*.
sliding scale *n* scala mobile.
slight [slīt] *a* (*slim*) snello(a), sottile; (*frail*) delicato(a), fragile; (*trivial*) insignificante; (*small*) piccolo(a) ♦ *n* offesa, affronto ♦ *vt* (*offend*) offendere, fare un affronto a; **the ~est** il minimo (*or* la minima); **not in the ~est** affatto, neppure per sogno.
slightly [slīt'lē] *ad* lievemente, un po'; **~ built** esile.
slim [slim] *a* magro(a), snello(a) ♦ *vi* dimagrire, fare (*or* seguire) una dieta dimagrante.
slime [slīm] *n* limo, melma; viscidume *m*.
slimming [slim'ing] *a* (*diet*, *pills*) dimagrante.
slimy [slī'mē] *a* (*also fig*: *person*) viscido(a); (*covered with mud*) melmoso(a).
sling [sling] *n* (*MED*) benda al collo ♦ *vt* (*pt*, *pp* **slung** [slung]) lanciare, tirare; **to have one's arm in a ~** avere un braccio al collo.
slingshot [sling'shât] *n* (*US*) catapulta, fionda.
slink, *pt*, *pp* **slunk** [slingk, slungk] *vi*: **to ~ away**, **~ off** svignarsela.
slip [slip] *n* scivolata, scivolone *m*; (*mistake*)

errore *m*, sbaglio; (*underskirt*) sottoveste *f*; (*paper*) bigliettino, talloncino ♦ *vt* (*slide*) far scivolare ♦ *vi* (*slide*) scivolare; (*move smoothly*): **to ~ into/out of** scivolare in/via da; (*decline*) declinare; **to give sb the ~** sfuggire qn; **a ~ of paper** un foglietto; **a ~ of the tongue** un lapsus linguae; **to ~ sth on/off** infilarsi/togliersi qc; **to let a chance ~ by** lasciarsi scappare un'occasione; **it ~ped from her hand** le sfuggì di mano.
slip away *vi* svignarsela.
slip in *vt* introdurre casualmente.
slip out *vi* uscire furtivamente.
slip-on [slip'ân] *a* (*gen*) comodo(a) da mettere; (*shoes*) senza allacciatura.
slipped disc [slipt disk] *n* spostamento delle vertebre.
slipper [slip'ûr] *n* pantofola.
slippery [slip'ûrē] *a* scivoloso(a).
slip road *n* (*Brit*: *to freeway*) rampa di accesso.
slipshod [slip'shâd] *a* sciatto(a), trasandato(a).
slip-up [slip'up] *n* granchio (*fig*).
slipway [slip'wā] *n* scalo di costruzione.
slit [slit] *n* fessura, fenditura; (*cut*) taglio; (*tear*) strappo ♦ *vt* (*pt*, *pp* **slit**) tagliare; **to ~ sb's throat** tagliare la gola a qn.
slither [slith'ûr] *vi* scivolare, sdrucciolare.
sliver [sliv'ûr] *n* (*of glass*, *wood*) scheggia; (*of cheese*, *sausage*) fettina.
slob [slâb] *n* (*col*) sciattone/a.
slog [slâg] *n* faticata ♦ *vi* lavorare con accanimento, sgobbare.
slogan [slō'gən] *n* motto, slogan *m inv*.
slop [slâp] *vi* (*also*: **~ over**) traboccare; versarsi ♦ *vt* spandere; versare ♦ *npl*: **~s** acqua sporca; sbobba.
slope [slōp] *n* pendio; (*side of mountain*) versante *m*; (*of roof*) pendenza; (*of floor*) inclinazione *f* ♦ *vi*: **to ~ down** declinare; **to ~ up** essere in salita.
sloping [slō'ping] *a* inclinato(a).
sloppy [slâp'ē] *a* (*work*) tirato(a) via; (*appearance*) sciatto(a); (*movie etc*) sdolcinato(a).
slosh [slâsh] *vi* (*col*): **to ~ around** (*person*) squazzare; (*liquid*) guazzare.
slot [slât] *n* fessura; (*fig*: *in timetable*, *RADIO*, *TV*) spazio ♦ *vt*: **to ~ into** introdurre in una fessura.
sloth [slôth] *n* (*vice*) pigrizia, accidia; (*ZOOL*) bradipo.
slot machine *n* (*for amusement*) slot-machine *f inv*; (*Brit*: *vending machine*) distributore *m* automatico.
slouch [slouch] *vi* (*when walking*) camminare dinoccolato(a); **she was ~ed in a chair** era sprofondata in una poltrona.
    slouch about, **slouch around** *vi* (*laze*) oziare.

slovenly [sluv'ənlē] *a* sciatto(a), trasandato(a).

slow [slō] *a* lento(a); (*watch*): **to be ~** essere indietro ♦ *ad* lentamente ♦ *vt, vi* (*also*: **~ down, ~ up**) rallentare; **at a ~ speed** a bassa velocità; **to be ~ to act/decide** essere lento ad agire/a decidere; **my watch is 20 minutes ~** il mio orologio è indietro di 20 minuti; **business is ~** (*COMM*) gli affari procedono a rilento; **to go ~** (*driver*) andare piano; (*in industrial dispute*) fare uno sciopero bianco.

slow-acting [slō'ak'ting] *a* che agisce lentamente, ad azione lenta.

slowdown [slō'doun] *n* (*US*) rallentamento dei lavori (*per agitazione sindacale*).

slowly [slō'lē] *ad* lentamente; **to drive ~** andare piano.

slow motion *n*: **in ~** al rallentatore.

slowness [slō'nis] *n* lentezza.

slowpoke [slō'pōk] *n* (*col: dawdler*) lumaca.

sludge [sluj] *n* fanghiglia.

slue [slōō] *vi* (*US*) (*also*: **~ around**) girare.

slug [slug] *n* lumaca; (*bullet*) pallottola.

sluggish [slug'ish] *a* lento(a); (*business, market, sales*) stagnante, fiacco(a).

sluice [slōōs] *n* chiusa ♦ *vt*: **to ~ down** *or* **out** lavare (con abbondante acqua).

slum [slum] *n* catapecchia.

slumber [slum'bûr] *n* sonno.

slump [slump] *n* crollo, caduta; (*economic*) depressione *f*, crisi *f inv* ♦ *vi* crollare; **he was ~ed over the wheel** era curvo sul volante.

slung [slung] *pt, pp of* **sling.**

slunk [slungk] *pt, pp of* **slink.**

slur [slûr] *n* pronuncia indistinta; (*stigma*) diffamazione *f*, calunnia; (*MUS*) legatura; (*smear*): **~ (on)** macchia (su) ♦ *vt* pronunciare in modo indistinto; **to cast a ~ on sb** calunniare qn.

slurred [slûrd] *a* (*pronunciation*) inarticolato(a), disarticolato(a).

slush [slush] *n* neve *f* mista a fango.

slush fund *n* fondi *mpl* neri.

slushy [slush'ē] *a* (*snow*) che si scioglie; (*Brit: fig*) sdolcinato(a).

slut [slut] *n* donna trasandata, sciattona.

sly [slī] *a* furbo(a), scaltro(a); **on the ~** di soppiatto.

smack [smak] *n* (*slap*) pacca; (*on face*) schiaffo ♦ *vt* schiaffeggiare; (*child*) picchiare ♦ *vi*: **to ~ of** puzzare di; **to ~ one's lips** fare uno schiocco con le labbra.

smacker [smak'ûr] *n* (*col: kiss*) bacio; (: *US: dollar bill*) dollaro; (: *Brit: pound note*) sterlina.

small [smôl] *a* piccolo(a); (*in height*) basso(a); (*letter*) minuscolo(a) ♦ *n*: **the ~ of the back** le reni; **to get** *or* **grow ~er** (*stain, town*) rimpicciolire; (*debt, organization, numbers*) ridursi; **to make ~er** (*amount,*

income) ridurre; (*garden, object, garment*) rimpicciolire; **a ~ storekeeper** un piccolo negoziante.

small ads *npl* (*Brit*) piccoli annunci *mpl.*

small arms *npl* armi *fpl* portatili *or* leggere.

small change *n* moneta, spiccioli *mpl.*

smallholding [smôl'hōlding] *n* (*Brit*) piccola tenuta.

smallish [smô'lish] *a* piccolino(a).

small-minded [smôl'mīn'did] *a* meschino(a).

smallpox [smôl'pâks] *n* vaiolo.

small print *n* caratteri *mpl* piccoli; (*on document*) parte scritta in piccolo.

small-scale [smôl'skāl] *a* (*map, model*) in scala ridotta; (*business, farming*) modesto(a).

small talk *n* chiacchiere *fpl.*

small-time [smôl'tīm'] *a* (*col*) da poco; **a ~ thief** un ladro di polli.

smart [smârt] *a* elegante; (*clever*) intelligente; (*quick*) sveglio(a) ♦ *vi* bruciare; **the ~ set** il bel mondo; **to look ~** essere elegante; **my eyes are ~ing** mi bruciano gli occhi.

smart-ass [smârt'as] *n* (*US col*) sapientone/a.

smarten up [smâr'tən up] *vi* farsi bello(a) ♦ *vt* (*people*) fare bello(a); (*things*) abbellire.

smash [smash] *n* (*also*: **~-up**) scontro, collisione *f*; (*sound*) fracasso ♦ *vt* frantumare, fracassare; (*opponent*) annientare, schiacciare; (*hopes*) distruggere; (*SPORT: record*) battere ♦ *vi* frantumarsi, andare in pezzi.

smash up *vt* (*car*) sfasciare; (*room*) distruggere.

smash-hit [smash'hit] *n* successone *m.*

smattering [smat'ûring] *n*: **a ~ of** un'infarinatura di.

smear [smē'ûr] *n* macchia; (*MED*) striscio; (*insult*) calunnia ♦ *vt* ungere; (*fig*) denigrare, diffamare; **his hands were ~ed with oil/ink** aveva le mani sporche di olio/inchiostro.

smear campaign *n* campagna diffamatoria.

smell [smel] *n* odore *m*; (*sense*) olfatto, odorato ♦ *vb* (*pt, pp* **smelt** *or* **smelled** [smelt, smeld]) *vt* sentire (l')odore di ♦ *vi* (*food etc*): **to ~ (of)** avere odore (di); (*pej*) puzzare, avere un cattivo odore; **it ~s good** ha un buon odore.

smelly [smel'ē] *a* puzzolente.

smelt [smelt] *pt, pp of* **smell** ♦ *vt* (*ore*) fondere.

smile [smīl] *n* sorriso ♦ *vi* sorridere.

smiling [smī'ling] *a* sorridente.

smirk [smûrk] *n* sorriso furbo; sorriso compiaciuto.

smith [smith] *n* fabbro.

smithy [smith'ē] *n* fucina.

smitten [smit'ən] *a*: **~ with** colpito(a) da.

smock [smâk] *n* grembiule *m*, camice *m.*

smog [smâg] *n* smog *m.*

smoke [smōk] *n* fumo ♦ *vt, vi* fumare; **to have a ~** fumarsi una sigaretta; **do you ~?** fumi?; **to go up in ~** (*house etc*) bruciare, andare distrutto dalle fiamme; (*fig*) andare in fumo.

smoked |smōkt| *a* (*bacon, glass*) affumicato(a).

smokeless fuel |smōk'lis fyōō'əl| *n* carburante *m* che non da fumo.

smoker |smō'kûr| *n* (*person*) fumatore/trice; (*RAIL*) carrozza per fumatori.

smoke screen *n* cortina fumogena *or* di fumo; (*fig*) copertura.

smoking |smō'king| *n* fumo; **"no ~"** (*sign*) "vietato fumare"; **he's given up ~** ha smesso di fumare.

smoking car *n* carrozza (per) fumatori.

smoky |smō'kē| *a* fumoso(a); (*surface*) affumicato(a).

smolder |smōl'dûr| *vi* (*US*) covare sotto la cenere.

smooth |smōōth| *a* liscio(a); (*sauce*) omogeneo(a), (*flavor, whiskey*) amabile; (*cigarette*) leggero(a); (*movement*) regolare; (*person*) mellifluo(a); (*landing, take-off, flight*) senza scosse ♦ *vt* lisciare, spianare; (*also:* ~ **out:** *difficulties*) appianare.

smooth over *vt:* **to ~ things over** (*fig*) sistemare le cose.

smoothly |smōōth'lē| *ad* (*easily*) liscio; **everything went ~** tutto andò liscio.

smother |smuth'ûr| *vt* soffocare.

smoulder |smōl'dûr| *vi* (*Brit*) = **smolder**.

smudge |smuj| *n* macchia; sbavatura ♦ *vt* imbrattare, sporcare.

smug |smug| *a* soddisfatto(a), compiaciuto(a).

smuggle |smug'əl| *vt* contrabbandare; **to ~ in/out** (*goods etc*) far entrare/uscire di contrabbando.

smuggler |smug'lûr| *n* contrabbandiere/a.

smuggling |smug'ling| *n* contrabbando.

smut |smut| *n* (*grain of soot*) granello di fuliggine; (*mark*) segno nero; (*in conversation etc*) sconcezze *fpl*.

smutty |smut'ē| *a* (*fig*) osceno(a), indecente.

snack |snak| *n* spuntino; **to have a ~** fare uno spuntino.

snack bar *n* tavola calda, snack bar *m inv*.

snag |snag| *n* intoppo, ostacolo imprevisto.

snail |snāl| *n* chiocciola.

snake |snāk| *n* serpente *m*.

snap |snap| *n* (*sound*) schianto, colpo secco; (*photograph*) istantanea; (*game*) rubamazzo ♦ *a* improvviso(a) ♦ *vt* (*far*) schioccare; (*break*) spezzare di netto ♦ *vi* spezzarsi con un rumore secco; (*fig: person*) crollare; **to ~ at sb** rivolgersi a qn con tono brusco; (*subj: dog*) cercare di mordere qn; **to ~ open/shut** aprirsi/chiudersi di scatto; **to ~ one's fingers at** (*fig*) infischiarsi di; **a cold ~** (*of weather*) un'improvvisa ondata di freddo.

snap off *vt* (*break*) schiantare.

snap up *vt* afferrare.

snap fastener *n* bottone *m* automatico.

snappy |snap'ē| *a* rapido(a); **make it ~!** (*col: hurry up*) sbrigati!, svelto!

snapshot |snap'shât| *n* istantanea.

snare |snär| *n* trappola.

snarl |snârl| *vi* ringhiare ♦ *vt:* **to get ~ed up** (*wool, plans*) ingarbugliarsi; (*traffic*) intasarsi.

snatch |snach| *n* (*fig*) furto; (*small amount*): **~es of** frammenti *mpl* di ♦ *vt* strappare (con violenza); (*steal*) rubare.

snatch up *vt* raccogliere in fretta.

sneak |snēk| *vi:* **to ~ in/out** entrare/uscire di nascosto ♦ *vt:* **to ~ a look at sth** guardare di sottecchi qc.

sneakers |snē'kûrz| *npl* scarpe *fpl* da ginnastica.

sneaking |snē'king| *a:* **to have a ~ feeling/ suspicion that ...** avere la vaga impressione/ il vago sospetto che ....

sneaky |snē'kē| *a* falso(a), disonesto(a).

sneer |snēr| *n* ghigno, sogghigno ♦ *vi* ghignare, sogghignare; **to ~ at sb/sth** farsi beffe di qn/qc.

sneeze |snēz| *n* starnuto ♦ *vi* starnutire.

snicker |snik'ûr| *n* riso represso ♦ *vi* ridacchiare, ridere sotto i baffi.

snide |snīd| *a* maligno(a).

sniff |snif| *n* fiutata, annusata ♦ *vi* fiutare, annusare; tirare su col naso; (*in contempt*) arricciare il naso ♦ *vt* fiutare, annusare; (*glue, drug*) sniffare.

sniff at *vt fus:* **it's not to be ~ed at** non è da disprezzare.

snigger |snig'ûr| *n, vi* = **snicker**.

snip |snip| *n* pezzetto; (*bargain*) (buon) affare *m*, occasione *f* ♦ *vt* tagliare.

sniper |snī'pûr| *n* franco tiratore *m*, cecchino.

snippet |snip'it| *n* frammento.

snivelling |sniv'əling| *a* piagnucoloso(a).

snob |snâb| *n* snob *m/f inv*.

snobbery |snâb'ûrē| *n* snobismo.

snobbish |snâb'ish| *a* snob *inv*.

snooker |snōōk'ûr| *n* tipo di gioco del biliardo.

snoop |snōōp| *vi:* **to ~ on sb** spiare qn; **to ~ around** curiosare.

snooper |snōō'pûr| *n* ficcanaso *m/f*.

snooty |snōō'tē| *a* borioso(a), snob *inv*.

snooze |snōōz| *n* sonnellino, pisolino ♦ *vi* fare un sonnellino.

snore |snôr| *vi* russare.

snoring |snôr'ing| *n* russare *m*.

snorkel |snôr'kəl| *n* (*of swimmer*) respiratore *m* a tubo.

snort |snôrt| *n* sbuffo ♦ *vi* sbuffare ♦ *vt* (*drugs slang*) sniffare.

snotty |snât'ē| *a* moccioso(a).

snout |snout| *n* muso.

snow |snō| *n* neve *f* ♦ *vi* nevicare ♦ *vt:* **to be ~ed under with work** essere sommerso di lavoro.

snowball |snō'bôl| *n* palla di neve.

snowbound [snō'bound] *a* bloccato(a) dalla neve.

snowcapped [snō'kapt] *a* (*mountain*) con la cima coperta di neve; (*peak*) coperto(a) di neve.

snowdrift [snō'drift] *n* cumulo di neve (*ammucchiato dal vento*).

snowdrop [snō'dråp] *n* bucaneve *m inv*.

snowfall [snō'fól] *n* nevicata.

snowflake [snō'flāk] *n* fiocco di neve.

snowman [snō'man] *n* pupazzo di neve.

snowmobile [snō'mōbēl] *n* gatto delle nevi.

snowplow, (*Brit*) **snowplough** [snō'plou] *n* spazzaneve *m inv*.

snowshoe [snō'shōō] *n* racchetta da neve.

snowstorm [snō'stórm] *n* tormenta.

snowy [snō'ē] *a* nevoso(a).

SNP *n abbr* (*Brit* POL) = *Scottish National Party*.

snub [snub] *vt* snobbare ♦ *n* offesa, affronto.

snub-nosed [snub'nōzd] *a* dal naso camuso.

snuff [snuf] *n* tabacco da fiuto ♦ *vt* (*also: ~ out*: *candle*) spegnere.

snug [snug] *a* comodo(a); (*room, house*) accogliente, comodo(a); **it's a ~ fit** è attillato.

snuggle [snug'əl] *vi*: **to ~ down in bed** accovacciarsi a letto; **to ~ up to sb** stringersi a qn.

snugly [snug'lē] *ad* comodamente; **it fits ~** (*object in pocket etc*) entra giusto giusto; (*garment*) sta ben attillato.

SO *abbr* (BANKING) = **standing order.**

so [sō] *ad* (*degree*) così, tanto; (*manner: thus*) così, in questo modo ♦ *cj* perciò; **~ as to do** in modo da *or* così da fare; **~ that** (*purpose*) affinché + *sub*; (*result*) così che; **~ that's the reason!** allora è questo il motivo!, ecco perché!; **~ do I, ~ am I** *etc* anch'io *etc*; **~ it is!, ~ it does!** davvero!; **if ~** se è così; **I hope ~** spero di sì; **10 or ~** circa 10; **quite ~!** esattamente!; **even ~** comunque; **~ far** fin qui, finora; (*in past*) fino ad allora; **~ long!** arrivederci!; **~ many** tanti(e); **~ much** *ad* tanto ♦ *det* tanto(a); **~ to speak** per così dire; **~ (what)?** (*col*) e allora?, e con questo?

soak [sōk] *vt* inzuppare; (*clothes*) mettere a mollo ♦ *vi* inzupparsi; (*clothes*) essere a mollo; **to be ~ed through** essere fradicio.

soak in *vi* penetrare.

soak up *vt* assorbire.

soaking [sō'king] *a* (*also: ~ wet*) fradicio(a).

so-and-so [sō'ənsō] *n* (*somebody*) un tale; **Mr/Mrs ~** signor/signora tal dei tali.

soap [sōp] *n* sapone *m*.

soapflakes [sōp'flāks] *npl* sapone *m* in scaglie.

soap opera *n* soap opera *f inv*.

soap powder *n* detersivo.

soapsuds [sōp'sudz] *npl* saponata.

soapy [sō'pē] *a* insaponato(a).

soar [sór] *vi* volare in alto; (*price, morale, spi-*

rits) salire alle stelle.

sob [sâb] *n* singhiozzo ♦ *vi* singhiozzare.

s.o.b. *n abbr* (US *col!*: = *son of a bitch*) figlio di puttana (*!*).

sober [sō'bûr] *a* non ubriaco(a); (*sedate*) serio(a); (*moderate*) moderato(a); (*color, style*) sobrio(a).

sober up *vt* far passare la sbornia a ♦ *vi* farsi passare la sbornia.

sobriety [səbrī'ətē] *n* (*not being drunk*) sobrietà; (*seriousness, sedateness*) sobrietà, pacatezza.

Soc. *abbr* (= *society*) Soc.

so-called [sō'kóld] *a* cosiddetto(a).

soccer [sâk'ûr] *n* calcio.

soccer player *n* calciatore *m*.

sociable [sō'shəbəl] *a* socievole.

social [sō'shəl] *a* sociale ♦ *n* festa, serata.

social climber *n* arrampicatore/trice sociale, arrivista *m/f*.

social club *n* club *m inv* sociale.

Social Democrat *n* socialdemocratico/a.

socialism [sō'shəlizəm] *n* socialismo.

socialist [sō'shəlist] *a, n* socialista (*m/f*).

socialite [sō'shəlīt] *n* persona in vista nel bel mondo.

socialize [sō'shəlīz] *vi* frequentare la gente; farsi degli amici; **to ~ with** socializzare con.

socially [sō'shəlē] *ad* socialmente, in società.

social science *n* scienze *fpl* sociali.

social security *n* previdenza sociale; **Department of S~ S~ (DSS)** (*Brit*) ≈ Istituto di Previdenza Sociale.

social welfare *n* assistenza sociale.

social work *n* servizio sociale.

social worker *n* assistente *m/f* sociale.

society [səsī'ətē] *n* società *f inv*; (*club*) società, associazione *f*; (*also*: **high ~**) alta società ♦ *cpd* (*party, column*) mondano(a).

socioeconomic [sōsēōēkənâm'ik] *a* socioeconomico(a).

sociological [sōsēəlåj'ikəl] *a* sociologico(a).

sociologist [sōsēâl'əjist] *n* sociologo/a.

sociology [sōsēâl'əjē] *n* sociologia.

sock [sâk] *n* calzino ♦ *vt* (*hit*) dare un pugno a; **to pull one's ~s up** (*fig*) darsi una regolata.

socket [sâk'it] *n* cavità *f inv*; (*of eye*) orbita; (ELEC: *also*: **wall ~**) presa di corrente; (: *for light bulb*) portalampada *m inv*.

sod [sâd] *n* (*of earth*) zolla erbosa; (*Brit col!*) bastardo/a (*!*).

soda [sō'də] *n* (CHEM) soda; (*also*: **~ water**) acqua di seltz; (US: *also*: **~ pop**) gassosa.

sodden [sâd'ən] *a* fradicio(a).

sodium [sō'dēəm] *n* sodio.

sodium chloride [sō'dēəm klôr'īd] *n* cloruro di sodio.

sofa [sō'fə] *n* sofà *m inv*.

Sofia [sōfē'ə] *n* Sofia.

soft [sôft] *a* (*not rough*) morbido(a); (*not*

hard) soffice; (*not loud*) sommesso(a); (*kind*) gentile; (: *look, smile*) dolce; (*not strict*) indulgente; (*weak*) debole; (*stupid*) stupido(a).

soft-boiled [sôft'boild'] *a* (*egg*) alla coque.

soft drink *n* analcolico.

soft drugs *npl* droghe *fpl* leggere.

soften [sôf'ən] *vt* ammorbidire; addolcire; attenuare ♦ *vi* ammorbidirsi; addolcirsi; attenuarsi.

softener [sôf'ənûr] *n* ammorbidente *m*.

softhearted [sôft'hârt'id] *a* sensibile.

softly [sôft'lē] *ad* dolcemente; morbidamente.

softness [sôft'nis] *n* dolcezza; morbidezza.

soft sell *n* persuasione *f* all'acquisto.

soft toy *n* giocattolo di peluche.

software [sôft'wär] *n* software *m*.

software package *n* pacchetto di software.

soft water *n* acqua non calcarea.

soggy [sâg'ē] *a* inzuppato(a).

soil [soil] *n* (*earth*) terreno, suolo ♦ *vt* sporcare; (*fig*) macchiare.

soiled [soild] *a* sporco(a), sudicio(a).

sojourn [sō'jûrn] *n* (*formal*) soggiorno.

solace [sâl'is] *n* consolazione *f*.

solar [sō'lûr] *a* solare.

solarium, *pl* **solaria** [sōlär'ēəm, sōlär'ēə] *n* solarium *m inv*.

solar plexus [sō'lûr plek'səs] *n* (*ANAT*) plesso solare.

sold [sōld] *pt, pp of* **sell**.

solder [sâd'ûr] *vt* saldare ♦ *n* saldatura.

soldier [sōl'jûr] *n* soldato, militare *m*; **toy ~** soldatino.

sold out *a* (*COMM*) esaurito(a).

sole [sōl] *n* (*of foot*) pianta (del piede); (*of shoe*) suola; (*fish*: *pl inv*) sogliola ♦ *a* solo(a), unico(a); (*exclusive*) esclusivo(a).

solely [sōl'lē] *ad* solamente, unicamente; **I will hold you ~ responsible** la considererò il solo responsabile.

solemn [sâl'əm] *a* solenne; grave; serio(a).

sole trader *n* (*COMM*) commerciante *m* in proprio.

solicit [səlis'it] *vt* (*request*) richiedere, sollecitare ♦ *vi* (*prostitute*) adescare i passanti.

solicitor [səlis'itûr] *n* (*Brit: for wills etc*) ≈ notaio; (*in court*) ≈ avvocato.

solid [sâl'id] *a* (*not hollow*) pieno(a); (*strong, sound, reliable, not liquid*) solido(a); (*meal*) sostanzioso(a); (*line*) ininterrotto(a); (*vote*) unanime ♦ *n* solido; **to be on ~ ground** essere su terraferma; (*fig*) muoversi su terreno sicuro; **we waited 2 ~ hours** abbiamo aspettato due ore buone.

solidarity [sâlidar'itē] *n* solidarietà.

solidify [səlid'əfī] *vi* solidificarsi ♦ *vt* solidificare.

solidity [səlid'itē] *n* solidità.

solid-state [sâl'idstāt'] *a* (*ELEC*) a transistor.

soliloquy [səlil'əkwē] *n* soliloquio.

solitaire [sâl'itär] *n* (*game, gem*) solitario.

solitary [sâl'itärē] *a* solitario(a).

solitary confinement *n* (*LAW*): **to be in ~** essere in cella d'isolamento.

solitude [sâl'ətōōd] *n* solitudine *f*.

solo [sō'lō] *n* (*MUS*) assolo.

soloist [sō'lōist] *n* solista *m/f*.

Solomon Islands [sâl'əmən ī'ləndz] *n*: **the ~** le isole Salomone.

solstice [sâl'stis] *n* solstizio.

soluble [sâl'yəbəl] *a* solubile.

solution [səlōō'shən] *n* soluzione *f*.

solve [sâlv] *vt* risolvere.

solvency [sâl'vənsē] *n* (*COMM*) solvenza, solvibilità.

solvent [sâl'vənt] *a* (*COMM*) solvibile ♦ *n* (*CHEM*) solvente *m*.

solvent abuse *n* abuso di solventi.

Som. *abbr* (*Brit*) = *Somerset*.

Somali [sōmä'lē] *a* somalo(a).

Somalia [sōmä'lēə] *n* Somalia.

somber, (*Brit*) **sombre** [sâm'bûr] *a* scuro(a); (*mood, person*) triste.

some [sum] *a* (*a few*) alcuni(e), qualche; (*certain*) certi(e); (*a certain number or amount*) *see phrases below*; (*unspecified*) un(a) ... qualunque ♦ *pronoun* alcuni(e); un po' ♦ *ad*: **~ 10 people** circa 10 persone; **~ children came** sono venuti dei bambini; **have ~ tea/ice-cream/water** prendi un po' di tè/gelato/acqua; **there's ~ milk in the fridge** c'è un po' di latte nel frigo; **~ people say that ...** certa gente dice che ...; **I have ~ books** ho qualche libro o alcuni libri; **~ (of it) was left** ne è rimasto un po'; **could I have ~ of that cheese?** potrei avere un po' di quel formaggio?; **I've got ~** (*i.e. books etc*) ne ho alcuni; (*i.e. milk, money etc*) ne ho un po'; **after ~ time** dopo un po'; **at ~ length** a lungo; **in ~ form or other** in una forma o nell'altra.

somebody [sum'bâdē] *pronoun* qualcuno; **~ or other** qualcuno.

someday [sum'dā] *ad* uno di questi giorni, un giorno o l'altro.

somehow [sum'hou] *ad* in un modo o nell'altro, in qualche modo; (*for some reason*) per qualche ragione.

someone [sum'wun] *pronoun* = **somebody**.

someplace [sum'plās] *ad* (*US*) = **somewhere**.

somersault [sum'ûrsôlt] *n* capriola; (*in air*) salto mortale ♦ *vi* fare una capriola (*or* un salto mortale); (*car*) cappottare.

something [sum'thing] *pronoun* qualcosa; **~ interesting** qualcosa di interessante; **~ to do** qualcosa da fare; **~ like me** mi assomiglia un po'; **it's ~ of a problem** è un bel problema.

sometime [sum'tīm] *ad* (*in future*) una volta o l'altra; (*in past*): **~ last month** durante il mese scorso; **I'll finish it ~** lo finirò prima o poi.

sometimes [sum'tīmz] *ad* qualche volta.

somewhat [sum'wut] *ad* piuttosto.

somewhere [sum'wär] *ad* in *or* da qualche parte; ~ **else** da qualche altra parte.

son [sun] *n* figlio.

sonar [sō'när] *n* sonar *m*.

sonata [sənät'ə] *n* sonata.

song [sông] *n* canzone *f*.

songbook [sông'bŏŏk] *n* canzoniere *m*.

songwriter [sông'rī'tûr] *n* compositore/trice di canzoni.

sonic [sân'ik] *a* (*boom*) sonico(a).

son-in-law [sun'inlô] *n* genero.

sonnet [sân'it] *n* sonetto.

sonny [sun'ē] *n* (*col*) ragazzo mio.

soon [sōōn] *ad* presto, fra poco; (*early*) presto; ~ **afterwards** poco dopo; **very/quite** ~ molto/abbastanza presto; **as** ~ **as possible** prima possibile; **I'll do it as** ~ **as I can** lo farò appena posso; **how** ~ **can you be ready?** fra quanto tempo sarà pronto?; **see you** ~! a presto!

sooner [sōō'nûr] *ad* (*time*) prima; (*preference*): **I would** ~ **do** preferirei fare; ~ **or later** prima o poi; **no** ~ **said than done** detto fatto; **the** ~ **the better** prima è meglio è; **no** ~ **had we left than** ... eravamo appena partiti, quando ....

soot [sŏŏt] *n* fuliggine *f*.

soothe [sōōth] *vt* calmare.

soothing [sōō'thing] *a* (*ointment etc*) calmante; (*tone, words etc*) rassicurante.

SOP *n abbr* = standard operating procedure.

sop [sâp] *n*: **that's only a** ~ è soltanto un contentino.

sophisticated [səfis'tikātid] *a* sofisticato(a); raffinato(a); (*movie, mind*) sottile.

sophistication [səfis'tikā'shən] *n* raffinatezza; (*of machine*) complessità; (*of argument etc*) sottigliezza.

sophomore [sâf'əmôr] *n* (*US*) studente/essa del secondo anno.

soporific [sâpərif'ik] *a* soporifero(a).

sopping [sâp'ing] *a* (*also*: ~ **wet**) bagnato(a) fradicio(a).

soprano [səpran'ō] *n* (*voice*) soprano *m*; (*singer*) soprano *m/f*.

sorbet [sôrbā'] *n* sorbetto.

sorcerer [sôr'sərûr] *n* stregone *m*, mago.

sordid [sôr'did] *a* sordido(a).

sore [sôr] *a* (*painful*) dolorante; (*col*: *offended*) offeso(a) ♦ *n* piaga; **my eyes are** ~, **I have** ~ **eyes** mi fanno male gli occhi; ~ **throat** mal *m* di gola; **it's a** ~ **point** (*fig*) è un punto delicato.

sorely [sôr'lē] *ad* (*tempted*) fortemente.

sorrel [sôr'əl] *n* acetosa.

sorrow [sâr'ō] *n* dolore *m*.

sorrowful [sâr'ōfəl] *a* triste.

sorry [sâr'ē] *a* spiacente; (*condition, excuse*)

misero(a), pietoso(a); (*sight, failure*) triste; ~! scusa! (*or* scusi! *or* scusate!); **to feel** ~ **for sb** rincrescersi per qn; **I'm** ~ **to hear that** ... mi dispiace (sentire) che ...; **to be** ~ **about sth** essere dispiaciuto *or* spiacente di qc.

sort [sôrt] *n* specie *f*, genere *m*; (*make: of coffee, car etc*) tipo ♦ *vt* (*also*: ~ **out**: *papers*) classificare; ordinare; (: *letters etc*) smistare; (: *problems*) risolvere; (*COMPUT*) ordinare; **what** ~ **of car?** che tipo di macchina?; **I'll do nothing of the** ~! nemmeno per sogno!; **it's** ~ **of awkward** (*col*) è piuttosto difficile.

sortie [sôr'tē] *n* sortita.

sorting office [sôr'ting ôf'is] *n* ufficio *m* smistamento *inv*.

SOS [es'ō'es'] *n abbr* (= save our souls) S.O.S. *m inv*.

so-so [sō'sō'] *ad* così così.

soufflé [sōōflā'] *n* soufflé *m inv*.

sought [sôt] *pt, pp of* **seek.**

sought-after [sôt'af'tûr] *a* richiesto(a).

soul [sōl] *n* anima; **the poor** ~ **had nowhere to sleep** il poveraccio non aveva dove dormire; **I didn't see a** ~ non ho visto anima viva.

soul-destroying [sōl'distroiing] *a* demoralizzante.

soulful [sōl'fəl] *a* pieno(a) di sentimento.

soulless [sōl'lis] *a* senz'anima, inumano(a).

soul mate *n* anima gemella.

soul-searching [sōl'sûrching] *n*: **after much** ~ dopo un profondo esame di coscienza.

sound [sound] *a* (*healthy*) sano(a); (*safe, not damaged*) solido(a), in buono stato; (*reliable, not superficial*) solido(a); (*sensible*) giudizioso(a), di buon senso; (*valid: argument, policy, claim*) valido(a) ♦ *ad*: ~ **asleep** profondamente addormentato ♦ *n* (*noise*) suono; rumore *m*; (*GEO*) stretto ♦ *vt* (*alarm*) suonare; (*also*: ~ **out**: *opinions*) sondare ♦ *vi* suonare; (*fig: seem*) sembrare; **to be of** ~ **mind** essere sano di mente; **I don't like the** ~ **of it** (*fig: of movie etc*) non mi dice niente; (: *of news*) è preoccupante; **it** ~**s as if** ... ho l'impressione che ...; **it** ~**s like French** somiglia al francese; **that** ~**s like them arriving** mi sembra di sentirli arrivare.

sound off *vi* (*col*): **to** ~ **off (about)** (*give one's opinions*) fare dei grandi discorsi (su).

sound barrier *n* muro del suono.

sound effects *npl* effetti *mpl* sonori.

sound engineer *n* tecnico del suono.

sounding [soun'ding] *n* (*NAUT etc*) scandagliamento.

sounding board *n* (*MUS*) cassa di risonanza; (*fig*): **to use sb as a** ~ **for one's ideas** provare le proprie idee su qn.

soundly [sound'lē] *ad* (*sleep*) profondamente; (*beat*) duramente.

soundproof [sound'prōōf] *vt* insonorizzare,

isolare acusticamente ♦ *a* insonorizzato(a), isolato(a) acusticamente.

sound track *n (of movie)* colonna sonora.

sound wave *n (PHYSICS)* onda sonora.

soup [sōōp] *n* minestra; *(clear)* brodo; *(thick)* zuppa; **in the** ~ *(fig)* nei guai.

soup course *n* minestra.

soup kitchen *n* mensa per i poveri.

soup plate *n* piatto fondo.

soupspoon [sōōp'spōōn] *n* cucchiaio da minestra.

sour [sou'ûr] *a* aspro(a); *(fruit)* acerbo(a); *(milk)* acido(a), fermentato(a); *(fig)* acido(a); **to go** *or* **turn** ~ *(milk, wine)* inacidirsi; *(fig: relationship, plans)* guastarsi; **it's** ~ **grapes** *(fig)* è soltanto invidia.

source [sôrs] *n* fonte *f*, sorgente *f*; *(fig)* fonte; **I have it from a reliable** ~ **that** ... ho saputo da fonte sicura che ....

south [south] *n* sud *m*, meridione *m*, mezzogiorno ♦ *a* del sud, sud *inv*, meridionale ♦ *ad* verso sud; **(to the)** ~ **of** a sud di; **the S~ of France** il sud della Francia; **to travel** ~ viaggiare verso sud.

South Africa *n* Sudafrica *m*.

South African *a, n* sudafricano(a).

South America *n* Sudamerica *m*, America del sud.

South American *a, n* sudamericano(a).

southbound [south'bound'] *a (gen)* diretto(a) a sud; *(lane)* sud *inv*.

southeast [southēst'] *n* sud-est *m*.

Southeast Asia *n* Asia sudorientale.

southerly [suth'ûrlē] *a* del sud.

southern [suth'ûrn] *a* del sud, meridionale; *(wall)* esposto(a) a sud; **the** ~ **hemisphere** l'emisfero australe.

South Pole *n* Polo Sud.

South Sea Islands *npl:* **the** ~ le isole dei Mari del Sud.

South Seas *npl:* **the** ~ i Mari del Sud.

southward(s) [south'wûrd(z)] *ad* verso sud.

southwest [south'west] *n* sud-ovest *m*.

souvenir [sōōvənēr'] *n* ricordo, souvenir *m inv*.

sovereign [sâv'rin] *a, n* sovrano(a).

sovereignty [sâv'rəntē] *n* sovranità.

soviet [sō'vēit] *a* sovietico(a).

Soviet Union *n:* **the** ~ l'Unione *f* Sovietica.

sow *n* [sou] scrofa ♦ *vt* [sō] *(pt* ~**ed,** *pp* **sown** [sōd, sōn]) seminare.

soy [soi] *n* soia.

soya [soi'ə] *etc (Brit)* = **soy** *etc*.

soybean [soi'bēn] *n* seme *m* di soia.

soy sauce *n* salsa di soia.

spa [spâ] *n (resort)* stazione *f* termale; *(US: also:* **health** ~) centro di cure estetiche.

space [spās] *n* spazio; *(room)* posto; spazio; *(length of time)* intervallo ♦ *cpd* spaziale ♦ *vt (also:* ~ **out)** distanziare; **in a confined** ~ in un luogo chiuso; **to clear a** ~ **for sth** fare po-

sto per qc; **in a short** ~ **of time** in breve tempo; **(with)in the** ~ **of an hour/three generations** nell'arco di un'ora/di tre generazioni.

space bar *n (on typewriter)* barra spaziatrice.

spacecraft [spās'kraft] *n (pl inv)* veicolo spaziale.

spaceman [spās'man] *n* astronauta *m*, cosmonauta *m*.

spaceship [spās'ship] *n* astronave *f*, navicella spaziale.

space shuttle *n* shuttle *m inv*.

spacesuit [spās'sōōt] *n* tuta spaziale.

spacewoman [spās'wōōmən] *n* astronauta *f*, cosmonauta *f*.

spacing [spā'sing] *n* spaziatura; **single/double** ~ *(TYP etc)* spaziatura singola/doppia.

spacious [spā'shəs] *a* spazioso(a), ampio(a).

spade [spād] *n (tool)* vanga; pala; *(child's)* paletta; ~**s** *npl (CARDS)* picche *fpl*.

spadework [spād'wûrk] *n (fig)* duro lavoro preparatorio.

spaghetti [spəget'ē] *n* spaghetti *mpl*.

Spain [spān] *n* Spagna.

span [span] *pt of* **spin** ♦ *n (of bird, plane)* apertura alare; *(of arch)* campata; *(in time)* periodo; durata ♦ *vt* attraversare; *(fig)* abbracciare.

Spaniard [span'yûrd] *n* spagnolo/a.

spaniel [span'yəl] *n* spaniel *m inv*.

Spanish [span'ish] *a* spagnolo(a) ♦ *n (LING)* spagnolo; **the** ~ *npl* gli Spagnoli; ~ **omelet** frittata di cipolle, pomodori e peperoni.

spank [spangk] *vt* sculacciare.

spanner [span'ûr] *n (Brit)* chiave *f* inglese.

spar [spâr] *n* asta, palo ♦ *vi (BOXING)* allenarsi.

spare [spär] *a* di riserva, di scorta; *(surplus)* in più, d'avanzo ♦ *n (part)* pezzo di ricambio ♦ *vt (do without)* fare a meno di; *(afford to give)* concedere; *(refrain from hurting, using)* risparmiare; **to** ~ *(surplus)* d'avanzo; **to** ~ **no expense** non badare a spese; **can you** ~ **the time?** ha tempo?; **I've a few minutes to** ~ ho un attimino di tempo; **there is no time to** ~ non c'è tempo da perdere; **can you** ~ **(me) $10?** puoi prestarmi 10 dollari?

spare part *n* pezzo di ricambio.

spare room *n* stanza degli ospiti.

spare time *n* tempo libero.

spare tire, *(Brit)* **spare tyre** *n (AUT)* gomma di scorta.

spare wheel *n (AUT)* ruota di scorta.

sparing [spär'ing] *a (amount)* scarso(a); *(use)* parsimonioso(a); **to be** ~ **with** essere avaro(a) di..

sparingly [spär'inglē] *ad* moderatamente.

spark [spârk] *n* scintilla.

spark plug [spârk' plug] *n* candela.

sparkle [spâr'kəl] *n* scintillio, sfavillio ♦ *vi*

scintillare, sfavillare; (*bubble*) spumeggiare, frizzare.

sparkling |spár'kling| *a* scintillante, sfavillante; (*wine*) spumante.

sparrow |spar'ō| *n* passero.

sparse |spárs| *a* sparso(a), rado(a).

spartan |spár'tən| *a* (*fig*) spartano(a).

spasm |spaz'əm| *n* (*MED*) spasmo; (*fig*) accesso, attacco.

spasmodic |spazmád'ik| *a* spasmodico(a); (*fig*) intermittente.

spastic |spas'tik| *n* spastico/a.

spat |spat| *pt, pp of* **spit** ♦ *n* (*US*) battibecco.

spate |spāt| *n* (*fig*): ~ **of** diluvio *or* fiume *m* di; **in** ~ (*river*) in piena.

spatial |spā'shəl| *a* spaziale.

spatter |spat'ûr| *vt, vi* schizzare.

spatula |spach'ələ| *n* spatola.

spawn |spôn| *vt* deporre; (*pej*) produrre ♦ *vi* deporre le uova ♦ *n* uova *fpl*.

SPCA *n abbr* (*US*: = *Society for the Prevention of Cruelty to Animals*) ≈ E.N.P.A. *m* (= *Ente Nazionale per la Protezione degli Animali*).

SPCC *n abbr* (*US*) = *Society for the Prevention of Cruelty to Children*.

speak, *pt* **spoke,** *pp* **spoken** |spēk, spōk, spōk'ən| *vt* (*language*) parlare; (*truth*) dire ♦ *vi* parlare; **to** ~ **to sb/of** *or* **about sth** parlare a qn/di qc; ~ **up!** parli più forte!; **to** ~ **at a conference/in a debate** partecipare ad una conferenza/ad un dibattito; **~ing!** (*on telephone*) sono io!; **to** ~ **one's mind** dire quello che si pensa; **he has no money to** ~ **of** non si può proprio dire che sia ricco.

speak for *vt fus:* **to** ~ **for sb** parlare a nome di qn; **that picture is already spoken for** (*in store*) quel quadro è già stato venduto.

speaker |spē'kûr| *n* (*in public*) oratore/trice; (*also:* **loud~**) altoparlante *m*; (*POL*): **the S~** *il presidente dei Rappresentanti* (*US*) *or della Camera dei Comuni* (*Brit*); **are you a Welsh** ~? parla gallese?

speaking |spē'king| *a* parlante; **Italian-~ people** persone che parlano italiano; **to be on** ~ **terms** parlarsi.

spear |spi'ûr| *n* lancia.

spearhead |spē'r'hed| *n* punta di lancia; (*MIL*) reparto d'assalto ♦ *vt* (*attack etc*) condurre.

spearmint |spē'r'mint| *n* (*BOT etc*) menta verde.

special |spesh'əl| *a* speciale ♦ *n* (*train*) treno supplementare; **"on** ~**"** (*COMM*) "in offerta speciale"; **nothing** ~ niente di speciale; **take** ~ **care** siate particolarmente prudenti.

special agent *n* agente *m* segreto.

special correspondent *n* inviato speciale.

special delivery *n* (*MAIL*): **by** ~ per espresso.

specialist |spesh'əlist| *n* specialista *m/f*; **a heart** ~ (*MED*) un cardiologo.

speciality |speshēal'ətē| *n* (*Brit*) = **specialty**.

specialize |spesh'əlīz| *vi*: **to** ~ **(in)** specializzarsi (in).

specially |spesh'əlē| *ad* specialmente, particolarmente.

special offer *n* (*COMM*) offerta speciale.

specialty |spesh'əltē| *n* (*esp US*) specialità *f inv*.

species |spē'shēz| *n* (*pl inv*) specie *f inv*.

specific |spisif'ik| *a* specifico(a); preciso(a); **to be** ~ **to** avere un legame specifico con.

specifically |spisif'iklē| *ad* (*explicitly*: *state, warn*) chiaramente, esplicitamente; (*especially*: *design, intend*) appositamente.

specification |spesəfəkā'shən| *n* specificazione *f*; **~s** *npl* (*of car, machine*) dati *mpl* caratteristici; (*for building*) dettagli *mpl*.

specify |spes'əfī| *vt* specificare, precisare; **unless otherwise specified** salvo indicazioni contrarie.

specimen |spes'əmən| *n* esemplare *m*, modello; (*MED*) campione *m*.

specimen copy *n* campione *m*.

specimen signature *n* firma depositata.

speck |spek| *n* puntino, macchiolina; (*particle*) granello.

speckled |spek'əld| *a* macchiettato(a).

specs |speks| *npl* (*col*) occhiali *mpl*.

spectacle |spek'təkəl| *n* spettacolo; *see also* **spectacles**.

spectacles |spek'təkəlz| *npl* (*Brit*) occhiali *mpl*.

spectacular |spektak'yəlûr| *a* spettacolare ♦ *n* (*CINEMA etc*) film *m inv etc* spettacolare.

spectator |spek'tātûr| *n* spettatore/trice.

specter |spek'tûr| *n* (*US*) spettro.

spectra |spek'trə| *npl of* **spectrum**.

spectre |spek'tûr| *n* (*Brit*) = **specter**.

spectrum, *pl* **spectra** |spek'trəm, spek'trə| *n* spettro; (*fig*) gamma.

speculate |spek'yəlāt| *vi* speculare; (*try to guess*): **to** ~ **about** fare ipotesi su.

speculation |spekyəlā'shən| *n* speculazione *f*; congetture *fpl*.

speculative |spek'yəlātiv| *a* speculativo(a).

speculator |spek'yəlātûr| *n* speculatore/trice.

sped |sped| *pt, pp of* **speed**.

speech |spēch| *n* (*faculty*) parola; (*talk*) discorso; (*manner of speaking*) parlata; (*language*) linguaggio; (*enunciation*) elocuzione *f*.

speech day *n* (*Brit SCOL*) giorno della premiazione.

speech impediment *n* difetto di pronuncia.

speechless |spēch'lis| *a* ammutolito(a), muto(a).

speech therapy *n* cura dei disturbi del linguaggio.

speed |spēd| *n* velocità *f inv*; (*promptness*) prontezza; (*AUT: gear*) marcia ♦ *vi* (*pt, pp* **sped** |sped|): **to** ~ **along** procedere velocemente; **the years sped by** gli anni sono volati; (*AUT: exceed ~ limit*) andare a velocità eccessiva; **at full** *or* **top** ~ a tutta velocità; **at a ~ of 70 km/h** a una velocità di 70 km l'ora; **shorthand/typing** ~s numero di parole al minuto in stenografia/dattilografia; **five-~ transmission** cambio a cinque marce.

speed up, *pt, pp* ~**ed up** *vi, vt* accelerare.

speedboat [spēd'bōt] *n* motoscafo; fuoribordo *m inv*.

speedily [spē'dilē] *ad* velocemente; prontamente.

speeding [spē'ding] *n* (*AUT*) eccesso di velocità.

speed limit *n* limite *m* di velocità.

speedometer [spēdăm'itûr] *n* tachimetro.

speed trap *n* (*AUT*) *tratto di strada sul quale la polizia controlla la velocità dei veicoli.*

speedway [spēd'wā] *n* (*SPORT*) pista per motociclismo.

speedy [spē'dē] *a* veloce, rapido(a); (*reply*) pronto(a).

speleologist [spēlēăl'əjist] *n* speleologo/a.

spell [spel] *n* (*also*: **magic ~**) incantesimo; (*period of time*) (*breve*) periodo ♦ *vt* (*pt, pp* ~**ed** *or* **spelt**) (*in writing*) scrivere (lettera per lettera); (*aloud*) dire lettera per lettera; (*fig*) significare; **to cast a ~ on sb** fare un incantesimo a qn; **he can't ~** fa errori di ortografia; **how do you ~ your name?** come si scrive il suo nome?; **can you ~ it for me?** me lo può dettare lettera per lettera?

spellbound [spel'bound] *a* incantato(a), affascinato(a).

spelling [spel'ing] *n* ortografia.

spelt [spelt] *pt, pp of* **spell**.

spelunker [spēlung'kûr] *n* speleologo/a.

spend, *pt, pp* **spent** [spend, spent] *vt* (*money*) spendere; (*time, life*) passare; **to ~ time/ money/effort on sth** dedicare tempo/soldi/ energie a qc.

spending [spen'ding] *n*: **government ~** spesa pubblica.

spending money *n* denaro per le piccole spese.

spending power *n* potere *m* d'acquisto.

spendthrift [spend'thrift] *n* spendaccione/a.

spent [spent] *pt, pp of* **spend** ♦ *a* (*patience*) esaurito(a); (*cartridge, bullets*) usato(a).

sperm [spûrm] *n* sperma *m*.

sperm whale *n* capodoglio.

spew [spyōō] *vt* vomitare.

sphere [sfēr] *n* sfera.

spherical [sfär'ikəl] *a* sferico(a).

sphinx [sfingks] *n* sfinge *f*.

spice [spīs] *n* spezia ♦ *vt* aromatizzare.

spick-and-span [spik'ənspan'] *a* impeccabile.

spicy [spī'sē] *a* piccante.

spider [spī'dûr] *n* ragno; ~**'s web** ragnatela.

spiel [spēl] *n* (*col*) tiritera.

spike [spīk] *n* punta; ~**s** *npl* (*SPORT*) scarpe *fpl* chiodate.

spike heel *n* (*US*) tacco a spillo.

spiky [spī'kē] *a* (*bush, branch*) spinoso(a); (*animal*) ricoperto(a) di aculei.

spill, *pt, pp* ~**ed** *or* **spilt** [spil, -d, -t] *vt* versare, rovesciare ♦ *vi* versarsi, rovesciarsi; **to ~ the beans** (*col*) vuotare il sacco.

spill out *vi* riversarsi fuori.

spill over *vi*: **to ~ over (into)** (*liquid*) versarsi (in); (*crowd*) riversarsi (in).

spin [spin] *n* (*revolution of wheel*) rotazione *f*; (*AVIAT*) avvitamento; (*trip in car*) giretto ♦ *vb* (*pt* **spun, span**, *pp* **spun** [spun, span]) *vt* (*wool etc*) filare; (*wheel*) far girare; (*Brit: clothes*) mettere nella centrifuga ♦ *vi* girare; **to ~ a yarn** raccontare una storia.

spin out *vt* far durare.

spinach [spin'ich] *n* spinacio; (*as food*) spinaci *mpl*.

spinal [spī'nəl] *a* spinale.

spinal column *n* colonna vertebrale, spina dorsale.

spinal cord *n* midollo spinale.

spindly [spind'lē] *a* lungo(a) e sottile, filiforme.

spin-dry [spindrī'] *vt* asciugare con la centrifuga.

spin-dryer [spindrī'ûr] *n* (*Brit*) centrifuga.

spine [spīn] *n* spina dorsale; (*thorn*) spina.

spine-chilling [spīn'chiling] *a* agghiacciante.

spineless [spīn'lis] *a* invertebrato(a), senza spina dorsale; (*fig*) smidollato(a).

spinner [spin'ûr] *n* (*of thread*) tessitore/trice.

spinning [spin'ing] *n* filatura.

spinning top *n* trottola.

spinning wheel *n* filatoio.

spin-off [spin'ôf] *n* applicazione *f* secondaria.

spinster [spin'stûr] *n* nubile *f*; zitella.

spiral [spī'rəl] *n* spirale *f* ♦ *a* a spirale ♦ *vi* (*prices*) salire vertiginosamente; **the inflationary ~** la spirale dell'inflazione.

spiral staircase *n* scala a chiocciola.

spire [spī'ûr] *n* guglia.

spirit [spir'it] *n* (*soul*) spirito, anima; (*ghost*) spirito, fantasma *m*; (*mood*) stato d'animo, umore *m*; (*courage*) coraggio; ~**s** *npl* (*drink*) alcolici *mpl*; **in good** ~**s** di buon umore; **in low** ~**s** triste, abbattuto(a); **community** ~, **public** ~ senso civico.

spirit duplicator *n* duplicatore *m* a spirito.

spirited [spir'itid] *a* vivace, vigoroso(a); (*horse*) focoso(a).

spirit level *n* livella a bolla (d'aria).

spiritual [spir'ichōōəl] *a* spirituale ♦ *n* (*also*: **Negro ~**) spiritual *m inv*.

spiritualism [spir'ichōōəlizəm] *n* spiritismo.

spit [spit] *n* (*for roasting*) spiedo; (*spittle*) sputo; (*saliva*) saliva ♦ *vi* (*pt, pp* **spat**) sputare; (*fire, fat*) scoppiettare.

spite [spīt] *n* dispetto ♦ *vt* contrariare, far di-

spetto a; **in ~ of** nònostante, malgrado.
spiteful |spīt'fəl| a dispettoso(a); (tongue, re-mark) maligno(a), velenoso(a).
spitroast |spit'rōst| vt cuocere allo spiedo.
spitting |spit'ing| n: "**~ prohibited**" "vietato sputare" ♦ a: **to be the ~ image of sb** esse-re il ritratto vivente or sputato di qn.
spittle |spit'əl| n saliva; sputo.
splash |splash| n spruzzo; (sound) tonfo; (of color) schizzo ♦ vt spruzzare ♦ vi (also: ~ **about**) sguazzare; **to ~ paint on the floor** schizzare il pavimento di vernice.
splashdown |splash'doun| n ammaraggio.
splay |splā| a: **~ footed** che ha i piedi piatti.
spleen |splēn| n (ANAT) milza.
splendid |splen'did| a splendido(a), ma-gnifico(a).
splendor, (Brit) **splendour** |splen'dûr| n splendore m.
splice |splīs| vt (rope) impiombare; (wood) ca-lettare.
splint |splint| n (MED) stecca.
splinter |splin'tûr| n scheggia ♦ vi scheggiarsi.
splinter group n gruppo dissidente.
split |split| n spaccatura; (fig: division, quarrel) scissione f ♦ vb (pt, pp **split**) vt spaccare; (party) dividere; (work, profits) spartire, ripartire ♦ vi (divide) dividersi; **to do the ~s** fare la spaccata; **to ~ the differ-ence** dividersi la differenza.
  split up vi (couple) separarsi, rompere; (meeting) sciogliersi.
split-level |split'lev'əl| a (house) a piani sfalsa-ti.
split peas npl piselli mpl secchi spaccati.
split personality n doppia personalità.
split second n frazione f di secondo.
splitting |split'ing| a: **a ~ headache** un mal di testa da impazzire.
splutter |splut'ûr| vi = **sputter**.
spoil, pt, pp **~ed** or **spoilt** |spoil, spoild, spoilt| vt (damage) rovinare, guastare; (mar) sciu-pare; (child) viziare; (ballot paper) rendere nullo(a), invalidare; **to be ~ing for a fight** morire dalla voglia di litigare.
spoiler |spoi'lûr| n (AUT) spoiler m inv.
spoils |spoilz| npl bottino.
spoilsport |spoil'spôrt| n guastafeste m/f inv.
spoilt |spoilt| pt, pp of **spoil**.
spoke |spōk| pt of **speak** ♦ n raggio.
spoken |spō'kən| pp of **speak**.
spokesman |spōks'mən|, **spokeswoman** |spōks'wōōmən| n portavoce m/f inv.
sponge |spunj| n spugna; (CULIN: also: ~ **cake**) pan m di Spagna ♦ vt spugnare, pulire con una spugna ♦ vi: **to ~** scroccare a.
sponge bag n (Brit) nécessaire m inv.
sponge cake n pan m di Spagna.
sponger |spun'jûr| n (pej) parassita m/f, scroccone/a.
spongy |spun'jē| a spugnoso(a).

sponsor |spän'sûr| n (RADIO, TV, SPORT etc) sponsor m inv; (of enterprise, bill, for fund-raising) promotore/trice ♦ vt sponsorizzare; patrocinare; (POL: bill) presentare; **I ~ed him at 25¢ a mile** (in fund-raising race) ho offerto in beneficenza 25 centesimi per ogni miglio che fa.
sponsorship |spän'sûrship| n sponsorizzazione f; patrocinio.
spontaneity |späntənē'itē| n spontaneità.
spontaneous |späntā'nēəs| a spontaneo(a).
spooky |spōō'kē| a che fa accapponare la pelle.
spool |spōōl| n bobina.
spoon |spōōn| n cucchiaio.
spoon-feed |spōōn'fēd| vt nutrire con il cuc-chiaio; (fig) imboccare.
spoonful |spōōn'fool| n cucchiaiata.
sporadic |spôrad'ik| a sporadico(a).
sport |spôrt| n sport m inv; (person) persona di spirito; (amusement) divertimento ♦ vt sfoggiare; **indoor/outdoor ~s** sport mpl al chiuso/all'aria aperta; **to say sth in ~** dire qc per scherzo.
sporting |spôr'ting| a sportivo(a); **to give sb a ~ chance** dare a qn una possibilità (di vincere).
sports car |spôrts kâr| n automobile f sporti-va.
sport(s) coat n (US) giacca sportiva.
sports field n campo sportivo.
sports jacket n (Brit) = **sport(s) coat.**
sportsman |spôrts'mən| n sportivo.
sportsmanship |spôrts'mənship| n spirito sportivo.
sports page n pagina sportiva.
sportswear |spôrts'weûr| n abiti mpl sportivi.
sportswoman |spôrts'wōōmən| n sportiva.
sporty |spôr'tē| a sportivo(a).
spot |spät| n punto; (mark) macchia; (dot: on pattern) pallino; (pimple) foruncolo; (place) posto; (also: ~ **advertisement**) spot m inv; (small amount): **a ~ of** un po' di ♦ vt (no-tice) individuare, distinguere; **on the ~** sul posto; **to do sth on the ~** fare qc immedia-tamente or lì per lì; **to pay cash on the ~** (US) pagare a tamburo battente; **to put sb on the ~** mettere qn in difficoltà; **to come out in ~s** coprirsi di foruncoli.
spot check n controllo senza preavviso.
spotless |spät'lis| a immacolato(a).
spotlight |spät'līt| n proiettore m; (AUT) faro ausiliario.
spot price n (COMM) prezzo del pronto.
spotted |spät'id| a macchiato(a); a puntini, a pallini; **~ with** punteggiato(a) di.
spotty |spät'ē| a (Brit: face) foruncoloso(a).
spouse |spous| n sposo/a.
spout |spout| n (of jug) beccuccio; (of liquid) zampillo, getto ♦ vi zampillare.
sprain |sprān| n storta, distorsione f ♦ vt: **to ~**

one's ankle storcersi una caviglia.

sprang [spraŋ] *pt of* **spring**.

sprawl [sprôl] *vi* sdraiarsi (in modo scomposto) ♦ *n*: **urban** ~ sviluppo urbanistico incontrollato; **to send sb ~ing** mandare qn a gambe all'aria.

spray [sprā] *n* spruzzo; (*container*) nebulizzatore *m*, spray *m inv*; (*of flowers*) mazzetto ♦ *cpd* (*deodorant*) spray *inv* ♦ *vt* spruzzare; (*crops*) irrorare.

spread [spred] *n* diffusione *f*; (*distribution*) distribuzione *f*; (*PRESS, TYP: two pages*) doppia pagina; (*: across columns*) articolo a più colonne; (*CULIN*) pasta (da spalmare) ♦ *vb* (*pt, pp* **spread**) *vt* (*cloth*) stendere, distendere; (*butter etc*) spalmare; (*disease, knowledge*) propagare, diffondere ♦ *vi* stendersi, distendersi; spalmarsi; propagarsi, diffondersi; **middle-age** ~ pancetta; **repayments will be** ~ **over 18 months** i versamenti saranno scaglionati lungo un periodo di 18 mesi.

spread-eagled [spred'ēgəld] *a*: **to be** *or* **lie** ~ essere disteso(a) a gambe e braccia aperte.

spreadsheet [spred'shēt] *n* (*COMPUT*) foglio elettronico.

spree [sprē] *n*: **to go on a** ~ fare baldoria.

sprig [sprig] *n* ramoscello.

sprightly [sprīt'lē] *a* vivace.

spring [spriŋ] *n* (*leap*) salto, balzo; (*bounciness*) elasticità; (*coiled metal*) molla; (*season*) primavera; (*of water*) sorgente *f* ♦ *vi* (*pt* **sprang**, *pp* **sprung**) (*leap*) saltare, balzare ♦ *vt*: **to** ~ **a leak** (*pipe etc*) cominciare a perdere; **to walk with a** ~ **in one's step** camminare con passo elastico; **in** ~, **in the** ~ in primavera; **to** ~ **from** provenire da; **to** ~ **into action** entrare (rapidamente) in azione; **he sprang the news on me** mi ha sorpreso con quella notizia.

spring up *vi* (*problem*) presentarsi.

springboard [spriŋ'bôrd] *n* trampolino.

spring-clean [spriŋ'klēn] *n* (*also:* ~**ing**) grandi pulizie *fpl* di primavera.

spring onion *n* (*Brit*) cipollina.

springtime [spriŋ'tīm] *n* primavera.

springy [spriŋ'ē] *a* elastico(a).

sprinkle [spriŋ'kəl] *vt* spruzzare; spargere; **to** ~ **water** *etc* **on**, ~ **with water** *etc* spruzzare dell'acqua *etc* su; **to** ~ **sugar** *etc* **on**, ~ **with sugar** *etc* spolverizzare di zucchero *etc*; ~**d with** (*fig*) cosparso(a) di.

sprinkler [spriŋ'klûr] *n* (*for lawn etc*) irrigatore *m*; (*for fire-fighting*) sprinkler *m inv*.

sprinkling [spriŋ'kliŋ] *n* (*of water*) qualche goccia; (*of salt, sugar*) pizzico.

sprint [sprint] *n* scatto ♦ *vi* scattare; **the 200-meters** ~ i 200 metri piani.

sprinter [sprin'tûr] *n* velocista *m/f*.

sprite [sprīt] *n* elfo, folletto.

sprocket [sprâk'it] *n* (*on printer etc*) dente *m*, rocchetto.

sprout [sprout] *vi* germogliare.

sprouts [sprouts] *npl* (*also:* **Brussels** ~) cavolini *mpl* di Bruxelles.

spruce [sprōōs] *n* abete *m* rosso ♦ *a* lindo(a); azzimato(a).

spruce up *vt* (*tidy*) mettere in ordine; (*smarten up: room etc*) abbellire; **to** ~ **o.s. up** farsi bello(a).

sprung [spruŋ] *pp of* **spring**.

spry [sprī] *a* arzillo(a), sveglio(a).

SPUC *n abbr* (= *Society for the Protection of Unborn Children*) associazione anti-abortista.

spun [spun] *pt, pp of* **spin**.

spur [spûr] *n* sperone *m*; (*fig*) sprone *m*, incentivo ♦ *vt* (*also:* ~ **on**) spronare; **on the** ~ **of the moment** lì per lì.

spurious [spyōōr'ēəs] *a* falso(a).

spurn [spûrn] *vt* rifiutare con disprezzo, sdegnare.

spurt [spûrt] *n* getto; (*of energy*) esplosione *f* ♦ *vi* sgorgare; zampillare; **to put in** *or* **on a** ~ (*runner*) fare uno scatto; (*fig: in work etc*) affrettarsi, sbrigarsi.

sputter [sput'ûr] *vi* farfugliare; sputacchiare.

spy [spī] *n* spia ♦ *cpd* (*film, story*) di spionaggio ♦ *vi*: **to** ~ **on** spiare ♦ *vt* (*see*) scorgere.

spying [spī'iŋ] *n* spionaggio.

Sq. *abbr* (*in address*) = **square**.

sq. *abbr* (*MATH etc*) = **square**.

squabble [skwâb'əl] *n* battibecco ♦ *vi* bisticciarsi.

squad [skwâd] *n* (*MIL*) plotone *m*; (*POLICE*) squadra.

squad car *n* (*POLICE*) automobile *f* della polizia.

squadron [skwâd'rən] *n* (*MIL*) squadrone *m*; (*AVIAT, NAUT*) squadriglia.

squalid [skwâl'id] *a* sordido(a).

squall [skwôl] *n* burrasca.

squalor [skwâl'ûr] *n* squallore *m*.

squander [skwân'dûr] *vt* dissipare.

square [skwär] *n* quadrato; (*in town*) piazza; (*US: block*) blocco, isolato; (*instrument*) squadra ♦ *a* quadrato(a); (*honest*) onesto(a); (*col: ideas, person*) di vecchio stampo ♦ *vt* (*arrange*) regolare; (*MATH*) elevare al quadrato ♦ *vi* (*agree*) accordarsi; **a** ~ **meal** un pasto abbondante; **2 meters** ~ di 2 metri per 2; **1** ~ **meter** 1 metro quadrato; **we're back to** ~ **one** (*fig*) siamo al punto di partenza; **all** ~ pari; **to get one's accounts** ~ mettere in ordine i propri conti; **I'll** ~ **it with him** (*col*) sistemo io le cose con lui; **can you** ~ **it with your conscience?** (*reconcile*) puoi conciliarlo con la tua coscienza?

square bracket *n* (*TYP*) parentesi *f inv* quadra.

squarely [skwär'lē] *ad* (*directly*) direttamente; (*honestly, fairly*) onestamente.

square root *n* radice *f* quadrata.

squash [skwâsh] *n* (*vegetable*) zucca; (*SPORT*) squash *m*; (*Brit: drink*): **lemon/orange ~** sciroppo di limone/arancia ♦ *vt* schiacciare.

squat [skwât] *a* tarchiato(a), tozzo(a) ♦ *vi* accovacciarsi; (*on property*) occupare abusivamente.

squatter [skwât'ûr] *n* occupante *m/f* abusivo(a).

squawk [skwôk] *vi* emettere strida rauche.

squeak [skwēk] *vi* squittire ♦ *n* (*of hinge, wheel etc*) cigolio; (*of shoes*) scricchiolio; (*of mouse etc*) squittio.

squeal [skwēl] *vi* strillare.

squeamish [skwē'mish] *a* schizzinoso(a); disgustato(a).

squeeze [skwēz] *n* pressione *f*; (*also ECON*) stretta; (*credit ~*) stretta creditizia ♦ *vt* premere; (*hand, arm*) stringere ♦ *vi*: **to ~ in** infilarsi; **to ~ past/under sth** passare vicino/sotto a qc con difficoltà; **a ~ of lemon** una spruzzata di limone.
  squeeze out *vt* spremere.

squelch [skwelch] *vi* fare ciac; sguazzare.

squib [skwib] *n* petardo.

squid [skwid] *n* calamaro.

squint [skwint] *vi* essere strabico(a); (*in the sunlight*) strizzare gli occhi ♦ *n*: **he has a ~** è strabico; **to ~ at sth** guardare qc di traverso; (*quickly*) dare un'occhiata a qc.

squirm [skwûrm] *vi* contorcersi.

squirrel [skwûr'əl] *n* scoiattolo.

squirt [skwûrt] *n* schizzo ♦ *vi* schizzare; zampillare.

Sr *abbr* = **senior; sister** (*REL*).

Sri Lanka [srē lângk'ə] *n* Sri Lanka *m*.

SRO *abbr* (*US*: = *standing room only*) solo posti in piedi.

SS *abbr* = **steamship**.

SSA *n abbr* (*US*: = *Social Security Administration*) ≈ Previdenza Sociale.

SST *n abbr* (*US*) = *supersonic transport*.

St *abbr* = **saint; street**.

stab [stab] *n* (*with knife etc*) pugnalata; (*col: try*): **to take a ~ at (doing) sth** provare a fare qc ♦ *vt* pugnalare; **to ~ sb to death** uccidere qn a coltellate.

stabbing [stab'ing] *n*: **there's been a ~** qualcuno è stato pugnalato ♦ *a* (*pain, ache*) lancinante.

stability [stəbil'ətē] *n* stabilità.

stabilization [stābiləzā'shən] *n* stabilizzazione *f*.

stabilize [stā'bəlīz] *vt* stabilizzare ♦ *vi* stabilizzarsi.

stabilizer [stā'bəlīzûr] *n* (*AVIAT, NAUT*) stabilizzatore *m*.

stable [stā'bəl] *n* (*for horses*) scuderia; (*for cattle*) stalla ♦ *a* stabile; **riding ~s** maneggio.

stableboy [stā'bəlboi] *n* mozzo *or* garzone *m* di stalla.

staccato [stəkâ'tō] *ad* in modo staccato ♦ *a* (*MUS*) staccato(a); (*sound*) scandito(a).

stack [stak] *n* catasta, pila; (*col*) mucchio, sacco ♦ *vt* accatastare, ammucchiare.

stadium [stā'dēəm] *n* stadio.

staff [staf] *n* (*work force: gen*) personale *m*; (: *Brit: SCOL*) personale insegnante; (: *servants*) personale di servizio; (*MIL*) stato maggiore; (*stick*) bastone *m* ♦ *vt* fornire di personale.

Staffs *abbr* (*Brit*) = **Staffordshire**.

stag [stag] *n* cervo; (*Brit STOCK EXCHANGE*) rialzista *m/f* su nuove emissioni.

stage [stāj] *n* (*platform*) palco; (*in theater*) palcoscenico; (*profession*): **the ~** il teatro, la scena; (*point*) fase *f*, stadio ♦ *vt* (*play*) allestire, mettere in scena; (*demonstration*) organizzare; (*fig: perform: recovery etc*) effettuare; **in ~s** per gradi; a tappe; **in the early/final ~s** negli stadi iniziali/finali; **to go through a difficult ~** attraversare un periodo difficile.

stagecoach [stāj'kōch] *n* diligenza.

stage door *n* ingresso degli artisti.

stage fright *n* paura del pubblico.

stagehand [stāj'hand] *n* macchinista *m*.

stage-manage [stāj'man'ij] *vt* allestire le scene per; montare.

stage manager *n* direttore *m* di scena.

stagger [stag'ûr] *vi* barcollare ♦ *vt* (*person*) sbalordire; (*hours, vacation*) scaglionare.

staggering [stag'ûring] *a* (*amazing*) incredibile, sbalorditivo(a).

stagnant [stag'nənt] *a* stagnante.

stagnate [stag'nāt] *vi* (*also fig*) stagnare.

stagnation [stagnā'shən] *n* stagnazione *f*, ristagno.

stag party *n* festa di addio al celibato.

staid [stād] *a* posato(a), serio(a).

stain [stān] *n* macchia; (*coloring*) colorante *m* ♦ *vt* macchiare; (*wood*) tingere.

stained glass window *n* vetrata.

stainless [stān'lis] *a* (*steel*) inossidabile.

stain remover *n* smacchiatore *m*.

stair [stär] *n* (*step*) gradino; **~s** *npl* (*flight of ~s*) scale *fpl*, scala.

staircase [stär'kās], **stairway** [stär'wā] *n* scale *fpl*, scala.

stairwell [stär'wel] *n* tromba delle scale.

stake [stāk] *n* palo, piolo; (*BETTING*) puntata, scommessa ♦ *vt* (*bet*) scommettere; (*risk*) rischiare; (*also: ~ out: area*) delimitare con paletti; **to be at ~** essere in gioco; **to have a ~ in sth** avere un interesse in qc; **to ~ a claim (to sth)** rivendicare (qc).

stalactite [stəlak'tīt] *n* stalattite *f*.

stalagmite [stəlag'mīt] *n* stalagmite *f*.

stale [stāl] *a* (*bread*) raffermo(a), stantio(a); (*beer*) svaporato(a); (*smell*) di chiuso.

stalemate [stāl'māt] *n* stallo; (*fig*) punto morto.

stalk |stôk| *n* gambo, stelo ♦ *vt* inseguire ♦ *vi* camminare impettito(a).

stall |stôl| *n* (*in stable*) box *m inv* di stalla; (*Brit*: *in street, market etc*) bancarella ♦ *vt* (*AUT*) far spegnere ♦ *vi* (*AUT*) spegnersi, fermarsi; (*fig*) temporeggiare; **~s** *npl* (*Brit*: *in cinema, theater*) platea; **newspaper/flower ~** chiosco del giornalaio/del fioraio.

stallholder |stôl'hōldûr| *n* (*Brit*) bancarellista *m/f*.

stallion |stal'yən| *n* stallone *m*.

stalwart |stôl'wûrt| *n* membro fidato.

stamen |stā'mən| *n* stame *m*.

stamina |stam'inə| *n* vigore *m*, resistenza.

stammer |stam'ûr| *n* balbuzie *f* ♦ *vi* balbettare.

stamp |stamp| *n* (*postage ~*) francobollo; (*implement*) timbro; (*mark, also fig*) marchio, impronta; (*on document*) bollo; timbro ♦ *vi* (*also*: **~ one's foot**) battere il piede ♦ *vt* battere; (*letter*) affrancare; (*mark with a ~*) timbrare; **~ed addressed envelope (sae)** (*Brit*) busta affrancata per la risposta.

  stamp out *vt* (*fire*) estinguere; (*crime*) eliminare; (*opposition*) soffocare.

stamp album *n* album *m inv* per francobolli.

stamp collecting *n* filatelia.

stampede |stampēd'| *n* fuggi fuggi *m inv*; (*of cattle*) fuga precipitosa.

stamp machine *n* distributore *m* automatico di francobolli.

stance |stans| *n* posizione *f*.

stand |stand| *n* (*position*) posizione *f*; (*MIL*) resistenza; (*structure*) supporto, sostegno; (*at exhibition*) stand *m inv*; (*at market*) bancarella; (*booth*) chiosco; (*SPORT*) tribuna; (*also*: **music ~**) leggio *m* ♦ *vb* (*pt, pp* **stood** |stŏŏd|) *vi* stare in piedi; (*rise*) alzarsi in piedi; (*be placed*) trovarsi ♦ *vt* (*place*) mettere, porre; (*tolerate, withstand*) resistere, sopportare; **to make a ~** prendere posizione; **to take a ~ on an issue** prendere posizione su un problema; **to ~ for parliament** (*Brit*) presentarsi come candidato (per il parlamento); **to ~ guard** *or* **watch** (*MIL*) essere di guardia; **it ~s to reason** è logico; **as things ~** stando così le cose; **to ~ sb a drink/meal** offrire da bere/un pranzo a qn; **I can't ~ him** non lo sopporto.

  stand aside *vi* farsi da parte, scostarsi.

  stand by *vi* (*be ready*) tenersi pronto(a) ♦ *vt fus* (*opinion*) sostenere.

  stand down *vi* (*withdraw*) ritirarsi; (*LAW*) lasciare il banco dei testimoni.

  stand for *vt fus* (*signify*) rappresentare, significare; (*tolerate*) sopportare, tollerare.

  stand in for *vt fus* sostituire.

  stand out *vi* (*be prominent*) spiccare.

  stand up *vi* (*rise*) alzarsi in piedi.

  stand up for *vt fus* difendere.

  stand up to *vt fus* tener testa a, resistere a.

stand-alone |stand'əlōn'| *a* (*COMPUT*) stand-alone *inv*.

standard |stan'dûrd| *n* modello, standard *m inv*; (*level*) livello; (*flag*) stendardo ♦ *a* (*size etc*) normale, standard *inv*; (*practice*) normale; (*model*) di serie; **~s** *npl* (*morals*) principi *mpl*, valori *mpl*; **to be** *or* **come up to ~** rispondere ai requisiti; **below** *or* **not up to ~** (*work*) mediocre; **to apply a double ~** usare metri diversi (nel giudicare *or* fare *etc*); **~ of living** livello di vita.

standardization |standûrdəzā'shən| *n* standardizzazione *f*.

standardize |stan'dûrdīz| *vt* normalizzare, standardizzare.

standard lamp *n* (*Brit*) lampada a stelo.

standard time *n* ora ufficiale.

standby |stand'bī| *n* riserva, sostituto; **to be on ~** (*gen*) tenersi pronto(a); (*doctor*) essere di guardia.

stand-by generator *n* generatore *m* d'emergenza.

stand-by passenger *n* (*AVIAT*) passeggero/a in lista d'attesa.

stand-by ticket *n* (*AVIAT*) biglietto senza garanzia.

stand-in |stand'in| *n* sostituto/a; (*CINEMA*) controfigura.

standing |stan'ding| *a* diritto(a), in piedi; (*permanent: committee*) permanente; (: *rule*) fisso(a); (: *army*) regolare; (*grievance*) continuo(a); (*duration*): **of 6 months' ~** che dura da 6 mesi ♦ *n* rango, condizione *f*, posizione *f*; **it's a ~ joke** è diventato proverbiale; **he was given a ~ ovation** tutti si alzarono per applaudirlo; **a man of some ~** un uomo di una certa importanza; **"no ~"** (*US AUT*) "divieto di sosta".

standing committee *n* commissione *f* permanente.

standing order *n* (*Brit: at bank*) ordine *m* di pagamento (permanente); **~s** *npl* (*MIL*) regolamento.

standing room *n* posto all'impiedi.

standoffish |standôf'ish| *a* scostante, freddo(a).

standpat |stand'pat| *a* (*US*) irremovibile.

standpipe |stand'pīp| *n* fontanella.

standpoint |stand'point| *n* punto di vista.

standstill |stand'stil| *n*: **at a ~** fermo(a); (*fig*) a un punto morto; **to come to a ~** fermarsi; giungere a un punto morto.

stank |stangk| *pt of* **stink**.

stanza |stan'zə| *n* stanza (*poesia*).

staple |stā'pəl| *n* (*for papers*) graffetta; (*chief product*) prodotto principale ♦ *a* (*food etc*) di base; (*crop, industry*) principale ♦ *vt* cucire.

stapler |stā'plûr| *n* cucitrice *f*.

star |stâr| *n* stella; (*celebrity*) divo/a; (*principal actor*) vedette *f inv* ♦ *vi*: **to ~ (in)** essere il (or la) protagonista (di) ♦ vt (CINEMA) essere interpretato(a) da; **four-~ hotel** ≈ albergo di prima categoria; **4-~ petrol** (Brit) ≈ super f.

star attraction n numero principale.

starboard [står'bûrd] n dritta; **to ~ a dritta.**

starch [stårch] n amido.

starched [stårcht] a (collar) inamidato(a).

starchy [står'chē] a (food) ricco(a) di amido.

stardom [står'dəm] n celebrità.

stare [stär] n sguardo fisso ♦ vi: **to ~ at** fissare.

starfish [står'fish] n stella di mare.

stark [stårk] a (bleak) desolato(a); (simplicity, color) austero(a); (reality, poverty, truth) crudo(a) ♦ ad: **~ naked** completamente nudo(a).

starlet [står'lit] n (CINEMA) stellina.

starlight [står'līt] n: **by ~** alla luce delle stelle.

starling [står'ling] n storno.

starlit [står'lit] a stellato(a).

starry [står'ē] a stellato(a).

starry-eyed [står'ēid] a (idealistic, gullible) ingenuo(a); (from wonder) meravigliato(a).

star-studded [står'studid] a: **a ~ cast** un cast di attori famosi.

start [stårt] n inizio; (of race) partenza; (sudden movement) sobbalzo; (advantage) vantaggio ♦ vt cominciare, iniziare; (found: business, newspaper) fondare, creare ♦ vi cominciare; (on journey) partire, mettersi in viaggio; (jump) sobbalzare; **to ~ doing sth** (in)cominciare a fare qc; **at the ~** all'inizio; **for a ~** tanto per cominciare; **to make an early ~** partire di buon'ora; **to ~ (off) with ...** (firstly) per prima cosa ...; (at the beginning) all'inizio; **to ~ a fire** provocare un incendio.

start off vi cominciare; (leave) partire.

start over vi (US) ricominciare.

start up vi cominciare; (car) avviarsi ♦ vt iniziare; (car) avviare.

starter [står'tûr] n (AUT) motorino d'avviamento; (SPORT: official) starter m inv; (: runner, horse) partente m/f; (Brit CULIN) primo piatto; **for ~s** tanto per cominciare.

starting point [står'ting point] n punto di partenza.

starting price [står'ting prīs] n prezzo m base inv.

startle [står'təl] vt far trasalire.

startling [stårt'ling] a sorprendente, sbalorditivo(a).

starvation [stårvā'shən] n fame f, inedia; **to die of ~** morire d'inedia.

starve [stårv] vi morire di fame; soffrire la fame ♦ vt far morire di fame, affamare; **I'm starving** muoio di fame.

state [stāt] n stato; (pomp): **in ~** in pompa ♦ vt dichiarare, affermare; annunciare; **to be in a ~** essere agitato(a); **the ~ of the art** il livello di tecnologia (or cultura etc); **~ of emergency** stato di emergenza; **~ of mind** stato d'animo.

state control n controllo statale.

stated [stā'tid] a fissato(a), stabilito(a).

State Department n (US) Dipartimento di Stato, ≈ Ministero degli Esteri.

state highway n (US) strada statale.

stateless [stāt'lis] a apolide.

stately [stāt'lē] a maestoso(a), imponente.

statement [stāt'mənt] n dichiarazione f; (LAW) deposizione f; (FINANCE) rendiconto; **official ~** comunicato ufficiale; **~ of account, bank ~** estratto conto.

state-owned [stāt'ōnd'] a statalizzato(a).

States [stāts] npl: **the ~** (USA) gli Stati Uniti.

statesman [stāts'mən] n statista m.

statesmanship [stāts'mənship] n abilità politica.

static [stat'ik] n (RADIO) scariche fpl ♦ a statico(a); **~ electricity** elettricità statica.

station [stā'shən] n stazione f; (rank) rango, condizione f ♦ vt collocare, disporre; **action ~s** posti mpl di combattimento; **to be ~ed in** (MIL) essere di stanza in.

stationary [stā'shənärē] a fermo(a), immobile.

stationer [stā'shənûr] n cartolaio/a; **~'s shop** cartoleria.

stationery [stā'shənärē] n articoli mpl di cancelleria; (writing paper) carta da lettere.

station master n (RAIL) capostazione m.

station wagon n (US) giardinetta.

statistic [stətis'tik] n statistica; see also **statistics.**

statistical [stətis'tikəl] a statistico(a).

statistics [stətis'tiks] n (science) statistica.

statue [stach'ōō] n statua.

statuesque [stachōōesk'] a statuario(a).

statuette [stachōōet'] n statuetta.

stature [stach'ûr] n statura.

status [stā'təs] n posizione f, condizione f sociale; (prestige) prestigio; (legal, marital) stato.

status quo [stā'təs kwō] n: **the ~** lo statu quo.

status symbol n simbolo di prestigio.

statute [stach'ōōt] n legge f; **~s** npl (of club etc) statuto.

statute book n codice m.

statutory [stach'ōōtôrē] a stabilito(a) dalla legge, statutario(a); **~ meeting** (COMM) assemblea ordinaria.

staunch [stônch] a fidato(a), leale ♦ vt (flow) arrestare; (blood) arrestare il flusso di.

stave [stāv] n (MUS) rigo ♦ vt: **to ~ off** (attack) respingere; (threat) evitare.

stay [stā] n (period of time) soggiorno, permanenza ♦ vi rimanere; (reside) alloggiare, stare; (spend some time) trattenersi, soggiornare; **~ of execution** (LAW) sospensione f dell'esecuzione; **to ~ put** non muoversi; **to ~ with friends** stare presso amici; **to ~ the night** passare la notte.

stay behind *vi* restare indietro.

stay in *vi* (*at home*) stare in casa.

stay on *vi* restare, rimanere.

stay out *vi* (*of house*) rimanere fuori (di casa); (*strikers*) continuare lo sciopero.

stay up *vi* (*at night*) rimanere alzato(a).

staying power [stā'ing pou'ûr] *n* capacità di resistenza.

STD *n abbr* (= *sexually transmitted disease*) malattia venerea; (*Brit*: = *subscriber trunk dialling*) teleselezione *f*.

stead [sted] *n*: **in sb's ~** al posto di qn.

steadfast [sted'fast] *a* fermo(a), risoluto(a).

steadily [sted'ilē] *ad* continuamente; (*walk*) con passo sicuro.

steady [sted'ē] *a* stabile, solido(a), fermo(a); (*regular*) costante; (*boyfriend etc*) fisso(a); (*person*) calmo(a), tranquillo(a) ♦ *vt* stabilizzare; calmare; **to ~ o.s.** ritrovare l'equilibrio.

steak [stāk] *n* (*meat*) bistecca; (*fish*) trancia.

steakhouse [stāk'hous] *n* ristorante specializzato in bistecche.

steal, *pt* **stole**, *pp* **stolen** [stēl, stōl, stō'lən] *vt* rubare ♦ *vi* (*thieves*) rubare.

steal away, steal off *vi* svignarsela, andarsene alla chetichella.

stealth [stelth] *n*: **by ~** furtivamente.

stealthy [stel'thē] *a* furtivo(a).

steam [stēm] *n* vapore *m* ♦ *vt* trattare con vapore; (*CULIN*) cuocere a vapore ♦ *vi* fumare; (*ship*): **to ~ along** filare; **to let off ~** (*fig*) sfogarsi; **under one's own ~** (*fig*) da solo, con i propri mezzi; **to run out of ~** (*fig*: *person*) non farcela più.

steam up *vi* (*window*) appannarsi; **to get ~ed up about sth** (*fig*) andare in bestia per qc.

steam engine *n* macchina a vapore; (*RAIL*) locomotiva a vapore.

steamer [stē'mûr] *n* piroscafo, vapore *m*; (*CULIN*) pentola a vapore.

steam iron *n* ferro a vapore.

steamroller [stēm'rōlûr] *n* rullo compressore.

steamship [stēm'ship] *n* piroscafo, vapore *m*.

steamy [stē'mē] *a* pieno(a) di vapore; (*window*) appannato(a).

steed [stēd] *n* (*literary*) corsiero, destriero.

steel [stēl] *n* acciaio ♦ *cpd* di acciaio.

steel band *n* banda di strumenti a percussione (*tipica dei Caribi*).

steel industry *n* industria dell'acciaio.

steel mill *n* acciaieria.

steelworks [stēl'wûrks] *n* acciaieria.

steely [stē'lē] *a* (*determination*) inflessibile; (*gaze*) duro(a); (*eyes*) freddo(a) come l'acciaio.

steep [stēp] *a* ripido(a), scosceso(a); (*price*)

eccessivo(a) ♦ *vt* inzuppare; (*washing*) mettere a mollo.

steeple [stē'pəl] *n* campanile *m*.

steeplechase [stē'pəlchās] *n* corsa a ostacoli, steeplechase *m inv*.

steeplejack [stē'pəljak] *n* chi ripara campanili e ciminiere.

steer [stēr] *n* manzo ♦ *vt* (*ship*) governare; (*car*) guidare ♦ *vi* (*NAUT*: *person*) governare; (: *ship*) rispondere al timone; (*car*) guidarsi; **to ~ clear of sb/sth** (*fig*) tenersi alla larga da qn/qc.

steering [stē'ring] *n* (*AUT*) sterzo.

steering column *n* piantone *m* dello sterzo.

steering committee *n* comitato direttivo.

steering wheel *n* volante *m*.

stem [stem] *n* (*of flower*, *plant*) stelo; (*of tree*) fusto; (*of glass*) gambo; (*of fruit*, *leaf*) picciolo ♦ *vt* contenere, arginare.

stem from *vt fus* provenire da, derivare da.

stench [stench] *n* puzzo, fetore *m*.

stencil [sten'səl] *n* (*of metal*, *cardboard*) stampino, mascherina; (*in typing*) matrice *f*.

stenographer [stənâg'rəfûr] *n* (*US*) stenografo/a.

stenography [stənâg'rəfē] *n* (*US*) stenografia.

step [step] *n* passo; (*stair*) gradino, scalino; (*action*) mossa, azione *f* ♦ *vi*: **to ~ forward** fare un passo avanti; **~ by ~** un passo dietro l'altro; (*fig*) poco a poco; **to be in/out of ~ with** (*also fig*) stare/non stare al passo con.

step down *vi* (*fig*) ritirarsi.

step in *vi* fare il proprio ingresso.

step off *vt fus* scendere da.

step over *vt fus* scavalcare.

step up *vt* aumentare; intensificare.

stepbrother [step'bruthûr] *n* fratellastro.

stepchild [step'child] *n* figliastro/a.

stepdaughter [step'dôtûr] *n* figliastra.

stepfather [step'fäthûr] *n* patrigno.

stepladder [step'ladûr] *n* scala a libretto.

stepmother [step'muthûr] *n* matrigna.

stepping stone [step'ing stōn] *n* pietra di un guado; (*fig*) trampolino.

stepsister [step'sistûr] *n* sorellastra.

stepson [step'sun] *n* figliastro.

stereo [stär'ēō] *n* (*system*) sistema *m* stereofonico; (*record player*) stereo *m inv* ♦ *a* (*also*: **~phonic**) stereofonico(a); **in ~** in stereofonia.

stereotype [stär'ēətīp] *n* stereotipo.

sterile [stär'əl] *a* sterile.

sterility [stəril'ətē] *n* sterilità.

sterilization [stärələzā'shən] *n* sterilizzazione *f*.

sterilize [stär'əlīz] *vt* sterilizzare.

sterling [stûr'ling] *a* (*gold*, *silver*) di buona lega; (*fig*) autentico(a), genuino(a) ♦ *n* (*ECON*) (lira) sterlina; **a pound ~** una lira sterlina.

sterling area *n* area della sterlina.

stern [stûrn] *a* severo(a) ♦ *n* (*NAUT*) poppa.

sternum [stûr'nəm] n sterno.
steroid [stâr'oid] n steroide m.
stethoscope [steth'əskōp] n stetoscopio.
stew [stōō] n stufato ♦ vt, vi cuocere in umido; ~ed tea tè lasciato troppo in infusione; ~ed fruit frutta cotta.
steward [stōō'ûrd] n (AVIAT, NAUT, RAIL) steward m inv; (in club etc) dispensiere m; (shop ~) rappresentante m/f sindacale.
stewardess [stōō'ûrdis] n assistente f di volo, hostess f inv.
stewing steak [stōō'ing stāk] n (Brit) = stew meat.
stew meat n (US) carne f (di manzo) per stufato.
stewpan [stōō'pan] n casseruola.
St. Ex. abbr = stock exchange.
stg abbr = sterling.
stick [stik] n bastone m; (of rhubarb, celery) gambo ♦ vb (pt, pp stuck [stuk]) vt (glue) attaccare; (thrust): to ~ sth into conficcare or piantare or infiggere qc in; (col: put) ficcare; (: tolerate) sopportare ♦ vi conficcarsi; tenere; (remain) restare, rimanere; (get jammed: door, elevator) bloccarsi; to ~ to (one's word, promise) mantenere; (principles) tener fede a; it stuck in my mind mi è rimasto in mente.
stick around vi (col) restare, fermarsi.
stick out, stick up vi sporgere, spuntare ♦ vt: to ~ it out (col) tener duro.
stick up for vt fus difendere.
sticker [stik'ûr] n cartellino adesivo.
sticking plaster [stik'ing plas'tûr] n (Brit) cerotto adesivo.
stickleback [stik'əlbak] n spinarello.
stickler [stik'lûr] n: to be a ~ for essere pignolo(a) su, tenere molto a.
stick-on [stik'ân] a (label) adesivo(a).
stick-up [stik'up] n (col) rapina a mano armata.
sticky [stik'ē] a attaccaticcio(a), vischioso(a); (label) adesivo(a).
stiff [stif] a rigido(a), duro(a); (muscle) legato(a), indolenzito(a); (difficult) difficile, arduo(a); (cold: manner etc) freddo(a), formale; (strong) forte; (high: price) molto alto(a);' to be or feel ~ (person) essere or sentirsi indolenzito; to have a ~ neck/back avere il torcicollo/mal di schiena.
stiffen [stif'ən] vt irrigidire; rinforzare ♦ vi irrigidirsi; indurirsi.
stiffness [stif'nis] n rigidità; indolenzimento; difficoltà; freddezza.
stifle [stī'fəl] vt soffocare.
stifling [stīf'ling] a (heat) soffocante.
stigma, pl (BOT. MED) ~ta, (fig) ~s [stig'mə] n stigma m.
stigmata [stigmâ'tə] npl (REL) stigmate fpl.
stile [stīl] n cavalcasiepe m; cavalcasteccato.
stiletto [stilet'ō] n (also: ~ heel) tacco a

spillo.
still [stil] a fermo(a); (quiet) silenzioso(a); (Brit: orange juice etc) non gassato(a) ♦ ad (up to this time, even) ancora; (nonetheless) tuttavia, ciò nonostante ♦ n (CINEMA) fotogramma m; keep ~! stai fermo!; he ~ hasn't arrived non è ancora arrivato.
stillborn [stil'bôrn] a nato(a) morto(a).
still life n natura morta.
stilt [stilt] n trampolo; (pile) palo.
stilted [stil'tid] a freddo(a), formale; artificiale.
stimulant [stim'yələnt] n stimolante m.
stimulate [stim'yəlāt] vt stimolare.
stimulating [stim'yəlāting] a stimolante.
stimulation [stimyəlā'shən] n stimolazione f.
stimulus, pl **stimuli** [stim'yələs, stim'yəlī] n stimolo.
sting [sting] n puntura; (organ) pungiglione m; (col) trucco ♦ vt (pt, pp stung [stung]) pungere ♦ vi bruciare; my eyes are ~ing mi bruciano gli occhi.
stingy [stin'jē] a spilorcio(a), tirchio(a).
stink [stingk] n fetore m, puzzo ♦ vi (pt stank, pp stunk [stangk, stungk]) puzzare.
stinker [stingk'ûr] n (col) porcheria; (person) fetente m/f.
stinking [sting'king] a (col): a ~ ... uno schifo di ..., un(a) maledetto(a) ...; ~ rich ricco(a) da far paura.
stint [stint] n lavoro, compito ♦ vi: to ~ on lesinare su.
stipend [stī'pend] n stipendio, congrua.
stipendiary [stīpen'dēārē] a: ~ magistrate magistrato stipendiato.
stipulate [stip'yəlāt] vt stipulare.
stipulation [stipyəlā'shən] n stipulazione f.
stir [stûr] n agitazione f, clamore m ♦ vt rimescolare; (move) smuovere, agitare ♦ vi muoversi; to give sth a ~ mescolare qc; to cause a ~ fare scalpore.
stir up vt provocare, suscitare.
stirring [stûr'ing] a eccitante; commovente.
stirrup [stûr'əp] n staffa.
stitch [stich] n (SEWING) punto; (KNITTING) maglia; (MED) punto (di sutura); (pain) fitta ♦ vt cucire, attaccare; suturare.
stoat [stōt] n ermellino.
stock [stâk] n riserva, provvista; (COMM) giacenza, stock m inv; (AGR) bestiame m; (CULIN) brodo; (FINANCE) titoli mpl, azioni fpl; (RAIL: also: rolling ~) materiale m rotabile; (descent, origin) stirpe f ♦ a (fig: reply etc) consueto(a); solito(a), classico(a); (greeting) usuale; (COMM: goods, size) standard inv ♦ vt (have in stock) avere, vendere; well-~ed ben fornito(a); to have sth in ~ avere qc in magazzino; out of ~ esaurito(a); to take ~ (fig) fare il punto; ~s and shares valori mpl di borsa; government ~ titoli di Stato.
stock up vi: to ~ up (with) fare provvista

(di).

stockade [ståkād'] *n* palizzata.

stockbroker [ståk'brōkûr] *n* agente *m* di cambio.

stock control *n* gestione *f* magazzino.

stock cube *n* (*Brit CULIN*) dado.

stock exchange *n* Borsa (valori).

stockholder [ståk'hōldûr] *n* (*FINANCE*) azionista *m/f*.

Stockholm [ståk'hōm] *n* Stoccolma.

stocking [ståk'ing] *n* calza.

stock-in-trade [ståk'intrād'] *n* (*fig*): it's his ~ è la sua specialità.

stockist [ståk'ist] *n* (*Brit*) fornitore *m*.

stock market *n* Borsa, mercato finanziario.

stock phrase *n* cliché *m inv*.

stockpile [ståk'pīl] *n* riserva ♦ *vt* accumulare riserve di.

stockroom [ståk'rōōm] *n* magazzino.

stocktaking [ståk'tāking] *n* (*Brit COMM*) inventario.

stocky [ståk'ē] *a* tarchiato(a), tozzo(a).

stodgy [ståj'ē] *a* pesante, indigesto(a).

stoic [stō'ik] *n* stoico/a.

stoical [stō'ikəl] *a* stoico(a).

stoke [stōk] *vt* alimentare.

stoker [stō'kûr] *n* fochista *m*.

stole [stōl] *pt of* **steal** ♦ *n* stola.

stolen [stō'lən] *pp of* **steal**.

stolid [stål'id] *a* impassibile.

stomach [stum'ək] *n* stomaco; (*abdomen*) ventre *m* ♦ *vt* sopportare, digerire.

stomachache [stum'əkāk] *n* mal *m* di stomaco.

stomach pump *n* pompa gastrica.

stomach ulcer *n* ulcera allo stomaco.

stomp [ståmp] *vi*: to ~ in/out *etc* entrare/uscire *etc* con passo pesante.

stone [stōn] *n* pietra; (*pebble*) sasso, ciottolo; (*in fruit*) nocciolo; (*MED*) calcolo; (*Brit: weight*) = 6.348 kg.; 14 libbre ♦ *cpd* di pietra ♦ *vt* lapidare; **within a ~'s throw of the station** a due passi dalla stazione.

Stone Age *n*: the ~ l'età della pietra.

stone-cold [stōn'kōld'] *a* gelido(a).

stoned [stōnd] *a* (*col: drunk*) sbronzo(a); (*on drugs*) fuori *inv*.

stone-deaf [stōn'def'] *a* sordo(a) come una campana.

stonemason [stōn'māsən] *n* scalpellino.

stonework [stōn'wûrk] *n* muratura.

stony [stō'nē] *a* pietroso(a), sassoso(a).

stood [stōōd] *pt, pp of* **stand**.

stool [stōōl] *n* sgabello.

stoop [stōōp] *vi* (*also*: **have a ~**) avere una curvatura; (*bend*) chinarsi, curvarsi; to ~ to sth/doing sth abbassarsi a qc/a fare qc.

stop [ståp] *n* arresto; (*stopping place*) fermata; (*in punctuation*) punto ♦ *vt* arrestare, fermare; (*break off*) interrompere; (*also*: put a ~ to) porre fine a; (*prevent*) impedire

♦ *vi* fermarsi; (*rain, noise etc*) cessare, finire; to ~ doing sth cessare *or* finire di fare qc; to ~ sb (from) doing sth impedire a qn di fare qc; to ~ dead fermarsi di colpo; ~ it! smettila!, basta!

stop by *vi* passare, fare un salto.

stop off *vi* sostare brevemente.

stop up *vt* (*hole*) chiudere, turare.

stopcock [ståp'kåk] *n* rubinetto di arresto.

stopgap [ståp'gap] *n* (*person*) tappabuchi *m/f inv*; (*measure*) ripiego ♦ *cpd* (*measures, solution*) di fortuna.

stoplights [ståp'līts] *npl* (*AUT*) stop *mpl*.

stopover [ståp'ōvûr] *n* breve sosta; (*AVIAT*) scalo.

stoppage [ståp'ij] *n* arresto, fermata; (*of pay*) trattenuta; (*strike*) interruzione *f* del lavoro.

stopper [ståp'ûr] *n* tappo.

stop press *n* ultimissime *fpl*.

stopwatch [ståp'wåch] *n* cronometro.

storage [stôr'ij] *n* immagazzinamento; (*COMPUT*) memoria.

storage heater *n* (*Brit*) radiatore *m* elettrico che accumula calore.

store [stôr] *n* provvista, riserva; (*depot*) deposito; (*department ~*) grande magazzino; (*US: shop*) negozio ♦ *vt* mettere da parte; conservare; (*grain, goods*) immagazzinare; (*COMPUT*) registrare; to set great/little ~ by sth dare molta/poca importanza a qc; who knows what is in ~ for us? chissà cosa ci riserva il futuro?

store up *vt* mettere in serbo, conservare.

storehouse [stôr'hous] *n* magazzino, deposito.

storekeeper [stôr'kēpûr] *n* negoziante *m/f*.

storeroom [stôr'rōōm] *n* dispensa.

storey [stôr'ē] *n* (*Brit: floor*) piano.

stork [stôrk] *n* cicogna.

storm [stôrm] *n* tempesta; (*also*: **thunder~**) temporale *m* ♦ *vi* (*fig*) infuriarsi ♦ *vt* prendere d'assalto.

storm cloud *n* nube *f* temporalesca.

storm door *n* controporta.

stormy [stôr'mē] *a* tempestoso(a), burrascoso(a).

story [stôr'ē] *n* storia; racconto; (*PRESS*) articolo; (*US: floor*) piano.

storybook [stôr'ēbōōk] *n* libro di racconti.

storyteller [stôr'ētelûr] *n* narratore/trice.

stout [stout] *a* solido(a), robusto(a); (*brave*) coraggioso(a); (*fat*) corpulento(a), grasso(a) ♦ *n* birra scura.

stove [stōv] *n* (*for cooking*) fornello; (: *small*) fornelletto; (*for heating*) stufa; gas/electric ~ cucina a gas/elettrica.

stow [stō] *vt* mettere via.

stowaway [stō'əwā] *n* passeggero(a) clandestino(a).

straddle [strad'əl] *vt* stare a cavalcioni di.

strafe [strāf] *vt* mitragliare.

straggle [strag'əl] *vi* crescere (*or* estendersi)

disordinatamente; trascinarsi; rimanere indietro; **~d along the coast** disseminati(e) lungo la costa.

straggler |strag'lûr| *n* sbandato/a.

straggling |strag'ling|, **straggly** |strag'lē| *a* (*hair*) in disordine.

straight |strāt| *a* (*continuous, direct*) dritto(a); (*frank*) onesto(a), franco(a); (*plain, uncomplicated*) semplice; (*THEATER*: *part, play*) serio(a); (*col: heterosexual*) eterosessuale ♦ *ad* diritto; (*drink*) liscio ♦ *n*: **the ~** la linea retta; (*RAIL*) il rettilineo; (*SPORT*) la dirittura d'arrivo; **to put** *or* **get ~** mettere in ordine, mettere ordine in; **to be (all) ~** (*tidy*) essere a posto, essere sistemato; (*clarified*) essere chiaro; **ten ~ wins** dieci vittorie di fila; **~ away, ~ off** (*at once*) immediatamente; **~ off, ~ out** senza esitare; **I went ~ home** sono andato direttamente a casa.

straighten |strā'tən| *vt* (*also:* **~ out**) raddrizzare; **to ~ things out** mettere le cose a posto.

straight-faced |strāt'fāst| *a* impassibile, imperturbabile ♦ *ad* con il viso serio.

straightforward |strātfôr'wûrd| *a* semplice; (*frank*) onesto(a), franco(a).

strain |strān| *n* (*TECH*) sollecitazione *f*; (*physical*) sforzo; (*mental*) tensione *f*; (*MED*) strappo; (*streak, trace*) tendenza; elemento; (*breed*) razza; (*of virus*) tipo ♦ *vt* tendere; (*muscle*) slogare; (*ankle*) storcere; (*friendship, marriage*) mettere a dura prova; (*filter*) colare, filtrare ♦ *vi* sforzarsi; **~s** *npl* (*MUS*) note *fpl*; **she's under a lot of ~** è molto tesa, è sotto pressione.

strained |strānd| *a* (*laugh etc*) forzato(a); (*relations*) teso(a).

strainer |strā'nûr| *n* passino, colino.

strait |strāt| *n* (*GEO*) stretto; **to be in dire ~s** (*fig*) essere nei guai.

straitjacket |strāt'jakit| *n* camicia di forza.

strait-laced |strāt'lāst| *a* puritano(a).

strand |strand| *n* (*of thread*) filo.

stranded |stran'did| *a* nei guai; senza mezzi di trasporto.

strange |strānj| *a* (*not known*) sconosciuto(a); (*odd*) strano(a), bizzarro(a).

strangely |strānj'lē| *ad* stranamente.

stranger |strān'jûr| *n* (*unknown*) sconosciuto/a; (*from another place*) estraneo/a; **I'm a ~ here** non sono del posto.

strangle |strang'gəl| *vt* strangolare.

stranglehold |strang'gəlhōld| *n* (*fig*) stretta (mortale).

strangulation |stranggyəlā'shən| *n* strangolamento.

strap |strap| *n* cinghia; (*of slip, dress*) spallina, bretella ♦ *vt* legare con una cinghia; (*child etc*) punire (con una cinghia).

straphanging |strap'hanging| *n* viaggiare *m* in piedi (*su mezzi pubblici reggendosi a un sostegno*).

strapless |strap'lis| *a* (*bra, dress*) senza spalline.

strapping |strap'ing| *a* ben piantato(a).

Strasbourg |stras'bûrg| *n* Strasburgo *f*.

strata |strā'tə| *npl of* **stratum**.

stratagem |strat'əjəm| *n* stratagemma *m*.

strategic |stratē'jik| *a* strategico(a).

strategist |strat'ijist| *n* stratega *m*.

strategy |strat'ijē| *n* strategia.

stratosphere |strat'əsfēr| *n* stratosfera.

stratum, *pl* **strata** |strā'təm, strā'tə| *n* strato.

straw |strô| *n* paglia; (*drinking ~*) cannuccia; **that's the last ~!** è la goccia che fa traboccare il vaso!

strawberry |strô'bärē| *n* fragola.

stray |strā| *a* (*animal*) randagio(a) ♦ *vi* perdersi; allontanarsi, staccarsi (dal gruppo); **~ bullet** proiettile *m* vagante.

streak |strēk| *n* striscia; (*fig: of madness etc*): **a ~ of** una vena di ♦ *vt* striare, screziare ♦ *vi*: **to ~ past** passare come un fulmine; **to have ~s in one's hair** avere le mèche nei capelli; **a winning/losing ~** un periodo fortunato/sfortunato.

streaky |strē'kē| *a* screziato(a), striato(a).

streaky bacon *n* (*Brit*) ≈ pancetta.

stream |strēm| *n* ruscello; corrente *f*; (*of people*) fiume *m* ♦ *vi* scorrere; **to ~ in/out** entrare/uscire a fiotti; **against the ~** controcorrente.

streamer |strē'mûr| *n* (*of paper*) stella filante.

streamline |strēm'līn| *vt* dare una linea aerodinamica a; (*fig*) razionalizzare.

streamlined |strēm'līnd| *a* aerodinamico(a), affusolato(a); (*fig*) razionalizzato(a).

street |strēt| *n* strada, via; **the back ~s** le strade secondarie; **to walk the ~s** (*homeless*) essere senza tetto; (*as prostitute*) battere il marciapiede.

streetcar |strēt'kâr| *n* (*US*) tram *m inv*.

street light *n* lampione *m*.

street lighting *n* illuminazione *f* stradale.

street map, street plan *n* pianta (di una città).

street market *n* mercato all'aperto.

streetsweeper |strēt'swēp'ûr| *n* (*US: person*) spazzino.

streetwise |strēt'wīz| *a* (*col*) esperto(a) dei bassifondi.

strength |strengkth| *n* forza; (*of girder, knot etc*) resistenza, solidità; (*of chemical solution*) concentrazione *f*; (*of wine*) gradazione *f* alcolica; **on the ~ of** sulla base di, in virtù di; **below/at full ~** con gli effettivi ridotti/al completo.

strengthen |strengk'thən| *vt* rinforzare; (*muscles*) irrobustire; (*economy, currency*) consolidare.

strenuous |stren'yōōəs| *a* vigoroso(a), energico(a); (*tiring*) duro(a), pesante.

stress [strɛs] *n* (*force*, *pressure*) pressione *f*; (*mental strain*) tensione *f*; (*accent*) accento; (*emphasis*) enfasi *f* ♦ *vt* insistere su, sottolineare; **to be under** ~ essere sotto tensione; **to lay great** ~ **on sth** dare grande importanza a qc.

stressful [strɛs'fəl] *a* (*job*) difficile, stressante.

stretch [strɛch] *n* (*of sand etc*) distesa; (*of time*) periodo ♦ *vi* stirarsi; (*extend*): **to** ~ **to** *or* **as far as** estendersi fino a; (*be enough*: *money*, *food*): **to** ~ **(to)** bastare (per) ♦ *vt* tendere, allungare; (*spread*) distendere; (*fig*) spingere (al massimo); **at a** ~ ininterrottamente; **to** ~ **a muscle** tendere un muscolo; **to** ~ **one's legs** sgranchirsi le gambe.
   stretch out *vi* allungarsi, estendersi ♦ *vt* (*arm etc*) allungare, tendere; (*to spread*) distendere; **to** ~ **out for sth** allungare la mano per prendere qc.

stretcher [strɛch'ûr] *n* barella, lettiga.

stretcher-bearer [strɛch'ûrbärûr] *n* barelliere *m*.

stretch marks *npl* smagliature *fpl*.

strewn [strōōn] *a*: ~ **with** cosparso(a) di.

stricken [strik'ən] *a* provato(a); affranto(a); ~ **with** colpito(a) da.

strict [strikt] *a* (*severe*) rigido(a), severo(a); (: *order*, *rule*) rigoroso(a); (: *supervision*) stretto(a); (*precise*) preciso(a), stretto(a); **in** ~ **confidence** in assoluta confidenza.

strictly [strikt'lē] *ad* severamente; rigorosamente; strettamente; ~ **confidential** strettamente confidenziale; ~ **speaking** a rigor di termini; ~ **between ourselves** ... detto fra noi ....

stride [strīd] *n* passo lungo ♦ *vi* (*pt* **strode**, *pp* **stridden** [strid'ən]) camminare a grandi passi; **to take in one's** ~ (*fig*: *changes etc*) prendere con tranquillità.

strident [strīd'ənt] *a* stridente.

strife [strīf] *n* conflitto; litigi *mpl*.

strike [strīk] *n* sciopero; (*of oil etc*) scoperta; (*attack*) attacco ♦ *vb* (*pt*, *pp* **struck** [struk]) *vt* colpire; (*oil etc*) scoprire, trovare; (*produce*, *make*: *coin*, *medal*) coniare; (: *agreement*, *deal*) concludere ♦ *vi* far sciopero, scioperare; (*attack*) attaccare; (*clock*) suonare; **to go on** *or* **come out on** ~ mettersi in sciopero; **to** ~ **a match** accendere un fiammifero; **to** ~ **a balance** (*fig*) trovare il giusto mezzo.
   strike back *vi* (*MIL*) fare rappresaglie; (*fig*) reagire.
   strike down *vt* (*fig*) atterrare.
   strike off *vt* (*from list*) cancellare; (: *doctor etc*) radiare.
   strike out *vt* depennare.
   strike up *vt* (*MUS*) attaccare; **to** ~ **up a friendship with** fare amicizia con.

strikebreaker [strīk'brākûr] *n* crumiro/a.

striker [strī'kûr] *n* scioperante *m/f*; (*SPORT*) attaccante *m*.

striking [strī'king] *a* impressionante.

string [string] *n* spago; (*row*) fila; sequenza; catena; (*COMPUT*) stringa, sequenza; (*MUS*) corda ♦ *vt* (*pt*, *pp* **strung** [strung]): **to** ~ **out** disporre di fianco; **to** ~ **together** mettere insieme; **to** ~ **sb along** tenere qn in sospeso; **the** ~**s** *npl* (*MUS*) gli archi; ~ **of pearls** filo di perle; **with no** ~**s attached** (*fig*) senza vincoli, senza obblighi; **to get a job by pulling** ~**s** ottenere un lavoro a forza di raccomandazioni.

string bean *n* fagiolino.

string(ed) instrument [string(d)' in'strəmənt] *n* (*MUS*) strumento a corda.

stringent [strin'jənt] *a* rigoroso(a); (*reasons*, *arguments*) stringente, impellente.

string quartet *n* quartetto d'archi.

strip [strip] *n* striscia ♦ *vt* spogliare; (*also*: ~ **down**: *machine*) smontare ♦ *vi* spogliarsi.

stripe [strīp] *n* striscia, riga.

striped [strīpt] *a* a strisce *or* righe.

strip light *n* (*Brit*) tubo al neon.

stripper [strip'ûr] *n* spogliarellista.

striptease [strip'tēz] *n* spogliarello.

strive, *pt* **strove**, *pp* **striven** [strīv, strōv, striv'ən] *vi*: **to** ~ **to do** sforzarsi di fare.

strode [strōd] *pt of* **stride**.

stroke [strōk] *n* colpo; (*of piston*) corsa; (*MED*) colpo apoplettico; (*SWIMMING*: *style*) nuoto; (*caress*) carezza ♦ *vt* accarezzare; **at a** ~ in un attimo; **on the** ~ **of 5** alle 5 in punto, allo scoccare delle 5; **a** ~ **of luck** un colpo di fortuna; **two-**~ **engine** motore a due tempi.

stroll [strōl] *n* giretto, passeggiatina ♦ *vi* andare a spasso; **to go for a** ~ andare a fare un giretto or due passi.

stroller [strō'lûr] *n* (*US*) passeggino.

strong [strông] *a* (*gen*) forte; (*sturdy*: *table*, *fabric etc*) solido(a); (*concentrated*, *intense*: *bleach*, *acid*) concentrato(a); (*protest*, *letter*, *measures*) energico(a) ♦ *ad*: **to be going** ~ (*company*) andare a gonfie vele; (*person*) essere attivo(a); **they are 50** ~ sono in 50; ~ **language** (*swearing*) linguaggio volgare.

strong-arm [strông'ârm] *a* (*tactics*, *methods*) energico(a).

strongbox [strông'bâks] *n* cassaforte *f*.

strong drink *n* alcolici *mpl*.

stronghold [strông'hōld] *n* fortezza, roccaforte *f*.

strongly [strông'lē] *ad* fortemente, con forza; solidamente; energicamente; **to feel** ~ **about sth** avere molto a cuore qc.

strongman [strông'man] *n* personaggio di spicco.

strongroom [strông'rōōm] *n* camera di sicurezza.

strove [strōv] *pt of* **strive**.

struck [struk] *pt, pp of* **strike.**
structural [struk'chûrəl] *a* strutturale; (*CONSTR*) di costruzione; di struttura.
structurally [struk'chûrəlē] *ad* dal punto di vista della struttura.
structure [struk'chûr] *n* struttura; (*building*) costruzione *f*, fabbricato.
struggle [strug'əl] *n* lotta ♦ *vi* lottare; **to have a ~ to do sth** avere dei problemi per fare qc.
strum [strum] *vt* (*guitar*) strimpellare.
strung [strung] *pt, pp of* **string.**
strut [strut] *n* sostegno, supporto ♦ *vi* pavoneggiarsi.
strychnine [strik'nīn] *n* stricnina.
stub [stub] *n* mozzicone *m*; (*of ticket etc*) matrice *f*, talloncino ♦ *vt*: **to ~ one's toe (on sth)** urtare *or* sbattere il dito del piede (contro qc).
  stub out *vt*: **to ~ out a cigarette** spegnere una sigaretta.
stubble [stub'əl] *n* stoppia; (*on chin*) barba ispida.
stubborn [stub'ûrn] *a* testardo(a), ostinato(a).
stubby [stub'ē] *a* tozzo(a).
stucco [stuk'ō] *n* stucco.
stuck [stuk] *pt, pp of* **stick** ♦ *a* (*jammed*) bloccato(a); **to get ~** bloccarsi.
stuck-up [stuk'up'] *a* presuntuoso(a).
stud [stud] *n* bottoncino; borchia; (*of horses*) scuderia, allevamento di cavalli; (*also:* **~ horse**) stallone *m* ♦ *vt* (*fig*): **~ded with** tempestato(a) di.
student [stōō'dənt] *n* studente/essa; (*US: at school*) allievo/a ♦ *cpd* studentesco(a); universitario(a); degli studenti; **a law/medical ~** uno studente di legge/di medicina; **he's a ~ teacher** sta facendo tirocinio come insegnante.
student driver *n* (*US*) conducente *m/f* principiante; **he's a ~** sta imparando a guidare.
studied [stud'ēd] *a* studiato(a), calcolato(a).
studio [stōō'dēō] *n* studio.
studio apartment *n* appartamento monolocale.
studious [stōō'dēəs] *a* studioso(a); (*studied*) studiato(a), voluto(a).
studiously [stōō'dēəslē] *ad* (*carefully*) deliberatamente, di proposito.
study [stud'ē] *n* studio ♦ *vt* studiare; esaminare ♦ *vi* studiare; **to make a ~ of sth** fare uno studio su qc; **to ~ for an exam** prepararsi a un esame.
stuff [stuf] *n* (*substance*) roba; (*belongings*) cose *fpl*, roba ♦ *vt* imbottire; (*animal: for exhibition*) impagliare; (*CULIN*) farcire; **my nose is ~ed up** ho il naso chiuso; **get ~ed!** (*Brit col!*) va' a farti fottere! (*!*); **~ed toy** giocattolo di peluche.
stuffing [stuf'ing] *n* imbottitura; (*CULIN*) ripieno.

stuffy [stuf'ē] *a* (*room*) mal ventilato(a), senz'aria; (*ideas*) antiquato(a).
stumble [stum'bəl] *vi* inciampare; **to ~ across** (*fig*) imbattersi in.
stumbling block [stum'bling blâk] *n* ostacolo, scoglio.
stump [stump] *n* ceppo; (*of limb*) moncone *m* ♦ *vt*: **to be ~ed for an answer** essere incapace di rispondere.
stun [stun] *vt* stordire; (*amaze*) sbalordire.
stung [stung] *pt, pp of* **sting.**
stunk [stungk] *pp of* **stink.**
stunning [stun'ing] *a* (*piece of news etc*) sbalorditivo(a); (*girl, dress*) favoloso(a), stupendo(a).
stunt [stunt] *n* bravata; trucco pubblicitario; (*AVIAT*) acrobazia ♦ *vt* arrestare.
stunted [stun'tid] *a* stentato(a), rachitico(a).
stuntman [stunt'mən] *n* cascatore *m*.
stupefaction [stōōpəfak'shən] *n* stupefazione *f*, stupore *m*.
stupefy [stōō'pəfī] *vt* stordire; intontire; (*fig*) stupire.
stupendous [stōōpen'dəs] *a* stupendo(a), meraviglioso(a).
stupid [stōō'pid] *a* stupido(a).
stupidity [stōōpid'itē] *n* stupidità.
stupidly [stōō'pidlē] *ad* stupidamente.
stupor [stōō'pûr] *n* torpore *m*.
sturdy [stûr'dē] *a* robusto(a), vigoroso(a); solido(a).
sturgeon [stûr'jən] *n* storione *m*.
stutter [stut'ûr] *n* balbuzie *f* ♦ *vi* balbettare.
Stuttgart [stōōt'gârt] *n* Stoccarda.
sty [stī] *n* (*of pigs*) porcile *m*.
stye [stī] *n* (*MED*) orzaiolo.
style [stīl] *n* stile *m*; (*distinction*) eleganza, classe *f*; (*hair ~*) pettinatura; (*of dress etc*) modello, linea; **in the latest ~** all'ultima moda.
styli [stī'lē] *npl of* **stylus.**
stylish [stī'lish] *a* elegante.
stylist [stī'list] *n*: **hair ~** parrucchiere/a.
stylized [stī'līzd] *a* stilizzato(a).
stylus, *pl* **styli** *or* **styluses** [stī'ləs, stī'lē] *n* (*of record player*) puntina.
suave [swâv] *a* untuoso(a).
sub [sub] *n abbr* = **submarine; subscription.**
sub... *prefix* sub..., sotto....
subcommittee [sub'kəmitē] *n* sottocomitato.
subconscious [subkân'chəs] *a, n* subcosciente (*m*).
subcontinent [subkân'tənənt] *n*: **the (Indian) ~** il subcontinente (indiano).
subcontract *n* [subkân'trakt] subappalto ♦ *vt* [subkəntrakt'] subappaltare.
subcontractor [subkân'traktûr] *n* subappaltatore/trice.
subdivide [subdivīd'] *vt* suddividere.
subdivision [subdivizh'ən] *n* suddivisione *f*.

subdue [səbdoo'] *vt* sottomettere, soggiogare.

subdued [səbdood'] *a* pacato(a); (*light*) attenuato(a); (*person*) poco esuberante.

subject *n* [sub'jikt] soggetto; (*citizen etc*) cittadino/a; (*SCOL*) materia ♦ *a* (*liable*): ~ **to** soggetto(a) a ♦ *vt* [səbjekt']: **to ~ to** sottomettere a; esporre a; ~ **to confirmation in writing** a condizione di ricevere conferma scritta; **to change the ~** cambiare discorso.

subjection [səbjek'shən] *n* sottomissione *f*, soggezione *f*.

subjective [səbjek'tiv] *a* soggettivo(a).

subject matter *n* argomento; contenuto.

sub judice [sub joo'disē] *a* (*LAW*) sub iudice.

subjugate [sub'jəgāt] *vt* sottomettere, soggiogare.

subjunctive [səbjungk'tiv] *a* congiuntivo(a) ♦ *n* congiuntivo.

sublease [sublēs'] (*US*) *vt* effettuare un leaseback *inv* ♦ *n* lease-back *m inv*.

sublet [sublet'] *vt, vi irg* subaffittare.

sublime [səblīm'] *a* sublime.

subliminal [sublim'ənəl] *a* subliminale.

submachine gun [subməshēn' gun] *n* mitra *m inv*.

submarine [sub'mərēn] *n* sommergibile *m*.

submerge [səbmûrj'] *vt* sommergere; immergere ♦ *vi* immergersi.

submersion [səbmûr'zhən] *n* sommersione *f*; immersione *f*.

submission [səbmish'ən] *n* sottomissione *f*; (*to committee etc*) richiesta, domanda.

submissive [səbmis'iv] *a* remissivo(a).

submit [səbmit'] *vt* sottomettere; (*proposal, claim*) presentare ♦ *vi* sottomettersi.

subnormal [subnôr'məl] *a* subnormale.

subordinate [səbôr'dənit] *a, n* subordinato(a).

subpoena [səpē'nə] *n* (*LAW*) citazione *f*, mandato di comparizione ♦ *vt* (*LAW*) citare in giudizio.

subroutine [subrooten'] *n* (*COMPUT*) sottoprogramma *m*.

subscribe [səbskrīb'] *vi* contribuire; **to ~ to** (*opinion*) approvare, condividere; (*fund*) sottoscrivere; (*newspaper*) abbonarsi a; essere abbonato(a) a.

subscriber [səbskrīb'ûr] *n* (*to periodical, telephone*) abbonato/a.

subscript [sub'skript] *n* deponente *m*.

subscription [səbskrip'shən] *n* sottoscrizione *f*; abbonamento; **to take out a ~ to** abbonarsi a.

subsequent [sub'səkwənt] *a* (*later*) successivo(a); (*further*) ulteriore; ~ **to** in seguito a.

subsequently [sub'səkwəntlē] *ad* in seguito, successivamente.

subservient [səbsûr'vēənt] *a*: ~ **(to)** remissivo(a) (a), sottomesso(a) (a).

subside [səbsīd'] *vi* cedere, abbassarsi; (*flood*) decrescere; (*wind*) calmarsi.

subsidence [səbsīd'əns] *n* cedimento, abbassamento.

subsidiary [səbsid'ēārē] *a* sussidiario(a); accessorio(a); (*Brit SCOL: subject*) complementare ♦ *n* filiale *f*.

subsidize [sub'sidīz] *vt* sovvenzionare.

subsidy [sub'sidē] *n* sovvenzione *f*.

subsist [səbsist'] *vi*: **to ~ on sth** vivere di qc.

subsistence [səbsis'təns] *n* esistenza; mezzi *mpl* di sostentamento.

subsistence allowance *n* indennità *f inv* di trasferta.

subsistence level *n* livello minimo di vita.

substance [sub'stəns] *n* sostanza; (*fig*) essenza; **to lack ~** (*argument*) essere debole.

substandard [substan'dûrd] *a* (*goods, housing*) di qualità scadente.

substantial [səbstan'chəl] *a* solido(a); (*amount, progress etc*) notevole; (*meal*) sostanzioso(a).

substantially [səbstan'chəlē] *ad* sostanzialmente; ~ **bigger** molto più grande.

substantiate [səbstan'chēāt] *vt* comprovare.

substitute [sub'stitoot] *n* (*person*) sostituto/a; (*thing*) succedaneo, surrogato ♦ *vt*: **to ~ sth/sb for** sostituire qc/qn a.

substitute teacher *n* (*US*) supplente *m/f*.

substitution [substitoo'shən] *n* sostituzione *f*.

subterfuge [sub'tûrfyooj] *n* sotterfugio.

subterranean [subtərā'nēən] *a* sotterraneo(a).

subtitle [sub'tītəl] *n* (*CINEMA*) sottotitolo.

subtle [sut'əl] *a* sottile; (*flavor, perfume*) delicato(a).

subtlety [sut'əltē] *n* sottigliezza.

subtly [sut'lē] *ad* sottilmente; delicatamente.

subtotal [subtō'təl] *n* somma parziale.

subtract [səbtrakt'] *vt* sottrarre.

subtraction [səbtrak'shən] *n* sottrazione *f*.

suburb [sub'ûrb] *n* sobborgo; **the ~s** la periferia.

suburban [səbûr'bən] *a* suburbano(a).

suburbia [səbûr'bēə] *n* periferia, sobborghi *mpl*.

subversion [səbvûr'zhən] *n* sovversione *f*.

subversive [səbvûr'siv] *a* sovversivo(a).

subway [sub'wā] *n* (*US: underground*) metropolitana; (*Brit: underpass*) sottopassaggio.

subway station *n* (*US*) stazione *f* del metrò.

subzero [sub'zē'rō] *a*: ~ **temperatures** temperature *fpl* sotto zero.

succeed [səksēd'] *vi* riuscire, avere successo ♦ *vt* succedere a; **to ~ in doing** riuscire a fare.

succeeding [səksē'ding] *a* (*following*) successivo(a); ~ **generations** generazioni *fpl* future.

success [səkses'] *n* successo.

successful [səkses'fəl] *a* (*venture*) coronato(a) da successo, riuscito(a); **to be ~ (in doing)** riuscire (a fare).

successfully [səkses'fəlē] *ad* con successo.

succession [səksesh'ən] *n* successione *f*; **in ~** di seguito.

successive [səkses'iv] *a* successivo(a); consecutivo(a); **on 3 ~ days** per 3 giorni consecutivi *or* di seguito.

successor [səkses'ûr] *n* successore *m*.

succinct [səksingkt'] *a* succinto(a), breve.

succulent [suk'yələnt] *a* succulento(a) ♦ *n* (*BOT*): **~s** piante *fpl* grasse.

succumb [səkum'] *vi* soccombere.

such [such] *a* tale; (*of that kind*): **~ a book** un tale libro, un libro del genere; **~ books** tali libri, libri del genere; (*so much*): **~ courage** tanto coraggio ♦ *ad*: **~ a long trip** un viaggio così lungo; **~ good books** libri così buoni; **~ a lot of** talmente *or* così tanto(a); **making ~ a noise that** facendo un rumore tale che; **~ a long time ago** tanto tempo fa; **~ as** (*like*) come; **a noise ~ as to** un rumore tale da; **~ books as I have** quei pochi libri che ho; **as ~** come *or* in quanto tale; **I said no ~ thing** non ho detto niente del genere.

such-and-such [such'ənsuch] *a* tale (*after noun*).

suchlike [such'līk] *pronoun* (*col*): **and ~** e così via.

suck [suk] *vt* succhiare; (*subj: baby*) poppare; (: *pump, machine*) aspirare.

sucker [suk'ûr] *n* (*ZOOL, TECH*) ventosa; (*BOT*) pollone *m*; (*col*) gonzo/a, babbeo/a.

suckle [suk'əl] *vt* allattare.

suction [suk'shən] *n* succhiamento; (*TECH*) aspirazione *f*.

suction pump *n* pompa aspirante.

Sudan [soōdan'] *n* Sudan *m*.

Sudanese [soōdənēz'] *a*, *n* sudanese (*m/f*).

sudden [sud'ən] *a* improvviso(a); **all of a ~** improvvisamente, all'improvviso.

suddenly [sud'ənlē] *ad* bruscamente, improvvisamente, di colpo.

suds [sudz] *npl* schiuma (di sapone).

sue [soō] *vt* citare in giudizio ♦ *vi*: **to ~ (for)** intentare causa (per); **to ~ for divorce** intentare causa di divorzio; **to ~ sb for damages** citare qn per danni.

suede [swād] *n* pelle *f* scamosciata ♦ *cpd* scamosciato(a).

suet [soō'it] *n* grasso di rognone.

Suez [soōez'] *n*: **the ~ Canal** il Canale di Suez.

Suff. *abbr* (*Brit*) = Suffolk.

suffer [suf'ûr] *vt* soffrire, patire; (*bear*) sopportare, tollerare; (*undergo: loss, setback*) subire ♦ *vi* soffrire; **to ~ from** soffrire di; **to ~ from the effects of alcohol/a fall** risentire degli effetti dell'alcool/di una caduta.

sufferance [suf'ûrəns] *n*: **he was only there on ~** era più che altro sopportato lì.

sufferer [suf'ûrûr] *n* (*MED*): **~ (from)** malato/a (di).

suffering [suf'ûring] *n* sofferenza; (*hardship, deprivation*) privazione *f*.

suffice [səfīs'] *vi* essere sufficiente, bastare.

sufficient [səfish'ənt] *a* sufficiente; **~ money** abbastanza soldi.

sufficiently [səfish'əntlē] *ad* sufficientemente, abbastanza.

suffix [suf'iks] *n* suffisso.

suffocate [suf'əkāt] *vi* (*have difficulty breathing*) soffocare; (*die through lack of air*) asfissiare.

suffocation [sufəkā'shən] *n* soffocamento; (*MED*) asfissia.

suffrage [suf'rij] *n* suffragio.

suffuse [səfyoōz'] *vt*: **to ~ (with)** (*color*) tingere (di); (*light*) soffondere (di); **her face was ~d with joy** la gioia si dipingeva sul suo volto.

sugar [shoōg'ûr] *n* zucchero ♦ *vt* zuccherare.

sugar beet *n* barbabietola da zucchero.

sugar bowl *n* zuccheriera.

sugar cane *n* canna da zucchero.

sugar-coated [shoōg'ûrkō'tid] *a* ricoperto(a) di zucchero.

sugar cube *n* zolletta di zucchero.

sugar refinery *n* raffineria di zucchero.

sugary [shoōg'ûrē] *a* zuccherino(a), dolce; (*fig*) sdolcinato(a).

suggest [səgjest'] *vt* proporre, suggerire; (*indicate*) indicare; **what do you ~ I do?** cosa mi suggerisce di fare?

suggestion [səgjes'chən] *n* suggerimento, proposta.

suggestive [səgjes'tiv] *a* suggestivo(a); (*indecent*) spinto(a), indecente.

suicidal [soōisīd'əl] *a* suicida *inv*; (*fig*) fatale, disastroso(a).

suicide [soō'isīd] *n* (*person*) suicida *m/f*; (*act*) suicidio; **to commit ~** suicidarsi.

suicide attempt *n* tentato suicidio.

suit [soōt] *n* (*man's*) completo; (*woman's*) completo, tailleur *m inv*; (*law~*) causa; (*CARDS*) seme *m*, colore *m* ♦ *vt* andar bene a *or* per; essere adatto(a) a *or* per; (*adapt*): **to ~ sth to** adattare qc a; **to be ~ed to sth** (*suitable for*) essere adatto a qc; **well ~ed** (*couple*) fatti l'uno per l'altro; **to bring a ~ against sb** intentare causa a qn; **to follow ~** (*fig*) fare altrettanto.

suitable [soō'təbəl] *a* adatto(a); appropriato(a); **would tomorrow be ~?** andrebbe bene domani?; **we found somebody ~** abbiamo trovato la persona adatta.

suitably [soō'təblē] *ad* (*dress*) in modo adatto; (*thank*) adeguatamente.

suitcase [soōt'kās] *n* valigia.

suite [swēt] *n* (*of rooms*) appartamento; (*MUS*) suite *f inv*; (*furniture*): **bedroom/dining room ~** arredo *or* mobilia per la camera da letto/sala da pranzo; **a three-piece ~** un salotto comprendente un divano e due poltrone.

suitor [soō'tûr] *n* corteggiatore *m*, spasimante *m*.

sulfate [sul'fāt] n (US) solfato; **copper** ~ solfato di rame.

sulfur [sul'fûr] n (US) zolfo.

sulfuric [sulfyōōr'ik] a (US): ~ **acid** acido solforico.

sulk [sulk] vi fare il broncio.

sulky [sul'kē] a imbronciato(a).

sullen [sul'ən] a scontroso(a); cupo(a).

sulphate [sul'fāt] n (Brit) = **sulfate**.

sulphur [sul'fûr] etc (Brit) = **sulfur** etc.

sultan [sul'tən] n sultano.

sultana [sultan'ə] n (fruit) uva (secca) sultanina.

sultry [sul'trē] a afoso(a).

sum [sum] n somma; (SCOL etc) addizione f.

sum up vt riassumere; (evaluate rapidly) valutare, giudicare ♦ vi riassumere.

Sumatra [sōōmát'rə] n Sumatra.

summarize [sum'ərīz] vt riassumere, riepilogare.

summary [sum'ûrē] n riassunto ♦ a (justice) sommario(a).

summer [sum'ûr] n estate f ♦ cpd d'estate, estivo(a); **in (the)** ~ d'estate.

summer camp n (US) colonia (estiva).

summerhouse [sum'ûrhous] n (in garden) padiglione m.

summertime [sum'ûrtīm] n (season) estate f.

summer time n (by clock) ora legale (estiva).

summery [sum'ûrē] a estivo(a).

summing-up [sum'ingup'] n (LAW) ricapitolazione f del processo.

summit [sum'it] n cima, sommità; (POL) vertice m.

summit conference n conferenza al vertice.

summon [sum'ən] vt chiamare, convocare; **to ~ a witness** citare un testimone.

summon up vt raccogliere, fare appello a.

summons [sum'ənz] n ordine m di comparizione ♦ vt citare; **to serve a ~ on sb** notificare una citazione a qn.

sump [sump] n (Brit AUT) coppa dell'olio.

sumptuous [sump'chōōəs] a sontuoso(a).

Sun. abbr (= Sunday) dom.

sun [sun] n sole m; **in the** ~ al sole; **to catch the** ~ prendere sole; **they have everything under the** ~ hanno tutto ciò che possono desiderare.

sunbathe [sun'bāth] vi prendere un bagno di sole.

sunbeam [sun'bēm] n raggio di sole.

sunbed [sun'bed] n lettino solare.

sunburn [sun'bûrn] n (tan) abbronzatura; (painful) scottatura.

sunburned [sun'bûrnd] a abbronzato(a); (painfully) scottato(a) dal sole.

sundae [sun'dē] n coppa di gelato guarnita.

Sunday [sun'dā] n domenica; for phrases see also **Tuesday**.

Sunday school n ≈ scuola di catechismo.

sundial [sun'dīl] n meridiana.

sundown [sun'doun] n tramonto.

sundries [sun'drēz] npl articoli diversi, cose diverse.

sundry [sun'drē] a vari(e), diversi(e); **all and** ~ tutti quanti.

sunflower [sun'flouûr] n girasole m.

sung [sung] pp of **sing**.

sunglasses [sun'glasiz] npl occhiali mpl da sole.

sunk [sungk] pp of **sink**.

sunken [sung'kən] a sommerso(a); (eyes, cheeks) infossato(a); (bath) incassato(a).

sunlamp [sun'lamp] n lampada a raggi ultravioletti.

sunlight [sun'līt] n (luce f del) sole m.

sunlit [sun'lit] a assolato(a), soleggiato(a).

sunny [sun'ē] a assolato(a), soleggiato(a); (fig) allegro(a), felice; **it is** ~ c'è il sole.

sunrise [sun'rīz] n levata del sole, alba.

sunroof [sun'rōōf] n (on building) tetto a terrazzo; (AUT) tetto apribile.

sunset [sun'set] n tramonto.

sunshade [sun'shād] n parasole m.

sunshine [sun'shīn] n (luce f del) sole m.

sunspot [sun'spät] n macchia solare.

sunstroke [sun'strōk] n insolazione f, colpo di sole.

suntan [sun'tan] n abbronzatura.

suntan lotion n latte m solare.

suntanned [sun'tand] a abbronzato(a).

suntan oil n olio solare.

super [sōō'pûr] a (col) fantastico(a).

superannuation [sōōpûranyōōā'shən] n contributi mpl pensionistici; pensione f.

superb [sōōpûrb'] a magnifico(a).

supercilious [sōōpûrsil'ēəs] a sprezzante, sdegnoso(a).

superficial [sōōpûrfish'əl] a superficiale.

superficially [sōōpûrfish'əlē] ad superficialmente.

superfluous [sōōpûr'flōōəs] a superfluo(a).

superhuman [sōōpûrhyōō'mən] a sovrumano(a).

superimpose [sōōpûrimpōz'] vt sovrapporre.

superintend [sōōpûrintend'] vt dirigere, sovraintendere.

superintendent [sōōpûrinten'dənt] n direttore/trice; (Brit POLICE) ≈ commissario (capo).

superior [səpēr'ûr] a superiore; (COMM: goods, quality) di prim'ordine, superiore; (smug: person) che fa il superiore ♦ n superiore m/f; **Mother S**~ (REL) Madre f Superiora, Superiora.

superiority [səpērēôr'itē] n superiorità.

superlative [səpûr'lətiv] a superlativo(a), supremo(a) ♦ n (LING) superlativo.

superman [sōō'pûrman] n superuomo.

supermarket [sōō'pûrmârkit] n supermercato.

supernatural [sōōpûrnach'ûrəl] a soprannaturale.

superpower [sōōpúrpou'úr] *n* (*POL*) superpotenza.

superscript [sōō'púrskript] *n* esponente *m*.

supersede [sōōpúrsēd'] *vt* sostituire, soppiantare.

supersonic [sōōpúrsán'ik] *a* supersonico(a).

superstition [sōōpúrstish'ən] *n* superstizione *f*.

superstitious [sōōpúrstish'əs] *a* superstizioso(a).

superstore [sōō'púrstòr] *n* (*Brit*) grande supermercato.

supertanker [sōō'púrtangkúr] *n* superpetroliera.

supertax [sōō'púrtaks] *n* soprattassa.

supervise [sōō'púrvïz] *vt* (*person etc*) sorvegliare; (*organization*) soprintendere a.

supervision [sōōpúrvizh'ən] *n* sorveglianza, supervisione *f*; **under medical ~** sotto controllo medico.

supervisor [sōō'púrvïzûr] *n* sorvegliante *m/f*, soprintendente *m/f*; (*in shop*) capocommesso/a; (*at university*) relatore/trice.

supervisory [sōōpúrvï'zûrē] *a* di sorveglianza.

supine [sōō'pïn] *a* supino(a).

supper [sup'úr] *n* cena; **to have ~** cenare.

supplant [səplant'] *vt* soppiantare.

supple [sup'əl] *a* flessibile; agile.

supplement *n* [sup'ləmənt] supplemento ♦ *vt* [sup'ləment] completare, integrare.

supplementary [supləmen'tûrē] *a* supplementare.

supplementary benefit *n* (*Brit*) forma di indennità assistenziale.

supplier [səpli'úr] *n* fornitore *m*.

supply [səpli'] *vt* (*goods*): **to ~ sth (to sb)** fornire qc (a qn); (*people, organization*): **to ~ sb (with sth)** fornire a qn (qc); (*system, machine*): **to ~ sth (with sth)** alimentare qc (con qc); (*a need*) soddisfare ♦ *n* riserva, provvista; (*supplying*) approvvigionamento; (*TECH*) alimentazione *f*; **supplies** *npl* (*food*) viveri *mpl*; (*MIL*) sussistenza; **office supplies** forniture *fpl* per ufficio; **to be in short ~** scarseggiare, essere scarso(a); **the electricity/water/gas ~** l'erogazione *f* di corrente/d'acqua/di gas; **~ and demand** la domanda e l'offerta; **the car comes supplied with a radio** l'auto viene fornita completa di radio.

supply teacher *n* (*Brit*) supplente *m/f*.

support [səpôrt'] *n* (*moral, financial etc*) sostegno, appoggio; (*TECH*) supporto ♦ *vt* sostenere; (*financially*) mantenere; (*uphold*) sostenere, difendere; (*SPORT: team*) fare il tifo per; **they stopped work in ~ (of)** hanno smesso di lavorare per solidarietà (con); **to ~ o.s.** (*financially*) mantenersi.

supporter [səpôr'tûr] *n* (*POL etc*) sostenitore/trice, fautore/trice; (*SPORT*) tifoso/a.

supporting [səpôr'ting] *a* (*THEATER: role*) se-

condario(a), di secondo piano; (: *actor*) che ha un ruolo secondario.

suppose [səpōz'] *vt, vi* supporre; immaginare; **to be ~d to do** essere tenuto(a) a fare; **I don't ~ she'll come** non credo che venga; **he's ~d to be an expert** dicono che sia un esperto, passa per un esperto.

supposedly [səpō'zidlē] *ad* presumibilmente; (*seemingly*) apparentemente.

supposing [səpō'zing] *cj* se, ammesso che + *sub*.

supposition [supəzish'ən] *n* supposizione *f*, ipotesi *f inv*.

suppository [səpáz'itôrē] *n* supposta, suppositorio.

suppress [səpres'] *vt* reprimere; sopprimere; tenere segreto(a).

suppression [səpresh'ən] *n* repressione *f*; soppressione *f*.

suppressor [səpres'úr] *n* (*ELEC etc*) soppressore *m*.

supremacy [səprem'əsē] *n* supremazia.

supreme [səprēm'] *a* supremo(a).

Supreme Court *n* (*US*) Corte *f* suprema.

Supt. *abbr* (*POLICE*) = **superintendent**.

surcharge [sûr'chârj] *n* supplemento; (*extra tax*) soprattassa.

sure [shōōr] *a* sicuro(a); (*definite, convinced*) sicuro(a), certo(a) ♦ *ad* (*col: US*): **that ~ is pretty, that's ~ pretty** è veramente *or* davvero carino; **~!** (*of course*) senz'altro!, certo!; **~ enough** infatti; **to make ~ of** assicurarsi di; **to be ~ of sth** essere sicuro di qc; **to be ~ of o.s.** essere sicuro di sé; **I'm not ~ how/why/when** non so bene come/perché/quando + *sub*.

sure-footed [shōōr'fŏŏt'id] *a* dal passo sicuro.

surely [shōōr'lē] *ad* sicuramente; certamente; **~ you don't mean that!** non parlerà sul serio!

surety [shōōr'ətē] *n* garanzia; **to go** *or* **stand ~ for sb** farsi garante per qn.

surf [sûrf] *n* (*waves*) cavalloni *mpl*; (*foam*) spuma.

surface [sûr'fis] *n* superficie *f* ♦ *vt* (*road*) asfaltare ♦ *vi* risalire alla superficie; (*fig: person*) venire a galla, farsi vivo(a); **on the ~ it seems that ...** (*fig*) superficialmente sembra che ...

surface area *n* superficie *f*.

surface mail *n* posta ordinaria.

surfboard [sûrf'bôrd] *n* tavola per surfing.

surfeit [sûr'fit] *n*: **a ~ of** un eccesso di; un'indigestione di.

surfer [sûrf'úr] *n* chi pratica il surfing.

surfing [sûrf'ing] *n* surfing *m*.

surge [sûrj] *n* (*strong movement*) ondata; (*of feeling*) impeto; (*ELEC*) sovracorrente *f* transitoria ♦ *vi* (*waves*) gonfiarsi; (*ELEC: power*) aumentare improvvisamente; **to ~ forward** buttarsi avanti.

surgeon [sûr'jən] n chirurgo.
Surgeon General n (US) ≈ Ministro della Sanità.
surgery [sûr'jûrē] n chirurgia; (Brit MED: room) studio or gabinetto medico, ambulatorio; (: session) visita ambulatoriale; (Brit: of MP etc) incontri mpl con gli elettori; **to undergo** ~ subire un intervento chirurgico.
surgery hours npl (Brit) orario delle visite or di consultazione.
surgical [sûr'jikəl] a chirurgico(a).
surgical spirit n (Brit) alcool denaturato.
surly [sûr'lē] a scontroso(a), burbero(a).
surmise [sûrmīz'] vt supporre, congetturare.
surmount [sûrmount'] vt sormontare.
surname [sûr'nām] n cognome m.
surpass [sûrpas'] vt superare.
surplus [sûr'pləs] n eccedenza; (ECON) surplus m inv ♦ a eccedente, d'avanzo; **it is** ~ **to our requirements** eccede i nostri bisogni; ~ **stock** merce f in sovrappiù.
surprise [sûrprīz'] n sorpresa; (astonishment) stupore m ♦ vt sorprendere; stupire; **to take by** ~ (person) cogliere di sorpresa; (MIL: town, fort) attaccare di sorpresa.
surprising [sûrprī'zing] a sorprendente, stupefacente.
surprisingly [sûrprī'zinglē] ad sorprendentemente; **(somewhat)** ~, **he agreed** cosa (alquanto) sorprendente, ha accettato.
surrealism [sərē'əlizəm] n surrealismo.
surrealist [sərē'əlist] a, n surrealista (m/f).
surrender [sərcn'dûr] n resa, capitolazione f ♦ vi arrendersi ♦ vt (claim, right) rinunciare a.
surrender value n (COMM) valore m di riscatto.
surreptitious [sûrəptish'əs] a furtivo(a).
surrogate [sûr'əgit] n (substitute) surrogato ♦ a surrogato(a).
surrogate mother n madre f sostitutiva.
surround [səround'] vt circondare; (MIL etc) accerchiare.
surrounding [səroun'ding] a circostante.
surroundings [səroun'dingz] npl dintorni mpl; (fig) ambiente m.
surtax [sûr'taks] n soprattassa.
surveillance [sûrvā'ləns] n sorveglianza, controllo.
survey n [sûr'vā] (comprehensive view: of situation, development) quadro generale; (study) indagine f, studio; (Brit: in housebuying etc) perizia; (of land) rilevamento, rilievo topografico ♦ vt [sərvā'] osservare; esaminare; (Brit SURVEYING: building) fare una perizia di; (: land) fare il rilevamento di.
surveying [sûrvā'ing] n (of land) agrimensura.
surveyor [sûrvā'ûr] n perito; (of land) agrimensore m.
survival [sûrvī'vəl] n sopravvivenza; (relic) reliquia, vestigio.
survival course n corso di sopravvivenza.

survival kit n equipaggiamento di prima necessità.
survive [sûrvīv'] vi sopravvivere ♦ vt sopravvivere a.
survivor [sûrvī'vûr] n superstite m/f, sopravvissuto/a.
susceptible [səsep'təbəl] a: ~ **(to)** sensibile (a); (disease) predisposto(a) (a).
suspect a, n [sus'pekt] a sospetto(a) ♦ n persona sospetta ♦ vt [səspekt'] sospettare; (think likely) supporre; (doubt) dubitare di.
suspend [səspend'] vt sospendere.
suspended sentence [səspen'did sen'təns] n condanna con la condizionale.
suspender belt [səspen'dûr belt] n (Brit) reggicalze m inv.
suspenders [səspen'dûrz] npl (US) bretelle fpl; (Brit) giarrettiere fpl.
suspense [səspens'] n apprensione f; (in film etc) suspense m.
suspense account n (COMM) conto in sospeso.
suspension [səspen'chən] n (gen, AUT) sospensione f; (of driver's license) ritiro temporaneo.
suspension bridge n ponte m sospeso.
suspicion [səspish'ən] n sospetto; **to be under** ~ essere sospettato; **arrested on** ~ **of murder** arrestato come presunto omicida.
suspicious [səspish'əs] a (suspecting) sospettoso(a); (causing suspicion) sospetto(a); **to be** ~ **of** or **about sb/sth** nutrire sospetti nei riguardi di qn/qc.
suss out [sus out] vt (Brit col): **I've ~ed it/ him out** ho capito come stanno le cose/che tipo è.
sustain [səstān'] vt sostenere; sopportare; (suffer) subire.
sustained [səstānd'] a (effort) prolungato(a).
sustenance [sus'tənəns] n nutrimento; mezzi mpl di sostentamento.
suture [sōō'chûr] n sutura.
SW abbr (RADIO: = short wave) O.C.
swab [swâb] n (MED) tampone m ♦ vt (NAUT: also: ~ **down**) radazzare.
swagger [swag'ûr] vi pavoneggiarsi.
swallow [swâl'ō] n (bird) rondine f; (of food) boccone m; (of drink) sorso ♦ vt inghiottire; (fig: story) bere.
swallow up vt inghiottire.
swam [swam] pt of **swim**.
swamp [swâmp] n palude f ♦ vt sommergere.
swampy [swâmp'ē] a palludoso(a), pantanoso(a).
swan [swân] n cigno.
swank [swangk] vi (col: talk boastfully) fare lo spaccone; (: show off) mettersi in mostra.
swan song n (fig) canto del cigno.
swap [swâp] n scambio ♦ vt: **to** ~ **(for)** scambiare (con).
swarm [swôrm] n sciame m ♦ vi formicolare;

(bees) sciamare.

swarthy [swôr'thē] *a* di carnagione scura.

swashbuckling [swåsh'bukling] *a (role, hero)* spericolato(a).

swastika [swås'tikə] *n* croce *f* uncinata, svastica.

swathe [swåth] *n* fascio ♦ *vt:* **to ~ in** *(bandages, blankets)* avvolgere in.

swatter [swåt'ûr] *n (also:* **fly ~**) ammazzamosche *m inv.*

sway [swā] *vi (building)* oscillare; *(tree)* ondeggiare; *(person)* barcollare ♦ *vt (influence)* influenzare ♦ *n (rule, power):* **~ (over)** influenza (su); **to hold ~ over sb** dominare qn.

Swaziland [swå'zēland] *n* Swaziland *m.*

swear, *pt* **swore,** *pp* **sworn** [swe'ûr, swôr, swôrn] *vi (witness etc)* giurare; *(curse)* bestemmiare, imprecare ♦ *vt:* **to ~ an oath** prestare giuramento; **to ~ to sth** giurare qc.
   swear in *vt* prestare giuramento in.

swearword [swär'wûrd] *n* parolaccia.

sweat [swet] *n* sudore *m,* traspirazione *f* ♦ *vi* sudare; **in a ~** in un bagno di sudore.

sweatband [swet'band] *n (SPORT)* fascia elastica (per assorbire il sudore).

sweater [swet'ûr] *n* maglione *m.*

sweatshirt [swet'shûrt] *n* maglione *m* in cotone felpato.

sweatshop [swet'shåp] *n azienda o fabbrica dove i dipendenti sono sfruttati.*

sweat suit *n* tuta sportiva.

sweaty [swet'ē] *a* sudato(a); bagnato(a) di sudore.

Swede [swēd] *n* svedese *m/f.*

swede [swēd] *n (Brit)* rapa svedese.

Sweden [swēd'ən] *n* Svezia.

Swedish [swē'dish] *a* svedese ♦ *n (LING)* svedese *m.*

sweep [swēp] *n* spazzata; *(curve)* curva; *(expanse)* distesa; *(range)* portata; *(also:* **chimney ~**) spazzacamino ♦ *vb (pt, pp* **swept** [swept]) *vt* spazzare, scopare; *(subj: fashion, craze)* invadere ♦ *vi* camminare maestosamente; precipitarsi, lanciarsi; (e)stendersi.
   sweep away *vt* spazzare via; trascinare via.
   sweep past *vi* sfrecciare accanto; passare accanto maestosamente.
   sweep up *vt, vi* spazzare.

sweeping [swē'ping] *a (gesture)* ampio(a); *(changes, reforms)* ampio(a), radicale; **a ~ statement** un'affermazione generica.

sweepstake [swēp'stāk] *n* lotteria *(spesso abbinata alle corse dei cavalli).*

sweet [swēt] *n (Brit: dessert)* dolce *m;* (: *candy)* caramella ♦ *a* dolce; *(fresh)* fresco(a); *(kind)* gentile; *(cute)* carino(a) ♦ *ad:* **to smell/taste ~** avere un odore/sapore dolce; **~ and sour** *a* agrodolce.

sweetbread [swēt'bred] *n* animella.

sweetcorn [swēt'kôrn] *n* granturco dolce.

sweeten [swēt'ən] *vt* addolcire; zuccherare.

sweetener [swēt'ənûr] *n (CULIN)* dolcificante *m.*

sweetheart [swēt'hårt] *n* innamorato/a.

sweetly [swēt'lē] *ad* dolcemente.

sweetness [swēt'nis] *n* sapore *m* dolce; dolcezza.

sweet pea *n* pisello odoroso.

sweet potato *n* patata americana, patata dolce.

sweetshop [swēt'shåp] *n (Brit)* ≈ pasticceria.

sweet tooth *n:* **to have a ~** avere un debole per i dolci.

swell [swel] *n (of sea)* mare *m* lungo ♦ *a (col: excellent)* favoloso(a) ♦ *vb (pt* **~ed,** *pp* **swollen, ~ed** [sweld, swōlən]) *vt* gonfiare, ingrossare; *(numbers, sales etc)* aumentare ♦ *vi* gonfiarsi, ingrossarsi; *(sound)* crescere; *(MED)* gonfiarsi.

swelling [swel'ing] *n (MED)* tumefazione *f,* gonfiore *m.*

sweltering [swel'tûring] *a* soffocante.

swept [swept] *pt, pp of* **sweep.**

swerve [swûrv] *vi* deviare; *(driver)* sterzare; *(boxer)* scartare.

swift [swift] *n (bird)* rondone *m* ♦ *a* rapido(a), veloce.

swiftly [swift'lē] *ad* rapidamente, velocemente.

swiftness [swift'nis] *n* rapidità, velocità.

swig [swig] *n (col: drink)* sorsata.

swill [swil] *n* broda ♦ *vt (also:* **~ out, ~ down**) risciacquare.

swim [swim] *n:* **to go for a ~** andare a fare una nuotata ♦ *vb (pt* **swam,** *pp* **swum** [swam, swum]) *vi* nuotare; *(SPORT)* fare del nuoto; *(head, room)* girare ♦ *vt (river, channel)* attraversare *or* percorrere a nuoto; **to go ~ming** andare a nuotare; **to ~ a length** fare una vasca (a nuoto).

swimmer [swim'ûr] *n* nuotatore/trice.

swimming [swim'ing] *n* nuoto.

swimming baths *npl (Brit)* piscina.

swimming cap *n* cuffia.

swimming costume *n (Brit)* costume *m* da bagno.

swimming pool *n* piscina.

swimming trunks *npl* costume *m* da bagno (per uomo).

swimsuit [swim'sōōt] *n* costume *m* da bagno.

swindle [swin'dəl] *n* truffa ♦ *vt* truffare.

swindler [swind'lûr] *n* truffatore/trice.

swine [swin] *n (pl inv)* maiale *m,* porco; *(col!)* porco (!).

swing [swing] *n* altalena; *(movement)* oscillazione *f; (MUS)* ritmo; *(also:* **~ music**) swing *m* ♦ *vb (pt, pp* **swung** [swung]) *vt* dondolare, far oscillare; *(also:* **~ around**) far girare ♦ *vi* oscillare, dondolare; *(also:* **~ around**: *object)* roteare; (: *person)* girarsi, voltarsi;

to be in full ~ (*activity*) essere in piena attività; (*party etc*) essere nel pieno; **a** ~ **to the left** (*POL*) una svolta a sinistra; **to get into the** ~ **of things** entrare nel pieno delle cose; **the road** ~**s south** la strada prende la direzione sud.

swing bridge *n* (*Brit*) ponte *m* girevole.

swing door *n* (*Brit*) porta battente.

swingeing [swin'jing] *a* (*Brit: defeat*) violento(a); (: *price increase*) enorme.

swinging [swing'ing] *a* (*step*) cadenzato(a), ritmico(a); (*rhythm, music*) trascinante.

swinging door *n* (*US*) porta battente.

swipe [swīp] *n* forte colpo; schiaffo ♦ *vt* (*hit*) colpire con forza; dare uno schiaffo a; (*col: steal*) sgraffignare.

swirl [swûrl] *n* turbine *m*, mulinello ♦ *vi* turbinare, far mulinello.

swish [swish] *n* (*sound: of whip*) sibilo; (: *of skirts, grass*) fruscio ♦ *vi* sibilare.

Swiss [swis] *a, n* (*pl inv*) svizzero(a).

Swiss French *a* svizzero(a) francese.

Swiss German *a* svizzero(a) tedesco(a).

switch [swich] *n* (*for light, radio etc*) interruttore *m*; (*change*) cambiamento ♦ *vt* (*also:* ~ **around**, ~ **over**) cambiare; scambiare.

switch off *vt* spegnere.

switch on *vt* accendere; (*engine, machine*) mettere in moto, avviare; (*AUT: ignition*) inserire.

switchback [swich'bak] *n* montagne *fpl* russe.

switchblade [swich'blād] *n* (*also:* ~ **knife**) coltello a scatto.

switchboard [swich'bôrd] *n* centralino.

switchboard operator *n* centralinista *m/f*.

switch tower *n* (*US RAIL*) cabina di manovra.

switchyard [swich'yârd] *n* (*US*) scalo smistamento.

Switzerland [swit'sûrlənd] *n* Svizzera.

swivel [swiv'əl] *vi* (*also:* ~ **around**) girare.

swollen [swō'lən] *pp* of **swell** ♦ *a* (*ankle etc*) gonfio(a).

swoon [swōōn] *vi* svenire.

swoop [swōōp] *n* (*by police etc*) incursione *f*; (*of bird etc*) picchiata ♦ *vi* (*also:* ~ **down**) scendere in picchiata; (*police*): **to** ~ **(on)** fare un'incursione (in).

swop [swâp] *n, vt* = **swap**.

sword [sôrd] *n* spada.

swordfish [sôrd'fish] *n* pesce *m* spada *inv*.

swore [swôr] *pt* of **swear**.

sworn [swôrn] *pp* of **swear**.

swot [swât] (*Brit*) *vt* sgobbare su ♦ *vi* sgobbare.

swum [swum] *pp* of **swim**.

swung [swung] *pt,· pp* of **swing**.

sycamore [sik'əmôr] *n* sicomoro.

sycophant [sik'əfənt] *n* leccapiedi *m/f*.

sycophantic [sikəfan'tik] *a* ossequioso(a), adu-

latore(trice).

Sydney [sid'nē] *n* Sydney *f*.

syllable [sil'əbəl] *n* sillaba.

syllabus [sil'əbəs] *n* programma *m;* **on the** ~ in programma d'esame.

symbol [sim'bəl] *n* simbolo.

symbolic(al) [simbâl'ik(əl)] *a* simbolico(a); **to be** ~ **of sth** simboleggiare qc.

symbolism [sim'bəlizəm] *n* simbolismo.

symbolize [sim'bəlīz] *vt* simbolizzare.

symmetrical [simet'rikəl] *a* simmetrico(a).

symmetry [sim'itrē] *n* simmetria.

sympathetic [simpəthet'ik] *a* (*showing pity*) compassionevole; (*kind*) comprensivo(a); ~ **towards** ben disposto(a) verso; **to be** ~ **to a cause** (*well-disposed*) simpatizzare per una causa.

sympathetically [simpəthet'iklē] *ad* in modo compassionevole; con comprensione.

sympathize [sim'pəthīz] *vi*: **to** ~ **with sb** compatire qn; partecipare al dolore di qn; (*understand*) capire qn.

sympathizer [sim'pəthīzûr] *n* (*POL*) simpatizzante *m/f*.

sympathy [sim'pəthē] *n* compassione *f*; **in** ~ **with** d'accordo con; (*strike*) per solidarietà con; **with our deepest** ~ con le nostre più sincere condoglianze.

symphonic [simfân'ik] *a* sinfonico(a).

symphony [sim'fənē] *n* sinfonia.

symphony orchestra *n* orchestra sinfonica.

symposium [simpō'zēəm] *n* simposio.

symptom [simp'təm] *n* sintomo; indizio.

symptomatic [simptəmat'ik] *a*: ~ **(of)** sintomatico(a) (di).

synagogue [sin'əgâg] *n* sinagoga.

synchromesh [sing'krəmesh] *n* cambio sincronizzato.

synchronize [sing'krənīz] *vt* sincronizzare ♦ *vi*: **to** ~ **with** essere contemporaneo(a) a.

syncopated [sing'kəpātid] *a* sincopato(a).

syndicate [sin'dəkit] *n* sindacato; (*PRESS*) agenzia di stampa.

syndrome [sin'drōm] *n* sindrome *f*.

synonym [sin'ənim] *n* sinonimo.

synonymous [sinân'əməs] *a*: ~ **(with)** sinonimo(a) (di).

synopsis, *pl* **synopses** [sinâp'sis, sinâp'sēz] *n* sommario, sinossi *f inv*.

syntax [sin'taks] *n* sintassi *f inv*.

synthesis, *pl* **syntheses** [sin'thəsis, sin'thəsēz] *n* sintesi *f inv*.

synthesizer [sin'thisīzûr] *n* (*MUS*) sintetizzatore *m*.

synthetic [sinthet'ik] *a* sintetico(a) ♦ *n* prodotto sintetico; (*TEXTILES*) fibra sintetica.

syphilis [sif'əlis] *n* sifilide *f*.

syphon [sī'fən] *n, vb* = **siphon**.

Syria [sir'ēə] *n* Siria.

Syrian [sēr'ēən] *a, n* siriano(a).

syringe [sərinj'] *n* siringa.

syrup |sir'əp| *n* sciroppo; (*Brit*: *also*: **golden ~**) melassa raffinata.

syrupy |sir'əpē| *a* scirotoppso(a).

system |sis'təm| *n* sistema *m*; (*network*) rete *f*; (*ANAT*) apparato; **it was a shock to his ~** è stato uno shock per il suo organismo.

systematic |sistəmat'ik| *a* sistematico(a).

system disk *n* (*COMPUT*) disco del sistema.

systems analyst |sis'təmz an'əlist| *n* analista *m/f* di sistemi.

T

T, t |tē| *n* (*letter*) T, t *m or f inv*; **T for Tommy** ≈ T come Taranto.

ta |tä| *excl* (*Brit col*) grazie!

tab |tab| *n abbr* = **tabulator** ♦ *n* (*loop on coat etc*) laccetto; (*label*) etichetta; **to keep ~s on** (*fig*) tenere d'occhio.

tabby |tab'ē| *n* (*also*: **~ cat**) (gatto) soriano, gatto tigrato.

tabernacle |tab'úrnakəl| *n* tabernacolo.

table |tā'bəl| *n* tavolo, tavola; (*chart*) tabella; **to lay** *or* **set the ~** apparecchiare *or* preparare la tavola; **to clear the ~** sparecchiare; **~ of contents** indice *m*.

tablecloth |tā'bəlklóth| *n* tovaglia.

table d'hôte |tab'əl dōt'| *a* (*meal*) a prezzo fisso.

table lamp *n* lampada da tavolo.

tableland |tā'bəlland| *n* tavolato, altopiano.

tablemat |tā'bəlmat| *n* (*Brit*) sottopiatto.

table salt *n* sale *m* fino *or* da tavola.

tablespoon |tā'bəlspōōn| *n* cucchiaio da tavola; (*also*: **~ful**: *as measurement*) cucchiaiata.

tablet |tab'lit| *n* (*MED*) compressa; (: *for sucking*) pastiglia; (*for writing*) blocco; (*of stone*) targa.

table tennis *n* tennis *m* da tavolo, ping-pong ® *m*.

table wine *n* vino da tavola.

tabloid |tab'loid| *n* (*newspaper*) tabloid *m inv* (*giornale illustrato di formato ridotto*); **the ~s** i giornali popolari.

taboo |tabōō'| *a*, *n* tabù (*m inv*).

tabulate |tab'yəlāt| *vt* (*data, figures*) tabulare, disporre in tabelle.

tabulator |tab'yəlātûr| *n* tabulatore *m*.

tachograph |tak'əgraf| *n* tachigrafo.

tachometer |təkâm'ətûr| *n* tachimetro.

tacit |tas'it| *a* tacito(a).

taciturn |tas'itûrn| *a* taciturno(a).

tack |tak| *n* (*nail*) bulletta; (*stitch*) punto

d'imbastitura; (*NAUT*) bordo, bordata ♦ *vt* imbullettare; imbastire ♦ *vi* bordeggiare; **to change ~** virare di bordo; **on the wrong ~** (*fig*) sulla strada sbagliata; **to ~ sth on to (the end of) sth** (*of letter, book*) aggiungere qc alla fine di qc.

tackle |tak'əl| *n* (*equipment*) attrezzatura, equipaggiamento; (*for lifting*) paranco; (*RUGBY*) placcaggio; (*SOCCER*) contrasto ♦ *vt* (*difficulty*) affrontare; (*RUGBY*) placcare; (*SOCCER*) contrastare.

tacky |tak'ē| *a* colloso(a), appiccicaticcio(a); ancora bagnato(a); (*col*: *shabby*) scadente.

tact |takt| *n* tatto.

tactful |takt'fəl| *a* delicato(a), discreto(a); **to be ~** avere tatto.

tactfully |takt'fəlē| *ad* con tatto.

tactical |tak'tikəl| *a* tattico(a).

tactics |tak'tiks| *n*, *npl* tattica.

tactless |takt'lis| *a* che manca di tatto.

tactlessly |takt'lislē| *ad* senza tatto.

tadpole |tad'pōl| *n* girino.

taffy |taf'ē| *n* (*US*) caramella *f* mou *inv*.

tag |tag| *n* etichetta; **price/name ~** etichetta del prezzo/con il nome.

tag along *vi* seguire.

Tahiti |təhē'tē| *n* Tahiti *f*.

tail |tāl| *n* coda; (*of shirt*) falda ♦ *vt* (*follow*) seguire, pedinare; **to turn ~** voltare la schiena; *see also* **head**.

tail away, tail off *vi* (*in size, quality etc*) diminuire gradatamente.

tailback |tāl'bak| *n* (*Brit*) ingorgo.

tail coat *n* marsina.

tail end *n* (*of train, procession etc*) coda; (*of meeting etc*) fine *f*.

tailgate |tāl'gāt| *n* (*AUT*) portellone *m* posteriore.

taillight |tāl'līt| *n* (*AUT*) fanalino di coda.

tailor |tā'lûr| *n* sarto ♦ *vt*: **to ~ sth (to)** adattare qc (alle esigenze di); **~'s (shop)** sartoria (da uomo).

tailoring |tā'lûring| *n* (*cut*) taglio.

tailor-made |tā'lûrmād| *a* (*also fig*) fatto(a) su misura.

tailwind |tāl'wind| *n* vento di coda.

taint |tānt| *vt* (*meat, food*) far avariare; (*fig*: *reputation*) infangare.

tainted |tānt'id| *a* (*food*) guasto(a); (*water, air*) infetto(a); (*fig*) corrotto(a).

Taiwan |tī'wân'| *n* Taiwan *m*.

take |tāk| *vb* (*pt* **took**, *pp* **taken** |tōōk, tā'kən|) *vt* prendere; (*gain*: *prize*) ottenere, vincere; (*require*: *effort, courage*) occorrere, volerci; (*tolerate*) accettare, sopportare; (*hold*: *passengers etc*) contenere; (*accompany*) accompagnare; (*bring, carry*) portare; (*conduct*: *meeting*) condurre; (*exam*) sostenere, presentarsi a ♦ *vi* (*dye, fire etc*) prendere; (*plant*) attecchire ♦ *n* (*CINEMA*) ripresa; **I ~ it that** suppongo che; **to ~ for a**

walk (*child*, *dog*) portare a fare una passeggiata; **to ~ sb's hand** prendere qn per mano; **to ~ it upon o.s. to do sth** prendersi la responsabilità di fare qc; **to be ~n ill** avere un malore; **to be ~n with sb/sth** (*attracted*) essere tutto preso da qn/qc; **it won't ~ long** non ci vorrà molto tempo; **it ~s a lot of time/courage** occorre *or* ci vuole molto tempo/coraggio; **it will ~ at least 5 liters** contiene almeno 5 litri; **~ the first left** prenda la prima a sinistra; **to ~ Russian at the university** fare russo all'università; **I took him for a doctor** l'ho preso per un dottore.

take after *vt fus* assomigliare a.

take apart *vt* smontare.

take away *vt* portare via; togliere; **to ~ away (from)** sottrarre (da).

take back *vt* (*return*) restituire; riportare; (*one's words*) ritirare.

take down *vt* (*building*) demolire; (*dismantle*: *scaffolding*) smontare; (*letter etc*) scrivere.

take in *vt* (*lodger*) prendere, ospitare; (*orphan*) accogliere; (*stray dog*) raccogliere; (*SEWING*) stringere; (*deceive*) imbrogliare, abbindolare; (*understand*) capire; (*include*) comprendere, includere.

take off *vi* (*AVIAT*) decollare; (*leave*) svignarsela ♦ *vt* (*remove*) togliere; (*imitate*) imitare.

take on *vt* (*work*) accettare, intraprendere; (*employee*) assumere; (*opponent*) sfidare, affrontare.

take out *vt* portare fuori; (*remove*) togliere; (*license*) prendere, ottenere; **to ~ sth out of** tirare qc fuori da; estrarre qc da; **don't ~ it out on me!** non prendertela con me!

take over *vt* (*business*) rilevare ♦ *vi*: **to ~ over from sb** prendere le consegne *or* il controllo da qn.

take to *vt fus* (*person*) prendere in simpatia; (*activity*) prendere gusto a; (*form habit of*): **to ~ to doing sth** prendere *or* cominciare a fare qc.

take up *vt* (*one's story*) riprendere; (*dress*) accorciare; (*absorb*: *liquids*) assorbire; (*accept*: *offer*, *challenge*) accettare; (*occupy*: *time*, *space*) occupare; (*engage in*: *hobby etc*) mettersi a; **to ~ up with sb** fare amicizia con qn.

takeaway [tā'kəwā] *a* (*Brit*) = **takeout**.

take-home pay [tāk'hōm' pā] *n* stipendio netto.

taken [tā'kən] *pp of* **take**.

takeoff [tāk'óf] *n* (*AVIAT*) decollo.

takeout [tāk'out] *a* (*US*: *food*) da portar via.

takeover [tāk'ōvûr] *n* (*COMM*) assorbimento.

takeover bid *n* offerta di assorbimento.

takings [tā'kingz] *npl* (*COMM*) incasso.

talc [talk] *n* (*also*: **~um powder**) talco.

tale [tāl] *n* racconto, storia; (*pej*) fandonia; **to tell ~s** fare la spia.

talent [tal'ənt] *n* talento.

talented [tal'əntid] *a* di talento.

talent scout *n* talent scout *m/f inv*.

talk [tók] *n* discorso; (*gossip*) chiacchiere *fpl*; (*conversation*) conversazione *f*; (*interview*) discussione *f* ♦ *vi* parlare; (*chatter*) chiacchierare; **to give a ~** tenere una conferenza; **to ~ about** parlare di; (*converse*) discorrere *or* conversare su; **to ~ sb out of/into doing** dissuadere qn da/convincere qn a fare; **to ~ shop** parlare del lavoro *or* degli affari; **~ing of movies, have you seen ...?** a proposito di film, ha visto ...?

talk over *vt* discutere.

talkative [tó'kətiv] *a* loquace, ciarliero(a).

talking point [tó'king point] *n* argomento di conversazione.

talking-to [tó'kingtōō] *n*: **to give sb a good ~** fare una bella paternale a qn.

talk show *n* (*TV*, *RADIO*) intervista (informale), talk show *m inv*.

tall [tól] *a* alto(a); **to be 6 feet ~** ≈ essere alto 1 metro e 80; **how ~ are you?** quanto è alto?

tallboy [tól'boi] *n* (*Brit*) cassettone *m* alto.

tallness [tól'nis] *n* altezza.

tall story *n* panzana, frottola.

tally [tal'ē] *n* conto, conteggio ♦ *vi*: **to ~ (with)** corrispondere (a); **to keep a ~ of sth** tener il conto di qc.

talon [tal'ən] *n* artiglio.

tambourine [tam'bərēn] *n* tamburello.

tame [tām] *a* addomesticato(a); (*fig*: *story*, *style*) insipido(a), scialbo(a).

tamper [tam'pûr] *vi*: **to ~ with** manomettere.

tampon [tam'pân] *n* tampone *m*.

tan [tan] *n* (*also*: **sun~**) abbronzatura ♦ *vt* abbronzare ♦ *vi* abbronzarsi ♦ *a* (*color*) marrone rossiccio *inv*; **to get a ~** abbronzarsi.

tandem [tan'dəm] *n* tandem *m inv*.

tang [tang] *n* odore *m* penetrante; sapore *m* piccante.

tangent [tan'jənt] *n* (*MATH*) tangente *f*; **to go off at a ~** (*fig*) partire per la tangente.

tangerine [tanjərēn'] *n* mandarino.

tangible [tan'jəbəl] *a* tangibile; **~ assets** patrimonio reale.

Tangier [tanjiûr'] *n* Tangeri *f*.

tangle [tang'gəl] *n* groviglio ♦ *vt* aggrovigliare; **to get in(to) a ~** finire in un groviglio.

tango [tang'gō] *n* tango.

tank [tangk] *n* serbatoio; (*for processing*) vasca; (*for fish*) acquario; (*MIL*) carro armato.

tankard [tangk'ûrd] *n* boccale *m*.

tanker [tangk'ûr] *n* (*ship*) nave *f* cisterna *inv*; (*for oil*) petroliera; (*truck*) autobotte *f*, autocisterna.

tanned [tand] *a* abbronzato(a).

tannin [tan'in] n tannino.
tanning [tan'ing] n (of leather) conciatura.
tantalizing [tan'təlīzing] a allettante.
tantamount [tan'təmount] a: ~ **to** equivalente a.
tantrum [tan'trəm] n accesso di collera; **to throw a** ~ fare le bizze.
Tanzania [tanzənē'ə] n Tanzania.
Tanzanian [tanzənē'ən] a, n tanzaniano(a).
tap [tap] n (on sink etc) rubinetto; (gentle blow) colpetto ♦ vt dare un colpetto a; (resources) sfruttare, utilizzare; (telephone conversation) intercettare; (telephone) mettere sotto controllo; **on** ~ (beer) alla spina; (fig: resources) a disposizione.
tap-dancing [tap'dansing] n tip tap m.
tape [tāp] n nastro; (also: **magnetic** ~) nastro (magnetico) ♦ vt (record) registrare (su nastro); **on** ~ (song etc) su nastro.
tape deck n piastra di registrazione.
tape measure n metro a nastro.
taper [tā'pûr] n candelina ♦ vi assottigliarsi.
tape-record [tāp'rek'ûrd] vt registrare (su nastro).
tape recorder n registratore m (a nastro).
tape recording n registrazione f.
tapered [tā'pûrd], **tapering** [tā'pûring] a affusolato(a).
tapestry [tap'istrē] n arazzo; tappezzeria.
tapeworm [tāp'wûrm'] n tenia, verme m solitario.
tapioca [tapēō'kə] n tapioca.
tappet [tap'it] n punteria.
tar [târ] n catrame m; **low-/middle-~** cigarettes sigarette a basso/medio contenuto di nicotina.
tarantula [təran'chələ] n tarantola.
tardy [târ'dē] a tardo(a); tardivo(a).
target [târ'git] n bersaglio; (fig: objective) obiettivo; **to be on** ~ (project) essere nei tempi (di lavorazione).
target practice n tiro al bersaglio.
tariff [tar'if] n tariffa.
tariff barrier n barriera tariffaria.
tarmac [târ'mak] n (AVIAT) pista di decollo; (Brit: on road) macadam m al catrame ♦ vt (Brit) macadamizzare.
tarnish [târ'nish] vt offuscare, annerire; (fig) macchiare.
tarpaulin [târpô'lin] n tela incatramata.
tarragon [tar'əgən] n dragoncello.
tart [târt] n (CULIN) crostata; (Brit col: pej: woman) sgualdrina ♦ a (flavor) aspro(a), agro(a).
tart up vt (col): **to** ~ **o.s. up** farsi bello(a); (pej) agghindarsi.
tartan [târ'tən] n tartan m inv.
tartar [târ'tûr] n (on teeth) tartaro.
tartar sauce n salsa tartara.
task [task] n compito; **to take to** ~ rimproverare.

task force n (MIL, POLICE) unità operativa.
taskmaster [task'mastûr] n: **he's a hard** ~ è un vero tiranno.
Tasmania [tazmā'nēə] n Tasmania.
tassel [tas'əl] n fiocco.
taste [tāst] n gusto; (flavor) sapore m, gusto; (fig: glimpse, idea) idea ♦ vt gustare; (sample) assaggiare ♦ vi: **to** ~ **of** (fish etc) sapere di, avere sapore di; **what does it** ~ **like?** che sapore or gusto ha?; **it ~s like fish** sa di pesce; **you can** ~ **the garlic (in it)** (ci) si sente il sapore dell'aglio; **can I have a** ~ **of this wine?** posso assaggiare un po' di questo vino?; **to have a** ~ **of sth** assaggiare qc; **to have a** ~ **for sth** avere un'inclinazione per qc; **to be in bad** or **poor** ~ essere di cattivo gusto.
taste bud n papilla gustativa.
tasteful [tāst'fəl] a di buon gusto.
tastefully [tāst'fəlē] ad con gusto.
tasteless [tāst'lis] a (food) insipido(a); (remark) di cattivo gusto.
tasty [tās'tē] a saporito(a), gustoso(a).
tattered [tat'ûrd] a see **tatters**.
tatters [tat'ûrz] npl: **in** ~ (also: **tattered**) a brandelli, sbrindellato(a).
tattoo [tatōō'] n tatuaggio; (spectacle) parata militare ♦ vt tatuare.
tatty [tat'ē] a (Brit col) malandato(a).
taught [tôt] pt, pp of **teach**.
taunt [tônt] n scherno ♦ vt schernire.
Taurus [tôr'əs] n Toro; **to be** ~ essere del Toro.
taut [tôt] a teso(a).
tavern [tav'ûrn] n taverna.
tawdry [tô'drē] a pacchiano(a).
tawny [tô'nē] a fulvo(a).
tax [taks] n imposta, tassa; (on income) imposte fpl, tasse fpl ♦ vt tassare; (fig: strain: patience etc) mettere alla prova; **free of** ~ esentasse inv, esente da imposte; **before/after** ~ al lordo/netto delle tasse.
taxable [tak'səbəl] a imponibile.
tax allowance n detrazione f d'imposta.
taxation [taksā'shən] n tassazione f; tasse fpl, imposte fpl; **system of** ~ sistema m fiscale.
tax avoidance n l'evitare legalmente il pagamento di imposte.
tax collector n esattore m delle imposte.
tax disc n (Brit AUT) ≈ bollo.
tax evasion n evasione f fiscale.
tax exemption n esenzione f fiscale.
tax exile n chi ripara all'estero per evadere le imposte.
tax free a esente da imposte.
tax haven n paradiso fiscale.
taxi [tak'sē] n taxi m inv ♦ vi (AVIAT) rullare.
taxidermist [tak'sidûrmist] n tassidermista m/f.
taxi driver n tassista m/f.
taximeter [tak'simētûr] n tassametro.

tax inspector n (*Brit*) ispettore m delle tasse.
taxi stand, (*Brit*) **taxi rank** n posteggio dei taxi.
tax payer n contribuente m/f.
tax rebate n rimborso fiscale.
tax relief n sgravio fiscale.
tax return n dichiarazione f dei redditi.
tax shelter n paradiso fiscale.
tax year n anno fiscale.
TB n abbr (= *tuberculosis*) TBC f.
TD n abbr (*US*) = **Treasury Department**; (: *FOOTBALL*) = **touchdown.**
tea [tē] n tè m inv; (*Brit: snack: for children*) merenda; **high** ~ (*Brit*) cena leggera (*presa nel tardo pomeriggio*).
tea bag n bustina di tè.
tea break n (*Brit*) intervallo per il tè.
teach, pt, pp **taught** [tēch, tôt] vt: **to ~ sb sth, ~ sth to sb** insegnare qc a qn ♦ vi insegnare; **it taught him a lesson** (*fig*) gli è servito da lezione.
teacher [tē'chûr] n (*gen*) insegnante m/f; (*in high school*) professore/essa; (*in grade school*) maestro/a; **French** ~ insegnante di francese.
teacher training college n (*for grade schools*) ≈ istituto magistrale; (*for high schools*) scuola universitaria per l'abilitazione all'insegnamento nelle medie superiori.
teaching [tē'ching] n insegnamento.
teaching aids npl materiali mpl per l'insegnamento.
teaching hospital n clinica universitaria.
tea cosy n copriteiera m inv.
teacup [tē'kup] n tazza da tè.
teak [tēk] n teak m.
tea leaves npl foglie fpl di tè.
team [tēm] n squadra; (*of animals*) tiro.
  team up vi: **to ~ up (with)** mettersi insieme (a).
team games npl giochi mpl di squadra.
teamwork [tēm'wûrk] n lavoro di squadra.
tea party n tè m inv (*ricevimento*).
teapot [tē'pât] n teiera.
tear n [tär] strappo; [tēr] lacrima ♦ vb [tär] (*pt* **tore,** pp **torn** [tôr, tôrn]) vt strappare ♦ vi strapparsi; **in ~s** in lacrime; **to burst into ~s** scoppiare in lacrime; **to ~ to pieces** or **to bits** or **to shreds** (*also fig*) fare a pezzi or a brandelli.
  tear along vi (*rush*) correre all'impazzata.
  tear apart vt (*also fig*) distruggere.
  tear away vt: **to ~ o.s. away (from sth)** (*fig*) staccarsi (da qc).
  tear out vt (*sheet of paper, check*) staccare.
  tear up vt (*sheet of paper etc*) strappare.
tearaway [tär'əwā] n (*Brit col*) monello/a.
teardrop [tēr'drâp] n lacrima.
tearful [tēr'fəl] a piangente, lacrimoso(a).

tear gas n gas m lacrimogeno.
tearoom [tē'rōōm] n sala da tè.
tease [tēz] vt canzonare; (*unkindly*) tormentare; (*hair*) cotonare.
tea set n servizio da tè.
teashop [tē'shâp] n (*Brit*) sala da tè.
teaspoon [tē'spōōn] n cucchiaino da tè; (*also:* ~**ful**: *as measurement*) cucchiaino.
tea strainer n colino da tè.
teat [tēt] n capezzolo; (*of bottle*) tettarella.
teatime [tē'tīm] n ora del tè.
tea towel n (*Brit*) strofinaccio (per i piatti).
tea urn n bollitore m per il tè.
tech [tek] n abbr (*col*) = **technical college; technology.**
technical [tek'nikəl] a tecnico(a).
technical college n ≈ istituto tecnico.
technicality [teknikal'itē] n tecnicità; (*detail*) dettaglio tecnico; **on a legal** ~ grazie a un cavillo legale.
technically [tek'niklē] ad dal punto di vista tecnico.
technician [teknish'ən] n tecnico/a.
technique [teknēk'] n tecnica.
technocrat [tek'nəkrat] n tecnocrate m/f.
technological [teknəlâj'ikəl] a tecnologico(a).
technologist [teknâl'əjist] n tecnologo/a.
technology [teknâl'əjē] n tecnologia.
teddy (bear) [ted'ē (bär)] n orsacchiotto.
tedious [tē'dēəs] a noioso(a), tedioso(a).
tedium [tē'dēəm] n noia, tedio.
tee [tē] n (*GOLF*) tee m inv.
teem [tēm] vi abbondare, brulicare; **to ~ with** brulicare di.
teenage [tēn'āj] a (*fashions etc*) per giovani, per adolescenti.
teenager [tēn'ājûr] n adolescente m/f.
teens [tēnz] npl: **to be in one's** ~ essere adolescente.
tee shirt n = **T-shirt.**
teeter [tē'tûr] vi barcollare, vacillare.
teeth [tēth] npl of **tooth.**
teethe [tēth] vi mettere i denti.
teething ring [tē'thing ring] n dentaruolo.
teething troubles [tē'thing trub'əlz] npl (*fig*) difficoltà fpl iniziali.
teetotal [tētōt'əl] a astemio(a).
teetotaler, (*Brit*) **teetotaller** [tētōt'əlûr] n astemio/a.
TEFL [tef'əl] n abbr = *Teaching of English as a Foreign Language.*
Tehran [tēərân'] n Tehran f.
tel. abbr (= *telephone*) tel.
Tel Aviv [tel' əvēv'] n Tel Aviv f.
telecast [tel'əkast] vt, vi teletrasmettere.
telecommunications [teləkəmyōōnikā'shənz] n telecomunicazioni fpl.
telegram [tel'əgram] n telegramma m.
telegraph [tel'əgraf] n telegrafo.
telegraphic [teləgraf'ik] a telegrafico(a).
telegraph pole n palo del telegrafo.

telegraph wire n filo del telegrafo.
telepathic [telǝpath'ik] a telepatico(a).
telepathy [tǝlep'ǝthē] n telepatia.
telephone [tel'ǝfōn] n telefono ♦ vt (person) telefonare a; (message) telefonare; **to have a ~** (subscriber) avere il telefono; **to be on the ~** (be speaking) essere al telefono.
telephone booth, (Brit) **telephone box** n cabina telefonica.
telephone call n telefonata.
telephone directory n elenco telefonico.
telephone exchange n centralino telefonico.
telephone kiosk n (Brit) cabina telefonica.
telephone number n numero di telefono.
telephone operator n centralinista m/f.
telephone tapping [tel'ǝfōn tap'ing] n intercettazione f telefonica.
telephonist [tel'ǝfōnist] n (Brit) telefonista m/f.
telephoto lens [telǝfō'tō lenz] n teleobiettivo.
teleprinter [tel'ǝprintûr] n telescrivente f.
telescope [tel'ǝskōp] n telescopio ♦ vi chiudersi a telescopio; (fig: vehicles) accartocciarsi.
telescopic [teliskâp'ik] a telescopico(a); (umbrella) pieghevole.
teletext [tel'ǝtekst] n teletext m inv.
telethon [tel'ǝthán] n programma televisivo fiume a scopo di beneficenza.
televiewer [tel'ǝvyōōûr] n telespettatore/trice.
televise [tel'ǝvīz] vt teletrasmettere.
television [tel'ǝvizhǝn] n televisione f; **on ~** alla televisione.
television licence n (Brit) abbonamento alla televisione.
television program n programma m televisivo.
television set n televisore m.
telex [tel'eks] n telex m inv ♦ vt trasmettere per telex ♦ vi mandare un telex; **to ~ sb (about sth)** informare qn via telex (di qc).
tell, pt, pp **told** [tel, tōld] vt dire; (relate: story) raccontare; (distinguish): **to ~ sth from** distinguere qc da ♦ vi (have effect) farsi sentire, avere effetto; **to ~ sb to do** dire a qn di fare; **to ~ sb about sth** dire a qn di qc; raccontare qc a qn; **to ~ the time** leggere l'ora; **can you ~ me the time?** può dirmi l'ora?; **I'll ~ you what ...** so io che cosa fare ...; **I couldn't ~ them apart** non riuscivo a distinguerli.
tell off vt rimproverare, sgridare.
tell on vt fus (inform against) denunciare.
teller [tel'ûr] n (in bank) cassiere/a.
telling [tel'ing] a (remark, detail) rivelatore(trice).
telltale [tel'tāl] a (sign) rivelatore(trice) ♦ n malalingua, pettegolo/a.
telly [tel'ē] n abbr (Brit col: = television) tivù f inv.
temerity [tǝmär'itē] n temerarietà.

temp [temp] abbr (Brit col: = temporary) n impiegato(a) straordinario(a) ♦ vi lavorare come impiegato(a) straordinario(a).
temper [tem'pûr] n (nature) carattere m; (mood) umore m; (fit of anger) collera ♦ vt (moderate) temperare, moderare; **to be in a ~** essere in collera; **to keep one's ~** restare calmo; **to lose one's ~** andare in collera.
temperament [tem'pûrǝmǝnt] n temperamento.
temperamental [tempûrǝmen'tǝl] a capriccioso(a).
temperance [tem'pûrǝns] n moderazione f; (in drinking) temperanza nel bere.
temperate [tem'pûrit] a moderato(a); (climate) temperato(a).
temperature [tem'pûrǝchûr] n temperatura; **to have** or **run a ~** avere la febbre.
tempered [tem'pûrd] a (steel) temprato(a).
tempest [tem'pist] n tempesta.
tempestuous [tempes'chōōǝs] a (relationship, meeting) burrascoso(a).
tempi [tem'pē] npl of **tempo.**
template [tem'plit] n sagoma.
temple [tem'pǝl] n (building) tempio; (ANAT) tempia.
templet [tem'plit] n (US) = **template.**
tempo, ~s or **tempi** [tem'pō, tem'pē] n tempo; (fig: of life etc) ritmo.
temporal [tem'pûrǝl] a temporale.
temporarily [tempǝrär'ilē] ad temporaneamente.
temporary [tem'pǝrärē] a temporaneo(a); (job, worker) avventizio(a), temporaneo(a); **~ secretary** segretaria temporanea; **~ teacher** supplente m/f.
temporize [tem'pǝrīz] vi temporeggiare.
tempt [tempt] vt tentare; **to ~ sb into doing** indurre qn a fare; **to be ~ed to do sth** essere tentato di fare qc.
temptation [temptā'shǝn] n tentazione f.
tempting [temp'ting] a allettante, seducente.
ten [ten] num dieci ♦ n dieci; **~s of thousands** decine di migliaia.
tenable [ten'ǝbǝl] a sostenibile.
tenacious [tǝnā'shǝs] a tenace.
tenacity [tǝnas'itē] n tenacia.
tenancy [ten'ǝnsē] n affitto; condizione f di inquilino.
tenant [ten'ǝnt] n inquilino/a.
tend [tend] vt badare a, occuparsi di; (sick etc) prendersi cura di ♦ vi: **to ~ to do** tendere a fare; (color): **to ~ to** tendere a.
tendency [ten'dǝnsē] n tendenza.
tender [ten'dûr] a tenero(a); (sore) sensibile; (fig: subject) delicato(a) ♦ n (COMM: offer) offerta; (money): **legal ~** valuta (a corso legale) ♦ vt offrire; **to put in a ~ (for)** fare un'offerta (per); **to ~ one's resignation** presentare le proprie dimissioni.
tenderize [ten'dǝrīz] vt (CULIN) far intenerire.

tenderly |tɛn'dûrlē| *ad* teneramente.
tenderness |tɛn'dûrnis| *n* tenerezza; sensibilità.
tendon |tɛn'dən| *n* tendine *m*.
tenement |tɛn'əmənt| *n* casamento.
Tenerife |tɛnərēf'| *n* Tenerife *f*.
tenet |tɛn'it| *n* principio.
Tenn. *abbr* (*US*) = *Tennessee*.
tenner |tɛn'ûr| *n* (*col*: *US*) (banconota da) dieci dollari; (: *Brit*) (banconota da) dieci sterline *fpl*.
tennis |tɛn'is| *n* tennis *m*.
tennis ball *n* palla da tennis.
tennis court *n* campo da tennis.
tennis elbow *n* (*MED*) gomito del tennista.
tennis match *n* partita di tennis.
tennis player *n* tennista *m/f*.
tennis racket *n* racchetta da tennis.
tennis shoes *npl* scarpe *fpl* da tennis.
tenor |tɛn'ûr| *n* (*MUS, of speech etc*) tenore *m*.
tenpin bowling |tɛn'pin bō'ling| *n* (*Brit*) = **tenpins**.
tenpins |tɛn'pinz| *n* (*US*) bowling *m*.
tense |tɛns| *a* teso(a) ♦ *n* (*LING*) tempo ♦ *vt* (*tighten*: *muscles*) tendere.
tenseness |tɛns'nis| *n* tensione *f*.
tension |tɛn'chən| *n* tensione *f*.
tent |tɛnt| *n* tenda.
tentacle |tɛn'təkəl| *n* tentacolo.
tentative |tɛn'tətiv| *a* esitante, incerto(a); (*conclusion*) provvisorio(a).
tenterhooks |tɛn'tûrhŏōks| *npl*: **on ~** sulle spine.
tenth |tɛnth| *num* decimo(a).
tent peg *n* picchetto da tenda.
tent pole *n* palo da tenda, montante *m*.
tenuous |tɛn'yŏōəs| *a* tenue.
tenure |tɛn'yûr| *n* (*of property*) possesso; (*of job*) incarico; (*guaranteed employment*): **to have ~** essere di ruolo.
tepid |tɛp'id| *a* tiepido(a).
term |tûrm| *n* (*limit*) termine *m*; (*word*) vocabolo, termine; (*SCOL*) trimestre *m*; (*LAW*) sessione *f* ♦ *vt* chiamare, definire; **~s** *npl* (*conditions*) condizioni *fpl*; (*COMM*) prezzi *mpl*, tariffe *fpl*; **~ of imprisonment** periodo di prigionia; **during his ~ of office** durante il suo incarico; **in the short/long ~** a breve/lunga scadenza; **"easy ~s"** (*COMM*) "facilitazioni di pagamento"; **to be on good ~s with** essere in buoni rapporti con; **to come to ~s with** (*person*) arrivare a un accordo con; (*problem*) affrontare.
terminal |tûr'mənəl| *a* finale, terminale; (*disease*) nella fase terminale ♦ *n* (*ELEC, COMPUT*) terminale *m*; (*AVIAT, for oil, ore etc*) terminal *m inv*; (*Brit: also:* **coach ~**) capolinea *m*.
terminate |tûr'mənāt| *vt* mettere fine a ♦ *vi*: **to ~ in** finire in *or* con.
termination |tûrmənā'shən| *n* fine *f*; (*of con-*

tract) rescissione *f*; **~ of pregnancy** (*MED*) interruzione *f* della gravidanza.
termini |tûr'mənē| *npl of* **terminus**.
terminology |tûrmənál'əjē| *n* terminologia.
terminus, *pl* **termini** |tûr'mənəs, tûr'mənē| *n* (*for buses*) capolinea *m*; (*for trains*) stazione *f* terminale.
termite |tûr'mīt| *n* termite *f*.
Ter(r). *abbr* = **terrace**.
terrace |tär'əs| *n* terrazza; (*Brit: row of houses*) fila di case a schiera; **the ~s** *npl* (*Brit SPORT*) le gradinate.
terraced |tär'əst| *a* (*garden*) a terrazze; (*Brit: in a row: house, cottage etc*) a schiera.
terrain |tərān'| *n* terreno.
terrible |tär'əbəl| *a* terribile; (*weather*) bruttissimo(a); (*performance, report*) pessimo(a).
terribly |tär'əblē| *ad* terribilmente; (*very badly*) malissimo.
terrier |tär'ûr| *n* terrier *m inv*.
terrific |tərif'ik| *a* incredibile, fantastico(a); (*wonderful*) formidabile, eccezionale.
terrify |tär'əfī| *vt* terrorizzare; **to be terrified** essere atterrito(a).
territorial |täritôr'ēəl| *a* territoriale.
territorial waters *npl* acque *fpl* territoriali.
territory |tär'itôrē| *n* territorio.
terror |tär'ûr| *n* terrore *m*.
terrorism |tär'ərizəm| *n* terrorismo.
terrorist |tär'ûrist| *n* terrorista *m/f*.
terrorize |tär'ərīz| *vt* terrorizzare.
terse |tûrs| *a* (*style*) conciso(a); (*reply*) laconico(a).
tertiary |tûr'shēärē| *a* (*gen*) terziario(a).
Terylene |tär'əlēn| ® *n* (*Brit*) terital ® *m*, terilene ® *m*.
TESL |tɛs'əl| *n abbr* = *Teaching of English as a Second Language*.
test |tɛst| *n* (*trial, check*) prova; (: *of goods in factory*) controllo, collaudo; (*MED*) esame *m*; (*CHEM*) analisi *f inv*; (*exam: of intelligence etc*) test *m inv*; (: *in school*) compito in classe; (*also:* **driving ~**) esame *m* di guida ♦ *vt* provare; controllare, collaudare; esaminare; analizzare; sottoporre ad esame; **to put sth to the ~** mettere qc alla prova; **to ~ sth for sth** analizzare qc alla ricerca di qc; **to ~ sb in history** esaminare qn in storia.
testament |tɛs'təmənt| *n* testamento; **the Old/New T~** il Vecchio/Nuovo testamento.
test ban *n* (*also:* **nuclear ~**) divieto di esperimenti nucleari.
test case *n* (*LAW, fig*) caso che farà testo.
test flight *n* volo di prova.
testicle |tɛs'tikəl| *n* testicolo.
testify |tɛs'təfī| *vi* (*LAW*) testimoniare, deporre; **to ~ to sth** (*LAW*) testimoniare qc; (*gen*) comprovare or dimostrare qc; (*be sign of*) essere una prova di qc.
testimonial |tɛstimō'nēəl| *n* (*gift*) testimo-

nianza di stima; (*Brit*: *reference*) benservito.

testimony [tɛs'tɔmōnē] *n* (*LAW*) testimonianza, deposizione *f*.

testing [tɛs'ting] *a* (*difficult*: *time*) duro(a).

testing ground *n* terreno di prova.

test match *n* (*CRICKET*, *RUGBY*) partita internazionale.

test paper *n* (*SCOL*) interrogazione *f* scritta.

test pilot *n* pilota *m* collaudatore.

test tube *n* provetta.

test-tube baby [tɛst'tōōb bā'bē] *n* bambino(a) concepito(a) in provetta.

testy [tɛs'tē] *a* irritabile.

tetanus [tɛt'ɔnɔs] *n* tetano.

tetchy [tɛch'ē] *a* irritabile, irascibile.

tether [tɛth'ûr] *vt* legare ♦ *n*: **at the end of one's ~** (*Brit*) al limite (della pazienza).

Tex. *abbr* (*US*) = *Texas*.

text [tɛkst] *n* testo.

textbook [tɛkst'bŏŏk] *n* libro di testo.

textile [tɛks'tɔl] *n* tessile *m*; **~s** *npl* tessuti *mpl*.

texture [tɛks'chûr] *n* tessitura; (*of skin, paper etc*) struttura.

TGIF *abbr* (*col*) = *thank God it's Friday*.

Thai [tī] *a* tailandese ♦ *n* tailandese *m/f*; (*LING*) tailandese *m*.

Thailand [tī'lɔnd] *n* Tailandia.

thalidomide [thɔlid'ɔmīd] ® *n* talidomide ® *m*.

Thames [tɛmz] *n*: **the ~** il Tamigi.

than [than] *cj* che; (*with numerals, pronouns, proper names*): **more ~ 10/me/Maria** più di 10/me/Maria; **you know her better ~ I do** la conosce meglio di me *or* di quanto non la conosca io; **she has more apples ~ pears** ha più mele che pere; **it is better to phone ~ to write** è meglio telefonare che scrivere; **no sooner did he leave ~ the phone rang** non appena uscì il telefono suonò.

thank [thangk] *vt* ringraziare; **~ you (very much)** grazie (tante); **~ heavens/God!** grazie al cielo/a Dio!; *see also* **thanks.**

thankful [thangk'fɔl] *a*: **~ (for)** riconoscente (per); **~ for/that** (*relieved*) sollevato(a) da/dal fatto che.

thankfully [thangk'fɔlē] *ad* con riconoscenza; con sollievo; **~ there were few victims** grazie al cielo ci sono state poche vittime.

thankless [thangk'lis] *a* ingrato(a).

thanks [thangks] *npl* ringraziamenti *mpl*, grazie *fpl* ♦ *excl* grazie!; **~ to** *prep* grazie a.

Thanksgiving (Day) [thangksgiv'ing (dā')] *n* giorno del ringraziamento.

that [that, thɔt] *cj* che ♦ *a* (*pl* **those**) quel(quell', quello) *m*; quella(quell') *f* ♦ *pronoun* ciò; (*the one, not "this one"*) quello(a); (*relative*) che; *prep* + il(la) quale; (*with time*): **on the day ~ he came** il giorno in cui *or* quando venne ♦ *ad*: **~ high** così alto; alto così; **it's about ~ high** è alto circa così; **~**

one quello(a) (là); **~ one over there** quello là; **after ~** dopo; **what's ~?** cos'è?; **who's ~?** chi è?; **is ~ you?** sei tu?; **~'s what he said** questo è ciò che ha detto; **~ is ...** cioè ..., vale a dire ...; **at** *or* **with ~ she ...** con ciò lei ...; **do it like ~** fallo così; **not ~ I know of** non che io sappia; **I can't work ~ much** non posso lavorare così tanto.

thatched [thacht] *a* (*roof*) di paglia; **~ cottage** cottage *m inv* col tetto di paglia.

thaw [thô] *n* disgelo ♦ *vi* (*ice*) sciogliersi; (*food*) scongelarsi ♦ *vt* (*food*) (fare) scongelare; **it's ~ing** (*weather*) sta sgelando.

the [thɔ, thē] *definite article* il(lo, l') *m*; la(l') *f*; i(gli) *mpl*; le *fpl*; (*in titles*): **Richard ~ Second** Riccardo secondo ♦ *ad*: **~ more he works ~ more he earns** più lavora più guadagna; **700 lire to ~ dollar** 700 lire per un dollaro; **paid by ~ hour** pagato a ore; **~ sooner ~ better** prima è, meglio è.

theater [thē'ɔtûr] *n* (*US*) teatro.

theater-goer [thē'ɔtûrgōûr] *n* frequentatore/trice di teatri.

theatre [thē'ɔtûr] *etc* (*Brit*) = **theater** *etc*.

theatrical [thēat'rikɔl] *a* teatrale.

theft [thɛft] *n* furto.

their [thär] *a* il(la) loro, *pl* i(le) loro.

theirs [thärz] *pronoun* il(la) loro, *pl* i(le) loro; **it is ~** è loro; **a friend of ~** un loro amico.

them [thɛm, thɔm] *pronoun* (*direct*) li(le); (*indirect*) gli, loro (*after vb*); (*stressed, after prep*: *people*) loro; (: *people, things*) essi(e); **I see ~** li vedo; **give ~ the book** dà loro *or* dagli il libro; **give me a few of ~** dammene un po' *or* qualcuno.

theme [thēm] *n* tema *m*.

theme song *n* tema musicale.

themselves [thɔmsɛlvz'] *pl pronoun* (*reflexive*) si; (*emphatic*) loro stessi(e); (*after prep*) se stessi(e); **between ~** tra (di) loro.

then [thɛn] *ad* (*at that time*) allora; (*next*) poi, dopo; (*and also*) e poi ♦ *cj* (*therefore*) perciò, dunque, quindi ♦ *a*: **the ~ president** il presidente di allora; **from ~ on** da allora in poi; **until ~** fino ad allora; **and ~ what?** e poi?, e allora?; **what do you want me to do ~?** allora cosa vuole che faccia?

theologian [thēɔlō'jɔn] *n* teologo/a.

theological [thēɔläj'ikɔl] *a* teologico(a).

theology [thēäl'ɔjē] *n* teologia.

theorem [thēr'ɔm] *n* teorema *m*.

theoretical [thērɛt'ikɔl] *a* teorico(a).

theorize [thē'ɔrīz] *vi* teorizzare.

theory [thiûr'ē] *n* teoria; **in ~** in teoria.

therapeutic(al) [thärɔpyōō'tik(ɔl)] *a* terapeutico(a).

therapist [thär'ɔpist] *n* terapista *m/f*.

therapy [thär'ɔpē] *n* terapia.

there [thär] *ad* là, lì; **~, ~!** su, su!; **it's ~** è lì; **he went ~** ci è andato; **~ is** c'è; **~ are** ci sono; **~ has been** c'è stato; **~ he is** eccolo (là); **back** ~ là dietro; **down** ~ laggiù; **in** ~ là dentro; **on** ~ lassù; **over** ~ là; **through** ~ di là; **to go** ~ **and back** andarci e ritornare.

thereabouts [ᵗh̲är'əbouts] *ad* (*place*) nei pressi, da quelle parti; (*amount*) giù di lì, all'incirca.

thereafter [ᵗh̲äraf'tûr] *ad* da allora in poi.

thereby [ᵗh̲ärbī'] *ad* con ciò.

therefore [ᵗh̲är'fôr] *ad* perciò, quindi.

there's [ᵗh̲ärz] = **there is; there has.**

thereupon [ᵗh̲ärəpán'] *ad* (*at that point*) a quel punto; (*formal: on that subject*) in merito.

thermal [thûr'məl] *a* (*currents, spring*) termale; (*underwear, printer*) termico(a); (*paper*) termosensibile.

thermodynamics [thûrmōdīnam'iks] *n* termodinamica.

thermometer [thûrmâm'itûr] *n* termometro.

thermonuclear [thûrmōnōō'klēûr] *a* termonucleare.

Thermos [thûr'məs] ℝ *n* thermos ℝ *m inv.*

thermostat [thûr'məstat] *n* termostato.

thesaurus [thisôr'əs] *n* dizionario dei sinonimi.

these [ᵗh̲ēz] *pl pronoun, a* questi(e).

thesis, *pl* **theses** [ᵗh̲ē'sis, ᵗh̲ē'sēz] *n* tesi *f inv.*

they [ᵗh̲ā] *pl pronoun* essi(esse); (*people only*) loro; ~ **say that** ... (*it is said that*) si dice che ....

they'd [ᵗh̲ād] = **they would; they had.**

they'll [ᵗh̲āl] = **they will; they shall.**

they're [ᵗh̲är] = **they are.**

they've [ᵗh̲āv] = **they have.**

thick [thik] *a* spesso(a); (*crowd*) compatto(a); (*stupid*) ottuso(a), lento(a) ♦ *n*: **in the** ~ **of** nel folto di; **it's 20 cm** ~ ha uno spessore di 20 cm.

thicken [thik'ən] *vi* ispessire ♦ *vt* (*sauce etc*) ispessire, rendere più denso(a).

thicket [thik'it] *n* boscaglia.

thickly [thik'lē] *ad* (*spread*) a strati spessi; (*cut*) a fette grosse; (*populated*) densamente.

thickness [thik'nis] *n* spessore *m.*

thickset [thik'set'] *a* tarchiato(a), tozzo(a).

thickskinned [thik'skind'] *a* (*fig*) insensibile.

thief, *pl* **thieves** [ᵗh̲ēf, ᵗh̲ēvz] *n* ladro/a.

thieving [ᵗh̲ē'ving] *n* furti *mpl.*

thigh [thī] *n* coscia.

thighbone [thī'bōn] *n* femore *m.*

thimble [thim'bəl] *n* ditale *m.*

thin [thin] *a* sottile; (*person*) magro(a); (*soup*) poco denso(a); (*hair, crowd*) rado(a); (*fog*) leggero(a) ♦ *vt* (*hair*) sfoltire ♦ *vi* (*fog*) diradarsi; (*also:* ~ **out:** *crowd*) disperdersi; **to** ~ **(down)** (*sauce, paint*) diluire; **his hair is** ~**ning** sta perdendo i capelli.

thing [thing] *n* cosa; (*object*) oggetto; (*contraption*) aggeggio; ~**s** *npl* (*belongings*) cose *fpl;* **for one** ~ tanto per cominciare; **the best** ~ **would be to** la cosa migliore sarebbe di; **the** ~ **is** ... il fatto è che ...; **the main** ~

is to ... la cosa più importante è di ...; **first** ~ **(in the morning)** come *or* per prima cosa (di mattina); **last** ~ **(at night)** come *or* per ultima cosa (di sera); **poor** ~ poveretto/a; **she's got a** ~ **about mice** è terrorizzata dai topi; **how are** ~**s?** come va?

think, *pt, pp* **thought** [thingk, thôt] *vi* pensare, riflettere ♦ *vt* pensare, credere; (*imagine*) immaginare; **to** ~ **of** pensare a; **what did you** ~ **of them?** cosa ne ha pensato?; **to** ~ **about sth/sb** pensare a qc/qn; **I'll** ~ **about it** ci penserò; **to** ~ **of doing** pensare di fare; **I** ~ **so** penso *or* credo di sì; **to** ~ **well of** avere una buona opinione di; **to** ~ **aloud** pensare ad alta voce; ~ **again!** rifletti!, pensaci su!

think out *vt* (*plan*) elaborare; (*solution*) trovare.

think over *vt* riflettere su; **I'd like to** ~ **things over** vorrei pensarci su.

think through *vt* riflettere a fondo su.

think up *vt* ideare.

thinking [thingk'ing] *n*: **to my (way of)** ~ a mio parere.

think tank *n* gruppo di esperti.

thinly [thin'lē] *ad* (*cut*) a fette sottili; (*spread*) in uno strato sottile.

thinness [thin'is] *n* sottigliezza; magrezza.

third [thûrd] *num* terzo(a) ♦ *n* terzo/a; (*fraction*) terzo, terza parte *f.*

third-degree burns [thûrd'digrē bûrnz] *npl* ustioni *fpl* di terzo grado.

thirdly [thûrd'lē] *ad* in terzo luogo.

third party insurance *n* (*Brit*) assicurazione *f* contro terzi.

third-rate [thûrd'rāt'] *a* di qualità scadente.

Third World *n*: **the** ~ il Terzo Mondo.

thirst [thûrst] *n* sete *f.*

thirsty [thûrs'tē] *a* (*person*) assetato(a), che ha sete; **to be** ~ aver sete.

thirteen [thûr'tēn'] *num* tredici.

thirtieth [thûr'tēith] *num* trentesimo(a).

thirty [thûr'tē] *num* trenta.

this [ᵗh̲is] *a, pronoun* (*pl* **these**) questo(a) ♦ *ad*: ~ **high** alto così; così alto; **it's about** ~ **high** è alto circa così; ~ **one** questo(a) (qui); ~ **is what he said** questo è ciò che ha detto; **who/what is** ~**?** chi è/che cos'è questo?; ~ **is Mr Brown** (*in introductions, in photo*) questo è il signor Brown; (*on telephone*) sono il signor Brown; ~ **time** questa volta; ~ **time last year** l'anno scorso in questo periodo; ~ **way** (*in this direction*) da questa parte; (*in this fashion*) così; **they were talking of** ~ **and that** stavano parlando del più e del meno.

thistle [this'əl] *n* cardo.

thong [thông] *n* cinghia.

thorn [thôrn] *n* spina.

thorny [thôr'nē] *a* spinoso(a).

thorough [thûr'ō] *a* (*person*) preciso(a), accurato(a); (*search*) minuzioso(a); (*knowledge, research*) approfondito(a), profondo(a); (*cleaning*) a fondo.

thoroughbred [thûr'ōbred] *n* (*horse*) purosangue *m/f inv*.

thoroughfare [thûr'ōfär] *n* strada transitabile.

thoroughly [thûr'ōlē] *ad* accuratamente; minuziosamente; in profondità; a fondo; **he ~ agreed** fu completamente d'accordo.

thoroughness [thûr'ōnis] *n* precisione *f*.

those [thōz] *pl pronoun* quelli(e) ♦ *pl a* quei(quegli) *mpl*; quelle *fpl*.

though [thō] *cj* benché, sebbene ♦ *ad* comunque, tuttavia; **even ~ anche se; it's not so easy, ~** tuttavia non è così facile.

thought [thôt] *pt, pp of* **think** ♦ *n* pensiero; (*opinion*) opinione *f*; (*intention*) intenzione *f*; **after much ~** dopo molti ripensamenti; **I've just had a ~** mi è appena venuta un'idea; **to give sth some ~** prendere qc in considerazione, riflettere su qc.

thoughtful [thôt'fəl] *a* pensieroso(a), pensoso(a); ponderato(a); (*considerate*) premuroso(a).

thoughtfully [thôt'fəlē] *ad* (*pensively*) con aria pensierosa.

thoughtless [thôt'lis] *a* sconsiderato(a); (*behavior*) scortese.

thoughtlessly [thôt'lislē] *ad* sconsideratamente; scortesemente.

thousand [thou'zənd] *num* mille; **one ~** mille; **~s of** migliaia di.

thousandth [thou'zəndth] *num* millesimo(a).

thrash [thrash] *vt* picchiare; bastonare; (*defeat*) battere.

 thrash about *vi* dibattersi.

 thrash out *vt* dibattere, sviscerare.

thrashing [thrash'ing] *n*: **to give sb a ~** = **to thrash sb**.

thread [thred] *n* filo; (*of screw*) filetto ♦ *vt* (*needle*) infilare; **to ~ one's way between** infilarsi tra.

threadbare [thred'bär] *a* consumato(a), logoro(a).

threat [thret] *n* minaccia; **to be under ~ of** (*closure, extinction*) rischiare di; (*exposure*) essere minacciato(a) di.

threaten [thret'ən] *vi* (*storm*) minacciare ♦ *vt*: **to ~ sb with sth/to do** minacciare qn con qc/di fare.

threatening [thret'əning] *a* minaccioso(a).

three [thrē] *num* tre.

three-dimensional [thrē'dimen'chənəl] *a* tridimensionale.

three-piece [thrē'pēs]: **~ suit** *n* completo (con gilè); **~ suite** *n* salotto comprendente un divano e due poltrone.

three-ply [thrē'plī] *a* (*wood*) a tre strati; (*wool*) a tre fili.

three-quarters [thrē'kwôr'tûrz] *npl* tre quarti *mpl*; **~ full** pieno per tre quarti.

thresh [thresh] *vt* (*AGR*) trebbiare.

threshing machine [thresh'ing məshēn'] *n* trebbiatrice *f*.

threshold [thresh'ōld] *n* soglia; **to be on the ~ of** (*fig*) essere sulla soglia di.

threshold agreement *n* (*ECON*) ≈ scala mobile.

threw [thrōō] *pt of* **throw**.

thrift [thrift] *n* parsimonia.

thrifty [thrif'tē] *a* economico(a), parsimonioso(a).

thrill [thril] *n* brivido ♦ *vi* eccitarsi, tremare ♦ *vt* (*audience*) elettrizzare; **I was ~ed to get your letter** la tua lettera mi ha fatto veramente piacere.

thriller [thril'ûr] *n* film *m inv* (*or* dramma *m or* libro) del brivido.

thrilling [thril'ing] *a* (*book, play etc*) pieno(a) di suspense; (*news, discovery*) entusiasmante.

thrive, *pt* **thrived, throve,** *pp* **thrived, thriven** [thrived, throv, thriven] *vi* crescere *or* svilupparsi bene; (*business*) prosperare; **he ~s on it** gli fa bene, ne gode.

thriving [thrīv'ing] *a* (*industry etc*) fiorente.

throat [thrōt] *n* gola; **to have a sore ~** avere (un *or* il) mal di gola.

throb [thräb] *n* (*of heart*) battito; (*of engine*) vibrazione *f*; (*of pain*) fitta ♦ *vi* (*heart*) palpitare; (*engine*) vibrare; (*with pain*) pulsare; **my head is ~bing** mi martellano le tempie.

throes [thrōz] *npl*: **in the ~ of** alle prese con; in preda a; **in the ~ of death** in agonia.

thrombosis [thrämbō'sis] *n* trombosi *f*.

throne [thrōn] *n* trono.

throng [thrông] *n* moltitudine *f* ♦ *vt* affollare.

throttle [thrät'əl] *n* (*AUT*) valvola a farfalla; (*on motorbike*) (manopola del) gas ♦ *vt* strangolare.

through [thrōō] *prep* attraverso; (*time*) per, durante; (*by means of*) per mezzo di; (*owing to*) a causa di ♦ *a* (*ticket, train, passage*) diretto(a) ♦ *ad* attraverso; **(from) Monday ~ Friday** (*US*) da lunedì a venerdì; **I am halfway ~ the book** sono a metà libro; **to let sth ~** lasciar passare qn; **to put sb ~ to sb** (*TEL*) passare qn a qn; **to be ~** (*TEL*) ottenere la comunicazione; (*have finished*) avere finito; **"no ~ traffic"** (*US*) "divieto d'accesso"; **"no ~ road"** "strada senza sbocco".

throughout [thrōōout'] *prep* (*place*) dappertutto in; (*time*) per *or* durante tutto(a) ♦ *ad* dappertutto; sempre.

throughput [thrōō'pŏŏt] *n* (*of goods, materials*) materiale *m* in lavorazione; (*COMPUT*) volume *m* di dati immessi.

throve [thrōv] *pt of* **thrive**.

throw [thrō] *n* tiro, getto; (*SPORT*) lancio ♦ *vt* (*pt* **threw,** *pp* **thrown** [thrōō, thrōn]) tirare, gettare; (*SPORT*) lanciare; (*rider*) disarcionare; (*fig*) confondere; (*pottery*) formare al tornio; **to ~ a party** dare una festa; **to ~ open** (*doors, windows*) spalancare; (*house, gardens etc*) aprire al pubblico; (*competition, race*) aprire a tutti.

throw about *vt* (*Brit*) = **throw around**.

throw around *vt* (*litter etc*) spargere.

throw away *vt* gettare *or* buttare via.

throw off *vt* sbarazzarsi di.

throw out *vt* buttare fuori; (*reject*) respingere.

throw together *vt* (*clothes, meal etc*) mettere insieme; (*essay*) buttar giù.

throw up *vi* vomitare.

throwaway [thrō'əwā] *a* da buttare.

throwback [thrō'bak] *n*: **it's a ~ to** (*fig*) ciò risale a.

throw-in [thrō'in] *n* (*SPORT*) rimessa in gioco.

thrown [thrōn] *pp* of **throw**.

thru [thrōō] *prep, a, ad* (*US*) = **through**.

thrush [thrush] *n* (*ZOOL*) tordo; (*MED: esp in children*) mughetto; (*: Brit: in women*) candida.

thrust [thrust] *n* (*TECH*) spinta ♦ *vt* (*pt, pp* **thrust**) spingere con forza; (*push in*) conficcare.

thrusting [thrust'ing] *a* (*troppo*) intraprendente.

thud [thud] *n* tonfo.

thug [thug] *n* delinquente *m*.

thumb [thum] *n* (*ANAT*) pollice *m* ♦ *vt* (*book*) sfogliare; **to ~ a lift** fare l'autostop; **to give sb/sth the ~s up** dare la propria approvazione a qn/qc.

thumb index *n* indice *m* a rubrica.

thumbnail [thum'nāl] *n* unghia del pollice.

thumbnail sketch *n* descrizione *f* breve.

thumbtack [thum'tak] *n* (*US*) puntina da disegno.

thump [thump] *n* colpo forte; (*sound*) tonfo ♦ *vt* battere su ♦ *vi* picchiare, battere.

thunder [thun'dûr] *n* tuono ♦ *vi* tuonare; (*train etc*): **to ~ past** passare con un rombo.

thunderbolt [thun'dûrbōlt] *n* fulmine *m*.

thunderclap [thun'dûrklap] *n* rombo di tuono.

thunderous [thun'dûrəs] *a* fragoroso(a).

thunderstorm [thun'dûrstôrm] *n* temporale *m*.

thunderstruck [thun'dûrstruk] *a* (*fig*) sbigottito(a).

thundery [thun'dûrē] *a* temporalesco(a).

Thur(s). *abbr* (= *Thursday*) gio.

Thursday [thûrz'dā] *n* giovedì *m inv*; *for phrases see also* **Tuesday**.

thus [thus] *ad* così.

thwart [thwôrt] *vt* contrastare.

thyme [tīm] *n* timo.

thyroid [thī'roid] *n* tiroide *f*.

tiara [tēar'ə] *n* (*woman's*) diadema *m*.

Tiber [tī'bûr] *n*: **the ~** il Tevere.

Tibet [tibet'] *n* Tibet *m*.

Tibetan [tibet'ən] *a* tibetano(a) ♦ *n* tibetano/a; (*LING*) tibetano.

tibia [tib'ēə] *n* tibia.

tic [tik] *n* tic *m inv*.

tick [tik] *n* (*sound: of clock*) tic tac *m inv*; (*mark*) segno; spunta; (*ZOOL*) zecca ♦ *vi* fare tic tac ♦ *vt* spuntare; **to put a ~ against sth** fare un segno di fianco a qc.

tick off *vt* spuntare; (*person*) sgridare.

tick over *vi* (*Brit: engine*) andare al minimo.

ticker tape [tik'ûr tāp] *n* nastro di telescrivente; (*US: in celebrations*) stelle *fpl* filanti.

ticket [tik'it] *n* biglietto; (*in store: on goods*) etichetta; (*: from cash register*) scontrino; (*US POL*) lista dei candidati; **to get a (parking) ~** (*AUT*) prendere una multa (per sosta vietata).

ticket agency *n* (*THEATER*) agenzia di vendita di biglietti.

ticket collector *n* bigliettaio.

ticket holder *n* persona munita di biglietto.

ticket inspector *n* controllore *m*.

ticket office *n* biglietteria.

tickle [tik'əl] *n* solletico ♦ *vt* fare il solletico a, solleticare; (*fig*) stuzzicare; piacere a; far ridere.

ticklish [tik'lish] *a* che soffre il solletico; (*which tickles: blanket, cough*) che provoca prurito.

tidal [tīd'əl] *a* di marea.

tidal wave *n* onda anomala.

tidbit [tid'bit] *n* (*US: food*) leccornia; (*: news*) notizia ghiotta.

tiddlywinks [tid'lēwingks] *n* gioco della pulce.

tide [tīd] *n* marea; (*fig: of events*) corso ♦ *vt*: **will $20 ~ you over till Monday?** ti basteranno 20 dollari fino a lunedì?; **high/low ~** alta/bassa marea; **the ~ of public opinion** l'orientamento dell'opinione pubblica.

tidily [tī'dilē] *ad* in modo ordinato; **to arrange ~** sistemare; **to dress ~** vestirsi per benino.

tidiness [tī'dēnis] *n* ordine *m*.

tidy [tī'dē] *a* (*room*) ordinato(a), lindo(a); (*dress, work*) curato(a), in ordine; (*person*) ordinato(a); (*mind*) organizzato(a) ♦ *vt* (*also: ~ up*) riordinare, mettere in ordine; **to ~ o.s. up** rassettarsi.

tie [tī] *n* (*string etc*) legaccio; (*also:* **neck~**) cravatta; (*fig: link*) legame *m*; (*SPORT: draw*) pareggio (*: match*) incontro; (*US RAIL*) traversina ♦ *vt* (*parcel*) legare; (*ribbon*) annodare ♦ *vi* (*SPORT*) pareggiare; **"black/white ~"** "smoking/abito di rigore"; **family ~s** legami familiari; **to ~ sth in a bow** annodare qc; **to ~ a knot in sth** fare un nodo a qc.

tie down *vt* fissare con una corda; (*fig*): **to ~ sb down to** costringere qn ad accettare.

tie in *vi*: **to ~ in (with)** (*correspond*) corrispondere (a).

tie on vt (Brit: label etc) attaccare.

tie up vt (parcel, dog) legare; (boat) ormeggiare; (arrangements) concludere; **to be ~d up** (busy) essere occupato or preso.

tie-break(er) [tī'brāk(ûr)] n (TENNIS) tie-break m inv; (in quiz) spareggio.

tie-on [tī'án] a (Brit: label) volante.

tiepin [tī'pin] n (Brit) fermacravatta m inv.

tier [tēr] n fila; (of cake) piano, strato.

Tierra del Fuego [tēär'ɔ del fwā'gō] n Terra del Fuoco.

tie tack n (US) fermacravatta m inv.

tiff [tif] n battibecco.

tiger [tī'gûr] n tigre f.

tight [tīt] a (rope) teso(a), tirato(a); (clothes) stretto(a); (budget, schedule, bend) stretto(a); (control) severo(a), fermo(a); (col: drunk) sbronzo(a) ♦ ad (squeeze) fortemente; (shut) ermeticamente; **to be packed ~** (suitcase) essere pieno zeppo; (people) essere pigiati; **everybody hold ~!** tenetevi stretti!; see also **tights**.

tighten [tīt'ɔn] vt (rope) tendere; (screw) stringere; (control) rinforzare ♦ vi tendersi; stringersi.

tightfisted [tīt'fis'tid] a avaro(a).

tightly [tīt'lē] ad (grasp) bene, saldamente.

tightrope [tīt'rōp] n corda (da acrobata).

tightrope walker n funambolo/a.

tights [tīts] npl (Brit) collant m inv.

tigress [tī'gris] n tigre f (femmina).

tilde [til'dɔ] n tilde f.

tile [tīl] n (on roof) tegola; (on floor) mattonella; (on wall) piastrella ♦ vt (floor, bathroom etc) piastrellare.

tiled [tīld] a rivestito(a) di tegole; a mattonelle; a piastrelle.

till [til] n registratore m di cassa ♦ vt (land) coltivare ♦ prep, cj = **until**.

tiller [til'ûr] n (NAUT) barra del timone.

tilt [tilt] vt inclinare, far pendere ♦ vi inclinarsi, pendere ♦ n (slope) pendio; **to wear one's hat at a ~** portare il cappello sulle ventitré; **(at) full ~** a tutta velocità.

timber [tim'bûr] n (material) legname m; (trees) alberi mpl da legname.

time [tīm] n tempo; (epoch: often pl) epoca, tempo; (by clock) ora; (moment) momento; (occasion, also MATH) volta; (MUS) tempo ♦ vt (race) cronometrare; (program) calcolare la durata di; (remark etc): **to ~ sth well/badly** scegliere il momento più/meno opportuno per qc; **a long ~** molto tempo; **for the ~ being** per il momento; **from ~ to ~** ogni tanto; **~ after ~, ~ and again** mille volte; **in ~** (soon enough) in tempo; (after some time) col tempo; (MUS) a tempo; **at ~s** a volte; **to take one's ~** prenderla con calma; **in a week's ~** fra una settimana; **in no ~** in un attimo; **on ~** puntualmente; **to be 30 minutes behind/ahead of ~** avere 30 minuti di

ritardo/anticipo; **by the ~ he arrived** quando è arrivato; **5 ~s 5** 5 volte 5, 5 per 5; **what ~ is it?** che ora è?, che ore sono?; **to have a good ~** divertirsi; **they had a hard ~ of it** è stato duro per loro; **~'s up!** è (l')ora!; **to be behind the ~s** vivere nel passato; **I've no ~ for it** (fig) non ho tempo da perdere con cose del genere; **he'll do it in his own (good) ~** (without being hurried) lo farà quando avrà (un minuto di) tempo; **he'll do it on** or (Brit) **in his own ~** (out of working hours) lo farà nel suo tempo libero; **the bomb was ~d to explode 5 minutes later** la bomba era stata regolata in modo da esplodere 5 minuti più tardi.

time-and-motion study [tīm'ɔnmōshɔn' studē] n analisi f inv dei tempi e dei movimenti.

time bomb n bomba a orologeria.

time card n cartellino (da timbrare).

time clock n orologio m marcatempo inv.

time-consuming [tīm'kɔnsōōming] a che richiede molto tempo.

time difference n differenza di fuso orario.

time-honored [tīm'ânûrd] a consacrato(a) dal tempo.

timekeeper [tīm'kēpûr] n (SPORT) cronometrista m/f.

time lag n intervallo, ritardo; (in travel) differenza di fuso orario.

timeless [tīm'lis] a eterno(a).

time limit n limite m di tempo.

timely [tīm'lē] a opportuno(a).

time off n tempo libero.

timeout [tīm'out] n (US).

timer [tī'mûr] n (in kitchen) contaminuti m inv; (TECH) timer m inv, temporizzatore m.

timesaving [tīm'sāving] a che fa risparmiare tempo.

time scale n tempi mpl d'esecuzione.

time sharing [tīm' shäring] n (COMPUT) divisione f di tempo.

time sheet n = **time card**.

time signal n segnale m orario.

time switch n interruttore m a tempo.

timetable [tīm'tābɔl] n orario; (program of events etc) programma m.

time zone n fuso orario.

timid [tim'id] a timido(a); (easily scared) pauroso(a).

timidity [timid'itē] n timidezza.

timing [tī'ming] n sincronizzazione f; (fig) scelta del momento opportuno, tempismo; (SPORT) cronometraggio.

timing device n (on bomb) timer m inv.

timpani [tim'pɔnē] npl timpani mpl.

tin [tin] n stagno; (also: ~ **plate**) latta; (Brit: can) barattolo (di latta), lattina, scatola; (for baking) teglia.

tin foil n stagnola.

tinge [tinj] n sfumatura ♦ vt: **~d with** tinto(a)

di.

tingle [ting'gəl] *vi* (*cheeks, skin: from cold*) pungere, pizzicare; (: *from bad circulation*) formicolare.

tinker [tingk'ûr] *n* stagnino ambulante; (*gipsy*) zingaro/a.

tinker with *vt fus* armeggiare intorno a; cercare di riparare.

tinkle [ting'kəl] *vi* tintinnare ♦ *n* (*col*): **to give sb a** ~ dare un colpo di telefono a qn.

tin mine *n* miniera di stagno.

tinned [tind] *a* (*Brit: food*) in scatola.

tinny [tin'ē] *a* metallico(a).

tin-opener [tin'ōp'ənûr] *n* (*Brit*) apriscatole *m inv.*

tinsel [tin'səl] *n* decorazioni *fpl* natalizie (*argentate*).

tint [tint] *n* tinta; (*for hair*) shampoo *m inv* colorante ♦ *vt* (*hair*) fare uno shampoo colorante a.

tinted [tin'tid] *a* (*hair*) tinto(a); (*glass*) colorato(a).

T-intersection [tēintərsek'shən] *n* (*US*) incrocio a T.

tiny [tī'nē] *a* minuscolo(a).

tip [tip] *n* (*end*) punta; (*protective: on umbrella etc*) puntale *m*; (*gratuity*) mancia; (*advice*) suggerimento; (*Brit: for garbage*) immondezzaio ♦ *vt* (*waiter*) dare la mancia a; (*tilt*) inclinare; (*overturn: also:* ~ **over**) capovolgere; (*empty: also:* ~ **out**) scaricare; (*predict: winner*) pronosticare; (: *horse*) dare vincente.

tip off *vt* fare una soffiata a.

tip-off [tip'ôf] *n* (*hint*) soffiata.

tipped [tipt] *a* (*Brit: cigarette*) col filtro; **steel-**~ con la punta d'acciaio.

Tipp-Ex [tip'eks] ® *n* (*Brit*) liquido correttore.

tipple [tip'əl] (*Brit*) *vi* sbevazzare ♦ *n*: **to have a** ~ prendere un bicchierino.

tippy-toe [tip'ētō] *n* (*US*): **on** ~ in punta di piedi.

tipsy [tip'sē] *a* brillo(a).

tiptoe [tip'tō] *n* (*Brit*) = **tippy-toe**.

tiptop [tip'tâp] *a*: **in** ~ **condition** in ottime condizioni.

tire [tīûr'] *vt* stancare ♦ *vi* stancarsi ♦ *n* (*US*) pneumatico, gomma.

tire out *vt* sfinire, spossare.

tired [tīûrd'] *a* stanco(a); **to be/feel/look** ~ essere/sentirsi/sembrare stanco; **to be** ~ **of** essere stanco *or* stufo di.

tiredness [tīûrd'nis] *n* stanchezza.

tireless [tīûr'lis] *a* instancabile.

tire pressure *n* pressione *f* (delle) gomme.

tiresome [tīûr'səm] *a* noioso(a).

tiring [tīûr'ing] *a* faticoso(a).

tissue [tish'ōō] *n* tessuto; (*paper handkerchief*) fazzolettino di carta.

tissue paper *n* carta velina.

tit [tit] *n* (*bird*) cinciallegra; (*col: breast*)

tetta; **to give** ~ **for tat** rendere pan per focaccia.

titanium [tītā'nēəm] *n* titanio.

titbit [tit'bit] *n* (*Brit*) = **tidbit**.

titillate [tit'əlāt] *vt* titillare.

titivate [tit'əvāt] *vt* agghindare.

title [tīt'əl] *n* titolo; (*LAW: right*): ~ **(to)** diritto (a).

title deed *n* (*LAW*) titolo di proprietà.

title page *n* frontespizio.

title role *n* ruolo *or* parte *f* principale.

titter [tit'ûr] *vi* ridere scioccamente.

tittle-tattle [tit'əltatəl] *n* chiacchiere *fpl*, pettegolezzi *mpl.*

titular [tich'əlûr] *a* (*in name only*) nominale.

tizzy [tiz'ē] *n* (*col*): **to be in a** ~ essere in agitazione.

T-junction [tē' jung'kshən] *n* (*Brit*) = **T-intersection**.

TM *n abbr* (= *transcendental meditation*) M.T. *f*; (*COMM*) = **trademark**.

TN *abbr* (*US MAIL*) = *Tennessee.*

TNT *n abbr* (= *trinitrotoluene*) T.N.T. *m.*

to [tōō, tōō] *prep* (*gen, with expressions of time*) a; (*towards*) verso ♦ *with vb* (*simple infinitive*): **go/eat** andare/mangiare; (*following another vb*): **to want** ~ **do** voler fare; **to try** ~ **do** cercare di fare; (*purpose, result*) per; **to give sth** ~ **sb** dare qc a qn; **give it** ~ **me** dammelo; **the key** ~ **the front door** la chiave della porta d'ingresso; **it belongs** ~ **him** gli appartiene, è suo; **to go** ~ **France/Portugal** andare in Francia/Portogallo; **the road** ~ **Boston** la strada per Boston; **I went** ~ **Claudia's** sono andato da Claudia; **to go** ~ **town/school** andare in città/a scuola; **8 apples** ~ **the kilo** 8 mele in un chilo; **it's twenty-five** ~ **3** sono *or* mancano venticinque minuti alle 3, sono le 2 e trentacinque; **to pull/push the door** ~ tirare/spingere la porta; **to go** ~ **and fro** andare e tornare; **I don't want** ~ non voglio (farlo); **I have things** ~ **do** ho (delle cose) da fare; **ready** ~ **go** pronto a partire; **he did it** ~ **help you** l'ha fatto per aiutarti.

toad [tōd] *n* rospo.

toadstool [tōd'stōōl] *n* fungo (velenoso).

toady [tō'dē] *vi* adulare.

toast [tōst] *n* (*CULIN*) toast *m*, pane *m* abbrustolito; (*drink, speech*) brindisi *m inv* ♦ *vt* (*CULIN*) abbrustolire; (*drink to*) brindare a; **a piece** *or* **slice of** ~ una fetta di pane abbrustolito.

toaster [tōs'tûr] *n* tostapane *m inv.*

toastmaster [tōst'mastûr] *n* direttore *m* dei brindisi.

toast rack *n* portatoast *m inv.*

tobacco [təbak'ō] *n* tabacco; **pipe** ~ tabacco da pipa.

tobacconist [təbak'ənist] *n* tabaccaio/a; ~**'s (shop)** tabaccheria.

Tobago [tōbā'gō] *n see* **Trinidad**.

toboggan [təbág'ən] *n* toboga *m inv*; (*child's*) slitta.

today [tədā'] *ad, n* (*also fig*) oggi (*m inv*); **what day is it ~?** che giorno è oggi?; **what date is it ~?** quanti ne abbiamo oggi?; **~ is the 4th of March** (oggi) è il 4 di marzo; **~'s paper** il giornale di oggi; **two weeks (from) ~** quindici giorni a oggi.

toddler [tåd'lûr] *n* bambino/a che impara a camminare.

toddy [tåd'ē] *n* grog *m inv*.

to-do [tədōō'] *n* (*fuss*) storie *fpl*.

toe [tō] *n* dito del piede; (*of shoe*) punta ♦ *vt*: **to ~ the line** (*fig*) stare in riga, conformarsi; **big ~** alluce *m*; **little ~** mignolino.

toehold [tō'hōld] *n* punto d'appoggio.

toenail [tō'nāl] *n* unghia del piede.

toffee [tôf'ē] *n* caramella.

tofu [tō'fōō] *n* tofu *m*.

toga [tō'gə] *n* toga.

together [tōōgeth'ûr] *ad* insieme; (*at same time*) allo stesso tempo; **~ with** insieme a.

togetherness [tōōgeth'ûrnis] *n* solidarietà; intimità.

toggle switch [tåg'əl swich] *n* (*COMPUT*) tasto bistabile.

Togo [tō'gō] *n* Togo.

togs [tågz] *npl* (*col: clothes*) vestiti *mpl*.

toil [toil] *n* travaglio, fatica ♦ *vi* affannarsi; sgobbare.

toilet [toi'lit] *n* (*Brit: lavatory*) gabinetto ♦ *cpd* (*bag, soap etc*) da toletta; **to go to the ~** andare al gabinetto *or* al bagno.

toilet bag *n* (*Brit*) nécessaire *m inv* da toilette.

toilet bowl *n* vaso *or* tazza del gabinetto.

toilet paper *n* carta igienica.

toiletries [toi'litrēz] *npl* articoli *mpl* da toletta.

toilet roll *n* rotolo di carta igienica.

toilet water *n* acqua di colonia.

token [tō'kən] *n* (*sign*) segno; (*voucher*) buono ♦ *cpd* (*fee, strike*) simbolico(a); **by the same ~** (*fig*) per lo stesso motivo.

Tokyo [tō'kēyō] *n* Tokyo *f*.

told [tōld] *pt, pp of* **tell**.

tolerable [tål'ûrəbəl] *a* (*bearable*) tollerabile; (*fairly good*) passabile.

tolerably [tål'ûrəblē] *ad* (*good, comfortable*) abbastanza.

tolerance [tål'ûrəns] *n* (*also TECH*) tolleranza.

tolerant [tål'ûrənt] *a*: **~ (of)** tollerante (nei confronti di).

tolerate [tål'ərāt] *vt* sopportare; (*MED, TECH*) tollerare.

toleration [tålərā'shən] *n* tolleranza.

toll [tōl] *n* (*tax, charge*) pedaggio ♦ *vi* (*bell*) suonare; **the accident ~ on the roads** il numero delle vittime della strada.

tollbridge [tōl'brij] *n* ponte *m* a pedaggio.

toll-free [tōl'frē'] *a* (*US*): **toll-free (number)** ≈ numero verde.

tomato, **~es** [təmā'tō] *n* pomodoro.

tomb [tōōm] *n* tomba.

tomboy [tåm'boi] *n* maschiaccio.

tombstone [tōōm'stōn] *n* pietra tombale.

tomcat [tåm'kat] *n* gatto.

tomorrow [təmôr'ō] *ad, n* (*also fig*) domani (*m inv*); **the day after ~** dopodomani; **a week ~** domani a otto; **~ morning** domani mattina.

ton [tun] *n* tonnellata (*US = 907 kg; Brit = 1016 kg; 20 cwt; metric = 1000 kg*); (*NAUT: also:* **register ~**) tonnellata di stazza (*= 2.83 cu.m; 100 cu. ft*).

tonal [tō'nəl] *a* tonale.

tone [tōn] *n* tono; (*of musical instrument*) timbro ♦ *vi* intonarsi.

tone down *vt* (*color, criticism, sound*) attenuare.

tone up *vt* (*muscles*) tonificare.

tone-deaf [tōn'def] *a* che non ha orecchio (musicale).

toner [tō'nûr] *n* (*for photocopier*) colorante *m* organico, toner *m*.

Tonga [tång'gə] *n* isole *fpl* Tonga.

tongs [tôngz] *npl* tenaglie *fpl*; (*for coal*) molle *fpl*; (*for hair*) arricciacapelli *m inv*.

tongue [tung] *n* lingua; **~ in cheek** (*fig*) ironicamente.

tongue-tied [tung'tīd] *a* (*fig*) muto(a).

tongue twister [tung' twis'tûr] *n* scioglilingua *m inv*.

tonic [tân'ik] *n* (*MED*) ricostituente *m*; (*skin ~*) tonico; (*MUS*) nota tonica; (*also:* **~ water**) acqua tonica.

tonight [tənīt'] *ad* stanotte; (*this evening*) stasera ♦ *n* questa notte; questa sera; **I'll see you ~** ci vediamo stasera.

tonnage [tun'ij] *n* (*NAUT*) tonnellaggio, stazza.

tonne [tun] *n* (*Brit: metric ton*) tonnellata.

tonsil [tân'səl] *n* tonsilla; **to have one's ~s out** farsi operare di tonsille.

tonsillitis [tånsəlī'tis] *n* tonsillite *f*; **to have ~** avere la tonsillite.

too [tōō] *ad* (*excessively*) troppo; (*also*) anche; **it's ~ sweet** è troppo dolce; **I went ~** ci sono andato anch'io; **~ much** *ad* troppo ♦ *a* troppo(a); **~ many** *a* troppi(e); **~ bad!** tanto peggio!; peggio così!

took [tōōk] *pt of* **take**.

tool [tōōl] *n* utensile *m*, attrezzo; (*fig: person*) strumento ♦ *vt* lavorare con un attrezzo.

tool box *n* cassetta *f* portautensili *inv*.

tool kit *n* cassetta di attrezzi.

toot [tōōt] *vi* suonare; (*with car horn*) suonare il clacson.

tooth, *pl* **teeth** [tōōth, tēth] *n* (*ANAT, TECH*) dente *m*; **to clean one's teeth** lavarsi i denti; **to have a ~ pulled** *or* (*Brit*) **out** farsi togliere un dente; **by the skin of one's teeth**

per il rotto della cuffia.

toothache [tōōth'āk] *n* mal *m* di denti; **to have** ~ avere il mal di denti.

toothbrush [tōōth'brush] *n* spazzolino da denti.

toothpaste [tōōth'pāst] *n* dentifricio.

toothpick [tōōth'pik] *n* stuzzicadenti *m inv*.

tooth powder *n* dentifricio in polvere.

top [tâp] *n* (*of mountain, page, ladder*) cima; (*of box, cupboard, table*) sopra *m inv*, parte *f* superiore; (*lid: of box, jar*) coperchio; (: *of bottle*) tappo; (*US AUT*) capote *f*; (*toy*) trottola; (*DRESS: blouse etc*) camicia (*or* maglietta *etc*); (*of pajamas*) giacca ♦ *a* più alto(a); (*in rank*) primo(a); (*best*) migliore ♦ *vt* (*exceed*) superare; (*be first in*) essere in testa a; **on** ~ **of** sopra, in cima a; (*in addition to*) oltre a; **at the** ~ **of the stairs/page/ street** in cima alle scale/alla pagina/alla strada; **at** ~ **speed** a tutta velocità; **at the** ~ **of one's voice** (*fig*) a squarciagola; **over the** ~ (*col: behavior etc*) eccessivo(a); **to go over the** ~ (*Brit*) esagerare.

top off, (*Brit*) **top up** *vt* riempire.

topaz [tō'paz] *n* topazio.

topcoat [tâp'kōt] *n* soprabito.

topflight [tâp'flīt'] *a* di primaria importanza.

top floor *n* ultimo piano.

top hat *n* cilindro.

top-heavy [tâp'hevē] *a* (*object*) con la parte superiore troppo pesante.

topic [tâp'ik] *n* argomento.

topical [tâp'ikəl] *a* (*talks*) d'attualità.

topless [tâp'lis] *a* (*bather etc*) col seno scoperto; ~ **swimsuit** topless *m inv*.

top-level [tâp'lev'əl] *a* (*talks*) ad alto livello.

topmost [tâp'mōst] *a* il(la) più alto(a).

topography [təpâg'rəfē] *n* topografia.

topping [tâp'ing] *n* (*CULIN*) guarnizione *f*.

topple [tâp'əl] *vt* rovesciare, far cadere ♦ *vi* cadere; traballare.

top-ranking [tâp'rang'king] *a* di massimo grado.

top-secret [tâp'sē'krit] *a* segretissimo(a).

topsy-turvy [tâp'sētûr'vē] *a*, *ad* sottosopra (*inv*).

top-up [tâp'up] *n* (*Brit*): **would you like a** ~**?** vuole che le riempia il bicchiere (*or* la tazza *etc*)?

torch [tôrch] *n* torcia; (*Brit: electric*) lampadina tascabile.

tore [tôr] *pt of* **tear**.

torment *n* [tôr'ment] tormento ♦ *vt* [tôrment'] tormentare; (*fig: annoy*) infastidire.

torn [tôrn] *pp of* **tear** ♦ *a*: ~ **between** (*fig*) combattuto(a) tra.

tornado, ~**es** [tôrnā'dō] *n* tornado.

torpedo, ~**es** [tôrpē'dō] *n* siluro.

torpedo boat *n* motosilurante *f*.

torpor [tôr'pûr] *n* torpore *m*.

torque [tôrk] *n* coppia di torsione.

torrent [tôr'ənt] *n* torrente *m*.

torrential [tôren'chəl] *a* torrenziale.

torrid [tôr'id] *a* torrido(a); (*fig*) denso(a) di passione.

torso [tôr'sō] *n* torso.

tortoise [tôr'təs] *n* tartaruga.

tortoiseshell [tôr'təs-shel] *a* di tartaruga.

tortuous [tôr'chōōəs] *a* tortuoso(a).

torture [tôr'chûr] *n* tortura ♦ *vt* torturare.

torturer [tôr'chûrûr] *n* torturatore/trice.

Tory [tôr'ē] *a* tory *inv*, conservatore(trice) ♦ *n* tory *m/f inv*, conservatore/trice.

toss [tôs] *vt* gettare, lanciare; (*head*) scuotere ♦ *n* (*movement: of head etc*) movimento brusco; (*of coin*) lancio; **to win/lose the** ~ vincere/perdere a testa o croce; (*SPORT*) vincere/perdere il sorteggio; **to** ~ **a coin** fare a testa o croce; **to** ~ **and turn** (*in bed*) girarsi e rigirarsi.

tot [tât] *n* (*child*) bimbo/a; (*Brit: drink*) bicchierino.

total [tōt'əl] *a* totale ♦ *n* totale *m* ♦ *vt* (*add up*) sommare; (*amount to*) ammontare a; **in** ~ in tutto.

totalitarian [tōtalitär'ēən] *a* totalitario(a).

totality [tōtal·itē] *n* totalità.

totally [tō'təlē] *ad* completamente.

tote bag [tōt' bag] *n* sporta.

totem pole [tō'təm pōl] *n* totem *m inv*.

totter [tât'ûr] *vi* barcollare; (*object, government*) vacillare.

touch [tuch] *n* tocco; (*sense*) tatto; (*contact*) contatto; (*SOCCER*) fuori gioco *m* ♦ *vt* toccare; **a** ~ **of** (*fig*) un tocco di; un pizzico di; **to get in** ~ **with** mettersi in contatto con; **to lose** ~ (*friends*) perdersi di vista; **I'll be in** ~ mi farò sentire; **to be out of** ~ **with events** essere tagliato fuori; **the personal** ~ una nota personale; **to put the finishing** ~**es to sth** dare gli ultimi ritocchi a qc.

touch on *vt fus* (*topic*) sfiorare, accennare a.

touch up *vt* (*improve*) ritoccare.

touch-and-go [tuch'əngō'] *a* incerto(a); **it was** ~ **with the sick man** il malato era tra la vita e la morte.

touchdown [tuch'doun] *n* atterraggio; (*US FOOTBALL*) meta; (*on sea*) ammaraggio.

touched [tucht] *a* commosso(a); (*col*) tocco(a), toccato(a).

touching [tuch'ing] *a* commovente.

touchline [tuch'līn] *n* (*SPORT*) linea laterale.

touch-type [tuch'tīp] *vi* dattilografare (senza guardare i tasti).

touchy [tuch'ē] *a* (*person*) suscettibile.

tough [tuf] *a* duro(a); (*resistant*) resistente; (*meat*) duro(a), tiglioso(a); (*journey*) faticoso(a), duro(a); (*person: rough*) violento(a), brutale *n* (*gangster etc*) delinquente *m/f*; ~ **luck!** che sfortuna!

toughen [tuf'ən] *vt* indurire, rendere più resi-

stente.
toughness [tuf'nis] *n* durezza; resistenza.
toupee [tōōpā'] *n* parrucchino.
tour [tōōr] *n* viaggio; (*also:* **package** ~) viaggio organizzato *or* tutto compreso; (*of town, museum*) visita; (*by artist*) tournée *f inv* ♦ *vt* visitare; **to go on a ~ of** (*region, country*) fare il giro di; (*museum, castle*) visitare; **to go on ~** andare in tournée.
touring [tōō'ring] *n* turismo.
tourism [tōōr'izəm] *n* turismo.
tourist [tōōr'ist] *n* turista *m/f* ♦ *ad* (*travel*) in classe turistica ♦ *cpd* turistico(a); **the ~ trade** il turismo.
tourist office *n* pro loco *f inv.*
tournament [tōōr'nəmənt] *n* torneo.
tourniquet [tûr'nikit] *n* (*MED*) laccio emostatico, pinza emostatica.
tour operator [tōōr' âp'ərātûr] *n* (*Brit*) operatore *m* turistico.
tousled [tou'zəld] *a* (*hair*) arruffato(a).
tout [tout] *vi:* **to ~ for** procacciare, raccogliere; cercare clienti per ♦ *n* (*Brit: also:* **ticket ~**) bagarino.
tow [tō] *vt* rimorchiare ♦ *n* rimorchio; **"in ~",** (*Brit*) **"on ~"** (*AUT*) "veicolo rimorchiato"; **to give sb a ~** rimorchiare qn.
toward(s) [tôrd(z)] *prep* verso; (*of attitude*) nei confronti di; (*of purpose*) per; **~ noon/ the end of the year** verso mezzogiorno/la fine dell'anno; **to feel friendly ~ sb** provare un sentimento d'amicizia per qn.
towel [tou'əl] *n* asciugamano; **to throw in the ~** (*fig*) gettare la spugna.
towelling [tou'əling] *n* (*fabric*) spugna.
towel rack, (*Brit*) **towel rail** *n* portasciugamano.
tower [tou'ûr] *n* torre *f* ♦ *vi* (*building, mountain*) innalzarsi; **to ~ above** *or* **over sb/sth** sovrastare qn/qc.
tower block *n* (*Brit*) palazzone *m.*
towering [tou'ûring] *a* altissimo(a), imponente.
towline [tō'līn] *n* (cavo da) rimorchio.
town [toun] *n* città *f inv;* **to go to ~** andare in città; (*fig*) mettercela tutta; **in (the) ~** in città; **to be out of ~** essere fuori città.
town center *n* centro (città).
town clerk *n* segretario comunale.
town council *n* consiglio comunale.
town hall *n* ≈ municipio.
town planner *n* (*Brit*) urbanista *m/f.*
town planning *n* (*Brit*) urbanistica.
townspeople [tounz'pēpəl] *npl* cittadinanza, cittadini *mpl.*
towpath [tō'path] *n* alzaia.
towrope [tō'rōp] *n* (cavo da) rimorchio.
tow truck *n* (*US*) carro *m* attrezzi *inv.*
toxic [tâk'sik] *a* tossico(a).
toxin [tâk'sin] *n* tossina.
toy [toi] *n* giocattolo.

toy with *vt fus* giocare con; (*idea*) accarezzare, trastullarsi con.
toyshop [toi'shâp] *n* negozio di giocattoli.
trace [trās] *n* traccia ♦ *vt* (*draw*) tracciare; (*follow*) seguire; (*locate*) rintracciare; **without a ~** (*disappear*) senza lasciare traccia; **there was no ~ of it** non ne restava traccia.
trace element *n* oligoelemento.
trachea [trā'kēə] *n* (*ANAT*) trachea.
tracing paper [trā'sing pā'pûr] *n* carta da ricalco.
track [trak] *n* (*mark: of person, animal*) traccia; (*on tape, SPORT; path: gen*) pista; (: *of bullet etc*) traiettoria; (: *of suspect, animal*) pista, tracce *fpl;* (*RAIL*) binario, rotaie *fpl;* (*COMPUT*) traccia, pista ♦ *vt* seguire le tracce di; **to keep ~ of** seguire; **to be on the right ~** (*fig*) essere sulla buona strada.
track down *vt* (*prey*) scovare; snidare; (*sth lost*) rintracciare.
track events *npl* (*SPORT*) prove *fpl* su pista.
tracking station [trak'ing stā'shən] *n* (*SPACE*) osservatorio spaziale.
track record *n:* **to have a good ~** (*fig*) avere un buon curriculum.
tracksuit [trak'sōōt] *n* tuta sportiva.
tract [trakt] *n* (*GEO*) tratto, estensione *f;* (*pamphlet*) opuscolo, libretto; **respiratory ~** (*ANAT*) apparato respiratorio.
traction [trak'shən] *n* trazione *f.*
tractor [trak'tûr] *n* trattore *m.*
tractor feed *n* (*on printer*) trascinamento a trattore.
trade [trād] *n* commercio; (*skill, job*) mestiere *m;* (*industry*) industria, settore *m* ♦ *vi* commerciare; **to ~ with/in** commerciare con/in; **foreign ~** commercio estero; **Department of T~ and Industry** (**DTI**) (*Brit*) ≈ Ministero del Commercio.
trade in *vt* (*old car etc*) dare come pagamento parziale.
trade barrier *n* barriera commerciale.
trade deficit *n* bilancio commerciale in deficit.
trade discount *n* sconto sul listino.
trade fair *n* fiera campionaria.
trade-in [trād'in] *n:* **to take as a ~** accettare in permuta.
trade-in price [trād'in prīs] *n* prezzo di permuta.
trademark [trād'mārk] *n* marchio di fabbrica.
trade mission *n* missione *f* commerciale.
trade name *n* marca, nome *m* depositato.
trader [trā'dûr] *n* commerciante *m/f.*
trade secret *n* segreto di fabbricazione.
tradesman [trādz'mən] *n* fornitore *m;* (*storekeeper*) negoziante *m.*
trade union *n* sindacato.
trade unionist [trād yōōn'yənist] *n* sindacalista *m/f.*
trade wind *n* aliseo.

trading [trā'ding] *n* commercio.
trading estate *n* (*Brit*) zona industriale.
trading stamp *n* bollo premio.
tradition [trədish'ən] *n* tradizione *f*; ~**s** *npl* tradizioni, usanze *fpl*.
traditional [trədish'ənəl] *a* tradizionale.
traffic [traf'ik] *n* traffico ♦ *vi*: **to** ~ **in** (*pej*: *liquor, drugs*) trafficare in.
traffic circle *n* (*US*) isola rotatoria.
traffic island *n* salvagente *m*, isola *f* spartitraffico *inv*.
traffic jam *n* ingorgo (del traffico).
trafficker [traf'ikûr] *n* trafficante *m/f*.
traffic lights *npl* semaforo.
traffic offence *n* (*Brit*) = **traffic violation**.
traffic sign *n* cartello stradale.
traffic violation *n* (*US*) infrazione *f* al codice stradale.
traffic warden *n* (*Brit*) addetto/a al controllo del traffico e del parcheggio.
tragedy [traj'idē] *n* tragedia.
tragic [traj'ik] *a* tragico(a).
trail [trāl] *n* (*tracks*) tracce *fpl*, pista; (*path*) sentiero; (*of smoke etc*) scia ♦ *vt* trascinare, strascicare; (*follow*) seguire ♦ *vi* essere al traino; (*dress etc*) strusciare; (*plant*) arrampicarsi; strisciare; **to be on sb's** ~ essere sulle orme di qn.
trail away, trail off *vi* (*sound*) affievolirsi; (*interest, voice*) spegnersi a poco a poco.
trail behind *vi* essere al traino.
trailer [trā'lûr] *n* (*AUT*) rimorchio; (*US*) roulotte *f inv*; (*CINEMA*) prossimamente *m inv*.
trailer park *n* (*US*) campeggio per roulotte.
trailer truck *n* (*US*) autoarticolato.
train [trān] *n* treno; (*of dress*) coda, strascico; (*Brit*: *series*): ~ **of events** serie *f* di avvenimenti a catena ♦ *vt* (*apprentice, doctor etc*) formare; (*sportsman*) allenare; (*dog*) addestrare; (*memory*) esercitare; (*point*: *gun etc*): **to** ~ **sth on** puntare qc contro ♦ *vi* formarsi; allenarsi; (*learn a skill*) fare pratica, fare tirocinio; **to go by** ~ andare in *or* col treno; **one's** ~ **of thought** il filo dei propri pensieri; **to** ~ **sb to do sth** preparare qn a fare qc.
train attendant *n* (*US*) addetto/a ai vagoni letto.
trained [trānd] *a* qualificato(a); allenato(a); addestrato(a).
trainee [trānē'] *n* allievo/a; (*in trade*) apprendista *m/f*.
trainer [trā'nûr] *n* (*SPORT*) allenatore/trice; (*of dogs etc*) addestratore/trice; ~**s** *npl* (*shoes*) scarpe *fpl* da ginnastica.
training [trā'ning] *n* formazione *f*; allenamento; addestramento; **in** ~ (*SPORT*) in allenamento; (*fit*) in forma.
training college *n* istituto professionale.
training course *n* corso di formazione professionale.

training shoes *npl* scarpe *fpl* da ginnastica.
train station *n* stazione *f* ferroviaria.
traipse [trāps] *vi*: **to** ~ **in/out** *etc* entrare/ uscire *etc* trascinandosi.
trait [trāt] *n* tratto.
traitor [trā'tûr] *n* traditore *m*.
trajectory [trəjek'tûrē] *n* traiettoria.
tram [tram] *n* (*Brit*: *also*: ~**car**) tram *m inv*.
tramline [tram'līn] *n* linea tranviaria.
tramp [tramp] *n* (*person*) vagabondo/a; (*col*: *pej*: *woman*) sgualdrina ♦ *vi* camminare con passo pesante ♦ *vt* (*walk through*: *town, streets*) percorrere a piedi.
trample [tram'pəl] *vt*: **to** ~ (**underfoot**) calpestare.
trampoline [trampəlēn'] *n* trampolino.
trance [trans] *n* trance *f inv*; (*MED*) catalessi *f inv*; **to go into a** ~ cadere in trance.
tranquil [trang'kwil] *a* tranquillo(a).
tranquility, (*Brit*) **tranquillity** [trangkwil'itē] *n* tranquillità.
tranquilizer, (*Brit*) **tranquillizer** [trang'kwəlīzûr] *n* (*MED*) tranquillante *m*.
transact [transakt'] *vt* (*business*) trattare.
transaction [transak'shən] *n* transazione *f*; ~**s** *npl* (*minutes*) atti *mpl*; **cash** ~ operazione *f* in contanti.
transatlantic [transətlan'tik] *a* transatlantico(a).
transcend [transend'] *vt* trascendere; (*excel over*) superare.
transcendental [transenden'təl] *a*: ~ **meditation** meditazione *f* trascendentale.
transcribe [transkrīb'] *vt* trascrivere.
transcript [tran'skript] *n* trascrizione *f*.
transcription [transkrip'shən] *n* trascrizione *f*.
transept [tran'sept] *n* transetto.
transfer *n* [trans'fûr] (*gen, also SPORT*) trasferimento; (*POL*: *of power*) passaggio; (*picture, design*) decalcomania ♦ *vt* [transfûr'] trasferire; passare; decalcare; **by bank** ~ tramite trasferimento bancario; **to** ~ **the charges** (*Brit TEL*) telefonare con addebito al ricevente.
transferable [transfûr'əbəl] *a* trasferibile; **not** ~ non cedibile, personale.
transfix [transfiks'] *vt* trafiggere; (*fig*): ~**ed with fear** paralizzato dalla paura.
transform [transfôrm'] *vt* trasformare.
transformation [transfûrmā'shən] *n* trasformazione *f*.
transformer [transfôr'mûr] *n* (*ELEC*) trasformatore *m*.
transfusion [transfyōō'zhən] *n* trasfusione *f*.
transgress [transgres'] *vt* (*go beyond*) infrangere; (*violate*) trasgredire, infrangere.
tranship [tranship'] *vt* = **transship**.
transient [tran'shənt] *a* transitorio(a), fugace.
transistor [tranzis'tûr] *n* (*ELEC*) transistor *m inv*; (*also*: ~ **radio**) radio *f inv* a transistor.
transit [tran'sit] *n*: **in** ~ in transito.

transit camp n campo (di raccolta) profughi.
transition [tranzish'ən] n passaggio, transizione f.
transitional [tranzish'ənəl] a di transizione.
transitive [tran'sətiv] a (LING) transitivo(a).
transit lounge n (AVIAT) sala di transito.
transitory [tran'sitôrē] a transitorio(a).
translate [tranz'lāt] vt tradurre; **to ~ (from/into)** tradurre (da/in).
translation [tranzlā'shən] n traduzione f; (SCOL: as opposed to prose) versione f.
translator [translā'tûr] n traduttore/trice.
translucent [translōō'sənt] a traslucido(a).
transmission [transmish'ən] n trasmissione f.
transmit [transmit'] vt trasmettere.
transmitter [transmit'ûr] n trasmettitore m.
transom [tran'səm] n (US) lunetta.
transparency [transpär'ənsē] n (PHOT) diapositiva.
transparent [transpär'ənt] a trasparente.
transpire [transpīûr'] vi (happen) succedere; **it finally ~d that** ... alla fine si è venuto a sapere che ....
transplant vt [transplant'] trapiantare ♦ n [trans'plant] trapianto; **to have a heart ~** subire un trapianto cardiaco.
transport n [trans'pôrt] trasporto ♦ vt [transpôrt'] trasportare; **Department of T~** (Brit) Ministero dei Trasporti.
transportation [transpûrtā'shən] n (mezzo di) trasporto; (of prisoners) deportazione f; **public ~** mezzi mpl pubblici; **Department of T~** (US) Ministero dei Trasporti.
transport café n (Brit) trattoria per camionisti.
transpose [tranzpōz'] vt trasporre.
transship [transship'] vt trasbordare.
transverse [transvûrs'] a trasversale.
transvestite [transves'tīt] n travestito/a.
trap [trap] n (snare, trick) trappola; (carriage) calesse m ♦ vt prendere in trappola, intrappolare; (immobilize) bloccare; (jam) chiudere, schiacciare; **to set** or **lay a ~ (for sb)** tendere una trappola (a qn); **to ~ one's finger in the door** chiudersi il dito nella porta; **shut your ~!** (col) chiudi quella boccaccia!
trap door n botola.
trapeze [trapēz'] n trapezio.
trapper [trap'ûr] n cacciatore m di animali da pelliccia.
trappings [trap'ingz] npl ornamenti mpl; indoratura, sfarzo.
trash [trash] n (garbage) rifiuti mpl, spazzatura; (pej: goods) ciarpame m; (: nonsense) sciocchezze fpl ♦ vt (US col): **to ~ sb** sputtanare qn.
trash can n (US) secchio della spazzatura.
trauma [trou'mə] n trauma m.
traumatic [trômat'ik] a (PSYCH, fig) traumatico(a), traumatizzante.

travel [trav'əl] n viaggio; viaggi mpl ♦ vi viaggiare; (move) andare, spostarsi ♦ vt (distance) percorrere; **this wine doesn't ~ well** questo vino non resiste agli spostamenti.
travel agency n agenzia (di) viaggi.
travel agent n agente m di viaggio.
travel brochure n dépliant m di viaggi.
traveler, (Brit) **traveller** [trav'əlûr] n viaggiatore/trice; (COMM) commesso viaggiatore.
traveler's cheque, (Brit) **traveller's check** n assegno turistico.
traveling [trav'əling] (US) n viaggi mpl ♦ a (circus, exhibition) itinerante ♦ cpd (bag, clock) da viaggio; (expenses) di viaggio.
travelling [trav'əling] etc (Brit) = **traveling** etc.
travelling salesman n commesso viaggiatore.
travelog(ue) [trav'əlôg] n (book, film) diario or documentario di viaggio; (talk) conferenza sui viaggi.
travel sickness n mal m d'auto (or di mare or d'aria).
traverse [trav'ûrs] vt traversare, attraversare.
travesty [trav'istē] n parodia.
trawler [trô'lûr] n peschereccio (a strascico).
tray [trā] n (for carrying) vassoio; (on desk) vaschetta.
treacherous [trech'ûrəs] a traditore(trice); **road conditions today are ~** oggi il fondo stradale è pericoloso.
treachery [trech'ûrē] n tradimento.
treacle [trē'kəl] n (Brit) melassa.
tread [tred] n passo; (sound) rumore m di passi; (of tire) battistrada m inv ♦ vi (pt **trod,** pp **trodden** [trâd, trâd'ən]) camminare.
tread on vt fus calpestare.
treadle [tred'əl] n pedale m.
treas. abbr = **treasurer.**
treason [trē'zən] n tradimento.
treasure [trezh'ûr] n tesoro ♦ vt (value) tenere in gran conto, apprezzare molto; (store) custodire gelosamente.
treasure hunt n caccia al tesoro.
treasurer [trezh'ûrûr] n tesoriere/a.
treasury [trezh'ûrē] n tesoreria; (POL): **the T~ Department,** (Brit) **the T~** ≈ il Ministero del Tesoro.
treasury bill n buono del tesoro.
treat [trēt] n regalo ♦ vt trattare; (MED) curare; (consider) considerare; **it was a ~** mi (or ci etc) ha fatto veramente piacere; **to ~ sb to sth** offrire qc a qn; **to ~ sth as a joke** considerare qc uno scherzo.
treatise [trē'tis] n trattato.
treatment [trēt'mənt] n trattamento; **to have ~ for sth** (MED) farsi curare qc.
treaty [trē'tē] n trattato, patto.
treble [treb'əl] a triplo(a), triplice ♦ n (MUS) soprano m/f ♦ vt triplicare ♦ vi triplicarsi.
treble clef n chiave f di violino.

tree [trē] n albero.
tree-lined [trē'līnd] a fiancheggiato(a) da alberi.
treetop [trē'tâp] n cima di un albero.
tree trunk n tronco d'albero.
trek [trek] n (hike) spedizione f; (tiring walk) camminata sfiancante ♦ vi (as vacation) fare dell'escursionismo.
trellis [trel'is] n graticcio, pergola.
tremble [trem'bəl] vi tremare; (machine) vibrare.
trembling [trem'bling] n tremito ♦ a tremante.
tremendous [trimen'dəs] a (enormous) enorme; (excellent) meraviglioso(a), formidabile.
tremendously [trimen'dəslē] ad incredibilmente; **he enjoyed it** ~ gli è piaciuto da morire.
tremor [trem'úr] n tremore m, tremito m; (also: **earth** ~) scossa sismica.
trench [trench] n trincea.
trench coat n trench m inv.
trench warfare n guerra di trincea.
trend [trend] n (tendency) tendenza; (of events) corso; (fashion) moda; ~ **towards/away from** tendenza a/ad allontanarsi da; **to set the** ~ essere all'avanguardia; **to set a** ~ lanciare una moda.
trendy [tren'dē] a (idea) di moda; (clothes) all'ultima moda.
trepidation [trepidā'shən] n trepidazione f, agitazione f.
trespass [tres'pas] vi: **to** ~ **on** entrare abusivamente in; (fig) abusare di; **"no ~ing"** "proprietà privata", "vietato l'accesso".
trespasser [tres'pasúr] n trasgressore m; **"~s will be prosecuted"** "i trasgressori saranno puniti secondo i termini di legge".
tress [tres] n ciocca di capelli.
trestle [tres'əl] n cavalletto.
trestle table n tavola su cavalletti.
trial [trīl] n (LAW) processo; (test: of machine etc) collaudo; (hardship) prova, difficoltà f inv; (worry) cruccio; **~s** npl (ATHLETICS) prove fpl di qualificazione; **horse ~s** concorso ippico; **to be on** ~ essere sotto processo; ~ **by jury** processo penale con giuria; **to be sent for** ~ essere rinviato a giudizio; **to bring sb to** ~ **(for a crime)** portare qn in giudizio (per un reato); **by** ~ **and error** a tentoni.
trial balance n (COMM) bilancio di verifica.
trial basis n: **on a** ~ in prova.
trial run n periodo di prova.
triangle [trī'anggəl] n (MATH, MUS) triangolo; (US) squadra.
triangular [trīang'gyəlûr] a triangolare.
tribal [trī'bəl] a tribale.
tribe [trīb] n tribù f inv.
tribesman [trībz'mən] n membro della tribù.
tribulation [tribyəlā'shən] n tribolazione f.

tribunal [trībyōō'nəl] n tribunale m.
tributary [trib'yətārē] n (river) tributario, affluente m.
tribute [trib'yōōt] n tributo, omaggio; **to pay** ~ **to** rendere omaggio a.
trice [trīs] n: **in a** ~ in un attimo.
trick [trik] n trucco; (clever act) stratagemma m; (prank) tiro; (CARDS) presa ♦ vt imbrogliare, ingannare; **to play a** ~ **on sb** giocare un tiro a qn; **it's a** ~ **of the light** è un effetto ottico; **that should do the** ~ (col) vedrai che funziona; **to** ~ **sb into doing sth** convincere qn a fare qc con l'inganno; **to** ~ **sb out of sth** fregare qc a qn.
trickery [trik'úrē] n inganno.
trickle [trik'əl] n (of water etc) rivolo; gocciolio ♦ vi gocciolare; **to** ~ **in/out** (people) entrare/uscire alla spicciolata.
trick question n domanda f trabocchetto inv.
trickster [trik'stúr] n imbroglione/a.
tricky [trik'ē] a difficile, delicato(a).
tricycle [trī'sikəl] n triciclo.
trifle [trī'fəl] n sciocchezza; (Brit CULIN) ≈ zuppa inglese ♦ ad: **a** ~ **long** un po' lungo ♦ vi: **to** ~ **with** prendere alla leggera.
trifling [trī'fling] a insignificante.
trigger [trig'úr] n (of gun) grilletto.
trigger off vt dare l'avvio a.
trigonometry [trigənäm'ətrē] n trigonometria f.
trilby [tril'bē] n (Brit: also: ~ **hat**) cappello floscio di feltro.
trill [tril] n (of bird, MUS) trillo.
trillion [tril'yən] n (US) bilione m.
trilogy [tril'əjē] n trilogia.
trim [trim] a ordinato(a); (house, garden) ben tenuto(a); (figure) snello(a) ♦ n (haircut etc) spuntata, regolata; (embellishment) finiture fpl; (on car) guarnizioni fpl ♦ vt spuntare; (decorate): **to** ~ **(with)** decorare (con); (NAUT: a sail) orientare; **to keep in (good)** ~ mantenersi in forma.
trimmings [trim'ingz] npl decorazioni fpl; (extras: gen CULIN) guarnizione f.
Trinidad and Tobago [trin'idad and tōbā'gō] n Trinidad e Tobago m.
Trinity [trin'itē] n: **the** ~ la Trinità.
trinket [tring'kit] n gingillo; (piece of jewelry) ciondolo.
trio [trē'ō] n trio.
trip [trip] n viaggio; (excursion) gita, escursione f; (stumble) passo falso ♦ vi inciampare; (go lightly) camminare con passo leggero; **on a** ~ in viaggio.
trip up vi inciampare ♦ vt fare lo sgambetto a.
tripartite [trīpâr'tīt] a (agreement) tripartito(a); (talks) a tre.
tripe [trīp] n (CULIN) trippa; (pej: nonsense) sciocchezze fpl, fesserie fpl.
triple [trip'əl] a triplo(a) ♦ ad: ~ **the distance/the speed** tre volte più lontano/più

veloce.

triplets [trip'lits] *npl* bambini(e) trigemini(e).

triplicate [trip'lǝkit] *n*: **in** ~ in triplice copia.

tripod [trī'pád] *n* treppiede *m*.

Tripoli [trip'ǝlē] *n* Tripoli *f*.

tripwire [trip'wīŭr] *n fio in tensione che fa scattare una trappola, allarme etc*.

trite [trīt] *a* banale, trito(a).

triumph [trī'ǝmf] *n* trionfo ♦ *vi*: **to** ~ **(over)** trionfare (su).

triumphal [trīum'fǝl] *a* trionfale.

triumphant [trīum'fǝnt] *a* trionfante.

trivia [triv'ēǝ] *npl* banalità *fpl*.

trivial [triv'ēǝl] *a* (*matter*) futile; (*excuse, comment*) banale; (*amount*) irrisorio(a); (*mistake*) di poco conto.

triviality [trivēal'ǝtē] *n* frivolezza; (*trivial detail*) futilità.

trivialize [triv'ēǝlīz] *vt* sminuire.

trod [trâd] *pt of* **tread**.

trodden [trâd'ǝn] *pp of* **tread**.

trolley [trâl'ē] *n* (*Brit*) carrello.

trolley bus *n* filobus *m inv*.

trollop [trâl'ǝp] *n* prostituta.

trombone [trâmbōn'] *n* trombone *m*.

troop [trōōp] *n* gruppo; (*MIL*) squadrone *m*; ~**s** *npl* (*MIL*) truppe *fpl*.

troop in *vi* entrare a frotte.

troop out *vi* uscire a frotte.

troop carrier *n* (*plane*) aereo per il trasporto (di) truppe; (*NAUT*: *also*: **troopship**) nave *f* per il trasporto (di) truppe.

trooper [trōō'pûr] *n* (*US*: *police officer*) poliziotto (della polizia di stato); (*MIL*) soldato di cavalleria.

troopship [trōōp'ship] *n* nave *f* per il trasporto (di) truppe.

trophy [trō'fē] *n* trofeo.

tropic [trâp'ik] *n* tropico; **in the** ~**s** ai tropici; **T~ of Cancer/Capricorn** tropico del Cancro/Capricorno.

tropical [trâp'ikǝl] *a* tropicale.

trot [trât] *n* trotto ♦ *vi* trottare; **on the** ~ (*Brit fig*) di fila, uno(a) dopo l'altro(a).

trot out *vt* (*excuse, reason*) tirar fuori; (*names, facts*) recitare di fila.

trouble [trub'ǝl] *n* (*problems*) difficoltà *fpl*, problemi *mpl*; (*worry*) preoccupazione *f*; (*bother, effort*) sforzo; (*with sth mechanical*) noie *fpl*; (*POL*) conflitti *mpl*, disordine *m*; (*MED*): **stomach** *etc* ~ disturbi *mpl* gastrici *etc* ♦ *vt* disturbare; (*worry*) preoccupare ♦ *vi*: **to** ~ **to do** disturbarsi a fare; ~**s** *npl* (*POL etc*) disordini *mpl*; **to be in** ~ avere dei problemi; (*for doing wrong*) essere nei guai; **to go to the** ~ **of doing** darsi la pena di fare; **it's no** ~! di niente!; **what's the** ~? cosa c'è che non va?; **the** ~ **is** ... c'è che ..., il guaio è che ...; **to have** ~ **doing sth** avere delle difficoltà a fare qc; **please don't** ~ **yourself** non si disturbi.

troubled [trub'ǝld] *a* (*person*) preoccupato(a), inquieto(a); (*epoch, life*) agitato(a), difficile.

trouble-free [trub'ǝlfrē] *a* senza problemi.

troublemaker [trub'ǝlmākûr] *n* elemento disturbatore, agitatore/trice.

troubleshooter [trub'ǝlshōōtûr] *n* (*in conflict*) conciliatore *m*.

troublesome [trub'ǝlsǝm] *a* fastidioso(a), seccante.

trouble spot *n* zona calda.

trough [trôf] *n* (*also*: **drinking** ~) abbeveratoio; (*also*: **feeding** ~) trogolo, mangiatoia; (*channel*) canale *m*; ~ **of low pressure** (*METEOROLOGY*) depressione *f*.

trounce [trouns] *vt* (*defeat*) sgominare.

troupe [trōōp] *n* troupe *f inv*.

trouser press [trou'zûr pres] *n* (*Brit*) stirapantaloni *m inv*.

trousers [trou'zûrz] *npl* pantaloni *mpl*, calzoni *mpl*; **short** ~ (*Brit*) calzoncini *mpl*.

trouser suit *n* (*Brit*) completo *m or* tailleur *m inv* pantalone *inv*.

trousseau, *pl* ~**x** *or* ~**s** [trōō'sō, trōō'sōz] *n* corredo da sposa.

trout [trout] *n* (*pl inv*) trota.

trowel [trou'ǝl] *n* cazzuola.

truant [trōō'ǝnt] *n*: **to play** ~ marinare la scuola.

truce [trōōs] *n* tregua.

truck [truk] *n* autocarro, camion *m inv*; (*RAIL*) carro merci aperto; (*for luggage*) carrello *m* portabagagli *inv*.

truck driver *n* (*Brit*) = **trucker**.

trucker [truk'ûr] *n* (*US*) camionista *m/f*.

truck farm *n* (*US*) orto industriale.

trucking [truk'ing] *n* (*esp US*) autotrasporto.

trucking company *n* (*esp US*) impresa di trasporti.

truck stop *n* (*US*) trattoria per camionisti.

truculent [truk'yǝlǝnt] *a* aggressivo(a), brutale.

trudge [truj] *vi* trascinarsi pesantemente.

true [trōō] *a* vero(a); (*accurate*) accurato(a), esatto(a); (*genuine*) reale; (*faithful*) fedele; (*wall, beam*) a piombo; (*wheel*) centrato(a); **to come** ~ avverarsi; ~ **to life** verosimile.

truffle [truf'ǝl] *n* tartufo.

truly [trōō'lē] *ad* veramente; (*truthfully*) sinceramente; (*faithfully*) fedelmente; **yours** ~ (*in letter-writing*) distinti saluti.

trump [trump] *n* (*CARDS*) atout *m inv*; **to turn up** ~**s** (*fig*) fare miracoli.

trump card *n* atout *m inv*; (*fig*) asso nella manica.

trumped-up [trumpt'up'] *a* inventato(a).

trumpet [trum'pit] *n* tromba.

truncated [trung'kātid] *a* tronco(a).

truncheon [trun'chǝn] *n* sfollagente *m inv*.

trundle [trun'dǝl] *vt*, *vi*: **to** ~ **along** rotolare rumorosamente.

trunk [trungk] *n* (*of tree, person*) tronco; (*of*

elephant) proboscide *f*; (*case*) baule *m*; (*US AUT*) bagagliaio.

trunk road *n* (*Brit*) strada principale.

trunks [trungks] *npl* (*also*: **swimming ~**) calzoncini *mpl* da bagno.

truss [trus] *n* (*MED*) cinto erniario ♦ *vt*: **to ~ (up)** (*CULIN*) legare.

trust [trust] *n* fiducia; (*LAW*) amministrazione *f* fiduciaria; (*COMM*) trust *m inv* ♦ *vt* (*have confidence in*) fidarsi di; (*rely on*) contare su; (*entrust*): **to ~ sth to sb** affidare qc a qn; (*hope*): **to ~ (that)** sperare (che); **you'll have to take it on ~** deve credermi sulla parola; **in ~** (*LAW*) in amministrazione fiduciaria.

trust company *n* trust *m inv*.

trusted [trus'tid] *a* fidato(a).

trustee [trustē'] *n* (*LAW*) amministratore(trice) fiduciario(a); (*of school etc*) amministratore/trice.

trustful [trust'fəl] *a* fiducioso(a).

trust fund *n* fondo fiduciario.

trusting [trus'ting] *a* = **trustful**.

trustworthy [trust'wûrthē] *a* fidato(a), degno(a) di fiducia.

trusty [trus'tē] *a* fidato(a).

truth, ~s [trooth, troothz] *n* verità *f inv*.

truthful [trooth'fəl] *a* (*person*) sincero(a); (*description*) veritiero(a), esatto(a).

truthfully [trooth'fəlē] *ad* sinceramente.

truthfulness [trooth'fəlnis] *n* veracità.

try [trī] *n* prova, tentativo; (*RUGBY*) meta ♦ *vt* (*LAW*) giudicare; (*test*: *sth new*) provare; (*strain*: *patience, person*) mettere alla prova ♦ *vi* provare; **to ~ to do** provare a fare; (*seek*) cercare di fare; **to give sth a ~** provare qc; **to ~ one's (very) best** *or* **one's (very) hardest** mettercela tutta.

try on *vt* (*clothes*) provare, mettere alla prova; **to ~ it on** (*fig*) cercare di farla.

try out *vt* provare, mettere alla prova.

trying [trī'ing] *a* (*day, experience*) logorante, pesante; (*child*) difficile, insopportabile.

tsar [zâr] *n* zar *m inv*.

T-shirt [tē'shûrt] *n* maglietta.

T-square [tē'skwär] *n* riga a T.

TT *abbr* (*US MAIL*) = *Trust Territory* ♦ *a abbr* (*Brit col*) = **teetotal**.

tub [tub] *n* tinozza; mastello; (*bath*) bagno.

tuba [too'bə] *n* tuba.

tubby [tub'ē] *a* grassoccio(a).

tube [toob] *n* tubo; (*for tire*) camera d'aria; (*Brit*: *subway*) metropolitana; (*col*: *television*): **the ~** la tele.

tubeless [toob'lis] *a* (*tire*) senza camera d'aria.

tuber [too'bûr] *n* (*BOT*) tubero.

tuberculosis (TB) [toobûrkyəlō'sis] *n* tubercolosi *f*.

tube station [toob' stā'shən] *n* (*Brit*) stazione *f* del metrò.

tubing [too'bing] *n* tubazione *f*; **a piece of ~** un tubo.

tubular [too'byəlûr] *a* tubolare.

TUC *n abbr* (*Brit*: = *Trades Union Congress*) confederazione *f* dei sindacati britannici.

tuck [tuk] *n* (*SEWING*) piega ♦ *vt* (*put*) mettere.

tuck away *vt* riporre.

tuck in *vt* mettere dentro; (*child*) rimboccare ♦ *vi* (*eat*) mangiare di buon appetito; abbuffarsi.

tuck up *vt* (*child*) rimboccare.

Tue(s). *abbr* (= *Tuesday*) mar.

Tuesday [tooz'dā] *n* martedì *m inv*; **(the date) today is ~ 23rd March** oggi è martedì 23 marzo; **on ~** martedì; **on ~s** di martedì; **every ~** tutti i martedì; **every other ~** ogni due martedì; **last/next ~** martedì scorso/prossimo; **~ next** martedì prossimo; **the following ~** (*in past*) il martedì successivo; (*in future*) il martedì dopo; **a week on ~, ~ week** martedì fra una settimana; **the ~ before last** martedì di due settimane fa; **the ~ after next** non questo martedì ma il prossimo; **~ morning/lunchtime/afternoon/evening** martedì mattina/all'ora di pranzo/pomeriggio/sera; **~ night** martedì sera; (*overnight*) martedì notte; **~'s newspaper** il giornale di martedì.

tuft [tuft] *n* ciuffo.

tug [tug] *n* (*ship*) rimorchiatore *m* ♦ *vt* tirare con forza.

tug-of-war [tug'əvwôr'] *n* tiro alla fune.

tuition [tooish'ən] *n* (*US*: *fees*) tasse *fpl* scolastiche (*or* universitarie); (*Brit*: *lessons*) lezioni *fpl*.

tulip [too'lip] *n* tulipano.

tumble [tum'bəl] *n* (*fall*) capitombolo ♦ *vi* capitombolare, ruzzolare; (*somersault*) fare capriole ♦ *vt* far cadere; **to ~ to sth** (*col*) realizzare qc.

tumbledown [tum'bəldoun] *n* cadente, diroccato(a).

tumble dryer *n* (*Brit*) asciugatrice *f*.

tumbler [tum'blûr] *n* bicchiere *m* (senza stelo).

tummy [tum'ē] *n* (*col*) pancia.

tumor, (*Brit*) **tumour** [too'mûr] *n* tumore *m*.

tumult [too'məlt] *n* tumulto.

tumultuous [toomul'chooəs] *a* tumultuoso(a).

tuna [too'nə] *n* (*pl inv*) (*also*: **~ fish**) tonno.

tune [toon] *n* (*melody*) melodia, aria ♦ *vt* (*MUS*) accordare; (*RADIO, TV, AUT*) regolare, mettere a punto; **to be in/out of ~** (*instrument*) essere accordato(a)/scordato(a); (*singer*) essere intonato(a)/stonato(a); **to the ~ of** (*fig*: *amount*) per la modesta somma di; **in ~ with** (*fig*) in accordo con.

tune in *vi* (*RADIO, TV*): **to ~ in (to)** sintonizzarsi (su).

tune up *vi* (*musician*) accordare lo strumento.

tuneful |tōōn'fəl| *a* melodioso(a).

tuner |tōō'nûr| *n* (*radio set*) sintonizzatore *m*; **piano** ~ accordatore/trice di pianoforte.

tuner amplifier *n* amplificatore *m* di sintonia.

tungsten |tung'stən| *n* tungsteno.

tunic |tōō'nik| *n* tunica.

tuning |tōō'ning| *n* messa a punto.

tuning fork *n* diapason *m inv*.

Tunis |tōō'nis| *n* Tunisi *f*.

Tunisia |tōōnē'zhə| *n* Tunisia.

Tunisian |tōōnē'zhən| *a*, *n* tunisino(a).

tunnel |tun'əl| *n* galleria ♦ *vi* scavare una galleria.

tunny |tun'ē| *n* tonno.

turban |tûr'bən| *n* turbante *m*.

turbid |tûr'bid| *a* torbido(a).

turbine |tûr'bīn| *n* turbina.

turbojet |tûr'bōjet| *n* turboreattore *m*.

turboprop |tûr'bōpráp| *n* turboelica *m inv*.

turbot |tûr'bət| *n* (*pl inv*) rombo gigante.

turbulence |tûr'byələns| *n* turbolenza.

turbulent |tûr'byələnt| *a* turbolento(a); (*sea*) agitato(a).

tureen |tərēn'| *n* zuppiera.

turf |tûrf| *n* terreno erboso; (*clod*) zolla ♦ *vt* coprire di zolle erbose; **the T~** l'ippodromo.

turf out *vt* (*col*) buttar fuori.

turgid |tûr'jid| *a* (*speech*) ampolloso(a), pomposo(a).

Turin |tōō'rin| *n* Torino *f*.

Turk |tûrk| *n* turco/a.

Turkey |tûr'kē| *n* Turchia.

turkey |tûr'kē| *n* tacchino.

Turkish |tûr'kish| *a* turco(a) ♦ *n* (*LING*) turco.

Turkish bath *n* bagno turco.

Turkish delight *n* *gelatine ricoperte di zucchero a velo*.

turmeric |tûr'mûrik| *n* curcuma.

turmoil |tûr'moil| *n* confusione *f*, tumulto.

turn |tûrn| *n* giro; (*in road*) curva; (*tendency: of mind, events*) tendenza; (*performance*) numero; (*MED*) crisi *f inv*, attacco ♦ *vt* girare, voltare; (*milk*) far andare a male; (*shape: wood, metal*) tornire; (*change*): **to ~ sth into** trasformare qc in ♦ *vi* girare; (*person: look back*) girarsi, voltarsi; (*reverse direction*) girarsi indietro; (*change*) cambiare; (*become*) diventare; **to ~ into** trasformarsi in; **a good ~** un buon servizio; **a bad ~** un brutto tiro; **it gave me quite a ~** mi ha fatto prendere un bello spavento; **"no left ~"** (*AUT*) "divieto di svolta a sinistra"; **it's your ~** tocca a lei; **in ~** a sua volta; **a turno**; **to take ~s (at sth)** fare (qc) a turno; **at the ~ of the year/century** alla fine dell'anno/del secolo; **to take a ~ for the worse** (*situation, events*) volgere al peggio; (*patient, health*) peggiorare; **to ~ left/right** girare a sinistra/destra.

turn around *vi* girare; (*person*) girarsi.

turn away *vi* girarsi (dall'altra parte) ♦ *vt* (*reject: person*) mandar via; (: *business*) rifiutare.

turn back *vi* ritornare, tornare indietro.

turn down *vt* (*refuse*) rifiutare; (*reduce*) abbassare; (*fold*) ripiegare.

turn in *vi* (*col: go to bed*) andare a letto ♦ *vt* (*fold*) voltare in dentro; (*give in*) consegnare.

turn off *vi* (*from road*) girare, voltare ♦ *vt* (*light, radio, engine etc*) spegnere.

turn on *vt* (*light, radio etc*) accendere; (*engine*) avviare.

turn out *vt* (*light, gas*) chiudere, spegnere; (*produce: goods*) produrre; (: *novel, good pupils*) creare ♦ *vi* (*appear, attend: troops, doctor etc*) presentarsi; **to ~ out to be ...** rivelarsi ..., risultare ....

turn over *vi* (*person*) girarsi; (*car etc*) capovolgersi ♦ *vt* girare.

turn round (*Brit*) = **turn around**.

turn up *vi* (*person*) arrivare, presentarsi; (*lost object*) saltar fuori ♦ *vt* (*collar, sound, gas etc*) alzare.

turnaround |tûrn'əround| *n* (*fig*) dietrofront *m inv*.

turncoat |tûrn'kōt| *n* voltagabbana *m/f inv*.

turned-up |tûrnd'up| *a* (*nose*) all'insù.

turning |tûr'ning| *n* (*in road*) curva; (*side road*) strada laterale; **the first ~ on the right** la prima a destra.

turning circle *n* (*Brit*) = **turning radius**.

turning point *n* (*fig*) svolta decisiva.

turning radius *n* (*US*) diametro di sterzata.

turnip |tûr'nip| *n* rapa.

turnout |tûrn'out| *n* presenza, affluenza.

turnover |tûrn'ōvûr| *n* (*COMM: amount of money*) giro di affari; (: *of goods*) smercio; (*CULIN*): **apple** *etc* ~ sfogliatella alle mele *etc*; **there is a rapid ~ in staff** c'è un ricambio molto rapido di personale.

turnpike |tûrn'pīk| *n* (*US*) autostrada a pedaggio.

turn signal *n* (*US*) indicatore *m* di direzione, freccia.

turnstile |tûrn'stīl| *n* tornella.

turntable |tûrn'tābəl| *n* (*on record player*) piatto.

turn-up |tûrn'up| *n* (*Brit: on pants*) risvolto.

turpentine |tûr'pəntīn| *n* (*also*: **turps**) acqua ragia.

turquoise |tûr'koiz| *n* (*stone*) turchese *m* ♦ *a* color turchese; di turchese.

turret |tûr'it| *n* torretta.

turtle |tûr'təl| *n* testuggine *f*.

turtleneck (sweater) |tûr'təlnek (swet'ûr)| *n* maglione *m* con il collo alto.

Tuscan |tus'kən| *a*, *n* toscano(a).

Tuscany |tus'kənē| *n* Toscana.

tusk |tusk| *n* zanna.

tussle |tus'əl| *n* baruffa, mischia.

tutor [tōō'tûr] *n* (*in college*) docente *m/f* (*responsabile di un gruppo di studenti*); (*private teacher*) precettore *m*.

tutorial [tōōtôr'ēəl] *n* (*SCOL*) lezione *f* con discussione (*a un gruppo limitato*).

tuxedo [tuksē'dō] *n* smoking *m inv*.

TV [tēvē] *n abbr* (= *television*) tivù *f inv*.

TVP *n abbr* = *texturized vegetable protein*.

twaddle [twâd'əl] *n* scemenze *fpl*.

twang [twang] *n* (*of instrument*) suono vibrante; (*of voice*) accento nasale ♦ *vi* vibrare ♦ *vt* (*guitar*) pizzicare le corde di.

tweak [twēk] *vt* (*nose*) pizzicare; (*ear, hair*) tirare.

tweed [twēd] *n* tweed *m inv*.

tweezers [twē'zûrz] *npl* pinzette *fpl*.

twelfth [twelfth] *num* dodicesimo(a).

Twelfth Night *n* la notte dell'Epifania.

twelve [twelv] *num* dodici; **at** ~ alle dodici, a mezzogiorno; (*midnight*) a mezzanotte.

twentieth [twen'tēith] *num* ventesimo(a).

twenty [twen'tē] *num* venti.

twerp [twûrp] *n* (*col*) idiota *m/f*.

twice [twīs] *ad* due volte; ~ **as much** due volte tanto; ~ **a week** due volte alla settimana; **she is** ~ **your age** ha il doppio dei suoi anni.

twiddle [twid'əl] *vt, vi*: **to** ~ **(with)** sth giocherellare con qc; **to** ~ **one's thumbs** (*fig*) girarsi i pollici.

twig [twig] *n* ramoscello ♦ *vt, vi* (*col*) capire.

twilight [twī'līt] *n* (*evening*) crepuscolo; (*morning*) alba; **in the** ~ nella penombra.

twill [twil] *n* spigato.

twin [twin] *a, n* gemello(a).

twin beds *npl* letti *mpl* gemelli.

twin-carburetor [twinkârbərāt'ûr] *a* a doppio carburatore.

twine [twīn] *n* spago, cordicella ♦ *vi* (*plant*) attorcigliarsi; (*road*) serpeggiare.

twin-engined [twin'enjənd] *a* a due motori; ~ **aircraft** bimotore *m*.

twinge [twinj] *n* (*of pain*) fitta; **a** ~ **of conscience/regret** un rimorso/rimpianto.

twinkle [twing'kəl] *n* scintillio ♦ *vi* scintillare; (*eyes*) brillare.

twin town *n* città *f inv* gemella.

twirl [twûrl] *n* piroetta ♦ *vt* far roteare ♦ *vi* roteare.

twist [twist] *n* torsione *f*; (*in wire, cord*) storta; (*in story*) colpo di scena; (*bend*) svolta, piega ♦ *vt* attorcigliare; (*weave*) intrecciare; (*roll around*) arrotolare; (*fig*) deformare ♦ *vi* attorcigliarsi; arrotolarsi; (*road*) serpeggiare; **to** ~ **one's ankle/wrist** (*MED*) slogarsi la caviglia/il polso.

twisted [twis'tid] *a* (*wire, rope*) attorcigliato(a); (*ankle, wrist*) slogato(a); (*fig: logic, mind*) contorto(a).

twit [twit] *n* (*col*) minchione/a.

twitch [twich] *n* tiratina; (*nervous*) tic *m inv* ♦

vi contrarsi; avere un tic.

two [tōō] *num* due; ~ **by** ~, **in** ~s a due a due; **to put** ~ **and** ~ **together** (*fig*) trarre le conclusioni.

two-door [tōō'dôr] *a* (*AUT*) a due porte.

two-faced [tōō'fāst] *a* (*pej: person*) falso(a).

twofold [tōō'fōld] *ad*: **to increase** ~ aumentare del doppio ♦ *a* (*increase*) doppio(a); (*reply*) in due punti.

two-piece [tōō'pēs] *n* (*also*: ~ **suit**) due pezzi *m inv*; (*also*: ~ **swimsuit**) (costume *m* da bagno a) due pezzi *m inv*.

two-seater [tōō'sē'tûr] *n* (*plane*) biposto; (*car*) macchina a due posti.

twosome [tōō'səm] *n* (*people*) coppia.

two-stroke [tōō'strōk'] *n* (*engine*) due tempi *m inv* ♦ *a* a due tempi.

two-tone [tōō'tōn'] *a* (*color*) bicolore.

two-way [tōō'wā'] *a* (*traffic*) a due sensi; ~ **radio** radio *f inv* ricetrasmittente.

TX *abbr* (*US MAIL*) = *Texas*.

tycoon [tīkōōn'] *n*: (*business*) ~ magnate *m*.

type [tīp] *n* (*category*) genere *m*; (*model*) modello; (*example*) tipo; (*TYP*) tipo, carattere *m* ♦ *vt* (*letter etc*) battere (a macchina), dattilografare; **what** ~ **do you want**? che tipo vuole?; **in bold/italic** ~ in grassetto/corsivo.

type-cast [tīp'kast] *a* (*actor*) a ruolo fisso.

typeface [tīp'fās] *n* carattere *m* tipografico.

typescript [tīp'skript] *n* dattiloscritto.

typeset [tīp'set] *vt* comporre.

typesetter [tīp'sctûr] *n* compositore *m*.

typewriter [tīp'rītûr] *n* macchina da scrivere.

typewritten [tīp'ritən] *a* dattiloscritto(a), battuto(a) a macchina.

typhoid [tī'foid] *n* tifoidea.

typhoon [tīfōōn'] *n* tifone *m*.

typhus [tī'fəs] *n* tifo.

typical [tip'ikəl] *a* tipico(a).

typify [tip'əfī] *vt* essere tipico(a) di.

typing [tī'ping] *n* dattilografia.

typing error *n* errore *m* di battitura.

typing pool *n* ufficio *m* dattilografia *inv*.

typist [tī'pist] *n* dattilografo/a.

typo [tī'pō] *n abbr* (*col*: = *typographical error*) refuso.

typography [tīpâg'rəfē] *n* tipografia.

tyranny [tēr'ənē] *n* tirannia.

tyrant [tī'rənt] *n* tiranno.

tyre [tīûr'] *etc* (*Brit*) = **tire** *etc*.

Tyrol [tirōl'] *n* Tirolo.

Tyrolean [tīrō'lēən] *a, n* tirolese (*m/f*).

Tyrrhenian Sea [tīrē'nēən sē'] *n*: **the** ~ il mar Tirreno.

tzar [zâr] *n* = **tsar**.

U

U, u [yōō] *n* (*letter*) U, u *m or f inv*; **U for Uncle** ≈ U come Udine.

U [yōō] *n abbr* (*Brit CINEMA*: = *universal*) per tutti.

UAW *n abbr* (*US*: = *United Automobile Workers*) *sindacato degli operai automobilistici*.

U-bend [yōō'bend] *n* (*Brit: in pipe*) sifone *m*.

ubiquitous [yōōbik'witəs] *a* onnipresente.

UDA *n abbr* (*Brit*: = *Ulster Defence Association*) *organizzazione paramilitare protestante*.

udder [ud'ûr] *n* mammella.

UDI *abbr* (*Brit POL*) = *unilateral declaration of independence*.

UDR *n abbr* (*Brit*: = *Ulster Defence Regiment*) *reggimento dell'esercito britannico in Irlanda del Nord*.

UEFA [yōōā'fa] *n abbr* (= *Union of European Football Associations*) U.E.F.A. *f*.

UFO [yōōefō'] *n abbr* (= *unidentified flying object*) UFO *m inv*.

Uganda [yōōgan'də] *n* Uganda.

Ugandan [yōōgan'dən] *a, n* ugandese (*m/f*).

ugh [u] *excl* puah!

ugliness [ug'lēnis] *n* bruttezza.

ugly [ug'lē] *a* brutto(a).

UHF *abbr* = *ultra-high frequency*.

UHT *a abbr* (= *ultra-heat treated*): ~ **milk** *n* latte *m* UHT.

UK *n abbr see* **United Kingdom**.

ulcer [ul'sûr] *n* ulcera; **mouth** ~ afta.

Ulster [ul'stûr] *n* Ulster *m*.

ulterior [ultēr'ēûr] *a* ulteriore; ~ **motive** secondo fine *m*.

ultimata [ultəmā'tə] *npl of* **ultimatum**.

ultimate [ul'təmit] *a* ultimo(a), finale; (*authority*) massimo(a), supremo(a) ♦ *n*: **the ~ in luxury** il non plus ultra del lusso.

ultimately [ul'təmitlē] *ad* alla fine; in definitiva, in fin dei conti.

ultimatum, *pl* **~s** *or* **ultimata** [ultimā'təm, ultimā'tə] *n* ultimatum *m inv*.

ultralight [ultrəlīt'] *n* aereo privato superleggero.

ultrasonic [ultrəsân'ik] *a* ultrasonico(a).

ultrasound [ul'trəsound] *n* (*MED*) ecografia.

ultraviolet [ultrəvī'əlit] *a* ultravioletto(a).

umbilical [umbil'ikəl] *a*: ~ **cord** cordone *m* ombelicale.

umbrage [um'brij] *n*: **to take** ~ offendersi, impermalirsi.

umbrella [umbrel'ə] *n* ombrello; **under the** ~ **of** (*fig*) sotto l'egida di.

umpire [um'pîûr] *n* arbitro.

umpteen [ump'tēn'] *a* non so quanti(e); **for the ~th time** per l'ennesima volta.

UMW *n abbr* (= *United Mineworkers of America*) *unione dei minatori d'America*.

UN *n abbr see* **United Nations**.

unabashed [unəbasht'] *a* imperturbato(a).

unabated [unəbā'tid] *a* non diminuito(a).

unable [unā'bəl] *a*: **to be** ~ **to** non potere, essere nell'impossibilità di; (*not to know how to*) essere incapace di, non sapere.

unabridged [unəbrijd'] *a* integrale.

unacceptable [unaksep'təbəl] *a* (*proposal, behavior*) inaccettabile; (*price*) impossibile.

unaccompanied [unəkum'pənēd] *a* (*child, lady*) non accompagnato(a); (*singing, song*) senza accompagnamento.

unaccountably [unəkount'əblē] *ad* inesplicabilmente.

unaccounted [unəkoun'tid] *a*: **two passengers are** ~ **for** due passeggeri mancano all'appello.

unaccustomed [unəkus'təmd] *a* insolito(a); **to be** ~ **to sth** non essere abituato(a) a qc.

unacquainted [unəkwān'tid] *a*: **to be** ~ **with** (*facts*) ignorare, non essere al corrente di.

unadulterated [unədul'tərātid] *a* (*gen*) puro(a); (*wine*) non sofisticato(a).

unaffected [unəfek'tid] *a* (*person, behavior*) naturale, spontaneo(a); (*emotionally*): **to be** ~ **by** non essere toccato(a) da.

unafraid [unəfrād'] *a*: **to be** ~ non aver paura.

unaided [unā'did] *ad* senza aiuto.

unanimity [yōōnənim'itē] *n* unanimità.

unanimous [yōōnan'əməs] *a* unanime.

unanimously [yōōnan'əməslē] *ad* all'unanimità.

unanswered [unan'sûrd] *a* (*question, letter*) senza risposta; (*criticism*) non confutato(a).

unappetizing [unap'itīzing] *a* poco appetitoso(a).

unappreciative [unəprē'shēətiv] *a* che non apprezza.

unarmed [unârmd'] *a* (*person*) disarmato(a); (*combat*) senz'armi.

unashamed [unəshāmd'] *a* sfacciato(a); senza vergogna.

unassisted [unəsis'tid] *a, ad* senza nessun aiuto.

unassuming [unəsōō'ming] *a* modesto(a), senza pretese.

unattached [unətacht'] *a* senza legami, libero(a).

unattended [unəten'did] *a* (*car, child, luggage*) incustodito(a).

unattractive [unətrak'tiv] *a* privo(a) di attrattiva, poco attraente.

unauthorized [unôth'ərīzd] *a* non autorizzato(a).

unavailable [unəvā'ləbəl] *a* (*article, room, book*) non disponibile; (*person*) impegnato(a).

unavoidable [unəvoi'dəbəl] *a* inevitabile.

unavoidably [unəvoi'dəblē] *ad* (*detained*) per cause di forza maggiore.

unaware [unəwär'] *a*: **to be ~ of** non sapere, ignorare.

unawares [unəwärz'] *ad* di sorpresa, alla sprovvista.

unbalanced [unbal'ənst] *a* squilibrato(a).

unbearable [unbär'əbəl] *a* insopportabile.

unbeatable [unbē'təbəl] *a* imbattibile.

unbeaten [unbēt'ən] *a* (*team, army*) imbattuto(a); (*record*) insuperato(a).

unbecoming [unbikum'ing] *a* (*unseemly: language, behavior*) sconveniente; (*unflattering: garment*) che non dona.

unbeknown(st) [unbinōn(st)'] *ad*: **~ to** all'insaputa di.

unbelief [unbilēf'] *n* incredulità.

unbelievable [unbilē'vəbəl] *a* incredibile.

unbelievingly [unbilē'vinglē] *ad* con aria incredula.

unbend [unbend'] *vb* (*irg*) *vi* distendersi ♦ *vt* (*wire*) raddrizzare.

unbending [unben'ding] *a* (*fig*) inflessibile, rigido(a).

unbiased [unbī'əst] *a* obiettivo(a), imparziale.

unblemished [unblem'isht] *a* senza macchia.

unblock [unblâk'] *vt* (*pipe, road*) sbloccare.

unborn [unbôrn'] *a* non ancora nato(a).

unbounded [unboun'did] *a* sconfinato(a), senza limite.

unbreakable [unbrā'kəbəl] *a* infrangibile.

unbridled [unbrī'dəld] *a* sbrigliato(a).

unbroken [unbrō'kən] *a* (*intact*) intero(a); (*continuous*) continuo(a); (*record*) insuperato(a).

unbuckle [unbuk'əl] *vt* slacciare.

unburden [unbûr'dən] *vt*: **to ~ o.s.** sfogarsi.

unbutton [unbut'ən] *vt* sbottonare.

uncalled-for [unkôld'fôr] *a* (*remark*) fuori luogo *inv*; (*action*) ingiustificato(a).

uncanny [unkan'ē] *a* misterioso(a), strano(a).

unceasing [unsē'sing] *a* incessante.

unceremonious [unsârəmō'nēəs] *a* (*abrupt, rude*) senza tante cerimonie.

uncertain [unsûr'tən] *a* incerto(a); **it's ~ whether ...** non è sicuro se ...; **in no ~ terms** chiaro e tondo, senza mezzi termini.

uncertainty [unsûr'təntē] *n* incertezza.

unchallenged [unchal'injd] *a* incontestato(a); **to go ~** non venire contestato, non trovare opposizione.

unchanged [unchānjd'] *a* immutato(a).

uncharitable [unchar'itəbəl] *a* duro(a), severo(a).

uncharted [unchâr'tid] *a* inesplorato(a).

unchecked [unchekt'] *a* incontrollato(a).

uncivilized [unsiv'ilīzd] *a* (*gen*) selvaggio(a); (*fig*) incivile, barbaro(a).

uncle [ung'kəl] *n* zio.

unclear [unkliûr'] *a* non chiaro(a); **I'm still ~ about what I'm supposed to do** non ho ancora ben capito cosa dovrei fare.

uncoil [unkoil'] *vt* srotolare ♦ *vi* srotolarsi, svolgersi.

uncomfortable [unkumf'təbəl] *a* scomodo(a); (*uneasy*) a disagio, agitato(a); (*situation*) sgradevole.

uncomfortably [unkumf'təblē] *ad* scomodamente; (*uneasily: say*) con voce inquieta; (: *think*) con inquietudine.

uncommitted [unkəmit'id] *a* (*attitude, country*) neutrale.

uncommon [unkâm'ən] *a* raro(a), insolito(a), non comune.

uncommunicative [unkəmyōō'nikətiv] *a* poco comunicativo(a), chiuso(a).

uncomplicated [unkâm'plikātid] *a* semplice, poco complicato(a).

uncompromising [unkâm'prəmīzing] *a* intransigente, inflessibile.

unconcerned [unkənsûrnd'] *a* (*unworried*) tranquillo(a); **to be ~ about** non darsi pensiero di, non preoccuparsi di *or* per.

unconditional [unkəndish'ənəl] *a* incondizionato(a), senza condizioni.

uncongenial [unkənjēn'yəl] *a* (*work, surroundings*) poco piacevole.

unconnected [unkənek'tid] *a* (*unrelated*) senza connessione, senza rapporto; **to be ~ with** essere estraneo(a) a.

unconscious [unkân'chəs] *a* privo(a) di sensi, svenuto(a); (*unaware*) inconsapevole, inconscio(a) ♦ *n*: **the ~** l'inconscio; **to knock sb ~** far perdere i sensi a qn con un pugno.

unconsciously [unkân'chəslē] *ad* inconsciamente.

unconstitutional [unkânstitōō'shənəl] *a* incostituzionale.

uncontested [unkəntes'tid] *a* (*champion*) incontestato(a); (*POL: seat*) non disputato(a).

uncontrollable [unkəntrō'ləbəl] *a* incontrollabile, indisciplinato(a).

uncontrolled [unkəntrōld'] *a* (*child, dog, emotion*) sfrenato(a); (*inflation, price rises*) che sfugge al controllo.

unconventional [unkənven'chənəl] *a* poco convenzionale.

unconvinced [unkənvinst'] *a*: **to be** *or* **remain ~** non essere convinto(a).

unconvincing [unkənvin'sing] *a* non convincente, poco persuasivo(a).

uncork [unkôrk'] *vt* stappare.

uncorroborated [unkərâb'ərātid] *a* non convalidato(a).

uncouth [unkōōth'] *a* maleducato(a), grossolano(a).

uncover |unkuv'ûr| *vt* scoprire.
uncovered |unkuv'ûrd| *a* (*US*: *check*) a vuoto.
unctuous |ungk'chōōəs| *a* untuoso(a).
undamaged |undam'ijd| *a* (*goods*) in buono stato; (*fig*: *reputation*) intatto(a).
undaunted |undôn'tid| *a* intrepido(a).
undecided |undisī'did| *a* indeciso(a).
undelivered |undiliv'ûrd| *a* non recapitato(a); **if ~ return to sender** in caso di mancato recapito rispedire al mittente.
undeniable |undinī'əbəl| *a* innegabile, indiscutibile.
under |un'dûr| *prep* sotto; (*less than*) meno di; al disotto di; (*according to*) secondo, in conformità a ♦ *ad* (al) disotto; **from ~ sth** da sotto a *or* dal disotto di qc; **~ there** là sotto; **in ~ 2 hours** in meno di 2 ore; **~ anesthetic** sotto anestesia; **~ discussion** in discussione; **~ repair** in riparazione; **~ the circumstances** date le circostanze.
under... *prefix* sotto..., sub....
underage |un'dûrāj'| *a* minorenne.
underarm |un'dûrârm| *n* ascella ♦ *a* ascellare ♦ *ad* da sotto in su.
undercapitalized |undûrkap'itəlīzd| *a* carente di capitali.
undercarriage |un'dûrkarij| *n* (*Brit AVIAT*) carrello (d'atterraggio).
undercharge |undûrchârj'| *vt* far pagare di meno a.
underclothes |un'dûrklōz| *npl* biancheria (intima).
undercoat |un'dûrkōt| *n* (*paint*) mano *f* di fondo ♦ *vt* (*US AUT*) rendere stagno il fondo di.
undercover |undûrkuv'ûr| *a* segreto(a), clandestino(a).
undercurrent |un'dûrkûrənt| *n* corrente *f* sottomarina.
undercut |undûrkut| *vt irg* vendere a prezzo minore di.
underdeveloped |un'dûrdivel'əpt| *a* sottosviluppato(a).
underdog |un'dûrdôg| *n* oppresso/a.
underdone |un'dûrdun'| *a* (*CULIN*) poco cotto(a).
underemployment |undûremploi'mənt| *n* sottoccupazione *f*.
underestimate |undûres'təmāt| *vt* sottovalutare.
underexposed |undûrikspōzd'| *a* (*PHOT*) sottoesposto(a).
underfed |undûrfed'| *a* denutrito(a).
underfoot |undûrfoot'| *ad* sotto i piedi.
undergo |undûrgō'| *vt irg* subire; (*treatment*) sottoporsi a; **the car is ~ing repairs** la macchina è in riparazione.
undergraduate |undûrgraj'ōoit| *n* studente(essa) universitario(a) ♦ *cpd*: **~ courses** corsi *mpl* di laurea.
underground |un'dûrground| *n* (*POL*) movi-

mento clandestino; (*Brit*) metropolitana ♦ *a* sotterraneo(a); (*fig*) clandestino(a); (*ART*, *CINEMA*) underground *inv* ♦ *ad* sottoterra; clandestinamente.
undergrowth |un'dûrgrōth| *n* sottobosco.
underhanded |un'dûrhan'did| *a* (*fig*) furtivo(a), subdolo(a).
underinsured |undûrinshōōrd'| *a* non sufficientemente assicurato(a).
underlie |undûrlī'| *vt irg* essere alla base di; **the underlying cause** il motivo di fondo.
underline |un'dûrlīn| *vt* sottolineare.
underling |un'dûrling| *n* (*pej*) subalterno/a, tirapiedi *m/f inv*.
undermanning |un'dûrman'ing| *n* carenza di personale.
undermentioned |un'dûrmenchənd| *a* (riportato(a)) qui sotto *or* qui di seguito.
undermine |un'dûrmīn| *vt* minare.
underneath |undûrnēth'| *ad* sotto, disotto ♦ *prep* sotto, al di sotto di.
undernourished |undûrnûr'isht| *a* denutrito(a).
underpaid |undûrpād'| *a* mal pagato(a).
underpants |un'dûrpants| *npl* mutande *fpl*, slip *m inv*.
underpass |un'dûrpas| *n* sottopassaggio.
underpin |undûrpin'| *vt* puntellare; (*argument*, *case*) corroborare.
underplay |undûrplā'| *vt* minimizzare.
underpopulated |undûrpâp'yəlātid| *a* scarsamente popolato(a), sottopopolato(a).
underprice |undûrprīs'| *vt* vendere a un prezzo inferiore al dovuto.
underprivileged |undûrpriv'əlijd| *a* svantaggiato(a).
underrate |undərāt'| *vt* sottovalutare.
underscore |undûrskôr'| *vt* sottolineare.
underseal |un'dûrsēl| *vt* (*Brit*) rendere stagno il fondo di.
under secretary *n* sottosegretario.
undersell |undûrsel'| *vt irg* (*competitors*) vendere a prezzi più bassi di.
undershirt |un'dûrshûrt| *n* (*US*) maglietta.
undershorts |un'dûrshôrts| *npl* (*US*) mutande *fpl*, slip *m inv*.
underside |un'dûrsīd| *n* disotto.
undersigned |un'dûrsīnd| *a*, *n* sottoscritto(a).
underskirt |un'dûrskûrt| *n* sottoveste *f*.
understaffed |undûrstaft'| *a* a corto di personale.
understand |undûrstand'| *vb* (*irg*: *like* **stand**) *vt*, *vi* capire, comprendere; **I ~ that ...** sento che ...; credo di capire che ...; **to make o.s. understood** farsi capire.
understandable |undûrstan'dəbəl| *a* comprensibile.
understanding |undûrstan'ding| *a* comprensivo(a) ♦ *n* comprensione *f*; (*agreement*) accordo; **on the ~ that ...** a patto che *or* a condizione che ...; **to come to an ~ with sb**

giungere ad un accordo con qn.

understate |undûrstāt'| *vt* minimizzare, sminuire.

understatement |undûrstāt'mənt| *n*: **that's an ~!** a dire poco!

understood |undûrstŏod'| *pt, pp of* **understand ♦** *a* inteso(a); (*implied*) sottinteso(a).

understudy |un'dûrstudē| *n* sostituto/a, attore/trice supplente.

undertake |undûrtāk'| *vt irg* intraprendere; **to ~ to do sth** impegnarsi a fare qc.

undertaker |un'dûrtākûr| *n* impresario di pompe funebri.

undertaking |undûrtā'king| *n* impresa; (*promise*) promessa.

undertone |un'dûrtōn| *n* (*low voice*) tono sommesso; (*of criticism etc*) vena, sottofondo; **in an ~** sottovoce.

undervalue |undûrval'yōō| *vt* svalutare, sottovalutare.

underwater |un'dûrwòt'ûr| *ad* sott'acqua ♦ *a* subacqueo(a).

underwear |un'dûrwär| *n* biancheria (intima).

underweight |un'dûrwāt| *a* al di sotto del giusto peso; (*person*) sottopeso *inv*.

underworld |un'dûrwûrld| *n* (*of crime*) malavita.

underwrite |un'dərīt| *vt* (*FINANCE*) sottoscrivere; (*INSURANCE*) assicurare.

underwriter |un'dərītûr| *n* sottoscrittore/trice; assicuratore/trice.

undeserving |undizûr'ving| *a*: **to be ~ of** non meritare, non essere degno di.

undesirable |undizîûr'əbəl| *a* indesiderabile, sgradito(a).

undeveloped |undivel'əpt| *a* (*land, resources*) non sfruttato(a).

undies |un'dēz| *npl* (*col*) robina, biancheria intima da donna.

undiluted |undilōō'tid| *a* non diluito(a).

undiplomatic |undipləmat'ik| *a* poco diplomatico(a).

undischarged |undischârjd'| *a*: **~ bankrupt** fallito non riabilitato.

undisciplined |undis'əplind| *a* indisciplinato(a).

undisguised |undisgīzd'| *a* (*dislike, amusement etc*) palese.

undisputed |undispyōō'tid| *a* indiscusso(a).

undistinguished |undisting'gwisht| *a* mediocre, qualunque.

undisturbed |undistûrbd'| *a* tranquillo(a); **to leave sth ~** lasciare qc così com'è.

undivided |undivī'did| *a*: **I want your ~ attention** esigo tutta la sua attenzione.

undo |undōō'| *vt irg* disfare.

undoing |undōō'ing| *n* rovina, perdita.

undone |undun'| *pp of* **undo**; **to come ~** slacciarsi.

undoubted |undou'tid| *a* sicuro(a), certo(a).

undoubtedly |undou'tidlē| *ad* senza alcun

dubbio.

undress |undres'| *vi* spogliarsi.

undrinkable |undringk'əbəl| *a* (*unpalatable*) imbevibile; (*poisonous*) non potabile.

undue |undōō'| *a* eccessivo(a).

undulating |un'jəlāting| *a* ondeggiante; ondulato(a).

unduly |undōō'lē| *ad* eccessivamente.

undying |undī'ing| *a* imperituro(a).

unearned |unûrnd'| *a* (*praise, respect*) immeritato(a); **~ income** rendita.

unearth |unûrth'| *vt* dissotterrare; (*fig*) scoprire.

unearthly |unûrth'lē| *a* soprannaturale; (*hour*) impossibile.

uneasy |unē'zē| *a* a disagio; (*worried*) preoccupato(a); **to feel ~ about doing sth** non sentirsela di fare qc.

uneconomic(al) |unēkənăm'ik(əl)| *a* non economico(a), antieconomico(a).

uneducated |uncj'ōōkātid| *a* senza istruzione, incolto(a).

unemployed |uncmploid'| *a* disoccupato(a) ♦ *npl*: **the ~** i disoccupati.

unemployment |uncmploi'mənt| *n* disoccupazione *f*.

unemployment compensation, (*Brit*) **unemployment benefit** *n* sussidio di disoccupazione.

unending |uncn'ding| *a* senza fine.

unenviable |uncn'vēəbəl| *a* poco invidiabile.

unequal |unck'wəl| *a* (*length, objects*) disuguale; (*amounts*) diverso(a); (*division of labor*) ineguale.

unequaled, (*Brit*) **unequalled** |unck'wəld| *a* senza pari, insuperato(a).

unequivocal |unikwiv'əkəl| *a* (*answer*) inequivocabile; (*person*) esplicito(a), chiaro(a).

unerring |unûr'ing| *a* infallibile.

UNESCO |yōōnes'kō| *n abbr* (= *United Nations Educational, Scientific and Cultural Organization*) U.N.E.S.C.O. *f*.

unethical |uncth'ikəl| *a* (*methods*) poco ortodosso(a), non moralmente accettabile; (*doctor's behavior*) contrario(a) all'etica professionale.

uneven |uncʹvən| *a* ineguale; (*ground*) disuguale, accidentato(a); (*heartbeat*) irregolare.

uneventful |univcnt'fəl| *a* senza sorprese, tranquillo(a).

unexceptional |unikscp'shənəl| *a* che non ha niente d'eccezionale.

unexciting |uniksī'ting| *a* (*news*) poco emozionante; (*film, evening*) poco interessante.

unexpected |unikspck'tid| *a* inatteso(a), imprevisto(a).

unexpectedly |unikspck'tidlē| *ad* inaspettatamente.

unexplained |uniksplānd'| *a* inspiegato(a).

unexploded |uniksplō'did| *a* inesploso(a).

unfailing |unfā'ling| *a* (*supply, energy*) inesau-

ribile; (*remedy*) infallibile.
unfair [unfär'] *a*: ~ **(to)** ingiusto(a) (nei confronti di); **it's** ~ **that** ... non è giusto che ... + *sub*.
unfair dismissal *n* licenziamento ingiustificato.
unfairly [unfär'lē] *ad* ingiustamente.
unfaithful [unfāth'fəl] *a* infedele.
unfamiliar [unfəmil'yûr] *a* sconosciuto(a), strano(a); **to be** ~ **with** sth non essere pratico di qc, non avere familiarità con qc.
unfashionable [unfash'ənəbəl] *a* (*clothes*) fuori moda *inv*; (*district*) non alla moda.
unfasten [unfas'ən] *vt* slacciare; sciogliere.
unfathomable [unfath'əməbəl] *a* insondabile.
unfavorable [unfā'vûrəblē] *a* (*US*) sfavorevole.
unfavorably [unfā'vûrəblē] *ad*: **to look** ~ **upon** vedere di malocchio.
unfavourable [unfā'vûrəbəl] *etc* (*Brit*) = **unfavorable** *etc*.
unfeeling [unfē'ling] *a* insensibile, duro(a).
unfinished [unfin'isht] *a* incompiuto(a).
unfit [unfit'] *a* inadatto(a); (*ill*) non in forma; (*incompetent*): ~ **(for)** incompetente (in); (: *work*, MIL) inabile (a); ~ **for habitation** inabitabile.
unflagging [unflag'ing] *a* instancabile.
unflappable [unflap'əbəl] *a* calmo(a), composto(a).
unflattering [unflat'ûring] *a* (*dress*, *hairstyle*) che non dona.
unflinching [unflin'ching] *a* che non indietreggia, risoluto(a).
unfold [unfōld'] *vt* spiegare; (*fig*) rivelare ♦ *vi* (*view*) distendersi; (*story*) svelarsi.
unforeseeable [unfôrsē'əbəl] *a* imprevedibile.
unforeseen [unfôrsēn'] *a* imprevisto(a).
unforgettable [unfûrget'əbəl] *a* indimenticabile.
unforgivable [unfûrgiv'əbəl] *a* imperdonabile.
unformatted [unfôr'matid] *a* (*disk*, *text*) non formattato(a).
unfortunate [unfôr'chənit] *a* sfortunato(a); (*event*, *remark*) infelice.
unfortunately [unfôr'chənitlē] *ad* sfortunatamente, purtroppo.
unfounded [unfoun'did] *a* infondato(a).
unfriendly [unfrend'lē] *a* poco amichevole, freddo(a).
unfulfilled [unfŏŏlfild'] *a* (*ambition*) non realizzato(a); (*prophecy*) che non si è avverato(a); (*desire*) insoddisfatto(a); (*promise*) non mantenuto(a); (*terms of contract*) non rispettato(a); (*person*) frustrato(a).
unfurl [unfûrl'] *vt* spiegare.
unfurnished [unfûr'nisht] *a* non ammobiliato(a).
ungainly [ungān'lē] *a* goffo(a), impacciato(a).
ungodly [ungâd'lē] *a* empio(a); **at an** ~ **hour** a un'ora impossibile.

ungrateful [ungrāt'fəl] *a* ingrato(a).
unguarded [ungâr'did] *a*: **in an** ~ **moment** in un momento di distrazione.
unhappily [unhap'ilē] *ad* (*unfortunately*) purtroppo, sfortunatamente.
unhappiness [unhap'ēnis] *n* infelicità.
unhappy [unhap'ē] *a* infelice; ~ **with** (*arrangements etc*) insoddisfatto(a) di.
unharmed [unhärmd'] *a* incolume, sano(a) e salvo(a).
unhealthy [unhel'thē] *a* (*gen*) malsano(a); (*person*) malaticcio(a).
unheard-of [unhûrd'əv] *a* inaudito(a), senza precedenti.
unhelpful [unhelp'fəl] *a* poco disponibile.
unhesitating [unhez'itāting] *a* (*loyalty*) che non vacilla; (*reply*, *offer*) pronto(a), immediato(a).
unhook [unhŏŏk'] *vt* sganciare; sfibbiare.
unhurt [unhûrt'] *a* incolume, sano(a) e salvo(a).
unhygienic [unhījēen'ik] *a* non igienico(a).
UNICEF [yŏŏ'nisef] *n abbr* (= *United Nations International Children's Emergency Fund*) U.N.I.C.E.F. *m*.
unicolor, (*Brit*) **unicolour** [yŏŏnəkul'ûr] *a* monocolore.
unicorn [yŏŏ'nəkôrn] *n* unicorno.
unidentified [unīden'təfīd] *a* non identificato(a).
uniform [yŏŏ'nəfôrm] *n* uniforme *f*, divisa ♦ *a* uniforme.
uniformity [yŏŏnəfôr'mitē] *n* uniformità.
unify [yŏŏ'nəfī] *vt* unificare.
unilateral [yŏŏnəlat'ûrəl] *a* unilaterale.
unimaginable [unimaj'ənəbəl] *a* inimmaginabile, inconcepibile.
unimaginative [unimaj'ənətiv] *a* privo(a) di fantasia, a corto di idee.
unimpaired [unimpärd'] *a* intatto(a), non danneggiato(a).
unimportant [unimpôr'tənt] *a* senza importanza, di scarsa importanza.
unimpressed [unimprest'] *a* niente affatto impressionato(a).
uninhabited [uninhab'itid] *a* disabitato(a).
uninhibited [uninhib'itid] *a* senza inibizioni; senza ritegno.
uninjured [unin'jûrd] *a* incolume.
unintelligent [unintel'ijənt] *a* poco intelligente.
unintentional [uninten'chənəl] *a* involontario(a).
unintentionally [uninten'chənəlē] *ad* senza volerlo, involontariamente.
uninvited [uninvī'tid] *a* non invitato(a).
uninviting [uninvī'ting] *a* (*place*, *food*) non invitante, poco invitante; (*offer*) poco allettante.
union [yŏŏn'yən] *n* unione *f*; (*also*: **trade** ~) sindacato ♦ *cpd* sindacale; **the U**~ (*US*) gli stati dell'Unione.

unionize [yo͞on'yənīz] vt sindacalizzare, organizzare in sindacato.

Union Jack n bandiera nazionale britannica.

Union of Soviet Socialist Republics (USSR) n Unione f delle Repubbliche Socialiste Sovietiche (U.R.S.S.).

union shop n stabilimento in cui tutti gli operai sono tenuti ad aderire ad un sindacato.

unique [yo͞onēk'] a unico(a).

unisex [yo͞o'niseks] a unisex inv.

unison [yo͞o'nisən] n: **in** ~ all'unisono.

unit [yo͞o'nit] n unità f inv; (section: of furniture etc) elemento; (team, squad) reparto, squadra; **production** ~ reparto m produzione inv; **sink** ~ blocco m lavello inv.

unit cost n costo unitario.

unite [yo͞onīt'] vt unire ♦ vi unirsi.

united [yo͞oni'tid] a unito(a); (efforts) congiunto(a).

United Arab Emirates npl Emirati mpl Arabi Uniti.

United Kingdom (UK) n Regno Unito.

United Nations (Organization) (UN, UNO) n (Organizzazione f delle) Nazioni Unite (O.N.U.).

United States (of America) (US, USA) n Stati mpl Uniti (d'America) (USA).

unit price n prezzo unitario.

unit trust n (Brit COMM) fondo d'investimento.

unity [yo͞o'nitē] n unità.

Univ. abbr = **university**.

universal [yo͞onəvûr'səl] a universale.

universe [yo͞o'nəvûrs] n universo.

university [yo͞onəvûr'sitē] n università f inv ♦ cpd (student, professor, education) universitario(a); (year) accademico(a).

university degree n laurea.

unjust [unjust'] a ingiusto(a).

unjustifiable [unjus'tifīəbəl] a ingiustificabile.

unjustified [unjus'təfīd] a ingiustificato(a); (TYP) non allineato(a).

unkempt [unkempt'] a trasandato(a); spettinato(a).

unkind [unkīnd'] a poco gentile, villano(a).

unkindly [unkīnd'lē] ad (speak) in modo sgarbato; (treat) male.

unknown [unnōn'] a sconosciuto(a); ~ **to me** ... a mia insaputa ...; ~ **quantity** (MATH, fig) incognita.

unladen [unlā'dən] a (ship, weight) a vuoto.

unlawful [unlô'fəl] a illecito(a), illegale.

unleaded [unled'id] a senza piombo.

unleash [unlēsh'] vt sguinzagliare; (fig) scatenare.

unleavened [unlev'ənd] a non lievitato(a), azzimo(a).

unless [unles'] cj a meno che (non) + sub; ~ **otherwise stated** salvo indicazione contraria; ~ **I am mistaken** se non mi sbaglio.

unlicensed [unlī'sənst] a (Brit) senza licenza per la vendita di alcolici.

unlike [unlīk'] a diverso(a) ♦ prep a differenza di, contrariamente a.

unlikelihood [unlīk'lēho͞od] a improbabilità.

unlikely [unlīk'lē] a improbabile; (explanation) inverosimile.

unlimited [unlim'itid] a illimitato(a).

unlisted [unlis'tid] a (US TEL): **to be** ~ non essere sull'elenco; (STOCK EXCHANGE) non quotato(a).

unlit [unlit'] a (room) senza luce; (road) non illuminato(a).

unload [unlōd'] vt scaricare.

unlock [unlâk'] vt aprire.

unlucky [unluk'ē] a sfortunato(a); (object, number) che porta sfortuna, di malaugurio; **to be** ~ (person) essere sfortunato, non avere fortuna.

unmanageable [unman'ijəbəl] a (tool, vehicle) poco maneggevole; (situation) impossibile.

unmanned [unmand'] a (spacecraft) senza equipaggio.

unmannerly [unman'ûrlē] a maleducato(a).

unmarked [unmârkt'] a (unstained) pulito(a), senza macchie; ~ **police car** civetta della polizia.

unmarried [unmar'ēd] a non sposato(a); (man only) scapolo, celibe; (woman only) nubile.

unmarried mother n ragazza f madre inv.

unmask [unmask'] vt smascherare.

unmatched [unmacht'] a senza uguali.

unmentionable [unmen'chənəbəl] a (vice, topic) innominabile; (word) irripetibile.

unmerciful [unmûr'sifəl] a spietato(a).

unmistakable [unmistā'kəbəl] a indubbio(a); facilmente riconoscibile.

unmitigated [unmit'əgātid] a (disaster etc) totale, assoluto(a).

unnamed [unnāmd'] a (nameless) senza nome; (anonymous) anonimo(a).

unnatural [unnach'ûrəl] a innaturale; contro natura.

unnecessary [unnes'isārē] a inutile, superfluo(a).

unnerve [unnûrv'] vt (subj: accident) sgomentare; (: hostile attitude) bloccare; (: long wait, interview) snervare.

unnoticed [unnō'tist] a: **to go** or **pass** ~ passare inosservato(a).

UNO [o͞o'nō] n abbr see **United Nations Organization**.

unobservant [unəbzûr'vənt] a: **to be** ~ non avere spirito di osservazione.

unobtainable [unəbtā'nəbəl] a (TEL) non ottenibile.

unobtrusive [unəbtro͞o'siv] a discreto(a).

unoccupied [unâk'yəpīd] a (house) vuoto(a); (seat, MIL: zone) libero(a), non occupato(a).

unofficial [unəfish'əl] a non ufficiale; (strike) non dichiarato(a) dal sindacato.

unopened |unō'pənd| *a* (*letter*) non aperto(a); (*present*) ancora incartato(a).

unopposed |unəpōzd'| *a* senza incontrare opposizione.

unorthodox |unôr'thədáks| *a* non ortodosso(a).

unpack |unpak'| *vi* disfare la valigia (*or* le valigie).

unpaid |unpād'| *a* (*vacation*) non pagato(a); (*work*) non retribuito(a); (*bill, debt*) da pagare.

unpalatable |unpal'ətəbəl| *a* (*food*) immangiabile; (*drink*) imbevibile; (*truth*) sgradevole.

unparalleled |unpar'əleld| *a* incomparabile, impareggiabile.

unpatriotic |unpātrēăt'ik| *a* (*person*) poco patriottico(a); (*speech, attitude*) antipatriottico(a).

unplanned |unpland'| *a* (*visit*) imprevisto(a); (*baby*) non previsto(a).

unpleasant |unplez'ənt| *a* spiacevole; (*person, remark*) antipatico(a); (*day, experience*) brutto(a).

unplug |unplug'| *vt* staccare.

unpolluted |unpəlōō'tid| *a* non inquinato(a).

unpopular |unpäp'yəlûr| *a* impopolare; **to make o.s.** ~ **(with)** rendersi antipatico(a); (*subj: politician etc*) alienarsi le simpatie (di).

unprecedented |unpres'identid| *a* senza precedenti.

unpredictable |unpridik'təbəl| *a* imprevedibile.

unprejudiced |unprej'ədist| *a* (*not biased*) obiettivo(a), imparziale; (*having no prejudices*) senza pregiudizi.

unprepared |unpripärd'| *a* (*person*) impreparato(a); (*speech*) improvvisato(a).

unprepossessing |unprēpəzes'ing| *a* insulso(a).

unpretentious |unpriten'chəs| *a* senza pretese.

unprincipled |unprin'səpəld| *a* senza scrupoli.

unproductive |unprəduk'tiv| *a* improduttivo(a); (*discussion*) sterile.

unprofessional |unprəfesh'ənəl| *a*: ~ **conduct** scorrettezza professionale.

unprofitable |unprâf'itəbəl| *a* (*financially*) redditizio(a); (*job, deal*) poco lucrativo(a).

unprovoked |unprəvōkt'| *a* non provocato(a).

unpunished |unpun'isht| *a*: **to go** ~ restare impunito(a).

unqualified |unkwâl'əfīd| *a* (*worker*) non qualificato(a); (*in professions*) non abilitato(a); (*success*) assoluto(a), senza riserve.

unquestionably |unkwes'chənəblē| *ad* indiscutibilmente.

unquestioning |unkwes'chəning| *a* (*obedience, acceptance*) cieco(a).

unravel |unrav'əl| *vt* dipanare, districare.

unreal |unrēl'| *a* irreale.

unrealistic |unrēəlis'tik| *a* (*idea*) illusorio(a);

(*estimate*) non realistico(a).

unreasonable |unrē'zənəbəl| *a* irragionevole; **to make** ~ **demands on sb** voler troppo da qn.

unrecognizable |unrek'əgnīzəbəl| *a* irriconoscibile.

unrecognized |unrek'əgnīzd| *a* (*talent, genius*) misconosciuto(a); (*POL: regime*) non ufficialmente riconosciuto(a).

unrecorded |unrikôr'did| *a* non documentato(a), non registrato(a).

unrefined |unrifīnd'| *a* (*sugar, petroleum*) greggio(a); (*person*) rozzo(a).

unrehearsed |unrihûrst'| *a* (*THEATER etc*) improvvisato(a); (*spontaneous*) imprevisto(a).

unrelated |unrilā'tid| *a*: ~ **(to)** senza rapporto (con); (*by family*) non imparentato(a) (con).

unrelenting |unrilen'ting| *a* implacabile; accanito(a).

unreliable |unrilī'əbəl| *a* (*person, machine*) che non dà affidamento; (*news, source of information*) inattendibile.

unrelieved |unrilēvd'| *a* (*monotony*) uniforme.

unremitting |unrimit'ing| *a* incessante, infaticabile.

unrepeatable |unripē'təbəl| *a* (*offer*) unico(a).

unrepentant |unripen'tənt| *a* impenitente.

unrepresentative |unreprizen'tətiv| *a* atipico(a), poco rappresentativo(a).

unreserved |unrizûrvd'| *a* (*seat*) non prenotato(a), non riservato(a); (*approval, admiration*) senza riserve.

unresponsive |unrispân'siv| *a* che non reagisce.

unrest |unrest'| *n* agitazione *f.*

unrestricted |unristrik'tid| *a* (*power, time*) illimitato(a); (*access*) libero(a).

unrewarded |unriwôr'did| *a* non ricompensato(a).

unripe |unrīp'| *a* acerbo(a).

unrivaled, (*Brit*) **unrivalled** |unrī'vəld| *a* senza pari.

unroll |unrōl'| *vt* srotolare.

unruffled |unruf'əld| *a* (*person*) calmo(a) e tranquillo(a), imperturbato(a); (*hair*) a posto.

unruly |unrōō'lē| *a* indisciplinato(a).

unsafe |unsāf'| *a* pericoloso(a), rischioso(a); ~ **to drink** non potabile; ~ **to eat** non commestibile.

unsaid |unsed'| *a*: **to leave sth** ~ passare qc sotto silenzio.

unsalable, (*Brit*) **unsaleable** |unsā'ləbəl| *a* invendibile.

unsatisfactory |unsatisfak'tûrē| *a* che lascia a desiderare, insufficiente.

unsavory, (*Brit*) **unsavoury** |unsā'vûrē| *a* (*fig: person*) losco(a); (: *reputation, subject*) disgustoso(a), ripugnante.

unscathed |unskāthd'| *a* incolume.

unscientific |unsīəntif'ik| *a* poco scientifico(a).

unscrew |unskrōō'| *vt* svitare.

unscrupulous |unskrōō'pyələs| *a* senza scrupoli.

unsecured |unsikyōōrd'| *a*: ~ **creditor** creditore *m* chirografario.

unseemly |unsēm'lē| *a* sconveniente.

unseen |unsēn'| *a* (*person*) inosservato(a); (*danger*) nascosto(a).

unselfish |unsel'fish| *a* (*person*) altruista; (*act*) disinteressato(a).

unsettled |unset'əld| *a* (*person*, *future*) incerto(a); (*question*) non risolto(a); (*weather*, *market*) instabile; **to feel ~** sentirsi disorientato(a).

unsettling |unset'ling| *a* inquietante.

unshak(e)able |unshā'kəbəl| *a* irremovibile.

unshaven |unshā'vən| *a* non rasato(a).

unsightly |unsīt'lē| *a* brutto(a), sgradevole a vedersi.

unskilled |unskild'| *a*: ~ **worker** manovale *m*.

unsociable |unsō'shəbəl| *a* (*person*) poco socievole; (*behavior*) antipatico(a).

unsocial |unsō'shəl| *a*: ~ **hours** orario sconveniente.

unsold |unsōld'| *a* invenduto(a).

unsolicited |unsəlis'itid| *a* non richiesto(a).

unsophisticated |unsəfis'tikātid| *a* semplice, naturale.

unsound |unsound'| *a* (*health*) debole, cagionevole; (*in construction*: *floor*, *foundations*) debole, malsicuro(a); (*policy*, *advice*) poco sensato(a); (*judgment*, *investment*) poco sicuro(a).

unspeakable |unspē'kəbəl| *a* (*bad*) abominevole.

unspoken |unspō'kən| *a* (*words*) non detto(a); (*agreement*, *approval*) tacito(a).

unsteady |unsted'ē| *a* instabile, malsicuro(a).

unstinting |unstin'ting| *a* (*support*) incondizionato(a); (*generosity*) illimitato(a); (*praise*) senza riserve.

unstuck |unstuk'| *a*: **to come ~** scollarsi; (*fig*) fare fiasco.

unsubstantiated |unsəbstan'chēātid| *a* (*rumor*, *accusation*) infondato(a).

unsuccessful |unsəkses'fəl| *a* (*writer*, *proposal*) che non ha successo; (*marriage*, *attempt*) mal riuscito(a), fallito(a); **to be ~** (*in attempting sth*) non riuscire; non avere successo; (*application*) non essere considerato(a).

unsuccessfully |unsəkses'fəlē| *ad* senza successo.

unsuitable |unsōō'təbəl| *a* inadatto(a); (*moment*) inopportuno(a).

unsuited |unsōō'tid| *a*: **to be ~ for** *or* **to** non essere fatto(a) per.

unsupported |unsəpôr'tid| *a* (*claim*) senza fondamento; (*theory*) non dimostrato(a).

unsure |unshōōr'| *a*: ~ (**of** *or* **about**) incerto(a) (su); **to be ~ of o.s.** essere insicuro(a).

unsuspecting |unsəspek'ting| *a* che non sospetta niente.

unsweetened |unswēt'ənd| *a* senza zucchero.

unswerving |unswûr'ving| *a* fermo(a).

unsympathetic |unsimpəthet'ik| *a* (*attitude*) poco incoraggiante; (*person*) antipatico(a); ~ (**to**) non solidale (verso).

untangle |untang'gəl| *vt* sbrogliare.

untapped |untapt'| *a* (*resources*) non sfruttato(a).

untaxed |untakst'| *a* (*goods*) esente da imposte; (*income*) non imponibile.

unthinkable |unthingk'əbəl| *a* impensabile, inconcepibile.

untidy |untī'dē| *a* (*room*) in disordine; (*appearance*, *work*) trascurato(a); (*person*, *writing*) disordinato(a).

untie |untī'| *vt* (*knot*, *parcel*) disfare; (*prisoner*, *dog*) slegare.

until |until'| *prep* fino a; (*after negative*) prima di ♦ *cj* finché, fino a quando; (*in past*, *after negative*) prima che + *sub*, prima di + *infinitive*; ~ **now** finora; ~ **then** fino ad allora; **from morning ~ night** dalla mattina alla sera.

untimely |untīm'lē| *a* intempestivo(a), inopportuno(a); (*death*) prematuro(a).

untold |untōld'| *a* incalcolabile; indescrivibile.

untouched |untucht'| *a* (*not used etc*) non toccato(a), intatto(a); (*safe: person*) incolume; (*unaffected*): ~ **by** insensibile a.

untoward |untôrd'| *a* sfortunato(a), sconveniente.

untrammeled, (*Brit*) **untrammelled** |untram'əld| *a* illimitato(a).

untranslatable |untranz'lātəbəl| *a* intraducibile.

untrue |untrōō'| *a* (*statement*) falso(a), non vero(a).

untrustworthy |untrust'wûrᵗᵺē| *a* di cui non ci si può fidare.

unusable |unyōō'zəbəl| *a* inservibile, inutilizzabile.

unused |unyōōzd'| *a* (*new*) nuovo(a); (*not made use of*) non usato(a), non utilizzato(a); |unyōōst'|: **to be ~ to sth/to doing sth** non essere abituato(a) a qc/a fare qc.

unusual |unyōō'zhōōəl| *a* insolito(a), eccezionale, raro(a).

unusually |unyōō'zhōōəlē| *ad* insolitamente.

unveil |unvāl'| *vt* scoprire, svelare.

unwanted |unwôn'tid| *a* non desiderato(a).

unwarranted |unwôr'əntid| *a* ingiustificato(a).

unwary |unwär'ē| *a* incauto(a).

unwavering |unwā'vûring| *a* fermo(a), incrollabile.

unwelcome |unwel'kəm| *a* (*gen*) non gradito(a); **to feel ~** sentire che la propria presenza non è gradita.

unwell |unwel'| *a* indisposto(a); **to feel ~** non

sentirsi bene.

unwieldy |unwēl'dē| *a* poco maneggevole.

unwilling |unwil'ing| *a*: **to be ~ to do** non voler fare.

unwillingly |unwil'inglē| *ad* malvolentieri.

unwind |unwīnd'| *vb (irg) vt* svolgere, srotolare ♦ *vi (relax)* rilassarsi.

unwise |unwīz'| *a (decision, act)* avventato(a).

unwitting |unwit'ing| *a* involontario(a).

unworkable |unwûr'kəbəl| *a (plan etc)* inattuabile.

unworthy |unwûr'thē| *a* indegno(a); **to be ~ of sth/to do sth** non essere degno di qc/di fare qc.

unwrap |unrap'| *vt* disfare; *(present)* aprire.

unwritten |unrit'ən| *a (agreement)* tacito(a).

unzip |unzip'| *vt* aprire (la chiusura lampo di).

up |up| *prep*: **to go/be ~ sth** salire/essere su qc ♦ *ad* su, (di) sopra; in alto ♦ *vt (col: price)* alzare ♦ *vi (col)*: **she ~ped and left** improvvisamente se ne andò; **~ there** lassù; **~ above** al di sopra; **~ to** fino a; **to be ~** *(out of bed)* essere alzato(a); *(building)* essere terminato(a); *(tent)* essere piantato(a); *(drapes, shutters, wallpaper)* essere su; **"this side ~"** "alto"; **to be ~ (by)** *(in price, value)* essere andato(a) su (di); **when the year was ~** *(finished)* finito l'anno; **time's ~** il tempo è scaduto; **it is ~ to you** tocca a lei decidere; **what's ~?** *(col: wrong)* che c'è?; **what's ~ with him?** che ha?, che gli prende?; **what is he ~ to?** cosa sta tramando?; **he is not ~ to it** non ne è capace; **~s and downs** *npl (fig)* alti e bassi *mpl*.

up-and-coming |upənkum'ing| *a* pieno(a) di promesse, promettente.

upbeat |up'bēt| *n (MUS)* tempo in levare; *(in economy, prosperity)* incremento ♦ *a (col)* ottimistico(a).

upbraid |upbrād'| *vt* rimproverare.

upbringing |up'bringing| *n* educazione *f*.

update |updāt'| *vt* aggiornare.

upend |upend'| *vt* rovesciare.

upgrade |upgrād'| *vt* promuovere; *(job)* rivalutare; *(COMPUT)* far passare a potenza superiore.

upheaval |uphē'vəl| *n* sconvolgimento; tumulto.

uphill *a* |up'hil'| in salita; *(fig: task)* difficile ♦ *ad* |uphil'|: **to go ~** andare in salita, salire.

uphold |uphōld'| *vt irg* approvare; sostenere.

upholstery |uphōl'stûrē| *n* tappezzeria.

UPI *n abbr (US: = United Press International)* organizzazione commerciale di giornali negli USA e all'estero per lo scambio di notizie.

upkeep |up'kēp| *n* manutenzione *f*.

up-market |up'mâr'kit| *a (product)* che si rivolge ad una fascia di mercato superiore.

upon |əpán'| *prep* su.

upper |up'ûr| *a* superiore ♦ *n (of shoe)* tomaia; **the ~ class** ≈ l'alta borghesia.

upper-class |up'ûrklas'| *a* dell'alta borghesia; *(district)* signorile; *(accent)* aristocratico(a); *(attitude)* snob *inv*.

upper hand *n*: **to have the ~** avere il coltello dalla parte del manico.

uppermost |up'ûrmōst| *a* il(la) più alto(a); predominante; **it was ~ in my mind** è stata la mia prima preoccupazione.

Upper Volta |up'ûr vōl'tə| *n* Alto Volta *m*.

upright |up'rīt| *a* diritto(a); verticale; *(fig)* diritto(a), onesto(a) ♦ *n* montante *m*.

uprising |up'rīzing| *n* insurrezione *f*, rivolta.

uproar |up'rôr| *n* tumulto, clamore *m*.

uproot |uprōōt'| *vt* sradicare.

upset *n* |up'set| turbamento ♦ *vt* |upset'| *(irg: like set) (glass etc)* rovesciare; *(plan, stomach)* scombussolare; *(person: offend)* contrariare; *(: grieve)* addolorare; sconvolgere ♦ *a* |upset'| contrariato(a); addolorato(a); *(stomach)* scombussolato(a), disturbato(a); **to have a stomach ~** *(Brit)* avere lo stomaco in disordine *or* scombussolato; **to get ~** contrariarsi; addolorarsi.

upset price *n (US, Scottish)* prezzo di riserva.

upsetting |upset'ing| *a (saddening)* sconvolgente; *(offending)* offensivo(a); *(annoying)* fastidioso(a).

upshot |up'shát| *n* risultato; **the ~ of it all was that ...** la conclusione è stata che ....

upside down |up'sīd doun'| *ad* sottosopra; **to turn ~** capovolgere; *(fig)* mettere sottosopra.

upstairs |up'stärz| *ad, a* di sopra, al piano superiore ♦ *n* piano di sopra.

upstart |up'stârt| *n* parvenu *m inv*.

upstream |up'strēm| *ad* a monte.

upsurge |up'sûrj| *n (of enthusiasm etc)* ondata.

uptake |up'tāk| *n*: **he is quick/slow on the ~** è pronto/lento di comprendonio.

uptight |up'tīt| *a (col)* teso(a).

up-to-date |up'tədāt'| *a* moderno(a); aggiornato(a).

upturn |up'tûrn| *n (in luck)* svolta favorevole; *(in value of currency)* rialzo.

upturned |up'tûrnd'| *a (nose)* all'insù.

upward |up'wûrd| *a* ascendente; verso l'alto.

upward(s) |up'wûrd(z)| *ad* in su, verso l'alto.

URA *n abbr (US: = Urban Renewal Administration)* amministrazione per il rinnovamento urbano.

Ural Mountains |yoor'əl moun'tənz| *npl*: **the ~** *(also:* **the Urals***)* gli Urali, i Monti Urali.

uranium |yoorā'nēəm| *n* uranio.

Uranus |yoor'ānəs| *n (planet)* Urano.

urban |ûr'bən| *a* urbano(a).

urbane |ûrbān'| *a* civile, urbano(a), educato(a).

urbanization |ûrbənəzā'shən| *n* urbanizzazione *f*.

urchin |ûr'chin| *n* monello; **sea ~** riccio di

mare.

urge |ûrj| *n* impulso, stimolo ♦ *vt* (*caution etc*) raccomandare vivamente; **to ~ sb to do** esortare qn a fare, spingere qn a fare; raccomandare a qn di fare.
  urge on *vt* spronare.

urgency |ûr'jənsē| *n* urgenza; (*of tone*) insistenza.

urgent |ûr'jənt| *a* urgente; (*earnest*, *persistent*: *plea*) pressante; (: *tone*) insistente, incalzante.

urgently |ûr'jəntlē| *ad* d'urgenza, urgentemente; con insistenza.

urinal |yo͞or'ənəl| *n* (*Brit*: *building*) vespasiano; (: *vessel*) orinale *m*, pappagallo.

urinate |yo͞or'ənāt| *vi* orinare.

urine |yo͞or'in| *n* orina.

urn |ûrn| *n* urna; (*also*: **tea ~**) bollitore *m* per il tè.

Uruguay |yo͞o'rəgwā| *n* Uruguay *m*.

Uruguayan |yo͞orəgwā'ən| *a*, *n* uruguaiano(a).

US *n abbr see* **United States**.

us |us| *pronoun* ci; (*stressed*, *after prep*) noi.

USA *n abbr* (*GEO*) *see* **United States (of America)**; (*MIL*) = *United States Army*.

usable |yo͞o'zəbəl| *a* utilizzabile, usabile.

USAF *n abbr* = *United States Air Force*.

usage |yo͞o'sij| *n* uso.

USCG *n abbr* = *United States Coast Guard*.

USDA *n abbr* = *United States Department of Agriculture*.

USDI *n abbr* = *United States Department of the Interior*.

use *n* |yo͞os| uso; impiego, utilizzazione *f* ♦ *vt* |yo͞oz| usare, utilizzare, servirsi di; **she ~d to do it** lo faceva (una volta), era solita farlo; **in ~** in uso; **out of ~** fuori uso; **to be of ~** essere utile, servire; **to make ~ of sth** far uso di qc, utilizzare qc; **ready for ~** pronto per l'uso; **it's no ~** non serve, è inutile; **to have the ~ of** poter usare; **what's this ~d for?** a che serve?; **to be ~d to** avere l'abitudine di; **to get ~d to** abituarsi a, fare l'abitudine a.
  use up *vt* finire; (*supplies*) dare fondo a; (*left-overs*) utilizzare.

used |yo͞ozd| *a* (*car*) d'occasione.

useful |yo͞os'fəl| *a* utile; **to come in ~** fare comodo, tornare utile.

usefulness |yo͞os'fəlnis| *n* utilità.

useless |yo͞os'lis| *a* inutile; (*unusable*: *object*) inservibile.

user |yo͞o'zûr| *n* utente *m/f*; (*of gasoline*, *gas etc*) consumatore/trice.

user-friendly |yo͞o'zûrfrɛnd'lē| *a* orientato(a) all'utente.

USES *n abbr* = *United States Employment Service*.

usher |ush'ûr| *n* usciere *m*; (*in cinema*) maschera ♦ *vt*: **to ~ sb in** far entrare qn.

usherette |ushərɛt'| *n* (*in cinema*) maschera.

USIA *n abbr* = *United States Information Agency*.

USM *n abbr* = *United States Mint*; *United States Mail*.

USN *n abbr* = *United States Navy*.

USPHS *n abbr* = *United States Public Health Service*.

USPS *n abbr* = *United States Postal Service*.

USS *abbr* = *United States Ship*.

USSR *n abbr see* **Union of Soviet Socialist Republics**.

usu. *abbr* = **usually**.

usual |yo͞o'zho͞oəl| *a* solito(a); **as ~** come al solito, come d'abitudine.

usually |yo͞o'zho͞oəlē| *ad* di solito.

usurer |yo͞o'zhûrûr| *a* usuraio/a.

usurp |yo͞o'sûrp| *vt* usurpare.

UT *abbr* (*US MAIL*) = *Utah*.

utensil |yo͞otɛn'səl| *n* utensile *m*.

uterus |yo͞o'tûrəs| *n* utero.

utilitarian |yo͞otilitär'čən| *a* utilitario(a).

utility |yo͞otil'itē| *n* utilità; (*also*: **public ~**) servizio pubblico.

utility room *n locale adibito alla stiratura dei panni etc*.

utilization |yo͞otəlizā'shən| *n* utilizzazione *f*.

utilize |yo͞o'təliz| *vt* utilizzare; sfruttare.

utmost |ut'mōst| *a* estremo(a) ♦ *n*: **to do one's ~** fare il possibile *or* di tutto; **of the ~ importance** della massima importanza; **it is of the ~ importance that** ... è estremamente importante che ... + *sub*.

utter |ut'ûr| *a* assoluto(a), totale ♦ *vt* pronunciare, proferire; emettere.

utterance |ut'ûrəns| *n* espressione *f*; parole *fpl*.

utterly |ut'ûrlē| *ad* completamente, del tutto.

U-turn |yo͞o'tûrn| *n* inversione *f* a U; (*fig*) voltafaccia *m inv*.

V

V, v |vē| *n* (*letter*) V, v *m or f inv*; **V for Victor** ≈ V come Venezia.

v *abbr* (= *verse*; = *vide*: *see*) v.; (= *volt*) V.; (= *versus*) contro.

VA *abbr* (*US MAIL*) = *Virginia*.

vac |vak| *n abbr* (*Brit col*) = **vacation**.

vacancy |vā'kənsē| *n* (*job*) posto libero; (*room*) stanza libera; **"no vacancies"** "completo"; **have you any vacancies?** (*office*) avete bisogno di personale?; (*hotel*) avete una stanza?

vacant |vā'kənt| *a* (*job*, *seat etc*) libero(a);

(*expression*) assente.

vacant lot *n* terreno non occupato; (*for sale*) terreno in vendita.

vacate [vā'kāt] *vt* lasciare libero(a).

vacation [vākā'shən] *n* (*esp US*) vacanze *fpl*; **to take a** ~ prendere una vacanza, prendere le ferie; **on** ~ in vacanza, in ferie.

vacation course *n* corso estivo.

vacationer [vākā'shənûr] *n* (*US*) villeggiante *m/f*.

vacation pay *n* (*US*) stipendio delle ferie.

vacation season *n* (*US*) stagione *f* delle vacanze.

vaccinate [vak'sənāt] *vt* vaccinare.

vaccination [vak'sənā'shən] *n* vaccinazione *f*.

vaccine [vaksēn'] *n* vaccino.

vacuum [vak'yōōm] *n* vuoto ♦ *vt* pulire con l'aspirapolvere.

vacuum bottle *n* (*US*) thermos ® *m inv*.

vacuum cleaner *n* aspirapolvere *m inv*.

vacuum flask *n* (*Brit*) = **vacuum bottle**.

vacuum-packed [vak'yōōmpakt'] *a* confezionato(a) sottovuoto.

vagabond [vag'əbänd] *n* vagabondo/a.

vagary [vā'gûrē] *n* capriccio.

vagina [vəjī'nə] *n* vagina.

vagrancy [vā'grənsē] *n* vagabondaggio.

vagrant [vā'grənt] *n* vagabondo/a.

vague [vāg] *a* vago(a); (*blurred*: *photo*, *memory*) sfocato(a); **I haven't the** ~**st idea** non ho la minima *or* più pallida idea.

vaguely [vāg'lē] *ad* vagamente.

vain [vān] *a* (*useless*) inutile, vano(a); (*conceited*) vanitoso(a); **in** ~ inutilmente, invano.

valance [val'əns] *n* volant *m inv*, balza.

valedictory [validik'tûrē] *a* di commiato.

valentine [val'əntīn] *n* (*also*: ~ **card**) cartolina *or* biglietto di San Valentino.

valet [valā'] *n* cameriere *m* personale.

valet parking *n* *parcheggio effettuato da un dipendente (dell'albergo etc)*.

valet service *n* (*for clothes*) servizio di lavanderia; (*for car*) servizio completo di lavaggio.

valiant [val'yənt] *a* valoroso(a), coraggioso(a).

valid [val'id] *a* valido(a), valevole; (*excuse*) valido(a).

validate [val'idāt] *vt* (*contract*, *document*) convalidare; (*argument*, *claim*) comprovare.

validity [vəlid'itē] *n* validità.

valise [vəlēs'] *n* borsa da viaggio.

valley [val'ē] *n* valle *f*.

valor, (*Brit*) **valour** [val'ûr] *n* valore *m*.

valuable [val'yōōəbəl] *a* (*jewel*) di (grande) valore; (*time*) prezioso(a); ~**s** *npl* oggetti *mpl* di valore.

valuation [valyōōā'shən] *n* valutazione *f*, stima.

value [val'yōō] *n* valore *m* ♦ *vt* (*fix price*) valutare, dare un prezzo a; (*cherish*) apprezza-

re, tenere a; **to be of great** ~ **to sb** avere molta importanza per qn; **to lose (in)** ~ (*currency*) svalutarsi; (*property*) perdere (di) valore; **to gain (in)** ~ (*currency*) guadagnare; (*property*) aumentare di valore; **you get good** ~ **(for money) in that shop** si compra bene in quel negozio.

value added tax (VAT) *n* imposta sul valore aggiunto (I.V.A.).

valued [val'yōōd] *a* (*appreciated*) stimato(a), apprezzato(a).

valuer [val'yōōûr] *n* stimatore/trice.

valve [valv] *n* valvola.

vampire [vam'pīûr] *n* vampiro.

van [van] *n* (*AUT*) furgone *m*; (*Brit RAIL*) vagone *m*.

vandal [van'dəl] *n* vandalo/a.

vandalism [van'dəlizəm] *n* vandalismo.

vandalize [van'dəlīz] *vt* vandalizzare.

vanguard [van'gârd] *n* avanguardia.

vanilla [vənil'ə] *n* vaniglia ♦ *cpd* (*ice cream*) alla vaniglia.

vanish [van'ish] *vi* svanire, scomparire.

vanity [van'itē] *n* vanità.

vanity case *n* valigetta per cosmetici.

vantage [van'tij] *n*: ~ **point** posizione *f or* punto di osservazione; (*fig*) posizione vantaggiosa.

vapor [vā'pûr] *n* (*US*) vapore *m*.

vaporize [vā'pərīz] *vt* vaporizzare ♦ *vi* vaporizzarsi.

vapor trail *n* (*AVIAT*) scia.

vapour [vā'pûr] *etc* (*Brit*) = **vapor** *etc*.

variable [vär'ēəbəl] *a* variabile; (*mood*) mutevole ♦ *n* fattore *m* variabile, variabile *f*.

variance [vär'ēəns] *n*: **to be at** ~ **(with)** essere in disaccordo (con); (*facts*) essere in contraddizione (con).

variant [vär'ēənt] *n* variante *f*.

variation [värēā'shən] *n* variazione *f*; (*in opinion*) cambiamento.

varicose [var'əkōs] *a*: ~ **veins** varici *fpl*.

varied [vär'ēd] *a* vario(a), diverso(a).

variety [vərī'ətē] *n* varietà *f inv*; (*quantity*): **a wide** ~ **of** ... una vasta gamma di ...; **for a** ~ **of reasons** per una serie di motivi.

variety show *n* spettacolo di varietà.

various [vär'ēəs] *a* vario(a), diverso(a); (*several*) parecchi(e), molti(e); **at** ~ **times** in momenti diversi; (*several*) diverse volte.

varnish [vär'nish] *n* vernice *f* ♦ *vt* verniciare; **to** ~ **one's nails** mettersi lo smalto sulle unghie.

vary [vär'ē] *vt*, *vi* variare, mutare; **to** ~ **(with** *or* **according to)** variare (con *or* a seconda di).

varying [vär'ēing] *a* variabile.

vase [vās] *n* vaso.

vasectomy [vasek'təmē] *n* vasectomia.

vaseline [vas'əlēn] ® *n* vaselina.

vast [vast] *a* vasto(a); (*amount*, *success*)

enorme.
vastly [vast'lē] *ad* enormemente.
vastness [vast'nis] *n* vastità.
VAT [vat] *n abbr see* **value added tax**.
vat [vat] *n* tino.
Vatican [vat'ikən] *n*: **the ~** il Vaticano.
vault [vôlt] *n* (*of roof*) volta; (*tomb*) tomba; (*in bank*) camera blindata; (*jump*) salto ♦ *vt* (*also:* **~ over**) saltare (d'un balzo).
vaunted [vôn'tid] *a*: **much-~** tanto celebrato(a).
VC *n abbr* = **vice-chairman**.
VCR *n abbr* (= *video cassette recorder*) VCR *m inv*.
VD *n abbr see* **venereal disease**.
VDU *n abbr see* **visual display unit**.
veal [vēl] *n* vitello.
veer [vēr] *vi* girare; virare.
vegan [vē'gən] *n vegetariano che non mangia alcun alimento di derivazione animale*.
vegetable [vej'təbəl] *n* verdura, ortaggio ♦ *a* vegetale.
vegetable garden *n* orto.
vegetarian [vejitär'ēən] *a, n* vegetariano(a).
vegetate [vej'itāt] *vi* vegetare.
vegetation [vejitā'shən] *n* vegetazione *f*.
vehemence [vē'əməns] *n* veemenza, violenza.
vehement [vē'əmənt] *a* veemente, violento(a); profondo(a).
vehicle [vē'ikəl] *n* veicolo; (*fig*) mezzo.
vehicular [vēhik'yəlûr] *a*: **"no ~ traffic"** "chiuso al traffico di veicoli".
veil [vāl] *n* velo ♦ *vt* velare; **under a ~ of secrecy** (*fig*) protetto da una cortina di segretezza.
veiled [vāld] *a* (*also fig*) velato(a).
vein [vān] *n* vena; (*on leaf*) nervatura; (*fig: mood*) vena, umore *m*.
vellum [vel'əm] *n* (*writing paper*) carta patinata.
velocity [vəlâs'itē] *n* velocità *f inv*.
velvet [vel'vit] *n* velluto.
vending machine [ven'ding məshēn'] *n* distributore *m* automatico.
vendor [ven'dûr] *n* venditore/trice; **street ~** venditore ambulante.
veneer [vənēr'] *n* impiallacciatura; (*fig*) vernice *f*.
venerable [ven'ûrəbəl] *a* venerabile.
venereal disease (VD) [vənēr'ēəl di'zēz] *n* malattia venerea.
Venetian [vənē'shən] *a, n* veneziano(a).
Venetian blind [vənē'shən blīnd] *n* (tenda alla) veneziana.
Venezuela [venizwā'lə] *n* Venezuela *m*.
Venezuelan [venizwā'lən] *a, n* venezuelano(a).
vengeance [ven'jəns] *n* vendetta; **with a ~** (*fig*) davvero; furiosamente.
vengeful [venj'fəl] *a* vendicativo(a).
Venice [ven'is] *n* Venezia.
venison [ven'isən] *n* carne *f* di cervo.

venom [ven'əm] *n* veleno.
venomous [ven'əməs] *a* velenoso(a).
vent [vent] *n* foro, apertura; (*in dress, jacket*) spacco ♦ *vt* (*fig: one's feelings*) sfogare, dare sfogo a.
ventilate [ven'təlāt] *vt* (*room*) dare aria a, arieggiare.
ventilation [ventəlā'shən] *n* ventilazione *f*.
ventilation shaft *n* condotto di aerazione.
ventilator [ven'təlātûr] *n* ventilatore *m*.
ventriloquist [ventril'əkwist] *n* ventriloquo/a.
venture [ven'chûr] *n* impresa (rischiosa) ♦ *vt* rischiare, azzardare ♦ *vi* arrischiarsi, azzardarsi; **a business ~** un'iniziativa commerciale; **to ~ to do sth** azzardarsi a fare qc.
venture capital *n* capitale *m* di rischio.
venue [ven'yōō] *n* luogo di incontro; (*SPORT*) luogo (designato) per l'incontro.
Venus [vē'nəs] *n* (*planet*) Venere *m*.
veracity [vəras'itē] *n* veridicità.
veranda(h) [vəran'də] *n* veranda.
verb [vûrb] *n* verbo.
verbal [vûr'bəl] *a* verbale; (*translation*) letterale.
verbally [vûr'bəlē] *ad* a voce.
verbatim [vûrbā'tim] *ad, a* parola per parola.
verbose [vûrbōs'] *a* verboso(a).
verdict [vûr'dikt] *n* verdetto; (*opinion*) giudizio, parere *m*; **~ of guilty/not guilty** verdetto di colpevolezza/non colpevolezza.
verge [vûrj] *n* bordo, orlo; **on the ~ of doing** sul punto di fare.
verge on *vt fus* rasentare.
verger [vûr'jûr] *n* (*REL*) sagrestano.
verification [värəfəkā'shən] *n* verifica.
verify [vär'əfī] *vt* verificare; (*prove the truth of*) confermare.
veritable [vär'itəbəl] *a* vero(a).
vermin [vûr'min] *npl* animali *mpl* nocivi; (*insects*) insetti *mpl* parassiti.
vermouth [vûrmōōth'] *n* vermut *m inv*.
vernacular [vûrnak'yəlûr] *n* vernacolo.
versatile [vûr'sətəl] *a* (*person*) versatile; (*machine, tool etc*) (che si presta a molti usi).
verse [vûrs] *n* (*of poem*) verso; (*stanza*) stanza, strofa; (*in bible*) versetto; (*no pl: poetry*) versi *mpl*; **in ~** in versi.
versed [vûrst] *a*: **(well-)~ in** versato(a) in.
version [vûr'zhən] *n* versione *f*.
versus [vûr'səs] *prep* contro.
vertebra, pl ~e [vûr'təbrə, vûr'təbrā] *n* vertebra.
vertebrate [vûr'təbrāt] *n* vertebrato.
vertebrae [vûr'təbrā] *npl of* **vertebra**.
vertical [vûr'tikəl] *a, n* verticale (*m*).
vertically [vûr'tiklē] *ad* verticalmente.
vertigo [vûr'təgō] *n* vertigine *f*; **to suffer from ~** soffrire di vertigini.
verve [vûrv] *n* brio; entusiasmo.

very [vär'ē] *ad* molto ♦ *a*: **the ~ book which** proprio il libro che; **~ much** moltissimo; **~ well** molto bene; **~ little** molto poco; **at the ~ end** proprio alla fine; **the ~ last** proprio l'ultimo; **at the ~ least** almeno; **the ~ thought (of it) alarms me** il solo pensiero mi spaventa, sono spaventato solo al pensiero.

vespers [ves'pûrz] *npl* vespro.

vessel [ves'əl] *n* (*ANAT*) vaso; (*NAUT*) nave *f*; (*container*) recipiente *m*.

vest [vest] *n* (*US: waistcoat*) gilè *m inv*; (*Brit*) maglia; (: *sleeveless*) canottiera ♦ *vt*: **to ~ sb with sth, to ~ sth in sb** conferire qc a qn.

vested interest [ves'tid in'trist] *n*: **to have a ~ in doing** avere tutto l'interesse a fare; **~s** *npl* (*COMM*) diritti *mpl* acquisiti.

vestibule [ves'təbyōōl] *n* vestibolo.

vestige [ves'tij] *n* vestigio.

vestment [vest'mənt] *n* (*REL*) paramento liturgico.

vestry [ves'trē] *n* sagrestia.

Vesuvius [vəsōō'vēəs] *n* Vesuvio.

vet [vet] *n abbr* (= *veterinarian*) veterinario ♦ *vt* esaminare minuziosamente; (*text*) rivedere; **to ~ sb for a job** raccogliere delle informazioni dettagliate su qn prima di offrirgli un posto.

veteran [vet'ûrən] *n* veterano; (*also:* **war ~**) reduce *m* ♦ *a*: **she's a ~ campaigner for ...** lotta da sempre per ....

veteran car *n* auto *f inv* d'epoca (*anteriore al 1919*).

veterinarian [vetûrənär'ēən] *n* (*US*) veterinario/a.

veterinary [vet'ûrənärē] *a* veterinario(a).

veterinary surgeon *n* (*Brit*) = **veterinarian.**

veto [vē'tō] *n* (*pl* **~es**) veto ♦ *vt* opporre il veto a; **to put a ~ on** opporre il veto a.

vex [veks] *vt* irritare, contrariare.

vexed [vekst] *a* (*question*) controverso(a), dibattuto(a).

VFD *n abbr* (*US*) = *voluntary fire department*.

VHF *abbr* (= *very high frequency*) VHF.

VI *abbr* (*US MAIL*) = *Virgin Islands*.

via [vī'ə] *prep* (*by way of*) via; (*by means of*) tramite.

viability [vīəbil'ətē] *n* attuabilità.

viable [vī'əbəl] *a* attuabile; vitale.

viaduct [vī'ədukt] *n* viadotto.

vibrant [vī'brənt] *a* (*sound*) vibrante; (*color*) vivace, vivo(a).

vibrate [vī'brāt] *vi*: **to ~ (with)** vibrare (di); (*resound*) risonare (di).

vibration [vībrā'shən] *n* vibrazione *f*.

vicar [vik'ûr] *n* pastore *m*.

vicarage [vik'ûrij] *n* presbiterio.

vicarious [vīkär'ēəs] *a* sofferto(a) al posto di un altro; **to get ~ pleasure out of sth** trarre piacere indirettamente da qc.

vice [vīs] *n* (*evil*) vizio; (*TECH*) morsa.

vice- *prefix* vice....

vice-chairman [vīs'chär'mən] *n* vicepresidente *m*.

vice-chancellor [vīs'chan'səlûr] *n* (*Brit SCOL*) rettore *m* (*per elezione*).

vice-president [vīs'prez'idənt] *n* vicepresidente *m*.

vice-principal [vīs'prin'səpəl] *n* (*SCOL*) vicepreside *m/f*.

vice squad *n* (squadra del) buon costume *f*.

vice versa [vīs' vûr'sə] *ad* viceversa.

vicinity [visin'ətē] *n* vicinanze *fpl*.

vicious [vish'əs] *a* (*remark*) maligno(a), cattivo(a); (*blow*) violento(a); **a ~ circle** un circolo vizioso.

viciousness [vish'əsnis] *n* malignità, cattiveria; ferocia.

vicissitudes [visis'ətōōdz] *npl* vicissitudini *fpl*.

victim [vik'tim] *n* vittima; **to be the ~ of** essere vittima di.

victimization [viktiməzā'shən] *n* persecuzione *f*; rappresaglie *fpl*.

victimize [vik'təmīz] *vt* perseguitare; compiere delle rappresaglie contro.

victor [vik'tûr] *n* vincitore *m*.

Victorian [viktōr'ēən] *a* vittoriano(a).

victorious [viktôr'ēəs] *a* vittorioso(a).

victory [vik'tûrē] *n* vittoria; **to win a ~ over sb** riportare una vittoria su qn.

video [vid'ēō] *cpd* video... ♦ *n* (**~ film**) video *m inv*; (*also:* **~ cassette**) videocassetta; (*also:* **~ cassette recorder**) videoregistratore *m*.

video cassette *n* videocassetta.

video cassette recorder (VCR) *n* videoregistratore *m*.

video recording *n* registrazione *f* su video.

video tape *n* videotape *m inv*.

videotex [vid'ēōteks] *n* sistema di televideo.

vie [vī] *vi*: **to ~ with** competere con, rivaleggiare con.

Vienna [vēen'ə] *n* Vienna.

Vietnam, Viet Nam [vēetnâm'] *n* Vietnam *m*.

Vietnamese [vēetnâmēz'] *a* vietnamita ♦ *n* vietnamita *m/f*; (*LING*) vietnamita *m*.

view [vyōō] *n* vista, veduta; (*opinion*) opinione *f* ♦ *vt* (*situation*) considerare; (*house*) visitare; **on ~** (*in museum etc*) esposto(a); **to be in or within ~ (of sth)** essere in vista (di qc); **in full ~ of sb** sotto gli occhi di qn; **an overall ~ of the situation** una visione globale della situazione; **in my ~** a mio avviso, secondo me; **in ~ of the fact that** considerato che; **to take** *or* **hold the ~ that ...** essere dell'opinione che ...; **with a ~ to doing sth** con l'intenzione di fare qc.

viewdata [vyōō'dātə] *n* (*Brit*) *sistema di televideo*.

viewer [vyōō'ûr] *n* (*viewfinder*) mirino; (*small projector*) visore *m*; (*TV*) telespettatore/trice.

viewfinder [vyōō'findûr] *n* mirino.

viewpoint |vyōō'point| *n* punto di vista.
vigil |vij'əl| *n* veglia; **to keep** ~ vegliare.
vigilance |vij'ələns| *n* vigilanza.
vigilant |vij'ələnt| *a* vigile.
vigor |vig'ûr| *n* (*US*) vigore *m*.
vigorous |vig'ûrəs| *a* vigoroso(a).
vigour |vig'ûr| *n* (*Brit*) = **vigor.**
vile |vil| *a* (*action*) vile; (*smell*) disgustoso(a), nauseante; (*temper*) pessimo(a).
vilify |vil'əfī| *vt* diffamare.
villa |vil'ə| *n* villa.
village |vil'ij| *n* villaggio.
villager |vil'ijûr| *n* abitante *m/f* di villaggio.
villain |vil'in| *n* (*scoundrel*) canaglia; (*criminal*) criminale *m*; (*in novel etc*) cattivo.
VIN *n abbr* (*US*) = *vehicle identification number.*
vindicate |vin'dikāt| *vt* comprovare; giustificare.
vindication |vindikā'shən| *n*: **in** ~ **of** per giustificare; a discolpa di.
vindictive |vindik'tiv| *a* vendicativo(a).
vine |vīn| *n* vite *f*; (*climbing plant*) rampicante *m*.
vinegar |vin'əgûr| *n* aceto.
vine grower *n* viticoltore *m*.
vine-growing |vīn'grōing| *a* viticola(a) ♦ *n* viticoltura.
vineyard |vin'yûrd| *n* vigna, vigneto.
vintage |vin'tij| *n* (*year*) annata, produzione *f*; **the 1970** ~ il vino del 1970.
vintage car *n* auto *f inv* d'epoca.
vintage wine *n* vino d'annata.
vinyl |vī'nil| *n* vinile *m*.
viola |vēō'lə| *n* viola.
violate |vī'əlāt| *vt* violare.
violation |vīəlā'shən| *n* violazione *f*; **in** ~ **of** sth violando qc.
violence |vī'ələns| *n* violenza; (*POL etc*) incidenti *mpl* violenti.
violent |vī'ələnt| *a* violento(a); **a** ~ **dislike of sb/sth** una violenta avversione per qn/qc.
violently |vī'ələntlē| *ad* violentemente; (*ill, angry*) terribilmente.
violet |vī'əlit| *a* (*color*) viola *inv*, violetto(a) ♦ *n* (*plant*) violetta.
violin |vīəlin'| *n* violino.
violinist |vīəlin'ist| *n* violinista *m/f*.
VIP *n abbr* (= *very important person*) V.I.P. *m/f inv*.
viper |vī'pûr| *n* vipera.
virgin |vûr'jin| *n* vergine *f* ♦ *a* vergine *inv*; **she is a** ~ lei è vergine; **the Blessed V**~ la Beatissima Vergine.
virginity |vûrjin'ətē| *n* verginità.
virgin wool *n* (*US*) pura lana vergine.
Virgo |vûr'gō| *n* (*sign*) Vergine *f*; **to be** ~ essere della Vergine.
virile |vir'əl| *a* virile.
virility |vəril'ətē| *n* virilità.
virtual |vûr'chōōəl| *a* effettivo(a), vero(a);

(*COMPUT. PHYSICS*) virtuale; (*in effect*): **it's a** ~ **impossibility** è praticamente impossibile; **the** ~ **leader** il capo all'atto pratico.
virtually |vûr'chōōəlē| *ad* (*almost*) praticamente; **it is** ~ **impossible** è praticamente impossibile.
virtue |vûr'chōō| *n* virtù *f inv*; (*advantage*) pregio, vantaggio; **by** ~ **of** grazie a.
virtuoso |vûrchōō'sō| *n* virtuoso.
virtuous |vûr'chōōəs| *a* virtuoso(a).
virulent |vir'yələnt| *a* virulento(a).
virus |vī'rəs| *n* (*also:* **computer** ~) virus *m inv*.
visa |vē'zə| *n* visto.
vis-à-vis |vēzăvē'| *prep* rispetto a, nei riguardi di.
viscount |vī'kount| *n* visconte *m*.
viscous |vis'kəs| *a* viscoso(a).
vise |vīs| *n* (*US TECH*) morsa.
visibility |vizəbil'ətē| *n* visibilità.
visible |viz'əbəl| *a* visibile; ~ **exports/imports** esportazioni *fpl*/importazioni *fpl* visibili.
visibly |viz'əblē| *ad* visibilmente.
vision |vizh'ən| *n* (*sight*) vista; (*foresight, in dream*) visione *f*.
visionary |vizh'ənärē| *n* visionario/a.
visit |viz'it| *n* visita; (*stay*) soggiorno ♦ *vt* (*person*) andare a trovare; (*place*) visitare; **to pay a** ~ **to** (*person*) fare una visita a; (*place*) andare a visitare; **on a private/official** ~ in visita privata/ufficiale.
visiting |viz'iting| *a* (*speaker, professor, team*) ospite.
visiting card *n* biglietto da visita.
visiting hours *npl* orario delle visite.
visitor |viz'itûr| *n* visitatore/trice; (*guest*) ospite *m/f*.
visitors' book *n* libro d'oro; (*in hotel*) registro.
visor |vī'zûr| *n* visiera.
VISTA |vis'tə| *n abbr* (= *Volunteers in Service to America*) volontariato *in zone depresse degli Stati Uniti.*
vista |vis'tə| *n* vista, prospettiva.
visual |vizh'ōōəl| *a* visivo(a); visuale; ottico(a).
visual aid *n* sussidio visivo.
visual display unit (VDU) *n* unità *f inv* di visualizzazione.
visualize |vizh'ōōəlīz| *vt* immaginare, figurarsi; (*foresee*) prevedere.
visually |vizh'ōōəlē| *ad*: ~ **appealing** piacevole a vedersi; ~ **handicapped** con una menomazione della vista.
vital |vī'təl| *a* vitale; **of** ~ **importance (to sb/sth)** di vitale importanza (per qn/qc).
vitality |vītal'itē| *n* vitalità.
vitally |vī'təlē| *ad* estremamente.
vital statistics *npl* (*of population*) statistica demografica; (*col: woman's*) misure *fpl*.
vitamin |vī'təmin| *n* vitamina.

vitiate [vish'čāt] *vt* viziare.
vitreous [vit'rēəs] *a* (*rock*) vetroso(a); (*china, enamel*) vetrificato(a).
vitriolic [vitrēāl'ik] *a* (*fig*) caustico(a).
viva [vē'və] *n* (*also:* ~ **voce**) (esame *m*) orale.
vivacious [vivā'shəs] *a* vivace.
vivacity [vivas'itē] *n* vivacità.
vivid [viv'id] *a* vivido(a).
vividly [viv'idlē] *ad* (*describe*) vividamente; (*remember*) con precisione.
vivisection [vivisek'shən] *n* vivisezione *f*.
vixen [vik'sən] *n* volpe *f* femmina; (*pej: woman*) bisbetica.
viz *abbr* (= *videlicet: namely*) cioè.
VLF *abbr* (= *very low frequency*) bassissima frequenza.
V-neck [vē'nek] *n* maglione *m* con lo scollo a V.
VOA *n abbr* (= *Voice of America*) voce *f* dell'America (*alla radio*).
vocabulary [vōkab'yəlärē] *n* vocabolario.
vocal [vō'kəl] *a* (*MUS*) vocale; (*communication*) verbale; (*noisy*) rumoroso(a).
vocal cords *npl* corde *fpl* vocali.
vocalist [vō'kəlist] *n* cantante *m/f* (*in un gruppo*).
vocation [vōkā'shən] *n* vocazione *f*.
vocational [vōkā'shənəl] *a* professionale; ~ **guidance** orientamento professionale; ~ **training** formazione *f* professionale.
vociferous [vōsif'ûrəs] *a* rumoroso(a).
vodka [vâd'kə] *n* vodka *f inv*.
vogue [vōg] *n* moda; (*popularity*) popolarità, voga; **to be in** ~, **be the** ~ essere di moda.
voice [vois] *n* voce *f* ♦ *vt* (*opinion*) esprimere; **in a loud/soft** ~ a voce alta/bassa; **to give** ~ **to** esprimere.
void [void] *n* vuoto ♦ *a*: ~ **of** privo(a) di.
voile [voil] *n* voile *m*.
vol. *abbr* (= *volume*) vol.
volatile [vâl'ətəl] *a* volatile; (*fig*) volubile.
volcanic [vâlkan'ik] *a* vulcanico(a).
volcano, ~**es** [vâlkā'nō] *n* vulcano.
volition [vōlish'ən] *n*: **of one's own** ~ di propria volontà.
volley [vâl'ē] *n* (*of gunfire*) salva; (*of stones etc*) raffica, gragnola; (*TENNIS etc*) volata.
volleyball [vâl'ēbôl] *n* pallavolo *f*.
volt [vōlt] *n* volt *m inv*.
voltage [vōl'tij] *n* tensione *f*, voltaggio; **high/low** ~ alta/bassa tensione.
voluble [vâl'yəbəl] *a* loquace, ciarliero(a).
volume [vâl'yōōm] *n* volume *m*; (*of tank*) capacità *f inv*; ~ **one/two** (*of book*) volume primo/secondo; **his expression spoke** ~**s** la sua espressione lasciava capire tutto.
volume control *n* (*RADIO, TV*) regolatore *m* or manopola del volume.
volume discount *n* (*COMM*) vantaggio sul volume di vendita.
voluminous [vəlōō'minəs] *a* voluminoso(a).

(*notes etc*) abbondante.
voluntarily [vâləntär'ilē] *ad* volontariamente; gratuitamente.
voluntary [vâl'əntärē] *a* volontario(a); (*unpaid*) gratuito(a), non retribuito(a).
voluntary liquidation *n* (*COMM*) liquidazione *f* volontaria.
volunteer [vâləntēr'] *n* volontario/a ♦ *vi* (*MIL*) arruolarsi volontario; **to** ~ **to do** offrire (volontariamente) di fare.
voluptuous [vəlup'chōōəs] *a* voluttuoso(a).
vomit [vâm'it] *n* vomito ♦ *vt*, *vi* vomitare.
vote [vōt] *n* voto, suffragio; (*cast*) voto; (*franchise*) diritto di voto ♦ *vi* votare ♦ *vt* (*gen*) votare; (*sum of money etc*) votare a favore di; **to** ~ **to do sth** votare a favore di fare qc; **he was** ~**d secretary** è stato eletto segretario; **to put sth to the** ~, **to take a** ~ **on sth** mettere qc ai voti; ~ **for/against** voto a favore/contrario; **to pass a** ~ **of confidence/no confidence** dare il voto di fiducia/sfiducia; ~ **of thanks** discorso di ringraziamento.
voter [vō'tûr] *n* elettore/trice.
voting [vō'ting] *n* scrutinio.
voting right *n* diritto di voto.
vouch [vouch]: **to** ~ **for** *vt fus* farsi garante di.
voucher [vou'chûr] *n* (*for meal, gasoline*) buono; (*receipt*) ricevuta; **travel** ~ voucher *m inv*, tagliando.
vow [vou] *n* voto, promessa solenne ♦ *vi* giurare; **to take** *or* **make a** ~ **to do sth** fare voto di fare qc.
vowel [vou'əl] *n* vocale *f*.
voyage [voi'ij] *n* viaggio per mare, traversata.
VP *n abbr* (= *vice-president*) V.P.
vs *abbr* (= *versus*) contro.
VSO *n abbr* (*Brit:* = *Voluntary Service Overseas*) servizio volontario in paesi sottosviluppati.
VT *abbr* (*US MAIL*) = *Vermont*.
VTR *n abbr* (= *video tape recorder*) VTR *m inv*.
vulgar [vul'gûr] *a* volgare.
vulgarity [vulgar'itē] *n* volgarità.
vulnerability [vulnûrəbil'ətē] *n* vulnerabilità.
vulnerable [vul'nûrəbəl] *a* vulnerabile.
vulture [vul'chûr] *n* avvoltoio.

W

W, w [dub'əlyōō] *n* (*letter*) W, w *m or f inv*; **W for William** ≈ W come Washington.

W *abbr* (= *west*) O; (*ELEC*: = *watt*) w.
WA *abbr* (*US MAIL*) = *Washington*.
wad [wâd] *n* (*of absorbent cotton, paper*) tampone *m*; (*of banknotes etc*) fascio.
wadding [wâd'ing] *n* imbottitura.
waddle [wâd'əl] *vi* camminare come una papera.
wade [wād] *vi*: **to ~ through** camminare a stento in ♦ *vt* guadare.
wading pool [wād'ing pōōl] *n* (*US*) piscina per bambini.
wafer [wā'fûr] *n* (*CULIN*) cialda; (*REL*) ostia; (*COMPUT*) wafer *m inv*.
wafer-thin [wā'fûrthin'] *a* molto sottile.
waffle [wâf'əl] *n* (*CULIN*) cialda; (*col*) ciance *fpl*; riempitivo ♦ *vi* cianciare; parlare a vuoto.
waffle iron *n* stampo per cialde.
waft [waft] *vt* portare ♦ *vi* diffondersi.
wag [wag] *vt* agitare, muovere ♦ *vi* agitarsi; **the dog ~ged its tail** il cane scodinzolò.
wage [wāj] *n* (*also*: **~s**) salario, paga ♦ *vt*: **to ~ war** fare la guerra; **a day's ~s** un giorno di paga.
wage claim *n* rivendicazione *f* salariale.
wage differential *n* differenza di salario.
wage earner *n* salariato/a.
wage freeze *n* blocco dei salari.
wage packet *n* (*Brit*) busta *f* paga *inv*.
wager [wā'jûr] *n* scommessa.
waggle [wag'əl] *vt* dimenare, agitare ♦ *vi* dimenarsi, agitarsi.
wagon, (*Brit*) waggon [wag'ân] *n* (*horse-drawn*) carro; (*truck*) furgone *m*; (*Brit RAIL*) vagone *m* (merci).
wail [wāl] *n* gemito; (*of siren*) urlo ♦ *vi* gemere; urlare.
waist [wāst] *n* vita, cintola.
waistcoat [wāst'kōt] *n* (*Brit*) panciotto, gilè *m inv*.
waistline [wāst'līn] *n* (giro di) vita.
wait [wāt] *n* attesa ♦ *vi* aspettare, attendere; **to ~ for** aspettare; **to keep sb ~ing** far aspettare qn; **~ a moment!** (aspetti) un momento!; **"repairs while you ~"** "riparazioni lampo"; **I can't ~ to ...** (*fig*) non vedo l'ora di ...; **to lie in ~ for** stare in agguato a.
wait behind *vi* rimanere (ad aspettare).
wait on *vt fus* servire.
wait up *vi* restare alzato(a) (ad aspettare); **don't ~ up for me** non rimanere alzato per me.
waiter [wā'tûr] *n* cameriere *m*.
waiting list [wāt'ing list] *n* lista d'attesa.
waiting room [wāt'ing rōōm] *n* sala d'aspetto *or* d'attesa.
waitress [wā'tris] *n* cameriera.
waive [wāv] *vt* rinunciare a, abbandonare.
waiver [wā'vûr] *n* rinuncia.
wake [wāk] *vb* (*pt* **woke**, **~d**, *pp* **woken**, **~d** [wōk, wō'kən]) *vt* (*also*: **~ up**) svegliare ♦ *vi* (*also*: **~ up**) svegliarsi ♦ *n* (*for dead person*) veglia funebre; (*NAUT*) scia; **to ~ up to sth** (*fig*) rendersi conto di qc; **in the ~ of** sulla scia di; **to follow in sb's ~** (*fig*) seguire le tracce di qn.
waken [wā'kən] *vt, vi* = **wake**.
Wales [wālz] *n* Galles *m*.
walk [wôk] *n* passeggiata; (*short*) giretto; (*gait*) passo, andatura; (*path*) sentiero; (*in park etc*) sentiero, vialetto ♦ *vi* camminare; (*for pleasure, exercise*) passeggiare ♦ *vt* (*distance*) fare *or* percorrere a piedi; (*dog*) accompagnare, portare a passeggiare; **10 minutes' ~ from** 10 minuti di cammino *or* a piedi da; **to go for a ~** andare a fare quattro passi; andare a fare una passeggiata; **from all ~s of life** di tutte le condizioni sociali; **to ~ in one's sleep** essere sonnambulo(a); **I'll ~ you home** ti accompagno a casa.
walk out *vi* (*go out*) uscire; (*as protest*) uscire (in segno di protesta); (*strike*) scendere in sciopero; **to ~ out on sb** piantare in asso qn.
walker [wôk'ûr] *n* (*person*) camminatore/trice.
walkie-talkie [wô'kētō'kē] *n* walkie-talkie *m inv*.
walking [wô'king] *n* camminare *m*; **it's within ~ distance** ci si arriva a piedi.
walking shoes *npl* scarpe *fpl* da passeggio.
walking stick *n* bastone *m* da passeggio.
walk-on [wôk'ân] *a* (*THEATER*: *part*) da comparsa.
walkout [wôk'out] *n* (*of workers*) sciopero senza preavviso *or* a sorpresa.
walkover [wôk'ōvûr] *n* (*col*) vittoria facile, gioco da ragazzi.
walkway [wôk'wā] *n* passaggio pedonale.
wall [wôl] *n* muro; (*internal, of tunnel, cave*) parete *f*; **to go to the ~** (*fig*: *firm etc*) fallire.
wall in *vt* (*garden etc*) circondare con un muro.
wall cupboard *n* pensile *m*.
walled [wôld] *a* (*city*) fortificato(a).
wallet [wâl'it] *n* portafoglio.
wallflower [wôl'flouûr] *n* violacciocca; **to be a ~** (*fig*) fare da tappezzeria.
wall hanging *n* tappezzeria.
wallop [wâl'əp] *vt* (*col*) pestare.
wallow [wâl'ō] *vi* sguazzare, rotolarsi; **to ~ in one's grief** crogiolarsi nel proprio dolore.
wallpaper [wôl'pāpûr] *n* carta da parati.
wall-to-wall [wôl'təwôl'] *a*: **~ carpeting** moquette *f*.
walnut [wôl'nut] *n* noce *f*; (*tree*) noce *m*.
walrus, *pl* **~** *or* **~es** [wôl'rəs] *n* tricheco.
waltz [wôlts] *n* valzer *m inv* ♦ *vi* ballare il valzer.
wan [wân] *a* pallido(a), smorto(a); triste.
wand [wând] *n* (*also*: **magic ~**) bacchetta (magica).
wander [wân'dûr] *vi* (*person*) girare senza

meta, girovagare; (*thoughts*) vagare; (*river*) serpeggiare.

wanderer |wăn'dûrûr| *n* vagabondo/a.

wandering |wăn'dûring| *a* (*tribe*) nomade; (*minstrel, actor*) girovago(a); (*path, river*) tortuoso(a); (*glance, mind*) distratto(a).

wane |wān| *vi* (*moon*) calare; (*reputation*) declinare.

wangle |wang'gəl| (*col*) *vt* procurare (con l'astuzia) ♦ *n* astuzia.

want |wŏnt| *vt* volere; (*need*) aver bisogno di; (*lack*) mancare di ♦ *n* (*poverty*) miseria, povertà; ~**s** *npl* (*needs*) bisogni *mpl*; **for** ~ **of** per mancanza di; **to** ~ **to do** volere fare; **to** ~ **sb to do** volere che qn faccia; **you're** ~**ed on the phone** la vogliono al telefono; "**cook** ~**ed**" "cercasi cuoco".

want ads *npl* (*US*) piccoli annunci *mpl*.

wanting |wŏn'ting| *a*: **to be** ~ (**in**) mancare (di); **to be found** ~ non risultare all'altezza.

wanton |wăn'tən| *a* sfrenato(a); senza motivo.

war |wŏr| *n* guerra; **to go to** ~ entrare in guerra.

warble |wŏr'bəl| *n* (*of bird*) trillo ♦ *vi* trillare.

war cry *n* grido di guerra.

ward |wŏrd| *n* (*in hospital: room*) corsia; (*LAW: child*) pupillo/a.

ward off *vt* parare, schivare.

warden |wŏr'dən| *n* (*US: of prison*) direttore/trice; (*of institution*) direttore/trice; (*of park, game reserve*) guardiano/a; (*Brit: also:* **traffic** ~) addetto/a al controllo del traffico e del parcheggio.

warder |wŏr'dûr| *n* (*Brit*) guardia carceraria.

wardrobe |wŏrd'rōb| *n* (*closet*) guardaroba *m inv*, armadio; (*clothes*) guardaroba; (*THEATER*) costumi *mpl*.

warehouse |wär'hous| *n* magazzino.

wares |wärz| *npl* merci *fpl*.

warfare |wŏr'fär| *n* guerra.

war game *n* war game *m inv*.

warhead |wŏr'hed| *n* (*MIL*) testata, ogiva.

warily |wär'ilē| *ad* cautamente, con prudenza.

warlike |wŏr'līk| *a* guerriero(a).

warm |wŏrm| *a* caldo(a); (*welcome, applause*) caloroso(a); (*person, greeting*) cordiale; (*heart*) d'oro; (*supporter*) convinto(a); **it's** ~ fa caldo; **I'm** ~ ho caldo; **to keep sth** ~ tenere qc al caldo; **with my** ~**est thanks** con i miei più sentiti ringraziamenti.

warm up *vi* scaldarsi, riscaldarsi; (*athlete, discussion*) riscaldarsi ♦ *vt* scaldare, riscaldare; (*engine*) far scaldare.

warm-blooded |wŏrm'blud'id| *a* a sangue caldo.

war memorial *n* monumento ai caduti.

warm-hearted |wŏrm'här'tid| *a* affettuoso(a).

warmly |wŏrm'lē| *ad* caldamente; calorosamente; vivamente.

warmonger |wŏr'munggûr| *n* guerrafondaio.

warmongering |wŏr'munggûring| *n* bellici-

smo.

warmth |wŏrmth| *n* calore *m*.

warm-up |wŏrm'up| *n* (*SPORT*) riscaldamento.

warn |wŏrn| *vt* avvertire, avvisare; **to** ~ **sb not to do sth** *or* **against doing sth** avvertire qn di non fare qc.

warning |wŏr'ning| *n* avvertimento; (*notice*) avviso; **without (any)** ~ senza preavviso; **gale** ~ avviso di burrasca.

warning light *n* spia luminosa.

warning triangle *n* (*AUT*) triangolo.

warp |wŏrp| *n* (*TEXTILES*) ordito ♦ *vi* deformarsi ♦ *vt* deformare; (*fig*) corrompere.

warpath |wŏr'path| *n*: **to be on the** ~ (*fig*) essere sul sentiero di guerra.

warped |wŏrpt| *a* (*wood*) curvo(a); (*fig: character, sense of humor etc*) contorto(a).

warrant |wŏr'ənt| *n* (*LAW: to arrest*) mandato di cattura; (: *to search*) mandato di perquisizione ♦ *vt* (*justify, merit*) giustificare.

warrant officer (WO) *n* sottufficiale *m*.

warranty |wŏr'əntē| *n* garanzia; **under** ~ (*COMM*) in garanzia.

warren |wŏr'ən| *n* (*of rabbits*) tana.

warring |wŏ'ring| *a* (*interests etc*) opposto(a), in lotta; (*nations*) in guerra.

warrior |wŏr'ēûr| *n* guerriero/a.

Warsaw |wŏr'sŏ| *n* Varsavia.

warship |wŏr'ship| *n* nave *f* da guerra.

wart |wŏrt| *n* verruca.

wartime |wŏr'tīm| *n*: **in** ~ in tempo di guerra.

wary |wär'ē| *a* prudente; **to be** ~ **about** *or* **of doing sth** andare cauto nel fare qc.

was |wuz| *pt of* **be**.

Wash. *abbr* (*US*) = **Washington**.

wash |wŏsh| *vt* lavare; (*sweep, carry: sea etc*) portare, trascinare ♦ *vi* lavarsi ♦ *n*: **to give sth a** ~ lavare qc, dare una lavata a qc; **to have a** ~ lavarsi; **he was** ~**ed overboard** fu trascinato in mare (dalle onde).

wash away *vt* (*stain*) togliere lavando; (*subj: river etc*) trascinare via.

wash down *vt* lavare.

wash off *vi* andare via con il lavaggio.

wash up *vi* (*US: have a wash*) lavarsi; (*Brit: dishes*) lavare i piatti.

washable |wŏsh'əbəl| *a* lavabile.

washbasin |wŏsh'bāsin| *n* lavabo.

washcloth |wŏsh'klŏth| *n* (*US*) pezzuola (per lavarsi).

washer |wŏsh'ûr| *n* (*TECH*) rondella.

washing |wŏsh'ing| *n* (*Brit: linen etc*) bucato; **dirty** ~ biancheria da lavare.

washing line *n* (*Brit*) corda del bucato.

washing machine *n* lavatrice *f*.

washing powder *n* (*Brit*) detersivo (in polvere).

Washington |wŏsh'ingtən| *n* Washington *f*.

washing-up |wŏsh'ingup| *n* (*Brit: dishes*) piatti *mpl* sporchi; **to do the** ~ lavare i piatti, rigovernare.

washing-up liquid *n* (*Brit*) detersivo liquido (per stoviglie).

wash-out |wàsh'out| *n* (*col*) disastro.

washroom |wàsh'rōōm| *n* gabinetto.

wasn't |wuz'ənt| = **was not**.

Wasp, WASP *n* *abbr* (*US*: = *White Anglo-Saxon Protestant*) W.A.S.P. *m* (*protestante bianco anglosassone*).

wasp |wåsp| *n* vespa.

waspish |wås'pish| *a* litigioso(a).

wastage |wās'tij| *n* spreco; (*in manufacturing*) scarti *mpl*.

waste |wāst| *n* spreco; (*of time*) perdita; (*garbage*) rifiuti *mpl* ♦ *a* (*material*) di scarto; (*food*) avanzato(a); (*energy, heat*) sprecato(a); (*land, ground: in city*) abbandonato(a); (: *in country*) incolto(a) ♦ *vt* sprecare; (*time, opportunity*) perdere; ~s *npl* distesa desolata; **it's a** ~ **of money** sono soldi sprecati; **to go to** ~ andare sprecato; **to lay** ~ devastare.

waste away *vi* deperire.

wastebin |wāst'bin| *n* (*Brit*) bidone *m* or secchio della spazzatura.

wasteful |wāst'fəl| *a* sprecone(a); (*process*) dispendioso(a).

waste ground *n* (*Brit*) terreno incolto *or* abbandonato.

wasteland |wāst'land| *n* terra desolata.

wastepaper basket |wāst'pāpûr bas'kit| *n* cestino per la carta straccia.

waste products *n* (*INDUSTRY*) materiali *mpl* di scarto.

watch |wàch| *n* (*wrist*~) orologio; (*act of watching*) sorveglianza; (*guard: MIL. NAUT*) guardia; (*NAUT: spell of duty*) quarto ♦ *vt* (*look at*) osservare; (: *game, program*) guardare; (*spy on, guard*) sorvegliare, tenere d'occhio; (*be careful of*) fare attenzione a ♦ *vi* osservare; (*keep guard*) fare *or* montare la guardia; **to keep a close** ~ **on sb/sth** tener bene d'occhio qn/qc; ~ **how you drive/what you're doing** attento a come guidi/quel che fai.

watch out *vi* fare attenzione.

watchband |wàch'band| *n* (*US*) cinturino da orologio.

watchdog |wàch'dóg| *n* cane *m* da guardia; (*fig*) sorvegliante *m/f*.

watchful |wàch'fəl| *a* attento(a), vigile.

watchmaker |wàch'mākûr| *n* orologiaio/a.

watchman |wàch'mən| *n* guardiano; (*also*: **night** ~) guardiano notturno.

watch stem *n* (*US*) corona di carica.

watchstrap |wàch'strap| *n* cinturino da orologio.

watchword |wàch'wûrd| *n* parola d'ordine.

water |wô'tûr| *n* acqua ♦ *vt* (*plant*) annaffiare ♦ *vi* (*eyes*) piangere; **in British** ~s nelle acque territoriali britanniche; **I'd like a drink of** ~ vorrei un bicchier d'acqua; **to pass** ~

orinare; **to make sb's mouth** ~ far venire l'acquolina in bocca a qn.

water down *vt* (*milk*) diluire; (*fig: story*) edulcorare.

water closet *n* (*Brit*) W.C. *m inv*, gabinetto.

watercolor, (*Brit*) **watercolour** |wô'tûrkulûr| *n* (*picture*) acquerello; ~s *npl* colori *mpl* per acquerelli.

water-cooled |wô'tûrkōōld| *a* raffreddato(a) ad acqua.

watercress |wô'tûrkrɛs| *n* crescione *m*.

waterfall |wô'tûrfôl| *n* cascata.

waterfront |wô'tûrfrunt| *n* (*seafront*) lungomare *m*; (*at docks*) banchina.

water heater *n* scaldabagno.

water hole *n* pozza d'acqua.

watering can |wô'tûring kan| *n* annaffiatoio.

water level *n* livello dell'acqua; (*of flood*) livello delle acque.

water lily *n* ninfea.

waterline |wô'tûrlīn| *n* (*NAUT*) linea di galleggiamento.

waterlogged |wô'tûrlôgd| *a* saturo(a) d'acqua; imbevuto(a) d'acqua; (*football pitch etc*) allagato(a).

water main *n* conduttura dell'acqua.

watermark |wô'tûrmârk| *n* (*on paper*) filigrana.

watermelon |wô'tûrmɛlən| *n* anguria, cocomero.

water polo *n* pallanuoto *f*.

waterproof |wô'tûrprōōf| *a* impermeabile.

water-repellent |wô'tûripɛl'ənt| *a* idrorepellente.

watershed |wôt'ûrshɛd| *n* (*GEO. fig*) spartiacque *m*.

water-skiing |wô'tûrskēing| *n* sci *m* acquatico.

water softener *n* addolcitore *m*; (*substance*) anti-calcare *m*.

water tank *n* serbatoio d'acqua.

watertight |wô'tûrtīt| *a* stagno(a).

water vapor *n* vapore *m* acqueo.

waterway |wô'tûrwā| *n* corso d'acqua navigabile.

waterworks |wô'tûrwûrks| *npl* impianto idrico.

watery |wô'tûrē| *a* (*color*) slavato(a); (*coffee*) acquoso(a).

WATS *n* *abbr* (*US*: = *Wide Area Telecommunications Service*) *servizio di abbonamento telefonico a tariffa mensile fissa*.

watt |wàt| *n* watt *m inv*.

wattage |wàt'ij| *n* wattaggio.

wattle |wàt'əl| *n* graticcio.

wave |wāv| *n* onda; (*of hand*) gesto, segno; (*in hair*) ondulazione *f*; (*fig: of enthusiasm, strikes etc*) ondata ♦ *vi* fare un cenno con la mano; (*flag*) sventolare ♦ *vt* (*handkerchief*) sventolare; (*stick*) brandire; (*hair*) ondulare; **short/medium/long** ~ (*RADIO*) onde corte/medie/lunghe; **the new** ~ (*CINEMA. MUS*) la new wave; **to ~ sb goodbye, to ~ goodbye to sb** fare un cenno d'addio a qn; **he ~d us over to his table** ci invitò con un cenno al suo tavolo.

wave aside, wave away vt (person): **to ~ sb aside** fare cenno a qn di spostarsi; (fig: suggestion, objection) respingere, rifiutare; (: doubts) scacciare.

waveband [wāv'band] n gamma di lunghezze d'onda.

wavelength [wāv'lɛngkth] n lunghezza d'onda.

waver [wā'vûr] vi vacillare; (voice) tremolare.

wavy [wā'vē] a ondulato(a); ondeggiante.

wax [waks] n cera ♦ vt dare la cera a; (car) lucidare ♦ vi (moon) crescere.

wax paper n (US) carta oleata.

waxworks [waks'wûrks] npl cere fpl; museo delle cere.

way [wā] n via, strada; (path, access) passaggio; (distance) distanza; (direction) parte f, direzione f; (manner) modo, stile m; (habit) abitudine f; (condition) condizione f; **which ~?** — **this** ~ da che parte or in quale direzione? — da questa parte or per di qua; **to crawl one's ~ to ...** raggiungere ... strisciando; **he lied his ~ out of it** se l'è cavata mentendo; **to lose one's ~** perdere la strada; **on the ~** (en route) per strada; (expected) in arrivo; **you pass it on your ~ home** ci passi davanti andando a casa; **to be on one's ~** essere in cammino or sulla strada; **to be in the ~** bloccare il passaggio; (fig) essere tra i piedi or d'impiccio; **to keep out of sb's ~** evitare qn; **it's a long ~ away** è molto lontano da qui; **the village is rather out of the ~** il villaggio è abbastanza fuori mano; **to go out of one's ~ to do** (fig) mettercela tutta or fare di tutto per fare; **to be under ~** (work, project) essere in corso; **to make ~ (for sb/sth)** far strada (a qn/qc); (fig) lasciare il posto or far largo (a qn/qc); **to get one's own ~** fare come si vuole; **put it the right ~ up** (Brit) mettilo in piedi dalla parte giusta; **to be the wrong ~ around** essere al contrario; **he's in a bad ~** è ridotto male; **in a ~** in un certo senso; **in some ~s** sotto certi aspetti; **in the ~ of** come; **by ~ of** (through) attraverso; (as a sort of) come; **~ in** entrata, ingresso; **~ out** uscita; **the ~ back** la via del ritorno; **this ~ and that** di qua e di là; "**give ~**" (Brit AUT) "dare la precedenza"; **no ~!** (col) assolutamente no!

waybill [wā'bil] n (COMM) bolla di accompagnamento.

waylay [wālā'] vt irg tendere un agguato a; attendere al passaggio; (fig): **I got waylaid** ho avuto un contrattempo.

wayside [wā'sīd] n bordo della strada; **to fall by the ~** (fig) perdersi lungo la strada.

way station n (US RAIL) stazione f secondaria; (fig) tappa.

wayward [wā'wûrd] a capriccioso(a); testardo(a).

WC n abbr (Brit: = water closet) W.C. m inv, gabinetto.

WCC n abbr (= World Council of Churches) Consiglio Ecumenico delle Chiese.

we [wē] pl pronoun noi; **here ~ are** eccoci.

weak [wēk] a debole; (health) precario(a); (beam etc) fragile; (tea, coffee) leggero(a); **to grow ~(er)** indebolirsi.

weaken [wēlth] vi indebolirsi ♦ vt indebolire.

weak-kneed [wēk'nēd] a (fig) debole, codardo(a).

weakling [wēk'ling] n smidollato/a; debole m/f.

weakly [wēk'lē] a deboluccio(a), gracile ♦ ad debolmente.

weakness [wēk'nis] n debolezza; (fault) punto debole, difetto.

wealth [wɛlth] n (money, resources) ricchezza, richezze fpl; (of details) abbondanza, profusione f.

wealth tax n imposta sul patrimonio.

wealthy [wɛl'thē] a ricco(a).

wean [wēn] vt svezzare.

weapon [wɛp'ən] n arma.

wear [wär] n (use) uso; (deterioration through use) logorio, usura; (clothing): **sports/baby ~** abbigliamento sportivo/per neonati ♦ vb (pt **wore**, pp **worn** [wôr, wôrn]) vt (clothes) portare; mettersi; (look, smile, beard etc) avere; (damage: through use) consumare ♦ vi (last) durare; (rub etc through) consumarsi; **~ and tear** usura, consumo; **evening ~** abiti mpl or tenuta da sera; **to ~ a hole in sth** bucare qc a furia di usarlo.

wear away vt consumare; erodere ♦ vi consumarsi; essere eroso(a).

wear down vt consumare; (strength) esaurire.

wear off vi sparire lentamente.

wear on vi passare.

wear out vt consumare; (person, strength) esaurire.

wearable [wär'əbəl] a indossabile.

wearily [wē'rilē] ad stancamente.

weariness [wē'rēnis] n stanchezza.

wearisome [wē'rēsəm] a (tiring) estenuante; (boring) noioso(a).

weary [wēr'ē] a stanco(a); (tiring) faticoso(a) ♦ vt stancare ♦ vi: **to ~ of** stancarsi di.

weasel [wē'zəl] n (ZOOL) donnola.

weather [wɛth'ûr] n tempo ♦ vt (wood) stagionare; (storm, crisis) superare; **what's the ~ like?** che tempo fa?; **under the ~** (fig: ill) poco bene.

weather-beaten [wɛth'ûrbētən] a (person) segnato(a) dalle intemperie; (building) logorato(a) dalle intemperie.

weather cock n banderuola.

weather forecast n previsioni fpl del tempo,

bollettino meteorologico.
weatherman [weᵗʰ'ûrman] *n* meteorologo.
weatherproof [weᵗʰ'ûrprōōf] *a* (*garment*)
impermeabile.
weather report *n* bollettino meteorologico.
weather strip(ping) [weᵗʰ'ûr strip('ing)] *n*
strisciolina isolante (per finestre *etc*).
weather vane [weᵗʰ'ûr vān'] *n* = **weather
cock.**
weave, *pt* **wove,** *pp* **woven** [wēv, wōv, wō'vən]
vt (*cloth*) tessere; (*basket*) intrecciare ♦ *vi*
(*fig: pt, pp* ~**d**: *move in and out*) zigzagare.
weaver [wē'vûr] *n* tessitore/trice.
weaving [wē'ving] *n* tessitura.
web [web] *n* (*of spider*) ragnatela; (*on foot*)
palma; (*fabric, also fig*) tessuto.
webbed [webd] *a* (*foot*) palmato(a).
webbing [web'ing] *n* (*on chair*) cinghie *fpl*.
wed [wed] *vt* (*pt, pp* **wedded**) sposare ♦ *n*:
the newly-~s gli sposi novelli.
Wed. *abbr* (= *Wednesday*) mer.
we'd [wēd] = **we had; we would.**
wedded [wed'id] *pt, pp of* **wed.**
wedding [wed'ing] *n* matrimonio; **silver/
golden** ~ nozze *fpl* d'argento/d'oro.
wedding anniversary *n* anniversario di matrimonio.
wedding day *n* giorno delle nozze *or* del matrimonio.
wedding dress *n* abito nuziale.
wedding present *n* regalo di nozze.
wedding ring *n* fede *f*.
wedge [wej] *n* (*of wood etc*) cuneo; (*under
door etc*) zeppa; (*of cake*) spicchio, fetta ♦ *vt*
mettere una zeppa sotto (*or* in); **to ~ a door
open** tenere aperta una porta con un fermo.
wedge-heeled shoes [wej'hēld shōōz] *npl*
scarpe *fpl* con tacco a zeppa.
wedlock [wed'lâk] *n* vincolo matrimoniale.
Wednesday [wenz'dā] *n* mercoledì *m inv*; *for
phrases see also* **Tuesday.**
wee [wē] *a* (*Scottish*) piccolo(a).
weed [wēd] *n* erbaccia ♦ *vt* diserbare.
weed killer *n* diserbante *m*.
weedy [wē'dē] *a* (*man*) allampanato.
week [wēk] *n* settimana; **once/twice a** ~ una
volta/due volte alla settimana; **in 2 ~s' time**
fra 2 settimane, fra 15 giorni; **Tuesday ~, a**
~ **from Tuesday** martedì a otto.
weekday [wēk'dā] *n* giorno feriale; (*COMM*)
giornata lavorativa; **on ~s** durante la settimana.
weekend [wēk'end] *n* fine settimana *m or f
inv*, weekend *m inv*.
weekend case *n* borsa da viaggio.
weekly [wēk'lē] *ad* ogni settimana, settima-
nalmente ♦ *a, n* settimanale (*m*).
weep, *pt, pp* **wept** [wēp, wept] *vi* (*person*)
piangere; (*MED: wound etc*) essudare.
weeping willow [wē'ping wil'ō] *n* salice *m*
piangente.

weft [weft] *n* (*TEXTILES*) trama.
weigh [wā] *vt, vi* pesare; **to ~ anchor** salpare
or levare l'ancora; **to ~ the pros and cons**
valutare i pro e i contro.
weigh down *vt* (*branch*) piegare; (*fig:
with worry*) opprimere, caricare.
weigh out *vt* (*goods*) pesare.
weigh up *vt* valutare.
weighing machine [wā'ing məshēn'] *n* pesa.
weight [wāt] *n* peso; **sold by** ~ venduto(a) a
peso; ~**s and measures** pesi e misure; **to
put on/lose** ~ ingrassare/dimagrire.
weighting [wā'ting] *n*: ~ **allowance** indennità
f inv speciale (*per carovita etc*).
weightlessness [wāt'lisnis] *n* mancanza di
peso.
weightlifter [wāt'liftûr] *n* pesista *m*.
weighty [wā'tē] *a* pesante; (*fig*) importante,
grave.
weir [wēr] *n* diga.
weird [wērd] *a* strano(a), bizzarro(a); (*eerie*)
soprannaturale.
welcome [wel'kəm] *a* benvenuto(a) ♦ *n* accoglienza, benvenuto ♦ *vt* accogliere
cordialmente; (*also:* **bid** ~) dare il benvenuto a; (*be glad of*) rallegrarsi di; **to be** ~
essere il(la) benvenuto(a); **to make sb** ~
accogliere bene qn; **you're** ~ (*after thanks*)
prego; **you're** ~ **to try** provi pure.
welcoming [wel'kəming] *a* accogliente.
weld [weld] *n* saldatura ♦ *vt* saldare.
welder [weld'ûr] *n* (*person*) saldatore *m*.
welding [weld'ing] *n* saldatura (autogena).
welfare [wel'fär] *n* benessere *m*; **to be on** ~
(*US*) vivere del sussidio.
welfare state *n* stato assistenziale.
welfare work *n* assistenza sociale.
well [wel] *n* pozzo ♦ *ad* bene ♦ *a*: **to be** ~
(*person*) stare bene ♦ *excl* allora!; ma!;
ebbene!; ~ **done!** bravo(a)!; **get** ~ **soon!**
guarisci presto!; **to do** ~ **in sth** riuscire in
qc; **to be doing** ~ stare bene; **to think** ~ **of**
sb avere una buona opinione di qn; **I don't
feel** ~ non mi sento bene; **as** ~ (*in addition*)
anche; **X as** ~ **as Y** sia X che Y; **he did as
~ as he could** ha fatto come meglio poteva;
you might as ~ **tell me** potresti anche
dirmelo; **it would be as** ~ **to ask** sarebbe
bene chiedere; ~**, as I was saying** ... dunque,
come stavo dicendo ....
well up *vi* (*tears, emotions*) sgorgare.
we'll [wēl] = **we will, we shall.**
well-behaved [welbihāvd'] *a* ubbidiente.
well-being [wel'bē'ing] *n* benessere *m*.
well-bred [wel'bred'] *a* educato(a), beneduca-
to(a).
well-built [wel'bilt'] *a* (*person*) ben fatto(a).
well-chosen [wel'chō'zən] *a* (*remarks, words*)
ben scelto(a), appropriato(a).
well-developed [wel'divel'əpt] *a* sviluppa-
to(a).

well-disposed [wel'dispōzd'] *a*: ~ **to(wards)** bendisposto(a) verso.

well-dressed [wel'drest'] *a* ben vestito(a), vestito(a) bene.

well-earned [wel'ûrnd'] *a* (*rest*) meritato(a).

well-groomed [wel'grōōmd] *a* curato(a), azzimato(a).

well-heeled [wel'hēld'] *a* (*col*: *wealthy*) agiato(a), facoltoso(a).

well-informed [wel'infôrmd'] *a* ben informato(a).

Wellington [wel'ingtən] *n* Wellington *f*.

wellingtons [wel'ingtənz] *npl* (*also*: **wellington boots**) stivali *mpl* di gomma.

well-kept [wel'kept'] *a* (*house*, *grounds*, *secret*) ben tenuto(a); (*hair*, *hands*) ben curato(a).

well-known [wel'nōn'] *a* noto(a), famoso(a).

well-mannered [wel'man'ûrd] *a* ben educato(a).

well-meaning [wel'mē'ning] *a* ben intenzionato(a).

well-nigh [wel'nī'] *ad*: ~ **impossible** quasi impossibile.

well-off [wel'ôf'] *a* benestante, danaroso(a).

well-read [wel'red'] *a* colto(a).

well-spoken [wel'spō'kən] *a* che parla bene.

well-stocked [wel'ståkt'] *a* (*shop*, *larder*) ben fornito(a).

well-timed [wel'tīmd'] *a* opportuno(a).

well-to-do [wel'tədōō'] *a* abbiente, benestante.

well-wisher [wel'wishûr] *n* ammiratore/trice; **letters from** ~**s** lettere *fpl* di incoraggiamento.

Welsh [welsh] *a* gallese ♦ *n* (*LING*) gallese *m*; **the** ~ *npl* i gallesi.

Welshman, Welshwoman [welsh'mən, welsh'wōōmən] *n* gallese *m/f*.

Welsh rarebit [welsh rär'bit] *n* crostino al formaggio.

welter [wel'tûr] *n* massa, mucchio.

went [went] *pt of* **go**.

wept [wept] *pt*, *pp of* **weep**.

were [wûr] *pt of* **be**.

we're [wēr] = **we are**.

weren't [wûr'ənt] = **were not**.

werewolf, *pl* **-wolves** [wär'wōōlf, -wōōlvz] *n* licantropo, lupo mannaro (*col*).

west [west] *n* ovest *m*, occidente *m*, ponente *m* ♦ *a* (a) ovest *inv*, occidentale ♦ *ad* verso ovest; **the W**~ l'Occidente.

westbound [west'bound] *a* (*traffic*) diretto(a) a ovest; (*lane*) ovest *inv*.

West Country *n*: **the** ~ il sud-ovest dell'Inghilterra.

westerly [wes'tûrlē] *a* (*wind*) occidentale, da ovest.

western [wes'tûrn] *a* occidentale, dell'ovest ♦ *n* (*CINEMA*) western *m inv*.

westernized [wes'tûrnīzd] *a* occidentalizzato(a).

West German *a*, *n* tedesco(a) occidentale.

West Germany *n* Germania Occidentale.

West Indian *a* delle Indie Occidentali ♦ *n* abitante *m/f* (*or* originario/a) delle Indie Occidentali.

West Indies *npl*: **the** ~ le Indie Occidentali.

westward(s) [westwûrd(z)] *ad* verso ovest.

wet [wet] *a* umido(a), bagnato(a); (*soaked*) fradicio(a); (*rainy*) piovoso(a) ♦ *vt*: **to** ~ **one's pants** *or* **o.s.** farsi la pipì addosso; **to get** ~ bagnarsi; "~ **paint**" "vernice fresca".

wet blanket *n* (*fig*) guastafeste *m/f inv*.

wetness [wet'nis] *n* umidità.

wet suit *n* tuta da sub.

we've [wēv] = **we have**.

whack [wak] *vt* picchiare, battere.

whale [wāl] *n* (*ZOOL*) balena.

whaler [wā'lûr] *n* (*ship*) baleniera.

wharf, *pl* **wharves** [wôrf, wôrvz] *n* banchina.

what [wut] *excl* cosa!, come! ♦ *a* quale ♦ *pronoun* (*interrogative*) che cosa, cosa, che; (*relative*) quello che, ciò che; ~ **are you doing?** che *or* (che) cosa fa?; ~**'s happening?** che *or* (che) cosa succede?; ~**'s in there?** cosa c'è lì dentro?; **for** ~ **reason?** per quale motivo?; **I saw** ~ **you did/was on the table** ho visto quello che ha fatto/quello che era sul tavolo; **I don't know** ~ **to do** non so cosa fare; ~ **a mess!** che disordine!; ~ **is his address?** qual'è il suo indirizzo?; ~ **will it cost?** quanto sarà *or* costerà?; ~ **is it called?** come si chiama?; ~ **I want is a cup of tea** ciò che voglio adesso è una tazza di tè; ~ **about doing ...?** cosa ne diresti di fare ...; ~ **about me?** e io?

whatever [wutev'ûr] *a*: ~ **book** qualunque *or* qualsiasi libro + *sub* ♦ *pronoun*: **do** ~ **is necessary/you want** faccia qualunque *or* qualsiasi cosa sia necessaria/lei voglia; ~ **happens** qualunque cosa accada; **no reason** ~ *or* **whatsoever** nessuna ragione affatto *or* al mondo; ~ **it costs** costi quello che costi.

whatsoever [wutsōev'ûr] = **whatever**.

wheat [wēt] *n* grano, frumento.

wheat germ *n* germe *m* di grano.

wheatmeal [wēt'mēl] *n* farina integrale di frumento.

wheedle [wēd'əl] *vt*: **to** ~ **sb into doing sth** convincere qn a fare qc (con lusinghe); **to** ~ **sth out of sb** ottenere qc da qn (con lusinghe).

wheel [wēl] *n* ruota; (*AUT*: *also*: **steering** ~) volante *m*; (*NAUT*) (ruota del) timone *m* ♦ *vt* spingere ♦ *vi* (*also*: *Brit*: ~ **round**) girare.

wheelbarrow [wēl'barō] *n* carriola.

wheelbase [wēl'bās] *n* interasse *m*.

wheelchair [wēl'chär] *n* sedia a rotelle.

wheel clamp *n* (*Brit AUT*) morsetto *m* bloccaruota *inv*.

wheeler-dealer [wē'lûrdē'lûr] *n* trafficone *m*, maneggione *m*.

wheeling [wē'ling] *n*: ~ **and dealing** maneggi *mpl*.

wheeze [wēz] *n* respiro affannoso ♦ *vi* ansimare.

when [wen] *ad* quando ♦ *cj* quando, nel momento in cui; (*whereas*) mentre; **on the day** ~ il giorno in cui.

whenever [wenev'ûr] *ad* quando mai ♦ *cj* quando; (*every time that*) ogni volta che; **I go** ~ **I can** ci vado ogni volta che posso.

where [wâr] *ad*, *cj* dove; **this is** ~ è qui che; ~ **are you from?** di dov'è?; ~ **possible** quando è possibile, se possibile.

whereabouts [wâr'əbouts] *ad* dove ♦ *n*: **sb's** ~ luogo dove qn si trova.

whereas [wâraz'] *cj* mentre.

whereby [wârbī'] *ad* (*formal*) per cui.

whereupon [wârəpán'] *ad* al che.

wherever [wârev'ûr] *ad* dove mai ♦ *cj* dovunque + *sub*; **sit** ~ **you like** si sieda dove vuole.

wherewithal [wâr'withôl] *n*: **the** ~ **(to do sth)** i mezzi (per fare qc).

whet [wet] *vt* (*tool*) affilare; (*appetite etc*) stimolare.

whether [weth'ûr] *cj* se; **I don't know** ~ **to accept or not** non so se accettare o no; **it's doubtful** ~ è poco probabile che; ~ **you go or not** che lei vada o no.

whey [wā] *n* siero.

which [wich] *a* (*interrogative*) che, quale; ~ **one of you?** chi di voi?; **tell me** ~ **one you want** mi dica quale vuole ♦ *pronoun* (*interrogative*, *indirect*) quale; (*relative*: *subject*) che; (: *object*) che, *prep* + *cui*, il(la) quale; **I don't mind** ~ non mi importa quale; **the apple** ~ **you ate/~ is on the table** la mela che ha mangiato/che è sul tavolo; **the chair on** ~ **la sedia sulla quale** *or* su cui; **the book of** ~ il libro del quale *or* di cui; **he said he knew,** ~ **is true/I feared** disse che lo sapeva, il che è vero/ciò che temevo; **after** ~ dopo di che; **in** ~ **case** nel qual caso; **by** ~ **time** e a quel punto.

whichever [wichev'ûr] *a*: **take** ~ **book you prefer** prenda qualsiasi libro che preferisce; ~ **book you take** qualsiasi libro prenda; ~ **way you** ... in qualunque modo lei ... + *sub*.

whiff [wif] *n* odore *m*; **to catch a** ~ **of sth** sentire l'odore di qc.

while [wīl] *n* momento ♦ *cj* mentre; (*as long as*) finché; (*although*) sebbene + *sub*; **for a** ~ per un po'; **in a** ~ tra poco; **all the** ~ tutto il tempo; **we'll make it worth your** ~ faremo in modo che le valga la pena.

while away *vt* (*time*) far passare.

whilst [wīlst] *cj* = **while**.

whim [wim] *n* capriccio.

whimper [wim'pûr] *n* piagnucolio ♦ *vi* piagnucolare.

whimsical [wim'zikəl] *a* (*person*) capriccio-

so(a); (*look*) strano(a).

whine [wīn] *n* gemito ♦ *vi* gemere; uggiolare; piagnucolare.

whip [wip] *n* frusta; (*for riding*) frustino; (*POL*: *person*) capogruppo (*che sovrintende alla disciplina dei colleghi di partito*) ♦ *vt* frustare; (*CULIN*: *cream etc*) sbattere; (*snatch*) sollevare (*or* estrarre) bruscamente.

whip up *vt* (*cream*) montare, sbattere; (*col*: *meal*) improvvisare; (: *stir up*: *support*, *feeling*) suscitare, stimolare.

whiplash [wip'lash] *n* (*MED*: *also*: ~ **injury**) colpo di frusta.

whipped cream [wipt krēm] *n* panna montata.

whipping boy [wip'ing boi] *n* (*fig*) capro espiatorio.

whip-round [wip'round] *n* (*Brit*) colletta.

whirl [wûrl] *n* turbine *m* ♦ *vt* (*far*) girare rapidamente; (*far*) turbinare ♦ *vi* turbinare; (*dancers*) volteggiare; (*leaves*, *dust*) sollevarsi in un vortice.

whirlpool [wûrl'pōōl] *n* mulinello.

whirlwind [wûrl'wind] *n* turbine *m*.

whirr [wûr] *vi* ronzare.

whisk [wisk] *n* (*CULIN*) frusta; frullino ♦ *vt* sbattere, frullare; **to** ~ **sb away** *or* **off** portar via qn a tutta velocità.

whiskers [wis'kûrz] *npl* (*of animal*) baffi *mpl*; (*of man*) favoriti *mpl*.

whiskey (*US*, *Ireland*), **whisky** (*Brit*) [wis'kē] *n* whisky *m inv*.

whisper [wis'pûr] *n* bisbiglio, sussurro; (*rumor*) voce *f* ♦ *vt*, *vi* bisbigliare, sussurrare; **to** ~ **sth to sb** bisbigliare qc a qn.

whispering [wis'pûring] *n* bisbiglio.

whist [wist] *n* (*Brit*) whist *m*.

whistle [wis'əl] *n* (*sound*) fischio; (*object*) fischietto ♦ *vi* fischiare ♦ *vt* fischiare; **to** ~ **a tune** fischiettare un motivetto.

whistle-stop [wis'əlståp] *a*: ~ **tour** (*POL*, *fig*) rapido giro.

Whit [wit] *n* Pentecoste *f*.

white [wīt] *a* bianco(a); (*with fear*) pallido(a) ♦ *n* bianco; (*person*) bianco/a; **to turn** *or* **go** ~ (*person*) sbiancare; (*hair*) diventare bianco; **the** ~**s** (*washing*) i capi bianchi; **tennis** ~**s** completo da tennis.

whitebait [wīt'bāt] *n* bianchetti *mpl*.

white coffee *n* (*Brit*) caffellatte *m inv*.

white-collar worker [wīt'kâl'ûr wûr'kûr] *n* impiegato/a.

white elephant *n* (*fig*) oggetto (*or* progetto) costoso ma inutile.

white goods *npl* (*appliances*) elettrodomestici *mpl*; (*linens*) biancheria per la casa.

white-hot [wīt'hât'] *a* (*metal*) incandescente.

white lie *n* bugia pietosa.

whiteness [wīt'nis] *n* bianchezza.

white noise *n* rumore *m* bianco.

white paper *n* (*POL*) libro bianco.

itewash [wĭt'wâsh] n (paint) bianco di
calce ♦ vt imbiancare; (fig) coprire.

whiting [wī'ting] n (pl inv) merlango.

Whit Monday n lunedì m inv di Pentecoste.

Whitsun [wĭt'sən] n Pentecoste f.

whittle [wĭt'əl] vt: **to ~ away, ~ down** ridurre, tagliare.

whizz [wiz] vi passare sfrecciando.

whizz kid n (col) prodigio.

WHO n abbr (= World Health Organization)
O.M.S. f (= Organizzazione mondiale della
sanità).

who [hōō] pronoun (interrogative) chi; (relative) che.

whodunit [hōōdun'it] n (col) giallo.

whoever [hōōev'ûr] pronoun: **~ finds it**
chiunque lo trovi; **ask ~ you like** lo chieda a
chiunque vuole; **~ told you that?** chi mai
gliel'ha detto?

whole [hōl] a (complete) tutto(a), comple-
to(a); (not broken) intero(a), intatto(a) ♦ n
(total) totale m; (sth not broken) tutto; **the
~ lot (of it)** tutto; **the ~ lot (of them)** tutti;
the ~ of the time tutto il tempo; **the ~ of
the town** la città intera; **on the ~, as a ~**
nel complesso, nell'insieme; **~ villages were
destroyed** interi paesi furono distrutti.

wholefood [hōl'fōōd] n cibo integrale.

wholehearted [hōl'hâr'tid] a sincero(a).

wholemeal [hōl'mēl] a (Brit) = **wholewheat**.

whole milk n (US) latte m intero.

whole note n (US MUS) semibreve f.

wholesale [hōl'sāl] n commercio or vendita
all'ingrosso ♦ a all'ingrosso; (destruction) totale.

wholesaler [hōl'sālûr] n grossista m/f.

wholesome [hōl'səm] a sano(a); (climate) salubre.

wholewheat [hōl'wēt] a (flour, bread) integrale.

wholly [hō'lē] ad completamente, del tutto.

whom [hōōm] pronoun che, prep + il(la) quale; (interrogative) chi; **those to ~ I spoke** le
persone con le quali ho parlato.

whooping cough [wōō'ping kôf] n pertosse f.

whoosh [wōōsh] n: **it came out with a ~**
(sauce etc) è uscito di getto; (air) è uscito
con un sibilo.

whopper [wâp'ûr] n (col: lie) balla; (: large
thing) cosa enorme.

whopping [wâp'ing] a (col: big) enorme.

whore [hôr] n (pej) puttana.

whose [hōōz] a: **~ book is this?** di chi è questo libro?; **~ pencil have you taken?** di chi è
la matita che ha preso?; **the man ~ son you
rescued** l'uomo di cui or del quale ha salvato
il figlio; **the girl ~ sister you were speaking
to** la ragazza alla cui sorella or alla sorella
della quale stava parlando ♦ pronoun: **~ is
this?** di chi è questo?; **I know ~ it is** so di
chi è.

Who's Who [hōōz' hōō'] n elenco di personalità.

why [wī] ad, cj perché ♦ excl (surprise) ma
guarda un po'!; (remonstrating) ma (via)!;
(explaining) ebbene!; **~ not?** perché no?; **~
not do it now?** perché non farlo adesso?;
the reason ~ il motivo per cui.

whyever [wī'evûr] ad perché mai.

WI abbr (GEO) = **West Indies**; (US MAIL) =
Wisconsin.

wick [wik] n lucignolo, stoppino.

wicked [wik'id] a cattivo(a), malvagio(a);
(mischievous) malizioso(a); (terrible: prices,
weather) terribile.

wicker [wik'ûr] n vimine m; (also: **~work**)
articoli mpl di vimini.

wicket [wik'it] n (CRICKET) porta; area tra le
due porte.

wide [wīd] a largo(a); (region, knowledge) va-
sto(a); (choice) ampio(a) ♦ ad: **to open ~**
spalancare; **to shoot ~** tirare a vuoto or fuori bersaglio; **it is 3 meters ~** è largo 3 metri.

wide-angle lens [wīd'ang'gəl lenz'] n
grandangolare m.

wide-awake [wīd'əwāk'] a completamente
sveglio(a).

wide-eyed [wīd'īd] a con gli occhi spalancati.

widely [wīd'lē] ad (different) molto, completamente; (believed) generalmente; **~ spaced**
molto distanziati(e); **to be ~ read** (author)
essere molto letto; (reader) essere molto
colto.

widen [wī'dən] vt allargare, ampliare.

wideness [wīd'nis] n larghezza; vastità;
ampiezza.

wide open a spalancato(a).

wide-ranging [wīd'rān'jing] a (survey, report)
vasto(a); (interests) svariato(a).

widespread [wīdspred'] a (belief etc) molto or
assai diffuso(a).

widow [wid'ō] n vedova.

widowed [wid'ōd] a (che è rimasto(a)) vedo-
vo(a).

widower [wid'ôûr] n vedovo.

width [width] n larghezza; **it's 7 meters in ~**
è largo 7 metri.

widthwise [width'wiz] ad trasversalmente.

wield [wēld] vt (sword) maneggiare; (power)
esercitare.

wife, pl **wives** [wīf, wīvz] n moglie f.

wig [wig] n parrucca.

wiggle [wig'əl] vt dimenare, agitare ♦ vi
(loose screw etc) traballare; (worm)
torcersi.

wiggly [wig'lē] a (line) ondulato(a), sinuo-
so(a).

wild [wīld] a (animal, plant) selvatico(a);
(countryside, appearance) selvaggio(a);
(sea) tempestoso(a); (idea, life) folle; (col:
angry) arrabbiato(a), furibondo(a); (enthusiastic): **to be ~ about** andar pazzo(a) per ♦

n: **the** ~ la natura; **~s** *npl* regione *f* selvaggia.

wild card *n* (*COMPUT*) wild card *m inv*.

wildcat [wīld'kat] *n* gatto(a) selvatico(a).

wildcat strike *n* ≈ sciopero selvaggio.

wilderness [wil'dûrnis] *n* deserto.

wildfire [wīld'fîûr] *n*: **to spread like** ~ propagarsi rapidamente.

wild-goose chase [wīld'gōōs' chās] *n* (*fig*) pista falsa.

wildlife [wild'līf] *n* natura.

wildly [wīld'lē] *ad* (*applaud*) freneticamente; (*hit, guess*) a casaccio; (*happy*) follemente.

wiles [wīlz] *npl* astuzie *fpl*.

wilful [wil'fəl] *a* (*Brit*) = **willful**.

will [wil] *auxiliary vb*: **he** ~ **come** verrà ♦ *vt* (*pt, pp* **~ed**): **to** ~ **sb to do** pregare (tra sé) perché qn faccia; **he ~ed himself to go on** continuò grazie a un grande sforzo di volontà ♦ *n* volontà; (*LAW*) testamento; **you won't lose it,** ~ **you?** non lo perderai, vero?; **that** ~ **be the mailman** (*in conjectures*) sarà il postino; ~ **you sit down** (*politely*) prego, si accomodi; (*angrily*) vuoi metterti seduto!; **the car won't start** la macchina non parte; **against sb's** ~ contro la volontà or il volere di qn; **to do sth of one's own free** ~ fare qc di propria volontà.

willful [wil'fəl] *a* (*US: person*) testardo(a); ostinato(a); (: *action*) intenzionale; (: *crime*) premeditato(a).

willing [wil'ing] *a* volonteroso(a) ♦ *n*: **to show** ~ dare prova di buona volontà; ~ **to do** disposto(a) a fare.

willingly [wil'inglē] *ad* volentieri.

willingness [wil'ingnis] *n* buona volontà.

will-o'-the-wisp [wil'ōthəwisp'] *n* (*also fig*) fuoco fatuo.

willow [wil'ō] *n* salice *m*.

will power *n* forza di volontà.

willy-nilly [wil'ēnil'ē] *ad* volente o nolente.

wilt [wilt] *vi* appassire.

Wilts [wilts] *abbr* (*Brit*) = **Wiltshire**.

wily [wī'lē] *a* furbo(a).

wimp [wimp] *n* (*col*) mezza calzetta.

win [win] *n* (*in sports etc*) vittoria ♦ *vb* (*pt, pp* **won** [wun]) *vt* (*battle, prize*) vincere; (*money*) guadagnare; (*popularity*) conquistare; (*contract*) aggiudicarsi ♦ *vi* vincere.

win over, (*Brit*) **win round** *vt* convincere.

wince [wins] *n* trasalimento, sussulto ♦ *vi* trasalire.

winch [winch] *n* verricello, argano.

Winchester disk [win'chestûr disk] *n* (*COMPUT*) disco Winchester.

wind *n* [wind] vento; (*MED*) flatulenza, ventosità ♦ *vb* [wīnd] (*pt, pp* **wound** [wound]) *vt* attorcigliare; (*wrap*) avvolgere; (*clock, toy*) caricare; (*take breath away*: [wind]) far restare senza fiato ♦ *vi* (*road, river*) serpeggiare; **the ~(s)** (*MUS*) i fiati; **into** *or* **against the** ~ controvento; **to get** ~ **of sth** venire a sapere qc; **to break** ~ scoreggiare (*col*).

wind down *vt* (*car window*) abbassare; (*fig: production, business*) diminuire.

wind up *vt* (*clock*) caricare; (*debate*) concludere.

windbreak [wind'brāk] *n* frangivento.

windbreaker [wind'brākûr] *n* (*US*) giacca a vento.

windfall [wind'fôl] *n* colpo di fortuna.

winding [wīn'ding] *a* (*road*) serpeggiante; (*staircase*) a chiocciola.

wind instrument [wind in'strəmənt] *n* (*MUS*) strumento a fiato.

windmill [wind'mil] *n* mulino a vento.

window [win'dō] *n* (*gen, COMPUT*) finestra; (*in car, train*) finestrino; (*in store etc*) vetrina; (*also*: ~ **pane**) vetro.

window box *n* cassetta da fiori.

window cleaner *n* (*person*) pulitore *m* di finestre.

window dressing *n* allestimento della vetrina.

window envelope *n* busta a finestra.

window frame *n* telaio di finestra.

window ledge *n* davanzale *m*.

window pane *n* vetro.

window-shopping [win'dōshāping] *n*: **to go** ~ andare a vedere le vetrine.

windowsill [win'dōsil] *n* davanzale *m*.

windpipe [wind'pīp] *n* trachea.

windscreen [wind'skrēn] *etc* (*Brit*) = **windshield** *etc*.

windshield [wind'shēld] *n* parabrezza *m inv*.

windshield washer *n* lavacristallo.

windshield wiper *n* tergicristallo.

windswept [wind'swept] *a* spazzato(a) dal vento.

wind tunnel *n* galleria aerodinamica *or* del vento.

windy [win'dē] *a* ventoso(a); **it's** ~ c'è vento.

wine [wīn] *n* vino ♦ *vt*: **to** ~ **and dine sb** offrire un ottimo pranzo a qn.

wine cellar *n* cantina.

wineglass [wīn'glas] *n* bicchiere *m* da vino.

wine list *n* lista dei vini.

wine merchant *n* commerciante *m* di vino.

wine tasting *n* degustazione *f* dei vini.

wine waiter *n* sommelier *m inv*.

wing [wing] *n* ala; **~s** *npl* (*THEATER*) quinte *fpl*.

winger [wing'ûr] *n* (*Brit SPORT*) ala.

wing mirror *n* (*Brit*) specchietto retrovisore esterno.

wing nut *n* galletto.

wingspan [wing'span], **wingspread** [wing'spred] *n* apertura alare, apertura d'ali.

wink [wingk] *n* occhiolino, strizzatina d'occhi ♦ *vi* ammiccare, fare l'occhiolino.

winkle [win'kəl] *n* litorina.

winner [win'ûr] *n* vincitore/trice.

winning |win'ing| *a* (*team*) vincente; (*goal*) decisivo(a); (*charming*) affascinante; *see also* **winnings**.

winning post *n* traguardo.

winnings |win'ingz| *npl* vincite *fpl*.

winsome |win'səm| *a* accattivante.

winter |win'tûr| *n* inverno; **in** ~ d'inverno, in inverno.

winter sports *npl* sport *mpl* invernali.

wintry |win'trē| *a* invernale.

wipe |wīp| *n* pulita, passata ♦ *vt* pulire (strofinando); (*dishes*) asciugare; **to give sth a** ~ dare una pulita *or* una passata a qc; **to ~ one's nose** soffiarsi il naso.

wipe off *vt* cancellare; (*stains*) togliere strofinando.

wipe out *vt* (*debt*) pagare, liquidare; (*memory*) cancellare; (*destroy*) annientare.

wipe up *vt* asciugare.

wire |wī'ûr| *n* filo; (*ELEC*) filo elettrico; (*TEL*) telegramma *m* ♦ *vt* (*ELEC*: *house*) fare l'impianto elettrico di; (: *circuit*) installare; (*also*: ~ **up**) collegare, allacciare.

wire brush *n* spazzola metallica.

wire cutters *npl* tronchese *m or f*.

wire netting *n* rete *f* metallica.

wiretapping |wī'ûrtaping| *n* intercettazione *f* telefonica.

wiring |wiûr'ing| *n* (*ELEC*) impianto elettrico.

wiry |wiûr'ē| *a* magro(a) e nerboruto(a).

Wis., Wisc. *abbr* (*US*) = Wisconsin.

wisdom |wiz'dəm| *n* saggezza; (*of action*) prudenza.

wisdom tooth *n* dente *m* del giudizio.

wise |wīz| *a* saggio(a); (*advice*, *remark*) prudente; **I'm none the** ~r ne so come prima.

wise up *vi* (*col*): **to** ~ **up to** divenire più consapevole di.

wisecrack |wīz'krak| *n* battuta spiritosa.

wish |wish| *n* (*desire*) desiderio; (*specific desire*) richiesta ♦ *vt* desiderare, volere; **best** ~**es** (*on birthday etc*) i migliori auguri; **with best** ~**es** (*in letter*) cordiali saluti, con i migliori saluti; **give her my best** ~**es** le faccia i migliori auguri da parte mia; **to** ~ **sb goodbye** dire arrivederci a qn; **he** ~**ed me well** mi augurò di riuscire; **to** ~ **to do/sb to do** desiderare *or* volere fare/che qn faccia; **to** ~ **for** desiderare; **to** ~ **sth on sb** rifilare qc a qn.

wishful |wish'fəl| *a*: **it's** ~ **thinking** è prendere i desideri per realtà.

wishy-washy |wish'ēwâshē| *a* insulso(a).

wisp |wisp| *n* ciuffo, ciocca; (*of smoke, straw*) filo.

wistful |wist'fəl| *a* malinconico(a); (*nostalgic*) nostalgico(a).

wit |wit| *n* (*gen pl*) intelligenza; presenza di spirito; (*wittiness*) spirito, arguzia; (*person*) bello spirito; **to be at one's** ~**s' end** (*fig*) non sapere più cosa fare; **to have** *or* **keep**

one's ~**s about one** avere presenza di spirito; **to** ~ *ad* cioè.

witch |wich| *n* strega.

witchcraft |wich'kraft| *n* stregoneria.

witch doctor *n* stregone *m*.

witch-hunt |wich'hunt| *n* (*fig*) caccia alle streghe.

with |with, with| *prep* con; **red** ~ **anger** rosso dalla *or* per la rabbia; **covered** ~ **snow** coperto di neve; **the man** ~ **the gray hat** l'uomo dal cappello grigio; **to shake** ~ **fear** tremare di paura; **to stay overnight** ~ **friends** passare la notte da amici; **to be** ~ **it** (*fig*) essere al corrente; essere sveglio(a); **I am** ~ **you** (*I understand*) la seguo.

withdraw |withdrô'| *vb* (*irg*) *vt* ritirare; (*money from bank*) ritirare, prelevare ♦ *vi* ritirarsi; **to** ~ **into o.s.** chiudersi in se stesso.

withdrawal |withdrô'əl| *n* ritiro; prelievo; (*of army*) ritirata; (*MED*) stato di privazione.

withdrawal symptoms *npl* crisi *f* di astinenza.

withdrawn |withdrôn'| *pp of* **withdraw** ♦ *a* distaccato(a).

wither |with'ûr| *vi* appassire.

withered |with'ûrd| *a* appassito(a); (*limb*) atrofizzato(a).

withhold |withhōld'| *vt irg* (*money*) trattenere; (*permission*): **to** ~ (**from**) rifiutare (a); (*information*): **to** ~ (**from**) nascondere (a).

within |within'| *prep* all'interno di; (*in time, distances*) entro ♦ *ad* all'interno, dentro; ~ **sight of** in vista di; ~ **a mile of** entro un miglio da; ~ **the week** prima della fine della settimana; ~ **an hour from now** da qui a un'ora; **to be** ~ **the law** restare nei limiti della legge.

without |without'| *prep* senza; **to go** *or* **do** ~ **sth** fare a meno di qc; ~ **anybody knowing** senza che nessuno lo sappia.

withstand |withstand'| *vt irg* resistere a.

witness |wit'nis| *n* (*person*) testimone *m/f* ♦ *vt* (*event*) essere testimone di; (*document*) attestare l'autenticità di ♦ *vi*: **to** ~ **to sth/having seen sth** testimoniare qc/di aver visto qc; **to bear** ~ **to sth** testimoniare qc; ~ **for the prosecution/defense** testimone a carico/discarico.

witness stand, (*Brit*) **witness box** *n* banco dei testimoni.

witticism |wit'əsizəm| *n* spiritosaggine *f*.

witty |wit'ē| *a* spiritoso(a).

wives |wīvz| *npl of* **wife**.

wizard |wiz'ûrd| *n* mago.

wizened |wiz'ənd| *a* raggrinzito(a).

wk *abbr* = **week**.

Wm. *abbr* = **William**.

WO *n abbr* see **warrant officer**.

wobble |wâb'əl| *vi* tremare; (*chair*) traballare.

wobbly [wâb'lē] *a* (*hand*, *voice*) tremante; (*table*, *chair*) traballante; (*object about to fall*) che oscilla pericolosamente.

woe [wō] *n* dolore *m*; disgrazia.

woke [wōk] *pt of* **wake**.

woken [wō'kən] *pp of* **wake**.

wolf, *pl* **wolves** [wŏolf, wŏolvz] *n* lupo.

woman, *pl* **women** [wŏom'ən, wim'ən] *n* donna ♦ *cpd*: ~ **doctor** *n* dottoressa; ~ **friend** *n* amica; ~ **teacher** *n* insegnante *f*; **women's page** *n* (*PRESS*) rubrica femminile.

womanize [wŏom'əniz] *vi* essere un donnaiolo.

womanly [wŏom'ənlē] *a* femminile.

womb [wŏom] *n* (*ANAT*) utero.

women [wim'ən] *npl of* **woman**.

Women's (Liberation) Movement *n* (*also*: **Women's Lib**) Movimento per la Liberazione della Donna.

won [wun] *pt*, *pp of* **win**.

wonder [wun'dûr] *n* meraviglia ♦ *vi*: **to** ~ **whether** domandarsi se; **to** ~ **at** essere sorpreso(a) di; meravigliarsi di; **to** ~ **about** domandarsi di; pensare a; **it's no** ~ **that** c'è poco *or* non c'è da meravigliarsi che + *sub*.

wonderful [wun'dûrfəl] *a* meraviglioso(a).

wonderfully [wun'dûrfəlē] *ad* (+ *adjective*) meravigliosamente; (+ *verb*) a meraviglia.

wonky [wâng'kē] *a* (*Brit col*) traballante.

won't [wōnt] = **will not**.

woo [wŏo] *vt* (*woman*) fare la corte a.

wood [wŏod] *n* legno; (*timber*) legname *m*; (*forest*) bosco ♦ *cpd* di bosco, silvestre.

wood alcohol *n* (*US*) alcool *m* denaturato.

wood carving *n* scultura in legno, intaglio.

wooded [wŏod'id] *a* boschivo(a); boscoso(a).

wooden [wŏod'ən] *a* di legno; (*fig*) rigido(a); inespressivo(a).

woodland [wŏod'land] *n* zona boscosa.

woodpecker [wŏod'pekûr] *n* picchio.

wood pigeon *n* colombaccio, palomba.

woodwind [wŏod'wind] *npl* (*MUS*): **the** ~ i legni.

woodwork [wŏod'wûrk] *n* parti *fpl* in legno; (*craft*, *subject*) falegnameria.

woodworm [wŏod'wûrm] *n* tarlo del legno.

woof [wŏof] *n* (*of dog*) bau bau *m* ♦ *vi* abbaiare; ~, ~! bau bau!

wool [wŏol] *n* lana; **to pull the** ~ **over sb's eyes** (*fig*) fargliela a qn.

woolen, (*Brit*) **woollen** [wŏol'ən] *a* di lana ♦ *n*: ~**s** indumenti *mpl* di lana.

wooly, (*Brit*) **woolly** [wŏol'ē] *a* lanoso(a); (*fig*: *ideas*) confuso(a).

word [wûrd] *n* parola; (*news*) notizie *fpl* ♦ *vt* esprimere, formulare; ~ **for** ~ parola per parola, testualmente; **what's the** ~ **for "pen" in Italian?** come si dice "pen" in italiano?; **to put sth into** ~**s** esprimere qc a parole; **in other** ~**s** in altre parole; **to have a** ~ **with sb** scambiare due parole con qn; **to have** ~**s with sb** (*quarrel with*) avere un diverbio con

qn; **to break/keep one's** ~ non mantenere/mantenere la propria parola; **I'll take your** ~ **for it** la crederò sulla parola; **to send** ~ **of** avvisare di; **to leave** ~ **(with** *or* **for sb) that** ... lasciare detto (a qn) che.....

wording [wûr'ding] *n* formulazione *f*.

word-perfect [wûrd'pûrfikt] *a* (*speech etc*) imparato(a) a memoria.

word processing *n* word processing *m*, elaborazione *f* testi.

word processor *n* word processor *m inv*.

wordwrap [wûrd'rap] *n* (*COMPUT*) ritorno carrello automatico.

wordy [wûr'dē] *a* verboso(a), prolisso(a).

wore [wôr] *pt of* **wear**.

work [wûrk] *n* lavoro; (*ART. LITERATURE*) opera ♦ *vi* lavorare; (*mechanism*, *plan etc*) funzionare; (*medicine*) essere efficace ♦ *vt* (*clay*, *wood etc*) lavorare; (*mine etc*) sfruttare; (*machine*) far funzionare ♦ *cpd* (*day*) feriale; (*tools*, *conditions*) di lavoro; (*clothes*) da lavoro; **to be at** ~ **(on sth)** lavorare (a qc); **to set to** ~, **to start** ~ mettersi all'opera; **to go to** ~ andare al lavoro; **to be out of** ~ essere disoccupato(a); **to** ~ **one's way through a book** riuscire a leggersi tutto un libro; **to** ~ **one's way through college** lavorare per pagarsi gli studi; **to** ~ **hard** lavorare sodo; **to** ~ **loose** allentarsi; "~ **wanted**" (*US*) domandi di impiego; *see also* **works**.

work on *vt fus* lavorare a; (*principle*) basarsi su; **he's** ~**ing on the car** sta facendo dei lavori alla macchina.

work out *vi* (*plans etc*) riuscire, andare bene; (*SPORT*) allenarsi ♦ *vt* (*problem*) risolvere; (*plan*) elaborare; **it** ~**s out at $100** fa 100 dollari.

workable [wûr'kəbəl] *a* (*solution*) realizzabile.

workaholic [wûrkəhâl'ik] *n* stacanovista *m/f*.

workbench [wûrk'bench] *n* banco (da lavoro).

workbook [wûrk'bŏok] *n* quaderno.

work council *n* consiglio aziendale.

worked up [wûrkt up] *a*: **to get** ~ andare su tutte le furie; eccitarsi.

worker [wûr'kûr] *n* lavoratore/trice; (*esp AGR*, *INDUSTRY*) operaio/a; **office** ~ impiegato/a.

work force *n* forza lavoro.

working [wûr'king] *a* (*Brit*: *day*) feriale; (: *tools*, *conditions*) di lavoro; (: *clothes*) da lavoro; (*wife*) che lavora; (*partner*) attivo(a); **in** ~ **order** funzionante; ~ **knowledge** conoscenza pratica.

working capital *n* (*COMM*) capitale *m* d'esercizio.

working class *n* classe *f* operaia *or* lavoratrice ♦ *a*: **working-class** operaio(a).

working man *n* lavoratore *m*.

working model *n* modello operativo.

working week *n* (*Brit*) settimana lavorativa.

work-in-progress [wûrkinprâg'res] *n* (*products*) lavoro in corso; (*value*) valore *m* del manufatto in lavorazione.

workload [wûrk'lōd] *n* carico di lavoro.

workman [wûrk'mən] *n* operaio.

workmanship [wûrk'mənship] *n* (*of worker*) abilità; (*of thing*) fattura.

workmate [wûrk'māt] *n* collega *m/f*.

workout [wûrk'out] *n* (*SPORT*) allenamento.

work party *n* commissione *f*.

work permit *n* permesso di lavoro.

works [wûrks] *npl* (*of clock, machine*) meccanismo ♦ *n* (*Brit: factory*) fabbrica; **road ~** opere stradali.

work sheet *n* (*COMPUT*) foglio col programma di lavoro.

workshop [wûrk'shâp] *n* officina.

work station *n* stazione *f* di lavoro.

work study *n* studio di organizzazione del lavoro.

work-to-rule [wûrk'tərōōl'] *n* (*Brit*) sciopero bianco.

work week *n* (*US*) settimana lavorativa.

world [wûrld] *n* mondo ♦ *cpd* (*tour*) del mondo; (*record, power, war*) mondiale; **all over the ~** in tutto il mondo; **to think the ~ of sb** pensare un gran bene di qn; **out of this ~** (*fig*) formidabile; **what in the ~ is he doing?** che cavolo sta facendo?; **to do sb a ~ of good** fare un gran bene a qn; **W~ War One/Two** la prima/seconda guerra mondiale.

world champion *n* campione/essa mondiale.

World Cup *n* (*SOCCER*) Coppa del Mondo.

world-famous [wûrldfā'məs] *a* di fama mondiale.

worldly [wûrld'lē] *a* di questo mondo.

worldwide [wûrld'wīd'] *a* universale.

worm [wûrm] *n* verme *m*.

worn [wôrn] *pp of* **wear** ♦ *a* usato(a).

worn-out [wôrn'out'] *a* (*object*) consumato(a), logoro(a); (*person*) sfinito(a).

worried [wûr'ēd] *a* preoccupato(a); **to be ~ about sth** essere preoccupato per qc.

worrier [wûr'ēûr] *n* ansioso/a.

worrisome [wûr'ēsəm] *a* preoccupante.

worry [wûr'ē] *n* preoccupazione *f* ♦ *vt* preoccupare ♦ *vi* preoccuparsi; **to ~ about** *or* **over sth/sb** preoccuparsi di qc/per qn.

worrying [wûr'ēing] *a* preoccupante.

worse [wûrs] *a* peggiore ♦ *ad, n* peggio; **a change for the ~** un peggioramento; **to get ~, to grow ~** peggiorare; **he is none the ~ for it** non ha avuto brutte conseguenze; **so much the ~ for you!** tanto peggio per te!

worsen [wûr'sən] *vt, vi* peggiorare.

worse off *a* in condizioni (economiche) peggiori; (*fig*): **you'll be ~ this way** così sarà peggio per lei; **he is now ~ than before** ora è in condizioni peggiori di prima.

worship [wûr'ship] *n* culto ♦ *vt* (*God*) adorare, venerare; (*person*) adorare; **Your W~** (*to mayor*) signor sindaco; (*to judge*) signor giudice.

worshipper [wûr'shipûr] *n* adoratore/trice; (*in church*) fedele *m/f*, devoto/a.

worst [wûrst] *a* il(la) peggiore ♦ *ad, n* peggio; **at ~** al peggio, per male che vada; **to come off ~** avere la peggio; **if ~ comes to ~**, (*Brit*) **if the ~ comes to the ~** nel peggior dei casi.

worsted [wōōs'tid] *n*: (**wool**) **~** lana pettinata.

worth [wûrth] *n* valore *m* ♦ *a*: **to be ~** valere; **how much is it ~?** quanto vale?; **it's ~ it** ne vale la pena; **it's not ~ the trouble** non ne vale la pena; **$2 ~ of apples** 2 dollari di mele.

worthless [wûrth'lis] *a* di nessun valore.

worthwhile [wûrth'wīl'] *a* (*activity*) utile; (*cause*) lodevole; **a ~ book** un libro che vale la pena leggere.

worthy [wûr'thē] *a* (*person*) degno(a); (*motive*) lodevole; **~ of** degno di.

would [wōōd] *auxiliary vb*: **she ~ come** verrebbe; **he ~ have come** sarebbe venuto; **~ you like a cookie?** vuole *or* vorrebbe un biscotto?; **~ you close the door, please** chiuda la porta per favore; **he ~ go there on Mondays** ci andava il lunedì; **you** WOULD **say that, ~n't you!** (*emphatic*) doveva dirlo, vero!; **he ~n't behave** (*insistence*) non ha voluto comportarsi bene.

would-be [wōōd'bē'] *a* (*pej*) sedicente.

wound *vb* [wound] *pt, pp of* **wind** ♦ *n, vt* [wōōnd] *n* ferita ♦ *vt* ferire; **~ed in the leg** ferito(a) alla gamba.

wove [wōv] *pt of* **weave.**

woven [wō'vən] *pp of* **weave.**

WP *n abbr* = **word processing; word processor.**

WPC *n abbr* (*Brit*: = *woman police constable*) donna poliziotto.

wpm *abbr* (= *words per minute*) p.p.m.

wrangle [rang'gəl] *n* litigio ♦ *vi* litigare.

wrap [rap] *n* (*stole*) scialle *m*; (*cape*) mantellina ♦ *vt* (*also:* **~ up**) avvolgere; (*parcel*) incartare; **under ~s** segreto.

wrapper [rap'ûr] *n* (*on chocolate*) carta.

wrapping paper [rap'ing pā'pûr] *n* carta da pacchi; (*for gift*) carta da regali.

wrath [rath] *n* collera, ira.

wreak [rēk] *vt* (*destruction*) portare, causare; **to ~ vengeance on** vendicarsi su; **to ~ havoc on** portare scompiglio in.

wreath, ~s [rēth, rēthz] *n* corona.

wreck [rek] *n* (*sea disaster*) naufragio; (*ship*) relitto; (*pej: person*) rottame *m* ♦ *vt* demolire; (*ship*) far naufragare; (*fig*) rovinare.

wreckage [rek'ij] *n* rottami *mpl*; (*of building*) macerie *fpl*; (*of ship*) relitti *mpl*.

wrecker [rek'ûr] *n* (*US*) carro *m* attrezzi *inv*.

wren [ren] *n* (*ZOOL*) scricciolo.

wrench [rench] *n* (*TECH*) chiave *f*; (*tug*) torsione *f* brusca; (*fig*) strazio ♦ *vt* strappare; storcere; **to ~ sth from** strappare qc a _or_ da.

wrest [rest] _vt_: **to ~ sth from sb** strappare qc a qn.

wrestle [res'əl] _vi_: **to ~ (with sb)** lottare (con qn); **to ~ with** (_fig_) combattere _or_ lottare contro.

wrestler [res'lûr] _n_ lottatore/trice.

wrestling [res'ling] _n_ lotta.

wrestling match _n_ incontro di lotta (_or_ lotta libera).

wretch [rech] _n_ disgraziato/a, sciagurato/a; **little ~!** (_often humorous_) birbante!

wretched [rech'id] _a_ disgraziato(a); (_col: weather, vacation_) orrendo(a), orribile; (: _child, dog_) pestifero(a).

wriggle [rig'əl] _n_ contorsione _f_ ♦ _vi_ dimenarsi; (_snake, worm_) serpeggiare, muoversi serpeggiando.

wring _pt, pp_ **wrung** [ring, rung] _vt_ torcere; (_wet clothes_) strizzare; (_fig_): **to ~ sth out of** strappare qc a.

wringer [ring'ûr] _n_ strizzatoio (manuale).

wringing [ring'ing] _a_ (_also:_ **~ wet**) bagnato(a) fradicio(a).

wrinkle [ring'kəl] _n_ (_on skin_) ruga; (_on paper etc_) grinza ♦ _vt_ corrugare; raggrinzire ♦ _vi_ corrugarsi; raggrinzirsi.

wrinkled [ring'kəld], **wrinkly** [ring'klē] _a_ (_fabric, paper_) stropicciato(a); (_surface_) corrugato(a), increspato(a); (_skin_) rugoso(a).

wrist [rist] _n_ polso.

wristwatch [rist'wâch] _n_ orologio da polso.

writ [rit] _n_ ordine _m_; mandato; **to issue a ~ against sb, serve a ~ on sb** notificare un mandato di comparizione a qn.

write, _pt_ **wrote**, _pp_ **written** [rīt, rōt, ritən] _vt, vi_ scrivere; **to ~ sb a letter** scrivere una lettera a qn.

write away _vi_: **to ~ away for** (_information_) richiedere per posta; (_goods_) ordinare per posta.

write down _vt_ annotare; (_put in writing_) mettere per iscritto.

write off _vt_ (_debt_) cancellare; (_depreciate_) deprezzare; (_smash up: car_) distruggere.

write out _vt_ scrivere; (_copy_) ricopiare.

write up _vt_ redigere.

write-off [rīt'ôf] _n_ perdita completa; **the car is a ~** (_Brit_) la macchina va bene per il demolitore.

write-protect [rīt'prətekt'] _vt_ (_COMPUT_) proteggere contro scrittura.

writer [rī'tûr] _n_ autore/trice, scrittore/trice.

write-up [rīt'up] _n_ (_review_) recensione _f_.

writhe [rīth] _vi_ contorcersi.

writing [rī'ting] _n_ scrittura; (_of author_) scritto, opera; **in ~** per iscritto; **in my own ~** scritto di mio pugno.

writing case _n_ nécessaire _m inv_ per la corrispondenza.

writing desk _n_ scrivania, scrittoio.

writing paper _n_ carta da scrivere.

written [rit'ən] _pp of_ **write**.

wrong [rông] _a_ sbagliato(a); (_not suitable_) inadatto(a); (_wicked_) cattivo(a); (_unfair_) ingiusto(a) ♦ _ad_ in modo sbagliato, erroneamente ♦ _n_ (_evil_) male _m_; (_injustice_) torto ♦ _vt_ fare torto a; **to be ~** (_answer_) essere sbagliato; (_in doing, saying_) avere torto; **you are ~ to do it** ha torto a farlo; **you are ~ about that, you've got it ~** si sbaglia; **to be in the ~** avere torto; **what's ~?** cosa c'è che non va?; **there's nothing ~** va tutto bene; **what's ~ with the car?** cos'ha la macchina che non va?; **to go ~** (_person_) sbagliarsi; (_plan_) fallire, non riuscire; (_machine_) guastarsi; **it's ~ to steal, stealing is ~** è male rubare.

wrongful [rông'fəl] _a_ illegittimo(a); ingiusto(a); **~ dismissal** licenziamento ingiustificato.

wrongly [rông'lē] _ad_ (_accuse, dismiss_) a torto; (_answer, do, count_) erroneamente; (_treat_) ingiustamente.

wrong number _n_: **you have the ~** (_TEL_) ha sbagliato numero.

wrong side _n_ (_of cloth_) rovescio.

wrote [rōt] _pt of_ **write**.

wrought [rôt] _a_: **~ iron** ferro battuto.

wrung [rung] _pt, pp of_ **wring**.

wry [rī] _a_ storto(a).

wt. _abbr_ = **weight**.

WV _abbr_ (_US MAIL_) = _West Virginia_.

W.Va. _abbr_ (_US_) = _West Virginia_.

WY _abbr_ (_US MAIL_) = _Wyoming_.

Wyo. _abbr_ (_US_) = _Wyoming_.

WYSIWYG [wiz'ēwig] _abbr_ (_COMPUT_) = _what you see is what you get_.

X

X, x [eks] _n_ (_letter_) X, x _f or m inv_; **X for Xmas** ≈ X come Xeres.

Xerox [zē'râks] ® _n_ (_also:_ **~ machine**) fotocopiatrice _f_; (_photocopy_) fotocopia ♦ _vt_ fotocopiare.

XL _abbr_ = _extra large_.

Xmas [eks'mis] _n abbr_ = **Christmas**.

X-rated [eks'rātid] _a_ (_US: film_) ≈ vietato ai minori di 18 anni.

X-ray [eks'rā] _n_ raggio X; (_photograph_) radiografia _f or_ radiografare; **to have an ~** farsi fare una radiografia.

xylophone [zī'ləfōn] _n_ xilofono.

Y

Y, y [wī] *n* (*letter*) Y, y *f or m inv*; **Y for Yoke** ≈ Y come Yacht.

yacht [yât] *n* panfilo, yacht *m inv*.

yachting [yât'ing] *n* yachting *m*, sport *m* della vela.

yachtsman [yâts'mən] *n* yachtsman *m inv*.

yam [yam] *n* igname *m*; (*sweet potato*) patata dolce.

Yank [yangk], **Yankee** [yang'kē] *n* (*pej*) yankee *m/f inv*, nordamericano/a.

yank [yangk] *n* strattone *m* ♦ *vt* tirare, dare uno strattone a.

yap [yap] *vi* (*dog*) guaire.

yard [yârd] *n* (*US: garden*) giardino; (*of house etc*) cortile *m*; (*measure*) iarda (= *914 mm; 3 feet*); **builder's** ~ deposito di materiale da costruzione.

yardstick [yârd'stik] *n* (*fig*) misura, criterio.

yarn [yârn] *n* filato; (*tale*) lunga storia.

yawn [yôn] *n* sbadiglio ♦ *vi* sbadigliare.

yawning [yôn'ing] *a* (*gap*) spalancato(a).

yd. *abbr* = **yard**.

yeah [ye] *ad* (*col*) sì.

year [yēr] *n* (*gen*, *Brit SCOL*) anno; (*referring to harvest, wine etc*) annata; **every** ~ ogni anno, tutti gli anni; **this** ~ quest'anno; ~ **in**, ~ **out** anno dopo anno; **she's three** ~**s old** ha tre anni; **a** *or* **per** ~ all'anno.

yearbook [yēr'bŏŏk] *n* annuario.

yearly [yēr'lē] *a* annuale ♦ *ad* annualmente; **twice-**~ semestrale.

yearn [yûrn] *vi*: **to** ~ **for sth/to do** desiderare ardentemente qc/di fare.

yearning [yûr'ning] *n* desiderio intenso.

yeast [yēst] *n* lievito.

yell [yel] *n* urlo ♦ *vi* urlare.

yellow [yel'ō] *a* giallo(a).

yellow fever *n* febbre *f* gialla.

yellowish [yel'ōish] *a* giallastro(a), giallognolo(a).

Yellow Sea *n*: **the** ~ il mar Giallo.

yelp [yelp] *n* guaito, uggiolio ♦ *vi* guaire, uggiolare.

Yemen [yem'ən] *n* Yemen *m*.

yen [yen] *n* (*currency*) yen *m inv*; (*craving*): ~ **for/to do** gran voglia di/di fare.

yeoman [yō'mən] *n*: **Y**~ **of the Guard** guardiano della Torre di Londra.

yes [yes] *ad*, *n* sì (*m inv*); **to say** ~ (**to**) dire di sì (a), acconsentire (a).

yes man *n* tirapiedi *m inv*.

yesterday [yes'tûrdā] *ad*, *n* ieri (*m inv*); ~ **morning/evening** ieri mattina/sera; **the day before** ~ l'altro ieri; **all day** ~ ieri tutto il giorno.

yet [yet] *ad* ancora; già ♦ *cj* ma, tuttavia; **it is not finished** ~ non è ancora finito; **the best** ~ il migliore finora; **as** ~ finora; ~ **again** di nuovo; **a few days** ~ ancora qualche giorno.

yew [yōō] *n* tasso (*albero*).

YHA *n abbr* (*Brit*: = *Youth Hostels Association*) Y.H.A. *f*.

Yiddish [yid'ish] *n* yiddish *m*.

yield [yēld] *n* resa; (*of crops etc*) raccolto ♦ *vt* produrre, rendere; (*surrender*) cedere ♦ *vi* cedere; (*US AUT*) dare la precedenza; **a** ~ **of 5%** un profitto *or* un interesse del 5%.

YMCA *n abbr* (= *Young Men's Christian Association*) Y.M.C.A. *m*.

yodel [yōd'əl] *vi* cantare lo jodel *or* alla tirolese.

yoga [yō'gə] *n* yoga *m*.

yog(h)ourt, yog(h)urt [yō'gûrt] *n* iogurt *m inv*.

yoke [yōk] *n* giogo ♦ *vt* (*also:* ~ **together**: *oxen*) aggiogare.

yolk [yōk] *n* tuorlo, rosso d'uovo.

yonder [yân'dûr] *ad* là.

Yorks [yârks] *abbr* (*Brit*) = **Yorkshire**.

you [yōō] *pronoun* tu; (*polite form*) lei; (*pl*) voi; (: *very formal*) loro; (*complement: direct*) ti; la; vi; ti; (: *indirect*) ti; le; vi; gli; (*stressed*) te; lei; voi; loro; (*one*) si; **fresh air does** ~ **good** l'aria fresca fa bene; ~ **never know** non si sa mai; **I'll see** ~ **tomorrow** ti (*or* la *etc*) vedrò domani; **if I was** *or* **were** ~ se fossi in te (*or* lei *etc*).

you'd [yōōd] = **you had**; **you would**.

you'll [yōōl] = **you will**; **you shall**.

young [yung] *a* giovane ♦ *npl* (*of animal*) piccoli *mpl*; (*people*): **the** ~ i giovani, la gioventù; **a** ~ **man** un giovanotto; **a** ~ **lady** una signorina; **a** ~ **woman** una giovane donna; **the** ~**er generation** la nuova generazione; **my** ~**er brother** il mio fratello minore.

youngish [yung'ish] *a* abbastanza giovane.

youngster [yung'stûr] *n* giovanotto/a; (*child*) bambino/a.

your [yōōr] *a* il(la) tuo(a), *pl* i(le) tuoi(tue); (*polite form*) il(la) suo(a), *pl* i(le) suoi(sue); (*pl*) il(la) vostro(a), *pl* i(le) vostri(e); (: *very formal*) il(la) loro, *pl* i(le) loro.

you're [yōōr] = **you are**.

yours [yōōrz] *pronoun* il(la) tuo(a), *pl* i(le) tuoi(tue); (*polite form*) il(la) suo(a), *pl* i(le) suoi(sue); (*pl*) il(la) vostro(a), *pl* i(le) vostri(e); (: *very formal*) il(la) loro, *pl* i(le) loro; **sincerely** ~ (*in letter*) distinti saluti; **a friend of** ~ un tuo (*or* suo *etc*) amico; **is it** ~? è tuo (*or* suo *etc*)?

yourself [yōōrself'] *pronoun* (*reflexive*) ti; (: *polite form*) si; (*after prep*) te; se; (*emphatic*) tu stesso(a); lei stesso(a); **you** ~ **told**

me me l'hai detto proprio tu, tu stesso me l'hai detto.

yourselves [yŏŏrselvz'] *pl pronoun (reflexive)* vi; (: *polite form*) si; (*after prep*) voi; loro; (*emphatic*) voi stessi(e); loro stessi(e).

youth [yŏŏth] *n* gioventù *f*; (*young man: pl* ~s [yŏŏthz]) giovane *m*, ragazzo; **in my** ~ da giovane, quando ero giovane.

youth club *n* centro giovanile.

youthful [yŏŏth'fəl] *a* giovane; da giovane; giovanile.

youthfulness [yŏŏth'fəlnis] *n* giovinezza.

youth hostel *n* ostello della gioventù.

youth movement *n* movimento giovanile.

you've [yŏŏv] = **you have.**

yowl [youl] *n* (*of dog, person*) urlo; (*of cat*) miagolio ♦ *vi* urlare; miagolare.

yr *abbr* = **year.**

YT *abbr* (*Canada*) = *Yukon Territory.*

yuck [yuk] *excl* (*col*) puah!

Yugoslav [yŏŏ'gŏslâv'] *a*, *n* jugoslavo(a).

Yugoslavia [yŏŏ'gŏslâvēə] *n* Jugoslavia.

Yugoslavian [yŏŏ'gŏslâ'vēən] *a*, *n* jugoslavo(a).

Yule log [yŏŏl' lôg'] *n* ceppo nel caminetto a Natale.

yuppie [yup'ē] *a*, *n* (*col*) yuppie (*m/f*) *inv*.

YWCA *n* *abbr* (= *Young Women's Christian Association*) Y.W.C.A. *m*.

Z

Z, z [zē] *n* (*letter*) Z, z *f* or *m* *inv*; **Z for Zebra** ≈ Z come Zara.

Zaire [zâēr'] *n* Zaire *m*.

Zambia [zam'bēə] *n* Zambia *m*.

Zambian [zam'bēən] *a*, *n* zambiano(a).

zany [zā'nē] *a* un po' pazzo(a).

zap [zap] *vt* (*COMPUT*) cancellare.

zeal [zēl] *n* zelo; entusiasmo.

zealot [zel'ət] *n* zelota *m/f*.

zealous [zel'əs] *a* zelante; premuroso(a).

zebra [zēb'rə] *n* zebra.

zebra crossing *n* (*Brit*) (passaggio pedonale a) strisce *fpl*, zebre *fpl*.

zenith [zē'nith] *n* zenit *m* *inv*; (*fig*) culmine *m*.

zero [zē'rō] *n* zero; **5° below** ~ 5° sotto zero.

zero hour *n* l'ora zero.

zero-rated [zē'rōrā'tid] *a* (*Brit*) ad aliquota zero.

zest [zest] *n* gusto; (*CULIN*) buccia.

zigzag [zig'zag] *n* zigzag *m* *inv* ♦ *vi* zigzagare.

Zimbabwe [zimbâ'bwā] *n* Zimbabwe *m*.

Zimbabwean [zimbâ'bwāən] *a* dello Zimbabwe.

zinc [zingk] *n* zinco.

Zionism [zī'ənizəm] *n* sionismo.

Zionist [zī'ənist] *a* sionistico(a) ♦ *n* sionista *m/ f*.

zip [zip] *n* (*also:* ~**per**) chiusura *f* or cerniera *f* lampo *inv*; (*energy*) energia, forza ♦ *vt* (*also:* ~ **up**) chiudere con una cerniera lampo.

zip code *n* (*US*) codice *m* di avviamento postale.

zither [ziṭh'ûr] *n* cetra.

zodiac [zō'dēak] *n* zodiaco.

zombie [zâm'bē] *n* (*fig*): **like a** ~ come un morto che cammina.

zone [zōn] *n* zona.

zoo [zōō] *n* zoo *m* *inv*.

zoological [zōəlâj'ikəl] *a* zoologico(a).

zoologist [zōâl'əjist] *n* zoologo/a.

zoology [zōâl'əjē] *n* zoologia.

zoom [zōōm] *vi*: **to** ~ **past** sfrecciare; **to** ~ **in** (**on sb/sth**) (*PHOT*, *CINEMA*) zumare (su qn/ qc).

zoom lens *n* zoom *m* *inv*, obiettivo a focale variabile.

zucchini [zōōkē'nē] *n* (*pl inv*) (*US*) zucchina.

Zulu [zōō'lōō] *a*, *n* zulù (*m/f*) *inv*.

Zürich [zûr'ik] *n* Zurigo *f*.

1994

Sorelle dell'Estate
JUDY BLUME

Santa Maria Novella